THE CRITICS SALUTE
A STATION IN THE DELTA

"Cassidy has caught the atmosphere of the jungle war, the penetrations and betrayals, the casualness of the killing."

Library Journal

"Better than any other book I have ever read, it captures the loneliness, danger, excitement and action of the silent intelligence war."

Vernon A. Walters, Lt. Gen. U.S.A. ret.

"A good companion piece to Graham Greene's masterful 'The Quiet American' . . . a readable, intelligent novel."

Washington Post

"Really captures the feeling of loneliness and isolation which characterize the silent war intelligence fights."

Boston Herald American

Also by John Cassidy
Published by Ivy Books:

ASSASSINATION ON MAYA BAY

A STATION IN THE DELTA

A Novel

John Cassidy

IVY BOOKS • NEW YORK

To Mother,
who *listens*

Ivy Books
Published by Ballantine Books

Library of Congress Catalog Card Number: 79-9819

ISBN 0-8041-0497-2

This edition published by arrangement with
Charles Scribner's Sons

Manufactured in the United States of America

First Ballantine Books Edition: January 1981
Fourth Printing: June 1989

[1]

THE little plane banked for the approach, and Toby Busch peered across the cockpit and out through the window on the pilot's side at the airstrip among the rice paddies, and at the town beyond, which was to be his home for the next two years. He tried to shift his weight in the narrow seat to get a better view, but the Browning 9mm pistol kept getting in his way. The holster was new and stiff, and usually ended up on the seat under his hip. The pilot noticed his struggles and gave him a faint smile, but said nothing.

Throughout his career Toby had always arrived at new posts by air, but never before in a plane as small as this three-passenger Helio, nor at a landing field such as this one, which consisted of nothing more than a dusty strip of packed earth, palm trees at the far end, and a small shack, a revetment made of wooden ammunition boxes, two abandoned sheepsfoot rollers, one jeep, and two sport-shirted Americans at the near end.

This was his second flight with this pilot, in this plane. The pilot was Dino Gallup. The Helio was such a noisy plane that they had not been able to talk very much. Toby knew little about him except that Gallup was the Americanized version of Bacigalupi, and that Dino enjoyed flying and being Italian-American, and was good at both endeavors.

"You'd think," Dino shouted at him above the noise, "that when they make a landing strip they'd study the wind currents. This strip here at My Tho always has a ninety-degree crosswind. Should have been built *this* way." He took one hand off the wheel and gestured across the front of his chest. "I keep telling Air Ops in Saigon that for these short-takeoff and -landing planes, it would be easier to land *across* the runway when you've got a fifteen-knot crosswind, but they won't let me try it!" He laughed. The prospect obviously intrigued him.

"Would it really do it?"

"Almost all of these STOLs would come pretty near it. But because they're so moss-backed up there in Saigon, we always have to wedge into My Tho like a goddamned crab."

Toby squinted at the pilot's face, whose tone said that if he had been in Air Ops in Saigon, he would also have refused permission for such an insane action.

Toby was not a pilot, but he could sense the balance of forces at work on the airplane, and he noted with amusement that his right foot was already twitching in search of a brake pedal.

Dino brought them out of the turn, eased off on the throttle, and nosed the plane down sharply until it seemed that he would skim off the tops of the heads of the waiting men.

"Always like to make a steep approach in Vietnam," he explained. "There are uncouth persons on the ground who like to sit around on approach paths and shoot at airplanes."

In a motion like the rocking of a board swing, the airplane swung back to level flight from the quick descent, and Dino skimmed it steadily along a few inches above the runway. The nose was pointed wildly off to the left of the direction they were moving, but at the instant that the wheels touched the dirt with a gentle tap, Dino deftly swung the nose back toward the palm trees without a bounce or a lurch.

"Outstanding!" Toby exclaimed.

A smile curled Dino's lips, but he did not look away from his task. He reversed the pitch of the propeller, applied the throttle, and brought them to a stop. More adjustments, and he whirled the plane around until it pointed back toward the waiting men. He locked the brakes, left the engine idling, and turned to Toby.

"Toby," he said, "you and I are going to be seeing quite a bit of each other from now on."

"Yes, I suppose I will be flying with you once in a while. All of this is new to me, so I can't tell how often."

"It's not new to me, and I guarantee it'll be pretty often."

"You think so?"

"Yep. Not always with me, of course. Depends on where you go, or whether they give me assignments outside of the Delta Region. Some of the places you'll need a chopper, or if you got a lot of cargo it would need a Porter instead of one of these little Helios. But anyway, I'm going to be a good friend and tell you something right here at the start, even though it's none of my business."

"What's that?"

"That pistol you got on your belt there."

"Yeah?"

"You know who wears the Browning 9mm in Vietnam?"

"No, who?"

"The CIA."

"Yeah?"

"Yep. Nobody but the CIA. It makes you stand out a mile. I knew the minute I saw you at Than Son Nhut the other day that you were CIA—before I ever met you."

"Well, but you're an Air American pilot, so you would know. Who else would figure it out?"

"Everybody," said Dino evenly.

"Well, you know the reason." The reason was that the Browning ammunition was compatible with the Swedish K machine gun, and that all the province offices had been supplied with both weapons, which were judged to be superior to the Colt .45 pistol and its machine-gun counterpart, the famous grease gun.

"I know the reason," Dino said. "Of course, it's no skin off of my ass, but all of us round-eyes in Vietnam already run enough risks as it is—getting shot by a sniper or degutted by some kid with a grenade. But you, you're doubling your risk by telling the whole world you belong to that bad old intelligence agency. So, I just thought I'd give you a tip."

"Thanks."

"Excuse me for butting in?"

Toby laughed at the mild contrition in the dark eyes. "Dino, my business is collecting information. When somebody gives me valuable information without me even asking for it, I'd have to be a damned fool to get mad at him for it."

Dino's face recovered its expression of insouciance. "You're gonna be one of our good ones, Toby," he said happily, and eased the throttle forward.

They fanned up a cloud of dust behind them as they rolled along the strip to the other end. "That's Ski there with Ben," Dino shouted. "Guess he wants me to take him back home, although Can Tho didn't say anything to me about it. John Kunowski's his name. Stationed in Moc Hoa. Doesn't have much to do up there, and he gets lonesome, so he visits around."

Toby had never heard of Ski, but he did know about Ben Compton from the briefings and conversations in Can Tho. The two men came to the side of the plane, Ski carrying a small airline bag.

"Hi, Dino," said Ski, when Dino had throttled back. "How about a ride to Moc Hoa?"

"I'm supposed to go over to Cao Lanh from here. Did you check with Can Tho?"

"Yep. Called Jerry on the sideband a few minutes ago. He said to call in as soon as you're airborne, and he'll adjust your schedule for you."

"Hop in."

The man waited until Toby had removed his own luggage from behind the seat, two large suitcases, battered and labeled by much travel in Europe and South America.

"You're Toby Busch," he said, tossing his little bag into the plane.

"That's right."

"I'm Ski Kunowski." He extended his hand and Toby gripped it.

"Glad to meet you."

"I'm up in Moc Hoa. Come up and see me after you get settled in."

"I may do that," Toby replied. He was being polite. He didn't know whether he would have the opportunity or the desire to make such a visit. Ski wedged himself into the plane and closed the door, and half a minute later Dino had lifted them off the runway and left a welcome silence behind.

"I'm Ben Compton," said the other man, extending his hand.

"I've heard a lot about you," said Toby, returning the firm grip. He knew that Ben was an army major, detached for special civilian duty with the CIA for the pacification program. He had served in the Special Forces, the 82nd Airborne, and had been in Korea and many other insurgency areas in Southeast Asia.

He was tall, slim, blond, and blue-eyed. Pleasant-looking. Might even be called handsome by some, and he moved with the lightness of an athlete. He was neat as a pin, in spite of the dust and heat, and Toby thought that he did not look much like a professional warrior.

They stowed Toby's luggage in the back of the open jeep and clambered into the front seats. "You've kind of got the advantage of me," said Ben, "because I never heard of you until a couple of days ago, and nobody around here knows much about you."

He said this in a cheerful voice, as if he were looking forward to the process of getting acquainted.

"I'm not surprised," said Toby. "I didn't know I was coming to My Tho myself until a couple of days ago."

"Par for the course," murmured Ben. He started the motor and swung the jeep off the end of the runway to the dusty road, heading toward the town.

"All this is new to me," said Toby.

"You mean the Far East?"

"Well, yes, the Far East is new to me—but what I was talking about was the system of assignments. It's the first time in my whole career that I didn't know what job I would have, even before I left my previous post. You know how it is. You're stationed in Athens, and your tour is about up, and they ask you if you want to go to Cairo as . . . well, on some specific assignment." He remembered that this man was military, under contract to the CIA, and that he had no need to know any details of the organization of a station. Ben looked at him curiously.

"But here in Vietnam," Toby went on, "it's different. You arrive in Saigon, just a warm body, with some intelligence operations experience, they hope, and then they shop you around."

"Did they shop you long?"

"No, sir, they sure as hell didn't. I didn't let them. All the section heads at the station there were lined up to interview me, and they all said how good a job they knew I could do in their sections, but I had a good look at that station, and I said to myself, My God, this is just like a headquarters in the field, and I can do without headquarters duty. So, when they said My Tho needed a P officer, I said: 'I accept! Where's My Tho and what's a P officer?' "

Ben laughed delightedly.

"And here I am," Toby concluded, with an expansive sweep of his hand.

"My new boss."

Toby looked at him quickly, but saw that Ben had made the remark with a matter-of-fact good humor. Toby began to relax in the presence of his new associate.

He looked around at the countryside as they bounced down the road. It was flat delta land, with rice paddies, an occasional clump of trees, small thatched dwellings. A little child was sitting on a water buffalo off to their left, and brought him a flashback of a picture he had seen in his sixth-grade geography book. Cochin China.

"So, how are things in Can Tho?" Ben asked.

"Well, I guess they're all right, but I don't know what standard to use. I've never been there before. In fact, I've never been on this side of the Pacific before."

"You're a clean slate."

"Right."

"That can be an advantage."

"I suppose so."

"How do the people in Can Tho think we're doing out here in the provinces?"

"You mean in the pacification program and things like that?"

"Yeah."

"They seem to be fairly optimistic. Not too good, but not too bad."

Ben nodded thoughtfully. "And what do they think in Saigon?"

"The Saigon people seem to think we've got the VC on the run out in the provinces."

"That figures. Saigon says we're winning, Regional

Offices in Can Tho say we're doing fairly well. The picture seems to be colored by the distance."

"And what does the Provincial Pacification Officer from My Tho say?" asked Toby.

"I say we're gettin' our butt waxed."

"The hell you say."

"They're just kickin' the shit out of us here. And not only here, but all over the delta. I can't speak with any authority about the other regions, but the delta, Region Four, is in trouble. Ski is the only guy in the region that isn't as uneasy as hell, and that's because he's got almost no VC up there. Hell, Kien Tuong Province doesn't have much of *anything!*"

"Have all of you been reporting these things to Saigon and Can Tho?"

"They've got the same facts we have. They just interpret them differently."

"It doesn't seem possible that people would put such different interpretations on the same set of facts."

"They look at the statistics. They're at a distance. Statistics is a poor way to estimate your position in unconventional warfare. The closer you get to the action, the less the statistics mean to you."

"Well, they get action in Saigon too, don't they?"

"Oh, sure. They get grenades and bombs and things like that. But there's no doubt about who controls Saigon. And Can Tho, too. Can Tho gets mortared now and then, but they've got the Ninth ARVN close by. But we're out here trying to reclaim towns and hamlets from the VC. The statistics say we're doing it, but a ride around the countryside says like *hell* we are!"

"I've got my work cut out for me, then. We've got to get good intelligence in to Can Tho and Saigon."

"Right."

The countryside certainly didn't look like a battlefield. He saw a man and a woman squatting at work in a large vegetable garden. It was a big enough plot to be a supplier for a town market. The conical straw hats hid the laborers' faces, and gave them the appearance of motionless symbols of the peace that seemed to pervade the land. From the air he had seen the lines of craters made by the B-52 bombs, but from ground level among the rice paddies and vegetable gardens he saw none of the ravages of war. Saigon had seemed to be laced together with barbed wire, and Can Tho looked nearly as besieged as Saigon, but here, where the action was, there seemed to be no trace of it, no fear of it, and no preparations for it.

"You've not only got your work cut out for you, Toby, but you've got an obstacle in Can Tho. Did you know that?"

"You talking about Chet Wolleson?"

"Uh-huh."

"News travels fast." Toby had not known Chet was in Can Tho until he arrived there on his way to My Tho. He wondered whether he would have asked for the My Tho assignment if he had known that Chet would be in the chain of command between him and Saigon.

"Well, I don't really know much about it. The fact is, it's really only a kind of gossip. Little Jack, the PRU adviser, was in Can Tho yesterday. Maybe you saw him?"

"Not that I know of. I don't know the man."

"Well, he heard by the grapevine that Chet doesn't exactly think you're God's gift to the Far East."

"That's putting it mildly."

"How come?"

"We were stationed together in Frankfurt. Chet was my supervisor. A young German agent was killed in one of my operations, and Chet thinks I was either stupid or deceitful, or both. I'll tell you about it someday."

"Well, it's lucky he's just the Deputy Regional Officer in Charge. How does the ROIC himself feel about it?"

"I don't know, but he seems like a bright guy and a nice enough fellow. I have an idea he'll want to make his own judgments about me."

"From what I know of Bill Voigt, I think you're right."

They entered the edge of the town. Toby noted that My Tho was no more oriental in appearance than Saigon or Can Tho, although for that matter he had no idea what would make a city appear to be oriental. Ideographic signs on streets and shop windows? The Vietnamese used the alphabet introduced to them by the Portuguese. Pagoda roofs? One did see an occasional pagoda, and these were classically oriental, but most of the other structures could have been lifted out and placed in any other tropical city he had ever been in, without changing the appearance of the city in the slightest.

They turned in at the gate in a high masonry wall. Two massive panels of steel swung inward as they approached, and the jeep drove through without having to stop. Ben waved to the uniformed guards at the gate, and at the corners of the wall, and they saluted him respectfully.

"Nung guards," said Ben.

"Yeah. I noticed people were always talking about Nung guards in Saigon, as if I would know what they are."

"They're ethnic Chinese," said Ben, "that have lived in Vietnam for God knows how many generations. They're supposed to be more loyal to their families and who knows what else than they are to Vietnam, and very few of them ever join the Viet Cong. So we hire them as guards for our buildings and compounds."

"Are they good at it?"

"Seem dependable. You have to keep your eye on them or they tend to goof off, but they're pretty good."

There were sandbag bunkers at each corner inside the outer wall, and similar bunkers were placed strategically near doors to the main building.

"Looks like the place is expecting an attack," Toby commented.

"We get mortared now and then," Ben replied. "You never know when some sapper squad will come in after a mortar barrage and try to blow you up with a satchel charge."

Toby made no further comment, afraid that he might betray the sense of foreboding that had begun to gnaw at him. They took the luggage through the front door of a building that reflected a kind of Latin or Mediterranean style—plain, even severe, on the outside, but spacious, colorful, and artistic on the inside: the old Roman atrium, or the Latin American patio.

The room they now entered had a high ceiling, from which hung big fans that brought to mind Sidney Greenstreet and fezzes and restless natives. The fans were turning slowly. The air was noticeably cooler inside than it was outside. The floor was tiled in blue, and there were columns, pilasters, and ceiling moldings that spoke of its French colonial origins.

Placed neatly about the room were sofas and occasional chairs that Toby recognized as typical USAID bamboo-and-foam-rubber styles, with tables, lamps, and magazine racks to match. It was comfortable and clean, but far from cozy.

"This is a sort of common room," Ben said. "Then we've got the bar over there in that corner, and stereo equipment, and a movie setup, when we can get the film."

The bar corner relieved the severity of the decor to some extent. The bar was of dark wood with high stools. Small easy chairs and cocktail tables nearby gave the scene an appearance of intimacy and comfort.

"We don't try to air-condition this space," Ben went on. "It's too big, for one thing, and the way it's built, high ceiling and fans and all, it stays fairly cool."

"Seems very nice."

"Out in back there's another building. Used to be servants' quarters, I think. We built a breezeway that leads from that door over there back to the other building, and made that building into our office. Living spaces are upstairs."

There was a stairway to the right of the front entrance, and they ascended it to the second floor. Ben and Little Jack had rooms opposite one another at one end of the corridor, and shared a bathroom. There was a guest room farther along, and at the end was the room that T. C. James had occupied. That room would now be Toby's. It had a private bath.

Ben opened the door to Toby's new room, and a wave of chilled air struck them. There was a large window on the far side, but Toby could not see through the heavy, translucent curtains. The panes, he knew, would be made of Plexiglas, as most windows were in this warring land. An air conditioner throbbed in its niche at the base of the window, and beyond that, somewhere in the rear of the building, he could hear the persistent muffled roar of the diesel generator, a sound he had heard wherever he walked or stayed since he had arrived in Vietnam. The American presence was peppered through the country, and no local power supply, however adequate it might be for the modest needs of the Vietnamese, could begin to satisfy the American appetite for light, refrigeration, air conditioning, appliances, and gadgets. Wherever they settled, the Americans brought their appliances, and the power to run them.

They put the luggage on the low double bed and Toby looked around. There was a desk against one wall, a small table, an easy chair with a floor lamp, a big steel wardrobe, a chest of drawers, and a large mirror affixed to the wall. On another wall were a number of hooks, from which hung a Swedish K, with several magazines of ammunition in a satchel beneath it, a steel helmet, an M-2 carbine, a flak jacket, and miscellaneous web gear.

The sight of this battle paraphernalia made him uneasy again. He had coped with danger many times, but it had never been the danger of open combat. His was a profession of wits, and if your wits were sharper than your adversary's you could foresee the risks and avoid them. If you used your wits to avoid combat, you would be a coward. What would combat be like? How would he handle himself if it came?

"You've got your own bathroom, through that door there," Ben said. "Little Jack and I have got a big one at the other end of the hall."

"How is it between you and him?" Toby asked. "You being a major and him a sergeant, and both of you living in the same quarters and sharing a bathroom?"

"For this work we're civilians. He hasn't been here long, and I haven't been able to get a good judgment of his professional skills, but we get along OK. It's 'Ben' and 'Little Jack' while we're in this situation. The minute we got back in uniform, of course, we'd be military again."

"That makes sense."

"I'll leave you to get settled," Ben said. "When you're ready, or if you need anything in the meantime, I'll be in the office."

"Thanks. I'll be down shortly."

Ben went out and closed the door.

Toby had had the impulse to say to Ben that he had impressed him very much with his simplicity, directness, and intelligence, and that he had a conviction they would get along well and probably become fast friends. In the Tau Kappa Epsilon house at Iowa University years ago, he would have said so to a new friend. But in his years of clandestine operations he had had to learn to resist such impulses. There would be plenty of time for Ben to discover that Toby was well impressed with him, and was pleased to be associated with him. If, in the meantime, it turned out that Ben was not quite what a first impression showed him to be, Toby was not committed to him in any way.

He began to unpack. Gregarious by instinct, he hated these restrictions on human relationships. It was one of the parts of his profession that he found unvaryingly distasteful. His entire career was one of dealing with, and using, human beings, and he had had to train himself away from his instinctive reactions to them. He had seen too many cases, some of them involving himself, in which a charming agent, who seemed to be such a kindred spirit in ideas and philosophies, sincerely dedicated to the free and messy political life of nontotalitarian governments, would turn out to be nothing more than an expert con man who would give you false information, run nonexistent collection nets, and embezzle your money, at the same time slapping you on the back. If you had become close friends with the agent, you found yourself excusing him, justifying him, defending him—maybe even lying about him to headquarters, a deadly mistake in the intelligence business.

He smiled a little sadly as he put away the neatly ironed clothes. Mary Lynn was meticulous about keeping his clothing neatly arranged and spotless, and this care for his things had been so consistent and unfailing through the years that he had almost ceased to notice it. He noticed it now. Those swift and efficient hands reached all the way from Iowa to touch his heart with a little pang of loneliness as he unpacked. He wondered, with guilty amusement, if he had been married so long that he would miss her attention to his clothing as much as he would miss her attention to his sexual needs. No, it hadn't reached that point yet.

He did miss her already. She had gone with him through all the years and had borne up well under the pressures of secrecy and the irritations of making a home for a man who could never discuss his work, even with his wife, and who did a great deal of that work at outlandish hours of the night. He had depended on her, as well, to bring the children through the first years, when they could be told only his cover story, to an age where their watchful eyes and youthful curiosity would at last become more dangerous than their knowledge of the truth. Then, they were told the truth—just enough to satisfy their curiosity and compel their silence.

She had had the choice: a safe-haven residence in Taiwan or Hong Kong, or a separation allowance and residence in the United States. She did not hesitate. She was now in a small rented house in her hometown in Iowa. It had been a joy for her to move back to that tranquil town, a few blocks from her parents, their polyglot children adapting to Iowa schools as they had adapted to European and South American schools in the past.

He would now see them twice a year. He had never been away from them for such a long time, but they were comfortable and safe, and they were learning what it was like to have a grandma and grandpa. That was good.

He showered and put on one of the clean sport shirts, tan slacks, and brown loafers. Mary Lynn thought this had been a directed assignment. When you got a directed assignment, which was often talked about in the CIA but rarely happened, you had your choice. You went or you resigned. You agreed to those terms before you were ever hired.

But this assignment had been directed, not by the CIA, but by his own inner compulsions. He had volunteered for the duty. Even as sensible a woman as Mary Lynn would never have understood why. This was where the action was today, and a man in this business wanted action. The days of the cold war, when he had cut his operational teeth against the clandestine power of the Soviet bloc pushing against the eastern borders of Europe—those days were gone. The power was now pushing, indirectly but relentlessly, in Vietnam, and he wanted to be there.

Mary Lynn was afraid for him. She had cried when he left. He had not seen tears in those lovely hazel eyes in a long time, especially tears shed about him, and they had touched him deeply.

Another reason for volunteering was the question of his record. So far as he could tell, the Frankfurt incident, although a serious setback, had not blighted his career. He was sure that there were some big, unanswered questions in his file, and that in a pinch, where a promotion or a choice assignment might hang in the balance, that unresolved difficulty might swing the balance against him. If he could turn in a good performance, under conditions of danger and hardship, having volunteered for the duty, that would also be in his file, and would tend to resolve in his favor any doubts from previous duty.

He went down the stairs and across the common room, elated and vaguely apprehensive. He was about to plunge once more into the tangle of the work he loved, and this time the tangle was to be complicated by an oriental setting and a vicious war.

[2]

Toby opened the door to the breezeway, walked across the short distance to the other building, and entered the office. Ben was seated at a desk on one side of the large room, and there was an empty desk on the side opposite him, which Toby surmised would be his own. Behind those desks, in one corner, amid a clutter of file cabinets and typewriter tables, was a third, slightly smaller desk. It had manuals, ammo magazines, a carbine, and other oddments of military equipment on its surface or leaned against it. That one had to be Little Jack's desk.

One wall of the office was almost completely covered by a large relief map of the province. One thing a war did for a country, he thought, was map it down to the last detail.

In the other far corner was a secretary's desk, where a woman was seated with her back to them. She was slender, and had glossy black hair that flowed down her back to her waist, accentuating the pale blue sheen of her *ao dai*. Toby noted the perfect curve of her waistline under the garment, and could see why the *ao dai* was often called the best legacy the French had left to the Vietnamese. American women, who could look so ravishing and luscious in other garments, usually succeeded only in looking vulgar when they put on an *ao dai.*

The woman was concentrating on a long document in her typewriter and did not stop work. Something about her posture made Toby think she would be pretty, but then he thought once again about how wrong impulsive judgments can be, and he inwardly prepared himself to see a broad, coarse face, perhaps pleasant, but unrefined and plain.

"Get settled?" Ben asked.

"Yeah. Room seems fine. How about drinking water?"

"Mrs. Chao boils it for us. She's our cook. You'll find bottles of drinking water in the refrigerator in the kitchen, and in the one behind the bar too."

"Good."

Ben explained the office arrangements briefly, identifying desks and safes. It was expected that Toby would use T.C.'s desk.

"Where is Little Jack?" Toby asked, as they came to the cluttered area.

"He's out at the PRU compound. They're going out on an operation tonight. A VC printing press in a village to the north of here. They're going to try to capture it if they can—or destroy it, if not."

"Little Jack is infantry?"

"That's right. Master Sergeant John Horner. He was in Korea, and he's knocked around quite a bit since then. Special Forces, and so on."

"Is he good?"

"Well, let's put it this way," said Ben with a laugh. "Little Jack doesn't hide his light under a bushel. If you ask him, he'll tell you he's damned good, although he'll say it in a real modest way."

There was no rancor in Ben's voice, but Toby realized that his direct question had been evaded.

"And back here in this other corner," said Ben, leading Toby to where the woman was still busily typing, "is Therese. Therese, I'd like for you to meet our new boss, Mr. Busch."

The woman turned in her swivel chair, and Toby was barely able to suppress a gasp of surprise. Therese was beautiful. Her complexion was impeccable, her mouth soft and full, and her eyes had just enough of the oriental to make them the most inviting and bewitching eyes he had ever gazed into. When she arose, unsmiling, and bowed to him ever so slightly, the lines and movement of her body completed the picture of perfection. She was slender, but there was nothing boyish about her body.

"How do you do, Mr. Busch," she said. Her English seemed fluent, but there were traces of Vietnamese tonality in it.

"I am happy to meet you, Therese. But shouldn't I call you something besides a first name? You are obviously not a little girl."

She did not laugh or smile. She did not seem surly or even timid, but rather sad, and perhaps worried. "Yes," she replied, "I am not a little girl, Mr. Busch." He liked her voice, too. It was soft and sweet. "I am a war widow. But most Americans cannot pronounce my Vietnamese name, so I ask them to call me Therese. It is my Catholic name."

"You are Catholic, then?"

"Yes. I am from Hanoi. One of the refugees."

Hanoi! thought Toby with a start, then cursed himself. Why did he have to pin everybody to an ideological board the minute he met them?

"All right, then," he said. "Therese it is."

"I believe we do not worry so much about names as Americans do," she said quietly, and Toby thought there might be an ever-so-gentle rebuke in her tone.

"Perhaps not. Anyway, I'll let you get back to your work." She nodded politely and returned to her typewriter.

"Now, why don't I show you the rest of the establishment?" Ben suggested. Toby nodded, and Ben led him off to the other rooms and outbuildings of the little compound. One was the small warehouse where Ben kept the supplies for his pacification teams—black pajamas, weapons, ammunition, foodstuffs, first-aid kits, books, office supplies. Off in one corner of the main structure, heavily bunkered with sandbags, was their main storage area. It contained boxes of ammunition, jerry cans of fresh water and fuel, boxes of C rations, racks of rifles and submachine guns, grenades, helmets, and other equipment.

Seeing the weapons reminded Toby. "Dino told me I'd be better off without the Browning pistol," he said.

"Dino is absolutely right," Ben replied laconically.

"Here." He handed Toby a Colt .45 pistol in a leather holster. "You can find yourself a web belt for that over there on that rack."

"I've already got the belt."

"There's plenty of ammo in that case over there, and extra clips. Ever handle one of these cannons before?"

"A few times. Years ago."

"We can go over to the police firing range as often as we like, to keep ourselves sharp. I can refresh you on stripping and cleaning it."

"Thanks. I feel less like a billboard for the CIA already."

"Not everybody's sharp like Dino, but he's right. You're better off without the Browning. It's a great pistol, and packs a wallop, but not the wallop *that* big old monster does. That baby will stop a man cold."

"I hope it doesn't come to that," Toby said unthinkingly, and Ben gave him a puzzled look.

They climbed a small stairway to the roof of the house. The roof was flat, and the outer walls of the structure came up to form a parapet about a foot high all around it. The center was bare, but at each corner there was a small, low revetment of sandbags. In and around these revetments were various weapons, one fifty-caliber machine gun on a tripod with a canvas cover, a 57mm recoilless rifle, two M-2 rocket launchers, with boxes of rockets and grenades.

"Little Jack scrounged most of this stuff," Ben said with a mixture of amusement and exasperation. "You'd think he was getting ready to defend Fort Donelson against Grant."

"It looks like he could do it."

"Who knows, maybe it will come in handy some time. Anyway, we've got a drill in case of attack. Little Jack stands by the switches till I get in position on the roof. When I give him the signal, he turns on the floodlights. Then he mans that corner over there. You'll take another corner, and I'll have this one."

"That leaves one corner unmanned."

"Yep. But, hell, the best military units in the world are never up to complete strength in combat. There's always a corner unmanned somewhere. You just fight the battle as it develops."

Toby thought that the floodlights would be as much of an advantage to the Viet Cong as to the defenders, but Ben reassured him. The lights were halfway up the outer walls, and would not silhouette the men on the roof. They would give the defenders a first look at the area in case of an attack, and would destroy the enemy's night vision for the first crucial minutes. An assault force would shoot out the lights as soon as they could, but while they were doing so, the defenders would be shooting at *them*.

There was a house directly across the street, another at some distance on one side, a vacant lot on the other side, and a small canal or irrigation ditch along the back. The sides of the canal had been sloped in such a way that it offered no concealment from observation from the house.

Toby looked at the area, and at the weaponry and the emplacements, lost in thought for some time. "Jesus!" he exclaimed at last. "Is this house in that much danger?"

"How much danger do you mean?"

"So much that all this is necessary?"

"Toby," said Ben slowly, "I think I have kind of the same reaction in a way, because I'm not much on defensive warfare. But where you've got to centralize your activities in one spot in a combat zone, you just naturally prepare as much as you can for *anything*. It would be suicide not to be ready . . . and that may be one value of having all this stuff. They probably know we've got it, and they have to take it into consideration in any plans they may have for this place. They'll know that an assault against us is going to hurt a lot of people."

They went back down to the office, where Ben showed him through the files and extracted from the safes a number of briefing booklets, operational records, chronological files of cables and dispatches.

"I don't want to try to teach an expert how to suck eggs," said Ben, "but I have an idea that if you go through this material first, you'll find that seeing people and places around here will fit in a lot better. And here is one file you ought to study harder than anything else, because this is something that is going to be in our hair for a long time around here."

He handed Toby a thick folder, labeled YENAN BATTALION.

"Oh, yes, I've heard them talking about this in Saigon and Can Tho," said Toby. He sat down at his desk.

Ben perched on the edge of it, placed the folder on the desk, and tapped it with his finger. "This is a main force battalion, and it's usually about four hundred strong. And I wish to God I had an outfit like that fighting under *me.*"

"Good, huh?"

"Any way you look at them. Tough, savvy fighters. Elusive. Well led. They're tearing one part of this province to shreds, and we can't ever pin them down with a big enough force to destroy them."

"They don't operate anywhere except in one part of this province?"

"That's the way it looks. And they're so famous on both sides that they don't have any trouble getting local force battalions to cooperate with them when they need it."

"But I thought main force battalions are like regular army, and the local forces are a kind of militia."

"Yep."

"So how come the Yenan Battalion confines its operations to just one area like this?"

"Damned if I know. It sure isn't normal. The only thing we can figure out is that they're getting ready for something big. We're not sure what it is, but we know that an outfit like that, operating in one particular area, sending local forces on minor operations, ambushing people, assaulting our pacification teams—we know they're workin' on some kind of a plan. They're harrassing us, and at the same time they're training themselves."

"What for?"

"I wish to God I knew. I guess that'll be your department—finding out what they're up to."

"Thanks," said Toby drily.

"We've got some ideas, though. It's pretty certain that they'll have to do whatever it is before the next monsoon season. The pattern of their operations doesn't center on anything in particular, although in this province its heaviest against My Tho. I don't know details about other provinces, but they all seem to have similar patterns. Personally, I think something big is going to happen around Tet."

"What makes you think so?"

"Rumors. A report here and there that Tet is the target

date for something. Some people say that the VC wouldn't dare violate the sacred New Year celebration . . . but I don't know. The tempo of their operations seems to point that way."

Toby remembered that his first home leave came about a month after Tet. He made a mental calculation. "That's less than five months away."

"Right."

"Have we got any collection operations at all?"

"Intelligence collection operations?"

"Yes."

"You'd have to look in the files. I don't know much about intelligence operations. My guess is that we haven't got a thing."

"And only five months to go? My God, you can't start with nothing, without even knowing the language, and expect to set up a good collection operation and get anything authenticated and reliable out of it in less than five months. You might do it in peacetime in a European situation, but not here in a combat zone."

"If you don't, we'll be fighting blind," said Ben.

"Does Saigon know about this? Nobody up there mentioned it to me."

"They've probably got some indications. But a lot of what I've told you is something I've just sensed in my gut. How do you report that to Saigon? A lot of the other fellows around the country have got the same feeling, but it's just a feeling. Something big is coming. If we're not ready for it, we're going to get wiped out."

"Five months." Toby stared at the folder.

"This Yenan Battalion is under the command of a guy they call the Tiger. He is also sometimes referred to as Tu Binh, but that's not likely to be his real name. It's like Therese says. The Vietnamese take names kind of casually. But, anyway, the Tiger has got good collection operations, all right. He knows every move we make. Almost as if he had somebody sitting here listening to us."

With a jolt Toby thought of Therese, typing away busily, well within the range of their voices. He must speak to Ben about this casual discussion of confidential information.

"Most important," Ben was saying, "is that he is one of

the best tacticians and combat leaders I've ever been up against. He's great, and if he lives through whatever it is that's coming, he'll be one of the military leaders of North Vietnam eventually."

"A pro, huh?"

"Yes, sir. That man plans and executes military operations without a flaw. He swoops in, tears his target to pieces, and gets away fast, without losing more than one or two of his men at the most."

"Well, I'd better get to work then," said Toby.

"Yeah. I'll leave you to your reading. Tomorrow, I suggest we go over to meet the Province Senior Adviser, and then go on over to the Special Police Office and meet the head man."

"That's Colonel Manh?"

"Right. Your counterpart. You'll be in liaison with him, and he knows who you're with. He's a decent guy, and his men seem to be pretty good, but they're up against experts, and they don't know shit from Shinola about intelligence operations."

"They don't?"

"Nope. Neither do I, Toby. We sure have been needing somebody around here that does."

"But you had some training before you came here?"

"Yeah, but most of it was on the pacification program. Which, of course, is my job here. But I ought to know something about intelligence, too. We can't put these teams in contested villages blind—or anyway, we *shouldn't* do it. The VC can come in on them at will and cut them to pieces. Even a sloppy bunch of local forces can do it if they catch them by surprise."

"I can believe it."

"That's why I think the new ICEX program is so important."

The utterance of those secret initials, with the beautiful Northerner in the room, caused Toby's skin to prickle. "We'd better talk about that later, Ben," he said peremptorily, so as to cut off the talk immediately, and he sensed the instinctive military response—obedience. Ben stood up.

"If you need anything, let me know," he said quietly, and went back to his desk.

* * *

Toby spent the rest of the afternoon delving in the records and files of the office.

He was perplexed at much of what he saw. Nothing like this had ever happened to him before. A small office, deep in a country that, under other circumstances, would have had only moderate interest for his agency. In liaison with a Special Police force whose functions were an odd mixture of military and police operations. Collecting order-of-battle intelligence, which was outside the charter of the CIA and to a great extent beyond its competence. That was what the Defense Intelligence Agency was for.

Most worrisome of all was the prospect of working in clandestine operations in a culture that was new to him and a language that he could hardly count to ten in. He would have to work through an interpreter, or through agents who spoke English. European languages were only a matter of time and concentration, for they shared a common pool of origin. Oriental languages were different, and there would not be time for him to learn the language well enough to operate in it. French was becoming less and less helpful as years passed in Vietnam, so that even his rather pedestrian French would be of little use to him.

And not one single going operation for the collection of intelligence!

Whatever intelligence was in the files—and there was almost nothing worthy of the name—had come from casual informants, whose authenticity and worth were not established, or had been passed to them from the Special Police, derived from their own collection operations, about which this office knew almost nothing.

Well, he'd have to change all this.

At five o'clock Therese put away her work, closed and locked the safe by her desk, and moved toward the door. She paused by his desk.

"Will you need me for anything more today, sir?"

"No, nothing, thank you."

"You come to our country at a bad time," she said, "but I hope you will like it."

"I like it already, Therese."

"I hope you will be pleased with my work, also."

"I'm sure I will. I notice you don't waste time."

"Vietnam has no time to waste," she said, and with a slight bow she turned and walked out the door.

"She seems so solemn," Toby commented to Ben. "Doesn't she ever smile?"

"Not very often. She's a troubled young woman."

"Where does she live?"

"She lives in a kind of a slum or tenement district across town a little way. She's got a little motorbike she rides."

Even as he spoke they heard the buzz of a small motor, and the gates clanked as she was let out of the compound.

"She sure is a knockout," Toby mused.

"I figured you would notice that."

"The reason I clammed up a minute ago is that ICEX is a restricted program, and I'm sure she hasn't been cleared to hear about it."

"I guessed as much," said Ben, shortly.

"I don't know even whether she's been cleared properly for the job she does have. Do you?"

"All I know is that T.C. hired her. I guess he had her cleared. You could look it up. I never had access to the security papers."

"I'll look tomorrow. If there's any doubt about her, I want to get it cleared up right now, because if we have to let her go for some reason I want to do it before I fall in love and try to run away to the jungle with her."

Ben laughed gleefully. "Yes, sir, she sure makes the old juices run."

They went into the main building, and Ben put a record on the stereo while Toby mixed drinks. They sat at the bar talking quietly of inconsequential things until Mrs. Chao, a slight, rather wrinkled and graying woman, announced that dinner was ready.

The dinner was delicious, although Toby did not recognize most of the dishes. Ben named them for him. "Vietnamese. You can't get it in a restaurant, even in Vietnam, because Vietnamese cooking doesn't adapt itself well to restaurant service. This is Mrs. Chao's way of saying welcome."

Toby thanked Mrs. Chao and complimented her on the meal, and she beamed at him.

After dinner they sat at the bar again and talked, getting acquainted. From force of habit, Toby got most of the information and gave very little. His evasion of questions he did not want to answer was as smooth as it was unconscious on his part, and it did not dampen the cordiality of the moment.

Ben had been in Vietnam in one capacity or another for many years, and had been about to return to military duty in the United States when he was contacted by a CIA representative. He was signed up under a contract program, trained in the United States and in the pacification school at Vung Tau, and now had forty-two pacification teams under his supervision in Dinh Tuong Province. He had made one attempt at marriage, but his wife had found no way to domesticate the man or to steer him into a different profession, and the divorce had been amicable.

They spoke of Little Jack and the Provincial Reconnaissance Units. Armed intelligence collection squads. Night fighters. Man for man the best warriors in Vietnam, on either side. Many of them ex-Viet Cong, who had "rallied" to the government side, as the peculiar English of the war described it, under the Chieu Hoi program. Each province in Vietnam had one of these units, about a hundred strong, "advised" by an American.

Ben had no authority over Little Jack, since the PRU program was not within the structure of his pacification operations. They collaborated in the defense arrangements for the house, but did not work together. Little Jack would be Toby's responsibility to supervise.

Toby was interested in combat experiences, but on that subject Ben's evasive skill matched his own. He merely steered the conversation away from tales of battle. Toby wondered why.

A nightcap, and Toby noticed the first, familiar rumblings of a coming diarrhea. He was not surprised. It never failed. In fact, he was surprised that it had not come sooner. A couple of days of intestinal upset, perhaps with some medication to ease it if it got too severe, and his system would be adjusted to the intestinal flora of his new location. He was glad he had a bathroom to himself. He knew he'd spend some time there tonight, often in waves of nausea that would make him want above all to be alone.

He said good night to Ben, who was sitting pensively in an easy chair, toying with a glass of whisky and water, listening to a tape of Roger Williams. Toby was not sorry to leave. The arpeggios and filigrees of Roger Williams distressed and bored him. Amplified and purified as they were by this high-quality electronic equipment, they filled the room from wall to wall with cascades of sterile syrup. Ben obviously was lost in pleasure among them.

Toby's room was cool, so cool that by the time he had brushed his teeth and prepared for bed he was slightly chilly, and he pulled the light woolen blanket over him gratefully. The Vietnamese must think the Americans insane, to spend so much fuel and machinery to cool a room down in the tropic night, and then put on a blanket to keep warm. The diarrhea had not yet come, and he drifted pleasantly into sleep.

He knew that he had not been asleep long when the wrenching of his gut awoke him. He turned on the light by the bed, slipped his feet into two plastic zoris, walked to the bathroom, switched on the light there, and sat down for the first of what he knew would be several convulsive evacuations that night. This first one was violent enough to make him feel justified in taking Lomotil, and he resolved to get a couple of pills from his kit before he went back to bed.

The twisting and heaving of his bowels subsided and he turned to get paper, and cursed the empty cardboard tube on the roller. He would tear the hide off whoever was responsible for this. He looked around the room. There had to be spare rolls. Where would they be?

There was a cabinet on the far wall, and he got up and waddled over to it.

He felt, rather than heard, the tremendous explosion, and the next thing he knew he was lying flat on the floor, halfway out of the bathroom door, which had been blown from its hinges by the blast.

For several seconds he lay there, trying to collect his thoughts, taking a mental stock of his body.

Ben burst from his own room, carrying a carbine. His eyes darted here and there, and he stepped across Toby's prone form and looked at the bathroom.

There was a gaping hole in the outer wall, beside the stool, and another one in the opposite wall where the projectile had exited, The air was cloudy with plaster dust and the smell of explosive.

"B-forty," said Ben tersely.

The B-40 rocket, hand-launched. The old German *Panzerfaust*, smaller than the American bazooka, but with astounding powers of penetration. A favorite weapon of the VC—light and powerful.

Ben turned off all the lights in the room and bathroom, and shouted something in Vietnamese down the inner corridor.

"I sure hope that's the right word for floodlights," he muttered, "and I hope Mrs. Chao knows what switches I mean." He stepped into the bathroom again and flung open the window and stood waiting. The area around the house was suddenly bathed in a brilliant light. Toby staggered weakly to his feet and looked out the window in the direction Ben was staring. Ben had calculated the trajectory and knew exactly where to look.

There, on the slope of the canal, was a small figure clad in dark clothing. The figure was standing upright, intent upon fitting another round into his rocket launcher.

"I've got to remember to get a heavy rifle in my room," Ben murmured. "This thing will have to do for now." He raised the carbine to his shoulder, fired one round, and the figure in the ditch crumpled silently to the ground.

They waited for a time, motionless.

"What are we waiting for?" asked Toby.

"To see if any more of them are around."

"Oh."

Ben called something in Vietnamese through the open window, went back into the bedroom, and turned on the low bed lamp. "Are you all right?" he asked, coming back to where Toby was crouched in the bathroom.

"I think so," Toby replied. He was nervous to the point of making inane jokes. "It's a hell of a time to try to kill a man, right when he's taking a crap. I thought there was some kind of a gentlemen's agreement in war that that was one time you didn't fire on the enemy."

"Were you sitting on the can?" Ben asked, astonished.

"No, I was looking for toilet paper. Some idiot had left the paper holder empty."

Ben burst out laughing, and Toby glowered at him.

"Frankly," he said, "I don't see anything so goddamned funny about it. Ridiculous and stupid, yes, but not funny."

"I'm sorry, Toby. I couldn't help thinking that Chi Hai has just saved your life."

"Who?"

"Chi Hai. That's Mrs. Chao's daughter. She takes care of the bedrooms. If she had put paper there, half of you would still be sitting on that stool. Look." He switched on the light.

Toby saw with horror that he had been sitting squarely in the rocket's path. If he had not moved at that precise moment, it would have caught him slightly above the waist, and would surely have cut him in two.

Ben turned off the light.

"Are you going out to get the body?" Toby asked.

"The guards will handle things from here on."

"What will they do with it?"

"They'll take the weapons and leave the body."

"Leave it?"

"Yeah. His family will come to pick him up. No sense making it worse than it is. They'll come in the dark and they'll take care of him."

"His family? Do families travel with the VC?"

"This was a local kid. I've seen him before. Probably a member of the local force battalion or a sapper squad."

"Just decided he was going to come and shoot at us?"

"Make no mistake about it, Toby," said Ben, "that wasn't just a little adventure. The VC don't operate that way. It had a purpose. Probably just wanted to let us know that they knew you had arrived. Kill you if they could, but even if they didn't we'd know that they know who you are and where you sleep. It's part of the terror."

"You mean that rocket was really aimed at *me*, and not just the house?"

"No question about it. Why would he aim at the corner if he was just aiming at the house? That fellow has probably been out there in the shadows for some time getting ready to fire. When your light came on he knew what was up, and knew he shouldn't miss the opportunity."

"Christ, what a thing to tell a man that's already got the shits!" It had never occurred to him that the enemy might zero in on him, personally. As a part of their composite foe, yes, but as a single, personal enemy—it was frightening. Frightening, hell! It was terrifying!

"Yes, sir," said Ben lightly, "it is some initiation to Region Four."

"If it wasn't for the honor of the thing . . ." Toby began, but couldn't remember the rest of the quip. Then he remembered his condition. "Ben, will you get the hell out of here and let me clean myself up?"

"OK, Toby. Just don't turn the lights up any higher."

"I won't. But Ben . . ." he looked earnestly at Ben, who had turned at the door to face him, ". . . are you sure that kid's dead? Maybe . . ."

"He won't fire at you again, Toby."

"That's not what I mean. I mean, if he's only wounded, and out there on the ground."

"He's dead, Toby. I hit him right in the heart."

"How do you know?"

"That's where I aimed. At that distance, and with a stationary target, I don't miss."

Ben left, and Toby stood for a long time as if in a trance. His mind could not cope with, could not even accept as real, the events of the past five minutes.

Slowly he went back into the bathroom and drew some water and washed. He climbed back into bed, knowing that sleep was far away.

[3]

BILL Voigt sat in his office in the somewhat dilapidated building assigned to the CIA's Regional Officer in Charge within the CORDS compound in Can Tho, and studied the latest ICEX outline from Saigon. Groups of capital letters were peppered liberally all over the page, initials so pervasive and familiar that the people who dealt with them rarely pronounced the letters separately, but simply spoke most of them as the words they appeared to be.

A faint smile played about his lips as he began to read. Here he was, a ROIC sitting in a CORDS office studying an ICEX paper detailing a program to attack the VC by coordinated work between the MACV and the ARVN with the CIA doing the coordinating. Newcomers ought to be given a course in acronyms before they studied Vietnamese.

Come to think of it, you would need more than just a course in acronyms, because sometimes the full title told you no more than the initials did. Military Assistance Command, Vietnam, and Army of the Republic of Vietnam were straightforward and simple. But what in hell was meant by Civilian Operations and Revolutionary Development Support? Bill knew what CORDS was and did, but that title certainly didn't say it. Maybe just U.S. Civilian Operations, Vietnam?

As to the Intelligence Coordination and Exploitation program, whatever its name or cabalistic sign might be, it was one of the first really sensible approaches to the intelligence business he had seen since arriving in Vietnam. Here at last was a plan, something he and his fellow operations officers could put into effect in a logical and organized way. Not that he had many experienced operations officers in his region. None of the other regions did either, for that matter, but he thought he had a more valid complaint than the others, since the delta had about 40 percent of the population and more than half of the VC in South Vietnam. That was the reason he had been so pleased with the assignment of Toby Busch to Region IV, and the reason he had forthwith confirmed Toby's assignment to My Tho, in the province of Dinh Tuong. Dinh Tuong was the worst trouble spot of all the fourteen provinces in the region.

Toby would know what to do, or would soon learn. Of course, the other province officers would learn too, but they were not instructed by the years of previous experience that Toby had. Most of them were nonstaffers, contract men, hastily recruited, trained, and placed. But astonishingly good men for such a large and hurried effort. Ex-smoke-jumpers, ex-Green Berets, ex-policemen, almost any active, physically demanding profession might provide grist for the CIA's pacification mill.

He shook his head slowly as he read. Even the best schemes in the world have got to suffer the ministrations of the bureaucrats. Words like "neutralization," "dichotomies," "interface," and "thrust" leaped out at him from places where simple words would have sufficed, and he rubbed his forehead wearily.

Chet Wolleson poked his head in the door. "That pouch just came in from Saigon," he said. "We got the file on Busch."

"Good. Let me have a look at it."

Chet stepped in and placed a folder on his desk.

"It's a shame it can't be his complete personnel folder," said Bill.

"Yeah. But I've never known headquarters to trust a complete folder to a pouch or a field office."

"No. Will this one contain an account of the Frankfurt incident?"

"I doubt it. Most of that was never put in writing, anyway. But I can fill you in on it."

"Are you going to be able to give it to me without bias, Chet?"

"Yes, I can," said Chet in a cold, even tone. "I don't make any secret of the fact that I don't like him, but I wouldn't give you any account that wasn't true and factual."

"All right. Let me go through this, then we can talk."

Chet left, and Bill opened the file. He folded the top documents over and began reading from the bottom of the pile, which was the beginning.

Tolliver Busch. Bill smiled. He had wondered when he first saw that name in the cable the other day if the man would be nicknamed Tolly. He liked Toby better.

Graduate of Iowa University. Joined agency in 1954. Training records excellent. Cold war days. Tours in Athens, Budapest, Frankfurt, and Bogotá. One short assignment to headquarters. Frequent TDY assignments throughout Europe and Latin America. Temporary duty assignments of such frequency indicated that the man had something rather special in the way of operational skills and drive. People knew him, knew what he could do, and asked to have him sent to them when they needed to have it done, whatever it was. Languages: German, native fluency. Greek and Spanish good. Adequate French, and some Hungarian.

Fitness reports. Bill frowned. Annual fitness reports could be the most misleading documents in a man's file. The natural decency of most rating officers, and the requirements of the form, made for a lot of high-blown rhetoric. Few officers were rated below the *excellent* category, because the erosion of the ratings over the years had brought about a situation where any man who was rated *good* was really poor, and if he was rated *fair*, he was an unmitigated disaster. When a supervisor wanted to show a man to be truly and exceptionally good under this system, he had to use words and phrases that indicated a da Vinci-like mind, and a Christlike character.

Tolliver Busch's fitness reports showed that his supervisors had had an especially high regard for him, until one report from Frankfurt, which damned him roundly with some seemingly mild criticism. Subsequent reports were undoubtedly colored by that one. Supervisors were not supposed to see previous reports by other supervisors before making out their own, but it happened, and a bad report would naturally tend to soften or deflect the impulse to praise.

Or perhaps Busch *had* gone into a slump—a decline?

". . . in this instance showed operational judgment that was not as carefully reasoned as it might have been, and caused serious disruption in one particular operation, with repercussions in other operations of this station."

In the language of the fitness report, that phrase said that Tolliver Busch had done something incredibly stupid.

That report was signed by Chester Wolleson.

Names of other supervisors. Some of them Bill knew personally, some of them by name only, and some of them not at all. Fitness reports never included any operational details, however. He could not tell exactly what it was Toby had done.

He closed the file, drummed nervously on the desk for a moment, leaned back in his chair, and lit a cigarette.

Toby had volunteered for assignment to Vietnam. That could mean any number of things. Chet had been the key supervisor who had given him his bad fitness report. Had probably brought delays to otherwise merited promotion. Perhaps had set a ceiling on Toby's career that might never be lifted.

Chet Wolleson was a good operations officer. He came recommended highly, and Bill had been pleased at the way Chet had taken hold of his responsibilities. Chet wanted and demanded action, and he gave as good as he got.

On the other hand, he had less tact and sensitivity than a person needed in a supervisory position. Energetic himself, and dedicated to the job during every waking hour, he could not understand anyone who could take his mind off work for a time to relax. He tended to be impatient with associates who were not as unrelentingly serious about the job as he was.

Admittedly, his blunt and often brutal treatment of those in his charge was accompanied by an equally fierce loyalty to the same persons when outsiders were involved. He could flay a subordinate alive, and five minutes later send an acid cable defending that same subordinate against any questions or insinuations from headquarters.

Toby Busch might be an exception. He detested Busch.

What a can of worms! Bill crushed out his cigarette and pressed a button, and Laura came to the door. She was plump and dark, a pleasant young woman, and a surprisingly good secretary. The best ones were not usually offered, or would not accept, assignments to Vietnam.

"Will you ask Mr. Wolleson to come in, please?"

"Yes, sir."

He leafed idly through the file as he waited. He wondered what kind of an impression his own file would make on somebody higher up the line. Again the faint smile tugged at the corners of his mouth. It would certainly be a bigger file than this one, old-time intelligence whore that he was. OSS in Burma and the Philippines. Changeover to CIA, cold war, Korea, Japan, Thailand. For a man from Massachusetts, he had certainly managed to get his life hopelessly entwined and identified with the affairs of the Far East. And here he was in the latest of the seemingly endless oriental wars, trying to do the right thing.

In this one, however, his own son was also involved. The smile turned to a frown as he thought of Will. A lieutenant in the 25th Division, stationed in II Corps. Probably a good soldier. Had Bill's passion for Far Eastern affairs guided the boy inexorably to his present occupation and location? A man wants his son to be a good citizen, and a good soldier if it came to that, but in Will's case was it necessary?

Chet opened the door.

"Let's talk about Busch," said Bill.

Chet sat down in the bamboo-and-foam-rubber chair opposite the desk. He waited for Bill to begin.

"His file isn't really bad," Bill said.

"No, I suppose not." Chet replied noncommittally.

"Except for that report you gave him in Frankfurt."

"It was justified."

"He's had a lot of TDY's all over the world. He apparently has got something people know about and need. Know what it is?"

"Yeah. He's a recruiter. That fellow could recruit Mao Tse-tung if he could get ten minutes alone with him."

Bill whistled softly. No wonder they asked for him! If there was one single virtue that the agency coveted it was the ability to recruit agents. Everything the agency did was based on recruited agents.

"You bring Busch into a station," Chet continued tonelessly, "and give him a couple of hours with a file on the prospect, and then turn him loose. If the man is recruitable, he'll get him. If he isn't, he cools the approach out in such a way that there aren't any unpleasant repercussions."

"Sounds pretty impressive."

"It is."

"And yet you don't think much of him?"

"I would not have accepted him for the Delta Region if I had been ROIC."

"All because of something that happened in Frankfurt?"

"That, and his attitude at the time, and ever since."

"What happened?"

"Well, he came to Frankfurt out of Budapest. I was Foreign Intelligence Ops Chief in Frankfurt at that time. Operations are a bit different in a denied area, of course. He was pretty critical of some of our operational procedures in Frankfurt, but I figured it was just because he had come from a tight situation, and that he'd relax a little bit when he got used to Frankfurt. He was replacing

Ernie Free, and they just had two weeks overlap before Ernie had to leave. I don't know whether you know Ernie?"

"No, I don't think so."

"Well, Ernie's principal operation was one he was pretty proud of, and he'd been working for a long time to get it started. I thought it was damned good. It was a net based in Bad Neustadt for cross-border operations into East Germany, and it looked like it had good chances of developing operations into Soviet territory too, although that was still pretty far in the future.

"So, when Busch arrives he looks over this file, and Ernie starts making arrangements to hand over the principal agent, but Busch right there dug his heels in. He didn't like the sound of the principal agent, and said he didn't want to meet him personally, but wanted to work with him through a cut-out until he could test him and authenticate him.

"Now, this was an old ex-Gehlen man, and that's what bothered Busch. He said he didn't see how we could ever run a unilateral operation with an agent that used to belong to Gehlen. How could we be sure the guy was ours now, and not still Gehlen's? But Ernie had ironclad proof that the guy had really broken with Gehlen, and in fact, the Gehlen people sent us a mildly derogatory report on the guy when we sent his name buried in a list for name checks.

"So Busch and Ernie and I sat down and talked it over, and I said I didn't think we ought to waste time testing the guy any more. And so Busch said all right, he would do it, but he wanted me to know he didn't like it one bit, and he thought the operation had holes big enough to drive a tank through."

"Did he put that in writing?"

"No."

"That says something in his favor, it seems to me."

"Frankly, I don't think he would have dared to put it in writing, because Ernie Free is one of the best ops officers I've ever worked with, and the way he built that net and handled the paper and administrative processing was a classic. Perfect. He looked into every danger and every possibility of a flap, and either eliminated it or resolved it as well as possible and made the situation a matter of record. We were beginning to get some preliminary take from it, and it looked good.

"Now, after Ernie was gone, Busch came to me and said he still wanted to test this operation, even if he was already blown to the principal agent, and so I said all right, go ahead and test it, but for God's sake get the goddamned thing going and keep it moving.

"Busch had recruited a young German university student, and was going to put him into the net to report back directly to him. I thought it was a waste of time, but I gave him the OK, and he went to work.

"What I didn't know, and what he never told me, was that he intended to *dangle* that kid. He wasn't going to introduce him to the principal agent and have the agent put the kid to work. He was going to set him up so that the principal agent would 'discover' the kid and bring him into the net without knowing that Busch had anything to do with it. He was going to penetrate his own operation at the middle echelon."

"Well, Christ," said Bill, "there's nothing wrong with that. It's a pretty good way to test an operation if you've got the time and the operation is important enough. I've done it myself."

"Yes, but in this case he used an inexperienced kid, up against an old pro, and sent him in without enough training."

"What happened?"

"Busch found the kid on his front doorstep a few weeks later. The kid's body was a pulp from bullets. Busch was never able to contact the principal agent again, not even by emergency or fallback arrangements. That agent was telling us that if that was the way we wanted to play, we'd have to play without him and his friends."

"Maybe Busch was right? Maybe the net was an East German or a Soviet operation against us. Or maybe just a paper mill, pure and simple?"

"No, sir! During a couple of years after that, our people managed to pick up an agent or two who had been members of that net, and there is no question that it was legitimate. They weren't sure exactly what had happened, but they did know that the principal agent got pissed off as hell at the Americans and called the whole thing off.

"So Busch not only succeeded in getting the kid killed, he also wiped out a chance for our station to set up what might have been one of the best collection operations in Europe."

Bill sat and stared into the distance for a time. At last he sighed, got up, gathered the papers out of his in-box, put them in his safe and twisted the knob to lock it. He tugged at the drawers to make sure they were locked, inspected the office carefully for stray papers, then went to the door.

"It's past quitting time," he said. "Let's go have a drink."

"I'll have to secure my office first. See you down there in a minute."

Bill stopped at Laura's desk. "I'll be over at the bar, Laura. There are some papers in my out-box for you, but the rest of the office is secure."

"OK, Mr. Voigt."

He walked down the stairs and paused at the air operations counter, near the front door of the building. Jerry Burkholder was sitting there surrounded by his big wall charts, his communications equipment, clipboards, schedules, and other paraphernalia.

"What's up, Jer?" Bill asked.

"Nothing much, Bill. Dino took Ski back up to Moc Hoa, and then he had to make an emergency run over to Chau Doc to pick up a wounded PRU and bring him to the hospital here."

"Jesus, that little Helio isn't much of a thing to haul a wounded man in."

"It was the only thing we had within range, and he couldn't wait for anything bigger."

"Anything else?"

"Nope. Everything's quiet. Quieter than I've seen things for a couple or three years. I don't like it."

Bill shook his head resignedly. "I don't either." Chet joined him. "I'll be over in the bar for a while if anything comes up," Bill told Jerry.

"Right."

They walked across the paved driveway into the little space that served the Americans living and working in this compound as a bar and mess hall. The bar was dimly lighted, and the walls were covered with woven reeds, giving it an atmosphere of South Pacific informality. They sat at a table near the far wall. Bill ordered his usual gin and tonic and Chet his usual CC and water.

"Chet," Bill said as they sipped their drinks, "I'm going to give Busch every benefit of the doubt. I'm not going to restrict him in any way in his operations. I'll keep my eye on him, but officially I have no reason to doubt his abilities or his judgment except for that one fitness report, which has been followed by some other fitness reports that neither refute yours nor bear it out."

Chet nodded. "I hope you won't be sorry."

"By the way, where is this other guy, this Ernie Free, now?"

Chet hitched forward in his chair excitedly. "That's another thing that pisses me off. You see, I persuaded Ernie to come out here when I came, because I wanted him with me. He works like a demon and he's one of the best ops officers I know, as I told you. But when he got to Saigon they ignored my request to have him assigned down here, and sent him up to Nha Trang."

"What's he doing up there?"

"He's the P officer up there. Last I heard, he had set up a penetration of the Provincial Committee of Kanh Hoa Province. It's one of the few we've got anywhere in the country, and maybe the best. And to think we could have had him down here, if those bastards up in Saigon had done what I wanted."

Two USAID nurses came in, and Bill motioned them to the table beside him. They were followed almost immediately by Dino, and Jess Theodorides, a helicopter pilot for Air America.

With Dino at the table, serious conversation was almost out of the question. He leered ferociously at the tiny barmaid and made her laugh. He kidded Cynthia and Sheila, the nurses, deplored everything Greek, for Jess's benefit, and spoke scornfully of flying anything that had an upside-down ceiling fan sticking out the top.

Everyone joined in the banter except Chet, and Bill was mildly uncomfortable for him. Chet had no fund of small talk. He seemed not to be able to talk to anyone about anything except his work. When he had at last finished his drink and left to go back to his office, Bill wondered if he had any inkling that the cordial farewells from the table reflected nothing more than relief at his departure.

Bill sipped his drink and sat back happily. These gatherings occurred regularly, and he was glad. In Can Tho they had little else to do during leisure hours. They drank more than they should, but he knew of no alcohol problems among them. It was overindulgence, but it was civilized. It helped shut the door for a time on the grim things that were going on in the country around them.

He had lost the thread of the conversation.

"I was just saying," Dino informed him, "that King Agesilaus here agrees with me on one thing."

"What's that?"

"When you fly, the most likely place to get shot is right in the ass," Dino said, serious now. "But Jess and I signed contracts to fly civilian aircraft for a civilian organization. When there is combat going on, I don't fly where it is."

"Right," said Jess.

"The army can do the combat flying."

"Right."

"If the Charlies ever shoot *me* in the ass, they're going to have to get under an easy chair or a bar stool to do it."

[4]

TOBY came downstairs to breakfast, and found Ben already seated at the table with a cup of coffee before him.

"How'd you sleep?" Ben asked.

"I won't lie to you. I was pretty tense."

"Gut still rumbling?"

"I took a couple of Lomotils, and they fixed me up, I think. From long experience with this kind of thing, I would say that my insides feel like it's all over."

"Good."

"Is the body gone?"

"Yeah."

"That bothered me more than the diarrhea, I think."

"What, getting shot at?"

"Well, sure, but mainly thinking about that kid out there dead, and his family, and all."

"Oh." Ben nodded, but Toby sensed that he did not understand.

Mrs. Chao came in, immaculately clean and cheerful, and set a cup of coffee before him. It wasn't bothering her, obviously, although she had seen the action too. "Bacon and eggs . . . soon," she said, nodding vigorously. He smiled his thanks and she went back into the kitchen.

"Minnie'll be back pretty soon, and we'll get him to arrange for repairs to the bathroom."

"Who's Minnie?"

"Tran Van Minh. Not our famous friend, 'Big Minh.' This one is our general manager, and handyman, and interpreter, and adviser on things Vietnamese. He went out with Little Jack on last night's PRU operation."

"Is that part of his duties?"

"No. Nobody makes him do it. I think he senses that the PRUs would turn into a gang of chicken thieves pretty quickly if they aren't led right, and he likes to be along to help out. He wants the Vietnamese to fight their own war."

"Sounds like quite a guy."

"If we didn't have Minnie around we'd have to hire six other men to do the things he does."

"Tran would be his family name, and Minh would be his given name, if I remember the Vietnam familiarization course correctly."

"Right."

"So you would call him either Minnie, or just Minh, or Mr. Tran?"

"Wrong. There aren't that many family names in Vietnam. Once you've used Tran and Hoang and Ho and Nguyen and a dozen or so others, there aren't any more. All a family name does is tell you what ancestral tribe the person claims to belong to. The given name is the one that separates him from other people, and so they say Ong—Mr.—Minh, not Ong Tran, and we round-eyes follow suit in our various languages and say Mr. Thieu, for example, instead of Mr. Nguyen."

"And Mrs. Chao," said Toby with a smile, as that small person came in and laid plates of food on the table.

She smiled back at him, ducked her head quickly, and returned to the kitchen, and the two men began to eat. The bacon was crisp and the eggs done just right. This part of the duty, at least, was not going to be a hardship.

"That thing doesn't seem to bother you, Ben, even if it did kind of get to me."

"What thing?"

"Killing that fellow last night. It doesn't seem quite real that a person could kill a man and not have the slightest impulse or desire to talk about it afterwards. Do you know what I mean? It made a big impression on me, but it doesn't seem to have had any effect on you at all."

"It's part of my profession," said Ben quietly.

"Yeah. Sure."

Toby ate in silence. Ben's attitude was right and normal, of course. In a war you shoot to kill. You aim at the heart.

But his mind rebelled against it all. Even though that kid was an enemy, there was something immensely sad about the crumpling of that young body so swiftly and silently in response to the crack of the carbine. Seeing it huddled there, lifeless, alone in death, he had remembered young Gerd, huddled on his doorstep that morning.

"I didn't mean to sound like a preacher or a saint," he said.

"You didn't."

"I guess it must sound crazy to you, but I couldn't help feeling a little sorry for that kid."

"No, it doesn't sound crazy. But while you're feeling sorry for him, don't forget that he was trying to kill you."

Toby shook his head. "I guess I'll never forget that."

The noise of the gates opening brought them both to their feet. They went to the door and saw a dusty jeep pulling into the space beside the other two under the shed roof that slanted down from the inner side of the compound wall.

A big muscular man climbed from behind the wheel, picked up an M-16, pouches of clips, and a pair of binoculars from the back of the vehicle, and came toward them.

His passenger, a slight, erect Vietnamese, dressed in fatigues, retrieved an M-2 carbine from the vehicle and followed him.

"How'd it go, Little Jack?" asked Ben.

"We got ambushed," said Little Jack wearily.

"Bad?"

"No, we saw the situation before we were fully committed, and pulled out. One of the men got a couple of fragments from a claymore. That's all."

"That's lucky."

"Damn right."

"Little Jack, this is Toby Busch. Little Jack Horner, Toby."

"Hello," said Little Jack. "I saw you from a distance down at Can Tho the other day, but didn't get a chance to say hello." He crushed Toby's hand in a big paw. Toby could see why the nickname stuck. The name of the Mother Goose character was wildly inappropriate for this giant. He was about six feet four inches, and must have weighed two hundred twenty pounds, all of it bone and muscle.

"And this is Tran Van Minh," Ben continued.

The Vietnamese extended his comparatively small hand, and now it was Toby's turn to feel like a bear.

"How do you do, Mr. Busch," Minh greeted him.

"Everybody around here calls him Minnie," said Ben.

"Well, I . . . er . . . Mr. Minh . . ." Toby began.

"If you wish to call me Minnie, I will not mind," said the man.

"All right, then: Minnie."

Minnie had the smooth complexion of the Indochinese. His hair was cut short and parted on one side, with deep indentations on either side where the hairline was receding, although he seemed fairly young. His ears stuck out from his head, his teeth were large and perfect, and when he smiled a mass of laugh lines radiated from the corners of his eyes. The big ears and the big teeth would have given him a comical, perhaps even a clownish, appearance were it not for something in his eyes that spoke of a keen intellect and a serious character.

"What happened?" Ben asked, as they trooped through the house to the office.

"You know the village we were targeting?"

"I've never been there, but I know where it is."

"Well, we was coming up along this canal that leads in from the south, and we got to a place where a big high footbridge goes across it—right at the edge of the village. It was dark, and I couldn't see clear to the head of the line, but the point man tripped a claymore that was someplace close to the end of that footbridge."

"The man that tripped it was the one that was wounded?"

"Yeah. And then we come under fire from three sides all at once, but we bugged out before they could close the door behind us."

"They knew you were coming."

"They sure as hell did. It was that goddamned Yenan Battalion is what it was."

Ben frowned. "Doesn't sound like it to me."

"Whattaya mean? I was there. That ambush was set up by professionals."

"That claymore sure wasn't rigged by any professional."

"How do you figure that?"

"Figure it out for yourself. When a professional rigs a claymore, the man that trips it gets blown to pieces, not just nicked with a couple of fragments. If you were in my platoon and you rigged up a claymore that didn't do anything except nick the point man and alert the enemy and let them escape, I'd have you digging latrines for a year. The Yenan Battalion doesn't work that way. Sounds more like a local force battalion to me."

"It wouldn't of if you'd a been there," Little Jack huffed, and went into the dining room.

They heard the clank of the gates and the buzz of the motorbike. Therese came in, clad in a different *ao dai* from yesterday's. This one was a tunic of soft pink over trousers of satiny white. They were spotless.

She greeted them politely and went directly to her desk. Toby caught a faint fragrance as she moved past him, and suddenly realized that he was staring intently at that perfect body and the lovely, melancholy face. He looked away quickly.

"You can see what we're up against, Toby," said Ben, himself seemingly caught in the same trance as Toby. "Whatever it was that hit those guys last night, it was certainly a trap, and it was prepared before the PRUs ever got near them."

"Does it always happen that way?"

"Not always. Sometimes an operation will go off without a hitch, but when it does I always figure it wasn't because the VC didn't know about it, but probably because they just couldn't get forces in place in time to ambush them. Or maybe because they knew the operation wasn't worth ambushing."

"It's a hell of a note."

"Yeah, and Little Jack has got an almost unbroken string of these ambushes. I feel kind of sorry for him, in a way."

Toby sat at his desk and drummed on its surface with his fingers. "Ben," he said, "any way you look at it, there's only one answer to this problem. We've got to find out how the information is leaking out."

"You'll know how to do that," Ben replied. "I sure don't. Let me know if I can help."

Toby nodded and Ben left. Toby turned in his chair and looked at Therese, who, with her back to him, was working at her typewriter. Might as well start on the obvious suspect. But it wasn't going to be easy or pleasant. He got up and walked back to her desk.

"Therese, may I interrupt you for a minute?"

"Certainly, Mr. Busch," she said, turning quickly to face him.

"I want to find out something about the files that are kept here in the office."

"Yes, sir." She rose and opened the safe by her desk. "This is my safe." She flicked through the files, her fingers precise and delicate. He steeled himself against the nearness of her body and looked over the tabs on the file folders. Intelligence reports from the Special Police. PRU reports. Pacification reports, requisitions, records.

He was relieved to find that none of the material in her safe was exclusively agency material to which she should not have had access.

"Will you come and sit up here for a moment?" he said. "I want to talk to you about the office routines and procedures, especially about security."

"Very well." She moved behind him to his desk and sat down in the chair beside it, facing him.

"Is the office ever left empty during working hours?"

"Only during lunchtime."

"But you lock everything up when you all go out to lunch, don't you?"

"Yes."

"And it has been a rule that the office is never left untended with the safes open and papers out on the desks?"

"Yes, sir, that has always been the rule." She was obviously disturbed and apprehensive about this line of questioning.

"In other words, when the safes are open, either Mr. Horner or Mr. Compton is here?"

"Yes. Or me."

"They leave you here alone when their own safes are open?"

The concern in her eyes deepened. "Yes."

Toby felt as guilty as if he were physically abusing her. "Did Mr. James give you any instructions about security when he hired you?"

"Yes. He told me about the need-to-know, and locking safes, and security checks before leaving, and those things."

"And you understand that *all* of us are subject to security rules, including me?"

She nodded.

"And being in charge of this office, it is my responsibility to see that the security of the office and its work is protected, and that means that I must question and watch everybody who has access to our papers and conversations?"

Again she nodded.

"You have had access to almost everything in the office, more than you are authorized to have, and perhaps more than it is good for you to have."

"And you do not trust me?"

"I didn't say that."

"But it is true."

"In a sense it is. Until I can see proof that you are trustworthy, it *must* be so. I have no choice."

"I see."

"Therese," he said gently, "this is a part of my profession that I dislike very much. If my personal feelings in the matter could govern things, I would never question you. But I cannot report to my superiors that the office is secure because my personal feelings tell me that it is. I hope you understand that?"

"Yes," she said, looking down at her hands, "but I cannot prove anything about myself to you. I come from Hanoi, and all my records are there. I was married there, but my husband was . . . my husband was killed soon after we came south, and there are no records of us in South Vietnam."

"I see," he said. "In a sense that may be one point in your favor."

"I do not understand."

"Look at it this way. If the North Vietnamese or the Viet Cong were using you as an agent, they would certainly have fixed you up with some kind of documentation, wouldn't they?"

"I think so, perhaps," she said hesitantly.

Ben came striding rapidly into the office. "Toby," he said, "I just got word that the VC hit my team at An Loi last night and hurt it bad. I gotta get down there as soon as possible. Can we cancel the meeting with the PSA and Colonel Manh this morning so you can go along with me?"

"Sure."

Therese rose. "I will call them to cancel the appointments if you wish, sir."

"Thank you, Therese," said Ben, and turned to Toby. "Would you get on the sideband to Can Tho, while I load up the jeep? See if Jerry can get us a couple of choppers up there. There's going to be some wounded to be brought out."

"That's An Loi, right?"

"Right."

"What about a plane if they don't have choppers?"

"No good. There's no landing strip."

Toby went to the single sideband transceiver, which glowed and hummed twenty-four hours a day just inside the breezeway door. He looked up Jerry's call sign, unhooked the microphone, and called for Butane, identifying himself as Buffalo. Burkholder from Busch. Silly system that the VC would figure out almost as soon as it was instituted, if they thought it worthwhile.

"I've only got one chopper," Butane responded, "and he's in the air right now. I'll divert him to you as soon as possible."

"OK. Can you try to get another one, too?"

"I'll do what I can."

"Thanks. Buffalo out."

"Butane out."

An Loi was worse than Toby could have imagined. There were few buildings left standing, and bodies were scattered among the ruins, many of them badly cut up by bullets and fragments. Dozens of wounded had been gathered in the hot interior of the only building left relatively intact, a structure of concrete and corrugated iron.

Jess landed in his chopper shortly after Ben and Toby had arrived, with Minnie along to help. By the time the chopper was loaded with wounded, a second one had arrived, this one with a Vietnamese doctor and two nurses. Gritting his teeth, Toby helped load the wounded on board, hurting them as he did so, not being able to avoid hurting them. All afternoon they worked.

When the last of the wounded were airborne, on their way to the Ninth Evacuation Hospital, Ben stood and talked with the team leader for some time. They gestured toward a large mound of mud some hundreds of yards away, beyond the edge of the devastated village. Ben was highly agitated, and the team leader, exhausted and still in the grip of the violence of the night's action, shook his head and replied in a low voice.

At length Ben patted the man on the back, and returned to the jeep.

"The team really didn't do so bad," he said, "considering that it was the Yenan Battalion that hit them in full force."

"What's the problem about that mud thing?" Toby asked him.

"That's a mud fort. You see the goddamned things all over the country."

"What do they do with them?"

"They commit suicide. Those walls can't stop a B-Forty round, but there's always a few damned fools that just won't give up the habit of taking cover in them, or using them as strongpoints. It might have been all right before shaped charges and rockets, while the French were here. They learned it from the French. Came from Africa and the Foreign Legion, I suppose. But they're death traps in this day and age.

"A lot of those wounded we just loaded had taken cover in that one over there. But most of the people inside it were killed. Two B-Forty rounds is all it took."

"Were any of your team members in there?"

"One. He was trying to persuade all the others to come out. He was killed."

"For nothing," Toby commented softly.

"For nothing. Bill Voigt will blow up when he hears about it. He's a fanatic on the subject. He had a couple of experiences with that kind of a defensive philosophy in Burma. He thinks mud forts do something to the psychology of a people."

Minnie climbed into the jeep and Ben started it up. "Bill wrote a paper on mud forts," he continued. "Headquarters was impressed with it, I understand, and circulated it to the Pentagon. His idea is that the South Vietnamese seem to be getting more and more of a mud fort attitude about the war—you know, go inside where it's safe and maybe the enemy will go away. Bill's even seeing signs that the Americans are being infected by it. He says if he had his way he'd blow up every mud fort in the country, and then pull the fingernails out of anybody that ever built another one."

He put the jeep in gear and they moved slowly along the littered street. There was nothing more they could do here. Already the villagers, although still showing signs of shock, were at work clearing away the wreckage, collecting their belongings, and preparing meals over small fires here and there.

"Not all of them are mud fort enthusiasts," Ben said. "You'd be surprised at how soon these people will have this village put back together."

"You gotta admire them, don't you?" Toby replied, watching a small man hauling mightily upon a large wooden pole, to begin clearing away the wreckage of his home.

"Guts."

"That's it."

"North or South Vietnamese, Viet Cong or ARVN, or just villagers like these, they're a feisty people, aren't they, Minnie?"

Minnie leaned forward in his seat. "The word is new to me, sir. Feisty?"

"Yeah. Feisty. It means pugnacious. It means they never run away from a fight, and they fight hard. Maybe even that they get a certain kind of fulfillment, a certain joy, out of fighting."

"And the word for that is 'feisty'?"

"That's right."

"Then I would say yes. The Vietnamese are feisty."

"You see what I was telling you, Toby?" Ben continued, as they reached the edge of the village and picked up speed on the rough road. "That Yenan Battalion is tearing us apart in this area. They did lose four or five men, and that's a lot for an attack on a little village like this one, but it isn't an unacceptable loss for them."

"There's no question that it was the Yenan Battalion?"

"Nope. Some of the dead had the insignias. They knew exactly where to hit and when. They knew this team was new and still pretty weak. They figured they could hit it without much damage to themselves, and that news of what happened in An Loi would demoralize a lot of other teams."

"Will it?"

"It'll scare the shit out of them for a while."

"It sure as hell would make *me* nervous," Toby said fervently.

"The Viet Cong secret weapon. Terror."

"You understand it . . . after you see something like that."

"And these little villages have been the center of the war all along. The war is *about* them, and it's *in* them. Not the cities. Right from the start you could see what the Viet Cong was up to. What they wanted was to destroy the government of South Vietnam, and they knew they could do it without even touching Saigon. All they had to do was cut the lines of authority and communication from Saigon to the villages and hamlets. They didn't even have to destroy the middle echelons, the regional and provincial governments.

"I saw it happen time after time at the beginning. They would come into the villages, like An Loi, in the middle of the night, haul the village chief out of bed, along with the chief of police, the schoolteachers, the educated people —anybody in a position of respect or authority—shoot them in the back of the head, and line the corpses up in the street with notes pinned on them, so the villagers would have no doubt about who had done it.

"If anybody was crazy enough to try to take the place of any of the murdered people, they'd be laying out in the streets the next morning themselves, with a note pinned on them. That's terror as the professionals build it and use it.

"They did that to each village, and each time the central government lost contact and authority over one more unit. The VC didn't even have to occupy or police the villages. The terror was enough. Saigon was losing the war. There was nothing Saigon could concentrate its big army and firepower on. There still isn't."

"Yep," said Toby. "I wasn't here to see it, but I've read about it a lot. And I was briefed on the techniques and situation by everybody you could imagine—"

"And now by me," said Ben apologetically. "I'm sorry."

"No need to apologize. You're the first one I've talked to about it who has seen it from the start, down at the level where it happened. It's like reading about a famous battle, and then visiting the battlefield. It comes to life for you."

"It does for a fact," Ben said.

"For example, I remember the figures they gave us. Forty thousand people killed that way in these villages in less than a year."

"That's right. That was the main push. It's still going on, but not as many each year now."

"Forty thousand is just a figure when you get briefed on it. You hear the figure, but you don't . . ."

"You don't think people, you think numbers. When you're sitting in an office or in front of a television set, it's just a number. But when you see it happen on the spot, and know the people it happens to, then it means something. And even then, my God, forty thousand!"

They drove in silence for a time through the gathering dusk. "In spite of it all," Ben said thoughtfully, "the villages seem to welcome our teams when they come to try to reestablish the government structure. They know that having a team in a village may provoke an attack like this one today, but they welcome the team just the same. They don't give up, except for the few that duck into the mud forts. If you give them some help and a little bit of hope, they come back. Feisty people."

"Feisty," echoed Minnie, pleased with the new word.

[5]

TOBY transferred some papers from the files to his leather briefcase and locked his safe. Ben was busy at his desk, preparing a report for Saigon about An Loi.

"I hope you don't mind me not going with you, Toby?"

"No, you go ahead with your work. Minnie knows his way around over at the Special Police Offices, I'm sure."

"Sure. Better than I do, in fact."

Toby went out to the jeep, where Minnie was waiting, dressed in slacks and open-collared shirt.

They drove first to the office of the Province Senior Adviser, an army lieutenant colonel who had no desire to become involved in Toby's affairs, and let the fact be known in a wash of great cordiality. "Please let me know . . . All the best of luck. . . . It is extremely important . . . If there is ever anything . . . You fellows over there have no idea how much . . . Good to have talked with you. . . . Appreciate your call."

So much for him. It was like calling on the ambassador at an overseas post. Great puffs of wind that mean nothing at all. No complications here.

Under Minnie's directions, he drove to the center of town, to a large, square compound that occupied a city block. It was enclosed on all sides by a fence of vertical iron bars, on a base wall of concrete about three feet high. It would keep out intruders, but was not fortified against military attack, so far as his nonmilitary eyes could discern. Guards were at the gates, and some sandbag bunkers here and there.

"This is the compound of the provincial government," said Minnie. "Almost all of the provincial government offices are here. Special Police Offices are on the second floor, and that small building behind the main building is the Revolutionary Development Office."

"Revolutionary Development." The name must be an awkward translation of something meaningful in Vietnamese, or else had been dreamed up by somebody who knew Vietnamese psychology better than he; but to Toby's ears, "revolutionary development" was no more satisfactory or descriptive than "pacification," and both referred to the same thing. But then, the strange and illogical language probably reflected quite accurately the minds that produced it.

"The Revolutionary Development Office is where Ben comes to meet his counterparts, I guess?" he said.

"Yes."

They parked the jeep inside the compound and went up to the second floor, past a reception desk in the corridor, and were ushered into a large office that overlooked the front of the compound. A squarely built, stocky man, with close-clipped hair, rose from his desk to greet them. He was neatly dressed in the dark trousers, white open-collared shirt, and shoulder boards that were the official working uniform of the Special Police. His mouth was straight and rather severe, his nose broad and flat, and his eyes were framed by steel-rimmed spectacles with slightly tinted lenses.

Minnie introduced them, and Colonel Manh motioned them into comfortable chairs around a low table in one corner of the office. *Good manners,* Toby thought. Around a table, rather than across a desk. Minnie interpreted for them so skillfully and unobtrusively that they were soon talking directly to one another, almost as if Minnie were not there at all.

"You have come to replace Mr. James," Manh said. "We liked Mr. James very much."

"I did not know Mr. James," said Toby.

"He was a charming man."

"Did you find your joint work with him to be successful?"

Manh seemed puzzled by the question.

"It was most pleasant," he replied.

"And was it productive?"

"Oh, yes, quite productive."

"Colonel Manh," said Toby, "I believe I should tell you here at the beginning that I hope to do more with you and your office than just be cordial friends." Manh nodded and waited for Toby to continue.

"It is my idea that our governments have put us into liaison with one another to work together, not merely to exchange papers now and then."

Manh was cautious, but interested. Toby went on.

"Our two organizations are working on a new program that is going to involve you and me in a lot of hard work together."

"I have heard something of the program."

"I want to anticipate the start of it by getting Dinh Tuong Province ready now."

Colonel Manh smiled. "I would be pleased by such an early beginning. What do you propose?"

Toby opened his briefcase and extracted a sheaf of papers. "These are intelligence reports from your department."

Manh looked at the papers in Toby's hand, and waited.

"However well they may have served in the past," Toby went on, "they are not good enough for the new program."

"Not good enough?"

"No. Let me show you."

Toby motioned Minnie to inch forward a bit so that he could read and interpret as they went through the reports, but before he began, Manh stopped him and called a subordinate to bring the original Vietnamese reports from the files.

With these two versions of the reports, Toby proceeded

to show Manh what was wrong with the Special Police reports. He was impressed by Manh's quick understanding of his criticisms, and he was sure that Manh would see through the fiction that the reports "may have been good enough in the past." Those reports were never good for anything.

At length Manh sat back. "You have shown me enough. What do you propose?"

Toby was elated at the attitude of genuine interest on Manh's part. He was sure that this was the first time Manh had ever had any contact with an American adviser who intended to work hard at the liaison, and bring to it some experience and expertise.

"I want to train your people, Colonel Manh," he said.

"You want to train them?"

"Yes. I want to ask you to make them available to me for a course of instruction in the collection of information, and in the preparation of reports."

Manh was thoughtful. "It would be difficult to allow the men to be away from their work."

"I know the difficulties. The decision is yours, of course. But the need is great, and it is urgent. I want the intelligence from Dinh Tuong Province to go all the way to the top of the ARVN command and the American MACV forces, and to be respected and believed."

Manh gave him a broad grin. *That* was the kind of talk he obviously liked. "Before we go further in this, let me call Major Thieu," he said. He indicated by a gesture that Minnie should tell Toby who Thieu was.

"Major Thieu is the officer who sees that Manh's orders are carried out, and makes sure that everything is done, and acts for the colonel. There is a name for it in English." Minnie searched for the word.

"Executive officer?"

"Yes, executive officer." Minnie continued speaking in a tone and manner that would indicate to Manh a dispassionate description of Thieu. "I believe I should tell you about Thieu. He is a . . . a positive man. He believes that he speaks good English, and he will not use an interpreter. He is difficult for Americans to work with because of that, but if you want to work well with the Special Police in this province you must work with Major Thieu in whatever way he wishes to work, because he is in a powerful position. I will try to help all I can, but it must never appear that I am interpreting for him. You will see."

"I'll follow your lead, Minnie," said Toby.

Major Thieu came in. He was about Colonel Manh's height, but less sturdily built. He had large protruding eyes, which gave him an expression of mild and perpetual astonishment.

After the introductions, Thieu sat down in a chair next to Toby and drew it uncomfortably near.

"You wish to teach men?" he asked, and Toby was tempted to move back from him, because Thieu spoke with his face close to his own.

"Yes," Toby replied. He spoke slowly and as distinctly as he could form the words. "I want to teach them two hours a day."

Thieu nodded, but Toby was not sure he had understood.

"Here?"

"Yes."

"*You* will teach?"

"Yes."

"When?"

"As soon as possible." Toby had the sensation of being in the midst of a classroom drill in a foreign-language course.

"How many men?"

"All of them who are engaged in intelligence work." He realized that this was probably too complicated a sentence for Thieu, but Thieu looked at him wisely and smiled.

"Impossible," said Thieu politely. "Too many. But it is not important. I will bring all men who get information and all men who write information. They require teach. Others not."

Toby smiled. Thieu had agreed with him while believing that he was disagreeing. "How many will that be?"

Thieu made a mental calculation. "Twelve men."

"I would like to begin about a week from now."

"Yes, we have them," replied Thieu promptly.

Minnie stirred uncomfortably and Toby glanced innocently at him.

"What about blackboards, chalk, desks, paper, pencils?" Toby asked, certain that these words would be as familiar to Thieu as they are to any beginning student in any language. Thieu fielded the question with ill-concealed pride in his skill, and replied that such things would be easily provided.

"We will also need a four-drawer safe, but I could provide that; and we will need the names and some biographical information on all the men who will be involved, because they will be handling secret information, and our regulations require that they be cleared before we can give them that information."

Toby made this statement with the realization that Thieu would not understand it, but hoping that Minnie would notice that he was also directing his remarks toward Manh. Minnie did. Thieu made as if to study the question seriously, and Minnie translated for Manh. Toby could see that Thieu was listening intently, with a somewhat condescending expression for his superior officer, who did not understand the language. Thieu then spoke at some length with Manh, and Minnie translated, as if from Manh. "If you will give them a written list of the preparations they should make, they will attend to it."

"I'll have it over here to them this afternoon," Toby said. "That's the kind of response I like." They all arose and shook hands, and Toby and Minnie left.

"Minnie," Toby said, as they drove out of the compound, "you do an excellent job of interpreting. I'm not used to dealing through interpreters, but I can recognize an expert job when I see one."

"Thank you, Mr. Busch."

"I call you Minnie and you call me Mr. Busch. It doesn't seem right."

"Friendship does not depend on such things, does it? One can be equally charming with formality as with informality."

"But others who hear it might think I had a kind of contempt for you."

"They might also think that when I call you 'Mr. Busch,' it is because *I* have contempt for *you*."

Toby grinned at him ruefully.

"I am not disturbed by the names as we use them,"

Minnie went on. "If I am not troubled, I believe you do not need to be troubled."

"OK," Toby gave in. "So be it."

Back at the office, Toby called Can Tho on the single sideband and asked for a plane to take him down the following day. Jerry promised to give him a pick-up hour later that evening, when tomorrow's schedule would be firm.

Now to start the process of defining his security problems. He called Little Jack into the common room for a conference. It was inconvenient that he did not have a private office where he could discuss confidential matters, but there was no use worrying about it. He would just have to get accustomed to using the common room for that purpose.

He laid a tablet of yellow foolscap on the low table before him. "I want you," he said to Little Jack, "to name all the people who have access to the information about your operations ahead of time."

"All of them?"

"Every single one you can think of."

"Let's see now. There's me, and Ben and Minnie and the PRU sergeant, and you and Therese and Colonel Manh and Major Thieu. And then, there's a Special Police officer they send along with us, and he certainly would have to know ahead of time."

Toby was jotting down names and drawing lines as Little Jack spoke. He shook his head in dismay.

"Look at all these people and all the loose ends," he said. "Not only have we got too many people who know about these things in our own office, but we have no control over where the information goes after it reaches Manh's office." He doodled on the pad, lost in thought.

"What about the Province Senior Adviser's office?" he went on.

"Oh, yeah," Little Jack admitted with a start. "We have to send a written notice of each operation to the PSA office before we go out."

Toby remembered his meeting with the PSA, and decided that this particular gap would not be difficult to close. He could delay sending the reports, or just neglect to send them at all. Dangerous, if a flap occurred, but perhaps a risk he would have to take.

"Think of anybody else?"

"Not offhand."

Toby leaned back in his chair, studying his list. "Well, that's a start.

"That all?" Little Jack asked, getting up to go.

"One other thing, Little Jack. In questions of security, there is one hard and fast rule. *Don't talk.* Don't even mention the problem to anybody without checking with me first, OK?"

"Sure."

"And that means, don't say or even hint to anybody that we are even talking about the *leaks,* or plans to find the source of the leaks. You understand? If you alert the guilty person, he's going to start laying low, and we'll never catch him. We've got to make sure he keeps on operating while we're looking for him."

"Well," said Little Jack, "of course you can automatically eliminate anybody that would get hurt by the leak."

"I don't automatically eliminate anybody," Toby replied coolly. "I don't eliminate the PRU man, or Minnie, or Therese, or even you."

Little Jack bristled. "Me? I'd have to be some kind of a stupid son of a bitch to leak the information and then walk into the ambush."

"Yes. Pretty stupid. Or very brave."

"Well, in this case—"

"About half of the security leaks that are found turn out to be people you would automatically eliminate, if you were using that kind of logic."

"Yeah, but for Christ's sake—"

"You could be giving out information without realizing it, you know. Have you got Vietnamese friends you talk to a lot? Any girlfriends?"

Little Jack perceived that he was being coolly interrogated. "Well, hell," he said, "a man's gonna have women if there's women around. But I sure as shit don't talk about military operations when I'm in the sack with a broad."

"No, I don't suppose you do. But you can see what we have to think about when you consider how many people have the information as a matter of course?"

Little Jack nodded slowly. Then, seeing that Toby had dismissed him, he returned to the office.

Toby next called Ben away from his work, and showed him his list. "I think you've got everybody down," Ben told him. "It's a big enough list, at that."

"What about your own operations? Who knows about them?"

"Everybody in the country knows about my operations, at every stage of the game," said Ben. "I've been giving this a lot of thought since you got here, and I've come to the conclusion that the least likely place to get information about my pacification teams would be here in this office. The teams are known about, by everybody, from the very start—Vung Tau, the villages they're going to, the Revolutionary Development Offices, the Special Police. Everybody."

"But didn't you say that the Yenan Battalion knows everything about your teams? How good they are? Which ones are weak? Things like that?"

"That's right. But they could get that information from their own sources in the villages."

"I suppose you're right. We'll go on that assumption."

"I don't want to try to tell you how to run something like this. You're in the business, and I'm not."

"Things like this are more a question of study, and common sense, than they are of any special skill, Ben. Now I've got to sit down and make some kind of sense of this, and come up with an idea of what we ought to do—write up something to take down to Can Tho with me."

"That reminds me, are you going to be coming back from Can Tho tomorrow?"

"If Jerry gets me down there early enough in the morning to get all my business done, and then gets me a plane back after lunch, I'll be back. Why?"

"We're planning a kind of welcome-aboard party for you."

"Who's we?"

"Couple of nurses and a secretary from the PSA office. All Americans."

"That sounds good."

"Would you go to the PX while you're there and bring us some things?"

"You bet. What do you need?"

"Nuts and crackers, and things like that for the bar. Some booze. Mrs. Chao may want some things for the kitchen, too. I'll have a list for you."

Toby returned to his desk. He found it difficult to concentrate, and realized with some disgust that the reason was a vague sense of elation he felt about the party. It was sophomoric, really. A party with unattached females, and he was reacting as if he were preparing for his first high-school date.

It didn't take much introspection to discover the reason. It was freedom. He had, by coming to Vietnam, regained the freedom of the single male. He had consciously and willingly given up that freedom when he took a wife, but he had never quite forgotten it, or ceased, it would seem, to regret losing it.

[6]

ONE of the tasks Bill Voigt had as Regional Officer in Charge was to deal with the press when Washington or Saigon so instructed him. That was why he was now squinting worriedly at Wilbur Hamilton, the PRU adviser for Bill's Phong Dinh Province, who was sitting in the chair across the desk from him.

This was a new experience to Bill. Intelligence officers should not, by the very nature of their profession, give interviews to the press, or even maintain any contacts with the press, except where it was firmly understood that the information exchanged was not to be published. This was the way it had always been, and journalists he had known in the past had understood and accepted the situation as natural.

In Vietnam, however, with six hundred reporters on the scene, the press was too overwhelming a presence to be safely ignored or fended off. Bill had already been back to the States on home leave once, and had been dismayed at the picture of the war that television was showing the American public.

"That isn't the same war I'm involved in!" he kept repeating to family and friends, but he could see that they didn't believe him.

The cable on the desk before him spoke volumes in few words: ". . . Miss Alice Christopher . . . Midwest News Syndicate . . . all phases of our counterinsurgency operations which can be securely . . . your own judgment . . . refusal would prejudice . . . desirable she draw favorable conclusions, but no attempts to distort or falsify . . . frank and candid without . . ."

It was enough to make a veteran clandestine operator panic. Sort of like walking out your front door naked. Without any restrictions, reporters had seen the Pacification Training Camp at Vung Tau. They had seen pacification teams at work in the villages. They had rejoiced in playing with the word "pacification," which was a goddamned stupid way to name or describe what the program was really trying to do.

Now here came Miss Alice Christopher, who was the Vietnam War correspondent for a small Midwestern chain of papers, and she wanted to go out on a PRU operation!

And Saigon had authorized it. *Authorized?* Hell, they had *instructed* him to do it. And the only reason they would do that was that Washington had sent *them* the same instructions.

"It's crazy, Chet," he said, looking over at his deputy, who was standing in the door with a copy of the same cable in his hand. "Sending a woman out with a bunch of night fighters into a VC-controlled hamlet. She won't be able to see a thing, and she'll probably get herself killed, and maybe you think *that* wouldn't make the CIA popular in the States!"

"I wouldn't do it if I were you," said Chet. "I'd tell Saigon to stick it up their ass."

"I can't do that."

"The hell you can't! You know as well as I do that nobody in headquarters is going to dare question a decision of the man on the spot, if he puts it on the record that he can't do something securely. If they go ahead and order him to do it anyway, and things blow up, who gets the blame? *They* do, because he didn't want to do it and they made him. They know that. They sure as hell won't order you to do it if you cable a refusal for security reasons."

"But don't you see that Saigon is on the spot? You've read this cable. Put yourself in the place of the guy that wrote it, and figure out why he would have said things the way he did. They want us to handle this a certain way, and you can bet they've had instructions from headquarters, maybe even from the White House. They can't put into an official communication exactly what they want to tell us about this situation, but if you read it from Saigon's point of view you can get the message. And they're trusting us to read between the lines and do the right thing. Know what I mean?"

Chet nodded, but Bill knew that he did not understand. It was a flaw in Chet's mentality that he was going to have to deal with in a fitness report that would be due in a few weeks. Chet considered anybody at the other end of a line of communications to be an adversary. Chet believed in calling a spade a spade. Chet was an excellent deputy—he had been a deputy in his last three posts. He would be a calamity as a chief of anything. He would have told the reporter to get lost, and would have sent a cable to Saigon with unanswerable objections to the request, thus forcing Saigon to look for other means of accomplishing a delicate and difficult task. And Chet would have indelibly impressed himself upon the minds of a number of uper-level officers as being an intractable and inflexible officer.

Bill stared at the cable.

. . . TAKE THIS WOMAN OFF OUR HANDS. GIVE HER A STORY THAT WILL SATISFY HER, AND WILL MAKE HER A FRIEND OF OUR AGENCY. DO NOT SHOW HER OUR WORST OPERATIONS, BECAUSE SHE WOULD REPORT THEM AS THE NORM. DO NOT SHOW HER ONLY THE BEST, BECAUSE SHE WOULD SUSPECT A SNOW JOB, AND WOULD LOOK FOR WORSE, AND WOULD FIND IT. BUT BE HONEST. THE WHITE HOUSE IS WATCHING. WHEN YOU REPORT ON WHAT

YOU DO WITH HER, MAKE IT A ROUTINE, FACTUAL, EVEN DRY, ACCOUNT. WE REALIZE THIS IS A TURD WE ARE HANDING YOU, BUT DON'T TELL US YOUR OBJECTIONS TO IT, BECAUSE WE'VE ALREADY THOUGHT OF THEM ALL. WE ARE DEPENDING ON YOU.

Bill would have liked to send her to Toby Busch, because Busch was at least an experienced agency man. But he couldn't do that. Busch was still somewhat of an unknown quantity, and anyway his province was too much of a problem.

He had finally settled on Phong Dinh Province, the province in which his own regional office was located. She was going out with the PRU that night to a hamlet that was VC-controlled, but not far away from Can Tho. The Special Police had a report that a VC commo-liaison cadre was living in that hamlet. If you could get a commo-liaison cadre it was like plugging into their phone line, or reading their mail, or breaking their code. The Special Police wanted this man, and wanted him badly, to interrogate him about operations in the province. The PRU was going to try to capture him.

Chances were that they would run into a firefight in the hamlet, too, because these VC villages were always on their guard.

Wilbur might not understand the problems of upper-level bureaucracy, but Bill trusted his judgment and his abilities. A navy lieutenant (jg), member of Seal Team One, he was an educated and articulate man and a good leader. Most important of all, he loved combat. If he had not, he would never have volunteered for duty with the Seals, that offshoot of the old Underwater Demolition teams, who were trained in unconventional warfare, in fighting on and under the sea, on land, and in the air. Parachutists, divers, warriors.

Wilbur would keep her safe if anybody could.

Laura ushered into the office a young woman who was visibly relishing her appearance in baggy fatigues. "This is Miss Alice Christopher," said Laura, and the others introduced themselves to the reporter.

"We're not very used to this sort of thing, Miss Christopher," Bill began uneasily.

"Everybody calls me Chris," she said.

"All right, Chris."

"I'm sorry to put you to so much trouble."

"I'm going to be perfectly honest with you. We want to show you a good PRU operation, but we don't want you to get hurt or killed. So the one we're showing you isn't the most dangerous one you could imagine, but it isn't a walk in the moonlight, either. There is likely to be some shooting, maybe a lot of it."

"I understand."

"I'd be a fool if I didn't want to show you our best, but I'd be even more foolish if I tried to convince you that we never do anything that isn't brilliantly conceived and executed."

"Don't worry," she said. "I didn't come to do a sensational exposé of the CIA or the PRU. Unless what I see looks crazy or stupid, the story won't put you in a bad light. What I want is a story that will show the PRU in action. I think I've got to see it to be able to write about it."

"You won't carry a weapon?"

"That's right. My only protection as a journalist."

"It's going to be dark," said Wilbur. "The VC may have trouble seeing who is a journalist and who is a PRU. You sure you want to get into that kind of a situation?"

"I won't tell you I'm not scared, because I am. But I won't back out. And I won't get in your way, and I don't expect any special protection."

Wilbur stood up. "I don't approve of it all, Chris," he said, with a disarming smile, "but your bosses and my bosses seem to think it's OK. So, if we're going to do it, we better get going right away. We've got a lot of preparations to make before dark."

They moved toward the door.

"Good luck," Bill said.

As they filed out into the anteroom, Wilbur paused at the door and said in a soft aside to Bill, "Relax if you can, sir. She's my little chicken now, and I'll take care of her."

Bill put his hand on Wilbur's shoulder and gripped it in a gesture of gratitude. Wilbur understood.

"Mr. Busch just came in," said Laura, as he was returning to his desk.

"Oh, I'd almost forgotten he was coming down today. Tell him to come on up, please."

Toby came through the door a moment later, briefcase in hand, and Bill waved him into the chair Wilbur had just vacated.

"I didn't expect to see you again so soon, Toby."

"I didn't expect it either, but it doesn't take long to see the problems we've got in My Tho, and I need to touch base with you because I intend to start on them right now."

"Good. Cup of coffee?" Bill signaled to Laura, who brought them coffee from the urn near her desk.

"Ben is convinced there's something big brewing for about the time of Tet," said Toby, taking a tentative sip of the coffee.

"I've heard that from a lot of people, but we've got nothing solid on it, and Saigon discounts the rumors heavily."

"Why?"

"Their theory is that the VC are not so stupid as to try something they can't possibly accomplish. The VC aren't really strong enough for anything big, and they know it as well as we do."

"I see. The old theory that you can judge a Communist's intentions by finding out what his capabilities are?"

"Right."

"It makes me uneasy as hell."

"It's worked pretty well in Europe. It's a cinch that anything the Russians *can* do against us, they *will* do."

"I know," said Toby. "I've heard it all before, but it still seems to be a pretty unsatisfactory way to find out what an enemy's intentions are."

"How else could you do it? Hell, we don't even know what our own intentions are ten days in advance!"

"That's a fact." Toby grinned. "Well, anyway, I doubt if My Tho intelligence is going to help you even find out the VC capabilities, because we've got a total lack of information about anything that's going on in the province, except for what Ben's pacification teams pick up in the course of their work—and you can hardly call that intelligence. Can't evaluate it. So, in reality, we know nothing. Zilch!"

"That's the way I've seen your problems from here."

"And to add to the problem, we've got a bad security leak somewhere."

"What kind of a leak?" Bill was alarmed.

"Oh, it's none of our agency classified information, so far as I can tell. It's information about PRU operations mainly, and about our locations and comings and goings in My Tho. The PRU information would carry over into the ICEX operations when they get started."

"So, what do you intend to do?"

"I've got some tentative plans for both problems, and I want to start working on them right away," said Toby. "I wanted to let you know what I'm going to do before I start."

"Good."

"Seems an awful waste of time to have to fly up here to tell you. I guess there's no other way we can communicate securely is there?"

"We do have pouches."

"Not often enough."

"That's the only other way."

"Well, we'll just have to cope with it," Toby concluded, reaching for his briefcase.

"Before you start, Toby, I think we ought to talk about you and Chet."

"About me and Chet? Why?"

"I know you'll understand my position. I have fourteen P officers, like you, and fourteen O officers, like Ben, in addition to fourteen PRU advisers. I can't possibly handle them all personally, so I've got a regional officer for each category. Chet is the regional P officer."

Toby was dismayed.

"You understand," Bill went on, "that I couldn't make an exception and deal personally with your operations?"

"Sure," Toby replied hesitantly.

"The fact is, I would have less excuse with you than with the others because you're an old hand, and wouldn't need all that much supervision."

"I understand."

"I'm sorry I didn't make this clear to you before you went up to My Tho. I guess I just assumed that you would see the situation."

"I certainly should have seen it. I've been around long enough to know how things have to function."

"Toby, I've read your file, and I've heard Chet's story of the Frankfurt incident. As far as I can tell, that episode doesn't need to enter into our professional relationships here. But I haven't heard your side of the story. You didn't write any comment on the fitness report. You knew, of course, that you had the right to add a comment?"

"Certainly."

"Do you want to tell me your version?"

"No. And for the same reason that I didn't comment on that fitness report. You know what the propaganda analysis people always says—that if you get somebody in a position where he has to deny something, you've already got him convicted."

"Do you believe you've been convicted?"

"No. I just don't want to be put in the position of making excuses or alibis, and I don't know how to tell it without running the risk that it will sound just like an alibi."

"I think I could handle the distinction."

"Maybe. But you've got both of us in full view for a while, and I'd rather you would judge me by actions, and not explanations."

"All right. It's your decision."

"It may make my job a little harder, to have to deal directly with Chet, but we'll manage."

"So," said Bill, leaning back in his chair, "what have you got in mind for your problems?"

"Oh, do you want to hear my ideas anyway?"

"Sure. It's not all that rigid and formal. I always like to be up on what you fellows are doing, and I want you to come in and shoot the breeze whenever we've both got the time. The actual management of things will be Chet's responsibility."

Toby, visibly relieved, gave Bill a brief account of his problems, and his plans for dealing with them. Bill listened with interest, and with the understanding of a man who has been through similar experiences.

"Have you got any of this on paper?" he asked.

"All of it," Toby replied, patting the briefcase.

"Good. Why don't you go give it to Chet right now?

Whatever you may think of him, he won't let your papers sit in his in-box. He'll work on them for you."

"I know. I don't worry about that part of it." Toby got up to go.

"By the way, I hear you almost got your ass shot off," Bill remarked as Toby reached the door. Toby turned and looked at Bill's twinkling eyes.

"It was a real welcome," Toby said with a crooked smile.

He found Chet in his office, and sat down and opened his briefcase.

"Bill said that all my work goes through you."

"That's right."

"OK. I've got a rough draft of a message I'd like to send to Saigon."

He handed the draft to Chet, and Chet read it slowly.

"Let me get this straight, Busch," said Chet, after studying the paper intently. "You say here that the office has got a security leak, and you want to verify the clearances of all these people and then test the operations for a leak?"

"That's right," Toby said steadily. "How else would you do it?"

"You sure are a great one for testing. This sounds just like a replay of Frankfurt."

"Except that I *suspected* that Frankfurt net. I *know* I've got a leak in My Tho."

"You were pretty goddamned positive about Frankfurt, too, as I remember."

"I had no proof, but I was certain. I still am. That principal agent was a double. You could look at that operation and see, you could smell it a mile off. The Soviets were setting up a penetration of our operations in Frankfurt, and that agent was their foot in the door."

"Horse shit! Ernie Free set up that operation like a model. Damned near perfect."

"Naturally. If you were setting up a double agent against *them*, wouldn't you see to it that everything fell into place perfectly?"

"Busch, we've been through all this before, and there's no use doing it again. But I want to get something straight right now. Because of you, and that stupid operation of yours, I've been a deputy for my last three assignments.

Never a chief. Never the head of anything. 'Chet Wolleson?' they all say. 'Experienced man. Got some good ops in his background. But, wait a minute. Don't forget Frankfurt. Yeah, don't forget Frankfurt. We better not promote him just yet. And we better not give him his own station yet. One more tour as a deputy to a strong officer. Can't have things like Frankfurt!'

"The Frankfurt flap wasn't my fault, but it happened when the operations there were under my supervision, and the Chief of Station wouldn't go to bat for me.

"Well, let me tell you something, Mr. College Boy. It isn't going to happen again, because I'm going to watch you like a hawk. There's gonna be no half-ass school solution operations here, because they'll never get past me. Every plan you submit, every cable you send, every proposal you make, is gonna be looked at very carefully, and if I have the slightest reason to doubt, I'll stop you. Cold."

Toby looked him steadily in the eye. "I don't have to tell you that there are ways the lower echelon can put the upper echelon on the spot," he said.

"Are you making threats?"

"I'm just reminding you that you're not dealing with a junior officer trainee who doesn't know how the system works."

"All right then, I'll tell *you* something. I may not have a college degree, and of course that's another thing against me, but I got where I am by work, not by wavin' a goddamned sheepskin. And in those years of work I've learned a few things about the system, too. Don't try any out-of-channels crap on me, Busch. You do everything by the book, or by God I'll blow you right out of the water!"

[7]

DINO angled the plane into the usual attitude for a landing at the My Tho strip, and squinted in the late-afternoon sun. "I didn't mention it this morning," he said, "but I notice you changed your hardware." He looked down at the Colt .45 on Toby's belt.

"Yeah. Ben said you were right."

"Ben is a brilliant fellow."

"I'm sure he will treasure your good opinion."

"They all do."

Dino dropped the plane lightly to the ground and taxied up to where Ben was waiting.

"Hi, Ben," he shouted, as Toby unloaded the bags of PX supplies. "How's things here in My Tho?"

"The VC still seem to be kind of unfriendly, Dino," said Ben.

"You don't say. Imagine that!"

"But we're still trying to win their hearts and minds."

"That's the way to handle 'em. If they won't be friends, take an ax handle to 'em, is what I say." He leaned across the cockpit to secure the door. "Well," he concluded, "keep a tight ass-hole!"

"Same to you."

"I got a request in for a steel plate to put under mine."

He secured the latch, waved gaily at them, and had soon lifted his little plane free to fade into a faint dot and a mutter in the sky.

"Party still on?" Toby asked Ben, as they headed toward town.

"Yeah. I'm gonna pick up the girls about seven. It'll just be drinks and dinner. Maybe put on some records and dance."

"Coat and tie?"

"No. We never do for parties around here."

"Good."

"How'd things go in Can Tho?"

"Pretty good. I have to deal through Chet, of course. That may cause me a lot of extra worry and work."

"I wouldn't be surprised. When do you expect to start training the Special Police?"

"As soon as possible."

"Can I sit in on the classes?"

Toby was surprised. "Sure, but it's going to be pretty elementary. I'm sure you've already had courses that were more advanced than what I'll be teaching these people."

"I've got a reason for asking." Ben said. "The way I see it, this is probably going to be the last real war of any size we're going to fight for a long time. But we'll still have the same power against us, and we're going to have to fight it by other means—the means *you* know how to use. . . . So, I'm thinking about trying to get the CIA to hire me and resign from the army."

"They can't, Ben. You've got it backwards. You'd have to resign first, and then apply to the CIA. There's a rule about proselytizing among the services, you know."

"Yeah, I know. What I've got in mind is to do things in such a way as to get a hint about whether the agency would be interested in hiring me."

"It would have to be an awfully broad hint, because that's just as much proselytizing as giving you a signature on a piece of paper. Our personnel people handle things like that as if they were walking on eggs."

"Well, I think I'll give it a try."

"But why do you want to sit in on these classes?"

"It's like being a soldier. You know, you can take the best recruit in the world, and train him for months in the United States, but no matter how you train him, he still isn't a soldier. He becomes a soldier when he gets into action. Now, a soldier learns more about being a soldier in a few hours of combat, watching and learning from experienced combat men, that he could ever learn in a training camp."

"Yeah, I've always heard that."

"I have an idea the same is true for your profession. Now, here I am with an opportunity to watch an experienced intelligence officer at work in the field, and I don't want to miss it."

"You want to study *me,* instead of the course, is that it?"

"Exactly."

"I'm flattered."

"And I promise that if we get into a combat situation, I'll let you come along and study me."

"That sounds like a fair proposition." Toby laughed. "But I know you'll understand when I tell you that collecting on a deal like that would not be one of my favorite pastimes."

"Then it's all right if I sit in on the classes?"

"Sure."

Toby had just enough time to shower and change clothes before the guests arrived. Minnie's workmen had patched the brickwork of the bathroom wall, but had not yet put the finish on it. Ben had spoken of putting a heavy wire mesh as a stand-off net along the sides of the house, to detonate any future projectiles before they reached the walls of the building itself. They still had not made a final decision about that. The psychological impact of such a cocoon around the house was something to think about, both for the inhabitants of the house and for the VC. Ben thought that it might be best just to place the guards somewhat differently, and have them patrol the canal area every hour or so.

Whatever the solution, Toby thought, inspecting himself in the mirror before going downstairs, it wasn't going to guarantee anybody's safety or really solve any problem. It would be just coping; and just coping in a combat zone left an empty feeling in the gut.

Mrs. Chao and Chi Hai had prepared hors d'oeuvres and placed them here and there on the bar and the cocktail tables. There were festive arrangements of napkins, flowers in small vases, and bowls of fruit. Toby liked the looks of it. It was understated, but it was special and somehow just right.

Ben left in the jeep to pick up the women, and Little Jack came into the common room dressed in slacks and sport shirt. His clothes had probably been neatly ironed and folded five minutes ago, but they had now acquired the rumpled look that was characteristic of the man. He did not seem to be looking forward to the party.

"It ain't gonna be any go-go dance, Toby," he said disconsolately.

"Well, I don't know that I had a go-go dance in mind."

"I guess it depends on how you like your women."

"How do you like them?" Toby asked.

"I like to have fun with them, and then lay 'em," he said.

"And if you start out knowing that you won't be able to lay them, then you don't have any fun?"

"Oh, I guess it ain't quite that simple. As long as there's a *possibility*, it's fun, you know what I mean? I guess the most fun in the world is a woman that will just barely let you lay her."

Toby laughed. "I think you've got hold of a universal law there," he said.

"But in this case you know there's no possibility," Little Jack went on gloomily. "In this case it's gonna be feed her, give her a couple of drinks, maybe dance a little bit, and then take her home. Some fun evening!"

Toby was surprised at the vague feeling of disappointment Little Jack's comments had evoked. He realized that although he had laughed at the man's crude statement, he shared Little Jack's philosophy about women to a greater extent than he liked to admit to himself. Of course, Little Jack's seductive skills would probably confine his successes to a certain type of woman, a type that would be of little interest to Toby.

Moreover, there was no sense in doing himself an injustice. He did like to be around women just to talk with them, even if he knew that they wouldn't even barely let him lay them. He hoped that there would be some good man-woman talk tonight.

The jeep came through the gate, and they went to the door to meet the guests.

Little Jack pointed out Louise Kenney, who would be Toby's dinner partner. He looked her over, and was surprised and pleased to find that she was pretty. Her blond hair was done in a neat, fluffy style that set off her soft blue eyes. Those eye had a gentle, but lively, quality. She had splendid curves, much too exuberant for the blue *ao dai* she was wearing.

Little Jack's partner was Marie Claire, and as near as he could tell from Little Jack's pronunciation, her last name was Renondeau. She had a slender, Gallic look about her, although her English was perfectly colloquial American. Her hair was straight and cut in a boyish style, which accentuated her long and graceful neck. She was not a beautiful woman, but her body was more petite and better suited to the *ao dai* than Louise's.

The tomboy was for Ben. One could see from the first moment that Peggy Hall was fun to be around. She was slightly below medium height and build, and she had on slacks and a blouse that, while feminine and clean, were nevertheless not selected or worn with any idea of half-concealing and half-revealing the good things underneath. Her hair was in some disarray, and she either did not notice it or did not care. She was chattering away at Ben, her eyes dancing with fun and mischief, and Ben was grunting a reply now and then, enjoying the chatter. Peggy and Louise were nurses, part of an American medical team that had volunteered to come to Vietnam to help improve the medical services here. They worked in the Vietnamese hospital near the edge of town. Marie Claire was the secretary of the Province Senior Adviser, and it was only after they were introduced that Toby realized he had seen her before.

They mingled comfortably, and soon were gathered around the bar. Little Jack found relief for his own unease by serving as bartender.

"So you're Toby," said Peggy. "The man who had such a narrow escape on his first night in My Tho."

Toby looked at her sharply, and saw that she was teasing.

"Peggy," said Louise, "you're embarrassing the poor man."

"Does it embarrass you, Toby?" asked Peggy.

"Well, it's not the kind of a war story I'll be able to tell my grandchildren, that's for sure."

"Maybe you could dress it up a little," said Marie Claire. "Have it happen in the kitchen, or the bedroom."

"That's it," said Peggy. "You could say you had been frying an egg, and had just turned around to get a spatula when the rocket came through right above the stove."

Toby sipped his drink and frowned at her. "Brilliant!"

he muttered. She obviously knew the entire story. All the embarrassing details.

"But," she went on, raising a hand in warning, "then one day this rather gray-haired, bent old ex-nurse comes to the door and says to you, 'Busch, I know about your past. If you do not pay me ten thousand dollars immediately, I will tell your grandchildren about that rocket.' "

"Not a dime!" Toby exploded. "Not a thin dime. Remember, gray-haired old ex-nurses are not that big an element in our population. Who would notice if one of them disappeared without a trace? In fact, who would notice if one of them disappeared *before* she got gray-haired and old and bent?"

"I'm going to arm-wrestle him later on," Peggy said in a loud aside to Ben. "He needs to be taught a lesson."

"Watch her, Toby," said Ben. "She's little, but she's wiry."

Mrs. Chao announced that dinner was served. They trooped into the dining room, and Ben commanded Mrs. Chao and Chi Hai to stand nearby as they gathered around the table. Before they sat down, Ben handed each of them a glass of wine and lifted his own toward Toby.

"I am not a speechmaker," he said. "But I know everybody here feels like I do. When we say welcome, we really mean it. Welcome to My Tho, Toby!"

They drank the toast with smiles and words of approval. Toby sat down with them, suffused with the glow of cocktails and friendship.

Mrs. Chao and Chi Hai served a delicious meal of dishes and names that were new to him. Wine added its warmth to the easy talk; and even Little Jack was making rough attempts at sophisticated chatter, which were amusing to everybody, including himself.

After dinner, Ben put on some records, and they dutifully danced two or three numbers; but the surfeit of food and drink had unfitted them for even slow dancing, and they drifted back to the pleasant darkness of the bar to sit and talk. Toby realized that he had not relaxed this much since coming to Vietnam.

"I suppose," said Louise quietly to him, "that you have noticed how Peggy feels about Ben?"

"No," he admitted, "I hadn't noticed anything special."

"I'm surprised. I had an idea that people in your business would be quick to catch on to people's feelings."

"In my business?" he asked her with studied casualness.

"Yes, my dear," she said gently. "Don't be upset. Everybody knows."

"What about Peggy's feelings?" he said abruptly. He wanted to get her off the subject of his profession. It did not surprise him that everybody knew, but he did not want to confirm it, or talk about it. The experience and training of years forbade such talk on an occasion like this.

"She's so hopelessly in love with that man that she can hardly think of anything else, and the big lunk hasn't got a clue."

Toby looked at Peggy, chattering softly to Ben at the table near them. *What a charming picture,* he thought, realizing at the same time that the euphoria of the drinks could make almost anything charming to his foggy eyes.

"Let me fix us another drink," said Toby with a judicious air, "and as I do it, I will observe them. And then I will give you an opinion."

"Good," said Louise. "The thing needs a trained observer to observe it. So you go and observe it."

Toby went behind the bar and mixed the drinks, watching the other couple all the while with meticulous discretion. He spilled some liquor on the bar, and mopped it up studiously, then walked back to his own table, taking elaborate precautions against colliding with chairs and tables on the way.

"Well," he said carefully, "I will admit that there is a certain sparkle to the eye, and a certain amount of touching and giggling, but it looks more like high spirits than love to me."

"It's love," said Louise, taking a drink from her replenished glass. "L-O-V-E, love." She was impressed with the solemnity of her pronouncement.

"Are you sure of that?"

"I live with her."

"Oh, I didn't know that."

"Yes. All three of us live in a house on the far edge of town."

"By yourselves?"

"Well, there's a Vietnamese couple who serve as housekeeper and caretaker, and we have guards."

"But you don't have an American man living with you?" he asked, in a tone of shock and disbelief.

"Well, really, Mr. Busch!"

"You know what I mean."

"It's just the way I told you. We've got to live somewhere, and there is no American compound around here, or any dormitory. The Province Senior Adviser lives in a house not very far from us, so . . ."

"Well, it seems to me—"

"Let's not talk about our domestic arrangements. Let's talk about Peggy."

"All right." He drank some more. He gazed at her and felt the tug of that voluptuous body, so near his own. He forced the thoughts back with an effort. *Get thee behind me, Little Jack.*

"We worry about her," Louise went on. "Ben doesn't care for her in the same way. You can see that. She's bound to get her heart broken. And underneath that joking and playfulness is a very sensitive woman." She looked at him earnestly, but seemed to have a little trouble keeping her eyes focused on him.

"Really?"

"Yes. It's so sad." Louise sipped her drink, and her gentle blue eyes began to cloud over, as if she might cry.

"Hell, Louise," he said, "I don't see how a person can be that much in love with somebody that doesn't return the affection at all."

"I don't know about men, but it can sure happen to a woman. In fact, one of the surest ways to attract some women is to ignore them completely."

"He's a great guy, but somehow I don't think I would figure him as a romantic type."

"He's not. He hasn't got the slightest idea of what's going on. If you ever get the chance, let him know, will you? I know he wouldn't want to hurt her."

"Never advise other people about their love life," said Toby pompously. "You'll never be thanked for it, and you may get punched in the nose."

"Don't be silly! That's not what I mean. I mean, if you ever see a chance just to put in a casual word . . . don't you see? I don't mean to collar him and give him a birds-and-bees talk."

They sat and sipped their drinks, and Toby looked at her intently.

"Louise," he said, with the careful concentration of the slightly drunk. "I suppose you and I will be thrown together quite a bit in the next year or so."

"You make us sound like a mulligan stew. But I know what you mean. I'll be here at least a year. I think I'd go crazy if I couldn't get together with Americans now and then."

"I haven't had much experience with platonic relationships with women."

She smiled mysteriously.

"In fact," he went on, "I have never had any *desire* to have a platonic relationship with a woman."

"I suppose not."

"Anyway," he went on, "I can tell already that weeks and weeks without talking seriously to a woman, talking about things that matter, you know, and being in company with a woman . . . Well, what I mean is without the atmosphere of a woman's company . . ." He stopped and looked at her as if he had made a statement, and was awaiting, and expecting, her approval of it.

"Go on," she said quietly.

"Well," he said with great deliberation, "I just wanted to say that I'm glad you are around. You are a sweet woman."

"How nice!"

"I want to be good friends with you."

"I'd like that."

"You are not going to be easy to be just friends with."

"I think that is rather nice to hear, too," she said.

"I am a little drunk, and I'm going to shut up before I say something stupid."

"I think I must be in the same position—I mean condition . . . myself," she said, "because I have an urge to tell you something I probably wouldn't say otherwise."

"What's that?"

She leaned close to him, to emphasize the weight of her words. "Let's be friends!"

What a profound observation! He took another drink and blinked. It almost brought a lump to his throat. Here was a woman with a brain. He took another sip. As well as a body. He glanced quickly at her body, then beyond it as if his gaze were intended to encompass other things as well.

"Well!" he said.

They sat and beamed at each other, certain that the warmth they were basking in was platonic.

The party broke up about midnight. Ben explained mistily to one and all that while it might seem unchivalrous for just one male to escort all the ladies home, nevertheless to troop across town in three vehicles would be pointless, and he suggested that he be the escort, since everybody else was drunk.

There was some discussion about who was and who was not drunk, but in the end Ben drove out the gates with his precious cargo, and Toby climbed the stairs to his room.

He was unbuttoning his shirt when the first mortar projectile he had ever heard in his life exploded about a block away. The adrenalin flowed and brought a chill of sobriety to his brain. He did not know what the explosion was, but memories of the rocket still loomed large, and he knew that whatever it was, it was hostile. He stood fixed to the spot, undecided. Then the second round hit, no nearer, but in a slightly different direction.

He heard Little Jack burst from his room. "They're mortaring us, Toby!" Little Jack called, as he went by the door. "Get a weapon and get down to the common room."

Toby grabbed the grease gun from its peg on the wall, picked up a satchel of magazines, and sped down the stairs as the third round went off, this one significantly closer than the first two.

Little Jack was sitting in an overstuffed chair in the middle of the room. He was naked to the waist, and he had an M-16 lying on the floor beside the chair. He motioned to a chair near him.

"Mortar fire would come right through that roof if it hit directly," he explained. "We always come down here during a barrage. The windows are up at a level so that we're out of line of any fragments that would come from a ground detonation."

Toby sat down. He was under attack by an enemy, and his heart was pounding. He did not count the explosions as they came, but he could perceive that this house was evidently not a target. Only one round fell close. The rest of the explosions seemed to center three or four blocks away. He noticed with some surprise that he could hear a faint, deep pop before each explosion, and wondered if it was the sound of the mortar being fired.

Little Jack said that it was. "You can't always hear it. If the night is quiet and the wind is right, you can. You get so you know the sound, though, and once you do, the first one you hear of an evening will start you toward cover before the round ever arrives."

"When do we go up to the roof?" Toby asked, forcing a casual tone to his voice.

"As soon as they quit firing," said Little Jack. "They wouldn't try anything with troops or sapper squads while the firing is in progress."

"Firing is in progress" was not a natural phrase for a man like Little Jack, and Toby found it amusing that in the midst of this kind of violence, the man would utter such a ponderous phrase—the prescribed military terminology.

They continued to converse quietly between explosions, strangely detached from the world of noise and fire outside.

"I suppose Ben will take cover somewhere?"

"Sure. You'd have to be a goddamned fool to drive through the streets with this going on, unless you had to. He may be still over at the girls' house. Wherever he is, you can bet your ass he's under cover."

Little Jack's tone was strangely sharp.

"Sounds like you've got kind of a low opinion of Ben," said Toby.

Little Jack returned his gaze steadily. "No, it ain't that. I just don't have much of an opinion at all."

"What does that mean?"

"I don't know much about him."

"Well, you know his rank, and where he's been, and what he's done."

"I know what the record says."

"Could the record lie?"

"Can CIA's records lie about a man?"

Toby winced inwardly. That had hit a nerve.

"In the army," Little Jack went on, "a man's personal record can make a real hero out of a chicken shit."

"He's got medals, hasn't he?"

"All that takes is friends that will write up and endorse the recommendation, and when you're an officer you can get friends like that easy. Medals are cheap in the army. Shit, I've got some myself. They don't mean a goddamned thing."

Detonations a bit closer now. Toby was uneasy. He was astonished that two men could sit under fire, even sheltered as they were, and talk about something other than the attack itself. But he also realized that the conversation helped keep his nerves under control.

"You think Ben may not be much of a soldier?"

"I don't know one way or the other. He talks real good, but talk is cheap."

He lit a cigarette and leaned back in the chair. There was only one dim floor lamp to give them light, but Toby noticed a long scar that slashed downward from Little Jack's left shoulder across his chest.

"That's some scar," he said.

"Yeah," said Little Jack carelessly.

"Is that a combat wound?"

"Bayonet."

"Jesus!" Toby laughed nervously. "Somebody sure wanted to kill you!"

"He tried."

"Where did it happen?"

"In Korea."

The firing ceased, and they climbed to the roof. "You watch that side, Toby," said Little Jack. "I don't look for anything against this house, because nothing was aimed at us, but we'll watch for a few minutes."

Toby peered over the low parapet. He could see the shadowy forms of the guards as they came out of their sandbag bunkers and repositioned themselves around the wall.

They watched for about ten minutes, and then felt their way slowly back down the steps.

"I'm going down and wait for Ben, Little Jack," said Toby.

"I think I'll go down myself and have a drink before I hit the sack."

They went to the bar and sat on the high stools, a nightcap in hand.

"This is the first time I've ever had any association with professional soldiers in action. I've always thought that a guy would have to be a little bit out of his mind to be one, and looking at you and that scar makes me all the more certain. What is it that makes you stay with it?"

"Damned if I know. It's my life, that's all. I move around a lot, I see a lot of the world, I'm usually where the action is, you know what I mean? A man likes to be where the action is.

"Right now, for instance, the whole goddamned world is watching this war, and I'm right in the middle of it. Sounds like I'm a conceited son of a bitch, but hell, a guy wants to be important in something. I haven't got much in the way of other talents. You've seen my PRU reports, and you can tell I ain't ever gonna win no prize for writing."

"Yes, I have to admit that," said Toby, without malice.

"I couldn't stand going back and holding down some kind of a job in the States."

"Sure," Toby teased him. "It's a hell of a lot better to run around getting sliced up with a bayonet."

Little Jack laughed. "Hell, that's really just a scratch, Toby. I got scratches like that all over me. See this one here?" He indicated a white line up the back of his hand, which looked like a tendon ridge until one inspected it closely. "I never did know what caused that one. We was holdin' a line during those first days around Pusan, and there was so much going off all around us that the first thing I knew I felt a real sharp sting, and looked down and saw that something had creased the back of my hand. I got a couple of fragments in one leg, and a place down low on my belly where a bullet went clean through me."

"And you still want to keep on being a soldier?"

"Yep. There ain't any other life I'd want to live."

They sipped their drinks in silence.

"I'll admit," Little Jack said after a time, "there is one thing that I'd never want to go through again."

"What's that?"

"Gettin' captured. I was a prisoner of war in Korea. The Koreans are mean son of a bitches and when they saw my size they figured they'd have to break me down."

"Did they do it?"

"No, but they came closer to killing me than I ever been before or since."

"Didn't seem to do you any permanent damage."

"No. I got three of my front teeth bridged over. Got the real ones knocked out with a rifle butt. And I had the amoebas so bad I damned near had my gut eaten through."

Ben drove in. During the barrage he had stayed at the women's house, which had been some distance from the target area.

"Could you see what their target was, Ben?" Toby asked.

"Most of the fire fell in two separate places, as near as I could tell. One area was just up here in the next block or so, and the other was across town, somewhere around where Therese lives. Nothing military in either area. It was just harassment, I guess."

"Jesus, I hope Therese is all right."

"Yeah."

"Seems strange that they would harass the people they're supposed to be trying to win over."

"Yes, it's hard to figure out. Everything all right here?"

"No damage."

"Good." Ben turned his head and listened. "Here comes Spooky."

They went back up to the roof to watch. A C-47 had arrived over the area, and it now released flares that lighted the scene and the aircraft in a pale, intense glow.

"That old airplane may be as much as thirty years old," Ben mused.

As if squirting a stream of golden water, the plane fired lines of tracers into the area from which the mortar fire had come.

"Six thousand rounds a minute!" snorted Little Jack.

"Mini-guns," Ben explained to Toby. "They got 'em on those Spookies, and on the helicopter gunships, too."

"Hell of a way to fight a war," said Little Jack.

"You can say that again," Ben agreed.

"What's wrong with it?" Toby asked. He had already

sensed that something about this lumbering old airplane pouring fire at the ground was not quite right, but he couldn't say what it was.

"Shit, the VC know the routine better than those guys up there with the guns," said Little Jack. "They know exactly where that plane is parked, and how long it takes to get it in the air, and they know how long it will take to get it over whatever target they're gonna work on. So, they just time their fire. If they figure it will be ten minutes before the Spooky can get there, they figure on eight minutes of mortar fire, and two minutes to move over a couple hundred yards so they can watch them guys make fools of theirself."

"This one is a little late, though," Ben pointed out.

"Half the time they are," said Little Jack. "But they're never early, that's for goddamned sure."

"Well, they gave our friends a chance to get a good seat over in some other treeline to watch the show."

"You mean all that fire is not hitting anything?" Toby asked.

"Not any VC, that's for sure. They'll fly around up there for five or ten minutes and fire off twenty-five or thirty thousand rounds, and all they'll do is fill a little patch of ground with lead," Little Jack said.

"If we lose this war," Ben said in a low, troubled voice, "it's going to be because we fought it wrong. There's something insane about firing twenty-five thousand rounds at a squad of men with three or four mortars."

"Especially if you don't kill a one of them!" Little Jack added.

"But how can we help it?" Ben went on. "The generals know it's crazy. Or at least some of the generals do. But they've got all the firepower our country can produce, and so when they have to make a choice between sending in men or sending in fire, there's only one choice they can make. Even when they know, and their own soldiers know, that it would make more military sense to send in the men, they've got to send the Spookies and the B-Fifty bombers instead."

"Because otherwise they'd get men killed?"

"Yep."

"My God, I thought it was routine for generals to send men into combat to get killed."

"Routine's hardly the word for it, and they don't send them in with the idea of getting them killed," Ben said. "But usually they send them in with a clear conscience, because they know that war kills men, and they know that sometimes getting four men killed now may save fifty men later on. But in this war, their hands are tied by television."

"Television?"

"Ever see that TV scene where American soldiers are setting fire to a Vietnamese village?"

"Everybody has."

"You saw them setting the fire?"

"Yes."

"Do you know *why* they set it?"

"Well, they were . . ." Toby began, then stopped, puzzled. "No, I guess I don't know."

"Neither did that television crew. And what's more, they didn't give a damn. They're in a competitive industry, and they were beating the competition with a sensational film."

"That's a fact. They don't conceal their motives very well. They don't even try to conceal them."

"Say some colonel sends in a platoon of men after a mortar squad, and six of them get killed, and here comes a TV crew and shows shots of the six body bags there on the ground, and then pans over to some gunships or Spookies sitting still on a ramp, and the announcer says something like, 'And so, this officer had to make a command decision, whether to oppose the enemy with American flesh or American firepower. He chose the flesh.' Then they pan the picture back to the body bags."

"That's the way they do it, all right."

"And he hasn't given a fact that wasn't true, but he has assembled a whole set of facts so that they tell a lie."

"It's a hell of a situation, isn't it?" Toby mused.

"I'll tell you something else about those television crews. Some of them are the gutsiest men I've ever seen. Give me a platoon of *them,* with rifles instead of cameras, and I'll take on any three platoons in the world. But their guts is causing more bloodshed . . . Oh, hell, what's the use talking about it?"

They watched the Spooky cruise back and forth, hosing down the area with its torrent of fire and metal.

"You gotta admit it's quite a show," said Toby. The Spooky released another flare. More jets of fire at the ground. Six thousand rounds a minute was one hundred rounds a second. At that rate, you couldn't hear the individual reports, as you did from a normal machine gun. You could only hear a one-hundred-cycle tone, a low hum. The lowest sound the human ear could perceive, as he remembered it, was about thirty or forty cycles per second. What note were the mini-guns playing? he wondered. He'd have to remember to look it up someday.

He grinned in the darkness, and thought that what Spooky was doing was not shooting the enemy—he was trying to hum the enemy to death. Toby was on the point of mentioning this to his companions, but then considered that they would think him drunk or frivolous, so he kept the thought to himself.

The last flare sputtered out. The big plane turned and lumbered away toward its home, and the three men felt their way back down the darkened stairs.

[8]

CHRIS Christopher sat huddled in the sampan, a little forward and to one side of Wilbur, her eyes staring at the black water of the Bassac rushing past the side of the boat. They had come about eight of the ten miles they were to make under the power of outboard motors. Two more miles and they would head up a smaller stream, propelled by poles and paddles. The last mile to the target would be on foot. There was no moon, but the zodiacal light was sufficient for a dim perception of objects and persons.

Wilbur said something in Vietnamese in a low tone, and

a small man came aft from the bow and squatted beside them.

"This is Xuan," said Wilbur. "He's going to take care of you."

"But I don't want to interfere with your operations."

"That's why I'm giving him this job. I'm going to be too busy to stick with you myself. He'll watch you. He's got eyes like a cat. It'll be easy for you to panic in the dark, but just remember the enemy can't see any better than we can. At first, they won't even be able to see as well, because all of them except the perimeter guard will be in lighted houses.

"If you get separated for some reason, don't move. Stay exactly where you are, because Xuan will find you, or if he doesn't, somebody else will. If you're moving around in the dark, we'll lose you as sure as hell."

"I'll remember," she said, now thoroughly frightened by the whole prospect. When she had persuaded her editors to send her to Vietnam she had assumed that being in combat action would be frightening, but she had not imagined how fearful it would really be.

The boats turned into the mouth of a small tributary of the Bassac, and the motors fell silent. Silently, dark figures arose in the sampans, and they were propelled by poles against the sluggish current.

They did not talk now. When at last they squished into a reedy bank, the men, though heavily armed, climbed out with hardly a clink of metal. Xuan led Chris to a small clump of saplings at the water's edge, where he cut a small wand with a sheath knife that was razor sharp. In pantomine, he showed her that she was to hold one end and he would hold the other, so that they could stay together in the darkness. They moved off down a path in single file.

She wondered at these slight, wiry men, who seemed to have the eyes and feet of cats. She stumbled repeatedly where they walked steadily.

There was a whispered exchange among them, after which some of their number left the path and disappeared into the blackness, as if they had been snuffed out of existence.

The lights of a small village appeared ahead of them. Xuan struck out to the left, dragging her through tall grass that whipped about her and sawed at her hands and face. They came to a mound of earth that loomed above the grass, and after circling it carefully, Xuan pulled her to the top and signaled her to keep down.

She crouched and looked about her in the dim light. She recognized the appearance of the mound. It was a grave, and the large bulky object before her was a concrete tomb.

Squatting beside her, Xuan used his carbine in a vigorous pantomine to show her that if firing started she should take cover on the side of the tomb opposite the village.

They waited. She marveled that he could sit so calmly in the darkness. She tried to relax. Maybe this operation would be uneventful after all. She hoped so. It wouldn't make a very good story, but she would at least live through it.

But no, she must not think that way. What she must hope for was action—hot, bloody combat. She wanted, she had to have, a story that would get a big play in her papers, and perhaps be picked up for publication elsewhere. Chris knew that she was reasonably attractive, at least as pretty as any female television correspondent she had ever seen, and prettier than most of them. She had the looks. All she needed was the breaks.

Television news. That was the career she wanted, the career she had been dreaming of since her high-school days. This small newspaper syndicate was the best she could do for now, but she was determined to make it the stepping-stone into television. It could be that. It would be, if she could get stories with real action, sensational coverage, the kind of human interest that television craved and devoured.

There was a shout from one of the houses. A woman screamed. Xuan remained motionless, while the crack of rifles split the silence of the night and tiny points of flame stabbed the darkness from several of the houses.

The firing intensified. Chris noticed that the sound came to her ears in waves, or surges, as the battle progressed. It was punctuated by shouts, and what must be Vietnamese oaths.

A ghostly figure hurtled toward them through the grass, and with a little cry of terror Chris started to rise. Her nerves tingled with fright, and her heart was pounding as if it would burst from her breast.

Xuan grasped her arm and held her down with an iron grip. The fleeing figure rushed by the mound with a loud snort and a grunt. It was a hog. Xuan patted her hand and released her.

The firing gathered and concentrated around three houses at one end of the village. Xuan shook his head in dismay. He held up a grenade and pointed it toward the village. She guessed that he must be saying that grenades would be used now, but she had no idea which side would use them.

As if on cue from Xuan, there came an explosion near one of the houses, followed in quick succession by two more. Then there was a lull in the firing. Xuan became tense, she could not tell why. He muttered something to her in a barely audible whisper. She did not know what he had said, but knew that he was expecting something.

The pop of carbines and the angry snap of heavier rifles resumed, now much closer to them, and Xuan suddenly grasped her arm again and shoved her roughly around to the other side of the vault, just in time to escape the bullets that began to smack into the earth and concrete of their position. The battle had moved from the village into the grassy field around them, and it intensified into a storm of sound and darting light.

A figure appeared at the base of the mound. Chris thought at first that it must be one of the PRUs, but Xuan's reaction showed her that she was wrong. Again her heart pounded wildly. The figure made as if to climb the side of the mound, and she realized that only Xuan stood between her and a swift death.

Xuan drew his knife. Why didn't he use his gun? She resisted an impulse to reach for his carbine. Silently he slipped down the side of the mound. She heard a startled exclamation, a scuffle, and then a strangled groan as Xuan's knife came up from below into the man's heart.

The firing was still swirling around them, but gradually it died out in the distance in little spasms of sound. Xuan climbed back up to where she was, wiping his knife with a handful of grass. He replaced it in its sheath and held out the wand for her to grasp.

The village was now quiet, and they found Wilbur standing in the doorway of one of the thatched houses that had been at the center of most of the fighting. The interior was lighted by oil lamps.

"You all right?" Wilbur asked her.

"Yes. Is it all over?"

"Yeah," he said, in a tone of heavy irony. "The operation was a success, but the patient died."

"You mean the cadre was killed?"

Wilbur pointed to a body on the floor beyond the door. "I think that's him."

She peered into the interior of the house at the body lying sprawled on the dirt floor near the far wall. Two other bodies were nearer to the door. She caught her breath in an involuntary start at the sight of the bodies, bodies that had only minutes before been alive and unaware of impending violence.

Some of the PRUs, their carbines at the ready, were moving purposefully about the village, going into houses, searching the exterior parts of the area. The villagers clustered warily in small groups. They were frightened. The PRUs were questioning some of them sharply, but were not harming them physically.

One by one the black-clad figures came to gather around the door where Wilbur stood, and reported to him, while Xuan went through the pockets of the dead man by the far wall.

Xuan had finished when the last of the PRUs had reported in, and he gathered the papers and pocket litter into a small bundle and brought it to Wilbur. The two men examined some of the paper and talked in low tones.

"Yeah, he was our man all right," Wilbur concluded with a sigh. "God, I wish we could have taken him alive. What this guy could have told us!"

Xuan then wrapped the papers in an oilcloth and tied a string around them. He handed the bundle back to Wilbur, who tucked it under his belt.

"This is all we got out of the operation," he said disgustedly.

"Not the way you planned it," said Chris.

"Sure wasn't. We got through their perimeter without any problem, but before we could get to the house something happened to alert the whole place. I think it was a pig."

"It was," said Chris, laughing nervously. "We saw it."

"They took us under fire, and after that it wasn't likely that we'd ever take the guy alive. They knew what we were after. They backed up in the village, and then most of them got away. They found a gap in our blocking force that shouldn't have been there. Tomorrow I'm going to find out why."

Chris remembered that she was a professional reporter, and she forced herself to act the part, keeping her voice calm with great effort. "Many people killed?"

"Two of the VC were killed out there in the street, besides these in here. Some people were hurt, too. I don't know how many yet. I don't think we lost any. Maybe a nick here and there."

"That's good."

"I don't know if we got any of them after they bugged out."

"Xuan killed one," Chris said, suddenly remembering, the shock of the memory showing in her voice. Wilbur spoke to Xuan, and Xuan gave a laconic reply.

"Yeah, he did," Wilbur said.

Chris looked once more at the bodies in the room, and felt her lips quivering and the sting of tears in her eyes. This was not the way she had imagined it at all. This was so calm and ruthless. A rush of pity for those young men and their families had destroyed her pose of journalistic detachment. For a moment she hated these cool, efficient killers, whose assault had left those bodies so battered and lifeless.

Wilbur was regarding her thoughtfully. "I'm sorry," she said. "This is the first battle I ever saw. I didn't know it would be exactly like this. I don't know what I expected."

"We killed them because we had to, Chris," said Wilbur. "When an enemy starts a firefight in these cases, your plan to simply arrest a man goes down the drain. You fight because you have to."

"Of course," she replied, squaring her shoulders. "I understand. I'll get used to it."

They made preparations to leave. "Sometimes the fact that the PRUs are so good and so well known works against us," Wilbur went on. "The enemy is so scared of them his actions are unpredictable."

Xuan finished a perfunctory search of the other corpses, and shook his head at Wilbur.

"OK," said Wilbur. "That's it. Let's move out." He put a hand on Chris's arm. "Be sure to stick with Xuan, will you? This could be the most dangerous part of the operation, because the whole countryside knows we're here now, and they may ambush us or set booby traps."

Xuan extended the wand to her, and they filed out of the village and back along the path through the tall grass. It seemed an eternity to Chris before they reached the sampans, but they did so without incident, and were soon moving downstream.

Wilbur was relaxed now, and in a more conversational mood. "Ask anybody in Vietnam about the PRUs," he said, moving his arm in a broad gesture toward the men in the sampans, "and they'll tell you that they're the best fighters in the country. It takes all the training and discipline we can give them to make them understand and operate on our primary objective the way we want them to. It doesn't make sense to them to move in against an enemy just to pick up a man for questioning, or to capture a communications center intact, or to collect the papers and files of a district committee. The war isn't a question of papers and information to them. To them, it's men and guns, and when they make contact with men and guns, they want to fight."

"So I notice."

"They are strictly ordered not to fight unless there is no way to avoid it on these operations. We're teaching them slowly but surely. This one is a good unit. They're smart and unflappable."

Xuan moved back to where they were seated, replacing his knife in its sheath. He extended his hand toward Chris, and she grasped what he was offering without at first realizing that it was the wand. He spoke to her in a cheery voice.

"He stripped the bark off and carved the name of the village and the date on the stick," Wilbur told her. "He thought you might like to keep it as a souvenir."

Chris was touched by the gesture from this slightly built man, who had led her through the night and protected her from its dangers.

"Yes, I would," she said. "Thank you, Xuan, for taking care of me." She extended her hand to him, as Wilbur translated. Xuan took her hand in his own in a friendly grip, then patted it lightly with his free hand, as he had done by the tomb, and returned to his seat in the bow.

[9]

WHILE he was awaiting Saigon and headquarters action on the clearance documents and training materials, Toby instructed Therese in his own methods of office management. He tightened filing systems, updated logs and records that had been ignored or poorly handled in the past, and purged great quantities of material from the files.

"I want you to handle these things so that I won't have to worry about them," he told her. "If the typing load is too great, we may have to get a typist to help you out, but I want this office run with good routines and lean files. Do you think you can do it?"

"Yes, Mr. Busch."

"There is one rule that we must follow strictly from now on. In my safe there are some documents that pertain only to our agency's work, and should be seen only by authorized persons. Mr. Compton and I are the only ones authorized, and I have changed the combination of my safe, so that he and I are the only ones with access."

She was troubled.

"You do not trust me with everything?"

He smiled reassuringly. "It is because of strict regulations of my agency, which have been established as a result of long experience, and which seem to have been ignored in this office for a long time. Except for those things, I am trusting you with every part of the office. Most important of all, I want to be able to depend on you to handle deadlines, tickler systems, and routines of all sorts. If it turns out that you can do all this, you will be doing me the greatest service you can imagine."

He did not add, of course, that she would in so doing also be maintaining her access to the information that had been leaking out.

In her grasp of office management, Therese proved to be the equal of any secretary he had ever had or worked with. She watched his changes with approval, often making suggestions for more logical and simplified procedures. She voluntarily took tasks off his hands, always leaving him the means of assuming the work himself without embarrassment to either of them, if he desired.

He visited the Special Police Offices regularly to check on the preparations for the classes. He was surprised when Thieu gave him a list of the participants without delay. He had never had such a quick response to a bureaucratic procedure, even in the most advanced countries of Europe, and certainly not in Latin America.

Minnie hovered in the background during the meetings with Thieu, but Thieu did not try to conceal his distaste for the presence of an interpreter, and Toby found that by speaking slowly and searching for uncomplicated ideas expressed in simple phrases, he could communicate with the man. He did wish that Thieu did not feel compelled to stand so close to a person to talk. He found himself slowly backpedaling during each conversation, inexorably being forced into a chair or a corner before he gave up and allowed Thieu to set the distance between them. He had known Frenchmen who did this, and wondered if Thieu had caught it from the French.

The room that was to serve as a classroom had been supplied with a portable blackboard and writing tables and chairs. It had only two windows, which looked out into a shady portion of the compound, and was rather dark.

"It seems to me," he said, gesturing toward the windows, "that there is hardly enough light in here. We may want to ask for some additional lamps. Do you have any available?"

"Yes," Thieu replied without hesitation. "That is Mekong River. But only one part. Other parts go by Truc Giang and Phu Vinh. Can Tho River is Bassac."

"Ah, I see," said Toby wisely, and added, as if making a quip that only he and Thieu would appreciate, "Then we will assume that our budding spies are to carry out their lucubrations by the light of the Mekong?" He gave an unobtrusive laugh that invited Thieu to join in, which Thieu did with alacrity. Minnie looked at them blankly, and Toby blessed him for it. Thieu would not have appreciated peasant participation in their sophisticated badinage.

Toby went with Little Jack to the PRU compound, and looked over the living arrangements and the men. The arrangements were spartan. These men did not decorate their barracks with *Playboy* pictures, although much of the rest of South Vietnam seemed to be papered with centerfolds. In fact, the PRUs did not decorate their quarters at all. Simple cots, pegs and racks and shelves for weaponry, small lockers for clothing. Toby noted that there did not seem to be any undercurrent of communication or sentiment between Little Jack and these men. They seemed almost indifferent to him and to Toby, and Little Jack apparently returned the indifference. Toby was uneasy, but told himself that he must withhold judgment in a situation so new to him.

Bill Voigt flew up and spent three hours with Toby. Mrs. Chao prepared a delicious lunch, and Toby felt that the inspection, if that was what it was, had gone off well. Bill said that he was calling a regional meeting of all P officers one week from that day, to discuss the ICEX program. It had been approved, and had been given a different name. It would be called the Phoenix program from now on.

"Why Phoenix?" Toby asked. "Somebody just draw it out of a hat, or does it have some significance?"

"I wasn't there," Bill said, "but as near as I can tell, it was selected with some care. They wanted something that would appeal to the emotions and the imagination of everybody, Americans and Vietnamese. They wanted something that would imply a successful campaign starting from nothing. Well, they thought of things like Bootstrap, but the Vietnamese have no tradition of the self-made man, and no history of boots with straps. They tried a lot of other things—slang, mythology, and so on—and then somebody thought of the phoenix, and came to find out the Vietnamese have got a legendary bird something like that. It didn't rise from the ashes, but there is something extraordinary about its origins, and so that's what the program is called. It's Phoenix in English, and Phung Hoang in Vietnamese."

"Phung Hoang?"

"Right."

"My God!" Toby laughed. "How can you get serious about something called 'Phung Hoang'?"

Bill smiled. "The Vietnamese apparently can, and we have got to do it, too."

"This meeting in Can Tho will be the first time I've had a chance to meet any of the other P officers, except for Ski," Toby said.

"Yes, and my son is going to be in Can Tho at the same time," Bill said. "You'll also get a chance to meet him." He made no attempt to conceal his pleasure at the prospect.

"On leave?"

"Three days. You can imagine what a joy it will be for his mother to have me write to her that I've been with him."

"The joy obviously won't be confined to his mother."

"Nope."

There were no mortarings during those days. Little Jack took his PRUs on an operation to find a Viet Cong rice cache. The operation was uneventful. They found no rice, and Little Jack concluded that the tip had been false.

The An Loi replacements were flown in, and Ben took them in a small convoy down to An Loi. He spent the night there, and returned the next day full of optimism for the little village and its team.

"You wouldn't recognize the place," he said. "They've got it pretty well rebuilt, and you can hardly see any traces of the attack. I think the team has got itself back together pretty well."

Toby was beginning to feel some optimism himself. He had prepared for, or had already begun, the major tasks that would occupy his time during this tour of duty, and he found that operating thus independently, at a distance from the corporate structure of the agency, gave him a sense of freedom and exhilaration he had never had in his work before.

There were two problems he had not yet even begun to

attack. One of them was the Yenan Battalion, whose file he took from the safe time and again, for study and analysis. There had to be some way he could get a handle on it.

The other was his lack of any intelligence collection operations of his own. Such operations were, after all, the core of any intelligence officer's work, and lacking any of them at all, he could never feel right. To make the problem worse, he was in a new culture, hemmed in by unusual elements of security, language, and war, and he did not have the slightest idea how he was going to go about acquiring agents within the Viet Cong. He didn't even have the necessary elements to do a target study.

On this latter problem, help came from a totally unexpected source.

"Mr. Busch, may I speak with you alone?" Therese asked him one morning.

"Certainly. Shall we go in the house?"

They sat in the big chairs by the coffee table in the common room, Therese perching uneasily on the edge of hers, made to look tiny by its dimensions.

"Mr. Busch, I know that my position here is only to do work of the office, and not do any of the plans or other things."

"Well, of course—"

"Please, I am not complaining. I am apologizing if what I am going to say is not proper."

"Go ahead."

"You have only my word that I hate the Viet Cong," she continued, and Toby's face softened.

"Therese, I do not doubt your word." He realized that he meant it.

"I could not help hearing you mention sometimes that you do not have informants in the Viet Cong."

Toby's breath quickened. He knew from experience that this kind of a preliminary meant some prospect for recruitment. Therese misinterpreted his agitation.

"I cannot help hearing things in this office," she said. "Even those things you would not want me to hear."

"Never mind that. What is it you have in mind?"

"Where I live . . . it is a place in town. . . ."

"Yes, I've driven by that area. They mortared it the other evening, I think."

"Yes. That is the Viet Cong way."

"Go on."

"A family that lives in a house near mine, they have a son who is in the Viet Cong. He is not often at home, because he belongs to a local force battalion. But his mother has told me that her son has come to hate the Viet Cong."

"And you think he might be willing to . . . ?"

"Perhaps to be your informant."

"What I am looking for is an agent, not an informant," said Toby.

"I do not understand."

"It's really just a question of the meaning of words," he went on. "An informant would only tell me what he knows already. An agent would go look for information I want."

"I see."

"I ought to tell you that I wouldn't be very interested even in an agent, if he is nothing but a soldier in a local force battalion. What could he tell me or find out for me that would be worth the time and effort? He might be a way to get to other higher-level people, but operating that way has only a modest chance of success, and it takes a lot of time. Time is something we have very little of, as you said yourself."

"But he is not just a soldier. He is the commander of the battalion."

"The commander! Hey, that's different."

"He is visiting his mother now. He will leave after midnight. Do you wish to meet him before he leaves?"

Toby was elated, but he was now confronted with a dilemma. There were no hard-and-fast rules about approaching agent prospects, but every officer was expected to remember certain maxims that had proven valid in action. Before ever making a personal meeting, find out who the prospect is, what he knows, why he might be willing to tell it, where to meet him, and how to make certain that the meeting is secure and unobserved. Above all, have contingency plans in case it is a trap.

He could not possibly fulfill these requirements on such short notice.

But there was only one response he could make. He must meet the man tonight.

"Yes, I want to see him."

"You understand that I would be there," she reminded him hesitantly.

"I not only understand it, I want it. I *must* have you there." She already knew about the prospect, and Toby would have to assume that she would know much that went on eventually, even if he tried to cut her out of future operations. He needed an interpreter. She could be the interpreter and it would be unnecessary to bring an additional person in. His instincts approved of that.

"Very well," she replied.

"Furthermore, if this works out I will want you to continue in the operation with me at all times, to interpret. And to help."

"Very well. Then I will go home at lunchtime and make arrangements for the meeting."

"Has he told anybody else?"

"His mother knows that he is not happy."

"He must not tell anybody else. About that, or about the meeting tonight. Get that across to him, will you?"

"Very well."

"Even his mother should not know about this meeting, or his decision, or anything else."

"I will tell him."

"Now, about the meeting. It must be arranged so that it cannot be seen or heard by others. But it must be in a place that it would be natural for me to go. That is going to be difficult for a round-eyes like me in My Tho."

"Yes," she said thoughtfully. "That will be very difficult."

"Do you live alone, Therese?"

"Yes. I have a small house that is joined to another one. You would not call it a house in America, I think. I live alone, but my house is fastened to the house of another family. They are friends."

"How would you feel if your friends and neighbors got the idea that you were my mistress?"

"Your mistress?" She was unfamiliar with the word, but her confusion and hesitation showed that she sensed its meaning.

"My lover."

"I do not know." She was confused, embarrassed.

"Here is what I have in mind, Therese," he went on,

with such enthusiasm and lack of guile that she relaxed and listened with interest. "I brought a little SONY television set with me from Can Tho the other day. Do you have a set in your house?"

"No. There are no television sets in any of the houses near there. Television sets are very expensive."

"But you do have electricity?"

"It is not constant, but we have electricity."

"Good. Here is what we could do, if you are willing to put your reputation on the line, Therese. I'll go with you this evening with the television set. We will let people conclude that it is a gift from me, but we won't *tell* them so. People believe something that they conclude much more firmly than something that you tell them. You will see to it that everybody in the area comes to know that you have the set. Let them watch it. You'll know how to handle things so they'll draw the conclusion. I'll also give you other things—"

"But Mr. Busch, I could not accept gifts from you."

"They will not be gifts from me. I will charge them to operational expenses, and they will be accounted for all the way to Washington. Since you are an employee, they will be officially on loan to you, and will appear on the records that way, but you will keep them in your possession as long as necessary for the operation. Do you see what I mean?"

"Yes."

"I am asking for a great deal from you," said Toby, checking his enthusiasm for a moment at the sight of her thoughtful eyes. "I will certainly understand if you refuse. Perhaps we could figure out another way to do it." His tone clearly said that no other way would be nearly so satisfactory as this one.

"I will do it," she said.

"Someday, perhaps, we can explain to your friends and neighbors the real truth about what we are doing."

"Does it mean that you now trust me?"

Toby paused and searched for the right words. "Therese," he said slowly, "in my work I have been deceived and even trapped by people I liked and trusted. Trust is the golden key in this business. Once a person wins the trust of an intelligence agency, he is in a position of great power. So, intelligence agencies are always careful about bestowing that trust."

"Yes, I see," she said, an edge of sarcasm in her voice.

"Therese," he said, pausing for a moment until her eyes were directly on him, "I am violating the standard procedures of my agency by going to a strange place with you tonight, to meet an agent prospect, without knowing anything about him except what you have told me. If it is a deception, it could be the end of my career; and if it is a trap, it could be the end of my life. But I am going. Does that say anything to you about trust?"

She looked down at her hands. "Yes," she said faintly, and then raised her eyes to his again. A bashful smile had come to her lips, almost banishing the sadness from her eyes, and he knew that he had been forgiven.

"All right," he said brusquely, "now let's get the meeting arranged. First off, can this man get into your house without being seen?"

"I believe so."

"When you instruct him, tell him that we will be in your house alone at seven o'clock. He must wait at least fifteen minutes. Fix up a signal that will tell him if everything is all right for him to come in—something natural like a door being ajar."

"I could leave my shoes in the door."

"Good. If he doesn't see those shoes, he is not to come in. If the shoes are there, he must come as soon after seven fifteen as he can without being seen. All right?"

"Would it not be better for him to be there already?"

"No," said Toby gently. "Psychology is extremely important, especially at this stage. He comes to see *me*. I do not go to see *him*. It may sound silly, but it is important."

Again she smiled. "It does not sound silly. It sounds like a Vietnamese."

"Then the effect won't be lost on him."

"No."

"Now, here in the office, only you and I will know about this. Nobody else, American or Vietnamese, must be told."

"Very well."

"It means that Mr. Compton and Mr. Horner will both

draw the same conclusions that we expect others to draw about you and me."

"I understand."

"A good name is a great sacrifice to make."

"Mr. Busch, I will not worry about my good name. Other things are more important."

It was growing dark when he loaded her little motorbike into the back of the jeep, placed a cardboard container with the television set alongside it, and drove her across town. He drove without looking to right or left, as if he were making an unsuccessful effort to act naturally. Therese sat woodenly beside him. They came to the entrance to her area, a narrow path, passable to a motorbike being pushed but not to larger vehicles. He parked the jeep at the curb and lifted the motorbike out. She grasped the handlebars and headed along the path, pushing the bike as she moved through the gathering dusk. He followed her with the cardboard carton under his arm.

It was a slum by occidental standards, but it was not filthy. He could hardly believe that so many human beings could live in such a small space in such seeming order and harmony, and with so little refuse to litter public spaces. The pathway curved and turned to accommodate the haphazard placement of the tiny structures of thatch or wattle. At one point, he had to set his foot down on the path within about eighteen inches of a large bowl of rice around which a family was preparing to squat for their evening meal.

Expressionless eyes followed their progress down the path. Therese exchanged low greetings now and then with some of the onlookers. There were smiles on these occasions, somewhat formal, he thought, showing neither cordiality nor mirth, but not hostile either.

At last they came to a wattle-and-daub structure with a corrugated-iron shed-type roof, which had been built against another somewhat larger structure of the same material. The tin roof extended out beyond the front wall to form a narrow, porchlike shelter, supported by wooden posts at both corners. Therese fastened her motorbike to one of these posts with a chain and padlock. The door was secured by a simple warded lock, to which she produced a key from her purse. She opened the door, stepped inside, and motioned Toby to enter.

With a quick, graceful motion, she bent and removed her shoes and placed them precisely in front of the door. Toby could not suppress a smile, a smile of delight and affection, at the sight of those small shoes, so carefully positioned by their owner. By American standards, they were almost child-size.

The interior was in almost total darkness, until Therese switched on a bare bulb that hung on a dropcord from the ceiling. The bulb was small and did not light the room very well. Two lizards, conditioned to expect a meal of insects when the light went on, scurried across the ceiling.

The room was sparsely furnished. A low table, two chairs, a benchlike platform near the window at one end, which he realized was a Vietnamese bed, and a wardrobe against the wall near it. In another corner was a small oil cookstove, some modest utensils hanging from nails on the wall, and a jerry can that probably contained water.

Against the back wall were two shelves that were filled with books. He could make out French titles, English titles, and Vietnamese. There were hardcover and paperback books.

The floor was of wooden planks. It was spotless.

The air of the neighborhod was heavy with the odor of dishes being cooked in *nuoc mam*, the sauce of fermented fish that is Vietnam's national condiment. Although not exactly foul, the odor was sharp and persistent, even penetrating this home to some extent. Here, however, it was almost displaced by a faint fragrance, an elusive aura of the woman who lived in the home.

Toby set the carton on the table, opened it, and lifted the television set out. He pulled out the telescope antenna, unwound the power cord, and began to look for an outlet. Therese pointed to the dropcord, which had a European-style receptacle. Fortunately, the television set had come with an adapter. He plugged it into the receptacle and turned it on. A Can Tho station came in, broadcasting a Chinese opera, and he beckoned Therese close to him so that he could speak into her ear.

"We will leave this on, fairly loud, so that the conversation won't be overheard," he said. He noticed, with a rush of sensation over his whole body, that his lips were nearly touching that satiny cheek, and he drew back quickly.

"We should go on conversing," he went on, trying to keep a normal inflection in his voice, "just as if what everybody is thinking is true. Does anybody around here speak English except you?"

"I do not think so. But today one cannot be sure."

"We really ought to have the table to meet around, but with the television set on it . . ."

"Mr. Busch, may I suggest something?"

"Go ahead."

"Vietnamese do not sit in chairs very much, and do not eat off tables like this. This man will feel more at ease if we sit on the floor."

"I can sit on the floor," Toby said, grinning, "but my legs are not in any shape for squatting as a Vietnamese does. But first, I want to check some things." He walked to the door and peered out slowly and unobtrusively. Then to the window to examine the shutters, which she had not opened upon their arrival.

"Can one see inside through these shutters?"

"Perhaps through a crack. I do not know."

"We may want to turn the light off during the meeting."

"Yes."

Toby sat down on the floor and hugged his knees to him. Therese dropped lightly to the floor beside him, but on her knees, geisha-style, rather than squatting on her heels. He wondered if a French education had taught her that Occidentals do not perceive squatting to be very ladylike. Not that he knew anything about her education.

"Si vous êtes catholique, du nord, vous . . . devez parler français . . . n'est-ce pas?" he asked, aware of how hesitant and awkward his French was.

"Oui," she replied. "Je parle français mieux qu'anglais." Her French was automatic and graceful.

"Well, now you *have* got me on the spot," he said.

"What do you mean?"

"If I say no, that your English is better than your French, you may be offended, and if I say your French is better than your English, you may be offended. So, what do I say?"

She laughed, and rang little bells of pleasure all through him.

"I'll just settle for this," he said. "Your English is better than my French, so I think we must stick with English."

"Very well."

"How long have you been in the south, Therese?"

A faint veil of distress clouded the lovely face, and he smiled reassuringly at her. "I am not questioning you. I am making conversation. And I *am* interested in knowing about you just for my own pleasure, not for official reasons."

"I have been in the south for a little more than one year."

"You escaped from the north more than a year ago?"

"Yes."

"When was your husband . . . killed?"

"About six months ago."

"Was he killed in battle?"

"No."

"You don't want to talk about it?"

"Yes."

"You *do* want to talk about it?"

"I mean, yes, I do not want to talk about it."

"Is it because you don't trust me?"

At first she was surprised by the question, and then she was delighted. Once again she laughed aloud, and he thought that she must have the most contagious, bubbling laugh he had ever heard.

"I didn't intend to make you laugh, but I'm glad I did. I'm not sure what it is that is so funny."

"I had thought that you do not trust me, but about me trusting you, I had not thought," she said. "I brought you to my home without any question, because I did not doubt you."

"Do I seem so harmless to you?"

"You would not harm me."

"No."

"But you do not trust me. And you do not trust yourself, either, I believe."

"You may be right."

The door opened noiselessly, and a man in dark shorts and an open-collared shirt came in. He appeared to be about forty years old, although Toby could not be sure. His hair was graying slightly at the temples, and there were lines under his eyes, lines of fatigue. His mouth was a grim, straight line, his face otherwise an expressionless mask.

They stood up, and Therese introduced the newcomer, Hoang Duc Dang. Toby had considered taking the customary precaution of using a pseudonym in this first exploratory meeting, but had discarded the idea. He was already widely known in My Tho, and certainly to the Viet Cong. There was no point in complicating matters needlessly.

Toby and Therese resumed their seats on the floor, and Dang squatted beside them.

"Who are you, Mr. Dang?" Toby asked abruptly.

Therese interpreted. "He says he is Hoang Duc Dang, and he is commander of the Determination-to-Win Local Force Battalion."

"How do I know that? I have only his word."

"He says that your own intelligence reports will verify that he is the commander of that battalion."

So they believe we have good intelligence on their forces? He is sure I already know about him. Well, no need to destroy that illusion.

"That is not what I meant," Toby said suavely. "What I mean is, how do I know he is *that* Hoang Duc Dang?"

Dang sat and throught about this question. Then he said something brusquely to Therese.

"He says he carries no documents."

"I would not have expected him to."

"He asks how he can be sure you are Tolliver Busch?"

"He can't," said Toby, without batting an eye. He looked at Therese. "Let's turn off the light, Therese, and turn up the volume on the television."

Therese did as he asked, leaving the room faintly illuminated by the small screen of the television set, which was facing away from them, and filling the air with the sounds of the Chinese opera—unmelodic, cacophonic to Toby's ears.

"Now," Toby continued, "why has he come to meet with me? Does he want to work with me?"

Therese exchanged several remarks with Dang. "He says for two reasons he has come. First, his family have been asking him to rally to the government side under the Chieu Hoi program for some time, but he does not want to rally. He says that as a Hoi Chanh he would be nothing but one who gives up. He does not want to give up . . . to quit. He wants to be useful. He wants to work for Vietnam."

"Well, just between us, Therese, I think he may have a false impression of the Chieu Hoi program, because a lot of the Hoi Chanhs *are* working for us. But that's all right with me, because if he did become a Hoi Chanh, I couldn't touch him. He'd be lost to me. Not only that, he'd stop getting any new information the minute he rallied. Now that I think of it, why keep this between you and me? Tell him what I have said."

Therese did so.

"Now," Toby went on, "he gave me his first reason. What is the second?"

Therese consulted Dang.

"He says that he does not believe in the mass . . . the mass . . . I do not know the English word for this. In French it is *soulèvement*."

Toby wracked his brain. That would have something to do with rising, leavening, lightness, a . . . an uprising! He caught his breath.

"Uprising is the English word, I think," he said. "Let's see if what he says about it fits that meaning." He realized that Dang would note his surprise and excitement. It didn't matter. Dang should have the satisfaction of providing him with *some* information he didn't already know.

"He says that all the Viet Cong military units and civilian cadres are preparing for a mass uprising of the South Vietnamese people during Tet. This is to be the final struggle that will overthrow the Thieu régime and drive the Americans out of the country."

"And he doesn't believe in it?"

"He says that the Viet Cong leaders are making a bad interpretation of history. He says his own experience with the masses makes him believe that they will do nothing but wait. It will be a waste of Viet Cong soldiers, and will gain nothing."

"He knows history, it seems," Toby mused, "history beyond what the gospel of Marx and Lenin teaches."

"I believe so."

"Then in reality he is not disillusioned with the Viet Cong; only with these particular plans?"

Another detailed exchange between Therese and Dang. Toby cursed the difference in language. This was the guts of a recruitment, the exploration of motives and emotions, the search for a solid common ground.

"He does not wish to try to deceive you. He believes the Viet Cong programs are better than the Thieu and American ideas. But he believes that the Tet plans will be such a disaster for the Viet Cong that he wants to prevent them."

"How can he do that?"

"He says that if the ARVN forces and the American military become convinced that the plan exists and will be carried out, they will take actions to prepare for it. If they do that well enough, even the most fanatical Viet Cong leader must see that they cannot succeed, and will cancel the plan, or change it."

Toby gazed at the dim figures of the other two, his mind racing with details he must remember, actions he must take. This man was a walk-in—an agent prospect who seeks out the Americans to join their side. Walk-ins almost invariably admit only a partial dissatisfaction or disillusionment, not a total break. The human heart resists such total breaks with the faith of the past. But Toby felt that Dang's disillusionment was probably more profound than he was admitting, even to himself. The most impressive thing about him was that he assumed what most walk-ins do not even consider until they are asked—that is, that it was his duty to stay in place and work for what he thought was right. Most such agent prospects just wanted *out*.

"Tell him," Toby said to Therese, "that I am going to proceed on the basis that what he has told me is the exact truth. I want one more meeting with him here as soon as he can make it. Ask him when he can come back to My Tho."

Dang replied that he could return in two weeks. They set a date and time.

"Next, I want him to bring me all the information he can get about his own battalion, and about the Tet uprising."

Dang grunted his assent, but added that he intended to be selective about the information he gave. This was also standard for the new walk-in.

"That brings up another item," Toby continued. "I want him to think carefully about the implications of what he is doing. How will he continue with the Viet Cong after Tet? What if they win? What if they lose? He is going to have to make a hard decision sooner or later. I believe this first step may be really only the beginning of his disillusionment with the Viet Cong and its methods and ideas. I think he should study seriously what is really in his heart, and should face all the facts, no matter how unpleasant or disturbing they may seem to him."

Therese passed along this short homily, and Dang stared silently in the direction of Toby's dim figure, but Toby could not see his eyes.

"At our next meeting," Toby continued, "I will give him some instructions in clandestine work, especially communications. He and I cannot meet regularly. The danger is too great. I am much too visible. On the other hand, I do not want any third person between him and me. The fewer persons who know about this, the safer he and I will both be. So we will set up systems so that we can pass information, but will not have to meet personally, except in an emergency."

Therese was translating these remarks piecemeal, and Dang received them without comment.

"I am sure I need not tell him that he must not reveal to anybody, to his family—not even his mother—that we have had this meeting. So far as his family knows, he should continue to procrastinate about rallying."

Dang understood, and said that he had already resolved on just that course of action.

"And finally, we need an interim emergency communication system. So here is what he must do. There is a revetment at the airstrip made out of ammunition boxes. Starting from the end nearest the road, he should look for the fourth box from the end, and the fourth box counting up from the ground. That box has a loose end. He should slip whatever information or message he has in that box. After he has loaded the box, he is to make a scratch or a slash with a knife on the wooden pole at the northwest corner of the block our compound is in, like this." Toby drew out his penknife and lightly scratched a curved slash on the floor for Dang to see. "He should make this mark about shoulder high, so that it is visible from the sidewalk without my having to search for it and attract attention. I will look at the pole each morning, so that the material will not be in the box too long."

Dang asked if he would have any difficulty knowing the pole he was to mark. Toby took a three-by-five card out of his pocket and sketched the location of the pole for him, and Dang studied it carefully, then handed the card back.

"Does he understand?" Toby asked.

"Yes."

"Have him repeat the instructions to me, step by step, please."

Dang repeated the instructions exactly. Toby was encouraged by this sign of an incisive mind.

"Now, Therese, we've got the housekeeping done. I want him to tell me everything he knows now about this uprising, and the preparations that are being made for it."

For the next hour they sat in the semi-darkness while Dang described the Viet Cong plan as he knew it. Toby made notes as best he could in the dim light, and occasionally questioned and probed to get the full picture. Dang explained that he had obtained what information he had in a series of orientation talks for local force leaders, in Tay Ninh Province. He gave the dates and the names of the participants in these sessions. Toby's professional doubts were further allayed by this information. Dang was intelligent enough to know that specific dates could be checked. If these facts checked with other information, Dang was probably exactly what he said he was, and could be a source of a wealth of intelligence about the Viet Cong.

When Toby saw that Dang was beginning to get restless, he arose to signal the end of the meeting.

"Before he goes," Toby said to Therese, "I want some personal data about him so that I can submit a clearance request on him, to see if he is on record as being used as an agent by anybody else, see if he has ever been used before, if he has ever lied to us or deceived us, things like that."

Therese spoke to Dang, who replied abruptly, in a way that told Toby the answer before Therese interpreted the words.

"He will not tell you anything about himself," she said.

"I will trust him that much less."

"He says he regrets it, but it must be so."

They reconfirmed the meeting for two weeks from that night in this same location. Toby held out his hand; Dang grasped it fleetingly, and slipped out the door.

"We will wait for a while," Toby said to Therese. They sat down at the table in the dim light.

"How did you know about the box at the airfield?" she asked.

"Force of habit," he replied. "We call that a 'dead drop.' In this business you never know when you'll need one, and when you need one it's too late to go looking for one.

"Dang admired that."

"Good." Toby peered closely at her in the dim light. "Therese, I have a task for you, and it may be difficult, but I hope you will try."

"I will try. What is it you wish?"

"I need all the information I can get about Dang. I can't get it from him directly, at least not yet, but I can't really work properly with him until I can be reasonably sure he isn't a double agent for the Viet Cong, or a provocation, or that he isn't already working with somebody else and just wants to make a little more money."

"He has not asked for money," Therese pointed out.

"No. An intelligent man would not ask at the first meeting. And if he is good he will never ask, and won't accept if if we offer it. At some stage in our relationship we may offer him some, and he might accept, who knows? It's possible he has some desperate financial problems. Anyway, I have to check up on him as well as I can."

"Of course."

"You know Dang's mother. I want you to talk casually to her and find out whatever you can about him, but without letting her know what you are doing. This is more for precise information about him than to test him. No telling how many Hoang Duc Dangs there are in Vietnam. I need to know exactly where he was born, and what the date was. His mother's name and his father's name. Anything else you can get about him."

"Very well, sir."

"Thanks." He stood up and turned on the light, then resumed his seat and began going over his notes. He corrected the sometimes illegible scrawl while the conversation was still fresh in his memory, and he probed Therese's memory on points that were not clear. Satisfied, he put the cards back in his pocket and rose to go.

"Thank you, Therese, for everything," he said. "For putting your reputation on the line, for spending your time. If Dang works out, we may have begun the recruitment of a first-class agent, a really important one, and the credit will be mostly yours."

"I am happy if I have been of help."

Toby took her hand in both of his own, and held it for a moment. "Poor Therese," he murmured. "You have such sadness and pain in your eyes."

"Yes," she said softly. "Someday it will pass."

He opened the door reluctantly, illuminating the area before the little dwelling with the faint light from the bulb within. "Perhaps we ought to put on an act for prying eyes, here in the lighted doorway."

"An act?"

"Do Vietnamese lovers . . . do they kiss, as we Westerners do?"

"Yes."

"Then, Therese, if you will stand very still, I will now make a public demonstration."

She stood still, looking up at him. He leaned down and kissed her on the lips. He tried to make it look like the last, light punctuation to an hour of passionate lovemaking. Her lips were soft and slightly parted, and he realized that she was not simply receiving a carefully staged kiss. She was kissing him back.

He knew that the act was unnecessary, and was sure she must have realized it too.

"Good night," he whispered.

"Good night, sir."

[10]

Toby stood in the hot mid-morning sun, leaning against the revetment of ammo boxes. His pilot today would not be Dino. The gathering of all the provincial intelligence officers at Can Tho had forced Jerry to mobilize every one of his aircraft for several intensive hours, and Dino's little three-passenger Helio would be joined in the effort by a seven-passenger Porter and by Jess Theodorides's helicopter. Jess was to pick up Toby.

He looked at his watch, and began to pace casually about the end of the revetment as if he were lost in thought. A sidelong glance at the box satisfied him that his dead drop was still exactly as he had described it. There could not be anything in it yet. He did not go near it.

He would be gone for two nights, and he had charged Therese with the task of watching for the scratch signal on the pole during his absence.

He went back to the end of the revetment and stood by his luggage: a small airline overnight bag and a thin attaché case. Travel in this informal situation in the tropics was uncomplicated—shirts, slacks, socks, and underwear, shaving gear, an extra pair of shoes.

He hitched the .45 to a more comfortable position on his hip. He still hadn't gone to the firing range to practice. He must remember to do that when he got back. If he could find time. He thought of the things he had to do within the next month, and was contented with the burden and the challenge.

He had ached to go directly to his typewriter the moment he returned to the compound from his meeting with Dang. But he had resisted the temptation. Everybody in the household would know that he had driven out with Therese, and everybody would draw the conclusions he had planned for them to draw. If he had gone directly to his typewriter they might have modified those conclusions, and he must avoid that at all costs.

The following morning, when the moment came that it would look altogether normal, Toby had set to work on the task that fascinated him, one that he excelled at: the task of turning rough notes and recollections of an agent meeting into reports that would succinctly and completely deliver the information he had, and put on the record the details of what had happened at the meeting.

The operational report first. Details, precautions, checks, systems, times, schedules, and comments about the demeanor of the agent. He had set up a log for meetings with Dang, and wrote the first entry, and the first contact report. He prided himself on his contact reports. From them, any newcomer could reconstruct a complete and accurate history of any operation he had ever run.

He had hesitated about writing the intelligence report. He had been given extremely valuable information, but he had no approved or authenticated source and could not evaluate the material except by his gut instincts. The agency was not so rigid as to ignore the instincts of its officers, but it was extremely reluctant to circulate intelligence reports based on those instincts. The times when circumstances dictated such a dissemination were few and far between, and were invariably the occasion for an accompanying disclaimer that the source was new and untested, and that the accuracy of the information could not be judged.

He had written the report in spite of the difficulties he could foresee. It did tell of a massive plan by the Viet Cong, of strategic significance to the whole U.S. involvement in Vietnam. If the customers believed the report, they could begin preparing for the event at an early enough stage so that they could cope with it when it came. He was sure that any army commander with a feel for the situation would sense the truth of it. Ben and Little Jack and Dino and Bill Voigt had already shown him that they were uneasy, that something big seemed to be brewing. So far as he knew, his report was the first solid information from a Viet Cong source that seemed to confirm their suspicions.

The Viet Cong were preparing to blow the lid off. He couldn't prove it, but he knew it.

The rattle of the big fan of a Huey helicopter came to his ears, and he squinted into the sun to find the silhouette of the Air America chopper. Jess came in steeply, and gently settled the skids of the aircraft close by. Toby set his luggage on the floor and climbed into the seat just behind Jess. There were two Filipino technicians and a Vietnamese soldier sitting on the other side. They exchanged friendly nods with him, but did not speak.

"Hi, Toby," said Jess. "Haven't seen you since An Loi. How's things down there?"

"Pretty good, I guess," he replied. "I haven't been back down. Ben took replacements down and he thinks they'll do better than the original ones did. Of course, the VC probably won't hit that village again, at least not for a long time."

"Probably not," Jess, said, craning his neck to inspect his surroundings before lifting his ungainly machine off the ground. "They sure as hell kicked the shit out of it when they did, though."

He broke the skids free of the runway, set the helicopter in that peculiar scooping angle of the takeoff, and they zoomed forward, rattling and shaking. When they had cleared the tree-tops at the end of the runway, Jess quickly veered to the right in a sharp bank.

"They got some F-104s operating between here and Can Tho," he explained, "so we gotta give them a wide berth."

"What are they doing?"

"They've spotted a new battalion that's just moved into the My Tho perimeter," Jess replied. "They think they've got it cornered along a canal off there to our left, and they're working it over."

Toby could make out the darting jets against the sky off to his left, and could see puffs of smoke from the ground when they streaked toward the ground and fired their rockets. He could not hear any explosions over the sound of the big rotor over his head.

"They sure it's a new battalion?" he asked nonchalantly. There was no feeling of nonchalance in the pit of his stomach. This could not be Dang's battalion, because Dang had located his on the opposite side of My Tho.

"Yeah, but I don't know how they know. They sure as hell can't tell from up there in those jets. They might be rocketing a fishing party for all *they* know."

"I suppose so."

"But there's no question about it, the VC is moving around My Tho. You guys are in the bull's eye."

"It sure looks like it."

"Lots of other province towns are in the same boat, of course, except I don't think they got as much around them as you guys have got."

"You've made my day, Jess," said Toby drily.

"Thought that would interest you." Jess grinned back at him. "Of course you fellows can always call on the Ninth Division over there in Dong Tam."

"Yeah, but the Ninth just got in from the States not too long ago. They tell me it's still pretty green and body-count conscious. Ben thinks they might be worse than no help at all."

"Maybe Ben's right." Jess shrugged. "But as far as I'm concerned, anybody with a pair of shoes and a canteen and a gun is a help."

Again he banked the helicopter abruptly. "Christ, they're over here now!" he exclaimed. He unhooked his microphone and called the Can Tho tower, giving them his position. "There's some 104s working on a treeline right here," he said indignantly, "and nobody told me a goddamned thing about it! Isn't Paddy Control talking to you guys anymore?"

"Sorry," came the answer. "I guess you were on the ground when those planes were diverted."

Grumbling to himself, Jess switched back to Jerry's frequency and gave Jerry his estimated time of arrival in Can Tho.

"I still say a helicopter is not made for warfare," he said, replacing the microphone on its bracket. "Hell, they go so slow and maneuver so slow, you could hit one of them with a slingshot. They can put Mickey Rooney in one of them, and send him into some real heroic film situations in Korea, but they're not gonna get old Theodorides flying around in the bullets. I'm strictly a mercenary civilian. Passengers and freight. No guns. No combat."

Toby was not listening to Jess. His mind was racing

back over the meeting with Dang, to see if he could remember any hint that Dang might have known about this new battalion. No new recollection came to him. He must remember to include some questions about it in his list for the next meeting.

Dino and the pilot of the Porter had already landed their first loads at Can Tho and were taking off for another load when the helicopter approached the airfield. Bill had sent members of his office force to the airport to drive the visitors to the CORDS dormitory, in the same building that housed the bar.

Toby recognized Ski among the group, and spoke briefly with him. He did not know any of the other province officers personally. That could be because he was in an area of the world he had never visited before, but it was more likely because all these province officers were contract men, with only one or two years of work with the agency.

He put his overnight bag on the bed in the cramped room assigned to him and hurried across the driveway to the ROIC office spaces. Chet was at his desk. Across from him sat a figure that was familiar to Toby. They both got up when Toby entered, and Chet greeted him with an unusually bluff and hearty manner. Chet was feeling expansive.

"Toby," he said, shaking hands, "you remember Ernie Free."

"Sure. How you doing, Ernie?"

"He's down here partly to relax and partly to sit in on our conference. Nothing official. Just cruising around."

"Good to see you again, Toby," said Ernie. He was skinny and slightly stooped, and wore glasses with heavy black frames. Toby was sure they were intended to give him a studious, intellectual appearance.

"Haven't seen you since Frankfurt," Toby said. "I think we nearly crossed paths a couple of times there at headquarters, but somehow always missed."

"Yeah. Boy, I sure was sorry to hear about how that Frankfurt operation turned out."

"It was a real blow."

"I just couldn't believe that agent would do such a thing," Ernie said, his eyes wide with innocence. Toby caught an almost feline bite behind the words.

"Chet," Toby said, "sorry to break in on you like this, but I had a meeting the other night that may turn into a good operation. I've got the operational report in rough draft right here, and I've also got an intel written up on the information. I'd appreciate it if you'd have a look at them as soon as you can."

"OK," said Chet, taking the papers from him absently. He was more interested right now in talking with Ernie Free, but Toby noted that he had put the papers on the desk before him, rather than in his in-box. It implied that he would attend to them first, and Toby was sure that he would do so. As Bill Voigt had said, Chet would move papers when they came to him.

"Have you seen Laura yet?" Chet asked him.

"No."

"Better go in there right away. She'll give you a schedule and all the material you'll need for the meetings."

Toby joined a small group of recently arrived officers in Laura's office, and picked up a sheaf of papers. The schedule told him that he was free until one o'clock. He went to the admin offices and found several province officers there. He decided to wait until later to check on supplies for My Tho. He ambled by Jerry's counter, and Jerry greeted him cordially.

"The clan is beginning to gather in the bar," said Jerry.

"Where else?" Toby laughed. "Guess I'll go have a beer before lunch."

He entered the bar and ordered a beer. As he started to drink it, sitting on a stool at the bar, he caught inviting glances from a table nearby and went over to the group that was seated there. They introduced themselves. Walt Dewey, from An Xuyen Province, Delbert Cumber from Kien Phong, men from Bac Lieu, Chau Doc, and Kien Giang.

"You're a staff man," Cumber commented.

"Yep. An old whore."

"All of use here are under the contract program," Dewey explained.

"So I understand."

"We were just talking about the new informant Saigon is supposed to have."

"New informant?"

"Yeah. The guy that came down to talk to us about the Phoenix program was telling Chet that Saigon has just made a real breakthrough. They've got access to an informant on the COSVN staff."

The Central Office for South Vietnam ran all the VC and North Vietnamese operations in the south. Its composition and location were unknown to the ARVN and the American forces, although nobody doubted that the office did exist, and that it was located not far from Saigon. If Saigon did have a penetration of COSVN, it was a real victory.

"Did Chet say it was an *informant?*" Toby asked gently. "We don't use that word very much. Agent, or source, maybe but . . ."

"Christ, I don't remember the exact word," said Cumber. "Shows you what a pro *I* am. Whatever Chet called it, Saigon is excited about it."

Toby was uneasy about discussing a sensitive operation in a group like this. He was relieved when the Bac Lieu man changed the subject.

"How's things in My Tho?" Bac Lieu asked.

"Compared to what?" Toby said with a laugh. "We've got no intelligence collection operations. We've got a main force battalion that is out there worrying the province like a dog with an old rag, and we seem to have a lot of local force battalions gathering around My Tho for some reason or other."

"You could give just about the same speech for Rock Jaw," said the Kien Giang man, and Toby remembered that the capital of Kien Giang Province was Rach Gia.

The others agreed. The Viet Cong were slowly gathering forces for something, and seemed to be concentrating around the provincial capitals.

"They're not even in a staging position yet," said Cumber, obviously a man of military experience. "In fact, they seem to be training, more than anything else."

"But you don't *know?*"

"Hell no. We don't really *know* hardly anything at all. We've got rumors and some eyeball reports that are pretty definite. Those battalions are there all right, but how many of them, and what they've got, and what they're getting ready for, we haven't the slightest idea."

"All the other Americans around An Xuyen are laughing at us and razzing us all the time," said Dewey. "They say the CIA has got a special weejee board and things like that. They don't believe anything special is going on. Even the Province Senior Adviser's office feels that way."

"So, they're not getting ready?"

"Nope. They couldn't hold off a squad of Boy Scouts, and they couldn't last a day without going to the grocery store."

Ski walked in. He bought a beer and joined the group.

"Tanks, by God! I'm seeing tanks."

"Come on, Ski," the Rach Gia man laughed. "Even if the VC had tanks, why in hell would they put them in Kien Tuong? Nothing ever happens in Kien Tuong. There's nothing there to happen."

"Who the hell said they were VC tanks, and who said they were in Kien Tuong?" Ski snorted. "These are North Vietnamese, and they're across the border in Cambodia."

"The hell you say!"

"Yes, sir, by God. I got a guy to take me up in one of those little forward observation planes, and we could see the goddamned things just as plain as day."

"You should have got some pictures of them."

"I tried," said Ski, "but I don't know a goddamned thing about any camera, and the Japanese job I had was so complicated that the pictures came out with those tanks looking like bushes in a cow pasture."

"That's probably what they were, Ski. Maybe Moc Hoa's getting to you at last."

"OK, you bastards," Ski growled good-naturedly, "go ahead and laugh. You'll have a great big thigh-slappin' belly laugh the day those bushes start coming across the border and shooting at you."

"Don't worry about it, Ski," said Dewey seriously. "If they are North Vietnamese tanks, they're going to have a hell of a problem operating. Tanks can't live off of the land. They can't swim in Mao Tse-tung's sea of the people. Tanks have got to have support, especially supply lines of fuel."

Cumber joined in. "Yeah, and anyway, they wouldn't attack you there in Moc Hoa. They won't be headed south, they'll be going east, right through the Parrot's Beak, right to Saigon. Saigon may not be very good at unconventional warfare, but one thing ARVN has got the equipment for is conventional warfare, including tanks. Right down their alley."

"We hope," Dewey muttered.

"Well," said Ski, "I told Chet about it, so Saigon will know."

"You *told* them about it?" Toby asked.

"Yeah."

"What are they supposed to do, telephone the information to Saigon?"

"Well, they'll do whatever—"

"If you saw those things with your own eyes, you've got the makings of an important intelligence report, but the people that need it can't use it if it doesn't come to them in complete detail, through channels, from the guy that knows."

"Well, Christ, I gave it to Chet, and he never said nothing about it like that."

"Have you ever written an intelligence report, Ski?" Toby asked.

"No."

"In Kien Tuong?" Cumber laughed.

"After the sessions today, if you want to get together with me," Toby went on, "we'll find a typewriter and rough out a report to turn in to the regional reports officer. I'll show you how to do it."

"OK," said Ski. "Let's do it." He looked triumphantly around at the group. Here was one man, a professional, who didn't laugh at what he had seen.

At one o'clock the province officers convened in the conference room for the first session. Their enjoyment of the situation was almost juvenile. The work of the province officer, while unlike that of any other intelligence assignment that Toby had ever heard of, was a solitary task. It was not that the officer was isolated from other human beings, or even from his own countrymen. The aloneness came more from the lack of anybody to talk shop with.

These fourteen province officers, privileged on these rare occasions to discuss their work with others who had the same assignments and the same problems, reveled in the camaraderie and self-importance of the occasion.

"How's things in Chuong Thien?"

"Some days a fellow thinks things are in good shape, and then they hit one of our villages, and we can see they're gaining on us."

"Got any penetrations of the VC?"

"Special Police say they got some, but I don't know what they are, and I sure haven't seen any good information out of them."

"Hey, An Xuyen! They tell me you got a new ARVN regiment stationed down there."

"Sure have. Damned good one, too. It's Colonel Thanh. He's a wild man, and he doesn't want any of this horse shit about Spookies and B-Fifties. He goes in after 'em, and his regiment acts like a bunch of Texans, they're so proud of themselves."

". . . and so if you want a little vacation, just go visit Ski. . . ."

". . . the sons of bitches come in and kick the hell out of Chau Doc for about a half an hour or so, and then zoom right back across that canal into Cambodia, and the only thing we can do is sit there with our thumb up our ass and watch 'em relax. Can't even shoot at them, because by that time they're out of small-arms range."

". . . I disseminated ten reports last month. . . ."

"Ten? You wrote ten reports?"

"I didn't say that. I disseminated ten that the Special Police sent me."

"That's a pretty useless exercise, isn't it?"

Disseminated ten reports, thought Toby uneasily. Nice guy, but he didn't know what the word "disseminate" meant in this business. Who would he have sent those reports to, to call it that? Not anybody along official CIA channels, because they would not conform to CIA requirements for dissemination. He was tempted to look into it. But no, what the hell, he couldn't tidy up the whole country. He had his hands full in his own province.

The more he mingled with them and talked with them, the more he was convinced that this was an exceptional group of young men. Better, in many respects, than an equal number of staff intelligence officers. There were no prima donnas among them. They were humble about their intelligence skills, but it was obvious to Toby that they had military skills that few of his fellow intelligence officers could boast. They knew what to do to make their little establishments as militarily strong and safe as possible. If rumors and reports about a Tet uprising were true, those military skills might be many times more important than intelligence collection capabilities right now.

A mumble of voices began to pour into the room from two heavy speakers at opposite corners—a "cocktail party" tape, several voices taped simultaneously and replayed to form a background of sound in the room. It would not prevent normal conversation, but to a bug that might be planted in that space anything that was said would only add one more voice to the confusion.

Bill Voigt came in and sat down at the head of the big table. A murmur of greeting came from the assembled men, and Bill returned it with a quick smile. Ex-OSS as he was, experienced in insurgency and paramilitary operations, he had a high regard for these men, and they returned the affection. Now his face grew grave.

"Is there anybody here who hasn't heard about Saigon's new source?" he asked. They had all heard.

"I had an idea that was the case," Bill said, looking straight at Toby. "How does that information strike you, Toby?"

Toby shifted uneasily, and looked around at the other men apologetically. "It worries the hell out of me."

Bill had expected the response. The others were surprised.

"Why?"

"Well, if *I* had laid on an important operation like that, I'd hate to think everybody in the whole agency was gossiping about it in bars and offices."

Bill nodded, and looked slowly around at all the faces turned toward him. There was a dead silence, except for the muttering of the speakers.

"Think about that, gentlemen," Bill said. "Think about the case officer that is running that operation. Think about the agent he's got, in a situation where that agent is going to get killed if the VC begin to suspect him; but remember that he won't have the privilege of dying easily or quickly. He'll be leaned on very, very hard, first.

"I am not going to tell you or confirm to you any information you believe you've got. I realize that this business is still a little new to most of you, and that you figured it was all right to talk with each other because we're all cleared, and that the hours and hours of drilling you on security procedures seemed just like a formality. But, gentlemen, let me tell you, it is no formality. This is not a girls' boarding school. We can talk shop as long as we keep it general. But don't talk about specific operations, either your own or anybody else's, not even to a fellow province officer, unless the person you're talking to has got to know, for official reasons. Is that clear?"

There were nods and grunts of assent.

"All right. That's all I intend to say on the subject, and I am confident it's all I will ever have to say from now on."

Toby glanced around the room and thought that Bill was probably right. His message had sunk in.

Bill dealt with some minor administrative matters, and then called in their guest from Saigon, who would be in charge of training them for the new program.

The Saigon man set up an easel with a flip chart of chains of command, and areas of responsibility. He passed out instruction sheets. He lectured the men on what they must do to initiate the program, and how they were to keep it going. PRU advisers would be given a training program a week or so later, and the PRU men must be held closely accountable to this new program. It was a hard, rational, coordinated attack on the secret Viet Cong structure within the territory and society of the south. It would be the major CIA contribution to the war effort from this moment forward.

Toby was fascinated. In all his years of collecting intelligence, this was the first time he had ever been involved in an enterprise where the collection would be in large part done by armed teams of men who would move at night through the countryside. He wished that there had been a more liberal salting of experienced staff officers among this group, men who would know better what to do with the information once they got it. On the other hand, these men would know how to *get* the information in the first place, which was also of primary importance.

He was not the only one to have thought along those lines. Much of the time in the two-day course was scheduled for training the men in the processing of the information once it was obtained. It was all elementary to Toby, but he realized that it was new to the rest of them.

But he was also sure that these young men, who knew so well how to survive and function in an insurgency situation, were bright enough to learn quickly the skills of intelligence work.

Except, perhaps, for Ski.

In the interim between the last session and an informal reception on that first day, which Bill Voigt had organized in his quarters, Toby worked with Ski to produce a draft of an intelligence report on his sighting of tanks. They went with the draft to the office of the regional reports officer, who read it with interest and said it could be submitted pretty much exactly as it had been written.

Ski was jubilant. What would be a modest task to a man reasonably adept at assembling and writing down facts in an orderly report was a major triumph to this veteran rifleman, who had earned his sergeant's stripes by combat, not by literary efforts. Toby had found him to be so inept at organizing and writing down what he knew that there was never any likelihood he would produce intelligence reports on his own in the future. This would perhaps be his only real production for the entire tour in Kien Tuong, and he could have had a right to be elated. But there was no doubt that Kien Tuong, where nothing ever happened, was the place for Ski.

At Bill's reception, to which the Regional Senior Adviser and a number of his staff had been invited so that they could meet the province officers, Toby had only a brief opportunity to speak to Chet.

"I read your material," Chet said coolly. "I want to talk to you about it tomorrow. Come to my office during the sessions on reports writing. You don't need that training."

"OK."

Toby stood and watched Chet move off, with Ernie Free in tow, introducing Ernie to guests, and leaving no doubt that he thought the gaunt, bespectacled man was a paragon of all the important virtues. Toby wondered at the strange friendship. He knew of nobody else who considered himself to be a close personal friend of Chet. Chet was so abrasive and defensive that other men were not tempted to exchange gossip or intimate thoughts with him. It was almost as if Ernie had tapped as unsuspected well of regard and affection in the depths of that prickly personality, and Ernie seemed to soak up the results without tiring. He cracked jokes and made Chet laugh. He listened to Chet's talk with shining eyes.

Toby would have thought that a man as basically cynical as Chet would have caught on to Ernie's act—and Toby was certain that it *was* an act. Ernie either didn't care, or didn't know how, to disguise his sycophancy. His mental stature was reflected in the object of that adulation, Toby thought. What could Chet ever do for him in the agency? If you're going to be a brown-nose, you ought to pick somebody who can do something for you.

Bill passed around a clipping from a newspaper account written by Chris Christopher. It was a lively and laudatory account of the PRUs, organized on a framework of a typical PRU nighttime operation against a Viet Cong village. Toby had a chance to talk it over with Wilbur, whose name appeared in the story, and Wilbur was pleased with the results of his operation.

"She didn't care very much for the bloodshed," he said, "and I was afraid maybe she might concentrate too much on that, or maybe even blast us for it, but she didn't. It's a good story. I'm having it translated and circulated to my PRUs here in Can Tho. They're always so proud of any kind of recognition like this in the American press. This is going to be better than a raise in pay. Say, would you like to have a copy of the translation to show to your own unit down there? I imagine Little Jack would like that. If you think so, I'll send you some copies."

"Thanks. I'd appreciate that."

During the reports-writing session the following day, Toby went to Chet's office. Ernie Free was there. He made no move to leave. Toby would have preferred to discuss the matter alone with Chet, but did not want to raise an issue that would get in the way of his main objective.

"Busch, I'm not going to send in this intel," Chet began tonelessly. "You've been had. This information goes absolutely against what Saigon is getting from its new source, and we've got nothing to justify sending this in. You don't even have any positive identification of your source. Nobody has ever heard of any series of orientation lectures for local force battalion commanders in Tay Ninh, and frankly I doubt that the VC would do such a thing."

Toby fought to keep his temper. "But the Saigon source is the only thing you're basing this decision on?"

"Let's put it this way," Chet said. "What they've got is a high-level penetration—a hell of a lot higher level than a local force battalion commander, *if* that's what you've got."

"That's what I've got."

"Well, the reports from their sources say that all these so-called preparations for the big offensive at the time of Tet are just for the purpose of keeping the country off balance, keeping the pressure on the Thieu government. They know they haven't got the strength to take on the ARVN and the American forces in conventional battle."

"How come this battalion commander doesn't know that?"

"Hell, Busch, use your head!" Chet glanced at Ernie, as if inviting him to share in deprecating Toby's obtuseness. "If you were planning that kind of a deception, would you let all your people in the field know it was a deception?"

Toby's gorge was rising, and he gripped the arms of the chair to control himself. It was true that the information agreed with Dang's assessment of Viet Cong capabilities; they couldn't succeed in such an uprising. But a deception operation on such a massive scale, involving the mobilization and disposition of so much of their military strength, merely to intimidate their enemy, didn't make sense to him.

"You mean they're doing all this just for show?"

"Well, no, the source never said that. He has said that they intend to carry out a series of local attacks, one right after another, starting after Tet. You know, Tet is a sacred holiday to these people and the VC aren't likely to mess it up with an offensive on that day." Chet sat back smugly in his chair, as if he had delivered the final blow.

Ernie hitched forward in his chair. "I can sympathize with you, Toby," he said unctuously. "I've got a penetration of the provincial committee in my province"—he said this with such studied matter-of-factness that it came across as blatant boasting to Toby—"and even *they* don't know about these plans of COSVN, although I think they suspect something like it."

Toby looked for a moment at the innocent eyes behind their heavy black frames, then turned away.

"What you're saying," he said to Chet, "is that you are basing your decision not to disseminate this information on the fact that the report disagrees with other information?"

"It disagrees with information from an established and tested source, yes. Your information comes from somebody we haven't even identified yet."

"Well, let me tell you something. I don't believe the information from your 'established and tested source.' "

"Oh? You don't believe a penetration of COSVN knows what he's talking about?"

"I'm out in the province, and this thing just doesn't look like a bluff to me." Toby realized that he had allowed himself to be led into a position of defending his information from the strength of his emotions about it. Not a very professional way to deal with intelligence matters.

"Another one of your gut feelings?" Chet sneered, glancing at Ernie. Ernie shook his head and smiled.

"Not just *my* gut feeling. The gut feelings of everybody that gets out into the provinces. The pilots and the province officers and the PRU advisers and the pacification teams."

"What are we supposed to do, make an intelligence report by majority vote?"

"No, but we ought to keep our minds and our ears open."

"That includes your own mind and your own ears, I suppose?"

"It ought to include everybody's."

"The report doesn't go."

"I could ask . . ." Toby began, then paused.

"Ask Bill?" Chet retorted sharply. He was waiting for that. Toby knew that he did not have a solid enough case to warrant putting the decision up to Bill, and Chet knew it, too.

"Forget it," Toby said, and rose to leave.

"The operational report will go in, of course," Chet said. "But this one either goes back to you or into the burn bag."

"I'll pick it up before I leave," Toby said. The operational report was mainly for the record. It would be read with some interest and filed away to await further developments from the field. Not even a hint of it would ever reach a customer.

He walked out and went across the driveway to the bar. It was almost time for lunch anyway, and he could have a beer and get his nerves back under control before he did or said something foolish.

Dino and Jess were sitting at the bar, glasses of beer on the dark wooden counter before them, engaged in a Greco-Roman skirmish.

"Hey, Toby," Dino exclaimed, "reinforcements! This Balkan won't admit that he doesn't know a thing about wines."

"You think *I* do?" Toby asked, signaling the girl behind the bar that he wanted a beer.

"Well, only a little bit, maybe, because with a name like Busch you gotta be classified as a *tedesco;* but after all, the Germans have got *some* wines that are all right."

"On behalf of Germany, I thank you," said Toby, raising his glass.

"Fact is," said Jess, picking up his own glass and peering through the amber liquid at the lights behind the bar, "beer is what started the argument. Caesar Augustus here was just saying that it's a shame we live in a culture dominated by the northern European influence, because beer is their drink, instead of all those great eyetalian wines. He thinks eyetalian wines are best. Better even than the French."

"I know they are," Dino volunteered. "And I know something else. Nobody in the world puts turpentine in their wine, except the Greeks."

"Turpentine," said Jess disgustedly. "Only a dumb eyetalian can't taste the difference between turpentine and a good retsina."

"Jess," said Dino slowly, rotating his glass of beer in the light, "to speak of a good retsina is like talking about a pleasant plane crash. There ain't no such animal."

"Too bad that bullet didn't hit you in the head instead

of the wing," said Jess. "It wouldn't have done any damage there."

Toby was interested. "You get hit by a bullet?"

"Yeah," said Dino, becoming serious. "I don't know where or when it happened, exactly, but from the looks of it it was heavy stuff. Maybe fifty-caliber."

"That's something new, isn't it?"

"Well, in a way, yes. Our planes have been getting shot at now and then all along, but it's always been when they went low near VC territory."

"Which is where I never go," said Jess.

"But now it seems to be happening in places you never would have expected before. Jess damned near got racked by some tracers a couple of days ago."

"Boy, that stops being fun pretty quick," said Toby.

"Damn right," said Jess. "Much more of that, and I may just turn in my Texaco road map and go home."

"We don't agree about wines," said Dino, "but we agree about bullets."

But Dino could not be serious for long. He ordered another beer, and when the girl brought him his change he caught her tiny hand in his.

"I know you're saying to yourself that I'm drinking too much," he said fiercely. The twinkle in her eye revealed the extent of her fright.

"I do not say," she said.

"Do you know why I drink too much?"

She shook her head.

"Because"—his voice descended to a rasping whisper—"because I love you, and you will not run away with me. That's why. You don't love me, do you?"

"Yes."

"You do?" Dino was incredulous.

"Yes, I do not love you. My husband would not like it."

They all burst out laughing, except Dino, who could not credit what his ears had heard. "Your husband? Do you mean that a little bitty girl like you, practically a baby, is married?"

"I am twenty-seven, Mr. Dino," said the girl, lifting her chin high, as if it would make her diminutive body taller and more impressive.

"Your husband is a lucky man, darling. He must love you almost as much as I do."

The girl went back to her work, glancing now and then in fond amusement at Dino. He finished his beer and he and Jess went into the dining room.

The door opened, and the province officers trooped in for drinks and lunch. Ernie Free was among them. He sat down on the stool next to Toby.

"Havin' a little brew before lunch?" he asked, with that forced bonhomie that seemed to characterize his dealings with other men.

"Yeah," said Toby shortly.

Ernie ordered a beer.

"This new program looks awfully good to me," he went on, looking for a subject that would open communications between them. Toby relented. His anger had subsided, and after all, his quarrel wasn't with Ernie, no matter how the latter's mannerisms might irritate him.

"Yeah," he said, "it makes a lot of sense. First thing we've done in this country that does make sense, it seems to me."

"You can say that again," said Ernie, paying for his beer and lifting his glass. "You know, I guess you and I are among the three or four staff men in the provinces in the whole country."

"Sure looks that way. It's no wonder we haven't got much in the way of collection operations."

"I know what you mean! Even though it does look like operating here isn't so hard for anybody that knows how to do it." He pushed the heavy black-framed glasses up on his nose and took another drink of his beer with a studied nonchalance. Toby stole a glance at him. Whatever his operational skills might be, he was certainly no actor. He could not conceal his eagerness to tell Toby of his triumphs in Kanh Hoa Province. He was a man who could not live without the approval of everybody around him.

"You may be right," Toby replied. He could not bring himself to play the game.

"I hadn't been in Nha Trang more than a couple of days before I found a way to get access to the Kanh Hoa Provincial Committee." He spoke in a low tone that could not be overheard in the noisy bar, but he was nevertheless violating the rule about talking shop. The tone implied a modest judgment that this operation of his was such an elementary piece of business that any other operations officer would have done exactly the same thing if he had been in Ernie's shoes.

"Have you got an approved project on that?"

Ernie nodded. "It's a going operation. Producing good info."

"Congratulations."

"Thanks. I must say," he continued, with a transparent attempt to be disarmingly frank and professional, "that the info I get coincides with what Chet was saying. These preparations are a deception, an intimidation, not real preparations for battle."

"My source says the opposite."

"But you don't know yet if he—"

"No, he hasn't been cleared or approved yet."

Toby had the uneasy feeling that Ernie was trying to needle him rather than seek his approval, and he was relieved that just at that moment young Will Voigt came in. Toby beckoned him to a seat on the opposite side of him from Ernie. The young soldier bore himself proudly, his uniform spotless and starchy, his boots mirror-like.

"You've met so many of us these two days," said Toby, "that you won't remember our names, I know. I'm Toby Busch, and this is Ernie Free."

"You're right, Mr. Busch," he said, shaking hands with the two of them. "I remember seeing you and hearing your names, but I couldn't have called the names right at this minute."

"I think we're close enough together in age," said Toby, "that I'd feel comfortable if you called me Toby."

"Same here," said Ernie.

"All right," said the soldier.

"I'm province officer in My Tho, and Ernie is up at Nha Trang."

"Things pretty hot down here in the delta?"

"Tense is a better word, I think."

"I think you're right. That's what you feel in the air up in Two Corps, too. A lot of tension."

"Personally," said Ernie, "I think it's just a ploy of the

Viet Cong. Keep us uptight. Doesn't cost them much to do it, and it wears our side down."

Will looked at him curiously and shrugged. He did not seem to share Ernie's opinion.

"I've been looking forward to meeting you," Toby said. "Your father is so proud of you, it's all he can do to keep from telling every one of us we're not half the man his son is."

Will's eyes softened. "Yeah, I know. The old man is a dedicated patriot and flag-waver."

"You don't believe in waving the flag?"

"I'm even worse than he is."

"Very few men your age feel that way these days, it seems."

"Very few men my age have been raised the way I have, Toby. Ever since I was born I've been traveling and living all over the world."

"Yep. That's life in the CIA."

"I guess the son of an operations officer, ex-OSS, would have more travel under his belt when he reaches high school than almost any other kid in the world. I've been all over the Orient with the family, and in a way I'm more at home in this area than I am in the United States. I speak Japanese and pretty good Mandarin, and Tagalog, and I can get around in some other languages, too. I've grown up with Asians, and I know something about how they feel. All these kids beating their breasts in the States give me a pain in the ass, because they don't know a god-damned thing about the world they're so shook up about."

"That's what we CIA men do to our children," said Toby thoughtfully. "We make cosmopolitans out of them. Linguists. World travelers. World citizens. And maybe unhappy?"

Will pursed his lips. "Oh, it can be tough sometimes, but there are compensations. I know that when I used to go back to Dad's hometown and meet some of the kids, I'd wonder how they could be so ignorant about the world, and how they could ever be happy confined to a little old town like that, with nothing but their dad's cars and drive-in movies, and dragging Main Street. That was when I appreciated the life I've had."

Toby turned sideways abruptly and looked at the young soldier. "You volunteer for this duty?"

"How could I stay out, with the old man in it this way?"

Toby stared at the rings on the bar. "I wonder if I ought to find another profession before my own son reaches military age?"

"He might just get killed in a drag race on Main," Will laughed.

"Then you don't think we give our kids psychological problems?" Ernie asked him.

"Oh, I don't know. Maybe so. But who doesn't have some kind of psychological problems? Spook kids are different, that's all."

"I suppose so."

"Other kids have nightmares about falling, or about trying to run away from something and not being able to move their legs."

"Yeah."

"You know what the bad dream is of most kids that have moved all over the world all their lives?"

"No, what?"

"Ask your own kids sometime, maybe after they're in high school, and I'll bet they'll tell you they've had some variation on this dream. I've asked friends of mine, spook kids and diplomatic kids, and lots of them do. It's a dream where you leave your house in the morning and go to school, or go out to do something, you know? And then when you come back . . ." Will paused and looked at Toby intently, ". . . home isn't there anymore. The house isn't there. Nothing is there."

"It sounds worse than being chased."

"You wake up sweating."

They drank their beer in silence for a moment, then Ernie spoke. "What do you do up there in Two Corps?"

"I'm adviser to a platoon of Vietnamese Rangers."

"What're they like?"

"They're good. Give them good leaders and they fight. But giving them good leaders seems to turn out to be a pretty hard thing to do."

"It's the story of Vietnam, apparently," said Toby.

They finished their beer and went into the dining room.

They sat down at the table with Dino and Jess, who were already halfway through lunch, and partway through a heated discussion of why the Italians had not been able to subdue the Greeks without Hitler's help.

[11]

THE inauguration of the Phoenix program made it all the more urgent for Toby to begin the training of his Special Police class. He got prompt security clearance on the students, and although he had not received all the materials and equipment he had asked for, he convened the class and began to teach them with what he had.

They were young, neat men, of slight stature, attentive and respectful. One of them Toby immediately nicknamed Gabby to himself, because he kept the entire class amused during their leisure moments. Another one reminded him of a Charlie Chan movie, and he dubbed him Number One Son. Whatever their personalities, they were serious about the training. Ben sat among them, and they accepted him without question.

Minnie sat on the edge of the little platform, perched on a high stool, and interpreted with his usual speed and self-effacing skill.

These men had already had some training in intelligence work, and Toby did not waste time in preliminary orientation. He plunged directly into the first subject.

"Clandestine communications," he said, "are the thread, the cord, that all of our work is bound together by. Without communications, intelligence has no value whatsoever. In this course, I intend for you to learn how to communicate messages clandestinely in the presence of the enemy.

"Now, that does not necessarily mean to communicate without being seen. In fact, perhaps the best way to communicate clandestinely is in full view of the world, doing things the onlooker can observe without any idea that what he is seeing or hearing is a message from you to somebody else.

"When our adversary becomes suspicious of us, he has taken the first step toward uncovering us, and destroying us. Therefore, it is better for your adversary to be confident that he knows everything you are doing, rather than have him wondering about some gaps in your day, or some equipment you have that doesn't look right. In other words, keep your enemy happy while you go about kicking him in the ass."

He hoped that Minnie would be able to put that into Vietnamese with some effect, and he was not disappointed. There was a burst of appreciative laughter, and he grinned his thanks to Minnie. He was off to a good start.

He worked them hard. He taught them the techniques of surveillance, neighborhood checks, target analysis. Agent selection, assessment, development. Recruitment techniques.

He hurried them. Tet was beginning to loom.

He wrote a skit on recruiting, and used Minnie and Therese in it, with the students participating to learn. There was little enthusiasm or comment about the skit, and he wondered if role playing was a good way to teach them.

He read scornfully the comment from one of their own office's intelligence reports, in which the reporting officer had urged the military reader of his message to "destroy the battalion" which the report had described.

"Your function is to give information," he told them, "not to take or recommend action about that information. You can tell your customer what the battalion is doing, how big it is, how many guns, who belongs to it, and how you got the information, but you have no authority to tell him to attack the battalion or ignore it.

"Suppose you were selling eggs in a stall in the municipal market. You have the moral obligation to tell the customer, if he wants to know, when the eggs were laid, whether they are chicken eggs or duck eggs, and what your price is. After he buys them, you have no authority to tell him that he must go home and make an omelette with them."

Toby thought this analogy would be mildly amusing to

them, but he was disappointed. The students looked more puzzled than amused.

That afternoon, Minnie approached him after the class. "May I speak with you for a moment about the class, sir?"

"Sure."

"Let me invite you to have a beer."

"It'll be a pleasure."

They went to a small bar on the main street of the town and sat at a table on the sidewalk with bottles of San Miguel before them.

"You teach very well," Minnie began.

"It's nice of you to say so."

"Interpreting, I believe, ought to be more than just changing words from one language to another. It should make communications move between persons with full and correct meanings."

"No question about that."

"Then, I hope you will not be offended if I offer you some advice you have not asked for, and perhaps may feel that you do not need?"

"Go ahead. I won't be offended."

"I think perhaps some things about the Vietnamese mind, about his soul, have not yet become clear to you. Most Americans see the world from a very American point of view, and they cannot even conceive that there may be other ways to look at ordinary things. Of course, the same may be said of the Vietnamese. When this happens, I believe it to be the obligation of the more educated one to make the bridge between them."

"I certainly can't quarrel with that."

"Some of the things you teach are very American, or you teach them in a very American way. These men do not have backgrounds that help them see the difference, and so sometimes the communication is absent."

"I've had a feeling about that several times."

"Your class on recruitment, for example."

"Not very good? But they seemed attentive."

"They would not be ill-mannered."

"But, Minnie, believe me, I know something about recruitment. That part of the instruction is the part I feel the most confident about."

"I do not doubt that your techniques would succeed in

Europe. If Therese had been a German or a French woman in our little drama, I believe you could have convinced her that dictatorship is bad and democracy is good; but I do not believe you would ever succeed in approaching and recruiting a Vietnamese for these reasons, the theories of democracy against dictatorship or totalitarianism."

"My God, Minnie," Toby exclaimed, clearly skeptical. "Our experience all over the world through all the years, as far as I know, is that ideology is the most important motivation of all. I don't mean that other countries ought to imitate the United States. But men naturally want freedom and justice, and will usually fight for them. Money is important, but not the most important. Blackmail is the worst, and we don't use it."

"Blackmail is bad anywhere in the world, I believe," Minnie agreed, "and money is important, even to the Vietnamese." He smiled and took a drink of his beer. "But if you want to recruit a Vietnamese, look for connections and levers in his family."

"His family?"

"Yes. Family is what makes a Vietnamese fight, or become emotional, or join one side or the other."

"Nothing but family?"

"Of course, it is not that simple. Other things do matter. But the most important, the first consideration of all, is his feeling for his family. This I believe you do not have in the European societies."

"No, certainly not in that sense."

"Another thing is the story about the eggs."

Toby scratched his head ruefully. "What was the matter with that story?"

"It is that the Vietnamese mind and the American mind seem to be on two separate roads in this matter."

"How do you mean?"

"In this respect, I am very Vietnamese myself, Mr. Busch. I confess that I do not understand the value of the story. I have been told that it is because of our reaction to what you call 'the what-if.' You suggested that we think what we might do if we were sellers in the marketplace. But you see, we are *not* sellers in the marketplace. How can we know what a seller feels? I am sure the class were all thinking that what they would need to do would be to find a seller in the marketplace and ask *him* about these things."

"But it's just a question of using your imagination."

"Perhaps. But a Vietnamese does not use his imagination that way."

Toby studied Minnie's words. "You mean that I can never successfully illustrate a point by asking the students to make believe they are somebody else?"

"Yes."

"Yes, I cannot?"

"Yes, you cannot."

"That's another thing," Toby said with a grin. "I notice that when you ask a Vietnamese a negative question, and he wants to give you a negative answer, he says yes."

"I do not understand."

"If I ask you, for example, 'Minnie, you are not a secret Viet Cong agent, are you?' what would you say?"

"I would say yes."

"Meaning you are not a Viet Cong agent."

"Yes."

"Americans would say no. 'No, I am not a Viet Cong agent.' "

"Vietnamese would say, 'Yes, I am not a Viet Cong agent.' "

"Now I wonder why that is?"

"For the Vietnamese, it is impolite to disagree."

"Can't you disagree in a polite way?"

"No. You must give your opinion in such a way that it will not be a disagreement, or appear to be a disagreement. It is a matter of form, but it is important."

"Well, I can understand that. Form is important, sometimes even in our pragmatic old United States."

"There is another thing, Mr. Busch," Minnie went on. "I have seen you come near another thing that must not be done, and I wonder if you know about it. From the way you speak, I think not."

"What's that, Minnie?"

"It is the power of words. To say the words sometimes makes a thing happen."

"Now *I'm* the one who doesn't understand," said Toby.

"If you asked one of the students what he would do if

the Viet Cong captured and threatened his wife, he would be very frightened."

"He would? Why?"

"Because he believes that saying the words can cause the thing to happen. He thinks words have substance . . . force . . . power. So he does not say them, and does not want to have them said."

"But surely that is a superstition?"

"Call it what you like, it is very real. The Vietnamese believe that words have physical power."

"I appreciate your concern, and I won't forget," said Toby. He looked at his watch. "It's getting late."

Minnie put a hand on his arm to delay him. "That is one more thing, Mr. Busch, if you pardon me for just another moment."

"OK," said Toby, resuming his seat. "What is it?"

"Time. You hurry the students on. You tell them time is short."

"Sure. You have to have some kind of a time framework."

"That is true. But the framework is different for a Vietnamese."

"How?"

"You must have heard that the oriental concept of time is circular, the occidental concept linear? To you, time moves in a straight line, and never repeats."

"That's right. And I have heard of the circular concept, but I don't understand it at all."

"Neither can we Vietnamese understand your linear concept. To us, time is eternal and repeating. A man, a soul, does not just begin at a point and end at another point on a line. He moves from one existence to another, in a circle of thousands of centuries. What he does in this one is not final or irrevocable, because this is not his only chance, his only existence."

"That, Minnie, is completely beyond my understanding," said Toby.

"I believe that neither people can completely understand the other in this respect. But it is important for us to know about the concepts we do not share."

"You are a thoughtful man, Minnie."

"Vietnam needs men to be thoughtful as well as brave.

After this war we must make a society that will be just and free, and Vietnamese."

"Amen to that."

"We must be able to withstand and throw off the American influence."

Toby was startled. "Throw off . . ."

"Mr. Busch, the French have gone, but now the Americans have come. It is not the same thing, and their intentions are good, but their power and wealth are very great in a small country like Vietnam, and the Vietnamese admire and imitate and envy what they see. Especially the youth. But we cannot *become* Americans. Someday the Americans will leave, we hope"—Minnie smiled good-naturedly—"and when they do, we must be prepared to be Vietnamese once again. That is why our country needs thoughtful men. I want to help. I would even like to be one of the leaders when the time comes."

"I have an idea you will be. But if what you say is true, then it would mean that death shouldn't matter to a Vietnamese?"

"No, it does not mean that. You Christians believe in heaven, which is a glorious place, many times better than this earth, and yet death is a tragedy to Christians, is it not?"

"I see what you mean."

"You have seen death in Vietnam, Mr. Busch. Death is all around us, constantly, but no matter how much death is around, it is always tragic to those who remain behind."

"Yes."

"Someday we will look back at this time and see that we were just episodes, and that the war is just one episode on that circle of thousands of years." Minnie traced a large circle in the air with his index finger.

"Or," said Toby with a twinkle in his eye, "an episode along that straight line of thousands of years that stretches from there to there." He traced a straight line in the air with his finger.

Minnie grinned broadly at him. "There we have you," he said. "You will fall off the end of your line someday, and disappear into nothing. But we will still be here." Again he traced the circle in the air. "Moving around in our circle of time."

[12]

You know, Toby," said Ben, "if I conform to the normal schedule of my tour here, I'll be home on leave from about the middle of January till the second week in February."

"Yes, I know," Toby replied. He had been planning to bring the matter up with Ben, but had hoped that he would have some more reliable information about the Tet uprising.

Ben sat down across the desk from him, obviously exploring the subject, rather than making a request. "The same rumors and the same feelings are around about trouble during Tet, you know?"

"I know."

"Well, you also heard about the information Saigon has that it may be a bluff?"

"Yes."

"The VC are certainly capable of such a trick."

"I suppose they are."

"I sure as hell hate to think of postponing my leave, too. My folks are going to be expecting me, and all. After all, the only thing we've got is just kind of a feeling or a suspicion. A fellow can't plan his life just on the basis of feelings like that."

"Certainly not. But we do have to use our judgment," said Toby, trying to make his voice sound casual and neutral. He did not want to force a decision. It would be better if it came from Ben.

"I agree. The thing that bothers me is that it could happen that I would postpone my leave, and *then* when I did go on it, all hell would break loose."

Toby remembered the predictions of Chet and Ernie about a delayed offensive. They troubled him. "Ben, I know you're in a hell of a spot on this decision."

"I sure am. If I'm not here and my teams get into deep trouble . . ."

"It's a hell of a prospect, isn't it?"

"Have you got a preference about what I do?"

This was the direct question. Ben was leaving the decision to Toby.

"Yes," said Toby. "I want you to postpone it."

"Any particular reason, except for our feelings?"

"Yes."

"Can you tell me what it is?"

"No." Toby wished he could tell Ben about Dang, but steeled himself against the temptation.

Ben got up. He seemed disappointed, but also somehow strangely relieved. "So be it, boss. I'll put it off. I don't have to tell you that I sure would like to know anything you can tell me . . . whenever you can tell me."

"You can count on it."

"One thing more. If everything seems to be hanging together all right, will you mind if I arrange to take a few days around Christmas up at Vung Tau? Get out on the beach a little bit, and there really is quite a bit of legitimate work in the training camp that I can be doing."

"Go ahead and plan it," said Toby. Ben went out whistling tunelessly, and Toby returned his attention to the agenda he was preparing in his small notebook.

If only Ben and Little Jack could both be away from My Tho *tonight,* he thought. Once again he must drive out that gate with Therese, to make the second meeting with Dang. He knew what they would think, and he hated it. He had rehearsed all kinds of casual remarks to himself, to explain lightly to them that he was just taking Therese home because he had to go that way for this or that reason, or because she was going to help him select a gift for Mary Lynn in one of the shops in town; but he knew that such a casual remark, volunteered out of the blue, would be more likely to arouse their suspicions than allay them.

And so he did not even try to dissemble. He and Therese drove out the gate as if it were the normal and customary thing to do. He had no briefcase, although the little note book was tucked into the pocket of his trousers, to help him maintain an efficient structure for the coming meeting with Dang.

Again they walked down the path, Therese ahead, wheeling her motorbike, and he self-consciously carrying a small package. It contained some items of toiletry and perfumes, which Therese had agreed would be good gifts for their act.

"But soaps and perfumes are not like television, Mr. Busch. One consumes them."

"Don't give it a thought, Therese," he said. "Let's just say that these are payment for the overtime. You're not collecting any money for all these extra hours, you know."

How graceful she was, even at the awkward task of wheeling the bike down a crooked path. The flowing lines of her *ao dai* undulated enticingly from the waist outward over the woman-curve of her hips, and made a delightful contrast with the hard, ungainly lines of the bike.

She locked her bike to the post, put her shoes just outside the door, snugly together, pointing precisely at the door frame.

They sat on the floor in the light of the television screen and waited. Toby sat close to her, but at this point his mind had blanked out all thoughts except for the coming meeting.

He went over his agenda with her, questioning her on some parts of it, letting her know what he intended to do at certain points so that she would be prepared for the interpretation. For this business he wished that he could have had Minnie. He would have been more confident of the communications, and communication was everything in the case of an agent under development, such as Dang. Therese did well enough, but she still had not caught the ability to take herself completely out of the conversation, the ability to avoid the "he says" locution that makes the interpreter a part of the conversation instead of simply an impersonal channel for it.

He closed the little book and tucked it into his shirt pocket. He was ready now. Now, when he looked at her, she was a woman again, the girl on the path with the bike. Her eyes returned his gaze for a moment, then she looked away shyly. There was something so appealing, so irresistible about the sadness in those lovely eyes. He realized that he was coming to trust her without any substantial reason for it. He also realized that no matter how unprofessional such an attitude might be, he was not uncomfortable about it.

Dang came in. This time he was purposeful, unhesitating. His eyes looked tired, perhaps more tired than they had at the first meeting. He held a small bundle of papers, and Toby's hand darted out and grasped it the moment Dang stepped through the door. Toby prodded and poked the packet, and then handed it back to its owner. Dang understood.

"Mr. Dang, what have you brought me to prove that you *are* Hoang Du Dang?" Toby asked, as they assumed their places on the floor.

Dang untied the string from around the bundle of papers and extracted two sheets from it. "I have thought about this for a long time," he said. "To fight against a bad cause is good, but to betray comrades is bad."

Therese had benefited from the experience of the first night. Her interpreting was smoother now, and usually omitted the "he says."

"I understand," said Toby. "These are difficult decisions for a man to make."

"I have decided that it is more important that you should believe me now, without delay, than it is to avoid danger for my comrades. Our whole country is in danger."

"I believe that," said Toby. But the remark made him slightly uneasy. His experience with clandestine agents was that, probably because their lives of secrecy provide them with few other emotional outlets, they have frequent urges to harangue their case officer with long patriotic speeches. He is an outlet. He is the only one to whom they can say these things. Toby had always felt that these moments were good for the agent, and helpful to the case officer–agent relationship, and he listened sympathetically. But in this case he did not have enough time to let Dang ramble on and was searching his mind for a way to stem the tide before it began, when Dang himself seemed to awaken to what he was doing.

"We do not have time for explanations," said Dang. "I believe you understand."

"I understand."

"Here," said Dang, extending the document, two sheets of paper covered with closely written words, "is a list of all the men of the Determination-to-Win Battalion. That will show you that I am Hoang Duc Dang, their commander."

"It will help, Mr. Dang. But I must point out to you that even if you were merely a clerk, you could have brought me such a list."

Dang nodded. He had been expecting this reaction. "If you wish to select any single name on that list," said Dang, "I will see that he goes on a visit to his home at a certain time. You may set the date, although you must allow time for him to travel. You may arrest him and interrogate him. You will find that he is what the list says he is."

Toby nodded. "You would be willing to have one of your own men arrested?"

Dang smiled. "The sacrifice would be mine, not his, because we do not have men to spare. As to his own feelings, if he knows that he has not done anything to betray himself, that his arrest is only a misfortune and not his own fault, and of no shame to him or his honor, he may even be glad to be arrested. There is no war on Phu Quoc Island, and the food and conditions in the prison camp there are in many ways better than they are for the men of the Determination-to-Win Battalion in the field."

Toby looked at the list and consulted with Therese. He pointed to a name, and she circled it and noted the village the man came from.

"Have this man," said Toby to Dang, pointing to the name, "at his home on Saturday and Sunday of next week. We will find out if he is a Viet Cong soldier, but without arresting him." He did not know how Manh's men handled prisoners, and did not want to subject the man to torture just to establish Dang's bona fide.

Dang looked at him quizzically. *Good,* thought Toby. *He believes our intelligence on his battalion is good; let him think we also have capabilities along other lines that he is not aware of.*

"Mr. Dang," he went on, placing the list on the floor beside him and pulling his notebook out of his shirt pocket, "can you make it back here for one more meeting?"

"Yes."

"When can you make it."

"One month?"

"That is a long time. You cannot make it sooner?"

"No. It would be dangerous."

"All right. It will be the last meeting between us, unless an emergency comes up. At that meeting we will take a great deal of time to establish systems of communication and alert."

They set the time and date for the meeting, and changed the safety signal from the shoes by the door to one shutter slightly ajar.

"Mr. Dang, we will keep that box at the airfield as our principal dead drop for the time being. The signal will be the same."

Dang nodded. Toby then gave him two other dead drops as fallbacks, and systems of signals whereby they could alert each other to the need for a meeting. Dang would have to carry all these things in his memory, so Toby kept the arrangements simple.

"Now, one more item of housekeeping," Toby continued. "We need to set up an escape plan, a bug-out plan, for you, in case they—" Toby paused abruptly: *Remember, Mr. Busch, words have power. Saying the words sometimes makes a thing happen.* "In case you ever decide that you want to leave your battalion," he finished lamely. "Do you understand what I mean?"

Dang understood exactly what he had not said. "No plan will be necessary. I would never run away."

Nor would Dang take any electronic gear with him, for signaling or communication. Toby had known that this would be the case. He asked the question so that his records would show truthfully, not that he had assumed that Dang could not do so, but that he had asked Dang and that Dang had refused.

Dang showed that he understood the necessity for all these odds and ends of clandestine operations, and he helped get them out of the way quickly. When they were ready for the substance of this meeting, he began, "Will the ARVN and the Americans take action to stop these plans for Tet?"

"They will if we give them sufficient detail, and can convince them that the plans are real."

"I know much of the details for this province, and some

of the general plan, but I cannot tell you details for other provinces, or for Saigon."

"I understand that. But something else has come up, Mr. Dang. We have reports that all the preparations you are talking about are really taking place, but that they are only for the purpose of deceiving the Thieu government and the Americans . . . that the Viet Cong know the plans are unrealistic, and do not intend the big attack to take place."

Dang's tired eyes followed Therese's interpretation intently. He nodded grimly, and replied at some length.

"He says that one of the men at the training session in Tay Ninh gave them indications that COSVN would try to deceive the Americans and Thieu exactly that way. He does not know how it was to be done, but he says they intended to have the deception reach the highest levels of both governments, and they were confident that they could do this."

"And so," said Toby thoughtfully, "it will boil down to this: Do we believe Dang, or do we believe the other story?"

Therese interpreted, and Dang looked steadily in Toby's direction.

"Well," said Toby, "we should not waste our time here by worrying about that. Let's get down to information and requirements."

Dang gave Toby other papers, some in his own handwriting, some lifted from battalion records. They contained information on the present disposition of troops in the province, and plans for bringing in other forces. The new battalion on the other side of My Tho, at which the planes had been firing the other day, was the 23rd Local Force Battalion. Its target would probably be the South Vietnamese Ranger Battalion stationed on the outskirts of the town. Although all of these forces were highly mobile and could not carry heavy weapons, they were equipped with good lighter ordnance: the AK-47 assault rifle, grenades, B-40 rockets, mortars, and some 90mm rockets and heavy machine guns.

"That doesn't seem to me like a peasant army swimming on the sea of the people," said Toby. "Surely they can't bring weapons like that on foot down the Ho Chi Minh Trail!"

Dang smiled. "The Ho Ch Minh Trail is more for propaganda and for men than for weapons," he said. "The weapons come by ship to Cambodia, by truck from the port to our border, and by sampan from the border to us. Thousands of tons every month."

"Can you get me details of who is involved in that traffic, and the exact routes and transfer points?"

"No. You would have to find that out in Cambodia, or near the border. A border liaison cadre could tell you, if you could find one."

"Keep that in mind, will you? It is of the utmost importance that we find out how this transportation system works. If we could interdict it at a crucial moment, it would help in our primary objective of preventing this uprising. Anything you can give us, or any names you find out about people we could recruit to help us . . ."

Dang nodded.

The agenda took an hour and a half to cover.

"That's all I have, Mr. Dang," Toby said at last. "Is there anything you believe we should talk about?"

"No."

They arose.

"When the time comes, you will be required to join in the offensive?" Toby asked.

"Yes."

"What will your task be—the task of the Determination-to-Win Battalion?"

"We will attack My Tho. The exact battle plan is not yet ready. I will inform you of details when I get them."

"You will attack My Tho with your mother and family living here?"

"Yes."

For the first time, Toby saw a sign of real distress in Dang's response. But he must be careful. *Words have . . . force . . . power.*

"Is there anything I can do to help them be safe?"

"No. Help from you would be more dangerous to them than military action."

"You cannot move them out?"

"No. All our soldiers have families in the towns and villages. These families are to be part of the general uprising. It is their safety and protection."

"Safety and protection in the battlefield won't be easy," Toby began, and then was fearful of saying more. He changed the subject. "Mr. Dang, you are risking your life, and I believe I can understand something of what has made you do it, but only *you* know what this decision has cost you in peace of mind. Nobody can help you in this inner struggle, but I can at least assure you that I believe you, that I am convinced that you are doing a good thing, and that I will do my best to see that your information does good for Vietnam. And I also want you to believe that if the time ever comes when I can help you in any way within my power to do so, you can depend upon me."

He waited for Therese to interpret these words, then held out his hand. Dang grasped it firmly, and the grip told Toby more about Dang's response than Dang could have expressed in words.

Therese peered out the door and nodded. Dang slipped out quickly and silently.

Toby and Therese sat down on the floor once more to wait. His knees were aching from the unaccustomed position, and he now stretched them out and lolled on one elbow. Therese sat easily, her legs tucked under her. The tension of the meeting was dissipating slowly.

"Interpreting uses more muscles than laboring with an ax or a shovel," said Toby. "I know, because I have interpreted for others in other languages."

"It is true," she said. "At the time, one does not notice. But now I feel very tired."

"You did well."

"I am glad."

"The meeting went well."

"Yes. Mr. Dang is confident now. He knows that you are experienced in these things, and so he is not so afraid for his safety."

"I think you're right. And he is beginning to understand himself better, and understand exactly what it is he's doing. He was still deceiving himself to some extent at the first meeting."

"Yes. He is thinking."

They sat quietly. A lizard on the ceiling scrabbled for an insect. A dog barked in the distance. The night was otherwise still. He caught a faint fragrance in the still air.

"I've been wondering about something, Therese," he said idly.

"What is that, Mr. Busch?"

"It may be indiscreet of me to ask, and I hope you will not be offended."

"I will not be offended."

"I have noticed all over Vietnam something about the women who live in conditions that are frankly primitive by modern standards. This, for example," he gestured to the room about him, "is primitive, isn't it?"

"Yes. It is primitive."

"In other parts of the world, when people live in primitive conditions, they usually look rather primitive themselves, more or less untidy—sometimes just plain dirty. But here in Vietnam I have not seen that. Even living in such conditions, the women of Vietnam always seem to be spotless, as if their clothing had never been near anything that would soil them, as if they had just been put on fresh about five minutes before. How do you manage to do that?"

"We work hard to do it, Mr. Busch. We do not feel right unless we are clean. One should be tidy, whatever the circumstances."

"Do all Vietnamese women feel that way?"

"I believe so."

"Most Americans would agree, I think, although whether they could do it under these circumstances, I can't say. We do have huge industries devoted to nothing but keeping people clean and sweet-smelling."

"Yes. You brought some of those things tonight."

"Coals to Newcastle."

"I do not understand."

"It's an old English saying. It means doing something that is unnecessary, something that has already been done, like putting a scent on a woman who already smells like a flower."

"Oh."

"I must go," he said, realizing with uneasiness the direction he had given to the conversation. He got up and extended his hand to her, although her lithe body needed no assistance.

She stood before him, close to him, her hand still held tightly in his own.

"I hate to leave you alone," he said.

"I am not afraid. Nothing will harm me here."

"That's not what I mean. I mean that to leave you here by yourself in this room, so full of grief and loneliness . . ."

"I am accustomed . . ."

". . . and so beautiful." His free hand brushed lightly over her hair and came to rest on one flawless cheek. He raised her chin and she stood quietly.

He kissed her, and held her tightly.

"Therese," he whispered ."Oh, Therese!"

"Yes. Yes, Mr. Busch," she whispered.

"Stop calling me Mr. Busch!" he growled.

He felt her laughing. "But it sounds . . ." she said, "Toby is . . . I cannot . . ."

"Nevertheless, when I have you in my arms I forbid you to call me Mr. Busch." He kissed her again, his hands caressing and exploring, finding the young, bare flesh. She kissed him back.

"Toby . . . Toby . . ." she murmured, tentatively, testing the sound. "No, it must be Tho. I will call you Anh Tho."

He was unzipping her tunic. "What does that mean?" he asked.

"It means lover," she said. She pulled his head down and whispered in his ear, "It means I am your mistress."

They sank to the floor, and groped and grasped and coupled, consumed and made frantic and clumsy by the sudden desire.

It was over quickly. Toby felt a wave of disgust at himself as he pulled away from her. He sat on the floor and rubbed his eyes and his forehead, as if in pain.

"That was not good, Therese," he muttered. "Not good at all."

"You do not . . . You find me . . . ?" She was stricken by his words.

"Oh, God, no, not that," he said quickly. "You are perfect. You are a perfect, a beautiful, an irresistible woman. That's not what I meant. I meant that doing this the way I just did is not the way a man and a woman should make love. This was almost as if I were an animal. It should be more than that."

She got to her feet and began to dress. "But we did not know it was going to happen."

He rose and stood beside her once more. She bent to pick up her bra, and when she straightened up, still naked to the waist, he clasped her to him again. "I want it to happen again, Therese," he said. "But I want it to be an evening where love is the center, not just an accident at the end."

"Yes," she said. "I would like that." Still clutching the bra in one hand, she put her arms around his bare back, and nuzzled the fine hair on his chest.

"I live in a real fishbowl," he said, "but I will find a way. Soon."

"Yes, Mr. . . . Anh Tho."

She drew away from him until her small, firm breasts barely touched his skin, tickling him, making him tingle. He kissed her again, then pushed her away. "I must go now, before it happens again, right here," he said.

He dressed quickly and stepped to the door. He opened it slowly, peeping out carefully as he did so. The shoes caught his eye.

"Therese," he gasped, "look at that!"

"What is it?" she asked, puzzled.

"Your shoes. They were straight together when we came in. Look at them now!"

One of the small shoes was slightly askew. It was not as she had left it. Something had moved it.

"Perhaps Mr. Dang—"

"He came in from that direction, and anyway, he would not have moved the shoe in that direction coming *in*. I saw him go, and he was not near the shoes at any time."

"Perhaps somebody was watching us." Therese was deeply embarrassed.

"It could be either that, or that somebody was watching our meeting with Dang." Toby peered up and down the pathway, listening for a telltale sound. He looked around the doorway for other evidence, but could find none.

"Now I really am afraid to leave you here alone," he said.

"I am not afraid," she said.

"You must come with me," he insisted.

"No. I will stay."

"But, Therese, I can't leave you after seeing this."

"It is not logical that they would want to harm me," she said.

"Logic has nothing to do with it."

"Nevertheless I will not go."

He could see that nothing would shake her resolve to stay. Reluctantly, fearfully, he kissed her and went down the path to his jeep, his mind racing.

Why did he have to louse things up right at the crucial moment, always? Even if Frankfurt wasn't exactly his fault, things *had* come unglued under his direction. Now here he was in the midst of a delicate recruitment, an agent-in-place in the Viet Cong, and so what did he do? He rutted around on a woman while his agent prospect was under surveillance! Or maybe while he himself was under surveillance.

He did not even make the usual check for bombs or booby traps, but started the jeep motor absently and drove home. He was unsatisfied, troubled. His anger rose at the security problem he now had, and his blood raced when he recollected those moments on the floor.

He had never made love to a woman like her. He had never made love to an Oriental. But it wasn't her being an Oriental. There was a certain hesitant wantonness about her responses that had made him virtually explode. How can you describe that? Of course, he had not made love to any other woman since he had married Mary Lynn.

Guilt, remorse, struck him so suddenly that it took his breath away. He had never before deceived or betrayed her, and now, during this entire evening he had not even once thought of his wife, who didn't deserve this of him.

What was happening to him?

[13]

MAJOR Thieu was angry, so angry that his English was even more incomprehensible than usual.

"Mr. Busch, *you* not send officers to districts. *I* send! *I* send officers on travel!"

Toby paused at the door of the classroom, stopped dead in his tracks by the fury of Thieu's words.

"It is part of their training," he said.

"But I not said OK!"

"Well, I did not suppose that you would object," Toby replied. Thieu as usual stood so close that he found himself slowly backpedaling. Minnie and Ben, who had come to the classroom with him, kept in the background.

"I not wish. I order them not go!" Thieu insisted.

"Now, wait just a goddamned minute," Toby flared. "Whatever protocol I violated, or whatever quarrel you and I have, can be settled without disrupting the training." In his own anger Toby forgot and spoke words Thieu would not grasp.

"Exactly!" said Thieu. "That is why I tell them not go."

He had not understood. Toby held up his hand. "Major Thieu, let us go sit down and discuss this together, you and I."

This Thieu understood, and he backed off a pace. "We talk," he said, "but my men stay in My Tho."

They went into the empty classroom, and Toby motioned to a chair by the table at the front of the room. Thieu sat down, with Toby opposite him.

"Major Thieu," Toby began, "this is complicated. Can we not have Mr. Minh interpret for us?"

"No," Thieu retorted haughtily. "We will speak in English."

"All right." Toby glanced over at Minnie, who sat

down in a chair at the rear of the room and began to look over some papers. Ben sat in a chair beside him, his face expressionless.

"To send men to districts is disturb," Thieu said. "This must be done by my office. Men must not go to districts as *men* wish."

So that was at least part of the problem—Toby had given the men their choice of districts to visit. It was part of the training in observation and reporting. Target analysis, as well. They were to go to the districts and spend two days, then come back and write him a report on their observations, what they could find out about the Viet Cong presence by eliciting information from local citizens. They were to touch base with the district police office, but were to work on their own.

He was getting them off their butts and out in the street where the work was. He had been pleased at their reaction to the assignment. From what he had been able to observe, men in their positions in Vietnam often seemed to feel that their work was to be done at a desk. The results certainly showed it.

Not only was it good training; it would also tell him something about each man, and about the districts, and would serve as a basis for target studies throughout the province. And it would form a squad of men ready for the work of the Phoenix program, to supplement the work of the PRU. That was the way he wanted the program run in his province.

Thieu was reacting to what was a subtle usurpation of his authority. Thieu wanted to run the show, and he would not run it in Toby's way, nor would Toby be satisfied with Thieu's way.

"Major Thieu, I want those men to go to the districts," said Toby evenly.

"No," Thieu replied coldly.

"I have seen your office's intelligence reports."

"Yes, our intelligence reports."

"They are trash, crap, useless garbage . . . What's the word I want, Minnie?" Toby called across the room, aware that it would infuriate Thieu even further. Minnie uttered a sharp guttural sound, and Thieu started, in spite of himself.

"I understand your words, Mr. Busch," he said.

"When the Viet Cong strikes My Tho, and other towns, and Saigon asks, 'Why did not My Tho report about this many weeks ago?' what will you say, Major Thieu? Saigon will say, 'It is Colonel Manh's fault.' Will Colonel Manh say, 'Yes, it is my fault'? No, Colonel Manh will call Major Thieu, and he will say, 'Thieu, why did we not know about the Viet Cong attack? Why did your officers, that Mr. Busch trained, not tell us about the attack? Let us call Mr. Busch and ask him why.'

"Then Colonel Manh will call me and will ask, 'Mr. Busch, you spent many days training these officers, but they produced no information about the attack. Why is this so?'

"And then, what will Mr. Busch say? Mr. Busch will say, 'Colonel Manh, those men were trained. They were capable. But they did not produce information from the districts *because they were sitting on their ass in My Tho!*'" Toby's voice rose to a bellow of rage as he finished. He was not really angry. Impatient, yes, but more amused than furious. Thieu was a bully, and probably a liar. The only way to deal with a bully is to butt heads with him. He was doing it with a lot of words that Thieu would not grasp, but with a tone and an attitude that Thieu could not mistake.

Thieu was confused, but tried to maintain a dignified anger. "You do not frighten," he said.

"I do not intend to frighten," Toby lied. "All I want, and what I demand, is that those men go to the districts assigned to them."

Thieu seemed to be confronting something new to him, and was searching for a way out. He thought for a moment, looked judiciously at Toby as if weighing all factors with complete objectivity.

"You say travel is necessary for training?"

"Absolutely!"

"I would assign men to different districts?"

"No." Toby wondered if Thieu had any special reasons for balking at the freedom of choice he had given to the men, and then decided that it was nothing more than mulishness.

"They will go if I order." said Thieu.

"Major Thieu," said Toby quietly, certain that the moment had arrived to allow Thieu a graceful retreat, "I believe you should order it."

Thieu thought for a moment. Then he arose. "When men come today, I will come talk. *I* will instruct, and *I* will order travel."

"Good! That is all I want. Thank you."

Thieu left the room, and Toby hurried back and sat down in a chair close to Minnie and Ben. There was little time before the men arrived. Ben was watching developments with an intense interest.

"Minnie," said Toby, "we're going to outsmart Thieu, and I'm going to have to depend on you to help."

"I will do whatever I can, Mr. Busch."

"Thieu knows that I do not speak Vietnamese, and when he talks to the men he may give them a frank, or perhaps a subtle set of instructions that will negate what I am trying to do."

"I am sure that is what he intends to do," said Minnie.

"And if that's the case, he will also wait around while I speak to them through you, to make sure of what I tell them."

"I am sure he will."

"Then I won't wait around until afterward, while *he* talks to them," said Toby firmly. Minnie was puzzled. "I am going to speak to them first," Toby went on, "and they'll already have their instructions before he speaks. By then it won't make any difference what he tells them later."

Minnie began to comprehend. A smile came to his lips, and grew wider as Toby talked. "Then we will tell them . . ."

"Minnie," said Toby, "we are going to see if these students remember anything about clandestine communications."

The men assembled, and before they had settled into their seats Major Thieu entered and went to the platform. He sat down near Minnie and waited. The class fell silent immediately, curious.

"Gentlemen," Toby began, "Major Thieu has spoken to me about the assignments to the districts. He is unhappy about this, and I understand why. I arranged the assignments without going through the correct channels, which is not a good or polite thing to do, and for that reason I apologize to Major Thieu."

As Minnie caught up in the interpretation, Toby turned and inclined his head in Major Thieu's direction, and Major Thieu acknowledged the gesture with a similar noncommittal nod.

"The mistake may be attributable to my zeal in teaching you clandestine operations—especially communications," Toby went on. "A large and significant part of this exercise is devoted to practicing the art of carrying out clandestine communications before the enemy, as I have taught you from the very beginning of these sessions." Toby again bowed to Major Thieu, and Major Thieu nodded back. Toby watched the faces before him intently as Minnie translated the words. Minnie's voice was almost expressionless, which in itself was unusual, and Toby was elated to see the looks of comprehension that came to the eyes of the young men. Several mouths looked as if they were struggling not to smile.

"I have explained to Major Thieu what it is we expect to accomplish by this assignment, and he understands and agrees with that. But he points out, with complete justification, that the details of the assignment should not be my responsibility, nor yours. Major Thieu, himself, must make the decisions as to where each of you goes, and when. I am sure that Major Thieu will make an intelligent decision about the places and schedules we have been considering. In any event I know that we can trust him to do what he feels to be right, and that we can all trust you to be on the lookout for opportunities to thwart the enemy in this new training exercise. Thank you."

The men smiled and nodded vigorously. Toby turned to Major Thieu.

"Major, you undoubtedly will want to speak to your men now. Mr. Compton, Mr. Minh, and I will withdraw for a time. Suppose we say that we will reconvene here in half an hour?"

"Very well," said Thieu complacently.

Toby signaled the others to follow him, and they went out and headed for the bar down the street.

"Toby," said Ben admiringly, when they were out of earshot, "that was slick. You've just taken the command of those men away from Thieu."

Toby smiled happily. "What do you think, Minnie?"

"They understand," said Minnie. "You can depend on them. They do not like Major Thieu. He is not a very skillful officer, and not a likable man. They will listen to him politely, but they will deceive him for you from now on, I believe."

"Then you did a good job."

"I think it would be more correct to say that *I* also learned something about clandestine communications today, Mr. Busch."

[14]

WHEN they returned to the classroom, Major Thieu announced to Toby in a magnanimous voice that he had decided to authorize the men to make the training trips as planned. Toby thanked him ceremoniously, while at the same time observing the faces of the students. They could not understand the words, but they must be aware of the general content of the speeches.

"Men understand," Thieu said, "that reports come to me first. This is proper . . ." He could not think of the word. Toby went to his rescue.

"Of course, that is the proper procedure, Major Thieu. It is exactly what they should do." He looked at Minnie and the students, and then questioningly at Thieu, who with a wave of his hand gave regal permission for Minnie to interpret the words for the students.

There was little change of expression, but something about the slight shifts of bodies in the chairs, the way the eyes rested first on Thieu and then on him, made Toby know beyond doubt that the students had joined his conspiracy. He smiled at them. The Vietnamese, he concluded, were not only a feisty people, they were an astute people. He could not remember ever having worked with any other nationality, even one whose language he spoke fluently, who grasped a situation of this kind more quickly or intelligently than these young men seemed to be doing. They would make formal reports to Thieu, but he knew that when they had something really significant they would pass it along to him directly, by some means.

The students stood up as one man when Major Thieu walked toward the door. He turned and stared at them for a moment before he walked out, as if sealing with this glance his own conspiracy with them.

The class would gather for an hour the following morning for final instructions and briefing. Toby had one more task he must accomplish before they left. He had checked the plans to find out which of the men would be working in the district that contained the village where Dang's man would be on leave. He would have the student verify the visit.

But how to give the instructions? If he passed them along through Minnie, no matter how he managed it, it would have the effect of including Minnie, at least on the periphery, of the Dang operation. Minnie had a quick mind. He would be curious.

There was no natural way he could include Therese personally in the instruction process. A surreptitious meeting with that one student would be difficult to arrange, and would indicate to the student the importance and significance of the task—and that would bring the student into the edge of the Dang operation.

He decided to bury the name.

When he got to the office, he called Therese over to his desk. Nobody was in the room but the two of them for the moment, and he was intensely aware of her presence, but he resisted the temptation to speak intimately with her. Ben or Little Jack might walk through the door at any moment. He contented himself with a broad smile. She smiled back, and he noted with pleasure that the sadness was no longer there in her eyes.

"Therese," he said, "I want you to help me with a job here. Will you bring me the Viet Cong suspect file, please?"

She produced the thick file, and he went to work with

her comparing the names with the districts the students were traveling to. He assigned one VC suspect name to each student.

"We will have them use their training in neighborhood checks, you see? Each student will have one suspect to check in his district. They will consider this just a part of their training exercise. But in the case of the student going to *this* district, we'll give him the name Dang gave us. By burying this name among the rest, nobody will attach special significance to it."

"Do you believe the student can do this well?"

"I hope so. Only time will tell."

"Dang might find out that—"

"Yes, Dang might find out how we went about verifying the existence of his test soldier. But I have not told him how we would do it, and there is no real harm in this. Dang is a leader of men, and he must know that one has to train men. He will probably assume that I am just taking advantage of a real-life opportunity to do so, instead of using other, better means of checking up on him."

If the student verified that the soldier had in fact visited his home during the days designated, it would reassure Toby that Dang was still in place and functioning. Whether Dang was under surveillance or perhaps under control of the enemy security service was another question.

Meanwhile, all the information Dang had given Toby was sitting in Toby's safe, carefully drawn up in intelligence reports. Toby was committing the cardinal intelligence sin: sitting on information. But he had no choice. Chet would not pass his reports along until he was able to give reasonable evidence of who Dang was, and whether his information was trustworthy.

This test soldier should help.

By the time the list was ready, and individual slips were made up for the students, it was time to quit work. Therese left. Toby knew that he would not be able to keep his thoughts on business for the rest of the afternoon, and he secured his own desk and safe and got up to leave.

"You haven't forgotten that we're invited over to the girls' house for dinner this evening?" Ben reminded him.

"No, I haven't forgotten. I'm going in to shower and shave now."

He went upstairs. He noted with some wonderment that after that first half-hour or so of remorse and guilt, he had ceased to worry or blame himself about that moment on the floor with Therese. It had happened. Nobody knew except him and Therese. Nobody else need ever know. He had been keeping secrets all his life, most of them from his wife as well as from the rest of the world. One more secret need not be difficult, and would not add measurably to the burden.

But how did it happen that he didn't really consider this secret to be a burden among all the others? And how could he sit and pass along to her by means of one long smile all the electric thoughts that were coursing through his mind, without any hesitation or doubt?

What was happening, he realized, was that his conscience wasn't as strong as he had supposed. The thought that was now uppermost in his mind was not that he should not have done it once, but rather that he might as well be hanged for stealing a flock as for stealing a lamb. It would be no more difficult to keep twice from Mary Lynn than to keep once from her. Whatever the struggle might be, or might have been, in the upper levels of his soul, there was no denying that down there in the lower levels, in the pit of his stomach, the focus of his physical reactions, his desire for Therese had been fanned from a spark to a flame by that first encounter; and he now found his mind straying regularly to plans by which he could spend a night with her. His pulse quickened at the recollection that she wanted a night alone with him, too.

It was an abrupt reversal of all his habits of mind and action. Was it because the profession of spying had already forced him into a mildly schizoid existence? He had spent his entire professional life up to now coolly and consciously appearing as one thing to some people and as another to others. But, then, everybody in the world was slightly schizoid. The intelligence business merely formalized the characteristic, and polished and developed it for the business at hand.

Here on his nighttable were letters from Mary Lynn. Loving letters, newsy letters, with gossip about the town, stories about the kids, plans for what they would do when he got home on leave. She was not a dull wife. She could on occasion be as exciting as any woman he could imagine. And she was bright. They talked. They knew each other as only a man and wife could, and, although he could not expect that their bodies would invariably be a source of mutual joy, they had had enough moments of real passion to judge that their sex life was a good one, probably far better than average. His feeling for her had not changed one bit since Therese.

Had it?

Suppose he found that his response to Mary Lynn had been altered? Sexual stimulus and response can be a mysterious and elusive thing. Suppose she detected something new in him—a difference in his attitudes or his desires?

It could happen. He had discovered within the first few months of their marriage that Mary Lynn had an uncanny understanding of her husband. She read him like a book. In a sense it had always been somewhat of a comfort to him, because, paradoxically enough, it relieved him of the necessity to make any decision about being unfaithful to her. There was no decision to make. He knew that he could not even think of seeking or accepting consummation of any of those fleeting lascivious thoughts that came to him when he peered down a voluptuous décolletage, or watched the inimitable parabolas described by a pair of female hips moving away from him—because Mary Lynn would know. Mary Lynn knew that he had a normal charge of lust in his batteries, but she also knew that he had never gone any further than looking since he married her.

If she did sense something different in him, could he lead her to believe that she was observing the aftereffects, not of adultery, but of simply living in a war?

It was a different world, there was no doubt about that. It was another life, a separate life. What he did in this one had only the most tenuous connection with the other one.

And now, here he was, getting himself ready to spend the evening with still *another* woman! He felt so good about that that he found himself whistling as he dressed. For this woman was different. It would be a relief to spend the evening with a woman without complications. He had always been stimulated by conversations with intelligent women. Their range of interests never ceased to surprise him, and it seemed to him that they tended to be more eclectic than men of relatively equal intellect and education. Most men he knew had no inkling of this, because they never really explored the minds of the women around them. Too busy exploring everything else.

And then, of course, there was the sheer pleasure of talking with women, communicating with the only sex that could be mothers, sisters, concubines, or wives.

He liked Louise. She was a woman who put on no acts, had no hang-ups, talked intelligently about interesting things. You could be at ease with her. It would be a pleasant evening.

The three men—bathed, shaved, combed, and smelling of PX lotions—climbed into the jeep and drove out the gate.

As they slowed down for the intersection to the northwest of the house, he glanced up at the wooden utility pole out of force of habit. His heart skipped a beat. There on the pole, at about eye level, was the peculiar slash he had instructed Dang to make.

On the other edge of the town, the woman who put on no acts and had no hang-ups was toweling down after a shower. Out of habit, she made a brief inspection in the mirror, detected no sags or lumps, and was reassured once more. She still had a nice tan, from the last trip to Con Son Island. She always jumped at the chance, when there happened to be a seat on the weekly cargo plane. There was usually a nice crowd for a picnic on the torrid beach, and if it weren't for an occasional day there she would probably be as pale as a ghost from spending most of her daylight hours in the hospital.

She took one more quick look before beginning to dress. It could be, of course, that there were changes taking place so slowly that she wasn't detecting them. Certainly that body was a thirty-year-old body, not sixteen. And the sags would come. She had seen too much bare human flesh on hospital beds to ignore her own vulnerability to the passage of time.

Well, it did no good to worry about it. She began to dress. But she did care. She cared very much. She liked the way a man's eyes flickered when they swept over her body. She knew that when she did meet the man she would want to marry, the least of her problems would be to make him desire her physically. All she had to be alert for was the man whose heart was right, whose mind was in tune with hers, whose tastes were like hers, and who would laugh with her at things that were funny.

It bothered some women that so many men began to think of bed soon after meeting them. It didn't bother Louise. If the guy was a slob, you brushed him off quickly, even brutally if necessary. If he was a decent man, all you had to do was give him the right clues and responses, and he would keep a civilized control over his male equipment. And it was that very tension, the little interplay of clues and responses and control, that gave excitement and flavor to being in company with men.

She adjusted her skirt, and pulled a flowered blouse down over her head. She grinned at her own grinning face in the mirror. *You,* she thought, nodding accusingly at the image, *have on certain occasions given the clues and responses that could lead only to the bed.*

She had no regrets about those times. She was neither virginal nor promiscuous. When she did marry she would do so without guilt or regrets, and she knew that she would have no trouble being a satisfying and faithful wife.

She put on a necklace that set off the pattern of the blouse, and inspected the result critically. Just right.

One thing she was sure about, in this evening to come: Toby Busch was not the one. His eyes had flickered most satisfactorily, and he was a brainy man with a sense of humor, but he was married. She recoiled at the thought of involvement with another woman's husband. The mischief of such a thing was intriguing, of course, and if the wife in question were a shrew it would be less reprehensible. But there was something grubby and unattractive about being the co-respondent, and she was repelled by the idea of troubling or breaking up any marriage, good or bad.

And you could tell by talking with Toby Busch for just about five minutes that he took things seriously. He would not take lightly any liaison with another woman. It would be devastating to his marriage.

Would that intense man, who could be so distant one moment, his mind concentrating on something far away, only to return to you in the next instant with a flash of humor—would he have been the one if he were not married?

He could have been. His life was interesting, certainly. He would probably not take a woman for granted, no matter how long he lived with her. He was the type who would expect a woman to help him change a tire one minute, and then would write a poem to her the next.

She went downstairs. It was still early.

Peggy was arranging chairs, and placing ashtrays and chips and nuts. Bottles and glasses and ice were on a small table to one side. The meal would be buffet style.

"It looks very nice, Peggy," said Louise.

"Yeah, I think it's about as good as we can make this old place," Peggy replied. "This G.I. furniture isn't the easiest stuff in the world to make look homey and comfortable."

"Are you all ready?" Louise asked casually, hoping that Peggy would say no. Peggy was her usual slightly disheveled self, clean as a pin, but somehow not quite touched up and patted into place.

"Yep. All I need is a chair and a whip and we can let the lions in," she said.

"Well, of course," Louise teased her, "we'll let them all in, but there's only one of them that will interest you."

"Sure," said Peggy carelessly, "I always get assigned to that one, and I have to work with the material I get."

"About to get him tamed?"

Peggy looked around at her, shrugged, and sat down on the edge of one of the chairs. "I guess I don't hide it very well, do I?" she said.

"Not well enough for a couple of women who *live* with you."

"Marie Claire notices too, huh?"

"Yes. And we both worry."

"You worry? About Ben and me?"

"Yes."

"What in the world for?"

"About whether you . . . about . . . Gee, do I really have to tell you?"

Peggy sighed. "No. But you shouldn't worry. That thing about the lions isn't too far off the mark, you know? I got him nicely tamed—or maybe he was already tame when I got him, but I can't seem to *train* him to do what I want him to do. But, don't worry, I know what I'm doing—or not doing."

"He was married once before."

"I know. I don't think it had any effect on him at all. She didn't teach him a thing. Maybe she didn't know how to teach him. And he's the kind that never makes the same mistake twice."

"But why is it him? He's nice, but frankly I can't imagine . . ."

"God, I don't know. If I could explain it, maybe I could do something about it. It's got something to do with him being so self-sufficient, so confident, I think."

"But he seems so unapproachable, too. You can never get next to him, never talk on real intimate terms with him, You can kid around, but when you start getting serious he seems to clam up. You can never find out what's really inside of him. Or maybe *you* can?"

"Probably better than others. But still not very much."

"Then you can't really say you know him, can you?" Louise sat down in the chair near Peggy.

"I know him better than you think," said Peggy. "I know, for instance, that he is a rock-bound puritan. That's what makes him a good soldier. He's got his world neatly lined up in categories. He's got just as much dirty old man in him as any man in the world, but he keeps it in its proper military place. He believes there is a time and place for everything—killing, healing, planting, reaping, and sex. And sex is fenced into a special, very narrow cage."

"Really?"

"Yes. And that affects all his dealings with women. There are so few circumstances where it's all right to pull the pants off a woman that he won't ever do anything that might even look like he's thinking about doing it. His idea of courtship is something out of seventeenth-century New England, because he thinks nice girls don't do it, unless they're married, and then they just grit their teeth and think about babies."

"Surely he's not that stupid," Louise exclaimed. "What does he . . . ?"

"He goes somewhere else. I don't know where. But I'm

sure he buys it, from girls that aren't 'nice.' And I'll bet he's a real riot in a whorehouse. The time and the place, you know."

"I must say, I never thought of him that way."

"He's that way. But even when he's whoring, it's bound to be a neatly arranged part of his existence, all labeled and scheduled and under control."

"Sounds awful! Doesn't that make you feel any different toward him?" Louise persisted.

"Nope. Because I know Ben has never had a woman *in* his life. He's had women around the edges of it, but never a part of it, never a part of him. If that wall, that shell he's got around him ever gets broken down, he could find out what a woman is really like and she could become a part of his life. And it wouldn't be a bad life, because underneath that rigid outside there's a good man. And I want to be the woman that finds it."

"And you think you've got a chance?"

"I don't know. Sometimes when he looks me in the eye, I want to come right out and say to him, 'Why don't you reach back there and unfasten my bra, Ben?' Or, when we're dancing, you know, 'Go ahead and put your hand there, Ben; I won't fly out of the room like a rocket.' Do you understand what I mean, Louise?"

"No."

"No, I suppose not," Peggy said gloomily. "Maybe I haven't explained it right. Or maybe I don't understand it myself. But what you *can* understand, I'm sure, is that after a day in the hospital, having to be strong and self-sufficient and help other people, it's such a relief to be around a man who wouldn't accept help if you offered it to him."

Louise nodded. "That I can see."

"And Louise, he is a *man*."

"So is Little Jack."

"Little Jack is a gorilla. If he thought it would be fun, he'd grab you by the heels and bang you against a tree. But Ben is a guy that when you walk down the street hanging on to his arm, you know that if people even look sideways at you, this big goddamned puritan is just naturally going to deck their ass."

Louise burst out laughing. Peggy rolled this kind of thing

off her tongue very seldom, and always when you least expected it. Now she enjoyed the effect her words had had on Louise.

"I wish we had talked about this before," Louise said.

Peggy shrugged. "I guess maybe I didn't want to, before this. I guess I hadn't really thought it out before. In fact, I kind of thought it out just now while I was talking about it."

"I'm sort of relieved."

"Relieved? Why?"

"We thought you didn't realize what you were up against."

"I know what you mean, but you said it wrong," said Peggy. "It isn't what I'm up against, it's what I *can't* get up against."

The sound of the jeep coming into the driveway interrupted them, and they went to the door. Marie Claire came down the stairs and joined them just as the men trooped up the steps.

They came in like a prairie gust, full of bellowing good humor, moving in a swirl of the trivia of the first moments of such a gathering. Each man went to the table and fixed drinks for himself and his partner, and they settled one by one into the chairs in the living room.

"I was telling the fellows," Ben said, "that I don't like that little wall you've got around this house. It's made me uneasy ever since I first saw it."

"What's wrong with it?" asked Peggy.

"If I was to look over this neighborhood as a battlefield . . ."

"Good God, Ben," said Marie Claire, "is the whole world a battlefield to you?"

"Yeah," Louise put in. "I know we have to be careful about bombs and things like that—but a battlefield?"

Ben was not at all troubled by the critical tone of their voices. "Of course the whole world isn't a battlefield," he said. "But imagine the surprise of the people of Gettysburg that morning in July. If you had asked one of them a month before, or maybe even a day or so before, what kind of a battlefield his front yard would make, he would have laughed at you."

"You mean you think there's going to be a battle in My Tho?" Peggy asked, frightened.

"No," Ben said with a reassuring smile. "What I mean is that if you wait until it happens, it's too late to get ready.

"For instance, this wall you've got around the house is so low it looks like it must have been built for a rifleman —just the right height and thickness. It's not even waist high. And if you look at the field of fire, you can see that if any action ever concentrated on the Province Senior Adviser's house, this house is one of the most important points in the whole area."

"No kidding?"

"I'm going to get a recommendation through, somehow," Ben went on, "probably to the Province Senior Adviser, to have that wall built up to about seven or eight feet . . . That is, if you ladies won't mind me butting in?"

"Of course not," said Louise, "but what will be the good of that?"

"It will make the house defensible for itself, and less useful as a key point in the area."

"Ben," said Toby, "as long as we're talking along these lines, why don't we set up some communication with this house?"

"How do you mean?"

"I'm getting ready to order a radio net for us, one of the VHF nets, you know—a GE or a Motorola setup. We'll have the base station at the office, with a big enough antenna that we could reach the hand-held sets anywhere in town, and even a few miles beyond the edge of town. I'm going to put a set at the PRU barracks, and one over at the Special Police Office, and at the Revolutionary Development Office, and have one for the jeeps, too. We could put one of them in here."

"Hey, that's a great idea," said Ben. "I'm always kind of nervous for these women. Can you get the equipment, all right?"

"If there is one thing our agency is good at," said Toby, "it's coming up with equipment you need the minute you need it. Our life depends on that."

"I don't know a thing about radios," said Marie Claire. "Do you girls?"

The other two shook their heads.

"You don't have to know anything," said Toby. "You just have to listen, and when you want to talk, you push a button. That's all."

"But won't you be violating regulations or something, to put your equipment in our house? We don't belong to your organization," Louise pointed out.

"You're a taxpayer, though," said Toby. "I may be going against the letter of the regulations, but we've got plenty of the equipment, so we're not depriving anybody else of the use of it. Don't worry about it."

"OK. Whatever you say."

They ate dinner. Afterward they danced, then sat and talked. They knew each other well now, and they enjoyed these gatherings of their group. Even Little Jack seemed to be acquiring some measure of ease and comfort around Marie Claire. She was a quiet woman, and made few demands.

"Louise," said Toby when they were dancing. "I need your help."

"OK. What is it?"

"I've got to go out on some business, but I don't want people to think that it is business. I don't even want them wondering what it is. Would you go along with me, even if I can't tell you what it is?"

"Going to meet Doctor No?"

He laughed. "I've never met anybody even remotely like Doctor No, and I hope I never do."

"Well, whatever it is, I'll do it. Do we walk?"

"No, we'll have to take the jeep."

"Will it take long?"

"Maybe half an hour."

"I hate to desert my responsibilities as a hostess," she said.

"They'll get along. I'll tell them it's something I have to do over at the office, and that you're coming along for the ride."

"You know what they'll think," she said, arching her eyebrows at him. She didn't really care.

He smiled. "In the time we'll be gone, they'd have to think I'm Speedy Gonzales."

"When de we go?" Louise was intrigued by the idea of

going along for some spy work, and would not have said no under any circumstances.

"Now," he replied.

Toby told the others, and there were some good-natured remarks and some laughter, but no apparent suspicion. To Louise, they seemed to be taking it as quite a natural thing for a man in Toby's work to do such a thing, and just as normal that she would prefer to be with him rather than unattached in the living room.

They got into the jeep and Toby drove in at a brisk pace through the darkened streets. They went by the government compound, and Toby drove in a complete circle around it, peering carefully through the iron bars that made up the upper half of the fence. What he was looking for she could not tell, nor could she guess as to whether he had found it.

He headed out beyond the outskirts of the town, and drove to the airstrip, where he steered the jeep off the road and onto the end of the runway. He peered carefully through the dark toward the other end of the runway.

"Well," he said at length, "I guess that's it."

"That's it?"

"Yep. Except for one thing."

"What's that?"

"Before we start back I've got to use the restroom over there." He motioned toward the wall of boxes along the side of the runway. "Will you mind? I'll be out of sight, but not more than twenty-five yards away from you if you yell."

"Go ahead," she said, and watched as his figure grew dim in the gloom and disappeared around the end of the wall. "You can write me the poem when we get back."

"What's that?" His voice came to her out of the darkness.

"Nothing. Just talking to myself."

He reappeared, climbed back into the seat, and started the motor.

"Is this what you people do at night?" Louise asked him.

"Yeah! Isn't it exciting?"

"I think I would prefer Doctor No."

"After such an adventure as this?"

"And you can't tell me what it was we did?"

"You mean you don't know?"

"No."

"See? I told you I was Speedy Gonzales! Shall I do it again?"

Louise laughed with delight, and Toby sat grinning at her for a moment before putting the jeep in gear and heading for home.

[15]

As soon as Therese arrived the next morning, Toby called her into the common room and showed her the envelope with the single sheet of paper he had found in the dead drop the night before. The note was scrawled in pencil.

"It is not very clear," she said. "He must have written it quickly, or with others nearby . . ."

"Tell me what it says now, and then make a typewritten translation, will you please?" Toby asked her urgently.

Therese translated:

"I cannot meet you as planned. I was followed when I left. I am now under observation. I will elude observation once to deliver this message, but I must not do so again because it would confirm suspicions. I will get information and will send it same way as this message, if possible. Do not use other plans to communicate with me until I advise all is safe."

"Of all the goddamned bad luck!" Toby exploded. "Just when we had the guy developed to where he was going to really go to work for us, instead of just handing us a few crumbs!"

"Who is following him?" Therese wondered.

Toby stared at the floor for a moment. "The possibilities are almost limitless," he said slowly. "There didn't seem to be any surveillance of you or me afterward, so we can be pretty sure that the tail was just one person. He probably had specific orders about what to do, unless he was just inexperienced. But I doubt that. I think he knew what he was up to, and he was confident that they could find out about us some other way . . . Or maybe they already know about us."

"About us?"

"Yes. Who we are, and why we would be meeting Dang. Maybe what they are after, now that they have made this first observation, is simply to *nail him*, not discover a network. If that's what they have in mind, they are watching him for the next meeting, so they can have witnesses to it, or send a strong enough force to the meeting site to round up everybody involved."

"Then, if we had gone again to my home to meet him," said Therese, "that might have happened."

"It sure might have happened. And there is another thing we must do. We must cancel the neighborhood checks the Special Police students were going to make." She looked at him quizzically. "Under the circumstances," he explained, "this would be no test. If the man isn't there, we would have to consider that Dang might not dare to send him now. If he is there, it could be that any kind of an inquiry about him would be one more link in the chain of evidence against Dang."

"Then I will destroy the instructions?"

"Yes. Put them in the burn trash."

Disconsolately, Toby went back to his desk and made a notation in his log, then wrote out an operations report for the headquarters record.

He was sitting at the desk, lost in thought, when Ben approached.

"It's almost ten," Ben said.

Toby shook himself out of the trance. He had not realized it was getting so late, and he had to give the students their final briefing. With Minnie, they got into the jeep and drove toward the government compound.

"Toby," said Ben, "I was just now on the sideband with Al Mallory up at Vung Tau. He wants to know if I can come up there this afternoon and help them get a new team transported down to this new village we're opening up, just across the river from Vinh Long Province. The VC have been giving the village fits in the past, and this team is a little edgy. Al thinks it might settle them down if I'm up there to help them move out, and if I go with them to the village to help them set things up."

"Go ahead. Nothing to keep you here, is there?"

"Nothing, except that it will leave you alone, what with Little Jack going down to Can Tho this afternoon for the Phoenix training program."

"Yeah, I had forgotten about that."

"You could probably get some of his PRUs to come up and supplement the guards around the house. They won't be doing anything else."

"Do you think that's necessary?" Toby asked him evenly.

"It's whatever you want," Ben replied.

"That's not what I asked you. Does the safety of the house require extra men?"

"No."

"Then you thought I would want them because I'm scared?"

"Well, no." Ben was embarrassed, and Toby knew he had discovered the truth. "I was just thinking that if you feel uneasy about a lack of experience, or anything like that . . ."

"Forget it, Ben. I've been scared shitless in my life, but it doesn't paralyze me. If the Nung guards and one armed spook are enough to make the house reasonably safe, that's the way it will be."

"OK."

"Mr. Busch," said Minnie, "since there will be little to do after the class this morning, I would also like to leave afterwards, unless you need me for something else. I would like to go to my brother's home for one extra day this weekend."

"Your brother's home?"

"Yes. My brother and his family have a small rice farm north of My Tho. I spend most of my weekends there. This time, with Friday also, I will be able to help him with some repairs to his house."

"Sure, Minnie. You'll be back Monday?"

"Yes. Certainly. As usual."

"I have yet to see a rice farm from close up. Maybe someday you'd take a man who grew up in the corn land of America, to see how they raise rice in Vietnam?"

"I would be pleased to do that, sir. I would have to let

my brother know, because he would be embarrassed if a visitor came and we were not ready."

"I can understand that." Toby looked at him thoughtfully. "You are a cosmopolitan fellow, and well educated, and yet your brother is a rice farmer."

"Yes."

"Were you raised on a rice farm?"

"Yes."

The answers were so reticent that Toby wondered if he had hit a nerve of pride or place. He remembered that in Europe or Latin America an intellectual did not find it a matter of pride to come from peasant or middle-class stock. Perhaps it was the same in Vietnam.

A new thought wiped the uneasiness out of Toby's mind. He would be all alone in the house, all night. The guards would be there, and so would Mrs. Chao and Chi Hai, but he had almost come to regard these people as if they were furniture, and so he viewed the prospect as one of being alone.

Alone for one full night. With Therese.

It was with difficulty that he brought his mind to bear on the final briefing for the students, but once into the process, he had no thoughts for anything except the last-minute instructions, and some final advice on common sense and flexibility.

He finished with a short statement about how happy he was with the results of the training so far, and how high a regard he had come to have for them, and how he knew that their work in the future was going to be fruitful for themselves and for Vietnam.

He dismissed them, and they filed by to shake his hand. They were diffident, and tended to bow a great deal, but he caught a warmth, a respect, and an affection from them that he could not have resisted. He liked these young men very much. He muttered words of farewell and good luck, which they did not understand, and they muttered back to him as if they had.

He could detect no change in Minnie's demeanor during the briefing, nor later in the jeep, and he decided that his uneasiness had been needless. They dropped Minnie off at the center of town, where he could get one of the tiny three-wheeled Lambretta buses for the countryside. When Toby and Ben arrived at the house, Ben went immediately to the sideband and called Jerry Burkholder.

"I'm in luck," he told Toby. "Dino's coming along this way at one o'clock, so Jerry's going to have him stop here. He'll be through for the day, and he can take me directly over to Vung Tau. This way I can spend the afternoon with the team, and it will give me time for a little pub-crawling this evening."

"Does Vung Tau have that much in the way of pubs?"

"Night life is where you find it, Toby," said Ben with a grin.

Toby thought with a start that Ben must have gathered something about his own plans for the evening, but a second glance at Ben's face reassured him that the words had contained no hidden meaning.

Ben went to his room to get ready, and Toby opened his safe and put away his briefcase. Therese was typing steadily, her back to him. He looked at her, started toward her desk, hesitated, then sat down at his own desk.

He realized, with wry amusement, perhaps even astonishment, that he was nervous about asking her. Then it came to him that in all his life he had never gone boldly up to any woman and asked her to spend the night with him. Nights with women had occurred as a result of circumstances—usually circumstances that he had carefully engineered—but they had never begun with the bald request.

He fiddled with some papers. He searched in the drawer for a pencil. When he found it, he sharpened it. He replaced some stray paperclips in the little bowl on his desk. Finally, laughing inwardly at his own foolishness, he swiveled his chair around. She was still typing steadily.

He went to her desk and leaned over it.

"Therese," he said quietly.

She started at the suddenness of his voice, and turned to face him.

"I will be all alone in the house tonight," he said. "Will you have dinner with me?"

"Have dinner here?" Her attention had not yet fully shifted from her work to him.

"Yes, here. With me. Alone."

"Oh! Yes, I would like that," she said, almost shyly.

"And we can have the whole night together," he said, almost making it a question instead of a statement.

"Yes."

"Now that you have said yes, please stop looking at me like that, and turn around and go back to work immediately, or I may be on the floor with you again, right behind this desk."

She laughed and returned to her typewriter.

Toby was glad of the distractions that came. He had a light lunch with Ben, then drove him to the airport. Exactly as scheduled, Dino set his little plane down lightly on the runway, loaded his passenger on board with his usual voluble good humor, and lifted them back up into the sky.

Toby drove home and went to the kitchen. Mrs. Chao was lying on the table, composing herself for her afternoon nap. She jumped to the floor with an agility that belied her wrinkled features.

"Mrs. Chao," he said, "Mr. Compton and Mr. Horner will be gone tonight."

"Yes," she replied, bobbing her head. "Gone."

"Miss Therese will be having dinner with me. Miss Therese and I, for dinner," he repeated slowly, and held up two fingers.

"Miss Therese?" She was puzzled.

"Yes. Miss Therese. Secretary." He pantomimed typing. She would know Therese by her Vietnamese name, of course.

"Ah! Miss Therese!" Now she understood. "Dinner here?"

"Yes."

"Good! I fix!" She was grinning broadly.

"Make it one of your good dinners, Mrs. Chao," he said. "Best wine and everything."

"Yes, yes! I fix," she repeated happily. "Chi Hai help. We fix."

There was nothing faked about Mrs. Chao's pleasure. Toby walked out of the kitchen with a sense of well-being. He need not worry about the dinner—it would be excellent. Mrs. Chao and Chi Hai would fix.

Therese brought a small bundle with her when she came

back from lunch, and Toby guessed that it must contain nightclothes He quit work early to shower and shave, and to check over the bedroom and the common room and the bar.

He went back to his desk and tried to concentrate.

After what seemed to him like an eternity, Therese put her things away and picked up the package.

"I will change now," she said to Toby. She had brought something besides nightclothes, evidently.

"I'll be in the common room," Toby said. "Do you like daiquiris, Therese?"

"Daiquiris? What is daiquiris?"

"It's a cocktail. I'll fix one while you are changing. I think you will like it."

He locked up and went into the bar. He had filled the shaker with ice, lime juice, rum, and sugar syrup, and was preparing to shake the mixture when Therese reappeared. She was clad in an *ao dai* of rich red, delicately embroidered at collar and breast. It was perfectly fitted to her form. Its red glow set off the dark flow of hair that cascaded over her shoulders.

As she moved through the room toward the bar, he found himself holding his breath at the serene beauty that was coming into his presence. She sat on a stool opposite him, aware of his rapt gaze, accepting it placidly.

"You are beautiful," he said, still holding the shaker motionless in his two hands.

"I am glad that you think so," she said.

He shook the cocktail, staring happily at her all the while, knowing that the smile on his face must look foolish, and only turned away when it came time to strain the pale green mixture into the glasses on the tray before him.

"Let's go sit at a table."

He led her to one of the low cocktail tables, and extended the tray to her after she was seated. They sipped and looked silently at each other. She nodded that she liked this new taste, and he smiled back.

Chi Hai came in to place a small tray of hors d'oeuvres before them. There were the usual dips and chips from the PX, but the central tidbit was a dish of *cha gio*, little morsels of shrimp and crabmeat mixed with bean sprouts, pork, and spices, wrapped in a jacket of the filmy rice-gluten *banh trang,* and deep-fried to a crisp brown.

They sipped and munched and talked. Toby felt strangely unacquainted with her. It was almost as if that night at her house had not happened, as if this were a first date. She seemed to feel the same. They talked about the ingredients of daiquiris and of *cha gio* and about why the spirituous beverage of Vietnam was cognac instead of sake or whiskey. They talked about French bread and French cooking, about Fritos and potato chips, and about countless other things that were of no consequence to them. They did not know what they were talking about or why they were doing so.

Therese's eyes, which had already lost most of their look of sadness, now began to sparkle with life and fun, and Toby was so smitten with this new, crimson-clad, effervescent Therese that he did not notice the pasage of time.

The sudden tropical dusk descended, and Chi Hai came to announce that dinner was served. Toby offered his hand to Therese, to lift her to her feet, and they stood together in the dim light of the bar as if afraid to break a spell.

He led her to the dining room. Mrs. Chao had set the big table in such a way that they would be close together at one corner, with two candles to give them light. The dinner was exquisite, a delicate meal that seemed designed for the mood and the occasion. Mrs. Chao and Chi Hai bustled quietly about them, as they had never done on other occasions. They spoke in low tones to Therese, but there was no hint of secrets shared among them and kept from Toby. Toby could not understand the words, but he could see the pleasure they were taking in her presence at the table.

After dinner they went back into the common room, and sat on the sofa. Mrs. Chao brought coffee and liqueurs, and bade them good night. Toby poured a tiny glass of Cointreau for Therese, a splash of brandy for himself. They drank and talked some more.

Toby kissed her, a light tentative kiss. Her arms went around him tightly, and then he kissed her with more authority.

"Come on," he said. He switched off the lights, and arm in arm they went up the stairs to his bedroom.

Toby was surprised and amused when he opened the door. The covers of his double bed, usually turned down on one side at this time of night, had been turned down on both sides ready for double occupancy. The air conditioner had been set at a higher temperature, so that the air in the room was less arctic than usual. It would not chill bare flesh.

On his desk was a large vase of flowers, lovingly arranged.

"Mrs. Chao and Chi Hai knew," he said to Therese.

"Yes," she said. "They knew. They are glad."

"Glad? You mean that this matters to them?"

"Yes. They like you very much. They believe you need a woman."

"I'll bet it's more than that," he said. "They like you, too. They don't think I just need any old woman. They think I need *you.*"

"Perhaps that is so."

He kissed her again, and went about the room turning off all the lights except for a small one by the bed. She was undressing, and was almost naked when he had finished. His hands went unwilled to her body and he clasped her to him.

"You must undress, too," she said, pushing him away gently.

He did, and then they were locked together on the bed. There was intense desire, but it was not hurried. Deliberately, savoring every moment, steeping himself in every female curve and every soft hidden secret of her body, he made love to her, and she responded. He could not tell whether her pleasure was from her joy at pleasing him, or from the pure physical sensation of a man on and around and within her, but he did not care. Whatever it was that drove them, they were both abandoned for the time to the primitive, unthinking enjoyment of each other's bodies, to the touch of lips, breasts, bellies, and thighs, to the caress and the grip of hands that roamed incessantly, as if trying to discover and grasp each new ecstasy and hold it like a tangible thing.

Then he was sated for the moment and they were still, tranquilly awaiting the next wave of desire that would come to flood their senses.

Toby had no idea what time it was when they lay at last, spent and relaxed.

"Thank you, Anh Tho," said Therese in a soft, wondering voice.

It was so sudden and unexpected that Toby burst out laughing. He raised himself on one elbow and looked down at her smiling face, framed as it was by the silky hair in disarray on the pillow.

"In all my life," he teased her, "I have never been thanked by a woman for doing that. Is that a Vietnamese custom?"

"I thanked you because you have made love to me sweetly," she said. "It has been many months that I have not been with a man. I knew that I missed it, but I did not realize how much."

"Not since . . ."

"Since my husband died. At first it was the sadness, but then I was not sure whether it was still the sadness or whether it was wanting a man."

"And tonight you knew?"

"Even before I met you, I had come to know. There was still the sadness, of course, but now they were apart. I would long for this, for a man's arms, for his hands, for . . . for everything. But I could not go to just any man. It would have been horrible if the man had been—if he had not . . ." She could not find words.

"I think I understand," he said.

"Yes," she said, placing a hand on his cheek. "Yes, you understand."

"But I may have brought you more unhappiness in the long run, Therese."

"How?"

"Because this can't last. I can't stay forever in Vietnam, and I can't take you with me when I leave."

"I know that."

"And yet you are happy? Even though there is no future in it?"

"One cannot plan for any future in Vietnam," she said, looking away from him. "I am living now. And I am in bed with a man who is good and gentle. And I love him."

He kissed her cheek tenderly. "I love you, too, Therese.

I do love you." He was surprised at his own words. "I do love you, and yet . . ."

"You are thinking of your wife," she said calmly, turning her head to look into his eyes again.

"Yes."

"Because you love her?"

"Yes. I love her very much."

"You do not believe that a man can love two women?"

"Therese," he said, frowning thoughtfully, "any time the thought of being with another woman has occurred to me, it was only *wanting* her that I thought about. I didn't even consider the possibility of truly *loving* her."

"You were not thinking deeply, then?"

"No, it's just that in our culture—and I don't know how it is in Vietnam—but with us it is understood that you can only have one woman at a time. If you come to love another one, she has got to replace the first one, or she must move out of the picture."

"Why?"

"Well . . ." He was stumped.

"What do you think now?" she persisted.

"If we were in my country now, I would not be able to do this, because neither woman would put up with it for long, and even if they did, society wouldn't. It would destroy my marriage and ruin my home."

"I see."

"But somehow the distance from her seems to be more than a question of miles in this case. It's psychological, almost spiritual. Somehow I am sure that I can do this without its having any effect on my feeling for her, without its having any effect on that other world."

"I hope that is so."

"But on the other hand, I wonder if I will be able to make love to her when I go back without always remembering how you felt in my arms, and without even sometimes having the sensation that it *is* you, in my arms once again."

"I hope it will be that way."

"Even if it hurts my marriage?" Toby asked gently.

"Oh, no!" she exclaimed. "I do not want to harm you or her in any way, Anh Tho. I only hope that you will remember tonight, and remember me, all of me, with us . . . this way . . . because then I will know that I will always be your lover, wherever you are."

He looked down at her nude figure, a perfect, living sculpture lying motionless beside him.

"A night like this," he said, "becomes a part of a man for the rest of his life, whether he wants it to be or not. There is no way I could erase it now, even if I wanted to. For the rest of my life, you will always be my lover, and I will love you."

"And I will love you, Anh Tho," she said tenderly, yet with a sudden sadness, "for the rest of my life."

"You have many years ahead of you, Therese."

"Perhaps."

"Of course you do." His hands stroked her body slowly, from the delicate breasts downward. "My beautiful, my perfect, mistress," he whispered. His hand came to rest on the flat belly. "You are so young, and so perfect. You will have your choice of men when you decide to choose. And peace will come, and then this flat little tummy will some day grow and grow with a second beautiful little Therese, with big lovely eyes, and a round little body—"

He was cut short by the look of shock and awful hurt that came to her eyes.

"Therese!" he gasped. "You—you already have a child!"

She nodded.

"But, it doesn't seem possible. Your body seems barely beyond your own childhood, so smooth and fresh." He stroked the satiny, unmarked belly again. "I had no idea. Where is the child?"

"I had two little girls," she said. "They are dead."

"My God," he said in a strangled voice. "Oh, my God! Children, too!" The sparkle had gone from her eyes, replaced once again by the deep pain, and by the slight glint of tears.

"I know this must hurt unbearably," he went on after a long time, "but I want to know about them, and about your husband. You belong to me now. You will always belong to me, no matter where we are or what happens. Won't you tell me?"

"I cannot." She shook her head.

"Have you ever talked to *anybody* about them?"

Again she shook her head.

"Therese, you must do what you think is right for you, but I believe it might help you to bear the grief if you talk about it. Perhaps I have come along not only to help you fight your loneliness, and to be a man beside you once more, but perhaps also to help you deal with your sorrow. I would like to try."

She looked away from him again, and was still. He waited. She felt his hand, and he grasped her searching hand in both of his own, kissed it, and held it tightly.

At length she turned her face to him again, and said, "Then, I will tell you." She closed her eyes and drew a deep breath.

"My husband was a good man, a thoughtful and gentle man, and I loved him. I was happy with him. He was educated and seemed to have a good life before him. His family was well respected, and they had enough money to live well. But they were Catholic, and the Secret Police accused them of counter-revolutionary activities. Their money and property were taken from them slowly, and then they were taken to prison, although they had done nothing. My husband was then in danger, and we escaped with the help of a Catholic friend."

"That was when you came to the south?"

"Yes. We went to Truc Giang, because there were some friends of his family who had already escaped, who lived in Truc Giang, and they could help my husband find work. We were poor, but we had enough to eat, and we were free.

"We had two little girls. Chi Hai was almost three years old."

"Chi Hai?"

"Yes," she said. In spite of the glistening eyes, a warm smile of recollection came to her lips. "*Chi hai* means 'number one sister' in Vietnamese. The oldest girl in a family is called Chi Hai."

"I like that. It makes her special, doesn't it?"

"Yes. Our Chi Hai was just as you said, very large eyes, round body, and so happy. She always looked . . . looked surprised . . . because her eyes were . . ." Therese's lips quivered, and she had to pause to regain her composure.

"Little Chi Ba was one year old," she continued. "She was just beginning to walk."

"*Chi ba* is . . ."

"Number two sister."

Toby's throat tightened, and he swallowed hard.

"The Viet Cong had told neighbors that my husband was working against them, and that they would kill him someday. My husband told all the neighbors that this was not so, that he was not working in any political or revolutionary way at all—which was true. He said that the Viet Cong were just trying to frighten him and the neighbors, that this was just part of their terror, that they would not do anything to him. He was a brave man. He continued to live and work as usual, and he did not show fear.

"Our house was small. It was built partly out over the river on logs that stand on end, I do not know the word."

"Pilings."

"Yes. We all slept in the back room over the water. It was cool and quiet. One night, when the others were asleep, I heard something . . . a noise along the bank of the river, and I got out of bed and went to the other room. I could see nothing, and I stepped out the door to see if I could see better from the outside.

"The Viet Cong had put some plastic in a sampan."

"Plastic explosive?"

"Yes."

Toby was horrified. He knew what a small amount—a few ounces—of plastic could do.

"They were letting the sampan float down in the water under our house. They made it explode just as I went out the door. I do not remember the explosion, but I remember getting up from the ground many meters away and running back to the house. My husband was lying there . . . He could not possibly still be living.

"I never again saw little Chi Ba. After the explosion, there was no more Chi Ba.

Therese's voice was shaking, and tears were streaming from her eyes. "I found Chi Hai in one corner of the front room, covered with broken things. She was crying, and her arms and legs were crooked, and she was blind."

Toby waited, gripping her hand.

"I picked her up and held her," said Therese, "and then she died."

Toby could not speak. Therese lay still, her eyes tightly shut, her lips quivering; then from the depths of her came an unearthly wail, half groan, half sob.

"Oh! Oh!" she moaned. "Oh, my babies . . . my babies . . . my babies . . ."

He gathered her swiftly into his arms and held her close, held her while the storm of pain wracked her body and contorted her beautiful face, caressed her wordlessly, grieving with all his heart over a hurt he was so powerless to soothe.

He turned off the light, and for much of what remained of the night he held her to him while the passion of remembering and suffering spent itself, and left her at last lying quietly in his arms, shaken now and again by a small fluttering sigh, as a child will catch its breath when the weeping is over.

[16]

Of the twelve men Toby sent to the districts, three were killed and two were gravely wounded.

He watched in stunned silence as the three bodies were brought into the government compound, to be claimed by their families. The two wounded men had been taken directly to the My Tho hospital, their lives hanging by a thread.

Gabby had been killed. The other two were average, good guys whose faces had become so familiar to him, whose eyes had so often followed him intently as he lectured or demonstrated. The faces were still now, the eyes dead; as still as that other face, as dead as those other eyes he had seen that morning on his doorstep in Frankfurt.
had seen that morning on his doorstep in Frankfurt.

He wished there were something he could say to show their stricken families how he felt, but knew that he could not have expressed it in any language.

Colonel Manh was calm, but cool. With Therese interpreting, he gave Toby the story as he had heard it. Each man had acquired lodgings that first night as best he could, and had been shot from ambush when he emerged from those lodgings the following morning. The wounds were from heavy rifles, and there were many of them. Instead of individual snipers, apparently there had been a small squad assigned to attack each man, and they had fired devastating volleys from long range. The attackers had not been apprehended. They had not even been seen.

"The Viet Cong knew about their missions," Colonel Manh concluded, looking Toby steadily in the eye.

"So it seems," said Toby.

"We should have thought that they would."

"Yes." Toby had never in his life been so nearly immobilized by shock. This was not a chance ambush that could be shrugged off as the fortunes of war, the mischance of being in the wrong place at the wrong time. This was an enemy reply to his efforts in Dinh Tuong Province. *We take you seriously, and you had damned well better take us seriously. We will kill them when we choose, and we will kill you when the time comes.* He shivered.

Major Thieu strode into the office. "Five men!" he shouted in a fury. "Five!" He held up the fingers of one hand for all to see. He turned on Toby.

"*You* send men! *You* send, and Viet Cong kill!"

Manh spoke sharply to Thieu, and Thieu fired a stream of angry words at him, not disrespectful, but certainly forceful by their sound. He was waving in Toby's direction all the while.

Well, he was right, wasn't he? Toby's career seemed to be taking on a regular pattern of finding men, preparing them, and dispatching them into a storm of bullets. He *should* have considered the possibility that the Viet Cong would learn of this operation, and that they would decide to act. He should have had those young men prepared for such an assault. His European-style professionalism had undermined whatever training and instinct they might have had for an insurgency situation, to the point where they had forgotten the most rudimentary safety precautions.

Dazed as he was, Toby was nonetheless struck by something about Thieu's face. There was a subtle difference in this wrath of today and the tantrum Thieu had thrown over Toby's original plan. That first rage had been so genuine that Toby had thought the man might fall into a fit at any moment. This one today seemed almost to be staged, acted out solely for the effect it would have on the audience. Thieu was not really all that upset about losing those men!

When Thieu had subsided, Manh turned to Toby. "You will understand," he said with studied politeness, "that Major Thieu is extremely angry. We will all be able to think about this more calmly some other time. I agree with Major Thieu that there will be no more teaching."

It was a blow, although not unexpected. The implication was plain that not only would there be no more teaching, there would be no more direct contact between him and the remaining students. The liaison would from now on be with Thieu and Manh only.

Thieu made no attempt to conceal his triumphant, righteous indignation as Toby and Therese left them, to drive back to the office. Thieu had won, and he knew that Toby knew it.

When they got back to the office, Toby could hear the single sideband transceiver muttering in the breezeway entrance.

"Buffalo, Buffalo, this is Volleyball. Buffalo, Buffalo, this is Volleyball. Over." Pause. "Buffalo, Buffalo, this is Volleyball. Over."

Toby recognized Volleyball's voice as that of Bill Voigt. He went to the transceiver and answered the call.

"Buffalo," came Bill's voice, "the regional office of your friends here tells us you had a hell of a night last night up there in your province. Over."

"Volleyball, that's affirmative. Have they given you details? Over."

"A lot of details. I don't know how accurate. But it sure looks serious. Over."

"It is serious, Volleyball. Over."

"Well, we can't discuss it this way. All hell may be about to break loose, so you better get on down here right away. Over."

"I can't make it immediately, Volleyball. Cobbler is not here, and I can't get in touch with him very quickly. And you know where Holiday is. Over."

"Yeah, that's right. How soon can you make it? Over."

Toby thought rapidly. "I can make it on Monday. Over."

"All right. I'll tell Butane he's got to get you here as early as possible. Call him for a schedule later this afternoon. Over."

"Roger, Volleyball. Over."

"Buffalo . . ." Bill's voice was grave. "I say again—this is serious. I need facts, all of them. Everything. Do you understand? Over."

"I understand, Volleyball. Over."

"See you Monday. Volleyball out."

"Buffalo out."

Toby went back to his desk and sat down. He did not know where or how to begin, even to begin thinking things through. Nor did he have any urge to do so. His mind was a blank, his initiative gone.

He sat as if in a trance, until a movement near his desk caught his eye. Therese had come and sat down and was looking at him intently. They were alone in the office. He tried to smile at her.

"Now it is my turn," she said.

"Your turn?"

"Yes. Today it is you who need help."

He blinked and tried to organize his thoughts. "Oh, not really, Therese. I'll be all right. I was a damned fool, and so wrapped up in what *I* knew that I didn't stop to think that maybe somebody else might have figured out some things about this war that I didn't know."

"You believe you have been defeated?"

"Whether I believe so is not the point. I know damned good and well that my *agency* will think so. My agency will see that the enemy has defeated me here in Dinh Tuong, and my superior in Can Tho has been proved right, and these facts will reach Washington. You are now looking at a man who is as high up in his profession as he will ever go . . . a man who will be among the first to go when there is another RIF."

"Another RIF?"

"Reduction in force. When they dismiss a certain percentage of the people of our agency. It happened in the past. It will happen in the future."

"They would not be so foolish! They would not dismiss you!"

"You are prejudiced," he said with a weak smile.

"Yes, Anh Tho, of course I am prejudiced. Anybody who knows you as well as I do must be prejudiced for you."

"The people in Washington don't have quite the same kind of an acquaintance with me that you do, Little Mistress."

She took his hand in hers, pulled the fingers out of the clenched ball, and held the hand tightly. "You will see," she said.

"Thanks. I know better than to be optimistic, but I love you for trying to help."

"You will see."

He took her hand in both of his own, and sat quietly with her for a long time.

"I do not like to leave you alone, Anh Tho," she said at last, "but I must go."

"All right," he said reluctantly. "But couldn't you come back this evening?" They stood up and she put her arms around him.

"No," she said. "Not tonight. Tonight it would not be good."

He knew she was right.

"You will see," she said once again, and kissed him quickly. Then she pulled away from his arms and was gone.

His brain was in no condition to work. He knew that even if he forced himself to stay at his desk, he would accomplish nothing. He went into the house, sat at the bar, and had a beer. Mrs. Chao called him to lunch, and he went in and sat down listlessly at the table. Mrs. Chao was tending to her tasks with a high good humor that showed she had heard nothing of Toby's problems.

"You sleep well?" she asked with elaborate innocence.

The question momentarily lifted the veil of gloom, and Toby grinned at her and wagged his finger accusingly.

"Shame on you, Mrs. Chao! No, I did not sleep. I did not sleep at all!"

Mrs. Chao laughed with delight. "No. Not sleep. I know."

"Of course you knew, you oriental yenta," he scolded her affectionately.

She grew suddenly serious. "You good man for Therese. Therese sad. Therese not happy. You help Therese."

Toby wished he could communicate with this woman with fluency, instead of the pidgin English that gave her speech such a childish sound. He knew that she was an intelligent woman who would have been able to give him a rational and thoughtful explanation of her feelings.

One thing was clear, in spite of the language barrier: Mrs. Chao had not looked upon the night from the point of view of Toby's good, but of Therese's. He loved the wrinkled little woman for that, and Mrs. Chao seemed to understand his feelings. "Good man," she said, and went back out into the kitchen.

Toby picked at his lunch without appetite. Afterward, he went back to the common room and paced up and down. He had a drink, and then another one. He had never used alcohol to forget or to escape, and he was not doing so now. He was merely bored, yet too keyed up to read, or to work, or to do anything except pace and drink. He knew that once he had liquor humming in his veins he would not be able to think clearly even if he tried, but he did not want to try.

He spent the rest of the afternoon in a leaden flush of alcohol. It did not solve his problem, but it made the time pass.

Mrs. Chao was silent when she served his dinner, and he guessed that she had heard the news by some kind of grape-vine. By bedtime he was tired of the strain of the idle day, tired of the pacing, tired of the taste of booze in his mouth. He brushed his teeth in a sleepy fog and tumbled into bed. He thought dizzily that he had a right to be tired, after all. He had hardly slept last night—in fact, had expended more physical and emotional energy than a normal working day would require, only to be confronted with another shock when the night was over.

Maybe Therese was right. Maybe he would be able to . . . No, she was wrong. A man who consistently sent agents out to get shot . . . But on the other hand . . .

* * *

"Toby, wake up! Toby!"

An insistent hand was jogging his shoulder. He opened his eyes. Daylight was coming feebly through the heavy curtains, and Ben was standing by the bed.

"Ben!" he muttered groggily. "I didn't expect you back this morning .What's the matter?"

"The Yenan Battalion wiped out my team in Phu Binh last night."

"Wiped it out?"

"Killed over half of them," Ben continued bitterly. "Wounded all but three or four of the rest."

"But how did you get here this early?" Toby asked, looking at the clock on his night table.

"Jerry rousted Jess out way before daylight. Jess is waiting for me now. I gotta get stuff to take with me and get

"Give me five minutes to have a shower," said Toby.

up there as fast as I can."

He needed time and cold water to clear his head.

"OK," said Ben. "I'll see if Mrs. Chao has got a cup of coffee."

Toby knew, even as he stepped into the shower, that his mind was healed, even though a new disaster had struck. The events of these days might ultimately destroy him, but he would sit down at his desk and start the rational process of studying them, and trying to find out the causes, and his mistakes, and what action he must take.

Mrs. Chao had begun preparing bacon and eggs the moment Ben drove in, and he was now wolfing the breakfast down.

"If it's all right with you, Toby," he said between mouthfuls, "I'm going to go down to the PRU barracks and pick out about half a dozen men to take with me to the village. This was without any doubt the Yenan Battalion, and they did such a job on that village that there's a chance they'll still have people around to hit the rescue effort."

"Sure. Take whatever you need. Will they go just on your say-so?"

"Yeah."

"Can you wait till I have a bite, or will you come back by and get me?"

"Suit yourself," said Ben, "but if I were you I wouldn't leave this place empty. The hospital here is already sending a big team up there in a convoy with ARVN troops, and there's nothing you can do."

Toby thought about that. "You're right, Ben. I can't leave this place deserted. Have you heard about the Special Police students?"

"No, what about them?"

Toby told him the story, and Ben's jaw dropped. "Jesus! That was the night before last?"

"No, early morning. Just after daylight."

"What districts were those five visiting?"

Toby looked at Ben with sudden comprehension. "Come on," he said, "let's go look at the map."

They went into the office, and located the five districts. They were clustered in one area due north of My Tho. Phu Binh was in the midst of this cluster, although not exactly in the center.

"Would you look at that!" Ben mused.

"There's a solar plexus somewhere in that area, Ben," said Toby. "We were getting too close to something, and they decided to stop it cold and fast."

Ben studied the map for a time, then suddenly started. "Christ, I've got to get a move on," he said. He hurried out.

Toby studied the map. The excitement of untangling a puzzle was gripping him. He had a problem of terrain in the province that was his responsibility. He also had a unit of more than one hundred crack troops at his command. Their job was to collect intelligence in the province. Well, here was the granddaddy of all targets. He would get together with Little Jack, as soon as Little Jack got back, and draw up a plan to search that area thoroughly. Even if it meant a delay in getting the Phoenix program under way.

There was something in that area that somebody did not want uncovered, and by God he was going to uncover it.

[17]

BEN had not been gone more than ten minutes when the sound of a motorcycle entering the gate reached Toby's ears. He went to the door. It was Tran Van Qui, one of his Special Police students, the one whom Toby had spotted as perhaps the best mind in the class, although reticent and careful.

Mystified, Toby watched him park his motorcycle and unstrap a cardboard box from the carrier behind the seat. He came up the steps and handed the box to Toby.

"I bring from class," he said.

I'll be damned. He speaks some English, and I never had an inkling.

Toby looked into the box and saw a number of items of office supplies and equipment he had left in the classroom, to be picked up later. He still did not understand.

"We do clandestine communications now," the man continued, with a slight smile.

So that was it! The man wanted to talk to him, and had brought the box as a simple cover for his visit.

"Come in," he said quickly, and ushered the man into his office. "I cannot speak Vietnamese," he said, "and Mr. Minh is not here."

"I speak English," said the man. "Not good English, but we talk?"

"Of course," said Toby. "We talk. I think you speak English as well as Major Thieu."

"Better," said the man calmly, and Toby laughed. This man was quick-witted.

"Since you speak English," Toby said, "we can keep this clandestine communication just between you and me. We will not need anybody else. Not Mr. Minh, nor Therese. Just you and me."

"Good."

It was a struggle for them to get ideas across to one another, and they talked for more than an hour. Toby found himself using Vietnamese words, and learning some new ones, as well as some phrases. He had resolved to study the language eventually, and now he had a tutor for it.

Qui did speak better English than Thieu. He could listen to a fairly complicated English sentence and get the sense of it, although he could not construct complicated answers.

What he had to say added to the optimism Toby was already feeling. Qui had spoken with the two wounded men in the hospital. He could not speak long with them, because of the gravity of their wounds, and he had to be especially discreet because of other ears near their beds. They had told him of their conviction that the districts they had visited held some VC secret. Either a large cache of ammunition, or a secret hideout. Perhaps a transfer depot for the shipment of war supplies. They knew that at the center of this secrecy was the Yenan Battalion. They were certain that the ambushes had been laid by the Yenan Battalion.

Most important and most encouraging of all, they were not troubled by the assignments that had sent them into the ambushes. They saw the attacks as proof that they were right to be snooping around. They wanted the search and investigation to continue. They wanted to be in on the work, although in both cases they had many weeks of convalescence before them.

Qui had discussed the situation with the other students, and found them to be unanimous in the feeling that they must continue to look into the districts in that area. They knew that even if Thieu had been willing for them to do so, he would not have the skill to organize a rational plan of investigation. They wanted Toby to organize it. They had delegated Qui—or, thought Toby with an inward smile, Qui had delegated himself, with their consent—to act as their communications channel to Toby.

"Now, Mr. Qui," he said, "suppose I do draw up a step-by-step plan of action for the men? How can they travel to the districts? Thieu would know, and he would not permit it."

Qui nodded. "Thieu is a fool. But Manh is chief. Manh

good. You talk to Manh, show him. We go to villages get information. Information for Manh, not for Thieu."

Toby nodded back. "It might work."

"*You* ask Manh give *you* information."

"Yeah, if he is running things, he'll give me the information in an official liaison exchange, but . . ."

"We give Manh information—but then I come here."

Toby looked at Qui, and a grin slowly began to spread across his face, reflected by an equally wide grin on the face of Qui. Qui had just recruited himself as Toby's agent, without Toby's lifting a finger.

"Qui," he said, "this is great!"

"You see Manh?"

"Tomorrow. I will have a plan to discuss with him by then. I think we can use the PRUs and the Special Police together in this operation."

"Number one!" exclaimed Qui, the highest encomium a Vietnamese could bestow, Toby knew.

"You and I must set up a system for meetings," said Toby. "Clandestine communications between you and me."

Qui held up his hand. "No problem. I come see you after work. You teach me English, I teach you Vietnamese. You have books?"

"Yes. Tuesdays and Thursdays in the evening?"

"Tuesdays and Thursdays. Good."

"I will tell Manh that the men should not go to the villages at the same time. I will draw up a schedule of villages to be visited. I will give you a copy of the same schedule I give to Manh, but Manh will not know you have it."

"OK."

"The basic instructions will be the same for the time being. Talk to the villagers, find out what's going on in the areas, what the Viet Cong is doing. You understand?"

"I understand. Same as before."

"Right."

"I go now. I come back Tuesday."

"Tuesday evening. Thanks, Qui. Thanks very much."

Qui shook his hand and left.

Ben returned late that evening in a black mood.

"They destroyed the team, all right," he said. "Killed

more than half of them, wounded the rest. They concentrated mainly on the team, not on the villagers, and the ones that could move hauled ass out, except for six of them who tried to make a stand. Those six were captured, and the VC marched them out into the street and shot them in the back of the head."

"God, what a war!"

"It's a fact of life, Toby. The Viet Cong can't take prisoners, as a general rule. They've got no way to keep them."

"That doesn't make it any less barbaric."

"No, of course not. Those that weren't killed have been evacuated to Vung Tau or the hospital, and I doubt if you would get many of them to go back to any village, anywhere, with another team."

"You could hardly blame them for that."

"And of course the village people, those that are left, have had the be-Jesus scared out of them. ARVN is up there in force, looking for the Yenan Battalion, but with the Tiger in charge they've got about as much chance of finding it as a bunch of campfire girls. The ARVN also lifted a Ranger Battalion up there with choppers, but they'll have no better luck than the others.

"But all the government troops in the world aren't going to make those villagers feel a bit better, because you can tell when you talk to them that the Tiger made sure that each one of them was given the word. If they let another team come in, or if they have anything to do with the Saigon régime, they'll get picked off one by one, at night, or they'll be assaulted in force one night. Either way, they'd all be killed."

"They believe that, too, of course?"

"Of course! The VC have given them all the proof they need. They wouldn't talk to me, and they wouldn't talk to the soldiers. You can scratch one pacified village from our list, my friend. We've flat lost it. For good. The VC can claim that as their own territory from now on."

"Other teams will hear about that, too," said Toby.

"Damn right!" Ben exclaimed. "For the next couple of weeks, I'm going to have to be out visiting as many of them as I can. A thing like this could spook even the best ones."

"Ben," said Toby, "I'm about to make up some plans that are essentially military, and I need your advice."

"OK. What have you got in mind?"

Toby explained to Ben about Qui's visit, and Ben forgot his gloom for the moment. "Didn't I tell you you had taken those men away from Thieu?"

"What I want to do is carry out a systematic examination of this entire area," Toby went on, taking Ben over to the wall map. "I thought of using the Special Police investigators, under cover of some kind, without the local police office knowing about it. I thought I could coordinate their work with PRU operations in the same vicinity. I was thinking of setting up a couple of cordon-and-search operations every week, until we've covered this territory from end to end. Maybe coordinate the operations with some work by your teams, when there is a team in the area."

"I haven't got any within the area, Toby, but I've got a couple or three near the edges that might be of help. They're located here, and here and here." He pointed to the map.

"That ought to help some, anyway."

They got a smaller map and spread it out on the desk. "You can ask Little Jack," said Ben, "but I doubt if what you'll want to do is a full-scale cordon and search. They take a lot of time and work. I don't think you'd have time to do as many as need to be done in this situation, and anyway, what you're looking for is obviously something pretty damned big, not just a rice cache or a few rifles or boxes of ammo. Whatever it is is big and important. The Viet Cong have told us that pretty plainly. A sudden, plain patrol, a straight search, by the PRU, ought to be just as effective as a cordon and search, and it'll be a lot simpler. Two of those you could do in a week."

"Thanks, Ben," said Toby. "I'll talk it over with Little Jack when he gets back."

They were mortared that night. The barrage struck their neighborhood, in a fairly even pattern. It sounded like a full-scale battle to Toby, because there were detonations all around them. The only damage to the house, however, was some pockmarks in the masonry walls from fragments and a hole in the upper corner of the roof where a shell had made a direct hit. The sandbag bunker had absorbed most of the impact.

"Things seem to be heating up, Ben," said Toby, trying to hide his nervousness as they crouched on the roof afterward.

"Oh, not really," Ben replied easily. "This is really more normal. There's been a kind of a lull ever since you got here, but the action is about back to where it has been for a long time."

"Even the Phu Binh attack was normal?"

"I told you when you got here, that first day, that they're kicking the shit out of us. This is what I meant. They're hitting our programs and our installations hard, and they're keeping the pressure on the towns in the countryside."

Early Monday morning, Toby was in Bill Voigt's office, with Chet in a chair nearby. Chet was not angry this morning. He was triumphant, and Toby was not surprised.

"Five of them, Bill," Chet was saying. "Five out of twelve is almost half. That's a pretty goddamned high casualty rate for *any* kind of an action!"

"Toby," said Bill, "give me the story."

Toby told him what he knew, and Bill listened intently. When the account was finished, he spoke.

"The Regional Office of the Special Police is on me to shag your ass out of the delta," he said, "and maybe even out of Vietnam."

"I'm not surprised," said Toby with a shrug. He was not repentant, but he was worried that he might not be left in My Tho to vindicate himself.

"It might not be a bad idea," Bill continued.

"I think it would be a *good* idea," said Chet. "If all a man can do is send people out to get shot—"

"Hold it, Chet," said Bill quietly. "Personalities are not going to help us get at a decision." Chet subsided.

"I know it's going to sound like an alibi," said Toby, "but I think it might be pointed out to the regional people that Manh and Thieu agreed to the operation, and in fact it was Thieu that gave the order, not me."

"He got his version of it here ahead of you, Toby. He says you forced him into the decision by threatening to go all the way to Saigon with some story about how he wasn't cooperating with you."

"Oh, Christ!" said Toby.

"I *will* tell you, though," Bill went on, "that we've managed to calm things down a little, and Saigon is going to leave it up to me. Whatever I say, they'll back me up with the Saigon office of the Special Police. And I don't mind telling you that all my instincts tell me to transfer you out of here. It would solve our problem with the Vietnamese. Furthermore, you've got to consider the scapegoat factor. If you stay, they're likely to pile the blame on you for everything bad that happens from now on. Of course, we could fix it up for our own records so that it wouldn't look as bad for you as Thieu makes it sound."

"Sure," said Toby in a taut voice.

Bill looked at him steadily.

"You've got something in mind, haven't you?"

"Yes."

"Let's hear it."

"If you look at the map, you can see a pattern to these ambushes and the attack on Phu Binh. That's Yenan Battalion territory. Now, why would they set up ambushes on those five men in that particular pattern? The Viet Cong don't act out of whim. There must be something in that area they don't want us to see. Ordinarily, they'd be mobile enough so that they wouldn't be that nervous about any particular piece of real estate. But they're building up for their Tet offensive."

"Jesus, here we go again," said Chet.

Toby ignored him. "And whatever it is has got to stay in place there until that time."

"And what do you think it is?"

"It's got to be something big: a hideout, or a supply dump of some kind. We hear down there that they're bringing in thousands of tons of war materiel from Cambodia every month. It's got to go somewhere, and they haven't been using it all lately."

"So?" Bill was listening intently.

"I want to send those Special Police officers out again, and—"

"Why, you stupid son of a bitch!" Chet exploded.

Toby was on his feet in a split second and was reaching

for Chet's shirt front, with his other hand balled into a fist and cocked back, but Bill, with reflexes that would have done credit to a younger man, brought his arm down on Toby's with a sharp blow. He then grabbed Toby's other arm in an iron grip and shoved him back toward his chair.

"Chet," Toby rasped, "if you ever say anything like that to me again I'll break your goodamned back!"

"All right!" said Bill. "Now both of you simmer down. I've got enough problems without having to referee a Pier Six brawl."

"Bill," said Chet, "that's the craziest thing I ever heard of. This is the second time he's had men shot on his operations, and now he wants to turn right around and do the same thing all over."

"He's got a point there," said Bill.

Toby, rubbing his wrist where Bill's had struck it, explained his plans to Bill, his use of Manh, his recruitment of Qui, the coordination of all the factors in the search he had in mind.

"Do you think Manh will go along with it?" asked Bill.

"I don't know. I'm going to do my best to talk him into it."

"He'd be putting his own neck on the block, you know."

"I realize that. But this is a war we're in the middle of, and I don't think it's exactly the time to worry about nothing but covering your ass. If he can be shown that there is something big there to be found, maybe he will be willing to risk it."

Bill toyed with a letter opener on his desk and frowned. Chet and Toby were silent.

"All right," he said at last. "I'll go along, too, if Manh does. I'd hate for the VC to think that all they've got to do is shoot up three or four of our people to make us pull back and stop bothering them."

"Thanks," said Toby. "I realize what a risk you'll be running."

"Make no mistake about it, Toby," said Bill, leveling a cool gaze at him, "if this thing blows up, if anything happens anywhere near like what happened Saturday morning, there will be no way I could save your skin, even if I wanted to. And I'm not even sure I'd want to. So don't thank me. I may not be doing you any favor. I may be doing nothing more than giving you whatever rope you need to hang yourself with."

"I'm not asking for anything except a chance," said Toby.

The temptation was almost irresistible to tell Bill about Dang, but he knew that he must not do so. For that information to get to Bill, it would have to come from Chet. Otherwise, Chet would consider it to be out of channels. Bill might think that Toby was merely being spiteful against Chet, especially since he still had no solid proof about Dang. Even the surveillance and the use of the dead drop could be interpreted by a skeptic as skillful trickery by Dang. And, after all, didn't all his training and experience teach him to be skeptical—teach them *all* to be skeptical?

They left Bill's office, and Toby followed Chet into Chet's office, thinking that perhaps Chet might be glad of an opportunity to add one more nail to his coffin.

"Chet," Toby said, when they had closed the door, "whatever we think of each other, this is a point of communications, and we've got to make it work. I've got some more on Dang that I think you ought to consider, and ought to let me submit an intelligence report on."

"What's that?" Chet asked, regarding Toby with a look of frigid hostility.

Toby told him about the latest developments in the Dang operation.

"Busch," said Chet, when the account was finished, "they're playing you like a goddamned Ping-Pong ball. You really and truly believe you've got hold of a VC penetration there?"

"I know it."

"Well then, you just go on and play with it, and play with yourself too, if you feel like it, because one thing's just about as useful to the agency as the other."

"You won't go to Bill with it?"

"No."

"If it's as bad as you say, I'd think you'd jump at the chance to tell Bill about it, and add one more black mark against me."

"You don't know me very well, buddy," Chet sneered.

"I'm not going to go around snitching to Papa, because Bill Voigt would assume that's exactly what I was doing. Anyway, I don't need to help you slam the drawer on your own balls, because you're going to arrange that all by yourself, and before very long, too. If you want the story taken to him, you could do it yourself, you know."

"Sure."

"I'm even going to give you a break. When things do blow up in your face up there, I'm not going to even mention this so-called penetration agent of yours. You're gonna be sent to Siberia anyway, but if I told that one too, they'd send you to the funny farm instead."

"Thanks for everything, Chet," said Toby abruptly. He turned on his heel and walked out.

Toby was surprised and elated to find that Manh was an easy mark for the new plan. He could hardly believe his ears when, sitting with Minnie in Manh's office, he heard Manh acknowledge that he himself had figured things out essentially the way Toby had. It was more than just a terrible harassment of the Special Police. Manh was willing to allow his young men to participate, under Manh's personal direction, in a coordinated effort to find out what the Viet Cong were up to in that section of the province.

Toby told Manh that he felt that Manh should set the pattern and pace of the operations, although the rest of them could work out the specific details. Manh nodded.

"Are you aware that the Viet Cong has agreed to a Christmas truce and a Tet truce?"

"I had heard that there was something along those lines being discussed," Toby said.

"I am certain that your MACV forces will respect the truce, and we will join you in that, of course."

"Do you think the Viet Cong will abide by a truce during Tet?" asked Toby.

"Yes. Tet is a sacred holiday. I believe they will respect it."

"I hope you are right," said Toby, hypocritically, aware as he said it that he was now in the terrible position of wishing the worst for Vietnam in order to save his own skin.

"We will have time for perhaps two operations before Christmas," said Manh.

"Very well," said Toby. Together they studied the map, and Manh pointed to an area near the edge of the zone they intended to search. Toby noted the names and coordinates down in his notebook.

"Let us do this one on December 15," said Manh.

"Good," said Toby. Then he continued in a worried voice, "Colonel, there is one matter that makes me very uneasy. What about Major Thieu?"

"Mr. Busch, I will be frank with you. Major Thieu will be opposed to this plan. He will, I know, make certain that his opposition is known to our superiors in some discreet manner. If we are making a mistake, it will be very bad for me."

"I understand, sir," said Toby. "I am in exactly the same position myself." Manh nodded and smiled at him.

Little Jack, back from his Phoenix training, accepted the idea of the searches without comment. He and Minnie briefed his PRUs, and decided to move into each area at night, so as to take advantage of the element of surprise when they began the search at sunrise.

Meanwhile two of Manh's men, Toby's students, would be in one hamlet close to the village to be searched, and two others would be in a village on the other side.

Ben would be spending the night in a third, pacified village, also close to the search area.

And Toby would stay at home. He could not join the Special Police officers, of course, and he would be more of a handicap than a help to Ben or Little Jack.

Moreover, always lurking in the back of his mind was the thought that when the house was empty, he could once again spend a night in the arms of Therese. He felt guilty to be thinking of such illicit joys of the flesh while his associates took the field against the enemy. He had not thought himself capable of such blithe depravity. Now he knew that he was.

He comforted himself with the thought that while he was actually in bed with her, the others would just be getting into position—that whatever action there was would take place the following morning.

He had a crazy impulse to try to cross every finger and toe as he watched Little Jack and Minnie drive out the gate that Friday evening, to go to the PRU compound and get underway. Ben had choppered up to his village during the afternoon.

Therese had stayed, happily, matter-of-factly.

"You are happy again, Anh Tho," she said, as they sat sipping a drink in the common room.

"Yes, I am, Little Mistress," he said. "I am at last making things move, instead of merely sitting back and studying them. I have a chance to repair a lot of damage from the past."

"Yes. That is so."

"But let's not talk about business. Most of the happiness I'm feeling now is on account of us, tonight."

"Yes. I am happy, also."

"Good."

"Tonight will be good," she said with a shy smile.

"But it is a sad sort of happiness, I'm afraid, because whatever we do, we can't make it last forever."

"But, Anh Tho," she said, "you, yourself, have said that what we have *is* forever."

"Yes," he replied softly. "Yes, I did. And I meant it. And do you know something else? For some reason, I am almost comfortable with that. I wonder why?"

"Perhaps because it is not complicated?"

He thought about that. "By golly, I believe you are right!"

"I think so."

"*It* is not complicated. *You* are not complicated. That must be the reason. You are here with me. There is no doubt about us. We know exactly what we are doing and where it will lead, or not lead, and so we don't waste time or energy worrying about other days. We enjoy this one."

"Yes."

The meal was another study in moderation and good taste. The matter-of-fact attention of Mrs. Chao and Chi Hai somehow seemed to give this affair a rightness, a total acceptability, and Toby abandoned himself to the enjoyment of it.

In his room, which had once again been prepared by the affectionate schemers from the kitchen, Toby was happy to find that nothing had changed. They made love again, and the enchantment was still there.

"Anh Tho," said Therese afterward, snuggling close to him in the dark, "I have discovered something."

"Have you?"

"I have been thinking about it for many days. I have discovered it tonight."

"M-m-m-m. I wonder what it could be? There is certainly nothing about *me* that you haven't discovered and ravished completely by now." He patted her bare bottom.

"No," she said, settling her head more comfortably in the hollow of his arms, "it is about you and me."

"What is it?"

"I do not believe that I have ever loved a man as I love you."

"Haven't you, Little Mistress?"

"Yes."

"You are going to make me sad," he said softly, his lips near her ear.

"But it is not sad," she said quickly. "Why should I be sad to discover such a good thing?"

"I love you, too, Therese," he said hesitantly. "I love you in a way that—" Her small hand suddenly covered his mouth.

"Do not say it," she said. "I do not want you to say something just to make me happy, something you do not mean."

"All right. But if I just say, 'I love you,' will that be all right?"

"Yes."

"I love you. Little Mistress, I love you."

The operation on Saturday morning was uneventful. The PRU search revealed nothing. Elicitation by the Special Police officers brought only some names of suspected Viet Cong collaborators, which Toby incorporated into his new file of suspects.

On Tuesday, December 19, they repeated the operation in an area to the north of the first one. This time Little Jack's men discovered a rice cache, and exchanged a few shots with two men who were nearby, but there were no casualties.

At this point, the war strangely came to a halt. Peace and relaxation were in the air.

"It's the Christmas truce, Toby," said Ben. "Even the people in the villages are less uptight than usual."

No more military operations were scheduled for the Christmas season. Little Jack would leave on Thursday morning for Rest and Recreation in Hong Kong. From the look in his eye, it was evident that he expected this R & R to be a most satisfactory time of "having fun with 'em and then laying 'em." Ben would depart the same day for his own scheduled visit to Vung Tau, undoubtedly to do something similar to what Little Jack had in mind, although perhaps more elegantly described and less blatantly announced. Minnie, with almost no responsibilities left around the office, asked permission to take the days off to go to his brother's place.

It was as if the war were a grammar school, letting out for Christmas.

Toby's own R & R would be to be alone in the house. He had not been in the country long enough to be eligible for leave of any kind, and would not have felt comfortable going on leave so soon, in any event.

He was keenly aware, moreover, that being alone in the house would permit him to be alone with Therese again. Thus, in his own way, he thought guiltily to himself, he could be said to have plans not essentially different from those of Ben and Little Jack. But before he could broach the subject to Therese, she came to his desk with a request that dampened his spirits.

"Mr. Busch, I have been invited to Saigon to spend Christmas with a family of Catholic friends from the north," she said. He wondered at this formal approach, but decided that she must want others in the office to see that her leave was proper and formally arranged.

"When would you go, Therese?" he asked, with equal formality.

"I would leave Friday morning, with your permission."

"And you would be back . . . ?"

"I would come back the day you suggest."

"Would the twenty-seventh suit you?"

"Yes, certainly. I can come back sooner if you wish."

"No. Make it the twenty-seventh, Therese. And enjoy yourself."

She went back to her desk, and he turned and surveyed them all: Little Jack at his desk, Minnie at his side looking at some manuals, Ben at his desk, and Therese settling herself once again to work.

"Fine bunch of troops I've got," he chided them. "Every single one of you off to have a good time, leaving poor old Busch here all by himself!"

Ben looked up in surprise. "Hell, Toby, I don't have to go! I can put my trip off until—"

Toby laughed. "Not on your life! Give up Vung Tau for me?"

They all saw that he was joking, and his mock martyrdom had put them at their ease. The teacher was sending them away without any homework.

[18]

THERESE was alone with him in the office for the final two hours of the Thursday workday, but she was busy at her desk, and was so engrossed in whatever she was doing that Toby did not disturb her. He felt somewhat uneasy about it, but told himself that he should be pleased with an employee who lost herself in her work that way, even if she was his mistress.

When she finally put all her things away and rose to leave, she stopped by his desk.

"I am sorry to go, Anh Tho," she said.

"Sit down, Therese," he said, much relieved by her genuine reluctance to leave him.

She sat down in the chair by his desk. He was on the point of urging her to stay the night with him, but somehow he knew that it would not be right. The whole thing was already too much like smoking behind the barn, and for him to take her to bed at every slightest opportunity smacked more of pure appetite than love.

"I hope you will not be lonely," she said.

"I will be. But it's nice to know that you will miss me."

"These friends made plans for this Christmas many months ago, and I said that I would be there, and so I cannot . . ."

"I understand. You needn't apologize. But I must say that I didn't realize Christmas was so important to the Vietnamese."

"For the Catholics, it is," she said. "It will be especially . . . what is the word you use . . . touching?"

"Yes, touching."

"It will be especially touching for this group of Catholics, because we are all far away from our homes in the north."

"But it will be a good Christmas, anyway, with friends."

"Yes. It will be good. Except that I will be wishing that I were here with you."

"But you will be back next week," he said. "We still have many times together in the future."

"Yes."

They stood. Impulsively, she threw her arms around him and kissed him, then slipped quickly from his embrace and was gone.

An hour later Qui appeared for his first Thursday visit. He brought nothing new with him, beyond the official information which Manh had already passed to Toby, and that information was of little consequence. Qui said that the morale among his group was high, and that they were certain that after these two preliminary operations, which were by way of testing the water, they would be closing in on something important. They were enthusiastic about the prospects.

The rest of Qui's visit turned into the language lesson that the visits were purported to be, and Toby was glad to be doing something about his ignorance of the language, although he could tell that this oriental system of speech was going to be difficult to master.

Qui gone, and dinner over, Toby set himself to another task. He made a test of each of the instruments of the new Motorola radio net that had been delivered that week. The net consisted of his base station, a small flat console with a pedestal microphone, and eight handsets, each about the size of a lunch box, with a telephone-type receiver clamped to the handle on top.

He drew a chart of the net, which would consist of his base station in the office, a handset in each of the two jeeps—which would be taken to his and Ben's bedrooms at night—one in the Province Senior Adviser's office, one in the PRU barracks, one in the Special Police Office, one in the Revolutionary Development Office, and one in the house of the three women. He named his net Victory, and marked each set with its own call sign. His base station was Victory-1, his jeep set was Victory-2, the Province Senior Adviser's was Victory-3, and so on.

Friday morning he installed the spidery antenna for his base station on the roof. He led the coaxial cable down from the antenna along the inside walls and through the breezeway to the office, where the base station console was located on a small table near the door.

He loaded the remaining sets in the jeep and set out to deliver them. His first call was the Province Senior Adviser's office. Marie Claire was there, and she listened intently as Toby explained the radio net to the Deputy Province Senior Adviser, a young army lieutenant. The lieutenant had used such equipment before, and understood the mechanics of the network without much explanation.

"I'm putting one of these in the house where Marie Claire lives with two other women," Toby said to the lieutenant. "In a sense it's beyond my authorization, but I've got a spare set, and it might as well be in their house as sitting idle on a shelf."

"That's a great relief," said the lieutenant. "I've been worried about them in that house."

"One of my people had an idea to try to do something about that wall of theirs, too," Toby went on.

"What about it?"

"He thinks it ought to be built higher—about eight feet."

The lieutenant was interested, but had heard nothing. Perhaps Ben had forgotten.

"Well, anyway," Toby continued, "it is understood that this net has several Vietnamese stations, and it is strictly for business. No social calls."

"Of course."

"Is anybody at home over at your house, Marie Claire?" Toby asked. "I can go over and deliver it now."

"No, Peggy and Louise are at the hospital," she said. "Why don't you come over later on, some time this evening?"

"OK. What time would be best?"

"Why don't you just come for dinner?"

"Oh, I wouldn't want to put you to any trouble," Toby said, not even trying to hide his pleasure.

"It's no trouble. If you don't mind being alone with three women."

"Being alone with crowds of women is one of my favorite pastimes," said Toby. "If you ladies won't mind dividing me into three, I'll be there."

"Peggy and I will be lucky to get a tenth each," said Marie Claire.

At dinner, the women served him and made over him with smiling, outlandish concern, and he soaked it up with a self-satisfied expression on his face. It was a welcome change to be in a home where the feminine was in evidence wherever the eye came to rest, after a masculine dormitory such as their own house, with weapons and manuals and the easy blasphemy of male talk.

Peggy and Marie Claire made some gestures about leaving him alone with Louise, but they were easily talked out of it, and they ended the evening sitting in the living room, listening to soft music, sipping coffee and talking.

The Victory-5 set installed in their living room, with instructions to take it to their bedrooms at night, and some demonstrations in how to use the equipment, Toby was ready to leave.

"If I could be sure of an evening like this every time," Toby said, "I'd send all my associates away every few days."

"You're going to be kind of lonesome for a while, aren't you, Toby?" asked Louise.

"No," he lied. "I've got so much work piled up that I'm really glad of the opportunity to be by myself to do it."

"Well, if it gets to be more than you can bear, let us

know," said Peggy. "We'll come over and put cornflakes in your bed, or something."

"I'll remember that gracious offer," said Toby. "By the way, when I get home, I'll give you a call to see if the signal reaches both ways."

"Standing by, Victory-One," said Peggy.

The reception and transmission by Victory-5 proved to be loud and clear, and Toby went to bed, having passed his first day alone without feeling alone. But the coming days loomed large, especially Christmas. If his own family in Iowa had been feeling especially lonely, it might have been a rather perverse and selfish consolation to him, but they would be in the midst of the larger family, and although they would miss him, they were far from being lonely. Their Christmas would be joyous, old-fashioned, probably even white, whereas his would be spent in an empty French-colonial house with guards around it, and a generator roaring ceaselessly out in back.

He didn't even have the fear of attack to occupy his mind now, because of the Christmas truce.

After breakfast the next morning he began to realize what it was going to be like to be alone. He wandered into the office, went over some reports, read a mass of material that had come in some days before in the pouch, most of which he would have glanced at and thrown away at any other time, but which now provided a means to spend an hour or so.

After lunch, he looked through the disreputable collection of books that had accumulated in the house, more by accident than by design. Most of them were paperbacks, of the kind one forgets within an hour of finishing. In addition to these, he found hardbacks copies of Arthur Schlesinger's *The Coming of the New Deal* and Truman Capote's *In Cold Blood,* attesting to an unusual catholicity of tastes on the part of some collector.

He decided to try Schlesinger, and labored over the book for about an hour before giving up.

He wrote a letter to Mary Lynn. He had to be extremely careful not to let his mood show. By sunset he was looking forward to the warmth of a drink at the bar. But alcohol seemed only to sharpen his despondency. He ate his dinner, hardly noticing the food.

He took his coffee back into the common room, and sat gloomily in the emptiness. The selection of records and tapes on the shelf consisted of music that either irritated him or faded innocuously from his consciousness and went unnoticed soon after the first syrupy chords. He decided to forego music.

He made a decision, a minor decision, to be sure, but in a nothing day it took on the characteristics of urgency and importance. He went to the radio set and called, "Victory-Five, this is Victory-One. Victory-Five, this is Victory-One. Over." He repeated the call once more, and heard Louise's voice.

"Victory-One, this is Victory-Five."

"Victory-One, if it's convenient for you, I think I should repair that defect in your set immediately. Would it be convenient for me to do it right away?"

"Can you wait just a minute, Victory-One?"

"Victory-One standing by."

There was a pause, then Louise's voice returned to the air. "Victory-One, we all believe it's important to get it fixed right away. In fact, we're having a great deal of difficulty with it."

Her voice was flat and calm, but Toby knew her eyes would be dancing with fun. "I'll be over as soon as I can make a place in my schedule," he said, in a voice equally as flat. "Victory-One out."

"Victory-Five out."

His gloom gone, he drove across town. Louise met him at the door and led him into the living room.

"Where are the other two?" Toby asked, looking around the room.

"They're both in housecoats and bare faces," said Louise, "and they have no intention of letting a man see them that way."

"You mean, I drove them out of their living room?"

"Only about half an hour before they would have left anyway, Toby. They don't mind. In this country and this war, a woman has got to take any chance she can get to be with a man, and they're happy that you've come, even if it's just for my sake."

"Well, but I didn't intend to come just to see *you*—Er, that is, what I mean is . . ."

"What you mean is," said Louise dramatically, "that this is the end between you and me?"

Toby laughed. "Dammit, Louise," he said, "that is the one thing I would hate more than anything else I can think of, for this between you and me to end. What I meant was . . ."

"It's too late to apologize for such heartless cruelty as that remark shows," she said with a twinkle in her eye, "but I'll do my duty and try to be a gracious hostess, anyway. Can I fix you a drink?"

"If you're not too overwrought to be trusted with strong potions," said Toby, "I would like a gin and tonic."

"OK. You're the only man I know who drinks gin and tonic at any hour of the day or any season of the year."

"It's a rut I can't seem to get out of."

She went over to the portable bar and mixed drinks for them.

"By the way," she said, handing him the glass, and settling herself beside him with a small glass of whisky and water, "what set was it you came over to repair?" Her voice was expressionless, but there was laughter just below the surface.

"Louise," he said, with mock humility, "I have a confession to make."

"Tell me, my son," she said, blessing him with an upraised hand, "what have you done? Have you been using bad language? Have you been thinking impure thoughts? Have you been unfaithful to your wife?"

The remark hit Toby so suddenly that he almost lost his composure. "No," he said carelessly, "it's none of those things. Or, rather, I should say that in *addition* to those things, and almost everything else, I want to confess that there's nothing at all wrong with your set."

"Nothing wrong with my set?"

"Nothing. Not a thing."

"In other words, my set has been OK all along?"

Toby was grinning happily. "As far as I can tell, it's absolutely perfect."

"Then, sir, why did you come under such false pretenses?"

Toby turned to her, and was serious. "I came over because I was bored to death, and because it's the Christmas season."

"I'm glad you did, Toby," she said softly. "Do you know, I've never really had a chance to sit and talk with you quietly?"

"Yes," he said. "I *have* noticed."

"I have a thousand things I want to talk to you about."

"Me too," he said. He leaned bark in the sofa. "You first."

"OK. First, why did you come to Vietnam? The CIA isn't like the army, is it? They can't force you to take an assignment like this?"

"I'll try to give you a satisfactory answer," he said, "but first, I want to ask you a question. Why do you ask me that?"

"I have just wondered, that's all. Ben told Peggy you came over here because you wanted to. And that could mean that you're trying to get away from something, or prove something, or who knows what else?"

Toby told her as much as he could of the Frankfurt incident. "It's all in my record," he said. "In a bureaucracy—and even our agency is a bureaucracy—you don't attack a bad mark headlong. You try to make it less evident or less important by surrounding it with a consistent record of good marks."

"But it wasn't your fault?"

"No, but that's of very little consequence, sometimes, in the official record."

"I know you can do it if you get the chance," she said. "And I hope you get the chance."

"You are a sweet woman," he said. "Now tell me why *you* are here."

They talked until late, and Toby relaxed in a mood of ease and contentment. Louise had a way of massaging his ego, and showing her regard for him, by gentle, sometimes almost tender words and inflections, while at the same time she teased him playfully and kept him always aware that he was sitting beside a vibrant woman.

"I must go," he said, looking at his watch.

"Must you?" she asked, with genuine regret.

"Yes."

"What about tomorrow?"

"Tomorrow?"

"Tomorrow is Christmas Eve. If you were bored and lonely this evening, what will it be like tomorrow?"

"You've got a point there."

"Christmas Eve is a terrible time to be alone. The worst time of the year."

"What you are hinting at," he said, "is that you would like to be asked out tomorrow evening?"

"No," she replied. "As a matter of fact I wasn't hinting at all. I was frankly leading up to a direct request."

"Well, then, let me save your virtue by doing it in a gentlemanly way. Louise, will you have dinner with me tomorrow evening?"

"Yes."

"Have you ever been to the Soong Palace?"

"Yes."

"Like it?"

"Yes."

"Shall we go there tomorrow evening?"

"Yes."

"With you in such a positive mood, I don't think I'd better ask you any more questions tonight." He made as if to rise from the sofa, but she put a hand on his arm and stopped him.

"Stay for just a minute more, won't you?" she asked, turning toward him and tucking her legs under her. "There's one more thing I want to ask you."

"OK," he said, leaning back once more, smiling contentedly. "Shoot."

"I'm dying to know. Who is she?"

"Who is who?" Toby asked uneasily.

"Who is the woman? Is it that pretty girl in your office?"

"What are you talking about?" he asked sharply.

"Toby, you blushed almost purple when I asked that silly question a while ago."

"I've never blushed in my life."

"Then that blush a minute ago must have been all the more significant. It's nosey of me, isn't it? It's a question I shouldn't be asking, but I thought that you and I had somehow gotten on such good terms, and—well, I just couldn't resist."

"But, Louise," said Toby earnestly, "even if what you say is true, you wouldn't expect me to talk to other people about it, would you? What kind of an opinion would you have of me if I did?"

"But this is not 'talking to other people,' is it? This is talking to *me*."

"Do you know," he said slowly, his eyes searching hers, "I believe you're jealous!"

"Of course," she replied, returning his gaze steadily.

"Well, I'll be damned!" He sat still for a long time, thinking, staring into space. Finally, he looked around at her again with a plaintive expression. "Why couldn't this have happened to me when I was twenty?" he exclaimed.

Louise burst out laughing. "You're an impossible man!" she said. She leaned over and kissed him lightly on the lips. "Go home!"

[19]

TOBY got up late the following morning, and puttered and piddled, trying to keep busy. A boy from the PSA brought a big envelope of mail, and there was a letter from Mary Lynn, timed perfectly, as if she had controlled the delivery system from Iowa. A Christmas letter, with notes from the children. She listed the gifts she had bought for the children and other family members, to be given in both their names. They had prepared a box for him, but it had not yet come. The letter was more important, anyway. He was back in touch with his family, back in a state of normality. The kids were enjoying their new town and school, and were looking forward to his first family leave in February. So was Mary Lynn.

He sat for a long time with the letter in his hand, and thought about himself, and Therese and Mary Lynn. It was as if there were two Toby Busches, both of them nice enough fellows, but not connected with one another. He knew that he should be feeling guilt and shame, but he didn't. He knew that if he were as decent as he ought to be, he would not even be able to perform during those moments of illicit love. But he had performed, and he had reveled in it, and oddly enough, he even had a vague feeling that this affair was broadening him as a man, taking him out of a narrow life, making him more profound, somehow more aware. But what if it turned out to be at Mary Lynn's expense? That would be unbearable. She was as much a part of that other Toby Busch's life as his hands and his eyes, and he loved her and would do anything to keep from wounding her.

Anything, that is, except give up Therese.

He sighed, and went in to lunch. Afterward, he gathered up the Swedish K, the M-16, the grease gun, and his .45 pistol, with plenty of ammunition for all of the weapons, and a set of earplugs, and drove over to the police firing range. He worked with all the weapons, marveling at the perfection of the M-16. The Swedish K was a much more elegant and comfortable weapon to fire than the grease gun; he could understand why the agency had adopted it for their men in combat zones. He dropped some tin cans about halfway to the first target mound, and practiced snap shooting with the .45. It was surprising that one could do that well by just pointing, instead of aiming. With a little more practice, he knew that he could become a deadly shot using that system.

He spent the rest of the afternoon back at the house, happily stripping and cleaning the weapons. He had hunted a lot when he was a youngster back in Iowa, usually for quail or pheasant, and using shotguns. But he enjoyed the feel and the machined touch of any firearm under his fingers, and he was whistling tunelessly to himself as he went about the pleasant chore.

He was still a little clumsy at stripping the pistol. He had watched Little Jack do it, his great paws snapping and sliding the parts with an ease that was astonishing and pleasing to the eye. Little Jack had tried to show him how he did it so smoothly, but Toby knew that it was not a question of knowing a method, but rather of devoting hours to practice.

He put the cleaned and oiled weapons away, scrubbed the oil off his hands, and took a leisurely shower. He rubbed his jaw after toweling it dry, and decided that since he had shaved so late in the morning he need not shave again for this evening.

He pulled into the driveway of the women's house just as dusk was settling. He knew that underlying his uneasiness about Mary Lynn and Therese was also the fact of Louise, but he put that out of his mind. After all, it did not have to be complicated. A dinner in a restaurant—a Chinese dinner, which would occupy a good part of the evening—and then home. The very fact of Therese would keep him from making a serious pass at Louise. How about that, for irony? He smiled at the thought, just as Louise came down the stairs.

She was dressed in a silk cocktail dress, of the same intense blue as her eyes. It did not seem to be cut to be seductive, but somehow, with Louise inside of them, dresses had that effect anyway.

"You look lovely," he said.

"You are sweet to say so," she replied.

"I would say it more often," he said, "except that I forget. You see, I really love you just for your mind."

"Yes, I know."

"What about the other women?"

"We were all invited to a Christmas Eve party at the Province Senior Adviser's house," she said. "They're going."

"But did you want to go, too? Would you have preferred that?"

"Don't be silly!"

They drove to the Soong Palace, which was as grand a name as the restaurant was unpretentious. They were greeted by a young Chinese who spoke good English. He ushered them to a small table in one corner of the dining room, discreetly walled in, although not hidden, by plants and screens. He then helped them order the unfamiliar dishes.

"I just happened to think," said Toby, when the waiter had left. "This is our first real date."

"That's true," she said. "Although I did go out spying with you one evening."

"Being in the line of duty like that, it doesn't count."

"Have you been out in the streets at night since then?"

"Yes, but it isn't the same without you."

"I'd go with you again, but I'd want to know what it was you were doing."

"I'd never tell you. It would surprise you, and disillusion you, it's so dull."

They ate a meal of many small dishes, and finished with cups of fragrant tea. Toby paid the bill and looked at his watch.

"It's early yet. Shall we go to my place for a nightcap?"

"I'd love it."

They drove to the house, and he fixed them a drink. They settled down on one of the sofas in the common room. Toby put on a record, and they sat and looked at each other placidly.

"This is nice," she said.

"Yes. Nice."

"I'm curious about something."

"Now, Louise, I—"

"Don't worry, it's not what you're thinking."

"OK, what is it?"

"Have you ever written a poem?"

"That's a strange question. Why do you ask?"

"Don't answer a question with a question."

"It's part of my training and my profession," he said with a smile.

"Answer the question," she commanded.

"No," he said. "I never have. I've tried, though."

"You have?"

"Yes. But what comes out always sounds like an intelligence report written by Gilbert and Sullivan."

She giggled. "But the fact that you've tried proves my point."

"What point?"

"You're a romantic."

"I am?"

"Yes. I mean romantic in the classical sense, you know, not amorous."

"You think I'm not amorous?"

"On the contrary, I'll bet you're a regular fireball, but even for that you'd be a romantic. I'm sure of it."

"I'm not understanding you very clearly," he said, wrinkling his brow.

"I'll give you an example. Take Marlene Dietrich, on the observation platform of the Orient Express, putting on a man's hat and looking sultry. That's just super-romantic. *That* kind of a woman would just give a man like you a case of the fantods."

"Marlene Dietrich was before my time," he laughed, "but I think that train was the Shanghai Express, not the Orient Express."

"Well, whatever train it was."

"Come on now, Louise," he said, "I have never found myself getting one bit excited by a woman putting on a man's hat."

"Never?"

"Nope. And I have never lit two cigarettes and handed one to a woman with a masterful stare, either."

"All right," she said, "maybe you're not *quite* that romantic. Maybe Camille is not your ideal sweetheart. But what I want to know is, did you ever *play* with a woman?"

"Now that," he said with a wide grin, "is such a loaded question, and such a beautiful straight line, that I'm not even going to answer it."

"But I mean it," she said. "I'm sure you've had a fair amount of experience with women, including recently"—she stopped Toby as he was about to protest—"but I'll bet every one of them has been a case of grand passions and emotions, you know, making the earth move in a sleeping bag. But wtihout it really being very much fun."

"Well, now," he said, "I don't ever recollect being exactly bored by the experience, and I've certainly never done it just out of a sense of duty or self-sacrifice."

"Let me prove my point," she said. She took his glass out of his hand and set it down beside her own on the table. "This is what I mean." She put her arms around him and pressed her lips to his with an evident burst of passion. In an instantaneous reflex, Toby's arms locked around her, and then she began to tickle him. It jarred him loose from her with an explosion of laughter.

"Now," she said, "did you ever kiss a girl that way before?"

"I didn't really kiss the girl, you know. I was kissed."

"You're stalling!"

"No," he admitted. "I never did, that I can remember."

"See what I mean? You've never really played with a woman."

"Maybe not. I'm not exactly sure whether you mean the same thing I do when you say 'play.' Is what you have in mind Indian wrestling, and King-of-the-Hill, and two falls out of three? Things like that?"

"You're getting the general idea."

"You and me?"

"Yes."

"This is just going to play hell with out beautiful platonic relationship. You know that, don't you?"

"Yes. Won't that be a shame?"

"You don't want any more of that drink, do you?" he asked, nodding toward the half-empty glasses.

"No."

"Come with me. I'll bet I can pin your shoulders to the mat in ten seconds flat." He took her hand and led her to his room, shut the door behind them, and kissed her—a long, hungry kiss. She pulled away from him.

"There comes the grand passion," she said, "whistling down the track toward Istanbul."

"Shanghai," he corrected her, not letting her go. "Sorry, but there are some things a man just naturally gets serious about."

"You *have* got a lot to learn," she said, "But I'm here to teach you. And the first thing is to get into uniform. You mustn't play in your good clothes, you know." She began to unbutton his shirt.

"When I'm on the Shanghai—well, all right, the *Orient* Express," he said, "I don't waste any time with buttons and things. I just reach out with one hand and rip the clothes right off of old Marlene."

"This is one of my best dresses," she said, "and it will come off without ripping, and I know how to do it. You wait right here."

Toby undressed quickly, his eyes glued to her all the while. She went over to his desk and stood with her back to him, not out of modesty, but because she was putting her garments on the desk as she took them off.

She unzipped the dress and pulled it up over her head.

Then the slip came off, and his heart thumped with what he decided was the purest lust he had ever known. He was sitting now on the edge of the low bed, oblivious of everything around him except the body that was being uncovered before his eyes. The bra came off, and then the panties. This was not a striptease. It was simply a woman taking her clothes off, and it was infinitely more tantalizing than the unimaginative bumps and grinds of what few stripteases he had ever tried to sit through. He had mentally undressed Louise often in the past, but he could see now that even an imagination as active as his own could never have done justice to the real thing.

She turned and revealed the rest to his staring eyes. She had a golden tan, except for the parts of her that had been covered by a moderately brief bikini, and the unburned skin was fair and satiny. It said mutely: *This part is never shown to anybody. This part you can now look at—and touch—but only you, and only here, when we are alone.*

He was suddenly aware that she was standing there flat-footed, at ease under his rapt gaze, smiling unabashedly at the effect she was having on him.

"Well," she said, "do I pass inspection?"

"You most certainly do," he breathed. "I was just trying to figure out where to put the seal of approval."

"Oh," she said, "I thought you would know. It goes right here." She pointed to the border between tan and white, just below her navel, and walked to where he sat on the bed.

"Just the place for it," he agreed.

He put his hands on her hips, pulled her to him, and kissed the spot firmly.

"Ouch!" she exclaimed, and drew away quickly.

"What's the matter?"

"That beard," she said, feeling his jaw with her fingertips.

"Oh,"he said. "Sorry about that."

"Sorry isn't enough," she said. "I have no intention of being sandpapered down to the quick tonight. Come here." She grabbed his hand and led him over to the easy chair. "Now, you sit right there," she commanded him.

She went into the bathroom and came out with a basin of water, soap, a can of shaving foam, a towel, and his razor. He was so entranced with the movements of her nude figure about the room that he paid little heed to what she was doing until she pushed his head back and began to rub his beard with a soapy washcloth.

"You're going to shave me?" he asked, straightening up in the chair.

"What does it look like?"

"But what do you know about shaving? You'll scrape me raw!"

"I'm a nurse, my dear. I've shaved hundreds of men. Even in other places besides their jaws." She leered playfully down along the length of his body, and he covered himself quickly with his hands.

"The jaws will be quite enough, thanks," he said.

"Lean back and be still."

She lathered his face with the foam and began to shave him. He had to admit that it was not bad. Not as nicely done as a barber would do it, and her hands did pull and tug his head in strange ways, but she moved the razor gently with the grain of the beard, and it was not at all painful. It might even have been relaxing if the barber had been anything but a naked woman.

He opened one eye and peered down the length of one of her arms. There below, perfectly framed in his field of vision, was one creamy breast, floating and swaying ever so gently with the movement of the arm. He could no more have controlled his hand than he could floated in the air. The hand came up automatically, and his fingers brushed lightly across the coral tip.

"Didn't you see the sign on the wall, sir?" she asked sternly, without pausing in her work.

"What sign?"

"Touching the barber is not permitted."

"Oh, but this is an absolute necessity," he said. "I'm conducting a test."

"A test?"

"Yes." His hand moved across her body, out of his line of sight, and stopped. "Aha!" he exclaimed, through lips she was distorting to tighten the skin on his jaw, "I thought so!"

"What?"

"You've got another one!"

The breast he could see jiggled deliciously as the barber laughed under her breath. "I must remind you again, sir, about that sign," she said.

"It was the only way," he said in a tight voice, because she was pinching his nostrils together to shave around them, "that I could confirm what I told you last night."

"What was that?"

"You've got a perfect set."

Again the breast jiggled. Now she moved to the other side of him, and all of her was in his field of vision. His other hand took over the exploration, and traced the line of her waist, down over the hips, over the thighs, and back up to where the white skin began.

"If these were the days of the straight razor," she said, "you wouldn't dare defy the rules of the shop that way."

"Come back tomorrow with a straight razor and see," he challenged her. His fingertips were moving lightly across her lower abdomen now, and up to where the tanned skin began. There was the slightest difference in texture between the skin of the tan and the white areas, and the velvety feel of the forbidden zones sent tiny lightning bolts of anticipation through his fingers and coursing out along his entire frame.

She finished shaving him, took the things to the bathroom, and brought back a bottle of lotion. Almost suffocated by the sight of that voluptuous form, which he had not yet been suffered to enjoy, moving back and forth across his room, he did not notice what she was doing with her hands until she was uncapping the bottle.

"No lotion, please, Miss Barber," he said.

"No lotion?"

"No."

"But won't your face feel dry and tight?"

"Probably. But if you put that stuff on, the only thing my nose will detect for the next two hours will be lime shaving lotion. When I am in the altogether with a woman, I want every one of my senses at its best."

She stepped back from him, puzzled. Interested.

"You really mean that, don't you?"

"I certainly do. If there is ever a time when all of a man's faculties ought to be sending him signals, this is the time." He got up, took the bottle from her, and put it on the lamp table by the chair.

"This, for example," he said, touching her neck just below the ear, "is one of the nicest places to kiss that you can find on a woman, and when I kiss her there I like to catch the fragrance of her. Because it's always there." He took her in his arms and bent down to kiss the spot, which was just as he had expected, soft, and warm, and fragrant, with a wisp of fine golden hair to tickle his nose. "Yes," he murmured through the kiss, "it's here." One hand, stroking the curve of her flank, detected sudden gooseflesh as she stood strangely still in his arms.

Then she jumped away, and sat on her heels in the middle of the bed. "That's an illegal hold," she said. "If you do that again, I'll have to penalize you."

Toby never recollected being so aroused in his life. He lunged at her, and she giggled, and bit him lightly on the nose, and they rolled and wrestled and laughed.

And it was over in ten seconds.

"Well!" she exclaimed, sitting up on her heels beside him once more. "Speedy Gonzales is back in town!"

"You *knew* that was going to happen!" he said accusingly; and her laughter was so spontaneous and free of malice that it healed his slightly bruised male ego, and he laughed with her.

"I must say that I'm improving, though," she said.

"You're improving?" This was beyond him.

"Yes. Don't you remember the other evening in the jeep? It happened and I didn't even realize it?"

"That's right," he grinned. "I remember."

"Well, this time, do you know what? I had a strange sensation, there for a while. Maybe it was an intuition. But whatever it was, somehow I knew for a few seconds that *something was happening!*"

"Oh, hell!" he said disgustedly. "If this gets out, my reputation for speed will be shot."

"Señor Gonzales," she said, pulling his ear gently, "after tonight you're going to be known as Slow-Talkin' Jones."

"Hah!" he snorted. "Just wait till I get my wind back."

"For that," she said brightly, "I've got just the thing. You need yoga."

"I do?"

"Yes. Quiet meditation. Awareness. Deep breathing. Things like that."

She ordered him to assume the seated position, legs crossed like a buddha, which he did as well as he could with his long, muscular legs. She sat in the same fashion, facing him, her knees touching his, arms relaxed at her sides.

"Now," she said, "watch me while I show you how to breathe."

He watched her. She ordered him to meditate as he did so, and he tried, but found it impossible. The deep-breathing display before him was much too spectacular.

"You have to blank everything else out of your mind," she insisted.

"Yes," he said obediently, making his voice sound cavernous and far away. "I am blanking everything out of my mind."

"It would be obvious to anybody who looked at you right now that you are doing no such a thing," she scolded him. "Now, forget about everything else, and try to do as I say."

"I am trying," he intoned, in the same hollow voice.

"Hush up and meditate."

Their meditations were soon interrupted by the arrival of the Orient Express, and shortly thereafter, Louise, her voice muffled by a welter of pillows and sheets, announced that she was absolutely certain something was happening.

They played on, and Toby found that he too could invent silly games, and that she played his just as enthusiastically as she elaborated on her own, and seemed to welcome each new arrival of the train, until at last, in the early morning hours, they lay facing each other on opposite sides of the bed, panting and grinning. He was aching, almost trembling wtih fatigue, and drained dry of all physical desire.

"Ma'am," he said.

"Yes?"

"Ma'am," he said, in a painfully slow drawl, "my name is Jones, and I've got something I want to ask you."

"What is it?"

"First off, would you come over here, please? I'm too

tired to move, and I haven't got the strength to talk across all that distance."

She wiggled herself over to him and into his arms.

"Now," he continued, "I just wanted to tell you that I never knew games could be such fun. I've really enjoyed the ones we've played tonight, and I've learned things from my coach that I never dreamed of before."

"I told you so," she said, squeezing him gently.

"And now, I wonder if the coach would mind if I just held on to her like this for the rest of the night?"

"Give up?" she asked him sleepily.

"I give up."

"All right, then," she replied. "Let that be a lesson to you." She settled herself snugly against him, her tousled blond hair brushing his nostrils, and they slept quietly until dawn.

[20]

MONDAY, January 1, 1968. Toby still had not been able to set up a single test of his operations to discover the security leak; still had no idea where the leak might be; had still not found out anything significant about the Yenan Battalion; had not had any further word from Dang; had obtained no solid information from his Special Police students; had acquired nothing that he could label as real intelligence; had, in fact, accomplished nothing he was supposed and resolved to accomplish in Vietnam. Tet was four weeks away.

Four weeks. The Christmas truce was over. It had been observed by both sides, violated only sporadically by unintended skirmishes or clashes. The calm had extended through the following week, and seemed to have imbued every human soul in the delta with the hope that perhaps the war, itself, was winding down.

The search operations resumed after Christmas, but

Toby had the impression that he alone felt the sense of impending disaster, the need for speed. It was not that the other participants were unwilling to carry out the operations, or untinterested in the results. It was just that they approached the work as routine assignments, upon which, after all, nothing very important depended.

The first one after Christmas began on the evening of Tuesday, January 2, and it would be the only one for that week. Toby watched the men set off at dusk, to be in place and ready by dawn of the following day. He went back into his office and sat down, intensely aware of Therese's presence behind him, at her desk.

She had arrived back from Saigon on schedule, radiant at the prospect of being reunited with him. He did not know whether she detected any change in him, but he certainly felt changed, and he was uneasy about it.

Before driving Louise home early Christmas morning, he had paused by the door and taken her hand.

"You were right," he said. "I had never played with a woman. Never in my life had a night like that one. Let's play again, soon?" And then he laughed at his own words. "That's the dumbest-sounding proposition I've ever made to a woman."

She smiled, a rather strange smile, almost a sad one. "I'm not sure, Toby," she said. "I'm not sure I ought to, or want to."

"Not sure you want to?"

"That's right. And I'm not going to try to explain that to you." She put her arms around him, inviting him to bend and kiss her, which he did. It was a loving kiss, and was on the way to becoming a passionate kiss, but she turned her head then, and whispered, "Take me home, Toby."

He had slept a good part of that day, Christmas Day. As the exhaustion and aching gradually drained away, he had taken stock of himself in wonderment.

Somehow his life had become so tangled and topsy-turvy that it was *Therese* he felt guilty about deceiving, not Mary Lynn. Well, of course, Therese was right here, not twelve thousand miles away. But he knew that the reason was not that simple. Moreover, he knew that, whatever cultural conditioning Therese might have about a rather free and casual sex life on the part of her man, she would not easily forgive such a swift and insouciant move from her arms into the arms of another woman.

My God, this was something you only read about! A normal, decent man didn't have this kind of problem. Toby had always considered men who moved easily and quickly from one woman to another to be stupid, thoughtless, self-centered.

But he must do something like that now. He knew that even if he had no immediate desire for *any* woman, he had to take Therese to him again, as soon as the opportunity presented itself. If not, she would be confused and hurt.

This evening, the opportunity had come. The house was empty for the night. She was finishing her day's work. He had tried to show her by quiet glances and smiles since her return from Saigon that his feeling for her had not changed, but he was not sure that his signals had been very convincing.

A year ago, if anybody had told him that he would one day be suffering pangs of remorse and doubt about having committed adultery against his *mistress,* he would have laughed.

If the night with Louise had been simply a pickup, a call-girl kind of thing, induced and fueled by loneliness and alcohol, it would have presented little difficulty. But he knew that underneath the lighthearted romping, the hilarious games, the challenge of her flesh against his, there was a strong current of something else, something he had not examined, did not even want to examine. His life was already complicated enough as it was.

Therese closed her desk and safe, and came to where he sat. She paused. He turned to her. She looked puzzled, hesitant.

He took her hand. God, if only he didn't have such an active imagination, or conscience! The very thought of the word "conscience" in this context was so incongruous that it made him smile in spite of himself, and she smiled back.

"Will you stay, Therese?" he asked, trying to make it sound urgent. He must not *worry.* Worry would make him impotent, would grow on its own effects.

"Yes, Anh Tho," she replied.

"Come on," he said. He led her into the common room.

As they went through the door his arm automatically moved around her, and his hand came to rest on the curve of her waist just above the hip. The flexing of that curve as she walked beside him triggered a familiar tightening in his gut, and he knew that he would be all right—but he was torn between amusement and exasperation at his heretofore unsuspected priapic capacities.

The reaction was fleeting, nevertheless. As he walked by her side it came to him in a sudden insight that this small, slender woman had stealthily slipped into his heart, into his very being. He wanted to protect her, love her, possess her, belong to her. He had said as much while making love to her, and now he knew that the words had not been merely sparks struck by the physical contact. He meant them. He had fallen in love with Therese.

Whatever this might mean to his marriage, the damage was already done, and nothing could be gained by worrying about it now. He would live this love while he could, knowing that there would be a reckoning, a price to pay, and knowing that that price would in large part be paid by innocent people.

But that accounting was due in the future. Nothing was to be gained by worrying about it now. He would love Therese while he could.

As to the search operation that night, it was even more uneventful than the previous ones.

They carried out two more the following week, each time working inward in the territory toward a central point somewhat arbitrarily established on the map.

"Toby," said Ben. "It's not my place to butt in on Little Jack's business, and maybe he already knows it, but you might be wise to talk to him about the morale of his men."

"What's wrong with them?"

"Nothing that I have exactly detected, but if I know soldiers, this going out time after time for nothing but a walk in the sun is bound to affect their fighting capabilities. They tend to get loose and relaxed. They tend to start bickering among themselves."

Toby asked Little Jack.

"Oh," the big man answered with a shrug, "there's been little problems now and then, but they'll be all right."

Only one search operation was made the following week. Another walk in the sun. Toby began to wonder if their theories had been crazy. There didn't seem to be any Viet Cong in that area at all. No caches of food or ammunition, no evidence of bivouacs—nothing.

Minnie seemed puzzled also. "It is strange, Mr. Busch," he said, in answer to Toby's question. "Perhaps you are right. Perhaps the Viet Cong are not there. We never find anything at all, and that is unusual. But perhaps we are looking for a complicated explanation of a simple fact."

"You may be right," Toby said.

Ben did not believe that a simple explanation was possible. "There is something unusual going on there, Toby," Ben said. "Believe me, this lack of reaction is not normal."

It was Friday, the nineteenth. Tet was ten days away. Toby was now often troubled by a feeling almost of panic. He couldn't make things move as he wanted them to move. He couldn't find out things he must know. He couldn't get a grip on the situation.

He found solace in Therese's arms at each opportunity, aware that their love affair must by now be common knowledge among their friends and associates.

That same Friday, Qui came to him unexpectedly, off schedule.

"I know!" he exclaimed, when they were alone in the common room. "The secret! I know!"

"You found out what's there?"

"Yes."

"How? What is it? Tell me, for God's sake!"

Qui extracted a small map from his pocket, and pointed to a village near the center of their search area. Through much stumbling talk, Toby learned that Qui had spent a night in that village on his own, after having been there on assignment during a previous search. He had discovered that in a village near that one there was a cousin of one of his associates, and he had worked on that cousin all night. The cousin did not have information from personal observation, but he finally told Qui what was fairly common knowledge among the villagers, and among the farmers in that area—which they would never reveal, on pain of death at the hands of the Viet Cong.

The Viet Cong had an underground hideout there. The Yenan Battalion and many other troops spent most of their time holed up in the tunnels. Qui pointed on the map to where the main access to the maze of tunnels was said to be located. The access was inside a small structure supposedly used for rice storage.

Toby had thought that the entire delta area was too wet for underground concealment like that. Qui said that apparently the Viet Cong had had the advice of a hydraulic engineer, who had shown them a place where the groundwater was far enough below the surface to make tunneling feasible.

Toby knew that this was the breakthrough he had been looking for. All he had was a vague report of rumors about a village, but it coincided so well with the facts as he knew them that his mind simply would not doubt the accuracy of the report.

He thanked Qui, and Qui left with a look of happiness, of accomplishment, on his face. Toby wrote up an intelligence report. This would be a legitimate report, because it came from an agent whom he had already made a matter of record.

It was, of course, an intelligence report of interest only to his own province, and to the American and Vietnamese military forces in the area, and would not be disseminated beyond those customers. But at least he had begun to produce.

He told Ben about the report, without revealing to him the source.

"It could be," Ben replied, intrigued. "That would explain everything all right. They are not attacking the search operations because they don't want to tip their hand. They may think you'll figure there's nothing there, and quit searching. But the day the search hits *that* area is the day the shit hits the fan."

"Well," said Toby, "I'm going to persuade Manh that this is where we've got to run the next operation. That'll be on the twenty-sixth."

"It will have to be the last one before Tet, then?"

"Yeah. I don't see how we can do any more before the thirtieth."

"So this one will tell the tale, or not," Ben mused.

"Yes, and I'm going along this time."

"You're going along?"

"Yeah. I know what's there, but I don't intend to tell anybody until we get there. That way I'll know there won't be any leak."

"Christ," Ben said earnestly, "that's likely to turn into a real fight."

"I suppose it could. But with all my big talk about testing for leaks, this is the first real test I have made on our operations."

"Well, it's your funeral."

"That was not a very felicitous choice of words." Toby grinned at him.

"I intended it that way, my friend."

"Why don't you come along, too?" Toby suggested impulsively. "I've let you watch me be an intelligence officer, maybe you could let me watch you and learn how to be a combat soldier."

"No," said Ben. "Not this time. I don't think you're wise to go yourself, but that's your decision to make, not mine. At any rate, if you go, you'll have to go without me."

Toby was about to ask him why, but decided against it.

Little Jack was not altogether pleased with Toby's decision, especially since he could not be told the specific reason why Toby wanted to go along.

"The one thing I can tell you, Little Jack," he said, "is that this time we're going to hit a VC nerve. We may run into a real fight."

Little Jack shrugged. "That's what we're here for. But I'm not gonna lie to you. If we're going to a place where we'll have a fight, I don't want to have an inexperienced civilian around getting in the way."

"I won't get in your way," said Toby. "There's a reason I have to go along."

"You could get killed, you know."

"I know. And the idea of getting killed is not one of my favorite daydreams, but I've got to go with you."

"OK. Suit yourself."

Toby willed himself to work on other things that afternoon. He knew that the first few hours after making his decision would be the time of the most pressing doubt and uneasiness about it. He was certain that he was consciously, and with a calm logic, willing himself into a battle. Somehow, his life had become so much of a turmoil that the fear of battle become less urgent. When he worried, it was not out of fear of being hurt or killed, but rather from a fear that he would be less than a man when danger came.

There was a space of about two hours, right after lunch, when he was alone in the office with Therese, and she asked him if they might talk alone in the common room. Something about the intensity of her words made Toby wonder, and he forgot his thoughts of combat for the moment.

They settled themselves on the sofa. "What is it, Therese?" he asked.

"Anh Tho," she said with a smile, "I am going to have a baby."

"You're what?" His reaction was so sudden and explosive that it made her start with surprise.

"I am going to have a baby."

"Is it—is it *my . . .?"* Toby began, and caught the hurt that came fleetingly to her eyes. "I almost asked the stupidest question of my life, Little Mistress."

She smiled, but said nothing.

"But," he continued fretfully, "I had thought that you would, you know, that you would have taken some means to avoid it, Therese."

"No," she said, visibly disturbed by his reaction. "I did nothing."

"Well, then you must do something now."

"Do something now?"

"Yes. You must do something to get rid of it."

"Get rid of it?" she gasped. "Why?"

"But, Therese," he said, "don't you see? I have made love to you, and I love you, but I cannot be your husband. You will have a baby that is part of my flesh, and I could never acknowledge it. The child would never know his father. The idea that somewhere in the world I have left a part of myself that way, who will never know me, and I will never know, is something I don't even want to think about."

"But, Anh Tho," she said softly, her voice freighted with the shock of what she was hearing, "the baby will be mine, too. I will care for him, and he will grow to be a man you would be proud of."

"But a man I would never know."

"A man who will be the only part of his father that I can have as my own."

"A man who will show by his features that his mother went to bed with an American. A man who will be half European and half Asian. A man who will be illegitimate. A bastard." Toby shook his head stubbornly.

"I will not mind," she said. "If people wish to think bad things about me, I will not care, because I know that what I have done is not wrong."

Toby sat in silence. Dammit, he had assumed that Therese was taking some kind of precautions. It had never occurred to him that she might *want* a child by him. It was ironic that before he was married he had always been uneasy about fathering a child, for fear it might force him into a marriage he did not want or was not ready for. Now he had begotten a child in the body of a woman he *would* have married instantly, but *could* not.

As for Therese, he was afraid that she was not looking squarely at the problems she might encounter, at the prejudices she would face, during a period of reconstruction.

"Anh Tho," said Therese timidly, "is it that you are afraid that I will cause difficulties for you after you leave Vietnam?"

"Of course not!" he exclaimed. "You could never do such a thing."

"Then, *please*, Anh Tho," she pleaded with him, "please tell me that you want me to have our baby."

"I am sorry," he said gently. "I am so sorry, Little Mistress. I don't want to hurt you. But I can't tell you truthfully that I want you to have the baby. I want you *not* to have it. I will try to find out how and where you can have it taken care of, if you like, but . . ."

"No," she said. "I only want you to say that you want me to have your child, but you will not say it."

"I can't say it, Therese. It would not be the truth."

Therese got up and went back into the office. When he got back to his own desk, she was gone. She returned to her desk from the bathroom after a long time, her eyes red, her head ereet, staring straight ahead.

Well, goddammit, here is another *problem!*

But he didn't have time or energy to spare for this one right now. It could wait a few days. On Tuesday morning he spoke to Minnie about his plan.

"But why do you wish to go, Mr. Busch?" Minnie asked. He was obviously quite concerned about Toby's plan.

"I can't tell you exactly why I want to go on this specific operation, but I think the reason will be clear to you when we get there."

"Where is it to be?"

Toby pointed to the map on the wall. "It will be in this general area," he said. "This is the last operation before Tet, and the logic of the previous ones puts us right in the middle of the territory."

"That is true," said Minnie. "But I believe you should not go."

"Why not? Do you know something about the place that I don't know?"

"I do not *know* anything, but I have been drawing some conclusions from what has been happening in the past. Either we will find nothing, or we will find something that will cause a battle."

"I think you're right, but I intend to go."

"Of course, you must do what you believe to be right."

Thursday evening he dressed and armed himself under Ben's advice and instructions. He had a flak jacket hanging on a hook on his wall, but when he found that none of the others would be wearing one he abandoned all thought of taking it along. Foolish pride, perhaps, but in a company of eighty or ninety men he would not under any circumstances be the only one to wear protective armor.

On Ben's advice he left the pistol at home. He took along an M-16 rifle and a bandolier with a basic load of eighteen clips of ammunition.

"Knowing what you're going after," Ben told him, "I think you'll want to take a claymore sack full of grenades too. Ever use a grenade?"

"I had some training with them years ago."

"And take along a medical kit. Two canteens. Be sure

you wear a helmet. Anything else in the way of survival gear—knives, things like that."

"Survival gear I know about," Toby said.

"Little Jack and his men will undoubtedly take along plenty of smoke and CS," said Ben, "and they'll know how to use it."

He filled his canteens at the house, and took along a box of C rations for the morning.

He was nervous. Little shivers of fear caught up with his muscles once in a while, and coursed along his frame. He kept his mind busy with the mechanics of hauling his body around with the unaccustomed gear, and when the empty, bottomless feeling suddenly came, he turned his attention, by a sheer act of will, to other simple things in his immediate vicinity.

In the jeep, moving along a dark, rough road, with one of the PRU soldiers at the wheel, he had little that he could occupy himself with except the problem of keeping his seat. Three jeeps, followed by four two-and-a-half-ton trucks, carried their search force. They moved through the night with a purposeful rumble.

What in the name of God was he doing here? What kind of insanity had come over him some months ago to volunteer for this kind of duty in the first place, and what climactic bit of craziness had impelled him to come on this night's specific expedition into war? He could certainly have told Little Jack the secret. Or perhaps Minnie. He could have changed his mind ten minutes ago and told Minnie, who had been sitting beside him in the jeep from the start; but that would mean getting out of the jeep in front of all the other men and going back to his house. He could not have done that.

And Therese was pregnant. He had always prided himself on keeping his life free of unnecessary complications. In his business there were a lot of necessary ones you could not avoid, and things were always complicated enough without making them any more so. But he *had* made them more so. When confronted by a nude Therese, there was only one thing he could think about. In fact, even when he was only *imagining* a nude Therese . . .

He turned his thoughts elsewhere, in reaction to this antic lust that had suddenly taken possession of him.

And Louise? He had not even spoken to her since that night. He should have given her some kind of a call, or a note, or something. She might think that . . .But hell, she was much too intelligent to read anything into his silence except—except what? Why had he not communicated with her in any way?

Well, what would he have said? But, for Christ's sake, he should have said *something!*

He decided what he would do when he got back: He would go to her house in the evening, knock on the door, and have two cigarettes lighted in his mouth when she came to answer it, whereupon he would take one of them out and slowly place it between her lips, with a steady, lascivious stare. The image pleased him, and would, he knew, break Louise up, especially since she didn't smoke.

And then there came dancing before his eyes a picture of that incredible body, the gently swaying breast as she shaved him; the hips, white on tan, undulating as she moved away from him; her sudden moments of submission as they played riotously in the confusion of sheets and pillows.

They pulled the vehicles off the road and left three men to guard them. The rest of them set off on foot. They walked along the road for about three miles, then Little Jack halted them, and set up guards around their makeshift bivouac.

"We're gonna wait here till daylight," he said. "The target area is right ahead of us. Better get some sleep."

"I'll take my turn at guard duty," Toby offered.

"No," said Little Jack. "Let the men do it. They've had experience, and if what you say is true, we're probably in a pretty touchy area here."

"I want to do my share, though," Toby protested.

"Sure," said Little Jack absently. He held up one of his canteens. "Speaking of experience, you'd think I was a goddamned recruit myself. I came off without filling my canteens. I'm gonna have to take some water from that shell hole over there."

"You can share mine."

"It's gonna be hot, and you're gonna be in action. You'll use all that water, and still be thirsty."

"But the water in that hole may be—"

"Probably full of buffalo piss and everything else, but it's wet. I'll put iodine tablets in it, and it'll be all right."

He moved off toward the hole, and Toby lay down on the ground and tried to sleep. The sky was clear and moonless, and he stared off into infinity. He knew he would not sleep. He tossed and turned restlessly, his eyes wide, his mind alert. And yet, when the sky began to get light, he realized that the time had passed too quickly for him to have been awake throughout the night. He had certainly dozed now and then.

The PRU knew exactly what they had to do, and they started out with a minimum of talk. They moved swiftly in the spreading daylight, aware that their presence must already be known. Toby kept himself near the middle of their extended line. It did not look to him much like a rational formation, but he knew that these men were veterans of this kind of action, and he was sure that there was a method and a reason for the way they approached the target.

Minnie was among the men at the point. Toby could now clearly make out the line of thatched huts which was their target, structures that almost blended into invisibility in the treeline immediately behind them. He noted that the land was higher here—only a few feet, but perhaps enough to permit tunneling for concealment. The ridges of the thatched roofs were in some semblance of a line, although it was an up-and-down affair. The floors were on numerous short posts or pilings, allowing air to circulate underneath, and the walls were of woven mats, held in place by vertical bamboo slats. These walls were open under the eaves, allowing for the entrance of light and air.

He peered carefully at them, and decided that there could be no tunnel entrance from inside any of these huts, because he could see all the way under every floor. Behind the row, in a small indentation in the treeline, however, was another structure, which was enclosed by a bamboo fence, and he judged that if the entrance were in this little hamlet, it must be inside that fence.

And that was a frightening thought. Here was a company of men approaching what might turn out to be the front door of a Viet Cong stronghold.

As if his uneasy thoughts had given birth to the fact, there came a loud explosion at the point and several of the men crumpled before it. A claymore. He heard something swishing through the grass near him, and wondered dully if these were fragments from the mine, dropping from a high trajectory.

Evidently on signal from the claymore, Toby heard a sound like a giant motor starting up. In the split second he wondered what in the world there could be in this place with such an engine, and then he realized that the motor sound was really a blast of fire from rifles and machine guns along two lines—one line ahead of them, and another line off to one side of their own line. He fell to the ground in an automatic reflex, as had the others.

They had been ambushed! His hands trembling, he companions, although he could not see the enemy. He brought his rifle around and joined in the firing with his could tell where the hostile fire was coming from, however. The ambush was L-shaped, with the apex on the road, so that both lines could fire on the raiding party without danger to themselves.

Toby suddenly realized that his rifle was not firing, although he was holding the trigger down with desperate strength. He laughed hysterically at himself. He had put it on semi-automatic, and had fired one round, and was now holding the trigger down tight on a silent weapon, trained steadily on the enemy. He loosened the finger and began to work it back and forth to fire repeatedly.

For the second time in his life he heard B-40 rockets detonating near him. He was new to combat, but he was certain that they had struck an overwhelming enemy force.

Out of the corner of his eye he saw Minnie moving swiftly about near the point. Minnie was gesturing to some men who were carrying an M-60 machine gun and ammunition, and they took up a position facing the short end of the L. Other men crouched near Minnie, and Minnie suddenly led them in a dash toward the apex of the lines of fire. Toby saw the point of the maneuver instantly. If they could get close enough, the enemy could not fire at them without danger to the other line of the ambush. But he could also see that it was insane even to *try* to move through that intense concentration of fire.

"You goddamned fools!" he screamed at them.

The M-60 opened up a covering fire, but it seemed to have little effect. The firing from the ambush got heavier. Two of the men with Minnie threw grenades, and two others fell heavily and lay still. Then the others dropped to the ground, enveloped in a curtain of flying metal, far short of their objective.

A B-40 rocket struck the men with the machine gun, and sent gun and men flying apart. Toby was paralyzed with the impact and astonishment of the insane violence that had suddenly torn across the world around him.

One of the men to his left gestured to Toby that they were going to withdraw, firing as they did so, to hold the ambush in its position.

"What about Minnie?" Toby shouted at him.

The man looked questioningly at him.

"Tran Van Minh!" Toby shouted, gesturing toward the point where Minnie was lying. The man shrugged and shook his head.

"Well, by God I'm not going to leave them there without at least *trying* to do something!" Toby bellowed, more to himself than to his companions, who would not understand his words. Surely a comrade would not leave his fellows behind—combat has got to be something besides eighty individual battles.

He rose to a crouch and rushed forward, until he stumbled, or was knocked down by some instinctive bodily reaction. His move had provoked an increased chatter of firing, and he felt a sharp pain in his right arm near the shoulder. He could feel the bullets hitting the ground and slicing through the grass around him, and the pop of their individual little sonic booms as they sped through the air above him.

His sleeve had been torn by a bullet, and an oozing of blood had discolored it. He pulled the sleeve up and saw that the bullet had only grazed his arm, that the blood was, in fact, oozing and not flowing.

This was no good. Two of the men in Minnie's group began to wriggle on their bellies toward him, but the rustling of the grass brought a stream of bullets, and one of the men stiffened, half rose, and fell on his face.

Now Toby noticed an ominous change in the sound of

the firing before him. It was coming closer. He heard a different kind of explosion, and saw that it was the sound of PRU grenades being hurled at the advancing enemy. He threw two grenades himself, and then turned and ran to where he had been stretched out prone a moment before—and made it without being hit. The remaining PRUs were beginning a systematic process of firing and moving back. They worked in such a way that the firing from their retreating line was constant, although not all of them were firing at once. The advance of the ambushing forces had been halted for the moment. Toby fell into the rhythm of the retreat, aware suddenly of having become so engrossed in the action that he had lost the nervousness, the trembling, that had beset him before the engagement. Fear was still in him, but it was now fear that compelled him to act, that held up no logical measures of risk and safety.

He saw that the maneuver was going to pull them free of the ambush. The two lines could not close on them fast enough to catch them, although the firing was having a deadly effect, nevertheless; for as they moved back they left behind ever more of their number, dead or immobilized by wounds. He wished that he could help those who were hurt and still, but knew that if he stopped, both he and the object of his pity would be killed.

He wondered where Little Jack was, and whether he was leading or ordering the men in any way. There was no evidence of it. Toby was thirsty, but did not dare to make the moves that would have brought his canteen to his mouth.

A man beside him motioned toward the rear and gestured that they were going to make a run that way. Toby looked and guessed that a faint line he could see there in the grass must be a ditch of some kind, although he did not remember having crossed it when they moved up a few minutes ago. All the PRU opened fire at once, and Toby joined them. Then they turned and ran as fast as they could go. He was right. It was a shallow ditch, and they tumbled into it gratefully. Toby almost fell on top of Little Jack, who was lying on his side, doubled up in an agony of pain.

"Were you hit?" Toby exclaimed.

Little Jack opened his eyes, his face white as a sheet.

"No," he said. "It's my gut. I've never had a pain like this before in my life."

"Your gut?"

"Yeah," he replied, through clenched teeth. "I think it must of been that goddamned water I drank a while ago."

"Jesus Christ, Little Jack," he said, "we've got to bug out of here! Can you move?"

"Yeah," the big man gasped. "Yeah, I can move."

Toby was going to ask him what they should do, but saw that Little Jack was so wrapped up in his pain that he would be of no help.

"Come on," Toby said. "We're heading for that line of trees, and I'm about to run like hell!"

He shouted the last words at the top of his lungs as he sped out toward the rear. The rest of the company were with him, and he managed to stay slightly ahead of them. He was taller, had longer legs than they did, but he was encumbered with a bag of grenades, the canteens, and the bandolier, as well as the rifle, and none of these things seemed to find a good or comfortable place on his frame so that he could run properly.

He leaped another shallow ditch, which ran diagonally to his line of flight, and continued running pell-mell for the trees.

The gigantic motor started up again, dead ahead of him. A blocking force had moved in behind them, heavily armed and well concealed. The gate had been closed. They were trapped.

He knew, afterward, that it was a foolish thing to do, but instead of dropping to the ground he turned tail and ran back to the diagonal ditch. He could not believe that so much metal had flown at him without hitting him. He fell into the ditch and found that Little Jack had made it this far too, although he was still in agony. It had never occurred to Toby that a simple thing like a bellyache could even *happen* in a battle, to say nothing of affecting the outcome. He crouched in the ditch, trembling, wanting to weep with rage and frustration. They were obviously surrounded by a force many times larger than their own—probably at least a battalion, perhaps more—tough veterans, he was sure, to judge from the systematic and persistent way they had fired at him and his companions, and pursued them into the trap. It was a force that had not been reported in this area, and had no business being here. It had to be the Yenan Battalion. He had found the secret—found what he was looking for—and he was going to pay for it with his life.

He panted heavily, and watched the big man beside him grit his teeth against the pain. Most of the PRUs had taken cover in the ditch, and were spread out in a line along its length. One of them came crawling along, stared for a moment at Little Jack, shook his head, and gestured for Toby's benefit toward the line of the ditch.

No firing came from along the direction the ditch lay in. Surely the enemy would not have been stupid enough to leave that obvious exit open!

Two others joined this man, and Toby followed them. They inched forward along the line of the ditch, through manure and mud, paying no heed to either. Toby could hear the men behind him keeping up a steady fire at the enemy, holding the ambush line back. Grenades were once again exploding here and there along the line.

The ditch curved, and Toby for the first time actually got a glimpse of one of the enemy. It was a small man, lying prone in the ditch, facing them, a rifle at his shoulder, aimed toward them. The man in the lead fell like a stone as the rifle cracked, and the others moved back quickly to the protection of the curve.

One of the men behind Toby immediately pulled the pin on a grenade and threw it in the direction of the prone Viet Cong. They crouched and waited. The grenade exploded with a loud *whump!* and they moved quickly up to the curve. The grenade had landed in front of the man, and he had apparently tried to reach it before it exploded.

Firing broke out from beyond the dead man, but it was scattered and hesitant. The PRUs with Toby spoke softly to one another, passed a word urgently down the line, and presently they gathered in a tighter clump along the ditch. Toby could tell that they were preparing to assault those few rifles in front of them with a sudden rush. He knew that he would go with them. He didn't know where Little Jack was, but he had no time to spare for Little Jack now. If they were to have any chance of getting out of this alive, it was by an immediate rush, before the rest of the blocking force could move laterally to intercept them.

They sprang to their feet and ran, firing as they went. Their appearance seemed to catch the enemy by surprise, and once again Toby got a glimpse of the men who were firing at them. Even as they appeared before him, he fired his rifle, along with the PRUs charging with him, not aiming, not even sure what he was doing, or why. He thought he might have killed one, but others were firing as well and he would never be sure.

Their sudden rush had rolled over a small squad of men who had been placed at that point, and the rest of the PRUs came swiftly into the opening, rifles ready, Little Jack running among them.

And then Toby realized that they were free. Free of the trap. Not safe yet, but now with a better than even chance of getting away, for all the points of enemy fire were behind them. There was no enemy between them and their vehicles.

One of the PRUs, seeing that Little Jack was not going to take charge of their retreat, called the remaining force together quickly and gave some terse instructions. Tired and winded as they were, they accepted the orders without question and deployed themselves in a scattered line, similar to the one they had formed on their approach to the trees. The men bringing up the rear were doing so by a system of leapfrogging, so that there were always some riflemen in position, facing the rear, while the main party made good its retreat.

Out of a force of eighty men they had left eighteen behind, including Minnie. Remembering An Loi and Phu Binh, Toby knew what would happen to any of those left, if they were not already dead. If Minnie had not been killed in his futile assault, and if the Viet Cong knew who he was, they might try to keep him alive for questioning. But Toby knew that this was not likely. He had a conviction that Minnie was dead. He was still too stirred by the action to be able to comprehend the deaths it had included, but he knew that later he would feel the loss of Minnie very deeply.

They climbed into the vehicles and drove carefully over

the bumpy road, so as not to cause needless pain for such wounded men as had been able to run and escape.

Lassitude now began to spread through Toby's body. He had been in combat, and had given a reasonably good account of himself, although he was a far cry from a hero. He knew that what was behind this violent action was significant for his operations in the delta, but he also knew that an analysis of what it meant would have to wait until he could think with his brain, instead of his racing blood.

Might they have done something besides run away? He didn't see how. It was obvious, even to an inexperienced ear like his own, that the force that had ambushed them was large and well prepared. It was a daylight raid, and the PRU skills as night fighters gave them no advantages in this case. At any rate, the PRU soldiers themselves seemed in no doubt about the best course of action, and who was he to gainsay their judgments?

As for Little Jack, he had been worse than useless.

He wondered if a military unit ought to discipline a sergeant who forgot an elementary thing like a canteen and who, as a result, had taken himself out of action at the crucial moment. He might have felt lenient toward Little Jack if he had merely heard about the episode, instead of being involved in it, having his own hide risked by it; but the memory of those moments of danger, almost of panic, with the key soldier writhing in pain on the ground, served only to infuriate him right now.

But he must not take any action, or make any reprimands, while he was as wrought up as he was now. *Calm down, and take action from a cool and objective point of view, if any action is in fact necessary.*

They dropped Toby off at the house, and Little Jack went on with the rest to take stock of the situation and get details for the formal report of the action. His pain had subsided to some extent, he said, although he was still having occasional stabs in the belly. He would get some medication for it after he had tended to the business of his unit.

Ben had heard the vehicles coming down the street, and was waiting at the door.

"Eighteen," he exclaimed, with a low whistle. "If you

lost eighteen of those tough little characters, it means you ran into some ambush!"

"Well," said Toby, taking off the battle gear and piling it on the desk, "I've never been in any ambush before, but this one sure sounded like a big one to me."

"You got yourself nicked a little bit, too," said Ben.

"Yeah," he said, with a wry smile. "Only a hero would have lived through that."

Ben pulled up the sleeve and looked at it. "Well, even if you don't consider it crippling, it would be a good idea to put something on it. In this climate . . ."

"First," said Toby, "I'm going to drink two gallons of that lovely cold water in the refrigerator, and then I'm going to take a shower, and then I'm going to fix this horrible, gaping wound. First things first."

He blessed the feel of the hot water. It soaked the tension out of his body and made him feel clean and sane again. Ben came to the door of his room.

"You'll have trouble taking care of that with one hand," he said. "Let me fix it up for you."

He brought a medical kit and put some strong disinfectant on the wound, which was more of an abrasion than a cut. "Fact is," he said, "in the tropics, this kind of scratch is more likely to get infected than a deeper cut." Toby didn't know whether Ben was right, but the sting of the disinfectant was reassuring, and after Ben had taped a bandage over the wound, he put on his shirt and they went down to the office.

Toby gave him a full account of the action, and it was only then that Ben found out about Minnie.

"That's a shame," he said, genuinely moved by the loss. "That little man was a bright guy, and brave as they come."

"Well," said Toby thoughtfully, "I had never before had any doubts about his brain, but what he did this morning didn't look to me like a very bright thing to do." He told Ben how Minnie had reacted to the ambush.

"He jumped up and tried a head-on assault the first thing?" Ben asked.

"That's right. It couldn't have been more than half a minute after they first opened fire. He was on his feet, and got a machine gun going, hollered at the men around him, and ran right into the fire."

"Never had a chance, huh?"

"Not a chance."

"As I've said before," Ben remarked, "I never like to judge another man's battles if I wasn't there to see them, but what Minnie did may have been the best thing to do."

"I don't see how," said Toby, with a shake of his head.

"Usually the right thing to do in an ambush is just that: make an immediate assault on it, firing every weapon you've got as you go. The ambushing force is not bulletproof, and they're just as susceptible to surprise and fear as the raiding force. With good men like the PRUs, well led, you could break up a pretty good-sized ambush force."

"They weren't well led today," Toby reminded him. He had not spared Little Jack in his narrative of the action.

Ben shook his head in disgust. "Big dumb jackass," he said. "I'd bust his ass to private if he was in my company."

"Anyway," said Toby, not really interested at this moment in the big sergeant, "we've proved that the Yenan Battalion is there. And as far as I'm concerned, we saw enough to be sure that the entrance to their tunnels is right there." He went over to the map and pointed to the village. "Now we can report this, and the ARVN can go in there and clear it out. They probably don't realize that we've discovered where their hideout is. They'll still be there."

"Lotsa luck, Toby," said Ben.

"What do you mean?"

"You might get an air strike, or maybe some guns to fire a few rounds on the place, for whatever good that might do, but it would take a couple of days for the ARVN to set up an operation against that area, and a couple of days is going to put us right into the middle of the Tet truce."

"But if they don't do something, all those troops are going to be available to hit My Tho during Tet."

"You think they're going to do that?"

"I *know* they are. Believe me, I know something about intelligence, and the intelligence I've got is good. The Viet Cong are going to blast this country with everything they've got during Tet."

"From what I know of you," said Ben, "I'm inclined to

believe every word you say, but I doubt if other people will. All you can do is try."

"I'm sure as hell going to do that."

"And we can at least have our place ready. If it does come, we may be one of the prime targets."

[21]

THERESE was at her desk as usual the following morning, and Toby was dismayed to see that something of the old look of haunted sadness had returned to her eyes. He ached to have her alone, to talk with her, to comfort her. He had thought about it last night. He had been foolish and selfish. It was obvious that she was clinging to the idea of this child, that the pregnancy meant something out of the ordinary to her, anchored her in some way in a world that had used her badly.

Later this afternoon he would talk to her about it—repair the wrong between them, bridge the gulf, be her lover again in every way. But now he had other things to do, more urgent than that.

He went first to the Province Senior Adviser's office, to report on the action of yesterday, and to warn the PSA that he should prepare his people for an attack on My Tho at the time of Tet. The PSA was dubious.

"They're pledged to observe a truce during Tet, Toby," he said.

"They're going to violate it, sir," said Toby.

"Well . . ." The PSA did not believe it.

"Whether you believe it altogether or not," Toby went on, "I certainly would recommend that you alert all your people, and have plenty of emergency equipment, and food and water ready."

"Oh, yes, of course," said the PSA cordially. "We'll certainly do all that."

Toby asked if they had an interpreter he could borrow for an hour or so. They did, a serious-faced middle-aged man, who climbed into the jeep without a word and rode to Manh's office with Toby.

There Toby gave his report, making no apologies or boasts about it, but indicating clearly that it had been worth the effort. He had found out where the Yenan Battalion was holed up, and he could advise ARVN and the American forces in time to be on the alert for a move from that area during Tet.

Manh was also skeptical of the Tet danger.

"We are instructed to be liberal in granting our men leave to go to their homes for Tet," he said. "Many of them will be gone."

"You cannot cancel those leaves?"

"No."

"Colonel," said Toby earnestly, "I urge you to take every possible precaution with the men you will have left. There is going to be a massive attack, perhaps even a popular uprising, during Tet. If the Viet Cong catch us off guard they can do us tremendous damage."

"We will, of course, take customary precautions against surprise," said Manh.

Toby knew that this meant they would take no real precautions at all.

He went to Louise's house. None of the women was home, and he drove over to the hospital.

Louise came to the reception area to see him. He had never seen her in her uniform, but he was not surprised to note that the white blouse and slacks were no more successful that other garments in suppressing the richness of the lines underneath.

She gave him a quiet smile, almost shy. He felt equally as awkward at first.

"I just came to warn you," he said. "Nobody seems to believe me, but the Viet Cong are going to hit this city hard on the day of Tet. I think you women should plan to stay somewhere where you will have some kind of defense and protection."

"Where would that be?"

"You could come to our house. Or maybe the Province

Senior Adviser could make room for you. He at least has a more defensible place, and plenty of guards."

"The hospital is probably the safest place we could be, don't you suppose? Even the Viet Cong won't hit the hospital."

"Don't be too sure of that."

"Well, I'll talk it over with the others, and we'll let you know," she said.

"Don't let anybody persuade you that there's not going to be any trouble. Nobody believes what I'm saying, evidently, and they'll try to persuade you too."

"I believe you."

He turned to go, and then paused. "Louise," he said in a voice that was muffled by hesitation and doubt, "I want to see you again . . . and I'm not talking about wanting to play, either. I just want to be with you, to talk."

She smiled. "I guess I ought to be flattered. Someone wants me for my mind."

He couldn't help grinning back at her. "I'm not going to play around with words with you, ma'am," he said. "I can say it all very simply. I miss you."

"That's nice."

"I'll talk to you later this evening."

"All right."

He went with the interpreter to the PRU barracks. Little Jack was not there, which was just as well. He called to one side the man who had been near him during most of the action the day before. He explained that although they had had to run away, they had nonetheless succeeded in their mission, because they had found out something very important. He was sorry that it had cost the lives of so many good men, and wanted the rest of them to know how much he appreciated their good work.

The man nodded and acknowledged his remarks with a few words. Toby thought he was pleased, although there was little expression on his face.

"Be sure that you keep somebody posted by that radio from now on," Toby instructed him. "The Viet Cong, including those forces we met yesterday, are going to attack My Tho on the day of Tet. I don't know how your unit will be used or deployed, but this city is going to need every experienced fighting man it can call up. Mr. Horner will be advised, and may have to contact you by that radio."

The man acknowledged the instructions. Toby had a sense of triumph in this case, for this man seemed to believe his warning without any reservations.

Toby went back to the house and had lunch; afterward he sat at his desk and prepared reports about yesterday's action, and the significance he attached to it. He didn't know how he was going to get the information to Can Tho, but figured he would fly down and back, if necessary. He gave his rough draft to Therese to put into a clean copy, and went back to join Ben, who was checking their supplies of weapons, ammunition, food, fuel, and water. Ben might have some doubts about the information, but he was going to be ready anyway. He helped Ben rearrange the supplies, to make them more easily available in a hurry. They took some additional ammunition out, to have ready in their rooms and on the roof.

Toby realized that in the urgency of the day's business he had neglected to make his daily check for Dang's signal, and he strolled out the gates and took a walk around the block.

A new curved mark had been scratched in the post, just under the first one.

Dang had loaded the dead drop once again. The material might have been in there all day yesterday, since Toby had not checked it then.

He hurried back to the office and called Therese to tell her what he had found.

"I don't know how long the material has been there—maybe all day yesterday, since I didn't check for the signal yesterday."

"I looked," said Therese. "It was not there yesterday."

"Good girl!" he exclaimed, trying to cheer her up. "It will be dark in about two hours, and I will go bring the material back. Could you come back to work this evening to help me with it?"

"Of course," she said.

"If you would like to leave now and rest for a while," he suggested. "The work tonight might be long and hard."

"Then I will leave now."

Toby was distressed by the coolness in her voice, but felt

that after the work was out of the way this evening he could talk with her and bring her back to a happy mood.

He asked Mrs. Chao to prepare his dinner earlier this evening, so that by the time it got dark he would be free of all other activities. Mrs. Chao did as he asked willingly enough, but she was not her usual cheerful self, and Toby guessed that she must have heard, or sensed, Therese's troubles.

As soon as the streets were dark, he drove as fast as he could to the airstrip. In the dead drop he found a big bundle of papers, wrapped in a plastic sheet and tied with a string. He rushed back to the office and found Therese already waiting for him, her desk and typewriter ready for work.

They opened the bundle, and even Therese seemed to forget her troubles in the excitement of the moment.

"See if there is a note or any kind of a personal communication from Dang, first," he said.

"Yes. Here is a letter from him."

"Will you read that to me now, to see if it contains any instructions or explanations about the other material?"

Therese read:

"My Friend: I go soon to My Tho for final study of our target for Tet. There will be others in the city at the same time. I do not dare to meet with you. I will leave package of papers with information in the box as you directed.

"I conclude your officials have not understood or believed my information. They have not prepared against Tet attack, and it will therefore be carried out as planned. You must warn them, however. The attack is ready. It will be carried out all over South Vietnam. I do not know details of plans for other areas, but I give following general information about all of South Vietnam, in addition to the enclosed detailed plans about operations in Dinh Tuong Province:

"(a) The false information from COSVN has reached highest American and ARVN levels, and is believed.

"(b) At least one important American place will be attacked in Saigon. I do not know which place, but Americans should put extra defense at BOQs, at Than Son Nhut, and at Embassy.

"(c) Three officers of your agency are to be killed or captured, but I do not believe you are one of these targets. They are in the north.

"(d) The attack will begin early on morning of January 30. *All* Viet Cong forces will participate. *All!*"

Therese put the paper down on the desk.

"There's something significant about his attitude this time," said Toby. "He is intelligent enough to know that as late as it is we can't possibly take defensive measures that would show the Viet Cong we are ready in time for them to call it off. He knows that the attack is going to be made, that there is no stopping it now, and yet he has sent us information to help us *defeat* the attack. He has come over to our side, even if he hasn't yet admitted it to himself."

Therese set to work typing out a translation of all the other documents, and Toby took the notes he had made from her oral translation of the letter and typed up an intelligence report. *One more,* he thought grimly, *for Chet Wolleson to put in a file and forget.* Well, by God, he was going to see that this one was not put in a file, even if he did have to go out of channels and work around Chet.

Therese worked steadily, often asking Toby for a precise English word when it would not come to her, exploring their mutual knowledge of French where all else failed. The picture began to emerge of a comprehensive battle plan for the city of My Tho. Toby could see that the value of this information was not for the upper levels of the CIA, nor of either government, although its wealth of detail about the plan would add authenticity to Dang's general information about the rest of the country. The principal use of these meticulous details was going to be to prepare My Tho for the attack.

Toby knew that it was now time to bring Ben into the picture. He went into the house and asked Ben to come into the office. With Therese still hard at work on the translations, Toby gave Ben a brief account of the Dang operation: of the first reports, which were still sitting in Can Tho, and of the receipt of the material they were working on now.

Ben was interested and excited by the operation itself, but that interest was quickly replaced by an intense desire to study the details of the battle plan. He was impressed with the military skill that had devised it.

"There is only one thing wrong with it, Toby," he said. "Even if all the forces he lists are really available, they still aren't enough to capture and hold a city like My Tho. They can do a lot of damage, maybe hold parts of the place for a long time, but unless ARVN and our own people make some crazy mistakes, the VC haven't got a chance. And yet, here they are, coming out of hiding all at once for a face-to-face battle, in the open field."

"But they're expecting that this attack is going to be accompanied by a mass uprising of the people," said Toby.

"Oh, sure, they're talking about the struggle of the masses and all of that, but they always have that crap in their papers."

"If I had the time," said Toby, "I could show you that in this case what they're saying is not just Communist jargon and slogans, Ben. There's a difference that you don't catch, unless you've been studying and living with it for years. In this case what they're saying is not just a bunch of Marxist-Leninist catch phrases. These words mean exactly what they say. These guys are really depending on the people all over South Vietnam to rise up and help them fight."

Ben shook his head. "I didn't think they were that stupid. It'll never happen. You can't make a crowd of people fight a battle. You can't even make them fight back when you attack them, unless they're an organized military unit."

"That's what Dang says."

"All the more reason why you should trust Dang."

"That brings up a worrisome point," said Toby, fingering one of the translations. "I'm still a little uneasy about how Dang came to know all the things he gives us in these papers and his note. After all, he's just a battalion commander, and I doubt if the high command at COSVN takes him into their confidence. Especially about a thing they want to keep a secret."

"I wouldn't worry about it," said Ben cheerfully. "If he's got enough common sense to see the basic flaw in their whole plan, he's got enough common sense to find out a lot of things from the rest of those dummies. This information is so good, it's just *got* to be right."

The picture emerged clearly and completely. The Yenan Battalion would be charged with occupying the provincial government compound and the tactical operations center. One platoon would be detailed to go through the dense residential neighborhoods, to carry out missions of "control and security," whatever that meant. Whatever it was was bound to be unpleasant. The central command post for the Viet Cong attack on the city would be a big pagoda in the center of town. Supplies of weapons and ammunition had already been accumulating in the pagoda for many weeks. The 23rd Local Force Battalion would be responsible for the sector of the city in which their own house and office compound was located. The nearest specific target for a part of the 23rd was a house one block down the street from Toby's compound, which would be occupied by a platoon shortly after midnight. Its task would be to ambush a South Vietnamese Ranger Battalion, which would come along that street into the city at the first news of a Viet Cong attack. Dang's report indicated that the Viet Cong had detailed knowledge of the South Vietnamese military plans for the defense of the city. The rest of the 23rd would close the trap around the Ranger Battalion, and destroy it.

Dang's Determination-to-Win Battalion had the sector of the city near the airport. Other local force battalions had been moved into place and were assigned specific areas of the residential and business districts of the city. Infiltration of troops would begin the day before the attack was to be launched.

"Toby," Ben repeated, leaning back in his chair thoughtfully, "this information can't possibly be false, or a plant. It rings too true. You've got the truth here, and you've just got to persuade Can Tho and Saigon to believe it and spread it around. This whole goddamned country is about to blow up in our faces."

"OK. Now, we've got to make up an intelligence report from this that will give enough of the facts to help people get ready, but written so it won't point to Dang as the source. A report has got to go to Manh, and Manh's office is probably penetrated by the VC. If Dang comes through this alive, he may be able to get back in touch with us, and become a regular agent. In any event, I don't want to get him shot.

"It's too late for me to call Jerry to get a plane up here, and when I call him tomorrow I'm going to have to take pretty much what he'll let me have as a matter of routine."

"Christ, Toby, this is *urgent!* Tell him it is! He'll have a plane up here in an hour."

"I can't do that. If the VC aren't monitoring our single sideband transmissions they're more stupid than they've given any sign of being. Suppose you had an action like this scheduled, and then a person in my profession and location suddenly puts in a scream for immediate transportation, and then preparations start all over the country—"

"I get it," Ben stopped him with an upraised hand. "OK, so you get to Can Tho as soon as you can, and then beat it back up here, right? We're gonna be busy as hell around here, you know."

"I know. It'll be down and back for me, nothing more. When I get down there and can talk to Jerry in person, instead of on the air, I can persuade him how urgent my needs are."

They worked until the early hours of the morning, and at last Toby had reports prepared for Manh, and for Can Tho to put into the official channels for dissemination through Vietnam and back to Washington. Nothing more could be done until the working day began.

"Therese, it's late," said Toby. Ben was within earshot. "You could lie down and sleep somewhere in the house until daylight, if you like."

"No, Mr. Busch," she said. "I would prefer to go home."

"I'll take you in the jeep."

While she was putting things away, Toby called Louise on the Victory net. They double-talked briefly, and Louise managed to convey to him that she and Peggy would be at the hospital if trouble started. Not only would it be as safe or safer than other locations, but there was also their own usefulness and professional responsibility to be considered. Marie Claire could do as she wished, and woud be guided by her own supervisor. Toby could not argue with that. He hung up the microphone grudgingly, and went out to the jeep with Therese.

He was tired, and it was cool. He drove slowly, enjoying

the quietness of the nearly spent night, curiously relaxed and relieved now that they had done everything they could do at this stage of developments. Now he could speak to Therese about her pregnancy.

"Therese," he began, "will you forgive me for what I said about the baby?"

"It has . . . been difficult to—" she said, slowly, measuring her words.

"I wasn't thinking," Toby interrupted her. "Or, rather, I was thinking, but only of myself and my own feelings, and I see now that I was being terribly selfish. I still won't like the idea of being the father of a child I'll never know, even though you are the mother. But I do know that you will care for it well. What I'm trying to say now is what I refused to say for you the other night. Therese, I do want you to have our baby."

He had reached her pathway, and he drew the jeep to a halt by the curb. She sat still, staring straight ahead.

"What's the matter, Therese? Don't you understand what I've been saying?"

"It is too late," she said tonelessly.

"What do you mean, it's too late?"

"It is too late to save the baby. I have already done as you asked."

"You had an abortion? Already?" he gasped.

"Yes. Two days ago."

"Oh, God."

She turned and stared at him with burning eyes. "The Viet Cong killed my other babies," she said, with a harshness he had never before heard in her voice. "This one I killed myself."

Toby sat, thunderstruck, as she slipped out of the jeep and ran down the path into the gloom.

[22]

THE slackness of the season made it possible for Toby to get a plane for Can Tho promptly the following morning, and he was in the ROIC's office by ten o'clock.

But Bill Voigt was not there. He had gone to Saigon, and would be back late in the evening or early the following morning.

Toby swore to himself. It must be some kind of a macumba, or a hex—something that was conspiring to prevent him from getting his intelligence across to the right people and making them believe it.

Chet was still contemptuous. Chet had now reached a point where information that should have made him doubt and reexamine his position only made him all the more stubborn, more resolved not to let any of today's nonsense upset the logical conclusions of the past.

"Chet," Toby told him, "this information is accurate. It has *got* to get to Saigon and Washington!"

"Not until we've got an approved agent or project to attribute it to, it doesn't. How am I supposed to evaluate what you've got here? Do I say, 'Busch says this information is true'?"

"Don't give me that!" Toby retorted. "You know exactly how to word a report under circumstances like these, so it will get read and accepted."

"Sure," said Chet. "*If* I believed it myself—which I don't."

"But look at the details, goddammit!"

"So what we say, then, is: 'This report has got to be true because there's so much of it!' Right?"

"Oh, Christ!"

"Now, look at something else, Busch," Chet went on. "The high-level penetration Saigon is running against

COSVN says this is all a deception operation. These guys learned deception from the Soviets. They're good at it. We've got to be just as professional in our response to it. Do you think this office, or the station in Saigon, or headquarters, is going to want to circulate in official channels one report with detailed information that other reports in the same channels say is false?"

"It isn't false, goddammit."

"*You* say it isn't."

"Ben Compton has seen it. He believes it."

"Oh, well, that's different," said Chet, his voice heavy with sarcasm. "I didn't know that. Then all we've got to do is send it in with a little note at the end saying, 'Ben Compton believes this information.' "

"OK, Chet, have your fun," said Toby, getting up abruptly. "I've got to get back to My Tho, because I know what's coming and I intend to have my town ready for it. I'm leaving these reports right here on your desk. What you do with them is up to you. I've got copies of them in my safe in My Tho, and when I get back I'm going to note on those copies that I have delivered the originals to you at ten o'clock A.M. on January 29."

"Be my guest," Chet sneered.

"I would advise you to show those reports to Bill Voigt as soon as he comes back, if you're not going to transmit them electronically through channels before then. If you don't tell Bill, you're making a decision on your own that may haunt you for the rest of your life."

"I've done exactly that before, in your case, don't you remember?"

"Goddammit, can't you forget Frankfurt for one minute? This is Vietnam. This is the biggest action the Viet Cong have ever tried. This isn't one agent, this is a whole country, two whole armies!"

"Two whole armies and Ben Compton," Chet grinned.

Toby ignored the gibe. "Will you tell Bill?" he insisted.

"If he isn't too busy, I may."

Therese had not come to work when he got back, but Toby had other urgent matters on his mind, and he gave her absence only scant attention. She had worked late, after all, and she was emotionally overwrought, as he would be if he were to let himself stop and think about their problems. Let her have time to rest and think.

He picked up the reports they had made up for Colonel Manh. They were in orderly array, and impeccably neat, just as she had typed and arranged them. He drove to the PSA's office to borrow the interpreter once more.

How he did miss Minnie! The soft-spoken, quick-witted man had become such an indispensable part of his day and his work that his absence made a real physical gap. But it wasn't only that. It was the sadness—no, the tragedy—of the death of a man like Minnie. He was a loss to his American friends, and a loss to the Vietnamese.

And surprisingly brave. Toby had known that Minnie was courageous, but he had not expected the automatic, almost insane heroism of that moment of the ambush, when Minnie was the first to react, was the only one who had the automatic reflexes to oppose an enemy ambush with immediate, aggressive action.

The longer he lived, the more Toby perceived that the world is full of great men who are never recognized publicly for their greatness. He had to place Tran Van Minh among those unrecognized heroes. The only award or monument Minnie would ever have would be in the memories of the friends he had left behind. That was the case with many of the world's true heroes.

But why should that be the only recognition? He suddenly knew that there was something he could and must do. He must set the wheels in motion to have Minnie decorated posthumously for his bravery.

The idea awoke him to yet another thing, and he cursed his thoughtlessness. He had not taken any steps to notify anybody about Minnie's death, and it was *his* responsibility. The PRU had its own machinery for that, but Minnie was *his* employee, and it was up to him to advise the next of kin. He didn't know who that would be. Perhaps the brother he went to see. He would have Therese help him with that as soon as she came in.

He couldn't blame Therese if she hated him. But he couldn't believe that she ever would. Everything seemed to be piling up on him at once, and things were in such a process of telescoping urgency that he had little time to think calmly and sensibly about any single problem, or to try to deal with it serenely.

He and the interpreter got an immediate audience with Manh, and Toby gave him the reports about the preparations for the assault on My Tho. He apologized to Manh for not yet being able to reveal to him the exact source of the information, and lied to him that he hoped and expected to reveal that source to him in due course.

Manh gave the papers a quick glance, and Toby sensed with a sinking heart that he was not immediately impressed. He was seeing in the policeman the same reaction he had witnessed everywhere—what seemed to be an almost willful refusal to believe, a desire *not* to believe, buttressed by soothing press and governmental releases that the truce was to be observed.

Toby even toyed briefly with the idea of trying to go personally to the various unit commanders around the city, to alert them, but knew that even if they believed him, which they would not, they would never take orders from him or make preparations that were not in accordance with the orders and policies of their own chains of command.

All during the next day Toby thought repeatedly of the phrase "the calm before the storm," and decided that he had never before fully appreciated its significance. Everything around their house and office had taken on a tranquility and a slowness of movement and reaction that seemed to his keyed-up senses nothing short of surrealistic. And yet the day passed swiftly.

The first thing he did was to drive to the women's house before time for them to leave for their work. He repeated to them his warning of the impending attack, told them he had had additional confirmation of the information, and demanded from them a careful schedule of their plans for the following day. He wrote out this schedule on a sheet of paper and made a copy for them.

"If you're going to deviate from this in any significant way," he said, "call me on the Victory net. I'll try to be near a set all day, and I'll answer to Victory-One, whatever set I'm near."

The women were impressed by his seriousness, and

promised to do as he said. Marie Claire would be at work in the Province Senior Adviser's office during the morning, but they were scheduled to take the afternoon off because of the Tet holiday. The two nurses would be on duty from 8:00 A.M. at the hospital. They did not think that they would have any time off, but said that if they did, they would spend it at home, and would advise Toby.

The rest of the morning Toby and Ben spent in preparation of a map and a Viet Cong battle plan for the city of My Tho, based on the information supplied by Dang.

"Although," Toby said dubiously at one point, "I wonder what good it's going to do? We can sit here and watch the battle develop, but if Manh and Can Tho and Saigon don't believe the information, the plan will be carried out without a hitch. Very little we could do about it."

"You might be surprised," said Ben. "Having a complete set of the enemy's plans may be better than having several hundred troops."

"How do you figure that?"

Ben straightened up from the map on the desk. "Those Viet Cong troops are going to come out of the woodwork for the first time and stand up straight and fight a full-scale battle in the field. They've never done that before, and they're going to find it quite a bit different than hit-and-run attacks, ambushes, sapper squads, and things like that. In this case they're going to be committed to win, not just do damage and run. They're not going to be able to get away from us this time."

Toby looked narrowly at Ben. Ben's eyes were shining with an expression Toby had never seen in them before.

"Jesus, you really mean that!"

"About them not getting away from us?"

"Yes."

"Damn right! Tomorrow we're going to see if the VC are men or boys."

"Just you and me and Little Jack?"

"Yep, and anybody else that wants to get in on the fun."

Toby laughed mirthlessly. "You've got a weird idea of fun. With you in that kind of mood, I sure hope the ARVN and everybody else is ready. You're likely to get us killed."

* * *

Therese had not yet appeared by lunchtime, and Toby spoke to Mrs. Chao. Mrs. Chao was also concerned, and dispatched Chi Hai by cyclo to see what was the matter.

Ben and Toby had a light lunch, and then, after putting the finishing touches on the map, they set about cleaning and oiling every one of the weapons, from handguns to the heavy machine gun on the roof.

"The middle of a battle is no time to find out that a bolt on an automatic weapon won't slam back and fire the next round," Ben said. Toby had had one hands-on session years ago on the firing of the M-2 machine gun; so Ben took him to the roof and drilled him repeatedly on feeding ammunition, aiming, firing, handling.

"If it fails to fire," Ben told him, "wait for about five seconds, then pull the bolt back this way, let it go, re-lay the weapon, and fire it. You've always got to be sure this cover here is latched, and make sure the belt is straight. Got that?"

Toby nodded, and they went over the drills several more times.

Chi Hai returned. Therese was not feeling well, she said, and could not come to work today.

"Therese very sad," Mrs. Chao told him. "Therese sick here." She placed a hand over her heart.

"I know," said Toby. "I am sad, too."

"Today, she not want see you," Mrs. Chao went on. "I know. But one week, maybe two week, she feel right, she love you again. This very hard for woman."

"I know, Mrs. Chao. Thank you."

He sensed through the simple, halting speech a fund of sympathy for himself as well as for Therese, and silently blessed the little woman for understanding. He knew that she would be an ally when the time came to make amends.

He spoke to Little Jack about what they should do with the PRUs.

"We ought to wait," said Little Jack. "Manh has got first call on them, and if we give them an assignment beforehand he'll be madder'n hell. If he hasn't given them some mission when the attack comes, if it comes, then we can do anything we want to with 'em and always have the excuse that we saw he wasn't using them anyway. Know what I mean?"

"Yes. I guess it's the only thing we can do."

"Well," said Ben about the middle of the afternoon. "I think we've got things in pretty good shape. Now, to judge by past performance, Ski will be popping in on us before long."

"You think so?"

"Yep. Ski usually comes down here the day before a holiday, and I'm damned sure he will before this one. He missed Christmas and New Year's, and except for that dust-up you guys had with the ambush, things have been awfully quiet all over the delta. When the rest of the country is quiet, Moc Hoa is stonecold dead. Ski gets too bored up there to even play with himself, and so he comes down here, or goes over to Vinh Long, to drink and tell lies."

"Yeah, but when Bill Voigt saw that information I left," Toby said, "I'll lay you ten to one he sent word out to everybody in the provinces to be ready. Ski wouldn't leave Moc Hoa in that case, would he?"

"No, not Ski. He may not be the greatest brain in the world, but he would never leave his duty post during an emergency or an alert."

"Furthermore," Toby went on, "I don't know what he'd eat. Mrs. Chao and Chi Hai are going to spend the night with relatives and celebrate Tet with them tomorrow."

"If there's food around, Ski will take care of himself. He doesn't set that much store by elegance or good cooking."

They went over to the RD offices in the government compound to a Tet party. They went out of a sense of duty, a social obligation to Vietnamese counterparts and associates, and watched while a collection of small men drank themselves into a frenzy of camaraderie and good spirits with expensive French cognac. It didn't take long. An hour and a half later, Toby and Ben took their leave and returned to the office.

"Boy!" Toby exclaimed, "getting smashed on something like cognac—you know their heads are going to be busting tomorrow morning."

"Yep," Ben agreed.

"And I didn't see a sign of any preparation for the attack."

"No," Ben said. "But then, the attack is scheduled for tomorrow morning, so Manh may be waiting until later this evening, after dark, to get his forces organized."

"Do you think that's the case?"

"No."

Toby looked sharply at him, and Ben shrugged. "Toby, I don't think anybody in the whole country believes you. Those guys there today didn't act like they did, although I've passed the word through their upper echelons and I've tried to impress on them the necessity to be alert. Of course, they're not combat soldiers, so they don't have much sense of urgency, but they're going to be in the battle anyway."

As if to reinforce Ben's pessimism, they found Ski sitting at the bar when they got back to the house.

"Hey, Ski!" Ben greeted him airily. "VC chase you out of Kien Tuong?"

"Whattaya say, fellas," Ski said. "I helped myself to your beer, because I knew you'd want it that way."

"Didn't Can Tho tell you about the attack?" Toby asked him.

"What attack?"

"The Tet offensive."

"Tet offensive? Never heard of it. Hell, there's a Tet *truce* going on!"

Ben explained briefly to Ski, and led him into the office and showed him the map and the battle plan. Ski whistled softly.

"Christ, Toby, is this for real?"

"I got this from a good agent. It's for real."

"Then how in the hell come Can Tho didn't say nothing to me about it? My house up there in Moc Hoa has got nothing but a handful of Nungs, and with me gone God knows what kind of a watch they're going to keep on things. I gotta get back—" He strode to the single sideband by the breezeway door, then paused and looked back. "You're sure, Toby?" This is not just a 'maybe'?"

"No maybe about it."

"Because there sure ain't any sign that anybody else knows about it. Dino was happy as a clam on the way down—going to a big party up in Can Tho when he gets back. He's gonna love me for making him come back and get me. . . . God almighty, this don't hardly seem possible, that they got good information and nobody is doing anything."

"It's the history of the intelligence business," said Toby. "We never seem to have the effect we ought to have, and half the time it's because we don't have the information, and the rest of the time it's because we've got information and nobody believes it."

Ski grinned. "Like seeing tanks."

"Exactly."

"Yeah, and those tanks aren't there anymore, and now I know that nobody is ever gonna believe I really saw 'em."

"I believe you, Ski."

"Thanks. How can I doubt your information after that?" Ski laughed and called Jerry, and was troubled to find out that Jerry had no way to send for him before dark. Ski would have to wait until morning.

The four of them, Ski, Ben, Little Jack, and Toby, ate a cold supper Mrs. Chao had left, and sat at the bar with cans of beer, waiting. Explosions started up in the street, and Toby was on his feet in an instant.

"Relax, Toby," said Ben. "That's firecrackers. They keep it up all night during Tet."

Toby sat down with a feeble grin.

"Ben," said Ski, "the only weapon I brought is this pistol. You better fix me up with something, don't you think?"

"Sure, Ski, come on," Ben said. He led Ski out to the storeroom, and Toby went along. There was something reassuring about being in the presence of these two men, who knew what to do at times like this, who took so much in their stride the prospect of a battle in the morning. It calmed his own seething insides, gave him some measure of confidence.

But he knew that he would never again volunteer for an assignment "where the action is."

[23]

It was midnight, and the Tet party in Can Tho was at its peak. Bill Voigt stood by the bar of the little lounge in the compound and looked foggily at the crowd of merry-makers. Dino was dancing with one of the nurses. Jerry was shaking a set of liar's dice with Russ, the commo man. A couple of people from an Ohio State University Research Team that was quartered at the far end of the compound were sitting with several of the USAID public relations people, who also had offices in the area. All of Bill's regional staff were there, as well as the Phong Dinh Province staff, and Wilbur Hamilton.

Even Chet had unwound more than Bill had ever known him to do; had, in fact, gotten somewhat bagged on CC and water.

The Christmas truce had been peaceful, and things had been quiet ever since, except for that astonishing ambush Toby Busch's people had run into. No question about it, they had uncovered an important hideout, probably of the Yenan Battalion. He would make sure Toby got full credit for that. Although, on the other hand, Little Jack surely ought to have handled that search operation better than that. *Christ, eighteen men killed.*

He looked at Chet, who was leaning on the bar beaming at nothing.

"Looks like our uneasiness about Viet Cong action during Tet was off the mark, Chet," he said. "Everything's calm and peaceful."

"Yeah," Chet replied. "Except for Busch, I guess. He's got his own private Tet offensive going."

"His Tet offensive? What's he doing, planning another search operation right away?"

"No, it's what he says the VC are planning. He's hollering that the VC are going to attack us tomorrow."

"Oh?" responded Bill idly, toying with the glass on the bar before him. "What's he got, some kind of a crystal ball?"

"No," muttered Chet, with something that sounded like a cross between a snort and a giggle, "I don't think either one of his balls is made of crystal, but I think his head is made of Jell-O."

"Well, you gotta admit he found a VC hideout the other day."

"Yeah, and got eighteen more men killed."

Bill did not respond. There was no point in arguing with Chet, especially about something he had such unreasoning responses to, and most especially when he was drunk.

"Him and his goddamned penetration," said Chet, taking a drink from the nearly empty glass.

"Penetration?"

"Yeah. Wunnerful great big goddamned penetration he says he's got. Brings me all kinds of crap from it."

"What's he been bringing you?" Bill asked, suddenly sober. "I've never seen any of it."

" 'Course not! Why should you be bothered with it? It's a whole pisspot full of stuff, but he never was able to get enough information on his agent so we could clear him, and then he said the agent was under surveillance, and he was out of touch, and then he was back in touch with a dead drop, and he comes down here with a great big goddamned battle plan of the Viet Cong and expects me to put that out in an intel—at the same time the Saigon penetration operation is getting constant take, straight from the horse's mouth, that it's all a deception, and—"

"Chet, listen to me," said Bill sternly. "Did Busch bring reports in about a Tet attack—specific information?"

"Yeah."

"When?"

"Yesterday morning. I looked it over. Bunch of bullshit!"

"Where did he get the information?"

"I just told you. From some guy that says he's a local force battalion commander."

"Come on," said Bill. "I'm going with you to your office. I want you to get that stuff out and show me."

Chet shrugged and walked behind Bill across the driveway into the ROIC offices.

Ten minutes later Bill was leafing through the papers Toby had left, his eyes wide with astonishment, sweat starting from every pore.

"Chet," he said, looking intently at the other man, who was sitting drowsy-eyed across the desk, "at the very best, what you've done here is the stupidest thing I've ever seen, and at worst it's downright criminal!"

"Come on," said Chet indignantly. "That stuff—"

"This stuff may be true, or highly exaggerated, or even false, but it is intelligence that should have been disseminated with IMMEDIATE precedence the minute you got it. You've got all the elements necessary here for the customer to study the information and judge for himself. And yet *you* interposed your own judgment that it is false, and stopped it cold."

"It *is* false," said Chet.

"You'd better be saying prayers for the rest of the night that it is," said Bill, "and even if it is false, this action of yours of sitting on a report is going to go into your record. You've let a personal feeling about another officer distort your judgment and get in the way of your professional obligations."

"Now, just hold on a goddamned minute!" Chet exclaimed. "How in hell can they do anything to me for—"

"And," Bill continued, "if the information turns out to be true, you're going to spend the rest of your career running errands in headquarters, unless they decide to fire you. So, as I say, you better hope it isn't true.

"Now I want you to get every one of the officers in here, and Laura too. We're going to have a staff meeting, and I'm going to do as much as possible to get us ready and warn the rest of the country."

Chet rose and made as if to protest.

"Move!" Bill said coldly. "Move your ass like you've never moved it before!"

The staff assembled with the boisterous good humor of the party they had left, but Bill's steely purposefulness brought them around quickly. Each man was ordered to check the locations of the persons under his supervision, and do whatever he could to alert them, all over the delta. They must not give out any specific information over the single sideband, but the matter was urgent enough, and far enough along, that they would allow the Viet Cong monitors to conclude that something urgent was causing a great deal of traffic.

Having energized and dispatched his staff to alert the entire region, Bill dictated a paragraph that was to accompany the cabled intelligence report the reports officer was even now preparing.

"Make this FLASH precedence," he said to Laura.

Chet protested. "Christ, if you alert the whole world that way, and then it turns out—"

"Come here, Chet," Bill said, leading his deputy outside, where nobody could hear them. When they were alone, he grabbed Chet's arm.

"Next time you butt in on this," he rasped, "I'll say whatever I've got to say in front of anybody that's around. But this is one more time I'm going to answer you in private. If it hadn't been for your stupidity, I wouldn't be having to lay my own reputation on the line by putting out a FLASH message. This information could have gone with nothing but a priority, or maybe an immediate precedence if it had been handled the minute you got it. As it is, FLASH precedence may save something, maybe not much.

"Now, if you can be of any help around here, pitch in. If not, get the hell back to the bar, or to bed."

Bill marched back into his office and dictated the cable.

His reports officer was just coming in with the finished intelligence report when he was signing off on the operational information to go with it.

"Thank God Busch is a pro," said the reports officer. "That report was a beauty just as he turned it in. All I had to do was look up some references, and fix up the dissemination line."

"It looks serious, doesn't it?"

"I gotta say that that report is damned convincing. Chet must have been out of his mind—"

"Here is the ops information to go with your intel," Bill said, handing the page to the reports officer just as the commo man came in to pick up the material for transmission.

THE FOLLOWING INFORMATION WAS OBTAINED FROM A SOURCE AT THE MIDDLE LEVEL OF THE VIET CONG MILITARY COMMAND. HE IS A NEW SOURCE, AND UNTESTED. THE RELIABILITY OF HIS INFORMATION CANNOT BE JUDGED, AND WE REALIZE THAT IT CONTRADICTS THE VOLUMINOUS REPORTING SAIGON STATION HAS BEEN RECEIVING FROM A HIGH-LEVEL VIET CONG SOURCE IN THE PAST (SEE REFERENCES), BUT FIELD ASSESSMENT BOTH OF THIS AGENT AND OF HIS INFORMATION LEADS ROIC TO BELIEVE THAT THIS REPORT IS ACCURATE. THE WEALTH OF DETAILS WITHIN THE AREA OF AGENT'S KNOWLEDGE, THE TENOR OF HIS JUDGMENTS AND SPECULATIONS IN AREAS BEYOND HIS COMPETENCE, AND THE COINCIDENCE BETWEEN HIS INFORMATION AND THE RESULTS OF A RECENT SEARCH OPERATION IN DINH TUONG PROVINCE, WHICH THE AGENT COULD NOT HAVE KNOWN AT THE TIME OF HIS REPORT, ARE ELEMENTS THAT INVITE CAREFUL CONSIDERATION. THIS REPORT IS MORE, AND IT IS BETTER, THAN WOULD HAVE BEEN LOGICAL OR REQUIRED BY A DECEPTION OPERATION. ROIC BELIEVES IT TO BE TRUE, AND THIS REGION IS BEING PREPARED FOR ACTION AS WELL AS POSSIBLE AT THIS LATE HOUR.

FOR REASONS THAT WILL BE CLARIFIED ELSEWHERE THIS REPORT IS LATE GETTING INTO CHANNELS. IT IS FOR THIS REASON THAT IT IS BEING TRANSMITTED WITH FLASH PRECEDENCE.

"OK," said Bill, signing off on the documents and handing them to Russ. "Let's get this on the air, while the rest of us get some weapons issued and get set for whatever is coming."

[24]

TOBY was not sure whether it was good news or bad, when the single sideband began to chatter with messages back and forth across the delta. It was obvious that Can Tho had at last gone on the alert, which was good; but if they were so late that the warning was coming only now, it was bad.

Well, that was Bill's problem. From here on, Toby had to concentrate on My Tho.

"Toby," said Ben, "I think we ought to turn that generator off. It's like a beacon to anybody around."

"You're right," Toby replied. "Will you attend to it, please?"

Ben went out, and the deep roar of the diesel engine ceased abruptly. The lights went out, except for two or three small fixtures that were on the city circuits.

"I'm going up on the roof," Ben said, when he came back in. "I think we'll want to set up watches for the night, before any of us hits the sack."

"I couldn't sleep right now, anyway," said Toby. He followed Ben up the stairs. Little Jack and Ski stayed at the bar, cans of beer in their hands.

It was the night of the new moon, only the light of the stars and the zodical light to see by on the roof, although the streets were dimly lighted by streetlights. The two of them sat down on sandbags near one corner of the roof. Everything was quiet. They could make out the shadowy forms of the guards below, each in his place. Ben had seen to that.

"Sure doesn't seem like any attack can be coming right away," Toby murmured.

"No, but a good part of their forces were going to infiltrate during the day, remember. As far as I know, nobody has done a thing to prevent that."

"Not that you could tell."

"I don't think anybody even went over to look at that pagoda," Ben went on.

"No. I understand they're awfully touchy about messing around with pagodas," Toby said.

"Who, the VC?"

"No, the South Vietnamese government."

Ben shifted his weight and peered idly down the street. "I don't see any sign that that platoon has moved into the house down there," he said.

"No. No sign yet," Toby agreed.

They were silent for a time.

"You don't get nervous, or scared, when you know a battle is coming?" Toby asked.

"Oh, sure, you get nervous," Ben said. He understood and sympathized with Toby. "I'm always nervous until it starts, because up till then I don't know what's going to happen, or how or where. After it starts, you're too busy to be nervous."

"I'll try not to get you killed, but you're going to have to teach me. You remember we said I'd teach you intelligence work, and you could teach me combat?"

"Yeah."

"I was kidding at the time."

"I thought so."

"It's not a joke, though."

"No, but you'll be all right, Toby. I understand you did real well with the PRU ambush the other day."

Toby was pleased, but dubious. "I've been wondering ever since if I shouldn't have done something, instead of just firing a couple of rounds and running like hell."

"From what I hear," Ben said, "you all walked right into a real sweet ambush. By the time they pulled the chain there was only one smart thing to do, and that was get the hell out."

"I hope you're right."

"I'm pretty sure I am."

"It still leaves me feeling guilty and unsatisfied. We lost eighteen men, including Minnie."

"I know how you feel, Toby. No way to overcome those feelings. What I meant to say about it was that a man without experience couldn't be expected to make a judgment about what to do. The main thing was, you kept control of yourself, you didn't panic, you didn't bug out and leave a buddy exposed. Things like that."

"Running away isn't much of a test, though."

"Oh, well . . ."

"And there's not going to be any running away tomorrow."

"You're right, there, pardner. What we're gonna do tomorrow is run *at* 'em, not *away* from 'em."

"You know you're crazy, don't you?" Toby said. Ben chuckled. Then he straightened up.

"Toby, look!" he said softly.

There in the street more than a block away were shadowy figures moving toward them.

"That must be the platoon that'll occupy that house down there to ambush the Ranger platoon," said Toby.

"Yeah," Ben replied. "The problem is, they're coming on past the house they're supposed to take over."

Ben was right. The figures moved silently toward them, across the intersection.

"Keep an eye on them," said Ben. "I've got to make sure those guards don't open up on that bunch unless they start firing first, or unless we start it from the roof. I'll send Ski and Little Jack up."

Ben slipped away in the dark, and Toby chambered a round in his rifle. He sat motionless behind the low revetment, watching the enemy draw near.

The shadowy figures grew in number as their line snaked up the street. From what Toby could make out, they seemed to have no intention of doing anything to his own house, and it was a consoling thought. But that they were Viet Cong troops there was no doubt. He was now peering down at his enemy, a sizable number of armed men, bent on some business that Dang's report had not described.

The other three joined him on the roof, and he was greatly comforted by the presence of three combat-wise veterans.

The figures in the street formed a knot directly across the street, and then began to fade into the darkness around the big house that stood there.

"What the hell are they up to?" Toby whispered to Ben.

"Damned if I can figure it out. Wait a minute. That's the

platoon that ought to be occupying the house down the street, all right. They've got the wrong house!"

"Damned if I don't think you're right," Toby said.

"Maybe they were told to home in on our lights and generator, a block away, and didn't find them. Anyway, if they know anything about our house at all, they'll think we're a block farther up that way. They'll have no idea we're right across the street from them."

"So, what should we do?"

In answer, Ben quietly summoned the other two, and they sat close together and talked in low voices. "Fellows, that Ranger Battalion hasn't been alerted to this, it's a leadpipe cinch. They're gonna be coming up this street when the fighting starts, and they'll run into an amubush right here."

"I'll be goddamned!" exclaimed Ski.

"All right, then," Ben went on, "if that's the way it is, here's what we've got to do. We'll keep a constant watch on that house from now on. If we open fire on them we'll ruin their ambush, but they might get away."

"Jesus, Ben," said Ski, "you can't let the Rangers walk into an ambush."

"I don't intend to. We'll wait until we can see the Rangers coming down there, way down the street. As soon as they get to a certain point, we'll open up on that house with everything we've got. That'll alert the Rangers, and if I know that battalion they'll fan out and come on up here ready for some fun, and we'll just naturally pound the piss out of our friends over there."

"Yeah," said Ski. His voice was steady, but emotionless.

"And they won't get away," Ben added.

Ski and Little Jack moved to the far corner of the house, and Toby sat with Ben, their eyes keeping constant watch over the house opposite them. For a while they observed the arrival of dark figures, the movement around the forecourt of the house, the placement of a machine gun near the street. Toby could make out several of the men holding a well-known weapon faintly outlined in the dim light: B-40 rocket launchers. There was no doubt at all that this was the platoon they had spoken of, and that it had occupied the wrong house.

At last the enemy was prepared, and settled down to

wait. Toby could not fathom their obtuseness in not noticing that the house across the street from them was walled and bunkered, but then realized that most of the bunkering would not be visible from the other side, especially at night.

The minutes dragged by slowly. Ski came creeping up to where they were and whispered, "Wonder what happened to Little Jack?"

"Isn't he over there with you?"

"He had to go down and take a leak, but he didn't come back."

"Go down and see, will you?" Ben asked.

Ski moved away. He was back within minutes. "He's layin' down there on the couch. Got a bellyache!"

"A bellyache?" Toby exclaimed softly. "Christ, another one?" He went down to the common room. There was Little Jack, curled up on his side, just as he had been in the field the other day, his face pale with pain.

"Is it the same as the other day?" Toby asked him.

"Yeah. Hurts like hell."

"Did you take anything for it?"

"I took some aspirin, but it didn't do any good yet."

Toby went back up to the roof. Ben and Ski were sitting close together, conversing in low tones.

"It's just like it was the other day," said Toby. "He's out of action."

"I figured as much," said Ben.

"Hell of a note, isn't it?"

"I guess the pain is real enough," said Ben, "but I don't think it's caused by the belly. It's caused by the balls—or the lack of them."

"Doesn't seem possible," Toby replied. "A guy that's seen as much action as that."

"What action has he seen?"

"Well, he's got scars and he says he was in Korea, and was a prisoner."

"That's what he says," said Ben drily. "I'd want to look at his service record."

"Some things are beginning to clear up here," Toby mused. "His operations with the PRU, for example."

"Yeah."

"But I never heard of him getting a bellyache on those operations before."

"He never before seems to have gotten into a real fight on any of those operations. One shot and they bugged out."

"But how could a guy be a professional soldier all his life like that and get scarred up, and still . . . ?"

"Some of 'em are real artists," said Ben.

"Yep," said Ski. "You find one of 'em once in a while. You learn never to put too much trust in what a guy *says* about his soldierin'. If you depend on that, you can end up just like we did tonight. And that reminds me that I better get back over there to my side and start actin' like a soldier instead of an old woman." He crept over to the other corner and took up his position.

"Maybe I ought to go down and see if there isn't something Little Jack can do in this business," Toby suggested.

"Leave him alone," said Ben. "Even if he agreed to do something, you couldn't be sure he'd do it. Better to have nobody than somebody you can't depend on."

The hours of darkness dragged on. Ben made another tour of the premises, instructed the guards in what he expected to do, told them to open fire when the firing began from the roof.

About an hour before daylight, heavy explosions began to occur in other parts of the city. "Probably satchel charges," said Ben, "or maybe B-Forties. They won't use mortars much in this action, because they've got their own troops so scattered around the city. Our friends across the street don't have any satchel charges, apparently. They're not expecting to hit any buildings—they're just waiting for the Rangers."

Ski now moved over to the machine gun and checked it. He assumed a position behind it, businesslike, calm. Toby felt an impulsive surge of admiration and affection for these men, who knew what had to be done, set about doing it calmly and matter-of-factly. These were great men.

"Toby, can you throw a grenade that far?" Ben asked.

Toby measured the distance with his eye, was sure he could.

"All right then," Ben continued, "when Ski starts firing with that M-Two, they're gonna be real surprised. They won't react all at once. You put a grenade rght in the middle of that little yard, huh? Be sure to get down after you throw. We could get some fragments even up this high.

Then we'll open up on them with our rifles. Just keep up the fire is the main thing. Pattern your firing on Ski. OK?"

"OK," said Toby, his throat taut, his ribs tight with fear.

"You're gonna be all right," said Ben, settling himself against a sandbag, his rifle at the ready, his eyes glued to the scene across the street.

"I may die trying," said Toby, "but I'll never in all my life understand why a man would choose a profession that would subject him to this kind of a thing."

"A man doesn't have any other moments in his life that will compare with what's coming," said Ben quietly.

"You love combat, don't you?"

"I don't think you'd call it loving combat. But I do know that there's something about this, it's a kind of coming to life. You live more in a few minutes than most men live in a lifetime."

"Do you enjoy the killing?"

"You can't have combat without killing, but it's more than that. Right now, for instance, what's best about this thing is that they're going to fight. We've got the bastards where they can't get away. We're going to measure them."

"And measure ourselves."

"Yeah. And that's another good part of it. You measure yourself against another man. But this measure is the big one. The big test. You kill him or he kills you."

"I'll never understand it."

"I can say one thing," Ben went on, shifting his weight slightly to find a more comfortable position, "I could never be a pilot, or a gunship man, or I don't even think I'd like artillery. That all puts you at a distance, and then combat becomes a question of accidents."

"You want to kill each man personally?"

"I think a war where you don't look the man in the eye when you kill him is not war. It's just a kind of butchery. The side that kills the most wins."

"I'd think it would be the other way around. To be able to look a man in the eye, and then kill him . . ."

"If you have to kill him, you should honor him," said Ben.

"Honor him?"

"Yeah. For instance, Ski is about to kill that man over there with the machine gun. I've got two men in positions close to him that I'm going to kill. I don't hate them. I almost have a kind of an affection for them. Can you understand that?"

"No."

"Those men and you and I have a lot more in common than we have with the guys in the spookies and the F-104s and the gunships. If we sat down together and talked, we'd find them a lot easier to talk to, to get next to, than we'd find the pilots to be, even though they're our enemies and the pilots are on our side.

"And," Ben went on with a quick gesture of his hand, "I sure am glad as hell that there wasn't a newspaper reporter or a television team around to hear me say that."

"Yeah, I guess they wouldn't understand, even as well as I do."

"Understand?" Ben said derisively. "They wouldn't *try* to understand. They wouldn't even *care* about understanding. They'd just report it, and it would sound like hell, and they'd have a headline."

"Yep."

"Remember that thing about 'We had to destroy that village to save it'?"

"Sure. That's going to be just as famous as 'Remember the Maine!' or 'Damn the torpedoes!' "

"Don't you feel sorry for the poor bastard that said it?"

"Sorry for him? I never thought about it," said Toby, puzzled.

"Can you imagine any soldier, even the dumbest one in the army, being stupid enough to say something like that and meaning it just that way?"

"No, I guess not."

"If you stop to look at it, you can figure out exactly what happened."

"What?"

"Well, this guy has just burned a village down. I don't know what the real reason was, but I'll assume there was a legitimate military reason for it. I've been in exactly the same situation myself. Now, even the biggest prick in the world won't burn down people's houses without feeling something about it, some kind of regret, you know?"

"I wouldn't think so."

"So here's this guy, looking at the village he's just

burned down, feeling like eight kinds of a shit heel for it, and a reporter comes up to him and asks him how he feels —you know how they do, like they go up to a woman who's just had her husband killed in a car wreck and ask her how she feels about it?"

"Uh-huh."

"So the guy is upset, and he says those words, 'We had to destroy it to save it,' and he was being, you know, sarcastic, facetious . . . what's the word?"

"Ironic?"

"Ironic! That's the word. He's being ironic. Now, if you quote that statement in print, without any explanation, it sounds like the guy that said it must be a mindless, heartless son of a bitch. But you've quoted him exactly. See what I mean? What can he complain about? He said the words, and there they are in the paper. And then you have all kinds of editorials and commentators hollerin' about what a monstrous war this is when men can say things like that, and that isn't what the guy really said at all."

"It's a shame you can't get that across to the public."

"Yep."

"But not what you said about liking those guys across the street, and then killing them."

"No. You couldn't really explain that on the printed page," Ben continued. "We're going to kill them, and they would have killed us if it was the other way around, and we know exactly what kind of things they're feeling down there, waiting for the fight. It's almost like you were in church. We don't make the wars, but we fight them. We test ourselves against each other, and if we live through it . . . But then, I always know I'm going to live through it."

"You know?"

"Yeah. When the firing starts, there's a kind of a feeling of invulnerability that comes over me. Hell, I can't explain it."

"Never been wounded?"

"Oh, sure. That doesn't count."

"Doesn't hint to you that next time you might really get it?"

"Nope."

"I can explain it," said Toby.

"How?"

"You're out of your mind."

"I guess maybe I am," Ben chuckled softly.

There was enough daylight now to outline objects in the streets clearly, and they had to be extremely careful not to give themselves away to the enemy.

"Did you ever meet that Ranger Battalion commander?" Ben asked him.

"No."

"He's a little bit of a guy, with a voice like a foghorn. When he yells, you'd think the recoil from the voice would knock him on his back. But he's the fightingest ninety pounds of man you'll ever see. He wears a big forty-five revolver. I don't know where he got it. It isn't military, and it's a foolish weapon for combat, and especially for him—it's so long and he's so short that it almost drags the ground when he walks. But he'll size up the situation within half a minute after we start firing, and you'll see those Rangers deploy and come around that house like a swarm of hornets. You'll have a chance to see a good military operation."

As if on cue from Ben's words, they saw the first vehicles of the battalion appear far down the street. Ben moved over to the other corner. Toby extracted a grenade from the bag by his feet, and waited.

Ben watched as the vehicles drew near. "Now!" he shouted, and Ski began to fire. Toby saw the man behind the machine gun across the street start, kick slightly, and then lie still. Others were being hit, and all of them looked in astonished bewilderment in the direction of this murderous fire. Toby pulled the pin on a grenade, waited, then threw it. He watched long enough to satisfy himself that it would reach the yard, then ducked behind the sandbags. The crump of the grenade brought him up to look, and he could see more still bodies.

"Keep firing," Ben shouted. Toby brought his rifle up and began to fire. By now, they were receiving answering fire from the upper windows across the street, and Toby aimed at those windows. His ears rang. A B-40 rocket entered the room below them and exploded with a shattering crash. Grenades came from across the street and fell in their own courtyard, forcing the guards to crouch even farther down in their bunkers.

Another rocket struck the outer wall around their yard, and went into the guard bunker near the gate. Toby saw the explosion, but could only imagine how the men inside must have been mangled and macerated by it. A ricochet sang off the parapet near him, and he ducked reflexively. Just like Hopalong Cassidy. Even as a kid he had known that if you hear it, it's too late to duck it.

From the courtyard, a small squad of men came sprinting for the gate, to make a charge on the house, and at that same instant every weapon on the Viet Cong side opened up at once on Toby and his comrades.

"That's the way to fight, goddammit!" Ben bellowed. "Come on, Charlie, we're fightin' like men today!" Ski had to crouch down, away from his machine gun because of the intensity of the fire, but Ben threw a grenade at the gate opposite them. It slowed the squad only temporarily. Ski straightened for a moment at the explosion, fired off two short bursts at the approaching squad, and sought cover again. Toby saw that the fire was concentrated on Ski's part of the roof. Plaster and brick dust hung in the air from the metal that was striking the wall of the house up that high. Toby leaned around the edge of his own small revetment and fired at the squad, his rifle on semi-automatic. He hit two of them, before the fire from the upper window across the street veered over to his corner. He flattened himself behind the sandbags and felt the impact of the bullets on the bags.

"That's the way to do it, Toby," Ski roared. As the stream of fire left his location he straightened up, and his machine gun chattered again. Another of the squad fell, and the rest retreated back into the yard.

A lull came in the firing, interrupted only now and then by the pop of a single rifle from across the street or from the guards below. When the firing revived a moment later, it was with a new intensity, and from a different direction. Toby had paid no attention to the Rangers after the firing had started, and he realized now that the Ranger Battalion had read the situation accurately and had already come up behind the Viet Cong's ambush site. A heavy explosion struck the Viet Cong house from somewhere. Now a squad of Rangers came around the corner and moved toward the front of the house, but were driven back behind a low wall next to the house by heavy firing from within. They held there, and from that position kept up a constant fire.

More intense firing began at the rear of the VC house, and it was evident that a massive assault was being made from behind. The squad by the low wall now renewed its own attack, and was soon inside the building.

It was all over. Some of the Rangers came out with several prisoners, stripped to their shorts, and herded them into a truck. A jeep with a heavy machine gun fixed to a frame behind the driver's seat pulled up before the house, and a diminutive man stood up and waved up to Ben.

"Thank you, Major," the man roared, and Toby thought he was hearing an old movie of the booming voice of Eugene Pallette.

Ben shouted something in Vietnamese, and the little colonel laughed. With much waving and shouting, the Ranger convoy resumed its ride up the street.

[25]

WHEN they got downstairs they found the guards tending to their dead comrades. Three had been killed by the rocket. They were being carried gently to the rear of the house and covered with a tarpaulin. Two others had minor wounds.

Little Jack was sitting on the sofa, his face white, his jaw clenched.

Ben went into the office to look at the battle plan. "The government compound is one of the main targets, and it was supposed to be occupied by now," he said. "That will mean the Special Police Offices, the RD building, the works. If anybody believed you, Toby, they were ready for the VC down there, and may have given them a fight. Let's see if they were."

He went to the Victory base station and called the RD office. There was no response. He called the PRU barracks, and got no response.

"Jesus, sounds like they got the whole town," said Ski.

"No," said Ben. "They may have the compound, but not the PRUs, I'm sure. More than likely Manh went down to the PRU barracks and got all the men for himself. They'd be the quickest troops he could lay his hands on, and he'd be after them, first thing. But I am worried about that RD office."

He went to the storeroom and got more ammunition and grenades.

"According to our map," he said, "I can make almost a straight run down to the compound from here without hitting any VC. Toby, you stand by that base station until I get back, will you? Ski, will you get things squared away on the roof, in case we get hit again? The rest of that Twenty-Third Battalion is still down there somewhere wondering what the hell went wrong with their ambush, and they may decide to make our house a secondary objective."

Ski went to the storeroom for more ammunition for the roof, and Ben climbed into the jeep and sped out the gate. Toby went immediately to the Victory base station and picked up the microphone.

"Victory-Five, this is Victory-One. Victory-Five, this is Victory-One. Over."

There was no answer. He repeated the call, to no avail. He hoped that meant that the women were at work, but he was troubled. It was earlier than they should have left the house. If they were at work it was because somebody had summoned them early, which of course was possible in a day that was already full of battle.

Again he repeated the call. This time he was rewarded with two short blips, the breaking of the squelch, the sound that was made on the receiving end when the talk button was depressed on the other end. What could that mean?

"Victory-One, this is Victory-Seven," came Ben's voice. "I caught those blips. Something may be wrong over there. I'll drive by and see."

"Roger, Victory-Seven."

* * *

Louise and Peggy and Marie Claire were huddled in Louise's room, terrified, desperate. Louise had taken the radio set into her room before going to bed, as Toby had ordered, and she had been awakened at dawn by the sound of rifles and explosions she could not identify.

The other two women had burst into her room as she ran to the window, to see a squad of Viet Cong finishing off the four guards at the front of their house, and then calmly killing the last two, who came speeding thoughtlessly around the side of the house from the rear.

The Viet Cong squad had then entered the ground floor. The women heard gunfire, and presumed that the housekeeper and her husband had been killed. Then the trampling of feet as the invaders explored the house. They chattered to one another as they searched. They had entered the other rooms on the second floor, tried Louise's door, and found it locked. They paused awhile, exchanged words with somebody on the ground floor, then descended. There was the sound of other feet in the corridor now and then, and Louise was certain men were stationed upstairs, some probably near her door, but she could not believe that they even suspected the women's presence in her room.

Through the window she watched the Viet Cong preparations. It was as Ben had predicted. They were not interested in *this* house, except as a vantage point. Their attention was mainly centered on the Province Senior Adviser's house, which was already under attack. They took up positions behind the low wall, and elsewhere around the structure, she assumed, although from her window the only VC men she could see were those around the wall. She counted them. Six men, whom she could see, well armed, loaded down with ammunition.

Evidently the women were going to be safe, so long as the battle for the PSA house continued.

Peggy turned to her and began to speak, but Louise quickly clapped her hand on Peggy's mouth and shook her head frantically. They must not make any sound. Peggy pointed to the radio set. Again Louise shook her head. If they spoke, it would alert the Viet Cong to their presence. She was sure that the Viet Cong would eventually discover them, but their only hope was to delay that discovery.

Louise went to a drawer and took out a small pistol, and

held it up ruefully. It was the only weapon she had in the room.

They waited. Louise thought about the poor couple downstairs, killed without hesitation; about the guards, all of them killed in a sudden, surprise attack. She didn't remember that Toby had said anything in his intelligence reports about their own house being a target. If it had been, he certainly would have told them. But, on the other hand, Ben had said long ago that their house was a key point in the area.

The radio came to life, and she could hear Ben calling somebody. Quickly she silenced the speaker, and they waited tensely to see if there was any reaction from outside the door. There was none.

Louise held the telephone-type receiver to her ear and listened to Ben's futile calls. The temptation to speak was almost irresistible, but she knew that they would be dead before help could get to them.

He called another number, and she looked on the card. The PRU barracks. *Ben, for God's sake, call Victory-Five! Victory-Five!*

But what if he did? She couldn't answer. Well, if she didn't answer he would know something was wrong, wouldn't he?

She got out the schedule Toby had made her prepare. According to that schedule they should be right where they were, for at least another hour.

Now it was Toby's voice, and she looked at the other women and gestured with frantic joy. They understood.

Toby called twice, and she could tell by the tone of his voice that he had not reached any conclusion. Then she noticed that each time he began to speak there was a slight click or blip as the transmission began. It was when he pushed the talk button, obviously.

When he called the third time, she pressed the talk button twice. That caught their ear! Now it was Ben's voice replying, wondering about the blips. He was out in the street, apparently. He must be in the jeep with the radio set. And he was coming by.

She looked at the other two and formed the word "Ben" soundlessly with her lips, steering a car in pantomime with her two hands. They crept quickly to the window.

Minutes passed.

"Victory-One, this is Victory-Seven," came Ben's voice. "I have their place in sight now. They've got some Charlies around the front of it, and as near as I can tell the whole place has been taken."

"Victory-Seven, we did get that response from Victory-Five."

"But no voice," said Ben. "Just a couple of clicks. It could be anybody. Let me try again. Victory-Five, whoever you are, are you still on the air?"

Desperately, Louise pushed the button twice again.

"They're there, One," said Ben. "But who they are is another matter."

"Seven," Toby's voice sounded again, "will you stand by for a minute and let me give them a test. Victory-Five, I am going to give you a list of five names. When I come to the name of somebody you saw at Christmastime, give me two clicks. Do you understand, Victory-Five?"

Louise pressed the button twice.

"All right, Victory-Five. Do not break the squelch—that is, do not press the button until you hear the name of the man you saw. Here are the five names. Joseph Murphy . . . Mr. Clean . . . William Voigt . . . Señor Gonzales . . ."

In a rush of relief and silent, hyterical laughter, Louise pressed the button twice.

"Victory-Seven," came Toby's voice, "the goodies are in the package all right."

"Roger, One," Ben replied. "Stand by and let me talk to them now. Victory-Five, listen to me carefully and answer with the button. Twice for yes, and once for no. Understand?"

Louise pressed the button twice.

"Are all three of you together?" Two blips. "Are you upstairs?" Two blips. "Do the Charlies know you're there?" One blip. "Are there Charlies in the house?" Two blips.

"All right. They're busy now with their main target. We've got very little time. I'm coming to get you, and there's going to be some shooting. All of you get down flat on the floor and stay there. Don't make any noise, and don't come out until I tell you. Understand?"

Louise pressed the button twice.

Instead of lying flat on the floor, they all went to the window. Louise motioned them to keep back out of sight. Up the street they could barely make out the outline of the jeep. It was moving slowly in their direction.

The man was insane! He was all by himself, against this heavily armed house. He had been right about one thing, though: the Viet Cong she could see were all intently watching the PSA house. Nobody was paying the slightest attention to anything else, and Ben's approach went undetected.

From midway up the block Ben accelerated suddenly, then slammed on the brakes as he approached the wall, headed the jeep straight for it, was standing up in the seat as it struck with the front wheels. The momentum propelled Ben forward, but he was prepared for it, had calculated it, and he came over the hood of the little vehicle and leaped the wall all in one strenuous motion. He landed on his feet in the courtyard, spraying fire from his machine gun as his feet hit the ground. The men crouched behind the wall, astonished, struck dumb and motionless by the speed of the assault, turned their weapons inward, but too late. Five of them fell, one by one, under the long burst of fire, and the sixth started to crawl away behind a raised flowerbed. Ben strode toward him relentlessly, ruthlessly, and sprayed him with bullets. He paused, pulled the magazine from the machine gun, snapped a fresh one in place, and moved toward the door. He disappeared from view then. A loud explosion followed. A grenade, Louise guessed. Silence, and then a rush of footsteps and voices. Firing from machine guns and rifles. Another grenade.

All was still as death now, and the women waited, their hearts pounding. From near their door they heard a series of shots, a muffled shout from below. A bullet struck their door, and then another. The house was full of a violent storm of fire and metal.

A movement outside the window caught Louise's eye. One of the men Ben had first shot had arisen, and was running toward the door with his rifle ready. He was bleeding, but still active and ready for a fight. Louise was about to scream a warning, but before she could find her voice a rattle of gunfire from downstairs told her that the warning would have been too late, anyway.

There was a rustle of feet outside their door, then footsteps up and down the corridor, then silence. A silence that seemed to last an eternity.

A knock sounded on the door and they heard a familiar voice.

"Peggy! Louise! Are you all in there?"

"Ben!" Peggy screamed with joy and relief. She flew to the door, frantically fumbled with the key until she had unlocked it, and threw herself into his arms, oblivious of the fact that she was dressed only in very sheer short pajamas. The other two clustered joyously around their rescuer, dressed no more modestly, laughing and weeping, and clinging to him in the inexpressible relief of liberation.

"OK, ladies," Ben said soothingly, "it's all over. Everything's all right now. You're OK. You're safe." His arms had closed around Peggy, one hand still clasping the machine gun. His face was powdered with plaster dust, and the air around him was filled with the smell of ordnance and broken masonry.

"Come on, now," he said at last. "I'm going to take you somewhere safer than this."

Only then did Louise realize the state the three of them were in.

"First we've got to get some clothes on, Ben," she said, trying to draw the nightgown around her more modestly.

"I should say so," Ben laughed. "Give me that radio, and get yourselves fixed up and downstairs as fast as you can."

He took the radio downstairs, and stepped outside the door.

"Victory-One," he called, "the goodies are safe. I'll be back there shortly."

"That's good news, Seven," came Toby's voice. "Thanks."

[26]

"THE VC have got the government compound," Ben announced to the others upon his return to the house.

"What about the women?" Toby asked.

"I took them over to the hospital," Ben replied. "The nurses will be needed there, and Marie Claire wouldn't be safe at her office, even if I could have gotten her over there. So I left her at the hospital too."

"So now what, Ben?" asked Ski.

"That's what we've got to figure out. Whatever it is, we've got to do it quick. These guys are new at taking and holding positions, and they haven't had time to get themselves all set yet. Now is the time to hit them, and hit them hard. A few hours from now it will be too late."

"So?"

"OK. I'm going to take Toby with me. He fights like a tiger, but he's green, so he needs to be with somebody. I want you to stay here and get this house back in shape, and repel any attack that comes. I'm still uneasy about the rest of the Twenty-Third being around here somewhere."

"OK, Ben," Ski replied. He obviously would have preferred to go with Ben, but he did not question the orders. "Where are you going?"

"We'll go down to the government compound and see if we can help out. If they keep hold of that, they've psychologically got control of the provincial government, and that's bad. Let's go, Toby."

They loaded the jeep with weapons and ammunition and sped out the gate. It was a wild ride, with Ben at the wheel. Twice they came under fire from machine guns, and they were regularly shot at by individual riflemen. The vehicle was struck twice by bullets, but the two men came through without a scratch.

Ben stopped the jeep in a side street out of sight of the compound, and they went on foot to the street that bordered it. An ARVN officer whom Ben knew had taken cover inside a small store across the street, and Ben spoke to him, gesturing toward the compound.

"They're waiting for an ARVN regiment that's supposed to come and retake the place," Ben said to Toby, not concealing his disgust. They heard scattered firing from along the street to their left. Ben spoke again to the officer.

"Well, whattaya know?" he said, returning to Toby. "Our friend Thieu has got a little squad of men and he's checking out the houses around the square. Finding a sniper here and there, apparently."

Ben signaled to Toby, and they moved around the square from tree to tree, house to house, while Ben looked the situation over.

"Toby," Ben said at last, "those guys had a little bit of a firefight with somebody in there when they took the place over, and they're acting like the battle is over and it's a big, final victory. They haven't got set yet against any counterattack, probably because they know that the only units that could counterattack them are still way the hell outside the city."

"I'm afraid to ask you what you've got in mind, because I think I already know."

Ben grinned back at him, a bright gleam in his eyes. "You and I," he said, "are going to go in there and chase the bastards out."

"How come?" Toby asked sharply. "I thought you wouldn't want them to get away?"

Ben laughed. "Most of 'em won't."

"How many are there?"

"That lieutenant says about a hundred. That means there may be as many as fifty. What did Dang's report say?"

"He didn't specify any numbers, as far as I can remember."

"Come on," said Ben. He led Toby at a trot back to the jeep. Toby followed unwillingly. He was now deeply afraid. This battle-hungry man was going to lead him into a fight that they could not win—a fight that would surely get them both killed.

Although the fear was mounting, and seizing his chest,

threatening to suffocate him, his leg muscles kept churning. He knew that terrified as he might be, he would follow Ben. If he refused, he was joining Little Jack on the sofa. He would rather die than do that.

Ben slung a Swedish K over his shoulder, and instructed Toby to take more magazines for the Swedish K in his own hands. Ben then picked up an M-79 grenade launcher and a bag of grenades.

"We're gonna be looking 'em right in the eye this time, Toby," he said. "We want handy, automatic weapons and grenades. We're gonna hit 'em hard and fast."

Toby had never seen the grenade launcher in use, but he had heard much about it. It looked something like a single-barreled shotgun, but fired a projectile forty millimeters in diameter. In this projectile was a charge of a quarter-ounce of plastic explosive, wrapped in finely serrated wire. When it exploded, it filled the air with a lethal cloud of almost microscopic fragments of that wire, and nobody within five feet of such an explosion would live to tell about it. The fragments did not make wounds one could see, or count. They dusted a body with thousands of tiny punctures, and the blood and the life oozed out.

"Let's go," said Ben. "We don't want them to get set."

He started out at the same trotting pace, and darted across the street to a small gate in the rear of the compound. Toby had not known this gate even existed. It was locked.

"You've got a K ready," Ben said. "See if you can bust that hasp." Toby studied the angle for a moment, trying to figure whether a ricochet might come back to strike them. He fired a burst, and the hasp broke loose. They rushed through the gate and took cover behind a tree. Ben's target was a small, one-story building behind the RD offices. Its shutters were closed, at least on this side, which was the rear.

"Get over behind that tree," Ben said, pointing to a big tree nearby, "and give those windows a burst from your K. See if we can make them open one of the shutters. If we can, I'll drop a grenade in."

Toby darted over to the other tree, sprayed one of the shutters with bullets, and waited. The shutters opened almost immediately and Ben, with a wide grin, stepped out into the open for a moment, aimed his ungainly weapon carefully, and fired. He immediately reloaded, and before the occupants could have recovered from the first explosion, he had lobbed another of the deadly little projectiles into their midst.

"Come on," Ben shouted, "let's get around in the front."

His mind a blank to all sensations except the voice of Ben, and the need for speed, Toby raced around one side of the building, while Ben went around the other way. The front door was open, and Ben motioned Toby in frantically. Toby understood. He was the one who had a machine gun at the ready. He hurried in, went through a small anteroom, and came to the room that looked out over the back fence. Four men were peering cautiously out of the window, their back to Toby. Two others lay motionless on the floor.

The four heard him, all at the same time, and turned. For the fraction of a second, Toby looked full into the eyes of the men he was about to kill. He pulled the trigger and held it, and the Swedish K chattered. Three of the men fell. The fourth came toward Toby. Toby gave him a burst, and could see the impact of the bullets in the clothing over the man's belly, but he kept coming. Desperately, Toby fired again, emptying the magazine, but the man still moved toward him. Toby leaped back and grabbed for a new magazine from the satchel at his waist, and heard a burst of fire from his side. Ben had brought his own machine gun around, had fired at the man and finally brought him down.

"I don't think I'll bring these Ks to my next fight," Ben said grimly. "They don't seem to stop a man very well."

His Swedish K had killed the other three without any problems, Toby thought. It was just that one . . .

"OK, Toby," said Ben. "Now we're gonna clear out the RD cadre building. What I want you to do is find a place where you get a full view of the ground between the RD building and the main building. I'll work on it with this M-Seventy-Nine from a distance, but I want to make sure they don't get any reinforcements from the main building. I'll depend on you to keep up a fire that will keep them busy and keep their attention, and keep anybody from making it from one building to the other. OK?"

"OK, Ben," said Toby.

Ben had not told him exactly where to go. Ben now assumed that Toby could figure that out for himself.

Toby looked the terrain over. There were no trees that seemed to offer any view of the area he had to cover. A jeep was parked to one side of the building, which would have afforded cover, but somehow he didn't trust the vehicle to stop bullets. Then his eye fell on something he had never noticed before. There in front of the jeep was a greasepit, which the mechanics used to service the government vehicles. It afforded the field of fire he needed. He caught Ben's eye and motioned toward the pit. Ben nodded, pulled his Swedish K up, and fired at the building. Toby realized that this was covering fire for his own run, and he sprinted out the door. Somebody was shooting at him from the main building, and he heard Ben's gun continue its intermittent fire.

He reached the greasepit at a dead run, leaped into it, and fell heavily on a crush of living bodies. The greasepit was crowded with people, mostly women, unarmed, who must have been caught in the early-morning assault. Toby's fall had hurt some of them, and he apologized wordlessly to them as he gathered his wits. Carefully he positioned himself against the concrete wall, peered up over the edge of the pit, and saw Ben signal. Some of the shutters of the RD building were closed, but there were enough of them open to give Ben ample targets. He began to fire the grenade launcher, and as if on signal two men came running from the main building toward the RD building. Toby fired at them and they fell. For good measure, he fired several more rounds at the door they had come out of. That magazine was empty, and he snapped another one into place. While he was doing so, he heard firing from the upper floor of the main building, just as more men came from the lower door. The shots sounded like carbines. Two of the men fell, and the other one hesitated, then ran back into the main building. Ben had not fired, and neither had Toby. The carbines were in the hands of friends on the second floor.

"We got company, Ben," Toby shouted.

"We sure have," Ben shouted back. "Let's treat 'em nice!"

Now the lower floor of the main building seemed to burst into sound, and bullets splattered and sang around the rim of the greasepit. Every weapon in the main building was apparently trained on his greasepit, and the firing kept up. Fragments of cement splattered, one of them striking his cheek, and he felt the sharp sting and a trickle of blood. Some of the women around him were wailing in terror.

He thought with sudden fright of enemy grenades. If they threw one into this pit, nobody could live through it. Why hadn't he thought of such an elementary thing before he selected this hole in the ground? He forced his brain to consider the problem calmly, and decided that he was out of the range of grenades from the main building, although perhaps from the RD building . . .

A familiar tremendous crack shook the universe around him and left his ears ringing and dead. B-40. Now another one. They were trying to make the rockets strike the inner edge of the greasepit, but did not succeed.

Toby found that he had to make a choice: either keep down and be relatively safe from the firing, or take a look and reassure himself that his little concrete trench was not being approached by the enemy on foot.

He took a quick look, fired some more, then realized that the fire from the main building had turned to concentrate on Ben. This would not do. He sprayed the building with his machine gun, and ducked. More heavy fire struck around him, including more rockets.

The morning took on a dreamy quality—a nightmarish quality. He wanted to wake up. He must wake up. But he couldn't. He was trapped in an eternity of shooting and being shot at, of explosions that shook the world around him, of automatic responses that followed the orders he had been given. He was down to two magazines now, and some hand grenades, although what the hell he could do with hand grenades from this hole in the ground . . .

He realized that during his nightmare, Ben had been lobbing grenades into the building, one after another. Now, he also realized that the firing from within the RD building had ceased.

He peered out at Ben, who motioned with his hands. Ben wanted him to come to him! He was overcome with a sudden rage at that cool, smiling, killing machine, who had brought him into this mess and was now calmly instructing him to come out of his shelter and get killed.

"What I'm going to do, goddamn you," he muttered to himself, "is do exactly as you say, and if I get over there to you, I'm going to club you right in the goddamned head."

He looked around and noticed the jeep. A quick run to the shelter of its chassis, and he would be within another short dash to Ben. One thing he had caught from his smiling mentor throughout the morning: When you decide to do something, do it immediately and fast.

He ran up the steps at the rear of the pit, heard the firing begin and knew it was pointed at him, made the safety of the jeep, paused for a moment, and when the firing had ceased, made another spring and reached Ben's side.

Ben clapped him on the back and grinned. Toby knew that he didn't hate him after all.

They made a rush at the door of the RD building. There were few men alive inside, and those few were suffering from the shock of Ben's relentless grenade bombardment. They killed these men quickly and paused in the wreckage to take stock.

"Jesus," said Ben, "we're about out of ammunition. We haven't got enough left to take on that main building."

Yesterday, taking that main building full of Viet Cong, with just the two of them to assault it, would have struck Toby as mad. Now it seemed to be the logical thing to do. Of course they would assault the main building. They would capture it.

Ben was invulnerable.

Toby was invulnerable.

"What'll we do," Toby asked, "go out and get some more and then come back?"

"It's either that, or give up the job, I guess," said Ben. "But if we leave, it'll give them a chance to retake these places, and then we'll have a hell of a time getting back in through that gate."

"Maybe I could go and leave you to hold on here," Toby began, but he was interrupted by a familiar voice.

"Resupply!" came a cheerful call.

"Ski!" shouted Ben. "In here."

Staggering under a load of ammunition, Ski came through the door.

"Nothin' goin' on up at the house," he said. "So I came on down here. Brought a lot of stuff with me in the jeep, and I watched you fellows for a while from over yonder, and wondered how I could come in and help you without you shooting me by mistake. And then, the more I watched, the more I figured you must be running short of everything except the runnin' shit, so I come in with a few groceries for you."

"That's great," said Ben. He began to fill his satchels, and Toby followed suit.

"Ski," said Ben as he worked, "we got a couple of friends up on the top floor there. Don't fire at them."

"I noticed that," Ski replied. "What's next?"

"Let's have a look," Ben replied. He motioned Toby over to a window facing the main building. Toby crouched on one side of the window and Ben crouched on the other. Ski went to the next one. Before Ben could speak, a crackling, screaming *whoosh* sounded between Ben and Toby, and the wall on the other side of the room was shattered by an explosion.

"B-Forty," said Ben with a grin. Toby would swear for the rest of his life that the rocket had brushed his ear. Their enemy was still very much alive, and with a lot of fight left in him.

"Toby," he heard Ben say, above the ringing in his ears, "grenades, hand grenades, are what we want in there. What we'll do is this. Ski and I will take up positions so that between us we've got all four walls in sight. When we're ready, you get up there close to the walls of that building. They can't get to you then, and you can flip grenades in every window you can reach. Just keep the grenades going. Anybody that shows up to try to take a shot at you, Ski and I will get. OK?"

"OK," said Toby. "What about the ones upstairs?"

"If our friends up there can't take care of them, we'll have to do it later. They can't do too much to us right now."

Toby picked up a large sack, heavy with grenades. Quick action was important, as usual.

"Give us time to get set," Ben said. "Ready, Ski?"

"Let's go," Ski replied.

The two of them darted swiftly out the door, and moved to trees, to vehicles, around any object they could find to provide momentary cover. Their progress was followed with such a fierce fire that Toby wondered how they could survive it, and then remembered that he himself had survived it only a moment ago.

Ski was soon lost from sight around one corner of the building. Ben took up a prone position behind a small piece of statuary, a pagoda-like structure, a shrine evidently, off one corner of the building. Ben motioned to Toby, and Toby took a deep breath and shot out the door. He ran straight to the back wall of the main building, the heavy bag of grenades banging clumsily against his side, and he had a passing thought of what might happen if a bullet hit that bag.

He was soon pressed against the wall of the building. The windows were at a height so that the sills were about even with the top of his head if he stood erect, which he did not do. In a semi-crouch, he began a systematic progress around the building, searching for open windows, and at each one he lobbed in a grenade. He waited each time before throwing, waited longer than was really safe. He did not want to see one of his own grenades come flying back out the window. He was naked there, with no place to hide.

Almost in a rhythmic dance, he moved along and sent charges of explosives and metal into the ground floor of the building. Ben and Ski fired steadily at the windows above him, and he knew that they were holding the enemy back from striking at their tormentor below the windowsills. On and on he went, flipping grenades in—he lost count of how many. He was down to three or four and paused, his eye caught by a motion from Ben. Ben was crawling carefully on his belly from behind the stone shrine toward a big tree near the front of the building. Toby watched for a moment, and then realized that he had a duty to his friend. He tossed another grenade. And then another.

Ben made it to the tree, waved cheerily at Toby, and pulled his weapon around to begin firing.

Toby heard the angry *whang* of a heavy rifle from a

new direction, across the street from the compound, and at the same moment he saw Ben's form leap with the shock.

He waited, stunned by the knowledge that his friend had been hit. Ben lay quietly for a moment, then lifted his head, waved again at Toby, and began to fire at the building.

Ben was invulnerable, just as he had said, Toby thought, and picked out another grenade. Then the sound of the carbines upstairs began again, but he could tell that they were turned inward. Shouts and more firing, and suddenly it was all over. About a dozen men straggled out the front door of the building, unarmed, their hands clasped over their heads. Toby learned later that about a dozen more had escaped out the back way, the same direction from which Toby and Ben had mounted their attack.

Toby could not bring himself to believe that the battle was over. His ears rang, his whole body was tingling as the fear and the blood lust drained away. He was suddenly very tired.

He looked over at Ben, who brought the palms of his hands to the ground under his chest to push himself up, and then collapsed.

Toby rushed to his side and saw a hole in his trousers just over the left buttock, where a bright patch of blood was soaking the cloth in an ever-widening circle.

"Shot right in the ass," Ben murmured weakly. "First time in my life."

Once again Toby was confronted with a gravely wounded man and did not know what he should do. Before he could make a decision, a small figure, clad in white blouse and slacks, came running through the front gate and fell to her knees beside the prone man.

"I knew it had to be him," she said to Toby, "when they told me that some crazy Americans were attacking this place." She leaned over and looked at Ben's face, lying on one cheek in the dirt. "You goddamned oaf," she said. "Why do you always figure you have to fight the war all by yourself?"

"Hi, Peggy," said Ben drowsily. "I'm feeling kind of poorly."

She looked up at Toby. "Help me turn him over, will

you?" she said. Her voice broke slightly, and Toby could see the anguish in her eyes.

Gently they tugged at the limp body. A groan of pain escaped from Ben's throat, and a sobbing gasp from Peggy showed where the pain had struck home. "Easy now," she said. "Let's take it real easy. Don't hurt him! Don't hurt him! That's the way." They got him over on his back, away from a pool of blood that had gathered under his belly. The clothing was soaked and torn.

Peggy unbuckled his belt and Toby handed her a knife. Quickly she cleared the clothing from his belly.

"Holy Mother of God!" she cried, her voice choked with horror. "That bullet must have hit bone somewhere and tumbled."

It did not seem possible to Toby that one bullet could have caused such massive damage. Ben's entire abdomen was a greenish-blue, and there was a jagged tear in it beside the navel. Bits of intestine were protruding from the tear, and blood was flowing steadily.

Peggy jumped to her feet. "Ski," she said, "do you know where the hospital is?"

"Sure."

"Get in that jeep of yours and go over there and bring Dr. Greevey back with you, and dammit, don't you take no for an answer. You tell him I said it is the most important man in this province, and he's got a bad abdominal wound. Bring him, do you hear?"

"On my way!"

Peggy took some gauze from Ben's own first-aid kit, and began to try to staunch the flow of blood. Then she spied the morphine in the little packet. With a cry of joy, she extracted it and gave him an injection.

"Toby," she said, "I need gauze and tape, and everything else. Do you suppose there is any of it in these buildings?"

"There ought to be," said Toby. "I'll go see."

He went in the door as the last of the prisoners were being herded out, prodded by carbines in the hands of Qui and two of his associates.

"Qui!" exclaimed Toby. "It was you up there?"

"Yes, sir."

"Thanks for your help."

"*We* thank *you,*" said Qui. "If you had not—"

"Do you have medicines, bandages, cotton, things like that? Mr. Compton has been wounded."

"Mr. Compton? Yes. I bring."

Qui turned the prisoners over to his comrades and disappeared into the building. He came back with a big medical kit. Peggy grabbed it and went instantly to work. Ben was lying quietly, his eyes glazed with shock and morphine.

"You big dumb oaf," she crooned to him, as her hands cleaned and dressed the wound. "You hardheaded stubborn jackass. Had to go and get yourself shot in the behind didn't you? Too bad, because there's still a few Viet Cong around town that you haven't shot yet. But maybe we can patch you up so you can go take care of them, too. We don't want to spoil your fun, now, do we? Too bad they shot you in the butt and the belly. If they'd shot you in that hard head, the bullet would have bounced right off."

Qui caught Toby's attention. "You and your friends kill Tu Binh," he said.

"Tu Binh?" The name was familiar to Toby.

"Tiger," said Qui. "Commander. Yenan Battalion."

"Where?"

"Inside."

"Show me."

Qui led him into the building, and Toby had his first look at the devastation caused by the grenades. They went into a corner room, which was littered with corpses, and Qui motioned across the room at a figure propped against the far wall.

"Oh," said Qui, "not dead yet!" He brought his carbine up. Toby stepped over to the figure, his eyes wide with disbelief.

It was Minnie.

His body was so badly torn that Toby wondered how he could still be alive, and knew that he could not live long. Both legs were lifeless, blood-soaked. His chest had been crushed by something powerful. A grenade?

Blood streamed down one side of his face from a scalp wound.

"This isn't the Tiger, Qui. This is Tran Van Minh."

"Yes," said Qui politely. "Tu Binh. Tiger."

Minnie tried to smile.

"Is it true, Minnie?" asked Toby.

"Dang did not know?" Minnie asked, his voice faint and breathy.

"Dang? Minnie, you knew about Dang? That means it was *you* at Therese's house. It's been you all along?"

Minnie closed his eyes, as if to nod.

"Then, you didn't really *charge* that ambush; you were leading us into it."

"I did not . . . did not like to be . . . your enemy, Mr. Busch," said Minnie weakly. "It is so strange. You and I are friends . . ."

"Minnie, don't talk anymore. I'm standing around here like a fool, when you need help. I'll go get help."

"Go if you wish, but it is of no use. I will not be alive."

"And I'm the one who killed you," said Toby bitterly.

"Mr. Busch," said Minnie, "remember . . ." He managed a genuine smile, and traced a large circle in the air with his index finger.

Toby stood motionless for a long time, his heart thumping with grief and regret. Then he turned and ran out the door.

"Peggy, can I stay here and watch Ben for a minute while you have a look at Minnie?"

"Minnie?"

"He's inside. He's been a VC all along. Will you look at him?"

Something about his tone sent Peggy into the building. She had placed big swatches of gauze over Ben's wound, and there was nothing to do now but wait for the doctor.

Peggy was back in a moment.

"He's dead," she said.

A sudden burst of fire from an upper floor across the street made them all start. The firing came from the direction of the rifle shot that had sruck Ben, but this fire was within the building. Toby went to the fence and looked over. A figure appeared in the window, and Qui came to Toby's side.

"Major Thieu," said Qui.

"So I see," said Toby. How could you predict the fortunes of a battle? Thieu had killed the man who had shot Ben.

Ski slid his jeep to a stop, leaped out, and ran to Peggy and Ben.

"The doctor's coming," he said. "He said it would take him about three or four minutes before he could leave, but then he would come as fast as he could."

"Did he ask who it was?"

"No. He already knew."

"He already knew?" Peggy was astonished. "How?"

"I told him just what you said," said Ski. "I said that you had told me to tell him that the most important man in the province had been hurt, and right away he says, 'Ben's been hit? Where?' "

"Boy," said Peggy with a sheepish grin, "I don't hide it from *anybody*, do I?"

Toby sat down on the ground by Ben and waited. He felt suddenly weak with the letdown. A young American doctor sped up in a jeep and ran up to them, carrying a heavy black bag. He lifted the gauze and looked at Ben's belly. He prized Ben's body up slightly and explored the hip with his hands, feeling and prodding gently. He peered at Ben's eyes, felt his pulse.

"Did you give him anything?" he asked Peggy.

"Morphine," she said.

"All right," said the doctor. "Get him ready for plasma, will you? Everything you'll need is in the bag."

The doctor stood, and spoke to Toby. "You're his associate?"

"That's right, Doctor. Toby Busch." They shook hands.

"Toby," the doctor said gravely, "Ben is in danger. We don't have the means of handling a wound like that in this hospital. That bullet has tumbled all through his gut, and he's going to need extended surgery, probably some of it pretty delicate. I can't even get in there to stop the internal bleeding without putting him in a danger I can't cope with. Is there any way you could get him up to Dong Tam?"

"I don't know. I can try."

"You'll have to do better than try. If he isn't up there in an hour, two hours at the very most, it will be too late."

Peggy had heard, even as she was setting up the apparatus for the plasma, and for the first time Toby saw tears start to her eyes. He squeezed her gently. "We'll get him up there, don't worry."

Peggy nodded quickly and kept working.

"Come on, Ski," said Toby. "Let's go get on that single sideband."

They ran to Ski's jeep and went careening up the street. The battle for My Tho was still raging at other points of the city, and they came under fire once, but made it home, and Toby rushed to the shortwave radio. It was not working.

"Well, shit!" he bellowed. "Of all the times for this goddamned thing to be on the blink."

"No electricity, Toby," Ski pointed out. The generator was not running.

"Oh, Christ, I forgot," said Toby. "Do you know how to start that generator?"

"Sure," said Ski. He hurried out the back door.

With a rumble the big generator came to life, and lights came on all over the house, refrigerators began to hum. The indicator lights on the transceiver winked on, and Toby waited for the tubes to heat. Then he grabbed the microphone and began to call Jerry Burkholder in Can Tho.

[27]

NONE of the Vietnamese employees had come to work in the CORDS compound that morning, and Bill Voigt and his staff had made a big pot of coffee, and were trying to get things organized in the midst of the battle that was swirling in the streets of Can Tho. The Tactical Operations Center had almost been lost to the Viet Cong attack in the early hours of the morning, as well as Eakin Compound and some of the dormitories. ARVN 9th Division Headquarters had come under heavy attack, but there was never any danger of losing that.

The two nurses, Cynthia and Sheila, who had not been able to get to their hospital, went back into the kitchen at the compound dining room and discovered a plentiful supply of bacon and eggs, coffee, milk, and other staples. They set to work cooking a great quantity of scrambled eggs and bacon, and hungry people came from all over the compound to eat.

Dino and Jess were among them. No Air America planes were aloft today, and the pilots had been told to stay on the ground until Saigon advised that they could resume operations. Jess and Dino were not unhappy.

"The fraternity of the unmitigated cowards, that's us!" Dino said. "Our motto is 'We fly anytime except when the bullets do.' "

"Right!" Jess exclaimed. "And our song is 'Here we stay, out of the wild blue yonder . . .' "

Bill was worried about the unprotected flank of the compound, which fronted on the Bassac River. An assault could be launched by sampan, if the Viet Cong considered the compound to be a worthwhile objective, but there had been no sign of that yet.

Jerry came into the dining room. The breakfast had been so late that the coffee loiterers were almost into lunchtime by now.

"Bill," said Jerry. "My Tho is on the horn. They want to know if we can get a chopper up there to them."

"You told them no, of course. You told them everything's grounded until Saigon gives the word?"

"No, I didn't. Before I could tell them that, Toby told me that Ben's been wounded so badly the doctor says he's only got an hour or so to live if he doesn't get to Dong Tam."

"Ben!" Bill exclaimed, all attention now.

Dino and Jess looked at each other, and shifted nervously in their chairs. "What's the situation up there in My Tho for flying?" Dino asked.

"Toby says the airstrip is in Viet Cong hands, and there's pockets of 'em all over the town. They've got small anti-aircraft guns here and there around the town, too, to keep gunships and Spookies off. The fellows over at Paddy Control tell me they've already lost two gunships over My Tho."

"Wow!" said Jess softly.

"You say Ben will die . . ."

"That's what this American doctor up there says. He's got an hour to live, maybe two."

"And he called for help in plain English over that radio?" asked Jess unhappily.

"No other way to do it, Jess."

Jess and Dino looked at one another in silence.

"It's old Ben, Jess," said Dino, quietly.

Jess nodded, and looked at Jerry. "Tell Toby I'm on my way," he said.

"I'm going with you, Jess," said Dino.

"What the hell for? What do you know about choppers?"

"I always wanted to keep it a secret" Dino said, grinning, "but I had some hours in 'em once, before I decided they wouldn't fly. I could probably get us out in case you get shot in the ass."

"Come on, then," said Jess. They went out the door to a Bronco parked near the door. Before they could get in, Cynthia joined them and unobtrusively but unhesitantly climbed into the seat, a medical kit under her arm. They looked questioningly at her for a moment, then climbed in and drove away.

Bill and Jerry went into the little room off the air ops office where the single sideband transceiver sat. Jerry brought Toby back on the air and told him the chopper was on its way.

Bill grabbed the microphone. "This is Volleyball, Buffalo. How are things up there?"

"We're pretty well infested," said Toby. "But we cleared the government compound, and I think we're going to kick the hell out of them."

"Good."

"You got my reports?"

"Great stuff, Buffalo! I got to them late, but it wasn't your fault. It was a real godsend, all over the country. Things could have been a lot worse without them. I'll fill you in completely later on."

"OK, Volleyball. I'm going to get the hell on down there to the compound now. Buffalo out."

"Volleyball out."

Toby hooked the microphone back on the set and came through the dining room. Little Jack was sitting at the bar, staring into space, apparently drunk. Toby shook his head, and he and Ski got back into the jeep. Everything seemed calm enough here at the house. They drove recklessly through the streets, back to Ben's side.

Ben had been eased onto a stretcher. Plasma was dripping into his arms and his eyes were open. He was drowsy. Peggy was holding his hand, stroking it lightly, scolding him lovingly all the while.

The beat of the fan of a Huey reached their ears, and they soon saw the Air America helicopter, up high, directly above them. Suddenly, the awkward machine banked until the blade was almost vertical to the ground, and came tumbling down in a tight, dizzying spiral. Toby would not have believed a helicopter to be capable of such a maneuver.

"Boy," exclaimed Ski, "old Jess can really fly that thing!"

There was a sound of machine guns from several directions, and the helicopter came abruptly out of the bank and flew away.

"They chased him off," Toby muttered.

"Yeah, those crazy things will only go eighty miles an hour. You can't face antiaircraft fire with that kind of speed."

The clatter of the fans came closer once more, but they could not see it this time because of the trees. He was somewhat lower than before. They listened tensely, but heard the noise begin to fade after a moment. He had been driven off again.

"I guess he must have given up," said Ski sadly.

"Looks like it. You can't blame him, really. He won't do Ben any good by getting *himself* killed. Maybe he'll try to land somewhere else, and see if we can get Ben to him by car."

Without warning, they heard a deafening clatter, and the blades of the chopper were beating the air only a few yards above them. Jess had come barreling in from the edge of town, so low he was almost dragging the trees, and then had set the strange machine back on its tail in a Bugs Bunny stop. He set it down like a feather on the ground in front of them.

Ski and Toby grasped the stretcher handles and lifted their friend carefully, while Peggy walked beside him, holding the plasma bottle. The door slid back, and Cynthia and

Dino jumped to the ground. Dino helped ease Ben into position on the floor of the helicopter, and strapped him down securely.

"I thought it was just us fliers that got shot in the ass, old buddy," he said to Ben as he worked. "You got some explaining to do after we get you up to the repair shop." Ben smiled up at him dreamily.

"I'm almost sorry you came," Peggy said to Cynthia, as the two of them settled their patient comfortably and secured the plasma bag to the back of the front seat.

"Why?" Cynthia asked.

"I wanted to go with him. Now I've got no excuse. Our hospital has got people waiting in the corridors. I've got to stay here."

"We'll take care of this fellow," Cynthia said. "We'll have him in Dong Tam in a few minutes, and I won't leave him till he's safe in bed up there."

Peggy felt Ben's bare feet, and tucked the blanket around them snugly. Then she bent over and patted his cheek.

"You come back, do you hear me, you big jackass?" she whispered into his ear. "You and I have got some things to settle."

"Thanks . . . Peggy," he said. "Thanks for the help."

She kissed his pale forehead, and jumped down and ran out from under the whirling blades. She stood there quietly, her hands to her face, her shoulders heaving.

"You certainly had problems getting in, didn't you?" Toby asked Jess through the door on the pilot's side.

"Sure as hell did," Jess replied, watching attentively as Dino checked the passenger space, and settled himself in the copilot's seat beside him. "We took several rounds, and I think one of 'em hit a blade, but she still flies. All set, Dino?"

"All set."

"OK." Jess grinned at him. "We came in *that* way, but we're gonna fool 'em and go out *that* way." He gestured in the opposite direction. "So put your hands in your pockets and lift up, 'cause here we go!"

The blades whirled faster and began to generate the typical *slap-slap* of the Huey, and Jess set the blade angle to bite the air. The machine lurched upward and hung suspended for a moment. Then Jess pointed the nose down, and they darted away, seeming to scrape the leaves of the tall trees with their skids. The downdraft caused the branches to whirl and sway violently.

Toby listened until the sound faded away, and its gradual fading reassured him. They had made it. The Dong Tam airstrip would be no problem, right in the middle of the U.S. 9th Division as it was.

"I'll take you to the hospital, Peggy," he said.

"I can take her," said Ski. "You get on back to the house, why don't you?"

Toby was too bone-tired to argue. He climbed into the jeep he and Ben had left on the side street, and drove home. The fighting had died down for the moment, and he ran into no hostile fire on this trip.

Mrs. Chao and Chi Hai were there. They had come home from the Tet celebration that had never happened. Mrs. Chao's face was drawn with fear.

"Viet Cong try to find us," she said. "Viet Cong send many men, send everywhere. Find Vietnamese work for Americans, and kill. Look for us. We run!"

Toby was alarmed. "They are out looking for Vietnamese who work for Americans, you say?"

"Yes."

"To kill them?"

"Yes. Already kill twenty, thirty."

"Therese!"

Toby raced back out the door, his fatigue forgotten, his muscles in the grip of a new terror.

He did not even notice whether he was being fired at as he drove back across the town and pulled up in front of the familiar pathway. One of the small dwellings was on fire, just off the path by the street, and neighbors were trying to save what had been inside. Otherwise, the neighborhood did not seem to have been touched by the battle.

He ran down the path, his Swedish K grasped purposefully, the bolt back, ready to fire. He passed a small clump of people, the women weeping. A teen-age boy came hurtling down the path in the opposite direction, and sped past him.

The area he was entering now seemed deserted, and he slowed down to a walk. It was eerie. He edged slowly up to Therese's little house. It was empty. He walked on, seeing a small cleared area through some spaces between the houses. There were people standing dumbly at the edge of this clearing.

He came out into the clearing from between two shacks. There, in the little bare-earth plaza was a line of bodies, more than a dozen. They had fallen at different angles, but always forward on their faces. They had passed the last moments of their lives kneeling before their assassins, their hands tied behind their backs, a pistol at the base of their skulls.

A small black object caught his eye. It was resting on the back of the body at the near end of the ghastly line. He moved closer, and saw the object more clearly. It was a SONY television set, smashed and ruined, but still recognizable.

He went up to the body and stood looking down, his mind not yet receiving or accepting what his eyes saw. He laid aside his weapon. He did not know if there were any enemy around. He had forgotten the enemy.

He picked up the smashed plastic box and set it carefully to one side. As he did so, he noticed the shoes. They had come off in the last seconds of violence, and were lying askew nearby. She would have hated that. *One should be tidy, whatever the circumstances.* He picked them up with a tender smile and set them, neatly together, by the motionless feet. He straightened her tunic, and his swimming eyes fell on her hands, twisted and swollen because of the fetters fashioned from the television power cord, its European adapter plug still attached, dangling from the knot. It was hurting her. He pulled out his knife and cut the cord from the wrists. As he did so, he heard a faint moan from nearby, and looked up.

A middle-aged woman had come, and was squatting there. She was dressed in black rayon trousers and a white blouse. She was watching him intently, her cheeks wet with tears, her hands clasped tightly together. She was shaking her heard slowly and rhythmically. The neighbor in the next house, perhaps. Toby nodded and managed a faint smile at her.

He placed the arms carefully beside the body, and moved to straighten the hair. He stared vacantly at the horrible, gaping hole at the base of the skull, the fine hair around it matted with blood.

Gently, he turned her over and pulled her to him, heedless of the blood, cradling her head in his arms, kissing her soiled cheek, caressing her, kissing and caressing as if he could thus bring life back into the still, fragile form.

It was the Day of Wrath. He knew. The Day of Wrath, and now it began to cave in on him . . . the noise, the fire, the killing, the screams, the blood, the terror.

And it all ended here, on the hardpacked dirt of this clearing in a slum.

"Oh, God. Oh, my God. Therese, Little Mistress, what have they done? What have they done?"

He lifted his gaze and looked at the sobbing woman, and back down at the quiet face before him.

"God damn them, Therese," he said, his voice hoarse and deliberate. It was not an oath of exasperation, but a curse, a holy malediction, pronounced out of a limitless rage. The woman did not understand his words, but she knew what he was doing, and she joined her keening to his invocation of the powers of heaven and hell.

He looked up at the afternoon sky.

"Whoever did this, whatever man has done this, may God damn his soul to eternal hell!"

For some time he continued to stare at the sky, calling down curses on the enemy, curses on this war, and curses upon his own thoughtless, selfish soul for what he had done.

Then he bent his head, and buried his face against the breast of his dead mistress, and wept.

[28]

THE Tet offensive continued for many days, as the Viet Cong, with incredible, reckless bravery, dashed themselves to pieces against the greater numbers and firepower of the South Vietnamese and American military forces. The "masses," from whom they had expected enthusiastic help, had stood by and watched, or had cowered in fear in the midst of the battles and the destruction, or, toward the end, had for the first time in the history of this war begun to report to the government about the location and the operations of the insurgent forces.

As the days passed, Bill Voigt heard and read reports from the provincial offices under his supervision, and smiled with pleasure. These tough young men, wise in the ways of their enemy, unflappable in the face of attack, had stood like rocks throughout the delta, and had more often than not provided the one hard nucleus around which government forces began to re-form and halt the attacks, and destroy the attacking forces.

And especially Toby Busch, who wasn't even a soldier.

Bill had gone to Dong Tam two days after Ben had been taken there. Ben was weak, and under sedation, and soon to be flown to Tokyo for surgery, but he was cheerful and optimistic.

"Hell yes, Bill," he said. "I'm coming back to My Tho. Don't let anybody else have my programs. Unless you're not satisfied with my work?"

"Oh, for Christ's sake," Bill snorted.

"Because now is bound to be our best opportunity. After this big attack the VC are going to be as weak as kittens. We'll have them on the run. With them all chopped up, the Phoenix program is really going to pay off, because now the farmers and the villagers will tell us who the secret ones are, and we can round 'em up. The farmers won't be afraid of them anymore. I want to be there now that this is happening."

A nurse came by and scolded him for getting excited, and he waved her off with a grin.

"Toby has sent Little Jack out of his province," said Bill. "I'm sending him back to the States."

"Yeah," Ben nodded. "Poor bastard."

"He was paralyzed the whole time."

"Has the CIA got medals for bravery, Bill?" Ben asked him abruptly.

"Yes, we have."

"Get one for Toby. The highest you've got."

"I was already thinking about something for his reporting on the Tet offensive."

"Well, I'm no judge of that, but I can tell you that he's one of the finest combat men I've ever fought with."

"When you get back on your feet, if you'll give me an account of the action, I'll pass the recommendation along."

"Get me an army clerk or a stenographer in here tomorrow, and I'll dictate it while it's fresh," said Ben.

"Sure you're strong enough?"

"Yep." Ben lay back easily for a moment. "We finally got 'em out on the battlefield, toe to toe," he said contentedly, "and we kicked the shit out of them."

"We sure did," Bill agreed. He didn't tell Ben that the American public did not yet know about the victory; that the American news media, with their relentless determination to doubt everything except their own judgments, seemed to see only a violent attack against the American Embassy's sacred premises, not the lifeless bodies of the attackers strewn around the grounds; seemed to see only the devastation of cities throughout the country, not the countryside, which had at last been relieved of the burden of a ruthless insurgent army that had for years been hidden in its reluctant breast; semed to see only the mangled bodies of American soldiers, not the smashed and bleeding battalions of the rural insurgency forces, who had destroyed themselves in urban combat; seemed to see only the venality and treason of many South Vietnamese officials, instead of the steadiness and sacrifice of the ARVN soldiers; seemed to see only an unmitigated disaster in what was in reality, to any thoughtful man on the spot, the most important and significant victory of the American and South Vietnamese forces of the entire war.

Ben would find all this out soon enough.

In My Tho, Toby kept busy. He had to keep busy. He must not stop to think. He engaged in no further combat; for ARVN forces and the U.S. 9th Division took over the task of eliminating the pockets of Viet Cong that clung stubbornly to parts of the city, and Toby had only to tend to the repair and reestablishment of his office and home.

It dawned on him only gradually that he was the only one left. Except for the guards and Mrs. Chao and Chi

Hai, he had to start all over, although he had heard from Ben that he expected to be back at work within a couple of months.

He had met with Manh and Thieu, and restored amicable relations, even with an unexpected overlay of mutual admiration, and he had taken advantage of the moment of cordiality to ask to be permitted to hire Qui to replace Minnie. He knew that Thieu would suppose that Qui would constitute a penetration of his office, but he didn't care. Qui was a sharp man. He would be about as good a replacement for Minnie as one could find.

"We will learn each other's language together, Qui," he said.

"Yes. And learn also each other work," came Qui's quaint reply, which Toby understood.

Can Tho was sending an assistant regional plans officer to handle Toby's office while Toby was away on family visitation. Some North Vietnamese friends of Therese, whom he had met at the simple Catholic funeral, had sent him a timid young girl, who spoke good English and could type. She was rather pretty, but did not even approach the beauty of her predecessor, which, Toby thought sadly, was a good thing.

Now he was ready to go home to his family for three weeks. He looked forward to it with relief and trepidation. It would be heaven to spend some days in absolute relaxation in a small Iowa town—in a countryside at peace. The coming reunion with Mary Lynn presented his mind with so many unknowns that he didn't even like to think about it; in fact, he consciously blotted it out of his mind for the time being, to be coped with when the moment came.

Tomorrow the Can Tho officer would arrive, and Toby could brief him. Fortunately, the man already knew almost all he would need to know, from having been in the chain of command for these many months.

And tonight the women had invited Toby to a farewell dinner. He was glad. They were almost his only link with the days before Tet, the days that seemed almost like an ancient dream.

They were old comrades, and although the dinner was not the lively party that their past gatherings had been, it was pleasant. They spoke pityingly of Little Jack, and wonderingly of the pugnacious Ben Compton. Peggy was certain that she had at last begun to penetrate that outer shell of the reticent soldier, and she did not try to conceal her sense of triumph.

And then the other two had, without any apologies or dissimulation, left Toby and Louise alone.

"I won't be here when you get back, Toby," said Louise quietly, when they were alone.

"You won't? I thought you had another year here."

"I've asked for a transfer, and they're going to send me up to Two Corps."

"I guess I know why."

"Of course you do. But there are some things I want to explain to you, anyway." She tucked her feet under her on the sofa and sat facing him.

"I guess I ought to try to explain some things, too," he said.

"I know about them already."

He shook his head with a smile. "There doesn't seem to have been one single secret in My Tho in all the time I've been here."

"We can even say her name out loud," she said gently. "You loved Therese very much."

"Yes."

"And now you're worried about going home?"

"Terribly worried. I don't know how I will . . . This world is so far away, it's as if I had taken up a whole new existence that has no connection with that other world. But I know it has all made such a deep impression on me that going back home to Mary Lynn may turn out to be a problem for me, and may hurt her terribly."

"But you still love her?"

"Yes. In that other world, I love her more than I can ever say."

"I was sure of it. That's why I'm transferring out of here."

"I wish it didn't have to be that way."

[illegible]en I first met you, I could tell that you would take [illegible]riously. And I didn't even let myself *think* about [illegible] All I could do would be cause you trouble, [illegible]ever have you for myself."

He was surprised. "But I thought—I just had an idea that when we were playing, the way you—"

"You really didn't think I was serious?"

"No."

"Well, I hadn't intended to be, had thought I wouldn't be. But then I got jealous."

"I caught a little hint of that, but mostly I thought you were just kidding."

"I was kidding for real. You have no idea what it did to me when I found out about Therese. Here I had kept myself in a very careful relationship with you because I didn't want to be a part of anything that might make a mess of your life; and then I knew that you had made love to her, and I was sure you weren't doing it in any casual way. A man like you couldn't be casual about an affair like that."

"I think you're right. I don't believe I ever could be."

"And so I thought, Well, I can never have him, but as long as he's already taken that step toward problems at home, I might as well have at least one night of fun."

Toby gazed intently at her.

"I wanted to play that night, Toby," she said, "but there was nothing casual about it. I wanted to roll and laugh and have fun and forget everything in this whole horrible damned world, except just us, and the night, and the games, and the love."

"Yes," he said. "That's the way it was. That was exactly the way it was."

"And," she went on, "if I stayed here in My Tho, we'd do the same thing again."

"Yes. I could never resist it."

"And we must never do it again."

"I suppose you're right."

"But not just for the reason you're thinking about."

"No?"

"No. It's me that couldn't bear it. *I'm* the one who would be destroyed."

"You?"

"Yes. I let down the barriers, thinking I could share a little part of you without it mattering very much. What I was not admitting to myself was that I began to fall in love with you that very first night when we sat and talked nonsense to each other. And after that, every silly ga we played just pulled me in more and more hopelessly. And the same thing is happening to me right now." She looked away from him abruptly.

"Louise, I—" he began.

"You don't have to make any kind and gentle remarks," she said. "That's not what I'm telling you this for."

"Goddammit, listen to me," he said roughly. "You're acting as if I were some dumb pet that you had to handle in a certain way so as not to upset him. You said you didn't want to cause me trouble, but you haven't the faintest idea of exactly what it is that's troubling me."

"What do you mean?"

"I mean that those games weren't just a casual night of fun to me. I mean that I love you, too, and if that sounds like the craziest thing in the whole crazy world, I guess it is, but it's true. If we had been back in the United States I would never have found out, because I would never have allowed myself the opportunity. Tell me, do *you* think a man can love more than one woman at the same time?"

"I don't know. How could I know?"

"It's crazy. It's insane. Back in that other world I would never have believed it. I would have said he was just fooling himself, that he was reacting with his glands, not his heart. But here, in this world, I could look at Therese, and say to myself, 'If I had met her first, I would have married her, and would have been happy all my life, and considered myself to be the most fortunate of men.' And then I can look at you and say, with all my heart, 'Louise, if I had met you first, in that other world, you would have been my only love, for all my life.' "

"Why do you have to say that?" she exclaimed, tears glistening in her eyes. "Why don't you *help* me?"

"Because I've got just as much right to give you the burden as you have to give it to me."

"It's not right."

"Louise, the only thing we will have of one another from now on is remembering that we made love, and that we w[illegible] love, and that we said it to each other. I'm glad [illegible]"

[illegible]ed a tear from her cheek. "I think you'd better

They stood by the door and he held her in his arms. Then he drew back and smiled down at her.

"You asked me once if I had ever written a poem."

"Yes," she said, her eyes smiling back at him.

"Now is a time when I wish I could. More than any other time I can remember. Because I don't think there's any other way to express what I'm thinking now."

"What are you thinking now?"

"I've been thinking that that night with you told me something about myself that I had never realized, never seen in myself, never thought about. I tend to be serious and solemn most of the time, I guess, maybe even gloomy. And then I played that night with you, and you are so fair, and so bright, and so clear-eyed, and so luminous, that it made me seem stuffy and dull in comparison.

"If I could write a poem, it would be something about how impossible it is to hold sunshine in your arms, but how warm and good the sunshine makes you feel when you try."

Her breath caught in her throat, and she stopped him. "Please don't go on."

He kissed her gently and held her close, saying nothing, deeply moved by her silence and the trembling of her body.

"Señor Gonzales," she said at last, in a small, pinched voice, "something is definitely happening to me, and it's the most horrible thing in my life. Please leave, while I still have the strength to let go."

He left, and she stood for a time, leaning against the closed door. "Sunshine!" she whispered to herself. "Oh, damn you, Toby Busch, Damn you, damn you!"

[29]

Bill Voigt drove into the compound shortly after dawn. The Viet Cong had mortared Can Tho in the early hours. Mortar attacks against the towns were about all they had left in them now. He had not been able to get back to sleep. The house he shared with Chet, on the airport road, was not a target, and the noise was not what had kept him awake. He was worried almost to the point of illness. He had puttered around, brewed a pot of coffee. He almost wished Chet were around, although he had no regrets about having demanded Chet's immediate transfer back to headquarters.

As he drove through the gate, he realized that the neighborhood around the compound had been the target of the mortars. You could see some of the destruction.

He saw movement through the door of the dining room, unusual for this time of the morning, and he went in to investigate. Cynthia and Sheila were there, and Jerry. Jerry had had the guard duty last night. The three of them were scrubbing the floor and the tables, and setting things back to rights.

"What's up?" Bill asked.

"I never had a night like this in my life, Bill," said Jerry. His face was pale and drawn.

"What happened?"

"The mortars made a lot of direct hits across the streets. We had this place full of wounded. That American doctor that lives down the driveway there came in and everybody in those houses over there heard that he was here treating people. The worst was the woman that brought her family in. Four kids. One of them died, and one of them lost both feet. And there were others."

"Yeah," said Sheila. "We see it all the time at the hospital. But this was bad, all right."

"Bill," said Jerry, pausing in his work to look up at him, "I don't know whether I'll ever be able to eat off of these tables again. The doctor used them to work on. And I've actually been picking up *pieces* of those children off of the floor. Picking up *pieces* of children! Can you imagine that? We're all a bunch of goddamned sonofabitching animals, that's what we are! Blowing little kids to pieces!"

He went back to work.

Bill went into his own office. He knew how Jerry must feel, but his own personal worry was occupying all of his thoughts, and right now he could not manage Jerry's as well.

At the commo room, he found that Russ had just come in. "I'm bringing the machines up on the air right now," Russ told him. "Last night's traffic will start coming in on them pretty soon."

"Let me know the minute anything comes in, will you?"

"Sure."

He went to his office and opened his safe. There on top of his in-box was the cable that had occupied his thoughts for the past eighteen hours, almost to the exclusion of everything else.

FOR BILL VOIGT. ALL YOUR FRIENDS AND ASSOCIATES HERE IN FAR EAST DIVISION GRIEVED AT LOSS OF YOUR SON AND EXTEND HEARTFELT CONDOLENCES.

It had to be a mistake. The army might be inefficient, and mix-ups were always possible, but it was not conceivable that his friends in headquarters could have heard that kind of news without his having the slightest inkling of it yet. He had cabled immediately to ask about it, but had had no reply so far. The answer was undoubtedly in the night's traffic, which Russ was only now receiving on his machines.

Lying in the in-box, under the cable, was a galley proof of an article that was soon to appear in a national magazine. He did not know how Washington had gotten hold of the proof, but it was obvious why they had sent it to him. It was entitled *The PRU: The CIA's Murder Incorporated.* It was written by Chris Christopher. It had a picture of the author in her baggy fatigues, standing by Wilbur Hamilton and some of his men. There was also a picture of a small stick of wood, with a date on it, "carved," the caption said, "by a knife that had only moments before been sunk into the heart of a Viet Cong soldier."

The article left no doubt in the reader's mind that the primary mission, and virtually the only activity, of the PRU, was to move out into the countryside and murder people it suspected of being part of a Viet Cong cadre or sympathizers. He had not yet shown the article to Wilbur. It would be a blow to that fine young officer.

Russ came in with a message, and Bill could tell by his face what the message contained.

"I am very sorry, Bill," Russ said, and quickly left.

REGRET TO INFORM YOU THAT YOUR SON, WILLIAM VOIGT, JR., WAS KILLED IN ACTION ON FEBRUARY 26. ALL CONCERNED DEEPLY DISTRESSED THAT REFERENCE MESSAGE REACHED YOU BEFORE OFFICIAL NOTIFICATION, WHICH WAS INEXPLICABLY DELAYED.

The phone rang, and Bill picked it up with a trembling hand. It was the adjutant at the Regional Adviser's office. "Bill," he said, "I've just received a message from Two Corps . . ."

"Yes, Hank," said Bill. "I know what's in it. I've just had the news from my own people."

"I don't know why this was delayed."

"It's all right. Those things can happen."

"I'll send this one right over."

"I'll appreciate it. How did it happen, do you know?"

"Yes. Apparently he did a brave thing, and it's not just the blah-blah that usually comes in these messages."

"What did he do?"

"He was trying to rally a remnant of Rangers after a bad ambush, and he went into one of those mud forts to bring some of them out."

"He went into a mud fort?"

"Yeah. A B-Forty hit it. He was killed instantly."

Bill sat as if frozen, the phone still in his hand.

"You still there, Bill?"

"Yeah. Sorry. Yeah, I'm still here."

"You OK?"

"Sure."

"There's nothing a fellow can say, Bill. Awfully sorry to give you such news."

"That's OK. Listen, do you think arrangements could be made for me to take him home personally?"

"I'm sure it could be arranged, if that's what you want to do."

"Will you work on it, then? I'll have to get my own people's permission for leave of absence, but I don't think that will be any problem."

"Leave it to me, old friend. I'll see that this doesn't get delayed. I'll be in touch with you."

Bill hung up the phone and sat motionless. He was feeling nothing yet. It was too soon. Such a calamity takes time to begin shaking a man's soul. He had had experiences in the past. The worst time was yet to come. He would weep for Will later today and tomorrow, but the real trial would come when he went home to his wife, bringing her only son back to her in a coffin.

He called Laura in and dictated a cable asking headquarters' permission to accompany Will's body to Massachusetts for burial. He also cabled headquarters to ask that his closest friend through all the years, a man whom he and his wife had known and loved since the old Burma days, be the one to go to her now with the news.

Then he went to the dining room. It was back to normal now, and the Vietnamese employees were serving breakfast to a capacity crowd. Bill sat down at a table that he was sure was the one that had held the dying child. The crowd was unaware of what had been going on in this room only three or four hours ago.

Two navy public relations officers, whom he knew by sight, came to the table with another man and asked if they might sit there. Bill motioned them into the chairs. The other man was a reporter.

"My paper printed the story, and it looks like a couple of others might pick it up, too," he was saying. "But it wasn't really as bad as it sounded to you when I told you about it yesterday."

The navy men smiled politely.

"It was worse," the reporter continued, wanting to give everybody within earshot the benefit of his witty attempts to needle his hosts. Bill regarded him blankly, not really paying attention.

"And so, I went out on that carrier, you know, and what do I have to put up with but an escort. It was a young jg that wouldn't let me out of his sight."

"Well," said one of the public relations men, "that's standard operating procedure, you know."

"Yeah, I know. I also know that what they wanted

was to keep me from moving around the ship and talking to the people I wanted to talk to, and getting the story I was after. But I got away from the stupid son of a bitch anyway, and found just the guys I was looking for, and got the story I wanted."

"What was the story you wanted?"

"I wanted to find out what the morale really was like on that ship. Whether the guys were smoking a lot of marijuana, whether there were many of them that had deserted or wanted to desert."

Bill could not resist interjecting a comment. "I'd think you could find a better story where the fighting is still going on. There's plenty of it."

"You're wrong, my friend," said the reporter. "The news isn't here in Vietnam. The news is back home. People are sick and tired of this stupid war, and what the people are interested in hearing is that their army and navy feel the same way. These kids want out. Now.

"Canada and Sweden are full of 'em, you know. At least there are *some* young guys in our country that have got enough brains and guts to figure out what's right and do it."

Bill stood up as if to leave, but instead of turning to go, he brought his fist around in a crunching haymaker that caught the reporter full in the mouth. The reporter's head snapped back and he flew backward against a nearby table, knocking it over and scattering the startled occupants in all directions. Bill moved over to where the man sat, groggy from the force of the blow. Blood from a cut lip was dripping on his fatigues.

"You slimy bastard," Bill snarled. "You've got a war that's tearing millions of lives apart on land and what do you do? You go on board a ship to look for drugs and deserters. That's all this war means to a chicken shit like you—a chance to beat the competition with a story of how worthless and demoralized our soldiers are, and how great and noble the Viet Cong are. Money and fame, that's what you're after, and you don't care how you get them!"

Everybody in the dining room was sitting in silence, staring at the scene. The reporter made as if to rise.

"If you get up now," Bill said, "I'll finish the job on you. You better sit there and listen, because it looks like the only way the press is ever going to get the truth is to get their hard heads beaten in.

"You're sitting in the middle of a battle that's been won, won flat and hands down by us and our allies, but do you print that? No, you sure as hell don't, because that message, even though it's the God's truth, that everybody in this room knows, doesn't happen to agree with the gospel according to Saint Walter.

"Now, buster, if you want to tell your editors who punched you in the mouth, and who would be glad to kill you if you were worth killing, tell them it was the CIA Regional Officer in Charge, and that if they want to ask me why, I'll be glad to tell them.

"And what I'll tell them, you miserable chicken shit, is that our soldiers have won this battle, and this war, but you and your smart-ass friends, and your wiser-than-anybody editors, have lost it. And so every single death and every drop of blood through all these years, that you've had so much fun showing on the screens with your snide remarks, it's all been for nothing.

"And that is *your* fault!

"I hope you and your friends can live with that, because there is no forgiving it, and twenty years from now you're never going to be able to explain it."

He stalked out.

The rest of the people in the dining room, who had been frozen into immobility by this sudden violent drama, began to straighten up the furniture and get back to normal. The public relations men helped the reporter to his feet and took him into the bar, where Sheila brought a basin with some water and some first-aid supplies, and began to treat his cut lip.

"Jesus Christ," said the reporter through his swelling lips, "what kind of Neanderthal is that guy?"

"He's a very sweet man," said Sheila. "You just caught him at a bad time."

"I've known a lot of hawks in my time," said the reporter, "and I've seen a lot of love-it-or-leave-it-flag-wavers, but I never had one come at me that way, for nothing."

"He didn't like your remarks about the army and navy," said one of the public relations men.

"In case you gentlemen didn't know it," Sheila went on, still swabbing at the cut lip with a piece of gauze dipped in disinfectant, "that man about half an hour ago got word that his son was killed in action up in Two Corps, day before yesterday."

"His son was in the army?" the reporter asked.

"That's right."

"With his old man here, he wouldn't have had to come to Vietnam," the reporter mused.

"He came because he believed in it," Sheila replied. "He volunteered."

"The boy seems to have had about as much brains as the old man," said the reporter.

Sheila put the gauze down and stepped back. She looked the reporter in the eye.

"You know, you really *are* a chicken shit," she said and walked indignantly out of the bar.

"Toby," said Bill, later that afternoon, "this is the only bright spot in what has been a bad day for me."

Toby had arrived from My Tho, on his way to Saigon and home for his leave. He looked gaunt, and the killing and grief had left a dark shadow in his eyes. Bill was glad he could give this man something pleasant for a change. He handed Toby a manila folder.

"This has got a whole stack of messages to and from headquarters about you, some that are addressed directly to you, and some that are not to or about you, but that will interest you nevertheless. But I'm going to take the selfish pleasure of being the first to tell you right now, instead of letting you get it from the written messages.

"First off, kind of a sad note, that I think you already know. Ernie Free was captured and taken north. You knew that, didn't you?"

"Yes. I'd heard it."

"Your intelligence report sort of predicted it, in fact. He was in a daze. The Tet attack caught him with his pants down, almost literally, and he never recovered. He never fought, never resisted."

"Poor guy. Believed his own reports, I guess."

"Not only *he* believed them. *Everybody* believed them."

"Yeah, I guess so."

"But you don't know the big part of it. That so-called penetration of COSVN . . ."

Toby's eyes widened with a dawning realization. "You're not going to tell me that that high-level penetration was Ernie's?"

"It sure as hell was. But there's more. After about a week of the fighting, when COSVN began to wake up to the fact that they had lost the battle, and the masses hadn't risen up, and the VC had been destroyed in the south, well, one of their high-level leaders defected to our embassy, and this was a sure-enough defection. The station debriefed him for several days. That's how they confirmed that Gypsy-One was a deception operation.

"Ernie was their patsy. As soon as he hit Vietnam, the word came down along the VC channels that there was a guy that they had already worked a double-agent operation on in Europe. They sent along an analysis of just how to go about hooking him again. He fell for it, and built up such a convincing project proposal that after a couple of cycles of reporting and assessing, his product was considered to be extremely valuable, and extremely high level."

"Jesus, you don't suppose he was *theirs,* do you?"

"No," Bill replied, "and neither does headquarters. He was an easy mark, and they knew him, and knew exactly where he was, and knew he was vulnerable and gullible, and knew exactly how to play him. But he wasn't a traitor. They probably figured he'd be an ideal man to debrief on CIA operations, and that's why they decided to pick him up, alive, and take him with them. Headquarters figures he's in the Soviet Union by now. They're in the middle of a damage assessment, and they'll probably have a lot of questions to ask you about him."

"He may have been foolish," said Toby, "but he didn't deserve that."

"Well, this straightens out the Frankfurt incident," said Bill, "and I don't have to tell you that your fitness report from me will tell the complete story and get the record straight. Not that it will really be necessary, because there's also a cable of commendation in there from the director, which will go into your record."

Toby smiled, and nodded his head with pleasure.

"And there is an acknowledgment of my recommendation that you be awarded the Distinguished Intelligence Cross for your performance during Tet."

The highest award the agency could give! It took Toby by surprise; left him speechless.

"From the wording of that message," Bill continued, "the recommendation has got enough high-level support that the award could be made within a week or so. If so, they'll want you and your wife to go to Washington for the ceremony."

"What can I say, Bill?" said Toby. "Nothing like this has ever happened to me before. But what about Ski and Ben?"

"I've sent recommendations through army channels to give Ben the Distinguished Service Cross, and a Silver Star for Ski," said Bill, "and I understand that those recommendations will get immediate and unqualified endorsement all the way up the line."

"Good," said Toby. "Those are two of the greatest men . . . you know . . . the most . . ."

Bill smiled at his struggle for words. "Combat friends, Toby. Comrades in arms. You don't have to explain it to me."

"But, on the other hand," Toby said, suddenly sober, "somehow there is something kind of horrible about me getting a medal for killing people, and in the middle of all the destruction, and so many other people being involved in so many ways. Some of them are dead, and my staff down there pretty well wiped out . . ."

"Yes, I know about that, too," Bill said with a sympathetic smile. "I think I know quite a bit about your staff, and what you thought of them."

Toby looked at him closely. "Yes," he said, "I expect you do."

The door opened, and Dino poked his head in, then opened it wide and walked in.

"My supersonic Spad is waiting at the airfield, Toby," he said. "The propeller is spinning, the wings are waving, all just itching to take off for Saigon."

"Another of our resident heroes," said Bill to Toby, grinning affectionately at Dino.

"I heard about him," said Toby.

"Hell yes," said Dino. "I'm a certified hero. We're all heroes. There ain't anybody in this ROIC office that isn't a goddamned hero."

"OK, Dino," said Bill, "see if you can get this hero to Saigon without getting him shot."

"Oh, he may get nicked in the butt," said Dino. "But why should he be any better than anybody else?"

Dino went out, and Toby grasped the hand Bill proffered "I won't have time to read all this stuff, Bill. Can you hold it for me till I get back?"

"Sure. It'll wait. You get the hell on home."

"Bill," said Toby hesitantly, "I know this is going to be a terribly sad time for you. When you see your wife, if you think it's OK, tell her that I met your son, and had some good talk with him, and that I can't think of any better way to tell her how he impressed me than to say that I hope my own son will be half as good a man in every way."

"Thanks, Toby. I'll be sure to tell her. She'll like that."

Toby left, and Bill sat for a long time staring at the door. That young man had come through days of shock, and he probably had no inkling that others had had the same experiences: bloodshed, separation, loneliness, love affairs, emotional turmoil, bereavement. Bill understood, remembered. Toby and Ben would be back together in My Tho in a couple of months, taking up where they had left off, picking up some of the pieces of things that had shattered, starting afresh on a difficult and exciting task, not even dreaming that others had been down the same road before them.

Bill glanced at the file folder on his desk, and over at the newspaper clippings in his in-box. He shook his head. There was one road he had never been down that Ben and Toby were going to have to travel, and he wondered how they would cope with it.

For the next year or so, Ben and Toby would be fighting and winning a war that was already lost.

TIME ALMANAC 2004

with INFORMATION PLEASE®

BORGNA BRUNNER
EDITOR IN CHIEF

Information Please®
www.infoplease.com
a Pearson Education Company

Information Please®
www.infoplease.com
a Pearson Education Company

Editor in Chief *Borgna Brunner*
Editor *Beth Rowen*
Senior Contributing Editor *Christine Frantz*
Contributing Editor *Susan Hyde*
Production Director *Susan Hyde*
Production Editor *Christine Frantz*

Vice President *George Kane*
Proofreading and Fact-Checking *Elissa Haney, Elizabeth Olson*
Editorial Assistant *Melissa Sogard*
Graphics *Sean M. Dessureau*
Technical Support *Karl DeBisschop*

Time Inc.
HOME ENTERTAINMENT

Contributing Editor *Kelly Knauer*
Design *Anthony Kosner*
Pictures *Patricia Cadley*

President *Rob Gursha*
Vice President, Branded Businesses *David Arfine*
Vice President, New Product Development *Richard Fraiman*

Executive Director, Marketing Services *Carol Pittard*
Director, Retail & Special Sales *Tom Mifsud*
Director of Finance *Tricia Griffin*
Assistant Marketing Director *Ann Marie Doherty*
Prepress Manager *Emily Rabin*
Book Production Manager *Jonathan Polsky*
Associate Product Manager *Kristin Walker*

Special thanks to: *Victoria Alfonso, Bozena Bannett, Alex Bliss, Robert Dente, Gina Di Meglio, Anne-Michelle Gallero, Peter Harper, Suzanne Janso, Robert Marasco, Natalie McCrea, Mary Jane Rigoroso, Steven Sandonato, Grace Sullivan*

The *TIME Almanac* welcomes comments and suggestions from readers. We prefer hearing from you through email (ipa@infoplease.com), if possible. Although the editors carefully consider each suggestion, because of the volume of correspondence we receive we cannot respond personally to each writer. The *TIME Almanac* does not rule on bets or wagers.

Editorial Office
Information Please
Pearson Education
160 Gould Street
Needham, MA 02494
Email: ipa@infoplease.com

Customer Service
Attention: TIME Almanac
PO Box 11016
Des Moines, IA 50336-1016

ISBN: 1-931933-78-2 Paperback
ISBN: 1-931933-85-5 Hardcover
ISSN: 0073-7860

If you would like to order copies of TIME's hardcover Collector's Edition books, please call us at 1-800-327-6388 (Monday through Friday, 7:00 A.M.–8:00 P.M. or Saturday, 7:00 A.M.–6:00 P.M. Central Time).

Keyword Index

Section Index

Page numbers followed by "n" indicate information in footnotes.

A

D

G

H

I

J

K

L

M

Q

R

S

U

V

W

X

Y

Z

The News of 2003: Nation

Preemption and War

Citing the possession of weapons of mass destruction, links to terrorism, and Saddam Hussein's despotism as the *casus belli* for "regime change" in Iraq, President George W. Bush launched the first preemptive war in United States history on March 20, 2003. For some months, the United States had deferred to the United Nations' handling of Iraq after the passage of Security Council resolution 1441 in Nov. 2002, which initiated new weapons inspections—Iraq had spent the past decade attempting to thwart UN measures to regulate its arsenal. But by March 2003, the president concluded that the UN's patient strategy of containment and deterrence in the face of Iraq's continuing defiance was dangerously fainthearted. In the war against terrorism—and Bush had controversially identified Iraq as the next target in that battle—the United States could no longer stand by while a potential threat to its security grew into an actual one. The new U.S. defense doctrine, announced by the president in a June 2002 speech at West Point and codified in *The National Security Strategy of the United States* (Sept. 2002), expanded the justifications for war: "Legal scholars . . . often conditioned the legitimacy of preemption on the existence of an imminent threat—most often a visible mobilization of armies." But a non-conventional war against terrorism, the document argued, requires "taking anticipatory action to defend ourselves, even if uncertainty remains as to the time and place of the enemy's attack." Many expressed alarm at this aggressive shift in U.S. policy—an "international hunting license" is how one critic put it. The doctrine was strongly criticized by the UN and a number of world leaders, particularly France, Germany, and Russia, who were apprehensive about what they saw as the U.S.'s circumvention of international law and its disregard for international consensus. The doctrine declared that the country "will not hesitate to act alone, if necessary, to exercise our right of self-defense by acting preemptively against . . . terrorists."

Going It Alone

In place of a UN mandate for war (the U.S. and Britain, after intensive lobbying, gained only two supporters among the 15-member Security Council: Spain and Bulgaria), the United States gathered a "coalition of the willing." Although the group of 45 nations was little more than decorative, it allowed Secretary of Defense Donald Rumsfeld to claim that "it is larger than the coalition that existed during the Gulf War in 1991." The differences in genuine international support between the two Iraq wars could not have been more profound. In 2003, besides the U.S.'s 225,000 troops and Britain's 45,000, only Australia and Poland contributed combat soldiers (2,000 and 200, respectively), whereas the UN-sponsored coalition in the 1991 Gulf War included combat troops from 32 countries. In 2003, the U.S. assumed the bulk of the war's cost, amounting to $4 billion a month; in 1991, the U.S. share of the war's expenses was just 10%.

Operation Iraqi Freedom

Along with its steadfast ally, Britain, the U.S. launched Operation Iraqi Freedom on March 20, beginning with an unsuccessful "decapitation attack" meant to eliminate Saddam Hussein and short-circuit the war. The U.S. military's promise of a campaign of "shock and awe" was in reality far more muted, but by April 9, despite meeting greater-than-expected resistance, U.S. forces took control of Baghdad, signalling the collapse of Saddam Hussein's regime. Major fighting was declared over by May 1. The United States sustained a total of 138 casualties, 116 of those from combat, between March 20 and May 1. As of Oct. 1, Saddam Hussein's whereabouts remained unknown, but numerous high-ranking Baathists, including Hussein's two sons, were killed or captured in the months following the war.

Troubled Aftermath

Post-war reconstruction went far less smoothly than the war itself. After decades of Hussein's repression, economic hardship from years of UN sanctions, and its third war in 20 years, Iraq now found itself enveloped in violence and lawlessness. Many essential services, including electricity and water, had yet to be restored to pre-war levels. Iraqis strongly protested the delay in self-rule and the absence of a timetable to end the U.S. occupation. In July, diplomat Paul Bremer, whom the U.S. designated as the chief administrator of the occupation, appointed a 25-member Iraqi governing council, a first step toward transferring authority to Iraqis.

Coalition forces faced daily attacks; by August, more soldiers had died in the aftermath of the war than during the period of official combat. The U.S. launched several tough military campaigns to subdue the remaining Iraqi resistance, which also had the effect of further alienating the populace. Among the most destructive acts of organized violence were the sabotage of several oil pipelines, the destruction of UN headquarters in Baghdad by a car bomb, which killed top UN envoy Sérgio Vieira de Mello, and the assassinations of one of Iraq's most important Shi'ite leaders and a member of the Iraqi governing council. It is unclear who was responsible for what U.S. forces commander Gen. John P. Abizaid called "a classical guerrilla-type campaign." Donald Rumsfeld blamed "dead-enders, foreign terrorists, and criminal gangs," but U.S. intelligence has suggested that the most significant threat is now ordinary Iraqis, bridling under the occupation.

Lawmakers on both sides of the aisle questioned whether more U.S. troops beyond the 130,000 stationed in post-war Iraq should be deployed. In addition to a British force of 11,000, a 9,000-strong international stabilizing force led by Poland began arriving in July 2003 to help alleviate the strain (the U.S. largely footed the bill for the Polish force). In a coolly received speech at the UN in September, Bush asked the international community to provide more troops and money for Iraq, but made it clear that decision-making would remain in U.S. hands. He had already asked Congress for $87 billion on top of the $79 billion Congress approved in April to cover military and reconstruction spending for Iraq ($11 billion was to be set aside for Afghanistan). The solidly pro-war *Economist* remarked that "since the objective was regime change, not just regime toppling, no triumph can be declared until a durable new regime is in place."

The War's Shifting Justifications

Months of searching for Iraq's weapons of mass destruction—one of the central reasons the Bush and Blair administrations cited for launching the war—yielded no hard evidence, and both administrations and their intelligence agencies came under fire. There were also mounting allegations that the existence of these weapons was exaggerated or distorted to justify the war. In July, the Bush administration conceded that evidence claiming that Iraq was pursuing a nuclear weapons program by seeking to obtain uranium from Africa—cited in the president's State of the Union address and repeated by a number of top administration officials—had been discredited. Two months later Vice President Cheney reluctantly admitted, "we never had any evidence that [Hussein] had acquired a nuclear weapon."

With his most compelling argument for war still unsubstantiated, Bush emphasized other rationales: Hussein's brutal repression and human rights record, and Iraq as "the central front" in the war against terrorism. According to Deputy Defense Secretary Paul Wolfowitz, a functioning democracy in Iraq would "demonstrate especially to the Arab and Muslim world that there is a better way than the way of the terrorist."

President Bush's broad, all-purpose definition of terrorism blurred the distinctions between the Sept. 11 attacks, al-Qaeda, and Iraq, creating a widespread impression among the public of their direct connection. Bush's May 1 speech declaring the end of the fighting, for example, claimed that "the battle of Iraq is one victory in a war on terror that began on Sept. 11, 2001. . . . We've removed an ally of al-Qaeda." A *Washington Post* poll just prior to the second anniversary of Sept. 11 revealed that 69% of Americans believed that Saddam Hussein was "personally involved" in the Sept. 11 attacks, an allegation for which Bush himself has acknowledged there is "no evidence."

A number of supporters of the war argued that murky or flawed pre-war rationales do not undermine the enormous good achieved by the war. Britain's prime minister Tony Blair maintained that "history would forgive" the UK and U.S. "if we are wrong" about weapons of mass destruction—the end to the "inhuman carnage and suffering" caused by Saddam Hussein was justification enough for the war. But opponents argued that if Washington's preemptive war was not based on a real and imminent threat but simply on the perception of one, if the evidence presented was not unimpeachably credible, and if the case for war hinged on fluctuating rationales adjusted after the fact, then the grave decision to launch an invasion becomes so perilously arbitrary and lacking in transparency that it cannot be sanctioned in a democracy. At its best the doctrine of preemption permits, in President Bush's words, "the wisdom and the will to stop great threats before they arrive." At its worst, the doctrine becomes, in UN Secretary General Kofi Annan's words, "the unilateral and lawless use of force."

Tax Cuts and the Deficit

On the domestic front, President Bush unveiled a sweeping economic stimulus plan that characteristically centered around tax cuts. The plan in its original form was to cut taxes by $670 billion over ten years; Congress approved a $350 billion version in May (which will in fact rise to a $800 billion tax cut if its sunset clauses are cancelled). The plan strongly favored two groups: two-parent households with several children, and the wealthy—nearly half the proposed tax benefits were reserved for the richest 10% of American taxpayers. Critics argued that it was unsound to offer tax cuts in the midst of a jobless recovery (nearly 3 million jobs had been lost since Bush came to office), when the country was involved in an enormously expensive war, and when the federal budget deficit, according to the nonpartisan Congressional Budget Office, was expected to reach a record $480 billion in 2004. Bush continued to argue that his previous tax cuts (this was his third round) had managed to keep the recession shallow and were beginning to revive the economy.

Prospects remained bleak for the poor: the most recent statistics revealed that in 2002, 34.6 million (12% of the population) lived in poverty, up 1.7 million from the year 2001, and the percent of the population without health insurance rose to 15.2%, the largest increase in a decade.

Landmark Affirmative Action Ruling

In a landmark case involving the University of Michigan's affirmative action policies—one of the most important rulings on the issue in twenty-five years—the Supreme Court decisively upheld the right of affirmative action in higher education. The Court ruled on two cases: the University of Michigan's undergraduate program (*Gratz* v. *Bollinger*) and its law school (*Grutter* v. *Bollinger*). The Supreme Court (5–4) upheld the University of Michigan Law School's policy, ruling that race can be one of many factors considered by colleges when selecting their students because it "furthers a compelling interest in obtaining the educational benefits that flow from a diverse student body." But the Court ruled (6–3) that the more formulaic approach of the University of Michigan's undergraduate admissions program, which uses a point system that rates students and awards additional points to minorities, had to be modified since it did not provide the necessary "individualized consideration."

The Court held that the justification for affirmative action had evolved since its introduction in the 1960s—originally meant to redress past oppression and injustice, it now served to promote a "compelling state interest in diversity" that provided advantages for all races. A record number of "friend-of-court" briefs were filed in support of the case by hundreds of organizations representing academia, business, labor unions, and the military, arguing the benefits of broad racial representation at all levels of society. □

The News of 2003: World

Middle East: Road Map to Nowhere

In an attempt to restart the stalled Israeli-Palestinian peace process, Israel and the United States resolved to circumvent Palestinian leader Yasir Arafat, whom Israeli prime minister Ariel Sharon called "irrelevant" and an obstacle. Under U.S. pressure, Arafat reluctantly appointed a prime minister in April, who was to replace him in negotiating the peace process. Prime Minister Mahmoud Abbas, formerly Arafat's second-in-command, was well-respected internationally but had virtually no political base among Palestinians. Unlike Arafat, however, he unequivocally rejected the violence of the intifada. On May 1, the "Quartet" (the U.S., UN, EU, and Russia) unfurled the "road map" for peace, which ultimately envisioned the creation of a Palestinian state by 2005. Although Sharon publicly acknowledged the need for a Palestinian state and Abbas committed himself to ending Palestinian violence, the road map quickly led nowhere, with neither side honoring their obligations: Abbas, with little real political power, did not disable terrorist organizations, and Sharon did not dismantle settlements, much less prevent new ones from cropping up. Sharon also persisted in building the highly controversial security barrier dividing Israeli and Palestinian areas. Although three militant Palestinian groups (Hamas, Islamic Jihad, and Fatah) declared a cease-fire on June 29, attacks resumed within weeks.

Hopes for the road map were shattered in August with the suicide bombing of an Israeli bus that killed 20, including 6 children, and with Israel's assassination of senior Hamas leader Abu Shanab. As Israel stepped up its "targeted killings" and Palestinian attacks on Israeli civilians continued, Mahmoud Abbas resigned, frustrated with the constant power wrangling with Arafat and his untenable role. Considered a puppet by the Palestinians, he was expected to perform the impossible by the Quartet. In September, further exacerbating tensions and alarming much of the world, Israel announced that it was prepared to "remove" Arafat. Critics charged that to exile or assassinate the Palestinians' elected leader, however obstructionist he had become, was not only to renounce the pursuit of peace but to invite increased violence. About 2,400 Palestinians and 800 Israelis have been killed since the intifada began in Sept. 2000.

Liberia Freed of Kleptocracy

Charles Taylor, Liberia's warlord-turned-president, was finally forced out of office by rebel groups and regional peacekeeping forces in August. Taylor, who came to power after a bloody civil war, spent his six-year presidency arming his country while its ruined infrastructure languished. His foreign policy was similarly destructive, supporting brutal Revolutionary United Front (RUF) in Sierra Leone's horrific civil war, and fueling conflicts in Guinea and Cote d'Ivoire. By June 2003, the Liberians United for Reconciliation and Democracy (LURD) and other rebels controlled two-thirds of the country, and the increased fighting intensified an already dire humanitarian crisis. Taylor resisted stepping down until the arrival of ECOWAS, the Nigerian-led West African peacekeeping force (along with a handful of American marines). Gyude Bryant, a businessman seen as a coalition-builder, was selected by the various factions as the new president. By the time he went into exile in Nigeria, Taylor had bankrupted his own country, siphoning off $100 million, and leaving it, according to the *New York Times,* the world's poorest nation.

Afghanistan at the Brink

Two years after the U.S.-led war resulted in the collapse of the Taliban, Afghanistan remained in a desperately fragile state, ruled by warlords and coming under renewed attack by Taliban and al-Qaeda forces. The U.S. maintained 11,500 troops in the country to combat the Taliban and al-Qaeda insurgency, but with its efforts focused on Iraq, the U.S.'s commitment to securing Afghanistan's stability waned. Most-wanted terrorist Osama bin Laden, still at large, was rarely even mentioned publicly by the administration.

Although Afghanistan made modest progress toward developing a constitution and establishing an army, President Hamid Karzai had almost no control over his country beyond the capital. The 5,500-member international peacekeeping force was reluctant to venture beyond Kabul, given the country's violent lawlessness. In August, NATO assumed command of the peacekeeping troops (most of whom were German and Canadian), and promised a more effective operation. In September Washington also announced it would increase its security and reconstruction efforts in Afghanistan—with mounting post-war difficulties in Iraq, President Bush could ill afford a second precarious state on his watch.

Axis of Nuclear Provocation

Throughout 2003, North Korea's Kim Il Jong aggressively taunted the U.S. with threats of nuclear proliferation, culminating in an April announcement that the country already possessed nuclear weapons (a claim not verified). It was difficult for much of the world to decipher how Kim expected to accomplish his aims—economic aid for his impoverished nation and a safeguard against U.S. attack—through such reckless brinkmanship. Refusing to bow to North Korea's mercurial demands, the United States informed the nation's diplomats that it would not begin to negotiate until North Korea first dismantled its nuclear program. China took on the role of mediator between North Korea and the U.S., urging less inflexibility on both sides. A modest breakthrough occurred when officials from the U.S., North Korea, China, Russia, South Korea, and Japan met in August in Beijing, although nothing substantive resulted.

Iran's seemingly illicit nuclear ambitions surfaced in June when the International Atomic Energy Agency (IAEA) criticized the country's concealment of nuclear activities and later discovered traces of highly enriched uranium at two sites. This led to IAEA demands for rigorous oversight; subsequent stonewalling by Iran's hardliners amplified the crisis. □

What Happened in 2003: Month by Month

Below are highlights of key events of the year, organized month by month, in three categories for easy reference. For the year's major Supreme Court decisions, *see* p. 149. "Countries of the World" covers specific international events, country by country. *See also* "People in the News," pp. 1030–1034, and "2003 Deaths," pp. 1035–1039, for more current-events coverage.

January 2003

WORLD

Britain Arrests Terror Suspects (Jan. 5): Six arrested when police find traces of the toxic agent ricin in a London apartment. **(Jan. 14):** Three more arrested in Manchester. **(Jan. 21):** Seven more arrested in raid on a London mosque. Authorities believe suspects were planning to poison food supply of British troops.

Suicide Bombers Strike Tel Aviv (Jan. 5): Two attackers blow themselves up seconds apart in crowded downtown area, killing 22 other people and injuring more than 100. Al-Aksa Martyrs Brigade claims responsibility.

North Korea Withdraws from Arms Treaty (Jan. 9): Rejects Treaty on the Nonproliferation of Nuclear Weapons. **(Jan. 10)** North Korean representatives meet with New Mexico governor Bill Richardson to discuss crisis.

U.S. Deploys Troops to Persian Gulf (Jan. 10): Secretary of Defense Donald Rumsfeld dispatches about 62,000 troops in 24 hours. Brings total troops deployed to gulf to nearly 80,000.

Mexican Foreign Minister Resigns (Jan. 10): Jorge Castañeda steps down, expressing frustration that U.S. and Mexico failed to reach an accord on migration.

Empty Warheads Found in Iraq (Jan. 16): UN weapons inspectors discover 11 empty chemical warheads in southern Iraq, which claims they were listed in weapons declaration. **(Jan. 19):** Iraq tells weapons inspectors it has found four other empty chemical warheads.

France Says It Does Not Support Immediate War in Iraq (Jan. 20): Foreign Minister Dominique de Villepin announces country may use veto power in Security Council to thwart U.S. push for resolution justifying early action against Iraq. Germany signals similar reluctance. Both countries recommend giving weapons inspections more time.

Libya to Chair UN Human Rights Commission (Jan. 20): U.S., Canada, and Guatemala vote against move, citing Libya's own poor human-rights record.

Two Americans Shot in Kuwait (Jan. 21): Michael Rene Pouliot, a civilian contractor for the government, killed in ambush. Other man, David Caraway, a software engineer, wounded.

Carter Urges Compromise in Venezuela (Jan. 21): In an attempt to end seven-week general strike, former president recommends either reducing presidential term to four years from six or holding a referendum on leadership of President Hugo Chávez.

North Korea Says It Has No Plans for Nuclear Weapons (Jan. 22): In cabinet-level meeting with South Korea, North says in a statement, "Although we have withdrawn from the Nuclear Nonproliferation Treaty, we have no intention of producing nuclear weapons at this stage."

Arms Inspectors Report on Iraq (Jan. 27): Hans Blix, chief chemical and biological weapons inspector, says that Iraq is not fully cooperating with inspectors and has failed to prove it has destroyed its banned weapons. Atomic weapons inspector Mohamed ElBaradei, however, reports that his team did not turn up any evidence that Iraq has resumed production of nuclear weapons.

U.S. Troops Battle in Afghanistan (Jan. 28): Heaviest fighting in months as U.S. and allied troops confront rebel warlords loyal to Taliban.

Sharon Prevails in Israeli Election (Jan. 29): Prime Minister Ariel Sharon and his Likud Party resoundingly defeat Labor Party, led by Amram Mitzna. Likud takes 38 seats in the 120-seat parliament, while Labor emerges with 19 seats, losing 6 seats.

NATION

108th Congress Convenes (Jan. 7): Republicans begin new term in control of both houses. Democrat Nancy Pelosi becomes House minority leader, the first woman to ever lead a party in Congress. Senate passes bill to extend unemployment benefits.

Bush Proposes New Tax Cuts (Jan. 7): Plan eliminates tax on stock dividends, increases child-care tax credit to $1,000 from $600, and increases write-off for small businesses that buy new equipment. Proposal criticized as a boon to the wealthy.

Court Rules for Bush in Combatant Case (Jan. 8): Federal appeals court says wartime president can hold a U.S. citizen deemed an enemy combatant indefinitely, without access to a lawyer.

Bush Signs Law to Extend Unemployment Benefits (Jan. 8): Legislation, passed by Congress, extends benefits to about 2.5 million Americans.

Illinois Governor Commutes Death Sentences (Jan. 11): Republican governor George Ryan commutes sentences of 167 on death row, calling capital punishment fundamentally flawed.

White House Announces Huge Deficits (Jan. 15): Administration expects 2003 deficit to top $200 billion and $300 billion in 2004.

U.S. Begins Developing System to Monitor Germ Attacks (Jan. 22): System will detect when pathogens such as anthrax and smallpox are released into air.

Ridge Sworn In as Homeland Security Chief (Jan. 24): Former governor of Pennsylvania becomes nation's first secretary of Homeland Security. Department unites 22 agencies and 170,000 employees.

Bush Presents Case for War in Iraq (Jan. 28): In his second State of the Union speech, president says country must be prepared to attack Iraq, preferably with the backing of the United Nations. Bush also asserts that his $674 billion tax-cut package will help to boost economy and vows to make prescription drug coverage part of Medicare.

Shoe Bomber Sentenced (Jan. 30): Richard Reid sentenced to life in prison for trying, in December 2001, to blow up a plane with explosives hidden in his shoes.

BUSINESS/SCIENCE/SOCIETY

Commuter Plane Crashes in North Carolina (Jan. 8): All 21 aboard die when plane dives into building seconds after takeoff.

AOL Chairman Steps Down (Jan. 12): Stephen Case, founder of the online service, resigns amid falling stock prices and dissatisfaction of shareholders. Case had masterminded the 2001 merger of AOL and Time Warner. **(Jan. 17):** Richard Parsons, chief executive of AOL Time Warner, chosen to succeed Case. **(Jan. 29)** Ted Turner, vice chairman of media giant, resigns as company announces large fourth-quarter loss and writes down value of America Online by $35 billion.

Mexican Earthquake Kills Dozens (Jan. 22): President Vicente Fox declares state of emergency in Colima. Nearly 30 people killed and about 300 injured.

Scientists Report Finding of Winged Dinosaur Fossil (Jan. 23): Discovery of four-winged *Microraptor gui* in China helps to explain evolution of birds and flight.

North Carolina Factory Explodes (Jan. 29): Blast at medical-supply plant in Kinston kills 4 and wounds 36.

February 2003

WORLD

Strike Ends in Venezuela (Feb. 2): Opposition group Democratic Coordinator ends crippling general strike. Oil-industry workers, however, remain on strike.

Yugoslavia Gets New Name (Feb. 4): Parliament votes to name country Serbia and Montenegro. Move reflects Montenegro's drive for independence.

Powell Argues for War in Iraq (Feb. 5): U.S. secretary of state tells Security Council that Saddam Hussein is an imminent threat to world security, has continuously deceived UN weapons inspectors, has links to al-Qaeda, and possesses mobile biological weapons factories.

Kurdish Leader Killed (Feb. 8): Shawkat Hajji Mushir, member of parliament, assassinated in northern Iraq by members of militant Islamic group Ansar al-Islam. Two other government officials killed in the attack. U.S. believes group linked to al-Qaeda and Saddam Hussein.

Europeans Thwart Defense for Turkey (Feb. 10): France, Germany, and Belgium veto U.S. request to NATO to begin sending military hardware to Turkey as a defense in case of war with Iraq. **(Feb. 16):** Dispute settled in compromise that has NATO Defense Planning Council, which does not include France, making arrangements to arm Turkey with hardware for self-defense.

New Bin Laden Tape Broadcast (Feb. 11): In recording released by Al Jazeera television network, voice, believed to be of Osama bin Laden, warns of future attacks against the U.S. and encourages Iraq to defend against U.S.-led offensive. U.S. says recording evidence that al-Qaeda and Iraq are connected.

Arms Experts Say Iraq Missile Violates Range Limits (Feb. 12): Panel, appointed by the UN, concludes that Al Samoud 2 ballistic missiles exceed 90-mile range limit set by the Security Council.

Weapons Inspectors Report Modest Progress in Iraq (Feb. 14): Hans Blix and Mohamed ElBaradei, chief inspectors, say Iraq becoming slightly more cooperative and forthcoming about weapons programs and by allowing surveillance flights. Report intensifies opposition by France and Germany against military action.

Millions Gather to Protest War (Feb. 15): Marchers demonstrate in New York and other U.S. cities, in London, Melbourne, Paris, Seoul, and many other locations to rally against war in Iraq.

Sept. 11 Suspect Convicted in Germany (Feb. 19): Hamburg court finds Mounir el-Motassadeq, 28, guilty of 3,066 counts of being an accessory to murder, attempted murder, and of belonging to a terrorist organization. He's the first Sept. 11 suspect to be convicted.

Weapons Inspector Orders Iraq to Destroy Missiles (Feb. 22): Hans Blix tells Iraq to dismantle Al Samoud 2 missiles, whose range exceeds limit. **(Feb. 26):** In a televised interview with CBS News anchor Dan Rather, Saddam Hussein says missiles do not violate range limit. Iraqi president also denies any link to al-Qaeda. **(Feb. 27):** In a letter to Hans Blix, Hussein says he agrees "in principle" to begin dismantling missiles.

U.S., UK, and Spain Say Iraq Has Failed to Disarm (Feb. 22): In a draft resolution submitted to the UN Security Council, countries state that "Iraq has failed to take the final opportunity afforded to it in Resolution 1441," and that it is now time to authorize use of military force against the country. **(Feb. 24):** France, Germany, and Russia submit an informal counter-resolution to the UN Security Council that states that inspections should be intensified and extended.

Explosions Rock Venezuela (Feb. 25): Colombian consulate and Spanish embassy in Caracas targeted.

U.S. Says North Korea Has Restarted Reactor (Feb. 26): Reactivation of plant at Yongbyon allows country to convert nuclear waste into weapons-grade plutonium.

Former Bosnian President Sentenced (Feb. 27): Biljana Plavsic to serve 11 years in jail for the persecution of thousands of Muslims and Croats in Bosnia between 1992 and 1995. She's the only woman indicted for war crimes in former Yugoslavia.

Parliament Approves Israeli Government (Feb. 28): Prime Minister Ariel Sharon will preside over hawkish four-party coalition.

U.S. Says Hussein Must Leave Iraq (Feb. 28): In a policy shift, White House says Iraq must disarm and Hussein must go into exile to avoid war.

NATION

Space Shuttle Explodes (Feb. 1): *Columbia* breaks up as it reenters Earth's atmosphere on its way to Kennedy Space Center, killing all seven crew members. Victims are: Rick D. Husband, William C. McCool, Michael P. Anderson, David M. Brown, Kalpana Chawla, Laurel Clark, and the first Israeli astronaut, Ilan Ramon. **(Feb. 13):** Investigators think a hole in the left wing let superheated gas flow into the shuttle, contributing to crash.

Bush Sends Congress Budget (Feb. 3): Fiscal year 2004 budget totals $2.23 trillion and predicts record deficits in coming years.

U.S. Issues Disaster Preparation Advice (Feb. 10): Guidelines for coping with chemical or biological attack prompt millions to clear store shelves of duct tape and plastic sheeting.

Greenspan Casts Doubt on Stimulus Plan (Feb. 11): Chairman of the Federal Reserve tells Senate Banking, Housing, and Urban Affairs Committee that economy may not need stimulus package, which includes deep tax cuts. Also warns that deficits predicted under President Bush's stimulus package could hurt economy in the long term.

Bush Announces Reorganization of Intelligence Agencies (Feb. 14): Counterterrorism divisions of FBI and CIA moving to a central location to consolidate information gathering and analysis.

Stampede Kills 21 in Chicago (Feb. 17): Panic erupts after security guards spray Mace to break up a fight in hip-hop club called E2. More than 50 people wounded.

States File Suit Against EPA (Feb. 19): Attorneys general of Connecticut, Massachusetts, Maine, New Jersey, Rhode Island, Washington, and New York suing agency for not regulating carbon dioxide emissions under the Clean Air Act.

Club Fire Kills Dozens in Rhode Island (Feb. 21): Pyrotechnics display set off during concert by band Great White ignites an inferno that quickly engulfs entire building at West Warwick. Death toll reaches 100.

Court Upholds Ban on Word "God" (Feb. 28): Federal appeals court in San Francisco lets stand earlier ruling that recitation in public schools of the words "under God" in Pledge of Allegiance violates the separation of church and state.

BUSINESS/SCIENCE/SOCIETY

Unemployment Rate Falls (Feb. 7): Jobless rate dips to 5.7% in January, down from 6% in December 2002.

Astronomers Confirm Age of Universe (Feb. 11): A satellite called the Wilkinson Microwave Anisotropy Probe produced detailed map of universe, revealing that it is 13.7 billion years old, it is rapidly expanding, and its weight is 4% atoms, 23% dark matter, and 73% dark energy.

AIDS Vaccine Fails to Prevent Infection (Feb. 23): First AIDS vaccine to reach large-scale test stage. It does, however, seem to decrease infection rate of some minorities.

Design for Ground Zero Selected (Feb. 27): Plan, drafted by architect Daniel Libeskind, features recessed memorial to victims of Sept. 11, 2001, attack and a 1,776-foot tower.

March 2003

WORLD

Iraq Begins to Destroy Missiles (March 1): Reluctantly starts dismantling its Al Samoud missiles, as ordered by UN chief weapons inspector Hans Blix.

September 11 Suspect Arrested (March 1): Khalid Shaikh Mohammed, a top aide to Osama bin Laden who is accused of masterminding the 2001 terrorist attacks against the U.S., captured in Rawalpindi, Pakistan.

Parliament Rejects U.S. Troops in Turkey (March 1): Turkish lawmakers reject plan to have about 62,000 American troops based in Turkey in case of war with Iraq. A stunning defeat for the U.S.

Bomb Explodes in Philippines (March 4): Attack at airport in Davao kills 21 people, including an American missionary, William P. Hyde. Officials suspect Muslim separatist group, the Moro Islamic Liberation Front.

Suicide Bomber Strikes Bus (March 5): Hamas claims responsibility for attack in Haifa that kills 15 people, including a 14-year-old American girl.

ElBaradei Discredits Evidence Against Iraq (March 7): UN weapons inspector reports to Security Council that documents that said Iraq tried to buy uranium from Niger were forged. Bush administration had used the evidence to claim Iraq was constituting its nuclear weapons program.

Turkey Elects New Leader (March 9): In a special vote, Recep Tayyip Erdogan of the Justice and Development Party wins a seat in parliament and becomes prime minister. He was previously barred from government for "inciting religious hatred."

Palestinian Parliament Approves Prime Minister Post (March 10): Yasir Arafat nominates Mahmoud Abbas, second-in-command of the Palestine Liberation Organization. **(March 19):** Mahmoud Abbas formally accepts the position of prime minister. New post will diminish the power of Yasir Arafat.

International Criminal Court Opens (March 11): Hague-based court will prosecute human rights abuses. The U.S. did not sign the treaty that created the court.

Serb Prime Minister Assassinated (March 12): Prime Minister Zoran Djindjic gunned down outside his Belgrade office. Authorities suspect organized crime.

Mystery Illness Strikes Asia (March 15): World Health Organization calls virus, severe acute respiratory syndrome (SARS), a "worldwide health threat." **(March 19):** WHO reports illness may be caused by a virus in the paramyxoviridae family. **(March 25):** U.S.-based Centers for Disease Control and Prevention says it thinks a "previously unrecognized virus from the coronavirus family" is the root of the illness.

Chinese Leadership Changes Hands (March 15): President Jiang Zemin officially steps down. Hu Jintao succeeds him.

U.S., Britain, and Spain Withdraw Resolution (March 17): When it becomes clear that France will veto a joint UN resolution that authorizes use of force against Iraq, countries withdraw resolution and agree to invade without the backing of the Security Council.

Serbian Parliament Elects New Prime Minister (March 18): Pro-Western reformer Zoran Zivkovic chosen to replace slain leader Zoran Djindjic.

Cuban Plane Hijacked (March 19): Six men, armed with knives, commandeer a plane destined for Havana and redirect it to Key West, Fla. All six suspects arrested.

War in Iraq Begins (March 20): U.S. launches Operation Iraqi Freedom. Called a "decapitation attack," the predawn air strike targets Saddam Hussein and other Iraqi leaders in Baghdad. Ground troops enter the country, crossing into southern Iraq from Kuwait. **(March 21):** Major phase of war begins with heavy aerial attacks on Baghdad and other cities. Campaign, dubbed "shock and awe," intended to promptly overwhelm Iraqi forces. **(March 23):** Coalition troops encounter fierce resistance near the southern city of Nasiriya. Iraqi forces capture 12 members of the 507th Ordnance Maintenance Company. **(March 25):** U.S. modifies its ground strategy as Iraqi militias, called fedayeen, attack coalition ground troops as they advance on Baghdad. **(March 26):** About 1,000 paratroopers land in Kurdish-controlled northern Iraq to open a northern front. **(March 27):** U.S. bombards Baghdad, targeting government buildings. **(March 28):** With Umm Qasr freed of mines, first shipment of humanitarian aid arrives in Iraq. Iraqi suicide bomber strikes near Najaf, killing four U.S. soldiers from the Third Infantry Division. **(March 30):** Secretary of Defense Donald Rumsfeld deflects criticism that the U.S. has not deployed enough Army ground troops in Iraq. **(March 30):** U.S. Marines and Army troops launch first attack on Iraq's Republican Guard, about 65 miles outside Baghdad.

U.S. Troops Strike in Afghanistan (March 20): In the largest operation in more than a year, about 1,000 soldiers raid Kandahar, seeking out al-Qaeda members.

Hindus Slain in Kashmir (March 23): Twenty-four Hindu Brahmins executed in Nandimarg. India blames Pakistani militants for the attack.

Japan Launches Spy Satellites Over North Korea (March 28): Devices to monitor activity in North Korea, which warned that such a move could result in "disastrous consequences."

NATION

Bush Prepares Country for War (March 6): In nationally televised press conference, president says Saddam Hussein is a direct threat to the U.S. and that the country will attack Iraq unilaterally if necessary.

Air Force Announces Rape Investigations (March 6): Reports 54 allegations of rape over 10 years at the U.S. Air Force Academy in Colorado. **(March 25):** Air Force dismisses four top academy officers in scandal.

Utah Teen Reunited with Family (March 12): Elizabeth Smart found in Sandy, Utah, with her alleged kidnappers, Brian Mitchell and his wife, Wendy Barzee, nine months after being kidnapped. **(March 18):** Mitchell and Barzee each charged with aggravated sexual assault, burglary, and kidnapping.

Senate Passes Abortion Ban (March 13): Votes, 64–33, to outlaw intact dilation and extraction, also called partial-birth abortion, a procedure to end pregnancies in the second and third trimesters.

Bush Warns Hussein (March 17): In a televised address, president tells country that war will be avoided only if Iraqi president Saddam Hussein steps down within 48 hours.

Senate Votes Down Alaska Drilling (March 19): After a bitter fight, Senate votes, 52–48, against drilling for oil in the Arctic National Wildlife Refuge.

House Passes Budget Resolution (March 21): Plan calls for $2.2 trillion in spending and allows for President Bush's $726 billion tax cut. **(March 25):** Senate passes, 51–48, an amendment to nonbinding budget resolution that reduces president's proposed $726 billion tax cut to $350 billion.

BUSINESS/SCIENCE/SOCIETY

Broadway Musicians Strike (March 7): Many theaters go dark when stagehands and actors vote to support musicians' strike. Dispute over the number of musicians required to play at Broadway venues. **(March 11):** Strike ends after an all-night negotiating session.

Large Job Losses Recorded in February (March 7): Labor Department announces U.S. payrolls fell by 308,000 in February.

***Chicago* Nabs Top Oscar (March 23):** Musical named best picture. Roman Polanski wins best director for holocaust drama, *The Pianist.* Film's star, Adrien Brody, takes best actor honor.

April 2003

WORLD

Hijackers Strike in Cuba (April 1): Suspect, Adermis Wilson Gonzalez, commandeers plane bound for Havana and demands that it land in Key West, Fla. He's arrested by U.S. authorities. **(April 4):** Armed men who hijacked a government-run ferry on April 2 surrender to Cuban authorities. **(April 11):** Cuba executes three hijackers of the ferry. Four others are given life sentences. International condemnation follows.

Bomb Explodes in Southern Philippines (April 2): Sixteen people die near a ferry terminal in Davao. Second such attack in a month. Officials blame the Moro Islamic Liberation Front, a Muslim separatist group.

U.S. Commandos Rescue Army Soldier (April 2): Special operations forces rescue Pfc. Jessica Lynch from a hospital in Nasiriya. She was one of the 12 members of the 507th Ordnance Maintenance Company captured by Iraqi troops on March 23.

U.S. Forces Enter Baghdad (April 5): Tanks and other vehicles roll into the Iraqi capital and engage in firefights with Iraqi troops.

British Forces Take Control of Basra (April 7): Declare that Iraq's second-largest city has fallen.

Three Journalists Killed in Iraq (April 8): U.S. tanks, reportedly responding to sniper fire, strike Palestine Hotel, where many reporters were based. Also fire on the building that served as the Iraq bureau for the Al Jazeera network.

Baghdad Falls (April 9): U.S. forces take control of the city, but sporadic fighting continues throughout the capital. Looters pillage government buildings, museums, hospitals, and stores. Statue of Saddam Hussein symbolically toppled. National Museum of Iraq plundered of its most prized treasures.

Kirkuk Falls to Kurds (April 11): U.S. to assume control of the northern city, rich in oil, to allay Turkish fears that Kurdish independence movement will spread to within its borders.

POWs Found Alive (April 13): Marines discover five soldiers who were captured by Iraqi troops on March 23 in Nasiriya.

Bush Accuses Syria of Helping Iraqis (April 13): President suspects that top Iraqi officials escaped to Syria. Also claims "there are chemical weapons in Syria."

South Africa Agrees to Pay Families of Apartheid Victims (April 15): Government to give the families of more than 19,000 victims each $3,900. Reparations to total $85 million.

U.S. Forces Capture Terrorist Group Leader (April 15): Troops in Baghdad apprehend Abu Abbas, a leader of the Palestine Liberation Front, the group that seized the Italian cruise ship *Achille Lauro* in 1985.

European Union Expands (April 16): Leaders of ten nations meet at the Acropolis in Athens, Greece, and sign treaties to join the European Union.

China Admits Underreporting SARS Cases (April 20): Government reports number of victims much higher than originally stated.

U.S. Civil Administrator Arrives in Baghdad (April 21): Retired lieutenant general Jay Garner takes charge of reconstruction and humanitarian aid in post-war Iraq.

Nigerian President Reelected (April 22): Election commission declares that incumbent Olusegun Obasanjo prevailed over opposition leader Muhammadu Buhari.

Arafat Endorses Cabinet (April 23): Last-minute compromise with Prime Minister Mahmoud Abbas paves the way for the U.S. to introduce a new peace plan.

North Korea Reports It Has a Nuclear Bomb (April 24): Declaration comes during talks with U.S. and Chinese officials. First time the country has admitted that it actually possesses a nuclear bomb.

Iraqi Official Surrenders (April 24): Tariq Aziz, deputy prime minister of Iraq, turns himself in to the U.S.

IRA Promises to Disarm (April 27): Gerry Adams, president of Sinn Fein, announces Irish Republican Army will dismantle arsenal and ban paramilitary activity as long as other groups meet their commitments to the Good Friday peace agreement.

Palestinian Parliament Approves Cabinet (April 29): Swears in the cabinet of Prime Minister Mahmoud Abbas. At the 11th hour, Yasir Arafat reluctantly endorses government.

U.S. to Move Troops from Saudi Arabia (April 29): Announces plans to withdraw combat troops by the summer.

Peace Plan Proposed for Middle East (April 30): U.S. presents Israeli prime minister Ariel Sharon and Palestinian prime minister Mahmoud Abbas a "road map" for peace in the Middle East. The plan calls on both sides to make concessions and end the violence, and envisions the creation of a Palestinian state by 2005.

NATION

Bush Orders Quarantine of SARS Patients (April 4): Signs an executive order that adds severe acute respiratory syndrome to the list of diseases that merit quarantine.

FBI Agent and Informant Arrested (April 9): Retired agent James Smith charged with gross negligence. His informer, Katrina Leung, who was also his lover, allegedly passed on classified documents she received from Smith to China. She is charged with using a classified document to aid a foreign nation.

Congress Approves Amber Alert Bill (April 10): Both houses vote to create national system to promptly alert public of kidnappings.

Congress Passes Budget Plan (April 11): Vice President Dick Cheney casts tie-breaking Senate vote to approve $2.2 trillion budget resolution that limits President Bush's tax cut to $350 billion. Earlier in the day, House also approved a resolution, with $550 billion tax cut.

Congress Approves War Funding Bill (April 12): Passes $79 billion legislation to pay for war in Iraq.

Bush Scales Back Tax Cut Plan (April 15): Lowers goal to $550 billion from $726 billion, and signals confidence Congress will pass a generous package.

Army Secretary Resigns (April 24): Thomas White steps down after two years in the Pentagon. He was widely criticized for having served as a vice president of Enron prior to joining the Defense Department.

BUSINESS/SCIENCE/SOCIETY

SARS Genome Decoded (April 12): Scientists at the British Columbia Cancer Agency determine that a "completely new" coronavirus causes the illness. Milestone an important step in developing a test and vaccine for disease. **(April 14):** Centers for Disease Control also maps the genome of SARS and confirms a new coronavirus as its cause.

Bush Renominates Greenspan (April 22): Appoints chairman of the Federal Reserve Board to a fifth term. Current term expires in June 2004.

American Airlines Chairman Resigns (April 24): Donald Carty steps down after being criticized for his handling of negotiations with airline unions, in which workers took pay cuts while executives were rewarded.

Judge Rules in Favor of Online Services (April 25): In a stunning blow to music and movie industries, federal judge says Grokster and StreamCast Networks, services that allow users to swap movies and music over the Internet, do not violate copyright laws.

Wall Street Investment Firms Settle with U.S. (April 28): Ten companies and two analysts agree to pay $1.4 billion fine for releasing dubious research reports to investors. Also commit to new guidelines.

Virginia Acts Against Spam (April 30): Passes law to end the sending or receiving of unsolicited commercial email to or from the state.

May 2003

WORLD

Bush Says Combat Over in Iraq (May 1): In a speech from the aircraft carrier *Abraham Lincoln,* president announces U.S. victorious in war in Iraq.

U.S. Declares End to Combat in Afghanistan (May 1): Marks the formal transition from military operations to reconstruction and paves the way for international groups to participate.

U.S. Reports Hussein Ordered Large Sum Removed from Bank (May 5): Hours before U.S.-led war, Qusay Hussein, son of Saddam, took about $1 billion from Iraq's central bank.

Bush Names Special Envoy to Iraq (May 6): L. Paul Bremer, former diplomat and former chief of counterterrorism for the State Department, selected as top civilian administrator to oversee selection of interim Iraqi government. He replaces Jay Garner.

Suicide Blast Kills Dozens in Chechnya (May 12): Truck carrying explosives blows up near government complex in Znamenskoye in north. More than 40 die and several more seriously wounded.

Terrorists Strike in Saudi Arabia (May 12): Three coordinated attacks inside residential compounds in Riyadh kill 34 people, including 8 Americans. U.S. had warned Saudi Arabia of imminent terrorist threat days before the attack. Al Qaeda suspected.

Menem Drops Out of Presidential Race (May 14): Former Argentine president Carlos Saúl Menem withdraws from runoff, handing presidency to Néstor Kirchner.

Bush and South Korean President Discuss North (May 14): In first meeting, George Bush and Roh Moo Hyun focus on how to handle rogue North Korea and release vague statement of cooperation.

Self-Rule Postponed in Iraq (May 16): U.S. and British officials decide against allowing Iraqi opposition groups to form an interim government by the end of May.

Several Bombs Explode in Morocco (May 17): Five suicide bombers kill more than 40 people in Casablanca in coordinated attacks. Moroccan terrorist cell suspected.

Sharon and Abbas Meet (May 17): Israeli and Palestinian prime ministers discuss proposed peace plan, called the road map, but fail to make progress in ending the protracted conflict.

Indonesian President Declares Martial Law in Aceh (May 18): Megawati Sukarnoputri cracks down on separatist Free Aceh Movement after continued violence ends ceasefire. **(May 19):** More than 1,000 Indonesian troops arrive in Aceh, beginning offensive.

Security Council Votes to Lift Sanctions on Iraq (May 22): Nations vote unanimously to end 13 years of economic sanctions. Resolution 1483 also gives the U.S. and Britain broad power to run Iraq's government and economy until an Iraqi government is in place.

UN Names Representative for Iraq (May 23): Secretary General Kofi Annan appoints UN official Sérgio Vieira de Mello to coordinate aid from the UN and nongovernmental organizations, oversee return of refugees, and make sure human rights are upheld.

Israeli Government Accepts Peace Plan (May 25): Prime Minister Ariel Sharon convinces cabinet to endorse plan.

Rumsfeld Says Iraq May Have Destroyed Weapons (May 27): Secretary of Defense acknowledges for the first time that Saddam Hussein may have ordered all biological and chemical weapons be destroyed before the U.S.-led invasion began.

Saudis Arrest Bombing Suspects (May 28): Police arrest eight militants thought to be involved in organizing the May 12 bombings.

U.S., Britain Defend Intelligence Reports (May 30): In separate speeches, U.S. secretary of state Colin Powell and British prime minister Tony Blair deny that intelligence about Iraq's biological and chemical weapons was exaggerated to justify an attack on Iraq.

Burmese Opposition Leader Detained (May 30): Military regime announces it has put Aung San Suu Kyi and other members of Burma's National League for Democracy (NLD) in "protective custody."

NATION

House Passes AIDS Plan (May 1): Votes, 375–41, for $15 billion measure to fight disease globally. Includes provision that one-third of the money be used to encourage abstinence.

Federal Court Rules in Campaign Law (May 2): In mixed ruling, court upholds provisions in the McCain-Feingold law that prohibit national political parties from using soft money for issue ads, but say it is unconstitutional to restrict the spending of such money for voter registration drives and other similar activities.

Board Cites Wing Damage in Shuttle Disaster (May 6): Investigators suspect superheated gas penetrated the left wing through a small hole and melted it. Hole likely caused by a piece of foam insulation that broke off seconds after liftoff.

Senate Compromises on Antiterrorism Act (May 8): Votes, 90-4, to expand federal government's right to spy on suspected foreign terrorists living in the U.S. Republicans drop their demand to make permanent the Patriot Act, which is set to expire in 2005.

Immigrants Die in Smuggling Operation (May 14): Bodies of 18 people from Mexico, El Salvador, and Guatemala found in truck in south Texas.

Texas Republicans Back Down on Redistricting (May 15): State's Democratic representatives, who had fled state to prevent vote on legislation introduced by Republicans, claim victory as bill dies.

Senate Agrees to End Nuclear Weapons Ban (May 20): Votes, 51–43, to allow research and development of nuclear arms under five kilotons.

Whitman Resigns from EPA (May 21): Christine Whitman steps down as head of the Environmental Protection Agency.

House and Senate Agree on Tax Bill (May 21): Accord will slash taxes by $350 billion over 10 years, temporarily cut dividend taxes and reduce capital gains taxes, and increase the tax credit for children. Senate approved similar legislation on May 15. **(May 28):** Bush signs tax cut plan.

Olympic Bombing Suspect Arrested (May 31): Eric Rudolph, accused in the attack at the 1996 Atlanta Olympics, apprehended in North Carolina after spending five years on the lam. Also suspected of attacking abortion clinics and a gay nightclub.

BUSINESS/SCIENCE/SOCIETY

Earthquake Hits Southeastern Turkey (May 1): The 6.4 magnitude quake destroys a bridge and dozens of buildings and kills more than 100 people.

Unemployment Ticks Up (May 2): Labor Department reports rise in rate, to 6% from 5.8% in March.

Landmark Stone Face Falls from Mountain (May 2): Old Man of the Mountain, a 700-ton granite formation, falls from its perch at New Hampshire's Franconia Notch.

Tornadoes Ravage Central U.S. (May 5): At least 38 people die in a series of twisters in Kansas, Missouri, Arkansas, and Tennessee.

Earthquake Devastates Algeria (May 21): The 6.8 magnitude earthquake, which strikes near Algiers, kills more than 2,250 people and injures approximately 10,000. Most destructive earthquake in two decades

Researchers Clone Idaho Mule (May 29): Scientists create mule, named Idaho Gem, from a cell from a mule fetus and a horse egg.

AOL and Microsoft Strike Deal (May 29): Microsoft agrees to pay $750 million to AOL to settle an antitrust suit filed by Netscape, a division of AOL.

June 2003

WORLD

Bush Travels to France for Summit (June 1): At meeting of Group of 8 leading industrial countries, leaders discuss nuclear weapons programs of North Korea and Iraq. Bush's first encounter with French president Jacques Chirac since dispute over war in Iraq.

Experts Reviewing Report on Iraq Weapons (June 3): Former CIA analysts begin pouring over top-secret National Intelligence Estimate to determine if intelligence community exaggerated Iraq's biological and chemical weapons programs.

Bush Meets with Middle East Leaders (June 5): At a summit meeting in Aqaba, Jordan, Israeli prime minister Ariel Sharon and Palestinian prime minister Mahmoud Abbas commit to taking the first steps to implement the new peace plan, called the road map.

French Troops Begin Mission in Congo (June 6): Peacekeeping soldiers begin arriving in Bunia to try to stem brutal inter-tribal war between Lendus and Hema.

Suicide Bomber Attacks in Kabul (June 7): Strikes military bus, killing 4 German peacekeeping troops and wounding about 30. Al-Qaeda suspected.

Peace Plan Hits Snags (June 8): Hamas, Islamic Jihad, and Al-Aksa Martyrs Brigades, three Islamic militant groups, collaborate in attack on Israeli soldiers in Hebron. Four soldiers die. **(June 10):** Israel tries to assassinate Hamas leader Dr. Abdel Aziz Rantisi. President Bush criticizes move. **(June 11):** Palestinian suicide bomber blows himself up on a bus in Jerusalem, killing 16 and wounding more than 100.

Poles Approve Entry into EU (June 8): About 78% of voters in favor of joining European Union.

U.S. Troops Move Against Hussein Supporters (June 9): In Operation Desert Scorpion, a force of about 4,000 soldiers circles area north of Baghdad where resistance is still strong.

Ontario Approves Gay Marriage (June 10): Canadian court of appeals upholds lower-court ruling allowing same-sex marriages. First province to legalize such unions.

Student Protests Continue in Iran (June 14): Students attacked on fifth day of demonstrations against Islamic government. Officials blame paramilitary group, Ansar Hezbollah.

Czechs Vote to Join European Union (June 14): More than 77% vote yes in referendum to gain membership in 2004.

U.S. Catches Top Aide to Hussein (June 16): Abed Hamid Mahmud al-Tikriti, Saddam Hussein's presidential secretary and fourth on the most-wanted list in Iraq, apprehended near Tikrit.

Italy Gives Top Leaders Immunity (June 18): Legislation protects five most senior politicians, including Prime Minister Silvio Berlusconi, from prosecution while in office.

U.S. Foils Plan to Destroy Brooklyn Bridge (June 19): Justice Department announces that in May Iyman Faris had pleaded guilty to giving material support to al-Qaeda. He had planned to destroy the Brooklyn Bridge and to derail a train near Washington, DC.

Bush Speaks of Dangers in Iraq (June 21): In first comments about continuing deaths of U.S. soldiers in combat in Iraq, president says Hussein loyalists trying to "kill and intimidate" Americans.

U.S. Attacks Convoy in Iraq (June 22): Officials announce that Predator drone had destroyed convoy near Syrian border. They originally believed Saddam Hussein was traveling in one of the vehicles.

Bush Offers Aid to Pakistan (June 24): At meeting at Camp David, president offers Pakistani president Pervez Musharraf $3 billion package, but says he will not give Pakistan F-16 fighters it has long sought.

Israelis Agree to Pull Out of Gaza (June 27): Troops to begin leaving parts of Gaza Strip. Palestinians to assume security role and will work to intercept attacks by militants. First coordinated step in the peace process.

Palestinian Militant Groups Announce Ceasefire (June 29): Hamas and Islamic Jihad vow to end attacks on Israeli targets for three months. Al Fatah announces a six-month truce.

U.S. Troops Raid Areas in Central Iraq (June 29): Carry out about 20 attacks in Tigris River Valley, intending to end series of deadly attacks on U.S. and British troops.

NATION

Report Critical of Roundup of Immigrants (June 2): Internal review by Justice Department's inspector general says detention of illegal immigrants was highly problematic and left many people with no links to terrorism jailed under harsh circumstances. **(June 5):** Testifying before the House Judiciary Committee, Attorney General John Ashcroft says roundup of 762 illegal immigrants necessary to protect country. He also seeks broader power to track down other possible terrorists.

House Approves Ban on Abortion Procedure (June 4): Votes, 282-139, to outlaw intact dilation and extraction method.

Senate Votes to Extend Child Tax Credit (June 5): Acting in response to outrage that about 6.5 million families earning between $10,500 and $26,625 a year were denied the tax credit, Senate votes, 94–2, to give them credit of $400 per child.

Maine Approves Universal Health Care (June 13): State will offer low-cost coverage to all residents by 2009.

Federal Court Rules in Favor of Justice Department (June 17): Rules, 2–1, that department had legal right to withhold the names of people arrested for immigration violations after Sept. 11, 2001, attacks.

Bush Bars Racial Profiling, with Exceptions (June 17): New regulation prohibits federal agents from using race or ethnicity in typical investigations, but does allow agents to consider the characteristics when information they receive about suspects includes race or ethnicity.

House Votes to Eliminate Federal Estate Tax (June 18): Bill passes, 264–163. Uncertain future in Senate.

FTC Moves to Curb Telemarketers (June 27): Federal Trade Commission creates Do-Not-Call registry. Beginning in October, telemarketers are prohibited from calling numbers on the list.

Congress Passes Drug Plan (June 27): In bipartisan vote, Senate, 76–21, approves what could be the largest expansion of Medicare since it was launched in 1965. House votes 216–215 for the $400 billion plan.

BUSINESS/SCIENCE/SOCIETY

FCC Relaxes Media Ownership Rules (June 2): Votes, 3–2, to allow media companies to own as many as three TV stations, eight radio stations, a daily newspaper, and a cable company in one market.

Martha Stewart Indicted (June 4): Charged with conspiracy, obstruction of justice, and securities fraud from Dec. 2001 sale of shares in ImClone Systems.

***New York Times's* Editors Resign (June 5):** Executive editor Howell Raines and managing editor Gerald Boyd step down, a result of a scandal over plagiarism and sloppy fact-checking.

Unemployment Reaches Nine-Year High (June 6): Labor Department reports rate rose to 6.1% in May, highest level since 1994.

Clinton Memoir Hits Bookstores (June 9): Hillary Rodham Clinton's much-publicized *Living History* debuts to mixed reviews and record sales.

Robot Heads for Mars (June 10): A rover named *Spirit*, equipped with eight cameras and a robot arm to analyze samples of the red planet's geologic composition, takes off from Cape Canaveral, Florida.

Fed Cuts Rates Again (June 25): Federal Reserve cuts short-term interest rates by a quarter of a point, bringing rates to lowest level since 1958.

July 2003

WORLD

Thousands Protest Proposed Law in Hong Kong (July 1): About 500,000 people participate in march against antisubversion laws that would impose lengthy jail terms for sedition, secession, or treason.

Israeli and Palestinian Prime Ministers Meet (July 1): Ariel Sharon and Mahmoud Abbas make symbolic public appearance together and hold two-hour meeting to discuss peace plan. Israeli troops continue to withdraw from parts of Gaza and the West Bank.

Bush Considers Intervention in Liberia (July 3): Says embattled Liberian president Charles Taylor must step down before U.S. sends peacekeeping force to oversee cease-fire between rebels and government militia.

Suicide Bomber Strikes in Pakistan (July 4): Attack at Shi'ite mosque kills 48 Muslims in Quetta. Islamic militants suspected.

SARS Declared Under Control (July 5): World Health Organization declares illness has been contained. No new cases reported since June 15. Officials warn that it could be a seasonal problem.

Israel Votes to Release Palestinian Prisoners (July 6): Cabinet agrees to begin freeing about 300 detainees. Palestinians say many more, up to 5,500, must be freed for cease-fire to hold. **(July 27):** Israeli cabinet votes to release some members of Hamas and Islamic Jihad.

U.S. Team Arrives in Liberia (July 7): Defense Department officials in capital, Monrovia, to assess requirements for peace-keeping force.

Parliamentary Committee Clears Blair on Weapons Evidence (July 8): Foreign affairs committee reports that British prime minister did not tamper with evidence to justify a war in Iraq. It does say, however, that Blair did unknowingly mislead Parliament when he presented it a dossier in February that included unverified information about Iraq's weapons capabilities.

Bush Travels to Africa (July 8): Begins five-day, five-country trip to sub-Saharan Africa.

Estimated Cost of War Increases (July 9): Secretary of Defense Donald Rumsfeld tells Senate committee that price of war in Iraq is about $3.9 billion a month, nearly double the April estimate.

Interim Government Established in Iraq (July 13): Governing Council, a diverse group of 25 Iraqi leaders, meets in Baghdad.

North Korea Announces Plans for Six Nuclear Bombs (July 14): Bush administration reports that North Korea had informed U.S. that it plans to use weapons-grade plutonium, obtained from spent nuclear fuel rods, to build nuclear weapons. CIA says it cannot confirm the claim. **(July 19):** The *New York Times* reports that North Korea has built a second plutonium-processing plant.

U.S. Troops May Face Lengthy Tours in Iraq (July 16): Gen. John Abizaid, commander of allied forces in Iraq, calls continued attacks on coalition troops a "guerrilla-type campaign" and says soldiers who will replace current troops may be deployed for yearlong tours.

Blair Defends Intelligence (July 17): In Washington, British prime minister tells joint session of Congress that war in Iraq was justified even if no biological, chemical, or nuclear weapons are found.

Rebels Enter Liberian Capital (July 19): Opposition force, Liberians United for Reconciliation and Democracy, which seeks to topple President Charles Taylor, lays siege to Monrovia. **(July 28):** Another rebel group, Movement for Democracy in Liberia, captures Buchanan, Liberia's second-largest city.

Hussein's Sons Killed (July 22): Uday and Qusay Hussein die in firefight in a Mosul palace.

Palestinian Prime Minister Visits White House (July 25): Mahmoud Abbas meets with President Bush to discuss Middle East peace plan. Bush presses Abbas to move against Palestinian terrorist groups.

Bush Orders Marines to Liberian Coast (July 25): Under pressure from UN and international community, president deploys 2,300 marines to waters off Liberia.

Argentine President Lifts Immunity of Officers (July 25): Nestor Kirchner revokes decree that banned officials from extradition to countries that have charged them with human rights violations.

Sharon Refuses to Dismantle Barrier (July 29): At White House meeting with President Bush, Israeli prime minister says he plans to continue construction of security barrier that cuts through the West Bank.

NATION

Pope Appoints Bishop for Boston (July 1): Names Sean P. O'Malley, a Franciscan friar, as leader of the embattled archdiocese. He replaces Cardinal Bernard Law, who resigned the post in Dec. 2002 amid outrage in the diocese of his handling of the sexual-abuse scandal.

Bush Administration Admits Iraq Weapons Intelligence Was Flawed (July 7): Says evidence that Iraq was pursuing a nuclear weapons program by seeking to buy uranium from Africa, cited in January State of the Union address, was unsubstantiated and should not have been included in speech. President maintains war in Iraq was justified. **(July 11):** George Tenet, director of the CIA, takes responsibility for allowing sentence about Iraq's pursuit of uranium from Africa to be included in Bush's State of the Union speech. **(July 22):** Deputy National Security Adviser Stephen Hadley said he should have insisted sentence about Iraq trying to buy uranium from Africa be omitted from Bush's State of the Union speech.

White House Predicts Enormous Deficits (July 15): Office of Management and Budget says current year's deficit to reach $455 billion, or 4.2% of the total economy. Figure about $150 billion more than previous estimate.

Justice Department Report Details Allegations of Abuse (July 20): Internal investigation regarding enforcement of 2001's USA Patriot Act, presented earlier to Congress by department's inspector general Glenn Fine, accuses Justice Department, FBI, Drug Enforcement Agency, and INS of widespread civil rights and civil liberties abuses.

House Moves to Block New FCC Rule (July 23): Votes, 400–21, to roll back measure to increase the reach of media companies.

Report on 9/11 Critical of FBI and CIA (July 24): Report by a joint panel of the House and Senate intelligence committees says FBI and CIA had failed to take seriously enough warnings that al-Qaeda had planned imminent terrorist attacks against the U.S.

California Sets Date for Recall (July 24): Lieutenant Governor Cruz Bustamante sets the recall vote for Oct. 7.

Pentagon Market for Betting on Terrorism Shut Down (July 29): Officials from the Defense Advanced Research Projects Agency close planned terrorism futures market, called Policy Analysis Market, one day after it is publicized and widely criticized. Traders would have been able to bet on future terrorist attacks, assassinations, and coups.

BUSINESS/SCIENCE/SOCIETY

Unemployment Rate Up Again (July 3): Labor Department reports jobless rate increased to 6.4% in June, highest rate in nine years. More than 30,000 jobs lost.

New York Politician Shot (July 23): James Davis, councilman from Brooklyn, gunned down inside City Hall by a political rival, Othniel Askew, who was shot and killed by a police officer.

U.S. Prison Population Increases Again (July 28): Department of Justice reports that the number of people in jail increased by 2.6% in 2002 to nearly 2.2 million.

Two Banks Settle in Enron-Related Case (July 28): J. P. Morgan Chase and Citigroup agree to pay nearly $300 million in fines. Banks were accused of helping Enron to report misleading information in its financial reports.

August 2003

WORLD

Truck Bomb Destroys Russian Hospital (Aug. 1): Explosion at military hospital in Mozdok kills 35 and injures dozens. Russian officials blame Chechen separatists.

Peacekeepers Arrive in Liberia (Aug. 4): Nigerian troops land at airport in Monrovia. A force of about 3,250 West African soldiers anticipated to help control vicious fighting between government militia and rebels.

Bomb Destroys Indonesian Hotel (Aug. 6): Sport utility vehicle loaded with explosives blows up at Jakarta's J. W. Marriott Hotel. At least 16 people killed and 150 injured. Jemaah Islamiyah, a terrorist group linked with al-Qaeda, suspected.

Car Bomb Explodes in Baghdad (Aug. 7): Blast outside the Jordanian embassy kills 11 and wounds about 70 people. No American casualties.

Liberian President Resigns (Aug. 7): After promising for several weeks to do so, President Charles Taylor submits his resignation to Liberia's Congress. **(Aug. 11):** Charles Taylor leaves the country for Nigeria. **(Aug. 21):** Liberia's rival parties select businessman Gyude Bryant as chairman of the interim government until October 2005, when elections are scheduled.

Bali Bomber Sentenced (Aug. 7): Amrozi bin Nurhasyim, 41, smiles to the courtroom when he receives death sentence for his role in the 2002 nightclub bombing that killed 202 people. He's believed to be a member of the Islamic terrorist group Jemaah Islamiyah.

NATO Assumes Control in Afghanistan (Aug. 11): In its first mission outside Europe, North Atlantic Treaty Organization takes formal control of peacekeeping force. NATO had been supplying 90% of the troops policing the country.

Inquiry into Scientist's Death Begins in England (Aug. 11): Judge, Lord Hutton, opens investigation into the suicide of David Kelly, a defense-ministry scientist who committed suicide in July. The BBC claims that Kelly told journalist Andrew Gilligan that the government had "sexed up" intelligence about Iraq's alleged weapons of mass destruction to help justify war in Iraq. **(Aug. 28):** In testimony, Prime Minister Tony Blair says he would have resigned if the BBC report were true.

Violence Claims Dozens in Afghanistan (Aug. 13): More than 60 people die in guerrilla fighting over a 24-hour period, the most deadly in about a year.

High-Ranking Terror Suspect Captured (Aug. 14): Riduan Isamuddin, known as Hambali, seized in Thailand by the CIA and Thai police. He is a leading member of Jemaah Islamiyah, which is linked to al-Qaeda.

Libya Accepts Blame for Bombing Over Lockerbie (Aug. 15): Agrees to pay $2.7 billion to the families of the victims of the 1988 attack of Pan Am flight 103 that killed 270 people over Scotland. Admission paves the way for the UN to lift sanctions against Libya.

Bomb Destroys UN Compound in Iraq (Aug. 19): Suicide bomber drives truck to UN headquarters, killing 23 people, including Sergio Vieira de Mello, the UN's special representative to Iraq. More than 100 people injured in the attack, the deadliest on the UN in history.

Devastating Suicide Bombing Threatens Peace Plan (Aug. 19): Attack on a crowded bus in Jerusalem kills 20 people, including 6 children, and wounds more than 100. Militant groups Hamas and Islamic Jihad both claim responsibility. **(Aug. 21):** After Israel retaliates by killing a top member of Hamas, Ismali Abu Shanab, Hamas and Islamic Jihad formally withdraw from cease-fire. **(Aug. 24):** Airstrike in Gaza City kills four Palestinians, including an operations leader.

Two Bombs Explode in Bombay (Aug. 25): Twin blasts kill more than 50 people and injure about 150. Officials blame Lashkar-e-Taiba, a Pakistan-based militant Islamic group.

Talks with North Korea Begin in Beijing (Aug. 27): Officials from the U.S., North Korea, China, Russia, South Korea, and Japan meet to discuss North Korea's nuclear weapons program. **(Aug. 28):** North Korean officials tell other diplomats at summit that country plans to declare itself a nuclear power and may test an atomic bomb. **(Aug. 29):** Summit ends with plans to resume talks within two months. Participants urge North Korea to abandon its weapons program.

Bomb Kills Shi'ite Cleric in Iraq (Aug. 29): Car bomb explodes at shrine in Najaf, killing dozens, including Ayatollah Muhammad Bakr al-Hakim, a moderate cleric who opposed Saddam Hussein and had encouraged Shi'ites to support the U.S. occupation of Iraq.

NATION

Candidates Swarm to California Race (Aug. 6): Republican movie star Arnold Schwarzenegger announces on Jay Leno's *Tonight* show that he plans to run for governor in California's recall vote. **(Aug. 7):** California lieutenant governor Cruz Bustamante and Insurance Commissioner John Garamendi announce their candidacies for governor. **(Aug. 13):** California secretary of state certifies 135 candidates in recall election of Gov. Gray Davis.

Bush Nominates EPA Administrator (Aug. 11): Selects Utah governor Michael Leavitt to replace Christine Whitman as head of the Environmental Protection Agency. Senate must confirm nomination.

Massive Blackout Darkens Northeast and Midwest (Aug. 14): In the country's largest power failure in history, 50 million people in eight U.S. states and parts of Canada are without electricity. Cause unknown, but officials acknowledge that electricity grid is antiquated. **(Aug. 15):** Power restored to most areas after 29-hour blackout. **(Aug. 16):** Electricity restored in Detroit, the last metropolitan area left in the dark.

Congressman Involved in Fatal Accident (Aug. 16): Bill Janklow, Republican representative from South Dakota, runs a stop sign and hits a motorcycle, killing its driver, Randolph Scott. **(Aug. 29):** Janklow charged with second-degree manslaughter.

Report on Shuttle Critical of NASA (Aug. 26): Board that investigated the loss of space shuttle *Columbia* cites organizational problems at NASA that breed a "broken safety culture." Says future shuttles and astronauts will be lost unless the agency reforms itself.

Budget Deficit Expected to Sharply Increase (Aug. 26): Congressional Budget Office predicts federal deficit of $480 billion in 2004 and a cumulative total of $5.8 trillion by 2013.

Bush Administration Relaxes Environmental Rules (Aug. 27): New rule allows power plants, refineries, and other plants to upgrade systems without improving pollution controls and without violating the Clean Air Act.

BUSINESS/SCIENCE/SOCIETY

Unemployment Down Slightly in July (Aug. 1): Although unemployment rate fell to 6.2% from 6.4% in June, 44,000 people lost their jobs.

Episcopal Church Approves Gay Bishop (Aug. 5): Diocesan bishops vote 62–45 to confirm V. Gene Robinson as church's first openly gay bishop.

Virus Attacks Computers (Aug. 12): Program, called the Blaster worm, wreaks havoc with about 500,000 computers running recent versions of Microsoft Windows operating systems. **(Aug. 29):** Minnesota teenager, Jeffrey Lee Parson, arrested for allegedly creating a variant of the Blaster virus.

Fed Holds Rate (Aug. 12): Federal Reserve keeps overnight interest rate at 1%, lowest rate in 50 years.

Heatwave Claims Thousands (Aug. 29): Several weeks of temperatures rising above 100 degrees Fahrenheit in Europe cause more than 11,000 deaths in France alone.

September 2003

WORLD

Iraqi Governing Council Selects Cabinet (Sept. 1): Twenty-five member body will assume day-to-day control of government functions, such as foreign affairs, finance, and oil.

Islamic Cleric Receives Mixed Verdict in Bali Bombing (Sept. 2): Indonesian court acquits Abu Bakar Bashir of ordering the attack on a Bali nightclub, but finds him guilty of aiding and abetting treason.

Car Bomb Explodes at Baghdad Police Compound (Sept. 2): Police chief, the assumed target, spared in attack. One person killed and more than 25 wounded. Fourth car bomb to explode in a month in Iraq.

U.S. Seeks UN Help in Iraq (Sept. 3): In a shift in policy, the Bush administration introduces a draft resolution to UN Security Council calling for a multinational force, under U.S. command, to help in Iraq.

Palestinian Prime Minister Resigns (Sept. 6): Mahmoud Abbas steps down, saying Israeli prime minister Ariel Sharon and Palestinian leader Yasir Arafat undermined his authority. **(Sept. 7):** Arafat nominates Ahmed Qurei, speaker of Palestinian parliament, as prime minister.

Iran Faces Deadline on Nuclear Compliance (Sept. 9): Britain, France, and Germany submit a UN resolution demanding that Iran provide complete information on its nuclear material and allow UN inspectors free access to nuclear sites.

Bin Laden Appears on Videotape (Sept. 10): On eve of second anniversary of Sept. 11 terrorist attacks, Osama bin Laden and his deputy, Ayman al-Zawahiri, seen on Al Jazeera network.

Swedish Foreign Minister Slain (Sept. 11): Anna Lindh dies from stab wounds she received while shopping in a Stockholm department store.

Israeli Government Announces Plans to Remove Arafat (Sept. 11): Threatens to exile, jail, or kill Palestinian leader. Statement bolsters Arafat's popularity among Palestinians.

U.S. Troops Kill Iraqi Police Officers (Sept. 12): In firefight in Falluja, soldiers kill ten policemen and a Jordanian security guard. Some of the victims gunned down from close range. U.S., which said troops fired upon first, apologizes for deaths.

Trade Talks Collapse in Cancún (Sept. 14): Representatives from developing nations quit meeting of World Trade Organization, rejecting compromise on farm subsidies proposed by wealthier nations.

Gunmen Shoot Iraqi Leader (Sept. 20): Akila al-Hashimi, one of three women on the Iraqi Governing Council, critically wounded in assassination attempt. **(Sept. 25):** Hashimi dies of wounds to her pancreas.

Japanese Premier Overwhelmingly Reelected (Sept. 20): Prime Minister Junichiro Koizumi takes 60% of the vote in race for leader of the Liberal Democratic Party.

Bush Addresses the UN (Sept. 23): President calls on other nations to put aside differences on the U.S.-led invasion of Iraq and work together to rebuild the nation. In his speech, French president Jacques Chirac criticizes the preemptive invasion of Iraq.

Draft Report Says Inspectors Have Not Found WMD in Iraq (Sept. 24): Interim document states that arms-inspection team has not yet uncovered any unconventional weapons during its four-month search.

OPEC to Cut Production (Sept. 24): Members of the Organization of the Petroleum Exporting Countries announce that they will reduce output by 3.5% on Nov. 1, citing a weak world economy.

Russia to Continue to Help Iran Build Nuclear Reactor (Sept. 27): Russian president Vladimir Putin tells President Bush that he will not cancel contract to aid in Iran's purportedly civilian nuclear energy program.

NATION

Court Blocks New Media Regulations (Sept. 3): Federal appeals court votes to stop implementation of new rule, passed by Federal Communications Commission, expanding reach of media companies. **(Sept. 16):** Senate votes, 55–40, in favor of a resolution to repeal new media rules.

Foreign-Born Population Jumps (Sept. 3): Census Bureau reports the number of U.S. residents who were born in other countries grew to more than 33 million in 2002, an amount slightly larger than the entire population of Canada. The increase represents a 5% rise from 2001.

Bush Seeks $87 Billion to Help in Iraq (Sept. 7): In a nationally televised speech, president Bush asks Congress for $87 billion to aid military and reconstruction efforts in Iraq.

Bush Calls for Revision of Patriot Act (Sept. 10): President seeks to broaden subpoena powers, expand federal death penalty statute, and allow judges to deny bail for suspects in terrorism cases.

California Recall Postponed (Sept. 15): The 9th U.S. Circuit Court of Appeals blocks gubernatorial recall election until outmoded punch-card ballot machines—still used by six counties—are replaced. **(Sept. 23):** A federal appeals court unanimously overturns decision to delay recall vote. Election set for Oct. 7.

Clark Enters Presidential Race (Sept. 17): Retired U.S. Army general Wesley Clark, the former supreme allied commander of NATO, announces his candidacy for the Democratic presidential nomination.

Federal Court Blocks Curbs on Telemarketing Calls (Sept. 24): Ruling thwarts implementation of federal Do-Not-Call registry, which includes more than 50 million phone numbers. Court says Federal Trade Commission needs congressional approval to enforce program.

Number of Americans Living in Poverty Increases (Sept. 26): Census Bureau reports poverty rate increased to 12.1% in 2002, up from 11.7% in 2001. Figure represents an increase of 1.7 million people. At the same time, median household income dropped by 1.1% from 2001 to 2002.

Uninsured Americans Increased in 2002 (Sept. 29): The number of people without health insurance rose to 43.6 million, or 15.2%, up from 14.6% in 2001. Largest increase in 10 years.

Justice Dept. to Investigate Leak of Classified Information (Sept. 29): Department informs White House of probe into who revealed the identity of a CIA officer to a syndicated columnist. Former ambassador Joseph Wilson, the husband of the CIA operative, believes the Bush administration leaked his wife's name as punishment for his disclosure that Bush's claim that Iraq was trying to buy uranium from Niger was false.

BUSINESS/SCIENCE/SOCIETY

RIAA Sues Music Swappers (Sept. 8): The Recording Industry Association of America files civil lawsuits against 261 people who shared more than 1,000 music files on the Internet. **(Sept. 9):** Brianna LaHara, 12, settles with RIAA, agreeing to pay $2,000 in fines for illegally sharing songs over the Internet.

Boston Archdiocese Settles with Abuse Victims (Sept. 9): Church agrees to pay $85 million to settle about 550 lawsuits filed by people who said they were sexually assaulted by priests. Each victim to receive between $80,000 and $300,000.

NYSE Chairman Steps Down (Sept. 17): Richard Grasso resigns amid controversy over his lucrative $140 million pay package. **(Sept. 21):** NYSE names John S. Reed, former chief executive of Citicorp, interim chairman of exchange.

Hurricane Sweeps Through Mid-Atlantic States (Sept. 18): Isabel hits North Carolina, Virginia, and Washington, DC, with winds of 100 mph, and causes at least 23 deaths. Millions left without power.

Nobel Prizes

(For years not listed, no award was made.)

PEACE

1901 Henri Dunant (Switzerland); Frederick Passy (France)
1902 Elie Ducommun and Albert Gobat (Switzerland)
1903 Sir William R. Cremer (UK)
1904 Institut de Droit International (Belgium)
1905 Bertha von Suttner (Austria)
1906 Theodore Roosevelt (U.S.)
1907 Ernesto T. Moneta (Italy) and Louis Renault (France)
1908 Klas P. Arnoldson (Sweden) and Frederik Bajer (Denmark)
1909 Auguste M. F. Beernaert (Belgium) and Baron Paul H. B. B. d'Estournelles de Constant de Rebecque (France)
1910 Bureau International Permanent de la Paix (Switzerland)
1911 Tobias M. C. Asser (Holland) and Alfred H. Fried (Austria)
1912 Elihu Root (U.S.)
1913 Henri La Fontaine (Belgium)
1917 International Red Cross
1919 Woodrow Wilson (U.S.)
1920 Léon Bourgeois (France)
1921 Karl H. Branting (Sweden) and Christian L. Lange (Norway)
1922 Fridtjof Nansen (Norway)
1925 Sir Austen Chamberlain (UK) and Charles G. Dawes (U.S.)
1926 Aristide Briand (France) and Gustav Stresemann (Germany)
1927 Ferdinand Buisson (France) and Ludwig Quidde (Germany)
1929 Frank B. Kellogg (U.S.)
1930 Lars O. J. Söderblom (Sweden)
1931 Jane Addams and Nicholas M. Butler (U.S.)
1933 Sir Norman Angell (UK)
1934 Arthur Henderson (UK)
1935 Karl von Ossietzky (Germany)
1936 Carlos de S. Lamas (Argentina)
1937 Lord Cecil of Chelwood (UK)
1938 Office International Nansen pour les Réfugiés (Switzerland)
1944 International Red Cross
1945 Cordell Hull (U.S.)
1946 Emily G. Balch and John R. Mott (U.S.)
1947 American Friends Service Committee (U.S.) and British Society of Friends' Service Council (UK)
1949 Lord John Boyd Orr (Scotland)
1950 Ralph J. Bunche (U.S.)
1951 Léon Jouhaux (France)
1952 Albert Schweitzer (French Equatorial Africa)
1953 George C. Marshall (U.S.)
1954 Office of U.N. High Commissioner for Refugees
1957 Lester B. Pearson (Canada)
1958 Rev. Dominique Georges Henri Pire (Belgium)
1959 Philip John Noel-Baker (UK)
1960 Albert John Luthuli (South Africa)
1961 Dag Hammarskjöld (Sweden)
1962 Linus Pauling (U.S.)
1963 Intl. Comm. of Red Cross; League of Red Cross Societies (both Switzerland)
1964 Rev. Dr. Martin Luther King, Jr. (U.S.)
1965 UNICEF (United Nations Children's Fund)
1968 René Cassin (France)
1969 International Labour Organization
1970 Norman E. Borlaug (U.S.)
1971 Willy Brandt (West Germany)
1973 Henry A. Kissinger (U.S.); Le Duc Tho (North Vietnam)[1]
1974 Eisaku Sato (Japan); Sean MacBride (Ireland)
1975 Andrei D. Sakharov (USSR)
1976 Mairead Corrigan and Betty Williams (both Northern Ireland)
1977 Amnesty International
1978 Menachem Begin (Israel) and Anwar el-Sadat (Egypt)
1979 Mother Teresa of Calcutta (India)
1980 Adolfo Pérez Esquivel (Argentina)
1981 Office of the United Nations High Commissioner for Refugees
1982 Alva Myrdal (Sweden) and Alfonso García Robles (Mexico)
1983 Lech Walesa (Poland)
1984 Bishop Desmond Tutu (South Africa)
1985 International Physicians for the Prevention of Nuclear War
1986 Elie Wiesel (U.S.)
1987 Oscar Arias Sánchez (Costa Rica)
1988 UN Peacekeeping Forces
1989 Dalai Lama (Tibet)
1990 Mikhail S. Gorbachev (USSR)
1991 Daw Aung San Suu Kyi (Burma)
1992 Rigoberta Menchú (Guatemala)
1993 F. W. de Klerk and Nelson Mandela (both South Africa)
1994 Yasir Arafat (Palestine), Shimon Peres, and Yitzhak Rabin (both Israel)
1995 Joseph Rotblat and Pugwash Conference on Science and World Affairs (UK)
1996 Carlos Filipe Ximenes Belo and José Ramos-Horta (East Timor)
1997 International Campaign to Ban Landmines and Jody Williams (U.S.)
1998 John Hume and David Trimble (Northern Ireland)
1999 Doctors without Borders (France)
2000 Kim Dae Jung (South Korea)
2001 United Nations and Kofi Annan
2002 Jimmy Carter (U.S.)

1. Le Duc Tho refused prize, charging that peace had not yet really been established in South Vietnam.

LITERATURE

1901 René F. A. Sully Prudhomme (France)
1902 Theodor Mommsen (Germany)
1903 Björnstjerne Björnson (Norway)

1904 Frédéric Mistral (France) and José Echegaray (Spain)
1905 Henryk Sienkiewicz (Poland)
1906 Giosuè Carducci (Italy)
1907 Rudyard Kipling (UK)
1908 Rudolf Eucken (Germany)
1909 Selma Lagerlöf (Sweden)
1910 Paul von Heyse (Germany)
1911 Maurice Maeterlinck (Belgium)
1912 Gerhart Hauptmann (Germany)
1913 Rabindranath Tagore (India)
1915 Romain Rolland (France)
1916 Verner von Heidenstam (Sweden)
1917 Karl Gjellerup (Denmark) and Henrik Pontoppidan (Denmark)
1919 Carl Spitteler (Switzerland)
1920 Knut Hamsun (Norway)
1921 Anatole France (France)
1922 Jacinto Benavente (Spain)
1923 William B. Yeats (Ireland)
1924 Wladyslaw Reymont (Poland)
1925 George Bernard Shaw (Ireland)
1926 Grazia Deledda (Italy)
1927 Henri Bergson (France)
1928 Sigrid Undset (Norway)
1929 Thomas Mann (Germany)
1930 Sinclair Lewis (U.S.)
1931 Erik A. Karlfeldt (Sweden)
1932 John Galsworthy (UK)
1933 Ivan G. Bunin (Russia)
1934 Luigi Pirandello (Italy)
1936 Eugene O'Neill (U.S.)
1937 Roger Martin du Gard (France)
1938 Pearl S. Buck (U.S.)
1939 Frans Eemil Sillanpää (Finland)
1944 Johannes V. Jensen (Denmark)
1945 Gabriela Mistral (Chile)
1946 Hermann Hesse (Switzerland)
1947 André Gide (France)
1948 Thomas Stearns Eliot (UK)
1949 William Faulkner (U.S.)
1950 Bertrand Russell (UK)
1951 Pär Lagerkvist (Sweden)
1952 François Mauriac (France)
1953 Sir Winston Churchill (UK)
1954 Ernest Hemingway (U.S.)
1955 Halldór Kiljan Laxness (Iceland)
1956 Juan Ramón Jiménez (Spain)
1957 Albert Camus (France)
1958 Boris Pasternak (USSR) (declined)
1959 Salvatore Quasimodo (Italy)
1960 St. John Perse (Alexis Léger) (France)
1961 Ivo Andric (Yugoslavia)
1962 John Steinbeck (U.S.)
1963 Giorgios Seferis (Seferiades) (Greece)
1964 Jean-Paul Sartre (France) (declined)
1965 Mikhail Sholokhov (USSR)
1966 Shmuel Yosef Agnon (Israel) and Nelly Sachs (Sweden)
1967 Miguel Angel Asturias (Guatemala)
1968 Yasunari Kawabata (Japan)
1969 Samuel Beckett (Ireland)
1970 Aleksandr Solzhenitsyn (USSR)
1971 Pablo Neruda (Chile)
1972 Heinrich Böll (Germany)
1973 Patrick White (Australia)
1974 Eyvind Johnson and Harry Martinson (both Sweden)
1975 Eugenio Montale (Italy)
1976 Saul Bellow (U.S.)
1977 Vicente Aleixandre (Spain)
1978 Isaac Bashevis Singer (U.S.)
1979 Odysseus Elytis (Greece)
1980 Czeslaw Milosz (U.S.)
1981 Elias Canetti (Bulgaria)
1982 Gabriel García Márquez (Colombia)
1983 William Golding (UK)
1984 Jaroslav Seifert (Czechoslovakia)
1985 Claude Simon (France)
1986 Wole Soyinka (Nigeria)
1987 Joseph Brodsky (U.S.)
1988 Naguib Mahfouz (Egypt)
1989 Camilo José Cela (Spain)
1990 Octavio Paz (Mexico)
1991 Nadine Gordimer (South Africa)
1992 Derek Walcott (Trinidad)
1993 Toni Morrison (U.S.)
1994 Kenzaburo Oe (Japan)
1995 Seamus Heaney (Ireland)
1996 Wislawa Szymborska (Poland)
1997 Dario Fo (Italy)
1998 José Saramago (Portugal)
1999 Günter Grass (Germany)
2000 Gao Xingjian (China)
2001 V. S. Naipaul (UK)
2002 Imre Kertész (Hungary)
2003 J. M. Coetzee (South Africa)*

*Only a few awards were announced at press time.

PHYSICS

1901 Wilhelm K. Roentgen (Germany), for discovery of Roentgen rays
1902 Hendrik A. Lorentz and Pieter Zeeman (Netherlands), for work on influence of magnetism upon radiation
1903 A. Henri Becquerel (France), for work on spontaneous radioactivity; and Pierre and Marie Curie (France), for study of radiation
1904 John Strutt (Lord Rayleigh) (UK), for discovery of argon in investigating gas density
1905 Philipp Lenard (Germany), for work with cathode rays
1906 Sir Joseph Thomson (UK), for investigations on passage of electricity through gases
1907 Albert A. Michelson (U.S.), for spectroscopic and metrologic investigations
1908 Gabriel Lippmann (France), for method of reproducing colors by photography
1909 Guglielmo Marconi (Italy) and Ferdinand Braun (Germany), for development of wireless
1910 Johannes D. van der Waals (Netherlands), for work with the equation of state for gases and liquids
1911 Wilhelm Wien (Germany), for his laws governing the radiation of heat
1912 Gustaf Dalén (Sweden), for discovery of automatic regulators used in lighting lighthouses and light buoys
1913 Heike Kamerlingh-Onnes (Netherlands), for work leading to production of liquid helium
1914 Max von Laue (Germany), for discovery of diffraction of Roentgen rays passing through crystals
1915 Sir William Bragg and William L. Bragg (UK), for analysis of crystal structure by X rays
1917 Charles G. Barkla (UK), for discovery of Roentgen radiation of the elements
1918 Max Planck (Germany), discoveries in connection with quantum theory

1919 Johannes Stark (Germany), discovery of Doppler effect in Canal rays and decomposition of spectrum lines by electric fields
1920 Charles E. Guillaume (Switzerland), for discoveries of anomalies in nickel-steel alloys
1921 Albert Einstein (Germany), for discovery of the law of the photoelectric effect
1922 Niels Bohr (Denmark), for investigation of structure of atoms and radiations emanating from them
1923 Robert A. Millikan (U.S.), for work on elementary charge of electricity and photoelectric phenomena
1924 Karl M. G. Siegbahn (Sweden), for investigations in X-ray spectroscopy
1925 James Franck and Gustav Hertz (Germany), for discovery of laws governing impact of electrons upon atoms
1926 Jean B. Perrin (France), for work on discontinuous structure of matter and discovery of the equilibrium of sedimentation
1927 Arthur H. Compton (U.S.), for discovery of Compton phenomenon; and Charles T. R. Wilson (UK), for method of perceiving paths taken by electrically charged particles
1928 In 1929, the 1928 prize was awarded to Sir Owen Richardson (UK), for work on the phenomenon of thermionics and discovery of the Richardson Law
1929 Prince Louis Victor de Broglie (France), for discovery of the wave character of electrons
1930 Sir Chandrasekhara Raman (India), for work on diffusion of light and discovery of the Raman effect
1932 In 1933, the prize for 1932 was awarded to Werner Heisenberg (Germany), for creation of quantum mechanics
1933 Erwin Schrödinger (Austria) and Paul A. M. Dirac (UK), for discovery of new fertile forms of the atomic theory
1935 James Chadwick (UK), for discovery of the neutron
1936 Victor F. Hess (Austria), for discovery of cosmic radiation; and Carl D. Anderson (U.S.), for discovery of the positron
1937 Clinton J. Davisson (U.S.) and George P. Thomson (UK), for discovery of diffraction of electrons by crystals
1938 Enrico Fermi (Italy), for identification of new radioactivity elements and discovery of nuclear reactions effected by slow neutrons
1939 Ernest Orlando Lawrence (U.S.), for development of the cyclotron
1943 Otto Stern (U.S.), for detection of magnetic momentum of protons
1944 Isidor Isaac Rabi (U.S.), for work on magnetic movements of atomic particles
1945 Wolfgang Pauli (Austria), for work on atomic fissions
1946 Percy Williams Bridgman (U.S.), for studies and inventions in high-pressure physics
1947 Sir Edward Appleton (UK), for discovery of layer that reflects radio short waves in the ionosphere
1948 Patrick M. S. Blackett (UK), for improvement on Wilson chamber and discoveries in cosmic radiation
1949 Hideki Yukawa (Japan), for mathematical prediction, in 1935, of the meson
1950 Cecil Frank Powell (UK), for method of photographic study of atom nucleus, and for discoveries about mesons
1951 Sir John Douglas Cockcroft (UK) and Ernest T. S. Walton (Ireland), for work in 1932 on transmutation of atomic nuclei
1952 Edward Mills Purcell and Felix Bloch (U.S.), for work in measurement of magnetic fields in atomic nuclei
1953 Fritz Zernike (Netherlands), for development of "phase contrast" microscope
1954 Max Born (UK), for work in quantum mechanics; and Walther Bothe (Germany), for work in cosmic radiation
1955 Polykarp Kusch and Willis E. Lamb, Jr. (U.S.), for atomic measurements
1956 William Shockley, Walter H. Brattain, and John Bardeen (all U.S.), for developing electronic transistor
1957 Tsung Dao Lee and Chen Ning Yang (China), for disproving principle of conservation of parity
1958 Pavel A. Cherenkov, Ilya M. Frank, and Igor E. Tamm (all USSR), for work resulting in development of cosmic-ray counter
1959 Emilio Segre and Owen Chamberlain (both U.S.), for demonstrating the existence of the anti-proton
1960 Donald A. Glaser (U.S.), for invention of "bubble chamber" to study subatomic particles
1961 Robert Hofstadter (U.S.), for determination of shape and size of atomic nucleus; Rudolf Mössbauer (Germany), for method of producing and measuring recoil-free gamma rays
1962 Lev D. Landau (USSR), for his theories about condensed matter
1963 Eugene Paul Wigner, Maria Goeppert Mayer (both U.S.), and J. Hans D. Jensen (Germany), for research on structure of atom and its nucleus
1964 Charles Hard Townes (U.S.), Nikolai G. Basov, and Aleksandr M. Prochorov (both USSR), for developing maser and laser principle of producing high-intensity radiation
1965 Richard P. Feynman, Julian S. Schwinger (both U.S.), and Shinichiro Tomonaga (Japan), for research in quantum electrodynamics
1966 Alfred Kastler (France), for work on energy levels inside atom
1967 Hans A. Bethe (U.S.), for work on energy production of stars
1968 Luis Walter Alvarez (U.S.), for study of subatomic particles
1969 Murray Gell-Mann (U.S.), for study of subatomic particles
1970 Hannes Alfvén (Sweden), for theories in plasma physics; and Louis Néel (France), for discoveries in antiferromagnetism and ferromagnetism
1971 Dennis Gabor (UK), for invention of holographic method of three-dimensional imagery
1972 John Bardeen, Leon N. Cooper, and John Robert Schrieffer (all U.S.), for theory of superconductivity, where electrical resistance in certain metals vanishes above absolute zero temperature

1973 Ivar Giaever (U.S.), Leo Esaki (Japan), and Brian D. Josephson (UK), for theories that have advanced and expanded the field of miniature electronics
1974 Antony Hewish (UK), for discovery of pulsars; Martin Ryle (UK), for using radiotelescopes to probe outer space with precision
1975 James Rainwater (U.S.), Ben Mottelson, and Aage N. Bohr (both Denmark), for showing that the atomic nucleus is asymmetrical
1976 Burton Richter and Samuel C. C. Ting (both U.S.), for discovery of subatomic particles known as J and psi
1977 Philip W. Anderson, John H. Van Vleck (both U.S.), and Nevill F. Mott (UK), for work underlying computer memories and electronic devices
1978 Arno A. Penzias and Robert W. Wilson (both U.S.), for work in cosmic microwave radiation; Piotr L. Kapitsa (USSR), for basic inventions and discoveries in low-temperature physics
1979 Steven Weinberg, Sheldon L. Glashow (both U.S.), and Abdus Salam (Pakistan), for developing theory that electromagnetism and the "weak" force, which causes radioactive decay in some atomic nuclei, are facets of the same phenomenon
1980 James W. Cronin and Val L. Fitch (both U.S.), for work concerning the asymmetry of subatomic particles
1981 Nicolaas Bloembergen, Arthur L. Schawlow (both U.S.), and Kai M. Siegbahn (Sweden), for developing technologies with lasers and other devices to probe the secrets of complex forms of matter
1982 Kenneth G. Wilson (U.S.), for analysis of changes in matter under pressure and temperature
1983 Subrahmanyam Chandrasekhar and William A. Fowler (both U.S.), for complementary research on processes involved in the evolution of stars
1984 Carlo Rubbia (Italy) and Simon van der Meer (Netherlands), for their role in discovering three subatomic particles, a step toward developing a single theory to account for all natural forces
1985 Klaus von Klitzing (Germany), for developing an exact way of measuring electrical conductivity
1986 Ernst Ruska, Gerd Binnig (both Germany), and Heinrich Rohrer (Switzerland), for work on microscopes
1987 K. Alex Müller (Switzerland) and J. Georg Bednorz (Germany), for their discovery of high-temperature superconductors
1988 Leon M. Lederman, Melvin Schwartz, and Jack Steinberger (all U.S.), for research that improved the understanding of elementary particles and forces
1989 Norman F. Ramsey (U.S.), for work leading to development of the atomic clock, and Hans G. Dehmelt (U.S.) and Wolfgang Paul (Germany), for developing methods to isolate atoms and subatomic particles
1990 Richard E. Taylor (Canada), Jerome I. Friedman, and Dr. Henry W. Kendall (both U.S.), for their "breakthrough in our understanding of matter" that confirmed the reality of quarks
1991 Pierre-Gilles de Gennes (France), for his discoveries about the ordering of molecules in substances ranging from "super" glue to an exotic form of liquid helium
1992 George Charpak (France), for his inventions of particle detectors
1993 Joseph H. Taylor and Russell A. Hulse (both U.S.), for their discovery of a binary pulsar
1994 Clifford G. Shull (U.S.) and Bertram N. Brockhouse (Canada), for adapting beams of neutrons as probes to explore the atomic structure of matter
1995 Martin L. Perl and Frederick Reines (both U.S.), for their discoveries of "two of nature's most remarkable subatomic particles"—the tau and the neutrino
1996 David M. Lee, Robert C. Richardson, and Douglas D. Osheroff (all U.S.), for their discovery of superfluity in helium-3
1997 Steven Chu, William D. Phillips (both U.S.), and Claude Cohen-Tannoudji (France), for developing a method to cool and trap atoms using light from lasers
1998 Robert B. Laughlin (U.S.), Horst L. Störmer (Germany), and Daniel C. Tsui (U.S.), for their discovery of a new form of quantum fluid with fractionally charged excitations
1999 Gerardus 't Hooft (Netherlands) and Martinus J. G. Veltman (Netherlands), for their theory concerning the production of the Sun's energy
2000 Zhores I. Alferov (Russia), Herbert Kroemer, and Jack S. Kilby (both U.S.), for work in the development of transistors and microchip technology
2001 Wolfgang Ketterle (Germany), Eric A. Cornell, and Carl E. Wieman (both U.S.), for discovering Bose-Einstein condensate, a new state of matter
2002 Raymond Davis, Jr. (U.S.) and Masatoshi Koshiba (Japan), for the detection of cosmic neutrinos, and Riccardo Giacconi (U.S.), for contributions to astrophysics, which have led to the discovery of cosmic X-ray sources
2003 Alexei A. Abrikosov (Russia, U.S.), Anthony J. Leggett (UK, U.S.), and Vitaly L. Ginzburg (Russia), for theories concerning superconductivity

CHEMISTRY

1901 Jacobus H. van't Hoff (Netherlands), for laws of chemical dynamics and osmotic pressure in solutions
1902 Emil Fischer (Germany), for experiments in sugar and purin groups of substances
1903 Svante A. Arrhenius (Sweden), for his electrolytic theory of dissociation
1904 Sir William Ramsay (UK), for discovery and determination of place of inert gaseous elements in air
1905 Adolf von Baeyer (Germany), for work on organic dyes and hydroaromatic combinations
1906 Henri Moissan (France), for isolation of fluorine, and introduction of electric furnace
1907 Eduard Buchner (Germany), discovery of cell-less fermentation and investigations in biological chemistry
1908 Sir Ernest Rutherford (UK), for investigations into disintegration of elements

1909 Wilhelm Ostwald (Germany), for work on catalysis and investigations into chemical equilibrium and reaction rates
1910 Otto Wallach (Germany), for work in the field of alicyclic compounds
1911 Marie Curie (France), for discovery of elements radium and polonium
1912 Victor Grignard (France), for reagent discovered by him; and Paul Sabatier (France), for methods of hydrogenating organic compounds
1913 Alfred Werner (Switzerland), for linking up atoms within the molecule
1914 Theodore W. Richards (U.S.), for determining atomic weight of many chemical elements
1915 Richard Willstätter (Germany), for research into coloring matter of plants, especially chlorophyll
1918 Fritz Haber (Germany), for synthetic production of ammonia
1920 Walther Nernst (Germany), for work in thermochemistry
1921 Frederick Soddy (UK), for investigations into origin and nature of isotopes
1922 Francis W. Aston (UK), for discovery of isotopes in nonradioactive elements and for discovery of the whole number rule
1923 Fritz Pregl (Austria), for method of microanalysis of organic substances discovered by him
1925 In 1926, the 1925 prize was awarded to Richard Zsigmondy (Germany), for work on the heterogeneous nature of colloid solutions
1926 Theodor Svedberg (Sweden), for work on disperse systems
1927 In 1928, the 1927 prize was awarded to Heinrich Wieland (Germany), for investigations of bile acids and kindred substances
1928 Adolf Windaus (Germany), for investigations on constitution of the sterols and their connection with vitamins
1929 Sir Arthur Harden (UK) and Hans K. A. S. von Euler-Chelpin (Sweden), for research of fermentation of sugars
1930 Hans Fischer (Germany), for work on coloring matter of blood and leaves and for his synthesis of hemin
1931 Karl Bosch and Friedrich Bergius (both Germany), for invention and development of chemical high-pressure methods
1932 Irving Langmuir (U.S.), for work in realm of surface chemistry
1934 Harold C. Urey (U.S.), for discovery of heavy hydrogen
1935 Frédéric and Irène Joliot-Curie (both France), for synthesis of new radioactive elements
1936 Peter J. W. Debye (Netherlands), for investigations on dipole moments and diffraction of X-rays and electrons in gases
1937 Walter N. Haworth (UK), for research on carbohydrates and vitamin C; and Paul Karrer (Switzerland), for work on carotenoids, flavins, and vitamins A and B
1938 Richard Kuhn (Germany), for carotenoid study and vitamin research (declined)
1939 Adolf Butenandt (Germany), for work on sexual hormones (declined the prize); and Leopold Ruzicka (Switzerland), for work with polymethylenes
1943 Georg Hevesy De Heves (Hungary), for work on use of isotopes as indicators
1944 Otto Hahn (Germany), for work on atomic fission
1945 Artturi Illmari Virtanen (Finland), for research in the field of conservation of fodder
1946 James B. Sumner (U.S.), for crystallizing enzymes; John H. Northrop and Wendell M. Stanley (both U.S.), for preparing enzymes and virus proteins in pure form
1947 Sir Robert Robinson (UK), for research in plant substances
1948 Arne Tiselius (Sweden), for biochemical discoveries and isolation of mouse paralysis virus
1949 William Francis Giauque (U.S.), for research in thermodynamics, especially effects of low temperature
1950 Otto Diels and Kurt Alder (both Germany), for discovery of diene synthesis enabling scientists to study structure of organic matter
1951 Glenn T. Seaborg and Edwin H. McMillan (both U.S.), for discovery of plutonium
1952 Archer John Porter Martin and Richard Laurence Millington Synge (both UK), for development of partition chromatography
1953 Hermann Staudinger (Germany), for research in giant molecules
1954 Linus C. Pauling (U.S.), for study of forces holding together protein and other molecules
1955 Vincent du Vigneaud (U.S.), for work on pituitary hormones
1956 Sir Cyril Hinshelwood (UK) and Nikolai N. Semenov (USSR), for parallel research on chemical reaction kinetics
1957 Sir Alexander Todd (UK), for research with chemical compounds that are factors in heredity
1958 Frederick Sanger (UK), for determining molecular structure of insulin
1959 Jaroslav Heyrovsky (Czechoslovakia), for development of polarography, an electrochemical method of analysis
1960 Willard F. Libby (U.S.), for "atomic time clock" to measure age of objects by measuring their radioactivity
1961 Melvin Calvin (U.S.), for establishing chemical steps during photosynthesis
1962 Max F. Perutz and John C. Kendrew (UK), for mapping protein molecules with X-rays
1963 Karl Ziegler (Germany) and Giulio Natta (Italy), for work in uniting simple hydrocarbons into large molecular substances
1964 Dorothy Mary Crowfoot Hodgkin (UK), for determining structure of compounds needed in combatting pernicious anemia
1965 Robert B. Woodward (U.S.), for work in synthesizing complicated organic compounds
1966 Robert Sanderson Mulliken (U.S.), for research on bond holding atoms together in molecule
1967 Manfred Eigen (Germany), Ronald G. W. Norrish, and George Porter (both UK), for work in high-speed chemical reactions
1968 Lars Onsager (U.S.), for development of system of equations in thermodynamics
1969 Derek H. R. Barton (UK) and Odd Hassel (Norway), for study of organic molecules

1970 Luis F. Leloir (Argentina), for discovery of sugar nucleotides and their role in biosynthesis of carbohydrates
1971 Gerhard Herzberg (Canada), for contributions to knowledge of electronic structure and geometry of molecules, particularly free radicals
1972 Christian Boehmer Anfinsen, Stanford Moore, and William Howard Stein (all U.S.), for pioneering studies in enzymes
1973 Ernst Otto Fischer (W. Germany) and Geoffrey Wilkinson (UK), for work that could solve problem of automobile exhaust pollution
1974 Paul J. Flory (U.S.), for developing analytic methods to study properties and molecular structure of long-chain molecules
1975 John W. Cornforth (Australia) and Vladimir Prelog (Switzerland), for research on structure of biological molecules such as antibiotics and cholesterol
1976 William N. Lipscomb, Jr. (U.S.), for work on the structure and bonding mechanisms of boranes
1977 Ilya Prigogine (Belgium), for contributions to nonequilibrium thermodynamics, particularly the theory of dissipative structures
1978 Peter Mitchell (UK), for contributions to the understanding of biological energy transfer
1979 Herbert C. Brown (U.S.) and Georg Wittig (West Germany), for developing a group of substances that facilitate very difficult chemical reactions
1980 Paul Berg, Walter Gilbert (both U.S.), and Frederick Sanger (UK), for developing methods to map the structure and function of DNA, the substance that controls the activity of the cell
1981 Roald Hoffmann (U.S.) and Kenichi Fukui (Japan), for applying quantum-mechanics theories to predict the course of chemical reactions
1982 Aaron Klug (UK), for research in the detailed structures of viruses and components of life
1983 Henry Taube (U.S.), for research on how electrons transfer between molecules in chemical reactions
1984 R. Bruce Merrifield (U.S.), for research that revolutionized the study of proteins
1985 Herbert A. Hauptman and Jerome Karle (both U.S.), for their outstanding achievements in the development of direct methods for the determination of crystal structures
1986 Dudley R. Herschback, Yuan T. Lee (both U.S.), and John C. Polanyi (Canada), for their work on "reaction dynamics"
1987 Donald J. Cram, Charles J. Pedersen (both U.S.), and Jean-Marie Lehn (France), for wide-ranging research that has included the creation of artificial molecules that can mimic vital chemical reactions of the processes of life
1988 Johann Deisenhofer, Robert Huber, and Hartmut Michel (all West Germany), for unraveling the structure of proteins that play a crucial role in photosynthesis
1989 Thomas R. Cech and Sidney Altman (both U.S.), for their discovery, independently, that RNA could actively aid chemical reactions in the cells
1990 Elias James Corey (U.S.), for developing new ways to synthesize complex molecules ordinarily found in nature
1991 Richard R. Ernst (Switzerland), for refinements he developed in nuclear magnetic-resonance spectroscopy
1992 Rudolph A. Marcus (U.S.), for his mathematical analysis of how the overall energy in a system of interacting molecules changes and induces an electron to jump from one molecule to another
1993 Kary B. Mullis (U.S.) and Michael Smith (Canada), for their contributions to the science of genetics
1994 George A. Olah (U.S.), University of Southern California in Los Angeles, for research that opened new ways to break apart and rebuild compounds of carbon and hydrogen
1995 F. Sherwood Rowland, Mario Molina (both U.S.), and Paul Crutzen (Netherlands), for their pioneering work in explaining the chemical processes that deplete the earth's ozone shield
1996 Richard E. Smalley, Robert F. Curl, Jr. (both U.S.), and Harold W. Kroto (UK), for discovery of a new class of carbon molecule
1997 Paul D. Boyer (U.S.), Jens C. Skou (Denmark), and John E. Walker (UK), for discoveries about a molecule that allows the human body to store and transfer energy between cells
1998 Walter Kohn (U.S.) and John A. Pople (UK), for their developments in the study of the properties of molecules and the chemical processes in which they are involved
1999 Ahmed H. Zewail (Egypt and U.S.), for creating the world's fastest camera, which captures atoms in motion
2000 Alan J. Heeger, Alan G. MacDiarmid (both U.S.), and Hideki Shirakawa (Japan), for the discovery and development of conductive polymers
2001 William S. Knowles (U.S.) and Ryoji Noyori (Japan), for their work on chirally catalyzed hydrogenation reactions, and K. Barry Sharpless (U.S.), for his work on chirally catalyzed oxidation reactions
2002 John B. Fenn (U.S.) and Koichi Tanaka (Japan), for development of methods for analyses of biological macromolecules, and Kurt Wüthrich (Switzerland), for determining the three-dimensional structure of biological macromolecules in solution

PHYSIOLOGY OR MEDICINE

1901 Emil A. von Behring (Germany), for work on serum therapy against diphtheria
1902 Sir Ronald Ross (UK), for work on malaria
1903 Niels R. Finsen (Denmark), for his treatment of lupus vulgaris with concentrated light rays
1904 Ivan P. Pavlov (USSR), for work on the physiology of digestion
1905 Robert Koch (Germany), for work on tuberculosis
1906 Camillo Golgi (Italy) and Santiago Ramón y Cajal (Spain), for work on structure of the nervous system
1907 Charles L. A. Laveran (France), for work with protozoa in the generation of disease

1908 Paul Ehrlich (Germany) and Elie Metchnikoff (USSR), for work on immunity
1909 Theodor Kocher (Switzerland), for work on the thyroid gland
1910 Albrecht Kossel (Germany), for achievements in the chemistry of the cell
1911 Allvar Gullstrand (Sweden), for work on the dioptrics of the eye
1912 Alexis Carrel (France), for work on vascular ligature and grafting of blood vessels and organs
1913 Charles Richet (France), for work on anaphylaxy
1914 Robert Bárány (Austria), for work on physiology and pathology of the vestibular system
1919 Jules Bordet (Belgium), for discoveries in connection with immunity
1920 August Krogh (Denmark), for discovery of regulation of capillaries' motor mechanism
1922 In 1923, the 1922 prize was shared by Archibald V. Hill (UK), for discovery relating to heat-production in muscles; and Otto Meyerhof (Germany), for correlation between consumption of oxygen and production of lactic acid in muscles
1923 Sir Frederick Banting (Canada) and John J. R. Macleod (Scotland), for discovery of insulin
1924 Willem Einthoven (Netherlands), for discovery of the mechanism of the electrocardiogram
1926 Johannes Fibiger (Denmark), for discovery of the Spiroptera carcinoma
1927 Julius Wagner-Jauregg (Austria), for use of malaria inoculation in treatment of dementia paralytica
1928 Charles Nicolle (France), for work on typhus exanthematicus
1929 Christiaan Eijkman (Netherlands), for discovery of the antineuritic vitamins; and Sir Frederick Hopkins (UK), for discovery of growth-promoting vitamins
1930 Karl Landsteiner (U.S.), for discovery of human blood groups
1931 Otto H. Warburg (Germany), for discovery of the character and mode of action of the respiratory ferment
1932 Sir Charles Sherrington (UK) and Edgar D. Adrian (U.S.), for discoveries of the function of the neuron
1933 Thomas H. Morgan (U.S.), for discoveries on hereditary function of the chromosomes
1934 George H. Whipple, George R. Minot, and William P. Murphy (U.S.), for discovery of liver therapy against anemias
1935 Hans Spemann (Germany), for discovery of the organizer effect in embryonic development
1936 Sir Henry Dale (UK) and Otto Loewi (Germany), for discoveries on chemical transmission of nerve impulses
1937 Albert Szent-Györgyi von Nagyrapolt (Hungary), for discoveries on biological combustion
1938 Corneille Heymans (Belgium), for determining importance of sinus and aorta mechanisms in the regulation of respiration
1939 Gerhard Domagk (Germany), for antibacterial effect of prontocilate
1943 Henrik Dam (Denmark) and Edward A. Doisy (U.S.), for analysis of vitamin K
1944 Joseph Erlanger and Herbert Spencer Gasser (both U.S.), for work on functions of the nerve threads
1945 Sir Alexander Fleming, Ernst Boris Chain, and Sir Howard Florey (all UK), for discovery of penicillin
1946 Herman J. Muller (U.S.), for hereditary effects of X-rays on genes
1947 Carl F. and Gerty T. Cori (U.S.), for work on animal starch metabolism; Bernardo A. Houssay (Argentina), for study of pituitary
1948 Paul Mueller (Switzerland), for discovery of insect-killing properties of DDT
1949 Walter Rudolf Hess (Switzerland), for research on brain control of body; and Antonio Caetano de Abreu Freire Egas Moniz (Portugal), for development of brain operation
1950 Philip S. Hench, Edward C. Kendall (both U.S.), and Tadeus Reichstein (Switzerland), for discoveries about hormones of adrenal cortex
1951 Max Theiler (South Africa), for development of anti-yellow-fever vaccine
1952 Selman A. Waksman (U.S.), for discovery of streptomycin
1953 Fritz A. Lipmann (Germany-U.S.) and Hans Adolph Krebs (Germany-UK), for studies of living cells
1954 John F. Enders, Thomas H. Weller, and Frederick C. Robbins (all U.S.), for work with cultivation of polio virus
1955 Hugo Theorell (Sweden), for work on oxidation enzymes
1956 Dickinson W. Richards, Jr., André F. Cournand (both U.S.), and Werner Forssmann (Germany), for new techniques in treating heart disease
1957 Daniel Bovet (Italy), for development of drugs to relieve allergies and relax muscles during surgery
1958 Joshua Lederberg (U.S.), for work with genetic mechanisms; George W. Beadle and Edward L. Tatum (both U.S.), for discovering how genes transmit hereditary characteristics
1959 Severo Ochoa and Arthur Kornberg (both U.S.), for discoveries related to compounds within chromosomes that play a vital role in heredity
1960 Sir Macfarlane Burnet (Australia) and Peter Brian Medawar (UK), for discovery of acquired immunological tolerance
1961 Georg von Bekesy (U.S.), for discoveries about physical mechanisms of stimulation within cochlea
1962 James D. Watson (U.S.), Maurice H. F. Wilkins, and Francis H. C. Crick (both UK), for determining structure of deoxyribonucleic acid (DNA)
1963 Alan Lloyd Hodgkin, Andrew Fielding Huxley (both UK), and Sir John Carew Eccles (Australia), for research on nerve cells
1964 Konrad E. Bloch (U.S.) and Feodor Lynen (Germany), for research on mechanism and regulation of cholesterol and fatty-acid metabolism
1965 François Jacob, André Lwoff, and Jacques Monod (all France), for study of regulatory activities in body cells

1966 Charles Brenton Huggins (U.S.), for studies in hormone treatment of cancer of prostate; Francis Peyton Rous (U.S.), for discovery of tumor-producing viruses
1967 Haldan K. Hartline, George Wald (both U.S.), and Ragnar Granit (Sweden), for work on human eye
1968 Robert W. Holley, Har Gobind Khorana, and Marshall W. Nirenberg (all U.S.), for studies of genetic code
1969 Max Delbruck, Alfred D. Hershey, and Salvador E. Luria (all U.S.), for study of mechanism of virus infection in living cells
1970 Julius Axelrod (U.S.), Ulf S. von Euler (Sweden), and Sir Bernard Katz (UK), for studies of how nerve impulses are transmitted within the body
1971 Earl W. Sutherland, Jr. (U.S.), for research on how hormones work
1972 Gerald M. Edelman (U.S.), and Rodney R. Porter (UK), for research on the chemical structure and nature of antibodies
1973 Karl von Frisch, Konrad Lorenz (both Austria), and Nikolaas Tinbergen (Netherlands), for their studies of individual and social behavior patterns
1974 George E. Palade, Christian de Duve (both U.S.), and Albert Claude (Belgium), for contributions to understanding inner workings of living cells
1975 David Baltimore, Howard M. Temin, and Renato Dulbecco (all U.S.), for work in interaction between tumor viruses and genetic material of the cell
1976 Baruch S. Blumberg and D. Carleton Gajdusek (both U.S.), for discoveries concerning new mechanisms for the origin and dissemination of infectious diseases
1977 Rosalyn S. Yalow, Roger C. L. Guillemin, and Andrew V. Schally (all U.S.), for research in role of hormones in chemistry of the body
1978 Daniel Nathans, Hamilton Smith (both U.S.), and Werner Arber (Switzerland), for discovery of restriction enzymes and their application to problems of molecular genetics
1979 Allan McLeod Cormack (U.S.) and Godfrey Newbold Hounsfield (UK), for developing computed axial tomography (CAT scan) X-ray technique
1980 Baruj Benacerraf, George D. Snell (both U.S.), and Jean Dausset (France), for discoveries that explain how the structure of cells relates to organ transplants and diseases
1981 Roger W. Sperry, David H. Hubel (both U.S.), and Torsten N. Wiesel (Sweden), for studies vital to understanding the organization and functioning of the brain
1982 Sune Bergstrom, Bengt Samuelsson (both Sweden), and John R. Vane (UK), for research in prostaglandins, hormonelike substances involved in a wide range of illnesses
1983 Barbara McClintock (U.S.), for her discovery of mobile genes in the chromosomes of a plant that change the future generations of plants they produce
1984 Cesar Milstein (UK/Argentina), Georges J. F. Kohler (West Germany), and Niels K. Jerne (UK/Denmark), for their work in immunology
1985 Michael S. Brown and Joseph L. Goldstein (both U.S.), for their work, which has drastically widened our understanding of the cholesterol metabolism and increased our possibilities to prevent and treat atherosclerosis and heart attacks
1986 Rita Levi-Montalcini (dual U.S./Italy) and Stanley Cohen (U.S.), for their contributions to the understanding of substances that influence cell growth
1987 Susumu Tonegawa (Japan), for his discoveries of how the body can suddenly marshal its immunological defenses against millions of different disease agents that it has never encountered before
1988 Gertrude B. Elion, George H. Hitchings (both U.S.), and Sir James Black (UK), for their discoveries of important principles for drug treatment
1989 J. Michael Bishop and Harold E. Varmus (both U.S.), for their unifying theory of cancer development
1990 Joseph E. Murray and E. Donnall Thomas (both U.S.), for their pioneering work in transplants
1991 Erwin Neher and Bert Sakmann (both Germany), for their research, particularly for the development of a technique called patch clamp
1992 Edmond H. Fischer and Edwin G. Krebs (both U.S.), for their discovery of a regulatory mechanism affecting almost all cells
1993 Phillip A. Sharp (U.S.) and Richard J. Roberts (UK), for their independent discovery in 1977 of "split genes"
1994 Alfred G. Gilman and Martin Rodbell (both U.S.), for discovery of G-proteins that help cells respond to outside signals
1995 Edward B. Lewis, Eric F. Wieschaus (both U.S.), and Christiane Nüsslein-Volhard (Germany), for studies of the fruit fly that will help explain congenital malformations in humans
1996 Peter C. Doherty (Australia) and Rolf M. Zinkernagel (Switzerland), for discoveries about how the immune system recognizes virus-infected cells
1997 Stanley B. Prusiner (U.S.), for discovery of a new type of germ, called prions, that causes degenerative brain disorders
1998 Robert F. Furchgott, Louis J. Ignarro, and Ferid Murad (all U.S.), for discovering that nitric oxide acts as a signal in the cardiovascular system
1999 Günter Blobel (U.S.), for discovering that proteins have intrinsic signals that govern their transport and localization in the cell
2000 Arvid Carlsson (Sweden), Paul Greengard, and Eric R. Kandel (both U.S.), for discoveries concerning signal transduction in the nervous system
2001 Leland H. Hartwell (U.S.), R. Timothy Hunt, and Paul M. Nurse (both UK), for discoveries concerning control of the cell cycle, which may make new cancer treatments possible
2002 Sydney Brenner (UK), H. Robert Horvitz (U.S.), and John E. Sulston (UK), for discoveries concerning genetic regulation of organ development and programmed cell death

ECONOMIC SCIENCE

1969 Ragnar Frisch (Norway) and Jan Tinbergen (Netherlands), for work in econometrics (application of mathematics and statistical methods to economic theories and problems)
1970 Paul A. Samuelson (U.S.), for efforts to raise the level of scientific analysis in economic theory
1971 Simon Kuznets (U.S.), for developing concept of using a country's gross national product to determine its economic growth
1972 Kenneth J. Arrow (U.S.) and Sir John R. Hicks (UK), for theories that help to assess business risk and government economic and welfare policies
1973 Wassily Leontief (U.S.), for devising the input-output technique to determine how different sectors of an economy interact
1974 Gunnar Myrdal (Sweden) and Friedrich A. von Hayek (UK), for pioneering analysis of the interdependence of economic, social, and institutional phenomena
1975 Leonid V. Kantorovich (USSR) and Tjalling C. Koopmans (U.S.), for work on the theory of optimum allocation of resources
1976 Milton Friedman (U.S.), for work in consumption analysis and monetary history and theory, and for demonstration of complexity of stabilization policy
1977 Bertil Ohlin (Sweden) and James E. Meade (UK), for contributions to theory of international trade and international capital movements
1978 Herbert A. Simon (U.S.), for research into the decision-making process within economic organizations
1979 Sir Arthur Lewis (UK) and Theodore Schultz (U.S.), for work on economic problems of developing nations
1980 Lawrence R. Klein (U.S.), for developing models for forecasting economic trends and shaping policies to deal with them
1981 James Tobin (U.S.), for analyses of financial markets and their influence on spending and saving by families and businesses
1982 George J. Stigler (U.S.), for work on government regulation in the economy and the functioning of industry
1983 Gerard Debreu (U.S.), in recognition of his work on the basic economic problem of how prices operate to balance what producers supply with what buyers want
1984 Sir Richard Stone (UK), for his work to develop the systems widely used to measure the performance of national economics
1985 Franco Modigliani (U.S.), for his pioneering work in analyzing the behavior of household savers and the functioning of financial markets
1986 James M. Buchanan (U.S.), for his development of new methods for analyzing economic and political decision-making
1987 Robert M. Solow (U.S.), for seminal contributions to the theory of economic growth
1988 Maurice Allais (France), for his pioneering development of theories to better understand market behavior and the efficient use of resources
1989 Trygve Haavelmo (Norway), for his pioneering work in methods for testing economic theories
1990 Harry M. Markowitz, William F. Sharpe, and Merton H. Miller (all U.S.), whose work provided new tools for weighing the risks and rewards of different investments and for valuing corporate stocks and bonds
1991 Ronald Coase (U.S.), for his pioneering work in how property rights and the cost of doing business affect the economy
1992 Gary S. Becker (U.S.), for "having extended the domain of economic theory to aspects of human behavior which had previously been dealt with—if at all—by other social science disciplines"
1993 Robert W. Fogel and Douglass C. North (both U.S.), for their work in economic history
1994 John F. Nash, John C. Harsanyi (both U.S.), and Reinhard Selten (Germany), for their pioneering work in game theory
1995 Robert E. Lucas, Jr. (U.S.), for having had the greatest influence on macroeconomic research since 1970
1996 James A. Mirrlees (UK) and William Vickrey (U.S.), for their fundamental contributions to the economic theory of incentives
1997 Robert C. Merton and Myron S. Scholes (both U.S.), for developing a formula that determines the value of stock options and other derivatives
1998 Amartya Sen (India), for his contributions to welfare economics
1999 Robert A. Mundell (Canada), for his work on monetary dynamics and optimum currency areas
2000 James J. Heckman and Daniel L. McFadden (both U.S.), for developing methods used in statistical analysis of individual and household behavior
2001 George A. Akerlof, A. Michael Spence, and Joseph E. Stiglitz (all U.S.), for market analyses with asymmetric information
2002 Daniel Kahneman (U.S.), for having integrated insights from psychological research into economic science, and Vernon L. Smith (U.S.), for having established laboratory experiments as a tool in empirical economic analysis

Pulitzer Prizes

(For years not listed, no award was made.)

PULITZER PRIZES IN JOURNALISM

Meritorious Public Service

1918 *New York Times;* also special award to Minna Lewinson and Henry Beetle Hough
1919 *Milwaukee Journal*
1921 *Boston Post*
1922 *New York World*
1923 *Memphis Commercial Appeal*
1924 *New York World*
1926 *Columbus* (Ga.) *Enquirer Sun*
1927 *Canton* (Ohio) *Daily News*

1928 *Indianapolis Times*
1929 *New York Evening World*
1931 *Atlanta Constitution*
1932 *Indianapolis News*
1933 *New York World-Telegram*
1934 *Medford* (Ore.) *Mail Tribune*
1935 *Sacramento Bee*
1936 *Cedar Rapids* (Iowa) *Gazette*
1937 *St. Louis Post-Dispatch*
1938 *Bismarck* (N.D.) *Tribune*
1939 *Miami Daily News*
1940 *Waterbury* (Conn.) *Republican* and *American*
1941 *St. Louis Post-Dispatch*
1942 *Los Angeles Times*
1943 *Omaha World-Herald*
1944 *New York Times*
1945 *Detroit Free Press*
1946 *Scranton* (Pa.) *Times*
1947 *Baltimore Sun*
1948 *St. Louis Post-Dispatch*
1949 (Lincoln) *Nebraska State Journal*
1950 *Chicago Daily News;* and *St. Louis Post-Dispatch*
1951 *Miami Herald;* and *Brooklyn Eagle*
1952 *St. Louis Post-Dispatch*
1953 *Whiteville* (N.C.) *News Reporter;* and *Tabor City* (N.C.) *Tribune*
1954 *Newsday* (Garden City, N.Y.)
1955 *Columbus* (Ga.) *Ledger* and *Sunday Ledger-Enquirer*
1956 *Watsonville* (Calif.) *Register-Pajaronian*
1957 *Chicago Daily News*
1958 (Little Rock) *Arkansas Gazette*
1959 *Utica* (N.Y.) *Observer Dispatch* and *Utica Daily Press*
1960 *Los Angeles Times*
1961 *Amarillo* (Tex.) *Globe-Times*
1962 *Panama City* (Fla.) *News-Herald*
1963 *Chicago Daily News*
1964 *St. Petersburg* (Fla.) *Times*
1965 *Hutchinson* (Kans.) *News*
1966 *Boston Globe*
1967 *Louisville Courier-Journal* and *Milwaukee Journal*
1968 *Riverside* (Calif.) *Press-Enterprise*
1969 *Los Angeles Times*
1970 *Newsday* (Garden City, N.Y.)
1971 *Winston–Salem* (N.C.) *Journal and Sentinel*
1972 *New York Times*
1973 *Washington Post*
1974 *Newsday* (Garden City, N.Y.)
1975 *Boston Globe*
1976 *Anchorage* (Alaska) *Daily News*
1977 *Lufkin* (Tex.) *News*
1978 *Philadelphia Inquirer*
1979 *Point Reyes* (Calif.) *Light*
1980 Gannett News Service
1981 *Charlotte* (N.C.) *Observer*
1982 *Detroit News*
1983 *Jackson* (Miss.) *Clarion-Ledger*
1984 *Los Angeles Times*
1985 *Fort Worth Star-Telegram*
1986 *Denver Post*
1987 *Pittsburgh Press,* reporting by Andrew Schneider and Matthew Brelis
1988 *Charlotte* (N.C.) *Observer*
1989 *Anchorage Daily News*
1990 *Philadelphia Inquirer* and *Washington* (N.C.) *Daily News*
1991 *Des Moines Register,* reporting by Jane Schorer
1992 *Sacramento Bee* for "The Sierra in Peril" series by Tom Knudson
1993 *Miami Herald*
1994 *Akron* (Ohio) *Beacon Journal*
1995 *Virgin Islands Daily News*
1996 *News and Observer* (Raleigh, N.C.)
1997 *Times-Picayune* (New Orleans, La.)
1998 *Grand Forks* (N.D.) *Herald*
1999 *Washington Post*
2000 *Washington Post*
2001 *Oregonian*
2002 *New York Times*
2003 *Boston Globe*

Editorial

1917 *New York Tribune*
1918 *Louisville Courier-Journal*
1920 Harvey E. Newbranch *(Omaha Evening World-Herald)*
1922 Frank M. O'Brien *(New York Herald)*
1923 William Allen White *(Emporia* [Kan.] *Gazette)*
1924 *Boston Herald;* special prize: Frank I. Cobb *(New York World)*
1925 *Charleston* (S.C.) *News and Courier*
1926 Edward M. Kingsbury *(New York Times)*
1927 F. Lauriston Bullard *(Boston Herald)*
1928 Grover Cleveland Hall *(Montgomery* [Ala.] *Advertiser)*
1929 Louis Isaac Jaffe *(Norfolk Virginian-Pilot)*
1931 Charles S. Ryckman *(Fremont* [Neb.] *Tribune)*
1933 *Kansas City* (Mo.) *Star*
1934 E. P. Chase *(Atlantic* [Iowa] *News Telegraph)*
1936 Felix Morley *(Washington Post);* George B. Parker (Scripps–Howard Newspapers)
1937 John W. Owens *(Baltimore Sun)*
1938 W. W. Waymack *(Des Moines Register and Tribune)*
1939 Ronald G. Callvert *(Portland Oregonian)*
1940 Bart Howard *(St. Louis Post-Dispatch)*
1941 Reuben Maury *(New York Daily News)*
1942 Geoffrey Parsons *(New York Herald Tribune)*
1943 Forrest W. Seymour *(Des Moines Register and Tribune)*
1944 Henry J. Haskell *(Kansas City* [Mo.] *Star)*
1945 George W. Potter *(Providence* [R.I.] *Journal-Bulletin)*
1946 Hodding Carter ([Greenville, Miss.] *Delta Democrat-Times*)
1947 William H. Grimes *(Wall Street Journal)*
1948 Virginius Dabney *(Richmond Times-Dispatch)*
1949 John H. Crider *(Boston Herald);* Herbert Elliston *(Washington Post)*
1950 Carl M. Saunders *(Jackson* [Mich.] *Citizen Patriot)*
1951 William H. Fitzpatrick *(New Orleans States)*
1952 Louis LaCoss *(St. Louis Globe-Democrat)*
1953 Vermont C. Royster *(Wall Street Journal)*
1954 Don Murray *(Boston Herald)*
1955 Royce Howes *(Detroit Free Press)*
1956 Lauren K. Soth *(Des Moines Register and Tribune)*
1957 Buford Boone *(Tuscaloosa* [Ala.] *News)*
1958 Harry S. Ashmore *(Arkansas Gazette)*
1959 Ralph McGill *(Atlanta Constitution)*
1960 Lenoir Chambers *(Virginian-Pilot)*
1961 William J. Dorvillier *(San Juan* [P.R.] *Star)*
1962 Thomas M. Storke *(Santa Barbara* [Calif.] *News-Press)*

1963 Ira B. Harkey, Jr. (*Pascagoula* [Miss.] *Chronicle*)
1964 Hazel Brannon Smith (*Lexington* [Miss.] *Advertiser*)
1965 John R. Harrison (*Gainesville* [Fla.] *Daily Sun*)
1966 Robert Lasch (*St. Louis Post-Dispatch*)
1967 Eugene Patterson (*Atlanta Constitution*)
1968 John S. Knight (Knight Newspapers)
1969 Paul Greenberg (*Pine Bluff* [Ark.] *Commercial*)
1970 Phillip L. Geyelin (*Washington Post*)
1971 Horance G. Davis, Jr. (*Gainesville* [Fla.] *Sun*)
1972 John Strohmeyer (*Bethlehem* [Pa.] *Globe Times*)
1973 Roger Bourne Linscott (*Berkshire Eagle* [Pittsfield, Mass.])
1974 F. Gilman Spencer (*Trenton* [N.J.] *Trentonian*)
1975 John Daniell Maurice (*Charleston* [W. Va.] *Daily Mail*)
1976 Philip P. Kerby (*Los Angeles Times*)
1977 Warren L. Lerude, Foster Church, and Norman F. Cardoza (*Reno* [Nev.] *Gazette* and *Nevada State Journal*)
1978 Meg Greenfield (*Washington Post*)
1979 Edwin M. Yoder, Jr. (*Washington Star*)
1980 Robert L. Bartley (*Wall Street Journal*)
1982 Jack Rosenthal (*New York Times*)
1983 *Miami Herald*
1984 Albert Scardino (*Georgia Gazette*)
1985 Richard Aregood (*Philadelphia Daily News*)
1986 Jack Fuller (*Chicago Tribune*)
1987 Jonathan Freedman (*San Diego Tribune*)
1988 Jane E. Healy (*Orlando Sentinel*)
1989 Lois Wille (*Chicago Tribune*)
1990 Thomas J. Hylton (*Pottstown* [Pa.] *Mercury*)
1991 Ron Casey, Harold Jackson, and Joey Kennedy (*Birmingham* [Ala.] *News*)
1992 Maria Henson (*Lexington* [Ky.] *Herald-Leader*)
1994 R. Bruce Dold (*Chicago Tribune*)
1995 Jeffrey Good (*St. Petersburg* [Fla.] *Times*)
1996 Robert B. Semple, Jr. (*New York Times*)
1997 Michael Gartner (*Daily Tribune* [Ames, Iowa])
1998 Bernard L. Stein (*The Riverdale Press* [Bronx, N.Y.])
1999 Editorial Board (*Daily News* [New York, N.Y.])
2000 John C. Bersia (*The Orlando Sentinel* [Orlando, Fla.])
2001 David Moats (*Rutland Herald* [Rutland, Vt.])
2002 Alex Raksin and Bob Sipchen (*Los Angeles Times*)
2003 Cornelia Grumman (*Chicago Tribune*)

Correspondence

1929 Paul Scott Mowrer (*Chicago Daily News*)
1930 Leland Stowe (*New York Herald Tribune*)
1931 H. R. Knickerbocker (*Philadelphia Public Ledger* and *New York Evening Post*)
1932 Walter Duranty (*New York Times*); Charles G. Ross (*St. Louis Post-Dispatch*)
1933 Edgar Ansel Mowrer (*Chicago Daily News*)
1934 Frederick T. Birchall (*New York Times*)
1935 Arthur Krock (*New York Times*)
1936 Wilfred C. Barber (*Chicago Tribune*)
1937 Anne O'Hare McCormick (*New York Times*)
1938 Arthur Krock (*New York Times*)
1939 Louis P. Lochner (Associated Press)
1940 Otto D. Tolischus (*New York Times*)
1941 Group award[1]
1942 Carlos P. Romulo (*Philippines Herald*)
1943 Hanson W. Baldwin (*New York Times*)
1944 Ernie Pyle (Scripps–Howard Newspaper Alliance)
1945 Harold V. (Hal) Boyle (Associated Press)
1946 Arnaldo Cortesi (*New York Times*)
1947 Brooks Atkinson (*New York Times*)

1. For the public services and the individual achievements of American news reporters in the war zones.

Editorial Cartooning

1922 Rollin Kirby (*New York World*)
1924 Jay Norwood Darling (*New York Tribune*)
1925 Rollin Kirby (*New York World*)
1926 D. R. Fitzpatrick (*St. Louis Post-Dispatch*)
1927 Nelson Harding (*Brooklyn Eagle*)
1928 Nelson Harding (*Brooklyn Eagle*)
1929 Rollin Kirby (*New York World*)
1930 Charles R. Macauley (*Brooklyn Eagle*)
1931 Edmund Duffy (*Baltimore Sun*)
1932 John T. McCutcheon (*Chicago Tribune*)
1933 H. M. Talburt (*Washington Daily News*)
1934 Edmund Duffy (*Baltimore Sun*)
1935 Ross A. Lewis (*Milwaukee Journal*)
1937 C. D. Batchelor (*New York Daily News*)
1938 Vaughn Shoemaker (*Chicago Daily News*)
1939 Charles G. Werner (*Daily Oklahoman* [Oklahoma City])
1940 Edmund Duffy (*Baltimore Sun*)
1941 Jacob Burck (*Chicago Times*)
1942 Herbert L. Block (NEA Service)
1943 Jay Norwood Darling (*New York Herald Tribune*)
1944 Clifford K. Berryman (*Washington Evening Star*)
1945 Bill Mauldin (United Features Syndicate)
1946 Bruce Alexander Russell (*Los Angeles Times*)
1947 Vaughn Shoemaker (*Chicago Daily News*)
1948 Reuben L. Goldberg (*New York Sun*)
1949 Lute Pease (*Newark Evening News*)
1950 James T. Berryman (*Washington Evening Star*)
1951 Reg (Reginald W.) Manning (*Arizona Republic* [Phoenix])
1952 Fred L. Packer (*New York Mirror*)
1953 Edward D. Kuekes (*Cleveland Plain Dealer*)
1954 Herbert L. Block (*Washington Post* and *Times-Herald*)
1955 Daniel R. Fitzpatrick (*St. Louis Post-Dispatch*)
1956 Robert York (*Louisville Times*)
1957 Tom Little (*Nashville Tennessean*)
1958 Bruce M. Shanks (*Buffalo Evening News*)
1959 Bill Mauldin (*St. Louis Post-Dispatch*)
1961 Carey Orr (*Chicago Tribune*)
1962 Edmund S. Valtman (*Hartford Times*)
1963 Frank Miller (*Des Moines Register*)
1964 Paul Conrad (formerly of *Denver Post*, later of *Los Angeles Times*)
1966 Don Wright (*Miami News*)
1967 Patrick B. Oliphant (*Denver Post*)
1968 Eugene Gray Payne (*Charlotte* [N.C.] *Observer*)
1969 John Fischetti (*Chicago Daily News*)
1970 Thomas F. Darcy (*Newsday* [Garden City, N.Y.])
1971 Paul Conrad (*Los Angeles Times*)
1972 Jeffrey K. MacNelly (*Richmond* [Va.] *News Leader*)
1974 Paul Szep (*Boston Globe*)
1975 Garry Trudeau (Universal Press Syndicate)
1976 Tony Auth (*Philadelphia Inquirer*)
1977 Paul Szep (*Boston Globe*)

1978 Jeffrey K. MacNelly *(Richmond* [Va.] *News Leader)*
1979 Herbert L. Block *(Washington Post)*
1980 Don Wright *(Miami News)*
1981 Mike Peters *(Dayton* [Ohio] *Daily News)*
1982 Ben Sargent *(Austin* [Tex.] *American-Statesman)*
1983 Richard Locher *(Chicago Tribune)*
1984 Paul Conrad *(Los Angeles Times)*
1985 Jeff MacNelly *(Chicago Tribune)*
1986 Jules Feiffer *(Village Voice)*
1987 Berke Breathed *(Washington Post* Writers Group)
1988 Doug Marlette *(Atlanta Constitution* and *Charlotte* [N.C.] *Observer)*
1989 Jack Higgins *(Chicago Sun-Times)*
1990 Tom Toles *(Buffalo News)*
1991 Jim Borgman *(Cincinnati Inquirer)*
1992 Signe Wilkinson *(Philadelphia Daily News)*
1993 Stephen R. Benson *(Arizona Republic)*
1994 Michael P. Ramirez *(Commercial Appeal,* Memphis)
1995 Mike Luckovich *(Atlanta Constitution)*
1996 Jim Morin *(Miami Herald)*
1997 Walt Handelsman *(Times-Picayune)*
1998 Stephen P. Breen *(Asbury Park* [N.J.] *Press)*
1999 David Horsey *(Seattle Post-Intelligencer)*
2000 Joel Pett *(Lexington* [Ky.] *Herald-Leader)*
2001 Ann Telnaes (Los Angeles Times Syndicate)
2002 Clay Bennett *(Christian Science Monitor)*
2003 David Horsey (*Seattle Post-Intelligencer)*

News Photography

1942 Milton Brooks *(Detroit News)*
1943 Frank Noel (Associated Press)
1944 Frank Filan (Associated Press); Earle L. Bunker *(Omaha World-Herald)*
1945 Joe Rosenthal (Associated Press)
1947 Arnold Hardy
1948 Frank Cushing *(Boston Traveler)*
1949 Nat Fein *(New York Herald Tribune)*
1950 Bill Crouch *(Oakland Tribune)*
1951 Max Desfor (Associated Press)
1952 John Robinson and Don Ultang *(Des Moines Register & Tribune)*
1953 William M. Gallagher *(Flint* [Mich.] *Journal)*
1954 Mrs. Walter M. Schau
1955 John L. Gaunt, Jr. *(Los Angeles Times)*
1956 *New York Daily News*
1957 Harry A. Trask *(Boston Traveler)*
1958 William C. Beall *(Washington Daily News)*
1959 William Seaman *(Minneapolis Star)*
1960 Andrew Lopez (United Press International)
1961 Yasushi Nagao (Mainichi Newspapers, Tokyo)
1962 Paul Vathis (Harrisburg [Pa.] bureau of Associated Press)
1963 Hector Rondon *(La Republica,* Caracas, Venezuela)
1964 Robert H. Jackson *(Dallas Times Herald)*
1965 Horst Faas (Associated Press)
1966 Kyoichi Sawada (United Press International)
1967 Jack R. Thornell (Associated Press)
1968 News: Rocco Morabito *(Jacksonville* [Fla.] *Journal);* features: Toshio Sakai (United Press International)
1969 Spot news: Edward T. Adams (Associated Press); features: Moneta Sleet, Jr.
1970 Spot news: Steve Starr (Associated Press); features: Dallas Kinney *(Palm Beach Post)*
1971 Spot news: John Paul Filo *(Valley Daily News* and *Daily Dispatch* [Tarentum and New Kensington, Pa.]); features: Jack Dykinga *(Chicago Sun-Times)*
1972 Spot news: Horst Faas and Michel Laurent (Associated Press); features: Dave Kennerly (United Press International)
1973 Spot news: Huynh Cong Ut *(Associated Press);* features: Brian Lanker *(Topeka Capital-Journal)*
1974 Spot news: Anthony K. Roberts (Associated Press); features: Slava Veder (Associated Press)
1975 Spot news: Gerald H. Gay *(Seattle Times);* features: Matthew Lewis *(Washington Post)*
1976 Spot news: Stanley J. Forman *(Boston Herald-American);* features: photographic staff of *Louisville Courier-Journal* and *Times*
1977 Spot news: Neal Ulevich (Associated Press) and Stanley J. Forman *(Boston Herald-American);* features: Robin Hood *(Chattanooga News-Free Press)*
1978 Spot news: John Blair, freelance, Evansville, Ind.; features: J. Ross Baughman (Associated Press)
1979 Spot news: Thomas J. Kelly, 3rd *(Pottstown* [Pa.] *Mercury);* features: photographic staff of *Boston Herald-American*
1980 Features: Erwin H. Hagler *(Dallas Times Herald)*
1981 Spot news: Larry C. Price *(Fort Worth Star-Telegram);* features: Taro M. Yamasaki *(Detroit Free Press)*
1982 Spot news: Ron Edmonds (Associated Press); features: John H. White *(Chicago Sun-Times)*
1983 Spot news: Bill Foley (Associated Press); features: James B. Dickman *(Dallas Times Herald)*
1984 Spot news: Stan Grossfeld *(Boston Globe);* features: Anthony Suau *(Denver Post)*
1985 Spot news: photographic staff of *Register,* Santa Ana, Calif.; features: Stan Grossfeld *(Boston Globe)*
1986 Spot news: Michel duCille and Carol Guzy *(Miami Herald)*; features: Tom Gralish *(Philadelphia Inquirer)*
1987 Spot news: Kim Komenich *(San Francisco Examiner);* features: David Peterson *(Des Moines Register)*
1988 Spot news: Scott Shaw *(Odessa* [Texas] *American);* features: Michel duCille *(Miami Herald)*
1989 Spot news: Ron Olshwanger *(St. Louis Post-Dispatch);* features: Manny Crisostomo *(Detroit Free Press)*
1990 Spot news: *Oakland Tribune;* features: David C. Turnley *(Detroit Free Press)*
1991 Spot news: Greg Marinovich (Associated Press); features: William Snyder *(Dallas Morning News)*
1992 Spot news: Associated Press staff; features: John Kaplan *(Herald* [Monterey, Calif.] and *Pittsburgh Post–Gazette)*
1993 Spot news: William Snyder and Ken Geiger *(Dallas Morning News);* features: Associated Press
1994 Spot news: Paul Watson *(Toronto Star);* features: Kevin Carter, freelancer for *New York Times*
1995 Spot news: Carol Guzy *(Washington Post);* features: Associated Press staff

1996 Spot news: Charles Porter IV, freelance photographer for Associated Press; features: Stephanie Walsh, freelance photographer for Newhouse News Service
1997 Spot news: Annie Wells *(Press Democrat* [Santa Rosa, Calif.]); features: Alexander Zemlianichenko (Associated Press)
1998 Spot news: Martha Rial *(Pittsburgh Post–Gazette)*; features: Clarence Williams *(Los Angeles Times)*
1999 Spot news: Associated Press photo staff; features: Associated Press photo staff
2000 Breaking news: photographic staff of *Denver Rocky Mountain News*; features: Carol Guzy, Michael Williamson, and Lucian Perkins *(Washington Post)*
2001 Breaking news: Alan Diaz (Associated Press); features: Matt Rainey *(Star-Ledger* [Newark, N.J.])
2002 Breaking news: *New York Times* staff; features: *New York Times* staff
2003 Breaking news: *Rocky Mountain News* staff; features: Don Bartletti *(Los Angeles Times)*

National Telegraphic Reporting

1942 Louis Stark *(New York Times)*
1944 Dewey L. Fleming *(Baltimore Sun)*
1945 James Reston *(New York Times)*
1946 Edward A. Harris *(St. Louis Post-Dispatch)*
1947 Edward T. Folliard *(Washington Post)*

National Reporting

1948 Bert Andrews *(New York Herald Tribune);* Nat S. Finney *(Minneapolis Tribune)*
1949 C. P. Trussell *(New York Times)*
1950 Edwin O. Guthman *(Seattle Times)*
1952 Anthony Leviero *(New York Times)*
1953 Don Whitehead (Associated Press)
1954 Richard Wilson (Cowles Newspapers)
1955 Anthony Lewis *(Washington Daily News)*
1956 Charles L. Bartlett *(Chattanooga Times)*
1957 James Reston *(New York Times)*
1958 Relman Morin (Associated Press) and Clark Mollenhoff *(Des Moines Register & Tribune)*
1959 Howard Van Smith *(Miami News)*
1960 Vance Trimble (Scripps-Howard Newspaper Alliance)
1961 Edward R. Cony *(Wall Street Journal)*
1962 Nathan G. Caldwell and Gene S. Graham *(Nashville Tennessean)*
1963 Anthony Lewis *(New York Times)*
1964 Merriman Smith (United Press International)
1965 Louis M. Kohlmeier *(Wall Street Journal)*
1966 Haynes Johnson *(Washington Evening Star)*
1967 Stanley Penn and Monroe Karmin *(Wall Street Journal)*
1968 Howard James *(Christian Science Monitor);* Nathan K. (Nick) Kotz *(Des Moines Register* and *Minneapolis Tribune)*
1969 Robert Cahn *(Christian Science Monitor)*
1970 William J. Eaton *(Chicago Daily News)*
1971 Lucinda Franks and Thomas Powers (United Press International)
1972 Jack Anderson *(United Feature Syndicate)*
1973 Robert Boyd and Clark Hoyt *(Knight Newspapers)*
1974 Jack White *(Providence* [R.I.] *Journal-Bulletin);* James R. Polk *(Washington Star-News)*
1975 Donald L. Barlett and James B. Steele *(Philadelphia Inquirer)*
1976 James Risser *(Des Moines Register)*
1977 Walter Mears (Associated Press)
1978 Gaylord D. Shaw *(Los Angeles Times)*
1979 James Risser *(Des Moines Register)*
1980 Bette Swenson Orsini and Charles Stafford *(St. Petersburg Times)*
1981 John M. Crewdson *(New York Times)*
1982 Rick Atkinson *(Kansas City* [Mo.] *Times)*
1983 *Boston Globe*
1984 John N. Wilford *(New York Times)*
1985 Thomas J. Knudson *(Des Moines Register)*
1986 Craig Flournoy and George Rodrigue *(Dallas Morning News)* and Arthur Howe *(Philadelphia Inquirer)*
1987 *Miami Herald,* staff; *New York Times,* staff
1988 Tim Weiner *(Philadelphia Inquirer)*
1989 Donald L. Barlett and James B. Steele *(Philadelphia Inquirer)*
1990 Ross Anderson, Bill Dietrich, Mary Ann Gwinn, and Eric Nalder *(Seattle Times)*
1991 Marjie Lundstrom and Rochelle Sharpe (Gannett News Service)
1992 Jeff Taylor and Mike McGraw *(Kansas City Star)*
1993 David Marannis *(Washington Post)*
1994 Eileen Welsome *(Albuquerque* [N.M.] *Tribune)*
1995 Tony Horwitz *(Wall Street Journal)*
1996 Alix M. Freedman *(Wall Street Journal)*
1997 *Wall Street Journal* staff
1998 Russell Carollo and Jeff Nesmith *(Dayton* [Ohio] *Daily News)*
1999 *New York Times* staff
2000 *Wall Street Journal* staff
2001 *New York Times* staff
2002 *Washington Post* staff
2003 Alan Miller and Kevin Sack *(Los Angeles Times)*

International Telegraphic Reporting

1942 Laurence Edmund Allen (Associated Press)
1943 Ira Wolfert (North American Newspaper Alliance, Inc.)
1944 Daniel De Luce (Associated Press)
1945 Mark S. Watson *(Baltimore Sun)*
1946 Homer W. Bigart *(New York Herald Tribune)*
1947 Eddy Gilmore (Associated Press)

International Reporting

1948 Paul W. Ward *(Baltimore Sun)*
1949 Price Day *(Baltimore Sun)*
1950 Edmund Stevens *(Christian Science Monitor)*
1951 Keyes Beech and Fred Sparks *(Chicago Daily News);* Homer Bigart and Marguerite Higgins *(New York Herald Tribune);* Relman Morin and Don Whitehead (Associated Press)
1952 John M. Hightower (Associated Press)
1953 Austin C. Wehrwein *(Milwaukee Journal)*
1954 Jim G. Lucas (Scripps-Howard Newspapers)
1955 Harrison E. Salisbury *(New York Times)*
1956 William Randolph Hearst, Jr., and Frank Conniff (Hearst Newspapers); Kingsbury Smith (INS)
1957 Russell Jones (United Press)
1958 *New York Times*
1959 Joseph Martin and Philip Santora *(New York Daily News)*
1960 A. M. Rosenthal *(New York Times)*
1961 Lynn Heinzerling (Associated Press)
1962 Walter Lippmann (New York Herald Tribune Syndicate)
1963 Hal Hendrix *(Miami News)*

1964 Malcolm W. Browne (Associated Press); David Halberstam *(New York Times)*
1965 J. A. Livingston *(Philadelphia Bulletin)*
1966 Peter Arnett (Associated Press)
1967 R. John Hughes *(Christian Science Monitor)*
1968 Alfred Friendly *(Washington Post)*
1969 William Tuohy *(Los Angeles Times)*
1970 Seymour M. Hersh (Dispatch News Service)
1971 Jimmie Lee Hoagland *(Washington Post)*
1972 Peter R. Kann *(Wall Street Journal)*
1973 Max Frankel *(New York Times)*
1974 Hedrick Smith *(New York Times)*
1975 William Mullen and Ovie Carter *(Chicago Tribune)*
1976 Sydney H. Schanberg *(New York Times)*
1978 Henry Kamm *(New York Times)*
1979 Richard Ben Cramer *(Philadelphia Inquirer)*
1980 Joel Brinkley and Jay Mather *(Louisville Courier-Journal)*
1981 Shirley Christian *(Miami Herald)*
1982 John Darnton *(New York Times)*
1983 Thomas L. Friedman *(New York Times)*
1984 Karen E. House *(Wall Street Journal)*
1985 Josh Friedman, Dennis Bell, and Ozier Muhammad *(Newsday)*
1986 Lewis M. Simons, Pete Carey, and Katherine Ellison *(San Jose Mercury News)*
1987 Michael Parks *(Los Angeles Times)*
1988 Thomas L. Friedman *(New York Times)*
1989 Bill Keller *(New York Times);* Glenn Frankel *(Washington Post)*
1990 Nicholas D. Kristof and Sheryl WuDunn *(New York Times)*
1991 Caryle Murphy *(Washington Post);* Serge Schmemann *(New York Times)*
1992 Patrick J. Sloyan *(Newsday)*
1993 John F. Burns *(New York Times);* Roy Gutman *(Newsday)*
1994 *Dallas Morning News* team
1995 Mark Fritz (Associated Press)
1996 David Rohde *(Christian Science Monitor)*
1997 John F. Burns *(New York Times)*
1998 *New York Times* staff
1999 *Wall Street Journal* staff
2000 Mark Schoofs *(Village Voice* [New York, N.Y.])
2001 Ian Johnson *(Wall Street Journal)* and Paul Salopek *(Chicago Tribune)*
2002 Barry Bearak *(New York Times)*
2003 Kevin Sullivan and Mary Jordan *(Washington Post)*

Reporting

1917 Herbert B. Swope *(New York World)*
1918 Harold A. Littledale *(New York Evening Post)*
1920 John J. Leary, Jr. *(New York World)*
1921 Louis Seibold *(New York World)*
1922 Kirke L. Simpson (Associated Press)
1923 Alva Johnston *(New York Times)*
1924 Magner White *(San Diego Sun)*
1925 James W. Mulroy and Alvin H. Goldstein *(Chicago Daily News)*
1926 William Burke Miller *(Louisville Courier-Journal)*
1927 John T. Rogers *(St. Louis Post-Dispatch)*
1929 Paul Y. Anderson *(St. Louis Post-Dispatch)*
1930 Russell D. Owen *(New York Times);* special award: W. O. Dapping *(Auburn* [N.Y.] *Citizen)*
1931 A. B. MacDonald *(Kansas City* [Mo.] *Star)*
1932 W. C. Richards, D. D. Martin, J. S. Pooler, F. D. Webb, and J. N. W. Sloan *(Detroit Free Press)*
1933 Francis A. Jamieson (Associated Press)
1934 Royce Brier *(San Francisco Chronicle)*
1935 William H. Taylor *(New York Herald Tribune)*
1936 Lauren D. Lyman *(New York Times)*
1937 John J. O'Neill *(New York Herald Tribune);* William Leonard Laurence *(New York Times);* Howard W. Blakeslee (Associated Press); Gobind Behari Lal (Universal Service); David Dietz (Scripps–Howard Newspapers)
1938 Raymond Sprigle *(Pittsburg Post-Gazette)*
1939 Thomas L. Stokes *(New York World-Telegram)*
1940 S. Burton Heath *(New York World-Telegram)*
1941 Westbrook Pegler *(New York World-Telegram)*
1942 Stanton Delaplane *(San Francisco Chronicle)*
1943 George Weller *(Chicago Daily News)*
1944 Paul Schoenstein and associates *(New York Journal-American)*
1945 Jack S. McDowell *(San Francisco Call-Bulletin)*
1946 William Leonard Laurence *(New York Times)*
1947 Frederick Woltman *(New York World-Telegram)*
1948 George E. Goodwin *(Atlanta Journal)*
1949 Malcolm Johnson *(New York Sun)*
1950 Meyer Berger *(New York Times)*
1951 Edward S. Montgomery *(San Francisco Examiner)*
1952 George de Carvalho *(San Francisco Chronicle)*
1953 Editorial staff *(Providence Journal and Evening Bulletin);*[1] Edward J. Mowery *(New York World-Telegram and Sun)*[2]
1954 *Vicksburg* (Miss.) *Sunday Post-Herald;*[1] Alvin Scott McCoy *(Kansas City* [Mo.] *Star)*[2]
1955 Mrs. Caro Brown *(Alice* [Tex.] *Daily Echo);*[1] Roland Kenneth Towery *(Cuero* [Tex.] *Record)*[2]
1956 Lee Hills *(Detroit Free Press);*[1] Arthur Daley *(New York Times)*[2]
1957 *Salt Lake Tribune;*[1] Wallace Turner and William Lambert *(Portland Oregonian)*[2]
1958 *Fargo* [N.D.] *Forum;*[1] George Beveridge *(Washington* [D.C.] *Evening Star)*[2]
1959 Mary Lou Werner *(Washington* [D.C.] *Evening Star);*[1] John Harold Brislin *(Scranton* [Pa.] *Tribune & Scrantonian)*[2]
1960 Jack Nelson *(Atlanta Constitution);*[1] Miriam Ottenberg *(Washington Evening Star)*[2]
1961 Sanche de Gramont *(New York Herald Tribune);*[1] Edgar May *(Buffalo Evening News)*[2]
1962 Robert D. Mullins (*Deseret News,* Salt Lake City);[1] George Bliss *(Chicago Tribune)*[2]
1963 Sylvan Fox, Anthony Shannon, and William Longgood *(New York World-Telegram and Sun);*[1] Oscar Griffin, Jr. (former editor of *Pecos* [Tex.] *Independent and Enterprise,* now on staff of *Houston Chronicle)*[2]

1. Reporting under pressure of edition deadlines.
2. Reporting not under pressure of edition deadlines.

General Local Reporting

1964 Norman C. Miller *(Wall Street Journal)*
1965 Melvin H. Ruder (*Hungry Horse News,* Columbia Falls, Mont.)
1966 *Los Angeles Times* staff
1967 Robert V. Cox *(Chambersburg* [Pa.] *Public Opinion)*

1968 *Detroit Free Press* staff
1969 John Fetterman *(Louisville Times* and *Courier-Journal)*
1970 Thomas Fitzpatrick *(Chicago Sun-Times)*
1971 *Akron* (Ohio) *Beacon* staff
1972 Richard Cooper and John Machacek *(Rochester* [N.Y.] *Times-Union)*
1973 *Chicago Tribune*
1974 Arthur M. Petacque and Hugh F. Hough *(Chicago Sun-Times)*
1975 *Xenia* (Ohio) *Daily Gazette*
1976 Gene Miller *(Miami Herald)*
1977 Margo Huston *(Milwaukee Journal)*
1978 Richard Whitt *(Louisville Courier-Journal)*
1979 Staff of *San Diego* (Calif.) *Evening Tribune*
1980 Staff of *Philadelphia Inquirer*
1981 *Longview* (Wash.) *Daily News*
1982 *Kansas City* (Mo.) *Star* and *Kansas City* (Mo.) *Times*
1983 *Fort Wayne* (Ind.) *News-Sentinel*
1984 *Newsday*

General News Reporting

1985 Thomas Turcol *(Virginian-Pilot and Ledger-Star)*
1986 Edna Buchanan *(Miami Herald)*
1987 *Akron Beacon Journal* staff
1988 *Alabama Journal* (Montgomery) staff; *Lawrence* (Mass.) *Eagle-Tribune* staff
1989 *Louisville Courier-Journal* staff
1990 *San Jose* (Calif.) *Mercury News*

Spot News Reporting

1991 *Miami Herald* staff
1992 *New York Newsday* staff
1993 *Los Angeles Times* staff
1994 *New York Times* staff
1995 *Los Angeles Times* staff
1996 Robert D. McFadden *(New York Times)*
1997 *Newsday* staff (Long Island, N.Y.)

Breaking News Reporting

1998 *Los Angeles Times* staff
1999 *Hartford Courant* staff
2000 *Denver Post* staff
2001 *The Miami Herald* staff
2002 *Wall Street Journal* staff
2003 *The Eagle-Tribune* staff (Lawrence, Mass.)

Special Local Reporting

1964 James V. Magee, Albert V. Gaudiosi, and Frederick A. Meyer *(Philadelphia Bulletin)*
1965 Gene Goltz *(Houston Post)*
1966 John A. Frasca *(Tampa Tribune)*
1967 Gene Miller *(Miami Herald)*
1968 J. Anthony Lukas *(New York Times)*
1969 Albert L. Delugach and Denny Walsh *(St. Louis Globe-Democrat)*
1970 Harold Eugene Martin *(Montgomery Advertiser)*
1971 William Hugh Jones *(Chicago Tribune)*
1972 Timothy Leland, Gerard N. O'Neill, Stephen A. Kurkjian, and Ann DeSantis *(Boston Globe)*
1973 Sun Newspapers of Omaha, Neb.
1974 William Sherman *(New York Daily News)*
1975 *Indianapolis Star*
1976 *Chicago Tribune*
1977 Acel Moore and Wendell Rawls, Jr. *(Philadelphia Inquirer)*
1978 Anthony R. Dolan *(Stamford* [Conn.] *Advocate)*
1979 Gilbert M. Gaul and Elliot G. Jaspin *(Pottsville* [Pa.] *Republican)*
1980 Nils J. Bruzelius, Alexander B. Hawes, Jr., Stephen A. Kurkjian, Robert M. Porterfield, and Joan Vennochi *(Boston Globe)*
1981 Clark Hallas and Robert B. Lowe (*Arizona Daily Star,* Tucson)
1982 Paul Henderson *(Seattle Times)*
1983 Loretta Tofani *(Washington Post)*
1984 Kenneth Cooper, Joan FitzGerald, Jonathan Kaufman, Norman Lockman, Gary McMillan, Kirk Scharfenberg, and David Wessel *(Boston Globe)*

Investigative Reporting

1985 Lucy Morgan, Jack Reed *(St. Petersburg* [Fla.] *Times),* and William K. Marimow *(Philadelphia Inquirer)*
1986 Jeffrey A. Marx and Michael M. York *(Lexington* [Ky.] *Herald Leader)*
1987 Daniel R. Biddle, H. G. Bissinger, and Fredric N. Tulsky *(Philadelphia Inquirer)*
1988 Dean Baquet, William C. Gaines, and Ann Marie Lipinski *(Chicago Tribune)*
1989 Bill Dedman *(Atlanta Journal and Constitution)*
1990 Lou Kilzer and Chris Ison *(Minneapolis-St. Paul Star Tribune)*
1991 Joseph T. Hallinan and Susan M. Headden *(Indianapolis Star)*
1992 Lorraine Adams and Dan Malone *(Dallas Morning News)*
1993 Jeff Brazil and Steve Berry *(Orlando* [Fla.] *Sentinel)*
1994 *Providence* (R.I.) *Journal-Bulletin* staff
1995 Stephanie Saul and Brian Donovan *(Newsday)*
1996 *Orange County Register* staff (Santa Ana, Calif.)
1997 Eric Nalder, Deborah Nelson, and Alex Tizon *(Seattle Times)*
1998 Gary Cohn and Will Englund (*Baltimore Sun*)
1999 *The Miami Herald* staff
2000 Sang-Hun Choe, Charles J. Hanley, and Martha Mendoza (Associated Press)
2001 David Willman *(Los Angeles Times)*
2002 Sari Horwitz, Scott Higham, and Sarah Cohen *(Washington Post)*
2003 Clifford J. Levy *(New York Times)*

Feature Writing

1979 Jon D. Franklin *(Baltimore Evening Sun)*
1980 Madeleine Blais *(Miami Herald)*
1981 Teresa Carpenter (*Village Voice,* New York)
1982 Saul Pett (Associated Press)
1983 Nan Robertson *(New York Times)*
1984 Peter M. Rinearson *(Seattle Times)*
1985 Alice Steinbach *(Baltimore Sun)*
1986 John Camp *(St. Paul Pioneer Press and Dispatch)*
1987 Steve Twomey *(Philadelphia Inquirer)*
1988 Jacqui Banaszynski *(St. Paul Pioneer Press Dispatch)*
1989 David Zucchino *(Philadelphia Inquirer)*
1990 Dave Curtin *(Colorado Springs Gazette Telegraph)*
1991 Sheryl James *(St. Petersburg* [Fla.] *Times)*
1992 Howell Raines *(New York Times)*
1993 George Lardner, Jr. *(Washington Post)*
1994 Isabel Wilkerson *(New York Times)*
1995 Ron Suskind *(Wall Street Journal)*

1996 Rick Bragg *(New York Times)*
1997 Lisa Pollak *(Baltimore Sun)*
1998 Thomas French *(St. Petersburg* [Fla.] *Times)*
1999 Angelo B. Henderson *(Wall Street Journal)*
2000 J. R. Moehringer *(Los Angeles Times)*
2001 Tom Hallman, Jr. *(Oregonian)*
2002 Barry Siegel *(Los Angeles Times)*
2003 Sonia Nazario *(Los Angeles Times)*

Commentary

1970 Marquis W. Childs *(St. Louis Post-Dispatch)*
1971 William A. Caldwell (*Record* [Hackensack, N.J.])
1972 Mike Royko *(Chicago Daily News)*
1973 David S. Broder *(Washington Post)*
1974 Edwin A. Roberts, Jr. *(National Observer)*
1975 Mary McGrory *(Washington Star)*
1976 Walter W. (Red) Smith *(New York Times)*
1977 George F. Will (*Washington Post* Writers Group)
1978 William Safire *(New York Times)*
1979 Russell Baker *(New York Times)*
1980 Ellen H. Goodman *(Boston Globe)*
1981 Dave Anderson *(New York Times)*
1982 Art Buchwald (*Los Angeles Times* Syndicate)
1983 Claude Sitton *(Raleigh* [N.C.] *News & Observer)*
1984 Vermont Royster *(Wall Street Journal)*
1985 Murray Kempton *(Newsday)*
1986 Jimmy Breslin *(New York Daily News)*
1987 Charles Krauthammer (*Washington Post* Writers Group)
1988 Dave Barry *(Miami Herald)*
1989 Clarence Page *(Chicago Tribune)*
1990 Jim Murray *(Los Angeles Times)*
1991 Jim Hoagland *(Washington Post)*
1992 Anna Quindlen *(New York Times)*
1993 Liz Balmaseda *(Miami Herald)*
1994 William Raspberry *(Washington Post)*
1995 Jim Dwyer *(New York Newsday)*
1996 E. R. Shipp *(New York Daily News)*
1997 Eileen McNamara *(Boston Globe)*
1998 Mike McAlary *(New York Daily News)*
1999 Maureen Dowd *(New York Times)*
2000 Paul A. Gigot *(Wall Street Journal)*
2001 Dorothy Rabinowitz *(Wall Street Journal)*
2002 Thomas Friedman *(New York Times)*
2003 Colbert King *(Washington Post)*

Criticism

1970 Ada Louise Huxtable *(New York Times)*
1971 Harold C. Schonberg *(New York Times)*
1972 Frank Peters, Jr. *(St. Louis Post-Dispatch)*
1973 Ronald Powers *(Chicago Sun-Times)*
1974 Emily Genauer (Newsday Syndicate)
1975 Roger Ebert *(Chicago Sun-Times)*
1976 Alan M. Kriegsman *(Washington Post)*
1977 William McPherson *(Washington Post)*
1978 Walter Kerr *(New York Times)*
1979 Paul Gapp *(Chicago Tribune)*
1980 William A. Henry, 3rd *(Boston Globe)*
1981 Jonathan Yardley *(Washington Star)*
1982 Martin Bernheimer *(Los Angeles Times)*
1983 Manuela Hoelterhoff *(Wall Street Journal)*
1984 Paul Goldberger *(New York Times)*
1985 Howard Rosenberg *(Los Angeles Times)*
1986 Donal Henahan *(New York Times)*
1987 Richard Eder *(Los Angeles Times)*
1988 Tom Shales *(Washington Post)*
1989 Michael Skube *(News and Observer* [Raleigh, N.C.])
1990 Allan Temko *(San Francisco Chronicle)*
1991 David Shaw *(Los Angeles Times)*
1993 Michael Dirda *(Washington Post)*
1994 Lloyd Schwartz *(Boston Phoenix)*
1995 Margo Jefferson *(New York Times)*
1996 Robert Campbell *(Boston Globe)*
1997 Tim Page *(Washington Post)*
1998 Michiko Kakutani *(New York Times)*
1999 Blair Kamin *(Chicago Tribune)*
2000 Henry Allen *(Washington Post)*
2001 Gail Caldwell *(Boston Globe)*
2002 Justin Davidson *(Newsday* [Long Island, N.Y.])
2003 Stephen Hunter *(Washington Post)*

Explanatory Journalism

1985 Jon Franklin *(Baltimore Evening Sun)*
1986 *New York Times*
1987 Jeff Lyon and Peter Gorner *(Chicago Tribune)*
1988 Daniel Hertzberg and James B. Stewart *(Wall Street Journal)*
1989 David Hanners, William Snyder, and Karen Blessen *(Dallas Morning News)*
1990 David A. Vise and Steve Coll *(Washington Post)*
1991 Susan C. Faludi *(Wall Street Journal)*
1992 Robert S. Capers and Eric Lipton *(Hartford Courant)*
1993 Mike Toner *(Atlanta Journal–Constitution)*
1994 Ronald Kotulak *(Chicago Tribune)*
1995 Leon Dash and Lucian Perkins *(Washington Post)*
1996 Laurie Garrett *(Newsday* [Long Island, N.Y.])
1997 Michael Vitez, Ron Cortes, and April Saul *(Philadelphia Inquirer)*
1998 Paul Salopek *(Chicago Tribune)*
1999 Richard Read *(Oregonian* [Portland, Ore.])
2000 Eric Newhouse *(Great Falls* [Mont.] *Tribune)*
2001 *Chicago Tribune* staff
2002 *New York Times* staff
2003 *Wall Street Journal* staff

Specialized Reporting

1985 Randall Savage and Jackie Crosby *(Macon* [Ga.] *Telegraph and News)*
1986 Andrew Schneider and Mary Pat Flaherty *(Pittsburgh Press)*
1987 Alex S. Jones *(New York Times)*
1988 Walt Bogdanich *(Wall Street Journal)*
1989 Edward Humes *(Orange County Register)*
1990 Tamar Stieber *(Albuquerque* (N.M.) *Journal)*

Beat Reporting

1991 Natalie Angier *(New York Times)*
1992 Deborah Blum *(Sacramento Bee)*
1993 Paul Ingrassia and Joseph B. White *(Wall Street Journal)*
1994 Eric Freedman and Jim Mitzelfeld *(Detroit News)*
1995 David M. Shribman *(Boston Globe)*
1996 Bob Keeler *(Newsday* [Long Island, N.Y.])
1997 Byron Acohido *(Seattle Times)*
1998 Linda Greenhouse *(New York Times)*
1999 Chuck Philips and Michael A. Hiltzik *(Los Angeles Times)*
2000 George Dohrmann *(St. Paul Pioneer Press)*
2001 David Cay Johnston *(New York Times)*
2002 Gretchen Morgenson *(New York Times)*
2003 Diana K. Sugg *(Baltimore Sun)*

PULITZER PRIZES IN LETTERS

Fiction[1]

1918 *His Family,* Ernest Poole
1919 *The Magnificent Ambersons,* Booth Tarkington
1921 *The Age of Innocence,* Edith Wharton
1922 *Alice Adams,* Booth Tarkington
1923 *One of Ours,* Willa Cather
1924 *The Able McLaughlins,* Margaret Wilson
1925 *So Big,* Edna Ferber
1926 *Arrowsmith,* Sinclair Lewis
1927 *Early Autumn,* Louis Bromfield
1928 *The Bridge of San Luis Rey,* Thornton Wilder
1929 *Scarlet Sister Mary,* Julia Peterkin
1930 *Laughing Boy,* Oliver La Farge
1931 *Years of Grace,* Margaret Ayer Barnes
1932 *The Good Earth,* Pearl S. Buck
1933 *The Store,* T. S. Stribling
1934 *Lamb in His Bosom,* Caroline Miller
1935 *Now in November,* Josephine Winslow Johnson
1936 *Honey in the Horn,* Harold L. Davis
1937 *Gone With the Wind,* Margaret Mitchell
1938 *The Late George Apley,* John Phillips Marquand
1939 *The Yearling,* Marjorie Kinnan Rawlings
1940 *The Grapes of Wrath,* John Steinbeck
1942 *In This Our Life,* Ellen Glasgow
1943 *Dragon's Teeth,* Upton Sinclair
1944 *Journey in the Dark,* Martin Flavin
1945 *A Bell for Adano,* John Hersey
1947 *All the King's Men,* Robert Penn Warren
1948 *Tales of the South Pacific,* James A. Michener
1949 *Guard of Honor,* James Gould Cozzens
1950 *The Way West,* A. B. Guthrie, Jr.
1951 *The Town,* Conrad Richter
1952 *The Caine Mutiny,* Herman Wouk
1953 *The Old Man and the Sea,* Ernest Hemingway
1955 *A Fable,* William Faulkner
1956 *Andersonville,* MacKinlay Kantor
1958 *A Death in the Family,* James Agee
1959 *The Travels of Jaimie McPheeters,* Robert Lewis Taylor
1960 *Advise and Consent,* Allen Drury
1961 *To Kill a Mockingbird,* Harper Lee
1962 *The Edge of Sadness,* Edwin O'Connor
1963 *The Reivers,* William Faulkner
1965 *The Keepers of the House,* Shirley Ann Grau
1966 *Collected Stories of Katherine Anne Porter,* Katherine Anne Porter
1967 *The Fixer,* Bernard Malamud
1968 *The Confessions of Nat Turner,* William Styron
1969 *House Made of Dawn,* N. Scott Momaday
1970 *Collected Stories,* Jean Stafford
1972 *Angle of Repose,* Wallace Stegner
1973 *The Optimist's Daughter,* Eudora Welty
1975 *The Killer Angels,* Michael Shaara
1976 *Humboldt's Gift,* Saul Bellow
1978 *Elbow Room,* James Alan McPherson
1979 *The Stories of John Cheever,* John Cheever
1980 *The Executioner's Song,* Norman Mailer
1981 *A Confederacy of Dunces,* John Kennedy Toole
1982 *Rabbit Is Rich,* John Updike
1983 *The Color Purple,* Alice Walker
1984 *Ironweed,* William Kennedy
1985 *Foreign Affairs,* Alison Lurie
1986 *Lonesome Dove,* Larry McMurtry
1987 *A Summons to Memphis,* Peter Taylor
1988 *Beloved,* Toni Morrison
1989 *Breathing Lessons,* Anne Tyler
1990 *The Mambo Kings Play Songs of Love,* Oscar Hijuelos
1991 *Rabbit at Rest,* John Updike
1992 *A Thousand Acres,* Jane Smiley
1993 *A Good Scent From a Strange Mountain,* Robert Olen Butler
1994 *The Shipping News,* E. Annie Proulx
1995 *The Stone Diaries,* Carol Shields
1996 *Independence Day,* Richard Ford
1997 *Martin Dressler: The Tale of an American Dreamer,* Steven Millhauser
1998 *American Pastoral,* Philip Roth
1999 *The Hours,* Michael Cunningham
2000 *Interpreter of Maladies,* Jhumpa Lahiri
2001 *The Amazing Adventures of Kavalier & Clay,* Michael Chabon
2002 *Empire Falls,* Richard Russo
2003 *Middlesex,* Jeffrey Eugenides

1. Before 1948, award was for novels only.

History

1917 *With Americans of Past and Present Days,* J. J. Jusserand, Ambassador of France to United States
1918 *A History of the Civil War, 1861–1865,* James Ford Rhodes
1920 *The War With Mexico,* Justin H. Smith
1921 *The Victory at Sea,* William Sowden Sims, in collaboration with Burton J. Hendrick
1922 *The Founding of New England,* James Truslow Adams
1923 *The Supreme Court in United States History,* Charles Warren
1924 *The American Revolution—A Constitutional Interpretation,* Charles Howard McIlwain
1925 *A History of the American Frontier,* Frederic L. Paxson
1926 *The History of the United States,* Edward Channing
1927 *Pinckney's Treaty,* Samuel Flagg Bemis
1928 *Main Currents in American Thought,* Vernon Louis Parrington
1929 *The Organization and Administration of the Union Army, 1861–1865,* Fred Albert Shannon
1930 *The War of Independence,* Claude H. Van Tyne
1931 *The Coming of the War: 1914,* Bernadotte E. Schmitt
1932 *My Experiences in the World War,* John J. Pershing
1933 *The Significance of Sections in American History,* Frederick J. Turner
1934 *The People's Choice,* Herbert Agar
1935 *The Colonial Period of American History,* Charles McLean Andrews
1936 *The Constitutional History of the United States,* Andrew C. McLaughlin
1937 *The Flowering of New England,* Van Wyck Brooks
1938 *The Road to Reunion, 1865–1900,* Paul Herman Buck
1939 *A History of American Magazines,* Frank Luther Mott
1940 *Abraham Lincoln: The War Years,* Carl Sandburg
1941 *The Atlantic Migration, 1607–1860,* Marcus Lee Hansen
1942 *Reveille in Washington,* Margaret Leech
1943 *Paul Revere and the World He Lived In,* Esther Forbes

1944 *The Growth of American Thought,* Merle Curti
1945 *Unfinished Business,* Stephen Bonsal
1946 *The Age of Jackson,* Arthur M. Schlesinger, Jr.
1947 *Scientists Against Time,* James Phinney Baxter III
1948 *Across the Wide Missouri,* Bernard DeVoto
1949 *The Disruption of American Democracy,* Roy Franklin Nichols
1950 *Art and Life in America,* Oliver W. Larkin
1951 *The Old Northwest, Pioneer Period 1815–1840,* R. Carlyle Buley
1952 *The Uprooted,* Oscar Handlin
1953 *The Era of Good Feelings,* George Dangerfield
1954 *A Stillness at Appomattox,* Bruce Catton
1955 *Great River: The Rio Grande in North American History,* Paul Horgan
1956 *The Age of Reform,* Richard Hofstadter
1957 *Russia Leaves the War: Soviet–American Relations, 1917–1920,* George F. Kennan
1958 *Banks and Politics in America: From the Revolution to the Civil War,* Bray Hammond
1959 *The Republican Era: 1869–1901,* Leonard D. White, assisted by Jean Schneider
1960 *In the Days of McKinley,* Margaret Leech
1961 *Between War and Peace: The Potsdam Conference,* Herbert Feis
1962 *The Triumphant Empire: Thunder-Clouds Gather in the West,* Lawrence H. Gipson
1963 *Washington, Village and Capital, 1800–1878,* Constance McLaughlin Green
1964 *Puritan Village: The Formation of a New England Town,* Sumner Chilton Powell
1965 *The Greenback Era,* Irwin Unger
1966 *Life of the Mind in America,* Perry Miller
1967 *Exploration and Empire: The Explorer and Scientist in the Winning of the American West,* William H. Goetzmann
1968 *The Ideological Origins of the American Revolution,* Bernard Bailyn
1969 *Origins of the Fifth Amendment,* Leonard W. Levy
1970 *Present at the Creation: My Years in the State Department,* Dean Acheson
1971 *Roosevelt: The Soldier of Freedom,* James McGregor Burns
1972 *Neither Black Nor White: Slavery and Race Relations in Brazil and the United States,* Carl N. Degler
1973 *People of Paradox: An Inquiry Concerning the Origin of American Civilization,* Michael Kammen
1974 *The Americans: The Democratic Experience, Vol. 3,* Daniel J. Boorstin
1975 *Jefferson and His Time,* Dumas Malone
1976 *Lamy of Santa Fe,* Paul Horgan
1977 *The Impending Crisis: 1841–1861,* David M. Potter
1978 *The Invisible Hand: The Managerial Revolution in American Business,* Alfred D. Chandler, Jr.
1979 *The Dred Scott Case: Its Significance in Law and Politics,* Don E. Fehrenbacher
1980 *Been in the Storm So Long,* Leon F. Litwack
1981 *American Education: The National Experience; 1783–1876,* Lawrence A. Cremin
1982 *Mary Chesnut's Civil War,* C. Vann Woodward, editor
1983 *The Transformation of Virginia, 1740–1790,* Rhys L. Isaac
1985 *The Prophets of Regulation,* Thomas K. McCraw
1986 *The Heavens and the Earth: A Political History of the Space Age,* Walter A. McDougall
1987 *Voyagers to the West: A Passage in the Peopling of America on the Eve of the Revolution,* Bernard Bailyn
1988 *The Launching of Modern American Science 1846–1876,* Robert V. Bruce
1989 *Parting the Waters,* Taylor Branch; *Battle Cry of Freedom,* James M. McPherson
1990 *In Our Image: America's Empire in the Philippines,* Stanley Karnow
1991 *A Midwife's Tale: The Life of Martha Ballard, Based on Her Diary 1785–1812,* Laurel Thatcher Ulrich
1992 *The Fate of Liberty: Abraham Lincoln and Civil Liberties,* Mark E. Neely, Jr.
1993 *The Radicalism of the American Revolution,* Gordon S. Wood
1995 *No Ordinary Time: Franklin and Eleanor Roosevelt: The Home Front in World War II,* Doris Kearns Goodwin
1996 *William Cooper's Town: Power and Persuasion on the Frontier of the Early American Republic,* Alan Taylor
1997 *Original Meanings: Politics and Ideas in the Making of the Constitution,* Jack N. Rakove
1998 *Summer for the Gods: The Scopes Trial and America's Continuing Debate Over Science and Religion,* Edward J. Larson
1999 *Gotham: A History of New York City to 1898,* Edwin G. Burrows and Mike Wallace
2000 *Freedom from Fear: The American People in Depression and War, 1929–1945,* David M. Kennedy
2001 *Founding Brothers: The Revolutionary Generation,* Joseph J. Ellis
2002 *The Metaphysical Club: A Story of Ideas in America,* Louis Menand
2003 *An Army at Dawn: The War in North Africa, 1942–1943,* Rick Atkinson

Biography or Autobiography

1917 *Julia Ward Howe,* Laura E. Richards and Maude Howe Elliott, assisted by Florence Howe Hall
1918 *Benjamin Franklin, Self-Revealed,* William Cabell Bruce
1919 *The Education of Henry Adams,* Henry Adams
1920 *The Life of John Marshall,* Albert J. Beveridge
1921 *The Americanization of Edward Bok,* Edward Bok
1922 *A Daughter of the Middle Border,* Hamlin Garland
1923 *The Life and Letters of Walter H. Page,* Burton J. Hendrick
1924 *From Immigrant to Inventor,* Michael Idvorsky Pupin
1925 *Barrett Wendell and His Letters,* M. A. DeWolfe Howe
1926 *The Life of Sir William Osler,* Harvey Cushing
1927 *Whitman,* Emory Holloway
1928 *The American Orchestra and Theodore Thomas,* Charles Edward Russell
1929 *The Training of an American: The Earlier Life and Letters of Walter H. Page,* Burton J. Hendrick
1930 *The Raven,* Marquis James
1931 *Charles W. Eliot,* Henry James

1932 *Theodore Roosevelt,* Henry F. Pringle
1933 *Grover Cleveland,* Allan Nevins
1934 *John Hay,* Tyler Dennett
1935 *R. E. Lee,* Douglas S. Freeman
1936 *The Thought and Character of William James,* Ralph Barton Perry
1937 *Hamilton Fish,* Allan Nevins
1938 *Pedlar's Progress,* Odell Shepard; *Andrew Jackson,* Marquis James
1939 *Benjamin Franklin,* Carl Van Doren
1940 *Woodrow Wilson: Life and Letters,* Vols. VII and VIII, Ray Stannard Baker
1941 *Jonathan Edwards,* Ola E. Winslow
1942 *Crusader in Crinoline,* Forrest Wilson
1943 *Admiral of the Ocean Sea,* Samuel Eliot Morison
1944 *The American Leonardo: The Life of Samuel F. B. Morse,* Carleton Mabee
1945 *George Bancroft: Brahmin Rebel,* Russel Blaine Nye
1946 *Son of the Wilderness,* Linnie Marsh Wolfe
1947 *The Autobiography of William Allen White*
1948 *Forgotten First Citizen: John Bigelow,* Margaret Clapp
1949 *Roosevelt and Hopkins,* Robert E. Sherwood
1950 *John Quincy Adams and the Foundations of American Foreign Policy,* Samuel Flagg Bemis
1951 *John C. Calhoun: American Portrait,* Margaret Louise Coit
1952 *Charles Evans Hughes,* Merlo J. Pusey
1953 *Edmund Pendleton, 1721–1803,* David J. Mays
1954 *The Spirit of St. Louis,* Charles A. Lindbergh
1955 *The Taft Story,* William S. White
1956 *Benjamin Henry Latrobe,* Talbot F. Hamlin
1957 *Profiles in Courage,* John F. Kennedy
1958 *George Washington,* Douglas Southall Freeman (Vols. 1–6) and John Alexander Carroll and Mary Wells Ashworth (Vol. 7)
1959 *Woodrow Wilson, American Prophet,* Arthur Walworth
1960 *John Paul Jones,* Samuel Eliot Morison
1961 *Charles Sumner and the Coming of the Civil War,* David Donald
1963 *Henry James: Vol. II, The Conquest of London, 1870–1881; Vol. III, The Middle Years, 1881–1895,* Leon Edel
1964 *John Keats,* Walter Jackson Bate
1965 *Henry Adams* (3 Vols.), Ernest Samuels
1966 *A Thousand Days,* Arthur M. Schlesinger, Jr.
1967 *Mr. Clemens and Mark Twain,* Justin Kaplan
1968 *Memoirs, 1925–1950,* George F. Kennan
1969 *The Man From New York,* B. L. Reid
1970 *Huey Long,* T. Harry Williams
1971 *Robert Frost: The Years of Triumph, 1915–1938,* Lawrence Thompson
1972 *Eleanor and Franklin: The Story of Their Relationship Based on Eleanor Roosevelt's Private Papers,* Joseph P. Lash
1973 *Luce and His Empire,* W. A. Swanberg
1974 *O'Neill, Son and Artist,* Louis Sheaffer
1975 *The Power Broker: Robert Moses and the Fall of New York,* Robert A. Caro
1976 *Edith Wharton: A Biography,* Richard W. B. Lewis
1977 *A Prince of Our Disorder,* John E. Mack
1978 *Samuel Johnson,* Walter Jackson Bate
1979 *Days of Sorrow and Pain: Leo Baeck and the Berlin Jews,* Leonard Baker
1980 *The Rise of Theodore Roosevelt,* Edmund Morris
1981 *Peter the Great,* Robert K. Massie
1982 *Grant: A Biography,* William S. McFeely
1983 *Growing Up,* Russell Baker
1984 *Booker T. Washington,* Louis R. Harlan
1985 *The Life and Times of Cotton Mather,* Kenneth Silverman
1986 *Louise Bogan: A Portrait,* Elizabeth Frank
1987 *Bearing the Cross: Martin Luther King, Jr., and the Southern Christian Leadership Conference,* David J. Garrow
1988 *Look Homeward: A Life of Thomas Wolfe,* David Herbert Donald
1989 *Oscar Wilde,* Richard Ellmann
1990 *Machiavelli in Hell,* Sebastian de Grazia
1991 *Jackson Pollock: An American Saga,* Steven Naifeh and Gregory White Smith
1992 *Fortunate Son: The Healing of a Vietnam Vet,* Lewis B. Puller, Jr.
1993 *Truman,* David McCullough
1994 *W. E. B. Du Bois: Biography of a Race, 1868–1919,* David Levering Lewis
1995 *Harriet Beecher Stowe: A Life,* Joan D. Hedrick
1996 *God: A Biography,* Jack Miles
1997 *Angela's Ashes: A Memoir,* Frank McCourt
1998 *Personal History,* Katharine Graham
1999 *Lindbergh,* A. Scott Berg
2000 *Vera (Mrs. Vladimir Nabokov),* Stacy Schiff
2001 *W. E. B. DuBois: The Fight for Equality and the American Century, 1919–1963,* David Levering Lewis
2002 *John Adams,* David McCullough
2003 *Master of the Senate,* Robert A. Caro

Poetry[1]

1918 *Love Songs,* Sara Teasdale
1919 *Old Road to Paradise,* Margaret Widdemer; *Corn Huskers,* Carl Sandburg
1922 *Collected Poems,* Edwin Arlington Robinson
1923 *The Ballad of the Harp-Weaver; A Few Figs from Thistles;* eight sonnets in *American Poetry, 1922, A Miscellany,* Edna St. Vincent Millay
1924 *New Hampshire: A Poem With Notes and Grace Notes,* Robert Frost
1925 *The Man Who Died Twice,* Edwin Arlington Robinson
1926 *What's O'Clock,* Amy Lowell
1927 *Fiddler's Farewell,* Leonora Speyer
1928 *Tristram,* Edwin Arlington Robinson
1929 *John Brown's Body,* Stephen Vincent Benét
1930 *Selected Poems,* Conrad Aiken
1931 *Collected Poems,* Robert Frost
1932 *The Flowering Stone,* George Dillon
1933 *Conquistador,* Archibald MacLeish
1934 *Collected Verse,* Robert Hillyer
1935 *Bright Ambush,* Audrey Wurdemann
1936 *Strange Holiness,* Robert P. T. Coffin
1937 *A Further Range,* Robert Frost
1938 *Cold Morning Sky,* Marya Zaturenska
1939 *Selected Poems,* John Gould Fletcher
1940 *Collected Poems,* Mark Van Doren
1941 *Sunderland Capture,* Leonard Bacon
1942 *The Dust Which Is God,* William Rose Benét
1943 *A Witness Tree,* Robert Frost
1944 *Western Star,* Stephen Vincent Benét
1945 *V-Letter and Other Poems,* Karl Shapiro
1947 *Lord Weary's Castle,* Robert Lowell
1948 *The Age of Anxiety,* W. H. Auden

1949 *Terror and Decorum,* Peter Viereck
1950 *Annie Allen,* Gwendolyn Brooks
1951 *Complete Poems,* Carl Sandburg
1952 *Collected Poems,* Marianne Moore
1953 *Collected Poems, 1917–1952,* Archibald MacLeish
1954 *The Waking,* Theodore Roethke
1955 *Collected Poems,* Wallace Stevens
1956 *Poems—North & South,* Elizabeth Bishop
1957 *Things of This World,* Richard Wilbur
1958 *Promises: Poems, 1954–1956,* Robert Penn Warren
1959 *Selected Poems, 1928–1958,* Stanley Kunitz
1960 *Heart's Needle,* William Snodgrass
1961 *Times Three: Selected Verse From Three Decades,* Phyllis McGinley
1962 *Poems,* Alan Dugan
1963 *Pictures From Breughel,* William Carlos Williams
1964 *At the End of the Open Road,* Louis Simpson
1965 *77 Dream Songs,* John Berryman
1966 *Selected Poems,* Richard Eberhart
1967 *Live or Die,* Anne Sexton
1968 *The Hard Hours,* Anthony Hecht
1969 *Of Being Numerous,* George Oppen
1970 *Untitled Subjects,* Richard Howard
1971 *The Carrier of Ladders,* William S. Merwin
1972 *Collected Poems,* James Wright
1973 *Up Country,* Maxine Winokur Kumin
1974 *The Dolphin,* Robert Lowell
1975 *Turtle Island,* Gary Snyder
1976 *Self-Portrait in a Convex Mirror,* John Ashbery
1977 *Divine Comedies,* James Merrill
1978 *Collected Poems,* Howard Nemerov
1979 *Now and Then: Poems, 1976–1978,* Robert Penn Warren
1980 *Selected Poems,* Donald Rodney Justice
1981 *The Morning of the Poem,* James Schuyler
1982 *The Collected Poems,* Sylvia Plath
1983 *Selected Poems,* Galway Kinnell
1984 *American Primitive,* Mary Oliver
1985 *Yin,* Carolyn Kizer
1986 *The Flying Change,* Henry Taylor
1987 *Thomas and Beulah,* Rita Dove
1988 *Partial Accounts: New and Selected Poems,* William Meredith
1989 *New and Collected Poems,* Richard Wilbur
1990 *The World Doesn't End,* Charles Simic
1991 *Near Changes,* Mona Van Duyn
1992 *Selected Poems,* James Tate
1993 *The Wild Iris,* Louise Gluck
1994 *Neon Vernacular,* Yusef Komunyakaa
1995 *Simple Truth,* Philip Levine
1996 *The Dream of the Unified Field,* Jorie Graham
1997 *Alive Together: New and Selected Poems,* Lisel Mueller
1998 *Black Zodiac,* Charles Wright
1999 *Blizzard of One,* Mark Strand
2000 *Repair,* C. K. Williams
2001 *Different Hours,* Stephen Dunn
2002 *Practical Gods,* Carl Dennis
2003 *Moy Sand and Gravel,* Paul Muldoon

1. The poetry prize was established in 1922. The 1918 and 1919 awards were made from gifts provided by the Poetry Society.

General Nonfiction

1962 *The Making of the President, 1960,* Theodore H. White
1963 *The Guns of August,* Barbara W. Tuchman
1964 *Anti-Intellectualism in American Life,* Richard Hofstadter
1965 *O Strange New World,* Howard Mumford Jones
1966 *Wandering Through Winter,* Edwin Way Teale
1967 *The Problem of Slavery in Western Culture,* David Brion Davis
1968 *Rousseau and Revolution,* Will and Ariel Durant
1969 *So Human an Animal,* Rene Jules Dubos; *The Armies of the Night,* Norman Mailer
1970 *Gandhi's Truth,* Erik H. Erikson
1971 *The Rising Sun,* John Toland
1972 *Stilwell and the American Experience in China, 1911–1945,* Barbara W. Tuchman
1973 *Fire in the Lake: The Vietnamese and the Americans in Vietnam,* Frances FitzGerald; *Children of Crisis* (Vols. 1 and 2), Robert M. Coles
1974 *The Denial of Death,* Ernest Becker
1975 *Pilgrim at Tinker Creek,* Annie Dillard
1976 *Why Survive? Being Old in America,* Robert N. Butler
1977 *Beautiful Swimmers: Watermen, Crabs and the Chesapeake Bay,* William W. Warner
1978 *The Dragons of Eden,* Carl Sagan
1979 *On Human Nature,* Edward O. Wilson
1980 *Gödel, Escher, Bach: An Eternal Golden Braid,* Douglas R. Hofstadter
1981 *Fin-de-Siecle Vienna: Politics and Culture,* Carl E. Schorske
1982 *The Soul of a New Machine,* Tracy Kidder
1983 *Is There No Place on Earth for Me?,* Susan Sheehan
1984 *Social Transformation of American Medicine,* Paul Starr
1985 *The Good War: An Oral History of World War II,* Studs Terkel
1986 *Move Your Shadow: South Africa, Black and White,* Joseph Lelyveld; *Common Ground: A Turbulent Decade in the Lives of Three American Families,* J. Anthony Lukas
1987 *Arab and Jew: Wounded Spirits in a Promised Land,* David K. Shipler
1988 *The Making of the Atomic Bomb,* Richard Rhodes
1989 *A Bright Shining Lie,* Neil Sheehan
1990 *And Their Children After Them,* Dale Maharidge and Michael Williamson
1991 *The Ants,* Bert Holldobler and Edward O. Wilson
1992 *The Prize: The Epic Quest for Oil, Money and Power,* Daniel Yergin
1993 *Lincoln at Gettysburg: The Words That Remade America,* Garry Wills
1994 *Lenin's Tomb: The Last Days of the Soviet Empire,* David Remick
1995 *The Beak of the Finch: A Story of Evolution in Our Time,* Jonathan Weiner
1996 *The Haunted Land: Facing Europe's Ghosts After Communism,* Tina Rosenberg
1997 *Ashes to Ashes: America's Hundred-Year Cigarette War, the Public Health, and the Unabashed Triumph of Philip Morris,* Richard Kluger
1998 *Guns, Germs, and Steel: The Fates of Human Societies,* Jared Diamond
1999 *Annals of the Former World,* John McPhee
2000 *Embracing Defeat: Japan in the Wake of World War II,* John W. Dower

2001 *Hirohito and the Making of Modern Japan,* Herbert P. Bix
2002 *Carry Me Home: Birmingham, Alabama, the Climactic Battle of the Civil Rights Revolution,* Diane McWhorter
2003 *"A Problem from Hell:" America and the Age of Genocide,* Samantha Power

PULITZER PRIZES IN MUSIC

1943 *Secular Cantata No. 2, A Free Song,* William Schuman
1944 *Symphony No. 4* (Op. 34), Howard Hanson
1945 *Appalachian Spring,* Aaron Copland
1946 *The Canticle of the Sun,* Leo Sowerby
1947 *Symphony No. 3,* Charles Ives
1948 *Symphony No. 3,* Walter Piston
1949 *Louisiana Story* music, Virgil Thomson
1950 *The Consul,* Gian Carlo Menotti
1951 Music for opera *Giants in the Earth,* Douglas Stuart Moore
1952 *Symphony Concertante,* Gail Kubik
1954 *Concerto for Two Pianos and Orchestra,* Quincy Porter
1955 *The Saint of Bleecker Street,* Gian Carlo Menotti
1956 *Symphony No. 3,* Ernst Toch
1957 *Meditations on Ecclesiastes,* Norman Dello Joio
1958 *Vanessa,* Samuel Barber
1959 *Concerto for Piano and Orchestra,* John La Montaine
1960 *Second String Quartet,* Elliott Carter
1961 *Symphony No. 7,* Walter Piston
1962 *The Crucible,* Robert Ward
1963 *Piano Concerto No. 1,* Samuel Barber
1966 *Variations for Orchestra,* Leslie Bassett
1967 *Quartet No. 3,* Leon Kirchner
1968 *Echoes of Time and the River,* George Crumb
1969 *String Quartet No. 3,* Karel Husa
1970 *Time's Encomium,* Charles Wuorinen
1971 *Synchronisms No. 6 for Piano and Electronic Sound,* Mario Davidowsky
1972 *Windows,* Jacob Druckman
1973 *String Quartet No. 3,* Elliott Carter
1974 *Notturno,* Donald Martino
1975 *From the Diary of Virginia Woolf,* Dominick Argento
1976 *Air Music,* Ned Rorem
1977 *Visions of Terror and Wonder,* Richard Wernick
1978 *Déjà Vu for Percussion Quartet and Orchestra,* Michael Colgrass
1979 *Aftertones of Infinity,* Joseph Schwantner
1980 *In Memory of a Summer Day,* David Del Tredici
1982 *Concerto for Orchestra,* Roger Sessions
1983 *Three Movements for Orchestra,* Ellen T. Zwilich
1984 *Canti del Sole,* Bernard Rands
1985 *Symphony RiverRun,* Stephen Albert
1986 *Wind Quintet IV,* George Perle
1987 *The Flight Into Egypt,* John Harbison
1988 *12 New Etudes for Piano,* William Bolcom
1989 *Whispers Out of Time,* Roger Reynolds
1990 *Duplicates: A Concerto for Two Pianos and Orchestra,* Mel Powell
1991 *Symphony,* Shulamit Ran
1992 *The Face of the Night, The Heart of the Dark,* Wayne Peterson
1993 *Trombone Concerto,* Christopher Rouse
1994 *Of Reminiscences and Reflections,* Gunther Schuller
1995 *Stringmusic,* Morton Gould
1996 *Lilacs,* George Walker
1997 *Blood on the Field,* Wynton Marsalis
1998 *String Quartet No. 2, Musica Instrumentalis,* Aaron Jay Kernis
1999 *Concerto for Flute, Strings and Percussion,* Melinda Wagner
2000 *Life Is a Dream, Opera in Three Acts: Act II, Concert Version,* Lewis Spratlan
2001 *Symphony No. 2 for String Orchestra,* John Corigliano
2002 *Ice Field,* Henry Brant
2003 *On the Transmigration of Souls,* John Adams

PULITZER PRIZES IN DRAMA

1918 *Why Marry?,* Jesse Lynch Williams
1920 *Beyond the Horizon,* Eugene O'Neill
1921 *Miss Lulu Bett,* Zona Gale
1922 *Anna Christie,* Eugene O'Neill
1923 *Icebound,* Owen Davis
1924 *Hell-Bent Fer Heaven,* Hatcher Hughes
1925 *They Knew What They Wanted,* Sidney Howard
1926 *Craig's Wife,* George Kelly
1927 *In Abraham's Bosom,* Paul Green
1928 *Strange Interlude,* Eugene O'Neill
1929 *Street Scene,* Elmer L. Rice
1930 *The Green Pastures,* Marc Connelly
1931 *Alison's House,* Susan Glaspell
1932 *Of Thee I Sing,* George S. Kaufman, Morrie Ryskind, and Ira Gershwin
1933 *Both Your Houses,* Maxwell Anderson
1934 *Men in White,* Sidney Kingsley
1935 *The Old Maid,* Zöe Akins
1936 *Idiot's Delight,* Robert E. Sherwood
1937 *You Can't Take It with You,* Moss Hart and George S. Kaufman
1938 *Our Town,* Thornton Wilder
1939 *Abe Lincoln in Illinois,* Robert E. Sherwood
1940 *The Time of Your Life,* William Saroyan
1941 *There Shall Be No Night,* Robert E. Sherwood
1943 *The Skin of Our Teeth,* Thornton Wilder
1945 *Harvey,* Mary Chase
1946 *State of the Union,* Russel Crouse and Howard Lindsay
1948 *A Streetcar Named Desire,* Tennessee Williams
1949 *Death of a Salesman,* Arthur Miller
1950 *South Pacific,* Richard Rodgers, Oscar Hammerstein II, and Joshua Logan
1952 *The Shrike,* Joseph Kramm
1953 *Picnic,* William Inge
1954 *The Teahouse of the August Moon,* John Patrick
1955 *Cat on a Hot Tin Roof,* Tennessee Williams
1956 *The Diary of Anne Frank,* Frances Goodrich and Albert Hackett
1957 *Long Day's Journey into Night,* Eugene O'Neill
1958 *Look Homeward, Angel,* Ketti Frings
1959 *J. B.,* Archibald MacLeish
1960 *Fiorello!,* George Abbott, Jerome Weidman, Jerry Bock, and Sheldon Harnick
1961 *All the Way Home,* Tad Mosel
1962 *How to Succeed in Business without Really Trying,* Frank Loesser and Abe Burrows
1965 *The Subject Was Roses,* Frank D. Gilroy
1967 *A Delicate Balance,* Edward Albee

1969 *The Great White Hope,* Howard Sackler
1970 *No Place to Be Somebody,* Charles Gordone
1971 *The Effect of Gamma Rays on Man-in-the-Moon Marigolds,* Paul Zindel
1973 *That Championship Season,* Jason Miller
1975 *Seascape,* Edward Albee
1976 *A Chorus Line,* conceived by Michael Bennett
1977 *The Shadow Box,* Michael Cristofer
1978 *The Gin Game,* Donald L. Coburn
1979 *Buried Child,* Sam Shepard
1980 *Talley's Folly,* Lanford Wilson
1981 *Crimes of the Heart,* Beth Henley
1982 *A Soldier's Play,* Charles Fuller
1983 *'Night, Mother,* Marsha Norman
1984 *Glengarry Glen Ross,* David Mamet
1985 *Sunday in the Park with George,* Stephen Sondheim and James Lapine
1987 *Fences,* August Wilson
1988 *Driving Miss Daisy,* Alfred Uhry
1989 *The Heidi Chronicles,* Wendy Wasserstein
1990 *The Piano Lesson,* August Wilson
1991 *Lost in Yonkers,* Neil Simon
1992 *The Kentucky Cycle,* Robert Schenkkan
1993 *Angels in America: Millennium Approaches,* Tony Kushner
1994 *Three Tall Women,* Edward Albee
1995 *The Young Man from Atlanta,* Horton Foote
1996 *Rent,* Jonathan Larson
1998 *How I Learned to Drive,* Paula Vogel
1999 *Wit,* Margaret Edson
2000 *Dinner with Friends,* Donald Margulies
2001 *Proof,* David Auburn
2002 *Topdog/Underdog,* Suzan-Lori Parks
2003 *Anna in the Tropics,* Nilo Cruz

SPECIAL CITATIONS

1938 *Edmonton* [Alberta] *Journal,* special bronze plaque for editorial leadership in defense of freedom of the press in province of Alberta
1941 *New York Times,* for the public educational value of its foreign news report
1944 Byron Price, director of the Office of Censorship, for the creation and administration of the newspaper and radio codes; Mrs. William Allen White, for her husband's interest and services during the past seven years as a member of the Advisory Board of the Graduate School of Journalism, Columbia University; Richard Rodgers and Oscar Hammerstein II, for their musical *Oklahoma!*
1945 The cartographers of the American press, for their war maps
1947 (Pulitzer centennial year.) Columbia University and the Graduate School of Journalism, for their efforts to maintain and advance the high standards governing the Pulitzer Prize awards; the *St. Louis Post-Dispatch,* for its unswerving adherence to the public and professional ideals of its founder and its leadership in American journalism
1948 Dr. Frank D. Fackenthal, for his interest and service
1951 Cyrus L. Sulzberger *(New York Times),* for his exclusive interview with Archbishop Stepinac in a Yugoslav prison
1952 *Kansas City Star,* for coverage of 1951 floods; Max Kase *(New York Journal–American),* for exposures of bribery in basketball
1953 *New York Times,* for its 17-year publication of "Review of the Week," and Lester Markel, its founder
1957 Kenneth Roberts, for his historical novels
1958 Walter Lippmann *(New York Herald Tribune),* for his "wisdom, perception and high sense of responsibility" in his commentary on national and international affairs
1960 Garrett Mattingly, for *The Armada*
1961 *American Heritage Picture History of the Civil War,* as a distinguished example of American book publishing
1964 Gannett Newspapers, Rochester, N.Y.
1973 James Thomas Flexner, for his biography *George Washington*
1974 Roger Sessions, for his "life's work in music"
1976 John Hohenberg, for "services for 22 years as Administrator of the Pulitzer Prizes"; Scott Joplin, for his contributions to American music
1977 Alex Haley, for his novel, *Roots*
1978 E. B. White of *New Yorker* magazine and Richard L. Strout of *The Christian Science Monitor*
1982 Milton Babbitt, "for his life's work as a distinguished and seminal American composer"
1984 Theodor Seuss Geisel (Dr. Seuss), for "books full of playful rhymes, nonsense words and strange illustrations"
1985 William Schuman, for "more than half a century of contribution to American music as a composer and educational leader"
1987 Joseph Pulitzer, Jr., "for extraordinary services to American journalism and letters during his 31 years as chairman of the Pulitzer Prize Board and for his accomplishments as an editor and publisher"
1992 *Maus,* Art Spiegelman
1996 Herb Caen *(San Francisco Chronicle),* "for his extraordinary and continuing contribution as a voice and conscience of his city"
1998 George Gershwin
1999 Edward Kennedy "Duke" Ellington, who "made an indelible contribution to art and culture"

Academy Awards (Oscars)

1928

Picture: *Wings,* Paramount
Director: Frank Borzage, *Seventh Heaven;* Lewis Milestone, *Two Arabian Nights*
Actress: Janet Gaynor, *Seventh Heaven, Street Angel, Sunrise*
Actor: Emil Jannings, *The Way of All Flesh, The Last Command*

1929

Picture: *The Broadway Melody,* MGM
Director: Frank Lloyd, *The Divine Lady*
Actress: Mary Pickford, *Coquette*
Actor: Warner Baxter, *In Old Arizona*

1930

Picture: *All Quiet on the Western Front,* Universal
Director: Lewis Milestone, *All Quiet on the Western Front*
Actress: Norma Shearer, *The Divorcee*
Actor: George Arliss, *Disraeli*

1931
Picture: *Cimarron,* RKO Radio
Director: Norman Taurog, *Skippy*
Actress: Marie Dressler, *Min and Bill*
Actor: Lionel Barrymore, *A Free Soul*

1932
Picture: *Grand Hotel,* MGM
Director: Frank Borzage, *Bad Girl*
Actress: Helen Hayes, *The Sin of Madelon Claudet*
Actor: Fredric March, *Dr. Jekyll and Mr. Hyde,* and Wallace Beery, *The Champ*

1933
Picture: *Cavalcade,* Fox
Director: Frank Lloyd, *Cavalcade*
Actress: Katharine Hepburn, *Morning Glory*
Actor: Charles Laughton, *The Private Life of Henry VIII*

1934
Picture: *It Happened One Night,* Columbia
Director: Frank Capra, *It Happened One Night*
Actress: Claudette Colbert, *It Happened One Night*
Actor: Clark Gable, *It Happened One Night*

1935
Picture: *Mutiny on the Bounty,* MGM
Director: John Ford, *The Informer*
Actress: Bette Davis, *Dangerous*
Actor: Victor McLaglen, *The Informer*

1936
Picture: *The Great Ziegfeld,* MGM
Director: Frank Capra, *Mr. Deeds Goes to Town*
Actress: Luise Rainer, *The Great Ziegfeld*
Actor: Paul Muni, *The Story of Louis Pasteur*
Supporting Actress: Gale Sondergaard, *Anthony Adverse*
Supporting Actor: Walter Brennan, *Come and Get It*

1937
Picture: *The Life of Emile Zola,* Warner Bros.
Director: Leo McCarey, *The Awful Truth*
Actress: Luise Rainer, *The Good Earth*
Actor: Spencer Tracy, *Captains Courageous*
Supporting Actress: Alice Brady, *In Old Chicago*
Supporting Actor: Joseph Schildkraut, *The Life of Emile Zola*

1938
Picture: *You Can't Take It with You,* Columbia
Director: Frank Capra, *You Can't Take It with You*
Actress: Bette Davis, *Jezebel*
Actor: Spencer Tracy, *Boys Town*
Supporting Actress: Fay Bainter, *Jezebel*
Supporting Actor: Walter Brennan, *Kentucky*

1939
Picture: *Gone with the Wind,* Selznick MGM
Director: Victor Fleming, *Gone with the Wind*
Actress: Vivien Leigh, *Gone with the Wind*
Actor: Robert Donat, *Goodbye, Mr. Chips*
Supporting Actress: Hattie McDaniel, *Gone with the Wind*
Supporting Actor: Thomas Mitchell, *Stagecoach*

1940
Picture: *Rebecca,* Selznick-United Artists
Director: John Ford, *The Grapes of Wrath*
Actress: Ginger Rogers, *Kitty Foyle*
Actor: James Stewart, *The Philadelphia Story*
Supporting Actress: Jane Darwell, *The Grapes of Wrath*
Supporting Actor: Walter Brennan, *The Westerner*

1941
Picture: *How Green Was My Valley,* 20th Century–Fox
Director: John Ford, *How Green Was My Valley*
Actress: Joan Fontaine, *Suspicion*
Actor: Gary Cooper, *Sergeant York*
Supporting Actress: Mary Astor, *The Great Lie*
Supporting Actor: Donald Crisp, *How Green Was My Valley*

1942
Picture: *Mrs. Miniver,* MGM
Director: William Wyler, *Mrs. Miniver*
Actress: Greer Garson, *Mrs. Miniver*
Actor: James Cagney, *Yankee Doodle Dandy*
Supporting Actress: Teresa Wright, *Mrs. Miniver*
Supporting Actor: Van Heflin, *Johnny Eager*

1943
Picture: *Casablanca,* Warner Bros.
Director: Michael Curtiz, *Casablanca*
Actress: Jennifer Jones, *The Song of Bernadette*
Actor: Paul Lukas, *Watch on the Rhine*
Supporting Actress: Katina Paxinou, *For Whom the Bell Tolls*
Supporting Actor: Charles Coburn, *The More the Merrier*

1944
Picture: *Going My Way,* Paramount
Director: Leo McCarey, *Going My Way*
Actress: Ingrid Bergman, *Gaslight*
Actor: Bing Crosby, *Going My Way*
Supporting Actress: Ethel Barrymore, *None but the Lonely Heart*
Supporting Actor: Barry Fitzgerald, *Going My Way*

1945
Picture: *The Lost Weekend,* Paramount
Director: Billy Wilder, *The Lost Weekend*
Actress: Joan Crawford, *Mildred Pierce*
Actor: Ray Milland, *The Lost Weekend*
Supporting Actress: Anne Revere, *National Velvet*
Supporting Actor: James Dunn, *A Tree Grows in Brooklyn*

1946
Picture: *The Best Years of Our Lives,* Goldwyn-RKO Radio
Director: William Wyler, *The Best Years of Our Lives*
Actress: Olivia de Havilland, *To Each His Own*
Actor: Fredric March, *The Best Years of Our Lives*
Supporting Actress: Anne Baxter, *The Razor's Edge*
Supporting Actor: Harold Russell, *The Best Years of Our Lives*

1947
Picture: *Gentleman's Agreement,* 20th Century–Fox
Director: Elia Kazan, *Gentleman's Agreement*
Actress: Loretta Young, *The Farmer's Daughter*
Actor: Ronald Colman, *A Double Life*
Supporting Actress: Celeste Holm, *Gentleman's Agreement*
Supporting Actor: Edmund Gwenn, *Miracle on 34th Street*

1948
Picture: *Hamlet,* Rank-Two Cities-UI
Director: John Huston, *Treasure of Sierra Madre*
Actress: Jane Wyman, *Johnny Belinda*
Actor: Laurence Olivier, *Hamlet*
Supporting Actress: Claire Trevor, *Key Largo*
Supporting Actor: Walter Huston, *Treasure of Sierra Madre*

1949
Picture: *All the King's Men,* Rossen-Columbia
Director: Joseph L. Mankiewicz, *A Letter to Three Wives*
Actress: Olivia de Havilland, *The Heiress*
Actor: Broderick Crawford, *All the King's Men*
Supporting Actress: Mercedes McCambridge, *All the King's Men*
Supporting Actor: Dean Jagger, *Twelve O'Clock High*

1950
Picture: *All About Eve,* 20th Century–Fox
Director: Joseph L. Mankiewicz, *All About Eve*
Actress: Judy Holliday, *Born Yesterday*
Actor: José Ferrer, *Cyrano de Bergerac*
Supporting Actress: Josephine Hull, *Harvey*
Supporting Actor: George Sanders, *All About Eve*

1951
Picture: *An American in Paris,* MGM
Director: George Stevens, *A Place in the Sun*
Actress: Vivien Leigh, *A Streetcar Named Desire*
Actor: Humphrey Bogart, *The African Queen*

Supporting Actress: Kim Hunter, *A Streetcar Named Desire*
Supporting Actor: Karl Malden, *A Streetcar Named Desire*

1952

Picture: *The Greatest Show on Earth,* DeMille-Paramount
Director: John Ford, *The Quiet Man*
Actress: Shirley Booth, *Come Back, Little Sheba*
Actor: Gary Cooper, *High Noon*
Supporting Actress: Gloria Grahame, *The Bad and the Beautiful*
Supporting Actor: Anthony Quinn, *Viva Zapata!*

1953

Picture: *From Here to Eternity,* Columbia
Director: Fred Zinnemann, *From Here to Eternity*
Actress: Audrey Hepburn, *Roman Holiday*
Actor: William Holden, *Stalag 17*
Supporting Actress: Donna Reed, *From Here to Eternity*
Supporting Actor: Frank Sinatra, *From Here to Eternity*

1954

Picture: *On the Waterfront,* Horizon-American Corp., Columbia
Director: Elia Kazan, *On the Waterfront*
Actress: Grace Kelly, *The Country Girl*
Actor: Marlon Brando, *On the Waterfront*
Supporting Actress: Eva Marie Saint, *On the Waterfront*
Supporting Actor: Edmond O'Brien, *The Barefoot Contessa*

1955

Picture: *Marty,* Hecht and Lancaster, United Artists
Director: Delbert Mann, *Marty*
Actress: Anna Magnani, *The Rose Tattoo*
Actor: Ernest Borgnine, *Marty*
Supporting Actress: Jo Van Fleet, *East of Eden*
Supporting Actor: Jack Lemmon, *Mister Roberts*

1956

Picture: *Around the World in 80 Days,* Michael Todd Co., Inc.-United Artists
Director: George Stevens, *Giant*
Actress: Ingrid Bergman, *Anastasia*
Actor: Yul Brynner, *The King and I*
Supporting Actress: Dorothy Malone, *Written on the Wind*
Supporting Actor: Anthony Quinn, *Lust for Life*

1957

Picture: *The Bridge on the River Kwai,* Horizon Films, Columbia
Director: David Lean, *The Bridge on the River Kwai*
Actress: Joanne Woodward, *The Three Faces of Eve*
Actor: Alec Guinness, *The Bridge on the River Kwai*
Supporting Actress: Miyoshi Umeki, *Sayonara*
Supporting Actor: Red Buttons, *Sayonara*

1958

Picture: *Gigi,* Arthur Freed Productions, Inc., MGM
Director: Vincente Minnelli, *Gigi*
Actress: Susan Hayward, *I Want to Live!*
Actor: David Niven, *Separate Tables*
Supporting Actress: Wendy Hiller, *Separate Tables*
Supporting Actor: Burl Ives, *The Big Country*

1959

Picture: *Ben-Hur,* MGM
Director: William Wyler, *Ben-Hur*
Actress: Simone Signoret, *Room at the Top*
Actor: Charlton Heston, *Ben-Hur*
Supporting Actress: Shelley Winters, *The Diary of Anne Frank*
Supporting Actor: Hugh Griffith, *Ben-Hur*

1960

Picture: *The Apartment,* Mirisch Co., Inc., United Artists
Director: Billy Wilder, *The Apartment*
Actress: Elizabeth Taylor, *Butterfield 8*
Actor: Burt Lancaster, *Elmer Gantry*
Supporting Actress: Shirley Jones, *Elmer Gantry*
Supporting Actor: Peter Ustinov, *Spartacus*

1961

Picture: *West Side Story,* Mirisch Pictures, Inc., and B and P Enterprises, Inc., United Artists
Director: Robert Wise and Jerome Robbins, *West Side Story*
Actress: Sophia Loren, *Two Women*
Actor: Maximillian Schell, *Judgment at Nuremberg*
Supporting Actress: Rita Moreno, *West Side Story*
Supporting Actor: George Chakiris, *West Side Story*

1962

Picture: *Lawrence of Arabia,* Horizon Pictures, Ltd.-Columbia
Director: David Lean, *Lawrence of Arabia*
Actress: Anne Bancroft, *The Miracle Worker*
Actor: Gregory Peck, *To Kill a Mockingbird*
Supporting Actress: Patty Duke, *The Miracle Worker*
Supporting Actor: Ed Begley, *Sweet Bird of Youth*

1963

Picture: *Tom Jones,* A Woodfall Production, United Artists-Lopert Pictures
Director: Tony Richardson, *Tom Jones*
Actress: Patricia Neal, *Hud*
Actor: Sidney Poitier, *Lilies of the Field*
Supporting Actress: Margaret Rutherford, *The V.I.P.s*
Supporting Actor: Melvyn Douglas, *Hud*

1964

Picture: *My Fair Lady,* Warner Bros.
Director: George Cukor, *My Fair Lady*
Actress: Julie Andrews, *Mary Poppins*
Actor: Rex Harrison, *My Fair Lady*
Supporting Actress: Lila Kedrova, *Zorba the Greek*
Supporting Actor: Peter Ustinov, *Topkapi*

1965

Picture: *The Sound of Music,* Argyle Enterprises Production, 20th Century–Fox
Director: Robert Wise, *The Sound of Music*
Actress: Julie Christie, *Darling*
Actor: Lee Marvin, *Cat Ballou*
Supporting Actress: Shelley Winters, *A Patch of Blue*
Supporting Actor: Martin Balsam, *A Thousand Clowns*

1966

Picture: *A Man for All Seasons,* Highland Films, Ltd., Production, Columbia
Director: Fred Zinnemann, *A Man for All Seasons*
Actress: Elizabeth Taylor, *Who's Afraid of Virginia Woolf?*
Actor: Paul Scofield, *A Man for All Seasons*
Supporting Actress: Sandy Dennis, *Who's Afraid of Virginia Woolf?*
Supporting Actor: Walter Matthau, *The Fortune Cookie*

1967

Picture: *In the Heat of the Night,* Mirisch Corp. Productions, United Artists
Director: Mike Nichols, *The Graduate*
Actress: Katharine Hepburn, *Guess Who's Coming to Dinner*
Actor: Rod Steiger, *In the Heat of the Night*
Supporting Actress: Estelle Parsons, *Bonnie and Clyde*
Supporting Actor: George Kennedy, *Cool Hand Luke*

1968

Picture: *Oliver!,* Columbia Pictures
Director: Sir Carol Reed, *Oliver!*
Actress: Katharine Hepburn, *The Lion in Winter* and Barbra Streisand, *Funny Girl*
Actor: Cliff Robertson, *Charly*
Supporting Actress: Ruth Gordon, *Rosemary's Baby*
Supporting Actor: Jack Albertson, *The Subject Was Roses*

1969

Picture: *Midnight Cowboy,* Jerome Hellman-John Schlesinger Production, United Artists
Director: John Schlesinger, *Midnight Cowboy*
Actress: Maggie Smith, *The Prime of Miss Jean Brodie*

Actor: John Wayne, *True Grit*
Supporting Actress: Goldie Hawn, *Cactus Flower*
Supporting Actor: Gig Young, *They Shoot Horses, Don't They?*

1970
Picture: *Patton,* Frank McCarthy-Franklin J. Schaffner Production, 20th Century–Fox
Director: Franklin J. Schaffner, *Patton*
Actress: Glenda Jackson, *Women in Love*
Actor: George C. Scott, *Patton*
Supporting Actress: Helen Hayes, *Airport*
Supporting Actor: John Mills, *Ryan's Daughter*

1971
Picture: *The French Connection,* D'Antoni Productions, 20th Century–Fox
Director: William Friedkin, *The French Connection*
Actress: Jane Fonda, *Klute*
Actor: Gene Hackman, *The French Connection*
Supporting Actress: Cloris Leachman, *The Last Picture Show*
Supporting Actor: Ben Johnson, *The Last Picture Show*

1972
Picture: *The Godfather,* Albert S. Ruddy Production, Paramount
Director: Bob Fosse, *Cabaret*
Actress: Liza Minnelli, *Cabaret*
Actor: Marlon Brando, *The Godfather*
Supporting Actress: Eileen Heckart, *Butterflies Are Free*
Supporting Actor: Joel Gray, *Cabaret*

1973
Picture: *The Sting,* Universal-Bill/Phillips-George Roy Hill Production, Universal
Director: George Roy Hill, *The Sting*
Actress: Glenda Jackson, *A Touch of Class*
Actor: Jack Lemmon, *Save the Tiger*
Supporting Actress: Tatum O'Neal, *Paper Moon*
Supporting Actor: John Houseman, *The Paper Chase*

1974
Picture: *The Godfather, Part II,* Coppola Co. Production, Paramount
Director: Francis Ford Coppola, *The Godfather, Part II*
Actress: Ellen Burstyn, *Alice Doesn't Live Here Anymore*
Actor: Art Carney, *Harry and Tonto*
Supporting Actress: Ingrid Bergman, *Murder on the Orient Express*
Supporting Actor: Robert De Niro, *The Godfather, Part II*

1975
Picture: *One Flew Over the Cuckoo's Nest,* Fantasy Films Production, United Artists
Director: Milos Forman, *One Flew Over the Cuckoo's Nest*
Actress: Louise Fletcher, *One Flew Over the Cuckoo's Nest*
Actor: Jack Nicholson, *One Flew Over the Cuckoo's Nest*
Supporting Actress: Lee Grant, *Shampoo*
Supporting Actor: George Burns, *The Sunshine Boys*

1976
Picture: *Rocky,* Robert Chartoff-Irwin Winkler Production, United Artists
Director: John G. Avildsen, *Rocky*
Actress: Faye Dunaway, *Network*
Actor: Peter Finch, *Network*
Supporting Actress: Beatrice Straight, *Network*
Supporting Actor: Jason Robards, *All the President's Men*

1977
Picture: *Annie Hall,* Jack Rollins-Charles H. Joffe Production, United Artists
Director: Woody Allen, *Annie Hall*
Actress: Diane Keaton, *Annie Hall*
Actor: Richard Dreyfuss, *The Goodbye Girl*
Supporting Actress: Vanessa Redgrave, *Julia*
Supporting Actor: Jason Robards, *Julia*

1978
Picture: *The Deer Hunter,* Michael Cimino Film Production, Universal
Director: Michael Cimino, *The Deer Hunter*
Actress: Jane Fonda, *Coming Home*
Actor: Jon Voight, *Coming Home*
Supporting Actress: Maggie Smith, *California Suite*
Supporting Actor: Christopher Walken, *The Deer Hunter*

1979
Picture: *Kramer vs. Kramer,* Stanley Jaffe Production, Columbia Pictures
Director: Robert Benton, *Kramer vs. Kramer*
Actress: Sally Field, *Norma Rae*
Actor: Dustin Hoffman, *Kramer vs. Kramer*
Supporting Actress: Meryl Streep, *Kramer vs. Kramer*
Supporting Actor: Melvyn Douglas, *Being There*

1980
Picture: *Ordinary People,* Wildwood Enterprises Production, Paramount
Director: Robert Redford, *Ordinary People*
Actress: Sissy Spacek, *Coal Miner's Daughter*
Actor: Robert De Niro, *Raging Bull*
Supporting Actress: Mary Steenburgen, *Melvin and Howard*
Supporting Actor: Timothy Hutton, *Ordinary People*

1981
Picture: *Chariots of Fire,* Enigma Productions, Ladd Company/Warner Bros.
Director: Warren Beatty, *Reds*
Actress: Katharine Hepburn, *On Golden Pond*
Actor: Henry Fonda, *On Golden Pond*
Supporting Actress: Maureen Stapleton, *Reds*
Supporting Actor: John Gielgud, *Arthur*

1982
Picture: *Gandhi,* Indo-British Films Production/Columbia
Director: Richard Attenborough, *Gandhi*
Actress: Meryl Streep, *Sophie's Choice*
Actor: Ben Kingsley, *Gandhi*
Supporting Actress: Jessica Lange, *Tootsie*
Supporting Actor: Louis Gossett, Jr., *An Officer and a Gentleman*

1983
Picture: *Terms of Endearment,* Paramount
Director: James L. Brooks, *Terms of Endearment*
Actress: Shirley MacLaine, *Terms of Endearment*
Actor: Robert Duvall, *Tender Mercies*
Supporting Actress: Linda Hunt, *The Year of Living Dangerously*
Supporting Actor: Jack Nicholson, *Terms of Endearment*

1984
Picture: *Amadeus,* Orion
Director: Milos Forman, *Amadeus*
Actress: Sally Field, *Places in the Heart*
Actor: F. Murray Abraham, *Amadeus*
Supporting Actress: Dame Peggy Ashcroft, *A Passage to India*
Supporting Actor: Haing S. Ngor, *The Killing Fields*

1985
Picture: *Out of Africa,* Universal
Director: Sydney Pollack, *Out of Africa*
Actress: Geraldine Page, *The Trip to Bountiful*
Actor: William Hurt, *Kiss of the Spider Woman*
Supporting Actress: Anjelica Huston, *Prizzi's Honor*
Supporting Actor: Don Ameche, *Cocoon*

1986
Picture: *Platoon,* Orion
Director: Oliver Stone, *Platoon*
Actress: Marlee Matlin, *Children of a Lesser God*
Actor: Paul Newman, *The Color of Money*
Supporting Actress: Dianne Wiest, *Hannah and Her Sisters*
Supporting Actor: Michael Caine, *Hannah and Her Sisters*

1987
Picture: *The Last Emperor,* Columbia Pictures
Director: Bernardo Bertolucci, *The Last Emperor*
Actress: Cher, *Moonstruck*
Actor: Michael Douglas, *Wall Street*

Supporting Actress: Olympia Dukakis, *Moonstruck*
Supporting Actor: Sean Connery, *The Untouchables*

1988
Picture: *Rain Man,* United Artists
Director: Barry Levinson, *Rain Man*
Actress: Jodie Foster, *The Accused*
Actor: Dustin Hoffman, *Rain Man*
Supporting Actress: Geena Davis, *The Accidental Tourist*
Supporting Actor: Kevin Kline, *A Fish Called Wanda*

1989
Picture: *Driving Miss Daisy,* Warner Bros.
Director: Oliver Stone, *Born on the Fourth of July*
Actress: Jessica Tandy, *Driving Miss Daisy*
Actor: Daniel Day-Lewis, *My Left Foot*
Supporting Actress: Brenda Fricker, *My Left Foot*
Supporting Actor: Denzel Washington, *Glory*

1990
Picture: *Dances With Wolves,* Orion
Director: Kevin Costner, *Dances With Wolves*
Actress: Kathy Bates, *Misery*
Actor: Jeremy Irons, *Reversal of Fortune*
Supporting Actress: Whoopi Goldberg, *Ghost*
Supporting Actor: Joe Pesci, *Goodfellas*

1991
Picture: *The Silence of the Lambs,* Orion
Director: Jonathan Demme, *The Silence of the Lambs*
Actress: Jodie Foster, *The Silence of the Lambs*
Actor: Anthony Hopkins, *The Silence of the Lambs*
Supporting Actress: Mercedes Ruehl, *The Fisher King*
Supporting Actor: Jack Palance, *City Slickers*

1992
Picture: *Unforgiven,* Warner Bros.
Director: Clint Eastwood, *Unforgiven*
Actress: Emma Thompson, *Howards End*
Actor: Al Pacino, *Scent of a Woman*
Supporting Actress: Marisa Tomei, *My Cousin Vinny*
Supporting Actor: Gene Hackman, *Unforgiven*

1993
Picture: *Schindler's List,* Universal
Director: Steven Spielberg, *Schindler's List*
Actress: Holly Hunter, *The Piano*
Actor: Tom Hanks, *Philadelphia*
Supporting Actress: Anna Paquin, *The Piano*
Supporting Actor: Tommy Lee Jones, *The Fugitive*

1994
Picture: *Forrest Gump,* Paramount
Director: Robert Zemeckis, *Forrest Gump*
Actress: Jessica Lange, *Blue Sky*
Actor: Tom Hanks, *Forrest Gump*
Supporting Actress: Dianne Wiest, *Bullets Over Broadway*
Supporting Actor: Martin Landau, *Ed Wood*

1995
Picture: *Braveheart,* Paramount
Director: Mel Gibson, *Braveheart*
Actress: Susan Sarandon, *Dead Man Walking*
Actor: Nicolas Cage, *Leaving Las Vegas*
Supporting Actress: Mira Sorvino, *Mighty Aphrodite*
Supporting Actor: Kevin Spacey, *The Usual Suspects*

1996
Picture: *The English Patient,* Miramax
Director: Anthony Minghella, *The English Patient*
Actress: Frances McDormand, *Fargo*
Actor: Geoffrey Rush, *Shine*
Supporting Actress: Juliette Binoche, *The English Patient*
Supporting Actor: Cuba Gooding, Jr., *Jerry Maguire*

1997
Picture: *Titanic,* 20th Century–Fox and Paramount
Director: James Cameron, *Titanic*
Actress: Helen Hunt, *As Good As It Gets*
Actor: Jack Nicholson, *As Good As It Gets*
Supporting Actress: Kim Basinger, *L.A. Confidential*
Supporting Actor: Robin Williams, *Good Will Hunting*

1998
Picture: *Shakespeare in Love,* Miramax
Director: Steven Spielberg, *Saving Private Ryan*
Actress: Gwyneth Paltrow, *Shakespeare in Love*
Actor: Roberto Benigni, *Life Is Beautiful*
Supporting Actress: Judi Dench, *Shakespeare in Love*
Supporting Actor: James Coburn, *Affliction*

1999
Picture: *American Beauty,* DreamWorks SKG
Director: Sam Mendes, *American Beauty*
Actress: Hilary Swank, *Boys Don't Cry*
Actor: Kevin Spacey, *American Beauty*
Supporting Actress: Angelina Jolie, *Girl, Interrupted*
Supporting Actor: Michael Caine, *The Cider House Rules*

2000
Picture: *Gladiator,* DreamWorks and Universal
Director: Steven Soderbergh, *Traffic*
Actress: Julia Roberts, *Erin Brockovich*
Actor: Russell Crowe, *Gladiator*
Supporting Actress: Marcia Gay Harden, *Pollock*
Supporting Actor: Benicio Del Toro, *Traffic*

2001
Picture: *A Beautiful Mind,* Brian Grazer and Ron Howard, producers
Director: Ron Howard, *A Beautiful Mind*
Actress: Halle Berry, *Monster's Ball*
Actor: Denzel Washington, *Training Day*
Supporting Actress: Jennifer Connelly, *A Beautiful Mind*
Supporting Actor: Jim Broadbent, *Iris*

2002
Picture: *Chicago,* Martin Richards, producer
Director: Roman Polanski, *The Pianist*
Actress: Nicole Kidman, *The Hours*
Actor: Adrien Brody, *The Pianist*
Supporting Actress: Catherine Zeta-Jones, *Chicago*
Supporting Actor: Chris Cooper, *Adaptation*

Other Academy Awards for 2002

Art Direction: John Myhre, *Chicago*
Cinematography: Conrad L. Hall, *Road to Perdition*
Costume Design: Colleen Atwood, *Chicago*
Documentary (feature): *Bowling for Columbine* (Michael Moore and Michael Donovan)
Editing: Martin Walsh, *Chicago*
Foreign-Language Film: *Nowhere in Africa,* Germany
Makeup: John Jackson and Beatrice De Alba, *Frida*
Music (original score): Elliot Goldenthal, *Frida*
Best Original Song: Eminem, Jeff Bass, and Luis Resto, "Lose Yourself," *8 Mile*
Adapted Screenplay: Ronald Harwood, *The Pianist*
Original Screenplay: Pedro Almodóvar, *Talk to Her*
Short Subject (live action): *This Charming Man (Der er en Yndig Mand)* (Martin Strange-Hansen and Mie Andreasen)
Sound: Michael Minkler, Dominick Tavella, and David Lee, *Chicago*
Sound Effects Editing: Ethan Van der Ryn and Michael Hopkins, *The Lord of the Rings: The Two Towers*
Visual Effects: Jim Rygiel, Joe Letteri, Randall William Cook, and Alex Funke, *The Lord of the Rings: The Two Towers*
Honorary Award: Peter O'Toole, actor

2002 National Society of Film Critics Awards

Best Picture: *The Pianist*
Best Actor: Adrien Brody, *The Pianist*
Best Actress: Diane Lane, *Unfaithful*
Best Supporting Actor: Christopher Walken, *Catch Me If You Can*
Best Supporting Actress: Patricia Clarkson, *Far from Heaven*
Best Director: Roman Polanski, *The Pianist*
Best Screenplay: Ronald Harwood, *The Pianist*
Best Cinematography: Ed Lachman, *Far from Heaven*
Best Foreign Film: *Y Tu Mama Tambien*, Alfonso Cuarón (Mexico)
Best Non-Fiction Film: *Standing in the Shadows of Motown*, Paul Justman
Special Citation: UCLA's film and television archives
Film Heritage Award: Kino International, for releasing restored versions of *Metropolis* and D. W. Griffith's silent films

2002 National Board of Review Awards

Best Picture: *The Hours*
Best Foreign Film: *Talk to Her* (Spain)
Best Actor: Campbell Scott, *Roger Dodger*
Best Actress: Julianne Moore, *Far from Heaven*
Best Supporting Actor: Chris Cooper, *Adaptation*
Best Supporting Actress: Kathy Bates, *About Schmidt*
Best Ensemble: *Nicholas Nickleby*
Breakthrough Performances: Derek Luke, *Antwone Fisher* and Maggie Gyllenhaal, *Secretary*
Best Director: Phillip Noyce, *The Quiet American* and *Rabbit-Proof Fence*
Best Directorial Debut: Rob Marshall, *Chicago*
Screenwriter of the Year: Charlie Kaufman, *Adaptation, Confessions of a Dangerous Mind,* and *Human Nature*
Best Documentary: *Bowling for Columbine*
Best Animated Feature: *Spirited Away*
Special Award for Visionary Cinematic Achievement: George Lucas
Career Achievement Awards: Elmer Bernstein, Conrad Hall, and Christopher Plummer
Humanitarian Award: Sheila Nevins
William K. Everson Award for Film History: Annette Insdorf, *Indelible Shadows: Films and the Holocaust*
Special Recognition of Films that Reflect the Freedom of Expression: *Ararat, Bloody Sunday, The Grey Zone,* and *Rabbit-Proof Fence*
Special Mention for Excellence in Filmmaking: *Frailty, The Good Girl, The Guys, Heaven, Igby Goes Down, Max, Personal Velocity, Real Women Have Curves, Roger Dodger, Sunshine State, Tadpole,* and *Tully*

2003 Cannes Film Festival

Palme d'Or: *Elephant,* Gus Van Sant (United States)
Grand Prize: *Uzak,* Nuri Bilge Ceylan (Turkey)
Jury Prize: *Panj é Asr (Five in the Afternoon),* Samira Makhmalbaf (Iran)
Best Director: *Elephant,* Gus Van Sant (United States)
Best Actor (co-winners): Muzaffer Ozdemir and Mehmet Emin Toprak, *Uzak* (Turkey)
Best Actress: Marie Josée Croze, *Barbarian Invasions* (Quebec)
Screenplay: Denys Arcand, *Barbarian Invasions* (Quebec)
Caméra d'Or: *Reconstruction,* Christoffer Boe (Denmark)
Palme d'Or for Short Film: *Cracker Bag,* Glendyn Ivin (Australia)
Jury Prize for Short Film: *L'Homme sans Tête,* Juan Solanas (France)

2003 Golden Globe Awards

Film Awards

Best Motion Picture—Drama: *The Hours*
Best Actor in a Drama: Jack Nicholson, *About Schmidt*
Best Actress in a Drama: Nicole Kidman, *The Hours*
Best Motion Picture—Musical or Comedy: *Chicago*
Best Actor in a Musical or Comedy: Richard Gere, *Chicago*
Best Actress in a Musical or Comedy: Renee Zellweger, *Chicago*
Best Supporting Actor: Chris Cooper, *Adaptation*
Best Supporting Actress: Meryl Streep, *Adaptation*
Best Director: Martin Scorsese, *Gangs of New York*
Best Screenplay: Alexander Payne and Jim Taylor, *About Schmidt*
Best Original Score: Elliot Goldenthal, *Frida*
Best Original Song: "The Hands That Built America," U2, *Gangs of New York*
Best Foreign Film: *Talk to Her* (Spain)
Cecil B. DeMille Award: Gene Hackman

Television Awards

Best Series—Drama: *The Shield* (FX)
Best Actor in a Drama: Michael Chiklis, *The Shield*
Best Actress in a Drama: Edie Falco, *The Sopranos*
Best Series—Musical or Comedy: *Curb Your Enthusiasm* (HBO)
Best Actor in a Musical or Comedy Series: Tony Shalhoub, *Monk*
Best Actress in a Musical or Comedy Series: Jennifer Aniston, *Friends*
Best Miniseries or Movie Made for Television: *The Gathering Storm* (HBO)
Best Actor in a Miniseries or Movie Made for Television: Albert Finney, *The Gathering Storm*
Best Actress in a Miniseries or Movie Made for Television: Uma Thurman, *Hysterical Blindness*
Best Supporting Actor in a Series, Miniseries, or Movie Made for Television: Donald Sutherland, *Path to War*
Best Supporting Actress in a Series, Miniseries, or Movie Made for Television: Kim Cattrall, *Sex and the City*

2003 Tony (Antoinette Perry) Awards

Play: *Take Me Out*
Musical: *Hairspray*
Revival—Play: *Long Day's Journey into Night*
Revival—Musical: *Nine*
Actor—Play: Brian Dennehy, *Long Day's Journey into Night*
Actress—Play: Vanessa Redgrave, *Long Day's Journey into Night*
Actor—Musical: Harvey Fierstein, *Hairspray*
Actress—Musical: Marissa Jaret Winokur, *Hairspray*
Featured Actor—Play: Denis O'Hare, *Take Me Out*
Featured Actress—Play: Michele Pawk, *Hollywood Arms*
Featured Actor—Musical: Dick Latessa, *Hairspray*
Featured Actress—Musical: Jane Krakowski, *Nine*
Director—Play: Joe Mantello, *Take Me Out*
Director—Musical: Jack O'Brien, *Hairspray*
Book—Musical: Thomas Meehan and Mark O'Donnell, *Hairspray*
Score—Musical: Scott Whittman and Marc Shaiman, *Hairspray*
Orchestration: Stuart Malina and Billy Joel, *Movin' Out*
Scenic Designer: Catherine Martin, *La Bohème*
Costume Designer: William Ivey Long, *Hairspray*
Choreographer: Twyla Tharp, *Movin' Out*
Lighting Designer: Nigel Levings, *La Bohème*
Special Theatrical Event: *Russell Simmons' Def Poetry Jam on Broadway*
Regional Theater: The Children's Theatre Company
Special Award: Cy Feuer, for lifetime achievement
Tony Honors for Excellence in Theatre: The principal ensemble of *La Bohème,* Paul Huntley, Johnson-Liff Casting Associates, and The Acting Company

2003 Drama Desk Awards

Outstanding Play: *Take Me Out*
Outstanding Musical: *Hairspray*
Outstanding Musical Revival: *Nine*
Outstanding Play Revival: *Long Day's Journey into Night*
Best Actor in a Play: Eddie Izzard, *A Day in the Death of Joe Egg*
Best Actress in a Play: Vanessa Redgrave, *Long Day's Journey into Night*
Best Featured Actor in a Play: Denis O'Hare, *Take Me Out*
Best Featured Actress in a Play: Lynn Redgrave, *Talking Heads*
Best Actor in a Musical (tie): Antonio Banderas, *Nine* and Harvey Fierstein, *Hairspray*
Best Actress in a Musical: Marissa Jaret Winokur, *Hairspray*
Best Featured Actor in a Musical: Dick Latessa, *Hairspray*
Best Featured Actress in a Musical: Jane Krakowski, *Nine*
Best Director of a Play: Robert Falls, *Long Day's Journey into Night*
Best Director of a Musical: Jack O'Brien, *Hairspray*
Best Choreography: Twyla Tharp, *Movin' Out*
Best Book of a Musical: Mark O'Donnell and Thomas Meehan, *Hairspray*
Best Music: Marc Shaiman, *Hairspray*
Best Lyrics: Scott Wittman and Marc Shaiman, *Hairspray*
Outstanding Orchestrations: Harold Wheeler, *Hairspray*
Outstanding Set Design of a Play: John Lee Beatty, *Dinner at Eight*
Outstanding Set Design of a Musical: Catherine Martin, *La Bohème*
Outstanding Costume Design: William Ivey Long, *Hairspray*
Outstanding Lighting Design: Nigel Levings, *La Bohème*
Outstanding Sound Design: Acme Sound Partners, *La Bohème*
Outstanding Solo Performance: Tovah Feldshuh, *Golda's Balcony*
Unique Theatrical Experience: *The Exonerated*
Special Awards: Brooklyn Academy of Music for bringing works of distinction from around the world to New York audiences; Charles Busch for career achievement as performer and playwright; Geoffrey Johnson and Vincent Liff (posthumous) of Johnson-Liff Casting for career achievement

2002–2003 Obie Awards

The Obie Awards, presented by *The Village Voice*, honor superior off-Broadway theater.

Direction: Emily Mann, *All Over;* Deborah Warner, *Medea*
Performance: Kathleen Chalfant, Daniel Davis, Christine Ebersole, Valerie Mahaffey, Lynn Redgrave, Brenda Wehle, *Talking Heads;* Mos Def, *F***ing A;* Rosemary Harris, *All Over;* Ty Jones, *The Blacks: A Clown Show;* J. Kyle Manzay, *The Blacks: A Clown Show;* Stephen Mellor, *in Bitter Bierce or, The Friction We Call Grief;* Edward Norton, *Burn This;* Jim Norton, *Dublin Carol;* Denis O'Hare, *Take Me Out;* Jason Petty, *Hank Williams: Lost Highway;* Simon Russell Beale, *Uncle Vanya;* Fiona Shaw, *Medea;* Barry Del Sherman, *The Mystery of Attraction*
Design: Kimberly Glennon, costume design *The Blacks: A Clown Show*; Anne Lommel, mask design *The Blacks: A Clown Show;* Kenneth Posner, sustained excellence of lighting design; Anthony Ward, set design *Uncle Vanya*
Special Citations: Art Acuna, Loy Arcenas, Lonnie Carter, Ramon de Ocampo, Ron Domingo, Jojo Gonzalez, Orlando Pabotoy, Ralph B. Pena, *The Romance of Magno Rubio;* Brooklyn Academy of Music International Programming; Lisa D'Amour, Katie Pearl, Kathy Randels, *Nita and Zita;* David Greenspan, *She Stoops to Comedy;* Morgan Jenness, *Longtime Support of Playwrights;* John Kani and Winston Ntshona, *The Island;* Erika Munk, *Editorship of Theater;* Ellen Maddow, Paul Zimet, Diane Beckett, Gary Brownlee, Randolph Curtis Rand, Steven Rattazzi, Tina Shepard, Louise Smith, Nic Ularu, Kiki Smith, Carol Mullins, Karinne Keithley, "Blue" Gene Tyranny, *Talking Band's Painted Snake in a Painted Chair*
Lifetime Achievement: Mac Wellman
Grants: Collapsable Hole, Galapagos, The Immigrant Theatre Project
Ross Wetzsteon Award: Soho Think Tank's Ice Factory series at the Ohio Theatre

Major Grammy Awards for Recording in 2002

Record: "Don't Know Why," Norah Jones
Album: *Come Away with Me,* Norah Jones
Song: "Don't Know Why," Jesse Harris, songwriter (Norah Jones)
New Artist: Norah Jones
Female Pop Vocal: "Don't Know Why," Norah Jones
Male Pop Vocal: "Your Body Is a Wonderland," John Mayer
Pop Duo or Group with Vocals: "Hey Baby," No Doubt
Pop Collaboration with Vocals: "The Game of Love," Santana & Michelle Branch
Pop Instrumental: "Auld Lang Syne," B. B. King
Pop Vocal Album: *Come Away with Me,* Norah Jones
Dance Recording: "Days Go By," Dirty Vegas
Traditional Pop Vocal Album: *Playin' with My Friends: Bennett Sings the Blues,* Tony Bennett
Female Rock Vocal: "Steve McQueen," Sheryl Crow
Male Rock Vocal: "The Rising," Bruce Springsteen
Rock Duo or Group with Vocals: "In My Place," Coldplay
Hard Rock: "All My Life," Foo Fighters
Metal: "Here to Stay," Korn
Rock Instrumental: "Approaching Pavonis Mons by Balloon (Utopia Planitia)," The Flaming Lips
Rock Song: "The Rising," Bruce Springsteen, songwriter (Bruce Springsteen)
Rock Album: *The Rising,* Bruce Springsteen
Alternative Music Album: *A Rush of Blood to the Head,* Coldplay
Female R&B Vocal: "He Think I Don't Know," Mary J. Blige
Male R&B Vocal: "U Don't Have to Call, " Usher
R&B Duo or Group with Vocals: "Love's in Need of Love Today," Stevie Wonder & Take Six
Traditional R&B Vocal: "What's Going On," Chaka Khan & The Funk Brothers
Urban/Alternative Vocal: "Little Things," India.Arie
R&B Song: "Love of My Life (An Ode to Hip Hop)," Erykah Badu, Madukwu Chinwah, Rashid Lonnie Lynn, Robert Ozuna, James Poyser, Raphael Saadiq, Glen Standridge, songwriters (Erykah Badu featuring Common)
R&B Album: *Voyage to India,* India.Arie
Contemporary R&B Album: *Ashanti,* Ashanti
Female Rap Solo: "Scream, a k a Itchin'," Missy Elliott
Male Rap Solo: "Hot in Herre," Nelly
Rap Duo or Group: "The Whole World," OutKast featuring Killer Mike
Rap Sung/Collaboration: "Dilemma," Nelly featuring Kelly Rowland
Rap Album: *The Eminem Show,* Eminem
Female Country Vocal: "Cry," Faith Hill
Male Country Vocal: "Give My Love to Rose," Johnny Cash
Country Duo or Group with Vocals: "Long Time Gone," Dixie Chicks
Country Collaboration with Vocals: "Mendocino County Line," Willie Nelson with Lee Ann Womack
Country Instrumental: "Lil' Jack Slade," Dixie Chicks
Country Song: "Where Were You (When the World Stopped Turning)," Alan Jackson, songwriter (Alan Jackson)
Country Album: *Home,* Dixie Chicks
Bluegrass Album: *Lost in the Lonesome Pines,* Jim Lauderdale, Ralph Stanley & the Clinch Mountain Boys
New Age Album: *Acoustic Garden,* Eric Tingstad & Nancy Rumbel
Contemporary Jazz Album: *Speaking of Now,* Pat Metheny Group
Jazz Vocal Album: *Live in Paris,* Diana Krall
Jazz Instrumental, Solo: "My Ship," Herbie Hancock
Jazz Instrumental Album: *Directions in Music,* Herbie Hancock, Michael Brecker, and Roy Hargrove
Large Jazz Ensemble Album: *What Goes Around,* Dave Holland Big Band
Latin Jazz Album: *The Gathering,* Caribbean Jazz Project
Rock Gospel Album: *Come Together,* Third Day
Pop/Contemporary Gospel Album: *The Eleventh Hour,* Jars of Clay
Southern, Country, or Bluegrass Gospel Album: *We Called Him Mr. Gospel Music: The James Blackwood Tribute Album,* The Jordanaires, Larry Ford and the Light Crust Doughboys
Traditional Soul Gospel Album: *Higher Ground,* The Blind Boys of Alabama
Contemporary Soul Gospel Album: *Sidebars,* Eartha
Gospel Album by a Choir or Chorus: *Be Glad,* Carol Cymbala, choir director; The Brooklyn Tabernacle Choir
Latin Pop Album: *Caraluna,* Bacilos
Latin Rock/Alternative Album: *Revolución de Amor,* Maná
Tropical Latin Album: *El Arte del Sabor,* Bebo Valdés Trio with Israel López "Cachao" & Carlos "Patato" Valdés
Salsa Album: *La Negra Tiene Tumbao,* Celia Cruz
Merengue Album: *Latino,* Grupo Mania
Mexican/Mexican-American Album: *Lo Dijo El Corazón,* Joan Sebastian
Tejano Album: *Acuérdate,* Emilio Navaira
Traditional Blues Album: *A Christmas Celebration of Hope,* B. B. King
Contemporary Blues Album: *Don't Give Up On Me,* Solomon Burke
Traditional Folk Album: *Legacy,* Doc Watson, David Holt
Contemporary Folk Album: *This Side,* Nickel Creek
Native American Music Album: *Beneath the Raven Moon,* Mary Youngblood
Reggae Album: *Jamaican E.T,* Lee "Scratch" Perry
World Music Album: *Mundo,* Rubén Blades
Polka Album: *Top of the World,* Jimmy Sturr
Musical Album for Children: *Monsters, Inc.: Scream Factory Favorites,* Riders in the Sky
Spoken Word Album for Children: *There Was an Old Lady Who Swallowed a Fly,* Tom Chapin
Spoken Word Album: *A Song Flung Up to Heaven,* Maya Angelou
Spoken Comedy Album: *Robin Williams: Live 2002,* Robin Williams
Musical Show Album: *Hairspray,* Marc Shaiman, composer and lyricist; Scott Wittman, lyricist
Best Compilation Soundtrack Album for a Motion Picture, Television, or Other Visual Media: *Standing in the Shadows of Motown,* Various Artists
Best Score Soundtrack Album for a Motion Picture, Television, or Other Visual Media: *The Lord of the Rings: The Fellowship of the Ring,* Howard Shore, composer
Song Written for a Motion Picture, Television, or Other Visual Media: "If I Didn't Have You" (from *Monsters, Inc.*), Randy Newman, composer (Randy Newman)
Classical Album: *Vaughan Williams: A Sea Symphony (Symphony No. 1),* Robert Spano, conductor; Thomas C. Moore, producer
Orchestral Performance: *Mahler: Symphony No. 6,* Michael Tilson Thomas, conductor (San Francisco Symphony)
Opera Recording: *Wagner: Tannhäuser,* Daniel Barenboim, conductor
Choral Performance: *Vaughan Williams: A Sea Symphony (Symphony No. 1),* Robert Spano, conductor
Chamber Music: *Beethoven: String Quartets ("Razumovsky" Op. 59, 1–3; "Harp" Op. 74),* Takacs Quartet
Classical Vocal: *Bel Canto (Bellini, Donizetti, Rossini, Etc.),* Renee Fleming, soprano
Classical Crossover Album: *Previn Conducts Korngold (Sea Hawk; Captain Blood, Etc.),* Andre Previn, conductor; the London Symphony Orchestra
Music Video, Short Form: "Without Me," (Eminem), Joseph Kahn, director
Music Video, Long Form: *Westway to the World,* (The Clash), Don Letts, director

2002 Country Music Association Awards

Entertainer of the Year: Alan Jackson
Male Vocalist of the Year: Alan Jackson
Female Vocalist of the Year: Martina McBride
Horizon Award: Rascal Flatts
Vocal Group of the Year: Dixie Chicks
Vocal Duo of the Year: Brooks & Dunn
Single of the Year: "Where Were You (When the World Stopped Turning)," Alan Jackson
Album of the Year: *Drive,* Alan Jackson
Song of the Year: "Where Were You (When the World Stopped Turning)," Alan Jackson, songwriter
Vocal Event of the Year: "Mendocino County Line," Willie Nelson with Lee Ann Womack
Musician of the Year: Jerry Douglas—dobro
Music Video of the Year: "I'm Gonna Miss Her (The Fishin' Song)," Brad Paisley; Peter Zavadil, director

2002 National Book Awards

Fiction: *Three Junes,* Julia Glass (Pantheon Books)
Nonfiction: *Master of the Senate: The Years of Lyndon Johnson,* Robert A. Caro (Alfred A. Knopf)
Poetry: *In the Next Galaxy,* Ruth Stone (Copper Canyon Press)
Young People's Literature: *The House of the Scorpion,* Nancy Farmer (Atheneum)
Medal for Distinguished Contribution to American Literature: Philip Roth

2002 National Book Critics Circle Awards

Fiction: *Atonement,* Ian McEwan (Nan A. Talese/ Doubleday)
General Nonfiction: *"A Problem from Hell:" America and the Age of Genocide,* Samantha Power (New Republic/Basic Books)
Biography or Autobiography: *Charles Darwin: The Power of Place, Vol. II,* Janet Browne (Alfred A. Knopf)
Poetry: *Early Occult Memory Systems of the Lower Midwest,* B. H. Fairchild (W. W. Norton & Company)
Criticism: *Tests of Time,* William H. Gass (Alfred A. Knopf)
Ivan Sandrof Lifetime Achievement Award: Richard Howard
Nona Balakian Citation for Excellence in Reviewing: Maureen N. McLane

PEN/Faulkner Award

The PEN/Faulkner award is the largest annual juried prize for fiction in the United States. The winner receives $15,000.

1981 Walter Abish, *How German Is It?*
1982 David Bradley, *The Chaneysville Incident*
1983 Toby Olson, *Seaview*
1984 John Edgar Wideman, *Sent for You Yesterday*
1985 Tobias Wolff, *The Barracks Thief*
1986 Peter Taylor, *The Old Forest*
1987 Richard Wiley, *Soldiers in Hiding*
1988 T. Coraghessan Boyle, *World's End*
1989 James Salter, *Dusk*
1990 E. L. Doctorow, *Billy Bathgate*
1991 John Edgar Wideman, *Philadelphia Fire*
1992 Don Delillo, *Mao II*
1993 E. Annie Proulx, *Postcards*
1994 Philip Roth, *Operation Shylock*
1995 David Guterson, *Snow Falling on Cedars*
1996 Richard Ford, *Independence Day*
1997 Gina Berriault, *Women in Their Beds*
1998 Rafi Zabor, *The Bear Comes Home*
1999 Michael Cunningham, *The Hours*
2000 Ha Jin, *Waiting*
2001 Philip Roth, *The Human Stain*
2002 Ann Patchett, *Bel Canto*
2003 Sabina Murray, *The Caprices*

Man Booker Prize

Britain's most prestigious literary award, formerly called the "Booker Prize," honors the best full-length novel written in English by a citizen of a current or former British Commonwealth country.

1969 *Something to Answer For,* P. H. Newby
1970 *The Elected Member,* Bernice Rubens
1971 *In a Free State,* V. S. Naipaul
1972 *G.: A Novel,* John Berger
1973 *The Siege of Krishnapur,* J. G. Farrell
1974 (tie) *The Conservationist,* Nadine Gordimer
Holiday, Stanley Middleton
1975 *Heat and Dust,* Ruth Prawer Jhabvala
1976 *Saville,* David Storey
1977 *Staying On,* Paul Scott
1978 *The Sea, The Sea,* Iris Murdoch
1979 *Offshore,* Penelope Fitzgerald
1980 *Rites of Passage,* William Golding
1981 *Midnight's Children,* Salman Rushdie
1982 *Schindler's List,* Thomas Keneally
1983 *Life & Times of Michael K,* J. M. Coetzee
1984 *Hotel du Lac,* Anita Brookner
1985 *The Bone People,* Keri Hulme
1986 *The Old Devils,* Kingsley Amis
1987 *Moon Tiger,* Penelope Lively
1988 *Oscar and Lucinda,* Peter Carey
1989 *The Remains of the Day,* Kazuo Ishiguro
1990 *Possession: A Romance,* A. S. Byatt
1991 *The Famished Road,* Ben Okri
1992 (tie) *The English Patient,* Michael Ondaatje
Sacred Hunger, Barry Unsworth
1993 *Paddy Clarke, Ha Ha Ha,* Roddy Doyle
1994 *How Late It Was, How Late,* James Kelman
1995 *The Ghost Road,* Pat Barker
1996 *Last Orders,* Graham Swift
1997 *The God of Small Things,* Arundhati Roy
1998 *Amsterdam,* Ian McEwan
1999 *Disgrace,* J. M. Coetzee
2000 *The Blind Assassin,* Margaret Atwood
2001 *True History of the Kelly Gang,* Peter Carey
2002 *Life of Pi,* Yann Martel

Truman Capote Award for Literary Criticism

The award is administered for the Truman Capote estate by the University of Iowa Writers' Workshop. The $50,000 award is the largest cash prize for literary criticism in the English language.

1996 Helen Vendler, *The Given and the Made*
1997 John Felstiner, *Paul Celan: Poet, Survivor, Jew*
1998 John Kerrigan, *Revenge Tragedy*
1999 Charles Rosen, *Romantic Poets, Critics, and Other Madmen*
2000 Elaine Scarry, *Dreaming by the Book* and Philip Fisher, *Still the New World*
2001 Malcolm Bowie, *Proust Among the Stars*
2002 Declan Kiberd, *Irish Classics*
2003 Seamus Heaney, *Finders Keepers: Selected Prose 1971–2001*

Newbery Medal

The Newbery Medal is awarded annually by the American Library Association for the most distinguished contribution to American literature for children.

2003 Newbery Medal and Honor Books

Newbery Medal for Best Book: *Crispin: The Cross of Lead,* Avi (Hyperion)

Newbery Honor Books: *The House of the Scorpion,* Nancy Farmer (Atheneum); *Pictures of Hollis Woods,* Patricia Reilly Giff (Random House/Wendy Lamb Books); *Hoot,* Carl Hiassen (Knopf); *A Corner of the Universe,* Anne M. Martin (Scholastic); *Surviving the Applewhites,* Stephanie S. Tolan (HarperCollins)

1922–2002

1922 *The Story of Mankind,* Hendrick Willem Van Loon
1923 *The Voyages of Dr. Doolittle,* Hugh A. Lofting
1924 *The Dark Frigate,* Charles Boardman Hawes
1925 *Tales from Silver Lands,* Charles Joseph Finger
1926 *Shen of the Sea,* Arthur Bowie Chrisman
1927 *Smoky, the Cow Horse,* Will James
1928 *Gay-Neck, the Story of a Pigeon,* Dhan Gopal Mukerji
1929 *The Trumpeter of Krakow,* Eric P. Kelly
1930 *Hitty, Her First Hundred Years,* Rachel Field
1931 *The Cat Who Went to Heaven,* Elizabeth Jane Coatsworth
1932 *Waterless Mountain,* Laura Adams Armer
1933 *Young Fu of the Upper Yangtze,* Elizabeth Foreman Lewis
1934 *Invincible Louisa,* Cornelia Meigs
1935 *Dobry,* Monica Shannon
1936 *Caddie Woodlawn,* Carol Ryrie Brink
1937 *Roller Skates,* Ruth Sawyer
1938 *The White Stag,* Kate Seredy
1939 *Thimble Summer,* Elizabeth Enright
1940 *Daniel Boone,* James Henry Daugherty
1941 *Call It Courage,* Armstrong Sperry
1942 *The Matchlock Gun,* Walter Dumax Edmonds
1943 *Adam of the Road,* Elizabeth Janet Gray
1944 *Johnny Tremain,* Esther Forbes
1945 *Rabbit Hill,* Robert Lawson
1946 *Strawberry Girl,* Lois Lenski
1947 *Miss Hickory,* Carolyn Sherwin Bailey
1948 *The Twenty-One Balloons,* William Pène du Bois
1949 *King of the Wind,* Marguerite Henry
1950 *The Door in the Wall,* Marguerite de Angeli
1951 *Amos Fortune, Free Man,* Elizabeth Yates
1952 *Ginger Pye,* Eleanor Estes
1953 *Secret of the Andes,* Ann Nolan Clark
1954 *. . . And Now Miguel,* Joseph Krumgold
1955 *The Wheel on the School,* Meindert DeJong
1956 *Carry On, Mr. Bowditch,* Jean Lee Latham
1957 *Miracles on Maple Hill,* Virginia Eggertsen Sorensen
1958 *Rifles for Watie,* Harold Keith
1959 *The Witch of Blackbird Pond,* Elizabeth George Speare
1960 *Onion John,* Joseph Krumgold
1961 *Island of the Blue Dolphins,* Scott O'Dell
1962 *The Bronze Bow,* Elizabeth George Speare
1963 *A Wrinkle in Time,* Madeleine L'Engle
1964 *It's Like This, Cat,* Emily Cheney Neville
1965 *Shadow of a Bull,* Maia Wojciechowska
1966 *I, Juan de Pareja,* Elizabeth Borton de Treviño
1967 *Up a Road Slowly,* Irene Hunt
1968 *From the Mixed-Up Files of Mrs. Basil E. Frankweiler,* E. L. Konigsburg
1969 *The High King,* Lloyd Alexander
1970 *Sounder,* William H. Armstrong
1971 *Summer of the Swans,* Betsy Byars
1972 *Mrs. Frisby and the Rats of NIMH,* Robert C. O'Brien
1973 *Julie of the Wolves,* Jean Craighead George
1974 *The Slave Dancer,* Paula Fox
1975 *M. C. Higgins, the Great,* Virginia Hamilton
1976 *The Grey King,* Susan Cooper
1977 *Roll of Thunder, Hear My Cry,* Mildred D. Taylor
1978 *Bridge to Terabithia,* Katherine Paterson
1979 *The Westing Game,* Ellen Raskin
1980 *A Gathering of Days: A New England Girl's Journal, 1830–32,* Joan W. Blos
1981 *Jacob Have I Loved,* Katherine Paterson
1982 *A Visit to William Blake's Inn: Poems for Innocent and Experienced Travelers,* Nancy Willard
1983 *Dicey's Song,* Cynthia Voigt
1984 *Dear Mr. Henshaw,* Beverly Cleary
1985 *The Hero and the Crown,* Robin McKinley
1986 *Sarah, Plain and Tall,* Patricia MacLachlan
1987 *The Whipping Boy,* Sid Fleischman
1988 *Lincoln: A Photobiography,* Russell Freedman
1989 *Joyful Noise: Poems for Two Voices,* Paul Fleischman
1990 *Number the Stars,* Lois Lowry
1991 *Maniac Magee: a Novel,* Jerry Spinelli
1992 *Shiloh,* Phyllis Reynolds Naylor
1993 *Missing May,* Cynthia Rylant
1994 *The Giver,* Lois Lowry
1995 *Walk Two Moons,* Sharon Creech
1996 *The Midwife's Apprentice,* Karen Cushman
1997 *The View from Saturday,* E. L. Konigsburg
1998 *Out of the Dust,* Karen Hesse
1999 *Holes,* Louis Sachar
2000 *Bud, Not Buddy,* Christopher Paul Curtis
2001 *A Year Down Yonder,* Richard Peck
2002 *A Single Shard,* Linda Sue Park

Caldecott Medal

The Caldecott Medal is awarded annually by the American Library Association for the most distinguished American picture book for children.

2003 Caldecott Medal and Honor Books

Caldecott Medal for Best Picture Book: *My Friend Rabbit,* illustrated and written by Eric Rohmann (Roaring Brook Press/Millbrook Press)

Caldecott Honor Books: *The Spider and the Fly,* illustrated by Tony DiTerlizzi; written by Mary Howitt (Simon & Schuster); *Hondo & Fabian,* illustrated and written by Peter McCarty (Henry Holt); *Noah's Ark,* illustrated and written by Jerry Pinkney (Sea Star/North-South Books)

1938–2002

1938 *Animals of the Bible, a Picture Book,* text selected by Helen Dean Fish, illustrated by Dorothy P. Lathrop
1939 *Mei Li,* written and illustrated by Thomas Handforth
1940 *Abraham Lincoln,* written and illustrated by Ingri and Edgar Parin D'Aulaire
1941 *They Were Strong and Good,* written and illustrated by Robert Lawson
1942 *Make Way for Ducklings,* written and illustrated by Robert McCloskey
1943 *The Little House,* written and illustrated by Virginia Lee Burton
1944 *Many Moons,* written by James Thurber, illustrated by Louis Slobodkin
1945 *Prayer for a Child,* written by Elizabeth Orton Jones
1946 *The Rooster Crows,* written and illustrated by Maud and Miska Petersham
1947 *The Little Island,* written by Golden MacDonald, illustrated by Leonard Weisgard
1948 *White Snow, Bright Snow,* written by Alvin Tresselt, illustrated by Roger Duvoisin
1949 *The Big Snow,* written and illustrated by Berta and Elmer Hader
1950 *Song of the Swallows,* written and illustrated by Leo Politi
1951 *The Egg Tree,* written and illustrated by Katherine Milhous
1952 *Finders Keepers,* written by William Lipkind, illustrated by Nicolas Mordivinoff
1953 *The Biggest Bear,* written and illustrated by Lynd Ward
1954 *Madeline's Rescue,* written and illustrated by Ludwig Bemelmans
1955 *Cinderella, or, The Little Glass Slipper,* translated and illustrated by Marcia Brown
1956 *Frog Went A-Courtin',* retold by John Langstaff, illustrated by Feodor Rojankovsky
1957 *A Tree Is Nice,* written by Janice May Udry, illustrated by Marc Simont
1958 *Time of Wonder,* written and illustrated by Robert McCloskey
1959 *Chanticleer and the Fox,* adapted and illustrated by Barbara Cooney
1960 *Nine Days to Christmas,* written by Marie Hall Ets and Aurora Labastida, illustrated by Marie Hall Ets
1961 *Baboushka and the Three Kings,* written by Ruth Robbins, illustrated by Nicolas Sidjakov
1962 *Once a Mouse,* retold and illustrated by Marcia Brown
1963 *The Snowy Day,* written and illustrated by Ezra Jack Keats
1964 *Where the Wild Things Are,* written and illustrated by Maurice Sendak
1965 *May I Bring a Friend?,* written by Beatrice Schenk de Regniers, illustrated by Beni Montresor
1966 *Always Room for One More,* written by Sorche Nic Leodhas, illustrated by Nonny Hogrogian
1967 *Sam, Bangs and Moonshine,* written and illustrated by Evaline Ness
1968 *Drummer Hoff,* written by Barbara Emberley, illustrated by Ed Emberley
1969 *The Fool of the World and the Flying Ship,* retold by Arthur Ransome, illustrated by Uri Shulevitz
1970 *Sylvester and the Magic Pebble,* written and illustrated by William Steig
1971 *A Story, A Story: An African Tale,* retold and illustrated by Gail E. Haley
1972 *One Fine Day,* written and illustrated by Nonny Hogrogian
1973 *The Funny Little Woman,* retold by Arlene Mosel, illustrated by Blair Lent
1974 *Duffy and the Devil,* retold by Harve Zemach, illustrated by Margot Zemach
1975 *Arrow to the Sun: A Pueblo Indian Tale,* adapted and illustrated by Gerald H. McDermott
1976 *Why Mosquitos Buzz in People's Ears (An African Tale),* retold by Verna Aardema, illustrated by Leo and Diane Dillon
1977 *Ashanti to Zulu: African Traditions,* written by Margaret Musgrove, illustrated by Leo and Diane Dillon
1978 *Noah's Ark,* written by Jacob Revius, illustrated by Peter Spier
1979 *The Girl Who Loved Wild Horses,* written and illustrated by Paul Goble
1980 *Ox-Cart Man,* written by Donald Hall, illustrated by Barbara Cooney
1981 *Fables,* written and illustrated by Arnold Lobel
1982 *Jumanji,* written and illustrated by Chris Van Allsburg
1983 *Shadow,* translated and illustrated by Marcia Brown
1984 *The Glorious Flight: Across the Channel with Louis Blériot,* written and illustrated by Alice and Martin Provensen
1985 *St. George and the Dragon,* retold by Margaret Hodges, illustrated by Trina Schart Hyman
1986 *The Polar Express,* written and illustrated by Chris Van Allsburg
1987 *Hey, Al,* written by Arthur Yorinks, illustrated by Richard Egielski
1988 *Owl Moon,* written by Jane Yolen, illustrated by John Schoenherr
1989 *Song and Dance Man,* written by Karen Ackerman, illustrated by Stephen Gammell
1990 *Lon Po Po: A Red-Riding Hood Story from China,* by Ed Young
1991 *Black & White,* written and illustrated by David Macaulay
1992 *Tuesday,* written and illustrated by David Wiesner
1993 *Mirette on the High Wire,* written and illustrated by Emily Arnold McCully

1994 *Grandfather's Journey,* written and illustrated by Allen Say
1995 *Smoky Night,* written by Eve Bunting, illustrated by David Diaz
1996 *Officer Buckle and Gloria,* written and illustrated by Peggy Rathmann
1997 *Golem,* written and illustrated by David Wisniewski
1998 *Rapunzel,* illustrated and retold by Paul O. Zelinsky
1999 *Snowflake Bentley,* written by Jacqueline Briggs Martin, illustrated by Mary Azarian
2000 *Joseph Had a Little Overcoat,* illustrated by Simms Taback
2001 *So You Want to Be President?,* by Judith St. George, illustrated by David Small
2002 *The Three Little Pigs,* written and illustrated by David Wiesner

Other American Library Association Awards for Children's Books, 2003

Coretta Scott King Award, honoring black authors and illustrators: (author): *Bronx Masquerade,* Nikki Grimes (Dial Books); **(illustrator):** *Talkin' About Bessie: The Story of Aviator Elizabeth Coleman,* E. B. Lewis (Orchard Books)

Michael L. Printz Award for excellence in young adult literature: *Postcards from No Man's Land,* Aidan Chambers (Dutton Books/Penguin Putnam)

Robert F. Sibert Award for informational book: *The Life and Death of Adolf Hitler,* James Cross Giblin (Clarion)

Margaret A. Edwards Award for lifetime contribution in writing for young adults: Nancy Garden

Mildred L. Batchelder Award, for best book originally published in a foreign language in a foreign country: *The Thief Lord,* written by Cornelia Funke in German and translated by Oliver Latsch (The Chicken House)

May Hill Arbuthnot Honor Lecture Award: Ursula K. Le Guin

Laura Ingalls Wilder Award for lasting contributions to children's literature: Eric Carle

Andrew Carnegie Medal, for best children's video: *So You Want to Be President?,* based on the book by Judith S. George and illustrated by David Small, produced by Paul R. Gagne and Melissa Reilly of Weston Woods Studios

2003 National Magazine Awards

General Excellence:
Foreign Policy (circulation less than 100,000)
Architectural Record (circulation 100,000 to 250,000)
Texas Monthly (circulation 250,000 to 500,000)
The Atlantic Monthly (circulation 500,000 to 1,000,000)
ESPN The Magazine (circulation 1,000,000 to 2,000,000)
Parenting (circulation more than 2,000,000)
Personal Service: *Outside*
Leisure Interests: *National Geographic Adventure*
Reporting: *The New Yorker*
Public Interest: *The Atlantic Monthly*
Feature Writing: *Harper's Magazine*
Columns and Commentary: *The Nation*
Essays: *The American Scholar*
Reviews and Criticism: *Vanity Fair*
Profiles: *Sports Illustrated*
Single-Topic Issue: *Scientific American*
Design: *Details*
Photography: *Condé Nast Traveler*
Fiction: *The New Yorker*
General Excellence Online: *Slate*

Bollingen Prize in Poetry

The Bollingen Prize in Poetry is administered by the Yale University Library.

1949 Ezra Pound
1950 Wallace Stevens
1951 John Crowe Ransom
1952 Marianne Moore
1953 Archibald MacLeish and William Carlos Williams
1954 W. H. Auden
1955 Léonie Adams and Louise Bogan
1956 Conrad Aiken
1957 Allen Tate
1958 e. e. cummings
1959 Theodore Roethke
1960 Delmore Schwartz
1961 Yvor Winters
1962 John Hall Wheelock and Richard Eberhart
1963 Robert Frost
1965 Horace Gregory
1967 Robert Penn Warren
1969 John Berryman and Karl Shapiro
1971 Richard Wilbur and Mona Van Duyn
1973 James Merrill
1975 Archie Randolph Ammons
1977 David Ignatow
1979 W. S. Merwin
1981 Howard Nemerov and May Swenson
1983 Anthony Hecht and John Hollander
1985 John Ashbery and Fred Chappell
1987 Stanley Kunitz
1989 Edgar Bowers
1991 Laura Riding Jackson and Donald Justice
1993 Mark Strand
1995 Kenneth Koch
1997 Gary Snyder
1999 Robert Creeley
2001 Louise Glück
2003 Adrienne Rich

Kingsley Tufts Poetry Prize

1993 Susan Mitchell, *Rapture*
1994 Yusef Komunyakaa, *Neon Vernacular*
1995 Thomas Lux, *Split Horizon*
1996 Deborah Digges, *Rough Music*
1997 Campbell McGrath, *Spring Comes to Chicago*
1998 John Koethe, *Falling Water*
1999 B. H. Fairchild, *The Art of the Lathe*
2000 Robert Wrigley, *Reign of Snakes: Poems*
2001 Alan Shapiro, *The Dead Alive and Busy*
2002 Carl Phillips, *The Tether*
2003 Linda Gregerson, *Waterborne*

2003 NAACP Image Awards

MOTION PICTURE

Outstanding Motion Picture: *Antwone Fisher*
Outstanding Actress in a Motion Picture: Angela Bassett, *Sunshine State*
Outstanding Actor in a Motion Picture: Denzel Washington, *John Q*
Outstanding Supporting Actress in a Motion Picture: Halle Berry, *Die Another Day*
Outstanding Supporting Actor in a Motion Picture: Denzel Washington, *Antwone Fisher*

TELEVISION

Outstanding Comedy Series: *The Bernie Mac Show*
Outstanding Actress in a Comedy Series: Tisha Campbell-Martin, *My Wife and Kids*
Outstanding Actor in a Comedy Series: Bernie Mac, *The Bernie Mac Show*
Outstanding Supporting Actress in a Comedy Series: Terri J. Vaughn, *The Steve Harvey Show*
Outstanding Supporting Actor in a Comedy Series: Cedric the Entertainer, *The Proud Family*
Outstanding Drama Series: *Soul Food*
Outstanding Actress in a Drama Series: Vanessa Williams, *Soul Food*
Outstanding Actor in a Drama Series: Michael Beach, *Third Watch*
Outstanding Supporting Actress in a Drama Series: Loretta Devine, *Boston Public*
Outstanding Supporting Actor in a Drama Series: Gary Dourdan, *CSI: Crime Scene Investigation*
Outstanding Television Movie, Miniseries, or Dramatic Special: *The Rosa Parks Story*
Outstanding Actress in a Television Movie, Miniseries, or Dramatic Special: Angela Bassett, *The Rosa Parks Story*
Outstanding Actor in a Television Movie, Miniseries, or Dramatic Special: Charles S. Dutton, *10,000 Black Men Named George*
Outstanding Actress in a Daytime Drama Series: Victoria Rowell, *The Young & the Restless*
Outstanding Actor in a Daytime Drama Series: Kristoff St. John, *The Young & the Restless*
Outstanding Variety Series/Special: *BET's 8th Annual Walk of Fame: A Tribute to Stevie Wonder*
Outstanding News, Talk, or Information Series or Special: *BET Tonight with Ed Gordon:* "R. Kelly (Part 1)"
Outstanding Performance in a Youth or Children's Series/Special: Levar Burton, *Reading Rainbow*

RECORDING

Outstanding New Artist: Ashanti
Outstanding Female Artist: India.Arie
Outstanding Male Artist: LL Cool J
Outstanding Duo or Group: India.Arie & Stevie Wonder
Outstanding Jazz Artist: Natalie Cole
Outstanding Gospel Artist: Kirk Franklin
Outstanding Music Video: India.Arie, "Little Things"
Outstanding Song: Kirk Franklin, "Brighter Day"
Outstanding Album: Kirk Franklin, *The Rebirth of Kirk Franklin*

LITERARY WORK

Outstanding Literary Work, Fiction: *Quilting the Black-Eyed Pea,* Nikki Giovanni
Outstanding Literary Work, Nonfiction: *Keeping the Faith,* Tavis Smiley
Outstanding Literary Work, Children's: *Nelson Mandela's Favorite African Folktales,* Nelson Mandela

The Spingarn Medal

The Spingarn Medal is awarded annually by the National Association for the Advancement of Colored People for outstanding achievement by a black American.

1915 Ernest E. Just
1916 Charles Young
1917 Harry T. Burleigh
1918 William Stanley Braithwaite
1919 Archibald H. Grimke
1920 W. E. B. Du Bois
1921 Charles S. Gilpin
1922 Mary B. Talbert
1923 George Washington Carver
1924 Roland Hayes
1925 James Weldon Johnson
1926 Carter G. Woodson
1927 Anthony Overton
1928 Charles W. Chesnutt
1929 Mordecai Wyatt Johnson
1930 Henry A. Hunt
1931 Richard Berry Harrison
1932 Robert Russa Moton
1933 Max Yergan
1934 William T. B. Williams
1935 Mary McLeod Bethune
1936 John Hope
1937 Walter White
1938 No award
1939 Marian Anderson
1940 Louis T. Wright
1941 Richard Wright
1942 A. Philip Randolph
1943 William H. Hastie
1944 Charles Drew
1945 Paul Robeson
1946 Thurgood Marshall
1947 Percy Julian
1948 Channing H. Tobias
1949 Ralph J. Bunche
1950 Charles Hamilton Houston
1951 Mabel Keaton Staupers
1952 Harry T. Moore
1953 Paul R. Williams
1954 Theodore K. Lawless
1955 Carl Murphy
1956 Jackie Robinson
1957 Martin Luther King, Jr.
1958 Daisy Bates and the Little Rock Nine
1959 Edward Kennedy (Duke) Ellington
1960 Langston Hughes
1961 Kenneth B. Clark
1962 Robert C. Weaver
1963 Medgar Evers
1964 Roy Wilkins
1965 Leontyne Price
1966 John H. Johnson
1967 Edward W. Brooke III
1968 Sammy Davis, Jr.
1969 Clarence M. Mitchell, Jr.
1970 Jacob Lawrence
1971 Leon Howard Sullivan
1972 Gordon Parks
1973 Wilson C. Riles
1974 Damon Keith
1975 Hank Aaron
1976 Alvin Ailey
1977 Alex Haley
1978 Andrew Young
1979 Rosa L. Parks
1980 Rayford W. Logan
1981 Coleman Young
1982 Benjamin E. Mays
1983 Lena Horne
1984 Tom Bradley
1985 Bill Cosby
1986 Benjamin L. Hooks
1987 Percy Ellis Sutton
1988 Frederick Douglass Patterson
1989 Jesse Jackson
1990 L. Douglas Wilder
1991 Colin T. Powell
1992 Barbara Jordan
1993 Dorothy Irene Height
1994 Maya Angelou
1995 John Hope Franklin
1996 A. Leon Higginbotham, Jr.
1997 Carl Rowan
1998 Myrlie Evers-Williams
1999 Earl G. Graves, Sr.
2000 Oprah Winfrey
2001 Vernon E. Jordan, Jr.
2002 John Lewis
2003 Constance Baker Motley

2003 Major Emmy Awards

Drama Series: *The West Wing* (NBC)
Actress: Edie Falco, *The Sopranos*
Actor: James Gandolfini, *The Sopranos*
Supporting Actress: Tyne Daly, *Judging Amy*
Supporting Actor: Joe Pantoliano, *The Sopranos*
Guest Actor: Charles S. Dutton, *Without a Trace*
Guest Actress: Alfre Woodard, *The Practice*
Directing: Christopher Misiano, *The West Wing:* "25"
Writing: David Chase, Robin Green, and Mitchell Burgess, *The Sopranos:* "Whitecaps"
Comedy Series: *Everybody Loves Raymond* (CBS)
Actress: Debra Messing, *Will & Grace*
Actor: Tony Shalhoub, *Monk*
Supporting Actress: Doris Roberts, *Everybody Loves Raymond*
Supporting Actor: Brad Garrett, *Everybody Loves Raymond*
Guest Actress: Christina Applegate, *Friends*
Guest Actor: Gene Wilder, *Will & Grace*
Directing: Robert B. Weide, *Curb Your Enthusiasm:* "Krazee-Eyez Killa"
Writing: Mike Royce, *Everybody Loves Raymond:* "Counseling"
Variety, Music, or Comedy Series: *The Daily Show with Jon Stewart* (Comedy Central)
Variety, Music, or Comedy Special: *Cher: The Farewell Tour* (NBC)
Individual Performance, Variety, or Music Program: Wayne Brady, *Whose Line Is It Anyway?*
Directing in a Variety, Music, or Comedy Program: Glenn Weiss, *The 56th Annual Tony Awards*
Writing in a Variety, Music, or Comedy Program: *The Daily Show with Jon Stewart*
Miniseries or Special: *Steven Spielberg Presents Taken* (Sci Fi)
Actress: Maggie Smith, *My House in Umbria*
Actor: William H. Macy, *Door to Door*
Supporting Actress: Gena Rowlands, *Hysterical Blindness*
Supporting Actor: Ben Gazzara, *Hysterical Blindness*
Directing: Steven Schachter, *Door to Door*
Writing: William H. Macy and Steven Schachter, *Door to Door*
Made-for-Television Movie: *Door to Door* (TNT)
Outstanding Nonfiction Series (traditional): *American Masters* (PBS)
Outstanding Nonfiction Special (traditional): Benjamin Franklin (PBS)
Outstanding Nonfiction Program (reality): *The Amazing Race* (CBS)
Outstanding Nonfiction Program (alternative): *Cirque Du Soleil Fire Within* (Bravo)
Outstanding Children's Program: *Through a Child's Eyes: September 11, 2001* (HBO)
Outstanding Animated Program (one hour or less): *The Simpsons:* "Three Gays of the Condo" (Fox)

2002–2003 Daytime Emmy Awards

Outstanding Drama Series: *As the World Turns* (CBS)
Lead Actor in a Drama Series: Maurice Benard, *General Hospital* (ABC)
Lead Actress in a Drama Series: Susan Flannery, *The Bold and the Beautiful* (CBS)
Supporting Actor in a Drama Series: Benjamin Hendrickson, *As the World Turns* (CBS)
Supporting Actress in a Drama Series: Vanessa Marcil, *General Hospital* (ABC)
Younger Actor in a Drama Series: Jordi Vilasuso, *Guiding Light* (CBS)
Younger Actress in a Drama Series: Jennifer Finnigan, *The Bold and the Beautiful* (CBS)
Outstanding Pre-School Children's Series: *Sesame Street* (PBS)
Outstanding Children's Special: *Bang Bang You're Dead* (Showtime)
Outstanding Children's Animated Program: *Rugrats* (Nickelodeon)
Outstanding Special Class Children's Animated Program: *Disney's Teacher's Pet* (ABC)
Performer in a Children's Series: Shia LaBeouf, *Even Stevens* (Disney)
Performer in a Children's Special: Ben Foster, *Bang Bang You're Dead* (Showtime)
Performer in an Animated Program: Gregory Hines, *Little Bill* (Nickelodeon)
Outstanding Children's Series: *Reading Rainbow* (PBS)
Outstanding Special Class Series: *A Baby Story* (TLC)
Outstanding Special Class Special: *Hollywood Rocks the Movies: The 1970s with David Bowie* (AMC)
Outstanding Game/Audience Participation Show: *Jeopardy!* (syndicated)
Outstanding Game-Show Host: Alex Trebek, *Jeopardy!* (syndicated)
Outstanding Talk Show (tie): *The View* (ABC) and *The Wayne Brady Show* (syndicated)
Outstanding Talk-Show Host: Wayne Brady, *The Wayne Brady Show* (syndicated)
Outstanding Service Show: *Martha Stewart Living* (syndicated)
Outstanding Service-Show Host: Martha Stewart, *Martha Stewart Living* (syndicated)

2003 Alfred I. du Pont–Columbia University Awards in Television and Radio

GOLD BATON
Frontline (PBS), produced at WGBH, Boston, for a series about terrorism by Islamic militants
SILVER BATONS
ABC News for *Nightline:* "Heart of Darkness"
ABC News Television and Radio for coverage of 9/11 and *Answering Children's Questions*
CNN en Español and Jorge Gestoso for *La Doble Desaparecida*
Court TV and Lumiere Productions for *Ghosts of Attica*
HBO for *In Memoriam: New York City 9/11/01*
KPBS, San Diego, and Lee Harvey, for *Culture of Hate: Who Are We?*
National Public Radio for coverage of 9/11 and the war in Afghanistan
NBC News and Martin Fletcher for coverage of the Israeli-Palestinian conflict
P.O.V. (PBS) and Tasha Oldham for *The Smith Family*
American Experience (PBS), Steeplechase Films, Sierra Club Productions, and WGBH for *Ansel Adams—A Documentary Film*
WBUR-FM, Boston, for *Surviving Torture: Inside Out*
WCVB-TV, Boston, for *Chronicle: Beyond the Big Dig*
WFAA-TV, Dallas, Brett Shipp and Mark Smith for *Fake Drugs, Real Lives*

2002 George Foster Peabody Awards for Broadcasting

Terror on Tape: CNN Productions (Atlanta)
Bringing Down A Dictator: York Zimmerman, Inc., presented on PBS
48 Hours: "9/11," CBS, New York
The Sonic Memorial Project: Lost and Found Sound from the Kitchen Sisters Productions, presented on NPR, and SonicMemorial.org.
Nightline: "The Survivors," ABC News, New York
Frontline: "Shattered Dreams of Peace: The Road from Oslo," PBS, SET Productions, C-Films Productions for WGBH/Boston, in association with FRANCE 2, ABU DHABI Television, and Tel Ad Israel
File on 4: "Export Controls," BBC Radio 4
The Hepatitis C Epidemic: A 15-Year Government Cover-Up: Fuji Television Network, Inc., Japan
Sounding the Alarm: WISN-TV, Milwaukee, Wis.
Fake Drugs, Real Lives: WFAA-TV, Dallas, Tex.
DNA Protects Men of Dishonor: KPRC-TV, Houston, Tex.
Nightline: "Heart of Darkness," ABC News, New York
How High Is the Mountain: Public Television Service Foundation, Taiwan
The Yiddish Radio Project: NPR and Sound Portrait Productions
Stories of Home: WBEZ/Chicago Public Radio
EGG The Arts Show: Thirteen/WNET (New York)
The Complete Angler: ESPN and Lake Champlain Productions
Monkey Trial: Nebraska ETV and The American Experience, WGBH (Boston)
The Rise and Fall of Jim Crow: Thirteen/WNET (New York)
Bang Bang You're Dead: Showtime from Viacom Productions and A Jersey Guys Production, Inc.
Almost Strangers: BBC America with Talkback Productions, presented on BBC
Stage on Screen: "Beckett on Film," Thirteen/WNET (New York)
Russell Simmons Presents Def Poetry Jam: HBO and Simmons/Lathan TV
The Interrogation of Michael Crowe: Court TV from JB Media and Hearst Entertainment
Boomtown: NBC/NBC Studios Inc. in association with DreamWorks Television
ExxonMobil Masterpiece Theatre: "Othello," WGBH and London Weekend Television
ExxonMobil Masterpiece Theatre's American Collection: "Almost A Woman," WGBH and ALT Films
The Gathering Storm: HBO and Scott Free Productions
Boston Public: "Chapter 37," FOX from David E. Kelley Productions and 20th Century Fox Television Studios
Six Feet Under: HBO from Janollari Studios and Actual Size, Inc. in association with HBO Original Programming
Door to Door: TNT from Rosemont Productions International in association with Angel/Brown Productions

2003 Webby Awards

Activism: ActForChange: www.actforchange.com
Best Practices: Movable Type: www.movabletype.org
Broadband: CBC Radio 3: www.cbcradio3.com
Commerce: Amazon.com: www.amazon.com
Community: Meetup: www.meetup.com
Education: NASA Earth Observatory: earthobservatory.nasa.gov
Fashion: SHOWstudio: www.showstudio.com
Film: indieWIRE www.indiewire.com
Finance: PayPal: www.paypal.com
Games: Orisinal: www.orisinal.com
Government and Law: NASA: www.nasa.gov
Health: Planned Parenthood Golden Gate: www.ppgg.org
Humor: get your war on: www.mnftiu.cc /mnftiu.cc/war.html
Living: Do-It-Yourself Network: www.diynet.com
Music: Flaming Lips: www.flaminglips.com
Net Art: Listening Post: www.earstudio.com /projects/listeningPost.html
News: Google News: news.google.com
Personal Website: NobodyHere: www.nobodyhere.com
Politics: MoveOn.org: www.moveon.org
Print and Zines: AlterNet: www.alternet.org
Radio: Epitonic Radio: http://epitonic.com/radio.jsp
Science: exploreMarsnow: www.exploremarsnow.org
Services: eBay: www.ebay.com
Spirituality: Pluralism Project: www.pluralism.org
Sports: ESPN.com: www.espn.com
Technical Achievement: Apache Web Server: www.apache.org
Travel: Lonely Planet Online: www.lonelyplanet.com
TV: Nick.Com: www.nick.com
Weird: rathergood.com: www.rathergood.com
Youth: 3d&i: www.3d-i.org

Enrico Fermi Award

The $100,000 award is given in recognition of scientific and technical achievement in atomic energy. Awarded by the president, it is the U.S. government's oldest science and technology award.

1954 Enrico Fermi
1956 John von Neumann
1957 Ernest O. Lawrence
1958 Eugene P. Wigner
1959 Glenn T. Seaborg
1961 Hans A. Bethe
1962 Edward Teller
1963 J. Robert Oppenheimer
1964 Hyman G. Rickover
1966 Otto Hahn, Lise Meitner, and Fritz Strassman
1968 John A. Wheeler
1969 Walter H. Zinn
1970 Norris E. Bradbury
1971 Shields Warren and Stafford L. Warren
1972 Manson Benedict
1976 William L. Russell
1978 Harold M. Agnew and Wolfgang K. H. Panofsky
1980 Alvin M. Weinberg and Rudolf E. Peirls
1981 W. Bennett Lewis
1982 Herbert Anderson and Seth Neddermeyer
1983 Alexander Hollaender and John Lawrence
1984 Robert R. Wilson and Georges Vendryès
1985 Norman C. Rasmussen and Marshall N. Rosenblath
1986 Ernest D. Courant and M. Stanley Livingston
1987 Luis W. Alvarez and Gerald F. Tape
1988 Richard B. Setlow and Victor F. Weisskopf
1990 George A. Cowan and Robley D. Evans
1992 Leon M. Lederman, Harold Brown, and John S. Foster, Jr.
1993 Freeman J. Dyson and Liane B. Russell
1995 Ugo Fano and Martin Kamen
1996 Richard Garwin, Mortimer Elkind, and H. Rodney Withers
1998 Maurice Goldhaber and Michael E. Phelps
2000 Sidney Drell, Sheldon Datz, and Herbert York

Fields Medal Winners

The Fields Medal has been awarded quadrennially since 1936 by the International Congress of Mathematicians in Toronto to recognize outstanding mathematics achievement.

1936 Lars Valerian Ahlfors (Harvard University) and Jesse Douglas (Massachusetts Institute of Technology)

(Fields Medals were not awarded during World War II)

1950 Laurent Schwarts (University of Nancy) and Atle Selberg (Institute for Advanced Study, Princeton)

1954 Kunihiko Kodaira (Princeton University) and Jean-Pierre Serre (University of Paris)

1958 Klaus Friedrich Roth (University of London) and René Thom (University of Strasbourgh)

1962 Lars V. Hörmander (University of Stockholm) and John Willard Milnor (Princeton University)

1966 Michael Francis Atiyah (Oxford University), Paul Joseph Cohen (Stanford University), Alexander Grothendieck (University of Paris), and Stephen Smale (University of California, Berkeley)

1970 Alan Baker (Cambridge University), Heisuke Hironaka (Harvard University), Serge P. Novikov (Moscow University), and John Griggs Thompson (Cambridge University)

1974 Enrico Bombieri (University of Pisa) and David Bryant Mumford (Harvard University)

1978 Pierre René Deligne (Institut des Hautes Études Scientifiques), Charles Louis Fefferman (Princeton University), Gregori Alexandrovitch Margulis (Moscow University), and Daniel G. Quillen (Massachusetts Institute of Technology)

1982 Alain Connes (Institut des Hautes Études Scientifiques), William P. Thurston (Princeton University), and Shing-Tung Yau (Institute for Advanced Study, Princeton)

1986 Simon Donaldson (Oxford University), Gerd Faltings (Princeton University), and Michael Freedman (University of California, San Diego)

1990 Vladimir Drinfeld (Phys. Inst. Kharkov), Vaughan Jones (University of California, Berkeley), Shigefumi Mori (University of Kyoto), and Edward Witten (Institute for Advanced Study, Princeton)

1994 Pierre-Louis Lions (Université de Paris–Dauphine), Jean-Christophe Yoccoz (Université de Paris–Sud), Jean Bourgain (Institute for Advanced Study, Princeton), and Efim Zelmanov (University of Wisconsin)

1998 Richard E. Borcherds (Cambridge University), William T. Gowers (Cambridge University), Maxim Kontsevich (Institut des Hautes Études Scientifiques and Rutgers University), and Curtis T. McMullen (Harvard University)

2002 Laurent Lafforgue (Institut des Hautes Études Scientifiques) and Vladimir Voevodsky (Institute for Advanced Study, Princeton)

2002 MacArthur Foundation Awards

The MacArthur Foundation awards $500,000 over five years to each MacArthur Fellow.

Bonnie Bassler, 40, molecular ecobiologist; Princeton, N.J.
Ann Blair, 40, intellectual historian; Cambridge, Mass.
Katharine Boo, 37, journalist; Washington, DC
Paul Ginsparg, 46, physicist and Internet publisher; Ithaca, N.Y.
David Goldstein, 51, energy conservation specialist; San Francisco, Calif.
Karen Hesse, 50, novelist; Brattleboro, Vt.
Janine Jagger, 52, epidemiologist; Charlottesville, Va.
Daniel Jurafsky, 39, computational linguist; Boulder, Colo.
Toba Khedoori, 37, artist; Los Angeles, Calif.
Liz Lerman, 54, choreographer; Takoma Park, Md.
George Lewis, 50, trombonist and composer; La Jolla, Calif.
Liza Lou, 33, glass-bead artist; Los Angeles, Calif.
Edgar Meyer, 41, bassist and composer; Nashville, Tenn.
Jack Miles, 60, literary scholar and critic; Los Angeles, Calif.
Erik Mueggler, 40, anthropologist; Ann Arbor, Mich.
Sendhil Mullainathan, 29, economist; Cambridge, Mass.
Stanley Nelson, 48, documentary filmmaker; New York, N.Y.
Lee Ann Newsom, 45, paleoethnobotanist; University Park, Pa.
Daniela Rus, 39, roboticist; Hanover, N.H.
Charles Steidel, 39, cosmologist; Pasadena, Calif.
Brian Tucker, 56, seismologist and disaster-prevention specialist; Palo Alto, Calif.
Camilo Vergara, 58, urban archivist; New York, N.Y.
Paul Wennberg, 40, atmospheric chemist; Pasadena, Calif.
Colson Whitehead, 32, novelist; Brooklyn, N.Y.

Presidential Medal of Freedom

The Presidential Medal of Freedom, the nation's highest civilian award, recognizes exceptional meritorious service. (These are the medals awarded during President Bush's administration.)

2002 Hank Aaron (baseball player), Bill Cosby (comedian and actor), Plácido Domingo (tenor), Peter Drucker (management theorist), Katharine Graham* (newspaper publisher), Dr. D. A. Henderson (leader in eradication of smallpox), Irving Kristol (author and editor), Nelson Mandela (former South African president), Gordon Moore (Intel cofounder), Nancy Reagan (former first lady), Fred Rogers (children's television host), A. M. Rosenthal (editor and columnist)

2003 Jacques Barzun (writer and historian), Julia Child (chef), Roberto W. Clemente* (baseball player), Van Cliburn (pianist), Vaclav Havel (playwright and former president of Czech Republic), Charlton Heston (actor), Edward Teller (physicist), R. David Thomas* (Wendy's founder and adoption advocate), Byron R. White* (Supreme Court justice), James Q. Wilson (professor), John R. Wooden (basketball coach)

NOTE: An asterisk following a name denotes a posthumous award.

Recipients of Kennedy Center Honors

The Kennedy Center Honors recognize the lifetime achievements of selected American performing artists.

1978 Marian Anderson (contralto), Fred Astaire (dancer-actor), Richard Rodgers (Broadway composer), Arthur Rubinstein (pianist), George Balanchine (choreographer)

1979 Ella Fitzgerald (jazz singer), Henry Fonda (actor), Martha Graham (choreographer), Tennessee Williams (playwright), Aaron Copland (composer)

1980 James Cagney (actor), Leonard Bernstein (composer-conductor), Agnes de Mille (choreographer), Lynn Fontanne (actress), Leontyne Price (soprano)

1981 Count Basie (jazz composer-pianist), Cary Grant (actor), Helen Hayes (actress), Jerome Robbins (choreographer), Rudolf Serkin (pianist)

1982 George Abbott (Broadway producer), Lillian Gish (actress), Benny Goodman (jazz clarinetist), Gene Kelly (dancer-actor), Eugene Ormandy (conductor)

1983 Katherine Dunham (dancer-choreographer), Elia Kazan (director-author), James Stewart (actor), Virgil Thomson (music critic-composer), Frank Sinatra (singer)

1984 Lena Horne (singer), Danny Kaye (comedian-actor), Gian Carlo Menotti (composer), Arthur Miller (playwright), Isaac Stern (violinist)

1985 Merce Cunningham (dancer-choreographer), Irene Dunne (actress), Bob Hope (comedian), Alan Jay Lerner (lyricist-playwright), Frederick Loewe (composer), Beverly Sills (soprano)

1986 Lucille Ball (comedienne), Ray Charles (musician), Yehudi Menuhin (violinist), Antony Tudor (choreographer), Hume Cronyn and Jessica Tandy (husband-and-wife acting team)

1987 Perry Como (singer), Bette Davis (actress), Sammy Davis, Jr., (entertainer), Nathan Milstein (violinist), Alwin Nikolais (choreographer)

1988 Alvin Ailey (choreographer), George Burns (comedian-actor), Myrna Loy (actress), Alexander Schneider (violinist), Roger L. Stevens (theatrical producer and the Kennedy Center's founding chairman)

1989 Harry Belafonte (singer-actor), Claudette Colbert (actress), Alexandra Danilova (ballerina), Mary Martin (actress), William Schuman (composer)

1990 Dizzy Gillespie (jazz trumpeter), Katharine Hepburn (actress), Risë Stevens (mezzo-soprano), Jule Styne (composer), Billy Wilder (director)

1991 Roy Acuff (country songwriter and singer), Betty Comden and Adolph Green (co-authors of books and lyrics of musicals), the brothers Fayard and Harold Nicholas (dancers), Gregory Peck (actor), Robert Shaw (choral director)

1992 Lionel Hampton (jazz musician), Paul Newman (actor), Joanne Woodward (actress), Ginger Rogers (dancer-actress), Mstislav Rostropovich (cellist-conductor), Paul Taylor (choreographer)

1993 Johnny Carson (talk-show host), Arthur Mitchell (dancer and choreographer), Georg Solti (conductor), Stephen Sondheim (composer and lyricist), Marion Williams (gospel singer)

1994 Kirk Douglas (actor), Aretha Franklin (singer), Morton Gould (composer), Harold Prince (producer and director), Pete Seeger (folk singer)

1995 Jacques d'Amboise (choreographer), Marilyn Horne (mezzo soprano), B. B. King (blues singer), Sidney Poitier (actor), Neil Simon (playwright)

1996 Edward Albee (playwright), Benny Carter (jazz musician), Johnny Cash (musician), Jack Lemmon (actor), Maria Tallchief (ballerina)

1997 Lauren Bacall (actress), Bob Dylan (songwriter and singer), Charlton Heston (actor), Jessye Norman (soprano), Edward Villella (ballet dancer and director)

1998 Bill Cosby (actor and comedian), John Kander and Fred Ebb (Broadway composer and lyricist team), Willie Nelson (singer and songwriter), André Previn (composer and conductor), Shirley Temple Black (actress)

1999 Victor Borge (comedian and pianist), Sean Connery (actor), Judith Jamison (dancer and teacher), Jason Robards (actor), Stevie Wonder (singer and songwriter)

2000 Mikhail Baryshnikov (dancer), Plácido Domingo (tenor), Angela Lansbury (actress), Chuck Berry (rock 'n' roll musician), Clint Eastwood (actor, director, producer)

2001 Julie Andrews (actress), Van Cliburn (pianist), Quincy Jones (music producer and composer), Jack Nicholson (actor), Luciano Pavarotti (singer)

2002 James Earl Jones (actor), James Levine (conductor), Chita Rivera (dancer and actress), Paul Simon (singer), Elizabeth Taylor (actress)

2003 James Brown (soul singer), Carol Burnett (comedian and actress), Loretta Lynn (country singer), Mike Nichols (film and theater director), Itzhak Perlman (violinist)

Albany Medical Center Prize in Medicine and Biomedical Research

Each year the Albany Medical Center honors a physician, scientist, or group whose work has led to significant advances in the fields of health care and scientific research.

2001 Dr. Arnold J. Levine, president of Rockefeller University, for his seminal findings as codiscoverer of the p53 gene and his ongoing research and many other scientific contributions.

2002 Dr. Anthony S. Fauci, AIDS researcher and director of the National Institute of Allergy and Infectious Diseases, for his seminal research in AIDS and other diseases of the immune system, his overall contributions to the advancement of science, and his distinguished public service.

2003 Dr. Michael S. Brown and Dr. Joseph L. Goldstein, both distinguished chairs at the University of Texas Southwestern Medical School, for their research on how a family of proteins regulates cholesterol synthesis. Brown and Goldstein shared a 1985 Nobel Prize in Medicine.

U.S. Symphonies and Their Music Directors

(with expenses over $1,050,000)

Akron Symphony Orchestra: Ya-Hui Wang
Alabama Symphony Orchestra: Richard Westerfield
American Composers Orchestra: Steven Sloane
American Symphony Orchestra: Leon Botstein
Arkansas Symphony Orchestra: David Itkin
Aspen Chamber Symphony: David Zinman
Atlanta Symphony Orchestra: Robert Spano
Austin Symphony Orchestra: Peter Bay
Baltimore Symphony Orchestra: Yuri Temirkanov
Baton Rouge Symphony: Timothy Muffitt
Boca Pops (Florida Symphonic Pops): Crafton Beck
Boston Symphony Orchestra: James Levine
Boulder Philharmonic Orchestra: Theodore Kuchar
Brooklyn Philharmonic: Robert Spano
Buffalo Philharmonic Orchestra: JoAnn Falletta
Cedar Rapids Symphony: Christian Tiemeyer
Charleston Symphony Orchestra: David Stahl
Charlotte Symphony: Christof Perick
Chattanooga Symphony & Opera: Robert Bernhardt
Chicago Sinfonietta: Paul Freeman
Chicago Symphony Orchestra: Daniel Barenboim
Cincinnati Symphony Orchestra: Paavo Järvi
Cleveland Orchestra: Franz Welser-Möst
Dallas Symphony Orchestra: Andrew Litton
Dayton Philharmonic Orchestra: Neal Gittleman
Delaware Symphony Orchestra: David Amado
Des Moines Symphony: Joseph Giunta
Detroit Symphony Orchestra: Neeme Järvi
Elgin Symphony Orchestra: Robert L. Hanson
El Paso Symphony Orchestra: Gürer Aykal
Erie Philharmonic: Hugh Keelan
Evansville Philharmonic Orchestra: Alfred Savia
Florida Orchestra: Stefan Sanderling
Florida Philharmonic Orchestra: Joseph Silverstein (acting)
Florida West Coast Symphony: Leif Bjaland[1, 2]
Fort Wayne Philharmonic: Edvard Tchivzhel
Fort Worth Symphony Orchestra: Miguel Harth-Bedoya
Fresno Philharmonic Orchestra: Theodore Kuchar
Grand Rapids Symphony: David Lockington
Grant Park Symphony Orchestra (Chicago): Carlos Kalmar[2]
Greensboro Symphony Orchestra: Stuart Malina
Greenville Symphony Orchestra: Edvard Tchivzhel
Handel & Haydn Society: Grant Llewellyn
Harrisburg Symphony Orchestra: Stuart Malina
Hartford Symphony Orchestra: Edward Cumming
Honolulu Symphony Orchestra: Samuel Wong
Houston Symphony: Hans Graf
Indianapolis Symphony: Mario Venzago
Jacksonville Symphony Orchestra: Fabio Mechetti
Kalamazoo Symphony Orchestra: Raymond Harvey
Kansas City Symphony: Anne Manson
Kennedy Center Opera House Orchestra: Heinz Fricke
Knoxville Symphony Orchestra: Lucas Richman
Little Orchestra Society of New York: Dino Anagnost[1, 2]
Long Beach Symphony Orchestra: Enrique Arturo Diemecke
Long Island Philharmonic: David Wiley
Los Angeles Chamber Orchestra: Jeffrey Kahane
Los Angeles Philharmonic: Esa-Pekka Salonen
Louisiana Philharmonic Orchestra: Klauspeter Seibel
Louisville Orchestra: Uriel Segal
Madison Symphony Orchestra: John DeMain
Memphis Symphony Orchestra: David Loebel
Milwaukee Symphony Orchestra: Andreas Delfs
Minnesota Orchestra: Osmo Vänskä
Mississippi Symphony Orchestra: Crafton Beck
Monterey Symphony: Kate Tamarkin
Music of the Baroque Chorus & Orchestra: Thomas S. Wikman
Naples Philharmonic Orchestra: Christopher Seaman
Nashville Symphony: Kenneth Schermerhorn
National Symphony (DC): Leonard Slatkin
New Haven Symphony Orchestra: Jung-Ho Pak
New Jersey Symphony Orchestra: Zdenek Macal
New Mexico Symphony: Roger Melone
New West Symphony: Boris Brott
New World Symphony (Fla.): Michael Tilson Thomas[1]
New York Chamber Symphony: Gerard Schwarz
New York Philharmonic: Lorin Maazel
New York Pops: Skitch Henderson
North Carolina Symphony: Gerhardt Zimmermann
Northeastern Pennsylvania Philharmonic: Clyde Mitchell
Ohio Chamber Orchestra: David Lockington
Oklahoma City Philharmonic: Joel Levine
Omaha Symphony: Victor Yampolsky
Omaha Symphony Chamber Orchestra: Victor Yampolsky
Oregon Symphony: James DePreist
Pacific Symphony Orchestra (Calif.): Carl St. Clair
Palm Beach Pops: Bob Lappin
Philadelphia Orchestra: Wolfgang Sawallisch
Philharmonia Baroque Orchestra: Nicholas McGegan
Phoenix Symphony: Hermann Michael
Pittsburgh Symphony: Mariss Jansons
Portland Symphony Orchestra: Toshiyuki Shimada
Quad City Symphony Orchestra: Donald Schleicher
Rhode Island Philharmonic: Larry Rachleff
Richmond Symphony: Mark Russell Smith
River City Brass Band: Denis Colwell
Rochester Philharmonic Orchestra: Christopher Seaman
St. Louis Symphony: David Amado
St. Paul Chamber Orchestra: Andreas Delfs
San Antonio Symphony: Larry Rachleff
San Francisco Symphony: Michael Tilson Thomas
Santa Barbara Symphony Orchestra: Gisèle Ben-Dor
Santa Rosa Symphony: Jeffrey Kahane
Savannah Symphony: Philip Greenberg
Seattle Symphony: Gerard Schwarz
Shreveport Symphony: Dennis Simons
Spokane Symphony: Fabio Mechetti
Springfield Symphony (Mass.): Kevin Rhodes
Stamford Symphony Orchestra: Roger Nierenberg
Syracuse Symphony Orchestra: Daniel Hege
Toledo Symphony: Andrew Massey
Tucson Symphony Orchestra: George Hanson
Utah Symphony: Keith Lockhart
Virginia Symphony: JoAnn Falletta
Westchester Philharmonic: Paul Lustig Dunkel
West Virginia Symphony Orchestra: Grant Cooper[1, 2]
Wichita Symphony: Andrew Sewell
Winston-Salem Piedmont Triad Symphony: Peter J. Perret
Youngstown Symphony Orchestra: Isaiah Jackson

1. Artistic Director. 2. Principal Conductor.

U.S. Opera Companies

(budgets $2,000,000 and over)

American Musical Theatre of San Jose: Stewart Slater, exec. prod.
Arizona Opera Company: David Speers, gen. dir.
Aspen Opera Theater Center: Ed Berkeley, dir.
Atlanta Opera, The: William Fred Scott, art. dir.
Austin Lyric Opera: Joseph McClain, gen. dir.
Baltimore Opera Company: Michael Harrison, gen. dir.
Boston Lyric Opera Company: Janice Mancini DelSesto, gen. dir.
Central City Opera: Pelham G. Pearce, gen. dir.
Cincinnati Opera Association: Nicholas Muni, art. dir.
Civic Light Opera: Charles Gray, exec. dir.
Cleveland Opera: David Bamberger, gen. dir.
Dallas Opera, The: Karen Stone, gen. dir.
Florentine Opera Company: Dennis Hanthorn, gen. dir.
Florida Grand Opera: Robert M. Heuer, gen. dir.
Glimmerglass Opera: Joanne Cossa, gen. dir.
Goodspeed Opera House: Michael Price, exec. dir.
Hawaii Opera Theatre: George Sinclair, exec. dir.
Houston Grand Opera: R. David Gockley, gen. dir.
Kentucky Opera: Deborah Sandler, gen. dir.
Los Angeles Opera: Plácido Domingo, art. dir.
Lyric Opera of Chicago: William Mason, gen. dir.
Lyric Opera of Kansas City: Evan R. Luskin, gen. dir.
Metro Lyric Opera: Era M. Tognoli, art. dir.
Metropolitan Opera Association: James Levine, art. dir.
Michigan Opera Theatre: David DiChiera, gen. dir.
Minnesota Opera, The: Dale Johnson, art. dir.
New York City Opera: Paul Kellogg, gen. dir. and art. dir.
Ohio Light Opera: Steven Daigle, art. dir.
Opera Colorado: Peter Russell, gen. dir.
Opera Company of Philadelphia: Robert B. Driver, producing art. dir.
Opera Pacific: John DeMain, art. dir.
Opera Theatre of St. Louis: Charles MacKay, gen. dir.
Orlando Opera Company: Robert Swedberg, gen. dir.
Palm Beach Opera: Anton Guadagno, art. dir.
Pittsburgh Opera: Mark Weinstein, gen. dir.
Portland Opera Association: Christopher Mattaliano, gen. dir.
San Diego Civic Light Opera Association: Brian Wells, art. dir.
San Diego Opera: Ian D. Campbell, gen. dir.
San Francisco Opera: Pamela Rosenberg, gen. dir.
San Francisco Opera Center: Sheri Greenawald, dir.
Santa Fe Opera: Richard Gaddes, gen. dir.
Sarasota Opera Association: Victor DeRenzi, art. dir.
Seattle Opera Association: Speight Jenkins, gen. dir.
Utah Opera Company: Anne Ewers, gen. dir.
Virginia Opera: Peter Mark, gen dir. and art. dir.
Washington (DC) Opera, The: Plácido Domingo, art. dir.

Most Frequently Produced Operas in North America

(through 2002–2003 season)

Opera	Composer	Number of productions[1]
Top works of 2002–2003 season		
1. *La Bohème*	Puccini	27
2. *La Traviata*	Verdi	19
3. *Die Fledermaus*	Strauss, Jr.	15
Tosca	Puccini	15
5. *Carmen*	Bizet	13

Opera	Composer	Number of productions[1]
Top 5 works over past 10 seasons		
1. *La Bohème*	Puccini	192
2. *Madama Butterfly*	Puccini	176
3. *La Traviata*	Verdi	165
4. *Carmen*	Bizet	159
5. *The Barber of Seville*	Rossini	137

1. Represents the number of productions by professional member companies of Opera America, not the number of performances. *Source:* Opera America. Web: www.operaamerica.org.

U.S. Dance Companies

(budgets $2,500,000 and over)

Alvin Ailey American Dance Theatre (1958): Judith Jamison, art. dir.
American Ballet Theatre (1940): Kevin McKenzie, art. dir.
Atlanta Ballet Company (1929): John McFall, art. dir.
Ballet Florida (1986): Marie Hale, art. dir.
Ballet San Jose of Silicon Valley (1986): Dennis Nahat, art. dir.
BalletMet Columbus (1978): Gerard Charles, art. dir.
Ballet West (1968[1]): Jonas Kåge, art. dir.
Boston Ballet (1963): Mikko Nissinen, art. dir.
Cincinnati Ballet (1958): Victoria Morgan, art. dir.
Colorado Ballet (1961): Martin Fredmann, art. dir. and CEO
Merce Cunningham Dance Company (1953): Merce Cunningham, art. dir.
Dance Theater of Harlem (1969): Arthur Mitchell, art. dir.
Eliot Feld's Ballet Tech (1973): Eliot Feld, dir.
Fort Worth Dallas Ballet (1993): David Mallette, exec. dir.
Martha Graham Dance Company (1926): Terese Capucilli and Christine Dakin, art. dir.
Houston Ballet (1969): Ben Stevenson, art. dir.
Joffrey Ballet of Chicago (1956): Gerald Arpino, art. dir.
Bill T. Jones/Arnie Zane Dance Company (1982): Bill T. Jones, art. dir.
José Limón Dance Company (1946): Carla Maxwell, art. dir.
Miami City Ballet (1986): Edward Villella, art. dir. and CEO
Milwaukee Ballet (1970): Michael Pink, art. dir.
Mark Morris Dance Group (1980): Mark Morris, art. dir.
New York City Ballet (1948): Christopher Wheeldon, resident choreographer; Peter Martins, ballet-master-in-chief and art. dir.
Ocheami African Dance Company (1978): Kofi Anang, art. dir.
Pacific Northwest Ballet (1972): Kent Stowell and Francia Russell, art. dirs.
Pittsburgh Ballet Theater (1970): Terrence S. Orr, art. dir.
San Francisco Ballet (1933): Helgi Tomasson, art. dir.
Paul Taylor Dance Company (1954): Paul Taylor, dir.
Washington Ballet (1976): Septime Webre, art. dir.

NOTE: Year founded appears in parentheses after name. 1. Prior company founded 1963, name changed to Ballet West in 1968.

Best-Selling Books, 2002

Source: Publishers Weekly.

Hardcover Fiction

1. *The Summons,* John Grisham
2. *Red Rabbit,* Tom Clancy
3. *Remnant,* Jerry B. Jenkins and Tim LaHaye
4. *The Lovely Bones,* Alice Seybold
5. *Prey,* Michael Crichton
6. *Skipping Christmas,* John Grisham
7. *The Shelters of Stone,* Jean M. Auel
8. *Four Blind Mice,* James Patterson
9. *Everything's Eventual,* Stephen King
10. *The Nanny Diaries,* Emma McLaughlin and Nicola Kraus
11. *From a Buick 8,* Stephen King
12. *The Beach House,* James Patterson and Peter de Jonge
13. *Star Wars: Attack of the Clones,* R. A. Salvatore
14. *Nights in Rodanthe,* Nicholas Sparks
15. *Answered Prayers,* Danielle Steel

Hardcover Nonfiction

1. *Self Matters,* Phillip C. McGraw
2. *A Life God Rewards,* Bruce Wilkinson with David Kopp
3. *Let's Roll!,* Lisa Beamer with Ken Abraham
4. *Guinness World Records 2003,* Guinness World Records Ltd.
5. *Who Moved My Cheese?,* Spencer Johnson
6. *Leadership,* Rudolph W. Giuliani
7. *The Prayer of Jabez for Women,* Darlene Wilkinson
8. *Bush at War,* Bob Woodward
9. *Portrait of a Killer,* Patricia Cornwell
10. *Body for Life,* Bill Phillips
11. *I Hope You Dance,* Mark D. Sanders and Tia Sillers
12. *Stupid White Men,* Michael Moore
13. *Bringing Up Boys,* James Dobson
14. *Good to Great,* Jim Collins
15. *Get with the Program,* Bob Greene

Trade Paperback

1. *Fix-It and Forget-It Cookbook,* Dawn J. Ranck and Phyllis Pellman Good
2. *The Two Towers,* J.R.R. Tolkien
3. *The Lord of the Rings,* J.R.R. Tolkien
4. *The Return of the King,* J.R.R. Tolkien
5. *The Fellowship of the Ring,* J.R.R. Tolkien
6. *What to Expect When You're Expecting, 3rd ed.,* Heidi Murkoff, Arlene Eisenberg, and Sandee Hathaway
7. *Sula,* Toni Morrison
8. *Empire Falls,* Richard Russo
9. *Fast Food Nation,* Eric Schlosser
10. *The Last Time They Met,* Anita Shreve
11. *The Hobbit,* J.R.R. Tolkien
12. *A Common Life,* Jan Karon
13. *Suzanne's Diary for Nicholas,* James Patterson
14. *Chicken Soup for the Mother's Soul II,* edited by Canfield & Hansen *et al.*
15. *Fix-It and Forget-It Recipes for Entertaining,* Phyllis Pellman Good and Dawn J. Ranck

Mass Market Paperback

1. *The Summons,* John Grisham
2. *The Lord of the Rings: The Two Towers,* J.R.R. Tolkien
3. *Face the Fire,* Nora Roberts
4. *The Villa,* Nora Roberts
5. *Midnight Bayou,* Nora Roberts
6. *On the Street Where You Live,* Mary Higgins Clark
7. *The Lord of the Rings: The Fellowship of the Ring,* J.R.R. Tolkien
8. *The Hobbit,* J.R.R. Tolkien
9. *1st to Die,* James Patterson
10. *The Kiss,* Danielle Steel
11. *Violets Are Blue,* James Patterson
12. *Isle of Dogs,* Patricia Cornwell
13. *Table for Two,* Nora Roberts
14. *The Lord of the Rings: The Return of the King,* J.R.R. Tolkien
15. *The Black House,* Stephen King and Peter Straub

Best-Selling Children's Books, 2002

Source: Publishers Weekly.

Hardcover

1. *The Prayer of Jabez for Kids,* Bruce Wilkinson and Melody Carlson
2. *The Prayer of Jabez for Little Ones,* Bruce Wilkinson and Melody Carlson; illustrated by Alexi Natchev
3. *The Hostile Hospital (A Series of Unfortunate Events #8),* Lemony Snicket; illustrated by Brett Helquist
4. *The Ersatz Elevator (A Series of Unfortunate Events #6),* Lemony Snicket; illustrated by Brett Helquist
5. *The Vile Village (A Series of Unfortunate Events #7),* Lemony Snicket; illustrated by Brett Helquist
6. *Monsters, Inc.: Read-Aloud Storybook*
7. *Disney's 5-Minute Adventure Stories,* Sarah Heller
8. *Olivia Saves the Circus,* Ian Falconer
9. *Ripley's Believe It or Not*
10. *What's Wrong with Timmy?,* Maria Shriver; illustrated by Sandra Speidel

Paperback

1. *Harry Potter and the Prisoner of Azkaban,* J. K. Rowling
2. *Harry Potter and the Sorcerer's Stone,* J. K. Rowling
3. *Fantastic Beasts and Where to Find Them,* Newt Scamander (aka J. K. Rowling)
4. *Quidditch Through the Ages,* Kennilworthy Whisp (aka J. K. Rowling)
5. *Captain Underpants and the Wrath of the Wicked Wedgie Woman,* Dav Pilkey
6. *Harry Potter and the Sorcerer's Stone Poster Book*
7. *The Princess Diaries,* Meg Cabot
8. *Chicken Soup for the Teenage Soul: On Tough Stuff,* Jack Canfield, *et al.*
9. *Amelia Bedelia 4 Mayor,* Herman Parish; illustrated by Lynn Sweat
10. *Twister on Tuesday (Magic Tree House #23),* Mary Pope Osborne; illustrated by Sal Murdocca

All-Time Best-Selling Children's Books

Source: Publishers Weekly.

From the date of publication (in parentheses) through the end of 2000.

Hardcover

1. *The Poky Little Puppy,* Janette Sebring Lowrey (1942)
2. *The Tale of Peter Rabbit,* Beatrix Potter (1902)
3. *Tootle,* Gertrude Crampton (1945)
4. *Green Eggs and Ham,* Dr. Seuss (1960)
5. *Harry Potter and the Goblet of Fire,* J. K. Rowling (2000)
6. *Pat the Bunny,* Dorothy Kunhardt (1940)
7. *Saggy Baggy Elephant,* Kathryn and Byron Jackson (1947)
8. *Scuffy the Tugboat,* Gertrude Crampton (1955)
9. *The Cat in the Hat,* Dr. Seuss (1957)
10. *Harry Potter and the Chamber of Secrets,* J. K. Rowling (1999)

Paperback

1. *Charlotte's Web,* E. B. White, illustrated by Garth Williams (1974)
2. *The Outsiders,* S. E. Hinton (1968)
3. *Tales of a Fourth Grade Nothing,* Judy Blume (1976)
4. *Love You Forever,* Robert Munsch, illustrated by Sheila McGraw (1986)
5. *Where the Red Fern Grows,* Wilson Rawls (1973)
6. *Island of the Blue Dolphins,* Scott O'Dell (1971)
7. *Harry Potter and the Sorcerer's Stone,* J. K. Rowling (1999)
8. *Are You There, God? It's Me, Margaret,* Judy Blume (1972)
9. *Shane,* Jack Schaeffer (1972)
10. *The Indian in the Cupboard,* Lynne Reid Banks (1982)

The 100 Best English-Language Novels of the 20th Century

The Board of the Modern Library, a division of Random House, published its selections in July 1998.

1. *Ulysses,* James Joyce (1922)
2. *The Great Gatsby,* F. Scott Fitzgerald (1925)
3. *A Portrait of the Artist as a Young Man,* James Joyce (1916)
4. *Lolita,* Vladimir Nabokov (1958)
5. *Brave New World,* Aldous Huxley (1932)
6. *The Sound and the Fury,* William Faulkner (1929)
7. *Catch-22,* Joseph Heller (1961)
8. *Darkness at Noon,* Arthur Koestler (1941)
9. *Sons and Lovers,* D. H. Lawrence (1913)
10. *The Grapes of Wrath,* John Steinbeck (1939)
11. *Under the Volcano,* Malcolm Lowry (1947)
12. *The Way of All Flesh,* Samuel Butler (1903)
13. *1984,* George Orwell (1949)
14. *I, Claudius,* Robert Graves (1934)
15. *To the Lighthouse,* Virginia Woolf (1927)
16. *An American Tragedy,* Theodore Dreiser (1925)
17. *The Heart Is a Lonely Hunter,* Carson McCullers (1940)
18. *Slaughterhouse-Five,* Kurt Vonnegut (1969)
19. *Invisible Man,* Ralph Ellison (1952)
20. *Native Son,* Richard Wright (1940)
21. *Henderson the Rain King,* Saul Bellow (1959)
22. *Appointment in Samarra,* John O'Hara (1934)
23. *U.S.A.* (trilogy), John Dos Passos (1937—trilogy completed)
24. *Winesburg, Ohio,* Sherwood Anderson (1919)
25. *A Passage to India,* E. M. Forster (1924)
26. *The Wings of the Dove,* Henry James (1902)
27. *The Ambassadors,* Henry James (1903)
28. *Tender Is the Night,* F. Scott Fitzgerald (1934)
29. *The Studs Lonigan Trilogy,* James T. Farrell (1935)
30. *The Good Soldier,* Ford Madox Ford (1915)
31. *Animal Farm,* George Orwell (1946)
32. *The Golden Bowl,* Henry James (1904)
33. *Sister Carrie,* Theodore Dreiser (1900)
34. *A Handful of Dust,* Evelyn Waugh (1934)
35. *As I Lay Dying,* William Faulkner (1930)
36. *All the King's Men,* Robert Penn Warren (1946)
37. *The Bridge of San Luis Rey,* Thornton Wilder (1927)
38. *Howards End,* E. M. Forster (1910)
39. *Go Tell It on the Mountain,* James Baldwin (1953)
40. *The Heart of the Matter,* Graham Greene (1948)
41. *Lord of the Flies,* William Golding (1954)
42. *Deliverance,* James Dickey (1969)
43. *A Dance to the Music of Time* (series), Anthony Powell (1975—series completed)
44. *Point Counter Point,* Aldous Huxley (1928)
45. *The Sun Also Rises,* Ernest Hemingway (1926)
46. *The Secret Agent,* Joseph Conrad (1907)
47. *Nostromo,* Joseph Conrad (1904)
48. *The Rainbow,* D. H. Lawrence (1915)
49. *Women in Love,* D. H. Lawrence (1921)
50. *Tropic of Cancer,* Henry Miller (1934)
51. *The Naked and the Dead,* Norman Mailer (1948)
52. *Portnoy's Complaint,* Philip Roth (1969)
53. *Pale Fire,* Vladimir Nabokov (1962)
54. *Light in August,* William Faulkner (1932)
55. *On the Road,* Jack Kerouac (1957)
56. *The Maltese Falcon,* Dashiell Hammett (1930)
57. *Parade's End,* Ford Madox Ford (1950)
58. *The Age of Innocence,* Edith Wharton (1920)
59. *Zuleika Dobson,* Max Beerbohm (1911)
60. *The Moviegoer,* Walker Percy (1961)
61. *Death Comes for the Archbishop,* Willa Cather (1927)
62. *From Here to Eternity,* James Jones (1951)
63. *The Wapshot Chronicles,* John Cheever (1957)
64. *The Catcher in the Rye,* J. D. Salinger (1951)
65. *A Clockwork Orange,* Anthony Burgess (1962)
66. *Of Human Bondage,* W. Somerset Maugham (1915)
67. *Heart of Darkness,* Joseph Conrad (1902)
68. *Main Street,* Sinclair Lewis (1920)
69. *The House of Mirth,* Edith Wharton (1905)
70. *The Alexandria Quartet,* Lawrence Durrell (1960—series completed)
71. *A High Wind in Jamaica,* Richard Hughes (1929)
72. *A House for Mr. Biswas,* V. S. Naipaul (1961)
73. *The Day of the Locust,* Nathanael West (1939)
74. *A Farewell to Arms,* Ernest Hemingway (1929)
75. *Scoop,* Evelyn Waugh (1938)

76. *The Prime of Miss Jean Brodie*, Muriel Spark (1961)
77. *Finnegans Wake*, James Joyce (1939)
78. *Kim*, Rudyard Kipling (1901)
79. *A Room with a View*, E. M. Forster (1908)
80. *Brideshead Revisited*, Evelyn Waugh (1945)
81. *The Adventures of Augie March*, Saul Bellow (1953)
82. *Angle of Repose*, Wallace Stegner (1971)
83. *A Bend in the River*, V. S. Naipaul (1979)
84. *The Death of the Heart*, Elizabeth Bowen (1938)
85. *Lord Jim*, Joseph Conrad (1900)
86. *Ragtime*, E. L. Doctorow (1975)
87. *The Old Wives' Tale*, Arnold Bennett (1908)
88. *The Call of the Wild*, Jack London (1903)
89. *Loving*, Henry Green (1945)
90. *Midnight's Children*, Salman Rushdie (1981)
91. *Tobacco Road*, Erskine Caldwell (1933)
92. *Ironweed*, William Kennedy (1983)
93. *The Magus*, John Fowles (1966)
94. *Wide Sargasso Sea*, Jean Rhys (1966)
95. *Under the Net*, Iris Murdoch (1954)
96. *Sophie's Choice*, William Styron (1979)
97. *The Sheltering Sky*, Paul Bowles (1949)
98. *The Postman Always Rings Twice*, James M. Cain (1934)
99. *The Ginger Man*, J. P. Donleavy (1955)
100. *The Magnificent Ambersons*, Booth Tarkington (1918)

The 100 Best English-Language Nonfiction Books of the 20th Century

The Board of the Modern Library, a division of Random House, published its selections in April 1999.

1. *The Education of Henry Adams*, Henry Adams (1906)
2. *The Varieties of Religious Experience*, William James (1902)
3. *Up from Slavery*, Booker T. Washington (1901)
4. *A Room of One's Own*, Virginia Woolf (1929)
5. *Silent Spring*, Rachel Carson (1962)
6. *Selected Essays, 1917–1932*, T. S. Eliot (1932)
7. *The Double Helix*, James D. Watson (1968)
8. *Speak, Memory*, Vladimir Nabokov (1967)
9. *The American Language*, H. L. Mencken (1919)
10. *The General Theory of Employment, Interest, and Money*, John Maynard Keynes (1935–1936)
11. *The Lives of a Cell*, Lewis Thomas (1974)
12. *The Frontier in American History*, Frederick Jackson Turner (1920)
13. *Black Boy*, Richard Wright (1945)
14. *Aspects of the Novel*, E. M. Forster (1927)
15. *The Civil War*, Shelby Foote (1958–1974)
16. *The Guns of August*, Barbara Tuchman (1962)
17. *The Proper Study of Mankind*, Isaiah Berlin (1997)
18. *The Nature and Destiny of Man*, Reinhold Niebuhr (1941–1943)
19. *Notes of a Native Son*, James Baldwin (1955)
20. *The Autobiography of Alice B. Toklas*, Gertrude Stein (1933)
21. *The Elements of Style*, William Strunk and E. B. White (1959)
22. *An American Dilemma*, Gunnar Myrdal (1944)
23. *Principia Mathematica*, Alfred North Whitehead and Bertrand Russell (1910–1913)
24. *The Mismeasure of Man*, Stephen Jay Gould (1981)
25. *The Mirror and the Lamp*, Meyer Howard Abrams (1953)
26. *The Art of the Soluble*, Peter B. Medawar (1967)
27. *The Ants*, Bert Hoelldobler and Edward O. Wilson (1990)
28. *A Theory of Justice*, John Rawls (1971)
29. *Art and Illusion*, Ernest H. Gombrich (1961)
30. *The Making of the English Working Class*, E. P. Thompson (1963)
31. *The Souls of Black Folk*, W.E.B. Du Bois (1903)
32. *Principia Ethica*, G. E. Moore (1903)
33. *Philosophy and Civilization*, John Dewey (1927)
34. *On Growth and Form*, D'Arcy Thompson (1917)
35. *Ideas and Opinions*, Albert Einstein (1954)
36. *The Age of Jackson*, Arthur Schlesinger, Jr. (1945)
37. *The Making of the Atomic Bomb*, Richard Rhodes (1986)
38. *Black Lamb and Grey Falcon*, Rebecca West (1942)
39. *Autobiographies*, W. B. Yeats (1926)
40. *Science and Civilization in China*, Joseph Needham (1954–)
41. *Goodbye to All That*, Robert Graves (1929)
42. *Homage to Catalonia*, George Orwell (1938)
43. *The Autobiography of Mark Twain*, Mark Twain (1924)
44. *Children of Crisis*, Robert Coles (1967)
45. *A Study of History*, Arnold J. Toynbee (1934–1961)
46. *The Affluent Society*, John Kenneth Galbraith (1958)
47. *Present at the Creation*, Dean Acheson (1969)
48. *The Great Bridge*, David McCullough (1972)
49. *Patriotic Gore*, Edmund Wilson (1962)
50. *Samuel Johnson*, Walter Jackson Bate (1977)
51. *The Autobiography of Malcolm X*, Alex Haley and Malcolm X (1965)
52. *The Right Stuff*, Tom Wolfe (1979)
53. *Eminent Victorians*, Lytton Strachey (1918)
54. *Working*, Studs Terkel (1974)
55. *Darkness Visible*, William Styron (1990)
56. *The Liberal Imagination*, Lionel Trilling (1950)
57. *The Second World War*, Winston Churchill (1948–1953)
58. *Out of Africa*, Isak Dinesen (1937)
59. *Jefferson and His Time*, Dumas Malone (1948–1981)
60. *In the American Grain*, William Carlos Williams (1925)
61. *Cadillac Desert*, Marc Reisner (1986)
62. *The House of Morgan*, Ron Chernow (1990)
63. *The Sweet Science*, A. J. Liebling (1956)
64. *The Open Society and Its Enemies*, Karl Popper (1945)
65. *The Art of Memory*, Frances A. Yates (1966)
66. *Religion and the Rise of Capitalism*, R. H. Tawney (1926)
67. *A Preface to Morals*, Walter Lippmann (1929)
68. *The Gate of Heavenly Peace*, Jonathan D. Spence (1981)
69. *The Structure of Scientific Revolutions*, Thomas S. Kuhn (1962)
70. *The Strange Career of Jim Crow*, C. Vann Woodward (1955)
71. *The Rise of the West*, William H. McNeill (1963)
72. *The Gnostic Gospels*, Elaine Pagels (1979)
73. *James Joyce*, Richard Ellmann (1959)
74. *Florence Nightingale*, Cecil Woodham-Smith (1950)

75. *The Great War and Modern Memory,* Paul Fussell (1975)
76. *The City in History,* Lewis Mumford (1961)
77. *Battle Cry of Freedom,* James M. McPherson (1988)
78. *Why We Can't Wait,* Martin Luther King, Jr. (1964)
79. *The Rise of Theodore Roosevelt,* Edmund Morris (1979)
80. *Studies in Iconology,* Erwin Panofsky (1939)
81. *The Face of Battle,* John Keegan (1976)
82. *The Strange Death of Liberal England,* George Dangerfield (1935)
83. *Vermeer,* Lawrence Gowing (1952)
84. *A Bright Shining Lie,* Neil Sheehan (1988)
85. *West with the Night,* Beryl Markham (1942)
86. *This Boy's Life,* Tobias Wolff (1989)
87. *A Mathematician's Apology,* G. H. Hardy (1940)
88. *Six Easy Pieces,* Richard P. Feynman (1963)
89. *Pilgrim at Tinker Creek,* Annie Dillard (1974)
90. *The Golden Bough,* James George Frazer (1922) (1 vol. ed.)
91. *Shadow and Act,* Ralph Ellison (1964)
92. *The Power Broker,* Robert A. Caro (1974)
93. *The American Political Tradition,* Richard Hofstadter (1948)
94. *The Contours of American History,* William Appleman Williams (1966)
95. *The Promise of American Life,* Herbert Croly (1909)
96. *In Cold Blood,* Truman Capote (1965)
97. *The Journalist and the Murderer,* Janet Malcolm (1990)
98. *The Taming of Chance,* Ian Hacking (1990)
99. *Operating Instructions,* Anne Lamott (1994)
100. *Melbourne,* Lord David Cecil (1939 & 1954)

Best American Journalism of the 20th Century

The following works were chosen as the 20th century's best American journalism by a panel of experts assembled by New York University's journalism department.

1. **John Hersey:** "Hiroshima," *The New Yorker,* 1946
2. **Rachel Carson:** *Silent Spring,* book, 1962
3. **Bob Woodward and Carl Bernstein:** Investigation of the Watergate break-in, *The Washington Post,* 1972
4. **Edward R. Murrow:** *Battle of Britain,* CBS radio, 1940
5. **Ida Tarbell:** "The History of the Standard Oil Company," *McClure's,* 1902–1904
6. **Lincoln Steffens:** "The Shame of the Cities," *McClure's,* 1902–1904
7. **John Reed:** *Ten Days That Shook the World,* book, 1919
8. **H. L. Mencken:** Scopes "Monkey" trial, *The Sun* of Baltimore, 1925
9. **Ernie Pyle:** Reports from Europe and the Pacific during World War II, Scripps-Howard newspapers, 1940–1945
10. **Edward R. Murrow and Fred Friendly:** Investigation of Sen. Joseph McCarthy, CBS, 1954
11. **Edward R. Murrow, David Lowe, and Fred Friendly:** documentary "Harvest of Shame," CBS television, 1960
12. **Seymour Hersh:** Investigation of massacre by American soldiers at My Lai in Vietnam, Dispatch News Service, 1969
13. ***The New York Times:*** Publication of the Pentagon Papers, 1971
14. **James Agee and Walker Evans:** *Let Us Now Praise Famous Men,* book, 1941
15. **W.E.B. Du Bois:** *The Souls of Black Folk,* collected articles, 1903
16. **I. F. Stone:** *I. F. Stone's Weekly,* 1953–1967
17. **Henry Hampton:** "Eyes on the Prize," documentary, 1987
18. **Tom Wolfe:** *The Electric Kool-Aid Acid Test,* book, 1968
19. **Norman Mailer:** *The Armies of the Night,* book, 1968
20. **Hannah Arendt:** *Eichmann in Jerusalem: A Report on the Banality of Evil,* collected articles, 1963
21. **William Shirer:** *Berlin Diary: The Journal of a Foreign Correspondent, 1939–1941,* collected articles, 1941
22. **Truman Capote:** *In Cold Blood: A True Account of a Multiple Murder and Its Consequences,* book, 1965
23. **Joan Didion:** *Slouching Towards Bethlehem,* collected articles, 1968
24. **Tom Wolfe:** *The Kandy-Kolored Tangerine-Flake Streamline Baby,* collected articles, 1965
25. **Michael Herr:** *Dispatches,* book, 1977
26. **Theodore White:** *The Making of the President: 1960,* book, 1961
27. **Robert Capa:** Ten photographs from D-Day, 1944
28. **J. Anthony Lukas:** *Common Ground: A Turbulent Decade in the Lives of Three American Families,* book, 1985
29. **Richard Harding Davis:** Coverage of German march into Belgium, Wheeler Syndicate and magazines, 1914
30. **Dorothy Thompson:** Reports on the rise of Hitler, *Cosmopolitan* and *Saturday Evening Post,* 1931–1934
31. **John Steinbeck:** Reports on Okie migrant camp life, *The San Francisco News,* 1936
32. **A. J. Liebling:** *The Road Back to Paris,* collected articles, 1944
33. **Ernest Hemingway:** Reports on the Spanish Civil War, *The New Republic,* 1937–1938
34. **Martha Gellhorn:** *The Face of War,* collected articles, 1959
35. **James Baldwin:** *The Fire Next Time,* book, 1963
36. **Joseph Mitchell:** *Up in the Old Hotel and Other Stories,* collection of much older articles, 1992
37. **Betty Friedan:** *The Feminine Mystique,* book, 1963
38. **Ralph Nader:** *Unsafe at Any Speed: The Designed-In Dangers of the American Automobile,* book, 1965
39. **Herblock (Herbert Block):** Cartoons on McCarthyism, *The Washington Post,* 1950
40. **James Baldwin:** "Letter from the South: Nobody Knows My Name," *The Partisan Review,* 1959
41. **Nick Ut:** Photograph of a burning girl running from a napalm attack, The Associated Press, 1972
42. **Pauline Kael:** "Trash, Art, and the Movies," *Harper's,* 1969
43. **Gay Talese:** *Fame and Obscurity: Portraits by Gay Talese,* collected articles, 1970

44. **Randy Shilts:** Reports on AIDS, *The San Francisco Chronicle,* 1981–1985
45. **Janet Flanner (Genet):** *Paris Journals* chronicling Paris's emergence from the Occupation, *The New Yorker,* 1944–1945
46. **Neil Sheehan:** *A Bright Shining Lie: John Paul Vann and America in Vietnam,* book, 1988
47. **A. J. Liebling:** *The Wayward Pressman,* collected articles, 1947
48. **Tom Wolfe:** *The Right Stuff,* book, 1979
49. **Murray Kempton:** *America Comes of Middle Age: Columns 1950–1962,* collected articles, 1963
50. **Murray Kempton:** *Part of Our Time: Some Ruins and Monuments of the Thirties,* book, 1955
51. **Donald L. Barlett and James B. Steele:** "America: What Went Wrong?," *The Philadelphia Inquirer,* 1991
52. **Taylor Branch:** *Parting the Waters: America in the King Years, 1954–1963,* book, 1988
53. **Harrison Salisbury:** Reporting from the Soviet Union, *The New York Times,* 1949–1954
54. **John McPhee:** *The John McPhee Reader,* collected articles, 1976
55. **ABC:** Live television broadcast of Army-McCarthy hearings, 1954
56. **Frederick Wiseman:** *Titicut Follies,* documentary, 1967
57. **David Remnick:** *Lenin's Tomb: The Last Days of the Soviet Empire,* book, 1993
58. **Richard Ben Cramer:** *What It Takes: The Way to the White House,* book, 1992
59. **Jonathan Schell:** *The Fate of the Earth,* book, 1982
60. **Russell Baker:** "Francs and Beans," *The New York Times,* 1975
61. **Homer Bigart:** Account of being over Japan in a bomber when World War II came to an end, The New York *Herald-Tribune,* 1945
62. **Ben Hecht:** *1,001 Afternoons in Chicago,* collected articles, 1922
63. **Walter Cronkite:** Documentary on Vietnam, CBS television, 1968
64. **Walter Lippmann:** Early essays, *The New Republic,* 1914
65. **Margaret Bourke-White:** Photographs following the defeat of Germany, *Life* magazine, 1945
66. **Lillian Ross:** *Reporting,* collected articles, 1964
67. **Nicholas Lemann:** *The Promised Land: The Great Black Migration and How It Changed America,* book, 1991
68. **Joe Rosenthal:** Photograph of Marines raising an American flag on Mount Suribachi on the island of Iwo Jima, The Associated Press, 1945
69. **Hodding Carter Jr.:** "Go for Broke," editorial, Carter's *Delta Democrat-Times* (Greenville, Miss.), 1945
70. **The New Yorker:** *The New Yorker Book of War Pieces,* collected articles, 1947
71. **Meyer Berger:** Report on the murderer Howard Unruh, *The New York Times,* 1949
72. **Norman Mailer:** *The Executioner's Song,* book, 1979
73. **Robert Capa:** Spanish Civil War photos, *Life* magazine, 1936
74. **Susan Sontag:** "Notes on 'Camp'," *The Partisan Review,* 1964
75. **Bob Woodward and Carl Bernstein:** *All the President's Men,* book, 1974
76. **John Hersey:** *Here to Stay,* collected articles, 1963
77. **A. J. Liebling:** *The Earl of Louisiana,* book, 1961
78. **Mike Davis:** *City of Quartz: Excavating the Future in Los Angeles,* book, 1990
79. **Melissa Fay Greene:** *Praying for Sheetrock,* book, 1991
80. **J. Anthony Lukas:** "The Two Worlds of Linda Fitzpatrick," *The New York Times,* 1967
81. **Herbert Bayard Swope:** "Klan Exposed," *The New York World,* 1921
82. **William Allen White:** "To an Anxious Friend," *The Emporia* (Kan.) *Gazette,* 1922
83. **Edward R. Murrow:** Report of the liberation of Buchenwald, CBS radio, 1945
84. **Joseph Mitchell:** *McSorley's Wonderful Saloon,* collected articles, 1943
85. **Lillian Ross:** *Picture,* book, 1952
86. **Earl Brown:** Series of articles on race, *Harper's* and *Life* magazines, 1942–1944
87. **Greil Marcus:** *Mystery Train: Images of America in Rock 'n' Roll Music,* book, 1975
88. **Morley Safer:** Atrocities committed by American soldiers on the hamlet of Cam Ne in Vietnam, CBS television, 1965
89. **Ted Poston:** Coverage of the "Little Scottsboro" trial, *The New York Post,* 1949
90. **Leon Dash:** "Rosa Lee's Story," *The Washington Post,* 1994
91. **Jane Kramer:** *Europeans,* collected articles, 1988
92. **Eddie Adams and Vo Suu:** Associated Press photograph and NBC television footage of a Saigon execution, 1968
93. **Grantland Rice:** "Notre Dame's 'Four Horsemen'," The New York *Herald-Tribune,* 1924
94. **Jane Kramer:** *The Politics of Memory: Looking for Germany in the New Germany,* collected articles, 1996
95. **Frank McCourt:** *Angela's Ashes,* book, 1996
96. **Vincent Sheean:** *Personal History,* book, 1935
97. **W.E.B. Du Bois:** Columns on race during his tenure as editor of *The Crisis,* 1910–1934
98. **Damon Runyon:** Crime reporting, *The New York American,* 1926
99. **Joe McGinniss:** *The Selling of the President 1968,* book, 1969
100. **Hunter S. Thompson:** *Fear and Loathing on the Campaign Trail,* book, 1973

Poets Laureate of England

Edmund Spenser	1591–1599	Laurence Eusden	1718–1730	Alfred Austin	1896–1913
Samuel Daniel	1599–1619	Colley Cibber	1730–1757	Robert Bridges	1913–1930
Ben Jonson	1619–1637	William Whitehead	1757–1785	John Masefield	1930–1967
William Davenant	1638–1668	Thomas Warton	1785–1790	Cecil Day-Lewis	1967–1972
John Dryden[1]	1668–1689	Henry James Pye	1790–1813	Sir John Betjeman	1972–1984
Thomas Shadwell	1689–1692	Robert Southey	1813–1843	Ted Hughes	1984–1998
Nahum Tate	1692–1715	William Wordsworth	1843–1850	Andrew Motion	1999–
Nicholas Rowe	1715–1718	Alfred Lord Tennyson	1850–1892		

1. First to bear the title officially.

Poets Laureate of the United States

Robert Penn Warren	1986–1987	Rita Dove	1993–1995
Richard Wilbur	1987–1988	Robert Hass	1995–1997
Howard Nemerov	1988–1990	Robert Pinsky	1997–2000
Mark Strand	1990–1991	Stanley Kunitz	2000–2001
Joseph Brodsky	1991–1992	Billy Collins	2001–2003
Mona Van Duyn	1992–1993	Louise Glück	2003–

NOTE: The post was established in 1985. Appointment is for a one-year term, but is renewable.

Longest Broadway Runs

Show	Dates	Performances[1]
1. *Cats*	10/82–9/2000	7,485
2. *Les Misérables*	3/87–5/18/2003	6,680
3. *The Phantom of the Opera*	1/88–present	6,310
4. *A Chorus Line*	7/75–4/90	6,137
5. *Oh! Calcutta!* (revival)	9/76–8/89	5,959
6. *Miss Saigon*	4/91–1/2001	4,092
7. *Beauty and the Beast*	4/94–present	3,797
8. *42nd Street*	8/80–1/89	3,486
9. *Grease*	2/72–4/80	3,388
10. *Fiddler on the Roof*	9/64–7/72	3,242
11. *Life with Father*	11/39–7/47	3,224
12. *Tobacco Road*	12/33–5/41	3,182
13. *Rent*	4/96–present	3,025
14. *Hello, Dolly!*	1/64–12/70	2,844
15. *Chicago* (revival)	11/96–present	2,796
16. *My Fair Lady*	3/56–9/62	2,717
17. *Threepenny Opera*	9/55–12/61	2,611
18. *The Lion King*	11/97–present	2,388
19. *Annie*	4/77–1/83	2,377
20. *Man of La Mancha*	11/65–6/71	2,328
21. *Abie's Irish Rose*	5/22–10/27	2,327
22. *Oklahoma!*	3/43–5/48	2,212
23. *Cabaret* (revival)	3/98–present	2,202
24. *Smokey Joe's Cafe*	3/95–1/2000	2,037
25. *Pippin*	10/72–6/77	1,944

1. As of 8/6/03. *Source:* League of American Theatres and Producers, Inc.

Top 15 Concert Grosses of 2002

Billboard annually ranks domestic and international concert grosses and touring acts. (Headliner, supporting act, dates; gross ticket sales in U.S. dollars; total attendance; venue)

1. **Paul McCartney (11/11, 11/13, 11/14),** $14,406,218; 120,429; Tokyo Dome, Tokyo, Japan
2. **Billy Joel and Elton John (2/13, 2/15, 2/17, 2/19, 2/22, 2/24),** $12,986,840; 112,248; First Union Center, Philadelphia, Pa.
3. **Billy Joel and Elton John (1/22, 1/24, 1/29, 1/31, 9/20),** $9,072,225; 85,638; FleetCenter, Boston, Mass.
4. **Paul McCartney (11/17–11/18),** $8,208,891; 80,284; Osaka Dome, Osaka, Japan
5. **Billy Joel and Elton John (9/25, 9/27, 10/11, 10/13),** $7,168,453; 67,769; Nassau Veterans Memorial Coliseum, Uniondale, N.Y.
6. **Billy Joel and Elton John (2/4, 2/6, 2/8, 2/9),** $6,796,339; 62,900; Hartford Civic Center, Hartford, Conn.
7. **The Who, Robert Plant (7/31, 8/1, 8/3, 8/4),** $6,265,660; 61,510; Madison Square Garden, New York, N.Y.
8. **Billy Joel and Elton John (10/2, 10/4, 10/8),** $6,192,840; 59,688; Continental Airlines Arena, East Rutherford, N.J.
9. **Luis Miguel (3/6–3/10, 3/13, 3/17–3/20),** $6,178,203; 112,974; Auditorio Nacional, Mexico City, Mexico
10. **Billy Joel and Elton John (3/3, 3/5, 3/7),** $5,818,001; 58,226; Office Depot Center, Sunrise, Fla.
11. **Billy Joel and Elton John (1/13, 1/18, 1/20),** $5,768,205; 55,820; MCI Center, Washington, DC
12. **Paul McCartney (4/5, 4/6),** $5,591,700; 23,341; MGM Grand Garden Arena, Las Vegas, Nev.
13. **Paul McCartney (11/2, 11/3, 11/5),** $4,787,211; 52,451; Palacio de los Deportes, Mexico City
14. **Billy Joel and Elton John (3/15, 9/23),** $4,309,990; 37,433; Madison Square Garden, New York, N.Y.
15. **Billy Joel and Elton John (3/9, 9/13),** $4,255,180; 39,178; St. Pete Times Forum, Tampa, Fla.

Top 10 Classical Albums, 2002

1. *Sentimento,* Andrea Bocelli (Philips/Universal Classics Group)
2. *Billy Joel: Fantasies & Delusions,* Richard Joo (Columbia/Sony Classical)
3. *Classic Yo-Yo,* Yo-Yo Ma (Sony Classical)
4. *Verdi,* Andrea Bocelli (Philips/Universal Classics Group)
5. *The Best of the Three Tenors,* Carreras-Domingo-Pavarotti (Decca/Universal Classics Group)
6. *Romantica,* Luciano Pavarotti (Decca/UTV/Universal Classics Group)
7. *Bach: Morimur,* The Hilliard Ensemble/Christoph Poppen (ECM/Universal Classics Group)
8. *Yo-Yo Ma Plays the Music of John Williams,* Yo-Yo Ma (Williams) (Sony Classical)
9. *Christmas with Chanticleer,* Chanticleer featuring Dawn Upshaw (Teldec/AG)
10. *Bel Canto,* Renee Fleming (Decca/Universal Classics Group)

Top 10 Country Singles, 2002

1. "Can't Fight the Moonlight," LeAnn Rimes (Curb)
2. "God Bless the USA," Lee Greenwood (Curb)
3. "Where the Stars and Stripes and the Eagle Fly," Aaron Tippin (Lyric Street/Hollywood)
4. "Long Time Gone," Dixie Chicks (Monument/CRG)
5. "Osama-Yo' Mama," Ray Stevens (Curb)
6. "America Will Always Stand," Randy Travis (Relentless Nashville/Madacy)
7. "That's Just Jessie," Kevin Denney (Lyric Street/Hollywood)
8. "I Should Be Sleeping," Emerson Drive (DreamWorks/Interscope)
9. "The Impossible," Joe Nichols (Universal South)
10. "God Bless America," LeAnn Rimes (Curb)

Top 10 Country Albums, 2002

1. *O Brother, Where Art Thou?,* Soundtrack (Lost Highway/Mercury)
2. *Scarecrow,* Garth Brooks (Capitol)
3. *Drive,* Alan Jackson (Arista Nashville/RLG)
4. *Home,* Dixie Chicks (Monument/Columbia/CRG)
5. *No Shoes, No Shirt, No Problems,* Kenny Chesney (BNA/RLG)
6. *ELV1S: 30 #1 Hits,* Elvis Presley (RCA)
7. *Unleashed,* Toby Keith (DreamWorks/Interscope)
8. *Pull My Chain,* Toby Keith (DreamWorks/Interscope)
9. *Cry,* Faith Hill (Warner Bros./WRN)
10. *Greatest Hits,* Martina McBride (RCA/RLG)

Top 10 Pop Singles, 2002

1. "A Moment Like This," Kelly Clarkson (RCA)
2. "Uh Huh," B2K (Epic)
3. "Lights, Camera, Action!," Mr. Cheeks (Universal/UMRG)
4. "Hush Lil' Lady," Corey featuring Lil' Romeo (Noontime/Motown/UMRG)
5. "Girlfriend," 'N Sync featuring Nelly (Jive)
6. "A Thousand Miles," Vanessa Carlton (A&M/Interscope)
7. "How You Remind Me," Nickelback (Roadrunner/IDJMG)
8. "Can't Fight the Moonlight," LeAnn Rimes (Curb)
9. "The Star Spangled Banner," Whitney Houston (Arista)
10. "AM to PM," Christina Milian (Def Soul/IDJMG)

Top 10 Pop Albums, 2002

1. *The Eminem Show,* Eminem (Web/Aftermath/Interscope)
2. *Weathered,* Creed (Wind-up)
3. *Nellyville,* Nelly (Fo' Reel/Universal/UMRG)
4. *Misundaztood,* Pink (Arista)
5. *[Hybrid Theory],* Linkin Park (Warner Bros.)
6. *O Brother, Where Art Thou?,* Soundtrack (Lost Highway/Mercury/IDJMG)
7. *Silver Side Up,* Nickelback (Roadrunner/IDJMG)
8. *Britney,* Britney Spears (Jive/Zomba)
9. *Now 8,* Various Artists (EMI/Universal/Sony/Zomba/Virgin)
10. *Word of Mouf,* Ludacris (Disturbing Tha Peace/Def Jam South/IDJMG)

Top 10 R&B/Hip-Hop Singles, 2002

1. "Uh Huh," B2K (Epic)
2. "Lights, Camera, Action!," Mr. Cheeks (Universal/UMRG)
3. "Round and Round," Jonell and Method Man (Def Soul/Def Jam/IDJMG)
4. "Hush Lil' Lady," Corey featuring Lil' Romeo (Noontime/Motown)
5. "Dansin Wit Wolvez," Strik 9ine (Fade/ECMD)
6. "It's the Weekend," Lil' J (Hollywood)
7. "Feels Good (Don't Worry Bout a Thing"), Naughty by Nature featuring 3LW (TVT)
8. "Girlfriend," 'N Sync featuring Nelly (Jive)
9. "Ballin' Boy," No Good (ARTISTdirect)
10. "Family Affair," Mary J. Blige (MCA)

Top 10 R&B/Hip-Hop Albums, 2002

1. *The Eminem Show,* Eminem (Web/Aftermath/Interscope)
2. *Word of Mouf,* Ludacris (Disturbing Tha Peace/Def Jam South/IDJMG)
3. *Nellyville,* Nelly (Fo' Reel/Universal/UMRG)
4. *Ashanti,* Ashanti (Murder Inc./AJM/IDJMG)
5. *Stillmatic,* Nas (Ill Will/Columbia/CRG)
6. *Pain Is Love,* Ja Rule (Murder Inc./Def Jam/IDJMG)
7. *8701,* Usher (Arista)
8. *Invincible,* Michael Jackson (Epic)
9. *Genesis,* Busta Rhymes (J)
10. *P. Diddy & Bad Boy Records Present . . . We Invented the Remix,* Various Artists (Bad Boy/Arista)

Top 10 Rap Singles, 2002

1. "Hot in Herre," Nelly (Fo' Reel/Universal/UMRG)
2. "Always on Time," Ja Rule featuring Ashanti (Murder Inc./Def Jam/IDJMG)
3. "Dilemma," Nelly featuring Kelly Rowland (Fo' Reel/Universal/UMRG)
4. "What's Luv?," Fat Joe featuring Ashanti (Terror Squad/Atlantic)
5. "I Need a Girl (Part Two)," P. Diddy & Ginuwine featuring Loon, Mario Winans & Tammy Ruggeri (Bad Boy/Arista))
6. "Oh Boy," Cam'ron featuring Juelz Santana (Roc-A-Fella/Def Jam/IDJMG)
7. "Nothin'," N.O.R.E. (Def Jam/IDJMG)
8. "I Need a Girl (Part One)," P. Diddy featuring Usher & Loon (Bad Boy/Arista))
9. "Gangsta Lovin'," Eve featuring Alicia Keys (Ruff Ryders/Interscope)
10. "Move B***H," Ludacris featuring Mystikal & Infamous 2.0 (Disturbing Tha Peace/Def Jam South/IDJMG)

Source: © 2002/2003 VNU Business Media, Inc. The Billboard ® Charts are the exclusive property of VNU Business Media, Inc. and are fully protected by copyright and trademark laws. Any reproduction or copying, in whatever form, now or hereafter requires prior written approval from VNU Business Media, Inc.

The Recording Industry Association of America's Top-Selling Albums of All Time*

28 Million
Eagles Their Greatest Hits 1971–1975, Eagles (Elektra)

26 Million
Thriller, Michael Jackson (Epic)

23 Million
The Wall, Pink Floyd (Columbia)

22 Million
Led Zeppelin IV, Led Zeppelin (Swan Song)

21 Million
Greatest Hits Volumes I & II, Billy Joel (Columbia)

19 Million
Back in Black, AC/DC (Elektra)
The Beatles, The Beatles (Capitol)
Come On Over, Shania Twain (Mercury Nashville)

18 Million
Rumours, Fleetwood Mac (Warner Bros.)

17 Million
The Bodyguard (Soundtrack), Whitney Houston (Arista)

16 Million
Boston, Boston (Epic)
Cracked Rear View, Hootie & the Blowfish (Atlantic)
Hotel California, Eagles (Elektra)
Jagged Little Pill, Alanis Morissette (Maverick)
No Fences, Garth Brooks (Capitol Nashville)
The Beatles 1967–1970, The Beatles (Capitol)

15 Million
Appetite for Destruction, Guns 'N Roses (Geffen)
Born in the U.S.A., Bruce Springsteen (Columbia)
Dark Side of the Moon, Pink Floyd (Capitol)
Greatest Hits, Elton John (Rocket)
Physical Graffiti, Led Zeppelin (Swan Song)
Saturday Night Fever (Soundtrack), Bee Gees (Polydor/Atlas)
The Beatles 1962–1966, The Beatles (Capitol)
Double Live, Garth Brooks (Capitol Nashville)

14 Million
Backstreet Boys, Backstreet Boys (Jive)
Bat Out of Hell, Meat Loaf (Epic)
Ropin' the Wind, Garth Brooks (Capitol Nashville)
Supernatural, Santana (Arista)

13 Million
. . . Baby One More Time, Britney Spears (Jive)
Bruce Springsteen & the E Street Band Live 1975–1985 (Box set), Bruce Springsteen & the E Street Band (Columbia)
Millennium, Backstreet Boys (Jive)
Purple Rain (Soundtrack), Prince and the Revolution (Warner Bros.)
Simon & Garfunkel's Greatest Hits, Simon & Garfunkel (Columbia)
Whitney Houston, Whitney Houston (Arista)

12 Million
Abbey Road, The Beatles (Capitol)
Breathless, Kenny G (Arista)
Forrest Gump (Soundtrack) (Epic)
Hysteria, Def Leppard (Mercury)
II, Boyz II Men (Motown)
Kenny Rogers' Greatest Hits, Kenny Rogers (Capitol Nashville)
Led Zeppelin II, Led Zeppelin (Atlantic)
Metallica, Metallica (Elektra)
No Jacket Required, Phil Collins (Atlantic)
Slippery When Wet, Bon Jovi (Mercury)
The Woman in Me, Shania Twain (Mercury Nashville)
Yourself or Someone Like You, matchbox twenty (Atlantic)
Hot Rocks, The Rolling Stones (abkco)

11 Million
Eagles Greatest Hits, Vol. II, Eagles (Elektra)
Candle in the Wind 1997/Something About the Way You Look Tonight (Single), Elton John (Rocket)
CrazySexyCool, TLC (LaFace)
Dirty Dancing (Soundtrack) (RCA)
Houses of the Holy, Led Zeppelin (Atlantic)
James Taylor's Greatest Hits, James Taylor (Warner Bros.)
No Strings Attached, 'N Sync (Jive)
Pieces of You, Jewel (Atlantic)
Sgt. Pepper's Lonely Hearts Club Band, The Beatles (Capitol)
Ten, Pearl Jam (Epic)
Titanic (Soundtrack) (Sony Classical)
Wide Open Spaces, Dixie Chicks (Monument)
Falling into You, Celine Dion (550 Music)

*Through 11/01/2002.

Rock and Roll Hall of Fame

The Rock and Roll Hall of Fame honors musicians and music-industry figures who have contributed to the energy and evolution of rock music. To be eligible for inclusion, musicians and bands must have released a record at least 25 years prior to the year of induction.

1986
Chuck Berry
James Brown
Ray Charles
Sam Cooke
Fats Domino
The Everly Brothers
Buddy Holly
Jerry Lee Lewis
Elvis Presley
Little Richard
Nonperformers
Alan Freed
Sam Phillips
Early Influences
Robert Johnson
Jimmie Rodgers
Jimmy Yancey
Lifetime Achievement
John Hammond

1987
The Coasters
Eddie Cochran
Bo Diddley
Aretha Franklin
Marvin Gaye
Bill Haley
B.B. King
Clyde McPhatter
Ricky Nelson
Roy Orbison
Carl Perkins
Smokey Robinson
Joe Turner
Muddy Waters
Jackie Wilson
Nonperformers
Leonard Chess
Ahmet Ertegun
Jerry Leiber and Mike Stoller
Jerry Wexler
Early Influences
Louis Jordan
T-Bone Walker
Hank Williams

1988
The Beach Boys
The Beatles
The Drifters
Bob Dylan
The Supremes
Nonperformer
Berry Gordy, Jr.
Early Influences
Woody Guthrie
Leadbelly
Les Paul

1989
Dion
Otis Redding
The Rolling Stones
The Temptations
Stevie Wonder
Nonperformer
Phil Spector
Early Influences
The Ink Spots
Bessie Smith
The Soul Stirrers

1990
Hank Ballard
Bobby Darin
The Four Seasons
The Four Tops
The Kinks
The Platters
Simon and Garfunkel
The Who
Nonperformers
Gerry Goffin and Carole King
Brian Holland, Eddie Holland, and Lamont Dozier
Early Influences
Louis Armstrong
Charlie Christian
Ma Rainey

1991
LaVern Baker
The Byrds
John Lee Hooker
The Impressions
Wilson Pickett
Jimmy Reed
Ike and Tina Turner
Nonperformers
Dave Bartholomew
Ralph Bass
Early Influence
Howlin' Wolf
Lifetime Achievement
Nesuhi Ertegun

1992
Bobby "Blue" Bland
Booker T. and the MG's
Johnny Cash
Jimi Hendrix Experience
Isley Brothers
Sam and Dave
The Yardbirds
Nonperformers
Leo Fender
Bill Graham
Doc Pomus
Early Influences
Elmore James
Professor Longhair

1993
Ruth Brown
Cream
Creedence Clearwater Revival
The Doors
Etta James
Frankie Lymon and the Teenagers
Van Morrison
Sly and the Family Stone
Nonperformers
Dick Clark
Milt Gabler
Early Influence
Dinah Washington

1994
The Animals
The Band
Duane Eddy
The Grateful Dead
Elton John
John Lennon
Bob Marley
Rod Stewart
Nonperformer
Johnny Otis
Early Influence
Willie Dixon

1995
The Allman Brothers Band
Al Green
Janis Joplin
Led Zeppelin
Martha and the Vandellas
Neil Young
Frank Zappa
Nonperformer
Paul Ackerman
Early Influence
The Orioles

1996
David Bowie
Jefferson Airplane
Little Willie John
Gladys Knight and the Pips
Pink Floyd
The Shirelles
The Velvet Underground
Nonperformer
Tom Donahue
Early Influence
Pete Seeger

1997
The Bee Gees
Buffalo Springfield
Crosby, Stills and Nash
The Jackson Five
Joni Mitchell
Parliament-Funkadelic
The (Young) Rascals
Nonperformer
Syd Nathan
Early Influences
Mahalia Jackson
Bill Monroe

1998
The Eagles
Fleetwood Mac
Mamas and Papas
Lloyd Price
Santana
Gene Vincent
Nonperformer
Allen Toussaint
Early Influence
"Jelly Roll" Morton

1999
Billy Joel
Curtis Mayfield
Paul McCartney
Del Shannon
Dusty Springfield
Bruce Springsteen
The Staple Singers
Nonperformer
George Martin
Early Influences
Charles Brown
Bob Wills and His Texas Playboys

2000
Eric Clapton
Earth, Wind, and Fire
Lovin' Spoonful
The Moonglows
Bonnie Raitt
James Taylor
Nonperformer
Clive Davis
Early Influences
Nat King Cole
Billie Holiday
Side-Men
Hal Blaine
King Curtis
James Jamerson
Scotty Moore
Earl Palmer

2001
Aerosmith
Solomon Burke
The Flamingos
Michael Jackson
Queen
Paul Simon
Steely Dan
Ritchie Valens
Nonperformer
Chris Blackwell
Side-Men
James Burton
Johnnie Johnson

2002
Isaac Hayes
Brenda Lee
Tom Petty and the Heartbreakers
Gene Pitney
Ramones
Talking Heads
Nonperformer
Jim Stewart
Side-Men
Chet Atkins

2003
AC/DC
The Clash
Elvis Costello and the Attractions
The Police
The Righteous Brothers
Nonperformer
Mo Ostin
Side-Men
Benny Benjamin
Floyd Cramer
Steve Douglas

Country Music Hall of Fame

1961
Jimmie Rodgers
Fred Rose
Hank Williams

1962
Roy Acuff

1963
No candidate received enough votes for induction.

1964
Tex Ritter

1965
Ernest Tubb

1966
Eddy Arnold
James R. Denny
George D. Hay
Uncle Dave Macon

1967
Red Foley
J. L. Frank
Jim Reeves
Stephen H. Sholes

1968
Bob Wills

1969
Gene Autry

1970
Bill Monroe
Original Carter Family

1971
Arthur Edward Satherley

1972
Jimmie H. Davis

1973
Chet Atkins
Patsy Cline

1974
Owen Bradley
Frank "Pee Wee" King

1975
Minnie Pearl

1976
Paul Cohen
Kitty Wells

1977
Merle Travis

1978
Grandpa Jones

1979
Hubert Long
Hank Snow

1980
Johnny Cash
Connie B. Gay
Original Sons of the Pioneers

1981
Vernon Dalhart
Grant Turner

1982
Lefty Frizzell
Roy Horton
Marty Robbins

1983
Little Jimmy Dickens

1984
Ralph Sylvester Peer
Floyd Tillman

1985
Lester Flatt and Earl Scruggs

1986
Whitey Ford
Wesley H. Rose

1987
Rod Brasfield

1988
Loretta Lynn
Roy Rogers

1989
Jack Stapp
Cliffie Stone
Hank Thompson

1990
Tennessee Ernie Ford

1991
Boudleaux and Felice Bryant

1992
George Jones
Frances Williams Preston

1993
Willie Nelson

1994
Merle Haggard

1995
Roger Miller
Jo Walker-Meador

1996
Patsy Montana
Buck Owens
Ray Price

1997
Harlan Howard
Brenda Lee
Cindy Walker

1998
George Morgan
Elvis Presley
E. W. "Bud" Wendell
Tammy Wynette

1999
Johnny Bond
Dolly Parton
Conway Twitty

2000
Charley Pride
Faron Young

2001
Bill Anderson
The Delmore Brothers
The Everly Brothers
Don Gibson
Homer & Jethro
Waylon Jennings
The Jordanaires
Don Law
The Louvin Brothers
Ken Nelson
Sam Phillips
Webb Pierce

2002
Bill Carlisle
Porter Wagoner

Top 10 DVD Sales, 2002

1. *Monsters, Inc.* (Walt Disney Home Entertainment/Buena Vista Home Entertainment)
2. *Pearl Harbor: 60th Anniversary Commemorative Edition* (Touchstone Home Video/Buena Vista Home Entertainment)
3. *Shrek (Special Edition)* (DreamWorks Home Entertainment)
4. *The Fast and the Furious* (Universal Studios Home Video)
5. *Harry Potter and the Sorcerer's Stone (Pan & Scan)* (Warner Home Video)
6. *The Lord of the Rings: The Fellowship of the Ring (Widescreen)* (New Line Home Entertainment/Warner Home Video)
7. *Rush Hour 2* (New Line Home Entertainment/Warner Home Video)
8. *Black Hawk Down* (Columbia TriStar Home Entertainment)
9. *Harry Potter and the Sorcerer's Stone (Widescreen)* (Warner Home Video)
10. *Training Day* (Warner Home Video)

Top 10 Video Sales, 2002

1. *Shrek* (DreamWorks Home Entertainment)
2. *How the Grinch Stole Christmas* (Universal Studios Home Video)
3. *Harry Potter and the Sorcerer's Stone* (Warner Home Video)
4. *Monsters, Inc.* (Walt Disney Home Entertainment/Buena Vista Home Entertainment)
5. *Pearl Harbor: 60th Anniversary Commemorative Edition* (Touchstone Home Video/Buena Vista Home Entertainment)
6. *The Princess Diaries* (Walt Disney Home Entertainment/Buena Vista Home Entertainment)
7. *Cinderella II—Dreams Come True* (Walt Disney Home Entertainment/Buena Vista Home Entertainment)
8. *The Lord of the Rings: The Fellowship of the Ring* (New Line Home Entertainment/Warner Home Video)
9. *Atlantis: The Lost Empire* (Walt Disney Home Entertainment/Buena Vista Home Entertainment)
10. *Jurassic Park III* (Universal Studios Home Video)

Source: © 2002/2003 VNU Business Media, Inc. The Billboard ® Charts are the exclusive property of VNU Business Media, Inc. and are fully protected by copyright and trademark laws. Any reproduction or copying, in whatever form, now or hereafter requires prior written approval from VNU Business Media, Inc.

Top 10 Video Rentals, 2002

1. *Don't Say a Word* (FoxVideo)
2. *Training Day* (Warner Home Video)
3. *Ocean's Eleven* (Warner Home Video)
4. *The Fast and the Furious* (Universal Studios Home Video)
5. *Rush Hour 2* (New Line Home Entertainment/Warner Home Video)
6. *Pearl Harbor* (Touchstone Home Video/Buena Vista Home Entertainment)
7. *The Score* (Paramount Home Video)
8. *Rat Race* (Paramount Home Video)
9. *The Others* (Dimension Home Video/Buena Vista Home Entertainment)
10. *Domestic Disturbance* (Paramount Home Entertainment)

Source: © 2002/2003 VNU Business Media, Inc. The Billboard ® Charts are the exclusive property of VNU Business Media, Inc. and are fully protected by copyright and trademark laws. Any reproduction or copying, in whatever form, now or hereafter requires prior written approval from VNU Business Media, Inc.

Top 10 Kid Videos, 2002

1. *Cinderella II—Dreams Come True* (Walt Disney Home Entertainment/Buena Vista Home Entertainment)
2. *The Land Before Time: The Big Freeze* (Universal Studios Home Video)
3. *Mickey's Magical Christmas: Snowed in the House of Mouse* (Walt Disney Home Entertainment/Buena Vista Home Entertainment)
4. *Tarzan & Jane* (Walt Disney Home Entertainment/Buena Vista Home Entertainment)
5. *Barbie in the Nutcracker* (Artisan Home Entertainment)
6. *Peter Pan: Return to Neverland* (Walt Disney Home Entertainment/Buena Vista Home Entertainment)
7. *Mary-Kate & Ashley: Holiday in the Sun* (Dualstar Video/Warner Home Video)
8. *The Hunchback of Notre Dame II* (Walt Disney Home Entertainment/Buena Vista Home Entertainment)
9. *Spider-Man: The Ultimate Villain Showdown* (Buena Vista Home Entertainment)
10. *Scooby-Doo and the Reluctant Werewolf* (Warner Family Entertainment/Warner Home Video)

Source: © 2002/2003 VNU Business Media, Inc. The Billboard ® Charts are the exclusive property of VNU Business Media, Inc. and are fully protected by copyright and trademark laws. Any reproduction or copying, in whatever form, now or hereafter requires prior written approval from VNU Business Media, Inc.

Weekly TV Viewing by Age
(in hours and minutes)

	Time per week		
	Nov. 2002	**Nov. 2001**	**Nov. 2000**
Women 18–24	23 hr 52 min	23 hr 11 min	23 hr 21 min
Women 25–54	33 hr 56 min	33 hr 56 min	33 hr 54 min
Women 55+	44 hr 52 min	44 hr 11 min	44 hr 31 min
Men 18–24	23 hr 31 min	22 hr 00 min	23 hr 21 min
Men 25–54	31 hr 05 min	30 hr 44 min	31 hr 15 min
Men 55+	40 hr 29 min	39 hr 39 min	40 hr 40 min

	Time per week		
	Nov. 2002	**Nov. 2001**	**Nov. 2000**
Female teens 12–17	21 hr 30 min	21 hr 20 min	21 hr 20 min
Male teens 12–17	22 hr 20 min	22 hr 20 min	22 hr 40 min
Children 2–5	24 hr 32 min	24 hr 01 min	24 hr 22 min
Children 6–11	20 hr 10 min	20 hr 40 min	21 hr 40 min

Source: Nielsen Media Research. © 2003, Nielsen Media Research.

Television Set Ownership
Estimated total number of TV households: 106,700,000[1]

	1950	1955	1960	1965	1970	1975	1980	1985	1990	1995	2000	2001	2002
% of total households:													
TV households	10%	67%	87%	94%	96%	97%	98%	98%	98%	98%	98%	98%	98%
% of TV households:													
Multi-set	—	4	12	22	35	43	50	57	65	71	76	74	75
Color	—	—	—	7	41	74	83	91	98	99	99	100	100
VCR	—	—	—	—	—	—	—	14	66	79	86	91	92
Remote control	—	—	—	—	—	—	—	29	77	91	95	95	95
Wired pay cable	—	—	—	—	—	—	—	26	29	28	32	40	48
Wired cable	—	—	—	—	7	12	20	43	56	63	68	69	70

1. As of January 2003. *Source:* Nielsen Media Research. © 2003, Nielsen Media Research.

Top 10 Television Specials, 2002–2003[1]

Rank	Program name (network)	Rating (% of TV households)
1.	*Academy Awards* (ABC)	20.4%
2.	*American Idol Special* (Fox)	17.2
3.	*20/20 Special* (2/6/2003) (ABC)	16.8
4.	*Joe Millionaire Special* (Fox)	16.6
5.	*Everybody Loves Raymond Special* (CBS)	15.3
6.	*Grammy Awards* (CBS)	14.7%
7.	*Will & Grace Clip Show* (NBC)	14.5
8.	*My Big Fat Greek Life Special* (CBS)	14.3
9.	*Primetime Special Edition* (12/4/2002) (ABC)	13.8
10.	*Friends Special* (2/6/2003) (NBC)	13.6

NOTES: Each rating point represents 1,067,000 households using television. Does not include sports telecasts. 1. Sept. 23, 2002–May 25, 2003. *Source:* Nielsen Media Research. © 2003, Nielsen Media Research.

Top 10 Syndicated TV Programs, 2002–2003[1]

Rank	Program name	Rating (% of TV households)
1.	*Wheel of Fortune*	9.3%
2.	*Jeopardy*	7.3
3.	*Friends* (AT)	7.0
4.	*Seinfeld* (AT)	6.9
5.	*ESPN NFL Regular Season*	6.4
6.	*Everybody Loves Raymond* (AT)	6.2
7.	*Seinfeld* (weekend) (AT)	6.1
8.	*Oprah Winfrey Show* (AT)	5.9
9.	*Entertainment Tonight* (AT)	5.8
10.	*Seinfeld* (AT)	5.7
11.	*World Wrestling Ent.*	5.4
12.	*Judge Judy* (AT)	5.2
13.	*Seinfeld* (weekend) (AT)	5.1
13.	*ESPN NFL Regular Season 2*	5.1%
15.	*MMN Home Team Baseball*	5.0
16.	*Dr. Phil Show*	4.7
17.	*Wheel of Fortune* (weekend)	4.5
18.	*Will & Grace* (AT)	4.1
19.	*That 70s Show* (AT)	3.7
19.	*Warner Bros. Vol. 32*	3.7
21.	*Live with Regis and Kelly*	3.6
22.	*Entertainment Tonight* (weekend)	3.5
22.	*Judge Joe Brown* (AT)	3.5
24.	*Inside Edition*	3.4

NOTES: Each rating point represents 1,067,000 households using television. (AT) = Additional Telecasts. 1. Sept. 23, 2002–May 25, 2003. *Source:* Nielsen Media Research.

Top 10 Regularly Scheduled Network Programs, 2002–2003[1]

Rank	Program name (network)	Rating (% of TV households)
1.	*CSI* (CBS)	16.1%
2.	*Friends* (NBC)	13.8
3.	*Joe Millionaire* (Fox)	13.3
4.	*ER* (NBC)	12.9
5.	*American Idol—Tues.* (Fox)	12.6
6.	*American Idol—Wed.* (Fox)	12.5
7.	*Survivor: Thailand* (CBS)	12.1
8.	*Everybody Loves Raymond* (CBS)	11.9
9.	*Survivor: Amazon* (CBS)	11.7
9.	*Law & Order* (NBC)	11.7
11.	*NFL Monday Night Football* (ABC)	11.2
12.	*CSI: Miami* (CBS)	11.0
13.	*Will & Grace* (NBC)	10.9
14.	*The Bachelorette* (ABC)	10.7
15.	*Scrubs* (NBC)	10.3%
16.	*Law & Order: SVU* (NBC)	10.0
16.	*Without a Trace* (CBS)	10.0
18.	*The Bachelor* (ABC)	9.6
19.	*60 Minutes* (CBS)	9.5
19.	*Judging Amy* (CBS)	9.5
21.	*Still Standing* (CBS)	9.4
22.	*Law & Order: Criminal Intent—*10:00 P.M. (NBC)	9.3
22.	*Law & Order: Criminal Intent* (NBC)	9.3
24.	*West Wing* (NBC)	9.0
25.	*JAG* (CBS)	8.9

NOTE: Each rating point represents 1,067,000 households using television. 1. Sept. 23, 2002–May 25, 2003. *Source:* Nielsen Media Research.

Top 10 Sports Telecasts, 2002–2003[1]

Rank	Program name (network)	Rating (% of TV households)
1.	Super Bowl XXXVII (ABC)	40.7%
2.	Super Bowl Showcase (ABC)	35.3
3.	Super Bowl Post Gun (ABC)	33.1
4.	Super Bowl Kickoff III (ABC)	29.6
5.	AFC Championship (CBS)	24.6
6.	NFC Championship (Fox)	23.8
7.	Super Bowl Post Game (ABC)	23.4
8.	AFC Divisional Playoff—Sun. (CBS)	22.1
9.	AFC Championship Post Gun (CBS)	18.9
10.	NFC Playoff—Sun. (Fox)	18.3

NOTE: Each rating point represents 1,067,000 households using television. 1. Sept. 23, 2002–May 25, 2003. *Source:* Nielsen Media Research.

Top 100 Daily Newspapers in the United States

Rank	Newspaper	Circulation
1.	*USA Today* (Arlington, Va.)	2,136,068
2.	*Wall Street Journal* (New York, N.Y.)	1,800,607
3.	*Times* (New York, N.Y.)	1,113,000
4.	*Times* (Los Angeles)	925,135
5.	*Post* (Washington, DC)	746,724
6.	*Daily News* (New York, N.Y.)	715,070
7.	*Tribune* (Chicago)	679,327
8.	*Post* (New York, N.Y.)	590,061
9.	*Newsday* (Long Island, N.Y.)	578,809
10.	*Chronicle* (Houston)	552,052
11.	*Chronicle* (San Francisco)	512,129
12.	*Morning News* (Dallas)	505,724
13.	*Sun-Times* (Chicago)	479,584
14.	*Globe* (Boston)	467,745
15.	*Arizona Republic* (Phoenix)	448,782
16.	*Star-Ledger* (Newark, N.J.)	408,557
17.	*Inquirer* (Philadelphia)	373,892
18.	*Journal-Constitution* (Atlanta)	371,161
19.	*Free Press* (Detroit)	368,839
20.	*Plain Dealer* (Cleveland)	363,750
21.	*Oregonian* (Portland)	342,789
22.	*Star Tribune* (Minneapolis)	342,780
23.	*Union-Tribune* (San Diego)	342,447
24.	*Times* (St. Petersburg, Fla.)	333,557
25.	*Herald* (Miami)	315,340
26.	*Post* (Denver)	305,060

Rank	Newspaper	Circulation
27.	*Rocky Mountain News* (Denver)	304,949
28.	*Register* (Orange County, Calif.)	300,888
29.	*Sun* (Baltimore)	300,410
30.	*Post-Dispatch* (St. Louis)	287,424
31.	*Bee* (Sacramento, Calif.)	283,194
32.	*Mercury News* (San Jose, Calif.)	272,682
33.	*Star* (Kansas City, Mo.)	269,188
34.	*Investor's Business Daily* (Los Angeles)	264,699
35.	*Sentinel* (Orlando, Fla.)	256,520
36.	*Times-Picayune* (New Orleans)	255,994
37.	*Star* (Indianapolis)	254,624
38.	*Dispatch* (Columbus, Ohio)	251,557
39.	*Post-Gazette* (Pittsburgh, Pa.)	243,091
40.	*Herald* (Boston)	242,957
41.	*News* (Detroit)	242,391
42.	*Journal Sentinel* (Milwaukee)	242,234
43.	*Sun-Sentinel* (Fort Lauderdale, Fla.)	238,589
44.	*Observer* (Charlotte, N.C.)	235,759
45.	*Times* (Seattle)	224,140
46.	*News* (Buffalo, N.Y.)	223,957
47.	*Express-News* (San Antonio, Tex.)	220,998
48.	*Star-Telegram* (Fort Worth, Tex.)	218,975
49.	*Courier-Journal* (Louisville, Ky.)	217,396
50.	*Tribune* (Tampa, Fla.)	214,178
51.	*Daily Oklahoman* (Oklahoma City)	199,581
52.	*Virginian-Pilot* (Norfolk, Va.)	195,866
53.	*Pioneer Press* (St. Paul, Minn.)	194,870
54.	*Courant* (Hartford, Conn.)	190,312
55.	*World-Herald* (Omaha, Neb.)	190,218
56.	*Enquirer* (Cincinnati)	189,084
57.	*Times-Dispatch* (Richmond, Va.)	187,409
58.	*Democrat-Gazette* (Little Rock, Ark.)	185,709
59.	*Tennessean* (Nashville)	184,106
60.	*American-Statesman* (Austin, Tex.)	183,288
61.	*Contra Costa Times* (Walnut Creek, Calif.)	182,196
62.	*Press-Enterprise* (Riverside, Calif.)	178,994
63.	*Record* (Bergen County, N.J.)	178,962
64.	*Daily News* (Los Angeles)	178,217
65.	*Democrat and Chronicle* (Rochester, N.Y.)	172,124
66.	*Asbury Park Press* (Neptune, N.J.)	168,718
67.	*Times-Union* (Jacksonville, Fla.)	168,558
68.	*Post* (W. Palm Beach, Fla.)	167,531
69.	*Journal* (Providence, R.I.)	166,836
70.	*Review-Journal* (Las Vegas)	164,848
71.	*News & Observer* (Raleigh, N.C.)	163,460
72.	*Bee* (Fresno, Calif.)	158,286
73.	*Post-Intelligencer* (Seattle)	157,558
74.	*Commercial Appeal* (Memphis)	156,513
75.	*Register* (Des Moines, Iowa)	152,633
76.	*Daily News* (Philadelphia)	150,154
77.	*Daily Herald* (Chicago)	149,882
78.	*News* (Birmingham, Ala.)	145,571
79.	*Advertiser* (Honolulu)	143,696
80.	*Blade* (Toledo, Ohio)	140,628
81.	*Press* (Grand Rapids, Mich.)	140,135
82.	*World* (Tulsa, Okla.)	139,383
83.	*Journal News* (Westchester Co., N.Y.)	139,170
84.	*Tribune* (Salt Lake City)	134,777
85.	*Beacon Journal* (Akron, Ohio)	134,774
86.	*Daily News* (Dayton, Ohio)	131,435
87.	*News Tribune* (Tacoma, Wash.)	128,739
88.	*La Opinion* (Los Angeles, Calif.)	126,189
89.	*Post-Standard* (Syracuse, N.Y.)	123,836
90.	*Tribune-Review* (Greensburg, Pa.)	119,338
91.	*News Journal* (Wilmington, Del.)	119,163
92.	*Morning Call* (Allentown, Pa.)	118,859
93.	*State* (Columbia, S.C.)	115,959
94.	*News-Sentinel* (Knoxville, Tenn.)	112,017
95.	*Herald-Leader* (Lexington, Ky.)	108,892
96.	*Journal* (Albuquerque)	108,344
97.	*Herald-Tribune* (Sarasota, Fla.)	106,594
98.	*Telegram & Gazette* (Worcester, Mass.)	102,978
99.	*Spokesman-Review* (Spokane, Wash.)	102,805
100.	*Patriot-News* (Harrisburg, Pa.)	101,598

NOTES: By circulation, as of Sept. 30, 2002. Most circulations are based on partial-week averages, therefore above circulations do not reflect full-week circulations. *Source: Editor & Publisher International Year Book 2003*. Web: www.editorandpublisher.com.

Top 100 Consumer Magazines, 2002

Rank	Magazine	Total paid circulation
1.	*NRTA/AARP Bulletin*	21,703,580
2.	*AARP Modern Maturity*	17,360,979
3.	*Reader's Digest*	12,078,469
4.	*TV Guide*	9,067,124
5.	*Better Homes and Gardens*	7,605,204
6.	*National Geographic*	6,774,138
7.	*Good Housekeeping*	4,699,736
8.	*Family Circle*	4,634,069
9.	*Woman's Day*	4,205,049
10.	*TIME*	4,111,927
11.	*Ladies' Home Journal*	4,101,347
12.	*My Generation*	3,999,683
13.	*People*	3,625,427
14.	*Rosie*	3,420,788
15.	*Westways*	3,369,799
16.	*Home & Away*	3,312,075
17.	*Sports Illustrated*	3,249,418
18.	*Playboy*	3,215,454
19.	*Newsweek*	3,183,008
20.	*Prevention*	3,140,916
21.	*Cosmopolitan*	2,992,536
22.	*Guideposts*	2,702,124
23.	*Via Magazine*	2,643,896
24.	*American Legion Magazine*	2,639,097
25.	*Southern Living*	2,555,114
26.	*Maxim*	2,540,631
27.	*Seventeen*	2,445,539
28.	*Glamour*	2,406,859
29.	*Redbook*	2,387,297
30.	*Martha Stewart Living*	2,341,229
31.	*O, The Oprah Magazine*	2,268,585
32.	*ym*	2,231,752
33.	*AAA Going Places*	2,202,555
34.	*Parents*	2,092,113
35.	*Parenting Magazine*	2,087,873
36.	*Smithsonian*	2,042,862
37.	*U.S. News & World Report*	2,025,890
38.	*Money*	1,970,666
39.	*Ebony*	1,863,227
40.	*National Enquirer*	1,788,210

Rank	Magazine	Total paid circulation
41.	*Country Living*	1,735,170
42.	*V.F.W. Magazine*	1,686,452
43.	*Men's Health*	1,677,574
44.	*Shape*	1,668,253
45.	*In Style*	1,665,493
46.	*Entertainment Weekly*	1,640,989
47.	*Woman's World*	1,639,759
48.	*Teen People*	1,627,431
49.	*Cooking Light*	1,587,597
50.	*Golf Digest*	1,571,362
51.	*Endless Vacation*	1,549,971
52.	*ESPN The Magazine*	1,543,242
53.	*Field & Stream*	1,531,660
54.	*FamilyFun*	1,508,819
55.	*American Rifleman*	1,492,011
56.	*Popular Science*	1,477,129
57.	*Sunset*	1,461,921
58.	*First for Women*	1,460,999
59.	*Golf Magazine*	1,418,153
60.	*Star Magazine*	1,410,116
61.	*Health*	1,384,093
62.	*Car and Driver*	1,378,481
63.	*Boys' Life*	1,323,678
64.	*Self*	1,308,693
65.	*Bon Appetit*	1,292,856
66.	*Motor Trend*	1,277,657
67.	*Rolling Stone*	1,263,840
68.	*Vogue*	1,251,639
69.	*PC Magazine*	1,231,822
70.	*Popular Mechanics*	1,229,696
71.	*Fitness*	1,225,515
72.	*Scholastic Parent & Child*	1,223,634
73.	*Family Handyman*	1,154,551
74.	*Stuff*	1,150,511
75.	*Vanity Fair*	1,119,473
76.	*PC World*	1,106,573
77.	*American Hunter*	1,106,396
78.	*Country Home*	1,103,081
79.	*Real Simple*	1,094,148
80.	*US Weekly*	1,084,622
81.	*Elks Magazine*	1,078,955
82.	*Outdoor Life*	1,078,609
83.	*CosmoGIRL!*	1,062,271
84.	*Scouting*	1,061,718
85.	*FHM*	1,059,061
86.	*Essence*	1,057,303
87.	*Discover*	1,051,434
88.	*Kiplinger's Personal Finance*	1,048,670
89.	*Michigan Living*	1,041,626
90.	*Home*	1,019,284
91.	*Elle*	995,183
92.	*Soap Opera Digest*	987,525
93.	*BusinessWeek*	982,349
94.	*Victoria*	963,409
95.	*Travel & Leisure*	961,774
96.	*This Old House*	957,340
97.	*Food & Wine*	954,795
98.	*Jet*	953,646
99.	*Allure*	953,473
100.	*Marie Claire*	947,662
Top 100		**248,967,368**

Source: Audit Bureau of Circulations, tabulated by Magazine Publishers of America.

Selected Political and Cultural Magazines

Magazine	2002 total paid circulation
The New Yorker	931,974
Scientific American	684,986
Atlantic Monthly	514,713
Economist	405,660
American Heritage	347,093
Utne Reader	225,743
Harper's	224,932
Mother Jones[1]	201,233
National Review	155,392
The Nation	122,998
New York Review of Books	118,169
New Republic	85,069

1. Publisher's statements for second half 2002 not available; numbers for first six months only. *Source:* Audit Bureau of Circulations.

American Film Institute's 50 Greatest Screen Legends

The American Film Institute defines an American screen legend as "an actor or a team of actors with a significant screen presence in American feature-length films whose screen debut occurred in or before 1950, or whose screen debut occurred after 1950 but whose death has marked a completed body of work."

Men

1. Humphrey Bogart
2. Cary Grant
3. James Stewart
4. Marlon Brando
5. Fred Astaire
6. Henry Fonda
7. Clark Gable
8. James Cagney
9. Spencer Tracy
10. Charlie Chaplin
11. Gary Cooper
12. Gregory Peck
13. John Wayne
14. Laurence Olivier
15. Gene Kelly
16. Orson Welles
17. Kirk Douglas
18. James Dean
19. Burt Lancaster
20. The Marx Brothers
21. Buster Keaton
22. Sidney Poitier
23. Robert Mitchum
24. Edward G. Robinson
25. William Holden

Women

1. Katharine Hepburn
2. Bette Davis
3. Audrey Hepburn
4. Ingrid Bergman
5. Greta Garbo
6. Marilyn Monroe
7. Elizabeth Taylor
8. Judy Garland
9. Marlene Dietrich
10. Joan Crawford
11. Barbara Stanwyck
12. Claudette Colbert
13. Grace Kelly
14. Ginger Rogers
15. Mae West
16. Vivien Leigh
17. Lillian Gish
18. Shirley Temple
19. Rita Hayworth
20. Lauren Bacall
21. Sophia Loren
22. Jean Harlow
23. Carole Lombard
24. Mary Pickford
25. Ava Gardner

American Film Institute's 100 Greatest Movies of All Time

1. *Citizen Kane* (1941)
2. *Casablanca* (1942)
3. *The Godfather* (1972)
4. *Gone with the Wind* (1939)
5. *Lawrence of Arabia* (1962)
6. *The Wizard of Oz* (1939)
7. *The Graduate* (1967)
8. *On the Waterfront* (1954)
9. *Schindler's List* (1993)
10. *Singin' in the Rain* (1952)
11. *It's a Wonderful Life* (1946)
12. *Sunset Boulevard* (1950)
13. *The Bridge on the River Kwai* (1957)
14. *Some Like It Hot* (1959)
15. *Star Wars* (1977)
16. *All About Eve* (1950)
17. *The African Queen* (1951)
18. *Psycho* (1960)
19. *Chinatown* (1974)
20. *One Flew Over the Cuckoo's Nest* (1975)
21. *The Grapes of Wrath* (1940)
22. *2001: A Space Odyssey* (1968)
23. *The Maltese Falcon* (1941)
24. *Raging Bull* (1980)
25. *E.T. the Extra-Terrestrial* (1982)
26. *Dr. Strangelove* (1964)
27. *Bonnie and Clyde* (1967)
28. *Apocalypse Now* (1979)
29. *Mr. Smith Goes to Washington* (1939)
30. *The Treasure of the Sierra Madre* (1948)
31. *Annie Hall* (1977)
32. *The Godfather Part II* (1974)
33. *High Noon* (1952)
34. *To Kill a Mockingbird* (1962)
35. *It Happened One Night* (1934)
36. *Midnight Cowboy* (1969)
37. *The Best Years of Our Lives* (1946)
38. *Double Indemnity* (1944)
39. *Doctor Zhivago* (1965)
40. *North by Northwest* (1959)
41. *West Side Story* (1961)
42. *Rear Window* (1954)
43. *King Kong* (1933)
44. *The Birth of a Nation* (1915)
45. *A Streetcar Named Desire* (1951)
46. *A Clockwork Orange* (1971)
47. *Taxi Driver* (1976)
48. *Jaws* (1975)
49. *Snow White and the Seven Dwarfs* (1937)
50. *Butch Cassidy and the Sundance Kid* (1969)
51. *The Philadelphia Story* (1940)
52. *From Here to Eternity* (1953)
53. *Amadeus* (1984)
54. *All Quiet on the Western Front* (1930)
55. *The Sound of Music* (1965)
56. *M*A*S*H* (1970)
57. *The Third Man* (1949)
58. *Fantasia* (1940)
59. *Rebel Without a Cause* (1955)
60. *Raiders of the Lost Ark* (1981)
61. *Vertigo* (1958)
62. *Tootsie* (1982)
63. *Stagecoach* (1939)
64. *Close Encounters of the Third Kind* (1977)
65. *The Silence of the Lambs* (1991)
66. *Network* (1976)
67. *The Manchurian Candidate* (1962)
68. *An American in Paris* (1951)
69. *Shane* (1953)
70. *The French Connection* (1971)
71. *Forrest Gump* (1994)
72. *Ben-Hur* (1959)
73. *Wuthering Heights* (1939)
74. *The Gold Rush* (1925)
75. *Dances with Wolves* (1990)
76. *City Lights* (1931)
77. *American Graffiti* (1973)
78. *Rocky* (1976)
79. *The Deer Hunter* (1978)
80. *The Wild Bunch* (1969)
81. *Modern Times* (1936)
82. *Giant* (1956)
83. *Platoon* (1986)
84. *Fargo* (1996)
85. *Duck Soup* (1933)
86. *Mutiny on the Bounty* (1935)
87. *Frankenstein* (1931)
88. *Easy Rider* (1969)
89. *Patton* (1970)
90. *The Jazz Singer* (1927)
91. *My Fair Lady* (1964)
92. *A Place in the Sun* (1951)
93. *The Apartment* (1960)
94. *GoodFellas* (1990)
95. *Pulp Fiction* (1994)
96. *The Searchers* (1956)
97. *Bringing Up Baby* (1938)
98. *Unforgiven* (1992)
99. *Guess Who's Coming to Dinner* (1967)
100. *Yankee Doodle Dandy* (1942)

Movie Revenues

All-Time Box Office Grosses[1]

1.	*Titanic* (1997)	$600,788,188
2.	*Star Wars* (1977)[2]	460,998,007
3.	*E.T. the Extra-Terrestrial* (1982)[2]	434,949,459
4.	*Star Wars: Episode One: The Phantom Menace* (1999)	431,088,295
5.	*Spider-Man* (2002)	403,706,375
6.	*Jurassic Park* (1993)	357,067,947
7.	*Lord of the Rings: The Two Towers* (2002)	339,734,454[3]
8.	*Forrest Gump* (1994)[2]	329,694,499
9.	*The Lion King* (1994)[2]	328,539,505
10.	*Finding Nemo* (2003)	320,020,760[3]
11.	*Harry Potter and the Sorcerer's Stone* (2001)	317,575,550
12.	*The Lord of the Rings: The Fellowship of the Ring* (2001)	313,364,114
13.	*Star Wars: Episode II: Attack of the Clones* (2002)	310,675,583
14.	*Return of the Jedi* (1983)[2]	309,209,079
15.	*Independence Day* (1996)	306,169,255
16.	*The Sixth Sense* (1999)	293,506,292
17.	*The Empire Strikes Back* (1980)[2]	290,271,960
18.	*Home Alone* (1990)	285,761,243
19.	*The Matrix Reloaded* (2003)	277,084,749[3]
20.	*Shrek* (2001)	267,665,011
21.	*Harry Potter and the Chamber of Secrets* (2002)	261,970,615
22.	*Dr. Seuss' How the Grinch Stole Christmas* (2000)	260,031,035
23.	*Jaws* (1975)[2]	260,000,000
24.	*Monsters, Inc.* (2001)	255,870,172
25.	*Batman* (1989)	251,188,924

Top 25 Movies of 2002[4]

1.	*Spider-Man* (Sony)	$403,706,375
2.	*Lord of the Rings: The Two Towers* (New Line)	337,013,432[3]
3.	*Star Wars: Episode II—Attack of the Clones* (Fox)	310,670,131[3]
4.	*Harry Potter and the Chamber of Secrets* (Warner Bros.)	261,970,615[3]
5.	*My Big Fat Greek Wedding* (IFC Films)	241,437,427
6.	*Signs* (Buena Vista)	227,965,690
7.	*Austin Powers in Goldmember* (New Line)	213,117,789
8.	*Men in Black 2* (Sony)	190,418,803
9.	*Ice Age* (Fox)	176,387,405
10.	*Catch Me If You Can* (DreamWorks)	164,304,610[3]
11.	*Die Another Day* (MGM)	160,201,106
14.	*Chicago* (Miramax)	156,851,720[3]
12.	*Scooby-Doo* (Warner Bros.)	153,294,164
13.	*Lilo & Stitch* (Buena Vista)	145,771,527
15.	*XXX* (Sony)	141,204,016
16.	*The Santa Clause 2* (Buena Vista)	139,225,854
17.	*Minority Report* (Fox)	132,024,714
18.	*The Ring* (DreamWorks)	128,579,698
19.	*Sweet Home Alabama* (Buena Vista)	127,214,072
20.	*Mr. Deeds* (Sony)	126,293,452
21.	*The Bourne Identity* (Universal)	121,661,683
22.	*The Sum of All Fears* (Paramount)	118,501,173
23.	*8 Mile* (Universal)	116,724,075
24.	*Road to Perdition* (DreamWorks)	104,339,248
25.	*Panic Room* (Sony)	95,308,367

1. As of Aug. 3, 2003. 2. Including reissues. 3. Still tracking. 4. As of April 13, 2003. *Source:* Exhibitor Relations Co. Inc.

The One Hundred Eighth Congress

Composition of the 107th and 108th Congresses

108th Congress	Rep.	Dem.	Ind.	Male	Female
Senate	51	48	1	86	14
House	229	205	1	373	62

107th Congress	Rep.	Dem.	Ind.	Male	Female
Senate	50	50	—	87	13
House	221	212	2	376	59

The Senate

Dates in left column indicate term in office; birth dates are given in parentheses after party affiliation. All terms are for six years and expire in January. Senators listed in italics were elected or reelected in 2002.

Alabama
1987–2005 Richard Shelby (R) (1934)
1997–2009 Jeff Sessions (R) (1946)
Alaska
1969–2009 Ted Stevens (R) (1923)
2002–2005 Lisa Murkowski (R) (1957)[1]
Arizona
1987–2005 John McCain (R) (1936)
1995–2007 Jon Kyl (R) (1942)
Arkansas
2003–2009 Mark Pryor (D) (1963)
1999–2005 Blanche Lincoln (D) (1960)
California
1993–2007 Dianne Feinstein (D) (1933)
1993–2005 Barbara Boxer (D) (1940)
Colorado
1993–2005 Ben Nighthorse Campbell (R) (1933)
1997–2009 Wayne Allard (R) (1943)
Connecticut
1981–2005 Christopher J. Dodd (D) (1944)
1989–2007 Joseph I. Lieberman (D) (1942)
Delaware
1973–2009 Joseph R. Biden, Jr. (D) (1942)
2001–2007 Thomas R. Carper (D) (1947)
Florida
1987–2005 Bob Graham (D) (1936)
2001–2007 Bill Nelson (D) (1942)
Georgia
2003–2009 Saxby Chambliss (R) (1943)
2000–2005 Zell Miller (D) (1932)[2]
Hawaii
1963–2005 Daniel K. Inouye (D) (1924)
1990–2007 Daniel K. Akaka (D) (1924)
Idaho
1991–2009 Larry E. Craig (R) (1945)
1999–2005 Mike Crapo (R) (1951)
Illinois
1997–2009 Richard J. Durbin (D) (1944)
1999–2005 Peter G. Fitzgerald (R) (1960)
Indiana
1977–2007 Richard G. Lugar (R) (1932)
1999–2005 Evan Bayh (D) (1955)
Iowa
1981–2005 Chuck Grassley (R) (1933)
1985–2009 Tom Harkin (D) (1939)
Kansas
1997–2005 Sam Brownback (R) (1956)
1997–2009 Pat Roberts (R) (1936)
Kentucky
1985–2009 Mitch McConnell (R) (1942)
1999–2005 Jim Bunning (R) (1931)
Louisiana
1987–2005 John B. Breaux (D) (1944)
1997–2009 Mary L. Landrieu (D) (1955)
Maine
1995–2007 Olympia J. Snowe (R) (1947)
1997–2009 Susan M. Collins (R) (1952)

Maryland
1977–2007 Paul S. Sarbanes (D) (1933)
1987–2005 Barbara A. Mikulski (D) (1936)
Massachusetts
1963–2007 Edward M. Kennedy (D) (1932)
1985–2009 John F. Kerry (D) (1943)
Michigan
1979–2009 Carl Levin (D) (1934)
2001–2007 Debbie A. Stabenow (D) (1950)
Minnesota
2003–2009 Norm Coleman (R) (1949)
2001–2007 Mark Dayton (D) (1947)
Mississippi
1979–2009 Thad Cochran (R) (1937)
1989–2007 Trent Lott (R) (1941)
Missouri
1987–2005 Christopher S. "Kit" Bond (R) (1939)
2003–2009 James M. Talent (R) (1956)
Montana
1978–2009 Max Baucus (D) (1941)
1989–2007 Conrad Burns (R) (1935)
Nebraska
1997–2009 Charles Hagel (R) (1946)
2001–2007 Ben Nelson (D) (1941)
Nevada
1987–2005 Harry Reid (D) (1939)
2001–2007 John Ensign (R) (1958)
New Hampshire
1993–2005 Judd Gregg (R) (1947)
2003–2009 John E. Sununu (R) (1964)
New Jersey
2001–2007 Jon Corzine (D) (1947)
2003–2009 Frank R. Lautenberg (D) (1924)
New Mexico
1973–2009 Pete V. Domenici (R) (1932)
1983–2007 Jeff Bingaman (D) (1943)
New York
1999–2005 Charles E. Schumer (D) (1950)
2001–2007 Hillary Rodham Clinton (D) (1947)
North Carolina
1999–2005 John Edwards (D) (1953)
2003–2009 Elizabeth Dole (R) (1936)
North Dakota
1987–2007 Kent Conrad (D) (1948)
1993–2005 Byron L. Dorgan (D) (1942)
Ohio
1995–2007 Mike DeWine (R) (1947)
1999–2005 George Voinovich (R) (1936)
Oklahoma
1989–2005 Don Nickles (R) (1948)
1994–2009 James M. Inhofe (R) (1934)
Oregon
1996–2005 Ron Wyden (D) (1949)
1997–2009 Gordon H. Smith (R) (1952)
Pennsylvania
1981–2005 Arlen Specter (R) (1930)
1995–2007 Rick Santorum (R) (1958)

Rhode Island
1997–2009 Jack Reed (D) (1949)
1999–2007 Lincoln Chafee (R) (1953)
South Carolina
1966–2005 Ernest Hollings (D) (1922)
2003–2009 Lindsey Graham (R) (1955)
South Dakota
1987–2005 Thomas A. Daschle (D) (1947)
1997–2009 Tim Johnson (D) (1946)
Tennessee
1995–2007 William Frist (R) (1952)
2003–2009 Lamar Alexander (R) (1940)
Texas
1995–2007 Kay Bailey Hutchison (R) (1943)
2003–2009 John Cornyn (R) (1952)
Utah
1977–2007 Orrin G. Hatch (R) (1934)
1993–2005 Robert F. Bennett (R) (1933)
Vermont
1975–2005 Patrick Leahy (D) (1940)
1989–2007 James M. Jeffords (I) (1934)
Virginia
1979–2009 John Warner (R) (1927)
2001–2007 George Allen (R) (1952)
Washington
1993–2005 Patty Murray (D) (1950)
2001–2007 Maria Cantwell (D) (1958)
West Virginia
1959–2007 Robert C. Byrd (D) (1917)
1985–2009 John D. "Jay" Rockefeller IV (D) (1937)
Wisconsin
1989–2007 Herbert Kohl (D) (1935)
1993–2005 Russ Feingold (D) (1953)
Wyoming
1995–2007 Craig Thomas (R) (1933)
1997–2009 Michael B. Enzi (R) (1944)

1. Lisa Murkowski was appointed to serve out the remaining term of Frank H. Murkowski, who resigned to become governor. 2. Zell Miller was appointed and then elected to serve out the remaining term of Paul Coverdell, who died in July 2000.

The House of Representatives

In the following lists, the numeral indicates the congressional district represented; AL is for representatives at large. All terms run from Jan. 2003 to Jan. 2005.

Alabama
1. Jo Bonner (R)
2. Terry Everett (R)
3. Mike Rogers (R)
4. Robert B. Aderholt (R)
5. Robert E. "Bud" Cramer, Jr. (D)
6. Spencer Bachus (R)
7. Artur Davis (D)

Alaska
AL Don Young (R)

Arizona
1. Rick Renzi (R)
2. Trent Franks (R)
3. John Shadegg (R)
4. Ed Pastor (D)
5. J. D. Hayworth (R)
6. Jeff Flake (R)
7. Raul Grijalva (D)
8. Jim Kolbe (R)

Arkansas
1. Marion Berry (D)
2. Vic Snyder (D)
3. John Boozman (R)
4. Mike Ross (D)

California
1. Mike Thompson (D)
2. Wally Herger (R)
3. Doug Ose (R)
4. John T. Doolittle (R)
5. Robert T. Matsui (D)
6. Lynn C. Woolsey (D)
7. George Miller (D)
8. Nancy Pelosi (D)
9. Barbara Lee (D)
10. Ellen O. Tauscher (D)
11. Richard W. Pombo (R)
12. Tom Lantos (D)
13. Pete Stark (D)
14. Anna G. Eshoo (D)
15. Michael M. Honda (D)
16. Zoe Lofgren (D)
17. Sam Farr (D)
18. Dennis Cardoza (D)
19. George P. Radanovich (R)
20. Cal Dooley (D)
21. Devin Nunes (R)
22. Bill Thomas (R)
23. Lois Capps (D)
24. Elton Gallegly (R)
25. Howard P. "Buck" McKeon (R)
26. David Dreier (R)
27. Brad Sherman (D)
28. Howard L. Berman (D)
29. Adam B. Schiff (D)
30. Henry A. Waxman (D)
31. Xavier Becerra (D)
32. Hilda L. Solis (D)
33. Diane Watson (D)
34. Lucille Roybal-Allard (D)
35. Maxine Waters (D)
36. Jane Harman (D)
37. Juanita Millender-McDonald (D)
38. Grace F. Napolitano (D)
39. Linda T. Sanchez (D)
40. Ed Royce (R)
41. Jerry Lewis (R)
42. Gary G. Miller (R)
43. Joe Baca (D)
44. Ken Calvert (R)
45. Mary Bono (R)
46. Dana Rohrabacher (R)
47. Loretta Sanchez (D)
48. Christopher Cox (R)
49. Darrell Issa (R)
50. Randy "Duke" Cunningham (R)
51. Bob Filner (D)
52. Duncan Hunter (R)
53. Susan Davis (D)

Colorado
1. Diana DeGette (D)
2. Mark Udall (D)
3. Scott McInnis (R)
4. Marilyn Musgrave (R)
5. Joel Hefley (R)
6. Tom Tancredo (R)
7. Bob Beauprez (R)

Connecticut
1. John B. Larson (D)
2. Rob Simmons (R)
3. Rosa L. DeLauro (D)
4. Christopher Shays (R)
5. Nancy L. Johnson (R)

Delaware
AL Michael N. Castle (R)

Florida
1. Jeff Miller (R)
2. Allen Boyd (D)
3. Corrine Brown (D)
4. Ander Crenshaw (R)
5. Virginia Brown-Waite (R)
6. Cliff Stearns (R)
7. John L. Mica (R)
8. Ric Keller (R)
9. Michael Bilirakis (R)
10. C. W. Bill Young (R)
11. Jim Davis (D)
12. Adam Putnam (R)
13. Katherine Harris (R)
14. Porter J. Goss (R)
15. Dave Weldon (R)
16. Mark Foley (R)
17. Kendrick Meek (D)
18. Ileana Ros-Lehtinen (R)
19. Robert Wexler (D)
20. Peter Deutsch (D)
21. Lincoln Diaz-Balart (R)
22. E. Clay Shaw, Jr. (R)
23. Alcee L. Hastings (D)
24. Tom Feeney (R)
25. Mario Diaz-Balart (R)

Georgia
1. Jack Kingston (R)
2. Sanford D. Bishop, Jr. (D)
3. Jim Marshall (D)
4. Denise Majette (D)
5. John Lewis (D)
6. Johnny Isakson (R)
7. John Linder (R)
8. Mac Collins (R)
9. Charlie Norwood (R)
10. Nathan Deal (R)
11. Phil Gingrey (R)
12. Max Burns (R)
13. David Scott (D)

Hawaii
1. Neil Abercrombie (D)
2. Ed Case (D)

Idaho
1. C. L. "Butch" Otter (R)
2. Mike Simpson (R)

Illinois
1. Bobby L. Rush (D)
2. Jesse L. Jackson, Jr. (D)
3. William O. Lipinski (D)
4. Luis V. Gutierrez (D)
5. Rahm Emanuel (D)
6. Henry J. Hyde (R)
7. Danny K. Davis (D)
8. Philip M. Crane (R)

9. Janice Schakowsky (D)
10. Mark Steven Kirk (R)
11. Jerry Weller (R)
12. Jerry F. Costello (D)
13. Judy Biggert (R)
14. J. Dennis Hastert (R)
15. Timothy V. Johnson (R)
16. Donald Manzullo (R)
17. Lane Evans (D)
18. Ray LaHood (R)
19. John Shimkus (R)

Indiana
1. Peter J. Visclosky (D)
2. Chris Chocola (R)
3. Mark E. Souder (R)
4. Steve Buyer (R)
5. Dan Burton (R)
6. Mike Pence (R)
7. Julia Carson (D)
8. John Hostettler (R)
9. Baron P. Hill (D)

Iowa
1. Jim Nussle (R)
2. Jim Leach (R)
3. Leonard L. Boswell (D)
4. Tom Latham (R)
5. Steve King (R)

Kansas
1. Jerry Moran (R)
2. Jim Ryun (R)
3. Dennis Moore (D)
4. Todd Tiahrt (R)

Kentucky
1. Edward Whitfield (R)
2. Ron Lewis (R)
3. Anne M. Northup (R)
4. Ken Lucas (D)
5. Harold Rogers (R)
6. Ernie Fletcher (R)

Louisiana
1. David Vitter (R)
2. William J. Jefferson (D)
3. Billy Tauzin (R)
4. Jim McCrery (R)
5. Rodney Alexander (D)
6. Richard H. Baker (R)
7. Chris John (D)

Maine
1. Tom Allen (D)
2. Mike Michaud (D)

Maryland
1. Wayne T. Gilchrest (R)
2. C. A. "Dutch" Ruppersberger (D)
3. Benjamin L. Cardin (D)
4. Albert R. Wynn (D)
5. Steny H. Hoyer (D)
6. Roscoe G. Bartlett (R)
7. Elijah E. Cummings (D)
8. Chris Van Hollen (D)

Massachusetts
1. John W. Olver (D)
2. Richard E. Neal (D)
3. Jim McGovern (D)
4. Barney Frank (D)
5. Martin T. Meehan (D)
6. John F. Tierney (D)
7. Edward J. Markey (D)
8. Michael E. Capuano (D)
9. Stephen F. Lynch (D)
10. Bill Delahunt (D)

Michigan
1. Bart Stupak (D)
2. Peter Hoekstra (R)
3. Vernon J. Ehlers (R)
4. Dave Camp (R)
5. Dale Kildee (D)
6. Fred Upton (R)
7. Nick Smith (R)
8. Mike Rogers (R)
9. Joe Knollenberg (R)
10. Candice Miller (R)
11. Thaddeus McCotter (R)
12. Sander M. Levin (D)
13. Carolyn Cheeks Kilpatrick (D)
14. John Conyers, Jr. (D)
15. John D. Dingell (D)

Minnesota
1. Gil Gutknecht (R)
2. John Kline (R)
3. Jim Ramstad (R)
4. Betty McCollum (D)
5. Martin Olav Sabo (D)
6. Mark Kennedy (R)
7. Collin C. Peterson (D)
8. James L. Oberstar (D)

Mississippi
1. Roger Wicker (R)
2. Bennie Thompson (D)
3. Charles W. "Chip" Pickering (R)
4. Gene Taylor (D)

Missouri
1. William Lacy Clay (D)
2. Todd Akin (R)
3. Richard A. Gephardt (D)
4. Ike Skelton (D)
5. Karen McCarthy (D)
6. Sam Graves (R)
7. Roy Blunt (R)
8. Jo Ann Emerson (R)
9. Kenny Hulshof (R)

Montana
AL Denny Rehberg (R)

Nebraska
1. Doug Bereuter (R)
2. Lee Terry (R)
3. Tom Osborne (R)

Nevada
1. Shelley Berkley (D)
2. Jim Gibbons (R)
3. Jon Porter (R)

New Hampshire
1. Jeb Bradley (R)
2. Charles Bass (R)

New Jersey
1. Robert E. Andrews (D)
2. Frank A. LoBiondo (R)
3. Jim Saxton (R)
4. Christopher H. Smith (R)
5. Scott Garrett (R)
6. Frank Pallone, Jr. (D)
7. Mike Ferguson (R)
8. Bill Pascrell, Jr. (D)
9. Steven R. Rothman (D)
10. Donald M. Payne (D)
11. Rodney Frelinghuysen (R)
12. Rush D. Holt (D)
13. Robert Menendez (D)

New Mexico
1. Heather Wilson (R)
2. Steve Pearce (R)
3. Tom Udall (D)

New York
1. Tim Bishop (D)
2. Steve Israel (D)
3. Peter T. King (R)
4. Carolyn McCarthy (D)
5. Gary L. Ackerman (D)
6. Gregory W. Meeks (D)
7. Joseph Crowley (D)
8. Jerrold Nadler (D)
9. Anthony D. Weiner (D)
10. Edolphus Towns (D)
11. Major R. Owens (D)
12. Nydia M. Velázquez (D)
13. Vito J. Fossella (R)
14. Carolyn B. Maloney (D)
15. Charles B. Rangel (D)
16. José E. Serrano (D)
17. Eliot L. Engel (D)
18. Nita M. Lowey (D)
19. Sue W. Kelly (R)
20. John E. Sweeney (R)
21. Michael R. McNulty (D)
22. Maurice D. Hinchey (D)
23. John M. McHugh (R)
24. Sherwood L. Boehlert (R)
25. James T. Walsh (R)
26. Thomas M. Reynolds (R)
27. Jack Quinn (R)
28. Louise M. Slaughter (D)
29. Amo Houghton (R)

North Carolina
1. Frank Ballance (D)
2. Bob Etheridge (D)
3. Walter B. Jones (R)
4. David E. Price (D)
5. Richard Burr (R)
6. Howard Coble (R)
7. Mike McIntyre (D)
8. Robin Hayes (R)
9. Sue Myrick (R)
10. Cass Ballenger (R)
11. Charles H. Taylor (R)
12. Melvin L. Watt (D)
13. Brad Miller (D)

North Dakota
AL Earl Pomeroy (D)

Ohio
1. Steve Chabot (R)
2. Rob Portman (R)
3. Mike Turner (R)
4. Michael G. Oxley (R)
5. Paul E. Gillmor (R)
6. Ted Strickland (D)
7. David L. Hobson (R)
8. John A. Boehner (R)
9. Marcy Kaptur (D)
10. Dennis J. Kucinich (D)
11. Stephanie Tubbs Jones (D)
12. Pat Tiberi (R)
13. Sherrod Brown (D)
14. Steven C. LaTourette (R)
15. Deborah Pryce (R)
16. Ralph Regula (R)
17. Timothy J. Ryan (D)
18. Robert W. Ney (R)

Oklahoma
1. John Sullivan (R)
2. Brad Carson (D)
3. Frank D. Lucas (R)
4. Tom Cole (R)
5. Ernest Istook (R)

Oregon
1. David Wu (D)
2. Greg Walden (R)
3. Earl Blumenauer (D)
4. Peter A. DeFazio (D)
5. Darlene Hooley (D)

Pennsylvania
1. Robert A. Brady (D)
2. Chaka Fattah (D)
3. Phil English (R)
4. Melissa Hart (R)
5. John E. Peterson (R)
6. Jim Gerlach (R)
7. Curt Weldon (R)
8. James C. Greenwood (R)
9. Bill Shuster (R)
10. Donald L. Sherwood (R)
11. Paul E. Kanjorski (D)
12. John P. Murtha (D)
13. Joseph M. Hoeffel (D)
14. Mike Doyle (D)
15. Patrick J. Toomey (R)
16. Joe Pitts (R)
17. Tim Holden (D)
18. Tim Murphy (R)
19. Todd R. Platts (R)

Rhode Island
1. Patrick J. Kennedy (D)
2. James R. Langevin (D)

South Carolina
1. Henry E. Brown, Jr. (R)
2. Joe Wilson (R)
3. J. Gresham Barrett (R)
4. Jim DeMint (R)
5. John M. Spratt, Jr. (D)
6. James E. Clyburn (D)

South Dakota
AL William J. Janklow (R)

Tennessee
1. Bill Jenkins (R)
2. John J. "Jimmy" Duncan, Jr. (R)
3. Zach Wamp (R)
4. Lincoln Davis (D)
5. Jim Cooper (D)
6. Bart Gordon (D)
7. Marsha Blackburn (R)
8. John Tanner (D)
9. Harold E. Ford, Jr. (D)

Texas
1. Max Sandlin (D)
2. Jim Turner (D)
3. Sam Johnson (R)
4. Ralph M. Hall (D)
5. Jeb Hensarling (R)
6. Joe L. Barton (R)
7. John Culberson (R)
8. Kevin Brady (R)
9. Nick Lampson (D)
10. Lloyd Doggett (D)
11. Chet Edwards (D)
12. Kay Granger (R)
13. William "Mac" Thornberry (R)
14. Ron Paul (R)
15. Rubén Hinojosa (D)
16. Silvestre Reyes (D)
17. Charles W. Stenholm (D)
18. Sheila Jackson-Lee (D)
19. Randy Neugebauer (R)
20. Charlie Gonzalez (D)
21. Lamar S. Smith (R)
22. Tom DeLay (R)
23. Henry Bonilla (R)
24. Martin Frost (D)
25. Chris Bell (D)
26. Michael C. Burgess (R)
27. Solomon P. Ortiz (D)
28. Ciro D. Rodriguez (D)
29. Gene Green (D)
30. Eddie Bernice Johnson (D)
31. John R. Carter (R)
32. Pete Sessions (R)

Utah
1. Rob Bishop (R)
2. Jim Matheson (D)
3. Christopher B. Cannon (R)

Vermont
AL Bernard Sanders (I)

Virginia
1. Jo Ann S. Davis (R)
2. Ed Schrock (R)
3. Robert C. Scott (D)
4. Randy Forbes (R)
5. Virgil H. Goode, Jr. (R)
6. Robert W. Goodlatte (R)
7. Eric I. Cantor (R)
8. James P. Moran (D)
9. Rick Boucher (D)
10. Frank R. Wolf (R)
11. Thomas M. Davis III (R)

Washington
1. Jay Inslee (D)
2. Rick Larsen (D)
3. Brian Baird (D)
4. Doc Hastings (R)
5. George Nethercutt (R)
6. Norm Dicks (D)
7. Jim McDermott (D)
8. Jennifer Dunn (R)
9. Adam Smith (D)

West Virginia
1. Alan B. Mollohan (D)
2. Shelley Moore Capito (R)
3. Nick J. Rahall II (D)

Wisconsin
1. Paul D. Ryan (R)
2. Tammy Baldwin (D)
3. Ron Kind (D)
4. Gerald D. Kleczka (D)
5. F. James Sensenbrenner, Jr. (R)
6. Tom Petri (R)
7. David R. Obey (D)
8. Mark Green (R)

Wyoming
AL Barbara Cubin (R)

The Governors of the Fifty States

State	Governor	Current term[1]	State	Governor	Current term[1]
Ala.	*Robert Riley (R)*	*2003–2007*	Mont.	Judy Martz (R)	2001–2005
Alaska	*Frank H. Murkowski (R)*	*2002–2006*[2]	*Nebr.*	*Mike Johanns (R)*	*1999–2007*
Ariz.	*Janet Napolitano (D)*	*2003–2007*	*Nev.*	*Kenny Guinn (R)*	*2003–2007*
Ark.	*Mike Huckabee (R)*	*2003–2007*	*N.H.*	*Craig Benson (R)*	*2003–2005*
Calif.	*Gray Davis (D)*[3]	*2003–2007*	N.J.	Jim McGreevey (D)	2002–2006
Colo.	*Bill Owens (R)*	*2003–2007*	*N.M.*	*Bill Richardson (D)*	*2003–2007*
Conn.	*John G. Rowland (R)*	*2003–2007*	*N.Y.*	*George E. Pataki (R)*	*2003–2007*
Del.	Ruth Ann Minner (D)	2001–2005	N.C.	Mike Easley (D)	2001–2005
Fla.	*Jeb Bush (R)*	*2003–2007*	N.D.	John Hoeven (R)	2000–2004[2]
Ga.	*Sonny Perdue (R)*	*2003–2007*	*Ohio*	*Bob Taft (R)*	*2003–2007*
Hawaii	*Linda Lingle (R)*	*2002–2006*[2]	*Okla.*	*Brad Henry (D)*	*2003–2007*
Idaho	*Dirk Kempthorne (R)*	*2003–2007*	*Ore.*	*Ted Kulongoski (D)*	*2003–2007*
Ill.	*Rod R. Blagojevich (D)*	*2003–2007*	*Pa.*	*Ed Rendell (D)*	*2003–2007*
Ind.	Joseph E. Kernan[4] (D)	2001–2005	*R.I.*	*Don Carcieri (R)*	*2003–2007*
Iowa	*Tom Vilsack (D)*	*2003–2007*	*S.C.*	*Mark Sanford (R)*	*2003–2007*
Kans.	*Kathleen Sebelius (D)*	*2003–2007*	*S.D.*	*Mike Rounds (R)*	*2003–2007*
Ky.	Paul E. Patton (D)	1999–2003[2]	*Tenn.*	*Phil Bredesen (D)*	*2003–2007*
La.	Mike Foster (R)	2000–2004	*Tex.*	*Rick Perry (R)*	*2003–2007*
Maine	*John Baldacci (D)*	*2003–2007*	Utah	Michael O. Leavitt (R)	2001–2005
Md.	*Robert L. Ehrlich, Jr. (R)*	*2003–2007*	*Vt.*	*Jim Douglas (R)*	*2003–2005*
Mass.	*Mitt Romney (R)*	*2003–2007*	Va.	Mark Warner (D)	2002–2006
Mich.	*Jennifer Granholm (D)*	*2002–2007*	Wash.	Gary Locke (D)	2001–2005
Minn.	*Tim Pawlenty (R)*	*2003–2007*	W. Va.	Bob Wise (D)	2001–2005
Miss.	Ronnie Musgrove (D)	2000–2004	*Wis.*	*Jim Doyle (D)*	*2003–2007*
Mo.	Bob Holden (D)	2001–2005	*Wyo.*	*Dave Freudenthal (D)*	*2003–2007*

NOTE: Governors listed in italics were elected or reelected in 2002. 1. Except where indicated, all terms begin and end in January. 2. Term begins and ends in December. 3. A recall election was scheduled for Oct. 7, 2003. 4. Lt. Gov. Kernan was sworn in as governor in Sept. 2003, after Frank O'Bannon's death.

Presidential Election of 2000, Electoral and Popular Vote Summary

Principal Candidates for President and Vice President:
Republican—George W. Bush; Richard B. Cheney (winner)
Democratic—Albert A. Gore, Jr.; Joseph I. Lieberman
Green—Ralph Nader; Winona LaDuke

	George W. Bush		Albert A. Gore, Jr.		Ralph Nader		Electoral votes		
	Popular vote	%	Popular vote	%	Popular vote	%	R	D	G
Alabama	941,173	56%	692,611	42%	18,323	1%	9		
Alaska	167,398	59	79,004	28	28,747	10	3		
Arizona	781,652	51	685,341	45	45,645	3	8		
Arkansas	472,940	51	422,768	46	13,421	1	6		
California	4,567,429	42	5,861,203	53	418,707	4		54	
Colorado	883,748	51	738,227	42	91,434	5	8		
Connecticut	561,094	38	816,015	56	64,452	4		8	
Delaware	137,288	42	180,068	55	8,307	3		3	
DC	18,073	9	171,923	85	10,576	5		2[1]	
Florida	2,912,790	49	2,912,253	49	97,488	2	25		
Georgia	1,419,720	55	1,116,230	43	13,432[2]	.5	13		
Hawaii	137,845	37	205,286	56	21,623	6		4	
Idaho	336,937	67	138,637	28	12,292[2]	2	4		
Illinois	2,019,421	43	2,589,026	55	103,759	2		22	
Indiana	1,245,836	57	901,980	41	18,531[2]	.8	12		
Iowa	634,373	48	638,517	49	29,374	2		7	
Kansas	622,332	58	399,276	37	36,086	3	6		
Kentucky	872,492	57	638,898	41	23,192	2	8		
Louisiana	927,871	53	792,344	45	20,473	1	9		
Maine	286,616	44	319,951	49	37,127	6		4	
Maryland	813,797	40	1,145,782	56	53,768	3		10	
Massachusetts	878,502	33	1,616,487	60	173,564	6		12	
Michigan	1,953,139	46	2,170,418	51	84,165	2		18	
Minnesota	1,109,659	46	1,168,266	48	126,696	5		10	
Mississippi	572,844	58	404,614	41	8,122	.8	7		
Missouri	1,189,924	50	1,111,138	47	38,515	2	11		
Montana	240,178	58	137,126	33	24,437	6	3		
Nebraska	433,862	62	231,780	33	24,540	4	5		
Nevada	301,575	50	279,978	46	15,008	2	4		
New Hampshire	273,559	48	266,348	47	22,198	4	4		
New Jersey	1,284,173	40	1,788,850	56	94,554	3		15	
New Mexico	286,417	48	286,783	48	21,251	4		5	
New York	2,403,374	35	4,107,697	60	244,030	4		33	
North Carolina	1,631,163	56	1,257,692	43	—	—	14		
North Dakota	174,852	61	95,284	33	9,486	3	3		
Ohio	2,351,209	50	2,186,190	46	117,857	3	21		
Oklahoma	744,337	60	474,276	38	—	—	8		
Oregon	713,577	47	720,342	47	77,357	5		7	
Pennsylvania	2,281,127	46	2,485,967	51	103,392	2		23	
Rhode Island	130,555	32	249,508	61	25,052	6		4	
South Carolina	785,937	57	565,561	41	20,200	1	8		
South Dakota	190,700	60	118,804	38	—	—	3		
Tennessee	1,061,949	51	981,720	47	19,781	1	11		
Texas	3,799,639	59	2,433,746	38	137,994	2	32		
Utah	515,096	67	203,053	26	35,850	5	5		
Vermont	119,775	41	149,022	51	20,374	7		3	
Virginia	1,437,490	52	1,217,290	44	59,398	2	13		
Washington	1,108,864	45	1,247,652	50	103,002	4		11	
West Virginia	336,475	52	295,497	46	10,680	2	5		
Wisconsin	1,237,279	48	1,242,987	48	94,070	4		11	
Wyoming	147,947	68	60,481	28	4,625[2]	2	3		
Total	**50,456,002**	**47.87%**	**50,999,897**	**48.38%**	**2,882,955**	**2.74%**	**271**	**266**	

NOTE: Total electoral votes = 538. Total electoral votes needed to win = 270. Dash (—) indicates not on ballot. 1. The District of Columbia has 3 votes. There was 1 abstention. 2. Write-in votes. *Source:* Federal Election Commission.

Voting age population (Census Bureau Population Survey for Nov. 2000): 205,815,000
Percentage of voting age population casting a vote for president: 51.3%

How a President Is Nominated and Elected

The Conventions

The national conventions of both major parties are held during the summer of a presidential election year. Earlier, each party selects delegates by primaries, conventions, committees, etc.

At each convention, a temporary chairman is chosen. After a credentials committee seats the delegates, a permanent chairman is elected. The convention then votes on a platform, drawn up by the platform committee.

By the third or fourth day, presidential nominations begin. The chairman calls the roll of states alphabetically. A state may place a candidate in nomination or yield to another state.

Voting, again alphabetically by roll call of states, begins after all nominations have been made and seconded. A simple majority is required in each party, although this may require many ballots.

Finally, the vice-presidential candidate is selected. Although there is no law saying that the candidates *must* come from different states, it is, practically, necessary for this to be the case. Otherwise, according to the Constitution (*see* the 12th Amendment), electors from that state could vote for only one of the candidates and would have to cast their other vote for some person of another state. This could result in a presidential candidate's receiving a majority electoral vote and his or her running mate's failing to do so.

The Electoral College

The next step in the process is the nomination of electors in each state, according to its laws. These electors must not be federal office holders. In the November election, the voters cast their votes for electors, not for president. In some states, the ballots include only the names of the presidential and vice-presidential candidates; in others, they include only names of the electors. Nowadays, it is rare for electors to be split between parties. The last such occurrence was in North Carolina in 1968; the last before that, in Tennessee in 1948. On four occasions (1824, 1876, 1888, and 2000), the presidential candidate with the largest popular vote failed to obtain an electoral vote majority.

Each state has as many electors as it has senators and representatives. For the 2000 election, the total electors were 538, based on 100 senators and 435 representatives, plus 3 electoral votes from the District of Columbia as a result of the 23rd Amendment to the Constitution.

On the first Monday after the second Wednesday in December, the electors cast their votes in their respective state capitols. Constitutionally they may vote for someone other than the party candidate but usually they do not since they are pledged to one party and its candidate on the ballot. Should the presidential or vice-presidential candidate die between the November election and the December meetings, the electors pledged to vote for him or her could vote for whomever they pleased. However, it seems certain that the national committee would attempt to get an agreement among the state party leaders for a replacement candidate.

The votes of the electors, certified by the states, are sent to Congress, where the president of the Senate opens the certificates and has them counted in the presence of both houses on Jan. 6. The new president is inaugurated at noon on Jan. 20.

Should no candidate receive a majority of the electoral vote for president, the House of Representatives chooses a president from among the three highest candidates, voting, not as individuals, but as states, with a majority (now 26) needed to elect. Should no vice-presidential candidate obtain the majority, the Senate, voting as individuals, chooses from the highest two.

Electoral College Votes by State, 2004 Presidential Elections

(total electoral votes: 538; majority needed to elect: 270)

Alabama	9	Kentucky	8	North Dakota	3
Alaska	3	Louisiana	9	Ohio	20
Arizona	10	Maine	4	Oklahoma	7
Arkansas	6	Maryland	10	Oregon	7
California	55	Massachusetts	12	Pennsylvania	21
Colorado	9	Michigan	17	Rhode Island	4
Connecticut	7	Minnesota	10	South Carolina	8
Delaware	3	Mississippi	6	South Dakota	3
District of Columbia	3	Missouri	11	Tennessee	11
Florida	27	Montana	3	Texas	34
Georgia	15	Nebraska	5	Utah	5
Hawaii	4	Nevada	5	Vermont	3
Idaho	4	New Hampshire	4	Virginia	13
Illinois	21	New Jersey	15	Washington	11
Indiana	11	New Mexico	5	West Virginia	5
Iowa	7	New York	31	Wisconsin	10
Kansas	6	North Carolina	15	Wyoming	3

National Political Conventions Since 1856

Opening date	Party	Where held
June 17, 1856	Republican	Philadelphia
June 2, 1856	Democratic	Cincinnati
May 16, 1860	Republican	Chicago
April 23, 1860	Democratic	Charleston and Baltimore
June 7, 1864	Republican[1]	Baltimore
Aug. 29, 1864	Democratic	Chicago
May 20, 1868	Republican	Chicago
July 4, 1868	Democratic	New York City
June 5, 1872	Republican	Philadelphia
June 9, 1872	Democratic	Baltimore
June 14, 1876	Republican	Cincinnati
June 28, 1876	Democratic	St. Louis
June 2, 1880	Republican	Chicago
June 23, 1880	Democratic	Cincinnati
June 3, 1884	Republican	Chicago
July 11, 1884	Democratic	Chicago
June 19, 1888	Republican	Chicago
June 6, 1888	Democratic	St. Louis
June 7, 1892	Republican	Minneapolis
June 21, 1892	Democratic	Chicago
June 16, 1896	Republican	St. Louis
July 7, 1896	Democratic	Chicago
June 19, 1900	Republican	Philadelphia
July 4, 1900	Democratic	Kansas City
June 21, 1904	Republican	Chicago
July 6, 1904	Democratic	St. Louis
June 16, 1908	Republican	Chicago
July 7, 1908	Democratic	Denver
June 18, 1912	Republican	Chicago
June 25, 1912	Democratic	Baltimore
June 7, 1916	Republican	Chicago
June 14, 1916	Democratic	St. Louis
June 8, 1920	Republican	Chicago
June 28, 1920	Democratic	San Francisco
June 10, 1924	Republican	Cleveland
June 24, 1924[2]	Democratic	New York City
June 12, 1928	Republican	Kansas City
June 26, 1928	Democratic	Houston
June 14, 1932	Republican	Chicago
June 27, 1932	Democratic	Chicago
June 9, 1936	Republican	Cleveland
June 23, 1936	Democratic	Philadelphia
June 24, 1940	Republican	Philadelphia
July 15, 1940	Democratic	Chicago
June 26, 1944	Republican	Chicago
July 19, 1944	Democratic	Chicago
June 21, 1948	Republican	Philadelphia
July 12, 1948	Democratic	Philadelphia
July 17, 1948	([3])	Birmingham
July 22, 1948	Progressive	Philadelphia
July 7, 1952	Republican	Chicago
July 21, 1952	Democratic	Chicago
Aug. 20, 1956	Republican	San Francisco
Aug. 13, 1956	Democratic	Chicago
July 25, 1960	Republican	Chicago
July 11, 1960	Democratic	Los Angeles
July 13, 1964	Republican	San Francisco
Aug. 24, 1964	Democratic	Atlantic City
Aug. 5, 1968	Republican	Miami Beach
Aug. 26, 1968	Democratic	Chicago
July 10, 1972	Democratic	Miami Beach
Aug. 21, 1972	Republican	Miami Beach
July 12, 1976	Democratic	New York City
Aug. 16, 1976	Republican	Kansas City, Mo.
Aug. 11, 1980	Democratic	New York City
July 14, 1980	Republican	Detroit
Aug. 20, 1984	Republican	Dallas
July 16, 1984	Democratic	San Francisco
July 18, 1988	Democratic	Atlanta
Aug. 15, 1988	Republican	New Orleans
July 13, 1992	Democratic	New York City
Aug. 17, 1992	Republican	Houston
Aug. 10, 1996	Republican	San Diego
Aug. 26, 1996	Democratic	Chicago
July 29, 2000	Republican	Philadelphia
Aug. 14, 2000	Democratic	Los Angeles

1. The convention adopted name Union Party to attract War Democrats and others favoring prosecution of war. 2. In session until July 10, 1924. 3. States' Rights delegates from 13 southern states.

National Committee Chairs Since 1944

Chairman and (state)	Term
Republican	
Herbert Brownell, Jr. (N.Y.)	1944–1946
Carroll Reece (Tenn.)	1946–1948
Hugh D. Scott, Jr. (Pa.)	1948–1949
Guy G. Gabrielson (N.J.)	1949–1952
Arthur E. Summerfield (Mich.)	1952–1953
Wesley Roberts (Kan.)	1953
Leonard W. Hall (N.Y.)	1953–1957
Meade Alcorn (Conn.)	1957–1959
Thruston B. Morton (Ky.)	1959–1961
William E. Miller (N.Y.)	1961–1964
Dean Burch (Ariz.)	1964–1965
Ray C. Bliss (Ohio)	1965–1969
Rogers C. B. Morton (Md.)	1969–1971
Robert Dole (Kan.)	1971–1973
George H. Bush (Tex.)	1973–1974
Mary Louise Smith (Iowa)	1974–1977
William E. Brock III (Tenn.)	1977–1981
Richard Richards (Utah)	1981–1983
Frank J. Fahrenkopf, Jr. (Nevada)	1983–1989
Lee Atwater (S.C.)	1989–1991
Clayton K. Yeutter (Neb.)	1991–1992
Richard Bond (N.Y.)	1992–1993
Haley Barbour (Miss.)	1993–1997
Jim Nicholson (Colo.)	1997–2001
Jim Gilmore (Va.)	2001–2002
Marc Racicot (Mont.)	2002–2003
Ed Gillespie (DC)	2003–

Chairman and (state)	Term
Democratic	
Robert E. Hannegan (Mo.)	1944–1947
J. Howard McGrath (R.I.)	1947–1949
William M. Boyle, Jr. (Mo.)	1949–1951
Frank E. McKinney (Ind.)	1951–1952
Stephen A. Mitchell (Ill.)	1952–1954
Paul M. Butler (Ind.)	1955–1960
Henry M. Jackson (Wash.)	1960–1961
John M. Bailey (Conn.)	1961–1968
Lawrence F. O'Brien (Mass.)	1968–1969
Fred R. Harris (Okla.)	1969–1970
Lawrence F. O'Brien (Mass.)	1970–1972
Jean Westwood (Utah)	1972
Robert S. Strauss (Tex.)	1972–1977
Kenneth M. Curtis (Me.)	1977
John C. White (Tex.)	1977–1981
Charles T. Manatt (Calif.)	1981–1985
Paul G. Kirk, Jr. (Mass.)	1985–1989
Ronald H. Brown (D.C.)	1989–1993
David Wilhelm (Ill.)	1993–1994
Christopher J. Dodd (Conn.)	1995–1996
Steven Grossman (Mass.)	1996–1999
Joe Andrew (Ind.)	1999–2001
Terry McAuliffe (Va.)	2001–

Republican National Committee: 310 First St., SE, Washington, DC 20003. *Democratic National Committee:* 430 South Capitol St., SE, Washington, DC 20003.

Presidential Elections, 1789–2000

For the original method of electing the president and the vice president (elections of 1789, 1792, 1796, and 1800), *see* Article II, Section 1, of the Constitution. The election of 1804 was the first one in which the electors voted for president and vice president on separate ballots. (See Amendment XII to the Constitution.)

Year	Presidential candidate	Party	Electoral votes
1789[1]	George Washington	(no party)	69
	John Adams	(no party)	34
	Scattering	(no party)	35
	Votes not cast		8
1792	George Washington	Federalist	132
	John Adams	Federalist	77
	George Clinton	Anti-Federalist	50
	Thomas Jefferson	Anti-Federalist	4
	Aaron Burr	Anti-Federalist	1
	Votes not cast		6
1796	John Adams	Federalist	71
	Thomas Jefferson	Dem.-Rep.	68
	Thomas Pinckney	Federalist	59
	Aaron Burr	Dem.-Rep.	30
	Scattering		48
1800[2]	Thomas Jefferson	Dem.-Rep.	73
	Aaron Burr	Dem.-Rep.	73
	John Adams	Federalist	65
	Charles C. Pinckney	Federalist	64
	John Jay	Federalist	1

Year	Presidential candidate	Party	Electoral votes	Vice-presidential candidate	Party	Electoral votes
1804	Thomas Jefferson	Dem.-Rep.	162	George Clinton	Dem.-Rep.	162
	Charles C. Pinckney	Federalist	14	Rufus King	Federalist	14
1808	James Madison	Dem.-Rep.	122	George Clinton	Dem.-Rep.	113
	Charles C. Pinckney	Federalist	47	Rufus King	Federalist	47
	George Clinton	Dem.-Rep.	6	John Langdon	Ind. (no party)	9
	Votes not cast		1	James Madison	Dem.-Rep.	3
				James Monroe	Dem.-Rep.	3
				Votes not cast		1
1812	James Madison	Dem.-Rep.	128	Elbridge Gerry	Dem.-Rep.	131
	De Witt Clinton	Federalist	89	Jared Ingersoll	Federalist	86
	Votes not cast		1	Votes not cast		1
1816	James Monroe	Dem.-Rep.	183	Daniel D. Tompkins	Dem.-Rep.	183
	Rufus King	Federalist	34	John E. Howard	Federalist	22
	Votes not cast		4	James Ross	Ind (no party)	5
				John Marshall	Federalist	4
				Robert G. Harper	Ind. (no party)	3
				Votes not cast		4
1820	James Monroe	Dem-Rep	231	Daniel D. Tompkins	Dem.-Rep.	218
	John Quincy Adams	Ind. (no party)	1	Richard Stockton	Ind. (no party)	8
	Votes not cast		3	Daniel Rodney	Ind. (no party)	4
				Richard Rush	Ind. (no party)	1
				Robert G. Harper	Ind. (no party)	1
				Votes not cast		3
1824[3]	John Quincy Adams	(no party)	84	John C. Calhoun	(no party)	182
	Andrew Jackson	(no party)	99	Nathan Sanford	(no party)	30
	William H. Crawford	(no party)	41	Nathaniel Macon	(no party)	24
	Henry Clay	(no party)	37	Andrew Jackson	(no party)	13
				Martin Van Buren	(no party)	9
				Henry Clay	(no party)	2
				Votes not cast		1
1828	Andrew Jackson	Democratic	178	John C. Calhoun	Democratic	171
	John Quincy Adams	Natl. Rep.	83	Richard Rush	Natl. Rep.	83
				William Smith	Democratic	7
1832	Andrew Jackson	Democratic	219	Martin Van Buren	Democratic	189
	Henry Clay	Natl. Rep.	49	John Sergeant	Natl. Rep.	49
	John Floyd	Ind. (no party)	11	Henry Lee	Ind. (no party)	11
	William Wirt	Antimasonic[4]	7	Amos Ellmaker	Antimasonic	7
	Votes not cast		2	William Wilkins	Ind. (no party)	30
				Votes not cast		2
1836	Martin Van Buren	Democratic	170	Richard M. Johnson[5]	Democratic	147
	William H. Harrison	Whig	73	Francis Granger	Whig	77
	Hugh L. White	Whig	26	John Tyler	Whig	47
	Daniel Webster	Whig	14	William Smith	Ind. (no party)	23
	W. P. Mangum	Ind. (no party)	11			

Year	Presidential candidate	Party	Electoral votes	Vice-presidential candidate	Party	Electoral votes
1840	William H. Harrison[6]	Whig	234	John Tyler	Whig	234
	Martin Van Buren	Democratic	60	Richard M. Johnson	Democratic	48
				L. W. Tazewell	Ind. (no party)	11
				James K. Polk	Democratic	1
1844	James K. Polk	Democratic	170	George M. Dallas	Democratic	170
	Henry Clay	Whig	105	Theo. Frelinghuysen	Whig	105
1848	Zachary Taylor[7]	Whig	163	Millard Fillmore	Whig	163
	Lewis Cass	Democratic	127	William O. Butler	Democratic	127
1852	Franklin Pierce	Democratic	254	William R. King	Democratic	254
	Winfield Scott	Whig	42	William A. Graham	Whig	42
1856	James Buchanan	Democratic	174	John C. Breckinridge	Democratic	174
	John C. Fremont	Republican	114	William L. Dayton	Republican	114
	Millard Fillmore	American[8]	8	A. J. Donelson	American[8]	8
1860	Abraham Lincoln	Republican	180	Hannibal Hamlin	Republican	180
	John C. Breckinridge	Democratic	72	Joseph Lane	Democratic	72
	John Bell	Const. Union	39	Edward Everett	Const. Union	39
	Stephen A. Douglas	Democratic	12	H. V. Johnson	Democratic	12
1864	Abraham Lincoln[9]	Union[10]	212	Andrew Johnson	Union[10]	212
	George B. McClellan	Democratic	21	G. H. Pendleton	Democratic	21
1868	Ulysses S. Grant	Republican	214	Schuyler Colfax	Republican	214
	Horatio Seymour	Democratic	80	Francis P. Blair, Jr.	Democratic	80
	Votes not counted[11]		23	Votes not counted[11]		23

NOTE: Due to the communications constrictions of the time and the lack of formal political party organizations, the framers of the Constitution specified that the president and vice president be chosen based upon the votes cast by members of an electoral college rather than by a direct popular vote. Eventually, states began to change the method by which electors cast their votes. Today, all but two states, Maine and Nebraska, have a winner-take-all system in which a popular vote decides which candidates will be given all of a given state's electoral votes. The number of popular votes won by each presidential candidate are listed here for elections beginning in 1872.

Year	Presidential candidate	Party	Electoral votes	Popular votes	Vice-presidential candidate and party
1872	Ulysses S. Grant	Republican	286	3,597,132	Henry Wilson—R
	Horace Greeley	Dem., Liberal Rep.	([12])	2,834,125	B. Gratz Brown—D, LR—(47)
	Thomas A. Hendricks	Democratic	42		Scattering—(19)
	B. Gratz Brown	Dem., Liberal Rep.	18		Vote not counted—(14)
	Charles J. Jenkins	Democratic	2		
	David Davis	Democratic	1		
	Votes not counted		17		
1876[13]	Rutherford B. Hayes	Republican	185	4,033,768	William A. Wheeler—R
	Samuel J. Tilden	Democratic	184	4,285,992	Thomas A. Hendricks—D
	Peter Cooper	Greenback	0	81,737	Samuel F. Cary—G
1880	James A. Garfield[14]	Republican	214	4,449,053	Chester A. Arthur—R
	Winfield S. Hancock	Democratic	155	4,442,035	William H. English—D
	James B. Weaver	Greenback	0	308,578	B. J. Chambers—G
1884	Grover Cleveland	Democratic	219	4,911,017	Thomas A. Hendricks—D
	James G. Blaine	Republican	182	4,848,334	John A. Logan—R
	Benjamin F. Butler	Greenback	0	175,370	A. M. West—G
	John P. St. John	Prohibition	0	150,369	William Daniel—P
1888	Benjamin Harrison	Republican	233	5,440,216	Levi P. Morton—R
	Grover Cleveland	Democratic	168	5,538,233	A. G. Thurman—D
	Clinton B. Fisk	Prohibition	0	249,506	John A. Brooks—P
	Alson J. Streeter	Union Labor	0	146,935	Charles E. Cunningham—UL
1892	Grover Cleveland	Democratic	277	5,556,918	Adlai E. Stevenson—D
	Benjamin Harrison	Republican	145	5,176,108	Whitelaw Reid—R
	James B. Weaver	People's[15]	22	1,041,028	James G. Field—Peo
	John Bidwell	Prohibition	0	264,133	James B. Cranfill—P
1896	William McKinley	Republican	271	7,035,638	Garret A. Hobart—R
	William J. Bryan	Dem., People's[15]	176	6,467,946	Arthur Sewall—D—(149)
					Thomas E. Watson—Peo—(27)
	John M. Palmer	Natl. Dem.	0	133,148	Simon B. Buckner—ND
	Joshua Levering	Prohibition	0	132,007	Hale Johnson—P

Year	Presidential candidate	Party	Electoral votes	Popular votes	Vice-presidential candidate and party
1900	William McKinley[16]	Republican	292	7,219,530	Theodore Roosevelt—R
	William J. Bryan	Dem., People's[15]	155	6,358,071	Adlai E. Stevenson—D, Peo
	Eugene V. Debs	Social Democratic	0	94,768	Job Harriman—SD
1904	Theodore Roosevelt	Republican	336	7,628,834	Charles W. Fairbanks—R
	Alton B. Parker	Democratic	140	5,084,491	Henry G. Davis—D
	Eugene V. Debs	Socialist	0	402,400	Benjamin Hanford—S
1908	William H. Taft	Republican	321	7,679,006	James S. Sherman—R
	William J. Bryan	Democratic	162	6,409,106	John W. Kern—D
	Eugene V. Debs	Socialist	0	402,820	Benjamin Hanford—S
1912	Woodrow Wilson	Democratic	435	6,286,214	Thomas R. Marshall—D
	Theodore Roosevelt	Progressive	88	4,126,020	Hiram Johnson—Prog
	William H. Taft	Republican	8	3,483,922	Nicholas M. Butler—R[17]
	Eugene V. Debs	Socialist	0	897,011	Emil Seidel—S
1916	Woodrow Wilson	Democratic	277	9,129,606	Thomas R. Marshall—D
	Charles E. Hughes	Republican	254	8,538,221	Charles W. Fairbanks—R
	A. L. Benson	Socialist	0	585,113	G. R. Kirkpatrick—S
1920	Warren G. Harding[18]	Republican	404	16,152,200	Calvin Coolidge—R
	James M. Cox	Democratic	127	9,147,353	Franklin D. Roosevelt—D
	Eugene V. Debs	Socialist	0	917,799	Seymour Stedman—S
1924	Calvin Coolidge	Republican	382	15,725,016	Charles G. Dawes—R
	John W. Davis	Democratic	136	8,385,586	Charles W. Bryan—D
	Robert M. LaFollette	Progressive, Socialist	13	4,822,856	Burton K. Wheeler—Prog, S
1928	Herbert Hoover	Republican	444	21,392,190	Charles Curtis—R
	Alfred E. Smith	Democratic	87	15,016,443	Joseph T. Robinson—D
	Norman Thomas	Socialist	0	267,420	James H. Maurer—S
1932	Franklin D. Roosevelt	Democratic	472	22,821,857	John N. Garner—D
	Herbert Hoover	Republican	59	15,761,841	Charles Curtis—R
	Norman Thomas	Socialist	0	884,781	James H. Maurer—S
1936	Franklin D. Roosevelt	Democratic	523	27,751,597	John N. Garner—D
	Alfred M. Landon	Republican	8	16,679,583	Frank Knox—R
	Norman Thomas	Socialist	0	187,720	George Nelson—S
1940	Franklin D. Roosevelt	Democratic	449	27,244,160	Henry A. Wallace—D
	Wendell L. Willkie	Republican	82	22,305,198	Charles L. McNary—R
	Norman Thomas	Socialist	0	99,557	Maynard C. Krueger—S
1944	Franklin D. Roosevelt[19]	Democratic	432	25,602,504	Harry S. Truman—D
	Thomas E. Dewey	Republican	99	22,006,285	John W. Bricker—R
	Norman Thomas	Socialist	0	80,518	Darlington Hoopes—S
1948	Harry S. Truman	Democratic	303	24,179,345	Alben W. Barkley—D
	Thomas E. Dewey	Republican	189	21,991,291	Earl Warren—R
	J. Strom Thurmond	States' Rights Dem.	39	1,176,125	Fielding L. Wright—SR
	Henry A. Wallace	Progressive	0	1,157,326	Glen Taylor—Prog
	Norman Thomas	Socialist	0	139,572	Tucker P. Smith—S
1952	Dwight D. Eisenhower	Republican	442	33,936,234	Richard M. Nixon—R
	Adlai E. Stevenson	Democratic	89	27,314,992	John J. Sparkman—D
1956	Dwight D. Eisenhower	Republican	457	35,590,472	Richard M. Nixon—R
	Adlai E. Stevenson	Democratic	73[20]	26,022,752	Estes Kefauver—D
1960	John F. Kennedy[21]	Democratic	303	34,226,731	Lyndon B. Johnson—D
	Richard M. Nixon	Republican	219[22]	34,108,157	Henry Cabot Lodge—R
1964	Lyndon B. Johnson	Democratic	486	43,129,484	Hubert H. Humphrey—D
	Barry M. Goldwater	Republican	52	27,178,188	William E. Miller—R
1968	Richard M. Nixon	Republican	301	31,785,480	Spiro T. Agnew—R
	Hubert H. Humphrey	Democratic	191	31,275,166	Edmund S. Muskie—D
	George C. Wallace	American Independent	46	9,906,473	Curtis F. LeMay—AI
1972	Richard M. Nixon[23]	Republican	520[24]	47,169,911	Spiro T. Agnew—R
	George McGovern	Democratic	17	29,170,383	Sargent Shriver—D
	John G. Schmitz	American	0	1,099,482	Thomas J. Anderson—A
1976	Jimmy Carter	Democratic	297	40,830,763	Walter F. Mondale—D
	Gerald R. Ford	Republican	240[25]	39,147,973	Robert J. Dole—R
	Eugene J. McCarthy	Independent	0	756,631	None

Year	Presidential candidate	Party	Electoral votes	Popular votes	Vice-presidential candidate and party
1980	Ronald Reagan	Republican	489	43,899,248	George Bush—R
	Jimmy Carter	Democratic	49	36,481,435	Walter F. Mondale—D
	John B. Anderson	Independent	0	5,719,437	Patrick J. Lucey—I
1984	Ronald Reagan	Republican	525	54,455,075	George Bush—R
	Walter F. Mondale	Democratic	13	37,577,185	Geraldine A. Ferraro—D
1988	George H. Bush	Republican	426	48,886,097	J. Danforth Quayle—R
	Michael S. Dukakis	Democratic	111[26]	41,809,074	Lloyd Bentsen—D
1992	William J. Clinton	Democratic	370	44,909,889	Albert A. Gore, J.—D
	George H. Bush	Republican	168	39,104,545	J. Danforth Quayle—R
	H. Ross Perot	Independent	0	19,742,267	James B. Stockdale—I
1996	William J. Clinton	Democratic	379	47,402,357	Albert A. Gore, Jr.—D
	Robert J. Dole	Republican	159	39,198,755	Jack F. Kemp—R
	H. Ross Perot	Reform Party[27]	0	8,085,402	Pat Choate—RP[27]
2000	George W. Bush	Republican	271	50,456,002	Richard B. Cheney—R
	Albert A. Gore	Democratic	266[28]	50,999,897	Joseph I. Lieberman—D
	Ralph Nader	Green Party	0	2,882,955	Winona LaDuke—GP

1. Only 10 states participated in the election. The New York legislature chose no electors, and North Carolina and Rhode Island had not yet ratified the Constitution. 2. As Jefferson and Burr were tied, the House of Representatives chose the president. In a vote by states, 10 votes were cast for Jefferson, 4 for Burr; 2 votes were not cast. 3. As no candidate had an electoral-vote majority, the House of Representatives chose the president from the first three. In a vote by states, 13 votes were cast for Adams, 7 for Jackson, and 4 for Crawford. 4. The Antimasonic Party on Sept. 26, 1831, was the first party to hold a nominating convention to choose candidates for president and vice president. 5. As Johnson did not have an electoral-vote majority, the Senate chose him 33–14 over Granger, the others being legally out of the race. 6. Harrison died April 4, 1841, and Tyler succeeded him April 6. 7. Taylor died July 9, 1850, and Fillmore succeeded him July 10. 8. Also known as the Know-Nothing Party. 9. Lincoln died April 15, 1865, and Johnson succeeded him the same day. 10. Name adopted by the Republican National Convention of 1864. Johnson was a War Democrat. 11. 23 Southern electoral votes were excluded. 12. Greeley died Nov. 29, 1872, before his 66 electors voted; 63 of Greeley's votes were scattered among four of the other candidates. 13. Hayes was chosen by a special electoral commission since initially neither candidate had the requisite 185 electoral votes. 14. Garfield died Sept. 19, 1881, and Arthur succeeded him Sept. 20. 15. Members of People's Party were called Populists. 16. McKinley died Sept. 14, 1901, and Roosevelt succeeded him the same day. 17. James S. Sherman, Republican candidate for vice president, died Oct. 30, 1912, and the Republican electoral votes were cast for Butler. 18. Harding died Aug. 2, 1923, and Coolidge succeeded him Aug. 3. 19. Roosevelt died April 12, 1945, and Truman succeeded him the same day. 20. One electoral vote from Alabama was cast for Walter B. Jones. 21. Kennedy died Nov. 22, 1963, and Johnson succeeded him the same day. 22. Sen. Harry F. Byrd received 15 electoral votes. 23. Nixon resigned Aug. 9, 1974, and Gerald R. Ford succeeded him the same day. 24. One electoral vote from Virginia was cast for John Hospers, Libertarian Party. 25. One electoral vote from Washington was cast for Ronald Reagan. 26. One electoral vote from West Virginia was cast for Lloyd Bentsen. 27. Perot helped establish the Reform Party following his defeat in the 1992 election. 28. One elector from the District of Columbia left her ballot blank to protest the city's lack of representation in Congress, leaving Gore with 266 electoral votes instead of 267.

Plurality and Majority

In order to win a plurality, a candidate must receive a greater number of votes than anyone running against him. If he receives 50 votes, for example, and two other candidates receive 49 and 2, he will have a plurality of one vote over his closest opponent.

However, a candidate does not have a majority unless he receives more than 50% of the total votes cast. In the example above, the candidate does not have a majority, because his 50 votes are less than 50% of the 101 votes cast.

Presidents Elected Without a Majority

Fifteen candidates (three of them twice) have become president of the United States with a popular vote less than 50% of the total cast. It should be noted, however, that in elections before 1872, presidential electors were not chosen by popular vote in all states. Adams's election in 1824 was by the House of Representatives, which chose him over Jackson, who had a plurality of both electoral and popular votes, but not a majority in the electoral college.

The "minority" presidents are listed below.

Year	President	Electoral percent	Popular percent
1824	John Q. Adams	31.8%	29.8%
1844	James K. Polk (D)	61.8	49.3
1848	Zachary Taylor (W)	56.2	47.3
1856	James Buchanan (D)	58.7	45.3
1860	Abraham Lincoln (R)	59.4	39.9
1876	Rutherford B. Hayes (R)	50.1	47.9
1880	James A. Garfield (R)	57.9	48.3
1884	Grover Cleveland (D)	54.6	48.8
1888	Benjamin Harrison (R)	58.1	47.8

Year	President	Electoral percent	Popular percent
1892	Grover Cleveland (D)	62.4%	46.0%
1912	Woodrow Wilson (D)	81.9	41.8
1916	Woodrow Wilson (D)	52.1	49.3
1948	Harry S. Truman (D)	57.1	49.5
1960	John F. Kennedy (D)	56.4	49.7
1968	Richard M. Nixon (R)	56.1	43.4
1992	William J. Clinton (D)	68.8	43.0
1996	William J. Clinton (D)	70.4	49.0
2000	George W. Bush (R)	50.3	47.8

The Closest Presidential Races

Although the 2000 presidential race was extremely close, there have been others that were also too close to call immediately after the election. Indeed, the results of the Nov. 7 election in 1876 were not known until March 2, 1877, just three days before the inauguration. More recently, John F. Kennedy's defeat of Richard M. Nixon in 1960 wasn't official until noon the following day.

President	Electoral votes	Popular votes
1800[1]		
Thomas Jefferson (Dem.-Rep.)	73	—
Aaron Burr (Dem.-Rep.)	73	—
John Adams (Federalist)	65	—
Charles C. Pinckney (Federalist)	64	—
John Jay (Federalist)	1	—
1824[2]		
John Quincy Adams (no party)	84	—
Andrew Jackson (no party)	99	—
William H. Crawford (no party)	41	—
Henry Clay (no party)	37	—
1876		
Rutherford B. Hayes (R)	185	4,033,768
Samuel J. Tilden (D)	184	4,285,992
1880		
James A. Garfield (R)	214	4,449,053
Winfield S. Hancock (D)	155	4,442,035
1916		
Woodrow Wilson (D)	277	9,129,606
Charles E. Hughes (R)	254	8,538,221
1960		
John F. Kennedy (D)	303	34,226,731
Richard M. Nixon (R)	219	34,108,157
1968		
Richard M. Nixon (R)	301	31,785,480
Hubert H. Humphrey (R)	191	31,275,166
George C. Wallace (American Independent)	46	9,906,473
1976		
Jimmy Carter (D)	297	40,830,763
Gerald R. Ford (R)	240	39,147,973
2000		
George W. Bush (R)	271	50,455,156
Albert A. Gore (D)	266[3]	50,992,335

1. As Jefferson and Burr were tied, the House of Representatives chose the president. In a vote by states, 10 votes were cast for Jefferson, 4 for Burr; 2 votes were not cast. For the original method of electing the president and vice president (elections of 1789, 1792, 1796, and 1800), see Article II, Section 1, of the Constitution. 2. As no candidate had an electoral vote majority, the House of Representatives chose the president from the first three. In a vote by states, 13 votes were cast for Adams, 7 for Jackson, and 4 for Crawford. 3. One elector from the District of Columbia left her ballot blank to protest the city's lack of representation in Congress, leaving Gore with 266 electoral votes instead of 267.

National Voter Turnout in Federal Elections: 1964–2000

Year	Voting-age population	Voter registration	Voter turnout	Turnout of voting-age population (percent)
2000	**205,815,000**	**156,421,311**	**105,586,274**	**51.3%**
1998	200,929,000	141,850,558	73,117,022	36.4
1996	**196,511,000**	**146,211,960**	**96,456,345**	**49.1**
1994	193,650,000	130,292,822	75,105,860	38.8
1992	**189,529,000**	**133,821,178**	**104,405,155**	**55.1**
1990	185,812,000	121,105,630	67,859,189	36.5
1988	**182,778,000**	**126,379,628**	**91,594,693**	**50.1**
1986	178,566,000	118,399,984	64,991,128	36.4
1984	**174,466,000**	**124,150,614**	**92,652,680**	**53.1**
1982	169,938,000	110,671,225	67,615,576	39.8
1980	**164,597,000**	**113,043,734**	**86,515,221**	**52.6**
1978	158,373,000	103,291,265	58,917,938	37.2
1976	**152,309,190**	**105,037,986**	**81,555,789**	**53.6**
1974	146,336,000	96,199,020[1]	55,943,834	38.2
1972	**140,776,000**	**97,328,541**	**77,718,554**	**55.2**
1970	124,498,000	82,496,747[2]	58,014,338	46.6
1968	**120,328,186**	**81,658,180**	**73,211,875**	**60.8**
1966	116,132,000	76,288,283[3]	56,188,046	48.4
1964	**114,090,000**	**73,715,818**	**70,644,592**	**61.9**

n.a. = not available. NOTE: Presidential election years are in boldface. 1. Registrations from Iowa not included. 2. Registrations from Iowa and Mo. not included. 3. Registrations from Iowa, Kans., Miss., Mo., Nebr., and Wyo. not included. D.C. did not have independent status. *Source:* Federal Election Commission. Data drawn from Congressional Research Service reports, Election Data Services Inc., and State Election Offices.

Facts About Elections

Candidate with highest popular vote: Reagan (1984), 54,455,075.

Candidate with highest electoral vote: Reagan (1984), 525.

Candidate carrying most states: Nixon (1972) and Reagan (1984), 49.

Candidate running most times: Norman Thomas (Socialist Party), six (1928, 1932, 1936, 1940, 1944, 1948).

Candidate elected, defeated, then reelected: Cleveland (1884, 1888, 1892).

Presidents

	Name and (party)[1]	Term	State of birth	Born	Died	Religion	Age at inaug.	Age at death
1.	Washington (F)[2]	1789–1797	Va.	2/22/1732	12/14/1799	Episcopalian	57	67
2.	J. Adams (F)	1797–1801	Mass.	10/30/1735	7/4/1826	Unitarian	61	90
3.	Jefferson (DR)	1801–1809	Va.	4/13/1743	7/4/1826	Deist	57	83
4.	Madison (DR)	1809–1817	Va.	3/16/1751	6/28/1836	Episcopalian	57	85
5.	Monroe (DR)	1817–1825	Va.	4/28/1758	7/4/1831	Episcopalian	58	73
6.	J. Q. Adams (DR)	1825–1829	Mass.	7/11/1767	2/23/1848	Unitarian	57	80
7.	Jackson (D)	1829–1837	S.C.	3/15/1767	6/8/1845	Presbyterian	61	78
8.	Van Buren (D)	1837–1841	N.Y.	12/5/1782	7/24/1862	Reformed Dutch	54	79
9.	W. H. Harrison (W)[3]	1841	Va.	2/9/1773	4/4/1841	Episcopalian	68	68
10.	Tyler (W)	1841–1845	Va.	3/29/1790	1/18/1862	Episcopalian	51	71
11.	Polk (D)	1845–1849	N.C.	11/2/1795	6/15/1849	Methodist	49	53
12.	Taylor (W)[3]	1849–1850	Va.	11/24/1784	7/9/1850	Episcopalian	64	65
13.	Fillmore (W)	1850–1853	N.Y.	1/7/1800	3/8/1874	Unitarian	50	74
14.	Pierce (D)	1853–1857	N.H.	11/23/1804	10/8/1869	Episcopalian	48	64
15.	Buchanan (D)	1857–1861	Pa.	4/23/1791	6/1/1868	Presbyterian	65	77
16.	Lincoln (R)[4]	1861–1865	Ky.	2/12/1809	4/15/1865	Liberal	52	56
17.	A. Johnson (U)[5]	1865–1869	N.C.	12/29/1808	7/31/1875	([6])	56	66
18.	Grant (R)	1869–1877	Ohio	4/27/1822	7/23/1885	Methodist	46	63
19.	Hayes (R)	1877–1881	Ohio	10/4/1822	1/17/1893	Methodist	54	70
20.	Garfield (R)[4]	1881	Ohio	11/19/1831	9/19/1881	Disciples of Christ	49	49
21.	Arthur (R)	1881–1885	Vt.	10/5/1829	11/18/1886	Episcopalian	50	56
22.	Cleveland (D)	1885–1889	N.J.	3/18/1837	6/24/1908	Presbyterian	47	71
23.	B. Harrison (R)	1889–1893	Ohio	8/20/1833	3/13/1901	Presbyterian	55	67
24.	Cleveland (D)[7]	1893–1897	N.J.	3/18/1837	6/24/1908	Presbyterian	55	71
25.	McKinley (R)[4]	1897–1901	Ohio	1/29/1843	9/14/1901	Methodist	54	58
26.	T. Roosevelt (R)	1901–1909	N.Y.	10/27/1858	1/6/1919	Reformed Dutch	42	60
27.	Taft (R)	1909–1913	Ohio	9/15/1857	3/8/1930	Unitarian	51	72
28.	Wilson (D)	1913–1921	Va.	12/28/1856	2/3/1924	Presbyterian	56	67
29.	Harding (R)[3]	1921–1923	Ohio	11/2/1865	8/2/1923	Baptist	55	57
30.	Coolidge (R)	1923–1929	Vt.	7/4/1872	1/5/1933	Congregationalist	51	60
31.	Hoover (R)	1929–1933	Iowa	8/10/1874	10/20/1964	Quaker	54	90
32.	F. D. Roosevelt (D)[3]	1933–1945	N.Y.	1/30/1882	4/12/1945	Episcopalian	51	63
33.	Truman (D)	1945–1953	Mo.	5/8/1884	12/26/1972	Baptist	60	88
34.	Eisenhower (R)	1953–1961	Tex.	10/14/1890	3/28/1969	Presbyterian	62	78
35.	Kennedy (D)[4]	1961–1963	Mass.	5/29/1917	11/22/1963	Roman Catholic	43	46
36.	L. B. Johnson (D)	1963–1969	Tex.	8/27/1908	1/22/1973	Disciples of Christ	55	64
37.	Nixon (R)[8]	1969–1974	Calif.	1/9/1913	4/22/1994	Quaker	56	81
38.	Ford (R)	1974–1977	Neb.	7/14/1913	—	Episcopalian	61	—
39.	Carter (D)	1977–1981	Ga.	10/1/1924	—	Southern Baptist	52	—
40.	Reagan (R)	1981–1989	Ill.	2/6/1911	—	Disciples of Christ	69	—
41.	G.H.W. Bush (R)	1989–1993	Mass.	6/12/1924	—	Episcopalian	64	—
42.	Clinton (D)	1993–2001	Ark.	8/19/1946	—	Baptist	46	—
43.	G. W. Bush (R)	2001–	Conn.	7/6/46	—	Methodist	54	—

1. F—Federalist; DR—Democratic-Republican; D—Democratic; W—Whig; R—Republican; U—Union. 2. No party for first election. The party system in the U.S. made its appearance during Washington's first term. 3. Died in office. 4. Assassinated in office. 5. The Republican National Convention of 1864 adopted the name Union Party. It renominated Lincoln for president; for vice president it nominated Johnson, a War Democrat. Although frequently listed as a Republican vice president and president, Johnson undoubtedly considered himself strictly a member of the Union Party. When that party broke apart after 1868, he returned to the Democratic Party. 6. Johnson was not a professed church member; however, he admired the Baptist principles of church government. 7. Second nonconsecutive term. 8. Resigned Aug. 9, 1974.

Vice Presidents

	Name and (party)[1]	Term	State of birth	Birth and death dates	President served under
1.	John Adams (F)[2]	1789–1797	Massachusetts	1735–1826	Washington
2.	Thomas Jefferson (DR)	1797–1801	Virginia	1743–1826	J. Adams
3.	Aaron Burr (DR)	1801–1805	New Jersey	1756–1836	Jefferson
4.	George Clinton (DR)[3]	1805–1812	New York	1739–1812	Jefferson and Madison
5.	Elbridge Gerry (DR)[3]	1813–1814	Massachusetts	1744–1814	Madison
6.	Daniel D. Tompkins (DR)	1817–1825	New York	1774–1825	Monroe
7.	John C. Calhoun[4]	1825–1832	South Carolina	1782–1850	J. Q. Adams and Jackson
8.	Martin Van Buren (D)	1833–1837	New York	1782–1862	Jackson
9.	Richard M. Johnson (D)	1837–1841	Kentucky	1780–1850	Van Buren
10.	John Tyler (W)[5]	1841	Virginia	1790–1862	W. H. Harrison
11.	George M. Dallas (D)	1845–1849	Pennsylvania	1792–1864	Polk
12.	Millard Fillmore (W)[5]	1849–1850	New York	1800–1874	Taylor
13.	William R. King (D)[3]	1853	North Carolina	1786–1853	Pierce

	Name and (party)[1]	Term	State of birth	Birth and death dates	President served under
14.	John C. Breckinridge (D)	1857–1861	Kentucky	1821–1875	Buchanan
15.	Hannibal Hamlin (R)	1861–1865	Maine	1809–1891	Lincoln
16.	Andrew Johnson (U)[5]	1865	North Carolina	1808–1875	Lincoln
17.	Schuyler Colfax (R)	1869–1873	New York	1823–1885	Grant
18.	Henry Wilson (R)[3]	1873–1875	New Hampshire	1812–1875	Grant
19.	William A. Wheeler (R)	1877–1881	New York	1819–1887	Hayes
20.	Chester A. Arthur (R)[5]	1881	Vermont	1829–1886	Garfield
21.	Thomas A. Hendricks (D)[3]	1885	Ohio	1819–1885	Cleveland
22.	Levi P. Morton (R)	1889–1893	Vermont	1824–1920	B. Harrison
23.	Adlai E. Stevenson (D)	1893–1897	Kentucky	1835–1914	Cleveland
24.	Garrett A. Hobart (R)[3]	1897–1899	New Jersey	1844–1899	McKinley
25.	Theodore Roosevelt (R)[5]	1901	New York	1858–1919	McKinley
26.	Charles W. Fairbanks (R)	1905–1909	Ohio	1852–1918	T. Roosevelt
27.	James S. Sherman (R)[3]	1909–1912	New York	1855–1912	Taft
28.	Thomas R. Marshall (D)	1913–1921	Indiana	1854–1925	Wilson
29.	Calvin Coolidge (R)[5]	1921–1923	Vermont	1872–1933	Harding
30.	Charles G. Dawes (R)	1925–1929	Ohio	1865–1951	Coolidge
31.	Charles Curtis (R)	1929–1933	Kansas	1860–1936	Hoover
32.	John N. Garner (D)	1933–1941	Texas	1868–1967	F. D. Roosevelt
33.	Henry A. Wallace (D)	1941–1945	Iowa	1888–1965	F. D. Roosevelt
34.	Harry S. Truman (D)[5]	1945	Missouri	1884–1972	F. D. Roosevelt
35.	Alben W. Barkley (D)	1949–1953	Kentucky	1877–1956	Truman
36.	Richard M. Nixon (R)	1953-1961	California	1913–1994	Eisenhower
37.	Lyndon B. Johnson (D)[5]	1961–1963	Texas	1908–1973	Kennedy
38.	Hubert H. Humphrey (D)	1965–1969	South Dakota	1911–1978	L. B. Johnson
39.	Spiro T. Agnew (R)[6]	1969–1973	Maryland	1918–1996	Nixon
40.	Gerald R. Ford (R)[7]	1973–1974	Nebraska	1913–	Nixon
41.	Nelson A. Rockefeller (R)[8]	1974–1977	Maine	1908–1979	Ford
42.	Walter F. Mondale (D)	1977–1981	Minnesota	1928–	Carter
43.	George Bush (R)	1981–1989	Massachusetts	1924–	Reagan
44.	J. Danforth Quayle (R)	1989–1993	Indiana	1947–	G.H.W. Bush
45.	Albert A. Gore, Jr. (D)	1993–2001	Washington, D.C.	1948–	Clinton
46.	Richard B. Cheney (R)	2001–	Nebraska	1941–	G. W. Bush

1. F—Federalist; DR—Democratic-Republican; D—Democratic; W—Whig; R—Republican; U—Union. 2. No party for first election. The party system in the U.S. made its appearance during Washington's first term as president. 3. Died in office. 4. Democratic-Republican with J. Q. Adams; Democratic with Jackson. Calhoun resigned in 1832 to become a U.S. senator. 5. Succeeded to presidency on death of president. Prior to the passage of the 25th Amendment (ratified Feb. 10, 1967), there were no provisions for filling a vacancy in the vice presidency. In the event of a vacancy, the president pro tempore took over most of the vice president's duties. 6. Resigned Oct. 10, 1973, after pleading no contest to federal income tax evasion charges. 7. Nominated by Nixon on Oct. 12, 1973, under provisions of 25th Amendment. Confirmed by Congress on Dec. 6, 1973, and was sworn in same day. He became president Aug. 9, 1974, upon Nixon's resignation. 8. Nominated by Ford Aug. 20, 1974; confirmed by Congress on Dec. 19, 1974, and was sworn in same day.

Presidential Libraries

These are not traditional libraries, but rather repositories for preserving and making available the papers, records, and other historical materials of the presidents since Herbert Hoover. The presidential library system formally began in 1939, when President Franklin Roosevelt donated his personal and presidential papers to the federal government.

Hoover Library
210 Parkside Drive
P.O. Box 488
West Branch, IA 52358-0488
http://hoover.archives.gov

Roosevelt Library
4079 Albany Post Road
Hyde Park, NY 12538-1999
http://www.fdrlibrary.marist.edu/

Truman Library
500 West U.S. Highway 24
Independence, MO 64050-1798
http://www.trumanlibrary.org

Eisenhower Library
200 SE 4th Street
Abilene, KS 67410-2900
http://www.eisenhower.utexas.edu

Kennedy Library
Columbia Point
Boston, MA 02125-3398
http://www.jfklibrary.org

Johnson Library
2313 Red River Street
Austin, TX 78705-5702
http://www.lbjlib.utexas.edu

The Nixon Project[1]
National Archives at College Park
8601 Adelphi Road
College Park, MD 20740-6001
http://www.nixon.archives.gov/

Ford Library
1000 Beal Avenue
Ann Arbor, MI 48109-2114
http://www.ford.utexas.edu

Carter Library
441 Freedom Parkway
Atlanta, GA 30307-1498
http://www.jimmycarterlibrary.org/

Reagan Library
40 Presidential Drive
Simi Valley, CA 93065-0666
http://www.reagan.utexas.edu

Bush Library
1000 George Bush Drive West
College Station, TX 77845
http://bushlibrary.tamu.edu/

1. The Nixon Project is not affiliated with the Richard Nixon Library and Birthplace in Yorba Linda, Calif., a private institution that was established by Nixon in 1990. *Source:* National Archives and Records Administration. Web: www.archives.gov/.

Wives and Children of the Presidents

President	Wife's name	Year and place of wife's birth	Married	Wife died	Children[1] Sons	Daughters
Washington	Martha Dandridge Custis	1732, Va.	1759	1802	—	—
John Adams	Abigail Smith	1744, Mass.	1764	1818	3	2
Jefferson[2]	Martha Wayles Skelton	1748, Va.	1772	1782	1	5
Madison	Dorothy "Dolley" Payne Todd	1768, N.C.	1794	1849	—	—
Monroe	Elizabeth "Eliza" Kortright	1768, N.Y.	1786	1830	—	2
J. Q. Adams	Louisa Catherine Johnson	1775, England	1797	1852	3	1
Jackson	Rachel Donelson Robards	1767, Va.	1791	1828	—	—
Van Buren	Hannah Hoes	1788, N.Y.	1807	1819	4	—
W. H. Harrison	Anna Symmes	1775, N.J.	1795	1864	6	4
Tyler	Letitia Christian	1790, Va.	1813	1842	3	4
	Julia Gardiner	1820, N.Y.	1844	1889	5	2
Polk	Sarah Childress	1803, Tenn.	1824	1891	—	—
Taylor	Margaret Smith	1788, Md.	1810	1852	1	5
Fillmore	Abigail Powers	1798, N.Y.	1826	1853	1	1
	Caroline Carmichael McIntosh	1813, N.J.	1858	1881	—	—
Pierce	Jane Means Appleton	1806, N.H.	1834	1863	3	—
Buchanan	(Unmarried)	—	—	—	—	—
Lincoln	Mary Todd	1818, Ky.	1842	1882	4	—
A. Johnson	Eliza McCardle	1810, Tenn.	1827	1876	3	2
Grant	Julia Dent	1826, Mo.	1848	1902	3	1
Hayes	Lucy Ware Webb	1831, Ohio	1852	1889	7	1
Garfield	Lucretia Rudolph	1832, Ohio	1858	1918	5	2
Arthur	Ellen Lewis Herndon	1837, Va.	1859	1880	2	1
Cleveland	Frances Folsom	1864, N.Y.	1886	1947	2	3
B. Harrison	Caroline Lavinia Scott	1832, Ohio	1853	1892	1	1
	Mary Scott Lord Dimmick	1858, Pa.	1896	1948	—	1
McKinley	Ida Saxton	1847, Ohio	1871	1907	—	2
T. Roosevelt	Alice Hathaway Lee	1861, Mass.	1880	1884	—	1
	Edith Kermit Carow	1861, Conn.	1886	1948	4	1
Taft	Helen Herron	1861, Ohio	1886	1943	2	1
Wilson	Ellen Louise Axson	1860, Ga.	1885	1914	—	3
	Edith Bolling Galt	1872, Va.	1915	1961	—	—
Harding	Florence Kling DeWolfe	1860, Ohio	1891	1924	—	—
Coolidge	Grace Anna Goodhue	1879, Vt.	1905	1957	2	—
Hoover	Lou Henry	1875, Iowa	1899	1944	2	—
F. D. Roosevelt	(Anna) Eleanor Roosevelt	1884, N.Y.	1905	1962	5	1
Truman	Bess Wallace	1885, Mo.	1919	1982	—	1
Eisenhower	Mamie Geneva Doud	1896, Iowa	1916	1979	2	—
Kennedy	Jacqueline Lee Bouvier	1929, N.Y.	1953	1994	2	1
L. B. Johnson	Claudia Alta "Lady Bird" Taylor	1912, Tex.	1934	—	—	2
Nixon	Thelma Catherine "Pat" Ryan	1912, Nev.	1940	1993	—	2
Ford	Elizabeth "Betty" Bloomer Warren	1918, Ill.	1948	—	3	1
Carter	Rosalynn Smith	1928, Ga.	1946	—	3	1
Reagan	Jane Wyman	1914, Mo.	1940[3]	—	1[4]	1
	Nancy Davis	1921, N.Y.	1952	—	1	1
G.H.W. Bush	Barbara Pierce	1925, N.Y.	1945	—	4	2
Clinton	Hillary Rodham	1947, Ill.	1975	—	—	1
G. W. Bush	Laura Welch	1946, Tex.	1977	—	—	2

1. Includes children who died in infancy. 2. Number of children listed here reflects only children Jefferson had with Martha Wayles Skelton. Scientists and historians agree, based on DNA evidence, that Jefferson may have fathered at least one child with slave Sally Hemings. 3. Divorced in 1948. 4. Adopted.

Biographies of the Presidents

GEORGE WASHINGTON was born on Feb. 22, 1732 (Feb. 11, 1731/2, old style) in Westmoreland County, Va. While in his teens, he trained as a surveyor, and at the age of 20 he was appointed adjutant in the Va. militia. For the next three years, he fought in the wars against the French and Indians, serving as Gen. Edward Braddock's aide in the disastrous campaign against Ft. Duquesne. In 1759, he resigned from the militia, married Martha Dandridge Custis, a widow with children, and settled down as a gentleman farmer at Mount Vernon, Va.

As a militiaman, Washington had been exposed to the arrogance of the British officers, and his experience as a planter with British commercial restrictions increased his anti-British sentiment. He opposed the Stamp Act of 1765 and after 1770 became increasingly prominent in organizing resistance. A delegate to the Continental Congress, Washington was selected as commander in chief of the Continental Army and took command at Cambridge, Mass., on July 3, 1775.

Inadequately supported and sometimes covertly sabotaged by the Congress, in charge of troops who were inexperienced, badly equipped, and impatient of discipline, Washington conducted the war on the policy of avoiding major engagements with the British and wearing them down by harassing tactics. His able generalship, along with the French alliance and the growing weariness within Britain, brought the war to a conclusion with the surrender of Cornwallis at Yorktown, Va., on Oct. 19, 1781.

The chaotic years under the Articles of Confederation led Washington to return to public life in the hope of promoting the formation of a strong central government. He presided over the Constitutional Convention and yielded to the universal demand that he serve as first president. He was inaugurated on April 30, 1789, in New York, the first national capital. In office, he sought to unite the nation and establish the authority of the new government at home and abroad. Greatly distressed by the emergence of the Hamilton-Jefferson rivalry, Washington worked to maintain neutrality but actually sympathized more with Hamilton. Following his unanimous reelection in 1792, his second term was dominated by the Federalists. His Farewell Address on Sept. 17, 1796 (published but never delivered) rebuked party spirit and warned against "permanent alliances" with foreign powers.

He died at Mount Vernon on Dec. 14, 1799.

JOHN ADAMS born on Oct. 30 (Oct. 19, old style), 1735, at Braintree (now Quincy), Mass. A Harvard graduate, he considered teaching and the ministry but finally turned to law and was admitted to the bar in 1758. Six years later, he married Abigail Smith. He opposed the Stamp Act, served as lawyer for patriots indicted by the British, and by the time of the Continental Congresses, was in the vanguard of the movement for independence. In 1778, he went to France as commissioner. Subsequently he helped negotiate the peace treaty with Britain, and in 1785 became envoy to London. Resigning in 1788, he was elected vice president under Washington and was reelected in 1792.

Though a Federalist, Adams did not get along with Hamilton, who sought to prevent his election to the presidency in 1796 and thereafter intrigued against his administration. In 1798, Adams's independent policy averted a war with France but completed the break with Hamilton and the right-wing Federalists; at the same time, the enactment of the Alien and Sedition Acts, directed against foreigners and against critics of the government, exasperated the Jeffersonian opposition. The split between Adams and Hamilton resulted in Jefferson's becoming the next president. Adams retired to his home in Quincy. He and Jefferson died on the same day, July 4, 1826, the 50th anniversary of the adoption of the Declaration of Independence.

His *Defence of the Constitutions of Government of the United States* (1787) contains original and striking, if conservative, political ideas.

THOMAS JEFFERSON was born on April 13 (April 2, old style), 1743, at Shadwell in Goochland (now Albemarle) County, Va. A William and Mary graduate, he studied law, but from the start showed an interest in science and philosophy. His literary skills and political clarity brought him to the forefront of the revolutionary movement in Virginia. As delegate to the Continental Congress, he drafted the Declaration of Independence. In 1776, he entered the Virginia House of Delegates and initiated a comprehensive reform program for the abolition of feudal survivals in land tenure and the separation of church and state.

In 1779, he became governor, but constitutional limitations on his power, combined with his own lack of executive energy, caused an unsatisfactory administration, culminating in Jefferson's virtual abdication when the British invaded Virginia in 1781. He retired to his beautiful home at Monticello, Va., to his family. His wife, Martha Wayles Skelton, whom he married in 1772, died in 1782.

Jefferson's *Notes on Virginia* (1784–85) illustrate his many-faceted interests, his limitless intellectual curiosity, his deep faith in agrarian democracy. Sent to Congress in 1783, he helped lay down the decimal system and drafted basic reports on the organization of the western lands. In 1785 he was appointed minister to France, where the Anglo-Saxon liberalism he had drawn from John Locke, the British philosopher, was stimulated by contact with the thought that would soon ferment in the French Revolution. In 1789, Washington appointed him secretary of state. While favoring the Constitution and a strengthened central government, Jefferson came to believe that Hamilton contemplated the establishment of a monarchy. Growing differences resulted in Jefferson's resignation on Dec. 31, 1793.

Elected vice president in 1796, Jefferson continued to serve as spiritual leader of the opposition to Federalism, particularly to the repressive Alien and Sedition Acts. He was elected president in 1801 by the House of Representatives as a result of Hamilton's decision to throw the Federalist votes to him rather than to Aaron Burr, who had tied him in electoral votes. He was the first president to be inaugurated in Washington, which he had helped to design.

The purchase of Louisiana from France in 1803, though in violation of Jefferson's earlier constitutional scruples, was the most notable act of his administration. reelected in 1804, with the Federalist Charles C. Pinckney opposing him, Jefferson tried desperately to keep the United States out of the Napoleonic Wars in Europe, employing to this end the unpopular embargo policy.

After his retirement to Monticello in 1809, he developed his interest in education, founding the University of Virginia and watching its development with never-flagging interest. He died at Monticello on July 4, 1826. Jefferson had an enormous variety of interests and skills, ranging from education and science to architecture and music.

JAMES MADISON was born in Port Conway, Va., on March 16, 1751 (March 5, 1750/1, old style). A Princeton graduate, he joined the struggle for independence on his return to Virginia in 1771. In the 1770s and 1780s he was active in state politics, where he championed the Jefferson reform program, and in the Continental Congress. Madison was influential in the Constitutional Convention as leader of the group favoring a strong central government and as recorder of the debates; and he subsequently wrote, in collaboration with Alexander Hamilton and John Jay, the *Federalist* papers to aid the campaign for the adoption of the Constitution.

Serving in the new Congress, Madison soon emerged as the leader in the House of the men who opposed Hamilton's financial program and his pro-British leanings in foreign policy. Retiring from Congress in 1797, he continued to be active in Virginia and drafted the Virginia Resolution protesting the Alien and Sedition Acts. His intimacy with Jefferson made him the natural choice for secretary of state in 1801.

In 1809, Madison succeeded Jefferson as president, defeating Charles C. Pinckney. His wife, Dolley Payne Todd, whom he married in 1794, brought a new social sparkle to the executive mansion. In the meantime, increasing tension with Britain culminated in the War of 1812—a war for which the United States was unprepared and for which Madison lacked the executive talent to clear out incompetence and mobilize the nation's energies. Madison was reelected in 1812, running against the Federalist De Witt Clinton. In 1814, the British actually captured Washington and forced Madison to flee to Virginia.

Madison's domestic program capitulated to the Hamiltonian policies that he had resisted 20 years before and he now signed bills to establish a United States Bank and a higher tariff.

After his presidency, he remained in retirement in Virginia until his death on June 28, 1836.

JAMES MONROE was born on April 28, 1758, in Westmoreland County, Va. A William and Mary graduate, he served in the army during the first years of the Revolution and was wounded at Trenton. He then entered Virginia politics and later national politics under the sponsorship of Jefferson. In 1786, he married Elizabeth (Eliza) Kortright.

Fearing centralization, Monroe opposed the adoption of the Constitution and, as senator from Virginia, was highly critical of the Hamiltonian program. In 1794, he was appointed minister to France, where his ardent sympathies with the Revolution exceeded the wishes of the State Department. His troubled diplomatic career ended with his recall in 1796. From 1799 to 1802, he was governor of Virginia. In 1803, Jefferson sent him to France to help negotiate the Louisiana Purchase and for the next few years he was active in various negotiations on the Continent.

In 1808, Monroe flirted with the radical wing of the Republican Party, which opposed Madison's candidacy; but the presidential boom came to naught and, after a brief term as governor of Virginia in 1811, Monroe accepted Madison's offer to become secretary of state. During the War of 1812, he vainly sought a field command and instead served as secretary of war from September 1814 to March 1815.

Elected president in 1816 over the Federalist Rufus King, and reelected without opposition in 1820, Monroe, the last of the Virginia dynasty, pursued the course of systematic tranquilization that won for his administrations the name "the era of good feeling." He continued Madison's surrender to the Hamiltonian domestic program, signed the Missouri Compromise, acquired Florida, and with the able assistance of his secretary of state, John Quincy Adams, promulgated the Monroe Doctrine in 1823, declaring against foreign colonization or intervention in the Americas. He died in New York City on July 4, 1831, the third president to die on the anniversary of Independence.

JOHN QUINCY ADAMS was born on July 11, 1767, at Braintree (now Quincy), Mass., the son of John Adams, the second president. He spent his early years in Europe with his father, graduated from Harvard, and entered law practice. His anti-Paine newspaper articles won him political attention. In 1794, he became minister to the Netherlands, the first of several diplomatic posts that occupied him until his return to Boston in 1801. In 1797, he married Louisa Catherine Johnson.

In 1803, Adams was elected to the Senate, nominally as a Federalist, but his repeated displays of independence on such issues as the Louisiana Purchase and the embargo caused his party to demand his resignation and ostracize him socially. In 1809, Madison rewarded him for his support of Jefferson by appointing him minister to St. Petersburg. He helped negotiate the Treaty of Ghent in 1814, and in 1815 became minister to London. In 1817 Monroe appointed him secretary of state where he served with great distinction, gaining Florida from Spain without hostilities and playing an equal part with Monroe in formulating the Monroe Doctrine.

When no presidential candidate received a majority of electoral votes in 1824, Adams, with the support of Henry Clay, was elected by the House in 1825 over Andrew Jackson, who had the original plurality. Adams had ambitious plans of government activity to foster internal improvements and promote the arts and sciences, but congressional obstructionism, combined with his own unwillingness or inability to play the role of a politician, resulted in little being accomplished. After being defeated for reelection by Jackson in 1828, he successfully ran for the House of Representatives in 1830. There, though nominally a Whig, he pursued as ever an independent course. He led the fight to force Congress to receive antislavery petitions and fathered the Smithsonian Institution.

Adams had a stroke while on the floor of the House, and died two days later on Feb. 23, 1848. His long and detailed *Diary* gives a unique picture of the personalities and politics of the times.

ANDREW JACKSON was born on March 15, 1767, in what is now generally agreed to be Waxhaw, S.C. After a turbulent boyhood as an orphan and a British prisoner, he moved west to Tennessee, where he soon qualified for law practice but found time for such frontier pleasures as horse racing, cockfighting, and dueling. His marriage to Rachel Donelson Robards in 1791 was complicated by subsequent legal uncertainties about the status of her divorce. During the 1790s, Jackson served in the Tennessee Constitutional Convention, the United States House of Representatives and Senate, and on the Tennessee Supreme Court.

After some years as a country gentleman, living at the Hermitage near Nashville, Jackson in 1812 was given command of Tennessee troops sent against the Creeks. He defeated the Indians at Horseshoe Bend in 1814; subsequently he became a major general and won the Battle of New Orleans over veteran British troops, though after the treaty of peace had been signed at Ghent. In 1818, Jackson invaded Florida, captured Pensacola, and hanged two

Englishmen named Arbuthnot and Ambrister, creating an international incident. A presidential boom began for him in 1821, and to foster it, he returned to the Senate (1823–25). Though he won a plurality of electoral votes in 1824, he lost in the House when Clay threw his strength to Adams. Four years later, he easily defeated Adams.

As president, Jackson greatly expanded the power and prestige of the presidential office and carried through an unprecedented program of domestic reform, vetoing the bill to extend the United States Bank, moving toward a hard-money currency policy, and checking the program of federal internal improvements. He also vindicated federal authority against South Carolina with its doctrine of nullification and against France on the question of debts. The support given his policies by the workingmen of the East as well as by the farmers of the East, West, and South resulted in his triumphant reelection in 1832 over Clay.

After watching the inauguration of his handpicked successor, Martin Van Buren, Jackson retired to the Hermitage, where he maintained a lively interest in national affairs until his death on June 8, 1845.

MARTIN VAN BUREN was born on Dec. 5, 1782, at Kinderhook, N.Y. After graduating from the village school, he became a law clerk, entered practice in 1803, and soon became active in state politics as state senator and attorney general. In 1820, he was elected to the United States Senate. He threw the support of his efficient political organization, known as the Albany Regency, to William H. Crawford in 1824 and to Jackson in 1828. After leading the opposition to Adams's administration in the Senate, he served briefly as governor of New York (1828–1829) and resigned to become Jackson's secretary of state. He was soon on close personal terms with Jackson and played an important part in the Jacksonian program.

In 1832, Van Buren became vice president; in 1836, president. The Panic of 1837 overshadowed his term. He attributed it to the overexpansion of the credit and favored the establishment of an independent treasury as repository for the federal funds. In 1840, he established a 10-hour day on public works. Defeated by Harrison in 1840, he was the leading contender for the Democratic nomination in 1844 until he publicly opposed immediate annexation of Texas, and was subsequently beaten by the Southern delegations at the Baltimore convention. This incident increased his growing misgivings about the slave power.

After working behind the scenes among the antislavery Democrats, Van Buren joined in the movement that led to the Free-Soil Party and became its candidate for president in 1848. He subsequently returned to the Democratic Party while continuing to object to its pro-Southern policy. He died in Kinderhook on July 24, 1862. His *Autobiography* throws valuable sidelights on the political history of the times.

His wife, Hannah Hoes, whom he married in 1807, died in 1819.

WILLIAM HENRY HARRISON was born in Charles City County, Va., on Feb. 9, 1773. Joining the army in 1791, he was active in Indian fighting in the Northwest, became secretary of the Northwest Territory in 1798 and governor of Indiana in 1800. He married Anna Symmes in 1795. Growing discontent over white encroachments on Indian lands led to the formation of an Indian alliance under Tecumseh to resist further aggressions. In 1811, Harrison won a nominal victory over the Indians at Tippecanoe and in 1813 a more decisive one at the Battle of the Thames, where Tecumseh was killed.

After resigning from the army in 1814, Harrison had an obscure career in politics and diplomacy, ending up 20 years later as a county recorder in Ohio. Nominated for president in 1835 as a military hero whom the conservative politicians hoped to be able to control, he ran surprisingly well against Van Buren in 1836. Four years later, he defeated Van Buren but caught pneumonia and died in Washington on April 4, 1841, a month after his inauguration. Harrison was the first president to die in office.

JOHN TYLER was born in Charles City County, Va., on March 29, 1790. A William and Mary graduate, he entered law practice and politics, serving in the House of Representatives (1817–21), as governor of Virginia (1825–27), and as senator (1827–36). A strict constructionist, he supported Crawford in 1824 and Jackson in 1828, but broke with Jackson over his United States Bank policy and became a member of the Southern state-rights group that cooperated with the Whigs. In 1836, he resigned from the Senate rather than follow instructions from the Virginia legislature to vote for a resolution expunging censure of Jackson from the Senate record.

Elected vice president on the Whig ticket in 1840, Tyler succeeded to the presidency on Harrison's death. His strict-constructionist views soon caused a split with the Henry Clay wing of the Whig party and a stalemate on domestic questions. Tyler's more considerable achievements were his support of the Webster-Ashburton Treaty with Britain and his success in bringing about the annexation of Texas.

After his presidency he lived in retirement in Virginia until the outbreak of the Civil War, when he emerged briefly as chairman of a peace convention and then as delegate to the provisional Congress of the Confederacy. He died on Jan. 18, 1862. He married Letitia Christian in 1813 and, two years after her death in 1842, Julia Gardiner.

JAMES KNOX POLK was born in Mecklenburg County, N.C., on Nov. 2, 1795. A graduate of the University of North Carolina, he moved west to Tennessee, was admitted to the bar, and soon became prominent in state politics. In 1825, he was elected to the House of Representatives, where he opposed Adams and, after 1829, became Jackson's floor leader in the fight against the Bank. In 1835, he became Speaker of the House. Four years later, he was elected governor of Tennessee, but was beaten in tries for reelection in 1841 and 1843.

The supporters of Van Buren for the Democratic nomination in 1844 counted on Polk as his running mate, but when Van Buren's stand on Texas alienated Southern support, the convention swung to Polk on the ninth ballot. He was elected over Henry Clay, the Whig candidate. Rapidly disillusioning those who thought that he would not run his own administration, Polk proceeded steadily and precisely to achieve four major objectives—the acquisition of California, the settlement of the Oregon question, the reduction of the tariff, and the establishment of the independent treasury. He also enlarged the Monroe Doctrine to exclude all non-American intervention in American affairs, whether forcible or not, and he forced Mexico into a war that he waged to a successful conclusion.

His wife, Sarah Childress, whom he married in 1824, was a woman of charm and ability. Polk died in Nashville, Tenn., on June 15, 1849.

ZACHARY TAYLOR was born at Montebello, Orange County, Va., on Nov. 24, 1784. Embarking on a military career in 1808, Taylor fought in the War of 1812, the Black Hawk War, and the Seminole War, meanwhile holding garrison jobs on the frontier or desk jobs in Washington. A brigadier general as a result of his victory over the Seminoles at Lake Okeechobee (1837), Taylor held a succession of Southwestern commands and in 1846 established a base on the Rio Grande, where his forces engaged in hostilities that precipitated the war with Mexico. He captured Monterrey in Sept. 1846 and, disregarding Polk's orders to stay on the defensive, defeated Santa Anna at Buena Vista in Feb. 1847, ending the war in the northern provinces.

Though Taylor had never cast a vote for president, his party affiliations were Whiggish and his availability was increased by his difficulties with Polk. He was elected president over the Democrat Lewis Cass. During the revival of the slavery controversy, which was to result in the Compromise of 1850, Taylor began to take an increasingly firm stand against appeasing the South; but he died in Washington on July 9, 1850, during the fight over the Compromise. He married Margaret Mackall Smith in 1810. His bluff and simple soldierly qualities won him the name Old Rough and Ready.

MILLARD FILLMORE was born at Locke, Cayuga County, N.Y., on Jan. 7, 1800. A lawyer, he entered politics with the Anti-Masonic Party under the sponsorship of Thurlow Weed, editor and party boss, and subsequently followed Weed into the Whig Party. He served in the House of Representatives (1833–35 and 1837–43) and played a leading role in writing the tariff of 1842. Defeated for governor of New York in 1844, he became state comptroller in 1848, was put on the Whig ticket with Taylor as a concession to the Clay wing of the party, and became president upon Taylor's death in 1850.

As president, Fillmore broke with Weed and William H. Seward and associated himself with the pro-Southern Whigs, supporting the Compromise of 1850. Defeated for the Whig nomination in 1852, he ran for president in 1856 as candidate of the American, or Know-Nothing, Party, which sought to unite the country against foreigners in the alleged hope of diverting it from the explosive slavery issue. Fillmore opposed Lincoln during the Civil War. He died in Buffalo on March 8, 1874.

He was married in 1826 to Abigail Powers, who died in 1853, and in 1858 to Caroline Carmichael McIntosh.

FRANKLIN PIERCE was born at Hillsboro, N.H., on Nov. 23, 1804. A Bowdoin graduate, lawyer, and Jacksonian Democrat, he won rapid political advancement in the party, in part because of the prestige of his father, Gov. Benjamin Pierce. By 1831 he was Speaker of the New Hampshire House of Representatives; from 1833 to 1837, he served in the federal House and from 1837 to 1842 in the Senate. His wife, Jane Means Appleton, whom he married in 1834, disliked Washington and the somewhat dissipated life led by Pierce; in 1842 Pierce resigned from the Senate and began a successful law practice in Concord, N.H. During the Mexican War, he was a brigadier general.

Thereafter Pierce continued to oppose antislavery tendencies within the Democratic Party. As a result, he was the Southern choice to break the deadlock at the Democratic convention of 1852 and was nominated on the 49th ballot. In the election, Pierce overwhelmed Gen. Winfield Scott, the Whig candidate.

As president, Pierce followed a course of appeasing the South at home and of playing with schemes of territorial expansion abroad. The failure of his foreign and domestic policies prevented his renomination. He died in Concord on Oct. 8, 1869, in relative obscurity.

JAMES BUCHANAN was born near Mercersburg, Pa., on April 23, 1791. A Dickinson graduate and a lawyer, he entered Pennsylvania politics as a Federalist. With the disappearance of the Federalist Party, he became a Jacksonian Democrat. He served with ability in the House (1821–31), as minister to St. Petersburg (1832–33), and in the Senate (1834–45), and in 1845 became Polk's secretary of state. In 1853, Pierce appointed Buchanan minister to Britain, where he participated with other American diplomats in Europe in drafting the expansionist Ostend Manifesto.

He was elected president in 1856, defeating John C. Frémont, the Republican candidate, and former President Millard Fillmore of the American Party. The growing crisis over slavery presented Buchanan with problems he lacked the will to tackle. His appeasement of the South alienated the Stephen Douglas wing of the Democratic Party without reducing Southern militancy on slavery issues. While denying the right of secession, Buchanan also denied that the federal government could do anything about it. He supported the administration during the Civil War and died in Lancaster, Pa., on June 1, 1868.

The only president to remain a bachelor throughout his term, Buchanan used his charming niece, Harriet Lane, as White House hostess.

ABRAHAM LINCOLN was born in Hardin (now Larue) County, Ky., on Feb. 12, 1809. His family moved to Indiana and then to Illinois, and Lincoln gained what education he could along the way. While reading law, he worked in a store, managed a mill, surveyed, and split rails. In 1834, he went to the Illinois legislature as a Whig and became the party's floor leader. For the next 20 years he practiced law in Springfield, except for a single term (1847–49) in Congress, where he denounced the Mexican War. In 1855, he was a candidate for senator and the next year he joined the new Republican Party.

A leading but unsuccessful candidate for the vice-presidential nomination with Frémont, Lincoln gained national attention in 1858 when, as Republican candidate for senator from Illinois, he engaged in a series of debates with Stephen A. Douglas, the

Democratic candidate. He lost the election, but continued to prepare the way for the 1860 Republican convention and was rewarded with the presidential nomination on the third ballot. He won the election over three opponents.

From the start, Lincoln made clear that, unlike Buchanan, he believed the national government had the power to crush the rebellion. Not an abolitionist, he held the slavery issue subordinate to that of preserving the Union, but soon perceived that the war could not be brought to a successful conclusion without freeing the slaves. His administration was hampered by the incompetence of many Union generals, the inexperience of the troops, and the harassing political tactics both of the Republican Radicals, who favored a hard policy toward the South, and the Democratic Copperheads, who desired a negotiated peace. The Gettysburg Address of Nov. 19, 1863, marks the high point in the record of American eloquence. Lincoln's long search for a winning combination finally brought generals Ulysses S. Grant and William T. Sherman to the top; and their series of victories in 1864 dispelled the mutterings from both Radicals and Peace Democrats that at one time seemed to threaten Lincoln's reelection. He was reelected in 1864, defeating Gen. George B. McClellan, the Democratic candidate. His inaugural address urged leniency toward the South: "With malice toward none, with charity for all . . . let us strive on to finish the work we are in; to bind up the nation's wounds . . ." This policy aroused growing opposition on the part of the Republican Radicals, but before the matter could be put to the test, Lincoln was shot by the actor John Wilkes Booth at Ford's Theater, Washington, on April 14, 1865. He died the next morning.

Lincoln's marriage to Mary Todd in 1842 was often unhappy and turbulent, in part because of his wife's pronounced instability.

ANDREW JOHNSON was born at Raleigh, N.C., on Dec. 29, 1808. Self-educated, he became a tailor in Greeneville, Tenn., but soon went into politics, where he rose steadily. He served in the House of Representatives (1843–54), as governor of Tennessee (1853–57), and as a senator (1857–62). Politically he was a Jacksonian Democrat and his specialty was the fight for a more equitable land policy. Alone among the Southern Senators, he stood by the Union during the Civil War. In 1862, he became war governor of Tennessee and carried out a thankless and difficult job with great courage. Johnson became Lincoln's running mate in 1864 as a result of an attempt to give the ticket a nonpartisan and nonsectional character. Succeeding to the presidency on Lincoln's death, Johnson sought to carry out Lincoln's policy, but without his political skill. The result was a hopeless conflict with the Radical Republicans who dominated Congress, passed measures over Johnson's vetoes, and attempted to limit the power of the executive concerning appointments and removals. The conflict culminated with Johnson's impeachment for attempting to remove his disloyal secretary of war in defiance of the Tenure of Office Act, which required senatorial concurrence for such dismissals. The opposition failed by one vote to get the two thirds necessary for conviction.

After his presidency, Johnson maintained an interest in politics and in 1875 was again elected to the Senate. He died near Carter Station, Tenn., on July 31, 1875. He married Eliza McCardle in 1827.

ULYSSES SIMPSON GRANT was born (as Hiram Ulysses Grant) at Point Pleasant, Ohio, on April 27, 1822. He graduated from West Point in 1843 and served without particular distinction in the Mexican War. In 1848 he married Julia Dent. He resigned from the army in 1854, after warnings from his commanding officer about his drinking habits, and for the next six years held a wide variety of jobs in the Middle West. With the outbreak of the Civil War, he sought a command and soon, to his surprise, was made a brigadier general. His continuing successes in the western theaters, culminating in the capture of Vicksburg, Miss., in 1863, brought him national fame and soon the command of all the Union armies. Grant's dogged, implacable policy of concentrating on dividing and destroying the Confederate armies brought the war to an end in 1865. The next year, he was made full general.

In 1868, as Republican candidate for president, Grant was elected over the Democrat, Horatio Seymour. From the start, Grant showed his unfitness for the office. His cabinet was weak, his domestic policy was confused, and many of his intimate associates were corrupt. The notable achievement in foreign affairs was the settlement of controversies with Great Britain in the Treaty of London (1871), negotiated by his able secretary of state, Hamilton Fish.

Running for reelection in 1872, he defeated Horace Greeley, the Democratic and Liberal Republican candidate. The Panic of 1873 graft scandals close to the presidency created difficulties for his second term.

After retiring from office, Grant toured Europe for two years and returned in time to accede to a third-term boom, but was beaten in the convention of 1880. Illness and bad business judgment darkened his last years, but he worked steadily at the *Personal Memoirs,* which were to be successful when published after his death at Mount McGregor, near Saratoga, N.Y., on July 23, 1885.

RUTHERFORD BIRCHARD HAYES was born in Delaware, Ohio, on Oct. 4, 1822. A graduate of Kenyon College and the Harvard Law School, he practiced law in Lower Sandusky (now Fremont) and then in Cincinnati. In 1852 he married Lucy Webb. A Whig, he joined the Republican party in 1855. During the Civil War he rose to major general. He served in the House of Representatives from 1865 to 1867 and then confirmed a reputation for honesty and efficiency in two terms as governor of Ohio (1868–72). His election to a third term in 1875 made him the logical candidate for those Republicans who wished to stop James G. Blaine in 1876, and he was nominated.

The result of the election was in doubt for some time and hinged upon disputed returns from South Carolina, Louisiana, Florida, and Oregon. Samuel J. Tilden, the Democrat, had the larger popular vote but was adjudged by the strictly partisan decisions of the Electoral Commission to have one fewer electoral vote, 185 to 184. The national acceptance of this result was due in part to the general understanding that Hayes would pursue a conciliatory policy toward the South. He withdrew the troops from the South, took a conservative position on financial and labor issues, and urged civil service reform.

Hayes served only one term by his own wish and spent the rest of his life in various humanitarian endeavors. He died in Fremont on Jan. 17, 1893.

JAMES ABRAM GARFIELD, the last president to be born in a log cabin, was born in Cuyahoga County, Ohio, on Nov. 19, 1831. A Williams graduate, he taught school for a time and entered Republican politics in Ohio. In 1858, he married Lucretia Rudolph. During the Civil War, he had a promising career, rising to major general of volunteers; but he resigned in 1863, having been elected to the House of Representatives, where he served until 1880. His oratorical and parliamentary abilities soon made him the leading Republican in the House, though his record was marred by his unorthodox acceptance of a fee in the DeGolyer paving contract case and by suspicions of his complicity in the Crédit Mobilier scandal.

In 1880, Garfield was elected to the Senate, but instead became the presidential candidate on the 36th ballot as a result of a deadlock in the Republican convention. In the election, he defeated Gen. Winfield Scott Hancock, the Democratic candidate. Garfield's administration was barely under way when he was shot by Charles J. Guiteau, a disappointed office seeker, in Washington on July 2, 1881. He died in Elberton, N.J., on Sept. 19.

CHESTER ALAN ARTHUR was born at Fairfield, Vt., on Oct. 5, 1829. A graduate of Union College, he became a successful New York lawyer. In 1859, he married Ellen Herndon. During the Civil War, he held administrative jobs in the Republican state administration and in 1871 was appointed collector of the Port of New York by Grant. This post gave him control over considerable patronage. Though not personally corrupt, Arthur managed his power in the interests of the New York machine so openly that President Hayes in 1877 called for an investigation and the next year Arthur was suspended.

In 1880 Arthur was nominated for vice president in the hope of conciliating the followers of Grant and the powerful New York machine. As president upon Garfield's death, Arthur, stepping out of his familiar role as spoilsman, backed civil service reform, reorganized the cabinet, and prosecuted political associates accused of post office graft. Losing machine support and failing to gain the reformers, he was not nominated for a full term in 1884. He died in New York City on Nov. 18, 1886.

(STEPHEN) GROVER CLEVELAND was born at Caldwell, N.J., on March 18, 1837. He was admitted to the bar in Buffalo, N.Y., in 1859 and lived there as a lawyer, with occasional incursions into Democratic politics, for more than 20 years. He did not participate in the Civil War. As mayor of Buffalo in 1881, he carried through a reform program so ably that the Democrats ran him successfully for governor in 1882. In 1884 he won the Democratic nomination for president. The campaign contrasted Cleveland's spotless public career with the uncertain record of James G. Blaine, the Republican candidate, and Cleveland received enough Mugwump (independent Republican) support to win.

As president, Cleveland pushed civil service reform, opposed the pension grab and attacked the high tariff rates. While in the White House, he married Frances Folsom in 1886. Renominated in 1888, Cleveland was defeated by Benjamin Harrison, polling more popular but fewer electoral votes. In 1892, he was elected over Harrison. When the Panic of 1893 burst upon the country, Cleveland's attempts to solve it by sound-money measures alienated the free-silver wing of the party, while his tariff policy alienated the protectionists. In 1894, he sent troops to break the Pullman strike. In foreign affairs, his firmness caused Great Britain to back down in the Venezuela border dispute.

In his last years Cleveland was an active and much-respected public figure. He died in Princeton, N.J., on June 24, 1908.

BENJAMIN HARRISON was born in North Bend, Ohio, on Aug. 20, 1833, the grandson of William Henry Harrison, the ninth president. A graduate of Miami University in Ohio, he took up the law in Indiana and became active in Republican politics. In 1853, he married Caroline Lavinia Scott. During the Civil War, he rose to brigadier general. A sound-money Republican, he was elected senator from Indiana in 1880. In 1888, he received the Republican nomination for president on the eighth ballot. Though behind on the popular vote, he won over Grover Cleveland in the electoral college by 233 to 168.

As president, Harrison failed to please either the bosses or the reform element in the party. In foreign affairs he backed Secretary of State Blaine, whose policy foreshadowed later American imperialism. Harrison was renominated in 1892 but lost to Cleveland. His wife died in the White House in 1892 and Harrison married her niece, Mary Scott (Lord) Dimmick, in 1896. After his presidency, he resumed law practice. He died in Indianapolis on March 13, 1901.

WILLIAM MCKINLEY was born in Niles, Ohio, on Jan. 29, 1843. He taught school, then served in the Civil War, rising from the ranks to become a major. Subsequently he opened a law office in Canton, Ohio, and in 1871 married Ida Saxton. Elected to Congress in 1876, he served there until 1891, except for 1883–85. His faithful advocacy of business interests culminated in the passage of the highly protective McKinley Tariff of 1890. With the support of Mark Hanna, a shrewd Cleveland businessman interested in safeguarding tariff protection, McKinley became governor of Ohio in 1892 and Republican presidential candidate in 1896. The business community, alarmed by the progressivism of William Jennings Bryan, the Democratic candidate, spent considerable money to assure McKinley's victory.

The chief event of McKinley's administration was the war with Spain, which resulted in the United States' acquisition of the Philippines and other islands. With imperialism an issue, McKinley defeated Bryan again in 1900. On Sept. 6, 1901, he was shot at Buffalo, N.Y., by Leon F. Czolgosz, an anarchist, and he died there eight days later.

THEODORE ROOSEVELT was born in New York City on Oct. 27, 1858. A Harvard graduate, he was early interested in ranching, in politics, and in writing picaresque historical narratives. He was a Republican member of the New York Assembly in 1882–84, an unsuccessful candidate for mayor of

New York in 1886, a U.S. civil service commissioner under Benjamin Harrison, police commissioner of New York City in 1895, and assistant secretary of the Navy under McKinley in 1897. He resigned in 1898 to help organize a volunteer regiment, the Rough Riders, and take a more direct part in the war with Spain. He was elected governor of New York in 1898 and vice president in 1900, in spite of lack of enthusiasm on the part of the bosses.

Assuming the presidency of the assassinated McKinley in 1901, Roosevelt embarked on a wide-ranging program of government reform and conservation of natural resources. He ordered antitrust suits against several large corporations, threatened to intervene in the anthracite coal strike of 1902, which prompted the operators to accept arbitration, and, in general, championed the rights of the "little man" and fought the "malefactors of great wealth." He was also responsible for such progressive legislation as the Elkins Act of 1903, which outlawed freight rebates by railroads; the bill establishing the Department of Commerce and Labor; the Hepburn Act, which gave the I.C.C. greater control over the railroads; the Meat Inspection Act; and the Pure Food and Drug Act.

In foreign affairs, Roosevelt pursued a strong policy, permitting the instigation of a revolt in Panama to dispose of Colombian objections to the Panama Canal and helping to maintain the balance of power in the East by bringing the Russo-Japanese War to an end, for which he won the Nobel Peace Prize, the first American to achieve a Nobel prize in any category. In 1904, he decisively defeated Alton B. Parker, his conservative Democratic opponent.

Roosevelt's increasing coldness toward his successor, William Howard Taft, led him to overlook his earlier disclaimer of third-term ambitions and to reenter politics. Defeated by the machine in the Republican convention of 1912, he organized the Progressive Party (Bull Moose) and polled more votes than Taft, though the split brought about the election of Woodrow Wilson. From 1915 on, Roosevelt strongly favored intervention in the European war. He became deeply embittered at Wilson's refusal to allow him to raise a volunteer division. He died in Oyster Bay, N.Y., on Jan. 6, 1919. He was married twice: in 1880 to Alice Hathaway Lee, who died in 1884, and in 1886 to Edith Kermit Carow.

WILLIAM HOWARD TAFT was born in Cincinnati on Sept. 15, 1857. A Yale graduate, he entered Ohio Republican politics in the 1880s. In 1886 he married Helen Herron. From 1887 to 1890, he served on the Ohio Superior Court; 1890–92, as solicitor general of the United States; 1892–1900, on the federal circuit court. In 1900 McKinley appointed him president of the Philippine Commission and in 1901 governor general. Taft had great success in pacifying the Filipinos, solving the problem of the church lands, improving economic conditions, and establishing limited self-government. His period as secretary of war (1904–08) further demonstrated his capacity as administrator and conciliator, and he was Roosevelt's hand-picked successor in 1908. In the election, he polled 321 electoral votes to 162 for William Jennings Bryan, who was running for the presidency for the third time.

Though he carried on many of Roosevelt's policies, Taft got into increasing trouble with the progressive wing of the party and displayed mounting irritability and indecision. After his defeat in 1912, he became professor of constitutional law at Yale. In 1921 he was appointed chief justice of the United States Supreme Court. He died in Washington, DC, on March 8, 1930.

(THOMAS) WOODROW WILSON was born in Staunton, Va., on Dec. 28, 1856. A Princeton graduate, he turned from law practice to post-graduate work in political science at Johns Hopkins University, receiving his Ph.D. in 1886. He taught at Bryn Mawr, Wesleyan, and Princeton, and in 1902 was made president of Princeton. After an unsuccessful attempt to democratize the social life of the university, he welcomed an invitation in 1910 to be the Democratic gubernatorial candidate in New Jersey, and was elected. His success in fighting the machine and putting through a reform program attracted national attention.

In 1912, at the Democratic convention in Baltimore, Wilson won the nomination on the 46th ballot and went on to defeat Roosevelt and Taft in the election. Wilson proceeded under the standard of the New Freedom to enact a program of domestic reform, including the Federal Reserve Act, the Clayton Antitrust Act, the establishment of the Federal Trade Commission, and other measures designed to restore competition in the face of the great monopolies. In foreign affairs, while privately sympathetic with the Allies, he strove to maintain neutrality in the European war and warned both sides against encroachments on American interests.

Reelected in 1916 as a peace candidate, he tried to mediate between the warring nations; but when the Germans resumed unrestricted submarine warfare in 1917, Wilson brought the United States into what he now believed was a war to make the world safe for democracy. He supplied the classic formulations of Allied war aims and the armistice of Nov. 11, 1918, was negotiated on the basis of Wilson's Fourteen Points. In 1919 he strove at Versailles to lay the foundations for enduring peace. He accepted the imperfections of the Versailles Treaty in the expectation that they could be remedied by action within the League of Nations. He probably could have secured ratification of the treaty by the Senate if he had adopted a more conciliatory attitude toward the mild reservationists; but his insistence on all or nothing eventually caused the diehard isolationists and diehard Wilsonites to unite in rejecting a compromise.

In Sept. 1919 Wilson suffered a paralytic stroke that limited his activity. After leaving the presidency he lived on in retirement in Washington, dying on Feb. 3, 1924. He was married twice—in 1885 to Ellen Louise Axson, who died in 1914, and in 1915 to Edith Bolling Galt.

WARREN GAMALIEL HARDING was born in Morrow County, Ohio, on Nov. 2, 1865. After attending Ohio Central College, Harding became interested in journalism and in 1884 bought the *Marion* (Ohio) *Star.* In 1891 he married a wealthy widow, Florence Kling De Wolfe. As his paper prospered, he entered Republican politics, serving as state senator (1899–1903) and as lieutenant governor (1904–06). In 1910, he was defeated for governor, but in 1914 was elected to the Senate. His reputation as an orator made him the keynoter at the 1916 Republican convention.

When the 1920 convention was deadlocked between Leonard Wood and Frank O. Lowden, Harding became the dark-horse nominee on his solemn affirmation that there was no reason in his past that he should not be. Straddling the League question, Harding was easily elected over James M. Cox, his Democratic opponent. His cabinet contained some able men, but also some manifestly unfit for public office. Harding's own intimates were mediocre when they were not corrupt. The impending disclosure of the Teapot Dome scandal in the Interior Department and illegal practices in the Justice Department and Veterans' Bureau, as well as political setbacks, profoundly worried him. On his return from Alaska in 1923, he died unexpectedly in San Francisco on Aug. 2.

(JOHN) CALVIN COOLIDGE was born in Plymouth, Vt., on July 4, 1872. An Amherst graduate, he went into law practice at Northampton, Mass., in 1897. He married Grace Anna Goodhue in 1905. He entered Republican state politics, becoming successively mayor of Northampton, state senator, lieutenant governor and, in 1919, governor. His use of the state militia to end the Boston police strike in 1919 won him a somewhat undeserved reputation for decisive action and brought him the Republican vice-presidential nomination in 1920. After Harding's death Coolidge handled the Washington scandals with care and finally managed to save the Republican Party from public blame for the widespread corruption.

In 1924, Coolidge was elected without difficulty, defeating the Democrat, John W. Davis, and Robert M. La Follette running on the Progressive ticket. His second term, like his first, was characterized by a general satisfaction with the existing economic order. He stated that he did not choose to run in 1928.

After his presidency, Coolidge lived quietly in Northampton, writing an unilluminating autobiography and a syndicated column. He died there on Jan. 5, 1933.

HERBERT CLARK HOOVER was born at West Branch, Iowa, on Aug. 10, 1874, the first president to be born west of the Mississippi. A Stanford graduate, he worked from 1895 to 1913 as a mining engineer and consultant throughout the world. In 1899, he married Lou Henry. During World War I, he served with distinction as chairman of the American Relief Committee in London, as chairman of the Commission for Relief in Belgium, and as U.S. Food Administrator. His political affiliations were still too indeterminate for him to be mentioned as a possibility for either the Republican or Democratic nomination in 1920, but after the election he served Harding and Coolidge as secretary of commerce.

In the election of 1928, Hoover overwhelmed Gov. Alfred E. Smith of New York, the Democratic candidate and the first Roman Catholic to run for the presidency. He soon faced the worst depression in the nation's history, but his attacks upon it were hampered by his devotion to the theory that the forces that brought the crisis would soon bring the revival and then by his belief that there were too many areas in which the federal government had no power to act. In a succession of vetoes, he struck down measures proposing a national employment system or national relief, he reduced income tax rates, and only at the end of his term did he yield to popular pressure and set up agencies such as the Reconstruction Finance Corporation to make emergency loans to assist business.

After his 1932 defeat, Hoover returned to private business. In 1946, President Truman charged him with various world food missions; and from 1947 to 1949 and 1953 to 1955, he was head of the Commission on Organization of the Executive Branch of the Government. He died in New York City on Oct. 20, 1964.

FRANKLIN DELANO ROOSEVELT was born in Hyde Park, N.Y., on Jan. 30, 1882. A Harvard graduate, he attended Columbia Law School and was admitted to the New York bar. In 1910, he was elected to the New York State Senate as a Democrat. Reelected in 1912, he was appointed assistant secretary of the navy by Woodrow Wilson the next year. In 1920, his radiant personality and his war service resulted in his nomination for vice president as James M. Cox's running mate. After his defeat, he returned to law practice in New York. In Aug. 1921, Roosevelt was stricken with infantile paralysis while on vacation at Campobello, New Brunswick. After a long and gallant fight, he recovered partial use of his legs. In 1924 and 1928, he led the fight at the Democratic national conventions for the nomination of Gov. Alfred E. Smith of New York, and in 1928 Roosevelt was himself induced to run for governor of New York. He was elected, and was reelected in 1930.

In 1932, Roosevelt received the Democratic nomination for president and immediately launched a campaign that brought new spirit to a weary and discouraged nation. He defeated Hoover by a wide margin. His first term was characterized by an unfolding of the New Deal program, with greater benefits for labor, the farmers, and the unemployed, and the progressive estrangement of most of the business community.

At an early stage, Roosevelt became aware of the menace to world peace posed by totalitarian fascism, and from 1937 on he tried to focus public attention on the trend of events in Europe and Asia. As a result, he was widely denounced as a warmonger. He was reelected in 1936 over Gov. Alfred M. Landon of Kansas by the overwhelming electoral margin of 523 to 8, and the gathering international crisis prompted him to run for an unprecedented third term in 1940. He defeated Wendell L. Willkie.

Roosevelt's program to bring maximum aid to Britain and, after June 1941, to Russia was opposed, until the Japanese attack on Pearl Harbor restored national unity. During the war, Roosevelt shelved the New Deal in the interests of conciliating the business community, both in order to get full production during the war and to prepare the way for a united acceptance of the peace settlements after the war. A series of conferences with Winston Churchill and Joseph Stalin laid down the bases for the postwar world. In 1944 he was elected to a fourth term, running against Gov. Thomas E. Dewey of New York.

On April 12, 1945, Roosevelt died of a cerebral hemorrhage at Warm Springs, Ga., shortly after his return from the Yalta Conference. His wife, (Anna) Eleanor Roosevelt, whom he married in 1905, was a woman of great ability who made significant contributions to her husband's policies.

HARRY S. TRUMAN was born on a farm near Lamar, Mo., on May 8, 1884. During World War I, he served in France as a captain with the 129th Field Artillery. He married Bess Wallace in 1919. After engaging briefly and unsuccessfully in the haberdashery business in Kansas City, Mo., Truman entered local politics. Under the sponsorship of Thomas Pendergast, Democratic boss of Missouri, he held a number of local offices, preserving his personal honesty in the midst of a notoriously corrupt political machine. In 1934, he was elected to the Senate and was reelected in 1940. During his first term he was a loyal but quiet supporter of the New Deal, but in his second term, an appointment as head of a Senate committee to investigate war production brought out his special qualities of honesty, common sense, and hard work, and he won widespread respect.

Elected vice president in 1944, Truman became president upon Roosevelt's sudden death in April 1945 and was immediately faced with the problems of winding down the war against the Axis and preparing the nation for postwar adjustment. Germany surrendered on May 8, and in July Truman attended the Potsdam Conference to discuss the settlement plans for postwar Europe. To end the war with Japan, he authorized the dropping of atomic bombs on Hiroshima and Nagasaki on Aug. 6 and Aug. 9, 1945. Japan surrendered on Aug. 14. Although the action undoubtedly saved many American lives by bringing the war to an end, the morality of the decision is still debated.

The years 1947–48 were distinguished by civil-rights proposals, the Truman Doctrine to contain the spread of Communism, and the Marshall Plan to aid in the economic reconstruction of war-ravaged nations. Truman's general record, highlighted by a vigorous Fair Deal campaign, brought about his unexpected election in 1948 over the heavily favored Thomas E. Dewey.

Truman's second term was primarily concerned with the cold war with the Soviet Union, the implementing of the North Atlantic Pact, the United Nations police action in Korea, and the vast rearmament program with its accompanying problems of economic stabilization.

On March 29, 1952, Truman announced that he would not run again for the presidency. After leaving the White House, he returned to his home in Independence, Mo., to write his memoirs. He further busied himself with the Harry S. Truman Library there. He died in Kansas City, Mo., on Dec. 26, 1972.

DWIGHT DAVID EISENHOWER was born in Denison, Tex., on Oct. 14, 1890. His ancestors lived in Germany and emigrated to America, settling in Pennsylvania, early in the 18th century. His father, David, had a general store in Hope, Kans., which failed. After a brief time in Texas, the family moved to Abilene, Kan.

After graduating from Abilene High School in 1909, Eisenhower did odd jobs for almost two years. He won an appointment to the Naval Academy at Annapolis, but was too old for admittance. Then he received an appointment in 1910 to West Point, from which he graduated as a second lieutenant in 1915.

He did not see service in World War I, having been stationed at Fort Sam Houston, Tex. There he met Mamie Geneva Doud, whom he married in Denver on July 1, 1916, and by whom he had two sons: Doud Dwight (died in infancy) and John Sheldon Doud.

Eisenhower served in the Philippines from 1935 to 1939 with Gen. Douglas MacArthur. Afterward, Gen. George C. Marshall, the army chief of staff, brought him into the War Department's General Staff and in 1942 placed him in command of the invasion of North Africa. In 1944, he was made Supreme Allied Commander for the invasion of Europe.

After the war, Eisenhower served as army chief of staff from Nov. 1945 until Feb. 1948, when he was appointed president of Columbia University.

In Dec. 1950, President Truman recalled Eisenhower to active duty to command the North Atlantic Treaty Organization forces in Europe. He held his post until the end of May 1952.

At the Republican convention of 1952 in Chicago, Eisenhower won the presidential nomination on the first ballot in a close race with Sen. Robert A. Taft of Ohio. In the election, he defeated Gov. Adlai E. Stevenson of Illinois.

Through two terms, Eisenhower hewed to moderate domestic policies. He sought peace through Free World strength in an era of new nationalisms, nuclear missiles, and space exploration. He fostered alliances pledging the United States to resist "Red" aggression in Europe, Asia, and Latin America. The Eisenhower Doctrine of 1957 extended commitments to the Middle East.

At home, the popular president lacked Republican congressional majorities after 1954, but he was reelected in 1956 by 457 electoral votes to 73 for Stevenson.

While retaining most Fair Deal programs, he stressed "fiscal responsibility" in domestic affairs. A moderate in civil rights, he sent troops to Little Rock, Ark., to enforce court-ordered school integration.

With his wartime rank restored by Congress, Eisenhower returned to private life and the role of elder statesman, with his vigor hardly impaired by a heart attack, an ileitis operation, and a mild stroke suffered while in office. He died in Washington, DC, on March 28, 1969.

JOHN FITZGERALD KENNEDY was born in Brookline, Mass., on May 29, 1917. His father, Joseph P. Kennedy, was ambassador to Great Britain from 1937 to 1940.

Kennedy was graduated from Harvard University in 1940 and joined the navy the next year. He became skipper of a PT boat that was sunk in the Pacific by a Japanese destroyer. Although given up for lost, he swam to a safe island, towing an injured enlisted man.

After recovering from a war-aggravated spinal injury, Kennedy entered politics in 1946 and was elected to Congress. In 1952, he ran against Sen. Henry Cabot Lodge, Jr., of Massachusetts, and won.

Kennedy was married on Sept. 12, 1953, to Jacqueline Lee Bouvier, by whom he had three children: Caroline, John Fitzgerald, Jr. (died in a 1999 plane crash), and Patrick Bouvier (died in infancy).

In 1957 Kennedy won the Pulitzer Prize for a book he had written earlier, *Profiles in Courage*.

After strenuous primary battles, Kennedy won the Democratic presidential nomination on the first ballot at the 1960 Los Angeles convention. With a plurality of only 118,574 votes, he carried the election over Vice President Richard M. Nixon and became the first Roman Catholic president.

Kennedy brought to the White House the dynamic idea of a "New Frontier" approach in dealing with problems at home, abroad, and in the dimensions of space. Out of his leadership in his first few months in office came the 10-year Alliance for Progress to aid Latin America, the Peace Corps, and accelerated programs that brought the first Americans into orbit in the race in space.

Failure of the U.S.-supported Cuban invasion in April 1961 led to the entrenchment of the Communist-backed Castro regime, only 90 mi from United States soil. When it became known that Soviet offensive missiles were being installed in Cuba in 1962, Kennedy ordered a naval "quarantine" of the island and moved troops into position to eliminate this threat to U.S. security. The world seemed on the brink of a nuclear war until Soviet premier Khrushchev ordered the removal of the missiles.

A sudden "thaw," or the appearance of one, in the cold war came with the agreement with the Soviet Union on a limited test-ban treaty signed in Moscow on Aug. 6, 1963.

In his domestic policies, Kennedy's proposals for medical care for the aged and aid to education were defeated, but on minimum wage, trade legislation, and other measures he won important victories.

Widespread racial disorders and demonstrations led to Kennedy's proposing sweeping civil rights legislation. As his third year in office drew to a close, he also recommended an $11-billion tax cut to bolster the economy. Both measures were pending in Congress when Kennedy, looking forward to a second term, journeyed to Texas for a series of speeches.

While riding in an automobile procession in Dallas on Nov. 22, 1963, he was shot to death by an assassin firing from an upper floor of a building. The alleged assassin, Lee Harvey Oswald, was killed two days later in the Dallas city jail by Jack Ruby, owner of a strip-tease club.

At 46 years of age, Kennedy became the fourth president to be assassinated and the eighth to die in office.

LYNDON BAINES JOHNSON was born in Stonewall, Tex., on Aug. 27, 1908. On both sides of his family he had a political heritage mingled with a Baptist background of preachers and teachers. Both his father and his paternal grandfather served in the Texas House of Representatives.

After his graduation from Southwest Texas State Teachers College, Johnson taught school for two years. He went to Washington in 1932 as secretary to Rep. Richard M. Kleberg. During this time, he married Claudia Alta Taylor, known as "Lady Bird." They had two children: Lynda Bird and Luci Baines.

In 1935, Johnson became Texas administrator for the National Youth Administration. Two years later, he was elected to Congress as an all-out supporter of Franklin D. Roosevelt, and served until 1949. He was the first member of Congress to enlist in the armed forces after the attack on Pearl Harbor. He served in the navy in the Pacific and won a Silver Star.

Johnson was elected to the Senate in 1948 after he had captured the Democratic nomination by only 87 votes. He was 40 years old. He became the Senate Democratic leader in 1953. A heart attack in 1955 threatened to end his political career, but he recovered fully and resumed his duties.

At the height of his power as Senate leader, Johnson sought the Democratic nomination for president in 1960. When he lost to John F. Kennedy, he surprised even some of his closest associates by accepting second place on the ticket.

Johnson was riding in another car in the motorcade when Kennedy was assassinated in Dallas on Nov. 22, 1963. He took the oath of office in the presidential jet on the Dallas airfield.

With Johnson's insistent backing, Congress finally adopted a far-reaching civil-rights bill, a voting-rights bill, a Medicare program for the aged, and measures to improve education and conservation. Congress also began what Johnson described as "an all-out war" on poverty.

Amassing a record-breaking majority of nearly 16 million votes, Johnson was elected president in his own right in 1964, defeating Sen. Barry Goldwater of Arizona.

The double tragedy of a war in Southeast Asia and urban riots at home marked Johnson's last two years in office. Faced with disunity in the nation and challenges within his own party, Johnson surprised the country on March 31, 1968, with the announcement that he would not be a candidate for reelection. He died of a heart attack suffered at his LBJ Ranch on Jan. 22, 1973.

RICHARD MILHOUS NIXON was born in Yorba Linda, Calif., on Jan. 9, 1913, to Midwestern-bred parents, Francis A. and Hannah Milhous Nixon, who raised their five sons as Quakers.

Nixon was a high school debater and was undergraduate president at Whittier College in California, where he was graduated in 1934. As a scholarship student at Duke University Law School in North Carolina, he graduated third in his class in 1937.

After five years as a lawyer, Nixon joined the navy in August 1942. He was an air transport officer in the South Pacific and a legal officer stateside before his discharge in 1946 as a lieutenant commander.

Running for Congress in California as a Republican in 1946, Nixon defeated Rep. Jerry Voorhis. As a member of the House Un-American Activities Committee, he made a name as an investigator of Alger Hiss, a former high State Department official, who was later jailed for perjury. In 1950, Nixon defeated Rep. Helen Gahagan Douglas, a Democrat, for the Senate. He was criticized for portraying her as a Communist dupe.

Nixon's anti-Communism ideals, his Western roots, and his youth figured into his selection in 1952 to run for vice president on the ticket headed by Dwight D. Eisenhower. Demands for Nixon's withdrawal followed disclosure that California businessmen had paid some of his Senate office expenses. His televised rebuttal, known as "the

Checkers speech" (named for a cocker spaniel given to the Nixons), brought him support from the public and from Eisenhower. The ticket won easily in 1952 and again in 1956.

Eisenhower gave Nixon substantive assignments, including missions to 56 countries. In Moscow in 1959, Nixon won acclaim for his defense of U.S. interests in an impromptu "kitchen debate" with Soviet premier Nikita S. Khrushchev.

Nixon lost the 1960 race for the presidency to John F. Kennedy.

In 1962, Nixon failed in a bid for California's governorship and seemed to be finished as a national candidate. He became a Wall Street lawyer, but kept his old party ties and developed new ones through constant travels to speak for Republicans.

Nixon won the 1968 Republican presidential nomination after a shrewd primary campaign, then made Gov. Spiro T. Agnew of Maryland his surprise choice for vice president. In the election, they edged out the Democratic ticket headed by Vice President Hubert H. Humphrey by 510,314 votes out of 73,212,065 cast.

Committed to winding down the U.S. role in the Vietnamese War, Nixon pursued "Vietnamization"—training and equipping South Vietnamese to do their own fighting. American ground combat forces in Vietnam fell steadily from 540,000 when Nixon took office to none in 1973 when the military draft was ended. But there was heavy continuing use of U.S. air power.

Nixon improved relations with Moscow and reopened the long-closed door to mainland China with a good-will trip there in Feb. 1972. In May of that same year, he visited Moscow and signed agreements on arms limitation and trade expansion and approved plans for a joint U.S.–Soviet space mission in 1975.

Inflation was a campaign issue for Nixon, but he failed to master it as president. On Aug. 15, 1971, with unemployment edging up, Nixon abruptly announced a new economic policy: a 90-day wage-price freeze, stimulative tax cuts, a temporary 10% tariff, and spending cuts. A second phase, imposing guidelines on wage, price, and rent boosts, was announced Oct. 7.

The economy responded in time for the 1972 campaign, in which Nixon played up his foreign-policy achievements. Played down was the burglary on June 17, 1972, of Democratic national headquarters in the Watergate apartment complex in Washington. The Nixon–Agnew reelection campaign cost a record $60 million and swamped the Democratic ticket headed by Sen. George McGovern of South Dakota with a plurality of 17,999,528 out of 77,718,554 votes. Only Massachusetts, with 14 electoral votes, and the District of Columbia, with 3, went for McGovern.

In Jan. 1973, hints of a cover-up emerged at the trial of six men found guilty of the Watergate burglary. With a Senate investigation under way, Nixon announced on April 30 the resignations of his top aides, H. R. Haldeman and John D. Ehrlichman, and the dismissal of White House counsel John Dean III. Dean was the star witness at televised Senate hearings that exposed both a White House cover-up of Watergate and massive illegalities in Republican fund-raising in 1972.

The hearings also disclosed that Nixon had routinely tape-recorded his office meetings and telephone conversations.

On Oct. 10, 1973, Agnew resigned as vice president, then pleaded no-contest to a negotiated federal charge of evading income taxes on alleged bribes. Two days later, Nixon nominated the House minority leader, Rep. Gerald R. Ford of Michigan, as the new vice president. Congress confirmed Ford on Dec. 6, 1973.

In June 1974, Nixon visited Israel and four Arab nations. Then he met in Moscow with Soviet leader Leonid I. Brezhnev and reached preliminary nuclear arms limitation agreements.

But, in the month after his return, Watergate ended the Nixon regime. On July 24 the Supreme Court ordered Nixon to surrender subpoenaed tapes. On July 30, the Judiciary Committee referred three impeachment articles to the full membership. On Aug. 5, Nixon bowed to the Supreme Court and released tapes showing he halted an FBI probe of the Watergate burglary six days after it occurred. It was in effect an admission of obstruction of justice, and impeachment appeared inevitable.

Nixon resigned on Aug. 9, 1974, the first president ever to do so. A month later, President Ford issued an unconditional pardon for any offenses Nixon might have committed as president, thus forestalling possible prosecution.

In 1940, Nixon married Thelma Catherine (Pat) Ryan. They had two daughters, Patricia (Tricia) and Julie, who married Dwight David Eisenhower II, grandson of the former president.

He died on April 22, 1994, in New York City of a massive stroke.

GERALD RUDOLPH FORD was born Leslie King Jr. in Omaha, Neb., on July 14, 1913, the only child of Leslie and Dorothy Gardner King. His parents were divorced in 1915. His mother moved to Grand Rapids, Mich., and married Gerald R. Ford. The boy was renamed for his stepfather.

Ford captained his high school football team in Grand Rapids, and a football scholarship took him to the University of Michigan, where he starred as varsity center before his graduation in 1935. A job as assistant football coach at Yale gave him an opportunity to attend Yale Law School, from which he graduated in the top third of his class in 1941.

He returned to Grand Rapids to practice law, but entered the Navy in April 1942. He saw wartime service in the Pacific on the light aircraft carrier *Monterey* and was a lieutenant commander when he returned to Grand Rapids early in 1946 to resume law practice and dabble in politics.

Ford was elected to Congress in 1948 for the first of his 13 terms in the House. He was soon assigned to the influential Appropriations Committee and rose to become the ranking Republican on the subcommittee on Defense Department appropriations.

As a legislator, Ford described himself as "a moderate on domestic issues, a conservative in fiscal affairs, and a dyed-in-the-wool internationalist." He carried the ball for Pentagon appropriations, was a hawk on the war in Vietnam, and kept a low profile on civil-rights issues.

Ford was also dependable and hard-working and popular with his colleagues. In 1963, he was elected chairman of the House Republican Conference. He served in 1963–1964 as a member of the Warren Commission, which investigated the assassination of John F. Kennedy. A revolt by dissatisfied younger Republicans in 1965 made him minority leader.

On Oct. 12, 1973, Nixon nominated Ford to fill the vice presidency left vacant by Agnew's resignation under fire. It was the first use of the procedures for filling vacancies in the vice presidency laid down in the 25th Amendment to the Constitution, which Ford had helped enact. Once in office, he said he did not believe Nixon had been involved in the Watergate scandals, but he criticized Nixon's stubborn court battle against releasing tape recordings of Watergate-related conversations for use as evidence. The scandals led to Nixon's unprecedented resignation on Aug. 9, 1974, and Ford was sworn in immediately as the 38th president, the first to enter the White House without winning a national election.

Ford assured the nation when he took office that "our long national nightmare is over" and pledged "openness and candor" in all his actions. He won a warm response from the Democratic 93rd Congress when he said he wanted "a good marriage" rather than a honeymoon with his former colleagues. In Dec. 1974 congressional majorities backed his choice of former New York governor Nelson A. Rockefeller as his vice president.

The cordiality was chilled by Ford's announcement on Sept. 8, 1974, that he had granted an unconditional pardon to Nixon for any crimes he might have committed as president. Although no formal charges were pending, Ford said he feared "ugly passions" would be aroused if Nixon were brought to trial. The pardon was widely criticized.

To fight inflation, the new president first proposed fiscal restraints and spending curbs and a 5% tax surcharge that got nowhere in the Senate and House. Congress again rebuffed Ford in the spring of 1975 when he appealed for emergency military aid to help the governments of South Vietnam and Cambodia resist massive Communist offensives.

Politically, Ford's fortunes improved steadily in the first half of 1975. Badly divided Democrats in Congress were unable to muster votes to override his vetoes of spending bills that exceeded his budget. He faced some right-wing opposition in his own party, but moved to preempt it with an early announcement—on July 8, 1975—of his intention to be a candidate in 1976. During the election campaign, Ford was regarded as a caretaker president lacking in strength and vision. He was defeated in November by Jimmy Carter.

In 1948, Ford married Elizabeth Anne (Betty) Bloomer. They had four children, Michael Gerald, John Gardner, Steven Meigs, and Susan Elizabeth.

JAMES EARL CARTER, JR., was born in the tiny village of Plains, Ga., Oct. 1, 1924, and grew up on the family farm at nearby Archery. Both parents were fifth-generation Georgians. His father, James Earl Carter, was known as a segregationist, but treated his black and white workers equally. Carter's mother, Lillian Gordy, was a matriarchal presence in home and community and opposed the then-prevailing code of racial inequality. The future president was baptized in 1935 in the conservative Southern Baptist Church and spoke often of being a "born again" Christian, although committed to the separation of church and state.

Carter married Rosalynn Smith, a neighbor, in 1946. Their first child, John William, was born a year later in Portsmouth, Va. Their other children are James Earl III, born in Honolulu in 1950; Donnel Jeffrey, born in New London, Conn., in 1952; and Amy Lynn, born in Plains in 1967.

In 1946 Carter was graduated from the U.S. Naval Academy at Annapolis and served in the nuclear-submarine program under Adm. Hyman G. Rickover. In 1954, after his father's death, he resigned from the Navy to take over the family's flourishing warehouse and cotton gin, with several thousand acres for growing seed peanuts.

Carter was elected to the Georgia Senate in 1962. In 1966 he lost the race for governor, but was elected in 1970. His term brought a state government reorganization, sharply reduced agencies, increased economy and efficiency, and new social programs, all with no general tax increase. In 1972 the peanut farmer–politician set his sights on the presidency and in 1974 built a base for himself as he criss-crossed the country as chairman of the Democratic Campaign Committee, appealing for revival and reform. In 1975 he won the support of most of the old Southern civil-rights coalition after endorsement by Rep. Andrew Young, black Democrat from Atlanta, who had been the closest aide to the Rev. Martin Luther King, Jr. Having won 19 out of 31 primaries with a broad appeal to conservatives and liberals, black and white, poor and well-to-do, he defeated Gerald R. Ford in Nov. 1976.

In his one term, Carter fought hard for his programs against resistance from an independent-minded Democratic Congress that frustrated many pet projects although it overrode only two vetoes. Public dissatisfaction with the "stagflation" economy, staff problems, friction with Congress, long gasoline lines, and the months-long Iranian crisis, including the abortive sally in April 1980 to free the hostages also proved problematic for the administration. Yet, assessments of his record have noted many positive elements. There was, for one thing, peace throughout his term, with no American combat deaths and with a brake on the advocates of force. Regarded as perhaps his greatest personal achievements were the Camp David accords between Israel and Egypt and the resulting treaty—the first between Israel and an Arab neighbor. The treaty with China and the Panama Canal treaties were also major achievements. Carter worked for nuclear-arms control. His concern for international human rights was credited with saving lives and reducing torture, and he supported the British policy that ended internecine warfare in Rhodesia, now Zimbabwe. Domestically, his environmental record was a major accomplishment. His judicial appointments won acclaim, with 265 choices for the federal bench that included minority members and women.

In 1980 Carter was renominated on the first ballot after vanquishing Sen. Edward M. Kennedy of Massachusetts in the primaries. In the election campaign, he attacked his rivals, Ronald Reagan and John B. Anderson, independent, with the warning that a Reagan Republican victory would heighten the risk of war and impede civil rights and economic opportunity. In November Carter lost to Reagan, who won 489 electoral college votes and 51% of the popular tally, to 49 electoral votes and 41% for Carter. He was awarded the 2002 Nobel Peace Prize.

RONALD WILSON REAGAN rode to the presidency in 1980 on a tide of resurgent right-wing sentiment among an electorate longing for a distant, simpler era. He left office in Jan. 1989 with two-thirds of the American people approving his performance during his two terms. It was the highest rating for any retiring president since World War II.

Reagan, an actor turned politician, a New Dealer turned conservative, came to films and politics from a thoroughly Middle-American background—middle class, Middle West, and small town. He was born in Tampico, Ill., Feb. 6, 1911, the second son of John Edward Reagan and Nelle Wilson Reagan; the family later moved to Dixon, Ill. His father was a shop clerk and merchant with Democratic sympathies. It was an impoverished family; young Ronald sold homemade popcorn at high school games and worked as a lifeguard to earn money for his college tuition. When his father got a New Deal WPA job, the future president became an ardent Roosevelt Democrat.

Reagan earned a BA degree in 1932 from Eureka (Ill.) College, where a photographic memory aided in his studies and in debating and college theatricals. During the Depression, he made $100 a week as a sports announcer for radio station WHO in Des Moines, Iowa. His career as a film and TV actor stretched from 1937 to 1966, and his salary climbed to $3,500 a week. As a World War II captain in army film studios, Reagan recoiled from what he saw as the laziness of civil service workers, and moved to the Right. As president of the Screen Actors Guild, he resisted what he considered a Communist plot to subvert the film industry. With advancing age, Reagan left leading-man roles and became a television spokesman for the General Electric Company.

With oratorical skill as his trademark, Reagan became an active Republican. In 1966, at the behest of a small group of conservative businessmen, he ran for governor of California with a pledge to cut spending; he was elected by almost a million votes over the political veteran, Democratic governor Edmund G. Brown. Reelected to a second term, he served as governor until 1975.

In the 1980 election battle against Jimmy Carter, Reagan broadened his appeal by espousing moderate policies, gaining much of his support from disaffected Democrats and blue-collar workers. The incoming administration immediately set out to "turn the government around" with a new economic program. Over strenuous congressional opposition, Reagan pushed through his "supply side" economic program to stimulate production and control inflation through tax cuts and sharp reductions in government spending. However, in 1982, as the economy declined into the worst recession in 40 years, the president's popularity slipped and support for supply-side economics faded.

Barely three months into his first term, Reagan was the target of an assassin's bullet; his courageous comeback won public admiration. The president also won high acclaim for his nomination of Sandra Day O'Connor as the first woman on the Supreme Court. His later nominations met increasing opposition and did much to tilt the Court's orientation to the Right.

Internationally, Reagan confronted numerous problems in his first term. In an effort to establish order on the Caribbean island of Grenada and eliminate the Cuban military presence there, Reagan ordered an invasion of the tiny nation on Oct. 25, 1983. The troops met strong resistance from Cuban military personnel on the island but soon occupied it. Another military effort, in Lebanon, ended in failure, however. U.S. Marines engaged as part of a multinational peacekeeping force in Beirut were forced to withdraw in 1984 after a disastrous terrorist attack left 241 marines dead.

With the economy improving and inflation under control, the popular president won reelection in a landslide in 1984. Domestically, a tax reform bill that Reagan backed became law. But the constantly growing budget deficit remained an irritant, with the president and Congress persistently at odds over priorities in spending for defense and domestic programs. Congress was also increasingly reluctant to increase spending for the Nicaraguan "Contras." But even severe critics praised Reagan's restrained but decisive handling of the crisis following the hijacking of an American plane in Beirut by Muslim extremists. The attack on Libya in April 1986 galvanized the nation, although it drew scathing disapproval from the NATO alliance.

Reagan's popularity with the public dipped sharply in 1986 when the Iran-Contra scandal broke, shortly after the Democrats gained control of the Senate. The weeks-long congressional hearings in the summer of 1987 heard an array of administration officials, present and former, reveal a web of deceit and undercover maneuvering in the White House. Yet the president's personal reputation remained untouched; on Aug. 12, 1987, he told the nation that he had not known of questionable activities but agreed that he was ultimately accountable.

Reagan's place in history will rest, perhaps, on the short- and intermediate-range missile treaty consummated on a cordial visit to the Soviet Union that he had once reviled as an "evil empire." Its provisions, including a ground-breaking agreement on verification inspection, were formulated in four days of summit talks in Moscow in May 1988 with the Soviet leader, Mikhail S. Gorbachev. Reagan could point to numerous domestic achievements as well: sharp cuts in income tax rates, creating economic growth without inflation, and reducing the unemployment rate, among others. He failed, however, to win the "Reagan Revolution" on such issues as abortion and school prayer.

Reagan married his wife, Nancy, fours years after his divorce from the screen actress Jane Wyman. The children from his first marriage are Maureen, his daughter by Wyman, and Michael, an adopted son. He had two children by Nancy: Patricia and Ron. Reagan suffers from Alzheimer's disease, which he developed in the years following his presidency.

GEORGE HERBERT WALKER BUSH was born June 12, 1924, in Milton, Mass., to Prescott and Dorothy Bush. The family later moved to Connecticut. The youth studied at the elite Phillips Academy in Andover, Mass.

The future president joined the Navy after war broke out and at 18 became the Navy's youngest commissioned pilot, serving from 1942 to 1945, and was awarded the Distinguished Flying Cross. He fought the Japanese on 58 missions and was shot down once.

After the war, Bush earned an economics degree and a Phi Beta Kappa key in two and a half years at Yale University.

In 1945 Bush married Barbara Pierce of Rye, N.Y., daughter of a magazine publisher. With his bride, Bush moved to Texas instead of entering his father's investment banking business. There he founded his oil company and by 1980 reported an estimated wealth of $1.4 million.

Throughout his whole career, Bush had the backing of an established family, headed by his father, Prescott Bush, who was elected to the Senate from Connecticut in 1952. The family helped the young patrician become established in his early business ventures, a rich uncle raising most of the capital required for founding the oil company.

In the 1960s, Bush won two contests for a Texas Republican seat in the House of Representatives, but lost two bids for a Senate seat. After Bush's second race for the Senate, President Nixon appointed him U.S. delegate to the United Nations and he later became Republican National Committee chairman. He headed the U.S. liaison office in Beijing before becoming Director of Central Intelligence. In 1980 Bush became Reagan's running mate despite earlier criticism of Reagan "voodoo economics" and by the 1984 election had won acclaim for his devotion to Reagan's conservative agenda.

The vice president entered the 1988 presidential campaign and easily defeated Democrat Michael Dukakis. Bush's choice of Sen. Dan Quayle of Indiana as a running mate provoked criticism and ridicule that continued even after the administration was in office. Nonetheless Bush strongly defended his choice. George Herbert Walker Bush became president on Jan. 20, 1989, with his theme harmony and conciliation after the often-turbulent Reagan years.

Bush's early Cabinet choices reflected a pragmatic desire for an efficient, nonideological government. And with his usual cautious instinct, in 1990 he nominated to the Supreme Court the scholarly David H. Souter, with broadly conservative views.

In his first year, Bush was confronted with the Lebanese hostage crisis, the *Exxon Valdez* oil spill in Alaska, and the ongoing war against drug trafficking. His public approval soared following the invasion of Panama in late 1989. But a staggering budget deficit and the savings and loan crisis caused the president's popularity to dip sharply in his second year. This plunge followed Bush's recantation of his campaign "no new taxes" pledge as he sat down with congressional leaders to tame the budget deficit and deal with a faltering economy.

In 1991, the president emerged as the leader of an international coalition of Western democracies, Japan, and even some Arab states that came together to free Kuwait following an invasion of the country by Iraq in Aug. 1990. The coalition forces defeated Iraq in only a little more than a month after Operation Desert Storm was launched on Jan. 16–17, 1991, and a nation grateful at feeling the end of the "Vietnam syndrome" gave the president an 89% approval rating. However, the high rating fell as the year went on, as doubts persisted about the war's outcome—Iraqi president Saddam Hussein remained in power and persistently avoided complying with the terms of the peace treaty—and as concerns began to grow about the faltering U.S. economy and other domestic problems.

A major Bush accomplishment in 1991 was the Strategic Arms Reduction Treaty (START), signed in July with Soviet president Mikhail S. Gorbachev at their fourth summit conference, marking the end of the long weapons buildup.

In the 1992 presidential election, Bush was defeated by Gov. Bill Clinton of Arkansas.

The Bushes have four sons, George, Jeb, Neil, and Marvin, and a daughter, Dorothy. Another daughter, Robin, died at age three from leukemia. Son George served as governor of Texas from 1995 to 2000, when he was elected the 43rd U.S. president. Jeb Bush was elected governor of Florida in 1998.

WILLIAM JEFFERSON CLINTON was born William Jefferson Blythe IV in Hope, Ark., on Aug. 19, 1946. He was named for his father, who was killed in an automobile accident before Clinton's birth. Virginia Kelley, his mother, eventually married Roger Clinton, a car dealer, whose surname the future president later adopted.

In high school in Hot Springs, Ark., Clinton considered becoming a doctor, but politics beckoned after a meeting with President John F. Kennedy in Washington, DC, on a Boys' Nation trip. He earned a BS in international affairs in 1968 at Georgetown University, having spent his junior year working for Arkansas senator J. William Fulbright. He was a Rhodes scholar at Oxford between 1968 and 1970. He then attended Yale Law School, where he met his future wife, Hillary Rodham, a Wellesley graduate. The couple has one child, Chelsea.

Clinton taught at the University of Arkansas (1974–1976), was elected state attorney general (1976), and in 1979 became the nation's youngest governor. But he was defeated for reelection in 1980 by voters irate at a rise in the state's automobile license fees. In 1982 he was elected again. This time he reined in liberal tendencies to accommodate the conservative bent of the voters.

Clinton became the 42nd U.S. president following a turbulent political campaign. He overcame vigorous personal attacks on his character and on his actions during the Vietnam War, which he actively opposed. The "character issue" stemmed from allegations of infidelity, which Clinton refuted in a television interview in which he and Hillary avowed their relationship was solid. Throughout his term in office, Clinton was dogged by allegations relating to the Whitewater real estate deal in which he and Hillary were involved prior to the 1992 election. Though the Clintons were never accused of any wrongdoing, partners in the venture were convicted of fraud and conspiracy in a trial in 1996.

The problems faced by the new president were as daunting as they were varied. In Jan. 1993 he became embroiled with the military leadership over his campaign pledge to allow homosexuals to serve openly in the armed services. He ultimately agreed to a compromise, dubbed the "don't ask, don't tell" policy. Clinton's first year also saw him wrangling with Congress over the federal budget and economic policy.

In his second year, Clinton was faced with acrimonious battles over health care, welfare reform, and crime prevention. A health care reform package crafted by his wife failed to gain sufficient support. Clinton had to reduce his objective from massive overhaul to incremental reform.

Clinton won major victories with the passage of the North American Free Trade Agreement (NAFTA), which took effect Jan. 1, 1994, and the Global Agreement on Tariffs and Trade (GATT), which led to the establishment in 1995 of the World Trade Organization (WTO). Congress also approved a deficit reduction bill, rules allowing abortion counseling in federally funded clinics, a waiting period for handgun purchases (the Brady Bill), and a national service program.

Foreign affairs became a proving ground for Clinton, since he has been elected primarily on a domestic economic agenda. He improved his international image when the Israel–Jordan peace agreement was signed at the White House in the summer of 1994 by Israeli prime minister Yitzhak Rabin and Jordan's King Hussein. In the fall of that year, the administration succeeded in restoring Haiti's ousted president, Jean-Bertrand Aristide, to power. Clinton scored again by bolstering Russian president Boris Yeltsin's popularity with promises of economic aid.

The problems in Eastern Europe were Clinton's next big challenge. Though he wanted desperately to end the brutal ethnic cleansing in Bosnia, he did not want to commit American ground troops to do so. A peace accord involving American peacekeeping troops was ultimately signed in Dayton, Ohio, in Nov. 1995.

The 1994 elections resulted in a Republican-controlled Congress, and 1995 was largely a tug-of-war between the White House and Capitol Hill over budget-balancing and other key points of the GOP's "Contract with America," crafted by Speaker of the House Newt Gingrich.

In 1996, aided by a booming economy, Clinton won reelection to a second term, becoming the first Democratic president since Franklin D. Roosevelt to do so. The country's general prosperity also made it possible in 1997 for Clinton and the Republicans to reach an agreement to balance the federal budget in three decades.

However, the character issues that had followed Clinton for years soon began to emerge once again. A series of investigations was begun to determine whether Clinton and Vice President Gore had participated in questionable fund-raising practices in their 1996 campaign.

As his tenure wore on, Clinton came under increasing pressure from Kenneth Starr, the independent counsel who in 1994 took over the investigation of the Clintons' involvement in the Whitewater land deal. Over time, Starr's brief was expanded to include other matters, such as the death of White House lawyer Vincent Foster, the handling of firings in the White House travel office, and shocking allegations of sexual misconduct by Clinton.

In Jan. 1998, Clinton was called to testify in a long-pending sexual harassment suit brought against him by Paula Corbin Jones, a former Arkansas state employee. In his testimony, Clinton denied that he had had a sexual relationship with a young White House intern, Monica Lewinsky, and that he had attempted to cover it up. Although a federal judge in Arkansas threw out the Jones sexual harassment suit in April 1998, by this time the Lewinsky affair had become the focus of Kenneth Starr's investigation as well as a national obsession.

Finally, on Aug. 17, 1998, after relentless media attention, leaks, and news of Lewinsky's upcoming testimony, Clinton made history by becoming the first U.S. president to testify in front of a grand jury in an investigation of his own possibly criminal conduct. In an address to the nation that evening, he admitted to having had an "inappropriate relationship" with Lewinsky, but reaffirmed that he did not ask anyone to lie about or cover up the affair.

Paradoxically, however, in spite of the scandalous outcome of events, Clinton's overall popularity among Americans remained high. The country seemed willing to ignore his weaknesses in character, much as they did in the 1992 elections, as long as the economy was good, his policies were popular, and the United States remained strong abroad.

On Sept. 9, Starr—a conservative Republican whose investigation was seen by Clinton supporters as a politically inspired vendetta—delivered his report to the House of Representatives. While the report outlined 11 possible grounds for impeachment, none stemmed from the initial subjects of the investigation, including the Whitewater real estate deal. The real focus of the accusations seemed to be Clinton's moral conduct, and the "Starr Report" graphically detailed his sexual affair.

Despite the American population's general disapproval of a trial (which was reflected in poll after poll), Congress moved forward in its highly partisan impeachment proceedings and on Dec. 19, Clinton became the second president in American history to be impeached. Two of the four articles of impeachment passed (Article I, grand jury perjury, and Article III, obstruction of justice), the votes drawn along party lines. After a Senate trial in Jan.–Feb. 1999, Clinton was acquitted on both counts.

While the impeachment trial overshadowed all other activity in Washington for a good portion of 1998, Clinton was forced to respond to continued problems with Iraq at the end of the year. In December, Saddam Hussein blocked a weapons inspection by the United Nations. The UN responded with airstrikes that would continue on a nearly daily basis for the next three months, and then off and on through the spring and summer, as Iraq taunted the U.S. and its allies further by shooting at jets patrolling the no-fly zones set up after the Persian Gulf war.

In the spring of 1999, reports of continued ethnic cleansing in the Serbian province of Kosovo were growing. Clinton and his British counterpart, Tony Blair, led the push for NATO intervention, which resulted in a 78-day bombing campaign against Serbia that began in March. Although Clinton received some sharp criticism for holding back on the deployment of NATO ground troops, he was ultimately justified, as Serbian president Slobodan Milosevic finally agreed to a peace treaty, signed June 9.

In his final year of office, the president maintained a relatively low profile but took several major trips overseas, to South Asia, Europe, and Africa. He also prepared for the 2000 elections, lending his support not only to presidential hopeful Al Gore, but also to his wife, Hillary Clinton, who successfully ran for U.S. senator from New York.

On Jan. 19, 2001, the day before he left office, Clinton agreed to a five-year suspension of his Arkansas law license and his paying of a $25,000 fine to the Arkansas Bar Association. In exchange, Kenneth Starr's successor, Robert Ray, agreed to close the Whitewater probe, ending the threat of criminal liability for Mr. Clinton after he left office.

GEORGE WALKER BUSH was born on July 6, 1946, in New Haven, Conn., the first child of future president George H. W. Bush. In 1948, the family moved to Odessa, Tex., where the senior Bush went to work in the oil business. George W. grew up mainly in Midland, Tex., and Houston, and later attended two of his father's alma maters, Phillips Academy in Andover, Mass., and Yale.

After graduating from Yale with a history degree in 1968, Bush joined the Texas Air National Guard, where he served as a part-time fighter pilot until 1973. After receiving an MBA from Harvard Business School in 1975, he returned to Texas, where he established his own oil and gas business. In 1977 he met and married his wife, Laura Welch, a librarian. The couple has twin daughters, Jenna and Barbara, born in 1981.

Coming from a prominent political family—his grandfather Prescott Bush had been a senator from Connecticut and his father a U.S. congressman and political appointee—George W. had been immersed in politics since childhood. In 1977 he entered the fray himself, unsuccessfully running for U.S. Congress from the West Texas district that included his hometown of Midland.

Following his defeat, Bush returned to the oil business. In 1985, however, oil prices fell sharply, and Bush's company verged on collapse until it was acquired by a Dallas firm. Bush then headed to Washington to become a paid adviser to his father's successful 1988 presidential campaign. After the election, Bush returned to Texas and assembled a group of investors to buy the Texas Rangers.

Bush again entered politics in 1993, running for the Texas governorship. Although he had a tough opponent in the immensely popular incumbent Ann Richards, he created a clear agenda focused on issues such as education and juvenile justice and won with 53% of the vote. He was reelected in 1998, not long before he announced plans to run for president.

During the 2000 campaign, Bush characterized himself as a "compassionate conservative," a somewhat vague description meant to evoke a kinder, gentler Republican. On the core issues, however, Bush adhered closely to the traditional conservative line, favoring small government, tax cuts, a strong military, and opposing gun control and abortion. His choice of running mate, Dick Cheney, former secretary of defense during his father's administration, provided his campaign with the necessary Washington political experience and gravitas.

With the country in a state of general prosperity and the candidates divided along only narrowly differentiated ideological lines, the 2000 election between George W. Bush and Vice President Al Gore was perceived to be one of the least dynamic on issues. As it turned out, the race was one of the closest in the country's history. By early evening on election night, it was apparent that whoever won Florida would win the election. Bush's razor thin margin of about 1,200 votes prompted an automatic recount. On Nov. 11, after the mandatory machine recount revealed that the two candidates were only a few hundred votes apart, the election began its tortuous journey through the judicial system. The Bush camp sued in federal district court to prohibit manual recounts sought by Gore, and the case ultimately ended up in the U.S. Supreme Court.

Bush officially became the president-elect on Dec. 13, after the U.S. Supreme Court reversed a decision by the Florida Supreme Court to allow manual recounts of ballots in some Florida counties. With Florida in his column, Bush won the presidency with 271 electoral votes, just one more than he needed, although he lost the popular vote by half a million. It was the first time that the Supreme Court, and not the electorate, determined the outcome of the presidential election.

The top item on Bush's domestic agenda—a $1.35 trillion tax cut over 11 years—was pushed through in June 2001. In his first year in office, Bush withdrew the country from a number of international treaties, including the Kyoto treaty on global warming, which Bush contended would hurt the economy, and the 1972 Antiballistic Missile Treaty, the basis for the last three decades of nuclear stability with the Soviet Union. To replace the latter, President Bush championed an antimissile defense system, meant to intercept long-range missiles lobbed at U.S. shores. Opponents of the plan have argued that it is technologically unfeasible and astronomically expensive. Bush succeeded, however, in persuading Russia to agree to a landmark treaty that would cut U.S. and Russian nuclear weapons stockpiles by two-thirds over the next decade. Bush also alienated allies abroad by withdrawing from a conference to regulate the global small-arms trade, rejecting the biological weapons convention banning germ warfare, imposing high tariffs on steel imports (to protect the U.S. steel industry), and withdrawing from a treaty to establish an international war-crimes court.

The terrorist attacks on the World Trade Center and the Pentagon on Sept. 11, 2001, irrevocably altered the direction of the Bush presidency; his primary focus would be the war on international terrorism. On Oct. 7 the U.S. and Britain began air strikes against Afghanistan, after the Taliban government repeatedly refused to surrender Osama bin Laden—the mastermind of the Sept. 11 attacks—and other al-Qaeda leaders. The Taliban collapsed on Dec. 9, but despite this outstanding military success, Bin Laden remained at large. Bush shored up enormous support from the international community to fight terrorism worldwide through intelligence-sharing, freezing suspected terrorist financial assets, and apprehending al-Qaeda and other terrorist suspects.

National security efforts included creating the White House Office of Homeland Security, a cabinet-level domestic security agency that would consolidate 20 federal agencies in a massive government reorganization; implementing tighter airport security; and reforming the intelligence community. More controversial was the passage of the USA Patriot Act, anti-terrorism legislation that has presented law enforcement officials with sweeping new powers to conduct searches without warrants, monitor financial transactions, eavesdrop, and detain and deport individuals in secret.

President Bush's broad characterizations of the terrorist threat allowed him to expand the scope of his foreign policy from al-Qaeda and other terrorist organizations to any regimes hostile to the United States, regardless of their connection to the Sept. 11 attacks. Following the war in Afghanistan, Bush designated Iraq as the primary new threat to American security, shifting the focus away from Osama bin Laden, al-Qaeda, and other terrorist groups. He famously labeled Iraq, along with North Korea and Iran, as part of an "axis of evil." Over the course of 2002, President Bush announced that the U.S. foreign strategy of containment and deterrence was an outdated cold war policy. In an age of terrorism, he maintained, the United States could no longer wait by defensively until a potential threat to its security grew into an actual one—a preemptive strike was called for. Many world leaders expressed alarm at this shift in U.S. policy, which stressed unilateralism rather than international consensus. In Sept. 2002, Bush addressed the UN, challenging the organization to swiftly enforce its own resolutions against Iraq, or else the U.S. would have no choice but to act on its own. The alleged existence of weapons of mass destruction, the thwarting of UN weapons inspections, Iraq's links to terrorism, and Saddam Hussein's despotism and human rights abuses were the casus belli for "regime change." The UN Security Council unanimously approved a resolution imposing tough new arms inspections on Iraq, but after three months of inspections that resulted in modest Iraqi cooperation, U.S. patience ran out: on March 20, President Bush declared war on Iraq and U.S. troops, along with their British allies, began bombing Baghdad. By April 9, Baghdad had fallen, and by May 1, combat was officially declared over.

The war was swift; post-war reconstruction proved far more difficult. The country was enveloped in violence and chaos, its infrastructure in ruins, and coalition forces continued to meet Iraqi resistance and fighting. Iraqis strongly protested against the delay in self-rule and the absence of a timetable to end the U.S. occupation. As American casualties grew and costs mounted (the Pentagon estimated $1 billion per week), the U.S.'s hasty go-it-alone policy began to haunt them. Without a UN mandate and the U.S. insisting on ultimate authority in Iraq, the U.S. was able to recruit only about 10,000 troops from other countries.

Months of searching for Iraq's weapons of mass destruction—one of the prime reasons the Bush and Blair administrations cited for launching the war—yielded no hard evidence, and both administrations and their intelligence agencies came under fire. There were also mounting allegations that the existence of these weapons and their imminent threat to American security was exaggerated or distorted as a pretext to justify the war. In the summer of 2003, the Bush administration admitted that its repeated assertion that Iraq had purchased uranium from Africa to reconstitute its nuclear weapons program was discredited. With the continued absence of weapons of mass destruction, the Bush administration began emphasizing that the justification for war was bringing democracy to the Middle East, which would ultimately defeat terrorism. Continued difficulties in Iraq led to the president's announcement in September that $87 billion in additional military and construction spending is needed—in addition to the $79 billion that Congress approved in April.

North Korea, also part of the "axis of evil," grew increasingly belligerent. In Nov. 2002, North Korea admitted that it had violated a 1994 agreement freezing its nuclear-weapons program and had in fact been developing a nuclear bomb. Faced with North Korea's escalating defiance throughout 2003, the administration played down the North Korean crisis—some interpreted this as a strategic method of handling Kim Jong Il, who has often used inflammatory rhetoric and threats to extort aid and food; others saw the administration as refusing to allow its single-minded focus on Iraq to be clouded by other foreign policy concerns. The U.S. continued to insist that there would be no concessions made until North Korea had completely dismantled its nuclear program.

Early in his presidency, Bush disengaged the U.S. from the Palestinian-Israeli crisis, but following the war in Iraq, which had been fought in part to introduce democracy to the Middle East, Bush presented a "road map" for peace to Israel and the Palestinians in May 2003. But within months, the escalating violence on both sides made it clear that the road map was going nowhere. The Bush administration also renewed its waning interest in Afghanistan by allocating more funds for reconstruction and security; despite the U.S. intervention, the country remained virtually lawless and rife with warlords and al-Qaeda operatives.

On the domestic front, President Bush unveiled a sweeping economic stimulus plan in early Jan. 2003 that characteristically centered around tax cuts. The plan, in its original form, would cut taxes by $670 billion over ten years; Congress approved a $350 billion version. Although all workers would benefit from Bush's tax plan, it strongly favored two groups: two-parent households with several children and the wealthy—nearly half the proposed tax benefits were reserved for the richest 10% of American taxpayers. The classic ideological divisions in Washington quickly surfaced, with Republicans arguing that the greatest tax cuts should go to the wealthy because they pay the most taxes, and Democrats countering that the cuts should go to lower- and middle-income taxpayers, those who need it most. Critics of the plan argued that it was unsound to offer tax cuts while the country was involved in an expensive war and in the midst of a jobless recovery (nearly 3 million jobs had been lost since Bush came to office). In addition, the poverty roll had grown to almost 35 million and the federal budget deficit, according to the nonpartisan Congressional Budget Office, was expected to reach a record $480 billion in 2004. The president countered that his tax cuts had kept the recession shallow and were beginning to show signs of stimulating the economy.

Senate and House Standing Committees, 108th Congress

Committees of the Senate

Agriculture, Nutrition, and Forestry (21 members)
Chairman: Thad Cochran (Miss.)
Ranking Dem.: Tom Harkin (Iowa)

Appropriations (29 members)
Chairman: Ted Stevens (Alaska)
Ranking Dem.: Robert C. Byrd (W.Va.)

Armed Services (25 members)
Chairman: John Warner (Va.)
Ranking Dem.: Carl Levin (Mich.)

Banking, Housing, and Urban Affairs (21 members)
Chairman: Richard C. Shelby (Ala.)
Ranking Dem.: Paul S. Sarbanes (Md.)

Budget (23 members)
Chairman: Don Nickles (Okla.)
Ranking Dem.: Kent Conrad (N.D.)

Commerce, Science, and Transportation (23 members)
Chairman: John McCain (Ariz.)
Ranking Dem.: Ernest F. Hollings (S.C.)

Energy and Natural Resources (23 members)
Chairman: Pete V. Domenici (N.M.)
Ranking Dem.: Jeff Bingaman (N.M.)

Environment and Public Works (19 members)
Chairman: James M. Inhofe (Okla.)
Ranking Member: James Jeffords (Vt.)

Finance (21 members)
Chairman: Charles E. Grassley (Iowa)
Ranking Dem.: Max Baucus (Mont.)

Foreign Relations (19 members)
Chairman: Richard G. Lugar (Ind.)
Ranking Dem.: Joseph R. Biden, Jr. (Del.)

Governmental Affairs (17 members)
Chairman: Susan Collins (Maine)
Ranking Dem.: Joseph Lieberman (Conn.)

Health, Education, Labor, and Pensions (21 members)
Chairman: Judd Gregg (N.H.)
Ranking Dem.: Edward M. Kennedy (Mass.)

Judiciary (19 members)
Chairman: Orrin G. Hatch (Utah)
Ranking Dem.: Patrick J. Leahy (Vt.)

Rules and Administration (19 members)
Chairman: Trent Lott (Miss.)
Ranking Dem.: Christopher Dodd (Conn.)

Small Business (19 members)
Chairman: Olympia J. Snowe (Maine)
Ranking Dem.: John Kerry (Mass.)

Veterans' Affairs (15 members)
Chairman: Arlen Specter (Pa.)
Ranking Dem: Bob Graham (Fla.)

Senate Special or Select Committees

Aging (21 members)
Chairman: Larry Craig (Idaho)
Ranking Dem.: John B. Breaux (La.)

Ethics (6 members)
Chairman: George V. Voinovich (Ohio)
Ranking Dem.: Harry Reid (Nev.)

Indian Affairs (15 members)
Chairman: Ben Nighthorse Campbell (Colo.)
Ranking Dem.: Daniel K. Inouye (Hawaii)

Intelligence (17 members)
Chairman: Pat Roberts (Kans.)
Ranking Dem.: John D. Rockefeller IV (W. Va.)

Committees of the House

Agriculture (51 members)
Chairman: Bob Goodlatte (Va.)
Ranking Dem.: Charles W. Stenholm (Tex.)

Appropriations (65 members)
Chairman: C. W. Bill Young (Fla.)
Ranking Dem.: David R. Obey (Wis.)

Armed Services (60 members)
Chairman: Duncan Hunter (Calif.)
Ranking Dem.: Ike Skelton (Mo.)

Budget (43 members)
Chairman: Jim Nussle (Iowa)
Ranking Dem.: John M. Spratt, Jr. (S.C.)

Education and the Workforce (49 members)
Chairman: John A. Boehner (Ohio)
Ranking Dem.: George Miller (Calif.)

Energy and Commerce (57 members)
Chairman: W. J. Billy Tauzin (La.)
Ranking Dem.: John D. Dingell (Mich.)

Financial Services (70 members)
Chairman: Michael G. Oxley (Ohio)
Ranking Dem.: Barney Frank (Mass.)

Government Reform (44 members)
Chairman: Tom Davis (Va.)
Ranking Dem.: Henry A. Waxman (Calif.)

House Administration (9 members)
Chairman: Robert W. Ney (Ohio)
Ranking Dem.: Steny H. Hoyer (Md.)

International Relations (49 members)
Chairman: Henry J. Hyde (Ill.)
Ranking Dem.: Tom Lantos (Calif.)

Judiciary (37 members)
Chairman: F. James Sensenbrenner, Jr. (Wis.)
Ranking Dem.: John Conyers, Jr. (Mich.)

Resources (52 members)
Chairman: James V. Hansen (Utah)
Ranking Dem.: Nick J. Rahall II (W. Va.)

Rules (13 members)
Chairman: David Dreier (Calif.)
Ranking Dem.: Martin Frost (Tex.)

Science (47 members)
Chairman: Sherwood L. Boehlert (N.Y.)
Ranking Dem.: Ralph M. Hall (Tex.)

Small Business (36 members)
Chairman: Donald A. Manzullo (Ill.)
Ranking Dem.: Nydia M. Velázquez (N.Y.)

Standards of Official Conduct (10 members)
Chairman: Joel Hefley (Colo.)
Ranking Dem.: Alan B. Mollohan (W. Va.)

Transportation and Infrastructure (75 members)
Chairman: Don Young (Alaska)
Ranking Dem.: James L. Oberstar (Minn.)

Veterans' Affairs (31 members)
Chairman: Christopher H. Smith (N.J.)
Ranking Dem.: Lane Evans (Ill.)

Ways and Means (41 members)
Chairman: William M. Thomas (Calif.)
Ranking Dem.: Charles B. Rangel (N.Y.)

Speakers of the House of Representatives

Dates served	Congress	Name and state
1789–1791	1	Frederick A. C. Muhlenberg (Pa.)
1791–1793	2	Jonathan Trumbull (Conn.)
1793–1795	3	Frederick A. C. Muhlenberg (Pa.)
1795–1799	4–5	Jonathan Dayton (N.J.)[1]
1799–1801	6	Theodore Sedgwick (Mass.)
1801–1807	7–9	Nathaniel Macon (N.C.)
1807–1811	10–11	Joseph B. Varnum (Mass.)
1811–1814	12–13	Henry Clay (Ky.)[2]
1814–1815	13	Langdon Cheves (S.C.)
1815–1820	14–16	Henry Clay (Ky.)[3]
1820–1821	16	John W. Taylor (N.Y.)
1821–1823	17	Philip P. Barbour (Va.)
1823–1825	18	Henry Clay (Ky.)
1825–1827	19	John W. Taylor (N.Y.)
1827–1834	20–23	Andrew Stevenson (Va.)[4]
1834–1835	23	John Bell (Tenn.)
1835–1839	24–25	James K. Polk (Tenn.)
1839–1841	26	Robert M. T. Hunter (Va.)
1841–1843	27	John White (Ky.)
1843–1845	28	John W. Jones (Va.)
1845–1847	29	John W. Davis (Ind.)
1847–1849	30	Robert C. Winthrop (Mass.)
1849–1851	31	Howell Cobb (Ga.)
1851–1855	32–33	Linn Boyd (Ky.)
1855–1857	34	Nathaniel P. Banks (Mass.)
1857–1859	35	James L. Orr (S.C.)
1859–1861	36	Wm. Pennington (N.J.)
1861–1863	37	Galusha A. Grow (Pa.)
1863–1869	38–40	Schuyler Colfax (Ind.)
1869–1869	40	Theodore M. Pomeroy (N.Y.)[5]
1869–1875	41–43	James G. Blaine (Maine)
1875–1876	44	Michael C. Kerr (Ind.)[6]
1876–1881	44–46	Samuel J. Randall (Pa.)
1881–1883	47	J. Warren Keifer (Ohio)
1883–1889	48–50	John G. Carlisle (Ky.)
1889–1891	51	Thomas B. Reed (Maine)
1891–1895	52–53	Charles F. Crisp (Ga.)
1895–1899	54–55	Thomas B. Reed (Maine)
1899–1903	56–57	David B. Henderson (Iowa)
1903–1911	58–61	Joseph G. Cannon (Ill.)
1911–1919	62–65	Champ Clark (Mo.)
1919–1925	66–68	Frederick H. Gillett (Mass.)
1925–1931	69–71	Nicholas Longworth (Ohio)
1931–1933	72	John N. Garner (Tex.)
1933–1934	73	Henry T. Rainey (Ill.)[7]
1935–1936	74	Joseph W. Byrns (Tenn.)[8]
1936–1940	74–76	William B. Bankhead (Ala.)[9]
1940–1947	76–79	Sam Rayburn (Tex.)
1947–1949	80	Joseph W. Martin, Jr. (Mass.)
1949–1953	81–82	Sam Rayburn (Tex.)
1953–1955	83	Joseph W. Martin, Jr. (Mass.)
1955–1961	84–87	Sam Rayburn (Tex.)[10]
1963–1971	87–91	John W. McCormack (Mass.)[11]
1971–1977	92–94	Carl Albert (Okla.)[12]
1977–1987	95–99	Thomas P. O'Neill, Jr. (Mass.)[13]
1987–1989	100–101	James C. Wright, Jr. (Tex.)[14]
1989–1995	101–103	Thomas S. Foley (Wash.)
1995–1999	104–105	Newt Gingrich (Ga.)[15]
1999–	106–	Dennis Hastert (Ill.)

1. George Dent (Md.) was elected Speaker pro tempore for April 20 and May 28, 1798. 2. Resigned during second session of 13th Congress. 3. Resigned between first and second sessions of 16th Congress. 4. Resigned during first session of 23rd Congress. 5. Elected Speaker and served the day of adjournment. 6. Died between first and second sessions of 44th Congress. During first session, there were two Speakers pro tempore: Samuel S. Cox (N.Y.), appointed for Feb. 17, May 12, and June 19, 1876, and Milton Sayler (Ohio), appointed for June 4, 1876. 7. Died in 1934 after adjournment of second session of 73rd Congress. 8. Died during second session of 74th Congress. 9. Died during third session of 76th Congress. 10. Died between first and second sessions of 87th Congress. 11. Not a candidate in 1970 election. 12. Not a candidate in 1976 election. 13. Not a candidate in 1986 election. 14. Resigned during first session of 101st Congress. 15. Resigned Jan. 3, 1999, three days before the first session of the 106th Congress. *Source: Congressional Directory.*

Floor Leaders of the Senate

Democratic

- Gilbert M. Hitchcock, Neb. (Min. 1919–20)
- Oscar W. Underwood, Ala. (Min. 1920–23)
- Joseph T. Robinson, Ark. (Min. 1923–33, Maj. 1933–37)
- Alben W. Barkley, Ky. (Maj. 1937–46, Min. 1947–48)
- Scott W. Lucas, Ill. (Maj. 1949–50)
- Ernest W. McFarland, Ariz. (Maj. 1951–52)
- Lyndon B. Johnson, Tex. (Min. 1953–54, Maj. 1955–60)
- Mike Mansfield, Mont. (Maj. 1961–77)
- Robert C. Byrd, W. Va. (Maj. 1977–81, Min. 1981–86, Maj. 1987–88)
- George John Mitchell, Maine (Maj. 1989–1994)
- Thomas A. Daschle, S.D. (Min. 1995–2001, Maj. 2001–2002, Min. 2003–)

Republican

- Charles Curtis, Kan. (Maj. 1925–29)
- James E. Watson, Ind. (Maj. 1929–33)
- Charles L. McNary, Ore. (Min. 1933–44)
- Wallace H. White, Jr., Maine (Min. 1944–47, Maj. 1947–48)
- Kenneth S. Wherry, Neb. (Min. 1949–51)
- Styles Bridges, N.H. (Min. 1951–52)
- Robert A. Taft, Ohio (Maj. 1953)
- William F. Knowland, Calif. (Maj. 1953–54, Min. 1955–58)
- Everett M. Dirksen, Ill. (Min. 1959–69)
- Hugh Scott, Pa. (Min. 1969–1977)
- Howard H. Baker, Jr., Tenn. (Min. 1977–81, Maj. 1981–84)
- Robert J. Dole, Kan. (Maj. 1985–86, Min. 1987–94, Maj. 1995–96)
- Trent Lott, Miss. (Maj. 1996–2001, Min. 2001–2002)
- Bill Frist, Tenn. (Maj. 2003–)

NOTE: Min. = Minority Leader; Maj. = Majority Leader. *Source:* United States Senate, Secretary for the Majority.

Composition of Congress, by Political Party, 1855–2003

Congress	Years	Senate					House				
		Total	Dems	Reps	Others	Vacant	Total	Dems	Reps	Others	Vacant
34th	1855–1857	62	42	15	5	—	234	83	108	43	—
35th	1857–1859	64	39	20	5	—	237	131	92	14	—
36th	1859–1861	66	38	26	2	—	237	101	113	23	—
37th	1861–1863	50	11	31	7	1	178	42	106	28	2
38th	1863–1865	51	12	39	—	—	183	80	103	—	—
39th	1865–1867	52	10	42	—	—	191	46	145	—	—
40th	1867–1869	53	11	42	—	—	193	49	143	—	1
41st	1869–1871	74	11	61	—	2	243	73	170	—	—
42nd	1871–1873	74	17	57	—	—	243	104	139	—	—
43rd	1873–1875	74	19	54	—	1	293	88	203	—	2
44th	1875–1877	76	29	46	—	1	293	181	107	3	2
45th	1877–1879	76	36	39	1	—	293	156	137	—	—
46th	1879–1881	76	43	33	—	—	293	150	128	14	1
47th	1881–1883	76	37	37	2	—	293	130	152	11	—
48th	1883–1885	76	36	40	—	—	325	200	119	6	—
49th	1885–1887	76	34	41	—	1	325	182	140	2	1
50th	1887–1889	76	37	39	—	—	325	170	151	4	—
51st	1889–1891	84	37	47	—	—	330	156	173	1	—
52nd	1891–1893	88	39	47	2	—	333	231	88	14	—
53rd	1893–1895	88	44	38	3	3	356	220	126	10	—
54th	1895–1897	88	39	44	5	—	357	104	246	7	—
55th	1897–1899	90	34	46	10	—	357	134	206	16	1
56th	1899–1901	90	26	53	11	—	357	163	185	9	—
57th	1901–1903	90	29	56	3	2	357	153	198	5	1
58th	1903–1905	90	32	58	—	—	386	178	207	—	1
59th	1905–1907	90	32	58	—	—	386	136	250	—	—
60th	1907–1909	92	29	61	—	2	386	164	222	—	—
61st	1909–1911	92	32	59	—	1	391	172	219	—	—
62nd	1911–1913	92	42	49	—	1	391	228	162	1	—
63rd	1913–1915	96	51	44	1	—	435	290	127	18	—
64th	1915–1917	96	56	39	1	—	435	231	193	8	3
65th	1917–1919	96	53	42	1	—	435	210[1]	216	9	—
66th	1919–1921	96	47	48	1	—	435	191	237	7	—
67th	1921–1923	96	37	59	—	—	435	132	300	1	2
68th	1923–1925	96	43	51	2	—	435	207	225	3	—
69th	1925–1927	96	40	54	1	1	435	183	247	5	—
70th	1927–1929	96	47	48	1	—	435	195	237	3	—
71st	1929–1931	96	39	56	1	—	435	163	267	1	4
72nd	1931–1933	96	47	48	1	—	435	216[2]	218	1	—
73rd	1933–1935	96	59	36	1	—	435	313	117	5	—
74th	1935–1937	96	69	25	2	—	435	322	103	10	—
75th	1937–1939	96	75	17	4	—	435	333	89	13	—
76th	1939–1941	96	69	23	4	—	435	262	169	4	—
77th	1941–1943	96	66	28	2	—	435	267	162	6	—
78th	1943–1945	96	57	38	1	—	435	222	209	4	—
79th	1945–1947	96	57	38	1	—	435	243	190	2	—
80th	1947–1949	96	45	51	—	—	435	188	246	1	—
81st	1949–1951	96	54	42	—	—	435	263	171	1	—
82nd	1951–1953	96	48	47	1	—	435	234	199	2	—
83rd	1953–1955	96	46	48	2	—	435	213	221	1	—
84th	1955–1957	96	48	47	1	—	435	232	203	—	—
85th	1957–1959	96	49	47	—	—	435	234	201	—	—
86th	1959–1961	98	64	34	—	—	436[3]	283	153	—	—
87th	1961–1963	100	64	36	—	—	437[4]	262	175	—	—
88th	1963–1965	100	67	33	—	—	435	258	176	—	1
89th	1965–1967	100	68	32	—	—	435	295	140	—	—
90th	1967–1969	100	64	36	—	—	435	248	187	—	—
91st	1969–1971	100	58	42	—	—	435	243	192	—	—
92nd	1971–1973	100	54	44	2	—	435	255	180	—	—
93rd	1973–1975	100	56	42	2	—	435	242	192	1	—
94th	1975–1977	100	61	37	2	—	435	291	144	—	—
95th	1977–1979	100	61	38	1	—	435	292	143	—	—
96th	1979–1981	100	58	41	1	—	435	277	158	—	—
97th	1981–1983	100	46	53	1	—	435	242	192	1	—
98th	1983–1985	100	46	54	—	—	435	269	166	—	—
99th	1985–1987	100	47	53	—	—	435	253	182	—	—
100th	1987–1989	100	55	45	—	—	435	258	177	—	—
101st	1989–1991	100	55	45	—	—	435	260	175	—	—

Congress	Years	Senate Total	Senate Dems	Senate Reps	Senate Others	Senate Vacant	House Total	House Dems	House Reps	House Others	House Vacant
102nd	1991–1993	100	56	44	—	—	435	267	167	1	—
103rd	1993–1995	100	57	43	—	—	435	258	176	1	—
104th	1995–1997	100	48	52	—	—	435	204	230	1	—
105th	1997–1999	100	45	55	—	—	435	207	226	2	—
106th	1999–2001	100	45	55	—	—	435	211	223	1	—
107th	2001–2003	100	50	50	—	—	435	212	221	2	—
108th	2003–2005	100	48	51	1	—	435	205	229	1	—

NOTE: All figures reflect immediate results of elections. 1. Democrats organized House with help of other parties. 2. Democrats organized House due to Republican deaths. 3. Proclamation declaring Alaska a state issued Jan 3., 1959. 4. Proclamation declaring Hawaii a state issued Aug. 21, 1959. *Source:* Office of the Clerk of the House of Representatives. Web: http://clerkweb.house.gov/histrecs/history.htm.

Salaries of the President, Vice President, and Other U.S. Officials, 2002

(per year)

Position	Salary
President	
1789	$ 25,000
1873	50,000
1909	75,000
1949	100,000[1]
1969	200,000[1]
2001	400,000[1]

Position	Salary
Vice President	$192,600[2]
Senator	150,000
Representative	150,000
Majority and Minority Leaders	166,700
Speaker of the House	192,600
Chief Justice, U.S. Supreme Court	192,600
Assoc. Justice, U.S. Supreme Court	184,400

1. Plus $50,000 non-taxable expense allowance to assist in defraying expenses relating to or resulting from the discharge of his official duties. 2. Plus $10,000 taxable expense allowance. *Source:* Office of Personnel Management. Web: www.opm.gov/.

Congressional Apportionment, 2000

Source: U.S. Census Bureau

Apportionment is the process of dividing the 435 seats in the House of Representatives among the 50 states. The number of seats, or representatives, each state is entitled to is apportioned according to the new census figures that are compiled every 10 years. States with larger populations have more representatives than states with smaller populations. Each state must have at least one representative.

Once the number of seats is assigned to each state, it is up to the individual state legislatures to redraw new congressional districts. Each representative is elected by voters from a congressional district within their state.

Who Counts?

The population figure used to calculate the apportionment of House seats is based on the total resident population of the United States, including citizens and noncitizens, plus U.S. military personnel and federal civilian employees and their dependents living overseas. It excludes the populations of the District of Columbia, Puerto Rico, and other U.S. territories that do not have voting seats in the House of Representatives. The Census 2000 apportionment population was 281,424,177.

Congressional District Size

The number of representatives in the U.S. House of Representatives has remained constant at 435 since 1911, except for a temporary increase to 437 at the time of admission of Alaska and Hawaii as states in 1959. However, the apportionment based on the 1960 census, which took effect for the election of 1962, reverted to 435 seats.

The average size of a congressional district based on the Census 2000 apportionment population will be 646,952, more than triple the average district size of 193,167 based on the 1900 census apportionment, and about 74,486 more than the average size of 572,466 based on the 1990 census.

Congressional Seats Gained/Lost in the 108th Congress[1]

Seats gained: + 2 seats	Seats gained: +1 seat	Seats lost: –1 seat	Seats lost: –2 seats
Arizona (8)	California (53)	Connecticut (5)	New York (29)
Florida (25)	Colorado (7)	Illinois (19)	Pennsylvania (19)
Georgia (13)	Nevada (3)	Indiana (9)	
Texas (32)	North Carolina (13)	Michigan (15)	
		Mississippi (4)	
		Ohio (18)	
		Oklahoma (5)	
		Wisconsin (8)	

NOTE: The number of representatives based on Census 2000 is given in parentheses after each state. 1. Based on Census 2000. *Source:* U.S. Census Bureau, Census 2000. Web: www.census.gov.

How a Bill Becomes a Law

When a senator or a representative introduces a bill, he or she sends it to the clerk of his house, who gives it a number and title. This is the *first reading,* and the bill is referred to the proper committee.

The committee may decide the bill is unwise or unnecessary and *table* it, thus killing it at once. Or it may decide the bill is worthwhile and hold hearings to listen to facts and opinions presented by experts and other interested persons. After members of the committee have debated the bill and perhaps offered amendments, a vote is taken; and if the vote is favorable, the bill is sent back to the floor of the house.

The clerk reads the bill sentence by sentence to the house, and this is known as the *second reading.* Members may then debate the bill and offer amendments. In the House of Representatives, the time for debate is limited by a *cloture rule,* but there is no such restriction in the Senate for cloture, where 60 votes are required. This makes possible a *filibuster,* in which one or more opponents hold the floor to defeat the bill.

The *third reading* is by title only, and the bill is put to a vote, which may be by voice or roll call, depending on the circumstances and parliamentary rules. Members who must be absent at the time but who wish to record their vote may be paired if each negative vote has a balancing affirmative one.

The bill then goes to the other house of Congress, where it may be defeated, or passed with or without amendments. If the bill is defeated, it dies. If it is passed with amendments, a joint congressional committee must be appointed by both houses to iron out the differences.

After its final passage by both houses, the bill is sent to the president. If he approves, he signs it, and the bill becomes a law. However, if he disapproves, he *vetoes* the bill by refusing to sign it and sending it back to the house of origin with his reasons for the veto. The objections are read and debated, and a roll-call vote is taken. If the bill receives less than a two-thirds vote, it is defeated and goes no further. But if it receives a two-thirds vote or greater, it is sent to the other house for a vote. If that house also passes it by a two-thirds vote, the president's veto is *overridden,* and the bill becomes a law.

Should the president desire neither to sign nor to veto the bill, he may retain it for ten days, Sundays excepted, after which time it automatically becomes a law without signature. However, if Congress has adjourned within those ten days, the bill is automatically killed, that process of indirect rejection being known as a *pocket veto.*

Presidential Vetoes, 1789–2003

President	Coincident Congresses	Regular vetoes	Pocket vetoes	Total vetoes	Vetoes overridden
Washington	1st–4th	2	—	2	—
Adams	5th–6th	—	—	—	—
Jefferson	7th–10th	—	—	—	—
Madison	11th–14th	5	2	7	—
Monroe	15th–18th	1	—	1	—
J. Q. Adams	19th–20th	—	—	—	—
Jackson	21st–24th	5	7	12	—
Van Buren	25th–26th	—	1	1	—
W. H. Harrison	27th	—	—	—	—
Tyler	27th–28th	6	4	10	1
Polk	29th–30th	2	1	3	—
Taylor	31st	—	—	—	—
Fillmore	31st–32nd	—	—	—	—
Pierce	33rd–34th	9	—	9	5
Buchanan	35th–36th	4	3	7	—
Lincoln	37th–39th	2	5	7	—
A. Johnson	39th–40th	21	8	29	15
Grant	41st–44th	45	48	93	4
Hayes	45th–46th	12	1	13	1
Garfield	47th	—	—	—	—
Arthur	47th–48th	4	8	12	1
Cleveland	49th–50th	304	110	414	2
B. Harrison	51st–52nd	19	25	44	1
Cleveland	53rd–54th	42	128	170	5
McKinley	55th–57th	6	36	42	—
T. Roosevelt	57th–60th	42	40	82	1
Taft	61st–62nd	30	9	39	1
Wilson	63rd–66th	33	11	44	6
Harding	67th	5	1	6	—
Coolidge	68th–70th	20	30	50	4
Hoover	71st–72nd	21	16	37	3
F. D. Roosevelt	73rd–79th	372	263	635	9
Truman	79th–82nd	180	70	250	12
Eisenhower	83rd–86th	73	108	181	2
Kennedy	87th–88th	12	9	21	—
L. B. Johnson	88th–90th	16	14	30	—
Nixon	91st–93rd	26	17	43	7

President	Coincident Congresses	Regular vetoes	Pocket vetoes	Total vetoes	Vetoes overridden
Ford	93rd–94th	48	18	66	12
Carter	95th–96th	13	18	31	2
Reagan	97th–100th	39	39	78	9
G.H.W. Bush[1]	101st–102nd	29	15	44	1
Clinton	103rd–106th	36	1	37	2
G. W. Bush	107th–108th	—	—	—	—
Total		**1,484**	**1,066**	**2,550**	**106**

1. President Bush attempted to pocket veto two bills during intrasession recess periods. Congress considered the two bills enacted into law because of the president's failure to return the legislation. The bills are not counted as pocket vetoes in this table. *Source:* Office of the Clerk of the House. Web: http://clerk.house.gov.

Order of Presidential Succession

According to the Presidential Succession Act of 1792, the Senate president pro tempore[1] was next in line after the vice president to succeed to the presidency, followed by the Speaker of the House.

In 1886, however, Congress changed the order of presidential succession, replacing the president pro tempore and the Speaker with the cabinet officers. Proponents of this change argued that the congressional leaders lacked executive experience, and none had served as president, while six former secretaries of state had later been elected to that office.

The Presidential Succession Act of 1947, signed by President Harry Truman, changed the order again to what it is today. The cabinet members are ordered in the line of succession according to the date their offices were established.

Prior to the ratification of the 25th Amendment in 1967, there was no provision for filling a vacancy in the vice presidency. When a president died in office, the vice president succeeded him, and the vice presidency then remained vacant. The first vice president to take office under the new procedure was Gerald Ford, who was nominated by Nixon on Oct. 12, 1973, and confirmed by Congress the following Dec. 6.

1. The Vice President
2. Speaker of the House
3. President pro tempore of the Senate[1]
4. Secretary of State
5. Secretary of the Treasury
6. Secretary of Defense
7. Attorney General
8. Secretary of the Interior
9. Secretary of Agriculture
10. Secretary of Commerce
11. Secretary of Labor
12. Secretary of Health and Human Services
13. Secretary of Housing and Urban Development
14. Secretary of Transportation
15. Secretary of Energy
16. Secretary of Education
17. Secretary of Veterans Affairs
18. Secretary of Homeland Security[2]

NOTE: An official cannot succeed to the Presidency unless that person meets the Constitutional requirements. 1. The president pro tempore presides over the Senate when the vice president is absent. By tradition the position is held by the senior member of the majority party. 2. May move to number 8 on the list pending legislation.

Executive Departments and Agencies

Source: United States Government Manual, 2002–2003

Unless otherwise indicated, addresses shown are in Washington, DC. ZIP codes are in parentheses.

White House Offices and Agencies

Office of Administration
Eisenhower Executive Office Bldg., 725 17th St., NW (20503)
Established: Dec. 12, 1977
Director: Phillip D. Larsen

Office of National Drug Control Policy
Executive Office of the President (20503)
Established: Jan. 29, 1989
Director: John P. Walters

Council of Economic Advisers (CEA)
Old Executive Office Bldg. (20502)
Members: 3
Established: Feb. 20, 1946
Chair: Dr. N. Gregory Mankin

Council on Environmental Quality
722 Jackson Place, NW (20503)
Established: 1969
Chair: James Connaughton

Office of Management and Budget
Executive Office Bldg. (20503)
Established: July 1, 1939
Director: Joshua B. Bolten

Office of Science and Technology Policy
Eisenhower Executive Office Building (20502)
Established: May 11, 1976
Director: John H. Marburger III

National Security Council (NSC)
Eisenhower Executive Office Bldg. (20504)
Members: 4
Established: July 26, 1947
Chair: The President
National Security Adviser: Condoleezza Rice
Other members: Vice President; Secretary of State; Secretary of Defense

Office of the United States Trade Representative
600 17th St., NW (20508)
Established: Jan. 15, 1963
Trade Representative: Robert Zoellick

Executive Departments

Department of Agriculture
1400 Independence Ave., SW (20250)
Established: May 15, 1862. Administered by Commissioner of Agriculture until 1889, when it was made executive department.
Secretary: Ann Veneman

Department of Commerce
1401 Constitution Ave., NW (20230)

Established: Department of Commerce and Labor was created Feb. 14, 1903. On March 4, 1913, all labor activities were transferred out of Department of Commerce and Labor and it was renamed Department of Commerce.
Secretary: Donald L. Evans

Department of Defense
Office of the Secretary, The Pentagon (20301-1155)
Established: July 26, 1947, as National Military Establishment; name changed to Department of Defense on Aug. 10, 1949. Subordinate to Secretary of Defense are Secretaries of Army, Navy, Air Force.
Secretary: Donald H. Rumsfeld
Deputy Secretary: Paul D. Wolfowitz
Secretary of Army: Thomas E. White
Secretary of Navy: Gordon R. England
Secretary of Air Force: James G. Roche
Commandant of Marine Corps: Gen. James L. Jones
Joint Chiefs of Staff: Gen. Richard B. Myers, Air Force, Chairman; Gen. Peter Pace, Marine Corps, Vice Chairman; Gen. Eric K. Shinseki, Army; Adm. Vernon E. Clark, Navy; Gen. John P. Jumper, Air Force; Gen. James L. Jones, Marine Corps.

Department of Education
400 Maryland Ave., SW (20202)
Established: Oct. 17, 1979
Secretary: Roderick R. Paige

Department of Energy
1000 Independence Ave., SW (20585)
Established: Oct. 1, 1977
Secretary: Spencer Abraham

Department of Health and Human Services
200 Independence Ave., SW (20201)
Established: Department of Health, Education, and Welfare was created April 11, 1953, replacing Federal Security Agency created in 1939. On Oct. 17, 1979, the Department of Education became a separate department.
Secretary: Tommy G. Thompson
Surgeon General: Dr. Richard Carmona

Department of Homeland Security
Washington DC (20528)
Established: The most significant transformation of the U.S. government since 1947 was formed in the aftermath of Sept. 11, 2001, when 22 separate agencies were combined to become the cabinet-level Department of Homeland Security. It became an official cabinet department Jan. 24, 2003
Secretary: Tom Ridge

Department of Housing and Urban Development
451 7th St., SW (20410)
Established: Nov. 9, 1965, replacing Housing and Home Finance Agency created in 1947
Secretary: Melquiades R. Martinez

Department of the Interior
1849 C St., NW (20240)
Established: March 3, 1849
Secretary: Gale A. Norton

Department of Justice
950 Pennsylvania Ave., NW (20530)
Established: Office of Attorney General was created Sept. 24, 1789. Although one of the original cabinet members, the attorney general was not an executive department head until June 22, 1870, when the Department of Justice was established.
Attorney General: John Ashcroft
Solicitor General: Theodore B. Olson
Director of FBI: Robert S. Mueller, III

Department of Labor
200 Constitution Ave., NW (20210)
Established: Bureau of Labor was created in 1884 under Department of the Interior; later became independent department without executive rank. Returned to bureau status in Department of Commerce and Labor, but on March 4, 1913, became independent executive department under its present name.
Secretary: Elaine L. Chao

Department of State
2201 C St., NW (20520)
Established: 1781 as Department of Foreign Affairs; reconstituted, 1789, following adoption of Constitution; name changed to Department of State Sept. 15, 1789.
Secretary: Colin L. Powell
UN Ambassador: John D. Negroponte
Deputy UN Ambassador: James Cunningham

Department of Transportation
400 7th St., SW (20590)
Established: Oct. 15, 1966, as result of Department of Transportation Act, which became effective April 1, 1967.
Secretary: Norman Y. Mineta

Department of the Treasury
1500 Pennsylvania Ave., NW (20220)
Established: Sept. 2, 1789
Secretary: John Snow
Treasurer of the U.S.: Vacant

Department of Veterans' Affairs
810 Vermont Ave., NW (20420)
Established: March 15, 1989, replacing Veterans Administration created in 1930
Secretary: Anthony J. Principi

Major Independent Agencies

Central Intelligence Agency (CIA)
Washington, DC (20505)
Established: 1947
Director of Central Intelligence: George J. Tenet

U.S. Commission on Civil Rights
624 9th St., NW (20425)
Established: 1957
Staff Director: Les Jin

Consumer Product Safety Commission
East West Towers, 4330 East West Highway, Bethesda, Md. 20814
Established: Oct. 27, 1972
Chair: Harold D. Stratton

Corporation for National and Community Service
1201 New York Ave., NW (20525)
Established: Sept. 1993
CEO: Leslie Lenkowsky

Environmental Protection Agency (EPA)
1200 Pennsylvania Ave., NW (20460)
Established: Dec. 2, 1970
Acting Administrator: Marianne Lamont Horinko

Equal Employment Opportunity Commission (EEOC)
1801 L St., NW (20507)
Members: 5
Established: July 2, 1965
Chair: Cari M. Dominguez

Farm Credit Administration (FCA)
1501 Farm Credit Dr., McLean, Va. 22102-5090
Members: 13
Established: March 27, 1933
Chair: Michael M. Reyna

Federal Communications Commission (FCC)
445 Twelfth Street, SW (20554)
Established: 1934
Chair: Michael Powell

Federal Deposit Insurance Corporation (FDIC)
550 17th St., NW (20429)
Established: June 16, 1933
Chair: Donald E. Powell

Federal Election Commission (FEC)
999 E St., NW (20463)
Members: 6
Established: 1975
Chair: David M. Mason

Federal Maritime Commission
800 North Capitol St., NW (20573-0001)
Members: 5
Established: Aug. 12, 1961

Chair: Steven R. Blust

Federal Mediation and Conciliation Service (FMCS)
2100 K St., NW (20427)
Established: 1947
Director: Peter J. Hurtgen

Federal Reserve System (FRS), Board of Governors of
20th St. & Constitution Ave., NW (20551)
Members: 7
Established: Dec. 23, 1913
Chair: Alan Greenspan

Federal Trade Commission (FTC)
600 Pennsylvania Ave., NW (20580)
Members: 5
Established: Sept. 26, 1914
Chair: Timothy J. Muris

General Services Administration (GSA)
1800 F St., NW (20405)
Established: July 1, 1949
Administrator: Stephen A. Perry

U.S. International Trade Commission
500 E St., SW (20436)
Members: 6
Established: Sept. 8, 1916
Chair: Deanna Tanner Okun

National Aeronautics and Space Administration (NASA)
300 E St., SW (20546)
Established: 1958
Administrator: Sean O'Keefe

National Archives and Records Administration (NARA)
8601 Adelphi Road, College Park, Md. 20740-6001
Established: Oct. 19, 1984. NARA is the successor agency to the National Archives Establishment, which was created in 1934 and later incorporated into the General Services Administration as the National Archives and Records Service in 1949.
Archivist of the U.S.: John W. Carlin

National Foundation on the Arts and the Humanities
1100 Pennsylvania Ave., NW (20506-0001)
Established: 1965
Chairs: National Endowment for the Arts, Chair, Eileen Mason, Acting; National Endowment for the Humanities, Chair, Bruce Cole

National Labor Relations Board (NLRB)
1099 14th St., NW (20570)
Members: 5
Established: July 5, 1935
Chair: Robert J. Battista

National Mediation Board
Suite 250 East, 1301 K St., NW (20572)
Established: June 21, 1934
Chair: Francis J. Duggan

National Science Foundation (NSF)
4201 Wilson Blvd., Arlington, Va. 22230
Established: 1950
Director: Rita R. Colwell

National Transportation Safety Board
490 L'Enfant Plaza, SW (20594)
Members: 5
Established: April 1, 1967, as an independent agency supported by the Dept. of Transportation. Ties with Dept. of Transportation officially ended in 1975.
Chair: Ellen G. Engleman

Nuclear Regulatory Commission (NRC)
Washington, DC 20555
Members: 5
Established: Jan. 19, 1975
Chair: Richard A. Meserve

Office of Personnel Management (OPM)
1900 E St., NW (20415-0001)
Established: Jan. 1, 1979
Director: Kay Coles James

U.S. Postal Service
475 L'Enfant Plaza West, SW (20260-0010)
Established: In 1775 with the appointment of Benjamin Franklin as the first postmaster general under the Continental Congress. In 1970 became independent agency headed by 11-member board of governors.
Postmaster General: John E. Potter

Securities and Exchange Commission (SEC)
450 5th St., NW (20549)
Members: 5
Established: July 2, 1934
Chair: Harvey L. Pitt

Selective Service System (SSS)
National Headquarters, Arlington, Va., 22209-2425
Established: Sept. 16, 1940
Acting Director: Lewis Brodsky

Small Business Administration (SBA)
409 3rd St., SW (20416)
Established: July 30, 1953
Administrator: Hector V. Barreto

Tennessee Valley Authority (TVA)
400 West Summit Hill Drive, Knoxville, Tenn. 37902. Washington office: One Massachusetts Ave., NW (20444-0001)
Members of Board of Directors: 3
Established: May 18, 1933
Chairman: Glenn L. McCullough, Jr.

Other Independent Agencies

American Battle Monuments Commission—Courthouse Plaza II, Suite 500, 2300 Clarendon Blvd., Arlington, Va. (22201)
Appalachian Regional Commission—1666 Connecticut Ave., NW, Suite 700 (20235)
Commission of Fine Arts—441 F St., NW, Ste. 312 (20001)
Commodity Futures Trading Commission—1155 21st St., NW (20581)
Export-Import Bank of the United States—811 Vermont Ave., NW (20571)
Federal Emergency Management Agency—500 C St., SW (20472)
Federal Housing Finance Board—1777 F St., NW (20006)
Federal Labor Relations Authority—607 14th St., NW (20424-0001)
Inter-American Foundation—901 N. Stuart St., Arlington, Va. 22203
National Commission on Libraries and Information Science—1110 Vermont Ave., NW, Ste. 820 (20005-3552)
National Credit Union Administration—1775 Duke St., Alexandria, Va. 22314-3428
Occupational Safety and Health Review Commission—1120 20th St., NW (20036-3419)
U.S. Parole Commission—Dept. of Justice, 5550 Friendship Blvd., Ste. 420, Chevy Chase, Md. 20815
Peace Corps—1111 20th St., NW (20526)
Pension Benefit Guaranty Corporation—1200 K St., NW (20005-4026)
Postal Rate Commission—1333 H St., NW (20268-0001)
President's Council on Physical Fitness and Sports—Dept. W, 200 Independence Ave., SW, Room 738-H (20201-0004)
Railroad Retirement Board (RRB)—844 N. Rush St., Ninth Floor, Chicago, Ill. 60611-2092; Office of Legislative Affairs: 1310 G St., N.W, Ste. 500 (20005-3004).

Legislative Department

Architect of the Capitol—U.S. Capitol Building (20515)
General Accounting Office (GAO)—441 G St., NW (20548)
Government Printing Office (GPO)—732 North Capitol St., NW (20401)
Library of Congress—101 Independence Ave., SE (20540)
United States Botanic Garden—Office of Executive Director, 245 1st St., SW (20024)

Quasi-Official Agencies

American National Red Cross—430 17th St., NW (20006)

Legal Services Corporation—3333 K St., NW 3rd Fl. (20007-3522)

National Academy of Sciences, National Academy of Engineering, National Research Council, Institute of Medicine—2101 Constitution Ave., NW (20418)

National Railroad Passenger Corporation (Amtrak)—60 Massachusetts Ave., NE (20002)

Smithsonian Institution—PO Box 37012 SI Bldg., Rm. 153, MRC 010 (20013-7012)

Government Officials

Cabinet Members with Dates of Appointment

Although the Constitution made no provision for a president's advisory group, the heads of the three executive departments (State, Treasury, and War) and the attorney general were organized by Washington into such a group; and by about 1793, the name "cabinet" was applied to it. With the exception of the attorney general up to 1870 and the postmaster general from 1829 to 1872, cabinet members have been heads of executive departments.

Cabinet members are appointed by the president, subject to the confirmation of the Senate; and as their terms are not fixed, they may be replaced at any time by the president. At a change in administration, it is customary for cabinet members to resign, but they remain in office until successors are appointed.

The table of cabinet members lists only those members who actually served after being duly commissioned. The dates shown are those of appointment. "Cont." indicates that the term continued from the previous administration for a substantial amount of time.

Washington

Secretary of State	Thomas Jefferson, 1789
	Edmund Randolph, 1794
	Timothy Pickering, 1795
Secretary of the Treasury	Alexander Hamilton, 1789
	Oliver Wolcott, Jr., 1795
Secretary of War	Henry Knox, 1789
	Timothy Pickering, 1795
	James McHenry, 1796
Attorney General	Edmund Randolph, 1789
	William Bradford, 1794
	Charles Lee, 1795

J. Adams

Secretary of State	Timothy Pickering (Cont.)
	John Marshall, 1800
Secretary of the Treasury	Oliver Wolcott, Jr. (Cont.)
	Samuel Dexter, 1801
Secretary of War	James McHenry (Cont.)
	Samuel Dexter, 1800
Attorney General	Charles Lee (Cont.)
Secretary of the Navy	Benjamin Stoddert, 1798

Jefferson

Secretary of State	James Madison, 1801
Secretary of the Treasury	Samuel Dexter (Cont.)
	Albert Gallatin, 1801
Secretary of War	Henry Dearborn, 1801
Attorney General	Levi Lincoln, 1801
	Robert Smith, 1805
	John Breckinridge, 1805
	Caesar A. Rodney, 1807
Secretary of the Navy	Benjamin Stoddert (Cont.)
	Robert Smith, 1801

Madison

Secretary of State	Robert Smith, 1809
	James Monroe, 1811
Secretary of the Treasury	Albert Gallatin (Cont.)
	George W. Campbell, 1814
	Alexander J. Dallas, 1814
	William H. Crawford, 1816
Secretary of War	William Eustis, 1809
	John Armstrong, 1813
	James Monroe, 1814
	William H. Crawford, 1815
Attorney General	Caesar A. Rodney (Cont.)
	William Pinckney, 1811
	Richard Rush, 1814
Secretary of the Navy	Paul Hamilton, 1809
	William Jones, 1813
	B. W. Crowninshield, 1814

Monroe

Secretary of State	John Quincy Adams, 1817
Secretary of the Treasury	William H. Crawford (Cont.)
Secretary of War	John C. Calhoun, 1817
Attorney General	Richard Rush (Cont.)
	William Wirt, 1817
Secretary of the Navy	B. W. Crowninshield (Cont.)
	Smith Thompson, 1818
	Samuel L. Southard, 1823

J. Q. Adams

Secretary of State	Henry Clay, 1825
Secretary of the Treasury	Richard Rush, 1825
Secretary of War	James Barbour, 1825
	Peter B. Porter, 1828
Attorney General	William Wirt (Cont.)
Secretary of the Navy	Samuel L. Southard (Cont.)

Jackson

Secretary of State	Martin Van Buren, 1829
	Edward Livingston, 1831
	Louis McLane, 1833
	John Forsyth, 1834
Secretary of the Treasury	Samuel D. Ingham, 1829
	Louis McLane, 1831
	William J. Duane, 1833
	Roger B. Taney[1], 1833
	Levi Woodbury, 1834
Secretary of War	John H. Eaton, 1829
	Lewis Cass, 1831
Attorney General	John M. Berrien, 1829
	Roger B. Taney, 1831
	Benjamin F. Butler, 1833
Postmaster General[2]	William T. Barry, 1829
	Amos Kendall, 1835
Secretary of the Navy	John Branch, 1829
	Levi Woodbury, 1831
	Mahlon Dickerson, 1834

1. Not confirmed by the Senate. 2. The postmaster general did not become a cabinet member until 1829. Earlier postmasters general were: Samuel Osgood (1789), Timothy Pickering (1791), Joseph Habersham (1795), Gideon Granger (1801), Return J. Meigs, Jr. (1814), and John McLean (1823).

Van Buren

Secretary of State	John Forsyth (Cont.)
Secretary of the Treasury	Levi Woodbury (Cont.)
Secretary of War	Joel R. Poinsett, 1837
Attorney General	Benjamin F. Butler (Cont.)
	Felix Grundy, 1838
	Henry D. Gilpin, 1840

Postmaster General	Amos Kendall (Cont.)
	John M. Niles, 1840
Secretary of the Navy	Mahlon Dickerson (Cont.)
	James K. Paulding, 1838

W. H. Harrison

Secretary of State	Daniel Webster, 1841
Secretary of the Treasury	Thomas Ewing, 1841
Secretary of War	John Bell, 1841
Attorney General	John J. Crittenden, 1841
Postmaster General	Francis Granger, 1841
Secretary of the Navy	George E. Badger, 1841

Tyler

Secretary of State	Daniel Webster (Cont.)
	Abel P. Upshur, 1843
	John C. Calhoun, 1844
Secretary of the Treasury	Thomas Ewing (Cont.)
	Walter Forward, 1841
	John C. Spencer[1], 1843
	George M. Bibb, 1844
Secretary of War	John Bell (Cont.)
	John C. Spencer, 1841
	James M. Porter[1], 1843
	William Wilkins, 1844
Attorney General	John J. Crittenden (Cont.)
	Hugh S. Legaré, 1841
	John Nelson, 1843
Postmaster General	Francis Granger (Cont.)
	Charles A. Wickliffe, 1841
Secretary of the Navy	George E. Badger (Cont.)
	Abel P. Upshur, 1841
	David Henshaw[1], 1843
	Thomas W. Gilmer, 1844
	John Y. Mason, 1844

1. Not confirmed by the Senate.

Polk

Secretary of State	James Buchanan, 1845
Secretary of the Treasury	Robert J. Walker, 1845
Secretary of War	William L. Marcy, 1845
Attorney General	John Y. Mason, 1845
	Nathan Clifford, 1846
	Isaac Toucey, 1848
Postmaster General	Cave Johnson, 1845
Secretary of the Navy	George Bancroft, 1845
	John Y. Mason, 1846

Taylor

Secretary of State	John M. Clayton, 1849
Secretary of the Treasury	William M. Meredith, 1849
Secretary of War	George W. Crawford, 1849
Attorney General	Reverdy Johnson, 1849
Postmaster General	Jacob Collamer, 1849
Secretary of the Navy	William B. Preston, 1849
Secretary of the Interior	Thomas Ewing, 1849

Fillmore

Secretary of State	Daniel Webster, 1850
	Edward Everett, 1852
Secretary of the Treasury	Thomas Corwin, 1850
Secretary of War	Charles M. Conrad, 1850
Attorney General	John J. Crittenden, 1850
Postmaster General	Nathan K. Hall, 1850
	Samuel D. Hubbard, 1852
Secretary of the Navy	William A. Graham, 1850
	John P. Kennedy, 1852
Secretary of the Interior	Thos. M. T. McKennan, 1850
	Alex. H. H. Stuart, 1850

Pierce

Secretary of State	William L. Marcy, 1853
Secretary of the Treasury	James Guthrie, 1853
Secretary of War	Jefferson Davis, 1853
Attorney General	Caleb Cushing, 1853
Postmaster General	James Campbell, 1853
Secretary of the Navy	James C. Dobbin, 1853
Secretary of the Interior	Robert McClelland, 1853

Buchanan

Secretary of State	Lewis Cass, 1857
	Jeremiah S. Black, 1860
Secretary of the Treasury	Howell Cobb, 1857
	Philip F. Thomas, 1860
	John A. Dix, 1861
Secretary of War	John B. Floyd, 1857
	Joseph Holt, 1861
Attorney General	Jeremiah S. Black, 1857
	Edwin M. Stanton, 1860
Postmaster General	Aaron V. Brown, 1857
	Joseph Holt, 1859
	Horatio King, 1861
Secretary of the Navy	Isaac Toucey, 1857
Secretary of the Interior	Jacob Thompson, 1857

Lincoln

Secretary of State	William H. Seward, 1861
Secretary of the Treasury	Salmon P. Chase, 1861
	William P. Fessenden, 1864
	Hugh McCulloch, 1865
Secretary of War	Simon Cameron, 1861
	Edwin M. Stanton, 1862
Attorney General	Edward Bates, 1861
	James Speed, 1864
Postmaster General	Montgomery Blair, 1861
	William Dennison, 1864
Secretary of the Navy	Gideon Welles, 1861
Secretary of the Interior	Caleb B. Smith, 1861
	John P. Usher, 1863

A. Johnson

Secretary of State	William H. Seward (Cont.)
Secretary of the Treasury	Hugh McCulloch (Cont.)
Secretary of War	Edwin M. Stanton (Cont.)
	John M. Schofield, 1868
Attorney General	James Speed (Cont.)
	Henry Stanbery, 1866
	William M. Evarts, 1868
Postmaster General	William Dennison (Cont.)
	Alexander W. Randall, 1866
Secretary of the Navy	Gideon Welles (Cont.)
Secretary of the Interior	John P. Usher (Cont.)
	James Harlan, 1865
	Orville H. Browning, 1866

Grant

Secretary of State	Elihu B. Washburne, 1869
	Hamilton Fish, 1869
Secretary of the Treasury	George S. Boutwell, 1869
	William A. Richardson, 1873
	Benjamin H. Bristow, 1874
	Lot M. Morrill, 1876
Secretary of War	John A. Rawlins, 1869
	William W. Belknap, 1869
	Alphonso Taft, 1876
	James D. Cameron, 1876
Attorney General	Ebenezer R. Hoar, 1869
	Amos T. Akerman, 1870
	George H. Williams, 1871
	Edwards Pierrepont, 1875
	Alphonso Taft, 1876
Postmaster General	John A. J. Creswell, 1869
	Marshall Jewell, 1874
	James N. Tyner, 1876
Secretary of the Navy	Adolph E. Borie, 1869
	George M. Robeson, 1869
Secretary of the Interior	Jacob D. Cox, 1869
	Columbus Delano, 1870
	Zachariah Chandler, 1875

Hayes

Secretary of State	William M. Evarts, 1877
Secretary of the Treasury	John Sherman, 1877
Secretary of War	George W. McCrary, 1877 Alexander Ramsey, 1879
Attorney General	Charles Devens, 1877
Postmaster General	David M. Key, 1877 Horace Maynard, 1880 Richard W. Thompson, 1877 Nathan Goff, Jr., 1881
Secretary of the Interior	Carl Schurz, 1877

Garfield

Secretary of State	James G. Blaine, 1881
Secretary of the Treasury	William Windom, 1881
Secretary of War	Robert T. Lincoln, 1881
Attorney General	Wayne MacVeagh, 1881
Postmaster General	Thomas L. James, 1881
Secretary of the Navy	William H. Hunt, 1881
Secretary of the Interior	Samuel J. Kirkwood, 1881

Arthur

Secretary of State	James G. Blaine (Cont.) F. T. Frelinghuysen, 1881
Secretary of the Treasury	William Windom (Cont.) Charles J. Folger, 1881 Walter Q. Gresham, 1884 Hugh McCulloch, 1884
Secretary of War	Robert T. Lincoln (Cont.)
Attorney General	Wayne MacVeagh (Cont.) Benjamin H. Brewster, 1881
Postmaster General	Thomas L. James (Cont.) Timothy O. Howe, 1881 Walter Q. Gresham, 1883 Frank Hatton, 1884
Secretary of the Navy	William H. Hunt (Cont.) William E. Chandler, 1882
Secretary of the Interior	Samuel J. Kirkwood (Cont.) Henry M. Teller, 1882

Cleveland

Secretary of State	Thomas F. Bayard, 1885
Secretary of the Treasury	Daniel Manning, 1885 Charles S. Fairchild, 1887
Secretary of War	William C. Endicott, 1885
Attorney General	Augustus H. Garland, 1885
Postmaster General	William F. Vilas, 1885 Don M. Dickinson, 1888
Secretary of the Navy	William C. Whitney, 1885
Secretary of the Interior	Lucius Q. C. Lamar, 1885 William F. Vilas, 1888
Secretary of Agriculture	Norman J. Colman, 1889

B. Harrison

Secretary of State	James G. Blaine, 1889 John W. Foster, 1892
Secretary of the Treasury	William Windom, 1889 Charles Foster, 1891
Secretary of War	Redfield Proctor, 1889 Stephen B. Elkins, 1891
Attorney General	William H. H. Miller, 1889
Postmaster General	John Wanamaker, 1889
Secretary of the Navy	Benjamin F. Tracy, 1889
Secretary of the Interior	John W. Noble, 1889
Secretary of Agriculture	Jeremiah M. Rusk, 1889

Cleveland

Secretary of State	Walter Q. Gresham, 1893 Richard Olney, 1895
Secretary of the Treasury	John G. Carlisle, 1893
Secretary of War	Daniel S. Lamont, 1893
Attorney General	Richard Olney, 1893 Judson Harmon, 1895
Postmaster General	Wilson S. Bissell, 1893 William L. Wilson, 1895
Secretary of the Navy	Hilary A. Herbert, 1893
Secretary of the Interior	Hoke Smith, 1893 David R. Francis, 1896
Secretary of Agriculture	Julius Sterling Morton, 1893

McKinley

Secretary of State	John Sherman, 1897 William R. Day, 1898 John Hay, 1898
Secretary of the Treasury	Lyman J. Gage, 1897
Secretary of War	Russell A. Alger, 1897 Elihu Root, 1899
Attorney General	Joseph McKenna, 1897 John W. Griggs, 1898 Philander C. Knox, 1901
Postmaster General	James A. Gary, 1897 Charles E. Smith, 1898
Secretary of the Navy	John D. Long, 1897
Secretary of the Interior	Cornelius N. Bliss, 1897 Ethan A. Hitchcock, 1898
Secretary of Agriculture	James Wilson, 1897

T. Roosevelt

Secretary of State	John Hay (Cont.) Elihu Root, 1905 Robert Bacon, 1909
Secretary of the Treasury	Lyman J. Gage (Cont.) Leslie M. Shaw, 1902 George B. Cortelyou, 1907
Secretary of War	Elihu Root (Cont.) William H. Taft, 1904 Luke E. Wright, 1908
Attorney General	Philander C. Knox (Cont.) William H. Moody, 1904 Charles J. Bonaparte, 1906
Postmaster General	Charles E. Smith (Cont.) Henry C. Payne, 1902 Robert J. Wynne, 1904 George B. Cortelyou, 1905 George von L. Meyer, 1907
Secretary of the Navy	John D. Long (Cont.) William H. Moody, 1902 Paul Morton, 1904 Charles J. Bonaparte, 1905 Victor H. Metcalf, 1906 Truman H. Newberry, 1908
Secretary of the Interior	Ethan A. Hitchcock (Cont.) James R. Garfield, 1907
Secretary of Agriculture	James Wilson (Cont.)
Secretary of Commerce and Labor	George B. Cortelyou, 1903 Victor H. Metcalf, 1904 Oscar S. Straus, 1906

Taft

Secretary of State	Philander C. Knox, 1909
Secretary of the Treasury	Franklin MacVeagh, 1909
Secretary of War	Jacob M. Dickinson, 1909 Henry L. Stimson, 1911
Attorney General	George W. Wickersham, 1909
Postmaster General	Frank H. Hitchcock, 1909
Secretary of the Navy	George von L. Meyer, 1909
Secretary of the Interior	Richard A. Ballinger, 1909 Walter L. Fisher, 1911
Secretary of Agriculture	James Wilson (Cont.)
Secretary of Commerce and Labor	Charles Nagel, 1909

Wilson

Secretary of State	William J. Bryan, 1913 Robert Lansing, 1915 Bainbridge Colby, 1920
Secretary of the Treasury	William G. McAdoo, 1913 Carter Glass, 1918 David F. Houston, 1920
Secretary of War	Lindley M. Garrison, 1913 Newton D. Baker, 1916

Attorney General	James C. McReynolds, 1913
	Thomas W. Gregory, 1914
	A. Mitchell Palmer, 1919
Postmaster General	Albert S. Burleson, 1913
Secretary of the Navy	Josephus Daniels, 1913
Secretary of the Interior	Franklin K. Lane, 1913
	John B. Payne, 1920
Secretary of Agriculture	David F. Houston, 1913
	Edwin T. Meredith, 1920
Secretary of Commerce	William C. Redfield, 1913
	Joshua W. Alexander, 1919
Secretary of Labor	William B. Wilson, 1913

Harding

Secretary of State	Charles E. Hughes, 1921
Secretary of the Treasury	Andrew W. Mellon, 1921
Secretary of War	John W. Weeks, 1921
Attorney General	Harry M. Daugherty, 1921
Postmaster General	Will H. Hays, 1921
	Hubert Work, 1922
	Harry S. New, 1923
Secretary of the Navy	Edwin Denby, 1921
Secretary of the Interior	Albert B. Fall, 1921
	Hubert Work, 1923
Secretary of Agriculture	Henry C. Wallace, 1921
Secretary of Commerce	Herbert Hoover, 1921
Secretary of Labor	James J. Davis, 1921

Coolidge

Secretary of State	Charles E. Hughes (Cont.)
	Frank B. Kellogg, 1925
Secretary of the Treasury	Andrew W. Mellon (Cont.)
Secretary of War	John W. Weeks (Cont.)
	Dwight F. Davis, 1925
Attorney General	Harry M. Daughtery (Cont.)
	Harlan F. Stone, 1924
	John G. Sargent, 1925
Postmaster General	Harry S. New (Cont.)
Secretary of the Navy	Edwin Denby (Cont.)
	Curtis D. Wilbur, 1924
Secretary of the Interior	Hubert Work (Cont.)
	Roy O. West, 1928
Secretary of Agriculture	Henry C. Wallace (Cont.)
	Howard M. Gore, 1924
	William M. Jardine, 1925
Secretary of Commerce	Herbert Hoover (Cont.)
	William F. Whiting, 1928
Secretary of Labor	James J. Davis (Cont.)

Hoover

Secretary of State	Frank B. Kellogg (Cont.)
	Henry L. Stimson, 1929
Secretary of the Treasury	Andrew W. Mellon (Cont.)
	Ogden L. Mills, 1932
Secretary of War	James W. Good, 1929
	Patrick J. Hurley, 1929
Attorney General	William D. Mitchell, 1929
Postmaster General	Walter F. Brown, 1929
Secretary of the Navy	Charles F. Adams, 1929
Secretary of the Interior	Ray Lyman Wilbur, 1929
Secretary of Agriculture	Arthur M. Hyde, 1929
Secretary of Commerce	Robert P. Lamont, 1929
	Roy D. Chapin, 1932
Secretary of Labor	James J. Davis (Cont.)
	William N. Doak, 1930

F. D. Roosevelt

Secretary of State	Cordell Hull, 1933
	E. R. Stettinius, Jr., 1944
Secretary of the Treasury	William H. Woodin, 1933
	Henry Morgenthau, Jr., 1934
Secretary of War	George H. Dern, 1933
	Harry H. Woodring, 1936
	Henry L. Stimson, 1940
Attorney General	Homer S. Cummings, 1933
	Frank Murphy, 1939
	Robert H. Jackson, 1940
	Francis Biddle, 1941
Postmaster General	James A. Farley, 1933
	Frank C. Walker, 1940
Secretary of the Navy	Claude A. Swanson, 1933
	Charles Edison, 1940
	Frank Knox, 1940
	James Forrestal, 1944
Secretary of the Interior	Harold L. Ickes, 1933
Secretary of Agriculture	Henry A. Wallace, 1933
	Claude R. Wickard, 1940
Secretary of Commerce	Daniel C. Roper, 1933
	Harry L. Hopkins, 1938
	Jesse H. Jones, 1940
	Henry A. Wallace, 1945
Secretary of Labor	Frances Perkins, 1933

Truman

Secretary of State	E. R. Stettinius, Jr. (Cont.)
	James F. Byrnes, 1945
	George C. Marshall, 1947
	Dean Acheson, 1949
Secretary of the Treasury	Henry Morgenthau, Jr. (Cont.)
	Frederick M. Vinson, 1945
	John W. Snyder, 1946
Secretary of Defense	James Forrestal, 1947
	Louis A. Johnson, 1949
	George C. Marshall, 1950
	Robert A. Lovett, 1951
Attorney General	Francis Biddle (Cont.)
	Tom C. Clark, 1945
	J. Howard McGrath, 1949
	James P. McGranery, 1952
Postmaster General	Frank C. Walker (Cont.)
	Robert E. Hannegan, 1945
	Jesse M. Donaldson, 1947
Secretary of the Interior	Harold L. Ickes (Cont.)
	Julius A. Krug, 1946
	Oscar L. Chapman, 1949
Secretary of Agriculture	Claude R. Wickard (Cont.)
	Clinton P. Anderson, 1945
	Charles F. Brannan, 1948
Secretary of Commerce	Henry A. Wallace (Cont.)
	W. Averell Harriman, 1946
	Charles Sawyer, 1948
Secretary of Labor	Frances Perkins (Cont.)
	Lewis B. Schwellenbach, 1945
	Maurice J. Tobin, 1948
Secretary of War[1]	Henry L. Stimson (Cont.)
	Robert P. Patterson, 1945
	Kenneth C. Royall, 1947
Secretary of the Navy[1]	James Forrestal (Cont.)

1. On July 26, 1947, the Departments of War and of the Navy were incorporated into the Department of Defense.

Eisenhower

Secretary of State	John Foster Dulles, 1953
	Christian A. Herter, 1959
Secretary of the Treasury	George M. Humphrey, 1953
	Robert B. Anderson, 1957
Secretary of Defense	Charles E. Wilson, 1953
	Neil H. McElroy, 1957
	Thomas S. Gates, Jr., 1959
Attorney General	Herbert Brownell, Jr., 1953
	William P. Rogers, 1958
Postmaster General	Arthur E. Summerfield, 1953
Secretary of the Interior	Douglas McKay, 1953
	Frederick A. Seaton, 1956
Secretary of Agriculture	Ezra Taft Benson, 1953
Secretary of Commerce	Sinclair Weeks, 1953
	Lewis L. Strauss[1], 1958
	Frederick H. Mueller, 1959

Secretary of Health, Education, and Welfare	Oveta Culp Hobby, 1953
	Marion B. Folsom, 1955
	Arthur S. Flemming, 1958
Secretary of Labor	Martin P. Durkin, 1953
	James P. Mitchell, 1953

1. Not confirmed by the Senate.

Kennedy

Secretary of State	Dean Rusk, 1961
Secretary of the Treasury	C. Douglas Dillon, 1961
Secretary of Defense	Robert S. McNamara, 1961
Attorney General	Robert F. Kennedy, 1961
Postmaster General	J. Edward Day, 1961
	John A. Gronouski, 1963
Secretary of the Interior	Stewart L. Udall, 1961
Secretary of Agriculture	Orville L. Freeman, 1961
Secretary of Commerce	Luther H. Hodges, 1961
Secretary of Labor	Arthur J. Goldberg, 1961
	W. Willard Wirtz, 1962
Secretary of Health, Education, and Welfare	Abraham A. Ribicoff, 1961
	Anthony J. Celebrezze, 1962

L. B. Johnson

Secretary of State	Dean Rusk (Cont.)
Secretary of the Treasury	C. Douglas Dillon (Cont.)
	Henry H. Fowler, 1965
	Joseph W. Barr[1], 1968
Secretary of Defense	Robert S. McNamara (Cont.)
	Clark M. Clifford, 1968
Attorney General	Robert F. Kennedy (Cont.)
	N. de B. Katzenbach, 1965
	Ramsey Clark, 1967
Postmaster General	John A. Gronouski (Cont.)
	Lawrence F. O'Brien, 1965
	W. Marvin Watson, 1968
Secretary of the Interior	Stewart L. Udall (Cont.)
Secretary of Agriculture	Orville L. Freeman (Cont.)
Secretary of Commerce	Luther H. Hodges (Cont.)
	John T. Connor, 1964
	A. B. Trowbridge, 1967
	C. R. Smith, 1968
Secretary of Labor	W. Willard Wirtz (Cont.)
Secretary of Health, Education, and Welfare	Anthony J. Celebrezze (Cont.)
	John W. Gardner, 1965
	Wilbur J. Cohen, 1968
Secretary of Housing and Urban Development	Robert C. Weaver, 1966
	Robert C. Wood[1], 1969
Secretary of Transportation	Alan S. Boyd, 1966

1. Recess appointment.

Nixon

Secretary of State	William P. Rogers, 1969
	Henry A. Kissinger, 1973
Secretary of the Treasury	David M. Kennedy, 1969
	John B. Connally, 1971
	George P. Shultz, 1972
	William E. Simon, 1974
Secretary of Defense	Melvin R. Laird, 1969
	Elliot L. Richardson, 1973
	James R. Schlesinger, 1973
Attorney General	John N. Mitchell, 1969
	Richard G. Kleindienst, 1972
	Elliot L. Richardson, 1973
	William B. Saxbe, 1974
Postmaster General[1]	William M. Blount, 1969
Secretary of the Interior	Walter J. Hickel, 1969
	Rogers C. B. Morton, 1971
Secretary of Agriculture	Clifford M. Hardin, 1969
	Earl L. Butz, 1971
Secretary of Commerce	Maurice H. Stans, 1969
	Peter G. Peterson, 1972
	Frederick B. Dent, 1973
Secretary of Labor	George P. Shultz, 1969
	James D. Hodgson, 1970
	Peter J. Brennan, 1973
Secretary of Health, Education, and Welfare	Robert H. Finch, 1969
	Elliot L. Richardson, 1970
	Caspar W. Weinberger, 1973
Secretary of Housing and Urban Development	George Romney, 1969
	James T. Lynn, 1973
Secretary of Transportation	John A. Volpe, 1969
	Claude S. Brinegar, 1973

1. The postmaster general is no longer a cabinet member.

Ford

Secretary of State	Henry A. Kissinger (Cont.)
Secretary of the Treasury	William E. Simon (Cont.)
Secretary of Defense	James R. Schlesinger (Cont.)
	Donald H. Rumsfeld, 1975
Attorney General	William B. Saxbe (Cont.)
	Edward H. Levi, 1975
Secretary of the Interior	Rogers C. B. Morton (Cont.)
	Stanley K. Hathaway, 1975
	Thomas S. Kleppe, 1975
Secretary of Agriculture	Earl L. Butz (Cont.)
	John Knebel, 1976
Secretary of Commerce	Frederick B. Dent (Cont.)
	Rogers C. B. Morton, 1975
	Elliot L. Richardson, 1976
Secretary of Labor	Peter J. Brennan (Cont.)
	John T. Dunlop, 1975
	William J. Usery, Jr., 1976
Secretary of Health, Education, and Welfare	Caspar W. Weinberger (Cont.)
	F. David Mathews, 1975
Secretary of Housing and Urban Development	James T. Lynn (Cont.)
	Carla A. Hills, 1975
Secretary of Transportation	Claude S. Brinegar (Cont.)
	William T. Coleman, Jr., 1975

Carter

Secretary of State	Cyrus R. Vance, 1977
	Edmund S. Muskie, 1980
Secretary of the Treasury	W. Michael Blumenthal, 1977
	G. William Miller, 1979
Secretary of Defense	Harold Brown, 1977
Attorney General	Griffin B. Bell, 1977
	Benjamin R. Civiletti, 1979
Secretary of the Interior	Cecil D. Andrus, 1977
Secretary of Agriculture	Bob S. Bergland, 1977
Secretary of Commerce	Juanita M. Kreps, 1977
	Philip M. Klutznick, 1979
Secretary of Labor	F. Ray Marshall, 1977
Secretary of Health and Human Services[1]	Joseph A. Califano, Jr., 1977
	Patricia Roberts Harris, 1979
Secretary of Housing and Urban Development	Patricia Roberts Harris, 1977
	Moon Landrieu, 1979
Secretary of Transportation	Brock Adams, 1977
	Neil E. Goldschmidt, 1979
Secretary of Energy	James R. Schlesinger, 1977
	Charles W. Duncan, Jr., 1979
Secretary of Education	Shirley Mount Hufstedler, 1979

1. Known as Department of Health, Education, and Welfare until May 1980.

Reagan

Secretary of State	Alexander M. Haig, Jr., 1981
	George P. Shultz, 1982
Secretary of the Treasury	Donald T. Regan, 1981
	James A. Baker 3rd, 1985
	Nicholas F. Brady, 1988
Secretary of Defense	Caspar W. Weinberger, 1981
	Frank C. Carlucci, 1987
Attorney General	William French Smith, 1981
	Edwin Meese 3rd, 1985
	Richard L. Thornburgh, 1988
Secretary of the Interior	James G. Watt, 1981
	William P. Clark, 1983
	Donald P. Hodel, 1985
Secretary of Agriculture	John R. Block, 1981
	Richard E. Lyng, 1986

Attorney General	William French Smith, 1981 Edwin Meese 3rd, 1985 Richard L. Thornburgh, 1988
Secretary of the Interior	James G. Watt, 1981 William P. Clark, 1983 Donald P. Hodel, 1985
Secretary of Agriculture	John R. Block, 1981 Richard E. Lyng, 1986
Secretary of Commerce	Malcolm Baldrige, 1981 C. William Verity, Jr., 1987
Secretary of Labor	Raymond J. Donovan, 1981 William E. Brock, 1985 Ann Dore McLaughlin, 1987
Secretary of Health and Human Services	Richard S. Schweiker, 1981 Margaret M. Heckler, 1983 Otis R. Bowen, 1985
Secretary of Housing and Urban Development	Samuel R. Pierce, Jr., 1981
Secretary of Transportation	Andrew L. Lewis, Jr., 1981 Elizabeth H. Dole, 1983 James H. Burnley 4th, 1987
Secretary of Energy	James B. Edwards, 1981 Donald P. Hodel, 1983 John S. Herrington, 1985
Secretary of Education	T. H. Bell, 1981 William J. Bennett, 1985 Lauro F. Cavazos, 1988

G. H. W. Bush

Secretary of State	James A. Baker 3d, 1989 Lawrence S. Eagleburger, 1992
Secretary of the Treasury	Nicholas F. Brady (Cont.)
Secretary of Defense	Richard Cheney, 1989
Attorney General	Richard L. Thornburgh (Cont.) William P. Barr, 1992
Secretary of the Interior	Manuel Lujan Jr., 1989
Secretary of Agriculture	Clayton K. Yeutter, 1989 Edward Madigan, 1991
Secretary of Commerce	Robert A. Mosbacher Sr., 1989 Barbara H. Franklin, 1992
Secretary of Labor	Elizabeth H. Dole, 1989 Lynn Martin, 1991
Secretary of Health and Human Services	Louis W. Sullivan, 1989
Secretary of Housing and Urban Development	Jack F. Kemp, 1989
Secretary of Transportation	Samuel K. Skinner, 1989 Andrew Card, 1992
Secretary of Energy	James D. Watkins, 1989
Secretary of Education	Lauro F. Cavazos (Cont.) Lamar Alexander, 1991
Secretary of Veterans' Affairs	Edward J. Derwinski, 1989

Clinton

Secretary of State	Warren M. Christopher, 1993 Madeleine Albright, 1996
Secretary of the Treasury	Lloyd Bentsen, 1993 Robert E. Rubin, 1995–1999 Lawrence H. Summers, 1999
Secretary of Defense	Les Aspin, 1993 William J. Perry, 1994 William S. Cohen, 1997
Attorney General	Janet Reno, 1993
Secretary of the Interior	Bruce Babbitt, 1993
Secretary of Agriculture	Mike Espy, 1993 Dan Glickman, 1995
Secretary of Commerce	Ronald H. Brown, 1993 Mickey Kantor, 1996 William M. Daley, 1997 Norman Y. Mineta, 2000
Secretary of Labor	Robert B. Reich, 1993 Alexis Herman, 1997
Secretary of Health and Human Services	Donna E. Shalala, 1993
Secretary of Housing and Urban Development	Henry G. Cisneros, 1993 Andrew M. Cuomo, 1997
Secretary of Transportation	Federico F. Pena, 1993 Rodney Slater, 1997
Secretary of Energy	Hazel R. O'Leary, 1993 Frederico F. Pena, 1997 Bill Richardson, 1998
Secretary of Education	Richard W. Riley, 1993
Secretary of Veterans' Affairs	Jesse Brown, 1993 Togo D. West, Jr., 1998

G. W. Bush

Secretary of State	Gen. Colin L. Powell, 2001
Secretary of the Treasury	Paul H. O'Neill, 2001–2002 John Snow, 2003
Secretary of Defense	Donald H. Rumsfeld, 2001
Attorney General	John Ashcroft, 2001
Secretary of the Interior	Gale A. Norton, 2001
Secretary of Agriculture	Ann M. Veneman, 2001
Secretary of Commerce	Donald L. Evans, 2001
Secretary of Labor	Elaine L. Chao, 2001
Secretary of Health and Human Services	Tommy G. Thompson, 2001
Secretary of Homeland Security	Tom Ridge, 2003
Secretary of Housing and Urban Development	Melquiades R. Martinez, 2001
Secretary of Transportation	Norman Y. Mineta, 2001
Secretary of Energy	Spencer Abraham, 2001
Secretary of Education	Roderick R. Paige, 2001
Secretary of Veterans' Affairs	Anthony Principi, 2001

Impeachments of Federal Officials

Source: Congressional Directory

The procedure for the impeachment of federal officials is detailed in Article I, Section 3, of the Constitution. The Senate has sat as a court of impeachment in the following cases:

William Blount, senator from Tennessee; charges dismissed for want of jurisdiction, Jan. 14, 1799.

John Pickering, judge of the U.S. District Court for New Hampshire; removed from office March 12, 1804.

Samuel Chase, associate justice of the Supreme Court; acquitted March 1, 1805.

James H. Peck, judge of the U.S. District Court for Missouri; acquitted Jan. 31, 1831.

West H. Humphreys, judge of the U.S. District Court for the middle, eastern, and western districts of Tennessee; removed from office June 26, 1862.

Andrew Johnson, president of the United States; acquitted May 26, 1868.

William W. Belknap, secretary of war; acquitted Aug. 1, 1876.

Charles Swayne, judge of the U.S. District Court for the northern district of Florida; acquitted Feb. 27, 1905.

Robert W. Archbald, associate judge, U.S. Commerce Court; removed Jan. 13, 1913.

George W. English, judge of the U.S. District Court for eastern district of Illinois; resigned Nov. 4, 1926; proceedings dismissed.

Harold Louderback, judge of the U.S. District Court for the northern district of California; acquitted May 24, 1933.

Halsted L. Ritter, judge of the U.S. District Court for the southern district of Florida; removed from office April 17, 1936.

Harry E. Claiborne, judge of the U.S. District Court for the district of Nevada; removed from office Oct. 9, 1986.

Alcee L. Hastings, judge of the U.S. District Court for the southern district of Florida; removed from office Oct. 20, 1988.

Walter L. Nixon, judge of the U.S. District Court for Mississippi; removed from office Nov. 3, 1989.

William J. Clinton, president of the United States; acquitted Feb. 12, 1999.

Members of the Supreme Court of the United States

Mailing address for the Supreme Court: U.S. Supreme Court Building, 1 First Street NE Washington, DC 20543

Name, state	Service			Birth			
	Assoc. Justice	Chief Justice	Yrs	Place	Date	Died	Religion
John Jay , N.Y.		1789–1795	5	N.Y.	1745	1829	Episcopal
James Wilson, Pa.	1789–1798		8	Scotland	1742	1798	Episcopal
John Rutledge, S.C.*	1790–1791	1795	1	S.C.	1739	1800	Church of England
William Cushing, Mass.	1790–1810		20	Mass.	1732	1810	Unitarian
John Blair, Va.	1790–1796		5	Va.	1732	1800	Presbyterian
James Iredell, N.C.	1790–1799		9	England	1751	1799	Episcopal
Thomas Johnson, Md.	1792–1793		0	Md.	1732	1819	Episcopal
William Paterson, N.J.	1793–1806		13	Ireland	1745	1806	Protestant
Oliver Ellsworth, Conn.		1796–1800	4	Conn.	1745	1807	Congregational
Samuel Chase, Md.	1796–1811		15	Md.	1741	1811	Episcopal
Bushrod Washington, Va.	1799–1829		30	Va.	1762	1829	Episcopal
Alfred Moore, N.C.	1800–1804		3	N.C.	1755	1810	Episcopal
John Marshall, Va.		1801–1835	34	Va.	1755	1835	Episcopal
William Johnson, S.C.	1804–1834		30	S.C.	1771	1834	Presbyterian
Brockholst Livingston, N.Y.	1807–1823		16	N.Y.	1757	1823	Presbyterian
Thomas Todd, Ky.	1807–1826		18	Va.	1765	1826	Presbyterian
Gabriel Duval, Md.	1811–1835		23	Md.	1752	1844	French Protestant
Joseph Story, Mass.	1812–1845		33	Mass.	1779	1845	Unitarian
Smith Thompson, N.Y.	1823–1843		20	N.Y.	1768	1843	Presbyterian
Robert Trimble, Ky.	1826–1828		2	Va.	1777	1828	Protestant
John McLean, Ohio	1830–1861		31	N.J.	1785	1861	Methodist-Epis.
Henry Baldwin, Pa.	1830–1844		14	Conn.	1780	1844	Trinity Church
James M. Wayne, Ga.	1835–1867		32	Ga.	1790	1867	Protestant
Philip P. Barbour, Va.	1836–1841		4	Va.	1783	1841	Episcopal
Roger B. Taney, Md.		1836–1864	28	Md.	1777	1864	Roman Catholic
John Catron, Tenn.	1837–1865		28	Pa.	1786	1865	Presbyterian
John McKinley, Ala.	1837–1852		14	Va.	1780	1852	Protestant
Peter V. Daniel, Va.	1841–1860		18	Va.	1784	1860	Episcopal
Samuel Nelson, N.Y.	1845–1872		27	N.Y.	1792	1873	Protestant
Levi Woodbury, N.H.	1845–1851		5	N.H.	1789	1851	Protestant
Robert C. Grier, Pa.	1846–1870		23	Pa.	1794	1870	Presbyterian
Benjamin R. Curtis, Mass.	1851–1857		5	Mass.	1809	1874	(2)
John A. Campbell, Ala.	1853–1861		8	Ga.	1811	1889	Episcopal
Nathan Clifford, Maine	1858–1881		23	N.H.	1803	1881	(1)
Noah H. Swayne, Ohio	1862–1881		18	Va.	1804	1884	Quaker
Samuel F. Miller, Iowa	1862–1890		28	Ky.	1816	1890	Unitarian
David Davis, Ill.	1862–1877		14	Md.	1815	1886	(4)
Stephen J. Field, Calif.	1863–1897		34	Conn.	1816	1899	Episcopal
Salmon P. Chase, Ohio		1864–1873	8	N.H.	1808	1873	Episcopal
William Strong, Pa.	1870–1880		10	Conn.	1808	1895	Presbyterian
Joseph P. Bradley, N.J.	1870–1892		21	N.Y.	1813	1892	Presbyterian
Ward Hunt, N.Y.	1872–1882		9	N.Y.	1810	1886	Episcopal
Morrison R. Waite, Ohio		1874–1888	14	Conn.	1816	1888	Episcopal
John M. Harlan, Ky.	1877–1911		33	Ky.	1833	1911	Presbyterian
William B. Woods, Ga.	1880–1887		6	Ohio	1824	1887	Protestant
Stanley Matthews, Ohio	1881–1889		7	Ohio	1824	1889	Presbyterian
Horace Gray, Mass.	1882–1902		20	Mass.	1828	1902	(3)

Name, state	Service: Assoc. Justice	Service: Chief Justice	Yrs	Birth: Place	Birth: Date	Died	Religion
Melville W. Fuller, Ill.		1888–1910	21	Maine	1833	1910	Episcopal
David J. Brewer, Kan.	1889–1910		20	Asia Minor	1837	1910	Protestant
Henry B. Brown, Mich.	1890–1906		15	Mass.	1836	1913	Protestant
George Shiras, Jr., Pa.	1892–1903		10	Pa.	1832	1924	Presbyterian
Howell E. Jackson, Tenn.	1893–1895		2	Tenn.	1832	1895	Baptist
Edward D. White, La.*	1894–1910	1910–1921	26	La.	1845	1921	Roman Catholic
Rufus W. Peckham, N.Y.	1895–1909		13	N.Y.	1838	1909	Episcopal
Joseph McKenna, Calif.	1898–1925		26	Pa.	1843	1926	Roman Catholic
Oliver W. Holmes, Mass.	1902–1932		29	Mass.	1841	1935	Unitarian
William R. Day, Ohio	1903–1922		19	Ohio	1849	1923	Protestant
William H. Moody, Mass.	1906–1910		3	Mass.	1853	1917	Episcopal
Horace H. Lurton, Tenn.	1909–1914		4	Ky.	1844	1914	Episcopal
Charles E. Hughes, N.Y.*	1910–1916	1930–1941	16	N.Y.	1862	1948	Baptist
Willis Van Devanter, Wyo.	1910–1937		26	Ind.	1859	1941	Episcopal
Joseph R. Lamar, Ga.	1910–1916		4	Ga.	1857	1916	Ch. of Disciples
Mahlon Pitney, N.J.	1912–1922		10	N.J.	1858	1924	Presbyterian
James C. McReynolds, Tenn.	1914–1941		26	Ky.	1862	1946	Disciples of Christ
Louis D. Brandeis, Mass.	1916–1939		22	Ky.	1856	1941	Jewish
John H. Clarke, Ohio	1916–1922		5	Ohio	1857	1945	Protestant
William H. Taft, Conn.		1921–1930	8	Ohio	1857	1930	Unitarian
George Sutherland, Utah	1922–1938		15	England	1862	1942	Episcopal
Pierce Butler, Minn.	1923–1939		16	Minn.	1866	1939	Roman Catholic
Edward T. Sanford, Tenn.	1923–1930		7	Tenn.	1865	1930	Episcopal
Harlan F. Stone, N.Y.*	1925–1941	1941–1946	20	N.H.	1872	1946	Episcopal
Owen J. Roberts, Pa.	1930–1945		15	Pa.	1875	1955	Episcopal
Benjamin N. Cardozo, N.Y.	1932–1938		6	N.Y.	1870	1938	Jewish
Hugo L. Black, Ala.	1937–1971		34	Ala.	1886	1971	Baptist
Stanley F. Reed, Ky.	1938–1957		19	Ky.	1884	1980	Protestant
Felix Frankfurter, Mass.	1939–1962		23	Austria	1882	1965	Jewish
William O. Douglas, Conn.	1939–1975		36	Minn.	1898	1980	Presbyterian
Frank Murphy, Mich.	1940–1949		9	Mich.	1890	1949	Roman Catholic
James F. Byrnes, S.C.	1941–1942		1	S.C.	1879	1972	Episcopal
Robert H. Jackson, Pa.	1941–1954		13	N.Y.	1892	1954	Episcopal
Wiley B. Rutledge, Iowa	1943–1949		6	Ky.	1894	1949	Unitarian
Harold H. Burton, Ohio	1945–1958		13	Mass.	1888	1964	Unitarian
Frederick M. Vinson, Ky.		1946–1953	7	Ky.	1890	1953	Methodist
Tom C. Clark, Tex.	1949–1967		17	Tex.	1899	1977	Presbyterian
Sherman Minton, Ind.	1949–1956		7	Ind.	1890	1965	Roman Catholic
Earl Warren, Calif.		1953–1969	15	Calif.	1891	1974	Protestant
John M. Harlan, N.Y.	1955–1971		16	Ill.	1899	1971	Presbyterian
William J. Brennan, Jr., N.J.	1956–1990		33	N.J.	1906	1997	Roman Catholic
Charles E. Whittaker, Mo.	1957–1962		5	Kan.	1901	1973	Methodist
Potter Stewart, Ohio	1958–1981		23	Mich.	1915	1985	Episcopal
Byron R. White, Colo.	1962–1993		31	Colo.	1917	2002	Episcopal
Arthur J. Goldberg, Ill.	1962–1965		2	Ill.	1908	1990	Jewish
Abe Fortas, Tenn.	1965–1969		3	Tenn.	1910	1982	Jewish
Thurgood Marshall, N.Y.	1967–1991		24	Md.	1908	1993	Episcopal
Warren E. Burger, Va.		1969–1986	17	Minn.	1907	1995	Presbyterian
Harry A. Blackmun, Minn.	1970–1994		24	Ill.	1908	1999	Methodist
Lewis F. Powell, Jr., Va.	1972–1987		15	Va.	1907	1998	Presbyterian
William H. Rehnquist, Ariz.*	1972–1986	1986–	—	Wis.	1924	—	Lutheran
John Paul Stevens, Ill.	1975–		—	Ill.	1920	—	Protestant
Sandra Day O'Connor, Ariz.	1981–		—	Tex.	1930	—	Episcopal
Antonin Scalia, DC	1986–		—	N.J.	1936	—	Roman Catholic
Anthony M. Kennedy, Calif.	1988–		—	Calif.	1936	—	Roman Catholic
David H. Souter, N.H.	1990–		—	Mass.	1939	—	Episcopal
Clarence Thomas, DC	1991–		—	Ga.	1948	—	Roman Catholic
Ruth Bader Ginsburg, DC	1993–		—	N.Y.	1933	—	Jewish
Stephen G. Breyer, Mass.	1994–		—	Calif.	1938	—	Jewish

NOTE: **Bold=Chief Justice** *Served as both chief justice and associate justice. 1. Congregational; later Unitarian. 2. Unitarian; then Episcopal. 3. Unitarian or Congregational. 4. Not a member of any church.

Milestone Cases in Supreme Court History

1803 ***Marbury* v. *Madison*** was the first instance in which a law passed by Congress was declared unconstitutional. The decision greatly expanded the power of the Court by establishing its right to overturn acts of Congress, a power not explicitly granted by the Constitution. Initially the case involved Secretary of State James Madison, who refused to seat four judicial appointees although they had been confirmed by the Senate.

1824 ***Gibbons* v. *Ogden*** defined broadly Congress's right to regulate commerce. Aaron Ogden had filed suit in New York against Thomas Gibbons for operating a rival steamboat service between New York and New Jersey ports. Ogden had exclusive rights to operate steamboats in New York under a state law, while Gibbons held a federal license. Gibbons lost the case and appealed to the U.S. Supreme Court, which reversed the decision. The Court held that the New York law was unconstitutional, since the power to regulate interstate commerce, which extended to the regulation of navigation, belonged exclusively to Congress. In the 20th century, Chief Justice John Marshall's broad definition of commerce was used to uphold civil rights.

1857 ***Dred Scott* v. *Sanford*** was a highly controversial case that intensified the national debate over slavery. The case involved Dred Scott, a slave, who was taken from a slave state to a free territory. Scott filed a lawsuit claiming that because he had lived on free soil he was entitled to his freedom. Chief Justice Roger B. Taney disagreed, ruling that blacks were not citizens and therefore could not sue in federal court. Taney further inflamed antislavery forces by declaring that Congress had no right to ban slavery from U.S. territories.

1896 ***Plessy* v. *Ferguson*** was the infamous case that asserted that "equal but separate accommodations" for blacks on railroad cars did not violate the "equal protection under the laws" clause of the 14th Amendment. By defending the constitutionality of racial segregation, the Court paved the way for the repressive Jim Crow laws of the South. The lone dissenter on the Court, Justice John Marshall Harlan, protested, "The thin disguise of 'equal' accommodations . . . will not mislead anyone."

1954 ***Brown* v. *Board of Education of Topeka*** invalidated racial segregation in schools and led to the unraveling of de jure segregation in all areas of public life. In the unanimous decision spearheaded by Chief Justice Earl Warren, the Court invalidated the Plessy ruling, declaring "in the field of public education, the doctrine of 'separate but equal' has no place" and contending that "separate educational facilities are inherently unequal." Future Supreme Court justice Thurgood Marshall was one of the NAACP lawyers who successfully argued the case.

1963 ***Gideon* v. *Wainwright*** guaranteed a defendant's right to legal counsel. The Supreme Court overturned the Florida felony conviction of Clarence Earl Gideon, who had defended himself after having been denied a request for free counsel. The Court held that the state's failure to provide counsel for a defendant charged with a felony violated the Fourteenth Amendment's due process clause. Gideon was given another trial, and with a court-appointed lawyer defending him, he was acquitted.

1964 ***New York Times* v. *Sullivan*** extended the protection offered the press by the First Amendment. L.B. Sullivan, a police commissioner in Montgomery, Ala., had filed a libel suit against the *New York Times* for publishing inaccurate information about certain actions taken by the Montgomery police department. In overturning a lower court's decision, the Supreme Court held that debate on public issues would be inhibited if public officials could sue for inaccuracies that were made by mistake. The ruling made it more difficult for public officials to bring libel charges against the press, since the official had to prove that a harmful untruth was told maliciously and with reckless disregard for truth.

1966 ***Miranda* v. *Arizona*** was another case that helped define the due process clause of the 14th Amendment. At the center of the case was Ernesto Miranda, who had confessed to a crime during police questioning without knowing he had a right to have an attorney present. Based on his confession, Miranda was convicted. The Supreme Court overturned the conviction, ruling that criminal suspects must be warned of their rights before they are questioned by police. These rights are: the right to remain silent, to have an attorney present, and, if the suspect cannot afford an attorney, to have one appointed by the state. The police must also warn suspects that any statements they make can be used against them in court. Miranda was retried without the confession and convicted.

1973 ***Roe* v. *Wade*** legalized abortion and is at the center of the current controversy between "pro-life" and "pro-choice" advocates. The Court ruled that a woman has the right to an abortion without interference from the government in the first trimester of pregnancy, contending that it is part of her "right to privacy." The Court maintained that right to privacy is not absolute, however, and granted states the right to intervene in the second and third trimesters of pregnancy.

1978 ***Regents of the University of California* v. *Bakke*** imposed limitations on affirmative action to ensure that providing greater opportunities for minorities did not come at the expense of the rights of the majority. In other words, affirmative action was unfair if it lead to reverse discrimination. The case involved the University of Calif., Davis, Medical School and Allan Bakke, a white applicant who was rejected twice even though there were minority applicants admitted with significantly lower scores than his. A closely divided Court ruled that while race was a legitimate factor in school admissions, the use of rigid quotas was not permissible.

Notable Decisions of the U.S. Supreme Court, 2002–2003 Term

Court Upholds Copyright Extension (January 15, 2003): Justices, 7–2, rule that Congress acted with constitutional authority when it extended by 20 years all existing and future copyrights. Under 1998's Sonny Bono Copyright Term Extension Act, works for hire (such as television scripts) that are owned by companies have a 95-year copyright, and works owned by their authors or estates are protected for the life of the creator, plus an additional 50 years.

Three-Strikes Law Validated (March 5, 2003): In two separate decisions, the court, 5–4, upholds California's "three strikes and you're out" law that calls for long sentences when a person is convicted of a third offense. One defendant was sentenced to 25 years to life in prison for shoplifting golf clubs. The other was sentenced to 50 years without parole for stealing videos valued at $150. The court rejected the argument that such harsh sentences violated the Eighth Amendment's protection from cruel and unusual punishment. The 1994 law mandated sentences of 25 years to life in prison for a third felony conviction. Under the law, crimes that are otherwise considered misdemeanors can be treated as felonies for the third offense. Twenty-five other states have three-strikes laws, but California's is the most stringent.

Railway Workers Can Sue When Vulnerable to Illness (March 10, 2003): Justices, 5–4, rule that railway workers who were exposed to asbestos on the job and have developed asbestosis, a disease that makes them susceptible to cancer, can receive damages from their employers when they prove the risk of getting cancer is "genuine and serious."

Justices Set Guidelines on Punitive Damages (April 7, 2003): The court, 6–3, overturns a jury award of $145 million in punitive damages, saying the amount was far too high. Instead, the court rules that $1 million in compensatory damages, as set by a trial judge, was appropriate in a suit against State Farm insurance company brought by a client. In the majority opinion, Justice Kennedy said the ratio of 145:1 was "irrational and arbitrary," and that the Utah high court was wrong to attempt to punish State Farm for conduct outside the case at issue.

Court Gives States Authority to Ban Cross-Burning (April 7, 2003): Court, 6–3, rules that states can ban cross-burning provided that the law as written places the burden on prosecutors to prove that the action was intended to intimidate and threaten, and not simply a form of expression. In an overlapping ruling, seven justices declare unconstitutional a part of a Virginia law that asserts any instance of cross-burning is a form of intimidation.

U.S. Can Imprison Immigrants Set for Deportation (April 29, 2003): Justices, 5–4, uphold mandatory-detention provisions of 1996's immigration law, allowing the government to hold legal immigrants it seeks to deport without first giving them a hearing to determine if they pose a danger to the community or are a flight risk. The case was not terrorism-related. Instead, it centered on a section of the immigration law that deals with legal permanent residents who are convicted of drug and other "aggravated" offenses.

Court Rules Charities Can Be Charged with Fraud (May 5, 2003): Justices unanimously uphold states' rights to charge fund-raisers and telemarketers with fraud. Court says prosecutors must prove that a solicitor purposely made a false assertion about what percent of a contribution will go directly to the charity "with the intent to mislead the listener, and [succeed] in doing so."

Maine Prescription Drug Plan Gets Qualified Approval (May 19, 2003): Court, 6–3, lifts an injunction that had prevented the Maine Rx Program from going into effect. Maine sought to reduce the price of prescription drugs for the state's uninsured by acting as a pharmacy benefit manager and requiring drug companies to offer the state similar rebates that they give to the Medicaid program.

Court Expands Federal Authority (May 27, 2003): Justices, 6–3, rule that states are not immune from lawsuits when they violate state employees' rights to take time off for family emergencies under the federal Family and Medical Leave Act. The decision was a break from the court's recent tendency to expand states' rights.

Justices Restrict Medication of Defendants (June 16, 2003): Court, 6–3, imposes strict limits on the government's ability to forcibly use antipsychotic drugs on defendants to make them fit to stand trial. The court says defendants can only be involuntarily drugged when the medication is in the defendant's own best interest and when it's highly unlikely that the drugs will cause side effects that could compromise the trial.

Court Saves Affirmative Action Program (June 23, 2003): Justices, 5–4, uphold the University of Michigan Law School's consideration of race and ethnicity in admissions. In her majority opinion, Justice O'Connor said that the law school uses a "highly individualized, holistic review of each applicant's file." Race, she said, is not used in a "mechanical way." Therefore, the university's program is consistent with the requirement of "individualized consideration" set in 1978's *Bakke* case. "In order to cultivate a set of leaders with legitimacy in the eyes of the citizenry, it is necessary that the path to leadership be visibly open to talented and qualified individuals of every race and ethnicity," O'Connor said. However, the court, 6–3, rules that the University of Michigan's undergraduate admissions system, which awards 20 points to black, Hispanic, and American-Indian applicants, is "nonindividualized, mechanical," and thus unconstitutional.

Internet Filter Law Upheld (June 23, 2003): Justices, 6–3, rule that the Children's Internet Protection Act, which requires public libraries that receive federal money to install antipornography filters on computers that provide Internet access, does not violate the First Amendment. In the majority opinion, Chief Justice Rehnquist wrote, "Because public librarians have traditionally excluded pornographic material from their other collections, Congress could reasonably impose a parallel limitation on its Internet assistance programs."

Sodomy Laws Declared Unconstitutional (June 26, 2003): Court, 6–3, overrules a Texas sodomy law and votes 5–4 to overturn 1986's *Bowers* v. *Hardwick* decision, which held that there's no constitutional right to have homosexual relations in private. "The state cannot demean their [gays'] existence or control their destiny by making their private sexual conduct a crime," wrote Justice Kennedy in the majority opinion. In his dissent, Justice Scalia said the court has "largely signed on to the so-called homosexual agenda."

Court Throws Out Death Sentence of Convicted Killer (June 26, 2003): Justices, 7–2, rule that because public defenders for Kevin Wiggins, a Maryland man convicted of killing a 77-year-old woman, did not investigate his background, which included years of physical and sexual abuse, they failed to provide him adequate representation. The court said that had the jury been informed of the abuse, it may have sentenced him to life in prison rather than death.

U.S. History Timeline

NOTES: o.s. = old style (according to the Julian calendar). *See also*, States by Order of Entry into the Union; Presidential Elections 1789–2000; the Confederate States of America; National Censuses; Milestone Cases in Supreme Court History; World History; and Current Events.

1607 Jamestown, the first permanent English settlement in America, is established by the London Company in southeast Virginia (**May 14 o.s.**).

1619 The House of Burgesses, the first representative assembly in America, meets for the first time in Virginia (**July 30 o.s.**). The first African slaves are brought to Jamestown (**summer**).

1620 The Plymouth Colony in Massachusetts is established by Pilgrims from England (**Dec. 11 o.s.**). Before disembarking from their ship, the *Mayflower,* 41 male passengers sign the Mayflower Compact, an agreement that forms the basis of the colony's government.

1650 Colonial population is estimated at 50,400.

1752 Britain and the British colonies switch from the Julian to the Gregorian calendar (**Sept. 2**).

1754–1763 French and Indian War: Final conflict in the ongoing struggle between the British and French for control of eastern North America. The British win a decisive victory over the French on the Plains of Abraham outside Quebec (**Sept. 13, 1759**) and, by the Treaty of Paris (signed **Feb. 10, 1763**), formally gain control of Canada and all the French possessions east of the Mississippi.

1770 Boston Massacre: British troops fire into a mob, killing five men and leading to intense public protests (**March 5**).

1773 Boston Tea Party: Group of colonial patriots disguised as Mohawk Indians board three ships in Boston harbor and dump more than 300 crates of tea overboard as a protest against the British tea tax (**Dec. 16**).

1774 First Continental Congress meets in Philadelphia, with 56 delegates representing every colony except Georgia. Delegates include Patrick Henry, George Washington, and Samuel Adams (**Sept. 5–Oct. 26**).

1775–1783 American Revolution: War of independence fought between Great Britain and the 13 British colonies on the eastern seaboard of North America. Battles of Lexington and Concord, Mass., between the British Army and colonial minutemen, mark the beginning of the war (**April 19, 1775**). Battle-weary and destitute Continental army spends brutally cold winter and following spring at Valley Forge, Pa. (**Dec. 19, 1777–June 19, 1778**). British general Charles Cornwallis surrenders to Gen. George Washington at Yorktown, Va. (**Oct. 19, 1781**). Great Britain formally acknowledges American independence in the Treaty of Paris, which officially brings the war to a close (**Sept. 3, 1783**).

1776 Continental Congress adopts the Declaration of Independence in Philadelphia (**July 4**).

1777 Continental Congress approves the first official flag of the United States (**June 14**). Continental Congress adopts the Articles of Confederation, the first U.S. constitution (**Nov. 15**).

1786 Shays's Rebellion erupts (**Aug.**); farmers from New Hampshire to South Carolina take up arms to protest high state taxes and stiff penalties for failure to pay.

1787 Constitutional Convention, made up of delegates from 12 of the original 13 colonies, meets in Philadelphia to draft the U.S. Constitution (**May–Sept.**).

1789 George Washington is unanimously elected president of the United States in a vote by state electors (**Feb. 4**). U.S. Constitution goes into effect, having been ratified by nine states (**March 4**). U.S. Congress meets for the first time at Federal Hall in New York City (**March 4**). Washington is inaugurated as president at Federal Hall in New York City (**April 30**).

1790 U.S. Supreme Court meets for the first time at the Merchants Exchange Building in New York City (**Feb. 2**). The court, made up of one chief justice and five associate justices, hears its first case in 1792. The nation's first census shows that the population has climbed to nearly 4 million.

1791 First ten amendments to the Constitution, known as the Bill of Rights, are ratified (**Dec. 15**).

1793 Washington's second inauguration is held in Philadelphia (**March 4**).

1797 John Adams is inaugurated as the second president in Philadelphia (**March 4**).

1800 The U.S. capital is moved from Philadelphia to Washington, DC (**June 15**). U.S. Congress meets in Washington, DC, for the first time (**Nov. 17**).

1801 Thomas Jefferson is inaugurated as the third president in Washington, DC (**March 4**).

1803 Louisiana Purchase: United States agrees to pay France $15 million for the Louisiana Territory, which extends west from the Mississippi River to the Rocky Mountains and comprises about 830,000 sq mi (treaty signed **May 2**). As a result, the U.S. nearly doubles in size.

1804 Lewis and Clark set out from St. Louis, Mo., on expedition to explore the West and find a route to the Pacific Ocean. (**May 14**).

1805 Jefferson's second inauguration (**March 4**). Lewis and Clark reach the Pacific Ocean (**Nov. 15**).

1809 James Madison is inaugurated as the fourth president (**March 4**).

1812–1814 War of 1812: U.S. declares war on Britain over British interference with American maritime shipping and westward expansion (**June 18, 1812**). Madison's second inauguration (**March 4, 1813**). British capture Washington, DC, and set fire to White House and Capitol (**Aug. 1814**). Francis Scott Key writes *Star-Spangled Banner* as he watches British attack on Fort McHenry at Baltimore (**Sept. 13–14, 1814**). Treaty of Ghent is signed, officially ending the war (**Dec. 24, 1814**).

1817 James Monroe is inaugurated as the fifth president (**March 4**).

1819 Spain agrees to cede Florida to the United States (**Feb. 22**).

1820 Missouri Compromise: In an effort to maintain the balance between free and slave states, Maine (formerly part of Massachusetts) is admitted as a free state so that Missouri can be admitted as a slave state; except for Missouri, slavery is prohibited in the Louisiana Purchase lands north of latitude 36°30′ **(March 3).**

1821 Monroe's second inauguration **(March 5).**

1823 Monroe Doctrine: In his annual address to Congress, President Monroe declares that the American continents are henceforth off-limits for further colonization by European powers **(Dec. 2).**

1825 John Quincy Adams is inaugurated as the sixth president **(March 4).** Erie Canal, linking the Hudson River to Lake Erie, is opened for traffic **(Oct. 26).**

1828 Construction is begun on the Baltimore and Ohio Railroad, the first public railroad in the U.S. **(July 4).**

1829 Andrew Jackson is inaugurated as seventh president **(March 4).**

1830 President Jackson signs the Indian Removal Act, which authorizes the forced removal of Native Americans living in the eastern part of the country to lands west of the Mississippi River **(May 28).** By the late 1830s the Jackson administration has relocated nearly 50,000 Native Americans.

1833 Jackson's second inauguration **(March 4).**

1836 Texas declares its independence from Mexico **(March 1).** Texan defenders of the Alamo are all killed during siege by the Mexican Army **(Feb. 24–March 6).** Texans defeat Mexicans at San Jacinto **(April 21).**

1837 Martin Van Buren is inaugurated as the eighth president **(March 4).**

1838 More than 15,000 Cherokee Indians are forced to march from Georgia to Indian Territory in present-day Oklahoma. Approximately 4,000 die from starvation and disease along the "Trail of Tears."

1841 William Henry Harrison is inaugurated as the ninth president **(March 4).** He dies one month later **(April 4)** and is succeeded in office by his vice president, John Tyler.

1845 U.S. annexes Texas by joint resolution of Congress **(March 1).** James Polk is inaugurated as the 11th president **(March 4).** The term "manifest destiny" appears for the first time in a magazine article by John L. O'Sullivan **(July–August).** It expresses the belief held by many white Americans that the United States is destined to expand across the continent.

1846 Oregon Treaty fixes U.S.-Canadian border at 49th parallel; U.S. acquires Oregon territory **(June 15).**

1846–1848 Mexican War: U.S. declares war on Mexico in effort to gain California and other territory in Southwest **(May 13, 1846).** War concludes with signing of Treaty of Guadalupe Hidalgo **(Feb. 2, 1848).** Mexico recognizes Rio Grande as new boundary with Texas and, for $15 million, agrees to cede territory comprising present-day California, Nevada, Utah, most of New Mexico and Arizona, and parts of Colorado and Wyoming.

1848 Gold is discovered at Sutter's Mill in California **(Jan. 24)**; gold rush reaches its height the following year. Women's rights convention is held at Seneca Falls, N.Y. **(July 19–20).**

1849 Zachary Taylor is inaugurated as the 12th president **(March 5).**

1850 President Taylor dies **(July 9)** and is succeeded by his vice president, Millard Fillmore.

1853 Franklin Pierce is inaugurated as the 14th president **(March 4).** Gadsden Purchase treaty is signed; U.S. acquires border territory from Mexico for $10 million **(Dec. 30).**

1854 Congress passes the Kansas-Nebraska Act, establishing the territories of Kansas and Nebraska **(May 30).** The legislation repeals the Missouri Compromise of 1820 and renews tensions between anti- and proslavery factions.

1857 James Buchanan is inaugurated as the 15th president **(March 4).**

1858 Abraham Lincoln comes to national attention in a series of seven debates with Sen. Stephen A. Douglas during Illinois state election campaign **(Aug.–Oct.).**

1859 Abolitionist John Brown and 21 followers capture federal arsenal at Harper's Ferry, Va. (now W. Va.), in an attempt to spark a slave revolt **(Oct. 16).**

1860 Abraham Lincoln is elected president **(Nov. 6).** South Carolina secedes from the Union **(Dec. 20).**

1861 Mississippi, Florida, Alabama, Georgia, and Louisiana secede **(Jan.).** Confederate States of America is established **(Feb. 8).** Jefferson Davis is elected president of the Confederacy **(Feb. 9).** Texas secedes **(March 2).** Abraham Lincoln is inaugurated as the 16th president **(March 4).**

1861–1865 Civil War: Conflict between the North (the Union) and the South (the Confederacy) over the expansion of slavery into western states. Confederates attack Ft. Sumter in Charleston, S.C., marking the start of the war **(April 12, 1861).** Virginia, Arkansas, North Carolina, and Tennessee secede **(April–June).** Emancipation Proclamation is issued, freeing slaves in the Confederate states **(Jan. 1, 1863).** Gen. William T. Sherman captures Atlanta **(Sept. 2, 1864).** Lincoln's second inauguration **(March 4, 1865).** Gen. Ulysses S. Grant captures Richmond, Va., the capital of the Confederacy **(April 3).** Confederate general Robert E. Lee surrenders to Ulysses S. Grant at Appomattox Courthouse, Va., **(April 9).**

1863 Homestead Act becomes law, allowing settlers to claim land (160 acres) after they have lived on it for five years **(Jan. 1).**

1865 Lincoln is assassinated **(April 14)** by John Wilkes Booth in Washington, DC, and is succeeded by his vice president, Andrew Johnson. Thirteenth Amendment to the Constitution is ratified, prohibiting slavery **(Dec. 6).**

1867 U.S. acquires Alaska from Russia for the sum of $7.2 million (treaty concluded **March 30).**

1868 President Johnson is impeached by the House of Representatives **(Feb. 24),** but he is acquitted at his trial in the Senate **(May 26).** Fourteenth Amendment to the Constitution is ratified, defining citizenship **(July 9).**

1869 Ulysses S. Grant is inaugurated as the 18th president **(March 4).** Central Pacific and Union Pacific railroads are joined at Promontory, Utah, creating first transcontinental railroad **(May 10).**

1870 Fifteenth Amendment to the Constitution is ratified, giving blacks the right to vote **(Feb. 3).**

1871 Chicago fire kills 300 and leaves 90,000 people homeless **(Oct. 8–9).**

1872 Crédit Mobilier scandal breaks, involving several members of Congress **(Sept.).**

1873 Grant's second inauguration **(March 4).**

1876 Lt. Col. George A. Custer's regiment is wiped out by Sioux Indians under Sitting Bull at the Little Big Horn River, Mont. **(June 25).**

1877 Rutherford B. Hayes is inaugurated as the 19th president **(March 5).** The first telephone line is built from Boston to Somerville, Mass.; the following year, President Hayes has the first telephone installed in the White House.

1881 James A. Garfield is inaugurated as the 20th president **(March 4).** He is shot **(July 2)** by Charles Guiteau in Washington, DC, and later dies from complications of his wounds in Elberon, N.J. **(Sept. 19).** Garfield's vice president, Chester Alan Arthur, succeeds him in office.

1882 U.S. adopts standard time **(Nov. 18).**

1885 Grover Cleveland is inaugurated as the 22nd president **(March 4).**

1886 Statue of Liberty is dedicated **(Oct. 28).** American Federation of Labor is organized **(Dec.).**

1889 Benjamin Harrison is inaugurated as the 23rd president **(March 4).** Oklahoma is opened to settlers **(April 22).**

1890 National American Woman Suffrage Association (NAWSA) is founded, with Elizabeth Cady Stanton as president. Sherman Antitrust Act is signed into law, prohibiting commercial monopolies **(July 2).** Last major battle of the Indian Wars occurs at Wounded Knee, S.D. **(Dec. 29).** In reporting the results of the 1890 census, the Census Bureau announces that the West has been settled and the frontier is closed.

1892 Ellis Island becomes chief immigration station of the U.S. **(Jan. 1).**

1893 Grover Cleveland is inaugurated a second time, as the 24th president **(March 4).** He is the only president to serve two nonconsecutive terms.

1897 William McKinley is inaugurated as the 25th president **(March 4).**

1898 Spanish-American War: USS *Maine* is blown up in Havana harbor **(Feb. 15),** prompting U.S. to declare war on Spain **(April 25).** Treaty of Paris is signed, ending the Spanish-American War **(Dec. 10);** Spain gives up control of Cuba, which becomes an independent republic, and cedes Puerto Rico, Guam, and (for $20 million) the Philippines to the U.S.

1898 U.S. annexes Hawaii by an act of Congress **(July 7).**

1899 U.S. acquires American Samoa by treaty with Great Britain and Germany **(Dec. 2).**

1900 Galveston hurricane leaves an estimated 6,000 to 8,000 dead **(Sept. 8).** According to the census, the nation's population numbers nearly 76 million.

1901 McKinley's second inauguration **(March 4).** He is shot **(Sept. 6)** by anarchist Leon Czolgosz in Buffalo, N.Y., and later dies from his wounds **(Sept. 14).** He is succeeded by his vice president, Theodore Roosevelt.

1903 U.S. acquires Panama Canal Zone (treaty signed **Nov. 17**). Wright brothers make the first controlled, sustained flight in heavier-than-air aircraft at Kitty Hawk, N.C. **(Dec. 17).**

1905 Theodore Roosevelt's second inauguration **(March 4).**

1906 San Francisco earthquake leaves 500 dead or missing and destroys about 4 sq mi of the city **(April 18).**

1908 Bureau of Investigation, forerunner of the FBI, is established **(July 26).**

1909 William Howard Taft is inaugurated as the 27th president **(March 4).**

1913 Woodrow Wilson is inaugurated as the 28th president **(March 4).** Seventeenth Amendment to the Constitution is ratified, providing for the direct election of U.S. senators by popular vote rather than by the state legislatures **(April 8).**

1914–1918 World War I: U.S. enters World War I, declaring war on Germany **(April 6, 1917)** and Austria-Hungary **(Dec. 7, 1917)** three years after conflict began in 1914. Armistice ending World War I is signed **(Nov. 11, 1918).**

1914 Panama Canal opens to traffic **(Aug. 15).**

1915 First long distance telephone service, between New York and San Francisco, is demonstrated **(Jan. 25).**

1916 U.S. agrees to purchase Danish West Indies (Virgin Islands) for $25 million (treaty signed **Aug. 14).** Jeannette Rankin of Montana is the first woman elected to the U.S. House of Representatives **(Nov. 7).**

1917 Wilson's second inauguration **(March 5).** First regular airmail service begins between Washington, DC, and New York **(May 15).**

1918 Eighteenth Amendment to the Constitution is ratified, prohibiting the manufacture, sale, and transportation of liquor **(Jan. 16).** It is later repealed by the Twenty-First Amendment in 1933.

1919 League of Nations meets for the first time; U.S. is not represented **(Jan. 13).** Nineteenth Amendment to the Constitution is ratified, granting women the right to vote **(Aug. 18).** President Wilson suffers a stroke **(Sept. 26).** Treaty of Versailles, outlining terms for peace at the end of World War I, is rejected by the Senate **(Nov. 19).**

1921 Warren G. Harding is inaugurated as the 29th president **(March 4).** He signs resolution declaring peace with Austria and Germany **(July 2).**

1923 President Harding dies suddenly **(Aug. 2).** He is succeeded by his vice president, Calvin Coolidge. Teapot Dome scandal breaks, as Senate launches an investigation into improper leasing of naval oil reserves during Harding administration **(Oct.)**

1925 Coolidge's second inauguration **(March 4).** Tennessee passes a law against the teaching of evolution in public schools **(March 23),** setting the stage for the Scopes Monkey Trial **(July 10–25).**

1927 Charles Lindbergh makes the first solo nonstop transatlantic flight in his plane *The Spirit of St. Louis* **(May 20–21).**

1929 Herbert Hoover is inaugurated as the 31st president **(March 4).** Stock market crash precipitates the Great Depression **(Oct. 29).**

1931 *The Star-Spangled Banner* is adopted as the national anthem **(March 3).**

1932 Hattie Wyatt Caraway of Arkansas is the first woman elected to the U.S. Senate, to fill a vacancy caused by the death of her husband **(Jan. 12).** She is reelected in 1932 and 1938. Amelia Earhart completes first solo nonstop transatlantic flight by a woman **(May 21).**

1933 Twentieth Amendment to the Constitution, sometimes called the "Lame Duck Amendment," is ratified, moving the president's inauguration date from March 4 to Jan. 20 **(Jan. 23).** Franklin Roosevelt is inaugurated as the 32nd president **(March 4).** New Deal recovery measures are enacted by Congress **(March 9–June 16).** Twenty-First Amendment to the Constitution is ratified, repealing Prohibition **(Dec. 5).**

1935 Works Progress Administration is established **(April 8).** Social Security Act is passed **(Aug. 14).** Bureau of Investigation (established 1908) becomes the Federal Bureau of Investigation under J. Edgar Hoover.

1937 F. Roosevelt's second inauguration **(Jan. 20).**

1938 Fair Labor Standards Act is passed, setting the first minimum wage in the U.S. at 25 cents per hour **(June 25).**

1939–1945 World War II: U.S. declares its neutrality in European conflict **(Sept. 5, 1939).** F. Roosevelt's third inauguration **(Jan. 20, 1941).** He is the first and only president elected to a third term. Japan attacks Hawaii, Guam, and the Philippines **(Dec. 7, 1941).** U.S. declares war on Japan **(Dec. 8).** Germany and Italy declare war on the United States; U.S. reciprocates by declaring war on both countries **(Dec. 11).** Allies invade North Africa **(Oct.–Dec. 1942)** and Italy **(Sept.–Dec. 1943).** Allies invade France on D-Day **(June 6, 1944).** F. Roosevelt's fourth inauguration **(Jan. 20, 1945).** President Roosevelt, Churchill, and Stalin meet at Yalta in the USSR to discuss postwar occupation of Germany **(Feb. 4–11).** President Roosevelt dies of a stroke **(April 12)** and is succeeded by his vice president, Harry Truman. Germany surrenders unconditionally **(May 7).** First atomic bomb is detonated at Alamogordo, N.M. **(July 16).** President Truman, Churchill, and Stalin meet at Potsdam, near Berlin, Germany, to demand Japan's unconditional surrender and to discuss plans for postwar Europe **(July 17–Aug. 2).** U.S. drops atomic bomb on Hiroshima, Japan **(Aug. 6).** U.S. drops atomic bomb on Nagasaki, Japan **(Aug. 9).** Japan agrees to unconditional surrender **(Aug. 14).** Japanese envoys sign surrender terms aboard the USS *Missouri* in Tokyo harbor **(Sept. 2).**

1945 United Nations is established **(Oct. 24).**

1946 The Philippines, which had been ceded to the U.S. by Spain at the end of the Spanish-American War, becomes an independent republic **(July 4).**

1947 Central Intelligence Agency is established.

1948 Congress passes foreign aid bill including the Marshall Plan, which provides for European postwar recovery **(April 2).** Soviets begin blockade of Berlin in the first major crisis of the cold war **(June 24).** In response, U.S. and Great Britain begin airlift of food and fuel to West Berlin **(June 26).**

1949 Truman's second inauguration **(Jan. 20).** North Atlantic Treaty Organization (NATO) is established **(April 4).** Soviets end blockade of Berlin **(May 12),** but airlift continues until Sept. 30.

1950–1953 Korean War: Cold war conflict between Communist and non-Communist forces on Korean Peninsula. North Korean communists invade South Korea **(June 25, 1950).** President Truman, without the approval of Congress, commits American troops to battle **(June 27).** Armistice agreement is signed **(July 27, 1953).**

1950–1975 Vietnam War: Prolonged conflict between Communist forces of North Vietnam, backed by China and the USSR, and non-Communist forces of South Vietnam, backed by the United States. President Truman authorizes $15 million in economic and military aid to the French, who are fighting to retain control of French Indochina, including Vietnam. As part of the aid package, Truman also sends 35 military advisers **(May 1950).** North Vietnamese torpedo boats allegedly attack U.S. destroyer in Gulf of Tonkin off the coast of North Vietnam **(Aug. 2, 1964).** Congress approves Gulf of Tonkin resolution, authorizing President Johnson to take any measures necessary to defend U.S. forces and prevent further aggression **(Aug. 7).** U.S. planes begin bombing raids of North Vietnam **(Feb. 1965).** First U.S. combat troops arrive in South Vietnam **(March 8–9).** North Vietnamese army and Viet Cong launch Tet Offensive, attacking Saigon and other key cities in South Vietnam **(Jan.–Feb. 1968).** American soldiers kill 300 Vietnamese villagers in My Lai massacre **(March 16).** U.S. troops invade Cambodia **(May 1, 1970).** Representatives of North and South Vietnam, the Viet Cong, and the U.S. sign a cease-fire agreement in Paris **(Jan. 27, 1973).** Last U.S. troops leave Vietnam **(March 29).** South Vietnamese government surrenders to North Vietnam; U.S. embassy Marine guards and last U.S. civilians are evacuated **(April 30, 1975).**

1951 Twenty-Second Amendment to the Constitution is ratified, limiting the president to two terms **(Feb. 27).** President Truman speaks in first coast-to-coast live television broadcast **(Sept. 4).**

1952 Puerto Rico becomes a U.S. commonwealth **(July 25).** First hydrogen bomb is detonated by the U.S. on Eniwetok, an atoll in the Marshall Islands **(Nov. 1).**

1953 Dwight Eisenhower is inaugurated as the 34th president **(Jan. 20).** Julius and Ethel Rosenberg are executed for passing secret information about U.S. atomic weaponry to the Soviets **(June 19).**

1954 Sen. Joseph R. McCarthy accuses army officials, members of the media, and other public figures of being Communists during highly publicized hearings **(April 22–June 17).**

1957 Eisenhower's second inauguration **(Jan. 21).** President sends federal troops to Central High School in Little Rock, Ark., to enforce integration of black students **(Sept. 24).**

1958 *Explorer I,* first American satellite, is launched **(Jan. 31).**

1959 Alaska becomes the 49th state **(Jan. 3)** and Hawaii becomes the 50th **(Aug. 21).**

1961 U.S. severs diplomatic relations with Cuba **(Jan. 3).** John F. Kennedy is inaugurated as the 35th president **(Jan. 20).** Bay of Pigs invasion of Cuba fails **(April 17–20).** A mixed-race group of volunteers sponsored by the Committee on Racial Equality—the so-called Freedom Riders—travel on buses through the

South in order to protest racially segregated interstate bus facilities **(May)**.

1962 Lt. Col. John Glenn becomes first U.S. astronaut to orbit Earth **(Feb. 20)**. Cuban Missile Crisis: President Kennedy denounces Soviet Union for secretly installing missile bases on Cuba and initiates a naval blockade of the island **(Oct. 22–Nov. 20)**.

1963 Rev. Martin Luther King, Jr., delivers his "I Have a Dream" speech before a crowd of 200,000 during the civil rights march on Washington, DC **(Aug. 28)**. President Kennedy is assassinated in Dallas, Tex. **(Nov. 22)**. He is succeeded in office by his vice president, Lyndon B. Johnson.

1964 President Johnson signs the Civil Rights Act **(July 2)**.

1965 In his annual state of the Union address, President Johnson proposes his Great Society program **(Jan. 4)**. L. Johnson's second inauguration **(Jan. 20)**. State troopers attack peaceful demonstrators led by Rev. Martin Luther King, Jr., as they try to cross bridge in Selma, Ala. **(March 7)**. President Johnson signs the Voting Rights Act, which prohibits discriminatory voting practices **(Aug. 6)**. In six days of rioting in Watts, a black section of Los Angeles, 35 people are killed and 883 injured **(Aug. 11–16)**.

1967 Twenty-Fifth Amendment to the Constitution is ratified, outlining the procedures for filling vacancies in the presidency and vice presidency **(Feb. 10)**.

1968 Rev. Martin Luther King, Jr., is assassinated in Memphis, Tenn. **(April 4)**. Sen. Robert F. Kennedy is assassinated in Los Angeles, Calif. **(June 5–6)**.

1969 Richard Nixon is inaugurated as the 37th president **(Jan. 20)**. Astronauts Neil Armstrong and Edwin Aldrin, Jr., become the first men to land on the Moon **(July 20)**.

1970 Four students are shot to death by National Guardsmen during an antiwar protest at Kent State University **(May 1)**.

1971 The Twenty-Sixth Amendment to the Constitution is ratified, lowering the voting age from 21 to 18 **(July 1)**.

1972 Nixon makes historic visit to Communist China **(Feb. 21–27)**. U.S. and Soviet Union sign strategic arms control agreement known as SALT I **(May 26)**. Five men, all employees of Nixon's reelection campaign, are caught breaking into rival Democratic headquarters at the Watergate complex in Washington, DC **(June 17)**.

1973 Nixon's second inauguration **(Jan. 20)**. Senate Select Committee begins televised hearings to investigate Watergate cover-up **(May 17–Aug. 7)**. Vice President Spiro T. Agnew resigns over charges of corruption and income tax evasion **(Oct. 10)**. President Nixon nominates Gerald R. Ford as vice president **(Oct. 12)**. Ford is confirmed by Congress and sworn in **(Dec. 6)**.

1974 House Judiciary Committee recommends to full House that Nixon be impeached on grounds of obstruction of justice, abuse of power, and contempt of Congress **(July 27–30)**. Nixon resigns; he is succeeded in office by his vice president, Gerald Ford **(Aug. 9)**. Nixon is granted an unconditional pardon by President Ford **(Sept. 8)**. Five former Nixon aides go on trial for their involvement in the Watergate cover-up **(Oct. 15)**; H. R. Haldeman, John D. Ehrlichman, and John Mitchell eventually serve time in prison. Nelson Rockefeller is confirmed and sworn in as vice president **(Dec. 19)**.

1977 Jimmy Carter is inaugurated as the 39th president **(Jan. 20)**. President Carter signs treaty **(Sept. 7)** agreeing to turn control of Panama Canal over to Panama on Dec. 31, 1999.

1978 President Carter meets with Egyptian president Anwar Sadat and Israeli prime minister Menachem Begin at Camp David **(Sept. 6)**; Sadat and Begin sign Camp David Accord, ending 30-year conflict between Egypt and Israel **(Sept. 17)**.

1979 U.S. establishes diplomatic ties with mainland China for the first time since Communist takeover in 1949 **(Jan. 1)**. Malfunction at Three Mile Island nuclear reactor in Pennsylvania causes near meltdown **(March 28)**. Panama takes control of the Canal Zone, formerly administered by U.S. **(Oct. 1)**. Iranian students storm U.S. embassy in Teheran and hold 66 people hostage **(Nov. 4)**; 13 of the hostages are released **(Nov. 19–20)**.

1980 President Carter announces that U.S. athletes will not attend Summer Olympics in Moscow unless Soviet Union withdraws from Afghanistan **(Jan. 20)**. FBI's undercover bribery investigation, code named Abscam, implicates a U.S. senator, seven members of the House, and 31 other public officials **(Feb. 2)**. U.S. mission to rescue hostages in Iran is aborted after a helicopter and cargo plane collide at the staging site in a remote part of Iran and 8 servicemen are killed **(April 25)**.

1981 Ronald Reagan is inaugurated as the 40th president **(Jan. 20)**. U.S. hostages held in Iran are released after 444 days in captivity **(Jan. 20)**. President Reagan is shot in the chest by John Hinckley, Jr. **(March 30)**. Sandra Day O'Connor is sworn in as the first woman Supreme Court justice **(Sept. 25)**.

1982 Deadline for ratification of the Equal Rights Amendment to the Constitution passes without the necessary votes **(June 30)**.

1983 U.S. invades Caribbean island of Grenada after a coup by Marxist faction in the government **(Oct. 25)**.

1985 Reagan's second inauguration **(Jan. 21)**.

1986 Space shuttle *Challenger* explodes 73 seconds after liftoff, killing all seven crew members **(Jan. 28)**. It is the worst accident in the history of the U.S. space program. U.S. bombs military bases in Libya in effort to deter terrorist strikes on American targets **(April 14)**. Iran-Contra scandal breaks when White House is forced to reveal secret arms-for-hostages deals **(Nov.)**.

1987 Congress holds public hearings in Iran-Contra investigation **(May 5–Aug. 3)**. In a speech in Berlin, President Reagan challenges Soviet leader Mikhail Gorbachev to "tear down this wall" and open Eastern Europe to political and economic reform **(June 12)**. Reagan and Gorbachev sign INF treaty, the first arms-control agreement to reduce the superpowers' nuclear weapons **(Dec. 8)**.

1989 George H. W. Bush is inaugurated as the 41st president **(Jan. 20)**. Oil tanker *Exxon Valdez* runs aground in Prince William Sound, spilling more than 10 million gallons of oil **(March 24).** It is the largest oil spill in U.S. history. President Bush signs legislation to provide for federal bailout of nearly 800 insolvent savings and loan institutions **(Aug. 9).** U.S. forces invade Panama in an attempt to capture Gen. Manuel Noriega, who previously had been indicted in the U.S. on drug trafficking charges **(Dec. 20).**

1991 Persian Gulf War: U.S. leads international coalition in military operation (code named "Desert Storm") to drive Iraqis out of Kuwait **(Jan. 16–Feb. 28).** Iraq accepts terms of UN ceasefire, marking an end of the war **(April 6).**

1991 U.S. and Soviet Union sign START I treaty, agreeing to further reduce strategic nuclear arms **(July 31).** Senate Judiciary Committee conducts televised hearings to investigate allegations of past sexual harassment brought against Supreme Court nominee Clarence Thomas by Anita Hill, a law professor at the University of Oklahoma **(Oct. 11–13).**

1992 Following the breakup of the Soviet Union in Dec. 1991, President Bush and Russian president Boris Yeltsin meet at Camp David and formally declare an end to the cold war **(Feb. 1).** The acquittal of four white police officers charged in the 1991 beating of black motorist Rodney King in Los Angeles sets off several days of rioting, leading to more than 50 deaths, thousands of injuries and arrests, and $1 billion in property damage **(April 29).** President Bush authorizes sending U.S. troops to Somalia as part of UN relief effort **(Dec. 4).** President Bush grants pardons to six officials convicted or indicted in the Iran-Contra scandal, leading some to suspect a cover-up **(Dec. 24).**

1993 Bill Clinton is inaugurated as the 42nd president **(Jan. 20).** Bomb explodes in basement garage of World Trade Center, killing 6, injuring 1,000, and causing more than $500 million in damage **(Feb. 26).** After 51-day standoff with federal agents, Branch Davidian compound in Waco, Tex., burns to the ground, killing 80 cult members **(April 19).** President Clinton orders missile attack against Iraq in retaliation for alleged plot to assassinate former President Bush **(June 26).** Eighteen U.S. soldiers are killed in ambush by Somali militiamen in Mogadishu **(Oct. 3–4).** President Clinton signs North American Free Trade Agreement into law **(Dec. 8).**

1994 Paula Jones, a former Arkansas state employee, files a federal lawsuit against President Clinton for sexual harassment **(May 6).**

1995 Bombing of federal office building in Oklahoma City kills 168 people **(April 19).** U.S. establishes full diplomatic relations with Vietnam **(July 11).** President Clinton sends first 8,000 of 20,000 U.S. troops to Bosnia for 12-month peacekeeping mission **(Dec.).** Budget standoff between President Clinton and Congress results in partial shutdown of U.S. government **(Dec. 16–Jan. 6).**

1997 Clinton's second inauguration **(Jan. 20).**

1998 President Clinton denies having had a sexual relationship with a White House intern named Monica Lewinsky **(Jan. 17).** President Clinton releases 1999 federal budget plan; it is the first balanced budget since 1969 **(Feb. 2).** In televised address, President Clinton admits having had a sexual relationship with Monica Lewinsky **(Aug. 17).** U.S. launches missile attacks on targets in Sudan and Afghanistan following terrorist attacks on U.S. embassies in Kenya and Tanzania **(Aug. 20).** U.S. and Britain launch air strikes against weapons sites in Iraq **(Dec. 16).** House of Representatives votes to impeach President Clinton on charges of perjury and obstruction of justice **(Dec. 19).**

1999 Senate acquits Clinton of impeachment charges **(Feb. 12).** NATO wages air campaign against Yugoslavia over killing and deportation of ethnic Albanians in Kosovo **(March 24–June 10).** School shooting at Columbine High School in Littleton, Colo., leaves 14 students (including the 2 shooters) and 1 teacher dead and 23 others wounded **(April 20).**

2000 According to the census, the nation's population numbers more than 280 million **(April 1).** No clear winner is declared in close presidential election contest between Vice President Al Gore and Texas governor George W. Bush **(Nov. 7).** Bush's tiny lead prompts automatic recount of votes in Florida **(Nov. 8).** More than a month after presidential election, U.S. Supreme Court determines the outcome by ruling against a manual recount of ballots in certain Florida counties **(Dec. 12).** Bush formally accepts the presidency, having won a slim majority in the electoral college but not a majority of the popular vote **(Dec. 13).**

2001 George W. Bush is inaugurated as the 43rd president **(Jan. 20).** Two hijacked jetliners ram twin towers of World Trade Center in worst terrorist attack against U.S.; a third hijacked plane flies into the Pentagon, and a fourth crashes in rural Pennsylvania. More than 3,000 people die in the attacks **(Sept. 11).** U.S. and Britain launch air attacks against targets in Afghanistan after Taliban government fails to hand over Saudi terrorist Osama bin Laden, the suspected mastermind behind the Sept. 11 attacks **(Oct. 7).** Following air campaign and ground assault by Afghani opposition troops, the Taliban regime topples **(Dec. 9);** however, the hunt for bin Laden and other members of al-Qaeda terrorist organization continues.

2002 In his first State of the Union address, President Bush labels Iran, Iraq, and North Korea an "axis of evil" and declares that U.S. will wage war against states that develop weapons of mass destruction **(Jan. 29).** President Bush signs legislation creating new Cabinet Department of Homeland Security. He nominates Tom Ridge as secretary. **(Nov. 25).**

2003 President Bush presents case for Iraqi war in State of the Union speech **(Jan. 28).** Space shuttle *Columbia* explodes upon reentry into Earth's atmosphere, killing all seven astronauts on board **(Feb. 1).** War in Iraq begins with an air strike on Baghdad **(March 20).** U.S. forces enter Baghdad; city falls 4 days later **(April 5–9).** President declares victory in Iraq **(May 1).** Bush signs $350 billion tax-cut bill **(May 28).**

See What Happened in 2003: Month-by-Month, National News, pp. 36–44.

Firsts in America

This selection is based on our editorial judgment. Other sources may list different firsts.

Admiral in U.S. Navy: David Glasgow Farragut, 1866.

Airmail route, first transcontinental: Between New York City and San Francisco, 1920.

Assembly, representative: House of Burgesses, founded in Virginia, 1619.

Bank established: Bank of North America, Philadelphia, 1781.

Birth in America to English parents: Virginia Dare, born Roanoke Island, N.C., 1587.

Black newspaper: *Freedom's Journal,* 1827, edited by John B. Russworm.

Black U.S. diplomat: Ebenezer D. Bassett, 1869, minister-resident to Haiti.

Black elected governor of a state: L. Douglas Wilder, Virginia, 1990.

Black elected to U.S. Senate: Hiram Revels, 1870, Mississippi.

Black elected to U.S. House of Representatives: Jefferson Long, Georgia, 1870.

Black associate justice of U.S. Supreme Court: Thurgood Marshall, Oct. 2, 1967.

Black secretary of state: Gen. Colin Powell, appointed Dec. 2000.

Black U.S. cabinet minister: Robert C. Weaver, 1966, Secretary of the Department of Housing and Urban Development.

Botanic garden: Established by John Bartram in Philadelphia, 1728, and is still in existence in its original location.

College: Harvard, founded 1636.

College to establish coeducation: Oberlin College (Ohio), 1833.

Electrocution of a criminal: William Kemmler in Auburn Prison, Auburn, N.Y., Aug. 6, 1890.

Five and Dime store: Founded by Frank Woolworth, Utica, N.Y., 1879 (moved to Lancaster, Pa., same year).

Fraternity, Greek-letter: Phi Beta Kappa; founded Dec. 5, 1776, at College of William and Mary.

Gay and lesbian civil rights advocacy organization, national: National Gay and Lesbian Task Force, founded in New York City, 1973.

Lesbian, acknowledged, elected to high local office: Kathy Kozachenko, 1974, Ann Arbor City Council.

Gay man, acknowledged, elected to high local office: Harvey Milk, 1977, San Francisco Board of Supervisors.

Law to be declared unconstitutional by U.S. Supreme Court: Judiciary Act of 1789. Case: *Marbury* v. *Madison,* 1803.

Library, circulating: Philadelphia, 1731.

Newspaper published daily: *Pennsylvania Packet and General Advertiser,* Philadelphia, Sept. 1784.

Newspaper published over a continuous period: *The Boston News-Letter,* April 1704.

Oil well, commercial: Titusville, Pa., 1859.

Panel quiz show on radio: *Information Please,* May 17, 1938.

Postage stamps issued: 1847.

Public school: Boston Latin School, Boston, 1635.

Radio station licensed: KDKA, Pittsburgh, Pa., Oct. 27, 1920.

Railroad, transcontinental: Central Pacific and Union Pacific railroads, joined at Promontory, Utah, May 10, 1869.

Savings bank: The Provident Institute for Savings, Boston, 1816.

Science museum: Founded by Charleston (S.C.) Library Society, 1773.

Skyscraper: Home Insurance Co., Chicago, 1885 (10 floors, 2 added later).

Slaves brought into America: At Jamestown, Va., 1619, from a Dutch ship.

Sorority: Alpha Delta Pi, at Wesleyan Female College, 1851.

State to abolish capital punishment: Michigan, 1847.

State to enter Union after original 13: Vermont, 1791.

Steam-heated building: Eastern Hotel, Boston, 1845.

Steam railroad (carried passengers and freight): Baltimore & Ohio, 1830.

Strike on record by union: Journeymen Printers, New York City, 1776.

Subway: Opened in Boston, 1897.

"Tabloid" picture newspaper: *The Illustrated Daily News* (now *The Daily News*), New York City, 1919.

Vaudeville theater: Gaiety Museum, Boston, 1883.

Woman astronaut appointed shuttle commander: Lt. Col. Eileen Collins, *Columbia,* launched July 1999.

Woman astronaut to ride in space: Dr. Sally K. Ride, 1983.

Woman cabinet member: Frances Perkins, Secretary of Labor, 1933.

Woman candidate for president: Victoria Claflin Woodhull, nominated by National Woman's Suffrage Assn. on ticket of Nation Radical Reformers, 1872.

Woman candidate for vice president: Geraldine A. Ferraro, nominated on a major party ticket, Democratic Party, 1984.

Woman doctor of medicine: Elizabeth Blackwell; M.D. from Geneva Medical College of Western New York, 1849.

Woman elected governor of a state: Nellie Tayloe Ross, Wyoming, 1925.

Woman elected to U.S. Senate: Hattie Caraway, Arkansas; elected Nov. 1932.

Woman member of U.S. House of Representatives: Jeannette Rankin (Mont.); elected Nov. 1916.

Woman member of U.S. Senate: Rebecca Latimer Felton (Ga.); appointed Oct. 3, 1922.

Woman member of U.S. Supreme Court: Sandra Day O'Connor; appointed July 1981.

Woman secretary of state: Madeleine Albright, appointed Dec. 1996.

Woman suffrage granted: Wyoming Territory, 1869.

Written constitution: *Fundamental Orders of Connecticut,* 1639.

The Early Congresses

At the urging of Massachusetts and Virginia, the First Continental Congress met in Philadelphia on Sept. 5, 1774, and was attended by representatives of all the colonies except Georgia. Patrick Henry of Virginia declared: "The distinctions between Pennsylvanians, New Yorkers, and New Englanders are no more. I am not a Virginian but an American." This Congress, which adjourned Oct. 26, 1774, passed intercolonial resolutions calling for extensive boycott by the colonies against British trade.

The following year, most of the delegates from the colonies were chosen by popular election to attend the Second Continental Congress, which assembled in Philadelphia on May 10. As war had already begun between the colonies and England, the chief problems before the Congress were the procuring of military supplies, the establishment of an army and proper defenses, the issuing of continental bills of credit, etc. On June 15, 1775, George Washington was elected to command the Continental army. Congress adjourned Dec. 12, 1776.

Other Continental Congresses were held in Baltimore (1776–1777), Philadelphia (1777), Lancaster, Pa. (1777), York, Pa. (1777–1778), and Philadelphia (1778–1781).

In 1781, the Articles of Confederation, although establishing a league of the thirteen states rather than a strong central government, provided for the continuance of Congress. Known thereafter as the Congress of the Confederation, it held sessions in Philadelphia (1781–1783), Princeton, N.J. (1783), Annapolis, Md. (1783–1784), and Trenton, N.J. (1784). Five sessions were held in New York City between the years 1785 and 1789.

The Congress of the United States, established by the ratification of the Constitution, held its first meeting on March 4, 1789, in New York City. Several sessions of Congress were held in Philadelphia, and the first meeting in Washington, DC, was on Nov. 17, 1800.

Presidents of the Continental Congresses

Name	Elected	Birth and death dates	Name	Elected	Birth and death dates
Peyton Randolph, Va.	9/5/1774	c.1721–1775	John Hanson, Md.	11/5/1781	1715–1783
Henry Middleton, S.C.	10/22/1774	1717–1784	Elias Boudinot, N.J.	11/4/1782	1740–1821
Peyton Randolph, Va.	5/10/1775	c.1721–1775	Thomas Mifflin, Pa.	11/3/1783	1744–1800
John Hancock, Mass.	5/24/1775	1737–1793	Richard Henry Lee, Va.	11/30/1784	1732–1794
Henry Laurens, S.C.	11/1/1777	1724–1792	John Hancock, Mass.[1]	11/23/1785	1737–1793
John Jay, N.Y.	12/10/1778	1745–1829	Nathaniel Gorham, Mass.	6/6/1786	1738–1796
Samuel Huntington, Conn.	9/28/1779	1731–1796	Arthur St. Clair, Pa.	2/2/1787	1734–1818
Thomas McKean, Del.	7/10/1781	1734–1817	Cyrus Griffin, Va.	1/22/1788	1748–1810

1. Resigned May 29, 1786, never having served, because of continued illness.

States by Order of Entry into Union

State	Entered Union	Year settled	State	Entered Union	Year settled
1. Delaware	Dec. 7, 1787	1638	26. Michigan	Jan. 26, 1837	1668
2. Pennsylvania	Dec. 12, 1787	1682	27. Florida	Mar. 3, 1845	1565
3. New Jersey	Dec. 18, 1787	1660	28. Texas	Dec. 29, 1845	1682
4. Georgia	Jan. 2, 1788	1733	29. Iowa	Dec. 28, 1846	1788
5. Connecticut	Jan. 9, 1788	1634	30. Wisconsin	May 29, 1848	1766
6. Massachusetts	Feb. 6, 1788	1620	31. California	Sept. 9, 1850	1769
7. Maryland	Apr. 28, 1788	1634	32. Minnesota	May 11, 1858	1805
8. South Carolina	May 23, 1788	1670	33. Oregon	Feb. 14, 1859	1811
9. New Hampshire	June 21, 1788	1623	34. Kansas	Jan. 29, 1861	1727
10. Virginia	June 25, 1788	1607	35. West Virginia	June 20, 1863	1727
11. New York	July 26, 1788	1614	36. Nevada	Oct. 31, 1864	1849
12. North Carolina	Nov. 21, 1789	1660	37. Nebraska	Mar. 1, 1867	1823
13. Rhode Island	May 29, 1790	1636	38. Colorado	Aug. 1, 1876	1858
14. Vermont	Mar. 4, 1791	1724	39. North Dakota	Nov. 2, 1889	1812
15. Kentucky	June 1, 1792	1774	40. South Dakota	Nov. 2, 1889	1859
16. Tennessee	June 1, 1796	1769	41. Montana	Nov. 8, 1889	1809
17. Ohio	Mar. 1, 1803	1788	42. Washington	Nov. 11, 1889	1811
18. Louisiana	Apr. 30, 1812	1699	43. Idaho	July 3, 1890	1842
19. Indiana	Dec. 11, 1816	1733	44. Wyoming	July 10, 1890	1834
20. Mississippi	Dec. 10, 1817	1699	45. Utah	Jan. 4, 1896	1847
21. Illinois	Dec. 3, 1818	1720	46. Oklahoma	Nov. 16, 1907	1889
22. Alabama	Dec. 14, 1819	1702	47. New Mexico	Jan. 6, 1912	1610
23. Maine	Mar. 15, 1820	1624	48. Arizona	Feb. 14, 1912	1776
24. Missouri	Aug. 10, 1821	1735	49. Alaska	Jan. 3, 1959	1784
25. Arkansas	June 15, 1836	1686	50. Hawaii	Aug. 21, 1959	1820

Source: Compiled from various sources by the editors.

The Confederate States of America

	State	Seceded from Union	Readmitted to Union[1]
1.	South Carolina	Dec. 20, 1860	July 9, 1868
2.	Mississippi	Jan. 9, 1861	Feb. 23, 1870
3.	Florida	Jan. 10, 1861	June 25, 1868
4.	Alabama	Jan. 11, 1861	July 13, 1868
5.	Georgia	Jan. 19, 1861	July 15, 1870[2]
6.	Louisiana	Jan. 26, 1861	July 9, 1868
7.	Texas	March 2, 1861	March 30, 1870
8.	Virginia	April 17, 1861	Jan. 26, 1870
9.	Arkansas	May 6, 1861	June 22, 1868
10.	North Carolina	May 20, 1861	July 4, 1868
11.	Tennessee	June 8, 1861	July 24, 1866

NOTE: Four other slave states—Delaware, Maryland, Kentucky, and Missouri—remained in the Union. The latter two were actually represented on the Confederate flag, which, like the Stars and Stripes, featured a star for every state. 1. Date of readmission to representation in U.S. House of Representatives. 2. Second readmission date. First date was July 21, 1868, but the representatives were unseated March 5, 1869.

Territorial Expansion

Accession	Date	Area[1]
United States	—	3,717,796
Territory in 1790	—	891,364
Louisiana Purchase	1803	831,321
Florida	1819	69,866
Texas	1845	384,958
Oregon	1846	283,439
Mexican Cession	1848	530,706
Gadsden Purchase	1853	29,640
Alaska	1867	591,004
Hawaii	1898	6,471
Other territory		
Philippines[2]	1898	115,600
Puerto Rico	1899	3,508
Guam	1899	217
American Samoa	1900	90
Canal Zone[3]	1904	553
Virgin Islands of U.S.	1917	171
Trust Territory of Pacific Islands[4]	1947	241
Northern Mariana Islands	1986	189
All other	—	16
Total, 1990	—	**3,722,228**

1. Total area (land and water), in square miles. 2. Became independent in 1946. 3. Reverted to Panama in 1979. 4. Palau, the last remaining trust territory, became a sovereign state in 1994. *Source:* U.S. Bureau of the Census, Web: www.census.gov.

History of the American Flag

According to popular legend, the first American flag was made by Betsy Ross, a Philadelphia seamstress who was acquainted with George Washington, leader of the Continental Army, and other influential Philadelphians. In May 1776, so the story goes, General Washington and two representatives from the Continental Congress visited Ross at her upholstery shop and showed her a rough design of the flag. Although Washington initially favored using a star with six points, Ross advocated for a five-pointed star, which could be cut with just one quick snip of the scissors, and the gentlemen were won over.

Unfortunately, historians have never been able to verify this charming version of events, although it is known that Ross made flags for the navy of Pennsylvania. The story of Washington's visit to the flagmaker became popular about the time of the country's first centennial, after William Canby, a grandson of Ross, told about her role in shaping U.S. history in a speech given at the Philadelphia Historical Society in March 1870.

What is known is that the first unofficial national flag, called the Grand Union Flag or the Continental Colours, was raised at the behest of General Washington near his headquarters outside Boston, Mass., on Jan. 1, 1776. The flag had 13 alternating red and white horizontal stripes and the British Union Flag (a predecessor of the Union Jack) in the canton. Another early flag had a rattlesnake and the motto "Don't Tread on Me."

The first official national flag, also known as the Stars and Stripes, was approved by the Continental Congress on June 14, 1777. The blue canton contained 13 stars, representing the original 13 colonies, but the layout varied. Although nobody knows for sure who designed the flag, it may have been Continental Congress member Francis Hopkinson.

After Vermont and Kentucky were admitted to the Union in 1791 and 1792, respectively, two more stars and two more stripes were added in 1795. This 15-star, 15-stripe flag was the "star-spangled banner" that inspired lawyer Francis Scott Key to write the poem that later became the U.S. national anthem.

In 1818, after five more states had gained admittance, Congress passed legislation fixing the number of stripes at 13 and requiring that the number of stars equal the number of states. The last new star, bringing the total to 50, was added on July 4, 1960, after Hawaii became a state.

The Pledge of Allegiance to the Flag[1]

I pledge allegiance to the Flag of the United States of America, and to the Republic for which it stands, one Nation under God,[2] indivisible, with liberty and justice for all.

1. The original pledge was published in the Sept. 8, 1892, issue of *The Youth's Companion* in Boston. For years, the authorship was in dispute between James B. Upham and Francis Bellamy of the magazine's staff. In 1939, after a study of the controversy, the United States Flag Association decided that authorship be credited to Bellamy. 2. The phrase "under God" was added to the pledge on June 14, 1954.

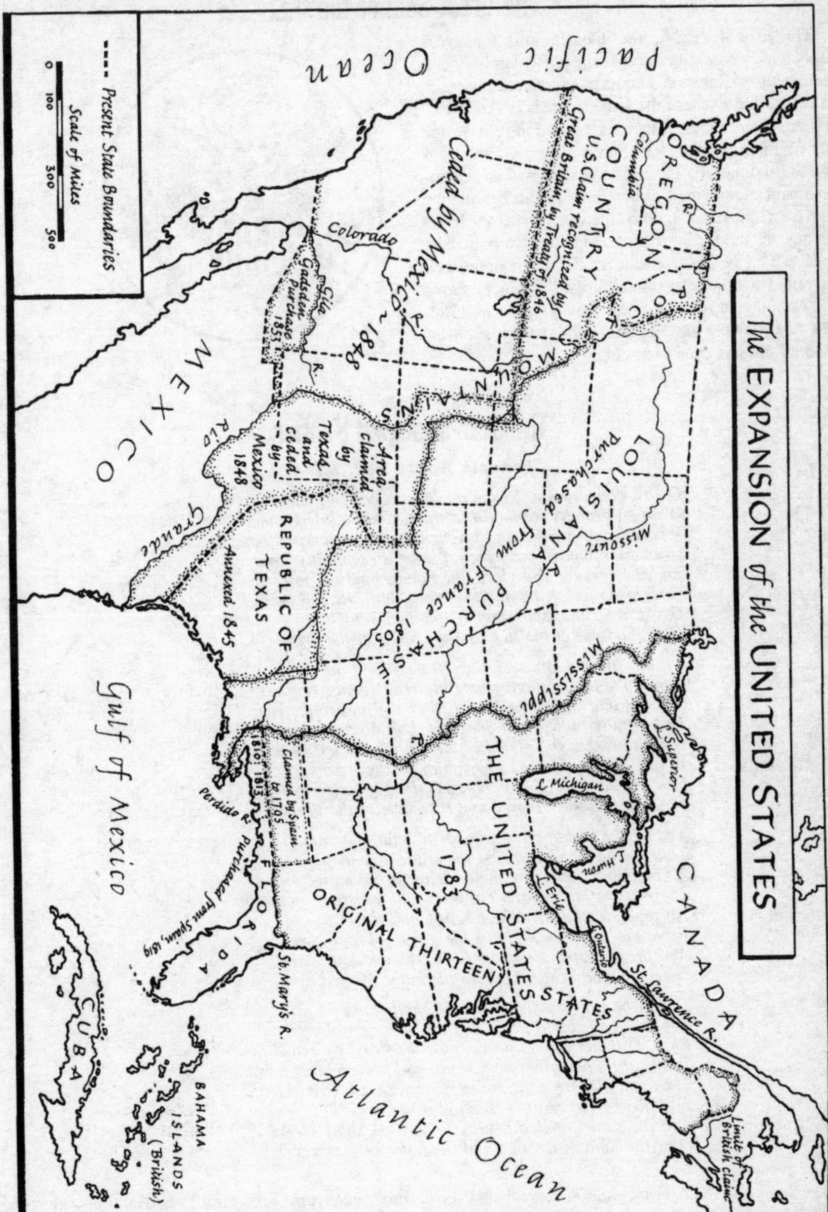

The EXPANSION of the UNITED STATES
Present State Boundaries
Scale of Miles
0 100 300 500
Pacific Ocean
OREGON COUNTRY
U.S. Claim recognized by Great Britain by Treaty of 1846
Columbia R.
Ceded by Mexico ~ 1848
Colorado
Gila R.
Gadsden Purchase 1853
Rocky Mountains
LOUISIANA PURCHASE
Purchased from France 1803
Missouri R.
Area claimed by Texas and ceded by Mexico 1848
REPUBLIC OF TEXAS
Annexed 1845
Rio Grande
MEXICO
Gulf of Mexico
Mississippi R.
THE UNITED STATES 1783
ORIGINAL THIRTEEN STATES
L. Superior
L. Michigan
L. Huron
L. Erie
L. Ontario
St. Lawrence R.
CANADA
Limit of British claim
Claimed by Spain to 1795
1810 1813
Perdido R.
FLORIDA
Purchased from Spain, 1819
St. Mary's R.
CUBA
BAHAMA ISLANDS (British)
Atlantic Ocean

The Great Seal of the U.S.

On July 4, 1776, the Continental Congress appointed a committee consisting of Benjamin Franklin, John Adams, and Thomas Jefferson "to bring in a device for a seal of the United States of America." After many delays, a verbal description of a design by William Barton was finally approved by Congress on June 20, 1782. The seal shows an American bald eagle with a ribbon in its mouth bearing the device *E pluribus unum* (One out of many). In its talons are the arrows of war and an olive branch of peace. On the reverse side it shows an unfinished pyramid with an eye (the eye of Providence) above it. Although this description was adopted in 1782, the first drawing was not made until four years later, and no die has ever been cut.

The Star-Spangled Banner

Francis Scott Key, 1814

O say, can you see, by the dawn's early light,
What so proudly we hail'd at the twilight's last gleaming?
Whose broad stripes and bright stars, thro' the perilous fight,
O'er the ramparts we watch'd, were so gallantly streaming?
And the rockets' red glare, the bombs bursting in air,
Gave proof thro' the night that our flag was still there.
O say, does that star-spangled banner yet wave
O'er the land of the free and the home of the brave?

On the shore dimly seen thro' the mists of the deep,
Where the foe's haughty host in dread silence reposes,
What is that which the breeze, o'er the towering steep,
As it fitfully blows, half conceals, half discloses?
Now it catches the gleam of the morning's first beam,
In full glory reflected, now shines on the stream:
'Tis the star-spangled banner: O, long may it wave
O'er the land of the free and the home of the brave!

And where is that band who so vauntingly swore
That the havoc of war and the battle's confusion,
A home and a country should leave us no more?
Their blood has wash'd out their foul footsteps' pollution.
No refuge could save the hireling and slave
From the terror of flight or the gloom of the grave:
And the star-spangled banner in triumph doth wave
O'er the land of the free and the home of the brave.

O thus be it ever when free-men shall stand
Between their lov'd home and the war's desolation;
Blest with vict'ry and peace, may the heav'n-rescued land
Praise the Pow'r that hath made and preserv'd us a nation!
Then conquer we must, when our cause it is just,
And this be our motto: "In God is our trust!"
And the star-spangled banner in triumph shall wave
O'er the land of the free and the home of the brave!

On Sept. 13, 1814, Francis Scott Key visited the British fleet in Chesapeake Bay to secure the release of Dr. William Beanes, who had been captured after the burning of Washington, DC. The release was secured, but Key was detained on ship overnight during the shelling of Fort McHenry, one of the forts defending Baltimore. In the morning, he was so delighted to see the American flag still flying over the fort that he began a poem to commemorate the occasion. First published under the title "Defense of Fort M'Henry," the poem soon attained wide popularity as sung to the tune "To Anacreon in Heaven." The origin of this tune is obscure, but it may have been written by John Stafford Smith, a British composer born in 1750. "The Star-Spangled Banner" was officially made the national anthem by Congress in 1931, although it already had been adopted as such by the army and the navy.

The Liberty Bell

The Liberty Bell was cast in England in 1752 for the Pennsylvania Statehouse (now named Independence Hall) in Philadelphia. It was recast in Philadelphia in 1753. It is inscribed with the words, "Proclaim liberty throughout all the land unto all the inhabitants thereof" (Lev. 25:10). The bell was rung on July 8, 1776, for the first public reading of the Declaration of Independence. Hidden in Allentown during the British occupation of Philadelphia, it was re-placed in Independence Hall in 1778. The bell cracked on July 8, 1835, while tolling the death of Chief Justice John Marshall. In 1976 the Liberty Bell was moved to a special exhibition building near Independence Hall.

The Declaration of Independence

On April 12, 1776, the legislature of North Carolina authorized its delegates to the Continental Congress to join with others in a declaration of separation from Great Britain; the first colony to instruct its delegates to take the actual initiative was Virginia on May 15. On June 7, 1776, Richard Henry Lee of Virginia offered a resolution to the Congress to the effect "that these United Colonies are, and of right ought to be, free and independent States. . . ." A committee consisting of Thomas Jefferson, John Adams, Benjamin Franklin, Robert R. Livingston, and Roger Sherman was organized to "prepare a declaration to the effect of the said first resolution." The Declaration of Independence was adopted on July 4, 1776. Most delegates signed the Declaration August 2, but George Wythe (Va.) signed August 27; Richard Henry Lee (Va.), Elbridge Gerry (Mass.), and Oliver Wolcott (Conn.) in September; Matthew Thornton (N.H.), not a delegate until September, in November; and Thomas McKean (Del.), although present on July 4, not until 1781 by special permission, having served in the army in the interim.

In Congress, July 4, 1776

The unanimous Declaration of the thirteen United States of America

When in the Course of human events it becomes necessary for one people to dissolve the political bands which have connected them with another, and to assume among the powers of the earth, the separate and equal station to which the Laws of Nature and of Nature's God entitle them, a decent respect to the opinions of mankind requires that they should declare the causes which impel them to the separation.

We hold these truths to be self-evident, that all men are created equal, that they are endowed by their Creator with certain unalienable Rights, that among these are Life, Liberty and the pursuit of Happiness.—That to secure these rights, Governments are instituted among Men, deriving their just powers from the consent of the governed.—That whenever any Form of Government becomes destructive of these ends, it is the Right of the People to alter or to abolish it, and to institute new Government, laying its foundation on such principles and organizing its powers in such form, as to them shall seem most likely to effect their Safety and Happiness. Prudence, indeed, will dictate that Governments long established should not be changed for light and transient causes; and accordingly all experience hath shewn that mankind are more disposed to suffer, while evils are sufferable, than to right themselves by abolishing the forms to which they are accustomed. But when a long train of abuses and usurpations, pursuing invariably the same Object evinces a design to reduce them under absolute Despotism, it is their right, it is their duty, to throw off such Government, and to provide new Guards for their future security.—Such has been the patient sufferance of these Colonies; and such is now the necessity which constrains them to alter their former Systems of Government. The history of the present King of Great Britain is a history of repeated injuries and usurpations, all having in direct object the establishment of an absolute Tyranny over these States. To prove this, let Facts be submitted to a candid world.

He has refused his Assent to Laws, the most wholesome and necessary for the public good.

He has forbidden his Governors to pass Laws of immediate and pressing importance, unless suspended in their operation till his Assent should be obtained; and when so suspended, he has utterly neglected to attend to them.

He has refused to pass other Laws for the accommodation of large districts of people, unless those people would relinquish the right of Representation in the Legislature, a right inestimable to them and formidable to tyrants only.

He has called together legislative bodies at places unusual, uncomfortable, and distant from the depository of their Public Records, for the sole purpose of fatiguing them into compliance with his measures.

He has dissolved Representative Houses repeatedly, for opposing with manly firmness his invasions on the rights of the people.

He has refused for a long time, after such dissolutions, to cause others to be elected; whereby the Legislative Powers, incapable of Annihilation, have returned to the People at large for their exercise; the State remaining in the mean time exposed to all the dangers of invasion from without, and convulsions within.

He has endeavoured to prevent the population of these States; for that purpose obstructing the Laws for Naturalization of Foreigners; refusing to pass others to encourage their migrations hither, and raising the conditions of new Appropriations of Lands.

He has obstructed the Administration of Justice, by refusing his Assent to Laws for establishing Judiciary Powers.

He has made Judges dependent on his Will alone, for the tenure of their offices, and the amount and payment of their salaries.

He has erected a multitude of New Offices, and sent hither swarms of Officers to harass our people, and eat out their substance.

He has kept among us, in times of peace, Standing Armies without the Consent of our legislatures.

He has affected to render the Military independent of and superior to the Civil Power.

He has combined with others to subject us to a jurisdiction foreign to our constitution, and unacknowledged by our laws; giving his Assent to their Acts of pretended Legislation:

For quartering large bodies of armed troops among us:

For protecting them, by a mock Trial, from punishment for any Murders which they should commit on the Inhabitants of these States:

For cutting off our Trade with all parts of the world:

For imposing Taxes on us without our Consent:

For depriving us in many cases, of the benefits of Trial by Jury:

For transporting us beyond Seas to be tried for pretended offences:

For abolishing the free System of English Laws in a neighbouring Province, establishing therein an Arbitrary government, and enlarging its Boundaries so as to render it at once an example and fit instrument for introducing the same absolute rule into these Colonies:

For taking away our Charters, abolishing our most valuable Laws and altering fundamentally the Forms of our Governments:

For suspending our own Legislatures, and declaring themselves invested with power to legislate for us in all cases whatsoever.

He has abdicated Government here, by declaring us out of his Protection and waging War against us.

He has plundered our seas, ravaged our Coasts, burnt our towns, and destroyed the lives of our people.

He is at this time transporting large Armies of foreign Mercenaries to compleat the works of death, desolation, and tyranny, already begun with circumstances of Cruelty & Perfidy scarcely paralleled in the most barbarous ages, and totally unworthy the Head of a civilized nation.

He has constrained our fellow Citizens taken Captive on the high Seas to bear Arms against their Country, to become the executioners of their friends and Brethren, or to fall themselves by their Hands.

He has excited domestic insurrections amongst us, and has endeavoured to bring on the inhabitants of our frontiers, the merciless Indian Savages, whose known rule of warfare, is an undistinguished destruction of all ages, sexes and conditions.

In every stage of these Oppressions We have Petitioned for Redress in the most humble terms: Our repeated Petitions have been answered only by repeated injury. A Prince, whose character is thus marked by every act which may define a Tyrant, is unfit to be the ruler of a free people.

Nor have We been wanting in attentions to our British brethren. We have warned them from time to time of attempts by their legislature to extend an unwarrantable jurisdiction over us. We have reminded them of the circumstances of our emigration and settlement here. We have appealed to their native justice and magnanimity, and we have conjured them by the ties of our common kindred to disavow these usurpations, which would inevitably interrupt our connections and correspondence. They too have been deaf to the voice of justice and of consanguinity. We must, therefore, acquiesce in the necessity, which denounces our Separation, and hold them, as we hold the rest of mankind, Enemies in War, in Peace Friends.

We, therefore, the Representatives of the United States of America, in General Congress, Assembled, appealing to the Supreme Judge of the world for the rectitude of our intentions, do, in the Name, and by Authority of the good People of these Colonies, solemnly publish and declare, That these United Colonies are, and of Right ought to be Free and Independent States; that they are Absolved from all Allegiance to the British Crown, and that all political connection between them and the State of Great Britain, is and ought to be totally dissolved; and that as Free and Independent States, they have full Power to levy War, conclude Peace, contract Alliances, establish Commerce, and to do all other Acts and Things which Independent States may of right do.—And for the support of this Declaration, with a firm reliance on the protection of Divine Providence, we mutually pledge to each other our Lives, our Fortunes and our sacred Honor.

—John Hancock

New Hampshire
Josiah Bartlett
Wm. Whipple
Matthew Thornton

Rhode Island
Step. Hopkins
William Ellery

Connecticut
Roger Sherman
Sam'el Huntington
Wm. Williams
Oliver Wolcott

New York
Wm. Floyd
Phil. Livingston
Frans. Lewis
Lewis Morris

New Jersey
Richd. Stockton
Jno. Witherspoon
Fras. Hopkinson
John Hart
Abra. Clark

Pennsylvania
Robt. Morris
Benjamin Rush
Benj. Franklin
John Morton
Geo. Clymer
Jas. Smith
Geo. Taylor
James Wilson
Geo. Ross

Massachusetts-Bay
Saml. Adams
John Adams
Robt. Treat Paine
Elbridge Gerry

Delaware
Caesar Rodney
Geo. Read
Tho. M'Kean

Maryland
Samuel Chase
Wm. Paca
Thos. Stone
Charles Carroll of Carrollton

Virginia
George Wythe
Richard Henry Lee
Th. Jefferson
Benj. Harrison
Ths. Nelson, Jr.
Francis Lightfoot Lee
Carter Braxton

North Carolina
Wm. Hooper
Joseph Hewes
John Penn

South Carolina
Edward Rutledge
Thos. Heyward, Junr.
Thomas Lynch, Junr.
Arthur Middleton

Georgia
Button Gwinnett
Lyman Hall
Geo. Walton

Constitution of the United States of America

(Historical text has been edited to conform to contemporary American usage. The bracketed words are designations for your convenience; they are not part of the Constitution.)

The oldest federal constitution in existence was framed by a convention of delegates from twelve of the thirteen original states in Philadelphia in May 1787, Rhode Island failing to send a delegate. George Washington presided over the session, which lasted until September 17, 1787. The draft (originally a preamble and seven Articles) was submitted to all thirteen states and was to become effective when ratified by nine states. It went into effect on the first Wednesday in March 1789, having been ratified by New Hampshire, the ninth state to approve, on June 21, 1788. The states ratified the Constitution in the following order:

Delaware	December 7, 1787	South Carolina	May 23, 1788
Pennsylvania	December 12, 1787	New Hampshire	June 21, 1788
New Jersey	December 18, 1787	Virginia	June 25, 1788
Georgia	January 2, 1788	New York	July 26, 1788
Connecticut	January 9, 1788	North Carolina	November 21, 1789
Massachusetts	February 6, 1788	Rhode Island	May 29, 1790
Maryland	April 28, 1788		

[Preamble]

We the people of the United States, in order to form a more perfect Union, establish justice, insure domestic tranquility, provide for the common defence, promote the general welfare, and secure the blessings of liberty to ourselves and our posterity, do ordain and establish this Constitution for the United States of America.

Article I

Section 1

[Legislative powers vested in Congress.] All legislative powers herein granted shall be vested in a Congress of the United States, which shall consist of a Senate and House of Representatives.

Section 2

[Composition of the House of Representatives.—1.] The House of Representatives shall be composed of members chosen every second year by the people of the several States, and the electors in each State shall have the qualifications requisite for electors of the most numerous branch of the State Legislature.

[Qualifications of Representatives.—2.] No Person shall be a Representative who shall not have attained to the age of twenty-five years, and been seven years a citizen of the United States, and who shall not, when elected, be an inhabitant of that State in which he shall be chosen.

[Apportionment of Representatives and direct taxes—census.[1]—3.] (Representatives and direct taxes shall be apportioned among the several States which may be included within this Union, according to their respective numbers, which shall be determined by adding to the whole number of free persons, including those bound to service for a term of years, and excluding Indians not taxed, three fifths of all other persons.) The actual enumeration shall be made within three years after the first meeting of the Congress of the United States, and within every subsequent term of ten years, in such manner as they shall by law direct. The number of Representatives shall not exceed one for every thirty thousand, but each State shall have at least one Representative; and until such enumeration shall be made, the State of New Hampshire shall be entitled to choose three, Massachusetts eight, Rhode-Island and Providence Plantations one, Connecticut five, New York six, New Jersey four, Pennsylvania eight, Delaware one, Maryland six, Virginia ten, North Carolina five, South Carolina five, and Georgia three.

[Filling of vacancies in representation.—4.] When vacancies happen in the representation from any State, the Executive Authority thereof shall issue writs of election to fill such vacancies.

[Selection of officers; power of impeachment.—5.] The House of Representatives shall choose their Speaker and other officers; and shall have the sole power of impeachment.

Section 3[2]

[The Senate.—1.] The Senate of the United States shall be composed of two Senators from each State, chosen by the Legislature thereof, for six years; and each Senator shall have one vote.

[Classification of Senators; filling of vacancies.—2.] Immediately after they shall be assembled in consequence of the first election, they shall be divided as equally as may be into three classes. The seats of the Senators of the first class shall be vacated at the expiration of the second year, of the second class at the expiration of the fourth year, and of the third class at the expiration of the sixth year, so that one-third may be chosen every second year; and if vacancies happen by resignation, or otherwise, during the recess of the Legislature of any State, the Executive thereof may make temporary appointments (until the next meeting of the Legislature, which shall then fill such vacancies).

[Qualification of Senators.—3.] No person shall be a Senator who shall not have attained to the age of thirty years, and been nine years a citizen of the United States, and who shall not, when elected, be an inhabitant of that State for which he shall be chosen.

[Vice President to be President of Senate.—4.] The Vice President of the United States shall be President of the Senate, but shall have no vote, unless they be equally divided.

[Selection of Senate officers; President pro tempore.—5.] The Senate shall choose their other

1. The clause included in parentheses is amended by the 14th Amendment, Section 2. 2. The first paragraph of this section and the part of the second paragraph included in parentheses are amended by the 17th Amendment.

officers, and also a President pro tempore, in the absence of the Vice President, or when he shall exercise the office of President of the United States.

[Senate to try impeachments.—6.] The Senate shall have the sole power to try all impeachments. When sitting for that purpose, they shall be on oath or affirmation. When the President of the United States is tried, the Chief Justice shall preside: and no person shall be convicted without the concurrence of two thirds of the members present.

[Judgment in cases of Impeachment.—7.] Judgment in cases of impeachment shall not extend further than to removal from office, and disqualification to hold and enjoy any office of honor, trust, or profit under the United States: but the party convicted shall nevertheless be liable and subject to indictment, trial, judgment and punishment, according to Law.

Section 4

[Control of congressional elections.—1.] The times, places, and manner of holding elections for Senators and Representatives, shall be prescribed in each State by the Legislature thereof; but the Congress may at any time by law make or alter such regulations, except as to the places of choosing Senators.

[Time for assembling of Congress[3]—2.] The Congress shall assemble at least once in every year, and such meeting shall be on the first Monday in December, unless they shall by law appoint a different day.

Section 5

[Each house to be the judge of the election and qualifications of its members; regulations as to quorum.—1.] Each House shall be the judge of the elections, returns, and qualifications of its own members, and a majority of each shall constitute a quorum to do business; but a smaller number may adjourn from day to day, and may be authorized to compel the attendance of absent members, in such manner, and under such penalties as each House may provide.

[Each house to determine its own rules.—2.] Each House may determine the rules of its proceedings, punish its members for disorderly behavior, and, with the concurrence of two thirds, expel a member.

[Journals and yeas and nays.—3.] Each House shall keep a journal of its proceedings, and from time to time publish the same, excepting such parts as may in their judgment require secrecy; and the yeas and nays of the members of either House on any question shall, at the desire of one fifth of those present, be entered on the journal.

[Adjournment.—4.] Neither House, during the session of Congress, shall, without the consent of the other, adjourn for more than three days, nor to any other place than that in which the two Houses shall be sitting.

Section 6

[Compensation and privileges of members of Congress.—1.] The Senators and Representatives shall receive a compensation for their services, to be ascertained by law, and paid out of the Treasury of the United States. They shall in all cases, except treason, felony, and breach of the peace, be privileged from arrest during their attendance at the session of their respective Houses, and in going to and returning from the same; and for any speech or debate in either House, they shall not be questioned in any other place.

[Incompatible offices; exclusions.—2.] No Senator or Representative shall, during the time for which he was elected, be appointed to any civil office under the authority of the United States, which shall have been created, or the emoluments whereof shall have been increased during such time; and no person holding any office under the United States shall be a member of either House during his continuance in office.

Section 7

[Revenue bills to originate in House.—1.] All bills for raising revenue shall originate in the House of Representatives; but the Senate may propose or concur with amendments as on other bills.

[Manner of passing bills; veto power of President.—2.] Every bill which shall have passed the House of Representatives and the Senate, shall, before it becomes a law, be presented to the President of the United States; if he approve he shall sign it, but if not he shall return it, with his objections to that House in which it shall have originated, who shall enter the objections at large on their journal, and proceed to reconsider it. If after such reconsideration two thirds of that House shall agree to pass the bill, it shall be sent, together with the objections, to the other House, by which it shall likewise be reconsidered, and if approved by two thirds of that House, it shall become a law. But in all such cases the votes of both Houses shall be determined by yeas and nays, and the names of the persons voting for and against the bill shall be entered on the journal of each house, respectively. If any bill shall not be returned by the President within ten days (Sundays excepted) after it shall have been presented to him, the same shall be a law, in like manner as if he had signed it, unless the Congress by their adjournment prevent its return, in which case it shall not be a law.

[Concurrent orders or resolutions, to be passed by President.—3.] Every order, resolution, or vote to which the concurrence of the Senate and House of Representatives may be necessary (except on a question of adjournment) shall be presented to the President of the United States; and before the same shall take effect, shall be approved by him, or being disapproved by him, shall be repassed by two thirds of the Senate and House of Representatives, according to the rules and limitations prescribed in the case of a bill.

Section 8

[General powers of Congress.[4]]

[Taxes, duties, imposts, and excises.—1.] The Congress shall have power to lay and collect taxes, duties, imposts and excises, to pay the debts and provide for the common defense and general welfare of the United States; but all duties, imposts and excises shall be uniform throughout the United States;

3. Amended by the 20th Amendment, Section 2. 4. By the 16th Amendment, Congress is given the power to lay and collect taxes on income.

[Borrowing of money.—2.] To borrow money on the credit of the United States;

[Regulation of commerce.—3.] To regulate commerce with foreign nations, and among the several States, and with the Indian tribes;

[Naturalization and bankruptcy.—4.] To establish a uniform rule of naturalization, and uniform laws on the subject of bankruptcies throughout the United States;

[Money, weights and measures.—5.] To coin money, regulate the value thereof, and of foreign coin, and fix the standard of weights and measures;

[Counterfeiting.—6.] To provide for the punishment of counterfeiting the securities and current coin of the United States;

[Post offices.—7.] To establish post offices and post roads;

[Patents and copyrights.—8.] To promote the progress of science and useful arts, by securing for limited times to authors and inventors the exclusive right to their respective writings and discoveries;

[Inferior courts.—9.] To constitute tribunals inferior to the Supreme Court;

[Piracies and felonies.—10.] To define and punish piracies and felonies committed on the high seas, and offences against the law of nations;

[War; marque and reprisal.—11.] To declare war, grant letters of marque and reprisal, and make rules concerning captures on land and water;

[Armies.—12.] To raise and support armies, but no appropriation of money to that use shall be for a longer term than two years;

[Navy.—13.] To provide and maintain a navy;

[Land and naval forces.—14.] To make rules for the government and regulation of the land and naval forces;

[Calling out militia.—15.] To provide for calling forth the militia to execute the laws of the Union, suppress insurrections, and repel invasions;

[Organizing, arming, and disciplining militia.—16.] To provide for organizing, arming, and disciplining, the militia, and for governing such part of them as may be employed in the service of the United States, reserving to the States, respectively, the appointment of the officers, and the authority of training the militia according to the discipline prescribed by Congress;

[Exclusive legislation over District of Columbia.—17.] To exercise exclusive legislation in all cases whatsoever, over such district (not exceeding ten miles square) as may, by cession of particular States, and the acceptance of Congress, become the seat of the Government of the United States, and to exercise like authority over all places purchased by the consent of the Legislature of the State in which the same shall be, for the erection of forts, magazines, arsenals, dock-yards, and other needful buildings;—And

[To enact laws necessary to enforce Constitution.—18.] To make all laws which shall be necessary and proper for carrying into execution the foregoing powers, and all other powers vested by this Constitution in the Government of the United States, or in any department or officer thereof.

Section 9

[Migration or importation of certain persons not to be prohibited before 1808.—1.] The migration or importation of such persons as any of the States now existing shall think proper to admit, shall not be prohibited by the Congress prior to the year one thousand eight hundred and eight, but a tax or duty may be imposed on such importation, not exceeding ten dollars for each person.

[Writ of habeas corpus not to be suspended; exception.—2.] The privilege of the writ of habeas corpus shall not be suspended, unless when in cases of rebellion or invasion the public safety may require it.

[Bills of attainder and ex post facto laws prohibited.—3.] No bill of attainder or ex post facto law shall be passed.

[Capitation and other direct taxes.—4.] No capitation, or other direct, tax shall be laid, unless in proportion to the census or enumeration herein before directed to be taken.[5]

[Exports not to be taxed.—5.] No tax or duty shall be laid on articles exported from any State.

[No preference to be given to ports of any States; interstate shipping.—6.] No preference shall be given by any regulation of commerce or revenue to the ports of one State over those of another: nor shall vessels bound to, or from, one State, be obliged to enter, clear, or pay duties in another.

[Money, how drawn from treasury; financial statements to be published.—7.] No money shall be drawn from the Treasury, but in consequence of appropriations made by law; and a regular statement and account of the receipts and expenditures of all public money shall be published from time to time.

[Titles of nobility not to be granted; acceptance by government officers of favors from foreign powers.—8.] No title of nobility shall be granted by the United States: and no person holding any office of profit or trust under them, shall, without the consent of the Congress, accept of any present, emolument, office, or title, of any kind whatever, from any king, prince, or foreign state.

Section 10

[Limitations of the powers of the several States.—1.] No State shall enter into any treaty, alliance, or confederation; grant letters of marque and reprisal; coin money; emit bills of credit; make any thing but gold and silver coin a tender in payment of debts; pass any bill of attainder, ex post facto law, or law impairing the obligation of contracts, or grant any title of nobility.

[State imposts and duties.—2.] No State shall, without the consent of the Congress, lay any imposts or duties on imports or exports, except what may be absolutely necessary for executing its inspection laws; and the net produce of all duties and imposts, laid by any State on imports or exports, shall be for the use of the Treasury of the United States; and all such laws shall be subject to the revision and control of the Congress.

[Further restrictions on powers of States.—3.] No State shall, without the consent of Congress, lay any duty of tonnage, keep troops, or ships of war in time of peace, enter into any agreement or compact

5. *See* the 16th Amendment.

with another state, or with a foreign power, or engage in war, unless actually invaded, or in such imminent danger as will not admit of delay.

Article II

Section 1

[The president; the executive power.—1.] The executive power shall be vested in a President of the United States of America. He shall hold his office during the term of four years, and, together with the Vice President, chosen for the same term, be elected, as follows

[Appointment and qualifications of presidential electors.—2.] Each State shall appoint, in such manner as the Legislature thereof may direct, a number of electors, equal to the whole number of Senators and Representatives to which the State may be entitled in the Congress: but no Senator or Representative, or person holding an office of trust or profit under the United States, shall be appointed an elector.

[Original method of electing the president and vice president.[6]] (The electors shall meet in their respective States, and vote by ballot for two persons, of whom one at least shall not be an inhabitant of the same State with themselves. And they shall make a list of all the persons voted for, and of the number of votes for each; which list they shall sign and certify, and transmit sealed to the seat of the Government of the United States, directed to the President of the Senate. The President of the Senate shall, in the presence of the Senate and House of Representatives, open all the certificates, and the votes shall then be counted. The person having the greatest number of votes shall be the President, if such number be a majority of the whole number of electors appointed; and if there be more than one who have such majority, and have an equal number of votes, then the House of Representatives shall immediately choose by ballot one of them for President; and if no person have a majority, then from the five highest on the list the said House shall in like manner choose the President. But in choosing the President, the votes shall be taken by States, the representation from each State having one vote; A quorum for this purpose shall consist of a member or members from two thirds of the States, and a majority of all the states shall be necessary to a choice. In every case, after the choice of the President, the person having the greatest number of votes of the electors shall be the Vice President. But if there should remain two or more who have equal votes, the Senate should choose from them by ballot the Vice President.)

[Congress may determine time of choosing electors and day for casting their votes.—3.] The Congress may determine the time of choosing the electors, and the day on which they shall give their votes; which day shall be the same throughout the United States.

[Qualifications for the office of president.[7]—4.] No person except a natural born citizen, or a citizen of the United States, at the time of the adoption of this Constitution, shall be eligible to the office of President; neither shall any person be eligible to that office who shall not have attained to the age of thirty-five years, and been fourteen years a resident within the United States.

[Filling vacancy in the office of president.[8]—5.] In case of the removal of the President from office, or of his death, resignation, or inability to discharge the powers and duties of the said office, the same shall devolve on the Vice President, and the Congress may by law provide for the case of removal, death, resignation or inability, both of the President and Vice President, declaring what officer shall then act as President, and such officer shall act accordingly, until the disability be removed, or a President shall be elected.

[Compensation of the president.—6.] The President shall, at stated times, receive for his services, a compensation, which shall neither be increased nor diminished during the period for which he shall have been elected, and he shall not receive within that period any other emolument from the United States, or any of them.

[Oath to be taken by the president.—7.] Before he enter on the execution of his office, he shall take the following oath or affirmation:—"I do solemnly swear (or affirm) that I will faithfully execute the office of President of the United States, and will to the best of my ability, preserve, protect, and defend the Constitution of the United States."

Section 2

[The president to be commander in chief of army and navy and head of executive departments; may grant reprieves and pardons.—1.] The President shall be Commander in Chief of the Army and Navy of the United States, and of the militia of the several States, when called into the actual service of the United States; he may require the opinion, in writing, of the principal officer in each of the executive departments, upon any subject relating to the duties of their respective offices, and he shall have power to grant reprieves and pardons for offences against the United States, except in cases of impeachment.

[President may, with concurrence of Senate, make treaties, appoint ambassadors, etc.; appointment of inferior officers, authority of Congress over.—2.] He shall have power, by and with the advice and consent of the Senate, to make treaties, provided two thirds of the Senators present concur; and he shall nominate, and by and with the advice and consent of the Senate, shall appoint ambassadors, other public ministers and consuls, judges of the Supreme Court, and all other officers of the United States, whose appointments are not herein otherwise provided for, and which shall be established by law: but the Congress may by law vest the appointment of such inferior officers, as they think proper, in the President alone, in the courts of law, or in the heads of departments.

[President may fill vacancies in office during recess of Senate.—3.] The President shall have power to fill up all vacancies that may happen during the recess of the Senate, by granting commissions which shall expire at the end of their session.

6. This clause has been superseded by the 12th Amendment. 7. For qualifications of the vice president, *see* the 12th Amendment. 8. Amended by the 20th Amendment, Sections 3 and 4.

Section 3

[President to give advice to Congress; may convene or adjourn it on certain occasions; to receive ambassadors, etc.; have laws executed and commission all officers.] He shall from time to time give to the Congress information of the state of the Union, and recommend to their consideration such measures as he shall judge necessary and expedient; he may, on extraordinary occasions, convene both Houses, or either of them, and in case of disagreement between them, with respect to the time of adjournment, he may adjourn them to such time as he shall think proper; he shall receive ambassadors and other public ministers: he shall take care that the laws be faithfully executed, and shall commission all the officers of the United States.

Section 4

[All civil officers removable by impeachment.] The President, Vice President, and all civil officers of the United States shall be removed from office on impeachment for, and conviction of, treason, bribery, or other high crimes and misdemeanors.

Article III

Section 1

[Judicial powers; how vested; term of office and compensation of judges.] The judicial Power of the United States, shall be vested in one Supreme Court, and in such inferior courts as the Congress may from time to time ordain and establish. The judges, both of the supreme and inferior courts, shall hold their offices during good behavior, and shall, at stated times, receive for their services, a compensation, which shall not be diminished during their continuance in office.

Section 2

[Jurisdiction of federal courts[9]—1.] The judicial power shall extend to all cases, in law and equity, arising under this Constitution, the laws of the United States, and treaties made, or which shall be made, under their authority; to all cases affecting ambassadors, other public ministers and consuls; to all cases of admiralty and maritime jurisdiction; to controversies to which the United States, shall be a party; to controversies between two or more States; between a State and citizens of another State; between citizens of different States; between citizens of the same State claiming lands under grants of different states, and between a State, or the citizens thereof, and foreign states, citizens, or subjects.

[Original and appellate jurisdiction of Supreme Court.—2.] In all cases affecting ambassadors, other public ministers and consuls, and those in which a State shall be party, the Supreme Court shall have original jurisdiction. In all the other cases before mentioned, the Supreme Court shall have appellate jurisdiction, both as to law and fact, with such exceptions, and under such regulations, as the Congress shall make.

[Trial of all crimes, except impeachment, to be by jury.—3.] The trial of all crimes, except in cases of impeachment, shall be by jury; and such trial shall be held in the State where the said crimes shall have been committed; but when not committed within any State, the trial shall be at such place or places as the Congress may by law have directed.

Section 3

[Treason defined; conviction of.—1.] Treason against the United States, shall consist only in levying war against them, or, in adhering to their enemies, giving them aid and comfort. No person shall be convicted of treason unless on the testimony of two witnesses to the same overt act, or on confession in open court.

[Congress to declare punishment for treason; proviso.—2.] The Congress shall have power to declare the punishment of treason, but no attainder of treason shall work corruption of blood, or forfeiture except during the life of the person attained.

Article IV

Section 1

[Each state to give full faith and credit to the public acts and records of other states.] Full faith and credit shall be given in each State to the public acts, records, and judicial proceedings of every other State. And the Congress may by general laws prescribe the manner in which such acts, records, and proceedings shall be proved, and the effect thereof.

Section 2

[Privileges of citizens.—1.] The citizens of each State shall be entitled to all privileges and immunities of citizens in the several States.

[Extradition between the several states.—2.] A person charged in any State with treason, felony, or other crime, who shall flee from justice, and be found in another State, shall on demand of the Executive authority of the State from which he fled, be delivered up, to be removed to the State having jurisdiction of the crime.

[Persons held to labor or service in one state, fleeing to another, to be returned.—3.] No person held to service or labor in one State, under the laws thereof, escaping into another, shall, in consequence of any law or regulation therein, be discharged from such service or labor, but shall be delivered up on claim of the party to whom such service or labor may be due.

Section 3

[New states.—1.] New States may be admitted by the Congress into this Union; but no new State shall be formed or erected within the jurisdiction of any other State; nor any State be formed by the junction of two or more States, or parts of States, without the consent of the Legislatures of the States concerned as well as of the Congress.

[Regulations concerning territory.—2.] The Congress shall have power to dispose of and make all needful rules and regulations respecting the territory or other property belonging to the United States; and nothing in this Constitution shall be so construed as to prejudice any claims of the United States, or of any particular State.

Section 4

[Republican form of government and protection guaranteed the several states.] The United States shall guarantee to every State in this Union a Republican form of government, and shall protect each of them against invasion; and on application of the Legislature, or of the Executive (when the Legislature cannot be convened) against domestic violence.

9. This section is abridged by the 11th Amendment.

Article V

[Ways in which the Constitution can be amended.] The Congress, whenever two thirds of both Houses shall deem it necessary, shall propose amendments to this Constitution, or, on the application of the Legislatures of two thirds of the several States shall call a convention for proposing amendments, which, in either case, shall be valid to all intents and purposes, as part of this Constitution, when ratified by the Legislatures of three fourths of the several States, or by conventions in three fourths thereof, as the one or the other mode of ratification may be proposed by the Congress; provided that no amendment which may be made prior to the year one thousand eight hundred and eight shall in any manner affect the first and fourth clauses in the ninth Section of the first Article; and that no State, without its consent, shall be deprived of its equal suffrage in the Senate.

Article VI

[Debts contracted under the confederation secured.—1.] All debts contracted and engagements entered into, before the adoption of this Constitution, shall be as valid against the United States under this Constitution, as under the Confederation.

[Constitution, laws, and treaties of the United States to be supreme.—2.] This Constitution, and the laws of the United States which shall be made in pursuance thereof; and all treaties made, or which shall be made, under the authority of the United States, shall be the supreme law of the land; and the judges in every State shall be bound thereby, any thing in the Constitution or laws of any State to the contrary notwithstanding.

[Who shall take constitutional oath; no religious test as to official qualification.—3.] The Senators and Representatives before mentioned, and the members of the several State Legislatures, and all executive and judicial officers, both of the United States and of the several States, shall be bound by oath or affirmation, to support this Constitution; but no religious test shall ever be required as a qualification to any office or public trust under the United States.

Article VII

[Constitution to be considered adopted when ratified by nine states.] The ratification of the conventions of nine States shall be sufficient for the establishment of this Constitution between the States so ratifying the same.

Done in convention by the unanimous consent of the States present the seventeenth day of September in the year of our Lord one thousand seven hundred and eighty seven and of the independence of the United States of America the Twelfth. In witness whereof we have hereunto subscribed our names.

George Washington
President and Deputy from Virginia

New Hampshire
John Langdon
Nicholas Gilman

Massachusetts
Nathaniel Gorham
Rufus King

Connecticut
Wm. Saml. Johnson
Roger Sherman

New York
Alexander Hamilton

New Jersey
Wil. Livingston
Wm. Paterson
David Brearley
Jona. Dayton

Pennsylvania
B. Franklin
Thomas Mifflin
Robt. Morris
Geo. Clymer
Thos. FitzSimons
Jared Ingersoll
James Wilson
Gouv. Morris

Delaware
Geo. Read
Gunning Bedford Jun.
John Dickinson
Richard Bassett
Jaco. Broom

Maryland
James McHenry
Dan. of St. Thos. Jenifer
Danl. Carroll

Virginia
John Blair
James Madison, Jr.

North Carolina
Wm. Blount
Richd Dobbs Spaight
Hu. Williamson

South Carolina
J. Rutledge
Charles Cotesworth Pinckney
Charles Pinckney
Pierce Butler

Georgia
William Few
Abr. Baldwin

Attest: William Jackson, Secretary

Amendments to the Constitution of the United States

(Amendments I to X inclusive, popularly known as the Bill of Rights, were proposed and sent to the states by the first session of the First Congress. They were ratified Dec. 15, 1791.)

Amendment I

[Freedom of religion, speech, of the press, and right of petition.] Congress shall make no law respecting an establishment of religion, or prohibiting the free exercise thereof; or abridging the freedom of speech, or of the press; or the right of the people peaceably to assemble, and to petition the Government for a redress of grievances.

Amendment II

[Right of people to bear arms not to be infringed.] A well regulated militia, being necessary to the security of a free State, the right of the people to keep and bear arms, shall not be infringed.

Amendment III

[Quartering of troops.] No soldier shall, in time of peace be quartered in any house, without the consent of the owner, nor in time of war, but in a manner to be prescribed by law.

Amendment IV

[Persons and houses to be secure from unreasonable searches and seizures.] The right of the people to be secure in their persons, houses, papers, and effects, against unreasonable searches and seizures, shall not be violated, and no warrants shall issue, but upon probable cause, supported by oath or affirmation, and particularly describing the place to be searched, and the persons or things to be seized.

Amendment V

[Trials for crimes; just compensation for private property taken for public use.] No person shall be held to answer for a capital, or otherwise infamous crime, unless on a presentment or indictment of a Grand Jury, except in cases arising in the land or naval forces, or in the militia, when in actual service in time of war or public danger; nor shall any person be subject for the same offence to be twice put in jeopardy of life or limb; nor shall be compelled in any criminal case to be a witness, against himself, nor be deprived of life, liberty, or property, without due process of law; nor shall private property be taken for public use, without just compensation.

Amendment VI

[Civil rights in trials for crimes enumerated.] In all criminal prosecutions, the accused shall enjoy the right to a speedy and public trial, by an impartial jury of the State and district wherein the crime shall have been committed, which district shall have been previously ascertained by law, and to be informed of the nature and cause of the accusation; to be confronted with the witnesses against him; to have compulsory process for obtaining witnesses in his favor, and to have the assistance of counsel for his defense.

Amendment VII

[Civil rights in civil suits.] In suits at common law, where the value in controversy shall exceed twenty dollars, the right of trial by jury shall be preserved, and no fact tried by a jury, shall be otherwise re-examined in any court of the United States, than according to the rules of the common law.

Amendment VIII

[Excessive bail, fines, and punishments prohibited.] Excessive bail shall not be required, nor excessive fines imposed, nor cruel and unusual punishments inflicted.

Amendment IX

[Reserved rights of people.] The enumeration in the Constitution, of certain rights, shall not be construed to deny or disparage others retained by the people.

Amendment X

[Powers not delegated, reserved to states and people respectively.] The powers not delegated to the United States by the Constitution, nor prohibited by it to the States, are reserved to the States, respectively, or to the people.

Amendment XI

(The proposed amendment was sent to the states Mar. 5, 1794, by the Third Congress. It was ratified Feb. 7, 1795.)

[Judicial power of United States not to extend to suits against a state.] The judicial power of the United States shall not be construed to extend to any suit in law or equity, commenced or prosecuted against one of the United States by citizens of another State, or by citizens or subjects of any foreign state.

Amendment XII

(The proposed amendment was sent to the states Dec. 12, 1803, by the Eighth Congress. It was ratified July 27, 1804.)

[Present mode of electing president and vice president by electors.[1]]

The electors shall meet in their respective states, and vote by ballot for President and Vice President, one of whom, at least, shall not be an inhabitant of the same state with themselves; they shall name in their ballots the person voted for as President, and in distinct ballots the person voted for as Vice President, and they shall make distinct lists of all persons voted for as President, and of all persons voted for as Vice President, and of the number of votes for each, which lists they shall sign and certify, and transmit sealed to the seat of the government of the United States, directed to the President of the Senate; the President of the Senate shall, in the presence of the Senate and House of Representatives, open all the certificates and the votes shall then be counted; the person having the greatest number of votes for President, shall be the President, if such number be a majority of the whole number of electors appointed; and if no person have such majority, then from the persons having the highest numbers not exceeding three on the list of those voted for as President, the House of Representatives shall choose immediately, by ballot, the President. But in choosing the President, the votes shall be taken by states, the representation from each State having one vote; a quorum for this purpose shall consist of a member or members from two thirds of the states, and a majority of all the states shall be necessary to a choice. And if the House of Representatives shall not choose a President whenever the right of choice shall devolve upon them, before the fourth day of March next following, then the Vice President shall act as President, as in the case of the death or other constitutional disability of the President. The person having the greatest number of votes as Vice President, shall be the Vice President, if such number be a majority of the whole number of electors appointed, and if no person have a majority, then from the two highest numbers on the list, the Senate shall choose the Vice President; a quorum for the purpose shall consist of two thirds of the whole

1. Amended by the 20th Amendment, Sections 3 and 4.

number of Senators, and a majority of the whole number shall be necessary to a choice. But no person constitutionally ineligible to the office of President shall be eligible to that of Vice President of the United States.

Amendment XIII

(The proposed amendment was sent to the states Feb. 1, 1865, by the Thirty-eighth Congress. It was ratified Dec. 6, 1865.)

Section 1

[Slavery prohibited.] Neither slavery nor involuntary servitude, except as a punishment for crime whereof the party shall have been duly convicted, shall exist within the United States, or any place subject to their jurisdiction.

Section 2

[Congress given power to enforce this article.] Congress shall have power to enforce this article by appropriate legislation.

Amendment XIV

(The proposed amendment was sent to the states June 16, 1866, by the Thirty-ninth Congress. It was ratified July 9, 1868.)

Section 1

[Citizenship defined; privileges of citizens.] All persons born or naturalized in the United States, and subject to the jurisdiction thereof, are citizens of the United States and of the State wherein they reside. No State shall make or enforce any law which shall abridge the privileges or immunities of citizens of the United States; nor shall any State deprive any person of life, liberty, or property, without due process of law; nor deny to any person within its jurisdiction the equal protection of the laws.

Section 2

[Apportionment of Representatives.] Representatives shall be apportioned among the several States according to their respective numbers, counting the whole number of persons in each State, excluding Indians not taxed. But when the right to vote at any election for the choice of electors for President and Vice President of the United States, Representatives in Congress, the executive and judicial officers of a State, or the members of the Legislature thereof, is denied to any of the male inhabitants of such State, being twenty-one years of age, and citizens of the United States, or in any way abridged, except for participation in rebellion, or other crime, the basis of representation therein shall be reduced in the proportion which the number of such male citizens shall bear to the whole number of male citizens twenty-one years of age in such State.

Section 3

[Disqualification for office; removal of disability.] No person shall be a Senator or Representative in Congress, or elector of President and Vice President, or hold any office, civil or military, under the United States, or under any State, who, having previously taken an oath, as a member of Congress, or as an officer of the United States, or as a member of any State Legislature, or as an executive or judicial officer of any State, to support the Constitution of the United States, shall have engaged in insurrection or rebellion against the same, or given aid or comfort to the enemies thereof. But Congress may, by a vote of two thirds of each House, remove such disability.

Section 4

[Public debt not to be questioned; payment of debts and claims incurred in aid of rebellion forbidden.] The validity of the public debt of the United States, authorized by law, including debts incurred for payment of pensions and bounties for services in suppressing insurrection or rebellion, shall not be questioned. But neither the United States nor any State shall assume or pay any debt or obligation incurred in aid of insurrection or rebellion against the United States, or any claim for the loss or emancipation of any slave; but all such debts, obligations, and claims shall be held illegal and void.

Section 5

[Congress given power to enforce this article.] The Congress shall have power to enforce, by appropriate legislation, the provisions of this article.

Amendment XV

(The proposed amendment was sent to the states Feb. 27, 1869, by the Fortieth Congress. It was ratified Feb. 3, 1870.)

Section 1

[Right of certain citizens to vote established.] The right of citizens of the United States to vote shall not be denied or abridged by the United States or by any State on account of race, color, or previous condition of servitude.

Section 2

[Congress given power to enforce this article.] The Congress shall have power to enforce this article by appropriate legislation.

Amendment XVI

(The proposed amendment was sent to the states July 12, 1909, by the Sixty-first Congress. It was ratified Feb. 3, 1913.)

[Taxes on income; Congress given power to lay and collect.] The Congress shall have power to lay and collect taxes on incomes, from whatever source derived, without apportionment among the several States, and without regard to any census or enumeration.

Amendment XVII

(The proposed amendment was sent to the states May 16, 1912, by the Sixty-second Congress. It was ratified April 8, 1913.)

[Election of U.S. senators; filling of vacancies; qualifications of electors.] The Senate of the United States shall be composed of two Senators from each State, elected by the people thereof, for six years; and each Senator shall have one vote. The electors in each State shall have the qualifications requisite for electors of the most numerous branch of the State Legislatures.

When vacancies happen in the representation of any State in the Senate, the executive authority of such State shall issue writs of election to fill such vacancies: Provided, that the legislature of any State may empower the executive thereof to make temporary appointment until the people fill the vacancies by election as the legislature may direct.

This amendment shall not be so construed as to affect the election or term of any Senator chosen before it becomes valid as part of the Constitution.

Amendment XVIII[2]

(The proposed amendment was sent to the states Dec. 18, 1917, by the Sixty-fifth Congress. It was ratified by three quarters of the states by Jan. 16, 1919, and became effective Jan. 16, 1920.)

Section 1

[Manufacture, sale, or transportation of intoxicating liquors, for beverage purposes, prohibited.] After one year from the ratification of this article the manufacture, sale, or transportation of intoxicating liquors within, the importation thereof into, or the exportation thereof from the United States and all territory subject to the jurisdiction thereof for beverage purposes is hereby prohibited.

Section 2

[Congress and the several states given concurrent power to pass appropriate legislation to enforce this article.] The Congress and the several States shall have concurrent power to enforce this article by appropriate legislation.

Section 3

[Provisions of article to become operative, when adopted by three fourths of the states.] This article shall be inoperative unless it shall have been ratified as an amendment to the Constitution by the legislatures of the several States, as provided in the Constitution, within seven years from the date of the submission hereof to the States by Congress.

Amendment XIX

(The proposed amendment was sent to the states June 4, 1919, by the Sixty-sixth Congress. It was ratified Aug. 18, 1920.)

[The right of citizens to vote shall not be denied because of sex.] The right of citizens of the United States to vote shall not be denied or abridged by the United States or by any State on account of sex.

[Congress given power to enforce this article.] Congress shall have power to enforce this article by appropriate legislation.

Amendment XX

(The proposed amendment, sometimes called the "Lame Duck Amendment," was sent to the states Mar. 3, 1932, by the Seventy-second Congress. It was ratified Jan. 23, 1933; but, in accordance with Section 5, Sections 1 and 2, did not go into effect until Oct. 15, 1933.)

Section 1

[Terms of president, vice president, senators, and representatives.] The terms of the President and Vice President shall end at noon on the twentieth day of January, and the terms of Senators and Representatives at noon on the third day of January, of the years in which such terms would have ended if this article had not been ratified; and the terms of their successors shall then begin.

Section 2

[Time of assembling Congress.] The Congress shall assemble at least once in every year, and such meeting shall begin at noon on the third day of January, unless they shall by law appoint a different day.

Section 3

[Filling vacancy in office of president.] If, at the time fixed for the beginning of the term of the President, the President-elect shall have died, the Vice President-elect shall become President. If a President shall not have been chosen before the time fixed for the beginning of his term, or if the President-elect shall have failed to qualify, then the Vice President shall have qualified; and the Congress may by law provide for the case wherein neither a President-elect nor a Vice President-elect shall have qualified, declaring who shall then act as President, or the manner in which one who is to act shall be selected, and such person shall act accordingly until a President or Vice President shall have qualified.

Section 4

[Power of Congress in presidential succession.] The Congress may by law provide for the case of the death of any of the persons from whom the House of Representatives may choose a President whenever the right of choice shall have devolved upon them, and for the case of the death of any of the persons from whom the Senate may choose a Vice President whenever the right of choice shall have devolved upon them.

Section 5

[Time of taking effect.] Sections 1 and 2 shall take effect on the 15th day of October following the ratification of this article.

Section 6

[Ratification.] This article shall be inoperative unless it shall have been ratified as an amendment to the Constitution by the legislatures of three fourths of the several States within seven years from the date of its submission.

Amendment XXI

(The proposed amendment was sent to the states Feb. 20, 1933, by the Seventy-second Congress. It was ratified Dec. 5, 1933.)

Section 1

[Repeal of Prohibition Amendment.] The eighteenth article of amendment to the Constitution of the United States is hereby repealed.

Section 2

[Transportation of intoxicating liquors.] The transportation or importation into any State, territory, or possession of the United States for delivery or use therein of intoxicating liquors, in violation of the laws thereof, is hereby prohibited.

Section 3

[Ratification.] This article shall be inoperative unless it shall have been ratified as an amendment to the Constitution by convention in the several States, as provided in the Constitution, within seven years from the date of the submission thereof to the States by the Congress.

Amendment XXII

(The proposed amendment was sent to the states Mar. 21, 1947, by the Eightieth Congress. It was ratified Feb. 27, 1951.)

2. Repealed by the 21st Amendment.

Section 1

[Limit to number of terms a president may serve.] No person shall be elected to the office of the President more than twice, and no person who has held the office of President, or acted as President, for more than two years of a term to which some other person was elected President shall be elected to the office of the President more than once. But this article shall not apply to any person holding the office of President when this article was proposed by the Congress, and shall not prevent any person who may be holding the office of President, or acting as President, during the term within which this article becomes operative from holding the office of President or acting as President during the remainder of such term.

Section 2

[Ratification.] This article shall be inoperative unless it shall have been ratified as an amendment to the Constitution by the legislatures of three fourths of the several States within seven years from the date of its submission to the States by the Congress.

Amendment XXIII

(The proposed amendment was sent to the states June 16, 1960, by the Eighty-sixth Congress. It was ratified March 29, 1961.)

Section 1

[Electors for the District of Columbia.] The District constituting the seat of Government of the United States shall appoint in such manner as the Congress may direct: A number of electors of President and Vice President equal to the whole number of Senators and Representatives in Congress to which the District would be entitled if it were a State, but in no event more than the least populous State; they shall be in addition to those appointed by the States, but they shall be considered, for the purposes of the election of President and Vice President, to be electors appointed by a State; and they shall meet in the District and perform such duties as provided by the twelfth article of amendment.

Section 2

[Congress given power to enforce this article.] The Congress shall have the power to enforce this article by appropriate legislation.

Amendment XXIV

(The proposed amendment was sent to the states Aug. 27, 1962, by the Eighty-seventh Congress. It was ratified Jan. 23, 1964.)

Section 1

[Payment of poll tax or other taxes not to be prerequisite for voting in federal elections.] The right of citizens of the United States to vote in any primary or other election for President or Vice President, for electors for President or Vice President, or for Senator or Representative in Congress, shall not be denied or abridged by the United States or any State by reasons of failure to pay any poll tax or other tax.

Section 2

[Congress given power to enforce this article.] The Congress shall have the power to enforce this article by appropriate legislation.

Amendment XXV

(The proposed amendment was sent to the states July 6, 1965, by the Eighty-ninth Congress. It was ratified Feb. 10, 1967.)

Section 1

[Succession of vice president to presidency.] In case of the removal of the President from office or of his death or resignation, the Vice President shall become President.

Section 2

[Vacancy in office of vice president.] Whenever there is a vacancy in the office of the Vice President, the President shall nominate a Vice President who shall take office upon confirmation by a majority vote of both Houses of Congress.

Section 3

[Vice president as acting president.] Whenever the President transmits to the President pro tempore of the Senate and the Speaker of the House of Representatives his written declaration that he is unable to discharge the powers and duties of his office, and until he transmits to them a written declaration to the contrary, such powers and duties shall be discharged by the Vice President as Acting President.

Section 4

[Vice president as acting president.] Whenever the Vice President and a majority of either the principal officers of the executive departments or of such other body as Congress may by law provide, transmit to the President pro tempore of the Senate and the Speaker of the House of Representatives their written declaration that the President is unable to discharge the powers and duties of his office, the Vice President shall immediately assume the powers and duties of the office as Acting President.

Thereafter, when the President transmits to the President pro tempore of the Senate and the Speaker of the House of Representatives his written declaration that no inability exists, he shall resume the powers and duties of his office unless the Vice President and a majority of either the principal officers of the executive department or of such other body as Congress may by law provide, transmit within four days to the President pro tempore of the Senate and the Speaker of the House of Representatives their written declaration that the President is unable to discharge the powers and duties of his office. Thereupon Congress shall decide the issue, assembling within forty-eight hours for that purpose if not in session. If the Congress, within twenty-one days after receipt of the latter written declaration, or, if Congress is not in session, within twenty-one days after Congress is required to assemble, determines by two thirds vote of both Houses that the President is unable to discharge the powers and duties of his office, the Vice President shall continue to discharge the same as Acting President; otherwise, the President shall resume the powers and duties of his office.

Amendment XXVI

(The proposed amendment was sent to the states Mar. 23, 1971, by the Ninety-second Congress. It was ratified July 1, 1971.)

Section 1

[Voting for 18-year-olds.] The right of citizens of the United States, who are 18 years of age or older, to vote shall not be denied or abridged by the United States or by any state on account of age.

Section 2

[Congress given power to enforce this article.] The Congress shall have power to enforce this article by appropriate legislation.

Amendment XXVII

(Ratified May 7, 1992.)

[Congressional raises.] No law, varying the compensation for the services of the Senators and Representatives, shall take effect, until an election of Representatives shall have intervened.

Lincoln's Gettysburg Address

The Battle of Gettysburg, one of the most noted battles of the Civil War, was fought on July 1–3, 1863. On Nov. 19, 1863, the field was dedicated as a national cemetery by President Lincoln in a two-minute speech that was to become immortal. At the time of its delivery the speech was relegated to the inside pages of the papers, while a two-hour address by Edward Everett, the leading orator of the time, caught the headlines.

> Fourscore and seven years ago our fathers brought forth on this continent a new nation conceived in liberty and dedicated to the proposition that all men are created equal. Now we are engaged in a great civil war testing whether that nation, or any nation so conceived and so dedicated, can long endure. We are met on a great battlefield of that war. We have come to dedicate a portion of that field as a final resting-place for those who here gave their lives that that nation might live. It is altogether fitting and proper that we should do this. But, in a larger sense, we cannot dedicate, we cannot consecrate, we cannot hallow this ground. The brave men, living and dead, who struggled here have consecrated it far above our poor power to add or detract. The world will little note nor long remember what we say here, but it can never forget what they did here. It is for us the living rather to be dedicated here to the unfinished work which they who fought here have thus far so nobly advanced. It is rather for us to be here dedicated to the great task remaining before us—that from these honored dead we take increased devotion to that cause for which they gave the last full measure of devotion—that we here highly resolve that these dead shall not have died in vain, that this nation under God shall have a new birth of freedom, and that government of the people, by the people, for the people shall not perish from the earth.

Assassinations and Attempts in U.S. Since 1865

Lincoln, Abraham (president of U.S.): Shot April 14, 1865, in Washington, DC, by John Wilkes Booth; died April 15.

Seward, William H. (secretary of state): Escaped assassination (though injured) April 14, 1865, in Washington, DC, by Lewis Powell (or Paine), accomplice of John Wilkes Booth.

Garfield, James A. (president of U.S.): Shot July 2, 1881, in Washington, DC, by Charles J. Guiteau; died Sept. 19.

McKinley, William (president of U.S.): Shot Sept. 6, 1901, in Buffalo by Leon Czolgosz; died Sept. 14.

Roosevelt, Theodore (ex-president of U.S.): Escaped assassination (though shot) Oct. 14, 1912, in Milwaukee while campaigning for president.

Cermak, Anton J. (mayor of Chicago): Shot Feb. 15, 1933, in Miami by Giuseppe Zangara, who attempted to assassinate Franklin D. Roosevelt; Cermak died March 6.

Roosevelt, Franklin D. (president-elect of U.S.): Escaped assassination unhurt Feb. 15, 1933, in Miami.

Long, Huey P. (U.S. senator from Louisiana): Shot Sept. 8, 1935, in Baton Rouge by Dr. Carl A. Weiss; died Sept. 10.

Truman, Harry S. (president of U.S.): Escaped assassination unhurt Nov. 1, 1950, in Washington, DC, as 2 Puerto Rican nationalists attempted to shoot their way into Blair House.

Kennedy, John F. (president of U.S.): Shot Nov. 22, 1963, in Dallas, Tex., allegedly by Lee Harvey Oswald; died same day. Injured was Gov. John B. Connally of Texas. Oswald was shot and killed two days later by Jack Ruby.

Malcolm X, also known as El-Hajj Malik El-Shabazz (black activist): Shot and killed in a New York City auditorium, Feb. 21, 1965; his killer(s) were never positively identified.

King, Martin Luther, Jr. (civil rights leader): Shot April 4, 1968, in Memphis by James Earl Ray; died same day.

Kennedy, Robert F. (U.S. senator from New York): Shot June 5, 1968, in Los Angeles by Sirhan Bishara Sirhan; died June 6.

Wallace, George C. (governor of Alabama): Shot and critically wounded in assassination attempt May 15, 1972, at Laurel, Md., by Arthur Herman Bremer. Wallace paralyzed from waist down.

Ford, Gerald R. (president of U.S.): Escaped assassination attempt Sept. 5, 1975, in Sacramento, Calif., by Lynette Alice (Squeaky) Fromme, who pointed but did not fire .45-caliber pistol. Escaped assassination attempt in San Francisco, Calif., Sept. 22, 1975, by Sara Jane Moore, who fired one shot from a .38-caliber pistol that was deflected.

Jordan, Vernon E., Jr. (civil rights leader): Shot and critically wounded in assassination attempt May 29, 1980, in Fort Wayne, Ind.

Reagan, Ronald (president of U.S.): Shot in left lung in Washington by John W. Hinckley, Jr., on March 30, 1981; three others also wounded.

Profile of the United States

This profile was created by the editors of the almanac from many data sources. Most figures are approximate. For additional details about the U.S., please refer to the appropriate sections of the almanac.

Geography

Number of states: 50
Territories: 14
Area (2000): total: 3,794,083 sq mi (9,826,675 sq km), land only: 3,537,438 sq mi (9,161,964 sq km), water: 256,645 sq mi (664,711 sq km). Share of world land area (1990): 6.2%
Northernmost point: Point Barrow, Alaska
Easternmost point: West Quoddy Head, Maine
Southernmost point: Ka Lae (South Cape), Hawaii
Westernmost point: Cape Wrangell, Alaska[1]
Geographic center (50 states): in Butte County, S.D. (44′ 58′ N. lat., 103′ 46′ W. long.)
Highest point: Mt. McKinley, Alaska (20,320 ft)
Lowest point: Death Valley, Calif. (282 ft below sea level)

1. The extreme points are measured from the geographic center of the United States (incl. Alaska and Hawaii), west of Castle Rock, S.D., 44° 58′ N. lat., 103° 46′ W. long. If measured from the prime meridian in Greenwich, England, Cape Wrangell, Alaska, would be the easternmost point.

Population

(Based on Census 2000 data unless otherwise noted.)

Total Resident Pop. (Sept. 2003 est.)[1]: 291,950,153
Population density: 79.6 people per sq mi
Mean center of population: 3 mi east of Edgar Springs in Phelps County, Mo.
Males: 138,053,563 (49.1% of pop.)
Females: 143,368,343 (50.9% of pop.)
White: 211,460,626 (75.1% of pop.)
Black: 34,658,190 (12.3% of pop.)
Asian: 10,242,998 (3.6% of pop.)
American Indian and Alaska Native: 2,475,956 (0.9% of pop.)
Hispanic/Latino[2]: 35,305,818 (12.5% of pop.)
Native Hawaiian and Other Pacific Islander: 398,835 (0.1% of pop.)
Median age: 35.3
Metropolitan population: 225,981,679
Nonmetropolitan population: 55,440,227
Families: 71,787,347
Average family size: 3.14
Homeownership (2000): 67.4% of pop.
Married couples (2000): 56,497,000
Never married (2000): 48,200,000
Divorced (2000): 19,800,000
Widowed (2000): 13,700,000

1. Excludes the U.S. Armed Forces overseas. 2. People of Hispanic or Latino origin may be of any race.

Vital Statistics

Births (2001): 4,025,933 (14.5 per 1,000 pop.)
Deaths (2001): 2,417,798 (8.5 per 1,000 pop.)
Marriages (2001): 2,327,000 (8.4 per 1,000 pop.)
Divorces (2001): 4.0 per 1,000 pop.[1]
Infant mortality rate (2000): 6.9 per 1,000 live births
Legal abortions (1999): 861,789
Life expectancy (2000): Total U.S., both sexes, 77.0; total men, 74.3; total women, 79.7; white men, 74.9; white women, 80.1; black men, 68.3; black women, 75.2

1. U.S. totals no longer available.

Civilian Labor Force

All (2002): 144,863,000 (5.8% unemployed)
Men (2002): 77,500,000 (5.9% unemployed)
Women (2002): 67,363,000 (5.6% unemployed)
Work at home (2001 est.): 19.8 million
Farms (2002): 2,158,090; total acres (2002): 941,480,000
Avg. weekly earnings of workers (2002): $609
Avg. weekly hours of workers (2000): 34.5

Income and Credit

GDP (2002): $10,446.2 billion
Fed. Budget (2002): total receipts, $1,853.2 billion; total outlays, $2,011.0 billion; (2003 est.): total receipts, $2,048.1 billion; total outlays, $2,128.2 billion
Personal income per capita (2002): $30,941
Median four-person family income (2001): $63,278
Consumer credit outstanding (2002): $1,762.3 billion
Number below poverty level (2001): total, 32,907,000; white, 22,739,000; black, 8,136,000; Hispanic, 7,997,000; Asian and Pacific Islander, 1,275,000

Education

Public elementary school pupils, pre-K–grade 8 (2001)[1]: 33,854,000
Public secondary school pupils, grades 9–12 (2001)[1]: 13,722,000
Private elementary school pupils, K–grade 8 (2001)[1]: 4,668,000
Private secondary school pupils, grades 9–12 (2001)[1]: 1,276,000
High school dropout rate, ages 16–24 (2001): 10.7%
Total 2- and 4-year colleges and universities (2001): 4,182
Total higher education enrollment (2001): 14,563,224
Undergraduate (2001): 12,681,231
Graduate (2001): 1,806,803
Professional (2001): 303,190

1. Estimated

Conveniences

Radio stations (Sept. 2002): AM, 4,804; FM, 6,161
Television stations (Sept. 2002): 1,714
Registered automobiles (2000): 133,621,000
Daily newspaper circulation (2001): 55,578,000
Total TV households (2003): 106,700,000
Percent households with a TV set (2003): 98%
Avg. number TV sets per household (2000): 2.4
Cable TV households (2003): 70%
Avg. number TV households with VCRs (2003): 92%
Percent households with a computer (2001): 56.5%
Percent households with Internet access (2001): 50.5%

Crime

Total arrests (2001): 9,306,587
State, federal, and local prison inmates (2002): 2,019,234
Prisoners under sentence of death (2002): 3,593
Persons executed under civil authority (2001): 71
Law enforcement officers killed (2000): 135
Total murder victims (2001): 13,752
Violent crimes per 100,000 people (2001): 504.4
Property crimes per 100,000 people (2001): 3,656.1
Homicides per 100,000 people (2001): 5.6
Hate crime victims (2001): 12,016

U.S. Census Timeline

1787 Article 1, Section 2 of the U.S. Constitution requires that a census of the population be conducted every ten years so that the representatives in Congress and direct taxes might be apportioned.

1790 Federal marshals conduct the first census by going door-to-door through the 13 states plus the districts of Maine, Vermont, Kentucky, and the Southwest Territory (Tennessee). The marshals record the name of every householder and count the occupants in each house. African-American slaves are counted as three-fifths of a person, and American Indians, who do not pay taxes, are excluded. The census is completed in 18 months at a cost of $45,000. The census counts 3.9 million people.

1830 The first printed forms are used for collecting census data. Prior to this, marshals used sheets of paper or notebooks.

1850 All free persons, rather than just the head of house, are recorded by name, along with their occupation and place of birth.

1868 The Fourteenth Amendment to the Constitution is ratified, ending the three-fifths counting rule for African Americans.

1870 Although individuals have been identified as white or black since the 1790 census, American Indians are first enumerated in the 1870 census. (However, those in the Indian Territory or on reservations are not included in the official U.S. population count used for congressional apportionment until 1890.) The Chinese population is also counted for the first time in the 1870 census.

1880 Congress establishes a census office in the Department of the Interior, and the U.S. marshals who have previously collected census data are replaced by professional enumerators.

1890 For the first time simple machines are used to tabulate census data.

1902 Congress authorizes a permanent census office, which is transferred the following year to the Department of Commerce and Labor. (In 1913, when Commerce and Labor become separate departments, the U.S. Census Bureau is placed in the Department of Commerce.)

1940 Statistical sampling techniques are introduced, which allow the Census Bureau to create a "long form" answered by only a subset of the population.

1950 For the first time an electronic computer, UNIVAC I, is used to help tabulate results.

1960 In an effort to move toward self-enumeration, census forms are mailed to urban households to be completed and mailed back to the Census Bureau.

1970 Mail-in forms take precedence over door-to-door enumerators. For the first time, respondents are asked to check off whether they are of Spanish or Hispanic origin or descent.

1980 Although 1980 census is considered one of the most accurate in recent decades, New York City and civil rights groups file numerous lawsuits challenging the final results.

1990 The 1990 census is the first to be less accurate than the one preceding it (an estimated 8.4 million people are missed while another 4.4 million are counted twice). The problem is partly blamed on declining census participation: the response rate for Census 1990 is only 65%.

1999 The Supreme Court rules that statistical sampling—which allows for the estimation of certain populations, such as the homeless or minorities—cannot not be used to apportion congressional seats, although it can be used for other purposes.

2000 Employing some 860,000 temporary workers and costing $6 billion, Census 2000 is the largest peacetime mobilization of resources and personnel. For the first time, the Census Bureau runs a nationwide advertising campaign to encourage people to fill out their forms.

Colonial Population Estimates

(in round numbers)

Year	Population	Year	Population
1610	350	1700	250,900
1620	2,300	1710	331,700
1630	4,600	1720	466,200
1640	26,600	1730	629,400
1650	50,400	1740	905,600
1660	75,100	1750	1,170,800
1670	111,900	1760	1,593,600
1680	151,500	1770	2,148,100
1690	210,400	1780	2,780,400

Covers years before the establishment of the U.S. Census in 1790.

National Censuses[1]

Year	Resident population[2]	Land area, sq mi	Pop. per sq mi	Year	Resident population[2]	Land area, sq mi	Pop. per sq mi
1790	3,929,214	864,746	4.5	1900	75,994,575	2,969,834	25.6
1800	5,308,483	864,746	6.1	1910	91,972,266	2,969,565	31.0
1810	7,239,881	1,681,828	4.3	1920	105,710,620	2,969,451	35.6
1820	9,638,453	1,749,462	5.5	1930	122,775,046	2,977,128	41.2
1830	12,866,020	1,749,462	7.4	1940	131,669,275	2,977,128	44.2
1840	17,069,453	1,749,462	9.8	1950	150,697,361	2,974,726	50.7
1850	23,191,876	2,940,042	7.9	1960	179,323,175	3,540,911	50.6
1860	31,443,321	2,969,640	10.6	1970	203,302,031	3,540,023	57.4
1870	39,818,449	2,969,640	13.4	1980	226,545,805	3,539,289	64.0
1880	50,155,783	2,969,640	16.9	1990	248,709,873	3,536,278	70.3
1890	62,947,714	2,969,640	21.2	2000	281,421,906	3,537,441	79.6

1. Beginning with 1960, figures include Alaska and Hawaii. 2. Excludes armed forces overseas. *Source:* U.S. Bureau of the Census. Web: www.census.gov.

Profile of General Demographic Characteristics, 2000

Subject	Number	Percent
Total population	281,421,906	100.0%
Sex and age		
Male	138,053,563	49.1
Female	143,368,343	50.9
Under 5 years	19,175,798	6.8
5 to 9 years	20,549,505	7.3
10 to 14 years	20,528,072	7.3
15 to 19 years	20,219,890	7.2
20 to 24 years	18,964,001	6.7
25 to 34 years	39,891,724	14.2
35 to 44 years	45,148,527	16.0
45 to 54 years	37,677,952	13.4
55 to 59 years	13,469,237	4.8
60 to 64 years	10,805,447	3.8
65 to 74 years	18,390,986	6.5
75 to 84 years	12,361,180	4.4
85 years and over	4,239,587	1.5
Median age (years)	35.3	n.a.
18 years and over	209,128,094	74.3
Male	100,994,367	35.9
Female	108,133,727	38.4
21 years and over	196,899,193	70.0
62 years and over	41,256,029	14.7
65 years and over	34,991,753	12.4
Male	14,409,625	5.1
Female	20,582,128	7.3
Race		
One race	274,595,678	97.6
White	211,460,626	75.1
Black or African American	34,658,190	12.3
American Indian and Alaska Native	2,475,956	0.9
Asian	10,242,998	3.6
Asian Indian	1,678,765	0.6
Chinese	2,432,585	0.9
Filipino	1,850,314	0.7
Japanese	796,700	0.3
Korean	1,076,872	0.4
Vietnamese	1,122,528	0.4
Other Asian[1]	1,285,234	0.5
Native Hawaiian and Other Pacific Islander	398,835	0.1
Native Hawaiian	140,652	—
Guamanian or Chamorro	58,240	—
Samoan	91,029	—
Other Pacific Islander[2]	108,914	—
Some other race	15,359,073	5.5
Two or more races	6,826,228	2.4
Race alone or in combination with one or more other races:[3]		
White	216,930,975	77.1
Black or African American	36,419,434	12.9
American Indian and Alaska Native	4,119,301	1.5
Asian	11,898,828	4.2
Native Hawaiian and Other Pacific Islander	874,414	0.3
Some other race	18,521,486	6.6

Subject	Number	Percent
Hispanic or Latino and race		
Total population	**281,421,906**	**100.0%**
Hispanic or Latino (of any race)	35,305,818	12.5
Mexican	20,640,711	7.3
Puerto Rican	3,406,178	1.2
Cuban	1,241,685	0.4
Other Hispanic or Latino	10,017,244	3.6
Not Hispanic or Latino	246,116,088	87.5
White alone	194,552,774	69.1
Relationship		
Total population	**281,421,906**	**100.0%**
In households	273,643,273	97.2
Householder	105,480,101	37.5
Spouse	54,493,232	19.4
Child	83,393,392	29.6
Own child under 18	64,494,637	22.9
Other relatives	15,684,318	5.6
Under 18	6,042,435	2.1
Nonrelatives	14,592,230	5.2
Unmarried partner	5,475,768	1.9
In group quarters	7,778,633	2.8
Institutionalized pop.	4,059,039	1.4
Noninstitutionalized pop.	3,719,594	1.3
Household by type		
Total households	**105,480,101**	**100.0**
Family households (families)	71,787,347	68.1
With own children under 18	34,588,368	32.8
Married-couple family	54,493,232	51.7
With own children under 18	24,835,505	23.5
Female householder, no husband present	12,900,103	12.2
With own children under 18	7,561,874	7.2
Nonfamily households	33,692,754	31.9
Householder living alone	27,230,075	25.8
Householder 65 and over	9,722,857	9.2
Households with individuals under 18	38,022,115	36.0
Households with individuals 65 and over	24,672,708	23.4
Average household size	2.59	n.a.
Average family size	3.14	n.a.
Housing occupancy		
Total housing units	**115,904,641**	**100.0**
Occupied housing units	105,480,101	91.0
Vacant housing units	10,424,540	9.0
For seasonal, recreational, or occasional use	3,578,718	3.1
Homeowner vacancy rate (%)	1.7	n.a.
Rental vacancy rate (%)	6.8	n.a.
Housing tenure		
Occupied housing units	**105,480,101**	**100.0**
Owner-occupied housing units	69,815,753	66.2
Renter-occupied housing units	35,664,348	33.8
Average household size of owner-occupied units	2.69	n.a.
Average household size of renter-occupied units	2.40	n.a.

NOTES: (—) represents zero or rounds to zero; n.a. = not applicable. 1. Other Asian alone, or two or more Asian categories. 2. Other Pacific Islander alone, or two or more Native Hawaiian and Other Pacific Islander categories. 3. In combination with one or more of the other races listed. The six numbers may add to more than the total population and the six percentages may add to more than 100% because individuals may report more than one race. *Source:* U.S. Census Bureau, Census 2000. Web: www.census.gov.

Population by State

State	July 2002 pop.	2000	1990	1950	1900	1790
Alabama	4,486,508	4,447,100	4,040,587	3,061,743	1,828,697	—
Alaska	643,786	626,932	550,043	128,643	63,592	—
Arizona	5,456,453	5,130,632	3,665,228	749,587	122,931	—
Arkansas	2,710,079	2,673,400	2,350,725	1,909,511	1,311,564	—
California	35,116,033	33,871,648	29,760,021	10,586,223	1,485,053	—
Colorado	4,506,542	4,301,261	3,294,394	1,325,089	539,700	—
Connecticut	3,460,503	3,405,565	3,287,116	2,007,280	908,420	237,946
Delaware	807,385	783,600	666,168	318,085	184,735	59,096
DC	570,898	572,059	606,900	802,178	278,718	—
Florida	16,713,149	15,982,378	12,937,926	2,771,305	528,542	—
Georgia	8,560,310	8,186,453	6,478,216	3,444,578	2,216,331	82,548
Hawaii	1,244,898	1,211,537	1,108,229	499,794	154,001	—
Idaho	1,341,131	1,293,953	1,006,749	588,637	161,772	—
Illinois	12,600,620	12,419,293	11,430,602	8,712,176	4,821,550	—
Indiana	6,159,068	6,080,485	5,544,159	3,934,224	2,516,462	—
Iowa	2,936,760	2,926,324	2,776,755	2,621,073	2,231,853	—
Kansas	2,715,884	2,688,418	2,477,574	1,905,299	1,470,495	—
Kentucky	4,092,891	4,041,769	3,685,296	2,944,806	2,147,174	73,677
Louisiana	4,482,646	4,468,976	4,219,973	2,683,516	1,381,625	—
Maine	1,294,464	1,274,923	1,227,928	913,774	694,466	96,540
Maryland	5,458,137	5,296,486	4,781,468	2,343,001	1,188,044	319,728
Massachusetts	6,427,801	6,349,097	6,016,425	4,690,514	2,805,346	378,787
Michigan	10,050,446	9,938,444	9,295,297	6,371,766	2,420,982	—
Minnesota	5,019,720	4,919,479	4,375,099	2,982,483	1,751,394	—
Mississippi	2,871,782	2,844,658	2,573,216	2,178,914	1,551,270	—
Missouri	5,672,579	5,595,211	5,117,073	3,954,653	3,106,665	—
Montana	909,453	902,195	799,065	591,024	243,329	—
Nebraska	1,729,180	1,711,263	1,578,385	1,325,510	1,066,300	—
Nevada	2,173,491	1,998,257	1,201,833	160,083	42,335	—
New Hampshire	1,275,056	1,235,786	1,109,252	533,242	411,588	141,885
New Jersey	8,590,300	8,414,350	7,730,188	4,835,329	1,883,669	184,139
New Mexico	1,855,059	1,819,046	1,515,069	681,187	195,310	—
New York	19,157,532	18,976,457	17,990,455	14,830,192	7,268,894	340,120
North Carolina	8,320,146	8,049,313	6,628,637	4,061,929	1,893,810	393,751
North Dakota	634,110	642,200	638,800	619,636	319,146	—
Ohio	11,421,267	11,353,140	10,847,115	7,946,627	4,157,545	—
Oklahoma	3,493,714	3,450,654	3,145,585	2,233,351	790,391[1]	—
Oregon	3,521,515	3,421,399	2,842,321	1,521,341	413,536	—
Pennsylvania	12,335,091	12,281,054	11,881,643	10,498,012	6,302,115	434,373
Rhode Island	1,069,725	1,048,319	1,003,464	791,896	428,556	68,825
South Carolina	4,107,183	4,012,012	3,486,703	2,117,027	1,340,316	249,073
South Dakota	761,063	754,844	696,004	652,740	401,570	—
Tennessee	5,797,289	5,689,283	4,877,185	3,291,718	2,020,616	35,691
Texas	21,779,893	20,851,820	16,986,510	7,711,194	3,048,710	—
Utah	2,316,256	2,233,169	1,722,850	688,862	276,749	—
Vermont	616,592	608,827	562,758	377,747	343,641	85,425
Virginia	7,293,542	7,078,515	6,187,358	3,318,680	1,854,184	747,610[2]
Washington	6,068,996	5,894,121	4,866,692	2,378,963	518,103	—
West Virginia	1,801,873	1,808,344	1,793,477	2,005,552	958,800	—
Wisconsin	5,441,196	5,363,675	4,891,769	3,434,575	2,069,042	—
Wyoming	498,703	493,782	453,588	290,529	92,531	—
Total U.S.	**288,368,698**	**281,421,906**	**248,709,873**	**151,325,798**	**76,212,168**	**3,929,214**

1. Includes population of Indian Territory, 1900: 392,960. 2. Until 1863, Virginia included what is now West Virginia. *Source:* U.S. Bureau of the Census. Web: www.census.gov.

Total U.S. Population

Area	2000	1990	1980
50 states[1]	281,421,906	248,709,873	226,545,805
48 coterminous[1]	279,583,437	247,051,601	225,179,263
Alaska	626,932	550,043	401,851
Hawaii	1,211,537	1,108,229	964,691
American Samoa	57,291	46,773	32,297
Guam	154,805	133,152	105,979
Johnston Atoll	(2)	(2)	327
Midway	(2)	(2)	453

Area	2000	1990	1980
N. Mariana Is.[3]	69,221	43,345	(4)
Puerto Rico	3,808,610	3,522,037	3,196,520
Trust Ter. of Pac. Is.	(4)	15,122[5]	132,929[5]
Virgin Is. of U.S.	108,612	101,809	96,569
Wake Island	(2)	(2)	302
Population abroad	576,367[6]	922,819	995,546
Armed forces	n.a.	910,611	515,408
Total	**286,196,812**	**253,451,585**	**231,106,727**

NOTE: n.a. = not available. 1. Includes the District of Columbia. 2. No indigenous population. 3. The Commonwealth of the Northern Mariana Islands (CNMI) became part of the United States in 1986. 4. Palau, the last remaining trust territory, became an independent country in 1994. 5. Palau only trust territory remaining. 6. Includes overseas U.S. military and federal civilian employees and their dependents living with them. *Source:* U.S. Bureau of the Census. Web: www.census.gov.

U.S. Population by Region, 1990–2002

Area	Population			Change, 1990–2000	
	April 1, 1990	April 1, 2000	March 2002	Number	Percent
United States	**248,709,873**	**281,421,906**	**282,082,000**	**32,712,033**	**13.2%**
Region[1]					
Northeast	50,809,229	53,594,378	53,300,000	2,785,149	5.5
Midwest	59,668,632	64,392,776	63,779,000	4,724,144	7.9
South	85,445,930	100,236,820	100,652,000	14,790,890	17.3
West	52,786,082	63,197,932	64,351,000	10,411,850	19.7

1. The Northeast region includes Connecticut, Maine, Massachusetts, New Hampshire, New Jersey, New York, Pennsylvania, Rhode Island, and Vermont. The Midwest includes Illinois, Indiana, Iowa, Kansas, Michigan, Minnesota, Missouri, Nebraska, North Dakota, Ohio, South Dakota, and Wisconsin. The South includes Alabama, Arkansas, Delaware, the District of Columbia, Florida, Georgia, Kentucky, Louisiana, Maryland, Mississippi, North Carolina, Oklahoma, South Carolina, Tennessee, Texas, Virginia, and West Virginia. The West includes Alaska, Arizona, California, Colorado, Hawaii, Idaho, Montana, Nevada, New Mexico, Oregon, Utah, Washington, and Wyoming. *Source:* U.S. Census Bureau, Census 2000; 1990 Census. Web: www.census.gov.

Resident Population—Selected Characteristics, 1790–2001

(in thousands)

Date	Male	Female	White	Black	Other			Hispanic origin[1]
					Total other	American Indian, Eskimo, Aleut	Asian and Pacific Islanders	
1790 (Aug. 2)[2]	n.a.	n.a.	3,172	757	n.a.	n.a.	n.a.	n.a.
1800 (Aug. 4)[2]	n.a.	n.a.	4,306	1,002	n.a.	n.a.	n.a.	n.a.
1850 (June 1)[2]	11,838	11,354	19,553	3,639	n.a.	n.a.	n.a.	n.a.
1900 (June 1)[2]	38,816	37,178	66,809	8,834	351	n.a.	n.a.	n.a.
1910 (Apr. 15)[2]	47,332	44,640	81,732	9,828	413	n.a.	n.a.	n.a.
1920 (Jan. 1)[2]	53,900	51,810	94,821	10,463	427	n.a.	n.a.	n.a.
1930 (Apr. 1)[2]	62,137	60,638	110,287	11,891	597	n.a.	n.a.	n.a.
1940 (Apr. 1)[2]	66,062	65,608	118,215	12,866	589	n.a.	n.a.	n.a.
1950 (Apr. 1)[2]	74,833	75,864	134,942	15,042	713	n.a.	n.a.	n.a.
1950 (Apr. 1)	75,187	76,139	135,150	15,045	1,131	n.a.	n.a.	n.a.
1960 (Apr. 1)	88,331	90,992	158,832	18,872	1,620	n.a.	n.a.	n.a.
1970 (Apr. 1)[3]	98,926	104,309	178,098	22,581	2,557	n.a.	n.a.	n.a.
1980 (Apr. 1)[4, 5]	110,053	116,493	194,713	26,683	5,150	1,420	3,729	14,609
1990 (Apr. 1)[4, 6]	121,271	127,494	208,727	30,511	9,527	2,065	7,462	22,372
2000 (Apr. 1)[4]	138,054	143,368	211,461	34,658	13,118	2,476	10,642	35,306
2001 (Apr. 1)[4]	139,813	144,984	230,290	36,247	14,185	2,726	11,459	36,972

NOTES: n.a. = not available. 1. Persons of Hispanic origin may be of any race. 2. Excludes Alaska and Hawaii. 3. The revised 1970 resident population count is 203,302,031, which incorporates changes due to errors found after tabulations were completed. The race and sex data shown here reflect the official 1970 census count. 4. The race data shown have been modified to be consistent with the guidelines in Federal Statistical Directive No. 15 issued by the Office of Management and Budget and are not comparable to data for earlier years. 5. Total population count has been revised since the 1980 census publications. Numbers by age, race, Hispanic origin, and sex have not been corrected. 6. The April 1, 1990, census count (248,765,170) includes count resolution corrections processed through Aug. 1997, and does not include adjustments for census coverage errors except for adjustments estimated for the 1995 Census Test in Oakland, Calif.; Paterson, N.J.; and six Louisiana parishes. These adjustments amounted to a total of 55,297 persons. *Source: Statistical Abstract of the United States* and Census 2000. Web (Census 2000): www.census.gov.

Ratio of Males to Females, by Age Group, 1950–2000

(number of males per 100 females, total resident population)

Age	1950	1960	1970	1980	1990[1]	2000
All ages	**98.6**	**97.1**	**94.8**	**94.5**	**95.1**	**96.3**
Under 14 years	103.7	103.4	103.9	104.6	104.9	104.9
14 to 24 years	98.2	98.7	98.7	101.9	104.6	105.1
25 to 44 years	96.4	95.7	95.5	97.4	98.9	100.2
45 to 64 years	100.1	95.7	91.6	90.7	92.5	94.8
65 years and over	89.6	82.8	72.1	67.6	67.2	70.8

NOTES: As of April 1 for all years. 1. The April 1, 1990, census count (248,765,170) includes count resolution corrections processed through August 1997, and does not include adjustments for census coverage errors except for adjustments estimated for the 1995 Census Test in Oakland, Calif.; Paterson, N.J.; and six Louisiana parishes. These adjustments amounted to a total of 55,297 persons. *Source:* U.S. Census Bureau, *Current Population Reports,* P25-1095 and P25-1130; and unpublished data. From *Statistical Abstract of the United States 1999.* 2000 data are from Census 2000.

Population Distribution by Age, Race, Nativity, and Sex Ratio

Year	Age: Total	Under 5	5–19	20–44	45–64	65 and over	Race and nativity: White[1] Total	White[1] Native born	White[1] Foreign born	Black	Other races[1]
Percent distribution											
1860[2]	100.0%	15.4%	35.8%	35.7%	10.4%	2.7%	85.6%	72.6%	13.0%	14.1%	0.3%
1870[2]	100.0	14.3	35.4	35.4	11.9	3.0	87.1	72.9	14.2	12.7	0.2
1880[2]	100.0	13.8	34.3	35.9	12.6	3.4	86.5	73.4	13.1	13.1	0.3
1890[3]	100.0	12.2	33.9	36.9	13.1	3.9	87.5	73.0	14.5	11.9	0.3
1900	100.0	12.1	32.3	37.7	13.7	4.1	87.9	74.5	13.4	11.6	0.5
1910	100.0	11.6	30.4	39.0	14.6	4.3	88.9	74.4	14.5	10.7	0.4
1920	100.0	10.9	29.8	38.4	16.1	4.7	89.7	76.7	13.0	9.9	0.4
1930	100.0	9.3	29.5	38.3	17.4	5.4	89.8	78.4	11.4	9.7	0.5
1940	100.0	8.0	26.4	38.9	19.8	6.8	89.8	81.1	8.7	9.8	0.4
1950	100.0	10.7	23.2	37.6	20.3	8.1	89.5	82.8	6.7	10.0	0.5
1960	100.0	11.3	27.1	32.2	20.1	9.2	88.6	83.4	5.2	10.5	0.9
1970[2]	100.0	8.4	29.5	31.7	20.6	9.8	87.6	83.4	4.3	11.1	1.4
1980	100.0	7.2	24.8	37.1	19.6	11.3	83.1	—	—	11.7	5.2
1990	100.0	7.6	21.3	40.1	18.6	12.5	83.9	—	—	12.3	3.8
2000	100.0	6.8	21.8	37.0	22.0	12.4	75.1[4]	—	—	12.3[4]	10.1[5]
Males per 100 females											
1860[2]	104.7	102.4	101.2	107.9	111.5	98.3	105.3	103.7	115.1	99.6	260.8
1870[2]	102.2	102.9	101.2	99.2	114.5	100.5	102.8	100.6	115.3	96.2	400.7
1880[2]	103.6	103.0	101.3	104.0	110.2	101.4	104.0	102.1	115.9	97.8	362.2
1890[3]	105.0	103.6	101.4	107.3	108.3	104.2	105.4	102.9	118.7	99.5	165.2
1900	104.4	102.1	100.9	105.8	110.7	102.0	104.9	102.8	117.4	98.6	185.2
1910	106.0	102.5	101.3	108.1	114.4	101.1	106.6	102.7	129.2	98.9	185.6
1920	104.0	102.5	100.8	102.8	115.2	101.3	104.4	101.7	121.7	99.2	156.6
1930	102.5	103.0	101.4	100.5	109.1	100.5	102.9	101.1	115.8	97.0	150.6
1940	100.7	103.2	102.0	98.1	105.2	95.5	101.2	100.1	111.1	95.0	140.5
1950	98.6	103.9	102.5	96.2	100.1	89.6	99.0	98.8	102.0	93.7	129.7
1960	97.1	103.4	102.7	95.6	95.7	82.8	97.4	97.6	94.2	93.3	109.7
1970[2]	94.8	104.0	103.3	95.1	91.6	72.1	95.3	95.9	83.8	90.8	100.2
1980	94.5	104.7	104.0	98.1	90.7	67.6	94.8	—	—	89.6	100.3
1990	95.1	104.8	105.0	99.8	92.5	67.2	95.9	—	—	89.8	96.5
2000	96.3	104.8	105.3	101.0	94.8	70.0	96.4[4]	—	—	90.5[4]	102.2[5]

NOTES: Data exclude armed forces overseas. Beginning in 1960, includes Alaska and Hawaii. (—) Data not available. 1. The 1980 and 1990 census data for white and other race categories are not directly comparable to those shown for the preceding years because of changes in the way some persons reported their race, as well as changes in procedures relating to racial classification. 2. Excludes persons for whom age is not available. 3. Excludes persons enumerated in the Indian Territory and on Indian reservations. 4. Includes only those claiming one race only. 5. Includes American Indian and Alaska Native, Asian, Native Hawaiian and other Pacific Islander, and some other races. *Source:* U.S. Bureau of the Census. Web: www.census.gov.

Households by Size, 1790–2000

Year	Number of households (in thousands)	Percent distribution of number of households: 1 person	2 persons	3 persons	4 persons	5 persons	6 persons	7 or more persons	Avg. pop. per household
1790 (Mar.)	558	3.7%	7.8%	11.7%	13.8%	13.9%	13.2%	35.8%	—
1890 (June)	12,690	3.6	13.2	16.7	16.8	15.1	11.6	23.0	4.93
1900 (Mar.)	15,964	5.1	15.0	17.6	16.9	14.2	10.9	20.4	—
1930 (Apr.)	29,905	7.9	23.4	20.8	17.5	12.0	7.6	10.9	4.11
1940 (Apr.)	34,949	7.1	24.8	22.4	18.1	11.5	6.8	9.3	3.67
1950 (Apr.)[1]	43,468	10.9	28.8	22.6	17.8	10.0	5.1	4.9	3.37
1955 (Mar.)	47,788	10.9	28.5	20.4	18.9	11.1	5.4	4.9	3.33
1960 (Mar.)[2]	52,610	13.1	27.8	18.9	17.6	11.5	5.7	5.4	3.35
1965 (Mar.)	57,251	15.0	28.1	17.9	16.1	11.0	5.8	6.1	3.32
1970 (Mar.)	62,874	17.0	28.8	17.3	15.8	10.4	5.6	5.1	3.14
1975 (Mar.)	71,120	19.6	30.6	17.4	15.6	9.0	4.3	3.5	2.04
1980 (Mar.)	80,776	22.7	31.3	17.5	15.7	7.5	3.1	2.2	2.76
1985 (Mar.)	86,789	23.7	31.6	17.8	15.7	7.0	2.6	1.5	2.69
1990 (Mar.)	93,347	24.6	32.2	17.2	15.5	6.7	2.3	1.4	2.63
1995 (Mar.)	98,990	25.0	32.1	17.0	15.5	6.7	2.3	1.4	2.65
2000 (Mar.)	104,705	25.5	33.1	16.4	14.6	6.7	2.3	1.4	2.62

1. Covers related persons only; therefore, not strictly comparable with other years. 2. Denotes first year for which figures include Alaska and Hawaii. *Source:* U.S. Census Bureau. Web: www.census.gov.

Households by Type, 1980–2002

Type of household	Households					
	Number				Percent distribution	
	1980	1990	2000	2002	1990	2000
Total households	**80,776,000**	**93,347,000**	**104,705,000**	**109,297,000**		
Family households	**59,550,000**	**66,090,000**	**72,025,000**	**74,329,000**	**100%**	**100%**
Married couple family	49,112,000	52,317,000	55,311,000	56,747,000	71	69
Male householder, no spouse present	1,733,000	2,884,000	4,028,000	4,438,000	56	53
Female householder, no spouse present	8,705,000	10,890,000	12,687,000	13,143,000	3	4
Nonfamily households	**21,226,000**	**27,257,000**	**32,680,000**	**34,969,000**	12	12
Living alone	18,296,000	22,999,000	26,724,000	28,775,000	**29**	**31**
Male householder	8,807,000	11,606,000	14,641,000	15,579,000	25	26
Living alone	6,966,000	9,049,000	11,181,000	12,004,000	12	14
Female householder	12,419,000	15,651,000	18,039,000	19,390,000	10	11
Living alone	11,330,000	13,950,000	15,543,000	16,771,000	17	17
					15	15

Source: U.S. Census Bureau, *Current Population Reports.* From *Statistical Abstract of the United States, 2002.*

Families by Type, Race, and Hispanic Origin, 2002

(in thousands, except as indicated)

Characteristic	All families	Married couple families				Female family householder[3]				Male family householder,[3] all races
		All races[1]	White	Black	Hispanic[2]	All races[1]	White	Black	Hispanic[2]	
All families	**74,329**	**56,747**	**49,605**	**4,233**	**5,778**	**13,143**	**8,639**	**3,838**	**1,922**	**4,438**
Without own children under 18	38,623	30,955	27,628	2,085	2,023	5,133	3,587	1,245	633	2,535
With own children under 18	35,705	25,792	21,978	2,148	3,754	8,010	5,052	2,593	1,259	1,903
Average per family with own children under 18	1.87	1.92	1.85	1.98	2.14	1.78	—	—	—	1.53
Marital status of householder:										
Married, spouse present	56,747	56,747	49,605	4,233	5,778	—	—	—	—	—
Married, spouse absent	703	—	—	—	—	480	298	132	128	223
Widowed	2,575	—	—	—	—	2,147	1,616	421	224	428
Divorced	6,051	—	—	—	—	4,639	3,590	824	486	1,412
Separated	1,880	—	—	—	—	1,515	993	443	351	365
Never married	6,372	—	—	—	—	4,363	2,142	2,019	731	2,010

NOTE: (—) = not applicable. 1. Includes other races not shown separately. 2. Persons of Hispanic origin may be of any race. 3. No spouse present. *Source:* U.S. Census Bureau. Web: www.census.gov

Young Adults Living at Home, 1960–2002

	Male			Female		
	Total population, 18–24 years old	Number living at home	Percent	Total population, 18–24 years old	Number living at home	Percent
1960	6,842,000	3,583,000	52%	7,876,000	2,750,000	35%
1970	10,398,000	5,641,000	54	11,959,000	4,941,000	41
1980	14,278,000	7,755,000	54	14,844,000	6,336,000	43
1990	12,450,000	7,232,000	58	12,860,000	6,135,000	48
2000	13,291,000	7,593,000	57	13,242,000	6,232,000	47
2002[1]	13,696,000	7,575,000	55	13,602,000	6,252,000	46

	Male			Female		
	Total population, 25–34 years old	Number living at home	Percent	Total population, 25–34 years old	Number living at home	Percent
1960	10,896,000	1,185,000	11%	11,587,000	853,000	7%
1970	11,929,000	1,129,000	10	12,637,000	829,000	7
1980	18,107,000	1,894,000	11	18,689,000	1,300,000	7
1990	21,462,000	3,213,000	15	21,779,000	1,774,000	8
2000	18,563,000	2,387,000	13	19,222,000	1,602,000	8
2002[1]	19,220,000	2,610,000	14	19,428,000	1,618,000	8

NOTE: Unmarried college students living in dorms are counted as living at home. 1. Data for March 2001 and later use population controls based on Census 2000 and an expanded sample of households designed to improve state estimates of children with health insurance. *Source:* U.S. Bureau of the Census, June 12, 2003.

Homeownership Rates by Race and Ethnicity of Householder

	1994	1995	1996	1997	1998	1999	2000	2002
U.S. total	**64.0**	**64.7**	**65.4**	**65.7**	**66.3**	**66.8**	**67.4**	**67.9**
White, total	67.7	68.7	69.1	69.3	70.0	70.5	71.1	71.8
White, non-Hispanic	70.0	70.9	71.7	72.0	72.6	73.2	73.8	74.5
Black, total	42.3	42.7	44.1	44.8	45.6	46.3	47.2	47.3
Other race[1]	47.7	47.2	51.0	52.5	53.0	53.7	53.5	54.7
American Indian, Aleut, Eskimo	51.7	55.8	51.6	51.7	54.3	56.1	56.2	54.6
Asian or Pacific Islander	51.3	50.8	50.8	52.8	52.6	53.1	52.8	54.7
Other	36.1	37.4	n.a.	n.a.	n.a.	n.a.	n.a.	n.a.
Hispanic	41.2	42.1	42.8	43.3	44.7	45.5	46.3	48.2
Non-Hispanic	65.9	66.7	67.4	67.8	68.3	68.9	69.5	70.0

NOTE: n.a. = not applicable. 1. Beginning in 1996, those answering "other" for race were allocated to one of the 4 race categories—white, black, American Indian, Aleut, or Eskimo (one category), or Asian or Pacific Islander. *Source:* U.S. Census Bureau. Web: www.census.gov.

Homeownership by State, 1990 and 2002

State	Homeownership rate (%)		State	Homeownership rate (%)		State	Homeownership rate (%)	
	1990	2002		1990	2002		1990	2002
U.S. total	**63.9%**	**67.9%**	Kentucky	65.8%	73.5%	Ohio	68.7%	72.0%
Alabama	68.4	73.5	Louisiana	67.8	67.1	Oklahoma	70.3	69.4
Alaska	58.4	67.3	Maine	74.2	73.9	Oregon	64.4	66.2
Arizona	64.5	65.9	Maryland	64.9	72.0	Pennsylvania	73.8	74.0
Arkansas	67.8	70.2	Massachusetts	58.6	62.7	Rhode Island	58.5	59.6
California	53.8	58.0	Michigan	72.3	76.0	South Carolina	71.4	77.3
Colorado	59.0	69.1	Minnesota	68.0	77.3	South Dakota	66.2	71.5
Connecticut	67.9	71.6	Mississippi	69.4	74.8	Tennessee	68.3	70.1
Delaware	67.7	75.6	Missouri	64.0	74.6	Texas	59.7	63.8
DC	36.4	44.1	Montana	69.1	69.3	Utah	70.1	72.7
Florida	65.1	68.7	Nebraska	67.3	68.4	Vermont	72.6	70.2
Georgia	64.3	71.7	Nevada	55.8	65.5	Virginia	69.8	74.3
Hawaii	55.5	57.4	New Hampshire	65.0	69.5	Washington	61.8	67.0
Idaho	69.4	73.0	New Jersey	65.0	67.2	West Virginia	72.0	77.0
Illinois	63.0	70.2	New Mexico	68.6	70.3	Wisconsin	68.3	72.0
Indiana	67.0	75.0	New York	53.3	55.0	Wyoming	68.9	72.8
Iowa	70.7	73.9	North Carolina	69.0	70.0			
Kansas	69.0	70.2	North Dakota	67.2	69.5			

Source: U.S. Census Bureau. Web: www.census.gov.

Characteristics of the Homeless, 1996

Characteristic	U.S. adult population (1996)	All homeless persons	Persons in homeless families	Single homeless persons
Sex:				
Male	48%	68%	16%	77%
Female	52	32	84	23
Race/ethnicity:				
White non-Hispanic	75	41	38	41
Black non-Hispanic	11	40	43	40
Hispanic	10	11	15	10
American Indian	1	8	3	8
Marital status:				
Never married	23	48	41	50
Married	60	9	23	7
Separated	(1)	15	23	14
Divorced	10	24	13	26
Widowed	7	3	0	4
Educational attainment:				
Less than high school	25	38	53	37
High school graduate/G.E.D.	30	34	21	36
More than high school	45	28	27	28
Veteran	13	23	5	26

NOTE: Numbers do not add up to 100% due to rounding. 1. Included in "married." *Source:* U.S. Bureau of the Census. From Interagency Council on the Homeless, *Homelessness: Programs and the People They Serve*, 1999.

Population Explosion Among Older Americans

The United States saw a rapid growth in its elderly population during the 20th century. The number of Americans aged 65 and older climbed above 34.9 million in 2000, compared with 3.1 million in 1900. For the same years, the ratio of elderly Americans to the total population jumped from 1 in 25 to 1 in 8. The trend is guaranteed to continue in the coming century as the baby-boom generation grows older. Between 1990 and 2020, the population aged 65 to 74 is projected to grow 74%.

The elderly population explosion is a result of impressive increases in life expectancy. When the nation was founded, the average American could expect to live to the age of 35. Life expectancy at birth had increased to 47.3 by 1900 and in 2000 stood at 76.9.

Along with the growth of the general elderly population has come a remarkable increase in the number of Americans reaching age 100. In 2000 there were 50,454 centenarians (people aged 100 or over), representing 1 out of every 5,578 people. In 1990 centenarians numbered 37,306 people, or 1 out of every 6,667 people.

Source: Based on U.S. Census Bureau data.

Population 65 Years and Over by Age, 1990 and 2000

Age	1990 Number	1990 Percent	2000 Number	2000 Percent	Percent of U.S. total 1990	Percent of U.S. total 2000	Percent change, 1990 to 2000
65 years and over	**31,241,831**	**100.0%**	**34,991,753**	**100.0%**	**12.6%**	**12.4%**	**12.0%**
65 to 74 years	18,106,558	58.0	18,390,986	52.6	7.3	6.5	1.6
65 to 69 years	10,111,735	32.4	9,533,545	27.2	4.1	3.4	–5.7
70 to 74 years	7,994,823	25.6	8,857,441	25.3	3.2	3.1	10.8
75 to 84 years	10,055,108	32.2	12,361,180	35.3	4.0	4.4	22.9
75 to 79 years	6,121,369	19.6	7,415,813	21.2	2.5	2.6	21.1
80 to 84 years	3,933,739	12.6	4,945,367	14.1	1.6	1.8	25.7
85 to 94 years	2,829,728	9.1	3,902,349	11.2	1.1	1.4	37.9
85 to 89 years	2,060,247	6.6	2,789,818	8.0	0.8	1.0	35.4
90 to 94 years	769,481	2.5	1,112,531	3.2	0.3	0.4	44.6
95 years and over	250,437	0.8	337,238	1.0	0.1	0.1	34.7

Source: U.S. Census Bureau, Census 2000; 1990 Census of Population, *General Population Characteristics, United States* (1990 CP-1-1). Web: www.census.gov.

Persons 65 Years Old and Over—Characteristics by Sex, 1980–2000

Characteristic	Total 1980	Total 1990	Total 2000	Male 1980	Male 1990	Male 2000	Female 1980	Female 1990	Female 2000
Total[1] (million)	**24.2**	**29.6**	**32.6**	**9.9**	**12.3**	**13.9**	**14.2**	**17.2**	**18.7**
White (million)	21.9	26.5	n.a.	9.0	11.0	n.a.	12.9	15.4	n.a.
Black (million)	2.0	2.5	n.a.	0.8	1.0	n.a.	1.2	1.5	n.a.
Percent below poverty level[2]	15.2%	11.4%	9.7%	11.1%	7.8%	6.9%	17.9%	13.9%	11.8%
Percent distribution									
Marital status:									
Single	5.5%	4.6%	3.9%	4.9%	4.2%	4.2%	5.9%	4.9%	3.6%
Married	55.4	56.1	57.2	78.0	76.5	75.2	39.5	41.4	43.8
Spouse present	53.6	54.1	54.6	76.1	74.2	72.6	37.9	39.7	41.3
Spouse absent	1.8	2.0	2.6	1.9	2.3	2.6	1.7	1.7	2.5
Widowed	35.7	34.2	32.1	13.5	14.2	14.4	51.2	48.6	45.3
Divorced	3.5	5.0	6.7	3.6	5.0	6.1	3.4	5.1	7.2
Years of school completed:									
8 years or fewer	43.1%	28.5%	16.7%	45.3%	30.0%	17.8%	41.6%	27.5%	15.9%
1 to 3 years of high school	16.2	16.1	13.8[3]	15.5	15.7	12.7[3]	16.7	16.4	14.7[3]
4 years of high school	24.0	32.9	35.9[4]	21.4	29.0	30.4[4]	25.8	35.6	39.9[4]
1 to 3 years of college	8.2	10.9	18.0[5]	7.5	10.8	17.8[5]	8.6	11.0	18.2[5]
4 years or more of college	8.6	11.6	15.6[6]	10.3	14.5	21.4[6]	7.4	9.5	11.4[6]
Labor force participation[7]:									
Employed	12.2%	11.5%	12.4%	18.4%	15.9%	16.9%	7.8%	8.4%	9.1%
Unemployed	0.4	0.4	0.4	0.6	0.5	0.6	0.3	0.3	0.3
Not in labor force	87.5	88.1	87.2	81.0	83.6	82.5	91.9	91.3	90.6

NOTES: n.a. = not available. 1. Includes other races, not shown separately. 2. Poverty status based on income in preceding year. 3. Represents those who completed 9th to 12th grade, but have no high school diploma. 4. High school graduate. 5. Some college or associate degree. 6. Bachelor's or advanced degree. 7. Annual averages of monthly figures (from U.S. Bureau of Labor Statistics, *Employment and Earnings,* January issues. Data beginning 1994 not directly comparable with earlier years). *Source:* Except as noted, U.S. Bureau of the Census, *Current Population Reports.* From *Statistical Abstract of the United States 2001.*

10 Places of 100,000 or More Population with the Highest Proportion of Their Population 65 and Over, 2000

Place[1]	Total population	Population 65 and over	Percent 65 and over
Clearwater, Fla.	108,787	23,357	21.5%
Cape Coral, Fla.	102,286	20,020	19.6
Honolulu, Hawaii[2]	371,657	66,257	17.8
St. Petersburg, Fla.	248,232	43,173	17.4
Hollywood, Fla.	139,357	24,159	17.3
Warren, Mich.	138,247	23,871	17.3
Miami, Fla.	362,470	61,768	17.0
Livonia, Mich.	100,545	16,988	16.9
Scottsdale, Ariz.	202,705	33,884	16.7
Hialeah, Fla.	226,419	37,679	16.6

1. Census 2000 showed 245 places in the United States with 100,000 or more population. They included 238 incorporated places (including 4 city-county consolidations) and 7 census designated places that were not legally incorporated. For a list of these places by state, see www.census.gov/population/www/cen2000/phc-t6.html. 2. Honolulu, Hawaii, is a census designated place and is not legally incorporated. Source: U.S. Census Bureau. Web: www.census.gov

Marital Status and Household Characteristics

Marriages and Divorces, 1900–2001

Year	Marriage Number	Marriage Rate[2]	Divorce[1] Number	Divorce[1] Rate[2]
1900	709,000	9.3	55,751	0.7
1910	948,166	10.3	83,045	0.9
1920	1,274,476	12.0	170,505	1.6
1930	1,126,856	9.2	195,961	1.6
1940	1,595,879	12.1	264,000	2.0
1950	1,667,231	11.1	385,144	2.6
1960	1,523,000	8.5	393,000	2.2
1965	1,800,000	9.3	479,000	2.5
1970	2,158,802	10.6	708,000	3.5
1975	2,152,662	10.1	1,036,000	4.9
1980	2,406,708	10.6	1,182,000	5.2
1982	2,495,000	10.8	1,180,000	5.1
1983	2,444,000	10.5	1,179,000	5.0
1984	2,487,000	10.5	1,155,000	4.9
1985	2,425,000	10.2	1,187,000	5.0
1986	2,400,000	10.0	1,159,000	4.8
1987	2,421,000	9.9	1,157,000	4.8
1988	2,389,000	9.7	1,183,000	4.8
1989	2,404,000	9.7	1,163,000	4.7
1990	2,448,000	9.8	1,175,000	4.7
1991	2,371,000	9.4	1,187,000	4.7
1992	2,362,000	9.2	1,215,000	4.8
1993	2,334,000	9.0	1,187,000	4.6
1994	2,362,000	9.1	1,191,000	4.6
1995	2,336,000	8.9	1,169,000	4.4
1996	2,344,000	8.8	1,150,000	4.3
1997	2,384,000	8.9	1,163,000	4.3
1998	2,256,000	8.4	1,135,000	4.2
1999	2,358,000	8.6	—	4.1
2000	2,329,000	8.5	—	4.1
2001	2,327,000	8.4	—	4.0

NOTE: (—) Data not available. Marriage and divorce figures for most years include some estimated data. Alaska is included beginning 1959, Hawaii beginning 1960. 1. Includes annulments. 2. Per 1,000 population. *Source:* U.S. Dept. of Health and Human Services, National Center for Health Statistics. Web: www.cdc.gov/nchs/.

Median Age at First Marriage

Year	Males	Females
1890	26.1	22.0
1900	25.9	21.9
1910	25.1	21.6
1920	24.6	21.2
1930	24.3	21.3
1940	24.3	21.5
1950	22.8	20.3
1960	22.8	20.3
1970	23.2	20.8
1980	24.7	22.0
1990	26.1	23.9
1995	26.9	24.5
1996	27.1	24.8
1997	26.8	25.0
1998	26.7	25.0
1999	26.9	25.1
2000	26.8	25.1
2001	26.9	25.1
2002	26.9	25.3

Source: U.S. Bureau of the Census; Web: www.census.gov.

Percent Never Married

Age	1970	1999	2000	2002
Male:				
20 to 24 years	35.8%	83.2%	83.7%	85.4%
25 to 29 years	10.5	52.1	51.7	53.7
30 to 34 years	6.2	30.7	30.0	34.0
35 to 39 years	5.4	21.1	20.3	21.1
40 to 44 years	4.9	15.8	15.7	16.7
Female:				
20 to 24 years	54.7%	72.3%	72.8%	74.0%
25 to 29 years	19.1	38.9	38.9	40.4
30 to 34 years	9.4	22.1	21.9	23.0
35 to 39 years	7.2	15.2	14.3	14.7
40 to 44 years	6.3	10.9	11.8	11.5

NOTE: Data apply to the U.S. *Source:* U.S. Bureau of the Census. From *Statistical Abstract of the United States 2001.*

Marital Status of the Population, 1980–2000

(numbers are in millions)

Marital status	Total 2000	Total 1995	Total 1990	Total 1980	Male 2000	Male 1995	Male 1990	Male 1980	Female 2000	Female 1995	Female 1990	Female 1980
Total	**201.8**	**191.6**	**181.8**	**159.5**	**96.9**	**92.0**	**86.9**	**75.7**	**104.9**	**99.6**	**95.0**	**83.8**
Never married	48.2	43.9	40.4	32.3	26.1	24.6	22.4	18.0	22.1	19.3	17.9	14.3
Married	120.1	116.7	112.6	104.6	59.6	57.7	55.8	51.8	60.4	58.9	56.7	52.8
Widowed	13.7	13.4	13.8	12.7	2.6	2.3	2.3	2.0	11.1	11.1	11.5	10.8
Divorced	19.8	17.6	15.1	9.9	8.5	7.4	6.3	3.9	11.3	10.3	8.8	6.0
Percent of total	100.0%	100.0%	100.0%	100.0%	100.0%	100.0%	100.0%	100.0%	100.0%	100.0%	100.0%	100.0%
Never married	23.9	22.9	22.2	20.3	27.0	26.8	25.8	23.8	21.1	19.4	18.9	17.1
Married	59.5	60.9	61.9	65.5	61.5	62.7	64.3	68.4	57.6	59.2	59.7	63.0
Widowed	6.8	7.0	7.6	8.0	2.7	2.5	2.7	2.6	10.5	11.1	12.1	12.8
Divorced	9.8	9.2	8.3	6.2	8.8	8.0	7.2	5.2	10.8	10.3	9.3	7.1

Source: U.S. Bureau of the Census, *Current Population Reports,* P20-491, and earlier reports; and unpublished data. From *Statistical Abstract of the United States 2001.*

Persons Living Alone, by Sex and Age

(in thousands)

Sex and age	2000 Number	2000 Percent	1995 Number	1995 Percent	1990 Number	1990 Percent	1980 Number	1980 Percent
Both sexes								
15 to 24 years	1,144	4%	1,196	5%	1,210	5%	1,726	9%
25 to 34 years	3,848	14	3,653	15	3,972	17	4,729[1]	26[1]
35 to 44 years	4,109	15	3,663	15	3,138	14	([1])	([1])
45 to 64 years	7,842	29	6,377	26	5,502	24	4,514	25
65 to 74 years	4,091	15	4,374	18	4,350	19	3,851	21
75 years and over	5,692	21	5,470	22	4,825	21	3,477	19
Total, 15 years and over	**26,724**	**100**	**24,732**	**100**	**22,999**	**100**	**18,296**	**100**
Male								
15 to 24 years	556	2	623	3	674	3	947	5
25 to 34 years	2,279	9	2,213	9	2,395	10	2,920[1]	16[1]
35 to 44 years	2,569	10	2,263	9	1,836	8	([1])	([1])
45 to 64 years	3,422	13	2,787	11	2,203	10	1,613	9
65 to 74 years	1,108	4	1,134	5	1,042	5	775	4
75 years and over	1,247	5	1,120	5	901	4	711	4
Total, 15 years and over	**11,181**	**42**	**10,140**	**41**	**9,049**	**39**	**6,966**	**38**
Female								
15 to 24 years	588	2	572	2	536	2	779	4
25 to 34 years	1,568	6	1,440	6	1,578	7	1,809[1]	10[1]
35 to 44 years	1,540	6	1,399	6	1,303	6	([1])	([1])
45 to 64 years	4,420	17	3,589	15	3,300	14	2,901	16
65 to 74 years	2,983	11	3,240	13	3,309	14	3,076	17
75 years and over	4,444	17	4,351	18	3,924	17	2,766	15
Total, 15 years and over	**15,543**	**58**	**14,592**	**59**	**13,950**	**61**	**11,330**	**62**

NOTE: As of March. 1. Data for persons 35 to 44 years old included with persons 25 to 34 years old. *Source:* U.S. Bureau of the Census, *Current Population Reports,* P20-491, and earlier reports; and unpublished data. From *Statistical Abstract of the United States 2001.*

Married-Couple and Unmarried-Partner Households for the U.S. and Regions, 2000

Area	Total number of coupled households[1]	Coupled households (% of all households)	Married couples (% of coupled households)	Unmarried partners (% of coupled households)	Opposite sex unmarried partners (% of coupled households)	Same-sex unmarried partners (% of coupled households)
United States	**59,969,000**	**56.9%**	**90.9%**	**9.1%**	**8.1%**	**1.0%**
Region						
Northeast	11,205,641	55.2	90.4	9.6	8.6	1.1
Midwest	14,222,533	57.5	91.1	8.9	8.1	0.7
South	21,549,582	56.7	91.6	8.4	7.4	1.0
West	12,991,244	57.9	89.8	10.2	9.0	1.2

NOTE: Totals may not add up due to rounding. 1. Coupled households represent total of married-couple and unmarried-partner households. *Source:* U.S. Census Bureau, Census 20000 Summary File 1.

Characteristics of Unmarried Partners and Married Spouses, 2000

(in thousands)

Characteristic	Number: Unmarried partners Men	Number: Unmarried partners Women	Number: Married spouses Men	Number: Married spouses Women	Percent: Unmarried partners Men	Percent: Unmarried partners Women	Percent: Married spouses Men	Percent: Married spouses Women
Total	**3,822**	**3,822**	**56,497**	**56,497**	**100.0%**	**100.0%**	**100.0%**	**100.0%**
Age:								
15 to 24 years old	597	937	1,321	2,386	15.6	24.5	2.3	4.2
25 to 34 years old	1,413	1,269	9,296	10,964	37.0	33.2	16.5	19.4
35 years old and over	1,811	1,616	45,881	43,146	47.4	42.3	81.2	76.4
Race and Hispanic origin								
White	3,127	3,147	49,668	49,581	81.8	82.3	87.9	87.8
Non-Hispanic	2,710	2,742	44,350	44,142	70.9	71.7	78.5	78.1
Black	562	498	4,294	4,097	14.7	13.0	7.6	7.3
Asian and Pacific Islander	63	105	2,118	2,393	1.6	2.7	3.7	4.2
Hispanic (of any race)	453	433	5,550	5,671	11.9	11.3	9.8	10.0
Education								
Less than high school	683	599	8,314	7,160	17.9	15.7	14.7	12.7
High school graduate	1,441	1,357	17,506	19,950	37.7	35.5	31.0	35.3
Some college	996	1,223	14,002	14,968	26.1	32.0	24.8	26.5
College graduate	702	643	16,674	14,419	18.4	16.8	29.5	25.5
Labor force status								
Employed	3,179	2,894	42,854	34,067	83.2	75.7	75.9	60.3
Unemployed	187	178	992	961	4.9	4.7	1.8	1.7
Not in labor force	453	747	12,650	21,468	11.9	19.5	22.4	38.0
Personal earnings								
Without earnings	402	642	11,353	19,368	10.5	16.8	20.1	34.3
With earnings	3,419	3,178	45,144	37,132	89.5	83.2	79.9	65.7
Under $5,000	184	373	1,874	4,683	4.8	9.8	3.3	8.3
$5,000 to $9,999	286	395	1,665	4,183	7.5	10.3	2.9	7.4
$10,000 to $14,999	360	445	2,401	4,497	9.4	11.6	4.2	8.0
$15,000 to $19,999	410	441	3,101	4,427	10.7	11.5	5.5	7.8
$20,000 to $24,999	401	397	3,561	4,249	10.5	10.4	6.3	7.5
$25,000 to $29,999	336	315	3,595	3,429	8.8	8.2	6.4	6.1
$30,000 to $39,999	548	405	7,492	4,954	14.3	10.6	13.3	8.8
$40,000 to $49,999	337	201	6,096	2,976	8.8	5.3	10.8	5.3
$50,000 to $74,999	370	137	8,703	2,683	9.7	3.6	15.4	4.7
$75,000 and over	187	69	6,656	1,051	4.9	1.8	11.8	1.9
Presence of children								
With children[1]	1,563	1,563	25,771	25,771	40.9	40.9	45.6	45.6

NOTE: Data are not shown separately for the American Indian and Alaska Native population because of the small sample size in the Current Population Survey in March 2000. 1. May be own children of either partner or both partners. Excludes ever married children under 18 years. *Source:* U.S. Census Bureau, Current Population Survey, March 2000.

Births

Gestational Age and Birthweight Characteristics by Plurality: United States 2001

	Singletons	Twins	Triplets	Quadruplets	Quintuplets/+
Number	3,897,216	121,246	6,885	501	85
Percent very preterm[1]	1.6%	11.8%	36.7%	64.5%	78.6%
Percent preterm[2]	10.4%	57.4%	92.4%	97.8%	91.7%
Mean gestational age (weeks)/ standard deviation	38.8 (2.5)	35.4 (3.7)	32.0 (4.0)	29.6 (4.1)	29.1 (3.9)
Percent very low birthweight[3]	1.1%	10.2%	34.8%	68.4%	77.4%
Percent low birthweight[4]	6.04%	64.9%	94.0%	98.4%	91.7%
Mean birthweight (grams)/ standard deviation	3,339 (573)	2,353 (647)	1,678 (574)	1,290 (549)	1,269 (676)

1. Very preterm is less than 32 completed weeks of gestation. 2. Preterm is less than 37 completed weeks of gestation. 3. Very low birthweight is less than 1,500 grams. 4. Low birthweight is less than 2,500 grams. *Source:* National Center for Health Statistics, *National Vital Statistics Reports,* vol. 51, no. 2, Dec. 18, 2002. Web: www.cdc.gov/nchs.

Births, Birth Rates, and Fertility Rates by State, 2001

State	Number of births	Birth rate[1]	Fertility rate[2]
United States[3]	4,025,933	14.5	66.9
Alabama	60,454	13.7	62.4
Alaska	10,003	16.0	75.5
Arizona	85,597	17.1	84.0
Arkansas	37,010	14.3	67.5
California	527,759	15.5	69.5
Colorado	67,007	15.9	74.6
Connecticut	42,648	12.9	61.0
Delaware	10,749	13.9	61.5
District of Columbia	7,625	14.8	63.9
Florida	205,793	13.2	67.0
Georgia	133,526	16.5	71.1
Hawaii	17,072	14.5	71.4
Idaho	20,688	16.0	75.4
Illinois	184,064	15.0	69.5
Indiana	84,459	14.4	66.1
Iowa	37,619	13.0	63.4
Kansas	38,869	14.5	68.1
Kentucky	54,658	13.6	62.3
Louisiana	65,352	14.9	67.2
Maine	13,759	10.9	50.0
Maryland	73,218	13.9	60.9
Massachusetts	81,077	13.0	59.1
Michigan	133,427	13.4	61.0
Minnesota	67,562	13.8	63.5
Mississippi	42,282	15.1	67.6
Missouri	75,464	13.6	63.2
Montana	10,970	12.3	61.8
Nebraska	24,820	14.8	69.7
Nevada	31,382	16.1	79.4
New Hampshire	14,656	11.9	52.0
New Jersey	115,795	14.0	66.3
New Mexico	27,128	15.4	72.8
New York	254,026	13.9	64.4
North Carolina	118,185	15.1	70.4
North Dakota	7,629	12.2	59.3
Ohio	151,570	13.4	61.9
Oklahoma	50,118	14.8	70.8
Oregon	45,322	13.5	65.3
Pennsylvania	143,495	12.0	57.7
Rhode Island	12,713	12.7	59.2
South Carolina	55,756	14.1	62.8
South Dakota	10,483	14.1	67.7
Tennessee	78,340	14.0	64.3
Texas	365,410	17.6	79.9
Utah	47,959	21.8	95.0
Vermont	6,366	10.6	47.9
Virginia	98,884	14.0	60.9
Washington	79,570	13.6	61.9
West Virginia	20,428	11.4	55.6
Wisconsin	69,072	12.9	60.2
Wyoming	6,115	12.7	62.0
Puerto Rico	55,866	14.2	61.2
Virgin Islands	1,669	13.7	63.4
Guam	3,564	22.6	113.7
American Samoa	1,655	24.7	113.9
Northern Marianas	1,449	19.4	57.5

NOTE: Data by place of residence. 1. Birth rates are live births per 1,000 estimated population in each area. 2. Fertility rates are live births per 1,000 women aged 15–44 years estimated in each area. 3. Excludes data for Puerto Rico, Virgin Islands, Guam, American Samoa, and Northern Marianas. *Source:* National Center for Health Statistics, *National Vital Statistics Reports,* vol. 51, no. 2, Dec. 18, 2002. Web: www.cdc.gov/nchs.

Live Births by Age and Race of Mother, 1940–2001

		Age of mother							
Year[1]/race	Total	Under 15	15–19	20–24	25–29	30–34	35–39	40–44	45–49[2]
1940	2,558,647	3,865	332,667	799,537	693,268	431,468	222,015	68,269	7,558
1945	2,858,449	4,028	298,868	832,746	785,299	554,906	296,852	78,853	6,897
1950	3,631,512	5,413	432,911	1,155,167	1,041,360	610,816	302,780	77,743	6,182
1955	4,014,112	6,181	493,770	1,290,939	1,133,155	732,540	352,320	89,777	5,430
1960	4,257,850	6,780	586,966	1,426,912	1,092,816	687,722	359,908	91,564	5,182
1965	3,760,358	7,768	590,894	1,337,350	925,732	529,376	282,908	81,716	4,614
1970	3,731,386	11,752	644,708	1,418,874	994,904	427,806	180,244	49,952	3,146
1975	3,144,198	12,642	582,238	1,093,676	936,786	375,500	115,409	26,319	1,628
1980	3,612,258	10,169	552,161	1,226,200	1,108,291	550,354	140,793	23,090	1,200
1985	3,760,561	10,220	467,485	1,141,320	1,201,350	696,354	214,336	28,334	1,162
1990	4,158,212	11,657	521,826	1,093,730	1,277,108	886,063	317,583	48,607	1,638
1995	3,899,589	12,242	499,873	965,547	1,063,539	904,666	383,745	67,250	2,727
1998	3,941,553	9,462	484,895	965,122	1,083,010	889,365	424,890	81,027	3,782[2]
1999	3,959,417	9,054	476,050	981,929	1,078,252	892,400	434,294	83,090	4,348[2]
2000	4,058,814	8,519[3]	468,990	1,017,806	1,087,547	929,278	452,057	90,013	4,604[2]
2001	4,025,933	7,781[3]	445,944	1,021,627	1,058,265	942,697	451,723	92,813	5,083[2]
White	3,177,626	4,095[3]	318,563	779,529	850,343	777,294	368,816	74,856	4,130[2]
Black	606,156	3,455[3]	110,843	199,221	137,400	94,660	49,065	11,001	511[2]
American Indian[3]	41,872	145[3]	7,939	14,071	9,878	6,190	2,940	674	35[2]
Asian or Pacific Islander	200,279	86[3]	8,599	28,806	60,644	64,553	30,902	6,282	407[2]
Hispanic origin[4]	851,851	2,555[3]	130,007	258,431	227,910	150,352	67,952	13,956	688[2]

NOTE: Data refer only to births occurring within the U.S. 1. Data for 1940–1955 are adjusted for under-registration. Beginning 1960, only registered births are shown. Data for 1960–1970 based on a 50% sample of births. For 1972–1984, based on 100% of births in selected states and on 50% sample in all other states. Beginning 1989, births are tabulated by race of mother; previously based on race of child. 2. Beginning 1998, ages 45–54. 3. Ages 10–14. 4. Includes births to Aleuts and Eskimos. 5. Persons of Hispanic origin may be any race. *Source:* National Center for Health Statistics, *National Vital Statistics Reports,* vol. 51, no. 4, Feb. 16, 2003. Web: www.cdc.gov/nchs.

Live Births by Sex and Sex Ratio

Year	Total[1, 2] Male	Female	Males per 1,000 females	White Male	Female	Males per 1,000 females	Black Male	Female	Males per 1,000 females
1985	1,927,983	1,832,578	1,052	1,536,646	1,454,727	1,056	308,575	299,618	1,030
1986	1,924,868	1,831,679	1,051	1,523,914	1,446,525	1,053	315,788	305,433	1,034
1987	1,951,153	1,858,241	1,050	1,535,517	1,456,971	1,054	325,259	316,308	1,028
1988	2,002,424	1,907,086	1,050	1,562,675	1,483,487	1,053	341,441	330,535	1,033
1989	2,069,490	1,971,468	1,050	1,606,757	1,525,234	1,053	360,131	349,264	1,031
1990	2,129,495	2,028,717	1,050	1,654,928	1,570,415	1,054	367,455	357,121	1,029
1991	2,101,518	2,009,389	1,046	1,659,077	1,582,196	1,049	346,455	336,147	1,031
1992	2,082,097	1,982,917	1,050	1,641,811	1,559,867	1,053	342,726	330,907	1,036
1993	2,048,861	1,951,379	1,050	1,616,332	1,533,501	1,054	333,984	324,891	1,028
1994	2,022,589	1,930,178	1,048	1,599,803	1,521,401	1,051	322,554	313,837	1,028
1995	1,996,355	1,930,234	1,049	1,588,427	1,510,458	1,052	308,115	297,024	1,031
1996	1,990,480	1,901,014	1,047	—	—	1,050	—	—	1,028
1997	1,985,596	1,895,298	1,048	—	—	1,052	—	—	1,031
1998	2,016,205	1,925,348	1,047	—	—	1,052	—	—	1,034
1999	2,026,854	1,932,563	1,049	—	—	1,052	—	—	1,031
2000	2,076,969	1,981,845	1,048	—	—	1,050	—	—	1,031
2001	2,057,922	1,968,011	1,046	—	—	1,047	—	—	1,032

NOTE: (—) Data not available. 1. Excludes births to nonresidents of U.S. 2. Includes races other than white and black. *Source:* National Center for Health Statistics, *National Vital Statistics Reports,* vol. 51, no. 2, Dec. 18, 2002. Web: www.cdc.gov/nchs.

Selected Characteristics of Births by Race of Mother, 2001

Characteristic	All races	White	Black	American Indian[1]	Asian or Pacific Islander	Hispanic origin[2]
Percentage of mothers who:						
Had prenatal care beginning in the first trimester	83.4%	85.2%	74.5%	69.3%	84.0%	75.7%
Had late or no prenatal care	3.7	3.2	6.5	8.2	3.4	5.9
Were tobacco users[3]	12.0	13.0	9.0	19.9	2.8	3.2
Were alcohol users[4]	0.9	0.8	1.0	2.8	0.3	0.5
Gained less than 16 lbs[5]	12.1	11.1	17.3	16.9	9.4	14.7
Median weight gain[5]	30.5	30.6	30.0	29.8	30.1	29.0
Had cesarean births	24.4	24.3	25.9	21.6	23.3	23.6
Percentage of infants who:						
Were born prior to 37 full weeks	11.9	11.0	17.5	13.2	10.3	11.4
Weighed less than 1,500 grams (3 lb 4 oz.)	1.4	1.2	3.0	1.3	1.0	1.1
Weighed less than 2,500 grams (5 lb 8 oz.)	7.7	6.7	13.0	7.3	7.5	6.5
Weighed 4,000 grams (8 lb 14 oz.) or more	9.4	10.4	5.2	11.6	5.5	8.7
Had five-minute Apgar scores of less than 7[6]	1.4	1.2	2.3	1.4	1.0	1.1

1. Includes births to Aleuts and Eskimos. 2. Hispanic origin may be of any race. 3. Excludes data for Calif., which did not report tobacco use on birth certificate. 4. Excludes data for Calif., which did not report alcohol use on birth certificate. 5. Excludes data for Calif., which did not report weight gain on birth certificate. Median weight gain shown in pounds. 6. Excludes data for Calif. and Tex., which did not report five-minute Apgar scores on birth certificate. Apgar scores are derived from evaluations of five major signs at one minute and five minutes after birth. Each sign is given a score of 0–2 for a total of ten possible points; scores of 7–10 are considered normal, 4–7 may require resuscitative measures, and 0–3 require immediate resuscitation. The signs and scores (0-1-2) are as follows: Activity or muscle tone (absent—arms and legs flexed—active movement); Pulse (absent—below 100 bpm—above 100 bpm); Grimace or reflex irritability (no response—grimace—sneeze, cough, pulls away); Appearance or skin color (blue-gray, pale all over—normal, except for extremities—normal over entire body); Respiration (absent—slow, irregular—good, crying). *Source:* National Center for Health Statistics, *National Vital Statistics Reports,* vol. 51, no. 2, Dec. 18, 2002. Web: www.cdc.gov/nchs.

Teen Birth Rates Continue to Decline

Source: Centers for Disease Control, National Center for Health Statistics, *National Vital Statistics Reports,* vol. 49, no. 10, Sept. 25, 2001.

Teenage childbearing has been on a long-term decline in the United States since the late 1950s, except for a brief, but steep, upward climb in the late 1980s through 1991. The 2000 rate (47.7 births per 1,000) is about half the peak rate recorded in 1957 (96 per 1,000). The declining teenage birth rate has had an impressive impact on the number of babies born to teenagers. If the birth rates by age had remained at 1991 levels throughout the 1990s instead of declining as they did, there would have been an additional 546,000 births to teenagers over the decade. Possible factors accounting for the decline include decreased sexual activity reflecting changing attitudes toward premarital sex, an increase in condom use, and the adoption of newly available hormonal contraception, implants, and injectables.

Despite the rates' reaching record lows in 2000, U.S. teenage birth rates remain substantially higher than rates for other developed countries. □

Teen Birth Rates in the U.S., Selected Years

(rates per 1,000 females in specified group)

Age	1980	1985	1990	1991	1993	1995	1998	2000	2001
All races									
10–14 years	1.1	1.2	1.4	1.4	1.4	1.3	1.0	0.9	0.8
15–19 years	53.0	51.0	59.9	62.1	59.6	56.8	51.1	47.7	45.8
White, total									
10–14 years	—	—	0.7	0.8	0.8	0.8	0.6	0.6	0.5
15–19 years	—	—	50.8	52.8	51.1	50.1	45.4	43.2	41.2
White, non-Hispanic									
10–14 years	0.4	—	0.5	0.5	0.5	0.4	0.3	0.3	0.3
15–19 years	41.2	—	42.5	43.4	40.7	39.3	35.2	32.6	30.3
Black									
10–14 years	4.3	4.5	4.9	4.8	4.6	4.2	2.9	2.3	2.0
15–19 years	97.8	95.4	112.8	115.5	108.6	96.1	85.4	77.4	71.8
American Indian[1]									
10–14 years	1.9	1.7	1.6	1.6	1.4	1.8	1.6	1.1	1.0
15–19 years	82.2	79.2	81.1	85.0	83.1	78.0	72.1	58.3	56.3
Asian/Pacific Islander									
10–14 years	0.3	0.4	0.7	0.8	0.6	0.7	0.4	0.3	0.2
15–19 years	26.2	23.8	26.4	27.4	27.0	26.1	23.1	20.5	19.8
Hispanic[2]									
10–14 years	1.7	—	2.4	2.4	2.7	2.7	2.1	1.7	1.6
15–19 years	82.2	—	100.3	106.7	106.8	106.7	93.6	87.3	86.4

NOTE: (—) = Data not available. 1. Includes births to Aleuts and Eskimos. 2. Persons of Hispanic origin may be of any race. *Source:* Centers for Disease Control, National Center for Health Statistics, *National Vital Statistics Reports*, vol. 51, no. 4, Feb. 6, 2003.

Births: Other Data for 2001

The source for the data on U.S. births, birth rates, and fertility rates in this section is the *National Vital Statistics Reports* series published by the National Center for Health Statistics, a part of the Centers for Disease Control and Prevention. The report issued on Feb. 12, 2002, showing final birth data for 2000 also highlighted these findings:

Births in the United States decreased 1% for 2001, to 4,025,933. This marks the first decline in the number of births following three consecutive years of increases. The **birth rate** declined from 14.7 to 14.5 births per 1,000 total population for 2001, matching record lows reported for 1997 and 1999. The **fertility rate,** which relates births to the number of women of childbearing age, also declined 1% for 2001, to 66.9 births per 1,000 women aged 15–44 years.

The **birth rate for teenagers** reached another historic low in 2001, falling to 45.8 births per 1,000 women aged 15–19 years, a record low for the nation.

The birth rates for women in their twenties declined in 2001. The rate for women ages 20–24 dropped 2% to 109.9 births per 1,000. The rate for 25–29 year olds was down very slightly to 121.3. The **birth rate for women in their thirties** increased in 2001. The rate for women ages 30–34 rose 1%, to 95.2 per 1,000, and that for women ages 35–39 years increased by 2%, to 41.3 per 1,000. Rates for these age groups have risen 20% and 30%, respectively, over the last decade. The birth rate for women 40–44 years increased to 8.1 per 1,000, matching the previous high in 1970.

In 2001, the **median age at first birth** increased to 24.8 years, from 24.6. The median age of first-time mothers has risen fairly consistently over the last three decades.

Cigarette smoking during pregnancy continued to fall in 2001, to 12.0%, a drop of 38% from 1989. As in previous years, women ages 18–24 were most likely to smoke during pregnancy. Smoking rates declined in 2001 for teenagers and women in age groups 25–54 years. A small increase was reported for women aged 20–24 years. Infant birth weight is seriously compromised by maternal smoking: In 2001, 11.9% of infants born to smokers weighed less than 2,500 grams (5 lb 8 oz), compared with 7.3% of infants born to nonsmokers.

The **cesarean delivery rate** increased for the fifth consecutive year, to 24.4% of all births. The 2001 rate is the highest since these data became available from birth certificates, in 1989. Following declines between 1989 and 1996, the rate has increased steadily.

The **preterm birth rate,** or percentage of infants born after less than 37 completed weeks of gestation, increased to 11.9% in 2001, up from 11.6% in 2000. The preterm birth rate has risen 27% since 1981.

The number and rate of **twin births** continued to climb for 2001, rising 3% to 30.1 per 1,000 total births, marking the first year in which the proportion of all births which are twins exceeded 3%. The twinning rate has risen 33% since 1990, and 59% since 1980. Following a 2-year decline, the rate of **triplet-plus births** rose 3% to 185.6 per 100,000, but remained lower than the 1998 peak. The triplet-plus birth rate has climbed more than 400% since 1980.

Adoption Trends

Background

Although adoption is mentioned in the legal codes and writings of many ancient peoples, including the Romans and Hebrews, no such laws existed in England or her colonies prior to the middle of the 19th century. Instead, indigent children were generally sent to public institutions known as almshouses until the age of six or seven, when they could be "put out" as indentured servants or apprentices. Families also sometimes took in children informally, especially in rural areas to help on the farm.

In the United States, these practices worked well enough until the early 19th century, when changes in economic conditions and the size of the population produced numbers of children the system couldn't cope with. At the same time, largely through the efforts of certain social reformers, society's attitude toward adoption began to change. Private agencies were established to place children in homes where they would be treated as members of the family rather than servants. And families who took in children increasingly petitioned state legislatures for private adoption acts to ensure the legal status and inheritance rights of adopted children.

Finally, as a result of pressure from individual families and to provide better care for destitute children, the state legislatures were prompted to take action. Between 1851 and 1873, 17 states enacted adoption legislation, and by 1929 all states had such laws. (England did not enact general adoption laws until 1926.) Under these new statutes, adoptions had to be approved by a judge, after which the adopted child assumed the same rights accorded any natural, legitimate child of the petitioners.

Adoption in the 20th Century

Despite the legislation, foundling homes continued to exist, and legal adoption was still relatively infrequent. Many people feared that poor, abandoned, or illegitimate children were doomed to grow into troubled adults. Infants in particular were undesirable because of high mortality rates and the lack of readily available breast milk.

Following World War I, however, the demand for babies began to grow. This was partly a response to the sharp drop in population caused by the war and the influenza epidemic of 1918, and partly also due to the development of a successful feeding formula. The number of adoptions exploded, and "closed" adoptions became the norm. In closed adoptions, the identities of the birth parents and adoptive parents were kept a secret because, it was thought, this helped the child bond to its new family and avoid the stigma of illegitimacy.

By the mid-1950s the demand for healthy infants began to exceed the number available. Agencies began screening prospective parents more selectively, and by 1975 many had stopped accepting applications for nondisabled white children altogether. Other agencies were obliged to put prospective parents on waiting lists, usually for an average of three to five years. Factors contributing to the decline in available infants included the increased availability of effective contraception, a rise in the abortion rate following *Roe* v. *Wade* in 1973, and an increase in the number of unmarried women keeping their babies rather than giving them up for adoption.

It was also during the 1970s that "open" adoption, in which adoptive and birth parents were known to each other, became more accepted. A growing number of prospective parents adopted through private placement, contacting a birth mother directly through an advertisement or through the services of a lawyer or other professional specializing in adoption.

More Recent Trends

Since the end of the 20th century, infertile couples and single people have increasingly turned to transracial and international adoptions, as well as new advanced medical techniques for treating infertility and providing alternative methods of reproduction. Meanwhile, the number of older special needs children waiting adoption has skyrocketed. These children often come from backgrounds of abuse and neglect, and finding appropriate placements for them is one of the most pressing concerns in child welfare today.

Source: Columbia Encyclopedia, 6th Edition. Web: www.infoplease.com. Sokoloff, Burton Z., "Antecedents of American Adoption" in *The Future of Children: Adoption,* vol. 3, no. 1. (David and Lucile Packard Foundation: Los Altos, Calif.) Spring 1993. Web: www.futureofchildren.org.

Top Countries of Origin for U.S. International Adoptions

	2002		2001	
Rank	Country of origin	Number[1]	Country of origin	Number[1]
1.	China (mainland)	5,053	China (mainland)	4,681
2.	Russia	4,939	Russia	4,279
3.	Guatemala	2,219	South Korea	1,870
4.	South Korea	1,779	Guatemala	1,609
5.	Ukraine	1,106	Ukraine	1,246
6.	Kazakhstan	819	Romania	782
7.	Vietnam	766	Vietnam	737
8.	India	466	Kazakhstan	672
9.	Colombia	334	India	543
10.	Bulgaria	260	Colombia	407
11.	Cambodia	254	Bulgaria	297
12.	Philippines	221	Cambodia	266
13.	Haiti	187	Philippines	219
14.	Belarus	169	Haiti	192
15.	Romania	168	Ethiopia	158
16.	Ethiopia	105	Belarus	129
17.	Poland	101	Poland	86
18.	Thailand	67	Thailand	74
19.	Peru	65	Mexico	73
20.	Mexico	61	Jamaica and Liberia	51
	Total[2]	**20,099**	**Total[2]**	**19,237**

1. Figures based on number of immigrant visas issued to orphans. 2. Figures for fiscal year. *Source:* U.S. State Department. Web: http://travel.state.gov/orphan_numbers.html.

Children in Foster Care

	Percent	Number
Total		**542,000**
Ages		
Under 1 year	4%	22,957
1–5 years	24	130,857
6–10 years	24	127,711
11–15 years	30	160,419
16–18 years	17	89,632
19 years and over	2	10,424
Gender		
Male	52	283,854
Female	48	258,146

	Percent	Number
Race/ethnicity		
White, non-Hispanic	37%	203,222
Black, non-Hispanic	38	204,973
Hispanic[1]	17	89,785
American Indian/Alaskan Native, non-Hispanic	2	10,106
Asian, non-Hispanic	1	3,649
Hawaiian/Pacific Islander, non-Hispanic	0	1,551
Unknown/unable to determine	3	17,235
Two or more races non-Hispanic	2	11,479

NOTE: Preliminary FY 2001 estimates as of March 2003. Percentages may not add up to 100% and numbers may not add up to totals due to rounding. 1. Hispanic can be of any race. *Source:* U.S. Dept. of Health and Human Services, Admin. for Children and Families, Adoption and Foster Care Analysis and Reporting System (AFCARS) Report #5. Web: www.acf.dhhs.gov/programs/cb.

Child Abuse and Neglect

Item	1990		1995		1999		2000	
	Number	Percent	Number	Percent	Number	Percent	Number	Percent
Types of substantiated maltreatment								
Victims, total[1, 2]	690,658	—	970,285	—	783,632	—	862,455	—
Neglect	338,770	49.1%	507,015	52.3%	439,094	56.0%	515,792	59.8%
Physical abuse	186,801	27.0	237,840	24.5	167,703	21.4	166,232	19.3
Sexual abuse	119,506	17.3	122,964	12.7	88,801	11.3	87,480	10.1
Emotional maltreatment	45,621	6.6	42,051	4.3	59,842	7.6	66,293	7.7
Medical neglect	n.a.	n.a.	28,541	2.9	18,809	2.4	25,450	3.0
Sex of victim								
Victims, total[2]	742,519	100.0	809,634	100.0	779,787	100.0	862,455	100.0
Male	323,339	43.5	381,075	47.1	371,588	47.7	412,074	47.8
Female	369,919	49.8	425,193	52.5	402,051	51.6	444,793	51.6
Age of victim								
Victims, total[2]	731,282	100.0	808,575	100.0	780,145	100.0	862,455	100.0
1 year and younger	97,101	13.3	103,335	12.8	109,597	14.1	132,267	15.3
2 to 5 years old	172,791	23.6	215,303	26.6	186,178	23.9	204,367	23.7
6 to 9 years old	157,681	21.6	195,400	24.2	196,639	25.2	210,463	24.4
10 to 13 years old	135,130	18.5	154,682	19.1	157,879	20.2	174,854	20.3
14 to 17 years old	103,383	14.1	121,548	15.0	117,436	15.1	125,370	14.5
18 years and over	4,880	0.7	7,506	0.9	4,101	0.5	995	0.1

NOTE: n.a. = not available. (—) = not applicable. 1. More than one type of maltreatment may be substantiated per child. Therefore, totals for this category will add up to more than 100 percent. Victim totals and maltreatment types are based on subset of states that reported both the number of child victims and maltreatment incidences by type for that year. 2. Includes other and unknown not shown separately. *Source: Statistical Abstract of the United States, 2002.*

Child-Care Arrangements for Preschool Children, 1999

Characteristic	Children		Type of nonparental arrangement[1]			
	Number (1,000s)	Percent distribution	Relative care	Nonrelative care	Center-based program[2]	Parental care only
Race/ethnicity						
White, non-Hispanic	5,296	61.9	18.8	19.3	59.4	23.6
Black, non-Hispanic	1,258	14.7	36.0	8.0	72.5	13.1
Hispanic	1,421	16.6	25.9	12.7	44.4	33.6
Other	574	6.7	31.0	9.9	66.0	17.5
Household income						
Less than $10,001	1,126	13.2	28.9	12.8	56.6	26.6
$10,001 to $20,000	1,395	16.3	29.5	12.9	51.1	28.1
$20,001 to $30,000	1,327	15.5	27.7	12.2	50.8	29.6
$30,001 to $40,000	1,050	12.3	23.3	14.9	54.5	25.3
$40,001 to $50,000	792	9.3	20.9	14.2	59.7	23.1
$50,001 to $75,000	1,351	15.8	17.3	20.5	65.5	19.0
$75,001 or more	1,509	17.7	16.2	21.9	74.0	13.4
Total	**8,549**	**100.0**	**23.3**	**15.9**	**59.3**	**23.3**

NOTES: Estimates are based on children three to five years old who have not entered kindergarten. 1. Columns do not add to total because some children participated in more than one type of nonparental arrangement. 2. Center-based programs include day-care centers, head-start programs, preschools, prekindergartens, and nursery schools. *Source: Statistical Abstract of the United States, 2001.*

Mortality

Life Expectancy by Age, 1850–2000

The expectation of life at a specified age is the average number of years that members of a hypothetical group of people of the same age would continue to live if they were subject throughout the remainder of their lives to the same mortality rate.

	Age								
Calendar period	0	10	20	30	40	50	60	70	80
White males									
1850[1]	38.3	48.0	40.1	34.0	27.9	21.6	15.6	10.2	5.9
1890[1]	42.50	48.45	40.66	34.05	27.37	20.72	14.73	9.35	5.40
1900–1902[2]	48.23	50.59	42.19	34.88	27.74	20.76	14.35	9.03	5.10
1909–1911[2]	50.23	51.32	42.71	34.87	27.43	20.39	13.98	8.83	5.09
1919–1921[3]	56.34	54.15	45.60	37.65	29.86	22.22	15.25	9.51	5.47
1929–1931	59.12	54.96	46.02	37.54	29.22	21.51	14.72	9.20	5.26
1939–1941	62.81	57.03	47.76	38.80	30.03	21.96	15.05	9.42	5.38
1949–1951	66.31	58.98	49.52	40.29	31.17	22.83	15.76	10.07	5.88
1959–1961[5]	67.55	59.78	50.25	40.98	31.73	23.22	16.01	10.29	5.89
1969–1971[6]	67.94	59.69	50.22	41.07	31.87	23.34	16.07	10.38	6.18
1979–1981	70.82	61.98	52.45	43.31	34.04	25.26	17.56	11.35	6.76
1990	72.7	63.5	54.0	44.7	35.6	26.7	18.7	12.1	7.1
2000[7]	74.8	65.4	55.7	46.4	37.1	28.2	20.0	13.0	7.6
White females									
1850[1]	40.5	47.2	40.2	35.4	29.8	23.5	17.0	11.3	6.4
1890[1]	44.46	49.62	42.03	35.36	28.76	22.09	15.70	10.15	5.75
1900–1902[2]	51.08	52.15	43.77	36.42	29.17	21.89	15.23	9.59	5.50
1909–1911[2]	53.62	53.57	44.88	36.96	29.26	21.74	14.92	9.38	5.35
1919–1921[3]	58.53	55.17	46.46	38.72	30.94	23.12	15.93	9.94	5.70
1929–1931	62.67	57.65	48.52	39.99	31.52	23.41	16.05	9.98	5.63
1939–1941	67.29	60.85	51.38	42.21	33.25	24.72	17.00	10.50	5.88
1949–1951	72.03	64.26	54.56	45.00	35.64	26.76	18.64	11.68	6.59
1959–1961[5]	74.19	66.05	56.29	46.63	37.13	28.08	19.69	12.38	6.67
1969–1971[6]	75.49	66.97	57.24	47.60	38.12	29.11	20.79	13.37	7.59
1979–1981	78.22	69.21	59.44	49.76	40.16	30.96	22.45	14.89	8.65
1990	79.4	70.1	60.3	50.6	41.0	31.6	23.0	15.4	9.0
2000[7]	80.0	70.5	60.7	50.9	41.3	32.0	23.2	15.5	9.1
All other males[4]									
1900–1902[2]	32.54	41.90	35.11	29.25	23.12	17.34	12.62	8.33	5.12
1909–1911[2]	34.05	40.65	33.46	27.33	21.57	16.21	11.67	8.00	5.53
1919–1921[3]	47.14	45.99	38.36	32.51	26.53	20.47	14.74	9.58	5.83
1929–1931	47.55	44.27	35.95	29.45	23.36	17.92	13.15	8.78	5.42
1939–1941	52.33	48.54	39.74	32.25	25.23	19.18	14.38	10.06	6.46
1949–1951	58.91	52.96	43.73	35.31	27.29	20.25	14.91	10.74	7.07
1959–1961[5]	61.48	55.19	45.78	37.05	28.72	21.28	15.29	10.81	6.87
1969–1971[6]	60.98	53.67	44.37	36.20	28.29	21.24	15.35	10.68	7.57
1979–1981	65.63	57.40	47.87	39.13	30.64	22.92	16.54	11.36	7.22
1990	67.0	58.5	49.0	40.3	31.9	23.9	17.0	11.4	7.0
2000[7]	68.3	59.6	50.0	41.1	32.3	24.3	17.5	11.8	7.4
All other females[4]									
1900–1902[2]	35.04	43.02	36.89	30.70	24.37	18.67	13.60	9.62	6.48
1909–1911[2]	37.67	42.84	36.14	29.61	23.34	17.65	12.78	9.22	6.05
1919–1921[3]	46.92	44.54	37.15	31.48	25.60	19.76	14.69	10.25	6.58
1929–1931	49.51	45.33	37.22	30.67	24.30	18.60	14.22	10.38	6.90
1939–1941	55.51	50.83	42.14	34.52	27.31	21.04	16.14	11.81	8.00
1949–1951	62.70	56.17	46.77	38.02	29.82	22.67	16.95	12.29	8.15
1959–1961[5]	66.47	59.72	50.07	40.83	32.16	24.31	17.83	12.46	7.66
1969–1971[6]	69.05	61.49	51.85	42.61	33.87	25.97	19.02	13.30	9.01
1979–1981	74.00	65.64	55.88	46.39	37.16	28.59	20.49	14.44	9.17
1990	75.2	66.6	56.8	47.3	38.1	29.2	21.3	14.5	8.8
2000[7]	75.0	66.2	56.4	46.8	37.6	29.0	21.0	14.1	8.7

1. Massachusetts only; white and nonwhite combined, the latter being about 1% of the total. *Source:* U.S. Dept. of Commerce, Bureau of the Census, *Historical Statistics of the United States.* 2. Original Death Registration States. 3. Death Registration States of 1920. 4. Data for periods 1900–1902, 1929–1931, and 2000 relate to blacks only. 5. Alaska and Hawaii included beginning in 1959. 6. Deaths of nonresidents of the United States excluded starting in 1970. 7. Preliminary. *Sources:* Department of Health and Human Services, National Center for Health Statistics. Web: www.dhhs.gov.

Life Expectancy at Birth by Race and Sex, 1940–2000

Year	All races			White			Black		
	Both sexes	Male	Female	Both sexes	Male	Female	Both sexes	Male	Female
2001[1]	77.2	74.4	79.8	77.7	75.0	80.2	72.2	68.6	75.5
2000	77.0	74.3	79.7	77.6	74.9	80.1	71.9	68.3	75.2
1999	76.7	73.9	79.4	77.3	74.6	79.9	71.4	67.8	74.7
1998	76.7	73.8	79.5	77.3	74.5	80.0	71.3	67.6	74.8
1997	76.5	73.6	79.4	77.2	74.3	79.9	71.1	67.2	74.7
1996	76.1	73.1	79.1	76.8	73.9	79.7	70.2	66.1	74.2
1995	75.8	72.5	78.9	76.5	73.4	79.6	69.6	65.2	73.9
1994	75.7	72.4	79.0	76.5	73.3	79.6	69.5	64.9	73.9
1993	75.5	72.2	78.8	76.3	73.1	79.5	69.2	64.6	73.7
1992	75.8	72.3	79.1	76.5	73.2	79.8	69.6	65.0	73.9
1991	75.5	72.0	78.9	76.3	72.9	79.6	69.3	64.6	73.8
1990	75.4	71.8	78.8	76.1	72.7	79.4	69.1	64.5	73.6
1989	75.1	71.7	78.5	75.9	72.5	79.2	68.8	64.3	73.3
1988	74.9	71.4	78.3	75.6	72.2	78.9	68.9	64.4	73.2
1987	74.9	71.4	78.3	75.6	72.1	78.9	69.1	64.7	73.4
1986	74.7	71.2	78.2	75.4	71.9	78.8	69.1	64.8	73.4
1985	74.7	71.1	78.2	75.3	71.8	78.7	69.3	65.0	73.4
1984	74.7	71.1	78.2	75.3	71.8	78.7	69.5	65.3	73.6
1983	74.6	71.0	78.1	75.2	71.6	78.7	69.4	65.2	73.5
1982	74.5	70.8	78.1	75.1	71.5	78.7	69.4	65.1	73.6
1981	74.1	70.4	77.8	74.8	71.1	78.4	68.9	64.5	73.2
1980	73.7	70.0	77.4	74.4	70.7	78.1	68.1	63.8	72.5
1979	73.9	70.0	77.8	74.6	70.8	78.4	68.5	64.0	72.9
1978	73.5	69.6	77.3	74.1	70.4	78.0	68.1	63.7	72.4
1977	73.3	69.5	77.2	74.0	70.2	77.9	67.7	63.4	72.0
1976	72.9	69.1	76.8	73.6	69.9	77.5	67.2	62.9	71.6
1975	72.6	68.8	76.6	73.4	69.5	77.3	66.8	62.4	71.3
1974	72.0	68.2	75.9	72.8	69.0	76.7	66.0	61.7	70.3
1973	71.4	67.6	75.3	72.2	68.5	76.1	65.0	60.9	69.3
1972[2]	71.2	67.4	75.1	72.0	68.3	75.9	64.7	60.4	69.1
1971	71.1	67.4	75.0	72.0	68.3	75.8	64.6	60.5	68.9
1970	70.8	67.1	74.7	71.7	68.0	75.6	64.1	60.0	68.3
1960	69.7	66.6	73.1	70.6	67.4	74.1	—	—	—
1950	68.2	65.6	71.1	69.1	66.5	72.2	—	—	—
1940	62.9	60.8	65.2	64.2	62.1	66.6	—	—	—

(—) Data not available. 1. Preliminary. 2. Deaths based on a 50% sample. *Source:* National Center for Health Statistics, *National Vital Statistics Reports,* vol. 49, no. 12, Oct. 9, 2001. Web: www.cdc.gov/nchs.

15 Leading Causes of Death in the U.S., 2001

Leading causes of death differ somewhat by age, sex, and race. In 2001, as in previous years, accidents were the leading cause of death for those under 34 years, while in older age groups chronic diseases such as cancer and heart disease were the leading causes. The top three causes for males and females—heart disease, cancer, and stroke—are exactly the same. However, suicide and chronic liver disease ranked 8th and 10th for males but were not ranked among the ten leading causes for females. Similarly, Alzheimer's disease ranked 7th for females but was not among the top ten for males. For white males aged 15–34, the top two causes were accidents and suicide, while for black males in the same age group, the top two causes of death were homicide and accidents.

Rank[1]	Causes of death	Number	Deaths per 100,000 population
	All causes	**2,417,798**	849.0
1.	Diseases of heart	699,697	245.7
2.	Malignant neoplasms (cancer)	553,251	194.3
3.	Cerebrovascular diseases	163,601	57.4
4.	Chronic lower respiratory diseases	123,974	43.5
5.	Accidents (unintentional injuries)	97,707	34.3
6.	Diabetes mellitus	71,252	25.0
7.	Influenza and pneumonia	62,123	21.8
8.	Alzheimer's disease	53,679	18.8
9.	Nephritis, nephrotic syndrome, and nephrosis	39,661	13.9
10.	Septicemia	32,275	11.3
11.	Suicide	29,423	10.3
12.	Chronic liver disease and cirrhosis	26,751	9.4
13.	Homicide	19,727	6.9
14.	Hypertension and hypertensive renal disease	19,054	6.7
15.	Pneumonitis due to solids and liquids	17,392	6.1
	All other causes	408,231	143.3

1. Rank based on number of deaths. *Source:* U.S. National Center for Health Statistics, *National Vital Statistics Report,* vol. 51, no. 5, March 14, 2003. Web: www.cdc.gov/nchs.

U.S. Annual Death Rates per 1,000 Population

Year	Rate	Year	Rate	Year	Rate	Year	Rate	Year	Rate	Year	Rate	Year	Rate
1900	17.2	1942	10.3	1952	9.6	1963	9.6	1973	9.3	1983	8.6	1993	8.8
1905	15.9	1943	10.9	1953	9.6	1964	9.4	1974	9.1	1984	8.6	1994	8.8
1910	14.7	1944	10.6	1954	9.2	1965	9.4	1975	8.8	1985	8.7	1995	8.8
1915	13.2	1945	10.6	1955	9.3	1966	9.5	1976	8.8	1986	8.7	1996	8.8
1920	13.0	1946	10.0	1956	9.4	1967	9.4	1977	8.6	1987	8.7	1997	8.6
1925	11.7	1947	10.1	1957	9.6	1968	9.7	1978	8.7	1988	8.8	1998	8.6
1930	11.3	1948	9.9	1958	9.5	1969	9.5	1979	8.5	1989	8.7	1999	8.8
1935	10.9	1949	9.7	1959	9.4	1970[1]	9.5	1980	8.7	1990	8.6	2000	8.7
1940	10.8	1950	9.6	1960	9.5	1971	9.3	1981	8.6	1991	8.5	2001	8.5
1941	10.5	1951	9.7	1962	9.5	1972	9.4	1982	8.5	1992	8.5		

NOTES: Includes only deaths occurring within the registration states. Beginning with 1933, area includes entire U.S.; with 1959 includes Alaska, and with 1960 includes Hawaii. Excludes fetal deaths. Rates as of April 1 for 1940, 1950, 1960, 1970, and 1980, and estimated as of July 1 for all other years. 1. First year for which deaths of nonresidents are excluded. *Source:* Department of Health and Human Services, National Center for Health Statistics. Web: www.dhhs.gov.

Infant Mortality Rates, 1950–2000

	Deaths per 1,000 live births					
		Neonatal				
Year	Infant	Under 28 days	Under 7 days	Postneonatal	Fetal mortality rate[1]	Late fetal mortality rate[2]
All races						
1950[3]	29.2	20.5	17.8	8.7	18.4	14.9
1960[3]	26.0	18.7	16.7	7.3	15.8	12.1
1970	20.0	15.1	13.6	4.9	14.0	9.5
1980	12.6	8.5	7.1	4.1	9.1	6.2
1985	10.6	7.0	5.8	3.7	7.8	4.9
1990	9.2	5.8	4.8	3.4	7.5	4.3
1991	8.9	5.6	4.6	3.4	7.3	4.1
1992	8.5	5.4	4.4	3.1	7.4	4.1
1993	8.4	5.3	4.3	3.1	7.1	3.8
1994	8.0	5.1	4.2	2.9	7.0	3.7
1995	7.6	4.9	4.0	2.7	7.0	3.6
1996	7.3	4.8	3.8	2.5	6.9	3.6
1997	7.2	4.8	3.8	2.5	6.8	3.5
1998	7.2	4.8	3.8	2.4	6.7	3.4
1999	7.1	4.7	3.8	2.3	6.7	3.4
2000	6.9	4.6	3.7	2.3	6.6	3.3
Race of child: white						
1950	26.8	19.4	17.1	7.4	16.6	13.3
1960	22.9	17.2	15.6	5.7	13.9	10.8
1970	17.8	13.8	12.5	4.0	12.3	8.6
1980	11.0	7.5	6.2	3.5	8.1	5.7
Race of mother: white						
1980	10.9	7.4	6.1	3.5	8.1	5.7
1985	9.2	6.0	5.0	3.2	6.9	4.5
1990	7.6	4.8	3.9	2.8	6.4	3.8
1995	6.3	4.1	3.3	2.2	5.9	3.3
1996	6.1	4.0	3.2	2.1	5.9	3.3
1997	6.0	4.0	3.2	2.0	5.8	3.2
1998	6.0	4.0	3.1	2.0	5.7	3.1
1999	5.8	3.9	3.1	1.9	—	—
Race of child: black						
1950	43.9	27.8	23.0	16.1	32.1	—
1960	44.3	27.8	23.7	16.5	—	—
1970	32.6	22.8	20.3	9.9	23.2	—
1980	21.4	14.1	11.9	7.3	14.4	8.9
Race of mother: black						
1980	22.2	14.6	12.3	7.6	14.7	9.1
1985	19.0	12.6	10.8	6.4	12.8	7.2
1990	18.0	11.6	9.7	6.4	13.3	6.7
1995	15.1	9.8	8.2	5.3	12.7	5.7
1996	14.7	9.6	7.8	5.1	12.5	5.5
1997	14.2	9.4	7.8	4.8	12.5	5.5
1998	14.3	9.5	7.8	4.8	12.3	5.3
1999	14.6	9.8	7.9	4.8	—	—

NOTES: "Infant" is defined as under 1 year of age; "neonatal" is under 28 days; "postneonatal" is 28 days–11 months. 1. Number of fetal deaths of 20 weeks or more gestation per 1,000 live births plus fetal deaths. 2. Number of fetal deaths of 28 weeks or more gestation per 1,000 live births plus late fetal deaths. 3. Includes birth and deaths of persons who were not residents of the 50 states and the District of Columbia. *Sources:* Centers for Disease Control and Prevention, National Center for Health Statistics. From *Health, United States, 2002.*

Deaths by Major Causes, 1960 to 2000

(age-adjusted death rates per 100,000 population)

Year	Heart disease	Cancer	Cerebro-vascular diseases	Chronic lower respiratory diseases	Accidents	Diabetes mellitus	Influenza and pneumonia	Suicide	Chronic liver disease and cirrhosis	Homicide
1960	559.0	193.9	177.9	12.5	63.1	22.5	53.7	12.5	13.3	5.2
1965	542.5	195.6	166.4	18.3	65.8	22.9	46.8	13.0	14.9	6.1
1970	492.7	198.6	147.7	21.3	62.2	24.3	41.7	13.1	17.8	9.0
1975	431.2	200.1	123.5	23.7	50.8	20.3	34.9	13.6	16.7	10.2
1980	412.1	207.9	96.4	28.3	46.4	18.1	31.4	12.2	15.1	10.5
1985	375.0	211.3	76.6	34.5	38.5	17.4	34.5	12.5	12.3	8.0
1990	321.8	216.0	65.5	37.2	36.3	20.7	36.8	12.5	11.1	9.5
1995	296.3	211.7	63.9	40.5	34.9	23.4	33.8	12.0	10.0	8.6
2000[1]	257.5	200.5	60.2	44.9	33.9	24.9	24.3	10.3	9.5	5.8

1. Preliminary data. *Source:* U.S. National Center for Health Statistics, *Vital Statistics of the United States*, annual. From *Statistical Abstract of the United States: 2002.*

Deaths by Firearms, 1979–2000

(per 100,000 population in specified group)

Year	All races[1]		White		Black	
	Number of deaths	Death rate[2]	Number of deaths	Death rate[2]	Number of deaths	Death rate[2]
1979	33,019	14.7	24,234	12.5	8,304	31.6
1980	33,780	14.9	24,849	12.8	8,505	31.9
1981	34,050	14.8	25,237	12.8	8,324	30.7
1982	32,957	14.2	25,071	12.7	7,415	27.0
1983	31,099	13.3	24,038	12.1	6,589	23.6
1984	31,331	13.3	24,419	12.2	6,449	22.9
1985	31,566	13.3	24,507	12.1	6,565	23.0
1986	33,373	13.9	25,339	12.5	7,494	25.9
1987	32,895	13.6	24,789	12.1	7,586	25.9
1988	33,989	13.9	24,892	12.1	8,475	28.5
1989	34,776	14.1	25,023	12.1	9,077	30.1
1990	37,155	14.9	26,299	12.6	10,175	33.4
1991	38,317	15.2	26,455	12.5	11,025	35.4
1992	37,776	14.8	26,120	12.3	10,906	34.5
1993	39,595	15.4	26,948	12.5	11,763	36.6
1994	38,505	14.8	26,403	12.2	11,223	34.4
1995	35,957	13.7	25,438	11.7	9,643	29.1
1996	34,040	12.8	24,114	11.0	9,175	27.4
1997	32,436	12.1	23,270	10.5	8,389	24.7
1998	30,708	11.4	22,480	10.1	7,503	21.8
1999	28,874	10.6	21,143	9.4	7,017	20.1
2000	28,663	10.4	20,945	9.3	7,054	20.0

1. Includes races other than black or white. 2. On an annual basis, per 100,000 population in specified group. *Source:* Centers for Disease Control and Prevention, *National Vital Statistics Reports*, vol. 50, no. 15, Sept. 16, 2002.

Death Rates for Suicide, 1950–2000

(deaths per 100,000 resident population)

Characteristic	1950[1]	1960[1]	1970	1980	1990	1996	1997	1998	1999	2000
All ages[2]	**13.6**	**12.5**	**13.1**	**12.2**	**12.0**	**11.7**	**11.4**	**11.3**	**10.7**	**10.7**
5 to 14 years	0.2	0.3	0.3	0.4	0.8	0.8	0.8	0.8	0.6	0.8
15 to 24 years	4.5	5.2	8.8	12.3	13.2	12.0	11.4	11.1	10.3	10.4
25 to 34 years	9.1	10.0	14.1	16.0	15.4	14.5	14.3	13.8	13.5	12.8
35 to 44 years	14.3	14.2	16.9	15.4	15.2	15.5	15.3	15.4	14.4	14.6
45 to 54 years	20.9	20.7	20.0	15.9	14.6	14.9	14.7	14.8	14.2	14.6
55 to 64 years	26.8	23.7	21.4	15.9	13.3	13.7	13.5	13.1	12.4	12.3
65 to 74 years	29.6	23.0	20.8	16.9	15.8	15.0	14.4	14.1	13.6	12.6
75 to 84 years	31.1	27.9	21.2	19.1	20.7	20.0	19.3	19.7	18.3	17.7
85 years and over	28.8	26.0	19.0	19.2	21.6	20.2	20.8	21.0	19.2	19.4
Male, all ages[2]	**21.2**	**20.0**	**19.8**	**19.9**	**20.6**	**20.0**	**19.4**	**19.2**	**18.2**	**17.5**
Female, all ages[2]	**5.6**	**5.6**	**7.4**	**5.7**	**4.4**	**4.3**	**4.4**	**4.3**	**4.1**	**4.1**

1. Includes deaths of persons who were not residents of the 50 states and the District of Columbia. 2. Data are age-adjusted. *Sources:* Centers for Disease Control and Prevention, National Center for Health Statistics. From *Health, United States, 2002.*

Miscellaneous

Expenditure per Consumer Unit for Entertainment and Reading

	Total	Percent of total expenditures	Fees and admissions	Television, radios, and sound equipment	Other equipment and services[1]	Reading
1985	$1,311	5.6%	$320	$371	$479	$141
1990	1,575	5.6	371	454	597	153
1995	1,775	5.5	433	542	637	163
2000	2,009	5.3	515	622	727	146
Age[2]						
Under 25 years old	1,148	5.1	271	473	348	57
25 to 34 years old	1,994	5.1	460	680	736	118
35 to 44 years old	2,615	5.8	715	789	960	151
45 to 54 years old	2,409	5.2	637	696	898	178
55 to 64 years old	2,134	5.4	509	581	865	179
65 to 74 years old	1,569	5.1	416	468	519	166
75 years old and over	835	3.8	214	325	167	128
Origin of reference person[2]						
Hispanic	1,245	3.8	262	545	380	59
Non-Hispanic	2,083	5.4	539	629	760	155
Race of reference person[2]						
White and other	2,137	5.4	561	629	791	157
Black	1,086	3.9	181	567	266	72
Region of residence[2]						
Northeast	2,087	5.4	577	627	711	172
Midwest	2,204	5.6	566	665	809	164
South	1,731	5.0	395	574	648	114
West	2,179	5.3	595	648	778	158

1. Other equipment and services includes pets, toys, and playground equipment; sports, exercise, and photographic equipment; and recreational vehicles. 2. Figures are for 2000. *Source:* U.S. Bureau of Labor Statistics, *Consumer Expenditure Survey,* annual. From *Statistical Abstract of the United States, 2002.*

Household Pet Ownership, 2001

Item	Dog	Cat	Pet bird	Horse
Percent of households owning companion pets[1]	36.1%	31.6%	4.6%	1.7%
Average number owned	1.6	2.1	2.1	3.0
Households obtaining veterinary care[2]	85.0%	66.8%	12.9%	56.7%
Average visits per household per year	2.8	1.9	0.3	2.2
Percent of households owning pets				
Annual household income:				
Under $20,000	29.7%	28.1%	5.1%	1.0%
$20,000 to $34,999	33.9	30.9	4.5	1.3
$35,000 to $54,999	37.9	32.2	4.8	2.0
$55,000 to $84,999	40.5	34.3	4.4	2.1
$85,000 and over	39.7	33.7	4.2	2.1
Household size:[1]				
One person	20.8	23.5	2.8	0.7
Two persons	34.3	31.3	4.0	1.6
Three persons	46.2	37.4	5.9	2.2
Four persons	50.6	38.2	6.3	2.3
Five or more persons	53.0	39.7	8.3	3.2

NOTE: Based on a sample survey of 80,000 households in 2001. 1. As of Dec. 31, 2001. 2. During 2001. *Source:* American Veterinary Medical Association, Schaumburg, Ill., *U.S. Pet Ownership and Demographics Sourcebook, 2002.* Reprinted with permission.

Most Popular Pet Names

The American Society for the Prevention of Cruelty to Animals (ASPCA) has conducted a veterinarian survey to find out which pet names are most popular in the United States today. Here are the top 30:

1. Max
2. Sam
3. Lady
4. Bear
5. Smokey
6. Shadow
7. Kitty
8. Molly
9. Buddy
10. Brandy
11. Ginger
12. Baby
13. Misty
14. Missy
15. Pepper
16. Jake
17. Bandit
18. Tiger
19. Samantha
20. Lucky
21. Muffin
22. Princess
23. Maggie
24. Charlie
25. Sheba
26. Rocky
27. Patches
28. Tigger
29. Rusty
30. Buster

Most Popular Given Names, 1880–2002

Boys

1880: John, William, Charles, George, James, Joseph, Frank, Henry, Thomas, Harry
1890: John, William, James, George, Charles, Joseph, Frank, Harry, Henry, Edward
1900: John, William, James, George, Charles, Joseph, Frank, Henry, Robert, Harry
1910: John, William, James, Robert, Joseph, Charles/George (tie), Edward, Frank, Henry
1920: John, William, James, Robert, Joseph, Charles, George, Edward, Thomas, Frank
1930: Robert, James, John, William, Richard, Charles, Donald, George, Joseph, Edward
1940: James, Robert, John, William, Richard, Charles, David, Thomas, Donald, Ronald
1950: John, James, Robert, William, Michael, David, Richard, Thomas, Charles, Gary
1960: David, Michael, John, James, Robert, Mark, William, Richard, Thomas, Steven
1970: Michael, David, John, James, Robert, Christopher, William, Mark, Richard, Brian
1980: Michael, Jason, Christopher, David, James, Matthew, John, Joshua, Robert, Daniel
1990: Michael, Christopher, Joshua, Matthew, David, Daniel, Andrew, Joseph, Justin, James
2000: Jacob, Michael, Matthew, Joshua, Christopher, Nicholas, Andrew, Joseph, Daniel, Tyler
2002: Jacob, Michael, Joshua, Matthew, Ethan, Joseph, Andrew, Christopher, Daniel, Nicholas

Girls

1880: Mary, Anna, Elizabeth, Margaret, Minnie, Emma, Martha, Alice, Marie, Annie/Sarah (tie)
1890: Mary, Anna, Elizabeth, Emma, Margaret, Rose, Ethel, Florence, Ida, Bertha/Helen (tie)
1900: Mary, Helen, Anna, Margaret, Ruth, Elizabeth, Marie, Rose, Florence, Bertha
1910: Mary, Helen, Margaret, Dorothy, Ruth, Anna, Mildred, Elizabeth, Alice, Ethel
1920: Mary, Dorothy, Helen, Margaret, Ruth, Virginia, Elizabeth, Anna, Mildred, Betty
1930: Mary, Betty, Dorothy, Helen, Barbara, Margaret, Maria, Patricia, Doris, Joan/Ruth (tie)
1940: Mary, Barbara, Patricia, Carol, Judith, Betty, Nancy, Maria, Margaret, Linda
1950: Linda, Mary, Patricia, Barbara, Susan, Maria, Sandra, Nancy, Deborah, Kathleen
1960: Mary, Susan, Maria, Karen, Lisa, Linda, Donna, Patricia, Debra, Deborah
1970: Jennifer, Lisa, Kimberly, Michelle, Angela, Maria, Amy, Melissa, Mary, Tracy
1980: Jennifer, Jessica, Amanda, Melissa, Sarah, Nicole, Heather, Amy, Michelle, Elizabeth
1990: Jessica, Ashley, Brittany, Amanda, Stephanie, Jennifer, Samantha, Sarah, Megan, Lauren
2000: Emily, Hannah, Madison, Ashley, Sarah, Alexis, Samantha, Jessica, Taylor, Elizabeth
2002: Emily, Madison, Hannah, Emma, Alexis, Ashley, Abigail, Sarah, Samantha, Olivia

NOTE: Represents the most frequently used given names for births, based on a sampling of Social Security Number card applications. *Source:* Social Security Administration. Web: www.ssa.gov/OACT/NOTES/note139/note139.html.

Most Common Last Names in the U.S.

Rank	Name	Frequency[1]	Rank	Name	Frequency[1]	Rank	Name	Frequency[1]
1.	Smith	1.01%	11.	Anderson	0.31%	21.	Clark	0.23%
2.	Johnson	0.81	12.	Thomas	0.31	22.	Rodriguez	0.23
3.	Williams	0.70	13.	Jackson	0.31	23.	Lewis	0.23
4.	Jones	0.62	14.	White	0.28	24.	Lee	0.22
5.	Brown	0.62	15.	Harris	0.28	25.	Walker	0.22
6.	Davis	0.48	16.	Martin	0.27	26.	Hall	0.20
7.	Miller	0.42	17.	Thompson	0.27	27.	Allen	0.20
8.	Wilson	0.34	18.	Garcia	0.25	28.	Young	0.19
9.	Moore	0.31	19.	Martinez	0.23	29.	Hernandez	0.19
10.	Taylor	0.31	20.	Robinson	0.23	30.	King	0.19

NOTE: Based on 1990 Census data. Numbers are rounded. 1. Percent of U.S. population sample. *Source:* U.S. Census Bureau. Web: www.census.gov/genealogy/names/dist.all.last.

2002 Charitable Contributions by Type of Recipient Organization

(in billions)

Type of organization	Amount contributed	Percent	Type of organization	Amount contributed	Percent
Total	**$240.92**	**100.0%**	Human services	$18.65	7.7%
Religion	84.28	35.0	Arts, culture, and humanities	12.22	5.1
Education	31.64	13.1	Public-society benefit	11.60	4.8
Unallocated giving	30.45	12.6	Environment/animals	6.59	2.7
Foundations[1]	22.00	9.1	International affairs	4.62	1.9
Health	18.87	7.8			

NOTE: All figures are rounded. Total may not be 100%. 1. Estimate. *Source:* AAFRC Trust for Philanthropy/*Giving USA 2003.*

2002 Charitable Contributions by Source of Contributions

(in billions)

Source	Amount contributed	Percent	Source	Amount contributed	Percent
Total	**$240.92**	**100.0%**	Bequests	$18.10	7.5%
Individuals	183.73	76.3	Corporations	12.19	5.1
Foundations	26.90	11.2			

NOTE: All figures are rounded. Total may not be 100%. *Source:* AAFRC Trust for Philanthropy/*Giving USA 2003.*

U.S. Charities Receiving Highest Donations in 2002

2002 rank	Charity	Private support	Year ending	2001 rank
1.	Salvation Army (Alexandria, Va.)	$1,391,073,000	9/30/2001	1.
2.	Fidelity Investments Charitable Gift Fund (Boston)	1,055,788,830	6/30/2001	2.
3.	Stowers Institute for Medical Research (Kansas City, Mo.)	950,297,058	12/31/2001	69.
4.	Lutheran Services in America (St. Paul)	848,657,502	6/30/2001	13.
5.	YMCA of the USA (Chicago)	791,376,000	12/31/2001	3.
6.	American Cancer Society (Atlanta)	756,507,000	8/31/2001	4.
7.	Harvard University (Cambridge, Mass.)	683,172,781	6/30/2001	8.
8.	Gifts In Kind International (Alexandria, Va.)	677,589,203	12/31/2001	6.
9.	American Red Cross (Washington)	663,637,966	6/30/2001	5.
10.	Metropolitan Museum of Art (New York)	499,161,764	6/30/2001	103.
11.	Stanford University (Palo Alto, Calif.)	468,966,495	8/31/2001	7.
12.	AmeriCares Foundation (New Canaan, Conn.)	462,764,787	6/30/2001	20.
13.	Catholic Charities USA (Alexandria, Va.)	461,942,580	12/31/2000	9.
14.	Nature Conservancy (Arlington, Va.)	461,001,831	6/30/2001	10.
15.	Feed the Children (Oklahoma City)	447,332,753	9/30/2001	16.
16.	Boys & Girls Clubs of America (Atlanta)	425,647,755	12/31/2001	11.
17.	America's Second Harvest (Chicago)	417,892,362	6/30/2001	12.
18.	American Heart Association (Dallas)	404,630,658	6/30/2001	15.
19.	Habitat for Humanity International (Americus, Ga.)	398,976,425	6/30/2001	18.
20.	World Vision (Federal Way, Wash.)	397,564,000	9/30/2001	17.
21.	Columbia University (New York)	358,682,692	6/30/2001	24.
22.	Yale University (New Haven, Conn.)	350,122,800	6/30/2001	19.
23.	Johns Hopkins University (Baltimore)	347,732,206	6/30/2001	23.
24.	Campus Crusade for Christ International (Orlando, Fla.)	332,659,000	8/31/2001	21.
25.	Cornell University (Ithaca, N.Y.)	309,472,937	6/30/2001	22.
26.	Indiana University System (Bloomington)	300,848,253	6/30/01	43.
27.	Emory University (Atlanta)	297,777,754	8/31/01	127.
28.	University of Wisconsin at Madison	292,428,950	6/30/01	27.
29.	Boy Scouts of America (Irving, Tex.)	290,181,000	12/31/01	28.
30.	Goodwill Industries International (Bethesda, Md.)	286,600,000	12/31/01	26.

Source: The Chronicle of Philanthropy, 2002. Reprinted with permission.

Percent of Adult Population Doing Volunteer Work, 2000

Age, sex, race, and Hispanic origin	Percent of population volunteering	Average hours volunteered per month
Total	**44.0%**	**15.1**
21–24 years	32.3	12.1
25–34 years	40.5	15.9
35–44 years	50.9	16.1
45–54 years	47.9	14.7
55–64 years	42.9	12.1
65–74 years	41.4	14.1
75 years and over	39.0	19.5
Male	41.2	14.6
Female	45.9	15.5
White	46.7	14.6
Black	36.9	18.4
Hispanic[1]	33.4	13.6

Educational attainment and household income	Percent of population volunteering	Average hours volunteered per month
Less than high school graudate	20.0%	17.1
High-school graduate	36.1	12.3
Technical, trade, or business school	46.9	16.3
4-year college degree	60.3	15.3
Some graduate school	58.4	16.7
Under $10,000	23.8	8.3
$10,000–19,999	27.2	13.1
$20,000–29,999	32.3	17.4
$30,000–39,999	37.3	12.5
$40,000–49,999	40.4	13.7
$50,000–59,999	48.3	13.0
$60,000–74,999	58.6	14.6
$75,000–99,999	57.0	16.5
$100,000 or more	55.5	18.6

Type of activity	Percent of population involved in activity
Arts, culture, humanities	2.1%
Education	7.7
Environment	2.1
Health	7.9
Human services	6.8
International, foreign	0.4
Political organizations	1.3

Type of activity	Percent of population involved in activity
Private, community foundations	2.2%
Public and societal benefit	4.0
Recreation—adults	1.5
Religion	19.1
Work-related organizations	1.0
Youth development	6.6

1. Hispanic persons may be of any race. NOTE: Covers persons 21 years and over. Volunteers are persons who worked in some way to help others for no monetary pay during the previous year. Based on a sample survey conducted during the spring of the following year and subject to sampling variability. *Source: Statistical Abstract of the United States: 2002.*

States

Data for state populations are the latest available from the U.S. Census Bureau. NOTE: Persons of Hispanic origin can be of any race. "American Indian" includes American Indians, Eskimos, and Aleuts. "Asian" includes Asian Indians, Chinese, Filipino, Japanese, Korean, and Vietnamese. Largest cities include incorporated places only, as defined by the U.S. Census Bureau. They do not include adjacent or suburban areas. Population data for U.S. cities are also the latest available from the U.S. Census Bureau.

For secession and readmission dates of the former Confederate states, *see* U.S. Government & History: The Confederate States of America. For a separate list of governors, and lists of senators and representatives elected to terms beginning in 2003, *see* U.S. Government & History: The Governors of the Fifty States, The Senate, and The House of Representatives. For U.S. Territories, *see* Countries of the World: United States.

Alabama

Capital: Montgomery
Governor: Bob Riley, R (to Jan. 2007)
Lieut. Governor: Lucy Baxley, D (to Jan. 2007)
Senators: Jeff Sessions, R (to Jan. 2009); Richard C. Shelby, R (to Jan. 2005)
Secy. of State: Nancy Worley, D (to Jan. 2007)
Treasurer: Kay Ivey, R (to Jan. 2007)
Atty. General: William Pryor, R (to Jan. 2007)
Organized as territory: March 3, 1817
Entered Union (rank): Dec. 14, 1819 (22)
Present constitution adopted: 1901
Motto: *Audemus jura nostra defendere* (We dare defend our rights)
State Symbols: flower, camellia (1959); **bird,** yellowhammer (1927); **song,** "Alabama" (1931); **tree,** Southern longleaf pine (1949, 1997); **salt water fish,** fighting tarpon (1955); **fresh water fish,** largemouth bass (1975); **horse,** racking horse (1975); **mineral,** hematite (1967); **rock,** marble (1969); **game bird,** wild turkey (1980); **dance,** square dance (1981); **nut,** pecan (1982); **fossil,** species *Basilosaurus Cetoides* (1984); **official mascot and butterfly,** eastern tiger swallowtail (1989); **insect,** monarch butterfly (1989); **reptile,** Alabama red-bellied turtle (1990); **gemstone,** star blue quartz (1990); **shell,** *scaphella junonia johnstoneae* (1990)
Nickname: Yellowhammer State
Origin of name: May come from Choctaw meaning "thicket-clearers" or "vegetation-gatherers"
10 largest cities (2000): Birmingham, 242,820; Montgomery, 201,568; Mobile, 198,915; Huntsville, 158,216; Tuscaloosa, 77,906; Hoover, 62,742; Dothan, 57,737; Decatur, 53,929; Auburn, 42,987; Gadsden, 38,978
Land area: 50,744 sq mi. (131,427 sq km)
Geographic center: In Chilton Co., 12 mi. SW of Clanton
Number of counties: 67
Largest county by population and area: Jefferson, 659,743 (2001); Baldwin, 1,596 sq mi.
State forests: 21 (48,000 ac.)
State parks: 22 (45,614 ac.)
Residents: Alabamian, Alabaman
2002 resident population est.: 4,486,508
2000 resident census population (rank): 4,447,100 (23). **Male:** 2,146,504 (48.3%); **Female:** 2,300,596 (51.7%). **White:** 3,162,808 (71.1%); **Black:** 1,155,930 (26.0%); **American Indian:** 22,430 (0.5%); **Asian:** 31,346 (0.7%); **Other race:** 28,998 (0.7%); **Two or more races:** 44,179 (1.0%); **Hispanic/Latino:** 75,830 (1.7%). **2000 percent population 18 and over:** 74.7; **65 and over:** 13.0; **median age:** 35.8.

Spanish explorers are believed to have arrived at Mobile Bay in 1519, and the territory was visited in 1540 by the explorer Hernando de Soto. The first permanent European settlement in Alabama was founded by the French at Fort Louis de la Mobile in 1702. The British gained control of the area in 1763 by the Treaty of Paris but had to cede almost all the Alabama region to the U.S. and Spain after the American Revolution. The Confederacy was founded at Montgomery in Feb. 1861, and, for a time, the city was the Confederate capital.

During the later 19th century, the economy of the state slowly improved with industrialization. At Tuskegee Institute, founded in 1881 by Booker T. Washington, Dr. George Washington Carver carried out his famous agricultural research.

In the 1950s and '60s, Alabama was the site of such landmark civil-rights actions as the bus boycott in Montgomery (1955–56) and the "Freedom March" from Selma to Montgomery (1965).

Today paper, chemicals, rubber and plastics, apparel and textiles, primary metals, and automobile manufacturing constitute the leading industries of Alabama. Continuing as a major manufacturer of coal, iron, and steel, Birmingham is also noted for its world-renowned medical center. The state ranks high in the production of poultry, soybeans, milk, vegetables, livestock, wheat, cattle, cotton, peanuts, fruits, hogs, and corn.

Points of interest include the Helen Keller birthplace at Tuscumbia, the Space and Rocket Center at Huntsville, the White House of the Confederacy, the restored state Capitol, the Civil Rights Memorial, the Rosa Parks Museum & Library, and the Shakespeare Festival Theater Complex in Montgomery; the Civil Rights Institute and the McWane Center in Birmingham; the Russell Cave near Bridgeport; the Bellingrath Gardens at Theodore; the USS *Alabama* at Mobile; Mound State Monument near Tuscaloosa; and the Gulf Coast area.

Famous natives and residents: Hank Aaron, baseball player; Ralph Abernathy, civil rights activist; Tallulah Bankhead, actress; Hugo L. Black, jurist; George Washington Carver, educator, agricultural chemist; Nat "King" Cole, entertainer; Lionel Hampton, jazz musician; W. C. Handy, composer; Courtney Cox-Arquette, actress; Helen Keller, author and educator; Coretta Scott King, civil rights leader; Harper Lee, writer; Joe Louis, boxer; Willie Mays, baseball player; Jim Nabors, actor; Jesse Owens, athlete; Rosa Parks, civil rights activist; Wayne Rogers, actor; Tascaluza, Choctaw chief; George Wallace, governor; William Weatherford (Red Eagle), Creek leader; Heather Whitestone, Miss America (1995).

Alaska

Capital: Juneau
Governor: Frank H. Murkowski, R (to Dec. 2006)
Lieut. Governor: Loren Leman, R (to Dec. 2006)
Senators: Lisa Murkowski, R (to Jan. 2005); Ted Stevens, R (to Jan. 2009)
Atty. General: Gregg D. Renkes, R (apptd. by gov.)
Organized as territory: 1912
Entered Union (rank): Jan. 3, 1959 (49)
Constitution ratified: April 24, 1956
Motto: North to the Future
State Symbols: flower, forget-me-not (1949); **tree,** sitka spruce (1962); **bird,** willow ptarmigan (1955); **fish,** king salmon (1962); **song,** "Alaska's Flag" (1955); **gem,** jade (1968); **marine mammal,** bowhead whale (1983); **fossil,** woolly mammoth (1986); **mineral,** gold (1968); **sport,** dog mushing (1972)
Nickname: The state is commonly called "The Last Frontier" or "Land of the Midnight Sun"
Origin of name: Corruption of Aleut word meaning "great land" or "that which the sea breaks against"
10 largest cities (2000): Anchorage, 260,283; Juneau, 30,711; Fairbanks, 30,224; Sitka, 8,835; Ketchikan, 7,922; Kenai, 6,942; Kodiak, 6,334; Bethel, 5,471; Wasilla, 5,469; Barrow, 4,581
Land area: 571,951 sq mi. (1,4 81,353 sq km)
Geographic center: 60 mi. NW of Mt. McKinley
Number of boroughs (counties): 27
Largest borough by population and area: Anchorage, 264,937 (2001); Yukon-Koyukuk, 157,121 sq mi.
State parks: more than 100 (3.5 million acres)
Residents: Alaskan
2002 resident population est.: 643,786
2000 resident census population (rank): 626,932 (48). **Male:** 324,112 (51.7%); **Female:** 302,820 (48.3%). **White:** 434,534 (69.3%); **Black:** 21,787 (3.5%); **American Indian and Alaska Native:** 98,043 (15.6%); **Asian:** 25,116 (4.0%); **Other race:** 9,997 (1.6%); **Two or more races:** 34,146 (5.4%); **Hispanic/Latino:** 25,852 (4.1%). **2000 percent population 18 and over:** 69.6; **65 and over:** 5.7; **median age:** 32.4.

Vitus Bering, a Dane working for the Russians, and Alexei Chirikov discovered the Alaskan mainland and the Aleutian Islands in 1741. The tremendous land mass of Alaska—equal to one-fifth of the continental U.S.—was unexplored in 1867 when Secretary of State William Seward arranged for its purchase from the Russians for $7,200,000. The transfer of the territory took place on Oct. 18, 1867. Despite a price of about two cents an acre, the purchase was widely ridiculed as "Seward's Folly." The first official census (1880) reported a total of 33,426 Alaskans, all but 430 being of aboriginal stock. The Gold Rush of 1898 resulted in a mass influx of more than 30,000 people. Since then, Alaska has contributed billions of dollars' worth of products to the U.S. economy.

In 1968, a large oil and gas reservoir near Prudhoe Bay on the Arctic Coast was found. The Prudhoe Bay reservoir, with an estimated recoverable 10 billion barrels of oil and 27 trillion cubic feet of gas, is twice as large as any other oil field in North America. The Trans-Alaska pipeline was completed in 1977 at a cost of $7.7 billion. Oil flows through the 800-mile-long pipeline from Prudhoe Bay to the port of Valdez.

Other important industries are fisheries, wood and wood products, furs, and tourism.

Denali National Park and Mendenhall Glacier in North Tongass National Forest are of interest, as is the large totem pole collection at Sitka National Historical Park. The Katmai National Park includes the "Valley of Ten Thousand Smokes," an area of active volcanoes.

The Alaska Native population includes Eskimos, Indians, and Aleuts. About half of all Alaska Natives are Eskimos. (*Eskimo* is used for Alaska Natives; *Inuit* is used for Eskimos living in Canada.) The two main Eskimo groups, Inupiat and Yupik, are distinguished by their language and geography. The former live in the north and northwest parts of Alaska and speak Inupiaq, while the latter live in the south and southwest and speak Yupik.

About a third of Alaska Natives are American Indians. The major tribes are the Alaskan Athabaskan in the central part of the state, and the Tlingit, Tsimshian, and Haida in the southeast.

The Aleuts, native to the Aleutian Islands, Kodiak Island, the lower Alaska and Kenai Peninsulas, and Prince William Sound, are physically and culturally related to the Eskimos. About 15% of Alaska Natives are Aleuts.

Famous natives and residents: Clarence L. Andrews, author; Aleksandr Baranov, first governor of Russian America; Margaret Elizabeth Bell, author; Benny Benson, designed state flag at age 13; Vitus Bering, explorer; Charles E. Bunnell, educator; Susan Butcher, sled-dog racer; William A. Egan, first state governor; Carl Ben Eielson, pioneer pilot; Henry E. Gruennig, political leader; B. Frank Heintzleman, territorial governor; Walter J. Hickel, governor; Sheldon Jackson, educator and missionary; Joe Juneau, prospector; Austin Lathrop, industrialist; Sydney Lawrence, painter; Ray Mala, actor; Virgil F. Partch, cartoonist; Joe Redington, Sr., sled-dog musher and promoter; Peter Trinble Rowe, first Episcopal bishop; Ivan Popov-Veniaminov (St. Innocent), Russian Orthodox missionary; Ferdinand Wrangel, educator; Samuel Hall Young, founder of first American church.

Arizona

Capital: Phoenix
Governor: Janet Napolitano, D (to Jan. 2007)
Senators: Jon Kyl, R (to Jan. 2007); John McCain, R (to Jan. 2005)
Secy. of State: Jan Brewer, R (to Jan. 2007)
Atty. General: Terry Goddard, D (to Jan. 2007)
Treasurer: David Petersen, R (to Jan. 2007)
Organized as territory: Feb. 24, 1863
Entered Union (rank): Feb. 14, 1912 (48)
Present constitution adopted: 1911
Motto: *Ditat Deus* (God enriches)
State Symbols: flower, flower of saguaro cactus (1931); **bird,** cactus wren (1931); **colors,** blue and old gold (1915); **song,** "Arizona" (1919); **tree,** palo verde (1954); **neckwear,** bola tie (1971); **fossil,** petrified wood (1988); **gemstone,** turquoise (1974); **mammal,** ringtail (1986); **reptile,** Arizona ridgenose rattlesnake (1986); **fish,** Arizona trout (1986); **amphibian,** Arizona tree frog (1986); **butterfly,** two-tailed swallowtail (2001)
Nickname: Grand Canyon State
Origin of name: From the Indian "Arizonac," meaning "little spring" or "young spring"
10 largest cities (2000): Phoenix, 1,321,045; Tucson, 486,699; Mesa, 396,375; Glendale, 218,812; Scottsdale, 202,705; Chandler, 176,581; Tempe, 158,625; Gilbert, 109,697; Peoria, 108,364; Yuma, 77,515
Land area: 113,635 sq mi. (294,315 sq km)
Geographic center: In Yavapai Co., 55 mi. ESE of Prescott
Number of counties: 15
Largest county by population and area: Maricopa, 3,194,798 (2001); Coconino, 18,562 sq mi.
State parks: 28

Residents: Arizonan, Arizonian
2002 resident population est.: 5,456,453
2000 resident census population (rank): 5,130,632 (20). **Male:** 2,561,057 (49.9%); **Female:** 2,569,575 (50.1%). **White:** 3,873,611 (75.5%); **Black:** 158,873 (3.1%); **American Indian:** 255,879 (5.0%); **Asian:** 92,236 (1.8%); **Other race:** 596,774 (11.6%); **Two or more races:** 146,526 (2.9%); **Hispanic/Latino:** 1,295,617 (25.3%). **2000 percent population 18 and over:** 73.4; **65 and over:** 13.0; **median age:** 34.2.

Marcos de Niza, a Spanish Franciscan friar, was the first European to explore Arizona. He entered the area in 1539 in search of the mythical Seven Cities of Gold. Although he was followed a year later by another gold seeker, Francisco Vásquez de Coronado, most of the early settlement was for missionary purposes. In 1775 the Spanish established Fort Tucson. In 1848, after the Mexican War, most of the Arizona territory became part of the U.S., and the southern portion of the territory was added by the Gadsden Purchase in 1853.

Arizona history is rich in legends of America's Old West. It was here that the great Indian chiefs Geronimo and Cochise led their people against the frontiersmen. Tombstone, Ariz., was the site of the West's most famous shoot-out—the gunfight at the O.K. Corral. Today, Arizona has one of the largest U.S. Indian populations; more than 14 tribes are represented on 20 reservations.

Manufacturing has become Arizona's most important industry. Principal products include electrical, communications, and aeronautical items. The state produces over half of the country's copper. Agriculture is also important to the state's economy. Top commodities are cattle and calves, dairy products, and cotton. In 1973 one of the world's most massive dams, the New Cornelia Tailings, was completed near Ajo.

State attractions include the Grand Canyon, the Petrified Forest, the Painted Desert, Hoover Dam, Lake Mead, Fort Apache, and the reconstructed London Bridge at Lake Havasu City.

Famous natives and residents: Apache Kid, Indian outlaw; Erma Bombeck, humorist and writer; Glen Campbell, singer; Lynda Carter, actress; Cesar Chavez, labor leader; Cochise, Apache chief; Alice Cooper, singer and songwriter; Wyatt Earp, marshall; Max Ernst, painter; Geronimo (Goyathlay), Apache chief; Barry Goldwater, politician; Zane Grey, novelist; Carl Trumbull Hayden, politician; George W. P. Hunt, first state governor; Bill Keane, cartoonist; Eusebio Kino, missionary; Percival Lowell, astronomer; Frank Luke, Jr., WWI fighter ace; Charles Mingus, jazz musician and composer; Carlos Montezuma, doctor and Indian spokesman; Stevie Nicks, singer; Sandra Day O'Connor, jurist; William O'Neill, frontier sheriff; Alexander M. Patch, general; William H. Pickering, astronomer; Linda Ronstadt, singer; Paolo Soleri, architect; Clyde W. Tombaugh, astronomer; Tanya Tucker, singer; Stewart Udall, secretary of the Interior; Frank Lloyd Wright, architect.

Arkansas

Capital: Little Rock
Governor: Mike Huckabee, R (to Jan. 2007)
Lieut. Governor: Winthrop Rockefeller, R (to Jan. 2007)
Senators: Mike Pryor, D (to Jan. 2009); Blanche Lambert Lincoln, D (to Jan. 2005)
Secy. of State: Charlie Daniels, D (to Jan. 2007)
Atty. General: Mike Beebe, D (to Jan. 2007)
Treasurer: Gus Wingfield, D (to Jan. 2007)
Organized as territory: March 2, 1819
Entered Union (rank): June 15, 1836 (25)
Present constitution adopted: 1874
Motto: *Regnat populus* (The people rule)
State Symbols: flower, apple blossom (1901); **tree,** pine (1939); **bird,** mockingbird (1929); **insect,** honeybee (1973); **song,** "Arkansas" (1963)
Nickname: The Natural State
Origin of name: From the Quapaw Indians
10 largest cities (2000): Little Rock, 183,133; Fort Smith, 80,268; North Little Rock, 60,433; Fayetteville, 58,047; Jonesboro, 55,515; Pine Bluff, 55,085; Springdale, 45,798; Conway, 43,167; Rogers, 38,829; Hot Springs, 35,750
Land area: 52,068 sq mi. (134,856 sq km)
Geographic center: In Pulaski Co., 12 mi. SW of Little Rock
Number of counties: 75
Largest county by population and area: Pulaski, 361,967 (2001); Union, 1,039 sq mi.
State parks: 50
Residents: Arkansan
2002 resident population est.: 2,710,079
2000 resident census population (rank): 2,673,400 (33). **Male:** 1,304,693 (48.8%); **Female:** 1,368,707 (51.2%). **White:** 2,138,598 (80.0%); **Black:** 418,950 (15.7%); **American Indian:** 17,808 (0.7%); **Asian:** 20,220 (0.8%); **Other race:** 40,412 (1.5%); **Two or more races:** 35,744 (1.3%); **Hispanic/Latino:** 86,866 (3.2%). **2000 percent population 18 and over:** 74.6; **65 and over:** 14.0; **median age:** 36.0.

Spaniard Hernando de Soto was among the early European explorers to visit the territory in the mid-16th century, but it was a Frenchman, Henri de Tonti, who in 1686 founded the first permanent white settlement—the Arkansas Post. In 1803 the area was acquired by the U.S. as part of the Louisiana Purchase.

Part of the Territory of Missouri from 1812, the area became a separate entity in 1819 after the first large wave of settlers arrived. The next several decades were marked by the development of the cotton industry and the spread of the Southern plantation system west into Arkansas. Arkansas joined the Confederacy in 1861, but from 1863 the northern part of the state was occupied by Union troops.

Food products are the state's largest employing sector, with lumber and wood products a close second. Arkansas is also a leader in the production of cotton, rice, and soybeans. It also has the country's only active diamond mine; located near Murfreesboro, it is operated as a tourist attraction.

Hot Springs National Park and Buffalo National River in the Ozarks are major state attractions. Blanchard Springs Caverns, the Historic Arkansas Museum at Little Rock, the William J. Clinton Birthplace in Hope, and the Arkansas Folk Center in Mountain View are also of interest.

Famous natives and residents: Maya Angelou, author and poet; Daisy Bates, social reformer; Dee Brown, author; Helen Gurley Brown, editor; Dale Bumpers, governor and senator; Glen Campbell, singer; Hattie Caraway, first elected woman senator; Johnny Cash, singer; Eldridge Cleaver, social activist; William Jefferson Clinton, former president; William Darby, founder of the Darby Rangers Dizzy Dean, baseball player; Orval Faubus, governor; John Gould Fletcher, poet; J. William Fulbright, former senator; John Grisham, author; Tess Harper, actress; John H. Johnson, publisher; E. Fay Jones, architect; Scott Joplin, composer; Douglas MacArthur, general; Patsy Montana, singer; Isaac C. Parker, judge; Albert Pike, pioneer teacher and lawyer; Mary Steenburgen, actress; Billy Bob Thornton, actor; Sam Walton, founder of Wal-Mart; William C. Warfield, concert singer and actor.

California

Capital: Sacramento
Governor: Gray Davis,[1] D (to Jan. 2007)
Lieut. Governor: Cruz M. Bustamante, D (to Jan. 2007)
Senators: Barbara Boxer, D (to Jan. 2005); Dianne Feinstein, D (to Jan. 2007)
Secy. of State: Kevin Shelley, D (to Jan. 2007)
Atty. General: Bill Lockyer, D (to Jan. 2007)
Treasurer: Phil Angelides, D (to Jan. 2007)
Entered Union (rank): Sept. 9, 1850 (31)
Present constitution adopted: 1879
Motto: *Eureka* (I have found it)
State Symbols: flower, golden poppy (1903); **tree,** California redwoods (*Sequoia sempervirens & Sequoiadendron giganteum)* (1937, 1953); **bird,** California valley quail (1931); **animal,** California grizzly bear (1953); **fish,** California golden trout (1947); **colors,** blue and gold (1951); **song,** "I Love You, California" (1951)
Nickname: Golden State
Origin of name: From a book, *Las Sergas de Esplandián,* by Garcia Ordóñez de Montalvo, c. 1500
10 largest cities (2000): Los Angeles, 3,694,820; San Diego, 1,223,400; San Jose, 894,943; San Francisco, 776,733; Long Beach, 461,522; Fresno, 427,652; Sacramento, 407,018; Oakland, 399,484; Santa Ana, 337,977; Anaheim, 328,014
Land area: 155,959 sq mi. (403,934 sq km)
Geographic center: In Madera Co., 38 mi. E of Madera
Number of counties: 58
Largest county by population and area: Los Angeles, 9,637,494 (2001); San Bernardino, 20,062 sq mi.
National forests: 18
State parks and beaches: 264
Residents: Californian
2002 resident population est.: 35,116,033
2000 resident census population (rank): 33,871,648 (1). **Male:** 16,874,892 (49.8%); **Female:** 16,996,756 (50.2%). **White:** 20,170,059 (59.5%); **Black:** 2,263,882 (6.7%); **American Indian:** 333,346 (1.0%); **Asian:** 3,697,513 (10.9%); **Other race:** 5,682,241 (16.8%); **Two or more races:** 1,607,646 (4.7%); **Hispanic/Latino:** 10,966,556 (32.4%). **2000 percent population 18 and over:** 72.7; **65 and over:** 10.6; **median age:** 33.3.

1. A recall election was scheduled for Oct. 7, 2003.

Although California was sighted by Spanish navigator Juan Rodríguez Cabrillo in 1542, its first Spanish mission (at San Diego) was not established until 1769. California became a U.S. territory in 1847 when Mexico surrendered it to John C. Frémont. On Jan. 24, 1848, James W. Marshall discovered gold at Sutter's Mill, starting the California Gold Rush and bringing settlers to the state in large numbers. By1964, California had surpassed New York to become the most populous state. One reason for this may be that more immigrants settle in California than any other state—more than one-third of the nation's total in 1994. Asians and Pacific Islanders led the influx.

Leading industries include agriculture, manufacturing (transportation equipment, machinery, and electronic equipment), biotechnology, aerospace-defense, and tourism. Principal natural resources include timber, petroleum, cement, and natural gas.

Death Valley, in the southeast, is 282 ft below sea level, the lowest point in the nation. Mt. Whitney (14,491 ft) is the highest point in the contiguous 48 states. Lassen Peak is one of two active U.S. volcanoes outside of Alaska and Hawaii; its last eruptions were recorded in 1917.

Other points of interest include Yosemite National Park, Disneyland, Hollywood, the Golden Gate Bridge, Sequoia National Park, San Simeon State Park, and Point Reyes National Seashore.

Famous natives and residents: Gertrude Atherton, author; David Belasco, playwright and producer; Shirley Temple Black, actress, ambassador; Dave Brubeck, musician; Luther Burbank, horticulturalist; Julia Child, chef; Joe DiMaggio, baseball player; James H. Doolittle, air force general; Isadora Duncan, dancer; John Frémont, explorer; Robert Frost, poet; Henry George, economist; Richard "Pancho" Gonzales, tennis player; George E. Hale, astronomer; Bret Harte, writer; William Randolph Hearst, publisher; Sidney Howard, playwright; Collis Potter Huntington, financier; Helen Hunt Jackson, writer; Robinson Jeffers, poet; Anthony M. Kennedy, jurist; Jack London, author; James W. Marshall, first discovered gold; Aimee Semple McPherson, evangelist; Marilyn Monroe, actress; John Muir, naturalist; Richard M. Nixon, president; Isamu Noguchi, sculptor; Frank Norris, novelist; Kathleen Norris, novelist; George S. Patton, Jr., general; Robert Redford, actor; Sally K. Ride, astronaut; William Saroyan, author; Junípero Serra, missionary; Upton Sinclair, novelist; Leland Stanford, railroad magnate; Lincoln Steffens, journalist, author; John Steinbeck, author; Adlai Stevenson, statesman; Johann Sutter, pioneer; Michael Tilson Thomas, conductor; Earl Warren, jurist.

Colorado

Capital: Denver
Governor: Bill Owens, R (to Jan. 2007)
Lieut. Governor: Jane Norton, R (to Jan. 2007)
Senators: Wayne A. Allard, R (to Jan. 2009); Ben Nighthorse Campbell, R (to Jan. 2005)
Secy. of State: Donetta Davidson, R (to Jan. 2007)
Treasurer: Mike Coffman, R (to Jan. 2007)
Atty. General: Ken Salazar, D (to Jan. 2007)
Organized as territory: Feb. 28, 1861
Entered Union (rank): Aug. 1, 1876 (38)
Present constitution adopted: 1876
Motto: *Nil sine Numine* (Nothing without Providence)
State Symbols: flower, Rocky Mountain columbine (1899); **tree,** Colorado blue spruce (1939); **bird,** lark bunting (1931); **animal,** Rocky Mountain bighorn sheep (1961); **gemstone,** aquamarine (1971); **colors,** blue and white (1911); **song,** "Where the Columbines Grow" (1915); **fossil,** stegosaurus (1991)
Nickname: Centennial State
Origin of name: From the Spanish, "ruddy" or "red"
10 largest cities (2000): Denver, 554,636; Colorado Springs, 360,890; Aurora, 276,393; Lakewood, 144,126; Fort Collins, 118,652; Arvada, 102,153; Pueblo, 102,121; Westminster, 100,940; Boulder, 94,673; Thornton, 82,384
Land area: 103,717 sq mi. (268,627 sq km)
Geographic center: In Park Co., 30 mi. NW of Pikes Peak
Number of counties: 63
Largest county by population and area: Denver, 554,446 (2001); Las Animas, 4,773 sq mi.
State forests: 1 (71,000 ac.)
State parks: 44 (160,000 ac.)
Residents: Coloradan, Coloradoan
2002 resident population est.: 4,506,542
2000 resident census population (rank): 4,301,261 (24). **Male:** 2,165,983 (50.4%); **Female:** 2,135,278 (49.6%). **White:** 3,560,005 (82.8%); **Black:** 165,063 (3.8%); **American Indian:** 44,241 (1.0%); **Asian:** 95,213 (2.2%); **Other race:** 309,931 (7.2%); **Two or more races:** 122,187 (2.8%); **Hispanic/Latino:** 735,601 (17.1%). **2000 percent population 18 and over:** 74.4; **65 and over:** 9.7; **median age:** 34.3.

First visited by Spanish explorers in the 1500s, the territory was claimed for Spain by Juan de

Ulibarri in 1706. The U.S. obtained eastern Colorado as part of the Louisiana Purchase in 1803, the central portion in 1845 with the admission of Texas as a state, and the western part in 1848 as a result of the Mexican War.

Colorado has the highest mean elevation of any state, with more than 1,000 Rocky Mountain peaks over 10,000 ft high and 54 towering above 14,000 ft. Pikes Peak, the most famous of these mountains, was discovered by U.S. Army lieutenant Zebulon M. Pike in 1806.

Once primarily a mining and agricultural state, Colorado's economy is now driven by the service industries, including medical providers and other business and professional services. Colorado's economy also has a strong manufacturing base. The primary manufactures are food products, printing and publishing, machinery, and electrical instruments. The state is also a communications and transportation hub for the Rocky Mountain region.

The farm industry, which is primarily concentrated in livestock, is also an important element of the state's economy. The primary crops in Colorado are corn, hay, and wheat.

Breathtaking scenery and world-class skiing make Colorado a prime tourist destination. The main tourist attractions in the state include Rocky Mountain National Park, Mesa Verde National Park, the Great Sand Dunes and Dinosaur National Monuments, Colorado National Monument, and the Black Canyon of the Gunnison National Monument.

Famous natives and residents: Tim Allen, actor and comedian; William E. Barrett, writer; William Bent, fur trader and pioneer; Charles F. Brannan, lawyer and public official; M. Scott Carpenter, astronaut; Lon Chaney, actor; Mary Coyle Chase, playwright; Jack Dempsey, boxer; John Evans, physician, educator; Douglas Fairbanks, actor; Eugene Fodor, violinist; Gene Fowler, writer; Erick Hawkins, choreographer; Helen Hunt Jackson, novelist and Indian rights activist; Homer Lea, soldier, writer; Ted Mack, TV host; Jaye P. Morgan, singer; Peg Murray, actress; Ouray, Ute Indian chief; Anne Parrish, writer; Barbara Rush, actress; Horace A. Tabor, silver king and lieut. governor; Lowell Thomas, commentator and author; Dalton Trumbo, screenwriter, novelist; Amy Van Dyken, athlete; Byron R. White, jurist; Paul Whiteman, conductor; Don Wilson, announcer.

Connecticut

Capital: Hartford
Governor: John G. Rowland, R (to Jan. 2007)
Lieut. Governor: M. Jodi Rell, R (to Jan. 2007)
Senators: Christopher J. Dodd, D (to Jan. 2005); Joseph I. Lieberman, D (to Jan. 2007)
Secy. of the State: Susan Bysiewicz, D (to Jan. 2007)
Treasurer: Denise Nappier, D (to Jan. 2007)
Atty. General: Richard Blumenthal, D (to Jan. 2007)
Entered Union (rank): Jan. 9, 1788 (5)
Present constitution adopted: Dec. 30, 1965
Motto: *Qui transtulit sustinet* (He who transplanted still sustains)
State Symbols: flower, mountain laurel (1907); **tree,** white oak (1947); **animal,** sperm whale (1975); **bird,** American robin (1943); **hero,** Nathan Hale (1985); **heroine,** Prudence Crandall (1995); **insect,** praying mantis (1977); **mineral,** garnet (1977); **song,** "Yankee Doodle" (1978); **ship,** USS *Nautilus* (1983); **shellfish,** eastern oyster (1989); **fossil,** *Eubrontes Giganteus* (1991); **composer,** Charles Edward Ives (1991)
Nickname: Constitution State (official, 1959); Nutmeg State
Origin of name: From an Indian word (Quinnehtukqut) meaning "beside the long tidal river"
10 largest cities (2000): Bridgeport, 139,529; New Haven, 123,626; Hartford, 121,578; Stamford, 117,083; Waterbury, 107,271; Norwalk, 82,951; Danbury, 74,848; New Britain, 71,538; West Hartford, 63,589; Greenwich, 61,101
Land area: 4,844 sq mi. (12,545 sq km)
Geographic center: In Hartford Co., at East Berlin
Number of counties: 8
Largest county by population and area: Fairfield, 885,368 (2001); Litchfield, 920 sq mi.
State forests: 30 (149,352 ac.)
State parks: 93 (32,960 ac.)
Residents: Connecticuter; Nutmegger
2002 resident population est.: 3,460,503
2000 resident census population (rank): 3,405,565 (29). **Male:** 1,649,319 (48.4%); **Female:** 1,756,246 (51.6%). **White:** 2,780,355 (81.6%); **Black:** 309,843 (9.1%); **American Indian:** 9,639 (0.3%); **Asian:** 82,313 (2.4%); **Other race:** 147,201 (4.3%); **Two or more races:** 74,848 (2.2%); **Hispanic/Latino:** 320,323 (9.4%). **2000 percent population 18 and over:** 75.3; **65 and over:** 13.8; **median age:** 37.4.

The Dutch navigator, Adriaen Block, was the first European of record to explore the area, sailing up the Connecticut River in 1614. In 1633, Dutch colonists built a fort and trading post near present-day Hartford but soon lost control to English Puritans from the Massachusetts Bay Colony. English settlements established in the 1630s at Windsor, Wethersfield, and Hartford united in 1639 to form the Connecticut Colony under the *Fundamental Orders*, the first modern constitution.

Connecticut played a prominent role in the Revolutionary War, serving as the Continental Army's major supplier. Sometimes called the "Arsenal of the Nation," the state became one of the most industrialized in the nation.

Today, Connecticut factories produce weapons, sewing machines, jet engines, helicopters, motors, hardware and tools, cutlery, clocks, locks, silverware, and submarines. Hartford has the oldest U.S. newspaper still being published—the *Hartford Courant,* established 1764—and is the insurance capital of the nation.

Connecticut leads New England in the production of eggs, pears, peaches, and mushrooms, and its oyster crop is the nation's second largest. Poultry and dairy products also account for a large portion of farm income.

Connecticut is a popular resort area with its 250-mile Long Island Sound shoreline and many inland lakes. Among the major points of interest are Yale University's Gallery of Fine Arts and Peabody Museum. Other famous museums include the P. T. Barnum, Winchester Gun, and American Clock and Watch. The town of Mystic features a re-created 19th-century New England seaport and the Mystic Marinelife Aquarium.

Famous natives and residents: Dean Acheson, statesman; Ethan Allan, American Revolutionary soldier; Benedict Arnold, American Revolutionary general; P. T. Barnum, showman; Henry Ward Beecher, clergyman; John Brown, abolitionist; Prudence Crandell, educator and reformer; Oliver Ellsworth, jurist; Eileen Farrell, soprano; Charles Goodyear, inventor; Nathan Hale, American Revolutionary officer; Dorothy Hamill, ice skater; Katharine Hepburn, actress; Charles Ives, composer; Edwin H. Land, inventor; John Pierpont Morgan, financier; Frederick Law Olmsted, landscape designer; Rosa Ponselle, soprano; Adam Clayton Powell, Jr., congressman; Benjamin Spock, pediatrician; Harriet Beecher Stowe, author; Mark Twain, author; Morris R. Waite, jurist; Noah Webster, lexicographer.

Delaware

Capital: Dover
Governor: Ruth Ann Minner, D (to Jan. 2005)
Lieut. Governor: John C. Carney, Jr., D (to Jan. 2005)
Senators: Joseph R. Biden, Jr., D (to Jan. 2009); Thomas R. Carper, D (to Jan. 2007)
Secy. of State: Harriet Smith Windsor, D (to Jan. 2007)
Treasurer: Jack Markell, D (to Jan. 2007)
Atty. General: M. Jane Brady, R (to Jan. 2007)
Entered Union (rank): Dec. 7, 1787 (1)
Present constitution adopted: 1897
Motto: Liberty and independence
State Symbols: colors, colonial blue and buff; **flower,** peach blossom (1895); **tree,** American holly (1939); **bird,** blue hen chicken (1939); **insect,** ladybug (1974); **butterfly,** tiger swallowtail (1999); **fish,** weakfish, *cynoscion regalis* (1981); **song,** "Our Delaware"; **beverage,** milk; **fossil,** belemnite
Nicknames: Diamond State; First State; Small Wonder
Origin of name: From Delaware River and Bay; named in turn for Sir Thomas West, Baron De La Warr
10 largest cities (2000): Wilmington, 72,664; Dover, 32,135; Newark, 28,547; Milford, 6,732; Seaford, 6,699; Middletown, 6,161; Elsmere, 5,800; Smyrna, 5,679; New Castle, 4,862; Georgetown, 4,643
Land area: 1,954 sq mi. (5,161 sq km)
Geographic center: In Kent Co., 11 mi. S of Dover
Number of counties: 3
Largest county by population and area: New Castle, 505,829 (2001); Sussex, 938 sq mi.
State forests: 3 (over 15,000 ac.)
State parks: 14
Residents: Delawarean
2002 resident population est.: 807,385
2000 resident census population (rank): 783,600 (45). **Male:** 380,541 (48.6%); **Female:** 403,059 (51.4%). **White:** 584,773 (74.6%); **Black:** 150,666 (19.2%); **American Indian:** 2,731 (0.3%); **Asian:** 16,259 (2.1%); **Other race:** 15,855 (2.0%); **Two or more races:** 13,033 (1.7%); **Hispanic/Latino:** 37,277 (4.8%). **2000 percent population 18 and over:** 75.2; **65 and over:** 13.0; **median age:** 36.0.

Henry Hudson, sailing under the Dutch flag, is credited with Delaware's discovery in 1609. The following year, Capt. Samuel Argall of Virginia named Delaware for his colony's governor, Thomas West, Baron De La Warr. An attempted Dutch settlement failed in 1631. Swedish colonization began at Fort Christina (now Wilmington) in 1638, but New Sweden fell to Dutch forces led by New Netherlands' governor Peter Stuyvesant in 1655.

England took over the area in 1664, and it was transferred to William Penn as the lower Three Counties in 1682. Semiautonomous after 1704, Delaware fought as a separate state in the American Revolution and became the first state to ratify the Constitution in 1787.

During the Civil War, although a slave state, Delaware did not secede from the Union.

In 1802, Ëleuthère Irénée du Pont established a gunpowder mill near Wilmington that laid the foundation for Delaware's huge chemical industry. Delaware's manufactured products now also include vulcanized fiber, textiles, paper, medical supplies, metal products, machinery, machine tools, and automobiles.

Delaware also grows a great variety of fruits and vegetables and is a U.S. pioneer in the food-canning industry. Corn, soybeans, potatoes, and hay are important crops. Delaware's broiler-chicken farms supply the big Eastern markets, and fishing and dairy products are other important industries.

Points of interest include the Fort Christina Monument, Hagley Museum, Holy Trinity Church (erected in 1698, the oldest Protestant church in the United States still in use), and Winterthur Museum, in and near Wilmington; central New Castle, an almost unchanged late 18th-century capital; and the Delaware Museum of Natural History.

Popular recreation areas include Cape Henlopen, Delaware Seashore, Trap Pond State Park, and Rehoboth Beach.

Famous natives and residents: Richard Allen, founder of the African Methodist Episcopal Church; Valerie Bertinelli, actress; Robert Montgomery Bird, writer and artist; Henry S. Canby, editor and author; Annie Jump Cannon, astronomer; Elizabeth Margaret Chandler, author; Felix Darley, artist; John Dickinson, statesman; E. I. du Pont, industrialist; Oliver Evans, inventor; Thomas Garrett, abolitionist; Henry Heimlich, surgeon, inventor; William Julius "Judy" Johnson, baseball player; J. P. Marquand, novelist; Howard Pyle, artist and author; George Read, jurist, signer of Declaration of Independence; Jay Saunders Redding, educator and author; Caesar Rodney, patriot, signer of Declaration of Independence; Frank Stephens, sculptor; Estelle Taylor, actress; George Alfred Townsend, journalist and author.

District of Columbia

See Washington, DC, listing in U.S. Cities.

Florida

Capital: Tallahassee
Governor: Jeb Bush, R (to Jan. 2007)
Lieut. Governor: Toni Jennings, R (to Jan. 2007)
Senators: Bob Graham, D (to Jan. 2005); Bill Nelson, D (to Jan. 2007)
Secy. of State: Glenda Hood , R (to Jan. 2007)
Atty. General: Charlie Crist, R (to Jan. 2007)
Organized as territory: March 30, 1821
Entered Union (rank): March 3, 1845 (27)
Present constitution adopted: 1969
Motto: In God we trust (1868)
State Symbols: flower, orange blossom (1909); **bird,** mockingbird (1927); **song,** "Suwannee River" (1935)
Nickname: Sunshine State (1970)
Origin of name: From the Spanish, meaning "feast of flowers" (Easter)
10 largest cities (2000): Jacksonville, 735,617; Miami, 362,470; Tampa, 303,447; St. Petersburg, 248,232; Hialeah, 226,419; Orlando, 185,951; Fort Lauderdale, 152,397; Tallahassee, 150,624; Hollywood, 139,357; Pembroke Pines, 137,427
Land area: 53,927 sq mi. (139,671 sq km)
Geographic center: In Hernando Co., 12 mi. NNW of Brooksville
Number of counties: 67
Largest county by population and area: Miami-Dade, 2,289,683 (2001); Palm Beach, 2,034 sq mi.
State forests: 31 (more than 890,000 ac.)
State parks: 151 (523,920 ac.)
Residents: Floridian, Floridan
2002 resident population est.: 16,713,149
2000 resident census population (rank): 15,982,378 (4). **Male:** 7,797,715 (48.8%); **Female:** 8,184,663 (51.2%). **White:** 12,465,029 (78.0%); **Black:** 2,335,505 (14.6%); **American Indian:** 53,541 (0.3%); **Asian:** 266,256 (1.7%); **Other race:** 477,107 (3.0%); **Two or more races:** 376,315 (2.4%); **Hispanic/Latino:** 2,682,715 (16.8%). **2000 percent population 18 and over:** 77.2; **65 and over:** 17.6; **median age:** 38.7.

In 1513, Ponce de León, seeking the mythical "Fountain of Youth," discovered and named Florida, claiming it for Spain. Later, Florida would be held at different times by Spain and England until Spain finally sold it to the United States in 1819. (Incidentally, France established a colony named Fort Caroline in 1564 in the state that was to become Florida.)

Florida's history in the early 19th century was marked by wars with the Seminole Indians, which did not end until 1842.

Florida's economy rests on a solid base of tourism, manufacturing, and agriculture. Leading the manufacturing sector are electrical equipment and electronics, printing and publishing, transportation equipment, food processing, and machinery. Oranges, grapefruit, and other citrus fruits lead Florida's agricultural products list, followed by potatoes, melons, strawberries, sugar cane, peanuts, dairy products, and cattle.

Major tourist attractions are Miami Beach, Palm Beach, St. Augustine (founded in 1565, thus the oldest permanent city in the U.S.), Daytona Beach, and Fort Lauderdale on the East Coast; Sarasota, Tampa, and St. Petersburg on the West Coast; and Key West off the southern tip of Florida. The Orlando area, where Disney World is located on a 27,000-acre site, is Florida's most popular tourist destination. Also drawing many visitors are the NASA Kennedy Space Center's Spaceport USA, Everglades National Park, and the Epcot Center.

Famous natives and residents: Julian "Cannonball" Adderley, jazz saxophonist; Pat Boone, singer; Fernando Bujones, ballet dancer; Steve Carlton, baseball player; Faye Dunaway, actress; Stepin Fetchit (Lincoln Theodore Perry), comedian; Lue Gim Gong, horticulturist; Dwight Gooden, baseball player; Zora Neale Hurston, writer; Daniel James, air force general; James Weldon Johnson, author and educator; Frances Langford, singer; Butterfly McQueen, actress; Jim Morrison, singer; Osceola, Seminole Indian leader; Sidney Poitier, actor; A. Philip Randolph, labor leader; Marjorie Kinnan Rawlings, author; Burt Reynolds, actor; Charles and John Ringling, circus entrepreneurs; Joseph W. Stilwell, army general; Norman E. Thargard, astronaut; Clarence Thomas, jurist; Ben Vereen, actor.

Georgia

Capital: Atlanta
Governor: Sonny Perdue, R (to Jan. 2007)
Lieut. Governor: Mark Taylor, D (to Jan. 2007)
Senators: Saxby Chambliss, R(to Jan. 2009); Zell Miller, D (to Jan. 2005)
Secy. of State: Cathy Cox, D (to Jan. 2007)
Chief Financial Officer: Tom Gallagher, R (to Jan. 2007)
Atty. General: Thurbert Baker, D (to Jan. 2007)
Entered Union (rank): Jan. 2, 1788 (4)
Present constitution adopted: 1977
Motto: Wisdom, justice, and moderation
State Symbols: flower, Cherokee rose (1916); **tree,** live oak (1937); **bird,** brown thrasher (1935); **song,** "Georgia on My Mind" (1922)
Nicknames: Peach State, Empire State of the South
Origin of name: In honor of George II of England
10 largest cities (2000): Atlanta, 416,474; Augusta-Richmond County[1], 199,775; Columbus[1], 186,291; Savannah, 131,510; Athens-Clarke County[1], 101,489; Macon, 97,255; Roswell, 79,334; Albany, 76,939; Marietta, 58,748; Warner Robins, 48,804
Land area: 57,906 sq mi. (149,977 sq km)
Geographic center: In Twiggs Co., 18 mi. SE of Macon
Number of counties: 159
Largest county by population and area: Fulton, 816,638 (2001); Ware, 903 sq mi.
State forests: 25,258,000 ac. (67% of total state area)
State parks: 53 (42,600 ac.)
Residents: Georgian
2002 resident population est.: 8,560,310
2000 resident census population (rank): 8,186,453 (10). **Male:** 4,027,113 (49.2%); **Female:** 4,159,340 (50.8%). **White:** 5,327,281 (65.1%); **Black:** 2,349,542 (28.7%); **American Indian:** 21,737 (0.3%); **Asian:** 173,170 (2.1%); **Other race:** 196,289 (2.4%); **Two or more races:** 114,188 (1.4%); **Hispanic/Latino:** 435,227 (5.3%). **2000 percent population 18 and over:** 73.5; **65 and over:** 9.6; **median age:** 33.4.

1. The city is part of a consolidated city-county government; the city and county are coextensive.

Hernando de Soto, the Spanish explorer, first traveled parts of Georgia in 1540. British claims later conflicted with those of Spain. After obtaining a royal charter, Gen. James Oglethorpe established the first permanent settlement in Georgia in 1733 as a refuge for English debtors. In 1742, Oglethorpe defeated Spanish invaders in the Battle of Bloody Marsh.

A Confederate stronghold, Georgia was the scene of extensive military action during the Civil War. Union general William T. Sherman burned Atlanta and destroyed a 60-mile-wide path to the coast, where he captured Savannah in 1864.

The largest state east of the Mississippi, Georgia is typical of the changing South with an ever-increasing industrial development. Atlanta, largest city in the state, is the communications and transportation center for the Southeast and the area's chief distributor of goods.

Georgia leads the nation in the production of paper and board, tufted textile products, and processed chicken. Other major manufactured products are transportation equipment, food products, apparel, and chemicals.

Important agricultural products are corn, cotton, tobacco, soybeans, eggs, and peaches. Georgia produces twice as many peanuts as the next leading state. From its vast stands of pine come more than half of the world's resins and turpentine and 74.4 percent of the U.S. supply. Georgia is a leader in the production of marble, kaolin, barite, and bauxite.

Principal tourist attractions in Georgia include the Okefenokee National Wildlife Refuge, Andersonville Prison Park and National Cemetery, Chickamauga and Chattanooga National Military Park, the Little White House at Warm Springs where Pres. Franklin D. Roosevelt died in 1945, Sea Island, the enormous Confederate Memorial at Stone Mountain, Kennesaw Mountain National Battlefield Park, and Cumberland Island National Seashore.

Famous natives and residents: Conrad Aiken, poet; James Bowie, soldier; James Brown, singer; Jim Brown, actor and athlete; Erskine Caldwell, writer; James E. Carter, former president; Ray Charles, singer; Lucius D. Clay, banker and general; Ty Cobb, baseball player; Ossie Davis, actor and writer; James Dickey, poet; Melvyn Douglas, actor; Rebecca Latimer Felton, first appointed woman U.S. senator; Roosevelt Grier, entertainer and former athlete; Oliver Hardy, comedian; Joel Chandler Harris, journalist and author; Larry Holmes, boxer; Miriam Hopkins, actress; Alan Jackson, singer; Harry James, trumpeter; Jasper Johns, painter and sculptor; Bobby Jones, golfer; Stacy Keach, actor; DeForest Kelley, actor; Martin Luther King, Jr., civil rights leader; Gladys Knight, singer; Joseph R. Lamar, jurist; Little Richard, singer; Juliette Gordon Low, U.S. Girl Scouts founder; Carson McCullers, novelist; Johnny Mercer, songwriter; Margaret Mitchell, novelist; Elijah Muhammad, religious leader; Jessye Norman, soprano; Otis Redding, singer; Burt Reynolds, actor; Jackie Robinson, baseball player; Dean Rusk, former secretary of state; Nipsey Russell, comedian; Travis Tritt, singer; Alice Walker, author; Joanne Woodward, actress. Trisha Yearwood, singer;

Hawaii

Capital: Honolulu (on Oahu)
Governor: Linda Lingle, R (to Dec. 2006)
Lieut. Governor: James "Duke" Aiona, R (to Dec. 2006)
Senators: Daniel K. Akaka, D (to Jan. 2007); Daniel K. Inouye, D (to Jan. 2005)
Atty. General: Mark J. Bennett (to Dec. 2006)
Organized as territory: 1900
Entered Union (rank): Aug. 21, 1959 (50)
Motto: *Ua Mau Ke Ea O Ka Aina I Ka Pono* (The life of the land is perpetuated in righteousness)
State Symbols: flower, hibiscus (yellow) (1988); **song,** "Hawaii Ponoi" (1967); **bird,** nene (Hawaiian goose) (1957); **tree,** kukui (candlenut) (1959)
Nickname: Aloha State (1959)
Origin of name: Uncertain. The islands may have been named by Hawaii Loa, their traditional discoverer. Or they may have been named after Hawaii or Hawaiki, the traditional home of the Polynesians.
10 largest cities[1] (2000): Honolulu, 371,657; Hilo, 40,759; Kailua, 36,513; Kaneohe, 34,970; Waipahu, 33,108; Pearl City, 30,976; Waimalu, 29,371; Mililani Town, 28,608; Kahului, 20,146; Kihei, 16,749
Land area: 6,423 sq mi. (16,637 sq km)
Geographic center: Between islands of Hawaii and Maui
Number of counties: 5 (Kalawao non-functioning)
Largest county by population and area: Honolulu, 881,295 (2001); Hawaii, 4,028 sq mi.
State parks and historic sites: 69
Residents: Hawaiian, also kamaaina (native-born nonethnic Hawaiian), malihini (newcomer)
2002 resident population est.: 1,244,898
2000 resident census population (rank): 1,211,537 (42). **Male:** 608,671 (50.2%); **Female:** 602,866 (49.8%). **White:** 294,102 (24.3%); **Black:** 22,003 (1.8%); **American Indian:** 3,535 (0.3%); **Asian:** 503,868 (41.6%); **Native Hawaiian and Other Pacific Islander:** 113,539 (9.4%); **Other race:** 15,147 (1.3%); **Two or more races:** 259,343 (21.4%); **Hispanic/Latino:** 87,699 (7.2%). **2000 percent population 18 and over:** 75.6; **65 and over:** 13.3; **median age:** 36.2.

1. Census Designated Places.

First settled by Polynesians sailing from other Pacific islands between A.D. 300 and 600, Hawaii was visited in 1778 by British captain James Cook, who called the group the Sandwich Islands.

Hawaii was a native kingdom throughout most of the 19th century, when the expansion of the sugar industry (pineapple came after 1898) meant increasing U.S. business and political involvement. In 1893, Queen Liliuokalani was deposed, and a year later the Republic of Hawaii was established with Sanford B. Dole as president. Following annexation (1898), Hawaii became a U.S. territory in 1900.

The Japanese attack on the naval base at Pearl Harbor on Dec. 7, 1941, was directly responsible for U.S. entry into World War II.

Hawaii, 2,397 mi west-southwest of San Francisco, is a 1,523-mile chain of islets and eight main islands—Hawaii, Kahoolawe, Maui, Lanai, Molokai, Oahu, Kauai, and Niihau. The Northwestern Hawaiian Islands, other than Midway, are administratively part of Hawaii.

The temperature is mild, and cane sugar, pineapple, and flowers and nursery products are the chief products. Hawaii also grows coffee beans, bananas, and macadamia nuts. The tourist business is Hawaii's largest source of outside income.

Hawaii's highest peak is Mauna Kea (13,796 ft). Mauna Loa (13,679 ft) is the largest volcanic mountain in the world by volume.

Among the major points of interest are Hawaii Volcanoes National Park (Hawaii), Haleakala National Park (Maui), Puuhonua o Honaunau National Historical Park (Hawaii), Polynesian Cultural Center (Oahu), the USS *Arizona* and USS *Missouri* Memorial at Pearl Harbor, The National Memorial Cemetery of the Pacific (Oahu), and Iolani Palace (the only royal palace in the U.S.), Bishop Museum, and Waikiki Beach (all in Honolulu).

Famous natives and residents: Salevaa Atisanoe (Konishiki), sumo wrestler; George Ariyoshi, first Japanese-American elected governor; Angela Perez Baraquio, Miss America (2001); Tia Carrere, singer, actress; Steve Case, business executive; Father Damien, priest; Hiram L. Fong, first Chinese-American senator; Don Ho, entertainer; Kaahumanu, Hawaiian queen; Duke Paoa Kahanamoku, Olympic swimming champion; Kamehameha I, first Hawaiian king; Kamehameha V, last of the dynasty; Liliuokalani, queen, last Hawaiian monarch; Bette Midler, singer; Ellison Onizuka, astronaut; Chad Rowan (Akebono), sumo wrestler; Carolyn Suzanne Sapp, Miss America (1991); John Waihee, first Hawaiian elected governor.

Idaho

Capital: Boise
Governor: Dirk Kempthorne, R (to Jan. 2007)
Lieut. Governor: Jim Risch, R (to Jan. 2007)
Senators: Larry E. Craig, R (to Jan. 2009); Mike Crapo, R (to Jan. 2005)
Secy. of State: Ben Ysursa, R (to Jan. 2007)
Atty. General: Lawrence Wasden, R (to Jan. 2007)
Treasurer: Ron G. Crane, R (to Jan. 2007)
Organized as territory: March 3, 1863
Entered Union (rank): July 3, 1890 (43)
Present constitution adopted: 1890
Motto: *Esto perpetua* (It is forever)
State Symbols: flower, syringa (1931); **tree,** white pine (1935); **bird,** mountain bluebird (1931); **horse,** Appaloosa (1975); **gem,** star garnet (1967); **song,** "Here We Have Idaho"; **folk dance,** square dance; **fish,** cutthroat trout (1990); **fossil,** Hagerman horse fossil (1988)
Nickname: Gem State
Origin of name: Though popularly believed to be an Indian word, it is an invented name whose meaning is unknown.
10 largest cities (2000): Boise, 185,787; Nampa, 51,867; Pocatello, 51,466; Idaho Falls, 50,730; Meridian, 34,919; Coeur d'Alene, 34,514; Twin Falls, 34,469; Lewiston, 30,904; Caldwell, 25,967; Moscow, 21,291
Land area: 82,747 sq mi. (214,315 sq km)
Geographic center: In Custer Co., at Custer, SW of Challis
Number of counties: 44, plus small part of Yellowstone National Park
Largest county by population and area: Ada, 312,337 (2001); Idaho, 8,485 sq mi.
State forests: 881,000 ac.
State parks: 27 (43,000+ ac.)
Residents: Idahoan
2002 resident population est.: 1,341,131
2000 resident census population (rank): 1,293,953 (39). **Male:** 648,660 (50.1%); **Female:** 645,293 (49.9%). **White:** 1,177,304 (91.0%); **Black:** 5,456 (0.4%); **American Indian:** 17,645 (1.4%); **Asian:** 11,889 (0.9%); **Other race:** 54,742 (4.2%); **Two or more races:** 25,609 (2.0%); **Hispanic/Latino:** 101,690 (7.9%). **2000 percent population 18 and over:** 71.5; **65 and over:** 11.3; **median age:** 33.2.

The region was explored by Meriwether Lewis and William Clark in 1805–1806. It was then a part of the Oregon country, held jointly by the United States and Great Britain. Boundary disputes with Great Britain were settled by the Oregon Treaty in 1846, and the first permanent U.S. settlement in Idaho was established by the Mormons at Franklin in 1860.

After gold was discovered at Orofino Creek in 1860, prospectors swarmed into the territory, but they left little more than a number of ghost towns.

In the 1870s, growing white occupation of Indian lands led to a series of battles between U.S. forces and the Nez Percé, Bannock, and Sheepeater tribes.

Mining and lumbering have been important for years. Idaho ranks high among the states in silver, antimony, lead, cobalt, garnet, phosphate rock, vanadium, zinc, and mercury.

Agriculture is a major industry: The state produces about one fourth of the nation's potato crop, as well as wheat, apples, corn, barley, sugar beets, and hops.

The 1990s saw a remarkable growth in the high technology industries, concentrated in the metropolitan Boise area.

With the growth of winter sports, tourism now outranks other industries in revenue. Idaho's many streams and lakes provide fishing, camping, and boating sites. The nation's largest elk herds draw hunters from all over the world, and the famed Sun Valley resort attracts thousands of visitors to its swimming, golfing, and skiing facilities.

Points of interest are the Craters of the Moon National Monument; Nez Percé National Historic Park, which includes many sites visited by Lewis and Clark; and the State Historical Museum in Boise. Other attractions are the Snake River Birds of Prey National Conservation Area south of Boise, Hells Canyon on the Idaho-Oregon border, and the Sawtooth National Recreation Area in south-central Idaho.

Famous natives and residents: Joe Albertson, grocery chain founder; Cecil Andrus, governor; T. H. Bell, educator; Ezra Taft Benson, secretary of Agriculture, pres. LDS church, marketing specialist; William E. Borah, senator; Gutzon Borglum, Mt. Rushmore sculptor; Carol R. Brink, author; Frank F. Church, senator; Fred Dubois, senator; Vardis Fisher, novelist; Lawrence H. Gipson, historian; Ernest Hemingway, author; Mariel Hemingway, actress; Chief Joseph, Nez Percé chief; Harmon Killebrew, baseball player; Jerry Kramer, football player, author; Ezra Pound, poet; Sacagawea, Shoshonean guide; J. R. Simplot, industrialist; Robert E. Smylie, political leader; Henry Spalding, missionary; Frank Steunenberg, governor; Picabo Street, skier; David Tompson, founded first trading post; Lana Turner, actress.

Illinois

Capital: Springfield
Governor: Rod R. Blagojevich, D (to Jan. 2007)
Lieut. Governor: Patrick Quinn, D (to Jan. 2007)
Senators: Richard J. Durbin, D (to Jan. 2009); Peter G. Fitzgerald, R (to Jan. 2005)
Atty. General: Lisa Madigan, D (to Jan. 2007)
Secy. of State: Jesse White, D (to Jan. 2007)
Treasurer: Judith Barr Topinka, R (to Jan. 2007)
Organized as territory: Feb. 3, 1809
Entered Union (rank): Dec. 3, 1818 (21)
Present constitution adopted: 1970
Motto: State sovereignty, national union
State Symbols: flower, violet (1908); **tree,** white oak (1973); **bird,** cardinal (1929); **animal,** white-tailed deer (1982); **fish,** bluegill (1987); **insect,** monarch butterfly (1975); **song,** "Illinois" (1925); **mineral,** fluorite (1965)
Nickname: Prairie State
Origin of name: Algonquin for "tribe of superior men"
10 largest cities (2000): Chicago, 2,896,016; Rockford, 150,115; Aurora, 142,990; Naperville, 128,358; Peoria, 112,936; Springfield, 111,454; Joliet, 106,221; Elgin, 94,487; Waukegan, 87,901; Cicero, 85,616
Land area: 55,584 sq mi. (143,963 sq km)
Geographic center: In Logan Co., 28 mi. NE of Springfield
Number of counties: 102
Largest county by population and area: Cook, 5,350,269 (2001); McLean, 1,184 sq mi.
Public use areas: 186 (275,000 ac.), incl. state parks, memorials, forests and conservation areas
Residents: Illinoisan
2002 resident population est.: 12,600,620
2000 resident census population (rank): 12,419,293 (5). **Male:** 6,080,336 (49.0%); **Female:** 6,338,957 (51.0%). **White:** 9,125,471 (73.5%); **Black:** 1,876,875 (15.1%); **American Indian:** 31,006 (0.2%); **Asian:** 423,603 (3.4%); **Other race:** 722,712 (5.8%); **Two or more races:** 235,016 (1.9%); **Hispanic/Latino:** 1,530,262 (12.3%). **2000 percent population 18 and over:** 73.9; **65 and over:** 12.1; **median age:** 34.7.

French explorers Jacques Marquette and Louis Joliet, in 1673, were the first Europeans of record to visit the region. In 1699 French settlers established the first permanent settlement at Cahokia, near present-day East St. Louis. Great Britain obtained the region at the end of the French and Indian Wars in 1763. The area figured prominently in frontier struggles during the Revolutionary War and in Indian wars during the early 19th century.

Significant episodes in the state's early history include the influx of settlers following the opening of the Erie Canal in 1825; the Black Hawk War, which virtually ended the Indian troubles in the area; and the rise of Abraham Lincoln from farm laborer to president.

Today, Illinois stands high in manufacturing, coal mining, agriculture, and oil production. The state's manufactures include food and agricultural products, transportation equipment, chemicals, industrial machinery, and computer equipment. The sprawling Chicago district (including a slice of Indiana) is a great iron and steel producer, meat packer, grain exchange, and railroad center. Chicago is also famous as a Great Lakes port.

Illinois is a leading producer of soybeans, corn, and hogs. Other agricultural commodities include cattle, wheat, oats, sorghum, and hay.

Central Illinois is noted for shrines and memorials associated with the life of Abraham Lincoln. In Springfield are the Lincoln Home, the Lincoln Tomb, and the restored Old State Capitol. Other points of interest are the home of Mormon leader Joseph Smith in Nauvoo and, in Chicago: the Art Institute, Field Museum, Museum of Science and Industry, Shedd Aquarium, Adler Planetarium, Merchandise Mart, and Chicago Portage National Historic Site.

Famous natives and residents: Franklin Pierce Adams, author; Jane Addams, social worker; Mary Astor, actress; Jack Benny, comedian; Black Hawk, Sauk Indian chief; Harry A. Blackmun, jurist; Ray Bradbury, author; William Jennings Bryan, orator and politician; Edgar Rice Burroughs, novelist; Gower Champion, choreographer; John Chancellor, TV commentator; Raymond Chandler, writer; Jimmy Connors, tennis champion; James Gould Cozzens, novelist; Richard J. Daley, mayor of Chicago; Miles Davis, musician; Peter DeVries, novelist; Everett Dirksen, senator; Walt Disney, film animator and producer; John Dos Passos, author; James T. Farrell, novelist; Dan Fogelberg, singer and songwriter; Betty Friedan, feminist; Benny Goodman, musician; John Gunther, author; Ernest Hemingway, author; Charlton Heston, actor; Wild Bill Hickok, scout; William Holden, actor; Rock Hudson, actor; Burl Ives, singer; James Jones, novelist; John Jones, civil rights leader; Quincy Jones, composer; Keokuk (Watchful Fox), chief of the Sac and Fox Indians; Walter Kerr, drama critic; Archibald MacLeish, poet; David Mamet, playwright; Robert A. Millikan, physicist; Sherrill Milnes, baritone; Bill Murray, actor; Bob Newhart, actor and comedian; William S. Paley, broadcasting executive; Drew Pearson, columnist; Richard Pryor, comedian and actor; Ronald Reagan, former president and actor; Carl Sandburg, poet; Sam Shepard, playwright; William L. Shirer, author and historian; John Paul Stevens, jurist; McLean Stevenson, actor; Preston Sturges, director; Gloria Swanson, actress; Carl Van Doren, writer and educator; Melvin Van Peebles, playwright; Irving Wallace, novelist; Alfred Wallenstein, conductor; Raquel Welch, actress; Oprah Winfrey, television talk show host and actress; Florenz Ziegfield, theatrical producer.

Indiana

Capital: Indianapolis
Governor: Joseph E. Kernan,[1] D (to Jan. 2005)
Lieut. Governor: Vacant
Senators: Evan Bayh, D (to Jan. 2005); Richard G. Lugar, R (to Jan. 2007)
Secy. of State: Todd Rokita, R (to Dec. 2004)
Treasurer: Tim Berry, R (to Feb. 2007)
Atty. General: Stephen Carter, R (to Jan. 2005)
Organized as territory: May 7, 1800
Entered Union (rank): Dec. 11, 1816 (19)
Present constitution adopted: 1851
Motto: The Crossroads of America
State Symbols: flower, peony (1957); **tree,** tulip tree (1931); **bird,** cardinal (1933); **song,** "On the Banks of the Wabash, Far Away" (1913); **river,** Wabash; **stone,** limestone
Nickname: Hoosier State
Origin of name: Meaning "land of Indians"
Official language: English
10 largest cities (2000): Indianapolis, 791,926; Fort Wayne, 205,727; Evansville, 121,582; South Bend, 107,789; Gary, 102,746; Hammond, 83,048; Bloomington, 69,291; Muncie, 67,430; Anderson, 59,734; Terre Haute, 59,614
Land area: 35,867 sq mi. (92,896 sq km)
Geographic center: In Boone Co., 14 mi. NNW of Indianapolis
Number of counties: 92
Largest county by population and area: Marion, 856,938 (2001); Allen, 657 sq mi.
State parks: 23 (56,409 ac.)
State historic sites: 17 (2,007 ac.)
Residents: Indianan, Indianian, Hoosier
2002 resident population est.: 6,159,068
2000 resident census population (rank): 6,080,485 (14). **Male:** 2,982,474 (49.0%); **Female:** 3,098,011 (51.0%); **White:** 5,320,022 (87.5%); **Black:** 510,034 (8.4%); **American Indian:** 15,815 (0.3%); **Asian:** 59,126 (1.0%); **Other race:** 97,811 (1.6%); **Two or more races:** 75,672 (1.2%); **Hispanic/Latino:** 214,536 (3.5%). **2000 percent population 18 and over:** 74.1; **65 and over:** 12.4; **median age:** 35.2.

1. Lt. Gov. Kernan was sworn in as governor in Sept. 2003, after Frank O'Bannon's death.

First explored for France by Robert Cavelier, Sieur de la Salle, in 1679–1680, the region figured importantly in the Franco-British struggle for North America that culminated with British victory in 1763. George Rogers Clark led American forces against the British in the area during the Revolutionary War and, prior to becoming a state, Indiana was the scene of frequent Indian uprisings until the victories of Gen. Anthony Wayne at Fallen Timbers in 1794 and Gen. William Henry Harrison at Tippecanoe in 1811.

During the 19th century, Indiana was the site of several experimental communities, including those established by George Rapp and Robert Owen at New Harmony.

Indiana's 41-mile Lake Michigan waterfront—one of the world's great industrial centers—turns out iron, steel, and oil products. Products include automobile parts and accessories, mobile homes and recreational vehicles, truck and bus bodies, aircraft engines, farm machinery, and fabricated structural steel. Wood office furniture and pharmaceuticals are also manufactured.

The state is a leader in agriculture with corn the principal crop. Hogs, soybeans, wheat, oats, rye, tomatoes, onions, and poultry also contribute heavily to Indiana's agricultural output.

Much of the building limestone used in the U.S. is quarried in Indiana, which is also a large producer of coal. Other mineral commodities include crushed stone, cement, and sand and gravel.

Wyandotte Cave, one of the largest in the U.S., is located in Crawford County in southern Indiana, and West Baden and French Lick are well known for their mineral springs. Other attractions include Indiana Dunes National Lakeshore, Indianapolis Motor Speedway, Lincoln Boyhood National Memorial, and the George Rogers Clark National Historical Park.

Famous natives and residents: George Ade, humorist; Leon Ames, actor; Anne Baxter, actress; Albert J. Beveridge, political leader; Larry Bird, basketball player; Bill Blass, fashion designer; Frank Borman, astronaut; Hoagy Carmichael, songwriter; James Dean, actor; Eugene V. Debs, Socialist leader; Lloyd C. Douglas, author; Theodore Dreiser, writer; Bernard F. Gimbel, merchant; Virgil Grissom, astronaut; Phil Harris, actor and band leader; John Milton Hay, statesman; James R. Hoffa, labor leader; Michael Jackson, singer; Buck Jones, actor; Alfred C. Kinsey, zoologist; David Letterman, TV host and comedian; Eli Lilly, pharmaceuticals manufacturer; Carole Lombard, actress; Shelley Long, actress; Marjorie Main, actress; James McCracken, tenor; Joaquin Miller, poet; Paul Osborn, playwright; Cole Porter, songwriter; Gene Stratton Porter, naturalist and author; Ernest Taylor Pyle, journalist; J. Danforth Quayle, former vice president; James Whitcomb Riley, poet; Knute Rockne, football coach; Ned Rorem, composer; Red Skelton, comedian; Rex Stout, mystery writer; Booth Tarkington, author; Twyla Tharp, dancer and choreographer; Forrest Tucker, actor; Harold C. Urey, physicist; Kurt Vonnegut, Jr., author; Dan Wakefield, author; Robert Wise, director; Jessamyn West, novelist; Wendell Willkie, lawyer; Wilbur Wright, inventor.

Iowa

Capital: Des Moines
Governor: Tom Vilsack, D (to Jan. 2007)
Lieut. Governor: Sally Pederson, D (to Jan. 2007)
Senators: Chuck Grassley, R (to Jan. 2005); Tom Harkin, D (to Jan. 2009)
Secy. of State: Chet Culver, D (to Jan. 2007)
Treasurer: Michael L. Fitzgerald, D (to Jan. 2007)
Atty. General: Tom Miller, D (to Jan. 2007)
Organized as territory: June 12, 1838
Entered Union (rank): Dec. 28, 1846 (29)
Present constitution adopted: 1857
Motto: Our liberties we prize and our rights we will maintain
State Symbols: flower, wild rose (1897); **bird,** eastern goldfinch (1933); **colors,** red, white, and blue (in state flag); **song,** "Song of Iowa"
Nickname: Hawkeye State
Origin of name: Probably from an Indian word meaning "this is the place" or "the Beautiful Land"

10 largest cities (2000): Des Moines, 198,682; Cedar Rapids, 120,758; Davenport, 98,359; Sioux City, 85,013; Waterloo, 68,747; Iowa City, 62,220; Council Bluffs, 58,268; Dubuque, 57,686; Ames, 50,731; West Des Moines, 46,403
Land area: 55,869 sq mi. (144,701 sq km)
Geographic center: In Story Co., 5 mi. NE of Ames
Number of counties: 99
Largest county by population and area: Polk, 379,029 (2001); Kossuth, 973 sq mi.
State forests: 8 (40,706 ac.)
State parks: 83 (53,000 ac.)
Residents: Iowan
2002 resident population est.: 2,936,760
2000 resident census population (rank): 2,926,324 (30). **Male:** 1,435,515 (49.1%); **Female:** 1,490,809 (50.9%). **White:** 2,748,640 (93.9%); **Black:** 61,853 (2.1%); **American Indian:** 8,989 (0.3%); **Asian:** 36,635 (1.3%); **Other race:** 37,420 (1.3%); **Two or more races:** 31,778 (1.1%); **Hispanic/Latino:** 82,473 (2.8%). **2000 percent population 18 and over:** 74.9; **65 and over:** 14.9; **median age:** 36.6.

The first Europeans to visit the area were the French explorers Jacques Marquette and Louis Joliet in 1673. The U.S. obtained control of the area in 1803 as part of the Louisiana Purchase, and during the first half of the 19th century, there was heavy fighting between white settlers and Indians. Lands were taken from the Indians after the Black Hawk War in 1832 and again in 1836 and 1837.

When Iowa became a state in 1846, its capital was Iowa City; the more centrally located Des Moines became the new capital in 1857. At that time, the state's present boundaries were also drawn.

Although Iowa produces a tenth of the nation's food supply, the value of Iowa's manufactured products is twice that of its agriculture. Major industries are food and associated products, non-electrical machinery, electrical equipment, printing and publishing, and fabricated products.

Iowa stands in a class by itself as an agricultural state. Its farms sell over $10 billion worth of crops and livestock annually. Iowa leads the nation in all corn, soybean, and hog marketings, and comes in third in total livestock sales. Iowa's forests produce hardwood lumber, particularly walnut, and its mineral products include cement, limestone, sand, gravel, gypsum, and coal.

Tourist attractions include the Herbert Hoover birthplace and library near West Branch; the Amana Colonies; Fort Dodge Historical Museum, Fort, and Stockade; the Iowa State Fair at Des Moines in August; and the Effigy Mounds National Monument, a prehistoric Indian burial site at Marquette.

Famous natives and residents: Bix Beiderbecke, jazz musician; Norman Borlaug, plant pathologist, geneticist, and Nobel Peace Prize winner; William "Buffalo Bill" F. Cody, scout; Johnny Carson, TV entertainer; Gardner Cowles, Jr., publisher; Simon Estes, bass-baritone; William Frawley, actor; George H. Gallup, poll taker; Susan Glaspell, writer; Herbert Hoover, president; MacKinlay Kantor, novelist; Charles A. Kettering, inventor; Ann Landers, columnist; Cloris Leachman, actress; John L. Lewis, labor leader; Glenn L. Martin, aviator and manufacturer; Elsa Maxwell, writer; Frederick L. Maytag, inventor and manufacturer; Glenn Miller, bandleader; Kate Mulgrew, actress; Harriet Nelson, actress; Nathan M. Pusey, educator; David Rabe, playwright; Harry Reasoner, TV commentator; Donna Reed, actress; Lillian Russell, soprano; Robert Schuller, evangelist; Wallace Stegner, novelist and critic; Billy Sunday, evangelist; James A. Van Allen, space physicist; Abigail Van Buren, columnist; Henry A. Wallace, statesman and vice president; John Wayne, actor; Andy Williams, singer; Meredith Willson, composer; Grant Wood, painter.

Kansas

Capital: Topeka
Governor: Kathleen Sebelius, D (to Jan. 2007)
Lieut. Governor: John E. Moore, D (to Jan. 2007)
Senators: Sam Brownback, R (to Jan. 2005); Pat Roberts, R (to Jan. 2009)
Secy. of State: Ron Thornburgh, R (to Jan. 2007)
Treasurer: Lynn Jenkins, R (to Jan. 2007)
Atty. General: Phill Kline, R (to Jan. 2007)
Organized as territory: May 30, 1854
Entered Union (rank): Jan. 29, 1861 (34)
Present constitution adopted: 1859
Motto: *Ad astra per aspera* (To the stars through difficulties)
State Symbols: flower, sunflower (1903); **tree,** cottonwood (1937); **bird,** western meadowlark (1937); **animal,** buffalo (1955); **song,** "Home on the Range" (1947)
Nicknames: Sunflower State; Jayhawk State
Origin of name: From a Sioux word meaning "people of the south wind"
10 largest cities (2000): Wichita, 344,284; Overland Park, 149,080; Kansas City, 146,866; Topeka, 122,377; Olathe, 92,962; Lawrence, 80,098; Shawnee, 47,996; Salina, 45,679; Manhattan, 44,831; Hutchinson, 40,787
Land area: 81,815 sq mi. (211,901 sq km)
Geographic center: In Barton Co., 15 mi. NE of Great Bend
Number of counties: 105
Largest county by population and area: Johnson, 465,058 (2001); Butler, 1,428 sq mi.
State parks: 22 (14,394 ac.)
Residents: Kansan
2002 resident population est.: 2,715,884
2000 resident census population (rank): 2,688,418 (32). **Male:** 1,328,474 (49.4%); **Female:** 1,359,944 (50.6%). **White:** 2,313,944 (86.1%); **Black:** 154,198 (5.7%); **American Indian:** 24,936 (0.9%); **Asian:** 46,806 (1.7%); **Other race:** 90,725 (3.4%); **Two or more races:** 56,496 (2.1%); **Hispanic/Latino:** 188,252 (7.0%). **2000 percent population 18 and over:** 73.5; **65 and over:** 13.3; **median age:** 35.2.

Spanish explorer Francisco de Coronado, in 1541, is considered the first European to have traveled this region. Sieur de la Salle's extensive land claims for France (1682) included present-day Kansas. Ceded to Spain by France in 1763, the territory reverted to France in 1800 and was sold to the U.S. as part of the Louisiana Purchase in 1803.

Lewis and Clark, Zebulon Pike, and Stephen H. Long explored the region between 1803 and 1819. The first permanent white settlements in Kansas were outposts—Fort Leavenworth (1827), Fort Scott (1842), and Fort Riley (1853)—established to protect travelers along the Santa Fe and Oregon Trails.

Just before the Civil War, the conflict between the pro- and anti-slavery forces earned the region the grim title of Bleeding Kansas.

Today, wheat fields, oil-well derricks, herds of cattle, and grain-storage elevators are chief features of the Kansas landscape. A leading wheat-growing state, Kansas also raises corn, sorghum, oats, barley, soybeans, and potatoes. Kansas stands high in petroleum production and mines zinc, coal, salt, and lead. It is also the nation's leading producer of helium.

Wichita is one of the nation's leading aircraft-manufacturing centers, ranking first in production of private aircraft. Kansas City is an important transportation, milling, and meat-packing center.

Points of interest include the Kansas History Center at Topeka, the Eisenhower boyhood home and the Eisenhower Memorial Museum and Presidential Library at Abilene, John Brown's cabin at Osawatomie, re-created Front Street in Dodge City, Fort Larned (an important military post on the Santa Fe Trail), Fort Leavenworth, and Fort Riley.

Famous natives and residents: Roscoe "Fatty" Arbuckle, actor; Clarence D. Batchelor, political cartoonist; Gwendolyn Brooks, poet; Walter P. Chrysler, auto manufacturer; Clark M. Clifford, secretary of defense; John Steuart Curry, painter; Charles Curtis, vice president; Robert Dole, senator; Amelia Earhart, aviator; Dwight D. Eisenhower, general and president; Milton S. Eisenhower, educator; Gary Hart, politician; William Inge, playwright; Walter Johnson, baseball pitcher; Osa L. Johnson, documentary film producer; Buster Keaton, comedian; Emmett Kelly, clown; Stan Kenton, jazz musician; James Lehrer, broadcast journalist; Edgar Lee Masters, poet; Mary McCarthy, actress; Hattie McDaniel, actress; Karl Menninger, psychiatrist; Carry A. Nation, temperance leader; Gordon Parks, film director; ZaSu Pitts, actress; Samuel Ramey, opera singer; Charles Robinson, statesman and first governor; Charles (Buddy) Rogers, actor; Damon Runyon, journalist; Gale Sayers, football player; Eugene W. Smith, photojournalist; Milburn Stone, actor; John Cameron Swayze, news commentator; William Allen White, journalist; Charles E. Whittaker, jurist; Jess Willard, boxer.

Kentucky

Capital: Frankfort
Governor: Paul E. Patton, D (to Dec. 2003)
Lieut. Governor: Stephen L. Henry, D (to Dec. 2003)
Senators: Jim Bunning, R (to Jan. 2005); Mitch McConnell, R (to Jan. 2009)
Secy. of State: John Y. Brown III, D (to Dec. 2003)
Treasurer: Jonathan Miller, D (to Dec. 2003)
Atty. General: A. B. "Ben" Chandler III, D (to Dec. 2003)
Entered Union (rank): June 1, 1792 (15)
Present constitution adopted: 1891
Motto: United we stand, divided we fall
State Symbols: tree, tulip poplar (1994); **flower,** goldenrod; **bird,** Kentucky cardinal; **song,** "My Old Kentucky Home"
Nickname: Bluegrass State
Origin of name: From an Iroquoian word "Ken-tah-ten" meaning "land of tomorrow"
10 largest cities (2000): Lexington-Fayette[1], 260,512; Louisville, 256,231; Owensboro, 54,067; Bowling Green, 49,296; Covington, 43,370; Hopkinsville, 30,089; Frankfort, 27,741; Henderson, 27,373; Richmond, 27,152; Jeffersontown, 26,633
Land area: 39,728 sq mi. (102,896 sq km)
Geographic center: In Marion Co., 3 mi. NNW of Lebanon
Number of counties: 120
Largest county by population and area: Jefferson, 692,910 (2001); Pike, 787 sq mi.
State forests: 4 (30,200 ac.)
State parks: 59
Residents: Kentuckian
2002 resident population est.: 4,092,891
2000 resident census population (rank): 4,041,769 (25). **Male:** 1,975,368 (48.9%); **Female:** 2,066,401 (51.1%). **White:** 3,640,889 (90.1%); **Black:** 295,994 (7.3%); **American Indian:** 8,616 (0.2%); **Asian:** 29,744 (0.7%); **Other race:** 22,623 (0.6%); **Two or more races:** 42,443 (1.1%); **Hispanic/Latino:** 59,939 (1.5%). **2000 percent population 18 and over:** 75.4; **65 and over:** 12.5; **median age:** 35.9.

1. Coextensive with Fayette County.

Kentucky was the first region west of the Allegheny Mountains to be settled by American pioneers. James Harrod established the first permanent settlement at Harrodsburg in 1774; the following year Daniel Boone, who had explored the area in 1767, blazed the Wilderness Trail through the Cumberland Gap and founded Boonesboro.

Politically, the Kentucky region was originally part of Virginia, but statehood was gained in 1792. Gen. Anthony Wayne's victory in 1794 at Fallen Timbers in Ohio marked the end of Native American resistance in the area and secured the Kentucky frontier.

As a slaveholding state with a considerable abolitionist population, Kentucky was caught in the middle during the Civil War, supplying both Union and Confederate forces with thousands of troops.

Kentucky prides itself on producing some of the nation's best tobacco, horses, and whiskey. Corn, soybeans, wheat, fruit, hogs, cattle, and dairy products are among the agricultural items produced.

Among the manufactured items produced in the state are motor vehicles, furniture, aluminum ware, brooms, apparel, lumber products, machinery, textiles, and iron and steel products. Kentucky also produces significant amounts of petroleum, natural gas, fluorspar, clay, and stone. However, coal accounts for 85% of the total mineral income.

Louisville is famous for the Kentucky Derby at Churchill Downs, and the Bluegrass country around Lexington is the home of some of the world's finest race horses. Other attractions are Mammoth Cave, the George S. Patton, Jr., Military Museum at Fort Knox, and Old Fort Harrod State Park.

Famous natives and residents: John Adair, pioneer and political leader; Muhammad Ali, boxer; Alben W. Barkley, vice president; Louis D. Brandeis, jurist; John Mason Brown, critic; Kit Carson, scout; Champ Clark, politician; George Clooney, actor; Rosemary Clooney, singer; Irvin S. Cobb, humorist; Jefferson Davis, president of the Confederacy; Johnny Depp, actor; Irene Dunne, actress; Crystal Gayle, singer; David W. Griffith, film producer; John M. Harlan, jurist; Elizabeth Hardwick, writer; Casey Jones, locomotive engineer; Ashley Judd, actress; Naomi Judd, singer; Wynona Judd, singer; Barbara Kingsolver, writer; Abraham Lincoln, president; Loretta Lynn, singer; Bill Monroe, bluegrass musician; Carry A. Nation, temperance leader; Patricia Neal, actress; George Reeves, actor; Wiley B. Rutledge, jurist; Diane Sawyer, broadcast journalist; Phil Simms, football player; Adlai Stevenson, vice president; Allen Tate, poet and critic; Hunter Thompson, writer; Frederick M. Vinson, jurist; Robert Penn Warren, novelist.

Louisiana

Capital: Baton Rouge
Governor: Murphy J. "Mike" Foster, R (to Jan. 2004)
Lieut. Governor: Kathleen Blanco, D (to Jan. 2004)
Senators: John B. Breaux, D (to Jan. 2005); Mary Landrieu, D (to Jan. 2009)
Secy. of State: W. Fox McKeithen, R (to Jan. 2004)
Treasurer: John Neely Kennedy, D (to Jan. 2004)
Atty. General: Richard P. Ieyoub, D (to Jan. 2004)
Organized as territory: March 26, 1804
Entered Union (rank): April 30, 1812 (18)
Present constitution adopted: 1974
Motto: Union, justice, and confidence
State Symbols: flower, magnolia (1900); **tree,** bald cypress (1963); **bird,** eastern brown pelican (1958); **songs,** "Give Me Louisiana" and "You Are My Sunshine"
Nickname: Pelican State
Origin of name: In honor of Louis XIV of France
10 largest cities (2000): New Orleans, 484,674; Baton Rouge, 227,818; Shreveport, 200,145; Lafayette, 110,257; Lake Charles, 71,757; Kenner, 70,517; Bossier City, 56,461; Monroe, 53,107; Alexandria, 46,342; New Iberia, 32,623

Land area: 43,562 sq mi. (112,826 sq km)
Geographic center: In Avoyelles Parish, 3 mi. SE of Marksville
Number of parishes (counties): 64
Largest parish by population and area: Orleans, 476,492 (2001); Vernon, 1,328 sq mi.
State forests: 1 (8,000 ac.)
State parks: 30 (13,932 ac.)
Residents: Louisianan, Louisianian
2002 resident population est.: 4,482,646
2000 resident census population (rank): 4,468,976 (22). **Male:** 2,162,903 (48.4%); **Female:** 2,306,073 (51.6%). **White:** 2,856,161 (63.9%); **Black:** 1,451,944 (32.5%); **American Indian:** 25,477 (0.6%); **Asian:** 54,758 (1.2%); **Other race:** 31,131 (0.7%); **Two or more races:** 48,265 (1.1%); **Hispanic/Latino:** 107,738 (2.4%). **2000 percent population 18 and over:** 72.7; **65 and over:** 11.6; **median age:** 34.0.

Louisiana has a rich, colorful historical background. Early Spanish explorers were Alvárez Piñeda, 1519; Álvar Núñez Cabeza de Vaca, 1528; and Hernando De Soto in 1541. Sieur de la Salle reached the mouth of the Mississippi and claimed all the land drained by it and its tributaries for Louis XIV of France in 1682.

Louisiana became a French crown colony in 1731 but was ceded to Spain in 1763 after the French and Indian Wars. (The portion east of the Mississippi came under British control in 1764.) Louisiana reverted to France in 1800 and was sold by Napoleon to the U.S. in 1803. The southern part, known as the territory of Orleans, became the state of Louisiana in 1812.

During the Civil War, Louisiana joined the Confederacy, but New Orleans was captured by Union Adm. David Farragut in April 1862. The state's economy suffered during Reconstruction; however, the situation improved at the turn of the 20th century, with the discovery of oil and natural gas and the growth of industry.

Louisiana is a leader in natural gas, salt, petroleum, and sulfur production. Much of the oil and sulfur comes from offshore deposits. The state also produces large crops of sweet potatoes, rice, sugar cane, pecans, soybeans, corn, and cotton. Leading manufactured items include chemicals, processed food, petroleum and coal products, paper, lumber and wood products, transportation equipment, and apparel.

The state has become a popular tourist destination. New Orleans is the major draw, known particularly for its picturesque French Quarter and the annual Mardi Gras celebration, held since 1838.

Other major points of interest include the Superdome in New Orleans, historic plantation homes near Natchitoches and New Iberia, Cajun country in the Mississippi Delta Region, Chalmette National Historic Park, and the state capital at Baton Rouge.

Famous natives and residents: Louis Armstrong, musician; Geoffrey Beene, fashion designer; Truman Capote, writer; Kitty Carlisle, singer and actress; Van Cliburn, concert pianist; Michael De Bakey, heart surgeon; Fats Domino, musician; Louis Moreau Gottschalk, pianist and composer; Bryant Gumbel, TV newscaster; Lillian Hellman, playwright; Al Hirt, trumpeter; Mahalia Jackson, gospel singer; Jean Laffite, privateer; Dorothy Lamour, actress; John A. Lejeune, Marine Corps general; Elmore Leonard, author; Jerry Lee Lewis, singer; Huey P. Long, politician; Wynton Marsalis, musician; Jelly Roll Morton, jazz musician and composer; Huey Newton, black activist; Paul Prudhomme, chef; Howard K. Smith, TV commentator; Ben Turpin, comedian; Ray Walston, actor; Edward Douglas White, jurist.

Maine

Capital: Augusta
Governor: John Baldacci, D (to Jan. 2007)
Senators: Susan Collins, R (to Jan. 2009); Olympia J. Snowe, R (to Jan. 2007)
Secy. of State: Dan A. Gwadosky, D (to Jan. 2007)
Treasurer: Dale McCormick (to Jan. 2007)
Atty. General: G. Steven Rowe, D (to Jan. 2007)
Entered Union (rank): March 15, 1820 (23)
Present constitution adopted: 1820
Motto: *Dirigo* (I lead)
State Symbols: flower, white pine cone and tassel (1895); **tree,** white pine tree (1945); **bird,** chickadee (1927); **fish,** landlocked salmon (1969); **mineral,** tourmaline (1971); **song,** "State of Maine Song" (1937); **animal,** moose (1979); **cat,** Maine coon cat (1985); **fossil,** *pertica quadrifaria* (1985); **insect,** honeybee (1975)
Nickname: Pine Tree State
Origin of name: First used to distinguish the mainland from the offshore islands. It has been considered a compliment to Henrietta Maria, queen of Charles I of England. She was said to have owned the province of Mayne in France.
10 largest cities (2000): Portland, 64,249; Lewiston, 35,690; Bangor, 31,473; South Portland, 23,324; Auburn, 23,203; Brunswick, 21,172; Biddeford, 20,942; Sanford, 20,806; Augusta, 18,560; Scarborough, 16,970
Largest town (1990 census): Brunswick, 20,906
Land area: 30,862 sq mi. (79,933 sq km)
Geographic center: In Piscataquis Co., 18 mi. N of Dover-Foxcroft
Number of counties: 16
Largest county by population and area: Cumberland, 266,988 (2001); Aroostook, 6,672 sq mi.
State forests: 1 (21,000 ac.)
State parks: 26 (247,627 ac.)
State historic sites: 18 (403 ac.)
Residents: Mainer
2002 resident population est.: 1,294,464
2000 resident census population (rank): 1,274,923 (40). **Male:** 620,309 (48.7%); **Female:** 654,614 (51.3%). **White:** 1,236,014 (96.9%); **Black:** 6,760 (0.5%); **American Indian:** 7,098 (0.6%); **Asian:** 9,111 (0.7%); **Other race:** 2,911 (0.2%); **Two or more races:** 12,647 (1.0%); **Hispanic/Latino:** 9,360 (0.7%); **2000 percent population 18 and over:** 76.4; **65 and over:** 14.4; **median age:** 38.6.

John Cabot and his son, Sebastian, are believed to have visited the Maine coast in 1498. However, the first permanent English settlements were not established until more than a century later, in 1623.

The first naval action of the Revolutionary War occurred in 1775 when colonials captured the British sloop *Margaretta* off Machias on the Maine coast. In that same year, the British burned Falmouth (now Portland).

Long governed by Massachusetts, Maine became the 23rd state as part of the Missouri Compromise in 1820.

Maine produces 98% of the nation's low-bush blueberries. Farm income is also derived from apples, potatoes, dairy products, and vegetables, with poultry and eggs the largest selling items.

The state is one of the world's largest pulp-paper producers. With almost 89% of its area forested, Maine turns out wood products from boats to toothpicks. Maine also leads the world in the production of the familiar flat tins of sardines, producing more than 75 million of them annually. In 2001, Maine lobstermen landed nearly 48 million pounds of lobster, compared with an estimated 53 million pounds in 2000.

A scenic seacoast, beaches, lakes, mountains, and resorts make Maine a popular vacationland. There are more than 2,500 lakes and 5,000 streams, plus 26 state parks to attract hunters, fishermen, skiers, and campers.

Major points of interest are Bar Harbor, Acadia National Park, Allagash National Wilderness Waterway, the Wadsworth-Longfellow House in Portland, Roosevelt Campobello International Park, and the St. Croix Island National Monument.

Famous natives and residents: F. Lee Bailey, defense attorney; Charles F. Browne (Artemus Ward), humorist; Cyrus Curtis, publisher; Dorothea Dix, civil rights reformer; John Ford, film director; Melville Fuller, jurist; Marsden Hartley, painter; Henry Wadsworth Longfellow, poet; Sarah Orne Jewett, author; Stephen King, writer; Linda Lavin, actress; Edna St. Vincent Millay, poet; Marston Morse, mathematician; Frank Munsey, publisher; Walter Piston, composer; George Putnam, publisher; Kenneth Roberts, historical novelist; Edwin Arlington Robinson, poet; Margaret Chase Smith, politician; Samantha Smith, peacemaker and actress; John Hay Whitney, publisher.

Maryland

Capital: Annapolis
Governor: Robert L. Ehrlich, Jr., R (to Jan. 2007)
Lieut. Gov.: Michael Steele, R (to Jan. 2007)
Senators: Barbara A. Mikulski, D (to Jan. 2005); Paul S. Sarbanes, D (to Jan. 2007)
Secy. of State: R. Karl Aumann, R (to Jan. 2007)
Treasurer: Nancy K. Kopp, D
Atty. General: J. Joseph Curran, Jr., D (to Jan. 2007)
Entered Union (rank): April 28, 1788 (7)
Present constitution adopted: 1867
Motto: *Fatti maschii, parole femine* (Manly deeds, womanly words)
State Symbols: bird, Baltimore oriole (1947); **boat,** skipjack (1985); **crustacean,** Maryland blue crab (1989); **dinosaur,** Astrodon johnstoni (1998); **dog,** Chesapeake Bay retriever (1964); **beverage,** milk (1998); **flower,** black-eyed susan (1918); **fish,** rockfish (1965); **folk dance,** square dance (1994); **fossil shell,** *ecphora gardnerae gardnerae* (Wilson) (1994); **insect,** Baltimore checkerspot butterfly (1973); **reptile,** Diamondback terrapin (1994); **song,** "Maryland! My Maryland!" (1939); **sport,** jousting (1962); **tree,** white oak (1941)
Nicknames: Free State; Old Line State
Origin of name: In honor of Henrietta Maria (queen of Charles I of England)
10 largest cities (2000): Baltimore, 651,154; Frederick, 52,767; Gaithersburg, 52,613; Bowie, 50,269; Rockville, 47,388; Hagerstown, 36,687; Annapolis, 35,838; College Park, 24,657; Salisbury, 23,743; Cumberland, 21,518
Land area: 9,774 sq mi. (25,315 sq km)
Geographic center: In Prince Georges Co., 4½ mi. NW of Davidsonville
Number of counties: 23, and 1 independent city
Largest county by population and area: Montgomery, 891,347 (2001); Frederick, 663 sq mi.
State forests: 13 (132,944 ac.)
State parks: 47 (87,670 ac.)
Residents: Marylander
2002 resident population est.: 5,458,137
2000 resident census population (rank): 5,296,486 (19). **Male:** 2,557,794 (48.3%); **Female:** 2,738,692 (51.7%). **White:** 3,391,308 (64.0%); **Black:** 1,477,411 (27.9%); **American Indian:** 15,423 (0.3%); **Asian:** 210,929 (4.0%); **Other race:** 95,525 (1.8%); **Two or more races:** 103,587 (2.0%); **Hispanic/Latino:** 227,916 (4.3%). **2000 percent population 18 and over:** 74.4; **65 and over:** 11.3; **median age:** 36.0.

In 1608, Capt. John Smith explored Chesapeake Bay. Charles I granted a royal charter for Maryland to Cecil Calvert, Lord Baltimore, in 1632, and English settlers, many of whom were Roman Catholic, landed on St. Clement's (now Blakistone) Island in 1634. Religious freedom, granted all Christians in the Toleration Act passed by the Maryland assembly in 1649, was ended by a Puritan revolt, 1654–1658.

From 1763 to 1767, Charles Mason and Jeremiah Dixon surveyed Maryland's northern boundary line with Pennsylvania. In 1791, Maryland ceded land to form the District of Columbia.

In 1814, during the British attempt to capture Baltimore, the bombardment of Fort McHenry inspired Francis Scott Key to write the words to "The Star-Spangled Banner." During the Civil War, Maryland was a slave state but remained in the Union. Consequently, Marylanders fought on both sides and many families were divided.

Maryland's Eastern Shore and Western Shore embrace the Chesapeake Bay, and the many estuaries and rivers create one of the longest waterfronts of any state. The Bay produces more seafood—oysters, crabs, clams, fin fish—than any comparable body of water. Important agricultural products are greenhouse and nursery products, chickens, dairy products, eggs, and soybeans. Stone, coal, sand, gravel, cement, and clay are the chief mineral products.

Manufacturing industries include food products, chemicals, computer and electronic products, transportation equipment, and primary metals. Baltimore, home of the Johns Hopkins University and Hospital, ranks as the nation's second port in foreign tonnage. The capital, Annapolis, is the site of the U.S. Naval Academy.

Among the popular attractions in Maryland are the Fort McHenry National Monument; Harpers Ferry and Chesapeake and Ohio Canal National Historic Parks; Antietam National Battlefield; National Aquarium, USS *Constellation*, and Maryland Science Center at Baltimore's Inner Harbor; Historic St. Mary's City; Jefferson Patterson Historical Park and Museum at St. Leonard; U.S. Naval Academy in Annapolis; Goddard Space Flight Center at Greenbelt; Assateague Island National Park Seashore; Ocean City beach resort; and Catoctin Mountain, Fort Frederick, and Piscataway parks.

Famous natives and residents: Benjamin Banneker, mathematician and astronomer; John Barth, writer; Eubie Blake, musician; John Wilkes Booth, actor and Lincoln assassin; Francis X. Bushman, actor; James M. Cain, writer; Samuel Chase, jurist; Frederick Douglass, abolitionist; John Fletcher Hurst, Methodist bishop and educator; Christopher Gist, frontiersman; Philip Glass, composer; John Hanson, president of Continental Congress; Matthew Henson, polar explorer; Billie Holiday, jazz-blues singer; Johns Hopkins, financier; Reverdy Johnson, lawyer and statesman; Thomas Johnson, political leader; Francis Scott Key, lawyer and poet; Thurgood Marshall, jurist; H. L. Mencken, writer; Hezekiah Niles, journalist; Charles Willson Peale, painter; Frank Perdue, farmer, businessman; James R. Randall, journalist and writer of the state song; Babe Ruth, baseball player; Upton Sinclair, novelist; Roger B. Taney, jurist; George Alfred Townsend (Gath), journalist; Harriet Tubman, abolitionist; Leon Uris, novelist; Frank Zappa, singer.

Massachusetts

Capital: Boston
Governor: Mitt Romney, R (to Jan. 2007)
Lieut. Governor: Kerry Healy, R (to Jan. 2007)
Senators: Edward M. Kennedy, D (to Jan. 2007); John F. Kerry, D (to Jan. 2009)
Secy. of the Commonwealth: William F. Galvin, D (to Jan. 2007)
Treasurer: Timothy P. Cahill, D (to Jan. 2007)
Atty. General: Thomas F. Reilly, D (to Jan. 2007)
Present constitution drafted: 1780 (oldest U.S. state constitution in effect today)
Entered Union (rank): Feb. 6, 1788 (6)
Motto: *Ense petit placidam sub libertate quietem* (By the sword we seek peace, but peace only under liberty)
State Symbols: flower, mayflower (1918); **tree,** American elm (1941); **bird,** chickadee (1941); **song,** "All Hail to Massachusetts" (1966); **beverage,** cranberry juice (1970); **insect,** ladybug (1974); **cookie,** chocolate chip (1997); **muffin,** corn muffin (1986); **dessert,** Boston cream pie (1996)
Nicknames: Bay State; Old Colony State
Origin of name: From Massachusett tribe of Native Americans, meaning "at or about the great hill"
10 largest cities (2000): Boston, 589,141; Worcester, 172,648; Springfield, 152,082; Lowell, 105,167; Cambridge, 101,355; Brockton, 94,304; New Bedford, 93,768; Fall River, 91,938; Lynn, 89,050; Quincy, 88,025
Land area: 7,840 sq mi. (20,306 sq km)
Geographic center: In Worcester Co., in N part of city of Worcester
Number of counties: 14
Largest county by population and area: Middlesex, 1,463,454 (2001); Worcester, 1,513 sq mi.
State forests and parks: 144 (300,000 ac.)[1]
Residents: Bay Stater
2002 resident population est.: 6,427,801
2000 resident census population (rank): 6,349,097 (13). **Male:** 3,058,816 (48.2%); **Female:** 3,290,281 (51.8%). **White:** 5,367,286 (84.5%); **Black:** 343,454 (5.4%); **American Indian:** 15,015 (0.2%); **Asian:** 238,124 (3.8%); **Other race:** 236,724 (3.7%); **Two or more races:** 146,005 (2.3%); **Hispanic/Latino:** 428,729 (6.8%). **2000 percent population 18 and over:** 76.4; **65 and over:** 13.5; **median age:** 36.5.

1. The Metropolitan District Commission, an agency of the Commonwealth serving municipalities in the Boston area, has about 20,000 acres of woodlands, wetlands, and urban parks under its jurisdiction.

Massachusetts has played a significant role in American history since the Pilgrims, seeking religious freedom, founded Plymouth Colony in 1620. As one of the most important of the 13 colonies, Massachusetts became a leader in resisting British oppression. In 1773, the Boston Tea Party protested unjust taxation. The Minute Men started the American Revolution by battling British troops at Lexington and Concord on April 19, 1775.

During the 19th century, Massachusetts was famous for the intellectual activity of its writers and educators and for its expanding commercial fishing, shipping, and manufacturing interests. Massachusetts pioneered the manufacture of textiles and shoes. Today, these industries have been replaced in importance by the electronics and communications equipment fields.

The state's cranberry crop is the nation's second-largest (after Wisconsin). Also important are dairy and poultry products, nursery and greenhouse produce, vegetables, and fruit.

Tourism has become an important factor in the economy of the state because of its numerous recreational areas and historical landmarks. Cape Cod has beaches, summer theaters, and an artists' colony at Provincetown. The Berkshires, in the western part of the state, is the site of Tanglewood, the summer home of the Boston Symphony; art museums, including Mass MoCA and the Clark Institute; and Jacob's Pillow, a world renowned dance center.

Among the many other points of interest are Old Sturbridge Village in Sturbridge, Minute Man National Historical Park between Lexington and Concord, and Plimoth Plantation in Plymouth. In Boston there are many places of historical interest, including Old North Church, Old State House, Faneuil Hall, the USS *Constitution,* and the John F. Kennedy Library and Museum.

Famous natives and residents: John Adams, president; John Quincy Adams, president; Samuel Adams, patriot; Bronson Alcott, educator and social reformer; Louisa May Alcott, writer; Horatio Alger, novelist; Susan B. Anthony, woman suffragist; Clara Barton, American Red Cross founder; Leonard Bernstein, conductor; George H. W. Bush, president; William Cullen Bryant, poet and editor; Luther Burbank, horticulturalist; John Cheever, novelist; John Singleton Copley, painter; e.e. cummings, poet; Jacques d'Amboise, ballet dancer; Bette Davis, actress; Cecil B. DeMille, film director; Emily Dickinson, poet; Ralph Waldo Emerson, philosopher and poet; Geraldine Farrar, soprano, actress; Benjamin Franklin, statesman and scientist; Buckminster Fuller, architect and educator; Robert Goddard, father of modern rocketry; John Hancock, statesman; Nathaniel Hawthorne, novelist; Oliver Wendell Holmes, jurist; Winslow Homer, painter; Elias Howe, inventor; John F. Kennedy, president; Amy Lowell, poet; James Russell Lowell, poet; Robert Lowell, poet; Horace Mann, educator; Cotton Mather, clergyman; Herman Melville, writer; Samuel F. B. Morse, painter and inventor; Edgar Allan Poe, writer; Paul Revere, silversmith and Revolutionary War figure; Norman Rockwell, artist; Dr. Seuss (Theodore Geisel), author and illustrator; David Souter, jurist; Lucy Stone, woman suffragist; Louis Henry Sullivan, architect; Henry David Thoreau, author; Barbara Walters, TV commentator; James McNeill Whistler, painter; Eli Whitney, inventor; John Greenleaf Whittier, poet.

Michigan

Capital: Lansing
Governor: Jennifer Granholm, D (to Jan. 2007)
Lieut. Governor: John D. Cherry, D (to Jan. 2007)
Senators: Carl Levin, D (to Jan. 2009); Debbie A. Stabenow, D (to Jan. 2007)
Secy. of State: Terri Lynn Land, R (to Jan. 2007)
Atty. General: Mike Cox, R (to Jan. 2007)
Treasurer: Jay B. Rising (apptd. by governor)
Organized as territory: Jan. 11, 1805
Entered Union (rank): Jan. 26, 1837 (26)
Present constitution adopted: April 1, 1963, (effective Jan. 1, 1964)
Motto: *Si quaeris peninsulam amoenam circumspice* (If you seek a pleasant peninsula, look around you)
State Symbols: flower, apple blossom (1897); **bird,** robin (1931); **mammal,** white-tailed deer (1997); **fishes,** trout (1965), brook trout (1988); **gem,** isle royal greenstone (chlorastrolite) (1972); **stone,** petoskey stone (1965); **tree,** white pine (1955); **soil,** kalkaska soil series (1990); **reptile,** painted turtle (1995); **flag,** "Blue charged with the arms of the state" (1911); **wildflower,** Dwarf Lake iris (1998)
Nickname: Wolverine State
Origin of name: From Indian word "Michigana" meaning "great or large lake"
10 largest cities (2000): Detroit, 951,270; Grand Rapids, 197,800; Warren, 138,247; Flint, 124,943; Sterling Heights, 124,471; Lansing, 119,128; Ann

Arbor, 114,024; Livonia, 100,545; Dearborn, 97,775; Westland, 86,602
Land area: 56,804 sq mi. (147,122 sq km)
Geographic center: In Wexford Co., 5 mi. NNW of Cadillac
Number of counties: 83
Largest county by population and area: Wayne, 2,045,473 (2001); Marquette, 1,821 sq mi.
State parks and recreation areas: 96 (265,000 ac.)
Residents: Michigander, Michiganite
2002 resident population est.: 10,050,446
2000 resident census population (rank): 9,938,444 (8). **Male:** 4,873,095 (49.0%); **Female:** 5,065,349 (51.0%). **White:** 7,966,053 (80.2%); **Black:** 1,412,742 (14.2%); **American Indian:** 58,479 (0.6%); **Asian:** 176,510 (1.8%); **Other race:** 129,552 (1.3%); **Two or more races:** 192,416 (1.9%); **Hispanic/Latino:** 323,877 (3.3%). **2000 percent population 18 and over:** 73.9; **65 and over:** 12.3; **median age:** 35.5.

Indian tribes were living in the Michigan region when the first European, Étienne Brulé of France, arrived in 1618. Other French explorers, including Jacques Marquette, Louis Joliet, and Sieur de la Salle, followed, and the first permanent settlement was established in 1668 at Sault Ste. Marie. France was ousted from the territory by Great Britain in 1763, following the French and Indian Wars.

After the Revolutionary War, the U.S. acquired most of the region, which remained the scene of constant conflict between the British and U.S. forces and their respective Indian allies through the War of 1812.

Bordering on four of the five Great Lakes, Michigan is divided into Upper and Lower peninsulas by the Straits of Mackinac, which link lakes Michigan and Huron. The two parts of the state are connected by the Mackinac Bridge, one of the world's longest suspension bridges. To the north, connecting lakes Superior and Huron, are the busy Sault Ste. Marie Canals.

While Michigan ranks first among the states in production of motor vehicles and parts, it is also a leader in many other manufacturing and processing lines, including prepared cereals, machine tools, airplane parts, refrigerators, hardware, and furniture.

The state produces important amounts of iron, copper, iodine, gypsum, bromine, salt, lime, gravel, and cement. Michigan's farms grow apples, cherries, beans, pears, grapes, potatoes, and sugar beets. Michigan's forests contribute significantly to the state's economy, supporting thousands of jobs in the wood-product, tourism, and recreation industries. With 10,083 inland lakes and 3,288 mi of Great Lakes shoreline, Michigan is a prime area for both commercial and sport fishing.

Points of interest are the automobile plants in Dearborn, Detroit, Flint, Lansing, and Pontiac; Mackinac Island; Pictured Rocks and Sleeping Bear Dunes National Lakeshores; Greenfield Village in Dearborn; and the many summer resorts along both the inland lakes and Great Lakes.

Famous natives and residents: Nelson Algren, novelist; Tim Allen, actor and comedian; Anita Baker, singer; William Boeing, Sr., airplane manufacturer; Ralph J. Bunche, statesman; Ellen Burstyn, actress; Bruce Catton, historian; Roger Chaffee, astronaut; Francis Ford Coppola, film director; Thomas E. Dewey, politician; Edna Ferber, novelist; Gerald Ford, former president; Henry Ford, industrialist; Ali Haji-Sheikh, football player; Julie Harris, actress; Earvin "Magic" Johnson, basketball player; Casey Kasem, radio personality; John Harvey Kellogg, surgeon and health reformer; Ring Lardner, writer; Charles A. Lindbergh, aviator; Madonna, singer; Dick Martin, comedian; Terry McMillan, author; John N. Mitchell, attorney general; Ted Nugent, singer; Chief Pontiac, Ottawa chief; Iggy Pop, musician; Gilda Radner, comedienne; Della Reese, singer; Jason Robards, Sr., actor; Diana Ross, singer; Steven Seagal, actor; Bob Seger, singer; Tom Selleck, actor; Thomas Schippers, conductor; Potter Stewart, jurist; Lily Tomlin, actress; Danny Thomas, entertainer; William E. Upjohn, pharmaceuticals manufacturer; Margaret Whiting, singer; Robin Williams, comedian and actor; Stevie Wonder, singer.

Minnesota

Capital: St. Paul
Governor: Tim Pawlenty, R (to Jan. 2007)
Lieut. Governor: Carol Molnau, R (to Jan. 2007)
Senators: Norm Coleman, R (to Jan. 2009)
Mark Dayton, D (to Jan. 2007)
Secy. of State: Mary Kiffmeyer, R (to Jan. 2007)
Atty. General: Mike Hatch, D (to Jan. 2007)
Commissioner of Finance: Laura M. King
Organized as territory: March 3, 1849
Entered Union (rank): May 11, 1858 (32)
Present constitution adopted: 1858
Motto: L'Étoile du Nord (The North Star)
State Symbols: flower, lady slipper (1902); **tree,** red (or Norway) pine (1953); **bird,** common loon (also called great northern diver) (1961); **song,** "Hail Minnesota" (1945); **fish,** walleye (1965); **mushroom,** morel (1984)
Nicknames: North Star State; Gopher State; Land of 10,000 Lakes
Origin of name: From a Dakota Indian word meaning "sky-tinted water"
10 largest cities (2000): Minneapolis, 382,618; St. Paul, 287,151; Duluth, 86,918; Rochester, 85,806; Bloomington, 85,172; Brooklyn Park, 67,338; Plymouth, 65,894; Eagan, 63,557; Coon Rapids, 61,607; Burnsville, 60,220
Land area: 79,610 sq mi. (206,190 sq km)
Geographic center: In Crow Wing Co., 10 mi. SW of Brainerd
Number of counties: 87
Largest county by population and area: Hennepin, 1,114,977 (2001); St. Louis, 6,226 sq mi.
State forests: 55
State parks: 66 (226,000 ac.)
Residents: Minnesotan
2002 resident population est.: 5,019,720
2000 resident census population (rank): 4,919,479 (21). **Male:** 2,435,631 (49.5%); **Female:** 2,483,848 (50.5%). **White:** 4,400,282 (89.4%); **Black:** 171,731 (3.5%); **American Indian:** 54,967 (1.1%); **Asian:** 141,968 (2.9%); **Other race:** 65,810 (1.3%); **Two or more races:** 82,742 (1.7%); **Hispanic/Latino:** 143,382 (2.9%). **2000 percent population 18 and over:** 73.8; **65 and over:** 12.1; **median age:** 35.4.

Following the visits of several French explorers, fur traders, and missionaries, including Jacques Marquette, Louis Joliet, and Robert Cavelier, Sieur de la Salle, the region was claimed for Louis XIV by Daniel Greysolon, Sieur Duluth, in 1679.

The U.S. acquired eastern Minnesota from Great Britain after the Revolutionary War and 20 years later bought the western part from France in the Louisiana Purchase of 1803. Much of the region was explored by U.S. Army lieutenant Zebulon M. Pike before the northern strip of Minnesota bordering Canada was ceded by Britain in 1818.

The state is rich in natural resources. A few square miles of land in the north in the Mesabi, Cuyuna, and Vermilion ranges produce more than 75% of the nation's iron ore. The state's farms rank high in yields of corn, wheat, rye, alfalfa, and sugar beets. Other leading farm products include butter, eggs, milk, potatoes, green peas, barley, soybeans, oats, and livestock.

Minnesota's factories produce nonelectrical machinery, fabricated metals, flour-mill products, plastics, electronic computers, scientific instruments, and processed foods. The state is also a leader in the printing and paper-products industries.

Minneapolis is the trade center of the Midwest, and the headquarters of the world's largest supercomputer and grain distributor. St. Paul is the nation's biggest publisher of calendars and law books. These "twin cities" are the nation's third-largest trucking center. Duluth has the nation's largest inland harbor and now handles a significant amount of foreign trade. Rochester is home to the Mayo Clinic, a world-famous medical center.

Tourism is a major revenue producer in Minnesota, with arts, fishing, hunting, water sports, and winter sports bringing in millions of visitors each year.

Among the most popular attractions are the St. Paul Winter Carnival; the Tyrone Guthrie Theatre, the Institute of Arts, Walker Art Center, and Minnehaha Park, in Minneapolis; Boundary Waters Canoe Area; Voyageurs National Park; North Shore Drive; the Minnesota Zoological Gardens; and the state's more than 10,000 lakes.

Famous natives and residents: LaVerne, Maxene, and Patti Andrews, singers; Warren E. Burger, jurist; William E. Colby, CIA director; William Demarest, actor; William O. Douglas, jurist; Bob Dylan, singer and composer; F. Scott Fitzgerald, novelist; Judy Garland, singer and actress; J. Paul Getty, oil executive; Cass Gilbert, architect; Duane Hanson, sculptor; Hubert H. Humphrey, senator and vice president; Jessica Lange, actress; Sinclair Lewis, novelist; Cornell MacNeil, baritone; Roger Maris, baseball player; E. G. Marshall, actor; Charles H. Mayo, surgeon; William J. Mayo, surgeon; Eugene J. McCarthy, former senator; Kate Millett, feminist; Walter F. Mondale, former vice president; Gen. Lauris Norstad, NATO commander; Westbrook Pegler, columnist; John Sargent Pillsbury, businessman; Marion Ross, actress; Jane Russell, actress; Harrison E. Salisbury, journalist; Charles M. Schulz, cartoonist; Max Shulman, novelist; Maurice H. Stans, secretary of commerce; Harold E. Stassen, government official; Michael Todd, producer; Frederick Weyerhaeuser, businessman; Gig Young, actor.

Mississippi

Capital: Jackson
Governor: Ronnie Musgrove, D (to Jan. 2004)
Lieut. Governor: Amy Tuck, R (to Jan. 2004)
Senators: Thad Cochran, R (to Jan. 2009); Trent Lott, R (to Jan. 2007)
Secy. of State: Eric Clark, D (to Jan. 2004)
Treasurer: Marshall Bennett, D (to Jan. 2004)
Atty. General: Mike Moore, D (to Jan. 2004)
Organized as territory: April 7, 1798
Entered Union (rank): Dec. 10, 1817 (20)
Present constitution adopted: 1890
Motto: *Virtute et armis* (By valor and arms)
State Symbols: flower, flower or bloom of the magnolia or evergreen magnolia (1952); **wildflower,** coreopsis (1991); **tree,** magnolia (1938); **bird,** mockingbird (1944); **song,** "Go, Mississippi" (1962); **stone,** petrified wood (1976); **fish,** largemouth or black bass (1974); **insect,** honeybee (1980); **shell,** oyster shell (1974); **water mammal,** bottlenosed dolphin or porpoise (1974); **fossil,** prehistoric whale (1981); **land mammal,** white-tailed deer (1974), red fox (1997); **waterfowl,** wood duck (1974); **beverage,** milk (1984); **butterfly,** spicebush swallowtail (1991); **dance,** square dance (1995)
Nickname: Magnolia State
Origin of name: From an Indian word meaning "Father of Waters"
10 largest cities (2000): Jackson, 184,256; Gulfport, 71,127; Biloxi, 50,644; Hattiesburg, 44,779; Greenville, 41,663; Meridian, 39,968; Tupelo, 34,211; Southhaven, 28,977; Vicksburg, 26,407; Pascagoula, 26,200
Land area: 46,907 sq mi. (121,489 sq km)
Geographic center: In Leake Co., 9 mi. WNW of Carthage
Number of counties: 82
Largest county by population and area: Hinds, 249,495 (2001); Yazoo, 920 sq mi.
State forests: 1 (1,760 ac.)
State parks: 29 (24,521 ac.)
Residents: Mississippian
2002 resident population est.: 2,871,782
2000 resident census population (rank): 2,844,658 (31). **Male:** 1,373,554 (48.3%); **Female:** 1,471,104 (51.7%). **White:** 1,746,099 (61.4%); **Black:** 1,033,809 (36.3%); **American Indian:** 11,652 (0.4%); **Asian:** 18,626 (0.7%); **Other race:** 13,784 (0.5%); **Two or more races:** 20,021 (0.7%); **Hispanic/Latino:** 39,569 (1.4%). **2000 percent population 18 and over:** 72.7; **65 and over:** 12.1; **median age:** 33.8.

First explored for Spain by Hernando De Soto, who discovered the Mississippi River in 1540, the region was later claimed by France. In 1699, a French group under Sieur d'Iberville established the first permanent settlement near present-day Ocean Springs.

Great Britain took over the area in 1763 after the French and Indian Wars, ceding it to the U.S. in 1783 after the Revolution. Spain did not relinquish its claims until 1798, and in 1810 the U.S. annexed West Florida from Spain, including what is now southern Mississippi.

For a little more than one hundred years, from shortly after the state's founding through the Great Depression, cotton was the undisputed king of Mississippi's largely agrarian economy. Over the last half-century, however, Mississippi has diversified its economy by balancing agricultural output with increased industrial activity.

Today, agriculture continues as a major segment of the state's economy. For almost four decades soybeans occupied the most acreage, while cotton remained the largest cash crop. In 2001, however, more acres of cotton were planted than soybeans, and Mississippi jumped to second in the nation in cotton production (exceeded only by Texas). The state's farmlands also yield important harvests of corn, peanuts, pecans, rice, sugar cane, and sweet potatoes as well as poultry, eggs, meat animals, dairy products, feed crops, and horticultural crops. Mississippi remains the world's leading producer of pond-raised catfish.

The state abounds in historical landmarks and is the home of the Vicksburg National Military Park. Other National Park Service areas are Brices Cross Roads National Battlefield Site, Tupelo National Battlefield, and part of Natchez Trace National Parkway. Pre–Civil War mansions are the special pride of Natchez, Oxford, Columbus, Vicksburg, and Jackson.

Famous natives and residents: Red Barber, sportscaster; Jimmy Buffett, singer and songwriter; Craig Claiborne, columnist and restaurant critic; Bo Diddley, guitarist;

Charles Evers, civil rights leader; Medgar Evers, civil rights leader; William Faulkner, novelist; Brett Favre, football player; Shelby Foote, historian; Richard Ford, novelist; John Grisham, novelist; Barry Hannah, novelist; Beth Henley, playwright and actress; Jim Henson, puppeteer; James Earl Jones, actor; B. B. King, guitarist; Steve McNair, football player; Mary Ann Mobley, actress; Willie Morris, writer; Elvis Presley, singer and actor; Leontyne Price, soprano; William Raspberry, columnist; Jerry Rice, football player; Jimmie Rodgers, singer; Sela Ward, actress; Muddy Waters, singer and guitarist; Eudora Welty, novelist; Tennessee Williams, playwright; Oprah Winfrey, talk-show host and actress; Richard Wright, novelist; Tammy Wynette, singer.

Missouri

Capital: Jefferson City
Governor: Bob Holden, D (to Jan. 2005)
Lieut. Governor: Joe Maxwell, D (to Jan. 2005)
Senators: Christopher S. Bond, R (to Jan. 2005); James M. Talent, R (to Jan. 2009)
Secy. of State: Matt Blunt, R (to Jan. 2005)
Auditor: Claire C. McCaskill, D (to Jan. 2003)
Treasurer: Nancy Farmer, D (to Jan. 2005)
Atty. General: Jeremiah "Jay" W. Nixon, D (to Jan. 2005)
Organized as territory: June 4, 1812
Entered Union (rank): Aug. 10, 1821 (24)
Present constitution adopted: 1945
Motto: *Salus populi suprema lex esto* (The welfare of the people shall be the supreme law)
State Symbols: flower, hawthorn (1923); **bird,** bluebird (1927); **aquatic animal,** paddlefish (1997); **fish,** channel catfish (1997); **song,** "Missouri Waltz" (1949); **fossil,** crinoid (1989); **musical instrument,** fiddle (1987); **rock,** mozarkite (1967); **mineral,** galena (1967); **insect,** honeybee (1985); **tree,** flowering dogwood (1955); **tree nut,** eastern black walnut (1990); **animal,** mule (1995); **dance,** square dance (1995); **Missouri Day,** third Wednesday in October (1969)
Nickname: Show-me State
Origin of name: Named after the Missouri Indian tribe. "Missouri" means "town of the large canoes."
10 largest cities (2000): Kansas City, 441,545; St. Louis, 348,189; Springfield, 151,580; Independence, 113,288; Columbia, 84,531; St. Joseph, 73,990; Lee's Summit, 70,700; St. Charles, 60,321; St. Peter's, 51,381; Florissant, 50,497
Land area: 68,886 sq mi. (178,415 sq km)
Geographic center: In Miller Co., 20 mi. SW of Jefferson City
Number of counties: 114, plus 1 independent city
Largest county by population and area: St. Louis, 1,015,417 (2001); Texas, 1,179 sq mi.
Conservation areas[1]**:** leased, 315 (197, 661 ac.); owned, 775 (770,574 ac.)
Conservation accesses: leased, 77; owned, 237
State parks and historic sites: 81
Residents: Missourian
2002 resident population est.: 5,672,579
2000 resident census population (rank): 5,595,211 (17). **Male:** 2,720,177 (48.6%); **Female:** 2,875,034 (51.4%). **White:** 4,748,083 (84.9%); **Black:** 629,391 (11.2%); **American Indian:** 25,076 (0.4%); **Asian:** 61,595 (1.1%); **Other race:** 45,827 (0.8%); **Two or more races:** 82,061 (1.5%); **Hispanic/Latino:** 118,592 (2.1%). **2000 percent population 18 and over:** 74.5; **65 and over:** 13.5; **median age:** 36.1.

1. Includes wildlife areas, natural history areas, state forests, and tower sites.

Hernando De Soto visited the Missouri area in 1541. France's claim to the entire region was based on Sieur de la Salle's travels in 1682. French fur traders established Ste. Genevieve in 1735, and St. Louis was first settled in 1764.

The U.S. gained Missouri from France as part of the Louisiana Purchase in 1803, and the territory was admitted as a state following the Missouri Compromise of 1820. Throughout the pre–Civil War period and during the war, Missourians were sharply divided in their opinions about slavery and in their allegiances, supplying both Union and Confederate forces with troops. However, the state itself remained in the Union.

Historically, Missouri played a leading role as a gateway to the West, St. Joseph being the eastern starting point of the Pony Express, while the much-traveled Santa Fe and Oregon trails began in Independence.

Missouri's economy is highly diversified. Service industries provide more income and jobs than any other segment, and include a growing tourism and travel sector. Wholesale and retail trade, manufacturing, and agriculture also play significant roles in the state's economy.

Missouri is a leading producer of transportation equipment (including automobile manufacturing and auto parts), beer and beverages, and defense and aerospace technology. Food processing is the state's fastest-growing industry.

Missouri mines produce 90% of the nation's principal (non-recycled) lead supply. Other natural resources include iron ore, zinc, barite, limestone, and timber.

The state's top agricultural products include grain, sorghum, hay, corn, soybeans, and rice. Missouri also ranks high among the states in cattle and calves, hogs, and turkeys and broilers. A vibrant wine industry also contributes to the economy.

Tourism draws hundreds of thousands of visitors to a number of Missouri points of interest: the country-music shows of Branson; Bass Pro Shops national headquarters (Springfield); the Gateway Arch at the Jefferson National Expansion (St. Louis); Mark Twain's boyhood home (Hannibal); the Harry S Truman home and library (Independence); the scenic beauty of the Ozark National Scenic Riverways; and the Pony Express and Jesse James museums (St. Joseph). The state's different lake regions also attract fishermen and sun-seekers from throughout the Midwest.

Famous natives and residents: Robert Altman, film director; Burt Bacharach, songwriter; Josephine Baker, singer and dancer; Wallace Beery, actor; Robert Russell Bennett, composer; Yogi Berra, baseball player; Thomas Hart Benton, painter; Bill Bradley, basketball player and N.J. senator; Omar N. Bradley, general; Grace Bumbry, soprano; William Burroughs, writer; Sarah Caldwell, opera director and conductor; Martha Jane Canary (Calamity Jane), frontierswoman; George Washington Carver, scientist; Don Cheadle, actor; Walter Cronkite, TV newscaster; Robert Cummings, actor; Jane Darwell, actress; Walt Disney, artist; T. S. Eliot, poet; Redd Foxx, actor and comedian; Betty Grable, actress; Dick Gregory, comic and activist; Jean Harlow, actress; Coleman Hawkins, jazz musician; George Hearn, actor; Edwin Hubble, astronomer; Langston Hughes, poet; John Huston, film director; Jesse James, outlaw; Scott Joplin, composer; Marianne Moore, poet; Geraldine Page, actress; James C. Penney, merchant; John Joseph Pershing, general; Vincent Price, actor; Joseph Pulitzer, journalist; Ginger Rogers, dancer and actress; Casey Stengel, baseball player; Gladys Swarthout, soprano; Sara Teasdale, poet; Virgil Thomson, composer; Harry S. Truman, president; Mark Twain, author; Dick Van Dyke, actor; Ruth Warrick, actress; Dennis Weaver, actor; Mary Wickes, actress; Laura Ingalls Wilder, author; Roy Wilkins, civil rights leader.

Montana

Capital: Helena
Governor: Judy Martz, R (to Jan. 2005)
Lieut. Governor: Karl Ohs, R (to Jan. 2005)
Senators: Max Baucus, D (to Jan. 2009); Conrad R. Burns, R (to Jan. 2007)
Secy. of State: Bob Brown, R (to Jan. 2005)
Auditor: John Morrison, D (to Jan. 2005)
Atty. General: Mike McGrath, D (to Jan. 2005)
Organized as territory: May 26, 1864
Entered Union (rank): Nov. 8, 1889 (41)
Present constitution adopted: 1972
Motto: *Oro y plata* (Gold and silver)
State Symbols: flower, bitterroot (1895); **tree,** ponderosa pine (1949); **stones,** sapphire and agate (1969); **bird,** Western meadowlark (1981); **song,** "Montana" (1945)
Nickname: Treasure State
Origin of name: Chosen from Latin dictionary by J. M. Ashley. It is a Latinized Spanish word meaning "mountainous."
10 largest cities (2000): Billings, 89,847; Missoula, 57,053; Great Falls, 56,690; Butte-Silver Bow[1], 34,606; Bozeman, 27,509; Helena, 25,780; Kalispell, 14,223; Havre, 9,621; Anaconda–Deer Lodge County, 9,417; Miles City, 8,487
Land area: 145,552 sq mi. (376,980 sq km)
Geographic center: In Fergus Co., 11 mi. W of Lewistown
Number of counties: 56
Largest county by population and area: Yellowstone, 130,398 (2001); Beaverhead, 5,543 sq mi.
State forests: 7 (214,000 ac.)
State parks and recreation areas: 110 (18,273 ac.)
Residents: Montanan
2002 resident population est.: 909,453
2000 resident census population (rank): 902,195 (44). **Male:** 449,480 (49.8%); **Female:** 452,715 (50.2%). **White:** 817,229 (90.6%); **Black:** 2,692 (0.3%); **American Indian:** 56,068 (6.2%); **Asian:** 4,691 (0.5%); **Other race:** 5,315 (0.6%); **Two or more races:** 15,730 (1.7%); **Hispanic/Latino:** 18,081 (2.0%). **2000 percent population 18 and over:** 74.5; **65 and over:** 13.4; **median age:** 37.5.

1. The city is part of a consolidated city-county government and is coextensive with Silver Bow County.

First explored for France by François and Louis-Joseph Verendrye in the early 1740s, much of the region was acquired by the U.S. from France as part of the Louisiana Purchase in 1803. Before western Montana was obtained from Great Britain in the Oregon Treaty of 1846, American trading posts and forts had been established in the territory.

The major Indian Wars (1867–1877) included the famous 1876 Battle of the Little Big Horn, better known as "Custer's Last Stand," in which Cheyenne and Sioux defeated George A. Custer and more than 200 of his men in southeast Montana.

Much of Montana's early history was concerned with mining, with copper, lead, zinc, silver, coal, and oil as principal products. Butte is the center of the area that once supplied half of the U.S. copper.

Fields of grain cover much of Montana's plains. It ranks high among the states in wheat and barley, with rye, oats, flaxseed, sugar beets, and potatoes as other important crops. Sheep and cattle raising make significant contributions to the economy.

Tourist attractions include hunting, fishing, skiing, and dude ranching. Glacier National Park, on the Continental Divide, has 60 glaciers, 200 lakes, and many streams with good trout fishing. Other major points of interest include the Little Bighorn Battlefield National Monument, Virginia City, Yellowstone National Park, Fort Union Trading Post and Grant-Kohr's Ranch National Historic Sites, and the Museum of the Plains Indians at Browning.

Famous natives and residents: Dorothy Baker, author; Dirk Benedict, actor; W. A. (Tony) Boyle, labor union official; Gary Cooper, actor; John Cowan, prospector and founder of Last Chance Gulch (now Helena); Alfred Bertram Guthrie, Pulitzer Prize–winning author; Chet Huntley, TV newscaster; Will James, writer and artist; Dorothy Johnson, author; Evel Knievel, daredevil motorcyclist; Myrna Loy, actress; David Lynch, filmmaker; Mike Mansfield, senator; George Montgomery, actor; Jeannette Rankin, first woman elected to Congress; Martha Raye, actress; Charles M. Russell, painter; Michael Smuin, choreographer; Lester C. Thurow, economist and educator.

Nebraska

Capital: Lincoln
Governor: Mike Johanns, R (to Jan. 2007)
Lieut. Governor: David Heineman, R (to Jan. 2007)
Senators: Charles Hagel, R (to Jan. 2009); Ben Nelson, D (to Jan. 2007)
Secy. of State: John Gale, R (to Jan. 2007)
Atty. General: Jon Bruning, R (to Jan. 2007)
Treasurer: Lorelee Byrd, R (to Jan. 2007)
Organized as territory: May 30, 1854
Entered Union (rank): March 1, 1867 (37)
Present constitution adopted: Oct. 12, 1875 (extensively amended 1919–20)
Motto: Equality before the law
State Symbols: flower, goldenrod (1895); **fish,** channel catfish (1997); **American folk dance,** square dance (1997); **ballad,** "A Place Like Nebraska" (1997); **tree,** cottonwood (1972); **bird,** Western meadowlark (1929); **insect,** honeybee (1975); **gemstone,** blue agate (1967); **rock,** prairie agate (1967); **fossil,** mammoth (1967); **song,** "Beautiful Nebraska" (1967); **soil,** typic argiustolls, holdreges series (1979); **mammal,** whitetail deer (1981); **grass,** little bluestem (1969); **beverage,** milk (1998)
Nicknames: Cornhusker State (1945); Beef State
Origin of name: From an Oto Indian word meaning "flat water"
10 largest cities (2000): Omaha, 390,007; Lincoln, 225,581; Bellevue, 44,382; Grand Island, 42,940; Kearney, 27,431; Fremont, 25,174; Hastings, 24,064; North Platte, 23,878; Norfolk, 23,516; Columbus, 20,971
Land area: 76,872 sq mi. (199,098 sq km)
Geographic center: In Custer Co., 10 mi. NW of Broken Bow
Number of counties: 93
Largest county by population and area: Douglas, 465,683 (2001); Cherry, 5,961 sq mi.
State parks: 85 areas, historical and recreational; 8 major areas
Residents: Nebraskan
2002 resident population est.: 1,729,180
2000 resident census population (rank): 1,711,263 (38). **Male:** 843,351 (49.3%); **Female:** 867,912 (50.7%). **White:** 1,533,261 (89.6%); **Black:** 68,541 (4.0%); **American Indian:** 14,896 (0.9%); **Asian:** 21,931 (1.3%); **Other race:** 47,845 (2.8%); **Two or more races:** 23,953 (1.4%); **Hispanic/Latino:** 94,425 (5.5%). **2000 percent population 18 and over:** 73.7; **65 and over:** 13.6; **median age:** 35.3.

French fur traders first visited Nebraska in the late 1600s. Part of the Louisiana Purchase in 1803, eastern Nebraska was explored by Lewis and Clark in 1804–1806. A few years later, Robert Stuart pioneered the Oregon Trail across Nebraska in 1812–

1813, and the first permanent white settlement was established at Bellevue in 1823.

Western Nebraska was acquired by treaty following the Mexican War in 1848. The Union Pacific began its transcontinental railroad at Omaha in 1865. In 1937, Nebraska became the only state in the Union to have a unicameral (one-house) legislature. Members are elected to it without party designation.

Nebraska is a leading grain-producer with bumper crops of sorghum, corn, and wheat. More varieties of grass, valuable for forage, grow in this state than in any other in the nation. The state's sizable cattle and hog industries make Dakota City and Lexington among the nation's largest meat-packing centers.

Manufacturing has become diversified: Firms making electronic components, auto accessories, pharmaceuticals, and mobile homes have joined such older industries as clothing, farm machinery, chemicals, and transportation equipment. Oil was discovered in 1939 and natural gas in 1949.

Among the principal attractions are Agate Fossil Beds, Homestead, and Scotts Bluff National Monuments; Chimney Rock National Historic Site; a re-created pioneer village at Minden; SAC Museum near Ashland; the Stuhr Museum of the Prairie Pioneer Grand Island; Boys Town; the Sheldon Memorial Art Gallery and the Lied Center for the Performing Arts at the University of Nebraska in Lincoln; the State Capitol in Lincoln; the Joslyn Art Museum in Omaha; the Henry Doorly Zoo in Omaha; Museum of Nebraska Art in Kearney; Museum of Nebraska History in Lincoln; and the University of Nebraska State Museum in Lincoln.

Famous natives and residents: Grace Abbott, social worker; Bess Streeter Aldrich, author; Grover Cleveland Alexander, baseball pitcher; Fred Astaire, dancer and actor; Max Baer, boxer; Bil Baird, puppeteer; George Beadle, geneticist; Marlon Brando, actor; William Jennings Bryan, political leader; Warren Buffett, investor; Johnny Carson, TV host; Willa Cather, author; Dick Cavett, TV entertainer; Richard B. Cheney, vice president; Montgomery Clift, actor; James Coburn, actor; William "Buffalo Bill" Cody, showman; Sandy Dennis, actress; Mignon Eberhart, author; Harold "Doc" Edgerton, inventor; Ruth Etting, singer and actress; Fr. Edward J. Flanagan, founder of Boys Town; Henry Fonda, actor; Gerald Ford, former president; Bob Gibson, baseball player; Howard Hanson, conductor; Leland Hayward, producer; Robert Henri, painter; David Janssen, actor; Francis La Flesche, ethnologist; Melvin Laird, politician; Frank W. Leahy, football coach; Harold Lloyd, actor; Malcolm X, civil rights advocate; Dorothy McGuire, actress; Julius Sterling Morton, politician and journalist; John G. Neihardt, epic poet; Nick Nolte, actor; George W. Norris, senator; John J. Pershing, army general; Nathan Roscoe Pound, educator and botanist; Red Cloud, Indian rights advocate; Mari Sandoz, author; Standing Bear, Indian rights advocate; Robert Taylor, actor; Susette La Flesche Tibbles, Omaha Indian activist; Paul Williams, singer, composer, and actor; Julie Wilson, singer and actress; Darryl F. Zanuck, film producer.

Nevada

Capital: Carson City
Governor: Kenny Guinn, R (to Jan. 2007)
Lieut. Governor: Lorraine Hunt, R (to Jan. 2007)
Senators: Harry Reid, D (to Jan. 2005); John Ensign, R (to Jan. 2007)
Secy. of State: Dean Heller, R (to Jan. 2007)
Treasurer: Brian Krolicki, R (to Jan. 2007)
Atty. General: Brian Sandoval, R (to Jan. 2003)
Organized as territory: March 2, 1861
Entered Union (rank): Oct. 31, 1864 (36)
Present constitution adopted: 1864
Motto: All for Our Country
State Symbols: flower, sagebrush (1959); **trees,** single-leaf pinon (1953) and bristlecone pine (1987); **bird,** mountain bluebird (1967); **animal,** desert bighorn sheep (1973); **colors,** silver and blue (1983); **song,** "Home Means Nevada" (1933); **rock,** sandstone (1987); **precious gemstone,** virgin valley black fire opal (1987); **semiprecious gemstone,** Nevada turquoise (1987); **grass,** Indian ricegrass (1977); **metal,** silver (1977); **fossil,** ichthyosaur (1977); **fish,** lahontan cutthroat trout (1981); **reptile,** desert tortoise (1989); **state artifact,** tule duck decoy (1995)
Nicknames: Sagebrush State; Silver State; Battle Born State
Origin of name: Spanish: "snowcapped"
10 largest cities (2000): Las Vegas, 478,434; Reno, 180,480; Henderson, 175,381; North Las Vegas, 115,488; Sparks, 66,346; Carson City, 52,457; Elko, 16,708; Boulder City, 14,966; Mesquite, 9,389; Fallon, 7,536
Land area: 109,826 sq mi. (284,449 sq km)
Geographic center: In Lander Co., 26 mi. SE of Austin
Number of counties: 16, plus 1 independent city
Largest county by population and area: Clark, 1,464,653 (2001); Nye, 18,147 sq mi.
State parks: 20 (150,000 ac., including leased lands)
Residents: Nevadan, Nevadian
2002 resident population est.: 2,173,491
2000 resident census population (rank): 1,998,257 (35). **Male:** 1,018,051 (50.9%); **Female:** 980,206 (49.1%). **White:** 1,501,886 (75.2%); **Black:** 135,477 (6.8%); **American Indian:** 26,420 (1.3%); **Asian:** 90,266 (4.5%); **Other race:** 159,354 (8.0%); **Two or more races:** 76,428 (3.8%); **Hispanic/Latino:** 393,970 (19.7%). **2000 percent population 18 and over:** 74.4; **65 and over:** 11.0; **median age:** 35.0.

Trappers and traders, including Jedediah Smith and Peter Skene Ogden, entered the Nevada area in the 1820s. In 1843–1845, John C. Frémont and Kit Carson explored the Great Basin and Sierra Nevada. The U.S. obtained the region in 1848 following the Mexican War, and the first permanent settlement was a Mormon trading post near present-day Genoa.

The driest state in the nation, with an average annual rainfall of only about 7 in., much of Nevada is uninhabited, sagebrush-covered desert. The wettest part of the state receives about 40 in. of precipitation per year, while the driest spot has less than 4 in. per year.

Nevada was made famous by the discovery of the Comstock Lode, the richest known U.S. silver deposit, in 1859, and its mines have produced large quantities of gold, silver, copper, lead, zinc, mercury, barite, and tungsten. Oil was discovered in 1954. Gold now far exceeds all other minerals in value of production.

In 1931, the state created two industries, divorce and gambling. For many years, Reno and Las Vegas were the "divorce capitals of the nation." More liberal divorce laws in many states have ended this distinction, but Nevada is still the gambling capital of the U.S. and a leading entertainment center. State gambling taxes account for 34.1% of general fund tax revenues.

The state's leading agricultural industry is cattle and calves. Agricultural crops consist mainly of hay, alfalfa seed, barley, wheat, and potatoes.

Nevada manufactures gaming equipment; lawn and garden irrigation devices; titanium products; seismic and machinery monitoring devices; and specialty printing.

Lake Tahoe, Reno, and Las Vegas are major resorts. Recreation areas include Pyramid Lake, Lake Tahoe, and Lake Mead and Lake Mohave, both in Lake Mead National Recreation Area. Other attractions are Hoover Dam, Virginia City, and Great Basin National Park (includes Lehman Caves).

Famous natives and residents: Eva Adams, director of U.S. Mint; Andre Agassi, tennis player; Raymond T. Baker, director of U.S. Mint; Helen Delich Bentley, government official and newspaperwoman; Robert Caples, painter; Walter Van Tilburg Clark, writer; Henry Comstock, prospector; Abby Dalton, actress; Michele Greene, actress; Sarah Winnemucca Hopkins, author and Paiute interpreter and peacemaker; Jack Kramer, tennis player; Paul Laxalt, politician; Robert Laxalt, writer; William Lear, aviation inventor; Robert C. Lynch, surgeon; John W. Mackay, benefactor, one of Big Four of Comstock Lode; Emma Nevada, opera singer; Thelma "Pat" Nixon, first lady; James W. Nye, territory governor and senator; Lute Pease, cartoonist and Pulitzer Prize winner; Edna Purviance, actress; Patty Sheehan, golfer; Jack Wilson, Paiute Indian prophet; George Wingfield, mining millionaire.

New Hampshire

Capital: Concord
Governor: Craig Benson, R (to Jan. 2005)
Senators: Judd Gregg, R (to Jan. 2005); John E. Sununu, R (to Jan. 2009)
Treasurer: Michael Ablowich, R (to Dec. 2004)
Secy. of State: William M. Gardner, D (to Dec. 2004)
Atty. General: Peter Heed, R (to Jan. 2005)
Entered Union (rank): June 21, 1788 (9)
Present constitution adopted: 1784
Motto: Live free or die
State Symbols: flower, purple lilac (1919); **tree,** white birch (1947); **animal,** white-tailed deer (1983); **insect,** ladybug (1977); **saltwater fish,** striped bass (1994); **freshwater fish,** brook trout (1995); **amphibian,** spotted newt (1985); **butterfly,** karner blue (1992); **bird,** purple finch (1957); **songs,** "Old New Hampshire" (1949) and "New Hampshire, My New Hampshire" (1963)
Nickname: Granite State
Origin of name: From the English county of Hampshire
10 largest cities (2000): Manchester, 107,006; Nashua, 86,605; Concord, 40,687; Derry, 34,021; Rochester, 28,461; Salem, 28,112; Dover, 26,884; Merrimack, 25,119; Londonderry, 23,236; Hudson, 22,928
Land area: 8,968 sq mi. (23,227 sq km)
Geographic center: In Belknap Co., 3 mi. E of Ashland
Number of counties: 10
Largest county by population and area: Hillsborough, 387,674 (2001); Coos, 1,801 sq mi.
State parks: 65 (50,000+ ac.)
Residents: New Hampshirite
2002 resident population est.: 1,275,056
2000 resident census population (rank): 1,235,786 (41). **Male:** 607,687 (49.2%); **Female:** 628,099 (50.8%). **White:** 1,186,851 (96.0%); **Black:** 9,035 (0.7%); **American Indian:** 2,964 (0.2%); **Asian:** 15,931 (1.3%); **Other race:** 7,420 (0.6%); **Two or more races:** 13,214 (1.1%); **Hispanic/Latino:** 20,489 (1.7%). **2000 percent population 18 and over:** 75.0; **65 and over:** 12.0; **median age:** 37.1.

Under an English land grant, Capt. John Smith sent settlers to establish a fishing colony at the mouth of the Piscataqua River, near present-day Rye and Dover, in 1623. Capt. John Mason, who participated in the founding of Portsmouth in 1630, gave New Hampshire its name.

After a 38-year period of union with Massachusetts, New Hampshire was made a separate royal colony in 1679. As leaders in the revolutionary cause, New Hampshire delegates received the honor of being the first to vote for the Declaration of Independence on July 4, 1776. New Hampshire gained a measure of international attention in 1905 when Portsmouth Naval Base played host to the signing of the treaty ending the Russo-Japanese War, known as the Treaty of Portsmouth.

Abundant water power turned New Hampshire into an industrial state early on, and manufacturing is the principal source of income. The most important industrial products are electrical and other machinery, textiles, pulp and paper products, and stone and clay products. Dairy and poultry, and growing fruit, truck vegetables, corn, potatoes, and hay are the major agricultural pursuits.

Because of New Hampshire's scenic and recreational resources, tourism now brings over $3.5 billion into the state annually.

Vacation attractions include Lake Winnipesaukee, largest of 1,300 lakes and ponds; the 724,000-acre White Mountain National Forest; Daniel Webster's birthplace near Franklin; and Strawbery Banke, restored buildings of the original settlement at Portsmouth. In 2003, the famous "Old Man of the Mountain" granite head profile, the state's official emblem, fell from its perch in Franconia.

Famous natives and residents: Sherman Adams, former governor and presidential advisor; Salmon P. Chase, jurist; Charles Anderson Dana, editor; Mary Baker Eddy, founder of the Christian Science Church; Dustin Farnum, actor; Thomas Green Fessenden, journalist and satirical poet; Daniel Chester French, sculptor; Robert Frost, poet; Horace Greeley, journalist and politician; Sarah J. Hale, editor; John Irving, writer; Benjamin F. Keith, theater entrepreneur; Jackson Hall Kelly, promoter of Oregon settlement; John Langdon, political leader; Sharon Christa McAuliffe, teacher and astronaut; Franklin Pierce, former president; Augustus Saint-Gaudens, sculptor; Alan Shepard, astronaut; Harlan F. Stone, jurist; Daniel Webster, statesman; Henry Wilson, politician and former vice president; Noah Worcester, clergyman and pacifist.

New Jersey

Capital: Trenton
Governor: Jim McGreevey, D (to Jan. 2006)
Senators: Frank R. Lautenberg, D (to Jan. 2009); Jon Corzine, D (to Jan. 2007)
Secy. of State: Regena L. Thomas (to Jan. 2006)
Treasurer: John E. McCormac
Atty. General: Peter C. Harvey, I (to Jan. 2006)
Entered Union (rank): Dec. 18, 1787 (3)
Present constitution adopted: 1947
Motto: Liberty and prosperity
State Symbols: flower, purple violet (1913); **bird,** eastern goldfinch (1935); **insect,** honeybee (1974); **tree,** red oak (1950); **animal,** horse (1977); **colors,** buff and blue (1965); **folk dance,** square dance; **dinosaur,** hadrosaurus foulkii; **fish,** brook trout; **shell,** knobbed whelk
Nickname: Garden State
Origin of name: From the Channel Isle of Jersey
10 largest cities (2000): Newark, 273,546; Jersey City, 240,055; Paterson, 149,222; Elizabeth, 120,568; Edison, 97,687; Woodbridge, 97,203; Dover, 89,706; Hamilton, 87,109; Trenton, 85,403; Camden, 79,904
Land area: 7,417 sq mi. (19,210 sq km)
Geographic center: In Mercer Co., 5 mi. SE of Trenton
Number of counties: 21
Largest county by population and area: Bergen, 886,680 (2001); Burlington, 805 sq mi.

State forests: 11
State parks: 35 (67,111 ac.)
Residents: New Jerseyite, New Jerseyan
2002 resident population est.: 8,590,300
2000 resident census population (rank): 8,414,350 (9). **Male:** 4,082,813 (48.5%); **Female:** 4,331,537 (51.5%). **White:** 6,104,705 (72.6%); **Black:** 1,141,821 (13.6%); **American Indian:** 19,492 (0.2%); **Asian:** 480,276 (5.7%); **Other race:** 450,972 (5.4%); **Two or more races:** 213,755 (2.5%); **Hispanic/Latino:** 1,117,191 (13.3%). **2000 percent population 18 and over:** 75.2; **65 and over:** 13.2; **median age:** 36.7.

New Jersey's early colonial history was involved with that of New York (New Netherlands), of which it was a part. One year after the Dutch surrender to England in 1664, New Jersey was organized as an English colony under Gov. Philip Carteret.

In 1676 the colony was divided between Carteret and a company of English Quakers who had obtained the rights belonging to John, Lord Berkeley. New Jersey became a united crown colony in 1702, administered by the royal governor of New York. Finally, in 1738, New Jersey was separated from New York under its own royal governor, Lewis Morris. Because of its key location between New York City and Philadelphia, New Jersey saw much fighting during the American Revolution.

Today, New Jersey, an area of wide industrial diversification, is known as the Crossroads of the East. Products from over 15,000 factories can be delivered overnight to almost 60 million people, representing 12 states and the District of Columbia. The greatest single industry is chemicals; New Jersey is one of the foremost research centers in the world. Many large oil refineries are located in northern New Jersey. Other important manufactured items are pharmaceuticals, instruments, machinery, electrical goods, and apparel.

Productive farmland covers nearly one million acres, about 20% of New Jersey's land area. The state ranks high in the production of almost all garden vegetables, as well as cranberries, blueberries, and peaches. Poultry, dairy products, and seafood are also top commodities.

Tourism is the second-largest industry in New Jersey. The state has numerous resort areas on 127 mi of Atlantic coastline. In 1977, New Jersey voters approved legislation allowing legalized casino gambling in Atlantic City. Points of interest include the Delaware Water Gap, the Edison National Historic Site in West Orange, Princeton University, Liberty State Park, Jersey City, and the N.J. State Aquarium in Camden.

Famous natives and residents: Bud Abbott, comedian; Charles Addams, cartoonist; Edwin Aldrin, astronaut; Count Basie, band leader; Joan Bennett, actress; Jon Bon Jovi, musician; William J. Brennan, jurist; Aaron Burr, political leader; James Fenimore Cooper, novelist; Lou Costello, comedian; Stephen Crane, writer; Helen Gahagan Douglas, representative; Allen Ginsberg, poet; William Frederick Halsey, Jr., admiral; Alfred Joyce Kilmer, poet; Ernie Kovacs, comedian; Jerry Lewis, comedian and film director; Anne Morrow Lindbergh, author; Norman Mailer, novelist; Patricia McBride, ballerina; Richard Nixon, president; Dorothy Parker, author; Joe Piscopo, comedian and actor; Paul Robeson, singer and actor; Philip Roth, novelist; Ruth St. Denis, dancer and choreographer; Antonin Scalia, jurist; H. Norman Schwarzkopf, general; Frank Sinatra, singer and actor; Bruce Springsteen, musician; Alfred Stieglitz, photographer; Albert Payson Terhune, journalist and novelist; Sarah Vaughan, singer; William Carlos Williams, physician and poet; Bruce Willis, actor; Edmund Wilson, literary critic and author.

New Mexico

Capital: Santa Fe
Governor: Bill Richardson, D (to Jan. 2007)
Lieut. Governor: Diane Denish, D (to Jan. 2007)
Senators: Jeff Bingaman, D (to Jan. 2007); Pete V. Domenici, R (to Jan. 2009)
Secy. of State: Rebecca Vigil-Giron, D (to Jan. 2007)
Atty. General: Patricia A. Madrid, D (to Jan. 2007)
State Treasurer: Robert E. Vigil, D (to Jan. 2007)
Organized as territory: Sept. 9, 1850
Entered Union (rank): Jan. 6, 1912 (47)
Present constitution adopted: 1911
Motto: *Crescit eundo* (It grows as it goes)
State Symbols: flower, yucca (1927); **tree,** pinon (1949); **animal,** black bear (1963); **bird,** roadrunner (1949); **fish,** cutthroat trout (1955); **vegetables,** chili and frijol (1965); **gem,** turquoise (1967); **song,** "O Fair New Mexico" (1917); **Spanish-language song,** "Asi Es Nuevo Méjico" (1971); **poem,** A Nuevo México (1991); **grass,** blue gramma (1973); **fossil,** coelophysis (1981); **cookie,** bizcochito (1989); **insect,** tarantula hawk wasp (1989); **ballad,** "Land of Enchantment" (1989); **bilingual song,** "New Mexico—Mi Lindo Nuevo Mexico", (1995); **question,** "Red or Green?" (1999)
Nickname: Land of Enchantment (1999)
Origin of name: From the country of Mexico
10 largest cities (2000): Albuquerque, 448,607; Las Cruces, 74,267; Santa Fe, 62,203; Rio Rancho, 51,765; Roswell, 45,293; Farmington, 37,844; Alamogordo, 35,582; Clovis, 32,667; Hobbs, 28,657; Carlsbad, 25,625
Land area: 121,356 sq mi. (314,312 sq km)
Geographic center: In Torrance Co., 12 mi. SSW of Willard
Number of counties: 33
Largest county by population and area: Bernalillo, 562,458 (2001); Catron, 6,928 sq mi.
State-owned forested land: 933,000 ac.
State parks: 31 (267,302 ac.)
Residents: New Mexican
2002 resident population est.: 1,855,059
2000 resident census population (rank): 1,819,046 (36). **Male:** 894,317 (49.2%); **Female:** 924,729 (50.8%). **White:** 1,214,253 (66.8%); **Black:** 34,343 (1.9%); **American Indian:** 173,483 (9.5%); **Asian:** 19,255 (1.1%); **Other race:** 309,882 (17.0%); **Two or more races:** 66,327 (3.6%); **Hispanic/Latino:** 765,386 (42.1%). **2000 percent population 18 and over:** 72.0; **65 and over:** 11.7; **median age:** 34.6.

Francisco Vásquez de Coronado, a Spanish explorer searching for gold, traveled the region that became New Mexico in 1540–1542. In 1598 the first Spanish settlement was established on the Rio Grande River by Juan de Onate; in 1610 Santa Fe was founded and made the capital of New Mexico.

The U.S. acquired most of New Mexico in 1848, as a result of the Mexican War, and the remainder in the 1853 Gadsden Purchase. Union troops captured the territory from the Confederates during the Civil War. With the surrender of Geronimo in 1886, the Apache Wars and most of the Indian conflicts in the area were ended.

Since 1945, New Mexico has been a leader in energy research and development with extensive experiments conducted at Los Alamos Scientific Laboratory and Sandia Laboratories in the nuclear, solar, and geothermal areas.

Minerals are the state's richest natural resource, and New Mexico is one of the U.S. leaders in output of uranium and potassium salts. Petroleum, natural gas, copper, gold, silver, zinc, lead, and molybdenum also contribute heavily to the state's income.

The principal manufacturing industries include food products, chemicals, transportation equipment, lumber, electrical machinery, and stone-clay-glass products. More than two-thirds of New Mexico's farm income comes from livestock products, especially sheep. Cotton, pecans, and sorghum are the most important field crops. Corn, peanuts, beans, onions, chilies, and lettuce are also grown.

Tourist attractions include the Carlsbad Caverns National Park, Inscription Rock at El Morro National Monument, the ruins at Fort Union, Billy the Kid mementos at Lincoln, the White Sands and Gila Cliff Dwellings National Monuments, Bandelier National Monument, and the Chaco Culture National Historical Park.

Famous natives and residents: Kathy Baker, actress; Notah Begay III, golfer; Judy Blume, author; Ernest L. Blumenshein, artist; William "Billy the Kid" Bonney, outlaw; Richard Bradford, author; Ralph Bunche, Nobel Peace Prize winner; Bruce Cabot, actor; Glen Campbell, singer; Kit Carson, army scout and trapper; Dennis Chavez, former senator; John Chisum, cattle king; Mangus Coloradas, Apache leader; Edward Condon, physicist; Bill Daily, actor; John Denver, singer; Bo Diddley, blues guitarist; Patrick Garrett, lawman; Greer Garson, actress; Sid Gutierrez, astronaut; William Hanna, animator; Neil Patrick Harris, actor; Carl Hatch, senator; Tony Hillerman, author; Conrad Hilton, hotel executive; Dennis Hopper, actor; Peter Hurd, artist; Preston Jones, playwright and actor; Ralph Kiner, baseball player and sportscaster; Nancy Lopez, golfer; Maria Martínez, San Ildefonso Pueblo potter; Demi Moore, actress; Jim Morrison, singer and songwriter; Bill Mauldin, political cartoonist; Popé, San Juan Pueblo medicine man and leader; Georgia O'Keeffe, painter; Harrison Schmitt, astronaut and representative; Kim Stanley, actress; Slim Summerville, actor; Clyde Tombaugh, astronomer; Al Unser, Bobby Unser, auto racers; Victorio, Apache chief; Linda Wertheimer, NPR correspondent; Kathy Whitworth, golfer.

New York

Capital: Albany
Governor: George E. Pataki, R (to Jan. 2007)
Lieut. Governor: Mary Donohue, R (to Jan. 2007)
Senators: Charles E. Schumer, D (to Jan. 2005); Hillary Rodham Clinton, D (to Jan. 2007)
Secy. of State: Randy A. Daniels, R (apptd. by governor)
Comptroller: Alan G. Hevesi, D (to Jan. 2007)
Atty. General: Eliot Spitzer, D (to Jan. 2007)
Entered Union (rank): July 26, 1788 (11)
Present constitution adopted: 1777 (last revised 1938)
Motto: *Excelsior* (Ever upward)
State Symbols: animal, beaver (1975); **fish,** brook trout (1975); **gem,** garnet (1969); **flower,** rose (1955); **tree,** sugar maple (1956); **bird,** bluebird (1970); **insect,** ladybug (1989); **song,** "I Love New York" (1980)
Nickname: Empire State
Origin of name: In honor of the Duke of York
10 largest cities (2000): New York, 8,008,278; Buffalo, 292,648; Rochester, 219,773; Yonkers, 196,086; Syracuse, 147,306; Albany, 95,658; New Rochelle, 72,182; Mount Vernon, 68,381; Schenectady, 61,821; Utica, 60,651
Land area: 47,214 sq mi. (122,284 sq km)
Geographic center: In Madison Co., 12 mi. S of Oneida and 26 mi. SW of Utica
Number of counties: 62
Largest county by population and area: Kings, 2,465,286 (2001); St. Lawrence, 2,686 sq mi.
State forest preserves: Adirondacks, 2,500,000 ac.; Catskills, 250,000 ac.
State parks: 152
Residents: New Yorker
2002 resident population est.: 19,157,532
2000 resident census population (rank): 18,976,457 (3). **Male:** 9,146,748 (48.2%); **Female:** 9,829,709 (51.8%). **White:** 12,893,689 (67.9%); **Black:** 3,014,385 (15.9%); **American Indian:** 82,461 (0.4%); **Asian:** 1,044,976 (5.5%); **Other race:** 1,341,946 (7.1%); **Two or more races:** 590,182 (3.1%); **Hispanic/Latino:** 2,867,583 (15.1%). **2000 percent population 18 and over:** 75.3; **65 and over:** 12.9; **median age:** 35.9.

Giovanni da Verrazano, an Italian-born navigator sailing for France, discovered New York Bay in 1524. Henry Hudson, an Englishman employed by the Dutch, reached the bay and sailed up the river now bearing his name in 1609, the same year that northern New York was explored and claimed for France by Samuel de Champlain.

In 1624 the first permanent Dutch settlement was established at Fort Orange (now Albany). One year later Peter Minuit purchased Manhattan Island from the Indians for trinkets worth about 60 Dutch guilders and founded the Dutch colony of New Amsterdam (now New York City), which was surrendered to the English in 1664.

New York's extremely rapid commercial growth may be partly attributed to Gov. De Witt Clinton, who pushed through the construction of the Erie Canal (Buffalo to Albany), which was opened in 1825. Today, the 641-mile Gov. Thomas E. Dewey Thruway connects New York City with Buffalo and with Connecticut, Massachusetts, and Pennsylvania express highways. Two toll-free superhighways, the Adirondack Northway (linking Albany with the Canadian border) and the North-South Expressway (crossing central New York from the Pennsylvania border to the Thousand Islands), have been opened.

The great metropolis of New York City is the nerve center of the nation. It is a leader in manufacturing, foreign trade, commerce and banking, book and magazine publishing, and theatrical production. A leading seaport, its John F. Kennedy International Airport is one of the busiest airports in the world. New York is also home to the New York Stock Exchange, the largest in the world. The printing and publishing industry is the city's largest manufacturing employer, with the apparel industry second.

Nearly all the rest of the state's manufacturing is done on Long Island, along the Hudson River north to Albany, and through the Mohawk Valley, Central New York, and Southern Tier regions to Buffalo. The St. Lawrence seaway and power projects have opened the North Country to industrial expansion and have given the state a second seacoast.

The state ranks seventh in the nation in manufacturing, with 805,200 employees in 2002. The principal industries are printing and publishing, industrial machinery and equipment, electronic equipment, and instruments. The convention and tourist business is also an important source of income.

New York farms produce cattle and calves, corn and poultry, and vegetables and fruits. The state is a leading wine producer.

Major points of interest are Castle Clinton, Fort Stanwix, and Statue of Liberty National Monuments; Niagara Falls; U.S. Military Academy at West Point; National Historic Sites that include homes of Franklin D. Roosevelt at Hyde Park and Theodore Roosevelt in Oyster Bay and New York City; the Women's Rights National Historical Park in Seneca Falls; National Memorials, including

Grant's Tomb and Federal Hall in New York City; Fort Ticonderoga; the Baseball Hall of Fame in Cooperstown; and the United Nations, skyscrapers, museums, theaters, and parks in New York City.

Famous natives and residents: Kareem Abdul-Jabbar, basketball player; Lucille Ball, actress; Humphrey Bogart, actor; James Cagney, actor; Maria Callas, opera singer; Benjamin N. Cardozo, jurist; Paddy Chayefsky, playwright; Peter Cooper, industrialist and philanthropist; Aaron Copland, composer; Tom Cruise, actor; Sammy Davis, Jr., actor and singer; Agnes de Mille, choreographer; Eamon De Valera, president of Ireland; George Eastman, inventor; Millard Fillmore, president; Lou Gehrig, baseball player; George Gershwin, composer; Learned Hand, jurist; Edward Hopper, painter; Julia Ward Howe, poet and reformer; Charles Evans Hughes, jurist; Washington Irving, author; Henry James, novelist; John Jay, jurist; Michael Jordan, basketball player; Jerome Kern, composer; Rockwell Kent, painter; Vince Lombardi, football coach; Chico, Groucho, Harpo, and Zeppo Marx, comedians; Herman Melville, author; Ethel Merman, singer and actress; Ogden Nash, poet; Rosie O'Donnell, comedian; Eugene O'Neill, playwright; Red Jacket, Seneca chief; John D. Rockefeller, industrialist; Norman Rockwell, painter and illustrator; Mickey Rooney, actor; Anna Eleanor Roosevelt, reformer and humanitarian; Franklin D. Roosevelt, president; Theodore Roosevelt, president; Jonas Salk, polio researcher; Margaret Sanger, birth control advocate; Beverly Sills, opera singer; Barbara Stanwyck, actress; Risë Stevens, opera singer; Joe Torre, baseball player and manager; Richard Tucker, tenor; Martin Van Buren, president; Mae West, actress; Walt Whitman, poet; Edith Wharton, novelist.

North Carolina

Capital: Raleigh
Governor: Mike Easley, D (to Jan. 2005)
Lieut. Governor: Beverly Perdue, D (to Jan. 2005)
Senators: John Edwards, D (to Jan. 2005); Elizabeth Dole, R (to Jan. 2009)
Secy. of State: Elaine F. Marshall, D (to Jan. 2005)
Treasurer: Richard H. Moore, D (to Jan. 2005)
Atty. General: Roy Cooper, D (to Jan. 2005)
Entered Union (rank): Nov. 21, 1789 (12)
Present constitution adopted: 1971
Motto: *Esse quam videri* (To be rather than to seem)
State Symbols: flower, dogwood (1941); **tree,** pine (1963); **bird,** cardinal (1943); **mammal,** gray squirrel (1969); **insect,** honeybee (1973); **reptile,** eastern box turtle (1979); **gemstone,** emerald (1973); **shell,** scotch bonnet (1965); **historic boat,** shad boat (1987); **beverage,** milk (1987); **rock,** granite (1979); **dog,** plott hound (1989); **song,** "The Old North State" (1927); **colors,** red and blue (1945); **fruit,** scuppernong grape (2001)
Nickname: Tar Heel State
Origin of name: In honor of Charles I of England
10 largest cities (2000): Charlotte, 540,828; Raleigh, 276,093; Greensboro, 223,891; Durham, 187,035; Winston-Salem, 185,776; Fayetteville, 121,015; Cary, 94,536; High Point, 85,839; Wilmington, 75,838; Asheville, 68,889
Land area: 48,711 sq mi. (126,161 sq km)
Geographic center: In Chatham Co., 10 mi. NW of Sanford
Number of counties: 100
Largest county by population and area: Mecklenburg, 716,407 (2001); Robeson, 949 sq mi.
State forests: 6
State parks: 33 (125,000 ac.)
Residents: North Carolinian
2002 resident population est.: 8,320,146
2000 resident census population (rank): 8,049,313 (11). **Male:** 3,942,695 (49.0%); **Female:** 4,106,618 (51.0%). **White:** 5,804,656 (72.1%); **Black:** 1,737,545 (21.6%); **American Indian:** 99,551 (1.2%); **Asian:** 113,689 (1.4%); **Other race:** 186,629 (2.3%); **Two or more races:** 103,260 (1.3%); **Hispanic/Latino:** 378,963 (4.7%). **2000 percent population 18 and over:** 75.6; **65 and over:** 12.0; **median age:** 35.3.

English colonists, sent by Sir Walter Raleigh, unsuccessfully attempted to settle Roanoke Island in 1585 and 1587. Virginia Dare, born there in 1587, was the first child of English parentage born in America.

In 1653 the first permanent settlements were established by English colonists from Virginia near the Roanoke and Chowan rivers. The region was established as an English proprietary colony in 1663–1665 and in its early history was the scene of Culpepper's Rebellion (1677), the Quaker-led Cary Rebellion (1708), the Tuscarora Indian War (1711–1713), and many pirate raids.

During the American Revolution, there was relatively little fighting within the state, but many North Carolinians saw action elsewhere. Despite considerable pro-Union, antislavery sentiment, North Carolina joined the Confederacy during the Civil War.

North Carolina is the nation's largest furniture, tobacco, brick, and textile producer. Metalworking, chemicals, and paper are also important industries. The major agricultural products are tobacco, corn, cotton, hay, peanuts, and vegetable crops. The state is the country's leading producer of mica and lithium.

Tourism is also important, with visitors spending more than $1 billion annually. Sports include year-round golfing, skiing at mountain resorts, both fresh- and salt-water fishing, and hunting.

Among the major attractions are the Great Smoky Mountains, the Blue Ridge National Parkway, the Cape Hatteras and Cape Lookout National Seashores, the Wright Brothers National Memorial at Kitty Hawk, Guilford Courthouse and Moores Creek National Military Parks, Carl Sandburg's home near Hendersonville, and the Old Salem Restoration in Winston-Salem.

Famous natives and residents: David Brinkley, TV newscaster; Howard Cosell, sportscaster; Virginia Dare, first person born in America to English parents; Elizabeth Dole, government official; James B. Duke, industrialist; Donna Fargo, singer; Roberta Flack, singer; Ava Gardner, actress; Richard Gatling, inventor; Billy Graham, evangelist; Kathryn Grayson, singer and actress; Andy Griffith, actor; Jesse Helms, politician; O. Henry, writer; Barbara Howar, broadcaster and writer; Andrew Johnson, president; Charles Kuralt, TV journalist; Sugar Ray Leonard, boxer; Dolley Madison, first lady; Ronnie Milsap, singer; Thelonious Monk, pianist; Alfred Moore, jurist; Edward R. Murrow, commentator and government official; Walter Hines Page, journalist and ambassador; Floyd Patterson, boxer; Richard Petty, auto racer; James K. Polk, president; Soupy Sales, comedian; Earl Scruggs, bluegrass musician; Randy Travis, musician; John Scott Trotter, orchestra leader; Thomas Wolfe, novelist.

North Dakota

Capital: Bismarck
Governor: John Hoeven, R (to Dec. 15, 2004)
Lieut. Governor: Jack Dalrymple, R (to Dec. 15, 2004)
Senators: Kent Conrad, D (to Jan. 2007); Byron L. Dorgan, D (to Jan. 2005)
Secy. of State: Alvin A. Jaeger, R (to Dec. 31, 2004)
Treasurer: Kathi Gilmore, D (to Dec. 31, 2004)
Atty. General: Wayne Stenehjem, R (to Dec. 31, 2004)
Organized as territory: March 2, 1861
Entered Union (rank): Nov. 2, 1889 (39)
Present constitution adopted: 1889

Motto: Liberty and union, now and forever: one and inseparable
State Symbols: tree, American elm (1947); **bird,** western meadowlark (1947); **song,** "North Dakota Hymn" (1947); **fish,** northern pike (1969); **grass,** western wheatgrass (1977); **fossil,** teredo petrified wood (1967); **beverage,** milk (1983); **state march,** Spirit of the Land (1975); **flower,** wild prairie rose (1907); **equine,** Nokota horse (1993); **dance,** square dance (1995)
Nickname: Sioux State; Flickertail State; Peace Garden State; Rough Rider State
Origin of name: From the Sioux tribe, meaning "allies"
10 largest cities (2000): Fargo, 90,599; Bismarck, 55,532; Grand Forks, 49,321; Minot, 36,567; Mandan, 16,718; Dickinson, 16,010; Jamestown, 15,527; West Fargo, 14,940; Williston, 12,512; Wahpeton, 8,586
Land area: 68,976 sq mi. (178,648 sq km)
Geographic center: In Sheridan Co., 5 mi. SW of McClusky
Number of counties: 53
Largest county by population and area: Cass, 124,021 (2001); McKenzie, 2,742 sq mi.
State parks: 20 (14,822 ac.)
Residents: North Dakotan
2002 resident population est.: 634,110
2000 resident census population (rank): 642,200 (47). **Male:** 320,524 (49.9%); **Female:** 321,676 (50.1%). **White:** 593,181 (92.4%); **Black:** 3,916 (0.6%); **American Indian:** 31,329 (4.9%); **Asian:** 3,606 (0.6%); **Other race:** 2,540 (0.4%); **Two or more races:** 7,398 (1.2%); **Hispanic/Latino:** 7,786 (1.2%). **2000 percent population 18 and over:** 75.0; **65 and over:** 14.7; **median age:** 36.2.

North Dakota was explored in 1738–1740 by French Canadians led by Sieur de la Verendrye. In 1803, the U.S. acquired most of North Dakota from France in the Louisiana Purchase. Lewis and Clark explored the region in 1804–1806, and the first settlements were made at Pembina in 1812 by Scottish and Irish families while this area was still in dispute between the U.S. and Great Britain. In 1818, the U.S. obtained the northeast part of North Dakota by treaty with Great Britain and took possession of Pembina in 1823. However, the region remained largely unsettled until the construction of the railroad in the 1870s and 1880s.

North Dakota is the most rural of all the states, with farms covering more than 90% of the land. North Dakota ranks first in the nation's production of spring and durum wheat; other agricultural products include barley, rye, sunflowers, dry edible beans, honey, oats, flaxseed, sugar beets, hay, beef cattle, sheep, and hogs.

Recently, manufacturing industries have grown, especially food processing and farm equipment. The state's coal and oil reserves are plentiful, and it also produces natural gas, lignite, clay, sand, and gravel.

The Garrison Dam on the Missouri River provides extensive irrigation and produces 400,000 kilowatts of electricity for the Missouri Basin areas.

Known for its waterfowl, grouse, pheasant, and deer hunting and bass, trout, and pike fishing, North Dakota has 20 state parks and recreation areas. Points of interest include the International Peace Garden near Dunseith, Fort Union Trading Post National Historic Site near Williston, Knife River Indian Villages National Historic Site in Stanton, the State Capitol at Bismarck, the Badlands, Theodore Roosevelt National Park, and Fort Abraham Lincoln State Park.

Famous natives and residents: Lynn Anderson, singer; Maxwell Anderson, playwright; Elizabeth Bodine, humanitarian; Dr. Anne Carlsen, educator; Warren Christopher, statesman; Ronald N. Davies, jurist; Angie Dickinson, actress; Ivan Dmitre, artist; Carl Ben Eielson, aviator; Phyllis Frelich, actress; Bertin C. Gamble, founder of Gamble-Skogmo; William H. Gass, writer and philosopher; Brynhild Haugland, state legislator; Phil D. Jackson, basketball player and coach; Dr. Leon O. Jacobson, researcher and educator; Harold K. Johnson, general; David C. Jones, general; Louis L'Amour, author; Peggy Lee, singer; William Lemke, representative; Roger Maris, baseball player; Marquis de Mores, cattleman who established Medora; Gerald P. Nye, senator; Casper Oimoen, skier; William A. Owens, admiral; Arthur Peterson, radio and TV actor; Cliff (Fido) Purpur, hockey player and coach; James Rosenquist, painter; Harold Schafer, founder of Gold Seal Co.; Eric Sevareid, TV commentator; Ann Sothern, actress; Dorothy Stickney, actress; Edward K. Thompson, editor; Era Bell Thompson, editor; Tommy Tucker, band leader; Lawrence Welk, band leader; Larry Woiwode, writer.

Ohio

Capital: Columbus
Governor: Bob Taft II, R (to Jan. 2007)
Lieut. Governor: Jennette Bradley, R (to Jan. 2007)
Senators: Mike DeWine, R (to Jan. 2007); George V. Voinovich, R (to Jan. 2005)
Secy. of State: J. Kenneth Blackwell, R (to Jan. 2007)
Treasurer: Joseph T. Deters, R (to Jan. 2007)
Atty. General: Jim Petro, R (to Jan. 2007)
Entered Union (rank): March 1, 1803 (17)
Present constitution adopted: 1851
Motto: With God all things are possible
State Symbols: flower, scarlet carnation (1904); **tree,** buckeye (1953); **bird,** cardinal (1933); **insect,** ladybug (1975); **gemstone,** flint (1965); **song,** "Beautiful Ohio" (1969); **beverage,** tomato juice (1965); **fossil,** trilobite (1985); **animal,** white-tailed deer (1988); **wildflower,** large white trillium (1987)
Nickname: Buckeye State
Origin of name: From an Iroquoian word meaning "great river"
10 largest cities (2000): Columbus, 711,470; Cleveland, 478,403; Cincinnati, 331,285; Toledo, 313,619; Akron, 217,074; Dayton, 166,179; Parma, 85,655; Youngstown, 82,026; Canton, 80,806; Lorain, 68,652
Land area: 40,948 sq mi. (106,055 sq km)
Geographic center: In Delaware Co., 25 mi. NNE of Columbus
Number of counties: 88
Largest county by population and area: Cuyahoga, 1,380,421 (2001); Ashtabula, 703 sq mi.
State forests: 20 (more than 183,000 ac.)
State parks: 73 (more than 204,000 ac.)
Residents: Ohioan
2002 resident population est.: 11,421,267
2000 resident census population (rank): 11,353,140 (7). **Male:** 5,512,262 (48.6%); **Female:** 5,840,878 (51.4%). **White:** 9,645,453 (85.0%); **Black:** 1,301,307 (11.5%); **American Indian:** 24,486 (0.2%); **Asian:** 132,633 (1.2%); **Other race:** 88,627 (0.8%); **Two or more races:** 157,885 (1.4%); **Hispanic/Latino:** 217,123 (1.9%). **2000 percent population 18 and over:** 74.6; **65 and over:** 13.3; **median age:** 36.2.

First explored for France by Robert Cavelier, Sieur de la Salle, in 1669, the Ohio region became British property after the French and Indian Wars. Ohio was acquired by the U.S. after the Revolutionary War in 1783. In 1788, the first permanent settlement was established at Marietta, capital of the Northwest Territory.

The 1790s saw severe fighting with the Indians in Ohio; a major battle was won by Maj. Gen. Anthony

Wayne at Fallen Timbers in 1794. In the War of 1812, Commodore Oliver H. Perry defeated the British in the Battle of Lake Erie on Sept. 10, 1813.

Ohio is one of the nation's industrial leaders, ranking third in manufacturing employment nationwide. Important manufacturing centers are located in or near Ohio's major cities. Akron is known for rubber; Canton for roller bearings; Cincinnati for jet engines and machine tools; Cleveland for auto assembly, auto parts, and steel; Dayton for office machines, refrigeration, and heating and auto equipment; Youngstown and Steubenville for steel; and Toledo for glass and auto parts.

The state's fertile soil produces soybeans, corn, oats, greenhouse and nursery products, wheat, hay, and fruit, including apples, peaches, strawberries, and grapes. More than half of Ohio's farm receipts come from dairy farming and sheep and hog raising. Ohio ranks fourth among the states in lime production and also ranks high in sand and gravel and crushed stone production.

Tourism is a valuable revenue producer, bringing in $25.7 billion in 2000. Attractions include the Rock and Roll Hall of Fame, Indian burial grounds at Mound City Group National Monument, Perry's Victory International Peace Memorial, the Pro Football Hall of Fame at Canton, and the homes of presidents Grant, Taft, Hayes, Harding, and Garfield.

Famous natives and residents: Neil Armstrong, astronaut; Kathleen Battle, soprano; George Bellows, painter and lithographer; Ambrose Bierce, journalist; Erma Bombeck, columnist; Bill Boyd (Hopalong Cassidy), actor; Milton Caniff, cartoonist; Hart Crane, poet; George Armstrong Custer, army officer; Dorothy Dandridge, actress; Doris Day, singer and actress; Clarence Darrow, lawyer; Ruby Dee, actress; Rita Dove, poet; Hugh Downs, TV broadcaster; Thomas A. Edison, inventor; Clark Gable, actor; James A. Garfield, president; Lillian Gish, actress; John Glenn, astronaut and senator; Ulysses S. Grant, president; Warren G. Harding, president; Rutherford Hayes, president; Benjamin Harrison, president; William Dean Howells, novelist and critic; Zane Grey, author; Robert Henri, painter; Kenisaw Mountain Landis, first baseball commissioner; Dean Martin, singer and actor; William McKinley, president; Paul Newman, actor; Jack Nicklaus, golfer; Annie Oakley, markswoman; Norman Vincent Peale, clergyman; Tyrone Power, actor; Judith Resnik, astronaut; Eddie Rickenbacker, aviator; Roy Rogers, actor and singer; Arthur M. Schlesinger, Jr., historian; William Tecumseh Sherman, army general; Gloria Steinem, feminist; William H. Taft, president; Tecumseh, Shawnee Indian chief; Lowell Thomas, explorer and commentator; James Thurber, author and cartoonist; Orville Wright, inventor; Cy Young, baseball player.

Oklahoma

Capital: Oklahoma City
Governor: Brad Henry, D (to Jan. 2007)
Lieut. Governor: Mary Fallin, R (to Jan. 2007)
Senators: James M. Inhofe, R (to Jan. 2009); Don Nickles, R (to Jan. 2005)
Secy. of State: M. Susan Savage, D (to Jan. 2007)
Treasurer: Robert Butkin, D (to Jan. 2007)
Atty. General: W. A. Drew Edmondson, D (to Jan. 2007)
Organized as territory: May 2, 1890
Entered Union (rank): Nov. 16, 1907 (46)
Present constitution adopted: 1907
Motto: *Labor omnia vincit* (Labor conquers all things)
State Symbols: flower, mistletoe (1893); **tree,** redbud (1937); **bird,** scissor-tailed flycatcher (1951); **animal,** bison (1972); **reptile,** mountain boomer lizard (1969); **stone,** rose rock (barite rose) (1968); **colors,** green and white (1915); **song,** "Oklahoma" (1953); **beverage,** milk; **butterfly,** black swallowtail; **fish,** white or sand bass; **folk dance,** square dance; **furbearer,** raccoon; **game animal,** white-tailed deer; **grass,** Indiangrass; **insect,** honeybee; **musical instrument,** fiddle; **poem,** "Howdy Folks," David Randolph Milsten; **waltz,** "Oklahoma Wind"; **wildflower,** Indian blanket
Nickname: Sooner State
Origin of name: From two Choctaw Indian words meaning "red people"
10 largest cities (2000): Oklahoma City, 506,132; Tulsa, 393,049; Norman, 95,694; Lawton, 92,757; Broken Arrow, 74,859; Edmond, 68,315; Midwest City, 54,088; Enid, 47,045; Moore, 41,138; Stillwater, 39,065
Land area: 68,667 sq mi. (177,848 sq km)
Geographic center: In Oklahoma Co., 8 mi. N of Oklahoma City
Number of counties: 77
Largest county by population and area: Oklahoma, 662,153 (2001); Osage, 2,251 sq mi.
State parks: 51 (72,000 ac.)
Residents: Oklahoman
2002 resident population est.: 3,493,714
2000 resident census population (rank): 3,450,654 (27). **Male:** 1,696,895 (49.1%); **Female:** 1,754,759 (50.9%). **White:** 2,628,434 (76.2%); **Black:** 260,968 (7.6%); **American Indian:** 273,230 (7.9%); **Asian:** 46,767 (1.4%); **Other race:** 82,898 (2.4%); **Two or more races:** 155,985 (4.5%); **Hispanic/Latino:** 179,304 (5.2%). **2000 percent population 18 and over:** 74.1; **65 and over:** 13.2; **median age:** 35.5.

Francisco Vásquez de Coronado first explored the region for Spain in 1541. The U.S. acquired most of Oklahoma in 1803 in the Louisiana Purchase from France; the Western Panhandle region became U.S. territory with the annexation of Texas in 1845.

Set aside as Indian Territory in 1834, the region was divided into Indian Territory and Oklahoma Territory on May 2, 1890. The two were combined to make a new state, Oklahoma, on Nov. 16, 1907.

On April 22, 1889, the first day homesteading was permitted, 50,000 people swarmed into the area. Those who tried to beat the noon starting gun were called "Sooners," hence the state's nickname.

Oil made Oklahoma a rich state, but natural-gas production has now surpassed it. Oil refining, meat packing, food processing, and machinery manufacturing (especially construction and oil equipment) are important industries. Minerals produced in Oklahoma include helium, gypsum, zinc, cement, coal, copper, and silver.

Oklahoma's rich plains produce bumper yields of wheat, as well as large crops of sorghum, hay, cotton, and peanuts. More than half of Oklahoma's annual farm receipts are contributed by livestock products, including cattle, dairy products, swine, and broilers.

Tourist attractions include the National Cowboy Hall of Fame in Oklahoma City, the Will Rogers Memorial in Claremore, the Cherokee Cultural Center with a restored Cherokee village, the restored Fort Gibson Stockade near Muskogee, the Lake Texoma recreation area, pari-mutuel horse racing at Remington Park in Oklahoma City, and Blue Ribbon Downs in Sallisaw.

Famous natives and residents: Johnny Bench, baseball player; John Berryman, poet; Garth Brooks, singer; Iron Eyes Cody, Cherokee actor; L. Gordon Cooper, astronaut; Ralph Ellison, writer; James Garner, actor; Owen K. Garriott, astronaut; Vince Gill, singer; Chester Gould, cartoonist; Woody Guthrie, singer and composer; Roy Harris, composer; Paul Harvey, broadcaster; Van Heflin, actor; Ron Howard, actor and director; Ben Johnson, actor; Jennifer Jones, actress; Jeane Kirkpatrick, educator and public-affairs spokesperson; Shannon Lucid, astronaut; Wilma P. Mankiller, principal chief of the Cherokee Nation of Oklahoma; Mickey Mantle, baseball player; Reba McEntire, singer; Shannon Miller, Olympic gymnast; Bill Moyers, journalist; Daniel Patrick Moynihan, N.Y. senator; Patti Page, singer; Mary Kay Place, actress and writer; Tony Randall, actor; Oral Roberts, evangelist; Dale Robertson, actor; Will Rogers, humorist; Dan Rowan, comedian; Thomas P. Stafford, astronaut; Maria Tallchief, ballerina; Jim Thorpe, athlete; Alfre Woodard, actress.

Oregon

Capital: Salem
Governor: Ted Kulongoski, D (to Jan. 2007)
Senators: Gordon Smith, R (to Jan. 2009); Ron Wyden, D (to Jan. 2005)
Secy. of State: Bill Bradbury, D (to Jan. 2005)
Treasurer: Randall Edwards, D (to Jan. 2005)
Atty. General: Hardy Myers, D (to Jan. 2005)
Organized as territory: Aug. 14, 1848
Entered Union (rank): Feb. 14, 1859 (33)
Present constitution adopted: 1859
Motto: *Alis volat Propriis* (She flies with her own wings) (1987)
State Symbols: flower, Oregon grape (1899); **tree,** douglas fir (1939); **animal,** beaver (1969); **bird,** western meadowlark (1927); **fish,** chinook salmon (1961); **rock,** thunderegg (1965); **colors,** navy blue and gold (1959); **song,** "Oregon, My Oregon" (1927); **insect,** swallowtail butterfly (1979); **dance,** square dance (1977); **nut,** hazelnut (1989); **gemstone,** sunstone (1987); **seashell,** Oregon hairy triton (1991); **beverage,** milk (1997); **mushroom,** Pacific golden chanterelle (1999)
Nickname: Beaver State
Origin of name: Unknown. However, it is generally accepted that the name, first used by Jonathan Carver in 1778, was taken from the writings of Maj. Robert Rogers, an English army officer.
10 largest cities (2000): Portland, 529,121; Eugene, 137,893; Salem, 136,924; Gresham, 90,205; Beaverton, 76,129; Hillsboro, 70,186; Medford, 63,154; Springfield, 52,864; Bend, 52,029; Corvallis, 49,322
Land area: 95,997 sq mi. (248,632 sq km)
Geographic center: In Crook Co., 25 mi. SSE of Prineville
Number of counties: 36
Largest county by population and area: Multnomah, 665,810 (2001); Harney, 10,135 sq mi.
State forests: 820,000 ac.
State parks: 240 (93,330 ac.)
Residents: Oregonian
2002 resident population est.: 3,521,515
2000 resident census population (rank): 3,421,399 (28). **Male:** 1,696,550 (49.6%); **Female:** 1,724,849 (50.4%). **White:** 2,961,623 (86.6%); **Black:** 55,662 (1.6%); **American Indian:** 45,211 (1.3%); **Asian:** 101,350 (3.0%); **Other race:** 144,832 (4.2%); **Two or more races:** 104,745 (3.1%); **Hispanic/Latino:** 275,314 (8.0%). **2000 percent population 18 and over:** 75.3; **65 and over:** 12.8; **median age:** 36.3.

Spanish and English sailors are believed to have sighted the Oregon coast in the 1500s and 1600s. Capt. James Cook, seeking the Northwest Passage, charted some of the coastline in 1778. In 1792, Capt. Robert Gray, in the *Columbia,* discovered the river named after his ship and claimed the area for the U.S.

In 1805 the Lewis and Clark expedition explored the area. John Jacob Astor's fur depot, Astoria, was founded in 1811. Disputes for control of Oregon between American settlers and the Hudson Bay Company were finally resolved in the 1846 Oregon Treaty, in which Great Britain gave up claims to the region.

Oregon has a $3.3 billion lumber and wood products industry, and an $859 million paper and allied manufacturing industry. Its salmon-fishing industry is one of the world's largest.

In agriculture, the state leads in growing peppermint, cover seed crops, blackberries, boysenberries, loganberries, black raspberries, and hazelnuts. It is second in raising hops, red raspberries, prunes, snap beans, and onions.

With the low-cost electric power provided by dams, Oregon has developed steadily as a manufacturing state. Leading manufactured items are lumber and plywood, metalwork, machinery, aluminum, chemicals, paper, food packing, and electronic equipment.

Crater Lake National Park, Mount Hood, and Bonneville Dam on the Columbia are major tourist attractions. Other points of interest include the Oregon Dunes National Recreation Area, Oregon Caves National Monument, Cape Perpetua in Siuslaw National Forest, Columbia River Gorge between The Dalles and Troutdale, Hells Canyon, Newberry Volcanic National Monument, and John Day Fossil Beds National Monument.

Famous natives and residents: James Beard, food expert; Raymond Carver, writer and poet; Homer C. Davenport, political cartoonist; David Douglas, botanist; Abigail Scott Duniway, women's suffrage advocate; Robert Gray, sea captain and discoverer of Columbia River; Matt Groening, cartoonist; Mark Hatfield, senator; Donald P. Hodel, secretary of the Interior; Chief Joseph, Nez Percé chief; Dave Kingman, baseball player; Ursula LeGuin, writer; Edwin Markham, poet; Phyllis McGinley, author; Linus Pauling, chemist; Jane Powell, actress and singer; John Reed, poet and author; Harvey W. Scott, editor; Doc Severinsen, band leader; Norton Simon, business executive; Paul M. Simon, Illinois senator; William E. Stafford, poet; Sally Struthers, actress.

Pennsylvania

Capital: Harrisburg
Governor: Ed Rendell, D (to Jan. 2007)
Lieut. Governor: Catherine Baker Knoll, D (to Jan. 2007)
Senators: Rick Santorum, R (to Jan. 2007); Arlen Specter, R (to Jan. 2005)
Acting Secy. of the Commonwealth: Pedro Cortes, D (at the pleasure of the governor)
Treasurer: Barbara Hafer, R (to Jan. 2005)
Atty. General: Mike Fisher, R (to Jan. 2005)
Entered Union (rank): Dec. 12, 1787 (2)
Present constitution adopted: 1968
Motto: Virtue, liberty, and independence
State Symbols: flower, mountain laurel (1933); **tree,** hemlock (1931); **bird,** ruffed grouse (1931); **dog,** Great Dane (1965); **colors,** blue and gold (1907); **song,** "Pennsylvania" (1990)
Nickname: Keystone State
Origin of name: In honor of Adm. Sir William Penn, father of William Penn. It means "Penn's Woodland."
10 largest cities (2000): Philadelphia, 1,517,550; Pittsburgh, 334,563; Allentown, 106,632; Erie, 103,717; Upper Darby, 81,821; Reading, 81,207; Scranton, 76,415; Bethlehem, 71,329; Lower Merion, 59,850; Bensalem, 58,434
Land area: 44,817 sq mi. (116,076 sq km)
Geographic center: In Centre Co., 2½ mi. SW of Bellefonte
Number of counties: 67

Largest county by population and area: Philadelphia, 1,491,812 (2001); Lycoming, 1,235 sq mi.
State forests: over 2 mil. ac.
State parks: 116
Residents: Pennsylvanian
2002 resident population est.: 12,335,091
2000 resident census population (rank): 12,281,054 (6). **Male:** 5,929,663 (48.3%); **Female:** 6,351,391 (51.7%). **White:** 10,484,203 (85.4%); **Black:** 1,224,612 (10.0%); **American Indian:** 18,348 (0.1%); **Asian:** 219,813 (1.8%); **Other race:** 188,437 (1.5%); **Two or more races:** 142,224 (1.2%); **Hispanic/Latino:** 394,088 (3.2%). **2000 percent population 18 and over:** 76.2; **65 and over:** 15.6; **median age:** 38.0.

Rich in historic lore, Pennsylvania territory was disputed in the early 1600s among the Dutch, the Swedes, and the English. England acquired the region in 1664 with the capture of New York, and in 1681 Pennsylvania was granted to William Penn, a Quaker, by King Charles II.

Philadelphia was the seat of the federal government almost continuously from 1776 to 1800; there the Declaration of Independence was signed in 1776 and the U.S. Constitution drawn up in 1787. Valley Forge, of Revolutionary War fame, and Gettysburg, site of the pivotal battle of the Civil War, are both in Pennsylvania. The Liberty Bell is located in a glass pavilion across from Independence Hall in Philadelphia.

The nation's first oil well was dug at Titusville in 1859, and the mining of iron ore and coal led to the development of the state's steel industry. More recently Pennsylvania's industry has diversified, although the state still leads the country in the production of specialty steel. The service, retail trade, and manufacturing sectors provide the most jobs; Pennsylvania is a leader in the production of chemicals and pharmaceuticals, food products, and electronic equipment.

Pennsylvania's 59,000 farms (occupying nearly 8 million acres) are the backbone of the state's economy, producing a wide variety of crops. Leading commodities are dairy products, cattle and calves, mushrooms, greenhouse and nursery products, poultry and eggs, a variety of fruits, sweet corn, potatoes, maple syrup, and Christmas trees.

Pennsylvania's rich heritage draws billions of tourist dollars annually. Among the chief attractions are the Gettysburg National Military Park, Valley Forge National Historical Park, Independence National Historical Park in Philadelphia, the Pennsylvania Dutch region, the Eisenhower farm near Gettysburg, and the Delaware Water Gap National Recreation Area.

Famous natives and residents: Louisa May Alcott, novelist; Marian Anderson, contralto; Maxwell Anderson, dramatist; Samuel Barber, composer; John Barrymore, actor; Donald Barthelme, author; Stephen Vincent Benét, poet and story writer; Daniel Boone, frontiersman; Ed Bradley, TV anchorman; James Buchanan, former president; Alexander Calder, sculptor; Rachel Carson, biologist and author; Mary Cassatt, painter; Henry Steele Commager, historian; Bill Cosby, actor; Stuart Davis, painter; Jimmy and Tommy Dorsey, band leaders; W. C. Fields, comedian; Stephen Foster, composer; Robert Fulton, inventor; Grace, Princess of Monaco; Martha Graham, choreographer; Alexander Haig, secretary of state; Marilyn Horne, mezzo-soprano; Lee Iacocca, auto executive; Reggie Jackson, baseball player; Gene Kelly, dancer and actor; Gelsey Kirkland, ballerina; S. S. Kresge, merchant; Mario Lanza, actor and singer; George C. Marshall, general; George McClellan, general; Margaret Mead, anthropologist; Andrew Mellon, financier; Tom Mix, actor; Arnold Palmer, golfer; Robert E. Peary, explorer; Man Ray, painter; Mary Roberts Rinehart, novelist; Betsy Ross, flagmaker; B. F. Skinner, psychologist; John Sloan, painter; Gertrude Stein, author; James Stewart, actor; John Updike, novelist; Honus Wagner, baseball player; Fred Waring, band leader; Ethel Waters, singer and actress; Anthony Wayne, military officer; August Wilson, poet, writer, and playwright; Wallis Warfield, Duchess of Windsor; Andrew Wyeth, painter.

Rhode Island

Capital: Providence
Governor: Don Carcieri, R (to Jan. 2007)
Lieut. Governor: Charles J. Fogarty, D (to Jan. 2007)
Senators: Jack Reed, D (to Jan. 2009); Lincoln Chafee, R (to Jan. 2007)
Secy. of State: Matt Brown, D (to Jan. 2007)
Atty. General: Patrick Lynch, D (to Jan. 2007)
General Treasurer: Paul J. Tavares, D (to Jan. 2007)
Entered Union (rank): May 29, 1790 (13)
Present constitution adopted: 1843
Motto: Hope
State Symbols: flower, violet (unofficial) (1968); **tree,** red maple (official) (1964); **bird,** Rhode Island red hen (official) (1954); **shell,** quahog (official); **mineral,** bowenite (1966); **stone,** cumberlandite (1966); **colors,** blue, white, and gold (in state flag); **song,** "Rhode Island" (1946)
Nickname: The Ocean State
Origin of name: From the Greek Island of Rhodes
10 largest cities (2000): Providence, 173,618; Warwick, 85,808; Cranston, 79,269; Pawtucket, 72,958; East Providence, 48,688; Woonsocket, 43,224; Coventry, 33,668; North Providence, 32,411; Cumberland, 31,840; West Warwick, 29,581
Land area: 1,045 sq mi. (2,706 sq km)
Geographic center: In Kent Co., 1 mi. SSW of Crompton
Number of counties: 5
Largest county by population and area: Providence, 627,314 (2001); Providence, 413 sq mi.
State forests: 11 (20,900 ac.)
State parks: 14
Residents: Rhode Islander
2002 resident population est.: 1,069,725
2000 resident census population (rank): 1,048,319 (43). **Male:** 503,635 (48.0%); **Female:** 544,684 (52.0%). **White:** 891,191 (85.0%); **Black:** 46,908 (4.5%); **American Indian:** 5,121 (0.5%); **Asian:** 23,665 (2.3%); **Other race:** 52,616 (5.0%); **Two or more races:** 28,251 (2.7%); **Hispanic/Latino:** 90,820 (8.7%). **2000 percent population 18 and over:** 76.4; **65 and over:** 14.5; **median age:** 36.7.

From its beginnings, Rhode Island has been distinguished by its support for freedom of conscience and action: Clergyman Roger Williams founded the present state capital, Providence, after being exiled by the Massachusetts Bay Colony Puritans in 1636. Williams was followed by other religious exiles who founded Pocasset, now Portsmouth, in 1638 and Newport in 1639.

Rhode Island's rebellious, authority-defying nature was further demonstrated by the burnings of the British revenue cutters *Liberty* and *Gaspee* prior to the Revolution; by its early declaration of independence from Great Britain in May 1776; by its refusal to participate actively in the War of 1812; and by Dorr's Rebellion of 1842, which protested property requirements for voting.

Rhode Island, smallest of the fifty states, is densely populated and highly industrialized. It is a major center for jewelry manufacturing. Electronics, metal, plastic products, and boat and ship construction are other important industries. Non-manufacturing employment includes research in health, medicine, and the ocean environment. Providence is a wholesale distribution center for New England.

Fishing ports are at Galilee and Newport. Rural areas of the state support small-scale farming, including grapes for local wineries, turf grass, and nursery stock. Tourism generates over a billion dollars a year in revenue.

Newport became famous as the summer capital of high society in the mid-19th century. Touro Synagogue (1763) is the oldest in the U.S. Other points of interest include the Roger Williams National Memorial in Providence, Samuel Slater's Mill in Pawtucket, the General Nathanael Greene Homestead in Coventry, and Block Island.

Famous natives and residents: Harry Anderson, actor; George M. Cohan, actor and dramatist; Eddie Dowling, actor and stage producer; Nelson Eddy, baritone and actor; Ann Smith Franklin, printer and almanac publisher; Charles Gorham, silversmith; Spalding Gray, writer, performance artist; Bobby Hackett, trumpeter; David Hartman, TV newscaster; Ruth Hussey, actress; Anne Hutchinson, religious leader; Thomas H. Ince, film producer; Wilbur John, Quaker leader; Van Johnson, actor; Clarence King, first director of the U.S. Geological Survey; Galway Kinnell, poet; Oliver La Farge, writer; Irving R. Levine, news correspondent; H. P. Lovecraft, author; Ida Lewis, lighthouse keeper; John McLaughlin, political commentator, broadcaster; Dana C. Munro, educator and historian; Matthew C. Perry, naval officer; Oliver Hazard Perry, naval officer; King Philip (Metacomet), Indian leader; Anthony Quinn, actor; Gilbert Stuart, painter; Sarah Helen (Power) Whitman, poet; Jemima Wilkinson, religious leader; Roger Williams, clergyman and founder of Rhode Island; Leonard Woodcock, labor union official; James Woods, actor.

South Carolina

Capital: Columbia
Governor: Mark Sanford, R (to Jan. 2007)
Lieut. Governor: R. Andre Bauer, R (to Jan. 2007)
Senators: Ernest Hollings, D (to Jan. 2005); Lindsey Graham, R (to Jan. 2009)
Secy. of State: Mark Hammond, R (to Jan. 2007)
Treasurer: Grady L. Patterson, Jr. , D (to Jan. 2007)
Atty. General: Henry McMaster, R (to Jan. 2007)
Entered Union (rank): May 23, 1788 (8)
Present constitution adopted: 1895
Mottoes: *Animis opibusque parati* (Prepared in mind and resources) and *Dum spiro spero* (While I breathe, I hope)
State Symbols: flower, Carolina yellow jessamine (1924); **tree,** palmetto tree (1939); **bird,** Carolina wren (1948); **song,** "Carolina" (1911)
Nickname: Palmetto State
Origin of name: In honor of Charles I of England
10 largest cities (2000): Columbia, 116,278; Charleston, 96,650; North Charleston, 79,641; Greenville, 56,002; Rock Hill, 49,765; Mount Pleasant, 47,609; Spartanburg, 39,673; Sumter, 39,643; Hilton Head Island, 33,862; Florence, 30,248
Land area: 30,109 sq mi. (77,982 sq km)
Geographic center: In Richland Co., 13 mi. SE of Columbia
Number of counties: 46
Largest county by population and area: Greenville, 386,693 (2001); Horry, 1,134 sq mi.
State forests: 4 (124,052 ac.)
State parks: 50 (61,726 ac.)
Residents: South Carolinian
2002 resident population est.: 4,107,183
2000 resident census population (rank): 4,012,012 (26). **Male:** 1,948,929 (48.6%); **Female:** 2,063,083 (51.4%). **White:** 2,695,560 (67.2%); **Black:** 1,185,216 (29.5%); **American Indian:** 13,718 (0.3%); **Asian:** 36,014 (0.9%); **Other race:** 39,926 (1.0%); **Two or more races:** 39,950 (1.0%); **Hispanic/Latino:** 95,076 (2.4%). **2000 percent population 18 and over:** 74.8; **65 and over:** 12.1; **median age:** 35.4.

Following exploration of the coast in 1521 by Francisco de Gordillo, the Spanish tried unsuccessfully to establish a colony near present-day Georgetown in 1526, and the French also failed to colonize Parris Island near Fort Royal in 1562. The first English settlement was made in 1670 at Albemarle Point on the Ashley River, but poor conditions drove the settlers to the site of Charleston (originally called Charles Town).

South Carolina, officially separated from North Carolina in 1729, was the scene of extensive military action during the Revolution and again during the Civil War. The Civil War began in 1861 as South Carolina troops fired on federal Fort Sumter in Charleston Harbor, and the state was the first to secede from the Union.

Once primarily agricultural, South Carolina today has many large textile and other mills that produce several times the output of its farms in cash value. Charleston makes asbestos, wood, pulp, steel products, chemicals, machinery, and apparel.

Farms have become fewer but larger in recent years. South Carolina ranks third in peach production; it ranks fourth in overall tobacco production. Other top agricultural commodities include nursery and greenhouse products, watermelons, peanuts, broilers and turkeys, and cattle and calves. The only commercial tea plantation in America is 20 mi south of Charleston on Wadmalaw Island.

Points of interest include Fort Sumter National Monument, Fort Moultrie, Fort Johnson, and aircraft carrier USS *Yorktown* in Charleston Harbor; the Middleton, Magnolia, and Cypress Gardens in Charleston; Cowpens National Battlefield; the Hilton Head resorts; and the Riverbanks Zoo and Botanical Garden in Columbia.

Famous natives and residents: Bernard Baruch, statesman; Mary McLeod Bethune, educator; James F. Byrnes, senator, jurist and secretary of state; John C. Calhoun, statesman; Mark Clark, general; Joe Frazier, prize fighter; Althea Gibson, tennis champion; Dizzy Gillespie, jazz trumpeter; DuBose Heyward, poet, playwright, and novelist; Andrew Jackson, president; Jesse Jackson, civil rights leader; Eartha Kitt, singer; Francis Marion ("Swamp Fox"), Revolutionary general; Ronald McNair, astronaut; John Rutledge, jurist; Strom Thurmond, politician; Charles Townes, physicist; William Westmoreland, general; Vanna White, TV personality.

South Dakota

Capital: Pierre
Governor: Mike Rounds, R (to Jan. 2007)
Lieut. Governor: Dennis Daugaard, R (to Jan. 2007)
Senators: Thomas A. Daschle, D (to Jan. 2005); Tim Johnson, D (to Jan. 2009)
Atty. General: Larry Long, R (to Jan. 2007)
Secy. of State: Chris Nelson, R (to Jan. 2007)
Treasurer: Vernon L. Larson, R (to Jan. 2007)
Organized as territory: March 2, 1861
Entered Union (rank): Nov. 2, 1889 (40)
Present constitution adopted: 1889
Motto: Under God the people rule
State Symbols: flower, American pasqueflower (1903); **grass,** Western wheat grass (1970); **soil,** houdek (1990); **tree,** black hills spruce (1947); **bird,**

ring-necked pheasant (1943); **insect,** honeybee (1978); **animal,** coyote (1949); **mineral stone,** rose quartz (1966); **gemstone,** fairburn agate (1966); **colors,** blue and gold (in state flag); **song,** "Hail! South Dakota" (1943); **fish,** walleye (1982); **musical instrument,** fiddle (1989); **dessert,** kuchen (2000)
Nicknames: Mount Rushmore State; Coyote State
Origin of name: From the Sioux tribe, meaning "allies"
10 largest cities (2000): Sioux Falls, 123,975; Rapid City, 59,607; Aberdeen, 24,658; Watertown, 20,237; Brookings, 18,504; Mitchell, 14,558; Pierre, 13,876; Yankton, 13,528; Huron, 11,893; Vermillion, 9,765
Land area: 75,885 sq mi. (196,542 sq km)
Geographic center: In Hughes Co., 8 mi. NE of Pierre
Number of counties: 66 (64 county governments)
Largest county by population and area: Minnehaha, 150,327 (2001); Meade, 3,471 sq mi.
State forests: None[1]
State parks: 12 plus 39 recreational areas (87,269 ac.)[2]
Residents: South Dakotan
2002 resident population est.: 761,063
2000 resident census population (rank): 754,844 (46). **Male:** 374,558 (49.6%); **Female:** 380,286 (50.4%). **White:** 669,404 (88.7%); **Black:** 4,685 (0.6%); **American Indian:** 62,283 (8.3%); **Asian:** 4,378 (0.6%); **Other race:** 3,677 (0.5%); **Two or more races:** 10,156 (1.3%); **Hispanic/Latino:** 10,903 (1.4%). **2000 percent population 18 and over:** 73.2; **65 and over:** 14.3; **median age:** 35.6.

1. No designated state forests; about 13,000 ac. of state land is forestland. 2. Acreage includes 39 recreation areas and 80 roadside parks, in addition to 12 state parks.

Exploration of this area began in 1743 when Louis-Joseph and François Verendrye came from France in search of a route to the Pacific.

The U.S. acquired the region as part of the Louisiana Purchase in 1803, and it was explored by Lewis and Clark in 1804–1806. Fort Pierre, the first permanent settlement, was established in 1817.

Settlement of South Dakota did not begin in earnest until the arrival of the railroad in 1873 and the discovery of gold in the Black Hills in 1874.

Agriculture is a cultural and economic mainstay, but it no longer leads the state in employment or share of gross state product. Durable-goods manufacturing and private services have evolved as the drivers of the economy. Tourism is also a booming industry in the state, generating over a billion dollars' worth of economic activity each year.

South Dakota is the second-largest producer of flaxseed and sunflower seed in the nation. It is the third-largest producer of hay and rye.

The Black Hills are the highest mountains east of the Rockies. Mt. Rushmore, in this group, is famous for the likenesses of Washington, Jefferson, Lincoln, and Theodore Roosevelt, which were carved in granite by Gutzon Borglum. A memorial to Crazy Horse is also being carved in granite near Custer.

Other tourist attractions include the Badlands; the World's Only Corn Palace, in Mitchell; and the city of Deadwood, where Wild Bill Hickok was killed in 1876 and where gambling was recently legalized.

Famous natives and residents: Sparky Anderson, baseball manager; Gertrude Bonnin (Zitkala-Sa), Sioux writer and pan-Indian activist; Tom Brokaw, TV newscaster; Robert Casey, writer; Myron Floren, accordionist; Joseph J. Foss, WW II Marine fighter ace; Mary Hart, TV host; Crazy Horse, Oglala chief; Oscar Howe, Sioux artist; Hubert H. Humphrey, vice president; Cheryl Ladd, actress; Ernest Orlando Lawrence, physicist; Russell Means, American Indian activist; George McGovern, politician; Arthur C. Mellette, first governor; Dorothy Provine, actress; Rain-in-the-Face, Hunkpapa Sioux chief; Red Cloud, chief of the Oglala Sioux; Ben Reifel, Brulé Sioux congressman; Ole Edvart Rølvaag, writer; Sitting Bull, chief of Hunkpappa Sioux; Norm Van Brocklin, football player; Mamie Van Doren, actress.

Tennessee

Capital: Nashville
Governor: Phil Bredesen, D (to Jan. 2007)
Lieut. Governor: John S. Wilder, D (to Jan. 2007)
Senators: Lamar Alexander, R (to Jan. 2009); William Frist, R (to Jan. 2007)
Secy. of State: Riley C. Darnell, D (to Jan. 2005)
Atty. General: Paul G. Summers, D (to Feb. 2007)
Treasurer: Steve Adams, D (to Jan. 2007)
Comptroller: John G. Morgan (to Jan. 2003)
Entered Union (rank): June 1, 1796 (16)
Present constitution adopted: 1870; amended 1953, 1960, 1966, 1972, 1978
Motto: Agriculture and Commerce (1987)
Slogan: Tennessee—America at its best! (1965)
State Symbols: flower, iris (1933); **tree,** tulip poplar (1947); **bird,** mockingbird (1933); **horse,** Tennessee walking horse; **animal,** raccoon (1971); **wild flower,** passion flower (1973); **songs,** "Tennessee Waltz" (1965); "My Homeland, Tennessee" (1925); "When It's Iris Time in Tennessee" (1935); "My Tennessee" (1955); "Rocky Top" (1982); "Tennessee" (1992);
Nickname: Volunteer State
Origin of name: Of Cherokee origin; the exact meaning is unknown
10 largest cities (2000): Memphis, 650,100; Nashville-Davidson [1], 569,891; Knoxville, 173,890; Chattanooga, 155,554; Clarksville, 103,455; Murfreesboro, 68,816; Jackson, 59,643; Johnson City, 55,469; Kingsport, 44,905; Franklin, 41,842
Land area: 41,217 sq mi. (106,752 sq km)
Geographic center: In Rutherford Co., 5 mi. NE of Murfreesboro
Number of counties: 95
Largest county by population and area: Shelby, 896,013 (2001); Shelby, 755 sq mi.
State forests: 5
State parks: 80
Residents: Tennessean, Tennesseean
2002 resident population est.: 5,797,289
2000 resident census population (rank): 5,689,283 (16). **Male:** 2,770,275 (48.7%); **Female:** 2,919,008 (51.3%). **White:** 4,563,310 (80.2%); **Black:** 932,809 (16.4%); **American Indian:** 15,152 (0.3%); **Asian:** 56,662 (1.0%); **Other race:** 56,036 (1.0%); **Two or more races:** 63,109 (1.1%); **Hispanic/Latino:** 123,838 (2.2%). **2000 percent population 18 and over:** 75.4; **65 and over:** 12.4; **median age:** 35.9.

1. The city is part of a consolidated city-county government and is coextensive with Davidson County.

First visited by the Spanish explorer Hernando de Soto in 1540, the Tennessee area would later be claimed by both France and England as a result of the 1670s and 1680s explorations of Jacques Marquette and Louis Joliet, Sieur de la Salle, and James Needham and Gabriel Arthur. Great Britain obtained the area after the French and Indian Wars in 1763.

During 1784–1787, the settlers formed the "state" of Franklin, which was disbanded when the region was allowed to send representatives to the North Carolina legislature. In 1790 Congress organized the territory south of the Ohio River, and Tennessee joined the Union in 1796.

Although Tennessee joined the Confederacy during the Civil War, there was much pro-Union sentiment in the state, which was the scene of extensive military action.

The state is now predominantly industrial; the majority of its population lives in urban areas. Among the most important products are chemicals, textiles, apparel, electrical machinery, furniture, and leather goods. Other lines include food processing, lumber, primary metals, and metal products. The state ranks high in the production of marble, zinc, pyrite, and ball clay.

Tennessee is a leading tobacco-producing state. Other farming income is derived from livestock and dairy products, as well as greenhouse and nursery products and cotton.

With six other states, Tennessee shares the extensive federal reservoir developments on the Tennessee and Cumberland River systems. The Tennessee Valley Authority operates a number of dams and reservoirs in the state.

Among the major points of interest are the Andrew Johnson National Historic Site at Greeneville, the American Museum of Atomic Energy at Oak Ridge, Great Smoky Mountains National Park, the Hermitage (home of Andrew Jackson near Nashville), Rock City Gardens near Chattanooga, and three National Military Parks.

Famous natives and residents: James Agee, writer; Eddy Arnold, singer; Chet Atkins, guitarist; Julian Bond, Georgia legislator; Davy Crockett, frontiersman; David G. Farragut, first American admiral; Lester Flatt, bluegrass musician; Tennessee Ernie Ford, singer; Abe Fortas, jurist; Aretha Franklin, singer; Nikki Giovanni, poet; Al Gore, Jr., vice president; Red Grooms, artist; Isaac Hayes, composer; Benjamin L. Hooks, civil rights activist; Cordell Hull, secretary of state; Andrew Jackson, president; Andrew Johnson, president; Estes Kefauver, legislator; Anita Kerr, singer; Grace Moore, soprano; Dolly Parton, singer; Minnie Pearl, singer and comedienne; James K. Polk, president; Grantland Rice, sportswriter; Carl Rowan, journalist; Wilma Rudolph, sprinter; Sequoyah, Cherokee scholar and educator; Cybil Shepherd, actress; Dinah Shore, actress and singer; Tina Turner, singer; Alvin York, World War I hero.

Texas

Capital: Austin
Governor: Rick Perry, R (to Jan. 2007)
Lieut. Governor: David Dewhurst, R (to Jan. 2007)
Senators: John Cornyn, R (to Jan. 2009); Kay Bailey Hutchison, R (to Jan. 2007)
Secy. of State: Gwyn Shea, R (apptd. by gov.)
Comptroller: Carole Keeton Rylander, R (to Jan. 2007)
Atty. General: Greg Abbott, R (to Jan. 2007)
Entered Union (rank): Dec. 29, 1845 (28)
Present constitution adopted: 1876
Motto: Friendship
State Symbols: flower, bluebonnet (1901); **tree,** pecan (1919); **bird,** mockingbird (1927); **song,** "Texas, Our Texas" (1929); **fish,** guadalupe bass (1989); **seashell,** lightning whelk (1987); **dish,** chili (1977); **folk dance,** square dance (1991); **fruit,** Texas red grapefruit (1993); **gem,** Texas blue topaz (1969); **gemstone cut,** Lone Star cut (1977); **grass,** sideoats grass (1971); **reptile,** horned lizard (1993); **stone,** petrified palmwood (1969); **plant,** prickly pear cactus; **insect,** monarch butterfly; **pepper,** jalapeño pepper; **mammal,** longhorn; **small mammal,** armadillo; **flying mammal,** Mexican free-tailed bat
Nickname: Lone Star State
Origin of name: From an Indian word meaning "friends"
10 largest cities (2000): Houston, 1,953,631; Dallas, 1,188,580; San Antonio, 1,144,646; Austin, 656,562; El Paso, 563,662; Fort Worth, 534,694; Arlington, 332,969; Corpus Christi, 277,454; Plano, 222,030; Garland, 215,768
Land area: 261,797 sq mi. (678,054 sq km)
Geographic center: In McCulloch Co., 15 mi. NE of Brady
Number of counties: 254
Largest county by population and area: Harris, 3,460,589 (2001); Brewster, 6,193 sq mi.
State forests: 5 (7,314 ac.)
State parks[1]: 125 (587,216 ac.)
Residents: Texan
2002 resident population est.: 21,779,893
2000 resident census population (rank): 20,851,820 (2). **Male:** 10,352,910 (49.6%); **Female:** 10,498,910 (50.4%). **White:** 14,799,505 (71.0%); **Black:** 2,404,566 (11.5%); **American Indian:** 118,362 (0.6%); **Asian:** 562,319 (2.7%); **Other race:** 2,438,001 (11.7%); **Two or more races:** 514,633 (2.5%); **Hispanic/Latino:** 6,669,666 (32.0%). **2000 percent population 18 and over:** 71.8; **65 and over:** 9.9; **median age:** 32.3.

1. Includes state parks and natural areas, two state fishing piers, and one county park.

Spanish explorers, including Álvar Núñez Cabeza de Vaca and Francisco Vásquez de Coronado, were the first to visit the region in the 16th and 17th centuries, settling at Ysleta near El Paso in 1682. In 1685, Robert Cavelier, Sieur de la Salle, established a short-lived French colony at Matagorda Bay.

Americans, led by Stephen F. Austin, began to settle along the Brazos River in 1821 when Texas was controlled by Mexico, recently independent from Spain. In 1836, following a brief war between the American settlers in Texas and the Mexican government, the Independent Republic of Texas was proclaimed with Sam Houston as president. This war was famous for the battles of the Alamo and San Jacinto. After Texas became the a state in 1845, border disputes led to the Mexican War of 1846–1848.

Possessing enormous natural resources, Texas is a major agricultural state and an industrial giant. Second only to Alaska in land area, it leads all other states in such categories as oil, cattle, sheep, and cotton. Texas ranches and farms also produce poultry and eggs, dairy products, greenhouse and nursery products, wheat, hay, rice, sugar cane, and peanuts, and a variety of fruits and vegetables.

Sulfur, salt, helium, asphalt, graphite, bromine, natural gas, cement, and clays are among the state's valuable resources. Chemicals, oil refining, food processing, machinery, and transportation equipment are among the major Texas manufacturing industries.

Millions of tourists spend well over $20.6 billion annually visiting more than 100 state parks, recreation areas, and points of interest such as the Gulf Coast resort area, the Lyndon B. Johnson Space Center in Houston, the Alamo in San Antonio, the state capital in Austin, and the Big Bend and Guadalupe Mountains National Park.

Famous natives and residents: Alvin Ailey, choreographer; Mary Kay Ash, cosmetics entrepreneur; Stephen Fuller Austin, founding father of Texas; Gene Autry, singer and actor; Carol Burnett, comedienne; George W. Bush, president and governor; Cyd Charisse, actress and dancer; Denton A. Cooley, heart surgeon; Joan Crawford, actress; Dwight David Eisenhower, president and general; A. J. Foyt, auto racer; Ben Hogan, golfer; Sam Houston, general and statesman; Howard Hughes, industrialist and film producer; Jack Johnson, boxer; Lyndon B. Johnson, president; George Jones, singer; Tommy Lee Jones, actor; Janis Joplin, singer; Scott Joplin, composer; Trini Lopez, singer; Mary Martin, singer and actress; Spanky McFarland, actor; Audie Murphy, actor and war hero; Chester Nimitz, admiral; Sandra Day O'Connor, jurist; Buck Owens, singer; Selena Pérez, singer; Lou Diamond Phillips, actor; Katherine Anne Porter, novelist; Wiley Post, aviator; Dan Rather, TV newscaster; Robert Rauschenberg, painter; Tex Ritter, singer; Rip Torn, actor and director; Tommy Tune, dancer and choreographer; Stevie Ray Vaughan, guitarist and singer; Lupe Velez, actress; Dooley Wilson, actor and musician; Babe Didrikson Zaharias, athlete and golfer.

Utah

Capital: Salt Lake City
Governor: Michael O. Leavitt, R (to Jan. 2005)
Lieut. Governor: Olene Walker, R (to Jan. 2005)
Senators: Robert F. Bennett, R (to Jan. 2005); Orrin G. Hatch, R (to Jan. 2007)
Treasurer: Edward T. Alter, R. (Jan. 2005)
Auditor: Auston G. Johnson, R (Jan. 2005)
Atty. General: Mark Shurtleff, R (to Jan. 2005)
Organized as territory: Sept. 9, 1850
Entered Union (rank): Jan. 4, 1896 (45)
Present constitution adopted: 1896
Motto: Industry
State Symbols: flower, sego lily (1911); **tree,** blue spruce (1933); **bird,** California gull (1955); **emblem,** beehive (1959); **song,** "Utah, We Love Thee" (1953); **gem,** topaz; **animal,** Rocky Mountain elk (1971); **insect,** honeybee (1983); **grass,** Indian rice grass (1990); **fossil,** allosaurus (1988); **cooking pot,** dutch oven (1997); **fish,** Bonneville cutthroat trout (1997); **fruit,** cherry (1997); **mineral,** copper; **rock,** coal (1991)
Nickname: Beehive State
Origin of name: From the Ute tribe, meaning "people of the mountains"
10 largest cities (2000): Salt Lake City, 181,743; West Valley City, 108,896; Provo, 105,166; Sandy, 88,418; Orem, 84,324; Ogden, 77,226; West Jordan, 68,336; Layton, 58,474; Taylorsville, 57,439; St. George, 49,663
Land area: 82,144 sq mi. (212,753 sq km)
Geographic center: In Sanpete Co., 3 mi. N. of Manti
Number of counties: 29
Largest county by population and area: Salt Lake, 904,331 (2001); San Juan, 7,821 sq mi.
National parks: 5
National monuments: 7
State parks/forests: 45 (64,097 ac.)
Residents: Utahan, Utahn
2002 resident population est.: 2,316,256
2000 resident census population (rank): 2,233,169 (34). **Male:** 1,119,031 (50.1%); **Female:** 1,114,138 (49.9%). **White:** 1,992,975 (89.2%); **Black:** 17,657 (0.8%); **American Indian:** 29,684 (1.3%); **Asian:** 37,108 (1.7%); **Other race:** 93,405 (4.2%); **Two or more races:** 47,195 (2.1%); **Hispanic/Latino:** 201,559 (9.0%). **2000 percent population 18 and over:** 67.8; **65 and over:** 8.5; **median age:** 27.1.

The region was first explored for Spain by Franciscan friars Escalante and Dominguez in 1776. In 1824 the famous American frontiersman Jim Bridger discovered the Great Salt Lake.

Fleeing religious persecution in the East and Midwest, the Mormons arrived in 1847 and began to build Salt Lake City. The U.S. acquired the Utah region in the treaty ending the Mexican War in 1848, and the first transcontinental railroad was completed with the driving of a golden spike at Promontory Summit in 1869.

Mormon difficulties with the federal government about polygamy did not end until the Mormon Church renounced the practice in 1890, six years before Utah became a state.

Rich in natural resources, Utah has long been a leading producer of copper, gold, silver, lead, zinc, and molybdenum. Oil has also become a major product. Utah shares rich oil shale deposits with Colorado and Wyoming. Utah also has large deposits of low sulphur coal.

The state's top agricultural commodities include cattle and calves, dairy products, hay, greenhouse and nursery products, and hogs.

Utah's traditional industries of agriculture and mining are complemented by increased tourism and growing aerospace, biomedical, and computer-related businesses.

Utah is a great vacationland with 11,000 mi of fishing streams and 147,000 acres of lakes and reservoirs. Among the many tourist attractions are Arches, Bryce Canyon, Canyonlands, Capitol Reef, and Zion National Parks; Cedar Breaks, Dinosaur, Hovenweep, Natural Bridges, Rainbow Bridge, Timpanogos Cave, and Grand Staircase (Escalante) National Monuments; the Mormon Tabernacle in Salt Lake City; and Monument Valley. Salt Lake City hosted the 2002 Winter Olympics.

Famous natives and residents: Maude Adams, actress; Roseanne, actress; Frank Borzage, film director and producer; John M. Browning, inventor; Butch Cassidy, outlaw; Laraine Day, actress; Bernard De Voto, writer; Avard Fairbanks, sculptor; Philo Farnsworth, television pioneer; Jake Garn, senator; John Gilbert, actor; J. Willard Marriott, restaurant and hotel chain founder; Peter Skene Ogden, fur trader and trapper; Merlin Olsen, football player; Donny Osmond, Marie Osmond, singers; Ivy Baker Priest, U.S. treasurer; Lee Greene Richards, painter; Leroy Robertson, composer; Brent Scowcroft, business executive and consultant; Reed Smoot, first Mormon elected to U.S. Senate; Mack Swain, actor; Everett Thorpe, painter; Robert Walker, actor; James Woods, actor; Brigham Young, territory governor and religious leader; Loretta Young, actress.

Vermont

Capital: Montpelier
Governor: Jim Douglas, R (to Jan. 2005)
Lieut. Governor: Brian Dubie, R (to Jan. 2005)
Senators: James M. Jeffords, I (to Jan. 2007); Patrick Leahy, D (to Jan. 2005)
Secy. of State: Deborah L. Markowitz, D (to Jan. 2007)
Treasurer: Jeb Spaulding, D (to Jan. 2007)
Atty. General: William Sorrell, D (to Jan. 2007)
Entered Union (rank): March 4, 1791 (14)
Present constitution adopted: 1793
Motto: Vermont, Freedom and Unity
State Symbols: flower, red clover (1894); **tree,** sugar maple (1949); **bird,** hermit thrush (1941); **animal,** Morgan horse (1961); **insect,** honeybee (1978); **song,** "These Green Mountains" (2000)
Nickname: Green Mountain State
Origin of name: From the French "vert mont," meaning "green mountain"
10 largest cities (2000): Burlington, 38,889; Essex, 18,626; Rutland, 17,292; Colchester, 16,986; South Burlington, 15,814; Bennington, 15,737; Brattleboro, 12,005; Hartford, 10.367; Milton, 9,479; Barre, 9,291
Land area: 9,250 sq mi. (23,958 sq km)
Geographic center: In Washington Co., 3 mi. E of Roxbury
Number of counties: 14
Largest county by population and area: Chittenden, 147,591 (2001); Windsor, 971 sq mi.
State forests: 38 (167,769.5 ac.)
State parks: 59 (47,756.5 ac.)
Residents: Vermonter
2002 resident population est.: 616,592
2000 resident census population (rank): 608,827 (49). **Male:** 298,337 (49.0%); **Female:** 310,490 (51.0%).

White: 589,208 (96.8%); **Black:** 3,063 (0.5%); **American Indian:** 2,420 (0.4%); **Asian:** 5,217 (0.9%); **Other race:** 1,443 (0.2%); **Two or more races:** 7,335 (1.2%); **Hispanic/Latino:** 5,504 (0.9%). **2000 percent population 18 and over:** 75.8; **65 and over:** 12.7; **median age:** 37.7.

The Vermont region was explored and claimed for France by Samuel de Champlain in 1609, and the first French settlement was established at Fort Ste. Anne in 1666. The first English settlers moved into the area in 1724 and built Fort Dummer on the site of present-day Brattleboro. England gained control of the area in 1763 after the French and Indian Wars.

First organized to drive settlers from New York out of Vermont, the Green Mountain Boys, led by Ethan Allen, won fame by capturing Fort Ticonderoga from the British on May 10, 1775, in the early days of the Revolutionary War. In 1777 Vermont adopted its first constitution, abolishing slavery and providing for universal male suffrage without property qualifications.

Vermont leads the nation in the production of monument granite, marble, and maple syrup. It is also a leader in the production of talc. Vermont's rugged, rocky terrain discourages extensive agricultural farming, but is well suited to raising fruit trees and to dairy farming.

Principal industrial products include electrical equipment, fabricated metal products, printing and publishing, and paper and allied products.

Tourism is a major industry in Vermont. Vermont's many famous ski areas include Stowe, Killington, Mt. Snow, Bromley, Jay Peak, and Sugarbush. Hunting and fishing also attract many visitors to Vermont each year. Among the many points of interest are the Green Mountain National Forest, Bennington Battle Monument, the Calvin Coolidge Homestead at Plymouth, and the Marble Exhibit in Proctor.

Famous natives and residents: Chester A. Arthur, president; Orson Bean, actor; Calvin Coolidge, president; George Dewey, admiral; John Dewey, philosopher and educator; Stephen A. Douglas, politician; James Fisk, financial speculator; Willbur Fisk, clergyman and educator; Richard Morris Hunt, architect; William Morris Hunt, painter; Elisha Otis, inventor; Moses Pendleton, choreographer; Joseph Smith, religious leader; Ernest Thompson, actor and writer; Rudy Vallee, singer and band leader; Henry Wells, pioneer entrepreneur (Wells Fargo & Co.); Brigham Young, religious leader.

Virginia

Capital: Richmond
Governor: Mark Warner, D (to Jan. 2006)
Lieut. Governor: Tim Kaine, D (to Jan. 2006)
Senators: John Warner, R (to Jan. 2009); George Allen, R (to Jan. 2007)
Secy. of the Commonwealth: Anita Rimler, D (apptd. by gov.)
Treasurer: Jody M. Wagner, R
Atty. General: Jerry W. Kilgore (to Jan. 2006)
Entered Union (rank): June 25, 1788 (10)
Present constitution adopted: 1970
Motto: *Sic semper tyrannis* (Thus always to tyrants)
State Symbols: flower, American dogwood (1918); **bird,** cardinal (1950); **dog,** American foxhound (1966); **shell,** oyster shell (1974); **tree,** dogwood (1956)
Nicknames: The Old Dominion; Mother of Presidents
Origin of name: In honor of Elizabeth "Virgin Queen" of England
10 largest cities (2000): Virginia Beach, 425,257; Norfolk, 234,403; Chesapeake, 199,184; Richmond, 197,790; Newport News, 180,150; Hampton, 146,437; Alexandria, 128,283; Portsmouth, 100,565; Roanoke, 94,911; Lynchburg, 65,269
Land area: 39,594 sq mi. (102,558 sq km)
Geographic center: In Buckingham Co., 5 mi. SW of Buckingham
Number of counties: 95, plus 40 independent cities
Largest county by population and area: Fairfax, 985,161 (2001); Augusta, 972 sq mi.
State forests: 15 (50,869 ac.)
State parks: 34 (plus 33 natural areas)
Residents: Virginian
2002 resident population est.: 7,293,542
2000 resident census population (rank): 7,078,515 (12). **Male:** 3,471,895 (49.0%); **Female:** 3,606,620 (51.0%). **White:** 5,120,110 (72.3%); **Black:** 1,390,293 (19.6%); **American Indian:** 21,172 (0.3%); **Asian:** 261,025 (3.7%); **Other race:** 138,900 (2.0%); **Two or more races:** 143,069 (2.0%); **Hispanic/Latino:** 329,540 (4.7%). **2000 percent population 18 and over:** 75.4; **65 and over:** 11.2; **median age:** 35.7.

The history of America is closely tied to that of Virginia, particularly during the Colonial period. Jamestown, founded in 1607, was the first permanent English settlement in North America and slavery was introduced there in 1619. The surrenders ending both the American Revolution (Yorktown) and the Civil War (Appomattox) occurred in Virginia. The state is called the "Mother of Presidents" because eight U.S. presidents were born there.

Today, the service sector provides one-third of all jobs in Virginia, generating as much income as the manufacturing and retail industries combined in 1999 and accounting for 23% of gross state product. (The largest component of the service sector is business services, which includes computer and data processing services.)

Virginia has a large number of manufacturing industries, including transportation equipment, food processing, electronic and other electrical equipment, chemicals, textiles and apparel, lumber and wood products, and furniture.

Agriculture remains an important sector, and the state ranks among the top ten in a variety of agricultural products, including tomatoes, tobacco, peanuts, apples, summer potatoes, sweet potatoes, snap beans, and turkeys and broilers. Virginia also has a large dairy industry.

Virginia is one of the top ten coal producers in the U.S. Coal accounts for roughly 70% of Virginia's mineral value; crushed stone, sand and gravel, lime, and kyanite are also mined.

Points of interest include Mt. Vernon, home of George Washington; Monticello, home of Thomas Jefferson; Stratford, home of the Lees; Richmond, capital of the Confederacy and of Virginia; and Williamsburg, the restored Colonial capital.

Other attractions are the Shenandoah National Park, Colonial National Historical Park, Fredericksburg and Spotsylvania National Military Park, the Booker T. Washington birthplace near Roanoke, Arlington House (the Robert E. Lee Memorial), Luray Caverns, the Skyline Drive, and the Blue Ridge National Parkway.

Famous natives and residents: Richard Arlen, actor; Arthur Ashe, tennis player; Pearl Bailey, singer; Russell Baker, columnist; Warren Beatty, actor; George Bingham, painter; Richard E. Byrd, polar explorer; Willa Cather, novelist; Roy Clark, country music artist; William Clark, explorer; Henry Clay, statesman; Joseph Cotten, actor; Ella Fitzgerald, singer; William H. Harrison, president; Patrick Henry, statesman; Sam Houston, political leader; Thomas Jefferson, president; Robert E. Lee, Confederate general; Meriwether Lewis, explorer; Shirley MacLaine, actress; James Madison, president; Moses Malone, basketball player; John Marshall, jurist; Cyrus McCormick, inventor; James Monroe, president; Opechancanough, Powhatan leader; John Payne, actor; Walter Reed, army surgeon; Matthew Ridgway, general; Bill "Bojangles" Robinson, dancer; George C. Scott, actor; Sam Snead, golfer; James "Jeb" Stuart, Confederate army officer; Thomas Sumter, general; Zachary Taylor, president; Nat Turner, leader of slave uprising; John Tyler, president; Booker T. Washington, educator; George Washington, first president; James E. West,, inventor; Woodrow Wilson, president; Tom Wolfe, journalist.

Washington

Capital: Olympia
Governor: Gary Locke, D (to Jan. 2005)
Lieut. Governor: Brad Owen, D (to Jan. 2005)
Senators: Patty Murray, D (to Jan. 2005); Maria Cantwell, D (to Jan. 2007)
Secy. of State: Sam Reed, R (to Jan. 2005)
Treasurer: Michael J. Murphy, D (to Jan. 2005)
Atty. General: Christine Gregoire, D (to Jan. 2005)
Auditor: Brian Sonntag, D (to Jan. 2005)
Organized as territory: March 2, 1853
Entered Union (rank): Nov. 11, 1889 (42)
Present constitution adopted: 1889
Motto: *Al-Ki* (Indian word meaning "by and by")
State Symbols: flower, coast rhododendron (1892); **tree,** western hemlock (1947); **bird,** willow goldfinch (1951); **fish,** steelhead trout (1969); **gem,** petrified wood (1975); **colors,** green and gold (1925); **song,** "Washington, My Home" (1959); **folk song,** "Roll On Columbia, Roll On" (1987); **dance,** square dance (1979); **grass,** bluebunch wheatgrass (1989); **insect,** blue darner dragonfly (1997); **fossil,** Columbian mammoth (1998); **fruit,** apple (1989)
Nicknames: Evergreen State
Origin of name: In honor of George Washington
10 largest cities (2000): Seattle, 563,374; Spokane, 195,629; Tacoma, 193,556; Vancouver, 143,560; Bellevue, 109,569; Everett, 91,488; Federal Way, 83,259; Kent, 79,524; Yakima, 71,845; Bellingham, 67,171
Land area: 66,544 sq mi. (172,349 sq km)
Geographic center: In Chelan Co., 10 mi. WSW of Wenatchee
Number of counties: 39
Largest county by population and area: King, 1,741,785 (2001); Okanogan, 5,268 sq mi.
State forest lands: 2.1 million ac.
State parks: 215 (260,000 ac.)[1]
Residents: Washingtonian
2002 resident population est.: 6,068,996
2000 resident census population (rank): 5,894,121 (15). **Male:** 2,934,300 (49.8%); **Female:** 2,959,821 (50.2%). **White:** 4,821,823 (81.8%); **Black:** 190,267 (3.2%); **American Indian:** 93,301 (1.6%); **Asian:** 322,335 (5.5%); **Other race:** 228,923 (3.9%); **Two or more races:** 213,519 (3.6%); **Hispanic/Latino:** 441,509 (7.5%). **2000 percent population 18 and over:** 74.3; **65 and over:** 11.2; **median age:** 35.3.

1. Parks and undeveloped areas administered by State Parks and Recreation Commission. Dept. of Wildlife administers wildlife and recreation areas totaling 428,989.5 acres.

As part of the vast Oregon Country, Washington territory was visited by Spanish, American, and British explorers—Bruno Heceta for Spain in 1775, the American Capt. Robert Gray in 1792, and Capt. George Vancouver for Britain in 1792–1794. Lewis and Clark explored the Columbia River region and coastal areas for the U.S. in 1805–1806.

Rival American and British settlers and conflicting territorial claims threatened war in the early 1840s. However, in 1846 the Oregon Treaty set the boundary at the 49th parallel and war was averted.

Washington is a leading lumber producer. Its rugged surface is rich in stands of Douglas fir, hemlock, ponderosa and white pine, spruce, larch, and cedar. The state holds first place in apples, lentils, dry edible peas, hops, pears, red raspberries, spearmint oil, and sweet cherries, and ranks high in apricots, asparagus, grapes, peppermint oil, and potatoes. Livestock and livestock products make important contributions to total farm revenue and the commercial fishing catch of salmon, halibut, and bottomfish makes a significant contribution to the state's economy.

Manufacturing industries in Washington include aircraft and missiles, shipbuilding and other transportation equipment, lumber, food processing, metals and metal products, chemicals, and machinery.

Washington has over 1,000 dams, including the Grand Coulee, built for a variety of purposes including irrigation, power, flood control, and water storage. Its abundance of electrical power makes Washington one of the nation's major producers of refined aluminum.

Among the major points of interest: Mt. Rainier, Olympic, and North Cascades National Parks. Mount St. Helens, a peak in the Cascade Range, erupted in May 1980. Also of interest are Whitman Mission and Fort Vancouver National Historic Sites; and the Pacific Science Center and the Space Needle, in Seattle.

Famous natives and residents: Earl Anthony, professional bowler; Mildred Bailey, singer; Bob Barker, TV host; Dyan Cannon, actress; Raymond Carver, writer; Carol Channing, actress; Ray Charles, singer and musician; Kurt Cobain, rock musician; Judy Collins, singer; Chris Cornell, rock musician; Fred Couples, professional golfer; Bing Crosby, singer and actor; Bob Crosby, musician; Merce Cunningham, choreographer; Howard Duff, actor; Frances Farmer, actress; Kenny G., saxophonist; Bill Gates, software executive; Jimi Hendrix, guitarist; Frank Herbert, writer; Robert Joffrey, choreographer; Chuck Jones, animator; Quincy Jones, music producer; Hank Ketcham, cartoonist; Gary Larson, cartoonist; Gypsy Rose Lee, entertainer; Kenny Loggins, rock musician; Mary McCarthy, novelist; Guthrie McClintic, theatrical producer and director; John McIntire, actor; Steve Miller, rock musician; Robert Motherwell, artist; Patrice Munsel, soprano; Craig T. Nelson, actor; Ella Raines, actress; Ahmad Rashad, football player; Ann Reinking, dancer and actress; Tom Robbins, novelist; Ann Rule, writer; Francis Scobee, astronaut; Seattle, Suquamish chief; Smohalla, Indian prophet and chief; Hillary Swank, actress; Julia Sweeney, actress; Adam West, actor; Audrey Wurdemann, poet.

West Virginia

Capital: Charleston
Governor: Bob Wise, D (to Jan. 2005)
Senators: Robert C. Byrd, D (to Jan. 2007); John D. "Jay" Rockefeller IV, D (to Jan. 2009)
Secy. of State: Joe Manchin, D (to Jan. 2005)
Treasurer: John D. Perdue, D (to Jan. 2005)
Atty. General: Darrell V. McGraw, Jr., D (to Jan. 2005)
Entered Union (rank): June 20, 1863 (35)
Present constitution adopted: 1872
Motto: *Montani semper liberi* (Mountaineers are always free)
State Symbols: flower, rhododendron (1903); **tree,** sugar maple (1949); **bird,** cardinal (1949); **animal,** black bear (1973); **colors,** blue and gold (official) (1863); **songs,** "West Virginia, My Home Sweet Home," "The West Virginia Hills," and "This Is My

West Virginia" (adopted by Legislature in 1947, 1961, and 1963 as official state songs);
Nickname: Mountain State
Origin of name: In honor of Elizabeth, "Virgin Queen" of England
10 largest cities (2000): Charleston, 53,421; Huntington, 51,475; Parkersburg, 33,099; Wheeling, 31,419; Morgantown, 26,809; Weirton, 20,411; Fairmont, 19,097; Beckley, 17,254; Clarksburg, 16,743; Martinsburg, 14,972
Land area: 24,077 sq mi. (62,359 sq km)
Geographic center: In Braxton Co., 4 mi. E of Sutton
Number of counties: 55
Largest county by population and area: Kanawha, 197,338 (2001); Randolph, 1,040 sq mi.
State forests: 9 (79,502 ac.)
State parks: 37 (74,508 ac.)
Residents: West Virginian
2002 resident population est.: 1,801,873
2000 resident census population (rank): 1,808,344 (37). **Male:** 879,170 (48.6%); **Female:** 929,174 (51.4%). **White:** 1,718,777 (95.0%); **Black:** 57,232 (3.2%); **American Indian:** 3,606 (0.2%); **Asian:** 9,434 (0.5%); **Other race:** 3,107 (0.2%); **Two or more races:** 15,788 (0.9%); **Hispanic/Latino:** 12,279 (0.7%). **2000 percent population 18 and over:** 77.7; **65 and over:** 15.3; **median age:** 38.9.

West Virginia's early history from 1609 until 1863 is largely shared with Virginia, of which it was a part until Virginia seceded from the Union in 1861. The delegates of the 40 western counties who opposed secession formed their own government, which was granted statehood in 1863.

In 1731 Morgan Morgan established the first permanent white settlement on Mill Creek in present-day Berkeley County. Coal, a mineral asset that would figure significantly in West Virginia's history, was discovered in 1742. Other important natural resources are oil, natural gas, and hardwood forests, which cover about 75% of the state's area.

The state's rapid industrial expansion began in the 1870s, drawing thousands of European immigrants and African Americans into the region. Miners' strikes between 1912 and 1921 required the intervention of state and federal troops to quell the violence.

Today, the state ranks second in total coal production, with about 15% of the U.S. total. It is also a leader in steel, glass, aluminum, and chemical manufactures. Major agricultural commodities are poultry and eggs, dairy products, and apples.

Tourism is increasingly popular in mountainous West Virginia. More than a million acres have been set aside in 37 state parks and recreation areas and in 9 state forests and 2 national forests. Major points of interest include Harpers Ferry and New River Gorge National River, The Greenbrier and Berkeley Springs resorts, the scenic railroad at Cass, and the historic homes in the Eastern Panhandle.

Famous natives and residents: George Brett, baseball player; Pearl S. Buck, author; Phyllis Curtin, soprano; Martin R. Delany, first black army major; Billy Dixon, frontiersman and scout; Joanne Dru, actress; Thomas "Stonewall" Jackson, Confederate general; John S. Knight, publisher; Don Knotts, actor; Peter Marshall, TV host; Kathy Mattea, singer; Whitney D. Morrow, banker and diplomat; Mary Lou Retton, gymnast; Walter Reuther, labor leader; Eleanor Steber, soprano; Lewis L. Strauss, naval officer and scientist; Cyrus Vance, government official; Jerry West, basketball player; William Lyne Wilson, legislator and university president; Chuck Yeager, test pilot and Air Force general.

Wisconsin

Capital: Madison
Governor: Jim Doyle, D (to Jan. 2007)
Lieut. Governor: Barbara Lawton, D (to Jan. 2007)
Senators: Russell D. Feingold, D (to Jan. 2005); Herbert Kohl, D (to Jan. 2007)
Secy. of State: Douglas J. La Follette, D (to Jan. 2007)
State Treasurer: Jack C. Voight, R (to Jan. 2007)
Atty. General: Peg Lautenschlager, D (to Jan. 2007)
Superintendent of Public Instruction: Elizabeth Burmaster, Nonpartisan (to July 2005)
Organized as territory: July 4, 1836
Entered Union (rank): May 29, 1848 (30)
Present constitution adopted: 1848
Motto: Forward
State Symbols: flower, wood violet (1949); **tree,** sugar maple (1949); **grain,** corn (1990); **bird,** robin (1949); **animal,** badger; **wild life animal,** white-tailed deer (1957); **domestic animal,** dairy cow (1971); **insect,** honeybee (1977); **fish,** musky (muskellunge) (1955); **song,** "On Wisconsin"; **mineral,** galena (1971); **rock,** red granite (1971); **symbol of peace,** mourning dove (1971); **soil,** antigo silt loam (1983); **fossil,** trilobite (1985); **dog,** American Water Spaniel (1986); **beverage,** milk (1988); **dance,** polka (1994); **waltz,** "The Wisconsin Waltz" (2001); **ballad,** "Oh Wisconsin, Land of My Dreams" (2001)
Nickname: Badger State
Origin of name: French corruption of an Indian word whose meaning is disputed
10 largest cities (2000): Milwaukee, 596,974; Madison, 208,054; Green Bay, 102,313; Kenosha, 90,352; Racine, 81,855; Appleton, 70,087; Waukesha, 64,825; Oshkosh, 62,916; Eau Claire, 61,704; West Allis, 61,254
Land area: 54,310 sq mi. (140,673 sq km)
Geographic center: In Wood Co., 9 mi. SE of Marshfield
Number of counties: 72
Largest county by population and area: Milwaukee, 932,012 (2001); Marathon, 1,545 sq mi.
State forests: 12 (493,975 ac.)
State parks & scenic trails: 43 parks, 14 trails (68,355 ac.)
Residents: Wisconsinite
2002 resident population est.: 5,441,196
2000 resident census population (rank): 5,363,675 (18). **Male:** 2,649,041 (49.4%); **Female:** 2,714,634 (50.6%). **White:** 4,769,857 (88.9%); **Black:** 304,460 (5.7%); **American Indian:** 47,228 (0.9%); **Asian:** 88,763 (1.7%); **Other race:** 84,842 (1.6%); **Two or more races:** 66,895 (1.2%); **Hispanic/Latino:** 192,921 (3.6%). **2000 percent population 18 and over:** 74.5; **65 and over:** 13.1; **median age:** 36.0.

The Wisconsin region was first explored for France by Jean Nicolet, who landed at Green Bay in 1634. In 1660 a French trading post and Roman Catholic mission were established near present-day Ashland.

Great Britain obtained the region in settlement of the French and Indian Wars in 1763; the U.S. acquired it in 1783 after the Revolutionary War. However, Great Britain retained actual control until after the War of 1812. The region was successively governed as part of the territories of Indiana, Illinois, and Michigan between 1800 and 1836, when it became a separate territory.

Wisconsin is a leading state in milk and cheese production. Other important farm products are peas, beans, beets, corn, potatoes, oats, hay, and cranberries.

The chief industrial products of the state are automobiles, machinery, furniture, paper, beer, and processed foods. Wisconsin ranks second among the 47 paper-producing states. The state's mines produce copper, iron ore, lead, and zinc.

Wisconsin is a pioneer in social legislation, providing pensions for the blind (1907), aid to dependent children (1913), and old-age assistance (1925). In labor legislation, the state was the first to enact an unemployment compensation law (1932) and the first in which a workman's compensation law actually took effect. In 1984, Wisconsin became the first state to adopt the Uniform Marital Property Act.

The state has over 14,000 lakes, of which Winnebago is the largest. Water sports, ice-boating, and fishing are popular, as are skiing and hunting. Public parks and forests take up one-seventh of the land, with 43 state parks, 12 state forests, 14 state trails, 3 recreational areas, and 2 national forests.

Among the many points of interest are the Apostle Islands National Lakeshore; Ice Age National Scientific Reserve; the Circus World Museum at Baraboo; the Wolf, St. Croix, and Lower St. Croix national scenic riverways; and the Wisconsin Dells.

Famous natives and residents: Don Ameche, actor; Roy Chapman Andrews, naturalist and explorer; Walter Annenberg, media tycoon and philanthropist; Carrie Catt, woman suffragist; John R. Commons, economist; Tyne Daly, actress; August Derleth, author; Jeanne Dixon, seer; Zona Gale, novelist; Eric Heiden, skater; Woody Herman, band leader; Hildegarde, singer; Harry Houdini, magician; Hans V. Kaltenborne, journalist; Pee Wee King, singer; George F. Kennan, diplomat; Robert La Follette, politician; William D. Leahy, admiral; Liberace, pianist; Charles Litel, actor; Allen Ludden, TV host; Alfred Lunt, actor; Frederic March, actor; Jackie Mason, comedian; John Ringling North, circus director; Pat O'Brien, actor; Georgia O'Keeffe, painter; Charlotte Rae, actress; William H. Rehnquist, jurist; Gena Rowlands, actress; Tom Snyder, newscaster; Spencer Tracy, actor; Thorstein Veblen, economist; Orson Welles, actor and producer; Thornton Wilder, author; Charles Winninger, actor; Frank Lloyd Wright, architect.

Wyoming

Capital: Cheyenne
Governor: Dave Freudenthal, D (to Jan. 2007)
Senators: Michael B. Enzi, R (to Jan. 2009); Craig Thomas, R (to Jan. 2007)
Secy. of State: Joe Meyer, R (to Jan. 2007)
Treasurer: Cynthia M. Lummis, R (to Jan. 2007)
Atty. General: Patrick Crank, D (to Jan. 2007)
Organized as territory: May 19, 1869
Entered Union (rank): July 10, 1890 (44)
Present constitution adopted: 1890
Motto: Equal rights (1955)
State Symbols: flower, Indian paintbrush (1917); **tree,** cottonwood (1947); **bird,** western meadowlark (1927); **dinosaur,** *Triceratops* (1994); **fish,** cutthroat trout (1987); **fossil,** *Knightia* (1987); **gemstone,** jade (1967); **insignia,** bucking horse (unofficial); **mammal,** bison (1985); **reptile,** horned toad (1993); **soil,** Forkwood series (unofficial); **song,** "Wyoming" (1955)
Nickname: Equality State
Origin of name: From the Delaware Indian word, meaning "mountains and valleys alternating"; the same as the Wyoming Valley in Pennsylvania
10 largest cities (2000): Cheyenne, 53,011; Casper, 49,644; Laramie, 27,204; Gillette, 19,646; Rock Springs, 18,708; Sheridan, 15,804; Green River, 11,808; Evanston, 11,507; Riverton, 9,310; Cody, 8,835
Land area: 97,100 sq mi. (251,501 sq km)
Geographic center: In Fremont Co., 58 mi. ENE of Lander
Number of counties: 23, plus Yellowstone National Park
Largest county by population and area: Laramie, 81,958 (2001); Sweetwater, 10,426 sq mi.
State parks and historic sites: 23 (58,498 ac.)
Residents: Wyomingite
2002 resident population est.: 498,703
2000 resident census population (rank): 493,782 (50). **Male:** 248,374 (50.3%); **Female:** 245,408 (49.7%). **White:** 454,670 (92.1%); **Black:** 3,722 (0.8%); **American Indian:** 11,133 (2.3%); **Asian:** 2,771 (0.6%); **Other race:** 12,301 (2.5%); **Two or more races:** 8,883 (1.8%); **Hispanic/Latino:** 31,669 (6.4%). **2000 percent population 18 and over:** 73.9; **65 and over:** 11.7; **median age:** 36.2.

The U.S. acquired the land comprising Wyoming from France as part of the Louisiana Purchase in 1803. John Colter, a fur-trapper, is the first white man known to have entered the region. In 1807 he explored the Yellowstone area and brought back news of its geysers and hot springs.

Robert Stuart pioneered the Oregon Trail across Wyoming in 1812–1813 and, in 1834, Fort Laramie, the first permanent trading post in Wyoming, was built. Western Wyoming was obtained by the U.S. in the 1846 Oregon Treaty with Great Britain and as a result of the treaty ending the Mexican War in 1848.

When the Wyoming Territory was organized in 1869, Wyoming women became the first in the nation to obtain the right to vote. In 1925 Mrs. Nellie Tayloe Ross became the first woman governor in the United States.

Wyoming's towering mountains and vast plains provide spectacular scenery, grazing lands for sheep and cattle, and rich mineral deposits.

Mining, particularly oil and natural gas, is the most important industry. Wyoming has the world's largest sodium carbonate (natrona) deposits and has the nation's second largest uranium deposits.

In 2000 Wyoming ranked second among the states in wool production (exceeded only by Texas) and third in sheep and lambs (exceeded only by Texas and California); it also had 1,580,000 cattle. Principal crops include wheat, oats, sugar beets, corn, barley, and alfalfa.

Second in mean elevation to Colorado, Wyoming has many attractions for the tourist trade, notably Yellowstone National Park. Hikers, campers and skiers are attracted to Grand Teton National Park and Jackson Hole National Monument in the Teton Range of the Rockies. Cheyenne is famous for its annual "Frontier Days" celebration. Flaming Gorge, the Fort Laramie National Historic Site, and Devils Tower and Fossil Butte National Monuments are other points of interest.

Famous natives and residents: James Bridger, trapper, guide, and storyteller; Dick Cheney, vice president; Buffalo Bill Cody, scout; John Colter, trader and first white man to enter Wyoming; June E. Downey, educator; Thomas Fitzpatrick, mountain man and guide; Curt Gowdy, sportscaster; Tom Horn, detective; Isabel Jewell, actress; Velma Linford, writer; Esther Morris, first woman judge; Ted Olson, writer; John "Portugee" Phillips, frontiersman; Jackson Pollock, painter; Nellie Tayloe Ross, first woman elected governor of a state; Alan K. Simpson, senator; Jedediah S. Smith, mountain man and first American to reach California from the East; Alan Swallow, publisher and author; Willis Van Devanter, jurist; Francis E. Warren, first state governor; Chief Washakie, chief of the Shoshone; James G. Watt, secretary of the Interior.

Tabulated Data on State Governments

	Governor		Legislature[1]						Highest Court[2]		
			Membership		Term, years						
State	Term, years	Annual salary	U[3]	L[4]	U[3]	L[4]	Salaries of members[5]		Members	Term, years	Annual salary
Alabama	4[6]	$ 94,655	35	105	4	4	$ 10	per diem	9	6	$185,376[7]
Alaska	4	85,779	20	40	4	2	24,012[8]	per annum	5	3[9]	109,908[7]
Arizona	4	95,000	30	60	2	2	25,000	per annum	5	6[14]	126,525[7]
Arkansas	4	75,296	35	100	4	2	13,751[8]	per annum	7	8	126,054[7]
California	4	165,000	40	80	4	2	99,000	per annum	7	12	162,409[7]
Colorado	4	90,000	35	65	4	2	30,000	per annum	7	10	79,500[7]
Connecticut	4	78,000	36	151	2	2	28,000[8]	per annum	7	8	129,404[7]
Delaware	4[10]	114,000	21	41	4	2	34,100	per annum	5	12	144,100[7]
Florida	4[6]	120,171	40	120	4[6]	2[11]	29,328[8]	per annum	7	6[14]	153,750
Georgia	4[6]	127,303	56	180	2	2	16,200	per session	7	6	153,086
Hawaii	4	94,780	25	51	4	2	32,000[8]	per annum	5	10	115,547[7]
Idaho	4	95,500	35	70	2	2	15,646[8]	per annum	5	6	102,125[7]
Illinois	4	151,771	59	118	4-2	2	57,619	per annum	7	10	159,235
Indiana	4[6]	95,000	50	100	4	2	11,600	per annum	5	2[9]	115,000
Iowa	4	107,482	50	100	4	2	21,381	per annum	9	8	116,600[7]
Kansas	4	94,036	40	125	4	2	76	per diem[12]	7	6	109,756[7]
Kentucky	4	104,619	38	100	4	2	164	per diem[13]	7	8	123,335[7]
Louisiana	4	95,000	39	105	4	4	16,800	per annum	7	10	85,000
Maine	4	70,000	35	151	2	2	18,803	per biennium	7	7	96,000
Maryland	4[6]	135,000	47	141	4	4	31,509[8]	per annum	7	10	131,600[7]
Massachusetts	4	135,000	40	160	2	2	46,410[8]	per annum	7	([14])	95,880[7]
Michigan	4	172,000	38	110	4	2	79,650	per annum	7	8	164,610
Minnesota	4	120,303	67	134	4[15]	2	31,140	per annum	7	6	125,897[7]
Mississippi	4	125,500	52	122	4	4	10,000	per session	9	8	102,300[7]
Missouri	4[10]	120,086	34	163	4[16]	2	31,351	per annum	7	12	123,000[7]
Montana	4	88,190	50	100	4	2	55	per diem	7	8	83,550
Nebraska	4[6]	85,000	49[17]	—	4[17]	—	12,000	per annum	7	6	119,276
Nevada	4[6]	117,000	21	42	4	2	7,800	per biennium	7	6	140,000
New Hampshire	2	100,690	24	([18])	2	2	200	per biennium	5	([14])	111,045[7]
New Jersey	4[6]	157,000	40	80	4[15]	2	49,000	per annum	7	7[19]	158,500[7]
New Mexico	4[6]	110,000	42	70	4	2	136	per diem	5	8	96,283[7]
New York	4	179,000	61	150	2	2	79,500	per annum	7	14	151,200[7]
North Carolina	4[6]	118,430	50	120	2	2	13,951[8]	per annum	7	8	115,336[7]
North Dakota	4	85,506	47	94	4	4	125	per diem[20]	5	10	99,122[7]
Ohio	4	130,292	33	99	4	2	53,018[8]	per annum	7	6	127,600[7]
Oklahoma	4	101,140	48	101	4	2	38,400	per annum	([21])	6	106,706[7]
Oregon	4[6]	99,200	30	60	4	2	1,092	per month	7	6[22]	105,200[7]
Pennsylvania	4[6]	138,270	50	203	4	2	63,629	per annum	7	10	137,386[7]
Rhode Island	4	95,000	38	75	2	2	12,407[23]	per annum	5	([24])	152,000[7]
South Carolina	4	106,078	46	124	4	2	10,400	per annum	5	10	106,061[7]
South Dakota	4[6]	95,389	35	70	2	2	6,000	per annum	5	3[25]	100,671[7]
Tennessee	4	85,000	33	99	4	2	16,500	per annum	5	8	101,820
Texas	4	99,122	31	150	4	2	7,200	per annum	9	6	94,686[7]
Utah	4	100,600	29	75	4	2	120[8]	per diem	5	3[22]	114,050[7]
Vermont	2	125,572	30	150	2	2	536[26]	per week	5	6	103,019[7]
Virginia	4	124,855	40	100	4	2	17,640[27]	per annum	7	12	132,523[7]
Washington	4[28]	139,087	49	98	4[11]	2	32,801[8]	per annum	9	6	134,584
West Virginia	4[6]	90,000	34	100	4	2	15,000	per annum	5	12	95,000
Wisconsin	4	122,406	33	99	4	2	44,233	per annum	7	10	122,418[7]
Wyoming	4	150,000	30	60	4	2	125	per diem	5	8	105,000

NOTE: Salaries are rounded to nearest dollar. 1. Known as *General Assembly* in Ark., Colo., Conn., Del., Ga., Ill., Iowa, Ind., Ky., Md., Mo., N.C., Ohio, Pa., R.I., S.C., Tenn., Vt., Va.; *Legislative Assembly* in N.D., Ore.; *General Court* in Mass., N.H.; *Legislature* in other states. Meets biennially in Ark., Ky., Mont., Nev., N.D., Ore., Texas. Wyoming Legislature has regular general session on odd-numbered years and a budget session on even-numbered years. Arkansas General Assembly meets every other year for 60 days in odd numbered years. Ohio General Assembly meets when deemed necessary. Legislative bodies meet annually in other states. 2. Known as *Court of Appeals* in Md., N.Y.; *Supreme Court of Virginia* in Va.; *Supreme Judicial Court* in Maine, Mass.; *Supreme Court* in other states. 3. Upper house: *Senate* in all states except Neb., which has a single-house legislative body, "the Legislature." 4. Lower house: *Assembly* in Calif., Nev., N.Y., Wis.; *House of Delegates* in Md., Va., W.Va.; *General Assembly* in N.J.; *House of Representatives* in other states. 5. Base salary. Does not include additional payments for expenses, mileage, special sessions, etc., or additional per diem payments. 6. May not serve third consecutive term. 7. Chief justice receives a higher salary. 8. Leaders receive a higher salary. 9. Initial term; thereafter elected popularly for 10-year term. 10. May serve only two terms, consecutive or otherwise. 11. Have term limitations. 12. When in session, plus $85 per day for expenses. There is also an out-of-session expense allowance of $5,400. Leaders receive an additional sum. 13. For days worked whether or not legislature is in session. 14. Until 70 years old. 15. Every 10 years (the year after census) term is only for 2 years. 16. Legislators may serve only 8 years in each house, 16 combined. 17. Unicameral legislature. 18. Constitutional number: 375-400. 19. Second term receive tenure, mandatory retirement at 70. 20. When in session, plus $250 per month when not in session. 21. Nine members in Supreme Court, highest in civil cases; five in Court of Criminal Appeals. 22. Until 75 years old. 23. Upper house receives slightly lower salary. 24. Term of good behavior. 25. Subsequent terms, eight years. 26. To limit of $13,000 per biennium; $105 per diem for Special Session. 27. Upper house receives higher salary. 28. No person is eligible who would have served during 8 of the previous 14 years. *Source:* questionnaires to the states.

Land and Water Area of States, 2000

(in square miles)

State	Rank (total area)	Land[1] area	Water[2] area	Total area
Alabama	30	50,744.00	1,675.01	52,419.02
Alaska	1	571,951.26	91,316.00	663,267.26
Arizona	6	113,634.57	363.73	113,998.30
Arkansas	29	52,068.17	1,110.45	53,178.62
California	3	155,959.34	7,736.23	163,695.57
Colorado	8	103,717.53	376.04	104,093.57
Connecticut	48	4,844.80	698.53	5,543.33
Delaware	49	1,953.56	535.71	2,489.27
Dist. of Columbia	—	61.4	6.94	68.34
Florida	22	53,926.82	11,827.77	65,754.59
Georgia	24	57,906.14	1,518.63	59,424.77
Hawaii	43	6,422.62	4,508.36	10,930.98
Idaho	14	82,747.21	822.87	83,570.08
Illinois	25	55,583.58	2,330.79	57,914.38
Indiana	38	35,866.90	550.83	36,417.73
Iowa	26	55,869.36	402.2	56,271.55
Kansas	15	81,814.88	461.96	82,276.84
Kentucky	37	39,728.18	680.85	40,409.02
Louisiana	31	43,561.85	8,277.85	51,839.70
Maine	39	30,861.55	4,523.10	35,384.65
Maryland	42	9,773.82	2,632.86	12,406.68
Massachusetts	44	7,840.02	2,714.55	10,554.57
Michigan	11	56,803.82	39,912.28	96,716.11
Minnesota	12	79,610.08	7,328.79	86,938.87
Mississippi	32	46,906.96	1,523.24	48,430.19
Missouri	21	68,885.93	818.39	69,704.31
Montana	4	145,552.43	1,489.96	147,042.40
Nebraska	16	76,872.41	481.31	77,353.73
Nevada	7	109,825.99	734.71	110,560.71
New Hampshire	46	8,968.10	381.84	9,349.94
New Jersey	47	7,417.34	1,303.96	8,721.30
New Mexico	5	121,355.53	233.96	121,589.48
New York	27	47,213.79	7,342.22	54,556.00
North Carolina	28	48,710.88	5,107.63	53,818.51
North Dakota	19	68,975.93	1,723.86	70,699.79
Ohio	34	40,948.38	3,876.53	44,824.90
Oklahoma	20	68,667.06	1,231.13	69,898.19
Oregon	9	95,996.79	2,383.85	98,380.64
Pennsylvania	33	44,816.61	1,238.63	46,055.24
Rhode Island	50	1,044.93	500.12	1,545.05
South Carolina	40	30,109.47	1,910.73	32,020.20
South Dakota	17	75,884.64	1,231.85	77,116.49
Tennessee	36	41,217.12	926.15	42,143.27
Texas	2	261,797.12	6,783.70	268,580.82
Utah	13	82,143.65	2,755.18	84,898.83
Vermont	45	9,249.56	364.7	9,614.26
Virginia	35	39,594.07	3,180.13	42,774.20
Washington	18	66,544.06	4,755.58	71,299.64
West Virginia	41	24,077.73	152.03	24,229.76
Wisconsin	23	54,310.10	11,187.72	65,497.82
Wyoming	10	97,100.40	713.16	97,813.56
U.S. total		**3,537,438.44**	**256,644.62**	**3,794,083.06**

1. Dry land and land temporarily or partially covered by water, such as marshland, swamps, etc.; streams and canals under one-eighth statute mile wide; and lakes, reservoirs, and ponds under 40 acres. 2. Permanent inland water surface, such as lakes, reservoirs, and ponds having an area of 40 acres or more; streams, sloughs, estuaries, and canals one-eighth statute mile or more in width; deeply indented embayments and sounds, and other coastal waters behind or sheltered by headlands or islands separated by less than 1 nautical mile of water, and islands under 40 acres in area. Excludes areas of oceans, bays, sounds, etc. lying within U.S. jurisdiction but not defined as inland water. *Source:* Department of Commerce, Bureau of the Census.

State Capitals and Largest Cities

State	Capital	Largest city
Alabama	Montgomery	Birmingham
Alaska	Juneau	Anchorage
Arizona	Phoenix	Phoenix
Arkansas	Little Rock	Little Rock
California	Sacramento	Los Angeles
Colorado	Denver	Denver
Connecticut	Hartford	Bridgeport
Delaware	Dover	Wilmington
Florida	Tallahassee	Jacksonville
Georgia	Atlanta	Atlanta
Hawaii	Honolulu	Honolulu
Idaho	Boise	Boise
Illinois	Springfield	Chicago
Indiana	Indianapolis	Indianapolis
Iowa	Des Moines	Des Moines
Kansas	Topeka	Wichita
Kentucky	Frankfort	Lexington
Louisiana	Baton Rouge	New Orleans
Maine	Augusta	Portland
Maryland	Annapolis	Baltimore
Massachusetts	Boston	Boston
Michigan	Lansing	Detroit
Minnesota	St. Paul	Minneapolis
Mississippi	Jackson	Jackson
Missouri	Jefferson City	Kansas City
Montana	Helena	Billings
Nebraska	Lincoln	Omaha
Nevada	Carson City	Las Vegas
New Hampshire	Concord	Manchester
New Jersey	Trenton	Newark
New Mexico	Santa Fe	Albuquerque
New York	Albany	New York City
North Carolina	Raleigh	Charlotte
North Dakota	Bismarck	Fargo
Ohio	Columbus	Columbus
Oklahoma	Oklahoma City	Oklahoma City
Oregon	Salem	Portland
Pennsylvania	Harrisburg	Philadelphia
Rhode Island	Providence	Providence
South Carolina	Columbia	Columbia
South Dakota	Pierre	Sioux Falls
Tennessee	Nashville	Memphis
Texas	Austin	Houston
Utah	Salt Lake City	Salt Lake City
Vermont	Montpelier	Burlington
Virginia	Richmond	Virginia Beach
Washington	Olympia	Seattle
West Virginia	Charleston	Charleston
Wisconsin	Madison	Milwaukee
Wyoming	Cheyenne	Cheyenne

Source: U.S. Bureau of the Census, 2000 figures.

50 Largest Cities of the United States

Data supplied by U.S. Census Bureau and by the cities in response to questionnaires. Per capita personal income data are given for the Metropolitan Statistical Area (MSA), the Primary Metropolitan Statistical Area (PMSA), the New England County Metropolitan Area (NECMA), or the Consolidated Metropolitan Statistical Area (CMSA), as noted. NOTE: Persons of Hispanic origin may be of any race.

Albuquerque, N.M.

Mayor: Martin Chavez (to Nov. 2005)
2000 census population (rank): 448,607 (35); **% change:** 16.6; **Male:** 217,887 (48.6%); **Female:** 230,720 (51.4%); **White:** 321,179 (71.6%); **Black:** 13,854 (3.1%); **American Indian and Alaska Native:** 17,444 (3.9%); **Asian:** 10,068 (2.2%); **Other race:** 66,292 (14.8%); **Two or more races:** 19,318 (4.3%); **Hispanic/Latino:** 179,075 (39.9%). **2000 percent population 18 and over:** 75.5%; **65 and over:** 12.0%; **median age:** 34.9.
Land area: 181 sq mi. (469 sq km); **Alt.:** 4,958 ft.
Avg. daily temp.: Jan., 34.2° F; July, 78.5° F
Churches: 211; **City-owned parks:** 189; **Radio stations:** 43 (AM, 17; FM, 26); **Television stations:** 11
Civilian Labor Force (MSA) 2002: 385,630; **Unemployed:** 18,284, **Percent:** 4.7; **Per capita personal income (MSA) 2001:** $27,030
Chamber of Commerce: Greater Albuquerque Chamber of Commerce, 401 2nd St. N.W., Albuquerque, N.M. 87125. Albuquerque Hispanic Chamber of Commerce, 202 Central Ave. S.E., Albuquerque, N.M. 87102

Albuquerque is the largest city in New Mexico and the seat of Bernalillo County. It is situated in west-central New Mexico on the upper Rio Grande.

Spanish settlers arrived in the mid-1600s, but they retreated from the area in 1680 after the Pueblo revolt. The old town was founded in 1706 by Don Francisco Cuervo y Valdés, the governor of New Mexico, and named after the Duke of Alburquerque, the viceroy of New Spain.

The opening of the Santa Fe Trail in the early 19th century brought an influx of settlers, and an army post was established following U.S. occupation in 1846. Albuquerque remained loyal to the Union during the Civil War, although it was briefly occupied by Confederate forces in 1862. The new town was laid out in 1880 after the Santa Fe Railroad was built one mile east of the original plaza. The Spanish old town and the mission church of San Felipe de Neri (1706) were soon enveloped by the new construction but survive today.

The city is noted as a center for health and medical services in the region, and government agencies, nuclear research, banking, and tourism are important to the economy. There is a growing high-tech center in Albuquerque, and Intel Corp.'s largest manufacturing facility is located there.

Albuquerque is the seat of the University of New Mexico (1889). Its numerous attractions include the Albuquerque Biological Park, the Indian Pueblo Cultural Center, the National Atomic Museum, Petroglyph National Monument, and the Sandia Mountain Wilderness.

Famous natives: Annabeth Gish, actress; Fred Haney, baseball player; Ernie Pyle, war correspondent; Al and Bobby Unser, auto racers.

Atlanta, Ga.

Mayor: Shirley Franklin (to Jan. 2006)
2000 census population (rank): 416,474 (39); **% change:** 5.7; **Male:** 206,725 (49.6%); **Female:** 209,749 (50.4%); **White:** 138,352 (33.2%); **Black:** 255,689 (61.4%); **American Indian and Alaska Native:** 765 (0.2%); **Asian:** 8,046 (1.9%); **Other race:** 8,272 (2.0%); **Two or more races:** 5,177 (1.2%); **Hispanic/Latino:** 18,720 (4.5%). **2000 percent population 18 and over:** 77.7%; **65 and over:** 9.7%; **median age:** 31.9.
City land area: 132 sq mi. (341 sq km); **Alt.:** Highest, 1,050 ft.; lowest, 940 ft.
Avg. daily temp.: Jan., 41.0° F; July, 78.8° F
Churches: 1,500; **City-owned parks:** 277 (3,178 ac.); **Radio stations:** AM, 7; FM, 20; **Television stations:** 8 commercial; 2 PBS
Civilian Labor Force (MSA) 2002: 2,378,289; **Unemployed:** 126,346, **Percent:** 5.3; **Per capita personal income (MSA) 2001:** $33,769
Chamber of Commerce: Metro Atlanta Chamber of Commerce, 235 International Blvd., Atlanta, Ga. 30303

Atlanta, the largest city and capital of Georgia, is the seat of Fulton County. It is situated in the northwest part of the state at the base of the Blue Ridge Mountains near the Chattahoochee River. The first European settler was Hardy Ivy, who built a cabin there in 1833.

Founded as Terminus in 1837, the town served as the end of the Georgia railroad line (Western and Atlantic Railroad) and later became incorporated as Marthasville in 1843 in honor of ex-governor Lumpkin's daughter Martha. It was renamed Atlanta in 1845 and incorporated as a city in 1847. The name was suggested by the railroad's chief engineer, J. Edgar Thomson, and was derived from its location at the end of the Georgia and Atlantic railroad line. The city became the capital of Georgia in 1868.

During the Civil War, the city was burned and almost completely destroyed while occupied by Gen. William T. Sherman's troops in Nov. 1864. It was rebuilt after the war and grew rapidly due to the expansion of the railroads in the southwest.

Today, Atlanta is the major commercial and transportation hub of the southeast United States, and its international airport is one of the busiest in the world. The city's economy is led by the service, communications, retail trade, manufacturing, finance, and insurance industries. The convention business is also important, and Atlanta is home to many major corporations, including Coca-Cola, which was founded there in 1892.

Atlanta is also a major educational center, with many prestigious universities and colleges, including Emory University (1836), Georgia Institute of Technology (1885), and Georgia State University

(1913). Morehouse College (1867), Spelman College (1881), and Clark Atlanta University (1865; 1869) are important historically black colleges.

Major attractions include Martin Luther King, Jr., National Historic Site, Grant Park, and the Carter Presidential Center. The 1996 Summer Olympics were held in Atlanta.

Famous natives: Hank Aaron, baseball player; Arrested Development, recording artists; Jimmy Carter, former president; Ray Charles, singer; James Dickey, poet; Mattivilda Dobbs, soprano; Walt Frazier, basketball player; Oliver Hardy, comedian; Evander Holyfield, boxer; Allan Jackson, singer; Bobby Jones, golfer; DeForest Kelley, actor; Martin Luther King, Jr., civil rights leader and Nobel Peace Prize winner; Gladys Knight, singer; Kriss Kross, recording artists; Margaret Mitchell, novelist; Bert Parks, entertainer; Eric Roberts, actor; Julia Roberts, actress; Doug Stone, singer; Gwen Torrence, Olympic athlete; Lee Tracy, actor; Travis Tritt, singer; Ted Turner, TBS and CNN founder; Jane Withers, actress; Joanne Woodward, actress; Andrew Young, civil rights activist.

Austin, Tex.

Mayor: Will Wynn (to June 15, 2006)
2000 census population (rank): 656,562 (16); **% change:** 41.0; **Male:** 337,569 (51.4%); **Female:** 318,993 (48.6%); **White:** 429,100 (65.4%); **Black:** 65,956 (10.0%); **American Indian and Alaska Native:** 3,889 (0.6%); **Asian:** 30,960 (4.7%); **Other race:** 106,538 (16.2%); **Two or more races:** 19,650 (3.0%); **Hispanic/Latino:** 200,579 (30.5%). **2000 percent population 18 and over:** 77.5%; **65 and over:** 6.7%; **median age:** 29.6
Land area: 252 sq mi. (653 sq km); **Alt.:** From 425 ft. to over 1000 ft.
Avg. daily temp.: Jan., 48.8° F; July, 84.5° F
Churches: 353 churches, representing 45 denominations; **City-owned parks and playgrounds:** 169 (11,800 ac.); **Radio stations:** AM, 12; FM, 27; **Television stations:** 7 commercial; 1 PBS; 1 independent
Civilian Labor Force (MSA) 2002: 768,643[1]; **Unemployed:** 43,594[1], **Percent:** 5.7[1]; **Per capita personal income (MSA) 2001:** $31,511[1]
Chamber of Commerce: Greater Austin Chamber of Commerce, P.O. Box 1967, Austin, Tex. 78767

1. Austin–San Marcos, Tex.

Austin, the state capital of Texas and seat of Travis County, is the fourth-largest city in Texas. It is situated in the south-central part of the state on the Colorado River.

The site was called Waterloo in 1838, and in 1839 it was incorporated as a city and chosen as the capital of the independent Republic of Texas. Waterloo was renamed Austin in honor of Stephen F. Austin, the founder of the Texas Republic. It became the permanent capital of the state of Texas in 1870.

Austin's growth was spurred by several developments after the Civil War—the railroads reached the city in the 1870s; it was crossed by the important Chisholm cattle trail; and it became the seat of the state university in 1883.

Austin has a growing commercial and diversified manufacturing sector. Civilian government employment is 20% of the labor force and is important to the economy. As home to the University of Texas, Austin is a major center for research and development and is nationally recognized as a high-technology center.

Austin's visitor attractions include the Austin Museum of Art, the Lyndon B. Johnson Library and Museum, the Lady Bird Johnson Wildflower Center, and the Austin Zoo.

Famous natives: Don Baylor, baseball player and manager; Earl Campbell, football player; Liz Carpenter, author; Dabney Coleman, actor; Ben Crenshaw, golfer; Michael Dell, founder Dell Computer Corp.; Tobe Hooper, film director; Lady Bird Johnson, former first lady; Tom Kite, golfer; James Michener, author; Willie Nelson, musician; Amado Pena, artist; Darrell Royal, football coach; Zachary Scott, actor; Jerry Jeff Walker, musician; Dalhart Windberg, artist.

Baltimore, Md.

Mayor: Martin O'Malley (to Dec. 2003)
2000 census population (rank): 651,154 (17); **% change:** –11.5; **Male:** 303,687 (46.6%); **Female:** 347,467 (53.4%); **White:** 205,982 (31.6%); **Black:** 418,951 (64.3%); **American Indian and Alaska Native:** 2,097 (0.3%); **Asian:** 9,985 (1.5%); **Other race:** 4,363 (0.7%); **Two or more races:** 9,554 (1.5%); **Hispanic/Latino:** 11,061 (1.7%). **2000 percent population 18 and over:** 75.2%; **65 and over:** 13.2%; **Median age:** 35.0.
Land area: 81 sq mi. (210 sq km); **Alt.:** Highest, 490 ft.; lowest, sea level
Avg. daily temp.: Jan., 31.8° F; July, 77.0° F
Churches: Roman Catholic, 72; Jewish, 50; Protestant and others, 344; **City-owned parks:** 347 park areas and tracts (6,314 ac.); **Radio stations:** AM, 10; FM, 11; **Television stations:** 7
Civilian Labor Force (PMSA) 2002: 1,346,803; **Unemployed:** 65,055, **Percent:** 4.8; **Per capita personal income (PMSA) 2001:** $34,039
Chamber of Commerce: Baltimore City Chamber of Commerce, 3 W. Baltimore, Baltimore, Md. 21202

Baltimore, the largest city in Maryland, is situated in the northern part of the state on the Patapsco River estuary, an arm of Chesapeake Bay. The city is independent and does not fall within any county.

The site was settled in the early 17th century and founded as a town in 1729. The town was named after Lord Baltimore, the founder of Maryland, and was incorporated as a city in 1797. It has an excellent harbor and has been a principal port since the 18th century. Baltimore was a pioneer shipbuilding center, and the Baltimore clipper was used extensively in world trade.

The city has been greatly affected by the nation's wars. During the War of 1812, the British bombarded nearby Fort McHenry, inspiring Francis Scott Key to write the *Star-Spangled Banner.* And although Maryland never seceded from the Union, Baltimore was occupied by Union troops throughout the Civil War. The city was also an important shipbuilding and supply center during the World Wars.

Baltimore's economy is very diverse, with strong financial, legal, and nonprofit service industries. The city also leads in scientific research and development through two highly acclaimed medical institutions, Johns Hopkins Hospital and University of Maryland Hospital. There is also a significant tourist sector. Major attractions include the the National Aquarium, Harborplace, the Maryland Science Center, the Babe Ruth Museum, Fort McHenry National Monument, and Pimlico Race Course, site of the Preakness.

Famous natives: Larry Adler, musician; John Astin, actor; Eubie Blake, pianist; Francis X. Bushman, actor; Charlie Chase, actor; Hans Conried, actor; Mildred Dunnock, actress; "Mama" Cass Elliot, singer; Barry Farber, broadcaster; Paul Ford, actor; Philip Glass, composer; Billie Holiday, singer; Barry Levinson, director; H. L. Mencken, writer; Babe Ruth, baseball player; Upton Sinclair, novelist; Leon Uris, novelist; John Waters, film director, writer, and actor; Frank Zappa, musician.

Boston, Mass.

Mayor: Thomas Menino (to Jan. 2006)
2000 census population (rank): 589,141 (20); **% change:** 2.6; **Male:** 283,588 (48.1%); **Female,** 305,553 (51.9%); **White:** 320,944 (54.5%); **Black:** 149,202 (25.3%); **American Indian and Alaska Native:** 2,365 (0.4%); **Asian:** 44,284 (7.5%); **Other race:** 46,102 (7.8%); **Two or more races:** 25,878 (4.4%); **Hispanic/Latino:** 85,089 (14.4%). **2000 percent population 18 and over:** 80.2%; **65 and over:** 10.4%; **median age:** 31.1.
Land area: 48 sq mi. (124 sq km); **Alt.:** Highest, 330 ft.; lowest, sea level
Avg. daily temp.: Jan., 28.6° F; July, 73.5° F
Churches: Protestant, 187; Roman Catholic, 70; Jewish, 13; others, 100; **City-owned parks, playgrounds, etc.:** 2,260 ac.; **Radio stations**[1]: AM, 24; FM, 22; **Television stations**[1]: 27
Civilian Labor Force (PMSA) 2002: 1,922,942; **Unemployed:** 93,024, **Percent:** 4.8; **Per capita personal income (NECMA) 2001:** $39,873[2]
Chamber of Commerce: Greater Boston Chamber of Commerce, 72 State St., 2nd Fl., Boston, Mass. 02109

1. Metropolitan area. 2. Boston–Worcester–Lawrence–Lowell–Brockton, Mass.–N.H.

Boston is the state capital, the seat of Suffolk County, and the largest city in Massachusetts. It is located in the eastern part of the state on Massachusetts Bay. It was incorporated as a city in 1822. No city in the U.S. is richer in historical associations than Boston, and no city has retained more of its original buildings as memorials to America's past.

The first European settler was Rev. William Blackstone, who arrived in 1623, just three years after the Pilgrims had landed at Plymouth in 1620. He was joined by Puritans from England in 1630. They named their new town Boston, after the former home of many of them in Lincolnshire, England. Fourteen years later, the pioneer Bostonians set aside the first public park in the U.S.—the Boston Common. The following year, 1635, they opened the first free public school in America. Today, the Boston area is home to 68 colleges and universities.

Boston is a major industrial, financial, and educational hub and has one of the finest ports in the world. The city's banking and financial services, insurance, and real estate sectors continue to drive Boston's economy. Boston is also a leading city in health care, with 25 inpatient hospitals and numerous community health centers. The city's unique cultural and historic heritage makes it a center of tourism, and its hotel industry ranks among the highest in the nation in occupancy. Boston's other businesses are in high technology, biotechnology, software, and electronics.

The city's tourist attractions include Faneuil Hall Marketplace, the JFK Library and Museum, the Museum of Fine Arts, the New England Aquarium, the USS *Constitution,* and many historic buildings and neighborhoods.

Famous natives: Samuel Adams, patriot; Louisa May Alcott, author; John Singleton Copley, painter; Ralph Waldo Emerson, philosopher and poet; Arthur Fiedler, conductor; Benjamin Franklin, statesman and scientist; Edward Everett Hale, clergyman and author; Oliver Wendell Holmes, Supreme Court justice; Winslow Homer, painter; Joseph P. Kennedy, financier; Jack Lemmon, actor; Robert Lowell, poet; Edgar Allan Poe, writer; Paul Revere, patriot and silversmith; John L. Sullivan, boxer; Barbara Walters, TV journalist.

Charlotte, N.C.

Mayor: Pat McCrory (to Nov. 2003)
2000 census population (rank): 540,828 (26); **% change:** 36.6; **Male:** 264,978 (49.0%); **Female:** 275,850 (51.0%); **White:** 315,061 (58.3%); **Black:** 176,964 (32.7%); **American Indian and Alaska Native:** 1,863 (0.3%); **Asian:** 18,418 (3.4%); **Other race:** 19,242 (3.6%); **Two or more races:** 8,997 (1.7%); **Hispanic/Latino:** 39,800 (7.4%). **2000 percent population 18 and over:** 75.3%; **65 and over:** 8.8%; **median age:** 32.7.
Land area: 242 sq mi. (627 sq km); **Alt.:** 765 ft.
Avg. daily temp.: Jan., 39.3° F; July, 79.3° F
Churches: Protestant, over 500; Roman Catholic, 13; Jewish, 3; Greek Orthodox, 1; **City-owned parks and parkways:** 130; **Radio stations:** AM, 10; FM, 19; **Television stations:** 6 commercial; 1 PBS
Civilian Labor Force (MSA) 2002: 859,919[1]; **Unemployed:** 53,957[1], **Percent:** 6.3[1]; **Per capita personal income (MSA) 2001:** $31,526[1]
Chamber of Commerce: Charlotte Chamber, P.O. Box 32785, Charlotte, N.C., 28232

1. Charlotte–Gastonia–Rock Hill, N.C.–S.C.

Charlotte, North Carolina's largest city and the seat of Mecklenburg County, is located in the southern part of the state near the South Carolina border. It was named for King George III of England's wife, Charlotte Sophia of Mecklenburg-Strelitz.

Settled about 1750, Charlotte was incorporated as a city in 1768 and made the county seat in 1774. From 1800 to 1848, Charlotte was the center of U.S. gold production. A branch of the U.S. mint operated there from 1837 to 1913. Charlotte was a leading Confederate city during the Civil War and was the last meeting place of the full Confederate cabinet.

Charlotte is the second-largest banking center in the United States, and two of the nation's top banks, Wachovia and Bank of America, are headquartered there. Other major employers are the education, health care, government, technology, and communications sectors. The city is a hub for US Airways.

Charlotte is the home of the University of North Carolina at Charlotte (1946) as well as the Carolina Panthers (football) and Lowe's Motor Speedway.

Famous natives: Romare Bearden, artist; Billy Graham, evangelist; Charles Gwathmey, architect; Hamilton Jordan, government official; Randolph Scott, actor.

Chicago, Ill.

Mayor: Richard M. Daley (to April 2007)
2000 census population (rank): 2,896,016 (3); **% change:** 4.0; **Male:** 1,405,107 (48.5%); **Female:** 1,490,909 (51.5%); **White:** 1,215,315 (42.0%); **Black:** 1,065,009 (36.8%); **American Indian and Alaska Native:** 10,290 (0.4%); **Asian:** 125,974 (4.3%); **Other race:** 393,203 (13.6%); **Two or more races:** 84,437 (2.9%); **Hispanic/Latino:** 753,644 (26.0%). **2000 percent population 18 and over:** 73.8%; **65 and over:** 10.3%; **median age:** 31.5.
Land area: 227 sq mi. (588 sq km); **Alt.:** Highest, 672 ft.; lowest, 578.5 ft.
Avg. daily temp.: Jan., 22.4° F; July, 75.1° F
Churches: Protestant, 850; Roman Catholic, 252; Jewish, 51; **City-owned parks:** 551; **Radio stations:** AM, 21; FM, 37; **Television stations:** 31
Civilian Labor Force (PMSA) 2002: 4,277,052; **Unemployed:** 287,378, **Percent:** 6.7; **Per capita personal income (PMSA) 2001:** $36,624
Chamber of Commerce: Chicagoland Chamber of Commerce, One IBM Plaza, 330 N. Wabash, Suite 2800, Chicago, Ill. 60611

Chicago is the largest city in Illinois and the seat of Cook County. It stretches for 22 mi along the southwest shore of Lake Michigan in the northeast part of the state.

The first white men known to have visited the region were Louis Joliet and Jacques Marquette in 1673. The first permanent white settler was John Kinzie, who is sometimes called the Father of Chicago. He took over a trading post in 1796 that had been established in 1791 by Jean-Baptiste Point du Sable, a black fur trapper. Fort Dearborn, a blockhouse and stockade, was built in 1804 but was evacuated in 1812, at which time more than half of its garrison was massacred by Potawatomi and Ottawa Indians loyal to the British.

The name Chicago is thought to come from an Algonquian word meaning "onion" or "skunk."

Laid out in 1830, Chicago was incorporated as a village in 1833 and as a city in 1837. In the Great Chicago Fire of 1871, an area of the city about 4 mi long and nearly a mile wide—more than two thousand acres—was totally destroyed. However, much of the city, including the railroads and stockyards, survived intact, and from the ashes of the old wooden structures there arose more modern constructions in steel and stone.

Today, Chicago is a major Great Lakes port and the commercial, financial, industrial, and cultural center of the Midwest. The manufacturing industries dominate the wholesale and retail trade, and trade in agricultural commodities is important to the economy. The Chicago Board of Trade is the largest agricultural futures market in the world.

Among Chicago's many attractions are the Art Institute of Chicago, the Field Museum of Natural History, the Jane Addams–Hull House Museum, Navy Pier, and numerous architectural landmarks such as the Sears Tower and Frank Lloyd Wright's Robie House.

Famous natives: Jack Benny, comedian; Edgar Rice Burroughs, author; Raymond Chandler, author; Hillary Rodham Clinton, U.S. senator, lawyer, and former first lady; Michael Crichton, author; Walt Disney, filmmaker; John Dos Passos, author; Bobby Fischer, chess player; Bob Fosse, choreographer and director; Benny Goodman, clarinetist; Dorothy Hamill, figure skater; Quincy Jones, composer; Gene Krupa, drummer; David Mamet, playwright; Bob Newhart, comedian; Kim Novak, actress; Donald O'Connor, actor; William L. Shirer, journalist and historian; Gloria Swanson, actress; Melvin Van Peebles, playwright; Alfred Wallenstein, conductor; Robin Williams, comedian and actor; Robert Young, actor.

Cleveland, Ohio

Mayor: Jane Campbell (to Jan. 2006)
2000 census population (rank): 478,403 (33); **% change:** –5.4; **Male:** 226,550 (47.4%); **Female:** 251,853 (52.6%); **White:** 198,510 (41.5%); **Black:** 243,939 (51.0%); **American Indian and Alaska Native:** 1,458 (0.3%); **Asian:** 6,444 (1.3%); **Other race:** 17,173 (3.6%); **Two or more races:** 10,701 (2.2%); **Hispanic/Latino:** 34,728 (7.3%). **2000 percent population 18 and over:** 71.5%; **65 and over:** 12.5%; **median age:** 33.0.
Land area: 78 sq mi. (202 sq km); **Alt.:** Highest, 1048 ft.; lowest, 573 ft.
Avg. daily temp.: Jan., 24.8° F; July, 71.9° F
Churches [1]: Protestant, 980; Roman Catholic, 187; Jewish, 31; Eastern Orthodox, 22; **City-owned parks:** 41 (1,930 ac.); **Radio stations:** AM, 9; FM, 19; **Television stations:** 22
Civilian Labor Force (PMSA) 2002: 1,113,034[1]; **Unemployed:** 72,688[1], **Percent:** 6.5[1]; **Per capita personal income (PMSA) 2001:** $31,807[1]
Chamber of Commerce: Greater Cleveland Growth Association, 200 Tower City Center, Cleveland, Ohio 44113

1. Cleveland–Lorain–Elyria, Ohio.

Cleveland is the second-largest city in Ohio and the seat of Cuyahoga County. It is located in the northeast part of the state on Lake Erie.

In the colonial era, the Cleveland area was known as the Connecticut Western Reserve, part of a land grant made to Connecticut by King Charles II in 1662. The city was founded in 1796 by Gen. Moses Cleaveland, who was the head surveyor of the Connecticut Land Company. This company had bought 3 million acres in what is now northern Ohio. A permanent settlement was founded in 1799, named after the general, and the spelling was shortened to Cleveland. The city was incorporated in 1836.

Cleveland's industrial growth was stimulated by the opening of the Ohio and Erie canals in 1832 and, later, by the advent of the Civil War, with the increasing demand for machinery, railroad equipment, ships, and other items. Today, the port of Cleveland is the largest overseas general cargo port on Lake Erie.

Greater Cleveland has long been famous as a durable goods manufacturing area. Following the national trend, however, Cleveland has been shifting to a more services-based economy. Greater Cleveland is a world corporate center for leading national and multinational companies in industries ranging from transportation, insurance, retailing, and utilities, to commercial banking and finance.

The city's cultural attractions include the Cleveland Museum of Art and the Cleveland Orchestra, one of the country's most highly acclaimed symphony orchestras. Jacobs Field, a new major league ballpark, and the Rock & Roll Hall of Fame also draw thousands of visitors to the city.

Famous natives: Jim Backus, actor; Drew Carey, actor and comedian; Dorothy Dandridge, actress; Ruby Dee, actress; Phil Donahue, talk-show host; Joel Grey, actor; Arsenio Hall, talk-show host; Margaret Hamilton, actress; Philip Johnson, architect; Henry Mancini, composer; Burgess Meredith, actor; Paul Newman, actor; Carl Stokes, jurist.

Colorado Springs, Colo.

Mayor: Lionel Rivera (to April 2007)
2000 census population (rank): 360,890 (48); **% change:** 28.4; **Male:** 178,469 (49.5%); **Female:** 182,421 (50.5%); **White:** 291,095 (80.7%); **Black:** 23,677 (6.6%); **American Indian and Alaska Native:** 3,175 (0.9%); **Asian:** 10,179 (2.8%); **Other race:** 18,091 (5.0%); **Two or more races:** 13,909 (3.9%); **Hispanic/Latino:** 43,330 (12.0%). **2000 percent population 18 and over:** 73.5%; **65 and over:** 9.6%; **median age:** 33.6.
Land area: 186 sq mi. (482 sq km); **Alt.:** 6,035 ft.
Avg. daily temp.: Jan., 28.8° F; July, 70.8° F
Churches: Protestant, 400+; Roman Catholic, 20; Jewish, 3; others, **City parks and playgrounds:** 156 (10,762 ac.); **Radio stations:** AM, 7; FM, 17; **Television stations:** 7
Civilian Labor Force (MSA) 2002: 279,833; **Unemployed:** 18,354, **Percent:** 6.6; **Per capita personal income (MSA) 2001:** $29,280
Chamber of Commerce: Colorado Springs Chamber of Commerce, 2 N. Cascade Ave., Suite 110, Colorado Springs, Colo. 80903

Colorado Springs is the second-largest city in Colorado, after Denver. It is the seat of El Paso County, making up about three-quarters of the county's population. It is located on the edge of the Rocky Mountains, with Pikes Peak (14,110 ft) towering beside it to the west. To the east begin the Great Plains.

The city was founded in 1871. Gen. William Jackson Palmer, a Pennsylvania-born Civil War veteran, came across the scenic spot in his railroad travels and was inspired to begin a new resort community there. The subsequent development of Colorado Springs was influenced in part by an influx of English tourists later in the 1870s and by the discovery of gold in nearby Cripple Creek in the 1890s. Millionaire businessmen and philanthropists, such as Spencer Penrose, Charles Tutt, and Winfield Scott Stratton, helped to establish the city's infrastructure and shape its popularity as a tourist destination.

During World War II, Colorado Springs sold a large amount of land just south of the city to the military. The U.S. Army established Fort Carson as a training facility. The military presence in Colorado Springs continued to grow with the establishment of the U.S. Air Force Academy there in the 1950s, and later, the construction of Peterson Air Force Base, Falcon Air Force Base, and Cheyenne Mountain Air Force Base. The bases are all home to space command centers (with Cheyenne Mountain housing the headquarters for the North American Aerospace Defense Command [NORAD]) and have collectively earned Colorado Springs its national reputation as the leading center for military space operations.

The city's economy is still based heavily on tourism, although in more recent years, Colorado Springs has gained a strong foothold in the electronics, high-technology, and manufacturing industries. The city is the headquarters of the U.S. Olympic Committee and Olympic Training Center facility.

Famous natives: Bert Andrews, journalist; Kelly Bishop, actress; Spring Byington, actress; Lon Chaney, actor; Marjorie Daw, actress; Marceline Day, actress; Rich "Goose" Gossage, baseball player; Helen Hunt Jackson, writer and poet; Chase Masterson, actress; Sherry Stringfield, actress.

Columbus, Ohio

Mayor: Michael B. Coleman (to Nov. 2003)
2000 census population (rank): 711,470 (15); **% change:** 12.4; **Male:** 345,878 (48.6%); **Female:** 365,592 (51.4%); **White:** 483,332 (67.9%); **Black:** 174,065 (24.5%); **American Indian and Alaska Native:** 2,090 (0.3%); **Asian:** 24,495 (3.4%); **Other race:** 8,292 (1.2%); **Two or more races:** 18,829 (2.6%); **Hispanic/Latino:** 17,471 (2.5%). **2000 percent population 18 and over:** 75.8%; **65 and over:** 8.9%; **median age:** 30.6.
Land area: 210 sq mi. (544 sq km); **Alt.:** Highest, 902 ft.; lowest, 702 ft.
Avg. daily temp.: Jan., 26.4° F; July, 73.2° F
Churches: Protestant, 436; Roman Catholic, 62; Jewish, 5; Other, 8; **City-owned parks:** 203 (12,891 ac.); **Radio stations:** AM, 10; FM, 16; **Television stations:** 9 commercial, 3 PBS
Civilian Labor Force (MSA) 2002: 882,860; **Unemployed:** 38,958, **Percent:** 4.4; **Per capita personal income (MSA) 2001:** $31,343
Chamber of Commerce: Columbus Area Chamber of Commerce, 37 N. High St., Columbus, Ohio 43215

Columbus, the largest city in Ohio, is the state capital and the seat of Franklin County. It is located in central Ohio on the Scioto River.

The first structures near the site of downtown Columbus were earthen mounds constructed by Indian tribes known as Mound Builders. Native Americans lived undisturbed in Central Ohio until the 1700s, when the first white explorers entered the Midwest. The first permanent white settlement in the area was founded by a surveyor from Kentucky, Lucas Sullivant, in 1797 and was named Franklinton. The state capital was laid out nearby in 1812 and named after Christopher Columbus. It became the capital in 1816. Columbus was chartered as a city in 1834 and annexed Franklinton in 1870. The city's growth was stimulated by the development of transportation facilities—a feeder to the Ohio Canal completed in 1832, the National Road in 1833, and the arrival of the railroad in 1850.

Columbus is a port of entry and a major commercial, distribution, and cultural center. It is the seat of Ohio State University (1870). The city has enjoyed steady growth over the years due to its economic diversity, and no single activity dominates the economy.

Famous natives: Warner Baxter, actor; George Bellows, painter; Michael Feinstein, singer and pianist; Eileen Heckart, actress; Jack Nicklaus, golfer; Tom Poston, actor; Eddie Rickenbacker, aviator; Arthur M. Schlesinger, historian; James Thurber, writer and cartoonist; Nancy Wilson, singer.

Dallas, Tex.

Mayor: Laura Miller (to May 2007)
City Manager: Teodoro J. Benavides
2000 census population (rank): 1,188,580 (8); **% change:** 18.0; **Male:** 598,991 (50.4%); **Female:** 589,589 (49.6%); **White:** 604,209 (50.8%); **Black:** 307,957 (25.9%); **American Indian and Alaska Native:** 6,472 (0.5%); **Asian:** 32,118 (2.7%); **Other race:** 204,883 (17.2%); **Two or more races:** 32,351 (2.7%); **Hispanic/Latino:** 422,587 (35.6%). **2000 percent population 18 and over:** 73.4%; **65 and over:** 8.6%; **median age:** 30.5.
Land area: 343 sq mi. (888 sq km); **Alt.:** Highest, 750 ft.; lowest, 375 ft.
Avg. daily temp.: Jan., 44.6° F; July, 85.9° F
Churches: 1,974 (in Dallas Co.); **City-owned parks:** 406 (22,743 ac.); **Radio stations:** AM, 19; FM, 30; **Television stations:** 10 commercial, 1 PBS
Civilian Labor Force (PMSA) 2002: 2,038,627; **Unemployed:** 145,274, **Percent:** 7.1; **Per capita personal income (PMSA) 2001:** $34,697
Chamber of Commerce: Greater Dallas Chamber of Commerce, 700 N. Pearl St., Ste. 1200, Dallas, Tex. 75201

Dallas is the second-largest city in Texas and the seat of Dallas County. It is situated 185 mi northeast of Austin on the Trinity River near the junction of its three forks.

Dallas was first settled by Tennessee lawyer John Neely Bryan as a trading post on the Trinity River in 1841. Many historians believe that Bryan named the city after George Mifflin Dallas, vice president under James K. Polk, but there is no official agreement on this. It was incorporated as a town in 1856 and as a city in 1871. Located in the chief cotton-producing region of Texas, the city developed as a cotton market in the 1870s.

The economy is highly diversified, and the city is the leading commercial, marketing, and industrial center of the southwest. The insurance business is important, and the service sector has experienced rapid growth. Dallas is also a popular tourist and convention city.

Famous natives: Tex Avery, animator and director; Robby Benson, actor; Ernie Banks, baseball player; Bebe Daniels, actress; Linda Darnell, actress; Lee Elder, golfer; Morgan Fairchild, actress; Trini Lopez, singer; Aaron Spelling, producer; Stephen Stills, singer; Sharon Tate, actress; Lee Trevino, golfer.

Denver, Colo.

Mayor: John Hickenlooper (to June 30, 2007)
2000 census population (rank): 554,636 (25); **% change:** 18.6; **Male:** 280,207 (50.5%); **Female:** 274,429 (49.5%); **White:** 362,180 (65.3%); **Black:** 61,649 (11.1%); **American Indian and Alaska Native:** 7,290 (1.3%); **Asian:** 15,611 (2.8%); **Other race:** 86,464 (15.6%); **Two or more races:** 20,794 (3.7%); **Hispanic/Latino:** 175,704 (31.7%); **2000 percent population 18 and over:** 78.0%; **65 and over:** 11.3%; **median age:** 33.1.
Land area: 153 sq mi. (396 sq km); **Alt.:** Highest, 5,494 ft.; lowest, 5,140 ft.
Avg. daily temp.: Jan., 29.7° F; July, 73.5° F
Churches[1]: Protestant, 859; Roman Catholic, 60; Jewish, 13; **City-owned parks:** 205 (4,166 ac.); **City-owned mountain parks:** 40 (13,600 ac.); **Radio stations[1]:** AM, 23; FM, 20; **Television stations[1]:** 10
Civilian Labor Force (PMSA) 2002: 1,215,905; **Unemployed:** 71,657, **Percent:** 5.9; **Per capita personal income (PMSA) 2001:** $38,513
Chamber of Commerce: Denver Metro Chamber of Commerce, 1445 Market Street, Denver, Colo. 80202

1. Metropolitan area.

Denver is the largest city in Colorado, the state capital, and the seat of Denver County. It lies at the foot of the Rocky Mountains at the junction of the South Platte River and Cherry Creek.

The city was born in 1858, when gold was discovered in the sands of Cherry Creek, at first just a tough village of cabins, shacks, and tents. It was incorporated as a city in 1861 and became the territorial capital in 1867. The city is named for James W. Denver, governor of the Kansas Territory, which included part of Colorado. The city prospered following the opening of the famous gold and silver mines of the 1870s and 1880s.

Today, Denver is an important communications, transportation, manufacturing, and agribusiness hub. Telecommunications and biomedical technology are two of the largest industries; construction, real estate, and retail trade are among the fastest-growing industries. The city is also home to many environmental organizations, including federal government agencies such as the Environmental Protection Agency and the National Oceanic and Atmospheric Administration.

Denver International Airport, the first major new airport constructed in the U.S. in 21 years, opened to passenger traffic in 1995. At 53 sq mi, it is the largest airport in North America.

The city's tourist attractions include the Denver Zoo, the Six Flags Elitch Gardens amusement park, the Red Rocks Amphitheatre, the Coors Brewery, and nearby Rocky Mountain National Park.

Famous natives: Tim Allen, comedian and actor; Ward Bond, actor; Douglas Fairbanks, Sr., actor; John Hart, newsman; Pat Hingle, actor; Ted Mack, TV host; Barbara Rush, actress; Alan K. Simpson, U.S. senator; Paul Whiteman, bandleader; Don Wilson, announcer.

Detroit, Mich.

Mayor: Kwame Kilpatrick (to Jan. 2006)
2000 census population (rank): 951,270 (10); **% change:** –7.5; **Male:** 448,319 (47.1%); **Female:** 502,951 (52.9%); **White:** 116,599 (12.3%); **Black:** 775,772 (81.6%); **American Indian and Alaska Native:** 3,140 (0.3%); **Asian:** 9,268 (1.0%); **Other race:** 24,199 (2.5%); **Two or more races:** 22,041 (2.3%); **Hispanic/Latino:** 47,167 (5.0%). **2000 percent population 18 and over:** 68.9%; **65 and over:** 10.4%; **median age:** 30.9.
Land area: 139 sq mi. (360 sq km); **Alt.:** Highest, 685 ft.; lowest, 574 ft.
Avg. daily temp.: Jan., 24.7° F; July, 74.2° F
Churches[1]: Protestant, 1,165; Roman Catholic, 89; Jewish, 2; **City-owned parks:** 56 parks (3,843 ac.); 393 sites (5,838 ac.); **Radio stations:** AM, 27; FM, 30 (includes 3 in Windsor, Ont.); **Television stations:** 8[2] (includes 1 in Windsor, Ont.)
Civilian Labor Force (PMSA) 2002: 2,220,245; **Unemployed:** 136,871, **Percent:** 6.2; **Per capita personal income (PMSA) 2001:** $34,035
Chamber of Commerce: Detroit Regional Chamber of Commerce, One Woodward Avenue, P.O. Box 33840, Detroit MI 48232-0840

1. Six-county metropolitan area. 2. Within four counties of Metro Detroit.

Detroit, the largest city in Michigan, is situated in the southeast part of the state on the Detroit River. The seat of Wayne County, Detroit was incorporated as a city in 1815 and reincorporated in 1824.

Detroit is the oldest city of any size west of the seaboard colonies, having been founded by Antoine de la Mothe Cadillac on July 24, 1701, more than a century before Chicago was founded. The French were the first settlers, and they gave the city its name from their word meaning "strait," referring to the 27-mile-long Detroit River, which connects Lake Erie and Lake St. Clair. The river forms part of the international boundary, and marks the only point where Canada lies directly south of U.S. territory.

Because of its strategic location, Detroit was fought over by the French, the British, and the Indians during the French and Indian Wars. It was the headquarters for the British forces in the Northwest Territory during the American Revolutionary War.

The first steam vessel, the *Walk-in-the-Water*, made its appearance on the Great Lakes in 1818, and Detroit was the western terminus for most of its voyages from Buffalo. Its link to all the important cities on the Great Lakes made it a major exporting center.

Detroit is one of the largest manufacturing cities in the U.S. and is the center of the automobile manufacturing industry, which has experienced a decline due to foreign competition in the past decade. The health and medical care sector is important to the economy, and employment in the finance, insurance, and real-estate industries has inched up in the Detroit metropolitan area since the early 1990s.

Famous natives: Anita Baker, singer; Sonny Bono, congressman and singer; Ralph Bunche, statesman; Ellen Burstyn, actress; Francis Ford Coppola, director; Aretha Franklin, singer; Casey Kasem, radio personality; Charles Lindbergh, aviator; Madonna, singer and actress; John Mitchell, former U.S. attorney general; Harry Morgan, actor; Rosa Parks, activist; George Peppard, actor; Gilda Radner, comedian; Della Reese, singer; Smokey Robinson, singer; Sugar Ray Robinson, boxer; Diana Ross, singer; George C. Scott, actor; Tom Selleck, actor; Lily Tomlin, comedian and actress; Margaret Whiting, singer.

El Paso, Tex.

Mayor: Joe Wardy (to May 2005)
2000 census population (rank): 563,662 (23); **% change:** 9.4; **Male:** 267,651 (47.5%); **Female:** 296,011 (52.5%); **White:** 413,061 (73.3%); **Black:** 17,586 (3.1%); **American Indian and Alaska Native:** 4,601 (0.8%); **Asian:** 6,321 (1.1%); **Other race:** 102,320 (18.2%); **Two or more races:** 19,190 (3.4%); **Hispanic/Latino:** 431,875 (76.6%). **2000 percent population 18 and over:** 69.0%; **65 and over:** 10.7%; **median age:** 31.1
Land area: 249 sq mi. (645 sq km); **Alt.:** 4,000 ft.
Avg. daily temp.: Jan., 42.8° F; July, 82.3° F
Churches: Protestant, 320; Roman Catholic, 39; Jewish, 3; others, 20; **City-owned parks:** 145 (2,150 ac.)[1]; **Radio Stations:** AM, 18; FM, 17; **Television stations:** 6
Civilian Labor Force (MSA) 2002: 292,494; **Unemployed:** 25,345, **Percent:** 8.7; **Per capita personal income (MSA) 2001:** $19,186
Chamber of Commerce: Greater El Paso Chamber of Commerce, Hispanic Chamber of Commerce, Black Chamber of Commerce, and Korean Chamber of Commerce, 10 Civic Center Plaza, El Paso, Tex. 79944

1. Includes 129 developed and 16 undeveloped parks.

El Paso, the fifth-largest city in Texas and the seat of El Paso County, is located in the far western part of the state on the north bank of the Rio Grande, opposite the Mexican city of Ciudad Juárez on the south bank.

On April 30, 1598, Juan de Oñate took formal possession of the area for King Philip II of Spain. Subsequently he crossed the Rio Grande near a site west of present downtown El Paso, which he called "El Paso del Rio del Norte," meaning the crossing of the river—the first use of the name "El Paso." In 1659, the mission of Nuestra Señora de Guadalupe was founded on a site that is present-day downtown Ciudad Juárez; the mission is still in use today. In 1682, Spanish colonists from Mexico founded the settlement of Ysleta on the site of the present-day city. However, it wasn't until 1827 that the first permanent settlement at El Paso was established by Juan María Ponce de León. The city's real growth started with the arrival of the Southern Pacific Railroad in 1881. El Paso was incorporated as a city in 1873.

In 1888, Mexico changed the name of Paso del Norte to Ciudad Juárez in honor of Benito Juárez. Later, in 1967, the U.S. agreed to cede a long-disputed part of El Paso to Mexico due to changes in the course of the Rio Grande, which forms the international boundary between the two countries. El Paso and its sister city of Ciudad Juárez across the U.S./Mexico border are inexorably joined by culture and economy. El Paso and Juárez make up the largest international metroplex in the world.

El Paso is an important port of entry to the U.S. from Mexico. The high technology, medical device manufacturing, plastics, refining, automotive, food processing, and defense-related industries are important to the economy. El Paso's service sector has experienced healthy growth since the 1980s. El Paso is also a major tourist resort.

Famous natives: Manuel Acosta, artist; Don Bluth, animation director; Vicki Carr, singer; Jose Cisneros, artist; Sam Donaldson, newsman; Albert Fall, government official; Judith Ivey, actress; Guy Kibbee, actor; Sandra Day O'Connor, Supreme Court justice; Debbie Reynolds, actress; Irene Ryan, actress.

Fort Worth, Tex.

Mayor: Mike Moncrief (to May 2005)
City Manager: Gary W. Jackson
2000 census population (rank): 534,694 (27); **% change:** 19.5; **Male:** 263,720 (49.3%); **Female:** 270,974 (50.7%); **White:** 319,159 (59.7%); **Black:** 108,310 (20.3%); **American Indian and Alaska Native:** 3,144 (0.6%); **Asian:** 14,105 (2.6%); **Other race:** 75,100 (14.0%); **Two or more races:** 14,535 (2.7%); **Hispanic/Latino:** 159,368 (29.8%). **2000 percent population 18 and over:** 71.7%; **65 and over:** 9.6%; **median age:** 30.9.
Land area: 293 sq mi. (759 sq km); **Alt.:** Highest, 780 ft.; lowest, 520 ft.
Avg. daily temp.: Jan., 43.4° F; July, 85.3° F
Churches: 1,032, representing 72 denominations; **City-owned parks:** 222 (10,380 ac.); **Radio stations**[1]**:** AM, 29; FM, 48; **Television stations:** 13
Civilian Labor Force (PMSA) 2002: 957,996[2]; **Unemployed:** 58,389[2], **Percent:** 6.1[2]; **Per capita personal income (PMSA) 2001:** $30,230[2]
Chamber of Commerce: Fort Worth Chamber of Commerce, 777 Taylor Street, Suite 900, Fort Worth, Tex. 76102

1. Dallas–Fort Worth area. 2. Fort Worth–Arlington, Tex.

Fort Worth, seat of Tarrant County, is situated in the north-central part of Texas on the Trinity River.

The city was founded by Maj. Ripley Arnold in 1849 as a military outpost on the Trinity River to protect settlers moving westward from frequent Indian attacks. It was named after Gen. William J. Worth, the commander of the Texas army. Fort Worth was incorporated in 1873. Its growth was stimulated in the 1870s by its proximity to the Chisholm cattle trail. It prospered as a meat-packing and shipping center when the Texas and Pacific Railway arrived in 1876 and later experienced a new boom when oil was discovered nearby in 1917. The establishment of military installations in the area during both world wars also spurred the economy.

Fort Worth has traditionally been a diverse center of manufacturing and is not dependent on the oil or financial sectors. The city's industries range from clothing and food products to jet fighters, helicopters, computers, pharmaceuticals, and plastics. Fort Worth is a national leader in aviation products, electronic equipment, and refrigeration equipment. It is home to a multitude of major corporate headquarters, offices, and distribution centers.

Famous natives: Robert Bass, financier; Mark Brooks, golfer; Betty Buckley, singer and actress; Kate Capshaw, actress; Ornette Coleman, composer; Sandra Haynie, golfer; Patricia Highsmith, writer; Spanky McFarland, actor; R. Bruce Merrifield, Nobelist in chemistry; Roger Miller, singer; Fess Parker, actor; Bill Paxton, actor; Rex Reed, critic; Johnny Rutherford, auto racer; Liz Smith, columnist.

Fresno, Calif.

Mayor: Alan Autry (to Jan. 2005)
City Manager: Daniel G. Hobbs
2000 census population (rank): 427,652 (37); **% change:** 20.7; **Male:** 210,107 (49.1%); **Female:** 217,545 (50.9%); **White:** 214,556 (50.2%); **Black:** 35,763 (8.4%); **American Indian and Alaska Native:** 6,763 (1.6%); **Asian:** 48,028 (11.2%); **Other race:** 99,898 (23.4%); **Two or more races:** 22,061 (5.2%); **Hispanic/Latino:** 170,520 (39.9%). **2000 percent population 18 and over:** 67.1%; **65 and over:** 9.3%; **median age:** 28.5.
Land area: 104 sq mi. (269 sq km); **Alt.:** 328 ft.
Avg. daily temp.: Jan., 45.7° F; July, 81.9° F

Churches: 450 (approximate); **City-owned parks:** 38 (690 ac.); **Radio stations:** AM, 11[1]; FM, 13[1]; Bilingual 1; **Television stations:** 8[1]
Civilian Labor Force (PMSA) 2002: 456,782; **Unemployed:** 64,395, **Percent:** 14.1; **Per capita personal income (MSA) 2001:** $21,463
Chamber of Commerce: Fresno Chamber of Commerce, 2331 Fresno St., Fresno, Calif. 93721

1. Metropolitan area.

Fresno is located in central California, 184 mi southeast of San Francisco and 222 mi northwest of Los Angeles. It is the seat of Fresno County. Fresno was incorporated as a city in 1885.

Fresno began as a station for the Central Pacific Railroad in 1872 and was made the seat of Fresno County in 1874. The city's name is Spanish for the ash trees that the early explorers found in the area.

Fresno is a leading agribusiness hub, with 250 different crops produced by 7,500 farmers on 1.9 million irrigated acres, worth $3 billion a year. Fresno County's top agricultural products are grapes, cotton, tomatoes, cattle and calves, and turkeys.

The city is also a distribution and manufacturing center. Its diverse industries include agricultural chemicals, farm equipment, canned fruit and vegetables, clothing, computer software, electric wire, pumps, glass, and plastic products.

Famous natives: Mike Connors, actor; Maynard Dixon, painter; Bruce Furniss, swimmer; Jon Hall, actor; Daryle Lamonica, football player; Sam Peckinpah, director; William Saroyan, novelist; Tom Seaver, baseball player.

Honolulu, Hawaii

Mayor: Jeremy Harris (to Jan. 2005)
2000 census population (rank)[1]: 371,657 (46); **% change:** 1.7; **Male:** 182,628 (49.1%); **Female:** 189,029 (50.9%); **White:** 73,093 (19.7%); **Black:** 6,038 (1.6%); **American Indian and Alaska Native:** 689 (0.2%); **Asian:** 207,588 (55.9%); **Native Hawaiian and Other Pacific Islander:** 25,457 (6.8%); **Other race:** 3,318 (0.9%); **Two or more races:** 55,474 (14.9%); **Hispanic/Latino:** 16,229 (4.4%). **2000 percent population 18 and over:** 80.8%; **65 and over:** 17.8%; **median age:** 39.7
Land area: 85.7 sq mi. (221.9 sq km)[1]; **Alt.:** Highest, 2,013 ft.[1]; lowest, sea level
Avg. daily temp.: Jan., 71.4° F; July, 78.9° F
Churches: Roman Catholic, 39; Buddhist, 51; Jewish, 2; Protestant and others, 402; **City-owned parks[1]:** 2,056 ac.; **Radio stations[1]:** AM, 17; FM, 11; **Television stations[1]:** 12
Civilian Labor Force (MSA) 2002: 412,083[2]; **Unemployed:** 16,014[2], **Percent:** 3.9[2]; **Per capita personal income (MSA) 2001:** $31,115[2]
Chamber of Commerce: Chamber of Commerce of Hawaii, 1132 Bishop St., Suite 402, Honolulu, Hawaii 96813

1. Census Designated Place, approximately Salt Lake to Hawaii Kai. 2. City and county.

Honolulu is the capital and largest city of Hawaii, on the southeast coast of the island of Oahu. The city is legally coextensive with the county of Honolulu, which includes the entire island of Oahu and most of the Northwest Hawaiian Islands, from Nihoa to Kure Atoll, except Midway. The population of Oahu makes up 73% of the state's total population. It is situated in the central Pacific Ocean 2,397 mi west-southwest of San Francisco. Honolulu's name derives from the native words *hono,* meaning "a bay," and *lulu,* meaning "sheltered."

Honolulu's early history was one of turbulence and conflict. One of the last areas on the globe to be explored and exploited by Europeans (it was first visited by British captain James Cook in 1778), Hawaii was subject to strong pressures from many forces, including American missionaries, who arrived in 1820, and opportunistic whalers. These whalers were among those who built Honolulu originally, bringing trade, commerce, and prosperity that led to expansion into the sugar and pineapple industries.

As early as 1814, Russia tried to move in, and Russian soldiers built a bastion at the harbor's edge. The British flag was raised in 1843 and French forces occupied Honolulu in 1849. Each time control was returned to the independent native kingdom without bloodshed. In 1898, a group of Americans completed a project attempted at intervals during the previous 65 years—annexation to the United States. Honolulu was incorporated as a city in 1907.

The Honolulu area was bombed by Japan in a surprise attack on the unprepared U.S. naval base at Pearl Harbor on Dec. 7, 1941. This action forced the United States to enter World War II. "Remember Pearl Harbor" became a famous American wartime slogan.

Hawaiian statehood in 1959 and the viability of commercial air travel to the island brought boom times to Honolulu. Tourism is the city's principal industry, followed by federal defense expenditures and agricultural exports (chiefly pineapples).

Famous natives: Hiram Bingham, explorer; Jean Erdman, dancer and choreographer; Hiram Fong, senator; Daniel Inouye, senator; Duke Kahanamoku, surfer and Olympian swimmer; Bette Midler, actress and singer; Kelly Preston, actress; Louise Morgan Sill, author; Don Stroud, actor; Merlin D. Tuttle, biologist and wildlife photographer.

Houston, Tex.

Mayor: Lee P. Brown (to Dec. 31, 2003)
2000 census population (rank): 1,953,631 (4); **% change:** 19.8; **Male:** 975,551 (49.9%); **Female:** 978,080 (50.1%); **White:** 962,610 (49.3%); **Black:** 494,496 (25.3%); **American Indian and Alaska Native:** 8,568 (0.4%); **Asian:** 103,694 (5.3%); **Other race:** 321,603 (16.5%); **Two or more races:** 61,478 (3.1%); **Hispanic/Latino:** 730,865 (37.4%). **2000 percent population 18 and over:** 72.5%; **65 and over:** 8.4%; **median age:** 30.9.
Land area: 579 sq mi. (1,500 sq km); **Alt.:** Highest, 120 ft.; lowest, sea level
Avg. daily temp.: Jan., 52.2° F; July, 83.5° F
Churches[1]: 1,750; **City-owned parks:** 293 (32,733 ac.); **Radio stations[1]:** AM, 23; FM, 32; **Television stations:** 15 commercial, 1 PBS
Civilian Labor Force (PMSA) 2002: 2,278,017; **Unemployed:** 133,445, **Percent:** 5.9; **Per capita personal income (PMSA) 2001:** $35,872
Chamber of Commerce: Greater Houston Partnership, 1200 Smith, Suite 700, Houston, Tex. 77002-4400

1. Harris County.

Houston, the largest city in Texas and seat of Harris County, is located in the southeast part of the state near the Gulf of Mexico.

Sam Houston was the commander-in-chief of the Texas troops who fought a successful war of rebellion against Mexico, which had been in possession of Texas. On April 21, 1836, Houston's men won a decisive victory in which the Mexican dictator, Gen. Santa Anna, was taken prisoner and forced to sign the treaty that launched the Republic of Texas. In September, a constitution was ratified, and Houston was elected president. The Texas Republic was recognized by the U.S. and by the major European powers. The present city of Houston was incorporated in 1837 and named after Sam Houston; it was the Republic's first capital.

The port of Houston ranks high among U.S. ports in foreign tonnage handled. The city is a major business, financial, science, and technology center. Houston is outstanding in oil and natural-gas production and is the energy capital of the world. It is the home of one of the largest medical facilities in the world—the Texas Medical Center—and the focus of the aerospace industry. The Lyndon B. Johnson Space Center is the nation's headquarters for staffed spaceflight.

Among the city's many visitor attractions are Space Center Houston, the Houston Arboretum and Nature Center, Six Flags AstroWorld, George Ranch Historical Park, the Astrodome baseball stadium, and nearby San Jacinto Battlefield.

Famous natives: Debbie Allen, choreographer; Lance Alworth, football player; Denton Cooley, heart surgeon; Jim Demaret, golfer; Allen Drury, novelist; Shelly Duvall, actress; A. J. Foyt, auto racer; Howard Hughes, industrialist and film producer; Barbara C. Jordan, educator, lawyer, and politician; Barbara Mandrell, singer; Annette O'Toole, actress; Dennis and Randy Quaid, actors; Kenny Rogers, singer; Patrick Swayze, actor and dancer.

Indianapolis, Ind.

Mayor: Bart Peterson (to Dec. 31, 2003)
2000 census population (rank): 781,870 (12); **% change:** 6.7; **Male:** 378,310 (48.4%); **Female:** 403,560 (51.6%); **White:** 540,212 (69.1%); **Black:** 199,412 (25.5%); **American Indian and Alaska Native:** 1,985 (0.3%); **Asian:** 11,161 (1.4%); **Other race:** 15,921 (2.0%); **Two or more races:** 12,857 (1.6%); **Hispanic/Latino:** 30,636 (3.9%). **2000 percent population 18 and over:** 74.3%; **65 and over:** 11.0%; **median age:** 33.5.
Land area: 366 sq mi. (948 sq km); **Alt.:** Highest, 840 ft.; lowest, 700 ft.
Avg. daily temp.: Jan., 25.5 F; July, 75.4° F
Churches[1]: 1,191; **City-owned parks:** 172 (10,174 ac.); **Radio stations[2]:** AM, 8; FM, 17; **Television stations[1]:** 7
Civilian Labor Force (MSA) 2002: 892,570; **Unemployed:** 41,174, **Percent:** 4.6; **Per capita personal income (MSA) 2001:** $31,960
Chamber of Commerce: Indianapolis Chamber of Commerce, 320 N. Meridian St., Indianapolis, Ind. 46204

1. Marion County. 2. Metropolitan area.

Indianapolis, the largest city in Indiana and seat of Marion County, is located in the central part of the state on the West Fork of the White River. Its name derives from combining "Indiana" with "polis," the Greek word for city.

Indianapolis was settled in 1820, and five years later it was chosen as the state capital. It was incorporated as a city in 1832 and reincorporated in 1838. The city's growth began when the railroad reached it in 1847. Toward the end of the 19th century, the discovery of nearby natural gas and the start of the automobile industry hastened its industrial expansion. In 1970, Indianapolis merged with surrounding Marion County.

Indianapolis is at the center of a rich agricultural region and is a major grain and livestock market. It is also a focal point of commerce, transportation, and manufacturing for the region. Some leading industries are electronics, pharmaceuticals, and food processing. The financial sector and service and insurance industries are growing rapidly.

Indianapolis is the site of the world-famous 500-mile automobile race and the Indiana State Fair.

Famous natives: Monte Blue, actor; David Letterman, TV host; Steve McQueen, actor; Jane Pauley, TV newscaster; Booth Tarkington, author; Kurt Vonnegut, Jr., author; Harry Von Zell, announcer; Clifton Webb, actor.

Jacksonville, Fla.

Mayor: John Peyton (to June 30, 2005)
2000 census population (rank): 735,617 (14); **% change:** 15.8; **Male:** 356,284 (48.4%); **Female:** 379,333 (51.6%); **White:** 474,307 (64.5%); **Black:** 213,514 (29.0%); **American Indian and Alaska Native:** 2,474 (0.3%); **Asian:** 20,427 (2.8%); **Other race:** 9,816 (1.3%); **Two or more races:** 14,631 (2.0%); **Hispanic/Latino:** 30,594 (4.2%). **2000 percent population 18 and over:** 73.3%; **65 and over:** 10.3%; **median age:** 33.8.
Land area: 758 sq mi. (1,963 sq km); **Alt.:** Highest, 71 ft.; lowest, sea level
Avg. daily temp.: Jan., 52.4° F; July, 81.6° F
Churches: Protestant, 794; Roman Catholic, 21; Jewish, 5; others, 22; **City-owned parks and playgrounds:** 19 (7,404 ac.); **Radio stations:** AM, 14; FM, 16; **Television stations:** 6 commercial, 1 PBS, 1 religious
Civilian Labor Force (MSA) 2002: 591,156; **Unemployed:** 31,273, **Percent:** 5.3; **Per capita personal income (MSA) 2001:** $29,625
Chamber of Commerce: Jacksonville Area Chamber of Commerce, 3 Independent Dr., Jacksonville, Fla. 32202

Jacksonville, Florida's largest city, is located in Duval County in the northeast corner of Florida, on the banks of the St. Johns River and adjacent to the Atlantic Ocean. It is the largest metropolitan area in northeast Florida and southeast Georgia.

Starting in the 16th century, French, Spanish, and English explorers and colonists were attracted to the region by the St. Johns River. The site was settled by Lewis Hogans in 1816. Jacksonville was laid out in 1822 and was named after Gen. Andrew Jackson, the first military governor of Florida. It was incorporated as a city in 1832.

During the Civil War, much of the city was destroyed by Union forces, who occupied Jacksonville four times. The city was rebuilt and, following the development of its harbor and the railroads, quickly became the transportation hub and leading industrial city in Florida by the 1880s. In 1968, the city and county governments consolidated.

Jacksonville is the leading transportation and distribution hub in the state. However, the strength of the city's economy lies in its broad diversification. The area's economy is balanced among distribution, financial services, biomedical technology, consumer goods, information services, manufacturing, and other industries. Jacksonville has the largest deep-water port in the South Atlantic and is a leading port in the U.S. for automobile imports.

Famous natives: Pat Boone, singer; Judy Canova, comedian; Harold Carmichael, football player; Billy Daniels, vocalist; Storm Davis, athlete; Bob Hayes, athlete; Wanda Hendrix, actress; James Weldon Johnson, author and educator; John Rosamond Johnson, musician and composer; Mark McCumber, pro golfer; Ray Mercer, boxer; Charles "Hoss" Singleton, songwriter; Bill Terry, baseball player and manager; Donnie Van Zant, rock musician; Ronnie Van Zant, rock musician; Leeroy Yarbrough, auto racer.

Kansas City, Mo.

Mayor: Kay Barnes (to April 2007)
City Manager: Wayne Cauthen (apptd. April 2003)
2000 census population (rank): 441,545 (36); **% change:** 1.5; **Male:** 213,141 (48.3%); **Female:** 228,404 (51.7%); **White:** 267,931 (60.7%); **Black:** 137,879 (31.2%); **American Indian and Alaska Native:** 2,122 (0.5%); **Asian:** 8,182 (1.9%); **Other race:** 14,158 (3.2%); **Two or more races:** 10,780 (2.4%); **Hispanic/Latino:** 30,604 (6.9%). **2000 percent population 18 and over:** 74.6%; **65 and over:** 11.7%; **median age:** 34.0.
Land area: 314 sq mi. (813 sq km); **Alt.:** Highest, 1,014 ft.; lowest, 722 ft.
Avg. daily temp.: Jan., 25.7° F; July, 78.5° F
Churches: 1,100 churches of all denominations[1]; **City-owned parks and playgrounds:** 189 (10,647 ac.); **Radio stations[1]:** AM, 14; FM, 19; **Television stations[1]:** 7
Civilian Labor Force (MSA) 2002: 1,002,897[2]; **Unemployed:** 57,388[2], **Percent:** 5.7[2]; **Per capita personal income (MSA) 2001:** $32,693[2]
Chamber of Commerce: Greater Kansas City Chamber of Commerce, 911 Main St., Kansas City, Mo. 64105

1. Metropolitan area. 2. Kansas City, Mo.–Kan.

Kansas City is the largest city in Missouri. It is located in the western part of the state, at the junction of the Missouri and Kansas rivers. Kansas City is located in Jackson, Clay, Platte, and Cass counties.

In 1821, the year Missouri entered the Union, French trader François Chouteau came from St. Louis to establish a trading post on the site of the present city to take advantage of the growing fur trade with the Kansa, Osage, Wyandotte, and other tribes. In 1833, a settlement called Westport Landing was laid out by John Calvin McCoy and developed. The community became the Town of Kansas and was incorporated as a city in 1850 and renamed Kansas City in 1889. The city's name reflects its Native American heritage—its site was within the territory of the Kansa, or Kaw, Indians.

The city grew rapidly in the mid-1880s as the starting point for gold prospectors and settlers heading westward. The coming of the Missouri-Pacific Railroad in 1865 and the spanning of the Missouri River by the Hannibal Bridge in 1869 also contributed to the city's growth. It also prospered as a center for the nation's cattle business.

The Kansas City metropolitan area, once known primarily for agriculture and manufacturing, has expanded its economic base to include strong growth in areas of telecommunications, banking and finance, and the service industry. A transportation hub since the 1800s, the area enjoys a national and regional prominence as a distribution and manufacturing center. Kansas City ranks nationally as first in greeting-card publishing (Hallmark Cards is located there), frozen food storage and distribution, and hard winter-wheat marketing; second in wheat flour production; and third in auto and truck assembly. The area is one of ten federal regional centers, and the federal, state, and local governments are among the top employers. The city is also a regional center for health care.

Famous natives: Robert Altman, director; Edward Asner, actor; Burt Bacharach, composer; Noah and Wallace Beery, actors; Robert Russell Bennett, composer; Jeanne Eagels, actress; Jean Harlow, actress; Ted Shawn, dancer and choreographer; Casey Stengel, baseball player; Virgil Thompson, composer; Tom Watson, golfer.

Las Vegas, Nev.

Mayor: Oscar Goodman (to May 2007)
2000 census population (rank): 478,434 (32); **% change:** 85.2; **Male:** 243,077 (50.8%); **Female:** 235,357 (49.2%); **White:** 334,230 (69.9%); **Black:** 49,570 (10.4%); **American Indian and Alaska Native:** 3,570 (0.7%); **Asian:** 22,879 (4.8%); **Other race:** 46,643 (9.7%); **Two or more races:** 19,397 (4.1%); **Hispanic/Latino:** 112,962 (23.6%); **2000 percent population 18 and over:** 74.1%; **65 and over:** 11.6%; **median age:** 34.5.
Land area: 113 sq mi. (293 sq km); **Alt.:** 2,174 ft.
Avg. daily temp.: Jan., 45.5° F; July, 91.1° F
Churches: over 500 churches and synagogues; **Radio stations:** AM, 4; FM, 8; **Television stations:** 7
Civilian Labor Force (MSA) 2002: 886,049[1]; **Unemployed:** 50,282[1], **Percent:** 5.7[1]; **Per capita personal income (MSA) 2001:** $27,916[1]
Chamber of Commerce: 3720 Howard Hughes Parkway, Las Vegas, NV 89109

1. Las Vegas, Nev.–Ariz.

Las Vegas, seat of Clark County in southeast Nevada, is the largest city in the state and one of the fastest-growing cities in the United States. Between April 1990 and April 2000, the Las Vegas metropolitan area population increased by 83%, growing from 852,737 to 1,563,282.

The area was discovered by Spanish explorers in 1829. The site of Las Vegas ("The Meadows" in Spanish) was originally a watering place for travelers on their way to southern California. It was first settled by Mormons in 1855, who were attracted by its artesian springs. They abandoned their settlement two years later in 1857, and the U.S. Army established Fort Baker there in 1864. In 1867, Las Vegas was detached from the Arizona Territory and joined with Nevada.

The town was established and started to grow with the arrival of the railroad in 1905. However, its growth did not really take off until shortly after 1931, when the Nevada legislature legalized gambling in an effort to lift the state from the Great Depression. The construction of nearby Hoover Dam aided the area economically as well.

The Las Vegas that we know today basically began after World War II, when the idea of large hotels along the brand new "strip" was developed. Las Vegas is the "marriage capital" of America; there are 50 wedding chapels in the city. Tourism and the convention industry are the city's major sources of income. In addition, manufacturing, government, warehousing, and trucking are major sources of employment. Many high-technology companies are also located in Las Vegas.

Las Vegas has a favorable business climate: taxes are relatively low, and there are neither city nor state income taxes. This is because gambling and sales taxes, paid by tourists, have allowed the city and state governments to avoid personal and corporate income taxes.

Popular nearby tourist attractions are Hoover Dam and Lake Mead (the largest man-made lake in the U.S.), Lake Mojave, the Mt. Charleston Recreation Area, Red Rock Canyon, and the Death Valley National Monument.

Famous natives: Andre Agassi, tennis player; Clara Bow, actress; Jack Kramer, tennis player; Phyllis McGuire, singer; Benjamin Siegel, hotel-casino promoter; Orson Welles, actor and producer; Joe Williams, jazz singer.

Long Beach, Calif.

Mayor: Beverly O'Neill (to April 2006)
City Manager: Gerald Miller
2000 census population (rank): 461,522 (34); **% change:** 7.5; **Male:** 226,718 (49.1%); **Female:** 234,804 (50.9%); 1996 est. population breakdown: **White:** 208,410 (45.2%); **Black:** 68,618 (14.9%); **American Indian and Alaska Native:** 3,881 (0.8%); **Asian:** 55,591 (12.0%); **Other race:** 95,107 (20.6%); **Two or more races:** 24,310 (5.3%); **Hispanic/Latino:** 165,092 (35.8%). **2000 percent population 18 and over:** 70.8%; **65 and over:** 9.1%; **median age:** 30.8.
Land area: 50 sq mi. (130 sq km); **Alt.:** Highest, 170 ft.; lowest, sea level
Avg. daily temp.: Jan., 55.9° F; July, 73.1° F
Churches: 236; **City-owned parks:** 58 (plus 5 golf courses); **Radio stations:** AM, 2; FM, 2; **Television stations:** 8 (metro area)
Civilian Labor Force (PMSA) 2002: 4,696,143[1]; **Unemployed:** 318,061[1], **Percent:** 6.8[1]; **Per capita personal income (PMSA) 2001:** $30,611[1]
Chamber of Commerce: Long Beach Area Chamber of Commerce, One World Trade Center, Suite 206, Long Beach, Calif. 90831-0350

1. Los Angeles–Long Beach, Calif.

Long Beach is the fifth-largest city in California and is situated on San Pedro Bay, south of Los Angeles, in Los Angeles County.

The town was laid out and settled in 1881 by developer W. E. Willmore, who sold lots on the site as a seaside resort community called Willmore City. It was renamed Long Beach for its 8½-mile beach in 1884. The city was incorporated in 1888 and reincorporated in 1897.

Long Beach is a major industrial port, ranked second-busiest in the U.S. and tenth-busiest in the world. In addition to international trade through the port, high technology has also been an important economic engine for the Long Beach area. Major technology and aerospace corporations such Gulfstream and Raytheon have large facilities in Long Beach, and Boeing continues to be the top employer, with over 17,000 employees.

Tourism is also important to the economy. Major attractions are the RMS *Queen Mary,* the Aquarium of the Pacific, whale watching tours, and water sports.

Famous natives: Jack Anderson, journalist; Jennifer Bartlett, artist; Barbara Britton, actress; Nicholas Cage, actor; Spike Jones, orchestra leader; Sally Kellerman, actress; Billie Jean King, tennis player; Martha Rae Watson, track star; Heather Watts, dancer.

Los Angeles, Calif.

Mayor: James K. Hahn (to June 2005)
2000 census population (rank): 3,694,820 (2); **% change:** 6.0; **Male:** 1,841,805 (49.8%); **Female:** 1,853,015 (50.2%); **White:** 1,734,036 (46.9%); **Black:** 415,195 (11.2%); **American Indian and Alaska Native:** 29,412 (0.8%); **Asian:** 369,254 (10.0%); **Other race:** 949,720 (25.7%); **Two or more races:** 191,288 (5.2%); **Hispanic/Latino:** 1,719,073 (46.5%). **2000 percent population 18 and over:** 73.4%; **65 and over:** 9.7%; **median age:** 31.6.
Land area: 469 sq mi. (1,215 sq km); **Alt.:** Highest, 5,081 ft.; lowest, sea level
Avg. daily temp.: Jan., 58.3° F; July, 74.3° F
Churches: 2,000 of all denominations; **City-owned parks:** 355 (15,357 ac.); **Radio stations:** AM, 35; FM, 53; **Television stations:** 19
Civilian Labor Force (PMSA) 2002: 4,696,143[1]; **Unemployed:** 318,061[1], **Percent:** 6.8[1]; **Per capita personal income (PMSA) 2001:** $30,611[1]
Chamber of Commerce: Los Angeles Chamber of Commerce, 404 S. Bixel St., Los Angeles, Calif. 90017

1. Los Angeles–Long Beach, Calif.

Los Angeles is the largest city in California and the second-largest urban area in the nation. It is located in the southern part of the state on the Pacific Ocean. It is the seat of Los Angeles County. Geographically, it extends more than 40 mi from the mountains to the sea.

The Spanish explorer Gaspar de Portolá visited the site in 1769. On Sept. 4, 1781, the Mexican provincial governor, Filipe de Neve, founded "El Pueblo de Nuestra Señora la Reina de Los Angeles," meaning "The Village of Our Lady, the Queen of the Angels." The pueblo became the capital of the Mexican province, Alta California, and it was the last place to surrender to the United States at the time of the American occupation in 1847. By the Treaty of Guadalupe Hidalgo in 1848, Mexico ceded California to the United States, and Los Angeles was incorporated as a city in 1850.

The city's phenomenal growth was brought about by its equable climate, which attracted people and industry from all parts of the nation; the development of its citrus-fruit industry; the discovery of oil in the area during the early 1890s; the development of its man-made harbor—its port is one of the busiest in the United States; and the growth of the motion picture industry in the early 20th century. Today, Hollywood is a suburb of Los Angeles.

Los Angeles is a major hub of shipping, manufacturing, industry, and finance, and is world-renowned in the entertainment and communications fields. It is a favorite vacation destination and attracts millions of tourists to the area each year from all over the world. Apart from the movie studios and other landmarks associated with the movie industry, points of interest include the J. Paul Getty Museum, the Los Angeles County Museum of Art, the La Brea Tar Pits (famous for Ice Age fossils), Disneyland (Anaheim), and the Santa Anita and Hollywood racetracks.

Los Angeles County is the nation's largest manufacturing center, and the ports of Los Angeles and Long Beach are second only to New York as the largest customs district in the United States. Major employers in the Los Angeles Five-County area are in the business and management sector. Growth in the key wholesale industries—apparel and textiles, furniture, jewelry, and toys—and the boom in industrial trade were the trend for the region in the 1990s. Other important sectors are health services and international trade and investment. After some lean years, the aerospace industry is making a modest comeback as a result of increased federal defense spending.

Famous natives: Busby Berkeley, choreographer and director; Marge Champion, dancer and choreographer; Jackie Coogan, actor; Jackie Cooper, actor; Linda Fratianne, figure skater; Jodie Foster, actress and director; John Gavin, actor and diplomat; Pancho Gonzalez, tennis player; Cynthia Gregory, ballerina; Jerome Hines, basso; Dustin Hoffman, actor; Theodore Harold Maiman, laser inventor; Marilyn Monroe, actress; Isamu Noguchi, sculptor; Leonard Slotkin, conductor; Duke Snider, baseball player; Adlai E. Stevenson, statesman; Madeleine Stowe, actress; Darryl Strawberry, baseball player.

Memphis, Tenn.

Mayor: W. W. Herenton (to Dec. 2003)
2000 census population (rank): 650,100 (18); **% change:** 6.5; **Male:** 307,643 (47.3%); **Female:** 342,457 (52.7%); **White:** 223,728 (34.4%); **Black:** 399,208 (61.4%); **American Indian and Alaska Native:** 1,217 (0.2%); **Asian:** 9,482 (1.5%); **Other race:** 9,438 (1.5%); **Two or more races:** 6,788 (1.0%); **Hispanic/Latino:** 19,317 (3.0%). **2000 percent population 18 and over:** 72.1%; **65 and over:** 10.9%; **median age:** 31.9.
Land area: 279 sq mi. (723 sq km); **Alt.:** Highest, 417 ft.
Avg. daily temp.: Jan., 39.7° F; July, 82.6° F
Churches: 2000+; **Parks and playgrounds:** 230 (13,291 ac.); **Radio stations:** AM, 17; FM, 25; **Television stations:** 6
Civilian Labor Force (MSA) 2002: 581,588[1]; **Unemployed:** 30,430[1]; **Percent:** 5.2[1]; **Per capita personal income (MSA) 2001:** $30,559[1]
Chamber of Commerce: Memphis Area Chamber of Commerce, P.O. Box 224, Memphis, Tenn. 38103

1. Memphis, Tenn.–Ark.–Miss.

Memphis, the largest city in Tennessee and the seat of Shelby County, is located in the southwest corner of the state, on the Mississippi River near the borders of Arkansas and Mississippi.

The first settlers of Memphis were the Chickasaw Indians, who had a village named Chisca there on the bluffs overlooking the Mississippi River. Hernando de Soto, in 1541, is said to have had his first glimpse of the Mississippi from the site of Memphis; in the next century, Louis Joliet and Jacques Marquette stopped there to trade with the Indians. The French explorer Robert Cavelier, Sieur de La Salle, tried to claim the region for France in 1682 and built Fort Prudhomme on the site.

The area was ceded to the United States by the Chickasaw Indians in 1818. Memphis was officially established in 1819 by three enterprising businessmen from Nashville, James Winchester, John Overton, and future president Andrew Jackson. Jackson named it after the ancient Egyptian city because of its site on the Nile-like Mississippi River. Memphis was incorporated as a city in 1826 and became an important Mississippi River port.

During the Civil War, Memphis was a Confederate military center. In 1862, federal forces won a gunboat battle on the river at Memphis, and General Sherman was able to take the city. After the war, Memphis's population was devastated by several yellow-fever epidemics during the 1870s. As a result, the city fell into decline and went bankrupt, losing its charter in 1879. However, owing to its superior location, the city was able to recover economically, and a new city charter was granted in 1893.

Memphis is known as "America's Distribution Center," serving the northeast, southeast, and southwest regions of the country. The city has one of the country's largest inland ports and is the national headquarters for the Fed Ex air-courier company. Health care and related activities such as medical education and biomedical research are Memphis's largest industries, bringing over $5 billion a year to the local economy. Also important are high-technology communications.

Many of the city's tourist attractions are landmarks associated with the great Memphis music legends, such as Graceland, Elvis Presley's home.

Famous natives: Kathy Bates, actress; Dixie Carter, actress; Rosalind Cash, singer; Abe Fortas, jurist; Aretha Franklin, singer; Morgan Freeman, actor; Al Green, singer; George Hamilton, actor; Anfernee "Penny" Hardaway, basketball player; Isaac Hayes, singer; Hal Holbrook, actor; Benjamin Hooks, organization official; Elvis Presley, singer and actor; Charlie Rich, singer; Cybill Shepherd, actress; Robert Siodmak, director; Fred Smith, business executive; Rufus Thomas, singer; Kemmons Wilson, business executive.

Mesa, Ariz.

Mayor: Keno Hawker (to June 2004)
City Manager: Mike Hutchinson
2000 census population (rank): 396,375 (42); **% change:** 37.6; **Male:** 196,378 (49.5%); **Female:** 199,997 (50.5%); **White:** 323,655 (81.7%); **Black:** 9,977 (2.5%); **American Indian and Alaska Native:** 6,572 (1.7%); **Asian:** 5,917 (1.5%); **Other race:** 38,271 (9.7%); **Two or more races:** 11,051 (2.8%); **Hispanic/Latino:** 78,281 (19.7%). **2000 percent population 18 and over:** 72.7%; **65 and over:** 13.3%; **median age:** 32.0
Land area: 125 sq mi. (324 sq km); **Alt.:** 1,241 ft.
Avg. daily temp.: Jan., 52.9° F; July, 91.2° F
City-owned parks: 55; **Radio stations:** AM, 23; FM, 12; **Television stations:** 7
Civilian Labor Force (MSA) 2002: 1,790,972[1]; **Unemployed:** 101,629[1], **Percent:** 5.7[1]; **Per capita personal income (MSA) 2001:** $28,337[1]
Chamber of Commerce: 120 N. Center St., P.O. Box 5820, Mesa, Ariz. 85201

1. Phoenix–Mesa, Ariz.

Mesa is the third-largest city in Arizona and is located in the south-central portion of the state in Maricopa County. Sitting atop a plateau overlooking the Valley of the Sun, the city gets its name from the Spanish word for "tabletop."

Prior to the arrival of Europeans, the area had been inhabited for centuries by native peoples, including the Hohokam and later the Pima. The Hohokam culture developed an extensive system of irrigation canals, some of which are still used today.

Controlled by Spain and then by Mexico, the area was ceded to the U.S. following the Mexican War (1846–1848). Mormon settlers arrived on the site in 1878 and used the old irrigation canals for farming in the Salt River valley. Mesa was incorporated as a town in 1883 and as a city in 1930.

Falcon Field Airport and Williams Air Force Base were built in 1941 to train fighter pilots during World War II. After the war, the city grew rapidly, as many military families decided to settle in Mesa permanently, and tourism also became a major force. Williams AFB closed in the early 1990s, but Falcon Field has become one of the ten largest U.S. airports in terms of based aircraft and supports more than 30 aviation-related businesses.

Currently Mesa is one of the fastest-growing cities in the United States, due to its excellent climate and strong local economy, which boasts some of the country's top manufacturers. Electronics, automotive testing, propulsion equipment, aerospace, and heavy machinery firms are among the most significant in the region.

With 313 days of sunshine a year, Mesa has been an ideal choice for several major-league baseball spring training camps.

Famous natives: Danielle Fishel, actress; Liz Reney, actress; John J. Rhodes, politician; Keri Russell, actress.

Miami, Fla.

Mayor: Manuel A. Diaz (to Nov. 2005)
City Manager: Joe Arriola
2000 census population (rank): 362,470 (47); **% change:** 1.1; **Male:** 180,194 (49.7%); **Female:** 182,276 (50.3%); **White:** 241,470 (66.6%); **Black:** 80,858 (22.3%); **American Indian and Alaska Native:,** 810 (0.2%); **Asian:** 2,376 (0.7%); **Other race:** 19,644 (5.4%); **Two or more races:** 17,182 (4.7%); **Hispanic/Latino:** 238,351 (65.8%). **2000 percent population 18 and over:** 78.3%; **65 and over:** 17.0%; **median age:** 37.7.
Land area: 36 sq mi. (93 sq km); **Water area:** 19.5 sq mi.; **Alt.:** Average, 12 ft.
Avg. daily temp.: Jan., 67.2° F; July, 82.6° F
Churches[1]: Protestant, 850; Roman Catholic, 61; Jewish, 64; **City-owned parks:** 109; **Radio stations[1]:** 29; **Television stations[1]:** 9 TV, 1 Cable
Civilian Labor Force (PMSA) 2002: 1,120,950; **Unemployed:** 86,527, **Percent:** 7.7; **Per capita personal income (PMSA) 2001:** $26,594
Chamber of Commerce: Greater Miami Chamber of Commerce, 1601 Biscayne Blvd., Miami, Fla. 33132

1. Dade County.

Miami, the second-largest city in Florida and seat of Miami-Dade County, is located in the southeast part of the state, on Biscayne Bay.

The area was once the home of the Tequesta Indians until they were nearly wiped out by European diseases and warfare brought on by two centuries of Spanish control of Florida. Miami was founded in 1870 near the site of Ft. Dallas, built in 1835 during the Seminole Indian wars. The city's name is probably derived from "Mayaimi," an Indian word for "big water."

Miami is the only U.S. city to have been planned by a woman. Julia Tuttle, a Clevelander, arrived there in 1891 and bought several hundred acres on the bank of the Miami River. She convinced New York financier Henry M. Flagler of the area's vast potential and persuaded him to extend his Florida East Coast Railroad to Miami in 1896, the year the city was incorporated. Flagler dredged Miami Harbor, built the renowned Royal Palm Hotel, and promoted the area as a winter playground. Tourists flocked there, and by 1910 the city was a thriving recreational area. Miami survived the collapse of a land speculation boom in the 1920s and severe hurricanes in 1926 and 1935 and continued to grow. It experienced a monumental population boost during the 1960s, when about 260,000 Cuban refugees arrived on its shore. They made a great impact on Miami, which is now a bilingual metropolis.

Miami is an international banking and finance center and has the greatest concentration of international and Edge Act banks (banks making only foreign loans and deposits) in North America; these constitute a major employment base. Greater Miami has a highly diversified economy with numerous multinational and Fortune 500 companies. It is a national leader in biomedical technology, and the health care sector is a major industry. Greater Miami is also part of an area known as the Computer Coast of Florida, and its growing technologies include computers, electrical engineering, and plastics manufacturing.

Miami is one of the world's leading year-round resort centers. The city is a major transportation hub, and the port of Miami is the world's largest cruise port and a major seaport for cargo. The famous island resort of Miami Beach, incorporated in 1915, is connected to Miami by four causeways.

Famous natives: Fernando Bujones, dancer; Steve Carlton, baseball player; Debbie Harry, singer; Dick Howser, baseball player and manager; Sidney Poitier, actor; Janet Reno, former attorney general of the U.S.; Ben Vereen, actor; Ellen Zwilich, composer.

Milwaukee, Wis.

Acting Mayor: Marvin Pratt (to April 2004)
2000 census population (rank): 596,974 (19); **% change:** –5.0; **Male:** 285,363 (47.8%); **Female:** 311,611 (52.2%); **White:** 298,379 (50.0%); **Black:** 222,933 (37.3%); **American Indian and Alaska Native:** 5,212 (0.9%); **Asian:** 17,571 (2.9%); **Other race:** 36,428 (6.1%); **Two or more races:** 16,150 (2.7%); **Hispanic/Latino:** 71,646 (12.0%). **2000 percent population 18 and over:** 71.4%; **65 and over:** 10.9%; **median age:** 30.6.
Land area: 96 sq mi. (249 sq km); **Alt.:** 580.60 ft.
Avg. daily temp.: Jan., 19.9° F; July, 73.6° F
Churches: 411; **County-owned parks:** 14,785 ac.; **Radio stations:** AM, 6; FM, 13; **Television stations:** 11
Civilian Labor Force (PMSA) 2002: 816,677[1]; **Unemployed:** 48,741[1]; **Percent:** 6.0[1]; **Per capita personal income (PMSA) 2001:** $33,780[1]
Chamber of Commerce: Metropolitan Milwaukee Association of Commerce, 756 N. Milwaukee St., Milwaukee, Wis. 53202; Milwaukee Minority Chamber of Commerce, 509 W. Wisconsin Ave. #606, Milwaukee, Wis. 53203; Hispanic Chamber of Commerce, 816 W. National Ave., Milwaukee, Wis. 53204

1. Milwaukee–Waukesha, Wis.

Milwaukee, the largest city in Wisconsin and seat of Milwaukee County, is located in the southeast part of the state on Lake Michigan.

French missionaries visited the site of Milwaukee in the 17th century, but it was not until 1795 that Jacques Vieau established a fur-trading post there. The first permanent white settler, Vieau's son-in-law, Solomon Juneau, an agent of the American Fur Company, made his home there in 1818. The settlement merged with several neighboring villages in 1838 to form Milwaukee, and the city was incorporated in 1846. A large wave of German immigrants arrived after 1848 and contributed greatly to the city's political, economic, and cultural development.

The origins of the word "Milwaukee" are disputed; it may come from the Potawatomi "Mahn-ah-wauk," meaning council grounds of the Potawatomi; "Mah-an-wauk-seepe," meaning gathering place of rivers; or the Algonquian "Milo-aki," meaning beautiful land.

Milwaukee is one of the great industrial centers in the country and one of the largest Great Lakes ports. Manufacturing remains strong, and Milwaukee manufacturers are national leaders in lithographic commercial printing and the production of medical diagnostic instruments, small gasoline engines, malt beverages, iron and steel forgings, mining machinery, and robotics. Milwaukee's high-tech manufacturing community is one of the largest among the nation's major metropolitan areas.

Though Milwaukee was once known as a "beer town," only a small percentage of its workforce is now involved in beer production. However, beer still plays an important role, and almost 11% of the nation's malt beverage is produced there.

Famous natives: Donald Gramm, bass-baritone; Woody Herman, band leader; Al Jarreau, singer; Kristen Johnston, actress; George F. Kennan, diplomat; Alfred Lunt, actor; Douglas MacArthur, army general; Pat O'Brien, actor; Tom Snyder, TV personality; Speech, member of the rap group "Arrested Development"; Spencer Tracy, actor; Gene Wilder, actor; Jerry and David Zucker, film producers.

Minneapolis, Minn.

Mayor: R. T. Rybak (to Jan. 2006)
2000 census population (rank): 382,618 (45); **% change:** 3.9; **Male:** 192,232 (50.2%); **Female:** 190,386 (49.8%); **White:** 249,186 (65.1%); **Black:** 68,818 (18.0%); **American Indian and Alaska Native:** 8,378 (2.2%); **Asian:** 23,455 (6.1%); **Other race:** 15,798 (4.1%); **Two or more races:** 16,694 (4.4%); **Hispanic/Latino:** 29,175 (7.6%). **2000 percent population 18 and over:** 78.0%; **65 and over:** 9.1%; **median age:** 31.2
Land area: 55 sq mi. (142 sq km); **Alt.:** Highest, 945 ft.; lowest, 695 ft.
Avg. daily temp.: Jan., 11.8° F; July, 73.6° F
Churches: 419; **City-owned parks:** 153; **Radio stations[1]:** AM, 17; FM, 15; **Television stations[1]:** 6
Civilian Labor Force (MSA) 2002: 1,832,816[2]; **Unemployed:** 77,912[2], **Percent:** 4.3[2]; **Per capita personal income (MSA) 2001:** $38,131[2]
Chamber of Commerce: Minneapolis Regional Chamber of Commerce, Young Quinlan Building, 81 S. Ninth St., Suite 200, Minneapolis, Minn. 55402-3223

1. Metropolitan area. 2. Minneapolis–St. Paul, Minn.–Wis.

Minneapolis, the largest city in Minnesota and the seat of Hennepin County, is located in the southeast central part of the state on the Mississippi River. It is adjacent to its "twin city" of St. Paul.

In 1680, Father Louis Hennepin visited the future site of Minneapolis and gave the Falls of St. Anthony their name. Lt. Zebulon Pike made a treaty with the Sioux Indians in 1805–1806, by which they ceded to the whites much land, including the Falls of St. Anthony and the site of Minneapolis. Fort Snelling was built in 1819–1820, and in 1823 the government built a lumber and flour mill. Flour milling became the major industry of early Minneapolis and made the city the milling capital of the world. The town of St. Anthony was established on the east bank of the Mississippi in 1848, and the town of Minneapolis grew up on the opposite bank of the river. The name Minneapolis is a combination of the Dakota Sioux word "minna," for water, and the Greek word "polis," for city. Minneapolis was incorporated as a city in 1867, and in 1872 the city of St. Anthony (chartered in 1860) was annexed to it. After the spread of the railroads in the 1870s, Minneapolis became the gateway to the Northern Great Plains.

Minneapolis is a center of industry and commerce serving a large agricultural region. During the 20th century, manufacturing, food processing, milling, computers, health services, and graphic arts developed as Minneapolis's major industries. Fifteen Fortune 500 companies are headquartered in the Minneapolis–St. Paul metropolitan area. The city is the headquarters of the Ninth Federal Reserve Bank.

The Twin Cities are known for their wide array of cultural attractions, and Minneapolis is home to many fine museums, including the Minneapolis Institute of Arts, the Walker Center, and the Frederick R. Weisman Art Museum at the University of Minnesota's Minneapolis campus.

Famous natives: La Verne, Maxene, and Patti Andrews, singers; James Arness, actor; Lew Ayres, actor; Patty Berg, golfer; Virginia Bruce, actress; J. Paul Getty, oil executive; Peter Graves, actor; George Roy Hill, director; Cornell MacNeil, baritone; Ralph Meeker, actor; Westbrook Pegler, columnist; Prince, singer; Harrison Salisbury, journalist; Charles Schulz, cartoonist; Anne Tyler, writer; Bud Wilkinson, football coach; David Winfield, baseball player.

Nashville-Davidson, Tenn.

Mayor: Bill Purcell (to Oct. 2003)
2000 census population (rank)[1]: 545,524 (22); **% change:** 11.6; **Male:** 264,095 (48.4%); **Female:** 281,429 (51.6%); **White:** 359,581 (65.9%); **Black:** 146,235 (26.8%); **American Indian and Alaska Native:** 1,639 (0.3%); **Asian:** 12,992 (2.4%); **Other race:** 13,677 (2.5%); **Two or more races:** 11,000 (2.0%); **Hispanic/Latino:** 25,774 (4.7%). **2000 percent population 18 and over:** 77.9%; **65 and over:** 11.0%; **median age:** 33.9.
Land area: 502 sq mi. (1,300 sq km); **Altitude:** Highest, 1,100 ft.; lowest, approx. 400 ft.
Avg. daily temp.: Jan., 36.2° F; July, 79.3° F
Churches: Protestant, 781; Roman Catholic, 18; Jewish, 3; **City-owned parks:** 76 (6,650 ac.); **Radio stations:** AM, 15; FM, 19; **Television stations:** 11
Civilian Labor Force (MSA) 2002: 696,254; **Unemployed:** 27,899, **Percent:** 4.0; **Per capita personal income (MSA) 2001:** $32,338
Chamber of Commerce: Nashville Area Chamber of Commerce, 211 Commerce Street, Suite 100, Nashville, Tenn. 37201

1. Nashville-Davidson city is consolidated with Davidson County.

Nashville-Davidson is the state capital and second-largest city in Tennessee and is located in the north-central part of the state on the Cumberland River. It is coextensive with Davidson County.

During the winter of 1779–1780, James Robertson and John Donelson founded a settlement at Big Salt Lick by the Cumberland River at the present site of the city. They built forts on both sides of the river, naming one of them Fort Nashborough in honor of Francis Nash, a Revolutionary War general. In 1784, the town was named Nashville, and it was incorporated as a city in 1806.

Nashville became the capital of Tennessee in 1843 and was the seat of Davidson County until 1963, when it merged with the county to become Nashville-Davidson.

The city is a port of entry and an important industrial and commercial center serving the Upper South. Its economy is based on a number of industries, including automobiles, apparel, publishing, insurance, and banking. Health care services are the largest sector, but Nashville is best known for its music industry. It is a major recording center, especially for country music.

Nashville is home to several religious organizations and is a major tourist attraction and convention center. Its many institutions of higher education include Vanderbilt University, Fisk University, and the University of Tennessee.

Famous natives: Roy Acuff, singer; Gregg Allman, singer; Pat Boone, singer; Rita Coolidge, singer; Jeff Gordon, race car driver; Al Gore, former vice president; Red Grooms, artist; Alex Haley, author; Barbara Howar, hostess and writer; Brenda Lee, singer; Minnie Pearl, comedienne; Annie Potts, actress; Paula Robeson, flutist; Wilma Rudolph, athlete; Dinah Shore, actress and singer; Tina Turner, singer; Oprah Winfrey, entertainer.

New Orleans, La.

Mayor: C. Ray Nagin (to May 2006)
2000 census population (rank): 484,674 (31); **% change:** –2.5; **Male:** 227,094 (46.9%); **Female:** 257,580 (53.1%); **White:** 135,956 (28.1%); **Black:** 325,947 (67.3%); **American Indian and Alaska Native:** 991 (0.2%); **Asian:** 10,972 (2.3%); **Other race:** 4,498 (0.9%); **Two or more races:** 6,201 (1.3%); **Hispanic/Latino:** 14,826 (3.1%). **2000 percent population 18 and over:** 73.3%; **65 and over:** 11.7%; **median age:** 33.1.
Land area: 181 sq mi. (469 sq km); **Alt.:** Highest, 15 ft.; lowest, –4 ft.
Avg. daily temp.: Jan., 51.3° F; July, 81.9° F
Churches: 712; **City-owned parks:** 165 (299 ac.); **Radio stations:** AM, 12; FM, 14; **Television stations:** 7
Civilian Labor Force (MSA) 2002: 593,433; **Unemployed:** 32,093, **Percent:** 5.4; **Per capita personal income (MSA) 2001:** $28,048
Chamber of Commerce: New Orleans Regional Chamber of Commerce, 601 Poydras St., Suite 1700, New Orleans, La. 70130

New Orleans, the largest city in Louisiana, is located in the southeast part of the state, between the Mississippi River and Lake Ponchartrain. It is coextensive with Orleans Parish.

One of the few cities of the nation that has been under three flags, New Orleans has belonged to Spain, France, and the United States. The French founded it in 1718 and named it in honor of the Duke of Orleans. In 1762, France ceded the city and the territory to Spain. In 1800, the territory was returned to France, but government authorities did not take over until 1803, just 20 days before the region became part of the United States in the Louisiana Purchase.

New Orleans is famous for its French Quarter, with its mixture of French, Spanish, and native architectural styles. The Mardi Gras—a week of carnival held in New Orleans before the beginning of Lent—is the most spectacular festival in the U.S. and is a popular tourist attraction. Tourism has grown rapidly in recent years, and New Orleans hosts more than seven million visitors annually.

New Orleans has one of the world's greatest international ports, one of the largest in the nation, and it is a major focus of the city's economy. New Orleans is home to the corporate offices of oil companies with major offshore operations in the Gulf of Mexico, as well as the distribution and service centers of offshore equipment suppliers and fabricators.

The manufacturing industry is a significant part of the economy, with petroleum, petrochemical, shipbuilding, and aerospace industries all playing a role. The New Orleans region also functions as a mining, processing, and transportation center for other minerals, principally sulfur. Service industries are playing a larger role, with health care and telecommunications leading the way. The New Orleans region is widely regarded as a leading center of medicine and health care in the South.

Famous natives: Louis Armstrong, musician; Truman Capote, author; Fats Domino, musician; Louis Gottschalk, pianist and composer; Bryant Gumbel, TV personality; Lillian Hellman, playwright and author; Al Hirt, musician; Mahalia Jackson, singer; Dorothy Lamour, actress; Wynton Marsalis, musician; Huey Newton, activist; Marguerite Piazza, soprano; Rusty Staub, baseball player; Ben Turpin, comedian; Shirley Verrett, mezzo-soprano; Carl Weathers, actor; Del Williams, football player.

New York, N.Y.

Mayor: Michael R. Bloomberg (to Dec. 2005)
Borough Presidents: Bronx, Adolfo Carrion; Brooklyn, Marty Markowitz; Manhattan, C. Virginia Fields; Queens, Helen M. Marshall; Staten Island, James P. Molinaro
2000 census population (rank): 8,008,278 (1); **% change:** 9.4; **Male:** 3,794,204 (47.4%); **Female:** 4,214,074 (52.6%); **White:** 3,576,385 (44.7%); **Black:** 2,129,762 (26.6%); **American Indian and Alaska Native:** 41,289 (0.5%); **Asian:** 787,047 (9.8%); **Other race:** 1,074,406 (13.4%); **Two or more races:** 393,959 (4.9%); **Hispanic/Latino:** 2,160,554 (27.0%). **2000 percent population 18 and over:** 75.8%; **65 and over:** 11.7%; **median age:** 34.2.
Land area: 303 sq mi. (785 sq km) (Queens, 109; Brooklyn, 71; Staten Island, 58; Bronx, 42; Manhattan, 23); **Alt.:** Highest, 426 ft.; lowest, sea level
Avg. daily temp.: Jan., 31.5° F; July, 76.8° F
Churches: Protestant, 1,766; Jewish, 1,256; Roman Catholic, 437; Orthodox, 66; **City-owned parks:** 1,701 (28,312 ac.); **Radio stations:** AM, 13; FM, 18; **Television stations:** 6 commercial, 1 public
Civilian Labor Force (PMSA) 2002: 4,430,974; **Unemployed:** 323,427, **Percent:** 7.3; **Per capita personal income (PMSA) 2001:** $40,450
Chamber of Commerce: Greater New York Chamber of Commerce and Industry, 172 Madison Ave., New York, N.Y. 10016

New York City is the largest city in the United States. It is located in the southern part of New York State, at the mouth of the Hudson River (also known as North River as it passes Manhattan Island).

In 1609, Henry Hudson, who worked for the Dutch East India Company, sailed up the river that now bears his name and went as far as Albany. Five years later, a permanent settlement was established at what is now New York, but it was originally called New Amsterdam by the Dutch governors. One of them, Peter Minuit, was said to have bought Manhattan Island from the Indians in exchange for beads, buttons, and trinkets. In 1664, Great Britain's Duke of York sent a fleet that quietly seized the settlement from the Dutch without bloodshed and rechristened the colony in honor of the duke.

Control of New York passed to the young U.S. at the end of the Revolutionary War, and George Washington was inaugurated president in New York's old City Hall. Congress met in New York from 1785 to 1790.

In 1898, when Greater New York was chartered, the city expanded to include the following five boroughs, which are also counties in New York State: Manhattan (New York County); Brooklyn (Kings County); Bronx (Bronx County); Queens (Queens County); and Staten Island (Richmond County).

"The Big Apple" is a major world capital and a world leader in finance, the arts, and communications. The port of New York is one of the finest in the world and ranks as the largest port complex on the East Coast. The city is the home of the United Nations and is headquarters for some of the world's largest corporations. The city is also the center of advertising, fashion, publishing, and radio broadcasting in the United States.

The city suffered incredible devastation in Sept. 2001, when terrorist hijackers crashed two commercial jets into the World Trade Center in lower Manhattan, causing the complete destruction of the twin towers and major loss of life.

Famous natives: Kareem Abdul-Jabbar, basketball player; Woody Allen, actor and director; Lauren Bacall, actress; James Baldwin, novelist; Harry Belafonte, singer and actor; Humphrey Bogart, actor; James Cagney, actor; Maria Callas, soprano; Aaron Copland, composer; Sammy Davis, Jr., singer and actor; Agnes de Mille, choreographer; Robert De Niro, actor; Eamon De Valera, former president of Ireland; Gertrude Elion, Nobel Prize winner in medicine; Lou Gehrig, baseball player; George Gershwin, composer; Ira Gershwin, lyricist; Jackie Gleason, actor; Rita Hayworth, actress; Lena Horne, singer; Julia Ward Howe, poet and reformer; Washington Irving, author; Henry James, novelist; Michael Jordan, basketball player; Sandy Koufax, baseball player; Roy Lichtenstein, painter; Vince Lombardi, football player and coach; Chico, Groucho, Harpo, and Zeppo Marx, comedians; Herman Melville, novelist; Yehudi Menuhin, violinist; James Michener, novelist; Arthur Miller, playwright; Eugene O'Neill, playwright; J. Robert Oppenheimer, nuclear physicist; Al Pacino, actor; Jerome Robbins, choreographer; Eleanor Roosevelt, reformer and humanitarian; Theodore Roosevelt, former president; Jonas Salk, polio researcher; Beverly Sills, soprano; Neil Simon, playwright; Barbra Streisand, singer and actress; Ed Sullivan, TV personality; Mae West, actress; Edith Wharton, novelist.

Oakland, Calif.

Mayor: Jerry Brown (to Jan. 2007)
City Manager: Robert C. Bobb
2000 census popultion (rank): 399,484 (41); **% change:** 7.3; **Male:** 192,757 (48.3%); **Female:** 206,727 (51.7%); **White:** 125,013 (31.3%); **Black:** 142,460 (35.7%); **American Indian and Alaska Native:** 2,655 (0.7%); **Asian:** 60,851 (15.2%); **Other race:** 46,592 (11.7%); **Two or more races:** 19,911 (5.0%); **Hispanic/Latino:** 87,467 (21.9%). **2000 percent population 18 and over:** 75.0%; **65 and over:** 10.5%; **median age:** 33.3.
Land area: 56 sq mi. (145 sq km); **Alt.:** Highest, 1,700 ft.; lowest, sea level
Avg. daily temp.: Jan., 49.9° F; July, 62.1° F
Churches: 374, representing over 78 denominations in the city; over 500 churches in Alameda County; **City-owned parks:** 2,196 ac.; **Radio stations:** AM, 1; **Television stations:** 1 commercial, 1 government access, 2 education access, 1 local
Civilian Labor Force (PMSA) 2002: 1,290,855; **Unemployed:** 79,253, **Percent:** 6.1; **Per capita personal income (PMSA) 2001:** $39,963
Chamber of Commerce: Oakland Chamber of Commerce, 475 Fourteenth St., Oakland, Calif. 94612

Oakland is located in the west-central part of California on the east side of San Francisco Bay. It is the seat of Alameda County.

Don Luis Peralta first settled the site of Oakland in 1820 when he established the Rancho San Antonio. The gold rush of 1849 attracted more people to the area, and the city's population continued to grow after a ferry service to San Francisco was started in 1851. Oakland was incorporated as a town in 1852 and as a city in 1854. It was named after the numerous oak trees found in the area. Oakland became the western terminus of the Central Pacific Railroad in 1869 and the seat of Alameda County in 1873.

In the latter part of the 19th century and also in 1910, additional territory was annexed to Oakland and the city assumed its present size. In 1906, thousands of people fled to Oakland in the aftermath of the San Francisco earthquake and settled there permanently, furthering the city's growth. Oakland's economic development continued to rise with the opening of the San Francisco–Oakland Bay Bridge in 1936.

Oakland is a major center of culture and commerce. It is an important container shipping port and the terminus of three transcontinental railroads. Oakland's industries include food processing, transportation, software, telecommunications, pharmaceuticals, and electrical and high technology manufacturing. The city is the headquarters of many national and international corporations.

Famous natives: Buster Crabbe, actor; Frederick Cottrell, inventor; Clint Eastwood, actor and director; Dennis Eckersley, athlete; Mark Hamill, singer, dancer, and songwriter; Hammer, actor; Tom Hanks, actor; Rod McKuen, singer and composer; Russ Meyer, producer and director; Eddie (Anderson) Rochester, actor; George Stevens, director; Amy Tan, writer; Jo Van Fleet, actress.

Oklahoma City, Okla.

Mayor: Kirk Humphreys (to April 2006)
City Manager: James D. Couch
2000 census population (rank): 506,132 (29); **% change:** 13.8; **Male:** 247,313 (48.9%); **Female:** 258,819 (51.1%); **White:** 346,226 (68.4%); **Black:** 77,810 (15.4%); **American Indian and Alaska Native:** 17,743 (3.5%); **Asian:** 17,595 (3.5%); **Other race:** 26,705 (5.3%); **Two or more races:** 19,693 (3.9%); **Hispanic/Latino:** 51,368 (10.1%). **2000 percent population 18 and over:** 74.5%; **65 and over:** 11.5%; **median age:** 34.0.
Land area: 607 sq mi. (1,572 sq km); **Alt.:** Highest, 1,320 ft.; lowest, 1,140 ft.
Avg. daily temp.: Jan., 35.9° F; July, 82.0° F
Churches: Roman Catholic, 25; Jewish, 4; Protestant and others, 741; **City-owned parks:** 144 (5,225 ac.); **Radio stations:** AM, 10; FM, 14; **Television stations:** 8
Civilian Labor Force (MSA) 2002: 574,342; **Unemployed:** 23,798, **Percent:** 4.1; **Per capita personal income (MSA) 2001:** $26,970
Chamber of Commerce: Greater Oklahoma City Chamber of Commerce, 123 Park Ave., Oklahoma City, Okla. 73102

Oklahoma City, the state capital and seat of Oklahoma County, is the largest city in Oklahoma. It is located in the central part of the state on the North Canadian River.

Oklahoma City sprang into being almost overnight. On April 22, 1889, the U.S. government opened the territory for settlement, and there was a rush across the border line to stake claims. A sprawling tent city sprang up near the Santa Fe railroad tracks, and within a short time Oklahoma City was a bustling town of 10,000. The city was incorporated in 1890 and replaced Guthrie as the state capital in 1910. Oil was discovered in the city in 1928, and petroleum production became a mainstay of the city's economy.

Oklahoma City is the wholesale and distributing center for the state, and the city's stockyards are the largest stocker and feeder cattle market in the world. Following the decline of the energy sector, Oklahoma City is fostering a private entrepreneurial environment and a more diversified economy. Within the service sector, health services are projected to grow, followed by retail trade and business services. Nearby Tinker Air Force Base, one of the world's largest air depots, is a major city employer.

In 1995 the city was the scene of a devastating terrorist bombing, which destroyed a federal office building and killed 168 people.

Famous natives: Johnny Bench, baseball player; Lon Chaney, Jr., actor; Ralph Ellison, writer; Kay Francis, actress; Vince Gill, country singer; Dale Robertson, actor; Ted Shackleford, actor; Pamela Tiffin, actress.

Omaha, Neb.

Mayor: Michael Fahey (to June 2005)
2000 census population (rank): 390,007 (44); **% change:** 16.1; **Male:** 190,032 (48.7%); **Female:** 199,975 (51.3%); **White:** 305,745 (78.4%); **Black:** 51,917 (13.3%); **American Indian and Alaska Native:** 2,616 (0.7%); **Asian:** 6,773 (1.7%); **Other race:** 15,250 (3.9%); **Two or more races:** 7,478 (1.9%); **Hispanic/Latino:** 29,397 (7.5%). **2000 percent population 18 and over:** 74.4%; **65 and over:** 11.8%; **median age:** 33.5.
Land area: 116 sq mi. (300 sq km); **Alt.:** Highest, 1,270 ft.
Avg. daily temp.: Jan., 21.1° F; July, 76.9° F
Churches: Protestant, 192; Roman Catholic, 44; Jewish, 4; **City-owned parks:** 192 (over 8,000 ac.); **Radio stations:** AM, 7; FM, 13; **Television stations:** 4
Civilian Labor Force (MSA) 2002: 415,442[1]; **Unemployed:** 15,857[1], **Percent:** 3.8[1]; **Per capita personal income (MSA) 2001:** $33,249[1]
Chamber of Commerce: Omaha Chamber of Commerce, 1301 Harney St., Omaha, Neb. 68102

1. Omaha, Neb.–Iowa.

Omaha, the largest city in Nebraska and the seat of Douglas County, is located in the eastern part of the state on the west bank of the Missouri River, opposite Council Bluffs, Iowa.

The Lewis and Clark expedition visited the area in 1804, and the U.S. Army built Ft. Atkinson nearby in 1819. Pierre Cabanne established a fur-trading post at the site in 1825. The first Mormon migrants wintered there in 1846–1847 on their way to Utah. The city grew rapidly as the most northerly supply point for overland wagons to the Far West.

The city was officially founded in 1854 after the Nebraska Territory was opened for settlement. It was named for the Omaha Indians living nearby, whose tribal name means "those who go upstream or against the current." Omaha was incorporated as a city in 1857 and was the capital of the Nebraska Territory from 1855 to 1867. The city continued to thrive as a point of entry and a major transportation center when the Union Pacific transcontinental railroad arrived in 1869.

Omaha is a major market for grain and livestock, food processing, telecommunications, and insurance. Other important industries include electrical equipment and finance as well as printing and publishing. It continues to be a major railroad hub.

Famous natives: Fred Astaire, dancer and actor; Max Baer, boxer; Robert Boozer, basketball player; Marlon Brando, actor; Montgomery Clift, actor; Gerald Ford, former president; Bob Gibson, baseball player; Swoosie Kurtz, actress; Melvin Laird, former secretary of defense; Dorothy McGuire, actress; Nick Nolte, actor; Gale Sayers, football player; Malcolm X, political activist; Paul Williams, singer and composer.

Philadelphia, Pa.

Mayor: John F. Street (to Jan. 2004)
2000 census population (rank): 1,517,550 (5); **% change:** –4.3; **Male:** 705,107 (46.5%); **Female:** 812,443 (53.5%); **White:** 683,267 (45.0%); **Black:** 655,824 (43.2%); **American Indian and Alaska Native:** 4,073 (0.3%); **Asian:** 67,654 (4.5%); **Other race:** 72,429 (4.8%); **Two or more races:** 33,574 (2.2%); **Hispanic/Latino:** 128,928 (8.5%). **2000 percent population 18 and over:** 74.7%; **65 and over:** 14.1%; **median age:** 34.2.
Land area: 135 sq mi. (350 sq km); **Alt.:** Highest, 440 ft.; lowest, sea level
Avg. daily temp.: Jan., 30.4° F; July, 76.7° F
Churches: Roman Catholic, 133; Jewish, 55; Protestant and others, 830; **City-owned parks:** 630 (10,252 ac.); **Radio stations**[1]: AM, 40; FM, 43; **Television stations:** 14
Civilian Labor Force (PMSA) 2002: 2,649,257[2]; **Unemployed:** 146,907[2], **Percent:** 5.5[2]; **Per capita personal income (PMSA) 2001:** $35,192[2]
Chamber of Commerce: Philadelphia Chamber of Commerce, 200 South Broad St., Suite 700, Philadelphia, Pa. 19102

1. Metropolitan area. 2. Philadelphia, Pa.–N.J.

Philadelphia, the largest city in Pennsylvania, is located in the southeast part of the state at the junction of the Schuylkill and Delaware Rivers. It is coextensive with Philadelphia County.

Philadelphia, the City of Brotherly Love, was settled in 1681 by Capt. William Markham, who, with a small band of colonists, had been sent out by his cousin, William Penn. Penn arrived the following year with the intention of creating a refuge for the Quakers.

In the period before the American Revolution, the city outstripped all others in the colonies in education, arts, science, industry, and commerce. In 1774–1776, the First and Second Continental Congresses met in Philadelphia, and, from 1781–1783, the city was the capital of the United States under the Articles of Confederation. In 1790, it became the nation's capital under the Constitution and remained so until the seat of the federal government moved to Washington in 1800.

Within a half-century of the founding of the nation at Independence Hall, Philadelphia had emerged as a leader in America's Industrial Revolution. Today the steam locomotives and hat factories of the 19th century have been replaced by diverse manufacturing specialties such as chemicals (including pharmaceuticals), medical devices, transportation equipment, and printing and publishing. In the services sector, Philadelphia leads in subsectors such as health services, insurance carriers, legal services, and architecture and engineering services. Philadelphia is also home to branches of the U.S. Mint, the Federal Reserve System, and the Internal Revenue Service.

The city's harbor, one of the largest freshwater ports in the world, is the centerpiece of the Ameri-Port facility in south Philadelphia, a major shipping center with rail links to the Midwest and Canada.

The city abounds in landmarks of early American history, including Independence Hall, where the Declaration of Independence was signed, and the Liberty Bell. Other significant tourist attractions are the Philadelphia Museum of Art, the Franklin Institute Science Museum, and the Philadelphia Zoological Gardens.

Famous natives: Marian Anderson, contralto; Frankie Avalon, singer and actor; John, Lionel, and Ethel Barrymore, actors; Kevin Bacon, actor; Boyz II Men, R&B group; Mary Cassatt, artist; Wilt Chamberlain, basketball player; Chubby Checker, singer; Bill Cosby, actor; Stuart Davis, painter; Thomas Eakins, painter and sculptor; W. C. Fields, comedian; Benjamin Franklin, inventor and statesman; Grace (Kelly), actress and princess of Monaco; Walt Kelly, cartoonist; Patti LaBelle, singer; Mario Lanza, singer and actor; George McClellan, general; Margaret Mead, anthropologist; Edgar Allen Poe, author; Anna Quindlen, writer and Pulitzer Prize winner; Man Ray, painter; Betsy Ross, flagmaker; Will Smith, actor; Jacqueline Susann, novelist; Robert Venturi, architect.

Phoenix, Ariz.

Mayor: Skip Rimsza (to Oct. 2003)
2000 census population (rank): 1,321,045 (6); **% change:** 34.3; **Male:** 671,760 (50.9%); **Female:** 649,285 (49.1%); **White:** 938,853 (71.1%); **Black:** 67,416 (5.1%); **American Indian and Alaska Native:** 26,696 (2.0%); **Asian:** 26,449 (2.0%); **Other race:** 216,589 (16.4%); **Two or more races:** 43,276 (3.3%); **Hispanic/Latino:** 449,972 (34.1%). **2000 percent population 18 and over:** 71.1%; **65 and over:** 8.1%; **median age:** 30.7.
Land area: 475 sq mi. (1,230 sq km); **Alt.:** Highest, 2,740 ft.; lowest, 1,017 ft.
Avg. daily temp.: Jan., 53.6° F; July, 93.5° F
City-owned parks: 170 (25,235 ac.); **Radio stations:** AM, 20; FM, 20; **Television stations:** 9 commercial; 1 PBS
Civilian Labor Force (MSA) 2002: 1,790,972[1]; **Unemployed:** 101,629[1], **Percent:** 5.7[1]; **Per capita personal income (MSA) 2001:** $28,337[1]
Chamber of Commerce: Phoenix Chamber of Commerce, 201 N. Central, Phoenix, Ariz. 85073

1. Phoenix–Mesa, Ariz.

Phoenix, the capital of Arizona and seat of Maricopa County, is the largest city in the state. It is located in the center of Arizona, on the Salt River.

The prehistoric Hohokam Indians first settled the area about 300 B.C. and dug a system of extensive irrigation canals for farming. The Indian culture mysteriously broke up in the 1400s.

The site was permanently resettled by Jack Swilling and "Lord Darrell" Duppa about 1867. Because the city was founded on the ruins of the ancient civilization, it was named Phoenix after the legendary bird that could regenerate itself. The irrigation canals were restored for farming, and ranching and prospecting began in the surrounding area. The city quickly grew as an important trading center. Phoenix was incorporated as a city in 1881 and was made the territorial capital in 1889. It became the state capital when Arizona was admitted to the Union in 1912.

Partly owing to its warm, dry climate, the city developed rapidly in the decades after World War II. Between 1950 and 1990 the population increased from 100,000 to 980,000. And Phoenix continues to be one of the fastest growing cities in the U.S.; between 1990 and 2000, its population increased another 34%, to 1.3 million.

Phoenix is a commercial and manufacturing center in an agricultural region. Major industries include government, agricultural products, aerospace technology, electronics, air-conditioning, leather goods, and Indian arts and crafts. Mining, timbering, and tourism also contribute to the economy.

Famous natives: Lynda Carter, actress; Alice Cooper, musician; Arthur A. Fletcher, government official; Barry Goldwater, politician; Stevie Nicks, musician; Charles S. Robb, politician; Mare Winningham, actress.

Portland, Ore.

Mayor: Vera Katz (to Dec. 2004)
2000 census population (rank): 529,121 (28); **% change:** 21.0; **Male:** 261,565 (49.4%); **Female:** 267,556 (50.6%); **White:** 412,241 (77.9%); **Black:** 35,115 (6.6%); **American Indian and Alaska Native:** 5,587 (1.1%); **Asian:** 33,470 (6.3%); **Other race:** 18,760 (3.5%); **Two or more races:** 21,955 (4.1%); **Hispanic/Latino:** 36,058 (6.8%). **2000 percent population 18 and over:** 78.9%; **65 and over:** 11.6%; **median age:** 35.2.
Land area: 134 sq mi. (347 sq km); **Alt.:** Highest, 1073 ft.; lowest, sea level
Avg. daily temp.: Jan., 39.6° F; July, 68.2° F
Churches: Protestant, 450; Roman Catholic, 48; Jewish, 9; Buddhist, 6; other, 190; **City-owned parks:** 200 (over 9,400 ac.); **Radio stations:** AM: 14, FM: 14; **Television stations:** 5 commercial, 1 public
Civilian Labor Force (PMSA) 2002: 1,092,232[1]; **Unemployed:** 85,474[1], **Percent:** 7.8[1]; **Per capita personal income (PMSA) 2001:** $31,971[1]
Chamber of Commerce: Portland Chamber of Commerce, 221 NW 2nd Ave., Portland, Ore. 97209

1. Portland–Vancouver, Ore.–Wash.

Portland, the largest city in Oregon and seat of Multnomah County, is located in the northwest part of the state on the Willamette River.

Lewis and Clark camped at the site of Portland in 1805 on their expedition across the continent. Portland was founded in 1845 and was almost called Boston after the city in Massachusetts. Founders Amos Lovejoy from Massachusetts and Francis Pettygrove from Maine flipped a coin to decide the name of the new town. Pettygrove won the toss and named the place Portland after his hometown. Portland was incorporated as a city in 1851.

In the 1850s Portland served as a supply base for the California gold rush, and it grew with the development of its salmon and lumber industries and the arrival of the railroad in 1883. The city continued to grow from 1879 to 1900 as a supply point for the Alaska gold rush and as the site of the Lewis and Clark Centennial Exposition in 1905.

The port of Portland leads the West in grain exports and is among the top five auto-import centers in the United States.

Portland has a diverse economy with a broad base of manufacturing, distribution, wholesale and retail trade, regional government, and business services. Major manufacturing industries include machinery, electronics, metals, transportation equipment, and lumber and wood products. Technology is a thriving part of Portland's economy, with over 1,700 high-tech companies located in the metropolitan area. Tourism is also important to Portland's economy, drawing more than 7 million visitors annually.

Famous natives: James Beard, food expert; Pietro Belluschi, architect; Richard Fosbury, high jumper; Matt Groening, cartoonist; Margaux Hemingway, actress; Phil Knight, founder of Nike; Terrance Knox, actor; Jeff Lorber, jazz musician; Linus Pauling, chemist; Jane Powell, singer and actress; Ahmad Rashad, football player and sportscaster; Susan Ruttan, actress; Doc Severinson, band leader; Norton Simon, business executive; Sally Ann Struthers, actress; Gus Van Sant, film director; Lindsay Wagner, actress; Mitch Williams, baseball pitcher.

Sacramento, Calif.

Mayor: Heather Fargo (to Nov. 2004)
City Manager: Robert P. Thomas
2000 census population (rank): 407,018 (40); **% change:** 10.2; **Male:** 197,784 (48.6%); **Female:** 209,234 (51.4%); **White:** 196,549 (48.3%); **Black:** 62,968 (15.5%); **American Indian and Alaska Native:** 5,300 (1.3%); **Asian:** 67,635 (16.6%); **Other race:** 44,627 (11.0%); **Two or more races:** 26,078 (6.4%); **Hispanic/Latino:** 87,974 (21.6%). **2000 percent population 18 and over:** 72.7%; **65 and over:** 11.4%; **median age:** 32.8.
Land area: 97 sq mi. (251 sq km)
Avg. daily temp.: Jan., 45.2° F; July, 75.7° F
City park & recreational facilities: 134+ (1,427+ ac.); **Television stations:** 7

Civilian Labor Force (PMSA) 2002: 863,806; **Unemployed:** 45,328, **Percent:** 5.2; **Per capita personal income (PMSA) 2001:** $30,906
Chamber of Commerce: Sacramento Chamber of Commerce, 917 7th St., Sacramento, Calif. 95814; West Sacramento Chamber of Commerce, 834-C Jefferson Blvd., Sacramento, Calif. 95691

Sacramento is the capital of California and the seat of Sacramento County. It is located in the north-central part of the state at the confluence of the Sacramento and American rivers.

In 1839, German-born Swiss citizen John Augustus Sutter obtained a grant from the Mexican governor to establish a colony for fellow Swiss emigrants on a large tract of land that he named New Helvetia (New Switzerland). He established Fort Sutter there as a trading post.

After gold was discovered on Sutter's property in 1848, the settlement rapidly expanded as the prominent supply point for gold prospectors coming from the East. Sacramento was laid out in 1848 and named after California's principal river, which ran beside it. The river's name in Spanish honors the Holy Sacrament. It became incorporated as a city in 1849 and was made the state capital in 1854. Sacramento was the terminus of the first railroad in 1856 and the western terminus of the Pony Express in 1860.

The city has always been a hub of river transportation and is a major deep-water port connected to the Pacific Ocean. Sacramento's economy is highly diversified and, along with state government and military installations, its industries include aerospace, high technology, furniture, chemicals, pharmaceuticals, meat packing, and food processing of crops from the Central Valley.

Famous natives: Joan Didion, author; Mark Goodson, TV producer; Tom Hanks, actor; Henry Hathaway, director; Anthony M. Kennedy, Supreme Court justice; Molly Ringwald, actress.

St. Louis, Mo.

Mayor: Francis G. Slay (to April 2005)
2000 census population (rank): 348,189 (49); **% change:** –12.2; **Male:** 163,567 (47.0%); **Female:** 184,622 (53.0%); **White:** 152,666 (43.8%); **Black:** 178,266 (51.2%); **American Indian and Alaska Native:** 950 (0.3%); **Asian:** 6,891 (2.0%); **Other race:** 2,783 (0.8%); **Two or more races:** 6,539 (1.9%); **Hispanic/Latino:** 7,022 (2.0%). **2000 percent population 18 and over:** 74.3%; **65 and over:** 13.7%; **median age:** 33.7.
Land area: 62 sq mi. (161 sq km); **Alt.:** Highest, 616 ft.; lowest, 413 ft.
Avg. daily temp.: Jan., 28.4° F; July, 78.4° F
Churches: 900[1]; **City-owned parks:** 106 (3,136 ac.); **Radio stations:** AM, 21; FM 27[1]; **Television stations:** 6 commercial; 1 PBS
Civilian Labor Force (MSA) 2002: 1,379,502[2]; **Unemployed:** 78,855[2], **Percent:** 5.7[2]; **Per capita personal income (MSA) 2001:** $32,666[2]
Chamber of Commerce: St. Louis Regional Chamber and Growth Association, One Metropolian Square, Suite 1300, St. Louis, Mo. 63102

1. Metropolitan area. 2. St. Louis, Mo.–Ill.

St. Louis, the second-largest city in Missouri, is located in the east central part of the state on the Mississippi River. The city is independent and is not part of any county.

St. Louis was founded by the French in 1764 when Auguste Chouteau established a fur-trading post and Pierre Laclède Liguest, a New Orleans merchant, founded a town at the present site. They named it after King Louis XV of France and his patron saint, Louis IX. From 1770 to 1803, St. Louis was a Spanish possession, but it was ceded back to France in 1803 in accordance with the Treaty of San Ildefonso (1800), only to be acquired by the U.S. as part of the Louisiana purchase later that year.

The town was incorporated in 1809. From 1812 to 1821, St. Louis was the capital of the Missouri Territory, and it was incorporated as a city in 1822.

John Jacob Astor opened the Western branch of the American Fur Company in 1819, and the city prospered during the early part of the 19th century as a commercial center for the fur trade. St. Louis continued to grow as a major transportation hub with the development of steamboat traffic and the later expansion of the railroads in the 1850s. The world-famous Louisiana Purchase Exposition was held here in 1904.

Manufacturing is important to the city's economy, and its highly developed industries include automobiles, aircraft and space technology, metal fabrication, beer, steelmaking, chemicals, food processing, and storage and distribution.

The giant stainless steel Gateway Arch, 630 ft high, standing on the banks of the Mississippi, symbolizes St. Louis as the Gateway to the West.

Famous natives: Josephine Baker, singer; Yogi Berra, baseball player; Chuck Berry, singer and guitarist; Grace Bumbry, mezzo-soprano; T. S. Eliot, poet; Eugene Field, poet; Redd Foxx, comedian; Joe Garagiola, baseball player; John Goodman, actor; Betty Grable, actress; Dick Gregory, comedian; Al Hirschfeld, cartoonist; Kevin Kline, actor; David Merrick, producer; Vincent Price, actor; Judy Rankin, golfer; Leon Spinks, boxer; Herbert Bayard Swope, journalist; Sara Teasdale, poet; Helen Traubel, soprano; Roy Wilkins, civil rights leader.

San Antonio, Tex.

Mayor: Ed Garza (to May 2005)
City Manager: Terry M. Brechtel
2000 census population (rank): 1,144,646 (9); **% change:** 22.3; **Male:** 553,245 (48.3%); **Female:** 591,401 (51.7%); **White:** 774,708 (67.7%); **Black:** 78,120 (6.8%); **American Indian and Alaska Native:** 9,584 (0.8%); **Asian:** 17,934 (1.6%); **Other race:** 221,362 (19.3%); **Two or more races:** 41,871 (3.7%); **Hispanic/Latino:** 671,394 (58.7%). **2000 percent population 18 and over:** 71.5%; **65 and over:** 10.4%; **median age:** 31.7.
Land area: 408 sq mi. (1,057 sq km); **Alt.:** 700 ft.
Avg. daily temp.: Jan., 49.3° F; July, 85.0° F
City-owned parks: 6,717 ac.; **Radio stations:** AM, 20; FM, 22; **Television stations:** 9
Civilian Labor Force (MSA) 2002: 812,331; **Unemployed:** 42,174, **Percent:** 5.2; **Per capita personal income (MSA) 2001:** $26,887
Chamber of Commerce: Greater San Antonio Chamber of Commerce, 602 E. Commerce, San Antonio, Tex. 78296

San Antonio, the third-largest city in Texas and the seat of Bexar County, is located in the south-central part of the state, on the San Antonio River.

The site of San Antonio was first visited in 1691 by a Franciscan friar on the feast day of St. Anthony and was named San Antonio de Padua in his honor. San Antonio was permanently settled on May 1, 1718, when the Spanish governor of Coahuila and Texas, Martin de Alarcón, founded the presidio (a fort) of San Antonio de Bejar (Bexar) and the mission of San Antonio de Valero (later called the

Alamo) on the site of a Coahuiltecan Indian village. San Antonio remained almost continuously under Spanish rule until 1812, when Mexico won its independence from Spain.

During the outbreak of the Texas revolution (1835) against the tyranny of Mexican dictator General Santa Anna, San Antonio was captured by a small band of rebels who occupied the fortified mission of the Alamo in Dec. 1835. The historic battle of the Alamo was fought there (Feb. 24 to March 6, 1836), and its 183 besieged defenders were massacred by Santa Anna's troops. Their heroism aroused the anger and fighting spirit of Texans and led them to shout their famous battle cry "Remember the Alamo!" and defeat the Mexicans six weeks later (April 21, 1836) at the battle of San Jacinto. Texas became an independent republic in 1836, and San Antonio was incorporated as a city on Jan. 5, 1837.

After the Civil War, with the arrival of the railroad in 1877, San Antonio prospered as a major shipping point for cattle. The city has been an important military center since World War II and is the home to five of the largest military installations in the nation, including Fort Sam Houston, constructed in 1876. San Antonio is a leading livestock center and one of the largest produce exchange markets. The city's industries are highly diversified, and tourism is also important to the economy.

Famous natives: Carol Burnett, comedienne; Cody Carlson, football player; Henry G. Cisneros, secretary of HUD; Joan Crawford, actress; Cito Gaston, baseball manager; Ann Harding, actress; Jesse James Leija, boxer; Emilio Navaira, Tejano music singer; Oliver North, military officer and government official; Suzy Parker, model and actress; Paula Prentiss, actress; Kyle Rote, football player; David R. Scott, astronaut; John Silber, university president; Patsy Torres, Tejano music singer; Edward H. White, astronaut.

San Diego, Calif.

Mayor: Dick Murphy (to Dec. 2004)
City Manager: Michael Uberuaga (apptd. Nov. 1997)
2000 census population (rank): 1,223,400 (7); **% change:** 10.2; **Male:** 616,884 (50.4%); **Female:** 606,516 (49.6%); **White:** 736,207 (60.2%); **Black:** 96,216 (7.9%); **American Indian and Alaska Native:** 7,543 (0.6%); **Asian:** 166,968 (13.6%); **Other race:** 151,532 (12.4%); **Two or more races:** 59,081 (4.8%); **Hispanic/Latino:** 310,752 (25.4%). **2000 percent population 18 and over:** 76.0%; **65 and over:** 10.5%; **median age:** 32.5.
Land area: 324 sq miles (839 sq km); **Alt.:** Highest, 1,591 ft.; lowest, sea level
Avg. daily temp.: Jan., 57.4° F; July, 71.0° F
Churches: Roman Catholic, 39; Jewish, 9; Protestant, 334; Eastern Orthodox, 8; other, 18; **City park and recreation facilities:** 164 (17,207 ac.); **Radio stations:** AM, 14; FM, 25; **Television stations:** 9
Civilian Labor Force (MSA) 2002: 1,468,248; **Unemployed:** 62,983, **Percent:** 4.3; **Per capita personal income (MSA) 2001:** $33,883
Chamber of Commerce: San Diego Chamber of Commerce, 402 West Broadway, Suite 1000, San Diego, Calif. 92101

San Diego is the second-largest city in California. It is located in the southwest part of the state, on San Diego Bay.

Portuguese navigator Juan Rodríguez Cabrillo claimed the bay for Spain in 1542. The site was named San Miguel by Cabrillo. On Nov. 12, 1602, Don Sebastian de Viscaíno came ashore with his party on the day of St. Didacus (San Diego in Spanish) and celebrated a mass in the saint's honor. By coincidence, Viscaíno's flagship was named *San Diego*. He renamed the place San Diego after the 15th-century saint.

In 1769, Franciscan father Junípero Serra established the first California mission there—San Diego del Alcala. In 1822, Mexico won control of the town after declaring its independence from Spain. In 1846, during the Mexican War, San Diego was seized by the U.S., and it was incorporated as a city in 1850, just after California joined the Union.

Today, San Diego's excellent natural harbor is a busy commercial port and a hub of U.S. naval operations (although the naval training center at San Diego has closed due to defense cutbacks). Other leading industries are electronics, aerospace and missiles, medical and scientific research, oceanography, and agriculture. Its magnificent climate and proximity to Mexico have made tourism a significant part of the city's economy.

Famous natives: Billy Casper, golfer; Florence Chadwick, swimmer; Dennis Conner, yacht racer; Ted Danson, actor; Robert Duvall, actor; Nanette Fabray, actress; Margaret O'Brien, actress; Carol Vaness, soprano; Ted Williams, baseball player; Mickey Wright, golfer.

San Francisco, Calif.

Mayor: Willie L. Brown, Jr. (to Jan. 2004)
2000 census population (rank): 776,733 (13); **% change:** 7.3; **Male:** 394,828 (50.8%); **Female:** 381,905 (49.2%); **White:** 385,728 (49.7%); **Black:** 60,515 (7.8%); **American Indian and Alaska Native:** 3,458 (0.4%); **Asian:** 239,565 (30.8%); **Other race:** 50,368 (6.5%); **Two or more races:** 33,255 (4.3%); **Hispanic/Latino:** 109,504 (14.1%). **2000 percent population 18 and over:** 85.5%; **65 and over:** 13.7%; **median age:** 36.5.
Land area: 47 sq mi. (122 sq km); **Alt.:** Highest, 925 ft.; lowest, sea level
Avg. daily temp.: Jan., 51.1° F; July, 59.1° F
Churches: 540 of all denominations; **City-owned parks and squares:** 225; **Radio stations:** 29; **Television stations:** 10
Civilian Labor Force (PMSA) 2002: 939,576; **Unemployed:** 55,466, **Percent:** 5.9; **Per capita personal income (PMSA) 2001:** $57,714
Chamber of Commerce: San Francisco Chamber of Commerce, 235 Montgomery St., San Francisco, Calif. 94104

San Francisco, the fourth-largest city in California, is coextensive with San Francisco County. It is located in the northern part of the state between the Pacific Ocean and San Francisco Bay on a narrow arm of land that embraces San Francisco Bay, the largest land-locked harbor in the world.

A Franciscan father who was sailing with Sebastián Rodríguez Cermeño named the bay San Francisco on Nov. 7, 1595. In 1776, the Spaniards established a presidio, or military post, and a Franciscan mission on the end of the beautiful peninsula. In the following year, a little town was founded around the mission. It was called Yerba Buena, Spanish for "Good Herb," because mint grew in abundance there. In 1846, during the Mexican War, Yerba Buena was taken over by the United States. It was renamed San Francisco in 1847 and became incorporated as a city in 1850.

When gold was discovered in California in 1848, the city's population jumped to 10,000, and it experienced turbulent years until order was established by Vigilance Committees, first in 1851, and again in 1856. Then followed a period of more orderly growth, and the foundations of the great commerce and industry of today were laid.

In 1906, San Francisco experienced the nation's most destructive earthquake, which, together with the fire that followed, practically destroyed the city. The city was quickly rebuilt and grew rapidly as a leading transportation, industrial, and cultural center. In the 19th century, the American explorer and soldier John C. Frémont, known as The Pathfinder, named the entrance to the bay the Golden Gate, and the famous bright orange Golden Gate Bridge was dedicated in May 1937.

A vital part of the economic and cultural fabric of northern California, the port of San Francisco covers 7½ mi of waterfront. The port is home to a broad range of commercial, maritime, and public activities. Its major shipping terminals serve shipping lines from around the world. Fisherman's Wharf, Alcatraz, Hyde St. Pier, and Pier 39 all make the port of San Francisco one of the world's leading visitor destinations.

The electronics and biotechnology industries are well represented throughout the Bay Area. With nearly 30% of the worldwide biotechnology labor force and 360 biotech firms, the Bay Area has been appropriately called "Bionic Bay."

Tourism is one of San Francisco's largest industries and the largest employer of city residents. In 2000, more than 17 million people visited San Francisco, and visitor spending was $7.6 billion, providing 82,000 jobs.

San Francisco is also the banking and financial center of the West and is home to a Federal Reserve Bank and a United States Mint. More than 60 foreign banks maintain offices there.

Famous natives: Gracie Allen, comedienne; Luis Walter Alvarez, Nobel Prize winner in physics; David Belasco, dramatist and producer; Mel Blanc, actor and voice specialist; Rosemary Casals, tennis player; Isadora Duncan, dancer; Clint Eastwood, actor; Robert Frost, poet; Rube Goldberg, cartoonist; William Randolph Hearst, publisher; Bruce Lee, actor; Mervyn LeRoy, director; Jack London, novelist; Johnny Mathis, singer; Lloyd Nolan, actor; O. J. Simpson, football player; Robert G. Sproul, educator; Irving Stone, novelist; Natalie Wood, actress.

San Jose, Calif.

Mayor: Ron Gonzales (to March 2006)
City Manager: Del D. Borgsdorf
2000 census population (rank): 894,943 (11); **% change:** 14.4; **Male:** 454,798 (50.8%); **Female:** 440,145 (49.2%); **White:** 425,017 (47.5%); **Black:** 31,349 (3.5%); **American Indian and Alaska Native:** 6,865 (0.8%); **Asian:** 240,375 (26.9%); **Other race:** 142,691 (15.9%); **Two or more races:** 45,062 (5.0%); **Hispanic/Latino:** 269,989 (30.2%). **2000 percent population 18 and over:** 73.6%; **65 and over:** 8.3%; **median age:** 32.6.
Land area: 175 sq mi. (453 sq km); **Alt.:** Highest, 4,372 ft.; lowest, sea level
Avg. daily temp.: Jan., 49.4° F; July, 69.5° F
Churches: 403; **City-owned parks and playgrounds:** 152 (3,136 ac.); **Radio stations:** 14; **Television stations:** 4
Civilian Labor Force (PMSA) 2002: 958,155; **Unemployed:** 80,590, **Percent:** 8.4; **Per capita personal income (PMSA) 2001:** $51,579
Chamber of Commerce: San Jose Chamber of Commerce, 310 S. First St., San Jose, Calif. 95113

San Jose, the third-largest city in California and seat of Santa Clara County, is located in the northern part of the state in the Santa Clara Valley, 50 mi south of downtown San Francisco.

San Jose was founded on Nov. 29, 1777, by Spanish colonizers who named the settlement Pueblo de San José de Guadalupe in honor of Saint Joseph and after the Guadalupe River on which the pueblo (town) was situated. San Jose was the first city to be established in California.

After California became a U.S. territory in 1847, San Jose was the state capital from 1849 to 1852 and was incorporated as a city in 1850. It developed commercially as a supply base for gold prospectors and, when the railroad connected it with San Francisco in 1864, it became the distribution point for agricultural products from the Santa Clara Valley.

Today, the city continues to be the distribution and food-processing center for the surrounding rich agricultural region, which produces seasonal fruits and grapes. More than 50 wineries grace the valley.

San Jose is the capital of Silicon (Santa Clara) Valley, where many high-tech companies are located. The area is also one of the world's leading centers for medical treatment and research. Heart transplants, gene splicing, and transportable baby incubators were developed there.

San Jose has healthy retail, transportation, and tourism industries and is the primary center for real estate and industrial development in the area. In 2001, it ranked second in the U.S. based on the median household income of $71,000.

Famous natives: "Fatty" Arbuckle, actor; Cesar Chavez, labor leader; Peggy Fleming, figure skater; Farley Granger, actor; Edmund Lowe, actor; Jim Plunkett, football player.

Seattle, Wash.

Mayor: Greg Nickels (to Dec. 31, 2005)
2000 census population (rank): 563,374 (24); **% change:** 9.1; **Male:** 280,973 (49.9%); **Female:** 282,401 (50.1%); **White:** 394,889 (70.1%); **Black:** 47,541 (8.4%); **American Indian and Alaska Native:** 5,659 (1.0%); **Asian:** 73,910 (13.1%); **Other race:** 13,423 (2.4%); **Two or more races:** 25,148 (4.5%); **Hispanic/Latino:** 29,719 (5.3%). **2000 percent population 18 and over:** 84.4%; **65 and over:** 12.0%; **median age:** 35.4.
Land area: 84 sq mi. (218 sq km); **Alt.:** Highest, 521 ft.; lowest, sea level
Avg. daily temp.: Jan., 40.1° F; July, 65.2° F
Churches: Roman Catholic, 35; Jewish, 12; Protestant, 447; others, 42; **City-owned parks, playgrounds, etc.:** 397 (6,000+ ac.); **Radio stations:** AM, 15; FM, 22; **Television stations:** 6
Civilian Labor Force (PMSA) 2002: 1,395,899[1]; **Unemployed:** 94,801[1], **Percent:** 6.8[1]; **Per capita personal income (PMSA) 2001:** $41,229[1]
Chamber of Commerce: Greater Seattle Chamber of Commerce, 1301 5th Ave., Suite 2400, Seattle, Wash. 98101-2603

1. Seattle–Bellevue–Everett, Wash.

Seattle is the largest city in Washington and the seat of King County. A city of steep hills, Seattle lies in western Washington between two bodies of water—Puget Sound on the west and Lake Washington on the east. Its fine landlocked harbor has made Seattle one of the major ports in the United States.

Seattle was first settled by five pioneer families from Illinois at Alki Point at the south end of Elliott Bay in 1851. They moved in 1852 to the eastern shore of the bay and laid out a town in 1853. It was named Seattle after a friendly Suquamish Indian chief (Seattle is only an approximation of his name).

Seattle successfully withstood an Indian attack in 1856 and was incorporated as a city in 1869. A disastrous fire almost destroyed the entire business district in 1889. When the Great Northern Railway arrived in 1893, the city became a major rail terminus and it grew rapidly. It was a boom town during the Alaska gold rush of 1897 and continued to prosper as a major Pacific port of entry with the opening of the Panama Canal in 1914.

Seattle is the region's commercial and transportation hub and the center of manufacturing, trade, and finance. Its important diversified industries include aircraft, lumber and forest products, fishing, high technology, food processing, boat building, machinery, fabricated metals, chemicals, pharmaceuticals, and apparel.

Famous natives: Chester Carlson, Xerox inventor; Carol Channing, actress; Judy Collins, singer; Fred Couples, golfer; Gail Devers, athlete; Frances Farmer, actress; William Gates, Microsoft founder; June Havoc, actress; Jimi Hendrix, guitarist; Robert Joffrey, choreographer; Gypsy Rose Lee, entertainer; Mary Livingstone, comedienne; Kevin McCarthy, actor; Mary McCarthy, novelist; Jeff Smith, food expert; Martha Wright, singer.

Tucson, Ariz.

Mayor: Bob Walkup (to Dec. 2003)
2000 census population (rank): 486,699 (30); **% change:** 20.1; **Male:** 238,408 (49.0%); **Female:** 248,291 (51.0%); **White:** 341,424 (70.2%); **Black:** 21,057 (4.3%); **American Indian and Alaska Native:** 11,038 (2.3%); **Asian:** 11,959 (2.5%); **Other race:** 81,988 (16.8%); **Two or more races:** 18,437 (3.8%); **Hispanic/Latino:** 173,868 (35.7%). **2000 percent population 18 and over:** 75.4%; **65 and over:** 11.9%; **median age:** 32.1.
Land area: 195 sq mi. (505 sq km); **Alt.:** 2,400 ft.
Avg. daily temp.: Jan., 51.3° F; July, 86.6° F
Churches: Protestant, 340; Roman Catholic, 42; other, 150; **City-owned parks and parkways:** (25,349 ac.); **Radio stations:** AM, 15; FM, 17; **Television stations:** 3 commercial; 1 educational; 3 other
Civilian Labor Force (MSA) 2002: 428,117; **Unemployed:** 20,774, **Percent:** 4.9; **Per capita personal income (MSA) 2001:** $24,767
Chamber of Commerce: Tucson Metropolitan Chamber of Commerce, 465 W. St. Mary's Rd., Tucson, Ariz. 85701

Tucson is the second-largest city in Arizona and the seat of Pima County. It is located in the southeast part of the state on the Santa Cruz River.

The site was originally settled by the prehistoric Hohokam Indians (300 B.C.–A.D.1400s). The first Europeans to visit the area were Spanish missionaries in the 17th century. In 1700, the Jesuit missionary explorer Father Eusebio Francisco Kino founded the mission of San Xavier del Bac close by the Papago Indian village of Stjukshon (later called Tucson). Stjukshon is an Indian word meaning "village of the dark spring at the foot of the mountain." The Papago Indians are descendants of the ancient Hohokam peoples.

In 1776, Spanish colonists from Mexico constructed a presidio (fort) at Tucson as protection against the hostile Apache Indians and also established the mission of San Jose de Tucson nearby. Tucson remained a military outpost under Spanish and later Mexican control until the area was sold to the United States as part of the Gadsden Purchase in 1853. Tucson was the capital of the Arizona Territory from 1867 to 1877. It was incorporated as a city in 1877. The town grew rapidly when the Southern Pacific Railroad arrived in 1880 and silver and copper deposits were discovered nearby.

Tucson is a popular vacation and health resort due to its sunny, mild, dry climate and unique desert location. Tourism is important to the city's economy. Major industries include aerospace and missile production, high technology, optics, biotechnology, environmental technology, software, and electronics. Tucson is also the commercial center for the surrounding area's agricultural and mining industries. The city is the home of the University of Arizona.

Famous natives: Rose E. Bird, jurist; Dennis De Concini, senator; Barbara Eden, actress; Linda Ronstadt, singer.

Tulsa, Okla.

Mayor: Bill LaFortune (to April 2006)
2000 census population (rank): 393,049 (43); **% change:** 7.0; **Male:** 189,937 (48.3%); **Female:** 203,112 (51.7%); **White:** 275,488 (70.1%); **Black:** 60,794 (15.5%); **American Indian and Alaska Native:** 18,551 (4.7%); **Asian:** 7,150 (1.8%); **Other race:** 13,564 (3.5%); **Two or more races:** 17,300 (4.4%); **Hispanic/Latino:** 28,111 (7.2%). **2000 percent population 18 and over:** 75.2%; **65 and over:** 12.9%; **median age:** 34.5.
Land area: 183 sq mi. (474 sq km); **Alt.:** 674 ft.
Avg. daily temp.: Jan., 35.2° F; July, 83.3° F
Churches: Protestant, 290; Roman Catholic, 40; Jewish, 3; others, 4; **City parks and playgrounds:** 140 (6,000 ac.); **Radio stations:** AM, 10; FM, 16; **Television stations:** 7 commercial; 1 PBS; 123 cable
Civilian Labor Force (MSA) 2002: 431,810; **Unemployed:** 21,053, **Percent:** 4.9; **Per capita personal income (MSA) 2001:** $30,650
Chamber of Commerce: Metropolitan Tulsa Chamber of Commerce, 2 West Second St., Ste. 150, Tulsa, Okla. 74103

Tulsa, the second-largest city in Oklahoma and seat of Tulsa County, is located in the northeast part of the state on the Arkansas River.

Tulsa was settled in the 1830s by Creek Indians from Alabama who were forcibly sent to the area (then part of Indian Territory) under the Indian Removal Act of 1830. Creek medicine men planted ashes from their old home at the new site, and the Creeks named their new village "Tulsy," meaning old town, in memory of their former home in Tallassee, Ala. In time, the village became the town of Tulsa.

The coming of the first railroad in 1882 attracted white settlers to Tulsa, and the town developed into a cattle-shipping center. When enormous oil deposits were discovered at nearby Red Fork in 1901 and at Glenn Pool in 1905, the city experienced rapid growth as a center of a booming petroleum industry. Tulsa was incorporated as a city in 1898 and chartered in 1908.

Tulsa is the center of the state's petroleum and telecommunications industries and has a diversified economy. Other important industries include aerospace, chemicals, computer parts, automobile glass, fabricated metals, and industrial machinery. The city became a major inland port when the Tulsa port of Catoosa opened in 1971.

Famous natives: Garth Brooks, singer; Blake Edwards, director; Paul Harvey, commentator; Jennifer Jones, actress; Henry R. Kravis, investment banker; Daniel Patrick Moynihan, senator; Tony Randall, actor; Alfre Woodard, actress; Judy Woodruff, journalist.

Virginia Beach, Va.

Mayor: Meyera E. Oberndorf (to June 2004)
2000 census population (rank): 425,257 (38); **% change:** 8.2; **Male:** 210,524 (49.5%); **Female:** 214,733 (50.5%); **White:** 303,681 (71.4%); **Black:** 80,593 (19.0%); **American Indian and Alaska Native:** 1,619 (0.4%); **Asian:** 20,869 (4.9%); **Other race:** 6,402 (1.5%); **Two or more races:** 11,677 (2.7%); **Hispanic/Latino:** 17,770 (4.2%); **2000 percent population 18 and over:** 72.5%; **65 and over:** 8.4%; **median age:** 32.7.
Land area: 248 sq mi. (642 sq km); **Alt.:** 12 ft.
Avg. daily temp.: Jan., 39.1° F; July, 78.2° F
Churches: Protestant, 235; Catholic, 13; Jewish, 5;
City-owned parks: 182 (1,748 ac.); **Radio stations:** AM 13, FM 31; **Television stations:** 8 commercial, 1 PBS, 1 cable
Civilian Labor Force (MSA) 2002: 778,889[1]; **Unemployed:** 32,510[1], **Percent:** 4.2[1]; **Per capita personal income (MSA) 2001:** $27,452[1]
Chamber of Commerce: Hampton Roads Chamber of Commerce, 420 Bank St., Norfolk, Va. 23510

1. Norfolk–Virginia Beach–Newport News, Va.–N.C.

Virginia Beach, the most populous city in Virginia, is located in the southeast part of the state on the Atlantic coastline. It is independent and is not part of any county.

The first English settlers to set foot in America landed at Cape Henry at the tip of Virginia Beach on April 29, 1607. They were led by John Smith on his way to establishing Jamestown. The first permanent settlement within the city limits was made at Lynnhaven Bay in 1621. Cape Henry became an important port for British merchant ships calling on America, and it was here that the French fleet led by Admiral Comte de Grasse blockaded the British fleet during the American Revolution.

Virginia Beach gained its reputation as a famous vacation resort in the 19th century, following the building of a railroad connecting its oceanfront with Norfolk and the construction of its first hotel in 1883. Virginia Beach was incorporated as a town in 1906 and as a city in 1952.

Tourism is a mainstay of the economy; more than 3 million people visit Virginia Beach each year. Virginia Beach's economy is also supported by four military bases and diverse industries, including agriculture, computer software, engineering, and technical services.

Famous natives and residents: V. C. Andrews, novelist; D. J. Dozier, football and baseball player; George Eastman, inventor; Juice Newton, singer; Kenneth S. Reightler, Jr., astronaut; Pat Robertson, evangelist; Henry Walke, naval officer; Pernell "Sweet Pea" Whitaker, boxer; Skip Wilkins, wheelchair athlete.

Washington, DC

Created municipal corporation: Feb. 21, 1871
Mayor: Anthony Williams (to Jan. 2007)
Motto: *Justitia omnibus* (Justice to all)
Flower: American beauty rose; **Tree:** Scarlet oak
2000 census population (rank): 572,059 (21); **% change:** –5.7; **Male:** 269,366 (47.1%); **Female:** 302,693 (52.9%); **White:** 176,101 (30.8%); **Black:** 343,312 (60.0%); **American Indian and Alaska Native:** 1,713 (0.3%); **Asian:** 15,189 (2.7%); **Other race:** 21,950 (3.8%); **Two or more races:** 13,446 (2.4%); **Hispanic/Latino:** 44,953 (7.9%); **2000 percent population 18 and over:** 79.9%; **65 and over:** 12.2%; **median age:** 34.6.
Land area: 61 sq mi. (158 sq km); **Alt.:** Highest, 420 ft.; lowest, sea level
Avg. daily temp.: Jan., 34.6° F; July, 80.0° F
Churches: Protestant, 610; Roman Catholic, 132; Jewish, 9; **City parks:** 753 (7,725 ac.); **Radio stations:** AM, 9; FM, 38; **Television stations:** 19
Civilian Labor Force (PMSA) 2002: 2,823,018[1]; **Unemployed:** 103,241[1], **Percent:** 3.7[1]; **Per capita personal income (PMSA) 2001:** $41,754[1]
Board of Trade: Greater Washington Board of Trade, 1129 20th Street N.W., Washington, DC 20036
Chamber of Commerce: DC Chamber of Commerce, 1213 K St. NW, Washington, DC 20005

1. Washington, DC–Md.–Va.–W.Va.

The District of Columbia—identical with the city of Washington—is the capital of the United States. It is located between Virginia and Maryland on the Potomac River. The district is named after Columbus.

DC history began in 1790 when Congress directed selection of a new capital site, 100 sq mi, along the Potomac. When the site was determined, it included 30.75 sq mi on the Virginia side of the river. In 1846, however, Congress returned that area to Virginia, leaving the 68.25 sq mi ceded by Maryland in 1788. The seat of government was transferred from Philadelphia to Washington on Dec. 1, 1800, and President John Adams became the first resident in the White House.

The city was planned and partly laid out by Maj. Pierre Charles L'Enfant, a French engineer. This work was perfected and completed by Maj. Andrew Ellicott and Benjamin Banneker, a freeborn black man who was an astronomer and mathematician. In 1814, during the War of 1812, a British force burned the capital including the White House.

Until Nov. 3, 1967, the District of Columbia was administered by three commissioners appointed by the president. On that day, a government consisting of a mayor-commissioner and a 9-member council, all appointed by the president with the approval of the Senate, took office. On May 7, 1974, the citizens of the District of Columbia approved a Home Rule Charter, giving them an elected mayor and 13-member council—their first elected municipal government in more than a century. The district also has one nonvoting member in the House of Representatives and an elected Board of Education.

On Aug. 22, 1978, Congress passed a proposed constitutional amendment to give Washington, DC, voting representation in the Congress. The amendment had to be ratified by at least 38 state legislatures within seven years to become effective. It died in 1985. A petition asking for the district's admission to the Union as the 51st state was filed in Congress on Sept. 9, 1983, and new statehood bills were introduced in 1993. The district is continuing this drive for statehood.

The federal government and tourism are the mainstays of the city's economy, and many unions, business, professional, and nonprofit organizations are headquartered there. Among the city's many educational institutions are the Catholic University of America, Georgetown University, Howard University, and Gallaudet University. Cultural attractions include the National Gallery of Art, the Smithsonian Institution, the John F. Kennedy Center for the Performing Arts, and the Folger Shakespeare Library.

Famous natives: Edward Albee, playwright; Billie Burke, comedienne; Ina Claire, actress; John Foster Dulles, statesman; Duke Ellington, musician; Jane Greer, actress; Goldie Hawn, actress; Helen Hayes, actress; J. Edgar

Hoover, former director of the F.B.I.; William Hurt, actor; Noor al-Hussein, queen of Jordan; Michael Learned, actress; Roger Mudd, newscaster; Eleanor Holmes Norton, government official; Chita Rivera, dancer and actress; Leonard Rose, cellist; John Philip Sousa, composer; Frances Sternhagen, actress.

Wichita, Kans.

Mayor: Carlos Mayans (to April 2007)
City Manager: Chris Cherches
2000 census population (rank): 344,284 (50); **% change:** 13.2; **Male:** 169,604 (49.3%); **Female:** 174,680 (50.7%); **White:** 258,900 (75.2%); **Black:** 39,325 (11.4%); **American Indian and Alaska Native:** 3,986 (1.2%); **Asian:** 13,647 (4.0%); **Other race:** 17,566 (5.1%); **Two or more races:** 10,662 (3.1%); **Hispanic/Latino:** 33,112 (9.6%); **2000 percent population 18 and over:** 72.9%; **65 and over:** 11.9%; **median age:** 33.4.
Land area: 136 sq mi. (352 sq km); **Alt.:** 1,333 ft.
Avg. daily temp.: Jan., 29.5° F; July, 81.4° F
Churches: Protestant, 512; Roman Catholic, 20; Jewish, 2; other, 66; **City parks:** 110 (4,388 ac.); **Radio stations:** 22; **Television stations:** 7
Civilian Labor Force (MSA) 2002: 287,135; **Unemployed:** 18,167, **Percent:** 6.3; **Per capita personal income (MSA) 2001:** $29,386
Chamber of Commerce: Wichita Chamber of Commerce, 350 W. Douglas, Wichita, Kans. 67202

Wichita is the largest city in Kansas and the seat of Sedgwick County. It is located in the south-central part of the state, at the confluence of the Arkansas and Little Arkansas rivers. Incorporated as a city in 1870, Wichita is the chief commercial and industrial center of southern Kansas.

More or less uninhabited at the time of Kansas's entry into the Union in 1861, the area was first settled by Wichita Indians, who came north from Texas and Oklahoma during the Civil War. At about the same time (during the mid-1860s) a number of trading posts were established at or near the river junction. One of the traders, Jesse Chisholm, pioneered the Chisholm Trail, which passed through Wichita and was the main cattle-drive route from Texas to the railroad in Abilene. After the railroad was extended to Wichita in 1872, the city boomed first as a cow town and then later as the trading center in an agricultural and livestock region. Although the city experienced an economic slump at the end of the 19th century, oil was discovered nearby in 1915, and subsequently the population almost doubled.

Aircraft manufacturing began in the 1920s, and Wichita remains a center of the aircraft industry today. In addition, the city also has flour mills, meatpacking plants, and oil refineries. Major manufactures include camping equipment, heaters and air conditioners, and electronics. Wichita has a number of art and historical museums, a zoo, and a planetarium. It is the site of several universities, including Wichita State University (1895). McConnell Air Force Base is nearby.

Famous natives: Kirstie Alley, actress; Alan Fudge, actor; Dan Glickman, former congressman and U.S. secretary of agriculture; Laurel Goodwin, actress; Stan Kenton, musician; Jim Lehrer, news anchor; Fred, Thomas, and Edwin McConnell, WWII pilots; Hattie McDaniel, actress; Barry Sanders, football player; Gale Sayers, football player; Arlen Specter, U.S. senator from Pennsylvania; Ron Wyden, U.S. senator from Oregon.

U.S. Cities and Metro Areas: Census 2000

Source: U.S. Census Bureau

Overall, cities expanded rapidly during the 1990s, growing nearly twice as fast as in the 1980s. Western and southern cities grew the fastest, while urban industrial centers in the Midwest and Northeast declined in population. New York remained the country's largest city, however, passing the 8 million mark.

In 2000, 80.3% of Americans (226 million people) lived in metropolitan areas, up slightly from 79.8% (198.4 million people) in 1990. (A metropolitan area is a city plus the adjacent communities to which it is linked economically.) All of the metropolitan areas with populations of at least 5 million grew over the period, ranging from 29% for the Dallas metropolitan area to 5% for Philadelphia. The total population within metropolitan areas increased by 14%, while the nonmetropolitan population grew by 10%.

Top Ten U.S. Cities by Percent Population Change, 1990–2000

Rank	Place name	Population		Change, 1990 to 2000	
		April 1, 2000	April 1, 1990	Number	Percent
1.	Augusta-Richmond County[1], Ga.	199,775	44,639	155,136	347.5%
2.	Gilbert, Ariz.	109,697	29,188	80,509	275.8
3.	Vancouver, Wash.	143,560	46,380	97,180	209.5
4.	Henderson, Nev.	175,381	64,942	110,439	170.1
5.	North Las Vegas, Nev.	115,488	47,707	67,781	142.1
6.	Athens-Clark County[2], Ga.	101,489	45,734	55,755	121.9
7.	Peoria, Ariz.	108,364	50,618	57,746	114.1
8.	Pembroke Pines, Fla.	137,427	65,452	71,975	110.0
9.	Chandler, Ariz.	176,581	90,533	86,048	95.0
10.	Las Vegas, Nev.	478,434	258,295	220,139	85.2

1. In 2000, Richmond County and the incorporated place of Augusta-Richmond County are coextensive. The 1990 population is for the incorporated place of Augusta city before consolidation of the city and county governments. 2. In 2000, Clarke County and the incorporated place of Athens-Clarke County are coextensive. The 1990 population is for the incorporated place of Athens city before consolidation of the city and county governments. *Source:* U.S. Census Bureau, Census 2000; 1990 Census. Web: www.census.gov.

The Five Fastest-Growing Metropolitan Areas, 1990–2000

Metropolitan area	Population		Change, 1990–2000	
	April 1, 1990	April 1, 2000	Number	Percent
Las Vegas, Nev., Ariz.	852,737	1,563,282	710,545	83.3%
Naples, Fla.	152,099	251,377	99,278	65.3
Yuma, Ariz.	106,895	160,026	53,131	49.7
McAllen-Edinburg-Mission, Tex.	383,545	569,463	185,918	48.5
Austin-San Marcos, Tex.	846,227	1,249,763	403,536	47.7

Source: U.S. Census Bureau, Census 2000; 1990 Census. Web: www.census.gov.

Top 50 Cities in the U.S. by Population and Rank, 1990 and 2000

	4/1/2000 census population	4/1/1990 census population	Numeric population change 1990–2000	Percent population change 1990–2000	Size rank 1990	Size rank 2000
New York, N.Y.	8,008,278	7,322,564	685,714	9.4	1	1
Los Angeles, Calif.	3,694,820	3,485,398	209,422	6.0	2	2
Chicago, Ill.	2,896,016	2,783,726	112,290	4.0	3	3
Houston, Tex.	1,953,631	1,630,553	323,078	19.8	4	4
Philadelphia, Pa.	1,517,550	1,585,577	–68,027	–4.3	5	5
Phoenix, Ariz.	1,321,045	983,403	337,642	34.3	10	6
San Diego, Calif.	1,223,400	1,110,549	112,851	10.2	6	7
Dallas, Tex.	1,188,580	1,006,877	181,703	18.0	8	8
San Antonio, Tex.	1,144,646	935,933	208,713	22.3	9	9
Detroit, Mich.	951,270	1,027,974	–76,704	–7.5	7	10
San Jose, Calif.	894,943	782,248	112,695	14.4	11	11
Indianapolis, Ind.	791,926	741,952	49,974	6.7	13	12
San Francisco, Calif.	776,733	723,959	52,774	7.3	14	13
Jacksonville, Fla.	735,617	635,230	100,387	15.8	15	14
Columbus, Ohio	711,470	632,910	78,560	12.4	16	15
Austin, Tex.	656,562	465,622	190,940	41.0	25	16
Baltimore, Md.	651,154	736,014	–84,860	–11.5	12	17
Memphis, Tenn.	650,100	610,337	39,763	6.5	18	18
Milwaukee, Wis.	596,974	628,088	–31,114	–5.0	17	19
Boston, Mass.	589,141	574,283	14,858	2.6	20	20
Washington, DC	572,059	606,900	–34,841	–5.7	19	21
Nashville-Davidson, Tenn.[1]	569,891	510,784	59,107	11.6	26	22
El Paso, Tex.	563,662	515,342	48,320	9.4	22	23
Seattle, Wash.	563,374	516,259	47,115	9.1	21	24
Denver, Colo.	554,636	467,610	87,026	18.6	28	25
Charlotte, N.C.	540,828	395,934	144,894	36.6	33	26
Fort Worth, Tex.	534,694	447,619	87,075	19.5	29	27
Portland, Ore.	529,121	437,319	91,802	21.0	27	28
Oklahoma City, Okla.	506,132	444,719	61,413	13.8	30	29
Tucson, Ariz.	486,699	405,390	81,309	20.1	34	30
New Orleans, La.	484,674	496,938	–12,264	–2.5	24	31
Las Vegas, Nev.	478,434	258,295	220,139	85.2	63	32
Cleveland, Ohio	478,403	505,616	–27,213	–5.4	23	33
Long Beach, Calif.	461,522	429,433	32,089	7.5	32	34
Albuquerque, N.M.	448,607	384,736	63,871	16.6	40	35
Kansas City, Mo.	441,545	435,146	6,399	1.5	31	36
Fresno, Calif.	427,652	354,202	73,450	20.7	48	37
Virginia Beach, Va.	425,257	393,069	32,188	8.2	39	38
Atlanta, Ga.	416,474	394,017	22,457	5.7	38	39
Sacramento, Calif.	407,018	369,365	37,653	10.2	37	40
Oakland, Calif.	399,484	372,242	27,242	7.3	35	41
Mesa, Ariz.	396,375	288,091	108,284	37.6	53	42
Tulsa, Okla.	393,049	367,302	25,747	7.0	44	43
Omaha, Neb.	390,007	335,795	54,212	16.1	47	44
Minneapolis, Minn.	382,618	368,383	14,235	3.9	43	45
Honolulu CDP,[2] Hawaii	371,657	365,272	6,385	1.7	41	46
Miami, Fla.	362,470	358,548	3,922	1.1	46	47
Colorado Springs, Colo.	360,890	281,140	79,750	28.4	54	48
St. Louis, Mo.	348,189	396,685	–48,496	–12.2	42	49
Wichita, Kans.	344,284	304,011	40,273	13.2	51	50

1. Nashville-Davidson city is consolidated with Davidson County. 2. Honolulu Census Designated Place; by agreement with the State of Hawaii, the Census Bureau does not show data separately for the city of Honolulu, which is coextensive with Honolulu County. *Source:* U.S. Census Bureau. Web: www.census.gov.

Tabulated Data on City Governments

City	Mayor: Term, years	Mayor: Salary[1]	City manager's salary[1,2]	Council or Commission: Name	Members	Term, years	Salary[1,3]
Albuquerque, N.M.	4	$ 90,314	$115,003	Council	9	4	$ 9,027
Atlanta, Ga.	4	141,490	—	Council	18	4	32,473
Austin, Tex.	3	60,000	188,115	Council	7	3	45,011
Baltimore, Md.	4	125,000	—	Council	19	4	48,000
Boston, Mass.	4	125,000	—	Council	13	2	62,500
Charlotte, N.C.	2	18,262	153,773	Council	11	2	13,044
Chicago, Ill.	4	192,100	—	Council	50	4	85,000
Cleveland, Ohio	4	115,108	—	Council	21	4	47,751
Colorado Springs, Colo.	4	6,250	137,000	Council	9	4	6,200
Columbus, Ohio	4	120,000	—	Council	7	4	35,000
Dallas, Tex.	4	60,000	263,000	Council	15[5]	2	37,500
Denver, Colo.	4	122,784	—	Council	13	4	62,304
Detroit, Mich.	4	176,176	—	Council	9	4	81,312
El Paso, Tex.	2	25,000	—	Council	9[5]	2	15,000
Fort Worth, Tex.	2	75[4]	189,010	Council	9[5]	2	75[4]
Fresno, Calif.	4	99,360	149,004	Council	7	4	44,511
Honolulu, Hawaii	4	112,200	107,100[6]	Council	9	4	43,350
Houston, Tex.	2	165,816	—	Council	14	2	44,218
Indianapolis, Ind.	4	95,000	—	Council	29	4	11,400
Jacksonville, Fla.	2	150,000	105,000[7]	Council	19	4	24,000
Kansas City, Mo.	4	89,988	151,740	Council	13[5]	4	44,988
Las Vegas, Nev.	4	53,422	167,747	Council	6	4	40,664
Long Beach, Calif.	4	98,935	199,500	Council	9	4	24,734
Los Angeles, Calif.	4[8]	177,091	210,178[6]	Council	15	4[8]	136,224
Memphis, Tenn.	4	140,000	107,000[6]	Council	13	4	20,100
Mesa, Ariz.	4	34,450	152,880	Council	6	4	17,238
Miami, Fla.	4	97,000	157,538	Commission	5	4	5,000
Milwaukee, Wis.	4	124,625	—	Council	17	4	61,934
Minneapolis, Minn.	4	86,288	119,606	Council	13	4	65,679
Nashville, Tenn.	4	75,000	8,900[9]	Council	40	4	6,900
New Orleans, La.	4	110,000	57,900	Council	7	4	42,500
New York, N.Y.	4	195,000	156,000[9]	Council	51	4	90,000
Oakland, Calif.	4	115,371	224,416[10]	Council	9[5]	4	60,000[11]
Oklahoma City, Okla.	4	24,000	133,500	Council	8	4	12,000
Omaha, Neb.	4	95,205	—	Council	7	4	27,813
Philadelphia, Pa.	4	130,000	140,000[7]	Council	17	4	80,000
Phoenix, Ariz.	4	56,000	190,672	Council	9[5]	4	35,999
Portland, Ore.	4	100,901	—	Council	4	4	84,989
Sacramento, Calif.	4	95,000	151,715	Council	9	4	2,300[12]
St. Louis, Mo.	4	116,142	—	Board of Alderman	29	4	28,745
San Antonio, Tex.	2	3,000[12]	200,000	Council	11[5]	2	20[4]
San Diego, Calif.	4	95,680	208,653	Council	8	4	71,796
San Francisco, Calif.	4	161,538	163,725	Bd. of Supvrs.	11	4	37,584
San Jose, Calif.	4	105,000	209,181	Council	11	4	75,000
Seattle, Wash.	4	136,158	—	Council	9	4	84,800
Tucson, Ariz.	4	42,000	163,200	Council	7[5]	4	24,000
Tulsa, Okla.	4	105,000	—	Council	9	2	18,000
Virginia Beach, Va.	4	20,000	167,200	Council	11[5]	4	18,000
Washington, DC	4	138,200	135,000	Council	13	4	92,520
Wichita, Kans.	4	65,240	141,260	Council	7[5]	4	24,850

1. Annual salary unless otherwise indicated; does not include additional payments for expenses, special sessions, etc. 2. City manager's term is indefinite and at will of council (or mayor). 3. In some cities, leaders receive a higher salary. 4. Per council meeting, with an annual cap. 5. Including mayor. 6. Appointed by mayor, approved by council. 7. Appointed by mayor; not subject to council confirmation. 8. Limited to 2 terms per city charter. 9. No city manager; salary is for deputy or vice mayor. 10. Denotes average based on range. 11. Council also serves as the Redevelopment Agency for which there is additional compensation. 12. Plus council pay. *Source:* Questionnaires to the cities.

U.S. Cities with Population over 100,000

ZIP codes provided below indicate the primary ZIP code for each city. Consult a ZIP code directory to find the appropriate ZIP code for a particular address, or try the U.S. Postal Service's online "ZIP Code Lookup," www.usps.gov/zip4/.

City	2000 Pop.	2000 Rank	ZIP Code
Alabama			
Birmingham	242,820	72	35203
Huntsville	158,216	130	35813
Mobile	198,915	94	36601
Montgomery	201,568	89	36119
Alaska			
Anchorage	260,283	66	99599
Arizona			
Chandler	176,581	116	85225
Gilbert	109,697	208	85296
Glendale	218,812	81	85302
Mesa	396,375	43	85201
Peoria	108,364	214	85381
Phoenix	1,321,045	6	85026
Scottsdale	202,705	88	85251
Tempe	158,625	129	85282
Tucson	486,699	30	85726
Arkansas			
Little Rock	183,133	112	72202
California			
Anaheim	328,014	56	92803
Bakersfield	247,057	70	93380
Berkeley	102,743	231	94704
Burbank	100,316	243	91505
Chula Vista	173,556	122	91910
Concord	121,780	181	94520
Corona	124,966	174	91718
Costa Mesa	108,724	213	92628
Daly City	103,621	227	94015
Downey	107,323	216	90241
El Monte	115,965	196	91734
Escondido	133,559	164	92025
Fontana	128,929	167	92335
Fremont	203,413	87	94537
Fresno	427,652	37	93706
Fullerton	126,003	173	92834
Garden Grove	165,196	127	92842
Glendale	194,973	100	91205
Hayward	140,030	154	94544
Huntington Beach	189,594	103	92647
Inglewood	112,580	204	90301
Irvine	143,072	150	92619
Lancaster	118,718	188	93534
Long Beach	461,522	34	90802
Los Angeles	3,694,820	2	90052
Modesto	188,856	104	95350
Moreno Valley	142,381	152	92553
Norwalk	103,298	229	90650
Oakland	399,484	42	94612
Oceanside	161,029	128	92054
Ontario	158,007	131	91761
Orange	128,821	168	92863
Oxnard	170,358	124	93030
Palmdale	116,670	194	93550
Pasadena	133,936	163	91103
Pomona	149,473	141	91769
Rancho Cucamonga	127,743	171	91729
Riverside	255,166	68	92507
Sacramento	407,018	41	95813
Salinas	151,060	138	93907
San Bernardino	185,401	110	92401
San Buenaventura (Ventura)	100,916	240	93001
San Diego	1,223,400	7	92199
San Francisco	776,733	13	94188
San Jose	894,943	11	95101
Santa Ana	337,977	52	92711
Santa Clara	102,361	232	95050
Santa Clarita	151,088	137	91355
Santa Rosa	147,595	144	95402
Simi Valley	111,351	206	93065
Stockton	243,771	71	95208
Sunnyvale	131,760	165	94086
Thousand Oaks	117,005	192	91362
Torrance	137,946	159	90503
Vallejo	116,760	193	94590
West Covina	105,080	224	91793
Colorado			
Arvada	102,153	235	80004
Aurora	276,393	62	80017
Colorado Springs	360,890	49	80903
Denver	554,636	25	80202
Fort Collins	118,652	189	80525
Lakewood	144,126	148	80202
Pueblo	102,121	236	81003
Westminster	100,940	239	80030
Connecticut			
Bridgeport	139,529	156	06602
Hartford	121,578	183	06101
New Haven	123,626	179	06511
Stamford	117,083	191	06904
Waterbury	107,271	217	06702
District of Columbia			
Washington[1]	572,059	21	20090
Florida			
Cape Coral	102,286	234	33909
Clearwater	108,787	212	33990
Coral Springs	117,549	190	33075
Fort Lauderdale	152,397	134	33310
Hialeah	226,419	76	33010
Hollywood	139,357	157	33022
Jacksonville	735,617	14	32203
Miami	362,470	48	33152
Orlando	185,951	107	32802
Pembroke Pines	137,427	161	33024
St. Petersburg	248,232	69	33730
Tallahassee	150,624	139	32301
Tampa	303,447	58	33630
Georgia			
Athens-Clarke County[2]	101,489	237	30608
Atlanta	416,474	40	30304
Augusta-Richmond County[3]	199,775	91	30901
Columbus	186,291	106	31908
Savannah	131,510	166	31402
Hawaii			
Honolulu CDP[4]	371,657	47	96820
Idaho			
Boise	185,787	108	83708
Illinois			
Aurora	142,990	151	60505
Chicago	2,896,016	3	60607
Joliet	106,221	221	60436
Naperville	128,358	169	60540
Peoria	112,936	203	61601
Rockford	150,115	140	61125
Springfield	111,454	205	62703
Indiana			
Evansville	121,582	182	47708
Fort Wayne	205,727	85	46802
Gary	102,746	230	46401
Indianapolis	791,926	12	46206
South Bend	107,789	215	46624
Iowa			
Cedar Rapids	120,758	185	52401
Des Moines	198,682	95	50318

City	2000 Pop.	2000 Rank	ZIP Code
Kansas			
Kansas City	146,866	146	66106
Overland Park	149,080	143	66204
Topeka	122,377	180	66603
Wichita	344,284	51	67276
Kentucky			
Lexington-Fayette	260,512	65	40511
Louisville	256,231	67	40231
Louisiana			
Baton Rouge	227,818	75	70826
Lafayette	110,257	207	70509
New Orleans	484,674	31	70113
Shreveport	200,145	90	71102
Maryland			
Baltimore	651,154	17	21202
Massachusetts			
Boston	589,141	20	02205
Cambridge	101,355	238	02139
Lowell	105,167	222	01853
Springfield	152,082	135	01101
Worcester	172,648	123	01613
Michigan			
Ann Arbor	114,024	199	48104
Detroit	951,270	10	48233
Flint	124,943	175	48502
Grand Rapids	197,800	96	49501
Lansing	119,128	187	48924
Livonia	100,545	242	48150
Sterling Heights	124,471	177	48311
Warren	138,247	158	48090
Minnesota			
Minneapolis	382,618	46	55401
St. Paul	287,151	60	55109
Mississippi			
Jackson	184,256	111	39205
Missouri			
Independence	113,288	202	64052
Kansas City	441,545	36	64108
St. Louis	348,189	50	63155
Springfield	151,580	136	65801
Nebraska			
Lincoln	225,581	77	68501
Omaha	390,007	45	68108
Nevada			
Henderson	175,381	118	89015
Las Vegas	478,434	32	89199
North Las Vegas	115,488	198	89030
Reno	180,480	114	89510
New Hampshire			
Manchester	107,006	218	03103
New Jersey			
Elizabeth	120,568	186	07208
Jersey City	240,055	73	07302
Newark	273,546	64	07102
Paterson	149,222	142	07510
New Mexico			
Albuquerque	448,607	35	87101
New York			
Buffalo	292,648	59	14240
New York	8,008,278	1	10199
Rochester	219,773	80	14692
Syracuse	147,306	145	13220
Yonkers	196,086	98	10701
North Carolina			
Charlotte	540,828	26	28228
Durham	187,035	105	27701
Fayetteville	121,015	184	28302
Greensboro	223,891	78	27420
Raleigh	276,093	63	27613
Winston-Salem	185,776	109	27102
Ohio			
Akron	217,074	82	44309
Cincinnati	331,285	55	45225
Cleveland	478,403	33	44101
Columbus	711,470	15	43216
Dayton	166,179	126	45401
Toledo	313,619	57	43601
Oklahoma			
Oklahoma City	506,132	29	73125
Tulsa	393,049	44	74107
Oregon			
Eugene	137,893	160	97401
Portland	529,121	28	97208
Salem	136,924	162	97309
Pennsylvania			
Allentown	106,632	219	18101
Erie	103,717	226	16515
Philadelphia	1,517,550	5	19104
Pittsburgh	334,563	53	15290
Rhode Island			
Providence	173,618	121	02904
South Carolina			
Columbia	116,278	195	29201
South Dakota			
Sioux Falls	123,975	178	57104
Tennessee			
Chattanooga	155,554	132	37421
Clarksville	103,455	228	37043
Knoxville	173,890	119	37950
Memphis	650,100	18	38101
Nashville-Davidson[5]	569,891	22	37230
Texas			
Abilene	115,930	197	79604
Amarillo	173,627	120	79120
Arlington	332,969	54	76004
Austin	656,562	16	78710
Beaumont	113,866	200	77707
Brownsville	139,722	155	78520
Carrollton	109,576	209	75006
Corpus Christi	277,454	61	78469
Dallas	1,188,580	8	75260
El Paso	563,662	23	79910
Fort Worth	534,694	27	76161
Garland	215,768	83	75040
Grand Prairie	127,427	172	75051
Houston	1,953,631	4	77201
Irving	191,615	102	75061
Laredo	176,576	117	78041
Lubbock	199,564	92	79402
McAllen	106,414	220	78501
Mesquite	124,523	176	75149
Pasadena	141,674	153	77501
Plano	222,030	79	75074
San Antonio	1,144,646	9	78284
Waco	113,726	201	76702
Wichita Falls	104,197	225	76307
Utah			
Provo	105,166	223	84601
Salt Lake City	181,743	113	84199
West Valley City	108,896	211	84199
Virginia			
Alexandria	128,283	170	22314
Chesapeake	199,184	93	23320
Hampton	146,437	147	23670
Newport News	180,150	115	23607
Norfolk	234,403	74	23501
Portsmouth	100,565	241	23707
Richmond	197,790	97	23232
Virginia Beach	425,257	38	23450
Washington			
Bellevue	109,569	210	98009
Seattle	563,374	24	98108

City	2000 Pop.	2000 Rank	ZIP Code
Spokane	195,629	99	99201
Tacoma	193,556	101	98413
Vancouver	143,560	149	98668
Wisconsin			
Green Bay	102,313	233	54303
Madison	208,054	84	53714
Milwaukee	596,974	19	53203

1. Washington city is coextensive with the District of Columbia. 2. In 2000, Clarke County and the incorporated place of Athens-Clarke County are coextensive. 3. In 2000, Richmond County and the incorporated place of Augusta-Richmond County are coextensive. 4. Honolulu Census Designated Place; data are not given separately for the city of Honolulu, which is coextensive with Honolulu County. 5. Nashville-Davidson city is consolidated with Davidson County. *Source:* U.S. Census Bureau. Web: www.census.gov.

Area Codes: United States, Canada, Caribbean

Area codes	Selected cities
UNITED STATES	
Alabama	
205	Birmingham, Tuscaloosa
251	Jackson, Mobile
256	Huntsville, Florence
334	Montgomery, Dothan, Selma
Alaska	
907	Entire state
Arizona	
480	Chandler, Scottsdale
520	Tucson
602	Phoenix
623	Sun City, Peoria
928	Flagstaff, Yuma
Arkansas	
479	Fayetteville, Fort Smith
501	Hot Springs, Little Rock
870	Jonesboro, Texarkana
California	
209	Stockton, Modesto
213, 323	Los Angeles
310	Santa Monica, Beverly Hills, Torrance
408	San Jose
415	San Francisco, San Rafael
510	Oakland, Berkeley
530	Redding, Davis
559	Fresno
562	Long Beach, Whittier
619	San Diego
626	Pasadena, Azusa
650	Palo Alto, San Mateo
661	Bakersfield
707	Vallejo, Eureka, Santa Rosa
714	Orange, Anaheim, Huntington Beach
760	Barstow, Palm Springs
805	San Luis Obispo, Santa Barbara, Simi Valley
818	San Fernando, Burbank
831	Santa Cruz, Salinas
858	Poway
909	Pomona, Riverside
916	Sacramento
925	Concord, Walnut Creek
949	Irvine, Newport Beach
Colorado	
303, 720	Denver, Boulder
719	Colorado Springs, Pueblo
970	Aspen, Fort Collins
Connecticut	
203	Bridgeport, New Haven, Danbury
860	Hartford, Norwich, New London
Delaware	
302	Entire state
District of Columbia	
202	Entire district
Florida	
239	Fort Myers, Naples
305	Miami, Key West
321	Orlando, Cape Canaveral
352	Gainesville, Ocala
386	Daytona Beach
407	Kissimmee, Orlando
561	West Palm Beach, Boca Raton
727	Clearwater, St. Petersburg
772	Fort Pierce, Port St. Lucie
786	Miami, Homestead
813	Tampa
850	Tallahassee, Pensacola
863	Lakeland, Winter Haven
904	Jacksonville
941	Port Charlotte, Sarasota
954, 754	Ft. Lauderdale
Georgia	
229	Albany, Valdosta
404	Atlanta
478	Macon
678, 770	Atlanta, Smyrna, Marietta
706	Athens, Augusta
912	Savannah
Hawaii	
808	Entire state
Idaho	
208	Entire state
Illinois	
217	Springfield, Champaign
224	Evanston, Schaumburg
309	Peoria, Bloomington
312, 773	Chicago
618	Carbondale, East St. Louis
630	Aurora, Naperville
708	Chicago Heights, Cicero
815	Rockford, Joliet
847	Waukegan, Skokie
Indiana	
219	Gary
260	Fort Wayne
317	Indianapolis
574	South Bend, La Porte, Elkhart
765	Lafayette, Muncie, Kokomo
812	Bloomington, Terre Haute
Iowa	
319	Cedar Rapids, Burlington
515	Des Moines, Ames
563	Dubuque, Davenport
641	Mason City, Ottumwa
712	Sioux City, Council Bluffs
Kansas	
316	Wichita
620	Dodge City, Emporia
785	Topeka, Lawrence
913	Kansas City, Leavenworth
Kentucky	
270	Owensboro, Bowling Green
502	Frankfort, Louisville
606	Ashland
859	Lexington, Covington
Louisiana	
225	Baton Rouge
318	Shreveport
337	Lafayette, Lake Charles
504	New Orleans, Metairie
985	Houma, Slidell
Maine	
207	Entire state
Maryland	
240, 301	Frederick, Hagerstown, Bethesda
410, 443	Baltimore, Salisbury, Annapolis
Massachusetts	
413	Springfield, Northampton
508, 774	Worcester, New Bedford
617, 857	Boston, Cambridge
781, 339	Waltham, Lynn
978, 351	Lowell, Gloucester
Michigan	
231	Muskegon, Shelby
248, 947	Troy, Pontiac
269	Kalamazoo, Battle Creek
313	Detroit, Dearborn
517	Lansing, Jackson
586	Warren, St. Clair Shores
616	Grand Rapids, Holland
734	Ann Arbor, Monroe, Ypsilanti
810	Flint, Port Huron
906	Sault Ste. Marie
989	Saginaw, Midland
Minnesota	
218	Duluth, Moorhead
320	St.Cloud
507	Rochester, Mankato
612	Minneapolis
651	St. Paul
763	Maple Grove, Coon Rapids
952	Bloomington, Edina
Mississippi	
228	Gulfport, Biloxi
601	Jackson, Vicksburg
662	Tupelo, Greenville
Missouri	
314	St. Louis, Webster Groves
417	Springfield, Joplin

Area codes	Selected cities
573	Jefferson City, Columbia
636	Chesterfield, St. Charles
660	Sedalia
816	Kansas City, Independence
Montana	
406	Entire state
Nebraska	
308	Grand Island, Kearney
402	Lincoln, Omaha
Nevada	
702	Las Vegas, Henderson
775	Carson City, Reno
New Hampshire	
603	Entire state
New Jersey	
201, 551	Jersey City, Hackensack
609	Trenton, Atlantic City
732, 848	New Brunswick, Long Branch
856	Cherry Hill, Vineland, Camden
908	Elizabeth, Summit
973, 862	Newark, Paterson
New Mexico	
505	Entire state
New York	
212, 646	Manhattan
315	Syracuse, Utica
347, 718	Bronx, Brooklyn, Queens, Staten Island
516	Mineola, Hicksville
518	Albany, Troy
585	Rochester
607	Binghamton, Elmira
631	Riverhead, Islip
716	Buffalo, Niagara Falls
845	Poughkeepsie, Kingston
914	White Plains, Yonkers
917	Manhattan, Bronx, Queens, Staten Island, Brooklyn
North Carolina	
252	Greenville, Rocky Mount
336	Winston-Salem, Greensboro
704, 980	Charlotte, Gastonia
828	Asheville, Hickory
910	Fayetteville, Wilmington
919	Raleigh, Chapel Hill
North Dakota	
701	Entire state
Ohio	
216	Cleveland, Shaker Heights
234, 330	Akron, Youngstown
419, 567	Toledo, Sandusky
440	Ashtabula, Lorain
513	Cincinnati
614	Columbus
740	Chillicothe, Zanesville
937	Dayton, Xenia
Oklahoma	
405	Oklahoma City, Shawnee
580	Enid, Lawton
918	Tulsa, Muskogee
Oregon	
503, 971	Salem, Portland
541	Eugene, Corvallis

Area codes	Selected cities
Pennsylvania	
215, 267	Philadelphia, Levittown
412, 878	Pittsburgh, McKeesport
484, 610	Allentown, Reading
570	Scranton, Williamsport
717	Harrisburg, Lancaster
724, 878	Uniontown, New Castle
814	Erie, State College
Rhode Island	
401	Entire state
South Carolina	
803	Columbia, Aiken
843	Charleston, Myrtle Beach
864	Greenville, Spartanburg
South Dakota	
605	Entire state
Tennessee	
423	Chattanooga, Johnson City
615	Nashville, Gallatin
731	Jackson
865	Knoxville, Oak Ridge
901	Memphis
931	Columbia, Clarksville
Texas	
210	San Antonio
214, 469, 972	Dallas, Plano
254	Waco, Killeen
281, 713, 832	Houston
325	Abilene
361	Corpus Christi, Victoria
409	Galveston, Port Arthur
432	Midland, Odessa
512	Austin
682, 817	Fort Worth, Arlington
806	Lubbock, Amarillo
830	Uvalde, Seguin
903, 430	Tyler, Texarkana, Paris
915	El Paso
936	Huntsville, Nacogdoches
940	Wichita Falls, Denton
956	Laredo, Brownsville
979	Bryan, College Station
Utah	
435	Moab, St. George
801	Salt Lake City, Provo
Vermont	
802	Entire state
Virginia	
276	Abingdon, Wytheville
434	Danville, Lynchburg, Charlottesville
540	Roanoke, Harrisonburg
571, 703	Alexandria, Mount Vernon
757	Norfolk, Virginia Beach
804	Richmond, Hopewell
Washington	
206	Seattle, Bainbridge Island
253	Tacoma, Auburn
360	Olympia, Bellingham
425	Bellevue, Redmond
509	Spokane, Yakima
West Virginia	
304	Entire state

Area codes	Selected cities
Wisconsin	
262	Racine, Kenosha
414	Milwaukee, Wauwatosa
608	Madison, Beloit
715	Eau Claire, Wausau
920	Green Bay, Oshkosh
Wyoming	
307	Entire state
U.S. TERRITORIES	
684	American Samoa
671	Guam
670	Marianas Islands
787, 939	Puerto Rico
340	U.S. Virgin Islands
CANADA	
Alberta	
403	Calgary
780	Edmonton
British Columbia	
250	Victoria
604, 778	Vancouver
Manitoba	
204	Entire province
New Brunswick	
506	Entire province
Newfoundland	
709	Entire province
Nova Scotia	
902	Nova Scotia, Prince Edward Island
Ontario	
289, 905	Hamilton
416, 647	Toronto
519	Windsor
613	Ottawa
705	Sudbury
807	Thunder Bay
Quebec	
418	Quebec
450	Laval
514	Montreal
819	Trois-Rivieres
Saskatchewan	
306	Entire province
Yukon, Northwest Territories, & Nunavut	
867	All provinces
CARIBBEAN AND ATLANTIC ISLANDS	
264	Anguilla
268	Antigua and Barbuda
242	Bahamas
246	Barbados
441	Bermuda
284	British Virgin Islands
345	Cayman Islands
809	Dominican Republic
767	Dominica
473	Grenada
876	Jamaica
664	Montserrat
869	St. Kitts & Nevis
758	St. Lucia
784	St. Vincent & the Grenadines
868	Trinidad & Tobago
649	Turks & Caicos

Source: North American Numbering Plan Administration. Web: www.nanpa.com.

U.S. Postal Rates and Fees

Domestic Rates, last revised by the U.S. Postal Service on June 30, 2002

First-Class Mail

First-Class Mail includes all personal correspondence, all bills and statements of accounts, all matter sealed or otherwise closed against inspection, and matter wholly or partly in writing or typewriting. Any mailable items may be sent as First-Class Mail. Each piece must weigh 13 oz or less. Pieces over 13 oz can be sent as Priority Mail.

Single-Piece Letter/Flat Rates

1st oz	$0.37
Each additional oz	0.23

Weight not over (oz)	Rate	Weight not over (oz)	Rate
1*	$0.37	9	$2.21
2	0.60	10	2.44
3	0.83	11	2.67
4	1.06	12	2.90
5	1.29	13	3.13
6	1.52	Over 13 oz, *see* Priority Mail.	
7	1.75		
8	1.98		

*Nonstandard surcharge may apply to pieces weighing 1 oz or less based on size.

Card Rates

Single postcard (commercial)	$0.23
Single postal card sold by United States Postal Service	0.25

Postcard Dimensions: Not larger than 4¼ by 6 in. by 0.016 in. thick. Not smaller than 3½ by 5 in. by 0.007 in. thick.

Express Mail

Express Mail is the fastest service, with next day delivery by 12 noon to most destinations. Express Mail is delivered 365 days a year—with no extra charge for Saturday, Sunday, or holiday delivery. Items must weigh 70 lbs or less and measure 108 in. or less in combined length and girth.

Customer Service—1-800-222-1811. Order Express Mail supplies and labels, arrange pickup service, obtain delivery information between ZIP Codes, and determine delivery status.

Post Office to Addressee Service

Up to 8 oz	$13.65
Up to 2 lbs	17.85
Up to 3 lbs	21.05
Up to 4 lbs	24.20
Up to 5 lbs	27.30
Up to 6 lbs	30.40
Up to 7 lbs	33.45

Over 7 lbs, see postmaster.

Express Mail Flat-Rate Envelope

$13.65, regardless of weight or destination, for matter sent in a flat-rate envelope provided by the Postal Service.

Priority Mail

Priority Mail offers 2-day service to most domestic destinations. Items must weigh 70 lbs or less and measure 108 in. or less in combined length and girth. Items that weigh less than 15 lbs but measure more than 84 in. (combined length and girth) are charged the 15 lb rate ($11.05)*.

Single-Piece Rates*

Up to 1 lb	$3.85
Up to 2 lbs	3.95
Up to 3 lbs	4.75
Up to 4 lbs	5.30
Up to 5 lbs	5.85

Over 5 pounds, see postmaster.

*Rates are given for zones local through 3.

Priority Mail Flat-Rate Envelope

$3.85, regardless of weight or destination, for matter sent in a flat-rate envelope provided by the Postal Service.

Media Mail (Book Rate)

Generally used for books (at least eight pages), film (16 mm or narrower), printed music, printed test materials, sound recordings, play scripts, printed educational charts, loose-leaf pages and binders consisting of medical information, and computer-readable media. Advertising restrictions apply. Packages must measure 108 in. or less in combined length and girth.

Weight not over (lbs)	Rate	Weight not over (lbs)	Rate
1	$1.42	9	$4.54
2	1.84	10	4.84
3	2.26	11	5.14
4	2.68	12	5.44
5	3.10	13	5.74
6	3.52	14	6.04
7	3.94	15	6.34
8	4.24	16	6.64

Special Services (Domestic Mail)

Certificate of Mailing

Provides evidence of mailing only. Certificate of mailing does not provide a record of delivery. Must be purchased at time of mailing. Available for First-Class Mail, Priority Mail, Parcel Post, Bound Printed Matter, and Media Mail.

Fee, in addition to postage—$0.90

Certified Mail

Provides the sender with a mailing receipt. A delivery record is maintained by the USPS. No insurance provided. Available with First-Class Mail and Priority Mail. For an additional fee, certified mail may be combined with restricted delivery or return receipt.

Fee, in addition to postage—$2.30

Insurance

Provides coverage against loss or damage. Coverage up to $5,000 for Parcel Post, Bound Printed Matter, and Media Mail matter as well as merchandise mailed at Priority Mail or First-Class Mail rates. Items must not be insured for more than their value. Insured mail must be presented to a retail employee at a post office or a rural carrier.

Liability	Fee, in addition to postage
$.01 to $50.00	$1.30
$50.01 to $100.00	2.20
$100.01 to $200.00	3.20
$200.01 to $300.00	4.20
$300.01 to $400.00	5.20
$400.01 to $500.00	6.20
$500.01 to $600.00	7.20
$600.01 to $5,000	*

*$7.00 plus $1.00 for each $100 or fraction over $600 in declared value.

Money Orders

Provides safe transmission of money. Available in amounts up to $1,000.
Fee up to $500, in addition to postage—$0.90
Fee up to $1,000, in addition to postage—$1.25

Registered Mail

Provides maximum protection and security for valuables. Provides sender with mailing receipt and a delivery record is maintained by the USPS. A record of mailing is maintained at the mailing post office. Available only for items paid at Priority Mail and First-Class Mail rates.

	Declared Value	Fee, in addition to postage
Without Insurance	$0.00	$ 7.50
With Insurance	$0.01 to $100	8.00
	$100.01 to $500.00	8.85
	$500.01 to $1,000.00	9.70
	$1,000.01 to $2,000.00	10.55

For higher values, consult your postmaster.

Restricted Delivery

Permits a mailer to direct delivery only to the addressee or addressee's authorized agent. The addressee must be an individual specified by name. Available for First-Class Mail, Priority Mail, Parcel Post, Bound Printed Matter, and Media Mail that is sent certified mail, COD, mail insured for more than $50, or registered mail.
Fee, in addition to postage—$3.50

Return Receipt

Available only for Express Mail, Certified Mail, COD, Insured Mail for more than $50.00, or Registered Mail.

Requested at time of mailing:
Showing to whom (signature), date, and addressee's address (in conjunction with another service) $1.75
Requested after mailing:
Showing to whom (signature) and date delivered $3.25

Special Handling

Provides preferential handling, but not preferential delivery, to extent practicable in dispatch and transportation. Available for First-Class Mail, Priority Mail, Parcel Post, Bound Printed Matter, and Media Mail.

Fee, in addition to postage:
Pieces weighing not more than 10 pounds—$5.95
Pieces weighing more than 10 pounds—$8.25

Collect on Delivery (COD)

Allows mailers to collect the price of goods and/or postage on merchandise ordered by addressee when it is delivered. Fees include insurance. Maximum amount $1,000; see postmaster for details.

Sizes for Domestic Mail

Mail must meet these standards:

• Thickness—No less than 0.007 in. thick. Pieces that are ¼ in. thick or less must be at least 3½ in. high, 5 in. long, and rectangular in shape.

• Combined length and girth—No more than 108 in.

• Weight—No more than 70 lbs.

Postcards must be:

• Minimum 3½ in. high, 5 in. long by .007 in. thick.

• Maximum 4¼ in. high, 6 in. long by .016 in. thick.

The Mail-Order Merchandise Rule

The mail-order rule adopted by the Federal Trade Commission in October 1975 provides that when you order by mail:

• You must receive the merchandise when the seller says you will.

• If you are not promised delivery within a certain time period, the seller must ship the merchandise to you no later than 30 days after your order comes in.

• If you don't receive it shortly after that 30-day period, you can cancel your order and get your money back.

ZIP Codes

The ZIP Code was instituted in 1963 and allows for electronic processing and delivery of mail. An envelope that does not include a ZIP Code in the delivery address must be manually sorted, which increases the cost of sorting the mail and causes mail to be delayed en route to the delivery address. ZIP Code directories are available for use or sale at your local post office, or you can look up ZIP Codes on-line: www.usps.gov/ncsc/.

In 1983, the Postal Service began to use an expanded ZIP Code called ZIP+4. It is composed of the original five-digit code plus a four-digit add-on. The four-digit add-on number identifies a geographic segment within the five-digit delivery area such as a city block, an office building, an individual high-volume receiver of mail, or any other unit that would aid efficient mail sorting and delivery.

Postal Information Websites

United States Postal Service: http://www.usps.gov/
ZIP Code Lookup: http://www.usps.gov/zip4/
U.S. Postal Service Rate Calculators:
domestic: http://postcalc.usps.gov/
international: http://ircalc.usps.gov/
business: http://dbcalc.usps.gov/

International Postal Rates

Last revised by the U.S. Postal Service on June 30, 2002

Single Piece Letter-Post

Weight not over (oz)	Canada	Mexico	Western Europe and Israel	Australia, Japan, New Zealand	Other countries
1	$ 0.60	$ 0.60	$ 0.80	$ 0.80	$ 0.80
2	0.85	0.85	1.60	1.70	1.55
3	1.10	1.25	2.40	2.60	2.30
4	1.35	1.65	3.20	3.50	3.05
5	1.60	2.05	4.00	4.40	3.80
6	1.85	2.45	4.80	5.30	4.55
7	2.10	2.85	5.60	6.20	5.30
8	2.35	3.25	6.40	7.10	6.05
12	3.10	4.00	7.55	8.40	7.65
16	3.75	5.15	8.70	9.70	9.25
20	4.40	6.30	9.85	11.00	10.85
24	5.05	7.45	11.00	12.30	12.45
28	5.70	8.60	12.15	13.60	14.05
32	6.35	9.75	13.30	14.90	15.65
36	7.00	10.95	14.50	16.25	17.35
40	7.65	12.15	15.70	17.60	19.05
44	8.30	13.35	16.90	18.95	20.75
48	8.95	14.55	18.10	20.30	22.45
52	9.65	15.80	19.35	21.70	24.20
56	10.35	17.05	20.60	23.10	25.95
60	11.05	18.30	21.85	24.50	27.70
64	11.75	19.55	23.10	25.90	29.45

Maximum weight: 64 oz. **Postcards and Postal Rates:** Canada and Mexico—$0.50; all others—$0.70.

All-Time Top 10 Most Popular Commemorative Stamps

Issue	No. saved (millions)
Elvis '93	124.0
Wildflowers '92	76.2
Rock and Roll '93	75.8
Civil War '95	46.6
Legends of the West '94	46.5
Marilyn Monroe '95	46.3
Bugs Bunny '97	45.3
Summer Olympics '92	39.6
The World of Dinosaurs	38.5
Centennial Olympic Games '96	38.1

Source: U.S.P.S., 1998; latest data available. Popularity of stamps is measured by number saved, not used.

Postal Workers Bitten by Dogs, by District

District	Dog bites
1. Greater Indiana	87
2. Gateway (Missouri, southern Illinois)	77
3. Long Beach	76
4. South Florida	73
5. Houston	72
6. Santa Anna	71
7. Northern Illinois	65
8. San Diego, Connecticut[1]	64
9. Triboro (Staten Island, Brooklyn, Queens)	62
10. Van Nuys	61

1. Ties. *Source:* U.S.P.S., 2002. A total of 3,070 postal workers were bitten by dogs in FY2002.

State Abbreviations and State Postal Codes

State	Abbreviation	Postal code	State	Abbreviation	Postal code	State	Abbreviation	Postal code
Alabama	Ala.	AL	Kentucky	Ky.	KY	Ohio	Ohio	OH
Alaska	Alaska	AK	Louisiana	La.	LA	Oklahoma	Okla.	OK
Arizona	Ariz.	AZ	Maine	Maine	ME	Oregon	Ore.	OR
Arkansas	Ark.	AR	Maryland	Md.	MD	Pennsylvania	Pa.	PA
California	Calif.	CA	Massachusetts	Mass.	MA	Puerto Rico	P.R.	PR
Colorado	Colo.	CO	Michigan	Mich.	MI	Rhode Island	R.I.	RI
Connecticut	Conn.	CT	Minnesota	Minn.	MN	South Carolina	S.C.	SC
Delaware	Del.	DE	Mississippi	Miss.	MS	South Dakota	S.D.	SD
Dist. of Columbia	D.C.	DC	Missouri	Mo.	MO	Tennessee	Tenn.	TN
Florida	Fla.	FL	Montana	Mont.	MT	Texas	Tex.	TX
Georgia	Ga.	GA	Nebraska	Nebr.	NE	Utah	Utah	UT
Guam	Guam	GU	Nevada	Nev.	NV	Vermont	Vt.	VT
Hawaii	Hawaii	HI	New Hampshire	N.H.	NH	Virginia	Va.	VA
Idaho	Idaho	ID	New Jersey	N.J.	NJ	Virgin Islands	V.I.	VI
Illinois	Ill.	IL	New Mexico	N.M.	NM	Washington	Wash.	WA
Indiana	Ind.	IN	New York	N.Y.	NY	West Virginia	W.Va.	WV
Iowa	Iowa	IA	North Carolina	N.C.	NC	Wisconsin	Wis.	WI
Kansas	Kans.	KS	North Dakota	N.D.	ND	Wyoming	Wyo.	WY

Timely Travel Tips

Online forums tell you what vacation guides can't—or would prefer not to

By ANITA HAMILTON TIME

Gary Eisenberg has climbed mountains in Sri Lanka and scuba dived in Thailand. He has worked in a boatyard in Turkey and bartended in Portugal. He has roamed Egypt, Morocco, and New Guinea. Yet this seasoned traveler—who globe-trotted for a decade before settling (at least for now) in New York City as a corporate lawyer—rarely takes a guidebook along. "As soon as a place gets listed," he explains, "everybody goes there. The quality drops, and it is hard to get in."

Instead, Eisenberg, 39, relies on online travel forums for advice. While printed guides may offer good cultural and historical information, the listings are typically a year old by the time the books hit store shelves. Online forums, in contrast, are buzzing with timely tips from fellow travelers—many of whom have just returned from a trip or, better still, are logging on from a cybercafe abroad.

AOL members can visit the bulletin boards at Keyword: Travel Community. Web wanderers can check out these sites:

thorntree.lonelyplanet.com With more than 7,000 new messages posted each day, Thorn Tree is the best one-stop shop. And because discussions are moderated by Lonely Planet staff, offensive posts are rare.

groups.google.com Type "rec.travel" in the search box to pull up 15 different newsgroups. The nonmoderated forums are peppered with commercial listings but full of useful advice too.

virtualtourist.com This free community site allows users to build their own travel Web pages and dish out advice. The pervasive ads are annoying, but the member pages, many with photos, must-see activities, and tips on tourist traps to avoid, are heartfelt and fun. □

Distinctive Destinations from the National Trust for Historic Preservation

Source: National Trust for Historic Preservation.

From a Georgia island once home to a who's who of Gilded Age glitterati to an antebellum southern town as charming and untouched today as it was in its heyday, and a California resort where Wallis Simpson met a prince and fell in love, America offers alternative vacation destinations that symbolize an increasing dedication to historic preservation. The National Trust for Historic Preservation, the country's largest private, nonprofit preservation organization, offers an annual list of "Dozen Distinctive Destinations," featuring unique and lovingly preserved communities in the United States that make interesting alternatives to the homogenization of many other vacation spots. The cities and towns on the 2003 list of America's Dozen Distinctive Destinations are:

Burlington, Vt. (pop. 38,889): On the shores of beautiful Lake Champlain, Burlington boasts an active arts scene, a rich architectural legacy, and a number of internationally known museums, making this both a convenient gateway to northern New England and the perfect getaway.

Coronado, Calif. (pop. 24,100): For more than a century, this charming seaside village and its opulent fantasy hotel, "The Del," have lured both jet-setters (including the Duke and Duchess of Windsor) and everyday visitors with an irresistible combination of natural beauty, history, and over-the-top elegance.

Edenton, N.C. (pop. 5,394): Steeped in history, Edenton inspired some of the country's earliest female political action. Today it showcases three centuries of architecture, a number of prominent African-American historic sites, waterfront parks, a canoe and kayak trail, and a National Fish Hatchery.

Galveston, Tex. (pop. 57,247): This city that rose from ruin after a devastating hurricane is still charming visitors, who find Galveston's cache of historic buildings, restaurants, shops, art galleries, and kid-friendly adventures—including an offshore oil rig and a historic sailing ship.

Georgetown, Colo. (pop. 1,088): Nestled among some of the West's most majestic peaks, Georgetown still beguiles those who come to ski, fish, hike, bike, raft, or soak in the ambience of an authentic, yet largely undiscovered, silver-mining town.

Jekyll Island, Ga. (pop. 1,000): Six miles off Georgia's coast, the island that was purchased by America's wealthiest industrialists in 1886 still glitters today with unspoiled beaches, the ruins of a former cotton plantation, and traces of early Native-American inhabitants who called this place "golden."

Keene, N.H. (pop. 22,563): Chartered in 1753, tiny Keene is a Currier & Ives landscape come to life, where pristine local landmarks, Revolutionary War reenactments, and bucolic rolling hills provide a perfect spot for family fun.

Mackinac Island, Mich. (pop. 500 year-round): Reachable only by ferry, 8-mile-long Mackinac Island's breathtaking scenery, richly detailed architecture, well-preserved historic sites, and striking natural wonders have been captivating visitors for centuries.

Natchez, Miss. (pop. 18,464): A richly preserved antebellum town, Natchez is a feast for the eyes with a treasure trove of distinctive architectural styles, year-round festivals, and diverse historic sites that celebrate the community's African-American and Native-American heritage.

New Harmony, Ind. (pop. 916): A southern Indiana jewel, New Harmony was founded by German religious refugees in 1814 and is today a living museum, where perfectly preserved historic structures and year-round festivals are reminders of the 19th-century dream of creating a perfect society.

Portland, Maine (pop. 64,249): On a rocky coastline decorated with fine sand beaches, Portland is a destination rich in historical significance and inherent beauty, with a bustling waterfront, vibrant arts district, and a collection of remarkable buildings.

Vancouver, Wash. (pop. 143,560): Located just across the Columbia River from Portland, Ore., with carefully preserved historic sites and spectacular nearby natural wonders such as Columbia Gorge and Mount St. Helens, Vancouver is an ideal family destination.

U.S. Passport Information

With a few exceptions, a passport is required for all U.S. citizens to depart and enter the United States and to enter most foreign countries. Persons who travel to a country where a U.S. passport is not required should be in possession of documentary evidence of their U.S. citizenship and identity to facilitate reentry into the United States. Travelers should check passport and visa requirements with consular officials of the countries to be visited well in advance of their departure date.

Application for a passport may be made at a passport agency, many federal and state courts, probate courts, some county and municipal offices, and some post offices. The thirteen major cities with U.S. passport agencies are Boston, Chicago, Honolulu, Houston, Los Angeles, Miami, New Orleans, New York, Norwalk, Conn., Philadelphia, San Francisco, Seattle, and Washington, DC.

All persons are required to obtain individual passports in their own names. Neither spouses nor children may be included in each other's passports. Applicants age 14 years and older must appear in person before the clerk or agent executing the application if it is their first time applying. For children age 13 and under, a parent or legal guardian may execute an application for them.

If you would like more information about obtaining or renewing a passport, visit the State Dept. website (http://travel.state.gov) or call the National Passport Information Center, 1-888-362-8668.

Visas

Some countries require visas for entry. These should be obtained from the appropriate foreign consular representative before proceeding abroad. Allow sufficient time for processing your visa application, especially if you are applying by mail. Most foreign consular representatives are located in principal cities, and in many instances, a traveler may be required to obtain visas from the consular office in the area of his/her residence. Processing and visa fees vary. Consult the embassy or consulate of the country you plan to visit for specific details.

Immunizations

Under the International Health Regulations adopted by the World Health Organization, a country may require International Certificates of Vaccination against yellow fever, especially if you are traveling from an area of the world that is infected with yellow fever. Check with health care providers or your records to ensure other immunizations (e.g. tetanus and polio) are up-to-date. Prophylactic medication for malaria and certain other preventive measures are advisable for travel to some countries. No immunizations are required to return to the United States. Detailed health information is included in Health Information for International Travel, available from the U.S. Government Printing Office (address on page 20) for $20 or may be obtained from your local health department or physician or by contacting the Centers for Disease Control and Prevention, telephone 1-877-FYI-TRIP (1-877-394-8747), toll-free autofax: 1-888-CDC-FAXX (1-888-232-3299), or Internet: www.cdc.gov.

A Safe Trip Abroad

The U.S. Department of State offers the following tips for safe travel abroad:

- Dress conservatively. Thieves often target tourists, so avoid wearing anything that will make you stand out, and leave your expensive jewelry at home.
- Travel light. You will be able to move more quickly and will be more likely to have a free hand. Also, you will be less tired and less likely to set your luggage down and leave it unattended.
- Conceal your valuables. Leave your passport, cash, and credit cards locked in a hotel safe if possible. When you carry them on you, conceal them in several different places rather than all in one wallet, pocket, or bag. Avoid using handbags, fanny packs, and outside pockets that are easy targets for thieves.
- If you wear glasses, pack an extra pair. Pack your glasses and any medicines you need in your carry-on luggage.
- Keep medicines in their original labeled containers. This will help you to avoid problems when passing through customs. Bring copies of your prescriptions and the generic names for the drugs. If a medication contains narcotics, carry a letter from your doctor attesting to your need to take the drug. If you have any doubt about the legality of

carrying a certain drug into a foreign country, consult the embassy or consulate of that country first.

- Bring travelers' checks and a major credit card instead of cash.
- Leave a copy of the serial numbers of your travelers' checks with a friend or relative at home. Carry your copy with you in a separate place, and as you cash the checks, cross them off the list.
- Bring an extra set of passport photos and a photocopy of your passport information page. This will make it easier to get a replacement if your passport is lost or stolen.
- Put your name, address, and telephone number inside each piece of luggage. Use covered luggage tags to avoid casual observation of your name, address, and nationality. Always lock your luggage.
- Consider getting a telephone calling card that can be used from overseas locations. Access numbers to U.S. operators are published in many international papers, but find out your access number before you go.

Source: U.S. Dept. of State, Bureau of Consular Affairs. Web: http://travel.state.gov.

Average Daily Temperatures (°F) in Tourist Cities

(For U.S. cities, *see* Climate of Selected U.S. Cities, pp. 599–600)

	January		April		July		October	
Location	**High**	**Low**	**High**	**Low**	**High**	**Low**	**High**	**Low**
Acapulco (Mexico)	87	72	87	73	89	77	89	77
Amsterdam (Netherlands)	41	34	53	40	69	55	57	46
Athens (Greece)	54	42	67	52	90	72	74	60
Auckland (New Zealand)	73	60	67	56	56	46	63	52
Bangkok (Thailand)	89	69	94	78	91	77	89	76
Beijing (China)	35	15	68	44	87	71	67	44
Belgrade (Yugoslavia)	38	28	62	43	81	60	64	46
Berlin (Germany)	35	26	55	38	74	55	55	41
Bombay (India)	83	67	89	76	85	77	89	76
Cairo (Egypt)	65	47	83	57	96	70	86	65
Calcutta (India)	80	55	97	75	89	79	89	74
Cape Town (South Africa)	69	56	66	54	60	50	65	53
Caracas (Venezuela)	75	56	81	60	78	61	79	61
Copenhagen (Denmark)	36	29	50	37	72	55	53	42
Dublin (Ireland)	47	35	54	38	67	51	57	43
Glasgow (Scotland)	43	34	53	38	66	52	54	43
Hamilton (Bermuda)	68	58	71	59	85	73	79	69
Helsinki (Finland)	27	17	43	31	71	57	45	37
Hong Kong (China)	67	51	79	67	90	78	84	70
Istanbul (Turkey)	48	36	59	45	78	64	66	53
Jerusalem (Israel)	55	41	73	50	87	63	81	59
Kingston (Jamaica)	86	67	87	70	90	73	88	73
Lagos (Nigeria)	88	74	89	77	82	74	85	74
Lisbon (Portugal)	56	46	64	52	79	63	69	57
London (United Kingdom)	44	35	56	40	73	55	58	44
Madrid (Spain)	50	34	63	43	89	61	67	48
Mexico City (Mexico)	66	42	77	51	73	53	70	50
Montreal (Canada)	22	6	51	33	79	60	56	39
Moscow (Russia)	21	9	47	31	76	55	46	34
Nairobi (Kenya)	77	53	75	57	69	51	77	54
Nassau (Bahamas)	77	65	81	69	88	75	85	73
Oslo (Norway)	30	20	50	34	73	56	49	37
Paris (France)	42	32	60	41	76	55	59	44
Prague (Czech Republic)	34	25	55	40	74	58	54	44
Quebec (Canada)	19	3	45	30	77	58	51	37
Rio de Janeiro (Brazil)	84	73	80	69	75	63	77	66
Rome (Italy)	54	39	68	46	88	64	73	53
San José (Costa Rica)	75	58	79	62	77	62	77	60
San Juan (Puerto Rico)	81	70	83	72	86	76	86	75
Seoul (Korea)	33	17	62	42	84	70	67	47
Singapore	86	73	89	75	87	75	88	74
Stockholm (Sweden)	31	23	45	32	70	55	48	39
Sydney (Australia)	79	65	73	57	62	44	72	55
Taipei (Taiwan)	66	54	77	63	92	76	81	67
Tokyo (Japan)	48	31	64	48	84	71	70	56
Toronto (Canada)	30	17	51	35	79	60	57	42
Vancouver (Canada)	42	32	55	41	71	55	57	44
Vienna (Austria)	34	26	57	41	75	59	55	44
Zurich (Switzerland)	36	26	60	41	77	56	57	43

The World's Top Tourism Destinations

(international tourist arrivals)

2001 rank	Country	Arrivals (million) 2000	Arrivals (million) 2001	Percent change 2000/2001	2001 market share
1.	France	75.6	76.5	1.2	11.0%
2.	Spain	47.9	49.5	3.4	7.1
3.	United States	50.9	45.5	−10.7	6.6
4.	Italy	41.2	39.1	−5.2	5.6
5.	China	31.2	33.2	6.2	4.8
6.	United Kingdom	25.2	22.8	−9.4	3.3
7.	Russian Fed.	21.2	—	—	—
8.	Mexico	20.6	19.8	−4.0	2.9
9.	Canada	19.7	19.7	0.2	2.8%
10.	Austria	18.0	18.2	1.1	2.6
11.	Germany	19.0	17.9	−5.9	2.6
12.	Hungary	15.6	15.3	−1.5	2.2
13.	Poland	17.4	15.0	−13.8	2.2
14.	Hong Kong (China)	13.1	13.7	5.1	2.0
15.	Greece	13.1	—	—	—

Source: World Tourism Organization (WTO). Web: www.world-tourism.org.

Top International Destinations of American Tourists

(numbers in thousands)

2000 rank	Country[1]	2000 travelers
1.	Mexico	18,849
2.	Canada	15,114
3.	United Kingdom	4,189
4.	France	2,927
5.	Germany	2,309
6.	Italy	2,148
7.	Japan	1,262
7.	Spain	1,262
8.	Netherlands	1,101
9.	Switzerland	994
10.	Bahamas	913
11.	Jamaica	886
12.	Hong Kong	832
13.	Republic of Korea	779
14.	Ireland	725
15.	Australia	698
16.	Brazil	671
16.	Taiwan	671
17.	China	644
18.	Israel	618
19.	Austria	564
20.	Philippines	457
20.	Belgium	457
20.	Greece	457
20.	India	457
20.	New Zealand	457
20.	Singapore	457

1. Ranked by 2000 visitation volume. *Source:* U.S. Dept. of Commerce, International Trade Administration.

Top States and Cities Visited by Overseas Travelers, 2000

State	Overseas visitors (thousands)	Market share (percent)
Total overseas travelers[1]	**25,975**	**100.0%**
California	6,364	24.5
Florida	6,026	23.2
New York	5,922	22.8
Hawaiian Islands	2,727	10.5
Nevada	2,364	9.1
Massachusetts	1,429	5.5
Illinois	1,377	5.3
Guam	1,325	5.1
Texas	1,169	4.5
New Jersey	909	3.5
Arizona	883	3.4
Georgia	805	3.1
Pennsylvania	649	2.5
Colorado	519	2.0

City	Overseas visitors (thousands)	Market share (percent)
Total overseas travelers[1]	**25,975**	**100.0%**
New York, N.Y.	5,714	22.0
Los Angeles, Calif.	3,533	13.6
Orlando, Fla.	3,013	11.6
Miami, Fla.	2,935	11.3
San Francisco, Calif.	2,831	10.9
Las Vegas, Nev.	2,260	8.7
Oahu/Honolulu, Hawaii	2,234	8.6
Washington, DC	1,481	5.7
Chicago, Ill.	1,351	5.2
Boston, Mass.	1,325	5.1
San Diego, Calif.	701	2.7
Atlanta, Ga.	701	2.7
Tampa/St. Petersburg, Fla.	519	2.0
San Jose, Calif.	494	1.9

NOTE: Includes travelers for business and pleasure, international travelers in transit through the United States, and students; excludes travel by international personnel and international businessmen employed in the United States. 1. Includes other states and cities, not shown separately. *Source:* U.S. Dept. of Commerce, International Trade Administration. From *Statistical Abstract of the United States, 2001.*

Top Nationalities of Travelers to the U.S.

2000 rank	Country of residence	2000 total	Percent of total travelers to U.S.
1.	Canada	14,594,000	29%
2.	Mexico	10,322,000	20
3.	Japan	5,061,377	10
4.	United Kingdom	4,703,008	9
5.	Germany	1,786,045	4
6.	France	1,087,087	2
7.	Brazil	737,245	1
8.	South Korea	661,844	1
9.	Italy	612,357	1%
10.	Venezuela	576,663	1
11.	Netherlands	553,297	1
12.	Australia	539,559	1
13.	Argentina	533,936	1
14.	Taiwan	457,302	—
15.	Colombia	417,065	—

NOTE: (—) = less than 1%. *Source:* U.S. Dept. of Commerce, International Trade Administration.

Tourism by World Region

Worldwide tourism experienced a 0.6% decrease in 2001, which is somewhat less than what was feared after Sept. 11, 2001. The Americas suffered the most (6.0% decrease), followed by South Asia (4.5%), and the Middle East (down 2.5%). Europe also experienced a slight decrease of 0.7%, but it remains the world's top tourism region.

	Arrivals (in millions)		Percent change	2001 market
	2000	2001	2000/2001	share
World	**696.8**	**692.6**	**–0.6%**	**100.0%**
Africa	27.2	28.4	4.3	4.1
Americas	128.5	120.8	–6.0	17.4
East Asia and the Pacific	109.2	115.2	5.5	16.6
Europe	402.5	399.7	–0.7%	57.7%
Middle East	23.2	22.7	–2.5	3.3
South Asia	6.1	5.8	–4.5	0.8

Source: World Tourism Organization (WTO). Web: www.world-tourism.org.

Africa

Africa experienced a 4.6% increase in international tourism in 2001. South Africa remains the most important destination, despite suffering a 1.5% decrease in arrivals. The countries enjoying the biggest growth last year were Namibia, Tanzania, and Nigeria.

	Arrivals (in thousands)		Percent change	2001 market
Region and country	2000	2001	2000/2001	share
Africa	**27,223**	**28,405**	**4.3%**	**100.0%**
South Africa	6,001	5,908	–1.5	20.8
Tunisia	5,057	5,387	6.5	19.0
Morocco	4,113	4,223	2.7	14.9
Zimbabwe	1,866	—	—	—
Botswana	995	—	—	—
Kenya	899	841	–6.5%	3.0%
Algeria	866	901	4.1	3.2
Nigeria	813	955	17.5	3.4

Source: World Tourism Organization (WTO). Web: www.world-tourism.org.

Americas

All of the Americas, excluding Central America, suffered declines in international tourism in 2001, especially the United States (10.7% decrease). The Caribbean countries did not repeat the success they had in 2000.

	Arrivals (in thousands)		Percent change	2001 market
Region and country	2000	2001	2000/2001	share
Americas	**128,497**	**120,840**	**–6.0%**	**100.0%**
United States	50,945	45,490	–10.7	37.6
Mexico	20,641	19,811	–4.0	16.4
Canada	19,663	19,697	0.2	16.3
Brazil	5,313	4,773	–10.2	3.9
Puerto Rico	3,341	3,551	6.3%	2.9%
Dominican Republic	2,973	2,778	–6.6	2.3
Argentina	2,909	2,629	–9.6	2.2
Uruguay	1,968	1,892	–3.9	1.6

Source: World Tourism Organization (WTO). Web: www.world-tourism.org.

Europe

Europe failed to repeat the record results posted in the Jubilee Year of 2000. But in relative terms, the decrease of 0.7% does not appear that bad. Southern and Eastern Europe are growing steadily, with Serbia and Montenegro, Croatia, Slovakia, and Slovenia welcoming the return of market demand. Bulgaria was a success story in 2001, while Poland suffered a decline of 13.8%. The greatest decline was experienced by Israel, 50.5%, due to the Palestinian conflict.

	Arrivals (in thousands)		Percent change	2001 market
Region and country	2000	2001	2000/2001	share
Europe	**402,539**	**399,711**	**–0.7%**	**100.0%**
France	75,580	76,508	1.2	19.1
Spain	47,898	49,519	3.4	12.4
Italy	41,181	39,055	–5.2	9.8
United Kingdom	25,211	22,833	–9.4%	5.7%
Germany	18,983	17,861	–5.9	4.5
Poland	17,400	15,000	–13.8	3.8
Hungary	15,571	15,340	–1.6	3.8

Source: World Tourism Organization (WTO). Web: www.world-tourism.org.

Middle East

On average, international arrivals were down 2.5% from the year before. The greatest success was experienced in Lebanon and Jordan, while Egypt suffered a decline of 14.8%.

Region and country	Arrivals (in thousands) 2000	2001	Percent change 2000/2001	2001 market share
Middle East	**23,237**	**22,653**	**–2.5%**	**100.0%**
Egypt	5,116	4,357	–14.8	19.2
Jordan	1,427	1,478	3.6	6.5
Syria	1,416	1,318	–6.9%	5.8%
Lebanon	742	837	12.9	3.7

Source: World Tourism Organization (WTO). Web: www.world-tourism.org.

East Asia and the Pacific

In contrast to the Americas, East Asia and the Pacific continued with strong growth, as seen in 2001, averaging 5.5%. China, together with Hong Kong and Macau, is becoming the unrivaled leader of Asian tourism, followed by Malaysia and Thailand.

Region and country	Arrivals (in thousands) 2000	2001	Percent change 2000/2001	2001 market share
East Asia and the Pacific	**109,171**	**115,156**	**5.5%**	**100.0%**
China	31,229	33,167	6.2	28.8
Hong Kong (China)	13,059	13,725	5.1	11.9
Malaysia	10,222	12,775	25.0	11.1
Thailand	9,579	10,133	5.8%	8.8%
Singapore	6,917	6,726	–2.8	5.8
Korea, Republic of	5,322	5,147	–3.3	4.5
Indonesia	5,084	5,154	1.8	4.5
Japan	4,757	4,772	0.3	4.1

Source: World Tourism Organization (WTO). Web: www.world-tourism.org.

South Asia

South Asia felt the impact of the increased tension between India and Pakistan and the war in Afghanistan. Arrivals were down 4.5%, with Nepal, Pakistan, and Sri Lanka suffering the biggest declines.

Region and country	Arrivals (in thousands) 2000	2001	Percent change 2000/2001	2001 market share
South Asia	**6,091**	**5,818**	**–4.5%**	**100.0%**
India	2,649	2,537	–4.2	43.6
Iran	1,342	1,402	4.5	24.1
Pakistan	557	500	–10.2	8.6
Maldives	467	461	–1.3%	7.9%
Nepal	464	363	–21.8	6.2
Sri Lanka	400	337	–15.9	5.8

Source: World Tourism Organization (WTO). Web: www.world-tourism.org.

Current Travel Warnings for U.S. Citizens[1]

Travel Warnings are issued when the State Department recommends that Americans avoid a certain country. The countries listed below are currently on that list. In addition to this list, the State Department issues Consular Information Sheets for every country of the world with information on such matters as the health conditions, crime, unusual currency or entry requirements or any areas of instability.

Country	Most recent warning issued
Afghanistan	7/28/03
Algeria	9/5/03
Angola	3/24/03
Bahrain	2/12/03
Bosnia and Herzegovina	6/4/02
Burundi	8/12/93
Central African Republic	4/7/03
Colombia	6/16/03
Côte d'Ivoire	8/13/03
Dem. Rep. of the Congo (formerly Zaire)	4/7/03
East Africa	5/14/03
Hong Kong	4/1/03
Indonesia	8/28/03
Iran	5/12/03
Iraq	8/22/03
Israel	4/17/03
Jordan	2/7/03
Kenya	5/16/03
Kuwait	3/16/03
Lebanon	5/6/03
Liberia	6/6/03
Libya	10/7/02
Macedonia	5/21/02
Nigeria	6/26/03
Oman	3/10/03
Pakistan	3/28/03
Qatar	2/12/03
Saudi Arabia	8/13/03
Somalia	3/4/03
Sudan	3/26/03
Syria	3/16/03
Tajikistan	12/20/02
Turkey	3/19/03
United Arab Emirates	3/10/03
Venezuela	2/19/02
Vietnam	3/22/03
Yemen	3/28/03
Zimbabwe	1/27/03

NOTE: In the wake of the terrorist attacks on the World Trade Center and the Pentagon on Sept. 11, 2001, the State Department issued a worldwide caution for U.S. citizens traveling abroad. 1. As of Sept. 2003. *Source:* U.S. Department of State. Web: http://travel.state.gov.

State and Territory Tourism Offices

The following is a selected list of state tourism office Web addresses and phone numbers. Where a toll-free 800 or 888 number is available, it is given. However, the numbers are subject to change.

Alabama
1-800-ALABAMA
www.touralabama.org

Alaska
907-929-2200
www.travelalaska.com

Arizona
1-888-520-3434
www.arizonaguide.com

Arkansas
1-800-NATURAL
www.arkansas.com

California
1-800-GOCALIF
www.gocalif.ca.gov

Colorado
1-800-COLORADO
www.colorado.com

Connecticut
1-800-CT-BOUND
www.ctbound.org

Delaware
1-866-2-VISIT-DE
www.visitdelaware.net

District of Columbia (Washington, DC)
202-789-7000
www.washington.org

Florida
888-7FLA-USA
www.flausa.com

Georgia
1-800-VISIT-GA
www.georgiaonmymind.org

Guam
671-646-5278/9
www.visitguam.org

Hawaii
1-800-GO-HAWAII
www.gohawaii.com

Idaho
1-800-635-7820
www.visitid.org

Illinois
1-800-2-CONNECT
www.enjoyillinois.com

Indiana
1-888-ENJOY-IN
www.enjoyindiana.com

Iowa
1-888-472-6035
www.traveliowa.com/

Kansas
1-800-2-KANSAS
www.travelks.com

Kentucky
1-502-223-8687
www.tourky.com

Louisiana
1-800-677-4082
www.louisianatravel.com

Maine
1-888-MAINE-45
www.visitmaine.com

Maryland
1-800-MDISFUN
www.mdisfun.org

Massachusetts
1-800-227-MASS
www.massvacation.com

Michigan
1-888-78-GREAT
www.michigan.org

Minnesota
1-800-657-3700
www.exploreminnesota.com

Mississippi
1-800-WARMEST
www.visitmississippi.org

Missouri
1-800-810-5500
www.missouritourism.org

Montana
1-800-VISIT-MT
www.visitmt.com

Nebraska
1-877-NEBRASKA
www.visitnebraska.org

Nevada
1-800-NEVADA-8
www.travelnevada.com

New Hampshire
1-800-FUN-IN-NH
www.visitnh.gov

New Jersey
1-800-VISIT-NJ
www.state.nj.us/travel

New Mexico
1-800-733-6396
www.newmexico.org

New York
1-800-CALL-NYS
www.iloveny.com

North Carolina
1-800-VISIT-NC
www.visitnc.com

North Dakota
1-800-HELLO-ND
www.ndtourism.com

Ohio
1-800-BUCKEYE
www.ohiotourism.com

Oklahoma
1-800-654-8240
www.touroklahoma.com

Oregon
1-800-547-7842
www.traveloregon.com

Pennsylvania
1-800-VISIT-PA
www.experiencepa.com

Puerto Rico
1-800-866-7827
www.gotopuertorico.com

Rhode Island
1-800-556-2484
www.visitrhodeisland.com

South Carolina
1-800-SCSMILE
www.travelsc.com

South Dakota
1-800-S-DAKOTA
www.travelsd.com

Tennessee
1-800-610-2-TENN
www.tourism.state.tn.us/

Texas
1-800-452-9292
www.traveltex.com

U.S. Virgin Islands
1-800-372-USVI
www.usvi.org/tourism/

Utah
1-800-UTAH-FUN
www.state.ut.us/visiting/travel.html

Vermont
1-800-VERMONT
www.1-800-vermont.com

Virginia
1-800-321-3244
www.virginia.org

Washington
360-725-5052
www.tourism.wa.gov

Washington, DC
See District of Columbia

West Virginia
1-800-CALL-WVA
www.callwva.com

Wisconsin
1-800-432-TRIP
www.travelwisconsin.com

Wyoming
1-800-225-5996
www.wyomingtourism.org

World's 25 Busiest Airports by Passengers and Cargo, 2002

Airport	Total passengers[1]	2001–2002 percent change	Airport	Total cargo[1]	2001–2002 percent change
1. Atlanta, Hartsfield (ATL)	76,876,128	1.3%	Memphis (MEM)	3,390,299	28.8%
2. Chicago, O'Hare (ORD)	66,501,496	–1.3	Hong Kong (HKG)	2,516,441	19.9
3. London, Heathrow (LHR)	63,338,649	4.3	Anchorage (ANC)[2]	2,027,754	16.8
4. Tokyo, Haneda (HND)	61,079,478	4.7	Tokyo, Narita (NRT)	2,001,824	19.1
5. Los Angeles (LAX)	56,198,447	–8.8	Los Angeles (LAX)	1,757,974	–1.9
6. Dallas/Ft. Worth (DFW)	52,826,304	–4.2	Seoul (ICN)	1,705,880	43.2
7. Frankfurt-Main (FRA)	48,450,357	–0.2	Singapore (SIN)	1,660,404	8.5
8. Paris, Charles de Gaulle (CDG)	48,303,439	0.6	Frankfurt-Main (FRA)	1,631,489	1.1
9. Amsterdam, Schiphol (AMS)	40,736,009	3.0	Miami (MIA)	1,624,240	–0.9
10. Denver (DEN)	35,651,098	–1.2	New York (JFK)	1,574,462	–1.1
11. Phoenix, Sky Harbor (PHX)	35,534,463	0.3	Louisville (SDF)	1,523,880	2.9
12. Las Vegas (LAS)	35,009,011	–0.5	Paris, Charles de Gaulle (CDG)	1,397,000	2.2
13. Houston (IAH)	33,946,484	–2.2	Taipei (TPE)	1,380,748	16.0
14. Madrid (MAD)	33,903,553	–0.4	London, Heathrow (LHR)	1,310,615	3.7
15. Hong Kong (HKG)	33,876,000	4.1	Amsterdam, Schiphol (AMS)	1,288,624	4.4
16. Minneapolis/St. Paul (MSP)	32,630,177	–3.3	Chicago, O'Hare (ORD)	1,279,176	–0.1
17. Detroit (DTW)	32,436,999	–0.5	Bangkok (BKK)	957,176	13.7
18. Bangkok (BKK)	32,177,245	5.1	Indianapolis (IND)	866,014	–23.4
19. San Francisco (SFO)	31,447,750	–9.2	Newark (EWR)	821,537	–7.6
20. Miami (MIA)	30,060,241	–5.1	Osaka (KIX)	805,432	–7.5
21. London, Gatwick (LGW)	29,628,441	–5.0	Dubai (DXB)	784,997	24.2
22. Singapore (SIN)	28,979,344	3.2	Atlanta, Hartsfield (ATL)	732,532	–1.2
23. Newark (EWR)	28,972,253	–6.9	Tokyo, Haneda (HND)	707,074	–2.6
24. Tokyo, Narita (NRT)	28,894,925	13.9	Dallas/Ft. Worth (DFW)	669,507	–11.9
25. New York (JFK)	28,888,686	–1.8	Beijing (PEK)	668,733	14.4

NOTES: Total passengers enplaned and deplaned, passengers in transit counted once. Total cargo loaded and unloaded, freight and mail (in metric tons). 1. Results are preliminary. 2. Includes transit freight. *Source:* Airports Council International World Headquarters, Geneva, Switzerland. Web: www.airports.org.

Consumer Complaints[1] Against Major U.S. Airlines by Airline,[2] 2002

Rank	Airline	Complaints	System-wide passenger boardings[3]	Complaints per 100,000 passenger boardings[3]
1.	United	1,172	68,639,794	1.71
2.	America West	318	19,453,645	1.63
3.	Northwest	765	52,752,116	1.45
4.	Continental	563	39,995,273	1.41
5.	Delta	1,231	89,866,513	1.37
6.	American	1,212	94,084,633	1.29
7.	U.S. Airways	532	47,167,570	1.13
8.	Alaska	129	14,153,286	0.91
9.	American Eagle	71	11,840,772	0.60
10.	Southwest	236	72,541,238	0.33
	Total	**6,229**	**510,494,840**	**1.22**

1. Consumer complaints filed with the U.S. Department of Transportation. Complaints range from flight problems and oversales to baggage and customer service. 2. Includes U.S. airlines with at least 1% of total domestic scheduled-service passenger revenues. 3. Refers to individual passenger boardings. *Source:* Office of Aviation Enforcement and Proceedings, U.S. Dept. of Transportation, *Air Travel Consumer Report.*

Consumer Complaints[1] Against Foreign Airlines, 2002

Foreign airlines	Total complaints	Foreign airlines	Total complaints	Foreign airlines	Total complaints
Aer Lingus	23	British Airways	127	Lufthansa	46
Aeroflot	14	BWIA	14	Mexicana	31
Aeromexico	11	Cathay Pacific Airways	10	Pakistan Int'l Airlines	12
Air Canada	50	El Al	14	Qantas Airways	13
Air France	175	EVA Airways	19	Royal Air Maroc	10
Air India	20	Ghana Airways	14	SAS	11
Air Jamaica	58	Iberia Airlines	24	Swissair	17
Alitalia Airlines	75	KLM	37	TACA Airlines	51
Allegro Airlines	16	Korean Air Lines	17	Virgin Atlantic	44
Austrian Airlines	23	Kuwait Airways	10	Other foreign airlines	299

1. Consumer complaints filed with the U.S. Department of Transportation. The complaints range from flight problems and oversales to baggage and customer service. The validity of the complaints has not been determined. *Source:* Office of Aviation Enforcement and Proceedings, U.S. Dept. of Transportation, *Air Travel Consumer Report.*

Getting to Work in the City

Commuting characteristics for the 15 largest U.S. cities by population, 2000

2000 rank	City of residence	Total workers 16 years and over	Means of transportation (%) Drove alone	Carpool	Public transit	Walked	Other means	Worked at home	Average travel time to work (min.)
1.	New York, N.Y.	3,332,698	24.1%	6.4%	56.3%	9.3%	1.4%	2.5%	39.0
2.	Los Angeles, Calif.	1,592,463	67.1	14.9	9.5	2.9	1.6	4.0	28.1
3.	Chicago, Ill.	1,252,949	50.5	12.8	27.6	5.6	0.9	2.5	33.1
4.	Houston, Tex.	919,762	72.9	14.7	6.0	2.6	1.2	2.6	25.9
5.	Philadelphia, Pa.	587,156	47.6	10.4	28.0	10.4	1.7	1.9	29.2
6.	Phoenix, Ariz.	589,860	71.9	17.0	3.6	1.9	2.5	3.2	24.7
7.	San Diego, Calif.	579,615	78.5	10.4	4.6	2.3	1.2	2.9	22.6
8.	Dallas, Tex.	560,913	73.4	14.5	5.1	2.2	2.3	2.5	25.2
9.	San Antonio, Tex.	490,076	78.7	13.9	3.6	1.6	0.9	1.4	21.5
10.	Detroit, Mich.	317,179	76.4	12.8	6.2	2.3	1.2	1.0	24.2
11.	San Jose, Calif.	450,093	73.0	16.9	4.9	1.7	0.8	2.7	26.4
12.	Indianapolis, Ind.	407,377	81.9	10.2	2.2	2.5	1.5	1.7	21.6
13.	San Francisco, Calif.	419,601	41.1	9.3	32.1	8.8	3.9	4.8	29.6
14.	Jacksonville, Fla.	350,797	81.9	11.4	1.9	1.5	1.5	1.8	22.6
15.	Columbus, Ohio	353,192	82.5	9.3	3.0	2.0	0.7	2.5	20.7
	Total for U.S.	**127,448,586**	**76.3**	**11.2**	**5.2**	**2.7**	**1.4**	**3.2**	**24.3**

NOTES: Percentages may not add up to 100%, due to rounding. *Source:* U.S. Bureau of the Census. Web: www.census.gov/.

Principal Means of Transportation to Work

	1985		1993		2001	
	Number (thousands)	Percent	Number (thousands)	Percent	Number (thousands)	Percent
All workers	99,592	100.0%	103,741	100.0%	120,191	100.0%
Automobile	86,148	86.5	91,301	88.0	105,586	87.8
Drives self	72,137	72.4	79,449	76.6	93,942	78.2
Carpool	14,011	14.1	11,852	11.4	11,644	9.7
2-person	10,381	10.4	9,105	8.8	9,036	7.5
3-person	2,024	2.0	1,684	1.6	1,635	1.4
4+ person	1,606	1.6	1,063	1.0	973	0.8
Public transportation[1]	5,091	5.1	4,740	4.6	5,627	4.7
Taxicab	129	0.1	117	0.1	133	0.1
Bicycle or motorcycle	958	1.0	744	0.7	847	0.7
Walks only	4,032	4.0	3,227	3.1	3,408	2.8
Other means[2]	286	0.3	474	0.5	1,049	0.9
Works at home	2,947	3.0	3,137	3.0	3,401	2.8

NOTE: Principal means of transportation refers to the mode used most often. 1. Public transportation refers to bus, streetcar, subway, or elevated trains. 2. Other means include ferryboats, surface trains, and van service. *Source:* U.S. Department of Housing and Urban Development, *American Housing Survey* (Washington, DC: various years).

Fatalities by Transportation Mode, 1970–2001

Mode	1970	1980	1990	2000	2001
Air					
U.S. air carrier[1]	146	1	39	92	531
Commuter carrier[2]	n.a.	37	6	5	13
On-demand air taxi[3]	n.a.	105	51	71	60
General aviation[4]	1,310	1,239	767	593	563[P]
Highway					
Passenger car occupants	n.a.	27,449	24,092	20,699[R]	20,233
Motorcyclists	2,280	5,144	3,244	2,897[R]	3,181
Truck occupants[5]					
Light	n.a.	7,486	8,601	11,526[R]	11,677
Large	n.a.	1,262	705	754[R]	704
Bus occupants	n.a.	46	32	22	34

Mode	1970	1980	1990	2000	2001
Pedestrians	8,950	8,070	6,482	4,763[R]	4,882
Pedalcyclists	760	965	859	693[R]	728
Other[6]	40,637	669	584	591[R]	677
Railroad					
Highway-rail grade crossing	1,440	833	698	425	421
Railroad	785	584	599	512	548
Waterborne[7]					
Vessel-related	178	206	85	32	n.a.
Not related to vessel casualties	420	281	101	87	n.a.
Recreational boating	1,418	1,360	865	701	n.a.

NOTES: n.a. = not available; P = preliminary data; R = revised data. 1. Carriers with 10 or more seats. 2. Carriers with fewer than 10 seats. 3. Nonscheduled service. 4. All other operations. 5. Large trucks are defined as trucks over 10,000 pounds gross vehicle weight. Light trucks are defined as trucks of 10,000 pounds gross vehicle weight rating or less, including pickups, vans, truck-based station wagons, and utility vehicles. 6. Includes occupants of other vehicle types and other nonmotorists. For 1960–1970, the U.S. Department of Transportation, National Highway Traffic Safety Administration did not break out fatality data to the same level of detail as in later years, so fatalities for those years also include occupants of passenger cars, trucks, and buses. 7. Vessel-related casualties include those involving damage to vessels such as collisions or groundings. Fatalities not related to vessel casualties include deaths from falling overboard or from accidents involving onboard equipment. *Source:* U.S. Dept. of Transportation, Bureau of Transportation Statistics, *National Transportation Statistics, 2002.*

Traffic Congestion in U.S. Cities, 2002

Rank	Urban area	Annual delay per person in hours	Rank	Urban area	Annual delay per person in hours
1.	Los Angeles, Calif.	136	26.	Albuquerque, N.M.	45
2.	San Francisco-Oakland, Calif.	92	28.	Nashville, Tenn.	44
3.	Washington, DC-Md.-Va.	84	29.	Cincinnati, Ohio-Ky.	43
4.	Seattle-Everett, Wash.	82	29.	W. Palm Beach-Boca Raton-Delray Beach, Fla.	43
5.	Houston, Tex.	75	29.	Indianapolis, Ind.	43
6.	San Jose, Calif.	74	29.	San Antonio, Tex.	43
6.	Dallas-Fort Worth, Tex.	74	29.	St. Louis, Mo.-Ill.	43
8.	New York, N.Y.-Northeastern N.J.	73	34.	Sacramento, Calif.	42
9.	Atlanta, Ga.	70	34.	Philadelphia, Pa.-N.J.	42
10.	Miami-Hialeah, Fla.	69	36.	Providence-Pawtucket, R.I.-Mass.	41
11.	Chicago, Ill.-Northwestern Ind.	67	37.	Las Vegas, Nev.	38
11.	Boston, Mass.	67	38.	Columbus, Ohio	36
11.	Denver, Colo.	67	39.	Tacoma, Wash.	34
14.	Orlando, Fla.	66	39.	Memphis, Tenn.-Ark.-Miss.	34
15.	San Bernardino-Riverside, Calif.	64	41.	Milwaukee, Wis.	32
16.	Ft. Lauderdale-Hollywood-Pompano Beach, Fla.	61	41.	Jacksonville, Fla.	32
16.	Austin, Tex.	61	43.	Birmingham, Ala.	31
18.	Phoenix, Ariz.	59	44.	Colorado Springs, Colo.	27
19.	Detroit, Mich.	55	45.	Charleston, S.C.	26
20.	Minneapolis-St. Paul, Minn.	54	46.	Tucson, Ariz.	25
21.	San Diego, Calif.	51	46.	Norfolk-Newport News-Virginia Beach, Va.	25
22.	Baltimore, Md.	50	46.	Omaha, Neb.-Iowa	25
23.	Portland-Vancouver, Ore.-Wash.	47	49.	Fresno, Calif.	24
23.	Charlotte, N.C.	47	49.	Honolulu, Hawaii	24
25.	Louisville, Ky.-Ind.	46	49.	Pensacola, Fla.	24
26.	Tampa-St. Petersburg-Clearwater, Fla.	45			

NOTE: Study conducted in 75 urbanized areas. *Source:* Texas Transportation Institute, the Texas A&M University System. *The 2002 Urban Mobility Report,* David Schrank and Tim Lomax. Web: http://mobility.tamu.edu.

Improper Driving as a Factor in Accidents

Kind of improper driving	Fatal accidents 1995	Fatal accidents 1999	Fatal accidents 2000	Injury accidents 1995	Injury accidents 1999	Injury accidents 2000	All accidents 1995	All accidents 1999	All accidents 2000
Improper driving	**68.1%**	**72.6%**	**61.6%**	**73.5%**	**67.2%**	**60.3%**	**75.5%**	**62.2%**	**57.8%**
Speed too fast or unsafe	19.8	23.0	23.7	13.9	13.0	16.3	14.0	10.6	13.6
Right of way	15.2	20.1	18.6	25.5	25.8	19.9	22.9	22.9	20.1
Failed to yield	10.2	10.8	10.1	18.1	19.2	15.0	17.0	13.8	12.7
Disregarded signal	3.0	4.7	4.6	5.0	4.9	3.6	4.0	5.9	5.3
Passed stop sign	2.2	4.6	3.8	2.4	1.7	1.3	1.9	3.2	2.2
Drove left of center	9.1	9.6	8.2	2.4	1.7	1.1	2.2	1.3	1.0
Made improper turn	2.3	1.2	0.7	2.8	2.4	2.0	4.2	3.0	2.4
Improper overtaking	1.5	1.1	0.9	1.3	0.9	0.6	1.5	1.2	0.9
Followed too closely	0.5	0.5	0.5	7.0	3.4	4.3	7.2	6.3	5.7
Other improper driving	19.7	17.1	9.0	20.7	20.3	16.1	23.6	16.9	14.1
No improper driving stated	**31.9**	**27.4**	**38.4**	**26.5**	**32.8**	**39.7**	**24.5**	**37.8**	**42.2**
Total	**100.0%**	**100.0%**	**100.0%**	**100.0%**	**100.0%**	**100.0%**	**100.0%**	**100.0%**	**100.0%**

NOTE: Based on reports from seven state traffic authorities. *Source:* National Safety Council, *Injury Facts, 2001 Edition.* Web: www.nsc.org.

U.S. Driving Fatalities, Total and Alcohol-Related

Year	Fatalities Total	Fatalities Alcohol-related	Percent	Year	Fatalities Total	Fatalities Alcohol-related	Percent
1982	43,945	26,173	60%	1992	39,250	18,290	47%
1983	42,589	24,635	58	1993	40,150	17,908	45
1984	44,257	24,762	56	1994	40,716	17,308	43
1985	43,825	23,167	53	1995	41,817	17,732	42
1986	46,087	25,017	54	1996	42,065	17,749	42
1987	46,390	24,094	52	1997	42,013	16,711	40
1988	47,087	23,833	51	1998	41,501	16,673	40
1989	45,582	22,424	49	1999	41,717	16,572	40
1990	44,599	22,587	51	2000	41,945	17,380	41
1991	41,508	20,159	49	2001	42,116	17,448	41

Source: 1982–2000 (Final) FARS Files and 2001 FARS Annual Report File, FHWA's Highway Statistics Annual Series, from the National Center for Statistics and Analysis.

Alcohol-Related Traffic Fatalities on Holidays, 2001

Holiday 2001	Total traffic fatalities	Total fatalities alcohol-related	Percent fatalities alcohol-related	Time period monitored
New Year's Eve (2000)	82	35	42.1%	12/31/00
New Year's Day	120	66	55.1	1/1/01
New Year's Holiday	357	181	50.7	6:00 p.m. 12/29/00–5:59 a.m. 1/2/01
Super Bowl Sunday	142	73	51.7	1/28/01–5:59 a.m. 1/29/01
St. Patrick's Day	162	99	61.4	3/17/01–5:59 a.m. 3/18/01
Memorial Day	515	284	55.1	6 p.m. 5/25/01–5:59 a.m. 5/29/01
Fourth of July	206	127	61.8	6 p.m. 7/3/01–5:59 a.m. 7/5/01
Labor Day weekend	482	252	52.2	6 p.m. 8/31/01–5:59 a.m. 9/4/01
Halloween	206	84	40.9	10/31/01–11/1/01
Thanksgiving	585	283	48.4	6 p.m. 11/21/01–5:59 a.m. 11/26/01
Thanksgiving–New Year's	4,943	2,053	41.5	11/21/01–12/31/01
Christmas	601	281	46.7	6 p.m. 12/21/01–5:59 a.m. 12/26/01
New Year's Eve (2001)	115	45	37.0	12/31/01

Source: Mothers Against Drunk Driving (MADD). Web: www.madd.org.

Age and Gender Distribution of U.S. Licensed Drivers, 2001

	Male drivers		Female drivers		Total drivers	
Age	Number	Percent of total drivers	Number	Percent of total drivers	Number	Percent of total drivers
Under 16	13,032	0.0%	12,357	0.0%	25,389	0.0%
19 and under	4,853,569	5.1	4,567,073	4.8	9,420,642	4.9
20–24	8,268,148	8.6	7,965,862	8.3	16,234,010	8.5
25–29	8,666,590	9.0	8,323,503	8.7	16,990,093	8.9
30–34	9,715,290	10.1	9,394,903	9.8	19,110,193	10.0
35–39	10,272,494	10.7	10,139,736	10.6	20,412,230	10.7
40–44	10,523,249	11.0	10,568,191	11.1	21,091,440	11.0
45–49	9,674,579	10.1	9,783,629	10.2	19,458,208	10.2
50–54	8,655,786	9.0	8,740,169	9.2	17,395,955	9.1
55–59	6,677,201	7.0	6,682,470	7.0	13,359,671	7.0
60–64	5,110,323	5.3	5,120,180	5.4	10,230,503	5.3
65–69	4,193,804	4.4	4,242,470	4.4	8,436,274	4.4
70–74	3,650,960	3.8	3,813,865	4.0	7,464,825	3.9
75–79	2,825,231	2.9	3,087,055	3.2	5,912,286	3.1
80–84	1,723,275	1.8	1,929,998	2.0	3,653,273	1.9
85 and over	981,746	1.0	1,124,370	1.2	2,106,116	1.1
Total	**95,792,245**	**100.0**	**95,483,474**	**100.0**	**191,275,719**	**100.0**

Source: U.S. Department of Transportation, Federal Highway Administration, *Highway Statistics 2001.*

Licensed Drivers and Vehicle Registrations

Year	Resident population (millions)	Drivers (millions)	Motor vehicles (millions)	Year	Resident population (millions)	Drivers (millions)	Motor vehicles (millions)
1960	180	87	74	1981	230	147	158
1961	183	89	76	1982	232	150	160
1962	186	91	79	1983	234	154	164
1963	188	94	83	1984	236	155	166
1964	191	95	86	1985	239	157	172
1965	194	99	90	1986	241	159	176
1966	196	101	94	1987	243	161	179
1967	197	103	97	1988	246	163	184
1968	199	105	101	1989	248	166	187
1969	201	108	105	1990	248	167	189
1970	204	112	108	1991	252	169	188
1971	207	114	113	1992	255	173	190
1972	209	118	119	1993	258	173	194
1973	211	122	126	1994	260	175	198
1974	213	125	130	1995	263	177	202
1975	215	130	133	1996	265	180	206
1976	218	134	139	1997	268	183	208
1977	220	138	142	1998	270	185	208
1978	222	141	148	1999	273	187	212
1979	225	143	152	2000	281	191	218
1980	227	145	156	2001	281	191	226

Source: U.S. Department of Transportation, Federal Highway Administration, *Highway Statistics 2001.*

Driving Laws, 2003

Currently all states plus DC have child safety seat laws and enforce a drinking age of 21. As of July 2003, 34 states had blood alcohol concentration (bac) limits of 0.08—there have been concerted state and national efforts to lower the rate from 0.10. A national speed limit of 55 mph was imposed in 1974, and in 1987 it was modified to allow 65-mile-per-hour speeds on some rural freeways. The federal law was entirely repealed in 1995, giving states the right to set their own limits. Montana, which had been the only state with no speed limit, imposed a 75-mile-an-hour limit in 1999. As of Jan. 2000, graduated licensing laws were in effect in 40 states, 30 of which prohibit young drivers from driving during high-risk nighttime and early morning hours.

State	Minimum age for driver's license[1]	License revocation for alcohol offenses since	Blood alcohol concentration limit[2]	Alcohol ignition interlock device[3]	Mandatory belt-use law seating positions	Motorcycle helmet law[4]	Maximum allowable speed limit	
							1995[5]	1999
Alabama	17	1996	0.08	no	front	yes	65	70
Alaska	16	1983	0.08	yes	all	18[6]	—	65
Arizona	16	1992	0.08	yes	front	18	55	75
Arkansas	16	1995	0.08	yes	front	21	65	70
California	17	1989	0.08	yes	all	yes	55	70
Colorado	17	1983	0.10	yes	front[7]	no	65	75
Connecticut	16 + 4 mo.	1990	0.08	no	front[7]	18	55	65
Delaware	16 + 10 mo.	yes	0.10	yes	front	19[8]	—	65
DC	18	yes	0.08	no	all	yes	—	—
Florida	18	1990	0.08	yes	front	21	65	70
Georgia	18	1995	0.08	yes	front[7]	yes	55	70
Hawaii	16	1990	0.08	no	front	18	—	60
Idaho	16	1994	0.08	yes	front	18	65	75
Illinois	17	1986	0.08	yes	front	no	65	65
Indiana	18	yes	0.10	yes	front	18	65	65
Iowa	17	1982	0.10	yes	front	no	55	65
Kansas	16	1988	0.08	yes	front	18	65	70
Kentucky	18	no	0.08	no	all	21[9, 10, 11]	65	65
Louisiana	17	1984	0.10	yes	front[7]	18[9]	65	70
Maine	16	1984	0.08	yes	all	15	65	65
Maryland	17 + 7 mo.	1989	0.08	yes	front[7]	yes	55	65
Massachusetts	18	1994	0.08	no	all	yes	55	65
Michigan	17	no	0.10	yes	front[7]	yes	55	70
Minnesota	16	1976	0.10	no	front[7]	18	65	70
Mississippi	16	1983	0.08	no	front	yes	65	70
Missouri	18	1987	0.08	yes	front[7]	yes	70	70
Montana	15	no	0.10	yes	all	18	65	75
Nebraska	17	1993	0.08	yes	front[7]	yes	65	75
Nevada	16	1983	0.10	yes	all	yes	55	75
New Hampshire	18	1994	0.08	no	—	18	65	65
New Jersey	18	no	0.10	yes	front	yes	—	65
New Mexico	16 + 6 mo.	1984	0.08	yes	all	18	65	75
New York	17	1994	0.10	yes	front[7]	yes	55	65
North Carolina	16 + 6 mo.	1983	0.08	yes	front[7]	yes	55	70
North Dakota	16	1983	0.10	yes	front	18	65	70
Ohio	17	1993	0.10	yes	front	18[11]	65	65
Oklahoma	16	1983	0.08	yes	front	18	65	75
Oregon	17	1983	0.08	yes	all	yes	65	65
Pennsylvania	17	no	0.10	no	front	yes	55	65
Rhode Island	17 + 6 mo.	no	0.08	yes	all	21[6, 11]	55	65
South Carolina	16 + 6 mo.	1998	0.10	no	all	18	65	70
South Dakota	16	no	0.08	no	front	18	65	75
Tennessee	16	no	0.08	yes	front[7]	yes	65	70
Texas	16 + 6 mo.	1995	0.08	yes	front[7]	21[9]	65	70
Utah	17	1983	0.08	yes	all	18	55	75
Vermont	16	1969	0.08	no	all	yes	65	65
Virginia	18	1995	0.08	yes	front	yes	65	65
Washington	17	1998	0.08	yes	all	yes	55	70
West Virginia	17	1981	0.10	yes	front[7]	yes	65	70
Wisconsin	16 + 9 mo.	1988	0.10	yes	all	18[10]	65	65
Wyoming	16	1973	0.08	no	all	18	65	75

1. Refers to minimum age for unrestricted driver's license. 2. Blood alcohol concentration that constitutes the threshold of legal intoxication. 3. Legislation for instruments designed to prevent drivers from starting their cars when breath alcohol content is at or above a set point. 4. Presence of law, or age below which riders are required to wear helmet. 5. In 1995, Congress repealed the national 55-miles-per-hour speed limit. 6. All passengers required to wear helmet. 7. Required for certain ages at all seating positions. 8. Helmet must also be carried on the motorcycle, whether or not it is worn, for persons 19 and older. 9. Helmet optional for those over listed age if they have proper insurance. 10. Helmets must be worn by cyclists holding learners' permits. 11. First-year novices required to wear helmet. *Sources:* National Safety Council, *Injury Facts, 2000 Edition;* Web: www.nsc.org. U.S. Dept. of Transportation, National Highway Traffic Safety Administration, *Traffic Safety Facts, 2001;* Web: www.nhtsa.dot.gov. Insurance Institute for Highway Safety; Web: www.hwysafety.org.

Most Popular Car Colors, 2001–2002

(Percentage of vehicles manufactured during 2002 model year in North America)

Luxury	2002	2001	Sport/Compact	2002	2001
1. Silver	32.1%	18.4%	1. Silver	24.6%	25.4%
2. White Met.	17.7	n.a.	2. Black	14.3	14.5
3. White	11.8	9.0	3. Med./Dk. Blue	12.9	11.3
4. Med./Dk. Blue	8.6	9.4	4. White	8.8	9.8
5. Black	8.5	11.1	5. Bright Red	6.9	5.3
6. Med./Dk. Gray	7.2	n.a.	6. Med./Dk. Gray	6.7	2.0
7. Med. Red	6.0	6.0	7. Med. Red	5.5	7.4
8. Gold	3.0	5.4	8. Lt. Brown	4.3	6.2
9. Med./Dk. Green	1.8	3.1	9. Gold	4.1	n.a.
10. Lt. Brown	1.7	n.a.	10. Dk. Red	2.6	2.6

Full/Intermediate	2002	2001	SUV/Truck/Van	2002	2001
1. Silver	28.1%	24.9%	1. White	19.3%	19.6%
2. White	11.8	14.1	2. Silver	18.0	17.8
3. Lt. Brown	11.6	8.1	3. Black	12.4	11.2
4. Black	11.2	9.8	4. Med./Dk. Blue	11.4	10.4
5. Med./Dk. Blue	9.5	8.9	5. Med/Dk. Gray	7.5	2.5
6. Med. Red	7.6	4.8	6. Med. Red	7.1	8.4
7. Med./Dk. Gray	6.2	n.a.	7. Med./Dk. Green	6.7	7.4
8. Med./Dk. Green	5.3	10.0	8. Lt. Brown	5.1	4.6
9. Gold	3.4	7.2	9. Bright Red	4.5	5.3
10. Dk. Red	2.6	4.9	10. Gold	4.5	3.8

Source: DuPont Herberts Automotive Systems, Troy, Mich. 2002 DuPont Automotive Color Popularity Survey Results. Web: www.dupont.com.

Top-Selling Light Trucks in the U.S., 1999–2001

Rank	1999	Number	2000	Number	2001	Number
1.	Ford F Series	806,579	Ford F Series	820,248	Ford F Series	1,330,230
2.	Chevy Silverado	533,177	Chevy Silverado	634,118	Ford Explorer	611,766
3.	Dodge Ram Pickup	428,930	Ford Explorer	445,157	Dodge Ram Pickup	539,877
4.	Ford Explorer	428,772	Dodge Ram Pickup	380,874	Ford Ranger	386,274
5.	Ford Ranger	348,358	Ford Ranger	330,125	Dodge Caravan	386,174
6.	Jeep Grand Cherokee	300,031	Dodge Caravan	285,739	Jeep Grand Cherokee	326,910
7.	Dodge Caravan	293,100	Jeep Grand Cherokee	271,723	GMC Sierra	306,580
8.	Chevrolet S10 Pickup	233,669	Chevrolet S Blazer	225,948	Chevy Tahoe	301,777
9.	Ford Expedition	233,125	Ford Windstar	222,298	Ford Windstar	257,247
10.	Chevrolet S Blazer	232,140	Ford Expedition	213,483	Ford Expedition	253,200

Source: Ward's AutoInfoBank. Web: www.wardsauto.com.

Top-Selling Passenger Cars in the U.S., 1999–2001

Rank	1999	Number	2000	Number	2001	Number
1.	Toyota Camry	448,162	Toyota Camry	422,961	Toyota Camry	616,054
2.	Honda Accord	404,192	Honda Accord	404,515	Honda Accord	596,321
3.	Ford Taurus	368,327	Ford Taurus	382,035	Ford Taurus	517,523
4.	Honda Civic	318,308	Honda Civic	324,528	Honda Civic	487,336
5.	Chevrolet Cavalier	272,122	Ford Focus	286,166	Ford Focus	381,748
6.	Ford Escort	260,486	Chevrolet Cavalier	236,803	Chevy Cavalier	372,909
7.	Toyota Corolla	249,128	Toyota Corolla	230,156	Toyota Corolla	338,534
8.	Pontiac Grand Am	234,936	Pontiac Grand Am	214,923	Chevy Impala	302,953
9.	Chevrolet Malibu	218,540	Chevrolet Malibu	207,376	Pontiac Grand Am	267,070
10.	Saturn S	207,977	Saturn S	177,355	Chevy Malibu	264,841

Source: Ward's AutoInfoBank. Web: www.wardsauto.com.

World's Largest Subway Systems

(by ridership)

City	Date system completed	Number of riders (year)	Length (km)	City	Date system completed	Number of riders (year)	Length (km)
Moscow	1935	3.2 bil (1997)	340	Paris	1900	1.2 bil (1998)	211
Tokyo	1927	2.6 bil (1997/98)	281+	Osaka	1933	957 mil (1997)	114
Seoul	1974	1.4 bil (1993)	278+	London	1863	866 mil (1999)	415
Mexico City	1969	1.4 bil (1996)	202	Hong Kong	1979	790 mil (1999)	82
New York City	1904	1.3 bil (2001)	371	St. Petersburg	1955	721 mil (1996)	110

Sources: Jane's Urban Transport Systems, 2002–2003 edition, and individual subway websites.

U.S. Railroad Ridership, 1989–2002

(millions)

	1989	1990	1991	1992	1993	1994	1995	1996	1997	1998	1999	2000	2001	2002
Amtrak system	21.4	22.2	22.0	21.3	22.1	21.2	20.7	19.7	20.2	21.1	21.5	22.5	23.5	23.4
Northeast Corridor	11.1	11.2	10.9	10.1	10.3	11.7	11.6	11.0	11.1	11.9	12.3	12.9	13.5	13.8
Intercity + West	10.3	11.0	11.1	11.2	11.8	9.4	9.1	8.7	9.1	9.2	9.2	9.6	10.0	9.6
Commuter trains[1]	17.4	18.0	18.1	20.3	32.9	39.5	42.2	45.9	48.5	54.0	58.3	61.6	n.a.	n.a.
Total	**38.8**	**40.2**	**40.1**	**41.6**	**55.0**	**60.7**	**62.9**	**65.6**	**68.7**	**75.1**	**79.8**	**84.1**	**n.a.**	**n.a.**

NOTE: n.a. = not available. 1. Includes only commuter trains run by Amtrak under contract. *Source:* National Assoc. of Railroad Passengers. Based on Amtrak annual reports. Web: www.narprail.org.

Two Centuries of Railroading

Source: Association of American Railroads. Web: www.aar.org.

1797 The steam locomotive is invented in England.

1823 The first public railway in the world opens in England.

1827 The first railroad in North America—the Baltimore & Ohio—is chartered by Baltimore merchants.

1830 The first regularly scheduled steam-powered rail passenger service in the U.S. begins operation in South Carolina, utilizing the U.S.-built locomotive *The Best Friend of Charleston.*

1833 Andrew Jackson travels from Baltimore to Ellicott's Mills, becoming the first sitting U.S. president to ride the rails.

1838 Five of the six New England states have rail service, as do such frontier states as Kentucky and Indiana.

1840 More than 2,800 miles of track are in operation.

1850 More than 9,000 miles of track are in operation in the U.S., as much as in the rest of the world combined.

1860 More than 30,000 miles of track are in operation in the U.S.

1862 President Abraham Lincoln signs the Pacific Railroad Act for the construction of the transcontinental railroad that will ultimately link California with the rest of the nation.

1865 The "golden age" of railroads begins. For nearly half a century, no other mode of transportation challenges railroads. During these years, the rail network grows from 35,000 to a peak of 254,000 miles in 1916.

1869 On May 10, at Promontory, in the Utah Territory, the "Golden Spike" joins the Union Pacific and Central Pacific railroads, marking completion of the first transcontinental railroad.

1917 The federal government seizes control of the railroads for the duration of World War I.

1900–1940 By the eve of World War II, automobiles, large buses, trucks, planes, and pipelines—supported by government subsidies and less burdened by regulation than railroads—have become full-fledged competitors to railroads.

1945–1970 Railroads enter the postwar era with a new sense of optimism that leads them to invest billions of dollars in new locomotives, freight equipment, and passenger trains. That investment would see retirement of the last steam locomotive by the late 1950s in favor of diesel engines. In spite of this modernization, the decline in rail market share that began before the war resumes.

1970–1975 Burdened by regulation and faced with subsidized competition, nine Class I railroads, representing almost one-quarter of the industry's trackage, file for bankruptcy protection.

1970 The Rail Passenger Service Act creates Amtrak to take over intercity rail passenger service.

1971 Amtrak officially begins service on May 1.

1980 The Staggers Rail Act reduces the Interstate Commerce Commission's regulatory jurisdiction over railroads and sparks competition that stimulates advances in technology and a restructuring of the industry.

1987 Conrail is privatized in what—at that time—was the largest share offering in U.S. history as investors pay $1.9 billion to buy shares in the railroad.

1996 After 108 years, the Interstate Commerce Commission is disbanded and replaced by the Surface Transportation Board, which assumes oversight responsibility for the railroads.

2000 U.S. freight railroads move 1.47 trillion ton-miles of freight, more than ever before, setting new safety records in the process.

PEOPLE

Many public figures not listed here may be found elsewhere in the almanac.

U.S. Presidents
U.S. Vice Presidents
Families of U.S. Presidents
U.S. Governors
U.S. Congress
U.S. Supreme Court Justices
U.S. Government Officials
British Prime Ministers
Rulers of England
Rulers of France
Rulers of Judah and Israel
Rulers of Prussia
Rulers of Russia
Sports Personalities

Names in parentheses indicate a person's original name or nickname. Locations in parentheses are the present-day name of the birthplace. Dates of birth appear as month/day/year. **Boldface** years in parentheses are dates of **(birth–death).**

Information has been gathered from many sources, including the individuals themselves. However, the almanac cannot guarantee the accuracy of every item.

A

Aalto, Alvar (architect); Kuortane, Finland **(1898–1976)**
Abbado, Claudio (orchestra conductor); Milan, Italy, 6/26/33
Abbott, Bud (William Abbott) (comedian); Asbury Park, N.J. **(1898–1974)**
Abbott, George (stage producer); Forestville, N.Y. **(1887–1995)**
Abelard, Peter (theologian); nr. Nantes, France **(1079–1142)**
Abernathy, Ralph (civil rights leader); Linden, Ala. **(1926–1990)**
Abraham, F(ahrid) Murray (actor); Pittsburgh, 10/24/39
Achebe, Chinua (writer); Ogidi, Nigeria, 11/16/30
Acheson, Dean (statesman); Middletown, Conn. **(1893–1971)**
Acuff, Roy Claxton (musician); nr. Maynardsville, Tenn. **(1903–1992)**
Adams, Abigail (First Lady, writer); Weymouth, Mass. **(1744–1818)**
Adams, Bryan (singer, songwriter); Kingston, Ont., Canada, 11/5/59
Adams, Charles Francis (diplomat); Boston **(1807–1886)**
Adams, Don (actor); New York City, 4/19/26
Adams, Edie (Edie Enke) (actress); Kingston, Pa., 4/16/29
Adams, Franklin Pierce (columnist, author); Chicago **(1881–1960)**
Adams, Gerry (political leader); West Belfast, Northern Ireland, 10/6/48
Adams, Henry Brooks (historian); Boston **(1838–1918)**
Adams, Joey (comedian); New York City **(1911–1999)**
Adams, John (2nd U.S. president); Braintree (Quincy), Mass. **(1735–1826)**
Adams, John Quincy (6th U.S. president); Braintree (Quincy), Mass. **(1767–1848)**
Adams, Maude (Maude Kiskadden) (actress); Salt Lake City **(1872–1953)**
Adams, Samuel (American Revolutionary patriot); Boston **(1722–1803)**
Adams, Scott (cartoonist); Catskill, N.Y., 6/8/57
Adamson, Joy (naturalist, writer); Troppau, Silesia **(1910–1980)**
Addams, Charles (cartoonist); Westfield, N.J. **(1912–1988)**
Addams, Jane (social worker, Nobel laureate); Cedarville, Ill. **(1860–1935)**
Adderley, Julian "Cannonball" (jazz saxophonist); Tampa, Fla. **(1928–1975)**
Ade, George (humorist); Kentland, Ind. **(1866–1944)**
Adenauer, Konrad (statesman); Cologne, Germany **(1876–1967)**
Adler, Alfred (psychoanalyst); Vienna **(1870–1937)**
Adler, Larry (musician); Baltimore **(1914–2001)**
Adler, Richard (songwriter); New York City, 8/3/21
Aeschylus (dramatist); Eleusis, Greece **(525–456 B.C.)**
Aesop (fabulist); Samos?, Greece, fl. c. 500 B.C.
Agnew, Spiro (political figure); Baltimore **(1905–1996)**
Aiello, Danny (actor); New York City, 6/20/33
Aiken, Conrad (poet); Savannah, Ga. **(1889–1973)**
Ailey, Alvin (choreographer); Rogers, Tex. **(1931–1989)**
Akhmatova, Anna (poet); Odessa, Ukraine **(1889–1966)**
Akihito, Tsugunomiya (Emperor of Japan); Tokyo, 12/23/33
Albanese, Licia (operatic soprano); Bari, Italy, 7/22/13
Albee, Edward (playwright); Washington, D.C., 3/12/28
Albers, Josef (painter); Bottrop, Germany **(1888–1976)**
Albert, Eddie (Edward Albert Heimberger) (actor); Rock Island, Ill., 4/22/08
Albert, Edward (actor); Los Angeles, 2/20/51
Albertson, Jack (actor); Malden, Mass. **(1907–1981)**
Albright, Madeleine (diplomat, U.S. secretary of state); Prague, Czechoslovakia, 5/15/37
Alcott, Louisa May (novelist); Germantown, Pa. **(1832–1888)**
Alda, Alan (actor); New York City, 1/28/36
Alden, John (American Pilgrim); England **(c. 1599–1687)**
Alexander, Jane (Quigley) (actress); Boston, 10/28/39
Alexander, Jason (Jay Scott Greenspan) (actor); Newark, N.J., 9/23/59
Alexander the Great (monarch, conqueror); Pella, Macedonia, Greece **(356–323 B.C.)**
Alger, Horatio (author); Revere, Mass. **(1834–1899)**
Algren, Nelson (novelist); Detroit **(1909–1981)**
Allen, Debbie (dancer-choreographer, actress); Houston, 1/16/50
Allen, Ethan (American Revolutionary soldier); Litchfield, Conn. **(1738–1789)**
Allen, Fred (John Florence Sullivan) (comedian); Cambridge, Mass. **(1894–1956)**
Allen, Gracie (Grace Ethel Cecile Rosalie Allen) (comedienne); San Francisco **(1906–1964)**
Allen, Joan (actress); Rochelle, Ill., 8/20/56
Allen, Mel (Melvin Israel) (sportscaster); Birmingham, Ala. **(1913–1996)**
Allen, Peter (actor, songwriter); Tenterfield, Australia **(1944–1992)**
Allen, Steve (TV entertainer); New York City **(1921–2000)**
Allen, Woody (Allen Stewart Konigsberg) (actor, writer, director); Brooklyn, N.Y., 12/1/35
Allende, Isabel (novelist); Lima, Peru, 8/2/42
Alley, Kirstie (actress); Wichita, Kans., 1/12/55
Allison, Fran (actress); LaPorte City, Iowa **(1908?–1989)**
Allman, Gregg (singer); Nashville, Tenn., 12/8/47
Allyson, June (Ella Geisman) (actress); New York City, 10/7/17
Alonso, Alicia (ballet dancer); Havana, 12/21/21?
Alpert, Herb (band leader); Los Angeles, 3/31/35?
Alsop, Joseph W., Jr. (journalist); Avon, Conn. **(1910–1989)**
Alsop, Stewart (journalist); Avon, Conn. **(1914–1974)**
Alt, Carol (model); Flushing, New York, 12/1/60
Altman, Robert (director); Kansas City, Mo., 2/20/25
Amanpour, Christiane (broadcast journalist); London, 1958
Amati, Nicola (violin maker); Cremona, Italy **(1596–1684)**
Ambler, Eric (suspense writer); London **(1909–1998)**
Ambrose, Stephen (author, historian); Whitewater, Wis. **(1936–2002)**
Ameche, Don (Dominic Amici) (actor); Kenosha, Wis. **(1908–1993)**
Amis, Kingsley (novelist); London **(1922–1995)**
Amis, Martin (novelist); Oxford, England, 8/25/49
Amory, Cleveland (conservationist); Nahant, Mass. **(1917–1998)**
Amos (Freeman F. Gosden) (radio comedian); Richmond, Va. **(1899–1982)**
Amos, John (actor); Newark, N.J., 12/27/41
Amos, Tori (singer); Newton, N.C., 8/22/63
Amsterdam, Morey (actor); Chicago **(1914–1996)**
Andersen, Hans Christian (author of fairy tales); Odense, Denmark **(1805–1875)**
Anderson, Eddie (Rochester) (actor); Oakland, Calif. **(1905–1977)**
Anderson, Gillian (actress); Chicago, 8/9/68
Anderson, Harry (actor); Newport, R.I., 10/14/52
Anderson, Ib (ballet dancer); Copenhagen, 12/14/54
Anderson, Jack (journalist); Long Beach, Calif., 10/19/22
Anderson, Dame Judith (actress); Adelaide, Australia **(1898–1992)**
Anderson, Lindsay (Gordon) (director); Bangalore, India **(1923–1994)**
Anderson, Loni (actress); St. Paul, Minn., 8/5/45
Anderson, Lynn (singer); Grand Forks, N.D., 9/26/47

Anderson, Marian (contralto); Philadelphia **(1897–1993)**
Anderson, Maxwell (dramatist); Atlantic, Pa. **(1888–1959)**
Anderson Lee, Pamela (Pamela Anderson) (model, actress); Ladysmith, B.C., Canada, 7/1/67
Anderson, Richard Dean (actor); Minneapolis, Minn., 1/23/50
Anderson, Robert (playwright); New York City, 4/28/17
Anderson, Sherwood (novelist); Camden, Ohio **(1876–1941)**
Andress, Ursula (actress); Bern, Switzerland, 3/19/38
Andrews, Julie (Julia Wells) (actress, singer); Walton-on-Thames, England, 10/1/35
Andrews, La Verne (singer); Minneapolis **(1916–1967)**
Andrews, Maxene (singer); Minneapolis **(1918–1995)**
Andrews, Patti (singer); Minneapolis, 2/16/20
Andy (Charles J. Correll) (radio comedian); Peoria, Ill. **(1890–1972)**
Angelico, Fra (Guido di Pietro; Giovanni de Fiesole) (painter); nr. Florence **(c. 1400–1455)**
Angelou, Maya (Marguerite Johnson) (poet, novelist); St. Louis, 4/4/28
Aniston, Jennifer (Jennifer Anistonapoulos) (actress); Sherman Oaks, Calif., 2/11/69
Anka, Paul (singer, composer); Ottawa, Ont., Canada, 7/30/41
Annan, Kofi (diplomat, UN secretary general); Kumasi, Ghana, 4/8/38
Ann-Margret (Ann-Margaret Olsson) (actress); Valsjobyn, Sweden, 4/28/41
Anouilh, Jean (playwright); Bordeaux, France **(1910–1987)**
Anthony, Susan Brownell (woman suffragist); Adams, Mass. **(1820–1906)**
Antonioni, Michelangelo (director); Ferrara, Italy, 9/29/12
Antony, Mark (Marcus Antonius) (statesman); Rome **(c. 83–30 B.C.)**
Anuszkiewicz, Richard (painter); Erie, Pa., 5/23/30
Apple, Fiona (singer); New York City, 4/8/68
Applegate, Christina (actress); Los Angeles, Calif., 11/25/71
Aquinas, St. Thomas (philosopher); nr. Aquino, Italy **(1225–1274)**
Arafat, Yasir (Mohammed Abdel-Raouf Arafat al Qudwa al Husseini) (chairman of the Palestine Liberation Organization); Cairo, Egypt, 8/24/29
Arbuckle, Roscoe "Fatty" (actor, director); Smith Center, Kans. **(1887–1933)**
Archimedes (physicist, mathematician); Syracuse, Sicily **(287–212 B.C.)**
Archipenko, Alexandre (sculptor); Kiev, Ukraine **(1887–1964)**
Arden, Elizabeth (Florence Nightingale Graham) (cosmetics executive); Woodbridge, Canada **(1878–1966)**
Arden, Eve (Eunice Quedens) (actress); Mill Valley, Calif. **(1912–1990)**
Arendt, Hannah (historian); Hanover, Germany **(1906–1975)**
Aristophanes (dramatist); Athens **(c. 448–c. 385 B.C.)**
Aristotle (philosopher); Stagirus, Macedonia **(384–322 B.C.)**
Arkin, Adam (actor); New York City, 8/19/57
Arkin, Alan (actor, director); New York City, 3/26/34
Arledge, Roone (TV executive); Forest Hills, N.Y. **(1931–2002)**
Arlen, Harold (Hyman Arluck) (composer); Buffalo, N.Y. **(1905–1986)**
Armani, Georgio (fashion designer); Piacenza, Italy, 7/11/34
Armstrong, Louis ("Satchmo") (musician); New Orleans **(1900–1971)**
Arnaz, Desi (Desiderio Alberto Araz y de Acha III) (actor, producer); Santiago, Cuba **(1917–1986)**
Arness, James (James Aurness) (actor); Minneapolis, 5/26/23
Arno, Peter (cartoonist); New York City **(1904–1968)**
Arnold, Benedict (American Revolutionary War general, charged with treason); Norwich, Conn. **(1741–1801)**
Arnold, Matthew (poet, critic); Laleham, England **(1822–1888)**
Arp, Jean (sculptor, painter); Strasbourg, France **(1887–1966)**
Arquette, Cliff (actor); Toledo, Ohio **(1905–1974)**
Arquette, Patricia (actress); Chicago, 4/8/68
Arquette, Rosanna (actress); New York City, 8/10/59
Arrau, Claudio (pianist); Chillán, Chile **(1903–1991)**
Arroyo, Martina (soprano); New York City, 2/2/40
Arthur, Bea (Bernice Frankel) (actress); New York City, 5/13/23
Arthur, Chester Alan (21st U.S. president); Fairfield, Vt. **(1829–1886)**
Ashcroft, John (U.S. attorney general); Chicago, Ill., 5/9/42
Ashcroft, Dame Peggy (actress); Croydon, England **(1907–1991)**
Ashkenazy, Vladimir (concert pianist); Gorki, U.S.S.R., 7/6/37
Ashley, Elizabeth (actress); Ocala, Fla., 8/30/39
Ashton, Sir Frederick William Mallandaine (choreographer); Guayaquil, Ecuador **(1904–1988)**
Asimov, Isaac (author); Petrovichi, Russia **(1920–1992)**
Asner, Edward (actor); Kansas City, Mo., 11/15/29
Assante, Armand (actor); New York City, 10/4/49
Astaire, Fred (Frederick Austerlitz) (dancer, actor); Omaha, Neb. **(1899–1987)**
Astin, John (actor, director); Baltimore, 3/30/30
Astor, Brooke (socialite, philanthropist); Portsmouth, N.H., 3/30/1902
Astor, John Jacob (financier); Waldorf, Germany **(1763–1848)**
Astor, Mary (Lucile Langhanke) (actress); Quincy, Ill. **(1906–1987)**
Ataturk, Kemal (Mustafa Kemal) (Turkish soldier, statesman); Salonika, Greece **(1881–1938)**
Atkins, Chet (guitarist); nr. Luttrell, Tenn. **(1924–2001)**
Atkinson, Rowan (actor); Newcastle-Upon-Tyne, England, 1/6/55
Attenborough, Richard (actor, director); Cambridge, England, 8/29/23
Attila (King of Huns); **(406?–453)**
Attucks, Crispus (American Revolutionary patriot); Boston **(c. 1723–1770)**
Auberjonois, Rene (actor); New York City, 6/1/40
Auchincloss, Louis (author); Lawrence, N.Y., 9/27/17
Auden, W(ystan) H(ugh) (poet); York, England **(1907–1973)**
Audubon, John James (naturalist, painter); Haiti **(1785–1851)**
Auer, Leopold (violinist, teacher); Veszprém, Hungary **(1845–1930)**
Augustine, Saint (Aurelius Augustinus) (theologian); Tagaste, Numidia, Algeria **(354–430)**
Augustus (Gaius Octavius) (Roman emperor); Rome **(63 B.C.– A.D. 14)**
Aung San Suu Kyi (human rights activist); Rangoon, Burma, 6/19/45
Austen, Jane (novelist); Steventon, England **(1775–1817)**
Autry, Gene (singer, actor); Tioga, Tex. **(1907–1998)**
Avalon, Frankie (singer); Philadelphia, 9/18/39
Avedon, Richard (photographer); New York City, 5/15/23
Avery, Milton (painter); Altmar, N.Y. **(1893–1965)**
Ax, Emanuel (pianist); Lvov, Ukraine, 6/8/49
Axelrod, George (playwright); New York City **(1922–2003)**
Ayckbourn, Alan (playwright); London, 4/12/39
Aykroyd, Dan (actor); Ottawa, Ont., Canada, 7/1/52
Ayres, Lew (actor); Minneapolis **(1908–1996)**

B

Bacall, Lauren (Betty Joan Perske) (actress); New York City, 9/16/24
Bach, Carl Phillipp Emanuel (composer); Weimar, Germany **(1714–1788)**
Bach, Johann Sebastian (composer); Eisenach, Germany **(1685–1750)**
Bacharach, Burt (songwriter); Kansas City, Mo., 5/12/29
Backus, Jim (actor); Cleveland **(1913–1989)**
Bacon, Francis (philosopher, essayist); London **(1561–1626)**
Bacon, Francis (painter); Dublin **(1910–1992)**
Bacon, Kevin (actor); Philadelphia, 7/8/58
Bacon, Roger (philosopher, scientist); Ilchester, England **(c. 1214–1294?)**
Badu, Erykah (Erykah Wright) (singer); Dallas, 1971
Baez, Joan (folk singer); Staten Island, N.Y., 1/9/41
Bailey, F. Lee (lawyer); Waltham, Mass., 6/10/33
Bailey, Pearl (singer); Newport News, Va. **(1918–1990)**
Bain, Conrad (actor); Lethbridge, Alba., Canada, 2/4/23
Baio, Scott (actor); Brooklyn, N.Y., 9/22/61
Baird, Bil (William B. Baird) (puppeteer); Grand Island, Neb. **(1904–1987)**
Baker, Anita (singer); Toledo, Ohio, 1958?
Baker, Carroll (actress); Johnstown, Pa., 5/28/31
Baker, Josephine (singer, dancer); St. Louis **(1906–1975)**
Baker, Russell (columnist); Loudoun County, Va., 8/14/25
Balanchine, George (choreographer); St. Petersburg, Russia **(1904–1983)**
Balboa, Vasco Nuñez de (explorer); Jerez de los Caballeros, Spain **(1475–1517)**
Baldwin, Alec (actor); Massapequa, N.Y., 4/3/58
Baldwin, James (novelist); New York City **(1924–1987)**
Bale, Christian (actor); Pembrokeshire, Wales, 1/30/74
Balenciaga, Cristóbal (fashion designer); Guetaria, Spain **(1895–1972)**
Ball, Lucille (Lucille Désirée Ball) (actress, producer); Celoron (nr. Jamestown), N.Y. **(1911–1989)**
Balsam, Martin (actor); Bronx, New York **(1919–1996)**
Balzac, Honoré de (novelist); Tours, France **(1799–1850)**
Bancroft, Anne (Annemarie Italiano) (actress); New York City, 9/17/31
Banderas, Antonio (José Antonio Dominguez Banderas) (actor, model); Málaga, Spain, 8/10/60
Bankhead, Tallulah (actress); Huntsville, Ala. **(1903–1968)**

Banks, Tyra (model); Los Angeles, 12/4/73
Banting, Fredrick Grant (physiologist); Alliston, Ont., Canada **(1891–1941)**
Bara, Theda (Theodosia Goodman) (actress); Cincinnati **(1890–1955)**
Barak, Ehud (former Israeli prime minister); Kibbutz Mishmar Hasharon, Israel, 2/12/42
Barbera, Joseph (animator, producer); New York City, 1911
Baraka, Imamu Amiri (LeRoi Jones) (playwright); Newark, N.J., 10/7/34
Baranski, Christine (actress); Buffalo, N.Y., 5/2/52
Barber, Red (Walter Lanier) (sportscaster); Columbus, Miss. **(1908–1992)**
Barber, Samuel (composer); West Chester, Pa. **(1910–1981)**
Barbie, Klaus (Nazi, "The Butcher of Lyon"); Bad Godesberg, Germany **(1913–1991)**
Bardem, Javier (actor); Gran Canaria, Spain, 5/1/69
Bardot, Brigitte (Camille Javal) (actress); Paris, 9/28/34
Barenboim, Daniel (concert pianist, conductor); Buenos Aires, 11/15/42
Barker, Bob (game-show host); Darrington, Wash., 12/12/23
Barkin, Ellen (actress); Bronx, N.Y., 4/16/54
Barnard, Christiaan N. (heart surgeon); Beauford West, South Africa **(1922–2001)**
Barnum, Phineas Taylor (showman); Bethel, Conn. **(1810–1891)**
Barrie, Sir James Matthew (author); Kirriemuir, Scotland **(1860–1937)**
Barry, John (naval officer); County Wexford, Ireland **(1745–1803)**
Barrymore, Diana (actress); New York City **(1921–1960)**
Barrymore, Drew (actress); Los Angeles, 2/22/75
Barrymore, Ethel (Ethel Blythe) (actress); Philadelphia **(1879–1959)**
Barrymore, Georgiana Drew (actress); Philadelphia **(1856–1893)**
Barrymore, John (John Blythe) (actor); Philadelphia **(1882–1942)**
Barrymore, Lionel (Lionel Blythe) (actor); Philadelphia **(1878–1954)**
Barrymore, Maurice (Herbert Blythe) (actor, playwright); Agra, India **(1847–1905)**
Barth, John (novelist); Cambridge, Md., 5/27/30
Barthelme, Donald (novelist); Philadelphia **(1931 –1989)**
Bartók, Béla (composer); Nagyszentmiklo, Hungary **(1881–1945)**
Barton, Clara (founder of American Red Cross); Oxford, Mass. **(1821–1912)**
Baruch, Bernard Mannes (statesman); Camden, S.C. **(1870–1965)**
Baryshnikov, Mikhail Nikolayevich (ballet dancer, artistic director); Riga, Latvia, 1/27/48
Basie, Count (William Basie) (band leader); Red Bank, N.J. **(1904–1984)**
Basinger, Kim (actress); Athens, Ga., 12/8/53
Bassett, Angela (actress); New York City, 8/16/58
Bassey, Shirley (singer); Cardiff, Wales, 1/8/37
Batchelor, Clarence Daniel (political cartoonist); Osage City, Kans. **(1888–1977)**
Bateman, Jason (actor); Rye, N.Y., 1/14/69
Bateman, Justine (actress); Rye, N.Y., 2/19/66
Bates, Alan (actor); Allestree, England, 2/17/34
Bates, Kathy (Kathleen Doyle Bates) (actress); Memphis, Tenn., 6/28/48
Battle, Kathleen (soprano); Portsmouth, Ohio, 8/13/48
Baudelaire, Charles Pierre (poet); Paris **(1821–1867)**
Baxter, Anne (actress); Michigan City, Ind. **(1923–1985)**
Baxter, Meredith (actress); Los Angeles, 6/21/47
Beardsley, Aubrey Vincent (illustrator); Brighton, England **(1872–1898)**
Beaton, Cecil (photographer, designer); London **(1904–1980)**
Beatty, Clyde (animal trainer); Bainbridge, Ohio **(1903–1965)**
Beatty, Warren (Henry Warren Beaty) (actor, producer); Richmond, Va., 3/30/37
Beaumont, Francis (dramatist); Grace-Dieu, England **(1584–1616)**
Becket, Thomas à (archbishop of Canterbury); London **(1118?–1170)**
Beckett, Samuel (playwright); Dublin **(1906–1989)**
Beckmann, Max (painter); Leipzig, Germany **(1884–1950)**
Bede, Saint ("The Venerable Bede") (scholar); Monkwearmouth, England **(673–735)**
Beecham, Sir Thomas (conductor); St. Helens, England **(1879–1961)**
Beecher, Henry Ward (clergyman); Litchfield, Conn. **(1813–1887)**
Beerbohm, Sir Max (author); London **(1872–1956)**
Beery, Noah (actor); Kansas City, Mo. **(1884–1946)**
Beery, Noah, Jr. (actor); New York City **(1913–1994)**
Beery, Wallace (actor); Kansas City, Mo. **(1886–1949)**
Beethoven, Ludwig van (composer); Bonn, Germany **(1770–1827)**
Begin, Menachem (Israeli prime minister); Brest-Litovsk, Belarus **(1913–1992)**
Begley, Ed (actor); Hartford, Conn. **(1901–1970)**
Beiderbecke, Bix (jazz musician); Davenport, Iowa **(1903–1931)**
Beineix, Jean-Jacques (director, producer, screenwriter) 1946
Belafonte, Harry (singer, actor); New York City, 3/1/27
Belafonte-Harper, Shari (actress); New York City, 9/22/54
Belasco, David (dramatist, producer); San Francisco **(1854–1931)**
Bel Geddes, Barbara (actress); New York City, 10/31/22
Bell, Alexander Graham (inventor); Edinburgh, Scotland **(1847–1922)**
Bell, Quentin (author, artist); England **(1910–1996)**
Bellamy, Edward (author); Chicopee Falls, Mass. **(1850–1898)**
Bellamy, Ralph (actor); Chicago **(1904–1991)**
Bellini, Giovanni (painter); Venice **(c. 1430–1516)**
Bellow, Saul (novelist); Lachine, Que., Canada, 6/10/15
Bellows, George Wesley (painter, lithographer); Columbus, Ohio **(1882–1925)**
Belushi, Jim (actor); Chicago, 6/15/54
Belushi, John (comedian, actor); Chicago **(1949–1982)**
Benchley, Peter Bradford (novelist); New York City, 5/8/40
Benchley, Robert Charles (humorist); Worcester, Mass. **(1889–1945)**
Bendix, William (actor); New York City **(1906–1964)**
Benedict, Ruth Fulton (anthropologist); New York City **(1887–1948)**
Benes, Eduard (statesman); Kozlany, former Czechoslovakia **(1884–1948)**
Benét, Stephen Vincent (poet, story writer); Bethlehem, Pa. **(1898–1943)**
Benét, William Rose (poet, novelist); Ft. Hamilton, Brooklyn, N.Y. **(1886–1950)**
Ben-Gurion, David (David Green) (statesman); Plónsk, Poland **(1886–1973)**
Benigni, Roberto (actor, director, screenwriter); Misericordia, Arezzo, Italy, 10/27/52
Bening, Annette (actress); Topeka, Kans., 5/29/58
Bennett, Enoch Arnold (novelist, dramatist); Hanley, England **(1867–1931)**
Bennett, James Gordon (editor); Keith, Scotland **(1795–1872)**
Bennett, Joan (actress); Palisades, N.J. **(1910–1990)**
Bennett, Robert Russell (composer); Kansas City, Mo. **(1894–1981)**
Bennett, Tony (Anthony Benedetto) (singer); Astoria, Queens, N.Y., 8/3/26
Benny, Jack (Benjamin Kubelsky) (comedian); Chicago **(1894–1974)**
Benson, Robby (Robert Segal) (actor); Dallas, 1/21/56
Bentham, Jeremy Heinrich (economist); London **(1748–1832)**
Benton, Thomas Hart (painter); Neosho, Mo. **(1889–1975)**
Berendt, John (writer); Syracuse, N.Y., 12/5/39
Berenger, Tom (actor); Chicago, 5/31/50
Berg, Alban (composer); Vienna **(1885–1935)**
Berg, Gertrude (writer, actress); New York City **(1899–1966)**
Bergen, Candice (actress); Beverly Hills, Calif., 5/9/46
Bergen, Edgar (ventriloquist); Chicago **(1903–1978)**
Bergen, Polly (Nellie Paulina Burgin) (actress, singer); Knoxville, Tenn., 7/14/30
Bergerac, Cyrano de (poet); Paris **(1619–1655)**
Bergman, Ingmar (film director); Uppsala, Sweden, 7/14/18
Bergman, Ingrid (actress); Stockholm **(1915–1982)**
Bergson, Henri (philosopher); Paris **(1859–1941)**
Berkeley, Busby (William Berkeley Enos) (choreographer, director); Los Angeles **(1895–1976)**
Berle, Milton (Milton Berlinger) (comedian); New York City **(1908–2002)**
Berlin, Irving (Israel Baline) (songwriter); Temum, Russia **(1888–1989)**
Berlioz, Louis Hector (composer); La Côte-Saint-André, France **(1803–1869)**
Berman, Lazar (concert pianist); Leningrad (St. Petersburg), Russia, 2/26/30
Bernardin, Joseph Cardinal (prelate); Columbia, S.C. **(1928–1996)**
Bernhard, Sandra (actress, comedian); Flint, Mich., 6/6/55
Bernhardt, Sarah (Rosine Bernard) (actress); Paris **(1844–1923)**
Bernini, Gian Lorenzo (sculptor, painter); Naples, Italy **(1598–1680)**
Bernoulli, Jacques (scientist); Basel, Switzerland **(1654–1705)**
Bernsen, Corbin (actor); North Hollywood, Calif., 7/7/54
Bernstein, Leonard (conductor); Lawrence, Mass. **(1918–1990)**
Berry, Chuck (Charles Edward Berry) (singer, guitarist); St. Louis, Mo., 10/19/26
Berry, Halle (actress, model); Cleveland, Ohio, 8/14/68
Berry, Ken (actor); Moline, Ill., 11/3/30
Berry, Richard (songwriter); Extension, S.C. **(1935–1997)**

Berryman, John (poet); McAlester, Okla. **(1914–1972)**
Bertinelli, Valerie (actress); Wilmington, Del., 4/23/60
Bertolucci, Bernardo (actor); Parma, Italy, 3/16/40
Bethune, Mary McLeod (educator); Mayesville, S.C. **(1875–1955)**
Betjeman, Sir John (poet laureate); London **(1906–1984)**
Bettelheim, Bruno (psychoanalyst); Vienna **(1903–1990)**
Bierce, Ambrose Gwinnett (journalist); Meigs County, Ohio **(1842–1914?)**
Bikel, Theodore (actor, folk singer); Vienna, 5/2/24
Bing, Sir Rudolf (opera manager); Vienna **(1902–1997)**
Bingham, George Caleb (painter); Augusta Co., Va. **(1811–1879)**
Binoche, Juliette (actress); Paris, 3/9/64
Bishop, Joey (Joseph Gottlieb) (comedian); New York City, 2/3/19
Bismarck-Schönhausen, Prince Otto Eduard Leopold von (statesman); Schönhausen, Germany **(1815–1898)**
Bisset, Jacqueline (actress); Weybridge, England, 9/13/44
Bixby, Bill (actor); San Francisco **(1934–1993)**
Bizet, Georges (Alexandre César Léopold Bizet) (composer); Paris **(1838–1875)**
Bjoerling, Jussi (tenor); Stora Tuna, Sweden **(1911–1960)**
Björk (Björk Gudmundsdottir) (pop musician, singer); Reykjavik, Iceland, 11/21/65
Black, Clint (singer, songwriter); Long Branch, N.J., 2/4/62
Black, Karen (Karen Ziegler) (actress); Park Ridge, Ill., 7/1/42
Black, Shirley Temple (child actress, former ambassador); Santa Monica, Calif., 4/23/28
Blackstone, Sir William (jurist); London **(1723–1780)**
Blackwell, Elizabeth (physician, educator); England **(1821–1910)**
Blades, Ruben (actor, musician, composer); Panama City, Panama, 7/16/48
Blair, Tony (British prime minister); Edinburgh, Scotland, 5/6/53
Blake, Amanda (Beverly Louise Neill) (actress); Buffalo, N.Y. **(1929–1989)**
Blake, Eubie (James Hubert) (pianist); Baltimore **(1883–1983)**
Blake, Robert (Michael Gubitosi) (actor); Nutley, N.J., 9/18/33
Blake, William (poet, artist); London **(1757–1827)**
Blanc, Mel (Melvin Jerome) (actor, voice specialist); San Francisco **(1908–1989)**
Blass, Bill (fashion designer); Fort Wayne, Ind. **(1922–2002)**
Bleeth, Yasmine (model, actress); New York City, 6/14/68
Blige, Mary J. (hip-hop singer); Bronx, N.Y., 1/11/71
Bloch, Ernest (composer); Geneva **(1880–1959)**
Bloom, Claire (actress); London, 2/15/31
Bloomberg, Michael (mayor of New York); Melrose, Mass., 2/14/1942
Bloomgarden, Kermit (producer); Brooklyn, N.Y. **(1904–1976)**
Blume, Judy (Judy Sussman) (young adult novelist); Elizabeth, N.J., 2/12/38
Bly, Nellie (pseud. for Elizabeth Seaman) (journalist); Cochrane Mills, Pa. **(1867–1922)**
Bly, Robert (poet, critic); Madison, Minn., 12/23/26
Boccaccio, Giovanni (author); Paris **(1313–1375)**
Boccherini, Luigi (Rodolfo) (composer); Lucca, Italy **(1743–1805)**
Boccioni, Umberto (painter, sculptor); Reggio di Calabria, Italy **(1882–1916)**
Bochco, Steven (TV producer, writer); New York City, 12/16/43
Bock, Jerry (composer); New Haven, Conn., 11/23/28
Bogarde, Dirk (Derek Van den Bogaerde) (film actor, director); London **(1921–1999)**
Bogart, Humphrey DeForest (actor); New York City **(1899–1957)**
Bogdanovich, Peter (producer, director); Kingston, N.Y., 7/30/39
Bogosian, Eric (playwright, screenwriter, actor, monologuist); Woburn, Mass., 4/24/53
Bohr, Niels (atomic physicist); Copenhagen **(1885–1962)**
Bok, Sissela (Sissela Ann Myrdal) (scholar); Stockholm, 12/2/34
Bolger, Ray (dancer, actor); Dorchester, Mass **(1904–1987)**
Bolivar, Simón (South American liberator); Caracas, Venezuela **(1783–1830)**
Bologna, Giovanni da (sculptor); Douai, France **(1529–1608)**
Bombeck, Erma (author, columnist); Dayton, Ohio **(1927–1996)**
Bonaparte, Napoléon (Emperor of the French); Ajaccio, Corsica, France **(1769–1821)**
Bond, Julian (Georgia legislator); Nashville, Tenn., 1/14/40
Bonet, Lisa (actress); San Francisco, 11/16/67
Bonham Carter, Helena (actress); London, 5/23/66
Bon Jovi, Jon (musician, songwriter); Sayreville, N.J., 3/2/62
Bonnard, Pierre (painter); Fontenayaux-Roses, France **(1867–1947)**
Bono (Paul Hewson) (singer, songwriter); Dublin, Ireland, 5/10/60
Bono, Sonny (Salvatore Bono) (singer, politician); Detroit **(1935–1998)**
Boone, Daniel (frontiersman); nr. Reading, Pa. **(1734–1820)**
Boone, Pat (Charles Boone) (singer); Jacksonville, Fla., 6/1/34
Boone, Richard (actor); Los Angeles **(1917–1981)**
Boorstin, Daniel (historian); Atlanta, 10/1/14
Booth, Edwin Thomas (actor); Bel Air, Md. **(1833–1893)**
Booth, Evangeline Cory (religious leader); London **(1865–1950)**
Booth, John Wilkes (actor; assassin of Lincoln); Harford County, Md. **(1838–1865)**
Booth, Shirley (Thelma Booth Ford) (actress); New York City **(1907–1992)**
Borden, Lizzie (Elizabeth Andrew Borden) (accused murderer); Fall River, Mass. **(1860–1927)**
Borge, Victor (pianist, comedian); Copenhagen **(1909–2000)**
Borgia, Cesare (nobleman, soldier); Rome **(1476–1507)**
Borgia, Lucrezia (Duchess of Ferrara); Rome **(1480–1519)**
Borgnine, Ernest (actor); Hamden, Conn., 1/24/17
Borromini, Francesco (architect); Bissone, Italy **(1599–1667)**
Bosch, Hieronymus (Hieronymus van Aeken) (painter); Hertogenbosch, Netherlands **(c. 1450–1516)**
Bosley, Tom (actor); Chicago, 10/1/27
Bostwick, Barry (actor); San Mateo, Calif., 2/24/45
Boswell, James (diarist, biographer); Edinburgh, Scotland **(1740–1795)**
Botticelli, Sandro (Alessandro di Mariano dei Filipepi) (painter); Florence, Italy **(1444–1510)**
Bottoms, Timothy (actor); Santa Barbara, Calif., 8/30/50
Boulez, Pierre (conductor); Montbrison, France, 3/26/25
Bourke-White, Margaret (photographer); New York City **(1906–1971)**
Boutros-Ghali, Boutros (ex-secretary general of the UN); Cairo, Egypt, 11/14/22
Bow, Clara (actress); Brooklyn, N.Y. **(1905–1965)**
Bowen, Catherine Drinker (biographer); Haverford, Pa. **(1897–1973)**
Bowie, David (David Robert Jones) (actor, musician); London, 1/8/47
Bowie, James (soldier); Burke County, Ga. **(1799–1836)**
Bowles, Chester (diplomat); Springfield, Mass. **(1901–1986)**
Boxleitner, Bruce (actor); Elgin, Ill., 5/12/50
Boyce, William (composer); London? **(1710–1779)**
Boyd, Bill ("Hopalong Cassidy") (actor); Cambridge, Ohio **(1895–1972)**
Boyd, Stephen (Stephen Millar) (actor); Belfast, Northern Ireland **(1928–1977)**
Boyer, Charles (actor); Figeac, France **(1897–1978)**
Boy George (George Alan O'Dowd) (singer); London, 6/14/61
Boyle, Peter (actor); Philadelphia, 10/18/33
Boyle, Robert (scientist); Lismore Castle, Munster, Ireland **(1627–1691)**
Bracken, Eddie (actor); Astoria, Queens, N.Y., 1920
Bradbury, Ray Douglas (science-fiction writer); Waukegan, Ill., 8/22/20
Bradlee, Benjamin C. (editor); Boston, 8/26/21
Bradley, Ed (broadcast journalist); Philadelphia, 6/22/41
Bradley, Omar N. (5-star general); Clark, Mo. **(1893–1981)**
Bradley, Thomas (mayor of Los Angeles); Calvert, Tex. **(1917–1998)**
Brady, Mathew (early photographer); Warren Co., N.Y. **(c. 1823–1896)**
Brahe, Tycho (astronomer); Knudstrup, Denmark **(1546–1601)**
Bragg, Billy (singer, songwriter); Barking, England, 12/20/57
Brahms, Johannes (composer); Hamburg, Germany **(1833–1897)**
Braille, Louis (teacher of blind); Coupvray, France **(1809–1862)**
Brailowsky, Alexander (pianist); Kiev, Ukraine **(1896–1976)**
Bramante, Donato D'Agnolo (architect); Monte Asdrualdo (now Fermignano), Italy **(1444–1514)**
Branagh, Kenneth (actor, director, writer, producer); Belfast, Northern Ireland, 12/10/60
Brancusi, Constantin (sculptor); Pestisansi, Romania **(1876–1957)**
Brandauer, Klaus Maria (Klaus Maria Steng) (actor); Bad Aussee, Steiermark, Austria , 6/22/44
Brando, Marlon (actor); Omaha, Neb., 4/3/24
Brandt, Willy (Herbert Frahm) (ex-chancellor); Lübeck, Germany **(1913– 1992)**
Brandy (Brandy Norwood) (actress, singer); McComb, Miss., 2/11/79
Braque, Georges (painter); Argenteuil, France **(1882–1963)**
Bratt, Benjamin (actor); San Francisco, 12/16/63
Braugher, André (actor); Chicago, 7/1/62
Braxton, Toni (R&B singer); Severn, Maryland, 10/7/67
Brazelton, T(homas) Berry II (pediatrician, writer); Waco, Tex., 5/10/18
Brecht, Bertolt (dramatist, poet); Augsburg, Bavaria **(1898–1956)**
Brel, Jacques (singer, composer); Brussels **(1929–1978)**
Brennan, Walter (actor); Lynn, Mass. **(1894–1974)**

Brennan, William J., Jr. (Supreme Court justice); Newark, N.J. **(1906–1997)**
Breslin, Jimmy (journalist); Jamaica, Queens, N.Y., 10/17/30
Breton, André (writer); Tinchebray, France **(1896–1966)**
Breuer, Marcel (architect, designer); Pécs, Hungary **(1902–1981)**
Brewster, Kingman, Jr. (ex-president of Yale); Longmeadow, Mass. **(1919–1988)**
Brezhnev, Leonid I. (Communist Party secretary); Dneprodzerzhinsk, Ukraine **(1906–1982)**
Brice, Fanny (Fannie Borach) (comedienne); New York City **(1892–1951)**
Bridges, Beau (actor); Los Angeles, 12/9/41
Bridges, Jeff (actor); Los Angeles, 12/4/49
Bridges, Lloyd (actor); San Leandro, Calif. **(1913–1998)**
Brinkley, Christie (model, actress); Malibu, Calif., 2/2/54
Brinkley, David (TV newscaster); Wilmington, N.C. **(1920–2003)**
Britten, Benjamin (composer); Lowestoft, England **(1913–1976)**
Broderick, Matthew (actor); New York City, 3/21/62
Brodsky, Joseph Alexandrovitch (poet); St. Petersburg, Russia **(1940–1996)**
Brody, Jane (journalist); Brooklyn, N.Y., 5/19/41
Brokaw, Tom (TV newscaster); Webster, S.D., 2/6/40
Brolin, James (actor); Los Angeles, 7/18/40
Bromfield, Louis (novelist); Mansfield, Ohio **(1896–1956)**
Bronson, Charles (Charles Buchinsky) (actor); Ehrenfield, Pa. **(1921–2003)**
Brontë, Charlotte (novelist); Thornton, England **(1816–1855)**
Brontë, Emily Jane (novelist); Thornton, England **(1818–1848)**
Bronzino, Agnolo (painter); Monticelli, Italy **(1503–1572)**
Brook, Peter (director); London, 3/21/25
Brooke, Rupert (poet); Rugby, England **(1887–1915)**
Brooks, Albert (Albert Einstein) (actor, writer, director); Beverly Hills, Calif., 7/22/47
Brooks, Avery (actor) 4/18/49
Brooks, Gwendolyn (poet); Topeka, Kans. **(1917–2000)**
Brooks, James L. (film and television producer); New York City, 5/9/40
Brooks, Mel (Melvin Kaminsky) (writer, film director); Brooklyn, N.Y., 6/28/26
Brosnan, Pierce (actor); County Meath, Ireland, 5/16/52
Brothers, Joyce (Bauer) (psychologist, author, radio-TV personality); New York City, 9/20/28
Broun, Matthew Heywood Campbell (journalist); Brooklyn, N.Y. **(1888–1939)**
Brown, Charles Brockden (novelist); Philadelphia **(1771–1810)**
Brown, Helen Gurley (editor, author); Green Forest, Ark., 2/18/22
Brown, James (singer); Augusta, Ga., 5/3/34
Brown, Joe E. (comedian); Holgate, Ohio **(1892–1973)**
Brown, John (abolitionist); Torrington, Conn. **(1800–1859)**
Brown, Les (band leader); Reinerton, Pa. **(1912–2000)**
Brown, Margaret Wise (children's author); Brooklyn, N.Y. **(1910–1952)**
Brown, Trisha (choreographer); Aberdeen, Wash., 11/25/36
Browne, Jackson (singer, guitarist); Heidelberg, Germany, 10/9/48
Browning, Elizabeth Barrett (poet); Durham, England **(1806–1861)**
Browning, Robert (poet); London **(1812–1889)**
Brubeck, Dave (musician); Concord, Calif., 12/6/20
Bruce, Lenny (comedian); Long Island, N.Y. **(1926–1966)**
Bruce, Nigel (actor); Ensenada, Mexico **(1895–1953)**
Brueghel, Pieter (painter); nr. Breda, Flanders, Netherlands **(c. 1520–1569)**
Bruhn, Erik (Belton Evers) (ballet dancer); Copenhagen **(1928–1986)**
Brunelleschi, Filippo (architect); Florence, Italy **(1377–1446)**
Bruno, Giordano (philosopher); Nola, Italy **(1548–1600)**
Brutus, Marcus Junius (Roman politician) **(85–42 B.C.)**
Bryan, William Jennings (orator, politician); Salem, Ill. **(1860–1925)**
Bryant, Anita (singer); Barnsdall, Okla., 3/25/40
Bryant, William Cullen (poet, editor); Cummington, Mass. **(1794–1878)**
Brynner, Yul (Taidje Khan) (actor); Sakhalin Island, Russia **(1920–1985)**
Brzezinski, Zbigniew (ex-presidential adviser); Warsaw, 3/28/28
Buber, Martin (philosopher, theologian); Vienna **(1878–1965)**
Buchanan, James (15th U.S. president); near Mercersburg, Pa. **(1791–1868)**
Buchanan, Pat (politician); Washington, D.C., 11/2/38
Buchholz, Horst (actor); Berlin, 12/4/33
Büchner, Georg (dramatist); Goddelau, Germany **(1813–1837)**
Buchwald, Art (Arthur Buchwald) (columnist); Mount Vernon, N.Y., 10/20/25
Buck, Pearl S(ydenstricker) (author); Hillsboro, W. Va. **(1892–1973)**
Buckley, Christopher (writer); New York City, 1952
Buckley, Jeff (singer, songwriter); Orange County, Calif. **(1966–1997)**
Buckley, William F., Jr. (journalist); New York City, 11/24/25
Buffalo Bill (William Frederick Cody) (scout); Scott County, Iowa **(1846–1917)**
Buffett, Jimmy (singer, writer); Pascogoula, Miss., 12/25/46
Buffett, Warren (investment expert); Omaha, Neb., 8/30/30
Bujold, Genevieve (actress); Montreal, 7/1/42
Bujones, Fernando (ballet dancer); Miami, Fla., 3/9/55
Bulgakov, Mikhail (novelist); Kiev, Ukraine **(1891–1940)**
Bullins, Ed (playwright); Philadelphia, 7/2/35
Bullock, Sandra (actress); Washington D.C., 7/26/65
Bunche, Ralph J. (statesman); Detroit **(1904–1971)**
Bundy, McGeorge (educator); Boston **(1919–1996)**
Bundy, William Putnam (editor); Washington, D.C. **(1917–2000)**
Buñuel, Luis (film director); Calanda, Spain **(1900–1983)**
Bunyan, John (preacher, author); Elstow, England **(1628–1688)**
Burbank, Luther (horticulturist); Lancaster, Mass. **(1849–1926)**
Burke, Adm. Arleigh A. (ex-chief of Naval Operations); Boulder, Colo. **(1901–1996)**
Burke, Billie (Mary William Ethelbert Appleton Burke) (comedienne); Washington, D.C. **(1885–1970)**
Burke, Delta (actress); Orlando, Fla., 7/30/56
Burke, Edmund (statesman); Dublin **(1729–1797)**
Burne-Jones, Edward Coley (painter); Birmingham, England **(1833–1898)**
Burnett, Carol (comedienne); San Antonio, 4/26/33
Burney, Fanny (Frances) (writer); King's Lynn, England **(1752–1840)**
Burns, Edward (actor, film director, screenwriter, producer); Long Island, N.Y., 1/29/68
Burns, George (Nathan Birnbaum) (comedian); New York City **(1896–1996)**
Burns, Ken (documentary filmmaker); Brooklyn, N.Y., 7/29/53
Burns, Robert (poet); Alloway, Scotland **(1759–1796)**
Burr, Aaron (political leader); Newark, N.J. **(1756–1836)**
Burr, Raymond (William Stacey Burr) (actor); New Westminster, B.C., Canada **(1917–1993)**
Burroughs, Edgar Rice (novelist); Chicago **(1875–1950)**
Burroughs, William S. (writer); St. Louis **(1914–1997)**
Burrows, Abe (playwright, director); New York City **(1910–1985)**
Burstyn, Ellen (Edna Rae Gillooly) (actress); Detroit, 12/7/32
Burton, LeVar (actor, director); Landsthul, Germany, 2/16/57
Burton, Richard (Richard Jenkins) (actor); Pontrhydfen, Wales **(1925–1984)**
Burton, Tim (filmmaker); Burbank, Calif., 8/25/58
Buscemi, Steve (actor); Brooklyn, N.Y., 12/13/57
Bush, George Herbert Walker (41st U.S. president); Milton, Mass., 6/12/24
Butkus, Dick (NFL linebacker, actor); Chicago, 12/9/42
Butler, Samuel (author); Langar, England **(1835–1902)**
Butterworth, Charles (actor); South Bend, Ind. **(1896–1946)**
Buttons, Red (Aaron Chwatt) (actor); New York City, 2/5/19
Buzzi, Ruth (comedienne); Westerly, R.I., 7/24/36
Byrd, Richard Evelyn (polar explorer); Winchester, Va. **(1888–1957)**
Byrne, David (composer, musician, director, actor); Dumbarton, Scotland, 5/14/52
Byrne, Gabriel (actor); Dublin, 5/12/50
Byron, George Gordon (6th Baron Byron) (poet); London **(1788–1824)**

C

Caan, James (actor); Queens, N.Y., 3/26/39
Caballé, Montserrat (soprano); Barcelona, Spain, 4/12/33
Cabot, John (Giovanni Caboto) (navigator); Genoa **(1450–1498)**
Cabot, Sebastian (navigator); Venice **(c. 1476–1557)**
Cadmus, Paul (painter, etcher); New York City **(1904–1999)**
Caesar, Irving (lyricist); New York City **(1895–1996)**
Caesar, Gaius Julius (statesman); Rome **(100–44 B.C.)**
Caesar, Sid (comedian); Yonkers, N.Y., 9/8/22
Cage, Nicolas (Nicolas Coppola) (actor); Long Beach, Calif., 1/7/64
Cagney, James (actor); New York City **(1899–1986)**
Cahn, Sammy (songwriter); New York City **(1913–1993)**
Caine, Michael (Maurice J. Micklewhite) (actor); London, 3/14/33
Calder, Alexander (sculptor); Lawnton, Pa. **(1898–1976)**
Calderón del al Barca, Pedro (dramatist); Madrid **(1600–1681)**
Caldwell, Erskine (novelist); White Oak, Ga. **(1903–1987)**
Caldwell, Sarah (opera director, conductor); Maryville, Mo., 3/6/24
Caldwell, Taylor (novelist); Manchester, England **(1900–1985)**
Caldwell, Zoe (actress); Hawthorn, Australia, 9/14/33
Calhoun, John Caldwell (statesman); nr. Calhoun Mills, S.C. **(1782–1850)**

Caligula Gaius Caesar (Roman emperor); Antium, Latium **(12–41)**
Calisher, Hortense (novelist); New York City, 12/20/11
Callas, Maria (Maria Calogeropoulos) (operatic soprano); New York City **(1923–1977)**
Calloway, Cab (Cabell Calloway) (band leader); Rochester, N.Y. **(1907–1994)**
Calvin, John (Jean Chauvin) (religious reformer); Noyon, Picardy **(1509–1564)**
Calvin, Melvin (chemist, Nobel laureate); St. Paul, Minn. **(1911–1997)**
Cambridge, Godfrey (comedian); New York City **(1933–1976)**
Cameron, James (director); Kapuskasing, Ont., Canada, 8/16/54
Cameron, Rod (Rod Cox) (actor); Calgary, Alba., Canada **(1912–1983)**
Campbell, Glen (singer); nr. Delight, Ark., 4/22/38
Campbell, Naomi (model); London, England, 5/22/70
Campbell, Neve (actress); Guelph, Ont., Canada, 10/3/73
Campion, Jane (director, screenwriter); Waikanae, New Zealand, 1954
Camus, Albert (author); Mondovi, Algeria **(1913–1960)**
Canaletto (Giovanni Antonio Canale) (painter); Venice **(1697–1768)**
Candy, John (actor, comedian); Toronto **(1950–1994)**
Caniff, Milton (cartoonist); Hillsboro, Ohio **(1907–1988)**
Cannon, Dyan (Samille Diane Friesen) (actress); Tacoma, Wash., 1/4/37
Cantinflas (Mario Moreno-Reyes) (comedian); Mexico City **(1911–1993)**
Cantor, Eddie (Edward Iskowitz) (actor); New York City **(1892–1964)**
Capone, Al(fonse) (gangster); Brooklyn, N.Y. **(1899–1947)**
Capote, Truman (Truman Streckfus Persons) (novelist); New Orleans **(1924–1984)**
Capp, Al (Alfred Gerald Caplin) (cartoonist); New Haven, Conn. **(1909–1979)**
Capra, Frank (film producer, director); Palermo, Italy **(1897–1991)**
Caputo, Phil (Philip Joseph Caputo) (author, journalist); Chicago, 6/10/41
Caravaggio, Michelangelo Merisi da (painter); Caravaggio, Italy **(1573–1610)**
Cardin, Pierre (fashion designer); nr. Venice, 7/7/22
Cardinale, Claudia (actress); Tunis, Tunisia, 4/15/39
Carey, Drew (actor, producer); Cleveland, 5/23/58
Carey, Harry (actor); New York City **(1878–1947)**
Carey, Macdonald (actor); Sioux City, Iowa **(1913–1994)**
Carlin, George (comedian); Bronx, N.Y., 5/12/37
Carlisle, Kitty (singer, actress); New Orleans, 9/3/15
Carlyle, Robert (actor); Glasgow, Scotland, 4/14/61
Carlyle, Thomas (essayist, historian); Ecclefechan, Scotland **(1795–1881)**
Carmichael, Hoagy (Hoagland Howard) (songwriter); Bloomington, Ind. **(1899–1981)**
Carne, Judy (Joyce Botterill) (singer, actress); Northampton, England, 4/27/39
Carnegie, Andrew (industrialist); Dunfermline, Scotland **(1835–1919)**
Carney, Art (actor); Mt. Vernon, N.Y., 11/4/18
Caron, Leslie (actress); Paris, 7/1/31
Carpenter, Mary Chapin (singer, songwriter); Princeton, N.J., 2/21/58
Carr, Vikki (Florencia Bisenta de Casillas Martinez Cardona) (singer); El Paso, Tex., 7/19/42
Carracci, Annibale (painter); Bologna, Italy **(1560–1609)**
Carracci, Lodovico (painter); Bologna, Italy **(1555–1619)**
Carradine, David (actor); Hollywood, Calif., 12/8/36
Carradine, John (actor); New York City **(1906–1988)**
Carradine, Keith (actor); San Mateo, Calif., 8/8/49
Carreras, José (tenor); Barcelona, Spain, 12/5/46
Carroll, Diahann (Carol Diahann Johnson) (singer, actress); Bronx, N.Y., 7/17/35
Carroll, Leo G. (actor); Weedon, England **(1892–1972)**
Carroll, Lewis (Charles Lutwidge Dodgson) (author, mathematician); Daresbury, England **(1832–1898)**
Carson, Johnny (TV entertainer); Corning, Iowa, 10/23/25
Carson, Kit (Christopher Carson) (scout); Madison County, Ky. **(1809–1868)**
Carson, Rachel (biologist, author); Springdale, Pa. **(1907–1964)**
Carter, Betty (jazz singer, composer); Flint, Mich. **(1930–1998)**
Carter, Chris (television and film writer, director, producer); Bellflower, Calif., 10/13/57
Carter, Dixie (actress); McLemoresville, Tenn., 5/25/39
Carter, Jack (comedian); New York City, 6/24/23
Carter, James Earl, Jr. (39th U.S. president); Plains, Ga., 10/1/24
Carter, Lynda (actress); Phoenix, Ariz., 7/24/51
Cartier, Jacques (explorer); Saint-Malo, Brittany, France **(1491–1557)**
Cartier-Bresson, Henri (photographer); Chanteloup, France, 8/22/08
Cartland, Barbara (author); England **(1901–2000)**
Caruso, Enrico (Errico Caruso) (tenor); Naples, Italy **(1873–1921)**
Carver, George Washington (botanist); Diamond Grove, Mo. **(1864–1943)**
Cary, Arthur Joyce Lunel (novelist); Londonderry, Ireland **(1888–1957)**
Casals, Pablo (cellist); Vendrell, Spain **(1876–1973)**
Casanova de Seingalt, Giovanni Jacopo (adventurer); Venice **(1725–1798)**
Case, Steve (business executive); Honolulu, 8/21/58
Cash, Johnny (singer); nr. Kingsland, Ark. **(1932–2003)**
Cass, Peggy (Mary Margaret Cass) (comedienne); Boston **(1924–1999)**
Cassatt, Mary (painter); Allegheny, Pa. **(1844–1926)**
Cassavetes, John (director); New York City **(1929–1989)**
Cassidy, David (singer); New York City, 4/12/50
Cassidy, Jack (actor); Richmond Hill, Queens, N.Y. **(1927–1976)**
Cassidy, Shaun (actor, television producer, singer); Los Angeles, 9/27/58
Cassini, Oleg (Oleg Lolewski-Cassini) (fashion designer); Paris, 4/11/13
Castagno, Andrea del (painter); San Martino a Corella, Italy **(c. 1421–1457)**
Castaneda, Carlos (cultural anthropologist, author); São Paulo, Brazil **(1931–1998)**
Castle, Irene (Irene Foote) (actress, dancer); New Rochelle, N.Y. **(1893–1969)**
Castle, Vernon Blythe (dancer, aviator); Norwich, England **(1887–1918)**
Castro Ruz, Fidel (premier); Mayari, Oriente, Cuba, 8/13/26
Cather, Willa Sibert (novelist); Winchester, Va. **(1873?–1947)**
Cato, Marcus Porcius (called Cato the Elder) (statesman); Tusculum, Italy **(234–149 B.C.)**
Catt, Carrie Lane Chapman (woman suffragist); Ripon, Wis. **(1859–1947)**
Catton, Bruce (historian); Petoskey, Mich. **(1899–1978)**
Catullus, Gaius Valerius (poet); Verona **(c. 84–c. 54 B.C.)**
Cavallaro, Carmen (band leader); New York City **(1913–1989)**
Cavett, Dick (Richard Cavett) (TV entertainer); Gibbon, Neb., 11/19/36
Ceausescu, Nicolae (head of state); Scorniscesti, Romania **(1918–1989)**
Céline, Louis Ferdinand (pseud. of Louis Fuch Destouches) (novelist); Paris **(1894–1961)**
Cellini, Benvenuto (goldsmith, sculptor); Florence, Italy **(1500–1571)**
Cervantes Saavedra, Miguel de (novelist); Alcalá de Henares, Spain **(1547–1616)**
Cézanne, Paul (painter); Aix-en-Provence, France **(1839–1906)**
Chagall, Marc (painter); Vitebsk, Russia **(1887–1985)**
Chaliapin, Feodor Ivanovitch (operatic basso); Kazan, Russia **(1873–1938)**
Chamberlain, Arthur Neville (statesman); Edgbaston, England **(1869–1940)**
Chamberlain, Richard (actor, producer); Los Angeles, 3/31/35
Champion, Gower (choreographer); Geneva, Ill. **(1921–1980)**
Champion, Marge (Marjorie Celeste Belcher) (actress, dancer); Los Angeles, 9/2/23
Champlain, Samuel de (explorer); nr. Rochefort, France **(1567–1635)**
Chan, Jackie (Chan Kwong Sang) (actor); Hong Kong, 4/7/54
Chancellor, John (TV commentator); Chicago **(1927–1996)**
Chandler, Jeff (Ira Grossel) (actor); Brooklyn, N.Y. **(1918–1961)**
Chandler, Raymond (writer); Chicago **(1883–1959)**
Chanel, "Coco" (Gabriel Bonheur) (fashion designer); Issoire, France **(1883–1971)**
Chaney, Lon (actor); Colorado Springs, Colo. **(1883–1930)**
Channing, Carol (actress); Seattle, 1/31/23
Channing, Stockard (Susan Stockard) (actress); New York City, 2/13/44
Chaplin, Geraldine (actress); Santa Monica, Calif., 7/31/44
Chaplin, Sir Charles (actor); London **(1889–1977)**
Charisse, Cyd (Tula Finklea) (dancer, actress); Amarillo, Tex., 3/8/21
Charlemagne (Holy Roman Emperor); birthplace unknown **(742–814)**
Charles, Ray (Ray Charles Robinson) (pianist, singer, songwriter); Albany, Ga., 9/23/30

Charo (Maria Rosario Pilar Martinez) (actress); Murcia, Spain, 1/15/51
Chase, Chevy (Cornelius Crane Chase) (comedian); New York City, 10/8/43
Chase, Lucia (founder Ballet Theatre [now American Ballet Theatre]); Waterbury, Conn. **(1907–1986)**
Chateaubriand, François René de (writer, statesman); St. Malo, France **(1768–1848)**
Chaucer, Geoffrey (poet); London **(c. 1340–1400)**
Chuan, Leekpai (prime minister of Thailand); Muang District, Thailand, 7/28/38
Chávez, Carlos (composer); nr. Mexico City **(1899–1978)**
Chavez, Cesar (labor leader); nr. Yuma, Ariz. **(1927–1993)**
Chayefsky, Paddy (Sidney Chayefsky) (playwright); New York City **(1923–1981)**
Checker, Chubby (Ernest Evans) (performer); Philadelphia, 10/3/41
Cheever, John (novelist); Quincy, Mass. **(1912–1982)**
Chekhov, Anton Pavlovich (dramatist, short-story writer); Taganrog, Russia **(1860–1904)**
Chen Shui-bian (president of Taiwan); Taiwan, 2/18/51
Cher (Cherilyn Sarkisian La Piere) (actress, singer); El Centro, Calif., 5/20/46
Cherubini, Luigi (composer); Florence **(1760–1842)**
Chesterton, Gilbert Keith (author); Kensington, England **(1874–1936)**
Chesnutt, Charles Waddell (author); Cleveland **(1858–1932)**
Chevalier, Maurice (entertainer); Paris **(1888–1972)**
Chiang Kai-shek (chief of state); Feng-hwa, China **(1887–1975)**
Child, Julia (food expert); Pasadena, Calif., 8/15/12
Chippendale, Thomas (cabinet-maker); Otley, England **(1718–1779)**
Chirac, Jacques (president of France); Paris, 11/29/32
Chirico, Giorgio de (painter); Vólos, Greece **(1888–1978)**
Chisholm, Shirley Anita St. Hill (U.S. representative); Brooklyn, N.Y., 11/30/24
Chlumsky, Anna (actress); Chicago, 12/3/80
Chomsky, (Avram) Noam (linguist, educator, activist); Philadelphia, 12/7/28
Chopin, Frédéric François (composer); nr. Warsaw **(1810–1849)**
Chopin, Kate O'Flaherty (author); St. Louis **(1851–1904)**
Chow, Yun-Fat (actor); Hong Kong, 5/18/55
Chrétien, Jean Joseph-Jacques (prime minister of Canada); Shawinigan, Que., Canada, 1/11/34
Christie, Agatha (mystery writer); Torquay, England **(1890–1976)**
Christie, Julie (actress); Chukua, India, 4/14/41
Chung, Connie (broadcast journalist); Washington, D.C., 8/20/46
Churchill, Sir Winston Leonard Spencer (statesman); Blenheim Palace, Oxfordshire, England **(1874–1965)**
Cicero, Marcus Tullius (orator, statesman); Arpinum, Italy **(106–43 B.C.)**
Cid, El (Rodrigo [or Ruy] Dìez de Bivar) (Spanish national hero); nr. Burgos, Spain **(c. 1043–1099)**
Cilento, Diane (actress); Queensland, Australia, 10/5/33
Cimabue, Giovanni (painter); Florence, Italy **(c. 1240–c. 1302)**
Cimino, Michael (director, writer, producer); New York City, 11/16/43
Claire, Ina (Ina Fagan) (actress); Washington, D.C. **(1895–1985)**
Clancy, Tom (novelist); Baltimore, 4/12/47
Clapton, Eric (singer, guitarist); Ripley, England, 3/30/45
Clark, Dick (TV personality); Mt. Vernon, N.Y., 11/30/29
Clark, Mary Higgins (writer); New York City, 12/24/31
Clark, Petula (singer); Epsom, England, 11/15/34
Clark, Roy (country music artist); Meherrin, Va., 4/15/33
Clark, William (explorer); Caroline County, Va. **(1770–1838)**
Clarke, Arthur C. (science fiction writer); Minehead, England, 12/16/17
Claude Lorrain (Claude Gellée) (painter); Champagne, France **(1600–1682)**
Clausewitz, Karl von (military strategist); Burg, Germany **(1780–1831)**
Clay, Henry (statesman); Hanover County, Va. **(1777–1852)**
Clay, Lucius D. (banker, ex-general); Marietta, Ga. **(1897–1978)**
Clayburgh, Jill (actress); New York City, 4/30/44
Cleary, Beverly (Beverly Atlee Bunn) (children's author); McMinnville, Ore., 1916
Cleaver, Eldridge (Leroy) (author, activist); Wabbaseka, Ark. **(1935–1998)**
Cleese, John (writer, actor); Weston-super-Mare, England, 10/27/39
Clemenceau, Georges (statesman); Mouilleron-en-Pareds, Vondée, France **(1841–1929)**
Cleopatra (queen of Egypt); Alexandria, Egypt **(69–30 B.C.)**
Cleveland, Stephen Grover (22nd & 24th U.S. president); Caldwell, N.J. **(1837–1908)**
Cliburn, Van (Harvey Lavan Cliburn, Jr.) (concert pianist); Shreveport, La., 7/12/34
Clift, Montgomery (actor); Omaha, Neb. **(1920–1966)**
Cline, Patsy (singer); Winchester, Va. **(1932–1963)**
Clinton, Hillary Rodham (ex-first lady, U.S. senator); Park Ridge, Ill., 10/26/47
Clinton, William Jefferson (42nd U.S. president); Hope, Ark., 8/19/46
Clooney, George (actor); Lexington, Ky., 5/6/61
Clooney, Rosemary (singer); Maysville, Ky. **(1928–2002)**
Close, Glenn (actress); Greenwich, Conn., 3/19/47
Cobain, Kurt (musician); Hoquiam, Wash. **(1967–1994)**
Cobb, Irvin Shrewsbury (humorist); Paducah, Ky. **(1876–1944)**
Cobb, Lee J. (Leo Jacob Cobb) (actor); New York City **(1911–1976)**
Coburn, Charles Douville (actor); Savannah, Ga. **(1877–1961)**
Coburn, James (actor); Laurel, Neb. **(1928–2002)**
Coca, Imogene (comedienne); Philadelphia **(1908–2001)**
Cocker, Jarvis (singer, songwriter); Sheffield, England, 9/19/63
Cocker, Joe (John Robert Cocker) (singer); Sheffield, England, 5/20/44
Coco, James (actor); New York City **(1929–1987)**
Cocteau, Jean (author); Maison-Lafitte, France **(1889–1963)**
Cohan, George Michael (actor, dramatist); Providence, R.I. **(1878–1942)**
Cohen, Leonard (composer); Montreal, Que., Canada, 9/21/34
Colbert, Claudette (Lily Chauchoin) (actress); Paris **(1903–1996)**
Cole, Nat "King" (singer); Montgomery, Ala. **(1919–1965)**
Cole, Natalie (singer); Los Angeles, 2/6/50
Cole, Thomas (painter); Lancashire, England **(1801–1848)**
Coleman, Dabney (actor); Austin, Tex., 1/3/32
Coleridge, Samuel Taylor (poet); Ottery St. Mary, England **(1772–1834)**
Colette (Sidonie-Gabrielle Colette) (novelist); St.-Sauveur, France **(1873–1954)**
Collingwood, Charles (TV commentator); Three Rivers, Mich. **(1917–1985)**
Collins, Joan (actress); London, 5/23/33
Collins, Judy (singer); Seattle, 5/1/39
Colman, Ronald (actor); Richmond, England **(1891–1958)**
Colonna, Jerry (comedian); Boston **(1905–1986)**
Coltrane, John (jazz musician); Hamlet, N.C. **(1926–1967)**
Columbus, Chris (director, screenwriter); Spangler, Pa., 9/10/58
Columbus, Christopher (Cristoforo Colombo) (explorer); Genoa, Italy **(1451–1506)**
Colvin, Shawn (folk singer); Vermillion, S.D., 1/10/58
Combs, Sean "Puffy" (singer, record producer); New York City, 11/9/69
Comden, Betty (writer); New York City, 5/3/19
Comenius, Johann Amos (educational reformer); Nivnice, Moravia, Czech Republic **(1592–1670)**
Commager, Henry Steele (historian); Pittsburgh **(1902–1998)**
Como, Perry (Pierino Como) (singer); Canonsburg, Pa. **(1912–2001)**
Compton, Karl Taylor (physicist); Wooster, Ohio **(1887–1954)**
Comte, Auguste (philosopher); Montpellier, France **(1798–1857)**
Conant, James B. (educator, statesman); Dorchester, Mass. **(1893–1978)**
Condon, Eddie (jazz musician); Goodland, Ind. **(1905–1973)**
Confucius (K'ung Fu-tzu) (philosopher); Shantung province, China **(c. 551– 479 B.C.)**
Congreve, William (dramatist); nr. Leeds, England **(1670–1729)**
Connelly, Marc (playwright); McKeesport, Pa. **(1890–1980)**
Connery, Sean (actor); Edinburgh, Scotland, 8/25/30
Connick, Jr., Harry (musician, actor); New Orleans, La., 9/11/67
Conniff, Ray (band leader); Attleboro, Mass. **(1916–2002)**
Connors, Chuck (actor); Brooklyn, N.Y. **(1921–1992)**
Connors, Mike (Krekor Ohanian) (actor); Fresno, Calif., 8/15/25
Conrad, Joseph (Teodor Jozef Konrad Korzeniowski) (novelist); Berdichev, Ukraine **(1857–1924)**
Conrad, Robert (Conrad Robert Falk) (actor); Chicago, 3/1/35
Conrad, William (actor); Louisville, Ky. **(1920–1994)**
Conried, Hans Georg, Jr. (actor); Baltimore **(1917–1982)**
Conroy, Pat (author); Atlanta, 10/26/45
Constable, John (painter); East Bergholt, Suffolk, England **(1776–1837)**
Constantine II (ex-king of Greece); Athens, 6/2/40
Constantine, Michael (actor); Reading, Pa., 5/22/27
Conte, Richard (actor); New York City **(1916–1975)**
Conti, Tom (actor); Paisley, Scotland, 11/22/41
Convy, Bert (actor, host); St. Louis **(1933–1991)**
Conway, Tim (comedian); Chagrin Falls, Ohio, 12/15/33
Coogan, Jackie (actor); Los Angeles **(1914–1984)**
Cook, Peter (actor, writer); Torquay, England **(1937–1995)**

Cooke, Alistair (Alfred Alistair) (TV narrator, journalist); Manchester, England, 11/20/08
Cooke, Jack Kent (business executive); Hamilton, Ont., Canada **(1912–1997)**
Cooley, Denton A(rthur) (heart surgeon); Houston, 8/22/20
Coolidge, (John) Calvin (30th U.S. president); Plymouth, Vt. **(1872–1933)**
Coolidge, Rita (singer); Nashville, Tenn., 5/1/45
Coolio (Artis Ivey, Jr.) (rap artist); Los Angeles, Calif., 8/1/63
Cooper, Alice (Vincent Furnier) (rock musician); Detroit, 2/4/48
Cooper, Gary (Frank James Cooper) (actor); Helena, Mont. **(1901–1961)**
Cooper, Dame Gladys (actress); Lewisham, England **(1898–1971)**
Cooper, Jackie (actor, director); Los Angeles, 9/15/22
Cooper, James Fenimore (novelist); Burlington, N.J. **(1789–1851)**
Cooper, Peter (industrialist, philanthropist); New York City **(1791–1883)**
Copernicus, Nicolaus (Mikolaj Kopernik) (astronomer); Thorn, Poland **(1473–1543)**
Copland, Aaron (composer); Brooklyn, N.Y. **(1900–1990)**
Copley, John Singleton (painter); Boston **(1738–1815)**
Copperfield, David (David Kotkin) (illusionist); Metuchen, N.J., 9/16/56
Coppola, Francis Ford (film director); Detroit, 4/7/39
Corelli, Arcangelo (composer); Fusignano, Italy **(1653–1713)**
Corelli, Franco (operatic tenor); Ancona, Italy, 4/8/23
Corgan, Billy (musician); Elk Grove, Ill., 3/17/67
Corneille, Pierre (dramatist); Rouen, France **(1606–1684)**
Cornell, Katharine (actress); Berlin **(1893–1974)**
Corot, Jean Baptiste Camille (painter); Paris **(1796–1875)**
Corella, Angel (ballet dancer); Madrid, Spain, 11/8/75
Correggio, Antonio Allegri da (painter); Correggio, Italy **(1494–1534)**
Corsaro, Frank (opera director); New York harbor, 12/22/24
Cortés (or Cortez), Hernando (explorer); Medellín, Spain **(1485–1547)**
Cosby, Bill (actor); Philadelphia, 7/12/37
Cosell, Howard (Howard Cohen) (sportscaster); Winston-Salem, N.C. **(1918–1995)**
Costello, Elvis (Declan Patrick McManus) (singer, musician, songwriter); London, 1954
Costello, Lou (Louis Cristillo) (comedian); Paterson, N.J. **(1908–1959)**
Costner, Kevin (actor); Los Angeles, 1/18/55
Cotten, Joseph (actor); Petersburg, Va. **(1905–1994)**
Couperin, François (composer); Paris **(1668–1733)**
Courbet, Gustave (painter); Ornans, France **(1819–1877)**
Couric, Katie (TV host); Arlington, Va., 1/7/57
Courtenay, Tom (actor); Hull, England, 2/25/37
Cousins, Norman (publisher); Union Hill, N.J. **(1915–1990)**
Cousteau, Jacques-Yves (marine explorer); St. André-de-Cubzac, France **(1910–1997)**
Covey, Stephen R. (author); Salt Lake City, 10/24/32
Coward, Sir Noel (playwright, actor); Teddington, England **(1899–1973)**
Cowles, Gardner, Jr. (newspaper publisher); Algona, Iowa **(1903–1985)**
Cowper, William (poet); Great Berkhamstead, England **(1731–1800)**
Cox, Archibald (Watergate prosecutor); Plainfield, N.J., 5/17/12
Cox, Courteney (actress); Birmingham, Ala., 6/15/64
Coyote, Peter (actor); New York City, 10/10/41
Cozzens, James Gould (novelist); Chicago **(1903–1978)**
Crabbe, Buster (Clarence Crabbe) (actor); Oakland, Calif. **(1908–1983)**
Cranach, Lucas, the elder (painter); Kronach, Germany **(1472–1553)**
Crane, Hart (poet); Garrettsville, Ohio **(1899–1932)**
Crane, Stephen (novelist, poet); Newark, N.J. **(1871–1900)**
Cranmer, Thomas (churchman); Aslacton, England **(1489–1556)**
Craven, Wes (director, producer, screenwriter); Cleveland, 8/2/39
Crawford, Broderick (actor); Philadelphia **(1911–1986)**
Crawford, Cheryl (stage producer); Akron, Ohio **(1902–1986)**
Crawford, Cindy (model, actress); De Kalb, Illinois, 2/20/66
Crawford, Joan (Lucille LeSueur) (actress, business executive); San Antonio **(1908–1977)**
Crazy Horse (Lakota Indian leader); nr. Bear Butte, S.D. **(1840?–1877)**
Crenna, Richard (actor); Los Angeles **(1927–2003)**
Crespin, Régine (operatic soprano); Marseilles, France, 2/23/29
Crichton, (John) Michael (novelist, film producer); Chicago, 10/23/42
Crick, Francis Harry Compton (scientist, Nobel laureate); Northampton, England, 6/8/16
Crisp, Donald (actor); London **(1880–1974)**
Croce, Benedetto (philosopher); Peseasseroli, Aquila, Italy **(1866–1952)**
Croce, Jim (singer); Philadelphia **(1942–1973)**
Crockett, Davy (David) (frontiersman); Greene County, Tenn. **(1786–1836)**
Cromwell, Oliver (statesman); Huntingdon, England **(1599–1658)**
Cronenberg, David (film director); Toronto, Canada, 3/15/43
Cronin, A. J. (Archibald J. Cronin) (novelist); Cardross, Scotland **(1896–1981)**
Cronkite, Walter (TV newscaster); St. Joseph, Mo., 11/4/16
Cronyn, Hume (actor); London, Ont., Canada, 7/18/11
Crosby, Bing (Harry Lillis) (singer, actor); Tacoma, Wash. **(1904–1977)**
Crosby, Bob (musician); Spokane, Wash. **(1913–1993)**
Crosby, Cathy Lee (actress); Los Angeles, 12/2/48
Crosby, Norm (comedian); Boston, 9/15/27
Cross, Ben (Bernard) (actor); Paddington, England, 12/16/47
Cross, Milton (opera commentator); New York City **(1897–1975)**
Crouse, Russell (playwright); Findlay, Ohio **(1893–1966)**
Crow, Sheryl (musician, record producer); Kennett, Mo., 2/11/62
Crowe, Russell (actor, musician); Auckland, New Zealand, 4/7/64
Crudup, Billy (actor); Manhasset, N.Y., 7/8/68
Cruise, Tom (Thomas Mapother IV) (actor, producer); Syracuse, N.Y., 7/3/62
Crystal, Billy (comedian, actor); Long Beach, N.Y., 3/14/47
Cugat, Xavier (band leader); Barcelona, Spain **(1900–1990)**
Cukor, George (film director); New York City **(1899–1983)**
Culkin, Macaulay (actor); New York City, 8/26/80
Cullen, Bill (William Lawrence Cullen) (radio and TV entertainer); Pittsburgh **(1920–1990)**
Cullen, Countee (poet); New York City **(1903–1946)**
Culp, Robert (actor); Berkeley, Calif., 8/16/30
cummings, e. e. (Edward Estlin Cummings) (poet); Cambridge, Mass. **(1894–1962)**
Cummings, Robert (actor); Joplin, Mo. **(1908–1990)**
Cunningham, Merce (choreographer); Centralia, Wash., 4/16/19
Curie, Marie (Marja Sklodowska) (physical chemist, Nobel laureate); Warsaw **(1867–1934)**
Curie, Pierre (physicist); Paris **(1859–1906)**
Curtin, Jane (actress); Cambridge, Mass., 9/6/47
Curtin, Phyllis (soprano); Clarksburg, W. Va., 12/3/27
Curtis, Jamie Lee (actress); Los Angeles, 11/22/58
Curtis, Tony (Bernard Schwartz) (actor); Bronx, N.Y., 6/3/25
Curzon, Clifford (concert pianist); London **(1907–1982)**
Cusack, Joan (actress); New York City, 10/11/62
Cusack, John (actor); Chicago, 6/28/66
Custer, George Armstrong (army officer); New Rumley, Ohio **(1839–1876)**

D

Dafoe, Willem (William Dafoe, Jr.) (actor); Appleton, Wis., 7/22/55
da Gama, Vasco (explorer); Sines, Portugal **(1460–1524)**
Daguerre, Louis (photographic pioneer); nr. Paris **(1787–1851)**
Dahl, Arlene (actress); Minneapolis, 8/11/28
Dahl, Roald (writer); Llandaff, Wales **(1916–1990)**
Dalai Lama (Tenzin Gyatso) (spiritual and temporal head of Tibet); Taktser, China, 1935
Daley, Richard J. (mayor of Chicago); Chicago **(1902–1976)**
Dali, Salvador (painter); Figueras, Spain **(1904–1989)**
Dalton, John (chemist); nr. Cockermouth, England **(1766–1844)**
Dalton, Timothy (actor); Colwyn Bay, Wales, U.K., 3/21/46
Daly, Tyne (actress); Madison, Wis., 2/21/46
d'Amboise, Jacques (ballet dancer); Dedham, Mass., 7/28/34
Damone, Vic (Vito Farinola) (singer); Brooklyn, N.Y., 6/12/28
Damrosch, Walter Johannes (orchestra conductor); Breslau, Poland **(1862–1950)**
Dana, Charles Anderson (editor); Hinsdale, N.H. **(1819–1897)**
Dandridge, Dorothy (actress); Cleveland **(1923–1965)**
Danes, Claire (actress); New York City, 4/12/79
Dangerfield, Rodney (Jacob Cohen) (actor, comedian); Babylon, N.Y., 11/22/22
Daniels, Jeff (actor); Chelsea, Mich., 2/19/55
Daniels, William (actor); Brooklyn, N.Y., 3/31/27
Danilova, Alexandra (ballet dancer); Peterhof, Russia **(1904–1997)**
Dannay, Frederic (novelist, pseudonym Ellery Queen); Brooklyn, N.Y. **(1905–1982)**
Danner, Blythe (actress); Philadelphia, 2/3/43
D'Annunzio, Gabriele (soldier, author); Francavilla at Mare, Pescara, Italy **(1863–1938)**

Danson, Ted (actor); San Diego, Calif., 12/29/47
Dante (or Durante) Alighieri (poet); Florence, Italy **(1265–1321)**
Danton, Georges Jacques (French Revolutionary leader); Arcis-sur-Aube, France **(1759–1794)**
Danza, Tony (actor); Brooklyn, N.Y., 4/21/51
Darren, James (actor); Philadelphia, 6/8/36
Darrow, Clarence Seward (lawyer); Kinsman, Ohio **(1857–1938)**
Darwin, Charles Robert (naturalist); Shrewsbury, England **(1809–1882)**
Dassin, Jules (film director); Middletown, Conn., 12/18/11
Daumier, Honoré (caricaturist); Marseilles, France **(1808–1879)**
David, Jacques-Louis (painter); Paris **(1748–1825)**
David (king of Israel and Judah;) died c. 973 B.C.
Davidson, John (singer, actor); Pittsburgh, 12/13/41
Davies, Marion (Marion Douras) (actress); New York City **(1897–1961)**
Davies, (William) Robertson (writer); Thamesville, Ont., Canada **(1913–1996)**
Davis, Angela (social activist); Birmingham, Ala., 1/26/44
Davis, Ann B. (actress); Schenectady, N.Y., 5/5/26
Davis, Lt. Gen. Benjamin O., Jr. (Air Force general); Washington, D.C. **(1912–2002)**
Davis, Brig. Gen. Benjamin O., Sr. (U.S. Army general); Washington, D.C. **(1877–1970)**
Davis, Bette (actress); Lowell, Mass. **(1908–1989)**
Davis, Geena (Virginia Davis) (actress); Wareham, Mass., 1/21/57
Davis, Jefferson (president of the Confederacy); Christian (now Todd) County, Ky. **(1808–1889)**
Davis, Judy (actress); Perth, Australia, 1955
Davis, Mac (singer); Lubbock, Tex., 1/21/42
Davis, Miles (jazz trumpeter); Alton, Ill. **(1926–1991)**
Davis, Ossie (actor, writer); Cogdell, Ga., 12/18/17
Davis, Sammy, Jr. (actor, singer); New York City **(1925–1990)**
Davis, Stuart (painter); Philadelphia **(1894–1964)**
Dawson, Richard (actor, host); Gosport, Hampshire, England, 11/20/32
Day, Doris (Doris von Kappelhoff) (singer, actress); Cincinnati, 4/3/24
Dayan, Moshe (ex-defense minister of Israel); Dagania, Palestine **(1915–1981)**
Day-Lewis, Daniel (actor); London, 4/29/58
Dean, James (actor); Marion, Ind. **(1931–1955)**
Dean, Jimmy (singer); Seth Ward, nr. Plainview, Tex., 8/10/28
De Bakey, Michael E. (heart surgeon); Lake Charles, La., 9/7/08
de Beauvoir, Simone (novelist, philosopher); Paris **(1908–1986)**
Debs, Eugene Victor (Socialist leader); Terre Haute, Ind. **(1855–1926)**
Debussy, Claude Achille (composer); St. Germain-en-Laye, France **(1862–1918)**
De Carlo, Yvonne (Peggy Yvonne Middleton) (actress); Vancouver, B.C., Canada, 9/1/24
Dee, Ruby (Ruby Ann Wallace) (actress); Cleveland, 10/27/24
Dee, Sandra (Alexandra Zuck) (actress); Bayonne, N.J., 4/23/42
Degas, Hilaire Germain Edgar (painter); Paris **(1834–1917)**
de Gaulle, Charles André Joseph Marie (soldier, statesman); Lille, France **(1890–1970)**
de Havilland, Olivia (actress); Tokyo, 7/1/16
de Kooning, Willem (artist); Rotterdam **(1904–1997)**
Delacroix, Eugène (painter); Charenton-St. Maurice, France **(1798–1863)**
Delany, Dana (actress); New York City, 3/15/56
de la Renta, Oscar (fashion designer); Santo Domingo, Dominican Republic, 7/22/32
Delaunay, Robert (painter); Paris **(1885–1941)**
De Laurentiis, Dino (film producer); Torre Annunziata, Bay of Naples, Italy, 8/8/18
della Robbia, Andrea (sculptor); Florence **(1435–1525)**
della Robbia, Luca (sculptor); Florence **(1400–1482)**
Delon, Alain (actor); Sceaux, France, 11/8/35
Del Toro, Benicio (actor); Santurce, Puerto Rico, 2/19/67
DeLuise, Dom (actor, comedian); Brooklyn, N.Y., 8/1/33
Demarest, William (actor); St. Paul, Minn. **(1892–1983)**
de Mille, Agnes (choreographer); New York City **(1905–1993)**
De Mille, Cecil Blount (film director); Ashfield, Mass. **(1881–1959)**
Demme, Jonathan (director, producer, screenwriter); Baldwin, N.Y., 2/22/44
Demosthenes (orator); Athens **(384?–322 B.C.)**
Dench, Dame Judi (film and stage actress); York, England, 12/9/34
Deneuve, Catherine (actress); Paris, 10/22/43
Deng Xiaoping (Chinese leader); Sichuan province, China **(1904–1997)**
De Niro, Robert (actor, director); New York City, 8/17/43
Dennehy, Brian (actor); Bridgeport, Conn., 7/9/39
Dennis, Sandy (actress); Hastings, Neb. **(1937–1992)**
Denny, Reginald (actor); Richmond, England **(1891–1967)**
Denver, John (Henry John Deutschendorf, Jr.) (singer, actor); Roswell, N.M. **(1943–1997)**
De Palma, Brian (film director); Newark, N.J., 9/11/40
Depp, Johnny (actor); Owensboro, Ky., 6/9/63
Derain, André (painter); Chatou, Seine-et-Oise, France **(1880–1954)**
Derek, John (Derek Harris) (actor, director); Los Angeles **(1926–1998)**
Dern, Bruce (actor); Winnetka, Ill., 6/4/36
Dern, Laura (actress); Los Angeles, 2/10/67
Dershowitz, Alan (lawyer); Brooklyn, N.Y., 9/1/38
Derrida, Jacques (philosopher); El-Biar, Algeria, 7/15/30
Descartes, René (philosopher, mathematician); La Haye, France **(1596–1650)**
De Seversky, Alexander P. (aviator); Tiflis (Tbilisi), Georgia **(1894–1974)**
De Sica, Vittorio (film director); Sora, Italy **(1901–1974)**
Desmond, Johnny (singer, composer); Detroit **(1921–1985)**
De Soto, Hernando (explorer); Barcarrota, Spain **(c. 1500–1542)**
De Valera, Eamon (ex-president of Ireland); New York City **(1882–1975)**
Devane, William (actor); Albany, N.Y., 9/5/39
Devine, Andy (actor); Flagstaff, Ariz. **(1905–1977)**
DeVito, Danny (Daniel Michael DeVito) (actor, director, producer); Neptune, N.J., 11/17/44
De Vries, Peter (novelist); Chicago **(1910–1993)**
de Waart, Edo (conductor); Amsterdam, the Netherlands, 6/1/41
Dewey, George (admiral); Montpelier, Vt. **(1837–1917)**
Dewey, John (philosopher, educator); Burlington, Vt. **(1859–1952)**
Dewey, Thomas E. (political figure); Owosso, Mich. **(1902–1971)**
Dewhurst, Colleen (actress); Montreal **(1926–1991)**
Dey, Susan (actress); Pekin, Ill., 12/10/52
Diaghilev, Sergei (ballet impressario); Novgorod, Russia **(1872–1929)**
Diamond, Neil (singer); Brooklyn, N.Y., 1/24/41
Diaz, Cameron (actress, model); San Diego, Calif., 8/30/72
DiCaprio, Leonardo (actor); Los Angeles, 11/11/74
Dichter, Misha (pianist); Shanghai, 9/27/45
Dickens, Charles John Huffam (novelist); Portsea, England **(1812–1870)**
Dickey, James (writer); Atlanta **(1923–1997)**
Dickinson, Angie (Angeline Brown) (actress); Kulm, N.D., 9/30/31
Dickinson, Emily Elizabeth (poet); Amherst, Mass. **(1830–1886)**
Diddley, Bo (Elias McDaniel) (guitarist); McComb, Miss., 12/30/28
Diderot, Denis (encyclopedist); Langres, France **(1713–1784)**
Dietrich, Marlene (Maria Magdalena von Losch) (actress); Berlin **(1901–1992)**
DiFranco, Ani (singer, songwriter); Buffalo, N.Y., 9/23/70
Diller, Phyllis (Phyllis Driver) (comedienne); Lima, Ohio, 7/17/17
Dillon, Matt (actor); New Rochelle, N.Y., 2/18/64
Dine, Jim (painter); Cincinnati, 6/16/35
Dinesen, Isak (Karen Blixen) (author); Rungsted, Denmark **(1885–1962)**
Dinkins, David (ex-mayor of New York City); Trenton, N.J., 7/10/27
Diogenes (philosopher); Sinope, Turkey **(c. 412–323 B.C.)**
Dion (Dion DiMucci) (singer); Bronx, N.Y., 7/18/39
Dion, Celine (musician); Charlemagne, Que., Canada, 3/30/68
Dior, Christian (fashion designer); Granville, France **(1905–1957)**
Disney, Walt(er) Elias (film animator, producer); Chicago **(1901–1966)**
Disraeli, Benjamin (Earl of Beaconsfield) (statesman); London **(1804–1881)**
Dix, Dorothea (civil rights reformer); Hampden, Maine **(1802–1887)**
Dixon, Jeane (Jeane Pinckert) (seer); Medford, Wis. **(1918–1997)**
Dobbs, Mattiwilda (soprano); Atlanta, 7/11/25
Doctorow, E(dgar) L(aurence) (novelist); New York City, 1/6/31
Dogg, Snoop Doggy (Calvin Broadus) (musician); Long Beach, Calif., 10/20/72
Doherty, Shannen (actress); Memphis, Tenn., 4/21/71
Dole, Elizabeth Hanford (public official); Salisbury, N.C., 7/29/36
Dole, Robert (political figure); Russell, Kans., 7/22/23
Dolin, Anton (dancer); Slinfold, England **(1904–1983)**
Domingo, Placido (tenor); Madrid, 1/21/41
Domino, Fats (Antoine) (musician); New Orleans, 2/26/28
Donahue, Phil (TV host); Cleveland, 12/21/35
Donahue, Troy (Merle Johnson) (actor); New York City **(1936–2001)**
Donaldson, Sam (broadcast journalist); El Paso, Tex., 3/11/34
Donat, Robert (actor); Withington, England **(1905–1958)**
Donatello (Donato Niccolò di Betto Bardi) (sculptor); Florence **(c. 1386–1466)**

Donlevy, Brian (actor); Portadown, Ireland **(1899–1972)**
Donne, John (poet); London **(1573–1631)**
Donner, Richard (director, producer); New York City, 1939
D'Onofrio, Vincent (actor); Brooklyn, N.Y., 6/30/59
Donovan (Donovan Leitch) (singer, songwriter); Glasgow, Scotland, 2/10/46
Doolittle, James H. (ex-Air Force general); Alameda, Calif. **(1896–1993)**
Doohan, James (actor); Vancouver, B.C., 3/20/20
Dorati, Antal (orchestra conductor); Budapest **(1906–1988)**
Dorn, Michael (actor); Luling, Tex., 12/9/52
Dorris, Michael (anthropologist, writer); Louisville, Ky. **(1945–1997)**
Dorsey, Jimmy (band leader); Shenandoah, Pa. **(1904–1957)**
Dorsey, Thomas Andrew (father of gospel music); Villa Rice, Ga. **(1899–1993)**
Dorsey, Tommy (band leader); Mahanoy Plane, Pa. **(1905–1956)**
Dos Passos, John (author); Chicago **(1896–1970)**
Dostoevski, Fyodor Mikhailovich (novelist); Moscow **(1821–1881)**
Dotrice, Roy (actor); Guernsey, Channel Islands, England, 5/26/23
Douglas, Aaron (painter); Topeka, Kans. **(1900–1979)**
Douglas, Helen Gahagan (ex-representative); Boonton, N.J. **(1900–1980)**
Douglas, Kirk (Issur Danielovitch) (actor); Amsterdam, N.Y., 12/9/16
Douglas, Melvyn (Melvyn Hesselberg) (actor); Macon, Ga. **(1901–1981)**
Douglas, Michael (actor, producer); New Brunswick, N.J., 9/25/44
Douglas, Mike (Michael D. Dowd, Jr.) (TV host); Chicago, 8/11/25
Douglas, Stephen Arnold (politician); Brandon, Vt. **(1813–1861)**
Douglass, Frederick (abolitionist, author, orator); Tuckahoe, Md. **(1817–1895)**
Dow, Charles (financier); Sterling, Conn. **(1851–1902)**
Down, Lesley-Ann (actress); London, 3/17/54
Downey, Robert, Jr. (actor, director); New York City, 4/4/65
Downs, Hugh (broadcast journalist); Akron, Ohio, 2/14/21
Doyle, Sir Arthur Conan (novelist, spiritualist); Edinburgh, Scotland **(1859–1930)**
Doyle, David (actor); Lincoln, Neb. **(1929–1997)**
Drake, Sir Francis (navigator); Tavistock, England **(1545–1596)**
Dr. Dre (Andre Young) (rap singer); Los Angeles, 2/18/66
Dreiser, Theodore (writer); Terre Haute, Ind. **(1871–1945)**
Drescher, Fran (television and film actress); New York City, 9/30/57
Dreyfus, Alfred (French army officer); Mulhouse, France **(1859–1935)**
Dreyfuss, Richard (actor); Brooklyn, N.Y., 10/29/47
Drury, Allen (novelist); Houston **(1918–1998)**
Dryden, John (poet); Northamptonshire, England **(1631–1700)**
Dryer, Fred (ex-NFL player, actor); Hawthorne, Calif., 7/6/46
Dubček, Alexander (ex-president of Czechoslovakia); Uhrovek, Slovakia **(1921–1992)**
Dubinsky, David (David Dobnievski) (labor leader); Brest-Litovsk, Belarus **(1892–1982)**
Du Bois, W(illiam) E(dward) B(urghardt) (scholar, civil rights activist); Great Barrington, Mass. **(1868–1963)**
Duchamp, Marcel (painter); Blainville, France **(1887–1968)**
Duchin, Eddy (pianist, bandleader); Cambridge, Mass. **(1909–1951)**
Duchin, Peter (pianist, band leader); New York City, 7/28/37
Duchovny, David (actor); New York City, 8/7/60
Dufay, Guillaume (composer); Cambrai, France **(c. 1400–1474)**
Duffy, Julia (actress); Minneapolis, Minn., 6/27/50
Dufy, Raoul (painter); Le Havre, France **(1877–1953)**
Dukakis, Olympia (actress); Lowell, Mass., 6/20/31
Duke, James B. (industrialist); nr. Durham, N.C. **(1856–1925)**
Duke, Patty (Anna Marie Duke) (actress); New York City, 12/14/46
Dulles, Allen Welsh (ex-director of CIA); Watertown, N.Y. **(1893–1969)**
Dulles, John Foster (political figure); Washington, D.C. **(1888–1959)**
Dumas, Alexandre (called Dumas fils) (novelist); Paris **(1824–1895)**
Dumas, Alexandre (called Dumas père) (novelist); Villers-Cotterets, France **(1802–1870)**
du Maurier, Daphne (novelist); London **(1907–1989)**
du Maurier, George Louis Palmella Busson (novelist); Paris **(1834–1896)**
Dumont, Margaret (actress); Brooklyn, N.Y. **(1889–1965)**
Dunaway, Faye (actress); Bascom, Fla., 1/14/41
Dunbar, Paul Laurence (poet, novelist); Dayton, Ohio **(1872–1906)**
Duncan, Isadora (dancer); San Francisco **(1878–1927)**
Duncan, Michael Clarke (actor); Chicago, 12/10/57
Duncan, Sandy (actress); Henderson, Tex., 2/20/46
Dunham, Katherine (dancer, choreographer); Chicago, 6/22/09
Dunne, Irene (actress); Louisville, Ky. **(1898–1990)**
Duns Scotus, John (theologian); Duns, Scotland **(1265–1303)**
Dunst, Kirsten (actress); Point Pleasant, N.J., 4/30/82
Du Pont, Pierre S. (economist); Paris **(1739–1817)**
Durante, Jimmy (comedian); New York City **(1893–1980)**
Duras, Marguerite (Donnadieu) (novelist, dramatist); Gia Dinh, Vietnam **(1914–1996)**
Durbin, Deanna (Edna Mae) (actress); Winnipeg, Canada, 12/4/21
Dürer, Albrecht (painter, engraver); Nürnberg, Germany **(1471–1528)**
Durning, Charles (actor); Highland Falls, N.Y., 2/28/23
Durrell, Lawrence George (novelist); Julundur, India **(1912–1990)**
Duse, Eleonora (actress); Chioggia, Italy **(1859–1924)**
Dussault, Nancy (actress); Pensacola, Fla., 6/30/36
Duvall, Robert (actor, director, producer); San Diego, Calif., 1/5/31
Duvall, Shelley (actress); Houston, 7/7/49
Dvořák, Antonin (composer); Nelahozeves, Czechoslovakia **(1841–1904)**
Dylan, Bob (Robert Zimmerman) (singer, songwriter, guitarist); Duluth, Minn., 5/24/41
Dysart, Richard (actor); Brighton, Mass., 3/30/29

E

Eakins, Thomas (painter, sculptor); Philadelphia **(1844–1916)**
Earhart, Amelia (aviator); Atchison, Kans. **(1897–1937)**
Earp, Wyatt (Berry Stapp) (sheriff, gunfighter); Monmouth, Ill. **(1848–1929)**
Eastman, George (camera inventor); Waterville, N.Y. **(1854–1932)**
Eastwood, Clint (actor, director, producer); San Francisco, 5/31/30
Ebert, Roger (film critic); Urbana, Ill., 6/18/42
Ebsen, Buddy (Christian Ebsen, Jr.) (actor); Belleville, Ill. **(1908–2003)**
Eckstine, Billy (singer); Pittsburgh **(1914–1993)**
Eddy, Mary Baker (founder of Christian Science Church); Bow, N.H. **(1821–1910)**
Eddy, Nelson (baritone, actor); Providence, R.I. **(1901–1967)**
Edel, Leon (author); Pittsburgh **(1907–1997)**
Edelman, Marian Wright (social activist); Bennettsville, S.C., 6/6/39
Eden, Sir Anthony (Earl of Avon) (ex-prime minister); Durham, England **(1897–1977)**
Eden, Barbara (Barbara Huffman) (actress); Tucson, Ariz., 8/23/34
Edison, Thomas Alva (inventor); Milan, Ohio **(1847–1931)**
Edwards, Anthony (actor); Santa Barbara, Calif., 7/19/62
Edwards, Blake (film writer, producer); Tulsa, Okla., 7/26/22
Edwards, Jonathan (theologian); East Windsor, Conn. **(1703–1758)**
Edwards, Ralph (TV and radio producer); Merino, Colo., 6/13/13
Edwards, Vincent (Vincent Edward Zoino) (actor); Brooklyn, N.Y. **(1928–1996)**
Eglevsky, André (ballet dancer); Moscow **(1917–1977)**
Egoyan, Atom (film director, writer, editor); Cairo, 7/19/60
Ehrlich, Paul (bacteriologist); Strzelin, Poland **(1854–1915)**
Eichmann, (Karl) Adolf (Nazi, mass murderer); Solingen, Germany **(1906–1962)**
Eikenberry, Jill (actress); New Haven, Conn., 1/21/47
Einstein, Albert (physicist); Ulm, Germany **(1879–1955)**
Eisner, Michael (entertainment executive); Mt. Kisco, N.Y., 3/7/42
Eisenhower, Dwight David (34th U.S. president); Denison, Tex. **(1890–1969)**
Eisenhower, Milton S. (educator); Abilene, Kans. **(1899–1985)**
Eisenstaedt, Alfred (photographer, photojournalist); Dirschau (Prussia, now Tczew), Poland **(1898–1995)**
Ekland, Britt (Britt-Marie) (actress); Stockholm, 10/6/42
Electra, Carmen (Tara Patrick) (model, actress); Cincinnati, Ohio, 4/20/73
Elfman, Jenna (Jennifer Mary Butala) (actress); Los Angeles, 9/30/71
Elgar, Sir Edward (composer); Worcester, England **(1857–1934)**
Elgart, Larry (band leader); New London, Conn., 3/20/22
El Greco (Domenicos Theotocopoulos) (painter); Candia, Crete, Greece **(c. 1541–1614)**
Elion, Gertrude B. (chemist, Nobel laureate); New York City **(1918–1999)**
Eliot, George (Mary Ann Evans) (novelist); Chilvers Coton, England **(1819–1880)**
Eliot, Thomas Stearns (poet); St. Louis **(1888–1965)**
Elizabeth I (queen of England); Greenwich, England **(1533–1603)**
Elizabeth II (queen of England); London, 4/21/26
Elizondo, Hector (actor); New York City, 12/22/36
Ellington, Duke (Edward Kennedy) (jazz musician); Washington, D.C. **(1899–1974)**
Elliot, "Mama" Cass (Ellen Naomi Cohen) (singer); Baltimore **(1941–1974)**
Elliott, Sam (actor); Sacramento, Calif., 8/9/44

Ellison, Lawrence J. (computer industry executive); New York City, 1944
Ellison, Ralph (novelist); Oklahoma City, Okla. **(1914–1994)**
Ellsberg, Daniel (activist); Chicago, 4/7/31
Elman, Mischa (violinist); Stalnoye, Ukraine **(1891–1967)**
Emerson, Ralph Waldo (philosopher, poet); Boston **(1803–1882)**
Enesco, Georges (composer); Dorohoi, Romania **(1881–1955)**
Engels, Friedrich (Socialist writer); Barmen, Germany **(1820–1895)**
Englund, Robert (actor); Glendale, Calif., 6/6/49
Entremont, Philippe (concert pianist); Rheims, France, 6/7/34
Ephron, Nora (writer, director); New York City, 5/19/41
Epicurus (philosopher); Samos, Greece **(341–270 B.C.)**
Epstein, Sir Jacob (sculptor); New York City **(1880–1959)**
Erasmus, Desiderius (Gerhard Gerhards) (scholar); Rotterdam **(1469–1536)**
Erdrich, (Karen) Louise (writer); Little Falls, Minn., 7/6/54
Erickson, Leif (actor); Alameda, Calif. **(1911–1986)**
Ericsson, Leif (navigator) c. 10th century A.D.
Erikson, Erik H. (psychoanalyst); Frankfurt, Germany **(1902–1994)**
Ernst, Max (painter); Bruhl, Germany **(1891–1976)**
Erté (Romain de Tirtoff) (artist, designer); St. Petersburg, Russia **(1892–1990)**
Estevez, Emilio (actor, director, screenwriter); New York City, 5/12/62
Eszterhas, Joe (screenwriter); Csakanydoroslo, Hungary, 11/23/44
Euclid (mathematician); Megara, Greece, fl. 300 B.C.
Euler, Leonhard (mathematician); Basel, Switzerland **(1707–1783)**
Euripides (dramatist); Salamis, Greece **(c. 484–407 B.C.)**
Evangelista, Linda (model); St. Catharines, Ont., Canada, 5/10/65
Evans, Dale (born Lucille Wood Smith but raised as Frances Octavia Smith) (actress, singer); Uvalde, Tex. **(1912–2001)**
Evans, Dame Edith (actress); London **(1888–1976)**
Evans, Linda (actress); Hartford, Conn., 11/18/42
Evans, Maurice (actor); Dorchester, England **(1901–1989)**
Everett, Chad (Raymond Lee Cramton) (actor); South Bend, Ind., 6/11/36
Everett, Rupert (actor, model, musician); Norfolk, England, 5/29/59
Everhart, Angie (model, actress); Akron, Ohio, 9/6/69
Evers, Charles (civil rights leader); Decatur, Miss., 9/14/22
Evers, Medgar (civil rights leader); Decatur, Miss. **(1925–1963)**
Evers-Williams, Myrlie (civil rights leader); Vicksburg, Miss., 3/17/33

F

Fabares, Shelley (actress); Santa Monica, Calif., 1/19/44
Fabian (Fabian Anthony Forte) (singer); Philadelphia, 2/6/43
Fabray, Nanette (Nanette Fabarés) (actress); San Diego, Calif., 10/27/22
Fahrenheit, Gabriel (German physicist); Danzig, Poland **(1686–1736)**
Fairbanks, Douglas (Douglas Ulman) (actor); Denver **(1883–1939)**
Fairbanks, Douglas, Jr. (actor); New York City **(1909–2000)**
Fairchild, Morgan (Patsy Ann McClenny) (actress); Dallas, 2/3/50
Faith, Percy (conductor); Toronto **(1908–1976)**
Falk, Peter (actor); New York City, 9/16/27
Falla, Manuel de (composer); Cadiz, Spain **(1876–1946)**
Faludi, Susan (journalist, writer); New York City, 4/18/59
Falwell, Jerry (fundamentalist preacher); Lynchburg, Va., 8/11/33
Faraday, Michael (physicist); Newington, England **(1791–1867)**
Farentino, James (actor); Brooklyn, N.Y., 2/24/38
Farley, Chris (actor, comedian); Madison, Wis. **(1964–1997)**
Farmer, James (civil rights leader); Marshall, Tex. **(1920–1999)**
Farnsworth, Richard (actor); Los Angeles **(1920–2000)**
Farr, Jamie (Jameel Joseph Farah) (actor); Toledo, Ohio, 7/1/34
Farrar, Geraldine (soprano, actress); Melrose, Mass. **(1882–1967)**
Farrell, Eileen (operatic soprano); Willimantic, Conn. **(1920–2002)**
Farrell, James T. (novelist); Chicago **(1904–1979)**
Farrell, Mike (actor); St. Paul, Minn., 2/6/39
Farrell, Perry (Perry Bernstein) (lead singer); Queens, N.Y., 3/29/59
Farrell, Suzanne (Roberta Sue Ficker) (ballet dancer); Cincinnati, 8/16/45
Farrow, Mia (actress); Los Angeles, 2/9/46
Fasanella, Ralph (painter); New York City **(1914–1997)**
Fassbinder, Rainer Werner (film, stage director); Bad Wörishofen, Germany **(1946–1982)**
Fast, Howard (novelist); New York City **(1914–2003)**
Faubus, Orval E(ugene) (governor of Arkansas); Combs, Ark. **(1910–1994)**
Faulkner, William (novelist); New Albany, Miss. **(1897–1962)**
Fauré, Gabriel Urbain (composer); Pamiers, France **(1845–1924)**
Fawcett, Farrah (Mary Farrah Leni Fawcett) (actress); Corpus Christi, Tex., 2/2/47
Faye, Alice (Ann Leppert) (actress); New York City **(1912–1998)**
Feiffer, Jules (cartoonist); New York City, 1/26/29
Feininger, Lyonel (painter); New York City **(1871–1956)**
Feldman, Marty (actor, screenwriter, director); London **(1938–1982)**
Feldon, Barbara (actress); Pittsburgh, 3/12/41
Feliciano, José (singer); Larez, Puerto Rico, 9/10/45
Felker, Clay S. (editor, publisher); St. Louis, 10/2/25
Fell, Norman (actor); Philadelphia **(1923–1998)**
Fellini, Federico (film director); Rimini, Italy **(1920–1993)**
Fender, Freddie (Baldemar Huerta) (singer); San Benito, Tex., 6/4/37
Ferber, Edna (novelist); Kalamazoo, Mich. **(1885–1968)**
Ferguson, Maynard (jazz trumpeter); Verdun, Que., Canada, 5/4/28
Ferlinghetti, Lawrence (poet, writer, translator); Yonkers, N.Y., 3/24/19
Fermi, Enrico (atomic physicist); Rome **(1901–1954)**
Fernandel (Fernand Joseph Desire Contandin) (actor); Marseilles, France **(1903–1971)**
Ferraro, Geraldine Anne (political figure); New York City, 8/26/35
Ferrer, José (actor, director); Santurce, Puerto Rico **(1912–1992)**
Ferrer, Mel (actor); Elberon, N.J., 8/25/17
Fiedler, Arthur (conductor); Boston **(1894–1979)**
Field, Eugene (poet); St. Louis **(1850–1895)**
Field, Marshall (merchant); nr. Conway, Mass. **(1834–1906)**
Field, Sally (actress); Pasadena, Calif., 11/6/46
Fielding, Henry (novelist); nr. Glastonbury, England **(1707–1754)**
Fields, W. C. (William Claude Dukenfield) (comedian); Philadelphia **(1880–1946)**
Fiennes, Joseph (actor); Salisbury, England, 5/27/70
Fiennes, Ralph (actor); Suffolk, England, 12/22/62
Fierstein, Harvey (Forbes) (playwright, actor); Brooklyn, 6/6/54
Figgis, Mike (director, screenwriter, composer, actor); Carlisle, England, 2/28/48
Filene, Edward A. (merchant) **(1860–1937)**
Fillmore, Millard (13th U.S. president); Locke, Cayuga County, N.Y. **(1800–1874)**
Finch, Peter (actor); Kensington, England **(1916–1977)**
Finney, Albert (actor); Salford, England, 5/9/36
Fiorentino, Linda (Clorinda Fiorentino) (actress); Philadelphia, 3/9/60
Firkusny, Rudolf (pianist); Napajedia, former Czechoslovakia **(1912–1994)**
Firth, Colin (actor); Grayshot, England, 9/10/60
Fischer-Dieskau, Dietrich (baritone); Berlin, 5/28/25
Fishburne, Laurence (actor); Augusta, Ga., 7/30/61
Fisher, Carrie (actress); Los Angeles, 10/21/56
Fisher, Eddie (Edwin) (singer); Philadelphia, 8/10/28
Fitzgerald, Barry (William Joseph Shields) (actor); Dublin **(1888–1961)**
Fitzgerald, Ella (singer); Newport News, Va. **(1917–1996)**
Fitzgerald, F. Scott (Francis Scott Key Fitzgerald) (novelist); St. Paul, Minn. **(1896–1940)**
Fitzgerald, Geraldine (actress); Dublin, 11/24/14
Fitzgerald, Pegeen (radio broadcaster); Norcatur, Kans. **(1910–1989)**
Flack, Roberta (singer); Black Mountain, N.C., 2/10/40
Flagstad, Kirsten (Wagnerian soprano); Hamar, Norway **(1895–1962)**
Flatt, Lester Raymond (bluegrass musician); Overton County, Tenn. **(1914–1979)**
Flaubert, Gustave (novelist); Rouen, France **(1821–1880)**
Fleming, Sir Alexander (bacteriologist); Lochfield, Scotland **(1881–1955)**
Fletcher, John (dramatist); Rye, Sussex, England **(1579–1625)**
Flockhart, Calista (actress); Freeport, Ill., 11/11/64
Flynn, Errol (actor); Hobart, Tasmania **(1909–1959)**
Fodor, Eugene (violinist); Turkey Creek, Colo., 3/5/50
Fokine, Michel (dancer, choreographer); St. Petersburg, Russia **(1880–1942)**
Fonda, Bridget (actress); Los Angeles, 1/27/64
Fonda, Henry (actor); Grand Island, Neb. **(1905–1982)**
Fonda, Jane (actress); New York City, 12/21/37
Fonda, Peter (actor); New York City, 2/23/39
Fontaine, Frank (singer, comedian); Cambridge, Mass. **(1920–1979)**
Fontaine, Joan (Joan de Havilland) (actress); Tokyo, 10/22/17
Fontanne, Lynn (actress); London **(1887–1983)**
Fonteyn, Dame Margot (Margaret Hookham) (ballet dancer); Reigate, England **(1919–1991)**
Foote, Shelby (historian); Greenville, Miss., 11/17/16
Forbes, Malcolm S(tevenson) (publisher, sportsman); Brooklyn, N.Y. **(1919–1990)**
Ford, Gerald Rudolph (38th U.S. president); Omaha, Neb., 7/14/13

Ford, Glenn (Gwyllyn Ford) (actor); Ste.-Christine, Que., Canada, 5/1/16
Ford, Harrison (actor); Chicago, 7/13/42
Ford, Henry (industrialist); Greenfield, Mich. **(1863–1947)**
Ford, John (film director); Cape Elizabeth, Maine **(1895–1973)**
Ford, Tennessee Ernie (Ernie Jennings Ford) (singer); Bristol, Tenn. **(1919–1991)**
Foreman, George (boxer, actor); Marshall, Tex., 1/10/49
Forrester, Maureen (contralto); Montreal, 7/25/30
Forsythe, John (John Lincoln Freund) (actor); Penn's Grove, N.J., 1/29/18
Fosdick, Harry Emerson (clergyman); Buffalo, N.Y. **(1878–1968)**
Fosse, Bob (Robert Louis Fosse) (choreographer, director); Chicago **(1927–1987)**
Foster, Jodie (Alicia Christian Foster) (actress, director, producer); Los Angeles, 11/19/62
Foster, Stephen Collins (composer); nr. Pittsburgh **(1826–1864)**
Fountain, Pete (jazz musician); New Orleans, 7/3/30
Fox, Matthew (actor); Crowheart, Wyo., 7/14/66
Fox, Michael J. (actor, producer); Edmonton, Alta., Canada, 6/9/61
Foxx, Redd (John Elroy Sanford) (actor, comedian); St. Louis **(1922–1991)**
Foy, Eddie, Jr. (dancer, actor); New Rochelle, N.Y. **(1905–1983)**
Fracci, Carla (ballet dancer); Milan, Italy, 8/20/36
Fragonard, Jean Honoré (painter); Grasse, France **(1732–1806)**
Frakes, Jonathan (actor); Bethlehem, Pa., 8/19/52
Frampton, Peter (rock musician); Beckenham, England, 4/20/50
France, Anatole (Jacques Anatole François Thibault) (author); Paris **(1844–1924)**
Francescatti, Zino (violinist); Marseilles, France **(1902–1991)**
Franciosa, Anthony (Anthony Papaleo) (actor); New York City, 10/25/28
Francis, Anne (actress); Ossining, N.Y., 7/16/30
Francis, Connie (Concetta Franconero) (singer); Newark, N.J., 12/12/38
Francis, Genie (actress); Englewood, N.J., 5/26/62
Francis of Assisi, Saint (Giovanni Francesco Barnardone) (founder of Franciscans); Assisi, Italy **(1182–1226)**
Franck, César Auguste (composer); Liège, Belgium **(1822–1890)**
Franco Bahamonde, Francisco (chief of state); El Ferrol, Spain **(1892–1975)**
Frankenheimer, John (movie director, producer); New York City, 1930
Frankenthaler, Helen (artist); New York City, 12/12/28
Frankl, Victor E. (psychiatrist); Vienna **(1905–1997)**
Franklin, Aretha (singer); Memphis, Tenn., 3/25/42
Franklin, Benjamin (statesman, scientist); Boston **(1706–1790)**
Franklin, Bonnie (actress); Santa Monica, Calif., 1/6/44
Franklin, John Hope (historian); Rentiesville, Okla., 1/2/15
Frann, Mary (actress); St. Louis **(1943–1998)**
Franz, Dennis (Dennis Schlachta) (actor); Chicago, 10/28/44
Fraser, Brendan (actor); Indianapolis, Indiana, 12/3/67
Frazer, Sir James George (anthropologist); Glasgow, Scotland **(1854–1941)**
Freeman, Morgan (actor); Memphis, Tenn., 6/1/37
Freud, Sigmund (psychoanalyst); Moravia, Czech Repubic **(1856–1939)**
Frey, Glenn (musician); Detroit, 11/6/48
Frick, Henry Clay (industrialist); Westmoreland Co., Pa. **(1849–1919)**
Friedan, Betty (Betty Naomi Goldstein) (feminist, writer); Peoria, Ill., 2/4/21
Fromm, Erich (psychoanalyst); Frankfurt-am-Main, Germany **(1900–1980)**
Frost, David (TV entertainer); Tenterden, England, 4/7/39
Frost, Robert Lee (poet); San Francisco **(1874–1963)**
Fry, Christopher (playwright); Bristol, England, 12/18/07
Fugard, Athol (playwright); Middleburg, South Africa, 6/11/32
Fulbright, J. William (politician); Sumner, Mo. **(1905–1995)**
Fuller, Charles (playwright); Philadelphia, 3/5/39
Fuller, R(ichard) Buckminster (Jr.) (architect, educator); Milton, Mass. **(1895–1983)**
Fulton, Robert (inventor); Lancaster County, Pa. **(1765–1815)**
Funicello, Annette (actress); Utica, N.Y., 10/22/42
Funt, Allen (TV producer); Brooklyn, N.Y. **(1914–1999)**

G

Gabin, Jean (actor); Paris **(1904–1976)**
Gable, (William) Clark (actor); Cadiz, Ohio **(1901–1960)**
Gabo, Naum (sculptor); Briansk, Russia **(1890–1977)**
Gabor, Eva (actress); Budapest **(1920–1995)**
Gabor, Zsa Zsa (Sari) (actress); Budapest, 2/6/17
Gabriel, Peter (musician); Cobham, England, 2/13/50
Gabrieli, Giovanni (composer); Venice **(c. 1557–1612)**
Gaddis, William (novelist); New York City **(1922–1998)**
Gainsborough, Thomas (painter); Sudbury, Suffolk, England **(1727–1788)**
Galbraith, John Kenneth (economist); Iona Station, Ont., Canada, 10/15/08
Galilei, Galileo (astronomer, physicist); Pisa, Italy **(1564–1642)**
Gallico, Paul (novelist); New York City **(1897–1976)**
Gallup, George H. (poll taker); Jefferson, Iowa **(1901–1984)**
Galsworthy, John (novelist, dramatist); Coombe, England **(1867–1933)**
Galway, James (flutist); Belfast, Northern Ireland, 12/8/39
Gambling, John A. (radio broadcaster); New York City, 1930
Gandhi, Indira (Indira Nehru) (former prime minister); Allahabad, India **(1917– 1984)**
Gandhi, Mohandas Karamchand (called Mahatma Gandhi) (Hindu leader); Porbandar, India **(1869–1948)**
Gannett, Frank E. (editor, publisher) **(1876–1957)**
Garagiola, Joe (Joseph Henry Garagiola) (sportscaster); St. Louis, 2/12/26
Garbo, Greta (Greta Gustafsson) (actress); Stockholm **(1905–1990)**
Garcia, Andy (Andres Arturo Garcia-Menendez) (actor); Havana, Cuba, 4/12/56
Garcia, Jerry (rock musician); San Francisco **(1942–1995)**
Garcia Lorca, Frederico (poet, dramatist); Fuente Vaqueros, Spain **(1898–1936)**
Garden, Mary (soprano); Aberdeen, Scotland **(1874–1967)**
Gardenia, Vincent (Vincente Scognamiglio) (actor); Naples, Italy **(1922–1992)**
Gardner, Ava (actress); Smithfield, N.C. **(1922–1990)**
Gardner, Erle Stanley (novelist); Malden, Mass. **(1889–1970)**
Garfield, James Abram (20th U.S. president); Cuyahoga County, Ohio **(1831–1881)**
Garfunkel, Art (Arthur) (singer); Newark, N.J., 11/5/41
Garibaldi, Giuseppe (Italian nationalist leader); Nice, France **(1807–1882)**
Garland, Judy (Frances Gumm) (actress, singer); Grand Rapids, Minn. **(1922–1969)**
Garner, Erroll (jazz pianist); Pittsburgh **(1921–1977)**
Garner, James (James Bumgarner) (actor); Norman, Okla., 4/7/28
Garofalo, Janeane (actress, comedienne); Newton, N.J., 9/28/64
Garr, Teri (actress); Lakewood, Ohio, 12/11/49
Garrison, William Lloyd (abolitionist); Newburyport, Mass. **(1805–1879)**
Garroway, Dave (TV host); Schenectady, N.Y. **(1913–1982)**
Garson, Greer (actress); County Down, Northern Ireland **(1903–1996)**
Garth, Jennie (actress); Urbana, Ill., 4/3/72
Garvey, Marcus Moziah (black nationalist leader); Jamaica **(1887–1940)**
Gassman, Vittorio (film actor, director); Genoa, Italy **(1922–2000)**
Gates, Bill (William Henry Gates III) (software pioneer); Seattle, 10/28/55
Gates, Henry Louis, Jr. (scholar); Keyser, W. Va., 9/16/50
Gaudí, Antonio (architect); Reus, Spain **(1852–1926)**
Gauguin, (Eugène Henri) Paul (painter); Paris **(1848–1903)**
Gautama Buddha (Prince Siddhartha) (philosopher); Kapilavastu, India **(c. 563–c. 483 B.C.)**
Gavin, John (actor, diplomat); Los Angeles, 4/8/35
Gavras, Konstantinos (Costa-Gavras) (film director); Loutra-Iraias, Greece, 2/13/33
Gaye, Marvin (singer); Washington, D.C. **(1939–1984)**
Gayle, Crystal (Brenda Gayle Webb) (singer); Paintsville, Ky., 1/9/51
Gaynor, Janet (actress); Philadelphia **(1906–1984)**
Gaynor, Mitzi (Francesca Mitzi Marlene de Czanyi von Gerber) (actress); Chicago, 9/4/31
Gazzara, Ben (Biagio Anthony Gazzara) (actor); New York City, 8/28/30
Gedda, Nicolai (tenor); Stockholm, 7/11/25
Gellar, Sarah Michelle (actress); New York City, 4/14/77
Genet, Jean (playwright); Paris **(1910–1986)**
Genghis Khan (Temujin) (conqueror); nr. Lake Baikal, Russia **(1162–1227)**
Gentry, Bobbie (Roberta Streeter) (singer); Chickasaw Co., Miss., 7/27/44
George, David Lloyd (statesman); Manchester, England **(1863–1945)**
George, Henry (economist, reformer); Philadelphia **(1839–1897)**
Gere, Richard (actor); Philadelphia, 8/31/49
Géricault, Jean Louis (painter); Rouen, France **(1791–1824)**

Geronimo (Goyathlay) (Apache chieftain); Arizona **(1829–1909)**
Gershwin, George (composer); Brooklyn, N.Y. **(1898–1937)**
Gershwin, Ira (lyricist); New York City **(1896–1983)**
Getty, J. Paul (oil executive); Minneapolis **(1892–1976)**
Getz, Stan (saxophonist); Philadelphia **(1927–1991)**
Ghiberti, Lorenzo (goldsmith, sculptor); Florence **(1378–1455)**
Ghostley, Alice (actress); Eve, Mo., 8/14/26
Giacometti, Alberto (sculptor); Switzerland **(1901–1966)**
Giannini, Giancarlo (actor); La Spezia, Italy, 8/1/42
Gibbon, Edward (historian); Putney, England **(1737–1794)**
Gibson, Charles Dana (illustrator); Roxbury, Mass. **(1867–1944)**
Gibson, Henry (actor, comedian); Germantown, Pa., 9/21/35
Gibson, Mel (actor, director, producer); Peekskill, N.Y., 1/3/56
Gide, André (author); Paris **(1869–1951)**
Gielgud, Sir John (actor); London **(1904–2000)**
Gifford, Kathie Lee (Kathie Lee Epstein) (talk show host); Paris, 8/16/53
Gilbert, Melissa (actress); Los Angeles, 5/8/64
Gilbert, Walter (chemist, Nobel laureate); Boston, 3/21/32
Gilbert, Sir William Schwenck (librettist); London **(1836–1911)**
Gilels, Emil (concert pianist); Odessa, Ukraine **(1916–1985)**
Gillespie, Dizzy (John Birks Gillespie) (jazz trumpeter); Cheraw, S.C. **(1917–1993)**
Gilligan, Carol (Friedman) (psychologist); New York City, 11/28/36
Gilpin, Peri (actress); Waco, Tex., 5/27/61
Gimbel, Bernard F. (merchant); Vincennes, Ind. **(1885–1966)**
Gingrich, Newt (politician); Harrisburg, Pa., 6/17/43
Ginsberg, Allen (poet); Newark, N.J. **(1926–1997)**
Giordano, Luca (painter); Naples, Italy **(1632–1705)**
Giorgione (painter); Castelfranco, Italy **(c. 1477–1510)**
Giotto di Bondone (painter); Vespignamo, Italy **(c. 1266–1337)**
Giovanni, Nikki (poet); Knoxville, Tenn., 6/7/43
Giroud, Françoise (French government official); Geneva, 9/21/16
Gish, Dorothy (actress); Massillon, Ohio **(1898–1968)**
Gish, Lillian (Lillian de Guiche) (actress); Springfield, Ohio **(1893–1993)**
Giuliani, Rudolph (public official); Brooklyn, N.Y., 5/24/44
Givenchy, Hubert (fashion designer); Beauvais, France, 2/21/27
Gladstone, William Ewart (statesman); Liverpool, England **(1809–1898)**
Glaser, Paul Michael (actor, director); Cambridge, Mass., 3/25/43
Glass, Philip (composer); Baltimore, 1/31/37
Gleason, Jackie (comedian); Brooklyn, N.Y. **(1916–1987)**
Glenn, John (legislator, astronaut); Cambridge, Ohio, 7/18/21
Gless, Sharon (actress); Los Angeles, 5/31/43
Glover, Danny (actor); San Francisco, 7/22/47
Gluck, Christoph Willibald (composer); Erasbach, Germany **(1714–1787)**
Gobel, George (comedian); Chicago **(1920–1991)**
Godard, Jean Luc (film director); Paris, 12/3/30
Goddard, Paulette (Marion Levy) (actress); Great Neck, N.Y. **(1911–1990)**
Goddard, Robert Hutchings (father of modern rocketry); Worcester, Mass. **(1882–1945)**
Godfrey, Arthur (entertainer); New York City **(1903–1983)**
Goebbels, Joseph Paul (Nazi leader); Rheydt, Germany **(1897–1945)**
Goering, Hermann (Nazi leader); Rosenheim, Germany **(1893–1946)**
Goethals, George Washington (engineer); Brooklyn, N.Y. **(1858–1928)**
Goethe, Johann Wolfgang von (poet, playwright, novelist); Frankfurt-am-Main, Germany **(1749–1832)**
Gogol, Nikolai Vasilievich (novelist); nr. Mirgorod, Ukraine **(1809–1852)**
Goldberg, Rube (cartoonist); San Francisco **(1883–1970)**
Goldberg, Whoopi (Caryn Johnson) (actress); New York City, 11/13/49
Goldblum, Jeff (actor); Pittsburgh, 10/22/52
Golden, Harry (Harry Goldhurst) (author); New York City **(1902–1981)**
Goldman, Emma (anarchist); Kovno, Lithuania **(1869–1940)**
Goldsmith, Oliver (dramatist, poet); County Longford, Ireland **(1728–1774)**
Goldwyn, Samuel (Schmuel Gelbfisz) (film producer); Warsaw **(1879–1974)**
Gompers, Samuel (labor leader); London **(1850–1924)**
Goodall, Jane (Baroness van Lawick-Goodall) (ethologist); London, 4/3/34
Gooding, Jr., Cuba (actor); Bronx, New York, 1/2/68
Goodman, Benny (clarinetist); Chicago **(1909–1986)**
Goodman, John (actor); St. Louis, 6/20/52
Goodwin, Doris (Helen) Kearns (historian); Rockville Center, N.Y., 1/4/43
Goodyear, Charles (inventor); New Haven, Conn. **(1800–1860)**
Gorbachev, Mikhail Sergeyevich (former Soviet leader); Privolnoye, Russia, 3/2/31
Gordimer, Nadine (novelist, short-story writer); Springs, South Africa, 12/20/23
Gordon, Dexter (jazz musician); Los Angeles **(1923–1990)**
Gordon, Ruth (actress); Wollaston, Mass. **(1896–1985)**
Gore, Albert, Jr. (ex-vice president of the U.S.); Washington, D.C., 3/31/48
Gordy, Berry, Jr. (record company executive); Detroit, 11/28/29
Gorey, Edward (St. John) (illustrator, author); Chicago **(1925–2000)**
Gorki, Maxim (Alexei Maximovich Peshkov) (author); Nizhni Novgorod, Russia **(1868–1936)**
Gorky, Arshile (painter); Armenia **(1904–1948)**
Gormé, Eydie (singer); Bronx, N.Y., 8/16/32
Gorshin, Frank (actor); Pittsburgh, 4/5/34
Gossett, Louis, Jr. (actor); Brooklyn, N.Y., 5/27/36
Gottschalk, Louis Moreau (pianist, composer); New Orleans **(1829–1869)**
Gould, Chester (cartoonist); Pawnee, Okla. **(1900–1985)**
Gould, Elliott (Elliott Goldstein) (actor); Brooklyn, N.Y., 8/29/38
Gould, Glenn (concert pianist); Toronto **(1932–1982)**
Gould, Morton (composer); Richmond Hill, Queens, N.Y. **(1913–1996)**
Gould, Stephen Jay (paleontologist, science writer); New York City **(1941–2002)**
Goulet, Robert (singer); Lawrence, Mass., 11/26/33
Gounod, Charles François (composer); Paris **(1818–1893)**
Goya y Lucientes, Francisco José de (painter); Fuendetodos, Spain **(1746–1828)**
Grable, Betty (actress); St. Louis **(1916–1973)**
Grace, Princess of Monaco (Grace Kelly) (ex-actress); Philadelphia **(1929–1982)**
Graham, Bill (Wolfgang Grajonca) (rock impresario); Berlin **(1930–1991)**
Graham, Billy (William F. Graham) (evangelist); Charlotte, N.C., 11/7/18
Graham, Katharine Meyer (newspaper publisher); New York City **(1917–2001)**
Graham, Martha (choreographer); Pittsburgh **(1894–1991)**
Grainger, Percy Aldridge (pianist, composer); Melbourne, Australia **(1882–1961)**
Gramm, Donald (Grambach) (bass-baritone); Milwaukee **(1927–1983)**
Grammer, Kelsey (actor); St. Thomas, V.I., 2/21/55
Granger, Stewart (James Stewart) (actor); London **(1913–1993)**
Grant, Cary (Alexander Archibald Leach) (actor); Bristol, England **(1904–1986)**
Grant, Hugh (actor); London, England, 9/9/60
Grant, Lee (Lyova Haskell Rosenthal) (actress); New York City, 10/31/30
Grant, Ulysses Simpson (18th U.S. president); Point Pleasant, Ohio **(1822–1885)**
Grass, Günter (novelist); Danzig, Poland, 10/16/27
Graves, Nancy (Stevenson) (artist); Pittsfield, Mass. **(1940–1996)**
Graves, Peter (Peter Aurness) (actor); Minneapolis, 3/18/26
Graves, Robert (writer); London **(1895–1985)**
Gray, Linda (actress); Santa Monica, Calif., 9/12/40
Gray, Thomas (poet); London **(1716–1771)**
Greco, José (dancer); Montorio nei Frentani, Italy **(1918–2000)**
Greeley, Horace (journalist, politician); Amherst, N.H. **(1811–1872)**
Green, Adolph (actor, lyricist); New York City **(1915–2002)**
Green, Al (singer); Forrest City, Ark., 4/13/46
Greene, Graham (novelist); Berkhamsted, England **(1904–1991)**
Greene, Lorne (actor); Ottawa, Ont., Canada **(1915–1987)**
Greene, Shecky (comedian, actor); Chicago, 4/8/25
Greenstreet, Sydney (actor); Sandwich, England **(1879–1954)**
Greenspan, Alan (chairman of the Federal Reserve); New York City, 3/6/26
Greer, Germaine (feminist, writer); Melbourne, Australia, 1/29/39
Gregory, Cynthia (ballet dancer); Los Angeles, 7/8/46
Gregory, Dick (comedian); St. Louis, 10/12/32
Gregory, Lady (Isabella) Augusta (playwright); Roxborough, Ireland **(1852–1932)**
Greuze, Jean-Baptiste (painter); Tournus, France **(1725–1805)**
Grey, Joel (Joel Katz) (actor, dancer); Cleveland, 4/11/32
Grey, Zane (author); Zanesville, Ohio **(1875–1939)**
Grieg, Edvard Hagerup (composer); Bergen, Norway **(1843–1907)**
Grier, Pam (actress); Winston-Salem, N.C., 5/26/49
Griffin, Merv (TV host, producer); San Mateo, Calif., 7/6/25
Griffith, Andy (actor); Mount Airy, N.C., 6/1/26

Griffith, David Lewelyn Wark (film producer); La Grange, Ky. **(1875–1948)**
Griffith, Melanie (actress); New York City, 8/9/57
Grigorovich, Yuri (choreographer); Leningrad (St. Petersburg), Russia, 1/1/27
Grimes, Tammy (actress); Lynn, Mass., 1/30/34
Grimm, Jacob (author of fairy tales); Hanau, Germany **(1785–1863)**
Grimm, Wilhelm (author of fairy tales); Hanau, Germany **(1786–1859)**
Gris, Juan (José Victoriano González) (painter); Madrid **(1887–1927)**
Grisham, John (attorney, author); Jonesboro, Ark., 2/8/55
Grodin, Charles (actor); Pittsburgh, 4/21/35
Groening, Matt (animator, producer); Portland, Ore., 2/14/54
Gromyko, Andrei A. (diplomat); Starye Gromyki, Russia **(1909–1989)**
Gropius, Walter (architect); Berlin **(1883–1969)**
Gropper, William (painter, illustrator); New York City **(1897–1977)**
Gross, Michael (actor); Chicago, 6/21/47
Grosz, George (painter); Germany **(1893–1959)**
Grove, Andrew (Andras Grof) (computer industry executive); Budapest, Hungary, 9/2/36
Grünewald, Matthias (Mathis Gothart Neithart) (painter); Würzburg, Germany **(c. 1470–1528)**
Guest, Christopher (Christopher Haden-Guest) (actor, writer, director); New York City, 2/5/48
Guggenheim, Meyer (capitalist); Langnau, Switzerland **(1828–1905)**
Guillaume, Robert (Robert Williams) (actor); St. Louis, 11/30/27
Guinness, Sir Alec (actor); London **(1914–2000)**
Guitry, Sacha (Alexandre Guitry) (actor, film director); St. Petersburg, Russia **(1885–1957)**
Gumbel, Bryant Charles (TV newscaster); New Orleans, 9/29/48
Gunther, John (author); Chicago **(1901–1970)**
Gutenberg, Johann (printer); Mainz, Germany **(c. 1397–1468)**
Guthrie, Arlo (singer); New York City, 7/10/47
Guthrie, Woody (folk singer, composer); Okemah, Okla. **(1912–1967)**
Gwenn, Edmund (actor); London **(1875–1959)**
Gwynne, Fred (actor); New York City **(1926–1993)**

H

Habibie, Bacharuddin, Jusuf (president of Indonesia); Pare-Pare, Indonesia, 6/25/36
Hackett, Bobby (trumpeter); Providence, R.I. **(1915–1976)**
Hackett, Buddy (Leonard Hacker) (comedian, actor); Brooklyn, N.Y. **(1924–2003)**
Hackman, Gene (actor); San Bernardino, Calif., 1/30/31
Hagen, Uta (actress); Göttingen, Germany, 6/12/19
Haggard, Merle (songwriter, singer); Bakersfield, Calif., 4/6/37
Hagman, Larry (Larry Hageman) (actor); Weatherford, Tex., 9/21/31
Haig, Alexander Meigs, Jr. (ex-secretary of state, ex-general); Bala-Cynwyd, Pa., 12/2/24
Haile Selassie (Ras Tafari Makonnen) (ex-emperor); Ethiopia **(1892–1975)**
Hailey, Arthur (novelist); Luton, England, 4/5/20
Halberstam, David (journalist); New York City, 4/10/34
Hale, Alan (actor, director); Washington, D.C. **(1892–1950)**
Hale, Barbara (actress); DeKalb, Ill., 4/18/21
Hale, Edward Everett (clergyman, author); Boston **(1822–1909)**
Hale, Nathan (American Revolutionary officer); Coventry, Conn. **(1755–1776)**
Halevi, Judah (Jewish poet); Toledo, Spain **(1085–1140)**
Haley, Alex (writer); Ithaca, N.Y. **(1921–1992)**
Haley, Jack (actor); Boston **(1899–1979)**
Hall, Anthony Michael (Michael Anthony Thomas Charles Hall) (actor, singer); Boston, 4/14/68
Hall, Arsenio (comedian, talk-show host); Cleveland, 2/12/58
Hall, Donald (Andrew, Jr.) (poet); New Haven, Conn., 9/20/28
Hall, Huntz (actor); New York City **(1919–1999)**
Hall, Jerry (model, actress); Mesquite, Texas, 7/2/56
Hall, Monty (TV personality); Winnipeg, Canada, 8/25/23
Halley, Edmund (astronomer); London **(1656–1742)**
Hals, Frans (painter); Antwerp, Netherlands **(c. 1580–1666)**
Halsey, William Frederick, Jr. (naval officer); Elizabeth, N.J. **(1882–1959)**
Hamel, Veronica (actress); Philadelphia, 11/20/43
Hamill, Mark (actor); Oakland, 9/25/52
Hamilton, Alexander (statesman); Nevis, British West Indies **(1755–1804)**
Hamilton, Alice (physician, reformer); New York City **(1869–1970)**
Hamilton, Edith (scholar); Dresden, Germany **(1867–1963)**
Hamilton, George (actor); Memphis, Tenn., 8/12/39
Hamlin, Harry (actor); Pasadena, Calif., 10/30/51
Hamlisch, Marvin (composer, pianist); New York City, 6/2/44
Hammarskjöld, Dag (UN secretary-general); Jönköping, Sweden **(1905–1961)**
Hammerstein, Oscar, II (librettist, stage producer); New York City **(1895–1960)**
Hampton, Lionel (vibraharpist, band leader); Birmingham, Ala. **(1913–2002)**
Hamsun, Knut (Knut Pedersen) (novelist); Lom, Norway **(1859–1952)**
Hancock, Herbie (jazz musician); Chicago, 4/12/40
Hancock, John (statesman); Braintree, Mass. **(1737–1793)**
Hand, Learned (jurist); Albany, N.Y. **(1872–1961)**
Handel, George Frideric (Georg Friedrich Händel) (composer); Halle, Germany **(1685–1759)**
Handy, William Christopher (blues composer); Florence, Ala. **(1873–1958)**
Hanks, Tom (actor, director, writer); Concord, Calif., 7/9/56
Hannah, Daryl (actress); Chicago, 12/19/60
Hannibal (Carthaginian general); North Africa **(247–182 B.C.)**
Hansberry, Lorraine (playwright); Chicago **(1930–1965)**
Hanson, Howard (conductor); Wahoo, Neb. **(1896–1981)**
Harburg, E. Y. "Yip" (songwriter); New York City **(1896–1981)**
Harden, Marcia Gay (actress); La Jolla, Calif., 8/14/59
Harding, Warren Gamaliel (29th U.S. president); Morrow County, Ohio **(1865–1923)**
Hardwicke, Sir Cedric (actor); Stourbridge, England **(1893–1964)**
Hardy, Oliver (comedian); Atlanta **(1892–1957)**
Hardy, Thomas (novelist); Dorsetshire, England **(1840–1928)**
Harkness, Edward S. (business executive); Cleveland **(1874–1940)**
Harlow, Jean (Harlean Carpenter) (actress); Kansas City, Mo. **(1911–1937)**
Harlow, Shalom (model, TV personality); Oshawa, Ontario, Canada, 12/5/73
Harmon, Mark (actor); Burbank, Calif., 9/2/51
Harnick, Sheldon (lyricist); Chicago, 4/30/24
Harper, Valerie (actress); Suffern, N.Y., 8/22/40
Harrell, Lynn (cellist); New York City, 1/30/44
Harrelson, Woody (actor); Midland, Tex., 7/23/61
Harriman, Pamela (ambassador); Farnborough, England **(1920–1997)**
Harriman, W. (William) Averell (ex-governor of New York); New York City **(1891–1986)**
Harrington, Pat, Jr. (actor, comedian); New York City, 8/13/29
Harris, Barbara (Sandra Markowitz) (actress); Evanston, Ill., 7/25/35
Harris, Ed (actor); Englewood, N.J., 11/28/50
Harris, Emmylou (singer); Birmingham, Ala., 4/2/47
Harris, Julie (actress); Grosse Pointe Park, Mich., 12/2/25
Harris, Phil (actor, band leader); Linton, Ind. **(1906–1995)**
Harris, Richard (actor); Limerick, Ireland **(1930–2002)**
Harris, Rosemary (actress); Ashby, England, 9/19/30
Harris, Roy (composer); Lincoln County, Okla. **(1898–1979)**
Harrison, Benjamin (23rd U.S. president); North Bend, Ohio **(1833–1901)**
Harrison, George (singer, songwriter); Liverpool, England **(1943–2001)**
Harrison, Gregory (actor); Avalon, Catalina Island, Calif., 5/31/50
Harrison, Sir Rex (Reginald Carey) (actor); Huyton, England **(1908–1990)**
Harrison, William Henry (9th U.S. president); Charles City County, Va. **(1773–1841)**
Harry, Deborah (Blondie) (musician); Miami, Fla., 7/1/45
Hart, Lorenz (lyricist); New York City **(1895–1943)**
Hart, Mary (Mary Johanna Harum) (host); Sioux Falls, S.D., 11/8/50
Hart, Melissa Joan (actress); Sayville, N.Y., 4/18/76
Hart, Moss (playwright); New York City **(1904–1961)**
Harte, Bret (Francis Brett Harte) (author); Albany, N.Y. **(1836–1902)**
Hartford, Huntington (George Huntington Hartford II) (A.&P. heir); New York City, 4/18/11
Hartford, John (singer, banjoist); New York City **(1937–2001)**
Hartley, Mariette (actress); New York City, 6/21/40
Hartman, David Downs (TV newscaster); Pawtucket, R.I., 5/19/35
Hartman, Phil (actor, comedian); Brantford, Ont., Canada **(1948–1998)**
Hartman Black, Lisa (actress); Houston, 6/1/56
Harvey, Laurence (Larushka Skikne) (actor); Joniskis, Lithuania **(1928–1973)**
Harvey, Polly Jean (PJ Harvey) (singer, songwriter); Yeovil, England, 10/9/69
Harvey, William (physician); Folkestone, England **(1578–1657)**
Hasselhoff, David (actor, producer); Baltimore, 7/17/52

Hatcher, Teri (actress); Sunnyvale, Calif., 12/8/64
Havel, Vaclav (political leader, dramatist, poet); Prague, 10/5/36
Havens, Richie (musician); Brooklyn, N.Y., 1/21/41
Hawke, Ethan (actor); Austin, Tex., 11/6/70
Hawking, Stephen (physicist, astronomer); Oxford, England, 1/8/42
Hawkins, Coleman (jazz musician); St. Joseph, Mo. **(1904–1969)**
Hawkins, Jack (actor); London **(1910–1973)**
Hawn, Goldie (actress, producer); Washington, D.C., 11/21/45
Haworth, Jill (actress); Sussex, England, 8/15/45
Hawthorne, Nathaniel (novelist); Salem, Mass. **(1804–1864)**
Hay, John Milton (statesman); Salem, Ind. **(1838–1905)**
Hayakawa, Sessue (actor); Honshu, Japan **(1890–1973)**
Hayden, Melissa (ballet dancer); Toronto, 4/25/23
Hayden, Sterling (Sterling Relyea Walter) (actor, writer); Montclair, N.J. **(1916–1986)**
Haydn, Franz Joseph (composer); Rohrau, Austria **(1732–1809)**
Hayek, Salma (actress); Coatzacoalcos, Mexico, 9/2/68
Hayes, Helen (Helen Hayes Brown) (actress); Washington, D.C. **(1900–1993)**
Hayes, Isaac (composer); Covington, Tenn., 8/20/42
Hayes, Peter Lind (comedian, singer); San Francisco **(1915–1998)**
Hayes, Rutherford Birchard (19th U.S. president); Delaware, Ohio **(1822–1893)**
Hayward, Leland (producer); Nebraska City, Neb. **(1902–1971)**
Hayward, Susan (Edythe Marrener) (actress); Brooklyn, N.Y. **(1918–1975)**
Hayworth, Rita (Margarita Cansino) (actress); New York City **(1918–1987)**
Head, Edith (costume designer); Los Angeles **(1907–1981)**
Heaney, Seamus (poet); Londonderry, Northern Ireland, 4/13/39
Hearst, Patricia (Campbell) (heiress); San Francisco, 2/20/54
Hearst, William Randolph (publisher); San Francisco **(1863–1951)**
Hearst, William Randolph, Jr. (publisher); New York City **(1908–1993)**
Heatherton, Joey (actress); Rockville Centre, N.Y., 9/14/44
Heche, Anne (actress); Aurora, Ohio, 5/25/69
Hecht, Ben (author); New York City **(1894–1964)**
Heckart, Eileen (actress); Columbus, Ohio **(1919–2001)**
Heflin, Van (Emmet Evan Heflin) (actor); Walters, Okla. **(1910–1971)**
Hefner, Hugh (publisher); Chicago, 4/9/26
Hegel, Georg Wilhelm Friedrich (philosopher); Stuttgart, Germany **(1770–1831)**
Heidegger, Martin (existentialist philosopher); Messkirch, Germany **(1889–1976)**
Heifetz, Jascha (concert violinist); Vilna, Russia **(1901–1987)**
Heine, Heinrich (Harry) (poet); Düsseldorf, Germany **(1797–1856)**
Heinemann, Gustav (ex-president of Germany); Schweim, Germany **(1899–1976)**
Heisenberg, Werner Karl (physicist); Würzburg, Germany **(1901–1976)**
Heller, Joseph (novelist); Brooklyn, N.Y. **(1923–1999)**
Hellman, Lillian (playwright); New Orleans **(1905–1984)**
Helmond, Katherine (actress); Galveston, Tex., 7/5/34
Helms, Jesse (politician); Monroe, N.C., 10/18/21
Helmsley, Harry Brakmann (business executive); New York City **(1909–1997)**
Hemingway, Ernest Miller (novelist); Oak Park, Ill. **(1899–1961)**
Hemingway, Margaux (actress); Portland, Ore. **(1955–1996)**
Hemmings, David (actor); Guilford, England, 11/2/41
Henderson, Florence (actress); Dale, Ind., 2/14/34
Henderson, Skitch (Lyle Russell Cedric) (conductor, pianist); Birmingham, England?, 1/27/18
Hendrix, Jimi (James Marshall Hendrix) (guitarist); Seattle **(1942–1970)**
Henley, Beth (playwright-actress); Jackson, Miss., 5/8/52
Henley, Don (musician); Linden, Tex., 7/22/47
Henner, Marilu (actress); Chicago, 4/6/52
Henning, Doug (magician, actor); Winnipeg, Canada **(1947–2000)**
Henri, Robert (painter); Cincinnati **(1865–1926)**
Henriksen, Lance (actor, screenwriter); New York City, 5/4/40
Henry VIII (king of England); Greenwich, England **(1491–1547)**
Henry, O. (William Sydney Porter) (story writer); Greensboro, N.C. **(1862–1910)**
Henry, Patrick (statesman); Hanover County, Va. **(1736–1799)**
Henson, Jim (puppeteer); Greenville, Miss. **(1936–1990)**
Hepburn, Audrey (actress); Brussels **(1929–1993)**
Hepburn, Katharine (actress); Hartford, Conn. **(1907–2003)**
Hepplewhite, George (furniture designer); England **(?–1786)**
Hepworth, Barbara (sculptor); Wakefield, England **(1903–1975)**
Herbert, George (poet); Montgomery Castle, Wales **(1593–1633)**
Herbert, Victor (composer); Dublin **(1859–1924)**
Herblock (Herbert L. Block) (political cartoonist); Chicago **(1909–2001)**
Herman, Pee-wee (Paul Rubenfeld) (comedian); Peekskill, N.Y., 8/27/52
Herman, Woody (Woodrow Charles Herman) (band leader); Milwaukee **(1913–1987)**
Herod (called Herod the Great) (king of Judea) **(73–4 B.C.)**
Herodotus (historian); Halicarnassus, Asia Minor (Turkey) **(c. 484–425 B.C.)**
Herrick, Robert (poet); London **(1591–1674)**
Herschbach, Dudley Robert (chemist, Nobel laureate); San Jose, Calif., 6/18/32
Herschel, William (Frederich Wilhelm Herschel) (astronomer); Hannover, Germany **(1738–1822)**
Hershey, Barbara (Barbara Herzstein) (actress); Hollywood, Calif., 2/5/48
Herzog, Chaim (Israeli statesman); Belfast, Northern Ireland **(1918–1997)**
Hesburgh, Theodore M. (educator); Syracuse, N.Y., 5/2/17
Hesseman, Howard (actor); Salem, Ore., 2/27/40
Heston, Charlton (actor); Evanston, Ill., 10/4/24
Heyerdahl, Thor (ethnologist, explorer); Larvik, Norway **(1914–2002)**
Hill, Anita (lawyer, professor); Lone Tree, Okla., 7/30/56
Hill, Benny (comedian); Southampton, England **(1925–1992)**
Hill, Lauryn (actress, musician); South Orange, N.J., 5/25/75
Hillary, Sir Edmund (mountain climber); New Zealand, 7/20/19
Hiller, Wendy (actress); Bramhall, England **(1912–2003)**
Hillerman, John (actor); Denison, Tex., 12/20/32
Hilton, Conrad (hotelier); San Antonio, N.M. **(1887–1979)**
Hindemith, Paul (composer); Hanau, Germany **(1895–1963)**
Hindenburg, Paul von (Paul Ludwig Hans Anton von Hindenburg und Beneckendorff) (German field marshal, president); Poznan, Poland **(1847– 1934)**
Hines, Earl "Fatha" (jazz pianist); Duquesne, Pa. **(1905–1983)**
Hines, Gregory (dancer, actor); New York City **(1946–2003)**
Hines, Jerome (Jerome Heinz) (basso); Los Angeles, 11/8/21
Hippocrates (physician); Cos, Greece **(c. 460–c. 377 B.C.)**
Hirohito (Emperor of Japan); Tokyo **(1901–1989)**
Hiroshige, Ando (painter); Edo, Tokyo **(1797–1858)**
Hirsch, Judd (actor); New York City, 3/15/35
Hirschfeld, Al (Albert) (cartoonist); St. Louis **(1903–2003)**
Hirschhorn, Joseph Herman (financier, speculator, art collector); Mitau, Latvia **(1899–1981)**
Hirt, Al (trumpeter); New Orleans **(1922–1999)**
Hiss, Alger (public official); Baltimore **(1904–1996)**
Hitchcock, Alfred J. (film director); London **(1899–1980)**
Hitler, Adolf (German dictator); Braunau, Austria **(1889–1945)**
Hobbes, Thomas (philosopher); Westport, England **(1588–1679)**
Hobson, Laura Z. (Laura K. Zametkin) (novelist); New York City **(1900–1986)**
Ho Chi Minh (Nguyen That Tranh) (Vietnamese nationalist leader); Kim Lien, Vietnam **(1890–1969)**
Hockney, David (artist); Bradford, England, 7/9/37
Hodgkin, Dorothy Mary Crowfoot (chemist, Nobel laureate); Cairo, Egypt **(1910–1994)**
Hoffa, "Jimmy" James R(iddle) (labor leader); Brazil, Ind. **(1913–1975?; presumed murdered.)**
Hoffman, Dustin (actor, director); Los Angeles, 8/8/37
Hoffman, Phillip Seymour (actor); Fairport, N.Y., 1968
Hofmann, Hans (painter); Germany **(1880–1966)**
Hoffmann, Roald (chemist, Nobel laureate); Zloczow, Poland, 7/18/37
Hofstadter, Richard (historian); Buffalo, N.Y. **(1916–1970)**
Hogan, Paul (actor); Lightning Ridge, N.S.W., Australia, 10/8/39
Hogarth, William (painter, engraver); London **(1697–1764)**
Hokusai, Katsushika (artist); Yedo, Japan **(1760–1849)**
Holbein, Hans (the Elder) (painter); Augsburg, Germany **(c. 1465–1524)**
Holbein, Hans (the Younger) (painter); Augsburg, Germany **(c. 1497–1543)**
Holbrook, Hal (actor); Cleveland, 2/17/25
Holden, William (William Franklin Beedle, Jr.) (actor); O'Fallon, Ill. **(1918–1981)**
Holder, Geoffrey (dancer); Port-of-Spain, Trinidad, 8/1/30
Holiday, Billie (Eleanora Fagan) (jazz-blues singer); Baltimore **(1915–1959)**
Holliman, Earl (Henry Earl Holliman) (actor); Delhi, La., 9/11/28
Holly, Buddy (singer); Lubbock, Tex. **(1936–1959)**
Holly, Lauren (actress); Geneva, N.Y., 10/28/63
Holm, Celeste (actress); New York City, 4/29/19
Holmes, Katie (actress); Toledo, Ohio, 12/18/78
Holmes, Oliver Wendell (jurist); Boston **(1841–1935)**
Home, Lord (Alexander Frederick Douglas-Home) (diplomat); London **(7/2/1903–10/9/1995)**

Homer, Winslow (painter); Boston **(1836–1910)**
Homer (Greek poet) fl. 850 B.C.
Honegger, Arthur (composer); Le Havre, France **(1892–1955)**
Hook, Sidney (philosopher); New York City **(1902–1989)**
Hooker, John Lee (blues guitarist, singer, songwriter); Clarksdale, Miss. **(1920–2001)**
Hoover, Herbert Clark (31st U.S. president); West Branch, Iowa **(1874–1964)**
Hoover, J. Edgar (FBI director); Washington, D.C. **(1895–1972)**
Hope, Bob (Leslie Townes Hope) (comedian); London **(1903–2003)**
Hopkins, Sir Anthony (actor); Port Talbot, Wales, 12/31/37
Hopkins, Gerald Manley (poet); Stratford, England **(1844–1899)**
Hopkins, Johns (financier); Anne Arundel County, Md. **(1795–1873)**
Hopper, Dennis (actor); Dodge City, Kans., 5/17/36
Hopper, Edward (painter); Nyack, N.Y. **(1882–1967)**
Horace (Quintus Horatius Flaccus) (poet); Venosa, Italy **(65–8 B.C.)**
Horne, Lena (singer); Brooklyn, N.Y., 6/30/17
Horne, Marilyn (mezzo-soprano); Bradford, Pa., 1/16/34
Horowitz, Vladimir (pianist); Kiev, Ukraine **(1903–1989)**
Horsley, Lee (actor); Muleshoe, Tex., 5/15/55
Horton, Edward Everett (comedian); Brooklyn, N.Y. **(1887–1970)**
Hoskins, Bob (actor); Bury St. Edmunds, England, 10/26/42
Houdini, Harry (Ehrich Weiss) (magician); Budapest, Hungary **(1874–1926)**
Houseman, John (Jacques Haussmann) (producer, director, actor); Bucharest **(1902–1988)**
Housman, A(lfred) E(dward) (poet); Fockburg, England **(1859–1936)**
Houston, Charles Hamilton (civil rights lawyer); Washington, D.C. **(1895–1950)**
Houston, Samuel (political leader); Rockbridge County, Va. **(1793–1863)**
Houston, Whitney (singer); Newark, N.J., 8/9/63
Howard, Ken (actor); El Centro, Calif., 3/28/44
Howard, Leslie (Leslie Stainer) (actor); London **(1893–1943)**
Howard, Ron (actor, producer, director); Duncan, Okla., 3/1/54
Howard, Trevor (actor); Kent, England **(1916–1988)**
Howe, Elias (inventor); Spencer, Mass. **(1819–1867)**
Howe, Irving (literary critic); New York City **(1920–1993)**
Howe, Julia Ward (poet, reformer); New York City **(1819–1910)**
Hudson, Henry (English navigator) **(fl. 1607–1611)**
Hudson, Rock (born Roy Scherer, Jr.; took Roy Fitzgerald as legal name) (actor); Winnetka, Ill. **(1925–1985)**
Huggins, Nathan Irvin (historian); Chicago **(1927–1989)**
Hughes, Charles Evans (jurist); Glens Falls, N.Y. **(1862–1948)**
Hughes, Howard (industrialist, film producer); Houston **(1905–1976)**
Hughes, Langston (poet); Joplin, Mo. **(1902–1967)**
Hughes, Ted (poet); Mytholmroyd, England **(1930–1998)**
Hugo, Victor Marie (author); Besançon, France **(1802–1885)**
Hulce, Tom (actor); Detroit, 12/6/53
Hume, David (philosopher); Edinburgh, Scotland **(1711–1776)**
Hume, Kirsty (model); Glasgow, Scotland, 9/4/76
Humperdinck, Engelbert (composer); Siegburg, Germany **(1854–1921)**
Humperdinck, Engelbert (Arnold Dorsey) (singer); Madras, India, 5/2/36
Hunt, Helen (actress); Los Angeles, 6/15/63
Hunt, Linda (actress); Morristown, N.J., 4/2/45
Hunter, Holly (actress); Atlanta, 3/20/58
Hunter, Kim (Janet Cole) (actress); Detroit **(1922–2002)**
Hunter, Tab (Arthur Andrew Gelien) (actor); New York City, 7/11/31
Hunter-Gault, Charlayne (activist, broadcast journalist); Due West, S.C., 2/27/42
Huntley, Chet (TV newscaster); Cardwell, Mont. **(1911–1974)**
Hurley, Elizabeth (actress, model); Backingstoke, England, 6/10/65
Hurok, Sol (Solomon Hurok) (impresario); Pogar, Russia **(1884–1974)**
Hurst, Fannie (novelist); Hamilton, Ohio **(1889–1968)**
Hurston, Zora Neale (author); Eatonville, Fla. **(1901–1960)**
Hurt, John (actor); Shirebrook, England, 1/22/40
Hurt, William (actor); Washington, D.C., 3/20/50
Hus, Jan (Bohemian religious reformer); Husinetz, nr. Budweis, Czech Republic **(c. 1369–1415)**
Husing, Ted (sportscaster); New York City **(1901–1962)**
Hussein I (king); Jordan **(1935–1999)**
Hussein, Saddam (al-Tikriti) (Iraqi president); Tikrit, Iraq, 4/28/37
Huston, Anjelica (actress); Los Angeles, 7/8/51
Huston, John (actor, director, writer); Nevada, Mo. **(1906–1987)**
Huston, Walter (Walter Houghston) (actor); Toronto **(1884–1950)**
Hutchins, Robert M. (educator); Brooklyn, N.Y. **(1899–1977)**
Hutton, Betty (Betty Thornburg) (actress); Battle Creek, Mich., 2/26/21
Hutton, Lauren (actress, model); Charleston, S.C., 11/17/43
Hutton, Timothy (actor); Los Angeles, 8/16/60
Huxley, Aldous (author); Godalming, England **(1894–1963)**
Huxley, Sir Julian S. (biologist, author); London **(1887–1975)**
Huxley, Thomas Henry (biologist); Ealing, England **(1825–1895)**
Hynde, Chrissie (singer); Akron, Ohio, 9/7/51

I

Iacocca, Lee (Lido Anthony) (business executive); Allentown, Pa., 10/15/24
Ian, Janis (singer); New York City, 5/7/51
Ibsen, Henrik (dramatist); Skien, Norway **(1828–1906)**
Ice Cube (O'Shea Jackson) (musician, actor); Los Angeles, 6/15/69
Ice-T (Tracy Morrow) (rap musician, actor); Newark, N.J., 2/16/68
Inge, William (playwright); Independence, Kans. **(1913–1973)**
Ingres, Jean Auguste Dominique (painter); Montauban, France **(1780–1867)**
Inness, George (painter); nr. Newburgh, N.Y. **(1825–1894)**
Ionesco, Eugene (playwright); Slatina, Romania **(1912–1994)**
Ireland, Jill (actress); London **(1936–1990)**
Ireland, Kathy (model, actress); Glendale, Calif., 3/8/63
Ireland, Patricia (feminist, social activist); Oak Park, Ill., 10/19/45
Irons, Jeremy (actor); Cowes, Isle of Wight, England, 9/19/48
Irving, Amy (actress); Palo Alto, Calif., 9/10/53
Irving, John (Winslow) (writer); Exeter, N.H., 3/2/42
Irving, Washington (author); New York City **(1783–1859)**
Isaak, Chris (musician, actor); Stockton, Calif., 6/26/56
Isherwood, Christopher (novelist, playwright); nr. Dilsey and High Lane, England **(1904–1986)**
Iturbi, José (concert pianist); Valencia, Spain **(1895–1980)**
Ives, Burl (Icle Ivanhoe) (singer); Hunt, Ill. **(1909–1995)**
Ives, Charles E(dward) (composer); Danbury, Conn. **(1874–1954)**
Ivins, Molly (journalist); Monterey, Calif., 8/30/44
Ivory, James (director, producer); Berkeley, Calif., 6/7/28

J

Jackson, Andrew (7th U.S. president); Waxhaw, S.C. **(1767–1845)**
Jackson, Anne (actress); Millvale, Pa., 9/3/26
Jackson, Glenda (actress); Cheshire, England, 5/9/36
Jackson, Janet (singer); Gary, Ind., 5/16/66
Jackson, Rev. Jesse (civil rights leader); Greenville, S.C., 10/8/41
Jackson, Kate (actress); Birmingham, Ala., 10/29/49
Jackson, Mahalia (gospel singer); New Orleans **(1911–1972)**
Jackson, Maynard (mayor of Atlanta); Dallas **(1938–2003)**
Jackson, Michael (singer); Gary, Ind., 8/29/58
Jackson, Peter (director); Wellington, New Zealand, Oct. 31, 1961
Jackson, Samuel L. (actor); Washington, D.C., 12/21/48
Jackson, Thomas Jonathan ("Stonewall") (general); Clarksburg, Va. (now W. Va.) **(1824–1863)**
Jacobi, Derek (actor); Leytonstone, England, 10/22/38
Jacobs, Jane (urbanologist); Scranton, Pa., 5/1/16
Jagger, Mick (Michael Phillip Jagger) (singer); Dartford, England, 7/26/43
James, Harry (trumpeter); Albany, Ga. **(1916–1983)**
James, Henry (novelist); New York City **(1843–1916)**
James, Jesse Woodson (outlaw); Clay County, Mo. **(1847–1882)**
James, William (psychologist); New York City **(1842–1910)**
Jameson, (Margaret) Storm (novelist); Whitby, England **(1897–1986)**
Janis, Byron (pianist); McKeesport, Pa., 3/24/28
Janis, Conrad (actor, musician); New York City, 2/11/28
Janssen, David (David Meyer) (actor); Naponee, Neb. **(1930–1980)**
Jaworkski, Leon (Watergate special prosecutor); Waco, Tex. **(1905–1982)**
Jay, John (statesman, jurist); New York City **(1745–1829)**
Jeanmaire, Renée (dancer); Paris, 4/29/24
Jefferson, Thomas (3rd U.S. president); Shadwell, Va. **(1743–1826)**
Jemison, Mae C. (astronaut, physician); Decatur, Ala., 10/17/56
Jenner, Edward (physician); Berkeley, England **(1749–1823)**
Jennings, Peter (news anchor); Toronto, 7/29/38
Jennings, Waylon (singer); Littlefield, Tex. **(1937–2002)**
Jessel, George (entertainer); New York City **(1898–1981)**
Jessup, Philip C. (diplomat); New York City **(1897–1986)**
Jillian, Ann (Ann Jura Nauseda) (actress); Cambridge, Mass., 1/29/51
Joan of Arc (Jeanne d'Arc) (saint, patriot); Domremy-la-Pucelle, France **(1412–1431)**
Jobs, Steven Paul (computer industry pioneer); San Francisco, 1955
Joel, Billy (singer); New York City, 5/9/49

Joffrey, Robert (Abdullah Jaffa Bey Khan) (choreographer); Seattle **(1930–1988)**
John, Elton (Reginald Kenneth Dwight) (singer, pianist); Pinner, England, 3/25/47
Johns, Jasper (painter, sculptor); Augusta, Ga., 5/15/30
Johnson, Andrew (17th U.S. president); Raleigh, N.C. **(1808–1875)**
Johnson, Don (actor); Flatt Creek, Mo., 12/15/49
Johnson, James Weldon (author, educator); Jacksonville, Fla. **(1871–1938)**
Johnson, Lyndon Baines (36th U.S. president); Stonewall, Tex. **(1908–1973)**
Johnson, Philip Cortelyou (architect); Cleveland, 7/8/06
Johnson, Samuel (lexicographer, author); Lichfield, England **(1709–1784)**
Johnson, Van (actor); Newport, R.I., 8/20/16
Johnson, Virginia (human sexuality expert); Springfield, Mo., 2/11/25
Jolie, Angelina (actress); Los Angeles, 6/5/75
Joliot-Curie, Frédéric (chemist, Nobel laureate); Paris **(1900–1958)**
Joliot-Curie, Irène (Irène Curie) (chemist, Nobel laureate); France **(1897–1956)**
Jolliet, Louis (Louis Joliet) (explorer); Beaupré, Canada **(1645–1700)**
Jolson, Al (Asa Yoelson) (actor, singer); St. Petersburg, Russia **(1886–1950)**
Jones, Dean (actor); Morgan County, Ala., 1/25/35
Jones, George (singer); Saratoga, Tex., 9/12/31
Jones, Inigo (architect); London **(1573–1652)**
Jones, James (novelist); Robinson, Ill. **(1921–1977)**
Jones, James Earl (actor); Arkabutla, Miss., 1/17/31
Jones, Jennifer (Phylis Isley) (actress); Tulsa, Okla., 3/2/19
Jones, John Paul (John Paul) (naval officer); Scotland **(1747–1792)**
Jones, Quincy (composer); Chicago, 3/14/33
Jones, Shirley (singer, actress); Smithtown, Pa., 3/31/34
Jones, Spike (host, orchestra leader); Long Beach, Calif. **(1911–1965)**
Jones, Tom (Thomas Jones Woodward) (singer); Pontypridd, Wales, 6/7/40
Jones, Tommy Lee (actor); San Saba, Tex., 9/15/46
Jong, Erica (writer); New York City, 3/26/42
Jonson, Ben (Benjamin Jonson) (poet, dramatist); Westminster, England **(1572–1637)**
Joplin, Janis (singer); Port Arthur, Tex. **(1943–1970)**
Joplin, Scott (ragtime pianist, composer); Texarkansas, Tex. **(1868–1917)**
Jordan, Barbara (U.S. representative); Houston **(1936–1996)**
Jordan, Neil (film director, screenwriter); Sligo, Ireland, 2/25/50
Joseph (Chief Joseph) (Nez Perce Indian leader); eastern Ore. **(1841–1904)**
Josquin des Prés (usually known as Josquin) (composer); Conde-sur-L'Escaut?, Hainaut, Belgium **(c. 1445–1521)**
Jovovich, Milla (actress, model, singer); Kiev, Ukraine, 12/19/75
Joyce, James (novelist); Dublin **(1882–1941)**
Juárez, Benito Pablo (statesman); Guelatao, Mexico **(1806–1872)**
Judd, Ashley (actress); Los Angeles, 4/19/68
Julia, Raul (Raúl Rafael Carlos Julia y Arcelay) (actor); San Juan, P.R. **(1940–1994)**
Jung, Carl Gustav (psychoanalyst); Basel, Switzerland **(1875–1961)**
Jurado, Katy (Maria Christina Jurado Garcia) (actress); Guadalajara, Mexico **(1924–2002)**

K

Kabalevsky, Dmitri (composer); St. Petersburg, Russia **(1904–1987)**
Kafka, Franz (author); Prague **(1883–1924)**
Kádár, János (Communist Party leader); Hungary **(1912–1989)**
Kahn, Gus (songwriter); Coblenz, Germany **(1886–1941)**
Kahn, Louis I. (architect); Oesel Island, Estonia **(1901–1974)**
Kahn, Madeline (actress); Boston **(1942–1999)**
Kandinsky, Wassily (painter); Moscow **(1866–1944)**
Kanin, Garson (playwright); Rochester, N.Y. **(1912–1999)**
Kant, Immanuel (philosopher); Königsberg (Kaliningrad), Russia **(1724–1804)**
Kantor, MacKinlay (novelist); Webster City, Iowa **(1904–1977)**
Kaplan, Justin (writer, editor); New York City, 9/5/25
Karan, Donna (fashion designer); Forest Hills, N.Y., 10/2/48
Karloff, Boris (William Henry Pratt) (actor); London **(1887–1969)**
Kasdan, Lawrence (film director, writer, actor, producer); Miami, 1/14/49
Kasem, Casey (disc jockey); Detroit, 4/27/32
Kaufman, Andy (actor, comedian); New York City **(1949–1984)**
Kaufman, George S. (playwright); Pittsburgh **(1889–1961)**
Kavner, Julie (actress); Los Angeles, 9/7/51
Kaye, Danny (David Daniel Kominski) (comedian); Brooklyn, N.Y. **(1913–1987)**
Kaye, Sammy (band leader); Cleveland **(1910–1987)**
Kazan, Elia (director); Constantinople, Turkey, 9/7/09
Kazan, Lainie (Levine) (singer); New York City, 5/15/40
Kazantzakis, Nikos (writer); Herakleion, Crete **(1883–1957)**
Keach, Stacy (actor); Savannah, Ga., 6/2/41
Keaton, Buster (Joseph Frank Keaton) (comedian); Piqua, Kans. **(1896–1966)**
Keaton, Diane (actress); Los Angeles, 1/5/46
Keaton, Michael (Michael Douglas) (actor); Robinson Township, Pa., 9/9/51
Keats, John (poet); London **(1795–1821)**
Keel, Howard (Harold Clifford Leek) (singer, actor); Gillespie, Ill., 4/13/19
Keeler, Ruby (Ethel Hilde Keeler) (actress, dancer); Halifax, N.S., Canada **(1910–1993)**
Keener, Catherine (actress); Miami, Fla., 1959(?)
Kefauver, Estes (legislator); Madisonville, Tenn **(1903–1963)**
Keitel, Harvey (actor); Brooklyn, N.Y., 5/13/39
Keith, Brian (Robert Brian Keith, Jr.) (actor); Bayonne, N.J. **(1921–1997)**
Keller, Helen Adams (author, educator); Tuscumbia, Ala. **(1880–1968)**
Kelley, DeForest (actor); Atlanta **(1920–1999)**
Kelly, Emmett (clown); Sedan, Kans. **(1898–1979)**
Kelly, Gene (dancer, actor); Pittsburgh **(1912–1996)**
Kelly, Grace (actress, Princess of Monaco); Philadelphia **(1929–1982)**
Kelly, R. (Robert Kelly) (singer, record producer, actor); Chicago, 1969
Kempis, Thomas à (mystic); Kempis, Prussia (Germany) **(1380–1471)**
Kendall, Henry W. (physicist, Nobel laureate); Boston **(1926–1999)**
Kennan, George F. (diplomat); Milwaukee, 2/16/04
Kennedy, Anthony (jurist); Sacramento, Calif., 7/23/36
Kennedy, Carolyn Bessette (socialite); White Plains, N.Y. **(1966–1999)**
Kennedy, George (actor); New York City, 2/18/25
Kennedy, John Fitzgerald (35th U.S. president); Brookline, Mass. **(1917–1963)**
Kennedy, John F., Jr. (publisher); Washington, D.C. **(1960–1999)**
Kennedy, Joseph P. (financier); Boston **(1888–1969)**
Kennedy, Robert Francis (legislator); Brookline, Mass. **(1925–1968)**
Kennedy, Rose Fitzgerald (president's mother); Boston **(1890–1995)**
Kent, Allegra (ballet dancer); Santa Monica, Calif., 8/11/38
Kent, Rockwell (painter); Tarrytown Heights, N.Y. **(1882–1971)**
Kenton, Stan (Stanley Newcomb) (jazz musician); Wichita, Kans. **(1912–1979)**
Kepler, Johannes (astronomer); Weil, Germany **(1571–1630)**
Kercheval, Ken (actor); Wolcottville, Ind., 7/15/35
Kerensky, Alexander Fedorovich (statesman); Simbirsk, Russia **(1881–1970)**
Kern, Jerome David (composer); New York City **(1885–1945)**
Kerns, Joanna (actress); San Francisco, 2/12/53
Kerouac, Jack (Jean-Louis Kerouac) (writer); Lowell, Mass. **(1922–1969)**
Kerr, Deborah (actress); Helensburgh, Scotland, 9/30/21
Kettering, Charles F. (engineer, inventor); nr. Loudonville, Ohio **(1876–1958)**
Kevorkian, Jack (medical pathologist); Pontiac, Mich., 3/26/28
Key, Francis Scott (lawyer, author of national anthem); Frederick (Carroll) County, Md. **(1779–1843)**
Keyes, Frances Parkinson (novelist); Charlottesville, Va. **(1885–1970)**
Keynes, John Maynard (1st Baron of Tilton) (economist); Cambridge, England **(1883–1946)**
Khachaturian, Aram (composer); Tiflis, Russia **(1903–1978)**
Khomeini, Ayatollah Ruhollah (Islamic religious leader); Iran **(1900–1989)**
Khrushchev, Nikita S. (Soviet leader); Kalinovka, nr. Kursk, Ukraine **(1894–1971)**
Kidd, Michael (Milton Greenwald) (choreographer); Brooklyn, N.Y., 8/12/19
Kidd, William (called Captain Kidd) (pirate); Greenock, Scotland **(c. 1645–1701)**
Kidder, Margot (actress); Yellowknife, N.W.T., Canada, 10/17/48
Kidman, Nicole (actress); Honolulu, 6/20/67
Kiepura, Jan (tenor); Sosnowiec, Poland **(1902–1966)**
Kieran, John (writer); New York City **(1892–1981)**
Kierkegaard, Sören Aalys (philosopher); Copenhagen **(1813–1855)**
Kiesinger, Kurt Georg (diplomat); Ebingen, Germany **(1904–1988)**

Kiley, Richard (actor, singer); Chicago **(1922–1999)**
Kilmer, Alfred Joyce (poet); New Brunswick, N.J. **(1886–1918)**
Kilmer, Val (actor); Los Angeles,, 12/31/59
King, Alan (Irwin Alan Kniberg) (entertainer); Brooklyn, N.Y., 12/26/27
King, B.B. (Riley King) (guitarist); Itta Bena, Miss., 9/16/25
King, Carole (singer, songwriter); Brooklyn, N.Y., 2/9/41
King, Coretta Scott (civil rights leader); Marion, Ala., 4/27/27
King, Larry (Lawrence Harvey Zeigler) (TV host); New York City, 11/19/33
King, Martin Luther, Jr. (civil rights leader); Atlanta **(1929–1968)**
King, Stephen (writer); Portland, Maine, 9/21/47
Kingsley, Ben (Krishna Bhanji) (actor); Snainton, England, 12/31/43
Kingsley, Sidney (Sidney Kirschner) (playwright); New York City **(1906–1995)**
Kingsolver, Barbara (writer); Annapolis, Md., 4/8/55
Kingston, Maxine Hong (novelist); Stockton, Calif., 10/27/40
Kinsey, Alfred Charles (human sexuality expert); Hoboken, N.J. **(1894–1956)**
Kinski, Nastassja (Nastassja Nakszynski) (actress); West Berlin, 1/24/61
Kipling, Rudyard (author); Bombay (Mumbai) **(1865–1936)**
Kipnis, Alexander (basso); Ukraine **(1891–1978)**
Kirby, George (comedian); Chicago **(1923–1995)**
Kirchner, Ernst Ludwig (painter); Aschaffenburg, Germany **(1880–1938)**
Kirk, Grayson (educator); Jeffersonville, Ohio **(1903–1997)**
Kirkland, Gelsey (ballet dancer); Bethlehem, Pa., 12/29/52
Kirkpatrick, Jeane Jordan (educator-public affairs); Duncan, Okla., 11/19/26
Kirkpatrick, Ralph (harpsichordist); Leominster, Mass. **(1911–1984)**
Kirstein, Lincoln (dance, theater executive); Rochester, N.Y. **(1907–1996)**
Kirsten, Dorothy (soprano); Montclair, N.J. **(1910–1992)**
Kissinger, Henry (Heinz Alfred Kissinger) (ex-U.S. secretary of state); Furth, Germany, 5/27/23
Kitt, Eartha (singer); North, S.C., 1/26/28
Klee, Paul (painter); Münchenbuchsee, nr. Bern, Switzerland **(1879–1940)**
Klein, Calvin (fashion designer); Bronx, N.Y., 11/19/42
Klein, Robert (comedian); New York City, 2/8/42
Kleist, Henrich von (poet); Frankfurt an der Oder, Germany **(1777–1811)**
Klemperer, Otto (conductor); Breslau, Poland **(1885–1973)**
Klemperer, Werner (actor); Cologne, Germany **(1920–2000)**
Klimt, Gustav (painter); Vienna **(1862–1918)**
Kline, Kevin (actor); St. Louis, 10/24/47
Klugman, Jack (actor); Philadelphia, 4/27/22
Knight, Gladys (singer); Atlanta, 5/28/44
Knight, John S. (publisher); Bluefield, W. Va. **(1894–1981)**
Knight, Ted (Tadeus Wladyslaw Konopka) (actor); Terryville, Conn. **(1923–1986)**
Knight, Wayne (actor); Cartersville, Ga., 8/7/55
Knopf, Alfred A. (publisher); New York City **(1892–1984)**
Knopfler, Mark (musician); Glasgow, Scotland, 8/12/49
Knotts, Don (actor); Morgantown, W. Va., 7/21/24
Knox, John (religious reformer); Haddington, East Lothian, Scotland **(1505–1572)**
Koch, Robert (physician); Klausthal, Germany **(1843–1910)**
Koenig, Walter (actor); Chicago, 9/14/36
Koestler, Arthur (novelist); Budapest **(1905–1983)**
Kokoschka, Oskar (painter); Póchlarn, Austria **(1886–1980)**
Kollwitz, Käthe (graphic artist, sculptor); Königsberg, Russia **(1867–1945)**
Koop, C. Everett (ex-surgeon general); Brooklyn, N.Y., 10/14/16
Kooper, Al (singer, pianist); Brooklyn, N.Y., 2/5/44
Kopell, Bernie (actor); New York City, 6/21/33
Koppel, Ted (broadcast journalist); Lancashire, England, 2/8/40
Korman, Harvey (actor); Chicago, 2/15/27
Kosciusko, Thaddeus (Tadeusz Andrzej Bonawentura Kosciuszko) (military officer and statesman) **(1746–1817)**
Kossuth, Lajos (patriot); Monok, Hungary **(1802–1894)**
Kostelanetz, André (orchestra conductor); St. Petersburg, Russia **(1901–1980)**
Kostunica, Vojislav (president of Yugoslavia); Belgrade, 3/24/44
Kosygin, Aleksei N. (premier); St. Petersburg, Russia **(1904–1980)**
Kotto, Yaphet (actor); New York City, 11/15/37
Koussevitzky, Serge (Sergei) Alexandrovitch (orchestra conductor); Vishni Volochek, Tver, Russia **(1874–1951)**
Kramer, Stanley E. (film producer, director); New York City **(1913–2001)**
Kraus, Lili (pianist); Budapest **(1905–1986)**
Kravitz, Lenny (musician); New York City, 5/26/64
Kreisler, Fritz (violinist, composer); Vienna **(1875–1962)**
Kresge, S. S. (merchant); Bald Mount, Pa. **(1867–1966)**
Krips, Josef (orchestra conductor); Vienna **(1902–1974)**
Kristofferson, Kris (singer); Brownsville, Tex., 6/22/36
Krupa, Gene (drummer); Chicago **(1909–1973)**
Krupp, Alfred (munitions magnate); Essen, Germany **(1812–1887)**
Kubelik, Rafael (conductor); Bychory, former Czechoslovakia **(1914–1996)**
Kublai Khan (Mongol conqueror) **(1216–1294)**
Kubrick, Stanley (film director, producer); New York City **(1928–1999)**
Kudrow, Lisa (actress); Encino, Calif., 7/30/63
Kuralt, Charles (TV journalist); Wilmington, N.C. **(1934–1997)**
Kurosawa, Akira (film director); Tokyo **(1910–1998)**
Kurtz, Efrem (conductor); St. Petersburg, Russia **(1900–1995)**
Kurtz, Swoosie (actress); Omaha, Neb., 9/6/44

L

LaBelle, Patti (singer, actress); Philadelphia, 5/24/44
Ladd, Cheryl (Cheryl Stoppelmoor) (actress); Huron, S.D., 7/12/51
Ladd, Diane (actress); Meridian, Miss., 11/29/32
Laden, Osama bin (terrorist); Riyadh, Saudi Arabia, c. 1957
Lafayette, Marquis de (Marie Joseph Paul Yves Roch Gilbert du Motier) (military officer); Auvergne, France **(1757–1834)**
Lafitte, Jean (pirate); Bayonne?, France **(1780–1826)**
La Follette, Robert Marin (politician); Primrose, Wis. **(1855–1925)**
La Fontaine, Jean de (poet); Château-Thierry, France **(1621–1695)**
La Guardia, Fiorello Henry (mayor of New York); New York City **(1882–1947)**
Lahti, Christine (actress, director); Birmingham, Mich., 4/4/50
Laine, Frankie (Frank Paul LoVecchio) (singer); Chicago, 3/30/13
Laird, Melvin (ex-secretary of defense); Omaha, Neb., 9/1/22
Lamarck, Chevalier de (Jean Baptiste Pierre Antoine de Monet) (naturalist); Bazantin, France **(1744–1829)**
Lamas, Lorenzo (actor); Los Angeles, 1/20/58
Lamb, Charles (Elia) (essayist); London **(1775–1834)**
L'Amour, Louis (author); Jamestown, N.D. **(1908–1988)**
Lancaster, Burt (actor); New York City **(1913–1994)**
Landau, Martin (actor); Brooklyn, N.Y., 6/20/31
Landers, Ann (Esther Pauline Friedman) (columnist); Sioux City, Iowa **(1918–2002)**
Landon, Michael (Eugene Maurice Orowitz) (actor, director, producer); Forest Hills, Queens, N.Y. **(1936–1991)**
Lane, Abbe (Abigail Francine Lassman) (singer); New York City, 1933
Lane, Burton (songwriter); New York City **(1912–1997)**
Lane, Nathan (Joseph Lane) (actor, singer); Jersey City, N.J., 2/3/56
Lang, Fritz (film director); Vienna **(1890–1976)**
Lange, Hope (actress); Redding Ridge, Conn., 11/28/33
Lange, Jessica (actress); Cloquet, Minn., 4/20/49
Langella, Frank (actor); Bayonne, N.J., 1/1/40
Langmuir, Irving (chemist); Brooklyn, N.Y. **(1881–1957)**
Langtry, Lillie (Emily Le Breton) (actress); Island of Jersey **(1852–1929)**
Lansbury, Angela (actress, producer); London, 10/16/25
Lansing, Robert (Robert Howell Brown) (actor); San Diego, Calif. **(1928–1994)**
Lanza, Mario (Alfred Arnold Cocozza) (singer, actor); Philadelphia **(1921–1959)**
Lao-tse (Li Erh) (philosopher); Honan Province, China **(c. 604–531 B.C.)**
Lardner, Ring (Ringgold Wilmar Lardner) (story writer); Niles, Mich. **(1885–1933)**
La Rouchefoucauld, Francois duc de (author); Paris **(1613–1680)**
Larroquette, John (actor); New Orleans, 11/25/47
Larson, Gary (cartoonist); Tacoma, Wash., 8/14/50
La Salle, Eriq (actor); Hartford, Conn., 7/23/62
La Salle, Sieur de (Robert Cavelier) (explorer); Rouen, France **(1643–1687)**
Lasch, Christopher (historian, social critic); Omaha, Neb. **(1932–1994)**
La Tour, Georges de (painter); Vic-sur-Seille, France **(1593–1652)**
Lauer, Matt (TV host); New York City, 12/20/57
Laughton, Charles (actor); Scarborough, England **(1899–1962)**
Lauper, Cyndi (singer); New York City, 6/20/53
Laurel, Stan (Arthur Jefferson) (comedian); Ulverston, England **(1890–1965)**
Laurents, Arthur (playwright); New York City, 7/14/18
Laurie, Piper (Rosetta Jacobs) (actress); Detroit, 1/22/32
Lavin, Linda (actress); Portland, Maine, 10/15/37

Lavoisier, Antoine-Laurent (chemist); Paris **(1743–1794)**
Lawford, Peter (actor); London **(1923–1984)**
Lawless, Lucy (Lucy Ryan) (actress); Auckland, New Zealand, 3/29/68
Lawrence, David Herbert (novelist); Nottingham, England **(1885–1930)**
Lawrence, Jacob (painter); Atantic City, N.J. **(1917–2000)**
Lawrence, Martin (actor); Frankfurt, Germany, 4/16/65
Lawrence, Sharon (actress); Charlotte, N.C., 6/29/62
Lawrence, Steve (Sidney Leibowitz) (singer); Brooklyn, N.Y., 7/8/35
Lawrence of Arabia (Thomas Edward Lawrence, later changed to Shaw) (author, soldier); Tremadoc, Wales **(1888–1935)**
Lawrence, Vicki (actress); Inglewood, Calif., 3/26/49
Leach, Penelope (Balchin) (child psychologist, writer); London, 11/19/37
Leach, Robin (host, producer); London, 8/29/41
Leachman, Cloris (actress); Des Moines, Iowa, 4/30/26
Leadbelly, (Huddie Ledbetter) (blues singer, guitarist); Mooringsport, La. **(1885–1949)**
Leakey, Louis Seymour Bazett (anthropologist); Kabete, Kenya **(1903–1972)**
Leakey, Mary (anthropologist); London **(1913–1996)**
Leakey, Richard (paleoanthropologist, wildlife conservationist); Kenya, 12/19/44
Lean, David (film director); Croydon, England **(1908–1991)**
Lear, Edward (nonsense poet); London **(1812–1888)**
Lear, Evelyn (Shulman) (soprano); Brooklyn, N.Y., 1/8/26
Lear, Norman (TV producer); New Haven, Conn., 7/27/22
Learned, Michael (actress); Washington, D.C., 4/9/39
Leary, Denis (actor, screenwriter, film director); Worcester, Mass., 8/18/57
Leary, Timothy (psychologist, LSD advocate); Springfield, Mass. **(1920–1996)**
Le Blanc, Matt (actor); Newton, Mass., 7/25/67
le Carré, John (David John Moore Cornwell) (novelist); Poole, England, 10/19/31
Le Corbusier (Charles Edouard Jeanneret) (architect); La Chaux-de-Fonds, Switzerland **(1887–1965)**
Lee, Ang (film director); Pingtung, Taiwan, 10/23/54
Lee, Christopher (actor); London, 5/27/22
Lee, Manfred B. (pseudonym Ellery Queen) (novelist); Brooklyn, N.Y. **(1905–1971)**
Lee, Peggy (Norma Engstrom) (singer); Jamestown, N.D. **(1920–2002)**
Lee, Robert E(dward) (Confederate general); Stratford Estate, Va. **(1807–1870)**
Lee, Spike (Shelton Jackson Lee) (actor, director, writer, producer); Atlanta, 3/20/57
Leeuwenhoek, Anton van (zoologist); Delft, Netherlands **(1632–1723)**
Lehár, Franz (composer); Komárom, Hungary **(1870–1948)**
Lehman, Herbert H. (governor, senator); New York City **(1878–1963)**
Lehmann, Lotte (soprano); Perleberg, Germany **(1888–1976)**
Lehrer, Jim (TV newscaster); Wichita, Kans., 5/19/34
Leibniz, Gottfried W. von (scientist); Leipzig, Germany **(1646–1716)**
Leibovitz, Annie (photographer); Westbury, Conn., 10/2/49
Leigh, Janet (Jeanette Helen Morrison) (actress); Merced, Calif., 7/6/27
Leigh, Jennifer Jason (Jennifer Morrow) (actress); Los Angeles, 2/5/62
Leigh, Mike (film director, screenwriter); Manchester, England, 2/20/43
Leigh, Vivien (Vivian Mary Hartley) (actress); Darjeeling, India **(1913–1967)**
Leinsdorf, Erich (conductor); Vienna **(1912–1993)**
Lemmon, Jack (actor); Boston **(1925–2001)**
Lenin, Vladimir (Vladimir Ilich Ulyanov) (Soviet leader); Simbirsk, Russia **(1870–1924)**
Lennon, John (singer, songwriter); Liverpool, England **(1940–1980)**
Leno, Jay (comedian, TV host); New Rochelle, N.Y., 4/28/50
Leonard, Sheldon (Sheldon Leonard Bershad) (actor, producer); New York City **(1907–1997)**
Leonardo da Vinci, (painter, scientist); Vinci, Tuscany, Italy **(1452–1519)**
Leoni, Téa (actress); New York City, 2/25/66
Lerner, Alan Jay (lyricist); New York City **(1918–1986)**
Lerner, Max (columnist); Minsk, Russia **(1902–1992)**
Lessing, Doris (novelist); Kermanshah, Iran, 10/22/19
Leto, Jared (actor); Bossier City, La., 12/26/71
Letterman, David (TV host, producer); Indianapolis, 4/12/47
Levant, Oscar (pianist); Pittsburgh **(1906–1972)**
Levenson, Sam (humorist); New York City **(1911–1980)**
Levi, Carlo (novelist); Turin, Italy **(1902–1975)**
Levine, James (artistic director, Metropolitan Opera); Cincinnati, 6/23/43
Levine, Joseph E. (film producer); Boston **(1905–1987)**
Levinson, Barry (screenwriter, director, producer, actor); Baltimore, 4/6/42
Lewis, C(live) S(taples) (author); Belfast, Northern Ireland **(1898–1963)**
Lewis, Gilbert Newton (chemist, Nobel laureate); Weymouth, Mass. **(1875–1946)**
Lewis, Jerry (Joseph Levitch) (comedian, film director); Newark, N.J., 3/16/26
Lewis, Jerry Lee (singer); Ferriday, La., 9/29/35
Lewis, John Llewellyn (labor leader); Lucas, Iowa **(1880–1969)**
Lewis, Juliette (actress); Los Angeles, 12/21/73
Lewis, Meriwether (explorer); Albemarle Co., Va. **(1774–1809)**
Lewis, (Percy) Wyndham (artist, writer); Bay of Fundy, Maine (at sea) **(1884–1957)**
Lewis, Shari (Shari Hurwitz) (puppeteer); New York City **(1934–1998)**
Lewis, Sinclair (novelist); Sauk Centre, Minn. **(1885–1951)**
Ley, Willy (science writer); Berlin **(1906–1969)**
Liberace (Wladziu Liberace) (pianist); West Allis, Wis. **(1919–1987)**
Lichtenstein, Roy (painter); New York City **(1923–1997)**
Lie, Trygve Halvdan (first U.N. secretary-general); Oslo **(1896–1968)**
Light, Judith (actress); Trenton, N.J., 2/9/49
Lightfoot, Gordon (singer, songwriter); Orillia, Ont., Canada, 11/17/38
Limbaugh, Rush (political commentator); Cape Girardeau, Mo., 1/12/51
Lin, Maya (architect, sculptor); Athens, Ohio, 10/5/59
Lin Yutang (author); Changchow, China **(1895–1976)**
Lincoln, Abraham (16th U.S. president); Hardin (Larue) County, Ky. **(1809–1865)**
Lind, Jenny (Johanna Maria Lind) (soprano); Stockholm **(1820–1887)**
Lindbergh, Anne Morrow (author); Englewood, N.J. **(1906–2001)**
Lindbergh, Charles A. (aviator); Detroit **(1902–1974)**
Linden, Hal (Harold Lipshitz) (actor); New York City, 3/20/31
Lindsay, Howard (playwright); Waterford, N.Y. **(1889–1968)**
Linkletter, Art (radio-TV personality); Moose Jaw, Sask., Canada, 7/17/12
Linnaeus, Carolus (Carl von Linné) (botanist); Råshult, Sweden **(1707–1778)**
Linney, Laura (actress); New York City, 2/5/64
Liotta, Ray (actor); Union, N.J., 12/18/55
Lipchitz, Jacques (sculptor); Druskieniki, Latvia **(1891–1973)**
Lippi, Fra Filippo (painter); Florence **(1406–1469)**
Lippmann, Walter (columnist, author, political analyst); New York City **(1889–1974)**
Lister, Joseph (1st Baron of Lyme Regis) (surgeon); Upton, England **(1827–1912)**
Liszt, Franz (composer, pianist); Raiding, Hungary **(1811–1886)**
Lithgow, John (actor); Rochester, N.Y., 6/6/45
Little, Rich (impressionist); Ottawa, Ont., Canada, 11/26/38
Livingstone, David (missionary, explorer); Lanarkshire, Scotland **(1813–1873)**
L. L. Cool J (James Todd Smith) (rap artist); New York City, 1/14/68
Llewellyn, Richard (novelist); St. David's, Wales **(1906–1983)**
Lloyd Webber, Andrew (composer); London, 3/22/48
Lloyd George, David (Earl of Dwyfor) (statesman); Manchester, England **(1863–1945)**
Lloyd, Jake (actor); Fort Collins, Colo., 3/5/89
Locke, Alain L. (philosopher); Philadelphia **(1886–1954)**
Locke, John (philosopher); Somersetshire, England **(1632–1704)**
Lockhart, June (actress); New York City, 6/25/25
Locklear, Heather (actress); Los Angeles, 9/25/61
Lodge, Henry Cabot (legislator); Boston **(1850–1924)**
Lodge, Henry Cabot, Jr. (diplomat); Nahant, Mass. **(1902–1985)**
Loesser, Frank (composer); New York City **(1910–1969)**
Loewe, Frederick (composer); Vienna **(1901–1988)**
Logan, Joshua (director, producer); Texarkana, Tex. **(1908–1988)**
Lollobrigida, Gina (Luigina Lollobrigida) (actress); Subiaco, Italy, 7/4/27
Lombard, Carole (Jane Alice Peters) (actress); Ft. Wayne, Ind. **(1908–1942)**
Lombardo, Guy (band leader); London, Ont., Canada **(1902–1977)**
London, George (baritone); Montreal **(1920–1985)**
London, Jack (John Griffith London) (novelist); San Francisco **(1876–1916)**
Long, Huey Pierce (politician); Winnfield, La. **(1893–1935)**
Long, Shelley (actress); Fort Wayne, Ind., 8/23/49

Longfellow, Henry Wadsworth (poet); Portland, Maine **(1807–1882)**
Longworth, Alice Roosevelt (social figure); New York City **(1884–1980)**
Loos, Anita (novelist); Sissons, Calif. **(1888–1981)**
Lopez, Jennifer (actress, singer); Bronx, N.Y., 7/24/70
Lopez, Trini (singer); Dallas, 5/15/37
Lopez, Vincent (band leader); Brooklyn, N.Y. **(1895–1975)**
Lord, Jack (John Joseph Ryan) (actor); New York City **(1920–1998)**
Loren, Sophia (Sofia Scicolone) (actress); Rome, 9/20/34
Lorenz, Konrad (ethologist); Vienna **(1903–1989)**
Lorre, Peter (Laszlo Löewenstein) (actor); Rosenberg, former Czechoslovakia **(1904–1964)**
Loudon, Dorothy (actress, singer); Boston, 9/17/33
Louis-Dreyfus, Julia (actress); New York City, 1/13/61
Louis XIV (King of France); St.-Germain-en-Laye, France **(1638–1715)**
Louise, Tina (actress); New York City, 2/11/37
Love, Susan (surgeon, oncologist, activist); Long Branch, N.J., 2/9/48
Lovecraft, Howard Phillips (author); Providence, R.I. **(1890–1937)**
Lovett, Lyle (country singer, songwriter); Klein, Tex., 11/1/56
Lowe, Rob (actor); Charlottesville, Va., 3/17/64
Lowell, Amy (poet); Brookline, Mass. **(1874–1925)**
Lowell, James Russell (poet); Cambridge, Mass. **(1819–1891)**
Lowell, Robert (poet); Boston **(1917–1977)**
Loy, Myrna (Myrna Williams) (actress); nr. Helena, Mont. **(1905–1993)**
Loyola, St. Ignatius of (Iñigo de Oñez y Loyola) (founder of Jesuits); Gúipuzcoa Province, Spain **(1491– 1556)**
Lubitsch, Ernst (film director); Berlin **(1892–1947)**
Lucas, George (film director); Modesto, Calif., 5/14/44
Lucci, Susan (actress); Scarsdale, N.Y., 12/23/46
Luce, Clare Boothe (playwright, former ambassador); New York City **(1903–1987)**
Luce, Henry Robinson (editor, publisher); Tengchow, China **(1898–1967)**
Ludlum, Robert (author); New York City **(1927–2001)**
Lugosi, Béla (Béla Blasko) (actor); Lugos, Hungary **(1888–1956)**
Lukas, J. Anthony (author); New York City **(1933–1997)**
Lukas, Paul (actor); Budapest **(1895–1971)**
Lully, Jean Baptiste (French composer); Florence **(1639–1687)**
Lumet, Sidney (director); Philadelphia, 6/25/24
Lunden, Joan (TV host); Fair Oaks, Calif., 9/19/50
Lunt, Alfred (actor); Milwaukee **(1892–1977)**
Lupino, Ida (actress, director); London **(1918–1995)**
LuPone, Patti (actress, singer); Northport, N.Y., 4/21/49
Luther, Martin (religious reformer); Eisleben, East Germany **(1483–1546)**
Lynch, David (film director); Missoula, Mont., 1/20/46
Lynn, Loretta (singer); Butcher's Hollow, Ky., 4/14/35

M

Ma, Yo-Yo (cellist); Paris, 10/7/55
Maazel, Lorin (conductor); Neuilly, France, 3/5/30
MacArthur, Charles (playwright); Scranton, Pa. **(1895–1956)**
MacArthur, Douglas (five-star general); Little Rock Barracks, Ark. **(1880–1964)**
MacArthur, James (actor); Los Angeles, 12/8/37
Macaulay, Thomas Babington (author); Rothley Temple, England **(1800–1859)**
MacDermot, Galt (composer); Montreal, 12/19/28
MacDonald, James Ramsay (statesman); Lossiemouth, Scotland **(1866–1937)**
MacDonald, Jeanette (actress, soprano); Philadelphia **(1907–1965)**
Macdonald, Ross (Kenneth Millar) (mystery writer); Los Gatos, Calif. **(1915–1983)**
MacDowell, Edward Alexander (composer); New York City **(1861–1908)**
MacDowell, Andie (Rosalie Anderson MacDowell) (actress); Gaffney, S.C., 4/21/58
MacFadden, Bernarr (physical culturist); nr. Mill Spring, Mo. **(1868–1955)**
Machaut, Guillaume de (composer); Marchault, France **(1300–1377)**
Machiavelli, Niccolò (political philosopher); Florence, Italy **(1469–1527)**
Mackie, Bob (designer); Monterey Park, Calif., 3/24/40
MacLaine, Shirley (Shirley MacLean Beaty) (actress); Richmond, Va., 4/24/34
MacLeish, Archibald (poet); Glencoe, Ill. **(1892–1982)**
Macmillan, Harold (ex-prime minister); London **(1894–1986)**
MacMurray, Fred (actor); Kankakee, Ill. **(1908–1991)**
MacNeil, Cornell (baritone); Minneapolis, 9/24/22
MacNeil, Robert (TV newscaster); Montreal, 1/19/31
MacNicol, Peter (actor); Dallas, 4/10/54
Macpherson, Elle (Eleanor Gow) (model, actress); Sydney, Australia, 3/29/64
MacRae, Gordon (singer, actor); East Orange, N.J. **(1921–1986)**
MacRae, Sheila (comedienne); London, 9/24/24
Madison, James (4th U.S. president); Port Conway, Va. **(1751–1836)**
Madonna (Madonna Louise Ciccone) (singer, actress); Bay City, Mich., 8/16/58
Maeterlinck, Count Maurice (author); Ghent, Belgium **(1862–1949)**
Magellan, Ferdinand (Fernando de Magalhaes) (navigator); Sabrosa, Portugal **(c. 1480–1521)**
Magliozzi, Ray ("Car Talk" host); Cambridge, Mass., 3/30/49
Magliozzi, Tom ("Car Talk" host); Cambridge, Mass., 6/28/37
Magritte, René (painter); Belgium **(1898–1967)**
Magsaysay, Ramón (statesman); Iba, Luzon, Philippines **(1907–1957)**
Maguire, Tobey (actor); Santa Monica, Calif., 6/27/75
Mahan, Alfred Thayer (naval historian); West Point, N.Y. **(1840–1914)**
Mahler, Gustav (composer, conductor); Kalischt, Czechoslovakia **(1860–1911)**
Mahoney, John (actor); Manchester, England, 6/20/40
Mailer, Norman (novelist); Long Branch, N.J., 1/31/23
Maillol, Aristide (sculptor); Banyuls-sur-Mer, Rousillion, France **(1861–1944)**
Maimonides, Moses (Jewish philosopher); Cordoba, Spain **(1135–1204)**
Mainbocher (Main Rousseau Bocher) (fashion designer); Chicago **(1891–1976)**
Majors, Lee (Harvey Lee Yeary) (actor); Wyandotte, Mich., 4/23/40
Makarova, Natalia (ballet dancer); Leningrad (St. Petersburg), Russia, 11/21/40
Makeba, Miriam (singer); Johannesburg, South Africa, 3/4/32
Malamud, Bernard (novelist); Brooklyn, N.Y. **(1914–1986)**
Malcolm X (Malcolm Little; el Hajj Malik el-Shabazz) (Black nationalist, religious leader); Omaha, Neb. **(1925–1965)**
Malden, Karl (Karl Mladen Sekulovich) (actor); Chicago, 3/22/13
Malkovich, John (actor); Christopher, Ill., 12/9/53
Mallarmé, Stephane (poet, essayist); Paris **(1842–1898)**
Malle, Louis (director); Thumeries, France **(1932–1995)**
Malraux, André (author); Paris **(1901–1976)**
Malthus, Thomas Robert (economist); nr. Dorking, England **(1766–1834)**
Maltin, Leonard (film critic and historian); New York City, 12/18/50
Mamet, David (playwright); Chicago, 11/30/47
Manchester, Melissa (singer); Bronx, N.Y., 2/15/51
Manchester, William (writer); Attleboro, Mass., 4/1/22
Mancini, Henry (composer, conductor); Cleveland **(1924–1994)**
Mandela, Nelson (Rolihlahla) (former president of South Africa); Umtata, Transkei, 7/18/18
Mandela, Winnie (Nomzamo) (South African political activist); Pondoland district of the Transkei, 1936?
Mandrell, Barbara (singer); Houston, 12/25/48
Manet, Edouard (painter); Paris **(1832–1883)**
Mangione, Chuck (hornist, pianist, composer); Rochester, N.Y., 11/29/40
Manheim, Camryn (actress); New York City, 3/8/61
Manilow, Barry (singer); Brooklyn, N.Y., 6/17/46
Mankiewicz, Frank F. (columnist); New York City, 5/16/24
Mankiewicz, Joseph L. (film writer, director); Wilkes-Barre, Pa. **(1909–1993)**
Mann, Horace (educator); Franklin, Mass. **(1796–1859)**
Mann, Thomas (novelist); Lübeck, Germany **(1875–1955)**
Mannes, Marya (writer); New York City **(1904–1990)**
Mansfield, Jayne (Jayne Palmer) (actress); Bryn Mawr, Pa. **(1932–1967)**
Mansfield, Katherine (story writer); Wellington, New Zealand **(1888–1923)**
Manson, Marilyn (Brian Warner) (rock musician); Canton, Ohio, 1/5/69
Mantegna, Andrea (painter); Isola di Carturo, Italy **(1431–1506)**
Mantegna, Joe (actor); Chicago, 11/13/47
Mantovani, Annunzio (conductor); Venice **(1905–1980)**
Mao Zedong (Tse-tung) (Chinese leader); Shao Shan, China **(1893– 1976)**
Mapplethorpe, Robert (photographer); Floral Park, Queens, N.Y. **(1946–1989)**
Marat, Jean Paul (French revolutionist); Boudry, Neuchâtel, Switzerland **(1743–1793)**
Marceau, Marcel (mime); Strasbourg, France, 3/22/23

Marceau, Sophie (actress); Paris, 11/17/66
March, Fredric (Frederick Bickel) (actor); Racine, Wis. **(1897–1975)**
Marchand, Nancy (actress); Buffalo, N.Y. **(1928–2000)**
Marconi, Guglielmo (inventor); Bologna, Italy **(1874–1937)**
Marcus Aurelius (Marcus Annius Verus) (Roman emperor); Rome **(121–180)**
Marcus, Rudolph Arthur (chemist, Nobel laureate); Montreal, 7/21/23
Marcuse, Herbert (philosopher); Berlin **(1898–1979)**
Margaret Rose (princess of England); Glamis Castle, Angus, Scotland, 8/21/30
Margrethe II (queen of Denmark); Copenhagen, 4/16/40
Margulies, Julianna (actress); Spring Valley, N.Y., 6/8/65
Marie Antoinette (Josephe Jeanne Marie Antoinette) (queen of France); Vienna **(1755 –1793)**
Marisol (Escobar) (Venezuelan-American sculptor); Paris, 1930
Markham, Edwin (poet); Oregon City, Ore. **(1852–1940)**
Markova, Dame Alicia (Lilian Alice Marks) (ballet dancer); London, 12/1/10
Marley, Bob (singer, songwriter); Kingston, Jamaica **(1945–1981)**
Marlowe, Christopher (dramatist); Canterbury, England **(1564–1593)**
Marquand, J(ohn) P(hillips) (novelist); Wilmington, Del. **(1893–1960)**
Marquette, Jacques (missionary, explorer); Laon, France **(1637–1675)**
Marriner, Neville (conductor); Lincoln, England, 4/15/24
Marsalis, Wynton (musician); New Orleans, 10/18/61
Marshall, E.G. (actor); Owatonna, Minn. **(1910–1998)**
Marshall, Garry (director, producer, screenwriter, actor); New York City, 11/13/34
Marshall, George Catlett (general); Uniontown, Pa. **(1880–1959)**
Marshall, Herbert (actor); London **(1890–1968)**
Marshall, John (jurist); nr. Germantown, Va. **(1755–1835)**
Marshall, Penny (Penny Marscharelli) (actress, director, producer); Bronx, N.Y., 10/15/42
Marshall, Thurgood (U.S. Supreme Court justice); Baltimore **(1908–1993)**
Martin, Dean (Dino Crocetti) (singer, actor); Steubenville, Ohio **(1917–1995)**
Martin, Mary (singer, actress); Weatherford, Tex. **(1913–1990)**
Martin, Steve (actor, writer, producer); Waco, Tex., 8/14/45
Martin, Tony (Alvin Morris) (singer); San Francisco, 12/25/12
Martinelli, Giovanni (tenor); Montagnana, Italy **(1885–1969)**
Martins, Peter (dancer, choreographer); Copenhagen, 10/27/45
Marvell, Andrew (poet); Winestead, England **(1621–1678)**
Marvin, Lee (actor); New York City **(1924–1987)**
Marx, Chico (Leonard) (comedian); New York City **(1887–1961)**
Marx, Groucho (Julius) (comedian); New York City **(1890–1977)**
Marx, Harpo (Arthur) (comedian); New York City **(1893–1964)**
Marx, Karl (Socialist writer); Treves, Germany **(1818–1883)**
Marx, Zeppo (Herbert) (comedian); New York City **(1901–1979)**
Mary Stuart (Mary, Queen of Scots) (queen of Scotland); Linlithgow, Scotland **(1542–1587)**
Masaccio, (Tommaso di Giovanni di Simone Cassai) (painter); San Giovanni Valdarno, Tuscany **(1401–c. 1428)**
Masaryk, Jan Garrigue (statesman); Prague **(1886–1948)**
Masaryk, Thomas Garrigue (statesman); Hodonin, Czech Republic **(1850–1937)**
Masefield, John (poet); Ledbury, England **(1878–1967)**
Masekela, Hugh (trumpeter); Wilbank, South Africa, 4/4/39
Mason, Jackie (Jacob Moshe Maza) (comedian); Sheboygan, Wis., 6/9/31
Mason, James (actor); Huddersfield, England **(1909–1984)**
Mason, Marsha (actress); St. Louis, 4/3/42
Massenet, Jules Emile Frédéric (composer); Montaud, France **(1842–1912)**
Massine, Léonide (choreographer); Moscow **(1895–1979)**
Masters, Edgar Lee (poet); Garnett, Kans. **(1869–1950)**
Masters, William (human sexuality expert); Cleveland **(1915–2001)**
Masterson, Mary Stuart (actress, writer, director); New York City, 6/28/66
Mastroianni, Marcello (actor); Fontana Liri, Italy **(1924–1996)**
Mather, Cotton (clergyman); Boston **(1663–1728)**
Mathis, Johnny (singer); Gilmer, Texas, 9/30/35
Matisse, Henri (painter); Le Cateau, France **(1869–1954)**
Matthau, Walter (Walter Matuschanskayasky) (actor); New York City **(1920–2000)**
Mature, Victor (actor); Louisville, Ky. **(1915–1999)**
Maugham, W(illiam) Somerset (author); Paris **(1874–1965)**
Mauldin, Bill (political cartoonist); Mountain Park, N.M., 10/29/21
Maupassant, Henri René Albert Guy de (story writer); Normandy, France **(1850–1893)**
Maurois, André (Emile Herzog) (author); Elbauf, France **(1885–1967)**
Maximilian (Ferdinand Maximilian Joseph) (emperor of Mexico); Vienna **(1832–1867)**
Maxwell, James Clerk (physicist); Edinburgh, Scotland **(1831–1879)**
Maxwell, (Ian) Robert (publisher); Selo Slatina, Czechoslavakia **(1923–1991)**
May, Elaine (Elaine Berlin) (entertainer, writer); Philadelphia, 4/21/32
May, Rollo (psychologist); Ada, Ohio **(1909–1994)**
Mayer, Louis B. (movie executive); Minsk, Russia **(1885–1957)**
Mayo, Charles H. (surgeon); Rochester, Minn. **(1865–1939)**
Mayo, Charles W. (surgeon); Rochester, Minn. **(1898–1968)**
Mayo, Virginia (Jones) (actress); St. Louis, 11/30/20
Mayo, William J. (surgeon); Le Sueur, Minn. **(1861–1939)**
Mayron, Melanie (actress); Philadelphia, 10/20/52
Mazzini, Giuseppe (patriot); Genoa **(1805–1872)**
McBride, Patricia (ballet dancer); Teaneck, N.J., 8/23/42
McCallum, David (actor); Glasgow, Scotland, 9/19/33
McCambridge, Mercedes (actress); Joliet, Ill., 3/17/18
McCarthy, Eugene J. (ex-senator); Watkins, Minn., 3/29/16
McCarthy, Joseph Raymond (senator); Grand Chute, Wis. **(1908–1957)**
McCarthy, Mary (novelist); Seattle **(1912–1989)**
McCartney, Linda (photographer, singer); New York City **(1941–1998)**
McCartney, Paul (singer, songwriter); Liverpool, England, 6/18/42
McClanahan, Rue (actress); Healdton, Okla., 2/21/35
McClellan, George Brinton (general); Philadelphia **(1826–1885)**
McClintock, Barbara (geneticist, Nobel laureate) **(1902–1992)**
McCloy, John J. (lawyer, banker); Philadelphia **(1895–1989)**
McCormack, John (tenor); Athlone, Ireland **(1884–1945)**
McCormack, John W. (ex-Speaker of House); Boston **(1891–1980)**
McCormick, Cyrus Hall (inventor); Rockbridge County, Va. **(1809–1884)**
McCourt, Frank (writer); Brooklyn, N.Y., 8/19/30
McCracken, James (dramatic tenor); Gary, Ind. **(1926–1988)**
McCrea, Joel (actor); Los Angeles **(1905–1990)**
McCullers, Carson (novelist); Columbus, Ga. **(1917–1967)**
McCullough, David (author, historian); Pittsburgh, 7/7/33
McDermott, Dylan (actor); Waterbury, Conn., 10/26/62
McDormand, Frances (actress); Illinois, 6/23/57
McDowall, Roddy (actor); London **(1928–1998)**
McDowell, Malcolm (actor); Leeds, England, 6/15/43
McFadden, Gates (actress); Cuyahoga Falls, Ohio, 3/2/49
McGavin, Darren (actor); San Joaquin, Calif., 5/7/22
McGillis, Kelly (actress); Newport Beach, Calif., 7/9/57
McGinley, Phyllis (poet, writer); Ontario, Ore. **(1905–1978)**
McGoohan, Patrick (actor); Astoria, Queens, N.Y., 3/19/28
McGovern, Elizabeth (actress); Evanston, Ill., 7/18/61
McGovern, Maureen (singer); Youngstown, Ohio, 7/27/49
McGregor, Ewan (actor); Crieff, Scotland, 3/31/71
McKellen, Ian (actor); Burnley, England, 5/25/39
McKinley, William (25th U.S. president); Niles, Ohio **(1843–1901)**
McKuen, Rod (singer, composer); Oakland, Calif., 4/29/33
McLachlan, Sarah (singer, songwriter); Halifax, N.S., 1/28/68
McLaughlin, John (guitarist); Yorkshire, England, 1/4/42
McLean, Don (singer, songwriter); New Rochelle, N.Y., 10/2/45
McLuhan, Marshall (Herbert Marshall) (communications writer); Edmonton, Alta., Canada **(1911–1980)**
McMahon, Ed (TV personality); Detroit, 3/6/23
McMurtry, Larry (novelist); Wichita Falls, Tex., 6/3/36
McQueen, Butterfly (Thelma) (actress); Tampa, Fla. **(1911–1995)**
McQueen, Steve (Terence Stephen McQueen) (actor); Beech Grove, Indiana **(1930–1980)**
McRaney, Gerald (actor); Collins, Miss., 8/19/47
McTeer, Janet (actress); York, England, 1962
Mead, Margaret (anthropologist); Philadelphia **(1901–1978)**
Meadows, Audrey (actress); Wu Chang, China **(1924–1996)**
Meadows, Jayne (actress); Wu Chang, China, 9/27/26
Meaney, Colm (actor); Dublin, 5/30/53
Meany, George (labor leader); New York City **(1894–1980)**
Meara, Anne (actress); New York City, 9/20/29
Medici, Lorenzo de' (called Lorenzo the Magnificent) (Florentine ruler); Florence, Italy **(1449–1492)**
Mehta, Zubin (conductor); Bombay (Mumbai), 4/29/36
Meir, Golda (Golda Myerson, nee Mabovitz) (ex-premier of Israel); Kiev, Ukraine **(1898–1978)**
Melba, Dame Nellie (Helen Porter Mitchell) (soprano); nr. Melbourne, Australia **(1861–1931)**
Melchior, Lauritz (Lebrecht Hommel) (heroic tenor); Copenhagen **(1890–1973)**

Mellon, Andrew William (financier); Pittsburgh **(1855–1937)**
Melville, Herman (novelist); New York City **(1819–1891)**
Mencken, Henry Louis (writer); Baltimore **(1880–1956)**
Mendel, Gregor Johann (geneticist); Heinzendorf, Austrian Silesia **(1822–1884)**
Mendeleyev, Dmitri Ivanovich (chemist); Tobolsk, Russia **(1834–1907)**
Mendelssohn-Bartholdy, Jakob Ludwig Felix (composer); Hamburg **(1809–1847)**
Mendès-France, Pierre (ex-Premier); Paris **(1905–1982)**
Mengele, Josef (Nazi, "Angel of Death"); Günzberg, Germany **(1911–1979)**
Mennin, Peter (Peter Mennini) (composer); Erie, Pa. **(1923–1983)**
Menninger, William C. (psychiatrist); Topeka, Kans. **(1899–1966)**
Menotti, Gian Carlo (composer); Cadegliano, Italy, 7/7/11
Menuhin, Yehudi (violinist, conductor); New York City **(1916–1999)**
Menzies, Robert Gordon (ex-prime minister); Jeparit, Australia **(1894–1978)**
Mercer, Johnny (songwriter); Savannah, Ga. **(1909–1976)**
Mercer, Mabel (singer); Burton-on-Trent, England **(1900–1984)**
Merchant, Ismail (Ismail Noormohamed Abdul Rehman) (film producer); Bombay (Mumbai), 12/25/36
Merchant, Natalie (singer, songwriter); Jamestown, N.Y., 10/26/63
Mercury, Freddie (Farookh Bulsara) (musician, singer); Zanzibar **(1946–1991)**
Meredith, Burgess (actor); Cleveland **(1908–1997)**
Meredith, James (author, civil-rights leader); Kosciusko, Miss., 6/26/23
Merman, Ethel (Ethel Zimmerman) (singer, actress); Astoria, Queens, N.Y. **(1909–1984)**
Merrick, David (David Margulois) (stage producer); St. Louis **(1912–2000)**
Merton, Thomas (clergyman, writer); France **(1915–1968)**
Mesmer, Franz Anton (physician); Itzmang, nr. Constance, Germany **(1733–1815)**
Mesta, Perle (social figure); Sturgis, Mich. **(1889–1975)**
Metacom, (King Philip) (Wampanoag Indian sachem); southeastern Mass. **(1640–1676)**
Metternich, Prince Klemens Wenzel Nepomuk Lothar von (statesman); Coblenz, Germany **(1773–1859)**
Mfume, Kweisi (Frizzell Gray) (politician, NAACP leader); Baltimore, 10/24/48
Michaels, Lorne (producer); Toronto, 11/17/44
Michelangelo Buonarroti (painter, sculptor, architect); Caprese, Italy **(1475–1564)**
Michener, James A. (novelist); New York City **(1907–1997)**
Mickiewicz, Adam (Polish poet); Zozie, Belorussia (Belarus) **(1798–1855)**
Midler, Bette (singer, actress, producer); Honolulu, 12/1/45
Mielziner, Jo (stage designer); Paris **(1901–1976)**
Mifune, Toshiro (actor, film producer); Tsingtao, China **(1920–1997)**
Mies van der Rohe, Ludwig (architect, designer); Aachen, Germany **(1886–1969)**
Mikoyan, Anastas I. (diplomat); Sanain, Armenia **(1895–1978)**
Milano, Alyssa (actress); Brooklyn, New York, 12/19/72
Milhaud, Darius (composer); Aix-en-Provence, France **(1892–1974)**
Mill, John Stuart (philosopher); London **(1806–1873)**
Milland, Ray (Reginald Truscott-Jones) (actor); Neath, Wales **(1907–1986)**
Millay, Edna St. Vincent (poet); Rockland, Maine **(1892–1950)**
Miller, Ann (Lucille Ann Collier) (dancer, actress); Cherino, Tex., 4/12/23
Miller, Arthur (playwright); New York City, 10/17/15
Miller, Glenn (band leader); Clarinda, Iowa **(1904–1944)**
Miller, Henry (novelist); New York City **(1891–1980)**
Miller, Jason (John Miller) (playwright, actor); New York City **(1939–2001)**
Miller, Mitch (Mitchell) (musician); Rochester, N.Y., 7/4/11
Miller, Roger (singer); Fort Worth **(1936–1992)**
Millet, Jean François (painter); Gruchy, France **(1814–1875)**
Millett, Kate (feminist, writer); St. Paul, Minn., 9/14/34
Millikan, Robert A. (physicist); Morrison, Ill. **(1869–1953)**
Mills, Donna (actress); Chicago, 12/11/41
Mills, Hayley (actress); London, 4/18/46
Mills, Juliet (actress); London, 11/21/41
Milne, A(lan) A(lexander) (author); London **(1882–1956)**
Milner, Martin (actor); Detroit, 12/28/31
Milnes, Sherrill (baritone); Downers Grove, Ill., 1/10/35
Milosevic, Slobodan (Yugoslav President); Pozarevac, Serbia, 8/29/41
Milstein, Nathan (concert violinist); Odessa, Ukraine **(1904–1992)**
Milton, John (poet); London **(1608–1674)**
Mingus, Charles (jazz composer); Nogales, Ariz. **(1922–1979)**
Minnelli, Liza (singer, actress); Hollywood, Calif., 3/12/46
Minnelli, Vincente (film director); Chicago **(1913–1986)**
Minuit, Peter (Governor of New Amsterdam); Wesel, Germany **(1580–1638)**
Miranda, Carmen (Maria do Carmo da Cunha) (singer, dancer); Lisbon **(1909–1955)**
Miró, Joan (painter); Barcelona **(1893–1983)**
Mirren, Helen (Ilynea Lydia Mironoff) (actress); London, 7/26/45
Mitchell, John N. (former Attorney General); Detroit **(1913–1988)**
Mitchell, Joni (Roberta Joan Anderson) (singer, songwriter); Ft. Macleod, Alb., Canada, 11/7/43
Mitchell, Margaret (novelist); Atlanta **(1900–1949)**
Mitchell, Maria (astronomer); Nantucket, Mass. **(1818–1889)**
Mitchum, Robert (actor); Bridgeport, Conn. **(1917–1997)**
Mitropoulos, Dimitri (orchestra conductor); Athens **(1896–1960)**
Mitterand, François (Maurice) (ex-prime minister of France); Jarnac, France **(1916–1996)**
Mix, Tom (actor); Mix Run, Pa. **(1880–1940)**
Mobutu Sese Seko (Zairean dictator); Lisala, Congo **(1930–1997)**
Modigliani, Amedeo (painter); Leghorn, Italy **(1884–1920)**
Moffo, Anna (soprano); Wayne, Pa., 6/27/34
Mohammed (prophet); Mecca, Saudi Arabia **(570–632)**
Molière (Jean Baptiste Poquelin) (dramatist); Paris **(1622–1673)**
Molina, Mario (chemist, Nobel laureate); Mexico City, 3/19/43
Moll, Richard (actor); Pasadena, Calif., 1/13/43?
Molnar, Ferenc (dramatist); Budapest **(1878–1952)**
Molotov, Vyacheslav M. (V. M. Skryabin) (diplomat); Kukarka, Russia **(1890–1986)**
Mondrian, Piet (painter); Amersfoort, Netherlands **(1872–1944)**
Monet, Claude (painter); Paris **(1840–1926)**
Monica Monica Arnold (singer); Atlanta, Ga., 10/24/80
Monk, Meredith (choreographer, composer, performing artist); Lima, Peru, 11/20/42
Monk, Thelonious (pianist); Rocky Mount, N.C. **(1918–1982)**
Monroe, James (5th U.S. president); Westmoreland County, Va. **(1758–1831)**
Monroe, Marilyn (Norma Jean Mortenson or Baker) (actress); Los Angeles **(1926–1962)**
Monsarrat, Nicholas (novelist); Liverpool, England **(1910–1979)**
Montaigne, Michel Eyquem de (essayist); nr. Bordeaux, France **(1533–1592)**
Montalban, Ricardo (actor); Mexico City, 11/25/20
Montand, Yves (Ivo Livi) (actor, singer); Florence, Italy **(1921–1991)**
Montesquieu, Charles-Louis de Secondat, baron de La Brède and de (philosopher); nr. Bordeaux, France **(1689–1755)**
Montessori, Maria (physician, educator); Chiaravalle, Italy **(1870–1952)**
Monteux, Pierre (conductor); Paris **(1875–1964)**
Monteverdi, Claudio (composer); Cremona Italy **(1567–1643)**
Montezuma II (Aztec emperor); Mexico **(1466–1520)**
Montgomery, Elizabeth (actress); Hollywood, Calif. **(1933–1995)**
Montgomery, Robert (Henry, Jr.) (actor); Beacon, N.Y. **(1904–1981)**
Montgomery of Alamein, 1st Viscount of Hindhead (Sir Bernard Law Montgomery) (military leader); London **(1887–1976)**
Montoya, Carlos (guitarist); Madrid **(1903–1993)**
Moore, Clayton (Jack Moore) (actor); Chicago **(1914–1999)**
Moore, Clement Clarke (author); New York City **(1779–1863)**
Moore, Demi (Demi Guynes) (actress); Roswell, N.M., 11/11/62
Moore, Dudley (actor, writer, musician); Dagenham, England **(1935–2002)**
Moore, Grace (soprano); Jellico, Tenn. **(1901–1947)**
Moore, Henry (sculptor); Castleford, England **(1898–1986)**
Moore, Julianne (actress); Fayetteville, N.C., 12/3/60
Moore, Marianne (poet); Kirkwood, Mo. **(1887–1972)**
Moore, Mary Tyler (actress); Brooklyn, N.Y., 12/29/36
Moore, Melba (Beatrice) (singer, actress); New York City, 10/27/45
Moore, Roger (actor); London, 10/14/27
Moore, Thomas (poet); Dublin **(1779–1852)**
Moorehead, Agnes (actress); Clinton, Mass. **(1906–1974)**
Moranis, Rick (actor); Toronto, 4/18/53
More, Henry (philosopher); Grantham, England **(1614–1687)**
More, Sir Thomas (statesman, author); London **(1478–1535)**
Moreno, Rita (Rosita Dolores Alverio) (actress); Humacao, P.R., 12/11/31
Morgan, Harry (Harry Bratsburg) (actor); Detroit, 4/10/15
Morgan, John Pierpont (financier); Hartford, Conn. **(1837–1913)**
Moriarty, Michael (actor); Detroit, 4/5/41
Morini, Erica (concert violinist); Vienna **(1904–1995)**
Morison, Samuel Eliot (historian); Boston **(1887–1976)**
Morita, Pat (Noriyuki Morita) (actor); Berkeley, Calif., 8/28/32
Morley, Christopher Darlington (novelist); Haverford, Pa. **(1890–1957)**
Morley, Robert (actor); Semley, England **(1908–1992)**

Morris, Mark (choreographer); Seattle, 8/29/56
Morris, William (poet, craftsman); Walthamstow, England **(1834–1896)**
Morrison, Jim (James Douglas Morrison) (singer, songwriter); Melbourne, Fla. **(1943–1971)**
Morrison, Toni (Chloe Anthony Wofford) (novelist); Lorain, Ohio, 2/18/31
Morrison, Van (singer); Belfast, Northern Ireland, 8/31/45
Morse, Marston (mathematician); Waterville, Maine **(1892–1977)**
Morse, Samuel Finley Breese (painter, inventor); Charlestown, Mass. **(1791–1872)**
Morton, Jelly Roll (Ferdinand Joseph La Menthe) (jazz composer); New Orleans **(1890–1941)**
Moseley-Braun, Carol (U.S. Senator); Chicago, 8/16/47
Moses, Grandma (Mrs. Anna Mary Robertson Moses) (painter); Greenwich, N.Y. **(1860–1961)**
Moses, Robert (urban planner); New Haven, Conn. **(1888–1981)**
Moss, Kate (model); London, England, 1/16/74
Mostel, Zero (Samuel Joel Mostel) (actor); Brooklyn, N.Y. **(1915–1977)**
Mother Teresa (Agnes Gonxha Bojaxhiu) (nun); Skopje, Macedonia **(1910–1997)**
Motherwell, Robert (artist, "action" painter); Aberdeen, Wash. **(1915–1991)**
Mott, Lucretia (Coffin) (feminist, reformer, abolitionist); Nantucket, Mass. **(1793–1880)**
Moussorgsky, Modest Petrovich (composer); Karev, Russia **(1839–1881)**
Moyers, Bill D. (Billy Don) (journalist); Hugo, Okla., 6/5/34
Moynihan, Daniel Patrick (New York senator); Tulsa, Okla. **(1927–2003)**
Mozart, Wolfgang Amadeus (Johannes Chrysostomus Wolfgangus Theophilus Mozart) (composer); Salzburg, Austria **(1756–1791)**
Mudd, Roger (TV newscaster); Washington, D.C., 2/9/28
Muggeridge, Malcolm (Thomas) (writer); Croydon, England **(1903–1990)**
Muhammad (founder of Islam); Mecca, Saudi Arabia **(c. 570–632)**
Muhammad, Elijah (Elijah Poole) (religious leader); Sandersville, Ga. **(1897–1975)**
Mulgrew, Kate (actress); Dubuque, Iowa, 4/29/55
Mulhare, Edward (actor); Ireland **(1923–1997)**
Mulliken, Robert Sanderson (chemist, Nobel laureate); Newburyport, Mass. **(1896–1986)**
Mulroney, Dermot (actor, musician, producer); Alexandria, Va., 10/31/63
Mumford, Lewis (cultural historian, city planner); Flushing, Queens, N.Y. **(1895–1990)**
Munch, Edvard (painter); Löten, Norway **(1863–1944)**
Munchhausen, Karl Friedrick Hieronymus, baron von (anecdotist); Hannover, Germany **(1720–1797)**
Muni, Paul (Muni Weisenfreund) (actor); Lemburg, Austria **(1895–1967)**
Muñoz Marin, Luis (ex-governor of Puerto Rico); San Juan, P.R. **(1898–1980)**
Munsel, Patrice (soprano); Spokane, Wash., 5/14/25
Murdoch, Iris (novelist); Dublin **(1919–1999)**
Murdoch, Rupert (publisher); Melbourne, Australia, 3/11/31
Murillo, Bartolomé Esteban (painter); Seville, Spain **(1617–1682)**
Murphy, Audie (actor, war hero); Kingston, Tex. **(1924–1971)**
Murphy, Eddie (actor, comedian); Brooklyn, N.Y., 4/3/61
Murphy, George (actor, dancer, ex-senator); New Haven, Conn. **(1902–1992)**
Murray, Arthur (dance teacher); New York City **(1895–1991)**
Murray, Bill (actor, comedian); Wilmette, Ill., 9/21/50
Murray, Kathryn (dance teacher); Jersey City, N.J. **(1906–1999)**
Murrow, Edward R. (commentator, government official); Greensboro, N.C. **(1908–1965)**
Musil, Robert (novelist); Klagenfurt, Austria **(1880–1942)**
Muskie, Edmund (political figure); Rumford, Maine **(1914–1996)**
Mussolini, Benito (Italian dictator); Dovia, Forli, Italy **(1883–1945)**
Muti, Riccardo (orchestra conductor); Naples, Italy, 7/28/41
Mutter, Anne-Sophie (violinist); Rheinfelden, Germany, 6/29/63
Myers, Mike (actor, writer, comedian); Scarborough, Ont., Canada, 5/25/63
Myerson, Bess (consumer advocate); Bronx, N.Y., 7/16/24
Myrdal, Gunnar (sociologist, economist); Gustaf Parish, Sweden **(1898–1987)**

N

Nabokov, Vladimir (novelist); St. Petersburg, Russia **(1899–1977)**
Nabors, Jim (actor, singer); Sylacauga, Ala., 6/12/32
Nader, Ralph (consumer advocate); Winsted, Conn., 2/27/34
Nair, Mira (director, screenwriter); Bhubaneswar, India, 10/15/57
Nash, Graham (singer); Blackpool, England, 1942
Nash, Ogden (poet); Rye, N.Y. **(1902–1971)**
Nasser, Gamal Abdel (statesman); Beni Mor, Egypt **(1918–1970)**
Nast, Thomas (cartoonist); Landau, Germany **(1840–1902)**
Nation, Carry Amelia (temperance leader); Garrard County, Ky. **(1846–1911)**
Natta, Giulio (chemist, Nobel laureate); Imperia, Italy **(1903–1979)**
Natwick, Mildred (actress); Baltimore **(1905–1994)**
Neagle, Anna (Marjorie Robertson) (actress); London **(1908–1986)**
Neal, Patricia (actress); Packard, Ky., 1/20/26
Neeson, Liam (William John) (actor); Ballymena, Northern Ireland, 6/7/52
Negri, Pola (Apolina Mathias-Chalupec) (actress); Bromberg, Poland **(1899–1987)**
Nehru, Jawaharlal (first prime minister of India); Allahabad, India **(1889–1964)**
Neill, Sam (Nigel Neill) (actor); Omagh, Northern Ireland, 9/14/47
Nelligan, Kate (actress); London, Ont., Canada, 3/16/51
Nelson, Barry (Robert Haakon Nielsen) (actor); San Francisco, 4/16/20
Nelson, David (actor); New York City, 10/24/36
Nelson, Harriet Hilliard (Peggy Lou Snyder) (actress); Des Moines, Iowa **(1909–1994)**
Nelson, Ozzie (Oswald) (actor); Jersey City, N.J. **(1907–1975)**
Nelson, Ricky (Eric) (singer, actor); Teaneck, N.J. **(1940–1985)**
Nelson, Viscount Horatio (naval officer); Burnham Thorpe, England **(1758–1805)**
Nelson, Willie (singer); Waco, Tex., 4/30/33
Nenni, Pietro (Socialist leader); Faenza, Italy **(1891–1980)**
Nero (Nero Claudius Caesar Drusus Germanicus) (Roman emperor); Antium, Italy **(37–68)**
Nero, Peter (pianist); New York City, 5/22/34
Netanyahu, Benjamin (Binyamin) (former Israeli prime minister); Tel Aviv, Israel, 10/21/49
Neuwirth, Bebe (Beatrice Neuwirth) (actress); Newark, N.J., 12/31/58
Nevelson, Louise (sculptor); Kiev, Russia **(1899–1988)**
Neville, Aaron (singer); New Orleans, 1/24/41
Newhart, Bob (actor); Chicago, 9/5/29
Newhouse, Samuel I. (publisher); New York City **(1895–1979)**
Newley, Anthony (actor, songwriter); London **(1931–1999)**
Newman, Edwin (news commentator); New York City, 1/25/19
Newman, John Henry (prelate); London **(1801–1890)**
Newman, Paul (actor, director); Cleveland, 1/26/25
Newman, Randy (singer); Los Angeles, 11/28/43
Newton, Huey (black activist); New Orleans **(1942–1989)**
Newton, Sir Isaac (mathematician, scientist); nr. Grantham, England **(1642–1727)**
Newton, Wayne (singer); Norfolk, Va., 4/3/42
Newton-John, Olivia (singer); Cambridge, England, 9/26/48
Nichols, Nichelle (actress); Robbins, Ill., 12/28/33
Nichols, Mike (Michael Peschkowsky) (stage and film director); Berlin, 11/6/31
Nicholson, Jack (actor, director, writer); Neptune, N.J., 4/22/37
Nicks, Stevie (Stephanie Lynn Nicks) (singer, songwriter); Phoenix, Ariz., 5/26/48
Nielsen, Leslie (actor); Regina, Sask., Canada, 2/11/26
Nietzsche, Friedrich Wilhelm (philosopher); nr. Lützen, Saxony, Germany **(1844–1900)**
Nightingale, Florence (nurse); Florence, Italy **(1820–1910)**
Nijinsky, Vaslav (ballet dancer); Warsaw **(1890–1950)**
Nilsson, Birgit (soprano); West Karup, Sweden, 5/17/23
Nilsson, Harry (singer, songwriter); Brooklyn, N.Y. **(1941–1994)**
Nimitz, Chester W. (naval officer); Fredericksburg, Tex. **(1885–1966)**
Nimoy, Leonard (actor, director, writer, producer); Boston, 3/26/31
Nin, Anais (author, diarist); Neuilly, France **(1903–1977)**
Niven, David (actor); Kirriemuir, Scotland **(1910–1983)**
Nixon, Richard Milhous (37th U.S. president); Yorba Linda, Calif. **(1913–1994)**
Nizer, Louis (lawyer, author); London **(1902–1994)**
Nobel, Alfred Bernhard (industrialist); Stockholm **(1833–1896)**
Noguchi, Isamu (sculptor); Los Angeles **(1904–1988)**
Nolan, Lloyd (actor); San Francisco **(1902–1985)**
Nolte, Nick (actor); Omaha, Neb., 2/8/40
Norell, Norman (Norman Levinson) (fashion designer); Noblesville, Ind. **(1900–1972)**
Norman, Jessye (soprano); Augusta, Ga., 9/15/45
Norman, Marsha (Marsha Williams) (playwright); Louisville, Ky., 9/21/47
Normand, Mabel (actress); Boston **(1894–1930)**

Norris, Chuck (Carlos Ray Norris) (actor, athlete); Ryan, Oklahoma, 3/10/40
Norstad, Gen. Lauris (ex-commander of NATO forces); Minneapolis **(1907–1988)**
North, John Ringling (circus director); Baraboo, Wis. **(1903–1985)**
North, Oliver (ex-military officer); San Antonio, 10/7/43
North, Sheree (actress); Los Angeles, 1/17/33
Norton, Edward (actor); Columbia, Md., 8/18/69
Norton, Eleanor Holmes (New York City government official, lawyer); Washington, D.C., 6/13/37
Nostradamus (Michel de Notredame) (astrologer); St. Rémy, France **(1503–1566)**
Novaes, Guiomar (pianist); São João de Boa Vista, Brazil **(1895–1979)**
Novak, Kim (Marilyn Novak) (actress); Chicago, 2/13/33
Novarro, Ramon (Ramon Samaniegoes) (actor); Durango, Mexico **(1899–1968)**
Novello, Ivor (actor, playwright, composer); Cardiff, Wales **(1893–1951)**
Nugent, Elliott (actor, director); Dover, Ohio **(1899–1980)**
Nureyev, Rudolf (ballet dancer); Siberia **(1938–1993)**
Nyro, Laura (singer, songwriter); Bronx, N.Y. **(1947–1997)**

O

Oakie, Jack (actor); Sedalia, Mo. **(1903–1978)**
Oakley, Annie (Phoebe Anne Oakley Mozee) (markswoman); Darke County, Ohio **(1860–1926)**
Oates, Joyce Carol (novelist); Lockport, N.Y., 6/16/38
Oberon, Merle (Estelle Merle O'Brien Thompson) (actress); Bombay, India **(1911–1979)**
Oberth, Hermann (rocketry and space flight pioneer); Nagyszeben, Austria-Hungary (Sibiu, Romania) **(1894–1989)**
O'Brian, Hugh (Hugh J. Krampe) (actor); Rochester, N.Y., 4/19/25
O'Brien, Conan (TV personality); Brookline, Mass., 4/18/63
O'Brien, Edmond (actor); New York City **(1915–1985)**
O'Brien, Margaret (Angela Maxine O'Brien) (actress); San Diego, Calif., 1/15/37
O'Brien, Pat (William Joseph O'Brien, Jr.) (actor); Milwaukee **(1899–1983)**
O'Brien, Tim (novelist); Austin, Minn., 10/1/46
Obuchi, Keizo (former prime minister of Japan); Nakanojo, Japan **(1937–2000)**
O'Casey, Sean (playwright); Dublin **(1881–1964)**
Ochs, Adolph Simon (publisher); Cincinnati **(1858–1935)**
O'Connor, Carroll (actor); New York City **(1924–2001)**
Odets, Clifford (playwright); Philadelphia **(1906–1963)**
Odetta (Odetta Holmes) (folk singer, actress); Birmingham, Ala., 12/31/30
O'Donnell, Chris (actor); Winnetka, Ill., 6/26/70
O'Donnell, Rosie (actress, talk show host); Commack, N.Y., 3/21/62
Offenbach, Jacques (composer); Cologne, Germany **(1819–1880)**
O'Hara, John (novelist); Pottsville, Pa. **(1905–1970)**
O'Hara, Maureen (Maureen FitzSimons) (actress); Dublin, 8/17/20
Ohlsson, Garrick (pianist); Bronxville, N.Y., 4/3/48
Oistrakh, David (concert violinist); Odessa, Russia **(1908–1974)**
O'Keeffe, Georgia (painter); Sun Prairie, Wis. **(1887–1986)**
Oland, Warner (actor); Umea, Sweden **(1880–1938)**
Oldenburg, Claes (painter); Stockholm, 1/28/29
Oldman, Gary (actor, director); London, 3/21/58
Olin, Lena (actress); Stockholm, 3/22/55
Oliphant, Patrick B. (editorial cartoonist); Adelaide, Australia, 7/24/35
Olivier, Sir Laurence (actor); Dorking, England **(1907–1989)**
Olmos, Edward James (actor); East Los Angeles, 2/24/47
Olmsted, Frederick Law (landscape architect); Hartford, Conn. **(1822–1903)**
Olsen, Ole (John Sigvard Olsen) (comedian); Peru, Ind. **(1892–1963)**
Omar Khayyam (poet, astronomer); Nishapur, Iran (died c. 1123)
Onassis, Aristotle (shipping executive); Smyrna, Turkey **(1906–1975)**
Onassis, Christina (shipping executive); New York City **(1950–1988)**
Onassis, Jacqueline Kennedy (Jacqueline Bouvier) (first lady); Southampton, N.Y. **(1929–1994)**
O'Neal, Ryan (Patrick) (actor); Los Angeles, 4/20/41
O'Neal, Tatum (actress); Los Angeles, 11/5/63
O'Neill, Eugene Gladstone (playwright); New York City **(1888–1953)**
O'Neill, Jennifer (actress); Rio de Janeiro, 2/20/49
Oppenheimer, J. Robert (nuclear physicist); New York City **(1904–1967)**
Orbach, Jerry (actor); New York City, 10/20/35
Orff, Carl (composer); Munich, Germany **(1895–1982)**
Orlando, Tony (Michael Anthony Orlando Cassavitis) (singer); New York City, 4/3/44
Ormandy, Eugene (conductor); Budapest **(1899–1985)**
Ormond, Julia (actress); Epsom, Surrey, England, 1/4/65
Orozco, José Clemente (painter); Zapotlán, Jalisco, Mexico **(1883–1949)**
Orwell, George (Eric Arthur Blair) (British author); Motihari, India **(1903–1950)**
Osborn, Paul (playwright); Evansville, Ind. **(1901–1988)**
Osborne, John (playwright); London **(1929–1994)**
Osbourne, Ozzy (John Osbourne) (singer); Birmingham, England, 12/3/48
Osler, Sir William (physician); Bondhead, Ont., Canada **(1849–1919)**
Osmond, Donny (singer, actor); Ogden, Utah, 12/9/57
Osmond, Marie (Olive Marie) (singer, actress); Ogden, Utah, 10/13/59
O'Sullivan, Maureen (actress); County Roscommon, Ireland **(1911–1998)**
Oswald, Lee Harvey (presumed assassin); New Orleans **(1939–1963)**
Otis, Elisha (inventor); Halifax, Vt. **(1811–1861)**
O'Toole, Peter (actor); Connemara, Ireland, 8/2/32
Ovid (Publius Ovidius Naso) (poet); Sulmona, Italy **(43 B.C.–A.D. 17)**
Ovitz, Michael (entertainment executive); Chicago, 12/14/46
Owens, Buck (Alvis Edgar Owens) (singer); Sherman, Tex., 8/12/29
Ozawa, Seiji (orchestra conductor); Fentian (Shenyan), Manchuria, 7/1/35

P

Paar, Jack (TV personality); Canton, Ohio, 5/1/18
Pacino, Al (Alfred) (actor); New York City, 4/25/40
Packard, Vance (author); Granville Summit, Pa. **(1914–1996)**
Paderewski, Ignace Jan (pianist, statesman); Kurylowka, Russian Podolia **(1860–1941)**
Paganini, Nicolò (violinist); Genoa, Italy **(1782–1840)**
Page, Geraldine (actress); Kirksville, Mo. **(1924–1987)**
Page, Jimmy (musician); Heston, Ireland, 1/9/44
Page, Patti (Clara Ann Fowler) (singer, entertainer); Claremore, Okla., 11/8/27
Pagels, Elaine Hiesey (religious scholar); Palo Alto, Calif., 2/13/43
Paglia, Camille (writer, social critic); Endicott, N.Y., 4/2/47
Paine, Thomas (political philosopher); Thetford, England **(1737–1809)**
Pakula, Alan J. (film director); New York City **(1928–1998)**
Palance, Jack (Walter Palanuik) (actor); Lattimer, Pa., 2/18/19
Palestrina, Giovanni Pierluigi da (composer); Palestrina, Italy **(1526–1594)**
Paley, William S. (broadcasting executive); Chicago **(1901–1990)**
Palladio, Andrea (architect); Padua or Vicenza, Italy **(1508–1580)**
Palmer, Robert (rock musician); Batley, England, 1/19/49
Palmerston, Henry John Templeton (3rd Viscount) (statesman); Broadlands, England **(1784–1865)**
Palminteri, Chazz (Calogero Lorenzo Palminteri) (actor, writer); Bronx, New York, 5/15/51
Paltrow, Gwyneth (actress); Los Angeles, 9/27/72
Papanicolaou, George N. (physician); Coumi, Greece **(1883–1962)**
Papas, Irene (Lelekou) (actress); Chiliomodian, Greece, 3/9/26
Papp, Joseph (Joseph Papirofsky) (stage producer, director); Brooklyn, N.Y. **(1921–1991)**
Paracelsus, Philippus (Aureolus Theophrastus Bombastus von Hohenheim) (physican); Einsiedeln, Switzerland **(1493–1541)**
Park, Chung Hee (ex-president of South Korea); Sangmo-ri, Korea **(1917–1979)**
Parker, Alan (director); London, 2/14/44
Parker, Charlie "Bird" (jazz musician); Kansas City, Kans. **(1920–1955)**
Parker, Dorothy (Dorothy Rothschild) (author); West End, N.J. **(1893–1967)**
Parker, Fess (actor); Fort Worth, Tex., 8/16/25
Parker, Sarah Jessica (actress); Nelsonville, Ohio, 3/25/65
Parker, Suzy (model, actress); San Antonio **(1933–2003)**
Parkinson, C(yril) Northcote (historian); Durham, England **(1909–1993)**
Parkman, Francis (historian); Boston **(1823–1893)**
Parks, Bert (Bert Jacobson) (entertainer); Atlanta **(1914–1992)**
Parks, Gordon (film director); Ft. Scott, Kans., 11/30/12
Parks, Rosa (civil rights activist); Tuskegee, Ala., 2/4/13
Parnell, Charles Stewart (statesman); Avondale, Ireland **(1846–1891)**
Parnis, Mollie (Mollie Parnis Livingston) (fashion designer); New York City **(1905?–1992)**
Parsons, Estelle (actress); Marblehead, Mass., 11/20/27

Parton, Dolly (singer); Locust Ridge, Tenn., 1/19/46
Pascal, Blaise (philosopher); Clermont, France **(1623–1662)**
Pasternak, Boris Leonidovich (author); Moscow **(1890–1960)**
Pasternak, Joseph (film producer); Szilagy-Somlyo, Hungary **(1901–1991)**
Pasteur, Louis (chemist); Dôle, France **(1822–1895)**
Pastor, Tony (Antonio) (actor, theater manager); New York City **(1837–1908)**
Pater, Walter (Horatio) (writer); London **(1839–1894)**
Patinkin, Mandy (Mandel) (actor, singer); Chicago, 11/30/52
Paton, Alan (author); Pietermaritzburg, South Africa **(1903–1988)**
Patric, Jason (actor); Queens, N.Y., 6/17/66
Patti, Adelina (soprano); Madrid **(1843–1919)**
Patton, George Smith, Jr. (general); San Gabriel, Calif. **(1885–1945)**
Paul, Alice (feminist, woman suffragist); Moorestown, N.J. **(1885–1977)**
Paul, Les (Lester William Polfus) (guitarist); Waukesha, Wis., 6/9/15
Paul VI (Giovanni Battista Montini) (Pope); Concesio, nr. Brescia, Italy **(1897–1978)**
Pauley, Jane (Margaret Jane Pauley) (TV newscaster); Indianapolis, 10/31/50
Pauling, Linus Carl (chemist, Nobel laureate); Portland, Ore. **(1901–1994)**
Pavarotti, Luciano (tenor); Modena, Italy, 10/12/35
Pavlov, Ivan Petrovich (physiologist); Ryazan district, Russia **(1849–1936)**
Pavlova, Anna (ballet dancer); St. Petersburg, Russia **(1885–1931)**
Paxton, Bill (actor); Fort Worth, Texas, 5/17/55
Peale, Norman Vincent (clergyman); Bowersville, Ohio **(1898–1993)**
Pearl, Minnie (Sarah Ophelia Colley Cannon) (comedienne, singer); Centerville, Tenn. **(1912–1996)**
Pears, Peter (tenor); Farnham, England **(1910–1986)**
Pearson, Drew (Andrew Russel Pearson) (columnist); Evanston, Ill. **(1897–1969)**
Pearson, Lester B. (statesman); Toronto **(1897–1972)**
Peary, Robert Edwin (explorer); Cresson, Pa. **(1856–1920)**
Peck, Gregory (Eldred Gregory Peck) (actor); La Jolla, Calif. **(1916–2003)**
Peckinpah, Sam (film director); Fresno, Calif. **(1925–1984)**
Peerce, Jan (tenor); New York City **(1904–1984)**
Pegler, (James) Westbrook (columnist); Minneapolis **(1894–1969)**
Pei, I(eoh) M(ing) (architect); Canton, China, 4/26/17
Penn, Arthur (director); Philadelphia, 9/27/22
Penn, Sean (actor, filmmaker); Los Angeles, 8/17/60
Penn, William (American colonist); London **(1644–1718)**
Penney, James C. (merchant); Hamilton, Mo. **(1875–1971)**
Peppard, George (actor); Detroit **(1928–1994)**
Pepys, Samuel (diarist); Bampton, England **(1633–1703)**
Perelman, S(idney) J(oseph) (writer); Brooklyn, N.Y. **(1904–1979)**
Perez, Rosie (actress, dancer, choreographer); Brooklyn, New York, 5/16/63
Pergolesi, Giovanni Battista (composer); Jesi, Italy **(1710–1736)**
Pericles (statesman); Athens died 429 B.C.
Perkins, Anthony (actor); New York City **(1932–1992)**
Perkins, Frances (social reformer); Boston **(1882–1965)**
Perlman, Itzhak (violinist); Tel Aviv, Israel, 8/31/45
Perlman, Rhea (actress); Brooklyn, N.Y., 3/31/48
Perón, Isabel (María Estela Martínez Cartas) (former chief of state); La Rioja, Argentina, 2/4/31
Perón, Juan D. (statesman); nr. Lobos, Argentina **(1895–1974)**
Perón, Maria Eva Duarte de (political leader); Los Toldos, Argentina **(1919–1952)**
Perot, H. Ross (business executive); Texarkana, Tex., 6/27/30
Perrine, Valerie (actress, dancer); Galveston, Tex., 9/3/43
Perry, Luke (Coy Luther Perry III) (actor); Fredericktown, Ohio, 10/11/66
Perry, Matthew (actor); Williamstown, Mass., 8/19/69
Pershing, John Joseph (general); Linn County, Mo. **(1860–1948)**
Pestalozzi, Johann (educator); Zurich, Switzerland **(1746–1827)**
Peters, Bernadette (Bernadette Lazzara) (actress); New York City, 2/28/48
Peters, Brock (actor, singer); New York City, 7/2/27
Peters, Jean (actress); Canton, Ohio **(1926–2000)**
Peters, Roberta (Roberta Peterman) (soprano); New York City, 5/4/30
Petit, Roland (choreographer, dancer); Villemombe, France, 1924
Petrarch (Francesco Petrarca) (poet); Arezzo, Italy **(1304–1374)**
Petty, Tom (folk/rock musician); Gainesville, Fla., 10/20/50
Pfeiffer, Michelle (actress); Santa Ana, Calif., 4/29/58
Philbin, Regis (talk show host); New York City, 8/25/33
Philip (Philip Mountbatten) (Duke of Edinburgh); Corfu, Greece, 6/10/21
Phillippe, Ryan (actor); New Castle, Del., 9/10/75
Phoenix, Joaquin (actor); San Juan, Puerto Rico, 10/28/74
Phoenix, River (actor); Madras, Ore. **(1970–1993)**
Piaf, Edith (Edith Gassion) (singer); Paris **(1916–1963)**
Piatigorsky, Gregor (cellist); Ekaterinoslav, Russia **(1903–1976)**
Piazza, Marguerite (soprano); New Orleans, 5/6/26
Picasso, Pablo (painter, sculptor); Málaga, Spain **(1881–1973)**
Pickett, Wilson (singer); Prattville, Ala., 3/18/41
Pickford, Mary (Gladys Mary Smith) (actress); Toronto **(1893–1979)**
Picon, Molly (actress); New York City **(1898–1992)**
Pidgeon, Walter (actor); East St. John, N.B., Canada **(1898–1984)**
Pierce, David Hyde (actor); Saratoga Springs, N.Y., 4/3/59
Pierce, Franklin (14th U.S. president); Hillsboro, N.H. **(1804–1869)**
Pileggi, Mitch (actor); Portland, Ore., 4/5/52
Pinkett-Smith, Jada (actress); Baltimore, 9/18/71
Pinsky, Robert (ex-poet laureate of the U.S.); Long Branch, N.J., 10/20/40
Pinochet (Ugarte), Augusto (former leader of Chile's military government); Valparaiso, Chile, 11/25/15
Pinter, Harold (playwright); London, 10/10/30
Pinza, Ezio (basso); Rome **(1892–1957)**
Pirandello, Luigi (dramatist, novelist); nr. Girgenti, Italy **(1867–1936)**
Piranesi, Giambattista (artist); Mestre, Italy **(1720–1778)**
Pissaro, Camille Jacob (painter); St. Thomas, U.S. Virgin Islands **(1830–1903)**
Piston, Walter (composer); Rockland, Maine **(1894–1976)**
Pitman, Sir [Isaac] James (educator, publisher); Bath, England **(1813–1897)**
Pitt, Brad (actor); Shawnee, Okla., 12/18/63
Pitt, William ("Younger Pitt") (statesman); nr. Bromley, England **(1759–1806)**
Pitts, ZaSu (actress); Parsons, Kans. **(1898–1963)**
Pius XII (Eugenio Pacelli) (Pope); Rome **(1876–1958)**
Pizarro, Francisco (explorer); Trujillo, Spain **(c. 1476–1541)**
Planck, Max (physicist); Kiel, Germany **(1858–1947)**
Plant, Robert (musician, singer, song writer); West Bromwich, Staffordshire, England , 8/20/48
Plath, Sylvia (poet); Boston **(1932–1963)**
Plato (Aristocles) (philosopher); Athens **(c. 427–347 B.C.)**
Pleasence, Donald (actor); Worksop, England **(1919–1995)**
Pleshette, Suzanne (actress); New York City, 1/31/37
Plimpton, George (author); New York City, 3/18/27
Plimpton, Martha (actress); New York City, 11/16/70
Plisetskaya, Maya (ballet dancer); Moscow, 11/20/25
Plowright, Joan (actress); Brigg, England, 10/28/29
Plummer, Christopher (actor); Toronto, 12/13/29
Plutarch (biographer); Chaeronea, Greece **(c. 46–c. 120)**
Pocahontas (Matoaka) (American Indian princess); Virginia **(c. 1595–1617)**
Podhoretz, Norman (author); Brooklyn, N.Y., 1/16/30
Poe, Edgar Allan (poet, story writer); Boston **(1809–1849)**
Poitier, Sidney (actor, director); Miami, Fla., 2/20/24
Polanski, Roman (director); Paris, 8/18/33
Polk, James Knox (11th U.S. president); Mecklenburg County, N.C. **(1795–1849)**
Pollack, Sydney (film director, producer, actor); Lafayette, Ind., 7/1/34
Pollard, Michael J. (actor); Passaic, N.J., 5/30/39
Pollock, Jackson (painter); Cody, Wyo. **(1912–1956)**
Polo, Marco (traveler); Venice **(c. 1254–1324)**
Pol Pot (Cambodian dictator); Kompong Thom, Cambodia **(1925–1998)**
Pompadour, Mme. de (Jeanne Antoinette Poisson) (courtesan); Versailles **(1721–1764)**
Pompey (Gnaeus Pompeius Magnus) (general); Rome **(106–48 B.C.)**
Ponce de León, Juan (explorer); Servas, Spain **(c. 1460–1521)**
Pons, Lily (coloratura soprano); Cannes, France **(1904–1976)**
Ponselle, Rosa (soprano); Meriden, Conn. **(1897–1981)**
Ponti, Carlo (director); Milan, Italy, 12/11/13
Pontormo, Jacopo da (painter); Pontormo, Italy **(1492–1557)**
Pope, Alexander (poet); London **(1688–1744)**
Porter, Cole (songwriter); Peru, Ind. **(1891–1964)**
Porter, Katherine Anne (novelist); Indian Creek, Tex. **(1891–1980)**
Portman, Natalie (actress); Jerusalem, 6/9/81
Posey, Parker (actress); Baltimore, 11/8/68
Post, Wiley (aviator); Grand Plain, Tex. **(1900–1935)**
Poston, Tom (actor); Columbus, Ohio, 10/17/27
Potëmkin, Grigori Aleksandrovich, Prince (statesman); Khizovo (Khizov), Belarus **(1739–1791)**
Potok, Chaim (author); New York City **(1929–2002)**
Potter, (Helen) Beatrix (author, illustrator); South Kensington, Middlesex, England **(1866–1943)**

Potts, Annie (actress); Nashville, Tenn., 10/28/52
Poulenc, Francis (composer); Paris **(1899–1963)**
Pound, Ezra (poet); Hailey, Idaho **(1885–1972)**
Poussin, Nicolas (painter); Villers, France **(1594–1665)**
Powell, Adam Clayton, Jr. (congressman); New Haven, Conn. **(1908–1972)**
Powell, Colin L. (secretary of state); New York City, 4/5/37
Powell, Dick (actor); Mt. View, Ark. **(1904–1963)**
Powell, Eleanor (actress, tap dancer); Springfield, Mass. **(1912–1982)**
Powell, Jane (Suzanne Burce) (actress, singer); Portland, Ore., 4/1/29
Powell, William (actor); Pittsburgh **(1892–1984)**
Power, Tyrone (actor); Cincinnati, Ohio **(1914–1958)**
Powers, Stefanie (Stefania Zofia Federkiewicz) (actress); Hollywood, Calif., 11/12/42
Praxiteles (sculptor); Athens **(c. 370–c. 330 B.C.)**
Preminger, Otto (director, producer); Vienna **(1906–1986)**
Prentiss, Paula (Paula Ragusa) (actress); San Antonio, 3/4/39
Presley, Elvis (singer, actor); Tupelo, Miss. **(1935–1977)**
Presley, Priscilla (actress); Brooklyn, N.Y., 5/24/45
Preston, Robert (Robert Preston Meservey) (actor); Newton Highlands, Mass. **(1918–1987)**
Previn, André (conductor); Berlin, 4/6/29
Price, Leontyne (Mary) (soprano); Laurel, Miss., 2/10/27
Price, Ray (country music artist); Perryville, Tex., 1/12/26
Price, Vincent (actor); St. Louis **(1911–1993)**
Pride, Charley (singer); Sledge, Miss., 3/18/38?
Priestley, Jason (actor, producer); Vancouver, B.C., Canada, 8/28/69
Priestley, J. B. (John B.) (author); Bradford, England **(1894–1984)**
Priestley, Joseph (chemist); nr. Leeds, England **(1733–1804)**
Primakov, Yevgeny (Russian political leader); Kiev, Ukraine, 10/29/29
Primrose, William (violist); Glasgow, Scotland **(1904–1982)**
Prince (Prince Rogers Nelson) (singer); Minneapolis, 6/7/58
Prince, Harold (stage producer); New York City, 1/30/28
Principal, Victoria (actress); Fukuoka, Japan, 1/3/45
Prinze, Freddie (actor); New York City **(1954–1977)**
Pritchett, V(ictor) S(awdon) (literary critic); Ipswich, England **(1900–1997)**
Procter, William (scientist); Cincinnati **(1872–1951)**
Prokofiev, Sergei Sergeevich (composer); St. Petersburg, Russia **(1891–1953)**
Proulx, E. Annie (novelist); Norwich, Conn., 8/22/35
Proust, Marcel (novelist); Paris **(1871–1922)**
Provine, Dorothy (actress); Deadwood, S.D., 1/20/37
Prowse, Juliet (actress, dancer); Bombay (Mumbai) **(1936–1996)**
Pryce, Jonathan (actor); Holywell, Wales, 6/1/47
Pryor, Richard (comedian); Peoria, Ill., 12/1/40
Ptolemy (Claudius Ptolemaeus) (astronomer, geographer); Ptolemais Hermii, Egypt, fl. 2nd cent.
Pucci, Emilio (Marchese di Barsento) (fashion designer); Naples, Italy **(1914–1992)**
Puccini, Giacomo (composer); Lucca, Italy **(1858–1924)**
Puente, Tito (band leader); New York City **(1923–2000)**
Pulaski, Casimir (military officer); Podolia, Poland **(1748–1779)**
Pulitzer, Joseph (publisher); Makó, Hungary **(1847–1911)**
Pullman, Bill (actor); Delphi, N.Y., 12/17/53
Pullman, George (inventor); Brockton, N.Y. **(1831–1897)**
Purcell, Henry (composer); London **(1658–1695)**
Pusey, Nathan M. (educator); Council Bluffs, Iowa **(1907–2001)**
Pushkin, Alexander Sergeevich (poet, dramatist); Moscow **(1799–1837)**
Putin, Vladimir (president of Russia); Leningrad, 1952
Puzo, Mario (novelist); New York City **(1920–1999)**
Pyle, Ernest Taylor (journalist); Dana, Ind. **(1900–1945)**
Pythagoras (mathematician, philosopher); Samos, Greece **(c. 582–c. 507A.D.)**

Q

Qaddafi, Muammar al- (Libyan leader); Libya, 1942
Quaid, Dennis (actor); Houston, 4/9/54
Quaid, Randy, (actor); Houston, 10/1/50
Quayle, Anthony (actor); Ainsdale, England **(1913–1989)**
Queen, Ellery: pen name of Frederic Dannay and Manfred B. Lee
Queen Latifah (Dana Owens) (rap musician, actress); Newark, New Jersey, 3/18/70
Queler, Eve (conductor); New York City, 1/1/36
Quennell, Sir Peter Courtney (biographer); Bromley, England **(1905–1993)**
Quindlen, Anna (writer); Philadelphia, 7/8/53
Quinn, Aidan (actor); Chicago, 3/8/59
Quinn, Anthony (Antonio Quiñones) (actor); Chihuahua, Mexico **(1915–2001)**

R

Rabe, David (playwright); Dubuque, Iowa, 3/10/40
Rabelais, François (satirist); nr. Chinon, France **(c. 1490–1553)**
Rabi, I(sidor) I(saac) (physicist); Rymanow, Poland **(1898–1988)**
Rabin, Yitzhak (former Israeli prime minister); Jerusalem **(1922–1995)**
Rachmaninoff, Sergei Wassilievitch (pianist, composer); Oneg Estate, Novgorod, Russia **(1873–1943)**
Racine, Jean Baptiste (dramatist); La Ferté-Milon, France **(1639–1699)**
Radner, Gilda (comedienne); Detroit **(1946–1989)**
Raft, George (actor); New York City **(1895–1980)**
Rainier III (Prince); Monaco, 5/31/23
Rains, Claude (actor); London **(1889–1967)**
Raitt, Bonnie (singer); Burbank, Calif., 11/8/49
Raitt, John (actor, singer); Santa Ana, Calif., 1/19/17
Raleigh, Sir Walter (courtier, navigator); London **(1552?–1618)**
Rambeau, Marjorie (actress); San Francisco **(1889–1970)**
Rameau, Jean-Philippe (composer); Dijon, France **(1683–1764)**
Rampal, Jean-Pierre (Louis) (flutist); Marseilles, France **(1922–2000)**
Rand, Ayn (novelist, philosopher); St. Petersburg, Russia **(1905–1982)**
Randall, Tony (Leonard Rosenberg) (actor); Tulsa, Okla., 2/26/20
Randolph, A(sa) Philip (labor leader); Crescent City, Fla. **(1889–1979)**
Rankin, Jeannette (politician, pacifist); Missoula, Mont. **(1880–1973)**
Raphael (Raffaello Santi) (painter, architect); Urbino, Italy **(1483–1520)**
Rasputin, Grigori Efimovich (monk); Tobolsk Province, Russia **(1872–1916)**
Rathbone, Basil (Philip St. John Basil Rathbone) (actor); Johannesburg, South Africa **(1892–1967)**
Rather, Dan (TV newscaster); Wharton, Tex., 10/31/31
Rattigan, Terence (playwright); London **(1911–1977)**
Ratzenberger, John (actor); Bridgeport, Conn., 4/6/47
Rauschenberg, Robert (painter); Port Arthur, Tex., 10/22/25
Ravel, Maurice Joseph (composer); Ciboure, France **(1875–1937)**
Ray, Aldo (DaRe) (actor); Pen Argyl, Pa. **(1926–1991)**
Ray, Gene Anthony (actor, dancer); Harlem, N.Y., 5/24/63
Ray, Man (painter); Philadelphia **(1890–1976)**
Ray, Satyajit (film director); Calcutta **(1921–1992)**
Raye, Martha (Margie Yvonne Reed) (comedienne, actress); Butte, Mont. **(1916–1994)**
Rea, Stephen (actor); Belfast, Ireland, 10/31/43
Reagan, Ronald Wilson (40th U.S. president, actor); Tampico, Ill., 2/6/11
Reasoner, Harry (TV commentator); Dakota City, Iowa **(1923–1991)**
Redding, Otis (singer); Dawson, Ga. **(1941–1967)**
Reddy, Helen (singer); Melbourne, Australia, 10/25/41
Redford, Robert (Charles Robert Redford, Jr.) (actor); Santa Monica, Calif., 8/18/37
Redgrave, Lynn (actress); London, 3/8/43
Redgrave, Sir Michael (actor); Bristol, England **(1908–1985)**
Redgrave, Vanessa (actress); London, 1/30/37
Redon, Odilon (artist); Bordeaux, France **(1840–1916)**
Reed, Donna (Donna Belle Mullenger) (actress); Denison, Iowa **(1921–1986)**
Reed, Lou (Lewis Allen Reed) (musician, guitarist, singer, song writer); Freeport, N.Y., 3/ 2/42
Reed, Rex (critic); Ft. Worth, 10/2/40
Reed, Walter (army surgeon); Belroi, Va. **(1851–1902)**
Reese, Della (Deloreese Patricia Early) (singer, actress); Detroit, 7/6/32
Reeve, Christopher (actor, activist); New York City, 9/25/52
Reeves, Jim (singer); Panola County, Tex. **(1923–1964)**
Reeves, Keanu (actor, musician); Beirut, Lebanon, 9/2/64
Reich, Robert (Clinton cabinet member); Scranton, Pa., 6/24/46
Reich, Steve (composer); New York City, 10/3/36
Reid, Wallace (actor); St. Louis **(1891–1923)**
Reiner, Carl (actor); New York City, 3/20/22
Reiner, Fritz (conductor); Budapest **(1888–1963)**
Reiner, Robert (actor, director, writer, producer); Bronx, N.Y., 3/6/45
Reinhardt, Max (Max Goldmann) (theater producer); nr. Vienna **(1873–1943)**
Reiser, Paul (actor, producer); New York City, 3/30/57
Remarque, Erich Maria (novelist); Osnabrük, Germany **(1898–1970)**

Rembrandt (Rembrandt Harmensz van Rijn) (painter); Leyden, Netherlands **(1605–1669)**
Remick, Lee (Ann) (actress); Boston **(1935–1991)**
Remnick, David (writer, editor); Hackensack, N.J., 10/29/58
Renfro, Brad (actor); Knoxville, Tenn., 7/25/82
Rennert, Günther (opera director, producer); Essen, Germany, 4/1/11
Rennie, Michael (actor); Bradford, England **(1909–1971)**
Reno, Janet (ex-U.S. attorney general); Miami, Fla., 7/21/38
Renoir, Jean (film director, writer); Paris **(1894–1979)**
Renoir, Pierre Auguste (painter); Limoges, France **(1841–1919)**
Resnais, Alain (film director); Vannes, France, 6/3/22
Resnik, Regina (mezzo-soprano); New York City, 8/30/22
Respighi, Ottorino (composer); Bologna, Italy **(1879–1936)**
Reston, James (journalist); Clydebank, Scotland **(1909–1995)**
Reuther, Walter (labor leader); Wheeling, W. Va. **(1907–1970)**
Revere, Paul (silversmith, hero of famous ride); Boston **(1735–1818)**
Revson, Charles (business executive); Boston **(1906–1975)**
Reynolds, Burt (actor, director, producer); Waycross, Ga., 2/11/36
Reynolds, Debbie (Marie Frances Reynolds) (actress); El Paso, Tex., 4/1/32
Reynolds, Sir Joshua (painter); nr. Plymouth, England **(1723–1792)**
Reynolds, Marjorie (Marjorie Goodspeed) (actress); Buhl, Idaho **(1921–1997)**
Reznor, Trent (musician); Mercer, Pa., 5/17/65
Rhodes, Cecil John (South African statesman); Bishop Stortford, England **(1853–1902)**
Ricci, Christina (actress); Santa Monica, Calif., 2/12/80
Rice, Anne (novelist); New Orleans, 10/14/41
Rice, Elmer (Elmer Leopold Reizenstein) (playwright); New York City **(1892–1967)**
Rice, Grantland (sports writer); Murfreesboro, Tenn. **(1880–1954)**
Rich, Buddy (Bernard) (drummer); Brooklyn, N.Y. **(1917–1987)**
Rich, Charlie (singer); Colt, Ark. **(1932–1995)**
Richard I the Lion-hearted (king of England); Oxford, England **(1157–1199)**
Richards, Ann (Dorothy Ann Willis) (ex-governor of Texas); Lakeview, Tex., 9/1/33
Richards, Keith (rock singer); Dartford, England, 12/18/43
Richards, Michael (actor); California, 7/21/48
Richardson, Elliot L. (ex-cabinet member); Boston **(1920–1999)**
Richardson, Sir Ralph (actor); Cheltenham, England **(1902–1983)**
Richardson, Tony (director); Shipley, England **(1928–1991)**
Richelieu, Duc de (Armand Jean du Plessis) (cardinal); Paris **(1585–1642)**
Richie, Lionel (singer, songwriter); Tuskegee, Ala., 6/20/49
Richter, Charles Francis (seismologist); Hamilton, Ohio **(1900–1985)**
Richter, Sviatoslav (pianist); Zhitomir, Ukraine **(1914–1997)**
Rickenbacker, Eddie (Edward V.) (aviator); Columbus, Ohio **(1890–1973)**
Rickles, Don (comedian); New York City, 5/8/26
Rickover, Vice Admiral Hyman G. (atomic energy expert); Russia **(1900–1986)**
Riddle, Nelson (composer); Hackensack, N.J. **(1921–1985)**
Ride, Sally K(risten) (astronaut, astrophysicist); Encino, Calif., 5/26/51
Ridgway, General Matthew B. (ex-Army chief of staff); Ft. Monroe, Va. **(1895–1993)**
Riemenschneider, Tilman (sculptor); Osterode, Germany **(c. 1460–1531)**
Rigg, Diana (actress); Doncaster, England, 7/20/38
Riley, James Whitcomb (poet); Greenfield, Ind. **(1849–1916)**
Rilke, Rainer Maria (poet); Prague **(1875–1926)**
Rimbaud, (Jean Nicolas) Arthur (poet); Charleville, France **(1854–1891)**
Rimes, LeAnn (singer); Jackson, Miss., 8/28/82
Rimsky-Korsakov, Nikolai Andreevich (composer); Tikhvin, Russia **(1844–1908)**
Rinehart, Mary (née Roberts) (novelist); Pittsburgh **(1876–1958)**
Ringwald, Molly (actress); Sacramento, Calif., 2/18/68
Ritchard, Cyril (actor, director); Sydney, Australia **(1898–1977)**
Ritter, John (Jonathan) (actor); Burbank, Calif. **(1948–2003)**
Ritter, Tex (Woodward Maurice Ritter) (singer); Panola County, Tex. **(1905–1973)**
Ritter, Thelma (actress); Brooklyn, N.Y. **(1905–1969)**
Rivera, Chita (Dolores Conchita Figuero del Rivero) (dancer, actress, singer); Washington, D.C., 1/23/33
Rivera, Diego (painter); Guanajuato, Mexico **(1886–1957)**
Rivera, Geraldo (Miguel Rivera) (TV host); New York City, 7/4/43
Rivers, Joan (comedienne); Brooklyn, N.Y., 6/8/33
Rivers, Larry (Yitzroch Loiza Grossberg) (painter); New York City **(1923–2002)**
Roach, Hal (film producer); Elmira, N.Y. **(1892–1992)**
Robards, Jason, Jr. (actor); Chicago **(1922–2000)**
Robards, Jason, Sr. (actor); Hillsdale, Mich. **(1892–1963)**
Robbins, Harold (Harold Rubin) (novelist); New York City **(1916–1997)**
Robbins, Jerome (Jerome Rabinowitz) (choreographer); New York City **(1918–1998)**
Robbins, Marty (singer); Glendale, Ariz. **(1925–1982)**
Robbins, Tim (Timothy Francis) (actor, director); West Covina, Calif., 10/16/58
Roberts, Cokie (Mary Martha Corinne Morrison Claiborne Boggs) (broadcast journalist); New Orleans, 12/27/43
Roberts, Eric (actor); Biloxi, Miss., 4/18/56
Roberts, Julia (actress); Smyrna, Ga., 10/28/67
Roberts, Oral (Granville) (evangelist, publisher); nr. Ada, Okla., 1/24/18
Robertson, Cliff (Clifford Parker Robertson III) (actor); La Jolla, Calif., 9/9/25
Robertson, Dale (Dayle) (actor); Oklahoma City, 7/14/23
Robeson, Paul (singer, actor); Princeton, N.J. **(1898–1976)**
Robespierre, Maximilien François Marie Isidore de (French Revolutionist); Arras, France **(1758–1794)**
Robinson, Bill "Bojangles" (Luther) (dancer); Richmond, Va. **(1878–1949)**
Robinson, Edward G. (Emanuel Goldenberg) (actor); Bucharest **(1893–1973)**
Robinson, Edwin Arlington (poet); Head Tide, Maine **(1869–1935)**
Robinson Peete, Holly (Holly Robinson) (actress); Philadelphia, 9/18/64
Robinson, Robert (chemist, Nobel laureate); Chesterfield, Derbyshire, England **(1885–1975)**
Robinson, Smokey (singer, songwriter); Detroit, 2/19/40
Rock, Chris (comedian, actor); Brooklyn, New York, 2/7/66
Rockefeller, David (banker); New York City, 6/12/15
Rockefeller, John Davison (business executive); Richford, N.Y. **(1839–1937)**
Rockefeller, John Davison, Jr. (industrialist); Cleveland **(1874–1960)**
Rockefeller, John D., 3rd (philanthropist); New York City **(1906–1978)**
Rockefeller, Laurance S. (conservationist); New York City, 5/26/10
Rockwell, Norman (painter, illustrator); New York City **(1894–1978)**
Roddenberry, Gene (creator of *Star Trek*); El Paso, Tex. **(1921–1991)**
Rodgers, Jimmie (singer); Meridian, Miss. **(1897–1933)**
Rodgers, Richard (composer); New York City **(1902–1979)**
Rodin, François Auguste René (sculptor); Paris **(1840–1917)**
Rodzinski, Artur (conductor); Spalato, Dalmatia **(1894–1958)**
Roeg, Nicolas (film director); London, 8/15/28
Roentgen, Wilhelm Konrad (physicist); Lennep, Prussia **(1845–1923)**
Roethke, Theodore (poet); Saginaw, Mich. **(1908–1963)**
Rogers, Buddy (Charles Rogers) (actor); Olathe, Kans. **(1904–1999)**
Rogers, Carl (psychologist); Oak Park, Ill. **(1902–1987)**
Rogers, Fred (TV producer, host); Latrobe, Pa. **(1928–2003)**
Rogers, Ginger (Virginia McMath) (dancer, actress); Independence, Mo. **(1911–1995)**
Rogers, Kenny (singer); Houston, 8/21/38
Rogers, Mimi (actress); Coral Gables, Fla., 1/27/56
Rogers, Roy (Leonard Frank Slye) (actor, singer); Cincinnati **(1911–1998)**
Rogers, Wayne (actor); Birmingham, Ala., 4/7/33
Rogers, Will (William Penn Adair Rogers) (humorist); Oologah, Okla. **(1879–1935)**
Rogers, William P. (ex-secretary of state); Norfolk, N.Y. **(1913–2001)**
Roland, Gilbert (Luis Antonio Damaso de Alonso) (actor); Juarez, Mexico **(1905–1994)**
Rolland, Romain (author); Clamecy, France **(1866–1944)**
Rollins, Sonny (saxophonist); New York City, 9/7/30
Romberg, Sigmund (composer); Szeged, Hungary **(1887–1951)**
Rome, Harold (composer); Hartford, Conn. **(1908–1993)**
Romero, Cesar (actor); New York City **(1907–1994)**
Romney, George W. (automobile executive, governor); Chihuahua, Mexico **(1907–1995)**
Romulo, Carlos P. (diplomat, educator); Manila **(1899–1985)**
Ronsard, Pierre de (poet); La Possonnière nr. Couture, France **(1524–1585)**
Ronstadt, Linda (singer); Tucson, Ariz., 7/30/46
Rooney, Andy (TV personality); Albany, N.Y., 1/14/19
Rooney, Mickey (Joe Yule, Jr.) (actor); Brooklyn, N.Y., 9/23/20
Roosevelt, (Anna) Eleanor (reformer, humanitarian); New York City **(1884–1962)**
Roosevelt, Franklin Delano (32nd U.S. president); Hyde Park, N.Y. **(1882–1945)**

Roosevelt, Theodore (26th U.S. president); New York City **(1858–1919)**
Rorem, Ned (composer); Richmond, Ind., 10/23/23
Rose, Billy (showman); New York City **(1899–1966)**
Rose, Leonard (concert cellist); Washington, D.C. **(1918–1984)**
Roseanne (Roseanne Barr) (actress); Salt Lake City, 11/3/52
Rosenberg, Ethel (spy); New York City **(1915–1953)**
Rosenberg, Julius (spy); New York City **(1918–1953)**
Ross, Betsy (Betsey Griscom) (flagmaker); Philadelphia **(1752–1836)**
Ross, Diana (singer); Detroit, 3/26/44
Ross, Katharine (actress); Hollywood, Calif., 1/29/42
Rossellini, Isabella (model, actress); Rome, Italy, 6/18/52
Rossellini, Roberto (film director); Rome **(1906–1977)**
Rossetti, Christina Georgina (poet); London **(1830–1894)**
Rossetti, Dante Gabriel (painter, poet); London **(1828–1882)**
Rossini, Gioacchino Antonio (composer); Pesaro, Italy **(1792–1868)**
Rosten, Leo (writer); Lódz, Poland **(1908–1997)**
Rostand, Edmond (dramatist); Marseilles, France **(1868–1918)**
Rostow, Walt Whitman (economist); New York City **(1916–2003)**
Rostropovich, Mstislav (cellist, conductor); Baku, Azerbaijan, 3/27/27
Roth, Henry (writer); Tysmenica, Ukraine **(1906–1995)**
Roth, Philip (novelist); Newark, N.J., 3/19/33
Roth, Tim (actor); London, 5/14/64
Rothko, Mark (Marcus Rothkovich) (painter); Russia **(1903–1970)**
Rouault, Georges (painter); Paris **(1871–1958)**
Roundtree, Richard (actor); New Rochelle, N.Y., 9/7/42
Rousseau, Henri (painter); Laval, France **(1844–1910)**
Rousseau, Jean Jacques (philosopher); Geneva **(1712–1778)**
Rovere, Richard H. (journalist); Jersey City, N.J., 5/5/15
Rowan, Carl Thomas (journalist); Ravenscroft, Tenn. **(1925–2000)**
Rowan, Dan (comedian); Beggs, Okla. **(1922–1987)**
Rowlands, Gena (actress); Cambria, Wis., 6/19/30
Rowling, J(oanne) K(athleen) (novelist); Chipping Sodbury, England, 7/31/65
Royko, Mike (columnist); Chicago **(1932–1997)**
Rubens, Sir Peter Paul (painter); Siegen, Germany **(1577–1640)**
Rubinstein, Arthur (concert pianist); Lódz, Poland **(1887–1982)**
Rubinstein, Helena (cosmetics executive); Kraków, Poland **(1870–1965)**
Rubinstein, John (actor, composer); Los Angeles, 12/8/46
Rucker, Darius (musician, singer, songwriter); Charleston, S.C., 5/13/66
Rudel, Julius (conductor); Vienna, 3/6/21
Ruffo, Titta (baritone); Italy **(1878–1953)**
Rumsfeld, Donald (sec. of defense); Chicago, 7/9/32
Runyon, (Alfred) Damon (journalist); Manhattan, Kans. **(1884–1945)**
Rush, Geoffrey (actor); Toowoomba, Australia, 7/6/51
Rushdie, (Ahmed) Salman (novelist); Bombay (Mumbai), 6/19/47
Rusk, Dean (ex-sec. of state); Cherokee County, Ga. **(1909–1994)**
Ruskin, John (art critic); London **(1819–1900)**
Russell, Keri (actress); Fountain Valley, Calif., 3/23/76
Russell, Lord Bertrand (Arthur William) (mathematician, philosopher); Trelleck, Wales **(1872–1970)**
Russell, Jane (actress); Bemidji, Minn., 6/21/21
Russell, Ken (film director); Southhampton, England, 4/3/27
Russell, Kurt (actor); Springfield, Mass., 3/17/51
Russell, Leon (pianist, singer); Lawton, Okla., 4/2/41
Russell, Lillian (Helen Louise Leonard) (soprano); Clinton, Iowa **(1861–1922)**
Russell, Mark (satirist); Buffalo, N.Y., 8/23/32
Russell, Nipsy (comedian); Atlanta, 10/13/24
Russell, Rosalind (actress); Waterbury, Conn. **(1912–1976)**
Russo, Rene (actress); Burbank, Calif., 2/17/54
Rustin, Bayard (civil rights leader); West Chester, Pa. **(1910–1987)**
Rutherford, Dame Margaret (actress); London **(1892–1972)**
Ryan, Meg (Margaret Mary Emily Anne Hyra) (actress); Fairfield, Conn., 11/19/61
Ryan, Robert (actor); Chicago **(1909–1973)**
Rydell, Bobby (Robert Ridarelli) (singer); Philadelphia, 4/26/42
Ryder, Winona (Winona Laura Horowitz) (actress); Winona, Minn., 10/29/71
Rysanek, Leonie (dramatic soprano); Vienna **(1928–1998)**

S

Saarinen, Eero (architect); Finland **(1910–1961)**
Sabin, Albert B. (polio researcher); Bialystok, Poland **(1906–1993)**
Sabu (Dastagir) (actor); Karapur, India **(1924–1963)**
Sacagawea (Shoshone Indian guide); Lemhi River valley (Idaho) **(c. 1786–1812)**
Sachs, Jeffrey D. (economist, educator); Michigan, 1954
Sadat, Anwar (former president); Egypt **(1918–1981)**
Sade, Marquis de (Donatien Alphonse François, Comte de Sade) (libertine, writer); Paris **(1740–1814)**
Safer, Morley (TV newscaster); Toronto, 11/8/31
Sagan, Carl (Edward) (astronomer, science writer); New York City **(1934–1996)**
Sagan, Françoise (novelist); Cajarc, France, 6/21/35
Sahl, Mort (Morton Lyon Sahl) (comedian); Montreal, 5/11/27
Saint, Eva Marie (actress); Newark, N.J., 7/4/24
St. Denis, Ruth (dancer, choreographer); Newark, N.J. **(1878–1968)**
St. James, Susan (Susan Miller) (actress); Los Angeles, 8/14/46
St. John, Jill (actress); Los Angeles, 8/19/40
St. Johns, Adela Rogers (journalist, author); Los Angeles **(1894–1988)**
Sainte-Marie, Buffy (Beverly) (folk singer); Craven, Sask., Canada, 2/20/41
Saint-Gaudens, Augustus (sculptor); Dublin **(1848–1907)**
Saint-Laurent, Yves (Henri Donat Mathieu) (fashion designer); Oran, Algeria, 8/1/36
Saint-Saens, Charles Camille (composer); Paris **(1835–1921)**
Sakharov, Andrei Dmitriyevich (nuclear physicist, peace activist); Russia **(1921–1989)**
Sales, Soupy (Milton Supman) (television entertainer); Franklinton, N.C., 1/6/26
Salinger, J(erome) D(avid) (novelist); New York City, 1/1/19
Salisbury, Harrison E. (journalist); Minneapolis **(1908–1993)**
Salk, Jonas (polio researcher); New York City **(1914–1995)**
Salk, Lee (psychologist); New York City **(1926–1992)**
Salomon, Haym (American Revolution financier); Leszno, Poland **(1740–1785)**
Sand, George (Amandine Lucille Aurore Dudevant, née Dupin) (novelist); Paris **(1804–1876)**
Sandburg, Carl (poet, biographer); Galesburg, Ill. **(1878–1967)**
Sanders, George (actor); St. Petersburg, Russia **(1906–1972)**
Sandler, Adam (comedian, musician, actor, screenwriter, singer); Brooklyn, N.Y., 9/9/66
Sands, Tommy (singer); Chicago, 8/27/37
Sanger, Margaret (birth-control advocate); Corning, N.Y. **(1879–1966)**
San Giacomo, Laura (actress); Hoboken, N.J., 11/14/62
Santayana, George (philosopher); Madrid **(1863–1952)**
Sappho (poet); Lesbos, Greece **(610 B.C.–580 B.C.)**
Sarandon, Susan (Susan Tomalin) (actress); New York City, 10/4/46
Sargent, John Singer (painter); Florence, Italy **(1856–1925)**
Sarnoff, David (radio executive); Minsk, Belarus **(1891–1971)**
Saroyan, William (novelist); Fresno, Calif. **(1908–1981)**
Sarto, Andrea del (Andrea Domenico d'Agnolo di Francesco) (painter); Florence, Italy **(1486–1531)**
Sartre, Jean-Paul (existentialist writer); Paris **(1905–1980)**
Sassoon, Vidal (hair stylist); London, 1/17/28
Satie, Erik (Alfred Leslie) (composer); Paris **(1866–1925)**
Saul (king of Israel) fl. 11th cent. B.C.
Savage, Fred (actor); Highland Park, Ill., 7/9/76
Savalas, Telly (Aristoteles) (actor); Garden City, N.Y. **(1924–1994)**
Savonarola, Girolamo (religious reformer); Ferrara, Italy **(1452–1498)**
Sawyer, Diane (broadcast journalist); Glasgow, Ky., 12/22/45
Sayão, Bidú (soprano); Rio de Janeiro **(1904–1999)**
Sayles, John (director, screenwriter, actor); Schenectady, N.Y., 9/28/50
Scarlatti, Alessandro (composer); Palermo, Italy **(1659–1725)**
Scarlatti, Domenico (composer); Naples, Italy **(1685–1757)**
Scavullo, Francesco (photographer); Staten Island, N.Y., 1/16/29
Schama, Simon (historian); London, 2/13/45
Schapiro, Meyer (Meir) (art historian); Siauliai, Lithuania **(1904–1996)**
Schary, Dore (producer, writer); Newark, N.J. **(1905–1980)**
Schell, Maximilian (actor); Vienna, 12/8/30
Schiaparelli, Elsa (fashion designer); Rome **(1890–1973)**
Schiff, Dorothy (newspaper publisher); New York City **(1903–1989)**
Schiffer, Claudia (model, actress); Rheinberg/Dusseldorf, Germany, 8/25/70
Schiller, Johann Christoph Friedrich von (dramatist, poet); Marbach, Germany **(1759–1805)**
Schipa, Tito (tenor); Lecce, Italy **(1890–1965)**
Schippers, Thomas (conductor); Kalamazoo, Mich. **(1930–1977)**
Schlegel, Friedrich von (philosopher); Hanover, Germany **(1772–1829)**
Schlesinger, Arthur M., Jr. (historian); Columbus, Ohio, 10/15/17
Schnabel, Artur (pianist, composer); Lipnik, Austria **(1882–1951)**

Schneider, Romy (Rose-Marie Albach-Retty) (actress); Vienna **(1938–1982)**
Schoenberg, Arnold (composer); Vienna **(1874–1951)**
Schomberg, Arthur (bibliophile, antiquarian); San Juan, P.R. **(1874–1938)**
Schopenhauer, Arthur (philosopher); Danzig, Poland **(1788–1860)**
Schröder, Gerhard (chancellor of Germany); Mossenberg, Germany, 4/7/44
Schubert, Franz Peter (composer); Vienna **(1797–1828)**
Schulberg, Budd (novelist); New York City, 3/27/14
Schulz, Charles M. (cartoonist); Minneapolis **(1922–2000)**
Schumacher, Joel (film director, producer, screenwriter); New York City, 8/29/39
Schuman, Robert (statesman); Luxembourg **(1886–1963)**
Schuman, William (composer); New York City **(1910–1992)**
Schumann, Robert Alexander (composer); Zwickau, Germany **(1810–1856)**
Schwartz, Arthur (songwriter); Brooklyn, N.Y. **(1900–1984)**
Schwarzenegger, Arnold (bodybuilder, actor); Graz, Austria, 7/30/47
Schwarzkopf, Elisabeth (soprano); Poznán, Poland, 12/9/15
Schwarzkopf, H. Norman (retired general); Trenton, N.J., 8/22/34
Schweitzer, Albert (humanitarian, Nobel laureate); Kaysersburg, Upper Alsace **(1875–1965)**
Schwimmer, David (actor); New York City, 11/12/66
Scofield, Paul (actor); Hurstpierpoint, England, 1/21/22
Scorsese, Martin (actor, writer, director, producer); Flushing, N.Y., 11/17/42
Scott, George C. (actor); Wise, Va. **(1927–1999)**
Scott, Hazel (singer, pianist); Port of Spain, Trinidad **(1920–1981)**
Scott, Lizabeth (Emma Matzo) (actress); Scranton, Pa., 9/29/23
Scott, Randolph (Randolph Crane) (actor); Orange County, Va. **(1898–1987)**
Scott, Robert Falcon (explorer); Devonport, England **(1868–1912)**
Scott, Sir Walter (novelist); Edinburgh, Scotland **(1771–1832)**
Scott, Zachary (actor); Austin, Tex. **(1914–1965)**
Scotto, Renata (operatic soprano); Savona, Italy, 2/24/36
Scruggs, Earl Eugene (bluegrass musician); Cleveland County, N.C., 1/6/24
Seaborg, Glenn Theodore (chemist, Nobel laureate); Ishpeming, Mich. **(1912–1999)**
Seagal, Steven (actor); Lansing, Mich., 4/10/52
Seal (Sealhenry Olumide Samuel) (singer, songwriter); London, England, 2/19/63
Seattle (Chief Seattle) (Suquamish Indian leader); Blake Island (Wash.) **(c. 1786–1866)**
Sebastian, John (composer, singer); New York City, 3/17/44
Seberg, Jean (actress); Marshalltown, Iowa **(1938–1979)**
Sedaka, Neil (singer); Brooklyn, N.Y., 3/13/39
Sedgwick, Kyra (actress); New York City, 8/19/65
Seeger, Pete (folk singer); New York City, 5/3/19
Segal, Erich (novelist); Brooklyn, N.Y., 6/16/37
Segal, George (actor); New York City, 2/13/36
Segovia, Andrés (guitarist); Linares, Spain **(1893–1987)**
Seinfeld, Jerry (comedian); Brooklyn, N.Y., 4/29/54
Selena (Selena Quintanilla Perez) (singer); Lake Jackson, Tex. **(1971–1995)**
Selleck, Tom (actor); Detroit, 1/29/45
Sellars, Peter (theater director); Pittsburgh, 1958?
Sellers, Peter (actor); Southsea, England **(1925–1980)**
Selznick, David O. (producer); Pittsburgh **(1902–1965)**
Sendak, Maurice (Bernard) (children's book author, illustrator); Brooklyn, N.Y., 6/10/28
Sennett, Mack (Michael Sinnott) (film producer); Richmond, Que., Canada **(1880–1960)**
Sequoyah (Cherokee linguist); Taskigi, Tenn. **(c. 1770–1843)**
Serkin, Peter (pianist); New York City, 7/24/47
Serkin, Rudolf (pianist); Eger, Czech Republic **(1903–1991)**
Serling, Rod (writer, TV host); Syracuse, N.Y. **(1924–1975)**
Sessions, Roger (composer); Brooklyn, N.Y. **(1896–1985)**
Seurat, Georges (painter); Paris **(1859–1891)**
Seuss, Dr. (Theodor Seuss Geisel) (author, illustrator); Springfield, Mass. **(1904–1991)**
Sevareid, Eric (TV commentator); Velva, N.D. **(1912–1991)**
Severinsen, Doc (Carl) (band leader); Arlington, Ore., 7/7/27
Sevigny, Chlöe (actress); Darien, Conn., 1975
Sewell, Rufus (actor, musician); London, 10/29/67
Sexton, Anne (poet); Newton, Mass. **(1928–1974)**
Seymour, Jane (Joyce Penelope Wilhelmina Frankenburg) (actress); Wimbledon, England, 2/15/51
Shabazz, Betty (Betty Sanders) (civil rights activist); Detroit **(1936–1997)**
Shaffer, Peter (playwright); Liverpool, England, 5/15/26
Shaham, Gil (violinist); Urbana, Ill., 1971
Shahn, Ben(jamin) (painter); Kaunas, Lithuania **(1898–1969)**
Shakespeare, William (dramatist); Stratford on Avon, England **(1564–1616)**
Shakur, Tupac (Amaru Shakur) (singer, actor); Brooklyn, N.Y. **(1971–1996)**
Shandling, Garry (comedian, actor, producer); Chicago, 11/29/49
Shange, Ntozake (Paulette Williams) (poet, playwright); Trenton, N.J., 10/18/48
Shankar, Ravi (sitar player); Benares, India, 4/7/20
Sharif, Omar (Michael Shalhoub) (actor); Alexandria, Egypt, 4/10/32
Shatner, William (actor); Montreal, 3/22/31
Shaw, Artie (Arthur Arshawsky) (band leader); New York City, 5/23/10
Shaw, George Bernard (dramatist); Dublin **(1856–1950)**
Shaw, Irwin (novelist); Brooklyn, N.Y. **(1913–1984)**
Shaw, Robert (actor); Lancashire, England **(1927–1978)**
Shaw, Robert (chorale conductor); Red Bluff, Calif. **(1916–1999)**
Shawn, Ted (Edwin Myers Shawn) (dancer, choreographer); Kansas City, Mo. **(1891–1972)**
Shawn, Wallace (actor); New York City, 11/12/43
Shearer, Moira (ballet dancer); Dunfermline, Scotland, 1/17/26
Shearer, Norma (actress); Montreal **(1900–1983)**
Shearing, George (pianist); London, 8/13/20
Sheedy, Ally (Alexandra Sheedy) (actress, writer); New York City, 6/12/62
Sheen, Charlie (actor); Los Angeles, 9/3/65
Sheen, Fulton J. (Peter Sheen) (Roman Catholic bishop); El Paso, Ill. **(1895–1979)**
Sheen, Martin (Ramon Estevez) (actor); Dayton, Ohio, 8/3/40
Shelley, Mary Wollstonecraft Godwin (writer); London **(1797–1851)**
Shelley, Percy Bysshe (poet); nr. Horsham, England **(1792–1822)**
Shelton, Henry (chairman of the Joint Chiefs of Staff); Tarboro, N.C., 1/2/42
Shepard, Sam (Samuel Shepard Rogers) (playwright); Ft. Sheridan, Ill., 11/5/43
Shepherd, Cybill (actress); Memphis, Tenn., 2/18/50
Sheraton, Thomas (furniture designer); Stockton-on-Tees, England **(1751–1806)**
Sheridan, Ann (Clara Lou Sheridan) (actress); Denton, Tex. **(1915–1967)**
Sheridan, Philip (army officer); Albany, N.Y. **(1831–1888)**
Sheridan, Richard Brinsley (dramatist); Dublin **(1751–1816)**
Sherman, William Tecumseh (army officer); Lancaster, Ohio **(1820–1891)**
Sherwood, Robert Emmet (playwright); New Rochelle, N.Y. **(1896–1955)**
Shevardnadze, Eduard Amvrosiyevich (State Council chairman, Georgia); Mamati, Georgia, 1/25/28
Shields, Brooke (actress); New York City, 5/31/65
Shire, Talia (Coppola) (actress); Lake Success, N.Y., 4/25/46
Shirer, William L. (journalist, historian); Chicago **(1904–1993)**
Sholokhov, Mikhail (novelist); Veshenskaya, Russia **(1905–1984)**
Shore, Dinah (Frances Rose Shore) (singer); Winchester,Tenn. **(1917–1994)**
Short, Bobby (Robert Waltrip Short) (singer, pianist); Danville, Ill., 9/15/24
Short, Martin (actor); Hamilton, Ont., Canada, 3/26/50
Shostakovich, Dmitri (composer); St. Petersburg, Russia **(1906–1975)**
Shriner, Herb (humorist, host); Toledo, Ohio **(1918–1970)**
Shriver, Maria (TV co-host); Chicago, 11/6/55
Shriver, Sargent (Robert Sargent Shriver, Jr.) (business executive); Westminster, Md., 11/9/15
Shue, Andrew (actor, soccer player); South Orange, N.J., 2/20/67
Shue, Elisabeth (actress); Wilmington, Del., 6/10/63
Shulman, Max (novelist); St. Paul, Minn. **(1919–1988)**
Sibelius, Jean (Johann Julius Christian Sibelius) (composer); Tavastehus, Finland **(1865–1957)**
Sidney, Sir Philip (poet); Penshurst, England **(1554–1586)**
Sidney, Sylvia (Sophia Kosow) (actress); New York City **(1910–1999)**
Siegfried and Roy (illusionists) **Siegfried Fischbacher**; Rosenheim, Bavaria, Germany, 1939 **Roy Uwe Ludwig Horn**; Nordenham, nr. Bremen, Germany, 1944
Siepi, Cesare (basso); Milan, Italy, 2/10/23
Signoret, Simone (Simone Kaminker) (actress); Wiesbaden, Germany **(1921–1985)**
Sihanouk, Norodom (king of Cambodia); Cambodia, 10/31/22
Sikorsky, Igor I. (inventor); Kiev, Ukraine **(1889–1972)**
Sills, Beverly (Belle Silverman) (soprano, opera director); Brooklyn, N.Y., 5/25/29

Sills, Milton (actor); Chicago **(1882–1930)**
Silone, Ignazio (Secondo Tranquilli) (novelist); Pescina del Marsi, Italy **(1900–1978)**
Silver, Ron (Ron Zimelman) (actor); New York City, 7/2/46
Silverheels, Jay (Harold J. Smith) (actor); Brantford, Ont., Canada **(1919–1980)**
Silverman, Fred (broadcasting executive); New York City, 9/13/37
Silvers, Phil (Philip Silversmith) (comedian); Brooklyn, N.Y. **(1912–1985)**
Silverstein, Shel (writer, poet); Chicago **(1932–1999)**
Silverstone, Alicia (actress); San Francisco, 10/4/76
Simenon, Georges (Georges Sim) (mystery writer); Liège, Belgium **(1903–1989)**
Simmons, Jean (actress); Crouch Hill, London, 1/31/29
Simon, Carly (singer, songwriter); New York City, 6/25/45
Simon, Neil (playwright); Bronx, N.Y., 7/4/27
Simon, Norton (business executive); Portland, Ore. **(1907–1993)**
Simon, Paul (singer, songwriter); Newark, N.J., 10/13/1941
Simone, Nina (Eunice Kathleen Waymoa) (singer, pianist); Tryon, N.C. **(1933–2003)**
Sinatra, Frank (Francis Albert Sinatra) (singer, actor); Hoboken, N.J. **(1915–1998)**
Sinbad (David Adkins) (actor, comedian); Benton Harbor, Mich., 11/10/56
Sinclair, Upton Beall (novelist); Baltimore **(1878–1968)**
Singer, Isaac Bashevis (novelist); Radzymin, Poland **(1904–1991)**
Singleton, John (writer, director); Los Angeles, 1/6/68
Sinise, Gary (actor, director); Chicago, 3/17/55
Siqueiros, David (painter); Chihuahua, Mexico **(1896–1974)**
Sirtis, Marina (actress); London, 3/29/59
Siskel, Gene (film critic); Chicago **(1946–1999)**
Sisley, Alfred (painter); Paris **(1839–1899)**
Sitting Bull (Prairie Sioux Indian chief); on Grand River, S.D. **(c. 1835–1890)**
Skelton, Red (Richard) (comedian); Vincennes, Ind. **(1913–1997)**
Skerritt, Tom (actor); Detroit, 8/25/43
Skinner, B(urrhus) F(rederic) (psychologist); Susquehanna, Pa. **(1904–1990)**
Skinner, Otis (actor); Cambridge, Mass. **(1858–1942)**
Slater, Christian (Christopher Hawkins) (actor); New York City, 8/18/69
Slatkin, Leonard (conductor); Los Angeles, 9/1/44
Sloan, Alfred P., Jr. (industrialist); New Haven, Conn. **(1875–1965)**
Sloan, John (painter); Lock Haven, Pa. **(1871–1951)**
Smalley, Richard E. (chemist, Nobel laureate); Akron, Ohio, 6/6/43
Smetana, Bedrich (composer); Litomysl, Czech Republic **(1824–1884)**
Smith, Adam (economist); Kirkaldy, Scotland **(1723–1790)**
Smith, Alexis (actress); Penticton, Canada **(1921–1993)**
Smith, Alfred Emanuel (politician); New York City **(1873–1944)**
Smith, Bessie (blues singer); Chattanooga, Tenn. **(1894–1937)**
Smith, Sir C. Aubrey (actor); London **(1863–1948)**
Smith, David (sculptor); Decatur, Ind. **(1906–1965)**
Smith, Harry (TV co-anchor); Hammond, Ind., 8/21/51
Smith, Howard K. (TV commentator); Ferriday, La. **(1914–2002)**
Smith, Jaclyn (actress); Houston, 10/26/47
Smith, John (American colonist); Willoughby, Lincolnshire, England **(1580–1631)**
Smith, Joseph (religious leader); Sharon, Vt. **(1805–1844)**
Smith, Kate (Kathryn) (singer); Greenville, Va. **(1909–1986)**
Smith, Kevin (director, screenwriter); Red Bank, N.J., 8/2/70
Smith, Dame Maggie (actress); Ilford, England, 12/28/34
Smith, Patti Lee (singer, songwriter); Chicago, 12/30/46
Smith, Red (Walter) (sports columnist); Green Bay, Wis. **(1905–1982)**
Smith, Will (actor, rap singer); Philadelphia, 9/25/68
Smits, Jimmy (actor); New York City, 7/9/55
Smollett, Tobias (novelist); Dalquhurn, Scotland **(1721–1771)**
Smothers, Dick (Richard) (comedian); New York City, 11/20/39
Smothers, Tom (Thomas) (comedian); New York City, 2/2/37
Snipes, Wesley (actor); Orlando, Fla., 7/31/62
Snow, Lord (Charles Percy) (author); Leicester, England **(1905–1980)**
Snowdon, Earl of (Anthony Armstrong-Jones) (photographer); London, 3/7/30
Snyder, Tom (TV personality); Milwaukee, 5/12/36
Socrates (philosopher); Athens **(469–399 B.C.)**
Soderbergh, Steven (film director, screenwriter); Atlanta, Ga., 1/14/63
Solomon (king of Israel); Jerusalem, fl. 950 B.C.
Solon (lawgiver); Salamis, Greece **(c. 630–559 B.C.)**
Solti, Sir Georg (conductor); Budapest **(1912–1997)**
Solzhenitsyn, Aleksandr (novelist); Kislovodsk, Russia, 12/11/18
Somers, Suzanne (Suzanne Mahoney) (actress); San Bruno, Calif., 10/16/46
Somes, Michael (ballet dancer); Horsley, England **(1917–1994)**
Sommer, Elke (Elke Schletz) (actress); Berlin, 11/5/42
Sondheim, Stephen (composer); New York City, 3/22/30
Sonnenfeld, Barry (cinematographer, film director); New York City, 4/1/53
Sontag, Susan (author, film director); New York City, 1/28/33
Sophocles (dramatist); nr. Athens **(c. 496–406 B.C.)**
Sorbo, Kevin (actor); Mound, Minn., 9/24/58
Sorvino, Mira (actress); Tenafly, N.J., 9/28/67
Sorvino, Paul (actor); Brooklyn, N.Y., 4/13/39
Sothern, Ann (Harriette Lake) (actress); Valley City, N.D. **(1909–2001)**
Soul, David (David Solberg) (actor); Chicago, 8/28/43
Sousa, John Philip (composer); Washington, D.C. **(1854–1932)**
Soyer, Raphael (painter); Borisoglebsk, Russia **(1899–1987)**
Spaak, Paul-Henri (statesman); Brussels **(1899–1972)**
Spacek, Sissy (Mary Elizabeth Spacek) (actress); Quitman, Tex., 12/25/49
Spacey, Kevin (actor); South Orange, N.J., 7/28/59
Spade, David (actor; comedian); Birmingham, Mich., 7/22/65
Spader, James (actor); Boston, 2/7/60
Spark, Muriel (novelist); Edinburgh, Scotland, 2/1/18
Spears, Britney (pop singer); Kentwood, La., 12/1/81
Spector, Phil (rock producer); Bronx, N.Y., 12/25/40
Spelling, Aaron (producer); Dallas, 4/22/28
Spelling, Tori (Victoria) (actress); Los Angeles, 5/16/73
Spencer, Herbert (philosopher); Derby, England **(1820–1903)**
Spender, Stephen (poet); nr. London **(1909–1995)**
Spengler, Oswald (philosopher); Blankenburg, Germany **(1880–1936)**
Spenser, Edmund (poet); London **(1552?–1599)**
Spewack, Bella (playwright); Hungary **(1899–1990)**
Spiegel, Sam (producer); Jaroslaw, Poland **(1901–1985)**
Spielberg, Steven (director, producer, writer, actor); Cincinnati, 12/18/47
Spillane, Mickey (Frank Spillane) (mystery writer); Brooklyn, N.Y., 3/9/18
Spiner, Brent (actor); Houston, 2/2/49
Spinoza, Baruch (philosopher); Amsterdam, Netherlands **(1632–1677)**
Spitalny, Phil (orchestra leader) **(1890–1970)**
Spivak, Lawrence (TV producer); Brooklyn, N.Y. **(1900–1994)**
Spock, Benjamin (pediatrician, writer); New Haven, Conn. **(1903–1998)**
Springsteen, Bruce (singer, songwriter); Freehold, N.J., 9/23/49
Sproul, Robert G. (educator); San Francisco **(1891–1975)**
Squanto (Wampanoag Indian emissary); Patuxet (Plymouth Bay, Mass.) **(c. 1590–1622)**
Stack, Robert (Robert Modini) (actor); Los Angeles **(1919–2003)**
Stafford, Jo (singer); Coalinga, Calif., 11/12/18
Stahl, Lesley (broadcast journalist); Lynn, Mass., 12/16/41
Stalin, Joseph Vissarionovich (Iosif V. Dzhugashvili) (Soviet leader); nr. Tiflis (Tbilisi), Georgia **(1879–1953)**
Stallone, Sylvester (actor, writer, director); New York City, 7/6/46
Stamp, Terence (actor); London, 1938
Stander, Lionel (actor); New York City **(1908–1994)**
Stanislavski (Konstantin Sergeevich Alekseev) (stage producer); Moscow **(1863–1938)**
Stanley, Sir Henry Morton (John Rowlands) (explorer); Denbigh, Wales **(1841–1904)**
Stanley, Kim (Patricia Reid) (actress); Tularosa, N.M. **(1925–2001)**
Stans, Maurice H. (ex-secretary of commerce); Shakope, Minn. **(1908–1998)**
Stanton, Elizabeth Cady (woman suffragist); Johnstown, N.Y. **(1815–1902)**
Stanton, Frank (broadcasting executive); Muskegon, Mich., 3/20/08
Stanwyck, Barbara (Ruby Stevens) (actress); Brooklyn, N.Y. **(1907–1990)**
Stapleton, Jean (Jeanne Murray) (actress); New York City, 1/19/23
Stapleton, Maureen (actress); Troy, N.Y., 6/21/25
Starker, Janós (cellist); Budapest, 7/5/26
Starr, Kay (Starks) (singer); Dougherty, Okla., 7/21/22
Starr, Kenneth (independent counsel for Whitewater investigation); Vernon, Tex., 7/21/46
Starr, Ringo (Richard Starkey) (singer, songwriter); Liverpool, England, 7/7/40
Stassen, Harold E. (ex-government official); West St. Paul, Minn. **(1907–2001)**
Staudinger, Hermann (chemist, Nobel laureate); Worms, Germany **(1881–1965)**
Steber, Eleanor (soprano); Wheeling, W. Va. **(1916–1990)**

Steegmuller, Francis (biographer); New Haven, Conn. **(1906–1994)**
Steel, Danielle (Danielle Fernande Schuelein-Steel) (novelist); New York City, 8/14/47
Steele, Tommy (singer); London, 12/17/36
Stefani, Gwen (singer); Orange County, Calif., 10/3/69
Stegner, Wallace (Earle) (novelist, critic); Lake Mills, Iowa **(1909–1993)**
Steichen, Edward Jean (photographer, artist); Luxembourg **(1879–1973)**
Steiger, Rod (Rodney) (actor); Westhampton, N.Y. **(1925–2002)**
Stein, Gertrude (author); Allegheny, Pa. **(1874–1946)**
Steinbeck, John Ernst (novelist); Salinas, Calif. **(1902–1968)**
Steinberg, David (comedian); Winnipeg, Man., Canada, 8/19/42
Steinberg, William (conductor); Cologne, Germany **(1899–1978)**
Steinem, Gloria (feminist, publisher); Toledo, Ohio, 3/25/34
Steinmetz, Charles (electrical engineer); Breslau, Poland **(1865–1923)**
Steenburgen, Mary (actress); Newport, Ark., 2/8/53
Stendhal (Marie Henri Beyle) (novelist); Grenoble, France **(1783–1842)**
Stern, Howard (radio personality); New York City, 1/2/54
Stern, Isaac (concert violinist); Kreminlecz, Russia **(1920–2001)**
Sterne, Laurence (novelist); Clonmel, Ireland **(1713–1768)**
Stevens, Cat (Steven Georgiou) (singer, songwriter); London, 7/21/47
Stevens, Connie (Concetta Ingolia) (singer); Brooklyn, N.Y., 8/8/38
Stevens, George (film director); Oakland, Calif. **(1905–1975)**
Stevens, Risë (mezzo-soprano); New York City, 6/11/13
Stevens, Wallace (poet); Reading, Pa. **(1879–1955)**
Stevenson, Adlai Ewing (statesman); Los Angeles **(1900–1965)**
Stevenson, McLean (actor); Bloomington, Ill. **(1929–1996)**
Stevenson, Parker (actor); Philadelphia, 6/4/52
Stevenson, Robert Louis Balfour (novelist, poet); Edinburgh, Scotland **(1850–1894)**
Stewart, James (actor); Indiana, Pa. **(1908–1997)**
Stewart, Jon (Jonathan Stewart Leibowitz) (comedian, actor); Trenton, N.J., 11/28/62
Stewart, Martha (entrepreneurial home stylist); Nutley, N.J., 8/3/41
Stewart, Patrick (actor); Mirfield, England, 7/13/40
Stewart, Rod (Roderick David) (singer); London, 1/10/45
Stieglitz, Alfred (photographer); Hoboken, N.J. **(1864–1946)**
Stiers, David Ogden (actor); Peoria, Ill., 10/31/42
Stiller, Ben (actor, director, comic); New York City, 11/30/65
Stiller, Jerry (actor); Brooklyn, N.Y., 6/8/29
Stills, Stephen (singer, songwriter); Dallas, 1/3/45
Stine, R. L. (Robert Lawrence Stine) (writer); Columbus, Ohio, 10/8/43
Sting (Gordon Matthew Sumner) (singer, composer); Wallsend, England, 10/2/51
Stipe, Michael (singer); Decatur, Ga., 1/4/60
Stockwell, Dean (actor); North Hollywood, Calif., 3/5/36
Stoker, Bram (novelist); Dublin **(1847–1912)**
Stokes, Carl (TV newscaster); Cleveland **(1927–1996)**
Stokowski, Leopold (conductor); London **(1882–1977)**
Stoltz, Eric (actor); Whittier, Calif., 9/30/61
Stone, Edward Durell (architect); Fayetteville, Ark. **(1902–1978)**
Stone, I(sidor) F(einstein) (journalist); Philadelphia **(1907–1989)**
Stone, Irving (Irving Tennenbaum) (novelist); San Francisco **(1903–1989)**
Stone, Lucy (woman suffragist); nr. West Brookfield, Mass. **(1818–1893)**
Stone, Oliver (director, writer, producer); New York City, 9/15/46
Stone, Robert (novelist); Brooklyn, N.Y., 8/21/37
Stone, Sharon (actress); Meadville, Pa., 3/10/58
Stone, Sly (Sylvester Stone) (rock musician) 1944
Stooges, The Three (comedy team) **Moe Howard** (Moses Horwitz); Brooklyn, N.Y. **(1897–1975;) Shemp Howard** (Samuel Horwitz); Brooklyn, N.Y. **(1900–1955;) Larry Fine** (Laurence Feinburg); Philadelphia **(1911–1974;) Curly Howard** (Jerome Horwitz); Brooklyn, N.Y. **(1906 –1952)**
Stoppard, Tom (Thomas Straussler) (playwright); Zlin, Slovakia, 7/3/37
Stout, Rex (mystery writer); Noblesville, Ind. **(1886–1975)**
Stowe, Harriet Elizabeth Beecher (novelist); Litchfield, Conn. **(1811–1896)**
Stowe, Madeleine (actress); Eagle Rock, Calif., 8/18/58
Strachey, (Giles) Lytton (biographer); London **(1880–1932)**
Stradivari, Antonio (violinmaker); Cremona, Italy **(1644–1737)**
Straight, Beatrice (actress); Old Westbury, N.Y. **(1918–2001)**
Strasberg, Lee (stage director); Budanov, Austria **(1901–1982)**
Strasberg, Susan (actress); New York City **(1938–1999)**
Stratas, Teresa (soprano); Toronto, 5/26/38
Straus, Oskar (composer); Vienna **(1870–1954)**
Strauss, Johann (composer); Vienna **(1825–1899)**
Strauss, Lewis L. (naval officer, scientist); Charleston, W. Va. **(1896–1974)**
Strauss, Peter (actor); New York City, 2/20/47
Strauss, Richard (composer); Munich, Germany **(1864–1949)**
Stravinsky, Igor (composer); Orlenbaum, Russia **(1882–1971)**
Streep, Meryl (Mary Louise) (actress); Summit, N.J., 6/22/49
Streisand, Barbra (singer, actress, director, producer, writer); Brooklyn, N.Y., 4/24/42
Strindberg, (Johan) August (dramatist); Stockholm **(1849–1912)**
Stritch, Elaine (actress); Detroit, 2/2/25
Struthers, Sally Ann (actress); Portland, Ore., 7/28/48
Stuart, Gilbert Charles (painter); Rhode Island **(1755–1828)**
Stuart, Gloria (film actress); Santa Monica, Calif., 7/4/10
Stuart, James Ewell Brown (known as Jeb) (Confederate army officer); Patrick County, Va. **(1833–1864)**
Sturges, Preston (Edmond P. Biden) (director, screenwriter, playwright); Chicago **(1898–1959)**
Stuyvesant, Peter (Governor of New Amsterdam); West Friesland, Netherlands **(1592–1672)**
Styne, Jule (Julius Kerwin Stein) (songwriter); London **(1905–1994)**
Styron, William (William Clark Styron, Jr.) (novelist); Newport News, Va., 6/11/25
Suharto (president of Indonesia); Sedaju-Godean, Java, 2/20/21
Sukarno (Indonesian leader); Surabaja, Java **(1901–1970)**
Sullavan, Margaret Brooke (actress); Norfolk, Va. **(1911–1960)**
Sullivan, Sir Arthur Seymour (composer); London **(1842–1900)**
Sullivan, Barry (Patrick Barry) (actor); New York City **(1912–1994)**
Sullivan, Ed (columnist, TV personality); New York City **(1901–1974)**
Sullivan, Frank (Francis John) (humorist); Saratoga Springs, N.Y. **(1892–1976)**
Sullivan, Louis Henry (architect); Boston **(1856–1924)**
Sulzberger, Arthur Ochs (newspaper publisher); New York City, 2/5/26
Sumac, Yma (singer); Ichocan, Peru, 9/10/27
Summer, Donna (La Donna Andrea Gaines) (singer); Boston, 12/31/48
Sun Ra (Herman "Sunny" Blount) (jazz composer); Birmingham, Ala. **(1914?–1993)**
Sun Tzu (writer, military strategist); China **(fl. c. 500–320 B.C.)**
Sun Yat-sen (statesman); nr. Macao **(1866–1925)**
Susann, Jacqueline (novelist); Philadelphia **(1918–1974)**
Susskind, David (TV producer); New York City **(1920–1987)**
Sutherland, Donald (actor); St. John, N.B., Canada, 7/17/34
Sutherland, Joan (soprano); Sydney, Australia, 11/7/26
Sutherland, Kiefer (actor); London, 12/18/66
Suzuki, Pat (actress); Cressey, Calif., 1931
Swados, Elizabeth (composer, playwright); Buffalo, N.Y., 2/5/51
Swank, Hilary (actress); Bellingham, Wash., 7/30/74
Swanson, Gloria (Gloria May Josephine Svensson) (actress); Chicago **(1899–1983)**
Swarthout, Gladys (soprano); Deepwater, Mo. **(1904–1969)**
Swayze, John Cameron (news commentator); Wichita, Kans. **(1906–1995)**
Swayze, Patrick (actor, dancer); Houston, 8/18/54
Swedenborg, Emanuel (scientist, philosopher, mystic); Stockholm **(1688–1772)**
Swift, Jonathan (satirist); Dublin **(1667–1745)**
Swinburne, Algernon Charles (poet); London **(1837–1909)**
Swit, Loretta (actress); Passaic, N.J., 11/4/37
Swope, Herbert Bayard (journalist); St. Louis **(1882–1958)**
Sydow, Max von (Carl Adolf von Sydow) (actor); Lund, Sweden, 4/10/29
Symons, Arthur (poet, critic); Milford Haven, Wales **(1865–1945)**
Synge, John Millington (dramatist); nr. Dublin **(1871–1909)**
Szilard, Leo (physicist); Budapest **(1898–1964)**

T

Taft, Robert Alphonso (legislator); Cincinnati **(1889–1953)**
Taft, William Howard (27th U.S. president); Cincinnati **(1857–1930)**
Tagore, Sir Rabindranath (poet); Calcutta **(1861–1941)**
Tallchief, Maria (ballet dancer); Fairfax, Okla., 1/24/25
Talleyrand-Pèrigord, Charles Maurice de (statesman); Paris **(1754–1838)**
Talmadge, Norma (actress); Niagara Falls, N.Y. **(1897–1957)**
Talvela, Martti (basso); Hiitola, Finalnd **(1935–1989)**
Tamerlane (Timur) (Mongol conqueror); nr. Samarkand, Turkestan **(c. 1336–1405)**
Tamiroff, Akim (actor); Baku, Azerbaijan **(1899–1972)**
Tan, Amy (novelist); Oakland, Calif., 2/19/52
Tanaka, Tomoyuki (film producer); Osaka, Japan **(1910–1997)**

Tandy, Jessica (actress); London **(1909–1994)**
Tarbell, Ida Minerva (author, muckraker); Erie Co., Pa. **(1857–1944)**
Tarkington, (Newton) Booth (novelist); Indianapolis **(1869–1946)**
Tartikoff, Brandon (television executive); Freeport, N.Y. **(1949–1997)**
Tate, Allen (John Orley) (poet, critic); Winchester, Ky. **(1899–1979)**
Tate, Sharon (actress); Dallas **(1943–1969)**
Taylor, Deems (composer); New York City **(1885–1966)**
Taylor, Elizabeth (actress); London, 2/27/32
Taylor, Harold (educator); Toronto, 9/28/14
Taylor, James (singer, songwriter); Boston, 3/12/48
Taylor, Laurette (Laurette Cooney) (actress); New York City **(1884–1946)**
Taylor, Lili (actress); Glenco, Ill., 2/20/67
Taylor, Gen. Maxwell D. (former Army chief of staff); Keytesville, Mo. **(1901–1987)**
Taylor, Niki (model); Pembroke Pines, Fla., 3/5/75
Taylor, Paul (choreographer); Wilkinsburg, Pa., 7/29/30
Taylor, Rod (actor); Sydney, Australia, 1/11/30
Taylor, Zachary (12th U.S. president); Montebello, Orange County, Va. **(1784–1850)**
Tchaikovsky, Peter (Pëtr) Ilich (composer); Votkinsk, Russia **(1840–1893)**
Teasdale, Sara (poet); St. Louis **(1884–1933)**
Tebaldi, Renata (lyric soprano); Pesaro, Italy, 1/2/22
Tecumseh (Shawnee Indian chief); nr. Springfield, Ohio **(1768–1813)**
Te Kanawa, Kiri (soprano); Gisborne, New Zealand, 3/6/44
Telemann, Georg Philipp (composer); Magdeburg, Germany **(1681–1767)**
Teller, Edward (atomic physicist); Budapest **(1908–2003)**
Templeton, Alec Andrew (pianist, composer); Cardiff, Wales **(1910–1963)**
Tennille, Toni (singer); Montgomery, Ala., 5/8/43
Tennyson, Alfred (1st Baron Tennyson) (poet); Somersby, England **(1809–1892)**
Tenskwatawa (Shawnee prophet); Old Piqua, Ohio **(c. 1770–c. 1835)**
Terhune, Albert Payson (novelist, journalist); Newark, N.J. **(1872–1942)**
Terkel, Studs (writer, interviewer); New York City, 5/16/12
Terry, Ellen Alicia (actress); Coventry, England **(1848–1928)**
Terry-Thomas (Thomas Terry Hoar Stevens) (actor); London **(1911–1990)**
Tesla, Nikola (electrical engineer, inventor); Smiljan, Lika, Croatia **(1856–1943)**
Thackeray, William Makepeace (novelist); Calcutta **(1811–1863)**
Thalberg, Irving G. (producer); Brooklyn, N.Y. **(1899–1936)**
Thant, U (U.N. statesman); Pantanaw, Burma **(1909–1974)**
Tharp, Twyla (dancer, choreographer); Portland, Ind., 7/1/42
Thatcher, Margaret (former prime minister); Grantham, England, 10/13/25
Thebom, Blanche (mezzo-soprano); Monessen, Pa., 9/19/19
Theodorakis, Mikis (composer); Chios, Greece, 7/29/25
Thicke, Alan (actor, composer); Kirland Lake, Ont., Canada, 3/1/47
Thieu, Nguyen Van (ex-president of South Vietnam); Trithuy, Vietnam, 4/5/23
Thomas, Danny (Amos Jacobs) (entertainer, TV producer); Deerfield, Mich. **(1912–1991)**
Thomas, Dylan Marials (poet); Carmarthenshire, Wales **(1914–1953)**
Thomas, JonathanTaylor (actor); Bethlehem, Pa., 9/8/81
Thomas, Kristen Scott (actress); Redruth, Cornwall, England, 1960
Thomas, Lowell (explorer, commentator); Woodington, Ohio **(1892–1981)**
Thomas, Marlo (actress); Detroit, 11/21/43
Thomas, Michael Tilson (conductor); Hollywood, Calif., 12/21/44
Thomas, Norman Mattoon (Socialist leader); Marion, Ohio **(1884–1968)**
Thomas, Philip Michael (actor); Columbus, Ohio, 5/26/49
Thomas, Richard (actor); New York City, 6/13/51
Thompson, Dorothy (writer); Lancaster, N.Y. **(1894–1961)**
Thompson, Emma (actress); London, 4/15/59
Thompson, Hunter (Stockton) (writer); Louisville, Ky., 7/18/39
Thompson, Lea (actress); Rochester, Minn., 5/31/61
Thompson, Sada (actress); Des Moines, Iowa, 9/27/29
Thomson, Virgil (Garnett) (composer); Kansas City, Mo. **(1896–1989)**
Thoreau, Henry David (naturalist, author); Concord, Mass. **(1817–1862)**
Thorndike, Dame Sybil (actress); Gainsborough, England **(1882–1976)**
Thorne-Smith, Courtney (actress); San Francisco, 11/8/67
Thornton, Billy Bob (actor, screenwriter); Hot Springs, Ark., 8/4/55
Thurber, James Grover (author, cartoonist); Columbus, Ohio **(1894–1961)**
Thurman, Robert A. F. (scholar, Indo-Tibetan Buddhist studies); New York City, 8/6/40
Thurman, Uma (actress); Boston, 4/29/70
Thurmond, (James) Strom (U.S. senator); Edgefield, S.C. **(1902–2003)**
Tibbett, Lawrence (baritone); Bakersfield, Calif. **(1896–1960)**
Tiberius Caesar Augustus (Roman emperor); Capri **(42 B.C.–A.D. 37)**
Tiegs, Cheryl (model, actress); Minnesota, 9/25/47
Tierney, Gene (actress); Brooklyn, N.Y. **(1920–1991)**
Tillich, Paul (philosopher, theologian); Starzeddel, Germany **(1886–1965)**
Tilly, Meg (Margaret Tilly) (actress); Texada Island, B.C., Canada, 2/14/60
Tintoretto, Il (Jacopo Robusti) (painter); Venice **(1518–1594)**
Tiny Tim (Herbert Khaury) (entertainer); New York City **(1932–1996)**
Tiomkin, Dmitri (composer); St. Petersburg, Russia **(1894–1979)**
Titian (Tiziano Vecelli) (painter); Pieve di Cadore, Italy **(1477–1576)**
Tito (Josip Broz or Brozovich) (president of Yugoslavia); Croatia (former Yugoslavia) **(1892–1980)**
Tocqueville, Alexis de (writer); Verneuil, France **(1805–1859)**
Todd, Michael (producer); Minneapolis **(1907–1958)**
Todd, Thelma (actress); Lawrence, Mass. **(1905–1935)**
Tolkien, J(ohn) R(onald) R(euel) (fantasy writer); Bloemfontein, South Africa **(1892–1973)**
Tolstoy, Count Leo (Lev) Nikolaevich (novelist); Tula Province, Russia **(1828–1910)**
Tomei, Marisa (actress); Brooklyn, N.Y., 12/4/64
Tomlin, Lily (actress, comedienne); Detroit, 9/1/36
Tone, Franchot (actor); Niagara Falls, N.Y. **(1905–1968)**
Tormé, Mel (Melvin) (singer); Chicago **(1925–1999)**
Torn, Rip (Elmore Torn, Jr.) (actor, director); Temple, Tex., 2/6/31
Torquamada, Tomásde (Spanish Inquisitor); Valladolid, Spain **(1420–1498)**
Toscanini, Arturo (orchestra conductor); Parma, Italy **(1867–1957)**
Totenberg, Nina (broadcast journalist); New York City, 1/14/44
Toulouse-Lautrec (Henri Marie Raymond de Toulouse-Lautrec Monfa) (painter); Albi, France **(1864–1901)**
Toynbee, Arnold J. (historian); London **(1889–1975)**
Tracy, Spencer (actor); Milwaukee **(1900–1967)**
Traubel, Helen (Wagnerian soprano); St. Louis **(1903–1972)**
Travanti, Daniel J. (actor); Kenosha, Wis., 3/7/40
Travolta, John (actor); Englewood, N.J., 2/18/54
Treacher, Arthur (actor); Brighton, England **(1894–1975)**
Tree, Sir Herbert Beerbohm (actor, manager); London **(1853–1917)**
Trevor, Claire (Wemlinger) (actress); New York City **(1909–2000)**
Trigère, Pauline (fashion designer); Paris, 11/4/12
Trilling, Diana (writer); New York City **(1905–1996)**
Trilling, Lionel (author, educator); New York City **(1905–1975)**
Trollope, Anthony (novelist); London **(1815–1882)**
Trotsky, Leon (Lev Davidovich Bronstein) (statesman); Elisavetgrad, Russia **(1879–1940)**
Troyanos, Tatiana (mezzo-soprano); New York City **(1938–1993)**
Trudeau, Garry (cartoonist); New York City, 1948
Trudeau, Pierre Elliott (former prime minister); Montreal **(1919–2000)**
Truffaut, François (film director); Paris **(1932–1984)**
Trujillo y Molina, Rafael Leonidas (dictator); San Cristóbal, Dominican Republic **(1891–1961)**
Truman, Harry S. (33rd U.S. president); near Lamar, Mo. **(1884–1972)**
Truman, Margaret (author); Independence, Mo., 2/17/24
Trump, Donald (business executive); New York City, 6/14/46
Truth, Sojourner (Isabella) (preacher, abolitionist); Ulster Co., N.Y. **(c. 1797–1883)**
Tryon, Thomas (actor, novelist); Hartford, Conn. **(1926–1991)**
Tsiolkovsky, Konstantin E. (father of cosmonautics); Izhevskoye, Russia **(1857–1935)**
Tsongas, Paul E. (politician); Lowell, Mass. **(1941–1997)**
Tubman, Harriet (Araminta) (abolitionist); Dorchester Co., Md. **(c. 1820–1913)**
Tuchman, Barbara (Wertheim) (historian, author); New York City **(1912–1989)**
Tucker, Forrest (actor); Plainfield, Ind. **(1919–1986)**
Tucker, Richard (tenor); New York City **(1914–1975)**
Tucker, Sophie (Sophia Kalish) (singer); Russia **(1884–1966)**
Tudor, Antony (choreographer); London **(1909–1987)**
Tune, Tommy (dancer, choreographer); Wichita Falls, Tex., 2/28/39
Turgenev, Ivan Sergeevich (novelist); Orel, Russia **(1818–1883)**
Turlington, Christy (model); San Francisco, 1/2/69
Turner, Frederick J. (historian); Portage, Wis. **(1861–1932)**

Turner, Ike (singer); Clarksdale, Miss., 11/5/31
Turner, Janine (actress); Lincoln, Neb., 12/6/62
Turner, Joseph M.W. (painter); London **(1775–1851)**
Turner, Kathleen (actress); Springfield, Mo., 6/19/54
Turner, Lana (Julia Jean Mildred Frances Turner) (actress); Wallace, Idaho **(1920–1995)**
Turner, Nat (civil rights leader); Southampton County, Va. **(1800–1831)**
Turner, Ted (business executive); Cincinnati, 11/19/38
Turner, Tina (Annie Mae Bullock) (singer); Nut Bush, Tenn., 11/26/39
Turpin, Ben (comedian); New Orleans **(1874–1940)**
Turturro, John (actor); Brooklyn, N.Y., 2/28/57
Twain, Mark (Samuel Langhorne Clemens) (author); Florida, Mo. **(1835–1910)**
Twain, Shania (Eileen Regina Twain) (country singer); Windsor, Ont., Canada, 8/28/65
Tweed, William Marcy (politician); New York City **(1823–1878)**
Twiggy (Leslie Hornby) (model); London, 9/19/49
Twining, Gen. Nathan F. (former Air Force chief of staff); Monroe, Wis. **(1897–1982)**
Twitty, Conway (Harold Lloyd Jenkins) (singer, guitarist); Friars Point, Miss. **(1933–1993)**
Tyler, John (10th U.S. president); Charles City County, Va. **(1790–1862)**
Tyler, Liv (actress, model); Portland, Maine, 7/1/77
Tyler, Steven (singer); New York City, 3/26/48
Tyson, Cicely (actress); New York City, 12/19/33

U

Uccello, Paolo (painter); Florence **(1397–1475)**
Udall, Stewart L. (ex-secretary of the interior); St. Johns, Ariz., 1/31/20
Uggams, Leslie (singer, actress); New York City, 5/25/43
Ulanova, Galina (ballet dancer); St. Petersburg, Russia **(1910–1998)**
Ullman, Tracey (actress, singer); Slough, England, 12/30/59
Ullmann, Liv (actress); Tokyo, 12/16/39
Ulrich, Skeet (actor, model); North Carolina, 1/20/70
Untermeyer, Louis (anthologist, poet); New York City **(1885–1977)**
Updike, John (novelist); Shillington, Pa., 3/18/32
Urey, Harold C. (chemist, Nobel laureate); Walkerton, Ind. **(1893–1981)**
Uris, Leon (novelist); Baltimore **(1924–2003)**
Ustinov, Peter (actor, producer); London, 4/16/21
Utrillo, Maurice (painter); Paris **(1883–1955)**

V

Vaccaro, Brenda (actress); Brooklyn, N.Y., 11/18/39
Vadim, Roger (Roger Vadim Plemiannikov) (film director); Paris **(1928–2000)**
Valentine, Karen (actress); Sabastopol, Calif., 5/25/47
Valentino, Rudolph (Rodolpho d'Antonguolla) (actor); Castellaneta, Italy **(1895–1926)**
Valentino (Valentino Garavani) (fashion designer); nr. Milan, Italy, 5/11/32
Valéry, Paul (Ambroise Toussaint Jules) (poet, critic); Sète, France **(1871–1945)**
Vallee, Rudy (Hubert Prior Rudy Vallée) (band leader, singer); Island Pond, Vt. **(1901–1986)**
Valli, Frankie (Frank Castellaccio) (singer); Newark, N.J., 5/3/37
Van Allen, James Alfred (space physicist); Mt. Pleasant, Iowa, 9/7/14
Van Buren, Abigail (Pauline Esther Friedman) (columnist); Sioux City, Iowa, 7/4/18
Van Buren, Martin (8th U.S. president); Kinderhook, N.Y. **(1782–1862)**
Vance, Vivian (Vivian Jones) (actress); Cherryvale, Kans. **(1909–1979)**
Van Der Beek, James (actor); Cheshire, Conn., 3/8/77
Vanderbilt, Alfred G. (sportsman); London **(1912–1999)**
Vanderbilt, Cornelius (financier); Port Richmond, N.Y. **(1794–1877)**
Vanderbilt, Gloria (fashion designer); New York City, 2/20/24
Van Doren, Carl (writer, educator); Hope, Ill. **(1885–1950)**
Van Doren, Mamie (actress); Rowena, S.D., 2/6/33
Vandross, Luther (R&B singer); New York City, 4/20/51
Van Dyke, Dick (actor); West Plains, Mo., 12/13/25
Vandyke (or Van Dyck), Sir Anthony (painter); Antwerp, Belgium **(1599–1641)**
Van Eyck, Jan (painter); Maeseyck, Belgium **(c. 1390–1441)**
Van Fleet, Jo (actress); Oakland, Calif. **(1915–1996)**
van Gogh, Vincent (painter); Groot Zundert, Brabant, The Netherlands **(1853–1890)**
van Hamel, Martine (ballet dancer); Brussels, 11/16/45
Van Heusen, Jimmy (Edward Chester Babcock) (songwriter); Syracuse, N.Y. **(1913–1990)**
Van Patten, Dick (actor); Richmond Hill, N.Y., 12/9/28
Van Peebles, Melvin (playwright); Chicago, 9/21/32
Vasari, Giorgio (art historian); Arezzo, Italy **(1511–1574)**
Vaughan, Sarah (singer); Newark, N.J. **(1924–1990)**
Vaughan Williams, Ralph (composer); Down Ampney, England **(1872–1958)**
Vaughn, Robert (actor); New York City, 11/22/32
Vaughn, Vince (actor); Minneapolis, 3/28/70
Veblen, Thorstein (economist, social critic); Cato Township, Wis. **(1857–1929)**
Veidt, Conrad (actor); Potsdam, Germany **(1893–1943)**
Velázquez, Diego Rodriguez de Silva y (painter); Seville, Spain **(1599–1660)**
Venturi, Robert (Charles) (architect); Philadelphia, 6/25/25
Verdi, Giuseppe (composer); Roncole, Italy **(1813–1901)**
Verdon, Gwen (actress); Culver City, Calif. **(1925–2000)**
Vereen, Ben (actor, singer); Miami, Fla., 10/10/46
Verlaine, Paul (poet); Metz, France **(1844–1896)**
Vermeer, Jan (or Jan van der Meer van Delft) (painter); Delft, Netherlands **(1632–1675)**
Verne, Jules (author); Nantes, France **(1828–1905)**
Veronese, Paolo (Paolo Cagliari) (painter); Verona, Italy **(1528–1588)**
Verrazano, Giovanni da (navigator); Florence, Italy **(c. 1485–1528)**
Verrett, Shirley (mezzo-soprano); New Orleans, 5/31/33
Versace, Gianni (fashion designer); Reggio di Calabria, Italy **(1946–1997)**
Vesalius, Andreas (anatomist); Brussels **(1515–1564)**
Vespucci, Amerigo (navigator); Florence, Italy **(1454–1512)**
Vico, Giovanni Battista (philosopher); Naples, Italy **(1668–1744)**
Victoria (queen of England); London **(1819–1901)**
Vidal, Gore (novelist); West Point, N.Y., 10/3/25
Vidor, King (film director, producer); Galveston, Tex. **(1895–1982)**
Vigoda, Abe (actor); New York City, 2/24/21
Villa, Pancho (Doroteo Arango) (revolutionary); Hacienda de Rio Grande, San Juan del Rio, Mexico **(1877–1923)**
Villella, Edward (ballet dancer); Bayside, Queens, N.Y., 10/1/36
Villon, François (François de Montcorbier) (poet); Paris **(1431–1463)**
Vinton, Bobby (singer); Canonsburg, Pa., 4/16/35
Virgil (or Vergil) (Publius Vergilius Maro) (poet); nr. Mantua, Italy **(70–19 B.C.)**
Vishnevskaya, Galina (soprano); St. Petersburg, Russia, 10/25/26
Vivaldi, Antonio (composer); Venice **(1678–1741)**
Vlaminck, Maurice de (painter); Paris **(1876–1958)**
Voight, Jon (actor); Yonkers, N.Y., 12/29/38
Volta, Alessandro (scientist); Como, Italy **(1745–1827)**
Voltaire (François Marie Arouet) (author); Paris **(1694–1778)**
von Braun, Wernher (rocket scientist); Wirsitz, Germany **(1912–1977)**
von Furstenberg, Betsy (Elizabeth Caroline Maria Agatha Felicitas Therese von Furstenberg-Hedringen) (actress); Nelheim-Heusen, Germany, 8/16/35
von Fürstenberg, Diane (Diane Simone Michelle Halfin) (fashion designer); Brussels, 12/31/46
von Hindenburg, Paul (statesman); Posen, Poland **(1847–1934)**
von Karajan, Herbert (conductor); Salzburg, Austria **(1908–1989)**
Vonnegut, Kurt, Jr. (novelist); Indianapolis, 11/11/22
Von Stade, Frederica (mezzo-soprano); Somerville, N.J., 6/1/45
Von Stroheim, Erich Oswald Hans Carl Maria von Nordenwall (actor, director); Vienna **(1885–1957)**
Von Zell, Harry (announcer); Indianapolis **(1906–1981)**
Vreeland, Diana (Diana Da Iziel) (fashion journalist, museum consultant); Paris **(1903?–1989)**

W

Wagner, Lindsay (actress); Los Angeles, 6/22/49
Wagner, Robert (actor); Detroit, 2/10/30
Wagner, Robert F. (ex-mayor of New York City); New York City **(1910–1991)**
Wagner, Wilhelm Richard (composer); Leipzig, Germany **(1813–1883)**
Wahlberg, Mark (actor, model, musician); Dorchester, Mass., 6/5/71
Waits, Tom (blues singer); Pomona, Calif., 12/7/49
Waldheim, Kurt (ex-UN secretary-general); St. Andrae-Wörden, Austria, 12/21/18

Walesa, Lech (Polish labor leader and ex-president); Popowo, Poland, 9/29/43
Walken, Christopher (actor); Queens, N.Y., 3/31/43
Walker, Alice (novelist, poet); Eatonon, Ga., 2/9/44
Walker, Nancy (Ann Myrtle Swoyer) (actress, comedienne); Philadelphia **(1922–1992)**
Walker, Robert (actor); Salt Lake City **(1918–1951)**
Walker, T-Bone (blues singer); Linden, Tex. **(1910–1975)**
Wallace, DeWitt (publisher); St. Paul, Minn. **(1889–1981)**
Wallace, George C. (ex-governor); Clio, Ala. **(1919–1998)**
Wallace, Irving (novelist); Chicago **(1916–1990)**
Wallace, Mike (Myron Wallace) (TV interviewer, commentator); Brookline, Mass., 5/9/18
Wallach, Eli (actor); Brooklyn, N.Y., 12/7/15
Wallenberg, Raoul (diplomat, humanitarian); Stockholm **(1912–1947)**
Wallenstein, Alfred (conductor); Chicago **(1898–1983)**
Waller, Thomas "Fats" (pianist); New York City **(1904–1943)**
Wallis, Hal (film producer); Chicago **(1899–1986)**
Walpole, Horace (statesman, novelist); London **(1717–1797)**
Walsh, J. T. (actor); San Francisco, Calif. **(1944–1998)**
Waltari, Mika (novelist); Helsinki **(1903–1979)**
Walter, Bruno (Bruno Walter Schlesinger) (orchestra conductor); Berlin **(1876–1962)**
Walters, Barbara (TV commentator); Boston, 9/25/31
Walton, Izaak (author); Stafford, England **(1593–1683)**
Wambaugh, Joseph (author, screenwriter); East Pittsburgh, 1/22/37
Wanamaker, John (merchant); Philadelphia **(1838–1922)**
Wanamaker, Sam (actor, director); Chicago **(1919–1993)**
Ward, Barbara (economist); York, England **(1914–1981)**
Ward, Rachel (actress); Cornwell Manor, England, 9/12/57
Warhol, Andy (Warhola) (artist); McKeesport, Pa. **(1928–1987)**
Waring, Fred (band leader); Tyrone, Pa. **(1900–1984)**
Warner, H. B. (Henry Bryan Warner Lickford) (actor); London **(1876–1958)**
Warren, Lesley Ann (actress); New York City, 8/16/46
Warren, Robert Penn (novelist); Guthrie, Ky. **(1905–1989)**
Warrick, Ruth (actress); St. Joseph, Mo., 6/29/15
Warwick, Dionne (singer); East Orange, N.J., 12/12/41
Washington, Booker T(aliaferro) (educator); Franklin County, Va. **(1856–1915)**
Washington, Denzel (actor); Mt. Vernon, N.Y., 12/28/54
Washington, George (1st U.S. president); Westmoreland County, Va. **(1732–1799)**
Washington, Harold (ex-mayor of Chicago); Chicago **(1922–1987)**
Waters, Ethel (actress, singer); Chester, Pa. **(1896–1977)**
Waters, Muddy (McKinley Morganfield) (singer, guitarist); Rolling Fork, Miss. **(1915–1983)**
Waterston, Sam (actor); Cambridge, Mass., 11/15/40
Watson, James Dewey (scientist, Nobel laureate); Chicago, 4/6/28
Watson, Thomas John (industrialist); Campbell, N.Y. **(1874–1956)**
Watt, James (inventor); Greenock, Scotland **(1736–1819)**
Watteau, Jean-Antoine (painter); Valanciennes, France **(1684–1721)**
Wattleton, Faye (family planning advocate); St. Louis, 7/8/43
Watts, André (concert pianist); Nuremberg, Germany, 6/20/46
Waugh, Alec (Alexander Raban Waugh) (novelist); London **(1898–1981)**
Waugh, Evelyn (novelist); London **(1903–1966)**
Wayans, Damon (actor, comedian, writer, producer); New York City, 9/4/60
Wayans, Keenan Ivory (actor, comedian, writer, director); New York City, 6/8/58
Wayne, Anthony (military officer); Waynesboro (family farm), nr. Paoli, Pa. **(1745–1796)**
Wayne, David (David McMeekan) (actor); Traverse City, Mich. **(1914–1995)**
Wayne, John (Marion Michael Morrison) (actor); Winterset, Iowa **(1907–1979)**
Weaver, Dennis (actor); Joplin, Mo., 6/4/25
Weaver, Fritz (actor); Pittsburgh, 1/19/26
Weaver, Sigourney (actress); New York City, 10/8/49
Webb, Clifton (Webb Parmelee Hollenbeck) (actor); Indianapolis **(1893–1966)**
Webb, Jack (actor, producer); Santa Monica, Calif. **(1920–1982)**
Weber, Karl Maria Friedrich Ernst von (composer); nr. Lübeck, Germany **(1786–1826)**
Webster, Daniel (statesman); Salisbury, N.H. **(1782–1852)**
Webster, Margaret (producer, director, actress); New York City **(1905–1973)**
Webster, Noah (lexicographer); West Hartford, Conn. **(1758–1843)**
Weill, Kurt (composer); Dessau, Germany **(1900–1950)**
Weir, Peter (director); Sydney, Australia, 8/21/44
Weissmuller, Johnny (Peter John Weissmuller) (actor, swimmer); Freidorf, Romania **(1904–1984)**
Weizmann, Chaim (statesman); Grodno Province, Russia **(1874–1952)**
Welch, Raquel (Raquel Tejada) (actress); Chicago, 9/5/40
Weld, Tuesday (Susan Ker Weld) (actress); New York City, 8/27/43
Welk, Lawrence (band leader); Strasburg, N.D. **(1903–1992)**
Welles, Orson (actor, director, producer); Kenosha, Wis. **(1915–1985)**
Wellington, Duke of (Arthur Wellesley) (statesman); Ireland **(1769–1852)**
Wells, H(erbert) G(eorge) (author); Bromley, England **(1866–1946)**
Wells, Ida Bell (Barnett) (journalist); Holly Springs, Miss. **(1862–1931)**
Welty, Eudora (novelist); Jackson, Miss. **(1909–2001)**
Wenner, Jann (publisher); New York City, 1/7/46
Werfel, Franz (novelist); Prague **(1890–1945)**
Werner, Oskar (Josef Schliessmayer) (actor, director); Vienna **(1922–1984)**
Wertheimer, Linda (radio journalist); Carlsbad, N.M., 3/19/43
Wertmueller, Lina (Arcanguela Felice Assunta W. von Elgg) (director); Rome, 8/14/28
Wesley, John (religious leader); Epworth Rectory, Lincolnshire, England **(1703–1791)**
West, Benjamin (painter); Springfield, Pa. **(1738–1820)**
West, Dame Rebecca (Cicily Fairfield) (novelist); County Kerry, Ireland **(1892–1983)**
West, Jessamyn (novelist); nr. North Vernon, Ind. **(1902–1984)**
West, Mae (actress); Brooklyn, N.Y. **(1893–1980)**
West, Nathanael (Nathan Weinstein) (novelist); New York City **(1902–1940)**
Westheimer, Dr. Ruth (Karola Ruth Siegel) (human sexuality expert); Frankfurt, Germany, 1928
Westinghouse, George (inventor); Central Bridge, N.Y. **(1846–1914)**
Westmoreland, William Childs (ex-Army chief of staff); Saxon, S.C., 3/26/14
Weyden, Roger van der (painter); Tournai, Belgium **(c. 1400–1464)**
Wharton, Edith Newbold (née Jones) (novelist); New York City **(1862–1937)**
Wheatley, Phillis (poet); Senegal **(c. 1753–1784)**
Wheeler, Bert (Albert Jerome Wheeler) (comedian); Paterson, N.J. **(1895–1968)**
Whistler, James Abbott McNeill (painter, etcher); Lowell, Mass. **(1834–1903)**
Whitaker, Forest (actor); Longview, Tex., 7/15/61
White, Betty (actress); Oak Park, Ill., 1/17/22
White, Edmund (writer); Cincinnati, Ohio, 1/13/40
White, E(lwyn) B(rooks) (author); Mt. Vernon, N.Y. **(1899–1985)**
White, Pearl (actress); Green Ridge, Mo. **(1889–1938)**
White, Stanford (architect); New York City **(1853–1906)**
White, Theodore H. (historian); Boston **(1915–1986)**
White, Vanna (TV personality); Conway, S.C., 2/18/57
White, William Allen (journalist); Emporia, Kans. **(1868–1944)**
Whitehead, Alfred North (mathematician, philosopher); Isle of Thanet, England **(1861–1947)**
Whiteman, Paul (band leader); Denver **(1891–1967)**
Whiting, Margaret (singer, actress); Detroit, 7/22/24
Whitman, Walt (Walter) (poet); West Hills, N.Y. **(1819–1892)**
Whitmore, James (actor); White Plains, N.Y., 10/1/21
Whitney, Cornelius Vanderbilt (sportsman); New York City **(1899–1992)**
Whitney, Eli (inventor); Westboro, Mass. **(1765–1825)**
Whitney, John Hay (publisher); Ellsworth, Maine **(1904–1982)**
Whittier, John Greenleaf (poet); Haverhill, Mass. **(1807–1892)**
Wideman, John Edgar (writer); Washington, D.C., 6/14/41
Widmark, Richard (actor); Sunrise, Minn., 12/26/14
Wiesel, Elie (Eliezer) (author); Signet, Romania, 9/30/28
Wiesenthal, Simon (Nazi hunter); Buchach, Ukraine, 12/31/08
Wilde, Cornel (film actor, producer); New York City **(1915–1989)**
Wilde, Oscar Fingal O'Flahertie Wills (author); Dublin **(1854–1900)**
Wilder, Billy (Samuel Wilder) (film producer, director); Vienna **(1906–2002)**
Wilder, Gene (Jerome Silberman) (actor, writer, director, producer); Milwaukee, 6/11/35
Wilder, Thornton (author); Madison, Wis. **(1897–1975)**
Wilkins, Roy (civil rights leader); St. Louis **(1901–1981)**
William, Prince (heir to British throne); London, 6/21/82
Williams, Andy (singer); Wall Lake, Iowa, 12/3/30
Williams, Anson (actor, director); Los Angeles, 9/25/49
Williams, Billy Dee (actor); New York City, 4/6/37
Williams, Cindy (actress); Van Nuys, Calif., 8/22/47
Williams, Edward Bennett (lawyer); Hartford, Conn. **(1920–1988)**
Williams, Emlyn (actor, playwright); Mostyn, Wales **(1905–1987)**
Williams, Esther (actress, swimmer); Los Angeles, 8/8/23
Williams, Gluyas (cartoonist); San Francisco **(1888–1982)**

Williams, Hank, Sr. (Hiram King Williams) (singer); Georgiana, Ala. **(1923–1953)**
Williams, Joe (singer); Cordele, Ga. **(1918–1999)**
Williams, John T. (composer, conductor); Queens, N.Y., 2/8/32
Williams, Lucinda (singer, songwriter); Lake Charles, La., 1/26/53
Williams, Paul (singer, composer, actor); Omaha, Neb., 9/19/40
Williams, Robin (actor, producer); Chicago, 7/21/52
Williams, Roger (clergyman); London **(1603?–1683)**
Williams, Tennessee (Thomas L. Williams) (playwright); Columbus, Miss. **(1911–1983)**
Williams, Treat (Richard Williams) (actor); Rowayton, Conn., 12/1/51
Williams, Vanessa (actress, singer); Milwood, N.Y., 3/18/63
Williams, William Carlos (physician, poet); Rutherford, N.J. **(1883–1963)**
Williamson, Nicol (actor); Hamilton, Scotland, 9/14/38
Willkie, Wendell Lewis (lawyer); Elwood, Ind. **(1892–1944)**
Willis, Bruce (actor); Germany, 3/19/55
Willson, Meredith (composer); Mason City, Iowa **(1902–1984)**
Wilson, August (poet, writer, playwright); Pittsburgh, 4/27/45
Wilson, Brian (musician); Inglewood, Calif., 6/20/42
Wilson, Don (radio and TV announcer); Lincoln, Neb. **(1900–1982)**
Wilson, Dooley (actor, musician); Tyler, Tex. **(1894–1953)**
Wilson, Edmund (literary critic, author); Red Bank, N.J. **(1895–1972)**
Wilson, Flip (Clerow Wilson) (comedian); Jersey City, N.J. **(1933–1998)**
Wilson, Harold (ex-prime minister); Huddersfield, England **(1916–1995)**
Wilson, Nancy (singer); Chillicothe, Ohio, 2/20/37
Wilson, Sloan (novelist); Norwalk, Conn., 5/8/20
Wilson, (Thomas) Woodrow (28th U.S. president); Staunton, Va. **(1856–1924)**
Winchell, Walter (columnist); New York City **(1897–1972)**
Windsor, Duchess of (Bessie Wallis Warfield) Blue Ridge Summit, Pa. **(1896–1986)**
Windsor, Duke of (formerly King Edward VIII of England); Richmond Park, England **(1894–1972)**
Winfrey, Oprah (TV host, producer); Kosciusko, Miss., 1/29/54
Winger, Debra (Mary Debra) (actress); Cleveland, 5/17/55
Winkler, Henry (actor, director, producer); New York City, 10/30/45
Winningham, Mare (actress); Phoenix, Ariz., 5/16/59
Winter, Johnny (guitarist); Leland, Miss., 2/23/44
Winters, Jonathan (comedian); Dayton, Ohio, 11/11/25
Winters, Shelley (Shirley Schrift) (actress); East St. Louis, Ill., 8/18/22
Winthrop, John (first governor, Massachusetts Bay Colony); Suffolk, England **(1588–1649)**
Wise, Stephen Samuel (rabbi); Budapest **(1874–1949)**
Withers, Jane (actress); Atlanta, 4/12/26
Witherspoon, Reese (actress); Nashville, 3/22/76
Wittig, Georg F. K. (chemist, Nobel laureate); Berlin, Germany **(1897–1987)**
Wittgenstein, Ludwig (Josef Johann) (philosopher); Vienna **(1889–1951)**
Wodehouse, P(elham) G(renville) (novelist); Guildford, England **(1881–1975)**
Wolf, Scott (actor); Boston, 6/4/68
Wolfe, Thomas Clayton (novelist); Asheville, N.C. **(1900–1938)**
Wolfe, Tom (journalist); Richmond, Va., 3/2/31
Wolff, Tobias (author); Birmingham, Ala., 6/19/45
Wolsey, Thomas (prelate, statesman); Ipswich, England **(c. 1475–1530)**
Wonder, Stevie (Steveland Judkins, later Steveland Morris) (singer, songwriter); Saginaw, Mich., 5/13/50
Wong, Anna May (Lu Tsong Wong) (actress); Los Angeles **(1907–1961)**
Woo, John (actor, film director, screenwriter); Guangzhou, Canton, China, 5/1/46
Wood, Elijah (actor); Cedar Rapids, Iowa, 1/28/81
Wood, Grant (painter); Anamosa, Iowa **(1892–1942)**
Wood, Natalie (Natasha Viparaeff) (actress); San Francisco **(1938–1981)**
Woods, James (actor); Vernal, Utah, 4/18/47
Woodhouse, Barbara (Blackburn) (dog trainer, author, TV personality); Rathfarnham, Ireland **(1910–1988)**
Woodruff, Judy (broadcast journalist); Tulsa, Okla., 11/20/46
Woodson, Carter G. (historian); New Canton, Va. **(1875–1950)**
Woodward, Edward (actor); Croydon, England, 6/1/30
Woodward, Joanne (actress); Thomasville, Ga., 2/27/30
Woodward, Robert Burns (chemist, Nobel laureate); Boston **(1917–1979)**
Woolf, (Adeline) Virginia (née Stephens) (novelist); London **(1882–1941)**
Woollcott, Alexander (author, critic); Phalanx, N.J. **(1887–1943)**
Woolley, Monty (Edgar Montillion Woolley) (actor); New York City **(1888–1963)**
Woolworth, Frank (merchant); Rodman, N.Y. **(1852–1919)**
Wopat, Tom (actor); Lodi, Wis., 9/9/50
Wordsworth, William (poet); Cockermouth, England **(1770–1850)**
Wouk, Herman (novelist); New York City, 5/27/15
Wovoka (Jack Wilson) (Paiute Indian religious leader); (western Nev.) **(c. 1858–1932)**
Wray, Fay (actress); nr. Cardston, Alb., Canada, 9/14/07
Wren, Sir Christopher (architect); East Knoyle, England **(1632–1723)**
Wright, Frank Lloyd (architect); Richland Center, Wis. **(1869–1959)**
Wright, Martha (singer); Seattle, 3/23/26
Wright, Orville (inventor); Dayton, Ohio **(1871–1948)**
Wright, Richard (novelist); nr. Natchez, Miss. **(1908–1960)**
Wright, Wilbur (inventor); Millville, Ind. **(1867–1912)**
Wyatt, Jane (actress); Campgaw, N.J., 8/12/12
Wycliffe, John (church reformer); Hipswell, England **(1320–1384)**
Wyeth, Andrew (painter); Chadds Ford, Pa., 7/12/17
Wyle, Noah (actor); Hollywood, Calif., 6/4/71
Wyler, William (director); Mulhouse, France **(1902–1981)**
Wyman, Jane (Sarah Jane Fulks) (actress); St. Joseph, Mo., 1/4/14
Wynette, Tammy (Virginia Wynette Pugh) (singer); Tupelo, Miss. **(1942–1998)**
Wynn, Ed (Isaiah Edwin Leopold) (comedian); Philadelphia **(1886–1966)**
Wynn, Keenan (actor); New York City **(1916–1986)**

X

Xavier, St. Francis (Jesuit missionary); Pamplona, Navarre, Spain **(1506–1552)**
Xenophon (soldier, historian, essayist); Athens **(c. 435–c. 355 B.C.)**
Xerxes, the Great (king); Persian Empire **(c. 519–465 B.C.)**

Y

Yeats, William Butler (poet); nr. Dublin **(1865–1939)**
Yeltsin, Boris (Russian president); Yekaterinburg (then Sverdlovsk), Russia, 2/1/31
Yevtushenko, Yevgeny (poet); Zima, Russia, 7/18/33
York, Michael (actor); Fulmer, England, 3/27/42
York, Susannah (Fletcher) (actress); London, 1/9/42
Yorty, Samuel W. (ex-mayor of Los Angeles); Lincoln, Neb. **(1909–1998)**
Yothers, Tina (actress); Whittier, Calif., 5/5/73
Young, Alan (actor); North Shield, England, 11/19/19
Young, Andrew (civil rights leader); New Orleans, 3/12/32
Young, Brigham (religious leader); Whitingham, Vt. **(1801–1877)**
Young, Gig (Byron Barr) (actor); St. Cloud, Minn. **(1917–1978)**
Young, Loretta (Gretchen Young) (actress); Salt Lake City **(1913–2000)**
Young, Neil (singer, songwriter); Toronto, 11/12/45
Young, Robert (actor); Chicago **(1907–1998)**
Youngman, Henny (comedian); Whitechapel, London **(1906–1998)**

Z

Zane, Billy (William George Zane, Jr.) (actor); Chicago, 2/24/66
Zanuck, Darryl F. (producer); Wahoo, Neb. **(1902–1979)**
Zappa, Frank (Francis Vincent Zappa, Jr.) (singer, songwriter); Baltimore **(1940–1993)**
Zeffirelli, Franco (director); Florence, Italy, 2/12/23
Zellweger, Renee (actress); Katy, Texas, 4/25/69
Zemeckis, Robert (filmmaker); Chicago, 1952
Zhou Enlai (premier); Hualyin, China **(1898–1976)**
Ziegfeld, Florenz (theatrical producer); Chicago **(1869–1932)**
Ziegler, Karl (chemist, Nobel laureate); Helsa, Germany **(1898–1973)**
Zimbalist, Efrem (violinist); Rostov-on-Don, Russia **(1889–1985)**
Zimbalist, Efrem, Jr. (actor); New York City, 11/30/23
Zimbalist, Stephanie (actress); New York City, 10/8/56
Zinnemann, Fred (director); Vienna **(1907–1997)**
Zola, Emile (novelist); Paris **(1840–1902)**
Zoroaster (religious leader); Persian Empire **(c. 628–c. 551 B.C.)**
Zucker, Jerry (film producer, director); Milwaukee, 3/11/50
Zukerman, Pinchas (violinist); Tel Aviv, Israel, 7/16/48
Zukor, Adolph (movie executive); Risce, Hungary **(1873–1976)**
Zurbarán, Francisco de (painter); Fuentes de Cantos, Spain **(1598–1664)**
Zweig, Stefan (author); Vienna **(1881–1942)**
Zwingli, Huldrych (humanist); Wildaus, Switzerland **(1484–1531)**

2004

January

S	M	T	W	T	F	S
				1	2	3
4	5	6	7	8	9	10
11	12	13	14	15	16	17
18	19	20	21	22	23	24
25	26	27	28	29	30	31

1—New Year's Day
6—Epiphany
19—Martin Luther King, Jr.'s birthday observed
22—Chinese New Year

February

S	M	T	W	T	F	S
1	2	3	4	5	6	7
8	9	10	11	12	13	14
15	16	17	18	19	20	21
22	23	24	25	26	27	28
29						

2—(Eid) al Adha*
2—Groundhog Day
12—Lincoln's Birthday
14—Valentine's Day
16—Washington's Birthday observed
22—First of Muharram*
22—Washington's Birthday
24—Shrove Tuesday
25—Ash Wednesday

March

S	M	T	W	T	F	S
	1	2	3	4	5	6
7	8	9	10	11	12	13
14	15	16	17	18	19	20
21	22	23	24	25	26	27
28	29	30	31			

7—Purim*
17—St. Patrick's Day
20—Spring begins (EST)**

April

S	M	T	W	T	F	S
				1	2	3
4	5	6	7	8	9	10
11	12	13	14	15	16	17
18	19	20	21	22	23	24
25	26	27	28	29	30	

4—Daylight Saving Time begins
4—Palm Sunday
6—1st Day of Passover*
9—Good Friday
11—Easter Sunday (Western and Orthodox)

May

S	M	T	W	T	F	S
						1
2	3	4	5	6	7	8
9	10	11	12	13	14	15
16	17	18	19	20	21	22
23	24	25	26	27	28	29
30	31					

2—Mawlid an-Nabi
9—Mother's Day
20—Ascension Day
26—1st Day of Shavuot*
30—Pentecost
31—Memorial Day observed

June

S	M	T	W	T	F	S
		1	2	3	4	5
6	7	8	9	10	11	12
13	14	15	16	17	18	19
20	21	22	23	24	25	26
27	28	29	30			

14—Flag Day
20—Father's Day
20—Summer begins (EDT)**

July

S	M	T	W	T	F	S
				1	2	3
4	5	6	7	8	9	10
11	12	13	14	15	16	17
18	19	20	21	22	23	24
25	26	27	28	29	30	31

1—Canada Day
4—Independence Day

August

S	M	T	W	T	F	S
1	2	3	4	5	6	7
8	9	10	11	12	13	14
15	16	17	18	19	20	21
22	23	24	25	26	27	28
29	30	31				

September

S	M	T	W	T	F	S
			1	2	3	4
5	6	7	8	9	10	11
12	13	14	15	16	17	18
19	20	21	22	23	24	25
26	27	28	29	30		

6—Labor Day
16—Rosh Hashanah*
22—Autumn begins (EDT)**
25—Yom Kippur*
30—Sukkot begins

October

S	M	T	W	T	F	S
					1	2
3	4	5	6	7	8	9
10	11	12	13	14	15	16
17	18	19	20	21	22	23
24	25	26	27	28	29	30
31						

8—Simchat Torah
11—Columbus Day observed
11—Thanksgiving Day (Canada)
15—1st Day of Ramadan*
31—Daylight Saving Time ends
31—Halloween

November

S	M	T	W	T	F	S
	1	2	3	4	5	6
7	8	9	10	11	12	13
14	15	16	17	18	19	20
21	22	23	24	25	26	27
28	29	30				

1—All Saints' Day
2—Election Day
11—Veterans Day
14—Ramadan ends (Eid al-Fitr)*
25—Thanksgiving Day (U.S.)
28—1st Sunday of Advent

December

S	M	T	W	T	F	S
			1	2	3	4
5	6	7	8	9	10	11
12	13	14	15	16	17	18
19	20	21	22	23	24	25
26	27	28	29	30	31	

8—1st Day of Hanukkah*
21—Winter begins (EST)**
25—Christmas Day
26—Kwanzaa begins

*All Jewish and Islamic holidays begin at sundown the day before they are listed here.
**See p. 325 for 2004 solstices and equinoxes.

2003

January

S	M	T	W	T	F	S
			1	2	3	4
5	6	7	8	9	10	11
12	13	14	15	16	17	18
19	20	21	22	23	24	25
26	27	28	29	30	31	

February

S	M	T	W	T	F	S
						1
2	3	4	5	6	7	8
9	10	11	12	13	14	15
16	17	18	19	20	21	22
23	24	25	26	27	28	

March

S	M	T	W	T	F	S
						1
2	3	4	5	6	7	8
9	10	11	12	13	14	15
16	17	18	19	20	21	22
23	24	25	26	27	28	29
30	31					

April

S	M	T	W	T	F	S
		1	2	3	4	5
6	7	8	9	10	11	12
13	14	15	16	17	18	19
20	21	22	23	24	25	26
27	28	29	30			

May

S	M	T	W	T	F	S
				1	2	3
4	5	6	7	8	9	10
11	12	13	14	15	16	17
18	19	20	21	22	23	24
25	26	27	28	29	30	31

June

S	M	T	W	T	F	S
1	2	3	4	5	6	7
8	9	10	11	12	13	14
15	16	17	18	19	20	21
22	23	24	25	26	27	28
29	30					

July

S	M	T	W	T	F	S
		1	2	3	4	5
6	7	8	9	10	11	12
13	14	15	16	17	18	19
20	21	22	23	24	25	26
27	28	29	30	31		

August

S	M	T	W	T	F	S
					1	2
3	4	5	6	7	8	9
10	11	12	13	14	15	16
17	18	19	20	21	22	23
24	25	26	27	28	29	30
31						

September

S	M	T	W	T	F	S
	1	2	3	4	5	6
7	8	9	10	11	12	13
14	15	16	17	18	19	20
21	22	23	24	25	26	27
28	29	30				

October

S	M	T	W	T	F	S
			1	2	3	4
5	6	7	8	9	10	11
12	13	14	15	16	17	18
19	20	21	22	23	24	25
26	27	28	29	30	31	

November

S	M	T	W	T	F	S
						1
2	3	4	5	6	7	8
9	10	11	12	13	14	15
16	17	18	19	20	21	22
23	24	25	26	27	28	29
30						

December

S	M	T	W	T	F	S
	1	2	3	4	5	6
7	8	9	10	11	12	13
14	15	16	17	18	19	20
21	22	23	24	25	26	27
28	29	30	31			

2005

January

S	M	T	W	T	F	S
						1
2	3	4	5	6	7	8
9	10	11	12	13	14	15
16	17	18	19	20	21	22
23	24	25	26	27	28	29
30	31					

February

S	M	T	W	T	F	S
		1	2	3	4	5
6	7	8	9	10	11	12
13	14	15	16	17	18	19
20	21	22	23	24	25	26
27	28					

March

S	M	T	W	T	F	S
		1	2	3	4	5
6	7	8	9	10	11	12
13	14	15	16	17	18	19
20	21	22	23	24	25	26
27	28	29	30	31		

April

S	M	T	W	T	F	S
					1	2
3	4	5	6	7	8	9
10	11	12	13	14	15	16
17	18	19	20	21	22	23
24	25	26	27	28	29	30

May

S	M	T	W	T	F	S
1	2	3	4	5	6	7
8	9	10	11	12	13	14
15	16	17	18	19	20	21
22	23	24	25	26	27	28
29	30	31				

June

S	M	T	W	T	F	S
			1	2	3	4
5	6	7	8	9	10	11
12	13	14	15	16	17	18
19	20	21	22	23	24	25
26	27	28	29	30		

July

S	M	T	W	T	F	S
					1	2
3	4	5	6	7	8	9
10	11	12	13	14	15	16
17	18	19	20	21	22	23
24	25	26	27	28	29	30
31						

August

S	M	T	W	T	F	S
	1	2	3	4	5	6
7	8	9	10	11	12	13
14	15	16	17	18	19	20
21	22	23	24	25	26	27
28	29	30	31			

September

S	M	T	W	T	F	S
				1	2	3
4	5	6	7	8	9	10
11	12	13	14	15	16	17
18	19	20	21	22	23	24
25	26	27	28	29	30	

October

S	M	T	W	T	F	S
						1
2	3	4	5	6	7	8
9	10	11	12	13	14	15
16	17	18	19	20	21	22
23	24	25	26	27	28	29
30	31					

November

S	M	T	W	T	F	S
		1	2	3	4	5
6	7	8	9	10	11	12
13	14	15	16	17	18	19
20	21	22	23	24	25	26
27	28	29	30			

December

S	M	T	W	T	F	S
				1	2	3
4	5	6	7	8	9	10
11	12	13	14	15	16	17
18	19	20	21	22	23	24
25	26	27	28	29	30	31

Astrological Signs

♈ **Aries (Ram):** March 21–April 19

♉ **Taurus (Bull):** April 20–May 20

♊ **Gemini (Twins):** May 21–June 20

♋ **Cancer (Crab):** June 21–July 22

♌ **Leo (Lion):** July 23–Aug. 22

♍ **Virgo (Virgin):** Aug. 23–Sept. 22

♎ **Libra (Scales):** Sept. 23–Oct. 22

♏ **Scorpio (Scorpion):** Oct. 23–Nov. 21

♐ **Sagittarius (Archer):** Nov. 22–Dec. 21

♑ **Capricorn (Goat):** Dec. 22–Jan. 19

♒ **Aquarius (Water Bearer):** Jan. 20–Feb. 18

♓ **Pisces (Fish):** Feb. 19–March 20

PERPETUAL CALENDAR

1800...4	1844...9	1888...8	1932.13	1976.12	2020.11
1801...5	1845...4	1889...3	1933...1	1977...7	2021...6
1802...6	1846...5	1890...4	1934...2	1978...1	2022...7
1803...7	1847...6	1891...5	1935...3	1979...2	2023...1
1804...8	1848.14	1892.13	1936.11	1980.10	2024...9
1805...3	1849...2	1893...1	1937...6	1981...5	2025...4
1806...4	1850...3	1894...2	1938...7	1982...6	2026...5
1807...5	1851...4	1895...3	1939...1	1983...7	2027...6
1808.13	1852.12	1896.11	1940...9	1984...8	2028.14
1809...1	1853...7	1897...6	1941...4	1985...3	2029...2
1810...2	1854...1	1898...7	1942...5	1986...4	2030...3
1811...3	1855...2	1899...1	1943...6	1987...5	2031...4
1812.11	1856.10	1900...2	1944.14	1988.13	2032.12
1813...6	1857...5	1901...3	1945...2	1989...1	2033...7
1814...7	1858...6	1902...4	1946...3	1990...2	2034...1
1815...1	1859...7	1903...5	1947...4	1991...3	2035...2
1816...9	1860...8	1904.13	1948.12	1992.11	2036.10
1817...4	1861...3	1905...1	1949...7	1993...6	2037...5
1818...5	1862...4	1906...2	1950...1	1994...7	2038...6
1819...6	1863...5	1907...3	1951...2	1995...1	2039...7
1820.14	1864.13	1908.11	1952.10	1996...9	2040...8
1821...2	1865...1	1909...6	1953...5	1997...4	2041...3
1822...3	1866...2	1910...7	1954...6	1998...5	2042...4
1823...4	1867...3	1911...1	1955...7	1999...6	2043...5
1824.12	1868.11	1912...9	1956...8	2000.14	2044.13
1825...7	1869...6	1913...4	1957...3	2001...2	2045...1
1826...1	1870...7	1914...5	1958...4	2002...3	2046...2
1827...2	1871...1	1915...6	1959...5	2003...4	2047...3
1828.10	1872...9	1916.14	1960.13	2004.12	2048.11
1829...5	1873...4	1917...2	1961...1	2005...7	2049...6
1830...6	1874...5	1918...3	1962...2	2006...1	2050...7
1831...7	1875...6	1919...4	1963...3	2007...2	2051...1
1832...8	1876.14	1920.12	1964.11	2008.10	2052...9
1833...3	1877...2	1921...7	1965...6	2009...5	2053...4
1834...4	1878...3	1922...1	1966...7	2010...6	2054...5
1835...5	1879...4	1923...2	1967...1	2011...7	2055...6
1836.13	1880.12	1924.10	1968...9	2012...8	2056.14
1837...1	1881...7	1925...5	1969...4	2013...3	2057...2
1838...2	1882...1	1926...6	1970...5	2014...4	2058...3
1839...3	1883...2	1927...7	1971...6	2015...5	2059...4
1840.11	1884.10	1928...8	1972.14	2016.13	2060.12
1841...6	1885...5	1929...3	1973...2	2017...1	2061...7
1842...7	1886...6	1930...4	1974...3	2018...2	2062...1
1843...1	1887...7	1931...5	1975...4	2019...3	2063...2

DIRECTIONS: The number given with each year in the key above is the number of the calendar to use for that year.

1

JANUARY

S	M	T	W	T	F	S
1	2	3	4	5	6	7
8	9	10	11	12	13	14
15	16	17	18	19	20	21
22	23	24	25	26	27	28
29	30	31				

FEBRUARY

S	M	T	W	T	F	S
			1	2	3	4
5	6	7	8	9	10	11
12	13	14	15	16	17	18
19	20	21	22	23	24	25
26	27	28				

MARCH

S	M	T	W	T	F	S
			1	2	3	4
5	6	7	8	9	10	11
12	13	14	15	16	17	18
19	20	21	22	23	24	25
26	27	28	29	30	31	

APRIL

S	M	T	W	T	F	S
						1
2	3	4	5	6	7	8
9	10	11	12	13	14	15
16	17	18	19	20	21	22
23	24	25	26	27	28	29
30						

MAY

S	M	T	W	T	F	S
	1	2	3	4	5	6
7	8	9	10	11	12	13
14	15	16	17	18	19	20
21	22	23	24	25	26	27
28	29	30	31			

JUNE

S	M	T	W	T	F	S
				1	2	3
4	5	6	7	8	9	10
11	12	13	14	15	16	17
18	19	20	21	22	23	24
25	26	27	28	29	30	

JULY

S	M	T	W	T	F	S
						1
2	3	4	5	6	7	8
9	10	11	12	13	14	15
16	17	18	19	20	21	22
23	24	25	26	27	28	29
30	31					

AUGUST

S	M	T	W	T	F	S
		1	2	3	4	5
6	7	8	9	10	11	12
13	14	15	16	17	18	19
20	21	22	23	24	25	26
27	28	29	30	31		

SEPTEMBER

S	M	T	W	T	F	S
					1	2
3	4	5	6	7	8	9
10	11	12	13	14	15	16
17	18	19	20	21	22	23
24	25	26	27	28	29	30

OCTOBER

S	M	T	W	T	F	S
1	2	3	4	5	6	7
8	9	10	11	12	13	14
15	16	17	18	19	20	21
22	23	24	25	26	27	28
29	30	31				

NOVEMBER

S	M	T	W	T	F	S
			1	2	3	4
5	6	7	8	9	10	11
12	13	14	15	16	17	18
19	20	21	22	23	24	25
26	27	28	29	30		

DECEMBER

S	M	T	W	T	F	S
					1	2
3	4	5	6	7	8	9
10	11	12	13	14	15	16
17	18	19	20	21	22	23
24	25	26	27	28	29	30
31						

2

JANUARY

S	M	T	W	T	F	S
	1	2	3	4	5	6
7	8	9	10	11	12	13
14	15	16	17	18	19	20
21	22	23	24	25	26	27
28	29	30	31			

FEBRUARY

S	M	T	W	T	F	S
				1	2	3
4	5	6	7	8	9	10
11	12	13	14	15	16	17
18	19	20	21	22	23	24
25	26	27	28			

MARCH

S	M	T	W	T	F	S
				1	2	3
4	5	6	7	8	9	10
11	12	13	14	15	16	17
18	19	20	21	22	23	24
25	26	27	28	29	30	31

APRIL

S	M	T	W	T	F	S
1	2	3	4	5	6	7
8	9	10	11	12	13	14
15	16	17	18	19	20	21
22	23	24	25	26	27	28
29	30					

MAY

S	M	T	W	T	F	S
		1	2	3	4	5
6	7	8	9	10	11	12
13	14	15	16	17	18	19
20	21	22	23	24	25	26
27	28	29	30	31		

JUNE

S	M	T	W	T	F	S
					1	2
3	4	5	6	7	8	9
10	11	12	13	14	15	16
17	18	19	20	21	22	23
24	25	26	27	28	29	30

JULY

S	M	T	W	T	F	S
1	2	3	4	5	6	7
8	9	10	11	12	13	14
15	16	17	18	19	20	21
22	23	24	25	26	27	28
29	30	31				

AUGUST

S	M	T	W	T	F	S
			1	2	3	4
5	6	7	8	9	10	11
12	13	14	15	16	17	18
19	20	21	22	23	24	25
26	27	28	29	30	31	

SEPTEMBER

S	M	T	W	T	F	S
						1
2	3	4	5	6	7	8
9	10	11	12	13	14	15
16	17	18	19	20	21	22
23	24	25	26	27	28	29
30						

OCTOBER

S	M	T	W	T	F	S
	1	2	3	4	5	6
7	8	9	10	11	12	13
14	15	16	17	18	19	20
21	22	23	24	25	26	27
28	29	30	31			

NOVEMBER

S	M	T	W	T	F	S
				1	2	3
4	5	6	7	8	9	10
11	12	13	14	15	16	17
18	19	20	21	22	23	24
25	26	27	28	29	30	

DECEMBER

S	M	T	W	T	F	S
						1
2	3	4	5	6	7	8
9	10	11	12	13	14	15
16	17	18	19	20	21	22
23	24	25	26	27	28	29
30	31					

3

JANUARY

S	M	T	W	T	F	S
		1	2	3	4	5
6	7	8	9	10	11	12
13	14	15	16	17	18	19
20	21	22	23	24	25	26
27	28	29	30	31		

FEBRUARY

S	M	T	W	T	F	S
					1	2
3	4	5	6	7	8	9
10	11	12	13	14	15	16
17	18	19	20	21	22	23
24	25	26	27	28		

MARCH

S	M	T	W	T	F	S
					1	2
3	4	5	6	7	8	9
10	11	12	13	14	15	16
17	18	19	20	21	22	23
24	25	26	27	28	29	30
31						

APRIL

S	M	T	W	T	F	S
	1	2	3	4	5	6
7	8	9	10	11	12	13
14	15	16	17	18	19	20
21	22	23	24	25	26	27
28	29	30				

MAY

S	M	T	W	T	F	S
			1	2	3	4
5	6	7	8	9	10	11
12	13	14	15	16	17	18
19	20	21	22	23	24	25
26	27	28	29	30	31	

JUNE

S	M	T	W	T	F	S
						1
2	3	4	5	6	7	8
9	10	11	12	13	14	15
16	17	18	19	20	21	22
23	24	25	26	27	28	29
30						

JULY

S	M	T	W	T	F	S
	1	2	3	4	5	6
7	8	9	10	11	12	13
14	15	16	17	18	19	20
21	22	23	24	25	26	27
28	29	30	31			

AUGUST

S	M	T	W	T	F	S
				1	2	3
4	5	6	7	8	9	10
11	12	13	14	15	16	17
18	19	20	21	22	23	24
25	26	27	28	29	30	31

SEPTEMBER

S	M	T	W	T	F	S
1	2	3	4	5	6	7
8	9	10	11	12	13	14
15	16	17	18	19	20	21
22	23	24	25	26	27	28
29	30					

OCTOBER

S	M	T	W	T	F	S
		1	2	3	4	5
6	7	8	9	10	11	12
13	14	15	16	17	18	19
20	21	22	23	24	25	26
27	28	29	30	31		

NOVEMBER

S	M	T	W	T	F	S
					1	2
3	4	5	6	7	8	9
10	11	12	13	14	15	16
17	18	19	20	21	22	23
24	25	26	27	28	29	30

DECEMBER

S	M	T	W	T	F	S
1	2	3	4	5	6	7
8	9	10	11	12	13	14
15	16	17	18	19	20	21
22	23	24	25	26	27	28
29	30	31				

4

JANUARY

S	M	T	W	T	F	S
			1	2	3	4
5	6	7	8	9	10	11
12	13	14	15	16	17	18
19	20	21	22	23	24	25
26	27	28	29	30	31	

FEBRUARY

S	M	T	W	T	F	S
						1
2	3	4	5	6	7	8
9	10	11	12	13	14	15
16	17	18	19	20	21	22
23	24	25	26	27	28	

MARCH

S	M	T	W	T	F	S
						1
2	3	4	5	6	7	8
9	10	11	12	13	14	15
16	17	18	19	20	21	22
23	24	25	26	27	28	29
30	31					

APRIL

S	M	T	W	T	F	S
		1	2	3	4	5
6	7	8	9	10	11	12
13	14	15	16	17	18	19
20	21	22	23	24	25	26
27	28	29	30			

MAY

S	M	T	W	T	F	S
				1	2	3
4	5	6	7	8	9	10
11	12	13	14	15	16	17
18	19	20	21	22	23	24
25	26	27	28	29	30	31

JUNE

S	M	T	W	T	F	S
1	2	3	4	5	6	7
8	9	10	11	12	13	14
15	16	17	18	19	20	21
22	23	24	25	26	27	28
29	30					

JULY

S	M	T	W	T	F	S
		1	2	3	4	5
6	7	8	9	10	11	12
13	14	15	16	17	18	19
20	21	22	23	24	25	26
27	28	29	30	31		

AUGUST

S	M	T	W	T	F	S
					1	2
3	4	5	6	7	8	9
10	11	12	13	14	15	16
17	18	19	20	21	22	23
24	25	26	27	28	29	30
31						

SEPTEMBER

S	M	T	W	T	F	S
	1	2	3	4	5	6
7	8	9	10	11	12	13
14	15	16	17	18	19	20
21	22	23	24	25	26	27
28	29	30				

OCTOBER

S	M	T	W	T	F	S
			1	2	3	4
5	6	7	8	9	10	11
12	13	14	15	16	17	18
19	20	21	22	23	24	25
26	27	28	29	30	31	

NOVEMBER

S	M	T	W	T	F	S
						1
2	3	4	5	6	7	8
9	10	11	12	13	14	15
16	17	18	19	20	21	22
23	24	25	26	27	28	29
30						

DECEMBER

S	M	T	W	T	F	S
	1	2	3	4	5	6
7	8	9	10	11	12	13
14	15	16	17	18	19	20
21	22	23	24	25	26	27
28	29	30	31			

5

JANUARY

S	M	T	W	T	F	S
				1	2	3
4	5	6	7	8	9	10
11	12	13	14	15	16	17
18	19	20	21	22	23	24
25	26	27	28	29	30	31

FEBRUARY

S	M	T	W	T	F	S
1	2	3	4	5	6	7
8	9	10	11	12	13	14
15	16	17	18	19	20	21
22	23	24	25	26	27	28

MARCH

S	M	T	W	T	F	S
1	2	3	4	5	6	7
8	9	10	11	12	13	14
15	16	17	18	19	20	21
22	23	24	25	26	27	28
29	30	31				

APRIL

S	M	T	W	T	F	S
			1	2	3	4
5	6	7	8	9	10	11
12	13	14	15	16	17	18
19	20	21	22	23	24	25
26	27	28	29	30		

MAY

S	M	T	W	T	F	S
					1	2
3	4	5	6	7	8	9
10	11	12	13	14	15	16
17	18	19	20	21	22	23
24	25	26	27	28	29	30
31						

JUNE

S	M	T	W	T	F	S
	1	2	3	4	5	6
7	8	9	10	11	12	13
14	15	16	17	18	19	20
21	22	23	24	25	26	27
28	29	30				

JULY

S	M	T	W	T	F	S
			1	2	3	4
5	6	7	8	9	10	11
12	13	14	15	16	17	18
19	20	21	22	23	24	25
26	27	28	29	30	31	

AUGUST

S	M	T	W	T	F	S
						1
2	3	4	5	6	7	8
9	10	11	12	13	14	15
16	17	18	19	20	21	22
23	24	25	26	27	28	29
30	31					

SEPTEMBER

S	M	T	W	T	F	S
		1	2	3	4	5
6	7	8	9	10	11	12
13	14	15	16	17	18	19
20	21	22	23	24	25	26
27	28	29	30			

OCTOBER

S	M	T	W	T	F	S
				1	2	3
4	5	6	7	8	9	10
11	12	13	14	15	16	17
18	19	20	21	22	23	24
25	26	27	28	29	30	31

NOVEMBER

S	M	T	W	T	F	S
1	2	3	4	5	6	7
8	9	10	11	12	13	14
15	16	17	18	19	20	21
22	23	24	25	26	27	28
29	30					

DECEMBER

S	M	T	W	T	F	S
		1	2	3	4	5
6	7	8	9	10	11	12
13	14	15	16	17	18	19
20	21	22	23	24	25	26
27	28	29	30	31		

6

JANUARY

S	M	T	W	T	F	S
					1	2
3	4	5	6	7	8	9
10	11	12	13	14	15	16
17	18	19	20	21	22	23
24	25	26	27	28	29	30
31						

FEBRUARY

S	M	T	W	T	F	S
	1	2	3	4	5	6
7	8	9	10	11	12	13
14	15	16	17	18	19	20
21	22	23	24	25	26	27
28						

MARCH

S	M	T	W	T	F	S
	1	2	3	4	5	6
7	8	9	10	11	12	13
14	15	16	17	18	19	20
21	22	23	24	25	26	27
28	29	30	31			

APRIL

S	M	T	W	T	F	S
				1	2	3
4	5	6	7	8	9	10
11	12	13	14	15	16	17
18	19	20	21	22	23	24
25	26	27	28	29	30	

MAY

S	M	T	W	T	F	S
						1
2	3	4	5	6	7	8
9	10	11	12	13	14	15
16	17	18	19	20	21	22
23	24	25	26	27	28	29
30	31					

JUNE

S	M	T	W	T	F	S
		1	2	3	4	5
6	7	8	9	10	11	12
13	14	15	16	17	18	19
20	21	22	23	24	25	26
27	28	29	30			

JULY

S	M	T	W	T	F	S
				1	2	3
4	5	6	7	8	9	10
11	12	13	14	15	16	17
18	19	20	21	22	23	24
25	26	27	28	29	30	31

AUGUST

S	M	T	W	T	F	S
1	2	3	4	5	6	7
8	9	10	11	12	13	14
15	16	17	18	19	20	21
22	23	24	25	26	27	28
29	30	31				

SEPTEMBER

S	M	T	W	T	F	S
			1	2	3	4
5	6	7	8	9	10	11
12	13	14	15	16	17	18
19	20	21	22	23	24	25
26	27	28	29	30		

OCTOBER

S	M	T	W	T	F	S
					1	2
3	4	5	6	7	8	9
10	11	12	13	14	15	16
17	18	19	20	21	22	23
24	25	26	27	28	29	30
31						

NOVEMBER

S	M	T	W	T	F	S
	1	2	3	4	5	6
7	8	9	10	11	12	13
14	15	16	17	18	19	20
21	22	23	24	25	26	27
28	29	30				

DECEMBER

S	M	T	W	T	F	S
			1	2	3	4
5	6	7	8	9	10	11
12	13	14	15	16	17	18
19	20	21	22	23	24	25
26	27	28	29	30	31	

7

JANUARY

S	M	T	W	T	F	S
						1
2	3	4	5	6	7	8
9	10	11	12	13	14	15
16	17	18	19	20	21	22
23	24	25	26	27	28	29
30	31					

FEBRUARY

S	M	T	W	T	F	S
		1	2	3	4	5
6	7	8	9	10	11	12
13	14	15	16	17	18	19
20	21	22	23	24	25	26
27	28					

MARCH

S	M	T	W	T	F	S
		1	2	3	4	5
6	7	8	9	10	11	12
13	14	15	16	17	18	19
20	21	22	23	24	25	26
27	28	29	30	31		

APRIL

S	M	T	W	T	F	S
					1	2
3	4	5	6	7	8	9
10	11	12	13	14	15	16
17	18	19	20	21	22	23
24	25	26	27	28	29	30

MAY

S	M	T	W	T	F	S
1	2	3	4	5	6	7
8	9	10	11	12	13	14
15	16	17	18	19	20	21
22	23	24	25	26	27	28
29	30	31				

JUNE

S	M	T	W	T	F	S
			1	2	3	4
5	6	7	8	9	10	11
12	13	14	15	16	17	18
19	20	21	22	23	24	25
26	27	28	29	30		

JULY

S	M	T	W	T	F	S
					1	2
3	4	5	6	7	8	9
10	11	12	13	14	15	16
17	18	19	20	21	22	23
24	25	26	27	28	29	30
31						

AUGUST

S	M	T	W	T	F	S
	1	2	3	4	5	6
7	8	9	10	11	12	13
14	15	16	17	18	19	20
21	22	23	24	25	26	27
28	29	30	31			

SEPTEMBER

S	M	T	W	T	F	S
				1	2	3
4	5	6	7	8	9	10
11	12	13	14	15	16	17
18	19	20	21	22	23	24
25	26	27	28	29	30	

OCTOBER

S	M	T	W	T	F	S
						1
2	3	4	5	6	7	8
9	10	11	12	13	14	15
16	17	18	19	20	21	22
23	24	25	26	27	28	29
30	31					

NOVEMBER

S	M	T	W	T	F	S
		1	2	3	4	5
6	7	8	9	10	11	12
13	14	15	16	17	18	19
20	21	22	23	24	25	26
27	28	29	30			

DECEMBER

S	M	T	W	T	F	S
				1	2	3
4	5	6	7	8	9	10
11	12	13	14	15	16	17
18	19	20	21	22	23	24
25	26	27	28	29	30	31

8

JANUARY

S	M	T	W	T	F	S
1	2	3	4	5	6	7
8	9	10	11	12	13	14
15	16	17	18	19	20	21
22	23	24	25	26	27	28
29	30	31				

FEBRUARY

S	M	T	W	T	F	S
			1	2	3	4
5	6	7	8	9	10	11
12	13	14	15	16	17	18
19	20	21	22	23	24	25
26	27	28	29			

MARCH

S	M	T	W	T	F	S
				1	2	3
4	5	6	7	8	9	10
11	12	13	14	15	16	17
18	19	20	21	22	23	24
25	26	27	28	29	30	31

APRIL

S	M	T	W	T	F	S
1	2	3	4	5	6	7
8	9	10	11	12	13	14
15	16	17	18	19	20	21
22	23	24	25	26	27	28
29	30					

MAY

S	M	T	W	T	F	S
		1	2	3	4	5
6	7	8	9	10	11	12
13	14	15	16	17	18	19
20	21	22	23	24	25	26
27	28	29	30	31		

JUNE

S	M	T	W	T	F	S
					1	2
3	4	5	6	7	8	9
10	11	12	13	14	15	16
17	18	19	20	21	22	23
24	25	26	27	28	29	30

JULY

S	M	T	W	T	F	S
1	2	3	4	5	6	7
8	9	10	11	12	13	14
15	16	17	18	19	20	21
22	23	24	25	26	27	28
29	30	31				

AUGUST

S	M	T	W	T	F	S
			1	2	3	4
5	6	7	8	9	10	11
12	13	14	15	16	17	18
19	20	21	22	23	24	25
26	27	28	29	30	31	

SEPTEMBER

S	M	T	W	T	F	S
						1
2	3	4	5	6	7	8
9	10	11	12	13	14	15
16	17	18	19	20	21	22
23	24	25	26	27	28	29
30						

OCTOBER

S	M	T	W	T	F	S
	1	2	3	4	5	6
7	8	9	10	11	12	13
14	15	16	17	18	19	20
21	22	23	24	25	26	27
28	29	30	31			

NOVEMBER

S	M	T	W	T	F	S
				1	2	3
4	5	6	7	8	9	10
11	12	13	14	15	16	17
18	19	20	21	22	23	24
25	26	27	28	29	30	

DECEMBER

S	M	T	W	T	F	S
						1
2	3	4	5	6	7	8
9	10	11	12	13	14	15
16	17	18	19	20	21	22
23	24	25	26	27	28	29
30	31					

9

JANUARY

S	M	T	W	T	F	S
	1	2	3	4	5	6
7	8	9	10	11	12	13
14	15	16	17	18	19	20
21	22	23	24	25	26	27
28	29	30	31			

FEBRUARY

S	M	T	W	T	F	S
				1	2	3
4	5	6	7	8	9	10
11	12	13	14	15	16	17
18	19	20	21	22	23	24
25	26	27	28	29		

MARCH

S	M	T	W	T	F	S
					1	2
3	4	5	6	7	8	9
10	11	12	13	14	15	16
17	18	19	20	21	22	23
24	25	26	27	28	29	30
31						

APRIL

S	M	T	W	T	F	S
	1	2	3	4	5	6
7	8	9	10	11	12	13
14	15	16	17	18	19	20
21	22	23	24	25	26	27
28	29	30				

MAY

S	M	T	W	T	F	S
			1	2	3	4
5	6	7	8	9	10	11
12	13	14	15	16	17	18
19	20	21	22	23	24	25
26	27	28	29	30	31	

JUNE

S	M	T	W	T	F	S
						1
2	3	4	5	6	7	8
9	10	11	12	13	14	15
16	17	18	19	20	21	22
23	24	25	26	27	28	29
30						

JULY

S	M	T	W	T	F	S
	1	2	3	4	5	6
7	8	9	10	11	12	13
14	15	16	17	18	19	20
21	22	23	24	25	26	27
28	29	30	31			

AUGUST

S	M	T	W	T	F	S
				1	2	3
4	5	6	7	8	9	10
11	12	13	14	15	16	17
18	19	20	21	22	23	24
25	26	27	28	29	30	31

SEPTEMBER

S	M	T	W	T	F	S
1	2	3	4	5	6	7
8	9	10	11	12	13	14
15	16	17	18	19	20	21
22	23	24	25	26	27	28
29	30					

OCTOBER

S	M	T	W	T	F	S
		1	2	3	4	5
6	7	8	9	10	11	12
13	14	15	16	17	18	19
20	21	22	23	24	25	26
27	28	29	30	31		

NOVEMBER

S	M	T	W	T	F	S
					1	2
3	4	5	6	7	8	9
10	11	12	13	14	15	16
17	18	19	20	21	22	23
24	25	26	27	28	29	30

DECEMBER

S	M	T	W	T	F	S
1	2	3	4	5	6	7
8	9	10	11	12	13	14
15	16	17	18	19	20	21
22	23	24	25	26	27	28
29	30	31				

10

JANUARY

S	M	T	W	T	F	S
		1	2	3	4	5
6	7	8	9	10	11	12
13	14	15	16	17	18	19
20	21	22	23	24	25	26
27	28	29	30	31		

FEBRUARY

S	M	T	W	T	F	S
					1	2
3	4	5	6	7	8	9
10	11	12	13	14	15	16
17	18	19	20	21	22	23
24	25	26	27	28	29	

MARCH

S	M	T	W	T	F	S
						1
2	3	4	5	6	7	8
9	10	11	12	13	14	15
16	17	18	19	20	21	22
23	24	25	26	27	28	29
30	31					

APRIL

S	M	T	W	T	F	S
		1	2	3	4	5
6	7	8	9	10	11	12
13	14	15	16	17	18	19
20	21	22	23	24	25	26
27	28	29	30			

MAY

S	M	T	W	T	F	S
				1	2	3
4	5	6	7	8	9	10
11	12	13	14	15	16	17
18	19	20	21	22	23	24
25	26	27	28	29	30	31

JUNE

S	M	T	W	T	F	S
1	2	3	4	5	6	7
8	9	10	11	12	13	14
15	16	17	18	19	20	21
22	23	24	25	26	27	28
29	30					

JULY

S	M	T	W	T	F	S
		1	2	3	4	5
6	7	8	9	10	11	12
13	14	15	16	17	18	19
20	21	22	23	24	25	26
27	28	29	30	31		

AUGUST

S	M	T	W	T	F	S
					1	2
3	4	5	6	7	8	9
10	11	12	13	14	15	16
17	18	19	20	21	22	23
24	25	26	27	28	29	30
31						

SEPTEMBER

S	M	T	W	T	F	S
	1	2	3	4	5	6
7	8	9	10	11	12	13
14	15	16	17	18	19	20
21	22	23	24	25	26	27
28	29	30				

OCTOBER

S	M	T	W	T	F	S
			1	2	3	4
5	6	7	8	9	10	11
12	13	14	15	16	17	18
19	20	21	22	23	24	25
26	27	28	29	30	31	

NOVEMBER

S	M	T	W	T	F	S
						1
2	3	4	5	6	7	8
9	10	11	12	13	14	15
16	17	18	19	20	21	22
23	24	25	26	27	28	29
30						

DECEMBER

S	M	T	W	T	F	S
	1	2	3	4	5	6
7	8	9	10	11	12	13
14	15	16	17	18	19	20
21	22	23	24	25	26	27
28	29	30	31			

11

JANUARY

S	M	T	W	T	F	S
			1	2	3	4
5	6	7	8	9	10	11
12	13	14	15	16	17	18
19	20	21	22	23	24	25
26	27	28	29	30	31	

FEBRUARY

S	M	T	W	T	F	S
						1
2	3	4	5	6	7	8
9	10	11	12	13	14	15
16	17	18	19	20	21	22
23	24	25	26	27	28	29

MARCH

S	M	T	W	T	F	S
1	2	3	4	5	6	7
8	9	10	11	12	13	14
15	16	17	18	19	20	21
22	23	24	25	26	27	28
29	30	31				

APRIL

S	M	T	W	T	F	S
			1	2	3	4
5	6	7	8	9	10	11
12	13	14	15	16	17	18
19	20	21	22	23	24	25
26	27	28	29	30		

MAY

S	M	T	W	T	F	S
					1	2
3	4	5	6	7	8	9
10	11	12	13	14	15	16
17	18	19	20	21	22	23
24	25	26	27	28	29	30
31						

JUNE

S	M	T	W	T	F	S
	1	2	3	4	5	6
7	8	9	10	11	12	13
14	15	16	17	18	19	20
21	22	23	24	25	26	27
28	29	30				

JULY

S	M	T	W	T	F	S
			1	2	3	4
5	6	7	8	9	10	11
12	13	14	15	16	17	18
19	20	21	22	23	24	25
26	27	28	29	30	31	

AUGUST

S	M	T	W	T	F	S
						1
2	3	4	5	6	7	8
9	10	11	12	13	14	15
16	17	18	19	20	21	22
23	24	25	26	27	28	29
30	31					

SEPTEMBER

S	M	T	W	T	F	S
		1	2	3	4	5
6	7	8	9	10	11	12
13	14	15	16	17	18	19
20	21	22	23	24	25	26
27	28	29	30			

OCTOBER

S	M	T	W	T	F	S
				1	2	3
4	5	6	7	8	9	10
11	12	13	14	15	16	17
18	19	20	21	22	23	24
25	26	27	28	29	30	31

NOVEMBER

S	M	T	W	T	F	S
1	2	3	4	5	6	7
8	9	10	11	12	13	14
15	16	17	18	19	20	21
22	23	24	25	26	27	28
29	30					

DECEMBER

S	M	T	W	T	F	S
		1	2	3	4	5
6	7	8	9	10	11	12
13	14	15	16	17	18	19
20	21	22	23	24	25	26
27	28	29	30	31		

12

JANUARY

S	M	T	W	T	F	S
				1	2	3
4	5	6	7	8	9	10
11	12	13	14	15	16	17
18	19	20	21	22	23	24
25	26	27	28	29	30	31

FEBRUARY

S	M	T	W	T	F	S
1	2	3	4	5	6	7
8	9	10	11	12	13	14
15	16	17	18	19	20	21
22	23	24	25	26	27	28
29						

MARCH

S	M	T	W	T	F	S
	1	2	3	4	5	6
7	8	9	10	11	12	13
14	15	16	17	18	19	20
21	22	23	24	25	26	27
28	29	30	31			

APRIL

S	M	T	W	T	F	S
				1	2	3
4	5	6	7	8	9	10
11	12	13	14	15	16	17
18	19	20	21	22	23	24
25	26	27	28	29	30	

MAY

S	M	T	W	T	F	S
						1
2	3	4	5	6	7	8
9	10	11	12	13	14	15
16	17	18	19	20	21	22
23	24	25	26	27	28	29
30	31					

JUNE

S	M	T	W	T	F	S
		1	2	3	4	5
6	7	8	9	10	11	12
13	14	15	16	17	18	19
20	21	22	23	24	25	26
27	28	29	30			

JULY

S	M	T	W	T	F	S
				1	2	3
4	5	6	7	8	9	10
11	12	13	14	15	16	17
18	19	20	21	22	23	24
25	26	27	28	29	30	31

AUGUST

S	M	T	W	T	F	S
1	2	3	4	5	6	7
8	9	10	11	12	13	14
15	16	17	18	19	20	21
22	23	24	25	26	27	28
29	30	31				

SEPTEMBER

S	M	T	W	T	F	S
			1	2	3	4
5	6	7	8	9	10	11
12	13	14	15	16	17	18
19	20	21	22	23	24	25
26	27	28	29	30		

OCTOBER

S	M	T	W	T	F	S
					1	2
3	4	5	6	7	8	9
10	11	12	13	14	15	16
17	18	19	20	21	22	23
24	25	26	27	28	29	30
31						

NOVEMBER

S	M	T	W	T	F	S
	1	2	3	4	5	6
7	8	9	10	11	12	13
14	15	16	17	18	19	20
21	22	23	24	25	26	27
28	29	30				

DECEMBER

S	M	T	W	T	F	S
			1	2	3	4
5	6	7	8	9	10	11
12	13	14	15	16	17	18
19	20	21	22	23	24	25
26	27	28	29	30	31	

13

JANUARY

S	M	T	W	T	F	S
					1	2
3	4	5	6	7	8	9
10	11	12	13	14	15	16
17	18	19	20	21	22	23
24	25	26	27	28	29	30
31						

FEBRUARY

S	M	T	W	T	F	S
	1	2	3	4	5	6
7	8	9	10	11	12	13
14	15	16	17	18	19	20
21	22	23	24	25	26	27
28	29					

MARCH

S	M	T	W	T	F	S
		1	2	3	4	5
6	7	8	9	10	11	12
13	14	15	16	17	18	19
20	21	22	23	24	25	26
27	28	29	30	31		

APRIL

S	M	T	W	T	F	S
					1	2
3	4	5	6	7	8	9
10	11	12	13	14	15	16
17	18	19	20	21	22	23
24	25	26	27	28	29	30

MAY

S	M	T	W	T	F	S
1	2	3	4	5	6	7
8	9	10	11	12	13	14
15	16	17	18	19	20	21
22	23	24	25	26	27	28
29	30	31				

JUNE

S	M	T	W	T	F	S
			1	2	3	4
5	6	7	8	9	10	11
12	13	14	15	16	17	18
19	20	21	22	23	24	25
26	27	28	29	30		

JULY

S	M	T	W	T	F	S
					1	2
3	4	5	6	7	8	9
10	11	12	13	14	15	16
17	18	19	20	21	22	23
24	25	26	27	28	29	30
31						

AUGUST

S	M	T	W	T	F	S
	1	2	3	4	5	6
7	8	9	10	11	12	13
14	15	16	17	18	19	20
21	22	23	24	25	26	27
28	29	30	31			

SEPTEMBER

S	M	T	W	T	F	S
				1	2	3
4	5	6	7	8	9	10
11	12	13	14	15	16	17
18	19	20	21	22	23	24
25	26	27	28	29	30	

OCTOBER

S	M	T	W	T	F	S
						1
2	3	4	5	6	7	8
9	10	11	12	13	14	15
16	17	18	19	20	21	22
23	24	25	26	27	28	29
30	31					

NOVEMBER

S	M	T	W	T	F	S
		1	2	3	4	5
6	7	8	9	10	11	12
13	14	15	16	17	18	19
20	21	22	23	24	25	26
27	28	29	30			

DECEMBER

S	M	T	W	T	F	S
				1	2	3
4	5	6	7	8	9	10
11	12	13	14	15	16	17
18	19	20	21	22	23	24
25	26	27	28	29	30	31

14

JANUARY

S	M	T	W	T	F	S
						1
2	3	4	5	6	7	8
9	10	11	12	13	14	15
16	17	18	19	20	21	22
23	24	25	26	27	28	29
30	31					

FEBRUARY

S	M	T	W	T	F	S
		1	2	3	4	5
6	7	8	9	10	11	12
13	14	15	16	17	18	19
20	21	22	23	24	25	26
27	28	29				

MARCH

S	M	T	W	T	F	S
			1	2	3	4
5	6	7	8	9	10	11
12	13	14	15	16	17	18
19	20	21	22	23	24	25
26	27	28	29	30	31	

APRIL

S	M	T	W	T	F	S
						1
2	3	4	5	6	7	8
9	10	11	12	13	14	15
16	17	18	19	20	21	22
23	24	25	26	27	28	29
30						

MAY

S	M	T	W	T	F	S
	1	2	3	4	5	6
7	8	9	10	11	12	13
14	15	16	17	18	19	20
21	22	23	24	25	26	27
28	29	30	31			

JUNE

S	M	T	W	T	F	S
				1	2	3
4	5	6	7	8	9	10
11	12	13	14	15	16	17
18	19	20	21	22	23	24
25	26	27	28	29	30	

JULY

S	M	T	W	T	F	S
						1
2	3	4	5	6	7	8
9	10	11	12	13	14	15
16	17	18	19	20	21	22
23	24	25	26	27	28	29
30	31					

AUGUST

S	M	T	W	T	F	S
		1	2	3	4	5
6	7	8	9	10	11	12
13	14	15	16	17	18	19
20	21	22	23	24	25	26
27	28	29	30	31		

SEPTEMBER

S	M	T	W	T	F	S
					1	2
3	4	5	6	7	8	9
10	11	12	13	14	15	16
17	18	19	20	21	22	23
24	25	26	27	28	29	30

OCTOBER

S	M	T	W	T	F	S
1	2	3	4	5	6	7
8	9	10	11	12	13	14
15	16	17	18	19	20	21
22	23	24	25	26	27	28
29	30	31				

NOVEMBER

S	M	T	W	T	F	S
			1	2	3	4
5	6	7	8	9	10	11
12	13	14	15	16	17	18
19	20	21	22	23	24	25
26	27	28	29	30		

DECEMBER

S	M	T	W	T	F	S
					1	2
3	4	5	6	7	8	9
10	11	12	13	14	15	16
17	18	19	20	21	22	23
24	25	26	27	28	29	30
31						

History of the Calendar

The purpose of the calendar is to reckon past or future time, to show how many days until a certain event takes place—the harvest or a religious festival—or how long since something important happened. The earliest calendars must have been strongly influenced by the geographical location of the people who made them. In colder countries, the concept of the year was determined by the seasons, specifically by the end of winter. But in warmer countries, where the seasons are less pronounced, the Moon became the basic unit for time reckoning; an old Jewish book says that "the Moon was created for the counting of the days."

Most of the oldest calendars were lunar calendars, based on the time interval from one new moon to the next—a so-called lunation. But even in a warm climate there are annual events that pay no attention to the phases of the Moon. In some areas it was a rainy season; in Egypt it was the annual flooding of the Nile River. The calendar had to account for these yearly events as well.

The Egyptian Calendar

The ancient Egyptians used a calendar with 12 months of 30 days each, for a total of 360 days per year. About 4000 B.C. they added five extra days at the end of every year to bring it more into line with the solar year.[1] These five days became a festival because it was thought to be unlucky to work during that time.

The Egyptians had calculated that the solar year was actually closer to 365¼ days, but instead of having a single leap day every four years to account for the fractional day (the way we do now), they let the one-quarter day accumulate. After 1,460 years, or four periods of 365 years, they added an entire leap year of 365 days. This means that as the years passed, the Egyptian months fell out of sync with the seasons, so that the summer months eventually fell during winter. Only once every 1,460 years did their calendar year coincide precisely with the solar year.

In addition to the civic calendar, the Egyptians also had a religious calendar that was based on the 29½-day lunar cycle and was more closely linked with agricultural cycles and the movements of the stars.

Lunar Calendars

During antiquity the lunar calendar that best approximated a solar-year calendar was based on a 19-year period, with 7 of these 19 years having 13 months. In all, the period contained 235 months. Still using the lunation value of 29½ days, this made a total of 6,932½ days, while 19 solar years added up to 6,939.7 days, a difference of just one week per period and about five weeks per century.

Even the 19-year period required adjustment, but it became the basis of the calendars of the ancient Chinese, Babylonians, Greeks, and Jews. This same calendar was also used by the Arabs, but Muhammad later forbade shifting from 12 months to 13 months, so that the Islamic calendar, even today, has a lunar year of 354 days. As a result, the months of the Islamic calendar, as well as the Islamic religious festivals, migrate through all the seasons of the year.

The Roman Calendar

When Rome emerged as a world power, the difficulties of making a calendar were well known, but the Romans complicated their lives because of their superstition that even numbers were unlucky. Hence their months were 29 or 31 days long, with the exception of February, which had 28 days. However, four months of 31 days, seven months of 29 days, and one month of 28 days added up to only 355 days. Therefore the Romans invented an extra month called Mercedonius of 22 or 23 days. It was added every second year.

Even with Mercedonius, the Roman calendar eventually became so far off that **Julius Caesar,** advised by the astronomer Sosigenes, ordered a sweeping reform in 45 B.C. One year, made 445 days long by imperial decree, brought the calendar back in step with the seasons. Then the solar year (with the value of 365 days and 6 hours) was made the basis of the calendar. The months were 30 or 31 days in length, and to take care of the 6 hours, every fourth year was made a 366-day year. Moreover, Caesar decreed the year began with the first of January, not with the vernal equinox in late March.

This calendar was named the **Julian calendar,** after Julius Caesar, and it continues to be the calendar of the Eastern Orthodox churches to this day. However, despite the correction, the Julian calendar is still 11½ minutes longer than the actual solar year, and after a number of centuries, even 11½ minutes adds up.

The Gregorian Reform

By the 15th century the Julian calendar had drifted behind the solar calendar by about a week, so that the vernal equinox was falling around March 12 instead of around March 20. Pope Sixtus IV (who reigned from 1471 to 1484) decided that another reform was needed and called the German astronomer Regiomontanus to Rome to advise him. Regiomontanus arrived in 1475, but unfortunately he died shortly afterward, and the pope's plans for reform died with him.

Then in 1545, the Council of Trent authorized Pope Paul III to reform the calendar once more. Most of the mathematical and astronomical work was done by Father Christopher Clavius, S.J. The immediate correction, advised by Father Clavius and ordered by Pope Gregory XIII, was that Thursday, Oct. 4, 1582, was to be the last day of the Julian calendar. The next day would be Friday, Oct. 15. For long-range accuracy, a formula suggested by the Vatican librarian Aloysius Giglio was adopted: every fourth year is a leap year *unless* it is a century year like 1700 or 1800. Century years can be leap years *only* when they are divisible by 400 (e.g., 1600 and 2000). This rule eliminates three leap years in four centuries, making the calendar sufficiently accurate.

For in spite of the revised leap year rule, an average calendar year is still about 26 seconds longer than the Earth's orbital period. But this discrepancy will need 3,323 years to build up to a single day.

1. The correct figures are lunation: 29 d, 12 h, 44 min, 2.8 sec (29.530585 d); solar year: 365 d, 5 h, 48 min, 46 sec (365.242216 d); 12 lunations: 354 d, 8 h, 48 min, 34 sec (354.3671 d).

Adoption of the Gregorian Calendar

Year	Country	Year	Country	Year	Country
1582	Catholic states of Italy, Portugal, Spain, Belgium, Holland, and Poland	1700	German, Swiss, and Dutch Protestant States, Denmark, and Norway	1873	Japan
1584	German and Swiss Catholic states	1753	Great Britain and its possessions (including the American colonies)	1875	Egypt
1587	Hungary			1918	Russia
				1926	Turkey

Reform Adopted Gradually

The Gregorian reform was not adopted throughout the West immediately. Most Catholic countries quickly changed to the Pope's new calendar in 1582. But Europe's Protestant princes chose to ignore the papal bull and continued with the Julian calendar. It was not until 1700 that the Protestant rulers of Germany and the Netherlands changed to the new calendar. In Great Britain (and its colonies) the shift did not take place until 1752, and in Russia a revolution was needed to introduce the Gregorian calendar in 1918. In Turkey, the Islamic calendar was used until 1926.

A Better Calendar?

Despite its widespread use, the Gregorian calendar has a number of weaknesses. It cannot be divided into equal halves or quarters; the number of days per month is haphazard; and months and years may begin on any day of the week. Holidays pegged to specific dates may also fall on any day of the week, and few Americans can predict when Thanksgiving will occur next year. Since Gregory XIII, many other proposals for calendar reform have been made, but none has been permanently adopted. In the meantime, the Gregorian calendar keeps the calendar dates in reasonable unison with astronomical events. □

Time Measurement, Time Zones, and the International Date Line

The two natural cycles on which time measurements are based are the year and the day. The year is defined as the time required for Earth to complete one revolution around the Sun, while the day is the time required for Earth to complete one turn upon its axis. Earth needs 365 days plus about six hours to go around the Sun once, so a year does not consist of a round number of days; the fractional day has to be taken care of by an extra day every fourth year.

But because Earth, while turning upon its axis, also moves around the Sun, there are two kinds of days. A day may be defined as the interval between the highest point of the Sun in the sky on two successive days. This, averaged out over the year, produces the customary 24-hour day. But one might also define a day as the time interval between the moments when a certain point in the sky, say a conveniently located star, is directly overhead. This is called:

Sidereal time. A sidereal day is the time that it takes the Earth to complete one rotation on its axis so that a particular star can be observed twice at the meridian that runs directly overhead. Because the Earth is moving around the Sun as it rotates on its axis, the sidereal day is about four minutes shorter than the solar day, being equivalent to 23 hours, 56 minutes, and 4 seconds in mean solar time. As a result, a star will appear to rise about four minutes earlier every night, and different stars will be visible at different times of the year. Astronomers use a point that they call the "vernal equinox" to determine local sidereal time.

Apparent solar time is the time based directly on the Sun's position in the sky. In ordinary life the day runs from midnight to midnight. It begins when the Sun is invisible by being 12 hours from its zenith.

Mean solar time, rather than apparent solar time, is the basis for local civil and standard time. The mean solar time is based on the position of a fictitious "mean sun." The reason why this fictitious sun has to be introduced is the following: Earth turns on its axis regularly; it needs the same number of seconds regardless of the season. But the movement of Earth around the Sun is not regular because Earth's orbit is an ellipse. This has the result (as explained in the section on the seasons below) that Earth moves faster in January and slower in July. Though it is Earth that changes velocity, it looks to us as if the Sun does. In January, when Earth moves faster, the *apparent* movement of the Sun looks faster. The mean sun of time measurements, then, is a sun that moves regularly all year round; the real Sun will be either ahead of or behind the mean sun. The difference between the real Sun and the fictitious mean sun is called the *equation of time.*

Time zones. But if all clocks were actually set by mean solar time we would be plagued by a welter of time differences that would be "correct" but a major nuisance. A clock on Long Island, correctly showing mean solar time for its location (this would be *local civil time*), would be slightly ahead of a clock in Newark, N.J. The Newark clock would be slightly ahead of a clock in Trenton, N.J., which, in turn, would be ahead of a clock in Philadelphia. This condition prevailed until 1884, when a system of standard time was adopted by the International Meridian Conference. Earth's surface was divided into 24 zones. The standard time of each zone is the mean astronomical time of one of 24 meridians, 15 degrees apart, beginning at the Greenwich, England, meridian and extending east and west around the globe to the International Date Line. (This system was actually put into use a year earlier by the railroad companies of the U.S. and Canada who, until then, had to contend with some 100 conflicting local sun times observed in terminals across the land.)

For practical purposes, this convention is sometimes altered. For example, Alaska, for a time, consisted of four of the eight U.S. time zones: the Pacific standard time zone (east of Juneau) and the

6th (Juneau), 7th (Anchorage), and 8th (Nome) zones, encompassing the 135°, 150°, and 165° meridians, respectively. In 1983, by act of Congress, the entire state (except the westernmost Aleutians) was united into the 6th zone, Alaska standard time.

The eight U.S. standard time zones are: Atlantic (includes Puerto Rico and the Virgin Islands), eastern, central, mountain, Pacific, Alaska, Hawaii-Aleutian (includes all of Hawaii and those Aleutians west of the Fox Islands), and Samoa standard time.

The Date Line. While the time zones are based on the natural event of the Sun crossing a meridian, the date must be an arbitrary decision. The meridians are traditionally counted from the meridian of the observatory of Greenwich, in England, which is called the zero meridian. The logical place for changing the date is 12 hours, or 180°, from Greenwich. Fortunately, the 180th meridian runs mostly through the open Pacific. The Date Line makes a zigzag in the north to incorporate the eastern tip of Siberia into the Siberian time system and then another one to incorporate a number of islands into the Hawaii-Aleutian time zone. In the south there is a similar zigzag for the purpose of tying a number of British-owned islands to the New Zealand time system. Otherwise, the Date Line is the same as 180° from Greenwich. At points to the east of the Date Line the calendar is one day earlier than at points to the west of it. A traveler going eastward across the Date Line from one island to another would not have to reset his watch because he would stay inside the time zone, but it would be the same time of the *previous* day.

For world and U.S. time zone map, *see* p. 523.

The Names of the Months

January: named after Janus, the god of doors and gates
February: named after Februalia, a time period when sacrifices were made to atone for sins
March: named after Mars, the god of war
April: from *aperire,* Latin for "to open" (buds)
May: named after Maia, the goddess of growth of plants
June: from *junius,* Latin for the goddess Juno
July: named after Julius Caesar in 44 B.C.
August: named after Augustus Caesar in 8 B.C.
September: from *septem,* Latin for "seven"
October: from *octo,* Latin for "eight"
November: from *novem,* Latin for "nine"
December: from *decem,* Latin for "ten"

NOTE: The earliest Latin calendar was a 10-month one, beginning with March; thus, September was the seventh month, October, the eighth, etc. July was originally called Quintilis, meaning fifth; August was originally called Sextilis, meaning sixth.

The Names of the Days of the Week

Latin	Old English	English	German	French	Italian	Spanish
Dies Solis	Sunnandaeg	Sunday	Sonntag	dimanche	domenica	domingo
Dies Lunae	Monandaeg	Monday	Montag	lundi	lunedì	lunes
Dies Martis	Tiwesdaeg	Tuesday	Dienstag	mardi	martedì	martes
Dies Mercurii	Wodnesdaeg	Wednesday	Mittwoch	mercredi	mercoledì	miércoles
Dies Jovis	Thunresdaeg	Thursday	Donnerstag	jeudi	giovedì	jueves
Dies Veneris	Frigedaeg	Friday	Freitag	vendredi	venerdì	viernes
Dies Saturni	Saeternesdaeg	Saturday	Samstag	samedi	sabato	sábado

NOTE: The seven-day week originated in ancient Mesopotamia and became part of the Roman calendar in A.D. 321. The names of the days are based on the seven celestial bodies (the Sun, the Moon, Mars, Mercury, Jupiter, Venus, and Saturn), believed at that time to revolve around Earth and influence its events. Most of Western Europe adopted the Roman nomenclature. The Germanic languages substituted Germanic equivalents for the names of four of the Roman gods: Tiw, the god of war, replaced Mars; Woden, the god of wisdom, replaced Mercury; Thor, the god of thunder, replaced Jupiter; and Frigg, the goddess of love, replaced Venus.

Daylight Saving Time

The United States. Daylight Saving Time, also called "summer time," is the practice of advancing clocks forward by one hour in the spring and setting them back by one hour in the fall in order to gain additional daylight during the early evening. The U.S. federal law that established "daylight time" in this country does not require its observance. Arizona, Hawaii, and the territories of Puerto Rico, Virgin Islands, and American Samoa do not use DST. These areas receive so much sun throughout the year that gaining another hour of sunlight in the summertime is not seen as a benefit.

Indiana. Indiana has a unique and complex time system. Not only is it split between two time zones (Eastern Standard and Central Standard), but parts of the state observe Daylight Saving Time while others do not. Currently, 77 of the state's 92 counties are in the Eastern Time Zone but do not switch to daylight time in April. Instead they remain on standard time all year. That is, except for two counties near Cincinnati, Ohio, and Louisville, Ky., which do use daylight time. Indiana's system is rooted in its once farming-dominated economy. Farmers prefer early daylight to dry their fields and an early sunset to end their work at a reasonable hour. Further complicating Indiana timekeeping are the Indiana counties in the northwest corner of the state (near Chicago) and the southwestern tip (near Evansville), which fall in the Central Time Zone: these counties switch to daylight time each April.

So you can find yourself in quite a mess when you ask, "What time is it?" in Indiana in the warmer months. The Hoosier Daylight Coalition, a group made up of business leaders, parents, teachers, and police, is trying to organize legislation that would simplify things in Indiana. Its hope is that a change will bring new business to the area. But since polls show that half of Indiana residents like things the way they are, it won't be an easy sell.

Around the World. About 70 countries around the world observe Daylight Saving Time in some form. Here are some interesting facts:

• In Canada, every province except Saskatchewan observes DST. It remains on standard time all year long.

• It wasn't until 1996 that our NAFTA neighbors in Mexico adopted DST. Now all three Mexican time zones are on the same schedule as the United States.

• Also in 1996, members of the European Union agreed to observe a "summer-time period" from the last Sunday in March to the last Sunday in October.

• In the winter months, Russia, which spans over 11 time zones, is always one hour ahead of standard time. In the summer, Russians turn their clocks ahead one more hour.

• Most countries near the equator don't deviate from standard time.

• In the Southern Hemisphere, where summer arrives in what we in the Northern Hemisphere consider the winter months, DST is observed from late October to late March.

• Three large regions in Australia do not participate in DST. Western Australia, the Northern Territory, and Queensland stay on standard time all year. The remaining south-central and southeastern sections of the continent (which is where Sydney and Melbourne are found) make the switch. This results in both vertical and horizontal time zones Down Under during the summer months

• China, which spans five time zones, is always eight hours ahead of Greenwich Mean Time and it does not observe DST.

• There is no DST period in Japan either.

U.S. Daylight Saving Time Schedule

Clocks are set forward one hour on the first Sunday in April at 2:00 a.m. local time and are set back one hour the last Sunday in October, also at 2:00 a.m.

2003	April 6	October 26
2004	April 4	October 31
2005	April 3	October 30

The Seasons

The seasons are caused by the tilt of Earth's axis (23.4°) and not by the fact that Earth's orbit around the Sun is an ellipse. The average distance of Earth from the Sun is 93 million miles; the difference between aphelion (farthest away from the Sun) and perihelion (closest to the Sun) is 3 million miles, so that perihelion is about 91.4 million miles from the Sun. Earth goes through the perihelion point a few days after New Year's Day, just when the Northern Hemisphere has winter. Aphelion is passed during the first days of July. This by itself shows that the distance from the Sun is not important within these limits. What is important is that when Earth passes through perihelion, the northern end of Earth's axis happens to tilt away from the Sun, so that the areas beyond the Tropic of Cancer receive only slanting rays from a Sun low in the sky.

The tilt of Earth's axis is responsible for four lines you find on every globe. When, say, the North Pole is tilted away from the Sun as much as possible, the farthest points in the North which can still be reached by the Sun's rays are 23.5° from the pole. This is the Arctic Circle. The Antarctic Circle is the corresponding limit 23.4° from the South Pole; the Sun's rays cannot reach beyond this point when we have midsummer in the North.

When the Sun is vertically above the equator, the day is of equal length all over Earth. This happens twice a year, and these are the "equinoxes" in March and in September. After having been over the equator in March, the Sun will seem to move northward. The northernmost point where the Sun can be straight overhead is 23.4° north of the equator. This is the Tropic of Cancer; the Sun can never be vertically overhead to the north of this line. Similarly the Sun cannot be vertically overhead to the south of a line 23.4° south of the equator—the Tropic of Capricorn.

This explains the climatic zones. In the belt (the Greek word *zone* means "belt") between the Tropic of Cancer and the Tropic of Capricorn, the Sun can be straight overhead; this is the tropical zone. The two zones where the Sun cannot be overhead but will be above the horizon every day of the year are the two temperate zones; the two areas where the Sun will not rise at all for varying lengths of time are the two polar areas, Arctic and Antarctic. □

Seasons for the Northern Hemisphere, 2004

Vernal Equinox: Mar. 20, 1:49 A.M. EST (06:49 UT*), Sun enters sign of Aries; spring begins.

Summer Solstice: June 20, 8:57 P.M. EDT (June 21, 00:57 UT*), Sun enters sign of Cancer; summer begins.

Autumnal Equinox: Sept. 22, 12:30 P.M. EDT (16:30 UT*), Sun enters sign of Libra; fall begins.

Winter Solstice: Dec. 21, 7:42 A.M. EST (12:42 UT*), Sun enters sign of Capricorn; winter begins.

Universal Time (UT), also known as Greenwich Mean Time (GMT). *See* p. 422 for a conversion table of Universal Time.

The Islamic (Hijri) Calendar

The Islamic calendar is based on the lunar year of 354 days. The number of days each month is adjusted according to the lunar cycle, beginning about two days after the new moon. The months drift backward over the seasons, beginning again on the same day every 32½ years. The Islamic year begins on the first day of Muharram, and is counted from the year of the Hegira (*anno Hegirae*)—the year in which Muhammad emigrated from Mecca to Medina (A.D. 622). The year 2004 translates to A.H. 1424–1425.

Months	Number of days	Months	Number of days	Months	Number of days	Months	Number of days
Muharram	29 or 30	Rabi II	29 or 30	Rajab	29 or 30	Shawwal	29 or 30
Safar	29 or 30	Jumada I	29 or 30	Sha'ban	29 or 30	Dhu'l-Qa'dah	29 or 30
Rabi I	29 or 30	Jumada II	29 or 30	Ramadan	29 or 30	Dhu'l-Hijjah	29 or 30

The Jewish Calendar

The Jewish calendar is based on both solar and lunar years. The average lunar year of 354 days is adjusted to the solar year by the addition of a leap year and an intercalary month. Nisan is considered the first month, although the new year begins with Rosh Hashanah, on the first of Tishri, which is in fact the seventh month—the calendar has different starting points for different purposes. The year 2004 translates to the Jewish year 5764–5765.

Months	Number of days	Months	Number of days	Months	Number of days
Nisan (March–April)*	30	Tishri (Sept.–Oct.)	30	Shevat (Jan.–Feb.)	30
Iyar (April–May)	29	Heshvan (Oct.–Nov.)	29	Adar (Feb.–March)	29
Sivan (May–June)	30	in some years	30	in some years	30
Tammuz (June–July)	29	Kislev (Nov.–Dec.)	29	Adar Sheni	29
Av (July–Aug.)	30	in some years	30	(intercalary month	
Elul (Aug.–Sept.)	29	Tevet (Dec.–Jan.)	29	in leap year only)	

*The months correspond approximately to those of the Gregorian calendar.

The Hindu (Indian National) Calendar

The Indian National Calendar, often called the "Hindu Calendar," is based on both lunar and solar years. This calendar was introduced in 1957 in a government push for all of India to use the same calendar, but various traditional calendars are also used. The start of the Indian National Calendar year coincides with March 22, except in a leap year, when it coincides with March 21. The year is counted from the first year of the Saka era, in A.D. 78. The year 2004 translates to Saka era 1925–1926.

Month	Number of days	Month	Number of days	Month	Number of days	Month	Number of days
Caitra	30*	Asadha	31	Asvina	30	Pausa	30
Vaisakha	31	Sravana	31	Kartika	30	Magha	30
Jyaistha	31	Bhadra	31	Agrahayana	30	Phalguna	30

* In a leap year Caitra has 31 days.

The Chinese Calendar

The Chinese lunar year is divided into 12 months of 29 or 30 days. The calendar is adjusted to the length of the solar year by the addition of extra months at regular intervals. The years are arranged in major cycles of 60 years. Each successive year is named after one of 12 animals. These 12-year cycles are continuously repeated. The Chinese New Year is celebrated at the second new moon after the winter solstice and falls between January 21 and February 19 on the Gregorian calendar. The year 2004 translates to the Chinese year 4701–4702.

Rat	Ox	Tiger	Rabbit	Dragon	Snake	Horse	Sheep (Goat)	Monkey	Rooster	Dog	Pig
1900	1901	1902	1903	1904	1905	1906	1907	1908	1909	1910	1911
1912	1913	1914	1915	1916	1917	1918	1919	1920	1921	1922	1923
1924	1925	1926	1927	1928	1929	1930	1931	1932	1933	1934	1935
1936	1937	1938	1939	1940	1941	1942	1943	1944	1945	1946	1947
1948	1949	1950	1951	1952	1953	1954	1955	1956	1957	1958	1959
1960	1961	1962	1963	1964	1965	1966	1967	1968	1969	1970	1971
1972	1973	1974	1975	1976	1977	1978	1979	1980	1981	1982	1983
1984	1985	1986	1987	1988	1989	1990	1991	1992	1993	1994	1995
1996	1997	1998	1999	2000	2001	2002	2003	2004	2005	2006	2007
2008	2009	2010	2011	2012	2013	2014	2015	2016	2017	2018	2019

Holidays

Religious and Secular, 2004

In the United States, there are ten federal holidays set by law. Four are set by date (New Year's Day, Independence Day, Veterans Day, and Christmas Day). The other six are set by a day of the week and month: Martin Luther King, Jr.'s Birthday, Washington's Birthday, Memorial Day, Labor Day, Columbus Day, and Thanksgiving. All but the last are celebrated on Mondays to create three-day weekends for federal employees. All Jewish and Islamic holidays begin at sundown the day before they are listed here.

New Year's Day, Thurs., Jan. 1. A federal holiday in the United States, New Year's Day has its origin in Roman times, when sacrifices were offered to Janus, the two-faced Roman deity who looked back on the past and forward to the future.

Epiphany (from Greek *epiphaneia,* "manifestation"), Tues., Jan. 6. Falls on the 12th day after Christmas and commemorates the manifestation of Jesus Christ to the Gentiles, as represented by the Magi, the baptism of Jesus, and the miracle of the wine at the marriage feast at Cana. One of the three major Christian festivals, along with Christmas and Easter. Epiphany originally marked the beginning of the carnival season preceding Lent, and the evening preceding it is known as Twelfth Night.

Martin Luther King, Jr.'s Birthday, Mon., Jan. 19. (The actual date of his birthday is Jan. 15.) A federal holiday observed on the third Monday in January that honors the late civil rights leader. It became a federal holiday in 1986. In 1999, New Hampshire became the last state to officially honor the holiday.

Groundhog Day, Mon., Feb. 2. Legend has it that if the groundhog sees his shadow, he'll return to his hole, and winter will last another six weeks.

Eid al-Adha, Mon., Feb. 2. Eid al-Adha, or the Feast of Sacrifice, commemorates Abraham's willingness to obey God by sacrificing his son. Lasting for three days, it concludes the annual Hajj, or pilgrimage to Mecca. Muslims worldwide sacrifice a lamb or other animal and distribute the meat to relatives or the needy.

Lincoln's Birthday, Thurs., Feb. 12. A holiday in many states, this day was first formally observed in Washington, DC, in 1866, when both houses of Congress gathered for a memorial address in tribute to the assassinated president.

St. Valentine's Day, Sat., Feb. 14. This day is the festival of two third-century martyrs, both named St. Valentine. It is not known why this day is associated with lovers. It may derive from an old pagan festival about this time of year, or it may have been inspired by the belief that birds mate on this day.

Washington's Birthday, Mon., Feb. 16. (The actual date of his birthday is Feb. 22.) A federal holiday observed the third Monday in February. It is a common misperception that the federal holiday was changed to "Presidents' Day" and now celebrates both Washington and Lincoln. Only Washington is commemorated by the federal holiday; 12 states, however, officially celebrate "Presidents' Day."

First Day of Muharram, Sun., Feb. 22. The month of Muharram marks the beginning of the Islamic liturgical year. On the tenth day of the month, many Muslims may observe a day of fasting, known as Ashurah.

Shrove Tuesday, Feb. 24. Falls the day before Ash Wednesday and marks the end of the carnival season, which once began on Epiphany but is now usually celebrated the last three days before Lent. In France, the day is known as Mardi Gras (Fat Tuesday), and Mardi Gras celebrations are also held in several American cities, particularly in New Orleans. The day is sometimes called Pancake Tuesday by the English because fats, which were prohibited during Lent, had to be used up.

Ash Wednesday, Feb. 25. The seventh Wednesday before Easter and the first day of Lent, which lasts 40 days. Having its origin sometime before A.D. 1000, it is a day of public penance and is marked in the Roman Catholic Church by the burning of the palms blessed on the previous year's Palm Sunday. With the ashes from the palms the priest then marks a cross with his thumb upon the forehead of each worshipper. The Anglican Church and a few Protestant groups in the United States also observe the day, but generally without the use of ashes.

Purim (Feast of Lots), Sun., March 7. A day of joy and feasting celebrating the deliverance of the Jews from a massacre planned by the Persian minister Haman. According to the Book of Esther, the Jewish queen Esther interceded with her husband, King Ahasuerus, to spare the life of her uncle, Mordecai, and Haman was hanged on the same gallows he had built for Mordecai. The holiday is marked by the reading of the Book of Esther (The Megillah), and by the exchange of gifts, donations to the poor, and the presentation of Purim plays.

St. Patrick's Day, Weds., March 17. St. Patrick, patron saint of Ireland, has been honored in America since the first days of the nation. Perhaps the most notable part of the observance is the annual St. Patrick's Day parade in New York City.

Palm Sunday, April 4. Observed the Sunday before Easter to commemorate the entry of Jesus into Jerusalem. The procession and the ceremonies introducing the benediction of palms probably had their origins in Jerusalem.

First Day of Passover (Pesach), Tues., April 6. The Feast of the Passover, also called the Feast of Unleavened Bread, commemorates the escape of the Jews from Egypt. As the Jews fled, they ate unleavened bread, and from that time the Jews have allowed no leavening in their houses during Passover, bread being replaced by matzoh.

Good Friday, April 9. The Friday before Easter, it commemorates the Crucifixion, which is retold during services from the Gospel according to St. John. A feature in Roman Catholic churches is the Liturgy of the Passion; there is no Consecration, the Host having been consecrated the previous day. The eating of hot-cross buns on this day is said to have started in England.

Easter Sunday, April 11. Observed in all Western Christian churches, Easter commemorates the Resurrection of Jesus. It is celebrated on the first Sunday after the full moon that occurs on or next after the vernal equinox (fixed at March 21) and is therefore celebrated between March 22 and April 25 inclusive. This date was fixed by the Council of Nicaea in A.D. 325.

Orthodox Easter (Pascha), Sun., April 11. The Orthodox church uses the same formula to calculate Easter as the Western church, but bases it on the traditional Julian calendar instead of the more contemporary Gregorian calendar. For this reason Orthodox Easter generally falls on a different date than the Western Christian Easter.

Mawlid an-Nabi, Sun., May 2. This holiday celebrates the birthday of Muhammad, the founder of Islam. It is fixed as the 12th day of the month of Rabi I in the Islamic calendar.

Mother's Day, Sun., May 9. Observed the second Sunday in May, as proposed by Anna Jarvis of Philadelphia in 1907. West Virginia was the first state to recognize the holiday in 1910, and President Woodrow Wilson officially proclaimed Mother's Day a national holiday in 1914.

Ascension Day, Thurs., May 20. The Ascension of Jesus took place in the presence of His apostles 40 days after the Resurrection. It is traditionally thought to have occurred on Mount Olivet in Bethany.

First Day of Shavuot (Hebrew Pentecost), Weds., May 26. This festival, sometimes called the Feast of Weeks, or of Harvest, or of the First Fruits, falls 50 days after Passover and originally celebrated the end of the seven-week grain-harvesting season. In later tradition, it also celebrated the giving of the Law to Moses on Mount Sinai.

Pentecost (Whitsunday), May 30. This day commemorates the descent of the Holy Ghost upon the apostles 50 days after the Resurrection. The sermon by the apostle Peter, which led to the baptism of 3,000 who professed belief, originated the ceremonies that have since been followed. "Whitsunday" is believed to have come from "white Sunday" when, among the English, white robes were worn by those baptized on the day.

Memorial Day, Mon., May 31. Memorial Day became a federal holiday in 1971 that is observed on the last Monday in May. It originated in 1868, when Union General John A. Logan designated a day in which the graves of Civil War soldiers would be decorated. Originally known as Decoration Day, the holiday was changed to Memorial Day within twenty years, becoming a holiday dedicated to the memory of all war dead.

Flag Day, Mon., June 14. This day commemorates the adoption by the Continental Congress on June 14, 1777, of the Stars and Stripes as the U.S. flag. Although it is a legal holiday only in Pennsylvania, President Truman, on Aug. 3, 1949, signed a bill requesting the president to call for its observance each year by proclamation.

Father's Day, Sun., June 20. Observed the third Sunday in June. The exact origin of the holiday is not clear, but it was first celebrated June 19, 1910, in Spokane, Wash. In 1966 President Lyndon Johnson signed a proclamation making Father's Day official.

Independence Day, Sun., July 4. The day of the adoption of the Declaration of Independence in 1776, celebrated in all states and territories. The observance began the next year in Philadelphia.

Labor Day, Mon., Sept. 6. A federal holiday observed the first Monday in September. Labor Day was first celebrated in New York in 1882 under the sponsorship of the Central Labor Union, following the suggestion of Peter J. McGuire, of the Knights of Labor, that the day be set aside in honor of labor.

First Day of Rosh Hashanah (Jewish New Year), Thurs., Sept. 16. This day marks the beginning of the Jewish year 5765 and opens the Ten Days of Penitence, which close with Yom Kippur.

Yom Kippur (Day of Atonement), Sat., Sept. 25. This day marks the end of the Ten Days of Penitence that began with Rosh Hashanah. It is described in Leviticus as a "Sabbath of rest," and synagogue services begin the preceding sundown, resume the following morning, and continue to sundown.

First Day of Sukkot (Feast of Tabernacles), Thurs., Sept. 30. This festival, also known as the Feast of the Ingathering, originally celebrated the fruit harvest, and the name comes from the booths or tabernacles in which the Jews lived during the harvest, although one tradition traces it to the shelters used by the Jews in their wandering through the wilderness. During the festival many Jews build small huts in their backyards or on the roofs of their houses.

Simchat Torah (Rejoicing of the Law), Fri., Oct. 8. This joyous holiday falls on the eighth day of Sukkot. It marks the end of the year's reading of the Torah (Five Books of Moses) in the synagogue every Saturday and the beginning of the new cycle of reading.

Columbus Day, Mon., Oct. 11. A federal holiday, observed the second Monday in October, it commemorates Christopher Columbus's landing in the New World in 1492. Quite likely the first celebration of Columbus Day was that organized in 1792 by the Society of St. Tammany, or the Columbian Order, widely known as Tammany Hall.

First Day of Ramadan, Fri., Oct. 15. This day marks the beginning of a month-long fast that all Muslims must keep during the daylight hours. It commemorates the first revelation of the Qur'an. Following the last day of Ramadan, **Eid al-Fitr** is celebrated on Sun., Nov. 14.

Halloween, Sun., Oct. 31. Eve of All Saints' Day, formerly called All Hallows and Hallowmass. Halloween is traditionally associated in some countries with customs such as bonfires, masquerading, and the telling of ghost stories. These are old Celtic practices marking the beginning of winter.

All Saints' Day, Mon., Nov. 1. A Roman Catholic and Anglican holiday celebrating all saints, known and unknown.

Election Day (legal holiday in certain states), Tues., Nov. 2. Since 1845, by act of Congress, the first Tuesday after the first Monday in November is the date for choosing presidential electors. State elections are also generally held on this day.

Veterans Day, Thurs., Nov. 11. Armistice Day, a federal holiday, was established in 1926 to commemorate the signing in 1918 of the armistice ending World War I. On June 1, 1954, the name was changed to Veterans Day to honor all men and women who have served America in its armed forces.

Thanksgiving, Thurs., Nov. 25. A federal holiday observed the fourth Thursday in November by act of Congress (1941), it was the first such national proclamation issued by President Lincoln in 1863, on the urging of Mrs. Sarah J. Hale, editor of *Godey's Lady's Book.* Most Americans believe that the holiday dates back to the day of thanks ordered by Governor Bradford of Plymouth Colony in New England in 1621, but scholars point out that days of thanks stem from ancient times.

First Sunday of Advent, Nov. 28. Advent is the season in which the faithful must prepare themselves for the coming, or advent, of the Savior on Christmas. The four Sundays before Christmas are marked by special church services.

First Day of Hanukkah (Festival of Lights), Weds., Dec. 8. This festival was instituted by Judas Maccabaeus in 165 B.C. to celebrate the purification of the Temple of Jerusalem, which had been desecrated three years earlier by Antiochus Epiphanes, who set up a pagan altar and offered sacrifices to Zeus Olympius. In Jewish homes, a light is lighted on each night of the eight-day festival.

Christmas (Feast of the Nativity), Sat., Dec. 25. The most widely celebrated holiday of the Christian year, Christmas is observed as the anniversary of the birth of Jesus. Christmas customs are centuries old. The mistletoe, for example, comes from the Druids, who, in hanging the mistletoe, hoped for peace and good fortune. Comparatively recent is the Christmas tree, first set up in Germany in the 17th century. Colonial Manhattan Islanders introduced the name Santa Claus, a corruption of the Dutch name St. Nicholas, who lived in fourth-century Asia Minor.

Christian and Secular Holidays, 2003–2005

Year	Ash Wednesday	Easter	Pentecost	Labor Day	Election Day	Thanksgiving	1st Sun. Advent
2003	March 5	April 20	June 8	Sept. 1	Nov. 4	Nov. 27	Nov. 30
2004	Feb. 25	April 11	May 30	Sept. 6	Nov. 2	Nov. 25	Nov. 28
2005	Feb. 2	March 27	May 15	Sept. 5	Nov. 8	Nov. 24	Nov. 28

Shrove Tuesday: 1 day before Ash Wednesday. Palm Sunday: 7 days before Easter. Maundy Thursday: 3 days before Easter. Good Friday: 2 days before Easter. Holy Saturday: 1 day before Easter. Ascension Day: 10 days before Pentecost. Trinity Sunday: 7 days after Pentecost. Corpus Christi: 11 days after Pentecost.

Orthodox Holidays, 2003–2006

Year	Great Lent Begins	Pascha (Easter)	Ascension	Pentecost
2003	March 10	April 27	June 5	June 15
2004	Feb. 22	April 11	May 20	May 30
2005	Feb. 10	May 1	June 2	June 19
2006	March 6	April 23	June 1	June 11

Jewish Holidays, 2003–2005

Year	Purim[1]	1st day Passover[2]	1st day Shavuot[3]	1st day Rosh Hashanah[4]	Yom Kippur[5]	1st day Sukkot[6]	Simchat Torah[7]	1st day Hanukkah[8]
2003	March 18	April 17	June 6	Sept. 27	Oct. 6	Oct. 11	Oct. 19	Dec. 20
2004	March 7	April 6	May 26	Sept. 16	Sept. 25	Sept. 30	Oct. 8	Dec. 8
2005	March 25	April 24	June 13	Oct. 4	Oct. 13	Oct. 18	Oct. 26	Dec. 25

1. Feast of Lots. 2. Feast of Unleavened Bread. 3. Hebrew Pentecost; or Feast of Weeks, or of Harvest, or of First Fruits. 4. Jewish New Year. 5. Day of Atonement. 6. Feast of Tabernacles, or of the Ingathering. 7. Rejoicing of the Law. In Israel, Simchat Torah is celebrated on the day before the date given. 8. Festival of Lights.

Length of Jewish holidays (O=Orthodox, C=Conservative, R=Reform): Passover: O & C, 8 days (holy days: first 2 and last 2); R, 7 days (holy days: first and last). Shavuot: O & C, 2 days; R, 1 day. Rosh Hashanah: O & C, 2 days; R, 1 day. Yom Kippur: All groups, 1 day. Sukkot: All groups, 7 days (holy days: O & C, first 2; R, first only); O & C observe 2 additional days: Shemini Atseret (Eighth Day of the Feast) and Simchat Torah; R observes Shemini Atseret but not Simchat Torah. Hanukkah: All groups, 8 days. NOTE: All holidays begin at sundown on the evening before the date given.

Islamic Holidays, 2002–2006 (A.H. 1423–1426)

In the Year of the Hegira	Muharram (Islamic New Year)	Mawlid al-Nabi (Muhammad's Birthday)	Ramadan begins	Eid al-Fitr (Ramadan ends)	Eid al-Adha (Festival of Sacrifice)
A.H. 1423	March 15, 2002	May 24, 2002	Nov. 6, 2002	Dec. 6, 2002	Feb. 12, 2003
A.H. 1424	March 5, 2003	May 14, 2003	Oct. 27, 2003	Nov. 26, 2003	Feb. 2, 2004
A.H. 1425	Feb. 22, 2004	May 2, 2004	Oct. 15, 2004	Nov. 14, 2004	Jan. 21, 2005
A.H. 1426	Feb. 10, 2005	April 21, 2005	Oct. 4, 2005	Nov. 3, 2005	Jan. 10, 2006

NOTE: All holidays begin at sundown on the evening before the date given. Islamic holidays are based on the lunar calendar and thus may vary by one or two days. Dates apply to North America.

Hindu Festival Dates, 2004

Source: Indian Calendars for the 21st Century, by Pal Singh Purewal

Jan. 14	Makar Sankranti
Jan. 26	Vasant Panchami
Feb. 18	Maha Shivaratri Vrat (fast)
March 6	Holi (last day)
March 21	Bikrami Samvat (2061 begins)
March 21	Chetra Navratras begin
March 30	Rama Navmi
April 13	Vaisakhi (solar new year)
Aug. 30	Raksha Bandhan
Sept. 6	Sri Krishna Jayanti
Sept. 17	Ganesh Chaturathi
Sept. 28	Saradhas begin
Oct. 15	Asuj Navratras begin
Oct. 22	Dassehra
Oct. 31	Karva Chauth Vrat (fast)
Nov. 12	Diwali (Festival of Lights)

Sikh Festival Dates, 2004

Source: Indian Calendars for the 21st Century, by Pal Singh Purewal

Jan. 5	Birthday of Guru Gobind Singh Sahib
Jan. 13	Maghi
March 7	Hola Mohalla
March 14	New Year's Day (Nanakshahi Era 536 begins)
April 14	Vaisakhi (birth anniversary of Khalsa)
June 16	Martyrdom of Guru Arjan Dev Sahib
Sept. 1	First Parkash Guru Granth Sahib
Oct. 20	Installation of Holy Scriptures as Guru Granth Sahib
Nov. 12	Bandi Chhor Divas (Diwali)
Nov. 26	Birthday of Guru Nanak Dev Sahib
Nov. 24	Martyrdom of Guru Tegh Bahadur Sahib

NOTE: Dates for Sikh holidays are determined according to the date of their observance in India.

Jain Festival Dates, 2004

Source: Indian Calendars for the 21st Century, by Pal Singh Purewal

April 3	Sri Mahavir Jyanti
April 22	Akshya Tritiya
Sept. 17	Samvatatsari
Oct. 21	Oli begins
Oct. 28	Oli ends
Nov. 16	Jnana Panchami
Nov.26	Rathayatra

Chinese New Year

2000	Feb. 5
2001	Jan. 24
2002	Feb. 12
2003	Feb. 1
2004	Jan. 22
2005	Feb. 9
2006	Jan. 29
2007	Feb. 18
2008	Feb. 7
2009	Jan. 26
2010	Feb. 14
2011	Feb. 3

State Holidays

Jan. 6, Three Kings' Day: P.R.
Jan. 8, Battle of New Orleans Day: La.
Jan. 11, De Hostos's Birthday: P.R.
Jan. 19, Robert E. Lee's Birthday: Ark., Fla., Ky., La., S.C.; **(third Mon.):** Ala., Miss.
Jan. 19, Confederate Heroes Day: Tex.
Jan. (third Mon.), Lee-Jackson-King Day: Va.
Jan. 30, F. D. Roosevelt's Birthday: Ky.
Feb. 15, Susan B. Anthony's Birthday: Fla., Minn.
March (first Tues.), Town Meeting Day: Vt.
March 2, Texas Independence Day: Tex.
March (first Mon.), Casimir Pulaski's Birthday: Ill.
March 17, Evacuation Day: Mass. (in Suffolk County)
March 20 (first day of spring), Youth Day: Okla.
March 22, Abolition Day: P.R.
March 25, Maryland Day: Md.
March 26, Prince Jonah Kuhio Kalanianaole Day: Hawaii
March (last Mon.), Seward's Day: Alaska
April 2, Pascua Florida Day: Fla.
April 13, Thomas Jefferson's Birthday: Ala., Okla.
April 16, De Diego's Birthday: P.R.
April (third Mon.), Patriots' Day: Maine, Mass.
April 21, San Jacinto Day: Tex.
April 22, Arbor Day: Nebr.
April 22, Oklahoma Day: Okla.
April 26, Confederate Memorial Day: Fla., Ga.
April (fourth Mon.), Fast Day: N.H.
April (last Mon.), Confederate Memorial Day: Ala., Miss.
May 1, Bird Day: Okla.
May 8, Truman Day: Mo.
May 11, Minnesota Day: Minn.
May 20, Mecklenburg Independence Day: N.C.
June (first Mon.), Jefferson Davis's Birthday: Ala., Miss.
June 3, Jefferson Davis's Birthday: Fla., S.C.
June 3, Confederate Memorial Day: Ky., La.
June 9, Senior Citizens Day: Okla.
June 11, King Kamehameha I Day: Hawaii
June 15, Separation Day: Del.
June 17, Bunker Hill Day: Mass. (in Suffolk County)
June 19, Emancipation Day: Tex.
June 20, West Virginia Day: W.Va.
July 17, Muñoz Rivera's Birthday: P.R.
July 24, Pioneer Day: Utah
July 25, Constitution Day: P.R.
July 27, Barbosa's Birthday: P.R.
Aug. (first Sun.), American Family Day: Ariz.
Aug. (first Mon.), Colorado Day: Colo.
Aug. (second Mon.), Victory Day: R.I.
Aug. 16, Bennington Battle Day: Vt.
Aug. (third Friday), Admission Day: Hawaii
Aug. 27, Lyndon B. Johnson's Birthday: Tex.
Aug. 30, Huey P. Long Day: La.
Sept. 9, Admission Day: Calif.
Sept. 12, Defenders' Day: Md.
Sept. 16, Cherokee Strip Day: Okla.
Sept. (first Sat. after full moon), Indian Day: Okla.
Oct. 10, Leif Eriksson Day: Minn.
Oct. 10, Oklahoma Historical Day: Okla.
Oct. 18, Alaska Day: Alaska
Oct. 31, Nevada Day: Nev.
Nov. 4, Will Rogers Day: Okla.
Nov. (week of the 16th), Oklahoma Heritage Week: Okla.
Nov. 19, Discovery Day: P.R.
Dec. 7, Delaware Day: Del.

Birthstones

Month	Stone	Month	Stone	Month	Stone
January	Garnet	June	Pearl, Alexandrite, or Moonstone	October	Opal or Tourmaline
February	Amethyst	July	Ruby or Star Ruby	November	Topaz or Citrine
March	Aquamarine or Bloodstone	August	Peridot or Sardonyx	December	Turquoise, Lapis Lazuli, Blue Zircon, or Blue Topaz
April	Diamond	September	Sapphire or Star Sapphire		
May	Emerald				

Source: Jewelry Industry Council.

Traditional Wedding Anniversary Gift List

Anniv.	Gift	Anniv.	Gift	Anniv.	Gift	Anniv.	Gift
1st	Paper	7th	Copper, wool	13th	Lace	35th	Coral
2nd	Cotton	8th	Bronze, pottery	14th	Ivory	40th	Ruby
3rd	Leather	9th	Pottery, willow	15th	Crystal	45th	Sapphire
4th	Fruit, flowers	10th	Tin	20th	China	50th	Gold
5th	Wood	11th	Steel	25th	Silver	55th	Emerald
6th	Sugar	12th	Silk, linen	30th	Pearl	60th	Diamond

National Holidays Around the World

Afghanistan, Aug. 19
Albania, Nov. 28
Algeria, Nov. 1
Andorra, Sept. 8
Angola, Nov. 11
Antigua and Barbuda, Nov. 1
Argentina, May 25
Armenia, Sept. 21
Australia, Jan. 26
Austria, Oct. 26
Azerbaijan, May 28
Bahamas, July 10
Bahrain, Dec. 16
Bangladesh, March 26
Barbados, Nov. 30
Belarus, July 3
Belgium, July 21
Belize, Sept. 21
Benin, Aug. 1
Bhutan, Dec. 17
Bolivia, Aug. 6
Bosnia and Herzegovina, March 1
Botswana, Sept. 30
Brazil, Sept. 7
Brunei, Feb. 23
Bulgaria, March 3
Burkina Faso, Aug. 4
Burma, Jan. 4
Burundi, July 1
Cambodia, Nov. 9
Cameroon, May 20
Canada, July 1
Cape Verde, July 5
Central African Rep., Dec. 1
Chad, Aug. 11
Chile, Sept. 18
China, People's Rep. of, Oct. 1
Colombia, July 20
Comoros, July 6
Congo, Aug. 15
Congo, Dem. Rep. of, June 30
Costa Rica, Sept. 15
Côte d'Ivoire, Aug. 7
Croatia, June 25
Cuba, Jan. 1
Cyprus, Oct. 1
Czech Rep., May 8
Denmark, June 5
Djibouti, June 27
Dominica, Nov. 3
Dominican Rep., Feb. 27
East Timor, Nov. 28
Ecuador, Aug. 10
Egypt, July 23
El Salvador, Sept. 15
Equatorial Guinea, Oct. 12
Eritrea, May 24
Estonia, Feb. 24
Ethiopia, May 28
Fiji, Oct. 10
Finland, Dec. 6
France, July 14
Gabon, Aug. 17
Gambia, The, Feb. 18
Georgia, May 26
Germany, Oct. 3
Ghana, March 6
Greece, March 25
Grenada, Feb. 7
Guatemala, Sept. 15
Guinea, April 3
Guinea-Bissau, Sept. 10
Guyana, Feb. 23
Haiti, Jan. 1
Honduras, Sept. 15
Hungary, Aug. 20
Iceland, June 17
India, Jan. 26
Indonesia, Aug. 17
Iran, April 1
Iraq, July 17
Ireland, March 17
Israel, April or May[1]
Italy, June 2
Jamaica, Aug.[1]
Japan, Dec. 23
Jordan, May 25
Kazakhstan, Oct. 25
Kenya, Dec. 12
Kiribati, July 12
Korea (North), Sept. 9
Korea (South), Aug. 15
Kuwait, Feb. 25
Kyrgyzstan, Aug. 31
Laos, Dec. 2
Latvia, Nov. 18
Lebanon, Nov. 22
Lesotho, Oct. 4
Liberia, July 26
Libya, Sept. 1
Liechtenstein, Aug. 15
Lithuania, Feb. 16
Luxembourg, June 23
Macedonia, Sept. 8
Madagascar, June 26
Malawi, July 6
Malaysia, Aug. 31
Maldives, July 26
Mali, Sept. 22
Malta, Sept. 21
Marshall Islands, May 1
Mauritania, Nov. 28
Mauritius, March 12
Mexico, Sept. 16
Micronesia, Federated States of, May 10
Moldova, Aug. 27
Monaco, Nov. 19
Mongolia, July 11
Morocco, March 3
Mozambique, June 25
Namibia, March 21
Nauru, Jan. 31
Nepal, Dec. 28
Netherlands, April 30
New Zealand, Feb. 6
Nicaragua, Sept. 15
Niger, Dec. 18
Nigeria, Oct. 1
Norway, May 17
Oman, Nov. 18
Pakistan, March 23
Palau, July 9
Panama, Nov. 3
Papua New Guinea, Sept. 16
Paraguay, May 14–15
Peru, July 28
Philippines, June 12
Poland, May 3
Portugal, June 10
Qatar, Sept. 3
Romania, Dec. 1
Russia, June 12
Rwanda, July 1
St. Kitts and Nevis, Sept. 19
St. Lucia, Feb. 22
St. Vincent and the Grenadines, Oct. 27
Samoa, June 1
San Marino, Sept. 3
São Tomé and Príncipe, July 12
Saudi Arabia, Sept. 23
Senegal, April 4
Serbia and Montenegro, April 27
Seychelles, June 18
Sierra Leone, April 27
Singapore, Aug. 9
Slovakia, Sept. 1
Slovenia, June 25
Solomon Islands, July 7
Somalia, July 1
South Africa, April 27
Spain, Oct. 12
Sri Lanka, Feb. 4
Sudan, Jan. 1
Suriname, Nov. 25
Swaziland, Sept. 6
Sweden, June 6
Switzerland, Aug. 1
Syria, April 17
Taiwan, Oct. 10
Tajikistan, Sept. 9
Tanzania, April 26
Thailand, Dec. 5
Togo, April 27
Tonga, June 4
Trinidad and Tobago, Aug. 31
Tunisia, March 20
Turkey, Oct. 29
Turkmenistan, Oct. 27
Tuvalu, Oct. 1
Uganda, Oct. 9
Ukraine, Aug. 24
United Arab Emirates, Dec. 2
United Kingdom, June[1]
United States, July 4
Uruguay, Aug. 25
Uzbekistan, Sept. 1
Vanuatu, July 30
Vatican, Oct. 22
Venezuela, July 5
Vietnam, Sept. 2
Yemen, May 22
Zambia, Oct. 24
Zimbabwe, April 18

1. Variable holidays, falling on a different date each year. *Source:* CIA World Factbook.

Major Religions of the World

There are twelve classical world religions—those religions most often included in history of world religion surveys and studied in world religions classes: Baha'i, Buddhism, Christianity, Confucianism, Hinduism, Islam, Jainism, Judaism, Shinto, Sikhism, Taoism, and Zoroastrianism. Here are overviews of the nine largest of these classical religions.

Judaism

Judaism is the oldest of the monotheistic faiths. It affirms the existence of one God, Yahweh, who entered into covenant with the descendants of Abraham, God's chosen people. Judaism's holy writings reveal how God has been present with them throughout their history. These writings are known as the Torah, specifically the five books of Moses, but most broadly conceived as the Hebrew Scriptures (traditionally called the Old Testament by Christians) and the compilation of oral tradition known as the Talmud (which includes the Mishnah, the oral law).

According to Scripture, the Hebrew patriarch Abraham (20th century? B.C.) founded the faith that would become known as Judaism. He obeyed the call of God to depart northern Mesopotamia and travel to Canaan. God promised to bless his descendants if they remained faithful in worship. Abraham's line descended through Isaac, then Jacob (also called Israel; his descendants came to be called Israelites). According to Scripture, 12 families that descended from Jacob migrated to Egypt, where they were enslaved. They were led out of bondage (13th century? B.C.) by Moses, who united them in the worship of Yahweh. The Hebrews returned to Canaan after a 40-year sojourn in the desert, conquering from the local peoples the "promised land" that God had provided for them.

The 12 tribes of Israel lived in a covenant association during the period of the judges (1200?–1000? B.C.), leaders known for wisdom and heroism. Saul first established a monarchy (r. 1025?–1005? B.C.); his successor, David (r. 1005?–965? B.C.), unified the land of Israel and made Jerusalem its religious and political center. Under his son, Solomon (r. 968?–928? B.C.), a golden era culminated in the building of a temple, replacing the portable sanctuary in use until that time. Following Solomon's death, the kingdom was split into Israel in the north and Judah in the south. Political conflicts resulted in the conquest of Israel by Assyria (721 B.C.) and the defeat of Judah by Babylon (586 B.C.). Jerusalem and its temple were destroyed, and many Judeans were exiled to Babylon.

During the era of the kings, the prophets were active in Israel and Judah. Their writings emphasize faith in Yahweh as God of Israel and of the entire universe, and they warn of the dangers of worshiping other gods. They also cry out for social justice.

The Judeans were permitted to return in 539 B.C. to Judea, where they were ruled as a Persian province. Though temple and cult were restored in Jerusalem, during the exile a new class of religious leaders had emerged—the scribes. They became rivals to the temple hierarchy and would eventually evolve into the party known as the Pharisees.

Persian rule ended when Alexander the Great conquered Palestine in 332 B.C. After his death, rule of Judea alternated between Egypt and Syria. When the Syrian ruler Antiochus IV Epiphanes tried to prevent the practice of Judaism, a revolt was led by the Maccabees (a Jewish family), winning Jewish independence in 128 B.C. The Romans conquered Jerusalem in 63 B.C.

During this period the Sadducees (temple priests) and the Pharisees (teachers of the law in the synagogues) offered different interpretations of Judaism. Smaller groups that emerged were the Essenes, a religious order; the Apocalyptists, who expected divine deliverance led by the Messiah; and the Zealots, who were prepared to fight for national independence. Hellenism also influenced Judaism at this time.

When the Zealots revolted, the Roman armies destroyed Jerusalem and its temple (A.D. 70). The Jews were scattered in the Diaspora (dispersion) and experienced much persecution. Rabbinic Judaism, developed according to Pharisaic practice and centered on Torah and synagogue, became the primary expression of faith. The Scriptures became codified,

Top Ten Organized Religions of the World

Statistics of the world's religions are only very rough approximations. Aside from Christianity, few religions, if any, attempt to keep statistical records; and even Protestants and Catholics employ different methods of counting members.

Religion	Members	Percentage	Religion	Members	Percentage
Christianity	1.9 billion	33.0%	Judaism	14 million	0.2
Islam	1.1 billion	20.0	Baha'ism	6.1 million	0.1
Hinduism	781 million	13.0	Confucianism	5.3 million	0.1
Buddhism	324 million	6.0	Jainism	4.9 million	0.1
Sikhism	19 million	0.4	Shintoism	2.8 million	0.0

NOTE: This list includes only organized religions and excludes more loosely defined groups such as Chinese or African traditional religions. *Sources:* Encyclopedia Britannica; www.adherents.com.

and the Talmud took shape. In the 12th century Maimonides formulated the influential 13 Articles of Faith, including belief in God, God's oneness and lack of physical or other form, the changelessness of Torah, restoration of the monarchy under the Messiah, and resurrection of the dead.

Two branches of European Judaism developed during the Middle Ages: the Sephardic, based in Spain and with an affinity to Babylonian Jews; and the Ashkenazic, based in Franco-German lands and affiliated with Rome and Palestine. Two forms of Jewish mysticism also arose at this time: medieval Hasidism and attention to the Kabbalah (a mystical interpretation of Scripture).

After a respite during the 18th-century Enlightenment, anti-Semitism again plagued European Jews in the 19th century, sparking the Zionist movement that culminated in the founding of the state of Israel in 1948. The Holocaust of World War II took the lives of more than 6 million Jews.

Jews today continue synagogue worship, which includes readings from the Law and the Prophets and prayers, such as the Shema (Hear, O Israel) and the Amidah (the 18 Benedictions). Religious life is guided by the commandments of the Torah, which include the practice of circumcision and Sabbath observance.

Present-day Judaism has three main expressions: Orthodox, Conservative, and Reform. Reform movements, resulting from the Haskala (Jewish Enlightenment) of the 18th century, began in western Europe but took root in North America. Reform Jews do not hold the oral law (Talmud) to be a divine revelation, and they emphasize ethical and moral teachings. Orthodox Jews follow the traditional faith and practice with great seriousness. They follow a strict kosher diet and keep the Sabbath with care. Conservative Judaism, which developed in the mid-18th century, holds the Talmud to be authoritative and follows most traditional practices, yet tries to make Judaism relevant for each generation, believing that change and tradition can complement each other. Because the Torah assumes belief in God but does not require it, a strong secular movement also exists within Judaism, including atheist and agnostic elements.

In general, Jews do not proselytize, but they do welcome newcomers to their faith.

Christianity

Christianity is a monotheistic religion founded by the followers of Jesus of Nazareth. Jesus, a Jew, was born in about 7 B.C. and assumed his public life, probably after his 30th year, in Galilee. The New Testament Gospels describe Jesus as a teacher and miracle worker. He proclaimed the kingdom of God, a future reality that is at the same time already present. Jesus set the requirements for participation in the kingdom of God as a change of heart and repentance for sins, love of God and neighbor, and concern for justice. Circa A.D. 30 he was executed on a cross in Jerusalem, a brutal form of punishment for those considered a political threat to the Roman Empire.

After his death his followers came to believe in him as the Christ, the Messiah. The Gospels report his resurrection and how the risen Jesus was witnessed by many of his followers. The apostle Paul helped spread the new faith in his missionary travels. Historically, Christianity arose out of Judaism and claims that Jesus fulfilled many of the promises of the Hebrew Scripture (often referred to as the Old Testament).

The new religion spread rapidly throughout the Roman Empire. In its first two centuries, Christianity began to take shape as an organization, developing distinctive doctrine, liturgy, and ministry. By the fourth century the Christian church had taken root in countries stretching from Spain in the West to Persia and India in the East. Christians had been subject to persecution by the Roman state, but gained tolerance under Constantine the Great (A.D. 313). The church became favored under his successors, and in 380 the emperor Theodosius proclaimed Christianity the state religion. Other religions were suppressed.

Because differences in doctrine threatened to divide the church, a standard Christian creed was formulated by bishops at successive ecumenical councils, the first of which was held in A.D. 325 (Nicaea). Important doctrines were defined concerning the Trinity—in other words, that there is one God in three persons: Father, Son, and Holy Spirit (Constantinople, A.D. 381), and the nature of Christ as both divine and human (Chalcedon, A.D. 541). Christians came to accept both Hebrew Scripture and the New Testament as authoritative. The New Testament comprises four Gospels (narratives of Jesus' life), 21 Epistles, The Acts of the Apostles, and Revelation.

Because of differences between Christians of the East and West, the unity of the church was broken in 1054. The religious center for the Eastern Orthodox Church was Constantinople, and the Roman

Largest 25 U.S. Churches,[1] 2002

Denomination name	Members
The Roman Catholic Church	63,683,030
Southern Baptist Convention	15,960,308
The United Methodist Church	8,340,954
The Church of God in Christ	5,499,875
The Church of Jesus Christ of Latter-Day Saints	5,208,827
Evangelical Lutheran Church in America	5,125,919
National Baptist Convention of America, Inc.	3,500,000
Presbyterian Church (U.S.A.)	3,485,332
Assemblies of God	2,577,560
The Lutheran Church—Missouri Synod (LCMS)	2,554,088
Progressive National Baptist Convention, Inc.	2,500,000
African Methodist Episcopal Church	2,500,000
National Missionary Baptist Convention of America	2,500,000
Episcopal Church	2,311,398
Greek Orthodox Archdiocese of America	1,500,000
Pentecostal Assemblies of the World, Inc.	1,500,000
Churches of Christ	1,500,000
American Baptist Churches in the U.S.A.	1,436,909
United Church of Christ	1,377,320
African Methodist Episcopal Zion Church	1,296,662
Baptist Bible Fellowship International	1,200,000
Christian Churches and Churches of Christ	1,071,616
The Orthodox Church in America	1,000,000
Jehovah's Witnesses	998,166
Church of God (Cleveland, Tenn.)	895,536

1. The National Baptist Convention U.S.A., Inc., one of the ten largest churches in the U.S., is currently at work producing an actual count to be available in subsequent editions. *Source: Yearbook of American & Canadian Churches,* 2002.

Catholic Church defined doctrine and practice for Christians in the West. In 1517 the Reformation began, which ultimately caused a schism in the Western church. Reformers wished to correct certain practices within the Roman church, but they also came to view the Christian faith in a distinctly new way. The major Protestant denominations (Lutheran, Presbyterian, Reformed, and Anglican [Episcopalian]) thus came into being. Over the centuries, numerous denominations have broken with these major traditions, resulting in a spectrum of Christian expression.

In the 21st century, many Christians hope to regain a sense of unity through dialogue and cooperation among different traditions. The ecumenical movement led to the formation of the World Council of Churches in 1948 (Amsterdam), which has since been joined by many denominations.

Through its missionary activity Christianity has spread to most parts of the globe.

Eastern Orthodoxy

Eastern Orthodoxy comprises the faith and practices stemming from ancient churches in the eastern part of the Roman Empire. It encompasses Orthodox churches in communion with the see of Constantinople.

The Orthodox, Catholic, Apostolic Church is the direct descendant of the Byzantine state church and consists of independent national churches that are united by doctrine, liturgy, and hierarchical organization (church leaders include deacons and priests, who may either be married or be monks before ordination, and bishops, who must be celibates). The heads of these churches are called patriarchs or metropolitans. Rivalry between the pope of Rome and the patriarch of Constantinople, as well as differences that existed for centuries between the eastern and western parts of the empire, led to a schism in 1054. The mutual excommunication pronounced in that year was lifted in 1965, however, and a climate of better understanding has ensued. Orthodox churches belong to the World Council of Churches.

The Eastern Orthodox churches recognize only the canons of the seven ecumenical councils (325–787) as binding for faith, and they reject doctrines that have been added in the West.

The central worship service is called the Liturgy, which is understood as representing God's acts of salvation. Its center is the celebration of the Eucharist, or Lord's Supper. Icons (sacred pictures) have a special place in Orthodox worship. The mother of Christ, angels, and saints are venerated. The Orthodox Church and the Western Catholic Church recognize the same number of sacraments.

Orthodox churches are found in Greece, Turkey, Russia, the Balkans, and other parts of the former Soviet Union. In this century Orthodox faith has spread to western Europe and other parts of the world, particularly North America.

Eastern Rite Churches

These include the Uniate Churches that recognize the authority of the pope but keep their own traditional liturgies and those churches dating back to the fifth century that emancipated themselves from the Byzantine state church. They include the Melchites, Syrian Catholics, Maronites (Arab Christians in Lebanon), Catholic Copts and Ethiopians, the autonomous Nestorian Church, and others.

Roman Catholicism

Roman Catholicism comprises the beliefs and practices of the Roman Catholic Church. It stands under the authority of the bishop of Rome, the pope, and is led by him and bishops who are held to be, through ordination, successors of Peter and the apostles. Doctrine and sacraments are administered by the hierarchy of archbishops, bishops, priests, and deacons. As successor to Peter, the pope is considered the Vicar of Christ. Roman Catholics believe their church to be the one, holy, catholic, and apostolic church, possessing all the properties of the one, true church of Christ.

The faith of the church is understood to be identical with that taught by Christ and his apostles and contained in the Bible and tradition. New definitions of doctrines, such as the Immaculate Conception of Mary (1854) and the bodily Assumption of Mary (1950), have been declared by popes, however. At Vatican Council I (1870) the pope was proclaimed "endowed with infallibility, *ex cathedra,* in other words, when exercising the office of pastor and teacher of all Christians."

The center of Roman Catholic worship is the celebration of the Mass, the Eucharist, which is the commemoration of Christ's sacrificial death and resurrection. Other sacraments are baptism, confirmation, penance, matrimony, anointing of the sick (formerly known as extreme unction), and holy orders.

Roman Catholic Church Hierarchy

The Catholic clergy is organized in a strict, sometimes overlapping hierarchy:

Pope: Head of the church, he is based at the Vatican. The pope is infallible in defining matters of faith and morals.

Cardinal: Appointed by the pope, the 178 cardinals worldwide, including 13 in the U.S., make up the College of Cardinals. As a body, it advises the pope and, on his death, elects a new pope.

Archbishop: An archbishop is a bishop of a main or metropolitan diocese, also called an archdiocese. A cardinal can concurrently hold the title. The U.S. has 45 archbishops.

Bishop: A bishop, like a priest, is ordained to this station. He is a teacher of church doctrine, a priest of sacred worship, and a minister of church government. The U.S. has 290 active bishops; 194 head dioceses.

Priest: An ordained minister who can administer most of the sacraments, including the Eucharist, baptism, and marriage. He can be with a particular religious order or committed to serving a congregation.

Deacon: A transitional deacon is a seminarian studying for the priesthood. A permanent deacon can be married and assists a priest by performing some of the sacraments.

Source: Time Magazine.

The Virgin Mary and the other saints, and their relics, are venerated, and prayers are made to them to intercede with God, in whose presence they are believed to dwell.

The Roman Catholic Church is the largest Christian organization in the world, found in most countries.

Vatican Council II (1962–1965) sought to "update" the church, bringing about changes in practice and more deeply involving the laity. The immensely popular Pope John Paul II (1978–) has taken a more conservative course and has reached out to Catholics worldwide through his extensive travels.

Protestantism

Protestantism encompasses the Christian churches that separated from Rome during the Reformation in the 16th century. This movement was initiated by an Augustinian monk, Martin Luther. The term *Protestant* was originally applied to followers of Luther, who protested at the Diet of Spires (1529) against the decree that prohibited all further ecclesiastical reforms. Other influential reformers included John Calvin, Ulrich Zwingli, and John Knox. Protestantism rejected attempts to tie God's revelation to earthly institutions and strictly adhered to the Word of God as sole authority in matters of faith and practice *(sola scriptura)*. Central in the reformers' understanding of the biblical message is the justification of the sinner by faith alone. The church is understood as a fellowship, and the priesthood of all believers is stressed.

The Augsburg Confession (1530) was the principal statement of Lutheran faith and practice. It became a model for other Protestant confessions of faith. Major Protestant denominations include the Lutheran, Reformed (Calvinist), Presbyterian, and Anglican (Episcopalian). Innumerable sects and denominations sprang from these roots, including Quakers, Baptists, Pentecostals, Congregationalists, Methodists, and nondenominational assemblies.

Since the latter part of the 19th century, national councils of churches have been established in many countries, for example, the Federal Council of Churches of Christ in America in 1908. Churches of a particular denomination have joined in federations and world alliances, beginning with the Anglican Lambeth Conference in 1867.

Protestant missionary activity, particularly strong in the 19th century, resulted in the founding of many churches in Asia and Africa. The ecumenical movement, which originated with Protestant missions, aims at unity among Christians and churches.

U.S. Protestant Groups

According to the Hartford Institute for Religious Research, U.S. Protestant groups are commonly divided into four broad categories:

Liberal Protestant: Episcopal, Presbyterian, Unitarian Universalist, United Church of Christ

Moderate Protestant: American Baptist, Disciples of Christ, Evangelical Lutheran, Mennonite, Reformed Church in America, United Methodist

Evangelical Protestant: Assemblies of God, Christian Reformed, Nazarene, Churches of Christ, Independent Christian Churches (Instrumental), Mega-churches, Nondenominational Protestant, Seventh-day Adventist, Southern Baptist

Historically Black Protestant denominations

Islam

Islam, one of the three major monotheistic faiths, was founded in Arabia by Muhammad between 610 and 632. There are an estimated 5.5 million Muslims in North America and 1 billion Muslims worldwide.

Muhammad was born in A.D. 570 at Mecca and belonged to the Quraysh tribe, which was active in the caravan trade. At the age of 25 he joined the trade from Mecca to Syria in the employment of a rich widow, Khadija, whom he later married. Critical of the lax moral standards and polytheistic practices of the inhabitants of Mecca, he began to lead a contemplative life in the desert. In a dramatic religious vision, the angel Gabriel announced to Muhammad that he was to be a prophet. Encouraged by Khadija, he devoted himself to the reform of religion and society. Polytheism was to be abandoned. But leaders of the Quraysh generally rejected his teaching, and Muhammad gained only a small following and suffered persecution. He eventually fled Mecca.

The Hegira *(Hijra,* meaning "emigration") of Muhammad from Mecca, where he was not honored, to Medina, where he was well received, occurred in 622 and marks the beginning of the Muslim era. After a number of military conflicts with Mecca, in 630 he marched on Mecca and conquered it. Muhammad died at Medina in 632. His grave there has since been a place of pilgrimage.

Muhammad's followers, called Muslims, revered him as the prophet of Allah (God), the only God. Muslims consider Muhammad to be the last in the line of prophets that included Abraham and Jesus. Islam spread quickly, stretching from Spain in the west to India in the east within a century after the prophet's death. Sources of the Islamic faith are the Qur'an (Koran), regarded as the uncreated, eternal Word of God, and tradition *(hadith)* regarding sayings and deeds of the prophet.

Islam means "surrender to the will of Allah," the all-powerful, who determines humanity's fate. Good deeds will be rewarded at the Last Judgment in paradise, and evil deeds will be punished in hell.

The Five Pillars, or primary duties, of Islam are profession of faith; prayer, to be performed five times a day; almsgiving to the poor and the mosque (house of worship); fasting during daylight hours in the month of Ramadan; and pilgrimage to Mecca (the *hajj*) at least once in a Muslim's lifetime, if it is physically and financially possible. The pilgrimage includes homage to the ancient shrine of the Ka'aba, the most sacred site in Islam.

Muslims gather for corporate worship on Fridays. Prayers and a sermon take place at the mosque, which is also a center for teaching of the Qur'an. The community leader, the *imam*, is considered a teacher and prayer leader.

Islam succeeded in uniting an Arab world of separate tribes and castes, but disagreements concerning the succession of the prophet caused a division in Islam between two groups, Sunnis and Shi'ites. The Shi'ites rejected the first three successors to Muhammad as usurpers, claiming the fourth, Muhammad's son-in-law Ali, as the rightful leader.

Countries with the Largest Muslim Populations

1. Indonesia	6. Iran
2. Pakistan	7. Egypt
3. India	8. Nigeria
4. Bangladesh	9. Algeria
5. Turkey	10. Morocco

The Sunnis (from the word *tradition*), the largest division of Islam (today more than 80%), believe in the legitimacy of the first three successors. Among these, other sects arose (such as the conservative Wahhabi of Saudi Arabia), as well as different schools of theology. Another development within Islam, beginning in the eighth and ninth centuries, was Sufism, a form of mysticism. This movement was influential for many centuries and was instrumental in the spread of Islam in Asia and Africa.

Islam has expanded greatly under Muhammad's successors. It is the principal religion of the Middle East, Asia, and the northern half of Africa.

Hinduism

Hinduism is the major religion of India, practiced by more than 80% of the population. In contrast to other religions, it has no founder. Considered the oldest religion in the world, it dates back, perhaps, to prehistoric times.

No single creed or doctrine binds Hindus together. Intellectually there is complete freedom of belief, and one can be monotheist, polytheist, or atheist. Hinduism is a syncretic religion, welcoming and incorporating a variety of outside influences.

The most ancient sacred texts of the Hindu religion are written in Sanskrit and called the *Vedas* (*vedah* means "knowledge"). There are four Vedic books, of which the Rig-Veda is the oldest. It discusses multiple gods, the universe, and creation. The dates of these works are unknown (1000 B.C.?). Present-day Hindus rarely refer to these texts but do venerate them.

The Upanishads (dated 1000–300 B.C.), commentaries on the Vedic texts, speculate on the origin of the universe and the nature of deity, and *atman* (the individual soul) and its relationship to *Brahman* (the universal soul). They introduce the doctrine of *karma* and recommend meditation and the practice of yoga.

Further important sacred writings include the Epics, which contain legendary stories about gods and humans. They are the Mahabharata (composed between 200 B.C. and A.D. 200) and the Ramayana. The former includes the Bhagavad-Gita (Song of the Lord), an influential text that describes the three paths to salvation. The Puranas (stories in verse, probably written between the 6th and 13th centuries) detail myths of Hindu gods and heroes and also comment on religious practice and cosmology.

According to Hindu beliefs, Brahman is the principle and source of the universe. This divine intelligence pervades all beings, including the individual soul. Thus the many Hindu deities are manifestations of the one Brahman. Hinduism is based on the concept of reincarnation, in which all living beings, from plants on earth to gods above, are caught in a cosmic cycle of becoming and perishing.

Life is determined by the law of karma—one is reborn to a higher level of existence based on moral behavior in a previous phase of existence. Life on earth is regarded as transient and a burden. The goal of existence is liberation from the cycle of rebirth and death and entrance into the indescribable state of *moksha* (liberation).

The practice of Hinduism consists of rites and ceremonies centering on birth, marriage, and death. There are many Hindu temples, which are considered to be dwelling places of the deities and to which people bring offerings. Places of pilgrimage include Benares on the Ganges, the most sacred river in India. Of the many Hindu deities, the most popular are the cults of Vishnu, Shiva, and Shakti, and their various incarnations. Also important is Brahma, the creator god. Hindus also venerate human saints.

Orthodox Hindu society in India was divided into four major hereditary classes: (1) the Brahmin (priestly and learned class); (2) the Kshatriya (military, professional, ruling, and governing occupations); (3) the Vaishya (landowners, merchants, and business occupations); and (4) the Sudra (artisans, laborers, and peasants). Below the Sudra was a fifth group, the Untouchables (lowest menial occupations and no social standing). The Indian government banned discrimination against the Untouchables in the constitution of India in 1950. Observance of class and caste distinctions varies throughout India.

In modern times work has been done to reform and revive Hinduism. One of the outstanding reformers was Ramakrishna (1836–1886), who inspired many followers, one of whom founded the Ramakrishna mission. The mission is active both in India and in other countries and is known for its scholarly and humanitarian works.

Buddhism

Buddhism was founded in the fourth or fifth century B.C. in northern India by a man known traditionally as Siddhartha (meaning "he who has reached the goal") Gautama, the son of a warrior prince. Some scholars believe that he lived from 563 to 483 B.C., though his exact life span is uncertain. Troubled by the inevitability of suffering in human life, he left home and a pampered life at the age of 29 to wander as an ascetic, seeking religious insight and a solution to the struggles of human existence. He passed through many trials and practiced extreme self-denial. Finally, while meditating under the bodhi tree ("tree of perfect knowledge"), he reached enlightenment and taught his followers about his new spiritual understanding.

Gautama's teachings differed from the Hindu faith prevalent in India at the time. Whereas in Hinduism the Brahmin caste alone performed religious functions and attained the highest spiritual understanding, Gautama's beliefs were more egalitarian, accessible to all who wished to be enlightened. At the core of his understanding were the Four Noble Truths: (1) all living beings suffer; (2) the origin of this suffering is desire—for material possessions, power, and so on; (3) desire can be overcome; and (4) there is a path that leads to release from desire. This way is called the Noble Eightfold Path: right views, right intention, right speech, right action, right livelihood, right effort, right concentration, and right ecstasy.

Gautama promoted the concept of *anatman* (that a person has no actual self) and the idea that existence is characterized by impermanence. This realization helps one let go of desire for transient things. Still, Gautama did not recommend extreme self-denial but rather a disciplined life called the Middle Way. Like the Hindus, he believed that existence consisted of reincarnation, a cycle of birth and death. He held that it could be broken only by reaching complete detachment from worldly cares. Then the soul could be released into *nirvana* (literally "blowing out")—an indescribable state of total transcendence. Gautama traveled to preach the *dharma* (sacred truth) and was recognized as the Buddha (enlightened one). After his death his followers continued to develop doctrine and practice, which came to center on the Three Jewels: the *dharma* (the sacred teachings of Buddhism), the *sangha* (the community of followers, which now includes nuns, monks, and laity), and the Buddha. Under the patronage of the Mauryan emperor Ashoka (third century B.C.), Buddhism spread throughout India and to other parts of Asia. Monasteries were established, as well as temples dedicated to Buddha; at shrines his relics were venerated. Though by the fourth century A.D. Buddhist presence in India had dwindled, it flourished in other parts of Asia.

Numerous Buddhist sects have emerged. The oldest, called the Theravada (Way of the Elders) tradition, interprets Buddha as a great sage but not a deity. It emphasizes meditation and ritual practices that help the individual become an *arhat*, an enlightened being. Its followers emphasize the authority of the earliest Buddhist scriptures, the Tripitaka (Three Baskets), a compilation of sermons, rules for celibates, and doctrine. This sect is prevalent in Southeast Asia and Sri Lanka. It is sometimes called the Hinayana (Lesser Vehicle) tradition (once considered a pejorative term).

Between the second century B.C. and the second century A.D., the Mahayana (Greater Vehicle) tradition refocused Buddhism to concentrate less on individual attainment of enlightenment and more on concern for humanity. It promotes the ideal of the *bodhisattva* (enlightened being), who shuns entering nirvana until all sentient beings can do so as well, willingly remaining in the painful cycle of birth and death to perform works of compassion. Members of this tradition conceive of Buddha as an eternal being to whom prayers can be made; other Buddhas are revered as well, adding a polytheistic dimension to the religion. Numerous sects have developed from the Mahayana tradition, which has been influential in China, Korea, and Japan.

A third broad tradition, variously called Vajrayana (Diamond Vehicle), Mantrayana (Vehicle of the Mantra), or Tantric Buddhism, offers a quicker, more demanding way to achieve nirvana. Because of its level of challenge—enabling one to reach enlightenment in one lifetime—it requires the guidance of a spiritual leader. It is most prominent in Tibet and Mongolia.

Zen Buddhism encourages individuals to seek the Buddha nature within themselves and to practice a disciplined form of sitting meditation in order to reach *satori*—spiritual enlightenment.

Sikhism

A major religion of India and the fifth-largest faith in the world, Sikhism emerged in the Punjab under the guidance of the guru Nanak (1469–1539?). This region had been influenced by the Hindu *bhakti* movement, which promoted both the idea that God comprises one reality alone as well as the practice of devotional singing and prayer. The Muslim mystical tradition of Sufism, with its emphasis on meditation, also had some prominence there. Drawing on these resources, Nanak forged a new spiritual path.

In his youth, Nanak began to compose hymns. At the age of 29, he had a mystical experience that led him to proclaim "There is no Hindu; there is no Muslim." A strict monotheist, he rejected Hindu polytheism but accepted the Hindu concept of life as a cycle of birth, death, and rebirth; *moksha,* release from this cycle into unity with God, could be achieved only with the help of a guru, or spiritual teacher. Nanak believed that communion with God could be gained through devotional repetition of the divine name, singing of hymns and praises, and adherence to a demanding ethical code. He rejected idols and the Hindu caste system; it became a custom for Sikhs of all social ranks to take meals together. These beliefs are still central to modern Sikhism.

Nanak was first in a line of ten gurus who shaped and inspired Sikhism. The fifth, Arjun (1563–1606), compiled hymns and other writings by earlier Sikh gurus, as well as medieval Hindu and Muslim saints, in the *Adi Granth* (First Book), or *Guru Granth Sahib* (the Granth Personified). This book became the sacred scripture of Sikhism. In addition to his spiritual leadership, Arjun wielded considerable secular power as he grappled with leaders of the Mughal Empire.

The tenth guru, Gobind Singh (1666–1708), was both a scholar and a military hero. He established the Khalsa (community of pure ones), an order that combined spiritual devotion, personal discipline, and ideals of military valor. Baptism initiates new members into the Khalsa. The *Adi Granth* took its final form under the supervision of Gobind Singh, as did the *Dasam Granth* (Tenth Book), a collection of prayers, poetry, and narrative. After the deaths of his four sons, Gobind Singh declared the line of gurus at an end. The *Adi Granth* would instead be reverenced in houses of worship, taking the place of a living guru.

Today, Sikhs worship at *gurdwaras* (temples), where the *Adi Granth* is the object of devotion. This book is consulted regarding questions of faith and practice. On certain occasions, it is recited in its entirety (requiring more than a day) or carried in procession; offerings may be placed before it. Worshipful singing, meditation, and focus on the divine name remain essential to spiritual life. Some Sikhs undertake pilgrimages to historical *gurdwaras,* such as the Golden Temple of Amritsar, that are associated with the gurus. Some become disciples of living saints. There is no established Sikh priesthood.

Confucianism

Confucius (K'ung Fu-tzu), born in the state of Lu (northern China), lived from 551 to 479 B.C. He was a brilliant teacher, viewing education not merely as the accumulation of knowledge but as a means of self-transformation. His legacy was a system of thought emphasizing education, proper behavior, and loyalty. His effect on Chinese culture was immense.

The teachings of Confucius are contained in the *Analects*, a collection of his sayings as remembered by his students. They were further developed by philosophers such as Mencius (Meng Tse, fl. 400 B.C.). Confucianism is little concerned with metaphysical discussion of religion or with spiritual attainments. It instead emphasizes moral conduct and right relationships in the human sphere.

Cultivation of virtue is a central tenet of Confucianism. Two important virtues are *jen*, a benevolent and humanitarian attitude, and *li*, maintaining proper relationships and rituals that enhance the life of the individual, the family, and the state. The "five relations," between king and subject, father and son, man and wife, older and younger brother, and friend and friend, are of utmost importance. These relationships are reinforced by participation in rituals, including the formal procedures of court life and religious rituals such as ancestor worship.

Confucius revolutionized educational thought in China. He believed that learning was not to be focused only on attaining the skills for a particular profession, but for growth in moral judgment and self-realization. Confucius's standards for the proper conduct of government shaped the statecraft of China for centuries. Hundreds of temples in honor of Confucius testify to his stature as sage and teacher.

Confucianism was far less dominant in 20th-century China, at least on an official level. The state cult of Confucius was ended in 1911. Still, Confucian traditions and moral standards are part of the cultural essence of China and other East Asian countries.

Shinto

Shinto comprises the religious ideas and practices indigenous to Japan. Ancient Shinto focused on the worship of the *kami*, a host of supernatural beings that could be known through forms (objects of nature, remarkable people, abstract concepts such as justice) but were ultimately mysterious. Shinto has no formal dogma and no holy writ, though early collections of Japanese religious thought and practice (*Kojiki*, "Records of Ancient Matters," A.D. 712, and *Nihon shoki*, "Chronicles of Japan," A.D. 720) are highly regarded.

Shinto has been influenced by Confucianism and by Buddhism, which was introduced in Japan in the 6th century. Syncretic schools (such as Ryobu Shinto) emerged, as did other sects that rejected Buddhism (such as Ise Shinto).

Under the reign of the emperor Meiji (1868–1912), Shinto became the official state religion. State Shinto, the national cult, emphasized the divinity of the emperor, whose succession was traced back to the first emperor, Jimmu (660 B.C.), and beyond him to the sun goddess Amaterasu-o-mi-kami. State Shinto was disestablished after World War II.

Sect Shinto, deriving from sects that developed during the 19th and 20th centuries, continues to thrive in Japan. Shrines dedicated to particular *kami* are visited by parishioners for prayer and traditional ceremonies, such as presenting a newborn child to the *kami*. Traditional festivals celebrated at the shrines include purification rites, presentation of food offerings, prayer, sacred music and dance, and a feast.

No particular day of the week is set aside for prayer. A person may visit a shrine at will, entering through the *torii* (gateway). It is believed that the *kami* can respond to prayer and can offer protection and guidance.

A variety of Shinto sects and practices exist today. Ten-rikyo emphasizes faith healing. Folk Shinto is characterized by veneration of roadside shrines and rites related to agriculture. Buddhist priests serve at many Shinto shrines, and many families keep a small shrine, or god-shelf, at home. Veneration of ancestors and pilgrimage are also common practices.

Taoism

Taoism, one of the major religions of China, is based on ancient philosophical works, primarily the Tao Te Ching, "Classic of Tao and Its Virtue." Traditionally, this book was thought to be the work of Lao-tzu, a quasi-historical philosopher of the 6th century B.C.; scholars now believe that the book dates from about the 3rd century B.C. The philosopher Chuang Tzu (4th–3rd centuries B.C.) also contributed to the seminal ideas of Taoism.

Tao, "the Way," is the ultimate reality of the universe, according to Taoism. It is a creative process, and humans can live in harmony with it by clearing the self of obstacles. By cultivating *wu-wei*, a type of inaction characterized by humility and prudence, a person can participate in the simplicity and spontaneity of Tao. Striving to attain virtue or achievement is counterproductive and unnecessary. Taoism values mystical contemplation and balance. The human being is viewed as a microcosm of the universe, and the Chinese principle of *yin-yang*, complementary duality, is a model of harmony.

The religious practices of Taoism emerged from these ancient philosophies and from Chinese shamanistic tradition; by the 2nd century A.D., it constituted an organized religion. Longevity and immortality were sought through regulating the energies of the body through breathing exercises, meditation, and use of medicinal plants, talismans, and magical formulas. A cult of immortals, including the divinized Lao-tzu, also developed. Influenced by Buddhism, Taoists organized monastic orders. Temple worship and forms of divination, including the *I ching*, were practiced.

Since its beginnings, many sects have arisen within Taoism. All subscribe to the philosophical origins of the religion; some have emphasized faith healing, exorcism, the worship of the immortals, meditation, or alchemy. Buddhism and Confucianism influenced some sects; some operated as secret societies.

Though the present Chinese government has tried to suppress it, Taoism is still practiced in mainland China, Taiwan, and Hong Kong. It profoundly influenced Chinese art and literature, and Taoist ideas have become popular in the West.

U.S. Religious Sects Originating in the 19th Century

The United States was the setting for new developments in religion in the 19th century. Sects and movements of many types arose, inspired variously by new interpretations of the Bible, the teachings of new prophets and thinkers, the expectation of Christ's second coming, and the social, scientific, and philosophical questions of the time. Sects that have thrived for over 100 years include the Christian Scientists, the Mormons, the Seventh-day Adventists, and the Jehovah's Witnesses.

Christian Scientists

Founded by Mary Baker Eddy (1821–1910) in the 1860s and 1870s, Christian Science views creation as entirely spiritual. The church holds the Bible as authoritative yet interprets it in a distinct way, focusing on the life of Jesus as a model of healing by prayer, a necessary element of spiritual growth. According to the Christian Science concept of Mind-healing, physical illness and injury result from error or wrong belief and can be healed through one's own prayer or the ministrations of a Christian Science practitioner. Worship services focus on readings from the Bible and *Science and Health with Key to the Scriptures,* Eddy's definitive textbook. Christian Science is based at the Mother Church in Boston, Massachusetts. *The Christian Science Monitor,* established under the direction of Eddy, has long been recognized for excellence in journalism.

Mormons

The Church of Jesus Christ of Latter-day Saints was established by Joseph Smith Jr. (1805–1844) of New York. He described an encounter with an angel who gave him the text that would become the *Book of Mormon,* which, together with the Bible and other texts, forms the Mormon scriptures (Mormon is an ancient American prophet noted in the book). Smith organized a church in 1830; due to persecution, church members searched for a place to practice their faith, finally settling in Utah. Salt Lake City, Utah, is home to institutions such as the Family History Library, the world's largest collection of genealogical information. Mormons believe that the Godhead consists of three separate personages (Father, Son, Holy Spirit), that souls preexist this life, and that the faithful will gain eternal life as gods. These rites can be undertaken by proxy for one's dead forebears. In the Mormon view, the second coming of Christ will lead to a chain of events culminating in a final resurrection, after which earth will become a celestial home for all people.

Seventh-day Adventists

Seventh-day Adventists trace their beginnings to the preacher William Miller (1782–1849), who expounded the idea that the second coming of Christ would occur between March 21, 1843, and March 21, 1844. His followers, called Adventists, had to rethink their convictions when that event did not occur. Some believed that Miller's dates designated the beginning of God's examination of the Book of Life, which would soon culminate in the final judgment and Christ's reign on earth. In 1863 they established the Seventh-day Adventist denomination, appointing Saturday (the seventh day) for worship and rest. Seventh-day Adventists practice vegetarianism and avoid alcohol and caffeine. They accept the Bible as the word of God and await the second coming. Among their leaders, Ellen Harmon White (1827–1915) was particularly influential; some consider her writings prophetic. Other Adventist groups hold to somewhat different views.

Jehovah's Witnesses

This sect grew out of the International Bible Students Association, founded in 1872 in Pittsburgh, Pennsylvania, by Charles Taze Russell (1852–1916). After intensive study of the Bible, he concluded that the invisible return of Christ had occurred in 1874, that the Gentile period would cease in 1914, and that, following a war, the kingdom of God would be established on earth. Jehovah's Witnesses no longer set such specific dates but believe that God's kingdom, the Theocracy, will follow Armageddon, the great war described in prophetic books of the Bible. They believe that biblical prophecies are being fulfilled in world events and that Jesus was created by God and acts as his agent. Jehovah's Witnesses worship at meeting places called Kingdom Halls. Because they believe that secular governments are unknowingly entangled with Satan, they do not salute flags or join the military. Jehovah's Witnesses actively seek converts; members are expected to spread the message. Their publishing efforts include the magazines *Watchtower* and *Awake!*

Roman Catholic Pontiffs

Name	Birthplace	Reigned From	Reigned To
St. Peter	Bethsaida	42?	67?
St. Linus	Tuscia	c. 67	76
St. Anacletus (Cletus)	Rome	76	88
St. Clement	Rome	88	97
St. Evaristus	Greece	97	105
St. Alexander I	Rome	105	115
St. Sixtus I	Rome	115	125
St. Telesphorus	Greece	125	136
St. Hyginus	Greece	136	140
St. Pius I	Aquileia	140	155
St. Anicetus	Syria	155	166
St. Soter	Campania	166	175
St. Eleutherius	Epirus	175	189
St. Victor I	Africa	189	199
St. Zephyrinus	Rome	199	217
St. Callistus I	Rome	217	222
St. Urban I	Rome	222	230
St. Pontian	Rome	230	235
St. Anterus	Greece	235	236
St. Fabian	Rome	236	250
St. Cornelius	Rome	251	253
St. Lucius I	Rome	253	254
St. Stephen I	Rome	254	257

Name	Birthplace	Reigned From	To
St. Sixtus II	Greece	257	258
St. Dionysius	Unknown	259	268
St. Felix I	Rome	269	274
St. Eutychian	Luni	275	283
St. Caius	Dalmatia	283	296
St. Marcellinus	Rome	296	304
St. Marcellus I	Rome	308	309
St. Eusebius	Greece	309[1]	309[1]
St. Meltiades	Africa	311	314
St. Sylvester I	Rome	314	335
St. Marcus	Rome	336	336
St. Julius I	Rome	337	352
Liberius	Rome	352	366
St. Damasus I	Spain	366	384
St. Siricius	Rome	384	399
St. Anastasius I	Rome	399	401
St. Innocent I	Albano	401	417
St. Zozimus	Greece	417	418
St. Boniface I	Rome	418	422
St. Celestine I	Campania	422	432
St. Sixtus III	Rome	432	440
St. Leo I (the Great)	Tuscany	440	461
St. Hilary	Sardinia	461	468
St. Simplicius	Tivoli	468	483
St. Felix III (II)[2]	Rome	483	492
St. Gelasius I	Africa	492	496
Anastasius II	Rome	496	498
St. Symmachus	Sardinia	498	514
St. Hormisdas	Frosinone	514	523
St. John I	Tuscany	523	526
St. Felix IV (III)	Samnium	526	530
Boniface II	Rome	530	532
John II	Rome	533	535
St. Agapitus I	Rome	535	536
St. Silverius	Campania	536	537
Vigilius	Rome	537	555
Pelagius I	Rome	556	561
John III	Rome	561	574
Benedict I	Rome	575	579
Pelagius II	Rome	579	590
St. Gregory I (the Great)	Rome	590	604
Sabinianus	Tuscany	604	606
Boniface III	Rome	607	607
St. Boniface IV	Marsi	608	615
St. Deusdedit (Adeodatus I)	Rome	615	618
Boniface V	Naples	619	625
Honorius I	Campania	625	638
Severinus	Rome	640	640
John IV	Dalmatia	640	642
Theodore I	Greece	642	649
St. Martin I	Todi	649	655
St. Eugene I[3]	Rome	654	657
St. Vitalian	Segni	657	672
Adeodatus II	Rome	672	676
Donus	Rome	676	678
St. Agatho	Sicily	678	681
St. Leo II	Sicily	682	683
St. Benedict II	Rome	684	685
John V	Syria	685	686
Conon	Unknown	686	687
St. Sergius I	Syria	687	701
John VI	Greece	701	705
John VII	Greece	705	707
Sisinnius	Syria	708	708
Constantine	Syria	708	715
St. Gregory II	Rome	715	731
St. Gregory III	Syria	731	741
St. Zachary	Greece	741	752
Stephen II (III)[4]	Rome	752	757
St. Paul I	Rome	757	767
Stephen III (IV)	Sicily	768	772
Adrian I	Rome	772	795
St. Leo III	Rome	795	816
Stephen IV (V)	Rome	816	817
St. Paschal I	Rome	817	824
Eugene II	Rome	824	827
Valentine	Rome	827	827
Gregory IV	Rome	827	844
Sergius II	Rome	844	847
St. Leo IV	Rome	847	855
Benedict III	Rome	855	858
St. Nicholas I (the Great)	Rome	858	867
Adrian II	Rome	867	872
John VIII	Rome	872	882
Marinus I	Gallese	882	884
St. Adrian III	Rome	884	885
Stephen V (VI)	Rome	885	891
Formosus	Portus	891	896
Boniface VI	Rome	896	896
Stephen VI (VII)	Rome	896	897
Romanus	Gallese	897	897
Theodore II	Rome	897	897
John IX	Tivoli	898	900
Benedict IV	Rome	900	903
Leo V	Ardea	903	903
Sergius III	Rome	904	911
Anastasius III	Rome	911	913
Landus	Sabina	913	914
John X	Tossignano	914	928
Leo VI	Rome	928	928
Stephen VII (VIII)	Rome	928	931
John XI	Rome	931	935
Leo VII	Rome	936	939
Stephen VIII (IX)	Rome	939	942
Marinus II	Rome	942	946
Agapitus II	Rome	946	955
John XII	Tusculum	955	964
Leo VIII[5]	Rome	963	965
Benedict V[5]	Rome	964	966
John XIII	Rome	965	972
Benedict VI	Rome	973	974
Benedict VII	Rome	974	983
John XIV	Pavia	983	984
John XV	Rome	985	996
Gregory V	Saxony	996	999
Sylvester II	Auvergne	999	1003
John XVII	Rome	1003	1003
John XVIII	Rome	1004	1009
Sergius IV	Rome	1009	1012
Benedict VIII	Tusculum	1012	1024
John XIX	Tusculum	1024	1032
Benedict IX[6]	Tusculum	1032	1044
Sylvester III	Rome	1045	1045
Benedict IX (2nd time)	Tusculum	1045	1045
Gregory VI	Rome	1045	1046
Clement II	Saxony	1046	1047
Benedict IX (3rd time)	Tusculum	1047	1048
Damasus II	Bavaria	1048	1048
St. Leo IX	Alsace	1049	1054
Victor II	Germany	1055	1057

Name	Birthplace	Reigned From	Reigned To
Stephen IX (X)	Lorraine	1057	1058
Nicholas II	Burgundy	1059	1061
Alexander II	Milan	1061	1073
St. Gregory VII	Tuscany	1073	1085
Bl. Victor III	Benevento	1086	1087
Bl. Urban II	France	1088	1099
Paschal II	Ravenna	1099	1118
Gelasius II	Gaeta	1118	1119
Callistus II	Burgundy	1119	1124
Honorius II	Flagnano	1124	1130
Innocent II	Rome	1130	1143
Celestine II	Città di Castello	1143	1144
Lucius II	Bologna	1144	1145
Bl. Eugene III	Pisa	1145	1153
Anastasius IV	Rome	1153	1154
Adrian IV	England	1154	1159
Alexander III	Siena	1159	1181
Lucius III	Lucca	1181	1185
Urban III	Milan	1185	1187
Gregory VIII	Benevento	1187	1187
Clement III	Rome	1187	1191
Celestine III	Rome	1191	1198
Innocent III	Anagni	1198	1216
Honorius III	Rome	1216	1227
Gregory IX	Anagni	1227	1241
Celestine IV	Milan	1241	1241
Innocent IV	Genoa	1243	1254
Alexander IV	Anagni	1254	1261
Urban IV	Troyes	1261	1264
Clement IV	France	1265	1268
Bl. Gregory X	Piacenza	1271	1276
Bl. Innocent V	Savoy	1276	1276
Adrian V	Genoa	1276	1276
John XXI[7]	Portugal	1276	1277
Nicholas III	Rome	1277	1280
Martin IV[8]	France	1281	1285
Honorius IV	Rome	1285	1287
Nicholas IV	Ascoli	1288	1292
St. Celestine V	Isernia	1294	1294
Boniface VIII	Anagni	1294	1303
Bl. Benedict XI	Treviso	1303	1304
Clement V	France	1305	1314
John XXII	Cahors	1316	1334
Benedict XII	France	1334	1342
Clement VI	France	1342	1352
Innocent VI	France	1352	1362
Bl. Urban V	France	1362	1370
Gregory XI	France	1370	1378
Urban VI	Naples	1378	1389
Boniface IX	Naples	1389	1404
Innocent VII	Sulmona	1404	1406
Gregory XII	Venice	1406	1415
Martin V	Rome	1417	1431
Eugene IV	Venice	1431	1447
Nicholas V	Sarzana	1447	1455
Callistus III	Jativa	1455	1458
Pius II	Siena	1458	1464
Paul II	Venice	1464	1471
Sixtus IV	Savona	1471	1484
Innocent VIII	Genoa	1484	1492
Alexander VI	Jativa	1492	1503
Pius III	Siena	1503	1503
Julius II	Savona	1503	1513
Leo X	Florence	1513	1521
Adrian VI	Utrecht	1522	1523
Clement VII	Florence	1523	1534
Paul III	Rome	1534	1549
Julius III	Rome	1550	1555
Marcellus II	Montepulciano	1555	1555
Paul IV	Naples	1555	1559
Pius IV	Milan	1559	1565
St. Pius V	Bosco	1566	1572
Gregory XIII	Bologna	1572	1585
Sixtus V	Grottammare	1585	1590
Urban VII	Rome	1590	1590
Gregory XIV	Cremona	1590	1591
Innocent IX	Bologna	1591	1591
Clement VIII	Florence	1592	1605
Leo XI	Florence	1605	1605
Paul V	Rome	1605	1621
Gregory XV	Bologna	1621	1623
Urban VIII	Florence	1623	1644
Innocent X	Rome	1644	1655
Alexander VII	Siena	1655	1667
Clement IX	Pistoia	1667	1669
Clement X	Rome	1670	1676
Bl. Innocent XI	Como	1676	1689
Alexander VIII	Venice	1689	1691
Innocent XII	Spinazzola	1691	1700
Clement XI	Urbino	1700	1721
Innocent XIII	Rome	1721	1724
Benedict XIII	Gravina	1724	1730
Clement XII	Florence	1730	1740
Benedict XIV	Bologna	1740	1758
Clement XIII	Venice	1758	1769
Clement XIV	Rimini	1769	1774
Pius VI	Cesena	1775	1799
Pius VII	Cesena	1800	1823
Leo XII	Genga	1823	1829
Pius VIII	Cingoli	1829	1830
Gregory XVI	Belluno	1831	1846
Pius IX	Senegallia	1846	1878
Leo XIII	Carpineto	1878	1903
St. Pius X	Riese	1903	1914
Benedict XV	Genoa	1914	1922
Pius XI	Desio	1922	1939
Pius XII	Rome	1939	1958
John XXIII	Sotto il Monte	1958	1963
Paul VI	Concesio	1963	1978
John Paul I	Forno di Canale	1978	1978
John Paul II	Wadowice, Poland	1978	

1. Or 310. 2. He should be called Felix II, and his successors of the same name should be numbered accordingly. The discrepancy was caused by the erroneous insertion in some lists of the name of St. Felix of Rome, Martyr. 3. He was elected during the exile of St. Martin I, who endorsed him as pope. 4. After St. Zachary died, a Roman priest named Stephen was elected but died before his consecration as bishop of Rome. His name is not included in all lists for this reason. In view of this historical confusion, the *National Catholic Almanac* lists the true Stephen II as Stephen II (III), the true Stephen III as Stephen III (IV), etc. 5. Confusion exists concerning the legitimacy of claims. If the deposition of John was invalid, Leo was an antipope until after the end of Benedict's reign. If the deposition of John was valid, Leo was the legitimate pope and Benedict an antipope. 6. If the triple removal of Benedict IX was not valid, Sylvester III, Gregory VI, and Clement II were antipopes. 7. Elimination was made of the name of John XX in an effort to rectify the numerical designation of popes named John. The error dates back to the time of John XV. 8. The names of Marinus I and Marinus II were construed as Martin. In view of these two pontificates and the earlier reign of St. Martin I, this pontiff was called Martin IV. *Source: National Catholic Almanac,* from *Annuarto Pontificio.*

The Books of the Bible

Below is the Protestant canon of the Bible (New Revised Standard Version). The Roman Catholic canon also includes the Deuterocanonical books as part of the Old Testament (these are considered apocryphal by most Protestants). The Hebrew Bible recognizes the books referred to as the Old Testament in the Protestant Bible, but not the Apocryphal/Deuterocanonical books or the New Testament.

The Old Testament with the Apocryphal/ Deuterocanonical Books

The Hebrew Scriptures

Genesis
Exodus
Leviticus
Numbers
Deuteronomy
Joshua
Judges
Ruth
1 Samuel
2 Samuel
1 Kings
2 Kings
1 Chronicles
2 Chronicles
Ezra
Nehemiah
Esther
Job
Psalms
Proverbs
Ecclesiastes
Song of Solomon
Isaiah
Jeremiah
Lamentations
Ezekiel
Daniel
Hosea
Joel
Amos
Obadiah
Jonah
Micah
Nahum
Habakkuk
Zephaniah
Haggai
Zechariah
Malachi

The Apocryphal/ Deuterocanonical Books

Tobit
Judith
Additions to the Book of Esther
Wisdom of Solomon
Ecclesiasticus, or the Wisdom of Jesus Son of Sirach
Baruch
The Letter of Jeremiah
The Prayer of Azariah and the Song of the Three Jews
Susanna
Bel and the Dragon
1 Maccabees
2 Maccabees
1 Esdras
Prayer of Manasseh
Psalm 151
3 Maccabees
2 Esdras
4 Maccabees

The New Testament

Matthew
Mark
Luke
John
Acts of the Apostles
Romans
1 Corinthians
2 Corinthians
Galatians
Ephesians
Philippians
Colossians
1 Thessalonians
2 Thessalonians
1 Timothy
2 Timothy
Titus
Philemon
Hebrews
James
1 Peter
2 Peter
1 John
2 John
3 John
Jude
Revelation

The Ten Commandments

The Ten Commandments, also called the Decalogue (Greek, "ten words"), were divine laws revealed to Moses by God on Mt. Sinai. Appearing in both Exodus (Ex. 20: 2–17) and Deuteronomy (Deut. 5:6–21), the commandments are numbered differently depending on whether they appear in a Catholic, Protestant, or Hebrew Bible. The following is the version given in the Revised Standard Version of the Bible.

You shall have no other gods before me.

You shall not make for yourself a graven image, or any likeness of anything that is in heaven above, or that is in the earth beneath, or that is in the water under the earth; you shall not bow down to them or serve them; for I the Lord your God am a jealous God, visiting the iniquity of the fathers upon the children to the third and the fourth generation of those who hate me, but showing steadfast love to thousands of those who love me and keep my commandments.

You shall not take the name of the Lord your God in vain; for the Lord will not hold him guiltless who takes his name in vain.

Remember the Sabbath day, to keep it holy. Six days you shall labor, and do all your work; but the seventh day is a Sabbath to the Lord your God; in it you shall not do any work, you, or your son, or your daughter, your manservant, or your maidservant, or your cattle, or the sojourner who is within your gates; for in six days the Lord made heaven and earth, the sea, and all that is in them, and rested the seventh day; therefore the Lord blessed the Sabbath day and hallowed it.

Honor your father and your mother, that your days may be long in the land which the Lord your God gives you.

You shall not kill.

You shall not commit adultery.

You shall not steal.

You shall not bear false witness against your neighbor.

You shall not covet your neighbor's wife, or his manservant, or his maidservant, or his ox, or his ass, or anything that is your neighbor's.

Source: Revised Standard Version of the Bible (Ex. 20: 2–17)

The Seven Deadly Sins

In Christianity, the seven deadly sins are considered "deadly" because it is believed they can do terrible damage to the soul. The now-famous list does not appear in the Bible and may have been formulated by Gregory the Great (540–604). The deadly sins are sometimes known as "capital" or "cardinal" sins: pride, greed, lust, envy, gluttony, anger, and sloth.

Selected Worldwide Religious Sites

Amritsar, India: Site of the Golden Temple (Sikhism).

Axum, Ethiopia: Church of St. Mary of Zion (Ethiopian Orthodox), where the Ark of the Covenant is believed to be kept.

Bethlehem, Israel: Birthplace of Jesus.

Black Hills, South Dakota: Sacred to the Lakota Indian tribe, who traditionally go on vision quests in the hills.

Bodhi Gaya, India: Place where the Buddha reached enlightenment.

Canterbury, England: Seat of the archbishop of Canterbury (Anglican).

Czestochowa, Poland: Chapel of Our Lady of Czestochowa, the Black Madonna of Poland. This painting is said to have been made by St. Luke.

Dharamsala, India: Seat of the Dalai Lama in exile (Tibetan Buddhism).

Fatima, Portugal: Site of several visions of the Virgin Mary in 1917. A major pilgrimage site for Catholics.

Ganges River, India: Sacred to Hindus (Mother Ganges is a Hindu goddess); immersion in the Ganges symbolizes spiritual purification.

Haifa, Israel: Seat of the Baha'i faith.

Istanbul, Turkey: Seat of the patriarchate of Constantinople (Eastern Orthodox).

Jerusalem, Israel: Major holy site for Judaism, Christianity, and Islam. The Temple Mount compound is believed to be both the site of the First and Second Temples of Judaism and the place where redemption will occur when the Messiah arrives. The same area is also called Haram al-Sharif (The Noble Sanctuary) and is of significance to Muslims. Nearby is the Dome of the Rock, the spot from which Muhammad ascended into heaven. Just below Temple Mount is the Western Wall, a remnant of the Second Temple and the holiest site in Judaism, where Jews come to pray. The Wall is part of a larger wall that encloses the Dome of the Rock and the al-Aksa mosque. The al-Aksa mosque, one of the holiest mosques in Islam, was originally the site toward which Muslims bowed to pray. The Holy Sepulchre, in which Jesus was buried, and from which he returned from the dead, is in the northwest corner of the Old City.

Knock, Ireland: Pilgrimage site for Catholics where 15 people claimed to see a vision of the Virgin Mary, St. Joseph, and St. John the Evangelist in 1879. About 1½ million pilgrims visit the site annually.

Kusinara, India: Site of the Buddha's death.

Lhasa, Tibet: Potala Palace, historical abode of the Dalai Lama (Tibetan Buddhism).

Loch Derg, Ireland: Site of St. Patrick's purgatory, pilgrimage destination; pilgrims walk barefoot around the lake, praying, like St. Patrick did.

Lourdes, France: In 1858, the Virgin Mary is said to have appeared to St. Bernadette at Lourdes in seven visions. It is now a Catholic pilgrimage site with a spring that some believe has curative properties.

Lumbini, Nepal: Birthplace of the Buddha.

Mecca, Saudi Arabia: The center of Islam and the birthplace of Muhammad, Mecca is the place toward which Muslims bow to pray five times a day. Mecca is the destination of the *hajj*, the pilgrimage which all Muslims who are financially and physically able must make in their lifetime. An estimated one million Muslims make the *hajj* annually. The focus of their worship is the Great Mosque at the center of Mecca. It encloses the Ka'aba, a small building that, according to the Qu'ran, was erected by Abraham and his son Ishmael.

Medina, Saudi Arabia: Muhammad lived in Medina after escaping Mecca in A.D. 622; it is now a holy city that only Muslims may enter.

Medjugorje, Bosnia-Herzegovina: Catholic pilgrimage site where many have claimed visions of the Virgin Mary.

Mt. Athos, Greece: Pilgrimage site for Eastern Orthodox males; site of many monasteries.

Mt. Fuji, Japan: Sacred to Buddhists and Shintos.

Mt. Tai Shan, China: Sacred to Taoists and Buddhists, this mountain with many beautiful temples is thought to be a center of living energy.

Nazareth, Israel: Place where Jesus lived and began teaching.

Palitana, India: The most important pilgrimage site for Jains, Palitana boasts 863 temples on one mountain, Shatrunjaya Hill.

Salt Lake City, Utah: Seat of Church of Jesus Christ of Latter-day Saints.

Santiago de Compostela, Spain: One of the most important medieval pilgrimage sites; the pilgrimage route of Santiago de Compostela passes through France and Spain before ending up at the city's cathedral. Santiago is Saint James, who was martyred at Jerusalem c. A.D. 44.

Sarnath, India: Place where the Buddha preached his first sermon in the deer park.

Sea of Galilee, Israel: Place where Jesus performed the miracle of the loaves and the fishes and preached the Sermon on the Mount.

Sri Pada (Adam's Peak), Sri Lanka: Sacred to some Buddhists, Hindus, Muslims, and Christians, the temple on the top of Adam's Peak contains a large footprint believed to belong to either the Buddha, Shiva, Adam, or St. Thomas.

Tepeyac, Mexico City, Mexico: Site of the appearance of the Virgin of Guadalupe to Juan Diego in 1531; now home to the Basilica of the Virgin, one of the most-visited churches in the world.

Turin, Italy: Place where the Holy Shroud of Turin (linen cloth believed to bear the visage of Jesus Christ) is housed.

Uluru (Ayer's Rock), Australia: Sacred site of the aborigines of Australia. Now a major tourist attraction, though the aborigine people ask that tourists not climb the rock.

Varanasi, India: City on the banks of the Ganges River; those who die there reach instant enlightenment.

The Vatican: Seat of the papacy (Catholicism).

See Calendar and Holidays for listings of religious holidays.

U.S. Education

Highest Level of Educational Attainment of U.S. Population, 2001

Some high school	15.7%	**Some college**	17.5%	**Bachelor's degree**	17.4%	**Doctoral degree**	1.2%
High school graduate	32.6%	**Associate's degree**	8.2%	**Master's degree**	6.0%	**Professional degree**	1.5%

NOTE: Persons 25 years and older (177 million). Percentage total exceeds 100% due to rounding. *Source:* U.S. Dept. of Commerce, Bureau of the Census, *Current Population Survey,* March 2001.

Educational Attainment by Race and Hispanic Origin, 1940–2001

(percent of population ages 25 and older, by years of school completed)

	White[1]			Black[1]			Hispanic		
Age and year	Less than 5 years of elementary school	High school completion or higher[2]	4 or more years of college[3]	Less than 5 years of elementary school	High school completion or higher[2]	4 or more years of college[3]	Less than 5 years of elementary school	High school completion or higher[2]	4 or more years of college[3]
April 1940	10.9%	26.1%	4.9%	41.8%	7.7%	1.3%	—	—	—
April 1950	8.9	36.4	6.6	32.6	13.7	2.2	—	—	—
April 1960	6.7	43.2	8.1	23.5	21.7	3.5	—	—	—
March 1970	4.2	57.4	11.6	14.7	36.1	6.1	—	—	—
March 1980	1.9	71.9	18.4	9.1	51.4	7.9	15.8%	44.5%	7.6%
March 1985	1.4	77.5	20.8	6.1	59.9	11.1	13.5	47.9	8.5
March 1990	1.1	81.4	23.1	5.1	66.2	11.3	12.3	50.8	9.2
March 1995	0.7	85.9	23.4	2.5	73.8	13.3	10.6	53.4	9.3
March 1996	0.6	86.0	25.9	2.2	74.6	13.8	10.4	53.1	9.3
March 1997	0.6	86.3	26.2	2.0	75.3	13.3	9.4	54.7	10.3
March 1998	0.6	87.1	26.6	1.7	76.4	14.8	9.3	55.5	11.0
March 1999	0.6	87.7	27.7	1.8	77.4	15.5	9.0	56.1	10.9
March 2000	0.5	88.4	28.1	1.6	78.9	16.6	8.7	57.0	10.6
March 2001	0.5	88.7	28.6	1.3	79.5	16.1	9.3	56.5	11.2

NOTE: Total includes other racial/ethnic groups not shown separately. 1. Includes persons of Hispanic origin for years prior to 1980. 2. Data for years prior to 1993 include all persons with at least 4 years of high school. 3. Data for 1993 and later years are for persons with a bachelor's or higher degree. *Source:* U.S. Department of Commerce, Burearu of the Census, U.S. Census of Population, 1960, Vol. 1, part 1; *Current Population Reports,* Series P-20 and unpublished data; and *1960 Census Monograph,* "Education of the American Population," by John K. Folger and Charles B. Nam. From U.S. Dept. of Education, National Center for Education Statistics, *Digest of Education Statistics 2002.*

Educational Attainment by Sex, 1910–2001

(percent of population ages 25 and older)

	Both sexes			Male			Female		
Year	Less than 5 years of elementary school	High school completion or higher[1]	4 or more years of college[2]	Less than 5 years of elementary school	High school completion or higher	4 or more years of college	Less than 5 years of elementary school	High school completion or higher	4 or more years of college
1910[3]	23.8%	13.5%	2.7%	—	—	—	—	—	—
1920[3]	22.0	16.4	3.3	—	—	—	—	—	—
1930[3]	17.5	19.1	3.9	—	—	—	—	—	—
April 1940	13.7	24.5	4.6	15.1%	22.7%	5.5%	12.4%	26.3%	3.8%
April 1950	11.1	34.3	6.2	12.2	32.6	7.3	10.0	36.0	5.2
April 1960	8.3	41.1	7.7	9.4	39.5	9.7	7.4	42.5	5.8
March 1970	5.3	55.2	11.0	5.9	55.0	14.1	4.7	55.4	8.2
March 1980	3.4	68.6	17.0	3.6	69.2	20.9	3.2	68.1	13.6
March 1990	2.5	77.6	21.3	2.7	77.7	24.4	2.2	77.5	18.4
March 1995	1.9	81.7	23.0	2.0	81.7	26.0	1.7	81.6	20.2
March 1996	1.8	81.7	23.6	1.9	81.9	26.0	1.7	81.6	21.4
March 1997	1.7	82.1	23.9	1.8	82.0	26.2	1.6	82.2	21.7
March 1998	1.7	82.8	24.4	1.7	82.8	26.5	1.6	82.9	22.4
March 1999	1.6	83.4	25.2	1.6	83.5	27.5	1.6	83.4	23.1
March 2000	1.6	84.1	25.6	1.6	84.2	27.8	1.5	84.0	23.6
March 2001	1.6	84.3	26.1	1.6	84.4	28.0	1.5	84.2	24.3

NOTE: (—) = not available. 1. Data for years prior to 1993 include all persons with at least 4 years of high school. 2. Data for 1993 and later years are for persons with a bachelor's degree or higher. 3. Estimates based on Bureau of the Census retrojection of 1940 Census data on education by age. *Source:* Based on data from the U.S. Department of Commerce, Bureau of the Census, *U.S Census of Population, 1960,* Vol. 1, part 1; *Current Population Reports,* Series P-20 and unpublished data; and *1960 Census Monograph,* "Education of the American Population," by John K. Folger and Charles B. Nam. From U.S. Dept. of Education, National Center for Education Statistics, *Digest of Education Statistics 2002.*

Enrollment in Educational Institutions, 1970–2001

(in thousands)

	Public elementary and secondary schools			Private elementary and secondary schools[1]			Degree-granting institutions[2]		
Year	Total	Pre-K through grade 8	Grades 9 through 12	Total	K through grade 8	Grades 9 through 12	Total	Public	Private
Fall 1970	45,894	32,558	13,336	5,363	4,052	1,311	8,581	6,428	2,153
Fall 1980	40,877	27,647	13,231	5,331	3,992	1,339	12,097	9,457	2,640
Fall 1990	41,217	29,878	11,338	5,234	4,084	1,150	13,819	10,845	2,974
Fall 1998	46,539	33,346	13,193	5,937[3]	4,702[3]	1,235[3]	14,507	11,138	3,369
Fall 1999	46,857	33,488	13,369	6,018	4,765	1,254	14,791	11,309	3,482
Fall 2000	47,223	33,709	13,514	5,944[3]	4,678[3]	1,266[3]	15,312	11,753	3,560
Fall 2001[4]	47,576	33,854	13,722	5,944	4,668	1,276	15,442	11,864	3,578

NOTE: Elementary and secondary enrollment excludes home-schooled children. Higher education enrollment includes students in colleges, universities, professional schools, and 2-year colleges. 1. Beginning in fall 1980, data include estimates for an expanded universe of private schools. Therefore, direct comparisons with earlier years should be avoided. 2. Two- and four-year institutions eligible to participate in Title IV federal financial aid programs. 3. Estimated. 4. Projected. *Source:* U.S. Department of Education, National Center for Education Statistics, *Digest of Education Statistics 2002.*

High School Dropout Rates by Sex, 1960–2001

Year	Total	Male	Female
1960	27.2%	27.8%	26.7%
1970	15.0	14.2	15.7
1980	14.1	15.1	13.1
1985	12.6	13.4	11.8
1990	12.1	12.3	11.8
1995	12.0	12.2	11.7
1996	11.1	11.4	10.9
1997	11.0	11.9	10.1
1998	11.8	13.3	10.3
1999	11.2	11.9	10.5
2000	10.9	12.0	9.9
2001	10.7	12.2	9.3

High School Dropout Rates by Race/Ethnicity, 1960–2001

Year	White	Black	Hispanic
1960	—	—	—
1970	13.2%	27.9%	—
1980	11.4	19.1	35.2%
1985	10.4	15.2	27.6
1990	9.0	13.2	32.4
1995	8.6	12.1	30.0
1996	7.3	13.0	29.4
1997	7.6	13.4	25.3
1998	7.7	13.8	29.5
1999	7.3	12.6	28.6
2000	6.9	13.1	27.8
2001	7.3	10.9	27.0

NOTE: (—) = not available. Data apply to persons ages 16–24. Because of changes in data collection procedures, data for 1992–2000 may not be comparable with figures for earlier years. *Source:* U.S. Dept. of Education, National Center for Education Statistics, *Digest of Education Statistics 2002.*

Students with Disabilities

	Percent of all students served by federally supported programs for students with disabilities[1]						
Type of disability	1976–1977	1980–1981	1990–1991	1995–1996	1998–1999	1999–2000	2000–2001
All disabilities	**8.32%**	**10.14%**	**11.55%**	**12.43%**	**13.01%**	**13.21%**	**13.33%**
Specific learning disabilities	1.80	3.58	5.17	5.75	5.99	6.04	6.02
Speech or language impairments	2.94	2.86	2.39	2.28	2.29	2.30	2.30
Mental retardation	2.17	2.03	1.30	1.27	1.28	1.28	1.27
Emotional disturbance	0.64	0.85	0.95	0.98	1.00	1.00	—
Hearing impairments	0.20	0.19	0.14	0.15	0.15	0.15	0.15
Orthopedic impairments	0.20	0.14	0.12	0.14	0.15	0.15	0.15
Other health impairments	0.32	0.24	0.13	0.30	0.47	0.54	0.62
Visual impairments	0.09	0.08	0.06	0.06	0.06	0.06	0.05
Multiple disabilities	—	0.17	0.23	0.21	0.23	0.24	0.26
Deaf–blindness	—	0.01	(2)	(2)	(2)	(2)	—
Developmental delay	—	—	—	—	0.03	0.04	0.06
Autism and traumatic brain injury	—	—	—	0.09	0.14	0.17	0.20
Preschool disabled[3]	.44	.57	1.07	1.21	1.22	1.24	1.25

NOTE: Because of rounding, details may not add to totals. 1. Based on the enrollment in public schools, kindergarten through 12th grade, including a relatively small number of prekindergarten students. Includes students ages 3 to 21. 2. Less than .05%. 3. Includes preschool children 3–5 years and 0–5 years served under Chapter I of the Elementary and Secondary Education Act and the Individuals with Disabilities Education Act (IDEA). *Source:* U.S. Department of Education, National Center for Education Statistics, *Digest of Education Statistics 2002.*

Current Expenditure per Pupil in Public Elementary and Secondary Schools

1959–60	1969–70	1979–80	1989–90	1993–94	1994–95	1995–96	1996–97	1997–98	1998–99	1999–2000
$375	$816	$2,272	$4,980	$5,767	$5,989	$6,147	$6,393	$6,676	$7,013	$7,392

Source: U.S. Dept. of Education, National Center for Education Statistics, *Digest of Education Statistics 2002.*

Funding for Public Elementary and Secondary Schools, 1919–1920 to 1999–2000

(in thousands, except percent)

School year	Total	Federal	State	Local	% Federal	% State	% Local
1919–1920	$ 970,121	$ 2,475	$ 160,085	$ 807,561	0.3%	16.5%	83.2%
1929–1930	2,088,557	7,334	353,670	1,727,553	0.4	16.9	82.7
1939–1940	2,260,527	39,810	684,354	1,536,363	1.8	30.3	68.0
1949–1950	5,437,044	155,848	2,165,689	3,115,507	2.9	39.8	57.3
1959–1960	14,746,618	651,639	5,768,047	8,326,932	4.4	39.1	56.5
1969–1970	40,266,923	3,219,557	16,062,776	20,984,589	8.0	39.9	52.1
1979–1980	96,881,165	9,503,537	45,348,814	42,028,813	9.8	46.8	43.4
1989–1990	208,547,573	12,700,784	98,238,633	97,608,157	6.1	47.1	46.8
1999–2000	372,864,603	27,097,866	184,613,352	161,153,385	7.3	49.5	43.2

Source: U.S. Department of Education, National Center for Education Statistics, *Digest of Education Statistics 2002.*

Public and Private Elementary and Secondary Pupil-Teacher Ratios, 1955–2001

Year	Total	Public	Private	Year	Total	Public	Private
1955	27.4	26.9	31.7[1]	**1985**	17.6	17.9	16.2
1960	26.4	25.8	30.7[1]	**1990**	16.9	17.2	14.7[1]
1965	25.1	24.7	28.3	**1995**	17.0	17.3	14.9
1970	22.4	22.3	23.0	**2000**	15.9	16.0	15.2[1]
1980	18.6	18.7	17.7	**2001**	15.8	15.9	15.2

1. Estimated. *Source:* U.S. Department of Education, National Center for Education Statistics 2002, *Digest of Education Statistics.* From *Statistical Abstract of the United States, 2002.*

General Educational Development (GED) Credentials Issued, 1971–2001

(in thousands)

Year	Number of credentials issued	Year	Number of credentials issued	Year	Number of credentials issued	Year	Number of credentials issued	Year	Number of credentials issued	Year	Number of credentials issued
1971	227	**1976**	333	**1981**	489	**1986**	428	**1991**	462	**1997**	460
1972	245	**1977**	332	**1982**	486	**1987**	444	**1992**	457	**1998**	481
1973	249	**1978**	381	**1983**	465	**1988**	410	**1993**	469	**1999**	498
1974	294	**1979**	426	**1984**	427	**1989**	357	**1994**	491	**2000**	487
1975	340	**1980**	479	**1985**	413	**1990**	410	**1995**	504	**2001**	648

Source: American Council on Education, General Educational Development Testing Service, *Who took the GED? Statistical Report,* various years.

Average SAT Scores[1]

	Verbal score					Mathematical score				
School year	Total	Male	Female	White	Black	Total	Male	Female	White	Black
1966–1967	543	540	545	n.a.	n.a.	516	535	495	n.a.	n.a.
1970–1971	532	531	534	n.a.	n.a.	513	529	494	n.a.	n.a.
1976–1977	507	509	505	n.a.	n.a.	496	520	474	n.a.	n.a.
1980–1981	502	508	496	n.a.	n.a.	492	516	473	n.a.	n.a.
1986–1987	507	512	502	524	428	501	523	481	514	411
1990–1991	499	503	495	518	427	500	520	482	513	419
1995–1996	505	507	503	526	434	508	527	492	523	422
1996–1997	505	507	503	526	434	511	530	494	526	423
1997–1998	505	509	502	n.a.	n.a.	512	531	496	n.a.	n.a.
1998–1999	505	509	502	527	434	511	531	495	528	422
1999–2000	505	507	504	528	434	514	533	498	530	426
2000–2001	506	509	502	529	433	514	533	498	531	426
2001–2002	504	507	502	527	430	516	534	500	533	427

NOTE: n.a. = not available. 1. Scholastic Assessment Test, formerly known as the Scholastic Aptitude Test. Minimum score 200; maximum score 800. *Source:* U.S. Dept. of Education, National Center for Education Statistics, *Digest of Education Statistics 2002.*

Cost of Higher Education, 1986–2002[1]

Year	All institutions	4-year institutions	2-year institutions
Public institutions			
1986–1987	$3,805	$4,138	$2,989
1991–1992	5,138	5,693	3,623
1995–1996	6,256	7,014	4,217
1996–1997	6,530	7,334	4,404
1997–1998	6,813	7,673	4,509
1998–1999	7,107	8,027	4,604
1999–2000	7,310	8,275	4,720
2000–2001	7,586	8,653	4,839
2001–2002[2]	8,046	9,199	5,137
Private institutions			
1986–1987	$ 9,676	$10,039	$ 6,384
1991–1992	13,892	14,258	9,632
1995–1996	17,208	17,612	11,563
1996–1997	18,039	18,442	11,954
1997–1998	18,516	19,070	12,921
1998–1999	19,368	19,929	13,319
1999–2000	20,186	20,706	13,965
2000–2001	21,368	21,856	14,788
2001–2002[2]	22,520	22,968	15,879

1. Average undergraduate tuition, fees, and room and board. 2. Preliminary data based on fall 2000 enrollment weights. *Source:* U.S. Department of Education, National Center for Education Statistics, *Digest of Education Statistics 2002.*

Median Annual Income, by Level of Education, 1990–2000

	Elementary/secondary			College					
Sex and year	Less than 9th grade	9th to 12th grade, no completion[1]	High school completion (includes equivalency)[2]	Some college, no degree[3]	Associate degree[4]	Bachelor's[5]	Master's[4]	Profes-sional[4]	Doc-torate[4]
Men									
1990	$17,394	$20,902	$26,653	$31,734	—	$39,328	—	—	—
1992	17,294	21,274	27,280	32,103	$33,433	41,355	$49,973	$ 76,220	$57,418
1994	17,532	22,048	28,037	32,279	35,794	43,663	53,500	75,009	61,921
1995	18,354	22,185	29,510	33,883	35,201	45,266	55,216	79,667	65,336
1997	19,291	24,726	31,215	35,945	38,022	48,616	61,690	85,011	76,234
1998	19,380	23,958	31,477	36,934	40,274	51,405	62,244	94,737	75,078
1999	20,429	25,035	33,184	39,221	41,638	52,985	66,243	100,000	81,687
2000	20,789	25,095	34,303	40,337	41,952	56,334	68,322	99,411	80,250
Women									
1990	$12,251	$14,429	$18,319	$22,227	—	$28,017	—	—	—
1992	12,958	14,559	19,427	23,157	$25,624	30,326	$36,037	$ 46,257	$45,790
1994	12,430	15,133	20,373	23,514	25,940	31,741	39,457	50,615	51,119
1995	13,577	15,825	20,463	23,997	27,311	32,051	40,263	50,000	48,141
1997	14,161	16,697	22,067	26,335	28,812	35,379	44,949	61,051	53,037
1998	14,467	16,482	22,780	27,420	29,924	36,559	45,283	57,565	57,796
1999	15,098	17,015	23,061	27,757	30,919	37,993	48,097	59,904	60,079
2000	15,978	17,919	24,970	28,697	31,071	40,415	50,139	58,957	57,081

NOTE: Year-round, full-time workers 25 years and older. (—) = not available. 1. Includes 1 to 3 years high school for 1990. 2. Includes 4 years of high school for 1990, and equivalency certificates for the other years. 3. Includes 1 to 3 years of college and associate degrees for 1990. 4. Not reported separately for 1990. 5. Includes 4 years of college for 1990. *Source:* U.S. Dept. of Commerce, Bureau of the Census, Current Population Reports, Series P-60, "Money Income of Households, Families, and Persons in the United States," "Income, Poverty, and Valuation of Noncash Benefits," various years; and Series P-60, "Money Income in the United States," various years. (This table was prepared March 2003.) From *Digest of Education Statistics 2002.*

College and University Endowments, 2002

Rank	Institution	Endowment[1]
1.	Harvard Univ. (Cambridge, Mass.)	$17,518,021,000
2.	Yale Univ. (New Haven, Conn.)	10,442,036,000
3.	Princeton Univ. (Princeton, N.J.)	8,320,000,000
4.	Univ. of Texas System Administration (Austin, Tex.)	8,259,705,297
5.	Stanford Univ. (Stanford, Calif.)	7,612,767,540
6.	Mass. Inst. of Tech. (Cambridge, Mass.)	5,359,400,000
7.	Columbia Univ. (New York, N.Y.)	4,238,168,000
8.	Emory Univ. (Atlanta, Ga.)	4,053,692,441
9.	Washington Univ. (St. Louis, Mo.)	3,633,057,000
10.	Univ. of Michigan (Ann Arbor, Mich.)	3,435,163,000
11.	Univ. of Pennsylvania (Philadelphia, Pa.)	3,393,297,284
12.	Northwestern Univ. (Evanston, Ill.)	3,203,837,250
13.	Univ. of Chicago (Chicago, Ill.)	3,111,626,000
14.	Cornell Univ. (Ithaca, N.Y.)	$3,034,769,000
15.	Rice Univ. (Houston, Tex.)	2,940,000,000
16.	Texas A&M Univ. (College Station, Tex.)	2,928,537,601
17.	Univ. of Notre Dame (Notre Dame, Ind.)	2,606,000,000
18.	Duke Univ. (Durham, N.C.)	2,440,878,348
19.	Dartmouth Coll. (Hanover, N.H.)	2,423,762,690
20.	Univ. of Southern California (Los Angeles, Calif.)	2,130,977,000
21.	Vanderbilt Univ. (Nashville, Tenn.)	1,989,692,450
22.	Univ. of Calif., Berkeley (Berkeley, Calif.)	1,774,200,000
23.	Johns Hopkins Univ. (Baltimore, Md.)	1,695,150,000
24.	Univ. of Virginia (Charlottesville, Va.)	1,654,291,673
25.	Mayo Foundation (Rochester, Minn.)	1,571,801,000

Rank	Institution	Endowment[1]
26.	Univ. of Minnesota (Minneapolis, Minn.)	$1,517,858,136
27.	Brown Univ. (Providence, R.I.)	1,434,666,000
28.	Univ. of Texas at Austin (Austin, Tex.)	1,350,815,842
29.	Case Western Reserve Univ. (Cleveland, Ohio)	1,347,100,000
30.	Rockefeller Univ. (New York, N.Y.)	1,338,754,978
31.	Univ. of California, Los Angeles (Los Angeles, CA)	1,224,018,000
32.	Williams Coll. (Williamstown, Mass.)	1,186,151,056
33.	New York Univ. (New York, N.Y.)	1,177,704,000
34.	Univ. of Rochester (Rochester, N.Y.)	1,131,554,397
35.	Boston Coll. (Chestnut Hill, Mass.)	1,125,964,000
36.	Univ. of Washington (Seattle, Wash.)	1,111,726,000
37.	Univ. of Pittsburgh (Pittsburgh, Pa.)	1,103,082,000
38.	Purdue Univ. (West Lafayette, Ind.)	1,098,939,000
39.	Georgia Univ. of Tech. (Atlanta, Ga.)	$1,091,470,138
40.	Univ. of N. Carolina at Chapel Hill (Chapel Hill, N.C.)	1,085,663,552
41.	Calif. Inst. of Tech. (Pasadena, Calif.)	1,083,873,000
42.	Grinnell Coll. (Grinnell, Iowa)	1,075,153,000
43.	Wellesley Coll. (Wellesley, Mass.)	1,032,464,639
44.	Pomona Coll. (Claremont, Calif.)	1,021,846,732
45.	Univ. of Wisc.-Madison (Madison, Wis.)	1,000,856,684
46.	Univ. of Richmond (University of Richmond, Va.)	998,193,000
47.	Ohio State Univ. (Columbus, Ohio)	960,079,365
48.	Baylor Coll. of Medicine (Houston, Tex.)	959,284,162
49.	Indiana Univ. (Bloomington, Ind.)	955,991,407
50.	Penn. State Univ. (University Park, Pa.)	942,829,960

NOTES: List includes only institutions that participated in the 2002 Voluntary Support of Education Survey. State systems that submitted combined endowments above the current cut-off are not included. 1. Endowment is market value at fiscal year-end 2002. *Source:* Council for Aid to Education, a subsidiary of RAND.

Top Fundraising Colleges and Universities, in Total Amount Raised, 2002

Rank	College or University	Amount raised
1.	University of Southern California (Los Angeles, Calif.)	$585,161,932
2.	Harvard University (Cambridge, Mass.)	477,617,144
3.	Stanford University (Stanford, Calif.)	454,769,878
4.	Cornell University (Ithaca, N.Y.)	363,031,766
5.	University of Pennsylvania (Philadelphia, Pa.)	319,742,070
6.	Johns Hopkins University (Baltimore, Md.)	318,687,392
7.	University of Wisconsin-Madison (Madison, Wis.)	307,213,842
8.	Univ. of California, Los Angeles (Los Angeles, Calif.)	282,343,369
9.	Columbia University (New York, N.Y.)	271,231,231
10.	Duke University (Durham, N.C.)	264,580,048
11.	Yale University (New Haven, Conn.)	256,342,000
12.	University of Virginia (Charlottesville, Va.)	255,043,646
13.	New York University (New York, N.Y.)	251,407,906
14.	University of Minnesota (Minneapolis, Minn.)	233,338,357
15.	University of Washington (Seattle, Wash.)	231,814,108
16.	Univ. of California, Berkeley (Berkeley, Calif.)	223,260,969
17.	Massachusetts Institute of Technology (Cambridge, Mass.)	220,572,527
18.	Michigan State University (East Lansing, Mich.)	211,629,395
19.	Emory University (Atlanta, Ga.)	210,372,283
20.	Univ. of California, San Francisco (San Francisco, Calif.)	207,227,552

Source: Council for Aid to Education, a subsidiary of RAND. Web: www.cae.org.

Top Fundraising Preparatory Schools, in Total Amount Raised, 2002

Rank	School	Amount raised
1.	Phillips Exeter Academy (Exeter, N.H.)	$39,810,637
2.	Phillips Academy (Andover, Mass.)	30,415,728
3.	Deerfield Academy (Deerfield, Mass.)	24,570,984
4.	Middlesex School (Concord, Mass.)	23,014,904
5.	Episcopal Academy (Merion, Pa.)	21,684,961
6.	Choate Rosemary Hall (Wallingford, Conn.)	17,433,016
7.	Lawrenceville School (Lawrenceville, N.J.)	15,213,809
8.	Loomis Chaffee School (Windsor, Conn.)	14,837,012
9.	Hackley School (Tarrytown, N.Y.)	14,808,545
10.	Mercersburg Academy (Mercersburg, Pa.)	13,005,304
11.	Greenwich Academy (Greenwich, Conn.)	12,002,530
12.	Taft School (Watertown, Conn.)	11,529,250
13.	The Culver Educational Foundation (Culver, Ind.)	11,368,100
14.	Hotchkiss School (Lakeville, Conn.)	11,139,080
15.	Groton School (Groton, Mass.)	10,704,832
16.	Berkshire School (Sheffield, Mass.)	9,948,230
17.	Friends Academy (Locust Valley, N.Y.)	9,610,056
18.	Lovett School (Atlanta, Ga.)	9,468,269
19.	Milton Academy (Milton, Mass.)	9,383,566
20.	Brunswick School (Greenwich, Conn.)	9,197,378

Source: Council for Aid to Education, a subsidiary of RAND. Web: www.cae.org.

Number of U.S. Colleges and Universities and Degrees Awarded[1]

	Number	Enrollment
Public 4-year institutions	622	5,969,950
Private 4-year institutions	1,828	3,228,575
Public 2-year institutions	1,076	5,339,449
Private 2-year institutions	656	253,250
Total	**4,182**	**14,791,224**
Undergraduate		12,681,231
Graduate		1,806,803
Professional		303,190

	Number
Degrees awarded:	
Associate	564,933
Bachelor's	1,237,875
Master's	457,056
Doctorate	44,808
Professional	80,057

1. 2001 figures. *Source: Chronicle of Higher Education.*

Accredited U.S. Senior Colleges and Universities

Schools are listed alphabetically within each state and are accredited four-year institutions offering at least a bachelor's degree.

Source: Peterson's Database, copyright 2002. Peterson's, a part of the Thomson Corporation. Web: http://petersons.com/.

Institution name; city	Public or private	Students	Percent Accepted	Percent Women
ALABAMA				
Alabama Agricultural and Mechanical University; Normal	Public	4,380	24%	52%
Alabama State University; Montgomery	Public	4,348	62	58
American College of Computer & Information Sciences; Birmingham	Private	1,204		
Auburn University; Auburn	Public	18,326	85	48
Auburn University Montgomery; Montgomery	Public	4,098		63
Birmingham-Southern College; Birmingham	Private	1,395	98	59
Faulkner University; Montgomery	Private	2,327	68	59
Huntingdon College; Montgomery	Private	705	73	62
International Bible College; Florence	Private		85	
Jacksonville State University; Jacksonville	Public	6,649	50	56
Judson College; Marion	Private	321	81	98
Oakwood College; Huntsville	Private	1,767	46	57
Samford University; Birmingham	Private	2,870	88	62
Southeastern Bible College; Birmingham	Private	217	52	
Southern Christian University; Montgomery	Private	134		25
Spring Hill College; Mobile	Private	1,227	89	62
Talladega College; Talladega	Private	460	22	
Troy State University; Troy	Public	4,602	64	60
Troy State University Dothan; Dothan	Public	1,564	76	63
Troy State University Montgomery; Montgomery	Public	2,643		64
Tuskegee University; Tuskegee	Private	2,467	71	58
University of Alabama; Tuscaloosa	Public	15,318	86	52
University of Alabama at Birmingham; Birmingham	Public	10,331	90	59
University of Alabama in Huntsville; Huntsville	Public	5,220	92	51
University of West Alabama; Livingston	Public	1,595	69	55
University of Mobile; Mobile	Private	1,724	98	68
University of Montevallo; Montevallo	Public	2,557	77	68
University of North Alabama; Florence	Public	4,944	83	59
University of South Alabama; Mobile	Public	9,232	94	58
Virginia College at Birmingham; Birmingham	Private	1,143		
ALASKA				
Alaska Bible College; Glennallen	Private	44	96	30
Alaska Pacific University; Anchorage	Private	480	80	63
Sheldon Jackson College; Sitka	Private	94	100	
University of Alaska Anchorage; Anchorage	Public	14,235		
University of Alaska Fairbanks; Fairbanks	Public	6,358	86	60
University of Alaska Southeast; Juneau	Public	2,799		
ARIZONA				
Arizona State University; Tempe	Public	33,985	77	52
Arizona State University East; Mesa	Public	1,529	83	49
Art Institute of Phoenix; Phoenix	Private	1,000	100	0
DeVry Institute of Technology; Phoenix	Private	3,705	62	25
Grand Canyon University; Phoenix	Private	1,563	76	64
International Baptist College; Tempe	Private	53		
Northern Arizona University; Flagstaff	Public	13,905	81	59
Prescott College; Prescott	Private	757		59
Southwestern College; Phoenix	Private	257	59	43
University of Advancing Computer Technology; Tempe	Private	1,055		19
University of Arizona; Tucson	Public	26,404	84	53
University of Phoenix–Phoenix Campus; Phoenix	Private	46,473		
University of Phoenix–Southern Arizona Campus; Tucson	Private	46,473		56
Western International University; Phoenix	Private	2,004		42

Institution name; city	Public or private	Students	Percent	
			Accepted	Women
ARKANSAS				
Arkansas Baptist College; Little Rock	Private	201		
Arkansas State University; Jonesboro	Public	9,289	65%	58%
Arkansas Tech University; Russellville	Public	4,841	54	53
Central Baptist College; Conway	Private	381	87	48
Harding University; Searcy	Private	3,982	81	55
Henderson State University; Arkadelphia	Public	3,078	67	55
Hendrix College; Conway	Private	1,130	87	54
John Brown University; Siloam Springs	Private	1,421	80	52
Lyon College; Batesville	Private	476	85	57
Ouachita Baptist University; Arkadelphia	Private	1,714	83	54
Philander Smith College; Little Rock	Private	932	100	61
Southern Arkansas University–Magnolia; Magnolia	Public	2,781	92	57
University of Arkansas; Fayetteville	Public	12,502	90	49
University of Arkansas at Little Rock; Little Rock	Public	8,383	62	
University of Arkansas at Pine Bluff; Pine Bluff	Public	2,926	71	55
University of Central Arkansas; Conway	Public	7,453	62	
University of the Ozarks; Clarksville	Private	622	74	52
Williams Baptist College; Walnut Ridge	Private	660	75	60
CALIFORNIA				
Academy of Art College; San Francisco	Private	5,294	45	43
Armstrong University; Oakland	Private	36		
Art Center College of Design; Pasadena	Private	1,358	63	39
Art Institute of California; San Diego	Private	450	85	47
Art Institute of Southern California; Laguna Beach	Private	280	93	46
Azusa Pacific University; Azusa	Private	3,453	73	64
Bethesda Christian University; Anaheim	Private	171	91	70
Biola University; La Mirada	Private	2,622	82	63
California Baptist University; Riverside	Private	1,524	80	63
California Christian College; Fresno	Private	90	100	34
California College for Health Sciences; National City	Private	4,093		0
California College of Arts and Crafts; San Francisco	Private	1,116	72	59
California Institute of Technology; Pasadena	Private	929	13	32
California Institute of the Arts; Valencia	Private	804	40	44
California Lutheran University; Thousand Oaks	Private	1,816	79	56
California Maritime Academy; Vallejo	Public	583	76	17
California Polytechnic State University, San Luis Obispo; San Luis Obispo	Public	15,867	45	44
California State Polytechnic University, Pomona; Pomona	Public	16,450	70	44
California State University, Chico; Chico	Public	13,904	91	53
California State University, Dominguez Hills; Carson	Public	7,733	77	70
California State University, Fresno; Fresno	Public	15,414	67	56
California State University, Fullerton; Fullerton	Public	23,385	72	59
California State University, Hayward; Hayward	Public	9,337	62	64
California State University, Long Beach; Long Beach	Public	25,153	86	58
California State University, Los Angeles; Los Angeles	Public	13,476	50	61
California State University, Northridge; Northridge	Public	22,553	78	58
California State University, Sacramento; Sacramento	Public	19,343	41	56
California State University, San Bernardino; San Bernardino	Public	10,273		
California State University, San Marcos; San Marcos	Public	5,005	66	62
California State University, Stanislaus; Turlock	Public	5,353	73	65
Chapman University; Orange	Private	2,968	63	55
Charles R. Drew Univ. of Medicine and Science; Los Angeles	Private	210	25	
Christian Heritage College; El Cajon	Private	675	79	65
Claremont McKenna College; Claremont	Private	1,002	28	43
Cogswell Polytechnical College; Sunnyvale	Private	500	85	
Columbia College–Hollywood; Tarzana	Private	100	88	
Concordia University; Irvine	Private	1,192	31	69
Design Institute of San Diego; San Diego	Private	350		
DeVry Institute of Technology; Fremont	Private	2,149	60	23
DeVry Institute of Technology; Long Beach	Private	2,877	65	29
DeVry Institute of Technology; Pomona	Private	3,674	68	27
DeVry Institute of Technology; West Hills	Private	886	58	23
Dominican University of California; San Rafael	Private	946	73	80
Fresno Pacific University; Fresno	Private	884	72	67
Golden Gate University; San Francisco	Private	1,302	97	58
Harvey Mudd College; Claremont	Private	717	35	29
Holy Names College; Oakland	Private	592	71	81
Hope International University; Fullerton	Private	703	42	53
Humboldt State University; Arcata	Public	6,469	73	54
John F. Kennedy University; Orinda	Private	196		81
LIFE Bible College; San Dimas	Private	488	94	48
Loma Linda University; Loma Linda	Private	967		75
Loyola Marymount University; Los Angeles	Private	4,851	62	57
Master's College and Seminary; Santa Clarita	Private	1,105	79	52

Institution name; city	Public or private	Students	Percent Accepted	Percent Women
Menlo College; Atherton	Private	662	73%	43%
Mills College; Oakland	Private	691	75	
Mount St. Mary's College; Los Angeles	Private	1,708	54	95
Mt. Sierra College; Monrovia	Private	1,222	73	34
National Hispanic University; San Jose	Private	350	82	
National University; La Jolla	Private	7,040	100	55
New College of California; San Francisco	Private	234		
Newschool of Architecture & Design; San Diego	Private	9	100	22
Notre Dame de Namur University; Belmont	Private	991	79	
Occidental College; Los Angeles	Private	1,697	57	58
Otis College of Art and Design; Los Angeles	Private	898	61	62
Pacific States University; Los Angeles	Private	25		24
Pacific Union College; Angwin	Private	1,453		56
Patten College; Oakland	Private	635	68	39
Pepperdine University; Malibu	Private	1,849	35	91
Pitzer College; Claremont	Private	924	56	62
Point Loma Nazarene University; San Diego	Private	2,312	75	59
Pomona College; Claremont	Private	1,565	30	49
Saint Mary's College of California; Moraga	Private	3,038	76	61
Samuel Merritt College; Oakland	Private	278	71	92
San Diego State University; San Diego	Public	25,658	65	57
San Francisco Art Institute; San Francisco	Private	493	61	51
San Francisco Conservatory of Music; San Francisco	Private	136	64	55
San Francisco State University; San Francisco	Public	20,365	67	60
San Jose Christian College; San Jose	Private	400	42	
San Jose State University; San Jose	Public	21,292	72	51
Santa Clara University; Santa Clara	Private	4,308	62	54
Scripps College; Claremont	Private	787	68	100
Shasta Bible College; Redding	Private	295	100	67
Sonoma State University; Rohnert Park	Public	6,211	92	65
Southern California Institute of Architecture; Los Angeles	Private	218		
St. John's Seminary College; Camarillo	Private	95	75	1
Stanford University; Stanford	Private	7,886	13	52
Thomas Aquinas College; Santa Paula	Private	277	77	47
Touro University International; Los Alamitos	Private	176	64	31
United States International University; San Diego	Private	522	62	56
University of California, Berkeley; Berkeley	Public	22,593	27	51
University of California, Davis; Davis	Public	20,418	63	56
University of California, Irvine; Irvine	Public	16,223	57	52
University of California, Los Angeles; Los Angeles	Public	25,011	29	55
University of California, Riverside; Riverside	Public	11,436	85	54
University of California, San Diego; La Jolla	Public	16,496	38	52
University of California, Santa Barbara; Santa Barbara	Public	17,538	65	54
University of California, Santa Cruz; Santa Cruz	Public	11,616	80	57
University of Judaism; Bel Air	Private	96	100	67
University of La Verne; La Verne	Private	1,349	74	58
University of Phoenix–No. Calif. Campus; Pleasanton	Private	46,473		56
University of Phoenix–Sacramento Campus; Sacramento	Private	46,473		56
University of Phoenix–San Diego Campus; San Diego	Private	46,473		56
University of Phoenix–So. Calif. Campus; Fountain Valley	Private	46,473		56
University of Redlands; Redlands	Private	1,734	78	56
University of San Diego; San Diego	Private	4,793	50	59
University of San Francisco; San Francisco	Private	4,084		
University of Southern California; Los Angeles	Private	15,705	34	50
University of the Pacific; Stockton	Private	3,093	76	58
Vanguard University of Southern California; Costa Mesa	Private	1,475	88	61
Westmont College; Santa Barbara	Private	1,269	70	62
Whittier College; Whittier	Private	1,296	89	56
Woodbury University; Burbank	Private	1,135	85	55
Yeshiva Ohr Elchonon Chabad/West Coast Talmudical Seminary; Los Angeles	Private	62		0
COLORADO				
Adams State College; Alamosa	Public	2,011	96	57
Art Institute of Colorado; Denver	Private	2,090	74	44
Colorado Christian University; Lakewood	Private	1,926	75	54
Colorado College; Colorado Springs	Private	1,919	62	54
Colorado School of Mines; Golden	Public	2,503	81	25
Colorado State University; Fort Collins	Public	19,075	78	52
Colorado Technical University Denver Campus; Greenwood Village	Private	227	65	28
Denver Technical College; Denver	Private	864		31
Fort Lewis College; Durango	Public	4,289	88	47
Johnson & Wales University; Denver	Private	325	81	43
Metropolitan State College of Denver; Denver	Public	17,688	84	57
Naropa University; Boulder	Private	434	93	68

Institution name; city	Public or private	Students	Percent Accepted	Percent Women
National American University; Colorado Springs	Private	325		
National American University; Denver	Private	380		
Nazarene Bible College; Colorado Springs	Private	473	60%	30%
Regis University; Denver	Private	1,022	84	
United States Air Force Academy; Colorado Springs	Public	4,319	18	15
University of Colorado at Boulder; Boulder	Public	23,342	86	48
University of Colorado at Colorado Springs; Colorado Springs	Public	5,054	75	61
University of Colorado at Denver; Denver	Public	8,478	73	56
University of Denver; Denver	Private	3,992	78	57
University of Northern Colorado; Greeley	Public	10,134	79	60
University of Phoenix–Colorado Campus; Lone Tree	Private	46,473		56
University of Phoenix–Southern Colorado Campus; Colorado Springs	Private	46,473		56
University of Southern Colorado; Pueblo	Public	5,122	81	57
Western State College of Colorado; Gunnison	Public	2,366	66	42
CONNECTICUT				
Albertus Magnus College; New Haven	Private	1,873	89	66
Central Connecticut State University; New Britain	Public	9,443	67	51
Charter Oak State College; New Britain	Public	1,453		52
Connecticut College; New London	Private	1,814	32	57
Eastern Connecticut State University; Willimantic	Public	4,821	64	57
Fairfield University; Fairfield	Private	4,173	63	55
Hartford College for Women; Hartford	Private	178	64	98
Holy Apostles College and Seminary; Cromwell	Private			
Lyme Academy of Fine Arts; Old Lyme	Private	191	97	63
Paier College of Art, Inc.; Hamden	Private	282	78	58
Quinnipiac University; Hamden	Private	4,843	75	64
Sacred Heart University; Fairfield	Private	4,029	74	62
Saint Joseph College; West Hartford	Private	1,227	83	98
Southern Connecticut State University; New Haven	Public	8,080	71	59
Teikyo Post University; Waterbury	Private	1,356	71	64
Trinity College; Hartford	Private	2,100	30	50
United States Coast Guard Academy; New London	Public	879	6	26
University of Bridgeport; Bridgeport	Private	1,212	78	53
University of Connecticut; Storrs	Public	13,251	67	52
University of Hartford; West Hartford	Private	5,369	71	52
University of New Haven; West Haven	Private	2,536	82	40
Wesleyan University; Middletown	Private	2,722	27	52
Western Connecticut State University; Danbury	Public	4,881	69	55
Yale University; New Haven	Private	5,440	16	50
DELAWARE				
Delaware State University; Dover	Public	2,855	74	58
Goldey-Beacom College; Wilmington	Private		84	
University of Delaware; Newark	Public	17,314	49	59
Wesley College; Dover	Private	1,416	72	54
Wilmington College; New Castle	Private		99	
DISTRICT OF COLUMBIA				
American University; Washington	Private	5,705	72	61
Catholic University of America; Washington	Private	2,609	87	54
Corcoran College of Art and Design; Washington	Private	341	58	
Gallaudet University; Washington	Private	1,244	67	54
Georgetown University; Washington	Private	6,418	22	54
George Washington University; Washington	Private	8,837	49	57
Southeastern University; Washington	Private	483	66	68
Strayer University; Washington	Private	10,279		57
Trinity College; Washington	Private	910	73	100
University of the District of Columbia; Washington	Public	5,008	86	62
FLORIDA				
American College of Prehospital Medicine; Navarre	Private	200	100	
American InterContinental University; Plantation	Private	429		
Baptist College of Florida; Graceville	Private	583	96	36
Barry University; Miami Shores	Private	5,777	72	65
Bethune-Cookman College; Daytona Beach	Private	2,745	74	57
Clearwater Christian College; Clearwater	Private	652	86	
DeVry Institute of Technology; Orlando	Private	349	51	20
Eckerd College; St. Petersburg	Private	1,572	73	55
Embry-Riddle Aeronautical University; Daytona Beach	Private	4,525	74	15
Flagler College; St. Augustine	Private	1,830	41	63
Florida Agricultural and Mechanical University; Tallahassee	Public	10,707	65	57
Florida Atlantic University; Boca Raton	Public	17,016	72	61
Florida Christian College; Kissimmee	Private	223	66	48
Florida College; Temple Terrace	Private	555	91	52
Florida Gulf Coast University; Fort Myers	Public	2,977	72	65
Florida Institute of Technology; Melbourne	Private	2,033	80	30
Florida International University; Miami	Public	26,222	54	56

Institution name; city	Public or private	Students	Percent Accepted	Percent Women
Florida Metropolitan Univ.–Brandon Campus; Tampa	Private	680		
Florida Metropolitan Univ.–Fort Lauderdale College; Fort Lauderdale	Private	896	84%	54%
Florida Metropolitan Univ.–Melbourne Campus; Melbourne	Private	544	68	68
Florida Metropolitan Univ.–Orlando College, North; Orlando	Private	826		66
Florida Metropolitan Univ.–Orlando College, South; Orlando	Private	1,250		
Florida Metropolitan Univ.–Tampa College; Tampa	Private	1,125		61
Florida Southern College; Lakeland	Private	1,755	80	61
Florida State University; Tallahassee	Public	27,014	54	56
Hobe Sound Bible College; Hobe Sound	Private	151	91	48
International Academy of Design & Technology; Tampa	Private	1,359		59
International College; Naples	Private	961	87	63
International Fine Arts College; Miami	Private	1,060		
Jacksonville University; Jacksonville	Private	1,817	72	51
Jones College; Jacksonville	Private	654		73
Lynn University; Boca Raton	Private	1,823	81	
New College of the University of South Florida; Sarasota	Public	649	70	63
New World School of the Arts; Miami	Public	339	62	53
Northwood University, Florida Campus; West Palm Beach	Private	969	69	47
Nova Southeastern University; Fort Lauderdale	Private	4,110	74	74
Ringling School of Art and Design; Sarasota	Private	958	43	45
Rollins College; Winter Park	Private	1,598	68	60
Saint Leo University; Saint Leo	Private	1,366	71	57
Schiller International University; Dunedin	Private	190		
Southeastern College of the Assemblies of God; Lakeland	Private	1,232	68	53
St. Thomas University; Miami	Private	1,035	75	55
Stetson University; DeLand	Private	2,155	75	57
Trinity Baptist College; Jacksonville	Private	362	83	46
Trinity College of Florida; New Port Richey	Private	157	77	47
University of Central Florida; Orlando	Public	28,252	63	55
University of Florida; Gainesville	Public	32,680	62	53
University of Miami; Coral Gables	Private	8,955	53	55
University of North Florida; Jacksonville	Public	10,663	72	58
University of Phoenix–Fort Lauderdale Campus; Plantation	Private	46,473		56
University of Phoenix–Jacksonville Campus; Jacksonville	Private	46,473		56
University of Phoenix–Orlando Campus; Maitland	Private	46,473		56
University of Phoenix–Tampa Campus; Tampa	Private	46,473		56
University of South Florida; Tampa	Public	27,384	58	59
University of Tampa; Tampa	Private	2,999	76	61
University of West Florida; Pensacola	Public	6,753	82	58
Warner Southern College; Lake Wales	Private	999	54	59
Webber College; Babson Park	Private	419	52	50
GEORGIA				
Agnes Scott College; Decatur	Private	892	72	100
Albany State University; Albany	Public	3,129	29	67
American InterContinental University; Atlanta	Private	860		60
Armstrong Atlantic State University; Savannah	Public	5,040		69
Atlanta Christian College; East Point	Private	385	73	51
Atlanta College of Art; Atlanta	Private	379	62	
Augusta State University; Augusta	Public	4,440	72	63
Beacon College; Columbus	Private	57	96	39
Berry College; Mount Berry	Private	1,825	79	
Beulah Heights Bible College; Atlanta	Private	585	90	
Brenau University; Gainesville	Private	613	85	100
Clark Atlanta University; Atlanta	Private	3,980	72	72
Clayton College & State University; Morrow	Public	4,455	63	64
Columbus State University; Columbus	Public	4,454	69	62
Covenant College; Lookout Mountain	Private	1,083	98	58
Dalton State College; Dalton	Public	3,139	67	
DeVry Institute of Technology; Alpharetta	Private	1,513	62	32
DeVry Institute of Technology; Decatur	Private	2,916	51	42
Emmanuel College; Franklin Springs	Private	782	51	55
Emory University; Atlanta	Private	6,215	45	55
Fort Valley State University; Fort Valley	Public	2,212	49	57
Georgia Baptist College of Nursing of Mercer Univ.; Atlanta	Private	312	46	97
Georgia College and State University; Milledgeville	Public	3,980	74	62
Georgia Institute of Technology; Atlanta	Public	10,745	57	29
Georgia Southern University; Statesboro	Public	12,648	79	53
Georgia Southwestern State University; Americus	Public	1,981	65	64
Georgia State University; Atlanta	Public	16,439	59	62
Kennesaw State University; Kennesaw	Public	11,664	73	
LaGrange College; LaGrange	Private	876	83	64
Luther Rice Bible College and Seminary; Lithonia	Private	1,300		
Macon State College; Macon	Public	4,118		66
Mercer University; Macon	Private	4,305	73	64

Institution name; city	Public or private	Students	Percent Accepted	Percent Women
Morehouse College; Atlanta	Private	2,970	75%	0%
Morris Brown College; Atlanta	Private	2,787	58	58
North Georgia College & State University; Dahlonega	Public	3,144	47	64
Oglethorpe University; Atlanta	Private	1,169	70	67
Paine College; Augusta	Private	858	54	70
Piedmont College; Demorest	Private	1,026	72	63
Reinhardt College; Waleska	Private	1,078	89	63
Savannah College of Art and Design; Savannah	Private	4,249	84	43
Savannah State University; Savannah	Public			
Shorter College; Rome	Private	1,889	87	65
South College; Savannah	Private	483		75
Southern Polytechnic State University; Marietta	Public	2,943	64	17
Spelman College; Atlanta	Private	1,952	53	
State University of West Georgia; Carrollton	Public	7,109	73	61
Thomas University; Thomasville	Private	543	100	66
Toccoa Falls College; Toccoa Falls	Private	926	64	56
University of Georgia; Athens	Public	24,213	62	
Valdosta State University; Valdosta	Public	7,511	65	60
Wesleyan College; Macon	Private	583	78	100
HAWAII				
Brigham Young University–Hawaii Campus; Laie	Private	2,358	55	60
Chaminade University of Honolulu; Honolulu	Private	1,905	69	58
Hawaii Pacific University; Honolulu	Private	6,988	84	52
University of Hawaii at Hilo; Hilo	Public	2,646	63	60
University of Hawaii at Manoa; Honolulu	Public	11,721	71	55
University of Phoenix–Hawaii Campus; Honolulu	Private	46,473		56
IDAHO				
Albertson College of Idaho; Caldwell	Private	812	97	53
Boise State University; Boise	Public	14,749	86	55
Idaho State University; Pocatello	Public	11,768	75	
Lewis-Clark State College; Lewiston	Public	2,702	62	62
Northwest Nazarene University; Nampa	Private	1,110	73	55
University of Idaho; Moscow	Public	8,759	83	46
ILLINOIS				
American Academy of Art; Chicago	Private	398	100	32
Augustana College; Rock Island	Private	2,261	72	57
Aurora University; Aurora	Private	1,316	62	59
Barat College; Lake Forest	Private	746	62	73
Benedictine University; Lisle	Private	2,007	81	59
Blackburn College; Carlinville	Private	540	72	
Blessing-Rieman College of Nursing; Quincy	Private	126	100	94
Bradley University; Peoria	Private	5,116	79	54
Columbia College Chicago; Chicago	Private	8,577	90	50
Concordia University; River Forest	Private	1,280	30	68
DePaul University; Chicago	Private	12,436	73	59
DeVry Institute of Technology; Addison	Private	4,006	65	23
DeVry Institute of Technology; Chicago	Private	4,095	66	36
DeVry Institute of Technology; Tinley Park	Private	1,010	95	26
Dominican University; River Forest	Private	1,127	79	69
Eastern Illinois University; Charleston	Public	9,344	73	58
Elmhurst College; Elmhurst	Private	2,484	71	64
Eureka College; Eureka	Private	441	78	
Greenville College; Greenville	Private	1,144	97	50
Illinois College; Jacksonville	Private	909	74	55
Illinois Institute of Art; Chicago	Private	1,250		
Illinois Institute of Art-Schaumburg; Schaumburg	Private	850	100	
Illinois Institute of Technology; Chicago	Private	1,736	65	25
Illinois State University; Normal	Public	18,025	76	58
Illinois Wesleyan University; Bloomington	Private	2,102	60	57
International Academy of Design & Technology; Chicago	Private	1,739	68	65
Judson College; Elgin	Private	1,111	76	58
Kendall College; Evanston	Private	600	83	
Knox College; Galesburg	Private	1,199	72	57
Lake Forest College; Lake Forest	Private	1,251	71	60
Lewis University; Romeoville	Private	3,327	70	56
Lincoln Christian College; Lincoln	Private	653	81	52
Loyola University Chicago; Chicago	Private	7,141	80	64
MacMurray College; Jacksonville	Private	727	69	51
McKendree College; Lebanon	Private	1,993	69	62
Millikin University; Decatur	Private	2,307	99	58
Monmouth College; Monmouth	Private	1,069	78	57
Moody Bible Institute; Chicago	Private	1,294	41	46
National-Louis University; Evanston	Private	3,482	77	
North Central College; Naperville	Private	2,117	76	58
North Park University; Chicago	Private	1,655	74	62

Institution name; city	Public or private	Students	Percent	
			Accepted	Women
Northeastern Illinois University; Chicago	Public	8,324	70%	62%
Northern Illinois University; De Kalb	Public	17,151	65	53
Northwestern University; Evanston	Private	7,724	33	52
Olivet Nazarene University; Bourbonnais	Private	1,874	83	59
Principia College; Elsah	Private	560	86	54
Quincy University; Quincy	Private	1,041	98	56
Robert Morris College; Chicago	Private	4,938	71	67
Rockford College; Rockford	Private	1,100	63	65
Roosevelt University; Chicago	Private	4,665	51	62
Saint Xavier University; Chicago	Private	2,611	73	73
School of the Art Institute of Chicago; Chicago	Private	2,053	76	63
Southern Illinois University Carbondale; Carbondale	Public	17,788	71	43
Southern Illinois University Edwardsville; Edwardsville	Public	9,576	86	58
St. Augustine College; Chicago	Private	1,543		79
Trinity Christian College; Palos Heights	Private	854	99	63
Trinity International University; Deerfield	Private	1,136	86	57
University of Chicago; Chicago	Private	4,008	44	49
University of Illinois at Chicago; Chicago	Public	16,131	60	55
University of Illinois at Urbana–Champaign; Urbana	Public	27,914	64	49
University of St. Francis; Joliet	Private	1,471	71	69
VanderCook College of Music; Chicago	Private	87	59	
Western Illinois University; Macomb	Public	10,656	65	51
Wheaton College; Wheaton	Private	2,418	58	53
INDIANA				
Anderson University; Anderson	Private	2,090	76	57
Ball State University; Muncie	Public	16,350	79	53
Bethel College; Mishawaka	Private	1,534	68	65
Butler University; Indianapolis	Private	3,313	84	63
DePauw University; Greencastle	Private	2,225	61	56
Earlham College; Richmond	Private	1,104	85	56
Franklin College of Indiana; Franklin	Private	1,020	77	51
Goshen College; Goshen	Private	1,084	68	57
Grace College; Winona Lake	Private	923	88	58
Hanover College; Hanover	Private	1,142	83	55
Huntington College; Huntington	Private	857	93	62
Indiana Institute of Technology; Fort Wayne	Private	1,951	14	51
Indiana State University; Terre Haute	Public	9,537	83	52
Indiana University Bloomington; Bloomington	Public	29,383	82	53
Indiana University East; Richmond	Public	2,262	64	69
Indiana University Kokomo; Kokomo	Public	2,381	91	70
Indiana University Northwest; Gary	Public	4,101	75	70
Indiana University South Bend; South Bend	Public	5,897	84	64
Indiana University Southeast; New Albany	Public	5,655	91	62
Indiana Univ.–Purdue University Fort Wayne; Fort Wayne	Public	9,773	94	57
Indiana Univ.–Purdue University Indianapolis; Indianapolis	Public	20,211	80	59
Indiana Wesleyan University; Marion	Private	5,101	78	63
Manchester College; North Manchester	Private	1,091	81	55
Marian College; Indianapolis	Private	1,411	89	75
Oakland City University; Oakland City	Private	1,492	100	51
Purdue University; West Lafayette	Public	30,899	78	43
Purdue University Calumet; Hammond	Public	7,784	99	56
Purdue University North Central; Westville	Public	3,416	98	60
Rose-Hulman Institute of Technology; Terre Haute	Private	1,581	77	17
Saint Joseph's College; Rensselaer	Private	935	74	56
Saint Mary's College; Notre Dame	Private	1,449	83	100
Saint Mary-of-the-Woods College; Saint Mary-of-the-Woods	Private	1,385	88	100
Taylor University; Upland	Private	1,886	67	
Taylor University, Fort Wayne Campus; Fort Wayne	Private	477	84	56
Tri-State University; Angola	Private	1,267	81	31
University of Evansville; Evansville	Private	2,785	91	60
University of Indianapolis; Indianapolis	Private	2,856	82	66
University of Notre Dame; Notre Dame	Private	8,038	34	46
University of Saint Francis; Fort Wayne	Private	1,390	83	67
University of Southern Indiana; Evansville	Public	8,539	95	60
Valparaiso University; Valparaiso	Private	2,980	81	54
Wabash College; Crawfordsville	Private	852	65	0
IOWA				
Allen College; Waterloo	Private	248	53	93
Briar Cliff College; Sioux City	Private	917	80	65
Buena Vista University; Storm Lake	Private	1,278	86	51
Central College; Pella	Private	1,336	88	57
Clarke College; Dubuque	Private	976	73	67
Coe College; Cedar Rapids	Private	1,256	81	55
Cornell College; Mount Vernon	Private	987	74	59
Dordt College; Sioux Center	Private	1,420	95	56

Institution name; city	Public or private	Students	Percent Accepted	Percent Women
Drake University; Des Moines	Private	3,544	87%	61%
Emmaus Bible College; Dubuque	Private	293	100	53
Faith Baptist Bible Coll. and Theological Sem.; Ankeny	Private	382	65	55
Graceland University; Lamoni	Private	2,952	69	
Grand View College; Des Moines	Private	1,380	63	65
Grinnell College; Grinnell	Private	1,344	64	56
Hamilton Technical College; Davenport	Private	380		
Iowa State University of Science and Technology; Ames	Public	22,087	91	45
Iowa Wesleyan College; Mount Pleasant	Private	777	82	60
Loras College; Dubuque	Private	1,626	79	53
Luther College; Decorah	Private	2,621	84	60
Maharishi University of Management; Fairfield	Private	239		50
Marycrest International University; Davenport	Private	387	68	53
Mercy College of Health Sciences; Des Moines	Private	409	25	92
Morningside College; Sioux City	Private	968	77	64
Mount Mercy College; Cedar Rapids	Private	1,363	90	68
Mount St. Clare College; Clinton	Private	560	78	55
Northwestern College; Orange City	Private	1,243	88	61
Palmer College of Chiropractic; Davenport	Private	60	100	78
Simpson College; Indianola	Private	1,912	86	57
St. Ambrose University; Davenport	Private	2,116	86	60
University of Dubuque; Dubuque	Private	669	82	41
University of Iowa; Iowa City	Public	19,284	83	54
University of Northern Iowa; Cedar Falls	Public	12,413	82	58
Upper Iowa University; Fayette	Private	697	75	39
Wartburg College; Waverly	Private	1,600	89	57
William Penn University; Oskaloosa	Private	1,353	76	42
KANSAS				
Baker University; Baldwin City	Private	923	81	58
Barclay College; Haviland	Private	193	42	53
Benedictine College; Atchison	Private	1,323	92	56
Bethany College; Lindsborg	Private	611	63	46
Bethel College; North Newton	Private	502	79	52
Emporia State University; Emporia	Public	4,191	100	59
Fort Hays State University; Hays	Public	4,427	99	54
Friends University; Wichita	Private	2,668	93	
Haskell Indian Nations University; Lawrence	Public	915		
Kansas State University; Manhattan	Public	18,252	61	47
Kansas Wesleyan University; Salina	Private	697	70	
Manhattan Christian College; Manhattan	Private	400	94	56
McPherson College; McPherson	Private	463	69	51
MidAmerica Nazarene University; Olathe	Private	1,302	58	52
Newman University; Wichita	Private	1,557	98	65
Ottawa University; Ottawa	Private	433	68	45
Pittsburg State University; Pittsburg	Public	5,222		48
Saint Mary College; Leavenworth	Private	506	83	65
Southwestern College; Winfield	Private	1,114	96	51
Sterling College; Sterling	Private	439	66	51
Tabor College; Hillsboro	Private	572	68	47
University of Kansas; Lawrence	Public	20,157	76	53
Washburn University of Topeka; Topeka	Public	4,888	100	62
Wichita State University; Wichita	Public	11,377	75	56
KENTUCKY				
Alice Lloyd College; Pippa Passes	Private	558	66	
Asbury College; Wilmore	Private	1,338	82	59
Bellarmine University; Louisville	Private	1,682	95	
Berea College; Berea	Private	1,590	34	58
Brescia University; Owensboro	Private	688		61
Campbellsville University; Campbellsville	Private	1,502	84	60
Centre College; Danville	Private	1,057	88	53
Clear Creek Baptist Bible College; Pineville	Private	190	83	15
Cumberland College; Williamsburg	Private	1,554	68	53
Eastern Kentucky University; Richmond	Public	12,676	71	58
Kentucky Christian College; Grayson	Private	569	90	55
Kentucky Mountain Bible College; Vancleve	Private	87	52	43
Kentucky State University; Frankfort	Public	2,129	45	56
Kentucky Wesleyan College; Owensboro	Private	680	79	54
Lindsey Wilson College; Columbia	Private	1,366	83	63
Mid-Continent College; Mayfield	Private	455	65	46
Midway College; Midway	Private	834	92	89
Morehead State University; Morehead	Public	6,750	74	60
Murray State University; Murray	Public	7,487	87	58
Northern Kentucky University; Highland Heights	Public	10,838	98	59
Pikeville College; Pikeville	Private	917	100	59
Spalding University; Louisville	Private	1,014	71	77

Institution name; city	Public or private	Students	Percent Accepted	Percent Women
Sullivan University; Louisville	Private			
Thomas More College; Crestview Hills	Private	1,273	79%	55%
Transylvania University; Lexington	Private	1,083	91	58
Union College; Barbourville	Private	653	75	48
University of Kentucky; Lexington	Public	16,897	61	52
University of Louisville; Louisville	Public	14,464	89	54
Western Kentucky University; Bowling Green	Public	13,235	87	58
LOUISIANA				
Centenary College of Louisiana; Shreveport	Private	858	89	61
Dillard University; New Orleans	Private	1,953	72	78
Grantham College of Engineering; Slidell	Private	967		
Louisiana State University and Agricultural and Mechanical College; Baton Rouge	Public	26,121	78	53
Louisiana State Univ. Health Sciences Center; New Orleans	Public	767		
Louisiana State University in Shreveport; Shreveport	Public	3,422	100	61
Louisiana Tech University; Ruston	Public	8,921	93	48
Loyola University New Orleans; New Orleans	Private	3,688	74	64
McNeese State University; Lake Charles	Public	6,703	72	59
Nicholls State University; Thibodaux	Public	6,556	93	62
Northwestern State University of Louisiana; Natchitoches	Public	7,972	98	62
Our Lady of Holy Cross College; New Orleans	Private	1,148	45	76
Saint Joseph Seminary College; Saint Benedict	Private		100	
Southeastern Louisiana University; Hammond	Public	12,916	77	63
Southern University and Agricultural and Mechanical College; Baton Rouge	Public	7,775		57
Tulane University; New Orleans	Private	7,382	73	53
University of Louisiana at Lafayette; Lafayette	Public	14,091	78	56
University of Louisiana at Monroe; Monroe	Public	8,037	95	62
University of New Orleans; New Orleans	Public	12,260	83	57
University of Phoenix-Louisiana Campus; Metairie	Private	46,473		56
MAINE				
Bates College; Lewiston	Private	1,694	29	52
Bowdoin College; Brunswick	Private	1,609	28	51
Colby College; Waterville	Private	1,814	37	54
College of the Atlantic; Bar Harbor	Private	278	80	64
Husson College; Bangor	Private	1,626	97	66
Maine College of Art; Portland	Private	413	87	60
Maine Maritime Academy; Castine	Public	707	81	15
New England School of Communications; Bangor	Private	135	41	28
Saint Joseph's College; Standish	Private	832	84	67
Thomas College; Waterville	Private	598	96	56
Unity College; Unity	Private	512	69	34
University of Maine; Orono	Public	8,229	83	52
University of Maine at Augusta; Augusta	Public	5,617	67	
University of Maine at Farmington; Farmington	Public	2,413	66	68
University of Maine at Fort Kent; Fort Kent	Public	886	89	63
University of Maine at Machias; Machias	Public	927	87	67
University of Maine at Presque Isle; Presque Isle	Public	1,427	88	63
University of New England; Biddeford	Private	1,869	72	81
University of Southern Maine; Portland	Public	8,726	78	60
MARYLAND				
Baltimore International College; Baltimore	Private	456	49	46
Bowie State University; Bowie	Public	3,109	44	60
Capitol College; Laurel	Private	684	80	27
College of Notre Dame of Maryland; Baltimore	Private	1,930	80	95
Columbia Union College; Takoma Park	Private	1,030	54	59
Frostburg State University; Frostburg	Public	4,430	73	53
Goucher College; Baltimore	Private	1,195	82	73
Griggs University; Silver Spring	Private	322		
Hood College; Frederick	Private	861	77	88
Johns Hopkins University; Baltimore	Private	3,910	32	42
Loyola College in Maryland; Baltimore	Private	3,476	61	56
Maryland Institute, College of Art; Baltimore	Private	1,154	45	58
Morgan State University; Baltimore	Public	5,685		59
Mount Saint Mary's College and Seminary; Emmitsburg	Private	1,500	87	59
Peabody Conservatory of Music of The Johns Hopkins University; Baltimore	Private	332	42	52
Salisbury State University; Salisbury	Public	5,883	21	57
Sojourner-Douglass College; Baltimore	Private	844		83
St. John's College; Annapolis	Private	476	79	47
St. Mary's College of Maryland; St. Mary's City	Public	1,547	74	59
Towson University; Towson	Public	13,905	62	60
United States Naval Academy; Annapolis	Public	4,172	15	15
University of Maryland Eastern Shore; Princess Anne	Public	2,969	66	58
University of Maryland University College; Adelphi	Public	13,226	100	58

Institution name; city	Public or private	Students	Percent Accepted	Percent Women
University of Maryland, Baltimore County; Baltimore	Public	9,101	66%	50%
University of Maryland, College Park; College Park	Public	24,638	51	49
University of Phoenix–Maryland Campus; Columbia	Private	46,473		56
Villa Julie College; Stevenson	Private	2,185		72
Washington Bible College; Lanham	Private	313	56	44
Washington College; Chestertown	Private	1,165	88	60
Western Maryland College; Westminster	Private	1,611	77	56
MASSACHUSETTS				
American International College; Springfield	Private	1,084	79	55
Amherst College; Amherst	Private	1,682	19	48
Anna Maria College; Paxton	Private	797	83	63
Art Institute of Boston at Lesley University; Boston	Private	791	49	58
Assumption College; Worcester	Private	2,455	71	64
Atlantic Union College; South Lancaster	Private	680	42	61
Babson College; Wellesley	Private	1,751	39	36
Bay Path College; Longmeadow	Private	764	67	100
Becker College; Worcester	Private	1,163	87	77
Bentley College; Waltham	Private	4,316	49	44
Berklee College of Music; Boston	Private	3,361	78	
Boston Architectural Center; Boston	Private	458	95	27
Boston College; Chestnut Hill	Private	8,930	32	52
Boston Conservatory; Boston	Private	350	47	67
Boston University; Boston	Private	17,819	49	59
Brandeis University; Waltham	Private	3,169	48	57
Bridgewater State College; Bridgewater	Public	7,080	81	61
Cambridge College; Cambridge	Private	350	100	
Clark University; Worcester	Private	2,124	70	59
College of Our Lady of the Elms; Chicopee	Private	740	85	88
College of the Holy Cross; Worcester	Private	2,826	41	53
Curry College; Milton	Private	2,218	76	50
Eastern Nazarene College; Quincy	Private	1,209	69	59
Emerson College; Boston	Private	3,168	52	58
Emmanuel College; Boston	Private	1,360	83	89
Endicott College; Beverly	Private	1,553	70	67
Fitchburg State College; Fitchburg	Public	3,238	66	58
Framingham State College; Framingham	Public	4,165	62	65
Gordon College; Wenham	Private	1,528	80	64
Hampshire College; Amherst	Private	1,172	62	56
Harvard University; Cambridge	Private	6,660	11	
Hebrew College; Brookline	Private			
Hellenic College; Brookline	Private	47	48	28
Lasell College; Newton	Private	841	79	76
Lesley University; Cambridge	Private	553	79	100
Massachusetts College of Art; Boston	Public	2,214	46	65
Massachusetts College of Liberal Arts; North Adams	Public	1,392	70	61
Massachusetts College of Pharmacy and Health Sciences; Boston	Private	446	76	65
Massachusetts Institute of Technology; Cambridge	Private	4,258	16	41
Massachusetts Maritime Academy; Buzzards Bay	Public	831	72	13
Merrimack College; North Andover	Private	2,568	70	52
Montserrat College of Art; Beverly	Private	402	84	57
Mount Holyoke College; South Hadley	Private	2,065	55	100
Mount Ida College; Newton Centre	Private	1,471	80	59
New England Conservatory of Music; Boston	Private	407	48	45
Nichols College; Dudley	Private	1,159	85	47
Northeastern University; Boston	Private	13,671	70	50
Pine Manor College; Chestnut Hill	Private	369	78	100
Regis College; Weston	Private	884	89	98
Saint John's Seminary College of Liberal Arts; Brighton	Private	32	73	0
Salem State College; Salem	Public	11,132	58	63
School of the Museum of Fine Arts; Boston	Private			
Simmons College; Boston	Private	1,224	65	100
Simon's Rock College of Bard; Great Barrington	Private	387	70	57
Smith College; Northampton	Private	2,630	53	100
Springfield College; Springfield	Private		58	
Stonehill College; Easton	Private	2,637	44	59
Suffolk University; Boston	Private	3,555	79	58
Tufts University; Medford	Private	4,863	26	53
University of Massachusetts Amherst; Amherst	Public	19,061	67	51
University of Massachusetts Boston; Boston	Public	10,442	59	57
University of Massachusetts Dartmouth; North Dartmouth	Public	6,423	73	53
University of Massachusetts Lowell; Lowell	Public	9,566	67	
Wellesley College; Wellesley	Private	2,267	43	100
Wentworth Institute of Technology; Boston	Private	3,152	67	20
Western New England College; Springfield	Private	3,136	69	

Institution name; city	Public or private	Students	Percent Accepted	Percent Women
Westfield State College; Westfield	Public	4,279	64%	55%
Wheaton College; Norton	Private	1,474	65	64
Wheelock College; Boston	Private	637	83	94
Williams College; Williamstown	Private	2,020	24	48
Worcester Polytechnic Institute; Worcester	Private	2,817	77	23
Worcester State College; Worcester	Public	4,569	52	
MICHIGAN				
Adrian College; Adrian	Private	1,082	86	54
Albion College; Albion	Private	1,522	85	58
Alma College; Alma	Private	1,409	82	59
Andrews University; Berrien Springs	Private	1,736	54	56
Aquinas College; Grand Rapids	Private	2,021	83	61
Ave Maria College; Ypsilanti	Private	135		53
Baker College of Auburn Hills; Auburn Hills	Private	1,910	100	67
Baker College of Cadillac; Cadillac	Private	864	100	72
Baker College of Clinton Township; Clinton Township	Private	2,560	46	77
Baker College of Flint; Flint	Private	3,901	100	67
Baker College of Jackson; Jackson	Private	1,201	100	75
Baker College of Muskegon; Muskegon	Private	2,727	75	68
Baker College of Owosso; Owosso	Private	1,905	100	69
Baker College of Port Huron; Port Huron	Private	1,230	100	78
Calvin College; Grand Rapids	Private	4,263	99	55
Center for Creative Studies; Detroit	Private	1,086	82	41
Central Michigan University; Mount Pleasant	Public	18,550	83	59
Cleary College; Howell	Private	848		62
Concordia College; Ann Arbor	Private	590	85	60
Cornerstone University; Grand Rapids	Private	1,592	93	60
Davenport University; Dearborn	Private	2,924	100	74
Davenport University; Grand Rapids	Private	2,144	100	65
Davenport University; Kalamazoo	Private	1,081		
Davenport University; Lansing	Private	1,140		71
Davenport University; Warren	Private	2,465	100	77
Eastern Michigan University; Ypsilanti	Public	18,131	73	61
Ferris State University; Big Rapids	Public	9,235	87	44
Finlandia University; Hancock	Private	380	73	67
Grace Bible College; Grand Rapids	Private	140	81	52
Grand Valley State University; Allendale	Public	15,221	77	60
Hillsdale College; Hillsdale	Private	1,138	84	50
Hope College; Holland	Private	3,015	89	60
Kalamazoo College; Kalamazoo	Private	1,322	70	57
Kendall College of Art and Design; Grand Rapids	Private	738		57
Kettering University; Flint	Private	2,642	72	19
Lake Superior State University; Sault Sainte Marie	Public	3,068	89	53
Lawrence Technological University; Southfield	Private	2,979	78	
Madonna University; Livonia	Private	3,066	66	78
Marygrove College; Detroit	Private	914	58	
Michigan State University; East Lansing	Public	34,342	69	53
Michigan Technological University; Houghton	Public	5,666	94	26
Northern Michigan University; Marquette	Public	7,244	85	54
Northwood University; Midland	Private	3,645	96	50
Oakland University; Rochester	Public	12,002	78	64
Olivet College; Olivet	Private	918	80	48
Reformed Bible College; Grand Rapids	Private	280	55	48
Rochester College; Rochester Hills	Private	830		54
Sacred Heart Major Seminary; Detroit	Private	275	100	
Saginaw Valley State University; University Center	Public	6,262		
Saint Mary's College of Ave Maria University; Orchard Lake	Private	479	81	44
Siena Heights University; Adrian	Private	1,658	73	
Spring Arbor University; Spring Arbor	Private	2,125	90	69
University of Michigan; Ann Arbor	Public	23,904	55	52
University of Michigan–Dearborn; Dearborn	Public	6,694	74	
University of Michigan–Flint; Flint	Public	5,786	82	65
University of Phoenix–Grand Rapids Campus; Grand Rapids	Private	46,473		56
University of Phoenix–Metro Detroit Campus; Troy	Private	46,473		56
Wayne State University; Detroit	Public	18,093	78	60
Western Michigan University; Kalamazoo	Public	22,756	85	53
William Tyndale College; Farmington Hills	Private	625	99	52
MINNESOTA				
Augsburg College; Minneapolis	Private	2,913	75	60
Bemidji State University; Bemidji	Public	4,368	77	57
Bethel College; St. Paul	Private	2,652	77	63
Carleton College; Northfield	Private	1,936	44	52
College of Saint Benedict; Saint Joseph	Private	2,024	80	100
College of St. Catherine; St. Paul	Private	3,555	85	98
College of St. Scholastica; Duluth	Private	1,438	36	

Institution name; city	Public or private	Students	Percent Accepted	Percent Women
College of Visual Arts; St. Paul	Private	278	65%	56%
Concordia College; Moorhead	Private	2,826	84	62
Concordia University; St. Paul	Private	1,504	67	59
Crown College; St. Bonifacius	Private	882	65	58
Gustavus Adolphus College; St. Peter	Private	2,560	76	57
Hamline University; St. Paul	Private	1,851	81	65
Macalester College; St. Paul	Private	1,794	53	60
Martin Luther College; New Ulm	Private	1,026		50
Metropolitan State University; St. Paul	Public	5,328		60
Minneapolis College of Art and Design; Minneapolis	Private	598	71	42
Minnesota Bible College; Rochester	Private	116	68	47
Minnesota State University, Mankato; Mankato	Public	10,442		53
Minnesota State University, Moorhead; Moorhead	Public	7,060	91	
North Central University; Minneapolis	Private	1,163	77	
Northwestern College; St. Paul	Private	2,084	75	62
Oak Hills Christian College; Bemidji	Private	155	80	50
Saint John's University; Collegeville	Private	1,880	85	1
Saint Mary's University of Minnesota; Winona	Private	1,682	91	52
Southwest State University; Marshall	Public	4,147	48	59
St. Cloud State University; St. Cloud	Public	13,942	83	55
St. Olaf College; Northfield	Private	3,014	74	57
University of Minnesota, Crookston; Crookston	Public	2,464	95	55
University of Minnesota, Duluth; Duluth	Public	8,606	78	51
University of Minnesota, Morris; Morris	Public	1,944	87	58
University of Minnesota, Twin Cities Campus; Minneapolis	Public	31,824	75	53
University of St. Thomas; St. Paul	Private	5,469	82	53
Winona State University; Winona	Public	6,739	68	
MISSISSIPPI				
Alcorn State University; Alcorn State	Public	2,398		60
Belhaven College; Jackson	Private	1,467	70	64
Blue Mountain College; Blue Mountain	Private	371	79	85
Delta State University; Cleveland	Public	3,356		60
Jackson State University; Jackson	Public	5,471	26	55
Magnolia Bible College; Kosciusko	Private	37	100	41
Millsaps College; Jackson	Private	1,191	88	54
Mississippi College; Clinton	Private	2,440	98	58
Mississippi State University; Mississippi State	Public	13,307	71	46
Mississippi University for Women; Columbus	Public	2,660	79	
Mississippi Valley State University; Itta Bena	Public	2,358	45	64
Rust College; Holly Springs	Private	852	40	65
Southeastern Baptist College; Laurel	Private		100	
Tougaloo College; Tougaloo	Private	1,000	99	72
University of Mississippi; Oxford	Public	9,608	82	52
University of Southern Mississippi; Hattiesburg	Public	12,144	65	61
MISSOURI				
Avila College; Kansas City	Private	1,123	97	70
Baptist Bible College; Springfield	Private	796	100	
Central Bible College; Springfield	Private	849	93	42
Central Christian College of the Bible; Moberly	Private	133		
Central Methodist College; Fayette	Private	1,172	85	61
Central Missouri State University; Warrensburg	Public	9,150	82	53
College of the Ozarks; Point Lookout	Private	1,404	17	56
Columbia College; Columbia	Private	782	97	59
Conception Seminary College; Conception	Private	91	100	3
Culver-Stockton College; Canton	Private	821	77	55
Deaconess College of Nursing; St. Louis	Private	220	37	96
DeVry Institute of Technology; Kansas City	Private	2,708	70	23
Drury University; Springfield	Private	1,438	88	56
Evangel University; Springfield	Private	1,488	92	56
Fontbonne College; St. Louis	Private	1,376	81	70
Global University of the Assemblies of God; Springfield	Private	2,674		32
Hannibal-LaGrange College; Hannibal	Private	1,104	41	
Harris-Stowe State College; St. Louis	Public	1,100	66	
Jewish Hospital Coll. of Nursing and Allied Health; St. Louis	Private	349	100	86
Kansas City Art Institute; Kansas City	Private	527	77	51
Kansas City College of Legal Studies; Kansas City	Private	102		
Lester L. Cox College of Nursing and Health Sciences; Springfield	Private	294	69	93
Lincoln University; Jefferson City	Public	3,128	80	58
Lindenwood University; St. Charles	Private	3,991		54
Maryville University of Saint Louis; St. Louis	Private	2,573	78	73
Messenger College; Joplin	Private	90	100	46
Missouri Baptist College; St. Louis	Private	2,574	75	63
Missouri Southern State College; Joplin	Public	5,785	91	57
Missouri Valley College; Marshall	Private	1,641	84	41
Missouri Western State College; St. Joseph	Public	5,089	100	61

Institution name; city	Public or private	Students	Percent Accepted	Percent Women
National American University; Kansas City	Private	380		
Northwest Missouri State University; Maryville	Public	5,568	90%	56%
Ozark Christian College; Joplin	Private	750	100	50
Park University; Parkville	Private	1,242	77	61
Research College of Nursing; Kansas City	Private	212	78	96
Rockhurst University; Kansas City	Private	2,034	88	58
Saint Louis University; St. Louis	Private	9,847	67	56
Southeast Missouri State University; Cape Girardeau	Public	7,758	48	58
Southwest Baptist University; Bolivar	Private	1,822	86	
Southwest Missouri State University; Springfield	Public	14,699	87	55
St. Louis Christian College; Florissant	Private	192	91	43
St. Louis College of Pharmacy; St. Louis	Private	826	79	65
Stephens College; Columbia	Private	634	82	93
Truman State University; Kirksville	Public	5,812	79	58
University of Missouri–Kansas City; Kansas City	Public	8,091	71	58
University of Missouri–Rolla; Rolla	Public	3,698	92	23
University of Missouri–St. Louis; St. Louis	Public	12,737	57	60
University of Phoenix–St. Louis Campus; Maryland Heights	Private	46,473		56
Washington University in St. Louis; St. Louis	Private	6,695	30	51
Webster University; St. Louis	Private	4,483	63	61
Westminster College; Fulton	Private	686	86	43
William Jewell College; Liberty	Private	1,153	87	59
William Woods University; Fulton	Private	1,011	84	
MONTANA				
Carroll College; Helena	Private	1,251	89	60
Montana State University–Billings; Billings	Public	3,826	88	64
Montana State University–Bozeman; Bozeman	Public	10,458	84	45
Montana State University–Northern; Havre	Public	1,367	100	52
Montana Tech of The University of Montana; Butte	Public	1,978	97	45
Rocky Mountain College; Billings	Private	792	99	
University of Great Falls; Great Falls	Private	970	100	
University of Montana–Missoula; Missoula	Public	10,666	86	53
Western Montana College; Dillon	Public	1,160	79	59
NEBRASKA				
Bellevue University; Bellevue	Private	2,815	94	50
Chadron State College; Chadron	Public	2,331	100	58
Clarkson College; Omaha	Private	274	72	89
College of Saint Mary; Omaha	Private	947	99	97
Concordia University; Seward	Private	1,180	92	55
Creighton University; Omaha	Private	3,765	89	59
Dana College; Blair	Private	583	97	47
Doane College; Crete	Private	1,517	89	53
Grace University; Omaha	Private	510	47	55
Hastings College; Hastings	Private	1,090	87	51
Midland Lutheran College; Fremont	Private	1,025	95	59
Nebraska Christian College; Norfolk	Private	162	65	49
Nebraska Methodist College; Omaha	Private	370	86	92
Nebraska Wesleyan University; Lincoln	Private	1,675	94	57
Peru State College; Peru	Public	1,454	63	55
Union College; Lincoln	Private	801	43	54
University of Nebraska at Kearney; Kearney	Public	5,502	93	55
University of Nebraska at Omaha; Omaha	Public	10,694	87	53
University of Nebraska–Lincoln; Lincoln	Public	17,968	92	47
Wayne State College; Wayne	Public	2,982	100	58
York College; York	Private	497	56	
NEVADA				
Sierra Nevada College; Incline Village	Private	354	96	52
University of Nevada, Las Vegas; Las Vegas	Public	17,327	79	55
University of Nevada, Reno; Reno	Public	10,134	91	55
University of Phoenix–Nevada Campus; Las Vegas	Private	46,473		56
NEW HAMPSHIRE				
Colby-Sawyer College; New London	Private	845	84	65
Daniel Webster College; Nashua	Private	1,099	84	31
Dartmouth College; Hanover	Private	4,057	21	48
Franklin Pierce College; Rindge	Private	1,489	75	49
Keene State College; Keene	Public	4,297	77	58
Magdalen College; Warner	Private	75	67	47
New England College; Henniker	Private	724	92	51
Notre Dame College; Manchester	Private	685	88	
Plymouth State College; Plymouth	Public	3,472	79	50
Rivier College; Nashua	Private	764	70	
Saint Anselm College; Manchester	Private	1,985	73	56
Southern New Hampshire University; Manchester	Private	3,878	80	56
Thomas More College of Liberal Arts; Merrimack	Private	72	66	56
University of New Hampshire; Durham	Public	10,927	76	58

Institution name; city	Public or private	Students	Percent Accepted	Percent Women
University of New Hampshire at Manchester; Manchester	Public	1,016	73%	62%
University System College for Lifelong Learning; Concord	Public			
White Pines College; Chester	Private	129	83	55
NEW JERSEY				
Bloomfield College; Bloomfield	Private	1,771	55	69
Caldwell College; Caldwell	Private	1,844	74	69
Centenary College; Hackettstown	Private	1,202	77	81
College of New Jersey; Ewing	Public	6,008	50	59
College of Saint Elizabeth; Morristown	Private	1,338	79	91
DeVry College of Technology; North Brunswick	Private	3,779	57	23
Drew University; Madison	Private	1,537	71	60
Fairleigh Dickinson University, Florham-Madison Campus; Madison	Private	2,526	76	55
Fairleigh Dickinson University, Teaneck–Hackensack Campus; Teaneck	Private	4,034	69	59
Felician College; Lodi	Private	1,254	66	73
Georgian Court College; Lakewood	Private	1,621	94	91
Kean University; Union	Public	9,299	62	65
Monmouth University; West Long Branch	Private	4,193	84	57
Montclair State University; Upper Montclair	Public	10,188	23	62
New Jersey City University; Jersey City	Public	6,355	51	62
New Jersey Institute of Technology; Newark	Public	5,270	57	22
Princeton University; Princeton	Private	4,663	12	47
Rabbinical College of America; Morristown	Private	250	100	
Ramapo College of New Jersey; Mahwah	Public	4,906	48	59
Richard Stockton College of New Jersey; Pomona	Public	5,976	48	
Rider University; Lawrenceville	Private	4,178	81	58
Rowan University; Glassboro	Public	8,051	30	58
Rutgers, The State Univ. of New Jersey, Camden; Camden	Public	3,706	59	59
Rutgers, The State Univ. of New Jersey, New Brunswick; New Brunswick	Public	27,939	58	53
Rutgers, The State Univ. of New Jersey, Newark; Newark	Public	5,873	52	58
Saint Peter's College; Jersey City	Private	2,687	84	
Seton Hall University; South Orange	Private	5,403	76	
Stevens Institute of Technology; Hoboken	Private	1,564	54	23
Thomas Edison State College; Trenton	Public	7,975		46
Westminster Choir College of Rider University; Princeton	Private	343	68	59
William Paterson University of New Jersey; Wayne	Public	8,454	51	59
NEW MEXICO				
College of Santa Fe; Santa Fe	Private	1,312	83	61
College of the Southwest; Hobbs	Private	568	55	69
Eastern New Mexico University; Portales	Public	2,942	47	60
National American University; Albuquerque	Private			
New Mexico Highlands University; Las Vegas	Public	1,972	79	
New Mexico Institute of Mining and Technology; Socorro	Public	1,236	68	36
New Mexico State University; Las Cruces	Public	12,453	61	54
St. John's College; Santa Fe	Private	433	81	43
University of New Mexico; Albuquerque	Public	15,803	85	
University of Phoenix–New Mexico Campus; Albuquerque	Private	46,473		56
NEW YORK				
Adelphi University; Garden City	Private	3,099	70	69
Albany College of Pharmacy of Union University; Albany	Private	628	80	63
Alfred University; Alfred	Private	2,085	76	52
Audrey Cohen College; New York	Private	1,087	68	83
Bard College; Annandale-on-Hudson	Private	1,264	48	56
Barnard College; New York	Private	2,268	37	100
Bernard M. Baruch College of the City University of New York; New York	Public	13,025	23	57
Boricua College; New York	Private	1,468	47	
Briarcliffe College; Bethpage	Private	1,790	65	52
Brooklyn College of the City University of New York; Brooklyn	Public	10,094		61
Canisius College; Buffalo	Private	3,349	83	53
Cazenovia College; Cazenovia	Private	962	100	73
City College of the City University of New York; New York	Public	8,232	74	52
Clarkson University; Potsdam	Private	2,539	83	26
Colgate University; Hamilton	Private	2,773	38	51
College of Aeronautics; Flushing	Private	1,301	88	8
College of Insurance; New York	Private	246	52	49
College of Mount Saint Vincent; Riverdale	Private	1,202	70	79
College of New Rochelle; New Rochelle	Private	5,164	55	87
College of Saint Rose; Albany	Private	2,726	75	73
College of Staten Island of the City University of New York; Staten Island	Public	9,746	100	59
Columbia College; New York	Private	3,913	13	51
Columbia University, School of General Studies; New York	Private	1,117	45	55
Concordia College; Bronxville	Private	578	83	57

Institution name; city	Public or private	Students	Percent Accepted	Percent Women
Cooper Union for the Advancement of Science and Art; New York	Private	878	13%	36%
Cornell University; Ithaca	Private	13,590	31	48
Culinary Institute of America; Hyde Park	Private	2,028	41	32
D'Youville College; Buffalo	Private	976	75	75
Daemen College; Amherst	Private	1,704	74	77
DeVry Institute of Technology; Long Island City	Private	1,652	47	20
Dominican College; Orangeburg	Private	1,564	86	72
Dowling College; Oakdale	Private	3,954	89	63
Elmira College; Elmira	Private	1,440	78	70
Eugene Lang College, New School University; New York	Private	518	56	68
Excelsior College; Albany	Private	17,886	100	60
Fashion Institute of Technology; New York	Public	10,708	41	81
Five Towns College; Dix Hills	Private	907	88	37
Fordham University; New York	Private	6,989	63	59
Globe Institute of Technology; New York	Private	662	90	41
Hamilton College; Clinton	Private	1,767	39	52
Hartwick College; Oneonta	Private	1,419	89	
Hilbert College; Hamburg	Private	893	89	65
Hobart and William Smith Colleges; Geneva	Private	1,854	72	53
Hofstra University; Hempstead	Private	9,346	80	54
Houghton College; Houghton	Private	1,409	88	63
Hunter College of the City University of New York; New York	Public	15,422	53	70
Iona College; New Rochelle	Private	3,422	78	52
Ithaca College; Ithaca	Private	5,906	70	56
Jewish Theological Seminary of America; New York	Private	177	60	63
John Jay College of Criminal Justice of the City University of New York; New York	Public	9,493	73	
Juilliard School; New York	Private	494	8	51
Kehilath Yakov Rabbinical Seminary; Brooklyn	Private		75	
Keuka College; Keuka Park	Private	952	86	72
Laboratory Institute of Merchandising; New York	Private	285	74	98
Le Moyne College; Syracuse	Private	2,399	84	59
Lehman College of the City University of New York; Bronx	Public	7,228		
Long Island University, Brooklyn Campus; Brooklyn	Private	5,554	79	71
Long Island University, C.W. Post Campus; Brookville	Private	6,548	85	
Long Island University, Southampton College; Southampton	Private	2,528	76	60
Machzikei Hadath Rabbinical College; Brooklyn	Private			
Manhattan College; Riverdale	Private	2,593	63	47
Manhattan School of Music; New York	Private	360	32	50
Manhattanville College; Purchase	Private	1,400	66	
Mannes College of Music, New School University; New York	Private	134	16	63
Marist College; Poughkeepsie	Private	4,713	53	58
Marymount College; Tarrytown	Private	938	81	96
Marymount Manhattan College; New York	Private	2,497	65	79
Medaille College; Buffalo	Private	1,444	70	70
Medgar Evers College of the City University of New York; Brooklyn	Public	4,700		78
Mercy College; Dobbs Ferry	Private	6,943		
Molloy College; Rockville Centre	Private	1,994	90	77
Mount Saint Mary College; Newburgh	Private	1,598	82	
Nazareth College of Rochester; Rochester	Private	1,810	78	74
New York Institute of Technology; Old Westbury	Private	5,290	75	39
New York School of Interior Design; New York	Private	686		86
New York University; New York	Private	18,628	29	60
Niagara University; Niagara Falls	Private	2,473	84	62
Nyack College; Nyack	Private	1,724	65	59
Pace University, New York City Campus; New York	Private	5,755	75	62
Pace University, Pleasantville/Briarcliff; Pleasantville	Private	3,394	82	57
Parsons School of Design, New School Univ.; New York	Private	2,433	41	73
Plattsburgh State University of New York; Plattsburgh	Public	5,377	63	57
Polytechnic University, Brooklyn Campus; Brooklyn	Private	1,775	66	19
Practical Bible College; Bible School Park	Private	252	53	40
Pratt Institute; Brooklyn	Private	2,922	43	51
Purchase College, State University of New York; Purchase	Public	3,941	33	56
Queens College of the City University of New York; Flushing	Public	11,566	49	63
Rabbinical Academy Mesivta Rabbi Chaim Berlin; Brooklyn	Private		100	
Rabbinical College Bobover Yeshiva B'nei Zion; Brooklyn	Private		81	
Rabbinical Seminary Adas Yereim; Brooklyn	Private			
Rensselaer Polytechnic Institute; Troy	Private	5,167	73	24
Roberts Wesleyan College; Rochester	Private	1,208	92	65
Rochester Institute of Technology; Rochester	Private	11,100	74	33
Russell Sage College; Troy	Private	819	76	100
Sarah Lawrence College; Bronxville	Private	1,139	38	75
School of Visual Arts; New York	Private	4,986	60	54

Institution name; city	Public or private	Students	Percent Accepted	Percent Women
Siena College; Loudonville	Private	3,306	67%	52%
Skidmore College; Saratoga Springs	Private	2,451	43	61
St. Bonaventure University; St. Bonaventure	Private	2,203	89	54
St. Francis College; Brooklyn Heights	Private	2,332	75	60
St. John Fisher College; Rochester	Private	2,175	73	62
St. John's University; Jamaica	Private	14,229	80	57
St. Joseph's College, New York; Brooklyn	Private	1,256	56	78
St. Joseph's College, Suffolk Campus; Patchogue	Private	3,115	75	78
St. Lawrence University; Canton	Private	1,969	69	53
St. Thomas Aquinas College; Sparkill	Private	2,015	75	
State University of New York at Albany; Albany	Public	11,780	58	49
State University of New York at Binghamton; Binghamton	Public	9,858	42	54
State University of New York at Farmingdale; Farmingdale	Public	5,045	69	44
State University of New York at New Paltz; New Paltz	Public	6,028	46	64
State University of New York at Oswego; Oswego	Public	6,999	57	54
State University of New York College at Brockport; Brockport	Public	6,751	54	58
State University of New York College at Buffalo; Buffalo	Public	9,386	59	58
State University of New York College at Cortland; Cortland	Public	5,648	62	58
State University of New York College at Fredonia; Fredonia	Public	4,743	60	59
State University of New York College at Geneseo; Geneseo	Public	5,197	47	66
State University of New York College at Old Westbury; Old Westbury	Public	2,992	56	60
State University of New York College at Oneonta; Oneonta	Public	5,341	71	60
State University of New York College at Potsdam; Potsdam	Public	3,580	69	60
State University of New York College of Agriculture and Technology at Cobleskill; Cobleskill	Public	2,301	34	46
State University of New York College of Environmental Science and Forestry; Syracuse	Public	1,166	57	39
State University of New York College of Technology at Canton; Canton	Public	2,126	90	50
State University of New York Empire State College; Saratoga Springs	Public	7,672		54
State University of New York Maritime College; Throggs Neck	Public	623	76	
Stony Brook University, State University of New York; Stony Brook	Public	13,257	56	49
Syracuse University; Syracuse	Private	10,740	58	54
Talmudical Seminary Oholei Torah; Brooklyn	Private			
Touro College; New York	Private	6,119	74	69
Union College; Schenectady	Private	2,124	47	48
United States Merchant Marine Academy; Kings Point	Public	921	24	10
United States Military Academy; West Point	Public	4,088	14	16
University at Buffalo, The State Univ. of New York; Buffalo	Public	16,683	68	46
University of Rochester; Rochester	Private	4,528	50	46
Utica College of Syracuse University; Utica	Private	2,105	82	62
Vassar College; Poughkeepsie	Private	2,400	35	61
Wadhams Hall Seminary-College; Ogdensburg	Private	21	100	0
Wagner College; Staten Island	Private	1,668	69	
Webb Institute; Glen Cove	Private	74	41	19
Wells College; Aurora	Private	462	89	100
Yeshiva Karlin Stolin Rabbinical Institute; Brooklyn	Private	38		0
Yeshiva University; New York	Private	2,529	79	44
York College of the City University of New York; Jamaica	Public	5,389	71	70
NORTH CAROLINA				
Appalachian State University; Boone	Public	12,112	70	51
Barber-Scotia College; Concord	Private	543	31	
Barton College; Wilson	Private	1,202	87	69
Belmont Abbey College; Belmont	Private	918	31	56
Bennett College; Greensboro	Private	619	16	100
Brevard College; Brevard	Private	710	89	46
Campbell University; Buies Creek	Private	2,360	75	53
Catawba College; Salisbury	Private	1,323	83	51
Chowan College; Murfreesboro	Private	773	71	45
Davidson College; Davidson	Private	1,679	36	50
Duke University; Durham	Private	6,325	26	48
East Carolina University; Greenville	Public	15,018	74	58
Elizabeth City State University; Elizabeth City	Public	1,920	27	
Elon University; Elon College	Private	3,900	61	61
Gardner-Webb University; Boiling Springs	Private	2,474	81	64
Greensboro College; Greensboro	Private	973	75	52
Guilford College; Greensboro	Private	1,246	78	53
Heritage Bible College; Dunn	Private	76		25
High Point University; High Point	Private	2,623	86	61
John Wesley College; High Point	Private	172	64	42
Johnson C. Smith University; Charlotte	Private	1,585	33	60
Lees-McRae College; Banner Elk	Private	712	92	54
Lenoir-Rhyne College; Hickory	Private	1,353	85	

Institution name; city	Public or private	Students	Percent Accepted	Percent Women
Livingstone College; Salisbury	Private	917	71%	48%
Mars Hill College; Mars Hill	Private	1,224	90	57
Meredith College; Raleigh	Private	2,432	80	100
Methodist College; Fayetteville	Private	2,134	65	46
Montreat College; Montreat	Private	1,064	86	57
Mount Olive College; Mount Olive	Private	1,713	87	54
North Carolina Agricultural and Technical State University; Greensboro	Public	6,850	93	53
North Carolina Central University; Durham	Public	4,057	74	64
North Carolina School of the Arts; Winston-Salem	Public	692	42	41
North Carolina State University; Raleigh	Public	21,990	65	42
North Carolina Wesleyan College; Rocky Mount	Private	1,956	91	56
Peace College; Raleigh	Private	604	83	100
Pfeiffer University; Misenheimer	Private	985	84	57
Piedmont Baptist College; Winston-Salem	Private	302	59	40
Queens College; Charlotte	Private	1,156	77	76
Roanoke Bible College; Elizabeth City	Private	159	62	43
Saint Augustine's College; Raleigh	Private	1,465	45	
Salem College; Winston-Salem	Private	898	81	98
Shaw University; Raleigh	Private	2,394	67	66
St. Andrews Presbyterian College; Laurinburg	Private	638	81	60
University of North Carolina at Asheville; Asheville	Public	3,187	64	57
University of North Carolina at Chapel Hill; Chapel Hill	Public	15,608	37	61
University of North Carolina at Charlotte; Charlotte	Public	14,388	71	54
University of North Carolina at Greensboro; Greensboro	Public	10,121	75	67
University of North Carolina at Pembroke; Pembroke	Public	3,076	86	63
University of North Carolina at Wilmington; Wilmington	Public	9,138	61	60
Wake Forest University; Winston-Salem	Private	3,946	49	51
Warren Wilson College; Asheville	Private	728	81	63
Western Carolina University; Cullowhee	Public	5,611	87	52
Wingate University; Wingate	Private	1,179	83	49
Winston-Salem State University; Winston-Salem	Public	2,704	67	67
NORTH DAKOTA				
Dickinson State University; Dickinson	Public	2,012	100	58
Jamestown College; Jamestown	Private	1,195	99	58
Mayville State University; Mayville	Public	776	96	55
Minot State University; Minot	Public	2,907	97	63
North Dakota State University; Fargo	Public	8,965	78	43
Trinity Bible College; Ellendale	Private	360	55	49
University of Mary; Bismarck	Private	1,908		
University of North Dakota; Grand Forks	Public	9,122	59	48
Valley City State University; Valley City	Public	1,090	94	55
OHIO				
Antioch College; Yellow Springs	Private	618	80	66
Art Academy of Cincinnati; Cincinnati	Private	230	83	58
Ashland University; Ashland	Private	2,819	90	57
Baldwin-Wallace College; Berea	Private	4,043	82	62
Bluffton College; Bluffton	Private	1,000	86	54
Bowling Green State University; Bowling Green	Public	15,494	88	57
Bryant and Stratton College; Cleveland	Private	205	93	40
Capital University; Columbus	Private	2,738	81	63
Case Western Reserve University; Cleveland	Private	3,434	71	39
Cedarville University; Cedarville	Private	2,849	74	54
Central State University; Wilberforce	Public	1,101	34	54
Cincinnati Bible College and Seminary; Cincinnati	Private	639	97	44
Circleville Bible College; Circleville	Private	216	65	45
Cleveland College of Jewish Studies; Beachwood	Private	17	75	88
Cleveland Institute of Music; Cleveland	Private	221	29	
Cleveland State University; Cleveland	Public	10,132	86	55
College of Mount St. Joseph; Cincinnati	Private	2,056	85	71
College of Wooster; Wooster	Private	1,837	74	53
Columbus College of Art and Design; Columbus	Private	1,546	70	51
David N. Myers College; Cleveland	Private	1,158	65	70
Defiance College; Defiance	Private	868	78	55
Denison University; Granville	Private	2,108	68	57
DeVry Institute of Technology; Columbus	Private	3,570	62	25
Franciscan University of Steubenville; Steubenville	Private	1,701	90	60
Franklin University; Columbus	Private	4,323	100	
God's Bible School and College; Cincinnati	Private	238		
Heidelberg College; Tiffin	Private	1,367	87	53
Hiram College; Hiram	Private	1,199	87	57
John Carroll University; University Heights	Private	3,525	87	54
Kent State University; Kent	Public	17,580	92	60
Kenyon College; Gambier	Private	1,599	65	55
Lake Erie College; Painesville	Private	560	83	77

Institution name; city	Public or private	Students	Percent Accepted	Percent Women
Lourdes College; Sylvania	Private	1,270	66%	81%
Malone College; Canton	Private	1,945	84	62
Marietta College; Marietta	Private	1,212	94	52
Miami University; Oxford	Public	14,914	69	55
Mount Carmel College of Nursing; Columbus	Private	335		
Mount Union College; Alliance	Private	2,334	84	57
Mount Vernon Nazarene College; Mount Vernon	Private	1,888	88	58
Muskingum College; New Concord	Private	1,562	85	52
Notre Dame College of Ohio; South Euclid	Private	728	55	
Oberlin College; Oberlin	Private	2,932	43	59
Ohio Dominican College; Columbus	Private	2,085	67	69
Ohio Northern University; Ada	Private	2,668	95	50
Ohio State University; Columbus	Public	35,749	72	49
Ohio State University at Lima; Lima	Public	1,482	72	63
Ohio State University–Mansfield Campus; Mansfield	Public	1,583	94	
Ohio State University–Newark Campus; Newark	Public		97	
Ohio University; Athens	Public	16,511	77	55
Ohio University–Chillicothe; Chillicothe	Public	1,638	94	
Ohio University–Eastern; St. Clairsville	Public	931		68
Ohio University–Lancaster; Lancaster	Public	1,409		
Ohio University–Zanesville; Zanesville	Public	1,188	100	68
Ohio Wesleyan University; Delaware	Private	1,880	81	52
Otterbein College; Westerville	Private	2,525	85	64
Pontifical College Josephinum; Columbus	Private	50	86	
Shawnee State University; Portsmouth	Public	3,280	100	63
Tiffin University; Tiffin	Private	1,299	80	52
Union Institute; Cincinnati	Private	690	83	66
University of Akron; Akron	Public	18,583	90	54
University of Cincinnati; Cincinnati	Public	20,039	82	49
University of Dayton; Dayton	Private	7,122	79	51
University of Findlay; Findlay	Private	3,459	81	57
University of Phoenix–Ohio Campus; Independence	Private	46,473		56
University of Rio Grande; Rio Grande	Private	1,934	100	
University of Toledo; Toledo	Public	15,950	99	52
Urbana University; Urbana	Private	1,310	73	51
Ursuline College; Pepper Pike	Private	1,016	94	93
Walsh University; North Canton	Private	1,404	82	60
Wilberforce University; Wilberforce	Private	908	22	59
Wilmington College; Wilmington	Private	1,262	81	54
Wittenberg University; Springfield	Private	2,274	88	57
Wright State University; Dayton	Public	11,344	91	57
Xavier University; Cincinnati	Private	4,019	88	59
Youngstown State University; Youngstown	Public	10,619	62	53
OKLAHOMA				
American Bible College and Seminary; Oklahoma City	Private	292		45
Cameron University; Lawton	Public	4,458	91	56
East Central University; Ada	Public	3,427		60
Hillsdale Free Will Baptist College; Moore	Private	256		37
Langston University; Langston	Public	3,354	18	58
Mid-America Bible College; Oklahoma City	Private	613	100	48
Northeastern State University; Tahlequah	Public	7,215	74	60
Northwestern Oklahoma State University; Alva	Public	1,746	100	54
Oklahoma Baptist University; Shawnee	Private	1,993	86	56
Oklahoma Christian University; Oklahoma City	Private	1,735	90	
Oklahoma City University; Oklahoma City	Private	2,062	82	58
Oklahoma Panhandle State University; Goodwell	Public	1,178	100	53
Oklahoma State University; Stillwater	Public	16,659	92	48
Oklahoma Wesleyan College; Bartlesville	Private	731		
Oral Roberts University; Tulsa	Private	3,064	81	58
Rogers State University; Claremore	Public	2,620	100	64
Southeastern Oklahoma State University; Durant	Public	3,438	77	54
Southwestern College of Christian Ministries; Bethany	Private	128		45
Southwestern Oklahoma State University; Weatherford	Public	4,256	93	
St. Gregory's University; Shawnee	Private	754	77	53
University of Central Oklahoma; Edmond	Public	11,752	95	56
University of Oklahoma; Norman	Public	17,707	86	48
University of Phoenix–Oklahoma City; Oklahoma City	Private	46,473		56
University of Phoenix–Tulsa; Tulsa	Private	46,473		56
University of Science and Arts of Oklahoma; Chickasha	Public	1,409	83	64
University of Tulsa; Tulsa	Private	2,874	75	52
OREGON				
Art Institute of Portland; Portland	Private	668		55
Cascade College; Portland	Private	321	100	53
Concordia University; Portland	Private	924	67	64
Eastern Oregon University; La Grande	Public	2,549	92	58

Institution name; city	Public or private	Students	Percent Accepted	Percent Women
Eugene Bible College; Eugene	Private	210	60%	47%
George Fox University; Newberg	Private	1,709	90	59
Lewis & Clark College; Portland	Private	1,709	68	60
Linfield College; McMinnville	Private	1,534	92	56
Multnomah Bible College and Biblical Seminary; Portland	Private	590	80	46
Northwest Christian College; Eugene	Private	463	100	
Oregon College of Art and Craft; Portland	Private	95	67	73
Oregon Institute of Technology; Klamath Falls	Public	2,831	77	43
Oregon State University; Corvallis	Public	13,776	87	46
Pacific Northwest College of Art; Portland	Private	317	86	61
Pacific University; Forest Grove	Private	1,094	86	61
Portland State University; Portland	Public	13,625	86	56
Reed College; Portland	Private	1,366	74	53
Southern Oregon University; Ashland	Public	4,879	96	57
University of Oregon; Eugene	Public	14,076	90	53
University of Phoenix–Oregon Campus; Portland	Private	46,473		56
University of Portland; Portland	Private	2,512	88	57
Warner Pacific College; Portland	Private	634	79	64
Western Baptist College; Salem	Private	696	72	58
Western Oregon University; Monmouth	Public	4,201	93	60
Willamette University; Salem	Private	1,749	90	55
PENNSYLVANIA				
Albright College; Reading	Private	1,728	76	57
Allegheny College; Meadville	Private	1,904	76	52
Alvernia College; Reading	Private	1,506	76	66
Arcadia University; Glenside	Private	1,628	76	74
Baptist Bible College of Pennsylvania; Clarks Summit	Private	592	79	59
Bloomsburg University of Pennsylvania; Bloomsburg	Public	6,843	61	61
Bryn Athyn College of the New Church; Bryn Athyn	Private	129	100	58
Bryn Mawr College; Bryn Mawr	Private	1,358	61	99
Bucknell University; Lewisburg	Private	3,426	42	48
Cabrini College; Radnor	Private	1,654	87	66
California University of Pennsylvania; California	Public	5,004	78	53
Carlow College; Pittsburgh	Private	1,631	70	93
Carnegie Mellon University; Pittsburgh	Private	5,224	36	37
Cedar Crest College; Allentown	Private	1,554	73	95
Chatham College; Pittsburgh	Private	587	87	99
Chestnut Hill College; Philadelphia	Private	936	75	85
Cheyney University of Pennsylvania; Cheyney	Public	1,132	82	56
Clarion University of Pennsylvania; Clarion	Public	5,687	86	61
College Misericordia; Dallas	Private	1,640	84	73
Curtis Institute of Music; Philadelphia	Private	148	7	
Delaware Valley College; Doylestown	Private	1,838	82	51
DeSales University; Center Valley	Private	1,869	72	57
Dickinson College; Carlisle	Private	2,115	64	61
Duquesne University; Pittsburgh	Private	5,499	84	58
Eastern College; St. Davids	Private	1,400	84	
Edinboro University of Pennsylvania; Edinboro	Public	6,486	80	57
Elizabethtown College; Elizabethtown	Private	1,825	77	65
Franklin and Marshall College; Lancaster	Private	1,892	56	50
Gannon University; Erie	Private	2,470	90	59
Geneva College; Beaver Falls	Private	2,047	78	56
Gettysburg College; Gettysburg	Private	2,218	68	52
Gratz College; Melrose Park	Private	11	75	64
Grove City College; Grove City	Private	2,326	51	50
Gwynedd-Mercy College; Gwynedd Valley	Private	1,665	79	75
Haverford College; Haverford	Private	1,135	32	52
Holy Family College; Philadelphia	Private	1,882	89	77
Immaculata College; Immaculata	Private	2,587	86	86
Indiana University of Pennsylvania; Indiana	Public	11,735	58	56
Juniata College; Huntingdon	Private	1,291	81	57
King's College; Wilkes-Barre	Private	2,090	86	52
Kutztown University of Pennsylvania; Kutztown	Public	7,068	73	60
La Roche College; Pittsburgh	Private	1,627	86	63
La Salle University; Philadelphia	Private	3,961	72	57
Lancaster Bible College; Lancaster	Private	686	82	54
Lebanon Valley College; Annville	Private	1,853	73	60
Lehigh University; Bethlehem	Private	4,722	46	41
Lincoln University; Lincoln University	Public	1,454	53	59
Lock Haven University of Pennsylvania; Lock Haven	Public	3,996	77	57
Lycoming College; Williamsport	Private	1,402	79	56
Mansfield University of Pennsylvania; Mansfield	Public	2,890	78	59
Marywood University; Scranton	Private	1,609	81	73
MCP Hahnemann University; Philadelphia	Private	588	69	65
Mercyhurst College; Erie	Private	3,058	80	60

Institution name; city	Public or private	Students	Percent Accepted	Percent Women
Messiah College; Grantham	Private	2,797	78%	61%
Millersville University of Pennsylvania; Millersville	Public	6,497	71	58
Moore College of Art and Design; Philadelphia	Private	530	57	100
Moravian College; Bethlehem	Private		69	
Mount Aloysius College; Cresson	Private	1,297	53	71
Muhlenberg College; Allentown	Private	2,470	44	58
Neumann College; Aston	Private	1,445	87	67
Peirce College; Philadelphia	Private	2,334	64	81
Pennsylvania College of Technology; Williamsport	Public	5,320	57	33
Pennsylvania State University Abington College; Abington	Public	3,048	81	50
Pennsylvania State University Altoona College; Altoona	Public	3,749	84	50
Pennsylvania State University, The Behrend College; Erie	Public	3,606	73	38
Pennsylvania State University Berks Campus of the Berks–Lehigh Valley College; Reading	Public	2,186	85	39
Pennsylvania State University Harrisburg Campus of the Capital College; Middletown	Public	1,865	100	52
Pennsylvania State University Lehigh Valley Campus of the Berks-Lehigh Valley College; Fogelsville	Public	665	83	38
Pennsylvania State University Schuylkill Campus of the Capital College; Schuylkill Haven	Public	1,096	89	54
Pennsylvania State University University Park Campus; State College	Public	34,406	48	47
Philadelphia Biblical University; Langhorne	Private	1,069	67	53
Philadelphia University; Philadelphia	Private	2,809	79	65
Point Park College; Pittsburgh	Private	2,417	81	54
Robert Morris College; Moon Township	Private	3,814	72	49
Rosemont College; Rosemont	Private	892	97	90
Saint Francis University; Loretto	Private	1,174	87	
Saint Joseph's University; Philadelphia	Private	4,517	60	56
Saint Vincent College; Latrobe	Private	1,206	84	49
Seton Hill College; Greensburg	Private	1,141	79	83
Shippensburg University of Pennsylvania; Shippensburg	Public	5,990	65	54
Slippery Rock University of Pennsylvania; Slippery Rock	Public	6,294	83	57
St. Charles Borromeo Seminary, Overbrook; Wynnewood	Private	298	100	55
Susquehanna University; Selinsgrove	Private	1,829	75	58
Swarthmore College; Swarthmore	Private	1,428	24	53
Temple University; Philadelphia	Public	18,394	71	58
Thiel College; Greenville	Private	1,039	78	53
University of Pennsylvania; Philadelphia	Private	9,687	23	48
University of Phoenix–Philadelphia Campus; Wayne	Private	46,473		56
University of Phoenix–Pittsburgh Campus; Pittsburgh	Private	46,473		56
University of Pittsburgh; Pittsburgh	Public	17,424	62	53
University of Pittsburgh at Bradford; Bradford	Public	1,204	82	59
University of Pittsburgh at Greensburg; Greensburg	Public	1,587	80	55
University of Pittsburgh at Johnstown; Johnstown	Public	3,031	83	55
University of Scranton; Scranton	Private	3,970	84	58
University of the Arts; Philadelphia	Private	1,919	54	53
University of the Sciences in Philadelphia; Philadelphia	Private	2,042	82	67
Ursinus College; Collegeville	Private	1,290	72	54
Villanova University; Villanova	Private	7,069	52	50
Washington & Jefferson College; Washington	Private	1,241	79	49
Waynesburg College; Waynesburg	Private	1,385	91	54
West Chester University of Pennsylvania; West Chester	Public	10,326	57	60
Widener University; Chester	Private	2,235	76	45
Wilkes University; Wilkes-Barre	Private	1,762	84	48
Wilson College; Chambersburg	Private	818	90	79
York College of Pennsylvania; York	Private	5,073	67	59
RHODE ISLAND				
Brown University; Providence	Private	6,029	16	53
Bryant College; Smithfield	Private	2,901	73	41
Johnson & Wales University; Providence	Private	8,533	82	48
Providence College; Providence	Private	4,405	57	58
Rhode Island College; Providence	Public	6,917	72	68
Rhode Island School of Design; Providence	Private	1,829	35	61
Roger Williams University; Bristol	Private	3,676	86	51
Salve Regina University; Newport	Private	1,835	67	69
University of Rhode Island; Kingston	Public	10,647	75	56
SOUTH CAROLINA				
Allen University; Columbia	Private	466	81	60
Anderson College; Anderson	Private	1,398	78	62
Charleston Southern University; Charleston	Private	2,315	93	59
Citadel, The Military College of South Carolina; Charleston	Public	1,995	81	7
Claflin University; Orangeburg	Private	1,315	56	
Clemson University; Clemson	Public	14,066	64	45
Coastal Carolina University; Conway	Public	4,405	72	56

Institution name; city	Public or private	Students	Percent Accepted	Percent Women
Coker College; Hartsville	Private	445	88%	64%
College of Charleston; Charleston	Public	9,750	67	63
Columbia College; Columbia	Private	1,205	79	
Columbia International University; Columbia	Private	549	61	55
Converse College; Spartanburg	Private	725	81	100
Erskine College; Due West	Private	502	78	61
Francis Marion University; Florence	Public	2,795	77	61
Furman University; Greenville	Private	2,789	60	56
Lander University; Greenwood	Public	2,436	81	63
Limestone College; Gaffney	Private	1,967	70	56
Morris College; Sumter	Private	940	48	66
Newberry College; Newberry	Private	727	86	46
North Greenville College; Tigerville	Private	1,282	66	46
Presbyterian College; Clinton	Private	1,147	82	55
South Carolina State University; Orangeburg	Public	3,639	59	
Southern Methodist College; Orangeburg	Private	82		
Southern Wesleyan University; Central	Private	1,724	66	62
University of South Carolina; Columbia	Public	15,266	69	55
University of South Carolina Aiken; Aiken	Public	3,148	64	66
University of South Carolina Spartanburg; Spartanburg	Public	3,585	62	65
Voorhees College; Denmark	Private	677	80	
Winthrop University; Rock Hill	Public	4,650	72	69
Wofford College; Spartanburg	Private	1,087	83	47
SOUTH DAKOTA				
Augustana College; Sioux Falls	Private	1,728	83	64
Black Hills State University; Spearfish	Public	3,549	66	62
Colorado Technical Univ. Sioux Falls Campus; Sioux Falls	Private	773	97	56
Dakota State University; Madison	Public	1,632	91	49
Dakota Wesleyan University; Mitchell	Private	676	87	61
Huron University; Huron	Private	598	39	52
Mount Marty College; Yankton	Private	1,044	93	67
National American University; Rapid City	Private	1,005		47
Northern State University; Aberdeen	Public	2,861	91	60
Oglala Lakota College; Kyle	Public			
Presentation College; Aberdeen	Private	462	100	
Sinte Gleska University; Rosebud	Private	907		
South Dakota School of Mines and Technology; Rapid City	Public	2,023	95	30
South Dakota State University; Brookings	Public	7,504	94	51
University of Sioux Falls; Sioux Falls	Private	1,070	94	56
University of South Dakota; Vermillion	Public	5,148		57
TENNESSEE				
American Baptist College of American Baptist Theological Seminary; Nashville	Private	106	100	
Aquinas College; Nashville	Private	435	9	
Austin Peay State University; Clarksville	Public	6,658	48	59
Belmont University; Nashville	Private	2,507	74	62
Bethel College; McKenzie	Private	776	62	50
Bryan College; Dayton	Private	562	37	
Carson-Newman College; Jefferson City	Private	1,994	90	58
Christian Brothers University; Memphis	Private	1,710	82	55
Crichton College; Memphis	Private	973	63	62
East Tennessee State University; Johnson City	Public	9,125	79	57
Fisk University; Nashville	Private	839	41	70
Free Will Baptist Bible College; Nashville	Private	318		
Freed-Hardeman University; Henderson	Private	1,438	71	54
Johnson Bible College; Knoxville	Private	548	85	48
King College; Bristol	Private	602	64	55
Lambuth University; Jackson	Private	979	72	57
Lane College; Jackson	Private	702	55	49
Lee University; Cleveland	Private	3,236	91	57
LeMoyne-Owen College; Memphis	Private	1,013	100	66
Lincoln Memorial University; Harrogate	Private	886	77	69
Lipscomb University; Nashville	Private	2,307	83	56
Martin Methodist College; Pulaski	Private	582	97	62
Maryville College; Maryville	Private	982	81	56
Memphis College of Art; Memphis	Private	255	83	52
Middle Tennessee State University; Murfreesboro	Public	17,247	79	54
Milligan College; Milligan College	Private	790	69	60
Rhodes College; Memphis	Private	1,537	70	57
Southern Adventist University; Collegedale	Private	1,939	72	54
Tennessee State University; Nashville	Public	7,142	54	62
Tennessee Technological University; Cookeville	Public	6,876	94	47
Tennessee Temple University; Chattanooga	Private	757	99	
Tennessee Wesleyan College; Athens	Private	795	29	63
Trevecca Nazarene University; Nashville	Private	1,021	82	59

Institution name; city	Public or private	Students	Percent Accepted	Percent Women
Tusculum College; Greeneville	Private	1,377	88%	55%
Union University; Jackson	Private	1,971	83	61
University of Memphis; Memphis	Public	15,296	71	58
University of Tennessee; Knoxville	Public	20,009	62	51
University of Tennessee at Chattanooga; Chattanooga	Public	6,993	56	57
University of Tennessee at Martin; Martin	Public	5,478	61	57
University of the South; Sewanee	Private	1,385	68	53
Vanderbilt University; Nashville	Private	5,935	55	53
TEXAS				
Abilene Christian University; Abilene	Private	4,231	72	55
Angelo State University; San Angelo	Public	5,899	76	55
Arlington Baptist College; Arlington	Private	220	100	37
Austin College; Sherman	Private	1,196	84	55
Baylor University; Waco	Private	11,806	84	58
Concordia University at Austin; Austin	Private	785	64	55
Criswell College; Dallas	Private	336		
Dallas Baptist University; Dallas	Private	3,190	43	62
Dallas Christian College; Dallas	Private	254	64	47
DeVry Institute of Technology; Irving	Private	3,462	64	29
East Texas Baptist University; Marshall	Private	1,402	92	55
Hardin-Simmons University; Abilene	Private	1,910	45	54
Houston Baptist University; Houston	Private	1,867	70	70
Howard Payne University; Brownwood	Private	1,480	80	47
Lamar University; Beaumont	Public	7,215	74	59
LeTourneau University; Longview	Private	2,708	86	47
Lubbock Christian University; Lubbock	Private	1,511	77	58
McMurry University; Abilene	Private	1,344	70	50
Midwestern State University; Wichita Falls	Public	5,151	62	57
Northwood University, Texas Campus; Cedar Hill	Private	1,014	68	56
Our Lady of the Lake Univ. of San Antonio; San Antonio	Private	2,233	65	77
Paul Quinn College; Dallas	Private		72	
Prairie View A&M University; Prairie View	Public	5,285	97	56
Rice University; Houston	Private	2,658	23	47
Sam Houston State University; Huntsville	Public	10,882	81	57
Schreiner University; Kerrville	Private	762	72	60
Southern Methodist University; Dallas	Private	5,662	82	55
Southwest Texas State University; San Marcos	Public	19,412	64	55
Southwestern Adventist University; Keene	Private	1,156	62	57
Southwestern Assemblies of God University; Waxahachie	Private	1,666		
Southwestern Christian College; Terrell	Private		90	
Southwestern University; Georgetown	Private	1,312	59	58
St. Edward's University; Austin	Private	3,105	78	55
Stephen F. Austin State University; Nacogdoches	Public	10,046	71	57
Sul Ross State University; Alpine	Public	1,463	99	
Tarleton State University; Stephenville	Public	6,345	71	54
Texas A&M International University; Laredo	Public	2,239	92	64
Texas A&M University; College Station	Public	36,229	66	49
Texas A&M University at Galveston; Galveston	Public	1,363	90	51
Texas A&M University–Commerce; Commerce	Public	4,314	60	57
Texas A&M University–Corpus Christi; Corpus Christi	Public	5,329	87	60
Texas Christian University; Fort Worth	Private	6,675	76	59
Texas Lutheran University; Seguin	Private	1,506	81	53
Texas Southern University; Houston	Public	5,124	49	56
Texas Tech University; Lubbock	Public	20,518	70	46
Texas Wesleyan University; Fort Worth	Private	2,015	79	65
Trinity University; San Antonio	Private	2,356	65	52
University of Dallas; Irving	Private	1,200	76	
University of Houston; Houston	Public	24,350	81	53
University of Houston–Downtown; Houston	Public	8,932	100	59
University of Mary Hardin-Baylor; Belton	Private	2,401	60	62
University of North Texas; Denton	Public	21,059	75	55
University of St. Thomas; Houston	Private	1,904	78	65
University of Texas at Arlington; Arlington	Public	15,449	86	53
University of Texas at Austin; Austin	Public	38,162	62	50
University of Texas at Dallas; Richardson	Public	6,560	49	47
University of Texas at El Paso; El Paso	Public	12,955	93	54
University of Texas at San Antonio; San Antonio	Public	16,026	99	55
University of Texas at Tyler; Tyler	Public	2,602	45	66
University of Texas of the Permian Basin; Odessa	Public	1,656	89	64
University of Texas–Pan American; Edinburg	Public	11,187	76	58
University of the Incarnate Word; San Antonio	Private	3,003	94	68
Wayland Baptist University; Plainview	Private	4,637	99	42
West Texas A&M University; Canyon	Public	5,623	72	55
Wiley College; Marshall	Private	552	71	56

Institution name; city	Public or private	Students	Percent Accepted	Percent Women
UTAH				
Brigham Young University; Provo	Private	29,688	64%	51%
Southern Utah University; Cedar City	Public	5,729	84	56
University of Phoenix–Utah Campus; Salt Lake City	Private	46,473		56
University of Utah; Salt Lake City	Public	20,963	94	46
Utah State University; Logan	Public	17,903	98	52
Weber State University; Ogden	Public	15,854	100	52
Western Governors University; Salt Lake City	Private	357		
Westminster College; Salt Lake City	Private	1,878	86	63
VERMONT				
Bennington College; Bennington	Private	545	70	69
Castleton State College; Castleton	Public	1,507	85	58
Champlain College; Burlington	Private	2,530	77	55
College of St. Joseph; Rutland	Private	371	95	66
Goddard College; Plainfield	Private	335	75	63
Green Mountain College; Poultney	Private	672	65	49
Johnson State College; Johnson	Public	1,284	83	61
Lyndon State College; Lyndonville	Public	1,153	93	45
Marlboro College; Marlboro	Private	321	70	59
Middlebury College; Middlebury	Private	2,278	25	51
Norwich University; Northfield	Private	2,180	89	39
Saint Michael's College; Colchester	Private	2,073	71	55
Southern Vermont College; Bennington	Private	479	75	64
Sterling College; Craftsbury Common	Private	74	77	49
University of Vermont; Burlington	Public	8,618	80	56
Vermont Technical College; Randolph Center	Public	1,145	71	31
VIRGINIA				
American Military University; Manassas Park	Private	802	95	14
Art Institute of Washington; Arlington	Private			
Averett University; Danville	Private	1,707	82	60
Bridgewater College; Bridgewater	Private	1,223	92	57
Christendom College; Front Royal	Private	286	82	57
Christopher Newport University; Newport News	Public	5,101	59	61
College of William and Mary; Williamsburg	Public	5,585	41	57
Eastern Mennonite University; Harrisonburg	Private	1,086	83	58
Emory & Henry College; Emory	Private	975	74	53
Ferrum College; Ferrum	Private	920	81	41
George Mason University; Fairfax	Public	15,185	61	56
Hampden-Sydney College; Hampden-Sydney	Private	976	72	0
Hampton University; Hampton	Private	4,891	48	61
Hollins University; Roanoke	Private	796	81	100
James Madison University; Harrisonburg	Public	14,280	64	58
Liberty University; Lynchburg	Private	5,403	60	51
Longwood College; Farmville	Public	3,387	77	65
Lynchburg College; Lynchburg	Private	1,748	82	
Mary Baldwin College; Staunton	Private	1,388	93	95
Mary Washington College; Fredericksburg	Public	4,103	56	69
Marymount University; Arlington	Private	2,004	78	72
Norfolk State University; Norfolk	Public	5,890	82	64
Old Dominion University; Norfolk	Public	12,786	70	57
Radford University; Radford	Public	7,622	76	60
Randolph-Macon College; Ashland	Private	1,171	72	51
Randolph-Macon Woman's College; Lynchburg	Private	748	82	100
Roanoke College; Salem	Private	1,677	81	61
Saint Paul's College; Lawrenceville	Private	531	88	
Shenandoah University; Winchester	Private	1,339	97	57
Sweet Briar College; Sweet Briar	Private	749	89	95
University of Richmond; Richmond	Private	2,910	42	51
University of Virginia; Charlottesville	Public	13,712	39	54
University of Virginia's College at Wise; Wise	Public	1,447	73	56
Virginia Commonwealth University; Richmond	Public	16,505	76	60
Virginia Intermont College; Bristol	Private	835	69	75
Virginia Military Institute; Lexington	Public	1,300	66	5
Virginia Polytechnic Institute and State Univ.; Blacksburg	Public	21,419	63	41
Virginia State University; Petersburg	Public	3,473	89	56
Virginia Union University; Richmond	Private	1,500		
Virginia Wesleyan College; Norfolk	Private	1,421	95	68
Washington and Lee University; Lexington	Private	1,736	35	46
WASHINGTON				
Central Washington University; Ellensburg	Public	7,604	85	54
Cornish College of the Arts; Seattle	Private	659	79	61
Eastern Washington University; Cheney	Public	7,149	89	58
Evergreen State College; Olympia	Public	3,901	87	57
Gonzaga University; Spokane	Private	2,853	82	55
Henry Cogswell College; Everett	Private	249	100	16

Institution name; city	Public or private	Students	Percent Accepted	Percent Women
Heritage College; Toppenish	Private	754	9%	80%
Northwest College; Kirkland	Private	1,096	53	56
Pacific Lutheran University; Tacoma	Private	3,246	82	61
Saint Martin's College; Lacey	Private	1,197	92	52
Seattle Pacific University; Seattle	Private	2,692	91	66
Seattle University; Seattle	Private	3,241	80	60
Trinity Lutheran College; Issaquah	Private	129	77	63
University of Phoenix–Washington Campus; Seattle	Private	46,473		56
University of Puget Sound; Tacoma	Private	2,621	72	61
University of Washington; Seattle	Public	25,982	78	52
Walla Walla College; College Place	Private	1,580	83	49
Washington State University; Pullman	Public	17,469	84	50
Western Washington University; Bellingham	Public	11,050	86	56
Whitman College; Walla Walla	Private	1,424	50	58
Whitworth College; Spokane	Private	1,807	90	60
WEST VIRGINIA				
Appalachian Bible College; Bradley	Private	302		51
Bethany College; Bethany	Private	750	71	46
Bluefield State College; Bluefield	Public	2,648	99	60
Concord College; Athens	Public	2,955	98	57
Davis & Elkins College; Elkins	Private	658	94	56
Fairmont State College; Fairmont	Public	6,496	100	56
Glenville State College; Glenville	Public	2,198	100	59
Marshall University; Huntington	Public	9,624	74	55
Mountain State University; Beckley	Private	2,076	50	
Ohio Valley College; Vienna	Private	417	45	53
Salem International University; Salem	Private	564	83	44
Shepherd College; Shepherdstown	Public	4,603	94	58
University of Charleston; Charleston	Private	1,219	72	64
West Liberty State College; West Liberty	Public	2,606	96	55
West Virginia State College; Institute	Public	4,823	100	59
West Virginia University; Morgantown	Public	15,463	94	46
West Virginia Univ. Institute of Technology; Montgomery	Public	2,313	99	
West Virginia Wesleyan College; Buckhannon	Private	1,581	82	57
Wheeling Jesuit University; Wheeling	Private	1,264	86	59
WISCONSIN				
Alverno College; Milwaukee	Private	1,754	70	99
Beloit College; Beloit	Private	1,254	67	58
Cardinal Stritch University; Milwaukee	Private	3,089	77	68
Carroll College; Waukesha	Private	2,681	85	66
Carthage College; Kenosha	Private	2,147	89	57
Concordia University Wisconsin; Mequon	Private	3,852	82	64
Edgewood College; Madison	Private	1,535	48	72
Lakeland College; Sheboygan	Private	3,328	76	61
Lawrence University; Appleton	Private	1,289	73	54
Marian College of Fond du Lac; Fond du Lac	Private	1,114	79	69
Marquette University; Milwaukee	Private	7,496	84	55
Milwaukee Institute of Art and Design; Milwaukee	Private	656	86	51
Milwaukee School of Engineering; Milwaukee	Private	2,279	82	18
Mount Mary College; Milwaukee	Private	1,089	63	95
Mount Senario College; Ladysmith	Private	830	64	36
Northland College; Ashland	Private	531	87	36
Ripon College; Ripon	Private	862	83	53
Silver Lake College; Manitowoc	Private	727	86	71
St. Norbert College; De Pere	Private	2,041	88	59
University of Wisconsin–Eau Claire; Eau Claire	Public	10,101	74	60
University of Wisconsin–Green Bay; Green Bay	Public	5,334	81	65
University of Wisconsin–La Crosse; La Crosse	Public	8,487	67	58
University of Wisconsin–Madison; Madison	Public	28,493	64	
University of Wisconsin–Milwaukee; Milwaukee	Public	19,246	69	55
University of Wisconsin–Oshkosh; Oshkosh	Public	9,124	78	59
University of Wisconsin–Parkside; Kenosha	Public	4,672	94	59
University of Wisconsin–River Falls; River Falls	Public	6,060	43	61
University of Wisconsin–Stevens Point; Stevens Point	Public	8,380	58	57
University of Wisconsin–Stout; Menomonie	Public	7,162	81	49
University of Wisconsin–Whitewater; Whitewater	Public	9,420	79	53
Viterbo University; La Crosse	Private	1,686	88	75
Wisconsin Lutheran College; Milwaukee	Private	634	89	61
WYOMING				
University of Wyoming; Laramie	Public	8,490	97	53

The American Gay Rights Movement: A Timeline

1924 The Society for Human Rights in Chicago becomes the country's earliest known gay rights organization.

1948 Alfred Kinsey publishes *Sexual Behavior in the Human Male,* revealing to the public that homosexuality is far more widespread than was commonly believed.

1951 The Mattachine Society, the first national gay rights organization, is formed by Harry Hay, considered by many to be the founder of the gay rights movement.

1956 The Daughters of Bilitis, a pioneering national lesbian organization, is founded.

1962 Illinois becomes the first state in the U.S. to decriminalize homosexual acts between consenting adults in private.

1969 The Stonewall riots transform the gay rights movement from one limited to a small number of activists into a widespread protest for equal rights and acceptance. Patrons of a gay bar in New York's Greenwich Village, the Stonewall Inn, fight back during a police raid on June 27, sparking three days of riots.

1973 The American Psychiatric Association removes homosexuality from its official list of mental disorders.

1982 Wisconsin becomes the first state to outlaw discrimination on the basis of sexual orientation.

1993 The "Don't Ask, Don't Tell" policy is instituted for the U.S. military, permitting gays to serve in the military but banning homosexual activity. President Clinton's original intention to revoke the prohibition against gays in the military was met with stiff opposition; this compromise, which has led to the discharge of thousands of men and women in the armed forces, was the result.

1996 In *Romer* v. *Evans*, the Supreme Court strikes down Colorado's Amendment 2, which denied gays and lesbians protections against discrimination, calling them "special rights." According to Justice Anthony Kennedy, "We find nothing special in the protections Amendment 2 withholds. These protections . . . constitute ordinary civil life in a free society."

2000 Vermont becomes the first state in the country to legally recognize civil unions between gay or lesbian couples. The law states that these "couples would be entitled to the same benefits, privileges, and responsibilities as spouses." It stops short of referring to same-sex unions as marriage, which the state defines as heterosexual.[1]

2003 The U.S. Supreme Court rules in *Lawrence* v. *Texas* that sodomy laws in the U.S. are unconstitutional. Justice Anthony Kennedy wrote, "Liberty presumes an autonomy of self that includes freedom of thought, belief, expression, and certain intimate conduct."

1. Internationally, Denmark became the first country to legalize same-sex partnerships in 1989. Within two years, Norway, Sweden, Iceland, and France followed suit. In 2001, the Netherlands became the first country legalizing same-sex marriages; Belgium followed in 2003. The Canadian provinces of Ottawa and British Columbia legalized same-sex marriage in 2003; sanctioning it on a federal level will be voted on in 2004.

Same-Sex Partners Sharing Households, U.S.

Nationwide, 594,391 same-sex partner households represented 1% of all coupled households, according to the 2000 Census. Of these, 301,026 were male partners and 293,365 were female partners.

Metropolitan Areas with the Highest Percentage of Same-Sex Households, 2000

Same-sex partner households by area	Number	Percent of all households in specified city	Same-sex partner households by area	Number	Percent of all households in specified city
San Francisco, Calif.	8,902	2.7%	Atlanta, Ga.	2,833	1.7%
Fort Lauderdale, Fla.	1,418	2.1	Minneapolis, Minn.	2,622	1.6
Seattle, Wash.	4,965	1.9	Washington, DC	3,678	1.5
Oakland, Calif.	2,650	1.8	Long Beach, Calif.	2,266	1.4
Berkeley, Calif.	788	1.8	Portland, Ore.	3,017	1.3

Source: Married-Couple and Unmarried-Partner Households: 2000, U.S. Census Bureau, Census 2000.

Percent of Same-Sex Households with Children Under 18 Years, 2000

Region	Male partners: Own children[1]	Male partners: Own and/or unrelated children[2]	Female partners: Own children[1]	Female partners: Own and/or unrelated children[2]
United States	21.8%	22.3%	32.7%	34.3%
Region				
Northeast	21.3	21.7	31.2	32.6
Midwest	22.3	22.9	32.8	34.7
South	22.1	23.9	34.4	36.1
West	20.6	21.1	31.5	33.1

1. Refers to own sons/daughters of the householder. 2. Refers to own sons/daughters of the householder and other children not related to the householder. *Source: Married-Couple and Unmarried-Partner Households: 2000,* U.S. Census Bureau, Census 2000.

Gender of Sexual Partners in the United States

(sexually active only)

	Same gender		Both genders		Opposite gender	
	Men	Women	Men	Women	Men	Women
1988	2.3%	0.2%	0.3%	0.0%	97.4%	99.8%
1989	1.4	1.2	0.3	0.4	98.3	98.4
1990	1.1	0.5	0.9	0.0	98.0	99.5
1991	2.0	0.3	0.7	0.1	97.3	99.6
1993	1.8	1.8	0.3	0.4	97.9	97.8
1994	2.1	2.1	0.5	0.4	97.5	97.5
1996	3.5	2.1	0.6	0.9	96.0	97.0

Source: General Social Survey (GSS), National Opinion Research Center, University of Chicago, 1996.

Key Events in the Women's Rights Movement

1848 The first women's rights convention is held in Seneca Falls, New York. A Declaration of Sentiments, which outlines grievances and sets the agenda for the women's rights movement, is signed by 68 women and 32 men.

1850 The first National Women's Rights Convention takes place in Worcester, Mass., attracting more than 1,000 participants. National conventions are held yearly (except for 1857) through 1860.

1869 In May, Susan B. Anthony and Elizabeth Cady Stanton form the National Woman Suffrage Association. Its primary goal is to achieve voting rights for women by means of a congressional amendment to the Constitution.

In November Lucy Stone, Henry Blackwell, and others form the American Woman Suffrage Association, which focuses exclusively on gaining voting rights for women through amendments to individual state constitutions.

In December the territory of Wyoming passes the first women's suffrage law. In 1870, women begin serving on juries in the territory.

1890 The National Woman Suffrage Association and the American Woman Suffrage Association merge to form the National American Woman Suffrage Association (NAWSA). As the movement's mainstream organization, NAWSA wages state-by-state campaigns to obtain voting rights for women.

1893 Colorado is the first state to adopt an amendment granting women the right to vote. Utah and Idaho follow suit in 1896, Washington State in 1910, California in 1911, Oregon, Kansas, and Arizona in 1912, Alaska and Illinois in 1913, Montana and Nevada in 1914, New York in 1917, Michigan, South Dakota, and Oklahoma in 1918.

1896 The National Association of Colored Women is formed, bringing together more than 100 black women's clubs. Leaders in the black women's club movement include Josephine St. Pierre Ruffin, Mary Church Terrell, and Anna Julia Cooper.

1913 Alice Paul and Lucy Burns form the Congressional Union to work toward the passage of a federal amendment to give women the vote. The group is later renamed the National Women's Party. Members picket the White House and practice other forms of civil disobedience.

1919 The federal woman suffrage amendment, originally written by Susan B. Anthony and introduced in Congress in 1878, is passed by the House of Representatives and the Senate. It is then sent to the states for ratification.

1920 On Aug. 26, the 19th Amendment to the Constitution, granting women the right to vote, is signed into law.

1921 Margaret Sanger founds the American Birth Control League, which evolves into the Planned Parenthood Federation of America in 1942.

1936 The federal law prohibiting the dissemination of contraceptive information through the mail is modified, and birth control information is no longer classified as obscene. Throughout the 1940s and 1950s, birth control advocates are engaged in numerous legal suits.

1961 President John F. Kennedy establishes the President's Commission on the Status of Women and appoints Eleanor Roosevelt as chairwoman. The report issued by the commission in 1963 documents substantial discrimination against women in the workplace and urges reform, including fair hiring practices, paid maternity leave, and affordable child care.

1963 Betty Friedan publishes her highly influential book *The Feminine Mystique,* which becomes a best-seller and galvanizes the modern women's rights movement.

In June Congress passes the Equal Pay Act, making it illegal for employers to pay a woman less than what a man would receive for the same job.

1964 Title VII of the Civil Rights Act bars discrimination in employment on the basis of race and sex. At the same time it establishes the Equal Employment Opportunity Commission (EEOC) to investigate complaints and impose penalties.

1965 In *Griswold* v. *Connecticut,* the Supreme Court strikes down the one remaining state law prohibiting the use of contraceptives by married couples.

1966 The National Organization for Women (NOW) is founded. The largest women's rights group in the United States, NOW seeks to end sexual discrimination by means of legislative lobbying, litigation, and public demonstrations.

1967 Executive Order 11375 expands President Lyndon Johnson's affirmative action policy of 1965 to cover discrimination based on gender.

1968 The EEOC rules that sex-segregated help wanted ads in newspapers are illegal. This ruling is upheld in 1973 by the Supreme Court, opening the way for women to apply for higher-paying jobs hitherto open only to men.

1969 California becomes the first state to adopt a "no fault" divorce law, which allows couples to divorce by mutual consent. By 1985 every state has adopted a similar law. Laws are also passed regarding the equal division of common property.

1971 *Ms.* magazine is first published as a sample insert in *New York* magazine; 300,000 copies are sold out in 8 days. The first regular issue is published in July 1972. The magazine becomes the major forum for feminist voices and turns cofounder and editor Gloria Steinem into an icon of the modern feminist movement.

In *Eisenstadt* v. *Baird* the Supreme Court rules that the right to privacy includes an unmarried person's right to use contraceptives.

1972 The Equal Rights Amendment (ERA) is passed by Congress and sent to the states for ratification. Originally drafted by Alice Paul in 1923, the amendment reads: "Equality of rights under the law shall not be denied or abridged by the United States or by any State on account of sex." The amendment died in 1982 when it failed to achieve ratification by a minimum of 38 states.

Title IX of the Education Amendments bans sex discrimination in schools. As a result, the enrollment of women in athletics programs and professional schools increases dramatically.

1973 As a result of *Roe* v. *Wade,* the Supreme Court establishes a woman's legal right to abortion, overriding the antiabortion laws of many states.

1974 The Equal Credit Opportunity Act prohibits discrimination in consumer credit practices on the basis of sex, race, marital status, religion, national origin, age, or receipt of public assistance.

1978 The Pregnancy Discrimination Act bans employment discrimination against pregnant women.

1984 EMILY's List (Early Money Is Like Yeast) is established as a financial network for pro-choice Democratic women running for national political office. The organization makes a significant impact on the increasing number of women elected to Congress.

1986 In *Meritor Savings Bank* v. *Vinson,* the Supreme Court finds that sexual harassment is a form of illegal job discrimination.

1994 The Violence Against Women Act tightens federal penalties for sex offenders, funds services for victims of rape and domestic violence, and provides for special training of police officers.

Domestic Violence

Type of victimization over lifetime	Percent		Number	
	Women	Men	Women	Men
Rape	7.7%	0.3%	7,753,669	278,244
Physical assault	22.1	7.4	22,254,037	6,863,352
Rape and/or physical assault	24.8	7.6	24,972,856	7,048,848
Stalking	4.8	0.6	4,833,456	556,488
Total victimized	25.5	7.9	25,677,735	7,327,092

NOTE: Survey consisted of telephone interviews with a nationally representative sample of 8,000 U.S. women and 8,000 men. **Definitions:** Rape includes completed or attempted forced vaginal, oral, or anal sex. Physical assault includes a range of behaviors from slapping and hitting to using a gun. Stalking involves repeated acts of harassment and intimidation with the victim reporting a high level of fear. *Source:* National Violence Against Women Survey, National Institute of Justice and Centers for Disease Control, July 2000.

The Wage Gap

Source: National Women's Law Center.

The wage gap is a statistical indicator often used as an index of the status of women's earnings relative to men's. It is also used to compare the earnings of other races and ethnicities to those of white males, a group generally not subject to race- or sex-based discrimination. The wage gap is expressed as a percentage (e.g., in 2001, women earned 76% as much as men) and is calculated by dividing the median annual earnings for women by the median annual earnings for men.

The Equal Pay Act was signed in 1963, making it illegal for employers to pay unequal wages to men and women who hold the same job and do the same work. At the time of the EPA's passage, women earned just 58 cents for every dollar earned by men. By 2001, nearly 40 years later, that rate had only increased to 76 cents, an improvement of less than half a penny a year. Minority women fare the worst. African-American women earn just 64 cents to every dollar earned by white men, and for Hispanic women that figure drops to merely 52 cents per dollar.

The wage gap between women and men cuts across a wide spectrum of occupations. The Bureau of Labor Statistics reported in 1999 that female physicians earned 62.5% of the median weekly wages of male physicians, and women in sales occupations earned just 59.9% of men's wages in equivalent positions.

If working women earned the same as men (those who work the same number of hours; have the same education, age, and union status; and live in the same region of the country), their annual family incomes would rise by $4,000 and poverty rates would be cut in half.

Women's Earnings as a Percentage of Men's, 1951–2002

(for year-round, full-time work)

Year	Percent	Year	Percent	Year	Percent	Year	Percent	Year	Percent
1951	63.9%	1962	59.3%	1973	56.6%	1984	63.7%	1995	71.4%
1952	63.9	1963	58.9	1974	58.8	1985	64.6	1996	73.8
1953	63.9	1964	59.1	1975	58.8	1986	64.3	1997	74.2
1954	63.9	1965	59.9	1976	60.2	1987	65.2	1998	73.2
1955	63.9	1966	57.6	1977	58.9	1988	66.0	1999	72.2
1956	63.3	1967	57.8	1978	59.4	1989	68.7	2000	73.0
1957	63.8	1968	58.2	1979	59.7	1990	71.6	2001	76.0
1958	63.0	1969	58.9	1980	60.2	1991	69.9	2002	76.0
1959	61.3	1970	59.4	1981	59.2	1992	70.8		
1960	60.7	1971	59.5	1982	61.7	1993	71.5		
1961	59.2	1972	57.9	1983	63.6	1994	72.0		

Source: U.S. Women's Bureau and the National Committee on Pay Equity.

Wage Gap, Selected European Countries

Country and year	Women/men wage ratio	Country and year	Women/men wage ratio	Country and year	Women/men wage ratio
Austria[1]		**Greece**[3]		**Norway**	
1987	99%	1987	65%	1987	84%
1990	99	1990	68	1990	87
1996	99	1995	68	1996	87
Denmark[2]		**Iceland**[4]		**United Kingdom**[5]	
1987	82	1988	69	1987	73
1990	83	1990	67	1990	77
1991	84	1995	71	1996	80

1. Permanent workers. 2. Adults 3. Manufacturing establishments with more than ten employees. 4. Skilled workers, mainly manufacturing. 5. Full time adults. *Source:* The Norwegian Centre for Gender Equality.

20 Leading Occupations of Employed Women, U.S.

(2001 annual averages)

Occupations	Total employed (women) (in thousands)	Total employed (men and women) (in thousands)	Percent women	Women's median usual weekly earnings[1]	Ratio of women's earnings to men's earnings
Total, 16 years and over	62,992	135,073	46.6%	$511	76.0%
Managers and administrators, n.e.c.[2]	2,486	8,018	31.0	762	65.6
Secretaries	2,366	2,404	98.4	475	n.a.
Cashiers	2,288	2,974	76.9	292	89.3
Sales supervisors and proprietors	1,990	4,836	44.1	502	70.5
Registered nurses	2,013	2,162	93.1	820	87.9
Elementary school teachers	1,828	2,216	82.5	731	94.9
Nursing aides, orderlies, and attendants	1,874	2,081	90.0	356	89.7
Bookkeepers, accounting, and auditing clerks	1,506	1,621	92.9	474	93.7
Waiters and waitresses	1,029	1,347	76.4	317	87.3
Sales workers, retail, and personal services[3]	1,023	2,311	44.3	n.a.	n.a.
Receptionists	1,015	1,047	96.9	401	n.a.
Sales workers, other commodities[3]	925	1,426	64.9	351	82.0
Accountants and auditors	975	1,657	58.8	687	72.0
Cooks	881	2,073	42.5	305	87.9
Investigators and adjusters, excluding insurance	878	1,171	75.0	487	89.4
Janitors and cleaners	779	2,166	36.0	318	81.7
Secondary school teachers	763	1,304	58.5	759	91.9
Hairdressers and cosmetologists	772	854	90.4	374	n.a.
General office clerks	756	903	83.7	462	96.0
Administrative support occupations	779	1,020	76.4	512	82.3

NOTE: n.a. = not available. Median not available where base is less than 50,000 male workers. 1. Wage and salary for full-time workers. 2. Not elsewhere classified. 3. Includes foods, drugs, health, and other commodities. *Source:* U.S. Dept. of Labor, Bureau of Labor Statistics.

Affirmative Action Timeline

In its tumultuous, nearly 40-year history, affirmative action has been both praised and pilloried as an answer to racial inequality. The policy was introduced in 1965 by President Johnson as a method of redressing discrimination that had persisted in spite of civil rights laws and constitutional guarantees. Focusing in particular on education and jobs, affirmative action policies required active measures to ensure that blacks and other minorities enjoyed the same opportunities for promotions, salary increases, career advancement, school admissions, scholarships, and financial aid that had been the nearly exclusive province of whites. From the outset, affirmative action was envisioned as a temporary remedy that would end once there was a "level playing field" for all Americans. By the late '70s, however, flaws in the policy began to show up amid its good intentions. Reverse discrimination became a passionate issue, symbolized by the famous *Bakke* case in 1978. The backlash against affirmative action grew, with "preferential treatment" and "quotas" becoming expressions of contempt. In the '90s the tide turned against affirmative action both in the courts and on a state level—California and Washington went as far as abolishing the policy in 1997 and 1998, respectively.

The Supreme Court has been divided in its opinions in affirmative action cases, partially because of opposing political ideologies but also because the issue is simply so complex. The Court has approached most of the cases in a piecemeal fashion, focusing on narrow aspects of policy rather than grappling with the whole. But in a landmark 2003 case involving the University of Michigan's affirmative action policies—one of the most important rulings on the issue in 25 years—the Supreme Court decisively upheld the right of affirmative action in higher education, ruling that although it was no longer justified as a way of redressing past oppression and injustice, it promoted a "compelling state interest" in diversity at all levels of society. A record number of "friend-of-the-court" briefs were filed in support of Michigan's affirmative action case by hundreds of organizations representing academia, business, labor unions, and the military, arguing the benefits of broad racial representation. As Sandra Day O'Connor wrote for the majority, "in order to cultivate a set of leaders with legitimacy in the eyes of the citizenry, it is necessary that the path to leadership be visibly open to talented and qualified individuals of every race and ethnicity."

March 6, 1961: Executive Order 10925 made the first reference to "affirmative action." President John F. Kennedy issued Executive Order 10925, which created the Committee on Equal Employment Opportunity and mandated that projects financed with federal funds "take affirmative action" to ensure that hiring and employment practices are free of racial bias.

July 2, 1964: Civil Rights Act signed by President Lyndon Johnson. The most sweeping civil rights legislation since Reconstruction, the Civil Rights Act prohibits discrimination of all kinds based on race, color, religion, or national origin.

June 4, 1965: Speech defining concept of affirmative action. In a speech to the graduating class at Howard University, President Johnson framed the concept underlying affirmative action, asserting that civil rights laws alone were not enough to remedy discrimination: "You do not wipe away the scars of centuries by saying: 'now, you are free to go where you want, do as you desire, and choose the leaders you please.' You do not take a man who for years has been hobbled by chains, liberate him, bring him to the starting line of a race, saying, 'you are free to compete with all the others,' and still justly believe you have been completely fair. . . . This is the next and more profound stage of the battle for civil rights. We seek not just freedom but opportunity—not just legal equity but human ability—not just equality as a right and a theory, but equality as a fact and as a result."

Sept. 24, 1965: Executive Order 11246 enforced affirmative action for the first time. Issued by President Johnson, the executive order required government contractors to "take affirmative action" toward prospective minority employees in all aspects of hiring and employment. Contractors must take specific measures to ensure equality in hiring and must document these efforts. On Oct. 13, 1967, the order was amended to cover discrimination on the basis of gender.

1969: The Philadelphia Order. Initiated by President Richard Nixon, the "Philadelphia Order" was the most forceful plan thus far to guarantee fair hiring practices in construction jobs. Philadelphia was selected as the test case because, as Assistant Secretary of Labor Arthur Fletcher explained, "The craft unions and the construction industry are among the most egregious offenders against equal opportunity laws . . . openly hostile toward letting blacks into their closed circle." The order included definite "goals and timetables." As President Nixon asserted, "We would not impose quotas, but would require federal contractors to show 'affirmative action' to meet the goals of increasing minority employment."

June 28, 1978: *Regents of the University of California* v. *Bakke*. This landmark Supreme Court case imposed limitations on affirmative action to ensure that providing greater opportunities for minorities did not come at the expense of the rights of the majority—affirmative action was unfair if it led to reverse discrimination. The case involved the University of California at Davis Medical School, which had two separate admissions pools, one for standard applicants, and another for minority and economically disadvantaged students. The school reserved 16 of its 100 places for this latter group. Allan Bakke, a white applicant, was rejected twice even though there were minority applicants admitted with significantly lower scores than his. Bakke maintained that judging him on the basis of his race was a violation of the Equal Protection Clause of the Fourteenth Amendment. The Supreme Court ruled that while race was a legitimate factor in school admissions, the use of such inflexible quotas as the medical school had set aside was not. The Supreme Court, however, was split 5–4 in its decision on the *Bakke* case and addressed only a minimal number of the many complex issues that had sprung up about affirmative action.

July 2, 1980: *Fullilove* v. *Klutznick*. While *Bakke* struck down strict quotas, in *Fullilove* the Supreme Court ruled that some modest quotas were perfectly constitutional. The Court upheld a federal law requiring that 15% of funds for public works be set aside for qualified minority contractors. The "narrowed focus and limited extent" of the affirmative action program did not violate the equal rights of nonminority contractors, according to the Court—there was no "allocation of federal funds according to inflexible percentages solely based on race or ethnicity."

May 19, 1986: *Wygant* v. *Jackson Board of Education*. This case challenged a school board's policy of protecting minority employees by laying off nonminority teachers first, even though the nonminority employees had seniority. The Supreme Court ruled against the school board, maintaining that the injury suffered by nonminorities could not justify the benefits to minorities.

Feb. 25, 1987: *United States* v. *Paradise*. In July 1970, a federal court found that the State of Alabama Department of Public Safety systematically discriminated against blacks in hiring: "in the 37-year history of the patrol there has never been a black trooper." The court ordered that the state reform its hiring practices to end "pervasive, systematic, and obstinate discriminatory exclusion of blacks." A full 12 years and several lawsuits later, the department still had not promoted any blacks above entry level. In response, the court ordered specific racial quotas to correct the situation. For every white hired or promoted, one black would also be hired or promoted until at least 25% of the upper ranks of the department were composed of blacks. The *Paradise* case challenged this use of numerical quotas. The Supreme Court, however, upheld the use of strict quotas in this case as one of the only means of combating the department's overt racism.

Jan. 23, 1989: *City of Richmond* v. *Croson*. Affirmative action on the state and local levels was challenged in this case involving a Richmond, Va., program setting aside 30% of city construction funds for black-owned firms. For the first time, affirmative action was judged as a "highly suspect tool." The Supreme Court ruled that an "amorphous claim that there has been past discrimination in a particular industry cannot justify the use of an unyielding racial quota." It maintained that affirmative action must be subject to "strict scrutiny" and is unconstitutional unless racial discrimination can be proven to be "widespread throughout a particular industry."

June 12, 1995: *Adarand Constructors, Inc.* v. *Peña*. What *Croson* was to state- and local-run affirmative action programs, *Adarand* was to federal programs. The Court again called for "strict scrutiny" in determining whether discrimination existed before implementing a federal affirmative action program. "Strict scrutiny" meant that affirmative action programs fulfilled a "compelling governmental interest," and were "narrowly tailored" to fit the particular situation. Although two of the judges (Scalia and Thomas) felt that there should be a complete ban on affirmative action, the majority of judges asserted that "the unhappy persistence of both the practice and the lingering effects of racial discrimination against minority groups in this country" justified the use of race-based remedial measures in some circumstances.

July 19, 1995: White House guidelines on affirmative action. President Clinton asserted in a speech that while *Adarand* set "stricter standards to mandate reform of affirmative action, it actually reaffirmed the need for affirmative action and reaffirmed the continuing existence of systematic discrimination in the United States." In a White House memorandum on the same day, he called for the elimination of any program that "(a) creates a quota; (b) creates preferences for unqualified individuals; (c) creates reverse discrimination; or (d) continues even after its equal opportunity purposes have been achieved."

March 18, 1996: *Hopwood* v. *University of Texas Law School*. Four white law-school applicants at the University of Texas challenged the school's affirmative action program, asserting that they were rejected because of unfair preferences toward less qualified minority applicants. As a result, the 5th U.S. Court of Appeals suspended the university's affirmative action admissions program and ruled that the 1978 *Bakke* decision was invalid—while *Bakke* rejected racial quotas, it maintained that race could serve as a factor in admissions. In addition to remedying past discrimination, *Bakke* maintained that the inclusion of minority students would create a diverse student body, and that was beneficial to the educational environment as a whole. *Hopwood*, however, rejected the legitimacy of diversity as a goal, asserting that "educational diversity is not recognized as a compelling state interest." The Supreme Court allowed the ruling to stand.

Nov. 3, 1997: Proposition 209 enacted in California. A state ban on all forms of affirmative action was passed in California: "The state shall not discriminate against, or grant preferential treatment to, any individual or group on the basis of race, sex, color, ethnicity, or national origin in the operation of public employment, public education, or public contracting." Proposed in 1996, the controversial ban had been delayed in the courts for almost a year before it went into effect.

Dec. 3, 1998: Initiative 200 enacted in Washington State. Washington became the second state to abolish state affirmative action measures when it passed "I 200," which was similar to California's Proposition 209.

Feb. 22, 2000: Florida banned race as factor in college admissions. Florida legislature approved education component of Gov. Jeb Bush's "One Florida" initiative, aimed at ending affirmative action in the state.

Dec. 13, 2000: Univ. of Michigan's undergraduate affirmative action policy. In *Gratz* v. *Bollinger*, a federal judge ruled that the use of race as a factor in admissions at the university was constitutional. The gist of the university's argument was as follows: just as preference is granted to children of alumni, scholarship athletes, and other groups for reasons deemed beneficial to the university, so too does the affirmative action program serve "a compelling interest" by providing educational benefits derived from a diverse student body.

March 27, 2001: Univ. of Michigan Law School's affirmative action policy. In *Grutter* v. *Bollinger,* a case similar to the University of Michigan undergraduate lawsuit, a different judge drew an opposite conclusion, invalidating the law school's policy and ruling that "intellectual diversity bears no obvious or necessary relationship to racial diversity." But on May 14, 2002, the decision was reversed on appeal, ruling that the admissions policy was, in fact, constitutional.

June 23, 2003: Supreme Court upholds affirmative action in university admissions. In the most important affirmative action decision since the 1978 Bakke case, the Supreme Court rules on the two recent University of Michigan cases, *Gratz* v. *Bollinger,* and *Grutter* v. *Bollinger.* The Court (5-4) upholds the University of Michigan Law School's policy, ruling that race can be one of many factors considered by colleges when selecting their students because it furthers "a compelling interest in obtaining the educational benefits that flow from a diverse student body." The Supreme Court, however, rules (6–3) that the more formulaic approach of the University of Michigan's undergraduate admissions program, which uses a point system that rates students and awards additional points to minorities, has to be modified. The undergraduate program, unlike the law school's, does not provide the "individualized consideration" of applicants deemed necessary in previous Supreme Court decisions on affirmative action.

Population of the United States by Race and Hispanic/Latino Origin, Census 2000 and July 1, 2002

Race and Hispanic/Latino origin	July 1, 2002, population	Percent of population	Census 2000, population	Percent of population
Total Population	**288,368,698**	**100.0%**	**281,421,906**	**100.0%**
Single race				
White	232,646,619	80.7	211,460,626	75.1
Black or African American	36,746,012	12.7	34,658,190	12.3
American Indian and Alaska Native	2,752,158	1.0	2,475,956	0.9
Asian	11,559,027	4.0	10,242,998	3.6
Native Hawaiian and other Pacific Islander	484,314	0.2	398,835	0.1
Two or more races	n.a.	1.5	6,826,228	2.4
Some other race	n.a.	n.a.	15,359,073	5.5
Hispanic or Latino	38,761,370	13.4	35,305,818	12.5

NOTE: Percentages add up to more than 100% because Hispanics may be of any race and are therefore counted under more than one category. *Source:* U.S. Census Bureau, Cenus 2000 Brief, March 2001, and National Population Estimates, June 18, 2003.

Black or African-American Population for the U.S. by Region, 2002

Area	Percent of black population	Percent of total population	Area	Percent of black population	Percent of total population
United States	**100.0%**	**12.7%**	Midwest	18.1%	10.2%
Region			South	55.3	19.8
Northeast	18.1	12.2	West	8.6	4.8

Source: U.S. Census Bureau, *Current Population Survey,* March 2002.

U.S. Hispanic/Latino Population, 2000

National origin	Population	Percent	National origin	Population	Percent
Total	**35,305,818**	**100.0%**	**South American**	**1,353,562**	**3.8%**
Mexican	**20,640,711**	**58.5**	Argentinean	100,864	0.3
Puerto Rican	**3,406,178**	**9.6**	Bolivian	42,068	0.1
Cuban	**1,241,685**	**3.5**	Chilean	68,849	0.2
Dominican (Dominican Republic)	**764,945**	**2.2**	Colombian	470,684	1.3
Central American (excludes Mexican)	**1,686,937**	**4.8**	Ecuadorian	260,559	0.7
			Paraguayan	8,769	(1)
Costa Rican	68,588	0.2	Peruvian	233,926	0.7
Guatemalan	372,487	1.1	Uruguayan	18,804	0.1
Honduran	217,569	0.6	Venezuelan	91,507	0.3
Nicaraguan	177,684	0.5	Other South American	57,532	0.2
Panamanian	91,723	0.3	**All other Hispanic or Latino**	**6,211,800**	**17.6**
Salvadoran	655,165	1.9			
Other Central American	103,721	0.3			

NOTE: Hispanics may be of any race. 1. Less than 0.1%. *Source:* U.S. Census Bureau, Census 2000.

U.S. Asian Population, 2000

National origin	Population[1]	Percent	National origin	Population[1]	Percent
Total[2]	**11,898,828**	**100.0%**	Korean	1,228,427	10.3%
Asian Indian	1,899,599	16.0	Laotian	198,203	1.7
Bangladeshi	57,412	0.5	Malaysian	18,566	0.2
Bhutanese	212	(3)	Maldivian	51	(3)
Burmese	16,720	0.1	Nepalese	9,399	0.1
Cambodian	206,052	1.7	Okinawan	10,599	0.1
Chinese, except Taiwanese	2,734,841	23.0	Pakistani	204,309	1.7
Filipino	2,364,815	19.9	Singaporean	2,394	(3)
Hmong	186,310	1.6	Sri Lankan	24,587	0.2
Indo Chinese	199	(3)	Taiwanese	144,795	1.2
Indonesian	63,073	0.5	Thai	150,283	1.3
Iwo Jiman	78	(3)	Vietnamese	1,223,736	10.3
Japanese	1,148,932	9.7	Other Asian, not specified	369,430	3.1

1. The numbers by national origin do not add up to the total population figure because respondents may have put down more than one country. Respondents reporting several countries are counted several times. 2. Total includes Asians alone or in combination with one or more other races or other Asian groups. The Asian population alone in 2000 was 10,242,998. 3. Less than 0.1%. *Source:* U.S. Census Bureau, Census 2000.

Native Hawaiian and Other U.S. Pacific Islander Population, 2000

National origin	Population[1]	Percent	National origin	Population[1]	Percent
Total[2]	**874,414**	**100.0%**	Kosraean	226	(3)
Polynesian			Pohnpeian	700	0.1%
Native Hawaiian	401,162	45.9	Chuukese	654	0.1
Samoan	133,281	15.2	Yapese	368	(3)
Tongan	36,840	4.2	Marshallese	6,650	0.8
Tahitian	3,313	0.4	I-Kiribati	175	(3)
Tokelauan	574	0.1	Micronesian, not specified	9,940	1.1
Polynesian, not specified	8,796	1.0	**Melanesian**		
Micronesian			Fijian	13,581	1.6
Guamanian or Chamorro	92,611	10.6	Papua New Guinean	224	(3)
Mariana Islander	141	(3)	Solomon Islander	25	(3)
Saipanese	475	0.1	Ni-Vanuatu	18	(3)
Palauan	3,469	0.4	Melanesian, not specified	315	(3)
Carolinian	173	(3)	Other Pacific Islander	174,912	20.0

1. The numbers by national origin do not add up to the total population figure because respondents may have put down more than one country. Respondents reporting several countries are counted several times. 2. Total includes Native Hawaiian and other Pacific Islanders alone or in combination with other races or groups. Native Hawaiian and Pacific Islander population alone in 2000 was 398,835. 3. Less than 0.1%. *Source:* U.S. Census Bureau, Census 2000.

American Indian and Alaska Native Population by Selected Tribes, 2000

Tribe	Population[1]	Tribe	Population[1]
Total[2]	**4,119,301**	Pima	11,493
Apache	96,833	Potawatomi	25,595
Blackfeet	85,750	Pueblo	74,085
Cherokee	729,533	Puget Sound Salish	14,631
Cheyenne	18,204	Seminole	27,431
Chickasaw	38,351	Shoshone	12,026
Chippewa	149,669	Sioux	153,360
Choctaw	158,774	Tohono O'odham	20,087
Colville	9,393	Ute	10,385
Comanche	19,376	Yakama	10,851
Cree	7,734	Yaqui	22,412
Creek	71,310	Yuman	8,976
Crow	13,394	Other specified American Indian tribes	357,658
Delaware	16,341	American Indian tribe, not specified	195,902
Houma	8,713	Alaska Athabascan	18,838
Iroquois	80,822	Aleut	16,978
Kiowa	12,242	Eskimo	54,761
Latin American Indian	180,940	Tlingit-Haida	22,365
Lumbee	57,868	Other specified Alaska Native tribes	3,973
Menominee	9,840	Alaska Native tribe, not specified	8,702
Navajo	298,197	American Indian or Alaska Native tribe, not specified	1,056,457
Osage	15,897		
Ottawa	10,677		
Paiute	13,532		

1. The numbers by American Indian and Alaska Native tribe do not add up to the total population figure because respondents may have put down more than one tribe. Respondents reporting several tribes are counted several times. 2. Total includes American Indian and Alaska Natives alone or in combination with other tribal groups or races. Indian and Alaskan Native population alone in 2000 was 2,475,956. *Source:* U.S. Census Bureau, Census 2000.

Ten Largest American Indian Tribes, 2000

Name	Population
Cherokee	729,533
Navajo	298,197
Latin American Indian	180,940
Choctaw	158,774
Sioux	153,360
Chippewa	149,669
Apache	96,833
Blackfeet	85,750
Iroquois	80,822
Pueblo	74,085

Source: U.S. Census Bureau, Census 2000 Summary File 1.

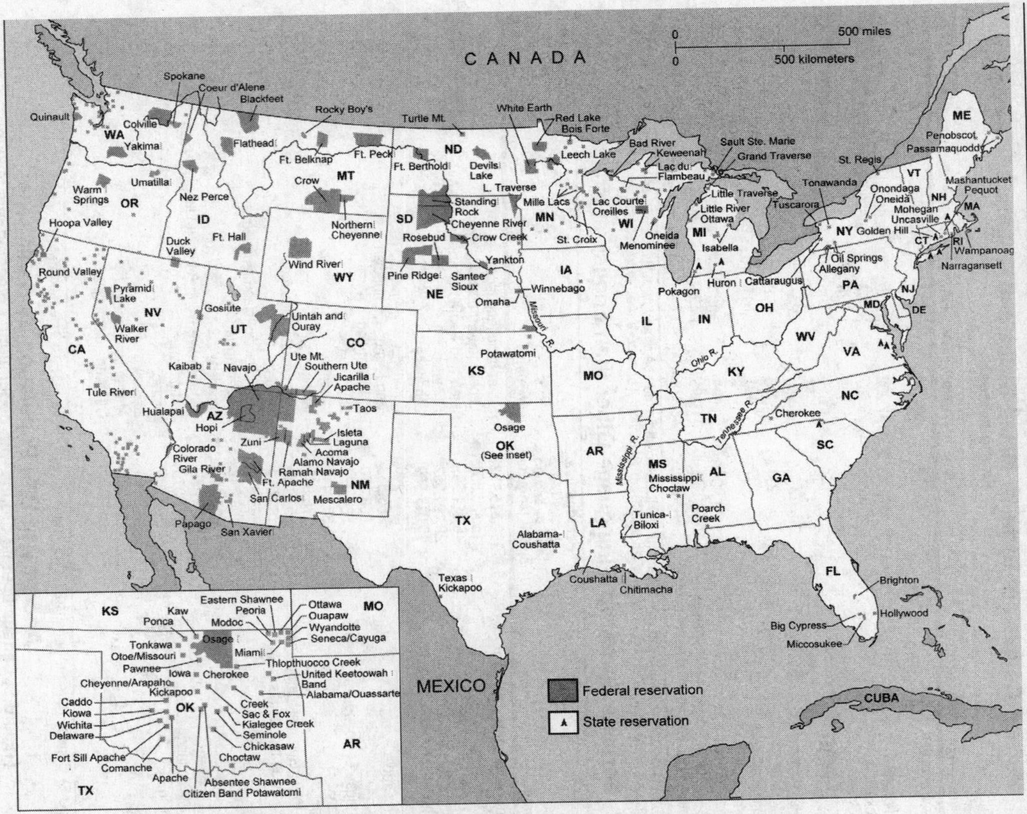

U.S. Federal and State Indian Reservations

Married Couples of Same or Mixed Races and Origins, 1980–2000
(in thousands)

Race and origin of spouse	1980	1990	1995	1998	1999	2000
Married couples, total	**49,714**	**53,256**	**54,937**	**55,305**	**55,849**	**56,497**
Race						
White/white	44,910	47,202	48,030	48,050	48,455	48,917
Black/black	3,354	3,687	3,703	3,839	3,868	3,989
Black/white	167	211	328	330	364	363
Black husband/white wife	122	150	206	210	240	268
White husband/black wife	45	61	122	120	124	95
White/other race[1]	450	720	988	975	1,086	1,051
Black/other race[1]	34	33	76	43	31	50
All other couples[1]	799	1,401	1,811	2,068	2,045	2,127
Hispanic origin						
Hispanic/Hispanic	1,906	3,085	3,857	4,279	4,480	4,739
Hispanic/other origin (not Hispanic)	891	1,193	1,434	1,662	1,647	1,742
All other couples (not of Hispanic origin)	46,917	48,979	49,646	49,363	49,722	50,016

NOTE: Persons 15 years old and over. Persons of Hispanic origin may be of any race. 1. Excluding white and black. *Source:* U.S. Census Bureau, *Current Population Reports.* From *Statistical Abstract of the United States 2001.*

Persons Speaking a Language Other than English at Home, 2000

Language	Persons five years old and over who speak language
Population, 5 years and over	**262,375,152**
Speak only English	215,423,557
Speak other language	46,951,595
Spanish or Spanish Creole	28,101,052
Other Indo-European languages	**10,017,989**
French (inc. Patois, Cajun)	1,643,838
French Creole	453,368
Italian	1,008,370
Portuguese or Portuguese Creole	564,630
German	1,383,442
Yiddish	178,945
Other West Germanic languages	251,135
Scandinavian languages	162,252
Greek	365,436
Russian	706,242
Polish	667,414
Serbo-Croatian	233,865
Other Slavic languages	301,079
Armenian	202,708
Persian	312,085
Gujarathi	235,988
Hindi	317,057
Urdu	262,900
Other Indic languages	439,289
Other Indo-European languages	327,946
Asian and Pacific Island languages	**6,960,065**
Chinese	2,022,143
Japanese	477,997
Korean	894,063
Mon-Khmer, Cambodian	181,889
Miao, Hmong	168,063
Thai	120,464
Laotian	149,303
Vietnamese	1,009,627
Other Asian languages	398,434
Tagalog	1,224,241
Other Pacific Island languages	313,841
Other languages	**1,872,489**
Navajo	178,014
Other Native North American languages	203,466
Hungarian	117,973
Arabic	614,582
Hebrew	195,374
African languages	418,505
Other and unspecified	144,575

Source: U.S. Census Bureau, Census 2000, Summary File 3, Table PCT 10, released Feb. 25, 2003.

Ancestry of U.S. Population by Rank
(1990 U.S. Census figures; groups with populations exceeding one million)

1990 Rank	Ancestry group	Percent
1.	German	23.2%
2.	Irish	15.6
3.	English	13.1
4.	African	9.6
5.	Italian	5.9
6.	American	5.0
7.	Mexican	4.7
8.	French	4.1
9.	Polish	3.8
10.	American Indian	3.5
11.	Dutch	2.5
12.	Scotch-Irish	2.3%
13.	Scottish	2.2
14.	Swedish	1.9
15.	Norwegian	1.6
16.	Russian	1.2
17.	French Canadian	0.9
18.	Welsh	0.8
19.	Spanish	0.8
20.	Puerto Rican	0.8
21.	Slovak	0.8
22.	White	0.7
23.	Danish	0.7%
24.	Hungarian	0.6
25.	Chinese	0.6
26.	Filipino	0.6
27.	Czech	0.5
28.	Portuguese	0.5
29.	British	0.4
30.	Hispanic	0.4
31.	Greek	0.4
32.	Swiss	0.4
33.	Japanese	0.4

NOTE: 2000 Census data on ancestry were not available at press time. Data are based on a sample and subject to sampling variability. Since persons who reported multiple ancestries were included in more than one group, the sum of the persons reporting the ancestry is greater than the total; for example, a person reporting "English-French" was tabulated in both the "English" and "French" categories. Ancestry groups such as "American" or "White" were self-identified. *Source:* U.S. Census Bureau.

Immigrants Admitted by Region and Selected Country of Birth, 2001

Region and country of birth	Number	Percent
All countries	**1,064,318**	**100.0%**
Africa	53,948	5.1
Asia	349,776	32.9
Europe	175,371	16.5
North America	**407,888**	**38.3**
Caribbean	103,546	9.7
Central America	75,914	7.1
Other North America	228,428	21.5
Oceania	6,113	0.6
South America	68,888	6.5
Unknown	2,334	0.2
Specific countries		
1. Mexico	206,426	19.4%
2. India	70,290	6.6
3. China, People's Republic	56,426	5.3
4. Philippines	53,154	5.0
5. Vietnam	35,531	3.3
6. El Salvador	31,272	2.9%
7. Cuba	27,703	2.6
8. Haiti	27,120	2.5
9. Bosnia-Herzegovina	23,640	2.2
10. Canada	21,933	2.1
11. Dominican Republic	21,313	2.0
12. Ukraine	20,975	2.0
13. Korea	20,742	1.9
14. Russia	20,413	1.9
15. Nicaragua	19,896	1.9
16. United Kingdom	18,436	1.7
17. Colombia	16,730	1.6
18. Pakistan	16,448	1.5
19. Jamaica	15,393	1.4
20. Guatemala	13,567	1.3
Subtotal	**737,408**	**69.3**
Other and unknown	**326,910**	**30.7**

Source: Legal Immigration, Fiscal Year 2001, U.S. Dept. of Justice, Immigration and Naturalization Service.

Countries of Birth of the Foreign-Born Population, 1850–2000

(resident population)

Ten leading countries by rank[1]	1850	1880	1900	1930	1960
1.	**Ireland** 962,000	**Germany** 1,967,000	**Germany** 2,663,000	**Italy** 1,790,000	**Italy** 1,257,000
2.	**Germany** 584,000	**Ireland** 1,855,000	**Ireland** 1,615,000	**Germany** 1,609,000	**Germany** 990,000
3.	**Great Britain** 379,000	**Great Britain** 918,000	**Canada** 1,180,000	**United Kingdom** 1,403,000	**Canada** 953,000
4.	**Canada** 148,000	**Canada** 717,000	**Great Britain** 1,168,000	**Canada** 1,310,000	**United Kingdom** 833,000
5.	**France** 54,000	**Sweden** 194,000	**Sweden** 582,000	**Poland** 1,269,000	**Poland** 748,000
6.	**Switzerland** 13,000	**Norway** 182,000	**Italy** 484,000	**Soviet Union** 1,154,000	**Soviet Union** 691,000
7.	**Mexico** 13,000	**France** 107,000	**Russia** 424,000	**Ireland** 745,000	**Mexico** 576,000
8.	**Norway** 13,000	**China** 104,000	**Poland** 383,000	**Mexico** 641,000	**Ireland** 339,000
9.	**Holland** 10,000	**Switzerland** 89,000	**Norway** 336,000	**Sweden** 595,000	**Austria** 305,000
10.	**Italy** 4,000	**Bohemia** 85,000	**Austria** 276,000	**Czechoslovakia** 492,000	**Hungary** 245,000

Ten leading countries by rank[1]	1970	1980	1990	2000
1.	**Italy** 1,009,000	**Mexico** 2,199,000	**Mexico** 4,298,000	**Mexico** 7,841,000
2.	**Germany** 833,000	**Germany** 849,000	**China** 921,000	**China** 1,391,000
3.	**Canada** 812,000	**Canada** 843,000	**Philippines** 913,000	**Philippines** 1,222,000
4.	**Mexico** 760,000	**Italy** 832,000	**Canada** 745,000	**India** 1,007,000
5.	**United Kingdom** 686,000	**United Kingdom** 669,000	**Cuba** 737,000	**Cuba** 952,000
6.	**Poland** 548,000	**Cuba** 608,000	**Germany** 712,000	**Vietnam** 863,000
7.	**Soviet Union** 463,000	**Philippines** 501,000	**United Kingdom** 640,000	**El Salvador** 765,000
8.	**Cuba** 439,000	**Poland** 418,000	**Italy** 581,000	**Korea** 701,000
9.	**Ireland** 251,000	**Soviet Union** 406,000	**Korea** 568,000	**Dominican Republic** 692,000
10.	**Austria** 214,000	**Korea** 290,000	**Vietnam** 543,000	**Canada** 678,000

1. In general, countries as reported at each census. Data are not totally comparable over time due to changes in boundaries for some countries. Great Britain excludes Ireland. United Kingdom includes Northern Ireland. China in 1990 includes Hong Kong and Taiwan. *Source: Profile of the Foreign-Born Population in the United States: 2000,* U.S. Census Bureau, 2001.

Prison Population Exceeds Two Million

According to a Justice Department report released in July 2003, the U.S. prison population surpassed 2 million for the first time—2,166,260 people were incarcerated in prisons or jails at the end of 2002 (the latest statistics available). Since 1990, the U.S. prison population, already the world's largest, has almost doubled.

About two-thirds of prisoners were in state and federal prisons, while the rest were in local jails. The report does not count all juvenile offenders, but noted that there were more than 10,000 inmates under age 18 held in adult prisons and jails in 2002. The number of women in federal and state prisons reached 97,491.

About 10.4% of the entire African-American male population in the United States aged 25 to 29 was incarcerated, by far the largest racial or ethnic group—by comparison, 2.4% of Hispanic men and 1.2% of white men in that same age group were incarcerated. According to a report by the Justice Policy Institute in 2002, the number of black men in prison has grown to five times the rate it was twenty years ago. Today, more African-American men are in jail than in college. In 2000 there were 791,600 black men in prison and 603,032 enrolled in college. In 1980, there were 143,000 black men in prison and 463,700 enrolled in college.

U.S. Prisoners, 1990–2002

Year	Total inmates	Federal prisoners	State prisoners	Local jails
1990	1,148,702	58,838	684,544	405,320
1995	1,585,586	89,538	989,004	507,044
2000[1]	1,937,482	133,921	1,176,269	621,149
2002[1]	2,033,331	151,618	1,209,640	665,475

1. Total counts include federal inmates in non-secure privately operated facilities (6,143 in 2000 and 6,598 in 2002). *Source: Prisoners in 2002,* U.S. Bureau of Justice Statistics.

Federal Prison Inmates, by Most Serious Offense, 2001

Offense	Number of sentenced inmates in federal prisons
Total	**142,766**
Violent offenses	16,117
Homicide[1]	2,364
Robbery	10,218
Other violent	3,535
Property offenses	10,664
Burglary	642
Fraud	7,617
Other property	2,405
Drug offenses	78,501
Public-order offenses	36,443
Immigration	15,012
Weapons	12,539
Other public-order	8,892
Other/unknown[2]	1,041

1. Includes murder, nonnegligent manslaughter, and negligent manslaughter. 2. Includes offenses not classifiable. *Source: Prisoners in 2002,* U.S. Bureau of Justice Statistics.

State Prison Inmates, by Offense, Gender, Race, and Hispanic Origin, 2001

Most serious offense	All	Male	Female	White	Black	Hispanic
Total	1,208,700	1,132,500	76,200	424,200	548,800	205,300
Violent offenses	596,100	571,700	24,400	208,100	267,800	102,600
Murder[1]	159,200	150,700	8,500	51,500	77,100	27,800
Manslaughter	16,900	15,000	1,900	6,300	6,300	3,500
Rape	30,900	30,600	300	15,100	11,700	2,700
Other sexual assault	87,600	86,600	1,000	50,700	21,300	12,600
Robbery	155,300	150,100	5,200	34,100	91,100	26,200
Assault	118,800	113,100	5,600	38,700	50,300	25,300
Other violent	27,400	25,500	1,900	11,700	10,000	4,700
Property offenses	233,000	213,100	20,000	101,800	92,300	32,500
Burglary	104,700	101,300	3,400	45,700	41,200	14,700
Larceny	45,500	39,600	5,800	17,400	20,300	6,100
Motor vehicle theft	18,000	17,300	700	6,900	6,700	4,200
Fraud	33,700	25,400	8,300	17,100	13,000	3,100
Other property	31,100	29,500	1,600	14,700	11,100	4,500
Drug offenses	246,100	222,900	23,200	57,300	139,700	47,000
Public-order offenses[2]	129,900	121,600	8,300	56,000	47,300	22,300
Other/unspecified[3]	3,600	3,200	400	900	1,700	800

NOTE: Data are for inmates with a sentence of more than one year under the jurisdiction of state correctional authorities. 1. Includes nonnegligent manslaughter. 2. Includes weapons, drunk driving, court offenses, commercialized vice, morals and decency charges, liquor law violations, and other public-order offenses. 3. Includes juvenile offenses and unspecified felonies. *Source: Prisoners in 2002,* U.S. Bureau of Justice Statistics.

Number of Persons Executed[1] by Jurisdiction, 1930–2002

	Number executed since			Number executed since			Number executed since	
State	**1930**	**1977[2]**	**State**	**1930**	**1977[2]**	**State**	**1930**	**1977[2]**
Texas	586	289	Oklahoma	115	55	Delaware	25	13
Georgia	397	31	Kentucky	105	2	Oregon	21	2
New York	329	0	Illinois	102	12	Connecticut	21	0
California	302	10	Tennessee	94	1	Utah	19	6
North Carolina	286	23	New Jersey	74	0	Iowa	18	0
Florida	224	54	Maryland	71	3	Kansas	15	0
South Carolina	190	28	Arizona	60	22	New Mexico	9	1
Virginia	179	87	Washington	51	4	Montana	8	2
Ohio	177	5	Indiana	50	9	Wyoming	8	1
Louisiana	160	27	Colorado	48	1	Nebraska	7	3
Alabama	160	25	District of Columbia	40	0	Idaho	4	1
Mississippi	160	6	West Virginia	40	0	Vermont	4	0
Pennsylvania	155	3	Nevada	38	9	New Hampshire	1	0
Arkansas	142	24	Federal system	35	2	South Dakota	1	0
Missouri	121	59	Massachusetts	27	0	**U.S. total**	**4,679**	**820**

NOTE: 71 people were executed in 2002. 1. Executed under civil authority; military authorities carried out an additional 160 executions, 1930–1997. 2. In 1972 the Supreme Court ruled that capital punishment, as it was then administered, was "cruel and unusual" and therefore unconstitutional. On July 1, 1976, however, the Court overturned the ruling by a 7–2 decision, and capital punishment was reinstated. *Source: Capital Punishment, 2001,* U.S. Bureau of Justice Statistics, and Death Penalty Information Center, www.deathpenaltyinfo.org.

Characteristics of Prisoners Under Sentence of Death

Characteristic	1980	1990	2000	Characteristic	1980	1990	2000
Race and age				**Marital status**			
White	418	1,368	1,990	Never married	268	998	1,749
Black and other	270	978	1,603	Married	229	632	739
Under 20 years	11	8	11	Divorced[1]	217	726	1,105
20 to 24 years	173	168	237	**Time elapsed since sentencing**			
25 to 34 years	334	1,110	1,103	Less than 12 months	185	231	208
35 to 54 years	186	1,006	2,019	12 to 47 months	389	753	786
55 years and over	10	64	223	48 to 71 months	102	438	507
Years of schooling completed				72 months and over	38	934	2,092
7 years or less	68	178	214	**Legal status at arrest**			
8 years	74	186	233	Not under sentence	384	1,345	2,202
9 to 11 years	204	775	1,157	Parole or probation[2]	115	578	921
12 years	162	729	1,184	Prison or escaped	45	128	126
More than 12 years	43	209	315	Unknown	170	305	344
Unknown	163	279	490	**Total**	**688**	**2,346**	**3,593**

NOTE: Excludes prisoners under sentence of death confined in local correctional systems pending appeal or who have not been committed to prison. 1. Includes persons married but separated, widows, widowers, and unknown. 2. Includes persons on mandatory conditional release, work release, leave, AWOL, or bail. *Source:* U.S. Bureau of Justice Statistics, *Capital Punishment,* annual, from *Statistical Abstract of the United States, 2002.*

Death Row Exonerations, 1973–2002

Between 1973 and 2002, 102 inmates on death row have been exonerated and freed. The most common reasons for wrongful convictions are mistaken eyewitness testimony, the false testimony of informants and "incentivized witnesses," incompetent lawyers, defective or fraudulent scientific evidence, prosecutorial and police misconduct, and false confessions. In recent years, DNA played a role in overturning 12 of these wrongful death row convictions.

State	Number	State	Number	State	Number	State	Number
Florida	22	New Mexico	4	Massachusetts	2	Nebraska	1
Illinois	13	Pennsylvania	4	Missouri	2	Nevada	1
Oklahoma	7	Alabama	3	Ohio	2	Washington	1
Texas	7	California	3	Idaho	1	Virginia	1
Georgia	6	North Carolina	3	Kentucky	1	**Total**	**102**
Arizona	6	South Carolina	3	Maryland	1		
Louisiana	5	Indiana	2	Mississippi	1		

Source: The Death Penalty Information Center, www.deathpenaltyinfo.org.

Methods of Execution

State	Minimum age	Method
Alabama	16	Electrocution
Alaska	—	No death penalty
Arizona[1]	16	Lethal injection or gas
Arkansas[2]	16	Lethal injection or electrocution
California	18	Lethal injection or gas
Colorado	18	Lethal injection
Connecticut	18	Lethal injection
Delaware[3]	16	Lethal injection or hanging
DC	—	No death penalty
Florida	17	Lethal injection or electrocution
Georgia	17	Lethal injection
Hawaii	—	No death penalty
Idaho	16	Lethal injection or firing squad
Illinois	18	Lethal injection
Indiana	16	Lethal injection
Iowa	—	No death penalty
Kansas	18	Lethal injection
Kentucky[4]	16	Lethal injection or electrocution
Louisiana	16	Lethal injection
Maine	—	No death penalty
Maryland	18	Lethal injection
Massachusetts	—	No death penalty
Michigan	—	No death penalty
Minnesota	—	No death penalty
Mississippi[5]	16	Lethal injection
Missouri	16	Lethal injection or gas
Montana	18	Lethal injection
Nebraska	18	Electrocution
Nevada	16	Lethal injection
New Hampshire[6]	17	Lethal injection or hanging
New Jersey	18	Lethal injection
New Mexico	18	Lethal injection
New York	18	Lethal injection
North Carolina[7]	17	Lethal injection
North Dakota	—	No death penalty
Ohio	18	Lethal injection or electrocution
Oklahoma[8]	16	Lethal injection, electrocution, or firing squad
Oregon	18	Lethal injection
Pennsylvania	16	Lethal injection
Rhode Island	—	No death penalty
South Carolina	16	Lethal injection or electrocution
South Dakota[9]	16	Lethal injection
Tennessee[10]	18	Lethal injection or electrocution
Texas	17	Lethal injection
Utah	16	Lethal injection or firing squad
Vermont	—	No death penalty
Virginia[11]	16	Lethal injection or electrocution
Washington	18	Lethal injection or hanging
West Virginia	—	No death penalty
Wisconsin	—	No death penalty
Wyoming[12]	16	Lethal injection or gas
Federal system[13]	18	Lethal injection

1. Ariz. authorizes lethal injection for those sentenced after 11/15/92; before that date, methods available are lethal injection or lethal gas. 2. Ark. authorizes lethal injection for those whose capital offense occurred on or after 7/4/83; before that date, methods available are lethal injection or electrocution. 3. Del. authorizes lethal injection for those whose capital offense occurred after 6/13/86; before that date, methods available are lethal injection or hanging. 4. Ky. authorizes lethal injection for those sentenced on or after 3/31/98; before that date, methods available are lethal injection or electrocution. 5. Miss. minimum age defined by statute is 13. 6. N.H. authorizes hanging only if lethal injection cannot be given. 7. N.C.'s minimum age is 17, unless the person was already incarcerated for murder when the subsequent murder occurred; then the minimum age is 14. 8. Okla. authorizes electrocution if lethal injection is ever held to be unconstitutional and firing squad if both lethal injection and electrocution are held unconstitutional. 9. S.D. authorizes juveniles to possibly be transferred to adult court; age can be a mitigating factor. 10. Tenn. authorizes lethal injection for those whose capital offense occurred after 12/31/98; before that date, methods available are lethal injection or electrocution. 11. Va.'s minimum age for transfer to adult court by statute is 14. 12. Wyo. authorizes lethal gas if lethal injection is ever held to be unconstitutional. 13. The method of execution of federal prisoners is lethal injection. For offenses under the Violent Crime Control and Law Enforcement Act of 1994, the method is that of the state in which the conviction took place. *Source: Capital Punishment, 2001,* U.S. Bureau of Justice Statistics, and the Death Penalty Information Center.

Federal Prosecutions of Public Corruption

Prosecution status	2000	1999	1997	1996	1995	1994	1993	1990	1985	1980
Total: Indicted	1,000	1,134	1,057	984	1,051	1,165	1,371	1,176	1,157	727
Convicted	938	1,065	853	902	878	969	1,362	1,084	997	602
Federal officials: Indicted	441	480	459	456	527	571	627	615	563	123
Convicted	422	460	392	459	438	488	595	583	470	131
State officials: Indicted	92	115	51	109	61	99	113	96	79	72
Convicted	91	80	49	83	61	97	133	79	66	51
Local officials: Indicted	211	237	255	219	236	248	309	257	248	247
Convicted	183	219	169	190	191	202	272	225	221	168

NOTE: Figures are latest available. *Source:* U.S. Department of Justice, *Federal Prosecutions of Corrupt Public Officials, 1970–1980,* and *Report to Congress on the Activities and Operations of the Public Integrity Section,* annual,. From *Statistical Abstract of the United States, 2002.*

Law Enforcement Officers Killed or Assaulted[1]

	2000	1999	1997	1996	1995	1994	1993	1992	1990	1985	1980
Total officers killed	**135**	**107**	**132**	**112**	**133**	**141**	**129**	**129**	**133**	**145**	**164**
Officers assaulted											
Firearm	1,749	1,783	2,110	1,878	2,354	3,174	3,880	4,455	3,651	2,793	3,295
Knife or cutting instrument	1,015	990	971	871	1,356	1,510	1,486	2,095	1,647	1,715	1,653
Other dangerous weapon	8,132	7,392	5,800	5,069	6,414	7,197	7,155	8,604	7,423	5,263	5,415
Hands, fists, feet, etc.	47,502	44,861	43,268	38,790	47,638	53,086	50,412	66,098	59,370	51,953	47,484
Total assaulted	**58,398**	**55,026**	**52,149**	**46,608**	**57,762**	**64,967**	**62,933**	**81,252**	**72,091**	**61,724**	**57,847**

1. Covers officers killed feloniously and accidentally in line of duty; includes federal officers. NOTE: Data are latest available. *Source:* U.S. Federal Bureau of Investigation, *Law Enforcement Officers Killed and Assaulted,* annual. From *Statistical Abstract of the United States, 2002.*

Homicide Rate (per 100,000), 1950–2001

Year	Homicide rate	Year	Homicide rate	Year	Homicide rate	Year	Homicide rate	Year	Homicide rate
1950	4.6	1961	4.8	1972	9.0	1983	8.3	1994	9.0
1951	4.4	1962	4.6	1973	9.4	1984	7.9	1995	8.2
1952	4.6	1963	4.6	1974	9.8	1985	7.9	1996	7.4
1953	4.5	1964	4.9	1975	9.6	1986	8.6	1997	6.8
1954	4.2	1965	5.1	1976	8.8	1987	8.3	1998	6.3
1955	4.1	1966	5.6	1977	8.8	1988	8.4	1999	5.7
1956	4.1	1967	6.2	1978	9.0	1989	8.7	2000	5.5
1957	4.0	1968	6.9	1979	9.7	1990	9.4	2001	5.6
1958	4.8	1969	7.3	1980	10.2	1991	9.8		
1959	4.9	1970	7.9	1981	9.8	1992	9.3		
1960	5.1	1971	8.6	1982	9.1	1993	9.5		

Source: Crime in the United States, 2001, FBI, Uniform Crime Reports.

Murder Victims: by Race and Sex, 2001

Race and sex	Total no. victims	Percent distribution[1]	Race and sex	Total no. victims	Percent distribution[1]
Race			**Sex**		
White	6,750	49.1%	Male	10,503	76.4%
Black	6,446	46.9	Female	3,214	23.4
Other	368	2.7	Unknown	35	0.3
Unknown	188	1.4	**Total**	13,752	**100.0**

1. Because of rounding, percentages may not add up to 100. *Source: Crime in the United States, 2001,* FBI, Uniform Crime Reports.

Murder Victims: Types of Weapon Used, 2001

Type of weapon	Total no. victims	Percent distribution[1]	Type of weapon	Total no. victims	Percent distribution[1]
Firearms	8,719	63.4%	Explosives	4	—
Knives or cutting instruments	1,796	13.1	Fire	104	0.8%
Blunt objects (clubs, hammers, etc.)	661	4.8	Narcotics	34	0.2
Personal weapons (hands, fists, feet, etc.)[2]	925	6.7	Strangulation	152	1.1
Poison	10	0.1	Asphyxiation	112	0.8
			Other weapon or not stated[3]	1,235	9.0
			Total	**13,752**	**100.0**

1. Because of rounding, percentages may not add up to 100. 2. Pushed is included in personal weapons. 3. Includes drowning. *Source: Crime in the United States, 2001,* FBI, Uniform Crime Reports.

Violent Crime Victimization Rates, 1993–2001

	Number of violent crimes per 1,000 persons age 12 or older				Percent change, 1993–2001
	1993	1997	2000	2001	
Gender					
Male	59.8	45.8	32.9	27.3	–54.3%
Female	40.7	33.0	23.2	23.0	–43.5
Race and ethnicity					
White	47.9	38.3	27.1	24.5	–48.9
Black	67.4	49.0	35.3	31.2	–53.7
Hispanic	55.2	43.1	28.4	29.5	–46.6
Other	39.8	28.0	20.7	18.2	–54.3
Annual household income					
Less than $7,500	84.7	71.0	60.3	46.6	–45.0
$7,500–$14,999	56.4	51.2	37.8	36.9	–34.6
$15,000–$24,999	49.0	40.1	31.8	31.8	–35.1
$25,000–$34,999	51.0	40.2	29.8	29.1	–42.9
$35,000–$49,999	45.6	38.7	28.5	26.3	–42.3
$50,000–$74,999	44.0	33.9	23.7	21.0	–52.3
$75,000 or more	41.3	30.7	22.3	18.5	–55.2

NOTE: These rates are based on the collection year. Thus, the 1993, 1994, and 1995 rates differ from rates published in *Changes in Criminal Victimization, 1994–95* (March 1997, NCJ, 162032), which are based on data years. *Source: Criminal Victimization 2001,* U.S. Dept. of Justice.

Summary of Hate Crime Statistics, 2001

	Number of incidents	Number of offenses	Number of victims	Number of known offenders
Race	**4,366**	**5,289**	**5,544**	**4,494**
Anti-white	889	1,032	1,063	1,147
Anti-black	2,900	3,530	3,701	2,819
Anti-American Indian/Alaskan Native	80	95	100	103
Anti-Asian/Pacific Islander	280	349	363	271
Anti-multi-racial group	217	283	317	154
Ethnicity/national origin	**2,098**	**2,507**	**2,634**	**2,192**
Anti-Hispanic	597	755	812	941
Anti-other ethnicity/national origin	1,501	1,752	1,822	1,251
Religion	**1,828**	**2,004**	**2,118**	**917**
Anti-Jewish	1,043	1,117	1,196	389
Anti-Catholic	38	38	40	12
Anti-Protestant	35	36	36	45
Anti-Islamic	481	546	554	334
Anti-other religious group	181	211	235	102
Anti-multi-religious group	45	51	52	28
Anti-atheism/agnosticism/etc.	5	5	5	7
Sexual orientation	**1,392**	**1,591**	**1,663**	**1,576**
Anti-male homosexual	980	1,103	1,152	1,196
Anti-female homosexual	205	245	257	170
Anti-homosexual	173	207	217	179
Anti-heterosexual	18	20	21	17
Anti-bisexual	16	16	16	14
Disability	**33**	**35**	**35**	**39**
Anti-physical	12	12	12	16
Anti-mental	21	23	23	23
Multiple-bias incidents[1]	**9**	**21**	**22**	**13**
Total	**9,726**	**11,447**	**12,016**	**9,231**

1. A *multiple-bias incident* is a hate crime in which two or more offense types were committed as a result of two or more bias motivations. *Source: Crime in the United States, 2001,* FBI, Uniform Crime Reports.

Index of Crime, United States, 1979–2001

(rate per 100,000 inhabitants)

Year	Crime index total	Violent crime[1]	Property crime[2]	Murder and non-negligent man-slaughter	Forcible rape	Robbery	Aggravated assault	Burglary	Larceny-theft	Motor vehicle theft
1979	5,565.5	548.9	5,016.6	9.7	34.7	218.4	286.0	1,511.9	2,999.1	505.6
1980	5,950.0	596.6	5,353.3	10.2	36.8	251.1	298.5	1,684.1	3,167.0	502.2
1981	5,858.2	594.3	5,263.9	9.8	36.0	258.7	289.7	1,649.5	3,139.7	474.7
1982	5,603.6	571.1	5,032.5	9.1	34.0	238.9	289.2	1,488.8	3,084.8	458.8
1983	5,175.0	537.7	4,637.4	8.3	33.7	216.5	279.2	1,337.7	2,868.9	430.8
1984	5,031.3	539.2	4,492.1	7.9	35.7	205.4	290.2	1,263.7	2,791.3	437.1
1985	5,207.1	556.6	4,650.5	8.0	37.1	208.5	302.9	1,287.3	2,901.2	462.0
1986	5,480.4	617.7	4,862.6	8.6	37.9	225.1	346.1	1,344.6	3,010.3	507.8
1987	5,550.0	609.7	4,940.3	8.3	37.4	212.7	351.3	1,329.6	3,081.3	529.4
1988	5,664.2	637.2	5,027.1	8.4	37.6	220.9	370.2	1,309.2	3,134.9	582.9
1989	5,741.0	663.1	5,077.9	8.7	38.1	233.0	383.4	1,276.3	3,171.3	630.4
1990	5,820.3	731.8	5,088.5	9.4	41.2	257.0	424.1	1,235.9	3,194.8	657.8
1991	5,897.8	758.1	5,139.7	9.8	42.3	272.7	433.3	1,252.0	3,228.8	659.0
1992	5,660.2	757.5	4,902.7	9.3	42.8	263.6	441.8	1,168.2	3,103.0	631.5
1993	5,484.4	746.8	4,737.6	9.5	41.1	255.9	440.3	1,099.2	3,032.4	606.1
1994	5,373.5	713.6	4,660.0	9.0	39.3	237.7	427.6	1,042.0	3,026.7	591.3
1995	5,275.9	684.6	4,591.3	8.2	37.1	220.9	418.3	987.1	3,043.8	560.4
1996	5,086.6	636.5	4,450.1	7.4	36.3	201.9	390.9	944.8	2,797.7	525.6
1997	4,930.0	611.3	4,318.7	6.8	35.9	186.3	382.3	919.4	2,893.4	506.0
1998	4,619.3	567.5	4,051.8	6.3	34.5	165.4	361.3	863.0	2,729.0	459.8
1999	4,266.8	524.7	3,742.1	5.7	32.7	150.2	336.1	770.0	2,551.4	420.7
2000	4,124.0	506.1	3,617.9	5.5	32.0	144.9	323.6	728.4	2,475.3	414.2
2001	4,160.5	504.4	3,656.1	5.6	31.8	148.5	318.5	740.8	2,484.6	430.6

1. Violent crimes are offenses of murder, forcible rape, robbery, and aggravated assault. 2. Property crimes are offenses of burglary, larceny-theft, and motor vehicle theft. Data are not included for the property crime of arson. *Source: Crime in the United States,* 2001, FBI, Uniform Crime Reports.

Arrests by Race, 2001

Offense charged	White	Black	American Indian or Alaskan Native	Asian or Pacific Islander
	Percent distribution[1]			
Total	69.2%	28.5%	1.3%	1.0%
Murder[2]	48.9	48.8	1.1	1.2
Forcible rape	63.1	34.3	1.2	1.5
Robbery	46.0	52.5	0.6	0.9
Aggravated assault	64.4	33.3	1.1	1.2
Burglary	68.1	29.9	0.9	1.1
Larceny-theft	64.9	32.6	1.2	1.3
Motor vehicle theft	58.0	39.3	0.7	1.9
Arson	72.4	24.9	1.8	0.9
Other assaults	65.9	31.6	1.4	1.0
Forgery and counterfeiting	67.3	30.6	0.6	1.5
Fraud	67.7	31.0	0.6	0.7
Embezzlement	65.5	32.4	0.6	1.6
Stolen property—buying, receiving, possessing	59.8	38.4	0.7	1.0
Vandalism	71.0	26.5	1.5	0.9
Weapons—carrying, possessing, etc.	59.5	38.8	0.7	1.0
Prostitution and commercialized vice	57.2	40.1	0.5	2.1%
Sex offenses, except forcible rape and prostitution	74.3%	23.1%	1.1%	1.5
Drug abuse violation	63.2	35.6	0.5	0.7
Gambling	29.8	65.4	0.1	4.6
Offenses against family and children	66.9	30.2	1.2	1.7
Driving under the influence	87.4	10.3	1.4	1.0
Liquor laws	84.8	11.6	2.7	0.9
Drunkenness	83.7	13.5	2.3	0.5
Disorderly conduct	65.4	32.2	1.6	0.7
Vagrancy	60.1	36.6	2.7	0.6
All other offenses except traffic	64.9	32.5	1.4	1.2
Suspicion	59.7	38.7	0.5	1.1

NOTE: For arrests 18 years and older. Total number of estimated arrests: 7,751,236. 1. Because of rounding, the percentages may not add up to total. 2. Includes nonnegligent manslaughter. *Source: Crime in the United States, 2001,* FBI, Uniform Crime Reports.

Crime Index by State, 2001

State	Crime index total: Number	Crime index total: Rate per 100,000	Violent crime	Property crime	Murder[1]
Ala.	192,835	4,319.4	19,582	173,253	379
Alaska	26,895	4,236.2	3,735	23,160	39
Ariz.	322,549	6,077.4	28,675	293,874	400
Ark.	111,296	4,134.2	12,190	99,106	148
Calif.	1,346,557	3,902.9	212,855	1,133,702	2,206
Colo.	186,379	4,218.9	15,492	170,887	158
Conn.	106,791	3,117.9	11,492	95,299	105
Del.	32,267	4,052.8	4,868	27,399	23
DC	44,085	7,709.6	9,931	34,154	232
Fla.	913,230	5,569.7	130,713	782,517	874
Ga.	389,543	4,646.3	41,671	347,872	598
Hawaii	65,947	5,386.1	3,117	62,830	32
Idaho	41,392	3,133.4	3,211	38,181	30
Ill.[2]	511,494	4,097.8	79,504	431,990	986
Ind.	234,282	3,831.4	22,734	211,548	413
Iowa	96,499	3,301.2	7,865	88,634	50
Kans.	116,446	4,321.4	10,909	105,537	92
Ky.[2]	119,449	2,938.1	10,448	109,001	191
La.	238,371	5,338.1	30,678	207,693	501
Maine	34,588	2,688.2	1,434	33,154	18
Md.	261,600	4,866.8	42,088	219,512	446
Mass.	197,666	3,098.6	30,587	167,079	145
Mich.	407,777	4,081.5	55,424	352,353	672
Minn.	178,191	3,583.7	13,145	165,046	119
Miss.	119,615	4,185.2	10,006	109,609	282
Mo.	268,883	4,776.1	30,472	238,411	372
Mont.	33,362	3,688.7	3,187	30,175	34
Nebr.	74,177	4,329.6	5,214	68,963	43
Nev.	89,845	4,266.0	12,359	77,486	180
N.H.	29,233	2,321.6	2,144	27,089	17
N.J.	273,645	3,225.3	33,094	240,551	336
N.M.	97,383	5,324.0	14,288	83,095	99
N.Y.	556,106	2,925.1	98,103	458,003	960
N.C.	404,242	4,938.0	40,465	363,777	505
N.D.	15,339	2,417.7	505	14,834	7
Ohio	475,138	4,177.6	40,023	435,115	452
Okla.	159,405	4,607.0	17,726	141,679	185
Ore.	175,174	5,044.1	10,650	164,524	84
Pa.	363,840	2,961.1	50,432	313,408	651
P.R.	70,117	1,826.1	11,403	58,714	744
R.I.	39,020	3,684.9	3,278	35,742	39
S.C.	193,103	4,752.7	29,265	163,838	255
S.D.	17,644	2,332.0	1,171	16,473	7
Tenn.	295,770	5,152.8	42,778	252,992	425
Tex.	1,098,809	5,152.7	122,155	976,654	1,332
Utah	96,307	4,243.0	5,314	90,993	67
Vt.	16,978	2,769.3	644	16,334	7
Va.	228,445	3,178.3	20,939	207,506	364
Wash.	308,492	5,151.9	21,258	287,234	179
W. Va.	46,120	2,559.5	5,035	41,085	40
Wisc.	179,410	3,321.2	12,486	166,924	192
Wyo.	17,392	3,517.6	1,272	16,120	9

NOTE: The Crime Index is composed of the violent and property crime categories. Violent crimes are murder, forcible rape, robbery, and aggravated assault. Property crimes are burglary, larceny-theft, and auto-theft. Data are not included for the property crime of arson. 1. Includes nonnegligent manslaughter. 2. Limited data for 2001 were available for the states of Illinois and Kentucky; therefore, it was necessary that their crime counts be estimated. *Source: Crime in the United States, 2001,* FBI, Uniform Crime Reports.

Crime Rates for Selected Large Cities, 2000
(offenses known to the police per 100,000 inhabitants)

		Violent crime				Property crime		
City ranked by population size, 2000[1]	Crime index, total	Murder	Forcible rape	Robbery	Aggravated assault	Burglary	Larceny-theft	Motor vehicle theft
New York, N.Y.	3,600.2	8.4	20.4	406.6	509.9	463.4	1,744.0	447.6
Los Angeles, Calif.	4,886.2	14.9	39.5	420.2	885.2	661.0	2,063.3	802.2
Chicago, Ill.	(2)	21.8	(2)	668.0	916.6	978.1	3,664.6	1,026.5
Houston, Tex.	6,741.9	11.8	41.6	422.6	624.1	1,190.3	3,434.7	1,016.8
Philadelphia, Pa.	6,457.8	21.0	67.3	687.0	727.9	796.6	3,093.9	1,064.0
San Diego, Calif.	3,789.4	4.4	28.5	145.3	407.1	549.0	1,881.2	773.8
Phoenix, Ariz.	7,380.4	11.5	31.9	284.9	410.1	1,200.6	3,967.9	1,473.5
San Antonio, Tex.	7,542.2	7.4	39.8	148.4	495.2	1,013.8	5,325.0	512.6
Dallas, Tex.	8,838.3	19.4	53.3	592.8	684.2	1,707.9	4,272.1	1,508.6
Detroit, Mich.	10,066.6	41.6	85.3	827.1	1,370.5	1,663.9	3,356.5	2,721.8
Las Vegas, Nev.	4,470.2	8.5	41.8	317.4	231.0	899.1	2,083.3	889.2
San Jose, Calif.	2,548.5	2.1	37.7	75.6	435.2	298.3	1,407.4	292.2
Honolulu, Hawaii	5,324.5	2.3	27.4	112.3	120.7	792.6	3,674.2	595.0
Indianapolis, Ind.	4,710.3	12.1	55.8	321.4	472.8	1,019.8	2,074.4	754.0
San Francisco, Calif.	5,429.4	7.6	29.5	444.9	354.7	733.2	3,143.4	716.2
Jacksonville, Fla.	6,942.9	10.7	60.2	274.9	769.8	1,353.3	3,857.7	616.2
Columbus, Ohio	8,868.1	9.4	81.2	435.4	316.9	1,911.5	5,104.4	1,009.2
Baltimore, Md.	10,118.3	40.1	56.2	1,015.6	1,345.8	1,641.4	4.812.5	1.206.8
El Paso, Tex.	6,151.2	3.5	33.4	129.7	613.3	395.3	4,542.6	433.4
Memphis, Tenn.	9,170.9	22.6	88.3	628.7	739.6	2,298.6	4,055.5	1,337.6
Charlotte-Mecklenburg, N.C.	7,904.0	12.0	49.2	423.6	716.2	1,533.7	4,440.5	728.8
Milwaukee, Wisc.	7,385.9	20.4	50.8	506.1	379.4	1,065.9	4,011.7	1,351.7
Austin, Tex.	5,936.8	4.9	57.7	153.1	256.2	980.3	4,074.7	410.0
Boston, Mass.	6,088.5	6.6	55.2	416.0	765.0	687.6	2,924.3	1,233.8
Seattle, Wash.	8,040.8	6.4	32.1	293.4	437.2	1,092.9	4,690.3	1,488.5
Nashville, Tenn.	8,806.7	13.0	73.4	406.7	1,129.9	1,382.2	4,838.7	962.8
Washington, DC	7,272.7	41.8	43.9	621.1	800.4	829.5	3,782.3	1,153.7
Denver, Colo.	4,742.2	5.8	53.4	187.3	273.7	898.4	2,315.4	1,008.2
Portland, Ore.	7,737.9	3.6	69.7	273.3	730.3	1,050.8	4,719.1	891.1
Fort Worth, Tex.	7,133.6	11.4	60.8	245.7	395.7	1,356.1	4,299.8	764.0
Cleveland, Ohio	6,811.0	14.8	128.6	644.6	474.7	1,554.1	2,710.9	1,283.2
Oklahoma City, Okla.	9,453.1	7.5	76.7	195.6	500.9	1,438.4	6,522.4	711.7
Tucson, Ariz.	9,148.4	12.3	72.9	296.7	551.3	1,380.9	5,619.3	1,214.9
New Orleans, La.	6,979.1	42.1	46.8	499.5	475.2	1,079.1	3,213.5	1,622.9
Kansas City, Mo.	10,672.8	25.6	70.2	513.0	1,017.6	1,712.6	5,699.8	1,634.0
Virginia Beach, Va.	4,207.6	2.6	23.8	106.1	89.4	611.6	3,174.1	200.1
Long Beach, Calif.	3,828.0	10.6	24.7	329.1	332.4	684.7	1,671.4	775.0
Albuquerque, N.M.	8,793.2	7.4	53.3	344.8	739.4	1,587.1	5,091.8	969.4
Atlanta, Ga.	13,318.5	32.2	66.8	1,037.8	1,644.5	2,222.5	6,549.7	1,765.1
Sacramento, Calif.	6,716.7	9.6	36.1	346.9	373.2	1,145.2	3,609.2	1,196.5
Fresno, Calif.	7,685.7	5.6	37.6	304.9	550.4	1,055.5	4,380.2	1,351.3
Tulsa, Okla.	6,832.0	8.4	61.6	187.5	864.8	1,369.5	3,479.7	860.5
Miami, Fla.	10,968.1	18.2	32.6	848.9	1,273.5	2,014.8	5,201.5	1,578.6
Omaha, Neb.	6,876.5	9.5	48.5	224.4	529.0	864.9	4,333.8	866.7
Oakland, Calif.	6,273.1	20.0	80.1	482.9	678.1	877.6	2,916.8	1,217.6
Mesa, Ariz.	6,439.6	3.8	30.3	109.2	460.4	938.5	4,032.0	865.3
Minneapolis, Minn.	7,184.5	13.1	110.3	509.1	518.5	1,179.8	3,865.0	988.7
Colorado Springs, Colo.	4,967.2	4.2	58.5	118.3	274.0	851.8	3,316.8	343.6
Pittsburgh, Pa.	5,701.4	10.8	37.5	464.5	444.5	924.0	3,086.6	733.5
St. Louis, Mo.	14,547.6	35.6	32.2	925.9	1,285.5	2,303.3	7,714.8	2,250.2
Cincinnati, Ohio	6,704.8	6.6	85.7	423.8	323.9	1,497.2	3,755.1	612.5
Wichita, Kans.	6,293.9	9.0	51.1	172.8	371.5	1,091.3	4,111.1	487.1
Toledo, Ohio	7,661.2	3.8	52.0	328.4	374.7	1,627.8	4,401.8	872.7
Arlington, Tex.	6,451.1	4.2	28.8	178.7	436.1	943.3	4,236.4	623.5
Santa Ana, Calif.	3,092.5	5.0	25.4	263.0	247.6	369.0	1,575.3	607.1
Buffalo, N.Y.	6,918.9	13.3	60.1	531.4	644.8	1,433.1	3,359.3	876.8
Anaheim, Calif.	3,020.9	3.4	25.6	130.5	271.3	478.6	1,638.3	473.2
Tampa, Fla.	11,094.5	12.5	77.4	719.4	1,293.5	2,035.6	5,053.9	1,902.1
Corpus Christi, Tex.	7,211.6	6.1	69.6	157.5	525.1	1,274.8	4,677.9	500.6
Newark, N.J.	7,188.2	21.2	34.7	703.0	737.0	1,010.8	2,692.1	1,989.4
Riverside, Calif.	4,792.2	6.7	33.7	239.5	506.3	831.6	2,449.4	725.0
Raleigh, N.C.	7,035.3	9.4	32.2	278.5	422.0	1,460.7	4,311.6	520.8
St. Paul, Minn.	6,518.9	7.0	77.7	264.0	484.8	1,078.5	3,911.9	695.1
Anchorage, Alaska	4,943.1	3.8	74.9	132.9	373.8	589.0	3,380.6	388.0
Louisville, Ky.	5,877.9	15.2	26.5	421.1	332.9	1,249.7	2,931.7	900.7

1. Resident population estimated by the U.S. Census Bureau. 2. The rates for forcible rape and crime index are not shown because the forcible rape figures were not in accordance with national Uniform Crime Reporting guidelines. *Source:* U.S. Federal Bureau of Investigation, *Crime in the United States,* annual. From *Statistical Abstract of the United States, 2002.*

Fact Sheet: Operation Iraqi Freedom

Official length of combat operation: March 20–May 1, 2003.

Deployment: More than 300,000 coalition troops deployed to the Gulf region: about 255,000 U.S., 45,000 British, 2,000 Australian, and 200 Polish troops (60 of whom served as combat soldiers). About 140,000 U.S. and 11,000 British troops were stationed in Iraq following official end of hostilities, May 1.

Coalition names for Operation Iraqi Freedom: UK, Operation Telic; Australia, Operation Falconer.

Central Command, U.S. Forces (CENTCOM): Theater headquarters: Qatar. Troops stationed in Bahrain, Iraq, Kuwait, Oman, Saudi Arabia, United Arab Emirates, Diego Garcia, the Mediterranean, Arabian Sea, and Persian Gulf.

U.S. casualties: Deaths March 20–May 1 (official end of hostilities): combat, 116; noncombat, 23; total, 138. Deaths May 1–Aug. 9 (100 days after end of hostilities): combat, 57; noncombat, 60; total, 117. Deaths March 20–Aug. 9: combat, 173; noncombat, 82; total, 255.

U.S. wounded: More than 1,000 (March 20–July 10): 791 wounded during combat; 253 noncombat.[1]

American POWs: 8 (6 captured on March 23 in Nasiriya; 2 pilots shot down on March 24 near Karbala). All were rescued.

British casualties: 14 combat deaths (6 of which occurred after official end of combat, May 1); 29 noncombat deaths (4 of which occurred after May 1). Total as of Aug. 9, 2003, 100 days after end of combat: 43.

Australian casualties: 0

British and Australian POWs: 0

Journalists killed during war: 18 (as of Aug. 20)

U.S. cost of stationing troops in Iraq: $4 billion per month[1]

Iraqi troop estimate: 350,000; Republican Guard: 15,000

Iraqi combat deaths: 2,320 (as of May 1)[1]

Iraqi POWs: 7,300 (as of April 15)[1]

Iraqi civilian deaths: circa 6,000–7,700 (Aug. 5)[2]

Iraqi civilians wounded: 5,103 (April 3)[3]

1. U.S. government figures. 2. From Iraqbodycount.net, a group of academic analysts and peace activists. 3. Iraqi government figures, as of April 3, reported by the CBC. *Sources:* Canadian Broadcasting Corporation (CBC), CNN, BBC, U.S. Dept. of Defense.

Iraq War Timeline

Jan. 29, 2002: President George Bush's State of the Union address labels Iraq part of the "axis of evil," and vows that the U.S. "will not permit the world's most dangerous regimes to threaten us with the world's most destructive weapons."

June 2: President Bush publicly introduces the new defense doctrine of preemption in a speech at West Point. In some instances, the president asserts, the U.S. must strike first against another state to prevent a potential threat from growing into an actual one: "Our security will require all Americans . . . [to] be ready for preemptive action when necessary to defend our liberty and to defend our lives."

Sept. 12: President Bush addresses the UN, challenging the organization to swiftly enforce its own resolutions against Iraq. If not, Bush contends, the U.S. will have no choice but to act on its own against Iraq.

Oct. 11: Congress authorizes an attack on Iraq.

Nov. 8: The UN Security Council unanimously approves resolution 1441 imposing tough new arms inspections on Iraq.

Nov. 18: UN weapons inspectors return to Iraq for the first time in almost four years.

Dec. 21: President Bush approves the deployment of U.S. troops to the Gulf region.

Jan. 28, 2003: In his State of the Union address, President Bush announces that he is ready to attack Iraq even without a UN mandate.

Feb. 14: In a UN weapons inspections report on Iraq, chief inspector Hans Blix indicates that slight progress has been made in Iraq's cooperation with the weapons team. Anti-war nations interpret this as a sign that inspections are yielding modest results and should continue; pro-war nations see it as Iraq's continued defiance of the international community, which is viewed as a threat to world peace and can only be remedied through force.

Feb. 24–March 14: The U.S. and Britain's intense lobbying efforts among UN Security Council members to shore up support for a strike on Iraq yield only two additional supporters (Spain and Bulgaria).

March 20: The war against Iraq begins 5:30 a.m. Baghdad time (9:30 p.m. EST, March 19), when the U.S. launches Operation Iraqi Freedom. A "decapitation attack" attempts to target Saddam Hussein and other Iraqi leaders. A second round of air strikes is launched against Baghdad later that day, and U.S. ground troops enter the country, crossing into southern Iraq from Kuwait.

March 21: The major phase of the war begins with heavy aerial attacks on Baghdad and other cities. The campaign, publicized in advance by the Pentagon as an overwhelming barrage meant to instill "shock and awe," is actually more restrained.

March 24: Troops march within 50 miles of Baghdad. They encounter strong resistance from Iraqi soldiers and paramilitary fighters along the way, particularly in towns such as Nasiriya and Basra.

March 26: About 1,000 paratroopers land in Kurdish-controlled Iraq to open a northern front.

March 30: U.S. Marines and Army troops launch first attack on Iraq's Republican Guard, about 65 miles outside Baghdad. Secretary of Defense Donald Rumsfeld deflects criticism that the U.S. has not deployed enough Army ground troops in Iraq.

April 2: Special operations forces rescue Pfc. Jessica Lynch from a hospital in Nasiriya. She was one of 12 members of the 507th Ordnance Maintenance Company captured by Iraqi troops on March 23.

April 5: U.S. tanks roll into the Iraqi capital and engage in firefights with Iraqi troops. Resistance weaker than anticipated. Heavy Iraqi casualties.

April 7: British forces take control of Basra, Iraq's second-largest city.

April 9: Baghdad falls to U.S. forces, but sporadic fighting continues throughout the capital. Looters pillage government buildings, museums, hospitals, and stores. Statue of Saddam Hussein symbolically toppled.

April 11: Kirkuk falls to Kurdish fighters.

April 13: Marines rescue five U.S. soldiers captured by Iraqi troops on March 23 in Nasiriya, and two pilots who had been shot down on March 24 near Karbala.

April 14: Major fighting in Iraq is declared over by the Pentagon, after U.S. forces take control of Tikrit, Saddam Hussein's birthplace. Saddam Hussein's whereabouts remain unknown.

April 15: Gen. Jay Garner, appointed by the U.S. to run post-war Iraq, meets with various Iraqi leaders to begin planning the new Iraqi federal government.

May 1: The U.S. declares an end to major combat operations.

May 12: A new civil administrator takes over in Iraq. U.S. diplomat Paul Bremer replaces Jay Garner, who was seen as ineffective in stemming the continuing lawlessness and violence taking place throughout Iraq.

May 22: UN Security Council votes to lift 13 years of sanctions on Iraq. Resolution 1483 also gives the U.S. and Britain broad power to run Iraq's government and economy until an Iraqi government is in place.

May 30: In separate speeches, U.S. secretary of state Colin Powell and British prime minister Tony Blair deny that intelligence about Iraq's weapons of mass destruction was distorted or exaggerated to justify an attack on Iraq. Both administrations face mounting questions because no weapons of mass destruction (WMD) have been found. Each had claimed that Iraq's WMD were an imminent threat to world security.

July 13: Iraq's interim governing council, composed of 25 Iraqis appointed by American and British officials, is inaugurated. American administrator Paul Bremer, however, retains ultimate authority.

June 15–29: About 1,300 troops launch Operation Desert Scorpion, combatting organized Iraqi resistance against American troops near Faluja. U.S. and British troops face continued attacks; about one American soldier has been killed per day since the end of combat was declared. It is the largest of several offensives.

July 7: Bush administration concedes that evidence that Iraq was pursuing a nuclear weapons program by seeking to buy uranium from Africa, cited in January State of the Union address and elsewhere, was unsubstantiated and should not have been included in speech. Over summer Tony Blair faces even stronger criticism than his American counterpart concerning flawed intelligence.

July 16: Gen. John Abizaid, commander of allied forces in Iraq who replaced retiring general Tommy Franks on July 7, calls continued attacks on coalition troops a "guerrilla-type campaign" and says soldiers who will replace current troops may be deployed for year-long tours.

July 22: Saddam Hussein's sons, Uday and Qusay Hussein, die in firefight in a Mosul palace.

Aug. 9: U.S. combat and noncombat casualties reach 255 at 100-day mark after declared end of combat on May 1; 43 British have died.

Aug. 19: Suicide bombing destroys UN headquarters in Baghdad, killing 24, including top envoy Sergio Vieira de Mello, and wounding more than 100.

Aug. 29: A bomb kills one of Iraq's most important Shi'ite leaders, Ayatollah Muhammad Bakr al-Hakim, as well as about 80 others, and wounds 125.

Sept. 7: Continued violence and slow progress in Iraq lead to President Bush's announcement that $87 billion is needed to cover additional military and reconstruction costs.

Fighting Words: An Iraq War Glossary

Collateral damage: A military euphemism for civilian deaths.

Decapitation strike: To remove a regime's leadership and thereby curtail warfare. The U.S. military attempted a decapitation strike against Saddam Hussein at the war's outset. Also called a **target of opportunity.**

Embedded reporter: A journalist traveling with troops and reporting from the battlefield. The 2003 Iraq war was the first time "embeds" were used. Pros: unprecedented media access to the front. Cons: lack of distance and independence between reporters and their protectors. A **unilateral** was a reporter unattached to a military unit.

Fedayeen ("soldier of sacrifice"): A paramilitary group founded by Saddam Hussein's son Uday in 1995 and used against the regime's domestic enemies. They showed unexpected resistance against U.S. and British troops in the 2003 Iraq war.

MOAB: The largest non-nuclear bomb in existence made its debut in the Iraq war. The acronym stands for Massive Ordnance Air Burst, but it has been nicknamed the Mother of All Bombs.

Patriot missiles: Rockets that intercept other missiles before they reach their targets.

Peshmerga ("those who face death"): Kurdish fighters who have battled the Iraqi regime for generations. They fought with coalition troops on the northern front in the 2003 Iraqi war.

Regime change: A polite term for the overthrow of a government.

Republican Guard: Saddam Hussein's most elite troops, led by his son Qusay.

Shock and awe: American equivalent to the blitzkrieg, in which the enemy is treated to an overwhelming strike that leads to a swift surrender.

Smart bombs: Accurate bombs that are guided to their targets by Global Positioning Satellites, as opposed to **dumb bombs,** those without guidance systems.

Surgical strike: Military jargon that makes a precision bombing sound like a beneficial medical procedure.

Weapons of mass destruction (WMD): chemical, biological, and nuclear weapons. The *Washington Post* quoted historian Paul Fussell on the subject: "A machine gun, properly fired, is a weapon of mass destruction. We're pretending that only awful and sinister people own weapons of mass destruction. We own them, too. We just call them something else."

America's Wars: U.S. Casualties and Veterans

American Revolution (1775–1783)	
Total servicemembers	217,000
Battle deaths	4,435
Nonmortal woundings	6,188
War of 1812 (1812–1815)	
Total servicemembers	286,730
Battle deaths	2,260
Nonmortal woundings	4,505
Indian Wars (approx. 1817–1898)	
Total servicemembers	106,000[1]
Battle deaths	1,000[1]
Mexican War (1846–1848)	
Total servicemembers	78,718
Battle deaths	1,733
Other deaths in service (nontheater)	11,550
Nonmortal woundings	4,152
Civil War (1861–1865)	
Total servicemembers (Union)	2,213,363
Battle deaths (Union)	140,414
Other deaths in service (nontheater) (Union)	224,097
Nonmortal woundings (Union)	281,881
Total servicemembers (Conf.)	1,050,000
Battle deaths (Conf.)	74,524
Other deaths in service (nontheater) (Conf.)	59,297[2]
Nonmortal woundings (Conf.)	unknown
Spanish-American War (1898–1902)	
Total servicemembers	306,760
Battle deaths	385
Other deaths in service (nontheater)	2,061
Nonmortal woundings	1,662
World War I (1917–1918)	
Total servicemembers	4,734,991
Battle deaths	53,402
Other deaths in service (nontheater)	63,114
Nonmortal woundings	204,002
Living veterans	fewer than 500
World War II (1940–1945)	
Total servicemembers	16,112,566
Battle deaths	291,557
Other deaths in service (nontheater)	113,842
Nonmortal woundings	671,846
Living veterans	4,762,000[1]
Korean War (1950–1953)	
Total servicemembers	5,720,000
Serving in-theater	1,789,000
Battle deaths	33,741
Other deaths in service (theater)	2,827
Other deaths in service (nontheater)	17,730
Nonmortal woundings	103,284
Living veterans	3,734,000[1]
Vietnam War (1964–1975)	
Total servicemembers	8,744,000
Serving in-theater	3,403,000
Battle deaths	47,410
Other deaths in service (theater)	10,789
Other deaths in service (nontheater)	32,000
Nonmortal woundings	153,303
Living veterans	8,295,000[1]
Gulf War (1990–1991)	
Total servicemembers	2,183,000
Serving in-theater	665,476
Battle deaths	147
Other deaths in service (theater)	382
Other deaths in service (nontheater)	1,565
Nonmortal woundings	467
Living veterans	1,852,000[1]
America's Wars Total	
Military service during war	42,348,460
Battle deaths	651,008
Other deaths in service (theater)	13,998
Other deaths in service (nontheater)	525,256
Nonmortal woundings	1,431,290
Living war veterans	17,578,500[3]
Living veterans	25,038,459

1. Veterans Administration estimate as of Sept. 30, 2002. 2. Estimated figure. Does not include 26,000–31,000 who died in Union prisons. 3. Approximately 1,065,000 veterans had service in multiple conflicts. They are counted under each conflict, but only once in the total. *Source:* Department of Defense and Veterans Administration.

Post-Vietnam Combat Casualties[1]

Place	Dates	Casualties
Lebanon	Aug. 1982–Feb. 1984	254
Grenada	Oct.–Nov. 1983	18
Libya	April 10–16, 1986	2
Panama	Dec. 1989–Jan. 1990	23
Persian Gulf	Jan. 16–April 6, 1991	147
Somalia	Dec. 1992–May 1993	29
Haiti	Sept. 1994–April 1996	0
Yugoslavia	March–June 1999	0
Afghanistan	Oct. 2001–May 2003[2]	20
Iraq	March 20,–Aug. 9, 2003[3]	173

1. Defined as battle deaths. Does not include deaths from accidents. 2. As of May 1, 2003, the official end of combat. Accidental deaths totalled 44. 3. The Aug. 9 date is 100 days after the official end of combat, May 1. A total of 255 Americans have been killed, including 82 accidental deaths and other deaths not the result of hostile attacks. *Source:* U.S. Department of Defense.

American Prisoners of War

Congress defines a prisoner of war as a person who, while serving on active military, naval, or air service, is forcibly detained or interned in the line of duty by an enemy government or a hostile force.

	Total	WWI	WWII	Korea	Vietnam	Persian Gulf	Somalia	Iraq
Captured and interned	142,233	4,120	130,201	7,140	745	23	1	8
Returned to U.S. military control	125,208	3,973	116,129	4,418	661	23	1	8
Alive on Jan. 1, 1982	93,030	633	87,996	3,770	631	n.a.	n.a.	n.a.
Died while POW	17,004	147	14,072	2,701	84	0	0	0
Alive on Jan. 1, 2002	42,781	0	39,719	2,434	601	23	1	n.a.

NOTES: n.a. = not applicable. Not included are the more than 92,000 military personnel considered missing in action: WWI, 3,350; WWII, 78,773; Korea, 8,100; Vietnam, 1,912 (as of June 2002); and the Persian Gulf, 1. *Source:* U.S. Department of Veterans Affairs.

Highest-Ranking Officers in U.S. History

General and Commander-in-Chief[1]

George Washington (1732–1799), b. Westmoreland County, Va., unanimously voted by Congress on June 15, 1775, to the rank of general and commander-in-chief (of the Continental army).

General of the Armies[2]

John Joseph Pershing (1860–1948), b. Linn County, Mo., made permanent general of the armies, 1919.

General of the Army, General of the Air Force (Five-Stars)

George Catlett Marshall (1880–1959), b. Uniontown, Pa., promoted Dec. 1944.

Douglas MacArthur (1880–1964), b. Little Rock, Ark., promoted Dec. 1944.

Dwight David Eisenhower (1890–1969), b. Denison, Tex., promoted Dec. 1944.

Henry Harley Arnold (1866–1950), b. Gladwyne, Pa. Arnold had the unique distinction of being a five-star general twice—in 1944 as general of the army, and in June 1949 as general of the air force. He is the only air force general to have held the five-star rank.

Omar Nelson Bradley (1893–1981), b. Clark, Mo., promoted Sept. 1950.

Fleet Admiral (Five-Star)

William Daniel Leahy (1875–1959), b. Hampton, Iowa, promoted Dec. 1944.

Ernest Joseph King (1878–1956), b. Lorain, Ohio, promoted Dec. 1944.

Chester William Nimitz (1885–1966), b. Fredericksburg, Tex., promoted Dec. 1944.

William Frederick Halsey (1882–1959), b. Elizabeth, N.J., promoted Dec. 1945.

1. On March 15, 1978, George Washington was promoted posthumously to the newly created rank of General of the Armies of the United States. Congress authorized this title to make it clear that Washington was the army's senior general. 2. General Pershing was given the option of five stars but he declined. *Source:* Department of Defense and U.S. Army Historian, Research and Analysis Center.

The Joint Chiefs of Staff (JCS)

The Joint Chiefs of Staff consist of the chairman, the vice chairman, the chief of staff of the army, the chief of naval operations, the chief of staff of the air force, and the commandant of the Marine Corps.

The collective body of the JCS is headed by the chairman (or vice chairman in the chairman's absence), who sets the agenda and presides over JCS meetings. Their responsibilities take precedence over their duties as the Chiefs of Military Services. The chairman is the principal military adviser to the president, the secretary of defense, and the National Security Council (NSC); however, all JCS members are by law military advisers, and they may respond to a request or voluntarily submit, through the chairman, advice or opinions to the president, the secretary of state, or the NSC. The Joint Chiefs of Staff have no executive authority to commit combatant forces.

In addition to their responsibilities on the JCS, the military service chiefs are responsible to the secretaries of their military departments for management of the services. The service chiefs serve for four years. By custom the vice chiefs of the services act for their chiefs in most matters having to do with day-to-day operation of the services.

Joint Chiefs of Staff, 2003

Chairman of the Joint Chiefs of Staff, General Richard B. Myers, U.S. Air Force; vice chairman of the Joint Chiefs of Staff, General Peter Pace, Marine Corps; General Peter J. Schoomaker, chief of staff of the U.S. Army; Admiral Vern Clark, chief of naval operations; General John P. Jumper, chief of staff of the U.S. Air Force; and General Michael W. Hagee, commandant of the Marine Corps.

Past Chairmen of the JCS

General of the Army, Omar N. Bradley, 1949–1953
Adm. Arthur W. Radford, U.S. Navy, 1953–1957
Gen. Nathan F. Twining, U.S. Air Force, 1957–1960
Gen. Lyman L. Lemnitzer, U.S. Army, 1960–1962
Gen. Maxwell D. Taylor, U.S. Army, 1962–1964
Gen. Earle G. Wheeler, U.S. Army, 1964–1970
Adm. Thomas H. Moorer, U.S. Navy, 1970–1974
Gen. George S. Brown, U.S. Air Force, 1974–1978
Gen. David C. Jones, U.S. Air Force, 1978–1982
Gen. John W. Vessey, Jr., U.S. Army, 1982–1985
Adm. William J. Crowe, U.S. Navy, 1985–1989
Gen. Colin L. Powell, U.S. Army, 1989–1993
Gen. John M. Shalikashvili, U.S. Army, 1993–1997
Gen. Henry H. Shelton, U.S. Army, 1997–2001

U.S. Military Spending, 1946–2004

(billions of 2002 dollars)

Year	Spending	Year	Spending	Year	Spending	Year	Spending	Year	Spending	Year	Spending
1946	$556.9	1956	$356.2	1966	$356.2	1976	$283.8	1986	$426.6	1996	$307.4
1947	52.4	1957	360.9	1967	412.0	1977	286.2	1987	427.9	1997	305.3
1948	103.9	1958	352.9	1968	449.3	1978	286.5	1988	426.4	1998	296.7
1949	144.2	1959	352.5	1969	438.1	1979	295.6	1989	427.7	1999	298.4
1950	141.2	1960	344.3	1970	406.3	1980	303.4	1990	409.7	2000	311.7
1951	224.3	1961	344.0	1971	370.6	1981	317.4	1991	358.1	2001	307.8
1952	402.1	1962	363.4	1972	343.8	1982	339.4	1992	379.5	2002	328.7
1953	442.3	1963	368.0	1973	313.3	1983	366.7	1993	358.6	2003	379.3[1]
1954	420.9	1964	364.4	1974	299.7	1984	381.7	1994	338.6	2004	379.9[1,2]
1955	376.9	1965	333.1	1975	293.3	1985	405.4	1995	321.6		

1. Figures based on requested defense budget, not actual spending. 2. In addition, President Bush has asked Congress for $87 billion to fund the war and reconstruction effort in Iraq. *Source:* Center for Defense Information.

U.S. Military Ranks

Source: U.S. Department of Defense.

Pay Grade	Army and Marine Corps	Navy and Coast Guard[1]	Air Force	Total number[2]
Commissioned officers				
0-1	Second Lieutenant	Ensign	Second Lieutenant	27,529
0-2	First Lieutenant	Lieutenant Junior Grade	First Lieutenant	32,440
0-3	Captain	Lieutenant	Captain	66,036
0-4	Major	Lieutenant Commander	Major	44,264
0-5	Lieutenant Colonel	Commander	Lieutenant Colonel	28,328
0-6	Colonel	Captain	Colonel	11,656
0-7	Brigadier General	Rear Admiral	Brigadier General	439
0-8	Major General	Rear Admiral	Major General	280
0-9	Lieutenant General	Vice Admiral	Lieutenant General	124
0-10	General	Admiral	General	35
Special grades[3]				
(5 stars)	General of the Army	Fleet Admiral	General of the Air Force	
Warrant officers				
W-1	Warrant Officer. Grades W-2 to W-5 Chief Warrant Officer			
Enlisted personnel				
E-1	Recruit	Seaman Recruit	Recruit	50,438
E-2	Army Private/ Marine Private First Class	Seaman Apprentice	Airman	85,129
E-3	Army Private First Class/ Marine Lance Corporal	Seaman	Airman First Class	224,729
E-4	Corporal	Petty Officer, Third Class	Sergeant	265,134
E-5	Sergeant	Petty Officer, Second Class	Staff Sergeant	248,807
E-6	Staff Sergeant	Petty Officer, First Class	Technical Sergeant	171,411
E-7	Army Sergeant First Class Marine Gunnery Sergeant	Chief Petty Officer	First Sergeant	100,188
E-8	Master Sergeant	Senior Chief Petty Officer	First Sergeant	27,004
E-9	Sergeant Major	Master Chief Petty Officer	First Sergeant	10,824
Special grades[4]				
	Sergeant Major of the Army Sergeant Major of the Marine Corps	Master Chief Petty Officer of the Navy	Chief Master Sergeant of the Air Force	

1. During peacetime, the United States Coast Guard operates within the Department of Transportation rather than the Department of Defense. Upon declaration of war or order of the president, the Coast Guard falls under the Department of the Navy. The ranks of the U.S. Coast Guard are identical to those of the U.S. Navy. 2. As of May 30, 2003. 3. There are no living five-star commissioned officers. 4. Senior enlisted advisers. There is only one for each branch of service. *Source:* Dept. of Defense and Center for Defense Information.

U.S. Military Personnel on Active Duty in Selected Regions/Countries,[1] 2002

Region/Country	Personnel
United States and Territories	
Continental U.S.	969,215
Alaska	15,906
Hawaii	34,608
Guam	3,149
Puerto Rico	2,592
Transients	27,863
Europe	
Belgium*	1,458
Bosnia and Herzegovina	3,082
France*	74
Germany*	68,701
Greece*	593
Greenland*	88
Iceland*	1,665
Italy*	12,466
Macedonia	146
Netherlands*	629
Norway*	123
Portugal*	992
Russia	78
Serbia (includes Kosovo)	2,804
Spain*	2,621
Turkey*	1,587
United Kingdom*	10,258
Afloat	5,003
East Asia and Pacific	
Australia	171
China (includes Hong Kong)	61
Japan	41,848
Korea, Rep. of	37,743
Philippines	86
Singapore	167
Thailand	125
North Africa, Near East, and South Asia	
Afghanistan	n.a.
Bahrain	1,560
Bangladesh	35
Diego Garcia	548
Egypt	433
Israel	36
Jordan	32
Kuwait	567
Oman	31
Pakistan	31
Qatar	71
Saudi Arabia	776
Sub-Saharan Africa	
Kenya	43
South Africa	32
Western Hemisphere	
Canada	148
Colombia	39
Cuba (Guantanamo)	549
Dominican Republic	55
Ecuador	35
Honduras	402
Mexico	31
Peru	41
Total foreign countries[2]	**230,484**
Ashore	208,479
Afloat	22,005
NATO Countries	101,252
Total worldwide[2]	**1,411,634**
Ashore	1,261,862
Afloat	149,772

NOTES: n.a. = not available. *NATO countries. 1. Only countries with 30 or more U.S. military personnel are listed. 2. Includes all regions/countries, not simply those listed. *Source:* U.S. Department of Defense, *Selected Manpower Statistics, Annual.*

Active Duty Military Personnel, 1940–2002[1]

Year	Army	Air Force	Navy	Marine Corps	Total
1940	269,023		160,997	28,345	458,365
1945	8,266,373		3,319,586	469,925	12,055,884
1950	593,167	411,277	380,739	74,279	1,459,462
1955	1,109,296	959,946	660,695	205,170	2,935,107
1960	873,078	814,752	616,987	170,621	2,475,438
1965	969,066	824,662	669,985	190,213	2,653,926
1970	1,322,548	791,349	691,126	259,737	3,064,760
1975	784,333	612,751	535,085	195,951	2,128,120
1980	777,036	557,969	527,153	188,469	2,050,627
1985	780,787	601,515	570,705	198,025	2,151,032
1990	732,403	535,233	579,417	196,652	2,043,705
1991	710,821	510,432	570,262	194,040	1,985,555
1992	610,450	470,315	541,886	184,529	1,807,177
1993	572,423	444,351	509,950	178,379	1,705,103
1994	541,343	426,327	468,662	174,158	1,610,490
1995	508,559	400,409	434,617	174,639	1,518,224
1996	491,103	389,001	416,735	174,883	1,471,722
1997	491,707	377,385	395,564	173,906	1,438,562
1998	483,880	367,470	382,338	173,142	1,406,830
1999	479,426	360,590	373,046	172,641	1,385,703
2000	482,170	355,654	373,193	173,321	1,384,338
2001	480,801	353,571	377,810	172,934	1,385,116
2002	486,542	368,251	385,051	173,733	1,413,577

NOTE: Figures for 1998 through 2002 include cadets/midshipmen. 1. Military personnel on extended or continuous active duty. Excludes reserves on active duty for training. *Source:* Department of Defense.

The Medal of Honor

Often called the Congressional Medal of Honor, it is the nation's highest military award for "uncommon valor" by men and women in the armed forces. It is given for actions that are above and beyond the call of duty in combat against an armed enemy. The medal was first awarded by the army on March 25, 1863. More than 3,400 men have been awarded the medal, as well as one woman, Dr. Mary Walker, a surgeon in the Civil War.

Recipients of the medal are awarded $400 per month for life, a right to burial at Arlington National Cemetery, admission for them or their children to a service academy (if they qualify and quotas permit), and free travel on government aircraft to almost anywhere in the world, on a space-available basis. In 2003, there were 137 Medal of Honor recipients living.

Medal of Honor Recipients

	Total[1]	Army	Navy	Marines	Coast Guard	Air Force	Civilian
Civil War	1,522	1,196	305	17	—	—	4
Noncombat, 1865–1870	13	1	12	—	—	—	—
Indian Wars (1861–1898)	426	422	—	—	—	—	4
Korea (1871)	15	—	9	6	—	—	—
Noncombat, 1871–1899	106	—	104	2	—	—	—
Spanish-American War	110	31	64	15	—	—	—
Samoa	4	—	1	3	—	—	—
Philippines	80	69	5	6	—	—	—
China	59	4	22	33	—	—	—
Noncombat, 1901–1910	49	1	46	2	—	—	—
Philippines (1911)	6	1	5	—	—	—	—
Mexican Campaign (1914)	56	1	46	9	—	—	—
Haiti (1915)	6	—	—	6	—	—	—
Noncombat, 1915–1916	8	—	8	—	—	—	—
Dominican Republic	3	—	—	3	—	—	—
World War I	119	90	21	8	—	—	—
Haiti (1919–1920)	2	—	—	2	—	—	—
Nicaragua (1927–1933)	2	—	—	2	—	—	—
Noncombat, 1920–1940	17	1	15	1	—	—	—
World War II	464	324	57	82	1	—	—
Korean War	131	82	7	42	—	—	—
Vietnam War	245	159	16	57	—	13	—
Somalia (1993)	2	2	—	—	—	—	—
Unknown Soldiers	9	9	—	—	—	—	—
Total	**3,454**	**2,393**	**743**	**296**	**1**	**13**	**8**

1. These totals reflect the total number of Medals of Honor awarded through June 2003. Nineteen (19) men received a second award. *Sources:* The Congressional Medal of Honor Society, Mt. Pleasant, S.C. Web: www.cmohs.org and Home of Heroes. Web: www.homeofheroes.com/moh/history/history_statistics.html.

U.S. Service Academies

U.S. Air Force Academy
Colorado Springs, Colo.
Established 1958
www.usafa.edu

U.S. Coast Guard Academy
New London, Conn.
Established 1876
www.cga.edu

U.S. Merchant Marine Academy
Kings Point, N.Y.
Established 1943
www.usmma.edu

U.S. Military Academy
West Point, N.Y.
Established 1802
www.usma.edu

U.S. Naval Academy
Annapolis, Md.
Established 1845
www.usna.edu

Last Civil War Widows

The last-known Confederate widow, Alberta Martin, born Dec, 4, 1906, lives quietly in Dothan, Alabama. In 1927, at age 21, she married William Jasper Martin, then 81. Martin joined the Confederate army in May 1864 and served with the 4th Alabama Infantry Regiment. Upon her husband's death, she married his grandson from his first marriage.

The last-known Union widow, Gertrude Janeway, died in Jan. 2003, in the log cabin she shared with her husband in Tennessee. John Janeway joined the Union army in 1864, served with the 14th Illinois Cavalry, and was briefly a POW at Andersonville. The couple married in 1927, after waiting three years until Gertrude turned 18. John was 81.

Veterans of U.S. Wars and Their Dependents

Veterans' benefits have existed since the origins of the nation. As of Oct. 2002, 2,177,303 veterans, their dependents, and survivors of deceased veterans are receiving VA benefits and services.

	Veterans	Children[1]	Parents	Surviving spouses
Civil War	—	7	—	1
Indian Wars	—	1	—	—
Spanish-American War	—	198	—	262
Mexican Border	5	23	—	139
World War I	56	5,220	1	17,984
World War II	580,110	17,812	838	259,715
Korean Conflict	242,611	3,869	1,044	62,443
Vietnam Era	927,656	12,147	5,136	124,048
Gulf War[2]	426,865	9,332	366	7,663
Total wartime	**2,177,303**	**48,609**	**7,385**	**472,255**
Nonservice-connected	346,173	24,988	—	212,641
Service-connected	1,831,130	23,621	7,385	259,614
Total	2,177,303	58,609	7,385	472,255

1. Children connotes a minor or a helpless adult. 2. For VA benefits purposes, the Gulf War period of service remains open-ended and also includes those discharged from 1991 to date. *Source:* Department of Veterans Affairs and Department of Defense. Web: www.va.gov/pressrel/amwars01.htm.

Last Living Veterans of America's Wars

American Revolution (1775–1783)
- Last veteran, Daniel F. Bakeman, died 4/5/1869, age 109
- Last widow, Catherine S. Damon, died 11/11/06, age 92
- Last dependent, Phoebe M. Palmeter, died 4/25/11, age 90

War of 1812 (1812–1815)
- Last veteran, Hiram Cronk, died 5/13/05, age 105
- Last widow, Carolina King, died 6/28/36, age unknown
- Last dependent, Esther A. H. Morgan, died 3/12/46, age 89

Indian Wars (c. 1861–1898)
- Last veteran, Fredrak Fraske, died 6/18/73, age 101

Mexican War (1846–1848)
- Last veteran, Owen Thomas Edgar, died 9/3/29, age 98
- Last widow, Lena James Theobald, died 6/20/63, age 89
- Last dependent, Jesse G. Bivens, died 11/1/62, age 94

Civil War (1861–1865)
- Last Union veteran, Albert Woolson, died 8/2/56, age 109
- Last Confederate veteran, John Salling*, died 3/16/58, age 112

Spanish-American War (1898)
- Last veteran, Nathan E. Cook, died 9/10/92, age 106

*Disputed. *Source:* Department of Veterans Affairs and Department of Defense. Web: www.va.gov/pressrel/amwars01.htm.

For international military affairs, *see* p. 721.

Cosmic Fingerprint

The clearest picture yet of the Big Bang's echoes yields five numbers that explain the universe

By MICHAEL D. LEMONICK TIME

Cosmology is sometimes pooh-poohed as more philosophy than science. It asks deep questions about nature but provides unsatisfyingly vague answers. The cosmos may be 12 billion years old, but it could be as much as 15 billion. The stars began to shine 100 million years after the Big Bang, or maybe it's a billion. "Our ideas," acknowledges Max Tegmark of the University of Pennsylvania, "have been kind of wobbly."

But much of the wobble has been fixed, thanks to a satellite known as the Wilkinson Microwave Anisotropy Probe, or WMAP. Since July 2001, WMAP has been orbiting in deep space, a million miles from Earth, studying the most ancient light in existence. And in a dramatic reminder that important space science is almost always done by machines, not fragile humans, it reported a series of precision measurements in 2003 that will finally put cosmology on a firm foundation.

What the satellite found, says Princeton University's David Spergel, a theorist on the WMAP team, "is that the universe can be explained with five numbers." First, the cosmos is 13.7 billion years old, give or take a negligible couple of hundred million years. Second, the first stars turned on just 200 million years after the Big Bang. Finally, the universe is made of three things in the following proportions: 4% ordinary atoms; 23% "dark matter," whose nature is still unknown; and 73% "dark energy," the equally mysterious force whose antigravity effect is speeding up the cosmic expansion. "This," says astrophysicist John Bahcall, of the Institute for Advanced Study in Princeton, N.J., "is a rite of passage for cosmology, from speculation to precision science."

Five Easy Stats

How old is the universe? What is it made of? For the first time, scientists have clarity.

- **13.7 billion years:** Age of the universe
- **200 million years:** Interval between the Big Bang and the appearance of the first stars
- **4%:** Proportion of the universe that is ordinary matter
- **23%:** Proportion that is dark matter
- **73%:** Proportion that is dark energy

Matching Fingerprints

WMAP learned this and more by scrutinizing the faint whisper of microwaves left over from the Big Bang. Hidden in that radiation are patterns of warmer and cooler spots, marking places where matter was a little more or less dense than average—spots that would eventually evolve into the clusters of galaxies and empty spaces that we see today. These patterns were first detected in crude form by the Cosmic Background Explorer (COBE) satellite in 1992, but without enough detail for much to be said about them.

But with a resolution some 40 times as sharp as COBE's, WMAP has plenty to say. (The W was added in honor of David Wilkinson, the Princeton physicist who helped launch the project but died just before the findings were published.) "It's a lot like matching fingerprints," says Spergel. "We ran computer simulations based on many different values for all of the numbers, generated patterns for each and found the one that best matched what we actually saw."

Einstein Was Right

WMAP also confirmed what earlier experiments had suggested about a basic characteristic of the universe: the geometry of space-time, in the Einsteinian sense, is flat. That's consistent with a theory called inflation, which posits that the cosmos underwent a period of turbocharged expansion before it was a second old. "I have to admit," says Bahcall, "that I was skeptical of the picture theorists had put together. Inflation, dark matter, dark energy—it's all pretty implausible. But this implausible, crazy universe has now been confirmed with exquisite detail."

That's not to say that WMAP has answered every question. Nobody knows what dark matter and dark energy are, and the theory of inflation, while strengthened, is far from proved. Beyond that, there are some strange measurements in WMAP's data that might be mere statistical flukes—or might point to some major monkey wrench that could still throw cosmology into turmoil. "We should know better after we get in more data," says Charles Bennett of the Goddard Space Flight Center, who is the WMAP team leader.

But cosmologists won't be sitting around waiting. "You're going to see a thousand papers based on these results," says Pennsylvania's Tegmark, who is already working on several. "It's an exciting time to be in this field." □

Astronomical Terms

Aphelion: see **Orbit.**

Apogee: see **Orbit.**

Black hole: the theoretical end-product of the total gravitational collapse of a massive star or group of stars. Crushed even smaller than the incredibly dense neutron star, the black hole may become so dense that not even light can escape its gravitational field. In 1996, astronomers found strong evidence for a massive black hole at the center of the Milky Way. Recent evidence suggests that black holes are so common that they probably exist at the core of nearly all galaxies.

Conjunction: the alignment of two celestial objects at the same celestial longitude. Conjunction of the Moon and planets is often determined with reference to the Sun. For example, Saturn is said to be in conjunction with the Sun when Saturn and the Earth are aligned on opposite sides of the Sun.

Mercury and Venus, the two planets with orbits within Earth's orbit, have two positions of conjunction. Mercury, for example, is said to be in *inferior conjunction* when the Sun and the Earth are aligned on opposite sides of Mercury. Mercury is in *superior conjunction* when Mercury and the Earth are aligned on opposite sides of the Sun.

Elongation: the angular distance between two points in the sky as measured from a third point. The elongation of Mercury, for example, is the angular distance between Mercury and the Sun as measured from Earth. Planets whose orbits are outside the Earth's can have elongations between 0° and 180°. (When a planet's elongation is 0° it is at conjunction; when it is 180°, it is at opposition.) Because Mercury and Venus are within the Earth's orbit, their greatest elongations measured from the Earth are 28° and 47°, respectively.

Galaxy: gas and millions of stars held together by gravity. All that you can see in the sky (with a very few exceptions) belongs to our galaxy—a system of roughly 200 billion stars. The exceptions you can see are other galaxies. Our own galaxy, the rim of which we see as the "Milky Way," is about 100,000 light-years in diameter and about 10,000 light-years in thickness. Its shape is roughly that of a thick lens; more precisely, it is a *spiral nebula,* a term first used for other galaxies when they were discovered and before it was realized that these were separate and distinct galaxies. Astronomers have estimated that the universe could contain 40 to 50 billion galaxies.

Neutron star: an extremely dense star with a powerful gravitational pull. Some neutron stars pulse radio waves into space as they spin; these are known as pulsars.

Astronomy Websites

American Astronomical Society: www.aas.org
Asteroid and Comet Impact Hazards: http://impact.arc.nasa.gov/index.html
Center for Earth and Planetary Studies: www.nasm.si.edu/ceps
The International Astronomical Union: www.iau.org
NASA Home Page: www.nasa.gov
The Nine Planets: www.seds.org/billa/tnp
Planet Quest: http://planetquest.jpl.nasa.gov/
Space Telescope Science Institute (home of Hubble): www.stsci.edu/resources
U.S. Naval Observatory: www.usno.navy.mil

Occultation: the eclipse of one celestial object by another. For example, a star is occulted when the Moon passes between it and the Earth.

Opposition: the alignment of two celestial objects when their longitude differs by 180°. Opposition of the Moon and planets is often determined with reference to the Sun. For example, Saturn is said to be at opposition when Saturn and the Sun are aligned on opposite sides of the Earth. Only the planets whose orbits lie outside the Earth's can be in opposition to the Sun.

Orbit: the path traveled by an object in space. The term comes from the Latin *orbis,* which means "circle" or "disk," and *orbita,* "orbit." Theoretically, there are four mathematical figures, or models, of possible orbits: two are open (hyperbola and parabola) and two are closed (ellipse and circle), but in reality all closed orbits are ellipses. Ellipses can be nearly circular, as are the orbits of most planets, or very elongated, as are the orbits of most comets, but the orbit revolves around a fixed, or *focal,* point. In our solar system, the Sun's gravitational pull keeps the planets in their elliptical orbits; the planets hold their moons in place similarly. For planets, the point of the orbit closest to the Sun is the *perihelion,* and the point farthest from the Sun is the *aphelion.* For orbits around the Earth, the point of closest proximity is the *perigee;* the farthest point is the *apogee.* See also **Retrograde.**

Perigee: see **Orbit.**

Perihelion: see **Orbit.**

Planet: a celestial object in orbit around a star. Even in ancient times, it was known that a number of "stars" did not stay in the same position relative to the others. There were five such restless "stars" known—Mercury, Venus, Mars, Jupiter, and Saturn—and the Greeks referred to them as *planetes,* a word which means "wanderers." That Earth is one of the planets was realized later. The additional planets were discovered after the invention of the telescope.

In 1994, Dr. Alexander Wolszcan, an astronomer at Pennsylvania State University, presented convincing evidence of the first known planets to exist outside our solar system. They circle a pulsar, or exploded star, in the constellation *Virgo.*

In 1995, several of these *extrasolar planets* were discovered orbiting stars similar to our Sun. Swiss astronomers found a planet orbiting star 51 in the constellation *Pegasus,* about 40 light-years away. It is the first planet ever discovered to circle a normal Sun-like star. As of April 2003, more than 100 planets have been discovered.

Pulsar: a celestial object, believed to be a rapidly spinning neutron star, that emits intense bursts of radio waves at regular intervals.

Quasar: "quasi-stellar" object. Originally thought to be peculiar stars in our own galaxy, quasars are now believed to be the most remote objects in the universe. A quasar detected in March 2000 with a redshift of 5.8 is 12 billion light-years from Earth and is the most distant object ever observed to date.[1]

1. Redshift is the amount by which light from a distant object is shifted toward the red end of the spectrum by the expansion of the universe. The higher the redshift, the greater the distance and the younger the universe when the light was emitted.

Quasars emit tremendous amounts of light and microwave radiation. Although they are not much bigger than Earth's solar system, quasars pour out 100 to 1,000 times as much light as an entire galaxy containing a hundred billion stars. It is believed that quasars are powered by massive black holes that suck up billions of stars.

Retrograde: describes the clockwise orbit or rotation of a planet or other celestial object, which is in the direction opposite to the Earth and most celestial bodies. As viewed from a position in space north of the solar system (from some great distance above the Earth's North Pole), all the planets revolve counterclockwise around the Sun, and all but Venus, Uranus, and Pluto rotate counterclockwise on their own axes. These three planets have retrograde motion.

Sometimes *retrograde* is also used to describe apparent backward motion as viewed from Earth. This motion happens when two objects rotate at different speeds around another fixed object. For example, the planet Mars appears to be retrograde when the Earth overtakes and passes by it as they both move around the Sun.

Satellite (or **moon**): an object in orbit around a planet. Until the discovery of Jupiter's four main moons by Galileo Galilei, celestial objects in orbit around a planet were called *moons.* However, upon Galilei's discovery, Johannes Kepler (in a letter to Galileo) suggested *satellite* (from the Latin *satelles,* which means "attendant") as a general term for such objects. The word *satellite* is used interchangeably with *moon,* and astronomers speak and write about the moons of Neptune, Saturn, etc. The term *satellite* is also used to describe man-made devices of any size that are launched into orbit.

Star: a celestial object consisting of intensely hot gases held together by gravity. Stars derive their energy from nuclear reactions going on in their interiors, generating heat and light. Stars are very large. Our Sun has a diameter of 865,400 mi—a comparatively small star.

A dwarf star is a small star that is of relatively low mass and average or below average luminosity. The Sun is a *yellow dwarf,* which is in its main sequence, or prime of life. This means that nuclear reactions of hydrogen maintain its size and temperature. By contrast, a *white dwarf* is a star at the end of its life, with low luminosity, small size, and very high density.

A *red giant* is a star nearing the end of its life. When a star begins to lose hydrogen and burn helium instead, it gradually collapses, and its outer region begins to expand and cool. The light we see from these stars is red because of their cooler temperature.

Supernova: a celestial phenomenon in which a star explodes, releasing a great burst of light. There are two basic types of supernova. Type Ia happens when a white dwarf star draws large amounts of matter from a nearby star until it can no longer support itself and collapses. The second more well-known kind of supernova, type IIa, is the result of the collapse of a massive star. (Massive is a classification for a star that is at least eight times the size of our Sun.) Once the star's nuclear fuel is exhausted, if its core is heavy enough, the star will collapse in on itself, releasing a huge amount of energy (the supernova), which may be brighter than the star's host galaxy.

The Milky Way, the galaxy containing our solar system, is about 100,000 light-years in diameter and about 10,000 light-years thick.

Origin of the Universe

Before the universe as we now know it existed, there was no space or time. The Big Bang and its associated theories try to explain or describe the moment of change from nothingness and no time to the existence of the universe filled with space and marked by time. Many physicists describe this event as an explosion, or flash, hence the name *Big Bang.* The Big Bang is a process of expansion in our universe that is still active today.

The universe flashed into existence (according to the Big Bang theory) from a very small agglomeration of matter of extremely high density and temperatures. As a dense, hot globule of gas, containing nothing but hydrogen and a small amount of helium, it began expanding rapidly outward. There were no stars or planets. The first stars probably formed when the universe was about 200 million years old. Recent pictures taken with the Hubble telescope indicate that star births peaked sometime between 500 million and 1 billion years after the Big Bang, but this process continues. Our Sun was formed 4.5 billion years ago, and through telescopes we can now see stars forming out of compressed pockets of hydrogen in outer space.

A 2003 study pinpointed the universe's age at 13.7 billion years, with just a 1% margin or error.

Birth and Death of a Star

Astronomers think that a star begins to form as a dense cloud of gas in the arms of spiral galaxies. Individual hydrogen atoms fall with increasing speed and energy toward the center of the cloud under the force of the star's gravity. The increase in energy heats the gas. When this process has continued for some millions of years, the temperature reaches about 20 million degrees Fahrenheit. At this temperature, the hydrogen within the star ignites and burns in a continuing series of nuclear reactions. The onset of these reactions marks the birth of a star.

When a star begins to exhaust its hydrogen supply, its life nears an end. The first sign of a star's old age is a swelling and reddening of its outer regions. Such an aging, swollen star is called a *red giant.* The Sun, a middle-aged star, will probably swell to a red giant in 5 billion years, vaporizing Earth and

Astronomical Constants

Light-year (distance traveled by light in one year)	5,880,000,000,000 mi
Parsec (parallax of one second, or stellar distances)	3.259 light-years
Velocity of light	c. 186,282.4 mi/sec
Astronomical unit (A.U.), or mean distance Earth to Sun	ca. 93,000,000 mi[1]
Mean distance, Earth to Moon	238,860 mi
General precession	50′,.26
Obliquity of the ecliptic	23° 27′8′.26-0′.4684(t-1900)[2]
Equatorial radius of Earth	3963.34 statute mi
Polar radius of Earth	3949.99 statute mi
Earth's mean radius	3958.89 statute mi
Oblateness of Earth	1/297
Equatorial horizontal parallax of the moon	57′2′.70
Earth's mean velocity in orbit	18.5 mi/sec
Sidereal year	365d.2564
Tropical year	365d.2422
Sidereal month	27d.3217
Synodic month	29d.5306
Mean sidereal day	23h56m4s.091 of mean solar time
Mean solar day	24h3m56s.555 of sidereal time

1. Actual mean distance derived from radar bounces: 92,935,700 mi. The value of 92,897,400 mi (based on parallax of 8″.80) is used in calculations. 2. *t* refers to the year in question, for example, 2003.

any creatures that may be on its surface. When all its fuel has been exhausted, a star cannot generate sufficient pressure at its center to balance the crushing force of gravity. The star collapses under the force of its own weight; if it is a small star, it collapses gently and remains collapsed. Such a collapsed star, at its life's end, is called a *white dwarf.* The Sun will probably end its life in this way. A different fate awaits a large star. Its final collapse generates a violent explosion, blowing the innards of the star out into space. There, the materials of the exploded star mix with the primeval hydrogen of the universe. Later in the history of the galaxy, other stars are formed out of this mixture. The Sun is one of these stars. It contains the debris of countless other stars that exploded before the Sun was born.

Formation of the Solar System

Our solar system consists of one star (the Sun), nine planets and all their moons, several thousand minor planets called asteroids or planetoids, and an equally large number of comets. The Sun's age was calculated in 1989 to be 4.49 billion years old, less than the 4.7 billion years previously believed. It was formed from a cloud of hydrogen mixed with small amounts of other substances that had been produced in the bodies of other stars before the Sun was born. This was the parent cloud of the solar system. The dense, hot gas at the center of the cloud gave rise to the Sun; the outer regions of the cloud—cooler and less dense—gave birth to the planets.

The Sun

All the stars, including our Sun, are gigantic balls of superheated gas, kept hot by atomic reactions in their centers. In our Sun, this atomic reaction is hydrogen fusion: four hydrogen atoms are combined to form one helium atom. The temperature at the core of our Sun is thought to be 36,000,000°F, or about 20,000,000°C, and the surface temperature averages 11,000°F, or about 6,000°C. The diameter of the Sun is 865,400 mi, and its surface area is approximately 12,000 times that of Earth. Compared with other stars, our Sun is just a bit below average in size and temperature, and is a yellow dwarf star. It is about 4.5 billion years old, and its fuel supply (hydrogen) is estimated to be sufficient for another 5 billion years.

Our Sun is not motionless in space; in fact, it has two kinds of motion. One is a seemingly straight-line motion in the direction of the constellation Hercules at the rate of about 12 miles per second. But since the Sun is a part of the Milky Way system and since the whole system rotates slowly around its own center, the Sun also moves at the rate of 175 miles per second as part of the rotating Milky Way system.

In addition to this motion, the Sun rotates on its axis. Observations of the motion of sunspots (darkish areas that look like enormous whirling storms) and solar flares, which are usually associated with sunspots, have shown that the rotational period of the Sun is just short of 25 days. But this figure is valid for the Sun's equator only; the sections near the Sun's poles seem to have a rotational period of 34 days. Since the Sun generates its own heat and light, there is no temperature difference between poles and equator.

What we call the Sun's "surface" is scientifically known as the *photosphere.* Since the whole Sun is a ball of expanding hot gas, there is really no such thing as a surface; it is a question of visual impression. The layer outside the photosphere is known as the *chromosphere,* which extends several thousand miles beyond the photosphere. It is in steady motion, and often enormous prominences can be seen to burst from it, extending as much as 100,000 mi into space. Outside the chromosphere is the *corona.* The corona consists of very tenuous gases (essentially hydrogen) and makes a magnificent sight when the Sun is eclipsed.

In addition to heat and light, the Sun also generates solar wind, a stream of ionized particles that radiates outward through the solar system at high speeds. One of the effects of solar wind is that it forces the tails of comets to point away from the Sun. The solar wind also interacts with the Earth's

A Star's Magnitude

Magnitude is the degree of brightness of a star. In 1856, British astronomer Norman Pogson proposed a quantitative scale of stellar magnitudes, which was adopted by the astronomical community. He noted that we receive 100 times more light from a first magnitude star as from a sixth; thus with a difference of five magnitudes, there is a 100:1 ratio of incoming light energy, which is called *luminous flux.*

Because of the nature of human perception, equal intervals of brightness are actually equal ratios of luminous flux. Pogson's proposal was that one increment in magnitude be the fifth root of 100. This means that each increment in magnitude corresponds to an increase in the amount of energy by 2.512, approximately. A fifth magnitude star is 2.512 times as bright as a sixth, and a fourth magnitude star is 6.310 times as bright as a sixth, and so on. The naked eye, upon optimum conditions, can see down to around the sixth magnitude, that is +6. Under Pogson's system, a few of the brighter stars now have negative magnitudes. For example, Sirius is –1.5. The lower the magnitude number, the brighter the object. The full moon has a magnitude of about –12.5, and the sun is a bright –26.51!

The Brightest Stars

Star	Constellation	Mag.	Dist (l.-y.)
Sirius	Canis Major	-1.6	8
Canopus	Carina	-0.9	650
Alpha Centauri	Centaurus	+0.1	4
Vega	Lyra	0.1	23
Capella	Auriga	0.2	42
Arcturus	Boötes	0.2	32
Rigel	Orion	0.3	545
Procyon	Canis Minor	0.5	10
Achernar	Eridanus	0.6	70
Beta Centauri	Centaurus	0.9	130
Altair	Aquila	0.9	18
Betelgeuse	Orion	0.9	600
Aldebaran	Taurus	1.1	54
Spica	Virgo	1.2	190
Pollux	Gemini	1.2	31
Antares	Scorpius	1.2	170
Fomalhaut	Piscis Austrinus	1.3	27
Deneb	Cygnus	1.3	465
Regulus	Leo	1.3	70
Beta Crucis	Crux	1.5	465
Eta Carinae	Carina	1–7	—
Alpha-one Crucis	Crux	1.6	150
Castor	Gemini	1.6	44
Gamma Crucis	Crux	1.6	—
Epsilon Canis Majoris	Canis Major	1.6	325
Epsilon Ursae Majoris	Ursa Major	1.7	50
Bellatrix	Orion	1.7	215
Lambda Scorpii	Scorpius	1.7	205
Epsilon Carinae	Carina	1.7	325
Mira	Cetus	2–10	250

magnetic field, causing the auroras and other phenomena. Solar flares—eruptions of hydrogen gas on the surface of the Sun—can also cause disturbances in the Earth's magnetic field.

As the Sun ages, it gradually expands and heats. It is estimated that the Sun's brilliancy will increase by 10% over the next 1.1 billion years or more, and, in about 6.5 billion years, our aging star will have doubled its present luminosity. The extreme heat generated will be catastrophic for Earth: the oceans will boil away and life as we know it will end. Eight billion years from now, the Sun's radius will extend beyond the present orbit of Venus, causing the total destruction of Earth.

The Moon

Mercury and Venus do not have any moons. The planet that comes after the Earth, Mars, has two very small moons. Jupiter has 4 major moons and at least 57 minor ones. Saturn, the ringed planet, has 31 known moons, of which 1 (Titan) is larger than the planet Mercury. Uranus has at least 21 moons (4 of them large) as well as rings, while Neptune has 1 large and 10 small moons. Pluto has one moon, discovered in 1978. Some astronomers still consider Pluto to be a "runaway moon" of Neptune.

Our Moon, with a diameter of 2,160 mi, is one of the larger moons in our solar system and is especially large when compared with the planet that it orbits. In fact, the common center of gravity of the Earth–Moon system is only about 1,000 mi below Earth's surface. The closest the Moon can come to us (its perigee) is 221,463 mi; the farthest it can go away (its apogee) is 252,710 mi. The period of rotation of the Moon is equal to its period of revolution around Earth, so from Earth we can see only one hemisphere of the Moon. Both periods are 27 days, 7 hours, 43 minutes, and 11.47 seconds. But while the rotation of the Moon is constant, its velocity in its orbit is not, since it moves more slowly in apogee than in perigee. Consequently, some portions near the rim of the Moon that are not normally visible will appear briefly. This phenomenon is called *libration,* and by taking advantage of the librations, astronomers have succeeded in mapping approximately 59% of the lunar surface. The other 41% can never be seen from Earth but has been mapped by American and Russian Moon-orbiting spacecraft.

Though the Moon goes around Earth in the time mentioned, the interval from new moon to new moon is 29 days, 12 hours, 44 minutes, and 2.78 seconds. This delay of nearly two days is due to the fact that Earth is moving around the Sun, so that the Moon needs two extra days to reach a spot in its orbit where no part is illuminated by the Sun, as seen from Earth.

If the plane of Earth's orbit around the Sun (the ecliptic) and the plane of the Moon's orbit around Earth were the same, the Moon would be eclipsed by Earth every time it is full, and the Sun would be eclipsed by the Moon every time the Moon is "new" (it would be better to call it the "black moon" when it is in this position). But because the two orbits do not coincide, the Moon's shadow normally misses Earth and Earth's shadow misses the Moon. The inclination of the two orbital planes to each other is 5°.

The tides are caused by the Moon with the help of the Sun, but in the open ocean they are surprisingly low, amounting to about one yard. The very high tides that can be observed near the shore in some places are due to funneling effects of the shorelines. At new moon and at full moon the tides raised by the Moon are reinforced by the Sun; these are the *spring tides.* If the Sun's tidal power acts at right angles to that of the Moon (quarter moons) we get the low *neap tides.*

The *Lunar Prospector* spacecraft, launched in Jan. 1998, found that as much as three billion metric tons of water ice is hidden in the permanently shaded craters at the poles. The water probably came from interstellar comets that crashed into the Moon. *Lunar Prospector* also confirmed that the Moon has a small core, supporting the theory that the Moon was ripped away from the early Earth when an object the size of Mars collided with the Earth.

At the end of its mission, on July 31, 1999, the spacecraft was intentionally crashed into a permanently shadowed crater at the Moon's south pole in the hope of detecting a rising plume of water ice, but no cloud of water vapor molecules was observed by powerful Earth telescopes.

Earth

Earth, circling the Sun at an average distance of 93 million miles, is the fifth-largest planet and the third from the Sun. It orbits the Sun at a speed of 67,000 mph, making one revolution in 365 days, 5 hours, 48 minutes, and 45.51 seconds. Earth completes one rotation on its axis every 23 hours, 56 minutes, and 4.09 seconds. Actually a bit pear-shaped rather than a true sphere, Earth has a diameter of 7,927 mi at the equator and a few miles less at the poles. It has an estimated mass of about 6.6 sextillion tons, with an average density of 5.52 grams per cubic centimeter. Earth's surface area encompasses 196,949,970 sq mi of which about three-fourths is water.

Origin of Earth

Earth, along with the other planets, is believed to have been born 4.5 billion years ago as a solidified cloud of dust and gases left over from the creation of the Sun. For perhaps 500 million years, the interior of Earth stayed solid and relatively cool, perhaps 2,000°F. The main ingredients, according to the best available evidence, were iron and silicates, with small amounts of other elements, some of them radioactive. As millions of years passed, energy released by radioactive decay—mostly of uranium, thorium, and potassium—gradually heated Earth, melting some of its constituents. The iron melted before the silicates, and, being heavier, sank toward the center. This forced up the silicates that it found there. After many years, the iron reached the center, almost 4,000 mi deep, and began to accumulate. No eyes were around at that time to view the turmoil that must have taken place on the face of Earth—gigantic heaves and bubblings on the surface, exploding volcanoes, and flowing lava covering everything in sight. Finally, the iron in the center accumulated as the core. Around it, a thin but fairly stable crust of solid rock formed as Earth cooled. Depressions in the crust were natural basins in which water, rising from the interior of the planet through volcanoes and fissures, collected to form the oceans. Slowly, Earth acquired its present appearance.

Earth Today

As a result of radioactive heating over millions of years, Earth's molten *core* is probably fairly hot today, around 11,000°F. By comparison, lead melts at around 800°F. Most of Earth's 2,100-mile-thick core is liquid, but the center of the core is mostly solid iron. The liquid outer portion, about 95% of the core, is constantly in motion. The interaction between the solid inner core and the fluid outer core creates a hydromagnetic dynamo that generates the magnetic field around Earth. The magnetic field protects the Earth from harmful cosmic radiation and makes navigation by compass possible.

Within the last decade, scientists have made some important discoveries about Earth's solid-iron core. In 1996, geophysicists discovered that the core rotates slightly faster than the rest of the planet and gains a quarter-turn every century. This may help explain how Earth's magnetic field periodically reverses its polarity. X-ray images of the inside of the Earth show that the core is not a perfect sphere—there are vast mountains 6 to 7 mi high and deep valleys. These features are in an inverse, or upside-down, relationship to similar features on the Earth's surface.

Outside the core is Earth's *mantle,* 1,800 mi thick and extending nearly to the surface. The mantle is composed of heavy silicate rock, similar to that brought up by volcanic eruptions. It is somewhere between liquid and solid, slightly yielding, and therefore contributing to an active, moving Earth. Most of Earth's radioactive material is in the thin *crust* that covers the mantle, but some is in the mantle and continues to give off heat. The crust's thickness ranges from 5 to 25 mi.

Continental Drift

A great deal of evidence confirms the theory that the continents of Earth, made mostly of relatively light granite, float in the slightly yielding mantle, like logs in a pond. For many years it had been noticed that if North and South America could be pushed toward western and southern Europe and western Africa, they would fit like pieces in a jigsaw puzzle. Today, there is little question—the continents have drifted widely and continue to do so.

In 10 million years, the world as we know it may be unrecognizable, with California drifting out to sea, Florida joining South America, and Africa moving farther away from Europe and Asia.

Earth's Atmosphere

The thin blanket of atmosphere that envelops Earth extends several hundred miles into space. From sea level—the very bottom of the ocean of air—to a height of about 60 mi, the air in the atmosphere is made up of the same gases in the same ratio: about 78% nitrogen, 21% oxygen, and the remaining 1% a mixture of argon, carbon dioxide, and tiny amounts of neon, helium, krypton, xenon, and other gases. The atmosphere becomes less dense with increasing altitude: more than three-fourths of Earth's huge envelope is concentrated in the first 5 to 10 mi above the surface. At sea level, a cubic foot of atmosphere weighs about an ounce and a quarter. The entire atmosphere weighs 5,700 trillion tons, and the force with which gravity holds it in place causes it to exert a pressure of nearly 15 psi. Going out from Earth's surface, the atmosphere is divided into five regions. The regions, and the heights to which they extend, are: *troposphere,* 0 to 7 mi (at middle latitudes); *stratosphere,* 7 to 30 mi; *mesosphere,* 30 to 50 mi; *thermosphere,* 50 to 400 mi; and *exosphere,* above 400 mi. The boundaries between each of the regions are known respectively as the *tropopause, stratopause, mesopause,* and *thermopause.* Alternative terms often used for the layers above the troposphere are *ozonosphere* (for stratosphere) and *ionosphere* for the remaining upper layers.

The Seasons

Seasons are caused by the 23.4° tilt of Earth's axis, which alternately turns the North and South Poles toward the Sun. Times when the Sun's apparent path crosses the equator are known as *equinoxes.* Times when the Sun's apparent path is at the greatest distance from the equator are known as *solstices.* The lengths of the days are most extreme at each solstice. If Earth's axis were perpendicular to the plane of Earth's orbit around the Sun, there would be no seasons, and the days always would be equal in length. Since Earth's axis is at an angle, the Sun strikes Earth directly at the equator only twice a year: in March (vernal equinox) and September (autumnal equinox). In the Northern Hemisphere, spring begins at the vernal equinox, summer at the summer solstice, fall at the autumnal equinox, and winter at the winter solstice. The situation is reversed in the Southern Hemisphere.

Mercury

Mercury is the planet nearest the Sun. Appropriately named for the wing-footed Roman messenger of the gods, Mercury whizzes around the Sun at a speed of 30 miles per second, completing one circuit in 88 days. The days and nights are long on Mercury. It takes 59 Earth days for Mercury to make a single rotation. It spins at a rate of about 6 mph (about 10 km/h), measured at the equator, as compared to Earth's spin of about 1,000 mph (about 1,600 km/h) at the equator.

The photographs *Mariner 10* (1974–1975) radioed back to Earth revealed an ancient, heavily cratered surface on Mercury, closely resembling our own Moon. The pictures showed huge cliffs, or scarps, crisscrossing the planet. These apparently were created when Mercury's interior cooled and shrank, compressing the planet's crust. The cliffs are as high as 1.2 mi (2 km) and as long as 932 mi (1,500 km). Another unique feature is the Caloris Basin, a large impact crater about 808 mi (1,300 km) in diameter.

Mercury, like Earth, appears to have a crust of light silicate rock. Scientists believe it has a heavy iron-rich core that makes up about half of its volume.

Instruments onboard *Mariner 10* discovered that the planet has a weak magnetic field and a trace of atmosphere—a trillionth the density of Earth's and composed chiefly of argon, neon, and helium. The spacecraft reported temperatures ranging from 950°F (510°C) on Mercury's sunlit side to –346°F (–210°C) on the dark side. Mercury literally bakes in daylight and freezes at night.

Until the *Mariner 10* probe, little was known about the planet. Even the best telescopic views from Earth showed Mercury as an indistinct object lacking any surface detail. The planet is so close to the Sun that it is usually lost in the Sun's glare.

Radar images taken by astronomers at Jet Propulsion Laboratories and California Institute of Technology during the summer of 1991 suggest that the polar regions of Mercury may be covered with patches of water ice. Although this seems impossible due to the planet's sizzling heat, the polar regions receive very little sunlight and may get as cold as –235°F (–148°C). The radar images showed bright patterns at the poles that are characteristic of ice reflecting radar signals. Other explanations may be offered for this unexpected discovery.

In March or April 2004, NASA plans to launch a spacecraft, *Messenger*, that will orbit Mercury in April 2009. It will map the planet for one Earth year and search for water, a magnetic field, and other phenomena.

Mercury is visible to the naked eye at morning or evening twilight when it is at its greatest elongation.

Venus

Although Venus is Earth's closest neighbor, very little is known about the planet because it is permanently covered by thick clouds. In 1962, Soviet and American space probes, coupled with Earth-based radar and infrared spectroscopy, began slowly unraveling some of the mystery surrounding Venus. Twenty-eight years later, the *Magellan* spacecraft, sent by the United States, arrived at Venus in Aug. 1990 and began radar-mapping the planet's surface in greater detail.

According to the latest results, Venus's atmosphere exerts a pressure at the surface 94.5 times greater than Earth's. Walking on Venus would be as difficult as walking a half-mile beneath the ocean. Because of a thick blanket of carbon dioxide, a "greenhouse effect" exists on Venus. Venus intercepts twice as much of the Sun's light as does Earth. The light enters freely through the carbon dioxide gas and is changed to heat radiation in molecular collisions. But carbon dioxide prevents the heat from escaping. Consequently, the temperature of the surface of Venus is over 800°F (427°C), hot enough to melt lead.

The atmospheric composition of Venus is about 96% carbon dioxide, 4% nitrogen, and minor amounts of water, oxygen, and sulfur compounds. There are at least four distinct cloud and haze layers that exist at different altitudes above the planet's surface. The haze layers contain small aerosol particles, possibly droplets of sulfuric acid. A concentration of sulfur dioxide above the cloud tops has been observed to be decreasing since 1978. The source of sulfur dioxide at this altitude is unknown; it may be injected by volcanic explosions or atmospheric overturning.

Measurements of the Venusian atmosphere and its cloud patterns reveal nearly constant high-speed zonal winds, about 220 mph (100 meters per second) at the equator. The winds decrease toward the poles so that the atmosphere at cloud-top level rotates almost like a solid body. The wind speeds at the equator correspond to Venus's rotation period of four to five days at most latitudes. The circulation is always in the same direction—east to west—as Venus's slow retrograde motion. Earth's winds blow from west to east, the same direction as its rotation.

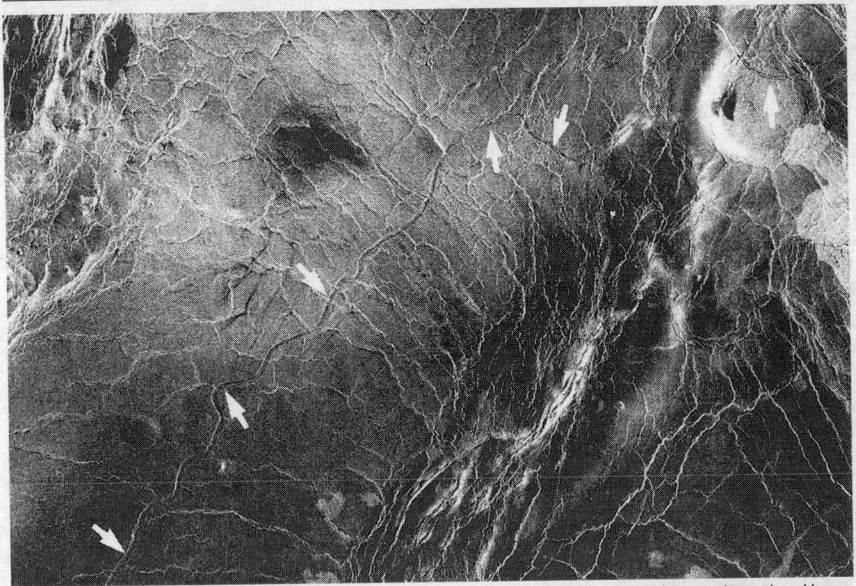

Largest Channel in the Solar System. *Magellan* took the above image of the largest known channel on Venus. At 4,200 mi (6,800 km) long and an average of 1.1 mi (1.8 km) wide, it is longer than the Nile River, Earth's longest river, making it the longest known channel in the solar system. The channel was originally discovered by the Soviet *Venery 15* and *16* spacecraft orbiters. *Source:* NASA.

Venus is round, very different from the other planets and from the Moon. Venus has neither polar flattening nor an equatorial bulge. The diameter of Venus is 7,519 mi (12,100 km). Venus has a retrograde axial rotation period of 243.1 Earth days. The surface atmospheric pressure is 1,396 psi (95 Earth atmospheres). The planet's mean distance from the Sun is 67.2 million miles (108.2 million kilometers). The period of its revolution around the Sun is 224.7 days.

The highest point on Venus is the summit of Maxwell Montes, 6.71 mi (10.8 km) above the mean level, more than a mile higher than Mount Everest. There is some evidence that this huge mountain is an active volcano. The lowest point is in the rift valley, Diana Chasma, 1.8 mi (2.9 km) below the mean level. This point is about one-fifth the greatest depth on Earth in the Marianas Trench.

Venus has an extreme lowland basin, Atalanta Planitia, which is about the size of Earth's North Atlantic Ocean basin. The smooth surface of the Atalanta Planitia resembles the mare basins of the Moon.

There are only two highland or continental masses on Venus: Ishtar Terra and Aphrodite Terra. Ishtar Terra is 6.8 mi (11 km) at its highest points (the highest peaks on Venus) and those of Aphrodite Terra rise to about 3.10 mi (5 km) above the planet. Ishtar Terra is about the size of the continental United States and Aphrodite Terra is about the size of Africa.

The unmanned NASA spacecraft *Magellan* was launched on May 4, 1989, from the shuttle *Atlantis* and arrived at Venus Aug. 10, 1990, to map most of the planet. Despite some problems with its radio transmissions, the results of the radar mapping delighted scientists and provided them with the sharpest images ever taken of the planet's surface. Images taken from *Magellan* show ten times more detail than ever seen before.

The radar images provided scientists with compelling evidence that the planet has been dominated by volcanism on a global scale. The photos also showed that the planet's second-highest mountain, Maat Mons, rising 5 mi (8 km) above the Venusian plains, appears to be covered with fresh lava and is possibly an active volcano.

Magellan discovered the longest known channel in the solar system on Venus. It is 4,200 mi (6,800 km) long and averages slightly over a mile (1.8 km) wide. Its origin is puzzling to scientists because high-temperature lava is unlikely to have caused such a long-distance flow on the surface, and there are no known substances that could remain liquid long enough under the planet's atmospheric pressure and temperature to have carved out this snakelike feature. The channel is slightly longer than the Nile River, the longest river on Earth.

Magellan ended its radar and emissions mapping in Sept. 1992 after covering 98% of the planet's surface. The spacecraft continued to gather data until Oct. 1994, when it was intentionally crashed into the planet's surface. The European Space Agency (ESA) plans a 2005 launch of the Venus Express to study the atmosphere and subsurface.

Venus is the brightest of all the planets and is often visible in the morning or evening, when it is frequently referred to as the Morning Star or Evening Star. At its brightest, it can sometimes be seen in full daylight with the naked eye, if one knows where to look.

Mars

Mars, on the other side of Earth from Venus, is Venus's direct opposite in terms of physical properties. Its atmosphere is cold, thin, and transparent, and readily permits observation of the planet's features. We know more about Mars than any other planet except Earth. Mars is a forbidding, rugged planet with huge volcanoes and deep chasms. The largest volcano, Olympus Mons (Olympic Mountain) rises 78,000 ft above the surface, higher than Mount Everest. The plains of Mars are pockmarked by the hits of thousands of meteors over the years.

Until the arrival of *Mars Pathfinder* and *Mars Global Surveyor* in 1997, most of our information about Mars came from the *Mariner* and *Viking* spacecrafts. *Mariner 9* orbited the planet in 1971 and photographed 100% of the planet, uncovering spectacular geological formations, including a Martian "Grand Canyon" that dwarfs the one on Earth. Called Valles Marineris (Mariner Valley), it stretches more than 3,000 mi along the equatorial region of Mars and is over 2.5 mi (4 km) deep in places and 50–62 mi (80 to 100 km) wide. The spacecraft's cameras also recorded what appeared to be dried riverbeds, suggesting the one-time presence of water on the planet. The latter idea gave encouragement to scientists looking for life on Mars, for where there is water, there may be life. However, to date, no evidence of life has been found. Temperatures range from 80°F at the equator during the day to –199°F at the poles at night.

Mars rotates upon its axis in nearly the same period as Earth—24 hours, 37 minutes—so that a Mars day is almost identical to an Earth day. Mars takes 687 days to make one trip around the Sun. Because of its eccentric orbit, Mars's distance from the Sun can vary by about 36 million miles. Its distance from Earth can vary by as much as 200 million miles. The atmosphere of Mars is much thinner than Earth's; atmospheric pressure is about 1% that of our planet. Its gravity is one-third of Earth's. Major constituents are carbon dioxide and nitrogen. Water vapor and oxygen are minor constituents. Mars's polar caps, composed mostly of frozen carbon dioxide (dry ice), recede and advance according to the Martian seasons.

Mars has four seasons like Earth, but they are much longer. For example, in the northern hemisphere, the Martian spring is 198 days, and the winter season lasts 158 days.

The *Mars Pathfinder* lander and its rover, *Sojourner*, set down on the edge of a boulder-strewn outflow channel known as *Ares Vallis* on July 4, 1997, and provided scientists with a wealth of information on the rocks, soils, and atmosphere of Mars. The lander sent back the first live pictures of the planet's topography, and its tiny rover explored a variety of rocks and analyzed their mineral composition with its cameras and on-board X-ray spectrometer.

In its three months of operation, the mission returned more than 16,000 images of the Martian landscape from the lander's camera and 550 images from the rover.

Analysis of the reddish surface soil pointed to the presence of oxidized iron, indicating that the planet's surface is rusting. *Sojourner* samples of soil taken from several sites found their composition similar to those analyzed by the two *Viking* landers in 1976, indicating that the Martian winds have distributed the soil evenly over the planet.

Scientists were surprised to learn how rapidly the Martian temperature fluctuates due to atmospheric turbulence. It can change by as much as 30°–40°F (17°–22°C) in a matter of minutes, possibly due to strong, gusty winds bringing warm air from one region or cold air from another.

Pictures and subsequent data from *Pathfinder* give the strongest evidence that Mars had an abundance of water millions of years ago. Scientists have inferred from the variety of rocks and sediments found in the *Ares* basin that the spacecraft landed in a channel that was once awash with torrential floods greater than any known on Earth. The diversity of rocks deposited there suggests their different origins, and it appears that they were washed down from the highlands at a time when great floods moved over the surface of Mars.

Before *Pathfinder*, knowledge of the kinds of rocks present on Mars was based mostly on the Martian meteorites found on Earth. Chemical analysis of the Martian rocks and soil found at *Ares Vallis* confirmed that these rocks have compositions distinct from those of the Martian meteorites found on Earth.

The *Sojourner* rover traveled a total of about 328 ft (100 m), performed more than 16 chemical analyses of rocks and soil, and explored 820 sq ft (250 sq m) of the planet's surface. Communications were lost with the lander on Sept. 27, 1997, after 83 days of relaying data.

NASA launched the *Mars Global Surveyor* spacecraft on Nov. 7, 1996, to provide detailed maps of the planet's surface, its distribution of minerals, and to monitor its weather. The spacecraft entered Mars's orbit on Sept. 11, 1997, and began mapping operations in mid-March 1999.

Surveyor discovered the first clear evidence of an ancient hydrothermal system near the equator. This implies that water was stable at or near the surface and that a thicker atmosphere existed in Mars's early history.

Surveyor's three-dimensional views of the planet's northern polar ice cap showed often striking canyons and spiral troughs in the water and carbon dioxide ice that can reach depths as great as 3,600 ft below the surface. Its data also showed that large areas of the ice cap were extremely smooth, with elevations varying only a few feet over many miles.

NASA's Mars exploration program suffered a setback with the loss of the *Climate Orbiter* as it entered the Martian atmosphere in Sept. 1999. The following December scientists also failed to establish contact with the *Polar Lander* after it reached Mars.

In 2000, NASA announced that the *Mars Global Surveyor* had observed features that looked like gullies carved out by flowing water and deposits of soil and rocks that were transported by the flow. Because gullies had never been seen before on Mars, the *Surveyor* images suggested that there might be current sources of liquid water at or near the surface.

In the spring of 2002, NASA released exciting news that large quantities of water ice had been found just below the surface of Mars. The discovery was made by NASA's *Mars Odyssey* spacecraft, which was launched in April 2001 and has been

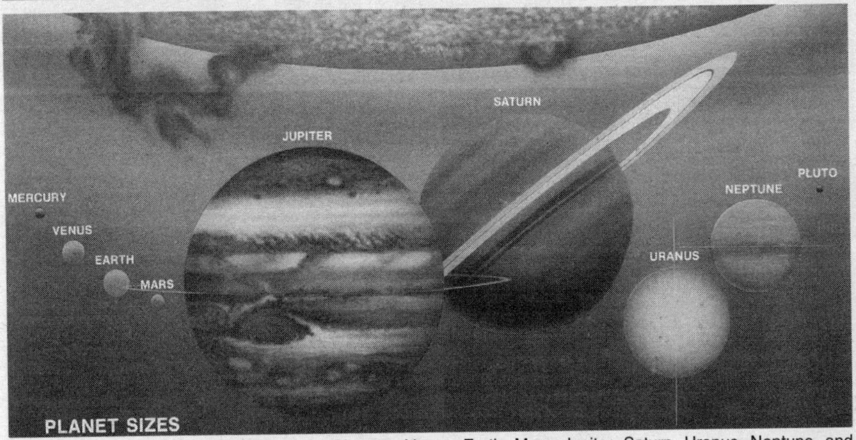

PLANET SIZES. Shown from left to right: Mercury, Venus, Earth, Mars, Jupiter, Saturn, Uranus, Neptune, and Pluto. *Copyright 1990 Hansen Planetarium, Salt Lake City, Utah. Reproduced with permission.*

collecting data since late 2001. Because water is necessary for life, the new findings are likely to spur further investigation. In 2003 the ESA launched a *Mars Express* mission and NASA launched two *Mars Exploration Rovers* to search for subsurface water and to study Mars's atmosphere and geology.

Mars was named for the Roman god of war, because when seen from Earth its distinct red color reminded the ancient people of blood. We know now that the reddish hue reflects the oxidized (rusted) iron in the surface material.

The Martian Moons

Mars has two very small elliptical-shaped moons, Deimos and Phobos—the Greek names for the companions of the god Mars: Deimos (Terror) and Phobos (Fear). They were discovered in Aug. 1877 by the American astronomer Asaph Hall (1829–1907) of the U.S. Naval Observatory in Washington, DC.

The inner satellite, Phobos, is 16.78 mi (27 km) long, and it revolves around the planet in 7.6 hours. The short orbital period of Phobos means that the satellite travels around Mars three times in a Martian day. The outer moon, Deimos, is 9.32 mi (15 km) long, and it circles the planet in 30.35 hours.

Phobos orbits Mars at a distance of only 5,627 mi (9,378 km) and is closer to its planet than any other moon in the solar system. Observation of Phobos has revealed that the moon's orbit is actually decreasing downward; in about 40 million years it will crash into the planet's surface or break up into a ring.

Meteorites from Mars

Twenty-eight meteorites, almost certainly from Mars, have been discovered as of Jan. 2003. They are known as SNCs[1] (named for the towns where the original 12 meteorites were found: Shergotty, India, in 1865; Nakhla, Egypt, in 1911; and Chassigny, France, in 1815). This hypothesis was based largely on the composition of noble gases (particularly argon and xenon) trapped in the meteorites, and the shergottites in particular, which resemble measurements of the Martian atmosphere made by the *Viking* spacecraft. Major element compositions of the SNCs are also similar to Martian soil analyses made by *Viking*.

The relatively young isotopic ages of the SNC meteorites (1.3 billion years or less) suggest that Mars has been volcanically active during its recent past.

A 40-pound meteorite that crashed to Earth in Nigeria in 1962 has been classified as coming from Mars. It was named Zagami for the region in which it was found. It is the largest single Martian meteorite ever found.

A 4-pound, 7-ounce (1.9-kilogram) meteorite, ALH 84001, found in the Allen Hills of Antarctica in 1984, was reclassified in 1993 as coming from the Red Planet, making it the tenth meteorite known to have originated from Mars. In 1996, NASA announced that meteorite ALH 84001 contained fossils of ancient Martian microbial life forms.

A 0.38-ounce (12-gram) meteorite (QUE 94201) found in Antarctica in 1995 became the 12th meteorite identified as having a Martian origin.

In 1997, the thirteenth known Martian meteorite, Dar al Gani 476, a 4.8-pound (2.2-kilogram) meteorite, was found in the Sahara Desert.

Two rock specimens weighing 8.6 oz (245.4 g) and 16 oz (452.6 g) that were found in the Mojave Desert about 20 years ago were classified in Feb. 2000 as the fourteenth Mars meteorite. The rocks are known as the Los Angeles meteorites.

It is estimated that some 20,000 meteorites fall to Earth every year, but only a few are from Mars. The most recent finds, mainly in 2000 and 2001, were discovered in Antarctica and the deserts of northern Africa, which have become the favored hunting grounds for meteorite collectors, since there is little or no ground cover to hide the rocks.

Jupiter

Jupiter is the largest planet in the solar system—a gaseous world as large as 1,300 Earths. Its equatorial diameter is 88,736 mi (142,800 km), while from pole to pole, Jupiter measures only 84,201 mi (133,500 km). For comparison, the diameter of Earth is 7,926.2 mi (12,756 km). The massive planet

1. Pronounced "snick."

Basic Planetary Data

	Mercury	Venus	Earth	Mars	Jupiter
Mean distance from Sun (millions of kilometers)	57.9	108.2	149.6	227.9	778.3
Mean distance from Sun (millions of miles)	36.0	67.24	92.9	141.71	483.88
Period of revolution	88 days	224.7 days	365.2 days	687 days	11.86 yrs
Rotation period	59 days	243 days retrograde	23 hr 56 min 4 sec	24 hr 37 min	9 hr 55 min 30 sec
Inclination of axis	Near 0°	3°	23°27′	25° 12′	3° 5′
Inclination of orbit to ecliptic	7°	3.4°	0°	1.9°	1.3°
Eccentricity of orbit	.206	.007	.017	.093	.048
Equatorial diameter (kilometers)	4,880	12,100	12,756	6,794	142,800
(miles)	3,032.4	7,519	7,926.2	4,194	88,736
Atmosphere (main components)	Virtually none	Carbon dioxide	Nitrogen oxygen	Carbon dioxide	Hydrogen helium
Satellites	0	0	1	2	61[1]
Rings	0	0	0	0	3

	Saturn	Uranus	Neptune	Pluto
Mean distance from Sun (millions of kilometers)	1,427	2,870	4,497	5,900
Mean distance from Sun (millions of miles)	887.14	1,783.98	2,796.46	3,666
Period of revolution	29.46 yrs	84 yrs	165 yrs	248 yrs
Rotation period	10 hr 40 min 24 sec	16.8 hr (?) retrograde	16 hr 11 min (?)	6 days 9 hr 18 mins retrograde
Inclination of axis	26°44′	97°55′	28°48′	60° (?)
Inclination of orbit to ecliptic	2.5°	0.8°	1.8°	17.2°
Eccentricity of orbit	.056	.047	.009	.254
Equatorial diameter (kilometers)	120,660	51,810	49,528	2,290 (?)
(miles)	74,978	32,193	30,775	1,423 (?)
Atmosphere (main components)	Hydrogen helium	Helium hydrogen methane	Hydrogen helium methane	None detected
Satellites	31[2]	21	11	1
Rings	1,000 (?)	11	4	?

1. Forty-three of these moons were discovered only recently, from 2000–2003. 2. Twelve of these moons, designated S/2000 S1 through S12, were discovered in late 2000. S/2003 S1 was discovered in early 2003. *Source:* Basic NASA data and other sources.

rotates at a dizzying speed—once every 9 hours and 55 minutes. It takes Jupiter almost 12 Earth years to complete a journey around the Sun.

The giant planet appears as a banded disk of turbulent clouds with all of its stripes running parallel to its bulging equator. Large dusky gray regions surround each pole. Darker gray or brown stripes called belts intermingle with lighter, yellow-white stripes called zones. The belts are regions of descending air masses and the zones are rising cloudy air masses. The strongest winds—up to 250 mph (400 km)—are found at boundaries between the belts and zones.

This uniquely colorful atmosphere is mainly 89% molecular hydrogen and 11% helium. It contains small amounts of methane, ammonia, ethane, and water.

Cloud-type lightning bolts similar to those on Earth have been found in the Jovian atmosphere. At the polar regions, auroras have been observed. A very thin ring of material less than 0.6 mi (1 km) in thickness and about 4,000 mi (6,000 km) in radial extent has been observed circling the planet about 35,000 mi (55,000 km) above the cloud tops.

The most prominent feature on Jupiter is its "Great Red Spot," an oval larger than the planet Earth. It is a tremendous atmospheric storm that rotates counterclockwise with one revolution every six days at the outer edge, while at the center almost no motion can be seen. The spot is about 16,000 mi (25,000 km) on its long axis, and would cover three Earths. Along the outer rim the winds blow at speeds reaching 225 mph (360 km/h).

Jupiter is circled by faint rings. They are very tenuous and contain many microscopic-sized particles. The rings are formed by dust kicked up as interplanetary meteoroids smash into the planet's four small inner moons.

Jupiter emits 67% more heat than it absorbs from the Sun. This heat is thought to have been accumulated during the planet's formation several billion years ago.

Twenty-one fragments of comet Shoemaker-Levy 9 bombarded the cloud-covered surface of Jupiter, July 16–22, 1994. It was the most violent event in the recorded history of our solar system. The impact of the comet fragments caused towering plumes of debris and hot gas to rise from the planet's surface.

On Dec. 7, 1995, the *Galileo* spacecraft released a probe into Jupiter's atmosphere to study the planet's physical and chemical properties. The probe lasted 57 minutes and early results indicated a lower abundance of water than was expected. *Galileo* data has shown that Jupiter has both wet and dry regions, just as Earth has tropics and deserts. This could explain why the probe found less water than anticipated. These dry spots cover less than 1% of the Jovian atmosphere. The *Galileo* mission is scheduled to end on Sept. 21, 2003, when the probe is to crash into the gas giant.

Jovian Moons

Jupiter has a total of 61 known satellites. The four great moons of Jupiter were discovered by Galileo Galilei (1564–1642) in Jan. 1610, and are called the Galilean satellites after their discoverer. Their names are Io, Europa, Ganymede, and Callisto. Like our Moon, the satellites always keep the same face turned toward the planet they circle. Jupiter's four largest moons all have thin atmospheres. A carbon dioxide atmosphere envelops Callisto; Europa and Ganymede each have thin oxygen atmospheres; and Io's contains sulfur dioxide.

Ganymede

Ganymede, 3,275 mi (5,270 km) in diameter, is Jupiter's largest moon, and it is also the largest satellite in the solar system. Ganymede is about one and one-half times the size of our Moon. It is heavily cratered and probably has the greatest variety of geologic process recorded on its surface. Ganymede is half water and half rock, resulting in a density about two-thirds that of Europa, an ice-coated satellite.

The first close-up photos of Ganymede, taken by the *Galileo* spacecraft during its June 1996 flyby, revealed a surface pockmarked with ancient craters and a landscape wrinkled and torn by the same forces that make mountains and move continents on Earth. *Galileo*'s findings also indicated that Ganymede is enveloped in its own magnetic field, possibly created by a molten iron core or even a thin layer of electricity-conducting salty water underneath its icy crust.

Ganymede is the first known moon with its own magnetosphere.

Europa

Europa, the brightest of Jupiter's satellites, is about 1,950 mi (3,160 km) in diameter or about the size of Earth's Moon. Its density is about three times that of water. The moon is covered with a thin ice crust and is crisscrossed with an amazingly complex network of ridges. Some of the fractures on its crust are more than 1,850 mi (3,000 km) long. Very few impact craters are visible on the surface. In fact, Europa is the smoothest object in the solar system. Its mostly flat surface doesn't exceed 0.62 mi (1 km) in height.

Galileo spacecraft photos taken at its closest flyby on Feb. 20, 1997, at a distance of 363 mi (586 km), showed the existence of ice flows on the surface that strongly suggest that the moon has a hidden subsurface ocean of water or ice-slush. The photos revealed chunky ice rafts that appear to be floating, comparable to icebergs on Earth. The presence of water and enough heat to keep water in a liquid state on Europa enhances the possibility that it could provide an environment for some form of extraterrestrial ocean life.

New evidence that a liquid ocean lies beneath Europa's crust was found when *Galileo* visited the moon in Jan. 2000. The spacecraft detected changes in Europa's magnetic field that are best explained by an electrically conducting (salty) body of water.

Definitive answers may not be possible for another decade, however. NASA scientists had proposed sending a spacecraft called the *Europa Ice Clipper* to the moon in 2001, but the mission was scrapped due to lack of funding.

Callisto

Callisto, 2,400 mi (4,800 km) in diameter, is the outermost and, apparently, the least geologically active of Jupiter's four major satellites. Its density is less than twice that of water. Callisto has the oldest body and most cratered face of any body yet observed in the solar system. Like Ganymede, it seems to have a rocky core surrounded by ice. Unlike Ganymede, the surface of Callisto is completely covered with scars left by tens of thousands of meteoric impacts. Scientists estimate that it would take several billion years to accumulate the number of craters found there. So Callisto is believed to be inactive for at least that long. Although it is the darkest of the Galilean satellites, it is twice as bright as Earth's Moon.

Data from the *Galileo* spacecraft in 1998 suggest that Callisto has a salty ocean beneath its crust, similar to Europa's.

Io

Io, 2,262 mi (3,640 km) in diameter, is the most spectacular of the Galilean moons. Its brilliant colors of red, orange, and yellow set it apart from any other moon or planet. Active volcanoes have been detected on Io, with some plumes extending up to 200 mi (320 km) above the surface. The relative smoothness of Io's surface and its volcanic activity suggest that it has the youngest surface of Jupiter's moons. Its surface is composed of large amounts of sulfur and sulfur-dioxide frost, which account for the primarily yellow-orange surface color.

The volcanoes seem to eject a sufficient amount of sulfur dioxide to form a doughnut-shaped ring (torus) of ionized sulfur and oxygen atoms around Jupiter near Io's orbit. Close-up views taken in 1999 and 2000 showed that Io had more than 100 erupting volcanoes, gigantic lava flows and lava lakes, and towering, collapsing mountains. The eruptions of Loki, the most powerful volcano in the solar system, can be seen by Earth telescopes.

Observations by *Galileo* during 1998 revealed dozens of volcanic vents on Io where lava is hotter than any surface temperatures recorded on any planetary body in our solar system. At one such volcanic vent, known as Pillan Patera, two of the spacecraft's instruments indicated that the lava temperature may have been 3,140°F.

In 1996, the *Galileo* spacecraft detected a huge iron core within Io that occupies half the moon's diameter. *Galileo* also discovered evidence that Io has its own magnetic field.

Amalthea

Amalthea, Jupiter's innermost satellite, was discovered in 1892. It is so small—165 mi (265 km) long and 90 mi (150 km) wide—that it is extremely difficult to observe from Earth. Amalthea is an elongated, irregularly shaped satellite of reddish color. It orbits the planet every 12 hours and is in synchronous rotation, with its long axis always oriented toward Jupiter.

Originally thought to be heavily cratered, late 2002 data from the *Galileo* mission indicated that Amalthea may be a loosely-packed pile of rubble. It

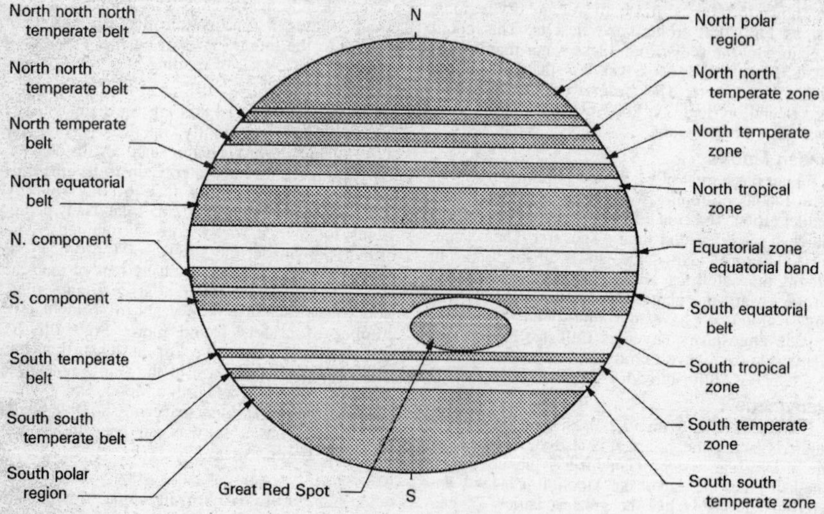

Schematic diagram of Jupiter's major features. *Source:* NASA.

was discovered that the satellite had an unexpected low density, close to the density of ice. Amalthea may originally have been one piece that was bombarded and broken into chunks now held together by the gravity of the pieces. The gaps between the boulder-like pieces may make up more of the moon's volume than the actual rocks. Amalthea may be mostly rock with some ice, rather than the rock and iron it was previously held to be.

Jupiter's other named moons are Adrasta, Metis, Thebe, Leda, Himalia, Lysithea, Elara, Ananke, Carne, Pasiphae, Sinope; those discovered in 1999 and 2000 are Themisto, Iocaste, Harpalyke, Praxidike, Taygete, Chaldene, Kalyke, Callirrhoe, Megaclite, Isonoe, and Erinome.

Between 2000 and early 2003, 43 moons were found, bringing Jupiter's satellite total to 61, the greatest in the solar system. The new moons were generally small with distant retrograde orbits (orbital movement opposite to the planet's spin). Most of the new moons were sighted using Hawaii's Mauna Kea telescopes. Some astronomers believe that Jupiter's moon count could reach 100.

The Magnetosphere of Jupiter

Perhaps the largest structure in the solar system is the magnetosphere of Jupiter. This is the region of space that is filled with Jupiter's magnetic field and is bounded by the interaction of that magnetic field with the solar wind, which is the Sun's outward flow of charged particles. The plasma of electrically charged particles that exists in the magnetosphere is flattened into a large disk more than 3 million miles (4.8 million kilometers) in diameter, is coupled to the magnetic field, and rotates around Jupiter. The Galilean satellites are located in the inner regions of the magnetosphere and are subjected to intense radiation bombardment.

The intense radiation field that surrounds Jupiter is fatal to humans. If astronauts were able to approach the planet as close as the *Voyager 1* spacecraft did, they would receive a dose of 400,000 rads, or roughly 1,000 times the lethal dose for humans.

Even when nearest Earth, Jupiter is still almost 400 million miles away. However, because of its size, it may rival Venus in brilliance when near. Jupiter's four large moons may be seen through field glasses moving rapidly around Jupiter and changing their positions from night to night.

Saturn

Saturn, the second-largest planet in the solar system, is the least dense. Its mass is 95 times the mass of Earth and its density is 0.70 gram per cubic centimeter, so that it would float in an ocean if there were one big enough to hold it.

Saturn radiates about 80% more energy than it receives from the Sun. However, the excess thermal energy cannot be primarily attributed to Saturn's primordial heat loss, as is speculated for Jupiter.

Saturn's diameter is 74,978 mi (120,660 km) but 10% less at the poles, a consequence of its rapid rotation. Its axis of rotation is tilted by 27° and the length of its day is 10 hours, 39 minutes, and 24 seconds.

Saturn is composed primarily of liquid metallic hydrogen (about 80%) and the second most common element is believed to be helium.

Saturn's atmospheric appearance is very similar to Jupiter's with dark and light cloud markings and swirls, eddies, and curling ribbons; the belts and zones are more numerous and a thick haze mutes the markings. Temperatures recorded by *Voyager II* ranged from 82°K (–312°F) to 143°K (–202°F).

Winds blow at extremely high speeds on Saturn. Near the equator, the *Voyagers* measured winds of about 1,100 mph (500 meters per second). The winds blow primarily in an eastward direction.

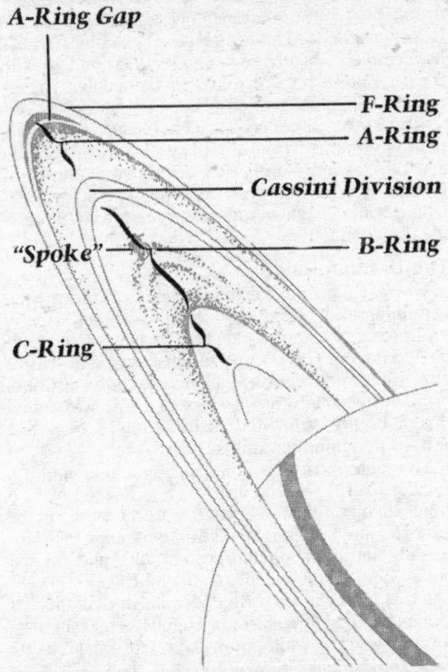

NASA illustration of the divisions in Saturn's ring system.

Saturn's Rings

Saturn's spectacular ring system is unique in the solar system, with uncountable billions of tiny particles of water ice (with traces of other material) in orbit around the planet. The ring particles range in size from smaller than grains of sugar to as large as a house. The main rings stretch out from about 4,350 mi (7,000 km) to above the atmosphere of the planet out to the F ring, a total span of 45,984 mi (74,000 km). Saturn's rings can be likened to a phonograph, rings within rings numbering in the hundreds, and spokes in the B rings, and shepherding satellites controlling the F ring.

The main rings are called the A, B, and C rings moving from outside to inside. The gap between the A and B rings is called Cassini's Division and is named for the Italian-French astronomer Gian Domenico Cassini, who discovered four of Saturn's major moons and the dark, narrow gap, Cassini's Division, splitting the planet's rings.

Saturn's magnetic field has well-defined north and south magnetic poles, and is aligned with Saturn's axis of rotation to within one degree.

Saturn's Moons

Saturn has 31 known moons, 12 of which were discovered in late 2000 and are known by the temporary designations S/2000 S1 through S12. S/2003 S1 was discovered in Feb. 2003. The five largest moons—Tethys, Dione, Rhea, Titan, and Iapetus—range from 650 to 3,200 mi (1,060 to 5,150 km) in diameter. The planet's outstanding satellite is Titan, first discovered by the Dutch astronomer Christiaan Huygens in 1656.

Titan

Titan is remarkable because it is the only known moon in the solar system that has a substantial atmosphere—largely nitrogen with a minor amount of methane and a rich variety of other hydrocarbons. Its surface is completely hidden from view (except at infrared and radio wavelengths) by a dense, hazy atmosphere.

The diameter of Titan is 3,200 mi (5,150 km), and it is the second-largest satellite in the solar system after Jupiter's Ganymede. Titan is larger than the planet Mercury.

Titan's surface temperature is about −280°F (−175°C), and its surface pressure is about 50% greater than the surface pressure of Earth. In 1990, radio telescope data showed that Titan reflects and scatters radio waves, suggesting that the satellite has a solid surface, possibly with small hydrocarbon lakes or ponds.

Infrared images of Titan taken in late 1999 by the W. M. Keck II telescope in Hawaii also revealed features that could be frozen land masses separated by frigid hydrocarbon seas and lakes. Other features might be highlands, and one dark area appeared to be a large impact crater or basin.

NASA is sending a scientific probe to the surface of Titan in 2004 as part of its *Cassini* mission. The probe will be provided by the European Space Agency (ESA).

Other Notable Saturnian Moons

The other four largest moons of Saturn are Tethys, Dione, Rhea, and Iapetus.

Tethys is 650 mi (1,060 km) in diameter. Its surface is heavily cratered, and it has a huge, globe-girdling canyon, Ithaca Chasma. Part of the canyon stretches over three-quarters of the satellite's surface. Ithaca Chasma is about 1,550 mi (2,500 km) long. It has an average width of about 62 mi (100 km) and a depth of 1.8 to 3.1 mi (3 to 5 km).

Tethys also has a huge impact crater named Odysseus that is 244 mi (4,400 km) in diameter, or more than one-third of the moon's diameter.

Dione is slightly larger than Tethys, 696 mi (1,120 km) in diameter, and is more than half composed of water ice. It has bright, wispy markings resembling thin veils covering its features.

Rhea, the largest of the inner satellites, is 951 mi (1,530 km) in diameter. It is composed mainly of water ice, causing its reflective surface to present an almost uniform white appearance.

Iapetus is the outermost of Saturn's icy satellites. Its appearance is unique because it has one dark and one bright hemisphere. The origin of the black coating of its dark face is unknown. Iapetus has a diameter of 907 mi (1,460 km).

Other notable moons of Saturn are Mimas, Enceladus, Hyperion, Phoebe, and Pan.

Mimas is small, only 244 mi (329 km) in diameter. It has a huge impact crater, Herschel, nearly one-third of its diameter. The crater is about 81 mi (130 km) wide and its icy peak rises almost 6.2 mi (10 km) above the floor.

Mimas is believed to be composed mainly of water and ice and to contain between 20% and 50% rock.

Enceladus is remarkable in that its surface shows signs of extensive and recent geological activity. There may be active water volcanism. The surface is extremely bright, reflecting more than 90% of incident sunlight. This suggests that its surface is composed of extremely pure ice without dust or rocks to contaminate it. Enceladus has a diameter of 310 mi (500 km).

Hyperion orbits between Iapetus and Titan. It is irregular in shape, measuring about 248 by 155 by 124 mi (400 by 250 by 200 km). It may be a remnant of a much larger object that was shattered by impact with another space body. It appears that Hyperion is composed primarily of water ice.

Hyperion orbits Saturn with an irregular motion ("chaotic tumbling").

Phoebe travels in a retrograde orbit at a distance of over 6.2 million miles (10 million kilometers) away from the planet. It is the darkest moon of Saturn and is the planet's only known satellite that does not keep the same face always turned to Saturn. It has been speculated that it is an asteroid that was captured by the planet. Phoebe rotates in about nine hours and orbits Saturn in 406 days. It has a diameter of 124 mi (200 km).

Pan was discovered in 1990 from *Voyager 2* photos taken in 1981. The satellite is estimated to be about 12.43 mi (20 km) in diameter, and it orbits within the Encke Gap, a 202-mile (325-kilometer) division in Saturn's A ring. It was identified by Johann Franz Encke (1791–1865) in 1837.

Saturn's other named moons are Atlas, Prometheus, Pandora, Epimetheus, Janus, Telesto, Calypso, and Helene. They are all nonspherical in shape and range from 15 to 120 mi (25 to 190 km) in diameter. In addition, 12 new moons were discovered in late 2000. Designated S/2000 S1 through S12, these new moons are quite small—only about 5 to 30 mi (10 to 50 km) in diameter—and have weak elliptical orbits.

NASA's *Cassini* mission to Saturn, launched in Oct. 1997, will shed more light on the planet's mysteries when it arrives there in 2004.

Saturn is the last of the planets visible to the naked eye. Saturn is never an object of overwhelming brilliance, but it looks like a bright star. The rings can be seen with a small telescope.

Uranus

Uranus, the first planet discovered in modern times by Sir William Herschel in 1781, is the seventh planet from the Sun, twice as far out as Saturn. Its mean distance from the Sun is 1,783 million miles (2,869 million km). Uranus's equatorial diameter is 32,200 mi (51,810 km). The axis of Uranus is tilted at 97°, so it goes around the Sun nearly lying on its side.

Due to Uranus's unusual inclination, the polar regions receive more sunlight during a Uranus year of 84 Earth years. Scientists had thought that the temperature of its poles would be warmer than that at its equator, but *Voyager 2* discovered that the equatorial temperatures were similar to the temperatures at the poles, –344°F (–209°C), implying that some redistribution of heat toward the equatorial region must occur within the atmosphere. The wind patterns on Uranus are much like Saturn's, flowing parallel to the equator in the direction of the planet's rotation.

Ninety-eight percent of the upper atmosphere is composed of hydrogen and helium; the remaining 2% is methane. Scientists speculate that the bulk of the lower atmosphere is composed of water (perhaps as much as 50%), methane, and ammonia. Methane is responsible for Uranus's blue-green color because it selectively absorbs red sunlight and condenses to form clouds of ice crystals in the cooler, higher regions of Uranus's atmosphere.

It was also discovered that the planet's magnetic field is 60° tilted from the planet's axis of rotation and offset from the planet's center by one-third of Uranus's radius. It may be generated at a depth where water is under sufficient pressure to be electrically conductive.

The Uranian Rings

Voyager 2 also expanded the body of information pertaining to the rings and moons of Uranus. *Voyager*'s cameras obtained the first images of 9 previously known narrow rings and discovered at least 2 new rings, one narrow and one broadly diffused, bringing the total known rings to 11. It was found that a highly structured distribution of fine dust exists throughout the ring system.

The outermost (epsilon) ring contains nothing smaller than fist-sized particles. It is flanked by two small moons discovered interior to the orbit of the Uranian moon Miranda. The moons exert a shepherding influence on the epsilon ring and on the outer edges of the gamma and delta rings.

All of the rings lie within one planetary radius[1] of Uranus's cloud tops. Most of Uranus's rings are narrow, ranging in width from 0.6 to 58 mi (1 to 93 km), and are only a few kilometers thick. The Uranian rings are colorless and extremely dark. The dark material may be either irradiated methane ice or organic-rich minerals mixed with water-impregnated, silicon-based compounds. There is evidence that incomplete rings, or "ring arcs," exist at Uranus.

The Uranian Moons

There are 21 known moons of Uranus. In order of decreasing distance from the planet, the moons are Setebos (1999 U1), Prospero (1999 U3), Sycorax, Stephano (1999 U2), Caliban, Oberon, Titania, Umbriel, Ariel, Miranda, Puck, 1986 U10, Belinda, Rosalind, Portia, Juliet, Desdemona, Cressida, Bianca, Ophelia, and Cordelia. Ten of the moons range in size from 16 to 67 mi (26 to 108 km) in diameter and, being closer to the planet, have faster periods of revolution (8–15 hours) than their more distant relatives.

Oberon and Titania

The two largest moons, Oberon, 942 mi (1,516 km) in diameter, and Titania, 982 mi (1,580 km) in diameter, are less than half the diameter of Earth's Moon. Titania, the reddest of Uranus's moons, may have endured global tectonics as evidenced by complex valleys and fault lines etched into its surface. Smooth sections indicate that volcanic resurfacing has taken place.

Umbriel and Ariel

Umbriel and Ariel are roughly three-fourths the size of Oberon and Titania. Umbriel is the darkest of the large moons, with huge craters peppering its surface. Umbriel has a paucity of what are known as bright ray craters, which are formed on an older,

1. The equatorial radius of Uranus is 15,880 mi (25,560 km) at a pressure of 1 bar.

darker surface when bright submerged ice is excavated and sprayed by meteoroid impacts.

In contrast, the surface of Ariel, the brightest of the Uranian moons, is relatively free of pockmarks due to volcanism that periodically erases the damage done by foreign projectiles. However, there are several extremely deep cuts on Ariel's surface.

Miranda

The smallest of Uranus's large moons, Miranda, 293 mi (472 km) in diameter, has been described as "the most bizarre body in the solar system," with the most geologically complex surface. Miranda's remarkable terrain consists of rolling, heavily cratered plains (the oldest known in the Uranian system) adjoined by three huge, 120- to 180-mile (200- to 300-kilometer) oval-to-trapezoidal regions known as coronae, which are characterized by networks of concentric canyons.

Puck

Puck was the first new moon discovered by *Voyager.* It is 96 mi (154 km) in diameter and makes a trip around Uranus every 18 hours. Puck is shaped somewhat like a potato, with a huge impact crater marring roughly one-fourth of its surface.

Caliban and Sycorax

In 1997, two new moons, the first with irregular, noncircular orbits, were discovered around Uranus. These far distant satellites were temporarily designated S/1997 U1 and S/1997 U2 and later named Caliban and Sycorax, respectively. Caliban has a diameter of 37 mi (60 km) and orbits Uranus at an average distance of 4.5 million miles (7.2 million kilometers). Sycorax has a diameter of 74.5 mi (120 km) and a much more elliptical orbit than Caliban, bringing it as close as 3.7 million miles (6 million km) to the planet.

New Uranian Moons Discovered

On May 18, 1999, the International Astronomical Union announced that Erich Karkoschka, a researcher at the Lunar and Planetary Lab of the University of Arizona in Tucson, had discovered the 18th moon orbiting Uranus.

Although the moon was found in 1999, it is designated as satellite S/1986 U10. According to its discoverer, the satellite is approximately 25 mi (40 km) in diameter, about the size of comet Hale-Bopp, and it may have a similar composition to the comet. It orbits 35,000 mi (51,000 km) from Uranus, circling the planet every 15 hours and 18 minutes, similar to the planet's rotational period of about 16.8 hours.

In Sept. 1999, Cornell University astronomers announced the discovery of three more satellites, bringing the total up to 21. The moons have been named Setebos, Stephano, and Prospero. The new satellites are about 12 mi (20 km) in diameter and orbit in distant, elliptical paths.

Uranus can—on rare occasions—become bright enough to be seen with the naked eye, if one knows exactly where to look; normally, a good set of field glasses or a small portable telescope is required.

Neptune

Little was known about Neptune until Aug. 1989, when NASA's *Voyager 2* became the first spacecraft to observe the planet. Passing about 3,000 mi (4,950 km) above Neptune's north pole, *Voyager 2* made its closest approach to any planet since leaving Earth 12 years prior. The spacecraft passed about 25,000 mi (40,000 km) from Neptune's largest moon, Triton, the last solid body that *Voyager 2* studied before continuing on to the outer boundary of the solar system.

Nearly 3 billion miles (4.5 billion kilometers) from the Sun, Neptune orbits the Sun once in 165 years, and therefore has made not quite a full circle around the Sun since it was discovered.[1]

With an equatorial diameter of 30,775 mi (49,528 km), Neptune is the smallest of our solar system's four gas giants, which also include Jupiter, Saturn, and Uranus.[2] Even so, its volume could hold nearly 60 Earths. Neptune is also denser than the other gas giants and about 64% heavier than if it were composed entirely of water.

Neptune has a blue color as a result of methane in its atmosphere. Methane preferentially absorbs the longer wavelengths of sunlight (those near the red end of the spectrum). What are left to be reflected are colors at the blue end of the spectrum. The atmosphere of Neptune is mainly composed of hydrogen, with helium and traces of methane and ammonia.

Neptune is a dynamic planet even though it receives only 3% as much sunlight as Jupiter does. *Voyager 2* discovered several large, dark spots that were prominent features on the planet. The largest spot was about the size of Earth and was designated the "Great Dark Spot" by its discoverers. It appeared to be an anticyclone similar to Jupiter's Great Red Spot. While Neptune's Great Dark Spot is comparable in size, relative to the planet, and at the same latitude (22°S latitude) as Jupiter's Great Red Spot, it was far more variable in size and shape than its Jovian counterpart. Bright, wispy "cirrus-type" clouds overlaid the Great Dark Spot at its southern and northeast boundaries.

At about 42°S latitude, a bright, irregularly shaped eastward-moving cloud circles much faster than did the Great Dark Spot, "scooting" around Neptune in about 16 hours. This "scooter" may have been a cloud plume rising between cloud decks.

Another spot, designated "D2," was located far to the south of the Great Dark Spot, at 55°S latitude. It is almond-shaped, with a bright central core, and moves eastward around the planet in about 16 hours.

In 1995, images taken by the Hubble Space Telescope showed that the Great Dark Spot has vanished. The great storm center has either dissipated or is obscured by other atmospheric conditions.

The atmosphere above Neptune's clouds is hotter near the equator, cooler in the mid-latitudes, and warm again at the south pole. Temperatures in the stratosphere were measured to be 750°K (900°F),

1. Astronomers have studied Neptune since Sept. 23, 1846, when Johann Gottfried Galle, of the Berlin Observatory, and Louis d'Arrest, an astronomy student, discovered the eighth planet on the basis of mathematical predictions by Urbain Jean Joseph Le Verrier. Similar predictions were made independently by John Couch Adams. Galileo Galilei had seen Neptune during several nights of observing Jupiter, in Jan. 1613, but didn't realize he was seeing a new planet.
2. These four planets are about 4 to 12 times greater in diameter than Earth. They have no solid surfaces, but possess massive atmospheres that contain substantial amounts of hydrogen and helium with traces of other gases.

while at the 100-millibar pressure level they were measured to be 55°K (–360°F).

Long, bright clouds, reminiscent of cirrus clouds on Earth, were seen high in Neptune's atmosphere. They appear to form above most of the methane, and consequently are not blue.

At northern low latitudes (27°N), *Voyager* captured images of cloud streaks casting their shadows on cloud decks estimated to be about 30 to 60 mi (50 to 100 km) below. The widths of these cloud streaks range from 30 to 125 mi (50 to 200 km). Cloud streaks were also seen in the southern polar regions (71°S) where the cloud heights were about 30 mi (50 km).

Most of the winds on Neptune blow in a westward direction, which is retrograde, or opposite to the rotation of the planet.

In Jan. 2000, astronomers announced taking the best Earth-based infrared images of Neptune, captured by the W. M. Keck II telescope in Hawaii. The images revealed giant 600-mph (966-km/hr) storms born of heat generated from the planet's still-contracting core. Storm features are pulled across the face of Neptune as it whirls through its 16-hour day.

The Magnetic Field of Neptune

Neptune's magnetic field is tilted 47° from the planet's rotation axis and is offset at least 0.55 radii, about 8,500 mi (13,500 km) from the physical center. The dynamo electric currents produced within the planet, therefore, must be relatively closer to the surface than for Earth, Jupiter, or Saturn. Because of its unusual orientation, and the tilt of the planet's rotation axis, Neptune's magnetic field goes through dramatic changes as the planet rotates in the solar wind.

Voyager's planetary radio astronomy instrument measured the periodic radio waves generated by the magnetic field and determined that the rotation rate of the interior of Neptune is 16 hours and 7 minutes.

Voyager also detected auroras, similar to the northern and southern lights on Earth, in Neptune's atmosphere. Unlike those on Earth, due to Neptune's complex magnetic field, the auroras are extremely complicated processes that occur over wide regions of the planet, not just near the planet's magnetic poles.

Neptune's Moons

Triton

The largest of Neptune's 11 known satellites, Triton was discovered in 1846 by British astronomer William Lassell. Triton circles Neptune in a tilted, circular, retrograde orbit, completing an orbit in 5.875 days at an average distance of 205,000 mi (330,000 km) above the planet's cloud tops.

Triton shows evidence of a remarkable geologic history, and *Voyager 2* images show active geyser-like eruptions spewing invisible nitrogen gas and dark dust particles 1 to 5 mi (2 to 8 km) into space.

Triton is about three-quarters the size of Earth's Moon and has a diameter of about 1,680 mi (2,705 km) and a mean density of about 2.066 grams per cubic centimeter. (The density of water is 1.0 grams per cubic centimeter.) This means that Triton contains more rock in its interior than the icy satellites of Saturn and Uranus.

The relatively high density and the retrograde orbit offer strong evidence that Triton did not originate near Neptune, but is a captured object.

An extremely thin atmosphere extends as much as 500 mi (800 km) above the satellite's surface. Tiny nitrogen ice particles may form thin clouds a few kilometers above the surface. Triton is very bright, reflecting 60% to 95% of the sunlight that strikes it. (By comparison, Earth's Moon reflects only 11%.)

The atmospheric pressure at Triton's surface is about 14 microbars, a mere 1/70,000th the surface pressure on Earth. Temperature at the surface is about 38°K (–391°F), making it the coldest surface of any body yet visited in the solar system.

Nereid

Nereid was discovered in 1949 through Earth-based telescopes. Little is known about Nereid, which is slightly smaller than Proteus, having a diameter of 211 mi (340 km). The satellite's surface reflects about 14% of the sunlight that strikes it. Nereid's orbit is the most eccentric in the solar system, ranging from about 841,100 mi (1,353,600 km) to 5,980,200 mi (9,623,700 km).

The Smaller Satellites

In addition to the previously known moons, Triton and Nereid, *Voyager 2* found six satellites in 1989. In 2003, astronomers using ground-based announced that 3 new moons had been discovered, bringing the total to 11.

Proteus

Proteus is one of the darkest objects in the solar system—"as dark as soot" is a good description. It reflects only 6% of the sunlight that strikes it. Proteus is an ellipsoid about 258 mi (416 km) in diameter, larger than Nereid. It circles Neptune at a distance of about 57,700 mi (92,800 km) above the cloud tops, and completes one orbit in 26 hours and 54 minutes. Scientists say that it is about as large as a satellite can be without being pulled into a spherical shape by its own gravity.

Proteus and its tiny companions are cratered and irregularly shaped—they are not round—and show no signs of any geologic modifications. All circle the planet in the same direction as Neptune rotates and remain close to Neptune's equatorial plane.

Larissa

This object is only about 30,300 mi (48,800 km) from Neptune and circles the planet in 13 hours and 18 minutes. Its diameter is 120 mi (190 km).

Despina

The satellite is 17,200 mi (27,700 km) from Neptune's clouds and makes one orbit every 8 hours. Its diameter is about 90 mi (150 km).

Galatea

It lies 23,100 mi (37,200 km) from Neptune. Its diameter is 110 mi (180 km), and it completes an orbit in 10 hours and 18 minutes.

Thalassa

Thalassa appears to be about 50 mi (80 km) in diameter. It orbits Neptune in 7 hours and 30 minutes some 15,700 mi (25,200 km) above the cloud tops.

Naiad

Naiad is about 37 mi (60 km) in diameter and orbits Neptune about 14,400 mi (23,200 km) above the clouds in 7 hours and 6 minutes.

The First Ten Minor Planets (Asteroids)

Name	Year of discovery	Mean distance from Sun (millions of mi)	Orbital period (years)	Diameter (mi)	Magnitude
1. Ceres	1801	257.0	4.60	485	7.4
2. Pallas	1802	257.4	4.61	304	8.0
3. Juno	1804	247.8	4.36	118	8.7
4. Vesta	1807	219.3	3.63	243	6.5
5. Astraea	1845	239.3	4.14	50	9.9
6. Hebe	1847	225.2	3.78	121	8.5
7. Iris	1847	221.4	3.68	121	8.4
8. Flora	1847	204.4	3.27	56	8.9
9. Metis	1848	221.7	3.69	78	8.9
10. Hygeia	1849	222.6	5.59	40(?)	9.5

New Neptunian Moons

In Jan. 2003, a team of astronomers from the Harvard-Smithsonian Center for Astrophysics and the National Research Council of Canada announced that three new moons had been discovered orbiting Neptune. Although S/2002 N1, S/2002 N2, and S2002 N3 are tiny, about 18–24 mi (30–40 km) in diameter, the astronomers made their discovery using ground-based telescopes in Chile and Hawaii.

Neptune's Rings

Voyager found four rings and evidence of ring *arcs* or incomplete rings. The "Main Ring" orbits Neptune at about 23,812.5 mi (38,100 km) above the cloud tops. The "Inner Ring" is about 17,750 mi (28,400 km) from Neptune's cloud tops. An "Inside Diffuse Ring"—a complete ring—is located about 10,687.5 mi (17,100 km) from the planet's cloud tops. Some scientists suspect that this ring may extend all the way down to Neptune's cloud tops. An area called "the Plateau" is a broad, diffuse sheet of fine material just outside the so-called Inner Ring. The fine material is approximately the size of smoke particles. All other rings contain a greater proportion of larger material.

Pluto

Pluto, the outermost and smallest planet in the solar system, is the only planet not visited by an exploring spacecraft. So little is known about it that it is difficult to classify. Its distance is so great that the Hubble Space Telescope cannot reveal its surface features. Appropriately named for the Roman god of the underworld, it must be frozen, dark, and dead. Pluto's mean distance from the Sun is 3,687.5 million miles (5,900 million kilometers).

In 1978, light-curve studies gave evidence of a moon revolving around Pluto within the same period as Pluto's rotation; therefore, it stays over the same point on Pluto's surface. In addition, it keeps the same face toward the planet. The satellite was later named Charon and is estimated to be about 789 mi (1,262.4 km) in diameter. Recent estimates indicate Pluto's diameter is about 1,441.6 mi (2,306.56 km), making the pair more like a double planet than any other in the solar system. Previously, the Earth–Moon system held this distinction. The density of Pluto is slightly greater than that of water.

There is evidence that Pluto has an atmosphere containing methane and polar ice caps that increase and decrease in size with the planet's seasons. It is not known to have water. The Hubble Space Telescope's faint-object camera revealed light and dark regions on Pluto indicating an ice cap at the planet's north pole. It is not known if there is an ice cap at Pluto's south pole.

Pluto was predicted by calculation when Percival Lowell (1855–1916) noticed irregularities in the orbits of Uranus and Neptune. Clyde Tombaugh (1906–1997) discovered the planet in 1930, precisely where Lowell predicted it would be. The name Pluto was chosen because the first two letters represent the initials of Percival Lowell.

Pluto has the most eccentric orbit in the solar system, bringing it at times closer to the Sun than Neptune. Pluto approached the perihelion of its orbit on Sept. 5, 1989, and until Feb. 1999 was closer to the Sun than Neptune. Even then, it could be seen only with a large telescope.

The Asteroids

Between the orbits of Mars and Jupiter are an estimated 30,000 pieces of rocky debris, known collectively as the asteroids, or planetoids. The first and, incidentally, the largest (Ceres), was discovered during the New Year's night of 1801 by the Italian astronomer Father Piazzi (1746–1826), and its orbit was calculated by the German mathematician Karl Friedrich Gauss (1777–1855). Gauss invented a new method of calculating orbits on that occasion. A few asteroids do not move in orbits beyond the orbit of Mars, but in orbits that cross the orbit of Mars. The first of them was named Eros because of this peculiar orbit. It had become the rule to bestow female names on the asteroids, but when it was found that Eros crossed the orbit of a major planet, it received a male name. These orbit-crossing asteroids are often referred to as the "male asteroids." A few of them—Albert, Adonis, Apollo, Amor, and Icarus—cross the orbit of Earth, and two of them may come closer than our Moon; but the crossing is like a bridge crossing a highway, not like two highways intersecting. Hence there is very little danger of collision from these bodies. They are all small, 3 to 5 mi (4.8 to 8.0 km) in diameter, and therefore very difficult objects to identify, even when quite close. Some scientists believe the asteroids represent the remains of an exploded planet.

On Oct. 29, 1991, the *Galileo* spacecraft took a historic photograph of asteroid 951 Gaspra from a distance of 10,000 mi (16,000 km) away. It was the first close-up photo ever taken of an asteroid in space. Gaspra is an irregular, potato-shaped object about 12.5 mi (20 km) by 7.5 mi (12 km) by 7 mi

(11.2 km) in size. Its surface is covered with a layer of loose rubble and its terrain is marked by several dozen small craters.

NASA's *Near-Earth Asteroid Rendezvous* spacecraft was launched on Feb. 17, 1996. (Near-Earth asteroids come within 121 million miles [195 million kilometers] of the Sun. Their orbits come close enough that one could eventually hit Earth.) It flew within 750 mi (1,200 km) of minor planet 253 Mathilde on June 27, 1997, and took spectacular images of the dark, crater-battered world. The asteroid's mean diameter was found to be 33 mi (52.8 km). The *NEAR* spacecraft discovered that the carbon-rich Mathilde is one of the darkest objects in the solar system, only reflecting about 3% of the Sun's light, making it twice as dark as a chunk of charcoal. The asteroid is almost completely cratered, and at least five of its craters just on the lighted side are larger than 12 mi (19.2 km).

On Feb. 14, 2000, NEAR successfully entered into orbit around Eros and remained in orbit for one year, taking photographs of the asteroid and gathering information about its composition, structure, size, and shape. The spacecraft landed safely on the surface of Eros in a controlled crash on Feb. 12, 2001. Against tremendous odds, it continued to relay information for another two weeks before being shut down.

NEAR measured Eros to be 21 mi (33.6 km) long by 8 mi (12.8 km) wide and 8 mi (12.8 km) deep. It rotates once every 5.27 hours and has no visible moons. NEAR data also showed that the asteroid's ancient surface is covered with craters, ridges, boulders, and other complex features.

NEAR was the first spacecraft to orbit an asteroid and the first craft to operate on solar power so far from the Sun. NEAR gathered about 160,000 images of Eros, about 10 times more than was planned. The spacecraft was renamed *NEAR-Shoemaker* in honor of geologist Dr. Eugene M. Shoemaker (1928–1997), who researched the influence of asteroids and comets in shaping planets.

In June 2002, scientists were caught unaware when an asteroid measuring about 300 ft across hurtled past Earth at a distance of only 75,000 mi—less than a third of the distance to the Moon. The asteroid, which was provisionally named 2002 MN, was only discovered three days after its closest approach. It is the sixth known asteroid to pass within the Moon's orbit.

Comets

Comets, according to the noted astronomer Fred L. Whipple (1906–), are enormous "snowballs" of frozen gases (mostly carbon dioxide, methane, and water vapor) and contain very little solid material. The whole behavior of comets can then be explained as the behavior of frozen gas being heated by the Sun. When the comet Kohoutek made its first appearance to human observers in 1973, its behavior seemed to confirm this theory, and later the international study by five spacecraft that encountered Halley's comet in March 1986 confirmed Whipple's idea of the make-up of comets.

Up until the middle of the 16th century, comets were believed to be phenomena of the upper atmosphere; they were usually explained as "burning vapors" which had risen from "distant swamps." That nobody had ever actually seen burning vapors rise from a swamp did not matter.

But a large comet that appeared in 1577 was carefully observed by Tycho Brahe (1546–1601), a Danish astronomer who is often, and with the best of reasons, called eccentric, but who insisted on precise measurements for everything. It was Tycho Brahe's accumulation of literally thousands of precise measurements that later enabled his younger collaborator, Johannes Kepler (1571–1630), to discover the laws of planetary motion. Measuring the motion of the comet of 1577, Brahe could show that it had been far beyond the atmosphere, even though he could not give figures for the distance. Brahe's work proved that comets were astronomical and not meteorological phenomena.

In 1682, the second Astronomer Royal of Great Britain, Dr. Edmond Halley (1656–1742), checked the orbit of a bright comet that was in the sky and then compared it with earlier comet orbits that were known in part. Halley found that the comet of 1682 was the third to move through what appeared to be the same orbit, and that the three appearances were roughly 76 years apart. Halley concluded that this was the same comet, moving around the Sun in a closed orbit, like the planets. He predicted that it would reappear in 1758 or 1759. Halley himself died in 1742, but a large comet appeared 16 years after his death as predicted and was immediately referred to as "Halley's comet."

Halley's comet appeared again in 1986, sparking a worldwide effort to study it up close. Five satellites in all took readings from the comet at various distances. Two Soviet craft, *Vega 1* and *Vega 2*, went in close to provide detailed pictures of the comet, including the first of the comet's core. The European Space Agency's craft, *Giotto*, entered the comet itself, coming to within 450 mi of the comet's center and successfully passing through its tail. In addition, two Japanese craft, the *Suisei* and the *Sakigake*, passed at a farther distance and analyzed the cloud and tail of the comet and the effect of solar radiation upon it.

Astronomers refer to comets as *periodic* or *non-periodic*, but the latter term does not mean that these comets have no period; it merely means that their period is not known. The actual periods of comets run from 3.3 years (the shortest known) to many thousands of years. Their orbits are elliptical, like those of the planets, but they are very eccentric, long, and narrow ellipses. Only comet Schwassmann-Wachmann has an orbit that has such a low eccentricity (for a cometary orbit) that it could be the orbit of a minor planet.

When a comet coming from deep space approaches the Sun, it is at first indistinguishable from a minor planet. Somewhere between the orbits of Mars and Jupiter, its outline becomes fuzzy; it is said to develop a *coma* (the word used here is the Latin word *coma*, which means "hair," not the phonetically identical Greek word that means "deep sleep"). Then, near the orbit of Mars, the comet develops its tail, which at first trails behind. This grows steadily as the comet comes closer and closer to the Sun. As it rounds the Sun (as first noticed by Girolamo Fracastoro, 1483–1553), the tail always points away from the Sun so that the comet, when moving away from the Sun, points its tail ahead like the landing lights of an airplane.

The reason for this behavior is that the tail is pushed in these directions by the radiation pressure of the Sun. It sometimes happens that a comet loses its tail at perihelion; it then grows another one. Although the tail is clearly visible against the black of the sky, it is very tenuous. It has been said that if the tail of Halley's comet could be compressed to the density of iron, it would fit into a small suitcase.

Although very low in mass, comets are among the largest members of the solar system. The nucleus of a comet may be up to 10,000 mi in diameter; its coma between 10,000 and 50,000 mi in diameter; and its tail as long as 28 million miles.

Comet Shoemaker-Levy 9 broke up into 21 fragments in July 1992 and crashed into the surface of Jupiter, July 16–22, 1994, in the most violent event in the recorded history of the solar system.

In 1951, Dutch astronomer Gerard Kuiper first suggested the existence of a disk-shaped swarm of short-period comets that begin beyond the orbit of Neptune and extend past Pluto. In 1995, the Hubble Space Telescope detected the long-sought Kuiper Belt and an estimated 200 million comets were discovered orbiting it.

In Sept. 2001, the *Deep Space 1* craft flew just 1,300 mi (2,200 km) from the Comet Borrelly and sent images and data about the comet's core. Scientists determined that the comet's nucleus and coma are more complex than previously thought. The *Stardust* mission, launched in 1999, is collecting space dust and plans to gather particles from the Comet Wild 2's nucleus in Jan. 2004. *Stardust* will return to Earth with the samples in 2006.

Meteors and Meteorites

The term *meteor* for what is usually called a *shooting star* bears an unfortunate resemblance to the term *meteorology,* the science of weather and weather forecasting. This resemblance is due to an ancient misunderstanding that wrongly considered meteors an atmospheric phenomenon. Actually, the streak of light in the sky that scientists call a meteor is essentially an astronomical phenomenon: the entry of a small piece of cosmic matter into our atmosphere.

The distinction between *meteors* and *fireballs* (formerly also called *bolides*) is merely one of convenience; a fireball is an unusually bright meteor. Incidentally, it also means that a fireball is larger than a faint meteor.

Objects that enter our atmosphere become visible when they are about 60 mi above the ground. The fact that they grow hot enough to emit light is not due to the "friction" of the atmosphere, as one often reads. The phenomenon responsible for the heating is one of compression. Unconfined air cannot move faster than the speed of sound. Since the entering meteorite moves with 30 to 60 times the speed of sound, the air simply cannot get out of the way. Therefore, it is compressed like the air in the cylinder of a diesel engine and is heated by compression. This heat—or part of it—is transferred to the moving object. The details of this process are now fairly well understood as a result of reentry tests with ballistic-missile nose cones.

The average weight of an object producing a faint *shooting star* is only a small fraction of an ounce. Even a bright fireball may not weigh more than 2 or 3 lb. Naturally, the smaller objects are worn to dust by the passage through the atmosphere; only rather large ones reach the ground. Those that are found are called meteorites. (The *meteor,* to repeat, is the term for the light streak in the sky.) Thousands of meteorites fall to Earth each year.

The largest meteorite known is still embedded in the ground near Grootfontein in southwest Africa and is estimated to weigh 70 tons. The second-largest known is the 34-ton Anighito (on exhibit in the Hayden Planetarium, New York), which was found by Admiral Peary in 1892 at Cape York in Greenland. The largest meteorite found in the United States is the Willamette meteorite (found in Oregon, weight ca. 15 tons), but large portions of this meteorite weathered away before it was found. Its weight as it struck the ground may have been 20 tons.

All these are iron meteorites (an iron meteorite normally contains about 7% nickel), which form one class of meteorites. The other class consists of the stony meteorites, and between them there are the so-called stony irons. Tektites consist of silica-rich glass similar to our volcanic glass obsidian, and because of the similarity, there is doubt in a number of cases whether the glass is of terrestrial or of extraterrestrial origin.

Though no meteorite larger than the Grootfontein is actually known, we do know that Earth has, on occasion, been struck by much larger bodies. Evidence for such hits are the meteorite craters, of which an especially good example is located near the Cañon Diablo in Arizona. Another meteor crater in the United States is a rather old crater near Odessa, Tex. Some scientists theorize that the mass extermination of dinosaurs from the face of Earth 65 million years ago was due to a large meteor that struck our planet at that time.

Meteor showers are caused by multitudes of very small bodies traveling in swarms. Earth travels in its orbit through these swarms like a car driving through falling snow. The point from which the meteors seem to emanate is called the *radiant* and is named for the constellation in that area. The Perseid meteor shower in August is the most spectacular of the year, boasting, at peak, roughly 60 meteors per hour under good atmospheric conditions.

The Constellations

Constellations are groupings of stars that form easily recognized and remembered patterns, such as Orion and the Big Dipper. The Big Dipper is actually an asterism, not a constellation, because it is only part of the constellation Ursa Major (the Big Bear). Actually, the stars in the majority of all constellations do not "belong together." Usually they are at greatly varying distances from Earth and just happen to lie more or less in the same line of sight as seen from our solar system. But in a few cases, the stars of a constellation are actually associated; most of the bright stars of the Big Dipper travel together and form what astronomers call an *open cluster.*

If you observe a planet, say Mars, for one complete revolution, you will see that it passes successively through 12 constellations. All planets (except Pluto at certain times) can be observed only in these 12 constellations, which form the so-called zodiac, and the Sun also moves through the zodiacal signs, though the Sun's apparent movement is actually caused by the movement of Earth.

Although the constellations are due mainly to the optical accident of line of sight and have no real

The 88 Recognized Constellations

In astronomical works, the Latin names of the constellations are used. The letter N or S following the Latin name indicates whether the constellation is located to the north or south of the Zodiac. The letter Z indicates that the constellation is within the Zodiac.

Latin name	Letter	English version
Andromeda	N	Andromeda
Antlia	S	Airpump
Apus	S	Bird of Paradise
Aquarius	Z	Water Bearer
Aquila	N	Eagle
Ara	S	Altar
Aries	Z	Ram
Auriga	N	Charioteer
Boötes	N	Herdsmen
Caelum	S	Sculptor's Tool
Camelopardalis	N	Giraffe
Cancer	Z	Crab
Canes Venatici	N	Hunting Dogs
Canis Major	S	Great Dog
Canis Minor	S	Little Dog
Capricornus	Z	Goat (or Sea-Goat)
Carina	S	Keel (of Argo)[1]
Cassiopeia	N	Cassiopeia
Centaurus	S	Centaur
Cepheus	N	Cepheus
Cetus	S	Whale
Chameleon	S	Chameleon
Circinus	S	Compasses
Columba	S	Dove
Coma Berenices	N	Berenice's Hair
Corona Australis	S	Southern Crown
Corona Borealis	N	Northern Crown
Corvus	S	Crow (Raven)
Crater	S	Cup
Crux	S	Southern Cross
Cygnus	N	Swan
Delphinus	N	Dolphin
Dorado	S	Swordfish (Goldfish)
Draco	N	Dragon
Equuleus	N	Filly
Eridanus	S	Eridanus (river)
Fornax	S	Furnace
Gemini	Z	Twins
Grus	S	Crane
Hercules	N	Hercules
Horologium	S	Clock
Hydra	N	Sea Serpent
Hydrus	S	Water Snake
Indus	S	Indian
Lacerta	N	Lizard
Leo	Z	Lion
Leo Minor	N	Little Lion
Lepus	S	Hare
Libra	Z	Scales
Lupus	S	Wolf
Lynx	N	Lynx
Lyra	N	Lyre (Harp)
Mensa	S	Table (mountain)
Microscopium	S	Microscope
Monoceros	S	Unicorn
Musca	S	Southern Fly
Norma	S	Rule (straight-edge)
Octans	S	Octant
Ophiuchus	N	Serpent-Bearer
Orion	S	Orion
Pavo	S	Peacock
Pegasus	N	Pegasus
Perseus	N	Perseus
Phoenix	S	Phoenix
Pictor	S	Painter (or his Easel)
Pisces	Z	Fishes
Piscis Austrinus	S	Southern Fish
Puppis	S	Poop (of Argo)[1]
Pyxis	S	Mariner's Compass
Reticulum	S	Net
Sagitta	N	Arrow
Sagittarius	Z	Archer
Scorpius	Z	Scorpion
Sculptor	S	Sculptor
Scutum	N	Shield
Serpens	N	Serpent
Sextans	S	Sextant
Taurus	Z	Bull
Telescopium	S	Telescope
Triangulum	N	Triangle
Triangulum Australe	S	Southern Triangle
Tucana	S	Toucan
Ursa Major	N	Big Dipper[2]
Ursa Minor	N	Little Dipper[3]
Vela	S	Sail (of Argo)[1]
Virgo	Z	Virgin
Volans	S	Flying Fish
Vulpecula	N	Fox

1. The original constellation Argo Navis (the Ship Argo) has been divided into Carina, Puppis, and Vela. Normally the brightest star in each constellation is designated by alpha, the first letter of the Greek alphabet, the second brightest by beta, the second letter of the Greek alphabet, and so forth. But the Greek letters run through Carina, Puppis, and Vela as if it were still one constellation. 2. The Big Dipper is only a part of the constellation Ursa Major (Great Bear) and is not a constellation by itself. 3. The Little Dipper is called Ursa Minor (Little Bear).

significance, astronomers have retained them as reference areas. It is much easier to speak of a star in Orion than to give its geometrical position in the sky. During the Astronomical Congress of 1928, it was decided to recognize 88 constellations. A description of their agreed-upon boundaries was published at Cambridge, England, in 1930, under the title *Atlas Céleste.*

The Auroras

The "northern lights" *(Aurora borealis)* as well as the "southern lights" *(Aurora australis)* are upper-atmosphere phenomena of astronomical origin. The auroras center around the magnetic (not the geographical) poles of Earth, which explains why, in the Western Hemisphere, they have been seen as far to the south as New Orleans and Florida, while the equivalent latitude in the Eastern Hemisphere never sees an aurora. The northern magnetic pole happens to be in the Western Hemisphere.

The lower limit of an aurora is at about 50 mi (80 km). Upper limits have been estimated to be as high as 400 mi (640 km). Since about 1880, a connection between the auroras on Earth and sunspots has been suspected and has gradually come to be accepted. It was said that the sunspots probably eject "particles" (later the word *electrons* was substituted), which on striking Earth's atmosphere cause the auroras. But this explanation suffered from certain difficulties. Sometimes a very large sunspot group on the Sun, with individual spots bigger than Earth itself, would not cause an aurora. Moreover, even if a sunspot caused an aurora, the time that passed between the appearance of the one and the occurrence of the other was highly unpredictable.

This problem of the time lag is, in all probability, solved by the discovery of the Van Allen layer[1], a double layer of charged subatomic particles around Earth. The inner layer, with its center some 1,500 mi (2,400 km) from the ground, reaches from about 40°N to about 40°S and does not touch the atmosphere. The outer layer, much larger and with its center several thousand miles from the ground, does touch the atmosphere in the vicinity of the magnetic poles.

It seems probable that the "leakage" of electrons from the outer Van Allen layer causes the auroras. A new burst of electrons from the Sun seems to be caught in the outer layer first. Under the assumption that all electrons are first caught in the outer layer, the time lag can be understood. There has to be an "overflow" from the outer layer to produce an aurora.

1. Named after the American physicist, James Alfred Van Allen (1914–), who discovered the broad bands of intense radiation surrounding Earth in 1958.

The Atmosphere

Though reasonably transparent to visible light, the atmosphere may absorb as much as 60% of the visible and near-visible light. It is opaque to most other wavelengths, except certain fairly short radio waves. In addition to absorbing much light, our atmosphere bends light rays entering at a slant (for a given observer) so that the true position of a star close to the horizon is not what it seems to be. One effect is that we see the Sun above the horizon before it actually is. And the unsteady movement of the atmosphere causes the "twinkling" of the stars, which may be romantic, but is a nuisance when it comes to observing.

The composition of our atmosphere near the ground is 78% nitrogen and 21% oxygen, the remaining 1% consisting of other gases, most of it argon. The composition stays the same to an altitude of at least 70 mi (112 km) (except that higher up two impurities, carbon dioxide and water vapor, are missing), but the pressure drops very fast. At 18,000 ft, half of the total mass of the atmosphere is below, and at 100,000 ft, 99% of the mass of the atmosphere is below. The upper limit of the atmosphere is usually given as 120 mi (192 km); no definitive figure is possible, since there is no boundary line between the incredibly attenuated gases 120 mi (192 km) up and space.

Phenomena, 2004

Configurations of Sun, Moon, and Planets

NOTE: The hour listings are in Universal Time. For conversion to U.S. time zones, *see* Conversion of Universal Time to Civil Time, p. 422. Terms in boldface can be found on pp. 399–400.

JANUARY

Day	Phenomenon	Hour
3	Moon is at **apogee**.	2000
4	Jupiter appears to be motionless in the sky as it goes from direct motion to **retrograde** motion.	1500
4	Earth is at **perihelion**.	1800
6	Mercury appears to be motionless in the sky as it moves toward its greatest elongation west of the Sun from a position east of the Sun as viewed from Earth.	1400
7	Saturn is 5° south of the Moon.	0000
7	FULL MOON	1600
9	Ceres, the largest asteroid, is at **opposition**.	1400
12	Jupiter is 3° south of the Moon.	1100
15	Venus is 0° 9′ south of Uranus.	0100
15	LAST QUARTER	0500
17	Mercury is at its greatest **elongation**, at 24° west of the Sun.	1000
19	The Moon is at **perigee**.	1900
20	Mercury is 5° north of the Moon.	0300
21	NEW MOON	2100
23	Uranus is 4° north of the Moon.	2100
24	Venus is 4° north of the Moon.	1600
28	Mars is 3° north of the Moon.	0300
29	FIRST QUARTER	0600
31	Moon is at **apogee**.	1400

FEBRUARY

Day	Phenomenon	Hour
2	Neptune is in **conjunction** with the Sun.	0900
3	Saturn is 4° south of the Moon.	0400
6	FULL MOON	0900
8	Jupiter is 3° south of the Moon.	1400
13	LAST QUARTER	1400
15	Mercury is 2° south of Neptune.	0900
16	Moon is at **perigee**.	0800
19	Neptune is 5° north of the Moon.	0100
20	NEW MOON	0900
22	Uranus is in **conjunction** with the Sun.	0200
23	Venus is 5° north of the Moon.	1900
25	Ceres appears to be motionless in the sky as it goes from **retrograde** to direct motion.	2000
26	Mars is 0° 9′ north of the Moon. **Occultation** of Mars by the Moon.	0200
28	FIRST QUARTER	0300
28	Moon is at **apogee**.	1100

MARCH

Day	Phenomenon	Hour
1	Saturn is 5° south of the Moon.	1000
4	Mercury is in superior **conjunction**.	0200
4	Jupiter is at **opposition**.	0500
6	Jupiter is 3° south of the Moon.	1600
6	FULL MOON	2300
7	Saturn appears to be motionless in the sky as it goes from **retrograde** to direct motion.	1500
12	Moon is at **perigee**.	0400
13	LAST QUARTER	2100
17	Neptune is 5° north of the Moon.	0900
18	Uranus is 4° north of the Moon.	2000
20	Equinox	0700
20	NEW MOON	2300
22	Mercury is 4° north of the Moon.	0500
24	Venus is 2° north of the Moon.	2100
24	Pluto appears to be motionless in the sky as it goes from direct motion to **retrograde** motion.	2300
26	Mars is 0° 8′ south of the Moon. **Occultation** of Mars by the Moon.	0000
27	The Moon is at **apogee**.	0700
28	Saturn is 5° south of the Moon.	1900
29	FIRST QUARTER	0000
29	Mercury is at its greatest **elongation**, at 19° east of the Sun.	1200
29	Venus is at its greatest **elongation**, at 46° east of the Sun.	1700

APRIL

Day	Phenomenon	Hour
2	Jupiter is 3° south of the Moon.	1900
5	FULL MOON	1100
6	Mercury appears to be motionless in the sky as it moves from its greatest **elongation** east of the Sun back toward a position west of the Sun as viewed from Earth.	2100
7	Mars is 7° north of Aldebaran, the brightest star in the constellation Taurus.	0500
8	The Moon is at **perigee**.	0200
12	LAST QUARTER	0400
13	Neptune is 5° north of the Moon.	1600
15	Uranus is 4° north of the Moon.	0400
16	Venus is 10° north of Aldebaran, the brightest star in the constellation Taurus.	1000
17	Mercury is in inferior **conjunction**.	0100

Day	Phenomenon	Hour
19	NEW MOON. Partial eclipse of the Sun.	1300
23	Venus is 1° 5′ north of the Moon.	1000
23	Mars is 2° south of the Moon.	2100
24	The Moon is at **apogee**.	0000
25	Saturn is 5° south of the Moon.	0600
27	FIRST QUARTER	1800
29	Mercury appears to be motionless in the sky as it moves toward its greatest **elongation** west of the Sun from a position east of the Sun as viewed from Earth.	1000
30	Jupiter is 4° south of the Moon.	0200

MAY

Day	Phenomenon	Hour
2	Venus is at its greatest brilliancy.	0800
4	FULL MOON. Total eclipse of the Moon.	2100
5	Jupiter appears to be motionless in the sky as it goes from **retrograde** to direct motion.	1300
6	The Moon is at **perigee**.	0500
10	Neptune is 5° north of the Moon.	2200
11	LAST QUARTER	1100
12	Uranus is 4° north of the Moon.	1200
12	Vesta, the third-largest asteroid, is 1° 1′ north of the Moon. **Occultation** of Vesta by the Moon.	2200
14	Mercury is at its greatest **elongation**, at 26° west of the Sun.	2100
15	The asteroid Juno appears to be motionless in the sky as it goes from direct motion to **retrograde** motion.	0800
16	Mercury is 3° south of the Moon.	2300
17	Neptune appears to be motionless in the sky as it goes from direct motion to **retrograde** motion.	1500
18	Venus appears to be motionless in the sky as it moves from its greatest **elongation** east of the Sun back toward a position west of the Sun as viewed from Earth.	0000
19	NEW MOON	0500
21	The Moon is at **apogee.**	1200
	Venus is 0° 3′ south of the Moon. **Occultation** of Venus by the Moon.	
22	Mars is 3° south of the Moon.	1600
22	Saturn is 5° south of the Moon.	1800
24	Mars is 1° 6′ north of Saturn.	2300
27	FIRST QUARTER	0800
27	Jupiter is 4° south of the Moon.	1200

JUNE

Day	Phenomenon	Hour
3	FULL MOON	0400
3	The Moon is at **perigee**.	1300
7	Neptune is 5° north of the Moon.	0600
8	Venus is in inferior **conjunction**. Transit of Venus.	0900
8	Uranus is 4° north of the Moon.	1900
9	LAST QUARTER	2000
9	Vesta, the third-largest asteroid, is 1° 2′ south of the Moon. **Occultation** of Vesta by the Moon.	2300
11	Uranus appears to be motionless in the sky as it goes from direct motion to **retrograde** motion.	0000
11	Pluto is at **opposition**.	1200
14	Mars is 6° south of Pollux, the brightest star in the constellation Gemini.	1800
17	The Moon is at **apogee**.	1600
17	NEW MOON	2000
18	Mercury is in superior **conjunction**.	2100
19	Saturn is 5° south of the Moon.	0700
20	Mars is 4° south of the Moon.	0900
21	Solstice	0100
23	Jupiter is 3° south of the Moon.	2300
24	Venus is 2° north of Aldebaran, the brightest star in the constellation Taurus.	2100
25	FIRST QUARTER	1900
29	Venus appears to be motionless in the sky as it moves toward its greatest **elongation** west of the Sun from a position east of the Sun as viewed from Earth.	1400
30	Pallas, the second largest asteroid, is in **conjunction** with the Sun.	2000

JULY

Day	Phenomenon	Hour
1	Mercury is 5° south of Pollux, the brightest star in the constellation Gemini.	1100
1	The Moon is at **perigee**.	2300
2	FULL MOON	1100
4	Venus is 1° 1′ north of Aldebaran, the brightest star in the constellation Taurus.	1000
4	Neptune is 5° north of the Moon.	1500
5	Earth is at **aphelion**.	1100
6	Uranus is 4° north of the Moon.	0300
8	Saturn is in **conjunction** with the Sun.	1700
9	The asteroid Juno is at **opposition**.	0400
9	LAST QUARTER	0800
10	Mercury is 0° 2′ north of Mars.	2300
14	Venus is 8° south of the Moon.	0000
14	The Moon is at **apogee.**	2100
15	Venus is at its greatest brilliancy.	0100
17	NEW MOON	1100
19	Mars is 4° south of the Moon.	0200
19	Mercury is 5° south of the Moon.	1500
21	Jupiter is 3° south of the Moon.	1300
25	FIRST QUARTER	0400
26	Mercury is 1° 5′ south of Regulus, the brightest star in the constellation Leo.	0000
27	Mercury is at its greatest **elongation**, at 27° east of the Sun.	0300
30	The Moon is at **perigee**.	0600
31	FULL MOON	1800

AUGUST

Day	Phenomenon	Hour
1	Neptune is 5° north of the Moon.	0000
1	Vesta, the third largest asteroid, appears to be motionless in the sky as it goes from direct motion to **retrograde** motion.	1700
2	Uranus is 4° north of the Moon.	1200
6	Neptune is at **opposition**.	0300
7	LAST QUARTER	2200
9	Mercury appears to be motionless in the sky as it moves from its greatest **elongation** east of the sun back toward a position west of the Sun as viewed from Earth.	0500
11	The Moon is at **apogee.**	1000
11	Venus is 8° south of the Moon.	2300
13	Saturn is 5° south of the Moon.	0900
16	NEW MOON	0100
17	Mercury is 6° south of Mars.	0300
17	Venus is at its greatest **elongation,** at 46° west of the Sun.	1900
18	Jupiter is 3° south of the Moon.	0500
23	FIRST QUARTER	1000

Day	Phenomenon	Hour
23	Mercury is in inferior **conjunction**.	2100
27	The Moon is at **perigee**.	0600
27	Uranus is at **opposition**.	1900
28	Neptune is 5° north of the Moon.	0900
29	Uranus is 4° north of the Moon.	2000
30	FULL MOON	0200
31	The asteroid Juno appears to be motionless in the sky as it goes from **retrograde** to direct motion.	1400
31	Pluto appears to be motionless in the sky as it goes from **retrograde** to direct motion.	1700

SEPTEMBER

Day	Phenomenon	Hour
1	Venus is 1° 9′ south of Saturn.	0100
1	Mercury appears to be motionless in the sky as it moves toward its greatest **elongation** west of the Sun as viewed from Earth.	1800
2	Venus is 9° south of Pollux, the brightest star in the constellation Gemini.	0200
6	LAST QUARTER	1500
8	The Moon is at **apogee**.	0300
9	Mercury is at its greatest **elongation,** at 18° west of the Sun.	1400
9	Saturn is 5° south of the Moon.	2200
10	Mercury is 0° 6′ south of Regulus, the brightest star in the constellation Leo.	0500
10	Venus is 7° south of the Moon.	1600
12	Saturn is 7° south of Pollux, the brightest star in the constellation Gemini.	0400
13	Mercury is 4° south of the Moon.	0100
13	Ceres, the largest asteroid, is in **conjunction** with the Sun.	0500
13	Vesta, the third largest asteroid, is at **opposition**.	0700
14	NEW MOON	1400
15	Mars is in **conjunction** with the Sun.	1300
21	FIRST QUARTER	1600
22	Jupiter is in **conjunction** with the Sun.	0000
22	Equinox	1600
22	The Moon is at **perigee**.	2100
24	Neptune is 5° north of the Moon.	1500
26	Uranus is 4° north of the Moon.	0300
28	FULL MOON	1300

OCTOBER

Day	Phenomenon	Hour
3	Venus is 0° 2′ south of Regulus, the brightest star in the constellation Leo.	1600
5	Mercury is in superior **conjunction**.	1900
5	The Moon is at **apogee**.	2200
6	LAST QUARTER	1000
7	Saturn is 5° south of the Moon.	1000
10	Venus is 4° south of the Moon.	1900
12	Jupiter is 1° 6′ south of the Moon.	1900
14	NEW MOON. Partial eclipse of the Sun.	0300
18	The Moon is at **perigee**.	0000
20	FIRST QUARTER	2200
21	Neptune is 5° north of the Moon.	2100
23	Uranus is 4° north of the Moon.	0800
24	Neptune appears to be motionless in the sky as it goes from **retrograde** to direct motion.	1000
28	FULL MOON. Total eclipse of the Moon.	0300
31	Mars is 3° north of Spica, the brightest star in the constellation Virgo.	0800
31	Vesta, the third largest asteroid, appears to be motionless in the sky as it goes from **retrograde** to direct motion.	1100

NOVEMBER

Day	Phenomenon	Hour
2	The Moon is at **apogee.**	1800
3	Saturn is 5° south of the Moon.	2000
4	Venus is 0° 6′ north of Jupiter.	2100
5	LAST QUARTER	0600
8	Saturn appears to be motionless in the sky as it goes from direct motion to **retrograde** motion.	1100
9	Jupiter is 1° 0′ south of the Moon. **Occultation** of Jupiter by the Moon.	1600
10	Venus is 0° 2′ north of the Moon. **Occultation** of Venus by the Moon.	0200
11	Mars is 0° 5′ north of the Moon. **Occultation** of Mars by the Moon.	0400
11	Mercury is 2° north of Antares, the brightest star in the constellation Scorpius.	1000
12	Uranus appears to be motionless in the sky as it goes from **retrograde** to direct motion.	0200
12	NEW MOON	1400
14	Mercury is 0° 9′ north of the Moon. **Occultation** of Mercury by the Moon.	0300
14	The Moon is at **perigee.**	1400
16	Venus is 4° north of Spica, the brightest star in the constellation Virgo.	0900
18	Neptune is 5° north of the Moon.	0300
19	FIRST QUARTER	0600
19	Uranus is 4° north of the Moon.	1300
21	Mercury is at its greatest **elongation,** at 22° east of the Sun.	0100
26	FULL MOON	2000
30	The Moon is at **apogee**.	1100
30	Mercury appears to be motionless in the sky as it moves from its greatest **elongation** east of the Sun back toward a position west of the Sun as viewed from Earth.	1300

DECEMBER

Day	Phenomenon	Hour
1	Saturn is 5° south of the Moon.	0200
5	LAST QUARTER	0100
5	Venus is 1° 3′ north of Mars.	0700
7	Jupiter is 0° 3′ south of the Moon. Occultation of Jupiter by the Moon.	1100
10	Mars is 2° north of the Moon.	0000
10	Venus is 4° north of the Moon.	0500
10	Mercury is in inferior **conjunction**.	0800
12	NEW MOON	0100
12	The Moon is at **perigee**.	2100
13	Pluto is in **conjunction** with the Sun.	1700
15	Neptune is 5° north of the Moon.	1100
16	Uranus is 4° north of the Moon.	2100
18	FIRST QUARTER	1700
20	Mercury appears to be motionless in the sky as it moves from its greatest **elongation** west of the Sun back toward a position east of the Sun as viewed from Earth.	0700
21	Solstice	1300
23	Venus is 4° north of Antares, the brightest star in the constellation Scorpius.	2100
26	FULL MOON	1500
27	The Moon is at **apogee**.	1900
28	Saturn is 5° south of the Moon.	0600
29	Mercury is 1° 2′ north of Venus.	0500
29	Mercury is at its greatest **elongation**, at 22° west of the Sun.	2100

Conversion of Universal Time (UT) to Civil Time

UT	EDT[1]	EST[2]	CST[3]	MST[4]	PST[5]
00	*8P	*7P	*6P	*5P	*4P
01	*9P	*8P	*7P	*6P	*5P
02	*10P	*9P	*8P	*7P	*6P
03	*11P	*10P	*9P	*8P	*7P
04	M	*11P	*10P	*9P	*8P
05	1A	M	*11P	*10P	*9P
06	2A	1A	M	*11P	*10P
07	3A	2A	1A	M	*11P
08	4A	3A	2A	1A	M
09	5A	4A	3A	2A	1A
10	6A	5A	4A	3A	2A
11	7A	6A	5A	4A	3A
12	8A	7A	6A	5A	4A
13	9A	8A	7A	6A	5A
14	10A	9A	8A	7A	6A
15	11A	10A	9A	8A	7A
16	N	11A	10A	9A	8A
17	1P	N	11A	10A	9A
18	2P	1P	N	11A	10A
19	3P	2P	1P	N	11A
20	4P	3P	2P	1P	N
21	5P	4P	3P	2P	1P
22	6P	5P	4P	3P	2P
23	7P	6P	5P	4P	3P

NOTES: * denotes previous day. N = noon. M = midnight. 1. Eastern Daylight Time. 2. Eastern Standard Time, same as Central Daylight Time. 3. Central Standard Time, same as Mountain Daylight Time. 4. Mountain Standard Time, same as Pacific Daylight Time. 5. Pacific Standard Time.

Eclipses of the Sun and Moon, 2004

Note: The day of an eclipse is given in Universal Time (U.T.) and may start a day earlier or later depending on your time zone. (*See* Phenomena, 2004, pp. 419–421, to find time of eclipse.)

Apr. 19. Partial eclipse of the Sun. Visible in Antarctica, southeast Atlantic Ocean, southern half of Africa and Madagascar.

May 4. Total eclipse of the Moon. The beginning of the umbral phase visible in Asia except extreme northeast, Europe except western region, Africa except northwesern part, Indonesia, Australia, New Zealand, Antarctica except part of the peninsula, the eastern South Atlantic Ocean, the Indian Ocean, and the western Pacific Ocean; the end visible in Africa, Europe, western Asia, western Australia, Antactcia, South America except the southwestern part, the eastern North Atlantic Ocean, the South Atlantic Ocean, the Indian Ocean, and the extreme southeastern South Pacific Ocean.

Oct. 14. Partial eclipse of the Sun. Visible in Northeast Asia, Japan, western Pacific Ocean, Hawaiian Islands, and the western part of Alaska.

Oct. 28. Total eclipse of the Moon. The beginning of the umbral phase visible in Africa, Europe, Greenland, the Arctic region, North America except the extreme northwest, Central America, South America, extreme western Asia, part of Queen Maud Land and the peninsula of Antarctica, the Atlantic Ocean, the eastern South Pacific Ocean, and the western Indian Ocean; the end visible in North America, the Arctic region, Greenland, Central America, South America, Europe, western Africa, Antarctic peninsula, the eastern Pacific Ocean, and the Atlantic Ocean.

Visibility of Planets in Morning and Evening Twilight, 2004

Morning

Venus	June 15–December 31
Mars	October 30–December 31
Jupiter	January 1–March 4 October 5–December 31
Saturn	July 27–December 31

Evening

Venus	January 1–June 2
Mars	January 1–July 31
Jupiter	March 4–September 8
Saturn	January 1–June 20

Destination Mars

A three-ship fleet sets sail for the Red Planet in search of signs of life

By JEFFREY KLUGER TIME

For a planet so close to ours, Mars has proved strangely inhospitable to earthly visitors. Of the 33 missions to the Red Planet since 1960, 22 have crashed, broken up en route, or otherwise failed before they could complete their research. Undaunted, earthlings launched yet another assault on Mars in June and July 2003, when no fewer than three spacecraft—two from NASA, one from the European Space Agency (ESA)—took flight. If they deliver on even part of their promise, the missions could go a long way toward explaining the history, geology, and—most intriguing—biology of Mars.

The trio of ships will take about seven months to reach Mars (the moon, by contrast, is just a quick three-day hop) and will follow flight plans that are in many respects quite similar. All are traveling to deep basins or other formations on Mars that look as if they were once flooded with water, a key requirement for life. All will also reach the surface in the Rube Goldbergian fashion pioneered by NASA's Mars *Pathfinder* in the summer of 1997, slowing their fall with a combination of heat shields, parachutes, and, in the case of the U.S. landers, braking rockets. All will come to a bouncing landing swaddled in air bags.

Mars Cars

The ESA mission, launched on June 2, 2003, was the first off the blocks, but it is the U.S. missions, which lifted off on June 10 and July 7, that generated the most buzz—and not just because NASA has had 45 years to master the media spin cycle. What will make these expeditions stand out is that each will set loose on the Martian surface a remote-controlled rover even smarter and more photogenic than the miniature robot that captured the world's attention during the *Pathfinder* mission.

Pathfinder's rover was a toy-size machine. Barely 1 ft high and 2 ft long and weighing 24 lbs, it operated for three months and in all that time toddled across a stretch of Martian terrain little bigger than a football field. The new rovers, named *Spirit* and *Opportunity*, are much closer to true space cars. Measuring 5 ft tall from their wheels to the top of their camera masts, the 2003 models weigh about 400 lbs each and should be able to cover up to 3,000 ft in their 90 days of life—including many days they will spend standing around studying rocks. Each has a robot arm crowded with instruments: a rock-abrasion tool for boring into samples, a pair of spectrometers for analyzing mineral composition and measuring radioactive and electromagnetic radiation, and a microscopic imager. "The rovers are like field geologists going out to a new place," says Steve Squyres of Cornell University, NASA's principal investigator for the missions.

The first inflight instrumentation check in early August 2003, indicated that the Mössbauer spectrometer on *Spirit*, which analyzes information about iron atoms, was not performing to expectations. The same instrument on *Opportunity* was functioning properly. NASA hopes to fix *Spirit's* Mössbauer before landing.

Each rover carries an array of eight cameras, including one perched atop the mast for a you-are-there view. On the 1997 mission, the rover's camera was barely 10 in. off the ground. "It was like crawling around on your belly," says project scientist Joy Crisp of NASA's Jet Propulsion Laboratory.

European Edge

For all their sophistication, the rovers won't be especially good at addressing the question people ask most: Is there now, or might there ever have been, life on Mars? The devices can make inferences, looking for evidence of water or iron. And if the microscopic imager sent back a picture of a microbial fossil, that would settle the question. But even NASA acknowledges that when it comes to searching for life, the Europeans have the edge this time.

The ESA probe comes in two parts: an orbiter that will stay aloft to conduct atmospheric studies and a lander that will descend to the surface. Dubbed *Beagle 2*, after Charles Darwin's famous specimen-collecting ship, the lander is only 3 ft wide when packed for flight, but on the ground it will open like a flower and deploy an impressive array of equipment. Among the instruments are a drill capable of digging 5 ft below the surface, 12 ovens that can heat samples to some 1,600°F to generate carbon dioxide, and a mass spectrometer to identify carbon isotopes, along with other elements. The lander can also measure ultraviolet radiation, temperature, and atmospheric pressure, all variables that play a key role in biology. "If there is one mission capable of detecting past and present life, it will be ours," says planetary scientist Colin Pillinger, a professor at Britain's Open University and the man who dreamed up the project.

Whatever discoveries the trio of missions make, they are almost certain to rekindle some of the thrill of space exploration for a world that has seen precious little of it lately. Says Squyres: "Hey, if you can't have fun building spacecraft and sending them to Mars, give it up, man!" □

Major Space Explorations

Ongoing Missions

Voyager (U.S.)

Destination: Jupiter and Saturn. **Launched:** Aug. 20 *(Voyager 2)* and Sept. 5 *(Voyager 1)*, 1977. **Mission:** To explore Jupiter and the other outer planets. Launched in 1977, *Voyager 1* and *Voyager 2* passed Jupiter in 1979 and sent back surprising color TV images of that planet and its moons. *Voyager 1* passed Saturn in Nov. 1980. *Voyager 2* passed Saturn in Aug. 1981 and Uranus in Jan. 1986. *Voyager 2* encountered Neptune on Aug. 29, 1989, and made many discoveries. It found four rings around the planet, six new moons, a giant spot, and evidence of volcanic-like activity on its largest moon, Triton. The spacecraft sent back over 9,000 pictures of the planet and its system. *Voyager 2* remains the only spacecraft ever to have visited the worlds of Neptune and Uranus. On Feb. 13, 1990, at a distance of 3.7 billion miles, *Voyager 1* took its final pictures of the Sun and six of its planets as seen from deep space. NASA released the extraordinary images to the public on June 6, 1990. Only Mercury, Mars, and Pluto were not seen.

In its quarter-century of exploration, the *Voyager* project has returned immense amounts of information. *Voyager I*, at 8.3 billion mi from the Sun, is currently the most distant human-made object in the universe, and *Voyager 2* is 6.6 billion mi from the Sun. Both spacecraft currently constitute the Voyager Interstellar Mission (VIM), the study of the region of space beyond the Sun's influence (the heliopause), at the outer boundary of the solar system. Both spacecraft continue to relay news of their surroundings through the Deep Space Network (DSN).

Galileo (U.S.)

Destination: Jupiter. **Launched:** Oct. 18, 1989. **Achieved Orbit:** Dec. 7, 1995. **Mission:** To study the chemical composition and physical state of the largest planet in the solar system, its atmosphere, and four of its moons. During its 2-year prime mission, *Galileo* made 11 orbits around Jupiter and visited and photographed Jupiter's large moons Io, Callisto, Ganymede, and Europa. Originally slated to end its explorations in Dec. 1997, *Galileo* has been favored with a series of two-year extensions from NASA and Congress. The first extension, dubbed the Galileo Europa Mission (GEM), included eight flybys of Europa, four flybys of Callisto, and two flybys of Io by the end of 1999. The spacecraft also observed the smaller moons Amalthea, Thebe, and Metis on Jan. 3, 2000. After so many successful flybys, *Galileo* was granted another tour, the Galileo Millennium Mission, which collected data on Io and Europa. On Feb. 22, 2000, *Galileo* made the closest pass ever of Io at 124 mi (200 km). Two flybys of Ganymede were conducted May 20 and Dec. 28, 2000. Also in Dec. 2000, *Galileo* embarked on a joint scientific expedition with the Saturn-bound *Cassini* spacecraft to make simultaneous observations of the Jupiter system from two vantage points.

In May of 2002, *Galileo* finished its observations of Io; the results revealed Io—now known as the most active body in the solar system—to be more heavily populated by active volcanoes than had been expected. *Galileo*'s last flyby was a close brush with Amalthea, an inner satellite of Jupiter, on Nov. 5, 2002. Intense radiation caused a computer failure that forced a switch to backup circuits and a temporary shutdown, but Galileo was able to record significant scientific data. In Sept. 2003, *Galileo* will self-destruct in a final, fatal plunge into Jupiter's atmosphere. *Galileo* was named for the Italian astronomer Galileo Galilei, who discovered the four great moons of Jupiter that were the major targets of this mission.

Ulysses (U.S. and European Space Agency)

Destination: The Sun. **Launched:** Oct. 6, 1990. **Mission:** An international project to study the Sun and map the interstellar space above and below its poles. The spacecraft was put into orbit at right angles to the solar system's ecliptic plane. This special orbit enabled *Ulysses* to examine for the first time the Sun's north and south polar regions. Besides investigating the Sun, the spacecraft is also studying phenomena from the Milky Way and beyond. The spacecraft completed its first full orbit around the Sun on April 17, 1998, and continues to orbit the Sun. Its next major mission milestone will occur in Feb. 2004, when it makes its closest approach to Jupiter.

Mars Global Surveyor (U.S.)

Destination: Mars. **Launched:** Nov. 7, 1996. **Arrival:** Sept. 11, 1997. **Mission:** An orbiting spacecraft designed to provide detailed maps of the planet's surface and distribution of minerals, and to monitor the Martian weather. Six instruments are studying Martian surface, atmosphere, and gravitational and magnetic fields. *Surveyor*'s cameras are able to distinguish features as small as 10 ft across.

The primary mapping mission was delayed until March 1999, due to problems with the craft's solar panels. *MGS* completed its primary mission in Jan. 2001, and is currently in an extended mission phase. Having studied the planet's entire surface, atmosphere, and interior, *MGS* has returned more Mars data than all other Martian missions combined. Its most significant results include photographs of gullies and debris flow that suggest the presence of water at or near the planet's surface.

Cassini (U.S., the European Space Agency, and the Italian Space Agency)

Destination: Saturn. **Launched:** Oct. 15, 1997. **Arrival:** July 1, 2004. **Mission:** Will orbit Saturn for four years. While orbiting Saturn, *Cassini* will send a small probe named *Huygens* (after the Dutch astronomer Christiaan Huygens, who discovered Titan) to the surface of Saturn's largest moon, Titan, to learn more about its dense atmosphere and its surface state and composition. After relaying data to Earth from Titan, *Cassini* will continue with orbits of Saturn and flybys of the planet's moons. The spacecraft will also examine Saturn's equatorial zone and study the planet's polar regions. *Cassini* encountered Jupiter on Dec. 30, 2000, and flew down the giant planet's magnetotail, performing studies complementing the *Galileo* mission until March 31, 2001. The spacecraft flew by asteroid

2685 Masursky on Jan. 23, 2000. The *Cassini* mission is named for the Italian-French astronomer Gian Domenico Cassini, who discovered four of Saturn's major moons.

Nozomi ("Hope") (Japan)
Destination: Mars. **Launched:** July 4, 1998, from Kagoshima Space Center. **Arrival:** Jan. 2004. Engine problems forced fuel conservation measures and delayed its scheduled 1999 arrival at Mars until 2004. **Mission:** To send an orbiter around Mars to study the effect of the solar wind on the planet's atmosphere for one Martian year (687 days). Its cameras will provide photographic data on cloud distribution, polar haze, dust storms, polar ice, and the planet's surface. After its successful launch, the Planet-B spacecraft was renamed *Nozomi* (hope). Japan's new effort made it the third nation after the United States and Russia to conduct a mission to another planet.

Stardust (U.S.)
Destination: Comet Wild 2. **Launched:** Feb. 7, 1999. **Mission:** To fly through coma of Comet Wild 2 in 2004, capture particles spewing out of comet, and return comet dust samples to Earth in 2006. *Stardust* will be the first mission to return with comet samples. Additionally, the *Stardust* spacecraft will bring back samples of interstellar dust, which is believed to include remnants from the formation of the solar system. On April 18, 2002, *Stardust* reached the farthest distance from the Sun ever traveled by a solar-powered spacecraft, 2.72 AU (253 million mi or 407 million km).

2001 Mars Odyssey (U.S.)
Destination: Mars. **Launched:** April 7, 2001. **Arrival:** Oct. 24, 2001. **Mission:** To conduct mineralogical mapping of the planet and study the radiation risk to humans over the course of three years. A goal of the program is to determine if Mars's atmosphere could support life.

Mars Odyssey's primary mission will continue through Aug. 2004, mapping the amount and distribution of chemical elements and minerals that form the Martian surface and searching especially for evidence of hydrogen in the subsurface. In addition to its scientific mission, *Mars Odyssey* will provide support to other missions in the Mars Exploration Program, serving as the communications relay for U.S. and international spacecraft scheduled to arrive at Mars in 2003 and 2004. *Odyssey* data will also be used to identify potential landing sites for future Mars missions.

Wilkinson Microwave Anisotropy Probe (WMAP) (U.S.)
Destination: Solar orbit. **Launched:** June 30, 2001. **Arrival:** Oct. 1, 2001. **Mission:** To reveal conditions as they existed in the early universe by measuring the properties of cosmic microwave background radiation (CMB), the radiant heat left over from the Big Bang, over the full sky. Each sky scan takes approximately six months, and in April 2002, *WMAP* completed its first; the second followed in Oct. 2002. The full sky map will be updated as more data is received and analyzed. Data from *WMAP*'s first full sky scan was released in Feb. 2003. *See* "Cosmic Fingerprint," p. 398.

Genesis (U.S.)
Destination: The Sun. **Launched:** Aug. 8, 2001. **Mission:** Gather samples of charged particles of the solar wind and return them to Earth in Sept. 2004 for detailed analysis. The reentry vehicle will separate from the spacecraft and parachute its sample return capsule to a location in the Utah desert. The data to be obtained are crucial for improving theories about the origin of the Sun and planets that formed from the same primordial dust cloud.

Mars Express (European Space Agency)
Destination: Mars. **Launched:** June 2, 2003. **Arrival:** Dec. 26, 2003. **Mission:** Search for subsurface water from orbit and drop a lander on the Martian surface. Instruments on the orbiting spacecraft will study the atmosphere and the planet's structure and geology. The lander, *Beagle 2* (named after the ship on which Charles Darwin sailed), is scheduled to take photographs, gather soil samples, and examine rocks and soil microscopically—all in the search for signs of past life on Mars.

Mars Exploration Rovers (MER) (U.S.)
Destination: Mars. **Launched:** June 10, 2003 *(Spirit)* and July 7 *(Opportunity)*. **Arrival:** Jan. 2004. **Mission:** To deploy, in two different locations, *Spirit* and *Opportunity*, two identical long-range rovers (larger than *Pathfinder's Sojourner*) that can trek up to 300 yards (100 m) across the surface in a Martian day. The rovers' sophisticated instruments will enable them to act as mobile field geologists, taking color pictures, analyzing soil and rocks, and searching for past and present evidence of water. The rovers are designed to operate for 90 days but could continue longer.

Future Missions

(Note: Dates are tentative.)

Selene SELenological and Engineering Explorer (Japan)
Destination: The Moon. **Launch:** 2005. **Mission:** A spacecraft that will study the origin and evolution of the Moon, orbiting it for one year. It will map the entire surface and gather data on chemical and mineralogical composition, magnetic fields, and interior structure. After a year, the propulsion module of the orbiter will separate from the spacecraft and soft-land on the lunar surface to continue the mission for two more months.

Space Technology 5 (U.S.)
Destination: Earth's magnetosphere. **Launch:** 2004. **Mission:** Fourth deep-space mission of NASA's New Millennium program. The Nanosat Constellation Trailblazer, known as Space Technology 5 or ST5, will test methods for operating three miniature spacecraft as a single system. Each of the spacecraft is about 17 in. (42 cm) across by 8 in. (20 cm) high and weighs about 47 lb.

SPIDR (U.S.)
Destination: Earth orbit. **Launch:** 2005. **Mission:** Of NASA's two most recently announced missions, the Explorer for Spectroscopy and Photometry of the Intergalactic Medium's Diffuse Radiation Orbiter, or *SPIDR*, is hoped to help shed light on how galaxies form and evolve by mapping the distribution of hot gas filaments in the nearby universe.

AIM (U.S.)
Destination: Earth orbit. **Launch:** 2006. **Mission:** *AIM*, the Aeronomy of Ice in the Mesosphere mission, will be employed to help scientists investigate the causes of the recent rise in noctilucent (glow-in-the-dark) clouds, wispy swirls that form about 50 mi (80 km) above the surface of the earth. The presence of the clouds over the polar regions has increased markedly in recent decades, and is thought by many scientists to be related to higher concentrations of greenhouse gases in Earth's atmosphere.

New Horizons (U.S.)
Destination: Pluto-Kuiper Belt. **Launch:** Jan. 2006. **Arrival:** Summer 2015. **Mission:** To study the worlds at the edge of our solar system. *New Horizons* will be the first mission specifically designed to study Pluto and its moon Charon. Ths mission plans to map Pluto and Charon's surface appearances, study surface compositions, and probe their atmospheres. *New Horizons* then will go to the Kuiper Belt, located beyond Neptune's orbit, and examine Kuiper Belt objects, thought to be similar to the composition of the cores of the giant planets.

Herschel Space Observatory (European Space Agency)
Destination: Earth's magnetosphere. **Launch:** 2007. **Mission:** To study how the first stars and galaxies were formed and to search for water in space. Formerly called the Far Infrared and Submillimetre Telescope (FIRST), Herschel will be equipped with an infrared telescope, a high-resolution spectrograph, and two infrared cameras. Construction of the observatory began in the spring of 2002.

U.S. Unstaffed Planetary and Lunar Programs

Lunar Orbiter. Series of spacecraft designed to orbit the Moon, taking pictures and obtaining data in support of the subsequent staffed *Apollo* landings. The U.S. launched five *Lunar Orbiter*s between Aug. 10, 1966 and Aug. 2, 1967.

Mariner. Designation for a series of spacecraft designed to fly past or orbit the planets, particularly Mercury, Venus, and Mars. *Mariner*s provided the early information on Venus and Mars. *Mariner 9,* orbiting Mars in 1971, returned the most revealing photographs of that planet and helped pave the way for a *Viking* landing in 1976. *Mariner 10* explored Venus and Mercury in 1973 and was the first probe to use a planet's gravity to propel it toward another.

Pioneer. Designation for the United States' first series of sophisticated interplanetary spacecraft. *Pioneer*s *10* and *11* reached Jupiter in 1973 and 1974 and continued on to explore Saturn and the other outer planets. *Pioneer 11,* renamed *Pioneer Saturn,* examined the Saturn system in Sept. 1979. Significant discoveries were the finding of a small new moon and a narrow new ring. In 1986, *Pioneer 10* was the first man-made object to escape the solar system. *Pioneer Venus 1* and *2* reached Venus in 1978 and provided detailed information about that planet's surface and atmosphere.

Ranger. NASA's earliest Moon-exploration program. Spacecraft were designed for a crash landing on the Moon, taking pictures and returning scientific data up to the moment of impact. Provided the first close-up views of the lunar surface. The *Ranger*s provided more than 17,000 close-up pictures, giving us more information about the Moon in a few years than in all the time that had gone before.

Surveyor. Series of unstaffed spacecraft designed to land gently on the Moon and provide information on the surface in preparation for the staffed lunar landings. *Surveyor*'s legs were instrumented to return data on the surface hardness of the Moon. *Surveyor* dispelled the fear that *Apollo* spacecraft might sink several feet or more into the lunar dust.

Viking. Designation for two spacecraft designed to conduct detailed scientific examination of the planet Mars, including a search for life. *Viking 1* landed on July 20, 1976; *Viking 2,* Sept. 3, 1976. More was learned about the red planet in a few short months than in all previous missions, but the question of whether there is life on Mars remains unresolved.

Notable Unstaffed Lunar and Interplanetary Probes

Spacecraft	Launch date	Destination	Remarks
Pioneer 3 (U.S.)	Dec. 6, 1958	Moon	Max. alt.: 66,654 mi. Discovered outer Van Allen layer.
Luna 2 (USSR)	Sept. 12, 1959	Moon	Impacted on Sept. 14. First space vehicle to reach Moon.
Luna 3 (USSR)	Oct. 4, 1959	Moon	Flew around Moon and transmitted first pictures of lunar far side, Oct. 7.
Mariner 2 (U.S.)	Aug. 27, 1962	Venus	Venus probe. Successful mid-course correction. Passed 21,648 mi from Venus Dec. 14, 1962. Reported 800°F surface temp. Contact lost Jan. 3, 1963, at 54 million mi.
Ranger 7 (U.S.)	July 28, 1964	Moon	Impacted near Crater Guericke 68.5 hr after launch. Sent 4,316 pictures during last 15 min of flight as close as 1,000 ft above lunar surface.
Mariner 4 (U.S.)	Nov. 28, 1964	Mars	Transmitted first close-up pictures on June 14, 1965, from altitude of 6,000 mi.
Luna 9 (USSR)	Jan. 31, 1966	Moon	220 lb instrument capsule soft-landed Feb. 3, 1966. Sent back about 30 pictures.
Surveyor 1 (U.S.)	May 30, 1966	Moon	Landed June 2, 1966. Sent almost 10,400 pictures, a number after surviving the 14-day lunar night.
Lunar Orbiter 1 (U.S.)	Aug. 10, 1966	Moon	Orbited Moon Aug. 14. 21 pictures sent.
Surveyor 3 (U.S.)	April 17, 1967	Moon	Soft-landed on Oceanus Procellarum 65 hr after launch. Scooped and tested lunar soil.
Venera 4 (USSR)	June 12, 1967	Venus	Arrived Oct. 17. Instrument capsule sent temperature and chemical data.

Spacecraft	Launch date	Destination	Remarks
Surveyor 5 (U.S.)	Sept. 8, 1967	Moon	Landed near lunar equator Sept. 10. Radiological analysis of lunar soil. Mechanical claw for digging soil.
Surveyor 7 (U.S.)	Jan. 6, 1968	Moon	Landed near Crater Tycho Jan. 10. Soil analysis. Sent 3,343 pictures.
Pioneer 9 (U.S.)	Nov. 8, 1968	Sun	Achieved orbit. Six experiments returned solar radiation data.
Venera 5 (USSR)	Jan. 5, 1969	Venus	Landed May 16, 1969. Returned atmospheric data.
Mariner 6 (U.S.)	Feb. 24, 1969	Mars	Came within 2,000 mi of Mars July 31, 1969. Sent back data and TV pictures.
Luna 16 (USSR)	Sept. 12, 1970	Moon	Soft-landed Sept. 20, scooped up rock, returned to Earth Sept. 24.
Luna 17 (USSR)	Nov. 10, 1970	Moon	Soft-landed on Sea of Rains Nov. 17. *Lunokhod 1*, self-propelled vehicle, used for first time. Sent TV photos, made soil analysis, etc.
Mariner 9 (U.S.)	May 30, 1971	Mars	First craft to orbit Mars, Nov. 13. 7,300 pictures, 1st close-ups of one of Mars's moons. Transmission ended Oct. 27, 1972.
Luna 20 (USSR)	Feb. 14, 1972	Moon	Soft-landed Feb. 21 in Sea of Fertility. Returned Feb. 25 with rock samples.
Pioneer 10 (U.S.)	March 3, 1972	Jupiter	620-million-mi flight path through asteroid belt past Jupiter Dec. 3, 1973, to give man first close-up of planet. In 1986, it became first man-made object to escape solar system.
Luna 21 (USSR)	Jan. 8, 1973	Moon	Soft-landed Jan. 16. *Lunokhod 2* (moon-car) scooped up soil samples, returned them to Earth Jan. 27.
Mariner 10 (U.S.)	Nov. 3, 1973	Venus, Mercury	Passed Venus Feb. 5, 1974. Arrived Mercury March 29, 1974, for man's first close-up look at planet. First time gravity of one planet (Venus) used to propel spacecraft toward another (Mercury).
Viking 1 (U.S.)	Aug. 20, 1975	Mars	Carrying life-detection labs. Landed July 20, 1976, for detailed scientific research, including pictures. Designed to work for only 90 days, it operated for almost 6½ years before it went silent in Nov. 1982.
Viking 2 (U.S.)	Sept. 9, 1975	Mars	Like Viking 1. Landed Sept. 3, 1976. Functioned 3½ years.
Luna 24 (USSR)	Aug. 9, 1976	Moon	Soft-landed Aug. 18, 1976. Returned soil samples Aug. 22, 1976.
Voyager 2 (U.S.)	Aug. 20, 1977	Jupiter, Saturn, Uranus	Launched before *Voyager 1*. Encountered Jupiter in July 1979; flew by Saturn Aug. 1981; passed Uranus Jan. 1986; and passed Neptune in Aug. 1989.
Voyager 1 (U.S.)	Sept. 5, 1977	Jupiter, Saturn	Flyby mission. Reached Jupiter in March 1979; passed Saturn Nov. 1980; passed Uranus 1986.
Pioneer Venus 1 (U.S.)	May 20, 1978	Venus	Arrived Dec. 4 and orbited Venus, photographing surface and atmosphere. Crashed into planet's surface mid-Oct. 1992 after circling Venus for 14 years.
Pioneer Venus 2 (U.S.)	Aug. 8, 1978	Venus	Four-part multiprobe, landed Dec. 9.
Venera 13 (USSR)	Oct. 30, 1981	Venus	Landed March 1, 1982. Took first X-ray fluorescence analysis of the planet's surface. Transmitted data 2 hours, 7 minutes.
VEGA 1 (USSR)	Deployed on Venus, June 10, 1985	Halley's Comet	In flyby over Venus while en route to encounter Halley's Comet, *VEGA 1* and *2* dropped scientific capsules onto Venus to study atmosphere and surface material. Encountered Halley's Comet on March 6 and March 9, 1986. Took TV pictures and studied comet's dust particles.
VEGA 2 (USSR)	Deployed on Venus, June 14, 1985	Halley's Comet	See *VEGA 1* above.
Suisei (Japan)	Aug. 18, 1985	Halley's Comet	Spacecraft made flyby of comet and studied atmosphere with ultraviolet camera; observed rotation nucleus (March 8, 1986).
Sakigake (Japan)	Jan. 8, 1985	Halley's Comet	Spacecraft made flyby to study solar wind and magnetic fields; detected plasma waves (March 11, 1986).
Giotto (E.S.A.)	July 2, 1985	Halley's Comet	European Space Agency spacecraft made closest approach to comet (March 13, 1986). Studied atmosphere and magnetic fields. Sent back best pictures of nucleus. Flew by comet Grigg-Skjellerup July 10, 1992. Unable to send pictures.
Phobos Mission (USSR)	July 7 and July 12, 1988	Mars and Phobos	Two spacecraft to probe Martian moon Phobos starting April 1989. Were to study orbit and soil chemistry, and send TV pictures and data of planet. Contact was lost with *Phobos 1* in Aug. 1988 and with *Phobos 2* in March 1989 after it reached the Martian moon.
Magellan (U.S.)	May 4, 1989	Venus	Arrived at Venus on Aug. 10, 1990, and made a geologic map of planet with a powerful radar. Crashed into Venus Oct. 12, 1994.
Galileo (U.S.)	Oct. 18, 1989	Jupiter	To study Jupiter's atmosphere and its moons during 22-month mission.

Spacecraft	Launch date	Destination	Remarks
Ulysses (U.S., E.S.A.)	Oct. 6, 1990	Sun	To study the poles of the Sun and interstellar space above and below the poles. First solar encounter was in 1994, second encounter in 1995.
Gamma-Ray Observatory (U.S.)	April 7, 1991	Earth orbit	To make first survey of gamma-ray sources across the whole sky, studying explosive energy sources such as supernovae, quasars, neutron stars, pulsars, and black holes. Mission ended, it was deorbited and crashed into Pacific Ocean, June 4, 2000.
Clementine (U.S.)	Jan. 25, 1994	Moon and asteroid 1620 Geographos	Entered lunar orbit Feb. 21 and took close-up photos of lunar surface for two months. Computer malfunction prevented planned rendezvous with *Geographos.*
Near-Earth Asteroid Rendezvous (NEAR) (U.S.)	Feb. 17, 1996	Asteroid 433 Eros	Photographed asteroid 253 Mathilde June 27, 1997. Entered into orbit around Eros Feb. 14, 2000, and landed on surface in controlled crash Feb. 12, 2001. Took detailed measurements and generated about 160,000 images of Eros. Renamed NEAR-Shoemaker in honor of geologist Eugene M. Shoemaker. First craft to orbit an asteroid.
Mars Pathfinder (U.S.)	Dec. 5, 1996	Ares Vallis, Mars	Landed July 4, 1997. The spacecraft lander and its rover, *Sojourner,* provided a wealth of information on the Martian rocks, soil, and atmosphere. Sent back the first live pictures. All *Pathfinder*'s objectives were fulfilled and communications failed on Sept. 27, 1997.
Lunar Prospector (U.S.)	Jan. 6, 1998	Moon	Orbited Moon for one year, mapped chemical composition of lunar surface. Found frozen water at north and south poles. At end of its mission on July 31, 1999, it was intentionally crashed into south polar crater in hope of detecting plume of water ice, but no cloud of molecular water vapor was observed by powerful Earth telescopes.
Deep Space 1 (U.S.)	Oct. 24, 1998	Deep space	The first launch of NASA's New Millennium Program, a series of missions to test new technologies. Famous for its July 1999 photos of the near-Earth Braille asteroid and the first-ever photos of a comet nucleus when it staged a risky flyby of the comet Borelly in Sept. 2001. The second phase of New Millennium, *Deep Space 2,* was launched in 1999, but NASA lost contact with it in Dec. 1999.
Space Infrared Telescope Facility (SIRTF) (U.S.)	Aug. 25, 2003	Earth-trailing solar orbit	Final mission in NASA's Great Observatories Program which has four observatories studying the universe in different kinds of light—visible (Hubble Space Telescope), gamma rays (Compton Gamma-Ray Observatory), x-rays (Chandra X-Ray Observatory), and infrared (SIRTF).

U.S. Staffed Space Flight Programs

Mercury. *Project Mercury,* initiated in 1958 and completed in 1963, was the United States' first human-in-space program. It was designed to further knowledge about humanity's capabilities in space.

In April 1959, seven military-jet test pilots were introduced to the public as America's first astronauts. They were: Lt. M. Scott Carpenter, USN; Capt. L. Gordon Cooper, Jr., USAF; Lt. Col. John H. Glenn, Jr., USMC; Cap. Virgil I. Grissom, USAF; Lt. Cdr. Walter M. Schirra, Jr., USN; Lt. Cdr. Alan B. Shepard, Jr., USN; and Capt. Donald K. Slayton, USAF. Six of the original seven would make a Mercury flight. Slayton was grounded for medical reasons but remained a director of NASA's astronaut office. He returned to flight status in 1975 as Docking Module Pilot on the *Apollo-Soyuz* flight.

Flight Summary

Each astronaut named his capsule and added the numeral 7 to denote the teamwork of the original astronauts.

May 5, 1961. Alan B. Shepard, Jr., made a suborbital flight in *Freedom 7* and became the first American in space. Time: 15 minutes, 22 seconds.

July 21, 1961. Virgil I. Grissom made the second successful suborbital flight in *Liberty Bell 7,* but spacecraft sank shortly after splashdown. Time: 15 minutes, 37 seconds. Grissom was later killed in *Apollo 1* fire, Jan. 27, 1967.

Feb. 20, 1962. John H. Glenn, Jr., made a three-orbit flight in *Friendship 7* and became the first American in orbit. Time: 4 hours, 55 minutes.

May 24, 1962. M. Scott Carpenter duplicated Glenn's flight in *Aurora 7.* Time: 4 hours, 56 minutes.

Oct. 3, 1962. Walter M. Schirra, Jr., made a six-orbit engineering test flight in *Sigma 7.* Time: 9 hours, 13 minutes.

May 15–16, 1963. L. Gordon Cooper, Jr., performed the last *Mercury* mission and completed 22 orbits in *Faith 7* to evaluate effects of one day in space. Time: 34 hours, 19 minutes.

The Women in Space Program

In 1960, NASA also tested the first female trainees for astronaut duty in the *Mercury* program. Thirteen out of America's 25 top female civilian pilots (women weren't allowed to be military pilots then) passed the same rigorous testing that male candidates underwent in the *Mercury 7* space program. Although all the pilots proved fit to become *Mercury* astronauts, NASA suddenly canceled its testing of qualified women in July 1961, claiming that they required jet test-pilot training at Edwards Air Force Base. Unfortunately, instruction at

Edwards was closed to women. This new requirement ended America's chance to put the first women in space.

It is ironic that unlike her skilled American counterparts, Valentina Tereshkova, the first woman to fly in space, was a textile factory worker when she entered the Soviet space program. She had no experience as a pilot and her only qualification was that of an amateur parachute jumper before being trained as a cosmonaut in 1962.

These outstanding "Mercury 13" candidates deserve much credit for preparing the way for American women in space. They were: Jerrie Cobb, Rhea Allison, Jane Hart, Mary Wallace Funk, Jean Hixson, Myrtle Cagle, Irene Leverton, Sarah Gorelick, twins Jan and Marion Dietrich, Gene Stumbough, Bernice Steadman, and Gerry Sloan Truhill.

Gemini. *Gemini* was an extension of *Project Mercury,* to determine the effects of prolonged space flight on humans for two weeks or longer—the time it would take to reach the Moon and return. "Walks in space" provided invaluable information for astronauts' later walks on the Moon. The *Gemini* spacecraft, twice as large as the *Mercury* capsule, accommodated two astronauts. Its crew named the project *Gemini* for the third constellation of the Zodiac and its twin stars, Castor and Pollux. The capsule differed from the *Mercury* spacecrafts in that it had hatches above the capsules so that the astronauts could leave the spacecraft and perform spacewalks or extra-vehicular activities (EVAs).

There were 10 staffed flights in the *Gemini* program, starting with *Gemini 3* on March 23, 1965, and ending with the *Gemini 12* mission on Nov. 15, 1966. *Gemini 1* and *2* were unstaffed test flights of the equipment.

Apollo. *Apollo* was the designation for the United States' effort to land a person on the Moon and return him safely to Earth. The goal was successfully accomplished with *Apollo 11* on July 20, 1969, culminating eight years of rehearsal and centuries of dreaming. Astronauts Neil A. Armstrong and Col. Edwin E. Aldrin, Jr., scooped up and brought back the first lunar rocks ever seen on Earth—about 47 pounds.

Tragedy struck Jan. 27, 1967, on the launch pad during a preflight test of what would have become *Apollo 1,* the first staffed mission. Astronauts Lt. Col. Virgil "Gus" Grissom, Lt. Col. Edward H. White, and Lt. Cdr. Roger Chafee lost their lives when a fire swept through the command module.

Six *Apollo* flights followed, ending with *Apollo 17* in December 1972. The last three *Apollo*s carried mechanized vehicles called lunar rovers for wide-ranging surface exploration of the Moon by astronauts. The rendezvous and docking of an *Apollo* spacecraft with a Russian *Soyuz* craft in Earth orbit on July 18, 1975, closed out the *Apollo* program.

During the Apollo project, the following 12 astronauts explored the lunar terrain: Col. Edwin E. "Buzz" Aldrin, Jr., and Neil A. Armstrong, *Apollo 11;* Cdr. Alan L. Bean and Cdr. Charles "Pete" Conrad, Jr., *Apollo 12;* Edgar D. Mitchell and Alan B. Shepard, *Apollo 14;* Lt. Col. James B. Irwin and Col. David R. Scott, *Apollo 15;* Col. Charles M. Duke, Jr., and Capt. John W. Young, *Apollo 16;* and Capt. Eugene A. Cernan and Dr. Harrison H. Schmitt, *Apollo 17.*

Apollo was a three-part spacecraft: the command module (CM), the crew's quarters and flight control section; the service modules (SM) for the propulsion and spacecraft support systems (when together, the two modules were called CSM); and the lunar module (LM) that took two of the crew to the lunar surface, supported them on the Moon, and returned them to the CSM in orbit.

The third lunar attempt, *Apollo 13,* April 11–17, 1970, 5 days, 22.9 hours, was aborted after the service module oxygen tank ruptured. The *Apollo 13* crew members were James A. Lovell, Jr., John L. Swigert, Jr., and Fred W. Haise, Jr. The mission was classified as a "successful failure" because the crew was rescued.

Skylab. America's first Earth-orbiting space station was launched May 14, 1973. *Project Skylab* was designed to demonstrate that men can work and live in space for prolonged periods without ill effects. Originally the spent third stage of a *Saturn 5* Moon rocket, *Skylab* measured 118 ft from stem to stern, and carried the most varied assortment of experimental equipment ever assembled in a single spacecraft. Three three-man crews visited the space stations, spending more than 740 hours observing the Sun and bringing home more than 175,000 solar pictures. These were the first recordings of solar activity above Earth's obscuring atmosphere. *Skylab* also evaluated systems designed to gather information on Earth's resources and environmental conditions. *Skylab*'s biomedical findings indicated that humans adapt well to space for at least a period of three months, provided they have a proper diet and adequately programmed exercise, sleep, work, and recreation periods. *Skylab* orbited Earth at a distance of about 300 mi. Five years after the last *Skylab* mission, the 77-ton space station's orbit began to deteriorate faster than expected, owing to unexpectedly high sunspot activity. On July 11, 1979, the parts of *Skylab* that did not burn up in the atmosphere came crashing down on parts of Australia and the Indian Ocean. No one was hurt.

Space Shuttle. The space shuttle *Columbia* was successfully launched on April 12, 1981. The second shuttle, *Challenger,* made its maiden flight on April 4, 1983. The third shuttle, *Discovery,* made its first flight on Aug. 30, 1984. The fourth space shuttle, *Atlantis,* made its maiden flight on Oct. 3, 1985.

A tragedy occurred on Jan. 28, 1986, when the shuttle *Challenger* exploded, killing the crew of seven 73 seconds after takeoff.

The crew members who were killed were: Francis R. Scobee, shuttle commander; Cdr. Michael J. Smith, pilot; mission specialists Judith A. Resnik, Lt. Col. Ellison S. Onizuka, and Ronald E. McNair; and payload specialists Gregory B. Jarvis and Christa McAuliffe (who was to be the first civilian schoolteacher in space).

The cause of the explosion was a rupture in a seal on one of the booster rockets, which let a jet of flame escape, igniting the fuel. The weakness in the seal was caused by the cold air temperature when the shuttle was launched.

The first U.S. space mission since the *Challenger* disaster was launched 32 months later, on Sept. 29, 1988, with the flight of *Discovery.* It had a crew of five and deployed a communications satellite.

The fifth orbiter, *Endeavour,* was built as a replacement for *Challenger.* It was named after the

16th-century British explorer James Cook's first ship. *Endeavour* was launched on its maiden voyage on May 7, 1992, with a crew of seven astronauts. They made four spacewalks and retrieved a disabled *Intelsat-6* communications satellite. During the mission, Dr. Kathryn Thornton became the second American woman to walk in space (Kathy Sullivan was the first in 1984).

The crew of the 50th shuttle mission, aboard the *Endeavour,* launched Sept. 12, 1992, included the first black woman astronaut, Dr. Mae C. Jemison, and the first married couple to fly together in space, Air Force Lt. Col. Mark C. Lee and Dr. N. Jan Davis.

Lt. Col. Eileen M. Collins became the first woman to pilot a shuttle, *Discovery,* during the spacecraft's historic rendezvous with the Russian space station *Mir* on Feb. 6, 1995. The shuttle *Atlantis* made the first link-up with the *Mir* on June 29, 1995.

The shuttle *Columbia* spent a record 17 days, 15 hours in space, Nov. 19–Dec. 7, 1996.

Lt. Col. Collins became the first woman to command a space shuttle when *Columbia* was launched in July 1999 on a mission to deploy the Chandra X-ray Observatory (formerly called AXAF).

Senator John Glenn, 76, the first American to orbit the Earth, flew as a payload specialist on the Oct. 1998 *Discovery* mission. He studied the effects of aging and microgravity on the human body.

In recent years, many of NASA's human spaceflight expeditions have involved improvement of the International Space Station. On May 27, 1999, the space shuttle *Discovery* began Flight STS-96, the first shuttle docking to the International Space Station. Crewmembers brought new equipment to better operations between the Unity and Zarya modules, including nearly 1,360 kg of equipment for use by future ISS astronauts. In 2000, work on the ISS continued; two successive *Atlantis* missions spent several days making improvements. On Nov. 2, 2001, the ISS celebrated its first full year of continuous international human presence in space. On June 19, 2002, Capt. Daniel Bursch and Col. Carl Walz broke the U.S. record for space flight endurance, having spent 196 days aboard the International Space Station.

Space Websites

European Space Agency (ESA): www.esrin.esa.it
Liftoff to Space Exploration: liftoff.msfc.nasa.gov
Lunar Prospector: lunar.arc.nasa.gov
NASA Astronaut Biographies: www.jsc.nasa.gov/Bios/index.html
NASA homepage: www.nasa.gov
NASA Jet Propulsion Laboratory: www.jpl.nasa.gov
NASA Spaceflight page: www.spaceflight.nasa.gov
National Air & Space Museum: www.nasm.edu
National Space Society: www.nss.org
The Planetary Society: www.planetary.org
SETI Institute: www.seti-inst.edu
Skywatch: spaceflight.nasa.gov/realdata/sightings
SPACE.com: www.space.com
Space Research Institute (Russia): www.iki.rssi.ru
Students for the Exploration and Development of Space: www.seds.org
Planet Quest: planetquest.jpl.nasa.gov

The shuttle program's second tragedy occurred on Feb. 1, 2003, when the shuttle *Columbia* broke up upon reentry into the Earth's atmosphere.

All crew members were killed: Rick Husband, shuttle commander; William McCool, pilot; payload commander Michael Anderson; payload specialist Ilan Ramon, also the first Israeli astronaut; mission specialists David M. Brown, Laurel Blair Salton Clark, and Kalpana Chawla, the first Indian-American woman in space.

The shuttle was returning after a 16-day scientific mission and was only minutes away from landing. The Columbia Accident Investigation Board subsequently ascertained that a chunk of fuel-tank foam insulation slammed into the wing edge during liftoff, creating a hole that allowed hot gases to enter the shuttle on reentry into the atmosphere.

Soviet Staffed Space Flight Programs

Vostok. The Soviets's first staffed capsule, roughly spherical, used to place the first six cosmonauts in Earth orbit (1961–1965).

Voskhod. Adaptation of the *Vostok* capsule to accommodate two and three cosmonauts. *Voskhod 1* orbited three persons, and *Voskhod 2* orbited two persons, performing the world's first staffed extra-vehicular activity.

Soyuz. Late-model staffed spacecraft with provisions for three cosmonauts and a "working compartment" accessible through a hatch. Soyuz is the Russian word for "union." The *Soyuz* spacecraft routinely brought cosmonauts and their foreign "guests" to the *Mir* space station. *Soyuz 19,* launched July 15, 1975, docked with the American *Apollo* spacecraft.

Salyut. Earth-orbiting space stations intended for prolonged occupancy and revisitation by cosmonauts. They were usually launched by Soviet Proton rockets. *Salyut 1* was launched April 19, 1971. *Salyut 2,* launched April 3, 1973, malfunctioned in orbit and was never occupied. *Salyut 3* was launched June 25, 1974. *Salyut 4* was launched Dec. 26, 1974. *Salyut 5* was launched June 22, 1976. *Salyut 6* was launched on Sept. 29, 1977. *Salyut 7* was launched on April 19, 1982. A record-breaking Russian endurance flight was set (Feb. 8, 1984–Oct. 2, 1985) when Soviet astronauts spent 237 days in orbit aboard *Salyut 7. Salyut 7* reentered the atmosphere and crashed into the Atlantic Ocean on Feb. 6, 1991.

Mir. Soviet space station, launched into orbit on Feb. 20, 1986. The Russian government had planned to deorbit the abandoned *Mir* in early 2000 due to lack of funds, but the space station got a new lease on life when private investors provided the cash to keep the craft in orbit. The new Russian partners, MirCorp, a Netherlands-based company, funded cosmonauts Sergei Zaloytin and Alexander Kaleri's return mission to reopen and repair the *Mir,* April 4 to June 15, 2000. However, *Mir* was deorbited on March 23, 2001.

Since the deorbiting of *Mir,* Russia's space program has revolved around projects at the International Space Station. Financial problems continue to curb cosmonaut capabilities, forcing the Russian Space Agency to seek funds elsewhere: in 2001, American businessman Dennis Tito paid a reported $20 million to become the world's first space tourist aboard a Russian spacecraft.

Notable Staffed Space Flights

Designation and country	Date	Astronauts	Flight time	Remarks
Vostok 1 (USSR)	April 12, 1961	Yuri A. Gagarin	1hr, 48 min	First person in space.
MR III (U.S.)	May 5, 1961	Alan B. Shepard, Jr.	15 min	Range 486 km (302 mi), peak 187 km (116.5 mi); capsule recovered. First American in space.
Vostok 2 (USSR)	Aug. 6–7, 1961	Gherman S. Titov	25 hr, 18 min	First long-duration flight.
MA VI (U.S.)	Feb. 20, 1962	John H. Glenn, Jr.	4 hr, 55 min	First American in orbit.
MA IX (U.S.)	May 15–16, 1963	L. Gordon Cooper, Jr.	34 hr, 20 min	Longest *Mercury* flight.
Vostok 6 (USSR)	June 16–19, 1963	Valentina V. Tereshkova	2 days, 22 hr, 50 min	First woman in space.
Voskhod 1 (USSR)	Oct. 12, 1964	Vladimir M. Komarov, Konstantin P. Feoktistov, Boris G. Yegorov	24 hr, 17 min	First 3-person orbital flight; also first flight without space suits.
Voskhod 2 (USSR)	March 18, 1965	Alexei A. Leonov, Pavel I. Belyayev	26 hr, 2 min	First "space walk" (by Leonov), 10 min.
GT III (U.S.)	March 23, 1965	Virgil I. Grissom, John W. Young	4hr, 53 min	First American 2-person crew.
GT IV (U.S.)	June 3–7, 1965	James A. McDivitt, Edward H. White, II	4 days, 1 hr, 48 min	First American "space walk" (by White), lasting slightly over 20 min.
GT VIII (U.S.)	March 16–17, 1966	Neil A. Armstrong, David R. Scott	10 hr, 42 min	First docking between staffed spacecraft and an unstaffed space vehicle (an orbiting *Agena* rocket).
Apollo 7 (U.S.)	Oct. 11–22, 1968	Walter M. Schirra, Jr., Donn F. Eisele, R. Walter Cunningham	10 days, 19 hr, 9 min	First staffed test of *Apollo* command module; first live TV transmissions from orbit.
Soyuz 3 (USSR)	Oct. 26–30, 1968	Georgi T. Bergeovoi	3 days, 22 hr, 51 min	First staffed rendezvous and possible docking by Soviet cosmonaut.
Apollo 8 (U.S.)	Dec. 21–27, 1968	Frank Borman, James A. Lovell, Jr., William A. Anders	6 days, 3 hr	First spacecraft in circumlunar orbit; TV transmissions from this orbit. The three astronauts were also the first astronauts to view the whole Earth.
Apollo 9 (U.S.)	Mar. 3–13, 1969	James A. McDivitt, David R. Scott, Russell L. Schweikart	10 days, 1 hr, 1 min	First staffed flight of Lunar Module.
Apollo 10 (U.S.)	May 18–26, 1969	Thomas P. Stafford, Eugene A. Cernan, John W. Young	8 days, 3 min	First descent to within nine miles of Moon's surface by staffed craft.
Apollo 11 (U.S.)	July 16–24, 1969	Neil A. Armstrong, Edwin E. Aldrin, Jr., Michael Collins	8 days, 3 hr, 18 min	First staffed landing and EVA on Moon; soil and rock samples collected; experiments left on lunar surface.
Soyuz 6 (USSR)	Oct. 11–16, 1969	Gorgiy Shonin, Valriy Kabasov	4 days, 22 hr, 42 min	Three spacecraft and seven men put into Earth's orbit simultaneously for first time.
Apollo 12 (U.S.)	Nov. 14–24, 1969	Charles Conrad, Jr., Richard F. Gordon, Jr., Alan Bean	10 days, 4 hr, 36 min	Staffed lunar landing mission; investigated *Surveyor 3* spacecraft; collected lunar samples. EVA time: 15 hr, 30 min.
Apollo 13 (U.S.)	April 11–17, 1970	James A. Lovell, Jr., Fred W. Haise, Jr., John L. Swigert, Jr.	5 days, 22 hr, 54 min	Third staffed lunar landing attempt; aborted due to pressure loss in liquid oxygen in service module and failure of fuel cells.
Apollo 14 (U.S.)	Jan. 31–Feb. 9, 1971	Alan B. Shepard, Stuart A. Roosa, Edgar D. Mitchell	9 days, 42 min	Third staffed lunar landing: returned largest amount of lunar material.
Soyuz 11 (USSR)	June 6–30, 1971	Georgiy Tomofeyevich Dobrovolskiy, Vladislav Nikolayevich Volkov, Viktor Ivanovich Patsyev	23 days, 17 hrs, 40 min	Longest stay in space. Linked up with first space station, *Salyut 1*. Astronauts died just before reentry due to loss of pressurization in spacecraft.
Apollo 15 (U.S.)	July 26–Aug. 7, 1971	David R. Scott, James B. Irwin, Alfred M. Worden	12 days, 7 hr, 12 min	Fourth staffed lunar landing; first use of lunar rover propelled by Scott and Irwin; first live pictures of LM lift-off from Moon; exploration time: 18 hr.
Apollo 16 (U.S.)	April 16–27, 1972	John W. Young, Thomas K. Mattingly, Charles M. Duke, Jr.	11 days, 1 hr, 51 min	Fifth staffed lunar landing; second use of lunar rover vehicle, propelled by Young and Duke. Total exploration time on the Moon was 20 hr, 14 min, setting new record. Mattingly's in-flight "walk in space" was 1 hr, 23 min. Approximately 213 lb of lunar rock returned.
Apollo 17 (U.S.)	Dec. 7–19, 1972	Eugene A. Cernan, Ronald E. Evans, Harrison H. Schmitt	12 days, 13 hr, 51 mini	Sixth and last staffed lunar landing; third to carry lunar rover. Cernan and Schmitt, during three EVAs, completed total of 22 hr, 05 min, 3 sec. USS *Ticonderoga* recovered crew and about 250 lbs of lunar samples.
Skylab SL-2 (U.S.)	May 25–June 22, 1973	Charles Conrad, Jr., Joseph P. Kerwin, Paul J. Weitz	28 days, 50 min	First staffed *Skylab* launch. Established Skylab Orbital Assembly and conducted scientific and medical experiments.

Designation and country	Date	Astronauts	Flight time	Remarks
Skylab SL-3 (U.S.)	July 28–Sept. 25, 1973	Alan L. Bean, Jr., Jack R. Lousma, Owen K. Garriott	59 days, 11 hr, 9 min	Second staffed *Skylab* launch. New crew remained in space for 59 days, continuing scientific and medical experiments and Earth observations from orbit.
Skylab SL-4 (U.S.)	Nov. 16, 1973–Feb. 8, 1974	Gerald Carr, Edward Gibson, William Pogue	84 days, 1 hr, 16 min	Third staffed *Skylab* launch; obtained medical data on crew for use in extending the duration of staffed space flight; crews "walked in space" 4 times, totaling 44 hr, 40 min. Splashdown in Pacific, Feb. 9, 1974.
Apollo/Soyuz Test Project (U.S. and USSR)	July 15–24, 1975 (U.S.)	U.S.: Brig. Gen. Thomas P. Stafford, Vance D. Brand, Donald K. Slayton	9 days, 5 min	World's first international staffed rendezvous and docking in space; aimed at developing a space rescue capability.
Apollo/Soyuz Test Project (U.S. and USSR)	July 15–21, 1975 (USSR)	USSR: Col. A. A. Leonov, V. N. Kubasov	9 days, 7 hr, 35 min	*Apollo* and *Soyuz* docked and crewmen exchanged visits on July 17, 1975. Mission duration for *Soyuz:* 142 hr, 31 min. For *Apollo:* 217 hr, 28 min.
Columbia (U.S.)	April 12–14, 1981	Capt. Robert L. Crippen, John W. Young	2 days, 5 hr, 20 min	Maiden voyage of space shuttle.
Challenger (U.S.)	Jan. 28, 1986	Francis R. Scobee, Gregory Jarvis, Christa McAuliffe, Ronald McNair, Ellison Onizuka, Judith Resnik, Michael Smith	73 sec	Exploded upon takeoff from Kennedy Space Center, killing all 7 crew members. A booster lock ignited the fuel, causing the explosion.
Mir (USSR)	Dec. 21, 1987–Dec. 21, 1988	Col. Vladimir Titov, Musa Manarov	366 days	Set current record for Soviet team endurance flight in orbiting space station.
Endeavour (U.S.)	May 7–16, 1992	Richard J. Hieb, Maj. Thomas D. Akers, Cdr. Pierre J. Thugt	8 days, 23 hr, 17 min	The three mission specialists remained free of the *Endeavour* for 8 hr, 20 min on May 13 during the repair of communications satellite, setting an absolute record for extravehicular duration in space. First capture of a satellite using hands only.
Endeavour (U.S.)	Dec. 2–13, 1993	Col. Richard O. Covey, Cdr. Kenneth D. Bowersox, Lt. Col. Tom Akers, Dr. Jeffrey A. Hoffman, Dr. Story Musgrave, Claude Nicollier, Dr. Kathryn C. Thornton	10 days, 19 hr, 59 min	Repaired Hubble Space Telescope. Replaced gyroscopes, solar arrays, camera, electronics, and hardware. Installed COSTAR corrective optics to compensate for flaw in Hubble's primary mirror. Record five space walks in a single mission.
Mir-17 (Russia)	Jan. 8, 1994–Mar. 22, 1995	Dr. Valery Polyakov	439[1] days	Record single endurance flight in orbiting space station. Returned to Earth with crewmates, cosmonaut Helena Kondakova and commander Alexander Viktorenko, who spent 169 days each in *Mir.*
Discovery (U.S.)	Feb. 3–11, 1995	Cdr. James D. Wetherbee, Lt. Col. Eileen M. Collins, Dr. Janice Voss, Dr. Bernard A. Harris, Jr., Dr. C. Michael Foale, Russian cosmonaut Co. Vladimir G. Titov	8 days, 6 hr, 29 min	First rendezvous of U.S. spacecraft with a Russian space station *(Mir)*, Feb. 6. Lt. Col. Collins was first female shuttle pilot. Deployed and retrieved solar observatory satellite. Extravehicular activity to test new space suit modifications and practice space station assembly techniques. EVA time: 4 hr, 35 min.
Soyuz TM-21 (Russia)	March 14–22, 1995	Russian cosmonauts Lt. Col. Vladimir N. Dezhurov and Gennady M. Strekalov, and U.S. astronaut Dr. Norman E. Thagard		Dr. Thagard became the first American astronaut to fly aboard a *Soyuz* spacecraft with a Russian crew launched from Baikonur Space Center in Kazakhstan. He also became the first American to enter the *Mir* space station on March 16.
Atlantis (U.S.)	June 27–July 7, 1995	Lt. Col. Charles J. Prescourt, Capt. Robert L. (Hoot) Gibson, Dr. Eileen S. Baker, Gregory J. Harbaugh, Dr. Bonnie Dunbar; Russian cosmonauts: *Mir-19* commander Anatoly Y. Solovyev, Nikolai M. Budarin	10 days	Marked 100th human mission in U.S. space program and first shuttle link-up with *Mir:* docked June 29, undocked July 4. Joined spacecraft held a record 10 people: 6 Americans and 4 Russians. Three *Mir* crew (*Mir-18* commander Lt. Col. Vladimir N. Dezhurov, cosmonaut Grennady M. Strekalov, and U.S. astronaut Dr. Norman E. Thagard) returned to Earth aboard the *Atlantis.* Cosmonauts Solovyev and Budarin remained aboard *Mir.*

Designation and country	Date	Astronauts	Flight time	Remarks
Atlantis (U.S.)	Nov. 12–20, 1995	Col. Kenneth D. Cameron, Lt. Col. James D. Halsell, Jr., Col. Jerry L. Ross, Lt. Col. William S. McArthur, Jr., Canadian Major Chris A. Hadfield, who operated the robot arm	8 days, 4 hr, 31 min	Second docking with *Mir.* Carried 15-foot-long, Russian-made docking module and attached it to *Mir.* Brought 2 new solar-powered panels for *Mir* and also supplies and scientific equipment. U.S. and Russian astronauts spent 3 days together on *Mir* conducting experiments.
Endeavour (U.S.)	Jan. 11–20, 1996	Col. Brian Duffy, Brent Jett, Dr. Leroy Chiao, Capt. Winston E. Scott, Dr. Daniel T. Berry, and Japanese astronaut Koichi Wakata, who operated robot arm	8 days, 22 hr, 1 min	Deployed and retrieved NASA satellite, retrieved Japanese satellite. Two spacewalks performed to test spacesuit components and practice space station construction, tools, and techniques. Total EVA time: 13 hr.
Atlantis (U.S.)	March 22–31, 1996	Col. Kevin P. Chilton, Lt. Col. Richard A. Searfoss, Dr. Ronald M. Sega, Dr. Linda M. Goodwin, Lt. Col. Michael R. Clifford, Shannon W. Lucid	9 days, 5 hr, 15 min	Third link-up with *Mir* (March 22–27). Clifford and Goodwin conducted 6-hour spacewalk in shuttle cargo bay while docked with *Mir.* Lucid remained on board *Mir* for scheduled 140-day tour to conduct biomedical and material science experiments. Booster problems delayed her return until mid-September. Lucid was first American woman to live on *Mir.* On July 15, 1996, she broke the previous record for the longest U.S. manned space flight.
Endeavour (U.S.)	May 19–29, 1996	Col. John H. Casper, Lt. Col. Curtis L. Brown, Jr., Cdr. Daniel W. Bursch, Mario Runco, Jr., Dr. Andrew S. W. Thomas, Canadian astronaut Dr. Marc Garneau	10 days, 0 hr, 40 min	Made record of four satellite rendezvous, including three with small PAMS satellite to test the concept of a self-stabilizing satellite in orbit. Deployed and retrieved a Spartan satellite that carried an experimental inflatable antenna.
Columbia (U.S.)	June 20–July 7, 1996	Col. Terence T. Henricks, Kevin R. Kregel, Lt. Col. Susan J. Helms, Richard M. Linnehan, Cdr. Charles E. Brady, Jr., Dr. Jean-Jacques Favier (France), Dr. Robert Brent Thirsk (Canada)	16 days, 21 hr, 48 min	Studied the effects of weightlessness on people, plants, and animals, and material manufacturing in near-zero gravity.
Atlantis (U.S.)	Sept. 16–26, 1996	William F. Readdy, Terrence W. Wilcutt, Thomas D. Akers, John E. Blaha, Jerome Apt, Carl E. Walz. Download: Shannon W. Lucid	10 days, 3hr, 19 min	Fourth *Mir* docking. Carried a Spacelab module. Transferred supplies and equipment to *Mir.* After breaking all American and women's space endurance records (188 days, 5 hr, 0 min), Lucid returned with *Atlantis* crew. John E. Blaha remained on *Mir* for a four-month stay.
Columbia (U.S.)	Nov. 19–Dec. 7, 1996	Kenneth D. Cockrell, Cdr. Kent V. Romingel, Tamara E. Jernigan, Thomas D. Jones, Dr. F. Story Musgrave	17 days, 15 hr, 53 min	Deployed and recovered two free-flying satellites: an ultraviolet telescope and Wake Shield (semiconductor processing) Facility. Dr. Musgrave, 61, became first person to fly on all five space shuttles.
Atlantis (U.S.)	Jan. 12–22, 1997	Capt. Michael A. Baker, Cdr. Brent W. Jett, Jr., John M. Grunsfeld, Marsha S. Ivins, Peter J.K. Wiscoff, Dr. Jerry L. Linenger. Download: John E. Blaha	10 days, 4 hr, 6 min	Fifth *Mir* docking (Jan.14–19). Carried Spacehab double module. Transferred supplies to *Mir.* Conducted experiments in Spacehab and *Mir.* John E. Blaha returned with *Atlantis* crew after 128 days in space, 118 aboard *Mir.* Jerry Linenger remained aboard *Mir* for 4.5-month stay.
Discovery (U.S.)	Feb. 11–21, 1997	Cdr. Kenneth Bowersox, Lt. Col. Scott J. Harowitz, Col. Mark C. Lee, Steven A. Hawley, Gregory J. Harbaugh, Steven L. Smith, Joseph R. Tanner	9 days, 23 hr, 38 min	Second space telescope servicing mission. Installed new imaging spectrograph and infrared camera. Also patched torn telescope insulating cover. Deployed telescope at higher altitude: 335 x 321 nautical mile orbit. Mission required five spacewalks totaling 33 hr, 11 min.
Atlantis (U.S.)	May 15–24,1997	Col. Charles J. Precourt, Lt. Col. Eileen M. Collins, Edward T. Lu, Maj. Carlos I. Noriega, Jean-François Clervoy (France), Elena V. Kondakova (Russia), C. Michael Foale. Download: Dr. Jerry M. Linenger	9 days, 5 hr, 20 min	Sixth *Mir* docking (May 16–21). Carried a Spacehab double module. Transferred supplies and equipment. Jerry M. Linenger returned with *Atlantis* after 132 days in space. Michael Foale remained on *Mir* for a 4.5-month stay.

Designation and country	Date	Astronauts	Flight time	Remarks
Atlantis (U.S.)	Sept. 25–Oct. 6, 1997	James T. Wetherbee, Michael J. Boomfield, Col. Vladimir G Titov, Scott E. Parazynski, Jean-Loup J. M. Chretien (France), Wendy B. Lawrence. Up: Dr. David Wolf. Down: C. Michael Foale	10 days, 19 hr, 22 min	Seventh Mir docking (Sept. 27–Oct. 3). 5-hr spacewalks (Oct.1) retrieved U.S. experimental packages from *Mir* for return to Earth. Transferred supplies. Tested emergency jet packs for space station workers. Dr. David Wolf replaced Michael Foale on *Mir* for 4-month stay.
Endeavour (U.S.)	Jan. 22–31, 1998	Lt. Col. Terrence W. Wilcutt, Joe F. Edwards, Bonnie J. Dunbar, Maj. Michael P. Anderson, James F. Reilly, II, Salizhan S. Sharipov (Kyrgyzstan). Up: Andrew S. W. Thomas. Down: Dr. David Wol	8 days, 19 hr, 48 min	Eighth *Mir* docking (Jan. 24–29). Thomas replaced David Wolf after 128 days in orbit. Thomas is the seventh and last American to live aboard *Mir.*
Discovery (U.S.)	June 2–12, 1998	Col. Charles J. Precourt, Cmdr. Dominic L. Gorie, Cmdr. Wendy B. Lawrence, Franklin R. Chang-Diaz, Janet Kavandi, Valeriy Ruymin (Russia). Down: Andrew S. W. Thomas	9 days, 19 hr, 54 min	Ninth and final *Mir* docking mission concluded the joint U.S.–Russian program as a precursor to the International Space Station partnership. Thomas returned to Earth after a 4.5-month stay.
Discovery (U.S.)	Oct. 29–Nov.7, 1998	Lt. Col. Curtis L. Brown, Maj. Steven W. Lindsey, Stephen K. Robinson, Dr. Scott E. Parazynski, Pedro Duque (Spain), Dr. Chiaki Mukai (Japan), Sen. John H. Glenn, Jr.	8 days, 21 hr, 56 min	Deployed and retrieved *Spartan* solar observing satellite. Did research with Hubble Telescope Optical Systems Test Platform (HOST). Studied the effects of aging and microgravity in space.
Endeavour (U.S.)	Dec. 4–15, 1998	Col. Robert D. Cabana, Capt. Frederick W. Sturckow, Lt. Col. Nancy Currie, Col. Jerry L. Ross, James H. Newman, Sergei K. Krikalev (Russia)	11 days, 19 hr, 18 min	International Space Station assembly mission. Connected Node 1, "Unity," to Functional Cargo Block, "Zarya." Ross and Newman made three spacewalks, total EVA: 21 hr, 22 min.
Discovery (U.S.)	May 27–June 6, 1999	Cmdr. Ken V. Rominger, Rick D. Husband, Ellen Ochoa, Tamara E. Jernigan, Daniel T. Barry, Julie Payette (Canada), Valery Tokarev (Russia)	9 days, 19 hr, 13 min	Docked 5 days, 18 hr with uninhabited International Space Station. Readied it for arrival of first resident crew. Jernigan and Barry conducted space walks (7 hr, 55 min) for assembly work.
Columbia (U.S.)	July 22–27, 1999	Lt. Col. Eileen M. Collins, Capt. Jeffrey S. Ashby, Steven A. Hawley, Lt. Col. Catherine G. Coleman, Col. Michel Tognini (France)	4 days, 22 hr, 50 min	Deployed Chandra X-ray Observatory (formerly AXAF). Eileen Collins became the first female shuttle commander.
Discovery (U.S.)	Dec. 19–27, 1999	Col. Curtis L. Brown Jr., Lt. Cmdr. Scott J. Kelly, Steven L. Smith, C. Michael Foale, John M. Grunsfeld, Claude Nicollier (Switzerland), Jean-François Clervoy (France)	7 days, 23 hr, 10 min	Third Hubble Space Telescope servicing mission. Three EVAs totaled 24 hr, 33 min: Dec. 22, Smith and Grunsfeld, 8 hr, 15 min; Dec. 23, Foale and Nicollier, 8 hr, 10 min; Dec. 24, Smith and Grunsfeld, 8 hr, 8 min.
Endeavour (U.S.)	Feb.11–22, 2000	Cmdr. Dominic L. Pudwill Gorie, Janet Lynn Kavandi, Janet Voss, Kevin R. Kregel, Mamoru Mohri (Japan), Gerhard P. J. Thiele (Germany)	11 days, 5 hr, 38 min	Radar mapping obtained most detailed topographical map of Earth to date.
Atlantis (U.S.)	Sept. 8–18, 2000	Lt. Col. Terance Wilcutt, Lt. Cmdr. Scott Altman, Edward Tsang Lu, Richard Mastracchio, Lt. Cmdr. Dan Burbank, Col. Yuri I. Malenchenko (Russia), Boris Morukov (Russia)	10 days, 18 hr, 41 min	Prepared International Space Station for arrival of first resident crew. Outfitted *Zvezda* module.

Designation and country	Date	Astronauts	Flight time	Remarks
Discovery (U.S.)	Oct. 11–22, 2000	Col. Brian Duffy, Lt. Col. Pamela A. Melroy, Koichi Wakata (Japan), Peter J. K. Wisoff, Cmdr. Michael E. Lopez-Alegria, Col. William S. McArthur, Jr.	10 days, 19 hr, 28 min	Assembled Integrated Truss Structure on space station to allow solar arrays to be installed. 100th space shuttle flight.
Soyuz (Russia)	Oct. 31, 2000–March 18, 2001	William M. Shepherd, Yuri Gidzenko (Russia), Sergei Krikalev (Russia)	138 days, 18 hr, 39 min	Expedition One, first crew aboard International Space Station.
Discovery (U.S.)	March 8–21, 2001	Capt. James D. Wetherbee, Lt. Col. James M. Kelly, Andrew S. W. Thomas, Paul W. Richards, Yury Usachev (Russia), Jim Voss, Susan Helms	12 days, 19 hr, 49 min	Delivered Expedition Two crew (Usachev, Voss, Helms) to space station and returned Expedition One crew (Shepherd, Krikalev, Gidzenko) to Earth.
Discovery (U.S.)	Aug. 10–Aug. 22, 2001	Col. Scott J. Horowitz, Lt. Col. Frederick W. Sturckow, Col. Patrick G. Forrester, Daniel T. Barry, Frank Culbertson, Lt. Col. Vladimir Dezhurov (Russia), Mikhail Tyurin (Russia)	11 days, 21 hr, 13 min	Delivered Expedition Three crew (Culbertson, Dezhurov, Tyurin) to space station and returned Expedition Two crew (Usachev, Voss, Helms) to Earth.
Endeavour (U.S.)	Dec. 5–17, 2001	Capt. Dominic Gorie, Lt. Cmdr. Mark E. Kelly, Linda M. Godwin, Daniel M. Tani, Col. Yuri Onufrienko (Russia), Col. Carl E. Walz, Capt. Daniel W. Bursch	11 days, 19 hr, 36 min	Delivered Expedition Four crew (Onufrienko, Walz, Bursch) to space station and returned Expedition Three crew (Culbertson, Tyurin, Dezhurov) to Earth.
Columbia (U.S.)	March 1–12, 2002	Cmdr. Scott Altman, Lt. Col. Duane Carey, Nancy Currie, John Grunsfield, Richard Linnehan, Michael Massimino, James Newman	10 days, 22 hr, 10 min	Fourth Hubble Space Telescope servicing mission. The latest upgrades leave Hubble with a new power unit, camera, and solar arrays. Five EVAs lasted a total of 35 hr 55 min.
Atlantis (U.S.)	April 8–19, 2002	Lt. Col. Michael Bloomfield, Stephen Frick, Rex Walheim, Ellen Ochoa, Lee Morin, Jerry Ross, Steven Smith.	10 days, 19 hr, 42 min	Installed S0 (S-Zero) Truss, the backbone for future expansion, onto International Space Station. Prepared Mobile Transporter, first railroad in space, for use. Mission specialist Jerry Ross made two space walks, retaining U.S. record for most space walks (nine) and total space-walking time (58 hr, 18 min).
Endeavour (U.S.)	June 5–19, 2002	Kenneth D. Cockrell, Lt. Col. Paul Lockhart, Philippe Perrin (France), Franklin Chang-Diaz, Col. Valery Korzun (Russia), Peggy Whitson, Sergei Treschev (Russia).	13 days, 20 hr, 35 min	Delivered Expedition Five crew (Korzun, Whitson, Treschev) to space station and returned Expedition Four crew (Onufrienko, Walz, Bursch) to Earth. On June 19, Expedition Four flight engineers Carl Walz and Dan Bursch broke the U.S. space flight endurance record (previously held by Shannon Lucid, who spent 188 days in space in 1996). The two spent a total of 196 days in space.
Columbia (U.S.)	Jan. 16–Feb. 1, 2003	Rick Husband, William McCool, Michael Anderson, Kalpana Chawla, David Brown, Laurel B. Clark, Ilan Ramon	16 days	Exploded upon reentry into Earth's atmosphere, killing all 7 crew members.
Soyuz TM-2 (Russia)	Apr. 25, 2003[2]	Yuri Malenchenko (Russia), Ed Lu, Ken Bowersox, Don Pettit, Nikolai Budarin (Russia)	([2])	With shuttle flights grounded, *Soyuz TMA-2* delivered Expedition Seven crew (Malenchenko, Lu) to space station. Expedition Six crew (Bowersox, Pettit, Budarin) returned to Earth via *Soyuz TMA-1,* docked at space station since Dec. 1, 2002. On Aug. 10, Malenchenko became the first man to get married from space.

NOTES: EVA = Extravehicular Activity. The letters MR stand for Mercury (capsule) and Redstone (rocket); MA, for Mercury and Atlas (rocket); GT, for Gemini (capsule) and Titan-II (rocket). The first astronaut listed in the Gemini and Apollo flights is the command pilot. The Mercury capsules had names: MR-III was *Freedom 7,* MR-IV was *Liberty Bell 7,* MA-VI was *Friendship 7,* MA-VII was *Aurora 7,* MA-VIII was *Sigma 7,* and MA-IX was *Faith 7.* The figure 7 referred to the fact that the first group of U.S. astronauts numbered seven men. Only one Gemini capsule had a name: GT-III was called *Molly Brown* (after the Broadway musical *The Unsinkable Molly Brown*); thereafter the practice of naming the capsules was discontinued. 1. From launch to landing. 2. *Soyuz TMA-2* scheduled to return Oct. 2003, *Soyuz TMA-1* returned May 3, 2003.

Influential Figures in Aviation

By the TIME staff

Pioneers

Orville and Wilbur Wright (1871–1948), (1867–1912): On Dec. 17, 1903, Orville Wright climbed into a 600-pound flying machine and made his historic flight in Kitty Hawk, N.C. Three days before, with Wilbur as pilot, the Wrights had tried but failed to get off the ground. The 17th turned out to be the fateful day for the Akron, Ohio-born brothers who had tinkered for months before finally unlocking the key to powered flight. They made four flights that day—Orville's first lasted 12 seconds and spanned 120 feet; Wilbur's best was a 59 second-long, 852 foot leap. It wasn't long before the brothers had formed the Wright Company, which bought and sold airplanes.

Charles Lindbergh (1902–1974): In 1919, New York hotel owner Raymond Orteig offered $25,000 to the first person to pilot a plane from New York to Paris nonstop. No one claimed the bounty—though several died trying—until 25-year-old, Detroit-born Charles Lindbergh touched down the *Spirit of St. Louis* at Le Bourget Field near Paris at 10:21 P.M. local time on May 21, 1927. A hero was born, but the first-ever TIME Man of the Year was never comfortable with his legendary status. He was considered the first mass-media celebrity, albeit a reluctant one, and the famous kidnapping and murder of his 20-month-old son, Charles, Jr., caused the family to shun the spotlight.

Amelia Earhart (1897–1937): The most famous woman in aviation history, Earhart was dubbed "Lady Lindy," a moniker that fit well with her publicists' attempt to fashion her as a female version of Charles Lindbergh. In 1928, she was a passenger on a three-person plane that crossed the Atlantic, and four years later she became the first person since Lindbergh to make that trip solo. In 1934, she flew from Hawaii to California, a trip that had previously claimed the lives of ten other pilots. In 1937, while attempting an around-the-world flight from Florida to California, Earhart's plane was lost, believed to have gone down 35 to 100 miles off the coast of Howland Island.

Samuel Langley (1834–1906): One of America's leading scientists in the late 1880s, Langley worked for years to get a manned, powered plane in the air. As the Secretary of the Smithsonian Institution Langley had considerably more resources than the Wrights, but the brothers from Ohio beat him in the race to produce the first flying machine. Langley's failed attempts led to public humiliation, but his name lives on at NASA Langley Research Center. The United States' first aircraft carrier, built in the early 1920s, also bears his name.

Glenn Curtiss (1878–1930): Like the Wright brothers, Curtiss, a former bike shop owner and motorcycle manufacturer, went from working with wheels to wings when flying captured the attention of mechanics everywhere at the turn of the 20th century. He joined Alexander Graham Bell's Aerial Experiment Association in 1907 and was the leading aircraft manufacturer in the U.S. by 1914, producing some of the most influential aircrafts of the time, including the first flying boats and the first planes to take off and land from a ship. For his accomplishments, Curtiss is known as the "Father of Naval Aviation."

Military Pilots

Manfred von Richthofen: The Red Baron (1892–1918): Perhaps the most famous ace in the history of air warfare, Richthofen was a member of the German cavalry up until the outbreak of World War I. New rules of engagement limited the role of a cavalry, and Richthofen wasn't one to take a back seat to action. After being transferred to the air service in 1915, Richthofen quickly became a star pupil, and it didn't take long for The Red Baron to assume his role as Germany's ace. In 1917, he was appointed commander of the highly skilled Flying Circus. In all, he was credited with 80 kills, the highest number of the war, before being shot down and killed in 1918 over enemy lines.

James "Jimmy" Doolittle (1896–1993): While Doolittle earned his wings in World War I and led perhaps the most famous U.S. air mission of World War II, his most significant achievements in flying occurred between those two eras. Throughout the 1920s and '30s, Doolittle amazed as a test and stunt pilot with his feats of speed (the first transcontinental flight in under 24 hours) and daring (the first blind flight). On April 18, 1942, Doolittle led a force of 16 planes on a long-distance bombing raid on Japan that served as much of an emotional purpose as it did a tactical one. For his effort, he was decorated with the Congressional Medal of Honor and later played a key role in U.S. combat in Europe.

Arthur Harris (1892–1984): One of the most controversial figures in the history of air warfare, the South African-born Harris was a pilot in Britain's Royal Flying Corps in World War I before becoming head of Bomber Command in 1942. It was then he introduced a strategy called "area bombing" that no longer limited attacks to strictly military targets. German cities of Hamburg, Cologne, and Dresden were ravaged, and an estimated 600,000 civilians lost their lives. After the war, Harris came under a firestorm of protest from those who questioned his ruthlessness. Harris never wavered, however, contending all along that putting the Germans on the defensive saved many lives.

Francis "Gabby" Gabreski (1919–2002): One of only seven pilots to earn ace status in both World War II and the Korean War, Gabreski remains one of the most revered fighter pilots in American history. His military career got off to an inauspicious start, however, when he struggled through training and barely made it though an "elimination flight," which was his last chance to prove himself. He finished the war with 28 kills, making him America's leading ace, but not before crash landing behind enemy lines on an unsuccessful mission in 1944. He was taken prisoner of war and was liberated by the Russians in April 1945. Duty called again in Korea, where he is credited with shooting down 6½ MiGs.

Adolf Galland (1912–1996): A charismatic German ace pilot and general of the Luftwaffe, Galland is credited with over 100 kills. Galland's distinguishing characteristics were his slicked-back hair, ever-present cigars, and Mickey Mouse insignia adorned on his planes. He held a somewhat romantic view of flying, even during wartime, and that won him respect even among his World War II foes, some of whom he later lectured with in America. Galland disagreed famously with the decisions made by his boss, Hermann Goering, and was relieved of his duties in January 1945. Adolf Hilter intervened, and Galland was flying up until two weeks before the war's end. After the war, Galland served as a consultant for Argentina's air force and pursued his interest in commercial flying.

Entrepreneurs

William Boeing (1881–1956): College degrees aren't for everyone—just ask Bill Gates. Despite dropping out of Yale, Boeing lived to see his name stamped all over an industry that infatuated him from the start. He studied engineering before starting his own lumber company, then turned to building aircraft after buying one in 1914 and insisting that he could build a better model. With the help of his engineering friend, George Conrad Westervelt, Boeing produced the *B&W* seaplane that carried their initials. Inspired by its success, Boeing started the Pacific Aero Products, later renamed the Boeing Airplane Company, which built military planes during World War I. In the late 1920s, Boeing Air Transport moved mail and, by the 1930s, Boeing's companies were so successful that he was battling the Roosevelt Administration over antitrust laws. Since World War II, Boeing is perhaps best known for its commercial planes, the most visible of which are the jumbo jets of the 1970s and beyond.

Juan Trippe (1899–1991): Flight's most special gift was bringing to the masses an ability to travel great distances and explore the globe faster and easier than ever before, and one of the pioneers in that field was Juan Trippe. As a new Pan American boss in 1927, Trippe's focus was a mail route from Key West to Havana, but his vision for the future was transporting people, not just letters—and not just the wealthy. His sea planes ran the first commercial routes across the Atlantic and Pacific Oceans in the 1930s, setting the stage for a post-war intercontinental aviation world that Pan Am dominated. Trippe insisted that bigger was indeed better, and his legacy is putting into service the Boeing 707 and 747 jumbo jets. Richard Branson wrote of Trippe for the Builders and Titans section of the TIME 100: "He almost single-handedly built a world airline, Pan American, but often acted as if he owned the world. He also had a vision that would change it, at least as regards airline travel. While his Pan Am does not survive today, his vision does."

Henry Ford (1863–1947): A giant in the automobile industry, Ford never met a dollar he didn't like, so it was only natural when, in the early 1920s, he set his sights on aircraft. In 1923, Ford used all-metal single-engine monoplanes built by the Stout Metal Airplane Company to run the Ford Air Transport Service, which, in 1925, became the first commercial route run specifically for the needs of one company. That same year, Ford dedicated the first modern airport in Dearborn, Mich., and launched his own Stout Metal Airplane Division of the Ford Motor Company. By 1926, Ford was the world's largest manufacturer of commercial aircraft. Sales of his Tri-Motor model—known as the "Tin Goose"—plummeted in the early 1930s, but Ford's aircraft manufacturing was a key component to World War II, when his plants churned out B-24 "Liberator" bombers.

Donald Douglas (1892–1981): Armed with an aeronautical degree from M.I.T.—which he earned in two years instead of the usual four—Douglas bounced around a few aircraft manufacturing companies before setting up his own shop in California in 1920. It was there he was hired by a rich sportsman named David Davis for $40,000 to build the first plane to fly non-stop across the United States. The mission failed, but Douglas's Cloudster drew raves, and he was soon put to work building torpedo bombers for the U.S. Navy. In 1936, he developed what has come to be known as the first modern airliner, the spacious and speedy DC-3, whose C-47 military versions played a key role in World War II. Douglas's company was the leader in commercial flight until Boeing introduced the 707 superjet in the late 1950s. Douglas combatted with the DC-8 and, in 1965, with the twin-jet DC-9. Financial troubles eventually forced the company to merge with St. Louis-based McDonnell Aircraft Corp. in 1967.

William Powell Lear, Sr. (1902–1978): Though he would later put his stamp on the luxury end of commercial flight, Lear began his career in aviation by getting his hands dirty in the cockpit. After learning to fly in 1931, Lear, who invented the car radio and many years later the 8-track tape player, dedicated his time to improving the way planes were piloted. By 1950, he'd secured more than 100 patents for aircraft radios, communications, and navigation equipment. Among his greatest developments was the first autopilot for jet aircraft; fully automatic landings in low-visibility conditions were now reality. His signature plane was the Learjet, a super-sleek and speedy model that reigned supreme on the must-have lists of corporations and ultra-wealthy individuals. □

See also aviation pioneers in Inventors Hall of Fame, p. 579.

Famous Firsts in Aviation

1783 First balloon flight. Jacques and Joseph Montgolfier of Annonay, France, sent up a small smoke-filled balloon about mid-November.

First hydrogen-filled balloon flight. Jacques A. C. Charles, Paris physicist, supervised construction by A. J. and M. N. Robert of a 13-foot-diameter balloon that was filled with hydrogen. It got up to about 3,000 ft and traveled about 16 mi in a 45-minute flight (Aug. 27).

First human balloon flights. A Frenchman, Jean Pilâtre de Rozier, made the first captive-balloon ascension (Oct. 15). With the Marquis d'Arlandes, Pilâtre de Rozier made the first free flight, reaching a peak altitude of about 500 ft, and traveling about 5½ mi in 20 min. (Nov. 21).

1784 First powered balloon. Gen. Jean Baptiste Marie Meusnier developed the first propeller-driven and elliptically shaped balloon—the crew cranking three propellers on a common shaft to give the craft a speed of about 3 mph.

First balloon flight by a woman. Mme. Thible, a French opera singer (June 4).

1793 First balloon flight in America. Jean Pierre Blanchard, a French pilot, made it from Philadelphia to near Woodbury, N.J., in just over 45 min. (Jan. 9).

1794 First military use of the balloon. Jean Marie Coutelle, using a balloon built for the French Army, made two 4-hour observation ascents. The military purpose of the ascents seems to have been to damage the enemy's morale.

1797 First parachute jump. André-Jacques Garnerin dropped from about 6,500 ft over Monceau Park in Paris in a 23-foot-diameter parachute made of white canvas with a basket attached (Oct. 22).

1843 First air transport company. In London, William S. Henson and John Stringfellow filed articles of incorporation for the Aerial Transit Company (March 24). It failed.

1852 First dirigible. Henri Giffard, a French engineer, flew in a controllable (more or less) steam-engine-powered balloon, 144 ft long and 39 ft in diameter, inflated with 88,000 cu ft of coal gas. It reached 6.7 mph on a flight from Paris to Trappe (Sept. 24).

1860 First aerial photographers. Samuel Archer King and William Black made two photos of Boston, which are still in existence.

1872 First gas-engine-powered dirigible. Paul Haenlein, a German engineer, flew in a semi-rigid-frame dirigible, powered by a 4-cylinder internal-combustion engine running on coal gas drawn from the supporting bag.

1873 First transatlantic attempt. *The New York Daily Graphic* sponsored the attempt with a 400,000-cubic-foot balloon carrying a lifeboat. A rip in the bag during inflation brought the collapse of the balloon and the project.

1897 First successful metal dirigible. An all-metal dirigible, designed by David Schwarz, a Hungarian, took off from Berlin's Tempelhof Field and, powered by a 16-horsepower Daimler engine, got several miles before leaking gas caused it to crash (Nov. 13).

1900 First zeppelin flight. Germany's Count Ferdinand von Zeppelin flew the first of his long series of rigid-frame airships. It attained a speed of 18 mph and got 3½ mi before its steering gear failed (July 2).

1903 First successful heavier-than-air machine flight. Aviation was really born on the sand dunes at Kitty Hawk, N.C., when Orville Wright crawled to his prone position between the wings of the biplane he and his brother Wilbur had built, opened the throttle of their home-made 12-horsepower engine, and took to the air. He covered 120 ft in 12 sec. Later that day, in one of four flights, Wilbur stayed up 59 sec. and covered 852 ft (Dec. 17).

Wilbur and Orville Wright with their second powered machine; Huffman prairie, Dayton, Ohio. *Source:* Library of Congress.

1904 First airplane maneuvers. Orville Wright made the first turn with an airplane (Sept. 15); five days later his brother Wilbur made the first complete circle.

1905 First airplane flight over half an hour. Orville Wright kept his craft up 33 min., 17 sec. (Oct. 4).

1906 First European airplane flight. Alberto Santos-Dumont, a Brazilian, flew a heavier-than-air machine at Bagatelle Field, Paris (Sept. 13).

1908 First airplane fatality. Lt. Thomas E. Selfridge, U.S. Army Signal Corps, was in a group evaluating the Wright plane at Fort Myer, Va. He was up 75 ft with Orville Wright when the propeller hit a bracing wire and was broken, throwing the plane out of control, killing Selfridge and seriously injuring Wright (Sept. 17).

1909 First cross-Channel flight. Louis Blériot flew in a 25-horsepower Blériot VI monoplane from Les Baraques near Calais, France, to Dover Castle, England, in a 26.61-mi (38-kilometer) 37-min. flight across the English Channel (July 25).

First International Aviation Competition Meeting. American Glenn Curtiss narrowly beat France's Louis Blériot in the main event and won the Gordon Bennett Cup. Meet held at Rheims, France (Aug. 22–28).

1910 First licensed woman pilot. Baroness Raymonde de la Roche of France, who learned to fly in 1909, received ticket No. 36 on March 8.

First flight from shipboard. Lt. Eugene Ely, USN, took a Curtiss plane off from the deck of the cruiser *Birmingham* at Hampton Roads, Va., and flew to Norfolk (Nov. 14). The following January he reversed the process, flying from Camp Selfridge to the deck of the armored cruiser *Pennsylvania* in San Francisco Bay (Jan. 18).

First aircraft to take off from water. Henri Fabre in a Gnome-powered floatplane, at Martigues, France (March 28).

1911 First U.S. woman pilot. Harriet Quimby, a magazine writer, got ticket No. 37, making her the first licensed American female pilot.

1912 First woman's cross-Channel flight. Harriet Quimby flew from Dover, England, across the

English Channel and landed at Hardelot, France, in a Blériot monoplane loaned to her by Louis Blériot (April 16). She was later killed in a flying accident over Dorchester Bay during a Harvard-Boston aviation meet on July 1, 1912.

First parachute jump from a powered airplane. Albert Berry jumped in a test over Jefferson Barracks military post, St. Louis (March 1). Some sources credit Grant Morton as making first jump in 1911.

1913 First multi-engined aircraft. Built and flown by Igor Ivan Sikorsky while still in his native Russia.

1914 First aerial combat. In Aug., Allied and German pilots and observers started shooting at each other with pistols and rifles—with negligible results.

1915 First air raids on England. German zeppelins dropped bombs on four English communities (Jan. 19).

1918 First U.S. air squadron. The U.S. Army Air Corps made its first independent raids over enemy lines, in DH-4 planes (British-designed) powered with 400-hp American-designed Liberty engines (April 8).

First regular airmail service. Operated for the Post Office Department by the Army, the first regular service was inaugurated with one round trip a day (except Sunday) between Washington, DC, and New York City (May 15).

1919 First transatlantic flight. The NC-4, one of four Curtiss flying boats commanded by Lt. Comdr. Albert C. Read, reached Lisbon, Portugal (May 27), after hops from Trepassy Bay, Newfoundland, to Horta, Azores (May 16–17), to Ponta Delgada (May 20). The Liberty-powered craft was piloted by Walter Hinton.

First nonstop transatlantic flight. Capt. John Alcock and Lt. Arthur Whitten Brown, British World War I flyers, made the 1,900-mile trip from St. John's, Newfoundland, to Clifden, Ireland, in 16 hr., 12 min. in a Vickers-Vimy bomber with two 350-horsepower Rolls-Royce engines (June 15–16).

First lighter-than-air transatlantic flight. The British dirigible R-34, commanded by Maj. George H. Scott, left Firth of Forth, Scotland (July 2), and touched down at Mineola, L.I., 108 hr. later. The eastbound trip was made in 75 hr. (completed July 13).

First scheduled London–Paris passenger service (using airplanes). Aircraft Travel and Transport inaugurated London–Paris service (Aug. 25). Later the company started the first trans-Channel mail service on the same route (Nov. 10).

First free-fall parachute jump. Leslie Irvin jumped over McCook Field, Dayton, Ohio, to prove that one won't lose consciousness during a delayed free-fall using a manually operated parachute (April 28).

1921 First U.S. black female pilot. Bessie Coleman received license June 15. Was killed April 30, 1926, in flying accident.

First naval vessel sunk by aircraft. Two battleships being scrapped by treaty were sunk by bombs dropped from Army planes in demonstration put on by Brig. Gen. William S. Mitchell (July 21).

First helium balloon. The C-7, nonrigid Navy dirigible was first to use noninflammable helium as lifting gas, making a flight from Hampton Roads, Va., to Washington, D.C. (Dec. 1).

1922 First member of Caterpillar Club. Lt. (later Maj. Gen.) Harold Harris bailed out of a crippled plane he was testing at McCook Field, Dayton, Ohio (Oct. 20), and became the first man to join the Caterpillar Club—those whose lives have been saved by parachutes.

1923 First nonstop transcontinental flight. Lts. John A. Macready and Oakley Kelly flew a single-engine Fokker T-2 nonstop from New York to San Diego, a distance of just over 2,500 mi in 26 hr., 50 min. (May 2–3).

First autogyro flight. Juan de la Cierva, a brilliant Spanish mathematician, made the first successful flight in a rotary wing aircraft in Madrid (June 9).

1924 First round-the-world flight. Four Douglas Cruiser biplanes of the U.S. Army Air Corps took off from Seattle under command of Maj. Frederick Martin (April 6). 175 days later, two of the planes (Lt. Lowell Smith's and Lt. Erik Nelson's) landed in Seattle after a circuitous route—one source saying 26,345 mi, another saying 27,553 mi.

1926 First polar flight. Then–Lt. Cmdr. Richard E. Byrd, acting as navigator, and Floyd Bennett as pilot, flew a Trimotor Fokker from Kings Bay, Spitsbergen, over the North Pole and back in 15½ hr. (May 8–9).

1927 First solo nonstop transatlantic flight. Charles Augustus Lindbergh lifted his Wright-powered Ryan monoplane, *Spirit of St. Louis,* from Roosevelt Field, N.Y., to stay aloft 33 hr. 39 min. and travel 3,600 mi to Le Bourget Field outside Paris (May 20–21). Although 91 persons in 13 separate flights crossed the Atlantic before him, he flew directly between two great world cities and did it alone.

Orville Wright, Major John F. Curry, and Colonel Charles Lindbergh, who came to pay Orville a personal call at Wright field, Dayton, Ohio, June 22, 1927. *Source:* Library of Congress.

First transatlantic passenger. Charles A. Levine was piloted by Clarence D. Chamberlin from Roosevelt Field, N.Y., to Eisleben, Germany, in a Wright-powered Bellanca (June 4–5).

1928 First east–west transatlantic crossing. Baron Guenther von Huenefeld, piloted by German Capt. Hermann Koehl and Irish Capt. James Fitzmaurice, left Dublin for New York City (April 12) in a single-engine all-metal Junkers-monoplane. Some 37 hr. later, they crashed on Greely Island, Labrador. Rescued.

First U.S.–Australia flight. Sir Charles Kingsford-Smith and Capt. Charles T. P. Ulm, Australians, and two American navigators, Harry W. Lyon and James Warner, crossed the Pacific from Oakland to Brisbane. They went via Hawaii and the Fiji Islands in a trimotor Fokker (May 31–June 8).

First transarctic flight. Sir Hubert Wilkins, an Australian explorer, and Carl Ben Eielson, who served as pilot, flew from Point Barrow, Alaska, to Spitsbergen (mid-April).

1929 **First of the endurance records.** With Air Corps Maj. Carl Spaatz in command and Capt. Ira Eaker as chief pilot, an Army Fokker, aided by refueling in the air, remained aloft 150 hr. 40 min. at Los Angeles (Jan. 1–7).

First round-the-world airship flight. The LZ-127, known as the *Graf Zeppelin,* flew 21,300 mi in 20 days and 4 hr. Also set distance record (Aug.).

First blind flight. James H. Doolittle proved the feasibility of instrument-guided flying when he took off and landed entirely on instruments (Sept. 24).

First rocket-engine flight. Fritz von Opel, a German auto maker, stayed aloft in his small rocket-powered craft for 75 sec., covering nearly 2 mi (Sept. 30).

First South Pole flight. Comdr. Richard E. Byrd, with Bernt Balchen as pilot, Harold I. June, radio operator, and Capt. A. C. McKinley, photographer, flew a trimotor Fokker from the Bay of Whales, Little America, over the South Pole and back (Nov. 28–29).

1930 **First Paris–New York nonstop flight.** Dieudonné Costes and Maurice Bellonte, French pilots, flew a Hispano-powered Breguet biplane from Le Bourget Field to Valley Stream, L.I., in 37 hr., 18 min. (Sept. 2–3).

1931 **First flight into the stratosphere.** Auguste Piccard, a Swiss physicist, and Charles Knipfer ascended in a balloon from Augsburg, Germany, and reached a height of 51,793 ft in a 17-hr. flight that terminated on a glacier near Innsbruck, Austria (May 27).

First nonstop transpacific flight. Hugh Herndon and Clyde Pangborn took off from Sabishiro Beach, Japan, dropped their landing gear, and flew 4,860 mi to near Wenatchee, Wash., in 41 hr. 13 min. (Oct. 4–5).

1932 **First woman's transatlantic solo.** Amelia Earhart, flying a Pratt & Whitney Wasp-powered Lockheed Vega, flew alone from Harbor Grace, Newfoundland, to Ireland in approximately 15 hr. (May 20–21).

First westbound transatlantic solo. James A. Mollison, a British pilot, took a de Havilland Puss Moth from Portmarnock, Ireland, to Pennfield, New Brunswick (Aug. 18).

Amelia Earhart, 1897–1937.
Source: Library of Congress.

First woman airline pilot. Ruth Rowland Nichols, first woman to hold three international records at the same time—speed, distance, and altitude—was employed by N.Y.–New England Airways.

1933 **First round-the-world solo.** Wiley Post took a Lockheed Vega, *Winnie Mae,* 15,596 mi around the world in 7 days, 18 hr., 49½ min. (July 15–22).

1937 **First successful helicopter flight.** Hanna Reitsch, a German pilot, flew Dr. Heinrich Focke's FW-61 in free, fully controlled flight at Bremen (July 4). Ms. Reitsch was also the first woman civil and military aviation test pilot.

First woman known to fly combat. Sabiha Gokcen, Turkish female army pilot, bombed and strafed Kurdish tribesmen during a rebellion.

1939 **First turbojet flight.** Just before their invasion of Poland, the Germans flew a Heinkel He-178 plane powered by a Heinkel S3B turbojet (Aug. 27).

1940 **First wartime use of military gliders.** German commandos made a successful glider assault on Belgium's Fort Eben-Emael during WWII (May 10).

1941–1945 **Most combat missions flown by a pilot in any war.** Captain Hans-Ulrich Rudel of Germany flew 2,530 combat missions during WWII while flying a JU-87 Stuka dive bomber. He survived the war.

1942–1945 **Top-scoring fighter pilot of any war.** German Luftwaffe ace Maj. Erich Hartmann scored 352 victories all while flying a Messerschmitt BF 109 during WWII. He was involved in 800 dogfights, and flew 1,425 missions. Maj. Hartmann survived the war.

1942 **First enemy bombing of U.S. mainland.** During WWII, a floatplane launched from a Japanese submarine off Cape Blanco, Ore., dropped incendiary bombs on the Oregon forest in two attempts to start forest fires and terrorize American civilians, but the bombs did little damage (Sept. 9 and 29).

First American jet plane flight. Robert Stanley, chief pilot for Bell Aircraft Corp., flew the Bell XP-59 *Airacomet* at Muroc Army Base, Calif. (Oct. 1).

First woman fighter pilot to shoot down an enemy aircraft. Soviet Lieutenant Lilya Litvyak, flying a Yak-1 fighter of the women's 586th Fighter Aviation Regiment, shot down two German planes over Stalingrad (Sept. 13).

1944 **First production stage rocket-engine fighter plane.** The German Messerschmitt Me 163B *Komet* (test flown 1941) became operational in June 1944. Some 350 of these delta-wing fighters were built before WWII in Europe ended.

1947 **First piloted supersonic flight in an airplane.** Capt. Charles E. Yeager, U.S. Air Force, flew the X-1 rocket-powered research plane built by Bell Aircraft Corp., faster than the speed of sound at Muroc Air Force Base, Calif. (Oct. 14).

1949 **First round-the-world nonstop flight.** Capt. James Gallagher and USAF crew of 13 flew a Boeing B-50A Superfortress around the world nonstop from Ft. Worth, returning to same point: 23,452 mi in 94 hr., 1 min., with four aerial refuelings en route (Feb. 27–March 2).

Active Pilot Certificates Held

Year	Total	Airline transport	Commercial	Private
1970	720,028	31,442	176,585	299,491
1980	814,667	63,652	182,097	343,276
1985	722,376	79,192	155,929	320,086
1990	702,659	107,732	149,666	299,111
1995	639,184	123,877	133,980	261,399
2000	625,581	141,596	121,858	251,561
2001	612,274	144,702	120,502	243,823

NOTE: Includes student (97,359), glider (9,390), recreational (343), and other pilot categories. Also nonpilot, i.e., mechanic, parachute rigger, etc. *Source:* May 2002 FAA Fact Book.

1950 First nonstop transatlantic jet flight. Col. David C. Schilling (USAF) flew 3,300 mi from England to Limestone, Maine, in 10 hr., 1 min. (Sept. 22).

1951 First solo across North Pole. Charles F. Blair, Jr., flew a converted P-51 (May 29).

1952 First jetliner service. The De Havilland Comet flight was inaugurated by BOAC between London and Johannesburg, South Africa. Flight, including stops, took 23 hr., 38 min. (May 2).

First transatlantic helicopter flight. Capt. Vincent H. McGovern and 1st Lt. Harold W. Moore piloted two Sikorsky H-19s from Westover, Mass., to Prestwick, Scotland (3,410 mi). Trip was made in five stops, with a flying time of 42 hr., 25 min. (July 15–31).

First transatlantic round trip in same day. A British Canberra twin-jet bomber flew from Aldergrove, Northern Ireland, to Gander, Newfoundland, and back in 7 hr., 59 min. flying time (Aug. 26).

1955 First transcontinental round trip in same day. Lt. John M. Conroy piloted an F-86 Sabrejet across U.S. (Los Angeles–New York) and back—5,085 mi—in 11 hr., 33 min., 27 sec. (May 21).

1957 First round-the-world nonstop jet plane flight. Maj. Gen. Archie J. Old, Jr., USAF, led a flight of three Boeing B-52 bombers, powered with eight 10,000-pound-thrust Pratt & Whitney Aircraft J57 engines around the world in 45 hr., 19 min; distance 24,325 mi; average speed 525 mph (completed Jan. 18).

1958 First transatlantic jet passenger service. BOAC, New York to London (Oct. 4). Pan American started daily service, New York to Paris (Oct. 26).

First domestic jet passenger service. National Airlines inaugurated service between New York and Miami (Dec. 10).

1968 Prototype of world's first supersonic airliner. The Soviet-designed Tupolev Tu-144 made its first flight, Dec. 31. It first achieved supersonic speed on June 5, 1969.

1973 First female pilot of a major U.S. scheduled airline. Emily H. Warner became employed by Frontier Airlines on Jan. 29 as second officer on a Boeing 737.

1976 First regularly scheduled commercial supersonic transport (SST) flights begin. Air France and British Airways inaugurated service (Jan. 21). Air France flew the Paris–Rio de Janeiro route; B.A., the London–Bahrain. Both airlines began SST service to Washington, D.C. (May 24).

1977 First successful human-powered aircraft. Paul MacCready, an aeronautical engineer from Pasadena, Calif., was awarded the Kremer Prize for creating the world's first successful human-powered aircraft. The *Gossamer Condor* was flown by Bryan Allen over the required 3-mile course on Aug. 23.

1978 First successful transatlantic balloon flight. Three Albuquerque, N.M., men, Ben Abruzzo, Larry Newman, and Maxie Anderson, completed the crossing (Aug. 16.; landed, Aug. 17) in their helium-filled balloon, *Double Eagle II.*

1979 First man-powered aircraft to fly across the English Channel. The Kremer Prize for the Channel crossing was won by Bryan Allen, who flew the *Gossamer Albatross* from Folkestone, England, to Cap Gris-Nez, France, in 2 hr., 55 min. (June 12).

1980 First successful balloon flight over the North Pole. Sidney Conn and his wife, Eleanor, in hot-air balloon *Joy of Sound* (April 11).

First nonstop transcontinental balloon flight, and also record for longest overland voyage in a balloon. Maxie Anderson and his son, Kris, completed four-day flight from Fort Baker, Calif., to successful landing outside Matane, Quebec, in their helium-filled balloon, *Kitty Hawk* (May 12).

First long-distance solar-powered flight. Janice Brown, a 98-pound former teacher, flew a tiny experimental solar-powered aircraft, *Solar Challenger,* 6 mi in 22 min. near Marana, Ariz. (Dec. 3). The craft was powered by a 2.75-horsepower engine.

First solar-powered aircraft to fly across the English Channel. Stephen R. Ptacek flew the 210-pound *Solar Challenger* at an average speed of 30 mph from Cormeilles-en-Vexin near Paris to the Royal Manston Air Force Base in southeast England in 5 hr., 30 min. (July 7).

1984 First solo transatlantic balloon flight. Joe W. Kittinger landed Sept. 18 near Savona, Italy, in his helium-filled balloon, *Rosie O'Grady's Balloon of Peace,* after a flight of 3,535 mi from Caribou, Maine.

1986 First nonstop flight around the world without refueling. From Edwards AFB, Calif., Dick Rutan and Jeana Yeager flew in *Voyager* around the world (24,986.727 mi), returning to Edwards in 216 hr., 3 min., 44 sec. (Dec. 14–23).

1987 First transatlantic hot-air balloon flight. Richard Branson and Per Lindstrand flew 2,789.6 mi from Sugarloaf Mt., Maine, to Ireland in the hot-air balloon *Virgin Atlantic Flyer* (July 2–4).

1991 First transpacific hot-air balloon flight. Richard Branson and Per Lindstrand flew about 6,700 mi from Miyakonyo, Japan, to 150 mi west of Yellowknife, Northwest Territories, Canada (Jan. 15–17).

1993 First woman to copilot a commercial supersonic plane. Barbara Harmer, British Airways, flew as first officer on the Concorde from London to New York City (March 25).

1995 First solo transpacific balloon flight. Steve Fossett made a flight of more than 5,430 mi from Seoul, South Korea, to Leader, Saskatchewan, Canada, in a helium-filled balloon. Also set record for distance (Feb. 18–21, 1995).

1999 First nonstop round-the-world balloon flight. Bertrand Piccard (Switzerland) and Brian Jones (UK) flew 28,431 mi (45,755 km) from Chateaux d'Oex, Switzerland, to Dakhla, Egypt, in 19 days, 21 hr., and 55 min. (March 1–21).

2001 First solar-powered flight to shatter altitude records. NASA's solar-powered propeller-driven plane *Helios* reached an altitude of 96,500 ft during a flight over Hawaii, breaking not only the 80,200-foot record for propeller-driven aircraft, but the 85,068-foot mark for all nonrocket aircraft as well (Aug. 13–14).

2002 **First solo nonstop round-the-world balloon flight.** Steve Fossett (U.S.) flew from Northam, West Australia, to Lake Yamma Yamma, Queensland, Australia, landing after 14 days, 19 hrs. He broke three balloon records along the way: fastest time around the world, measured by crossing 117° East longitude (13 days, 3 min.), longest distance flown solo (20,483.25 mi; 32,963.35 km), and longest time flown solo (355 hrs, 50 min.) (June 19–July 3).

Absolute World Records

(maximum performance in any class)

Source: National Aeronautic Association

Speed around the World, Nonstop, Nonrefueled

Speed (mph)	Date	Plane	Pilots	Place
115.65	Dec. 14–23, 1986	*Voyager*	Dick Rutan & Jeana Yeager (U.S.)	Edwards AFB, Calif.—Edwards AFB, Calif.

Distance, Great Circle without Landing, also Distance, Closed Circuit without Landing

Distance (mi)	Date	Plane	Pilots	Place
24,986.727	Dec. 14–23, 1986	*Voyager*	Dick Rutan & Jeana Yeager (U.S.)	Edwards AFB, Calif.—Edwards AFB, Calif.

Speed over a Straight Course

Speed (mph)	Date	Plane type	Pilot	Place
2,193.16	July 28, 1976	Lockheed SR-71A	Capt. Eldon W. Joersz (USAF)	Beale AFB, Calif.

Speed over a Closed Circuit

Speed (mph)	Date	Plane type	Pilot	Place
2,092.294	July 27, 1976	Lockheed SR-71A	Maj. Adolphus H. Bledsoe, Jr. (USAF)	Beale AFB, Calif.

Altitude

Height (ft)	Date	Plane type	Pilot	Place
123,523.58	Aug. 31, 1977	MIG-25, E-266M	Alexander Fedotov (U.S.S.R.)	U.S.S.R.

Altitude in Horizontal Flight

Height (ft)	Date	Pilot	Place
85,068.997	July 28, 1976	Capt. Robert C. Helt (USAF)	Beale AFB, Calif.

Altitude, Aircraft Launched from a Carrier Airplane

Height (ft)	Date	Plane type	Pilot	Place
314,750.00	July 17, 1962	N. American X-15-1	Maj. Robert White (USAF)	Edwards AFB, Calif.

World-Class Helicopter Records

Selected records. *Source:* National Aeronautic Association

Great Circle Distance without Landing
International: 2,213.04 mi; 3,561.55 km.
Robert G. Ferry (U.S.) in Hughes YOH-6A helicopter powered by Allison T-63-A-5 engine; from Culver City, Calif., to Ormond Beach, Fla., April 6–7, 1966.

Distance, Closed Circuit without Landing
International: 1,739.96 mi; 2,800.20 km.
Jack Schweibold (U.S.) in Hughes YOH-6A helicopter powered by Allison T-63-A-5 engine; Edwards Air Force Base, Calif., March 26, 1966.

Altitude without Payload
International: 40,820 ft; 12,442 m.
Jean Boulet (France) in Alouette SA 315-001 *Lama* powered by Artouste IIIB 735 KW engine; Istres, France, June 21, 1972.

Speed around the World, Eastbound
40.99 mph; 65.97 kph.
Joe Ronald Bower (U.S.) pilot, in Bell JetRanger III, powered by one Allison 250-C20J (317 shp), covered 23,800 mi in 24 days, 4 hr., 36 min. June 28–July 22, 1994.

Speed around the World, Westbound
57.01 mph; 91.75 kph.
Joe Ronald Bower (U.S.) pilot, John W. Williams (U.S.), co-pilot in Bell 430 powered by 2 Allison 250–C40, (811 shp), Aug. 17–Sept. 3, 1996.

Absolute World Records, Balloons

Selected records. *Source:* National Aeronautic Association

Altitude
113,739.9 ft; 34,668 m.
Cmdr. M.D. Ross (U.S.) and Lt. Cmdr. V.A. Prather, *Lee Lewis Memorial,* Gulf of Mexico, May 4, 1961.

Distance
25,360 mi; 40,814 km.
Bertrand Piccard (Switzerland) and Brian Jones (UK), *Cameron Balloons R-650,* Château d'Oex, Switzerland, to Dakhla, Egypt, March 1–21, 1999.

Duration
477 hr., 47 min.
Bertrand Piccard (Switzerland) and Brian Jones (UK), *Cameron Balloons R-650,* Château d'Oex, Switzerland, to Dakhla, Egypt, March 1–21, 1999.

Fastest time around the world
312 hr., 3 min.
Steve Fossett (U.S.), Spirit of Freedom, Northam, Western Australia to Lake Yamma Yamma, Queensland, Australia. Flight, June 19–July 3; record broken on July 2, 2002.

The Seven Wonders of the World

Since ancient times, people have put together many "seven wonders" lists. The content of these lists tends to vary, and none is definitive. The seven wonders that are most widely agreed upon as being in the original list are the **Seven Wonders of the Ancient World.** (* indicates photo can be found in the Headline History section.)

The **Pyramids of Egypt*** are three pyramids at Giza, outside modern Cairo. The largest pyramid, built by Khufu (Cheops), a king of the fourth dynasty, had an original estimated height of 482 ft (now approximately 450 ft). The base has sides 755 ft long. It contains 2,300,000 blocks; the average weight of each is 2.5 tons. Estimated date of completion is 2680 B.C. Of all the Ancient Wonders, the pyramids alone survive.

The **Hanging Gardens of Babylon** were supposedly built by Nebuchadnezzar around 600 B.C. to please his queen, Amuhia. They are also associated with the mythical Assyrian queen, Semiramis. Archeologists surmise that the gardens were laid out atop a vaulted building, with provisions for raising water. The terraces were said to rise from 75 to 300 ft.

The **Statue of Zeus (Jupiter) at Olympia** was made of gold and ivory by the Greek sculptor Phidias (5th century B.C.). Reputed to be 40 ft high, the statue has been lost without a trace, except for reproductions on coins.

The **Temple of Artemis (Diana) at Ephesus** was begun about 350 B.C., in honor of a non-Hellenic goddess who later became identified with the Greek goddess of the same name. The temple, with Ionic columns 60 ft high, was destroyed by invading Goths in A.D. 262.

The **Mausoleum at Halicarnassus** was erected by Queen Artemisia in memory of her husband, King Mausolus of Caria in Asia Minor, who died in 353 B.C. Some remains of the structure are in the British Museum. This shrine is the source of the modern word "mausoleum."

The **Colossus at Rhodes** was a bronze statue of Helios (Apollo), about 105 ft high. The work of the sculptor Chares, who reputedly labored for 12 years before completing it in 280 B.C., it was destroyed during an earthquake in 224 B.C.

The **Pharos (Lighthouse) of Alexandria** was built by Sostratus of Cnidus during the 3rd century B.C. on the island of Pharos off the coast of Egypt. It was destroyed by an earthquake in the 13th century.

(Some lists include the Walls of Babylon in place of the second or seventh wonder.)

Famous Structures

Ancient

The **Great Sphinx** of Egypt, one of the wonders of ancient Egyptian architecture, adjoins the pyramids of Giza and has a length of 240 ft. Built in the fourth dynasty, it is approximately 4,500 years old. A 10-year $2.5 million restoration project was completed in 1998. Other Egyptian buildings of note include the *Temples of Karnak, Edfu,* and *Abu Simbel,* and the *Tombs at Beni Hassan.*

The **Parthenon*** of Greece, built on the Acropolis in Athens, was the chief temple to the goddess Athena. It was believed to have been completed by 438 B.C. The present temple remained intact until the 5th century A.D. Today, though the Parthenon is in ruins, its majestic proportions are still discernible.

Other great structures of ancient Greece were the *Temples at Paestum* (c. 540 and 420 B.C.); the famous *Erechtheum* (c. 421–405 B.C.), the *Temple of Athena Niké* (c. 426 B.C.), and the *Olympieum* (174 B.C.–A.D. 131) atop the Acropolis; the *Athenian Treasury* at Delphi (c. 515 B.C.); and the *Theater* at Epidaurus (c. 325 B.C.).

The **Colosseum** (Flavian Amphitheater) of Rome, the largest and most famous of the Roman amphitheaters, was opened for use A.D. 80. Elliptical in shape, it consisted of three stories and an upper gallery, rebuilt in stone in its present form in the third century A.D. It was principally used for gladiatorial combat and could seat between 40,000 and 50,000 spectators.

The **Pantheon** at Rome, begun by Agrippa in 27 B.C. as a temple, was rebuilt in its present circular form by Hadrian (A.D. 118–128). Literally the Pantheon was intended as a temple of "all the gods." It is remarkable for its perfect preservation today, and it has served continuously for 20 centuries as a place of worship.

Famous Roman triumphal arches, built to commemorate major military victories, include the **Arch of Titus** (c. A.D. 80) and the **Arch of Constantine** (c. A.D. 315).

Teotihuacán, located in central Mexico, was the largest city in the Americas at its height between A.D. 300 and 900. Built on a grid plan with a central avenue known as the Street of the Dead, it is the site of two enormous pyramid temples and the temple of the plumed serpent god Quetzalcoatl.

Later European

St. Mark's Cathedral in Venice (1063–1071), one of the great examples of Byzantine architecture, was begun in the 9th century. Partly destroyed by fire in 976, it was later rebuilt as a Byzantine edifice.

Other famous examples of Byzantine architecture are *St. Sophia* in Istanbul (532–537); *San Vitale* in Ravenna (542); and *Assumption Cathedral* in the Kremlin, Moscow (begun in 1475).

The cathedral group at Pisa (1067–1173), one of the most celebrated groups of structures built in Romanesque style, consists of the cathedral, the cathedral's baptistery, and the campanile (**Leaning Tower***). The campanile, a form of bell tower, is 180 ft high and now leans 13.5 ft out of the perpendicular.

Other examples of Romanesque architecture include the *Vézelay Abbey* in France (1130) and *Durham Cathedral* in England.

The **Alhambra** (1248–1354), located in Granada, Spain, is universally esteemed as one of the greatest masterpieces of Muslim architecture. Designed as a palace and fortress for the Moorish monarchs of Granada, it is surrounded by a heavily fortified wall more than a mile in perimeter. The location of the Alhambra in the Sierra Nevada provides a magnificent setting for this jewel of Moorish Spain.

The **Tower of London** is a group of buildings and towers covering 13 acres along the north bank of the Thames. The central *White Tower,* begun in 1078 during the reign of William the Conqueror, was originally a fortress and royal residence, but was later used as a prison. The *Bloody Tower* is associated with Anne Boleyn and other notables.

Westminster Abbey, in London, was begun in 1050 and completed in 1065. It was rebuilt and enlarged in several phases, beginning in 1245. With only two exceptions (Edward V and Edward VIII), every British monarch since William the Conqueror has been crowned in the abbey.

Notre-Dame de Paris (begun in 1163), one of the great examples of Gothic architecture, is a twin-towered church with a steeple over the crossing and immense flying buttresses supporting the masonry at the rear of the church.

Other famous Gothic structures are *Chartres Cathedral* (France; 12th century); *Sainte Chapelle* (Paris, France; 1246–1248); *Reims Cathedral* (France; 13th–14th centuries; rebuilt after its almost complete destruction in World War I); *Rouen Cathedral* (France; 13th–16th centuries); *Salisbury Cathedral* (England; 1220–1260); *York Minster* or the *Cathedral of St. Peter* (England; 1220–1472); *Milan Cathedral* (Italy; begun 1386); and *Cologne Cathedral* (Germany; 13th–19th centuries; damaged in World War II but completely restored).

The **Duomo*** (cathedral) in Florence, with its pink, white, and green marble façade, has become a symbol of the city and the Renaissance. Construction began in 1296, but it was not completed until nearly 200 years later, following the addition of Brunelleschi's massive dome. The adjacent baptistery is famous for its gilded bronze doors by Ghiberti.

The **Vatican** is a group of buildings in Rome comprising the official residence of the pope. The *Basilica of St. Peter,* the largest church in the Christian world, was begun in 1452, and it was rebuilt between 1506 and 1626. The *Sistine Chapel,* begun in 1473, is noted for the art masterpieces of Michelangelo, Botticelli, and others. To the southeast of Vatican City is the *Basilica of the Savior* (known as *St. John Lateran*). As the cathedral of the pope, it is the first-ranking Catholic Church in the world.

Other examples of Renaissance architecture are the *Palazzo Riccardi,* the *Palazzo Pitti,* and the *Palazzo Strozzi* in Florence; the *Farnese Palace* in Rome; *Palazzo Grimani* (completed about 1550) in Venice; the *Escorial* (1563–93) near Madrid; the *Town Hall* of Seville (1527–32); the *Louvre,* Paris; the *Château* at Blois, France; *St. Paul's Cathedral,* London (1675–1710; badly damaged in World War II); the *École Militaire,* Paris (1752); the *Pazzi Chapel,* Florence, designed by Brunelleschi (1429); and the *Palace of Fontainebleau* and the *Château de Chambord* in France.

The **Palace of Versailles** in France, containing the famous Hall of Mirrors, was built during the reign of Louis XIV in the 17th century and served as the royal palace until 1793. Built on the colossal scale typical of many works of baroque architecture, the palace is also noted for its gardens, which include some 1,400 fountains.

The **Eiffel Tower,** in Paris, was built for the Exposition of 1889 by Alexandre Gustave Eiffel. It is 984 ft high (1,056 ft including the television tower).

Asian, African, and American

The **Taj Mahal*** (1632–1650), at Agra, India, built by Shah Jahan as a tomb for his wife, is considered by some as the most perfect example of the Mogul style and by others as the most beautiful building in the world. Four slim white minarets flank the building, which is topped by a white dome; the entire structure is made of marble. Other examples of Indian architecture are the temples at Benares and Tanjore.

The **Dome of the Rock** (687–691) in Jerusalem is considered the first great work of Muslim architecture. It is noted for its beautiful mosaics of scrolling vines and flowers, and for its dome, which was originally covered in pure gold.

Another well-known Muslim edifice is the **Citadel**, located on an outcrop of limestone overlooking Cairo. Begun in 810, it was fortified (1176–1183) by Saladin during the Crusades.

Other famed Muslim edifices are the *Tombs of the Mamelukes* (15th century) in Cairo, the *Tomb of Humayun* in Delhi, the *Blue Mosque* (1468) at Tabriz, and the *Tamerlane Mausoleum* at Samarkand.

Angkor Wat, outside the city of Angkor Thom, Cambodia, is one of the most beautiful examples of Cambodian or Khmer architecture. The sanctuary was built during the 12th century.

The **Great Wall of China** (begun c. 214 B.C.), designed specifically as a defense against nomadic tribes, has large watch towers that could be called buildings. It was erected by Emperor Ch'in Shih Huang Ti and is 1,400 mi long. Built mainly of earth and stone, it varies in height between 18 and 30 ft.

The **Forbidden City** (1407–1420) in Beijing served as the seat of imperial power during the Ming and Qing dynasties (1368–1911). It is the world's largest palace complex, covering about 183 acres and including 9,999 buildings.

Typical of Chinese architecture are the pagodas or temple towers. Among some of the better-known pagodas are the *Great Pagoda of the Wild Geese* at Sian (founded in 652) and *Nan t'a* (11th century) at Fang Shan.

The painted wooden **Torii,** or Gateway, at Miyajima Island, Japan, stands in the tidal flats opposite the historic Itsukushima Shrine. Built in the traditional Shinto style, with two columns supporting a concave crosspiece on top, the gate serves to welcome the spirits of the dead as they come from across the Inland Sea.

Other famous Japanese buildings include the Buddhist temples of **Horyuji** (7th century) and **Todaiji** (8th century) at Nara.

Machu Picchu is an ancient Inca fortress in the Andes Mountains of Peru. Thought to have been built and occupied from the mid-15th century, it is surrounded on three sides by stepped agricultural terraces, which are connected to the main plazas and buildings by thousands of stone steps.

United States

The **Chrysler Building** in New York City is one of the finest examples of Art Deco style high-rise architecture. Built for the automotive magnate Walter P. Chrysler between 1928 and 1930, the building makes use of decorative elements borrowed from automobiles. At 1,046 ft it was briefly the tallest building in the world before the Empire State Building was completed the following year.

The **Empire State Building,** one of the most popular tourist attractions in the heart of Manhattan, was constructed between 1930 and 1931. Features include a tiered structure that recalls ancient Egyptian and Aztec pyramids and a mast at the top for mooring dirigibles. Rising to 1,250 ft (not including the mast), it remained the tallest building in the world until the 1970s.

The **Cathedral of St. John the Divine,** at 112th St. and Amsterdam Ave. in New York City, was begun in 1892 and is now in the final stages of completion. When completed, it will be the largest cathedral in the world: 601 ft long, 146 ft wide at the nave, 320 ft wide at the transept. The east end is designed in Romanesque-Byzantine style, and the nave and west end are Gothic.

The **Brooklyn Bridge,** built between 1869 and 1883, was the remarkable achievement of engineer John Roebling and his son, Washington Roebling. The first steel-wire suspension bridge in the world, it has a main span of 1,596 ft.

The **Sears Tower** in Chicago is, at 1,450 ft, the tallest building in the United States. Constructed between 1974 and 1976 for Sears, Roebuck and Company, the structure is composed of 75-foot square tubes that rise to varying levels.

San Francisco's **Golden Gate Bridge,** completed in 1937, is one of the most recognizable structures in the United States. Designed by Joseph B. Strauss, this elegant suspension bridge has a main span of 4,200 ft.

The Seattle **Space Needle** was planned as the central structure and symbol of the 1962 Seattle World's Fair, the theme of which was "Century 21." The Needle, which is 605 ft tall, is topped by an observation deck and a revolving restaurant.

* Photos of these structures can be found in the Headline History section.

World's Tallest Buildings[1]

Rank	Building, city	Year	Stories	Height m	Height ft.
1.	Taipei 101, Taipei, Taiwan	UC04	106	508	1,667
2.	Petronas Tower 1, Kuala Lumpur, Malaysia	1998	88	452	1,483
3.	Petronas Tower 2, Kuala Lumpur, Malaysia	1998	88	452	1,483
4.	Sears Tower, Chicago	1974	110	442	1,450
5.	Jin Mao Building, Shanghai	1999	88	421	1,381
6.	Two International Finance Center, Hong Kong	UC03	88	412	1,352
7.	Citic Plaza, Guangzhou, China	1996	80	391	1,283
8.	Shun Hing Square, Shenzhen, China	1996	69	384	1,260
9.	Empire State Building, New York	1931	102	381	1,250
10.	Central Plaza, Hong Kong	1992	78	374	1,227
11.	Bank of China Tower, Hong Kong	1989	70	369	1,209
12.	Emirates Tower One, Dubai	1999	55	355	1,165
13.	The Center, Hong Kong	1998	79	350	1,148
14.	T & C Tower, Kaohsiung, Taiwan	1997	85	348	1,140
15.	Aon Centre, Chicago	1973	80	346	1,136
16.	John Hancock Center, Chicago	1969	100	344	1,127
17.	Burj al Arab Hotel, Dubai	1999	60	321	1,053
18.	Chrysler Building, New York	1930	77	319	1,046
19.	Bank of America Plaza, Atlanta	1993	55	312	1,023
20.	Library Tower, Los Angeles	1990	75	310	1,018
21.	Telekom Malaysia Headquarters, Kuala Lumpur	1999	55	310	1,017
22.	Emirates Tower Two, Dubai	2000	56	309	1,014
23.	AT&T Corporate Center, Chicago	1989	60	307	1,007
24.	JP Morgan Chase Tower, Houston	1982	75	305	1,002
25.	Baiyoke Tower II, Bangkok	1997	85	304	997
26.	Two Prudential Plaza, Chicago	1990	64	303	995
27.	Kingdom Centre, Riyadh	2001	30	302	992
28.	Pyongyang Hotel, Pyongyang, N. Korea	1995	105	300	984
29.	First Canadian Place, Toronto	1975	72	298	978
30.	Wells Fargo Plaza, Houston	1983	71	296	972
31.	Landmark Tower, Yokohama, Japan	1993	70	296	971
32.	Bank of America Center, Seattle	1984	76	295	967
33.	311 South Wacker Drive, Chicago	1990	65	293	961
34.	SEG Plaza, Shenzhen	2000	72	292	957
35.	American International Building, New York	1932	67	290	952
36.	Cheung Kong Center, Hong Kong	1999	70	290	951
37.	Key Tower, Cleveland	1991	57	289	947
38.	Plaza 66, Shanghai	2001	62	288	945
39.	One Liberty Place, Philadelphia	1987	61	288	945
40.	Sunjoy Tomorrow Square, Shanghai	1999	59	285	934
41.	The Trump Building, New York	1930	72	283	927
42.	Bank of America Plaza, Dallas	1985	72	281	921
43.	Overseas Union Bank Centre, Singapore	1986	66	280	919
44.	United Overseas Bank Plaza, Singapore	1992	66	280	919
45.	Republic Plaza, Singapore	1995	66	280	919
46.	Citicorp Center, New York	1977	59	279	915
47.	Hong Kong New World Building, Shanghai	2001	58	278	913
48.	Scotia Plaza, Toronto	1989	68	275	902
49.	Williams Tower, Houston	1983	64	275	901

Rank	Building, city	Year	Stories	Height m	Height ft.
50.	Wuhan World Trade Tower,. Wuhan	1998	60	273	896
51.	Renaissance Tower, Dallas	1975	56	270	886
52.	Dapeng International Plaza, Guangzhou	UC03	56	269	883
53.	Al Faisaliah Center, Riyadh	2000	30	267	876
54.	900 North Michigan Ave., Chicago	1989	66	265	871
55.	Bank of America Center, Charlotte	1992	60	265	871
56.	SunTrust Plaza, Atlanta	1992	60	265	871
57.	Shenzhen Special Zone Daily Tower, Shenzhen	1998	42	264	866
58.	Tower Palace Three, Tower G, Seoul	UC04	73	264	865
59.	BCE Place–Canada Trust Tower, Toronto	1990	51	263	863
60.	Trump World Tower, New York	2001	72	262	861
61.	Water Tower Place, Chicago	1976	74	262	859
62.	Aon Center, Los Angeles	1974	62	262	858
63.	Post & Telecommunication Hub, Guangzhou	2002	66	260	853
64.	Transamerica Pyramid, San Francisco	1972	48	260	853
65.	G.E. Building, New York	1933	70	259	850
66.	Bank One Plaza, Chicago	1969	60	259	850
67.	Commerzbank Tower, Frankfurt	1997	56	259	850
68.	Two Liberty Place, Philadelphia	1990	58	258	848
69.	Philippine Bank of Communications, Makati	2000	52	258	848
70.	Park Tower, Chicago	2000	67	257	844
71.	Messeturm, Frankfurt	1990	70	257	843
72.	USX Tower, Pittsburgh	1970	64	256	841
73.	Sorrento 1, Hong Kong	UC03	75	256	840
74..	Mokdong Hyperion Tower A, Seoul	UC03	69	256	840
75.	Rinku Gate Tower, Osaka	1996	56	256	840
76.	Capital Tower, Singapore	2000	52	254	833
77.	Highcliffe, Hong Kong	2003	73	253	831
78.	Osaka World Trade Center, Osaka	1995	55	252	827
79.	Jiali Plaza, Wuhan	1997	61	251	824
80.	Rialto Tower, Melbourne	1985	63	251	823
81.	One Atlantic Center, Atlanta	1987	50	250	820
82.	Wisma 46, Jakarta	1995	46	250	820
83.	Korea Life Insurance Company, Seoul	1985	60	249	817
84.	Bear Stearns Headquarters Building, New York	2001	45	248	815
85.	CitySpire, New York	1989	75	248	814
86.	One Chase Manhattan Plaza, New York	1961	60	248	813
87.	Bank One Tower, Indianapolis	1989	48	247	811
88.	Royal Charoen Krung Tower, Bangkok	2001	68	247	810
89.	Conde Nast Building, New York	1999	48	247	809
90.	MetLife, New York	1963	59	246	808
91.	JR Central Towers, Nagoya	2000	51	245	804
92.	Shin Kong Life Tower, Taipei, Taiwan	1993	51	244	801
93.	Malayan Bank, Kuala Lumpur, Malaysia	1988	50	244	799
94.	The Tower, Dubai	2002	54	243	797
95.	Tokyo Metropolitan Government, Tokyo	1991	48	243	797
96.	City Gate Tower, Ramat-Gan	2001	67	242	794
97.	Dalian World Trade Center, Dalian	2000	55	242	794
98.	Woolworth Building, New York	1913	57	241	792
99.	Maxdo Centre, Shanghai	2002	55	241	792
100.	Mellon Bank Center, Philadelphia	1991	54	241	792

NOTES: Height is measured from sidewalk level of main entrance to structural top of building. Antennas and flag poles are not included. UC = under construction, number indicates year of expected completion. 1. World Trade Center twin towers of New York City ranked fifth and sixth (at 1,368 ft and 1,362 ft) on this list until their destruction on Sept. 11, 2001. *Source:* Council on Tall Buildings and Urban Habitat, Lehigh University, 2003.

World's Tallest Towers[1]

Tower, city	Year	Height (m)	Height (ft)
Canadian National Tower, Toronto, Canada	1975	553	1,815
Ostankino Tower, Moscow, Russia	1967	537	1,762
Oriental Pearl Tower, Shanghai, China	1995	468	1,535
Menara Kuala Lumpur, Kuala Lumpur, Malaysia	1996	421	1,403
Central Radio & TV Tower, Beijing, China	1992	417	1,369
Tianjin TV Tower, Tianjin, China	1991	415	1,362
LORAN-C Tower, Port Clarence, Alaska, U.S.	1962	411	1,350
Tashkent Tower, Tashkent, Uzbekistan	1985	375	1,230
Liberation Tower, Kuwait City, Kuwait	1996	370	1,214
Fernsehturm Tower, Berlin, Germany	1969	365	1,198
Stratosphere Tower, Las Vegas, United States	1996	350	1,149
Tokyo Tower, Tokyo, Japan	1959	333	1,092
Skytower, Auckland, New Zealand	1997	328	1,076
AMP Tower Centrepoint, Sydney, Australia	1981	305	1,001
Eiffel Tower, Paris, France	1889	300	984

NOTE: Height is to the structural top of the tower. This includes spires, but does not include television antennas, radio antennas, or flag poles. 1. A tower differs from a building in that the latter is considered to be a structure that is designed for residential, business, or manufacturing purposes. Also, an essential characteristic of a building is that it has floors. The structures listed here are principally telecommunications towers, and while they may have observation decks or restaurants, they do not have floors going all the way up. *Source*: Council on Tall Buildings and Urban Habitat, Lehigh University, and other sources.

Notable Modern Bridges

Name	Location	Length of main span feet	Length of main span meters	Year completed
Suspension	**United States**			
Verrazano-Narrows	Lower New York Bay	4,260	1,298	1964
Golden Gate	San Francisco Bay	4,200	1,280	1937
Mackinac	Mackinac Straits, Mich.	3,800	1,158	1957
George Washington	Hudson River at New York City	3,500	1,067	1931
Tacoma Narrows II	Puget Sound at Tacoma, Wash.	2,800	853	1950
San Francisco–Oakland Bay[1]	San Francisco Bay	2,310	704	1936
Bronx-Whitestone	East River, New York City	2,300	701	1939
Delaware Memorial[1]	Delaware River near Wilmington, Del.	2,150	655	1951, 1968
Seaway Skyway	St. Lawrence River at Ogdensburg, N.Y.	2,150	655	1960
Walt Whitman	Delaware River at Philadelphia	2,000	610	1957
Ambassador International	Detroit River at Detroit	1,850	564	1929
Throgs Neck	East River, New York City	1,800	549	1961
Benjamin Franklin	Delaware River at Philadelphia	1,750	533	1926
William Preston Lane, Jr.[1]	Chesapeake Bay, Md.	1,600	488	1952, 1973
Brooklyn Bridge	East River, New York City	1,596	486	1883
St. Johns Bridge	Portland, Ore.	1,207	368	1931
Royal Gorge	Arkansas River, Colo.	1,053	321	1929
Wheeling Bridge	Ohio River, Wheeling, W.Va.	1,010	308	1847
	International			
Akashi Kaikyo	Hyogo, Japan	6,529	1,990	1998
Izmit Bay	Marmara Sea, Turkey	5,472	1,668	UC
Storebælt	Denmark	5,328	1,624	1998
Humber	Humberside, England	4,626	1,410	1981
Jiangyin	Yangtze River, China	4,543	1,385	1999
Tsing Ma	Hong Kong	4,518	1,377	1997
Höga Kusten (High Coast)	Västernorrland, Sweden	3,969	1,210	1997
Minami Bisan-Seto	Japan	3,609	1,100	1988
Second Bosporus	Istanbul, Turkey	3,576	1,090	1988
First Bosporus	Istanbul, Turkey	3,524	1,074	1973
Third Kurushima	Japan	3,379	1,030	1999
Second Kurushima	Japan	3,346	1,020	1999
Ponte 25 de Abril	Tagus River at Lisbon, Portugal	3,323	1,013	1966
Forth Road	Queensferry, Scotland	3,300	1,006	1964
Kita Bisan-Seto	Japan	3,248	990	1988
Severn	Severn River at Beachley, England	3,240	988	1966
Yichang	Yangtze River, Hubei Province, China	3,150	960	2001
Shimotsui Straits	Japan	3,084	940	1988
Xiling Yangtze	Three Gorges Dam, China	2,952	900	1996
Tigergate (Humen)	Pearl River, Guangdong Province, China	2,913	888	1997
Ohnaruto	Japan	2,874	876	1988
Pierre Laporte	Quebec, Canada	2,190	668	1970
Cantilever	**United States**			
Commodore John Barry	Chester, Pa.	1,644	501	1974
Crescent City Connection[1]	Mississippi River, New Orleans, La.	1,576	480	1958, 1985
Transbay Bridge	San Francisco Bay	1,400	427	1936
	International			
Quebec Railway	Quebec, Canada	1,800	549	1917
Forth Railway[1]	Queensferry, Scotland	1,710	521	1890
Minato Ohashi	Osaka, Japan	1,673	510	1974
Howrah	Hooghly River at Calcutta, India	1,500	457	1943
Steel Arch	**United States**			
New River Gorge	Fayetteville, W. Va.	1,700	518	1977
Bayonne	Kill Van Kull at Bayonne, N.J.	1,675	510	1931
Fremont	Portland, Ore.	1,255	383	1973
Hell Gate	East River (Hell Gate), New York City	978	298	1916
	International			
Lupu Bridge	Shanghai, China	1,800	550	2003
Sydney Harbor	Sydney, Australia	1,670	509	1932
Zdákov	Vltava River, Czech Republic	1,244	380	1967
Port Mann	Fraser River at Vancouver, British Columbia	1,200	366	1964
Cable-Stayed	**United States**			
Dames Point	Jacksonville, Fla.	1,300	396	1988
Houston Ship Channel	Baytown, Tex.	1,250	381	1995

Name	Location	Length of main span feet	Length of main span meters	Year completed
Sidney Lanier	Brunswick River, Ga.	1,250	381	2003
Hale Boggs Memorial	Luling, La.	1,222	373	1983
Sunshine Skyway	Tampa, Fla.	1,200	366	1987
	International			
Tatara	Honshu-Shikoku, Japan	2,920	890	1999
Pont de Normandie	Le Havre, France	2,808	856	1995
Second Nanjing	Yangtze River, Nanjing, China	2,060	628	2001
Wuhan Third Yangtze	Wuhan, Hubei Province, China	2,028	618	2000
Qingzhou Minjiang	Fuzhou, China	1,985	605	1996
Yang Pu	Shanghai, China	1,975	602	1993
Xupu	Shanghai, China	1,936	590	1997
Meiko Chuo	Aichi, Japan	1,936	590	1997
Patras	Greece	1,837	560	UC04
Skarnsundet	near Trondheim, Norway	1,739	530	1991
Queshi	Guangdong Province, China	1,700	518	1999
Tsurumi Tsubasa	Kanagawa, Japan	1,673	510	1995
Jingzhou	Yangtze River, Hubei Province, China	1,640	500	2002
Oresund	Denmark/Sweden	1,614	492	2000
Ikuchi	Honshu-Shikoku, Japan	1,608	490	1991
Higashi Kobe	Hyogo, Japan	1,591	485	1994
Zhanjiang Bay	Guangdong Province, China	1,575	480	1998
Ting Kau	Hong Kong	1,558	475	1997
Seohae Grand	South Korea	1,542	470	2000
Alex Fraser	Vancouver, B.C., Canada	1,525	465	1986
Yokohama-ko-odan	Kanagawa, Japan	1,509	460	1989
Second Hooghly	Calcutta, India	1,500	457	1992
Second Severn Crossing	Severn River, England	1,496	456	1996
Dartford	Thames River, Dartford, England	1,476	450	1992
Dao Kanong	Chao Phraya River, Bangkok, Thailand	1,476	450	1987
Continuous Truss	**United States**			
Astoria	Columbia River, Ore.	1,232	376	1966
Croton Reservoir	Croton, N.Y.	1,052	321	1970
Ravenswood	Ohio River, Ravenswood, W. Va.	902	275	1981
Central	Ohio River, Newport, Ky.	850	259	1995
Dubuque	Mississippi River at Dubuque, Iowa	845	258	1943
	International			
Oshima	Oshima Island, Japan	1,066	325	1976
Tenmon	Kumamoto, Japan	984	300	1966
Kuronoseto	Nagashima-Kyushu, Japan	984	300	1974
Graf Spee	Germany	839	256	1936
Concrete Arch	**United States**			
Natchez Trace Pkwy.	Franklin, Tenn.	582	177	1994
Westinghouse	Pittsburgh, Pa.	460	140	1931
Jack's Run	Pittsburgh, Pa.	400	120	1930
Cappelen	Minneapolis, Minn.	400	120	1923
	International			
Wanxian	Wanxian, Sichuan Province, China	1,378	420	1997
Krk (I)	Krk, Croatia	1,280	390	1980
Jiangjiehe	Guizhou Province, China	1,083	330	1995
Gladesville	Parramatta River at Sydney, Australia	1,000	305	1964
Amizade	Paraná River at Foz do Iguassu, Brazil	951	290	1964
Bloukrans	Bloukrans River, South Africa	892	272	1983
Arrábida	Porto, Portugal	886	270	1963
Sandö	Angerman River at Kramfors, Sweden	866	264	1943
Confederation	Northumberland Strait, Canada	820	250	1997
Sibenik	Sibenik, Croatia	808	246	1966
Krk (II)	Krk, Croatia	800	244	1979
Fiumarella	Catanzaro, Italy	758	231	1961
Zaporozhe	Old Dnepr River, Ukraine	748	228	1952
Esla	Esla River at Zamora, Spain	645	197	1940
Segmental Construction	**United States**			
Jesse H. Jones Memorial	Houston Ship Channel, Tex.	750	228	1982

NOTES: UC = under construction in 2003. 1. Twin span. *Source:* Federal Highway Administration.

World's Highest Dams

Name	River, state, and country	Structural height: Feet	Structural height: Meters	Gross reservoir capacity: Thousands of acre feet	Gross reservoir capacity: Millions of cubic meters	Year completed
Rogun	Vakhsh, Tajikistan	1099	335	9,404	11,600	1985
Nurek	Vakhsh, Tajikistan	984	300	8,512	10,500	1980
Grande Dixence	Dixence, Switzerland	935	285	324	400	1962
Inguri	Inguri, Georgia	892	272	801	1,100	1984
Vaiont	Vaiont, Italy	859	262	137	169	1961
Manuel M. Torres	Grijalva, Mexico	856	261	1,346	1,660	1981
Tehri	Bhagirathi, India	856	261	2,869	3,540	UC
Alvaro Obregon	Mextiquic, Mexico	853	260	n.a.	n.a.	1926
Mauvoisin	Drance de Bagnes, Switzerland	820	250	146	180	1957
Alberto Lleras	Orinoco, Colombia	797	243	811	1,000	1989
Mica	Columbia, Canada	797	243	20,000	24,670	1972
Sayano-Shushensk	Yenisei, Russia	794	242	25,353	31,300	1980
Ertan	Yangtze/Yalong, China	787	240	4,702	5,800	1999
La Esmeralda	Batá, Colombia	778	237	661	815	1975
Kishau	Tons, India	774	236	1,946	2,400	1985
Oroville	Feather, Calif., U.S.	770	235	3,538	4,299	1968
El Cajón	Humuya, Honduras	768	234	4,580	5,650	1984
Chirkey	Sulak, Russia	764	233	2,252	2,780	1977
Bhakra	Sutlej, India	741	226	8,002	9,870	1963
Luzzone	Brenno di Luzzone, Switzerland	738	225	71	87	1963
Hoover	Colorado, Ariz./Nev., U.S.	732	223	28,500	35,154	1936
Contra	Verzasca, Switzerland	722	220	70	86	1965
Mratinje	Piva, Herzegovina	722	220	713	880	1973
Dworshak	North Fork Clearwater, Idaho, U.S.	717	219	3,453	4,259	1974
Glen Canyon	Colorado, Ariz., U.S.	710	216	27,000	33,304	1964

NOTES: UC = under construction in 2003. n.a. = not available. China's Three Gorges dam on the Yangtze River, begun in 1993 and expected to be completed in 2009, will be the world's largest and highest dam. *Source:* International Commission on Large Dams, *World Register of Dams 1998* and other sources.

World's Largest Dams

Dam	Location	Volume (thousands): Cubic meters	Volume (thousands): Cubic yards	Year completed
Syncrude Tailings	Canada	540,000	706,320	UC
Chapetón	Argentina	296,200	311,539	UC
Pati	Argentina	238,180	274,026	UC
New Cornelia Tailings	United States	209,500	274,026	1973
Tarbela	Pakistan	121,720	159,210	1976
Kambaratinsk	Kyrgyzstan	112,200	146,758	UC
Fort Peck	Montana	96,049	125,628	1940
Lower Usuma	Nigeria	93,000	121,644	1990
Cipasang	Indonesia	90,000	117,720	UC
Atatürk	Turkey	84,500	110,522	1990
Yacyretá-Apipe	Paraguay/Argentina	81,000	105,944	1998
Guri (Raul Leoni)	Venezuela	78,000	102,014	1986
Rogun	Tajikistan	75,500	98,750	1985
Oahe	South Dakota	70,339	92,000	1963
Mangla	Pakistan	65,651	85,872	1967
Gardiner	Canada	65,440	85,592	1968
Afsluitdijk	Netherlands	63,400	82,927	1932
Oroville	California	59,639	78,008	1968
San Luis	California	59,405	77,700	1967
Nurek	Tajikistan	58,000	75,861	1980
Garrison	North Dakota	50,843	66,500	1956
Cochiti	New Mexico	48,052	62,850	1975
Tabka (Thawra)	Syria	46,000	60,168	1976
Bennett W.A.C.	Canada	43,733	57,201	1967
Tucuruíi	Brazil	43,000	56,242	1984

NOTE: UC = under construction in 2003. China's Three Gorges dam on the Yangtze River, begun in 1993 and expected to be completed in 2009, will be the world's largest and highest dam. *Source:* Department of the Interior, Bureau of Reclamation and *International Water Power and Dam Construction*.

Famous Ship Canals

Name	Location	Length (miles)[1]	Width (feet)	Depth (feet)	Locks	Year opened
Albert	Belgium	80.0	53.0	16.5	6	1939
Amsterdam-Rhine	Netherlands	45.0	164.0	41.0	3	1952
Beaumont-Port Arthur	United States	40.0	200.0	34.0	—	1916
Canal du Midi	France	149.0	n.a.	n.a.	100	1692
Chesapeake and Delaware	United States	14.0	450.0	35.0	—	1829
Erie Canal	United States	363.0	70.0	7.0	82	1825
Grand Canal	China	1,085.0	n.a.	n.a.	n.a.	7th cent.
Gôta Canal	Sweden	240.0	n.a.	n.a.	58	1832
Houston	United States	50.0	(2)	40.0	—	1914
Kiel (Nord-Ostsee Kanal)	Germany	61.3	144.0	36.0	4	1895
Panama	Panama	50.7	110.0	41.0	12	1914
St. Lawrence Seaway	U.S. and Canada	2,400.0[3]	(4)	—	—	1959
Montreal to Prescott	U.S. and Canada	11.5	80.0	30.0	7	1959
Welland	Canada	27.5	80.0	27.0	8	1931
Sault Ste. Marie	Canada	1.2	60.0	16.8	1	1895
Sault Ste. Marie	United States	1.6	80.0	25.0	4	1915
Suez	Egypt	119.9[5]	1197.5	68.9	—	1869

1. Statute miles. 2. 300–400 ft. 3. From Montreal to Duluth. 4. 442–550 ft; there are 11.5 mi of locks, 80 ft wide and 30 ft deep. 5. From Port Said lighthouse to entrance channel in Suez roads. *Source:* American Society of Civil Engineers.

Notable Tunnels

Name	Location	Length mi	Length km	Year completed
Railroad, excluding subways				
Seikan	Tsugaru Strait, Japan	33.5	53.9	1988
Channel Tunnel[1]	English Channel, England–France	31.1	50.0	1994
Iwate Ichinohe	Tanigawa Mountains, Japan	16.0	25.8	2002
Daishimizu	Mikuni Mountain Range, Japan	13.8	22.2	1982
Simplon (I and II)	Alps, Switzerland–Italy	12.3	19.8	1906 & 1922
Vereina	Klosters–Sagliains, Switzerland	11.8	19.1	1999
Shin Kanmon	Kanmon Strait, Japan	11.6	18.7	1975
Apennine	Bologna–Florence, Italy	11.5	18.5	1934
Qinling I-II	Qinling Mountains, China	11.5	18.5	2002
Rokkô	Rokkô Mountain, Japan	10.1	16.3	1972
Furka Base	Andermatt–Brig, Switzerland	9.6	15.4	1982
Haruna	Gunma Prefecture, Japan	9.5	15.4	1982
Severomuyskiy	Baikal–Amur, Russia	9.5	15.3	2001
Gorigamine	Takasaki–Nagano, Japan	9.4	15.2	1997
Monte Santomarco	Paola–Cosenza, Italy	9.3	15.0	1987
St. Gotthard	Swiss Alps	9.3	15.0	1882
Nakayama	Nakayama Pass, Hokkaido, Japan	9.2	14.9	1982
Lötschberg	Swiss Alps	9.1	14.6	1913
Mount MacDonald	Rogers Pass, Glacier Nat'l Park, Canada	9.1	14.6	1989
Romeriksporten	Oslo–Gardermoen airport, Norway	9.1	14.6	1999
Vehicular				
Laerdal	Laerdal–Aurland, Norway	15.2	24.5	2000
St. Gotthard	Alps, Switzerland	10.2	16.4	1980
Arlberg	Austrian Alps	8.7	14.0	1979
Fréjus	French Alps	8.0	12.9	1980
Mt. Blanc	Alps, France–Italy	7.0	11.3	1965
Gudvanga	Bergen–Oslo, Norway	7.1	11.4	1991
Folgefonn	Odda–Gjerde, Norway	6.9	11.2	2001
Kanetsu (south-bound)	Tokyo–Niigata, Japan	6.9	11.1	1991
Kanetsu (north-bound)	Tokyo–Niigata, Japan	6.8	10.9	1985
Gran Sasso d'Italia (East)	Abruzzo, Italy	6.3	10.2	1984
Gran Sasso d'Italia (West)	Abruzzo, Italy	6.3	10.2	1995
Aqualine Expressway	Tokyo Bay, Japan	5.9	9.5	1997
Mt. Ena	Japan Alps, Japan	5.3	8.5	1976[2]
Westerschelde	Zeeuwsch-Vlaanderen–Zuid-Beveland, Netherlands	4.1	6.6	2003
Great St. Bernard	Alps, Switzerland-Italy	3.4	5.5	1964

1. Three-tunnel system including two rail tunnels (one carries passengers from England to France, the other from France to England) and a central service tunnel. 2. Parallel tunnel begun in 1976. *Source:* American Society of Civil Engineers and International Bridge, Tunnel & Turnpike Association, Wittiker's. Web: 222.home.no.net/lotsberg/data/rail.html.

Conversion Factors

To change	To	Multiply by	To change	To	Multiply by
acres	square feet	43,560	liters	quarts (liquid)	1.0567
acres	square miles	.001562	meters	feet	3.2808
atmospheres	cms. of mercury	76	meters	miles	.0006214
Btu	kilowatt-hour	.0002931	meters	yards	1.0936
Btu/hour	watts	.2931	metric tons	tons (long)	.9842
bushels	cubic inches	2150.4	metric tons	tons (short)	1.1023
centimeters	inches	.3937	miles	kilometers	1.6093
centimeters	feet	.03281	miles	feet	5280
cubic feet	cubic meters	.0283	miles (nautical)	miles (statute)	1.1516
cubic meters	cubic feet	35.3145	miles (statute)	miles (nautical)	.8684
cubic meters	cubic yards	1.3079	miles/hour	feet/minute	88
cubic yards	cubic meters	.7646	millimeters	inches	.0394
fathoms	feet	6.0	ounces (avdp)	grams	28.3495
feet	meters	.3048	ounces	pounds	.0625
feet	miles (nautical)	.0001645	ounces (troy)	ounces (avdp)	1.09714
feet	miles (statute)	.0001894	pecks	liters	8.8096
feet/second	miles/hour	.6818	pints (dry)	liters	.5506
furlongs	feet	660.0	pints (liquid)	liters	.4732
furlongs	miles	.125	pounds (ap or troy)	kilograms	.3732
gallons (U.S.)	liters	3.7853	pounds (avdp)	kilograms	.4536
grains	grams	.0648	pounds	ounces	16
grams	ounces (avdp)	.0353	quarts (dry)	liters	1.1012
grams	pounds	.002205	quarts (liquid)	liters	.9463
hectares	acres	2.4710	radians	degrees	57.30
hectoliters	bushels (U.S.)	2.8378	rods	meters	5.029
horsepower	watts	745.7	rods	feet	16.5
horsepower	Btu/hour	2,547	square feet	square meters	.0929
hours	days	.04167	square kilometers	square miles	.3861
inches	millimeters	25.4000	square meters	square feet	10.7639
inches	centimeters	2.5400	square miles	square kilometers	2.5900
kilograms	pounds (avdp or troy)	2.2046	square yards	square meters	.8361
kilometers	miles	.6214	tons (long)	metric tons	1.016
kilowatt-hour	Btu	3412	tons (short)	metric tons	.9072
knots	nautical miles/hour	1.0	tons (long)	pounds	2240
knots	statute miles/hour	1.151	tons (short)	pounds	2000
liters	gallons (U.S.)	.2642	watts	Btu/hour	3.4121
liters	pints (dry)	1.8162	watts	horsepower	.001341
liters	pints (liquid)	2.1134	yards	meters	.9144
liters	quarts (dry)	.9081	yards	miles	.0005682

NOTE: avdp = avoirdupois weight, ap = apothecaries' weight. *See also* p.539.

Fahrenheit and Celsius (Centigrade) Scales

°Celsius	°Fahrenheit	°Celsius	°Fahrenheit
–273.15	–459.67	30	86
–250	–418	35	95
–200	–328	40	104
–150	–238	45	113
–100	–148	50	122
–50	–58	55	131
–40	–40	60	140
–30	–22	65	149
–20	–4	70	158
–10	14	75	167
0	32	80	176
5	41	85	185
10	50	90	194
15	59	95	203
20	68	100	212
25	77		

Zero on the Fahrenheit scale represents the temperature produced by the mixing of equal weights of snow and common salt.

	°Fahrenheit	°Celsius
Boiling point of water	212°	100°
Freezing point of water	32°	0°
Absolute zero	–459.6°	–273.1°

Absolute zero is theoretically the lowest possible temperature, the point at which all molecular motion would cease.

To convert Fahrenheit to Celsius (Centigrade), subtract 32 and divide by 1.8.

To convert Celsius (Centigrade) to Fahrenheit, multiply by 1.8 and add 32.

Kelvin Scale

Absolute zero, –273.15° on the Celsius (Centigrade) scale, is 0 Kelvin. Thus, Kelvin is equivalent to Celsius plus 273.15. The freezing point of water, 0°C and 32°F, is 273.15K. The conversion formula is K = C° + 273.15.

Cardinal, Ordinal, and Nominal Numbers

Cardinal numbers, known as the "counting numbers," indicate quantity. **Ordinal numbers** indicate the order or rank of things in a set (e.g., sixth in line; fourth place). **Nominal numbers** name or identify something (e.g., a zip code or a player on a team.) They do not show quantity or rank.

Roman Numerals

Roman numerals are expressed by letters of the alphabet and are rarely used today except for formality or variety. There are four basic principles for reading Roman numerals:

1. A letter repeated once or twice repeats its value that many times (XXX = 30, CC = 200, etc.).
2. One or more letters placed after another letter of greater value increases the greater value by the amount of the smaller (VI = 6, LXX = 70, MCC = 1200, etc.).
3. A letter placed before another letter of greater value decreases the greater value by the amount of the smaller (IV = 4, XC = 90, CM = 900, etc.). Several rules apply for subtraction: (a) only subtract powers of ten (I, X, or C, but not V or L); (b) only subtract one number from another; (c) do not subtract a number from one that is more than 10 times greater (that is, you can subtract 1 from 10 [IX] but not from 20—there is no such number as IXX).
4. A bar placed on top of a letter or string of letters increases the numeral's value by 1,000 times (XV = 15, $\overline{XV}$ = 15,000).

Letter	Value	Letter	Value	Letter	Value	Letter	Value	Letter	Value
I	1	VII	7	XL	40	C	100	$\overline{C}$	100,000
II	2	VIII	8	L	50	D	500	$\overline{D}$	500,000
III	3	IX	9	LX	60	M	1,000	$\overline{M}$	1,000,000
IV	4	X	10	LXX	70	$\overline{V}$	5,000		
V	5	XX	20	LXXX	80	$\overline{X}$	10,000		
VI	6	XXX	30	XC	90	$\overline{L}$	50,000		

Mean and Median

The arithmetic mean, also called the average, of a series of quantities is obtained by finding the sum of the quantities and dividing it by the number of quantities. In the series 1, 3, 5, 18, 19, 20, 25, the mean or average is 13—in other words, 91 divided by 7.

The median of a series is that point which so divides it that half the quantities are on one side, half on the other. In the above series, the median is 18.

The median often better expresses the common-run, since it is not, as is the mean, affected by an excessively high or low figure. In the series 1, 3, 4, 7, 55, the median of 4 is a truer expression of the common-run than is the mean of 14.

Prime Numbers between 1 and 1,000

	2	3	5	7	11	13	17	19	23
29	31	37	41	43	47	53	59	61	67
71	73	79	83	89	97	101	103	107	109
113	127	131	137	139	149	151	157	163	167
173	179	181	191	193	197	199	211	223	227
229	233	239	241	251	257	263	269	271	277
281	283	293	307	311	313	317	331	337	347
349	353	359	367	373	379	383	389	397	401
409	419	421	431	433	439	443	449	457	461
463	467	479	487	491	499	503	509	521	523
541	547	557	563	569	571	577	587	593	599
601	607	613	617	619	631	641	643	647	653
659	661	673	677	683	691	701	709	719	727
733	739	743	751	757	761	769	773	787	797
809	811	821	823	827	829	839	853	857	859
863	877	881	883	887	907	911	919	929	937
941	947	953	967	971	977	983	991	997	(1009)

Portraits and Designs of U.S. Paper Currency

Currency[1]	Portrait	Design on back
$1	Washington	ONE between obverse and reverse of Great Seal of U.S.
$2[2]	Jefferson	Monticello
$2[3]	Jefferson	"The Signing of the Declaration of Independence"
$5[4]	Lincoln	Lincoln Memorial
$10[4]	Hamilton	U.S. Treasury Building
$20[5]	Jackson	White House
$50[6]	Grant	U.S. Capitol
$100[7]	Franklin	Independence Hall
$500	McKinley	Ornate FIVE HUNDRED
$1,000	Cleveland	Ornate ONE THOUSAND
$5,000	Madison	Ornate FIVE THOUSAND
$10,000	Chase	Ornate TEN THOUSAND
$100,000[8]	Wilson	Ornate ONE HUNDRED THOUSAND

1. Denominations of $500 and higher were discontinued in 1969. 2. Discontinued in 1966. 3. New issue, April 1976. 4. New issue, May 2000. 5. New issue, Sept. 1998. 6. New issue, fall 1997. 7. New issue, March 1996. 8. For use only in transactions between Federal Reserve System and Treasury Department.

New $20 Bill

The U.S. Treasury adopted a new design for the $20 dollar bill in fall 2003. The new bill incorporates security features introduced in the 1990s, including a watermark and a security thread—both visible when the bill is held up to the light—and color shifting ink. Other changes include the addition of background colors (green, peach, and light blue), and an enlargement of Andrew Jackson's portrait. The U.S. Treasury redesigns bills every 5 to 10 years to make counterfeiting more difficult. The government estimates that one out of every ten thousand bills is counterfeit, a low percentage, but that means upwards of $44 million dollars in use are fake. A redesigned $50, featuring Ulysses S. Grant, and a new $100, featuring Benjamin Franklin, will follow in 2004 and 2005.

New Quarters and Dollar Coin

The 50 State Quarters Program Act began in 1999 and is expected to run until 2008, with five new quarters released every year over ten years. The quarters are being released in the order that the states joined the union. 700 million copies of each quarter will be produced. Each quarter will feature a different state design on the back

In 2000, a new dollar coin, featuring the Shoshone guide Sacagawea, replaced the Susan B. Anthony coin, whose reserves are running low.

State	Date of statehood	Year of Issue	Design
Delaware	Dec. 7, 1787	1999	Caesar Rodney's horseback ride
Pennsylvania	Dec. 12, 1787	1999	Commonwealth statue, keystone, and outline of state
New Jersey	Dec. 18, 1787	1999	Washington crossing the Delaware River
Georgia	Jan. 2, 1788	1999	Peach, Live Oak, and outline of state
Connecticut	Jan. 9, 1788	1999	The Charter Oak
Massachusetts	Feb. 6, 1788	2000	Minuteman statue and outline of state
Maryland	April 28, 1788	2000	Maryland Statehouse and White Oak
South Carolina	May 23, 1788	2000	Palmetto tree, Carolina wren, and Yellow Jessamine
New Hampshire	June 21, 1788	2000	Old Man of the Mountain rock formation
Virginia	June 25, 1788	2000	First three ships to Jamestown
New York	July 26, 1788	2001	Statue of Liberty, state outline, the words, "Gateway to Freedom," 11 stars
North Carolina	Nov. 21, 1789	2001	First flight at Kitty Hawk
Rhode Island	May 29, 1790	2001	A sailboat on the open sea, commemorating the "Ocean State"
Vermont	March 4, 1791	2001	Camel's Hump Mountain, maple trees with sap buckets
Kentucky	June 1, 1792	2001	Federal Hill, or "My Old Kentucky Home," race horse behind a fence
Tennessee	June 1, 1796	2002	Fiddle, trumpet, guitar, and musical score
Ohio	March 1, 1803	2002	Early airplane, astronaut, and state outline
Louisiana	April 30, 1812	2002	Pelican, horn with musical notes, and outline of Louisiana Purchase
Indiana	Dec. 11, 1816	2002	Race car and state outline
Mississippi	Dec. 10, 1817	2002	Blossoms and leaves of two magnolias
Illinois	Dec. 3, 1818	2003	Abraham Lincoln and state outline
Alabama	Dec. 14, 1819	2003	Helen Keller, with name in English and Braille
Maine	March 15, 1820	2003	The Pemaquid Point Light House and a schooner
Missouri	Aug. 10, 1821	2003	Lewis and Clark travelling down the Missouri River
Arkansas	June 15, 1836	2003	Rice stalks, a diamond, and a mallard, representing the "Natural State"

Customary U.S. Weights and Measures

Linear Measure

12 inches (in.) = 1 foot (ft.)
3 feet = 1 yard (yd)
5½ yards = 1 rod (rd), pole, or perch (16½ ft.)
40 rods = 1 furlong (fur) = 220 yds = 660 ft.
8 furlongs = 1 statute mile (mi.) = 1,760 yds = 5,280 ft.
3 land miles = 1 league
5,280 feet = 1 statute or land mile
6,076.11549 feet = 1 international nautical mile

Area Measure

144 square inches = 1 sq ft.
9 square feet = 1 sq yd = 1,296 sq in.
30¼ square yards = 1 sq rd = 272¼ sq ft.
160 square rods = 1 acre = 4,840 sq yds = 43,560 sq ft.
640 acres = 1 sq mi.
1 mile square = 1 section (of land)
6 miles square = 1 township = 36 sections = 36 sq mi.

Cubic Measure

1,728 cubic inches = 1 cu ft.
27 cubic feet = 1 cu yd

Liquid Measure

When necessary to distinguish the liquid pint or quart from the dry pint or quart, the word "liquid" or the abbreviation "liq" should be used in combination with the name or abbreviation of the liquid unit.

4 gills (gi) = 1 pint (pt) (= 28.875 cu in.)
2 pints = 1 quart (qt) (= 57.75 cu in.)
4 quarts = 1 gallon (gal) (= 231 cu in.) = 8 pts = 32 gills

Apothecaries' Fluid Measure

60 minims (min.) = 1 fluid dram (fl dr) (= 0.2256 cu in.)
8 fluid drams = 1 fluid ounce (fl oz) (= 1.8047 cu in.)
16 fluid ounces = 1 pt (= 28.875 cu in.) = 128 fl drs
2 pints = 1 qt (= 57.75 cu in.) = 32 fl oz = 256 fl drs
4 quarts = 1 gal (= 231 cu in.) = 128 fl oz = 1,024 fl drs

Avoirdupois Weight

When necessary to distinguish the avoirdupois dram from the apothecaries' dram, or to distinguish the avoirdupois dram or ounce from the fluid dram or ounce, or to distinguish the avoirdupois ounce or pound from the troy or apothecaries' ounce or pound, the word "avoirdupois" or the abbreviation "avdp" should be used in combination with the name or abbreviation of the avoirdupois unit. (The "grain" is the same in avoirdupois, troy, and apothecaries' weights.)

27 11/32 grains = 1 dram (dr)
16 drams = 1 oz = 437½ grains
16 ounces = 1 lb = 256 drams = 7,000 grains
100 pounds = 1 hundredweight (cwt)[1]
20 hundredweights = 1 ton (tn) = 2,000 lbs[1]

In "gross" or "long" measure, the following values are recognized:

112 pounds = 1 gross or long cwt[1]
20 gross or long hundredweights = 1 gross or long ton = 2,240 lbs[1]

1. When the terms "hundredweight" and "ton" are used unmodified, they are commonly understood to mean the 100-pound hundredweight and the 2,000-pound ton, respectively; these units may be designated "net" or "short" when necessary to distinguish them from the corresponding units in gross or long measure.

Dry Measure

When necessary to distinguish the dry pint or quart from the liquid pint or quart, the word "dry" should be used in combination with the name or abbreviation of the dry unit.

2 pints = 1 qt (= 67.2006 cu in.)
8 quarts = 1 peck (pk) (= 537.605 cu in.) = 16 pts
4 pecks = 1 bushel (bu) (= 2,150.42 cu in.) = 32 qts

Apothecaries' Weight

20 grains = 1 scruple (s ap)
3 scruples = 1 dram apothecaries' (dr ap) = 60 grains
8 drams apothecaries' = 1 ounce apothecaries' (oz ap) = 24 scruples = 480 grains
12 ounces apothecaries' = 1 pound apothecaries' (lb ap) = 96 drams apothecaries' = 288 scruples = 5,760 grains

Units of Circular Measure

Second (″) = —
Minute (′) = 60 seconds
Degree (°) = 60 minutes
Right angle = 90 degrees
Straight angle = 180 degrees
Circle = 360 degrees

Troy Weight

24 grains = 1 pennyweight (dwt)
20 pennyweights = 1 ounce troy (oz t) = 480 grains
12 ounces troy = 1 pound troy (lb t) = 240 pennyweights = 5,760 grains

Gunter's or Surveyor's Chain Measure

7.92 inches = 1 link (li)
100 links = 1 chain (ch) = 4 rods = 66 ft.
80 chains = 1 statute mile = 320 rods = 5,280 ft.

The International System (Metric)

Source: Department of Commerce, National Bureau of Standards.

The International System of Units is a modernized version of the metric system, established by international agreement, that provides a logical and interconnected framework for all measurements in science, industry, and commerce. The system is built on a foundation of seven basic units, and all other units are derived from them. (Use of metric weights and measures was legalized in the United States in 1866, and our customary units of weights and measures are defined in terms of the meter and kilogram.)

Length. Meter. Up until 1983, the meter was defined as 1,650,763.73 wavelengths in a vacuum of the orange-red line of the spectrum of krypton-86. Since then, it is equal to the distance traveled by light in a vacuum in 1/299,792,45 of a second.

Time. Second. The second is defined as the duration of 9,192,631,770 cycles of the radiation associated with a specified transition of the cesium-133 atom.

Mass. Kilogram. The standard for the kilogram is a cylinder of platinum-iridium alloy kept by the International Bureau of Weights and Measures at Paris. A duplicate at the National Bureau of Standards serves as the mass standard for the United States. The kilogram is the only base unit still defined by a physical object.

Temperature. Kelvin. The Kelvin is defined as the fraction 1/273.16 of the thermodynamic temperature of the triple point of water; that is, the point at which water forms an interface of solid, liquid, and vapor. This is defined as 0.01°C on the Centigrade or Celsius scale and 32.02°F on the Fahrenheit scale. The temperature 0°K is called "absolute zero."

Electric Current. Ampere. The ampere is defined as that current that, if maintained in each of two long parallel wires separated by one meter in free space, would produce a force between the two wires (due to their magnetic fields) of 2×10^{-7} newton for each meter of length. (A newton is the unit of force that when applied to one kilogram mass would experience an acceleration of one meter per second per second.)

Luminous Intensity. Candela. The candela is defined as the luminous intensity of 1/600,000 of a square meter of a cavity at the temperature of freezing platinum (2,042°K).

Amount of Substance. Mole. The mole is the amount of substance of a system that contains as many elementary entities as there are atoms in 0.012 kilogram of carbon-12.

Tables of Metric Weights and Measures

Linear Measure

10 millimeters (mm) = 1 centimeter (cm)
10 centimeters = 1 decimeter (dm) = 100 millimeters
10 decimeters = 1 meter (m) = 1,000 millimeters
10 meters = 1 dekameter (dam)
10 dekameters = 1 hectometer (hm) = 100 meters
10 hectometers = 1 kilometer (km) = 1,000 meters

Volume Measure

10 milliliters (ml) = 1 centiliter (cl)
10 centiliters = 1 deciliter (dl) = 100 milliliters
10 deciliters = 1 liter (l) = 1,000 milliliters
10 liters = 1 dekaliter (dal)
10 dekaliters = 1 hectoliter (hl) = 100 liters
10 hectoliters = 1 kiloliter (kl) = 1,000 liters

Area Measure

100 square millimeters (mm^2) = 1 sq centimeter (cm^2)
10,000 square centimeters = 1 sq meter (m^2) = 1,000,000 sq millimeters
100 square meters = 1 are (a)
100 ares = 1 hectare (ha) = 10,000 sq meters
100 hectares = 1 sq kilometer (km^2) = 1,000,000 sq meters

Cubic Measure

1,000 cubic millimeters (mm^3) = 1 cu centimeter (cm^3)
1,000 cubic centimeters = 1 cu decimeter (dm^3) = 1,000,000 cu millimeters
1,000 cubic decimeters = 1 cu meter (m^3) = 1 stere = 1,000,000 cu centimeters = 1,000,000,000 cu millimeters

Weight

10 milligrams (mg) = 1 centigram (cg)
10 centigrams = 1 decigram (dg) = 100 milligrams
10 decigrams = 1 gram (g) = 1,000 milligrams
10 grams = 1 dekagram (dag)
10 dekagrams = 1 hectogram (hg) = 100 grams
10 hectograms = 1 kilogram (kg) = 1,000 grams
1,000 kilograms = 1 metric ton (t)

Metric and U.S. Equivalents

1 angstrom[1] (light wave measurement)	0.1 millimicron 0.000 1 micron 0.000 000 1 millimeter 0.000 000 004 inch
1 cable's length	120 fathoms 720 feet 219.456 meters
1 centimeter	0.3937 inch
1 decimeter	3.937 inches
1 dekameter	32.808 feet
1 fathom	6 feet 1.8288 meters
1 foot	0.3048 meter
1 furlong	10 chains (surveyor's) 660 feet 220 yards ⅛ statute mile 201.168 meters
1 inch	2.54 centimeters
1 kilometer	0.621 mile
1 league (land)	3 statute miles 4.828 kilometers
1 meter	39.37 inches 1.094 yards
1 micron	0.001 millimeter 0.000 039 37 inch
1 mil	0.001 inch 0.025 4 millimeter
1 mile (statute or land)	5,280 feet 1.609 kilometers
1 mile (nautical international)	1.852 kilometers 1.151 statute miles 0.999 U.S. nautical miles
1 millimeter	0.03937 inch
1 millimicron (m+GRKm)	0.001 micron 0.000 000 039 37 inch
1 nanometer	0.001 micrometer or 0.000 000 039 37 inch
1 point (typography)	0.013 837 inch 1⁄72 inch (approximately) 0.351 millimeter
1 rod, pole, or perch	16½ feet 5.0292 meters
1 yard	0.9144 meter

Areas or Surfaces

1 acre	43,560 square feet 4,840 square yards 0.405 hectare
1 are	119.599 square yards 0.025 acre
1 hectare	2.471 acres
1 square centimeter	0.155 square inch
1 square decimeter	15.5 square inches
1 square foot	929.030 square centimeters
1 square inch	6.4516 square centimeters
1 square kilometer	0.386 square mile 247.105 acres
1 square meter	1.196 square yards 10.764 square feet
1 square mile	258.999 hectares
1 square millimeter	0.002 square inch
1 square rod, square pole or square perch	25.293 square meters
1 square yard	0.836 square meters

Capacities or Volumes

1 barrel, liquid	31 to 42 gallons[2]
1 bushel (U.S.) struck measure[3]	2,150.42 cubic inches 35.238 liters
1 bushel, heaped (U.S.)	2,747.715 cubic inches 1.278 bushels, struck measure[4]
1 cord (firewood)	128 cubic feet
1 cubic centimeter	0.061 cubic inch
1 cubic decimeter	61.024 cubic inches
1 cubic foot	7.481 gallons 28.316 cubic decimeters
1 cubic inch	0.554 fluid ounce 4.433 fluid drams 16.387 cubic centimeters
1 cubic meter	1.308 cubic yards
1 cubic yard	0.765 cubic meter
1 cup, measuring	8 fluid ounces ½ liquid pint
1 dram, fluid or liquid (U.S.)	⅛ fluid ounces 0.226 cubic inch 3.697 milliliters 1.041 British fluid drachms
1 dekaliter	2.642 gallons 1.135 pecks
1 gallon (U.S.)	231 cubic inches 3.785 liters 0.833 British gallon 128 U.S. fluid ounces
1 gallon (British Imperial)	277.42 cubic inches 1.201 U.S. gallons 4.546 liters 160 British fluid ounces
1 hectoliter	26.418 gallons 2.838 bushels
1 liter	1.057 liquid quarts 0.908 dry quart 61.024 cubic inches
1 milliliter	0.271 fluid dram 16.231 minims 0.061 cubic inch
1 ounce, fluid or liquid (U.S.)	1.805 cubic inch 29.574 milliliters 1.041 British fluid ounces
1 peck	8.810 liters
1 pint, dry	33.600 cubic inches 0.551 liter
1 pint, liquid	28.875 cubic inches 0.473 liter
1 quart, dry (U.S.)	67.201 cubic inches 1.101 liters 0.969 British quart

1 quart, liquid (U.S.)	57.75 cubic inches 0.946 liter 0.833 British quart
1 quart (British)	69.354 cubic inches 1.032 U.S. dry quarts 1.201 U.S. liquid quarts
1 tablespoon, measuring	3 teaspoons 4 fluid drams ½ fluid ounce
1 teaspoon, measuring	⅓ tablespoon 1⅓ fluid drams
1 carat	200 milligrams 3.086 grains
1 dram, apothecaries'	60 grains 3.888 grams
1 dram, avoirdupois	27 11/32 (=27.344) grains 1.772 grams
1 grain	64.798 91 milligrams
1 gram	15.432 grains 0.035 avoirdupois ounce
1 kilogram	2.205 pounds
1 microgram (µg—the Greek letter mu in combination with the letter g)	0.000 001 gram
1 milligram	0.015 grain
1 ounce, avoirdupois	437.5 grains 0.911 troy or apothecaries' ounce 28.350 grams
1 ounce, troy or apothecaries'	480 grains 1.097 avoirdupois ounces 31.103 grams
1 pennyweight	1.555 grams
1 point	0.01 carat 2 milligrams
1 pound, avoirdupois	7,000 grains 1.215 troy or apothecaries' pounds 453.592 37 grams
1 pound, troy or apothecaries'	5,760 grains 0.823 avoirdupois pound 373.242 grams
1 ton, gross or long[5]	2,240 pounds 1.12 net tons 1.016 metric tons
1 ton, metric	2,204.623 pounds 0.984 gross ton 1.102 net tons
1 ton, net or short	2,000 pounds 0.893 gross ton 0.907 metric ton

1. The angstrom is basically defined as 10^{-10} meter. 2. There is a variety of "barrels" established by law or usage. For example, federal taxes on fermented liquors are based on a barrel of 31 gallons; many state laws fix the "barrel for liquids" at 31½ gallons; one state fixes a 36-gallon barrel for cistern measurement; federal law recognizes a 40-gallon barrel for "proof spirits"; by custom, 42 gallons compose a barrel of crude oil or petroleum products for statistical purposes, and this equivalent is recognized "for liquids" by four states. 3. "Struck measure" refers to a struck, or level, bushel. It is the only official bushel measure in the UK. 4. Frequently recognized as 1¼ bushels, struck measure. 5. The gross or long ton is used commercially in the United States to only a limited extent, usually in restricted industrial fields. These units are the same as the British "ton."

Definitions of Gold Terminology

The term "fineness" defines a gold content in parts per thousand. For example, a gold nugget containing 885 parts of pure gold, 100 parts of silver, and 15 parts of copper would be considered 885-fine.

The word "karat" indicates the proportion of solid gold in an alloy based on a total of 24 parts. Thus, 14-karat (14K) gold indicates a composition of 14 parts of gold and 10 parts of other metals.

The term "gold-filled" is used to describe articles of jewelry made of base metal that are covered on one or more surfaces with a layer of gold alloy. No article having a gold alloy portion of less than one twentieth by weight may be marked "gold-filled." Articles may be marked "rolled gold plate" provided the proportional fraction and fineness designations are also shown.

Electroplated jewelry items carrying at least 7 millionths of an inch of gold on significant surfaces may be labeled "electroplate." Plate thicknesses less than this may be marked "gold-flashed" or "gold-washed."

Bolts and Screws: Conversion from Fractions of an Inch to Millimeters

Inch	mm	Inch	mm	Inch	mm	Inch	mm
1/64	0.40	17/64	6.75	33/64	13.10	49/64	19.45
1/32	0.79	9/32	7.14	17/32	13.50	25/32	19.84
3/64	1.19	19/64	7.54	35/64	13.90	51/64	20.24
1/16	1.59	5/16	7.94	9/16	14.29	13/16	20.64
5/64	1.98	21/64	8.33	37/64	14.69	53/64	21.03
3/32	2.38	11/32	8.73	19/32	15.08	27/32	21.43
7/64	2.78	23/64	9.13	39/64	15.48	55/64	21.83
1/8	3.18	3/8	9.53	5/8	15.88	7/8	22.23
9/64	3.57	25/64	9.92	41/64	16.27	57/64	22.62
5/32	3.97	13/32	10.32	21/32	16.67	29/32	23.02
11/64	4.37	27/64	10.72	43/64	17.06	59/64	23.42
3/16	4.76	7/16	11.11	11/16	17.46	15/16	23.81
13/64	5.16	29/64	11.51	45/64	17.86	61/64	24.21
7/32	5.56	15/32	11.91	23/32	18.26	31/32	24.61
15/64	5.95	31/64	12.30	47/64	18.65	63/64	25.00
1/4	6.35	1/2	12.70	3/4	19.05	1	25.40

Cooking Measurement Equivalents

1 tablespoon (tbsp) = 3 teaspoons (tsp)
1/16 cup = 1 tablespoon
1/8 cup = 2 tablespoons
1/6 cup = 2 tablespoons + 2 teaspoons
1/4 cup = 4 tablespoons
1/3 cup = 5 tablespoons + 1 teaspoon
3/8 cup = 6 tablespoons
1/2 cup = 8 tablespoons
2/3 cup = 10 tablespoons + 2 teaspoons
3/4 cup = 12 tablespoons
1 cup = 48 teaspoons
1 cup = 16 tablespoons
8 fluid ounces (fl oz) = 1 cup
1 pint (pt) = 2 cups
1 quart (qt) = 2 pints
4 cups = 1 quart
1 gallon (gal) = 4 quarts
16 ounces (oz) = 1 pound (lb)
1 milliliter (ml) = 1 cubic centimeter (cc)
1 inch (in) = 2.54 centimeters (cm)

Source: United States Dept. of Agriculture (USDA).

U.S.–Metric Cooking Conversions

U.S. to Metric

Capacity		Weight	
1/5 teaspoon	1 milliliter	1 oz	28 grams
1 teaspoon	5 ml	1 pound	454 grams
1 tablespoon	15 ml		
1 fluid oz	30 ml		
1/5 cup	47 ml		
1 cup	237 ml		
2 cups (1 pint)	473 ml		
4 cups (1 quart)	.95 liter		
4 quarts (1 gal.)	3.8 liters		

Metric to U.S.

Capacity		Weight	
1 milliliter	1/5 teaspoon	1 gram	.035 ounce
5 ml	1 teaspoon	100 grams	3.5 ounces
15 ml	1 tablespoon	500 grams	1.10 pounds
100 ml	3.4 fluid oz	1 kilogram	2.205 pounds
240 ml	1 cup		35 oz
1 liter	34 fluid oz		
	4.2 cups		
	2.1 pints		
	1.06 quarts		
	0.26 gallon		

Prefixes and Multiples

Prefix	Suffix	Equivalent	Multiple/submultiple	Prefix	Suffix	Equivalent	Multiple/submultiple
atto	a	quintillionth part	10^{-18}	deci	d	tenth part	10^{-1}
femto	f	quadrillionth part	10^{-15}	deka	da	tenfold	10
pico	p	trillionth part	10^{-12}	hecto	h	hundredfold	10^{2}
nano	n	billionth part	10^{-9}	kilo	k	thousandfold	10^{3}
micro	µ	millionth part	10^{-6}	mega	M	millionfold	10^{6}
milli	m	thousandth part	10^{-3}	giga	G	billionfold	10^{9}
centi	c	hundredth part	10^{-2}	tera	T	trillionfold	10^{12}

Common Formulas

CIRCUMFERENCE

Circle: $C = \pi d$, in which π is 3.1416 and *d* the diameter.

AREA

Triangle: $A = \frac{ab}{2}$, in which *a* is the base and *b* the height.

Square: $A = a^2$, in which *a* is one of the sides.

Rectangle: $A = ab$, in which *a* is the base and *b* the height.

Trapezoid: $A = \frac{h(a+b)}{2}$, in which *h* is the height, *a* the longer parallel side, and *b* the shorter.

Regular pentagon: $A = 1.720a^2$, in which *a* is one of the sides.

Regular hexagon: $A = 2.598a^2$, in which *a* is one of the sides.

Regular octagon: $A = 4.828a^2$, in which *a* is one of the sides.

Circle: $A = \pi r^2$, in which π is 3.1416 and *r* the radius.

VOLUME

Cube: $V = a^3$, in which *a* is one of the edges.

Rectangular prism: $V = abc$, in which *a* is the length, *b* is the width, and *c* the depth.

Pyramid: $V = \frac{Ah}{3}$, in which *A* is the area of the base and *h* the height.

Cylinder: $V = \pi r^2 h$, in which π is 3.1416, *r* the radius of the base, and *h* the height.

Cone: $V = \frac{\pi r^2 h}{3}$, in which π is 3.1416, *r* the radius of the base, and *h* the height.

Sphere: $V = \frac{4 \pi r^3}{3}$, in which π is 3.1416 and *r* the radius.

TEMPERATURE SCALES

Degrees Fahrenheit to Degrees Celsius:

$$T_C = \frac{5}{9}(T_F - 32)$$

Degrees Celsius to Degrees Fahrenheit:

$$T_F = \frac{9}{5} T_C + 32$$

Degrees Celsius to Kelvin:

$$T_K = T_C + 273.15$$

MISCELLANEOUS

Distance in feet traveled by falling body:
$d = 16t^2$, in which *t* is the time in seconds.

Speed of sound in feet per second through any given temperature of air:

$V = \frac{1087\sqrt{273 + t}}{16.52}$, in which *t* is the temperature Celsius.

Cost in cents of operation of electrical device:

$C = \frac{Wtc}{1000}$, in which *W* is the number of watts, *t* the time in hours, and *c* the cost in cents per kilowatt-hour.

Conversion of matter into energy (Einstein's Theorem): $E = mc^2$, in which *E* is the energy in ergs, *m* the mass of the matter in grams, and *c* the speed of light in centimeters per second:

$$(c^2 = 9 \times 10^{20})$$

Decimal Equivalents of Common Fractions

1/2	.5000	1/10	.1000	2/7	.2857	3/11	.2727	5/9	.5556	7/11	.6364
1/3	.3333	1/11	.0909	2/9	.2222	4/5	.8000	5/11	.4545	7/12	.5833
1/4	.2500	1/12	.0833	2/11	.1818	4/7	.5714	5/12	.4167	8/9	.8889
1/5	.2000	1/16	.0625	3/4	.7500	4/9	.4444	6/7	.8571	8/11	.7273
1/6	.1667	1/32	.0313	3/5	.6000	4/11	.3636	6/11	.5455	9/10	.9000
1/7	.1429	1/64	.0156	3/7	.4286	5/6	.8333	7/8	.8750	9/11	.8182
1/8	.1250	2/3	.6667	3/8	.3750	5/7	.7143	7/9	.7778	10/11	.9091
1/9	.1111	2/5	.4000	3/10	.3000	5/8	.6250	7/10	.7000	11/12	.9167

First Aid for Crossword Puzzlers

We cannot begin to list all the odd words you might encounter in your daily and Sunday crossword puzzles, for such words run into the thousands. But we have tried to include those that turn up most frequently, as well as many others that should be of help to you when you are unable to go any further.

We do not guarantee that the definitions in your puzzle will be exactly the same as ours, although we have checked every word with a standard dictionary and have followed its definition.

In nearly every case, we have used as the key word the principal noun of the definition, rather than any adjective, adjective phrase, or noun used as an adjective. And, to simplify your searching, we have grouped the words according to the number of spaces you have to fill.

Words of Two Letters

Ambary, DA
And (French, Latin), ET
Article (Arabic), AL
  (French), LA, LE, UN
  (Spanish), EL, LA, UN
At the (French), AU
  (Spanish), AL
Behold, LO
Bird: Hawaiian, OO
Birthplace: Abraham's, UR
Bone, OS
Buddha, FO
Butterfly: Peacock, IO
Champagne, AY
Chaos, NU
Chief: Burmese, BO
Coin: Roman, AS
  Siamese, AT
Concerning, RE
Dialect: Chinese, WU
Double (Egy. relig.), KA
Drama: Japanese, NO
Egg (comb. form), OO
Esker, OS
Eye (Scottish), EE
Factor: Amplification, MU
Fifty (Greek), NU
Fish: Carplike, ID
Force, OD
Forty (Greek), MU
From (French, Latin, Spanish), DE
  (Latin prefix), AB
From the (French), DU
God: Babylonian, EA, ZU
  Egyptian sun, RA
  Hindu unknown, KA
  Semitic, EL
Goddess: Babylonian, AI
  Greek Earth, GE
Gold (heraldry), OR
Gulf: Arctic, OB
Heart (Egy. relig.), AB
Indian: South American, GE
King: Of Bashan, OG
Language: Artificial, RO
  Assamese, AO
Lava: Hawaiian, AA
Letter: Greek, MU, NU, PI, XI
  Hebrew, HE, PE
Lily: Palm, TI
Measure: Chinese, HO, HU, KO, LI, MU, PU, TO, TU
  Japanese, GO, JO, MO, RI, SE, TO
  Netherlands, EL
  Portuguese, PE
  Siamese, WA
  Swedish, AM
  Type, EM, EN
  Vietnamese, LY
Monk: Buddhist, BO
Month: Jewish, AB
Mouth, OS
Mulberry: Indian, AL
Native: Burmese, WA
Note: Of scale, DO, FA, MI, LA, RE, TI
Of (French, Latin, Spanish), DE
Of the (French), DU
One (Scottish), AE
Pagoda: Chinese, TA
Plant: East Indian fiber, DA
Ridge: Sandy, AS, OS
River: Russian, OB
Sloth: Three-toed, AI
Soul (Egy. relig.), BA
Sound: Hindu mystic, OM
Suffix: Comparative, ER
To the: French, AU
  Spanish, AL
Tree: Buddhist sacred, BO
Tribe: Assamese, AO
Type: Jumbled, PI
Weight: Chinese, LI
  Danish, ES
  Japanese, MO
  Roman, AS
  Vietnamese, TA
Whirlwind: Faeroe Is., OE
Yes (German), JA
  (Italian, Spanish), SI
  (Russian), DA

Words of Three Letters

Adherent, IST
Again, BIS
Age, ERA
Antelope: African, GNU, KOB
Apricot: Japanese, UME
Article (German), DAS, DEM, DEN, DER, DES, DIE, EIN
  (French), LES, UNE
  (Spanish), LAS, LOS, UNA
Banana: Polynesian, FEI
Barge, HOY
Bass: African, IYO
Beak, NEB, NIB
Beard: Grain, AWN
Beetle: June, DOR
Being, ENS
Berry: Hawthorn, HAW
Beverage: Hawaiian, AVA
Bird: Australian, EMU
  Crowlike, JAY
  Extinct, MOA
  Fabulous, ROC
  Frigate, IWA
  Parson, POE, TUE, TUI
  Sea, AUK
Blackbird, ANI, ANO
Born, NEE
Bronze: Roman, AES
Bugle: Yellow, IVA
By way of, VIA
Canton: Swiss, URI
Cap: Turkish, FEZ
Catnip, NEP
Character: In "Faerie Queene," UNA
Coin (Money of account):
  Afghan, PUL
  Albanian, LEK
  Bulgarian, LEV, LEW
  French, ECU, SOU
  Guyanese, BIT
  Indian, PIE
  Japanese, SEN, YEN
  Korean, WON
  Lithuanian, LIT
  Macao, Timor, AVO
  Palestinian, MIL
  Persian, PUL
  Peruvian, SOL
  Rumanian, BAN, LEU, LEY
  Scandinavian, ORE
  Siamese, ATT
Collection: Facts, ANA
Commune: Belgian, ANS, ATH
  Netherlands, EDE, EPE
Community: Russian, MIR
Constellation: Southern, ARA
Contraction: Poetic, EEN, EER, OER
Covering: Apex of roof, EPI
Crab: Fiddler, UCA
Crag: Rocky, TOR
Cry: Crow, rook, raven, CAW
Cup: Wine, AMA
Cymbal, Oriental, TAL, ZEL
Disease: Silkworm, UJI
Division: Danish territorial, AMT
  Geologic, EON
Doctrine, ISM
Dowry, DOT
Dry (French), SEC
Dynasty: Chinese, CHI, HAN, SUI, WEI, YIN
Eagle: Sea, ERN
Earth (comb. form), GEO
Egg: Louse, NIT
Eggs: Fish, ROE
Emmet, ANT
Enzyme, ASE
Equal (comb. form), ISO
Extension: building, ELL
Far (comb. form), TEL
Farewell, AVE
Fiber: Palm, TAL
Finial, EPI
Fish: Carplike, IDE
  Pikelike, GAR
Flatfish, DAB
Fleur-de-lis, LIS, LYS
Food: Hawaiian, POI
Formerly, NEE
Friend (French), AMI
Game: Card, LOO
Garment: Camel-hair, ABA
Gateway, DAR
Gazelle: Tibetan, GOA
Genus: Ducks, AIX
  Grasses, POA
  Grasses (maize), ZEA
  Herbs or shrubs, IVA
  Lizards, UTA
  Rodents (incl. house mice), MUS
  Ruminants (incl. cattle), BOS
  Swine, SUS
Gibbon: Malay, LAR
God: Assyrian, SIN
  Babylonian, ABU, ANU, BEL, HEA, SIN, UTU
  Irish sea, LER
  Phrygian, MEN
  Polynesian, ORO
Goddess: Babylonian, AYA
  Etruscan, UNI
  Hindu, SRI, UMA, VAC
  Teutonic, RAN
Governor: Algerian, DEY
  Turkish, BEY
Grampus, ORC
Grape, UVA
Grass: Meadow, POA
Gypsy, ROM
Hail, AVE
Hare: Female, DOE
Hawthorn, HAW
Hay: Spread for drying, TED
Herb: Japanese, UDO
  Perennial, PIA
  Used for blue dye, WAD
Herd: Whales, GAM, POD
Hero: Spanish, CID
High (music), ALT
Honey (pharm.), MEL
Humorist: American, ADE
I (Latin), EGO
I love (Latin), AMO
Indian: Algonquin, FOX, SAC, WEA
  Chimakuan, HOH
  Keresan, SIA
  Mayan, MAM
  Shoshonean, UTE
  Siouan, KAW, OTO
  South American, ITE, ONA, URO, URU, YAO
  Tierra del Fuego, ONA
  Wakashan, AHT
Ingot, PIG
Inlet: Narrow, RIA
Island: Cyclades, IOS
  Dodecanese, COS, KOS
  (French), ILE
  River, AIT
Jackdaw, DAW

John (Gaelic), IAN
Keelbill, ANI, ANO
Kiln, OST
King: British legendary, LUD
Kobold, NIS
Lace: To make, TAT
Lamprey, EEL
Language: Artificial, IDO
Bantu, ILA
Siamese, LAO, TAI
Leaf: Palm, OLA, OLE
Leaving, ORT
Left: Cause to turn, HAW
Letter: Greek, CHI, ETA, PHI, PSI, RHO, TAU
Hebrew, MEM, NUN, SIN, TAV, VAU
Lettuce, COS
Life (comb. form), BIO
Lily: Palm, TOI
Lizard, EFT
Louse: Young, NIT
Love (Anglo-Irish), GRA
Lute: Oriental, TAR
Macaw: Brazilian, ARA
Marble, TAW
Match: Shooting (French), TIR
Meadow, LEA
Measure: Abyssinian, TAT
Algerian, PIK
Arabian, DEN, SAA
Belgian, VAT
Bulgarian, OKA, OKE
Chinese, FEN, TOU, YIN
Cloth, ELL
Cyprus, OKA, OKE, PIK
Czech, LAN, SAH
Danish, FOD, MIL, POT
Dominican Republic, ONA
Dutch, old, AAM
East Indian, KIT
Egyptian, APT, HEN, PIK, ROB
Electric, MHO, OHM
Energy, ERG
English, PIN
Estonian, TUN
French, POT
German, AAM
Greek, PIK
Hebrew, CAB, HIN, KOR, LOG
Hungarian, AKO
Icelandic, FET
Indian, GAZ, GUZ, JOW, KOS
Japanese, BOO, CHO, KEN, RIN, SHO, SUN, TAN
Malabar, ADY
Metric (land), ARE
Netherlands, KAN, KOP, MUD, VAT, ZAK
Norwegian, FOT, POT
Persian, GAZ, GUZ, MOU, ZAR, ZER
Polish, CAL
Rangoon, DHA, LAN
Roman, PES, URN
Russian, FUT, LOF
Scottish, COP
Siamese, KEN, NIU, RAI, SAT, SEN, SOK, WAH, YOT
Somaliland, TOP
Spanish, PIE
Straits Settlements, PAU, TUN
Swedish, ALN, FOT, MIL, REF, TUM
Swiss, POT
Tunisian, SAA
Turkish, OKA, OKE, PIK
Vietnamese, GON, MAU, NGU, VUO, SAO, TAO, TAT
Wire, MIL
Württemberg, IMI
Yarn, LEA
Yugoslav, OKA, RIF
Milk, LAC
Milkfish, AWA
Moccasin, PAC
Money: Yap stone, FEI
Money of Account (also Coin):
Anglo-Saxon, ORA, ORE
French, SOU
Indian, LAC
Japanese, RIN
Oman, GAJ
Virgin Islands, BIT
Monkey: Capuchin, SAI
Morsel, ORT
Mother: Peer Gynt's, ASE
Mountain: Asia Minor, IDA
Mulberry: Indian, AAL, ACH, AWL
Muttonbird: New Zealand, OII
Nahoor, SNA
Native: Mindanao, ATA
Neckpiece, BOA
Newt, EFT
No (Scottish), NAE
Note: Guido's highest, ELA
Of scale, SOL
Nursemaid: Oriental, AMA, IYA
Ocher: Yellow, SIL
One (Scottish), YIN
Ornament: Pagoda, TEE
Oven: Polynesian, UMU
Ox: Tibetan, YAK
Pagoda: Chinese, TAA
Parrot: Hawk, HIA
New Zealand, KEA
Part: Footlike, PES
Particle: Electrified, ION
Pasha, DEY
Pass: Mountain, COL
Paste: Rice, AME
Pea: Indian split, DAL
Peasant: Philippine, TAO
Penpoint, NEB, NIB
Piece out, EKE
Pigeon, NUN
Pine: Textile screw, ARA
Pistol (slang), GAT
Pit: Baking, IMU
Plant: Pepper, AVA
Play: By Capek, RUR
Poem: Old French, DIT
Porgy: Japanese, TAI
Priest: Biblical high, ELI
Prince: Ethiopian, RAS
Pseudonym: Dickens', BOZ
Queen: Fairy, MAB
Quince: Bengal, BEL
Record: Ship's, LOG
Refuse: Flax (Scottish), PAB, POB
Resin, LAC
Resort, SPA
Revolver (slang), GAT
Right: Cause to turn, GEE
River: Scottish or English, DEE
(Spanish), RIO
Swiss, AAR
Room: Harem, ODA
Rootstock: Fern, ROI
Rose (Persian), GUL
Ruff: Female, REE
Rule: Indian, RAJ
Sailor, GOB, TAR
Saint: Female (abbr.), STE
Islamic, PIR
Salt, SAL
Sash: Japanese, OBI
Scrap, ORT
Seed: Poppy, MAW
Small, PIP
Self, EGO
Serpent: Vedic sky, AHI
Sesame, TIL
Sheep: Female, EWE
Indian, SHA
Male, RAM
Sheepfold (Scottish), REE
Shelter, LEE
Shield, ECU
Shooting match (French), TIR
Shrew: European, ERD
Shrub: Evergreen, YEW
Silkworm, ERI
Snake, ASP, BOA
Soak, RET
Son-in-law: Mohammed's, ALI
Sorrel: Wood, OCA
Spade: Long, narrow, LOY
Spirit: Malignant, KER
Spot: Playing-card, PIP
Spread for drying, TED
Spring: Mineral, SPA
Sprite: Water, NIX
Statesman: Japanese, ITO
Stern: Toward, AFT
Stomach: Bird's, MAW
Street (French), RUE
Summer (French), ETE
Sun, SOL
Swamp, BOG, FEN
Swan: Male, COB
Tea: Chinese, CHA
Temple: Shinto, SHA
Thing (law), RES
Title: Etruscan, LAR
Monk's, FRA
Portuguese, DOM
Spanish, DON
Turkish, AGA, BEY
Tool: Cutting, ADZ, AXE
Mining, GAD
Piercing, AWL
Tree: Candlenut, AMA
Central American, EBO
East Indian, SAJ, SAL
Evergreen, YEW
Hawaiian, KOA, KOU
Indian, BEL, DAR
Linden, LIN
New Zealand, AKE
Philippine, DAO, TUA, TUI
Rubber, ULE
South American, APA
Tribe: New Zealand, ATI
Turmeric, REA
Twice, BIS
Twin: Siamese, ENG
Uncle (dialect), EAM, EME
Veil: Chalice, AER, AIR
Vessel: Wine, AMA
Vestment: Ecclesiastical, ALB
Vetch: Bitter, ERS
Victorfish, AKU
Vine: New Zealand, AKA
Philippine, IYO
Wallaba, APA
Wapiti, ELK
Water (French), EAU
Waterfall, LIN
Watering place: Prussian, EMS
Weave: Designating plain, UNI
Weight: Bulgarian, OKA, OKE
Burmese, MOO, VIS
Chinese, FEN, HAO, KIN, SSU, TAN, YIN
Cyprus, OKA, OKE
Danish, LOD, ORT, VOG
East Indian, TJI
Egyptian, KAT, OKA, OKE
English, for wool, TOD
German, LOT
Greek, MNA, OKA, OKE
Indian, SER
Japanese, FUN, KIN, RIN, SHI
Korean, KON
Malacca, KIP
Mongolian, LAN
Netherlands, ONS
Norwegian, LOD
Polish, LUT
Rangoon, PAI
Roman, BES
Russian, LOT
Siamese, BAT, HAP, PAI
Swedish, ASS, ORT
Turkish, OKA, OKE
Vietnamese, CAN
Yugoslav, OKA, OKE
Whales: Herd, GAM, POD
Wildebeest, GNU
Wing, ALA
Witticism, MOT
Wolframite, CAL
Worm: African, LOA
Wreath: Hawaiian, LEI
Yale, ELI
Yam: Hawaiian, HOI
Yes (French), OUI
Young: Bring forth, EAN
Z (letter), ZED

Words of Four Letters

Aborigine: Borneo, DYAK
Agave, ALOE
Animal: Footless, APOD
Ant: White, ANAI, ANAY
Antelope: African, ASSE, BISA, GUIB, KOBA, KUDU, ORYX, POKU, PUKU, TOPI, TORA
Apoplexy: Plant, ESCA
Apple, POME
Apricot, ANSU
Ardor, ELAN
Armadillo, APAR, PEBA, PEVA, TATU
Ascetic: Islamic, SUFI
Association: Chinese, TONG
Astronomer: Persian, OMAR
Avatar: Of Vishnu, RAMA
Axillary, ALAR
Band: Horizontal (heraldry), FESS
Barracuda, SPET
Bark: Mulberry, TAPA
Base: Column, DADO
Bearing (heraldry), ORLE
Beer: Russian, KVAS
Beige, ECRU
Being, ESSE
Beverage: Japanese rice, SAKE
Bird: Asian, MINA, MYNA
Egyptian sacred, IBIS
Extinct, DODO, MAMO
Flightless, KIWI
Gull-like, TERN
Hawaiian, IIWI, MAMO
Parson, KOKO
Unfledged, EYAS
Birds: As class, AVES
Black, EBON
(French), NOIR
Blackbird: European, MERL
Boat: Flat-bottomed, DORY
Bone: Forearm, ULNA
Bones, OSSA
Box, Japanese, INRO

Bravo (rare), EUGE
Buffalo: Indian wild, ARNA
Bull (Spanish), TORO
Burden, ONUS
Cabbage: Sliced, SLAW
Caliph: Islamic, OMAR
Canoe: Malay, PRAU, PROA
Cap: Military, KEPI
Cape, NESS
Capital: Ancient Irish, TARA
Case: Article, ETUI
Cat: Wild, BALU, EYRA
Chalcedony, SARD
Chamber: Indian ceremonial, KIVA
Channel: Brain, ITER
Cheese: Dutch, EDAM
Chest: Sepulchral stone, CIST
Chieftain: Arab, EMIR
Church: Part of, APSE, NAVE
  (Scottish), KIRK
Claim (law), LIEN
Cluster: Flower, CYME
Coin: Chinese, TAEL, YUAN
  German, MARK
  Indian, ANNA
  Iranian, RIAL
  Italian, LIRA
  Moroccan, OKIA
  Siamese, BAHT
  South American, PESO
  Spanish, DURO, PESO
  Turkish, PARA
Commune: Belgian, AATH
Composition: Musical, OPUS
Compound: Chemical, DIOL
Constellation: Southern, PAVO
Council: Russian, DUMA
Counsel, REDE
Covering: Seed, ARIL
Cross: Egyptian, ANKH
Cry: Bacchanalian, EVOE
Cup (Scottish), TASS
Cupbearer, SAKI
Dagger, DIRK
  Malay, KRIS
Dam: River, WEIR
Dash, ELAN
Date: Roman, IDES
Dawn: Pertaining to, EOAN
Dean: English, INGE
Decay: In fruit, BLET
Deer: Sambar, MAHA
Disease: Skin, ACNE
Disk: Solar, ATEN
Dog: Hunting, ALAN
Drink: Hindu intoxicating, SOMA
Duck, SMEE, SMEW, TEAL
Dynasty: Chinese, CHEN, CHIN, CHOU,
  CHOW, HSIA, MING, SUNG, TANG,
  TSIN
  Mongol, YUAN
Eagle: Biblical, GIER
  Sea, ERNE
Ear: Pertaining to, OTIC
Egyptian: Christian, COPT
Entrance: Mine, ADIT
Esau, EDOM
Escutcheon: Voided, ORLE
Eskers, OSAR
Evergreen: New Zealand, TAWA
Fairy: Persian, PERI
Family: Italian, ESTE
Far (comb. form), TELE
Farewell, VALE
Father (French), PERE
Fennel: Philippine, ANIS
Fever: Malarial, AGUE
Fiber: East Indian, JUTE
Firn, NEVE
Fish: Carplike, DACE
  Hawaiian, ULUA
  Herringlike, SHAD
  Mackerellike, CERO
  Marine, HAKE
  Sea, LING, MERO, OPAH
  Spiny-finned, GOBY
Food: Tropical, TARO
Foot: Metric, IAMB
Formerly, ERST
Founder: Of Carthage, DIDO
France: Southern, MIDI
Furze, ULEX
Gaelic, ERSE
Gaiter, SPAT
Game: Card, FARO, SKAT
Garlic: European wild, MOLY
Garment: Hindu, SARI
  Roman, TOGA
Gazelle, CORA
Gem, JADE, ONYX, OPAL, RUBY
Genus: Amphibians (incl. frogs), RANA
  Amphibians (incl. tree toads), HYLA
  Antelopes, ORYX
  Auks, ALCA, URIA
  Bees, APIS
  Birds (American ostriches), RHEA
  Birds (cranes), CRUS
  Birds (magpies), PICA
  Birds (peacocks), PAVO
  Cetaceans, INIA
  Ducks (incl. mallards), ANAS
  Fishes (burbots), LOTA
  Fishes (incl. bowfins), AMIA
  Geese (snow geese), CHEN
  Gulls, XEMA
  Herbs, ARUM, GEUM
  Insects (water scorpions), NEPA
  Lilies, ALOE
  Mammals (humans), HOMO
  Orchids, DISA
  Owls, ASIO, BUBO, OTUS
  Palms, NIPA
  Sea birds, SULA
  Sheep, OVIS
  Shrubs, Eurasian, ULEX
  Shrubs (hollies), ILEX
  Shrubs (incl. Virginia Willow), ITEA
  Shrubs, tropical, EVEA
  Snakes (sand snakes), ERYX
  Swans, OLOR
  Trees, chocolate, COLA
  Trees (ebony family), MABA
  Trees (incl. maples), ACER
  Trees (olives), OLEA
  Trees, tropical, EVEA
  Turtles, EMYS
Goat: Wild, IBEX, KRAS, TAHR, TAIR,
  THAR
God: Assyrian, ASUR
  Babylonian, ADAD, ADDU, ENKI,
  ENZU, IRRA, NABU, NEBO, UTUG
  Celtic, LLEU, LLEW
  Hindu, AGNI, CIVA, DEVA, DEWA,
  KAMA, RAMA, SIVA, VAYU
  Phrygian, ATYS
  Semitic, BAAL
  Teutonic, HLER
Goddess: Babylonian, ERUA, GULA
  Hawaiian, PELE
  Hindu, DEVI, KALI, SHRI, VACH
Gooseberry: Hawaiian, POHA
Gourd, PEPO
Grafted (heraldry), ENTE
Grandfather (obsolete), AIEL
Grandparents: Pertaining to, AVAL
Grass: Hawaiian, HILO
Gray (French), GRIS
Green (heraldry), VERT
Groom: Indian, SYCE
Half (prefix), DEMI, HEMI, SEMI
Hamlet, DORP
Hammerhead: Part of, PEEN
Handle, ANSA
Harp: Japanese, KOTO
Hartebeest, ASSE, TORA
Hautboy, OBOE
Hawk: Taken from nest (falconry), EYAS
Hearing (law), OYER
Heater: For liquids, ETNA
Herb: Aromatic, ANET, DILL
  Fabulous, MOLY
  Perennial, GEUM, SEGO
  Pot, WORT
  Used for blue dye, WADE, WOAD
Hill: Flat-topped, MESA
  Sand, DENE, DUNE
Hoarfrost, RIME
Hog: Immature female, GILT
Holly, ILEX
House: Cow, BYRE
  (Spanish), CASA
Ice: Floating, FLOE
Image, ICON, IKON
Incarnation: Of Vishnu, RAMA
Indian: Algonquin, CREE, SAUK
  Central American, MAYA
  Iroquoian, ERIE
  Mexican, CORA
  Peruvian, CANA, INCA, MORO
  Shoshonean, HOPI
  Siouan, OTOE
  Southwestern, HOPI, PIMA, YUMA,
  ZUNI
Insect: Immature, PUPA
Instrument: Stringed, LUTE, LYRE
Ireland, EIRE, ERIN
Jacket: English, ETON
Jail (British), GAOL
Jar, OLLA
Judge: Islamic, CADI
Juniper: European, CADE
Kiln, OAST, OVEN
King: British legendary, LUDD, NUDD
Kiss, BUSS
Knife: Philippine, BOLO
Koran: Section of, SURA
Laborer: Spanish American, PEON
Lake: Mountain, TARN
  (Scottish), LOCH
Lamp: Miner's, DAVY
Landing place: Indian, GHAT
Language: Buddhist, PALI
  Japanese, AINU
Latvian, LETT
Layer: Of iris, UVEA
Leaf: Palm, OLAY, OLLA
Legislature: Ukrainian, RADA
Lemur, LORI
Leopard, PARD
Let it stand, STET
Letter: Greek, BETA, IOTA, ZETA
  Hebrew, AYIN, BETH, CAPH, KOPH,
  RESH, SHIN, TETH, YODH
  Papal, BULL
Lily, ALOE
Literature: Hindu sacred, VEDA
Lizard, GILA
  Monitor, URAN
Loquat, BIWA
Magistrate: Genoese or Venetian, DOGE
Man (Latin), HOMO
Mark: Omission, DELE
Marmoset: South American, MICO
Meadow: Fertile, VEGA
Measure: Electric, VOLT, WATT
  Force, DYNE
  Hebrew, OMER
  Printing, PICA
  Spanish or Portuguese, VARA
  Swiss land, IMMI
Medley, OLIO
Merganser, SMEW
Milk (French), LAIT
Molding, GULA
  Curved, OGEE
Mongoose: Crab-eating, URVA
Monk: Tibetan, LAMA
Monkey: African, MONA, WAAG
  Ceylonese, MAHA
  Cochin-China, DOUC
  South American, SAKI, TITI
Monkshood, ATIS
Month: Jewish, ADAR, ELUL, IYAR
Mother (French), MERE
Mountain: Thessaly, OSSA
Mouse: Meadow, VOLE
Mythology: Norse, EDDA
Nail (French), CLOU

Native: Philippine, MORO
Nest: Of pheasants, NIDE
Network, RETE
No (German), NEIN
Noble: Islamic, AMIR
Notice: Death, OBIT
Novel: By Zola, NANA
Nursemaid: Oriental AMAH, AYAH, EYAH
Nut: Philippine, PILI
Oak: Holm, ILEX
Oil (comb. form), OLEO
Ostrich: American, RHEA
Oven, KILN, OAST
Owl: Barn, LULU
Ox: Celebes wild, ANOE
Extinct wild, URUS
Palm, ATAP, NIPA, SAGO
Parliament, DIET
Parrot: New Zealand, KAKA
Pass: Indian mountain, GHAT
Passage: Closing (music), CODA
Peach: Clingstone, PAVY
Peasant: Indian, RYOT
Old English, CARL
Pepper: Australasian, KAVA
Perfume, ATAR
Persia, IRAN
Person: Extraordinary, ONER
Pickerel or pike, ESOX
Pitcher, EWER
Plant: Aromatic, NARD
Century, ALOE
Indigo, ANIL
Pepper, KAVA
Platform: Raised, DAIS
Plum: Wild, SLOE
Pods: Vegetable, OKRA, OKRO
Poem: Epic, EPOS
Poet: Persian, OMAR
Roman, OVID
Poison, BANE
Arrow, INEE
Porkfish, SISI
Portico: Greek, STOA
Premium, AGIO
Priest: Islamic, IMAM
Prima donna, DIVA
Prong: Fork, TINE
Pseudonym: Lamb's, ELIA
Queen: Carthaginian, DIDO
Hindu, RANI
Rabbit, CONY
Race: Of Japan, AINU
Rail: Ducklike, COOT
North American, SORA
Redshank, CLEE
Refuse: After pressing, MARC
Regiment: Turkish, ALAI
Reliquary, ARCA
Resort: Italian, LIDO
Ridges: Sandy, ASAR, OSAR
River: German, ELBE, ODER
Italian, ADDA
Siberian, LENA
Road: Roman, ITER
Rockfish: California, RENA
Rodent: Mouselike, VOLE
South American, PACA
Rootstock, TARO
Salamander, NEWT
Salmon: Silver, COHO
Young, PARR
Same (Greek), HOMO
(Latin), IDEM
Sauce: Fish, ALEC
School: English, ETON
Seaweed, AGAR, ALGA, KELP
Secular, LAIC
Sediment, SILT
Seed: Dill, ANET
Of vetch, TARE
Serf, ILOT
Sesame, TEEL
Settlement: Eskimo, ETAH
Shark: Atlantic, GATA
European, TOPE
Sheep: Wild, UDAD
Sheltered, ALEE
Shield, EGIS
Ship: Jason's, ARGO
Left side of, PORT
Two-masted, BRIG
Shrine: Buddhist, TOPE
Shrub: New Zealand, TUTU
Sign: Magic, RUNE
Silkworm, ERIA
Skin: Beaver, PLEW
Skink: Egyptian, ADDA
Slave, ESNE
Sloth: Two-toed, UNAU
Smooth, LENE
Snow: Glacial, NEVE
Soapstone, TALC
Society: African secret, EGBO, PORO
Son: Of Seth, ENOS
Song (German), LIED
Unaccompanied, GLEE
Sound: Lung, RALE
Sour, ACID
Sow: Young, GILT
Spike: Brad-shaped, BROB
Spirit: Buddhist evil, MARA
Stake: Poker, ANTE
Star: Temporary, NOVA
Starch: East Indian, SAGO
Stone: Precious, OPAL
Strap: Bridle, REIN
Strewn (heraldry), SEME
Sweetsop, ATES, ATTA
Sword: Fencing, EPEE, FOIL
Tambourine: African, TAAR
Tapir: Brazilian, ANTA
Tax, CESS
Tea: South American, MATE
Therefore (Latin), ERGO
Thing: Extraordinary, ONER
Three (dice, cards, etc.), TREY
Thrush: Hawaiian, OMAO
Tide, NEAP
Tipster: Racing, TOUT
Tissue, TELA
Title: Etruscan, LARS
Hindu, BABU
Indian, RAJA
Islamic, EMIR, IMAM
Persian, BABA
Spanish, DONA
Turkish, AGHA, BABA
Toad: Largest-known, AGUA
Tree, HYLA
Tool: Cutting, ADZE
Track: Deer, SLOT
Tract: Sandy, DENE
Tree: Apple, SORB
Central American, EBOE
East Indian, TEAK
Eucalyptus, YATE
Guyanese and Trinidadian, MORA
Javanese, UPAS
Linden, LIME, LINN, TEIL, TILL
Sandarac, ARAR
Sassafras, AGUE
Tamarisk salt, ATLE
Tribe: Moro, SULU
Trout, CHAR
Vessel: Arab, DHOW
Vestment: Ecclesiastical, COPE
Vetch, TARE
Vine: East Indian, SOMA
Violinist: Famous, AUER
Vortex, EDDY
Wampum, PEAG
Wapiti, STAG
Waste: Allowance for, TRET
Watchman: Indian, MINA
Water (Spanish), AGUA
Waterfall, LINN
Wavy (heraldry), ONDE, UNDE
Wax, CERE
Chinese, PELA
Weed: Biblical, TARE
Weight: Ancient, MINA
Danish (pl.), ESER
East Asian, TAEL
Greek, MINA
Siamese, BAHT
Well done (rare), EUGE
Whale, CETE
Killer, ORCA
White, HUSE, HUSO
Whirlpool, EDDY
Wife: Of Geraint, ENID
Willow: Virginia, ITEA
Wine, PORT
Winged, ALAR
(Heraldry), AILE
Wings, ALAE
Withered, SERE
Without (French), SANS
Wool: To comb, CARD
Work, OPUS
Wrong: Civil, TORT
Young: Bring forth, YEAN

Words of Five Letters

Abode of dead: Babylonian, ARALU
Aborigine: Borneo, DAYAK
Aftersong, EPODE
Aloe, AGAVE
Animal: Footless, APODE
Ant, EMMET
Antelope: African, ADDAX, BEISA, CAAMA, ELAND, GUIBA, ORIBI, TIANG
Goat, GORAL, SEROW
Indian, SASIN
Siberian, SAIGA
Arch: Pointed, OGIVE
Armadillo, APARA, POYOU, TATOU
Arrowroot, ARARU
Artery: Trunk, AORTA
Association: Russian, ARTEL
Secret, CABAL
Author: English, READE
Automaton, GOLEM, ROBOT
Award: Motion-picture, OSCAR
Basket: Fishing, CREEL
Beer: Russian, KVASS
Bible: Islamic, KORAN, QUR'AN
Bird: Asian, MINAH, MYNAH
Indian, SHAMA
Larklike, PIPIT
Loonlike, GREBE
Oscine, VIREO
South American, AGAMI
Swimming, GREBE
Black: (French), NOIRE
(Heraldry), SABLE
Blackbird: European, MERLE, OUSEL, OUZEL
Block: Glacial, SERAC
Blue (heraldry), AZURE
Boat: Eskimo, BIDAR, UMIAK
Bobwhite, COLIN, QUAIL
Bone (comb. form), OSTEO
Leg, TIBIA
Thigh, FEMUR
Broom: Twig, BESOM
Brother (French), FRERE
Moses, AARON
Canoe: Eskimo, BIDAR, KAYAK
Cape: Papal, FANON, ORALE
Caravansary, SERAI
Card: Old playing, TAROT
Caterpillar: New Zealand, AWETO
Catkin, AMENT
Cavity: Stone, GEODE
Cephalopod, SQUID
Cetacean, WHALE
Chariot, ESSED
Cheek: Pertaining to, MALAR
Chieftain: Arab, EMEER

Child (Scottish), BAIRN
Cigar, CLARO
Coating: Seed, TESTA
Cockatoo: Palm, ARARA
Coin: Costa Rican, COLON
Danish, KRONE
Ecuadorian, SUCRE
English, GROAT, PENCE
French, FRANC
German, KRONE, TALER
Hungarian, PENGO
Icelandic, KRONA
Indian, RUPEE
Iraqi, DINAR
Norwegian, KRONE
Polish, ZLOTY
Russian, COPEC, KOPEK, RUBLE
Swedish, KRONA
Turkish, ASPER
Yugoslav, DINAR
Collar: Papal, FANON, ORALE
Roman, RABAT
Commune: Italian, TREIA
Composition: Choral, MOTET
Compound: Chemical, ESTER
Conceal (law), ELOIN
Council: Ecclesiastical, SYNOD
Court: Anglo-Saxon, GEMOT
Inner, PATIO
Crest: Mountain, ARETE
Crown: Papal, TIARA
Cuttlefish, SEPIA
Date: Roman, NONES
Decree: Islamic, IRADE
Russian, UKASE
Deposit: Loam, LOESS
Desert: Gobi, SHAMO
Devilfish, MANTA
Disease: Cereals, ERGOT
Disk, PATEN
Dog: Wild, DHOLE, DINGO
Dormouse, LEROT
Drum, TABOR
Duck: Sea, EIDER
Dynasty: Chinese, CHING, LIANG, SHANG
Earthquake, SEISM
Eel, ELVER, MORAY
Ermine: European, STOAT
Ether: Crystalline, APIOL
Fabric: Velvetlike, PANNE
Fabulist, AESOP
Family: Italian, CENCI
Fiber: West Indian, SISAL
Fig: Smyrna, ELEME, ELEMI
Figure: Of speech, TROPE
Finch: European, SERIN
Fish: American small, KILLY
Flower: Garden, ASTER
Friend (Spanish), AMIGO
Fruit: Tropical, MANGO
Fungus: Rye, ERGOT
Furze, GORSE
Gateway, TORAN, TORII
Gem, AGATE, BERYL, PEARL, TOPAZ
Genus: Barnacles, LEPAS
Bears, URSUS
Birds (loons), GAVIA
Birds (nuthatches), SITTA
Cats, FELIS
Dogs, CANIS
Fishes (chiros), ELOPS
Fishes (perch), PERCA
Geese, ANSER
Grasses, STIPA
Grasses (incl. oats), AVENA
Gulls, LARUS
Hares, rabbits, LEPUS
Hawks, BUTEO
Herbs, old world, INULA
Herbs, trailing or climbing, APIOS
Herbs, tropical, TACCA, URENA
Horses, EQUUS
Insects (olive flies), DACUS
Lice, plant, APHIS
Lichens, USNEA
Lizards, AGAMA
Moles, TALPA
Mollusks, OLIVA
Monkeys, CEBUS
Palms, ARECA
Pigeons, GOURA
Plants (amaryllis family), AGAVE
Ruminants (goats), CAPRA
Shrubs, Asiatic, SABIA
Shrubs (heath), ERICA
Shrubs (incl. raspberry), RUBUS
Shrubs, tropical, IXORA, TREMA, URENA
Ticks, ARGAS
Trees (of elm family), TREMA, ULMUS
Trees, tropical, IXORA, TREMA
Goat: Bezoar, PASAN
God: Assyrian, ASHIR, ASHUR, ASSUR
Babylonian, DAGAN, SIRIS
Gaelic, DAGDA
Hindu, BHAGA, INDRA, SHIVA
Japanese, EBISU
Philistine, DAGON
Phrygian, ATTIS
Teutonic, AEGIR, GYMIR
Welsh, DYLAN
Goddess: Babylonian, ISTAR, NANAI
Hindu, DURGA, GAURI, SHREE
Group: Of six, HEXAD
Grove: Sacred to Diana, NEMUS
Growing out, ENATE
Guitar: Hindu, SITAR
Gull: PEWEE, PEWIT
Hartebeest, CAAMA
Headdress: Jewish or Persian, TIARA
Liturgical, MITER, MITRE
Heath, ERICA
Herb: Grasslike marsh, SEDGE
Heron, EGRET
Hog: Young, SHOAT, SHOTE
Image, EIKON
Indian: Cariban, ARARA
Iroquoian, HURON
Mexican, AZTEC, OPATA, OTOMI
Muskhogean, CREEK
Siouan, OSAGE, TETON
Spanish American, ARARA, CARIB
Inflorescence: Racemose, AMENT
Insect: Immature, LARVA
Intrigue, CABAL
Iris: Yellow, SEDGE
Juniper, GORSE, RETEM
Kidneys: Pertaining to, RENAL
King: British legendary, LLUDD
Kite: European, GLEDE
Kobold, NISSE
Land: Cultivated, ARADA, ARADO
Landholder (Scottish), LAIRD, THANE
Language: Dravidian, TAMIL
Lariat, LASSO, REATA
Laughing, RIANT
Lawgiver: Athenian, DRACO, SOLON
Leaf: Calyx, SEPAL
Fern, FROND
Lemur, LORIS
Letter: English, AITCH
Greek, ALPHA, DELTA, GAMMA, KAPPA, OMEGA, SIGMA, THETA
Hebrew, ALEPH, CHETH, GIMEL, SADHE, ZAYIN
Lichen, USNEA
Lighthouse, PHARE
Lizard: Old World, AGAMA
Loincloth, DHOTI
Louse: Plant, APHID
Macaw: Brazilian, ARARA
Mahogany: Philippine, ALMON
Mammal: Badgerlike, RATEL
Civetlike, GENET
Giraffelike, OKAPI
Raccoonlike, COATI
Man (French), HOMME
Marble, AGATE
Mark: Insertion, CARET
Market place: Greek, AGORA
Marsupial: Australian, KOALA
Measure: Electric, FARAD, HENRY
Energy, JOULE
Metric, LITER, STERE
Printing, AGATE
Russian, VERST
Mixture: Smelting, MATTE
Mohicans: Last of, UNCAS
Molding: Convex, OVOLO, TORUS
Mole, TALPA
Monkey: African, PATAS
Capuchin, SAJOU
Howling, ARABA
Monkshood, ATEES
Month: Jewish, NISAN, SIVAN, TEBET
Museum (French), MUSEE
Musketeer, ATHOS
Native: Aleutian, ALEUT
New Zealand, MAORI
Neckpiece: Ecclesiastical, AMICE
Nerve (comb. form), NEURO
Nest: Eagle's or hawk's, AERIE
Insect's, NIDUS
Net: Fishing, SEINE
Newsstand, KIOSK
Nitrogen, AZOTE
Noble: Islamic, AMEER
Nodule: Stone, GEODE
Nostrils, NARES
Notched irregularly, EROSE
Nymph: Islamic, HOURI
Official: Roman, EDILE
Oleoresin, ELEMI
Opening: Mouthlike, STOMA
Oration: Funeral, ELOGE
Ostiole, STOMA
Page: Left-hand, VERSO
Right-hand, RECTO
Palm, ARECA, BETEL
Park: Colorado, ESTES
Perfume, ATTAR
Philosopher: Greek, PLATO
Pillar: Stone, STELA, STELE
Pinnacle: Glacial, SERAC
Plain, LLANO
Plant: Century, AGAVE
Climbing, LIANA
Dwarf, CUMIN
East Asian perennial, RAMIE
Medicinal, SENNA
Mustard family, CRESS
Plate: Communion, PATEN
Poem: Lyric, EPODE
Point: Lowest, NADIR
Poplar, ABELE, ALAMO, ASPEN
Porridge: Spanish American, ATOLE
Post: Stair, NEWEL
Priest: Islamic, IMAUM
Protozoan, AMEBA
Queen: (French), REINE
Hindu, RANEE
Rabbit, CONEY
Rail, CRAKE
Red (heraldry), GULES
Religion: Moslem, Muslim, ISLAM
Resin, ELEMI
Revoke (law), ADEEM
Rich man, MIDAS, NABOB
Ridge: Sandy, ESKAR, ESKER
River: French, LOIRE, SEINE
Rockfish: California, REINA
Rootstock: Fragrant, ORRIS
Ruff: Female, REEVE
Sack: Pack, KYACK
Salt: Ethereal, ESTER
Saltpeter, NITER, NITRE
Salutation: Eastern, SALAM
Sandpiper: Old World, TEREK
Scented, OLENT
School: Fish, SHOAL
French public, LYCEE
Scriptures: Islamic, KORAN
Seaweeds, ALGAE
Seed: Aromatic, ANISE
Seraglio, HAREM, SERAI
Serf, HELOT
Sheep: Wild, AUDAD

Sheeplike, OVINE
Shield, AEGIS
Shoe: Wooden, SABOT
Shoots: Pickled bamboo, ACHAR
Shot: Billiard, CAROM, MASSE
Shrine: Buddhist, STUPA
Shrub: Burning bush, WAHOO
  Ornamental evergreen, TOYON
  Used in tanning, SUMAC
Silk: Watered, MOIRE
Sister (French), SOEUR
  (Latin), SOROR
Six: Group of, HEXAD
Skeleton: Marine, CORAL
Slave, HELOT
Snake, ABOMA, ADDER, COBRA, RACER
Soldier: French, POILU
  Indian, SEPOY
Sour, ACERB
Spirit: Air, ARIEL
Staff: Shepherd's, CROOK
Starwort, ASTER
Steel (German), STAHL
Stockade: Russian, ETAPE
Stop (nautical), AVAST
Storehouse, ETAPE
Subway: Parisian, METRO
Tapestry, ARRAS
Tea: Paraguayan, YERBA
Temple: Hawaiian, HEIAU
Terminal: Positive, ANODE
Theater: Greek, ODEON, ODEUM
Then (French), ALORS
Thread: Surgical, SETON
Thrush: Wilson's, VEERY
Title: Hindu, BABOO
  Indian, RAJAH, SAHEB, SAHIB
  Islamic, EMEER, IMAUM
Tree: Buddhist sacred, PIPAL
  East Indian cotton, SIMAL
  Hickory, PECAN
  Light-wooded, BALSA
  Malayan, TERAP
  Mediterranean, CAROB
  Mexican, ABETO
  Mexican pine, OCOTE
  New Zealand, MAIRE
  Philippine, ALMON
  Rain, SAMAN
  South American, UMBRA
  Tamarack, LARCH
  Tamarisk salt, ATLEE
  West Indian, ACANA
Trout, CHARR
Troy, ILION, ILIUM
Twin: Siamese, CHANG
Vestment: Ecclesiastical, STOLE
Violin: Famous, AMATI, STRAD
Volcano: Mud, SALSE
Wampum, PEAGE
War cry: Greek, ALALA
Wavy (heraldry), UNDEE
Weight: Jewish, GERAH
Wen, TALPA
Wheat, SPELT
Wheel: Persian water, NORIA
Whitefish, CISCO
Willow, OSIER
Window: Bay, ORIEL
Wine, MEDOC, RHINE, TINTA, TOKAY
Winged, ALATE
Woman (French), FEMME
Year: Excess of solar over lunar, EPACT
Zoroastrian, PARSI

Words of Six or More Letters

Agave, MAGUEY
Alkaloid: Crystalline, ESERIN, ESERINE
Alligator, CAYMAN
Amphibole, EDENITE, URALITE
Ant: White, TERMITE
Antelope: African, DIKDIK, DUIKER, GEMSBOK, IMPALA, KOODOO
  European, CHAMOIS
  Indian, NILGAI, NILGAU, NILGHAI, NILGHAU
Ape: Asian or East Indian, GIBBON
Appendage: Leaf, STIPEL, STIPULE
Armadillo, PELUDO, TATOUAY
Arrowroot, ARARAO
Ascetic: Jewish, ESSENE
Ass: Asian wild, ONAGER
Avatar: Of Vishnu, KRISHNA
Babylonian, ELAMITE
Badge: Shoulder, EPAULET
Baldness, ALOPECIA
Barracuda, SENNET
Bark: Aromatic, SINTOC
Bearlike, URSINE
Beetle, ELATER
Bible: Zoroastrian, AVESTA
Bird: Sea, PETREL
  South American, SERIEMA
  Wading, AVOCET, AVOSET
Bone: Leg, FIBULA
Branched, RAMATE
Brother (Latin), FRATER
Bunting: European, ORTOLAN
Call: Trumpet, SENNET
Canoe: Eskimo, BAIDAR, OOMIAK
Caravansary, IMARET
Cat: Asian or African, CHEETAH
  Leopardlike, OCELOT
Cenobite: Jewish, ESSENE
Centerpiece: Table, EPERGNE
Cetacean, DOLPHIN, PORPOISE
Chariot, ESSEDA, ESSEDE
Chief: Seminole, OSCEOLA
Claim: Release as (law), REMISE
Clock: Water, CLEPSYDRA
Cloud, CUMULUS, NIMBUS
Coach: French hackney, FIACRE
Coin: Czech, KORUNA
  Dutch, GUILDER
  Ethiopian, TALARI
  Finnish, MARKKA
  German, THALER
  Greek, DRACHMA
  Haitian, GOURDE
  Honduran, LEMPIRA
  Hungarian, FORINT
  Indo-Chinese, PIASTER
  Panamanian, BALBOA
  Paraguayan, GUARANI
  Portuguese, ESCUDO
  Russian, COPECK, KOPECK, ROUBLE
  Spanish, PESETA
  Venezuelan, BOLIVAR
Communion: Last holy, VIATICUM
Conceal (law), ELOIGN
Confection, PRALINE
Construction: Sentence, SYNTAX
Convexity: Shaft of column, ENTASIS
Court: Anglo-Saxon, GEMOTE
Cow: Sea, DUGONG, MANATEE
Cylindrical, TERETE
Dagger, STILETTO
  Malay, CREESE, KREESE
Date: Roman, CALENDS, KALENDS
Deer, CARIBOU, WAPITI
Disease: Plant, ERINOSE
Doorkeeper, OSTIARY
Dragonflies: Order of, ODANATA
Drink: Of gods, NECTAR
Drum: TABOUR
  Moorish, ATABAL, ATTABAL
Duck: Fish-eating, MERGANSER
  Sea, SCOTER
Dynasty: Chinese, MANCHU
Eel, CONGER
Edit, REDACT
Envelope: Flower, PERIANTH
Eskimo, AMERIND
Ether: Crystalline, APIOLE
Excuse (law), ESSOIN
Eyespots, OCELLI
Fabric, ESTAMENE, ESTAMIN, ETAMINE
Falcon: European, KESTREL
Figure: Used as column, CARYATID, TELAMON
Fine: For punishment, AMERCE
Fish: Asian fresh-water, GOURAMI
  Pikelike, BARRACUDA
Five: Group of, PENTAD
Fly: African, TSETSE
Foot: Metric, ANAPEST, IAMBUS
Foxlike, VULPINE
Frying pan, SPIDER
Fur, KARAKUL
Galley: Greek or Roman, BIREME, TRIREME
Game: Card, ECARTE
Garment: Greek, CHLAMYS
Gateway, GOPURA, TORANA
Genus: Birds (ravens, crows), CORVUS
  Eels, CONGER
  Fishes, ANABAS
  Foxes, VULPES
  Herbs, ANEMONE
  Insects, CICADA
  Lemurs, GALAGO
  Mints (incl. catnip), NEPETA
  Mollusks, ANOMIA, ASTARTE, TEREDO
  Mollusks (incl. oysters), OSTREA
  Monkeys (spider monkeys), ATELES
  Thrushes (incl. robins), TURDUS
  Trees (of elm family), CELTIS
  Trees (inc. dogwood), CORNUS
  Trees, tropical American, SAPOTA
  Wrens, NANNUS
Gibbon, SIAMANG, WOUWOU
Gland: Salivary, RACEMOSE
Goat: Bezoar, PASANG
Goatlike, CAPRINE
God: Assyrian, ASHSHUR, ASSHUR
  Babylonian, BABBAR, MARDUK, MERODACH, NANNAR, NERGAL, SHAMASH
  Hindu, BRAHMA, KRISHNA, VISHNU
  Tahitian, TAAROA
Goddess: Babylonian, ISHTAR
  Hindu, CHANDI, HAIMAVATI, LAKSHMI, PARVATI, SARASVATI, SARASWATI
Government, POLITY
Governor: Persian, SATRAP
Grandson (Scottish), NEPOTE
Group: Of five, PENTAD
  Of nine, ENNEAD
  Of seven, HEPTAD
Hare: in first year, LEVERET
Harpsichord, SPINET
Herb: Alpine, EDELWEISS
  Chinese, GINSENG
  South African, FREESIA
Hermit, EREMITE
Hero: Legendary, PALADIN
Heron, BITTERN
Horselike, EQUINE
Hound: Short-legged, BEAGLE
House (French), MAISON
Idiot, CRETIN
Implement: Stone, NEOLITH
Incarnation: Hindu, AVATAR
Indian, APACHE, COMANCHE, PAIUTE, SENECA
Inn: Turkish, IMARET
Insects: Order of, DIPTERA
Instrument: Japanese banjolike, SAMISEN
  Musical, CLAVIER, SPINET
Interstice, AREOLA
Ironwood, COLIMA
Juniper: Old Testament, RAETAM
Kettledrum, ATABAL
King: Fairy, OBERON
Kneecap, PATELLA
Knife, MACHETE
Langur: Sumatran, SIMPAI
Legislature: Spanish, CORTES

Lemur: African, GALAGO
Madagascar, AYEAYE
Letter: Greek, EPSILON, LAMBDA, OMICRON, UPSILON
Hebrew, DALETH, LAMEDH, SAMEKH
Lighthouse, PHAROS
Lizard, IGUANA
Llama, ALPACA
Lockjaw, TETANUS
Locust, CICADA, CICALA
Macaw: Brazilian, MARACAN
Maid: Of Astolat, ELAINE
Mammal: Madagascar, TENDRAC, TENREC
Man (Spanish), HOMBRE
Marmoset: South American, TAMARIN
Marsupial, BANDICOOT, WOMBAT
Massacre, POGROM
Mayor: Spanish, ALCALDE
Measure: Electric, AMPERE, COULOMB, KILOWATT
Medicine: Quack, NOSTRUM
Member: Religious order, CENOBITE
Molasses, TREACLE
Monkey: African, GRIVET, NISNAS
Asian, LANGUR
Philippine, MACHIN
South American, PINCHE, SAIMIRI, SAMIRI, SAPAJOU
Monster, CHIMERA, GORGON
(Comb. form), TERATO
Cretan, MINOTAUR
Month: Jewish, HESHVAN, KISLEV, SHEBAT, TAMMUZ, TISHRI, VEADAR
Mountain: Asia Minor, ARARAT
Mulct, AMERCE
Musketeer, ARAMIS, PORTHOS
Nearsighted, MYOPIC
Net, TRAMMEL
New York City, GOTHAM
Nine: Group of, ENNEAD
Nobleman: Spanish, GRANDEE
Official: Roman, AEDILE
Onyx: Mexican, TECALI
Order: Dragonflies, ODANATA
Insects, DIPTERA
Organ: Plant, PISTIL
Ornament: Shoulder, EPAULET
Overcoat: Military, CAPOTE
Ox: Wild, BANTENG
Oxidation: Bronze or copper, PATINA
Paralysis: Incomplete, PARESIS
Pear: Alligator, AVOCADO
Persimmon: Mexican, CHAPOTE
Pipe: Peace, CALUMET
Plaid (Scottish), TARTAN
Plain, PAMPAS, STEPPE, TUNDRA
Plant: Buttercup family, ANEMONE
Century, MAGUEY
On rocks, LICHEN
Plowing: Fit for, ARABLE
Poem: Heroic, EPOPEE
Six-lined, SESTET
Point: Highest, ZENITH
Potion: Love, PHILTER, PHILTRE
Protozoan, AMOEBA
Punish, AMERCE
Purple (heraldry), PURPURE
Queen: Fairy, TITANIA
Race: Skiing, SLALOM
Rat, BANDICOOT, LEMMING
Retort, RIPOST, RIPOSTE
Ring: Harness, TERRET
Little, ANNULET
Rodent: Jumping, JERBOA
Spanish American, AGOUTI, AGOUTY
Sailor: East Indian, LASCAR
Salmon: Young, GRILSE
Salutation: Eastern, SALAAM
Sandpiper, PLOVER
Sandy, ARENOSE
Sapodilla, SAPOTA, SAPOTE
Saw: Surgical, TREPAN
Seven: Group of, HEPTAD
Sexes: Common to both, EPICENE
Shawl: Mexican, SERAPE
Sheathing: Flower, SPATHE
Sheep: Wild, AOUDAD, ARGALI
Shipworm, TEREDO
Shoes: Mercury's winged, TALARIA
Shortening: Syllable, SYSTOLE
Shrub, SPIRAEA
Sickle-shaped, FALCATE
Silver (heraldry), ARGENT
Snake, ANACONDA
Speech: Loss of, APHASIA
Spiral, HELICAL
Staff: Bishop's, CROSIER, CROZIER
Stalk: Plant, PETIOLE
State: Swiss, CANTON
Studio, ATELIER
Swan: Young, CYGNET
Swimming, NATANT
Sword-shaped, ENSATE
Terminal: Negative, CATHODE
Third (music), TIERCE
Thrust: Fencing, RIPOST, RIPOSTE
Tile: Pertaining to, TEGULAR
Tomb: Empty, CENOTAPH
Tooth (comb. form), ODONTO
Tower: Islamic, MINARET
Tree: African timber, BAOBAB
Black gum, TUPELO
East Indian, MARGOSA
Locust, ACACIA
Malayan, SINTOC
Marmalade, SAPOTE
Urn: Tea, SAMOVAR
Vehicle, LANDAU, TROIKA
Verbose, PROLIX
Viceroy: Egyptian, KHEDIVE
Vulture: American, CONDOR
Warehouse (French), ENTREPOT
Whale: White, BELUGA
Whirlpool, VORTEX
Will: Addition to, CODICIL
Having left, TESTATE
Wind, CHINOOK, MONSOON, SIMOOM, SIMOON, SIROCCO
Window: In roof, DORMER
Wine, BARBERA, BURGUNDY, CABERNET, CHABLIS, CHIANTI, CLARET, MUSCATEL, RIESLING, SAUTERNE, SHERRY, ZINFANDEL
Wolfish, LUPINE
Woman: Boisterous, TERMAGANT
Woolly, LANATE
Workshop, ATELIER
Zoroastrian, PARSEE

Old Testament Names

We do not pretend that this list is all-inclusive. We list only those names that occur most often in crossword puzzles.

Aaron: First high priest of Jews; son of Amram; brother of Miriam and Moses; father of Abihu, Eleazer, Ithamar, and Nadab.
Abel: Son of Adam and Eve; slain by Cain.
Abigail: Wife of Nabal; later, wife of David.
Abihu: Son of Aaron.
Abimelech: King of Gerar.
Abner: Commander of army of Saul and Ishbosheth; slain by Joab.
Abraham (or Abram): Patriarch; forefather of the Jews; son of Terah; husband of Sarah; father of Isaac and Ishmael.
Absalom: Son of David and Maacah; revolted against David; slain by Joab.
Achish: King of Gath; gave refuge to David.
Achsa (or Achsah): Daughter of Caleb; wife of Othniel.
Adah: Wife of Lamech.
Adam: First man; husband of Eve; father of Cain, Abel, and Seth.
Adonijah: Son of David and Haggith.
Agag: King of Amalek; spared by Saul; slain by Samuel.
Ahasuerus: King of Persia; husband of Vashti and, later, Esther; sometimes identified with Xerxes the Great.
Ahijah: Prophet; foretold accession of Jeroboam.
Ahinoam: Wife of David.
Amasa: Commander of army of David; slain by Joab.
Amnon: Son of David and Ahinoam; raped Tamar; slain by Absalom.
Amram: Husband of Jochebed; father of Aaron, Miriam and Moses.
Asenath: Wife of Joseph.
Asher: Son of Jacob and Zilpah.
Balaam: Prophet; rebuked by his donkey for cursing God.
Barak: Jewish captain; associated with Deborah.
Baruch: Secretary to Jeremiah.
Bathsheba: Wife of Uriah; later, wife of David.
Belshazzar: Crown prince of Babylon.
Benaiah: Warrior of David; proclaimed Solomon King.
Ben-Hadad: Name of several kings of Damascus.
Benjamin: Son of Jacob and Rachel.
Bezaleel: Chief architect of Tabernacle.
Bilbah: Servant of Rachel; mistress of Jacob.
Bildad: Comforter of Job.
Boaz: Husband of Ruth; father of Obed.
Cain: Son of Adam and Eve; slayer of Abel; father of Enoch.
Cainan: Son of Enos.
Caleb: Spy sent out by Moses to visit Canaan; father of Achsa.
Canaan: Son of Ham.
Chilion: Son of Elimelech; husband of Orpah.
Cush: Son of Ham; father of Nimrod.
Dan: Son of Jacob and Bilhah.
Daniel: Prophet; saved from lions by God.
Deborah: Hebrew prophetess and judge; helped Israelites conquer Canaanites.
Delilah: Mistress and betrayer of Samson.
Elam: Son of Shem.
Eleazar: Son of Aaron; succeeded him as high priest.
Eli: High priest and judge; teacher of Samuel; father of Hophni and Phinehas.
Eliakim: Chief minister of Hezekiah.
Eliezer: Servant of Abraham.
Elihu: Comforter of Job.
Elijah (or Elias): Prophet; went to heaven in chariot of fire.

Elimelech: Husband of Naomi; father of Chilion and Mahlon.
Eliphaz: Comforter of Job.
Elisha (or Eliseus): Prophet; successor of Elijah.
Elkanah: Husband of Hannah; father of Samuel.
Enoch: Son of Cain.
Enoch: Father of Methuselah.
Enos: Son of Seth; father of Cainan.
Ephraim: Son of Joseph.
Esau: Son of Isaac and Rebecca; sold his birthright to his twin brother Jacob.
Esther: Jewish wife of Ahasuerus; saved Jews from Haman's plotting.
Eve: First woman; wife of Adam.
Ezra (or Esdras): Hebrew scribe and priest.
Gad: Son of Jacob and Zilpah.
Gehazi: Servant of Elisha.
Gideon: Israelite hero; defeated Midianites.
Goliath: Philistine giant; slain by David.
Hagar: Handmaid of Sarah; concubine of Abraham; mother of Ishmael.
Haggith: Mother of Adonijah.
Ham: Son of Noah; father of Cush, Mizraim, Phut, and Canaan.
Haman: Chief minister of Ahasuerus; hanged on gallows prepared for Mordecai.
Hannah: Wife of Elkanah; mother of Samuel.
Hanun: King of Ammonites.
Haran: Brother of Abraham; father of Lot.
Hazael: King of Damascus.
Hephzi-Bah: Wife of Hezekiah; mother of Mannaseh.
Hiram: King of Tyre.
Holofernes: General of Nebuchadnezzar; slain by Judith.
Hophni: Son of Eli.
Isaac: Hebrew patriarch; son of Abraham and Sarah; half brother of Ishmael; husband of Rebecca; father of Esau and Jacob.
Ishmael: Son of Abraham and Hagar; half brother of Isaac.
Issachar: Son of Jacob and Leah.
Ithamar: Son of Aaron.
Jabal: Son of Lamech and Adah.
Jabin: King of Hazor.
Jacob: Hebrew patriarch; founder of Israel; son of Isaac and Rebecca; husband of Leah and Rachel; father of sons Asher, Benjamin, Dan, Gad, Issachar, Joseph, Judah, Levi, Naphtali, Reuben, Simeon, and Zebulun, and daughter Dinah.
Jael: Slayer of Sisera.
Japheth: Son of Noah.
Jehoiada: High priest; husband of Jehoshabeath; revolted against Athaliah and made Joash King of Judah.
Jehoshabeath (or Jehosheba): Daughter of Jehoram of Judah; wife of Jehoiada.
Jephthah: Judge in Israel; sacrificed his only daughter because of vow.
Jesse: Son of Obed; father of David.
Jethro: Midianite priest; father of Zipporah.
Jezebel: Phoenician princess; wife of Ahab; mother of Ahaziah, Athaliah, and Jehoram.
Joab: Commander in chief under David; slayer of Abner, Absalom, and Amasa.
Job: Patriarch; underwent many afflictions; comforted by Bildad, Elihu, Eliphaz and Zophar.
Jochebed: Wife of Amram.
Jonah: Prophet; cast into sea and swallowed by great fish.
Jonathan: Son of Saul; friend of David.
Joseph: Son of Jacob and Rachel; sold into slavery by his brothers; husband of Asenath; father of Ephraim and Manassah.
Joshua: Successor of Moses; son of Nun.
Jubal: Son of Lamech and Adah.
Judah: Son of Jacob and Leah.
Judith: Slayer of Holofernes.
Kish: Father of Saul.
Laban: Father of Leah and Rachel.
Lamech: Son of Methuselah; father of Noah.
Lamech: Husband of Adah and Zillah; father of Jabal, Jubal, and Tubal-Cain.
Leah: Daughter of Laban; wife of Jacob; sister of Rachel.
Levi: Son of Jacob and Leah.
Lot: Son of Haran; escaped destruction of Sodom.
Maacah: Mother of Absalom and Tamar.
Mahlon: Son of Elimelech; first husband of Ruth.
Manasseh: Son of Joseph.
Melchizedek: King of Salem.
Methuselah: Patriarch; son of Enoch; father of Lamech.
Michal: Daughter of Saul; wife of David.
Miriam: Prophetess; daughter of Amram; sister of Aaron and Moses.
Mizraim: Son of Ham.
Mordecai: Uncle of Esther; with her aid, saved Jews from Haman's plotting.
Moses: Prophet and lawgiver; son of Amram; brother of Aaron and Miriam; husband of Zipporah.
Naaman: Syrian captain; cured of leprosy by Elisha.
Nabal: Husband of Abigail.
Naboth: Owner of vineyard; stoned to death because he would not sell it to Ahab.
Nadab: Son of Aaron.
Nahor: Father of Terah.
Naomi: Wife of Elimelech; mother-in-law of Ruth.
Naphtali: Son of Jacob and Bilhah.
Nathan: Prophet; reproved David for causing Uriah's death.
Nebuchadnezzar (or Nebuchadrezzar): King of Babylon; destroyer of Jerusalem.
Nehemiah: Jewish leader; empowered by Artaxerxes to rebuild Jerusalem.
Nimrod: Mighty hunter; son of Cush.
Noah: Patriarch; son of Lamech; escaped Deluge by building Ark; father of Ham, Japheth and Shem.
Nun (or Non): Father of Joshua.
Obed: Son of Boaz; father of Jesse.
Og: King of Bashan.
Orpah: Wife of Chilion.
Othniel: Kenezite; judge of Israel; husband of Achsa.
Phinehas: Son of Eleazer.
Phinehas: Son of Eli.
Phut (or Put): Son of Ham.
Potiphar: Egyptian official; bought Joseph.
Rachel: Wife of Jacob; mother of Joseph; sister of Leah.
Rebecca (or Rebekah): Wife of Isaac; mother of Esau and Jacob.
Reuben: Son of Jacob and Leah.
Ruth: Wife of Mahlon, later of Boaz; daughter-in-law of Naomi.
Samson: Judge of Israel; famed for strength; betrayed by Delilah.
Samuel: Hebrew judge and prophet; son of Elkanah.
Sarah (or Sara, Sarai): Wife of Abraham; mother of Isaac.
Sennacherib: King of Assyria.
Seth: Son of Adam; father of Enos.
Shem: Son of Noah; father of Elam.
Simeon: Son of Jacob and Leah.
Sisera: Canaanite captain; slain by Jael.
Tamar: Daughter of David and Maachah; raped by Amnon.
Terah: Son of Nahor; father of Abraham.
Tubal-Cain: Son of Lamech and Zillah.
Uriah: Husband of Bathsheba; sent to death in battle by David.
Vashti: Wife of Ahasuerus; set aside by him.
Zadok: High priest during David's reign.
Zebulun (or Zabulon): Son of Jacob and Leah.
Zillah: Wife of Lamech.
Zilpah: Servant of Leah; mistress of Jacob.
Zipporah: Daughter of Jethro; wife of Moses.
Zophar: Comforter of Job.

Kings of Judah and Israel

Kings Before Division of Kingdom

Saul: First King of Israel; son of Kish; father of Ish-Bosheth, Jonathan and Michal.
Ish-Bosheth (or Eshbaal): King of Israel; son of Saul.
David: King of Judah; later of Israel; son of Jesse; husband of Abigail, Ahinoam, Bathsheba, Michal, etc.; father of Absalom, Adonijah, Amnon, Solomon, Tamar, etc.
Solomon: King of Israel and Judah; son of David; father of Rehoboam.
Rehoboam: Son of Solomon; during his reign the kingdom was divided into Judah and Israel.

Kings of Judah (Southern Kingdom)

Rehoboam: First King.
Abijah (or Abijam or Abia): Son of Rehoboam.
Asa: Probably son of Abijah.
Jehoshaphat: Son of Asa.
Jehoram (or Joram): Son of Jehoshaphat; husband of Athaliah.
Ahaziah: Son of Jehoram and Athaliah.
Athaliah: Daughter of King Ahab of Israel and Jezebel; wife of Jehoram; only queen to occupy the throne of Judah.
Joash (or Jehoash): Son of Ahaziah.

Amaziah: Son of Joash.
Uzziah (or Azariah): Son of Amaziah.
Jotham: Regent, later King; son of Uzziah.
Ahaz: Son of Jotham.
Hezekiah: Son of Ahaz; husband of Hephzi-Bah.
Manasseh: Son of Hezekiah and Hephzi-Bah.
Amon: Son of Manasseh.
Josiah (or Josias): Son of Amon.
Jehoahaz (or Joahaz): Son of Josiah.
Jehoiakim: Son of Josiah.
Jehoiachin: Son of Jehoiakim.
Zedekiah: Son of Josiah; kingdom overthrown by Babylonians under Nebuchadnezzar.

Kings of Israel (Northern Kingdom)

Jeroboam I: Led secession of Israel.
Nadab: Son of Jeroboam I.
Baasha: Overthrew Nadab.
Elah: Son of Baasha.
Zimri: Overthrew Elah.
Omri: Overthrew Zimri.
Ahab: Son of Omri; husband of Jezebel.
Ahaziah: Son of Ahab.
Jehoram (or Joram): Son of Ahab.
Jehu: Overthrew Jehoram.
Jehoahaz (or Joahaz): Son of Jehu.
Jehoash (or Joash): Son of Jehoahaz.
Jeroboam II: Son of Jehoash.
Zechariah: Son of Jeroboam II.
Shallum: Overthrew Zechariah.
Menahem: Overthrew Shallum.
Pekahiah: Son of Menahem.
Pekah: Overthrew Pekahiah.
Hoshea: Overthrew Pekah; kingdom overthrown by Assyrians under Sargon II.

Prophets

Major. Isaiah, Jeremiah, Ezekiel, Daniel.
Minor. Hosea, Obadiah, Nahum, Haggai, Joel, Jonah, Habakkuk, Zechariah, Amos, Micah, Zephaniah, Malachi.

Greek and Roman Mythology

Most of the Greek deities were adopted by the Romans, although in many cases there was a change of name. In the list below, information is given under the Greek name; the name in parentheses is the Roman equivalent. However, all Latin names are listed with cross-references to the Greek ones. In addition, there are several deities that are exclusively Roman. **Bold** words within entries indicate cross references.

Acheron: One of several **Rivers of Underworld.**
Achilles: Greek warrior; slew Hector at Troy; slain by Paris, who wounded him in his vulnerable heel.
Actaeon: Hunter; surprised Artemis bathing; changed by her to stag; and killed by his dogs.
Admetus: King of Thessaly; his wife, Alcestis, offered to die in his place.
Adonis: Beautiful youth loved by Aphrodite.
Aeacus: One of three judges of dead in Hades; son of Zeus.
Aeëtes: King of Colchis; father of Medea; keeper of Golden Fleece.
Aegeus: Father of Theseus; believing Theseus killed in Crete, he drowned himself; Aegean Sea named for him.
Aegisthus: Son of Thyestes; slew Atreus; with Clytemnestra, his paramour, slew Agamemnon; slain by Orestes.
Aegyptus: Brother of Danaus; his sons, except Lynceus, slain by Danaides.
Aeneas: Trojan; son of Anchises and Aphrodite; after fall of Troy, led his followers eventually to Italy; loved and deserted Dido.
Aeolus: One of several **Winds.**
Aesculapius: *See* Asclepius.
Aeson: King of Ioclus; father of Jason; overthrown by his brother Pelias; restored to youth by Medea.
Aether: Personification of sky.
Aethra: Mother of Theseus.
Agamemnon: King of Mycenae; son of Atreus; brother of Menelaus; leader of Greeks against Troy; slain on his return home by Clytemnestra and Aegisthus.
Aglaia: One of several **Graces.**
Ajax: Greek warrior; killed himself at Troy because Achilles's armor was awarded to Odysseus.
Alcestis: Wife of Admetus; offered to die in his place but saved from death by Hercules.
Alcmene: Wife of Amphitryon; mother by Zeus of Hercules.
Alcyone: One of several **Pleiades.**
Alecto: One of several **Furies.**
Alectryon: Youth changed by Ares into cock.
Althaea: Wife of Oeneus; mother of Meleager.
Amazons: Female warriors in Asia Minor; supported Troy against Greeks.
Amor: *See* Eros.
Amphion: Musician; husband of Niobe; charmed stones to build fortifications for Thebes.
Amphitrite: Sea goddess; wife of Poseidon.
Amphitryon: Husband of Alcmene.
Anchises: Father of Aeneas.
Ancile: Sacred shield that fell from heavens; palladium of Rome.
Andraemon: Husband of Dryope.
Andromache: Wife of Hector.
Andromeda: Daughter of Cepheus; chained to cliff for monster to devour; rescued by Perseus.
Anteia: Wife of Proetus; tried to induce Bellerophon to elope with her.
Anteros: God who avenged unrequited love.
Antigone: Daughter of Oedipus; accompanied him to Colonus; performed burial rite for Polynices and hanged herself.
Antinoüs: Leader of suitors of Penelope; slain by Odysseus.
Aphrodite (Venus): Goddess of love and beauty; daughter of Zeus and Dione; mother of Eros.
Apollo: God of beauty, poetry, music; later identified with Helios as Phoebus Apollo; son of Zeus and Leto.
Aquilo: One of several **Winds.**
Arachne: Maiden who challenged Athena to weaving contest; changed to spider.
Ares (Mars): God of war; son of Zeus and Hera.
Argo: Ship in which Jason and followers sailed to Colchis for Golden Fleece.
Argus: Monster with hundred eyes; slain by Hermes; his eyes placed by Hera into peacock's tail.
Ariadne: Daughter of Minos; aided Theseus in slaying Minotaur; deserted by him on island of Naxos and married to Dionysus.
Arion: Musician; thrown overboard by pirates but saved by dolphin.
Artemis (Diana): Goddess of moon; huntress; twin sister of Apollo.
Asclepius (Aesculapius): Mortal son of Apollo; slain by Zeus for raising dead; later deified as god of medicine. Also known as Asklepios.
Astarte: Phoenician goddess of love; variously identified with Aphrodite, Selene, and Artemis.
Asterope: *See* Sterope.
Astraea: Goddess of Justice; daughter of Zeus and Themis.
Atalanta: Princess who challenged her suitors to a foot race; Hippomenes won race and married her.
Athena (Minerva): Goddess of wisdom; known poetically as Pallas Athene; sprang fully armed from head of Zeus.
Atlas: Titan; held world on his shoulders as punishment for warring against Zeus; son of Iapetus.
Atreus: King of Mycenae; father of Menelaus and Agamemnon; brother of Thyestes, three of whose sons he slew and served to him at banquet; slain by Aegisthus.
Atropos: One of several **Fates.**
Aurora: *See* Eos.
Auster: One of several **Winds.**
Avernus: Infernal regions; name derived from small vaporous lake near Vesuvius which was fabled to kill birds and vegetation.
Bacchus: *See* Dionysus.
Bellerophon: Corinthian hero; killed Chimera with aid of Pegasus; tried to reach Olympus on Pegasus and was thrown to his death.
Bellona: Roman goddess of war.
Boreas: One of several **Winds.**
Briareus: Monster of hundred hands; son of Uranus and Gaea.
Briseis: Captive maiden given to Achilles; taken by Agamemnon in exchange for loss of Chryseis, which caused Achilles to cease fighting, until death of Patroclus.
Cadmus: Brother of Europa; planter of dragon seeds from which first Thebans sprang.
Calliope: One of several **Muses.**

Calypso: Sea nymph; kept Odysseus on her island Ogygia for seven years.
Cassandra: Daughter of Priam; prophetess who was never believed; slain with Agamemnon.
Castor: One of **Dioscuri.**
Celaeno: One of several **Pleiades.**
Centaurs: Beings half man and half horse; lived in mountains of Thessaly.
Cephalus: Hunter; accidentally killed his wife Procris with his spear.
Cepheus: King of Ethiopia; father of Andromeda.
Cerberus: Three-headed dog guarding entrance to Hades.
Ceres: *See* Demeter.
Chaos: Formless void; personified as first of gods.
Charon: Boatman on Styx who carried souls of dead to Hades; son of Erebus.
Charybdis: Female monster; personification of whirlpool.
Chimera: Female monster with head of lion, body of goat, tail of serpent; killed by Bellerophon.
Chiron: Most famous of centaurs.
Chronos: Personification of time.
Chryseis: Captive maiden given to Agamemnon; his refusal to accept ransom from her father Chryses caused Apollo to send plague on Greeks besieging Troy.
Circe: Sorceress; daughter of Helios; changed Odysseus's men into swine.
Clio: One of several **Muses.**
Clotho: One of several **Fates.**
Clytemnestra: Wife of Agamemnon, whom she slew with aid of her paramour, Aegisthus; slain by her son Orestes.
Cocytus: One of several **Rivers of Underworld.**
Creon: Father of Jocasta; forbade burial of Polynices; ordered burial alive of Antigone.
Creüsa: Princess of Corinth, for whom Jason deserted Medea; slain by Medea, who sent her poisoned robe; also known as Glaüke.
Creusa: Wife of Aeneas; died fleeing Troy.
Cronus (Saturn): Titan; god of harvests; son of Uranus and Gaea; dethroned by his son Zeus.
Cupid: *See* Eros.
Cybele: Anatolian nature goddess; adopted by Greeks and identified with Rhea.
Cyclopes: Race of one-eyed giants (singular: Cyclops).
Daedalus: Athenian artificer; father of Icarus; builder of Labyrinth in Crete; devised wings attached with wax for him and Icarus to escape Crete.
Danae: Princess of Argos; mother of Perseus by Zeus, who appeared to her in form of golden shower.
Danaïdes: Daughters of Danaüs; at his command, all except Hypermnestra slew their husbands, the sons of Aegyptus.
Danaüs: Brother of Aegyptus; father of Danaïdes; slain by Lynceus.
Daphne: Nymph; pursued by Apollo; changed to laurel tree.
Decuma: One of several **Fates.**
Deino: One of several **Graeae.**
Demeter (Ceres): Goddess of agriculture; mother of Persephone.
Diana: *See* Artemis.
Dido: Founder and queen of Carthage; stabbed herself when deserted by Aeneas.
Diomedes: Greek hero; with Odysseus, entered Troy and carried off Palladium, sacred statue of Athena.
Diomedes: Owner of man-eating horses, which Hercules, as ninth labor, carried off.
Dione: Titan goddess; mother by Zeus of Aphrodite.
Dionysus (Bacchus): God of wine; son of Zeus and Semele.
Dioscuri: Twins Castor and Pollux; sons of Leda by Zeus.
Dis: *See* Pluto, Hades.
Dryads: Wood nymphs.
Dryope: Maiden changed to Hamadryad.
Echo: Nymph who fell hopelessly in love with Narcissus; faded away except for her voice.
Electra: Daughter of Agamemnon and Clytemnestra; sister of Orestes; urged Orestes to slay Clytemnestra and Aegisthus.
Electra: One of several **Pleiades.**
Elysium: Abode of blessed dead.
Endymion: Mortal loved by Selene.
Enyo: One of several **Graeae.**
Eos (Aurora): Goddess of dawn.
Epimetheus: Brother of Prometheus; husband of Pandora.
Erato: One of several **Muses.**
Erebus: Spirit of darkness; son of Chaos.
Erinyes: One of several **Furies.**
Eris: Goddess of discord.
Eros (Amor or Cupid): God of love; son of Aphrodite.
Eteocles: Son of Oedipus, whom he succeeded to rule alternately with Polynices; refused to give up throne at end of year; he and Polynices slew each other.
Eumenides: One of several **Furies.**
Euphrosyne: One of several **Graces.**
Europa: Mortal loved by Zeus, who, in form of white bull, carried her off to Crete.
Eurus: One of several **Winds.**
Euryale: One of several **Gorgons.**
Eurydice: Nymph; wife of Orpheus.
Eurystheus: King of Argos; imposed twelve labors on Hercules.
Euterpe: One of several **Muses.**
Fates: Goddesses of destiny; Clotho (Spinner of thread of life), Lachesis (Determiner of length), and Atropos (Cutter of thread); also called Moirae. Identified by Romans with their goddesses of fate; Nona, Decuma, and Morta; called Parcae.
Fauns: Roman deities of woods and groves.
Faunus: *See* Pan.
Favonius: One of several **Winds.**
Flora: Roman goddess of flowers.
Fortuna: Roman goddess of fortune.
Furies: Avenging spirits; Alecto, Megaera, and Tisiphone; known also as Erinyes or Eumenides.
Gaea: Goddess of earth; daughter of Chaos; mother of Titans; known also as Ge, Gea, Gaia, etc.
Galatea: Statue of maiden carved from ivory by Pygmalion; given life by Aphrodite.
Galatea: Sea nymph; loved by Polyphemus.
Ganymede: Beautiful boy; successor to Hebe as cupbearer of gods.
Glaucus: Mortal who became sea divinity by eating magic grass.
Golden Fleece: Fleece from ram that flew Phrixos to Colchis; Aeëtes placed it under guard of dragon; carried off by Jason.
Gorgons. Female monsters; Euryale, Medusa, and Stheno; had snakes for hair; their glances turned mortals to stone.
Graces: Beautiful goddesses: Aglaia (Brilliance), Euphrosyne (Joy), and Thalia (Bloom); daughters of Zeus.
Graeae. Sentinels for Gorgons.; Deino, Enyo, and Pephredo; had one eye among them, which passed from one to another.
Hades (Dis): Name sometimes given Pluto; also, abode of dead, ruled by Pluto.
Haemon: Son of Creon; promised husband of Antigone; killed himself in her tomb.
Hamadryads: Tree nymphs.
Harpies: Monsters with heads of women and bodies of birds.
Hebe (Juventas): Goddess of youth; cupbearer of gods before Ganymede; daughter of Zeus and Hera.
Hecate: Goddess of sorcery and witchcraft.
Hector: Son of Priam; slayer of Patroclus; slain by Achilles.
Hecuba: Wife of Priam.
Helen: Fairest woman in world; daughter of Zeus and Leda; wife of Menelaus; carried to Troy by Paris, causing Trojan War.
Heliades: Daughters of Helios; mourned for Phaëthon and were changed to poplar trees.
Helios (Sol): God of sun; later identified with Apollo.
Helle: Sister of Phrixos; fell from ram of Golden Fleece; water where she fell named Hellespont.
Hephaestus (Vulcan): God of fire; celestial blacksmith; son of Zeus and Hera; husband of Aphrodite.
Hera (Juno): Queen of heaven; wife of Zeus.
Hercules: Hero and strong man; son of Zeus and Alcmene; performed twelve labors or deeds to be free from bondage under Eurystheus; after death, his mortal share was destroyed, and he became immortal. Also known as Herakles or Heracles. Labors: (1) killing Nemean lion; (2) killing Lernaean Hydra; (3) capturing Erymanthian boar; (4) capturing Cerynean hind; (5) killing man-eating Stymphalian birds; (6) procuring girdle of Hippolyte; (7) cleaning Augean stables; (8) capturing Cretan bull; (9) capturing man-eating horses of Diomedes; (10) capturing cattle of Geryon; (11) procuring golden apples of Hesperides; (12) bringing Cerberus up from Hades.
Hermes (Mercury): God of physicians and thieves; messenger of gods; son of Zeus and Maia.
Hero: Priestess of Aphrodite; Leander swam Hellespont nightly to see her; drowned herself at his death.
Hesperus: Evening star.
Hestia (Vesta): Goddess of hearth; sister of Zeus.
Hippolyte: Queen of Amazons; wife of Theseus.
Hippolytus: Son of Theseus and Hippolyte; falsely accused by Phaedra of trying to kidnap her; slain by Poseidon at request of Theseus.
Hippomenes: Husband of Atalanta, whom he beat in race by dropping golden apples, which she stopped to pick up.

Hyacinthus: Beautiful youth accidentally killed by Apollo, who caused flower to spring up from his blood.
Hydra: Nine-headed monster in marsh of Lerna; slain by Hercules.
Hygeia: Personification of health.
Hyman: God of marriage.
Hyperion: Titan; early sun god; father of Helios.
Hypermnestra: Daughter of Danaüs; refused to kill her husband Lynceus.
Hypnos (Somnus): God of sleep.
Iapetus: Titan; father of Atlas, Epimetheus, and Prometheus.
Icarus: Son of Daedalus; flew too near sun with wax-attached wings and fell into sea and was drowned.
Io: Mortal maiden loved by Zeus; changed by Hera into heifer.
Iobates: King of Lycia; sent Bellerophon to slay Chimera.
Iphigenia: Daughter of Agamemnon; offered as sacrifice to Artemis at Aulis; carried by Artemis to Tauris where she became priestess; escaped from there with Orestes.
Iris: Goddess of rainbow; messenger of Zeus and Hera.
Ismene: Daughter of Oedipus; sister of Antigone.
Iulus: Son of Aeneas.
Ixion: King of Lapithae; for making love to Hera he was bound to endlessly revolving wheel in Tartarus.
Janus: Roman god of gates and doors; represented with two opposite faces.
Jason: Son of Aeson; to gain throne of Ioclus from Pelias, went to Colchis and brought back Golden Fleece; married Medea; deserted her for Creüsa.
Jocasta: Wife of Laius; mother of Oedipus; unwittingly became wife of Oedipus; hanged herself when relationship was discovered.
Juno: *See* Hera.
Jupiter: *See* Zeus.
Juventas: *See* Hebe.
Lachesis: One of several **Fates.**
Laius: Father of Oedipus, by whom he was slain.
Laocoön: Priest of Apollo at Troy; warned against bringing wooden horse into Troy; destroyed with his two sons by serpents sent by Athena.
Lares: Roman ancestral spirits protecting descendants and homes.
Latona: *See* Leto.
Lavinia: Wife of Aeneas after defeat of Turnus.
Leander: Swam Hellespont nightly to see Hero; drowned in storm.
Leda: Mortal loved by Zeus in form of swan; mother of Helen, Clytemnestra, Dioscuri.
Lethe: One of several **Rivers of Underworld.**
Leto (Latona): Mother by Zeus of Artemis and Apollo.
Lucina: Roman goddess of childbirth; identified with Juno.
Lynceus: Son of Aegyptus; husband of Hypermnestra; slew Danaüs.
Maia: Daughter of Atlas; mother of Hermes.
Maia: One of several **Pleiades.**
Manes: Souls of dead Romans, particularly of ancestors.
Mars: *See* Ares.
Marsyas: Shepherd; challenged Apollo to music contest and lost; flayed alive by Apollo.
Medea: Sorceress; daughter of Aeëtes; helped Jason obtain Golden Fleece; when deserted by him for Creüsa, killed her children and Creüsa.
Medusa: One of several **Gorgons.** slain by Perseus, who cut off her head.
Megaera: One of several **Furies.**
Meleager: Son of Althaea; his life would last as long as brand burning at his birth; Althaea quenched and saved it but destroyed it when Meleager slew his uncles.
Melpomene: One of several **Muses.**
Memnon: Ethiopian king; made immortal by Zeus; son of Tithonus and Eos.
Menelaus: King of Sparta; son of Atreus; brother of Agamemnon; husband of Helen.
Mentor: Tutor of Telemachus and friend of Odysseus. In the *Odyssey*, on several occasions, Athena assumes form of Mentor to give advice to Telemachus or Odysseus
Mercury: *See* Hermes.
Merope: One of several **Pleiades.** Merope is said to have hidden in shame for loving a mortal.
Mezentius: Cruel Etruscan king; ally of Turnus against Aeneas; slain by Aeneas.
Midas: King of Phrygia; given gift of turning to gold all he touched.
Minerva: *See* Athena.
Minos: King of Crete; after death, one of three judges of dead in Hades; son of Zeus and Europa.
Minotaur: Monster, half man and half beast, kept in Labyrinth in Crete; slain by Theseus.
Mnemosyne: Goddess of memory; mother by Zeus of Muses.
Moirae: One of several **Fates.**
Momus: God of ridicule.
Morpheus: God of dreams.
Mors: *See* Thanatos.
Morta: One of several **Fates.**
Muses: Goddesses presiding over arts and sciences: Calliope (epic poetry), Clio (history), Erato (lyric and love poetry), Euterpe (music), Melpomene (tragedy), Polymnia or Polyhymnia (sacred poetry), Terpsichore (choral dance and song), Thalia (comedy and bucolic poetry), Urania (astronomy); daughters of Zeus and Mnemosyne.
Naiads: Nymphs of waters, streams, and fountains.
Napaeae: Wood nymphs.
Narcissus: Beautiful youth loved by Echo; in punishment for not returning her love, he was made to fall in love with his image reflected in pool; pined away and became flower.
Nemesis: Goddess of retribution.
Neoptolemus: Son of Achilles; slew Priam; also known as Pyrrhus.
Neptune: *See* Poseidon.
Nereids: Sea nymphs; attendants on Poseidon.
Nestor: King of Pylos; noted for wise counsel in expedition against Troy.
Nike: Goddess of victory.
Niobe: Daughter of Tantalus; wife of Amphion; her children slain by Apollo and Artemis; changed to stone but continued to weep her loss.
Nona: One of several **Fates.**
Notus: One of several **Winds.**
Nox: *See* Nyx.
Nymphs: Beautiful maidens; minor deities of nature.
Nyx (Nox): Goddess of night.
Oceanids: Ocean nymphs; daughters of Oceanus.
Oceanus: Eldest of Titans; god of waters.
Odysseus (Ulysses): King of Ithaca; husband of Penelope; wandered ten years after fall of Troy before arriving home.
Oedipus: King of Thebes; son of Laius and Jocasta; unwittingly murdered Laius and married Jocasta; tore his eyes out when relationship was discovered.
Oenone: Nymph of Mount Ida; wife of Paris, who abandoned her; refused to cure him when he was poisoned by arrow of Philoctetes at Troy.
Ops: *See* Rhea.
Oreads: Mountain nymphs.
Orestes: Son of Agamemnon and Clytemnestra; brother of Electra; slew Clytemnestra and Aegisthus; pursued by Furies until his purification by Apollo.
Orion: Hunter; slain by Artemis and made heavenly constellation.
Orpheus: Famed musician; son of Apollo and Muse Calliope; husband of Eurydice.
Pales: Roman goddess of shepherds and herdsmen.
Palinurus: Aeneas' pilot; fell overboard in his sleep and was drowned.
Pan (Faunus): God of woods and fields; part goat; son of Hermes.
Pandora: Opener of box containing human ills; mortal wife of Epimetheus.
Parcae: One of several **Fates.**
Paris: Son of Priam; gave apple of discord to Aphrodite, for which she enabled him to carry off Helen; slew Achilles at Troy; slain by Philoctetes.
Patroclus: Great friend of Achilles; wore Achilles' armor and was slain by Hector.
Pegasus: Winged horse that sprang from Medusa's body at her death; ridden by Bellerophon when he slew Chimera.
Pelias: King of Ioclus; seized throne from his brother Aeson; sent Jason for Golden Fleece; slain unwittingly by his daughters at instigation of Medea.
Pelops: Son of Tantalus; his father cooked and served him to gods; restored to life; Peloponnesus named for him.
Penates: Roman household gods.
Penelope: Wife of Odysseus; waited faithfully for him for many years while putting off numerous suitors.
Pephredo: One of several **Graeae.**
Periphetes: Giant; son of Hephaestus; slain by Theseus.
Persephone (Proserpine): Queen of infernal regions; daughter of Zeus and Demeter; wife of Pluto.
Perseus: Son of Zeus and Danaë; slew Medusa; rescued Andromeda from monster and married her.
Phaedra: Daughter of Minos; wife of Theseus; caused the death of her stepson, Hippolytus.

Phaethon: Son of Helios; drove his father's sun chariot and was struck down by Zeus before he set world on fire.
Philoctetes: Greek warrior who possessed Hercules' bow and arrows; slew Paris at Troy with poisoned arrow.
Phineus: Betrothed of Andromeda; tried to slay Perseus but turned to stone by Medusa's head.
Phlegethon: One of several **Rivers of Underworld.**
Phosphor: Morning star.
Phrixos: Brother of Helle; carried by ram of Golden Fleece to Colchis.
Pirithous: Son of Ixion; friend of Theseus; tried to carry off Persephone from Hades; bound to enchanted rock by Pluto.
Pleiades: Alcyone, Celaeno, Electra, Maia, Merope, Sterope or Asterope, Taygeta; seven daughters of Atlas; transformed into heavenly constellation, of which six stars are visible (Merope is said to have hidden in shame for loving a mortal).
Pluto (Dis): God of Hades; brother of Zeus.
Plutus: God of wealth.
Pollux: One of **Dioscuri.**
Polyhymnia: *See* Polymnia.
Polymnia (Polyhymnia): One of several **Muses.**
Polynices: Son of Oedipus; he and his brother Eteocles killed each other; burial rite, forbidden by Creon, performed by his sister Antigone.
Polyphemus: Cyclops; devoured six of Odysseus's men; blinded by Odysseus.
Polyxena: Daughter of Priam; betrothed to Achilles, whom Paris slew at their betrothal; sacrificed to shade of Achilles.
Pomona: Roman goddess of fruits.
Pontus: Sea god; son of Gaea.
Poseidon (Neptune): God of sea; brother of Zeus.
Priam: King of Troy; husband of Hecuba; ransomed Hector's body from Achilles; slain by Neoptolemus.
Priapus: God of regeneration.
Procris: Wife of Cephalus, who accidentally slew her.
Procrustes: Giant; stretched or cut off legs of victims to make them fit iron bed; slain by Theseus.
Proetus: Husband of Anteia; sent Bellerophon to Iobates to be put to death.
Prometheus: Titan; stole fire from heaven for man. Zeus punished him by chaining him to rock in Caucasus where vultures devoured his liver daily.
Proserpine: *See* Persephone.
Proteus: Sea god; assumed various shapes when called on to prophesy.
Psyche: Beloved of Eros; punished by jealous Aphrodite; made immortal and united with Eros.
Pygmalion: King of Cyprus; carved ivory statue of maiden which Aphrodite gave life as Galatea.
Pyramus: Babylonian youth; made love to Thisbe through hole in wall; thinking Thisbe slain by lion, killed himself.
Python: Serpent born from slime left by Deluge; slain by Apollo.
Quirinus: Roman war god.
Remus: Brother of Romulus; slain by him.
Rhadamanthus: One of three judges of dead in Hades; son of Zeus and Europa.
Rhea (Ops): Daughter of Uranus and Gaea; wife of Cronus; mother of Zeus; identified with Cybele.
Rivers of Underworld. Acheron (woe), Cocytus (wailing), Lethe (forgetfulness), Phlegethon (fire), Styx (across which souls of dead were ferried by Charon).
Romulus: Founder of Rome; he and Remus suckled in infancy by she-wolf; slew Remus; deified by Romans.
Sarpedon: King of Lycia; son of Zeus and Europa; slain by Patroclus at Troy.
Saturn: *See* Cronus.
Satyrs: Hoofed demigods of woods and fields; companions of Dionysus.
Sciron: Robber; forced strangers to wash his feet, then hurled them into sea where tortoise devoured them; slain by Theseus.
Scylla: Female monster inhabiting rock opposite Charybdis; menaced passing sailors.
Selene: Goddess of moon.
Semele: Daughter of Cadmus; mother by Zeus of Dionysus; demanded Zeus appear before her in all his splendor and was destroyed by his lightning bolts.
Sibyis: Various prophetesses; most famous, Cumaean sibyl, accompanied Aeneas into Hades.
Sileni: Minor woodland deities similar to satyrs (singular: silenus). Sometimes Silenus refers to eldest of satyrs, son of Hermes or of Pan.
Silvanus: Roman god of woods and fields.
Sinis: Giant; bent pines, with which he hurled victims against side of mountain; slain by Theseus.
Sirens: Minor deities who lured sailors to destruction with their singing.
Sisyphus: King of Corinth; condemned in Tartarus to roll huge stone to top of hill; it always rolled back down again.
Sol: *See* Helios.
Somnus: *See* Hypnos.
Sphinx: Monster of Thebes; killed those who could not answer her riddle; slain by Oedipus. Name also refers to other monsters having body of lion, wings, and head and bust of woman.
Sterope (Asterope): One of several **Pleiades.**
Stheno: One of several **Gorgons.**
Styx: One of several **Rivers of Underworld.** The souls of the dead were ferried across the Styx by Charon.
Symplegades: Clashing rocks at entrance to Black Sea; Argo passed through, causing them to become forever fixed.
Syrinx: Nymph pursued by Pan; changed to reeds, from which he made his pipes.
Tantalus: Cruel king; father of Pelops and Niobe; condemned in Tartarus to stand chin-deep in lake surrounded by fruit branches; as he tried to eat or drink, water or fruit always receded.
Tartarus: Underworld below Hades; often refers to Hades.
Taygeta: One of several **Pleiades.**
Telemachus: Son of Odysseus; made unsuccessful journey to find his father.
Tellus: Roman goddess of earth.
Terminus: Roman god of boundaries and landmarks.
Terpsichore: One of several **Muses.**
Terra: Roman earth goddess.
Thalia: One of several **Graces.** Also one of several **Muses.**
Thanatos (Mors): God of death.
Themis: Titan goddess of laws of physical phenomena; daughter of Uranus; mother of Prometheus.
Theseus: Son of Aegeus; slew Minotaur; married and deserted Ariadne; later married Phaedra.
Thisbe: Beloved of Pyramus; killed herself at his death.
Thyestes: Brother of Atreus; Atreus killed three of his sons and served them to him at banquet.
Tiresias: Blind soothsayer of Thebes.
Tisiphone: One of several **Furies.**
Titans: Early gods from which Olympian gods were derived; children of Uranus and Gaea.
Tithonus: Mortal loved by Eos; changed into grasshopper.
Triton: Demigod of sea; son of Poseidon.
Turnus: King of Rutuli in Italy; betrothed to Lavinia; slain by Aeneas.
Ulysses: *See* Odysseus.
Urania: One of several **Muses.**
Uranus: Personification of Heaven; husband of Gaea; father of Titans; dethroned by his son Cronus.
Venus: *See* Aphrodite.
Vertumnus: Roman god of fruits and vegetables; husband of Pomona.
Vesta: *See* Hestia.
Vulcan: *See* Hephaestus.
Winds: Aeolus (keeper of winds), Boreas (Aquilo) (north wind), Eurus (east wind), Notus (Auster) (south wind), Zephyrus (Favonius) (west wind).
Zephyrus: One of several **Winds.**
Zeus (Jupiter): Chief of Olympian gods; son of Cronus and Rhea; husband of Hera.

Norse Mythology

Aesir: Chief gods of Asgard.
Andvari: Dwarf; robbed of gold and magic ring by Loki.
Angerbotha (Angrbotha): Giantess; mother by Loki of Fenrir, Hel, and Midgard serpent.
Asgard (Asgarth): Abode of gods.
Ask (Aske, Askr): First man; created by Odin, Hoenir, and Lothur.
Asynjur: Goddesses of Asgard.
Atli: Second husband of Gudrun; invited Gunnar and Hogni to his court, where they were slain; slain by Gudrun.
Audhumia (Audhumbla): Cow that nourished Ymir; created Buri by licking ice cliff.
Balder (Baldr, Baldur): God of light, spring, peace, joy; son of Odin; slain by Hoth at instigation of Loki.
Bifrost: Rainbow bridge connecting Midgard and Asgard.
Bragi (Brage): God of poetry; husband of Ithunn.

Branstock: Great oak in hall of Volsungs; into it, Odin thrust Gram, which only Sigmund could draw forth.
Brynhild: Valkyrie; wakened from magic sleep by Sigurd; married Gunnar; instigated death of Sigurd; killed herself and was burned on pyre beside Sigurd.
Bur (Bor): Son of Buri; father of Odin, Hoenir, and Lothur.
Buri (Bori): Progenitor of gods; father of Bur; created by Audhumla.
Embla: First woman; created by Odin, Hoenir, and Lothur.
Fafnir: Son of Rodmar, whom he slew for gold in Otter's skin; in form of dragon, guarded gold; slain by Sigurd.
Fenrir: Wolf; offspring of Loki; swallows Odin at Ragnarok and is slain by Vitharr.
Forseti: Son of Balder.
Frey (Freyr): God of fertility and crops; son of Njorth; originally one of **Vanir.**
Freya (Freyja): Goddess of love and beauty; sister of Frey; originally one of **Vanir.**
Frigg (Frigga): Goddess of sky; wife of Odin.
Garm: Watchdog of Hel; slays, and is slain by, Tyr at Ragnarok.
Gimle: Home of blessed after Ragnarok.
Giuki: King of Nibelungs; father of Gunnar, Hogni, Guttorm, and Gudrun.
Glathsehim (Gladsheim): Hall of gods in Asgard.
Gram (meaning "Angry"): Sigmund's sword; rewelded by Regin; used by Sigurd to slay Fafnir.
Greyfell: Sigmund's horse; descended from Sleipnir.
Grimhild: Mother of Gudrun; administered magic potion to Sigurd which made him forget Brynhild.
Gudrun: Daughter of Giuki; wife of Sigurd; later wife of Atli and Jonakr.
Gunnar: Son of Giuki; in his semblance Sigurd won Brynhild for him; slain at hall of Atli.
Guttorm: Son of Giuki; slew Sigurd at Brynhild's request.
Heimdall (Heimdallr): Guardian of Asgard.
Hel: Goddess of dead and queen of underworld; daughter of Loki.
Hiordis: Wife of Sigmund; mother of Sigurd.
Hoenir: One of creators of Ask and Embla; son of Bur.
Hogni: Son of Giuki; slain at hall of Atli.
Hoth (Hoder, Hodur): Blind god of night and darkness; slayer of Balder at instigation of Loki.
Ithunn (Ithun, Iduna): Keeper of golden apples of youth; wife of Bragi.
Jonakr: Third husband of Gudrun.
Jormunrek: Slayer of Swanhild; slain by sons of Gudrun.
Jotunnheim (Jotunheim): Abode of giants.
Lif and Lifthrasir: First man and woman after Ragnarok.
Loki: God of evil and mischief; instigator of Balder's death.
Lothur (Lodur): One of creators of Ask and Embla.
Midgard (Midgarth): Abode of mankind; the earth.
Midgard Serpent: Sea monster; offspring of Loki; slays, and is slain by, Thor at Ragnarok.
Mimir: Giant; guardian of well in Jotunnheim at root of Yggdrasill; knower of past and future.
Mjollnir: Magic hammer of Thor.
Nagifar: Ship to be used by giants in attacking Asgard at Ragnarok; built from nails of dead men.
Nanna: Wife of Balder.
Nibelungs: Dwellers in northern kingdom ruled by Giuki.
Niflheim (Nifelheim): Outer region of cold and darkness; abode of Hel.
Njorth: Father of Frey and Freya; originally one of **Vanir.**
Norns: Demigoddesses of fate: Urth (Urdur) (past), Verthandi (Verdandi) (present), Skuld (future).
Odin (Othin): Head of **Aesir;** creator of world with Vili and Ve; equivalent to Woden (Wodan, Wotan) in Teutonic mythology.
Otter: Son of Rodmar; slain by Loki; his skin filled with gold hoard of Andvari to appease Rodmar.
Ragnarok: Final destruction of present world in battle between gods and giants; some minor gods will survive, and Lif and Lifthrasir will repeople world.
Regin: Blacksmith; son of Rodmar; foster-father of Sigurd.
Rerir: King of Huns; son of Sigi.
Rodmar: Father of Regin, Otter, and Fafnir; demanded Otter's skin be filled with gold; slain by Fafnir, who stole gold.
Sif: Wife of Thor.
Siggeir: King of Goths; husband of Signy; he and his sons slew Volsung and his sons, except Sigmund; slain by Sigmund and Sinflotli.
Sigi: King of Huns; son of Odin.
Sigmund: Son of Volsung; brother of Signy, who bore him Sinflotli; husband of Hiordis, who bore him Sigurd.
Signy: Daughter of Volsung; sister of Sigmund; wife of Siggeir; mother by Sigmund of Sinflotli.
Sigurd: Son of Sigmund and Hiordis; wakened Brynhild from magic sleep; married Gudrun; slain by Guttorm at instigation of Brynhild.
Sigyn: Wife of Loki.
Sinflotli: Son of Sigmund and Signy.
Skuld: One of several **Norns.**
Sleipnir (Sleipner): Eight-legged horse of Odin.
Surt (Surtr): Fire demon; slays Frey at Ragnarok.
Svartalfaheim: Abode of dwarfs.
Swanhild: Daughter of Sigurd and Gudrun; slain by Jormunrek.
Thor: God of thunder; oldest son of Odin; equivalent to Germanic deity Donar.
Tyr: God of war; son of Odin; equivalent to Tiu in Teutonic mythology.
Ull (Ullr): Son of Sif; stepson of Thor.
Urth: One of several **Norns.**
Valhalla (Valhall): Great hall in Asgard where Odin received souls of heroes killed in battle.
Vali: Odin's son: Ragnarok survivor.
Valkyries: Virgins, messengers of Odin, who selected heroes to die in battle and took them to Valhalla; generally considered as nine in number.
Vanir: Early race of gods; three survivors, Njorth, Frey, and Freya, are associated with **Aesir.**
Ve: Brother of Odin; one of creators of world.
Verthandi: One of several **Norns.**
Vili: Brother of Odin; one of creators of world.
Vingolf: Abode of goddesses in Asgard.
Vitharr (Vithar): Son of Odin; survivor of Ragnarok.
Volsung: Descendant of Odin, and father of Signy, Sigmund; his descendants were called Volsungs.
Yggdrasill: Giant ash tree springing from body of Ymir and supporting universe; its roots extended to Asgard, Jotunnheim, and Niffheim.
Ymir (Ymer): Primeval frost giant killed by Odin, Vili, and Ve; world created from his body; also, from his body sprang Yggdrasill.

Egyptian Mythology

Aaru: Abode of the blessed dead.
Amen (Amon, Ammdn): One of chief Theban deities; united with sun god under form of Amen-Ra; husband of Mut.
Amenti: Region of dead where souls were judged by Osiris.
Anubis: Guide of souls to Amenti; son of Osiris; jackal-headed.
Apis: Sacred bull, an embodiment of Ptah; identified with Osiris as Osiris-Apis or Serapis.
Geb (Keb, Seb): Earth god; father of Osiris; represented with goose on head.
Hathor (Athor): Goddess of love and mirth; cow-headed.
Horus: God of day; son of Osiris and Isis; hawk-headed.
Isis: Goddess of motherhood and fertility; sister and wife of Osiris.
Khepera: God of morning sun.
Khnemu (Khnum, Chnuphis, Chnemu, Chnum): Ram-headed god.
Khonsu (Khensu, Khuns): Son of Amen and Mut.
Mentu (Ment): Solar deity, sometimes considered god of war; falcon-headed.
Min (Khem, Chem): Principle of physical life.
Mut (Maut): Wife of Amen.
Nephthys: Goddess of the dead; sister and wife of Set.
Nu: Chaos from which world was created, personified as a god.
Nut: Goddess of heavens; consort of Geb.
Osiris: God of underworld and judge of dead; son of Geb and Nut; brother and husband of Isis.
Ptah (Phtha): Chief deity of Memphis.
Ra: God of the Sun, the supreme god; son of Nut; Pharaohs claimed descent from him; represented as lion, cat, or falcon.
Serapis: God uniting attributes of Osiris and Apis.
Set (Seth): God of darkness or evil; brother and enemy of Osiris; brother and husband of Nephthys.
Shu: Solar deity; son of Ra and Hathor.
Tem (Atmu, Atum, Tum): Solar deity.
Thoth (Dhouti): God of wisdom and magic; scribe of gods; ibis-headed.

A Concise Guide to Grammar and Style

This section discusses and illustrates the basic conventions of American capitalization, italicization, and punctuation.

Capitalization

Capitalize the following:

- **Proper nouns and adjectives derived from proper nouns:**

  Marie Curie — China, Chinese
  Smokey Robinson — Darwin, Darwinian

  But vocabulary words derived from proper nouns are generally lowercase:

  china cups — plaster of paris
  french fries — vienna sausage

- **The names of geographic divisions, regions, and localities and topographical features such as rivers, lakes, and mountains:**

  North Pole — Gulf States
  Middle East — Atlantic Ocean
  Southern Hemisphere — Rocky Mountains
  the North — Lake Tahoe
  Lower East Side — Erie Canal

  Do not capitalize directions: She lives 10 miles north of Boston.

- **The names of nationalities, ethnic groups, tribes, and languages:**

  Spanish — Bantu
  Asian American — Creole

- **Titles when preceding a name:**

  President Lincoln — Aunt Mary
  Queen Victoria — Doctor Johnson
  Senator Kennedy — Professor Davies

  Do not capitalize such terms elsewhere: a biography of the queen; the senator's speech; my aunt, Mary Wilson; the president's fundraising efforts; the residence of the vice president.

- **Epithets:** Ivan the Terrible; Lincoln is known as The Great Emancipator.

- **The names of political and judicial bodies, social organizations, councils, and departments:**

  U.S. Senate — Rotary Club
  Democratic Party — United Negro College Fund
  State Department — U.S. Supreme Court

- **The names for periods, events, and documents of historical importance:**

  Middle Ages — Constitution
  Renaissance — Treaty of Versailles
  Battle of Waterloo — Magna Carta

- **The names for streets, buildings, and monuments:**

  Fifth Avenue — World Trade Center
  Broadway — Statue of Liberty

- **The names for the supreme deity and sacred works:**

  God, the Father Almighty — Bible
  Yahweh — Talmud
  Allah — Qu'ran

- **The names for religious denominations and their members:**

  Buddhism, Buddhists
  Catholicism, Catholics
  Judaism, Jews
  Methodist Church, Methodists
  Society of Friends, Quakers

- **The days of the week, months of the year, holidays, and holy days:**

  Thursday — Labor Day
  December — Passover

- **The pronoun I:**

  I told her I didn't want to go.

- **The first word in the salutation and complimentary close of a letter:**

  My dear Carol . . .
  Very truly yours . . .

- **The first word of a sentence:**

  Are you hungry? Lunch will be served soon.

- **The first word of a direct quotation, except when the quotation is split:**

  I asked, "Do you really like bats?"
  "Yes," said Holly, "they're so cute."

- **The first word and all the key words in the title of a literary or other artistic work:**

  The Bluest Eye (novel)
  A Streetcar Named Desire (play)
  "The Road Not Taken" (poem)
  Starry Night (painting)
  "Only the Lonely" (song)

- **The names of ships, aircraft, and space vehicles:**

  USS *Maine*
  The Spirit of St. Louis
  space shuttle *Challenger*

- **The names of constellations, planets, and stars:**

  Milky Way — Saturn
  the asteroid Juno — Little Dipper

- **The names of geologic eras, periods, epochs, and names of prehistoric divisions:**

  Paleozoic Era — *Pleistocene*
  Quaternary Period — *Stone Age*

- **The genus but not the species name in binomial nomenclature:**

  Canis familiaris (dog)
  Malus pumila (apple tree)

Italicization

Italicize the following (or underline if writing by hand or using a typewriter):

- **The titles of books, plays, book-length poems, magazines, and newspapers:**

War and Peace	*TIME magazine*
Twelfth Night	*National Geographic*
Beowulf	*Miami Herald*

- **The titles of movies and radio and television programs:**

Finding Nemo	*Law & Order*
Car Talk	*Masterpiece Theater*

- **The titles of works of art, including paintings, sculptures, and major musical compositions:**

  Mona Lisa (painting)
  The Thinker (sculpture)
  Swan Lake (ballet)
  Porgy and Bess (opera)

  Do not italicize musical compositions named by number or key: Symphony No. 4; Quartet in E minor.

- **Words, letters, and numbers used as such:**

  How do you spell *ache*?
  Does your name end with a *c* or a *k*?
  The *6* looked like a *0*.

- **Foreign words and phrases that have not been assimilated into English:**

  Alex's *Weltanschauung* was gloomy.
  Ed made a *tarte au citron* for dessert.

- **Words and phrases that are being emphasized:**

  Paris was *the* place to be in the '20s.

- **The names of the plaintiff and defendant in legal citations:** *Johnson* v. *Smith.*

- **The names of ships, aircraft, and space vehicles:**

  USS *Maine*
  The Spirit of St. Louis
  space shuttle *Challenger*

- **The New Latin names of genera, species, subspecies, and varieties in botanical and zoological nomenclature:** *Quercus alba; Homo sapiens.*

Punctuation

End Marks

- **Use a period after a declarative or imperative statement:**

  I went to the library.
  Sign your name here.

- **Use a question mark after a direct question or to indicate uncertainty:**

  What is your name?
  Chaucer's dates are 1340?–1400.

  Do not use a question mark after an indirect question: I asked them what time they were leaving.

- **Use an exclamation point after an exclamatory or emphatic sentence or an interjection:**

  Give me a break!
  Hey! Ouch! Wow!

Comma

Use a comma:

- **To separate words in a list or series:**

  The baby likes grapes, bananas, and cantaloupe.

- **To separate two or more adjectives that come before a noun when *and* can be substituted without changing the meaning:**

  He had a kind, generous nature.
  The dog had thick, soft, shiny fur.

  Do not use the comma if the adjectives together express a single idea or the noun is a compound made up of an adjective and a noun:

  The kitchen had bright yellow curtains.
  A majestic bald eagle soared overhead.

- **To set off words or phrases in apposition to a noun:**

  George Eliot, the great 19th-century novelist, was born in 1819.

  Do not use commas when the appositive word or phrase is essential to the meaning of the sentence:

  The novelist George Eliot was born in 1819.

- **To set off nonessential phrases and clauses:**

  My French professor, who has an odd sense of humor, has been teaching for some 30 years.

  Do not use commas when the phrase or clause is essential to the meaning of the sentence:

  The professor who teaches my French class has an odd sense of humor.

- **To separate the independent clauses joined by a coordinating conjunction in a compound sentence:**

  He lives in New York, and she lives in London.

  Some people like golf, but others prefer tennis.

- **To set off interrupters such as *of course, however, I think,* and *by the way* from the rest of the sentence**:

  She knew, of course, that he was lying.
  By the way, I'll be away next week.

- **To set off an introductory word, phrase, or clause at the beginning of a sentence:**

  Yes, I'd like to go with you.
  After some years, we met again.
  Being tall, she often gets teased.

- **To set off a word in direct address:**

  Thanks, guys, for all your help.
  How was your trip, Kathy?

- **To set off a tag question:**

  You won't do that again, will you?

- **To introduce a short quotation:**

  The queen said, "Let them eat cake!"

- **To close the salutation in a personal letter and the complimentary close in a business or personal letter:**

  Dear Mary, . . . Sincerely, Fred

- **To set off titles and degrees:**

  Sarah Little, Ph.D. Robert Johnson, Jr.

- **To separate sentence elements that might be read incorrectly without the comma:**

  As they entered, in the shadows you could see a figure lurking.

- **To set off the month and day from the year in full dates:**

  The conference will be held on August 6, 2001.

  Do not use a comma when only the month and year appear:

  The conference will be held in August 2001.

- **To set off the city and state in an address:**

  Sam Green
  10 Joy Street
  Boston, MA 02116

  If the address is inserted into text, add a second comma after the state:

  Cincinnati, Ohio, is their home.

Colon

Use a colon:

- **To introduce a list, or words, phrases, and clauses that explain, enlarge upon, or summarize what has gone before:**

  Please provide the following: your name, address, and phone number.

  "No honest poet can ever feel quite sure of the permanent value of what he has written: He may have wasted his time and messed up his life for nothing."—T. S. Eliot

- **To introduce a long quotation:**

  In 1780 John Adams wrote: "English is destined to be in the next and succeeding centuries more generally the language of the world than Latin was in the last or French is in the present age . . . "

- **To separate hour and minute(s) in standard time notation:**

  The train arrives at 9:30.

- **To close the salutation in a business letter:**

  Dear Sir or Madam:

Semicolon

Use a semicolon:

- **To separate the independent clauses in a compound sentence not joined by a conjunction:**

  Only two seats were left; we needed three.

  The situation is hopeful; the storm may lift soon.

- **To separate two independent clauses, the second of which begins with an adverb such as *however, consequently, moreover,* and *therefore*:**

  We waited an hour; however, we couldn't hang around indefinitely.

- **To separate elements already punctuated with commas:**

  Invitations were mailed to the various professors, associate professors, and assistant professors; the secretary of the department; and some of the grad students.

Dashes & Hyphens

- **Use a dash to indicate a sudden break in continuity or to set off an explanatory, a defining, or an emphatic phrase:**

  The sky grew dark—where were the kids?

  Dairy foods—milk, cheese, yogurt—are a good source of calcium.

- **Use a hyphen to join the elements of a compound word or to join the elements of a compound modifier before a noun:**

well-wisher	ice-skating rink
fifty-three	college-age students

- **Use a hyphen to divide a word at the end of a line:**

  Rasputin is one of history's most enig-
  matic and intriguing figures.

Brackets & Parentheses

- **Use brackets to set off words or letters in quoted matter that have been added by someone other than the author:**

  "She [Willa Cather] is certainly one of the great American writers of the 20th century."

- **Use parentheses to set off nonessential information:**

  We spent an hour (more or less) cleaning up.

Apostrophe

Use an apostrophe to indicate:

- **The possessive case of singular and plural nouns, indefinite pronouns, and proper nouns:**

my sister's son	somebody's lunch
my two sisters' sons	Charles's house
the children's toys	the Rosses' friends

- **The plural of letters, numbers, symbols, and words used as such:**

too many *thus*'s	ten *5*'s in a row
spelled with two *e*'s	delete some &'s

- **Missing letters in contractions and missing numbers in dates:**

I'm (I am)	class of '95
ma'am (madam)	winter of '97–'98

Quotation Marks

Use quotation marks:

- **To set off direct quotations:**

  "Let's go to the beach," she suggested.

- **To set off titles of short stories, articles, chapters, essays, songs, poems, and individual radio and television programs:**

  Chapter 9, "The New Englishes"
  sang the "Star-Spangled Banner"
  "The Apparent Trap" episode of *Frasier*

- **To set off words and phrases that are being used in an unusual or questionable way or might be preceded by *so-called*:**

  Mari's "fine" was a day's volunteer work.

  According to the article, bees appear to "remember" landmarks.

Commonly Mispronounced Words

aegis: *ee-jis,* not *ay-jis*
asterisk: *as-ter-isk,* not *as-ter-ik*
alumnae: *a-lum-nee,* not *a-lum-nay*
archipelago: *ar-ki-PEL-a-go,* not *arch-i-pel-a-go*
athlete: *ath-leet,* not *ath-a-leet*
candidate: *kan-di-dayt,* not *kan-i-dayt*
chimera: *kiy-MEER-a,* not *CHIM-er-a*
disastrous: *di-zas-tres,* not *di-zas-ter-es*
electoral: *e-LEK-tor-al,* not *e-lek-TOR-al*
erudition: *ayr-yoo-dish-en,* not *ayr-a-dish-en*
espresso: *e-spres-o,* not *ex-pres-o*
etcetera: *et-set-er-a,* not *ek-set-er-a*
February: *Feb-roo-a-ree,* not *Feb-yoo-a-ree*
inaugural: *in-nawg-yoor-al,* not *in-nawg-a-ral*
hegemony: *he-JEM-o-nee,* not *HEJ-e-mo-nee*
lambaste: *lam-bayst,* not *lam-bast*
larvae: *lar-vee,* not *lar-vay*
library: *li-bra-ry,* not *li-bary*
mischievous: *MIS-che-vus,* not *mis-CHEE-vee-us*
mispronunciation: *mis-pro-nun-see-ay-shun,* not *mis-pro-nown-see-ay-shun*
nuclear: *noo-klee-ur,* not *noo-kyu-lur*
nuptial: *nup-shul,* not *nup-shoo-al*
primer: *prim-mer,* not *pry-mer*
picture: *pik-cher,* not *pit-cher*
prescription: *pre-skrip-shun,* not *per-skrip-shun*
prerogative: *pre-rog-a-tive,* not *per-rog-a-tive*
peremptory: *per-emp-tor-ee,* not *pre-emp-tor-ee*
probably: *prob-a-blee,* not *pra-lee* or *prob-lee*
realtor: *reel-ter,* not *ree-la-ter*
supposedly: *su-pos-ed-lee,* not *su-pos-ab-lee*
spurious: *spyoor-ee-us,* not *spur-ee-us*
ticklish: *tik-lish,* not *tik-i-lish*
triathlon: *try-ath-lon,* not *try-ath-a-lon*

Frequently Misspelled Words

absence
address
advice
all right
arctic
beginning
believe
bicycle
broccoli
bureau
calendar
camaraderie
ceiling
cemetery
changeable
conscientious
conscious
decease
deceive
definite
descent
desperate
device
disastrous
ecstasy
embarrass
exercise
fascinate
February
fiery
fluorescent
foreign
government
grateful
guarantee
harass
height
humorous
independent
jealous
jewelry
judgment
ketchup
knowledge
leisure
library
license
maintenance
mathematics
mediocre
millennium
miniature
miscellaneous
mischievous
misspell
mysterious
necessary
neighbor
nuclear
occasion
occurrence
odyssey
piece
pigeon
playwright
precede
prejudice
privilege
pumpkin
raspberry
receive
rhythm
sacrilegious
science
scissors
separate
sincerely
special
thorough
through
truly
until
Wednesday
weird
you're

National Spelling Bee

The National Spelling Bee was launched by the Louisville, Kentucky, *Courier-Journal* in 1925. With competitions, cash prizes, and a trip to the nation's capital, it was hoped the Bee would stimulate "general interest among pupils in a dull subject." The Scripps Howard News Service took over the Bee in 1941. Over the years the national finals have grown from a mere 9 contestants to about 250. In 2003, 13-year-old Dallas eighth-grader Sai Gunturi took home $12,000 cash, among other prizes, for correctly spelling *pococurante.* Here are the winning words that made past spellers into national champions.

1925	gladiolus
1926	abrogate
1927	luxuriance
1928	albumen
1929	asceticism
1930	fracas
1931	foulard
1932	knack
1933	propitiatory
1934	deteriorating
1935	intelligible
1936	interning
1937	promiscuous
1938	sanitarium
1939	canonical
1940	therapy
1941	initials
1942	sacrilegious
1943	NO BEE
1944	NO BEE
1945	NO BEE
1946	semaphore
1947	chlorophyll
1948	psychiatry
1949	dulcimer
1950	haruspex
1951	insouciant
1952	vignette
1953	soubrette
1954	transept
1955	custaceology
1956	condominium
1957	schappe
1958	syllepsis
1959	cacolet
1960	troche
1961	smaragdine
1962	esquamulose
1963	equipage
1964	sycophant
1965	eczema
1966	ratoon
1967	chihuahua
1968	abalone
1969	interlocutory
1970	croissant
1971	shalloon
1972	macerate
1973	vouchsafe
1974	hydrophyte
1975	incisor
1976	narcolepsy
1977	cambist
1978	deification
1979	maculature
1980	elucubrate
1981	sarcophagus
1982	psoriasis
1983	Purim
1984	luge
1985	milieu
1986	odontalgia
1987	staphylococci
1988	elegiacal
1989	spoliator
1990	fibranne
1991	antipyretic
1992	lyceum
1993	kamikaze
1994	antediluvian
1995	xanthosis
1996	vivisepulture
1997	euonym
1998	chiaroscurist
1999	logorrhea
2000	demarche
2001	succedaneum
2002	prospicience
2003	pococurante

Easily Confused or Misused Words

affect / effect *Effect* is usually a noun that means a result or the power to produce a result: "The sound of the falling rain had a calming effect, nearly putting me to sleep." *Affect* is usually a verb that means to have an influence on: "His loud humming was affecting my ability to concentrate." Note that *effect* can also be a verb meaning to bring about or execute: "The speaker's somber tone effected a dampening in the general mood of the audience."

all right / alright Although *alright* is widely used, it is considered nonstandard English. As the *American Heritage Dictionary* notes, it's not "all right to use alright."

allusion / illusion *Allusion* is a noun that means an indirect reference: "The speech made allusions to the final report." *Illusion* is a noun that means a misconception: "The policy is designed to give an illusion of reform."

alternately / alternatively *Alternately* is an adverb that means in turn; one after the other: "We alternately spun the wheel in the game." *Alternatively* is an adverb that means on the other hand; one or the other: "You can choose a large bookcase or, alternatively, you can buy two small ones."

beside / besides *Beside* is a preposition that means next to: "Stand here beside me." *Besides* is an adverb that means also: "Besides, I need to tell you about the new products my company offers."

bimonthly / semimonthly *Bimonthly* is an adjective that means every two months: "I brought the cake for the bimonthly office party." *Bimonthly* is also a noun that means a publication issued every two months: "The company publishes several popular bimonthlies." *Semimonthly* is an adjective that means happening twice a month: "We have semimonthly meetings on the 1st and the 15th."

capital / capitol The city or town that is the seat of government is called the *capital*; the building in which the legislative assembly meets is the *capitol*. The term *capital* can also refer to an accumulation of wealth or to a capital letter.

cite / site *Cite* is a verb that means to quote as an authority or example: "I cited several eminent scholars in my study of water resources." It also means to recognize formally: "The public official was cited for service to the city." It can also mean to summon before a court of law: "Last year the company was cited for pollution violations." *Site* is a noun meaning location: "They chose a new site for the factory just outside town."

complement / compliment *Complement* is a noun or verb that means something that completes or makes up a whole: "The red sweater is a perfect complement to the outfit." *Compliment* is a noun or verb that means an expression of praise or admiration: "I received compliments about my new outfit."

comprise / compose According to the traditional rule, the whole comprises the parts, and the parts compose the whole. Thus, the board comprises five members, whereas five members compose (or make up) the board. It is also correct to say that the board is composed (not comprised) of five members.

connote / denote *Connote* is a verb that means to imply or suggest: "The word 'espionage' connotes mystery and intrigue." *Denote* is a verb that means to indicate or refer to specifically: "The symbol for 'pi' denotes the number 3.14159."

discreet / discrete *Discreet* is an adjective that means prudent, circumspect, or modest: "Her discreet handling of the touchy situation put him at ease." *Discrete* is an adjective that means separate or individually distinct: "Each company in the conglomerate operates as a discrete entity."

disinterested / uninterested *Disinterested* is an adjective that means unbiased or impartial: "We appealed to the disinterested mediator to facilitate the negotiations." *Uninterested* is an adjective that means not interested or indifferent: "They seemed uninterested in our offer."

emigrant / immigrant *Emigrant* is a noun that means one who leaves one's native country to settle in another: "The emigrants spent four weeks aboard ship before landing in Los Angeles." *Immigrant* is a noun that means one who enters and settles in a new country: "Most of the immigrants easily found jobs." One emigrates *from* a place; one immigrates *to* another.

farther / further *Farther* is an adjective and adverb that means to or at a more distant point: "We drove 50 miles today; tomorrow, we will travel 100 miles farther." *Further* is an adjective and adverb that means to or at a greater extent or degree: "We won't be able to suggest a solution until we are further along in our evaluation of the problem." It can also mean in addition or moreover: "They stated further that they would not change the policy."

few / less *Few* is an adjective that means small in number. It is used with countable objects: "This department has few employees." *Less* is an adjective that means small in amount or degree. It is used with objects of indivisible mass: "Which jar holds less water?"

figuratively / literally *Figuratively* is an adverb that means metaphorically or symbolically: "Happening upon the shadowy figure, they figuratively jumped out of their shoes." *Literally* is an adverb that means actually: "I'm not exaggerating when I say I literally fell off my chair." It also means according to the exact meaning of the words: "I translated the Latin passage literally."

foreword / forward *Foreword* is a noun that means an introductory note or preface: "In my foreword I explained my reasons for writing the book." *Forward* is an adjective or adverb that means toward the front: "I sat in the forward section of the bus." "Please step forward when your name is called." *Forward* is also a verb that means to send on: "Forward the letter to the customer's new address."

founder / flounder In its primary sense *founder* means to sink below the surface of the water: "The ship foundered after colliding with an iceberg." By extension, *founder* means to fail utterly. *Flounder* means to move about clumsily, or to act with confusion. A good synonym for *flounder* is blunder: "After floundering through the first half of the course, Amy finally passed with the help of a tutor."

hanged / hung *Hanged* is the past tense and past participle of hang when the meaning is to execute by suspending by the neck: "They hanged the prisoner for treason." "The convicted killer was hanged at dawn." *Hung* is the past tense and participle of hang when the meaning is to suspend from above with no support from below: "I hung the painting on the wall." "The painting was hung at a crooked angle."

historic / historical In general usage, *historic* refers to what is important in history, while *historical* applies more broadly to whatever existed in the past whether it was important or not: "a historic summit meeting between the prime ministers;" "historical buildings torn down in the redevelopment."

i.e. / e.g. The abbreviation *e.g.* means for example (from Latin *exempli gratia)*: "Her talents were legion and varied (e.g., deep sea diving, speed reading, bridge, and tango dancing)." The abbreviation *i.e.* means that is or in other words (from Latin *id est):* "The joy of my existence (i.e., my stamp collection) embues my life with meaning."

it's / its *It's* is a contraction for it is, whereas *its* is the possessive form of it: "It's a shame that we cannot talk about its size."

laid / lain / lay *Laid* is the past tense and the past participle of the verb lay and not the past tense of lie. *Lay* is the past tense of the verb lie and *lain* is the past participle: "He laid his books down and lay down on the couch, where he has lain for an hour."

lend / loan Although some people feel *loan* should only be used as a noun, *lend* and *loan* are both acceptable as verbs in standard English: "Can you lend (loan) me a dollar?" However, only *lend* should be used in figurative senses: "Will you lend me a hand?"

nonplussed Meaning perplexed or bewildered, *nonplussed* is very often thought to mean just the opposite—calm, unruffled, cool-as-a-cucumber. A common mistake is to think the word means not "plussed," but no such word exists. *Nonplussed* originates from the Latin *non* (no) and *plus* (more, further), and means a state in which no more can be done—one is so perplexed that further action is impossible. "The lexicographer grew increasingly agitated and nonplussed by the frequency with which she noted the misuse of *nonplussed*."

passed / past *Passed* is the past tense and past participle of *pass. Past* refers to time gone by; it is also a preposition meaning beyond. "In the past decade, I passed over countless opportunities; I was determined not to let them get past me again."

penultimate Meaning "next to last," *penultimate* is often mistakenly used to mean "the very last," or the ultimate: "The perfectionist was crestfallen when he was awarded the penultimate prize; the grand prize went to another."

principal / principle *Principal* is a noun that means a person who holds a high position or plays an important role: "The school principal has 20 years of teaching experience." *Principal* is also an adjective that means chief or leading: "The necessity of moving to another city was the principal reason I turned down the job offer." *Principle* is a noun that means a rule or standard: "They refused to compromise their principles."

stationary / stationery *Stationary* is an adjective that means fixed or unmoving: "They maneuvered around the stationary barrier in the road." *Stationery* is a noun that means writing materials: "We printed the letters on company stationery."

their/there/they're *Their* is the possessive form of they; *there* refers to place; and *they're* is the contraction of *they are.* "They're going there because their mother insisted they become proficient in Serbo-Croatian."

who's / whose *Who's* is the contraction of *who is. Whose* is the possessive form of *who.* "Who's going to figure out whose job it is to clean the stables?"

Some Basic Phrases in Other Languages

	The language itself	hello	good bye	please	thank you	English	yes	no	traditional toast
German	Deutsch	hallo	auf Wiedersehen	bitte	danke	Englisch	ja	nein	prosit
Dutch	Nederlands	hallo	tot ziens	alstublieft	dankjewel	engels	ja	nee	proost
Danish	dansk	hej	farvel	(1)	tak	engelsk	ja	nej	skål
Swedish	svenska	hej	hejdå	tack	tack	engelska	ja	nej	skål
French	français	bonjour	au revoir	s'il vous plaît	merci	anglais	oui	non	santé
Spanish	español	hola	adiós	por favor	gracias	inglés	sí	no	salud
Italian	italiano	ciao	arrivederci	per favore	grazie	inglese	si	no	salute
Hebrew	ivrit	shalom	lehitraot	bevakasha	toda	anglit	ken	lo	le-chaim
Irish	Gaeilge	fáilte	slán	le do thoil	go raibh maith agat	Béarla	sea[2]	ní ha[3]	slainte
Swahili	Kiswahili	(4)	kwa heri	tafadhali	asante	Kingereza	ndiyo	siyo	—
Japanese	nihongo	konnichiwa	sayonara	kudasai	arigatou	eigo	hai	iie	kanpai
Finnish	suomi	päivää	näkemiin	ole hyvä	kiitos	englanti	kyllä	ei	kippis
Indonesian	bahasa Indonesia	selamat pagi	selamat tinggal[5]	tolong	terima kasih	bahasa Inggris	ya	tidak	—

1. There is no single word or expression that directly corresponds to "please." Polite requests are made in different ways. 2. Literally, "it is." This can only be used in answering a question with the verb "to be." In Irish there is no word for "yes" or "no." Instead, the speaker repeats the verb from the question in the affirmative or the negative: Did you sleep well? I did. Are you coming? I am not. 3. Literally, "it is not." See above. 4. There is no single word for "hello." Which greeting is used will depend on the relative ages, number (singular or plural), and/or race of the speakers. For example, "hujambo," reply "sijambo," would be used by two people of similar age and race, whereas "jambo," reply "jambo," would be used by a white person and a black person. 5. Said by the person leaving; "selamat jalan" is said by the person staying.

Foreign Words and Phrases

The English meanings given below are not necessarily literal translations. Foreign words and phrases should be set in italics (or underlined if written in longhand) if their meanings are likely to be unknown to the reader. Whether the expression is familiar or unfamiliar, however, is a matter of judgment. Below, all foreign words have been italicized for the sake of emphasis.

ad absurdum (ad ab-sir′dum) [Lat.]: to the point of absurdity. "He tediously repeated his argument *ad absurdum.*"

ad infinitum (ad in-fun-eye′tum) [Lat.]: to infinity. "The lecture seemed to drone on *ad infinitum.*"

ad nauseam (ad noz′ee-um) [Lat.]: to a sickening degree. "The politician uttered one platitude after another *ad nauseam.*"

aficionado (uh-fish′ya-nah′doh) [Span.]: an ardent devotee. "I was surprised at what a baseball *aficionado* she had become."

annus mirabilis (an′us muh-ra′buh-lis) [Lat.]: wonderful year. "Last year was the *annus mirabilis* for my company."

a priori (ah pree-or′ee) [Lat.]: based on theory rather than observation. "The fact that their house is in such disrepair suggests *a priori* that they are having financial difficulties."

au courant (oh′ koo-rahn′) [Fr.]: up-to-date. "The shoes, the hair, the clothes—every last detail of her dress, in fact—was utterly *au courant.*"

beau geste (boh zhest′) [Fr.]: a fine or noble gesture, often futile. "My fellow writers supported me by writing letters of protest to the publisher, but their *beau geste* could not prevent the inevitable."

beau monde (boh′ mond′) [Fr.]: high society. "Such elegant decor would impress even the *beau monde.*"

bête noire (bet nwahr′) [Fr.]: something or someone particularly disliked. "Talk of the good old college days way back when had become his *bête noire,* and he began to avoid his school friends."

bona fide (boh′na fide) [Lat.]: in good faith; genuine. "For all her reticence and modesty, it was clear that she was a *bona fide* expert in her field."

bon mot (bon moe′) [Fr.]: a witty remark or comment. "One *bon mot* after another flew out of his mouth, charming the audience."

bon vivant (bon vee-vahnt′) [Fr.]: a person who lives luxuriously and enjoys good food and drink. "It's true he's quite the *bon vivant,* but when he gets down to business he conducts himself like a Spartan."

carpe diem (kar′pay dee′um) [Lat.]: seize the day. "So what if you have an 8:00 a.m. meeting tomorrow and a full day of appointments? *Carpe diem!*"

carte blanche (kart blonsh′) [Fr.]: unrestricted power to act on one's own. "I may have *carte blanche* around the office, but at home I'm a slave to my family's demands."

cause célèbre (koz suh-leb′ruh) [Fr.]: a widely known controversial case or issue. "The Sacco and Vanzetti trial became an international *cause célèbre* during the 1920s."

caveat emptor (kav′ee-ot emp′tor) [Lat.]: let the buyer beware. "Before you leap at that real estate deal, *caveat emptor!*"

comme ci comme ça (kom see′ kom sah′) [Fr.]: so-so. "The plans for the party strike me as *comme ci comme ça.*"

comme il faut (kom eel foe′) [Fr.]: as it should be; fitting. "His end was truly *comme il faut.*"

coup de grâce (koo de grahss′) [Fr.]: finishing blow. "After an already wildly successful day, the *coup de grâce* came when she won best all-around athlete."

cri de coeur (kree′ de kur′) [Fr.]: heartfelt appeal. "About to leave the podium, he made a final *cri de coeur* to his people to end the bloodshed."

de rigueur (duh ree-gur′) [Fr.]: strictly required, as by etiquette, usage, or fashion. "Loudly proclaiming one's support for radical causes had become *de rigueur* among her crowd."

deus ex machina (day′us ex mahk′uh-nuh) [Lat.]: a contrived device to resolve a situation. "Stretching plausibility, the movie concluded with a *deus ex machina* ending in which everyone was rescued at the last minute."

dolce vita (dole′chay vee′tuh) [Ital.]: sweet life; the good life perceived as one of physical pleasure and self-indulgence. "My vacation this year is going to be two uninterrupted weeks of *dolce vita.*"

Doppelgänger* (dop′pul-gang-ur) [Ger.]: a ghostly double or counterpart of a living person. "I could not shake the sense that some shadowy *Doppelgänger* echoed my every move."

enfant terrible (ahn-fahn′ tay-reeb′luh) [Fr.]: an incorrigible child; an outrageously outspoken or bold person. "He played the role of *enfant terrible,* jolting us with his blunt assessment."

entre nous (ahn′truh noo′) [Fr.]: between ourselves; confidentially. "*Entre nous,* their marriage is on the rocks."

ex cathedra (ex kuh-thee′druh) [Lat.]: with authority; used especially of those pronouncements of the pope that are considered infallible. "I resigned myself to obeying; my father's opinions were *ex cathedra* in our household."

ex post facto (ex′ post fak′toh) [Lat.]: retroactively. "I certainly hope that the change in policy will be honored *ex post facto.*"

fait accompli (fate ah-kom-plee′) [Fr.]: an accomplished fact, presumably irreversible. "There's no use protesting—it's a *fait accompli.*"

faux pas (foh pah′) [Fr.]: a social blunder. "Suddenly, she realized she had unwittingly committed yet another *faux pas.*"

flagrante delicto (fla-grahn′tee di-lik′toh) [Lat.]: in the act. "The detective realized that without hard evidence he had no case; he would have to catch the culprit *flagrante delicto.*"

glasnost (glaz′nohst) [Rus.]: open and frank discussion: initiated by Mikhail Gorbachev in 1985 in the Soviet Union. "Once the old chairman retired, the spirit of *glasnost* pervaded the department."

hoi polloi (hoy′ puh-loy′) [Gk.]: the common people. "Marie Antoinette recommended cake to the *hoi polloi.*"

in loco parentis (in loh′koh pa-ren′tiss) [Lat.]: in the place of a parent. "The court appointed a guardian for the children, to serve *in loco parentis.*"

in situ (in sit′too) [Lat.]: situated in the original or natural position. "I prefer seeing statues *in situ* rather than in the confines of a museum."

in vino veritas (in vee′no vare′i-toss) [Lat.]: in wine there is truth. "By the end of the party, several of the guests had made a good deal of their private lives public, prompting the host to murmur to his wife, '*in vino veritas.*'"

ipso facto (ip′soh fak′toh) [Lat.]: by the fact itself. "An extremist, *ipso facto,* cannot become part of a coalition."

je ne sais quoi (zhun say kwah′) [Fr.]: I know not what; an elusive quality. "She couldn't explain it, but there was something *je ne sais quoi* about him that she found devastatingly attractive."

mano a mano (mah′no ah mah′no) [Span.]: directly or face-to-face in a confrontation or conflict. "'Stay out of it,' he admonished his friends, 'I want to handle this guy *mano a mano.*'"

mea culpa (may′uh kul′puh) [Lat.]: I am to blame. "His *mea culpa* was so offhand that I hardly think he meant it."

memento mori (muh-men′toh more′ee) [Lat.]: a reminder that you must die. "The skull rested on the mantlepiece as a *memento mori.*"

modus operandi (moh′dus op-er-an′dee) [Lat.]: a method of operating. "Her *modus operandi* is to sugarcoat the truth so thoroughly that the news almost seems welcome."

mot juste (moh zhoost′) [Fr.]: the exact, appropriate word. "'Rats!' screamed the defiant three-year-old, immensely proud of his *mot juste.*"

ne plus ultra (nee′ plus ul′truh) [Lat.]: the most intense degree of a quality or state. "Pulling it from the box, he realized he was face to face with the *ne plus ultra* of computers."

nom de plume (nom duh ploom′) [Fr.]: pen name. "Deciding it was time to sit down and begin a novel, the would-be writer spent the first several hours deciding upon a suitable *nom de plume.*"

nota bene (noh′tuh ben′nee) [Ital.]: note well; take notice. "Her postcard included a reminder, *nota bene,* I'll be returning on the 11 o'clock train."

persona non grata (per-soh′nuh non grah′tuh) [Lat.]: unacceptable or unwelcome person. "Once I was cut out of the will, I became *persona non grata* among my relatives."

pro bono (pro boh′noh) [Lat.]: done or donated without charge; free. "The lawyer's *pro bono* work gave him a sense of value that his work on behalf of the corporation could not."

quid pro quo (kwid′ pro kwoh′) [Lat.]: something for something; an equal exchange. "She vowed that when she had the means, she would return his favors *quid pro quo.*"

sans souci (sahn soo-see′) [Fr.]: carefree. "Their mood was definitely *sans souci.*"

savoir-faire (sav′wahr fair′) [Fr.]: the ability to say and do the correct thing. "She presided over the gathering with impressive *savoir-faire.*"

sine qua non (sin′ay kwah nohn′) [Lat.]: indispensable. "Lemon is the *sine qua non* of this recipe."

terra incognita (tare′uh in-kog-nee′tuh) [Lat.]: unknown territory. "When the conversation suddenly switched from contemporary fiction to medieval Albanian playwrights, he felt himself entering *terra incognita.*"

veni, vidi, vici (ven′ee vee′dee vee′chee) [Lat.]: I came, I saw, I conquered. "After the takeover the business mogul gloated, '*veni, vidi, vici.*'"

vox populi (voks pop′yoo-lie) [Lat.]: the voice of the people. "My sentiments echo those of the *vox populi.*"

Wanderjahr* (vahn′der-yahr) [Ger.]: a year or period of travel, especially following one's schooling. "The trio took off on their *Wanderjahr* soon after they graduated, to circle the globe by bicycle."

Weltschmerz* (velt′shmerts) [Ger.]: sorrow over the evils of the world. "His poetry expressed a certain *Weltschmerz,* or world-weariness."

Zeitgeist* (zite′guyst) [Ger.]: the spirit of the time; general trend of thought or feeling characteristic of a particular period of time. "She blamed it on the *Zeitgeist,* which encouraged hedonistic excess."

*German nouns are capitalized. A familiar German expression that is not italicized, however, should be lowercased, following the English conventions of not capitalizing common nouns. "His proclivities leaned more to the occult than to the philosophical: a poltergeist he could understand; the *Zeitgeist* he could not."

Most Widely Spoken Languages in the World

Language	Approx. number of speakers
1. Chinese (Mandarin)	1,075,000,000
2. English	514,000,000
3. Hindustani	496,000,000
4. Spanish	425,000,000
5. Russian	275,000,000
6. Arabic	256,000,000
7. Bengali	215,000,000
8. Portuguese	194,000,000
9. Malay-Indonesian	176,000,000
10. French	129,000,000

Source: Ethnologue, 13th Edition and other sources.

Most Studied Foreign Languages in the U.S.[1]

Language	Number of BA degrees awarded
1. Spanish	7,031
2. French	2,514
3. German	1,125
4. Russian	340
5. Japanese	321
6. Italian	237
7. Chinese	183
8. Latin	79
9. Portuguese	33
10. Ancient Greek	26

1. By number of bachelor degrees awarded in 1999–2000. *Source:* U.S. Dept. of Education, National Center for Education Statistics, *Digest of Education Statistics 2001.*

Latin and Greek Word Elements

English is a living language, and it is growing all the time. One way that new words come into the language is when words are borrowed from other languages. New words are also created when words or word elements, such as roots, prefixes, and suffixes, are combined in new ways.

Many English words and word elements can be traced back to Latin and Greek. Often you can guess the meaning of an unfamiliar word if you know the meaning.

A **word root** is a part of a word. It contains the core meaning of the word, but it cannot stand alone. A **prefix** is also a word part that cannot stand alone. It is placed at the beginning of a word to change its meaning. A **suffix** is a word part that is placed at the end of a word to change its meaning. Often you can guess the meaning of an unfamiliar word if you know the meaning of its parts; that is, the root and any prefixes or suffixes that are attached to it.

Latin Roots, Prefixes, and Suffixes

Latin was the language spoken by the ancient Romans. As the Romans conquered most of Europe, the Latin language spread throughout the region. Over time, the Latin spoken in different areas developed into separate languages, including Italian, French, Spanish, and Portuguese. These languages are considered "sisters," as they all descended from Latin, their "mother" language.

In 1066 England was conquered by William, duke of Normandy, which is in northern France. For several hundred years after the Norman invasion, French was the language of court and polite society in England. It was during this period that many French words were borrowed into English. Linguists estimate that some 60% of our common everyday vocabulary today comes from French. Thus many Latin words came into English indirectly through French.

Many Latin words came into English directly, though, too. Monks from Rome brought religious vocabulary as well as Christianity to England beginning in the 6th century. From the Middle Ages onward many scientific, scholarly, and legal terms were borrowed from Latin.

During the 17th and 18th centuries, dictionary writers and grammarians generally felt that English was an imperfect language whereas Latin was perfect. In order to improve the language, they deliberately made up a lot of English words from Latin words. For example, fraternity, from Latin fraternitas, was thought to be better than the native English word brotherhood.

Many English words and word parts can be traced back to Latin and Greek. The following table lists some common Latin roots.

Latin root	Basic meaning	Example words
-dict-	to say	contradict, dictate, diction, edict, predict
-duc-	to lead, bring, take	deduce, produce, reduce
-gress-	to walk	digress, progress, transgress
-ject-	to throw	eject, inject, interject, project, reject, subject
-pel-	to drive	compel, dispel, impel, repel
-pend-	to hang	append, depend, impend, pendant, pendulum
-port-	to carry	comport, deport, export, import, report, support
-scrib-, -script-	to write	describe, description, prescribe, prescription, subscribe, subscription, transcribe, transcription
-tract-	to pull, drag, draw	attract, contract, detract, extract, protract, retract, traction
-vert-	to turn	convert, divert, invert, revert

From the example words in the above table, it is easy to see how roots combine with prefixes to form new words. For example, the root *-tract-*, meaning "to pull," can combine with a number of prefixes, including *de-* and *re-*. Detract means literally "to pull away" (*de-*, "away, off") and retract means literally "to pull back" (*re-*, "again, back"). The following table gives a list of Latin prefixes and their basic meanings.

Latin prefix	Basic meaning	Example words
co-	together	coauthor, coedit, coheir
de-	away, off; generally indicates reversal or removal in English	deactivate, debone, defrost, decompress, deplane
dis-	not, not any	disbelief, discomfort, discredit, disrepair, disrespect
inter-	between, among	international, interfaith, intertwine, intercellular, interject
non-	not	nonessential, nonmetallic, nonresident, nonviolence, nonskid, nonstop
post-	after	postdate, postwar, postnasal, postnatal
pre-	before	preconceive, preexist, premeditate, predispose, prepossess, prepay
re-	again; back, backward	rearrange, rebuild, recall, remake, rerun, rewrite
sub-	under	submarine, subsoil, subway, subhuman, substandard
trans-	across, beyond, through	transatlantic, transpolar

Words and word roots may also combine with suffixes. Here are examples of some important English suffixes that come from Latin:

Latin suffix	Basic meaning	Example words
-able, -ible	forms adjectives and means "capable or worthy of"	likable, flexible
-ation	forms nouns from verbs	create, creation; civilize, civilization
-fy, -ify	forms verbs and means "to make or cause to become"	purify, acidify, humidify
-ment	forms nouns from verbs	entertain, entertainment; amaze, amazement
-ty, -ity	forms nouns from adjectives	subtlety, certainty, cruelty, frailty, loyalty, royalty; eccentricity, electricity, peculiarity, similarity, technicality

Greek Roots, Prefixes, and Suffixes

The following table lists some common Greek roots:

Greek root	Basic meaning	Example words
-anthrop-	human	misanthrope, philanthropy, anthropomorphic
-chron-	time	anachronism, chronic, chronicle, synchronize, chronometer
-dem-	people	democracy, demography, demagogue, endemic, pandemic
-morph-	form	amorphous, metamorphic, morphology
-path-	feeling, suffering	empathy, sympathy, apathy, apathetic, psychopathic
-pedo-, -ped-	child, children	pediatrician, pedagogue
-philo-, -phil-	having a strong affinity or love for	philanthropy, philharmonic, philosophy
-phon-	sound	polyphonic, cacophony, phonetics

The following table gives a list of Greek prefixes and their basic meanings:

Greek prefix	Basic meaning	Example words
a-, an-	without	achromatic, amoral, atypical, anaerobic
anti-, ant-	opposite; opposing	anticrime, antipollution, antacid
auto-	self, same	autobiography, automatic, autopilot
bio-, bi-	life, living organism; biology, biological	biology, biophysics, biotechnology, biopsy
geo-	Earth; geography	geography, geomagnetism, geophysics, geopolitics
hyper-	excessive, excessively	hyperactive, hypercritical, hypersensitive
micro-	small	microcosm, micronucleus, microscope
mono-	one, single, alone	monochrome, monosyllable, monoxide
neo-	new, recent	neonatal, neophyte, neoconservatism, neofascism, neodymium
pan-	all	panorama, panchromatic, pandemic, pantheism
thermo-, therm-	heat	thermal, thermometer, thermostat

Words and word roots may also combine with suffixes. Here are examples of some important English suffixes that come from Greek:

Greek suffix	Basic meaning	Example words
-ism	forms nouns and means "the act, state, or theory of"	criticism, optimism, capitalism
-ist	forms agent nouns from verbs ending in -ize or nouns ending in -ism and is used like -er	conformist, copyist, cyclist
-ize	forms verbs from nouns and adjectives	formalize, jeopardize, legalize, modernize, emphasize, hospitalize, industrialize, computerize
-gram	something written or drawn, a record	cardiogram, telegram
-graph	something written or drawn; an instrument for writing, drawing, or recording	monograph; phonograph, seismograph
-logue, -log	speech, discourse; to speak	monologue, dialogue, travelogue
-logy	discourse, expression; science, theory, study	phraseology, biology, dermatology
-meter, -metry	measuring device; measure	geometry, kilometer, parameter, perimeter
-oid	forms adjectives and nouns and means "like, resembling" or "shape, form"	humanoid, spheroid, trapezoid
-phile	one that loves or has a strong affinity for; loving	audiophile, Francophile
-phobe, -phobia	one that fears a specified thing; an intense fear of a specified thing	agoraphobe, agoraphobia, xenophobe, xenophobia
-phone	sound; device that receives or emits sound; speaker of a language	homophone, geophone, telephone, Francophone

American Sign Language

Sign language for the deaf was first systematized in France during the 18th century by Abbot Charles-Michel l'Epée. French Sign Language (FSL) was brought to the United States in 1816 by Thomas Gallaudet, founder of the American School for the Deaf in Hartford, Conn. He developed American Sign Language (ASL), a language of gestures and hand symbols that express words and concepts. It is the fourth most used language in the United States today.

In many respects, sign language is just like any spoken language, with a rich vocabulary and a highly organized, rule-governed grammar. But in sign language, information is processed through the eyes rather than the ears. Thus, facial expression and body movement play an important part in conveying information.

In spoken language, the relationship between most words and the objects and concepts they represent is arbitrary—there is nothing about the word "tree" that actually suggests a tree, either in the way it is spelled or pronounced. In the same way, in sign language most signs do not suggest, or imitate, the thing or idea they represent, and must be learned. Sign language may be acquired naturally as a child's first language, or it may be learned through study and practice.

"last year" or "one year ago"

Sign language shares other similarities with spoken languages. Like any living language, ASL grows and changes over time to accommodate native users' needs. ASL also has regional varieties, equivalent to spoken accents, with different signs being used in different parts of the country.

American Manual Alphabet

Along with sign language and lip reading, many deaf people also communicate with the manual alphabet, which uses finger positions that correspond to the letters of the alphabet to spell out words and names.

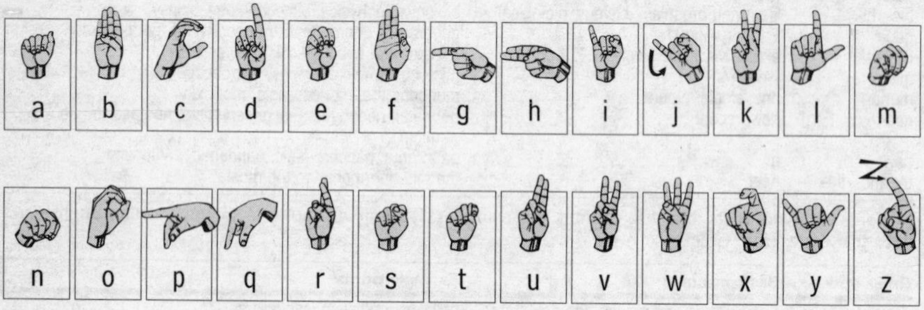

Braille Alphabet

Braille is a system of printing and writing for the blind created in 1824 by Louis Braille (1809–1852), a French inventor who went blind from an accident when he was three. Each character in Braille is made up of an arrangement of one-to-six raised points used in 63 possible combinations. Braille is read by passing the fingers over the raised characters. A universal Braille code for English-speaking countries was adopted in 1932.

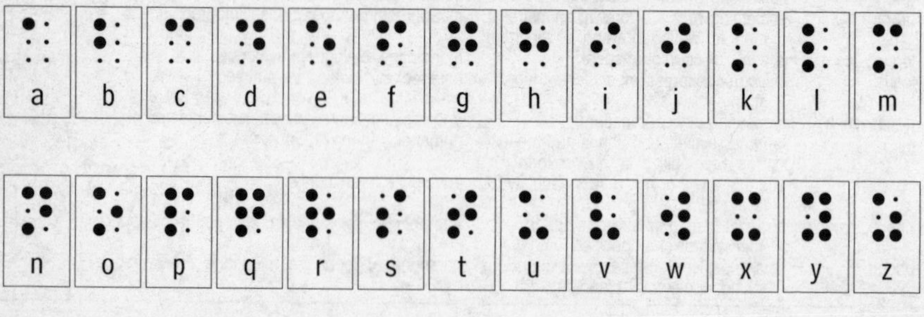

Geography Glossary

latitude lines Imaginary lines running horizontally around the globe. Also called parallels, latitude lines are equidistant from each other. Each degree of latitude is about 69 miles (110 km) apart. Zero degrees (0°) latitude is the equator, the widest circumference of the globe. Latitude is measured from 0° to 90° north and 0° to 90° south—90° north is the North Pole and 90° south is the South Pole.

longitude lines Imaginary lines, also called meridians, running vertically around the globe. Unlike latitude lines, longitude lines are not parallel. Meridians meet at the poles and are widest apart at the equator. Zero degrees longitude (0°) is called the prime meridian. The degrees of longitude run 180° east and 180° west from the prime meridian.

geographic coordinates Latitude and longitude lines form an imaginary grid over the Earth's surface. By combining longitude and latitude measurements, any location on earth can be determined. The units of measurement for geographic coordinates are degrees (°), minutes (′), and seconds (″). Like a circle, the Earth has 360 degrees. Each degree is divided into 60 minutes, which in turn is divided into 60 seconds. Latitude and longitude coordinates also include cardinal directions: north or south of the equator for latitude, and east or west of the prime meridian for longitude. The geographic coordinates of New York City, for example, are 40° N, 74° W, meaning that it is located 40 degrees north latitude and 74 degrees west longitude. Using minutes and seconds as well as degrees, the coordinates for New York would be 40°42′51″ N, 74°0′23″ W. (Latitude is always listed first.) A less common format for listing coordinates is in decimal degrees. The Tropic of Cancer, for example, can be expressed in degrees and minutes (23°30′ N) or in decimal degrees (23.5° N).

hemisphere A hemisphere is half the Earth's surface. The four hemispheres are the Northern and Southern hemispheres, divided by the equator (0° latitude), and the Eastern and Western hemispheres, divided by the prime meridian (0° longitude) and the International Date Line (180°).

equator Zero degrees latitude. The Sun is directly overhead the equator at noon on the two equinoxes (March and Sept. 20 or 21). The equator divides the globe into the Northern and Southern hemispheres. The equator appears halfway between the North and South poles, at the widest circumference of the globe. It is 24,901.55 miles (40,075.16 km) long.

prime meridian Zero degrees longitude (0°). The prime meridian runs through the Royal Greenwich Observatory in Greenwich, England (the location was established in 1884 by international agreement). The prime meridian divides the globe into the Western and Eastern hemispheres. The Earth's time zones are measured from the prime meridian. The time at 0° is called Universal Time (UT) or Greenwich Mean Time (GMT). With the Greenwich meridian as the starting point, each 15° east and west marks a new time zone. The 24 time zones extend east and west around the globe for 180° to the International Date Line. When it is noon along the prime meridian, it is midnight along the International Date Line.

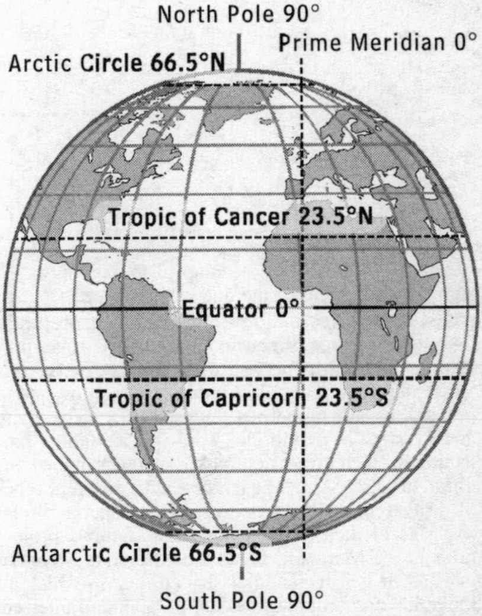

International Date Line Located at 180° longitude (180° E and 180° W are the same meridian). Regions to the east of the International Date Line are counted as being one calendar day earlier than the regions to the west. Although the International Date Line generally follows the 180° meridian (most of which lies in the Pacific Ocean), it does diverge in places. Since 180° runs through several countries, it would divide those countries not simply into two different time zones, but into two different calendar days. To avoid such unnecessary confusion, the date line dips and bends around countries to permit them to share the same time.

Tropic of Cancer A line of latitude located at 23°30' north of the equator. The Sun is directly overhead the Tropic of Cancer on the summer solstice in the Northern Hemisphere (June 20 or 21). It marks the northernmost point of the tropics, which falls between the Tropic of Cancer and the Tropic of Capricorn.

Tropic of Capricorn A line of latitude located at 23°30' south. The Sun is directly overhead the Tropic of Capricorn on the summer solstice in the Southern Hemisphere (Dec. 20 or 21). It marks the southernmost point of the tropics.

Arctic Circle A line of latitude located at 66°30' north, delineating the Northern Frigid Zone of the Earth.

Antarctic Circle A line of latitude located at 66°30' south, delineating the Southern Frigid Zone of the Earth.

Mercator Projection

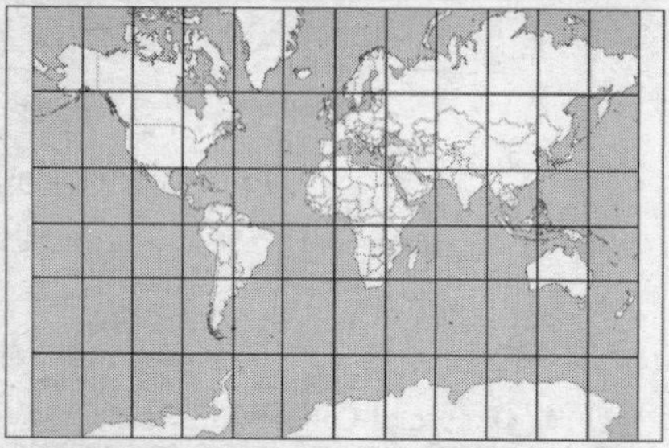

Robinson Projection

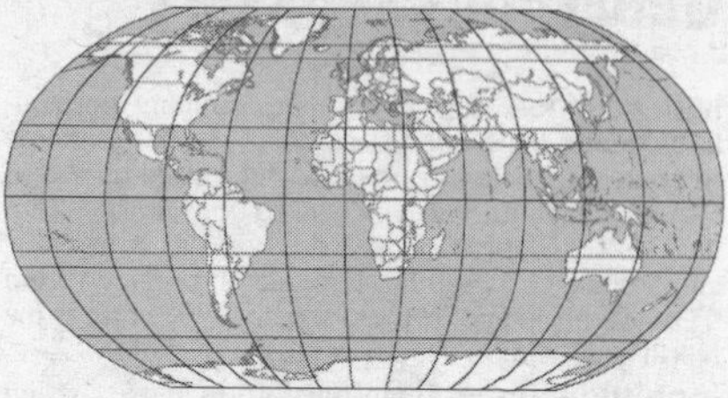

globe The most accurate map of the Earth, duplicating its spherical shape and relative size.

map projections Two-dimensional representations of the three-dimensional Earth. Because projections attempt to present the spherical Earth on a flat plane, they inevitably produce distortions. Map projections are numerous and complex (e.g., there are a variety of cylindrical, conic, or azimuthal projections). Each projection has advantages and serves different purposes, and each produces different types of distortions in direction, distance, shape, and relative size of areas. One of the most famous projections is the Mercator, created by Geradus Mercator in 1569. It is a rectangular-shaped map in which all longitude and latitude lines are parallel and intersect at right angles (on a globe, meridians are not parallel, but grow narrower, eventually converging at the poles). Near the equator, the scale of the Mercator is accurate, but the farther one moves toward the poles, the greater the distortion—Antarctica in the far south and Greenland in the far north, for example, appear gigantic. The Mercator projection was used well into the 20th century, but has now been superseded by others, including the widely used Robinson projection. The Robinson projection is an elliptical-shaped map with a flat top and bottom. Developed in 1963 by Arthur H. Robinson, it is an orthophanic ("right appearing") projection, which attempts to reflect the spherical appearance of the Earth. The meridians, for example, are curved arcs, which gives the flat map a three-dimensional appearance. But to convey the likeness of a curved, three-dimensional globe, the Robinson projection must in fact distort shape, area, scale, and distance. The Albers, Lambert, Mollweide, and Winkel Tripel are some of the other commonly used map projections.

Explorations

Country or place	Event	Explorer	Date
AFRICA			
Sierra Leone	Explored	Hanno, Carthaginian seaman	c. 520 B.C.
Zaire River (Congo)	Mouth visited[1]	Diogo Cão, Portuguese explorer	c. 1484
Cape of Good Hope	Rounded	Bartolomeu Diaz, Portuguese explorer	1488
Gambia River	Explored	Mungo Park, Scottish explorer	1795
Sahara	Crossed	Dixon Denham and Hugh Clapperton, English explorers	1822–1823
Zambezi River	Explored[1]	David Livingstone, Scottish explorer	1851
Sudan	Explored	Heinrich Barth, German explorer	1852–1855
Victoria Falls	Explored[1]	David Livingstone, Scottish explorer	1855
Lake Tanganyika	Explored[1]	Richard Burton and John Speke, British explorers	1858
Lake Victoria, identified as the source of the Nile	Explored	John Speke, British explorer	1858
Zaire River (Congo)	Traced	Sir Henry M. Stanley, British explorer	1877
ASIA			
Punjab (India)	Invaded	Alexander the Great, king of Macedonia	327 B.C.
China	Explored	Marco Polo, Italian traveler	c. 1272
Tibet	Visited	Odoric of Pordenone, Italian monk	c. 1325
Southern China	Explored	Niccolò dei Conti, Venetian traveler	c. 1440
India	Explored (Cape route)	Vasco da Gama, Portuguese navigator	1498
Japan	Visited	St. Francis Xavier of Spain, missionary	1549
Arabia	Explored	Carsten Niebuhr, German explorer	1762
China	Explored	Ferdinand Richthofen, German scientist	1868
Mongolia	Explored	Nikolai M. Przhevalsky, Russian explorer	1870–1873
Central Asia	Explored	Sven Hedin, Swedish scientist	1890–1908
EUROPE			
Shetland Islands	Visited	Pytheas of Massilia (Marseille), Greek navigator and geographer	c. 325 B.C.
North Cape	Rounded	Ottar, Norwegian explorer	c. 870

Country or place	Event	Explorer	Date
Iceland	Colonized	Norwegian noblemen	c. 890–900
NORTH AMERICA			
Greenland	Colonized	Eric the Red, Norwegian	c. 985
Labrador, Newfoundland, Nova Scotia (?)	Explored[1]	Leif Ericsson, Norse explorer	1000
West Indies	Explored[1]	Christopher Columbus, Italian	1492
North America	Coast explored[1]	Giovanni Caboto (John Cabot), for British	1497
Pacific Ocean	Sighted[1]	Vasco Núñez de Balboa, Spanish explorer	1513
Florida	Explored	Ponce de León, Spanish explorer	1513
Mexico	Conquered	Hernando Cortés, Spanish adventurer	1519–1521
St. Lawrence River	Explored[1]	Jacques Cartier, French navigator	1534
Southwest United States	Explored	Francisco Coronado, Spanish explorer	1540–1542
Colorado River	Explored[1]	Hernando de Alarcón, Spanish explorer	1540
Mississippi River	Explored[1]	Hernando de Soto, Spanish explorer	1541
Frobisher Bay	Explored[1]	Martin Frobisher, English seaman	1576
Maine Coast	Explored	Samuel de Champlain, French explorer	1604
Jamestown, Va.	Settled	John Smith, English colonist	1607
Hudson River	Explored	Henry Hudson, English navigator	1609
Hudson Bay (Canada)	Explored[1]	Henry Hudson	1610
Baffin Bay	Explored[1]	William Baffin, English navigator	1616
Lake Michigan	Navigated	Jean Nicolet, French explorer	1634
Arkansas River	Explored[1]	Jacques Marquette and Louis Jolliet, French explorers	1673
Mississippi River	Explored	Sieur de La Salle, French explorer	1682
Bering Strait	Explored[1]	Vitus Bering, Danish explorer	1728
Alaska	Explored[1]	Vitus Bering	1741
Mackenzie River (Canada)	Explored[1]	Sir Alexander Mackenzie, Scottish-Canadian explorer	1789
Northwest United States	Explored	Meriwether Lewis and William Clark, American explorers	1804–1806
Northeast Passage (Arctic Ocean)	Navigated	Nils Nordenskjöld, Swedish explorer	1879
Greenland	Explored	Robert E. Peary, American explorer	1892
Northwest Passage	Navigated	Roald Amundsen, Norwegian explorer	1906
SOUTH AMERICA			
Continent	Explored	Christopher Columbus, Italian	1498
Brazil	Explored[1]	Pedro Alvarez Cabral, Portuguese	1500
Peru	Conquered	Francisco Pizarro, Spanish explorer	1532–1533
Amazon River	Explored	Francisco Orellana, Spanish explorer	1541
Cape Horn	Explored[1]	Willem C. Schouten, Dutch navigator	1615
OCEANIA			
Papua New Guinea	Explored	Jorge de Menezes, Portuguese explorer	1526
Australia	Explored	Abel Janszoon Tasman, Dutch navigator	1642
Tasmania	Explored[1]	Abel Janszoon Tasman	1642
Australia	Crossed	John McDouall Stuart, English explorer	1862
Australia	Explored	Robert Burke and William Wills, Australian explorers	1861
New Zealand	Sighted (and named)	Abel Janszoon Tasman, Dutch navigator	1642
New Zealand	Explored	James Cook, English navigator	1769
ARCTIC, ANTARCTIC, AND MISCELLANEOUS			
Africa, Middle East, Asia, and Europe	Explored	Ibn Batuta, greatest Arab traveler	1325–1349
Ocean exploration	Expedition	Ferdinand Magellan's ships circled globe for Spain	1519–1522
Galápagos Islands	Explored	Diego de Rivadeneira, Spanish captain	1535
Spitsbergen	Explored	Willem Barents, Dutch navigator	1596
Antarctic Circle	Crossed	James Cook, English navigator	1773
Antarctica	Explored[1]	Nathaniel Palmer, American whaler (archipelago), and Fabian Gottlieb von Bellingshausen, Russian admiral (mainland)	1820–1821
Antarctica	Explored	Charles Wilkes, American explorer	1840
North Pole	Reached[2]	Robert E. Peary, American explorer	1909
South Pole	Reached	Roald Amundsen, Norwegian explorer	1911

1. First European to reach the area. 2. Admiral Peary's claim to have reached the Pole has been disputed from the beginning—as was the claim made by his former colleague, Dr. Frederick Cook, who has been generally dismissed as a charlatan. The credit ultimately went to Peary, a claim officially backed by the U.S. Congress. But recent scholarship, including evidence culled from the journals and diaries of both Cook and Peary, has cast doubt on both explorers' veracity. If it is the case that neither reached the Pole, then the credit goes to Joseph Fletcher, who landed a U.S. Air Force C-47 plane there in 1952.

The Continents

A continent is defined as a large unbroken land mass completely surrounded by water, although in some cases continents are (or were in part) connected by land bridges. The seven continents are North America, South America, Europe, Asia, Africa, Australia, and Antarctica. The island groups in the Pacific are often called Oceania but this name does *not* imply that scientists consider them the remains of a continent.

Political considerations have often overridden geographical facts when it came to naming continents. Geographically, Europe, including the British Isles, is a large western peninsula of the continent of Asia; and many geographers, when referring to Europe and Asia, speak of the Eurasian continent. But traditionally, Europe is counted as a separate continent, with the Ural and the Caucasus mountains forming the line of demarcation between Europe and Asia. To the south of Europe, Asia has an odd-shaped peninsula jutting westward, which has a large number of political subdivisions. The northern section is taken up by Turkey; to the south of Turkey there are Syria, Iraq, Israel, Jordan, Saudi Arabia, and a number of smaller Arab countries. All these are part of Asia. Traditionally, the island of Cyprus in the Mediterranean is also considered to be part of Asia. The Caribbean islands, Central America, and Greenland are considered part of North America.

Continental Drift and Plate-Tectonics Theory

Source: U.S. Dept. of the Interior, Geological Survey

According to the theory of continental drift, the world was made up of a single continent through most of geologic time. That continent eventually separated and drifted apart, forming into the seven continents we have today. The first comprehensive theory of continental drift was suggested by the German meteorologist Alfred Wegener in 1912. The hypothesis asserts that the continents consist of lighter rocks that rest on heavier crustal material—similar to the manner in which icebergs float on water. Wegener contended that the relative positions of the continents are not rigidly fixed but are slowly moving—at a rate of about one yard per century.

According to the generally accepted plate-tectonics theory, scientists believe that Earth's surface is broken into a number of shifting slabs or plates, which average about 50 miles in thickness. These plates move relative to one another above a hotter, deeper, more mobile zone at average rates as great as a few inches per year. Most of the world's active volcanoes are located along or near the boundaries between shifting plates and are called plate-boundary volcanoes.

World Land Areas and Elevations

Area	Approximate land area sq. km	Approximate land area sq. mi.	Percentage of total land area	Elevation, feet and meters	
				Highest	Lowest
WORLD	148,647,000	57,393,000	100.0%	Mt. Everest, Tibet-Nepal, 29,035 ft. (8,850 m)[1]	Dead Sea, Israel-Jordan, 1,349 ft. below sea level (–411 m)
AFRICA	30,065,000	11,608,000	20.2	Mt. Kilimanjaro, Tanzania, 19,340 ft. (5,895 m)	Lake Assal, Djibouti, 512 ft. below sea level (–156 m)
ANTARCTICA	13,209,000	5,100,000	8.9	Vinson Massif, Ellsworth Mts., 16,066 ft. (4,897 m)	Lowest land point hidden within Bentley Subglacial Trench[2]
ASIA (includes the Middle East)	44,579,000	17,212,000	30.0	Mt. Everest, Tibet-Nepal, 29,035 ft. (8,850 m)	Dead Sea, Israel-Jordan, 1,349 ft. below sea level (–411 m)
AUSTRALIA (includes Oceania)	8,112,000	3,132,000	5.3	Mt. Kosciusko, Australia, 7,310 ft. (2,228 m)	Lake Eyre, Australia, 52 ft. below sea level (–12 m)
EUROPE (the Ural Mountains in Russia form the boundary between Europe and Asia)	9,938,000	3,837,000	6.7	Mt. Elbrus, Russia/Georgia, 18,510 ft. (5,642 m)	Caspian Sea, Russia/Kazakhstan 92 ft. below sea level (–28 m)
NORTH AMERICA (includes Central America and the Caribbean)	24,474,000	9,449,000	16.5	Mt. McKinley, Alaska, 20,320 ft. (6,194 m)	Death Valley, Calif., 282 ft. below sea level (–86 m)
SOUTH AMERICA	17,819,000	6,879,000	12.0	Mt. Aconcagua, Argentina, 22,834 ft. (6,960 m)	Valdes Peninsula, Argentina 131 ft. below sea level (–40 m)

1. The 1954 elevation of Everest, 29,028 ft. (8,848 m) was revised on Nov. 11, 1999, and now stands at 29,035 ft. (8,850 m).
2. Bentley Subglacial Trench itself (ice, not land) is –8,327 ft. below sea level (–2,538 m). *Source:* WorldAtlas.com.

Volcanoes of the World

Source: U.S. Dept. of the Interior, Geological Survey

About 550 volcanoes have erupted on Earth's surface since recorded history; about 60 are active each year. Far more have erupted unobserved on the ocean floor. Most volcanoes exist at the boundaries of Earth's crustal plates, such as the famous Ring of Fire that surrounds the Pacific Ocean plate. Fifty volcanoes have erupted in the United States since recorded history, and the United States ranks third, behind Indonesia and Japan, in the number of historically active volcanoes.

The Nature of Volcanoes

Volcanoes are built by the accumulation of their own eruptive products—lava, bombs (crusted over ash flows), and tephra (airborne ash and dust). A volcano is most commonly a conical hill or mountain built around a vent that connects with reservoirs of molten rock below the surface of Earth. The term *volcano* also refers to the opening or vent through which molten rock and gases are expelled.

Driven by buoyancy and gas pressure, the molten rock, which is lighter than the surrounding solid rock, forces its way upward and may ultimately break though zones of weaknesses in Earth's crust. If so, an eruption begins, and the molten rock may pour from the vent as nonexplosive lava flows, or it may shoot violently into the air as dense clouds of lava fragments. Larger fragments fall back around the vent, and accumulations of fall-back fragments may move downslope as ash flows under the force of gravity. Some of the finer ejected materials may be carried by the wind and fall to the ground many miles away. The finest ash particles may be injected miles into the atmosphere and carried many times around the world by stratospheric winds before settling out.

Magma, Lava, and Pumice

Molten rock below the surface of Earth that rises in volcanic vents is known as magma, but after it erupts from a volcano it is called lava. Originating many tens of miles beneath the ground, the ascending magma commonly contains some crystals, fragments of surrounding (unmelted) rocks, and dissolved gases, but it is primarily a liquid composed of oxygen, silicon, aluminum, iron, magnesium, calcium, sodium, potassium, titanium, and manganese. Magmas also contain many other chemical elements in trace quantities. Upon cooling, the liquid magma may precipitate crystals of various minerals until solidification is complete to form an igneous or magmatic rock.

Lava is red-hot when it pours or blasts out of a vent but soon changes to dark red, gray, black, or some other color as it cools and solidifies. Very hot, gas-rich lava containing abundant iron and magnesium is fluid and flows like hot tar, whereas cooler, gas-poor lava high in silicon, sodium, and potassium flows sluggishly, like thick honey, or in other cases, like pasty, blocky masses.

All magmas contain dissolved gases, and as they rise to the surface to erupt, the confining pressures are reduced and the dissolved gases are liberated either quietly or explosively. If the lava is a thin fluid (not viscous), the gases may escape easily. But if the lava is thick and pasty (highly viscous), the gases will not move freely but will build up tremendous pressure and ultimately escape with explosive violence, throwing out great masses of solid rock as well as lava, dust, and ashes.

The violent separation of gas from lava may produce rock froth called pumice. Some of this froth is so light—because of the many gas bubbles—that it floats on water. In many eruptions the froth is shattered explosively into small fragments that are hurled high into the air in the form of volcanic cinders (red or black), volcanic ash (commonly tan or gray), and volcanic dust. □

Recent Volcanic Activity

(**Bold** indicates activity in 2003)

Volcano	Date of last eruption or activity
Adatara, Honshu, Japan	Sept. 15, 1997
Akutan, Alaska	March 10, 1996
Amukta, Alaska	Sept. 17, 1996
Anatahan, Mariana Islands	**June 26, 2003**
Arenal, Costa Rica	April 4, 2001
Asama, Honshu, Japan	**April 18, 2003**
Aso, Kyushu, Japan	**July 10, 2003**
Axial Seamount	Jan. 25–28, 1998
Bandai, Honshu, Japan	Aug. 16, 2000
Barren Island, Indian Ocean	**March 18, 2003**
Bezymianny, Kamchatka, Russia	March 15, 2000
Bromo, Java, Indonesia	Nov. 30, 2000
Mount Cameroon, Cameroon	June 7, 2000
Canlaon, Philippines	**July 11, 2003**
Cerro Azul, Galápagos Islands, Ecuador	Oct. 5, 1998
Cerro Negro, Nicaragua	Aug. 6, 1999
Chiginagak, Alaska	Nov. 7, 1997
Chikurachki, Kuril Islands, Russia	**June 2003**
Mt. Cleveland, Chuginadak, Alaska	March 20, 2001
Colima, Mexico	**July 17, 2003**
Copahue, Argentina and Chile	July 16, 2000
Dukono, Indonesia	**June 2, 2003**
Eastern Gemini Seamount, Vanuatu	Feb. 23, 1996
Erta Ale, Ethiopia	**Jan. 14, 2003**
Etna, Sicily, Italy	**June 7, 2003**
Fernandina, Galápagos	Jan. 25, 1995
Fogo, Cape Verde	April 2, 1995
Fuego, Guatemala	**July 9, 2003**
Grimsvotn, Iceland	Dec. 18–28, 1998
Guagua Pichincha, Ecuador	**April 17, 2003**
Hachijo-Jima, Izu Islands, Japan	Sept. 10, 2002
Hakkoda, Japan	July 12, 1997
Hekla, Iceland	Feb. 26, 2000
Mount Hili Aludo, Indonesia	May 13, 1997
Hosho, Kyushu, Japan	Oct. 12, 1995
Ijen, Java, Indonesia	Feb. 5, 2001
Iwate-san, Honshu, Japan	July 10, 1998
Jackson Segment, N. Gorda Ridge (nr. Oregon)	April 3, 2001
Kaba, Sumatra, Indonesia	Aug. 17, 2000
Mount Karangetang, Indonesia	**July 20, 2003**
Karymsky, Kamchatka, Russia	**May 27, 2003**

Volcano	Date of last eruption or activity
Kavachi Seamount, Solomon Islands	Jan. 13, 2002
Kelut, Java, Indonesia	Jan. 29, 2001
Kick-'em-Jenny (nr. Grenada)	**March 15, 2003**
Kilauea, Hawaii	**ongoing**
Kliuchevskoi, Kamchatka, Russia	**Jan. 2003**
Komagatake, Hokkaido, Japan	Nov. 8, 2000
Korovin, Alaska	June 30, 1998
Krakatau, Indonesia	March 27, 2001
Langila, New Britain	July 11, 2002
Lascar, Chile	July 20, 2000
Leroboleng, Indonesia	**July 14, 2003**
Mount Lewotobi, Indonesia	**May 30, 2003**
Llaima, Chile	**April 11, 2003**
Loihi Seamount, Hawaii	July 26, 1996
Lokon, Sulawesi, Indonesia	**April 1, 2003**
Long Valley caldera, California	April 2, 1996
Lopevi, Central Islands, Vanuatu	**June 14, 2003**
La Madera, Nicaragua	Sept. 27, 1996
Manam, Papua New Guinea	**May 27, 2003**
Maroa, New Zealand	March 30, 2001
Masaya, Nicaragua	April 23, 2001
Mauna Loa, Hawaii	**March 18, 2003**
Mayon, Philippines	**May 14, 2003**
McDonald Island, Australia	Dec. 1996
Merapi, Indonesia	March 3, 2002
Metis Shoal, Tonga	June 6, 1995
Momotombo, Nicaragua	April 4, 1996
Monowai Seamount, Kermadec Islands	Dec. 5, 1997
Nyamuragira, Congo (Dem. Rep.)	Feb. 6, 2001
Nyiragongo, Congo (Dem. Rep.)	**Feb. 2003**
Okmok, Alaska	May 2, 1997
Mount Oyama, Japan	April 2, 2002
Pacaya, Guatemala	**July 5, 2003**
Pago, Papua New Guinea	**March 13, 2003**
Papandayan, Java, Indonesia	Nov. 11, 2002
Pavlof, Alaska	June 3, 1997
Peuet Sague, Indonesia	April 27, 1998
Piparo, Trinidad	Feb. 22, 1997
Piton de la Fournaise, Réunion, Indian Ocean	**July 28, 2003**
Popocatepetl, Mexico	**July 19, 2003**
Rabaul, Papua New Guinea	**Jan. 2003**
Reventador, Ecuador	**Jan. 2003**
Rincon de la Vieja, Costa Rica	Feb. 16, 1998
Rotorua, New Zealand	Jan. 26, 2001
Ruapehu, New Zealand	Sept. 13, 1999
Ruby Seamount, Mariana Islands	Oct. 25, 1995
Mount St. Helens, Washington	July 1, 1998
Sakura-Jima, Japan	Oct. 9, 2000
San Cristobal, Nicaragua	May 10, 2001
Semeru, Java, Indonesia	**July 21, 2003**
Sheveluch, Kamchatka, Russia	**ongoing**
Shin-dake, Kuchinoerabujima Island, Japan	Aug. 26, 1999
Shishaldin, Unimak Island, Alaska	May 15, 2000
Soufriere Hills, Montserrat, West Indies	**ongoing**
South Sister, Oregon	May 8, 2001
Stromboli, Italy	Nov. 2002
Tavurvur, Papua New Guinea	Sept. 6, 2000
Taal, Philippines	Sept. 30, 1999
Telica, Nicaragua	Aug. 11, 1999
Terceira, Azores	Jan. 8, 1999
Tonga (unnamed volcano)	Jan. 18, 1999
Tungurahua, Ecuador	**ongoing**
Ulawun, Papua New Guinea	**June 10, 2003**
Usu, Japan	April 17, 2000
Veniaminof, Alaska	**Oct. 1, 2003**
Villarrica, Chile	Jan. 20–May 30, 2000
White Island, New Zealand	**July 27, 2000–ongoing**
Yellowstone, Wyoming	Jan. 9, 1998
Zacatecas, Mexico	June 1997

Source: Volcano World. Web: www.volcanoworld.org.

The Deadliest Volcanic Eruptions

Volcano	Year	Deaths	Major cause of deaths
Tambora, Indonesia	1815	92,000	Starvation
Krakatau, Indonesia	1883	36,417	Tsunami
Mount Pelee, Martinique	1902	29,025	Ash flows
Ruiz, Colombia	1985	25,000	Mudflows
Unzen, Japan	1792	14,300	Volcano collapse, tsunami
Laki, Iceland	1783	9,350	Starvation
Kelut, Indonesia	1919	5,110	Mudflows
Galunggung, Indonesia	1882	4,011	Mudflows
Vesuvius, Italy	1631	3,500	Mudflows, lava flows
Vesuvius, Italy	79	3,360	Ash flows, falls
Papandayan, Indonesia	1772	2,957	Ash flows
Lamington, Papua New Guinea	1951	2,942	Ash flows
El Chichon, Mexico	1982	2,000	Ash flows
Soufriere, St. Vincent	1902	1,680	Ash flows
Oshima, Japan	1741	1,475	Tsunami
Asama, Japan	1783	1,377	Ash flows, mudflows
Taal, Philippines	1911	1,335	Ash flows
Mayon, Philippines	1814	1,200	Mudflows
Agung, Indonesia	1963	1,184	Ash flows
Cotopaxi, Ecuador	1877	1,000	Mudflows
Pinatubo, Philippines	1991	800	Disease
Komagatake, Japan	1640	700	Tsunami
Ruiz, Colombia	1845	700	Mudflows
Hibok-Hibok, Philippines	1951	500	Ash flows

NOTE: All eruptions with more than 500 known human fatalities. Based on data in *Volcanic Hazards: A Sourcebook on the Effects of Eruptions* by Russell J. Blong (Academic Press, 1984). *Source:* Volcano World. Web: www.volcanoworld.org.

Earthquakes

The Severity of an Earthquake

Source: National Earthquake Information Center, U.S. Geological Survey

Earthquakes are the result of forces deep within Earth's interior that continuously affect its surface. The energy from these forces is stored in a variety of ways within the rocks. When this energy is released suddenly—by shearing movements along faults in the crust of Earth, for example—an earthquake results. The area of the fault where the sudden rupture takes place is called the focus or hypocenter of the earthquake. The point on Earth's surface directly above the focus is called the epicenter of the earthquake.

The severity of an earthquake can be expressed in terms of both intensity and magnitude. The two terms are quite different, however, and they are often confused. Intensity is based on the observed effects of ground shaking on people, buildings, and natural features. It varies from place to place within the disturbed region depending on the location of the observer with respect to the earthquake epicenter. Magnitude is related to the amount of seismic energy released at the hypocenter of the earthquake. It is based on the amplitude of the earthquake waves recorded on instruments, which have a common calibration. Magnitude is thus represented by a single, instrumentally determined value.

The Richter Magnitude Scale

Seismic waves are the vibrations from earthquakes that travel through Earth; they are recorded on instruments called seismographs. Seismographs record a zigzag trace that shows the varying amplitude of ground oscillations beneath the instrument. Sensitive seismographs, which greatly magnify these ground motions, can detect strong earthquakes from sources anywhere in the world. The time, location, and magnitude of an earthquake can be determined from the data recorded by seismograph stations.

The Richter magnitude scale was developed in 1935 by Charles F. Richter of the California Institute of Technology as a mathematical device to compare the size of earthquakes. The magnitude of an earthquake is determined from the logarithm of the amplitude of waves recorded by seismographs. Adjustments are included in the magnitude formula to compensate for the variation in the distance between the various seismographs and the epicenter of the earthquakes. On the Richter Scale, magnitude is expressed in whole numbers and decimal fractions. For example, a magnitude of 5.3 might be computed for a moderate earthquake, and a strong earthquake might be rated as magnitude 6.3. Because of the logarithmic basis of the scale, each whole number increase in magnitude represents a tenfold increase in measured amplitude; as an estimate of energy, each whole number step in the magnitude scale corresponds to the release of about 31 times more energy than the amount associated with the preceding whole number value. Although the Richter Scale has no upper limit, the largest known shocks have had magnitudes in the 8.8 to 8.9 range.

Why Are There So Many Earthquake Magnitude Scales?

Earthquake size, as measured by the Richter Scale, is a well-known, but not well understood, concept. What is even less well understood is the proliferation of magnitude scales and their relation to Richter's original magnitude scale. Richter's magnitude scale was first created for measuring the size of earthquakes occurring in southern California, using relatively high-frequency data from nearby seismograph stations. This magnitude scale was referred to as ML, with the L standing for local.

As more seismograph stations were installed around the world, it became apparent that the method developed by Richter was strictly valid only for certain frequency and distance ranges. In order to take advantage of the growing number of globally distributed seismograph stations, new magnitude scales that are an extension of Richter's original idea were developed. These include body-wave magnitude, "mb," and surface-wave magnitude, "MS." Each is valid for a particular frequency range and type of seismic signal. In its range of validity each is equivalent to the Richter magnitude.

Because of the limitations of all three magnitude scales—ML, mb, and MS—a new, more uniformly applicable extension of the magnitude scale, known as moment magnitude, or "MW," was developed. In particular, for very large earthquakes moment magnitude gives the most reliable estimate of earthquake size. New techniques that take advantage of modern telecommunications have recently been implemented, allowing reporting agencies to obtain rapid estimates of moment magnitude for significant earthquakes. So nowadays, when most seismologists announce a magnitude number, they are rarely referring to the Richter Scale.

The Modified Mercalli Intensity Scale

The effect of an earthquake on Earth's surface is called the intensity. The intensity scale consists of a series of certain key responses, such as people awakening, movement of furniture, damage to chimneys, and finally—total destruction. Although numerous intensity scales have been developed over the past several hundred years to evaluate the effects of earthquakes, the one currently used in the United States is the Modified Mercalli (MM) Intensity Scale. It was developed in 1931 by the American seismologists Harry Wood and Frank Neumann. This scale, composed of 12 increasing levels of intensity that range from imperceptible shaking to catastrophic destruction, is designated by Roman numerals. It does not have a mathematical basis; instead it is an arbitrary ranking based on observed effects. The Modified Mercalli Intensity value assigned to a specific site after an earthquake has a more meaningful measure of severity to the nonscientist than the magnitude because intensity refers to the effects actually experienced at that place.

Frequency of Earthquakes Worldwide[1]

Descriptor	Magnitude	Annual average
Great	8 or higher	1
Major	7–7.9	18
Strong	6–6.9	120
Moderate	5–5.9	800
Light	4–4.9	c. 6,200
Minor	3–3.9	c. 49,000
Very minor	2–3	c. 1,000[2]
Very minor	1–2	c. 8,000[2]

1. Since 1900. 2. Per day. *Source:* National Earthquake Information Center, U.S. Geological Survey.

Number of Earthquakes Worldwide, 1990–2003, and Mortality Figures

Magnitude	1990	1994	1995	1996	1997	1998	1999	2000	2001	2002	2003
8.0–9.9	0	2	3	1	0	2	0	4	1	0	0
7.0–7.9	12	13	22	21	20	14	23	16	14	13	8
6.0–6.9	115	161	185	160	125	113	123	153	127	134	82
5.0–5.9	1,635	1,542	1,327	1,223	1,118	979	1,106	1,345	1,210	1,059	558
4.0–4.9	4,493	4,544	8,140	8,794	7,938	7,303	7,042	8,045	8,129	8,728	4,358
3.0–3.9	2,457	5,000	5,002	4,869	4,467	5,945	5,521	4,784	6,148	6,998	4,353
2.0–2.9	2,364	5,369	3,838	2,388	2,397	4,091	4,201	3,758	4,138	6,443	4,002
1.0–1.9	474	779	645	295	388	805	715	1,028	946	1,137	1,084
0.1–0.9	0	17	19	1	4	10	5	5	1	10	33
No magnitude	5,062	1,944	1,826	2,186	3,415	2,426	2,096	3,120	2,871	2,953	1,646
Total	16,612	19,371	21,007	19,938	19,872	21,688	20,832	22,256	23,575	27,465[1]	16,124[1]
Estimated deaths	**51,916**	**1,038**	**7,949**	**419**	**2,907**	**8,928**	**22,711**	**231**	**21,357**	**1,712**	**2,776**

1. As of August 2003. *Source:* National Earthquake Information Center, U.S. Geological Survey.

Major Earthquakes around the World, 2003

Date	Location	Magnitude[1]
Jan. 20	Solomon Islands	7.3
Jan. 22	Colima, Mexico	7.6
March 17	Rat Islands, Aleutian Islands, Alaska	7.0
May 26	Near Honshu, Japan	7.0
May 26	Halmahera, Indonesia	7.0
June 20	Amazonas, Brazil	7.1
July 15	Carlsberg Ridge, Indian Ocean	7.6
Aug. 4	Scotia Sea, Canada	7.5
Aug. 21	South Island, New Zealand	7.2

NOTE: A major earthquake is defined here as having a magnitude of 7.0 or more. 1. Unless otherwise indicated, magnitudes listed are moment magnitudes, the newest, most uniformly applicable magnitude scale. *Source:* National Earthquake Information Center, U.S. Geological Survey.

Estimated Deaths from Earthquakes, 2003[1]

Date	Region	Magnitude	Number killed[2]
Jan. 21	Near the coast of Guatemala	6.5	1
Jan. 22	Colima, Mexico	7.6	29
Jan. 27	Turkey	6.1	1
Feb. 24	Southern Xinjiang, China	6.4	261
Feb. 25	Southern Xinjiang, China	5.3	5
March 25	Flores Region, Indonesia	6.5	4
March 29	Hindu Kush region, Afghanistan	5.9	1
May 1	Eastern Turkey	6.4	177
May 4	Southern Xinjiang, China	5.8	1
May 21	Northern Algeria	6.8	2,266
May 26	Halmahera, Indonesia	7.0	1
May 27	Northern Algeria	5.8	9
June 24	Western Iran	4.6	1
July 10	Southern Iran	5.7	1
July 21	Yunnan, China	6.0	16
July 26	India-Bangladesh border region	5.6	2
Total			**2,776**

1. As of August 2003. 2. Includes "missing and presumed dead." *Source:* National Earthquake Information Center, U.S. Geological Survey.

The Ten Largest[1] Earthquakes of the 20th Century

Location	Date	Magnitude[2]
1. Chile	May 22, 1960	9.5
2. Prince William Sound, Alaska	March 28, 1964[3]	9.2
3. Andreanof Islands, Aleutian Islands	March 9, 1957	9.1
4. Kamchatka	Nov. 4, 1952	9.0
5. Off the coast of Ecuador	Jan. 31, 1906	8.8
6. Rat Islands, Aleutian Islands	Feb. 4, 1965	8.7
7. India-China border	Aug. 15, 1950	8.6
8. Kamchatka	Feb. 3, 1923	8.5
9. Banda Sea, Indonesia	Feb. 1, 1938	8.5
10. Kuril Islands	Oct. 13, 1963	8.5

1. In terms of magnitude. 2. Moment magnitude. 3. March 28, 03:36:14 UT (March 27, 5:36 P.M. local time) *Source:* National Earthquake Information Center, U.S. Geological Survey.

Deadliest Earthquakes on Record

(50,000 deaths or more)

Date	Location	Deaths	Magnitude
Jan. 23, 1556	Shansi, China	830,000	n.a.
July 27, 1976	Tangshan, China	255,000[1]	8.0
Aug. 9, 1138	Aleppo, Syria	230,000	n.a.
May 22, 1927	near Xining, China	200,000	8.3
Dec. 22, 856[2]	Damghan, Iran	200,000	n.a.
Dec. 16, 1920	Gansu, China	200,000	8.6
March 23, 893[2]	Ardabil, Iran	150,000	n.a.
Sept. 1, 1923	Kwanto, Japan	143,000	8.3
Oct. 5, 1948	Ashgabat, Turkmenistan, USSR	110,000	7.3
Dec. 28, 1908	Messina, Italy	70,000–100,000[3]	7.5
Sept. 1290	Chihli, China	100,000	n.a.
Nov. 1667	Shemakha, Caucasia	80,000	n.a.
Nov. 18, 1727	Tabriz, Iran	77,000	n.a.
Nov. 1, 1755	Lisbon, Portugal	70,000	8.7
Dec. 25, 1932	Gansu, China	70,000	7.6
May 31, 1970	Peru	66,000	7.8
1268[4]	Silicia, Asia Minor	60,000	n.a.
Jan. 11, 1693	Sicily, Italy	60,000	n.a.
May 30, 1935	Quetta, Pakistan	30,000–60,000	7.5
Feb. 4, 1783	Calabria, Italy	50,000	n.a.
June 20, 1990	Iran	50,000	7.7

1. Official. Estimated death toll as high as 655,000. 2. Note that these dates are prior to A.D. 1000. No digit is missing. 3. Estimated. 4. No date available. *Source:* National Earthquake Information Center, U.S. Geological Survey. Data compiled from several sources.

The World's 14 Highest Mountain Peaks (above 8,000 meters)

All 14 of the world's 8,000-meter peaks are located in the Himalaya or the Karakoram ranges in Asia. According to Everestnews.com, only 10 climbers have reached the summits of all 14: Reinhold Messner (Italy) was first, followed by Jerzy Kukuczka (Poland), Ehardt Loretan (Switzerland), Carlos Carsolio (Mexico), Krzysztof Wielicki (Poland), Juan Oiarzabal (Spain), Sergio Martini (Italy), Park Young Seok (Korea), Hang-Gil Um (Korea), and Alberto Inurrategui (Spain).

Mountain	Location	Height Meters	Height Feet	First to summit (nationality)	Date
1. Everest[1]	Nepal/Tibet	8,850	29,035	Edmund Hillary (New Zealander, UK), Tenzing Norgay (Nepalese)	May 29, 1953
2. K2 (Godwin Austen)	Pakistan/China	8,611	28,250	A. Compagnoni, L. Lacedelli (Italian)	July 31, 1954
3. Kangchenjunga	Nepal/India	8,586	28,169	G. Band, J. Brown, N. Hardie, S. Streather (UK)	May 25, 1955
4. Lhotse	Nepal/Tibet	8,516	27,940	F. Luchsinger, E. Reiss (Swiss)	May 18, 1956
5. Makalu	Nepal/Tibet	8,463	27,766	J. Couzy, L. Terray, J. Franco, G. Magnone-Gialtsen, J. Bouier, S. Coupé, P. Leroux, A. Vialatte (French)	May 15, 1955
6. Cho Oyu	Nepal/Tibet	8,201	26,906	H. Tichy, S. Jöchler (Austrian), Pasang Dawa Lama (Nepalese)	Oct. 19, 1954
7. Dhaulagiri	Nepal	8,167	26,795	A. Schelbert, E. Forrer, K. Diemberger, P. Diener (Swiss), Nyima Dorji, Nawang Dorji (Nepalese)	May 13, 1960
8. Manaslu	Nepal	8,163	26,781	T. Imamishi, K. Kato, M. Higeta, (Japanese) G. Norbu (Nepalese)	May 9, 1956
9. Nanga Parbat	Pakistan	8,125	26,660	Hermann Buhl (Austrian)	July 3, 1953
10. Annapurna	Nepal	8,091	26,545	M. Herzog, L. Lachenal (French)	June 3, 1950
11. Gasherbrum I	Pakistan/China	8,068	26,470	P. K. Schoeing, A. J. Kauffman	July 4, 1958
12. Broad Peak	Pakistan/China	8,047	26,400	M. Schmuck, F. Wintersteller, K. Diemberger, H. Buhl (Austrian)	June 9, 1957
13. Gasherbrum II	Pakistan/China	8,035	26,360	F. Moravec, S. Larch, H. Willenpart (Austrian)	July 7, 1956
14. Shisha Pangma	Tibet	8,013	26,289	Hsu Ching and team of 9 (Chinese)	May 2, 1964

1. The 1955 elevation of Everest, 29,028 ft. (8,848 m), was revised on Nov. 11, 1999, and now stands at 29,035 ft. (8,850 m).

Highest Mountain Peaks of the World

(*See* p. 502 for U.S. peaks.)

Mountain peak	Range	Location	Height ft.	Height m
Annapurna II	Himalayas	Nepal	26,041	7,937
Gyachung Kang	Himalayas	Nepal	25,910	7,897
Disteghil Sar	Karakoram	Pakistan	25,858	7,882
Himalchuli	Himalayas	Nepal	25,801	7,864
Nuptse	Himalayas	Nepal	25,726	7,841
Nanda Devi	Himalayas	India	25,663	7,824
Masherbrum	Karakoram	Kashmir[1]	25,660	7,821
Rakaposhi	Karakoram	Pakistan	25,551	7,788
Kanjut Sar	Karakoram	Pakistan	25,461	7,761
Kamet	Himalayas	India/Tibet	25,446	7,756
Namcha Barwa	Himalayas	Tibet	25,445	7,756

Mountain peak	Range	Location	Height ft.	Height m
Gurla Mandhata	Himalayas	Tibet	25,355	7,728
Ulugh Muztagh	Kunlun	Tibet	25,340	7,723
Kungur	Muztagh Ata	China	25,325	7,719
Tirich Mir	Hindu Kush	Pakistan	25,230	7,690
Saser Kangri	Karakoram	India	25,172	7,672
Makalu II	Himalayas	Nepal	25,120	7,657
Minya Konka (Gongga Shan)	Daxue Shan	China	24,900	7,590
Kula Kangri	Himalayas	Bhutan	24,783	7,554
Chang-tzu	Himalayas	Tibet	24,780	7,553
Muztagh Ata	Muztagh Ata	China	24,757	7,546
Skyang Kangri	Himalayas	Kashmir	24,750	7,544
Ismail Samani Peak (formerly Communism Peak)	Pamirs	Tajikistan	24,590	7,495
Jongsong Peak	Himalayas	Nepal	24,472	7,459
Pobeda Peak	Tien Shan	Kyrgyzstan	24,406	7,439
Sia Kangri	Himalayas	Kashmir	24,350	7,422
Haramosh Peak	Karakoram	Pakistan	24,270	7,397
Istoro Nal	Hindu Kush	Pakistan	24,240	7,388
Tent Peak	Himalayas	Nepal	24,165	7,365
Chomo Lhari	Himalayas	Tibet/ Bhutan	24,040	7,327
Chamlang	Himalayas	Nepal	24,012	7,319
Kabru	Himalayas	Nepal	24,002	7,316
Alung Gangri	Himalayas	Tibet	24,000	7,315
Baltoro Kangri	Himalayas	Kashmir	23,990	7,312
Muztagh Ata (K-5)	Kunlun	China	23,890	7,282
Mana	Himalayas	India	23,860	7,273
Baruntse	Himalayas	Nepal	23,688	7,220
Nepal Peak	Himalayas	Nepal	23,500	7,163
Amne Machin	Kunlun	China	23,490	7,160
Gauri Sankar	Himalayas	Nepal/ Tibet	23,440	7,145
Badrinath	Himalayas	India	23,420	7,138
Nunkun	Himalayas	Kashmir	23,410	7,135
Lenin Peak	Pamirs	Tajikistan/ Kyrgyzstan	23,405	7,134
Pyramid	Himalayas	Nepal	23,400	7,132
Api	Himalayas	Nepal	23,399	7,132
Pauhunri	Himalayas	India/ China	23,385	7,128
Trisul	Himalayas	India	23,360	7,120
Korzhenevski Peak	Pamirs	Tajikistan	23,310	7,105
Kangto	Himalayas	Tibet	23,260	7,090
Nyainqentanglha	Nyainqentanglha Shan	China	23,255	7,088
Trisuli	Himalayas	India	23,210	7,074
Dunagiri	Himalayas	India	23,184	7,066
Revolution Peak	Pamirs	Tajikistan	22,880	6,974
Aconcagua	Andes	Argentina	22,834	6,960
Ojos del Salado	Andes	Argentina/ Chile	22,664	6,908
Bonete	Andes	Argentina/ Chile	22,546	6,872
Ama Dablam	Himalayas	Nepal	22,494	6,856
Tupungato	Andes	Argentina/ Chile	22,310	6,800
Moscow Peak	Pamirs	Tajikistan	22,260	6,785
Pissis	Andes	Argentina	22,241	6,779
Mercedario	Andes	Argentina/ Chile	22,211	6,770
Huascarán	Andes	Peru	22,205	6,768
Llullaillaco	Andes	Argentina/ Chile	22,057	6,723
El Libertador	Andes	Argentina	22,047	6,720
Cachi	Andes	Argentina	22,047	6,720
Kailas	Himalayas	Tibet	22,027	6,714
Incahuasi	Andes	Argentina/ Chile	21,720	6,620
Yerupaja	Andes	Peru	21,709	6,617
Kurumda	Pamirs	Tajikistan	21,686	6,610
Galan	Andes	Argentina	21,654	6,600
El Muerto	Andes	Argentina/ Chile	21,463	6,542
Sajama	Andes	Bolivia	21,391	6,520
Nacimiento	Andes	Argentina	21,302	6,493
Illampu	Andes	Bolivia	21,276	6,485
Illimani	Andes	Bolivia	21,201	6,462
Coropuna	Andes	Peru	21,083	6,426
Laudo	Andes	Argentina	20,997	6,400
Ancohuma	Andes	Bolivia	20,958	6,388
Cuzco (Ausangate)	Andes	Peru	20,945	6,384

1. Kashmir is divided between India, Pakistan, and China, and the three countries dispute the boundaries. *Source:* National Geographic Society.

Climbing the Seven Summits

About 75 mountaineers have climbed all "Seven Summits"—the highest peak on each of the seven continents. The first was Dick Bass, an American businessman, on April 30, 1985. The seven summits are Mt. Everest (Asia) 29,035 ft., Mt. Aconcagua (South America) 22,834 ft., Mt. McKinley (North America) 20,320 ft., Mt. Kilimanjaro (Africa) 19,340 ft., Mt. Elbrus (Europe) 18,510 ft., Vinson Massif (Antarctica) 16,066 ft., and Kosciusko (Australia) 7,310 ft. Some climbers believe that the true Seven Summits should include Carstensz Pyramid (16,023 ft.) in Irian Jaya, Indonesia, rather than Australia's Kosciusko. Carstensz is the highest summit in Australia/Oceania, but strictly speaking, Oceania is not a continent.

Climbing Mount Everest: A Timeline

1852 The Great Trigonometrical Survey of India establishes that "Peak XV" in the Himalayas, then thought to be 29,002 feet, is the highest mountain in the world.

1865 Called Chomolungma in Tibet and Sagarmatha in Nepal, the world's highest mountain is named after Sir George Everest, the British Surveyor General from 1830–1843.

1920 The 13th Dalai Lama opens Tibet to foreigners. British reconnaissance party leaves Darjeeling to explore a route to Mt. Everest from the Tibetan side.

1921 First attempt to climb Mt. Everest is made by a British team that includes George Mallory.

1922 The first recorded deaths on Everest occur when seven Sherpa porters, part of a British expedition, die in an avalanche.

1924 George Mallory, 38, and Andrew Irvine, 22, disappear on their way to the summit. They were last spotted by a member of the expedition, who reported they "were going strong for the top." Whether they reached the summit remains a mystery.

1952 Swiss climber Raymond Lambert and renowned Sherpa climber Tenzing Norgay, a Nepalese Sherpa from India, almost make it to the South Summit before turning back.

1953 First summit of Everest accomplished by Edmund Hillary, New Zealand, for the British Commonwealth, and Tenzing Norgay on May 29 at 11:00 A.M.

1955 The height of Mt. Everest is adjusted by 26 feet to 29,028 feet (8,848 m) from the original measurements of the 1852 Great Trigonometrical Survey of India.

1963 The first American, James Whittaker, summits Everest.

1975 Junko Tabei (Japan) becomes the first woman to summit.

1977 Reinhold Messner (Italy) and Peter Habeler (Austria) make the first ascent without supplemental oxygen.

1978 Reinhold Messner makes the first solo ascent of Everest (also without supplemental oxygen).

1996 Fifteen climbers died on Everest—the most casualties in a single year.

1999 George Mallory's body is found by a search expedition at 27,000 feet. Searchers had hoped to find a camera that might contain photos of Mallory and Irvine or some other proof that they summited Everest, but no evidence is found. On Nov. 11, the revised official elevation of Everest is announced by the National Geographic Society to be 29,035 feet (8,850 m).

2001 182 climbers make it to the summit—the most ever in a single year. Erik Weihenmayer (American) becomes the first blind person to summit Everest.

2003 At 70, Japanese climber Yuichiro Miura becomes the oldest person ever to reach Everest's summit, and a 15-year-old Sherpa girl from Nepal, Ming Kipa, becomes the youngest. Renowed climber Apa Sherpa summits for the 13th time, making him the person who has climbed Everest the most.

Measuring the World's Highest Peak

Mount Everest once went by the pedestrian name of Peak XV among Westerners. That was before surveyors established that it was the highest mountain on Earth, a fact that came as something of a surprise—Peak XV had seemed lost in the crowd of other formidable Himalayan peaks, many of which gave the illusion of greater height.

In 1852 the Great Trigonometrical Survey of India measured Everest's elevation as 29,002 feet above sea level. This figure remained the officially accepted height for more than one hundred years. In 1955 it was adjusted by a mere 26 feet to 29,028 (8,848 m).

The mountain received its official name in 1865 in honor of Sir George Everest, the British Surveyor General from 1830–1843 who had mapped the Indian subcontinent. He had some reservations about having his name bestowed on the peak, arguing that the mountain should retain its local appellation, the standard policy of geographical societies.

The Andes Muscle In On the Action

Before the Survey of India, a number of other mountains ranked supreme in the eyes of the world. In the 17th and 18th centuries, the Andean peak Chimborazo was considered the highest. At a relatively unremarkable 20,561 feet (6,310 m), it is in fact nowhere near the highest, surpassed by about thirty other Andean peaks and several dozen in the Himalayas. In 1809, the Himalayan peak Dhaulagiri (26,167 ft.; 8,167 m) was declared the ultimate, only to be shunted aside in 1840 by Kanchenjunga (28,169 ft.; 8,586 m), which today ranks third. Everest's status has been unrivaled for the last century-and-a-half, but not without a few threats.

K2 Tries to Take the Cake

The most recent challenge came from a 1986 American expedition climbing K2 (28,250 ft.; 8,611 m) in the Karakoram range in Pakistan. According to their measurements, K2 was actually 29,284 feet, beating Everest by a cool 256 feet. Had this figure been accepted, mountaineering history would have required drastic revision: Everest would have taken a back seat to K2, no longer the *ne plus ultra* of geographical extremes.

Everest Undergoes a Growth Spurt

K2 was left even further back in the clouds when Everest's official height was revised in 1999. On May 5, 1999, a team of nine climbers summited Everest, armed with state-of-the-art satellite measuring devices. Six months later the results of their survey were announced: Everest is in fact 29,035 feet (8,850 m)—six feet or two meters higher than the last official (1955) measurement.

It is remarkable how accurate all the official measurements of Everest have been. Conducted 147 years earlier, the Great Trigonometrical Survey of India in 1852 was a mere 33 feet off the 1999 mark.

Oceans and Seas

Name	Area sq. mi.	Area sq. km	Average depth ft.	Average depth m	Greatest known depth ft.	Greatest known depth m	Place of greatest known depth
Pacific Ocean	60,060,700	155,557,000	13,215	4,028	36,198	11,033	Mariana Trench
Atlantic Ocean	29,637,900	76,762,000	12,880	3,926	30,246	9,219	Puerto Rico Trench
Indian Ocean	26,469,500	68,556,000	13,002	3,963	24,460	7,455	Sunda Trench
Southern Ocean[1]	7,848,300	20,327,000	13,100–16,400	4,000–5,000	23,736	7,235	South Sandwich Trench
Arctic Ocean	5,427,000	14,056,000	3,953	1,205	18,456	5,625	77°45′N; 175°W
Mediterranean Sea[2]	1,144,800	2,965,800	4,688	1,429	15,197	4,632	Off Cape Matapan, Greece
Caribbean Sea	1,049,500	2,718,200	8,685	2,647	22,788	6,946	Off Cayman Islands
South China Sea	895,400	2,319,000	5,419	1,652	16,456	5,016	West of Luzon
Bering Sea	884,900	2,291,900	5,075	1,547	15,659	4,773	Off Buldir Island
Gulf of Mexico	615,000	1,592,800	4,874	1,486	12,425	3,787	Sigsbee Deep
Okhotsk Sea	613,800	1,589,700	2,749	838	12,001	3,658	146°10′E; 46°50′N
East China Sea	482,300	1,249,200	617	188	9,126	2,782	25°16′N; 125°E
Hudson Bay	475,800	1,232,300	420	128	600	183	Near entrance
Japan Sea	389,100	1,007,800	4,429	1,350	12,276	3,742	Central Basin
Andaman Sea	308,000	797,700	2,854	870	12,392	3,777	Off Car Nicobar Island
North Sea	222,100	575,200	308	94	2,165	660	Skagerrak
Red Sea	169,100	438,000	1,611	491	7,254	2,211	Off Port Sudan
Baltic Sea	163,000	422,200	180	55	1,380	421	Off Gotland

NOTE: For Caspian Sea, *see* Large Lakes of the World. 1. A decision by the International Hydrographic Organization in spring 2000 delimited a fifth world ocean. 2. Includes Black Sea and Sea of Azov.

Large Lakes of the World

Name and location	Area sq. mi.	Area km	Length mi.	Length km	Maximum depth ft.	Maximum depth m
Caspian Sea, Azerbaijan-Russia-Kazakhstan-Turkmenistan-Iran[1]	152,239	394,299	745	1,199	3,104	946
Superior, U.S.-Canada	31,820	82,414	383	616	1,333	406
Victoria, Tanzania-Uganda	26,828	69,485	200	322	270	82
Huron, U.S.-Canada	23,010	59,596	247	397	750	229
Michigan, U.S.	22,400	58,016	321	517	923	281
Aral, Kazakhstan-Uzbekistan	13,000	33,800	266	428	223	68
Tanganyika, Tanzania-Congo	12,700	32,893	420	676	4,708	1,435
Baikal, Russia	12,162	31,500	395	636	5,712	1,741
Great Bear, Canada	12,000	31,080	232	373	270	82
Nyasa, Malawi-Mozambique-Tanzania	11,600	30,044	360	579	2,316	706
Great Slave, Canada	11,170	28,930	298	480	2,015	614
Chad,[2] Chad-Niger-Nigeria	9,946	25,760	—	—	23	7
Erie, U.S.-Canada	9,930	25,719	241	388	210	64
Winnipeg, Canada	9,094	23,553	264	425	204	62
Ontario, U.S.-Canada	7,520	19,477	193	311	778	237
Balkhash, Kazakhstan	7,115	18,428	376	605	87	27
Ladoga, Russia	7,000	18,130	124	200	738	225
Onega, Russia	3,819	9,891	154	248	361	110
Titicaca, Bolivia-Peru	3,141	8,135	110	177	1,214	370
Nicaragua, Nicaragua	3,089	8,001	110	177	230	70
Athabaska, Canada	3,058	7,920	208	335	407	124
Rudolf, Kenya	2,473	6,405	154	248	—	—
Reindeer, Canada	2,444	6,330	152	245	—	—
Eyre, South Australia	2,400[3]	6,216	130	209	varies	varies
Issyk-Kul, Kyrgyzstan	2,394	6,200	113	182	2,297	700
Urmia,[2] Iran	2,317	6,001	81	130	49	15
Torrens, South Australia	2,200	5,698	130	209	—	—
Vänern, Sweden	2,141	5,545	87	140	322	98
Winnipegosis, Canada	2,086	5,403	152	245	59	18
Mobutu Sese Seko, Uganda	2,046	5,299	100	161	180	55
Nettilling, Baffin Island, Canada	1,950	5,051	70	113	—	—
Nipigon, Canada	1,870	4,843	72	116	—	—
Manitoba, Canada	1,817	4,706	140	225	22	7
Great Salt, U.S.	1,800	4,662	75	121	15–25	5–8
Kioga, Uganda	1,700	4,403	50	80	about 30	9

NOTE: area more than 1,700 sq. mi. 1. The Caspian Sea is called "sea" because the Romans, finding it salty, named it *Mare Caspium.* Many geographers, however, consider it a lake because it is land-locked. 2. Figures represent high-water data. 3. Varies with the rainfall of the wet season. It has been reported to dry up almost completely on occasion.

Principal Rivers of the World

(*See* pp. 500–501 for other U.S. rivers.)

River	Source	Outflow	Approx. length mi.	Approx. length km
Nile	Tributaries of Lake Victoria, Africa	Mediterranean Sea	4,180	6,690
Amazon	Glacier-fed lakes, Peru	Atlantic Ocean	3,912	6,296
Mississippi-Missouri-Red Rock	Source of Red Rock, Montana	Gulf of Mexico	3,710	5,970
Chang Jiang (Yangtze)	Tibetan plateau, China	China Sea	3,602	5,797
Ob	Altai Mts., Russia	Gulf of Ob	3,459	5,567
Huang Ho (Yellow)	Eastern part of Kunlan Mts., West China	Gulf of Chihli	2,900	4,667
Yenisei	Tannu-Ola Mts., western Tuva, Russia	Arctic Ocean	2,800	4,506
Paraná	Confluence of Paranaiba and Grande rivers	Río de la Plata	2,795	4,498
Irtish	Altai Mts., Russia	Ob River	2,758	4,438
Zaire (Congo)	Confluence of Lualab and Luapula rivers, Congo	Atlantic Ocean	2,716	4,371
Heilong (Amur)	Confluence of Shilka (Russia) and Argun (Manchuria) rivers	Tatar Strait	2,704	4,352
Lena	Baikal Mts., Russia	Arctic Ocean	2,652	4,268
Mackenzie	Head of Finlay River, British Columbia, Canada	Beaufort Sea (Arctic Ocean)	2,635	4,241
Niger	Guinea	Gulf of Guinea	2,600	4,184
Mekong	Tibetan highlands	South China Sea	2,500	4,023
Mississippi	Lake Itasca, Minnesota	Gulf of Mexico	2,348	3,779
Missouri	Confluence of Jefferson, Gallatin, and Madison rivers, Montana	Mississippi River	2,315	3,726
Volga	Valdai plateau, Russia	Caspian Sea	2,291	3,687
Madeira	Confluence of Beni and Maumoré rivers, Bolivia–Brazil boundary	Amazon River	2,012	3,238
Purus	Peruvian Andes	Amazon River	1,993	3,207
São Francisco	Southwest Minas Gerais, Brazil	Atlantic Ocean	1,987	3,198
Yukon	Junction of Lewes and Pelly rivers, Yukon Territory, Canada	Bering Sea	1,979	3,185
St. Lawrence	Lake Ontario	Gulf of St. Lawrence	1,900	3,058
Rio Grande	San Juan Mts., Colorado	Gulf of Mexico	1,885	3,034
Brahmaputra	Himalayas	Ganges River	1,800	2,897
Indus	Himalayas	Arabian Sea	1,800	2,897
Danube	Black Forest, Germany	Black Sea	1,766	2,842
Euphrates	Confluence of Murat Nehri and Kara Su rivers, Turkey	Shatt-al-Arab	1,739	2,799
Darling	Central part of Eastern Highlands, Australia	Murray River	1,702	2,739
Zambezi	11°21′S, 24°22′E, Zambia	Mozambique Channel	1,700	2,736
Tocantins	Goiás, Brazil	Pará River	1,677	2,699
Murray	Australian Alps, New South Wales	Indian Ocean	1,609	2,589
Nelson	Head of Bow River, western Alberta, Canada	Hudson Bay	1,600	2,575
Paraguay	Mato Grosso, Brazil	Paraná River	1,584	2,549
Ural	Southern Ural Mts., Russia	Caspian Sea	1,574	2,533
Ganges	Himalayas	Bay of Bengal	1,557	2,506
Amu Darya (Oxus)	Nicholas Range, Pamir Mts., Turkmenistan	Aral Sea	1,500	2,414
Japurá	Andes, Colombia	Amazon River	1,500	2,414
Salween	Tibet, south of Kunlun Mts.	Gulf of Martaban	1,500	2,414
Arkansas	Central Colorado	Mississippi River	1,459	2,348
Colorado	Grand County, Colorado	Gulf of California	1,450	2,333
Dnieper	Valdai Hills, Russia	Black Sea	1,419	2,284
Ohio-Allegheny	Potter County, Pennsylvania	Mississippi River	1,306	2,102
Irrawaddy	Confluence of Nmai and Mali rivers, northeast Burma	Bay of Bengal	1,300	2,092
Orange	Lesotho	Atlantic Ocean	1,300	2,092
Orinoco	Serra Parima Mts., Venezuela	Atlantic Ocean	1,281	2,062
Pilcomayo	Andes Mts., Bolivia	Paraguay River	1,242	1,999
Xi Jiang (Si Kiang)	Eastern Yunnan Province, China	China Sea	1,236	1,989
Columbia	Columbia Lake, British Columbia, Canada	Pacific Ocean	1,232	1,983
Don	Tula, Russia	Sea of Azov	1,223	1,968
Sungari	China–North Korea boundary	Amur River	1,215	1,955
Saskatchewan	Canadian Rocky Mts.	Lake Winnipeg	1,205	1,939
Peace	Stikine Mts., British Columbia, Canada	Great Slave River	1,195	1,923
Tigris	Taurus Mts., Turkey	Shatt-al-Arab	1,180	1,899

Large Islands of the World

Island	Location and political affiliation	Area sq. mi.	Area sq. km
Greenland	North Atlantic (Danish)	839,999	2,175,597
New Guinea	Southwest Pacific (West Papua [Irian Jaya], Indonesia, western part; Papua New Guinea, eastern part)	309,000	800,311
Borneo	West mid-Pacific (Indonesian, south part; Brunei and Malaysian, north part)	287,300	744,108
Madagascar	Indian Ocean (Malagasy Republic)	227,000	587,931
Baffin	North Atlantic (Canadian)	195,926	507,451
Sumatra	Northeast Indian Ocean (Indonesian)	182,859	473,605
Honshu	Sea of Japan–Pacific (Japanese)	89,176	230,966
Great Britain	Off coast of NW Europe (England, Scotland, and Wales)	88,795	229,979
Victoria	Arctic Ocean (Canadian)	83,896	217,291
Ellesmere	Arctic Ocean (Canadian)	75,767	196,236
Sulawesi (Celebes)	West mid-Pacific (Indonesian)	73,057	189,218
South Island	South Pacific (New Zealand)	58,384	151,215
Java	Indian Ocean (Indonesian)	51,038	132,189
North Island	South Pacific (New Zealand)	44,702	115,778
Cuba	Caribbean Sea (republic)	42,803	110,860
Newfoundland	North Atlantic (Canadian)	42,031	108,860
Luzon	West mid-Pacific (Philippines)	40,420	104,688
Iceland	North Atlantic (republic)	39,800	103,082
Mindanao	West mid-Pacific (Philippines)	36,537	94,631
Ireland	West of Great Britain (republic, south part; United Kingdom, north part)	32,597	84,426
Hokkaido	Sea of Japan–Pacific (Japanese)	32,245	83,515
Sakhalin (Karafuto)	North of Japan (Russian)	29,500	76,405
Hispaniola	Caribbean Sea (Dominican Republic, east part; Haiti, west part)	29,300	75,887
Banks	Arctic Ocean (Canadian)	27,038	70,028
Tasmania	South of Australia (Australian)	26,200	67,858
Sri Lanka (Ceylon)	Indian Ocean (republic)	24,900	64,491
Devon	Arctic Ocean (Canadian)	21,331	55,247

NOTE: Australia is not included in this list because it is defined as a continent rather than an island.

Highest Waterfalls of the World

Name(s) (foreign)	Location	Height Feet	Height Meters
Angel (Salto Angel)	Canaima Nat'l Park, Venezuela	3,212	979
Tugela	Natal Nat'l Park, South Africa	2,800	850
Utigord (Utigordsfoss)	Norway	2,625	800
Monge (Mongefoss)	Marstein, Norway	2,540	774
Mutarazi (Mtarazi)	Nyanga Nat'l Park, Zimbabwe	2,499	762
Yosemite	Yosemite Nat'l Park, California, U.S.	2,425	739
Pieman	Alpine Nat'l Park, Victoria, Australia	2,346	715
Espelands (Espelandsfoss)	Hardanger Fjord, Norway	2,307	703[1]
Lower Mar Valley (Østra Mardolafoss)	Eikesdal, Norway	2,151	655[2]
Tyssestrengene	Odda, Norway	2,123	647[2]
Cuquenan (Salto Kukenan)	Kukenan Tepuy, Venezuela	2,000	610
Sentinel	Yosemite Nat'l Park, California, U.S.	2,000	610
Dudhsagar	Goa/Karnataka, India	1,969	600
Sutherland	Milford Sound, New Zealand	1,904	580
Kjell (Kjellfossen)	Gudvanger, Norway	1,841	561
Kahiwa	Molokai, Hawaii, U.S.	1,750	533
Takkakaw	Yoho Nat'l Park, B.C., Canada	1,650	503
Ribbon	Yosemite Nat'l Park, California, U.S.	1,612	491
King George VI	Guyana	1,600	488
Upper Mar Valley (Mardalsfossen)	nr. Eikesdal, Norway	1,536	468
Kaliuwaa (Sacred)	Pahu, Hawaii, U.S.	1,520	463
Della	Strathcona Provincial Park, B.C., Canada	1,444	440
Gavarnie	nr. Lourdes, France	1,384	422
Cachoeira da Fumaça (Glass or Smoke)	Chapada Diamantia Nat'l Park, Brazil	1,378	420
Giessbach	Bern, Switzerland	1,312	400
Krimmler	Hohe Tauern Nat'l Park, Austria	1,250	381
Vettis (Vettisfoss)	Jotunheimen, Norway	1,215	370
Papalaua	Molokai, Hawaii, U.S.	1,200	366
Tin Mine	Kosciusko Nat'l Park, Australia	1,182	360

1. Unofficial (estimated) height. Subject to revision. 2. Incorporated in hydroelectric scheme. Greatly diminished flow. *Sources:* Merriam Webster's Geographical Dictionary, Third Edition (1997), www.britannica.com, www.waterfallsnorthwest.com, www.americanparknetwork.com, www.ga.gov.au/education/facts/landforms/waterfal.htm/, www.atlas.gc.ca/site/english/facts/waterfalls.html, The State of Hawaii Data Book 2001.

Polar Regions

Antarctica

The second smallest continent, mostly south of the Antarctic Circle.

Area: 14.2 million sq. km (5.5 million sq. mi.).

Geographic South Pole: Earth's southernmost point, at latitude 90°S, where all lines of longitude meet.

Magnetic South Pole: The magnetic South Pole shifts about 5 miles (km) a year and is now located at about 66°S and 139°E on the Adélie Coast of Antarctica.

Terrain: About 98% thick ice sheet and 2% barren rock; glaciers form ice shelves along about half of the coastline, and floating ice shelves constitute 11% of the area of the continent. **Ice sheet:** The continental ice sheet contains approximately 7 million cubic miles (30 million cu km) of ice, representing about 90% of the world's total. **Major ice shelves:** Amery, Filchner, Larsen, Ronne, Ross. Ice shelves make up about 10% of Antarctica's ice, and are floating sheets of ice attached to land that project out into coastal waters.

Climate: The coldest, windiest, driest continent.

Regions: East Antarctica (c. 3,000,000 sq. mi./7,770,000 sq. km), the largest portion of the continent, is a high, ice-covered plateau. West Antarctica (c. 2,500,000 sq. mi./6,475,000 sq. km), is an archipelago of mountainous islands connected by ice. A mountain range divides them.

Elevation extremes: *Lowest point:* Bentley Subglacial Trench –8,327 ft. below sea level (–2,538 m)—the lowest land elevation is hidden within the trench. *Highest point:* Vinson Massif 16,066 ft. (4,897 m), Ellsworth Mountains.

The Arctic

Region, primarily made up of the frozen Arctic Ocean, that surrounds the North Pole. Land masses include islands and the northern parts of the European, Asian, and North American continents.

Area: 14.056 million sq. km (5.4 million sq. mi.), largely frozen ocean.

Geographic North Pole: Northern end of Earth's axis, located at about latitude 90°N.

Magnetic North Pole: Continues to shift and is located at about 78°N and 104°W in the Queen Elizabeth Islands of northern Canada.

Terrain: Central surface covered by a perennial drifting polar icepack that averages about 3 meters in thickness; the icepack is surrounded by open seas during the summer, but more than doubles in size during the winter and extends to the encircling landmasses.

Climate: Polar climate characterized by persistent cold and relatively narrow annual temperature ranges; winters characterized by continuous darkness, cold and stable weather conditions, and clear skies; summers characterized by continuous daylight, damp and foggy weather, and weak cyclones with rain or snow.

Regions: The Arctic is divided by the summer isotherm, a climatic boundary between regions with summer temperatures averaging 50°F (or 10°C)—the subarctic—and colder regions (the true Arctic).

Elevation extremes: *Lowest point:* Fram Basin –4,665 m. *Highest point:* sea level 0 m.

Interesting Caves and Caverns of the World

Aggtelek. In village of same name, northern Hungary. Large stalactitic cavern about 5 mi. long.

Altamira Cave. Near Santander, Spain. Contains Stone Age animal paintings on roof and walls.

Antiparos. On island of same name in the Grecian Archipelago. Some stalactites are 20 ft. long. Brilliant colors and fantastic shapes.

Blue Grotto. On island of Capri, Italy. Sea cavern hollowed out in limestone by constant wave action. Now half filled with water because of sinking coast. Name derived from unusual blue light permeating the cave. Source of light is a submerged opening allowing light to pass through the water.

Carlsbad Caverns. Southeast New Mexico. Contains some of the largest and most impressive stalactities and stalagmites, particularly in the Lechuguilla Cave.

Fingal's Cave. On island of Staffa off coast of western Scotland. Penetrates about 200 ft. inland. Contains basaltic columns almost 40 ft. high.

Jenolan Caves. In Blue Mountain plateau, New South Wales, Australia. Beautiful stalactitic formations.

Kent's Cavern. Near Torquay, England. Source of much information on Paleolithic humans.

Lascaux Cave. Southwestern France. Features prehistoric cave paintings estimated to be tens of thousands of years old. Closed to the public.

Lubang Nasib Bagus. Sarawak, Malaysia. World's largest cave chamber: 2,300 ft. long, 1,480 ft. wide, and everywhere at least 230 ft. high.

Luray Caverns. Near Luray, Va. Has large stalactitic and stalagmitic columns of many colors.

Mogao Caves. Located along the old Silk Route in China, Mogao is composed of 492 cells and cave sanctuaries that are famous for their statues and wall paintings, spanning a thousand years of Buddhist art.

Mammoth Cave. This limestone cavern in central Kentucky is the longest cave system in the world. Cave area is about 10 mi. in diameter but has 345 mi. of irregular subterranean passageways at various levels, plus underground lakes and rivers.

Peak Cavern or Devil's Hole. Derbyshire, England. About 2,250 ft. into a mountain. Lowest part is about 600 ft. below the surface.

Postojna Grotto. Postojna, Slovenia. Largest cavern in Europe; numerous beautiful stalactites. Famous example of a karst cave—grooved and irregularly eroded limestone formations carved out by underground streams. Pivka River flows through part of it.

Singing Cave. Iceland. A lava cave; name derived from echoes of people singing in it.

Waitomo Cave. North Island, New Zealand. Glowworms on cave ceiling look like thousands of stars in the night sky.

Wind Cave. In Black Hills of South Dakota. Limestone caverns with stalactites and stalagmites almost entirely missing. Variety of crystal formations called "boxwork."

Wyandotte Cave. In Crawford County, southern Indiana. A limestone cavern with five levels of passages; one of the largest in North America. "Monumental Mountain," approximately 135 ft. high, is believed to be one of the world's largest underground "mountains."

Principal Deserts of the World

Deserts are arid regions, generally receiving less than ten inches of precipitation a year, or regions where the potential evaporation rate is twice as great as the precipitation.

The world's deserts are divided into four categories. **Subtropical deserts** are the hottest, with parched terrain and rapid evaporation. Although **cool coastal deserts** are located within the same latitudes as subtropical deserts, the average temperature is much cooler because of frigid offshore ocean currents. **Cold winter deserts** are marked by stark temperature differences from season to season, ranging from 100° F (38° C) in the summer to 10° F (–12° C) in the winter. **Polar regions** are also considered to be deserts because nearly all moisture in these areas is locked up in the form of ice.

Desert	Location	Size	Topography
SUBTROPICAL DESERTS			
Sahara	Morocco, Western Sahara, Algeria, Tunisia, Libya, Egypt, Mauritania, Mali, Niger, Chad, Ethiopia, Eritrea, Somalia	3.5 million sq. mi.	70% gravel plains, sand, and dunes. Contrary to popular belief, the desert is only 30% sand. The world's largest nonpolar desert gets its name from the Arabic word *Sahra'*, meaning desert
Arabian	Saudi Arabia, Kuwait, Qatar, United Arab Emirates, Oman, Yemen	1 million sq. mi.	Gravel plains, rocky highlands; one-fourth is the Rub al-Khali ("Empty Quarter"), the world's largest expanse of unbroken sand
Kalahari	Botswana, South Africa, Namibia	220,000 sq. mi.	Sand sheets, longitudinal dunes
Australian Desert			
Gibson	Australia (southern portion of the Western Desert)	120,000 sq. mi.	Sandhills, gravel, grass. These three regions of desert are collectively referred to as the Great Western Desert—otherwise known as "the Outback." Contains Ayers Rock, or Uluru, one of the world's largest monoliths
Great Sandy	Australia (northern portion of the Western Desert)	150,000 sq. mi.	
Great Victoria	Australia (southernmost portion of the Western Desert)	250,000 sq. mi.	
Simpson and Sturt Stony	Australia (eastern half of the continent)	56,000 sq. mi.	Simpson's straight, parallel sand dunes are the longest in the world—up to 125 mi. Encompasses the Stewart Stony Desert, named for the Australian explorer
Mojave	U.S.: Arizona, Colorado, Nevada, Utah, California	54,000 sq. mi.	Mountain chains, dry alkaline lake beds, calcium carbonate dunes
Sonoran	U.S.: Arizona, California; Mexico	120,000 sq. mi.	Basins and plains bordered by mountain ridges; home to the Saguaro cactus
Chihuahuan	Mexico; southwestern U.S.	175,000 sq. mi.	Shrub desert; largest in North America
Thar	India, Pakistan	175,000 sq. mi.	Rocky sand and sand dunes
COOL COASTAL DESERTS			
Namib	Angola, Namibia, South Africa	13,000 sq. mi.	Gravel plains
Atacama	Chile	54,000 sq. mi.	Salt basins, sand, lava; world's driest desert
COLD WINTER DESERTS			
Great Basin	U.S.: Nevada, Oregon, Utah	190,000 sq. mi.	Mountain ridges, valleys, 1% sand dunes
Colorado Plateau	U.S.: Arizona, Colorado, New Mexico, Utah, Wyoming	130,000 sq. mi.	Sedimentary rock, mesas, and plateaus—includes the Grand Canyon and is also called the "Painted Desert" because of the spectacular colors in its rocks and canyons
Patagonian	Argentina	260,000 sq. mi.	Gravel plains, plateaus, basalt sheets
Kara-Kum	Uzbekistan, Turkmenistan	135,000 sq. mi.	90% gray layered sand—name means "black sand"
Kyzyl-Kum	Uzbekistan, Turkmenistan, Kazakhstan	115,000 sq. mi.	Sands, rock—name means "red sand"
Iranian	Iran	100,000 sq. mi.	Salt, gravel, rock
Taklamakan	China	105,000 sq. mi.	Sand, dunes, gravel
Gobi	China, Mongolia	500,000 sq. mi.	Stony, sandy soil, steppes (dry grasslands)
POLAR			
Arctic	U.S., Canada, Greenland, Iceland, Norway, Sweden, Finland, Russia		Snow, glaciers, tundra
Antarctic	Antarctica	5.4 million sq. mi.	Ice, snow, bedrock

Latitude and Longitude of World Cities
(and time corresponding to 12:00 noon, Eastern Standard Time)

City	Latitude °	Latitude ′	Longitude °	Longitude ′	Time
Aberdeen, Scotland	57	9 N	2	9 W	5:00 p.m.
Adelaide, Australia	34	55 S	138	36 E	2:30 a.m.[1]
Algiers, Algeria	36	50 N	3	0 E	6:00 p.m.
Amsterdam, Netherlands	52	22 N	4	53 E	6:00 p.m.
Ankara, Turkey	39	55 N	32	55 E	7:00 p.m.
Asunción, Paraguay	25	15 S	57	40 W	1:00 p.m.
Athens, Greece	37	58 N	23	43 E	7:00 p.m.
Auckland, New Zealand	36	52 S	174	45 E	5:00 a.m.[1]
Bangkok, Thailand	13	45 N	100	30 E	midnight
Barcelona, Spain	41	23 N	2	9 E	6:00 p.m.
Beijing, China	39	55 N	116	25 E	1:00 a.m.[1]
Belém, Brazil	1	28 S	48	29 W	2:00 p.m.
Belfast, Northern Ireland	54	37 N	5	56 W	5:00 p.m.
Belgrade, Yugoslavia	44	52 N	20	32 E	6:00 p.m.
Berlin, Germany	52	30 N	13	25 E	6:00 p.m.
Birmingham, England	52	25 N	1	55 W	5:00 p.m.
Bogotá, Colombia	4	32 N	74	15 W	12:00 noon
Bombay, India	19	0 N	72	48 E	10:30 p.m.
Bordeaux, France	44	50 N	0	31 W	6:00 p.m.
Bremen, Germany	53	5 N	8	49 E	6:00 p.m.
Brisbane, Australia	27	29 S	153	8 E	3:00 a.m.[1]
Bristol, England	51	28 N	2	35 W	5:00 p.m.
Brussels, Belgium	50	52 N	4	22 E	6:00 p.m.
Bucharest, Romania	44	25 N	26	7 E	7:00 p.m.
Budapest, Hungary	47	30 N	19	5 E	6:00 p.m.
Buenos Aires, Argentina	34	35 S	58	22 W	2:00 p.m.
Cairo, Egypt	30	2 N	31	21 E	7:00 p.m.
Calcutta, India	22	34 N	88	24 E	10:30 p.m.
Canton, China	23	7 N	113	15 E	1:00 a.m.[1]
Cape Town, South Africa	33	55 S	18	22 E	7:00 p.m.
Caracas, Venezuela	10	28 N	67	2 W	1:00 p.m.
Cayenne, French Guiana	4	49 N	52	18 W	1:00 p.m.
Chihuahua, Mexico	28	37 N	106	5 W	11:00 a.m.
Chongqing, China	29	46 N	106	34 E	1:00 a.m.[1]
Copenhagen, Denmark	55	40 N	12	34 E	6:00 p.m.
Córdoba, Argentina	31	28 S	64	10 W	2:00 p.m.
Dakar, Senegal	14	40 N	17	28 W	5:00 p.m.
Darwin, Australia	12	28 S	130	51 E	2:30 a.m.[1]
Djibouti, Djibouti	11	30 N	43	3 E	8:00 p.m.
Dublin, Ireland	53	20 N	6	15 W	5:00 p.m.
Durban, South Africa	29	53 S	30	53 E	7:00 p.m.
Edinburgh, Scotland	55	55 N	3	10 W	5:00 p.m.
Frankfurt, Germany	50	7 N	8	41 E	6:00 p.m.
Georgetown, Guyana	6	45 N	58	15 W	1:15 p.m.
Glasgow, Scotland	55	50 N	4	15 W	5:00 p.m.
Guatemala City, Guatemala	14	37 N	90	31 W	11:00 a.m.
Guayaquil, Ecuador	2	10 S	79	56 W	12:00 noon
Hamburg, Germany	53	33 N	10	2 E	6:00 p.m.
Hammerfest, Norway	70	38 N	23	38 E	6:00 p.m.
Havana, Cuba	23	8 N	82	23 W	12:00 noon
Helsinki, Finland	60	10 N	25	0 E	7:00 p.m.
Hobart, Tasmania	42	52 S	147	19 E	3:00 a.m.[1]
Iquique, Chile	20	10 S	70	7 W	1:00 p.m.
Irkutsk, Russia	52	30 N	104	20 E	1:00 a.m.
Jakarta, Indonesia	6	16 S	106	48 E	0:30 a.m.[1]
Johannesburg, South Africa	26	12 S	28	4 E	7:00 p.m.
Kingston, Jamaica	17	59 N	76	49 W	12:00 noon
Kinshasa, Congo	4	18 S	15	17 E	6:00 p.m.
La Paz, Bolivia	16	27 S	68	22 W	1:00 p.m.
Leeds, England	53	45 N	1	30 W	5:00 p.m.
Lima, Peru	12	0 S	77	2 W	12:00 noon
Lisbon, Portugal	38	44 N	9	9 W	5:00 p.m.
Liverpool, England	53	25 N	3	0 W	5:00 p.m.
London, England	51	32 N	0	5 W	5:00 p.m.
Lyons, France	45	45 N	4	50 E	6:00 p.m.
Madrid, Spain	40	26 N	3	42 W	6:00 p.m.
Manchester, England	53	30 N	2	15 W	5:00 p.m.
Manila, Philippines	14	35 N	120	57 E	1:00 a.m.[1]
Marseilles, France	43	20 N	5	20 E	6:00 p.m.
Mazatlán, Mexico	23	12 N	106	25 W	10:00 a.m.
Mecca, Saudi Arabia	21	29 N	39	45 E	8:00 p.m.
Melbourne, Australia	37	47 S	144	58 E	3:00 a.m.[1]
Mexico City, Mexico	19	26 N	99	7 W	11:00 a.m.
Milan, Italy	45	27 N	9	10 E	6:00 p.m.
Montevideo, Uruguay	34	53 S	56	10 W	2:00 p.m.
Moscow, Russia	55	45 N	37	36 E	8:00 p.m.
Munich, Germany	48	8 N	11	35 E	6:00 p.m.
Nagasaki, Japan	32	48 N	129	57 E	2:00 a.m.[1]
Nagoya, Japan	35	7 N	136	56 E	2:00 a.m.[1]
Nairobi, Kenya	1	25 S	36	55 E	8:00 p.m.
Nanjing (Nanking), China	32	3 N	118	53 E	1:00 a.m.[1]
Naples, Italy	40	50 N	14	15 E	6:00 p.m.
Newcastle-on-Tyne, England	54	58 N	1	37 W	5:00 p.m.
Odessa, Ukraine	46	27 N	30	48 E	8:00 p.m.
Osaka, Japan	34	32 N	135	30 E	2:00 a.m.[1]
Oslo, Norway	59	57 N	10	42 E	6:00 p.m.
Panama City, Panama	8	58 N	79	32 W	12:00 noon
Paramaribo, Suriname	5	45 N	55	15 W	1:30 p.m.
Paris, France	48	48 N	2	20 E	6:00 p.m.
Perth, Australia	31	57 S	115	52 E	1:00 a.m.[1]
Plymouth, England	50	25 N	4	5 W	5:00 p.m.
Port Moresby, Papua New Guinea	9	25 S	147	8 E	3:00 a.m.[1]
Prague, Czech Republic	50	5 N	14	26 E	6:00 p.m.
Rangoon, Myanmar	16	50 N	96	0 E	11:30 p.m.
Reykjavík, Iceland	64	4 N	21	58 W	4:00 p.m.
Rio de Janeiro, Brazil	22	57 S	43	12 W	2:00 p.m.
Rome, Italy	41	54 N	12	27 E	6:00 p.m.
Salvador, Brazil	12	56 S	38	27 W	2:00 p.m.
Santiago, Chile	33	28 S	70	45 W	1:00 p.m.
St. Petersburg, Russia	59	56 N	30	18 E	8:00 p.m.
São Paulo, Brazil	23	31 S	46	31 W	2:00 p.m.
Shanghai, China	31	10 N	121	28 E	1:00 a.m.[1]
Singapore, Singapore	1	14 N	103	55 E	0:30 a.m.[1]
Sofia, Bulgaria	42	40 N	23	20 E	7:00 p.m.
Stockholm, Sweden	59	17 N	18	3 E	6:00 p.m.
Sydney, Australia	34	0 S	151	0 E	3:00 a.m.[1]
Tananarive, Madagascar	18	50 S	47	33 E	8:00 p.m.
Teheran, Iran	35	45 N	51	45 E	8:30 p.m.
Tokyo, Japan	35	40 N	139	45 E	2:00 a.m.[1]
Tripoli, Libya	32	57 N	13	12 E	7:00 p.m.
Venice, Italy	45	26 N	12	20 E	6:00 p.m.
Veracruz, Mexico	19	10 N	96	10 W	11:00 a.m.
Vienna, Austria	48	14 N	16	20 E	6:00 p.m.
Vladivostok, Russia	43	10 N	132	0 E	3:00 a.m.[1]
Warsaw, Poland	52	14 N	21	0 E	6:00 p.m.
Wellington, New Zealand	41	17 S	174	47 E	5:00 a.m.[1]
Zürich, Switzerland	47	21 N	8	31 E	6:00 p.m.

1. On the following day.

Miscellaneous Data for the United States

Highest point: Mount McKinley, Alaska	20,320 ft. (6,198 m)
Lowest point: Death Valley, Calif.	282 ft. (86 m) below sea level
Approximate mean elevation	2,500 ft. (763 m)
Points farthest apart (50 states): Log Point, Elliot Key, Fla., and Kure Island, Hawaii	5,859 mi. (9,429 km)
Geographic center (50 states): in Butte County, S.D. (west of Castle Rock)	44°58′N lat.103°46′W long.
Geographic center (48 conterminous states): in Smith County, Kan. (near Lebanon)	39°50′N lat. 98°35′W long.
Boundaries:	
Between Alaska and Canada	1,538 mi. (2,475 km)
Between the 48 conterminous states and Canada (incl. the Great Lakes)	3,987 mi. (6,416 km)
Between the United States and Mexico	1,933 mi. (3,111 km)

Source: U.S. Geological Survey.

Extreme Points of the United States (50 States)

Extreme point	Latitude	Longitude	Distance[1] mi.	km
Northernmost point: Point Barrow, Alaska	71°23′ N	156°29′ W	2,507	4,034
Easternmost point: West Quoddy Head, Maine	44°49′ N	66°57′ W	1,788	2,997
Southernmost point: Ka Lae (South Cape), Hawaii	18°55′ N	155°41′ W	3,463	5,573
Westernmost point: Cape Wrangell, Alaska (Attu Island)	52°55′ N	172°27′ E	3,625	5,833

1. From geographic center of United States (incl. Alaska and Hawaii), west of Castle Rock, S.D., 44°58′ lat., 103°46′ W long. If measured from the prime meridian in Greenwich, England, Cape Wrangell, Attu Island, Alaska, would be the easternmost point.

The Continental Divide

The Continental Divide is a ridge of high ground that runs irregularly north and south through the Rocky Mountains and separates eastward-flowing from westward-flowing streams. The waters that flow eastward empty into the Atlantic Ocean, chiefly by way of the Gulf of Mexico; those that flow westward empty into the Pacific. Every continent with the exception of Antarctica has a continental divide.

Rivers of the United States
(350 or more miles long)

Alabama-Coosa (600 mi.; 966 km): From junction of Oostanula and Etowah R. in Georgia to Mobile R.

Altamaha-Ocmulgee (392 mi.; 631 km): From junction of Yellow R. and South R., Newton Co. in Georgia to Atlantic Ocean.

Apalachicola-Chattahoochee (524 mi.; 843 km): From Towns Co. in Georgia to Gulf of Mexico in Florida.

Arkansas (1,459 mi.; 2,348 km): From Lake Co. in Colorado to Mississippi R. in Arkansas.

Brazos (923 mi.; 1,490 km): From junction of Salt Fork and Double Mountain Fork in Texas to Gulf of Mexico.

Canadian (906 mi.; 1,458 km): From Las Animas Co. in Colorado to Arkansas R. in Oklahoma.

Cimarron (600 mi.; 966 km): From Colfax Co. in New Mexico to Arkansas R. in Oklahoma.

Colorado (1,450 mi.; 2,333 km): From Rocky Mountain National Park in Colorado to Gulf of California in Mexico.

Colorado (862 mi.; 1,387 km): From Dawson Co. in Texas to Matagorda Bay.

Columbia (1,243 mi.; 2,000 km): From Columbia Lake in British Columbia to Pacific Ocean (entering between Oregon and Washington).

Colville (350 mi.; 563 km): From Brooks Range in Alaska to Beaufort Sea.

Connecticut (407 mi.; 655 km): From Third Connecticut Lake in New Hampshire to Long Island Sound in Connecticut.

Cumberland (720 mi.; 1,159 km): From junction of Poor and Clover Forks in Harlan Co. in Kentucky to Ohio R.

Delaware (390 mi.; 628 km): From Schoharie Co. in New York to Liston Point, Delaware Bay.

Gila (649 mi.; 1,044 km): From Catron Co. in New Mexico to Colorado R. in Arizona.

Green (360 mi.; 579 km): From Lincoln Co. in Kentucky to Ohio R. in Kentucky.

Green (730 mi.; 1,175 km): From Sublette Co. in Wyoming to Colorado R. in Utah.

Illinois (420 mi.; 676 km): From St. Joseph Co. in Indiana to Mississippi R. at Grafton in Illinois.

James (sometimes called *Dakota*) (710 mi.; 1,143 km): From Wells Co. in North Dakota to Missouri R. in South Dakota.

Kanawha-New (352 mi.; 566 km): From junction of North and South Forks of New R. in North Carolina, through Virginia and West Virginia (New R. becoming Kanawha R.), to Ohio R.

Kansas (743 mi.; 1,196 km): From source of Arikaree R. in Elbert Co., Colorado, to Missouri R. at Kansas City, Kansas.

Koyukuk (470 mi.; 756 km): From Brooks Range in Alaska to Yukon R.

Kuskokwim (724 mi.; 1,165 km): From Alaska Range in Alaska to Kuskokwim Bay.

Licking (350 mi.; 563 km): From Magoffin Co. in Kentucky to Ohio R. at Cincinnati in Ohio.

Little Missouri (560 mi.; 901 km): From Crook Co. in Wyoming to Missouri R. in North Dakota.

Milk (625 mi.; 1,006 km): From junction of forks in Alberta Province to Missouri R.

Mississippi (2,348 mi.; 3,779 km): From Lake Itasca in Minnesota to mouth of Southwest Pass in Louisiana.

Mississippi-Missouri-Red Rock (3,710 mi.; 5,970 km): From source of Red Rock R. in Montana to mouth of Southwest Pass in Louisiana.

Missouri (2,315 mi.; 3,726 km): From junction of Jefferson R., Gallatin R., and Madison R. in Montana to Mississippi R. near St. Louis.

Missouri-Red Rock (2,540 mi.; 4,090 km): From source of Red Rock R. in Montana to Mississippi R. near St. Louis.

Mobile-Alabama-Coosa (645 mi.; 1,040 km): From junction of Etowah R. and Oostanula R. in Georgia to Mobile Bay.

Neosho (460 mi.; 740 km): From Morris Co. in Kansas to Arkansas R. in Oklahoma.

Niobrara (431 mi.; 694 km): From Niobrara Co. in Wyoming to Missouri R. in Nebraska.

Noatak (350 mi.; 563 km): From Brooks Range in Alaska to Kotzebue Sound.

North Canadian (800 mi.; 1,290 km): From Union Co. in New Mexico to Canadian R. in Oklahoma.

North Platte (618 mi.; 995 km): From Jackson Co. in Colorado to junction with South Platte R. in Nebraska to form Platte R.

Ohio (981 mi.; 1,579 km): From junction of Allegheny R. and Monongahela R. at Pittsburgh to Mississippi R. between Illinois and Kentucky.

Ohio-Allegheny (1,306 mi.; 2,102 km): From Potter Co. in Pennsylvania to Mississippi R. at Cairo in Illinois.

Osage (500 mi.; 805 km): From east-central Kansas to Missouri R. near Jefferson City in Missouri.

Ouachita (605 mi.; 974 km): From Polk Co. in Arkansas to Red R. in Louisiana.

Pearl (411 mi.; 661 km): From Neshoba County in Mississippi to Gulf of Mexico (Mississippi-Louisiana).

Pecos (926 mi.; 1,490 km): From Mora Co. in New Mexico to Rio Grande in Texas.

Pee Dee-Yadkin (435 mi.; 700 km): From Watauga Co. in North Carolina to Winyah Bay in South Carolina.

Pend Oreille–Clark Fork (531 mi.; 855 km): Near Butte in Montana to Columbia R. on Washington-Canada border.

Platte (990 mi.; 1593 km): From source of Grizzly Creek in Jackson Co., Colorado, to Missouri R. south of Omaha, Nebraska.

Porcupine (569 mi.; 916 km): From Yukon Territory, Canada, to Yukon R. in Alaska.

Potomac (383 mi.; 616 km): From Garrett Co. in Maryland to Chesapeake Bay at Point Lookout in Maryland.

Powder (375 mi.; 603 km): From junction of forks in Johnson Co. in Wyoming to Yellowstone R. in Montana.

Red (1,290 mi.; 2,080 km): From source of Tierra Blanca Creek in Curry County, New Mexico, to Mississippi R. in Louisiana.

Red (also called *Red River of the North*) (545 mi.; 877 km): From junction of Otter Tail R. and Bois de Sioux R. in Minnesota to Lake Winnipeg in Manitoba, Canada.

Republican (445 mi.; 716 km): From junction of North Fork and Arikaree R. in Nebraska to junction with Smoky Hill R. in Kansas to form the Kansas R.

Rio Grande (1,900 mi.; 3,060 km): From San Juan Co. in Colorado to Gulf of Mexico.

Roanoke (380 mi.; 612 km): From junction of forks in Montgomery Co. in Virginia to Albemarle Sound in North Carolina.

Sabine (380 mi.; 612 km): From junction of forks in Hunt Co. in Texas to Sabine Lake between Texas and Louisiana.

Sacramento (377 mi.; 607 km): From Siskiyou Co. in California to Suisun Bay.

Saint Francis (425 mi.; 684 km): From Iron Co. in Missouri to Mississippi R. in Arkansas.

Salmon (420 mi.; 676 km): From Custer Co. in Idaho to Snake R.

San Joaquin (350 mi.; 563 km): From junction of forks in Madera Co. in California to Suisun Bay.

San Juan (360 mi.; 579 km): From Archuleta Co. in Colorado to Colorado R. in Utah.

Santee-Wateree-Catawba (538 mi.; 866 km): From McDowell Co. in North Carolina to Atlantic Ocean in South Carolina.

Smoky Hill (540 mi.; 869 km): From Cheyenne Co. in Colorado to junction with Republican R. in Kansas to form Kansas R.

Snake (1,038 mi.; 1,670 km): From Ocean Plateau in Wyoming to Columbia R. in Washington.

South Platte (424 mi.; 682 km): From Park Co. in Colorado to junction with North Platte R. in Nebraska to form Platte R.

Stikine (379 mi.; 610 km): From British Columbia in Canada to Stikine Strait near Wrangell, Alaska.

Susquehanna (444 mi.; 715 km): From Otsego Lake in New York to Chesapeake Bay in Maryland.

Tanana (659 mi.; 1,060 km): From Wrangell Mts. in Yukon Territory, Canada, to Yukon R. in Alaska.

Tennessee (652 mi.; 1,049 km): From junction of Holston R. and French Broad R. in Tennessee to Ohio R. in Kentucky.

Tennessee–French Broad (886 mi.; 1,417 km): From Transylvania Co. in North Carolina to Ohio R. at Paducah in Kentucky.

Tombigbee (525 mi.; 845 km): From junction of forks in Itawamba Co. in Mississippi to Mobile R. in Alabama.

Trinity (360 mi.; 579 km): From junction of forks in Dallas Co. in Texas to Galveston Bay.

Wabash (512 mi.; 824 km): From Darke Co. in Ohio to Ohio R. between Illinois and Indiana.

Washita (500 mi.; 805 km): From Hemphill Co. in Texas to Red R. in Oklahoma.

White (722 mi.; 1,160 km): From Madison Co. in Arkansas to Mississippi R.

Wisconsin (430 mi.; 692 km): From Vilas Co. in Wisconsin to Mississippi R.

Yellowstone (692 mi.; 1,110 km): From Park Co. in Wyoming to Missouri R. in North Dakota.

Yukon (1,979 mi.; 3,185 km): From source of McNeil R. in Yukon Territory, Canada, to Bering Sea in Alaska.

Coastline of the United States

State	Lengths, statute miles: General coastline[1]	Tidal shoreline[2]	State	Lengths, statute miles: General coastline[1]	Tidal shoreline[2]
Atlantic Coast:			**Gulf Coast:**		
Maine	228	3,478	Florida (Gulf)	770	5,095
New Hampshire	13	131	Alabama	53	607
Massachusetts	192	1,519	Mississippi	44	359
Rhode Island	40	384	Louisiana	397	7,721
Connecticut	—	618	Texas	367	3,359
New York	127	1,850	Total Gulf Coast	1,631	17,141
New Jersey	130	1,792	**Pacific Coast:**		
Pennsylvania	—	89	California	840	3,427
Delaware	28	381	Oregon	296	1,410
Maryland	31	3,190	Washington	157	3,026
Virginia	112	3,315	Hawaii	750	1,052
North Carolina	301	3,375	Alaska (Pacific)	5,580	31,383
South Carolina	187	2,876	Total Pacific Coast	7,623	40,298
Georgia	100	2,344	**Arctic Coast:**		
Florida (Atlantic)	580	3,331	Alaska (Arctic)	1,060	2,521
Total Atlantic Coast	2,069	28,673	Total Arctic Coast	1,060	2,521
			States Total	**12,383**	**88,633**

1. Figures are lengths of general outline of seacoast. Measurements are made with unit measure of 30 minutes of latitude on charts as near scale of 1:1,200,000 as possible. Coastline of bays and sounds is included to point where they narrow to width of unit measure, and distance across at such point is included. 2. Figures were obtained in 1939–1940 with recording instrument on the largest-scale maps and charts then available. Shoreline of outer coast, offshore islands, sounds, bays, rivers, and creeks is included to head of tidewater, or to point where tidal waters narrow to width of 100 feet. *Source:* Department of Commerce, National Oceanic and Atmospheric Administration, National Ocean Service.

Mountain Peaks in the United States Higher Than 14,000 Feet

Name	State	Height (ft.)	Name	State	Height (ft.)	Name	State	Height (ft.)
Mt. McKinley	Alaska	20,320	Castle Peak	Colo.	14,265	Windom Peak	Colo.	14,082
Mt. St. Elias	Alaska	18,008	Quandary Peak	Colo.	14,265	Mt. Columbia	Colo.	14,073
Mt. Foraker	Alaska	17,400	Mt. Evans	Colo.	14,264	Mt. Augusta	Alaska	14,070
Mt. Bona	Alaska	16,500	Longs Peak	Colo.	14,255	Missouri Mtn.	Colo.	14,067
Mt. Blackburn	Alaska	16,390	Mt. Wilson	Colo.	14,246	Humboldt Peak	Colo.	14,064
Mt. Sanford	Alaska	16,237	White Mtn.	Calif.	14,246	Mt. Bierstadt	Colo.	14,060
Mt. Vancouver	Alaska	15,979	North Palisade	Calif.	14,242	Sunlight Peak	Colo.	14,059
South Buttress	Alaska	15,885	Mt. Cameron	Colo.	14,238	Split Mtn.	Calif.	14,058
Mt. Churchill	Alaska	15,638	Mt. Shavano	Colo.	14,229	Handies Peak	Colo.	14,048
Mt. Fairweather	Alaska	15,300	Crestone Needle	Colo.	14,197	Culebra Peak	Colo.	14,047
Mt. Hubbard	Alaska	14,950	Mt. Belford	Colo.	14,197	Mt. Lindsey	Colo.	14,042
Mt. Bear	Alaska	14,831	Mt. Princeton	Colo.	14,197	Ellingwood Point	Colo.	14,042
East Buttress	Alaska	14,730	Mt. Yale	Colo.	14,196	Middle Palisade	Calif.	14,040
Mt. Hunter	Alaska	14,573	Mt. Bross	Colo.	14,172	Little Bear Peak	Colo.	14,037
Browne Tower	Alaska	14,530	Kit Carson Mtn.	Colo.	14,165	Mt. Sherman	Colo.	14,036
Mt. Alverstone	Alaska	14,500	Mt. Wrangell	Alaska	14,163	Redcloud Peak	Colo.	14,034
Mt. Whitney	Calif.	14,494[1]	Mt. Sill	Calif.	14,162	Mt. Langley	Calif.	14,027
University Peak	Alaska	14,470	Mt. Shasta	Calif.	14,162	Conundrum Peak	Colo.	14,022
Mt. Elbert	Colo.	14,433	El Diente Peak	Colo.	14,159	Mt. Tyndall	Calif.	14,019
Mt. Massive	Colo.	14,421	Point Success	Wash.	14,158	Pyramid Peak	Colo.	14,018
Mt. Harvard	Colo.	14,420	Maroon Peak	Colo.	14,156	Wilson Peak	Colo.	14,017
Mt. Rainier	Wash.	14,410	Tabeguache Mtn.	Colo.	14,155	Wetterhorn Peak	Colo.	14,015
Mt. Williamson	Calif.	14,370	Mt. Oxford	Colo.	14,153	North Maroon Peak	Colo.	14,014
La Plata Peak	Colo.	14,361	Mt. Sneffels	Colo.	14,150	San Luis Peak	Colo.	14,014
Blanca Peak	Colo.	14,345	Mt. Democrat	Colo.	14,148	Middle Palisade	Calif.	14,012
Uncompahgre Peak	Colo.	14,309	Capitol Peak	Colo.	14,130	Mt. Muir	Calif.	14,012
Crestone Peak	Colo.	14,294	Liberty Cap	Wash.	14,112	Mt. of the Holy Cross	Colo.	14,005
Mt. Lincoln	Colo.	14,286	Pikes Peak	Colo.	14,110	Huron Peak	Colo.	14,003
Grays Peak	Colo.	14,270	Snowmass Mtn.	Colo.	14,092	Thunderbolt Peak	Calif.	14,003
Mt. Antero	Colo.	14,269	Mt. Russell	Calif.	14,088	Sunshine Peak	Colo.	14,001
Torreys Peak	Colo.	14,267	Mt. Eolus	Colo.	14,083			

1. National Geodetic Survey. *Source:* U.S. Dept. of the Interior, Geological Survey.

Highest, Lowest, and Mean Elevations in the United States

State	Elevation (ft.)[1]	Highest point	Elevation (ft.)	Lowest point	Elevation (ft.)
Alabama	500	Cheaha Mountain	2,405	Gulf of Mexico	Sea level
Alaska	1,900	Mt. McKinley	20,320	Pacific Ocean	Sea level
Arizona	4,100	Humphreys Peak	12,633	Colorado River	70
Arkansas	650	Magazine Mountain	2,753	Ouachita River	55
California	2,900	Mt. Whitney	14,494	Death Valley	–282[2]
Colorado	6,800	Mt. Elbert	14,433	Arkansas River	3,350
Connecticut	500	Mt. Frissell, on south slope	2,380	Long Island Sound	Sea level
Delaware	60	Ebright Road, Del.–Pa. state line	448	Atlantic Ocean	Sea level
D.C.	150	Tenleytown, at Reno Reservoir	410	Potomac River	1
Florida	100	Sec. 30, T6N, R20W, Walton County	345	Atlantic Ocean	Sea level
Georgia	600	Brasstown Bald	4,784	Atlantic Ocean	Sea level
Hawaii	3,030	Puu Wekiu, Mauna Kea	13,796	Pacific Ocean	Sea level
Idaho	5,000	Borah Peak	12,662	Snake River	710
Illinois	600	Charles Mound	1,235	Mississippi River	279
Indiana	700	Franklin Township, Wayne County	1,257	Ohio River	320
Iowa	1,100	Sec. 29, T100N, R41W, Osceola County	1,670	Mississippi River	480
Kansas	2,000	Mt. Sunflower	4,039	Verdigris River	679
Kentucky	750	Black Mountain	4,139	Mississippi River	257
Louisiana	100	Driskill Mountain	535	New Orleans	–8[2]
Maine	600	Mt. Katahdin	5,267	Atlantic Ocean	Sea level
Maryland	350	Backbone Mountain	3,360	Atlantic Ocean	Sea level
Massachusetts	500	Mt. Greylock	3,487	Atlantic Ocean	Sea level
Michigan	900	Mt. Arvon	1,979	Lake Erie	572
Minnesota	1,200	Eagle Mountain	2,301	Lake Superior	600
Mississippi	300	Woodall Mountain	806	Gulf of Mexico	Sea level
Missouri	800	Taum Sauk Mountain	1,772	St. Francis River	230
Montana	3,400	Granite Peak	12,799	Kootenai River	1,800
Nebraska	2,600	Johnson Township, Kimball County	5,424	Missouri River	840
Nevada	5,500	Boundary Peak	13,140	Colorado River	479
New Hampshire	1,000	Mt. Washington	6,288	Atlantic Ocean	Sea level
New Jersey	250	High Point	1,803	Atlantic Ocean	Sea level
New Mexico	5,700	Wheeler Peak	13,161	Red Bluff Reservoir	2,842
New York	1,000	Mt. Marcy	5,344	Atlantic Ocean	Sea level
North Carolina	700	Mt. Mitchell	6,684	Atlantic Ocean	Sea level
North Dakota	1,900	White Butte	3,506	Red River	750
Ohio	850	Campbell Hill	1,549	Ohio River	455
Oklahoma	1,300	Black Mesa	4,973	Little River	289
Oregon	3,300	Mt. Hood	11,239	Pacific Ocean	Sea level
Pennsylvania	1,100	Mt. Davis	3,213	Delaware River	Sea level
Rhode Island	200	Jerimoth Hill	812	Atlantic Ocean	Sea level
South Carolina	350	Sassafras Mountain	3,560	Atlantic Ocean	Sea level
South Dakota	2,200	Harney Peak	7,242	Big Stone Lake	966
Tennessee	900	Clingmans Dome	6,643	Mississippi River	178
Texas	1,700	Guadalupe Peak	8,749	Gulf of Mexico	Sea level
Utah	6,100	Kings Peak	13,528	Beaverdam Wash	2,000
Vermont	1,000	Mt. Mansfield	4,393	Lake Champlain	95
Virginia	950	Mt. Rogers	5,729	Atlantic Ocean	Sea level
Washington	1,700	Mt. Rainier	14,410	Pacific Ocean	Sea level
West Virginia	1,500	Spruce Knob	4,861	Potomac River	240
Wisconsin	1,050	Timms Hill	1,951	Lake Michigan	579
Wyoming	6,700	Gannett Peak	13,804	Belle Fourche River	3,099
United States	**2,500**	**Mt. McKinley (Alaska)**	**20,320**	**Death Valley (California)**	**–282[2]**

1. Approximate mean elevation. 2. Below sea level. *Source:* U.S. Geological Survey.

Latitude and Longitude of U.S. and Canadian Cities
(and time corresponding to 12:00 noon, Eastern Standard Time)

City	Lat. °	Lat. ′	Long. °	Long. ′	Time	City	Lat. °	Lat. ′	Long. °	Long. ′	Time
Albany, N.Y.	42	40	73	45	12:00 noon	Memphis, Tenn.	35	9	90	3	11:00 a.m.
Albuquerque, N.M.	35	05	106	39	10:00 a.m.	Miami, Fla.	25	46	80	12	12:00 noon
Amarillo, Tex.	35	11	101	50	11:00 a.m.	Milwaukee, Wis.	43	2	87	55	11:00 a.m.
Anchorage, Alaska	61	13	149	54	8:00 a.m.	Minneapolis, Minn.	44	59	93	14	11:00 a.m.
Atlanta, Ga.	33	45	84	23	12:00 noon	Mobile, Ala.	30	42	88	3	11:00 a.m.
Austin, Tex.	30	16	97	44	11:00 a.m.	Montgomery, Ala.	32	21	86	18	11:00 a.m.
Baker, Ore.	44	47	117	50	9:00 a.m.	Montpelier, Vt.	44	15	72	32	12:00 noon
Baltimore, Md.	39	18	76	38	12:00 noon	Montreal, Que., Can.	45	30	73	35	12:00 noon
Bangor, Maine	44	48	68	47	12:00 noon	Moose Jaw, Sask., Can.	50	37	105	31	10:00 a.m.
Birmingham, Ala.	33	30	86	50	11:00 a.m.						
Bismarck, N.D.	46	48	100	47	11:00 a.m.	Nashville, Tenn.	36	10	86	47	11:00 a.m.
Boise, Idaho	43	36	116	13	10:00 a.m.	Nelson, B.C., Can.	49	30	117	17	9:00 a.m.
Boston, Mass.	42	21	71	5	12:00 noon	Newark, N.J.	40	44	74	10	12:00 noon
Buffalo, N.Y.	42	55	78	50	12:00 noon	New Haven, Conn.	41	19	72	55	12:00 noon
Calgary, Alba., Can.	51	1	114	1	10:00 a.m.	New Orleans, La.	29	57	90	4	11:00 a.m.
Carlsbad, N.M.	32	26	104	15	10:00 a.m.	New York, N.Y.	40	47	73	58	12:00 noon
Charleston, S.C.	32	47	79	56	12:00 noon	Nome, Alaska	64	25	165	30	8:00 a.m.
Charleston, W. Va.	38	21	81	38	12:00 noon	Oakland, Calif.	37	48	122	16	9:00 a.m.
Charlotte, N.C.	35	14	80	50	12:00 noon	Oklahoma City, Okla.	35	26	97	28	11:00 a.m.
Cheyenne, Wyo.	41	9	104	52	10:00 a.m.	Omaha, Neb.	41	15	95	56	11:00 a.m.
Chicago, Ill.	41	50	87	37	11:00 a.m.	Ottawa, Ont., Can.	45	24	75	43	12:00 noon
Cincinnati, Ohio	39	8	84	30	12:00 noon	Philadelphia, Pa.	39	57	75	10	12:00 noon
Cleveland, Ohio	41	28	81	37	12:00 noon	Phoenix, Ariz.	33	29	112	4	10:00 a.m.
Columbia, S.C.	34	0	81	2	12:00 noon	Pierre, S.D.	44	22	100	21	11:00 a.m.
Columbus, Ohio	40	0	83	1	12:00 noon	Pittsburgh, Pa.	40	27	79	57	12:00 noon
Dallas, Tex.	32	46	96	46	11:00 a.m.	Portland, Maine	43	40	70	15	12:00 noon
Denver, Colo.	39	45	105	0	10:00 a.m.	Portland, Ore.	45	31	122	41	9:00 a.m.
Des Moines, Iowa	41	35	93	37	11:00 a.m.	Providence, R.I.	41	50	71	24	12:00 noon
Detroit, Mich.	42	20	83	3	12:00 noon	Quebec, Que., Can.	46	49	71	11	12:00 noon
Dubuque, Iowa	42	31	90	40	11:00 a.m.	Raleigh, N.C.	35	46	78	39	12:00 noon
Duluth, Minn.	46	49	92	5	11:00 a.m.	Reno, Nev.	39	30	119	49	9:00 a.m.
Eastport, Maine	44	54	67	0	12:00 noon	Richfield, Utah	38	46	112	5	10:00 a.m.
Edmonton, Alb., Can.	53	34	113	28	11:00 a.m.	Richmond, Va.	37	33	77	29	12:00 noon
El Centro, Calif.	32	38	115	33	9:00 a.m.	Roanoke, Va.	37	17	79	57	12:00 noon
El Paso, Tex.	31	46	106	29	10:00 a.m.	Sacramento, Calif.	38	35	121	30	9:00 a.m.
Eugene, Ore.	44	3	123	5	9:00 a.m.	St. John, N.B., Can.	45	18	66	10	1:00 p.m.
Fargo, N.D.	46	52	96	48	11:00 a.m.	St. Louis, Mo.	38	35	90	12	11:00 a.m.
Flagstaff, Ariz.	35	13	111	41	10:00 a.m.	Salt Lake City, Utah	40	46	111	54	10:00 a.m.
Fort Worth, Tex.	32	43	97	19	11:00 a.m.	San Antonio, Tex.	29	23	98	33	11:00 a.m.
Fresno, Calif.	36	44	119	48	9:00 a.m.	San Diego, Calif.	32	42	117	10	9:00 a.m.
Grand Junction, Colo.	39	5	108	33	10:00 a.m.	San Francisco, Calif.	37	47	122	26	9:00 a.m.
Grand Rapids, Mich.	42	58	85	40	12:00 noon	San Jose, Calif.	37	20	121	53	9:00 a.m.
Havre, Mont.	48	33	109	43	10:00 a.m.	San Juan, P.R.	18	30	66	10	1:00 p.m.
Helena, Mont.	46	35	112	2	10:00 a.m.	Santa Fe, N.M.	35	41	105	57	10:00 a.m.
Honolulu, Hawaii	21	18	157	50	7:00 a.m.	Savannah, Ga.	32	5	81	5	12:00 noon
Hot Springs, Ark.	34	31	93	3	11:00 a.m.	Seattle, Wash.	47	37	122	20	9:00 a.m.
Houston, Tex.	29	45	95	21	11:00 a.m.	Shreveport, La.	32	28	93	42	11:00 a.m.
Idaho Falls, Idaho	43	30	112	1	10:00 a.m.	Sioux Falls, S.D.	43	33	96	44	11:00 a.m.
Indianapolis, Ind.	39	46	86	10	12:00 noon	Sitka, Alaska	57	10	135	15	8:00 a.m.
Jackson, Miss.	32	20	90	12	11:00 a.m.	Spokane, Wash.	47	40	117	26	9:00 a.m.
Jacksonville, Fla.	30	22	81	40	12:00 noon	Springfield, Ill.	39	48	89	38	11:00 a.m.
Juneau, Alaska	58	18	134	24	8:00 a.m.	Springfield, Mass.	42	6	72	34	12:00 noon
Kansas City, Mo.	39	6	94	35	11:00 a.m.	Springfield, Mo.	37	13	93	17	11:00 a.m.
Key West, Fla.	24	33	81	48	12:00 noon	Syracuse, N.Y.	43	2	76	8	12:00 noon
Kingston, Ont., Can.	44	15	76	30	12:00 noon	Tampa, Fla.	27	57	82	27	12:00 noon
Klamath Falls, Ore.	42	10	121	44	9:00 a.m.	Toledo, Ohio	41	39	83	33	12:00 noon
Knoxville, Tenn.	35	57	83	56	12:00 noon	Toronto, Ont., Can.	43	40	79	24	12:00 noon
Las Vegas, Nev.	36	10	115	12	9:00 a.m.	Tulsa, Okla.	36	09	95	59	11:00 a.m.
Lewiston, Idaho	46	24	117	2	9:00 a.m.	Vancouver, B.C., Can.	49	13	123	06	10:00 a.m.
Lincoln, Neb.	40	50	96	40	11:00 a.m.	Victoria, B.C., Can.	48	25	123	21	9:00 a.m.
London, Ont., Can.	43	2	81	34	12:00 noon	Virginia Beach, Va.	36	51	75	58	12:00 noon
Long Beach, Calif.	33	46	118	11	9:00 a.m.	Washington, D.C.	38	53	77	02	12:00 noon
Los Angeles, Calif.	34	3	118	15	9:00 a.m.	Wichita, Kan.	37	43	97	17	11:00 a.m.
Louisville, Ky.	38	15	85	46	12:00 noon	Wilmington, N.C.	34	14	77	57	12:00 noon
Manchester, N.H.	43	0	71	30	12:00 noon	Winnipeg, Man., Can.	49	54	97	7	11:00 a.m.

For more on U.S. geography, *see* National Parks, pp. 587–591.

ALL PHOTOS: AP—WIDE WORLD PHOTOS

"SHOCK AND AWE": U.S. bombs struck Baghdad for the second time in 12 years as U.S. president George W. Bush vowed to topple the regime of Iraqi strongman Saddam Hussein. The conflict began March 20 with a surprise, highly targeted missile strike on a specific site where U.S. intelligence indicated Saddam, his family, and key aides were hiding. The massive bombing campaign that followed aimed to instill "shock and awe" in Iraqis, the Pentagon said. U.S. troops occupied Iraq's capital on April 9.

ALLIES: President Bush argued that Saddam's regime aided al-Qaeda and possessed weapons of mass destruction. The U.N. and most nations did not agree; British prime minister Tony Blair, left, was one of the few major allies who supported the war.

TARGETS: Saddam Hussein's sons Uday, left, 38, and Qusay, right, 37, played key roles in the regime. On July 23, the two were besieged inside a palace in the northern city of Mosul. After a four-hour gunfight, both men had been killed. As of Sept. 1, Saddam was at large.

NO WAR! Protesters gather near the Washington Monument on March 15 to denounce war on Iraq. Massive demonstrations in major cities around the world were held on the same day, as the run-up to war divided the U.S. from many allies in Europe and the U.N.

ADVOCATE: U.S. secretary of state Colin Powell laid out the case for war against Iraq at the U.N. on Feb. 14, but the world body did not support the plan.

UNWILLING: From left, foreign ministers Joschka Fischer of Germany, Dominique de Villepin of France and Igor Ivanov of Russia all refused to take part in the war, in sharp contrast to the first Gulf War, which attracted a diverse international coalition of allies.

TOPPLED: A statue of Saddam Hussein in central Baghdad is pulled down by a U.S. Army tank on April 9. After the relatively easy victory, U.S. troops faced a grinding war of attrition against a host of loosely organized foes. By Aug. 27, 139 U.S. soldiers had died after the war's official end, more than were lost during the main phase of combat.

ATTACK: Terrorists exploded a car bomb at Baghdad's Canal Hotel, headquarters for the United Nations in Iraq, on Aug. 19, killing top U.N. envoy Sergio Vieira de Mello and 22 others. The deed underscored the fragility of the U.S. position in occupied Iraq.

MOST WANTED: Coalition forces were given playing cards to identify the key members of Iraq's regime.

VICTORY LAP: Secretary of Defense Donald Rumsfeld, a highly influential proponent of the war, visited U.S. troops in Iraq in April.

TOP GUN: On May 1, President Bush landed on the aircraft carrier U.S.S. *Abraham Lincoln* to declare "mission accomplished." But critics strongly questioned if he had an exit strategy for Iraq.

HOME AT LAST: Pfc. Jessica Lynch greets supporters after her return to West Virginia. Captured in Iraq, she was rescued by U.S. troops in a nighttime raid on the hospital where she was held.

TREMORS: A Republican drive to recall newly reelected California governor Gray Davis, left, a Democrat, succeeded in putting the question to voters on an Oct. 7 ballot. On Aug. 6, Austrian-born film action hero (and Kennedy-family in-law) Arnold Schwarzenegger declared on Jay Leno's *Tonight Show* that he would run for Gray's seat—joining some 130 other candidates.

LIGHTS OUT! New York City is darkened on Aug. 15, the day after the largest blackout in history left parts of eight U.S. states and two Canadian provinces without power. Some areas were dark for three days. Despite the inconvenience in a hot month, civility reigned. Human error and an aging, overladen power grid were blamed for the crisis.

OLD WOES: The U.S. road map to peace in the Middle East was on track when Palestine's newly named prime minister, Mahmoud Abbas, left, met Israel's PM, Ariel Sharon, on July 1. But after the suicide bombing of a Jerusalem bus in August, above, killed 20, Israel launched deadly raids against the militant group Hamas, and Abbas resigned, quenching hopes for peace.

NEW HOPE: North Korea's Kim Jong Il, center, meets with Russian diplomats in January. China, Japan, Russia, the U.S., and both Koreas began talks in August on a plan to disarm North Korea's nuclear weapons in exchange for economic aid.

NEW BOSS: Outgoing Chinese president Jiang Zemin, left, shares a photo-op with incoming leader Hu Jintao. The veteran Jiang retained his position as head of China's military, promising continuity in the populous nation's turn to capitalism.

LIBERIA LIBERATED: President Charles Taylor waves farewell on Aug. 11 as he boards an airplane that will take him to exile in Nigeria. The reluctant departure of the corrupt dictator followed a four-year revolt that left his nation impoverished and divided. President Bush sent a small task force of U.S. Marines to aid in the transfer of power.

NABBED: Indonesian terror chief Hambali was arrested in Thailand in August. Al-Qaeda's boss in Southeast Asia is believed to have plotted several bombings.

SAUDI BOMB: Al-Qaeda claimed it was behind a May 12 suicide bombing in a residential section of Riyadh that left 34 dead, including nine Americans. Saudi officials apprehended the blast's alleged mastermind in June.

AFFIRMED: Protesters supporting affirmative action rally outside the U.S. Supreme Court in April. The court ruled in June in favor of the limited use of racial considerations in college admissions in two cases involving procedures at the University of Michigan.

GAY RIGHTS: Openly gay priest Gene Robinson, above, was named a bishop at a divisive convocation of U.S. Episcopalians in August. The U.S. Supreme Court ruled 6 to 3 in June that a Texas law outlawing sodomy was unconstitutional. Also in June, two of Canada's provinces legalized same-sex marriages.

EPIDEMIC: Choirboys wearing surgical masks to ward off the SARS virus leave a Roman Catholic cathedral in Hong Kong on Good Friday. Fast-spreading and fatal in some 4% of cases, SARS (severe acute respiratory syndrome) originated in China's Guangdong province late in 2002. Chinese officials initially tried to hush up the outbreak, but it spread to Hong Kong in March, then to Canada and other nations. Quarantines managed to contain the epidemic—for the short run, at least.

TRAGEDY IN SPACE: Seven astronauts perished when the U.S. shuttle *Columbia* burned up on reentry on Feb. 1. The cause: a loose piece of insulating foam struck and damaged a wing on liftoff, right. The seven astronauts, from left: David Brown, Rick Husband, Laurel Clark, Kalpana Chawla, Michael Anderson, William McCool, and Israel's Ilan Ramon.

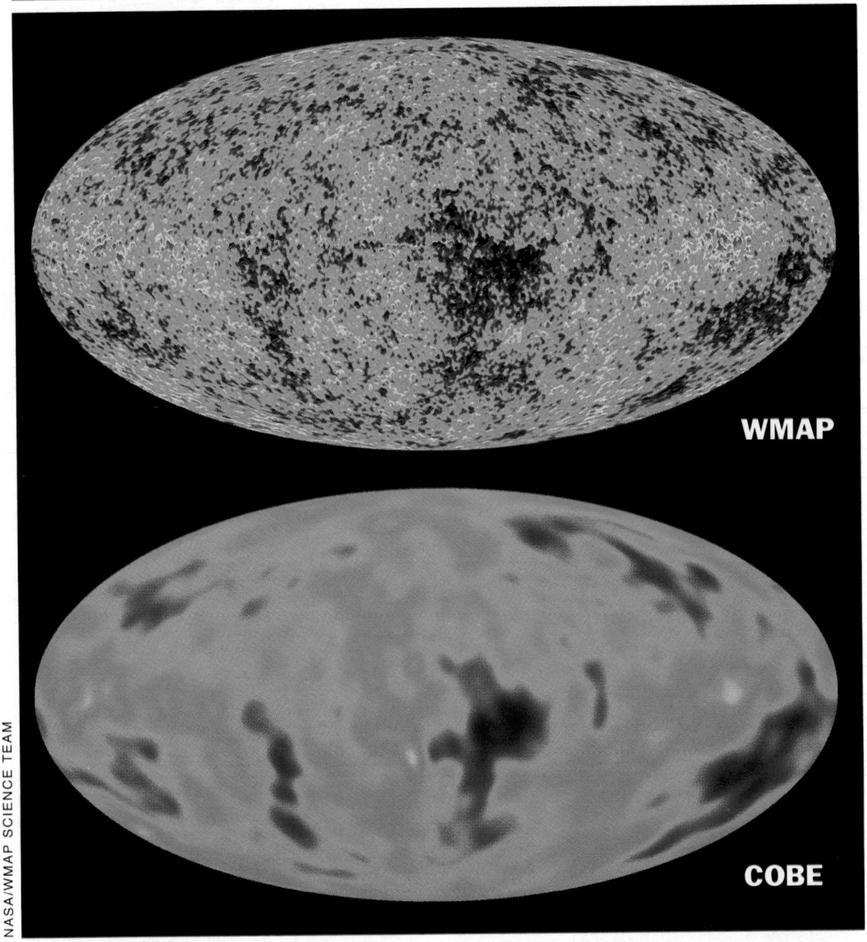

NASA/WMAP SCIENCE TEAM

BABY PICTURES: NASA's Wilkinson Microwave Anisotropy Probe (WMAP) satellite captured the portrait of the universe at top, which shows the afterglow of the Big Bang in the form of lingering microwaves. The map of the infant universe was far more detailed than the one taken in 1992 by NASA's COBE (Cosmic Background Explorer) satellite, bottom. The WMAP data placed the age of the universe at 13.7 billion years.

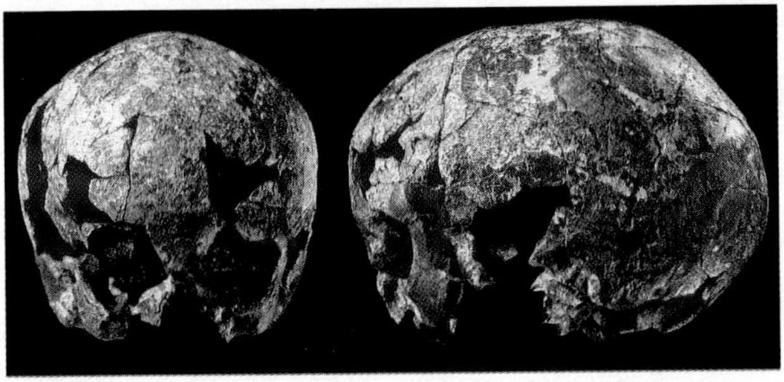

AFP—CORBIS

OLD BONES: This 160,000-year-old child's skull is one of three specimens found in the Awash Valley region of Ethiopia in 1997. In June, scientists identified them as the earliest examples of *Homo sapiens* yet unearthed.

TAKE TWO: Yankee ace Roger Clemens notched his 300th career win and 4,000th strike-out on the same night in June.

DANDY: Powered by his blazing 140-m.p.h. serve, American Andy Roddick, 21, beat Spain's Juan Ferrero to win the U.S. Open.

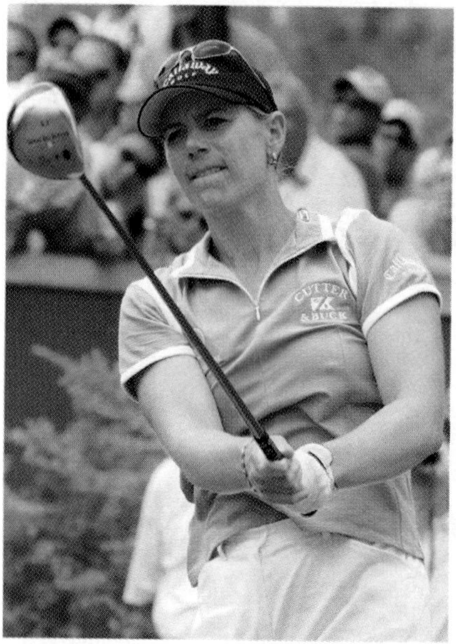

GUEST: Top woman pro Annika Sorenstam teed off in the PGA's Colonial Invitational on May 22, but she failed to make the cut.

BEN WHO? America's Ben Curtis won the British Open in a year when golf's four major trophies went to little-known pros.

PAGING ALL WIZARDS: The June publication of *Harry Potter and the Order of the Phoenix,* the fifth in J. K. Rowling's fantasy series on wizards-in-training, created an international sensation. Above, British fans dig into the first of the volume's 870 pages.

IDOLS: As America's love affair with reality TV and viewer polling continued, Fox scored with its knockoff of the old amateur-hour format, *American Idol.* A huge audience tuned in on May 21 and voted Ruben Stoddard, 25, right, the winner over Clay Aiken, 24.

GREGORY PECK, 87: His classic portrayal of lawyer Atticus Finch in *To Kill a Mockingbird* earned him an Oscar and a 2003 citation as the No. 1 hero in film history.

DAVID BRINKLEY, 82: With co-anchor Chet Huntley, he pioneered TV journalism at NBC in the 1960s, then created an influential Sunday-morning political show.

KATHARINE HEPBURN, 96: Her secret? Fans knew that the smart, no-nonsense heroines she played onscreen were simply stand-ins for the inimitable, original Kate.

BOB HOPE, 100: Born in Britain, the rapid-fire gagman conquered vaudeville, radio, TV and film. His travels abroad to entertain U.S. troops made him a legend.

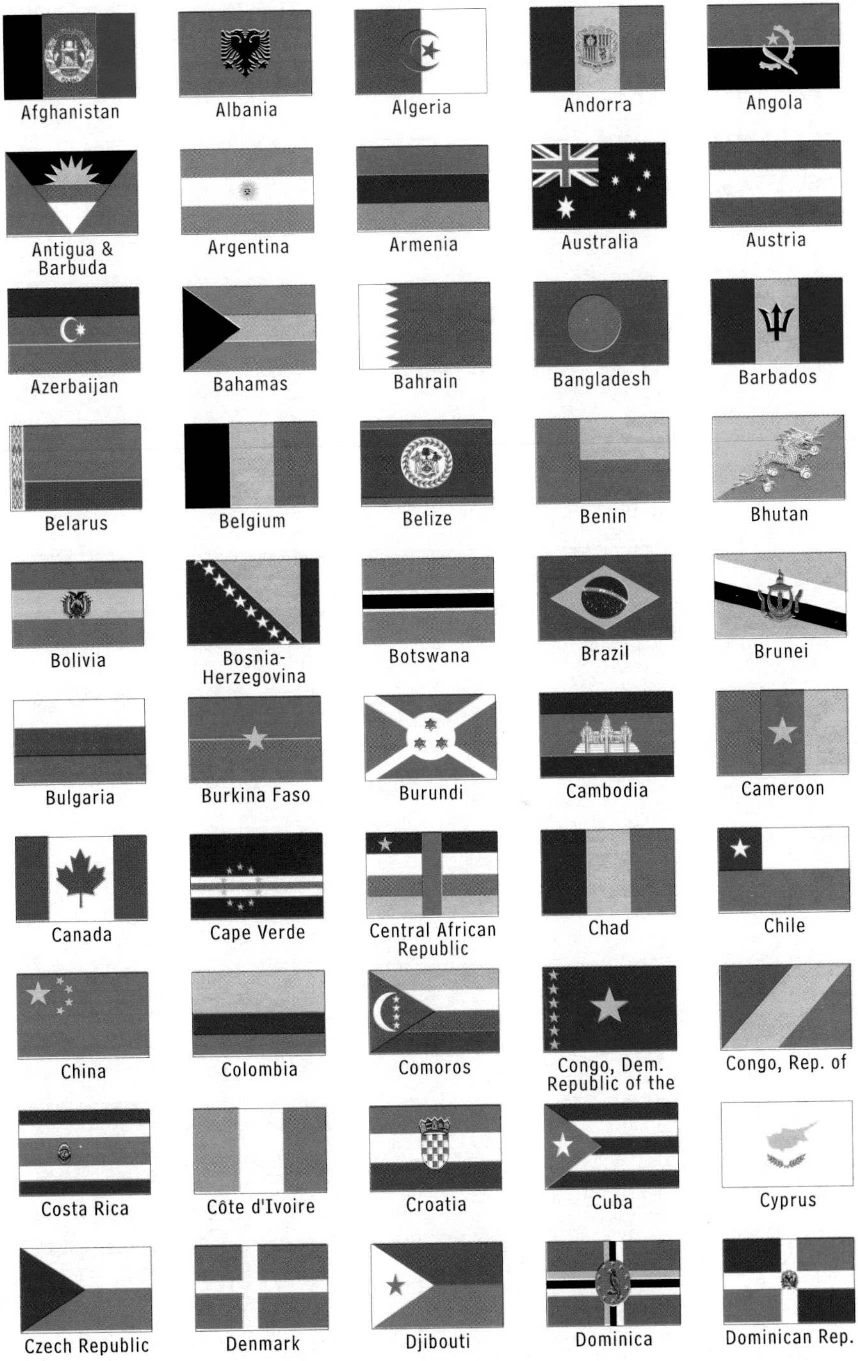
Afghanistan
Albania
Algeria
Andorra
Angola
Antigua & Barbuda
Argentina
Armenia
Australia
Austria
Azerbaijan
Bahamas
Bahrain
Bangladesh
Barbados
Belarus
Belgium
Belize
Benin
Bhutan
Bolivia
Bosnia-Herzegovina
Botswana
Brazil
Brunei
Bulgaria
Burkina Faso
Burundi
Cambodia
Cameroon
Canada
Cape Verde
Central African Republic
Chad
Chile
China
Colombia
Comoros
Congo, Dem. Republic of the
Congo, Rep. of
Costa Rica
Côte d'Ivoire
Croatia
Cuba
Cyprus
Czech Republic
Denmark
Djibouti
Dominica
Dominican Rep.

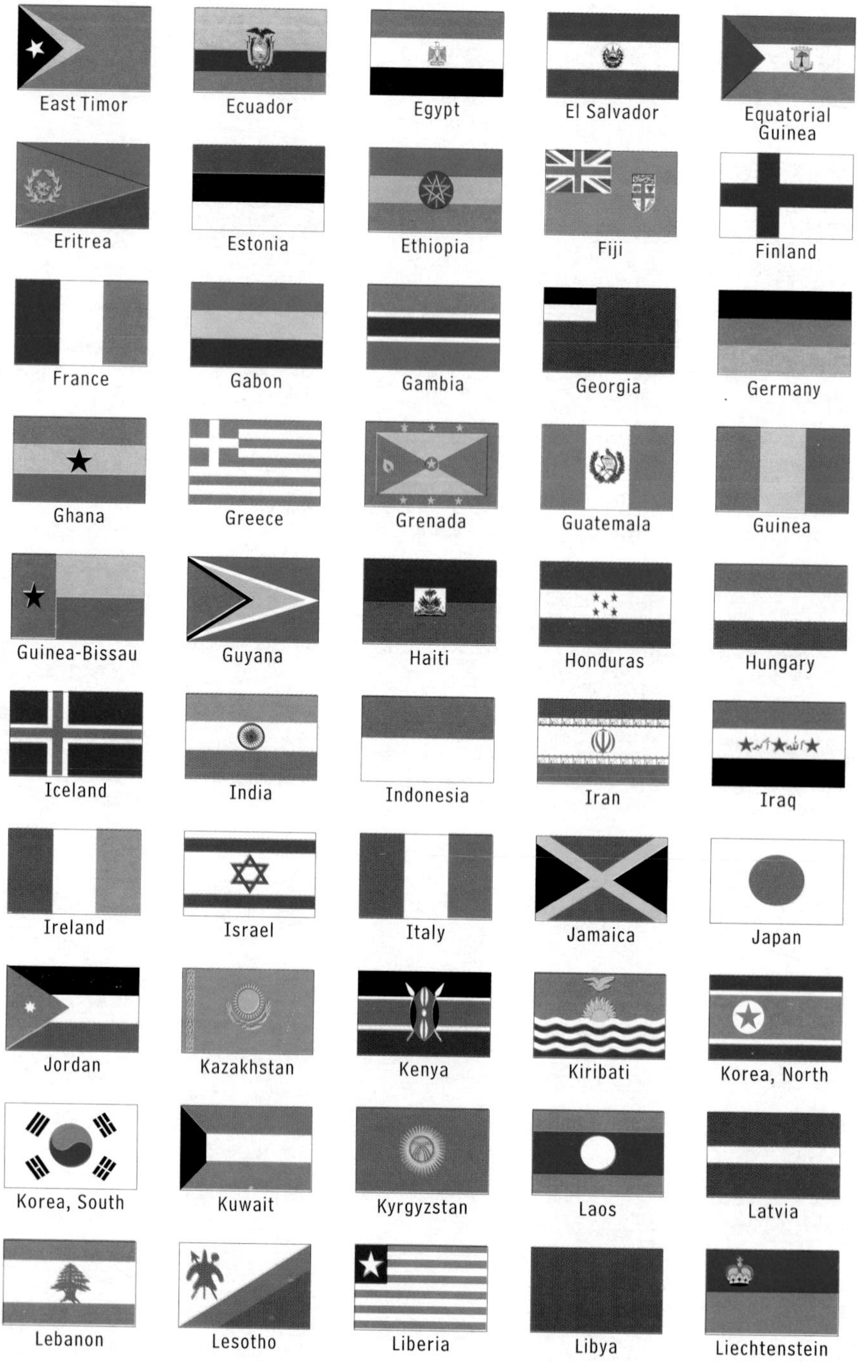
East Timor
Ecuador
Egypt
El Salvador
Equatorial Guinea
Eritrea
Estonia
Ethiopia
Fiji
Finland
France
Gabon
Gambia
Georgia
Germany
Ghana
Greece
Grenada
Guatemala
Guinea
Guinea-Bissau
Guyana
Haiti
Honduras
Hungary
Iceland
India
Indonesia
Iran
Iraq
Ireland
Israel
Italy
Jamaica
Japan
Jordan
Kazakhstan
Kenya
Kiribati
Korea, North
Korea, South
Kuwait
Kyrgyzstan
Laos
Latvia
Lebanon
Lesotho
Liberia
Libya
Liechtenstein

Lithuania Luxembourg Macedonia Madagascar Malawi

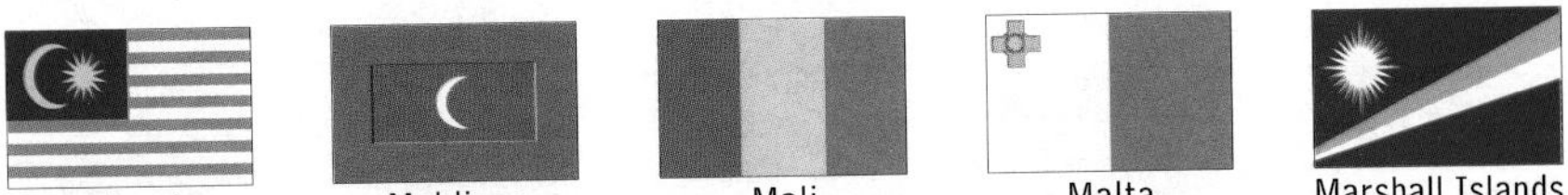

Malaysia Maldives Mali Malta Marshall Islands

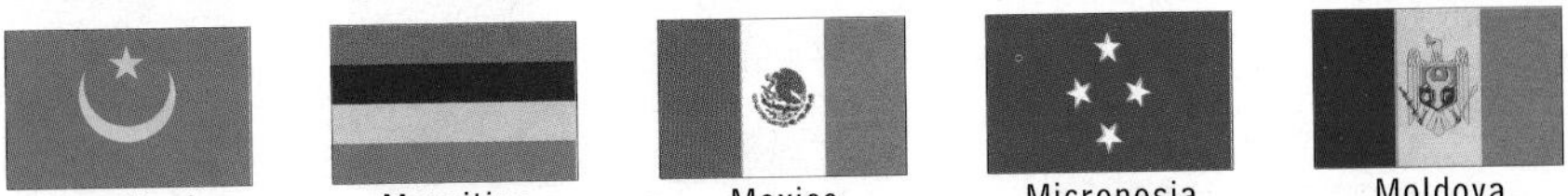

Mauritania Mauritius Mexico Micronesia Moldova

Monaco Mongolia Morocco Mozambique Myanmar

Namibia Nauru Nepal Netherlands New Zealand

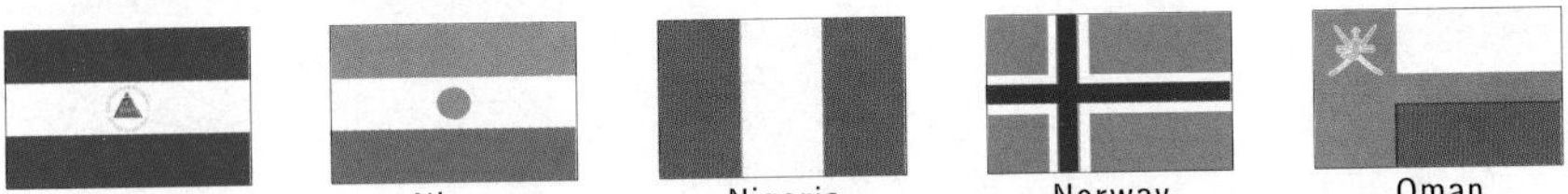

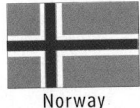

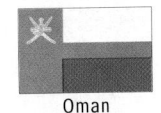

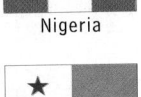

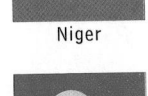

Nicaragua Niger Nigeria Norway Oman

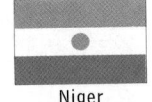

Pakistan Palau Panama Papua New Guinea Paraguay

Peru Philippines Poland Portugal Qatar

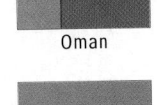

Romania Russia Rwanda St. Kitts & Nevis St. Lucia

St. Vincent & The Grenadines Samoa San Marino São Tomé & Príncipe Saudi Arabia

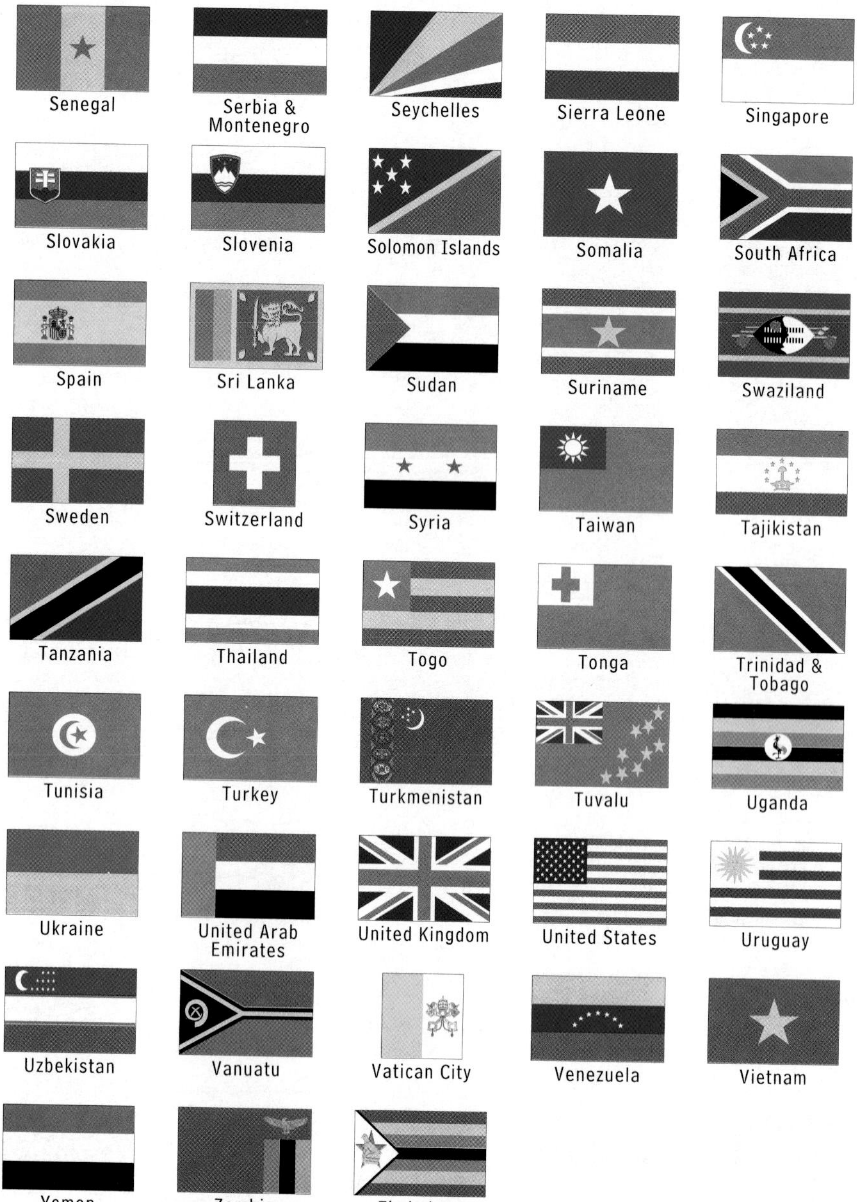

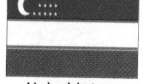

Senegal
Serbia & Montenegro
Seychelles
Sierra Leone
Singapore
Slovakia
Slovenia
Solomon Islands
Somalia
South Africa
Spain
Sri Lanka
Sudan
Suriname
Swaziland
Sweden
Switzerland
Syria
Taiwan
Tajikistan
Tanzania
Thailand
Togo
Tonga
Trinidad & Tobago
Tunisia
Turkey
Turkmenistan
Tuvalu
Uganda
Ukraine
United Arab Emirates
United Kingdom
United States
Uruguay
Uzbekistan
Vanuatu
Vatican City
Venezuela
Vietnam
Yemen
Zambia
Zimbabwe

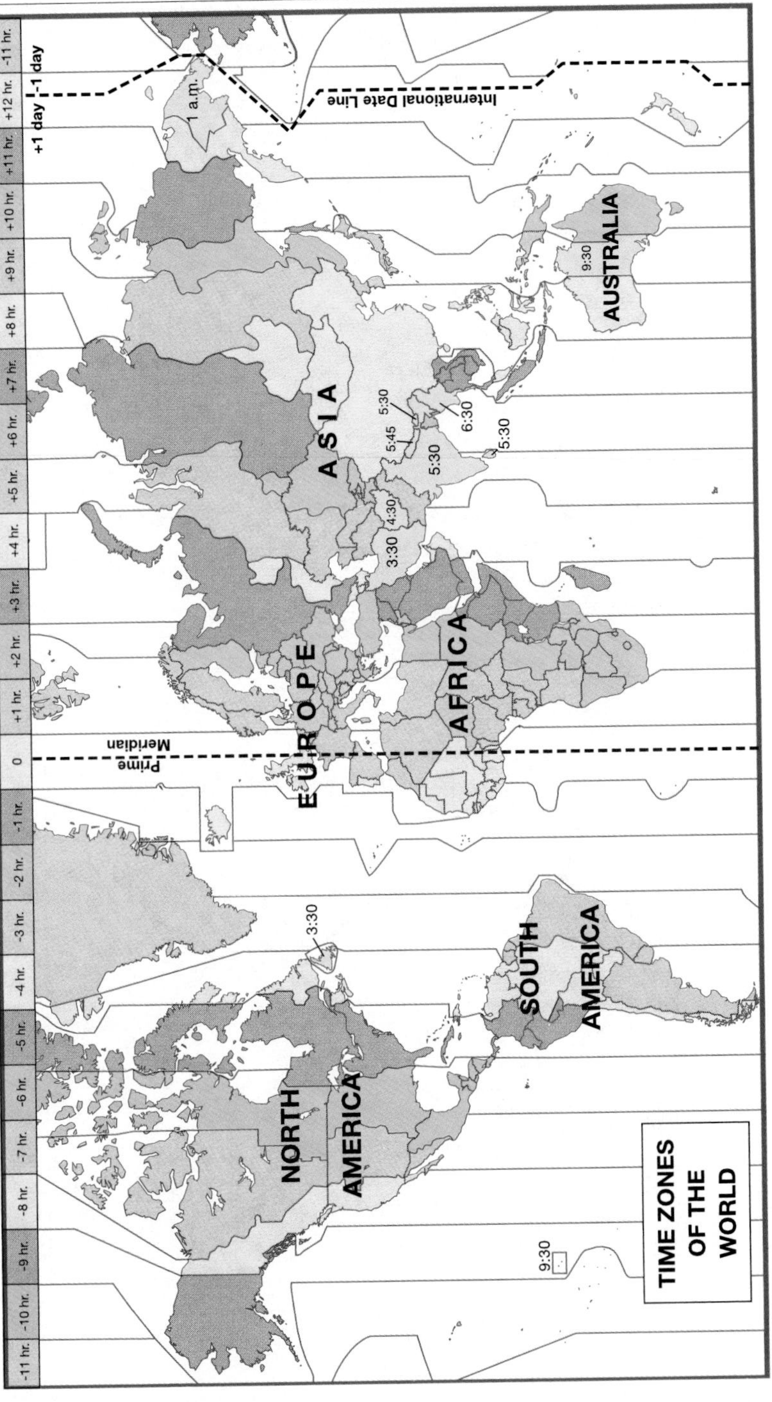
-11 hr.
-10 hr.
-9 hr.
-8 hr.
-7 hr.
-6 hr.
-5 hr.
-4 hr.
-3 hr.
-2 hr.
-1 hr.
0
+1 hr.
+2 hr.
+3 hr.
+4 hr.
+5 hr.
+6 hr.
+7 hr.
+8 hr.
+9 hr.
+10 hr.
+11 hr.
+12 hr.
-11 hr.
+1 day
-1 day
International Date Line
1 a.m.
Prime Meridian
NORTH AMERICA
SOUTH AMERICA
EUROPE
ASIA
AFRICA
AUSTRALIA
3:30
9:30
3:30
4:30
5:30
5:45
5:30
6:30
5:30
9:30
TIME ZONES OF THE WORLD

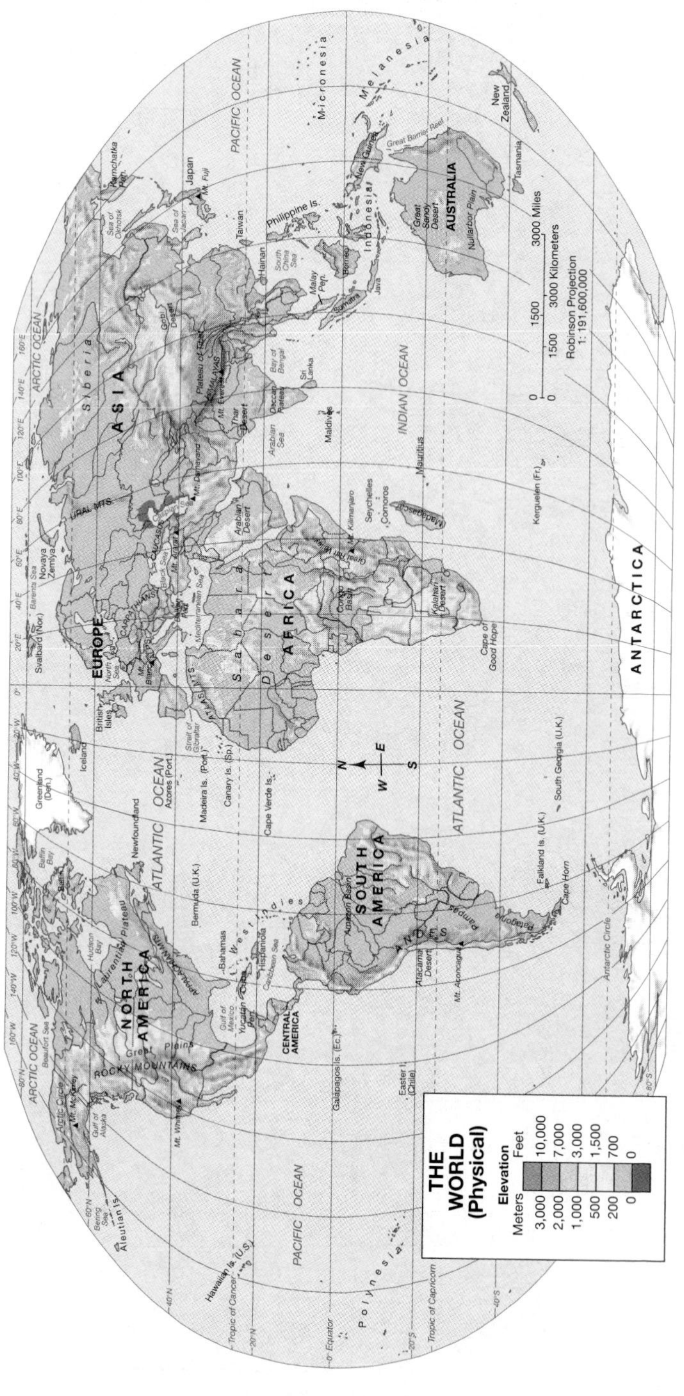
THE WORLD (Physical)
Elevation
Meters Feet
3,000 10,000
2,000 7,000
1,000 3,000
500 1,500
200 700
0 0
0 1500 3000 Miles
0 1500 3000 Kilometers
Robinson Projection
1: 191,600,000
N
W E
S
NORTH AMERICA
SOUTH AMERICA
CENTRAL AMERICA
EUROPE
ASIA
AFRICA
AUSTRALIA
ANTARCTICA
ARCTIC OCEAN
PACIFIC OCEAN
ATLANTIC OCEAN
INDIAN OCEAN
Arctic Circle
Tropic of Cancer
Equator
Tropic of Capricorn
Antarctic Circle
ROCKY MOUNTAINS
Great Plains
Laurentian Plateau
APPALACHIAN MTS.
Hudson Bay
Baffin Bay
Beaufort Sea
Gulf of Alaska
Bering Sea
Aleutian Is.
Mt. McKinley
Mt. Whitney
Gulf of Mexico
Yucatan Pen.
Bahamas
Cuba
Hispaniola
Caribbean Sea
West Indies
Bermuda (U.K.)
Newfoundland
Greenland (Den.)
Iceland
Hawaiian Is. (U.S.)
Galapagos Is. (Ec.)
Easter I. (Chile)
Polynesia
Amazon Basin
ANDES
Atacama Desert
Mt. Aconcagua
Pampas
Patagonia
Cape Horn
Falkland Is. (U.K.)
South Georgia (U.K.)
Azores (Port.)
Madeira Is. (Port.)
Canary Is. (Sp.)
Cape Verde Is.
Strait of Gibraltar
British Isles
North Sea
Mt. Blanc
ALPS
CARPATHIANS
Svalbard (Nor.)
Barents Sea
Novaya Zemlya
URAL MTS.
CAUCASUS
Black Sea
Caspian Sea
Mediterranean Sea
Balkan Pen.
Mt. Ararat
ATLAS MTS.
Sahara Desert
Arabian Desert
Mt. Damavand
Congo Basin
Mt. Kilimanjaro
Great Rift Valley
Kalahari Desert
Cape of Good Hope
Madagascar
Comoros
Seychelles
Mauritius
Kerguelen (Fr.)
Arabian Sea
Thar Desert
Deccan Plateau
Maldives
Sri Lanka
Bay of Bengal
Mt. Everest
HIMALAYAS
Plateau of Tibet
Gobi Desert
Siberia
Sea of Okhotsk
Kamchatka Pen.
Sea of Japan
Japan
Mt. Fuji
Taiwan
Hainan
South China Sea
Philippine Is.
Malay Pen.
Sumatra
Borneo
Java
Indonesia
New Guinea
Micronesia
Melanesia
Great Barrier Reef
Great Sandy Desert
Nullarbor Plain
Tasmania
New Zealand

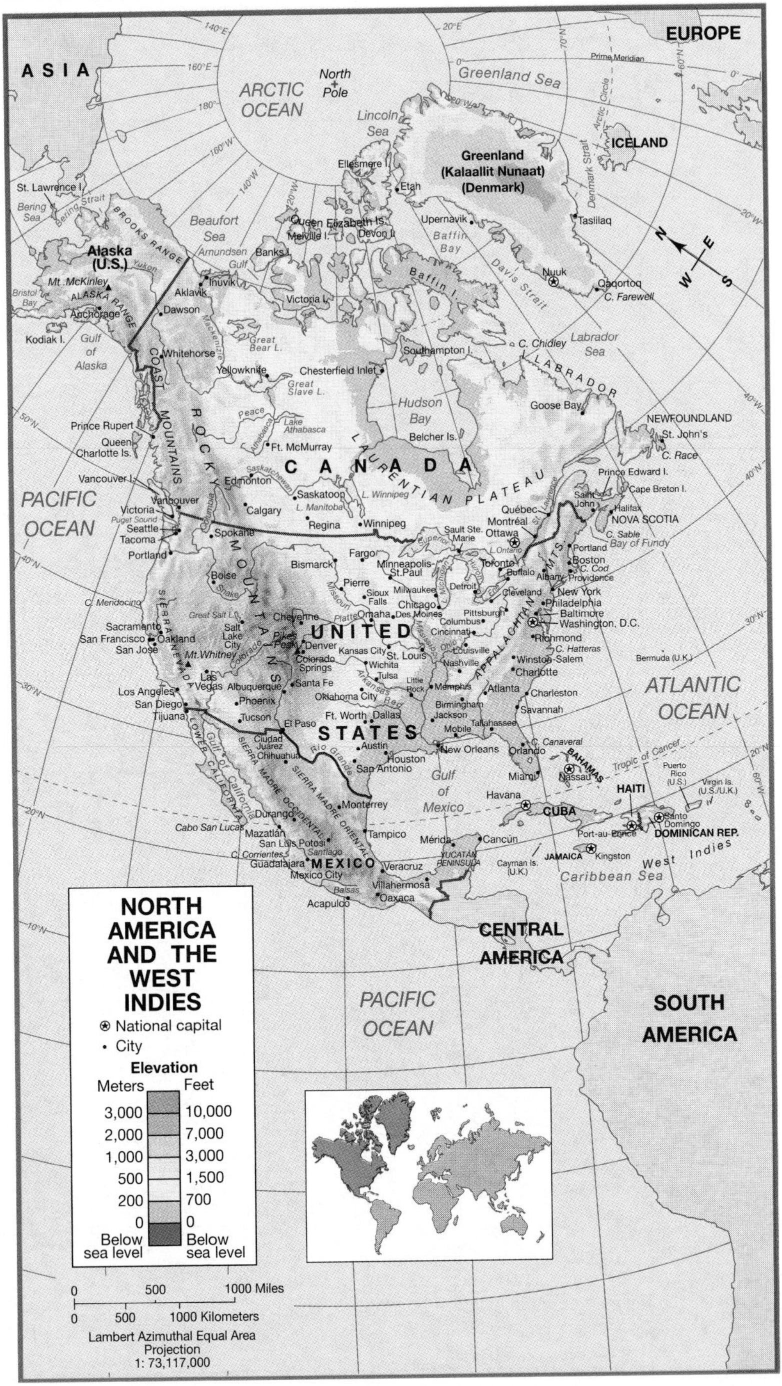
NORTH AMERICA AND THE WEST INDIES
National capital
City
Elevation
Meters
Feet
3,000
10,000
2,000
7,000
1,000
3,000
500
1,500
200
700
0
0
Below sea level
Below sea level
0 500 1000 Miles
0 500 1000 Kilometers
Lambert Azimuthal Equal Area Projection
1: 73,117,000
ASIA
EUROPE
ARCTIC OCEAN
North Pole
Greenland Sea
Lincoln Sea
Greenland (Kalaallit Nunaat) (Denmark)
ICELAND
Denmark Strait
Arctic Circle
Prime Meridian
Tasiilaq
Etah
Upernavik
Baffin Bay
Davis Strait
Nuuk
Qaqortoq
C. Farewell
Ellesmere I.
Queen Elizabeth Is.
Devon I.
Melville I.
Banks I.
Victoria I.
Baffin I.
Beaufort Sea
Amundsen Gulf
St. Lawrence I.
Bering Strait
Bering Sea
BROOKS RANGE
Alaska (U.S.)
Yukon
Mt. McKinley
ALASKA RANGE
Bristol Bay
Anchorage
Kodiak I.
Gulf of Alaska
Inuvik
Aklavik
Dawson
Mackenzie
Whitehorse
Yellowknife
Great Bear L.
Great Slave L.
Chesterfield Inlet
Southampton I.
C. Chidley
Labrador Sea
LABRADOR
Hudson Bay
Goose Bay
Belcher Is.
NEWFOUNDLAND
St. John's
C. Race
Prince Rupert
Queen Charlotte Is.
COAST MOUNTAINS
ROCKY MOUNTAINS
Peace
Athabasca
Lake Athabasca
Ft. McMurray
CANADA
LAURENTIAN PLATEAU
Vancouver I.
Edmonton
Saskatchewan
Saskatoon
L. Manitoba
L. Winnipeg
Prince Edward I.
Cape Breton I.
Saint John
Halifax
NOVA SCOTIA
C. Sable
Bay of Fundy
PACIFIC OCEAN
Vancouver
Victoria
Puget Sound
Seattle
Tacoma
Portland
Columbia
Calgary
Regina
Winnipeg
Spokane
Québec
Montréal
St. Lawrence
Ottawa
Sault Ste. Marie
Superior
L. Ontario
Toronto
Buffalo
Albany
Portland
Boston
C. Cod
Providence
New York
Philadelphia
Baltimore
Washington, D.C.
Richmond
C. Hatteras
Fargo
Bismarck
Minneapolis-St.Paul
Pierre
Sioux Falls
Milwaukee
Michigan
Huron
Detroit
Erie
Cleveland
Pittsburgh
Chicago
Des Moines
Omaha
Platte
Missouri
Mississippi
Ohio
Columbus
Cincinnati
Louisville
Nashville
Boise
Snake
C. Mendocino
SIERRA NEVADA
Great Salt L.
Salt Lake City
Cheyenne
UNITED STATES
APPALACHIAN MTS.
Sacramento
San Francisco
Oakland
San Jose
Mt. Whitney
Colorado
Pikes Peak
Denver
Colorado Springs
Kansas City
St. Louis
Wichita
Tulsa
Arkansas
Little Rock
Memphis
Winston-Salem
Charlotte
Atlanta
Charleston
Savannah
Bermuda (U.K.)
ATLANTIC OCEAN
Las Vegas
Los Angeles
San Diego
Tijuana
Albuquerque
Santa Fe
Phoenix
Tucson
Oklahoma City
Red
Birmingham
Jackson
Tallahassee
Mobile
Ft. Worth
Dallas
El Paso
Ciudad Juarez
Chihuahua
Rio Grande
Austin
Houston
San Antonio
New Orleans
C. Canaveral
Orlando
Miami
BAHAMAS
Nassau
Tropic of Cancer
Puerto Rico (U.S.)
Virgin Is. (U.S./U.K.)
HAITI
LOWER CALIFORNIA
Gulf of California
SIERRA MADRE OCCIDENTAL
SIERRA MADRE ORIENTAL
Gulf of Mexico
Havana
CUBA
Santo Domingo
Port-au-Prince
DOMINICAN REP.
Monterrey
Durango
Cabo San Lucas
Mazatlán
Tampico
San Luis Potosí
Santiago
C. Corrientes
Guadalajara
MEXICO
Mexico City
Veracruz
Mérida
Cancún
YUCATÁN PENINSULA
Cayman Is. (U.K.)
JAMAICA
Kingston
West Indies
Caribbean Sea
Villahermosa
Balsas
Oaxaca
Acapulco
CENTRAL AMERICA
PACIFIC OCEAN
SOUTH AMERICA

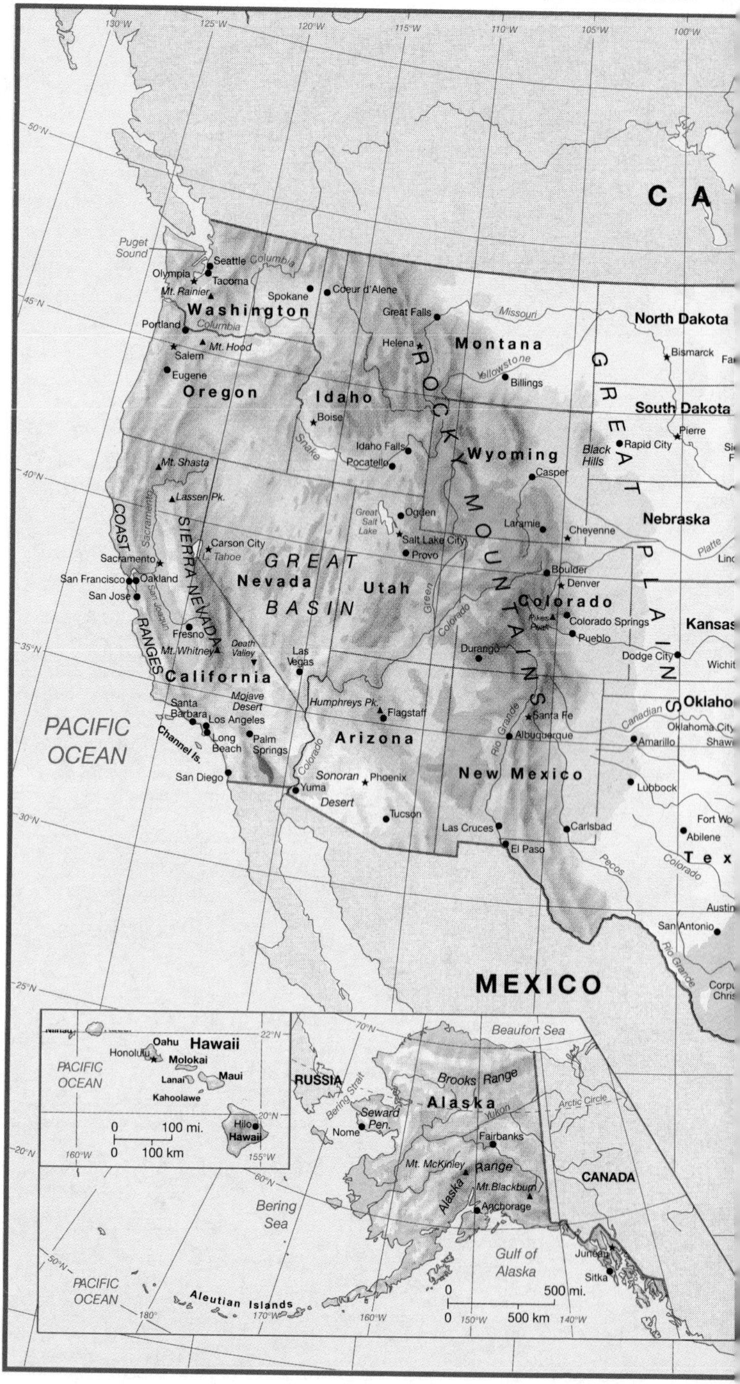

130°W
125°W
120°W
115°W
110°W
105°W
100°W
50°N
45°N
40°N
35°N
30°N
25°N
20°N
CA
Puget Sound
Seattle
Columbia
Olympia
Tacoma
Mt. Rainier
Spokane
Coeur d'Alene
Washington
Portland
Columbia
Mt. Hood
Salem
Eugene
Oregon
Great Falls
Missouri
Helena
Montana
Yellowstone
Billings
North Dakota
Bismarck
South Dakota
Pierre
Rapid City
Black Hills
Idaho
Boise
Snake
Idaho Falls
Pocatello
Wyoming
Casper
ROCKY MOUNTAINS
GREAT PLAINS
Mt. Shasta
Lassen Pk.
Great Salt Lake
Ogden
Salt Lake City
Provo
Laramie
Cheyenne
Nebraska
Platte
COAST RANGES
Sacramento
SIERRA NEVADA
Carson City
L. Tahoe
GREAT BASIN
Nevada
Utah
Sacramento
San Francisco
Oakland
San Jose
San Joaquin
Green
Colorado
Boulder
Denver
Colorado
Kansas
Pikes Peak
Colorado Springs
Pueblo
Fresno
Mt. Whitney
Death Valley
Las Vegas
Durango
Dodge City
California
Mojave Desert
Santa Barbara
Los Angeles
Long Beach
Palm Springs
Channel Is.
Humphreys Pk.
Flagstaff
Santa Fe
Canadian
Oklahoma City
Amarillo
Albuquerque
Rio Grande
PACIFIC OCEAN
Arizona
Colorado
Sonoran Desert
Phoenix
San Diego
Yuma
New Mexico
Lubbock
Tucson
Las Cruces
Carlsbad
El Paso
Abilene
Pecos
Colorado
San Antonio
Rio Grande
MEXICO
Niihau
Oahu
Hawaii
Honolulu
Molokai
PACIFIC OCEAN
Lanai
Maui
Kahoolawe
22°N
20°N
0 100 mi.
0 100 km
Hilo
Hawaii
160°W
155°W
70°N
Beaufort Sea
RUSSIA
Bering Strait
Brooks Range
Alaska
Yukon
Arctic Circle
Seward Pen.
Nome
Fairbanks
Mt. McKinley
Alaska Range
Mt. Blackburn
CANADA
60°N
Bering Sea
Anchorage
Gulf of Alaska
Juneau
Sitka
50°N
PACIFIC OCEAN
Aleutian Islands
0 500 mi.
0 500 km
180°
170°W
160°W
150°W
140°W

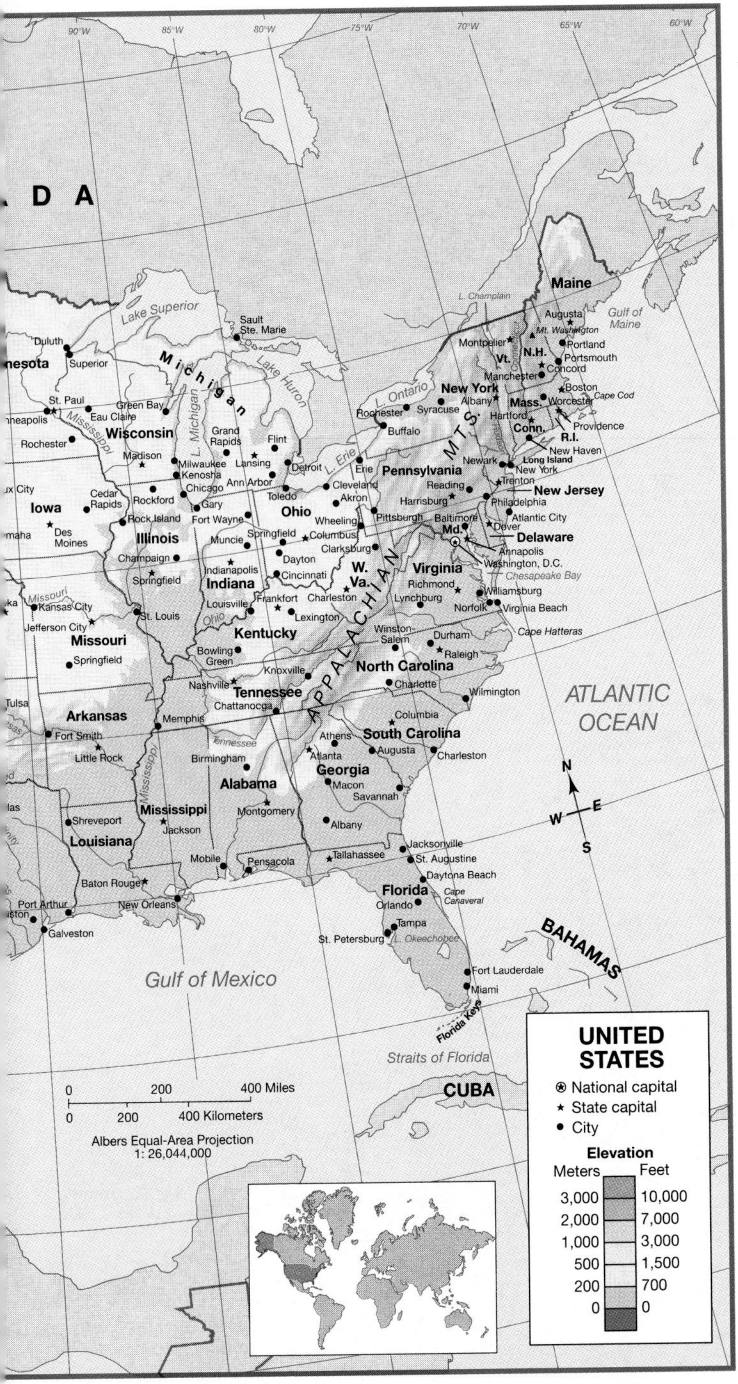
UNITED STATES
National capital
State capital
City
Elevation
Meters Feet
3,000 10,000
2,000 7,000
1,000 3,000
500 1,500
200 700
0 0
Albers Equal-Area Projection
1: 26,044,000
0 200 400 Miles
0 200 400 Kilometers
ATLANTIC OCEAN
Gulf of Mexico
Straits of Florida
CUBA
BAHAMAS
APPALACHIAN MTS.
Maine
Vt.
N.H.
Mass.
Conn.
R.I.
New York
Pennsylvania
New Jersey
Delaware
Md.
Virginia
W. Va.
Ohio
Michigan
Indiana
Illinois
Wisconsin
Iowa
Missouri
Kentucky
Tennessee
North Carolina
South Carolina
Georgia
Florida
Alabama
Mississippi
Louisiana
Arkansas
Lake Superior
Lake Huron
L. Michigan
L. Ontario
L. Erie
L. Champlain
Gulf of Maine
Cape Cod
Cape Hatteras
Chesapeake Bay
Cape Canaveral
L. Okeechobee
Florida Keys
Washington, D.C.

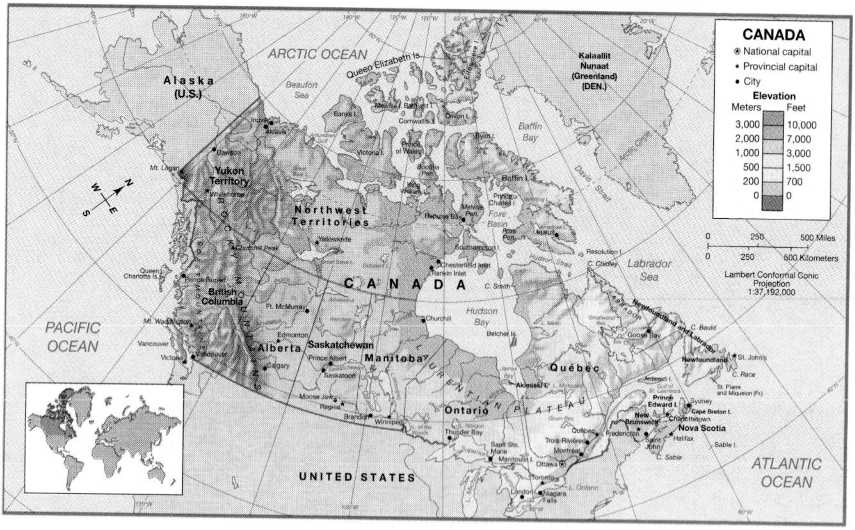
CANADA
National capital
Provincial capital
City
Elevation
Meters Feet
3,000 10,000
2,000 7,000
1,000 3,000
500 1,500
200 700
0 0
0 250 500 Miles
0 250 500 Kilometers
Lambert Conformal Conic Projection
1:37,192,000
ARCTIC OCEAN
Alaska (U.S.)
Kalaallit Nunaat (Greenland) (DEN.)
Yukon Territory
Northwest Territories
British Columbia
Alberta
Saskatchewan
Manitoba
Ontario
Québec
Newfoundland and Labrador
Nova Scotia
New Brunswick
Prince Edward I.
CANADA
PACIFIC OCEAN
ATLANTIC OCEAN
UNITED STATES
Hudson Bay
Labrador Sea
Baffin Bay
Beaufort Sea
Queen Elizabeth Is.
Ottawa
Toronto
Montreal
Québec
Vancouver
Victoria
Edmonton
Calgary
Regina
Winnipeg
Whitehorse
Yellowknife
Iqaluit
Halifax
Fredericton
Charlottetown
St. John's

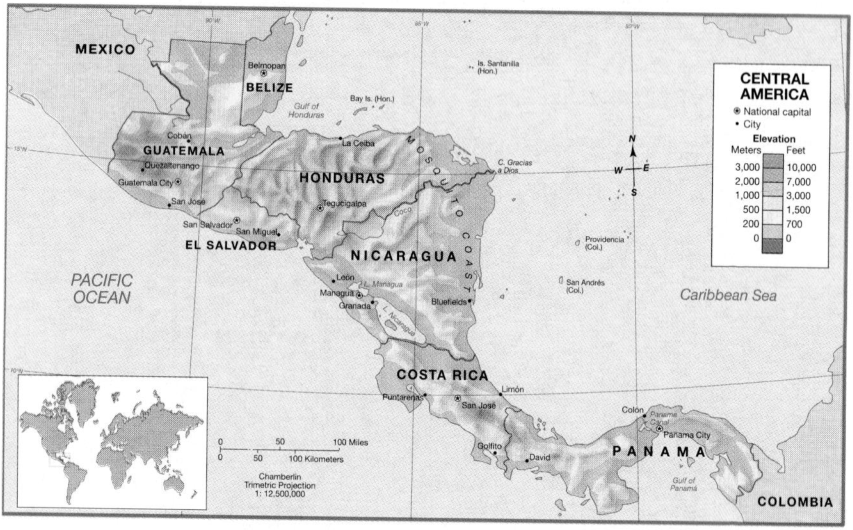
CENTRAL AMERICA
National capital
City
Elevation
Meters Feet
3,000 10,000
2,000 7,000
1,000 3,000
500 1,500
200 700
0 0
0 50 100 Miles
0 50 100 Kilometers
Chamberlin Trimetric Projection
1: 12,500,000
MEXICO
BELIZE
Belmopan
GUATEMALA
Guatemala City
HONDURAS
Tegucigalpa
EL SALVADOR
San Salvador
NICARAGUA
Managua
COSTA RICA
San José
PANAMA
Panama City
COLOMBIA
PACIFIC OCEAN
Caribbean Sea
Gulf of Honduras
MOSQUITO COAST
Gulf of Panamá

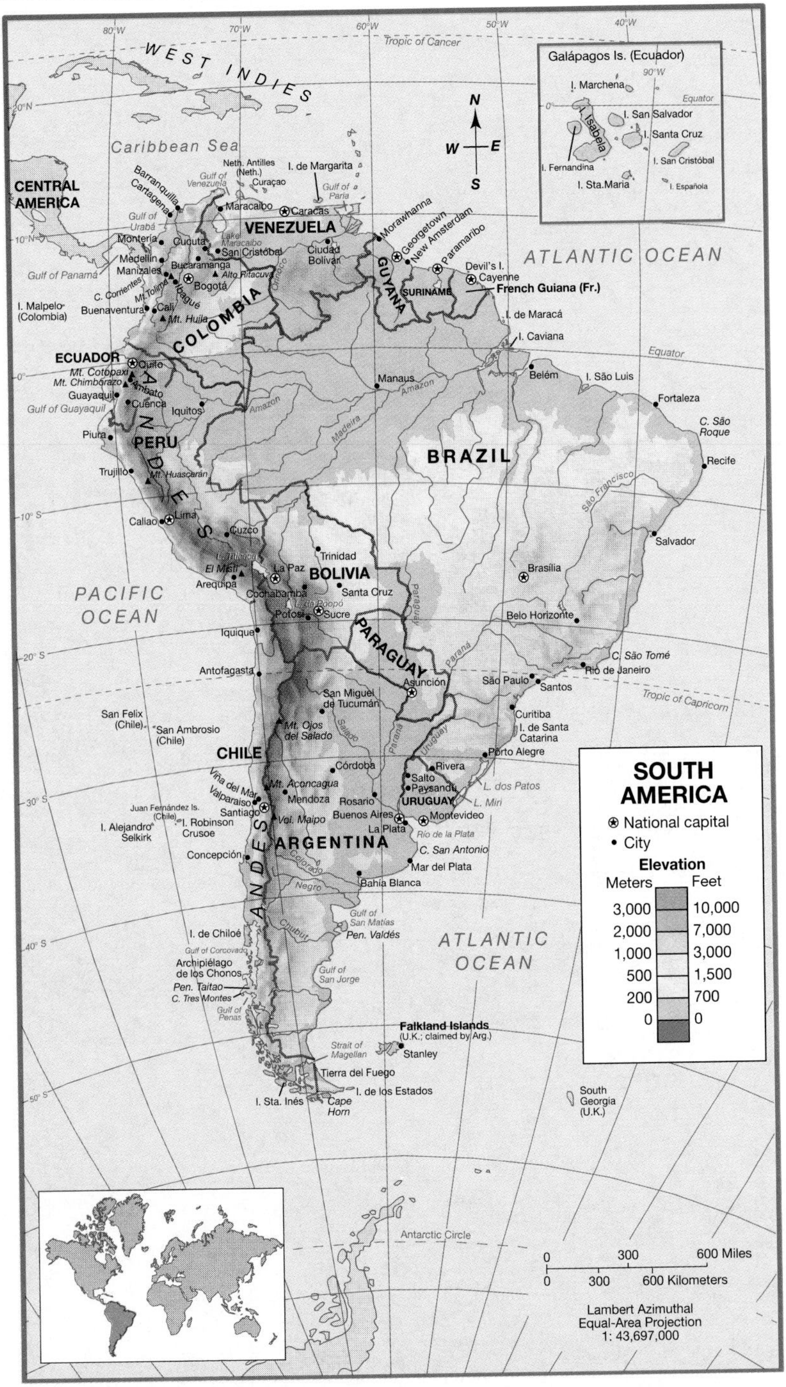
SOUTH AMERICA
National capital
City
Elevation
Meters
Feet
3,000
10,000
2,000
7,000
1,000
3,000
500
1,500
200
700
0
0
Galápagos Is. (Ecuador)
90° W
I. Marchena
Equator
I. San Salvador
I. Isabela
I. Santa Cruz
I. San Cristóbal
I. Fernandina
I. Sta.Maria
I. Española
80° W
70° W
60° W
50° W
40° W
Tropic of Cancer
WEST INDIES
20° N
10° N
0°
10° S
20° S
30° S
40° S
50° S
Caribbean Sea
CENTRAL AMERICA
Barranquilla
Cartagena
Gulf of Venezuela
Neth. Antilles (Neth.)
Curaçao
I. de Margarita
Gulf of Paria
Maracaibo
Caracas
Gulf of Urabá
VENEZUELA
Lake Maracaibo
Montería
Cúcuta
San Cristóbal
Ciudad Bolívar
Orinoco
Medellín
Bucaramanga
Manizales
Alto Ritacuva
Gulf of Panamá
C. Corrientes
Mt. Tolima
Ibagué
Bogotá
I. Malpelo (Colombia)
Buenaventura
Cali
Mt. Huila
COLOMBIA
Morawhanna
Georgetown
New Amsterdam
Paramaribo
GUYANA
SURINAME
Devil's I.
Cayenne
French Guiana (Fr.)
ATLANTIC OCEAN
I. de Maracá
I. Caviana
Equator
Belém
I. São Luis
Fortaleza
C. São Roque
Recife
ECUADOR
Quito
Mt. Cotopaxi
Mt. Chimborazo
Ambato
Guayaquil
Cuenca
Gulf of Guayaquil
Iquitos
Amazon
Manaus
Madeira
Piura
PERU
Trujillo
Mt. Huascarán
ANDES
Callao
Lima
Cuzco
BRAZIL
São Francisco
Salvador
Trinidad
L. Titicaca
El Misti
Arequipa
La Paz
BOLIVIA
Cochabamba
Santa Cruz
Brasília
PACIFIC OCEAN
L. de Poopó
Potosí
Sucre
Paraguay
Belo Horizonte
Iquique
PARAGUAY
Paraná
C. São Tomé
Rio de Janeiro
Antofagasta
Asunción
São Paulo
Santos
Tropic of Capricorn
San Felix (Chile)
San Ambrosio (Chile)
San Miguel de Tucumán
Curitiba
I. de Santa Catarina
Mt. Ojos del Salado
Salado
Uruguay
CHILE
Porto Alegre
Córdoba
Rivera
Viña del Mar
Salto
Paysandú
L. dos Patos
Valparaiso
Mt. Aconcagua
Mendoza
Rosario
URUGUAY
L. Mirí
Juan Fernández Is. (Chile)
Santiago
Buenos Aires
Montevideo
I. Alejandro Selkirk
I. Robinson Crusoe
Vol. Maipo
La Plata
Rio de la Plata
ARGENTINA
C. San Antonio
Concepción
Colorado
Mar del Plata
Negro
Bahía Blanca
Gulf of San Matías
Chubut
I. de Chiloé
Pen. Valdés
ATLANTIC OCEAN
Gulf of Corcovado
Archipiélago de los Chonos
Gulf of San Jorge
Pen. Taitao
C. Tres Montes
Gulf of Penas
Falkland Islands (U.K.; claimed by Arg.)
Strait of Magellan
Stanley
Tierra del Fuego
I. de los Estados
I. Sta. Inés
Cape Horn
South Georgia (U.K.)
Antarctic Circle
0
300
600 Miles
0
300
600 Kilometers
Lambert Azimuthal Equal-Area Projection
1: 43,697,000

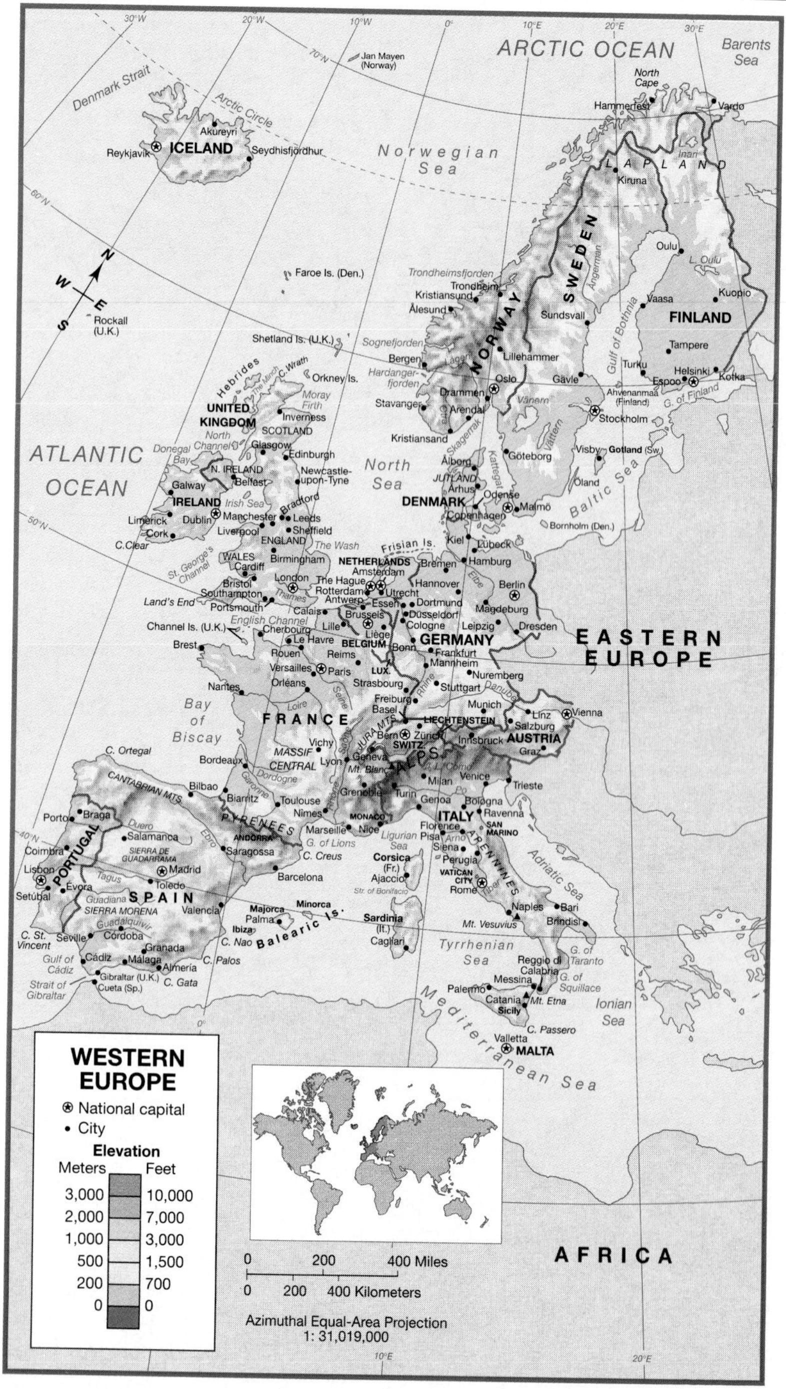
WESTERN EUROPE
National capital
City
Elevation
Meters
Feet
3,000
10,000
2,000
7,000
1,000
3,000
500
1,500
200
700
0
0
0
200
400 Miles
0
200
400 Kilometers
Azimuthal Equal-Area Projection
1: 31,019,000
ARCTIC OCEAN
Barents Sea
North Cape
Hammerfest
Vardø
Jan Mayen (Norway)
Denmark Strait
Arctic Circle
Akureyri
Reykjavík
ICELAND
Seydhisfjördhur
Norwegian Sea
LAPLAND
Inari
Kiruna
SWEDEN
Oulu
L. Oulu
Faroe Is. (Den.)
Trondheimsfjorden
Trondheim
Kristiansund
Ålesund
NORWAY
Ångerman
Vaasa
Kuopio
FINLAND
Sundsvall
Gulf of Bothnia
Rockall (U.K.)
Shetland Is. (U.K.)
Sognefjorden
Bergen
Lillehammer
Tampere
Turku
Helsinki
Espoo
Kotka
Hebrides
C. Wrath
The Minch
Orkney Is.
Hardangerfjorden
Oslo
Gävle
Ahvenanmaa (Finland)
G. of Finland
Moray Firth
Drammen
Stavanger
Arendal
Vänern
Stockholm
UNITED KINGDOM
Inverness
SCOTLAND
North Channel
Kristiansand
Skagerrak
Vättern
ATLANTIC OCEAN
Donegal Bay
Glasgow
Edinburgh
Göteborg
Visby
Gotland (Sw.)
N. IRELAND
Belfast
Newcastle-upon-Tyne
North Sea
Ålborg
JUTLAND
Århus
Kattegat
Öland
Galway
IRELAND
Irish Sea
Bradford
DENMARK
Odense
Malmö
Baltic Sea
Limerick
Dublin
Manchester
Leeds
Copenhagen
Bornholm (Den.)
Cork
Liverpool
Sheffield
C. Clear
ENGLAND
The Wash
Kiel
Lübeck
St. George's Channel
WALES
Birmingham
Frisian Is.
Hamburg
Cardiff
NETHERLANDS
Amsterdam
Bremen
Elbe
Bristol
London
The Hague
Rotterdam
Hannover
Berlin
Southampton
Thames
Utrecht
Land's End
Portsmouth
Antwerp
Essen
Dortmund
Calais
Brussels
Düsseldorf
Magdeburg
English Channel
Lille
Cologne
Leipzig
Dresden
Channel Is. (U.K.)
Cherbourg
Liège
Le Havre
BELGIUM
Bonn
GERMANY
EASTERN EUROPE
Brest
Rouen
Reims
Frankfurt
Mannheim
Versailles
Paris
LUX.
Nuremberg
Nantes
Orléans
Strasbourg
Stuttgart
Danube
Bay of Biscay
Loire
Seine
Rhine
Freiburg
Munich
FRANCE
Basel
LIECHTENSTEIN
Linz
Vienna
Salzburg
JURA MTS.
Bern
Zürich
SWITZ.
Innsbruck
AUSTRIA
C. Ortegal
Vichy
MASSIF CENTRAL
Graz
Bordeaux
Lyon
Geneva
Mt. Blanc
ALPS
L. Como
Dordogne
Garonne
Milan
Venice
Trieste
CANTABRIAN MTS.
Bilbao
Grenoble
Turin
Po
Biarritz
Toulouse
Genoa
Bologna
Porto
Braga
Nîmes
MONACO
ITALY
Ravenna
PYRENEES
Duero
Marseille
Nice
Florence
SAN MARINO
Ebro
ANDORRA
Ligurian Sea
Pisa
Arno
Salamanca
PORTUGAL
G. of Lions
Siena
APENNINES
Coimbra
SIERRA DE GUADARRAMA
Saragossa
C. Creus
Corsica (Fr.)
Perugia
Adriatic Sea
Lisbon
Madrid
Barcelona
Ajaccio
VATICAN CITY
Tagus
Toledo
Rome
Tiber
Setúbal
Évora
SPAIN
Str. of Bonifacio
Guadiana
SIERRA MORENA
Valencia
Minorca
Naples
Bari
Majorca
Palma
Sardinia (It.)
Guadalquivir
Balearic Is.
Mt. Vesuvius
Brindisi
Ibiza
C. St. Vincent
Seville
Córdoba
C. Nao
Cagliari
Tyrrhenian Sea
G. of Taranto
Granada
Gulf of Cádiz
Cádiz
Málaga
Almería
C. Palos
Reggio di Calabria
Strait of Gibraltar
Gibraltar (U.K.)
Cueta (Sp.)
C. Gata
Messina
G. of Squillace
Palermo
Catania
Mt. Etna
Ionian Sea
Sicily
Mediterranean Sea
C. Passero
Valletta
MALTA
AFRICA
30°W
20°W
10°W
0°
10°E
20°E
30°E
70°N
60°N
50°N
40°N
N
S
E
W

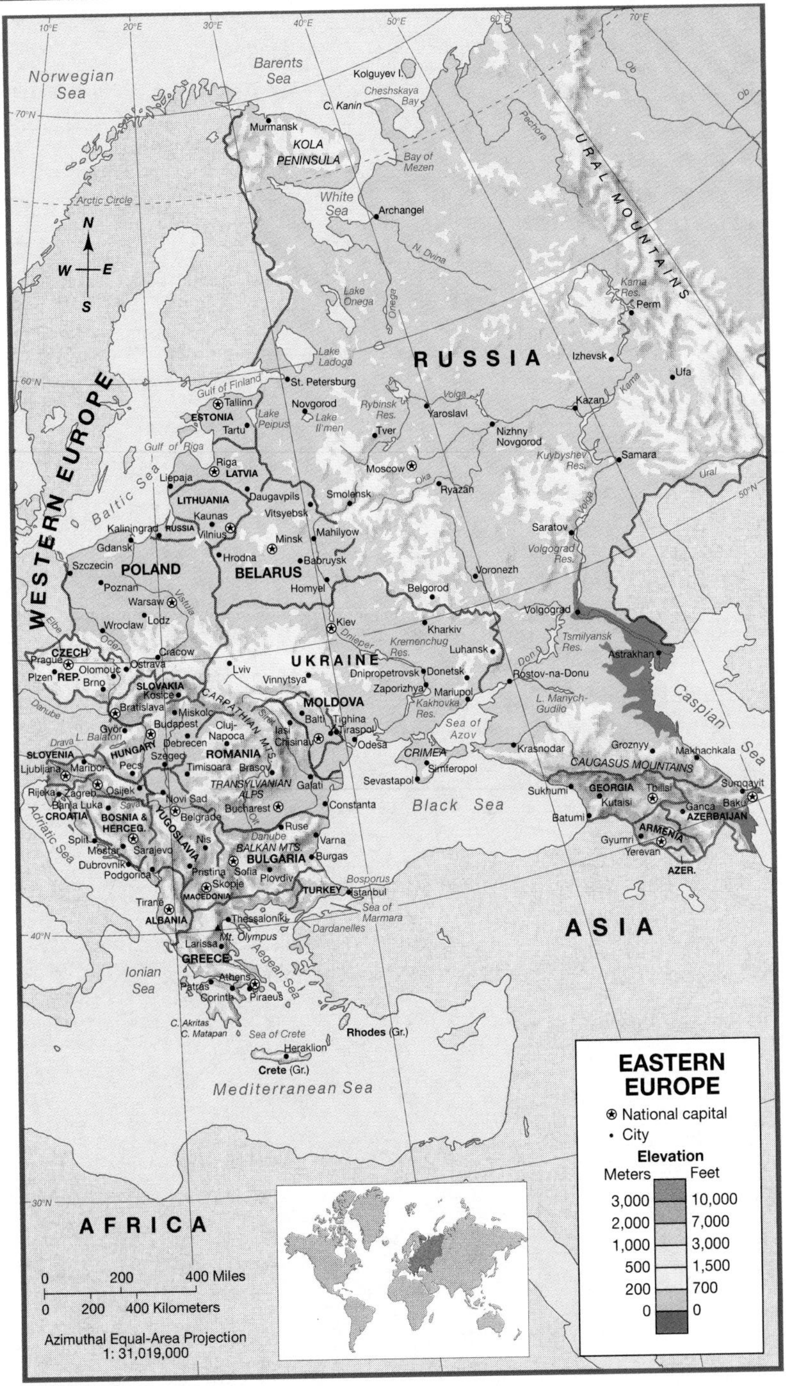
EASTERN EUROPE
National capital
City
Elevation
Meters
Feet
3,000
2,000
1,000
500
200
0
10,000
7,000
3,000
1,500
700
0
0 200 400 Miles
0 200 400 Kilometers
Azimuthal Equal-Area Projection
1: 31,019,000
10°E
20°E
30°E
40°E
50°E
60°E
70°E
70°N
60°N
50°N
40°N
30°N
N
W
E
S
Norwegian Sea
Barents Sea
Kolguyev I.
Cheshskaya Bay
C. Kanin
Murmansk
KOLA PENINSULA
Bay of Mezen
Arctic Circle
White Sea
Archangel
N. Dvina
Pechora
URAL MOUNTAINS
Ob
Lake Onega
Onega
Kama Res.
Perm
Lake Ladoga
RUSSIA
Izhevsk
Ufa
Kama
St. Petersburg
Gulf of Finland
Tallinn
ESTONIA
Tartu
Lake Peipus
Novgorod
Lake Il'men
Rybinsk Res.
Volga
Yaroslavl
Kazan
Tver
Nizhny Novgorod
Kuybyshev Res.
Samara
Gulf of Riga
Riga
LATVIA
Moscow
Oka
Ryazan
Ural
WESTERN EUROPE
Baltic Sea
Liepaja
LITHUANIA
Daugavpils
Smolensk
Kaunas
Vitsyebsk
Kaliningrad
RUSSIA
Vilnius
Mahilyow
Saratov
Gdansk
Minsk
Volgograd Res.
Szczecin
POLAND
Hrodna
Babruysk
BELARUS
Voronezh
Poznan
Homyel
Belgorod
Warsaw
Vistula
Volgograd
Elbe
Wroclaw
Lodz
Oder
Kiev
Kharkiv
Dnieper
Kremenchug Res.
Tsmilyansk Res.
Astrakhan
CZECH REP.
Prague
Cracow
Ostrava
Olomouc
Plzen
Brno
Luhansk
Don
Lviv
UKRAINE
Dnipropetrovsk
Donetsk
Rostov-na-Donu
Vinnytsya
Zaporizhya
Mariupol
SLOVAKIA
Kosice
Danube
Bratislava
CARPATHIAN MTS.
MOLDOVA
Kakhovka Res.
L. Manych-Gudilo
Caspian Sea
Miskolc
Siret
Balti
Tighina
Sea of Azov
Budapest
Cluj-Napoca
Iasi
Tiraspol
Gyor
Drava
L. Balaton
Debrecen
Chisinau
Odesa
Krasnodar
Groznyy
Makhachkala
SLOVENIA
HUNGARY
Szeged
ROMANIA
CRIMEA
Ljubljana
Maribor
Pecs
Timisoara
Brasov
Simferopol
CAUCASUS MOUNTAINS
Rijeka
Zagreb
Osijek
TRANSYLVANIAN ALPS
Galati
Sevastopol
Sukhumi
GEORGIA
Tbilisi
Sumqayit
Banja Luka
Sava
Novi Sad
Kutaisi
Baku
CROATIA
BOSNIA & HERCEG.
Belgrade
Bucharest
Constanta
Black Sea
Ganca
AZERBAIJAN
Batumi
Adriatic Sea
YUGOSLAVIA
Olt
Ruse
ARMENIA
Split
Nis
Danube
Varna
Gyumri
Mostar
Sarajevo
BALKAN MTS.
Yerevan
Dubrovnik
BULGARIA
Burgas
AZER.
Podgorica
Pristina
Sofia
Plovdiv
Skopje
Bosporus
MACEDONIA
TURKEY
Istanbul
Tirane
Sea of Marmara
ALBANIA
Thessaloniki
Dardanelles
Mt. Olympus
ASIA
Larissa
GREECE
Aegean Sea
Ionian Sea
Athens
Patras
Piraeus
Corinth
C. Akritas
C. Matapan
Sea of Crete
Rhodes (Gr.)
Heraklion
Crete (Gr.)
Mediterranean Sea
AFRICA

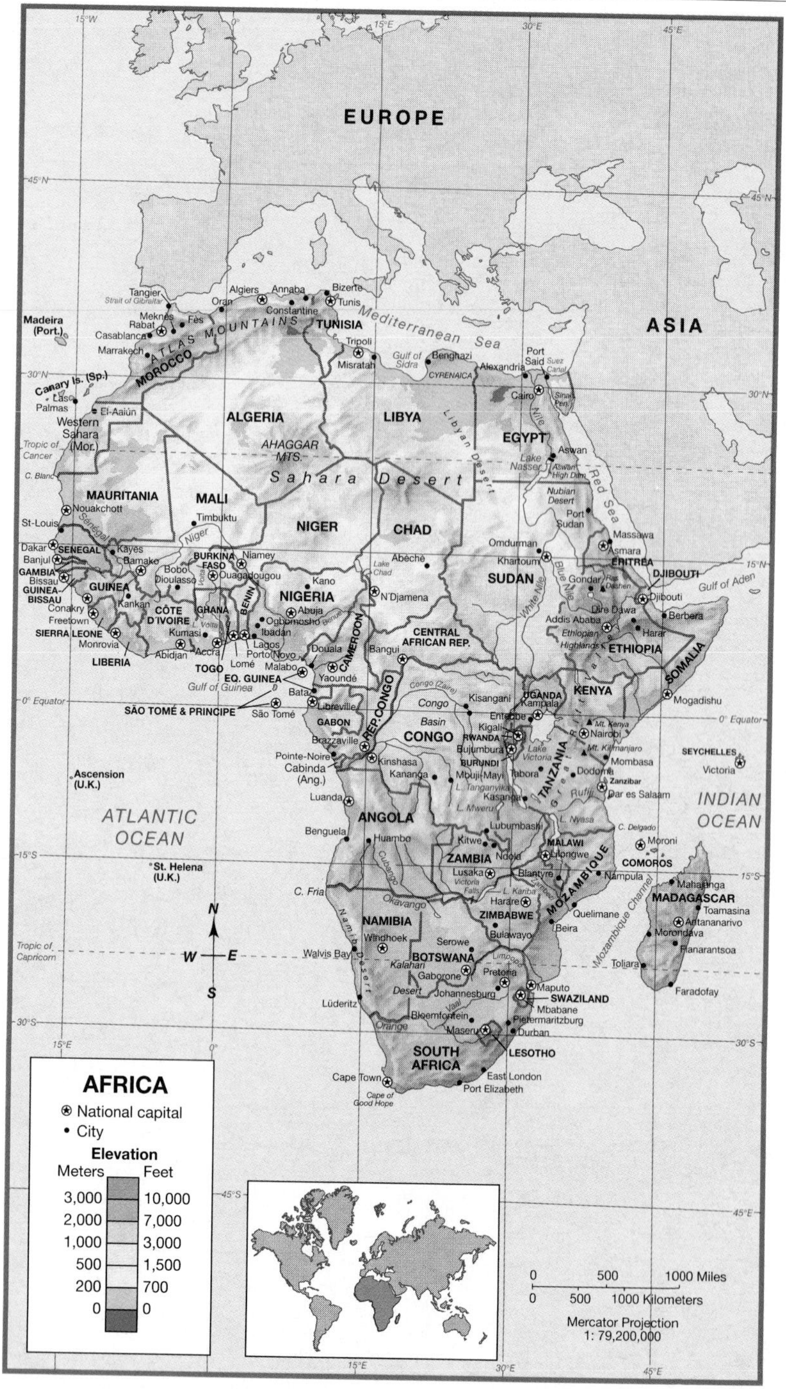
AFRICA
National capital
City
Elevation
Meters
Feet
3,000
10,000
2,000
7,000
1,000
3,000
500
1,500
200
700
0
0
EUROPE
ASIA
ATLANTIC OCEAN
INDIAN OCEAN
Mediterranean Sea
Red Sea
Gulf of Aden
Gulf of Guinea
Mozambique Channel
Sahara Desert
Libyan Desert
Nubian Desert
Namib Desert
Kalahari Desert
ATLAS MOUNTAINS
AHAGGAR MTS.
Ethiopian Highlands
Congo Basin
Strait of Gibraltar
Gulf of Sidra
CYRENAICA
Suez Canal
Sinai Pen.
Aswan High Dam
Lake Nasser
Lake Chad
Lake Victoria
L. Tanganyika
L. Mweru
L. Nyasa
L. Kariba
Victoria Falls
Nile
Blue Nile
White Nile
Niger
Senegal
Volta
Benue
Congo (Zaire)
Cubango
Okavango
Zambezi
Limpopo
Vaal
Orange
Rufiji
Mt. Kenya
Mt. Kilimanjaro
Ras Dashen
Madeira (Port.)
Canary Is. (Sp.)
Las Palmas
Western Sahara (Mor.)
El-Aaiún
Tropic of Cancer
C. Blanc
Tropic of Capricorn
0° Equator
15°W
0°
15°E
30°E
45°E
45°N
30°N
15°N
15°S
30°S
45°S
MOROCCO
Tangier
Rabat
Meknès
Fès
Casablanca
Marrakech
ALGERIA
Algiers
Oran
Annaba
Constantine
TUNISIA
Bizerte
Tunis
LIBYA
Tripoli
Misratah
Benghazi
EGYPT
Alexandria
Port Said
Cairo
Aswan
SUDAN
Port Sudan
Omdurman
Khartoum
ERITREA
Massawa
Asmara
DJIBOUTI
Djibouti
ETHIOPIA
Gondar
Addis Ababa
Dire Dawa
Harar
SOMALIA
Berbera
Mogadishu
MAURITANIA
Nouakchott
MALI
Timbuktu
Kayes
Bamako
NIGER
Niamey
CHAD
Abéché
N'Djamena
SENEGAL
St-Louis
Dakar
GAMBIA
Banjul
GUINEA-BISSAU
Bissau
GUINEA
Conakry
Kankan
SIERRA LEONE
Freetown
LIBERIA
Monrovia
CÔTE D'IVOIRE
Bobo Dioulasso
Abidjan
BURKINA FASO
Ouagadougou
GHANA
Kumasi
Accra
TOGO
Lomé
BENIN
Porto Novo
NIGERIA
Kano
Abuja
Ogbomosho
Ibadan
Lagos
CAMEROON
Douala
Yaoundé
CENTRAL AFRICAN REP.
Bangui
EQ. GUINEA
Malabo
Bata
SÃO TOMÉ & PRINCIPE
São Tomé
GABON
Libreville
REP. CONGO
Brazzaville
Pointe-Noire
Cabinda (Ang.)
CONGO
Kisangani
Kinshasa
Kananga
Mbuji-Mayi
Kasanga
Lubumbashi
UGANDA
Entebbe
Kampala
KENYA
Nairobi
Mombasa
RWANDA
Kigali
BURUNDI
Bujumbura
TANZANIA
Tabora
Dodoma
Zanzibar
Dar es Salaam
SEYCHELLES
Victoria
ANGOLA
Luanda
Benguela
Huambo
C. Fria
ZAMBIA
Kitwe
Ndola
Lusaka
MALAWI
Lilongwe
Blantyre
MOZAMBIQUE
C. Delgado
Nampula
Quelimane
Beira
Maputo
COMOROS
Moroni
MADAGASCAR
Mahajanga
Toamasina
Antananarivo
Morondava
Fianarantsoa
Toliara
Faradofay
ZIMBABWE
Harare
Bulawayo
NAMIBIA
Windhoek
Walvis Bay
Lüderitz
BOTSWANA
Serowe
Gaborone
SOUTH AFRICA
Pretoria
Johannesburg
Bloemfontein
Pietermaritzburg
Durban
East London
Port Elizabeth
Cape Town
Cape of Good Hope
SWAZILAND
Mbabane
LESOTHO
Maseru
Ascension (U.K.)
St. Helena (U.K.)
N
W
E
S
0
500
1000 Miles
0
500
1000 Kilometers
Mercator Projection
1: 79,200,000

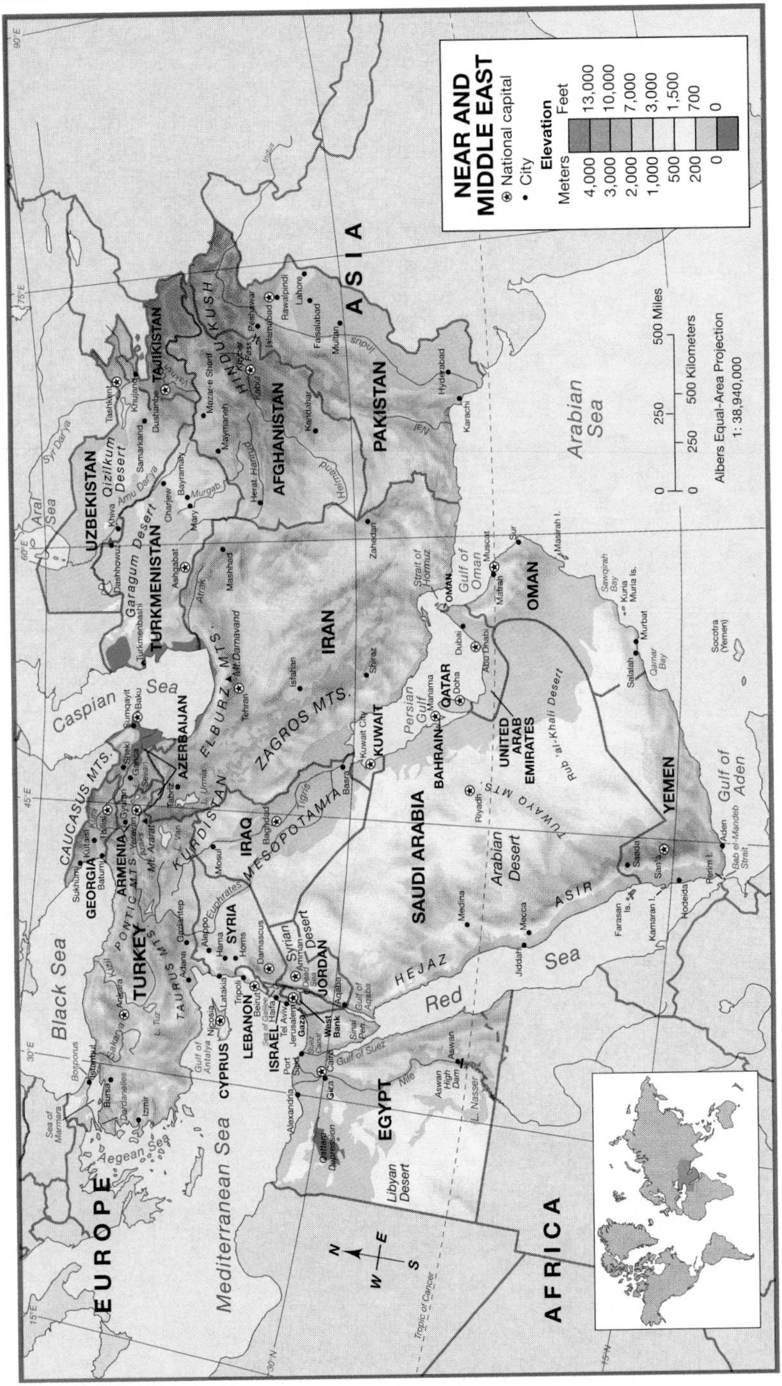
NEAR AND MIDDLE EAST
National capital
City
Elevation
Meters Feet
4,000 13,000
3,000 10,000
2,000 7,000
1,000 3,000
500 1,500
200 700
0 0
0 250 500 Miles
0 250 500 Kilometers
Albers Equal-Area Projection
1: 38,940,000
EUROPE
ASIA
AFRICA
Black Sea
Caspian Sea
Mediterranean Sea
Aegean Sea
Sea of Marmara
Red Sea
Persian Gulf
Gulf of Oman
Arabian Sea
Gulf of Aden
Aral Sea
TURKEY
GEORGIA
ARMENIA
AZERBAIJAN
SYRIA
IRAQ
IRAN
CYPRUS
LEBANON
ISRAEL
JORDAN
EGYPT
SAUDI ARABIA
KUWAIT
BAHRAIN
QATAR
UNITED ARAB EMIRATES
OMAN
YEMEN
TURKMENISTAN
UZBEKISTAN
TAJIKISTAN
AFGHANISTAN
PAKISTAN
CAUCASUS MTS.
PONTIC MTS.
TAURUS MTS.
ELBURZ MTS.
ZAGROS MTS.
HINDU KUSH
KURDISTAN
MESOPOTAMIA
HEJAZ
ASIR
TUWAYQ MTS.
Syrian Desert
Arabian Desert
Rub 'al-Khali Desert
Libyan Desert
Qattara Depression
Garagum Desert
Qizilkum Desert
Mt. Ararat
Mt. Damavand
Istanbul
Bursa
Izmir
Ankara
Adana
Gaziantep
Aleppo
Hama
Homs
Damascus
Beirut
Tripoli
Latakia
Nicosia
Haifa
Tel Aviv
Jerusalem
Gaza
Amman
Aqaba
Cairo
Giza
Alexandria
Port Said
Aswan
Aswan High Dam
L. Nasser
Nile
Suez Canal
Gulf of Suez
Gulf of Aqaba
Sinai Pen.
West Bank
Dead Sea
Sea of Galilee
Medina
Mecca
Jiddah
Riyadh
Sanaa
Aden
Hodeida
Perim I.
Bab el-Mandeb Strait
Kamaran I.
Farasan Is.
Salalah
Murbat
Qamar Bay
Kuria Muria Is.
Sawqirah Bay
Masirah I.
Sur
Muscat
Matrah
Abu Dhabi
Dubai
Doha
Manama
Kuwait City
Basra
Baghdad
Mosul
Tigris
Euphrates
Tabriz
L. Urmia
L. Van
Yerevan
Tbilisi
Gyumri
Ganca
Sheki
Baku
Sumqayit
Batumi
Kutaisi
Sukhumi
Tehran
Isfahan
Shiraz
Mashhad
Zahedan
Strait of Hormuz
Turkmenbashi
Ashgabat
Dashhowuz
Khiva
Charjew
Mary
Bayramaly
Samarkand
Tashkent
Khujand
Dushanbe
Amu Darya
Syr Darya
Murgab
Atrak
Herat
Mazar-e Sharif
Maymanah
Kabul
Kandahar
Helmand
Khyber Pass
Peshawar
Islamabad
Rawalpindi
Lahore
Faisalabad
Multan
Indus
Hyderabad
Karachi
Socotra (Yemen)
Tropic of Cancer
Bosporus
Dardanelles
Gulf of Antalya
30° N
15° N
15° E
30° E
45° E
60° E
75° E
90° E
N
S
E
W

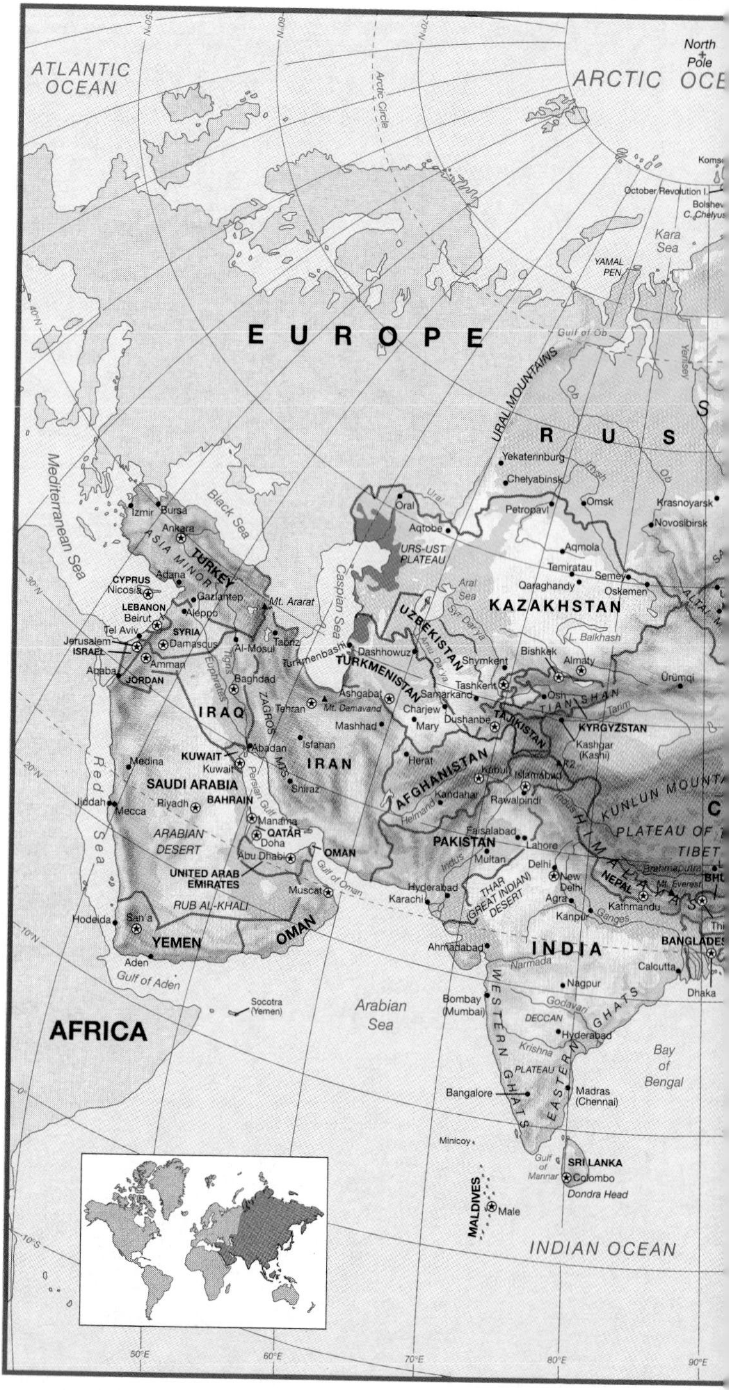

ATLANTIC OCEAN
ARCTIC OCE
North Pole
Arctic Circle
October Revolution I.
Kara Sea
YAMAL PEN.
Gulf of Ob
EUROPE
URAL MOUNTAINS
Ob
Yenisey
R U S S
Yekaterinburg
Chelyabinsk
Irtysh
Omsk
Petropavl
Krasnoyarsk
Novosibirsk
Oral
Ural
Aqtobe
URS-UST PLATEAU
Aqmola
Temirtau
Qaraghandy
Semey
Oskemen
Aral Sea
KAZAKHSTAN
UZBEKISTAN
Syr Darya
Amu Darya
L. Balkhash
Bishkek
Almaty
Shymkent
Tashkent
Ürümqi
Dashhowuz
Turkmenbashi
TURKMENISTAN
Ashgabat
Samarkand
Osh
TIAN SHAN
Tarim
Charjew
Dushanbe
TAJIKISTAN
KYRGYZSTAN
Mary
Mashhad
Kashgar (Kashi)
Herat
AFGHANISTAN
Kabul
Islamabad
K2
Kandahar
Rawalpindi
Helmand
Indus
KUNLUN MOUNTA
PLATEAU OF TIBET
HIMALAYAS
Brahmaputra
Mt. Everest
Faisalabad
Lahore
PAKISTAN
Multan
Delhi
New Delhi
NEPAL
Kathmandu
Agra
Kanpur
Ganges
Hyderabad
Karachi
THAR (GREAT INDIAN) DESERT
Ahmadabad
INDIA
BANGLADES
Narmada
Calcutta
Nagpur
Dhaka
Bombay (Mumbai)
Godavari
WESTERN GHATS
EASTERN GHATS
DECCAN
Hyderabad
Krishna
PLATEAU
Bay of Bengal
Bangalore
Madras (Chennai)
Minicoy
Gulf of Mannar
SRI LANKA
Colombo
Dondra Head
MALDIVES
Male
INDIAN OCEAN
Mediterranean Sea
Black Sea
Izmir
Bursa
Ankara
ASIA MINOR
TURKEY
CYPRUS
Nicosia
Adana
Gaziantep
Mt. Ararat
LEBANON
Beirut
Aleppo
SYRIA
Tel Aviv
Jerusalem
ISRAEL
Damascus
Amman
Aqaba
JORDAN
Al-Mosul
Tabriz
Caspian Sea
Tigris
Euphrates
Baghdad
IRAQ
ZAGROS MTS.
Tehran
Mt. Damavand
Isfahan
Abadan
KUWAIT
Kuwait
IRAN
Shiraz
Medina
SAUDI ARABIA
BAHRAIN
Persian Gulf
Jiddah
Mecca
Riyadh
Manama
QATAR
Doha
ARABIAN DESERT
Abu Dhabi
OMAN
UNITED ARAB EMIRATES
Gulf of Oman
Muscat
RUB AL-KHALI
Hodeida
San'a
YEMEN
OMAN
Aden
Gulf of Aden
Red Sea
Socotra (Yemen)
Arabian Sea
AFRICA
50°N
60°N
70°N
40°N
30°N
20°N
10°N
0°
10°S
50°E
60°E
70°E
80°E
90°E

ASIA
National capital
City
Great Wall of China
Elevation
Meters Feet
6,000 19,000
3,000 10,000
2,000 7,000
1,000 3,000
500 1,500
200 700
0 0
0 500 1000 Miles
0 500 1000 Kilometers
Lambert Azimuthal Equal-Area Projection
1:61,016,000
Bering Strait
C. Dezhnev
CHUKCHI PEN.
Wrangel I.
Gulf of Anadyr
Bering Sea
East Siberian Sea
Anadyr
New Siberian Is.
Lyakhov Is.
KOLYMA RANGE
Kolyma
KAMCHATKA PENINSULA
Commander Is.
Shelekhov Gulf
VERKHOYANSK RA.
Lena
Sea of Okhotsk
C. Lopatka
Yakutsk
C. Yelizaveta
Shantar Is.
Sakhalin
Kuril Is.
Tatar Strait
Amur
SIKHOTE-ALIN RA.
La Pérouse Strait
Kharbarovsk
Hokkaido
Sapporo
L. Baikal
GREATER KHINGAN RA.
Harbin
Vladivostok
Sendai
Ulaanbaatar
MANCHURIA
Sea of Japan
Honshu
GOLIA
JAPAN
Tokyo
Yokohama
Mt. Fuji
Shenyang
Yalu
NORTH KOREA
Nagoya
Kyoto
GOBI DESERT
P'yongyang
Kobe
Osaka
Seoul
Hiroshima
INNER MONGOLIA
Beijing
Tianjin
Dailan
SOUTH KOREA
Pusan
Shikoku
Great Wall of China
Qingdao
Fukuoka
Nagasaki
Kyushu
Taiyuan
Yellow Sea
Cheju
Huang (Yellow)
Lanzhou
Nanjing
Ryukyu Is.
Tropic of Cancer
Wei
Xian
Hangzhou
Shanghai
Wuhan
East China Sea
Okinawa
Chang (Yangtze)
Chengdu
Changsha
Chongqing
Fuzhou
Formosa Strait
Taipei
TAIWAN
PACIFIC OCEAN
Guilin
Kunming
Hongshui
Kaohsiung
Guangzhou
Xi
Red
Hong Kong
Macao (Port.)
C. Engaño
Hanoi
Haiphong
Luzon
PHILIPPINES
Philippine Sea
Haikou
Hainan
LAOS
Gulf of Tonkin
Vientiane
South China Sea
Manila
Mindoro
Chang Mai
Mekong
Da Nang
Cebu
Panay
THAILAND
VIETNAM
Qui Nhon
Bangkok
Angkor
CAMBODIA
Palawan
Sulu Sea
Mindanao
Davao
Nha Trang
Phnom Penh
Ho Chi Minh City (Saigon)
Gulf of Thailand
Talaud Is.
Cenderawasih Bay
C. Perkam
Biak
Jayapura
C. Camau
Kota Kinabalu
Celebes Sea
Halmahera
DOBERAI PENINSULA
Manokwari
MAOKE MTS.
New Guinea
Songkhla
Bandar Seri Begawan
BRUNEI
SABAH
Gulf of Tomini
Moluccas Is.
Miri
Natuna Is.
MALAYSIA
SARAWAK
Molucca Sea
Ceram
Aru Is.
Ipoh
Kuala Lumpur
Kuching
Makassar Strait
C. Vals
Yos Sudarsa
SINGAPORE
Borneo
Sulawesi
Sula Is.
Buru
Yamdena
Tanimbar Is.
Sumatra
BARISAN MTS.
Karimata Strait
Gulf of Bone
Banda Sea
Arafura Sea
Bangka
Billiton
Banjarmasin
Ujung Pandang
INDONESIA
Mentawai Is.
Palembang
Sunda Is.
Sumbawa
Timor
Jakarta
Java Sea
Madura
Flores Sea
Flores
Timor Sea
Sunda Strait
Java
Semarang
Surabaya
Lombok
Sumba
AUSTRALIA
Bandung
100°E
110°E
120°E
130°E
140°E
150°E
Equator
0°
10°S
10°N
20°N
30°N
40°N
50°N
60°N
70°N
80°N
N
E
W
S

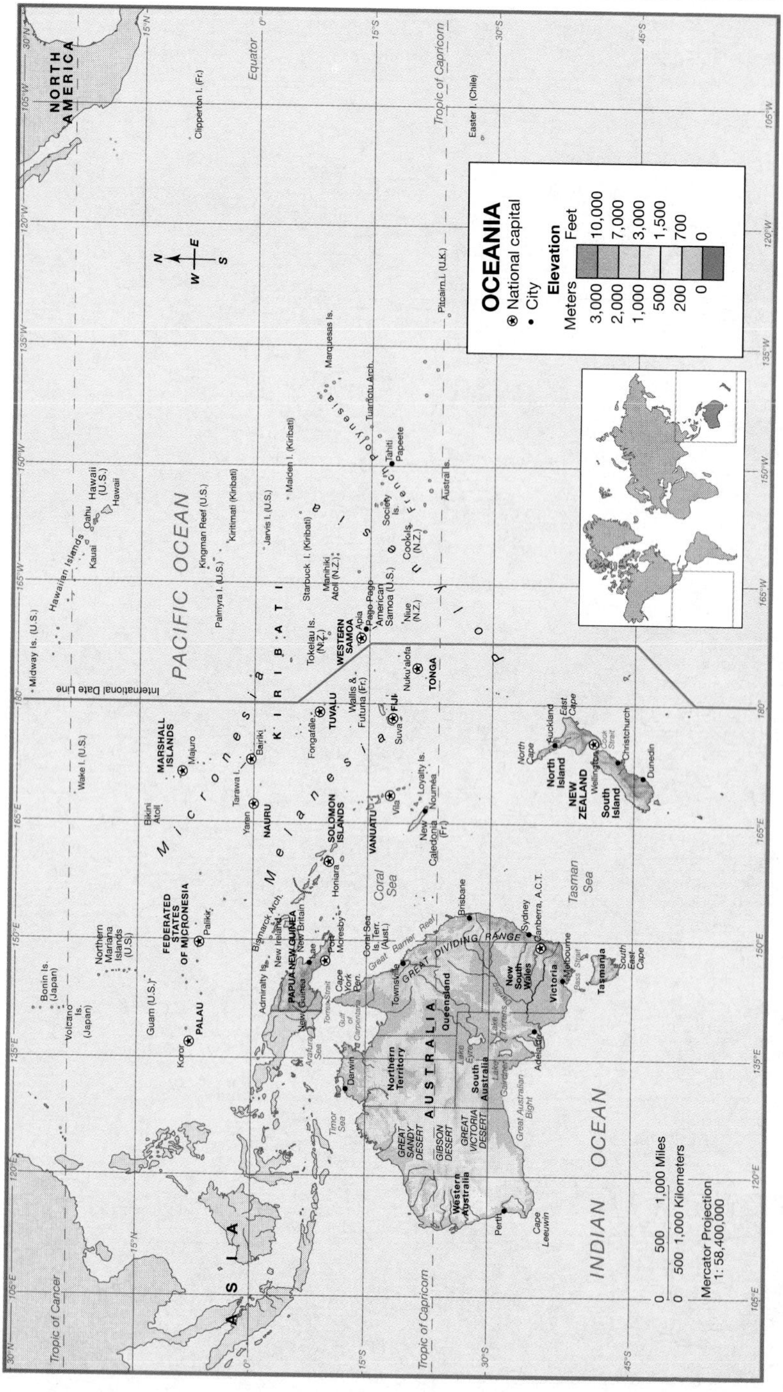
OCEANIA
National capital
City
Elevation
Meters Feet
3,000 10,000
2,000 7,000
1,000 3,000
500 1,500
200 700
0 0
0 500 1,000 Miles
0 500 1,000 Kilometers
Mercator Projection
1: 58,400,000
PACIFIC OCEAN
INDIAN OCEAN
NORTH AMERICA
ASIA
AUSTRALIA
Micronesia
Melanesia
Polynesia
French Polynesia
International Date Line
Equator
Tropic of Cancer
Tropic of Capricorn
Coral Sea
Tasman Sea
Timor Sea
Arafura Sea
Gulf of Carpentaria
Torres Strait
Bass Strait
Cook Strait
Great Australian Bight
Great Barrier Reef
GREAT DIVIDING RANGE
GREAT SANDY DESERT
GIBSON DESERT
GREAT VICTORIA DESERT
Lake Eyre
Lake Torrens
Lake Gairdner
Western Australia
Northern Territory
South Australia
Queensland
New South Wales
Victoria
Tasmania
Perth
Darwin
Adelaide
Melbourne
Canberra, A.C.T.
Sydney
Brisbane
Townsville
Cape York Pen.
Cape Leeuwin
South East Cape
NEW ZEALAND
North Island
South Island
Auckland
Wellington
Christchurch
Dunedin
North Cape
East Cape
PAPUA NEW GUINEA
New Guinea
Port Moresby
Lae
New Britain
New Ireland
Bismarck Arch.
Admiralty Is.
SOLOMON ISLANDS
Honiara
VANUATU
Vila
New Caledonia (Fr.)
Nouméa
Loyalty Is.
Coral Sea Is. Terr. (Aust.)
FIJI
Suva
TONGA
Nuku'alofa
WESTERN SAMOA
Apia
American Samoa (U.S.)
Pago Pago
TUVALU
Fongafale
Wallis & Futuna (Fr.)
Tokelau Is. (N.Z.)
Niue (N.Z.)
Cook Is. (N.Z.)
NAURU
Yaren
KIRIBATI
Bairiki
Tarawa I.
MARSHALL ISLANDS
Majuro
Bikini Atoll
FEDERATED STATES OF MICRONESIA
Palikir
PALAU
Koror
Guam (U.S.)
Northern Mariana Islands (U.S.)
Bonin Is. (Japan)
Volcano Is. (Japan)
Wake I. (U.S.)
Midway Is. (U.S.)
Hawaiian Islands
Kauai
Oahu
Hawaii (U.S.)
Hawaii
Palmyra I. (U.S.)
Kingman Reef (U.S.)
Kiritimati (Kiribati)
Jarvis I. (U.S.)
Starbuck I. (Kiribati)
Malden I. (Kiribati)
Manihiki Atoll (N.Z.)
Society Is.
Tahiti
Papeete
Austral Is.
Tuamotu Arch.
Marquesas Is.
Pitcairn I. (U.K.)
Easter I. (Chile)
Clipperton I. (Fr.)
N
E
S
W

Life-Saving Skills Summary

Skill	Adult (9 years and older)	Child (1 to 8 years)	Infant (birth to 1 year)
Rescue breathing (used when victim is not breathing)	Give 1 slow breath about every 5 seconds; about 1½ seconds per breath; 1 minute = about 10 to 12 breaths	Give 1 slow breath about every 3 seconds; about 1½ seconds per breath; 1 minute = about 20 breaths	Give 1 slow breath about every 3 seconds; about 1½ seconds per breath; 1 minute = about 20 breaths
CPR (used if victim is not breathing *and* does not have a heartbeat)	Depth of compression is about 2 inches; compressions are performed with both hands; complete 15 compressions in about 10 seconds; do cycles of 15 compressions and 2 breaths	Depth of compression is about 1½ inches; compressions are performed with 1 hand; complete 5 compressions in about 3 seconds; do cycles of 5 compressions and 1 breath	Depth of compression is about 1 inch; compressions are performed with 2 fingers; complete 5 compressions in about 3 seconds; do cycles of 5 compressions and 1 breath
Choking (conscious)	Determine if person is choking; stand behind person and deliver abdominal thrusts; repeat until object is expelled or victim loses consciousness	Determine if child is choking; stand or kneel behind child and deliver abdominal thrusts; repeat until object is expelled or child loses consciousness	Determine if infant is choking; give 5 back blows; give 5 chest thrusts; repeat until object is expelled or infant loses consciousness
Choking (unconscious)	Give 2 slow breaths; retilt head and give 2 slow breaths; give up to 5 abdominal thrusts; do finger sweep; give 2 slow breaths; repeat abdominal thrusts, finger sweep, and 2 slow breaths	Give 2 slow breaths; retilt head and give 2 slow breaths; give up to 5 abdominal thrusts; check for object in throat; do finger sweep if object is visible; give 2 slow breaths; repeat abdominal thrusts, foreign-body check/finger sweep, and 2 slow breaths	Give 2 slow breaths; retilt head and give 2 slow breaths; give 5 back blows; give 5 chest thrusts; check for object in throat; do finger sweep if object is visible; repeat back blows, chest thrusts, foreign-body check/finger sweep, and 2 slow breaths

Rescue Breathing

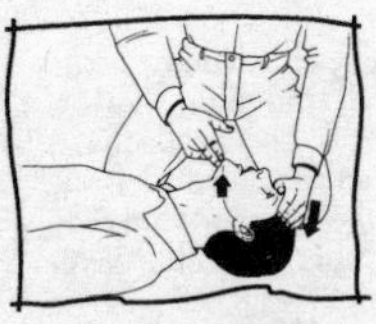

1. With head tilted back, pinch nose shut.

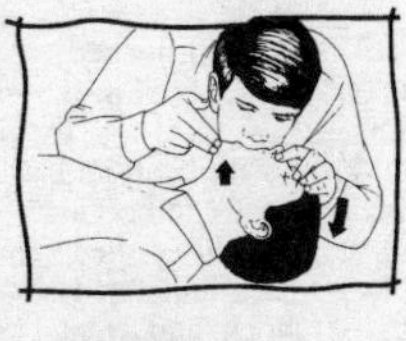

2. ADULT: Give 1 slow breath about every 5 seconds.

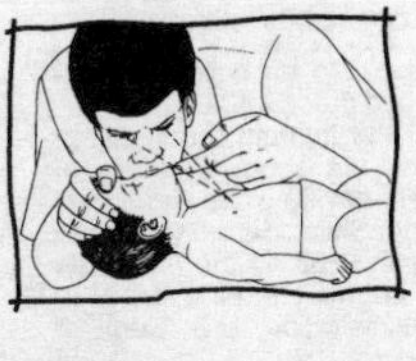

CHILD/INFANT: Give 1 slow breath about every 3 seconds.

CPR (Adult)

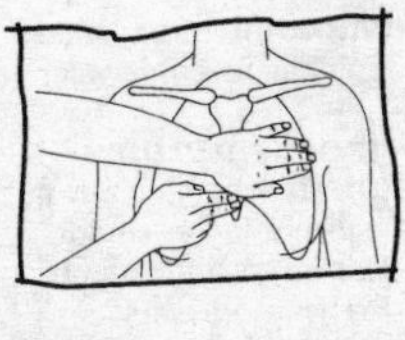

1. Find hand position.

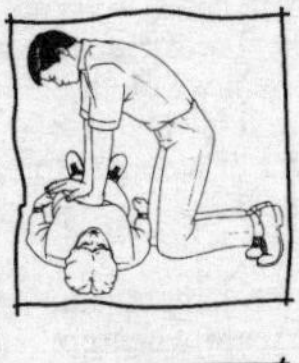

2. Position shoulders over hands. Compress chest 15 times.

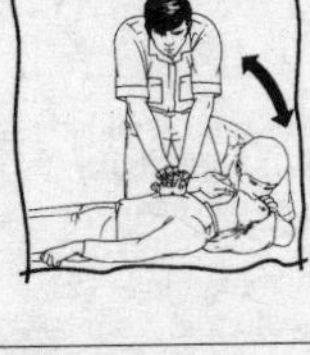

3. Give 2 slow breaths. Recheck pulse and breathing. If no pulse, continue sets of 15 compressions and 2 breaths.

Choking

If conscious but choking, give abdominal thrusts until object comes out.

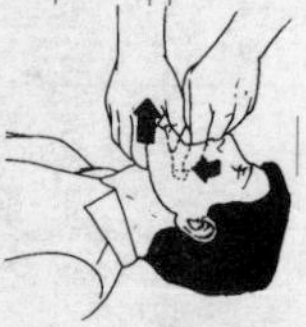

If a person becomes unconscious:

Step 1. Clear any object from mouth.

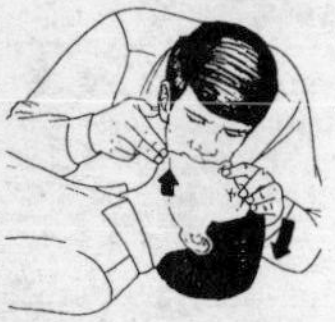

Step 2. Give 2 slow breaths.

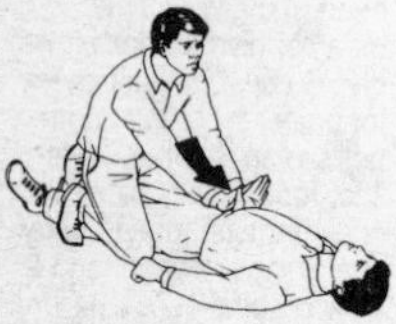

If air won't go in, give up to 5 abdominal thrusts.

Other Emergencies

Burns

First Degree: Signs/Symptoms—reddened skin. **Treatment**—Immerse quickly in cold water or apply ice until pain stops.

Second Degree: Signs/Symptoms—reddened skin, blisters. **Treatment**—(1) Cut away loose clothing. (2) Cover with several layers of cold moist dressings or, if limb is involved, immerse in cold water for relief of pain. (3) Treat for shock.

Third Degree: Signs/Symptoms—skin destroyed, tissues damaged, charring. **Treatment**—(1) Cut away loose clothing (do not remove clothing adhered to skin). (2) Cover with several layers of sterile, cold, moist dressings for relief of pain and to stop burning action. (3) Treat for shock.

Poisons

Treatment—(1) Dilute by drinking large quantities of water. (2) Induce vomiting except when poison is corrosive or a petroleum product. (3) Call the poison-control center or a doctor.

Shock

Shock may accompany any serious injury: blood loss, breathing impairment, heart failure, burns. Shock can kill—treat as soon as possible and continue until medical aid is available.

Signs/Symptoms—(1) Shallow breathing. (2) Rapid and weak pulse. (3) Nausea, collapse, vomiting. (4) Shivering. (5) Pale, moist skin. (6) Mental confusion. (7) Drooping eyelids, dilated pupils.

Treatment—(1) Establish and maintain an open airway. (2) Control bleeding. (3) Keep victim lying down. Exception: Head and chest injuries, heart attack, stroke, sun stroke. If no spine injury, victim may be more comfortable and breathe better in a semi-reclining position. If in doubt, keep the victim flat. Elevate the feet unless injury would be aggravated. Maintain normal body temperature. Place blankets under and over victim.

Frostbite

Most frequently frostbitten: toes, fingers, nose, and ears. It is caused by exposure to cold.

Signs/Symptoms—(1) Skin becomes pale or a grayish-yellow color. (2) Parts feel cold and numb. (3) Frozen parts feel doughy.

Treatment—(1) Victim should be wrapped in woolen cloth and kept dry. (2) Do not rub, chafe, or manipulate frostbitten parts. (3) Bring victim indoors. (4) Place affected parts in warm water (102°F to 105°F) and make sure water remains warm. Never thaw if the victim has to go back out into the cold, which may cause the affected area to be refrozen. (5) Do not use hot water bottles or a heat lamp, and do not place victim near a hot stove. (6) For serious frostbite, seek medical aid for thawing because pain will be intense and tissue damage extensive.

Heat Cramps

Affects people who work or do strenuous exercises in a hot environment. To prevent it, such people should drink large amounts of cool water and add a pinch of salt to each glass of water.

Signs/Symptoms—(1) Painful muscle cramps in legs and abdomen. (2) Faintness. (3) Profuse perspiration.

Treatment—(1) Move victim to a cool place. (2) Give victim sips of salted drinking water (one teaspoon of salt to one quart of water). (3) Apply manual pressure to the cramped muscle.

Heat Exhaustion

Signs/Symptoms—(1) Pale and clammy skin. (2) Profuse perspiration. (3) Rapid and shallow breathing. (4) Weakness, dizziness, and headache.

Treatment—(1) Care for victim as if he or she were in shock. (2) Remove victim to a cool area, do not allow chilling. (3) If body gets too cold, cover victim.

Heat Stroke

Signs/Symptoms—(1) Face is red and flushed. (2) Victim becomes rapidly unconscious. (3) Skin is hot and dry with no perspiration.

Treatment—(1) Lay victim down with head and shoulders raised. (2) Reduce the high body temperature as quickly as possible. (3) Apply cold applications to the body and head. (4) Use ice and fan if available. (5) Watch for signs of shock and treat accordingly. (6) Get medical aid as soon as possible.

NOTE: The almanac is not responsible for actions undertaken by anyone using these first-aid procedures. This information cannot substitute for a CPR or first-aid course. Contact your local Red Cross to find out about a variety of community programs that teach life-saving skills and safety information. *Sources:* "Life-saving Skills Summary" table and graphics from First Aid First © 1995 by the American Red Cross. "Other Emergencies" courtesy of First Aid, Mining Enforcement and Safety Administration, U.S. Dept. of the Interior.

Health and Medicine Update, A-Z

By DAVID BJERKLIE, ALICE PARK, and SORA SONG TIME

A

Atkins Diet The naysayers in the medical establishment got high-cholesterol egg on their faces in 2002. For three decades, the experts railed against Dr. Robert Atkins and his popular steak-heavy, high-fat, low-carb nutrition plan. (Atkins died in April 2003 after a fall.) Then came surprising new studies showing that the diet not only works (pound for pound, up to 100% better than low-fat diets) but also appears to be good for the heart, lowering triglycerides and raising HDL, the "good" cholesterol. Studies were small, however, and the results preliminary. The last word will probably have to wait for the big five-year, $2.5 million clinical trial, sponsored by the National Institutes of Health (NIH), that is tracking the health effects of the Atkins diet on 360 obese Americans. Meanwhile, the bottom line hasn't changed: you lose weight only when you burn more calories than you eat. (See E for Exercise.)

AIDS A UN report on the global AIDS epidemic made it painfully clear that 2002 was another bleak year for AIDS. Among its findings: 40 million people are infected with HIV, 3 million of them children. All told, more than 20 million have died of AIDS since 1981. Progress in the research labs has been slow and not that steady, but it has produced some results. Scientists discovered three proteins—alpha-defensins 1, 2, and 3—that may account for the so-called non-progressors, the 1% or 2% of people who contract HIV but never develop AIDS. Also, the Food and Drug Administration (FDA) approved a new rapid HIV test called OraQuick, which reliably detects HIV antibodies in a blood sample in less than 30 minutes.

B

Breast Cancer Things were confusing enough for breast-cancer patients, but in one regard doctors now have clarity: a lumpectomy followed by radiation, it has been definitively shown, is just as effective as a full mastectomy. Doctors and patients had long been concerned that simply removing a tumor instead of an entire breast might increase the chances of a relapse. But two studies, both published in the *New England Journal of Medicine,* that followed more than 2,500 women for at least 20 years found no difference in survival rates between those who had had mastectomies and those who had chosen the less drastic lumpectomy with radiation.

Bypass Surgery Doctors called it "pump head"—the mental decline suffered by 30% of heart-bypass patients in the days and weeks following their operations. The theory was that their difficulties in thinking, remembering, and paying attention were somehow caused by the heart-lung machines that oxygenate and circulate blood during surgery while the heart is stopped. However, a 2002 Dutch study found no long-term differences in cognitive decline between heart-lung-machine patients and "off-pump" patients, whose hearts were never stopped.

C

Cataracts Cataract operations have become routine—3 million are performed in the U.S. each year—but they are not perfect. In too many cases, the performance of the implanted lens is marred by imperfections caused by measurement errors or variations in the healing process. Solution: an implantable lens that can be recalibrated weeks after surgery. The new lens contains a photosensitive compound that is activated by a tiny beam of ultraviolet light, allowing doctors to fine-tune the power of the lens after it's in place. The lens is expected to be commercially available in Europe soon. Look for it in the U.S. by 2007.

C-Reactive Protein You still have to count your cholesterol, but the latest thing your doctor is watching is your CRP level. C-reactive protein is a blood chemical that provides a good measure of the degree of inflammation in your heart vessels. New studies have provided the strongest evidence yet that inflammation is a better predictor than cholesterol levels of your risk of heart disease. What won't change is your doctor's advice. CRP levels are lowered in the same ways by which cholesterol is reduced: diet, exercise, and statins.

D

Diabetes Close to 20 million Americans have diabetes, and nearly that many have a condition doctors have started to call prediabetes. Experts project that by the end of the decade, 10% of the U.S. will be diabetic. A big part of the problem is that cases of Type 2 diabetes, which used to be called adult-onset diabetes, are exploding among children and young adults. For kids at risk, drinking more milk might help. A study found that because the lactose in dairy products metabolizes slowly, it can help regulate blood-sugar levels. This doesn't mean kids should live on milk shakes and fried mozzarella sticks. They need milk, but they also also need to exercise, maintain a healthy weight, and eat a high-fiber diet.

E

Exercise What's a couch potato to think? First, researchers told us that even a 30-minute walk in the park a few times a week was enough to get the bulk of the cardiovascular benefit of exercise. Then other studies argued that intense activity was much better. Now the government has weighed in with new guidelines that call for an hour of exercise daily—double the previous recommendation. It's enough to make you throw up your hands and look for the TV remote. Don't. The message may be mixed, but it's really very simple: doing anything is always better than doing nothing. And doing more is even better. It's a lesson Americans seem to have missed; 25% get no regular exercise at all.

F

Fetal Hearts In a surgical first, doctors fixed a deadly heart-valve defect in a 5-month-old fetus. Guided by ultrasound, they angled a needle-thin catheter into the aortic valve, a spot one-eighth of an inch in diameter in a beating heart the size of a grape. A minuscule balloon was then inflated to enlarge the constricted valve, which had been obstructing the flow of blood to the body. Eleven weeks later, doctors induced early labor, anticipating the need for another operation, but the repair job had worked so well that the 5-lb. 8-oz. healthy baby boy didn't require a second procedure.

G

Gene Therapy When French doctors reported that they had successfully treated four boys for the devastating immune-system disorder known as bubble-boy disease, the news was hailed as the first clear victory for gene therapy. The researchers overcame their patients' genetic deficit by inserting a working version of a gene that enabled the boys to produce healthy infection-fighting cells. But only five months later, similar trials were halted in France and the U.S. when the experimental treatment was blamed for causing a leukemia-like illness in one child. It may be that retroviruses, used to ferry new genes into a patient's DNA, are triggering cancer by interfering with other genes. For now, the promise of gene therapy remains on hold.

H

Herbs The multimillion-dollar herbal-remedy market took a hit when new studies questioned the efficacy of two of its top sellers. A six-week trial of ginkgo biloba, used to enhance memory, found that ginkgo was no better than a placebo at improving memory, learning, or concentration. St.-John's-wort, which is supposed to lift your mood, didn't fare much better in a trial sponsored by the NIH. A separate study found that St.-John's-wort interferes with the effects of irinotecan, a widely prescribed chemotherapy drug.

Hormone Replacement Therapy For millions of women of a certain age, the news struck like a hot flash. In the summer of 2002 a huge, federally funded study of hormone-replacement therapy (HRT) involving more than 16,000 women was abruptly halted when researchers discovered that long-term use of estrogen and progestin was not lowering the risk of heart disease and stroke in postmenopausal women, as had been promised, but raising it, along with the risk of invasive breast cancer and blood clots. In 2003 the news got worse: further findings from the same study found that HRT not only fails to deter dementia, but older women who take it for long periods of time also double their risk of developing Alzheimer's and other cognitive problems. HRT is still the most widely effective medication available for the treatment of such menopausal symptoms as night sweats, hot flashes, and mood swings. It's fine to take it for that reason, experts say: just keep the dosage low, and take it for less than two years.

Hyperactivity Nobody knows what causes the impulsiveness and fidgetiness of attention-deficit/hyperactivity disorder (ADHD), but a brain-imaging study provided further evidence that the disorder is biologically hard-wired. A federally funded 10-year study of nearly 300 children ages 4 to 19 found that the brains of kids diagnosed with ADHD were 3% to 4% smaller in volume than those of normal children. While smaller brains don't necessarily mean lower IQs, brain size does appear to affect the severity of ADHD. In general, the smaller the brain, the greater the symptoms.

I

Infertility It has been 25 years—and a million births—since the arrival of Louise Joy Brown, the world's first test-tube baby, and you would think doctors would know by now if the procedure carried any extra risks. But only recently did studies show that babies conceived through in-vitro fertilization were more than twice as likely as naturally conceived babies to suffer major birth defects and nearly three times as likely to be born small, a significant risk factor for later cardiac and cognitive problems. It's doubtful either finding will deter many would-be parents who cannot conceive in the usual way.

K

Knee Surgery Arthroscopic knee surgery has been a popular treatment for people whose knees are racked by osteoarthritis. Minimally invasive, it flushes out debris in the joint and smooths bone surfaces without major surgery. But a surprising study showed that the operation is no more effective than a placebo. One in three patients reported improvement, whether having had real surgery or a sham operation with all the same pre- and post-op procedures but no actual treatment. Even if the placebo benefit is ignored, the study still casts doubt on surgery that succeeds only one-third of the time. Patients may be better off doing strengthening exercises and taking off a few pounds to ease the burden on their aching knees.

M

Mammography For two years, a bitter argument has raged over medical advice that most women thought was unimpeachable: routine mammograms save lives. The contrarians insist that the statistics don't bear this out. They also argue that mammograms miss 10% to 15% of breast cancers and that the vast majority of the abnormalities mammograms do spot are benign, which results in millions of unnecessary biopsies and countless anxious women. In a sharp repudiation of the critics, Health and Human Services Secretary Tommy Thompson declared that while mammograms are not perfect, they are "an important and effective tool that helps to save lives." The last word, for now.

Monkeypox At least a dozen people in six Midwestern states were hospitalized in the summer of 2003 by a close kin of the vanquished smallpox virus—monkeypox. The virus, African in origin, apparently entered the U.S. along with a shipment of giant pouched rats imported from Ghana by a Texas rare-pet dealer. At least one rat apparently passed the virus onto prairie dogs while in captivity. While less virulent than smallpox, which kills 30% of those it infects, monkeypox is nonetheless dangerous. Symptoms include high fever, headaches, dry cough, chills, and sweating, followed by eruptions of blister-like pimples filled with pus. The disease was effectively contained, said the Centers for Disease Control and Prevention.

N

Nicotine You can't smoke 'em if you got 'em in more and more public places, but what about licking 'em or drinking 'em? Not without the government's green light. The FDA warned pharmacists to stop mixing up nicotine-laden lollipops and lip balm, both of which the agency ruled were illegal drugs that could appeal to children. A few months later, the FDA dried up a California company's plans to douse the nation with nicotine water. The only nicotine products the agency okayed for over-the-counter sale were nicotine lozenges.

O

Osteoporosis Bone may look hard and static, but it's very much alive: new bone cells are constantly being made and old bone cells destroyed. With age, however, less bone gets made than destroyed. Result: 10 million Americans have dangerously low bone mass, or osteoporosis. This process can be reversed, however, and the FDA recently approved Forteo, the first treatment that does that. The drug contains part of the human parathyroid hormone, which builds up bone by boosting bone-making cells and suppressing bone destroyers. Studies show that postmenopausal women taking Forteo along with calcium and vitamin-D supplements significantly reduced their risk of fractures. Unfortunately, Forteo comes only in injectable form, which means daily shots in the thigh or abdomen.

P

Prostate Cancer Watchful waiting has become a byword for prostate-cancer patients, most of whom won't need aggressive surgery to remove their slow-growing tumors. But doctors have long felt uneasy about the tightrope they walked, trying to find the right balance between advising surgery for those men most likely to survive the cancer and counseling those with the slowest-growing tumors to watch and wait. Fresh guidance came from a large Scandinavian study, in which men randomly assigned to undergo surgery reduced by 50% their risk of dying from prostate cancer or having their cancer spread. It's not clear, however, how this applies to American men. In the Scandinavian group, most patients were found to have relatively advanced tumors, big enough to be felt in a doctor's manual exam. By contrast, in the U.S., 75% of men's tumors are discovered by a blood test, which picks up cancers long before they become noticeable.

S

Severe Acute Respiratory Syndrome (SARS) SARS, a new life-threatening disease, had much of the world on edge in late 2002 and into 2003, as it spread from China's Guangdong Province to all corners of the world. The first severe and readily transmissible new disease to emerge in the 21st century prompted many travelers to cancel trips to Asia. SARS causes a dry cough, shortness of breath, stiffness, fever, loss of appetite, and malaise. Scientists have identified a previously unknown virus in the coronavirus family as the primary cause of SARS. There is no cure for SARS; patients are given supportive care for their symptoms, such as ventilators and fluids. China and Hong Kong were hit hardest by the disease. China reported 5,327 probable cases and 348 deaths from SARS, and Hong Kong tallied 1,755 cases and 298 deaths. The U.S. reported 75 probable cases and zero deaths. The World Health Organization declared SARS contained in July 2003, but warned that it may be a seasonal illness and reappear in subsequent winters.

Smallpox The rise of terrorism and the anthrax attacks of 2001 have led to concern that this historic scourge, banished from the U.S. in 1949, could be reintroduced into the population. That's why the U.S. government has begun vaccinating military and health-care personnel and ordered enough vaccine to inoculate the entire U.S. population. It's the first smallpox-vaccination program since routine shots were discontinued in the U.S. in 1972. Should you get a smallpox shot when it becomes widely available, assuming the threat is still merely theoretical? Things to consider before you line up for a shot: many of the volunteers who tested the new vaccine experienced fevers, chills, and severe muscle aches. Those with weakened immune systems, such as AIDS and cancer patients, as well as people with a history of eczema or other skin conditions, probably shouldn't get vaccinated.

T

Tamoxifen Most women treated for breast cancer take tamoxifen to prevent the cancer from recurring, but it seems that for the drug to be most effective, timing is key. Until 2002, most women with early-stage, estrogen-sensitive breast cancer had surgery followed by chemotherapy and tamoxifen. Tamoxifen blocks estrogen's cancer-promoting effects, but it turns out that the drug keeps chemotherapy agents from penetrating cancer cells and destroying them. An eight-year study of breast-cancer patients showed that women who waited to take tamoxifen until after their chemotherapy cycles were complete were 18% more likely to survive without a recurrence of cancer than women who took the two treatments together.

V

Vaccines Why is autism 10 times as prevalent among young children today as it was in the 1980s? Many parents, noting that the onset of symptoms coincided with their child's vaccination against measles, mumps, and rubella (MMR), blame the mercury that's used as a preservative in the vaccine. But doctors have not been able to find a link, and now the results of a Danish survey of more than

500,000 children should finally put the theory to rest. The researchers found no difference in the incidence of autism between children who received MMR shots and those who did not. The more likely reasons for the increase: a broader definition of autism and greater awareness of its symptoms.

W

West Nile Virus Carried by birds on the wing, the West Nile virus continued its westward flight across the U.S. in 2002 and into 2003. Mosquitoes have been infecting birds and following them on their seasonal migration paths to 40 states. In 2002, the virus killed more than 200 people in the largest outbreak of West Nile encephalitis in the world. The trend continued into 2003, with 10 deaths and 470 cases by mid-August. Colorado was the hardest hit in 2003, reporting 247 of the 470 cases. Even more worrisome, doctors learned for the first time that the virus can be passed from an infected mother to her unborn child.

X

Xenotransplants Nobody likes the idea of taking organs from another species and putting them in people, a procedure known as xenotransplantation. But human organs are scarce, and pigs' body parts are similar in size and physiology to humans'. Researchers have even found a way to make pig organs less piglike (and thus less likely to be rejected by human immune systems): by removing one of the genes responsible for the most severe form of rejection. That doesn't mean that pig-to-human transplants are about to begin. The gene is probably one of several that trigger the human immune response, so the genetically engineered pigs are the first in what will probably be several generations of human friendly porkers.

Z

Zoloft For 5% of menstruating women, their time of the month can be emotionally and physically exhausting. Those who suffer from premenstrual dysphoric disorder (PMDD) are often debilitated by feelings of sadness and changes in their sleeping and eating habits. The FDA has approved a popular antidepressant, Zoloft, for treatment of PMDD. It works by keeping brain nerves bathed in the chemical serotonin. And unlike other PMDD treatments, such as hormones or psychotherapy, it has been studied in depth in clinical trials. □

Status of the World AIDS Epidemic, End of 2002

	Total	Adults	Women	Children under 15 years
People newly infected with HIV in 2002	5 million	4.2million	2 million	800,000
Number of people living with HIV/AIDS	42 million	38.6 million	19.2 million	3.2 million
AIDS deaths in 2002	3.1 million	2.5 million	1.2 million	610,000
Total number of AIDS deaths since beginning of epidemic	27.9 million	22.4 million	11.3 million	5.5 million

Source: World Health Organization; UNAIDS. Web: www.unaids.org.

HIV/AIDS Statistics and Features by World Region

(as of Dec. 2002)

World region	Epidemic started	Adults & children living with HIV/AIDS	Adults & children newly infected with HIV	Adult prevalence rate[1]	Percent of HIV-positive adults who are women	Main mode(s) of transmission for adults[2]
Sub-Saharan Africa	late '70s–early '80s	29.4 million	3.5 million	8.8%	58%	Hetero
North Africa & Middle East	late '80s	550,000	83,000	0.3%	55%	Hetero, IDU
South & Southeast Asia	late '80s	6.0 million	700,000	0.6%	36%	Hetero, IDU
East Asia & Pacific	late '80s	1.2 million	270,000	0.1%	24%	IDU, Hetero, MSM
Latin America	late '70s–early '80s	1.5 milion	150,000	0.6%	30%	MSM, IDU, Hetero
Caribbean	late '70s–early '80s	440,000	60,000	2.4%	50%	Hetero, MSM
Eastern Europe & Central Asia	early '90s	1.2 million	250,000	0.6%	27%	IDU
Western Europe	late '70s–early '80s	570,000	30,000	0.3%	25%	MSM, IDU
North America	late '70s–early '80s	980,000	45,000	0.6%	20%	MSM, IDU, Hetero
Australia & New Zealand	late '70s–early '80s	15,000	500	0.1%	7%	MSM
Total		**42 million**	**5 million**	**1.2%**	**50%**	

1. The proportion of adults (15 to 49 years of age) living with HIV/AIDS in 2002, using 2002 population numbers. 2. Hetero (heterosexual transmission), IDU (transmission through injecting drug use), MSM (sexual transmission among men who have sex with men). *Source:* World Health Organization, UNAID. Web: www.unaids.org.

Global Estimates[1] of the HIV/AIDS Epidemic as of End 2002

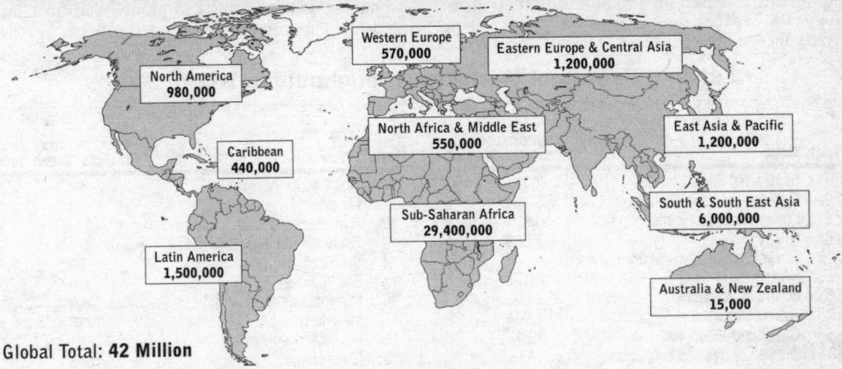

Note: 1. Number of people currently infected with HIV/AIDS. *Source:* World Health Organization, UNAIDS.

Understanding AIDS

Acquired Immune Deficiency Syndrome, or AIDS, was first reported in mid-1981 in the United States; it is believed to have originated in Sub-Saharan Africa. The human immunodeficiency virus (HIV) that causes AIDS was identified in 1983, and by 1985 tests to detect the virus were available. The credit for discovering the AIDS virus is jointly shared by Dr. Robert Gallo, a researcher at the National Cancer Institute, and Luc Montagnier of the Pasteur Institute, France.

Destruction of Immune System

A fatal and incurable disease caused by HIV, AIDS attacks and destroys the immune system, gradually leaving the individual defenseless against illnesses that lead to death. These illnesses are referred to as "opportunistic" infections or diseases: in AIDS patients the most common are Pneumocystis carinii pneumonia (PCP), a parasitic infection of the lungs, and a type of cancer known as Kaposi's sarcoma (KS). Other opportunistic infections include unusually severe infections with yeast, cytomegalovirus, herpes virus, and parasites such as Toxoplasma or Cryptosporidia. Milder infections with these organisms do not suggest immune deficiencies. Symptoms of full-blown AIDS include a persistent cough, fever, and difficulty in breathing. Multiple purplish blotches and bumps on the skin may indicate Kaposi's sarcoma. The virus can also cause brain damage.

People infected with the virus can have a wide range of symptoms—from none to mild to severe. At least a fourth to a half of those infected with HIV will develop AIDS within four to ten years. Many experts think the percentage will grow much higher.

Transmission

Although the first reported cases involved homosexual men in Los Angeles who were infected through sexual contact, the principal mode of transmission throughout the world is through the exchange of bodily fluids during heterosexual intercourse. According to the World Health Organization, extensive spread of HIV appears to have begun in the late 1970s and early 1980s. It spread in men and women with multiple sexual partners in East and Central Africa and among homosexual and bisexual men in certain urban areas of the Americas, Australasia, and Western Europe.

In addition to sexual contact, AIDS has been spread by intravenous drug users sharing infected hypodermic needles. The virus can also be passed on through transfused blood or its components. It may also be transmitted from infected mother to infant before, during, or shortly after birth.

Two major types of HIV have been recognized, HIV-1 and HIV-2. HIV-1 is the dominant type worldwide. HIV-2 is found principally in West Africa but cases have been reported in East Africa, Europe, Asia, and Latin America. There are at least ten different genetic subtypes of HIV-1, but their biological and epidemiological significance is unclear at present. Both HIV-1 and HIV-2 are transmitted in the same ways.

Pandemic

With no cure at present, prudence could save thousands of people who have yet to be exposed to the virus. Use of condoms lessens the possibility of transmission as does the elimination of sharing hypodermic needles. The fate of many will depend less on science than on the ability of large numbers of human beings to change their behavior in the face of growing danger.

The introduction of highly active antiretroviral therapy in 1996 was a turning point for hundreds of thousands of people with access to sophisticated health-care systems. Although they can't cure HIV/AIDS, antiretrovirals (ARVs) and their use in combination, "cocktails," have dramatically reduced mortality and morbidity and prolonged and improved the lives of sufferers. However, 95% of people with HIV/AIDS live in developing countries, where access to these medicines remains unacceptably limited. In addition, not everyone can tolerate the potent medications, which can have devastating side effects—including diabetes, anemia, and high cholesterol. Doctors are also reporting a significant increase of patients with drug-resistant HIV strains, prompting research to produce different drugs. Some 100 separate drugs are either in use or being tested for use against AIDS. Meanwhile, HIV has been spreading, with rising rates of infection in Eastern Europe, Russia, China, and Southeast Asia, prompting some scientists to grimly warn that the epidemic has only just begun.

Leading Causes of Mortality Throughout the World, 2001

Rank	Cause	All countries: Total deaths (in thousands)	All countries: % of total
1.	Ischaemic heart disease	7,181	12.7%
2.	Cerebrovascular disease	5,454	9.6
3.	Lower respiratory infections	3,871	6.8
4.	HIV/AIDS	2,866	5.1
5.	Chronic obstructive pulmonary disease	2,672	4.7
6.	diarrheal diseases	2,001	3.5
7.	Tuberculosis	1,644	2.9
8.	Childhood diseases	1,318	2.3
9.	Cancer of trachea/bronchus/ lung	1,213	2.1
10.	Road traffic accidents	1,194	2.1%
11.	Malaria	1,124	2.0
12.	Hypertensive heart disease	874	1.5
13.	Other unintentional injuries	874	1.5
14.	Stomach cancer	850	1.5
15.	Self-inflicted	849	1.5
16.	Cirrhosis of the liver	796	1.4
17.	Measles	745	1.3
18.	Nephritis/nephrosis	625	1.1
19.	Liver cancer	616	1.1
20.	Colon/rectum cancer	615	1.1

Source: The World Health Report, 2002, The World Health Organization (WHO).

Common Infectious Diseases Worldwide

Sources: The Centers for Disease Control (CDC); The World Health Organization (WHO).

The following is a list of the most common infectious diseases throughout the world today. Accurate caseload numbers are difficult to determine, especially because so many of these diseases are endemic to developing countries, where many people do not have access to modern medical care. Approximately half of all deaths caused by infectious diseases each year can be attributed to just three diseases: tuberculosis, malaria, and AIDS. Together, these diseases cause over 300 million illnesses and more than 5 million deaths each year.

African Trypanosomiasis ("sleeping sickness"): African trypanosomiasis is spread by the tsetse fly, which is common to many African countries. The World Health Organization (WHO) estimates that nearly 450,000 cases occur each year. Symptoms of the disease include fever, headaches, joint pains, and itching in the early stage, and confusion, sensory disturbances, poor coordination, and disrupted sleep cycles in the second stage. If the disease goes untreated in its first stage, it causes irreparable neurological damage; if it goes untreated in its second stage, it is fatal.

Cholera: Cholera is a disease spread mostly through contaminated drinking water and unsanitary conditions. It is endemic in the Indian subcontinent, Russia, and sub-Saharan Africa. It is an acute infection of the intestines with the bacterium *Vibrio cholerae.* Its main symptom is copious diarrhea. Between 5% and 10% of those infected with the disease will develop severe symptoms, which also include vomiting and leg cramps. In its severe form, cholera can cause death by dehydration. An estimated 200,000 cases are reported to WHO annually.

Cryptosporidiosis: Cryptosporidiosis has become one of the most common causes of waterborne disease in the United States in recent years; it is also found throughout the rest of the world. It is caused by a parasite that spreads when a water source is contaminated, usually with the feces of infected animals or humans. Symptoms include diarrhea, stomach cramps, an upset stomach, and slight fever. Some people do not exhibit any symptoms.

Dengue: WHO estimates that 50 million cases of dengue fever appear each year. It is spread through the bite of the *Aedes aegypti* mosquito. Recent years have seen dengue outbreaks all over Asia and Africa. Dengue fever can be mild to moderate, and occasionally severe, though it is rarely fatal. Mild cases, which usually affect infants and young children, involve a nonspecific febrile illness, while moderate cases, seen in older children and adults, display high fever, severe headaches, muscle and joint pains, and rash. Severe cases develop into dengue hemorrhagic fever, which involves high fever, hemorrhaging, and sometimes circulatory failure.

Hepatitis A: Hepatitis A is a highly contagious liver disease caused by the hepatitis A virus. Spread primarily by the fecal-oral route or by ingestion of contaminated water or food, the number of annual infections worldwide is estimated at 1.4 million. Symptoms include fever, fatigue, jaundice, and dark urine. Although those exposed usually develop lifelong immunity, the best protection against Hepatitis A is vaccination.

Hepatitis B: Approximately 2 billion people are infected with the hepatitis B virus (HBV), making it the most common infectious disease in the world today. Over 350 million of those infected never rid themselves of the infection. Hepatitis is an inflammation of the liver that causes symptoms such as jaundice, extreme fatigue, nausea, vomiting, and stomach pain; hepatitis B is the most serious form of the disease. Chronic infections can cause cirrhosis of the liver or liver cancer in later years.

Hepatitis C: Hepatitis C is a less common, and less severe, form of hepatitis. An estimated 170 million people worldwide are infected with hepatitis C virus (HCV); 3–4 million more are infected every year. The majority of HCV cases are asymptomatic, even in people who develop chronic infection.

HIV/AIDS: *See* pp. 542–544.

Influenza: Several influenza epidemics in the 20th century caused millions of deaths worldwide, including the worst epidemic in American history, the Spanish influenza outbreak that killed more than 500,000 in 1918. Today influenza is less of a public health threat, though it continues to be a serious disease that affects many people. Approximately 20,000 people die of the flu in the United States every year. The influenza virus attacks the human respiratory tract, causing symptoms such as fever, headaches, fatigue, coughing, sore throat, nasal congestion, and body aches.

Japanese Encephalitis: Japanese encephalitis is a mosquito-borne disease endemic in Asia. Around 50,000 cases occur each year; 25% to 30% of all cases are fatal.

Leishmaniasis: Leishmaniasis is a disease spread by the bite of the sandfly. It is found mostly in tropical countries. There are several types of leishmaniasis, and they vary in symptoms and severity. Visceral leishmaniasis (VL, or *kala azar*) is the most severe; left untreated, it is always fatal. Its symptoms include fever, weight loss, anemia, and a swelling of the spleen and liver. Mucocutaneous leishmaniasis (MCL, or *espundia*) produces lesions that affect the nose, mouth, and throat and can destroy their mucous membranes. Cutaneous leishmaniasis (CL) produces skin ulcers, sometimes as many as 200, that cause disability and extensive scarring. Diffuse cutaneous leishmaniasis (DCL) is similar to CL, and infected people are prone to relapses. Approximately 12 million cases of leishmaniasis exist today.

Malaria: Malaria is a mosquito-borne disease that affects 300–500 million people annually, causing nearly 3 million deaths. It is most common in tropical and subtropical climates and is found in over 100 countries, including many parts of Central and South America, Africa, Southeast Asia and the Indian subcontinent, and the Middle East. Symptoms include several stages of illness. The first stage consists of shaking and chills, the next stage involves high fever and severe headache, and in the final stage the infected person's temperature drops and he or she sweats profusely. Infected people also often suffer from anemia, weakness, and a swelling of the spleen. Malaria was almost eradicated 30 years ago; now it is on the rise again.

Measles: Measles is a disease that has seen a drastic reduction in countries where a vaccine is readily available, but it is still prevalent in developing countries, where most of the 777,000 deaths (out of 30 million cases) it caused in 2001 occurred. Symptoms include high fever, coughing, and a maculo-papular rash; common complications include diarrhea, pneumonia, and ear infections.

Meningitis: Meningitis, often known as spinal meningitis, is an infection of the spinal cord. It is usually the result of a viral or bacterial infection. Bacterial meningitis is more severe than viral meningitis and may cause brain damage, hearing loss, and learning disabilities. An estimated 1.2 million cases of bacterial meningitis occur every year, over a tenth of which are fatal. Symptoms include severe headache, fever, nausea, vomiting, lethargy, delirium, photophobia, and a stiff neck.

Onchocerciasis ("river blindness"): Onchocerciasis is caused by the larvae of *Onchocerca volvulus,* a parasitic worm that lives in the human body for years. It is endemic in Africa, where nearly all of the 18 million people infected with the disease live. Of those infected, over 6.5 million have developed dermatitis and 270,000 have gone blind. Symptoms include visual impairment, rashes, lesions, intense itching, skin depigmentation, and lymphadenitis.

Pneumonia: Pneumonia has many possible causes, but it is usually an infection of the streptococcus or mycoplasma bacteria. These bacteria can live in the human body without causing infection for years, and only surface when another illness has lowered the person's immunity to disease. *Streptococcus pneumoniae* causes streptococcal pneumonia, the most common kind, which is more severe than mycoplasmal pneumonia. *S. pneumoniae* is responsible for more than 100,000 hospitalizations for pneumonia annually, as well as 6 million cases of otitis media and over 60,000 cases of invasive diseases such as meningitis.

Rotavirus: Rotavirus is the most common cause of viral gastroenteritis worldwide. It kills more than 600,000 children each year, mostly in developing countries. Symptoms include vomiting, watery diarrhea, fever, and abdominal pain.

Schistosomiasis: Schistosomiasis is a parasitic disease that is endemic in many developing countries. Roughly 200 million people worldwide are infected with the flukeworm, whose eggs cause the symptoms of the disease. Some 120 million of those infected are symptomatic, and 20 million suffer severely from the infection. Symptoms include rash and itchiness soon after becoming infected, followed by fever, chills, coughing, and muscle aches.

Shigellosis: Shigella infection causes an estimated 600,000 deaths worldwide every year. It is most common in developing countries with poor sanitation. Shigella bacteria cause bacillary dysentery, or shigellosis. Symptoms include diarrhea with bloody stool, vomiting, and abdominal cramps.

Tuberculosis: Tuberculosis causes nearly 2 million deaths every year, and WHO estimates that nearly 1 billion people will be infected between 2000 and 2020 if more effective preventive procedures are not adopted. The TB bacteria are most often found in the lungs, where they can cause chest pain and a bad cough that brings up bloody phlegm. Other symptoms include fatigue, weight loss, appetite loss, chills, fever, and night sweats.

Typhoid: Typhoid fever causes an estimated 600,000 deaths annually, out of 12–17 million cases. It is usually spread through infected food or water. Symptoms include a sudden and sustained fever, severe headache, nausea, severe appetite loss, constipation, and sometimes diarrhea.

Yellow Fever: Yellow fever causes an estimated 30,000 deaths each year, out of 200,000 cases. The disease has two phases. In the "acute phase," symptoms include fever, muscle pain, headache, shivers, appetite loss, nausea, and vomiting. This lasts for 3–4 days, after which most patients recover. But 15% will enter the "toxic phase," in which fever reappears, along with other symptoms, including jaundice; abdominal pain; vomiting; bleeding from the mouth, nose, eyes, and stomach; and deterioration of kidney function (sometimes complete kidney failure). Half of all patients in the toxic phase die within two weeks; the other half recover.

Is It a Cold or the Flu?

Symptoms	Cold	Flu
fever	rare	characteristic, high (102°–104° F); lasts 3–4 days
headache	rare	prominent
general aches, pains	slight	usual; often severe
fatigue, weakness	quite mild	can last up to 2–3 weeks
extreme exhaustion	never	early and prominent
stuffy nose, sore throat	common	sometimes
Complications	sinus congestion or earache	bronchitis, pneumonia; can be life-threatening
Prevention	none	annual vaccination; antiviral medicines—see your doctor
Treatment	only temporary relief of symptoms	antiviral medicines—see your doctor

Source: National Institute of Allergy and Infectious Diseases.

The Common Cold

Source: National Institute of Allergy and Infectious Diseases, National Institutes of Health.

The problem. In the course of a year, individuals in the United States suffer one billion colds, according to some estimates. Adults average about two to four colds a year, although the range varies widely. Women, especially those aged 20–30 years, have more colds than men, possibly because of their closer contact with children. On average, individuals older than 60 have fewer than one cold a year. Colds are most prevalent among children, and seem to be related to youngsters' relative lack of resistance to infection and to contacts with other children in day-care centers and schools. Children have about six to ten colds a year. In families with children in school, the number of colds per child can be as high as 12 a year.

The causes: viruses. More than 200 different viruses are known to cause the symptoms of the common cold. **Rhinoviruses** (from the Greek *rhin,* meaning "nose") cause an estimated 30% to 35% of all adult colds, and are most active in early fall, spring and summer. More than 110 distinct rhinovirus types have been identified. **Coronaviruses** are believed to cause a large percentage of all adult colds. They induce colds primarily in the winter and early spring. Of the more than 30 isolated strains, three or four infect humans.

Does cold weather cause a cold? Although many people are convinced that a cold results from exposure to cold weather, or from getting chilled or overheated, these conditions in fact have little or no effect on the development or severity of a cold.

How cold viruses cause disease. Viruses cause infection by overcoming the body's complex defense system. The body's first line of defense is mucus, produced by the membranes in the nose and throat. Mucus traps the material we inhale: pollen, dust, bacteria, and viruses. When a virus penetrates the mucus and enters a cell, it commandeers the protein-making machinery to manufacture new viruses, which, in turn, attack surrounding cells.

How colds are spread. Depending on the virus type, any or all of the following routes of transmission may be common:

- Touching infectious respiratory secretions on the skin and on environmental surfaces and then touching the eyes or nose.
- Inhaling relatively large particles of respiratory secretions transported briefly in the air.
- Inhaling droplet nuclei, smaller infectious particles suspended in the air for long periods of time.

Prevention. Handwashing is the simplest and most effective way to keep from getting rhinovirus colds. Not touching the nose or eyes is another. Individuals with colds should always sneeze or cough into a facial tissue, and promptly throw it away. Because rhinoviruses can survive up to three hours outside the nasal passages on inanimate objects and skin, cleaning environmental surfaces with a virus-killing disinfectant might help prevent spread of infection.

Treatment. Only symptomatic treatment is available for uncomplicated cases of the common cold: bed rest, plenty of fluids, gargling with warm salt water, applying petroleum jelly to a raw nose, and taking aspirin or acetaminophen to relieve headache or fever. Nonprescription cold remedies, including decongestants and cough suppressants, may relieve some cold symptoms but will not prevent, cure, or even shorten the duration of illness.

Antibiotics do not kill viruses. These prescription drugs should be used only for rare bacterial complications, such as sinusitis or ear infections, that can develop as secondary infections. The use of antibiotics "just in case" will not prevent secondary bacterial infections.

Does vitamin C have a role? Many people are convinced that taking large quantities of vitamin C will prevent colds or relieve symptoms. To test this theory, several large-scale, controlled studies involving children and adults have been conducted. To date, no conclusive data have shown that large doses of vitamin C prevent colds. The vitamin may reduce the severity or duration of symptoms, but there is no definitive evidence.

National Transplant Data

Registered U.S. Patients Waiting for Transplants
(as of June 6, 2003)

Kidney	54,867	Lung	3,886	Heart/Lung	197
Liver	17,171	Kidney/Pancreas	2,393	Intestine	178
Heart	3,748	Pancreas	1,420	**Total patients**	**81,913[1]**

NOTE: Patients can be listed with more than one transplant center, thus the number of registrations is greater than the actual number of patients. 1. Some patients are waiting for more than one organ; therefore the total number of patients is less than the sum of patients waiting for each organ. *Source:* United Network for Organ Sharing.

Number of U.S. Transplants Per Year, 1988–2002

	1988	1990	1995	2000	2002
Heart	1,676	2,107	2,355	2,194	2,154
Heart/Lung	74	52	69	48	33
Intestine	—	5	46	79	108
Kidney	8,873	9,416	11,054	13,402	14,766
Kidney/Pancreas	170	459	919	913	905
Liver	1,713	2,690	3,931	4,961	5,329
Lung	33	203	872	956	1,042
Pancreas	79	69	107	436	553
Total:					
All organs	**12,618**	**15,001**	**19,353**	**22,989**	**24,890**

NOTE: Kidney-pancreas transplants are counted apart from kidney transplants and pancreas transplants and do not show up in the totals for the individual organs. Double kidney, double lung, and heart-lung transplants are each counted as one transplant. All other multi-organ transplants are included in the total for each individual organ. *Source:* National Organ Procurement and Transplantation Network.

Americans Without Health Insurance[1] by Characteristic, 2001

Characteristic	Percent
Total	**14.6%**
Race and ethnicity	
White	13.6
Non-Hispanic	10.0
Black	19.0
Asian and Pacific Islander	18.2
Hispanic[2]	33.2
Household income	
Less than $25,000	23.3
$25,000 to $49,999	17.7
$50,000 to $74.999	11.3
$75,000 or more	7.7
Age	
Under 18 years	11.7%
18 to 24 years	28.1
25 to 34 years	23.4
35 to 44 years	16.1
45 to 64 years	13.1
65 years and over	0.8
Nativity	
Native	12.2
Foreign born	33.4
Work experience (18 to 64 years old)	
Worked during year	17.0
Did not work	24.7

1. For the entire year. 2. Hispanics may be of any race. *Source:* U.S. Census Bureau, *Current Population Survey, 2001* and 2002 Annual Demographic Supplements.

Percent of Americans Without Health Insurance by State, 2001

State	Percent
Alabama	13.1%
Alaska	15.7
Arizona	17.9
Arkansas	16.1
California	19.5
Colorado	15.6
Connecticut	10.2
Delaware	9.2
DC	12.7
Florida	17.5
Georgia	16.6
Hawaii	9.6
Idaho	16.0
Illinois	13.6
Indiana	11.8
Iowa	7.5
Kansas	11.4
Kentucky	12.3
Louisiana	19.3%
Maine	10.3
Maryland	12.3
Massachusetts	8.2
Michigan	10.4
Minnesota	8.0
Mississippi	16.4
Missouri	10.2
Montana	13.6
Nebraska	9.5
Nevada	16.1
New Hampshire	9.4
New Jersey	13.1
New Mexico	20.7
New York	15.5
North Carolina	14.4
North Dakota	9.6
Ohio	11.2
Oklahoma	18.3%
Oregon	12.8
Pennsylvania	9.2
Rhode Island	7.7
South Carolina	12.3
South Dakota	9.3
Tennessee	11.3
Texas	23.5
Utah	14.8
Vermont	9.6
Virginia	10.9
Washington	13.1
West Virginia	13.2
Wisconsin	7.7
Wyoming	15.9
Total U.S.	**14.6**

NOTE: These estimates should not be used to rank the states. Results from different samplings could easily show different estimates and rankings because of small sampling sizes. *Source:* U.S. Census Bureau, *March 2002 Current Population Survey.*

Cancer: Estimated New Cases (2003) and Survival Rates

	Estimated new cases, 2003 (in thousands)			Five-year relative survival rates[1] (percent)					
				White		Black		All races	
Site	Total	Male	Female	1983–1985	1992–1998	1983–1985	1992–1998	1983–1985	1992–1998
All sites[2]	1,334	675	659	54%	64%	40%	53%	52%	62%
Lung	172	92	80	14	15	11	12	14	15
Breast[3]	213	1	211	79	88	63	73	78	86
Colon	106	49	57	58	63	49	53	58	62
Rectum	42	24	18	56	62	44	53	55	62
Prostate	221	221	n.a.	76	98	64	93	75	97
Bladder	57	42	15	78	82	60	65	78	82
Uterine corpus	40	n.a.	40	85	86	54	61	83	84
Non-Hodgkins lymphoma[4]	53	28	25	54	56	45	46	54	55
Oral cavity and pharynx	28	18	10	55	59	35	35	53	56
Leukemia[4]	31	18	13	42	47	34	38	41	46
Melanoma—skin	54	30	24	85	89	74	66	85	89
Pancreas	31	15	16	3	4	5	4	3	4
Kidney	32	20	12	56	62	55	60	56	62
Stomach	22	13	9	16	21	19	20	17	22
Ovary	25	n.a.	25	40	53	42	53	41	53
Uterine cervix	12	n.a.	12	71	72	60	60	69	71

NOTE: n.a. = not applicable. 1. The 5-year relative survival rate indicates that a person will not die from causes directly related to their cancer within 5 years. 2. Includes other sites not shown separately. 3. Survival rates for female only. 4. All types combined. *Source:* U.S. National Institutes of Health, National Cancer Institute.

What Is Cancer?

Source: National Cancer Institute.

Cancer is a group of many different diseases that have some important things in common. Cancer affects our cells, the body's basic unit of life.

To understand cancer, it is helpful to know what happens when normal cells become cancerous. Usually, cells grow, divide, and produce more cells as they are needed to keep the body healthy. Sometimes, however, the process goes astray—cells keep dividing when new cells are not needed. The mass of extra cells forms a growth or tumor.

Benign tumors are not cancer. They often can be removed and, in most cases, they do not come back. Cells in benign tumors do not spread to other parts of the body. Most important, benign tumors are rarely a threat to life.

Malignant tumors are cancer. Cells in malignant tumors are abnormal and divide without control or order. These cancer cells can invade and destroy the tissue around them. Cancer cells can also break away from a malignant tumor and enter the bloodstream or lymphatic system (these two networks of vessels carry blood and lymph throughout the body). The process by which cancer spreads from the original tumor to form new tumors in other parts of the body is called metastasis.

Sexually Transmitted Diseases (STDs)

More than 25 diseases are spread primarily through sexual activity. The latest estimates (1999) indicate that there are 15 million new sexually transmitted disease cases in the United States each year. Approximately one-fourth of these new infections are in teenagers. Nearly two-thirds of all STD cases occur in people younger than 25 years.

While some sexually transmitted diseases, such as syphilis, have been brought to all-time lows, others, like genital herpes, gonorrhea, and chlamydia, continue to resurge and spread through the population.

Not including HIV, the most common sexually transmitted diseases in the U.S. are chlamydia, gonorrhea, syphilis, genital herpes, human papillomavirus, hepatitis B, and trichomoniasis.

Sexually transmitted disease	Incidence (estimated number of new cases every year)	Prevalence[1] (estimated number of people currently infected)
Chlamydia	3 million	2 million
Gonorrhea	650,000	n.a.
Syphilis	70,000	n.a.
Herpes	1 million	45 million
Human papillomavirus (hpv)	5.5 million	20 million
Hepatitis B	120,000	417,000
Trichomoniasis	5 million	n.a.

NOTE: n.a. = not available. 1. No recent surveys on national prevalence for gonorrhea, syphilis, trichomoniasis, or bacterial vaginosis have been conducted. *Source:* Centers for Disease Control, 1999.

Abortion in the United States

Incidence of Abortion

- 49% of pregnancies among American women are unintended; almost half of these are terminated by abortion.
- In 2000, 1.31 million abortions took place, down from an estimated 1.36 million in 1996. From 1973 through 2000, more than 39 million legal abortions occurred.
- Each year, 2 out of every 100 women aged 15–44 have an abortion; 48% of them have had at least one previous abortion and 61% have had a previous birth.
- An estimated 43% of women will have at least one abortion by the time they are 45 years old.
- Each year, an estimated 46 million abortions occur worldwide. Of these, 20 million procedures are obtained illegally.

Who Has Abortions

- 52% of U.S. women obtaining abortions are younger than 25: Women aged 20–24 obtain 33% of all abortions, and teenagers obtain 19%.
- Black women are more than three times as likely as white women to have an abortion, and Hispanic women are two-and-a-half times as likely.
- Two-thirds of all abortions are among never-married women.
- On average, women give at least three reasons for choosing abortion: three-fourths say that having a baby would interfere with work, school, or other responsibilities; about two-thirds say they cannot afford a child; and half say they do not want to be a single parent or are having problems with their husband or partner.
- About 13,000 women have abortions each year following rape or incest.

Contraceptive Use

- 54% of women having abortions used a contraceptive method during the month they became pregnant.
- 8% of women having abortions have never used a method of birth control; nonuse is greatest among those who are young, unmarried, poor, black, Hispanic, or poorly educated.
- Nine in ten women at risk of unintended pregnancy are using a contraceptive method.
- 49% of the 6.3 million pregnancies that occur each year are unplanned.
- As much as 43% of the decline in abortion between 1994 and 2000 can be attributed to the use of emergency contraception.

Providers and Services

- In September 2000, the U.S. Food and Drug Administration approved the abortion drug mifepristone to be marketed in the U.S. as an alternative to surgical abortion.
- The number of abortion providers declined by 11% between 1996 and 2000 (from 2,042 to 1,819). 87% of all U.S. counties lacked an abortion provider in 2000. These counties were home to 34% of all 15–44-year-old women.
- 97% of abortion facilities provide abortion at eight weeks, and 86% provide services at 12 weeks, but provision drops off steeply after that, with only 13% of providers offering services at 24 weeks.
- A growing proportion of providers offers very early abortion (at four weeks gestation), an increase from 7% in 1993 to 37% in 2000.
- In 2000, the cost of a nonhospital abortion with local anesthesia at ten weeks of gestation ranged from $150 to $4,000, and the average amount paid was $372.
- Approximately 600 providers offered medical abortion in the first half of 2001.
- About 37,000 medical abortions were performed in the first half of 2001; these procedures involved the use of mifepristone and methotrexate.
- In nonhospital facilities offering mifepristone for use in medical abortion in 2000, the average cost of medical abortion was $490.

Source: Alan Guttmacher Institute, *Induced Abortion, Facts in Brief,* 2002. Web: www.guttmacher.org. Reprinted with permission.

Abortion Statistics, 1972–1999

	1972	1980	1985	1990	1995	1997	1999
Reported no. legal abortions	586,760	1,297,606	1,328,570	1,429,247	1,210,883	1,186,039	861,789
Abortion ratio[1]	180	359	354	344	311	306	256
Abortion rate[2]	13	25	24	24	20	20	17
				Percentage distribution			
Age group (yrs)							
≤19	32.6%	29.2%	26.3%	22.4%	20.1%	20.1%	19.2%
20–24	32.5	35.5	34.7	33.2	32.5	31.7	32.2
≥25	34.9	35.3	39.0	44.4	47.4	48.2	48.6
Marital status							
Married	29.7	23.1	19.3	21.7	19.7	19.0	19.2
Unmarried	70.3	76.9	80.7	78.3	80.3	81.0	80.8

NOTE: The number of areas reporting a given characteristic varied. 1. Number of legal induced abortions per 1,000 live births. 2. Number of legal induced abortions per 1,000 women aged 15–44 years. *Source:* U.S. Centers for Disease Control and Prevention. *Abortion Surveillance: Preliminary Analysis—United States, 1997.* Jan. 7, 2000.

Overview of Mental Illness

Source: Mental Health: A Report of the Surgeon General, 1999.

Mental illness is a term rooted in history that refers collectively to all of the diagnosable mental disorders. Mental disorders are characterized by abnormalities in cognition, emotion or mood, or the highest integrative aspects of behavior, such as social interactions or planning of future activities.

This overview of mental illness focuses on the most common of these disorders.

Anxiety

Anxiety is one of the most readily accessible and easily understood of the major symptoms of mental disorders. Each of us encounters anxiety in many forms throughout the course of our routine activities. Anxiety has evolved as a vitally important physiological response to dangerous situations that prepares one to evade or confront a threat in the environment. However, the mechanisms that regulate anxiety may break down in a wide variety of circumstances, leading to excessive or inappropriate expression of anxiety. Specific examples include phobias, panic attacks, and generalized anxiety. In phobias, high-level anxiety is aroused by specific situations or objects that may range from concrete entities such as snakes, to complex circumstances such as social interactions or public speaking. Panic attacks are brief and very intense episodes of anxiety that often occur without a precipitating event or stimulus. Generalized anxiety represents a more diffuse and nonspecific kind of anxiety that is most often experienced as excessive worrying, restlessness, and tension occurring with a chronic and sustained pattern. In each case, an anxiety disorder may be said to exist if the anxiety experienced is disproportionate to the circumstance, is difficult for the individual to control, or interferes with normal functioning.

In addition to these common manifestations of anxiety, obsessive-compulsive disorder and post-traumatic stress disorder are generally believed to be related to the anxiety disorders. In the case of obsessive-compulsive disorder, individuals experience a high level of anxiety that drives their obsessional thinking or compulsive behaviors. When such an individual fails to carry out a repetitive behavior such as hand washing or checking, there is an experience of severe anxiety. Post-traumatic stress disorder is produced by an intense and overwhelmingly fearful event that is often life-threatening in nature. The characteristic symptoms that result from such a traumatic event include the persistent reexperience of the event in dreams and memories, persistent avoidance of stimuli associated with the event, and increased arousal.

Psychosis

Disturbances of perception and thought process fall into a broad category of symptoms referred to as psychosis. The threshold for determining whether thought is impaired varies somewhat with the cultural context. Like anxiety, psychotic symptoms may occur in a wide variety of mental disorders. They are most characteristically associated with schizophrenia, but psychotic symptoms can also occur in severe mood disorders.

One of the most common groups of symptoms that result from disordered processing and interpretation of sensory information are hallucinations. Hallucinations are said to occur when an individual experiences a sensory impression that has no basis in reality. Hallucinations may be auditory, olfactory, gustatory, kinesthetic, tactile, or visual. For example, auditory hallucinations frequently involve the impression that one is hearing a voice. In each case, the sensory impression is falsely experienced as real.

A more complex group of symptoms resulting from disordered interpretation of information consists of delusions. A delusion is a false belief that an individual holds despite evidence to the contrary. A common example is paranoia, in which a person has delusional beliefs that others are trying to harm him or her. Attempts to convince the person that these beliefs are unfounded typically fail and may even result in the further entrenchment of the beliefs.

Hallucinations and delusions are among the most commonly observed psychotic symptoms. Symptoms of schizophrenia are divided into two broad classes: positive symptoms and negative symptoms. Positive symptoms generally involve the experience of something in consciousness that should not normally be present. For example, hallucinations and delusions represent perceptions or beliefs that should not normally be experienced. In addition to hallucinations and delusions, patients with psychotic disorders such as schizophrenia frequently have marked disturbances in the logical process of their thoughts. Specifically, psychotic thought processes are characteristically loose, disorganized, illogical,

Major diagnostic classes of mental disorders

The standard manual used for diagnosis of mental disorders in the United States, the *Diagnostic and Statistical Manual of Mental Disorders (DSM-IV)*, organizes mental disorders into 16 major diagnostic classes:

- Delirium, dementia, and amnestic and other cognitive disorders
- Mental disorders due to a general medical condition
- Substance-related disorders
- Schizophrenia and other psychotic disorders
- Mood disorders
- Anxiety disorders
- Somatoform disorders
- Factitious disorders
- Dissociative disorders
- Sexual and gender identity disorders
- Eating disorders
- Sleep disorders
- Impulse-control disorders
- Adjustment disorders
- Personality disorders
- Disorders of childhood and adolescence

or bizarre. The severe disturbances of thought content and process that comprise the positive symptoms often are the most recognizable and striking features of psychotic disorders such as schizophrenia or manic depressive illness.

However, in addition to positive symptoms, patients with schizophrenia and other psychoses have been noted to exhibit major deficits in motivation and spontaneity that are referred to as negative symptoms. While positive symptoms represent the presence of something not normally experienced, negative symptoms reflect the absence of thoughts and behaviors that would otherwise be expected. Concreteness of thought represents impairment in the ability to think abstractly. Blunting of affect refers to a general reduction in the ability to express emotion. Motivational failure and inability to initiate activities represent a major source of long-term disability in schizophrenia. Anhedonia reflects a deficit in the ability to experience pleasure and to react appropriately to pleasurable situations. Positive symptoms such as hallucinations are responsible for much of the acute distress associated with schizophrenia, but negative symptoms appear to be responsible for much of the chronic and long-term disability associated with the disorder.

Mood Disorders

Most of us have an immediate and intuitive understanding of the notion of mood. We readily comprehend what it means to feel sad or happy. These concepts are nonetheless very difficult to formulate in a scientifically precise and quantifiable way; the challenge is greater given the cultural differences that are associated with the expression of mood. Nevertheless, dysregulation of mood and the expression of mood, or affect, represent a major category among mental disorders.

Disturbances of mood characteristically manifest themselves as a sustained feeling of sadness or sustained elevation of mood. As with anxiety and psychosis, disturbances of mood may occur in a variety of patterns associated with different mental disorders. The disorder most closely associated with persistent sadness is major depression, while that associated with sustained elevation or fluctuation of mood is bipolar disorder. Along with the prevailing feelings of sadness or elation, disorders of mood are associated with a host of related symptoms that include disturbances in appetite, sleep patterns, energy level, concentration, and memory.

Disturbances of Cognition

Cognitive function refers to the general ability to organize, process, and recall information. Progressive deterioration of cognitive function is referred to as dementia. Dementia may be caused by a number of specific conditions including Alzheimer's disease. It is not uncommon to find profound disturbances of cognition in patients suffering from severe mood disturbances. More recently, cognitive deficits have been reported in schizophrenia and now have become a major new topic of research. Last, cognitive impairment frequently occurs in a host of chemical, metabolic, and infectious diseases that exert an impact on the brain.

Other Symptoms

Anxiety, psychosis, mood disturbances, and cognitive impairments are among the most common and disabling manifestations of mental disorders. It is important, however, to appreciate that mental disorders leave no aspect of human experience untouched. Other common manifestations include, for example, somatic or other physical symptoms and impairment of impulse control.

Overview of Drug Use in the United States

Source: Substance Abuse and Mental Health Services Administration.

The *National Household Survey on Drug Abuse,* an annual survey conducted by the Substance Abuse and Mental Health Services Administration, estimates the prevalence of illicit drug use in the United States. Some of the more notable statistics from the 2001 study follow.

• An estimated 15.9 million Americans age 12 years or older were current users of illicit drugs in 2001, meaning they used an illicit drug at least once during the 30 days prior to being interviewed. This represents 7.1% of the population 12 years or older. By comparison, in 2000 the survey found that 6.3% of this population were current illicit drug users. The survey also found statistically significant increases between 2000 and 2001 in the use of particular drugs or groups of drugs, such as marijuana (from 4.8% to 5.4%) and cocaine (0.5% to 0.7%), and the nonmedical use of pain relievers (1.2% to 1.6%) and tranquilizers (0.4% to 0.6%).

• Among youths aged 12–17 in 2001, 10.8% had used an illicit drug within the 30 days prior to being interviewed, compared to 9.7% in 2000. The rate was highest in 1979 (16.3%), declined to 5.3% in 1992, then increased to 10.9% in 1995.

• The number of persons reporting they had ever tried Ecstasy (MDMA) increased from 6.5 million in 2000 to 8.1 million in 2001. The number of current users was 786,000. The number of persons reporting use of Oxycontin for nonmedical purposes at least once in their lifetime increased fourfold from 1999 to 2001. The estimates were 221,000 in 1999; 399,000 in 2000; and 957,000 in 2001.

• Adults who used illicit drugs were twice as likely to have serious mental illness (SMI) as adults who did not use an illicit drug. Among adults who used an illicit drug in the past year, 16.6% had SMI during that period, while among adults who did not use an illicit drug the rate of SMI was 6.1%.

• Overall, an estimated 16.6 million persons age 12 or older were classified with dependence on or abuse of either alcohol or illicit drugs in 2001 (7.3% of the population). This was up from 14.5 million (6.5% of the population) in 2000. Of these, 2.4 million were classified with dependence or abuse of both alcohol and illicit drugs, 3.2 million were dependent on or abused illicit drugs but not alcohol, and 11.0 million were dependent on or abused alcohol but not illicit drugs.

Drug Use by Americans, 12 Years and Older

Type of drug	Ever used 1979	Ever used 1990	Ever used 2000	Ever used 2001	Current user 1979	Current user 1990	Current user 2000	Current user 2001
Any illicit drug[1]	n.a.	n.a.	38.9%	41.7%	n.a.	n.a.	6.3 %	7.1%
Marijuana and hashish	27.9 %	30.5 %	34.2	36.9	13.2 %	5.4%	4.8	5.4
Cocaine	8.6	11.2	11.2	12.3	2.6	0.9	0.5	0.7
Crack	n.a.	n.a.	2.4	2.8	n.a.	n.a.	0.1	0.2
Hallucinogens	8.9	7.9	11.7	12.5	1.9	0.4	0.4	0.6
LSD	n.a.	n.a.	8.8	9.0	n.a.	n.a.	0.2	0.1
PCP	n.a.	n.a.	2.6	2.7	n.a.	n.a.	0.0	0.0
Ecstasy	n.a.	n.a.	2.9	3.6	n.a.	n.a.	n.a.	0.3
Heroin	1.3	0.8	1.2	1.4	0.1	n.a.	0.1	0.1
Stimulants[2]	n.a.	5.5	6.6	7.1	n.a.	0.6	0.4	0.5
Methamphetamine	n.a.	n.a.	4.0	4.3	n.a.	n.a.	0.2	0.3
Sedatives[2]	n.a.	2.8	3.2	3.3	n.a.	0.2	0.1	0.1
Tranquilizers[2]	n.a.	4.0	5.8	6.2	n.a.	0.6	0.4	0.6

NOTE: Current users are those who used drugs at least once within month prior to this study. n.a. = not available. 1. Any illicit drug indicates use at least once of marijuana/hashish, cocaine (including crack), heroin, hallucinogens (including LSD and PCP), inhalants, or any prescription-type psychotherapeutic used nonmedically. 2. Nonmedical use; does not include over-the-counter drugs. *Source:* U.S. Substance Abuse and Mental Health Services Administration (SAMHSA), Office of Applied Studies, *National Household Survey on Drug Abuse.*

Smoking Prevalence Among U.S. Adults, 1965–2000
(as a percent of population, 18 years of age and older)

Year	Overall population	Males	Females	White male	Black male	White female	Black female
1965	41.9%	51.2%	33.7%	50.4%	58.8%	33.9%	31.8%
1985	29.9	32.2	27.9	31.3	40.2	27.9	30.9
1990	25.3	28.0	22.9	27.6	32.8	23.5	20.8
1995	24.6	26.5	22.7	26.2	29.4	23.4	23.5
2000	23.1	25.2	21.1	25.5	25.7	22.0	20.7

Source: Health, United States, 2002, Centers for Disease Control and Prevention.

Cigarette Consumption, United States, 1900–2002

Year	Total no. in billions	Year	Total no. in billions	Year	Total no. in billions	Year	Total no. in billions
1900	2.5	1930	119.3	1960	484.4	1990	525.0
1905	3.6	1935	134.4	1965	528.8	1995	487.0
1910	8.6	1940	181.9	1970	536.5	2000	430.0
1915	17.9	1945	340.6	1975	607.2	2001	425.0
1920	44.6	1950	369.8	1980	631.5	2002	420.0[2]
1925	79.8	1955	396.4	1985	594.0		

1. Preliminary. 2. Estimated. *Source: Tobacco Outlook Report,* Economic Research Service, U.S. Dept. of Agriculture.

Alcohol Consumption, 2000
(persons 18 years of age and over)

	Both sexes	Male	Female
Drinking status[1]			
All	100.0%	100.0%	100.0%
Lifetime abstainer	**24.1**	**17.5**	**29.9**
Former drinker	**14.4**	**14.9**	**14.2**
Infrequent	8.2	7.0	9.2
Regular	6.3	7.8	5.0
Current drinker	**61.5**	**67.7**	**55.8**
Infrequent	14.7	11.1	18.2
Regular	46.7	56.6	37.7

	Both sexes	Male	Female
Level of alcohol consumption in past year for current drinkers[2]			
All drinking levels	100.0%	100.0%	100.0%
Light	70.6	60.4	82.0
Moderate	22.2	32.0	11.5
Heavier	7.1	7.7	6.5
Number of days in the past year with 5 or more drinks			
All current drinkers	100.0%	100.0%	100.0%
No days	68.2	56.9	80.6
At least 1 day	31.8	43.1	19.4
1–11 days	17.4	21.2	13.3
12 or more days	14.4	21.9	6.1

1. Lifetime abstainers had fewer than 12 drinks in their lifetime. Former drinkers had at least 12 drinks in their lifetime and none in the past year. Former infrequent drinkers are former drinkers who had fewer than 12 drinks in any one year. Former regular drinkers are former drinkers who had at least 12 drinks in any one year. Current drinkers had 12 drinks in their lifetime and at least one drink in the past year. Current infrequent drinkers are current drinkers who had fewer than 12 drinks in the past year. Current regular drinkers are current drinkers who had at least 12 drinks in the past year. 2. Level of alcohol consumption categories are defined as follows: light drinkers, up to 3 drinks per week; moderate drinkers, 4–14 drinks per week for men and 4–7 drinks per week for women; heavier drinkers, more than 14 drinks per week for men and more than 7 drinks per week for women. *Source:* Centers for Disease Control and Prevention, *Health, United States, 2002.*

Caffeine Content of Selected Foods and Drugs

Product	Serving size[1]	Caffeine (mg)	Product	Serving size[1]	Caffeine (mg)
Over-the-counter drugs			**Soft drinks**		
Excedrin	2 tablets	130	Mountain Dew	12 ounces	55
Anacin	2 tablets	64	Diet Coke	12 ounces	47
Coffees			Coca-Cola	12 ounces	45
Coffee, brewed	8 ounces	135	Dr. Pepper	12 ounces	41
Coffee, instant	8 ounces	95	Sunkist Orange Soda	12 ounces	40
Coffee, decaffeinated	8 ounces	5	Pepsi-Cola	12 ounces	37
Teas			**Chocolates or candies**		
Tea, leaf or bag	8 ounces	50	Hershey Bar, 1 bar	1.5 ounces	10
Snapple Iced Tea	16-ounce bottle	48	Cocoa or hot chocolate	8 ounces	5
Tea, green	8 ounces	30			
Tea, instant	8 ounces	15			

1. Serving sizes are based on commonly eaten portions, pharmaceutical instructions, or the amount of the leading-selling container size. *Source:* Center for Science in the Public Interest. Reprinted/Adapted from *Nutrition Action Healthletter* (1875 Connecticut Ave., NW., Suite 300, Washington, DC 20009–5728).

The Food Pyramid: Healthy or Not?

The food pyramid, created by the U.S. Department of Agriculture (USDA), debuted in 1992. It is a guide to help people understand how to eat a healthy and balanced diet. In recent years, doctors and scientists have studied the food pyramid and have begun to question just how helpful—healthful—the guidelines really are. In fact, the USDA itself is reevaluating the food pyramid and may revise it in 2004.

The pyramid indicates that people should eat between 6 and 11 servings of grains a day. Grains include bread, pasta, and cereals. One serving equals one slice of bread or one-half cup of cooked rice or pasta. By recommending so many bread products, which are usually low in fat, the USDA has been promoting a low-fat diet. But many experts now believe that a low-fat diet that's high in sugar (most processed grains, such as white flour, are made out of forms of sugar like glucose and fructose) has actually led to an increase in obesity and heart problems.

Some doctors now contend that a diet higher in fat—with the fat coming from nuts, cheeses, some oils (such as olive oil), poultry, eggs, and a small amount of red meat—will keep people trimmer and healthier than a high-carbohydrate, low-fat diet.

So what should you eat? Eat a variety of foods from all five food groups: grains, vegetables, fruit, dairy (milk, yogurt, and cheese), and fats and oils. But when eating grains, try to avoid white bread and pasta and instead eat whole-grain foods, such as whole-wheat bread, oatmeal, whole-wheat crackers, and whole-wheat pasta. They contain more natural nutrients and are high in fiber. Fiber helps to lower cholesterol and may protect against some cancers.

Try to eat less red meat, such as hamburgers and steak, and more fish, nuts, and cheese. You won't go wrong eating lots of fruits and vegetables. Many vegetables have been found to reduce the risk of cancer, and fruits are a great source of many vitamins, such as vitamin C.

In addition, the USDA (United States Department of Agriculture) and HHS (Department of Health and Human Services) have developed seven guidelines to use along with the food pyramid:

1. Eat a variety of foods.
2. Exercise regularly and in proportion to the amount of food consumed.
3. Eat plenty of grains, vegetables, and fruits.
4. Keep intake of fat, saturated fat, and cholesterol low.
5. Keep intake of sugars moderate.
6. Keep intake of salt and sodium moderate.
7. Those who choose to drink alcoholic beverages should do so only in moderation.

Overweight and Obesity in the United States, 1960–2000

	Overweight[1] and obesity			Obesity[2]		
	1960–1962	1988–1994	1999–2000	1960–1962	1988–1994	1999–2000
Both sexes	**44.8%**	**56.0%**	**64.5%**	**13.3%**	**23.3%**	**30.9%**
Men	49.5	61.0	67.0	10.7	20.6	27.7
Women	40.2	51.2	62.0	15.7	26.0	34.0
White men	50.2	62.3	—	10.5	21.0	—
White women	37.5	49.4	—	14.2	24.3	—
Black men	43.9	58.0	—	14.0	21.1	—
Black women	59.2	68.5	—	26.8	39.0	—
Men						
20–34 yrs	42.7	47.5	58.0	9.2	14.1	24.1
35–44 yrs	53.5	65.5	67.6	12.1	21.5	25.2
45–54 yrs	53.9%	66.1%	71.3%	12.5%	23.2%	30.1%
55–64 yrs	52.2	70.5	72.5	9.2	27.2	32.9
65–74 yrs	47.8	68.5	77.2	10.4	24.1	33.4
75 and over	—	56.5	66.4	—	13.2	20.4
Women						
20–34 yrs	21.2	37.0	51.5	7.2	18.5	25.8
35–44 yrs	37.2	49.6	63.6	14.7	25.5	33.9
45–54 yrs	49.3	60.3	64.7	20.3	32.4	38.1
55–64 yrs	59.9	66.3	73.1	24.4	33.7	43.1
65–74 yrs	60.9	60.3	70.1	23.2	26.9	38.8
75 and over	—	52.3	59.6	—	19.2	25.1

Note: (—) = not available. 1. Body mass index (BMI) greater than or equal to 25. 2. BMI greater than or equal to 30. *Source: Health, United States, 2002,* Centers for Disease Control and Prevention.

Measuring Body Mass

Body mass index (BMI) is measure of body fat based on height and weight that applies to both adult men and adult women. To determine BMI, weight in kilograms is divided by height in meters, squared. To calculate your body mass index from the table below, locate your height in inches in the left-hand column, then follow it across until you locate your weight; the number at the very top is your body mass index. A BMI of less than 18.5 is considered underweight, 18.5 to 24.9 is considered normal weight, 25 to 29.9 is considered overweight, and one of 30 or above is considered obese.

Body Mass Index Chart

Height (inches)	19	20	21	22	23	24	25	26	27	28	29	30	31	32	33	34	35
	Body weight (pounds)																
58	91	96	100	105	110	115	119	124	129	134	138	143	148	153	158	162	167
59	94	99	104	109	114	119	124	128	133	138	143	148	153	158	163	168	173
60	97	102	107	112	118	123	128	133	138	143	148	153	158	163	168	174	179
61	100	106	111	116	122	127	132	137	143	148	153	158	164	169	174	180	185
62	104	109	115	120	126	131	136	142	147	153	158	164	169	175	180	186	191
63	107	113	118	124	130	135	141	146	152	158	163	169	175	180	186	191	197
64	110	116	122	128	134	140	145	151	157	163	169	174	180	186	192	197	204
65	114	120	126	132	138	144	150	156	162	168	174	180	186	192	198	204	210
66	118	124	130	136	142	148	155	161	167	173	179	186	192	198	204	210	216
67	121	127	134	140	146	153	159	166	172	178	185	191	198	204	211	217	223
68	125	131	138	144	151	158	164	171	177	184	190	197	203	210	216	223	230
69	128	135	142	149	155	162	169	176	182	189	196	203	209	216	223	230	236
70	132	139	146	153	160	167	174	181	188	195	202	209	216	222	229	236	243
71	136	143	150	157	165	172	179	186	193	200	208	215	222	229	236	243	250
72	140	147	154	162	169	177	184	191	199	206	213	221	228	235	242	250	258
73	144	151	159	166	174	182	189	197	204	212	219	227	235	242	250	257	265
74	148	155	163	171	179	186	194	202	210	218	225	233	241	249	256	264	272
75	152	160	168	176	184	192	200	208	216	224	232	240	248	256	264	272	279
76	156	164	172	180	189	197	205	213	221	230	238	246	254	263	271	279	287

Source: National Heart, Lung, and Blood Institute.

Prevalence of Overweight Among Children and Adolescents Ages 6-19 Years, 1963–2000

Age (years)[1]	1963–1965 1966–1970[2]	1971–1974	1976–1980	1988–1994	1999–2000
6–11	4%	4%	7%	11%	15%
12–19	5	6	5	11	15

1. Excludes pregnant women starting with 1971–1974. Pregnancy status not available for 1963–1965 and 1966–1970. 2. Data for 1963–1965 are for children 6–11 years of age; data for 1966–1970 are for adolescents 12–17 years of age, not 12–19 years. *Source:* Centers for Disease Control and Prevention, National Center for Health Statistics.

Physical Activity and Cardiovascular Health

- Cardiovascular disease (CVD) is the No. 1 killer in America. About 950,000 Americans died last year of CVD, accounting for over 40% of all deaths.
- Lack of physical activity is clearly shown to be a risk factor for coronary heart disease.
- Estimates are that up to 250,000 deaths per year in the U.S.—about 12% of total deaths—are due to a lack of regular physical activity.
- The relative risk of coronary heart disease associated with physical inactivity ranges from 1.5 to 2.4, an increase in risk comparable with that observed for high cholesterol, high blood pressure, and cigarette smoking.
- Less active, less fit persons have a 30–50% greater risk of developing high blood pressure.
- Participation in regular physical activity gradually increased during the 1960s, '70s, and early '80s, but seems to have leveled off in recent years.
- Surveys show that 28% of Americans age 18 or older aren't active at all. 44% of adults get some exercise, but they don't do it regularly or intensely enough to protect their hearts. Only 27% of American adults get enough leisure-time exercise to achieve cardiovascular fitness.
- People with lower incomes and less than a 12th grade education are more likely to be physically inactive.
- Of people age 55 and older, 38% report essentially sedentary lifestyles.
- Even low-to-moderate intensity activities, when done for as little as 30 minutes a day, can bring benefits. These activities include pleasure walking, climbing stairs, gardening, yard work, moderate-to-heavy housework, dancing, and home exercise.
- More vigorous aerobic activities, such as brisk walking, running, swimming, bicycling, roller skating, and jumping rope—done most days of the week for at least 30 minutes—are best for improving the fitness of the heart and lungs.

Percentage of Adults Engaging in Leisure Time Physical Activity, 2000

Characteristic	Persons who meet recom-mended activity[1]	Persons with insufficient activity[2]	Persons who are physically inactive[3]
Total	26.2%	46.2%	27.6%
Male	27.1	47.5	25.3
Female	25.5	44.8	29.7
White, non-Hispanic	27.5	48.3	24.2
Black, non-Hispanic	21.9	43.3	34.8
Hispanic	21.1	37.9	41.0
Other	27.3	42.9	29.8
Males			
18 to 29 years old	26.9	54.6	18.5
30 to 44 years old	23.7	52.2	24.2
45 to 64 years old	26.0	45.5	28.5
65 to 74 years old	33.7	38.7	27.6
75 years old and over	35.9	29.2	34.9
Females			
18 to 29 years old	25.4	49.3	25.3
30 to 44 years old	24.7%	47.1%	28.2%
45 to 64 years old	25.7	44.9	29.4
65 to 74 years old	24.6	40.9	34.4
75 years old and over	28.4	27.8	43.8
School years completed			
Less than 12 years	14.5	36.2	49.3
12 years	21.9	44.7	33.4
Some college	28.3	48.2	23.5
College	34.2	50.0	15.8
Household income			
Less than $10,000	18.9	36.7	44.5
$10,000 to $19,999	18.9	40.2	40.9
$20,000 to $34,999	23.3	44.3	32.4
$35,000 to $49,999	27.8	47.8	24.5
$50,000 and over	33.5	50.3	16.3

NOTE: Covers persons 18 years old and over. 1. Recommended activity is physical activity at least 5 times/week × 30 minutes/time or vigorous physical activity for 20 minutes at a time at least 3 times/week. 2. Persons whose reported physical activity does not meet recommended level. 3. Persons with no reported physical activity. *Source:* U.S. National Center for Chronic Disease Prevention and Health Promotion, "Nutrition and Physical Activity," and unpublished data. From *Statistical Abstract of the United States, 2002.*

Blood Types

Human blood is grouped into four types: A, B, AB, and O. Each letter refers to a kind of antigen, or protein, on the surface of red blood cells. For example, the surface of red blood cells in Type A blood has antigens known as A-antigens.

Each blood type is also grouped by its Rhesus factor, or Rh factor. Blood is either Rh positive (Rh+) or Rh negative (Rh-). About 85% of Americans have Rh+ blood.

Rhesus refers to another type of antigen, or protein, on the surface of red blood cells. The name Rhesus comes from Rhesus monkeys, in which the protein was discovered.

Blood types become very important when a blood transfusion is necessary. In a blood transfusion, a patient must receive a blood type that is compatible with his or her own blood type—that is, the donated blood must be accepted by the patient's own blood. If the blood types are not compatible, red blood cells will clump together, making clots that can block blood vessels and cause death.

Type O– blood is considered the "universal donor" because it can be donated to people of any blood type. Type AB+ blood is considered the "universal recipient" because people with this type can receive any blood type.

Blood type	Percent of Americans with this type	Who can receive this type
O+	37%	O+, A+, B+, AB+
O–	6	All blood types
A+	34	A+, AB+
A–	6	A+, A–, AB+, AB–
B+	10	B+, AB+
B–	2	B+, B–, AB+, AB–
AB+	4	AB+
AB–	1	AB+, AB–

Blood Pressure Explained

Blood pressure is the force of blood against the walls of arteries. Blood pressure is recorded as two numbers—the systolic pressure (as the heart beats) over the diastolic pressure (as the heart relaxes between beats). The measurement is written one above or before the other, with the systolic number on top and the diastolic number on the bottom. For example, a blood pressure measurement of 120/80 mm Hg (millimeters of mercury) is expressed verbally as "120 over 80."

Normal blood pressure is less than 120 mm Hg systolic and less than 80 mm Hg diastolic.

When systolic and diastolic blood pressures fall into different categories, the higher category should be used to classify blood pressure level. For example, 160/80 mm Hg would be stage 2 hypertension (high blood pressure).

	Blood pressure level (mm Hg)	
Category	Systolic	Diastolic
Normal	< 120	< 80
Prehypertension	120-139	80-89
High Blood Pressure		
Stage 1 hypertension	140-159	90-99
Stage 2 hypertension	≥160	≥100

NOTE: < means less than; ≥ means greater than or equal to. *Source:* National Heart, Lung, and Blood Institute.

It's All Free!

Music! Movies! TV shows! Millions of people download them every day. Is digital piracy killing the entertainment industry?

By LEV GROSSMAN TIME

James Phung saw *Phone Booth* before you did. What's more, he saw it for free, in the comfort of his private home-screening room. Phung isn't a movie star or a Hollywood insider; he's a junior at the University of Texas who makes $8 an hour at the campus computer lab. But many big-budget Hollywood movies have their North American premieres in his humble off-campus apartment. Like millions of other people, Phung downloads movies for free from the Internet, often before they hit theaters. "Basically," he says, "the world is at my fingertips."

Phung is the entertainment industry's worst nightmare, but he's very real, and there are a lot more like him. Quietly, with no sirens and no breaking glass, your friends and neighbors and colleagues and children are on a 24-hour virtual smash-and-grab looting spree, aided and abetted by the anonymity of the Internet. Every month they—or is it we?—download some 2.6 billion files illegally, and that's just music. That number doesn't include the movies, TV shows, software, and video games that circulate online. First-run films turn up online well before they hit the theaters. Albums debut on the Net before they have a chance to hit the charts. Somewhere along the line, Americans—indeed, computer users everywhere—have made a collective decision that since no one can make us pay for entertainment, we're not going to.

A Victimless Crime?

As crimes go, downloading has a distinctly victimless feel to it—can anything this fun be wrong?—but there are real consequences. Click by click, file by file, we are tearing the entertainment industry apart. CD shipments in 2002 were down 9%, on top of a 6% decline in 2001. A report by Internet services company Divine estimates pirates swap between 400,000 and 600,000 movies online every day. It's information-superhighway robbery.

If you ask the pirates, they'll say they're just fighting for their right to party. If you ask the suits, they'll say they're fighting for their lives. "If we let this stand, you're going to see the undoing of this society," says Jack Valenti, head of the Motion Picture Association of America (MPAA). "I didn't preside over this movie industry to see it disintegrate like the music industry." Them's fightin' words, and the battle lines are being drawn. Two recent landmark legal decisions, one in favor of the entertainment industry and one against it, will shape the way we deal with digital movies and music for years to come. The only thing left to decide is which side of those battle lines you're on.

It's easy to see why the pirates do what they do. Right now you can find thousands of free movies online if you know where to look. Just about every song ever released—as well as quite a few that haven't been—is available online for nothing more than the effort it takes to point and click. Record-industry types have a cute nickname for this phenomenon: "the celestial jukebox."

Most online piracy happens through what is called file-sharing software, such as Kazaa, Gnutella, and Direct Connect, that links millions of computers to one another over the Internet. File-sharing software takes advantage of the fact that music and movies are stored as digital data—they're not vinyl and celluloid anymore, but collections of disembodied, computerized bits and bytes that can be stored or played on a computer and transmitted over the Internet as easily as email. Using file-sharing software, people can literally browse through one another's digital music and movie collections, picking and choosing and swapping whatever they want. If you've never tried it, it's hard to describe how seductive it is. Start up a program like Kazaa, type in the name of your favorite rock band, and a list of song titles will instantly appear on your screen. See something you like, click on it, and it's yours. An average song might take two minutes to download to your computer if you have a broadband connection. Log on any night of the week and you'll find millions of users sharing hundreds of millions of songs, movies, and more.

Savvy Services Replace Napster

This isn't how it was supposed to be. A little more than three years ago the Recording Industry Association of America (RIAA), which represents most U.S. record labels, filed suit against Napster, the granddaddy of file-sharing services, for "contributory and vicarious copyright infringement." The RIAA won; Napster lost. A judge ordered its servers shut down. End of story?

Hardly. The file-sharing services didn't go away. They evolved, getting smarter and more decentralized and harder to shut down. Napster's network relied on a central server, an Achilles' heel that made it easier to unplug and shut down. But Kazaa, now the most popular file-sharing software, is built around a floating, distributed network of individual PCs that has no center. There's no single plug to pull. Kazaa has savvily chosen a decentralized business strategy too: it's a mirage of complicated partnerships with the official owner, Sharman Networks, tucked away on the South Pacific island of Vanuatu. So far, its diffuse structure has kept its management off U.S. soil and out of U.S. courtrooms.

It isn't just the file-sharing companies that are evolving; the Internet is too. Broadband Internet access has become cheaper and more widespread—analysts expect the number of households with broadband to jump 41% in 2003—and that means we can move bigger, fatter files in less and less time. Personal computers have also evolved. In 1992 the average hard drive was 120 megabytes. Now it's 40 gigabytes, 300 times as big—perfect for stashing whole libraries of audio and video. CD and DVD burners used to be expensive peripherals; now they come standard. Every new PC is a self-contained entertainment studio, right out of the box. What we have here is not a failure to communicate; it's a raging, runaway success.

CD Sales Take a Big Hit

For years people wondered whether all this downloading would actually affect the entertainment industry's bottom line. The figures provide the answer. According to Nielsen SoundScan, CD album sales slid from 712 million units in 2001 to 680 million in 2002. CD sales in the first quarter of 2003 were down 15 million units from 2002. Or look at it this way: in 2000 the top 10 albums in America sold 60 million copies; in 2001, 40 million; in 2002, 33 million. Nobody knows for sure exactly how much of the decline is caused by piracy, but it's safe to say the answer is somewhere between "some of it" and "most of it." Sure, the economy had a down year in 2002, but people found enough spare change in their couches to boost sales of MP3 players 56% over 2001. And while consumers bought about 680 million albums in 2002, they purchased 1.7 billion blank CDs—up 40% from the year before. The clear implication: users are downloading free music and burning it onto blank CDs.

Which isn't to say music executives are sitting around wringing their hands. It takes time for any corporation to recognize that its universe has changed, and major labels don't exactly turn on a dime.

Labels Fight Back

In 2001 EMI Music Publishing brought in new top management, including chairman of EMI Recorded Music Alain Levy, to help navigate the brave new digital world. The administration promptly laid off 1,800 employees (20% of EMI's staff), which helped absorb the impact when sales fell 10% in 2002—and created an executive position, global head of antipiracy. It also brought in executive vice president John Rose, an e-commerce ace from consulting firm McKinsey. "The fundamental premise of hiring someone like me," says Rose, "is that this industry needs to be re-engineered." EMI has held weekly three-hour lunch meetings with artists, managers, agents, and lawyers, a dozen at a time, to explain to them, as Rose puts it, "how the world needs to evolve."

First order of business: evolve some claws. Some labels (they're reluctant to identify themselves) hire professional counterhackers that specialize in electronic countermeasures such as "spoofing"—releasing dummy versions of popular songs onto file-sharing networks. To your average Kazaa user they look like the real thing, but when you download them, they turn out to be unplayable. Movie studios, meanwhile, staff screenings with ushers wearing night-vision goggles to suss out would-be pirates with camcorders. When Epic Records distributed review copies of the new Pearl Jam album in 2002, it sent them inside CD players that had been glued shut. The White Stripes went further: review copies of their new album *Elephant* were sent on good old-fashioned vinyl, which is trickier to copy. In the copy-protection wars, low tech is the new high tech.

Let the Legal Battles Begin

Of course, there's an even older-fashioned way to keep people from stealing your stuff. It's called the law. The legal landscape on which the war against piracy will be fought is being defined right now. In January 2003 a federal judge ruled that Verizon, a telephone company that is also an Internet service provider (ISP), must reveal the identity of one of its customers, a Kazaa user whom they suspect of downloading more than 600 songs.

The message is clear: If you're going to download music, don't expect to hide behind the anonymity of the Internet. On the other hand, if you're in the business of making file-sharing software, you have a lot less to worry about. In May 2003 a federal judge ruled that two companies—Grokster and StreamCast Networks, which makes a program called Morpheus—were not liable if users of their file-sharing software infringed on someone else's copyright. In his decision Judge Stephen Wilson cited the legal fuss that sprang up in the 1980s over Sony's Betamax technology. Like file sharing, it was a tool that could be used for both legal and illegal copying. Then, as now, the former was deemed to outweigh the latter.

The ruling tells us a lot about how the war against piracy will be fought. If file-sharing services won't sit still and be sued, individual users will make easier targets. Case in point: lawsuits filed in April 2003 against students at Princeton, Michigan Technological University, and Rensselaer Polytechnic Institute seek billions of dollars in damages—$150,000 for each pirated song. Nobody thinks piracy can be stopped by suing one user at a time, but if companies focus on major uploaders—people who make huge numbers of files available for others to download—a few high-profile busts may scare off some of the rest.

But the legal fight is far from a sure thing. Copyright laws are slippery and subjective—the judge in the Grokster case made a special plea in his ruling asking Congress to fix gaps in the laws that cover file sharing. Enforcing those laws is also tricky. Colleges, where a lot of the downloading goes on, like to think of themselves as bastions of privacy and free speech, not copyright police.

There's another problem with suing people: it doesn't make you popular with your customers—and Big Media are already fighting a major p.r. battle. Everybody who has ever watched VH1's *Behind the Music* has heard musicians bad-mouth their record labels, and no one is going to feel bad for ripping off the suits who ripped off their favorite rock star. But more and more artists have begun speaking out, and they stand a better chance of winning sympathy. Nelly, the Dixie Chicks, Brian Wilson, and the incontrovertibly cool Missy Elliott have delivered televised antipiracy scoldings.

The entertainment industry's grand plan for surviving piracy isn't just about the stick; there's a carrot too, a big one. The Internet offers a whole new way of selling music, and when music and movie executives are not expressing their outrage over downloading, they are salivating over a potentially massive revenue opportunity. There are already a couple of dozen legal, pay-to-play downloading services, including Apple's new iTunes Music Store, Pressplay, Listen.com's Rhapsody, and Music Net. Movie and TV downloading websites are sprouting up as well. Movielink, which is backed by five major Hollywood studios, features a library of more than 300 films. SoapCity.com offers online episodes of daytime serials.

A Future for Pay Services?

Until the spring of 2003, the future of online payment for downloading music seemed bleak. Take Pressplay, a pay service that offered upwards of 300,000 tracks. Membership started at $9.95 a month—and involved a mesh of restrictions that mired users in "can't-do" mode: Pressplay users can't download more than a limited number of songs, can't move the songs to a portable MP3 player, can't burn copies of them onto a CD, can't share them with friends unless they're also Pressplay subscribers. Miss a payment, and you can't download any more tunes.

Enter Apple Computer visionary Steve Jobs, who revitalized the hopes for online music payment with the debut of the Apple iTunes Music Store. The new program eliminated monthly fees and let people burn songs to an unlimited number of CDs and onto Apple's portable iPod music player. And users didn't have to download an entire album: they paid a basic rate of 99 cents per tune. In the first 18 hours after the Music Store went live on April 28, buyers paid for an estimated 275,000 songs, according to *Billboard* magazine.

The catch: 97% of America's computer users are on PCs, not Macs—and Apple's proprietary iTunes system, of course, works only on Macs. But there was no question that iTunes had broken new ground: here at last was a customer friendly, legal way to download music. The music industry and the PC world hastened to follow Apple's lead. If the retail music business is going to survive, this may be what it will look like.

Recorded entertainment has gone from an analog object to a disembodied digital spirit roaming the planet's information infrastructure at will, and all the litigation and legislation in the world won't change it back. The genie is out of the bottle, and we're fresh out of wishes. □

Unique Users of File-Sharing Applications

	Average month within quarter (thousands)			
	Napster	Kazaa	Audiogalaxy Satellite	Morpheus
1Q 2001	11,962	—	550	—
2Q 2001	8,264	519	719	808
3Q 2001	5,722	1,588	946	2,271
4Q 2001	2,960	2,998	1,832	4,884
1Q 2002	1,644	4,577	2,912	7,146
2Q 2002	1,060	7,278	3,132	3,758
3Q 2002	751	9,431	1,646	(1)

NOTE: File-sharing data indicate launch/usage of the stated services' client application by unique users at home. This table does not include all file-sharing applications. 1. Data not available. *Source:* comScore Media Metrix.

Online Activities by Age, 2002

Online activities	18–34	35–54	55+
Received and sent email	92%	93%	95%
Used a search engine	78	80	76
Participated in contests or sweepstakes	59	60	55
Gathered information on local events, restaurants, maps, or traffic	61	61	55
Sent electronic greeting/post card	49	54	57
Researched products and services	59	65	68
Used AOL Instant Messenger, ICQ, Yahoo Messenger, or similar instant message services	59%	49%	45%
Visited an online directory site to find addresses or phone numbers	46	45	46
Chatted online	48	38	31
Used the Internet to get the daily news	51	55	57
Travel research	41	47	54

Source: Jupiter Research.

Top Home Internet Access Providers

	Percentage of online users		
	Overall	Dial-up	Broadband
AOL	35%	39%	16%
MSN	14	14	8
Local Telco	9	8	20
Earthlink/Mindspring	6	6	4
AT&T	5	4	9
Free ISP	5%	5%	2%
CompuServe	3	3	1
RoadRunner	2	0	14
Other	21	20	28

Source: Jupiter Research.

Online Consumer Spending

(in millions of dollars)

Rank	Category	Full year 2002	Rank	Category	Full year 2002
1.	Travel	$30,246	6.	Event tickets	$2,116
2.	Computer hardware	10,107	7.	Home and garden	2,070
3.	Office	5,827	8.	Health and beauty	1,169
4.	Consumer electronics	3,735	9.	Sport and fitness	1,075
5.	Books	2,285	10.	Movies and video	956

NOTE: Ranking excludes auctions and large corporate purchases. *Source:* comScore Networks.

Percent of Households with Internet Access, 2001

	U.S.	Rural	Urban	Central cities
Total	**50.5%**	**48.7%**	**51.1%**	**45.7%**
Income				
Under $5,000	20.5	12.5	23.0	20.2
$5,000–$9,999	14.4	11.0	15.5	14.5
$10,000–$14,999	19.4	18.1	20.7	19.3
$15,000–$19,999	23.6	21.0	25.3	24.6
$20,000–$24,999	31.8	31.7	32.4	28.7
$25,000–$34,999	42.2	40.5	43.7	41.3
$35,000–$49,999	56.4	55.0	57.5	56.2
$50,000–$74,999	71.4%	70.6%	71.7%	70.5%
$75,000+	85.4	84.8	85.5	83.8
Race/Hispanic Origin				
White	55.4	51.0	56.8	54.8
Black	30.8	24.4	30.9	27.4
Asian American and Pacific Islander	68.1	68.2	64.1	63.1
Hispanic	32.0	29.9	32.6	29.8

Source: NTIA and ESA, U.S. Dept. of Commerce, using U.S. Bureau of the Census Current Population Survey supplements.

Internet Use from Any Location by Individuals Age Three and Older

	Internet use (percent of total U.S. population)			
	Oct. 1997	Dec. 1998	Aug. 2000	Sept. 2001
Total[1]	22.2%	32.7%	44.4%	53.9%
Gender				
Male	24.3	34.2	44.6	53.9
Female	20.2	31.4	44.2	53.8
Race/origin				
White	25.3	37.6	50.3	59.9
Black	13.2	19.0	29.3	39.8
Asian American & Pacific Islander	26.4	35.8	49.4	60.4
Hispanic	11.0	16.6	23.7	31.6
Family income				
Less than $15,000	9.2	13.7	18.9	25.0
$15,000–$24,999	11.6	18.4	25.5	33.4
$25,000–$34,999	17.1	25.3	35.7	44.1
$35,000–$49,999	22.8	34.7	46.5	57.1
$50,000–$74,999	32.3	45.5	57.7	67.3
$75,000 & above	44.5	58.9	70.1	78.9
Educational attainment[2]				
Less than high school	1.8%	4.2%	8.8%	12.8%
High school diploma or GED	9.7	19.2	30.6	39.8
Some college	24.8	38.6	54.2	62.4
Bachelor's degree	41.4	58.4	72.5	80.8
Beyond bachelor's degree	51.9	66.4	78.5	83.7
Age group				
Age 3–8	7.2	11.0	15.3	27.9
Age 9–17	33.2	43.0	53.4	68.6
Age 18–24	31.6	44.3	56.8	65.0
Age 25–49	27.1	40.9	55.4	63.9
Age 50+	11.2	19.3	29.6	37.1

1. U.S. population: 1997: 255,689,000; 1998: 258,453,000; 2000: 262,620,000; 2001: 265,180,000. 2. Age 25 and older. *Source:* U.S. Bureau of the Census, Current Population Survey supplements, Oct. 1997, Dec. 1998, Aug. 2000, and Sept. 2001.

U.S. Household PC Growth and Penetration

Year	PC households: Number (in millions)	Percent	Year	PC households: Number (in millions)	Percent
2001	71.1	67%	2005[1]	84.1	75%
2002	74.1	69	2006[1]	86.7	77
2003[1]	77.5	71	2007[1]	88.7	78
2004[1]	80.8	73			

1. Projected. *Source:* Jupiter Research.

Home Internet Connection Type

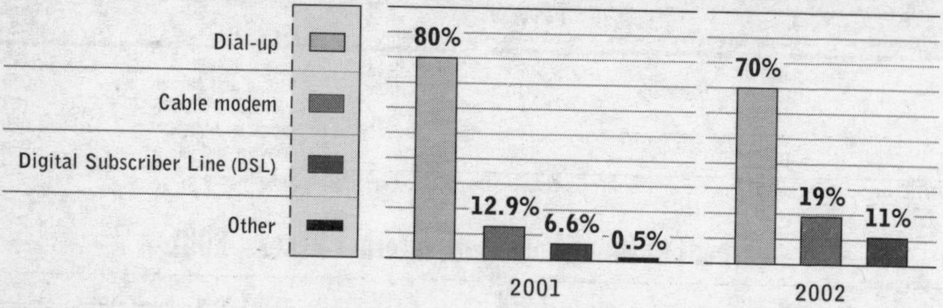

Sources: 2001: NTIA and ESA, U.S. Department of Commerce, using U.S. Census Bureau Current Population Survey supplements. 2002: Leichtman Research Group, Inc.

Percent of Households with a Computer, 1998 and 2001

	1998	2001
All	42.1%	56.5%
Race/Hispanic Origin		
White Non-Hispanic	46.6	61.1
Black Non-Hispanic	23.2	37.1
Asian American & Pacific Islander	55.0	72.7
Hispanic	25.5	40.0
Income		
Under $5,000	15.9	25.9
$5,000–9,999	12.3	19.2
$10,000-14,999	15.9	25.7
$15,000-19,999	21.2	31.8
$20,000-24,999	25.7	40.1
$25,000–34,999	35.8	49.7
$35,000–49,999	50.2%	64.3%
$50,000–74,999	66.3	77.7
$75,000 and above	79.9	89.0
Education		
Elementary	7.9	16.0
Some high school	15.7	28.2
High school graduate or GED	31.2	46.5
Some college	49.3	64.5
Bachelor's degree or more	68.7	79.8
Geographic location		
Rural	39.9	55.6
Urban	42.9	56.7
Central city	38.5	51.5

Source: U.S. Department of Commerce, National Telecommunications and Information Administration.

Top 15 Countries in Internet Usage, 2002

	Internet users (in thousands)	Share %
1. U.S.	160,700	24.13%
2. Japan	64,800	9.73
3. China	54,500	6.71
4. Germany	30,350	8.18
5. UK	27,150	4.08
6. South Korea	26,900	4.04
7. Italy	20,850	3.13
8. Canada	17,830	2.68
9. France	16,650	2.50
10. India	16,580	2.49%
11. Brazil	15,840	2.38
12. Russia	13,500	2.03
13. Australia	10,450	1.57
14. Spain	10,390	1.56
15. Taiwan	9,510	1.43
Top 15 Total	**496,000**	**74.48**
Worldwide Total	**665,910**	**100.00**

Source: Computer Industry Almanac Inc. Web: www.c-i-a.com. Reprinted with permission.

Largest Search Engines, January 2003

		Worldwide English speaking	United States
1.	Google	33%	23%
2.	Yahoo!	24	26
3.	MSN Search	19%	17%
4.	AOL	12	20

Note: Figures represent share of worldwide and U.S. consumer searches. *Source:* comScore Media Metrix.

Top Domains/Websites, April 2003

		Unique visitors (thousands)			
		Total	Home	Work	Colleges/universities
	Total Internet	**145,588**	**125,379**	**48,690**	**10,173**
1.	AOL Time Warner Network	109,766	86,844	34,403	8,295
2.	MSN-Microsoft sites	107,709	85,826	40,413	8,106
3.	Yahoo! sites	106,022	83,345	36,405	8,032
4.	eBay	55,740	40,557	20,664	4,152
5.	Google sites	55,100	41,104	20,055	4,951
6.	About/Primedia	46,658	30,450	17,049	3,952
7.	Terra Lycos	45,410	29,984	16,086	3,873
8.	Gator Network	36,228	22,876	13,686	3,200
9.	Amazon sites	35,267	23,019	13,002	2,830
10.	Viacom Online	27,124	18,006	8,901	2,107
11.	InfoSpace Network	26,552	16,663	9,930	1,837
12.	CNET networks	25,233	14,704	10,903	2,430
13.	Walt Disney Internet Group (WDIG)	25,051	16,839	9,033	1,492
14.	Real.com Network	23,143	13,178	9,809	1,677
15.	eUniverse Network	22,523	15,233	6,718	1,583
16.	AT&T properties	21,915	15,228	7,784	1,254
17.	Classmates.com sites	21,524	14,071	7,053	1,320
18.	Vivendi-Universal sites	20,742	12,532	7,350	1,777
19.	Excite Network	20,064	13,915	8,030	1,192
20.	The Weather Channel	19,523	12,930	8,289	1,558

NOTE: Audience: All persons at U.S. home/work/college-university locations. *Source:* comScore Media Metrix (comScore Media Metrix is a division of comScore Networks, Inc.).

Top Entertainment Sites, April 2003

		Unique visitors (thousands)			
		Total	Home	Work	Colleges/universities
	Total Internet	**145,588**	**125,379**	**48,690**	**10,173**
	Entertainment category	**116,388**	**92,129**	**39,721**	**8,432**
1.	Viacom Online	27,124	18,006	8,901	2,107
2.	WindowsMedia	25,564	14,133	9,994	2,500
3.	Real.com Network	23,143	13,178	9,809	1,677
4.	eUniverse Network	22,523	15,233	6,718	1,583
5.	Sony Online	16,498	10,562	5,583	1,302
6.	AOL Prop Entertainment	13,312	10,047	3,084	788
7.	MSN Entertainment	12,815	7,123	5,953	824
8.	Cox Enterprises Inc.	12,414	7,983	4,339	864
9.	Disney Online	12,271	8,927	3,386	520
10.	UGO networks	11,893	7,440	4,025	1,458

NOTE: Audience: All persons at U.S. home/work/college-university locations. *Source:* comScore Media Metrix (comScore Media Metrix is a division of comScore Networks, Inc.).

Top General News Sites, April 2003

		Unique visitors (thousands)			
		Total	Home	Work	Colleges/universities
	Total Internet	**145,588**	**125,379**	**48,690**	**10,173**
	General news category	**85,193**	**63,621**	**32,834**	**5,686**
1.	CNN	25,657	15,477	10,735	1,614
2.	MSNBC	25,479	14,505	12,503	1,359
3.	AOL Prop News	25,137	19,461	6,045	1,389
4.	Yahoo! News	21,417	13,315	9,642	1,327
5.	New York Times Digital	12,182	7,818	5,118	733
6.	ABC News Digital	8,768	4,847	4,004	497
7.	Knight Ridder Digital	7,181	4,315	3,210	477
8.	BBC Sites	6,412	3,410	2,876	515
9.	CBS Sites	6,190	3,667	2,409	387
10.	Foxnews.com	5,873	3,124	3,037	239

NOTE: Audience: All persons at U.S. home/work/college-university locations. *Source:* comScore Media Metrix (comScore Media Metrix is a division of comScore Networks, Inc.).

Top Travel Sites, April 2003

		Unique visitors (thousands)			
		Total	Home	Work	Colleges/universities
	Total Internet	**145,588**	**125,379**	**48,690**	**10,173**
	Travel category	**65,977**	**48,041**	**24,945**	**4,190**
1.	Mapquest.com	26,263	17,123	9,911	1,708
2.	Expedia Travel	14,716	9,095	6,085	741
3.	Orbitz.com	12,874	8,354	4,961	638
4.	Travelocity	11,123	7,332	4,339	498
5.	Trip Network Inc.	10,931	6,504	4,220	623
6.	AOL Prop Travel	6,759	5,097	1,437	349
7.	Southwest.com	5,870	3,753	2,166	301
8.	Priceline.com	5,411	3,435	1,960	310
9.	Hotwire.com	5,411	3,053	2,187	264
10.	Yahoo! Travel	4,717	2,844	1,843	264

NOTE: Audience: All persons at U.S. home/work/college-university locations. *Source:* comScore Media Metrix (comScore Media Metrix is a division of comScore Networks, Inc.).

Internet Timeline

1969 ARPA (Advanced Research Projects Agency) goes online in December, connecting four major U.S. universities. Designed for research, education, and government organizations, it provides a communications network linking the country in the event that a military attack destroys conventional communications systems.

1972 Electronic mail is introduced by Ray Tomlinson, a Cambridge, Mass., computer scientist. He uses the @ to distinguish between the sender's name and network name in the email address.

1973 Transmission Control Protocol/Internet Protocol (TCP/IP) is designed and in 1983 it becomes the standard for communicating between computers over the Internet. One of these protocols, FTP (File Transfer Protocol), allows users to log onto a remote computer, list the files on that computer, and download files from that computer.

1976 Presidential candidate Jimmy Carter and running mate Walter Mondale use email to plan campaign events.

Queen Elizabeth sends her first email. She's the first state leader to do so.

1982 The word "Internet" is used for the first time.

1984 Domain Name System (DNS) is established, with network addresses identified by extensions such as .com, .org, and .edu.

Writer William Gibson coins the term "cyberspace."

1985 Quantum Computer Services, which later changes its name to America Online, debuts. It offers email, electronic bulletin boards, news, and other information.

1988 A virus called the Internet Worm temporarily shuts down about 10% of the world's Internet servers.

1989 The World (world.std.com) debuts as the first provider of dial-up Internet access for consumers.

The first effort to index the Internet is created by Peter Deutsch at McGill University in Montreal, who devises Archie, an archive of FTP sites. Another indexing system, WAIS (Wide Area Information Server), is developed by Brewster Kahle of Thinking Machines Corp. Tim Berners-Lee of CERN (European Laboratory for Particle Physics) develops a new technique for distributing information on the Internet, which eventually is called the World Wide Web. The Web is based on hypertext, which permits the user to connect from one document to another at different sites on the Internet via hyperlinks (specially programmed words, phrases, buttons, or graphics). Unlike other Internet protocols, such as FTP and email, the Web is accessible through a graphical user interface.

1991 Gopher, which provides point-and-click navigation, is created at the University of Minnesota and named after the school mascot. Gopher becomes the most popular interface for several years.

1993 Mosaic is developed by Marc Andreeson at the National Center for Supercomputing Applications (NCSA). It becomes the dominant navigating system for the World Wide Web, which at this time accounts for merely 1% of all Internet traffic.

1994 The White House launches its website, www.whitehouse.gov.

Initial commerce sites are established and mass marketing campaigns are launched via email, introducing the term "spamming" to the Internet vocabulary.

Marc Andreessen and Jim Clark start Netscape Communications. They introduce the Navigator browser.

1995 CompuServe, America Online, and Prodigy start providing dial-up Internet access.

Sun Microsystems releases the Internet programming language called Java.

The Vatican launches its own website, www.vatican.va.

1996 Approximately 45 million people are using the Internet, with roughly 30 million of those in North America (United States and Canada), 9 million in Europe, and 6 million in Asia/Pacific (Australia, Japan, etc.). 43.2 million (44%) U.S. households own a personal computer, and 14 million of them are online.

1997 On July 8, 1997, Internet traffic records are broken as the NASA website broadcasts images taken by *Pathfinder* on Mars. The broadcast generates 46 million hits in one day.

1999 College student Shawn Fanning invents Napster, a computer application that allows users to swap music over the Internet.

The number of Internet users worldwide reaches 150 million by the beginning of 1999. More than 50% are from the United States.

"E-commerce" becomes the new buzzword as Internet shopping rapidly spreads.

2000 To the chagrin of the Internet population, deviant computer programmers begin designing and circulating viruses with greater frequency. "Love Bug" and "Stages" are two examples of self-replicating viruses that send themselves to people listed in a computer user's email address book. The heavy volume of email messages being sent and received forces many infected companies to temporarily shut down their clogged networks.

The Internet bubble bursts, as the fountain of investment capital dries up and the Nasdaq stock index plunges, causing the initial public offering (IPO) window to slam shut and many dotcoms to close their doors.

2001 Napster is dealt a potentially fatal blow when the 9th U.S. Circuit Court of Appeals in San Francisco rules that the company is violating copyright laws and orders it to stop distributing copyrighted music. The file-swapping company says it is developing a subscription-based service.

About 9.8 billion electronic messages are sent daily.

2002 As of January, 58.5% of the U.S. population (164.14 million people) uses the Internet. Worldwide there are 544.2 million users.

2003 It's estimated that Internet users illegally download about 2.6 billion songs each month.

Spam, unsolicited email, becomes a server-clogging menace. It accounts for about half of all emails.

Apple Computer introduces Apple iTunes Music Store, which allows people to download songs for 99 cents each.

Sources for this timeline include International Data Corporation, the W3C Consortium, Nielsen/NetRatings, and the Internet Society.

Top-Selling Software, 2002

Rank	Title	Publisher	Average price
1.	TurboTax 2001 Deluxe	Intuit	$38.88
2.	Norton Antivirus 2002 8.0	Symantec	44.42
3.	MS Campus Agreement 3.0 Lic	Microsoft	14.62
4.	TurboTax 2001	Intuit	19.88
5.	TurboTax 2001 Multi State 45	Intuit	29.41
6.	The Sims: Vacation Expansion Pack	Electronic Arts	$28.46
7.	Taxcut 2001 Deluxe	Block Financial	24.77
8.	The Sims: Unleashed Expansion Pack	Electronic Arts	27.96
9.	MS Windows XP Home Ed Upgr	Microsoft	97.91
10.	MS Windows 2000 Svr Clnt Acc OPEN Mnt Lic	Microsoft	16.69

Source: NPD Group/NPDTechworld. Web: www.npd.com.

Top-Selling Education Software, 2002

Rank	Title	Publisher	Average price
1.	Adventure Workshop 1st-3rd Grade	Riverdeep Interactive	$18.77
2.	Instant Immersion Spanish JC	Topics Entertainment	9.94
3.	Mavis Beacon Teaches Typing 12.0	Riverdeep Interactive	19.43
4.	Dora The Explorer Backpack Adventure	Infogrames Entertainment	17.76
5.	Adventure Workshop Preschool-1st Grade	Riverdeep Interactive	18.13
6.	Adventure Workshop 4th-6th Grade	Riverdeep Interactive	$18.62
7.	Instant Immersion Spanish	Topics Entertainment	18.04
8.	I Spy Treasure Hunt	Scholastic	20.77
9.	Blue's ABC Time Activities JC	Infogrames Entertainment	9.90
10.	Clifford Reading	Scholastic	18.53

Source: NPD Group/NPDTechworld. Web: www.npd.com.

Top-Selling Game Software, 2002

Rank	Title	Publisher	Average price
1.	The Sims: Vacation Expansion Pack	Electronic Arts	$28.46
2.	The Sims: Unleashed Expansion Pack	Electronic Arts	27.96
3.	Warcraft III: Reign Of Chaos	Vivendi Universal Publishing	54.28
4.	Medal Of Honor: Allied Assault	Electronic Arts	44.36
5.	The Sims	Electronic Arts	$41.93
6.	The Sims: Hot Date Expansion Pack	Electronic Arts	28.69
7.	The Sims Deluxe	Electronic Arts	40.74
8.	MS Zoo Tycoon	Microsoft	26.82
9.	Harry Potter & The Sorcerer's Stone	Electronic Arts	26.12
10.	Roller Coaster Tycoon 2	Infogrames Entertainment	27.29

Source: NPD Group/NPDTechworld. Web: www.npd.com.

The 160,000-Year-Old Man

New fossils prove that the first *Homo sapiens* looked like us, walked like us, and in some ways acted like us as well

By MICHAEL D. LEMONICK and ANDREA DORFMAN TIME

The village of Herto, in the Middle Awash region of Ethiopia, is surrounded by sparse patches of dry, scrubby vegetation, barely enough to sustain the sheep, cattle, and goat herds of the seminomadic Afar people who live there. But 160,000 years ago, conditions were far different: a shallow lake sat here, teeming with hippos, crocodiles, and catfish. The lush grasslands that surrounded its pebble-strewn shores were filled with lions, zebras, and antelopes as well as another creature, which traveled on two legs rather than four. Our distant ancestors had walked the earth for millions of years by this time, and although they stood upright, many looked more like apes than like us.

These hominids were different. Properly dressed, they could walk down New York City's Fifth Avenue without attracting a second glance. Many of the hallmarks of modern humanity, including art, culture, spoken language, and civilization, were probably still tens of thousands of years in the future. But for the first time in history, evolution had produced creatures that looked like us and—at least in some ways—acted like us as well.

Our First True Ancestors?

Until now, paleontologists could only speculate about the existence of such people. But an international research team co-directed by Tim White of the University of California, Berkeley, reported in *Nature* in June 2003, that it has finally unearthed the long-sought fossil remains of what could be the very first true *Homo sapiens,* dated to between 160,000 and 154,000 years ago. And because of the quality of the specimens and where they were discovered, they cast new light on several of paleontology's thorniest questions.

The discovery was largely an accident, one that never would have happened if not for El Niño. Back in 1997, the Pacific Ocean disturbance that affects much of the world's weather triggered punishing rains in Ethiopia. The deluges not only exposed buried fossils but also drove away the people of Herto and their livestock, which would have trampled the fragile bones. When White and the others happened to drive by the village, they noticed a fossil hippo skull poking out of the ancient sand. On closer examination, the skull bore marks indicating that the animal had been gashed with a stone tool. Clearly, human ancestors had once lived there.

When the scientists returned 11 days later, it took them only minutes to find the skulls of two adults, probably male. Six days after that, Berhane Asfaw of Ethiopia's Rift Valley Research Service found a third, the skull of a 6- or 7-year-old child, shattered into about 200 pieces. After years of painstaking cleaning, reassembly, and study, the team was confident enough to tell the world that it had found the earliest true remains of *Homo sapiens*—older by at least 1,000 generations than anything previously discovered. "It's not a modern human," says White, "but it's so close that there's no doubt it will become one. The child, in particular, is so like us that you couldn't distinguish it in a population of modern human children."

Out of Africa

White and his colleagues think these hominids are distinctive enough to merit their own subspecies, which the team has dubbed *Homo sapiens idaltu.* (*Idàltu* means elder in the Afar language.) But whether or not the nomenclature holds up, says paleoanthropologist G. Philip Rightmire of the State University of New York at Binghamton, "the key point is that they are from the right place at the right time to be, broadly speaking, the ancestor of modern people. It's as near as we're going to get."

The find lays to rest a long-standing dispute about another breed of hominid, the Neanderthals. "It's now clear," says White, "that there were anatomically modern humans in Africa long before there were classic Neanderthals in Europe." This means that the more primitive Neanderthals could not, as some have argued, have been our ancestors. They were almost certainly a side branch on the evolutionary tree, and that branch died out some 30,000 years ago.

Another controversial point has to do with where modern humans first appeared. Everyone agrees that a hominid called *Homo erectus* left its African home some 2 million years ago to populate the Middle East, Asia, and Europe. Long after that, argues one camp, *Homo sapiens* evolved, also in Africa, and began a second exodus. In contrast to this out-of-Africa scenario, the so-called multiregionalists say there was no second sojourn. The far-flung *Homo erectus* communities and their descendants, the multiregionalists believe, could have interbred enough that *Homo sapiens* appeared pretty much everywhere at once.

Genetic analysis tends to refute this claim. Among other things, Africans are more genetically diverse than any other people on Earth, which suggests that they have had longer to differentiate. And populations in eastern Africa, where most of the oldest hominid fossils have been found, are the most diverse of all. Finding this most ancient of *Homo sapiens* in Africa pretty much settles the argument. "It's not just another nail in the coffin for the multiregional view," says Rightmire. "It lowers the coffin into the ground." Declares White: "This is what stepped out of Africa."

Perhaps the most intriguing discovery, however, is that these ancestors behaved like us in at least one poignant way: all three skulls were deliberately tampered with after death, evidently as part of some sort of mortuary practice. "This," says White, "is the earliest evidence of hominids continuing to handle skulls long after the individual died."

"Handle" is an understatement. Cut marks on the skulls indicate that the overlying skin, muscles, nerves, and blood vessels were removed, probably with an obsidian flake. Then a stone tool was scraped back and forth, creating faint clusters of parallel lines. The modification of the child's skull is even more dramatic. The lower jaw was detached, and soft tissues at the base of the head were cut away, leaving fine, deep cut marks. Portions of the skull were smoothed and polished.

"The cut marks aren't a classic sign of cannibalism," White pointed out while showing the skulls to a TIME reporter in Addis Ababa. "If you wanted to get at the brain in order to eat it, you'd just smash open the skull." Instead, he suspects, the scratches might be a form of decoration. As for the polished areas, he says, "we know they weren't caused by the environment, because the marks go across the breaks between the recovered pieces. The child's skull looks as though it has been fondled repeatedly."

Despite this evidence of ritualistic behavior, *Homo sapiens* still had a long way to go. What may be the earliest art, for example—pieces of red ocher engraved with abstract designs found in South Africa—would not appear for nearly 80,000 more years, while the spectacular cave paintings in Spain and France would not be created for another 40,000 years after that. Clearly, being like us physically was not enough by itself to trigger the cultural complexity—innovation, creativity, symbolism, and perhaps spoken language—that distinguishes us from all other animals.

So what triggered those changes? Theories include hardships of the last Ice Age or random genetic mutations, but nobody really knows. Which is why paleontologists like White and Asfaw are going back to search for new clues in the ancient soil of eastern Africa. □

See also "Roundup of Recent Discoveries," pp. 572–574.

Major Discoveries About Human Ancestors

Living and extinct human beings and their near-human ancestors are called "hominids" and belong to the *Hominidae* family of primates. They should not be confused with "hominoids," which belong to the *Hominoidea* superfamily of primates and include apes and humans. Scientists theorize that the human and ape lines branched off from a common ancestor 8 million to 6 million years ago.

Years ago	Species	Discovered	Remarks
5.8–5.2 million	*Ardipithecus ramidus kadabba*	1997–1998 in Alayla, Ethiopia	Oldest known human ancestor. About the size of modern chimpanzees, or 4 ft tall standing. Walked upright
c. 4.4 million	*Ardipithecus ramidus ramidus*	1994 in Aramis, Ethiopia	Similar to *A. ramidus kadabba*
c. 4.2 million	*Australopithecus anamensis*	1995, two sites at Lake Turkana in Kenya: Kanapoi and Allia Bay	Possible ancestor of *A. afarensis* (Lucy). Walked upright
c. 3.2 million	*Australopithecus afarensis*	1974 at Hadar in the Afar triangle of eastern Ethiopia; Laetoli, Tanzania	Nicknamed "Lucy." Her skeleton was 3.5 ft (100 cm) tall. Had apelike skull. Walked fully upright. Lived in family groups throughout eastern Africa
c. 2.5 million	*Australopithecus africanus*	1924 at Taung, northern Cape Province, South Africa	Descendant of "Lucy." Lived in social groups
c. 2 million	*Australopithecus robustus*	1938 in Kromdraai, South Africa	Was related to *A. africanus*
c. 2 million	*Homo habilis* ("skillful" or "handy man")	1960 in Olduvai Gorge, Tanzania	First brain enlargement; is believed to have used stone tools
c. 1.8 million	*Homo erectus* ("upright man")	1891 at Trinil, Java, Indonesia	Brain size twice that of *australopithecine* species. "Java Man" may have been a direct ancestor of *Homo sapiens* or instead developed on a separate evolutionary track. He is the first hominid to use fire and the hand ax, and to live in caves
c. 160,000(?)	*Homo sapiens idaltu* ("knowing or wise elder man")	1997, Herto, Middle Awash region, Ethiopia	Anatomically modern humans
c. 100,000(?)	*Homo sapiens sapiens* ("knowing or wise man")	1868, Cro-Magnon, France	Anatomically modern humans

The Periodic Table

Although some elements, such as gold and iron, have been known to humans since prehistoric times, it wasn't until the 17th century that the first scientific discovery of an element (phosphorus) was made. Only 12 elements were known prior to 1700, but as more and more elements were discovered—by 1900 there were more than 80—scientists tried to find a way to organize them systematically, according to their physical and chemical properties.

Today, the periodic table (*see* opposite) organizes the elements in horizontal rows, or periods, by order of increasing atomic number, which equals the number of protons in the atomic nucleus of each element. The elements are also organized in vertical columns, or groups, based on similar physical characteristics and chemical behavior. This arrangement developed side by side with atomic theory over about 200 years, and it continues to evolve as new elements are discovered.

Early Attempts

One of the earliest attempts to organize the elements based on their chemical and physical properties was made by German chemist Johann Dobereiner. In 1817 Dobereiner noticed that certain elements that were chemically similar could be grouped together in threes, for example, calcium, strontium, and barium; lithium, sodium, and potassium; chlorine, bromine, and iodine. In each group of three, the atomic weight of one element fell halfway between the atomic weights of the other two elements. The pattern seemed too remarkable to be a coincidence. Based on his findings, Dobereiner proposed the Law of Triads in 1829. His work soon prompted other scientists to find patterns among even larger groups of elements.

Another attempt to systematically organize the elements based on their properties was made by the French geologist Alexandre-Émile Beguyer de Chancourtois in 1862. He devised a kind of spiral graph that was arranged on a cylinder, with the elements ordered by increasing atomic weight and with similar elements lined up vertically. De Chancourtois was the first to notice the periodicity of the elements, that is, when the elements were arranged according to their atomic weights, similar elements seemed to occur at regular intervals.

A year later, the English chemist John Newlands also attempted to classify the known elements of his day based on their atomic weight. Like de Chancourtois, he noticed a repeating pattern—every eighth element had similar properties. Newlands called this the Law of Octaves. Although the tables worked out by both de Chancourtois and Newlands were important precursors to the periodic table, neither received much attention at the time.

Mendeleev

The next milestone in the development of the periodic table was set by the Russian chemist Dmitri Mendeleev, who is generally acknowledged as the "father" of the modern periodic table. Mendeleev wrote out the names of the elements, along with their atomic weights and other properties, on cards, which he then laid out in rows and columns much like a game of solitaire. When the elements were ordered according to atomic weight, Mendeleev, like de Chancourtois and Newlands, could see that certain chemical properties were repeated periodically; however, not all the elements fit this pattern neatly. Mendeleev's solution was to move certain elements to new positions, despite their accepted weight, in order to group them with other elements sharing similar properties. (Nearly half a century later, after the periodic table was revised according to atomic number rather than atomic weight, these elements fell into place.)

Mendeleev's work on periodic law—which states that the properties of elements recur periodically as their atomic weights increase—was announced in 1869. At about the same time, a German chemist named Julius Lothar Meyer independently arrived at a periodic table that was remarkably similar to Mendeleev's. Unfortunately for Meyer, Mendeleev presented his work to the scientific community first. However, Mendeleev's table was also superior to Meyer's because he left a number of empty spaces to account for elements that were yet to be discovered.

20th-Century Revisions

The first major change to the periodic table occurred following the discovery of an entirely new group of elements, the noble gases, between 1895 and 1901. They were called the noble gases because they were believed to be inert—incapable of reacting with other elements to form compounds. (Today it is known that they do enter into chemical combinations, only reluctantly.) These elements were simply added on in a separate column under helium.

The first major revision of the entire periodic table was carried out by Henry Gwyn-Jeffries Moseley, an English physicist who began his research under Ernest Rutherford. In 1914, Moseley showed that each atomic nucleus could be assigned a number that was equal to the number of units of positive charge (later identified as "protons") associated with it. Once the periodic table was reorganized according to this atomic number instead of atomic weight, the few discrepancies in Mendeleev's system disappeared.

Over the years other revisions of the table have been made, including the incorporation of the rare-earth elements (lanthanide series) and the synthetic elements (technetium, promethium, and all the elements with atomic number 93 or higher). The actinides, which are radioactive and mainly synthetic, and the lanthanides do not fit into the same pattern of repeated properties as the other elements, so they are generally shown below the periodic table in separate rows. Most of these changes were the work of American chemist Glenn Seaborg, who codiscovered elements 94 (plutonium) through 102 (nobelium) between 1940 and 1958. Seaborg also suggested a superactinide series of elements, with atomic numbers 122 through 153, but so far none of these has been synthesized or detected. □

Periodic Table of Elements

Key: Group (1) · Number (1) · Period (1) · Symbol (H) · Name (Hydrogen) · Weight (1.00794)

Period	1	2	3	4	5	6	7	8	9	10	11	12	13	14	15	16	17	18
1	1 H Hydrogen 1.00794																	2 He Helium 4.002602
2	3 Li Lithium 6.941	4 Be Beryllium 9.012182											5 B Boron 10.811	6 C Carbon 12.0107	7 N Nitrogen 14.0067	8 O Oxygen 15.9994	9 F Flourine 18.9984032	10 Ne Neon 20.1797
3	11 Na Sodium 22.98977	12 Mg Magnesium 24.305											13 Al Aluminum 26.981538	14 Si Silicon 28.0855	15 P Phosphorus 30.973761	16 S Sulfur 32.065	17 Cl Chlorine 35.453	18 Ar Argon 39.948
4	19 K Potassium 39.0983	20 Ca Calcium 40.078	21 Sc Scandium 44.95591	22 Ti Titanium 47.867	23 V Vanadium 50.9415	24 Cr Chromium 51.9961	25 Mn Manganese 54.938049	26 Fe Iron 55.845	27 Co Cobalt 58.9332	28 Ni Nickel 58.6934	29 Cu Copper 63.546	30 Zn Zinc 65.39	31 Ga Gallium 69.723	32 Ge Germanium 72.64	33 As Arsenic 74.9216	34 Se Selenium 78.96	35 Br Bromine 79.904	36 Kr Krypton 83.8
5	37 Rb Rubidium 85.4678	38 Sr Strontium 87.62	39 Y Yttrium 88.90585	40 Zr Zirconium 91.224	41 Nb Niobium 92.90638	42 Mo Molybdenum 95.94	43 Tc Technetium 98[1]	44 Ru Ruthenium 101.07	45 Rh Rhodium 102.9055	46 Pd Palladium 106.42	47 Ag Silver 107.8682	48 Cd Cadmium 112.411	49 In Indium 114.818	50 Sn Tin 118.71	51 Sb Antimony 121.76	52 Te Tellurium 127.60	53 I Iodine 126.90447	54 Xe Xenon 131.293
6	55 Cs Cesium 132.90545	56 Ba Barium 137.327	*	72 Hf Hafnium 178.49	73 Ta Tantalum 180.9479	74 W Tungsten 183.84	75 Re Rhenium 186.207	76 Os Osmium 190.23	77 Ir Iridium 192.217	78 Pt Platinum 195.078	79 Au Gold 196.96655	80 Hg Mercury 200.59	81 Tl Thallium 204.3833	82 Pb Lead 207.2	83 Bi Bismuth 208.98038	84 Po Polonium 209[1]	85 At Astatine 210[1]	86 Rn Radon 222[1]
7	87 Fr Francium 223[1]	88 Ra Radium 226[1]	**	104 Rf Rutherfordium 261[1]	105 Db Dubnium 262[1]	106 Sg Seaborgium 266[1]	107 Bh Bohrium 264[1]	108 Hs Hassium 277[1]	109 Mt Meitnerium 268[1]	110 Uun Ununnilium 281[1]	111 Uuu Unununium 272[1]	112 Uub Ununbium 285[1]	113 – (-)	114 Uuq Ununquadium 289[1]	115 – (-)	116 – (-)	117 – (-)	118 – (-)

Alkali Metals ☐ Alkaline Earth Metals ☐ Transition Metals ☐ Other Metals ☐ Non-Metals ☐ Noble Gases ☐

Series	Period															
*Lanthanide Series	6	57 La Lanthanum 138.9055	58 Ce Cerium 140.116	59 Pr Praseodymium 140.90765	60 Nd Neodymium 144.24	61 Pm Promethium 145[1]	62 Sm Samarium 150.36	63 Eu Europium 151.964	64 Gd Gadolinium 157.25	65 Tb Terbium 158.92534	66 Dy Dysprosium 162.5	67 Ho Holmium 164.93032	68 Er Erbium 167.259	69 Tm Thulium 168.93421	70 Yb Ytterbium 173.04	71 Lu Lutetium 174.967
**Actinide Series	7	89 Ac Actinium 227[1]	90 Th Thorium 232.0381	91 Pa Protactinium 231.03588	92 U Uranium 238.02891	93 Np Neptunium 237[1]	94 Pu Plutonium 244[1]	95 Am Americium 243[1]	96 Cm Curium 247[1]	97 Bk Berkelium 247[1]	98 Cf Californium 251[1]	99 Es Einsteinium 252[1]	100 Fm Fermium 257[1]	101 Md Mendelevium 258[1]	102 No Nobelium 259[1]	103 Lr Lawrencium 262[1]

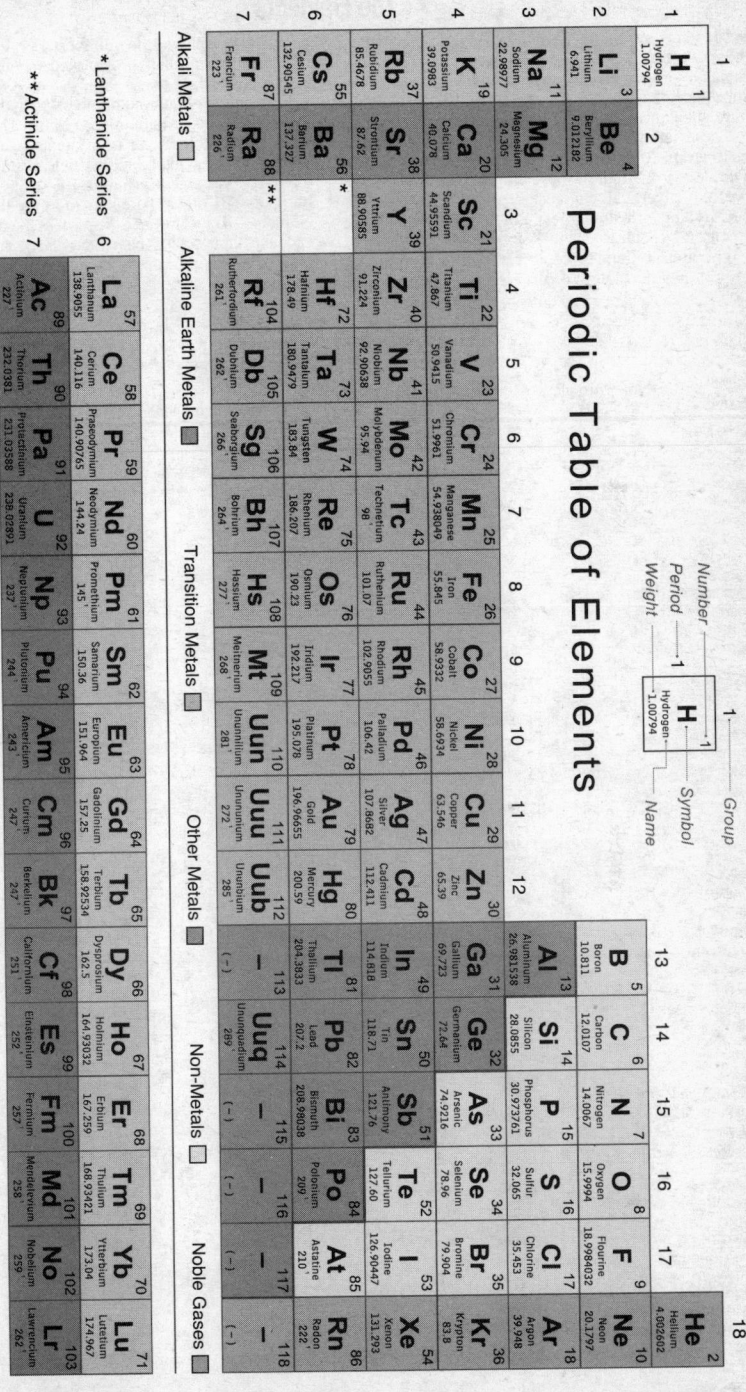

Notes: Elements 110, 111, 112, and 114 are under review. A temporary system of naming recommended by J. Chatt has been used above. 1. Mass number of the longest-lived isotope that is known. *Source*: International Union of Pure and Applied Chemistry (IUPAC). Web: http://www.chem.qmv.ac.uk/iupac/AtWt/

The Elements

Elements are the building blocks of nature. Water, for example, is a compound consisting of the elements hydrogen and oxygen. Each element is a pure substance that cannot be split up into any simpler pure substance.

The smallest particle of an element that can exist is an atom. An atom consists of subatomic particles. The most important of these are protons, which have positive electrical charges; electrons, which have negative electrical charges; and neutrons, which are electrically neutral.

The atomic number of an element is the number of protons in one atom of the element. Each element has a different atomic number. For example, the atomic numbers of hydrogen and oxygen are 1 and 8, respectively.

Elements with atomic numbers 1 (hydrogen) to 94 (plutonium) occur naturally on Earth. The remaining artificial elements have been created since 1940 by using nuclear reactors and particle accelerators. Element 100 is named fermium. Elements with atomic numbers 101 onward are known as the transfermium elements. They are also known as heavy elements because their atoms have very large masses compared with atoms of hydrogen, the lightest of all elements.

Chemical Elements

Element	Symbol	Atomic no.	Atomic wt.	Specific gravity	Melting point °C	Boiling point °C	No. of isotopes[1]	Discoverer	Year
Actinium	Ac	89	227[2]	10.07[3]	1051	3198	11	Debierne/Giesel	1899/1902
Aluminum	Al	13	26.981538	2.6989	660.32	2519	8	Wöhler	1827
Americium	Am	95	243[2]	13.67	1176	2011	13[4]	Seaborg et al.	1944
Antimony	Sb	51	121.76	6.61	630.63	1587	29	Early historic times	—
Argon	Ar	18	39.948	1.7837[5]	−189.35	−185.85	8	Rayleigh and Ramsay	1894
Arsenic (gray)	As	33	74.9216	5.73	817	603	14	Albertus Magnus	1250
Astatine	At	85	210[2]	—	302	—	21	Corson et al.	1940
Barium	Ba	56	137.327	3.5	727	1897	25	Davy	1808
Berkelium	Bk	97	247[2]	14.00[6]	1050 (α form)	—	8[4]	Seaborg et al.	1949
Beryllium	Be	4	9.012182	1.848	1287	2471	6	Vauquelin	1798
Bismuth	Bi	83	208.98038	9.747	271.40	1564	19	Geoffroy the Younger	1753
Bohrium	Bh	107	264[2]	—	—	—	—	Armbruster and Münzenberg	1981
Boron	B	5	10.811	2.37[7]	2075	4000	6	Gay-Lussac and Thénard; Davy	1808
Bromine	Br	35	79.904	3.12[5]	−7.2	58.8	19	Balard	1826
Cadmium	Cd	48	112.411	8.65	321.07	767	22	Stromeyer	1817
Calcium	Ca	20	40.078	1.55	842	1484	14	Davy	1808
Californium	Cf	98	251[2]	—	900	—	12[4]	Seaborg et al.	1950
Carbon	C	6	12.0107	1.8–3.5[8]	4492 (graphite)	3825	7	Prehistoric	—
Cerium	Ce	58	140.116	6.771	798	3443	19	Berzelius and Hisinger; Klaproth	1803
Cesium	Cs	55	132.90545	1.873	28.5	671	22	Bunsen and Kirchoff	1860
Chlorine	Cl	17	35.453	1.56[5]	−101.5	−34.04	11	Scheele	1774
Chromium	Cr	24	51.9961	7.18-7.20	1907	2671	9	Vauquelin	1797
Cobalt	Co	27	58.9332	8.9	1495	2927	14	Brandt	c.1735
Copper	Cu	29	63.546	8.96	1084.62	2562	11	Prehistoric	—
Curium	Cm	96	247[2]	13.51[3]	1345	3100	13[4]	Seaborg et al.	1944
Dubnium	Db	105	262[2]	—	—	—	—	Ghiorso et al.	1970
Dysprosium	Dy	66	162.5	8.540	1412	2567	21	de Boisbaudran	1886
Einsteinium	Es	99	252[2]	—	860	—	12[4]	Ghiorso et al.	1952
Erbium	Er	68	167.259	9.045	1529	2868	16	Mosander	1843
Europium	Eu	63	151.964	5.283	822	1529	21	Demarcay	1901
Fermium	Fm	100	257[2]	—	1527	—	10[4]	Ghiorso et al.	1953
Fluorine	F	9	18.9984032	1.108[5]	−219.67	−188.12	6	Moissan	1886
Francium	Fr	87	223[2]	—	27	—	21	Perey	1939
Gadolinium	Gd	64	157.25	7.898	1313	3273	17	de Marignac	1880
Gallium	Ga	31	69.723	5.904	29.76	2204	14	de Boisbaudran	1875
Germanium	Ge	32	72.64	5.323	938.25	2833	17	Winkler	1886
Gold	Au	79	196.96655	19.32	1064.18	2856	21	Prehistoric	—
Hafnium	Hf	72	178.49	13.31	2233	4603	17	Coster and von Hevesy	1923
Hassium	Hs	108	277[2]	—	—	—	—	Armbruster and Münzenberg	1983
Helium	He	2	4.002602	0.1785[5]	−272.2	−268.934	5	Janssen	1868
Holmium	Ho	67	164.93032	8.781	1474	2700	29	Delafontaine and Soret	1878
Hydrogen	H	1	1.00794	0.070[5]	−259.34	−252.87	3	Cavendish	1766
Indium	In	49	114.818	7.31	156.60	2072	34	Reich and Richter	1863
Iodine	I	53	126.90447	4.93	113.7	184.4	24	Courtois	1811
Iridium	Ir	77	192.217	22.42	2446	4428	25	Tennant	1804
Iron	Fe	26	55.845	7.894	1538	2861	10	Prehistoric	—
Krypton	Kr	36	83.8	3.733[5]	−157.38	−153.22	23	Ramsay and Travers	1898
Lanthanum	La	57	138.9055	6.166	918	3464	19	Mosander	1839
Lawrencium	Lr	103	262[2]	—	1627	—	20[4]	Ghiorso et al.	1961
Lead	Pb	82	207.2	11.35	327.46	1749	29	Prehistoric	—

Element	Symbol	Atomic no.	Atomic wt.	Specific gravity	Melting point °C	Boiling point °C	No. of isotopes[1]	Discoverer	Year
Lithium	Li	3	6.941	0.534	180.50	1342	5	Arfvedson	1817
Lutetium	Lu	71	174.967	9.835	1663	3402	22	Urbain/ von Welsbach	1907
Magnesium	Mg	12	24.305	1.738	650	1090	8	Black	1755
Manganese	Mn	25	54.938049	7.21–7.44[9]	1246	2061	11	Gahn, Scheele, and Bergman	1774
Meitnerium	Mt	109	268[2]	—	—	—	—	GSI, Darmstadt, West Germany	1982
Mendelevium	Md	101	258[2]	—	827	—	3[4]	Ghiorso et al.	1955
Mercury	Hg	80	200.59	13.546	–38.83	356.73	26	Prehistoric	—
Molybdenum	Mo	42	95.94	10.22	2623	4639	20	Scheele	1778
Neodymium	Nd	60	144.24	6.80 & 7.004[9]	1021	3074	16	von Welsbach	1885
Neon	Ne	10	20.1797	0.89990 (g/10°C/1 atm)	–248.59	–246.08	8	Ramsay and Travers	1898
Neptunium	Np	93	237[2]	20.25	644		15[4]	McMillan and Abelson	1940
Nickel	Ni	28	58.6934	8.902	1455	2913	11	Cronstedt	1751
Niobium (Columbium)	Nb	41	92.90638	8.57	2477	4744	24	Hatchett	1801
Nitrogen	N	7	14.0067	0.808[5]	–210.00	–195.79	8	Rutherford	1772
Nobelium	No	102	259[2]	—	827	—	7[4]	Ghiorso et al.	1958
Osmium	Os	76	190.23	22.57	3033	5012	19	Tennant	1803
Oxygen	O	8	15.9994	1.14[5]	–218.79	–182.95	8	Priestley/Scheele	1774
Palladium	Pd	46	106.42	12.02	1554.9	2963	21	Wollaston	1803
Phosphorous (white)	P	15	30.973761	1.82	44.15	280.5	7	Brand	1669
Platinum	Pt	78	195.078	21.45	1768.4	3825	32	Ulloa/Wood	1735/1741
Plutonium	Pu	94	244[2]	19.84	640	3228	16[4]	Seaborg et al.	1940
Polonium	Po	84	209[2]	9.32	254	962	34	Curie	1898
Potassium	K	19	39.0983	0.862	63.5	759	10	Davy	1807
Praseodymium	Pr	59	140.90765	6.772	931	3520	15	von Welsbach	1885
Promethium	Pm	61	145[2]	—	1042	3000	14	Marinsky et al.	1945
Protactinium	Pa	91	231.03588	15.37[3]	1572	—	14	Hahn and Meitner	1917
Radium	Ra	88	226[2]	5.0?	700	—	15	Pierre and Marie Curie	1898
Radon	Rn	86	222[2]	4.4[5]	–71	–61.7	20	Dorn	1900
Rhenium	Re	75	186.207	21.02	3186	5596	21	Noddack, Berg, and Tacke	1925
Rhodium	Rh	45	102.9055	12.41	1964	3695	20	Wollaston	1803
Rubidium	Rb	37	85.4678	1.532	39.30	688	20	Bunsen and Kirchoff	1861
Ruthenium	Ru	44	101.07	12.44	2334	4150	16	Klaus	1844
Rutherfordium	Rf	104	261[2]	—	—	—	—	Ghiorso et al.	1969
Samarium	Sm	62	150.36	7.536	1074	1794	17	Boisbaudran	1879
Scandium	Sc	21	44.95591	2.989	1541	2836	15	Nilson	1878
Seaborgium	Sg	106	266[2]	—	—	—	—	Ghiorso et al.	1974
Selenium (gray)	Se	34	78.96	4.79	220.5	685	20	Berzelius	1817
Silicon	Si	14	28.0855	2.33	1414	3265	8	Berzelius	1824
Silver	Ag	47	107.8682	10.5	961.78	2162	27	Prehistoric	—
Sodium	Na	11	22.98977	0.971	97.80	883	7	Davy	1807
Strontium	Sr	38	87.62	2.54	777	1382	18	Davy	1808
Sulfur	S	16	32.065	2.07[9]	95.3 (rhombic)	444.60	10	Prehistoric	—
Tantalum	Ta	73	180.9479	16.654	3017	5458	19	Ekeberg	1801
Technetium	Tc	43	98[2]	11.50[3]	2157	4265	23	Perrier and Segré	1937
Tellurium	Te	52	127.60	6.24	449.51	988	29	von Reichenstein	1782
Terbium	Tb	65	158.92534	8.234	1356	3230	24	Mosander	1843
Thallium	Tl	81	204.3833	11.85	304	1473	28	Crookes	1861
Thorium	Th	90	232.0381	11.72	1750	4788	12	Berzelius	1828
Thulium	Tm	69	168.93421	9.314	1545	1950	18	Cleve	1879
Tin (white)	Sn	50	118.71	7.31	231.93	2602	28	Prehistoric	—
Titanium	Ti	22	47.867	4.55	1668	3287	9	Gregor	1791
Tungsten	W	74	183.84	19.3	3422	5555	22	J. and F. d'Elhuyar	1783
Uranium	U	92	238.02891	19.05	1135	4131	15	Peligot	1841
Vanadium	V	23	50.9415	6.11	1910	3407	9	del Rio	1801
Xenon	Xe	54	131.293	3.52[5]	–111.79	–108.12	31	Ramsay and Travers	1898
Ytterbium	Yb	70	173.04	6.972	819	1196	16	Marignac	1878
Yttrium	Y	39	88.90585	4.457	1522	3345	21	Gadolin	1794
Zinc	Zn	30	65.39	7.133	419.5	907	15	Prehistoric	—
Zirconium	Zr	40	91.224	6.506[3]	1855	4409	20	Klaproth	1789

NOTES: Elements 110, 111, 112, and 114 are under review and are thus not included. ≈ means "approximately." < means "less than." 1. Isotopes are different forms of the same element having the same atomic number but different atomic weights. 2. Mass number of the longest-lived isotope that is known. 3. Calculated figure. 4. Artificially produced. 5. Liquid. 6. Estimated. 7. Amorphous. 8. Depending on whether amorphous, graphite, or diamond. 9. Depending on allotropic form.

Scientific Classification

Classification, or taxonomy, is a system of categorizing living things. There are seven divisions in the system: (1) Kingdom; (2) Phylum or Division; (3) Class; (4) Order; (5) Family; (6) Genus; (7) Species.

Kingdom is the broadest division. Most scientists support a four-kingdom (Animalia, Plantae, Protista, and Monera) or five-kingdom (Animalia, Plantae, Protista, Monera, and Fungi) system. The lowest division is species, which consists of organisms that are capable of interbreeding to produce fertile offspring. Species are identified by two names (binomial nomenclature). The first name is the genus, the second is the species.

For example, a lion is *Panthera leo,* a tiger is *Panthera tigris.* The first word is always capitalized, the second is not, and both should be italicized. Humans, of course, are *Homo sapiens.* The full classification for a lion would be: Kingdom, Animalia (animals); Phylum, Chordata (vertebrate animals); Class, Mammalia (mammals); Order, Carnivora (meat eaters); Family, Felidae (all cats); Genus, Panthera (great cats); Species, leo (lions).

Table of Geological Periods

It is generally assumed that planets are formed by the accretion of gas and dust in a cosmic cloud, but there is no way of estimating the length of this process. Our Earth acquired its present size, more or less, between 4 billion and 5 billion years ago. Life on Earth originated about 2 billion years ago, but there are no good fossil remains from periods earlier than the Cambrian, which began about 550 million years ago. The largely unknown past before the Cambrian Period is referred to as the Pre-Cambrian and is subdivided into the Lower (or older) and Upper (or younger) Pre-Cambrian—also called the Archaeozoic and Proterozoic Eras.

The known geological history of Earth since the Cambrian Period is subdivided into three eras, each of which includes a number of periods. They, in turn, are subdivided into subperiods. In a subperiod, a certain section may be especially well known because of rich fossil finds.

Paleozoic Era

This era began 570 million years ago and lasted for 325 million years. The name was compounded from Greek *palaios* (old) and *zoön* (animal).

Period	Duration[1]	Subperiods	Events
Cambrian (from *Cambria,* Latin name for Wales)	60	Lower Cambrian Middle Cambrian Upper Cambrian	Invertebrate sea life of many types proliferating during this and the following period
Ordovician (from Latin *Ordovices,* people of early Britain)	70	Lower Ordovician Upper Ordovician	First known fishes
Silurian (from Latin *Silures,* people of early Wales)	30	Lower Silurian Upper Silurian	Gigantic sea scorpions
Devonian (from Devonshire in England)	50	Lower Devonian Upper Devonian	Proliferation of fishes and other forms of sea life; land still largely lifeless
Carboniferous (from Latin *carbo* = coal + *fero* = to bear)	70	Lower or Mississippian Upper or Pennsylvanian	Period of maximum coal formation in swampy forests; early insects and first known amphibians
Permian (from district of Perm in Russia)	45	Lower Permian Upper Permian	Early reptiles and mammals; earliest form of turtles

1. In millions of years.

Mesozoic Era

This era began 245 million years ago and lasted for 180 million years. The name was compounded from Greek *mesos* (middle) and *zoön* (animal). Popular name: Age of Reptiles.

Period	Duration[1]	Subperiods	Events
Triassic (from *trias* = triad)	37	Lower or Buntsandstein (from German *bunt* = colorful + *sandstein* = sandstone). Middle or Muschelkalk (from German *muschel* = shell + *kalk* = limestone). Upper or Keuper (old miner's term)	Early saurians (reptiles that resemble lizards)
Jurassic (from Jura Mountains)	62	Lower or Black Jurassic, or Lias (from French *liais* = hard stone) Middle or Brown Jurassic, or Dogger (old provincial English for ironstone) Upper or White Jurassic, or Malm (Middle English for sand)	Many seagoing reptiles; early large dinosaurs; somewhat later, flying reptiles (pterosaurs), earliest known birds
Cretaceous (from Latin *creta* = chalk)	81	Lower Cretaceous Upper Cretaceous	Maximum development of dinosaurs; birds proliferating; opossumlike mammals

1. In millions of years.

Cenozoic Era

This era began 65 million years ago and includes the geological present. The name was compounded from Greek *kainos* (new) and *zoön* (animal). Popular name: Age of Mammals.

Period	Duration[1]	Subperiods	Events
Tertiary (originally thought to be the third of only three periods)	c. 65	Paleocene (from Greek *palaios* = old + *kainos* = new). Eocene (from Greek *eos* = dawn + *kainos* = new). Oligocene (from Greek *oligos* = few + *kainos* = new). Miocene (from Greek *meios* = less + *kainos* = new). Pliocene (from Greek *pleios* = more + *kainos* = new)	First mammals not marsupials. Formation of amber, rich insect fauna, early bats, steady increase of large mammals. Mammals closely resembling present types; protohumans
Pleistocene (from Greek *pleistos* = most + *kainos* = new) (popular name: Ice Age)	2.0	Four major glaciations, named Günz, Mindel, Riss, and Würm, originally the names of rivers. Last glaciation ended 10,000 to 15,000 years ago	Various forms of early humans
Holocene (from Greek *holos* = entire + *kainos* = new)	0.01	The last 10,000 years to the present	Earliest written documents c. 3200 B.C., Sumer

1. In millions of years.

Branches of Science

Science describes an area of knowledge, typically about something in the physical world, that can be explained in terms of scientific observation or the scientific method. The scientific method is a discovery process that has evolved over several hundred years and can be summarized as follows:

- a phenomenon in the physical world is observed
- an explanation, or hypothesis, for the phenomenon is formed
- the hypothesis is tested by means of objective, reproducible experiments

If the results of the experiments support the hypothesis, it becomes accepted as scientific theory. Later, if new information is found to contradict the hypothesis, it may be revised or abandoned in favor of a new hypothesis, which is then subjected to additional experiments.

The sciences that describe the physical universe are categorized in different ways. The largest distinction in science is whether a science is pure, or theoretical, or whether it is applied, or practical. Pure science explains a phenomenon, while applied science determines how a particular phenomenon may be put to use. In general, pure science is divided into the following categories:

- Physical sciences, which deal with matter and energy and allow us to describe the material universe in terms of weight, mass, volume, and other standard, objective measures.
- Earth sciences, which explain the phenomena of the Earth, its atmosphere, and the solar system to which it belongs.
- Life sciences, which describe living organisms, their internal processes, and their relationship to each other and the environment.

However, these three categories of pure science have areas of overlap, where one type of phenomenon may be associated with another. For example, light (studied in physics) is the energy source behind the (chemical) process of photosynthesis, or food production, in plants (studied in biology). For this reason, distinctions between pure sciences, and even between pure and applied sciences, can blur, and a new compound science can develop. An example of this is biochemistry, in which the chemical processes of living things (such as photosynthesis) are observed and explained.

Physical sciences	Life sciences	Earth sciences
Physics Kinetics Mechanics Electromagnetics Thermodynamics	Biology Botany Zoology	Geology Meteorology Astronomy
Chemistry Inorganic Chemistry Electrochemistry Analytical Chemistry		
	Examples of Overlapping Sciences	
Physics + Chemistry = Physical Chemistry	Biology + Chemistry = Biochemistry Organic Chemistry	Geology + Chemistry = Geochemistry
Astronomy + Physics = Astrophysics	Biology + Geology = Paleontology	Geology + Astronomy = Astrogeology
	Biology + Astronomy + Physics = Astronautics	

Roundup of Recent Discoveries

Vital Stats of the Universe

In one of the most important cosmological discoveries in years, NASA scientists have captured the most precise image of the universe, shedding light on its origins and age, and providing further evidence for the long-standing Big Bang and inflation theories. In Feb. 2003, a joint NASA–Princeton University satellite, the Wilkinson Microwave Anisotropy Probe (WMAP), produced a high-resolution map that captured the oldest light in the universe. This ancient light, called the cosmic microwave background, is the cooled remnant of the hot explosion known as the Big Bang. "The cosmic microwave light is a fossil," explained David Wilkinson, after whom the probe was named. "Just as we can study dinosaur bones and reconstruct their lives of millions of years ago, we can probe this ancient light and reconstruct the universe as it was." (Wilkinson died just before WMAP's remarkable findings were published.)

The age of the universe has now been accurately determined—with just a 1% margin of error—as 13.7 billion years old (previous estimates ranged between 8–20 billion years old). The birth of stars has been pinpointed to just 200 million years after the Big Bang, a surprise to most scientists (predictions had ranged from 500 million to 1 billion years after the cosmos formed). The WMAP image also revealed the contents of the universe: only 4% is made up of atoms, or the physical universe as we know it. The remainder is made up of poorly understood substances: dark energy (73%) and dark matter (23%). These findings are consistent with the Big Bang and inflation theories, which assert that the universe materialized in a "big bang" and immediately began cooling and expanding. "I think every astronomer will remember where they were when they heard these results," said John Bahcall, a Princeton University astrophysicist. "I certainly will. This announcement represents a rite of passage for cosmology from speculation to precision science." For a detailed discussion, *see* p. 398.

Violent Gamma Rays Apprehended

The mystery of gamma-ray bursts—the universe's most powerful explosions, which release as much energy as a billion trillion suns—has baffled scientists ever since they were first identified in 1973. Lasting only seconds and appearing at random, these maddeningly unpredictable flashes of astounding energy eluded the watchful eyes of the world's scientists—that is, until the early hours of March 29, 2003, when a satellite finally caught a particularly brazen one in *flagrante delecto*. This gamma-ray burst was particularly long-lasting (30 seconds), bright (a trillion times more luminous than the Sun), and tantalizingly close (just 2 billion, as opposed to the usual 10–12 billion, light-years away). The afterglow continued for an unprecedented two weeks, a lucky break that finally gave scientists the evidence they had been looking for.

Gamma-ray bursts, it turns out, are none other than supernovae—explosions associated with the violent deaths of massive stars, something that many scientists had suspected but could not prove. "We've been searching for a direct link for decades, and we finally got it," said NASA's Donald Kniffen. Astronomer Brian Lee of Lawrence Berkeley National Laboratory registered relief that the long hunt is finally over: "It just leaves one slightly stunned to be looking for an answer for 12 years, have so many hints and false guesses, and then one day just have the answer. There are still lots of questions, but no one is guessing about the main one any more."

Precocious Planet

The Hubble telescope has detected the oldest known planet—and it appears to have been formed billions of years earlier than astronomers thought possible. Nicknamed Methuselah after the aged biblical patriarch, the planet is an astonishing 12.7 billion years old. In contrast, all other known planets (including our own) were created about 8 billion years later, roughly 4.5 billion years ago. Methuselah's age is causing astronomers to reevaluate the prevalent theory of planet formation, which argues that the early universe did not contain sufficient heavy elements (e.g., carbon, silicon, and oxygen) to allow for planets to form. But Methuselah defies this theory, having debuted when the primordial universe had only one-thirtieth of the heavy elements existing when our own solar system was born.

160,000 Years Ago, Our Forefathers . . .

Three fossilized skulls discovered near the Ethiopian village of Herto in 1997 have now been identified as the oldest known remains of modern humans. Assigned to a new human subspecies called *Homo sapiens idaltu (idaltu* means elder in the Afar language of Ethiopia), the skulls are estimated to be about 160,000 years old—a good 50,000 years older than any previously discovered *Homo sapiens.* The Herto discovery helps resolve two major debates in paleontology: whether humans are related to Neanderthals and whether all modern humans originated in Africa or developed simultaneously in other regions of the world. These skulls suggest that modern humans existed thousands of years before the Neanderthals evolved in Europe, which would confirm that *Homo sapiens neanderthalis* was not a rung on the evolutionary ladder leading to *Homo sapiens sapiens* (that's us) but an entirely separate offshoot of hominid that eventually went extinct. The Herto find also supports the "Out of Africa" hypothesis, which contends that all modern humans developed within Africa and then migrated elsewhere, and refutes the multiregional hypothesis, which claims that modern humans developed in various parts of the world at roughly the same time. The earliest human fossils found outside Africa are much younger than the 160,000-year-old Herto skulls. Berkeley paleoanthroplogist Tim White, one of the find's principal scientists, is convinced that Herto is "the critical missing data" that supports the Out of Africa theory. "All people," he contends, "every one of us living today, is ultimately African." For a detailed discussion, *see* p. 564–565.

A Younger Mungo

After years of contentious debate, scientists have finally agreed on the age of Mungo Man, Australia's oldest *Homo sapien* discovery. Originally thought to be 62,000 years old, new testing released in Feb. 2003 has definitively shaved 22,000 years off his age. "The consensus was unanimous—Mungo Man was buried about 42,000 years ago, " says geologist Jim Bowler of the University of Melbourne, who discovered Mungo Man in 1974 in the dry bed of Lake Mungo in New South Wales. Mungo Man is the oldest ritually buried skeleton in the world—his body was painted with ochre.

Mungo Man's revised age is not merely a victory for the advancement of scientific testing, but it makes also an important contribution to the theories of human evolution. Had Mungo Man been 62,000 years old as originally determined, the multiregionalist view of human development would have received an important boost. Multiregionalists maintain that an early human ancestor, *Homo erectus,* left Africa between 1 and 2 million years ago and then evolved into modern *Homo sapiens* in various regions of the world. Since, as most paleontologists agree, early humans could not have migrated swiftly enough from Africa to arrive in Australia before 50,000 years ago, a 62,000-year-old Mungo suggests that modern humans had evolved independently in Australia. But a sprightly 42,000-year-old Mungo lends support to the "Out of Africa" hypothesis (the more prevalent view among paleontologists) that anatomically modern humans left Africa and arrived in Australia around 50,000 years ago. Mungo Man's *Homo sapien* ancestors from Africa would have had plenty of time to make their way to far-flung Australia before young Mungo appeared on the scene.

It's a Bird . . . It's a Dino . . . It's Microraptor!

Scientists have uncovered the fossil of a new species of flying dinosaur in northeastern China thought to have existed 120 million years ago. Discovered in Feb. 2003, it is the first dinosaur ever found with four wings. The Chinese team that found the dinosaur has named it *Microraptor gui,* after Chinese paleontologist Gu Zhiwei. The creature may have lived in trees, perhaps gliding from branch to branch. Related to the *Tyrannosaurus rex,* though much smaller—from head to tail the tiny raptor measures just 30 inches—it resembles a flying squirrel more than a formidable carnivore. Scientists hope *Microraptor gui* may prove the link between dinosaurs and birds—some scientists have hypothesized that birds evolved directly from dinosaurs, but thus far there hasn't been enough evidence to prove this. "It is a beautiful mix of dinosaur and bird . . . it's so unique," commented paleontologist Nick Czaplewski of the Sam Noble Oklahoma Museum of Natural History. "It's a very interesting critter no matter how it's classified."

The Dark Side of Dinosaurs

Scientists studying dinosaur bones from Madagascar have discovered a dinosaur who wasn't just a run-of-the-mill carnivore—the 65-million-year-old *Majungatholus atopus,* a two-legged dinosaur from the Cretaceous period, is believed to have feasted on members of its own species. After examining the jaws and teeth of other contemporaneous Madagascan dinosaurs for likely suspects, the researchers concluded that this had been a *Majungatholus*-on-*Majungatholus* crime. "With these other candidates eliminated, *Majungatholus atopus* stands accused of cannibalism and is presumed guilty until proven innocent, which, in my opinion, is unlikely to happen," said one of the scientists, David Krause of SUNY–Stony Brook. This is the first genuine evidence that a dinosaur species practiced cannibalism. But according to the journal *Nature,* the *Majungatholus* was hardly the only cannibal in the animal kingdom, and today cannibalism is practiced by a variety of creatures, ranging from mice to lions.

Life in the Underground

Far below the ocean floor thrives a world of microbes, according to scientists from Oregon State University. The scientists drilled 1,000 feet beneath the bottom of the ocean, first through 825 feet of ocean-floor sediment and then through 175 feet of basalt, deep within the Earth's 3.5 million-year-old crust. The samples they collected turned up a profusion of bacterial life within this seemingly hostile environment. Living amid basalt crevices in hot water reaching 149°F (65°C), these microscopic creatures survive on inorganic molecules such as sulphide, hydrogen, and carbon dioxide (most living beings consume organic molecules). "This is one of the best views we've ever had of this difficult-to-reach location in the Earth's crust and the life forms that live in it," said Michael Rappe, one of the researchers. "Until now we knew practically nothing about the biology of areas such as this, but we found about the same amount of bacteria in that water as you might find in surrounding seawater in the ocean. It was abundant."

"Rotting Y" Redeemed

In June 2003, scientists published the first comprehensive analysis of the genetic code of the Y chromosome. Geneticists have always been somewhat dismissive of the Y chromosome, which provides just 78 genes out of the estimated 30,000 in human DNA and makes few important contributions beyond determining gender (females have two X chromosomes; males have an X and a Y chromosome). Once the size of the X chromosome, which contains about 1,000 genes, the Y chromosome has been rapidly decaying over the course of human evolution, dwindling to a mere tenth of its former self. While the X chromosome comes in pairs and uses its partner to regenerate, the Y stands alone. Consequently, many scientists have subscribed to the "rotting Y" theory, which holds that the Y, unable to recombine, will continue to degenerate over the next 5 million years or so, eventually becoming extinct. But now scientists have gained a new respect for the Y's ingenuity and powers of survival—written off as a degenerate loner, the Y in fact shows impressive signs of pulling itself up by its bootstraps. The Y chromosome is in fact capable of repairing its most crucial genes, and it does so all on its own: "denied the benefits of recombining with the X, the Y recombines with itself." According to one of the lead researchers, Richard K. Wilson of the Genome Sequencing Center at Washington University School of Medicine in St. Louis, "This study shows that the Y chromosome has become very efficient at preserving its important genes. It's found different ways to do the things chromosomes must do to evolve, survive, and thrive." The news has gladdened another lead researcher, MIT geneticist David Page, who considers it his duty to "defend the honor of the Y chromosome in the face of a century of insults."

See also new medical discoveries, pp. 539–542.

Inventions & Discoveries

See also Famous Firsts in Aviation, Nobel Prizes.

Adrenaline: (isolation of) John Jacob Abel, U.S., 1897.
Aerosol can: Erik Rotheim, Norway, 1926.
Air brake: George Westinghouse, U.S., 1868.
Air conditioning: Willis Carrier, U.S., 1911.
Airship: (non-rigid) Henri Giffard, France, 1852; (rigid) Ferdinand von Zeppelin, Germany, 1900.
Aluminum manufacture: (by electrolytic action) Charles M. Hall, U.S., 1866.
Anatomy, human: (*De fabrica corporis humani,* an illustrated systematic study of the human body) Andreas Vesalius, Belgium, 1543; (comparative: parts of an organism are correlated to the functioning whole) Georges Cuvier, France, 1799–1805.
Anesthetic: (first use of anesthetic—ether—on humans) Crawford W. Long, U.S., 1842.
Antibiotics: (first demonstration of antibiotic effect) Louis Pasteur, Jules-François Joubert, France, 1887; (discovery of penicillin, first modern antibiotic) Alexander Fleming, Scotland, 1928; (penicillin's infection-fighting properties) Howard Florey, Ernst Chain, England, 1940.
Antiseptic: (surgery) Joseph Lister, England, 1867.
Antitoxin, diphtheria: Emil von Behring, Germany, 1890.
Appliances, electric: (fan) Schuyler Wheeler, U.S., 1882; (flatiron) Henry W. Seely, U.S., 1882; (stove) Hadaway, U.S., 1896; (washing machine) Alva Fisher, U.S., 1906.
Aqualung: Jacques-Yves Cousteau, Emile Gagnan, France, 1943.
Aspirin: Dr. Felix Hoffman, Germany, 1899.
Astronomical calculator: The Antikythera device, Greece, first century B.C.. Found off island of Antikythera in 1900.
Atom: (nuclear model of) Ernest Rutherford, England, 1911.
Atomic structure: (formulated nuclear model of atom, Rutherford model) Ernest Rutherford, England, 1911; (proposed current concept of atomic structure, the Bohr model) Niels Bohr, Denmark, 1913.
Atomic theory: (ancient) Leucippus, Democritus, Greece, c. 500 B.C.; Lucretius, Rome c.100 B.C.; (modern) John Dalton, England, 1808.
Automobile: (first with internal combustion engine, 250 rpm) Karl Benz, Germany, 1885; (first with practical high-speed internal combustion engine, 900 rpm) Gottlieb Daimler, Germany, 1885; (first true automobile, not carriage with motor) René Panhard, Emile Lavassor, France, 1891; (carburetor, spray) Charles E. Duryea, U.S., 1892.
Autopilot: (for aircraft) Elmer A. Sperry, U.S., c.1910, first successful test, 1912, in a Curtiss flying boat.
Avogadro's law: (equal volumes of all gases at the same temperature and pressure contain equal number of molecules) Amedeo Avogadro, Italy, 1811.
Bacteria: Anton van Leeuwenhoek, The Netherlands, 1683.
Balloon, hot-air: Joseph and Jacques Montgolfier, France, 1783.
Barbed wire: (most popular) Joseph E. Glidden, U.S., 1873.

Science Websites

National Science Foundation: www.nsf.gov
National Academy of Sciences: www.nas.edu
American Association for the Advancement of Science: www.aaas.org/
The Franklin Institute: www.fi.edu/tfi/welcome.html
Science News Online: www.sciencenews.org
Popular Science: www.popsci.com
Periodic Table of Elements: www.infoplease.com/periodictable.php
Dinosauria Online: www.dinosauria.com/
Discovery Channel Online: www.discovery.com
Fermi National Accelerator Lab: www.fnal.gov/
Cosmology 101: http://map.gsfc.nasa.gov/m_uni.html
American Museum of Natural History: www.amnh.org
Newton (for K–12 teachers and students): www.newton.dep.anl.gov
Science Blog: www.scienceblog.com/
Inventors Hall of Fame: www.invent.org/
The Smithsonian Web: www.si.edu
Scientific American: www.sciam.com

Bar codes (computer-scanned binary signal code): (retail trade use) Monarch Marking, U.S. 1970; (industrial use) Plessey Telecommunications, England, 1970.
Barometer: Evangelista Torricelli, Italy, 1643.
Bicycle: Karl D. von Sauerbronn, Germany, 1816; (first modern model) James Starley, England, 1884.
Big Bang theory: (the universe originated with a huge explosion) George LeMaitre, Belgium, 1927; (modified LeMaitre theory labeled "Big Bang") George A. Gamow, U.S., 1948; (cosmic microwave background radiation discovered, confirms theory) Arno A. Penzias and Robert W. Wilson, U.S., 1965.
Blood, circulation of: William Harvey, England, 1628.
Boyle's law: (relation between pressure and volume in gases) Robert Boyle, Ireland, 1662.
Braille: Louis Braille, France, 1829.
Bridges: (suspension, iron chains) James Finley, Pa., 1800; (wire suspension) Marc Seguin, Lyons, 1825; (truss) Ithiel Town, U.S., 1820.
Bullet: (conical) Claude Minié, France, 1849.
Calculating machine: (logarithms: made multiplying easier and thus calculators practical) John Napier, Scotland, 1614; (slide rule) William Oughtred, England, 1632; (digital calculator) Blaise Pascal, 1642; (multiplication machine) Gottfried Leibniz, Germany, 1671; (important 19th-century contributors to modern machine) Frank S. Baldwin, Jay R. Monroe, Dorr E. Felt, W. T. Ohdner, William Burroughs, all U.S.; ("analytical engine" design, included concepts of programming, taping) Charles Babbage, England, 1835.
Calculus: Isaac Newton, England, 1669; (differential calculus) Gottfried Leibniz, Germany, 1684.

Camera: (hand-held) George Eastman, U.S., 1888; (Polaroid Land) Edwin Land, U.S., 1948.
"Canals" of Mars: Giovanni Schiaparelli, Italy, 1877.
Carpet sweeper: Melville R. Bissell, U.S., 1876.
Car radio: William Lear, Elmer Wavering, U.S., 1929, manufactured by Galvin Manufacturing Co., "Motorola."
Cells: (word used to describe microscopic examination of cork) Robert Hooke, England, 1665; (theory: cells are common structural and functional unit of all living organisms) Theodor Schwann, Matthias Schleiden, 1838–1839.
Cement, Portland: Joseph Aspdin, England, 1824.
Chewing gum: (spruce-based) John Curtis, U.S., 1848; (chicle-based) Thomas Adams, U.S., 1870.
Cholera bacterium: Robert Koch, Germany, 1883.
Circuit, integrated: (theoretical) G.W.A. Dummer, England, 1952; (phase-shift oscillator) Jack S. Kilby, Texas Instruments, U.S., 1959.
Classification of plants: (first modern, based on comparative study of forms) Andrea Cesalpino, Italy, 1583; (classification of plants and animals by genera and species) Carolus Linnaeus, Sweden, 1737–1753.
Clock, pendulum: Christian Huygens, The Netherlands, 1656.
Coca-Cola: John Pemberton, U.S., 1886.
Combustion: (nature of) Antoine Lavoisier, France, 1777.
Compact disk: RCA, U.S., 1972.
Computers: (first design of analytical engine) Charles Babbage, 1830s; (ENIAC, Electronic Numerical Integrator and Calculator, first all-electronic, completed) John Presper Eckert, Jr., John Mauchly, U.S., 1945; (dedicated at University of Pennsylvania) 1946; (UNIVAC, Universal Automatic Computer, handled both numeric and alphabetic data) 1951; (personal computer) Steve Wozniak, U.S., 1976.
Concrete: (reinforced) Joseph Monier, France, 1877.
Condensed milk: Gail Borden, U.S., 1853.
Conditioned reflex: Ivan Pavlov, Russia, c.1910.
Conservation of electric charge: (the total electric charge of the universe or any closed system is constant) Benjamin Franklin, U.S., 1751–1754.
Contagion theory: (infectious diseases caused by living agent transmitted from person to person) Girolamo Fracastoro, Italy, 1546.
Continental drift theory: (geographer who pieced together continents into a single landmass on maps) Antonio Snider-Pellegrini, France, 1858; (first proposed in lecture) Frank Taylor, U.S. 1912; (first comprehensive detailed theory) Alfred Wegener, Germany, 1912.
Contraceptive, oral: Gregory Pincus, Min Chuch Chang, John Rock, Carl Djerassi, U.S., 1951.
Converter, Bessemer: William Kelly, U.S., 1851.
Cosmetics: Egypt, c. 4000 B.C.
Cosmic string theory: (first postulated) Thomas Kibble, UK, 1976.
Cotton gin: Eli Whitney, U.S., 1793.
Crossbow: China, c. 300 B.C.
Cyclotron: Ernest O. Lawrence, U.S., 1931.
Defibrillator: Dr. William Bennett Kouwenhoven, U.S., 1932; (implantable) M. Stephen Heilman, MD, Dr. Alois Langer, Morton Mower, MD, Michel Mirowski, MD, 1980.
Deuterium: (heavy hydrogen) Harold Urey, U.S., 1931.
Disease: (chemicals in treatment of) crusaded by Philippus Paracelsus, 1527–1541; (germ theory) Louis Pasteur, France, 1862–1877.
DNA: (deoxyribonucleic acid) Friedrich Meischer, Germany, 1869; (determination of double-helical structure) F. H. Crick, England and James D. Watson, U.S., 1953.
Dye: (aniline, start of synthetic dye industry) William H. Perkin, England, 1856.
Dynamite: Alfred Nobel, Sweden, 1867.
Electric cooking utensil: (first) patented by St. George Lane-Fox, England, 1874.
Electric generator (dynamo): (laboratory model) Michael Faraday, England, 1832; Joseph Henry, U.S., c.1832; (hand-driven model) Hippolyte Pixii, France, 1833; (alternating-current generator) Nikola Tesla, U.S., 1892.

Thomas Alva Edison (1847–1931) *Library of Congress*

Electric lamp: (arc lamp) Sir Humphrey Davy, England, 1801; (fluorescent lamp) A.E. Becquerel, France, 1867; (incandescent lamp) Sir Joseph Swann, England, Thomas A. Edison, U.S., contemporaneously, 1870s; (carbon arc street lamp) Charles F. Brush, U.S., 1879; (first widely marketed incandescent lamp) Thomas A. Edison, U.S., 1879; (mercury vapor lamp) Peter Cooper Hewitt, U.S., 1903; (neon lamp) Georges Claude, France, 1911; (tungsten filament) Irving Langmuir, U.S., 1915.
Electrocardiography: Demonstrated by Augustus Waller, Switzerland, 1887; (first practical device for recording activity of heart) Willem Einthoven, 1903, Netherlands.
Electromagnet: William Sturgeon, England, 1823.
Electron: Sir Joseph J. Thompson, England, 1897.
Electronic mail: Ray Tomlinson, U.S., 1972.
Elevator, passenger: (safety device permitting use by passengers) Elisha G. Otis, U.S., 1852; (elevator utilizing safety device) 1857.
$E = mc^2$: (equivalence of mass and energy) Albert Einstein, Switzerland, 1907.
Engine, internal combustion: No single inventor. Fundamental theory established by Sadi Carnot, France, 1824; (two-stroke) Etienne Lenoir, France, 1860; (ideal operating cycle for four-stroke) Alphonse Beau de Roche, France, 1862; (operating four-stroke) Nikolaus Otto, Germany, 1876; (diesel) Rudolf Diesel, Germany, 1892; (rotary) Felix Wankel, Germany, 1956.
Evolution: (organic) Jean-Baptiste Lamarck, France, 1809; (by natural selection) Charles Darwin, England, 1859.
Exclusion principle: (no two electrons in an atom can occupy the same energy level) Wolfgang Pauli, Germany, 1925.
Expanding universe theory: (first proposed) George LeMaitre, Belgium, 1927; (discovered first direct evidence that the universe is expanding) Edwin P. Hubble, U.S., 1929; (Hubble constant: a measure of the rate at which the universe is expanding) Edwin P. Hubble, U.S., 1929.
Falling bodies, law of: Galileo Galilei, Italy, 1590.
Fermentation: (microorganisms as cause of) Louis Pasteur, France, c.1860.
Fiber optics: Narinder Kapany, England, 1955.
Fibers, man-made: (nitrocellulose fibers treated to change flammable nitrocellulose to harmless cellulose, precursor of rayon) Sir Joseph Swann, England, 1883; (rayon) Count Hilaire de Chardonnet, France, 1889; (Celanese) Henry and Camille Dreyfuss, U.S., England, 1921; (research on polyesters and polyamides, basis for modern man-made fibers) U.S., England, Germany, 1930s; (nylon) Wallace H. Carothers, U.S., 1935.
Frozen food: Clarence Birdseye, U.S., 1924.

Gene transfer: (recombinant DNA organism) Herbert Boyer, Stanley Cohen, U.S., 1973; (human) Steven Rosenberg, R. Michael Blaese, W. French Anderson, U.S., 1989.

Geometry, elements of: Euclid, Alexandria, Egypt, c. 300 B.C.; (analytic) René Descartes, France; and Pierre de Fermat, Switzerland, 1637.

Gravitation, law of: Sir Isaac Newton, England, c.1665 (published 1687).

Gunpowder: China, c.700.

Gyrocompass: Elmer A. Sperry, U.S., 1905.

Gyroscope: Jean Léon Foucault, France, 1852.

Halley's Comet: Edmund Halley, England, 1705.

Heart implanted in human, permanent artificial: Dr. Robert Jarvik, U.S., 1982.

Heart, temporary artificial: Willem Kolff, Netherlands, U.S., 1957.

Helicopter: (double rotor) Heinrich Focke, Germany, 1936; (single rotor) Igor Sikorsky, U.S., 1939.

Helium first observed on sun: Sir Joseph Lockyer, England, 1868.

Heredity, laws of: Gregor Mendel, Austria, 1865.

Holograph: Dennis Gabor, England, 1947.

Home videotape systems (VCR): (Betamax) Sony, Japan, 1975; (VHS) Matsushita, Japan, 1975.

Ice age theory: Louis Agassiz, Swiss-American, 1840.

Induction, electric: Joseph Henry, U.S., 1828.

Insulin: (first isolated) Sir Frederick G. Banting and Charles H. Best, Canada, 1921; (discovery first published) Banting and Best, 1922; (Nobel Prize awarded for purification for use in humans) John Macleod and Banting, 1923; (first synthesized), China, 1966.

Intelligence testing: Alfred Binet, Theodore Simon, France, 1905.

Interferon: Alick Isaacs, England, Jean Lindemann, Switzerland, 1957.

Isotopes: (concept of) Frederick Soddy, England, 1912; (stable isotopes) J. J. Thompson, England, 1913; (existence demonstrated by mass spectrography) Francis W. Aston, England, 1919.

Jet propulsion: (engine) Sir Frank Whittle, England, Hans von Ohain, Germany, 1936; (aircraft) *Heinkel He 178,* 1939.

Kinetic theory of gases: (molecules of a gas are in a state of rapid motion) Daniel Bernoulli, Switzerland, 1738.

Laser: (theoretical work on) Charles H. Townes, Arthur L. Schawlow, U.S., N. Basov, A. Prokhorov, U.S.S.R., 1958; (first working model) T. H. Maiman, U.S., 1960.

Lawn mower: Edwin Budding, John Ferrabee, England, 1830–1831.

LCD (liquid crystal display): Hoffmann-La Roche, Switzerland, 1970.

Lens, bifocal: Benjamin Franklin, U.S., c.1760.

Leyden jar: (prototype electrical condenser) Canon E. G. von Kleist of Kamin, Pomerania, 1745; independently evolved by Cunaeus and P. van Musschenbroek, University of Leyden, Holland, 1746, from where name originated.

Light, nature of: (wave theory) Christian Huygens, The Netherlands, 1678; (electromagnetic theory) James Clerk Maxwell, England, 1873.

Light, speed of: (theory that light has finite velocity) Olaus Roemer, Denmark, 1675.

Lightning rod: Benjamin Franklin, U.S., 1752.

Lock, cylinder: Linus Yale, U.S., 1851.

Locomotive: (steam powered) Richard Trevithick, England, 1804; (first practical, due to multiple-fire-tube boiler) George Stephenson, England, 1829; (largest steam-powered) Union Pacific's "Big Boy," U.S., 1941.

Loom: (horizontal, two-beamed) Egypt, c. 4400 B.C.; (Jacquard drawloom, pattern controlled by punch cards) Jacques de Vaucanson, France, 1745, Joseph-Marie Jacquard, 1801; (flying shuttle) John Kay, England, 1733; (power-driven loom) Edmund Cartwright, England, 1785.

Benjamin Franklin (1706–1790)

Machine gun: (hand-cranked multibarrel) Richard J. Gatling, U.S., 1862; (practical single barrel, belt-fed) Hiram S. Maxim, Anglo-American, 1884.

Magnet, Earth is: William Gilbert, England, 1600.

Match: (phosphorus) François Derosne, France, 1816; (friction) Charles Sauria, France, 1831; (safety) J. E. Lundstrom, Sweden, 1855.

Measles vaccine: John F. Enders, Thomas Peebles, U.S., 1953.

Metric system: revolutionary government of France, 1790–1801.

Microphone: Charles Wheatstone, England, 1827.

Microscope: (compound) Zacharias Janssen, The Netherlands, 1590; (electron) Vladimir Zworykin et al., U.S., Canada, Germany, 1932–1939.

Microwave oven: Percy Spencer, U.S., 1947.

Motion, laws of: Isaac Newton, England, 1687.

Motion pictures: Thomas A. Edison, U.S., 1893.

Motion pictures, sound: Product of various inventions. First picture with synchronized musical score: *Don Juan,* 1926; with spoken dialogue: *The Jazz Singer,* 1927; both Warner Bros.

Motor, electric: Michael Faraday, England, 1822; (alternating-current) Nikola Tesla, U.S., 1892.

Motorcycle: (motor tricycle) Edward Butler, England, 1884; (gasoline-engine motorcycle) Gottlieb Daimler, Germany, 1885.

Moving assembly line: Henry Ford, U.S., 1913.

Neptune: (discovery of) Johann Galle, Germany, 1846.

Neptunium: (first transuranic element, synthesis of) Edward M. McMillan, Philip H. Abelson, U.S., 1940.

Neutron: James Chadwick, England, 1932.

Neutron-induced radiation: Enrico Fermi et al., Italy, 1934.

Nitroglycerin: Ascanio Sobrero, Italy, 1846.

Nuclear fission: Otto Hahn, Fritz Strassmann, Germany, 1938.

Nuclear reactor: Enrico Fermi, Italy, et al., 1942.

Ohm's law: (relationship between strength of electric current, electromotive force, and circuit resistance) Georg S. Ohm, Germany, 1827.

Oil well: Edwin L. Drake, U.S., 1859.

Oxygen: (isolation of) Joseph Priestley, England, 1774; Karl Scheele, Sweden, 1773.

Ozone: Christian Schönbein, Germany, 1839.

Pacemaker: (internal) Clarence W. Lillehie, Earl Bakk, U.S., 1957.

Paper: China, c.100 A.D.

Parachute: Louis S. Lenormand, France, 1783.

Pen: (fountain)Lewis E. Waterman, U.S., 1884; (ball-point, for marking on rough surfaces) John H. Loud, U.S., 1888; (ball-point, for handwriting) Lazlo Biro, Argentina, 1944.

Periodic law: (that properties of elements are functions of their atomic weights) Dmitri Mendeleev, Russia, 1869.

Periodic table: (arrangement of chemical elements based on periodic law) Dmitri Mendeleev, Russia, 1869.

Phonograph: Thomas A. Edison, U.S., 1877.

Photography: (first paper negative, first photograph, on metal) Joseph Nicéphore Niepce, France, 1816–1827; (discovery of fixative powers of hyposulfite of soda) Sir John Herschel, England, 1819; (first direct positive image on silver plate, the daguerreotype) Louis Daguerre, based on work with Niepce, France, 1839; (first paper negative from which a number of positive prints could be made) William Talbot, England, 1841. Work of these four men, taken together, forms basis for all modern photography. (First color images) Alexandre Becquerel, Claude Niepce de Saint-Victor, France, 1848–1860; (commercial color film with three emulsion layers, Kodachrome) U.S., 1935.

Photovoltaic effect: (light falling on certain materials can produce electricity) Edmund Becquerel, France, 1839.

Piano: (Hammerklavier) Bartolommeo Cristofori, Italy, 1709; (pianoforte with sustaining and damper pedals) John Broadwood, England, 1873.

Planetary motion, laws of: Johannes Kepler, Germany, 1609, 1619.

Plant respiration and photosynthesis: Jan Ingenhousz, Holland, 1779.

Plastics: (first material, nitrocellulose softened by vegetable oil, camphor, precursor to Celluloid) Alexander Parkes, England, 1855; (Celluloid, involving recognition of vital effect of camphor) John W. Hyatt, U.S., 1869; (Bakelite, first completely synthetic plastic) Leo H. Baekeland, U.S., 1910; (theoretical background of macromolecules and process of polymerization on which modern plastics industry rests) Hermann Staudinger, Germany, 1922; (polypropylene and low-pressure method for producing high-density polyethylene) Robert Banks, Paul Hogan, U.S., 1958.

Plate tectonics: Alfred Wegener, Germany, 1912–1915.

Plow, forked: Mesopotamia, before 3000 B.C.

Plutonium, synthesis of: Glenn T. Seaborg, Edwin M. McMillan, Arthur C. Wahl, Joseph W. Kennedy, U.S., 1941.

Polio, vaccine: (experimentally safe dead-virus vaccine-)Jonas E. Salk, U.S., 1952; (effective large-scale field trials) 1954; (officially approved) 1955; (safe oral live-virus vaccine developed) Albert B. Sabin, U.S., 1954; (available in the U.S.) 1960.

Johann Gutenberg (c. 1400–1468)

Positron: Carl D. Anderson, U.S., 1932.

Pressure cooker: (early version) Denis Papin, France, 1679.

Printing: (block) Japan, c.700; (movable type) Korea, c.1400, Johann Gutenberg, Germany, c.1450; (lithography, offset) Aloys Senefelder, Germany, 1796; (rotary press) Richard Hoe, U.S., 1844; (linotype) Ottmar Mergenthaler, U.S., 1884.

Probability theory: René Descartes, France, and Pierre de Fermat, Switzerland, 1654.

Proton: Ernest Rutherford, England, 1919.

Prozac: (antidepressant fluoxetine) Bryan B. Malloy, Scotland, and Klaus K. Schmiegel, U.S., 1972; (released for use in U.S.) Eli Lilly & Company, 1987.

Psychoanalysis: Sigmund Freud, Austria, c.1904.

Pulsars: Antony Hewish and Jocelyn Bell Burnel, England, 1967.

Quantum theory: (general) Max Planck, Germany, 1900; (sub-atomic) Niels Bohr, Denmark, 1913; (quantum mechanics) Werner Heisenberg, Erwin Schrödinger, Germany, 1925.

Quarks: Jerome Friedman, Henry Kendall, Richard Taylor, U.S., 1967.

Quasars: Marten Schmidt, U.S., 1963.

Rabies immunization: Louis Pasteur, France, 1885.

Radar: (limited to one-mile range) Christian Hulsmeyer, Germany, 1904; (pulse modulation, used for measuring height of ionosphere) Gregory Breit, Merle Tuve, U.S., 1925; (first practical radar—radio detection and ranging) Sir Robert Watson-Watt, England, 1934–1935.

Radio: (electromagnetism, theory of) James Clerk Maxwell, England, 1873; (spark coil, generator of electromagnetic waves) Heinrich Hertz, Germany, 1886; (first practical system of wireless telegraphy) Guglielmo Marconi, Italy, 1895; (first long-distance telegraphic radio signal sent across the Atlantic) Marconi, 1901; (vacuum electron tube, basis for radio telephony) Sir John Fleming, England, 1904; (triode amplifying tube) Lee de Forest, U.S., 1906; (regenerative circuit, allowing long-distance sound reception) Edwin H. Armstrong, U.S., 1912; (frequency modulation—FM) Edwin H. Armstrong, U.S., 1933.

Radioactivity: (X-rays) Wilhelm K. Roentgen, Germany, 1895; (radioactivity of uranium) Henri Becquerel, France, 1896; (radioactive elements, radium and polonium in uranium ore) Marie Sklodowska-Curie, Pierre Curie, France, 1898; (classification of alpha and beta particle radiation) Pierre Curie, France, 1900; (gamma radiation) Paul-Ulrich Villard, France, 1900.

Radiocarbon dating, carbon-14 method: (discovered) Willard F. Libby, U.S., 1947; (first demonstrated) U.S., 1950.

Radio signals, extraterrestrial: first known radio noise signals were received by U.S. engineer, Karl Jansky, originating from the Galactic Center, 1931.

Radio waves: (cosmic sources, led to radio astronomy) Karl Jansky, U.S., 1932.

Razor: (safety, successfully marketed) King Gillette, U.S., 1901; (electric) Jacob Schick, U.S., 1928, 1931.

Reaper: Cyrus McCormick, U.S., 1834.

Refrigerator: Alexander Twining, U.S., James Harrison, Australia, 1850; (first with a compressor device) the Domelse, Chicago, U.S., 1913.

Refrigerator ship: (first) the *Frigorifique,* cooling unit designed by Charles Teller, France, 1877.

Relativity: (special and general theories of) Albert Einstein, Switzerland, Germany, U.S., 1905–1953.

Revolver: Samuel Colt, U.S., 1835.

Richter scale: Charles F. Richter, U.S., 1935.

Rifle: (muzzle-loaded) Italy, Germany, c.1475; (breech-loaded) England, France, Germany, U.S., c.1866; (bolt-action) Paul von Mauser, Germany, 1889; (automatic) John Browning, U.S., 1918.

Rocket: (liquid-fueled) Robert Goddard, U.S., 1926.

Roller bearing: (wooden for cartwheel) Germany or France, c.100 B.C.

Rotation of Earth: Jean Bernard Foucault, France, 1851.

Royal Observatory, Greenwich: established in 1675 by Charles II of England; John Flamsteed first Astronomer Royal.

Rubber: (vulcanization process) Charles Goodyear, U.S., 1839.

Saccharin: Constantine Fuhlberg, Ira Remsen, U.S., 1879.

Safety pin: Walter Hunt, U.S., 1849.

Saturn, ring around: Christian Huygens, The Netherlands, 1659.

"Scotch" tape: Richard Drew, U.S., 1929.

Screw propeller: Sir Francis P. Smith, England, 1836; John Ericsson, England, worked independently of and simultaneously with Smith, 1837.

Seat belt: (three point) Nils Bohlin, Sweden, 1962.

Seismograph: (first accurate) John Milne, England, 1880.

Sewing machine: Elias Howe, U.S., 1846; (continuous stitch) Isaac Singer, U.S., 1851.

Solar energy: First realistic application of solar energy using parabolic solar reflector to drive caloric engine on steam boiler, John Ericsson, U.S., 1860s.

Solar system, universe: (Sun-centered universe) Nicolaus Copernicus, Warsaw, 1543; (establishment of planetary orbits as elliptical) Johannes Kepler, Germany, 1609; (infinity of universe) Giordano Bruno, Italian monk, 1584.

Spectrum: (heterogeneity of light) Sir Isaac Newton, England, 1665–1666.

Spectrum analysis: Gustav Kirchhoff, Robert Bunsen, Germany, 1859.

Spermatozoa: Anton van Leeuwenhoek, The Netherlands, 1683.

Spinning: (spinning wheel) India, introduced to Europe in Middle Ages; (Saxony wheel, continuous spinning of wool or cotton yarn) England, c.1500–1600; (spinning jenny) James Hargreaves, England, 1764; (spinning frame) Sir Richard Arkwright, England, 1769; (spinning mule, completed mechanization of spinning, permitting production of yarn to keep up with demands of modern looms) Samuel Crompton, England, 1779.

Star catalog: (first modern) Tycho Brahe, Denmark, 1572.

Steam engine: (first commercial version based on principles of French physicist Denis Papin) Thomas Savery, England, 1639; (atmospheric steam engine) Thomas Newcomen, England, 1705; (steam engine for pumping water from collieries) Savery, Newcomen, 1725; (modern condensing, double acting) James Watt, England, 1782; (high-pressure) Oliver Evans, U.S., 1804.

Steamship: Claude de Jouffroy d'Abbans, France, 1783; James Rumsey, U.S., 1787; John Fitch, U.S., 1790; (high-pressure) Oliver Evans, U.S., 1804. All preceded Robert Fulton, U.S., 1807, credited with launching first commercially successful steamship.

Stethoscope: René Laënnec, France, 1819.

Sulfa drugs: (parent compound, para-aminobenzene-sulfanomide) Paul Gelmo, Austria, 1908; (antibacterial activity) Gerhard Domagk, Germany, 1935.

Samuel F. B. Morse (1791–1872)
Library of Congress

Superconductivity: (theory) John Bardeen, Leon Cooper, John Scheiffer, U.S., 1957.

Symbolic logic: George Boule, 1854; (modern) Bertrand Russell, Alfred North Whitehead, England, 1910–1913.

Tank, military: Sir Ernest Swinton, England, 1914.

Tape recorder: (magnetic steel tape) Valdemar Poulsen, Denmark, 1899.

Teflon: DuPont, U.S., 1943.

Telegraph: Samuel F. B. Morse, U.S., 1837.

Telephone: Alexander Graham Bell, U.S., 1876.

Telescope: Hans Lippershey, The Netherlands, 1608; (astronomical) Galileo Galilei, Italy, 1609; (reflecting) Isaac Newton, England, 1668.

Television: (Iconoscope–T.V. camera table) Vladimir Zworykin, U.S., 1923, and also kinescope (cathode ray tube) 1928; (mechanical disk-scanning method) successfully demonstrated by J.L. Baird, Scotland, C.F. Jenkins, U.S., 1926; (first all-electric television image) Philo T. Farnsworth, U.S., 1927; (color, mechanical disk) Baird, 1928; (color, compatible with black and white) George Valensi, France, 1938; (color, sequential rotating filter) Peter Goldmark, U.S., first introduced, 1951; (color, compatible with black and white) commercially introduced in U.S., National Television Systems Committee, 1953.

Thermodynamics: (first law: energy cannot be created or destroyed, only converted from one form to another) Julius von Mayer, Germany, 1842; James Joule, England, 1843; (second law: heat cannot of itself pass from a colder to a warmer body) Rudolph Clausius, Germany, 1850; (third law: the entropy of ordered solids reaches zero at the absolute zero of temperature) Walter Nernst, Germany, 1918.

Thermometer: (open-column) Galileo Galilei, c.1593; (clinical) Santorio Santorio, Padua, c.1615; (mercury, also Fahrenheit scale) Gabriel D. Fahrenheit, Germany, 1714; (centigrade scale) Anders Celsius, Sweden, 1742; (absolute-temperature, or Kelvin, scale) William Thompson, Lord Kelvin, England, 1848.

Tire, pneumatic: Robert W. Thompson, England, 1845; (bicycle tire) John B. Dunlop, Northern Ireland, 1888.

Toilet, flush: Product of Minoan civilization, Crete, c. 2000 B.C. Alleged invention by "Thomas Crapper" is untrue.

Tractor: Benjamin Holt, U.S., 1900.

Transformer, electric: William Stanley, U.S., 1885.

Transistor: John Bardeen, Walter H. Brattain, William B. Shockley, U.S., 1947.

Tuberculosis bacterium: Robert Koch, Germany, 1882.

Typewriter: Christopher Sholes, Carlos Glidden, U.S., 1867.

Uncertainty principle: (that position and velocity of an object cannot both be measured exactly, at the same time) Werner Heisenberg, Germany, 1927.

Uranus: (first planet discovered in recorded history) William Herschel, England, 1781.

Vaccination: Edward Jenner, England, 1796.

Vacuum cleaner: (manually operated) Ives W. McGaffey, U.S., 1869; (electric) Hubert C. Booth, England, 1901; (upright) J. Murray Spangler, U.S., 1907.

Van Allen (radiation) Belt: (around Earth) James Van Allen, U.S., 1958.

Video disk: Philips Co., The Netherlands, 1972.

Vitamins: (hypothesis of disease deficiency) Sir F. G. Hopkins, Casimir Funk, England, 1912; (vitamin A) Elmer V. McCollum, M. Davis, U.S., 1912–1914; (vitamin B) McCollum, U.S., 1915–1916; (thiamin, B_1) Casimir Funk, England, 1912; (riboflavin, B_2) D. T. Smith, E. G. Hendrick, U.S., 1926; (niacin) Conrad Elvehjem, U.S., 1937; (B_6) Paul Gyorgy, U.S., 1934; (vitamin C) C. A. Hoist, T. Froelich, Norway, 1912; (vitamin D) McCollum, U.S., 1922; (folic acid) Lucy Wills, England, 1933.

Voltaic pile: (forerunner of modern battery, first source of continuous electric current) Alessandro Volta, Italy, 1800.

Wallpaper: Europe, 16th and 17th century.

Wassermann test: (for syphilis) August von Wassermann, Germany, 1906.

Wheel: (cart, solid wood) Mesopotamia, c.3800–3600 B.C.

Windmill: Persia, c.600.

World Wide Web: (developed while working at CERN) Tim Berners-Lee, England, 1989; (development of Mosaic browser makes WWW available for general use) Marc Andreeson, U.S., 1993.

Xerography: Chester Carlson, U.S., 1938.

Yellow Fever: (transmission of)Walter Reed, U.S., 1900.

Zero: India, c. 600; (absolute zero temperature, cessation of all molecular energy) William Thompson, Lord Kelvin, England, 1848.

Zipper: W. L. Judson, U.S., 1891.

The National Inventors Hall of Fame

The National Inventors Hall of Fame,™ established in 1973 and located in Akron, Ohio, honors the women and men responsible for the great technological advances that make human, social, and economic progress possible. The Class of 2003 inductees are all inventors in the field of aviation and aerospace.

George Carruthers, 1939–, *Far Electrograph Ultraviolet Camera.* The Far Ultraviolet Camera and Spectrograph uses ultraviolet light to study Earth's upper atmosphere, stars, and interstellar space. It went to the Moon on the *Apollo 16* lunar mission in 1972, and produced about 200 photos revealing new features of Earth's far-outer atmosphere.

Frank Cepollina, 1936–, *Satellite Servicing Techniques.* In 1970 Frank Cepollina led the effort to develop NASA's first spacecraft to be repaired in space. In 1993, he led the historic repair of the Hubble Space Telescope, which restored Hubble's vision. He also led three additional repair missions in 1997, 1999, and 2002.

Glenn Curtiss, 1878–1930, *Hydroaeroplane.* In Jan. 1911, Curtiss successfully flew from water to land and from land to water. He generated over 70 patents during his lifetime, including designs for dirigibles, airplanes, flying boats, and the aileron, which is a device for maintaining the lateral balance of airplanes. He founded the first company created specifically for manufacturing airplanes.

Maxime Faget, 1921–, *Space Capsule Design.* Max Faget conceptualized and designed the first space capsule, the Mercury Capsule, the Apollo command and service modules, and contributed to the space shuttle. His design allowed for the spacecraft to slow down in the upper part of the atmosphere, causing less friction and G-force.

Leroy Grumman, 1895–1982, *Retractable Landing Gear; Folding Wing.* In 1929, Grumman designed an aircraft featuring retractable landing gear. He went on to design several of the outstanding warplanes of World War II, including the Wildcat (which featured a unique folding wing), the Avenger, and the Hellcat.

Charles Kaman, 1919–, *Rotor Control Mechanism for Rotary Aircraft.* In 1947, Kaman revolutionized helicopter safety and stability with his aerodynamic "servo-controlled flaps," which could automatically adjust to provide stability. He also introduced the first helicopter powered by a gas turbine, the first twin-turbine helicopter, and the first remote controlled helicopter.

Paul Kollsman, 1900–1982, *Altimeter.* Prior to 1928, there was no reliable or accurate way for airplane pilots to know how far above the ground they were. The barometric altimeter, accurate within 20 feet, measured altitude by assessing barometric pressure and enabled pilots to fly "blind."

Edwin A. Link, 1904–1981, *Link Trainer/Simulator.* While working in his father's piano and organ factory, Link was inspired to use organ parts and compressed air to build the first flight simulator. During World War II, the Link Trainer, called "The Blue Box," was essential in training U.S. and Allied pilots.

Thomas Midgley, Jr., 1889–1944, *Ethyl Gasoline.* Knock was a destructive phenomenon that occurred in internal combustion engines and only became worse at high engine-compression ratios. In Dec. 1921, Midgley ran an engine test with a small amount of tetraethyl lead added to the fuel, completely eliminating knock.

John Northrop, 1895–1981, *Flying Wing Plane; All-Metal High-Wing Monocoque Airplane.* Northrup came up with the "Flying Wing" in the 1940's, although the bomber did not reach production until the 1990s in the B-2 Spirit stealth bomber. Northrop created more than 48 different aircraft throughout his career including the Vega, a one-engine plane with an all-metal molded monocoque (single-shell fuselage) and internal-braced wing.

John Pierce, 1910–2002, *Communications Satellite.* In 1936, Pierce joined Bell Telephone Laboratories and helped develop the traveling wave tube, an amplifier that facilitates satellite communication. In 1962 the first commercial communications satellite, Telstar 1, was launched into low-orbit and transmitted the first live television signals across the Atlantic.

Harold Rosen, 1926–, *Spin Stabilized Synchronous Communications Satellite.* With Don Williams and Tom Hudspeth, Rosen developed the first 24-hour communications satellite, enabling efficient international telephone communication and real-time television transmission.

Theodore von Kármán, 1881–1963, *Turbo Jet.* Theodore von Kármán observed the presence of eddies (counter-rotating currents) in the wake of a moving object, leading to the Kármán Vortex Trail, a scientific snapshot of the structure of a wake behind a moving body under certain conditions. Von Kármán's work paved the way for the development of supersonic jets, rockets, and guided missiles.

Hans J. P. von Ohain, 1911–1998, *Jet Engine 1939.* Hans von Ohain was the first to design and build an operational jet engine. In August 1939, near Rostock, Germany, von Ohain's liquid-filled engine, the HeS-3B, was installed in the HE 178 airplane, and the first turbojet-powered aircraft took flight.

Richard Whitcomb, 1921–, *Supercritical Wing.* Whitcomb designed a new aircraft wing that increased the range, speed, and fuel efficiency of the jet. A uniquely shaped airfoil yielded weaker shock waves and created less drag for more efficiency.

Sir Frank Whittle, 1907–1996, *Jet Engine 1941.* Whittle developed a propellerless aircraft that made its maiden flight in England in 1941.

Sam Williams, 1921–, *Small Fan-Jet Engine.* In 1954, Williams and his team began developing small gas turbine engines for a variety of applications. He then moved on to design small turbojet engines for target and reconnaissance drones, patenting the small fan-jet engine in 1968.

The Environmental Challenges We Face

Sustainable development as an avenue to a healthier future

By JEFFREY KLUGER and ANDREA DORFMAN TIME

With 6.1 billion people relying on the resources of the same small planet, we're coming to realize that we're drawing from a finite account. The amount of crops, animals, and other biomatter we extract from the Earth each year exceeds what the planet can replace by an estimated 20%, meaning it takes 14.4 months to replenish what we use in 12—deficit spending of the worst kind. Sustainable development—a concept that can be hard to implement but wonderfully simple to understand—works to reverse the flow, to expand the resource base and adjust how we use it so we're living off biological interest without ever touching principal. "The old environmental movement had a reputation of élitism," says Mark Malloch Brown, administrator of the United Nations Development Program (UNDP). "The key now is to put people first and the environment second, but also to remember that when you exhaust resources, you destroy people." Among a host of difficult issues that affect both people and the environment:

Population and Health

While the number of people on Earth is still rising rapidly, especially in the developing countries of Asia, the good news is that the growth rate is slowing. World population increased 48% from 1975 to 2000, compared with 64% from 1950 to 1975. As this gradual deceleration continues, the population is expected to level off eventually, perhaps at 11 billion sometime in the last half of this century.

Economic-development and family-planning programs have helped slow the tide of people, but in some places, population growth is moderating for all the wrong reasons. In the poorest parts of the world, most notably Africa, infectious diseases such as AIDS, malaria, cholera, and tuberculosis are having a Malthusian effect. Rural-land degradation is pushing people into cities, where crowded, polluted living conditions create the perfect breeding grounds for sickness. Worldwide, at least 68 million are expected to die of AIDS by 2020, including 55 million in sub-Saharan Africa. While any factor that eases population pressures may help the environment, the situation would be far less tragic if rich nations did more to help the developing world reduce birth rates and slow the spread of disease.

Efforts to provide greater access to family planning and health care have proved effective. Though women in the poorest countries still have the most children, their collective fertility rate is 50% lower than it was in 1969 and is expected to decline more by 2050. Other programs targeted at women include basic education and job training. Educated mothers not only have a stepladder out of poverty, but they also choose to have fewer babies.

Rapid development will require good health care for the young since there are more than 1 billion people ages 15 to 24. Getting programs in place to keep this youth bubble healthy could make it the most productive generation ever conceived. Says Thoraya Obaid, executive director of the U.N. Population Fund: "It's a window of opportunity to build the economy and prepare for the future."

Food

Though it's not always easy to see it from the well-fed West, up to a third of the world is in danger of starving. Two billion people lack reliable access to safe, nutritious food, and 800 million of them—including 300 million children—are chronically malnourished.

Agricultural policies now in place define the very idea of unsustainable development. Just 15 cash crops such as corn, wheat, and rice provide 90% of the world's food, but planting and replanting the same crops strips fields of nutrients and makes them more vulnerable to pests. Slash-and-burn planting techniques and overreliance on pesticides further degrade the soil.

Solving the problem is difficult, mostly because of the ferocious debate over how to do it. Biotech partisans say the answer lies in genetically modified crops—foods engineered for vitamins, yield, and robust growth. Environmentalists worry that fooling about with genes is a recipe for Frankensteinian disaster. There is no reason, however, that both camps can't make a contribution.

Better crop rotation and irrigation can help protect fields from exhaustion and erosion. Old-fashioned cross-breeding can yield plant strains that are heartier and more pest-resistant. But in a world that needs action fast, genetic engineering must still have a role—provided it produces suitable crops. Increasingly, those crops are being created not just by giant biotech firms but also by home-grown groups that know best what local consumers need.

The National Agricultural Research Organization of Uganda has developed corn varieties that are more resistant to disease and thrive in soil that is poor in nitrogen. Agronomists in Kenya are developing a sweet potato that wards off viruses. Also in the works are drought-tolerant, disease-defeating, and vitamin-fortified forms of such crops as sorghum and cassava—hardly staples in the West, but essentials elsewhere in the world. The key, explains economist Jeffrey Sachs, head of Columbia University's Earth Institute, is not to dictate food policy from the West but to help the developing world build its own biotech infrastructure so it can produce the things it needs the most. "We can't presume that our technologies will bail out poor people in Malawi," he says. "They need their own improved varieties of sorghum and millet, not our genetically improved varieties of wheat and soybeans."

Water

For a world that is 70% water, things are drying up fast. Only 2.5% of water is fresh, and only a fraction of that is accessible. Meanwhile, each of us requires about 50 quarts per day for drinking, bathing, cooking, and other basic needs. At present, 1.1 billion people lack access to clean drinking water and more than 2.4 billion lack adequate sanitation. "Unless we take swift and decisive action," says U.N. Secretary-General Kofi Annan, "by 2025, two-thirds of the world's population may be living in countries that face serious water shortages."

The answer is to get smart about how we use water. Agriculture accounts for about two-thirds of the fresh water consumed. A report prepared for the summit thus endorses the "more crop per drop" approach, which calls for more efficient irrigation techniques, planting of drought- and salt-tolerant crop varieties that require less water and better monitoring of growing conditions, such as soil humidity levels. Improving water-delivery systems would also help, reducing the amount that is lost en route to the people who use it.

One program winning quick support is dubbed WASH—for Water, Sanitation, and Hygiene for All—a global effort that aims to provide water services and hygiene training to everyone who lacks them by 2015.

Energy and Climate

In the U.S., people think of rural electrification as a long-ago legacy of the New Deal. In many parts of the world, it hasn't even happened yet. About 2.5 billion people have no access to modern energy services, and the power demands of developing economies are expected to grow 2.5% per year. But if those demands are met by burning fossil fuels such as oil, coal, and gas, more and more carbon dioxide and other greenhouse gases will hit the atmosphere. That, scientists tell us, will promote global warming, which could lead to rising seas, fiercer storms, severe droughts, and other climatic disruptions.

Of more immediate concern is the heavy air pollution caused in many places by combustion of wood and fossil fuels. A new U.N. Environment Program report warns of the effects of a haze across all southern Asia. Dubbed the "Asian brown cloud" and estimated to be 2 miles thick, it may be responsible for hundreds of thousands of deaths a year from respiratory diseases.

The better way to meet the world's energy needs is to develop cheaper, cleaner sources. In India there has been a boom in wind power because the government has made it easier for entrepreneurs to get their hands on the necessary technology and has then required the national power grid to purchase the juice that wind systems produce.

Other technologies can work their own little miracles. Micro-hydroelectric plants are already operating in numerous nations, including Kenya, Sri Lanka, and Nepal. The systems divert water from streams and rivers and use it to run turbines without complex dams or catchment areas. Each plant can produce as much as 200 kilowatts—enough to electrify 200 to 500 homes and businesses—and lasts 20 years. One plant in Kenya was built by 200 villagers, all of whom own shares in the cooperative that sells the power.

The Global Village Energy Partnership, which involves the World Bank, the UNDP, and various donors, wants to provide energy to 300 million people, as well as schools, hospitals, and clinics in 50,000 communities worldwide over 10 years. The key will be to match the right energy source to the right users. For example, solar panels that convert sunlight into electricity might be cost-effective in remote areas, while extending the power grid might be better in Third World cities.

Biodiversity

More than 11,000 species of animals and plants are known to be threatened with extinction, about a third of all coral reefs are expected to vanish in the next 30 years, and about 36 million acres of forest are being razed annually. In his new book, *The Future of Life,* Harvard biologist Edward O. Wilson writes of his worry that unless we change our ways, half of all species could disappear by the end of this century.

The damage being done is more than aesthetic. Many vanishing species provide humans with both food and medicine. What's more, once you start tearing out swaths of ecosystem, you upset the existing balance in ways that harm even areas you didn't intend to touch. Environmentalists have said this for decades, and now that many of them have tempered ecological absolutism with developmental realism, more people are listening.

The Equator Initiative, a public-private group, is publicizing examples of sustainable development in the equatorial belt. Among the projects already cited are one to help restore marine fisheries in Fiji and another that promotes beekeeping as a source of supplementary income in rural Kenya. The Global Conservation Trust hopes to raise $260 million to help conserve genetic material from plants for use by local agricultural programs. "When you approach sustainable development from an environmental view, the problems are global," says the U.N.'s Malloch Brown. "But from a development view, the front line is local, local, local." □

Human Access to Water Supplies, by Region, 2000

Region	Percent served: Urban	Rural	Total
Global	94%	71%	82%
Africa	85	47	81
Asia	93	75	81
Latin America/Caribbean	93	62	85
Oceania	98%	63%	88%
Europe	100	87	96
North America	100	100	100

Source: Global Water Supply and Sanitation Assessment 2000 Report, World Health Organization (WHO). Web: www.who.int.

World Energy Consumption and Carbon Dioxide Emissions, 1990–2025

Region	Energy consumption (quadrillion btu)				Carbon dioxide emissions (million metric tons)			
	1990	2001	2010	2025	1990	2001	2010	2025
Industrialized nations	**182.8**	**211.5**	**240.1**	**288.3**	**2,844**	**3,179**	**3,572**	**4,346**
Eastern Europe/Former Soviet Union	**76.3**	**53.3**	**65.9**	**82.3**	**1,337**	**856**	**1,038**	**1,267**
Developing nations								
Asia	52.5	85.0	110.1	174.6	1,089	1,640	2,075	3,263
Middle East	13.1	20.8	25.0	36.0	231	354	420	601
Africa	9.3	12.4	14.4	20.0	179	230	261	361
Central and South America	14.4	20.9	25.2	39.0	192	263	319	523
Total developing	**89.3**	**139.2**	**174.7**	**269.6**	**1,691**	**2,487**	**3,075**	**4,749**
Total world	**348.4**	**403.9**	**480.6**	**640.1**	**5,872**	**6,522**	**7,685**	**10,361**

Sources: 1990 and 2001: Energy Information Administration (EIA), *International Energy Annual 2001,* 2010, and 2025: EIA, System for the Analysis of Global Energy Markets (2003). Web: www.eia.doe.gov/iea/.

World Net Electricity Consumption by Selected Countries, 1990–2025

(billion kilowatt-hours)

Region	History			Projections				
	1990	2000	2001	2005	2010	2015	2020	2025	Average annual percent change, 2001–2025
United States	2,827	3,605	3,602	3,684	4,101	4,481	4,850	5,252	1.6%
France	324	406	415	446	482	519	572	626	1.7
Japan	765	944	964	989	1,073	1,154	1,229	1,302	1.3
Eastern Europe/ Former Soviet Union	1,906	1,504	1,528	1,768	1,982	2,204	2,423	2,642	2.3
China	551	1,189	1,312	1,545	1,966	2,428	2,986	3,596	4.3
India	257	477	497	528	662	802	958	1,104	3.4
Africa	286	388	396	442	521	611	705	800	3.0
Central and South America	463	724	721	782	925	1,081	1,302	1,577	3.3
Total industralized countries	**6,368**	**7,950**	**8,016**	**8,307**	**9,200**	**10,106**	**11,030**	**11,994**	**1.7**
Total developing countries	**2,272**	**4,175**	**4,390**	**4,886**	**5,962**	**7,172**	**8,555**	**10,038**	**3.5**
Total world	**10,546**	**13,629**	**13,934**	**14,960**	**17,144**	**19,482**	**22,009**	**24,673**	**2.4**

Sources: Energy Information Administration (EIA): *International Energy Outlook 2003.*

Greatest Oil Reserves by Country, 2002

2002 rank	Country	2002 proved reserves (billion barrels)	2002 rank	Country	2002 proved reserves (billion barrels)
1.	Saudi Arabia	261.7	6.	Russia	53.9
2.	Iraq	115.0	7.	Venezuela	50.2
3.	Iran	99.1	8.	Libya	30.0
4.	Kuwait	98.9		Nigeria	30.0
5.	United Arab Emirates	62.8	10.	China	29.5

NOTES: Figures for Russia are "explored reserves," which are understood to be proved plus some probable. All other figures are proved reserves recoverable with present technology and prices. *Source:* U.S. Energy Information Administration, *International Energy Annual 2001* (March 2003).

Greatest Gas Reserves by Country, 2002

2002 rank	Country	2002 proved reserves (trillion cu ft)	2002 rank	Country	2002 proved reserves (trillion cu ft)
1.	Russia	1,700.0	6.	United States	183.5
2.	Iran	939.4	7.	Algeria	175.0
3.	Qatar	757.7	8.	Nigeria	159.0
4.	Saudi Arabia	228.2	9.	Venezuela	149.2
5.	United Arab Emirates	204.1	10.	Iraq	112.6

NOTES: Figures for Russia are "explored reserves," which are understood to be proved plus some probable. All other figures are proved reserves recoverable with present technology and prices. *Source:* U.S. Energy Information Administration, *International Energy Annual 2001* (March 2003).

U.S. Emissions of Greenhouse Gases, 1990–2001

(million metric tons of gas)

Gas	1990	1994	1995	1996	1997	1998	1999	2000	2001
Carbon dioxide	4,969.4	5,224.4	5,273.5	5,454.8	5,533.0	5,540.0	5,630.7	5,805.5	5,789.0
Methane	31.7	31.0	31.1	29.9	29.6	28.9	28.7	28.2	28.0
Nitrous oxide	1.2	1.3	1.3	1.2	1.2	1.2	1.2	1.2	1.2

Source: Compiled by the U.S. Energy Information Administration. Web: www.eia.doe.gov/.

America's 25 Most Ozone-Polluted Metropolitan Areas

Metropolitan area	Rank 2003	Rank 2000
Los Angeles-Riverside-Orange County, Calif.	1	1
Fresno, Calif.	2	3
Bakersfield, Calif.	3	2
Visalia-Tulare-Porterville, Calif.	4	4
Houston-Galveston-Brazoria, Tex.	5	5
Sacramento-Yolo, Calif.	6	11
Merced, Calif.	7	10
Atlanta, Ga.	8	9
Knoxville, Tenn.	9	12
Charlotte-Gastonia-Rock Hill, N.C.-S.C.	10	8
Washington-Baltimore, DC-Md.-Va.-W. Va.	11	7
Dallas-Fort Worth, Tex.	12	14
Philadelphia-Wilmington-Atlantic City, Pa.-N.J.-Del.-Md.	13	13
New York-Northern New Jersey-Long Island, Conn.-N.J.-N.Y.	14	16
Phoenix-Mesa, Ariz.	15	19
Baton Rouge, La.	16	n.a.
Greensboro–Winston-Salem–High Point, N.C.	17	n.a.
Memphis, Tenn.-Ark.-Miss.	18	23
Birmingham, Ala.	18	24
San Diego, Calif.	20	6
Nashville, Tenn.	21	18
Raleigh-Durham-Chapel Hill, N.C.	22	17
Allentown-Bethlehem-Easton, Pa.	23	n.a.
Macon, Ga.	24	n.a.
Louisville, Ky.-Ind.	25	n.a.

Source: State of the Air: 2003, American Lung Association.

Major Air Pollutants

Pollutant	Sources	Effects
Ozone. A gas that can be found in two places. Near the ground (the troposphere), it is a major part of smog. Higher in the air (the stratosphere), it helps block radiation from the sun.	Ozone is not created directly, but is formed when nitrogen oxides and volatile organic compounds mix in sunlight. That is why ozone is mostly found in the summer. Nitrogen oxides come from burning gasoline, coal, or other fossil fuels. There are many types of volatile organic compounds, and they come from sources ranging from factories to trees.	Ozone near the ground can cause a number of health problems. Ozone can lead to more frequent asthma attacks in people who have asthma and can cause sore throats, coughs, and breathing difficulty. It may even lead to premature death. Ozone can also hurt plants and crops.
Carbon monoxide. A gas that comes from the burning of fossil fuels, mostly in cars. It cannot be seen or smelled.	Carbon monoxide is released when engines burn fossil fuels. Emissions are higher when engines are not tuned properly, and when fuel is not completely burned. Cars emit a lot of the carbon monoxide found outdoors.	Carbon monoxide makes it hard for body parts to get the oxygen they need to run correctly. Exposure to carbon monoxide makes people feel dizzy and tired and gives them headaches.
Nitrogen dioxide. A reddish-brown gas that comes from the burning of fossil fuels. It has a strong smell at high levels.	Nitrogen dioxide mostly comes from power plants and cars. Nitrogen dioxide is formed in two ways—when nitrogen in the fuel is burned, or when nitrogen in the air reacts with oxygen at very high temperatures.	People who are exposed to nitrogen dioxide for a long time have a higher chance of getting respiratory infections. Acid rain can hurt plants and animals and can make lakes dangerous to swim or fish in.
Particulate matter. Solid or liquid matter that is suspended in the air. To remain in the air, particles are usually less than 0.1 mm wide and can be as small as 0.00005 mm.	Particulate matter can be divided into two types—coarse particles and fine particles. Coarse particles are formed from sources like road dust, sea spray, and construction. Fine particles are formed when fuel is burned in automobiles and power plants.	Particulate matter that is small enough can enter the lungs and cause health problems. Some of these problems include more frequent asthma attacks, respiratory problems, and premature death.

Pollutant	Sources	Effects
Sulfur dioxide. A corrosive gas that cannot be seen or smelled at low levels but can have a "rotten egg" smell at high levels.	Sulfur dioxide mostly comes from the burning of coal or oil in power plants. It also comes from factories that make chemicals, paper, or fuel. Like nitrogen dioxide, sulfur dioxide also reacts in the atmosphere to form acid rain and particles.	Sulfur dioxide exposure can affect people who have asthma or emphysema by making it more difficult for them to breathe. It can also irritate people's eyes, noses, and throats. Sulfur dioxide can harm trees and crops, damage buildings, and make it harder for people to see long distances.
Lead. A blue-gray metal that is very toxic and is found in a number of forms and locations.	Outside, lead comes from cars in areas where unleaded gasoline is not used. Lead can also come from power plants and other industrial sources. Inside, lead paint is an important source of lead, especially in houses where paint is peeling.	High amounts of lead can be dangerous for small children and can lead to lower IQs and kidney problems. For adults, exposure to lead can increase the chance of having heart attacks or strokes.
Toxic air pollutants. A large number of chemicals that are known or suspected to cause cancer. Some important pollutants in this category include arsenic, asbestos, benzene, and dioxin.	Each toxic air pollutant comes from a slightly different source, but many are created in chemical plants or are emitted when fossil fuels are burned. Some toxic air pollutants, like asbestos and formaldehyde, can be found in building materials and can lead to indoor air problems. Many toxic air pollutants can also enter the food and water supply.	Toxic air pollutants can cause cancer. Some toxic air pollutants can also cause birth defects. Other effects depend on the pollutant, but can include skin and eye irritation and breathing problems.
Stratospheric ozone depleters. Chemicals that can destroy the ozone in the stratosphere. These chemicals include chlorofluorocarbons (CFCs), halons, and other compounds that include chlorine or bromine.	CFCs are used in air conditioners and refrigerators, since they work well as coolants. They can also be found in aerosol cans and fire extinguishers. Other stratospheric ozone depleters are used as solvents in industry.	If the ozone in the stratosphere is destroyed, people are exposed to more radiation from the sun (ultraviolet radiation). This can lead to skin cancer and eye problems. Higher ultraviolet radiation can also harm plants and animals.
Greenhouse gases. Gases that stay in the air for a long time and warm up the planet by trapping sunlight. This is called the "greenhouse effect" because the gases act like the glass in a greenhouse. Some of the important greenhouse gases are carbon dioxide, methane, and nitrous oxide.	Carbon dioxide is the most important greenhouse gas, and it comes from the burning of fossil fuels in cars, power plants, houses, and industry. Methane is released during the processing of fossil fuels, and also comes from natural sources like cows and rice paddies. Nitrous oxide comes from industrial sources and decaying plants.	The greenhouse effect can lead to changes in the climate of the planet. Some of these changes might include more temperature extremes, higher sea levels, changes in forest composition, and damage to land near the coast. Human health might be affected by diseases that are related to temperature or by damage to land and water.

Source: Jonathan Levy, Harvard School of Public Health. Based on information provided by the Environmental Protection Agency.

Largest Nuclear Power Plants in the U.S.

Plant	Operating utility	Capacity (net MW[e])[1]	Year operative
South Texas 2, Tex.	STP Nuclear Operating Co.	1,265	1989
South Texas 1, Tex.	STP Nuclear Operating Co.	1,264	1988
Palo Verde 3, Ariz.	Arizona Nuclear Power Project	1,247	1988
Palo Verde 1, Ariz.	Arizona Nuclear Power Project	1,243	1986
Palo Verde 2, Ariz.	Arizona Nuclear Power Project	1,243	1986
Perry 1, Ohio	FirstEnergy Nuclear Operating Co.	1,238	1987
Grand Gulf 1, Miss.	Entergy Nuclear	1,231	1985
Byron 1, Ill.	Exelon	1,194	1985
Braidwood 1, Ill.	Exelon	1,185	1988
Braidwood 2, Ill.	Exelon	1,177	1988
Wolf Creek, Kans.	Wolf Creek Nuclear Operating	1,170	1985
Byron 2, Ill.	Exelon	1,162	1987
Seabrook 1, N.H.	North Atlantic Energy Service Corp.	1,161	1990
Vogtle 2, Ga.	Southern Nuclear Operating Co.	1,149	1989
Vogtle 1, Ga.	Southern Nuclear Operating Co.	1,148	1987
Callaway 1, Mo.	AmerenUE	1,143	1984
Watts Bar 1, Tenn.	Tennessee Valley Authority	1,138	1996
Millstone 3, Conn.	Dominion Generation	1,136	1986

1. MG[e] = megawatts of electricity. *Source:* Department of Energy, Energy Information Administration, April 2003. Web: www.eia.doe.gov/cneaf/nuclear/page/nuc_reactors/operational.xls.

Animals and Nature

Animal Names: Male, Female, and Young

Animal	Male	Female	Young	Animal	Male	Female	Young	Animal	Male	Female	Young
Ass	Jack	Jenny	Foal	Duck	Drake	Duck	Duckling	Sheep	Ram	Ewe	Lamb
Bear	Boar	Sow	Cub	Elephant	Bull	Cow	Calf	Swan	Cob	Pen	Cygnet
Cat	Tom	Queen	Kitten	Fox	Dog	Vixen	Cub	Swine	Boar	Sow	Piglet
Cattle	Bull	Cow	Calf	Goose	Gander	Goose	Gosling	Tiger	Tiger	Tigress	Cub
Chicken	Rooster	Hen	Chick	Horse	Stallion	Mare	Foal	Whale	Bull	Cow	Calf
Deer	Buck	Doe	Fawn	Lion	Lion	Lioness	Cub	Wolf	Dog	Bitch	Pup
Dog	Dog	Bitch	Pup	Rabbit	Buck	Doe	Bunny				

Source: James G. Doherty, general curator, The Wildlife Conservation Society.

Gestation, Incubation, and Longevity of Certain Animals

Animal	Gestation or incubation, in days (average)	Longevity, in years (record exceptions)	Animal	Gestation or incubation, in days (average)	Longevity, in years (record exceptions)
Ass	365	18–20 (63)	Horse	329–345 (336)	20–25 (50+)
Bear	180–240[1]	15–30 (47)	Human	253–303	([2])
Cat	52–69 (63)	10–12 (26+)	Kangaroo	32–39[1]	4–6 (23)
Chicken	22	7–8 (14)	Lion	105–113 (108)	10 (29)
Cow	280	9–12 (39)	Monkey	139–270[1]	12–15[1] (29)
Deer	197–300[1]	10–15 (26)	Mouse	19–31[1]	1–3 (4)
Dog	53–71 (63)	10–12 (24)	Parakeet (Budgerigar)	17–20 (18)	8 (12+)
Duck	21–35[1] (28)	10 (15)	Pig	101–130 (115)	10 (22)
Elephant	510–730[1] (624)	30–40 (71)	Pigeon	11–19	10–12 (39)
Fox	51–63[1]	8–10 (14)	Rabbit	30–35 (31)	6–8 (15)
Goat	136–160 (151)	12 (17)	Rat	21	3 (5)
Groundhog	31–32	4–9	Sheep	144–152[1] (151)	12 (16)
Guinea pig	58–75 (68)	3 (6)	Squirrel	44	8–9 (15)
Hamster, golden	15–17	2 (8)	Whale	365–547[1]	n.a.
Hippopotamus	220–255 (240)	30 (49+)	Wolf	60–63	10–12 (16)

1. Depending on kind. 2. For human life expectancy charts, *see* Life Expectancy at Birth by Race and Sex, p. 192. *Source:* James G. Doherty, general curator, The Wildlife Conservation Society.

Speed of Animals

Most of the following measurements are for maximum speeds over approximate quarter-mile distances. Exceptions—which are included to give a wide range of animals—are the lion and elephant, whose speeds were clocked in the act of charging; the whippet, which was timed over a 200-yard course; the cheetah over a 100-yard distance; humans for a 15-yard segment of a 100-yard run; and the black mamba snake, six-lined race runner, spider, giant tortoise, three-toed sloth, and garden snail, which were measured over various small distances.

Animal	Speed (mph)	Animal	Speed (mph)	Animal	Speed (mph)
Peregrine falcon	200.00+	Zebra	40.00	Cat (domestic)	30.00
Cheetah	70.00	Mongolian wild ass	40.00	Human	27.89
Pronghorn antelope	61.00	Greyhound	39.35	Elephant	25.00
Wildebeest	50.00	Whippet	35.50	Black mamba snake	20.00
Lion	50.00	Rabbit (domestic)	35.00	Six-lined race runner	18.00
Thomson's gazelle	50.00	Mule deer	35.00	Squirrel	12.00
Quarter horse	47.50	Jackal	35.00	Pig (domestic)	11.00
Elk	45.00	Reindeer	32.00	Chicken	9.00
Cape hunting dog	45.00	Giraffe	32.00	House mouse	8.00
Coyote	43.00	Kangaroo	30.00	Spider (Tegenearia atrica)	1.17
Gray fox	42.00	White-tailed deer	30.00	Giant tortoise	0.17
Ostrich	40.00	Wart hog	30.00	Three-toed sloth	0.15
Hyena	40.00	Grizzly bear	30.00	Garden snail	0.03

Source: Natural History Magazine, March 1974, copyright 1974. The American Museum of Natural History; and James G. Doherty, general curator, The Wildlife Conservation Society.

Animal Group Terminology

Source: James G. Doherty, general curator, The Wildlife Conservation Society.

ants: colony
bears: sleuth, sloth
bees: grist, hive, swarm
birds: flight, volery
cats: clutter, clowder
cattle: drove
chicks: brood, clutch
clams: bed
cranes: sedge, seige
crows: murder
doves: dule
ducks: brace, team
elephants: herd
elks: gang
finches: charm
fish: school, shoal, draught
foxes: leash, skulk
geese: flock, gaggle, skein
gnats: cloud, horde
goats: trip
gorillas: band
hares: down, husk
hawks: cast
hens: brood
hogs: drift
horses: pair, team
hounds: cry, mute, pack
kangaroos: troop
kittens: kindle, litter
larks: exaltation
lions: pride
locusts: plague
magpies: tiding
mules: span
nightingales: watch
oxen: yoke
oysters: bed
parrots: company
partridges: covey
peacocks: muster, ostentation
pheasants: nest, bouquet
pigs: litter
ponies: string
quail: bevy, covey
rabbits: nest
seals: pod
sheep: drove, flock
sparrows: host
storks: mustering
swans: bevy, wedge
swine: sounder
toads: knot
turkeys: rafter
turtles: bale
vipers: nest
whales: gam, pod
wolves: pack, route
woodcocks: fall

Threatened and Endangered Species

Group	Endangered[1] U.S.	Endangered[1] Foreign	Threatened[2] U.S.	Threatened[2] Foreign	Total species	Species with recovery plans
Mammals	65	251	9	17	342	52
Birds	78	175	14	6	273	77
Reptiles	14	64	22	15	115	32
Amphibians	12	8	9	1	30	14
Fishes	71	11	44	0	126	96
Clams	62	2	8	0	72	57
Snails	21	1	11	0	33	22
Insects	35	4	9	0	48	29
Arachnids	12	0	0	0	12	5
Crustaceans	18	0	3	0	21	13
Animal subtotal	**388**	**516**	**129**	**39**	**1,072**	**397**
Flowering plants	571	1	144	0	716	572
Conifers and cycads	2	0	1	2	5	2
Ferns and allies	24	0	2	0	26	26
Lichens	2	0	0	0	2	2
Plant subtotal	**599**	**1**	**147**	**2**	**749**	**602**
Total	**987**	**517**	**276**	**41**	**1,821**[3]	**999**

NOTE: As of June 1, 2003. 1. *Endangered species* are those in danger of extinction. 2. *Threatened species* are those likely to become an endangered species within the foreseeable future. 3. Nine U.S. species have dual status. *Source:* U.S. Fish and Wildlife Service. Web: http://ecos.fws.gov/tess_public/html/boxscore.html.

Water Supply of the World

The Antarctic Icecap is the largest supply of fresh water, nearly 2% of the world's total of fresh and salt water. As can be seen from the table below, the amount of water in our atmosphere is over ten times as much as the water in all the rivers taken together. The fresh water actually available for human use in lakes and rivers and the accessible ground water amounts to only about one-third of 1% of the world's total water supply.

	Surface area (sq mi)	Volume (cu mi)	Percentage of total[1]
Salt water			
The oceans	139,500,000	317,000,000	97.2%
Inland seas and saline lakes	270,000	25,000	0.008
Fresh water			
Freshwater lakes	330,000	30,000	0.009
All rivers (average level)	—	300	0.0001
Antarctic Icecap	6,000,000	6,300,000	1.9
Arctic Icecap and glaciers	900,000	680,000	0.21
Water in the atmosphere	197,000,000	3,100	0.001
Ground water within half a mile from surface	—	1,000,000	0.31
Deep-lying ground water	—	1,000,000	0.31
Total (rounded)	—	**326,000,000**	**100.00**

1. All figures are estimated. *Source:* Department of the Interior, Geological Survey.

The National Park System

Source: Department of the Interior, National Park Service.

The National Park System of the United States is administered by the National Park Service, a bureau of the Department of the Interior. Started with the establishment of Yellowstone National Park on March 1, 1872, the system includes not only the most extraordinary and spectacular scenic exhibits in the United States, but also a large number of sites distinguished either for their historic or prehistoric importance or scientific interest, or for their superior recreational assets. The National Park System is made up of 375 areas covering more than 83 million acres in every state except Delaware. It also includes areas in the District of Columbia, American Samoa, Guam, Puerto Rico, and the Virgin Islands. A list of the areas follows. Note that the National Park System does not include the Affiliated Areas, National Heritage Areas, Wild and Scenic Rivers System, and the National Trails System. See also the excellent website of the Park Service: www.nps.gov.

NATIONAL PARKS

Name, location, and year authorized	Acreage	Outstanding characteristics
Acadia (Maine), 1919	47,548.94	Rugged seashore on Mt. Desert Island and adjacent mainland
Arches (Utah), 1971	76,518.98	Unusual stone arches, windows, pedestals caused by erosion (park was a National Monument 1929–1971)
Badlands (S.D.), 1978	242,755.94	Arid land of fossils, prairie, bison, deer, bighorn sheep, antelope (park was a National Monument 1929–1978)
Big Bend (Tex.), 1935	801,163.21	Mountains and desert bordering the Rio Grande
Biscayne (Fla.), 1980	172,924.07	Aquatic, coral reef park south of Miami (park was a National Monument, 1968–1980)
Bryce Canyon (Utah), 1924	35,835.08	Area of grotesque eroded rocks brilliantly colored
Canyonlands (Utah), 1964	337,597.83	Colorful wilderness with impressive red-rock canyons, spires, arches
Capitol Reef (Utah), 1971	241,904.26	Highly colored sedimentary rock formations in high, narrow gorges (park was a National Monument 1937–1971)
Carlsbad Caverns (N.M.), 1930	46,766.45	One of the world's largest known caves
Channel Islands (Calif.), 1980	249,561.00	Area is rich in marine mammals, sea birds, endangered species, and archeology (park was a National Monument 1938–1980)
Crater Lake (Ore.), 1902	183,224.05	Deep blue lake in heart of inactive volcano
Cuyahoga Valley (Ohio), 2000	32,860.73	Wilderness area offering recreational, historic, and cultural attractions, including scenic rail journeys (park was a National Recreation Area 1974–2000)
Death Valley (Calif.-Nev.), 1994	3,340,409.65	Largest desert, surrounded by high mountains, containing the lowest point in the Western Hemisphere (park was a National Monument 1933–1994)
Denali (Alaska), 1917	4,740,911.72	Contains Mt. McKinley, N. America's highest mountain (20,320 ft) (formerly Mt. McKinley National Park, 1917–1980)
Dry Tortugas (Fla.), 1992	64,701.22	Located 70 mi off Key West. Features an underwater nature trail (formerly Ft. Jefferson National Monument 1935–1992)
Everglades (Fla.), 1934	1,508,491.84	Subtropical area with abundant bird and animal life
Gates of the Arctic (Alaska), 1980	7,523,897.74	Diverse north central wilderness contains part of Brooks Range
Glacier (Mont.), 1910	1,013,572.41	Rocky Mountain scenery with many glaciers and lakes
Glacier Bay (Alaska), 1980	3,224,840.31	Popular for wildlife, whale-watching, glacier-calving, and scenery (park was a National Monument 1925–1980)
Grand Canyon (Ariz.), 1919	1,217,403.32	Mile-deep gorge, 4 to 18 mi wide, 217 mi long
Grand Teton (Wyo.), 1929	309,994.66	Picturesque range of high mountain peaks
Great Basin (Nev.), 1986	77,180.00	Exceptional scenic, biologic, and geologic attractions (formerly Lehman Caves National Monument 1922–1986)
Great Smoky Mts. (N.C.-Tenn.), 1926	521,495.36	Highest mountain range east of Black Hills; luxuriant plant life
Guadalupe Mountains (Tex.), 1966	86,415.97	Contains highest point in Texas: Guadalupe Peak (8,751 ft)
Haleakala (Hawaii), 1916	29,830.15	World-famous 10,023-foot Haleakala volcano (dormant) (formerly part of Hawaii National Park. Renamed in 1960)
Hawaii Volcanoes (Hawaii), 1916	209,695.38	Spectacular volcanic area; luxuriant vegetation at lower levels (formerly Hawaii National Park. Renamed in 1961)
Hot Springs (Ark.), 1921	5,550.25	47 mineral hot springs said to have therapeutic value
Isle Royale (Mich.), 1931	571,790.11	Largest wilderness island in Lake Superior; moose, wolves, lakes
Joshua Tree (Calif.), 1994	784,162.05	Desert region featuring Joshua trees and a great variety of plants and animals (park was a National Monument 1936–1994)
Katmai (Alaska), 1980	3,674,529.68	Expansion may assure brown bear's preservation. Park is known for fishing, 1912 eruption of Novarupta, bears (park was a National Monument 1918–1980)
Kenai Fjords (Alaska), 1980	669,982.99	Mountain goats, marine mammals, birdlife are features at this seacoast park near Seward (park was a National Monument 1978–1980)

Name, location, and year authorized	Acreage	Outstanding characteristics
Kings Canyon (Calif.), 1890	461,901.20	Huge canyons; high mountains; giant sequoias (formerly General Grant National Park 1890–1940)
Kobuk Valley (Alaska), 1980	1,750,736.82	Native culture and anthropology center around the broad Kobuk River in northwest Alaska (park was a National Monument 1978–1980)
Lake Clark (Alaska), 1980	2,619,733.21	Park provides scenic and wilderness recreation across Cook Inlet from Anchorage (park was a National Monument 1978–1980)
Lassen Volcanic (Calif.), 1916	106,372.36	Exhibits of impressive volcanic phenomena
Mammoth Cave (Ky.), 1926	52,830.19	Vast limestone labyrinth with underground river
Mesa Verde (Colo.), 1906	52,121.93	Best-preserved prehistoric cliff dwellings in United States
Mount Rainier (Wash.), 1899	235,625.00	Single-peak glacial system; dense forests, flowered meadows
National Park of American Samoa, 1988	9,000.00	Samoa National Park, American Samoa: two rain forest preserves and a coral reef on the island of Ofu are home to unique tropical animals. The park also includes several thousand acres on the islands of Tutuila and Ta'u
North Cascades (Wash.), 1968	504,780.94	Roadless Alpine landscape; jagged peaks; mountain lakes; glaciers
Olympic (Wash.), 1938	922,650.94	Finest Pacific Northwest rain forest; scenic mountain park
Petrified Forest (Ariz.), 1962	93,532.57	Extensive natural exhibit of petrified wood (park was a National Monument 1906–1962)
Redwood (Calif.), 1968	112,512.97	Coastal redwood forests; contains world's tallest known tree (369.2 ft)
Rocky Mountain (Colo.), 1915	265,765.03	Section of the Rocky Mountains; 107 named peaks over 10,000 ft
Saguaro (Ariz.), 1994	91,445.16	Giant saguaro cacti, unique to the Sonoran Desert, sometimes reach a height of 50 ft in this cactus forest (park was a National Monument 1933–1994)
Sequoia (Calif.), 1890	404,051.17	Giant sequoias; magnificent High Sierra scenery, including Mt. Whitney
Shenandoah (Va.), 1926	199,038.07	Tree-covered mountains; scenic Skyline Drive
Theodore Roosevelt (N.D.), 1978	70,446.89	Scenic valley of Little Missouri River; T.R. Ranch; wildlife (Theodore Roosevelt National Memorial Park 1947–1978)
Virgin Islands (U.S. V.I.), 1956	14,688.87	Beaches; lush hills; prehistoric Carib Indian relics
Voyageurs (Minn.), 1971	218,200.17	Wildlife, canoeing, fishing, and hiking
Wind Cave (S.D.), 1903	28,295.03	Limestone caverns in Black Hills; buffalo herd
Wrangell-St. Elias (Alaska), 1980	8,323,147.59	Largest Park System area has abundant wildlife, second highest peak in U.S. (Mt. St. Elias); adjoins Canadian park (park was a National Monument 1978–1980)
Yellowstone (Wyo.-Mont.-Idaho), 1872	2,219,790.71	World's greatest geyser area; abundant falls, wildlife, and canyons
Yosemite (Calif.), 1890	761,266.28	Mountains; inspiring gorges and waterfalls; giant sequoias
Zion (Utah), 1919	146,597.64	Multicolored gorge in heart of southern Utah desert

Name and location	*Total acreage*
National Historical Parks	
Adams (Mass.)	23.82
Appomattox Court House (Va.)	1,772.36
Boston (Mass.)	43.32
Cane River Creole (La.)	207.38
Cedar Creek and Belle Grove (Va.)	3,566.61
Chaco Culture (N.M.)	33,960,19
Chesapeake and Ohio Canal (Md.-W.Va.-DC)	19,575.25
Colonial (Va.)	9,452.41
Cumberland Gap (Ky.-Tenn.-Va.)	20,463.15
Dayton Aviation Heritage (Ohio)	86.46
George Rogers Clark (Ind.)	26.17
Harpers Ferry (W.Va.-Md.)	2,501.67
Hopewell Culture (Ohio)	1,169.96
Independence (Pa.)	44.80
Jean Lafitte (La.)	20,004.90
Kalaupapa (Hawaii)	10,778.88
Kaloko-Honokohau (Hawaii)	1,160.91
Keweenaw (Mich.)	1,869.40
Klondike Gold Rush (Alaska-Wash.)	13,191.35
Lowell (Mass.)	141.34
Lyndon B. Johnson (Tex.)	1,570.15
Marsh-Billings-Rockefeller (Vt.)	643.07
Minute Man (Mass.)	970.83
Morristown (N.J.)	1,711.36
Natchez (Miss.)	105.31
New Bedford Whaling (Mass.)	34.00
New Orleans Jazz (La.)	5.13
Nez Perce (Idaho)	2,494.59
Pecos (N.M.)	6,670.08
Pu'uhonua o Honaunau (Hawaii)	181.80
Rosie the Riveter/WW II Home Front (Calif.)	145.19
Salt River Bay and Ecological Preserve (U.S. V.I.)	947.75
San Antonio Missions (Tex.)	825.92
San Francisco Maritime (Calif.)	49.86
San Juan Island (Wash.)	1,751.99
Saratoga (N.Y.)	3,392.42
Sitka (Alaska)	113.17
Tumacacori (Ariz.)	46.28
Valley Forge (Pa.)	3,464.26
War in the Pacific (Guam)	2,036.98
Women's Rights (N.Y.)	7.44

Name and location	Total acreage
National Monuments	
Agate Fossil Beds (Neb.)	3,055.22
Alibates Flint Quarries (Tex.)	1,370.97
Aniakchak (Alaska)	137,176.00
Aztec Ruins (N.M.)	317.80
Bandelier (N.M.)	33,676.67
Black Canyon of the Gunnison (Colo.)	30,045.03
Booker T. Washington (Va.)	223.92
Buck Island Reef (U.S. V.I.)	19,015.47
Cabrillo (Calif.)	159.94
Canyon de Chelly (Ariz.)	83,840.00
Cape Krusenstern (Alaska)	649,085.04
Capulin Volcano (N.M.)	792.84
Casa Grande Ruins (Ariz.)	472.50
Castillo de San Marcos (Fla.)	20.21
Castle Clinton (N.Y.)	1.00
Cedar Breaks (Utah)	6,154.60
Chiricahua (Ariz.)	11,984.73
Colorado (Colo.)	20,533.93
Congaree Swamp (S.C.)	21,889.85
Craters of the Moon (Idaho)	304,727.05
Devils Postpile (Calif.)	798.46
Devils Tower (Wyo.)	1,346.91
Dinosaur (Utah-Colo.)	210,277.55
Effigy Mounds (Iowa)	2,526.39
El Malpais (N.M.)	114,276.95
El Morro (N.M.)	1,278.72
Florissant Fossil Beds (Colo.)	5,998.09
Fort Frederica (Ga.)	241.42
Fort Matanzas (Fla.)	300.11
Fort McHenry (Md.)	43.26
Fort Pulaski (Ga.)	5,623.10
Fort Stanwix (N.Y.)	15.52
Fort Sumter (S.C.)	199.57
Fort Union (N.M.)	720.60
Fossil Butte (Wyo.)	8,198.00
George Washington Birthplace (Va.)	550.23
George Washington Carver (Mo.)	210.00
Gila Cliff Dwellings (N.M.)	533.13
Governor's Island (N.Y.)	22.78
Grand Portage (Minn.)	709.97
Great Sand Dunes (Colo.)	42,272.18
Hagerman Fossil Beds (Idaho)	4,351.15
Hohokam Pima (Ariz.)	1,690.00
Homestead (Neb.)	195.11
Hovenweep (Utah-Colo.)	784.93
Jewel Cave (S.D.)	1,273.51
John Day Fossil Beds (Ore.)	14,056.73
Lava Beds (Calif.)	46,559.87
Little Big Horn Battlefield (Mont.)	765.34
Minidoka Internment (Idaho)	72.75
Montezuma Castle (Ariz.)	857.69
Muir Woods (Calif.)	553.55
Natural Bridges (Utah)	7,636.49
Navajo (Ariz.)	360.00
Ocmulgee (Ga.)	701.54
Oregon Caves (Ore.)	487.98
Organ Pipe Cactus (Ariz.)	330,688.86
Petroglyph (N.M.)	7,231.63
Pinnacles (Calif.)	17,614.05
Pipe Spring (Ariz.)	40.00
Pipestone (Minn.)	281.78
Poverty Point (La.)	910.85
Rainbow Bridge (Utah)	160.00
Russell Cave (Ala.)	310.45
Salinas Pueblo Missions (N.M.)	1,071.42

Name and location	Total acreage
Scotts Bluff (Neb.)	3,004.81
Statue of Liberty (N.Y.-N.J.)	58.38
Sunset Crater Volcano (Ariz.)	3,040.00
Timpanogos Cave (Utah)	250.00
Tonto (Ariz.)	1,120.00
Tuzigoot (Ariz.)	800.62
U.S. Virgin Islands Coral Reef (V.I.)	13,892.78
Walnut Canyon (Ariz.)	3,579.46
White Sands (N.M.)	143,732.92
Wupatki (Ariz.)	35,422.13
Yucca House (Colo.)	33.87
National Preserves	
Aniakchak (Alaska)	465,603.00
Bering Land Bridge (Alaska)	2,697,393.11
Big Cypress (Fla.)	720,565.67
Big Thicket (Tex.)	97,168.03
Denali (Alaska)	1,334,117.99
Gates of the Arctic (Alaska)	948,607.96
Glacier Bay (Alaska)	58,406.00
Great Sand Dunes (Colo.)	41,686.00
Katmai (Alaska)	418,699.22
Lake Clark (Alaska)	1,410,291.99
Little River Canyon (Ala.)	13,632.96
Mojave (Calif.)	1,531,831.60
Noatak (Alaska)	6,569,904.43
Tallgrass Prairie (Kans.)	10,894.00
Timucuan Ecological and Historic Preserve (Fla.)	46,286.91
Wrangell-St. Elias (Alaska)	4,852,753.10
Yukon-Charley Rivers (Alaska)	2,526,512.31
National Reserves	
City of Rocks (Idaho)	14,107.19
Ebey's Landing (Wash.)	19,323.99
National Military Parks	
Chickamauga and Chattanooga (Ga.-Tenn.)	8,266.34
Fredericksburg and Spotsylvania (Va.)	8,361.92
Gettysburg (Pa.)	5,990.31
Guilford Courthouse (N.C.)	228.59
Horseshoe Bend (Ala.)	2,040.00
Kings Mountain (S.C.)	3,945.29
Pea Ridge (Ark.)	4,300.35
Shiloh Nat. Park (Tenn.)	4,024.88
Vicksburg (Miss.)	1,753.16
National Battlefields	
Antietam (Md.)	3,244.37
Big Hole (Mont.)	1,010.61
Cowpens (S.C.)	841.56
Fort Donelson (Tenn.)	551.69
Fort Necessity (Pa.)	902.80
Little Big Horn (Mont.)	765.34
Monocacy (Md.)	1,647.01
Moores Creek (N.C.)	87.75
Petersburg (Va.)	2,659.19
Stones River (Tenn.)	709.36
Tupelo (Miss.)	1.00
Wilson's Creek (Mo.)	1,749.91
National Battlefield Parks	
Kennesaw Mountain (Ga.)	2,884.14
Manassas (Va.)	5,067.92
Richmond (Va.)	2,151.94

Name and location	Total acreage
National Battlefield Site	
Brices Cross Roads (Miss.)	1.00
National Historic Sites	
Abraham Lincoln Birthplace (Ky.)	344.50
Allegheny Portage Railroad (Pa.)	1,249.20
Andersonville (Ga.)	494.61
Andrew Johnson (Tenn.)	16.68
Bent's Old Fort (Colo.)	798.80
Boston African-American (Mass.)	0.59
Brown v. Board of Education (Kans.)	1.85
Carl Sandburg Home (N.C.)	263.65
Charles Pinckney (S.C.)	28.45
Christiansted (U.S. V.I.)	27.15
Clara Barton (Md.)	8.59
Edgar Allan Poe (Pa.)	0.52
Edison (N.J.)	21.25
Eisenhower (Pa.)	690.46
Eleanor Roosevelt (N.Y.)	180.50
Eugene O'Neill (Calif.)	13.19
First Ladies (Ohio)	0.33
Ford's Theatre (Lincoln Museum) (DC)	0.29
Fort Bowie (Ariz.)	999.45
Fort Davis (Tex.)	473.87
Fort Laramie (Wyo.)	832.85
Fort Larned (Kan.)	718.39
Fort Point (Calif.)	29.00
Fort Raleigh (N.C.)	512.93
Fort Scott (Kan.)	16.69
Fort Smith (Ark.-Okla.)	75.05
Fort Union Trading Post (N.D.-Mont.)	443.81
Fort Vancouver (Wash.)	208.89
Frederick Douglass Home (DC)	8.53
Frederick Law Olmsted (Mass.)	7.21
Friendship Hill (Pa.)	674.56
Golden Spike (Utah)	2,735.28
Grant-Kohrs Ranch (Mont.)	1,618.38
Hampton (Md.)	62.04
Harry S. Truman (Mo.)	6.67
Herbert Hoover (Iowa)	186.80
Home of F. D. Roosevelt (N.Y.)	799.98
Hopewell Furnace (Pa.)	848.06
Hubbell Trading Post (Ariz.)	160.09
James A. Garfield (Ohio)	7.82
Jimmy Carter (Ga.)	70.86
John F. Kennedy (Mass.)	0.09
John Muir (Calif.)	344.73
Knife River Indian Villages (N.D.)	1,758.35
Lincoln Home (Ill.)	12.24
Little Rock Central High School (Ark.)	27.28
Longfellow (Mass.)	1.98
Maggie L. Walker (Va.)	1.29
Manzanar (Calif.)	813.81
Martin Luther King, Jr. (Ga.)	38.66
Martin Van Buren (N.Y.)	39.55
Mary McLeod Bethune Council House (DC)	0.07
Minuteman Missile (S.D.)	15.00
Nicodemus (Kans.)	161.35
Ninety Six (S.C.)	989.14
Palo Alto Battlefield (Tex.)	3,407.46
Pennsylvania Avenue (DC)	0.00
Puukohola Heiau (Hawaii)	86.24
Ronald Reagan Boyhood Home (Ill.)	1.01
Sagamore Hill (N.Y.)	83.02
Saint-Gaudens (N.H.)	148.15
Saint Paul's Church (N.Y.)	6.13
Salem Maritime (Mass.)	9.02
San Juan (P.R.)	75.13
Saugus Iron Works (Mass.)	8.51
Springfield Armory (Mass.)	54.93
Steamtown (Pa.)	62.48
Theodore Roosevelt Birthplace (N.Y.)	0.11
Theodore Roosevelt Inaugural (N.Y.)	1.03
Thomas Stone (Md.)	328.25
Tuskegee Airmen (Ala.)	86.69
Tuskegee Institute (Ala.)	57.92
Ulysses S. Grant (Mo.)	9.60
Vanderbilt Mansion (N.Y.)	211.65
Washita Battlefield (Okla.)	315.20
Weir Farms (Conn.)	74.20
Whitman Mission (Wash.)	99.93
William Howard Taft (Ohio)	3.10
National Memorials	
Arkansas Post (Ark.)	746.88
Arlington House, the Robert E. Lee Memorial (Va.)	27.91
Chamizal (Tex.)	54.90
Coronado (Ariz.)	4,750.22
De Soto (Fla.)	26.84
Federal Hall (N.Y.)	0.45
Fort Caroline (Fla.)	138.39
Fort Clatsop (Ore.)	125.20
Franklin Delano Roosevelt Memorial (DC)	7.50
General Grant (N.Y.)	0.76
Hamilton Grange (N.Y.)	1.04
Jefferson National Expansion Memorial (Mo.)	192.83
Johnstown Flood (Pa.)	164.12
Korean War Veterans (DC)	2.20
Lincoln Boyhood (Ind.)	199.65
Lincoln Memorial (DC)	107.43
Lyndon Baines Johnson Memorial Grove on the Potomac (DC)	17.00
Mount Rushmore (S.D.)	1,278.45
Oklahoma City (Okla.)	6.24
Perry's Victory and International Peace Memorial (Ohio)	25.39
Roger Williams (R.I.)	4.56
Thaddeus Kosciuszko (Pa.)	0.02
Theodore Roosevelt Island (DC)	88.50
Thomas Jefferson Memorial (DC)	18.36
USS *Arizona* Memorial (Hawaii)	10.50
Vietnam Veterans Memorial (DC)	2.00
Washington Monument (DC)	106.01
Wright Brothers (N.C.)	428.44
National Seashores	
Assateague Island (Md.-Va.)	39,733.43
Canaveral (Fla.)	57,661.69
Cape Cod (Mass.)	43,604.94
Cape Hatteras (N.C.)	30,321.46
Cape Lookout (N.C.)	28,243.36
Cumberland Island (Ga.)	36,415.13
Fire Island (N.Y.)	19,579.47
Gulf Islands (Fla.-Miss.)	137,792.89
Padre Island (Tex.)	130,434.27
Point Reyes (Calif.)	71,067.66

Name and location	Total acreage
National Parkways	
Blue Ridge (Va.-N.C.)	91,813.23
George Washington Memorial (Va.-Md.)	7,342.48
John D. Rockefeller, Jr., Memorial (Wyo.)	23,777.22
Natchez Trace (Miss.-Tenn.-Ala.)	51,981.57
National Lakeshores	
Apostle Islands (Wis.)	69,371.89
Indiana Dunes (Ind.)	15,044.47
Pictured Rocks (Mich.)	73,235.53
Sleeping Bear Dunes (Mich.)	71,194.71
National Park System Rivers	
Alagnak Wild River (Alaska)	30,665.45
Big South Fork National River and Recreation Area (Ky.-Tenn.)	125,310.34
Bluestone National Scenic River (W. Va.)	4,309.51
Buffalo National River (Ark.)	94,293.31
Delaware National Scenic River (Pa.)	1,973.33
Great Egg Harbor Scenic and Recreational River (N.J.-Pa.)	43,311.42
Mississippi National River and Recreation Area (Minn.)	53,775.00
Missouri National Recreational River (Neb.)	45,350.00
New River Gorge National River (W.Va.)	70,465.89
Niobrara National Scenic Riverway (Neb.)	5,992.96
Obed Wild and Scenic River (Tenn.)	5,173.69
Ozark National Scenic Riverways (Mo.)	80,785.04
Rio Grande Wild and Scenic River (Tex.)	9,600.00
St. Croix National Scenic River (Minn.-Wis.)	67,460.31
Upper Delaware Scenic and Recreational River (Pa.)	74,999.56
National Recreation Areas	
Amistad (Tex.)	58,500.00
Bighorn Canyon (Wyo.-Mont.)	120,296.22
Boston Harbor Islands (Mass.)	1,482.25
Chattahoochee River (Ga.)	9,164.53
Chickasaw (Okla.)	9,888.83
Curecanti (Colo.)	41,972.42
Delaware Water Gap (Pa.-N.J.)	66,740.46
Gateway (N.Y.-N.J.)	26,606.63
Gauley River (W. Va.)	11,505.59
Glen Canyon (Ariz.-Utah)	1,254,306.19
Golden Gate (Calif.)	74,815.56
Lake Chelan (Wash.)	61,946.72
Lake Mead (Ariz.-Nev.)	1,495,664.00
Lake Meredith (Tex.)	44,977.63
Lake Roosevelt (Wash.)	100,390.31
Ross Lake (Wash.)	117,574.59
Santa Monica Mountains (Calif.)	153,672.77
Whiskeytown-Shasta-Trinity (Calif.)	42,503.46
National Scenic Trails	
Appalachian (Maine-N.H.-Vt.-Mass.-Conn.-N.Y.-N.J.- Pa.-Md.-W.Va.-Va.-N.C.-Tenn., Ga.)	222,613.24
Natchez Trace (Ala.-Miss.-Tenn.)	10,995.00
Potomac Heritage (DC-Md.-Va.-Pa.)	n.a.
International Historic Site	
Saint Croix Island (Maine)	44.90
National Cemeteries[1]	
Antietam (Md.)	11.36
Battleground (DC)	1.03
Chalmette Cemetery (La.)	17.5
Fort Donelson (Tenn.)	15.30
Fredericksburg (Va.)	12.00
Gettysburg (Pa.)	20.58
Poplar Grove (Va.)	8.72
Shiloh (Tenn.)	10.05
Stones River (Tenn.)	719.81
Vicksburg (Miss.)	116.28
Yorktown (Va.)	2.91

1. The National Cemeteries are not independent areas of the National Park System; each is part of a military park, battlefield, etc., except Battleground. Their acreage is kept separately. Arlington National Cemetery is under the Department of the Army.

Name and location	Total acreage
Other Parks	
Catoctin Mountain (Md.)	5,809.87
Constitution Gardens (DC)	52.00
Fort Washington Park (Md.)	341.00
Greenbelt (Md.)	1,175.99
National Capital Parks (DC)	6,629.42
National Mall (DC)	146.35
Piscataway (Md.)	4,624.91
Prince William Forest (Va.)	18,856.04
Rock Creek Park (DC)	1,754.70
White House (DC)	18.07
Wolf Trap Farm Park for the Performing Arts (Va.)	130.28

Ten Most Visited National Park Sites, 2002

Rank	Name and location	Number of visitors
1.	Blue Ridge Parkway, Va.-N.C.	21,538,760
2.	Golden Gate National Recreation Area, Calif.	13,961,267
3.	Great Smoky Mountains National Park, Tenn.	9,316,420
4.	Gateway National Recreation Area, N.Y.-N.J.	9,014,438
5.	Lake Mead National Recreation Area, Nev.-Ariz.	7,550,284
6.	George Washington Memorial Parkway, Va.-Md.-DC	7,419,375
7.	Delaware Water Gap National Recreation Area, Pa.-N.J.	5,165,415
8.	Gulf Islands National Seashore, Fla.-Miss.	4,561,862
9.	Cape Cod National Seashore, Mass.	4,455,931
10.	Grand Canyon National Park, Ariz.	4,001,974

Source: Based on data from the National Park Service. Web: www.nps.gov.

Zeus, Park Rangers, and the Probability of Being Struck by Lightning

Zeus, the Greek king of the gods, punished wayward mortals and miscreant gods by hurling thunderbolts at them. Sky deities from many world religions, including Zeus's Roman counterpart Jupiter, the Germanic Thor, the Mayan Chac, and the Slavic Perun, all used the thunderbolt as the paramount symbol of power.

Whether deserving the wrath of the gods or not, chances are slim that you'll meet your end from a bolt of lightning. Lightning causes only an average of 93 deaths and 300 injuries in the United States each year. The National Weather Service publication *Storm Data* recorded a total of 3,239 deaths and 9,818 injuries from lightning strikes between 1959 and 1994.

Dead Ringers

Whatever your strategy for avoiding lightning, be sure to stay clear of church bells. During the Middle Ages, their ringing was believed to diffuse lightning, and many medieval bells were engraved with *Fulgura frango* ("I break up the lightning"). This suspect theory was discredited by a medieval scholar who observed that over a 33-year period, there were 386 lightning strikes on church towers and 103 fatalities among bell ringers.

Shocking Humor

Should you live to tell the tale of being struck by lightning, you can join the Lightning Strike and Electric Shock Survivors International, Inc. (LSESSI), a non-profit support group for such survivors. With its motto, "Join us if it strikes you," and newsletter, *Hit or Miss,* the group emphasizes the necessity of a sense of humor in overcoming trauma.

One LSESSI member has been victimized both indoors and outdoors. The record holder, however, is Roy C. Sullivan, an ex-park ranger who survived seven different lightning strikes. According to the *Guinness Book of Records,* Sullivan was first hit by lightning in 1942, which caused him to lose his big toenail. Over the next 35 years, lightning burned off Sullivan's eyebrows, seared his left shoulders, set his hair on fire, struck his legs, injured his ankle, and burned his stomach and chest.

Safe Spots

The safest place to be during a thunderstorm is in a building, preferably one with a lightning rod. The rod offers protection by intercepting lightning—an electrical charge—and transmitting its current into the ground. Made out of metal so that it conducts the charge, it is usually located as high as possible because of lightning's tendency to strike the nearest object to it. (And yes, Benjamin Franklin did invent the lightning rod, as well as prove that lightning was actually electricity through his flying-a-kite-during-a-thunderstorm experiment.)

The other safe place is a car with the windows rolled up, as long as you don't touch any of the metal parts. If lightning strikes, the car's metal body will conduct the charge down to the ground—contrary to popular belief, the rubber of the wheels offers no protection. □

Costliest Hurricanes in the United States[1]

(U.S. Mainland)

Rank	Hurricane	Location	Year	Category[2]	Damage (in billions)
1.	Andrew	Fla./La.	1992	5[3]	$26.5
2.	Hugo	S.C.	1989	4	7.0
3.	Floyd	Mid Atlantic/ NE U.S.	1999	2	4.5
4.	Fran	N.C.	1996	3	3.2
5.	Opal	Fla./Ala.	1995	3	3.0
6.	Georges	Fla./Miss./ Ala.	1998	2	$2.31
7.	Frederic	Ala./Miss.	1979	3	2.3
8.	Agnes	Fla./NE U.S.	1972	1	2.1
9.	Alicia	Tex.	1983	3	2.0
10.	Bob	N.C./NE U.S.	1991	2	1.5
10.	Juan	La.	1985	1	1.5

NOTE: Damages are listed in U.S. dollars and are not adjusted for inflation. 1. 1900–2000. 2. Saffir-Simpson Hurricane scale: Cat. 1 = weak; Cat. 5 = devastating. 3. Hurricane Andrew was upgraded in Aug. 2002 from Cat. 4 to 5. *Source:* National Oceanic and Atmospheric Administration (NOAA).

Deadliest Hurricanes in the United States[1]

(U.S. Mainland)

Rank	Hurricane	Year	Category[2]	Deaths
1.	Galveston, Tex.	1900	4	8,000[3]
2.	Lake Okeechobee, Fla.	1928	4	1,836
3.	Florida Keys/S. Tex.	1919	4	600[4]
4.	New England	1938	3	600
5.	Florida Keys	1935	5	408
6.	Audrey (SW La./N. Tex.)	1957	4	390
7.	NE U.S.	1944	3	390[5]
8.	Grand Isle, La.	1909	4	350
9.	New Orleans, La.	1915	4	275
10.	Galveston, Tex.	1915	4	275

1. 1900–2000. 2. Saffir-Simpson Hurricane scale: Cat. 1 = weak; Cat. 5 = devastating. 3. May actually have been as high as 10,000 to 12,000. 4. Over 500 of these lost on ships at sea; 600–900 estimated deaths. 5. Some 344 of these lost on ships at sea. *Source:* National Oceanic and Atmospheric Administration (NOAA).

Most Intense[1] Hurricanes in the United States[2]

(U.S. Mainland)

Rank	Hurricane	Year	Category[3]	Rank	Hurricane	Year	Category[3]
1.	Florida Keys	1935	5	6.	Donna (Fla./Eastern U.S.)	1960	4
2.	Camille (Miss./La./Va.)	1969	5	7.	Galveston, Tex.	1900	4
3.	Andrew (Fla./La.)	1992	5[4]	8.	Grand Isle, La.	1909	4
4.	Florida Keys/Tex.	1919	4	9.	New Orleans, La.	1915	4
5.	Lake Okeechobee, Fla.	1928	4	10.	Carla (Tex.)	1961	4

1. Intensity is for time of landfall. May have been stronger at other times. 2. 1900–2000. 3. Saffir-Simpson Hurricane scale: Cat. 1 = weak; Cat. 5 = devastating. 4. Hurricane Andrew was upgraded in Aug. 2002 from Cat. 4 to 5. *Source:* National Oceanic and Atmospheric Administration (NOAA).

Atlantic Hurricane Names

Because hurricanes often occur at the same time, officials assign short, distinctive names to the storms to avoid confusion among weather stations, coastal bases, and ships at sea. Since 1953, Atlantic tropical storms have been named from lists created by the National Hurricane Center and now maintained and updated by an international committee of the World Meteorological Organization. The lists featured only women's names until 1979, when men's and women's names were alternated. Six lists are used in rotation. Thus, the 2003 list will be used again in 2009. A storm is given a name once its winds reach an intensity of 40 mph. In addition to the Atlantic list of names, there are ten other lists corresponding to other storm-prone regions of the world.

2003	2004	2005	2006	2007	2008
Ana	Alex	Arlene	Alberto	Andrea	Arthur
Bill	Bonnie	Bret	Beryl	Barry	Bertha
Claudette	Charley	Cindy	Chris	Chantal	Cristobal
Danny	Danielle	Dennis	Debby	Dean	Dolly
Erika	Earl	Emily	Ernesto	Erin	Edouard
Fabian	Frances	Franklin	Florence	Felix	Fay
Grace	Gaston	Gert	Gordon	Gabrielle	Gustav
Henri	Hermine	Harvey	Helene	Humberto	Hanna
Isabel	Ivan	Irene	Isaac	Ingrid	Isidore
Juan	Jeanne	Jose	Joyce	Jerry	Josephine
Kate	Karl	Katrina	Kirk	Karen	Kyle
Larry	Lisa	Lee	Leslie	Lorenzo	Lili
Mindy	Matthew	Maria	Michael	Melissa	Marco
Nicholas	Nicole	Nate	Nadine	Noel	Nana
Odette	Otto	Ophelia	Oscar	Olga	Omar
Peter	Paula	Philippe	Patty	Pablo	Paloma
Rose	Richard	Rita	Rafael	Rebekah	Rene
Sam	Shary	Stan	Sandy	Sebastien	Sally
Teresa	Tomas	Tammy	Tony	Tanya	Teddy
Victor	Virginie	Vince	Valerie	Van	Vicky
Wanda	Walter	Wilma	William	Wendy	Wilfred

Source: National Hurricane Center, National Oceanic and Atmospheric Administration (NOAA).

Retired Hurricane Names

When hurricanes are particularly destructive, their names are retired from the list of usable names. Any country affected by a particularly terrible storm can request that the name be retired by petitioning the World Meteorological Organization. Below is a list of infamous hurricanes that have settled into retirement.

Name	Year	Location(s) affected
Agnes	1972	Florida, Northeast U.S.
Alicia	1983	North Texas
Allen	1980	Antilles, Mexico, South Texas
Andrew	1992	Bahamas, South Florida, and Louisiana
Anita	1977	Mexico
Audrey	1957	Louisiana, North Texas
Betsy	1965	Bahamas, Southeast Florida, Southeast Louisiana
Beulah	1967	Antilles, Mexico, South Texas
Bob	1991	North Carolina, Northeast U.S.
Camille	1969	Louisiana, Mississippi, and Alabama
Carla	1961	Texas
Carmen	1974	Mexico
Carol	1954	Northeast U.S.
Celia	1970	South Texas
Cleo	1964	Lesser Antilles, Haiti, Cuba, Southeast Florida
Connie	1955	North Carolina
David	1979	Lesser Antilles, Hispanola, Florida, and Eastern U.S.
Diana	1990	Mexico
Diane	1955	Mid-Atlantic U.S. and Northeast U.S.
Donna	1960	Bahamas, Florida, and Eastern U.S.
Dora	1964	Northeast Florida
Elena	1985	Mississippi, Alabama, Western Florida
Ekiuse	1975	Antilles, Northwest Florida, Alabama
Flora	1963	Haiti, Cuba
Frederic	1979	Alabama and Mississippi
Gilbert	1988	Lesser Antilles, Jamaica, Yucatan Peninsula, Mexico
Gloria	1985	North Carolina, Northeast U.S.
Hattie	1961	Belize, Guatemala
Hazel	1954	Antilles, North and South Carolina
Hilda	1964	Louisiana

Name	Year	Location(s) affected
Hugo	1989	Antilles, South Carolina
Ione	1955	North Carolina
Inez	1966	Lesser Antilles, Hispanola, Cuba, Florida Keys, Mexico
Janet	1955	Lesser Antilles, Belize, Mexico
Joan	1988	Curacao, Venezuela, Colombia, Nicaragua (crossed Pacific and became Miriam)
Klaus	1990	Martinique
Luis	1995	Lesser Antilles
Marilyn	1995	Lesser Antilles, Puerto Rico
Mitch	1998	Central America, Nicaragua, Honduras
Opal	1995	Central America, Mexico, Florida
Roxanne	1995	Mexico

Source: National Hurricane Center, National Oceanic and Atmospheric Administration (NOAA).

The 20 Deadliest Tornadoes

Date	Location(s)	Deaths
1. March 18, 1925	Tri-State (Mo., Ill., Ind.)	689
2. May 6, 1840	Natchez, Miss.	317
3. May 27, 1896	St. Louis, Mo.	255
4. April 5, 1936	Tupelo, Miss.	216
5. April 6, 1936	Gainesville, Ga.	203
6. April 9, 1947	Woodward, Okla.	181
7. April 24, 1908	Amite La.; Purvis, Miss.	143
8. June 12, 1899	New Richmond, Wis.	117
9. June 8, 1953	Flint, Mich.	115
10. May 11, 1953	Waco, Tex.	114
10. May 18, 1902	Goliad, Tex.	114
12. March 23, 1913	Omaha, Neb.	103
13. May 26, 1917	Mattoon, Ill.	101
14. June 23, 1944	Shinnston, W. Va.	100
15. April 18, 1880	Marshfield, Mo.	99
16. June 1, 1903	Gainesville, Holland, Ga.	98
16. May 9, 1927	Poplar Bluff, Mo.	98
18. May 10, 1905	Snyder, Okla.	97
19. April 24, 1908	Natchez, Miss.	91
20. June 9, 1953	Worcester, Mass.	90

Source: Storm Prediction Center at the National Weather Service, National Oceanographic and Atmospheric Administration (NOAA). Web: www.spc.noaa.gov/archive/tornadoes/t-deadly.html.

2002 Tornado Fatality Information

Number of Deadly Tornadoes

State	Deadly tornadoes	Fatalities
Tennessee	5	17
Alabama	4	13
Ohio	3	5
Illinois	3	4
Texas	2	3
Louisiana	2	3
Missouri	3	3
Maryland	2	3
Kentucky	1	1
Pennsylvania	1	1
Mississippi	1	1
Arkansas	1	1
Total	**28**	**55**

Circumstances

Circumstance	Fatalities
Mobile home	37
Permanent home	10
Vehicle	4
Business	2
Other/unknown	2
Total	**55**

Source: Storm Prediction Center at the National Weather Service, National Oceanographic and Atmospheric Administration (NOAA). Web: www.spc.noaa.gov/climo/torn/2002deadlytorn.html.

Greatest Snowfalls in North America

	Place	Date	Inches	Centimeters
24 hours	Silver Lake, Colo.	April 14–15, 1921	76	195.6
1 month	Tamarack, Calif.	Jan. 1911	390	991
1 storm	Mt. Shasta Ski Bowl, Calif.	Feb. 13–19, 1959	189	480
1 season	Mount Baker, Wash.	1998–1999	1,140	2,895.6

Source: U.S. Army Corps of Engineers, Engineer Topographic Laboratories.

Recorded Weather Extremes

Highest average annual mean temperature (world): Dallol, Ethiopia (Oct. 1960–Dec. 1966), 94° F (34.4° C). **(U.S.):** Key West, Fla. (30-year normal), 78.2° F (25.7° C).

Lowest average annual mean temperature (world): Plateau Station, Antarctica, –70° F (–56.7° C). **(U.S.):** Barrow, Alaska (30-year normal), 9.3° F (–12.6° C).

Greatest average yearly rainfall (world): Cherrapunji, India (74-year avg), 450 in. (1,143 cm). **(U.S.):** Mt. Waialeale, Kauai, Hawaii (32-year avg), 460 in. (1,168 cm).

Minimum average yearly rainfall (world): Arica, Chile (59-year avg), 0.03 in. (0.08 cm) (no rainfall for 14 consecutive years). **(U.S.):** Death Valley, Calif. (42-year avg), 1.63 in. (4.14 cm). Bagdad, Calif., holds the U.S. record for the longest period with no measurable rain, 767 days, from Oct. 3, 1912 to Nov. 8, 1914.

Hottest summer average in Western Hemisphere (U.S.): Death Valley, Calif., 98° F (36.7° C).

Longest hot spell (world): Marble Bar, W. Australia, 100° F (37.8° C) (or above) for 162 consecutive days, Oct. 30, 1923 to Apr. 7, 1924.

Largest hailstone (U.S.): Aurora, Neb., 7 in. (17.8 cm) in diameter, 18.75 in. (47.6 cm) in circumference, June 22, 2003.

World and U.S. Extremes of Climate

Highest Recorded Temperatures

	Place	Date	Degrees Fahrenheit	Degrees Celsius
World (Africa)	El Azizia, Libya	Sept. 13, 1922	136	58
North America (U.S.)	Death Valley, Calif.	July 10, 1913	134	57
Asia	Tirat Tsvi, Israel	June 21, 1942	129	54
Australia	Cloncurry, Queensland	Jan. 16, 1889	128	53
Europe	Seville, Spain	Aug. 4, 1881	122	50
South America	Rivadavia, Argentina	Dec. 11, 1905	120	49
Canada	Midale and Yellow Grass, Saskatchewan, Canada	July 5, 1937	113	45
Oceania	Tuguegarao, Philippines	April 29, 1912	108	45.6
Persian Gulf (sea-surface)		Aug. 5, 1924	96	36
Antarctica	Vanda Station, Scott Coast	Jan. 5, 1974	59	15
South Pole		Dec. 27, 1978	7.5	–14

Lowest Recorded Temperatures

	Place	Date	Degrees Fahrenheit	Degrees Celsius
World (Antarctica)	Vostok	July 21, 1983	–129	–89
Asia	Oimekon, Russia	Feb. 6, 1933	–90	–68
	Verkhoyansk, Russia	Feb. 7, 1892	–90	–68
Greenland	Northice	Jan. 9, 1954	–87	–66
North America (excl. Greenland)	Snag, Yukon, Canada	Feb. 3, 1947	–81	–63
United States	Prospect Creek, Alaska	Jan. 23, 1971	–80	–62
U.S. (excl. Alaska)	Rogers Pass, Mont.	Jan. 20, 1954	–70	–56.5
Europe	Ust 'Shchugor, Russia	Jan.[1]	–67	–55
South America	Sarmiento, Argentina	June 1, 1907	–27	–33
Africa	Ifrane, Morocco	Feb. 11, 1935	–11	–24
Australia	Charlotte Pass, N.S.W.	June 29, 1994	–9	–22
Oceania	Haleakala Summit, Maui, Hawaii	Jan. 2, 1961	14	–10.8

1. Exact date unknown; lowest in 15-year period.

Greatest Rainfalls

	Place	Date	Inches	Centimeters
1 minute (World)	Unionville, Md.	July 4, 1956	1.23	3.1
20 minutes (World)	Curtea-de-Arges, Romania	July 7, 1889	8.1	20.5
42 minutes (World)	Holt, Mo.	June 22, 1947	12	30.5
12 hours (World)	Grand Ilet, La Réunion	Jan. 26, 1980	46	114
24 hours (World)	Foc-Foc, La Réunion	Jan. 7–8, 1966	72	182.5
24 hours (N. Hemisphere)	Paishih, Taiwan	Sept. 10–11, 1963	49	125
24 hours (Australia)	Bellenden Ker, Queensland	Jan. 4, 1979	44	114
24 hours (U.S.)	Alvin, Tex.	July 25–26, 1979	43	109
24 hours (Canada)	Ucluelet Brynnor Mines, British Columbia	Oct. 6, 1967	19	49
5 days (World)	Commerson, La Réunion	Jan. 23–28, 1980	156	395
1 month (World)	Cherrapunji, India	July 1861	366	930
12 months (World)	Cherrapunji, India	Aug. 1860–Aug. 1861	1,042	2,647
12 months (U.S.)	Kukui, Maui, Hawaii	Dec. 1981–Dec. 1982	739	1878

Lowest Average Annual Precipitation Extremes

Continent	Place	Lowest avg. (in.)	Elevation (ft)	Years of record
World (South America)	Arica, Chile	0.03	95	59
Africa	Wadi Halfa, Sudan	<0.10	410	39
Antarctica	Amundsen-Scott South Pole Station	0.80[1]	9,186	10
North America	Batagues, Mexico	1.20	16	14
Asia	Aden, Yemen	1.80	22	50
Australia	Mulka (Troudaninna), South Australia	4.05	160[2]	42
Europe	Astrakhan, Russia	6.40	45	25
Oceania	Puako, Hawaii, Hawaii	8.93	5	13

1. The value given is the average amount of solid snow accumulating in one year as indicated by snow markers. The liquid content of the snow is undetermined. 2. Approximate elevation. *Source:* U.S. Army Corps of Engineers, Engineer Topographic Laboratories.

Record Highest Temperatures by State

State	Temp. °F	Temp. °C	Date	Station	Elevation in feet
Alabama	112	44	Sept. 5, 1925	Centerville	345
Alaska	100	38	June 27, 1915	Fort Yukon	est. 420
Arizona	128	53	June 29, 1994	Lake Havasu City	505
Arkansas	120	49	Aug. 10, 1936	Ozark	396
California	134	57	July 10, 1913	Greenland Ranch	-178
Colorado	118	48	July 11, 1888	Bennett	5,484
Connecticut	106	41	July 15, 1995	Danbury	450
Delaware	110	43	July 21, 1930	Millsboro	20
D.C.	106	41	July 20, 1930	Washington	410
Florida	109	43	June 29, 1931	Monticello	207
Georgia	112	44	Aug. 20, 1983	Greenville	860
Hawaii	100	38	Apr. 27, 1931	Pahala	850
Idaho	118	48	July 28, 1934	Orofino	1,027
Illinois	117	47	July 14, 1954	E. St. Louis	410
Indiana	116	47	July 14, 1936	Collegeville	672
Iowa	118	48	July 20, 1934	Keokuk	614
Kansas	121	49	July 24, 1936[1]	Alton (near)	1,651
Kentucky	114	46	July 28, 1930	Greensburg	581
Louisiana	114	46	Aug. 10, 1936[1]	Plain Dealing	268
Maine	105	41	July 10, 1911[1]	North Bridgton	450
Maryland	109	43	July 10, 1936[1]	Cumberland & Frederick	623; 325
Massachusetts	107	42	Aug. 2, 1975	New Bedford & Chester	120; 640
Michigan	112	44	July 13, 1936	Mio	963
Minnesota	114	46	July 6, 1936[1]	Moorhead	904
Mississippi	115	46	July 29, 1930	Holly Springs	600
Missouri	118	48	July 14, 1954[1]	Warsaw & Union	705; 560
Montana	117	47	July 5, 1937	Medicine Lake	1,950
Nebraska	118	48	July 24, 1936[1]	Minden	2,169
Nevada	125	52	June 29, 1994	Laughlin	605
New Hampshire	106	41	July 4, 1911	Nashua	125
New Jersey	110	43	July 10, 1936	Runyon	18
New Mexico	122	50	June 27, 1994	Waste Isolat. Pilot Pit	3,418
New York	108	42	July 22, 1926	Troy	35
North Carolina	110	43	Aug. 21, 1983	Fayetteville	213
North Dakota	121	49	July 6, 1936	Steele	1,857
Ohio	113	45	July 21, 1934[1]	Gallipolis (near)	673
Oklahoma	120	49	June 27, 1994[1]	Tipton	1,350
Oregon	119	48	Aug. 10, 1898	Pendleton	1,074
Pennsylvania	111	44	July 10, 1936[1]	Phoenixville	100
Rhode Island	104	40	Aug. 2, 1975	Providence	51
South Carolina	111	44	June 28, 1954[1]	Camden	170
South Dakota	120	49	July 5, 1936	Gannvalley	1,750
Tennessee	113	45	Aug. 9, 1930[1]	Perryville	377
Texas	120	49	Aug. 12, 1936	Seymour	1,291
Utah	117	47	July 5, 1895	Saint George	2,880
Vermont	105	41	July 4, 1911	Vernon	310
Virginia	110	43	July 15, 1954	Balcony Falls	725
Washington	118	48	Aug. 5, 1961[1]	Ice Harbor Dam	475
West Virginia	112	44	July 10, 1936[1]	Martinsburg	435
Wisconsin	114	46	July 13, 1936	Wisconsin Dells	900
Wyoming	114	46	July 12, 1900	Basin	3,500

1. Also on earlier dates at the same or other places. *Source:* National Climatic Data Center, Asheville, N.C., and Storm Phillips, STORMFAX, INC.

Record Lowest Temperatures by State

State	Temp. °F	Temp. °C	Date	Station	Elevation in feet
Alabama	–27	–33	Jan. 30, 1966	New Market	760
Alaska	–80	–62	Jan. 23, 1971	Prospect Creek Camp	1,100
Arizona	–40	–40	Jan. 7, 1971	Hawley Lake	8,180
Arkansas	–29	–34	Feb. 13, 1905	Pond	1,250
California	–45	–43	Jan. 20, 1937	Boca	5,532
Colorado	–61	–52	Feb. 1, 1985	Maybell	5,920
Connecticut	–32	–36	Feb. 16, 1943	Falls Village	585
Delaware	–17	–27	Jan. 17, 1893	Millsboro	20
D.C.	–15	–26	Feb. 11, 1899	Washington	410
Florida	–2	–19	Feb. 13, 1899	Tallahassee	193
Georgia	–17	–27	Jan. 27, 1940	CCC Camp F-16	est. 1,000
Hawaii	12	–11	May 17, 1979	Mauna Kea	13,770
Idaho	–60	–51	Jan. 18, 1943	Island Park Dam	6,285
Illinois	–36	–38	Jan. 5, 1999	Congerville	635
Indiana	–36	–38	Jan. 19, 1994	New Whiteland	785
Iowa	–47	–44	Feb. 3, 1996	Elkader	770
Kansas	–40	–40	Feb. 13, 1905	Lebanon	1,812
Kentucky	–37	–38	Jan. 19, 1994	Shelbyville	730
Louisiana	–16	–27	Feb. 13, 1899	Minden	194
Maine	–48	–44	Jan. 19, 1925	Van Buren	510
Maryland	–40	–40	Jan. 13, 1912	Oakland	2,461
Massachusetts	–35	–37	Jan. 12, 1981	Chester	640
Michigan	–51	–46	Feb. 9, 1934	Vanderbilt	785
Minnesota	–60	–51	Feb. 2, 1996	Tower	1,460
Mississippi	–19	–28	Jan. 30, 1966	Corinth	420
Missouri	–40	–40	Feb. 13, 1905	Warsaw	700
Montana	–70	–57	Jan. 20, 1954	Rogers Pass	5,470
Nebraska	–47	–44	Feb. 12, 1899	Camp Clarke	3,700
Nevada	–50	–46	Jan. 8, 1937	San Jacinto	5,200
New Hampshire	–47	–44	Jan. 29, 1934	Mt. Washington	6,262
New Jersey	–34	–37	Jan. 5, 1904	River Vale	70
New Mexico	–50	–46	Feb. 1, 1951	Gavilan	7,350
New York	–52	–47	Feb. 18, 1979[1]	Old Forge	1,720
North Carolina	–34	–37	Jan. 21, 1985	Mt. Mitchell	6,525
North Dakota	–60	–51	Feb. 15, 1936	Parshall	1,929
Ohio	–39	–39	Feb. 10, 1899	Milligan	800
Oklahoma	–27	–33	Jan. 18, 1930	Watts	958
Oregon	–54	–48	Feb. 10, 1933[1]	Seneca	4,700
Pennsylvania	–42	–41	Jan. 5, 1904	Smethport	est. 1,500
Rhode Island	–23	–31	Jan. 11, 1942	Kingston	100
South Carolina	–19	–28	Jan. 21, 1985	Caesars Head	3,115
South Dakota	–58	–50	Feb. 17, 1936	McIntosh	2,277
Tennessee	–32	–36	Dec. 30, 1917	Mountain City	2,471
Texas	–23	–31	Feb. 8, 1933[1]	Seminole	3,275
Utah	–69	–56	Feb. 1, 1985	Peter's Sink	8,092
Vermont	–50	–46	Dec. 30, 1933	Bloomfield	915
Virginia	–30	–34	Jan. 22, 1985	Mountain Lake	3,870
Washington	–48	–44	Dec. 30, 1968	Mazama & Winthrop	2,120; 1,765
West Virginia	–37	–38	Dec. 30, 1917	Lewisburg	2,200
Wisconsin	–55	–48	Feb. 4, 1996	Couderay	1,300
Wyoming	–66	–54	Feb. 9, 1933	Riverside R.S.	6,500

1. Also on earlier dates at the same or other places. *Source:* National Climatic Data Center, Asheville, N.C., and Storm Phillips, STORMFAX, INC.

Record Monthly High and Low Temperatures in the United States

Source: National Climatic Data Center, Asheville, N.C., and Storm Phillips, STORMFAX, Inc.

January

The highest temperature ever recorded for the month of January occurred on January 17, 1936, and again in 1954, in Laredo, Tex. (elevation 421 ft), where the temperature reached 98°F.

The lowest temperature ever recorded for the month of January occurred on January 20, 1954, in Rogers Pass, Mont. (elevation 5,470 ft), where the temperature fell to –70°F.

February

The highest temperature ever recorded for the month of February occurred on February 3, 1963, in Montezuma, Ariz. (elevation 735 ft), where the temperature reached 105°F.

The lowest temperature ever recorded for the month of February occurred on February 1, 1985, at the Peters Sink station in Utah (elevation 8,095 ft), where the temperature fell to –69°F.

March

The highest temperature ever recorded for the month of March occurred on March 31, 1954, in Rio Grande City, Tex. (elevation 168 ft), where the temperature reached 108°F.

The lowest temperature ever recorded for the month of March occurred on March 17, 1906, in Snake River, Wyo. (elevation 6,862 ft), where the temperature dropped to –50°F.

April

The highest temperature ever recorded for the month of April occurred on April 25, 1898, at Volcano Springs, Calif. (elevation –220 ft), where the temperature reached 118°F.

The lowest temperature ever recorded for the month of April occurred on April 5, 1945, in Eagle Nest, N.M. (elevation 8,250 ft), where the temperature dropped to –36°F.

May

The highest temperature ever recorded for the month of May occurred on May 27, 1896, in Salton, Calif. (elevation –263 ft), where the temperature reached 124°F.

The lowest temperature ever recorded for the month of May occurred on May 7, 1964, in White Mountain 2, Calif. (elevation 12,470 ft), where the temperature dropped to –15°F.

June

The highest temperature ever recorded for the month of June occurred on June 23, 1902, at Volcano Springs, Calif. (elevation –220 ft), where the temperature reached 129°F.

The lowest temperature ever recorded for the month of June occurred on June 13, 1907, in Tamarack, Calif. (elevation 8,000 ft), where the temperature dropped to 2°F.

July

The highest temperature ever recorded for the month of July occurred on July 10, 1913, at Greenland Ranch, Calif. (elevation –178 ft), where the temperature reached 134°F.

The lowest temperature ever recorded for the month of July occurred on July 21, 1911, at Painter, Wyo. (elevation 6,800 ft), where the temperature fell to 10°F.

August

The highest temperature ever recorded for the month of August occurred on August 12, 1933, at Greenland Ranch, Calif. (elevation –178 ft), where the temperature reached 127°F.

The lowest temperature ever recorded for the month of August occurred on August 25, 1910, in Bowen, Mont. (elevation 6,080 ft), where the temperature fell to 5°F.

September

The highest temperature ever recorded for the month of September occurred on September 2, 1950, in Mecca, Calif. (elevation –175 ft), where the temperature reached 126°F.

The lowest temperature ever recorded for the month of September occurred on September 24, 1926, at Riverside Ranger Station, Mont. (elevation 6,700 ft), where the temperature fell to –9°F.

October

The highest temperature ever recorded for the month of October occurred on October 5, 1917, in Sentinel, Ariz. (elevation 685 ft), where the temperature reached 116°F.

The lowest temperature ever recorded for the month of October occurred on October 29, 1917, in Soda Butte, Wyo. (elevation 6,600 ft), where the temperature fell to –33°F.

November

The highest temperature ever recorded for the month of November occurred on November 12, 1906, in Craftonville, Calif. (elevation 1,759 ft), where the temperature reached 105°F.

The lowest temperature ever recorded for the month of November occurred on November 16, 1959, at Lincoln, Mont. (elevation 5,130 ft), where the temperature fell to –53°F.

December

The highest temperature ever recorded for the month of December occurred on December 8, 1938, in La Mesa, Calif. (elevation 539 ft), where the temperature reached 100°F.

The lowest temperature ever recorded for the month of December occurred on December 19, 1924, at Riverside Ranger Station, Mont. (elevation 6,700 ft), where the temperature fell to –59°F.

Climate of 100 Selected U.S. Cities

(For world cities, *see* p. 271)

	Average monthly temperature (°F)[1]				Precipitation Average annual		Snowfall Average annual	
City	Jan.	April	July	Oct.	(in.)[1]	(days)[2]	(in.)[2]	Years[2]
Albany, N.Y.	21.1	46.6	71.4	50.5	35.74	134	65.5	38
Albuquerque, N.M.	34.8	55.1	78.8	57.4	8.12	59	10.6	45
Anchorage, Alaska	13.0	35.4	58.1	34.6	15.20	115	69.2	41[3]
Asheville, N.C.	36.8	55.7	73.2	56.0	47.71	124	17.5	20
Atlanta, Ga.	41.9	61.8	78.6	62.2	48.61	115	1.9	50
Atlantic City, N.J.	31.8	51.0	74.4	55.5	41.93	112	16.4	40[3]
Austin, Texas	49.1	68.7	84.7	69.8	31.50	83	0.9	43
Baltimore, Md.	32.7	54.0	76.8	56.9	41.84	113	21.8	34
Baton Rouge, La.	50.8	68.4	82.1	68.2	55.77	108	0.1	34[3]
Billings, Mont.	20.9	44.6	72.3	49.3	15.09	96	57.2	50
Birmingham, Ala.	42.9	62.8	80.1	62.6	54.52	117	1.3	41
Bismarck, N.D.	6.7	42.5	70.4	46.1	15.36	96	40.3	45
Boise, Idaho	29.9	48.6	74.6	51.9	11.71	92	21.4	45
Boston, Mass.	29.6	48.7	73.5	54.8	43.81	127	41.8	49[3]
Bridgeport, Conn.	29.5	48.6	74.0	56.0	41.56	117	26.0	36
Buffalo, N.Y.	23.5	45.4	70.7	51.5	37.52	169	92.2	41
Burlington, Vt.	16.6	42.7	69.6	47.9	33.69	153	78.2	41
Caribou, Maine	10.7	37.3	65.1	43.1	36.59	160	113.3	45
Casper, Wyo.	22.2	42.1	70.9	47.1	11.43	95	80.5	34
Charleston, S.C.	47.9	64.3	80.5	65.8	51.59	113	0.6	42
Charleston, W.Va.	32.9	55.3	74.5	55.9	42.43	151	31.5	37
Charlotte, N.C.	40.5	60.3	78.5	60.7	43.16	111	6.1	45
Cheyenne, Wyo.	26.1	41.8	68.9	47.5	13.31	98	54.1	49
Chicago, Ill.	21.4	48.8	73.0	53.5	33.34	127	40.3	26
Cleveland, Ohio	25.5	48.1	71.6	53.2	35.40	156	53.6	43
Columbia, S.C.	44.7	63.8	81.0	63.4	49.12	109	1.9	37
Columbus, Ohio	27.1	51.4	73.8	53.9	36.97	137	28.3	37[3]
Concord, N.H.	19.9	44.1	69.5	48.3	36.53	125	64.5	43
Dallas-Ft. Worth, Texas	44.0	65.9	86.3	67.9	29.46	78	3.1	31
Denver, Colo.	29.5	47.4	73.4	51.9	15.31	88	59.8	50
Des Moines, Iowa	18.6	50.5	76.3	54.2	30.83	107	34.7	45
Detroit, Mich.	23.4	47.3	71.9	51.9	30.97	133	40.4	26
Dodge City, Kan.	29.5	54.3	80.0	57.7	20.66	78	19.5	42
Duluth, Minn.	6.3	38.3	65.4	44.2	29.68	135	77.4	41[3]
El Paso, Texas	44.2	63.6	82.5	63.6	7.82	47	5.2	45
Fairbanks, Alaska	−12.7	30.2	61.5	25.1	10.37	106	67.5	33
Fargo, N.D.	4.3	42.1	70.6	46.3	19.59	100	35.9	42
Grand Junction, Colo.	25.5	51.7	78.9	54.9	8.00	72	26.1	38
Grand Rapids, Mich.	22.0	46.3	71.4	50.9	34.35	143	72.4	21
Hartford, Conn.	25.2	48.8	73.4	52.4	44.39	127	50.0	30
Helena, Mont.	18.1	42.3	67.9	45.1	11.37	96	47.9	44
Honolulu, Hawaii	72.6	75.7	80.1	79.5	23.47	100	0.0	38[3]
Houston, Texas	51.4	68.7	83.1	69.7	44.76	105	0.4	50
Indianapolis, Ind.	26.0	52.4	75.1	54.8	39.12	125	23.1	53[3]
Jackson, Miss.	45.7	65.1	81.9	65.0	52.82	109	1.2	21
Jacksonville, Fla.	53.2	67.7	81.3	69.5	52.76	116	T	43
Juneau, Alaska	21.8	39.1	55.7	41.8	53.15	220	102.8	41
Kansas City, Mo.	28.4	56.9	80.9	59.6	29.27	98	20.0	43
Knoxville, Tenn.	38.2	59.6	77.6	59.5	47.29	127	12.3	42
Las Vegas, Nev.	44.5	63.5	90.2	67.5	4.19	26	1.4	36
Lexington, Ky.	31.5	55.1	75.9	56.8	45.68	131	16.3	40
Little Rock, Ark.	39.9	62.4	82.1	63.1	49.20	104	5.4	42
Long Beach, Calif.	55.2	60.9	72.8	67.5	11.54	32	T	41[3]
Los Angeles, Calif.	56.0	59.5	69.0	66.3	12.08	36	T	49
Louisville, Ky.	32.5	56.6	77.6	57.7	43.56	125	17.5	37
Madison, Wisc.	15.6	45.8	70.6	49.5	30.84	118	40.8	36
Memphis, Tenn.	39.6	62.6	82.1	62.9	51.57	107	5.5	34
Miami, Fla.	67.1	75.3	82.5	77.9	57.55	129	0.0	42
Milwaukee, Wisc.	18.7	44.6	70.5	50.9	30.94	125	47.0	44
Minneapolis–St. Paul, Minn.	11.2	46.0	73.1	49.6	26.36	115	48.9	46
Mobile, Ala.	50.8	68.0	82.2	68.5	64.64	123	0.3	43
Montgomery, Ala.	46.7	65.2	81.7	65.3	49.16	108	0.3	40
Mt. Washington, N.H.	5.1	22.4	48.7	30.5	89.92	209	246.8	52
Nashville, Tenn.	37.1	59.7	79.4	60.2	48.49	119	11.1	43
Newark, N.J.	31.2	52.1	76.8	57.2	42.34	122	28.2	43
New Orleans, La.	52.4	68.7	82.1	69.2	59.74	114	0.2	38[3]
New York, N.Y.	31.8	51.9	76.4	57.5	42.82	119	26.1	40[3]
Norfolk, Va.	39.9	58.2	78.4	61.3	45.22	115	7.9	36

City	Average monthly temperature (°F)[1] Jan.	April	July	Oct.	Precipitation Average annual (in.)[1]	(days)[2]	Snowfall Average annual (in.)[2]	Years[2]
Oklahoma City, Okla.	35.9	60.2	82.1	62.3	30.89	82	9.0	45
Olympia, Wash.	37.2	47.3	63.0	50.1	50.96	164	18.0	43
Omaha, Neb.	20.2	52.2	77.7	54.5	30.34	98	31.1	49[3]
Philadelphia, Pa.	31.2	52.9	76.5	56.5	41.42	117	21.9	42[3]
Phoenix, Ariz.	52.3	68.1	92.3	73.4	7.11	36	T	47[3]
Pittsburgh, Pa.	26.7	50.1	72.0	52.5	36.30	154	44.6	32
Portland, Maine	21.5	42.8	68.1	48.5	43.52	128	72.4	44
Portland, Ore.	38.9	50.4	67.7	54.3	37.39	154	6.8	44
Providence, R.I.	28.2	47.9	72.5	53.2	45.32	124	37.1	31
Raleigh, N.C.	39.6	59.4	77.7	59.7	41.76	112	7.7	40
Reno, Nev.	32.2	46.4	69.5	50.3	7.49	51	25.3	42
Richmond, Va.	36.6	57.9	77.8	58.6	44.07	113	14.6	47
Roswell, N.M.	41.4	61.9	81.4	61.7	9.70	52	11.4	37[3]
Sacramento, Calif.	45.3	58.2	75.6	63.9	17.10	58	0.1	36[3]
Salt Lake City, Utah	28.6	49.2	77.5	53.0	15.31	90	59.1	56
San Antonio, Texas	50.4	69.6	84.6	70.2	29.13	81	0.4	42
San Diego, Calif.	56.8	61.2	70.3	67.5	9.32	43	T	44
San Francisco, Calif.	48.5	54.8	62.2	60.6	19.71	63	T	57
Savannah, Ga.	49.1	66.0	81.2	66.9	49.70	111	0.3	34
Seattle-Tacoma, Wash.	39.1	48.7	64.8	52.4	38.60	158	12.8	40
Sioux Falls, S.D.	12.4	46.4	74.0	49.4	24.12	96	39.9	39
Spokane, Wash.	25.7	45.8	69.7	47.5	16.71	114	51.5	37
Springfield, Ill.	24.6	53.3	76.5	56.0	33.78	114	24.5	37
St. Louis, Mo.	28.8	56.1	78.9	57.9	33.91	111	19.8	48[3]
Tampa, Fla.	59.8	71.5	82.1	74.4	46.73	107	T	38
Toledo, Ohio	23.1	47.8	71.8	51.7	31.78	137	38.3	29
Tucson, Ariz.	51.1	64.9	86.2	70.4	11.14	52	1.2	44
Tulsa, Okla.	35.2	61.0	83.2	62.6	38.77	89	9.0	46
Vero Beach, Fla.	61.9	71.7	81.1	75.2	51.41	n.a.	n.a.	0
Washington, D.C.	35.2	56.7	78.9	59.3	39.00	112	17.0	41[3]
Wichita, Kan.	29.6	56.3	81.4	59.1	28.61	85	16.4	31
Wilmington, Del.	31.2	52.4	76.0	56.3	41.38	117	20.9	37

1. Based on 30-year period 1951–1980. Data latest available. 2. Data through 1984 based on number of years as indicated in Years column. 3. For snowfall data where number of years differs from that for precipitation data. T = trace. n.a. = not available. *Source:* National Oceanic and Atmospheric Administration (NOAA).

Revised Wind Chill Index

Source: The National Weather Service

The wind chill temperature index measures how cold people feel when outside. Wind chill is based on the rate of heat loss from exposed skin caused by wind and cold. As the wind increases, it draws heat from the body, driving down skin temperature and eventually the internal body temperature. The wind therefore makes it feel much colder. If the temperature is 0°F and the wind is blowing at 15 mph, the wind chill is –19°F. At this wind chill temperature, exposed skin can freeze in 30 minutes.

A revised wind chill table was introduced by the National Weather Service on Nov. 1, 2001. The new index was tested on human subjects and is based on heat loss from exposed skin. The old index, formulated in 1945 by Antarctic explorers, measured the cooling rate of water.

Wind speed (mph)	Temperature (°F) 40	35	30	25	20	15	10	5	0	–5	–10	–15	–20	–25	–30	–35	–40	–45
5	36	31	25	19	13	7	1	–5	–11	–16	**–22**	**–28**	**–34**	**–40**	**–46**	**–52**	*–57*	*–63*
10	34	27	21	15	9	3	–4	–10	–16	**–22**	**–28**	**–35**	**–41**	*–47*	*–53*	*–59*	*–66*	*–72*
15	32	25	19	13	6	0	–7	–13	**–19**	**–26**	**–32**	**–39**	*–45*	*–51*	*–58*	*–64*	***–71***	***–77***
20	30	24	17	11	4	–2	–9	–15	**–22**	**–29**	**–35**	*–42*	*–48*	*–55*	*–61*	***–68***	***–74***	***–81***
25	29	23	16	9	3	–4	–11	–17	**–24**	**–31**	*–37*	*–44*	*–51*	*–58*	***–64***	***–71***	***–78***	***–84***
30	28	22	15	8	1	–5	–12	**–19**	**–26**	**–33**	*–39*	*–46*	*–53*	***–60***	***–67***	***–73***	***–80***	***–87***
35	28	21	14	7	0	–7	–14	**–21**	**–27**	*–34*	*–41*	*–48*	***–55***	***–62***	***–69***	***–76***	***–82***	***–89***
40	27	20	13	6	–1	–8	–15	**–22**	**–29**	*–36*	*–43*	*–50*	***–57***	***–64***	***–71***	***–78***	***–84***	***–91***
45	26	19	12	5	–2	–9	–16	**–23**	**–30**	*–37*	*–44*	***–51***	***–58***	***–65***	***–72***	***–79***	***–86***	***–93***
50	26	19	12	4	–3	–10	–17	**–24**	**–31**	*–38*	*–45*	***–52***	***–60***	***–67***	***–74***	***–81***	***–88***	***–95***
55	25	18	11	4	–3	–11	**–18**	**–25**	*–32*	*–39*	*–46*	***–54***	***–61***	***–68***	***–75***	***–82***	***–89***	***–97***
60	25	17	10	3	–4	–11	**–19**	**–26**	*–33*	*–40*	***–48***	***–55***	***–62***	***–69***	***–76***	***–84***	***–91***	***–98***

Frostbite Times: **Bold = 30 minutes** *Italic = 10 Minutes* ***Bold italic = 5 minutes***

Formula: Wind Chill (°F) = $35.74 + 0.6215T - 35.75(V^{0.16}) + 0.4275T(V^{0.16})$
Where, T = Air Temperature (°F) V = Wind Speed (mph)

See Weights and Measures, p. 451, for Fahrenheit and Celsius scales.

The following lists are not all-inclusive due to space limitations. Only disasters involving great loss of life and/or property, historical interest, or unusual circumstances are listed. Data as of August 2003.
For other disasters *see* Current Events: What Happened in 2003, pp. 36–44.

WORST UNITED STATES DISASTERS

AIRCRAFT

1979 **May 25, Chicago:** American Airlines DC-10 crashed seconds after takeoff, killing all 272 people aboard and 3 on the ground.

AVALANCHE

1910 **March 1, Wellington, Wash.:** two trains snowbound in Stevens Pass in Cascade Range swept off tracks into canyon 150 ft below, killing 96.

DROUGHT

1930s **Many states:** longest drought of 20th century. Peak periods were 1930, 1934, 1936, 1939, and 1940. During 1934, dry regions stretched solidly from N.Y. and Pa. across the Great Plains to the Calif. coast. A great "dust bowl" covered 50 million acres in south-central plains during winter of 1935–1936.

EARTHQUAKE

1906 **April 18, San Francisco:** earthquake accompanied by fire razed more than 4 sq mi; more than 500 dead or missing.

EPIDEMIC

1918 **Nationwide:** Spanish influenza killed over 500,000 Americans.

EXPLOSION

1947 **April 16–18, Texas City, Tex.:** a fire and subsequent explosion on the French freighter *Grandcamp* destroyed most of the city; 516 killed.

FIRE

1871 **Oct. 8, Peshtigo, Wis.:** over 1,500 lives lost and 3.8 million acres burned in forest fire.

FLOOD

1889 **May 31, Johnstown, Pa.:** collapse of South Fork Dam left more than 2,200 dead.

HURRICANE

1900 **Sept. 8, Galveston, Tex.:** an estimated 6,000–8,000 dead, mostly from devastation due to tidal surge.

MARINE

1865 **April 27, Mississippi River, nr. Memphis, Tenn.:** explosion on steamboat *Sultana* killed 1,547.

MINE

1907 **Dec. 6, Monongah, W. Va.:** coal mine explosion killed 362.

OIL SPILL

1989 **March 24, Prince William Sound, Alaska:** tanker *Exxon Valdez* hit an undersea reef and released 10 million plus gallons of oil into the waters.

RAILROAD

1918 **July 9, Nashville, Tenn.:** 101 killed in a two-train collision near Nashville.

SUBMARINE

1963 **April 10, North Atlantic:** atomic-powered submarine *Thresher* sank; 129 dead.

TERRORIST ATTACK

2001 **Sept. 11, New York City, Arlington, Va., and Shanksville, Pa.:** hijackers crashed two commercial jets into twin towers of World Trade Center; two more hijacked jets were crashed into the Pentagon and a field in rural Pa. Total dead numbered 3,044, including the 19 hijackers. Islamic al-Qaeda terrorist group blamed.

TORNADO

1925 **March 18, Mo., Ill., and Ind.:** great "Tri-State Tornado"; 689 dead; over 2,000 injured. Property damage estimated at $16.5 million.

WINTER STORM

1888 **March 11–14, East Coast:** the "Blizzard of 1888." 400 people died; as much as 5 ft of snow. Damage was estimated at $20 million.

EARTHQUAKES AND VOLCANIC ERUPTIONS

A.D. 79 **Aug. 24, Italy:** eruption of Mt. Vesuvius buried cities of Pompeii and Herculaneum, killing thousands.

856 **Dec. 22, Damghan, Iran:** earthquake killed 200,000.

893 **March 23, Ardabil, Iran:** earthquake killed about 150,000 people.

1138 **Aug. 9, Aleppo, Syria:** deadly earthquake claimed lives of 230,000 people.

1290 **Sept., Chihli, China:** earthquake killed about 100,000 people.

1556 **Jan. 23, Shaanxi (Shensi) province, China:** most deadly earthquake in history; 830,000 killed.

1667 **Nov., Shemakha, Caucasia:** earthquake killed about 80,000 people.

1727 **Nov. 18, Tabriz, Iran:** about 77,000 victims killed in deadly earthquake.

1755 **Nov. 1, Portugal:** earthquake leveled Lisbon and was felt as far away as southern France and North Africa; 70,000 killed.

1783 **June 8, Iceland:** eruption of Laki volcano lasted until Feb. 1784. Haze from eruption resulted in loss of island's livestock and widespread crop failure; 9,350 deaths, mostly due to starvation.

1792 **May 21, Kyushu Island, Japan:** collapse of old lava dome during eruption of Unzen volcano caused avalanche and tsunami that killed an estimated 14,300 people. (Most were killed by the tsunami.) Japan's greatest volcano disaster.

1811 **Dec. 16, Mississippi Valley nr. New Madrid, Mo.:** earthquake reversed the course of the Mississippi River. Fatalities unknown due to sparse population in area. Aftershocks and tremors continued into 1812. It has been estimated that three of the series of earthquakes had surface-wave magnitudes of 8.6, 8.4, and 8.8 on the Richter scale. It is the largest series of earthquakes known to have occurred in North America.

1815 **April 5, 10–11, Netherlands Indies (Sumbawa, Indonesia):** eruption of Tambora largest in historic times. An estimated 92,000 people were killed, about 10,000 directly as a result of explosions and ash fall and about 82,000 indirectly by starvation and disease.

1877 **June 26, north-central Ecuador:** eruption of Mt. Cotopaxi caused severe mudflows that wiped out surrounding cities and valleys; 1,000 deaths.

1883 **Aug. 26–28, Netherlands Indies (Krakatau, Indonesia):** eruption of Krakatau; violent explosions destroyed two-thirds of island, leaving an estimated 36,000 dead. Sea waves occurred as far away as Cape Horn and possibly England.

1886 **Aug. 31, Charleston, S.C.:** 60 people killed and extensive damage to city. Earthquake's magnitude was 7.7 on the Richter scale.

1902 **May 7, St. Vincent, West Indies:** Soufrière volcano erupted, devastating one-third of the island and killing some 1,680 people.

May 8, Martinique, West Indies: Mt. Pelée erupted and wiped out city of St. Pierre; 40,000 dead.

1906 **April 18, San Francisco:** earthquake accompanied by fire razed more than 4 sq mi; more than 500 dead or missing.

1908 **Dec. 28, Messina, Sicily:** city totally destroyed by earthquake. Death toll 70,000–100,000 in Sicily and southern Italy.

1915 **Jan. 13, Avezzano, Italy:** earthquake left 29,980 dead.

1920 **Dec. 16, Gansu province, China:** magnitude 8.6 earthquake killed 200,000 in northwest China.

1923 **Sept. 1, Japan:** magnitude 8.3 earthquake destroyed one third of Tokyo and most of Yokohama. More than 140,000 killed.

1927 **May 22, nr. Xining, China:** magnitude 8.3 earthquake claimed approximately 200,000 victims.

1932 **Dec. 25, Gansu, China:** magnitude 7.6 earthquake killed approximately 70,000.

1935 **May 30, Pakistan:** earthquake at Quetta killed 30,000–60,000.

1939 **Jan. 24, Chile:** earthquake razed 50,000 sq mi; about 30,000 killed.

Dec. 27, northern Turkey: severe quakes destroyed city of Erzingan; about 100,000 casualties.

1950 **Aug. 15, India:** earthquake affected 30,000 sq mi in Assam; 20,000–30,000 believed killed.

1960 **Feb. 29, Agadir, Morocco:** 10,000–12,000 dead as earthquake set off tidal wave and fire, destroying most of city.

May 22, Chile: strongest earthquake ever recorded (9.5 magnitude) struck near the coast, killing more than 2,000, wounding 3,000.

1964 **March 28[1], Alaska:** strongest earthquake ever to strike North America (9.2 magnitude) hit 80 mi east of Anchorage; followed by seismic wave 50 ft high that traveled 8,445 mi at 450 mph; 117 killed.

1970 **Jan. 5, Yunnan province, China:** magnitude 7.7 quake killed 15,621.

May 31, Peru: earthquake left more than 50,000 dead, 17,000 missing.

1972 **Dec. 22, Managua, Nicaragua:** earthquake devastated city, leaving up to 6,000 dead.

1976 **Feb. 4, Guatemala:** quake left over 23,000 dead.

July 28, Tangshan, China: worst earthquake to hit China in 20th century; devastated 20 sq mi of city, leaving 242,000 dead (official). Estimated death toll as high as 655,000.

Aug. 17, Mindanao, Philippines: earthquake and tidal wave left up to 8,000 dead or missing.

1978 **Sept. 16, Tabas, Iran:** earthquake destroyed city in eastern Iran, leaving 25,000 dead.

1985 **Sept. 19–20, Mexico:** magnitude 8.1 earthquake devastated part of Mexico City and three coastal states; estimated 25,000 killed.

Nov. 14–16, Colombia: eruption of Nevada del Ruiz, 85 mi northwest of Bogotá. Mudslides buried most of the town of Armero and devastated Chinchiná; estimated 25,000 killed.

1988 **Dec. 7, Armenia:** earthquake measuring 6.9 in magnitude killed nearly 25,000, injured 15,000, and left at least 400,000 homeless.

1989 **Oct. 17, San Francisco Bay area:** earthquake measuring 7.1 in magnitude killed 67 and injured over 3,000. Over 100,000 buildings damaged or destroyed. Damage cost city billions of dollars.

1990 **June 21, northwest Iran:** earthquake measuring 7.7 in magnitude destroyed cities and villages in Caspian Sea area. At least 50,000 dead, over 60,000 injured, and 400,000 homeless.

July 16, northern Philippines: magnitude 7.7 quake killed nearly 2,000.

1991 **July 15, Luzon Island, Philippines:** eruption of Mt. Pinatubo buried over 300 sq mi under volcanic ash and resulted in more than 800 deaths.

1993 **Aug. 8, Guam:** earthquake measuring 8.1 in magnitude caused severe damage to many structures but no fatalities. Damages were estimated at nearly $300 million.

1994 **Jan. 17, San Fernando Valley, Calif.:** earthquake measuring 6.6 in magnitude killed 61 and injured over 8,000. Damage estimated at $13–20 billion.

1995 **Jan. 17, Osaka, Kyoto, and Kobe, Japan:** 5,100 killed and 26,800 injured; estimated damage $100 billion. Magnitude: 7.2.

1997 **May 12, northeast Iran:** severe earthquake measuring 7.1 in magnitude left more than 1,500 people dead and at least 4,460 injured.

June–Sept., southern Montserrat: ongoing eruption of Soufrière Hills volcano since July 1995; killed 20 people in major eruption on June 25, 1997, rendered southern two-thirds of Montserrat uninhabitable, and forced some 8,000 of the island's 12,000 residents to abandon the island.

1998 **May 30, northern Afghanistan:** magnitude 7.1 earthquake and aftershocks killed an estimated 5,000 and injured at least 1,500. A quake on Feb. 4 in same area had killed about 2,300.

1999 **Aug. 17, northwest Turkey:** magnitude 7.4 quake centered near Izmit killed over 17,000 and injured about 44,000. Damage estimated at $8.5 billion. Another severe 7.2 temblor killed more than 700 in Ducze and nearby towns in Nov.

Sept. 21, central Taiwan: severe 7.7 earthquake and aftershocks killed 2,295 and injured 8,729.

2001 **Jan. 13, El Salvador:** magnitude 7.7 earthquake set off some 185 landslides across El Salvador; at least 850 died and nearly 100,000 houses were destroyed.

Jan. 26, Bhuj, India: magnitude 7.7 earthquake rocked western Indian state of Gujarat, killing more than 20,000 people and leaving 600,000 homeless.

2002 **March 25, northeast Afghanistan:** series of earthquakes—the largest measuring 6.1 in magnitude—rattled an area 100 mi north of Kabul. Estimated 1,000 people killed and 7,000 families homeless. The city of Nahrin, a densely populated district capital, was completely razed.

2003 **May 21, Northern Algeria:** magnitude 6.8 earthquake caused the collapse of numerous buildings, killed more than 2,250 people, and injured 10,000. The epicenter was 40 miles east of Algiers, the capital city.

1. March 28, 03:36:14 UT (March 27, 5:36 P.M. local time).

MAJOR U.S. EPIDEMICS

1793 Philadelphia: more than 4,000 residents died from yellow fever.

1832 July–Aug., New York City: over 3,000 people killed in a cholera epidemic.

Oct., New Orleans: cholera took the lives of 4,340 people.

1848 New York City: more than 5,000 deaths caused by cholera.

1853 New Orleans: yellow fever killed 7,790.

1867 New Orleans: 3,093 perished from yellow fever.

1878 Southern states: over 13,000 people died from yellow fever in lower Mississippi Valley.

1916 Nationwide: over 7,000 deaths occurred and 27,363 cases were reported of polio (infantile paralysis) in America's worst polio epidemic.

1918 March–Nov., nationwide: outbreak of Spanish influenza killed over 500,000 people in the worst single U.S. epidemic.

1949 Nationwide: 2,720 deaths occurred from polio, and 42,173 cases were reported.

1952 Nationwide: polio killed 3,300; 57,628 cases reported; worst epidemic since 1916.

1981-Dec. 2001: total U.S. AIDS cases reported to Centers for Disease Control: 816,149; total AIDS deaths reported: 467,910. (Total world cases: 42 million; total AIDS deaths: 27.9 million.)

FLOODS, AVALANCHES, AND TIDAL WAVES

1228 Holland: 100,000 people reputedly drowned by sea flood in Friesland.

1642 China: rebels destroyed Kaifeng seawall; 300,000 drowned.

1889 May 31, Johnstown, Pa.: more than 2,200 died in flood after South Fork Dam collapsed.

1896 June 15, Sanriku, Japan: earthquake and tidal wave killed 27,000.

1910 March 1, Wellington, Wash.: avalanche in Cascade Range swept two trains into canyon, killing 96. Worst U.S. avalanche.

1928 March 12, Santa Paula, Calif.: collapse of St. Francis Dam left 450 dead.

1931 July–Aug., China: flood along Yangtze River left 3.7 million people dead from disease, starvation, or drowning.

1953 Jan. 31–Feb. 5, northwest Europe: storm followed by floods devastated North Sea coastal areas. Netherlands was hardest hit with 1,794 dead.

1954 Aug., Teheran, Iran: flood rains resulted in some 10,000 deaths.

1959 Dec. 2, Fréjus, France: flood caused by collapse of Malpasset Dam left 412 dead.

1962 Jan. 10, Peru: avalanche down extinct Huascaran volcano killed more than 3,000.

1963 Oct. 9, Italy: landslide into the Vaiont Dam; flood killed about 2,000.

1966 Oct. 21, Aberfan, Wales: avalanche of coal, waste, mud, and rocks killed 144 people, including 116 children in school.

1969 Jan. 18–26, southern Calif.: floods and mudslides from heavy rains caused widespread property damage; at least 100 dead. Another downpour (Feb. 23–26) caused further floods and mudslides; at least 18 dead.

1970 Nov. 13, East Pakistan: 200,000 killed by cyclone-driven tidal wave from Bay of Bengal. Over 100,000 missing.

1971 Aug., Hanoi, North Vietnam: heavy rains severely flooded the Red River Delta, killing 100,000.

1972 Feb. 26, Man, W. Va.: more than 118 died when slag-pile dam collapsed under pressure of torrential rains and flooded 17-mile valley.

June 9–10, Rapid City, S.D.: flash flood caused 237 deaths and $160 million in damage.

June 20, Eastern Seaboard: tropical storm Agnes, in ten-day rampage, caused widespread flash floods. Death toll 129; 115,000 left homeless; damage estimated at $3.5 billion.

1988 Aug.–Sept., Bangladesh: heaviest monsoon in 70 years inundated three-fourths of country, killing more than 1,300 and leaving 30 million homeless. Damage estimated at over $1 billion.

1993 June–Aug., Ill., Iowa, Kan., Ky., Minn., Mo., Neb., N.D., S.D., Wis.: two months of heavy rain caused Mississippi River and tributaries to flood; 50 deaths and about $12 billion in damage. Almost 70,000 left homeless.

1997 March, Ohio and Mississippi Valleys: flooding and tornadoes plagued Ark., Mo., Miss., Tenn., Ill., Ind., Ky., Ohio, and W.Va. 67 were killed and damage totaled approximately $1 billion.

1998 July 17, Papua New Guinea: three tsunamis, possibly spurred by an undersea landslide following an earthquake, wiped out entire villages in the northwest province of Sepik. At least 2,000 found or presumed dead.

Summer, central and northeast China: heaviest flooding of Yangtze and other rivers since 1954. More than 3,000 killed and 14 million left homeless. Estimated damages exceeded $20 billion.

1999 Summer, Asia: torrential downpours and flooding left more than 950 dead and millions homeless in S. Korea, China, Japan, the Philippines, and Thailand.

Oct., southwest Mexico: over a week of heavy rains killed at least 360 people in mudslides and flood waters.

Nov. and Dec., Vietnam: devastating floods caused $285 million in damage and killed more than 700 people.

Dec. 15–16, northern Venezuela: heavy rains caused catastrophic flooding and mudslides, killing an estimated 5,000 to 20,000 people. Country's worst modern-day natural disaster.

2000 Feb., southeast Africa: weeks of rain resulted in deadly floods in Mozambique and Zimbabwe. About 700 people were killed and more than 280,000 were left homeless.

2002 June–Aug., Asia: annual monsoons caused record floods and more than 2,000 deaths in China, India, Nepal, and Bangladesh.

Aug., Europe: record flooding across central and eastern Europe killed 108 people and caused billions of dollars of extensive infrastructure damage and deforestation.

MAJOR STORMS

Cyclones, hurricanes, and typhoons are the same kind of tropical storm but are called by different names in different areas of the world.

CYCLONES

1864 **Oct. 5, Calcutta, India:** 70,000 killed.

1942 **Oct. 16, Bengal, India:** about 40,000 lives lost.

1960 **Oct. 10, East Pakistan:** cyclone and tidal wave killed about 6,000.

1963 **May 28–29, East Pakistan:** cyclone killed about 22,000 along coast.

1965 **May 11–12 and June 1–2, East Pakistan:** cyclones killed about 47,000.

Dec. 15, Karachi, Pakistan: cyclone killed about 10,000.

1970 **Nov. 12–13, East Pakistan:** cyclone and tidal waves killed 200,000 and another 100,000 were reported missing.

1971 **Sept. 29, Orissa state, India:** cyclone and tidal wave off the Bay of Bengal killed as many as 10,000.

1974 **Dec. 25, Darwin, Australia:** cyclone destroyed nearly the entire city; 50 reported dead.

1977 **Nov. 19, Andhra Pradesh, India:** cyclone and tidal wave claimed lives of 20,000.

1991 **April 30, southeast Bangladesh:** cyclone killed over 131,000 and left as many as 9 million homeless. Thousands of survivors died from hunger and water-borne disease.

1999 **Oct. 29, Orissa state, India:** supercyclone swept in from Bay of Bengal, killing at least 9,573 and leaving over 10 million homeless.

U.S. HURRICANES

(U.S. deaths only, except where noted. Damages are actual cost in U.S. dollars, followed in parentheses by dollar figures adjusted to the year 2000.)

1776 **Sept. 2–9, N.C. to Nova Scotia:** called the "Hurricane of Independence," it is believed that 4,170 in the U.S. and Canada died in the storm.

1856 **Aug. 11, Last Island, La.:** 400 died.

1893 **Aug. 28, Savannah, Ga., Charleston, S.C., Sea Islands, S.C.:** at least 1,000 died.

1900 **Sept. 8, Galveston, Tex.:** an estimated 6,000–8,000 died in hurricane and tidal surge. The "Galveston Hurricane" is considered the deadliest in U.S. history.

1909 **Sept. 10–21, La. and Miss.:** 350 deaths.

1915 **Aug. 5–23, Galveston, Tex., and New Orleans, La.:** 275 killed.

1919 **Sept. 2–15, Fla. keys, La., and southern Tex.:** more than 600 killed, mostly lost on ships at sea.

1926 **Sept. 11–22, southeast Fla. and Ala.:** 243 deaths.

1928 **Sept. 6–20, Lake Okeechobee, southeast Fla.:** 1,836 deaths. Second-deadliest U.S. hurricane on record.

1935 **Aug. 29–Sept. 10, Fla. keys:** "Labor Day Hurricane"; 408 deaths.

1938 **Sept. 10–22, Long Island, N.Y., and southern New England:** "New England Hurricane"; 600 deaths.

1944 **Sept. 9–16, N.C. to New England:** 390 deaths, 344 of which were at sea.

1954 **Aug. 25–31, N.C. to New England:** "Carol" killed 60 in Long Island–New England area.

Oct. 5–18, S.C. to N.Y.: "Hazel" killed 95 in U.S.; about 400–1,000 in Haiti; 78 in Canada.

1955 **Aug. 7–21, N.C. to New England:** "Diane" took 184 lives and cost $8.3 million ($5.5 billion).

1957 **June 25–28, southwest La. and northern Tex.:** "Audrey" wiped out Cameron, La., causing 390 deaths.

1960 **Aug. 29–Sept. 13, Fla. to New England:** "Donna" killed 50 in the U.S.; 115 deaths in Antilles, mostly from flash floods in Puerto Rico.

1961 **Sept. 3–15, Tex. coast:** "Carla" devastated Tex. gulf cities, taking 46 lives.

1965 **Aug. 27–Sept. 12, southern Fla. and La.:** "Betsy" killed 75 people and cost more than $1.4 ($8.5) billion.

1969 **Aug. 14–22, Miss., La., Ala., Va., and W. Va.:** 256 killed as a result of "Camille." Damages estimated at $1.4 ($6.9) billion.

1972 **June 14–23, northwest Fla. to N.Y.:** "Agnes" caused 117 deaths (50 in Pa.). Damages estimated at over $2.1 ($8.6) billion. Still the worst natural disaster ever in Pa.

1979 **Aug. 29–Sept. 15, Ala. and Miss.:** "Frederic" devastated Mobile, Ala., and caused $2.3 ($4.9) billion in damage overall.

1985 **Oct. 6–Nov. 1:** "Juan" struck La. and the Southeast. Though only a category 1 hurricane, it caused severe flooding and $1.5 ($2.4) billion in damages; 63 lives were lost.

1989 **Sept. 10–22, Caribbean Sea, S.C., and N.C.:** "Hugo" claimed 86 lives (57 U.S. mainland). With damages estimated at over $7 ($9.7) billion, it is the second most costly U.S. hurricanes.

1991 **Oct. 30–Nov. 1, Eastern Atlantic seaboard:** an unnamed hurricane labeled the "perfect storm" caused extensive erosion and flooding along the Atlantic seaboard and created 39-foot waves.

1992 **Aug. 22–26, Bahamas, southern Fla., and La.:** Hurricane "Andrew" left 26 dead and more than 100,000 homes destroyed or damaged. With total U.S. damages estimated at $26.5 ($34.9) billion, it is the most costly hurricane in U.S. history.

1994 **Nov. 8–21, Caribbean and southern Fla.:** "Gordon" led to an estimated 1,122 deaths in Haiti. Eight died in Fla.

1995 **Nov. 29, Fla. panhandle and Ala.:** storm surge during "Opal" caused extensive damage to coastal areas. In U.S. death toll reached nine and damages $3 ($3.5) billion.

1996 **Sept. 5, N.C. and Va.:** "Fran" took 37 lives and caused more than $3.2 ($3.6) billion in damage.

1999 **Sept. 14–18, Bahamas to New England:** "Floyd" and associated flooding caused at least 57 deaths including one in the Bahamas. Hardest-hit N.C. suffered 36 "Floyd" related deaths. Damage estimated at $4.5 ($4.6) billion.

2001 **June 8–15, Gulf Coast to southern New England:** tropical storm "Allison" caused severe flooding, especially around Houston, where 20,000 residents were evacuated from their homes. Damage estimated at $5 billion (actual cost); 41 deaths, including 23 in Tex.

OTHER HURRICANES

1780 **Oct. 10–16, Barbados, West Indies:** "The Great Hurricane of 1780" killed 20,000–22,000 people and completely flattened the islands of Barbados, Martinique, and St. Eustatius; is the deadliest western hemisphere hurricane on record.

1926 **Oct. 20, Cuba:** powerful hurricane killed 650.

1930 **Sept. 3, Dominican Republic:** hurricane killed about 8,000 people.

1955 **Sept. 19, Mexico:** "Hilda" took 200 lives.
Sept. 22–28, Caribbean: "Janet" killed 200 in Honduras and 300 in Mexico.

1961 **Oct. 31, British Honduras:** "Hattie" devastated capital Belize, killed at least 400.

1963 **Oct. 2–7, Caribbean:** "Flora" killed about 7,200 in Haiti and Cuba.

1966 **Sept. 24–30, Caribbean area:** "Inez" killed 293.

1974 **Sept. 14–19, Honduras:** "Fifi" struck northern part of country, leaving 8,000 dead and 100,000 homeless.

1988 **Sept. 12–17, Caribbean Sea and Gulf of Mexico:** "Gilbert" took at least 260 lives and caused some 39 tornadoes in Tex.

1997 **Oct. 8–10, southern Mexico:** "Pauline" devastated resort city of Acapulco and villages along the coast in states of Oaxaca and Guerrero, leaving 217 dead and 20,000 homeless.

1998 **Sept. 20–29, Caribbean, Fla. Keys, and Gulf Coast:** "Georges" killed about 600 people, mostly in Dominican Republic. Damage estimated to be $5 billion, including $2 billion in Puerto Rico.
Oct. 26–Nov. 4, Honduras, Nicaragua, Guatemala: "Mitch" killed more than 11,000 people, becoming the deadliest Atlantic storm in 200 years. Two to three million people were left homeless; damages were more than $5 billion.

TYPHOONS

1906 **Sept. 18, Hong Kong:** typhoon with tsunami killed an estimated 10,000 people.

1934 **Sept. 21, Japan:** typhoon killed more than 4,000 on Honshu.

1949 **Dec. 5, off Korea:** typhoon struck fishing fleet; several thousand men reported dead.

1958 **Sept. 27, Honshu, Japan:** "Vera" left nearly 5,000 dead and 1.5 million homeless.

1959 **Aug. 20, Fukien province, China:** "Iris" killed 2,334.

1960 **June 9, Fukien province, China:** "Mary" caused at least 1,600 deaths.

1984 **Sept. 2–3, Philippines:** "Ike" hit seven major islands, leaving 1,300 dead.

1991 **Nov. 5, central Philippines:** flash floods triggered by tropical storm "Thelma" killed about 3,000 people. City of Ormoc on Leyte was worst hit.

RECENT HURRICANE-LIKE STORMS

1999 **Dec. 26–28, northern and western Europe:** two back-to-back hurricane-force storms left 97 people dead. Winds reaching 120 mph uprooted trees, disrupted transportation, and left millions of homes without power.

BLIZZARDS

1888 **Jan. 12, Dakota and Montana territories, Minn., Nebr., Kans., and Tex.:** "Schoolchildren's Blizzard" resulted in 235 deaths, many of which were children on their way home from school.
March 11–14, East Coast: "Blizzard of 1888" resulted in 400 deaths and as much as 5 ft of snow. Damage was estimated at $20 million.

1949 **Jan. 2–4, Nebr., Wyo., S.D., Utah, Colo., and Nev.:** Actually one of a series of winter storms between Jan. 1 and Feb. 22. Although only 1 ft to 30 in. of snow fell, fierce winds of up to 72 mph created drifts as high as 30 ft. Tens of thousands of cattle and sheep perished.

1950 **Nov. 25–27, eastern U.S.:** "Storm of the Century" generated heavy snow and hurricane-force winds across 22 states and claimed 383 lives. Damages estimated at $70 million.

1978 **Feb. 6–8, eastern U.S.:** "Blizzard of 1978" battered the East Coast, particularly the Northeast; claimed 54 lives and caused $1 billion in damage. Snowfall ranged from 2–4 ft in New England, plus nearly 2 ft of snow already on the ground from an earlier storm.

1993 **March 12–14, eastern U.S.:** "Superstorm" paralyzed the eastern seaboard, causing the deaths of some 270 people. Record snowfalls (with rates of 2–3 in. per hour) and high winds caused $3 billion to $6 billion in damage.

1996 **Jan. 6–8, eastern U.S.:** heavy snow paralyzed the Appalachians, the mid-Atlantic, and the Northeast. 187 were killed in the blizzard and in the floods that resulted after a sudden warm-up. Damages reached $3 billion.

U.S. TORNADOES

1840 **May 6, Natchez, Miss.:** tornado struck heart of the city, killing 317 and injuring over 1,000.

1880 **April 18, Marshfield, Mo.:** series of 24 tornadoes demolished city, killing 99 people.

1884 **Feb. 19, Miss., Ala., N.C., S.C., Tenn., Ky., Ind.:** series of 60 tornadoes caused estimated 800 deaths.

1896 **May 27, eastern Mo. and southern Ill.:** series of 18 tornadoes; 1 tornado destroyed large section of St. Louis, Mo., killing 255.

1899 **June 12, New Richmond, Wis.:** tornado struck while circus was in town, causing 117 deaths.

1902 **May 18, Goliad, Tex.:** tornado killed 114.

1903 **June 1, Gainesville, Holland, Ga.:** twister caused 98 deaths.

1905 **May 10, Snyder, Okla.:** tornado killed 97.

1908 **April 24–25, La., Miss., Ala., Ga.:** 18 tornadoes resulted in 310 deaths (143 of these caused by 1 tornado that moved from Amite, La., to Purvis, Miss.).
April 24, Natchez, Miss.: twister struck, causing 91 deaths.

1913 **March 23, eastern Nebr. and western Iowa:** Easter Sunday, 8 tornadoes resulted in 181 deaths (94 in Omaha, Nebr.).

1917 **May 26, Mattoon, Ill.:** tornado smashed area, causing 101 deaths.

1925 **March 18, Mo., Ill., Ind.:** the "Tri-State Tornado" was the most violent single twister in U.S. history. It caused the deaths of 689 people and injured over 2,000. Property damage was estimated at $16.5 million.

1927 **May 9, Poplar Bluff, Mo.:** twister killed 98.
Sept. 29, St. Louis, Mo.: a five-minute tornado ripped through the city and caused 79 deaths.

1932 **March 21–22, Ala., Miss., Ga., Tenn.:** outbreak of 33 tornadoes killed 334 (268 in Ala.).

1936 **April 5–6, Deep South:** series of 17 tornadoes; 216 killed in Tupelo, Miss., and 203 killed in Gainesville, Ga., a small mill town that was obliterated.

1944 **June 23, W.Va., Pa., Md.:** 4 tornadoes caused 153 deaths.

1947 **April 9, Woodward, Okla.:** tornado demolished town, killing 181.

1952 **March 21–22, Ark. and Tenn.:** 28 tornadoes caused 204 deaths.

1953 **May 11, Waco, Tex.:** a single tornado killed 114.
June 8, Flint, Mich.: tornado killed 116.

June 9, Worcester, Mass.: tornado hit town, causing 90 deaths.

1955 **May 25, Udall, Kans.:** tornado killed 80.

1965 **April 11–12, Midwest–Great Lakes region:** tornadoes in Iowa, Ill., Ind., Ohio, Mich., and Wis. caused 256 deaths.

1967 **April 21, northern Ill., also Mo., Iowa, lower Mich.:** series of 52 tornadoes caused 58 deaths.

1971 **Feb. 21, Miss., La., Ark., Tenn.:** series of 10 tornadoes resulted in 121 deaths.

1974 **April 3–4:** a series of 148 twisters within 16 hours comprised the deadly "Super Tornado Outbreak" that struck 13 states in the East, South, and Midwest. Before it was over, 330 died and 5,484 were injured in a damage path covering more than 2,500 mi.

1979 **April 10, northern Tex. and southern Okla.:** 11 tornadoes caused 59 deaths.

1985 **May 31, Pa. and Ohio:** 27 tornadoes resulted in 756 deaths. Estimated damages were $450 million.

1992 **Nov. 21–23, southeast Tex. to Mid-Atlantic and Ohio Valley:** total of 94 tornadoes caused 26 deaths and $291 million in damage.

1994 **March 27, Ala., Ga., and N.C.:** Palm Sunday tornado outbreak resulted in 42 deaths, 320 injuries, and $107 million in property damage. Twenty people died and 90 were injured when a tornado caused the roof of a church near Piedmont, Ala., to collapse.

1999 **May 3, Okla. and Kans.:** unusually large twister, thought to have been a mile wide at times, killed 44 people and injured at least 748 others in Okla. A separate tornado killed another 5 and injured about 150 in Kans. Damages totaled at least $1 billion.

2002 **Nov. 9–11, central and southeast U.S.:** series of more than 70 tornadoes across 9 states from Miss. to Pa. killed 36 people.

2003 **May 1–10: southern and midwestern U.S.:** a record-breaking number of more than 400 tornadoes in the first 10 days of May killed 42.

DROUGHTS AND HEAT WAVES

1930s **Many states:** longest drought of the 20th century. Peak periods were 1930, 1934, 1936, 1939, and 1940. A great "dust bowl" covered some 50 million acres in the south-central plains during the winter of 1935–1936.

1955 **Aug. 31–Sept. 7, Los Angeles:** 8-day run of 100°-plus heat left 946 people dead.

1972 **July 14–26, New York City:** 891 people died in 14-day heat wave.

1980 **June–Sept., central and eastern U.S.:** an estimated 10,000 people were killed during the summer in a long heat wave and drought. Damages totaled about $20 billion.

1982–1983 **worldwide:** El Niño caused wildly unusual weather in the U.S. and elsewhere throughout 1983. Drought in the western Pacific region led to disastrous forest fires in Indonesia and Australia. Overall loss to world economy was over $8 billion. Similar event in 1997–1998 resulted in estimated loss of $25–33 billion.

1988 **Summer, central and eastern U.S.:** a severe drought and heat wave killed an estimated 5,000–10,000 people, including heat stress-related deaths. Damages reached $40 billion.

1995 **July 12–17, Chicago:** 739 people died in record heat wave.

1998 **Summer, southern U.S.:** severe heat and drought spread across Tex. and Okla., all the way to N.C. and S.C. At least 200 were left dead and $6 billion to $9 billion of damage was estimated.

1999 **Summer, eastern U.S.:** rainfall shortages resulted in worst drought on record for Md., Del., N.J., and R.I. The state of W.Va. was declared a disaster area. 3.81 million acres were consumed by fire as of mid-Aug. Record heat throughout the country resulted in 502 deaths nationwide.

2000 **Spring–summer, southern U.S.:** severe drought and heat killed an estimated 140 people. Damages were estimated at $4 billion.

2003 **May–June, southern India:** a month-long intense heat wave claimed more than 1,500 lives.

Aug., Europe: drought conditions and a heat wave, one of the worst in 150 years, covered Europe, broke temperature records from London to Portugal, fueled deadly forest fires, ruined crops, and caused thousands of deaths. (French fatalities estimated at more than 10,000.)

NUCLEAR POWER PLANT ACCIDENTS

1952 **Dec. 12, Chalk River, nr. Ottawa, Canada:** a partial meltdown of the reactor's uranium fuel core resulted after the accidental removal of four control rods. Although millions of gallons of radioactive water accumulated inside the reactor, there were no injuries.

1957 **Oct. 7, Windscale Pile No. 1, north of Liverpool, England:** fire in a graphite-cooled reactor spewed radiation over the countryside, contaminating a 200-square-mile area.

South Ural Mountains: explosion of radioactive wastes at Soviet nuclear weapons factory 12 mi from city of Kyshtym forced the evacuation of over 10,000 people from a contaminated area. No casualties were reported by Soviet officials.

1976 **nr. Greifswald, East Germany:** radioactive core of reactor in the Lubmin nuclear power plant nearly melted down due to the failure of safety systems during a fire.

1979 **March 28, Three Mile Island, nr. Harrisburg, Pa.:** one of two reactors lost its coolant, which caused overheating and partial meltdown of its uranium core. Some radioactive water and gases were released.

1986 **April 26, Chernobyl, nr. Kiev, Ukraine:** explosion and fire in the graphite core of one of four reactors released radioactive material that spread over part of the Soviet Union, eastern Europe, Scandinavia, and later western Europe. 31 claimed dead. Total casualties are unknown. Worst such accident to date.

1999 **Sept. 30, Tokaimura, Japan:** uncontrolled chain reaction in a uranium-processing nuclear fuel plant spewed high levels of radioactive gas into the air, killing one worker and seriously injuring two others. Japan's worst nuclear accident.

FIRES AND EXPLOSIONS

1666 **Sept. 2, England:** "Great Fire of London" destroyed St. Paul's Cathedral, etc. Damage £10 million.

1835 **Dec. 16, New York City:** 530 buildings destroyed by fire.

1871 **Oct. 8, Chicago:** the "Chicago Fire" burned 17,450 buildings and killed 250 people; $196 million in damage.

1872 **Nov. 9, Boston:** fire destroyed 800 buildings; $75 million in damage.

1876 **Dec. 5, New York City:** fire in Brooklyn Theater killed more than 300.

1881 **Dec. 8, Vienna:** at least 620 died in fire at Ring Theatre.

1900 **June 30, Hoboken, N.J.:** piers of North German Lloyd Steamship line burned; 326 dead.

1903 **Dec. 30, Chicago:** Iroquois Theatre fire killed 602.

1904 **Feb. 7, Baltimore, Md.:** blaze spread through downtown Baltimore. More than 1,500 buildings were destroyed. Damages $150 million, but no lives lost.

1906 **March 10, France:** explosion in coal mine in Courrières killed 1,060.

1907 **Dec. 6, Monongah, W. Va.:** coal mine explosion killed 362.

Dec. 19, Jacobs Creek, Pa.: explosion in coal mine left 239 dead.

1908 **Jan. 13, Boyertown, Pa.:** fire in Rhoads Opera House killed 170 people who were attending church-sponsored stage performance.

1909 **Nov. 13, Cherry, Ill.:** explosion in coal mine killed 259.

1911 **March 25, New York City:** fire in Triangle Shirt-waist Factory fatal to 145.

1913 **Oct. 22, Dawson, N.M.:** coal mine explosion left 263 dead.

1917 **Dec. 6, Halifax Harbor, Nova Scotia:** Belgian steamer collided with ammunition ship *Mont Blanc*, which was carrying over 2,500 tons of explosives. Explosion leveled part of Halifax and left about 1,600 people dead.

1930 **April 21, Columbus, Ohio:** fire in Ohio State Penitentiary killed 320 convicts.

1937 **March 18, New London, Tex.:** explosion destroyed schoolhouse; 294 killed.

1942 **April 26, Manchuria:** explosion in Honkeiko Colliery killed 1,549.

Nov. 28, Boston, Mass.: Coconut Grove nightclub fire killed 491.

1944 **July 6, Hartford, Conn.:** fire and ensuing stampede in main tent of Ringling Brothers Circus killed 168, injured 487.

July 17, Port Chicago, Calif.: 322 killed when ammunition ships exploded.

1946 **Dec. 7, Atlanta:** fire in Winecoff Hotel killed 119.

1947 **April 16–18, Texas City, Tex.:** most of the city destroyed by a fire and subsequent explosion on the French freighter *Grandcamp*, which was carrying a cargo of ammonium nitrate. At least 516 were killed and over 3,000 injured.

1949 **Sept. 2, China:** fire on Chongqing (Chungking) waterfront killed 1,700.

1954 **May 26, off Quonset Point, R.I.:** explosion and fire aboard aircraft carrier *Bennington* killed 103 crewmen.

1956 **Aug. 7, Colombia:** about 1,100 reported killed when seven army ammunition trucks exploded at Cali.

Aug. 8, Belgium: 262 died in coal mine fire at Marcinelle.

1960 **Jan. 21, Coalbrook, South Africa:** coal mine explosion killed 437.

Nov. 13, Syria: 152 children killed in movie-house fire.

1961 **Dec. 17, Niteroi, Brazil:** circus fire fatal to 323.

1962 **Feb. 7, Saarland, West Germany:** coal mine gas explosion killed 298.

1963 **Nov. 9, Japan:** explosion in coal mine at Omuta killed 447.

1965 **May 28, India:** coal mine fire in state of Bihar killed 375.

June 1, nr. Fukuoka, Japan: coal mine explosion killed 236.

1967 **May 22, Brussels, Belgium:** fire in L'Innovation department store left 322 dead.

July 29, off North Vietnam: fire on U.S. carrier *Forrestal* killed 134.

1972 **June 6, Wankie, Rhodesia:** explosion in coal mine killed 427.

1973 **Nov. 29, Kumamoto, Japan:** fire in Taiyo department store killed 101.

1974 **Feb. 1, São Paulo, Brazil:** fire in upper stories of bank building killed 189 people, many of whom leaped to their deaths.

1975 **Dec. 27, Dhanbad, India:** explosion in coal mine followed by flooding from nearby reservoir left 372 dead.

1977 **May 28, Southgate, Ky.:** fire in Beverly Hills Supper Club; 167 dead.

1978 **Aug. 20, Abadan, Iran:** nearly 400 killed when arsonists set fire to crowded theater.

1986 **Dec. 31, San Juan, P.R.:** fire in Dupont Plaza Hotel set by three employees, killing 96 people.

1989 **June 3, Ural Mountains:** liquefied petroleum gas leaking from a pipeline running alongside the Trans-Siberian railway near Uta, 72 mi east of Moscow, exploded and destroyed two passing passenger trains. About 500 travelers were killed and 723 injured of an estimated 1,200 passengers on both trains.

1990 **March 25, New York City:** arson fire in the illegal Happy Land Social Club, in the Bronx, killed 87 people.

1993 **May 10, nr. Bangkok, Thailand:** fire in doll factory killed at least 187 people and injured 500 others. World's deadliest factory fire.

1999 **March 24, Chamonix, France:** Belgian truck carrying margarine and flour broke out in flames in the Mont Blanc tunnel, trapping dozens of cars. Death toll was at least 42.

2000 **Nov. 11, nr. Kaprun, Austria:** cable car transporting skiers to the Kitzsteinhorn glacier broke into flames while moving through mountain tunnel. Final death toll reached 156 in what was termed Austria's worst Alpine disaster.

Dec. 25, Luoyang, China: at least 309 people were killed in fire at shopping center. Most of the victims had been attending Christmas party at unlicensed disco in building.

2002 **Jan. 27, Lagos, Nigeria:** series of explosions at military depot triggered a stampede from the surrounding neighborhoods. More than 1,000 killed; many of the victims drowned in two muddy canals as they tried to flee.

June 20, Jixi, Heilongjian Province, China: gas explosion at the Chengzihe coal mine killed 111 people. China's mining industry is one of the deadliest; it is estimated that more than 5,000 mining-related deaths occurred in 2001.

2003 **Feb. 18, Daegu, South Korea:** subway fire, started by an arsonist, raced through two trains, killing 189 people and injuring more than 140.

Feb. 20, Warwick, R.I.: fire caused by a pyrotechnics display engulfed a Rhode Island nightclub, The Station, killing 100 and injuring more than 150.

WORST U.S. FOREST FIRES

1871 **Oct. 8–14, Peshtigo, Wis:** over 1,500 lives lost and 3.8 million acres burned in nation's worst forest fire.

1889 **June 6, Seattle, Wash.:** fire destroyed 64 acres of the city and killed 2 people. Damage was estimated at $15 million.

1894 **Sept. 1, Minn.:** forest fires ravaged over 160,000 acres and destroyed 6 towns; 600 killed, including 413 in town of Hinckley.

1902 **Sept., Wash. and Ore.:** Yacoult fire destroyed 1 million acres and left 38 dead.

1910 **Aug. 10, Idaho and Mont.:** fires burned 3 million acres of woods and killed 85 people.

1918 **Oct. 13–15, Minn. and Wis.:** forest fire struck towns in both states; 1,000 died, including 400 in town of Cloquet, Minn. About $1 million in losses.

1947 **Oct. 25–27, Maine:** forest fire destroyed part of Bar Harbor and damaged Acadia National Park. In all, 205,678 acres burned and 16 lives were lost.

1949 **Aug. 5, Mann Gulch, Mont.:** 12 smokejumpers—firefighters who parachuted near the fire—and 1 forest ranger died after being overtaken by a 200-ft wall of fire at the top of a gulch near Helena, Mont. Three smokejumpers survived.

1970 **Sept. 26, Laguna, Calif.:** large-scale brush fire burned 175,425 acres and 382 structures.

1988 **Aug.–Sept., western U.S.:** fires destroyed over 1.2 million acres in Yellowstone National Park and damaged Alaska woodlands.

1990 **June, Santa Barbara, Calif.:** Painted Cave fire consumed 4,900 acres and destroyed 641 structures.

1991 **Oct. 20–23, Oakland–Berkeley, Calif.:** brush fire in drought-stricken area destroyed over 3,000 homes and apartments. At least 24 people died; damage estimated at $1.5 billion.

1994 **July 2–11, South Canyon, Colo.:** relatively small fire (2,000 acres) resulted in deaths of 14 firefighters.

2000 **April–May, northern N.M.:** prescribed fire started by National Park Service raged out of control, destroying 235 structures and forcing evacuation of more than 20,000 people. Blaze consumed an estimated 47,000 acres and threatened Los Alamos National Laboratory.

Nov. 3, western U.S.: combination of hot, dry weather and plenty of dry vegetation led to one of the most destructive forest fire seasons in U.S. history. As of Nov. 3 about 7.2 million acres had burned nationwide, nearly double the 10-year average. States hardest hit included Alaska, Idaho, Mont., N.M., Nev., and Ore.

2002 **June–early July, mainly western U.S.:** Hayman fire in Pike National Forest destroyed 137,760 acres and 600 structures, making it the worst wildfire in Colorado history. In central Ariz., the 85,000-acre Rodeo fire, which had already been declared the worst in Arizona's history, merged with the Chediski fire to form an inferno that destroyed 468,638 acres and more than 400 structures. Large wildfires also burned in Alaska, southern Calif., N.M., Utah, Oregon, and Ga.

SHIPWRECKS

1833 **May 11, *Lady of the Lake:*** bound from England to Quebec, struck iceberg; 215 perished.

1853 **Sept. 29, *Annie Jane:*** emigrant vessel off coast of Scotland; 348 died.

1865 **April 27, *Sultana:*** boiler explosion on Mississippi River steamboat, near Memphis; 1,547 killed. Most of the dead were Union POWs finally heading home at the end of the Civil War.

1898 **Feb. 15, *Maine:*** U.S. battleship destroyed in Havana harbor by an explosion that killed 260 men. The incident led to the outbreak of the Spanish-American War in April 1898.

Nov. 26, *City of Portland:* 157 died nr. Cape Cod.

1904 **June 15, *General Slocum:*** excursion steamer burned in East River, N.Y.; 1,021 perished.

1912 **March 5, *Principe de Asturias:*** Spanish steamer struck rock off Sebastien Point; 500 drowned.

April 15, *Titanic:* supposedly unsinkable British ocean liner went down on maiden voyage after colliding with an iceberg. More than 1,500 people died.

1914 **May 29, *Empress of Ireland:*** sank after collision in St. Lawrence River; 1,024 perished.

1915 **July 24, *Eastland:*** Great Lakes excursion steamer overturned in Chicago River; 812 died.

1934 **Sept. 8, *Morro Castle:*** 134 killed in fire off Asbury Park, N.J.

1945 **Jan. 30, *Wilhelm Gustloff:*** cruise ship carrying German refugees and soldiers sunk by Soviet submarine in Baltic. It is thought that as many as 10,000 people were aboard, of which only about 900 survived.

1949 **Sept. 17, *Noronic:*** Canadian Great Lakes cruise ship burned at Toronto dock; about 130 died.

1952 **April 26, *Hobson:*** minesweeper collided with aircraft carrier *Wasp* and sank during night maneuvers in mid-Atlantic; 176 people lost.

1953 **Jan. 9, *Chang Tyong-Ho:*** South Korean ferry foundered off Pusan; 249 reported dead.

1954 **Sept. 26, *Toya Maru:*** more than 1,000 killed when commercial ferry sank in Tsugaru Strait, Japan.

1956 **July 25, *Andrea Doria:*** Italian liner collided with Swedish liner *Stockholm* off Nantucket Island, Mass., and sank the next day. At least 52 died or were unaccounted for.

1962 **April 8, *Dara:*** British liner exploded and sank in Persian Gulf; 236 dead. Caused by time bomb.

1963 **April 10, *Thresher:*** atomic-powered U.S. submarine sank in North Atlantic; 129 dead.

1968 **Late May, *Scorpion:*** U.S. nuclear submarine sank in Atlantic 400 mi southwest of Azores; 99 dead.

1975 **Nov. 10, *Edmund Fitzgerald:*** cargo vessel carrying 26,000 long tons of iron ore pellets sank in eastern Lake Superior; all 29 crew lost.

1983 **May 25, *10th of Ramadan:*** Nile steamer caught fire and sank in Lake Nasser, near Aswan, Egypt; 272 dead and 75 missing.

1987 **March 6, *Herald of Free Enterprise:*** British ferry capsized after leaving Belgian port of Zeebrugge with 500 aboard; 134 drowned.

Dec. 20, *Dona Paz:* over 4,000 killed when passenger ferry collided with oil tanker *Victor* off Mindoro Is., 110 mi south of Manila, Philippines.

1990 **April 7, *Scandinavian Star:*** suspected arson fire aboard Danish-owned North Sea ferry killed at least 110 passengers in Skagerrak Strait off Norway.

1991 **Dec. 15, *Salem Express:*** ferry carrying 569 passengers sank in Red Sea off coast of Safaga, Egypt, after hitting a coral reef. Over 460 people believed drowned.

1993 **Feb. 17, *Neptune:*** triple-deck ferry capsized off southern peninsula of Haiti during a squall. Over 1,000 passengers believed drowned. About 300 survived the sinking.

1994 **Sept. 28, *Estonia:*** passenger ferry capsized off coast of southwest Finland and sank in a stormy Baltic Sea. Only about 140 of the estimated 1,040 passengers aboard survived.

1996 **Jan. 21, *Gurita:*** overloaded ferry sank off the coast of northern Sumatra, killing 340.

1999 **Feb., *Harta Rimba:*** ship sank in the South China Sea, killing about 325 people. The ship had not been licensed for passenger use.

2000 **June 29, *Cahaya Bahari:*** ferry carrying refugees sank about 40 mi off the coast of Sulawesi. None of the 492 people aboard survived.

Aug. 12, *Kursk:* Russian nuclear submarine sank to bottom of Barents Sea following an explosion; 118 dead.

2001 **Feb. 9, *Ehime Maru:*** U.S. submarine *Greeneville* collided with Japanese fishing boat near Pearl Harbor, Hawaii. Twenty-six people aboard the *Ehime Maru* were rescued; nine others, including four students, were presumed dead.

2002 **Sept. 26, *Joola:*** overloaded Senegalese ferry capsized off the coast of Gambia, drowning 1,863 people. Only 64 passengers were rescued.

MYSTERIOUS DISAPPEARANCES

1872 ***Mary Celeste:*** the brigantine set sail from New York harbor for Genoa, Italy, on Nov. 5. A British brigantine, the *DeGratia,* discovered the ship derelict on Dec. 5 and boarded her. Everyone aboard the *Mary Celeste* had vanished—her captain, his family, and its 14-man crew. The ship was in perfect order with ample supplies and there was no sign of violence or trouble. The fate of the crew remains unknown.

1918 **USS *Cyclops:*** the navy coal ship, used to deliver fuel and other supplies to U.S. battlefleet during World War I, disappeared while en route from Brazil to Baltimore. The ship docked briefly at Barbados on March 3–4. When it failed to arrive in Baltimore on March 13, a search was made, but neither her wreck nor any of the 309 people aboard were ever found, and the cause of her loss remains unknown.

1928 ***Köbenhavn:*** five-masted Danish steel barque, a sail-training ship with a crew of 75 including 45 boy cadets, sailed from the River Plate for Melbourne, Australia, on Dec. 14. The last radio contact with the ship was made on Dec. 22 and all was well. The *Köbenhavn* and its crew disappeared without a trace and no one knows what happened to it.

AIRCRAFT CRASHES

(150 deaths or more, with exceptions. *See also* Terrorist Attacks, pp. 613–614.)

1921 **Aug. 24, England:** British dirigible *AR-2* broke in two on trial trip near Hull; 62 died.

1925 **Sept. 3, Caldwell, Ohio:** U.S. dirigible *Shenandoah* broke apart; 14 dead.

1930 **Oct. 5, Beauvais, France:** British dirigible *R 101* crashed, killing 47.

1933 **April 4, N.J.:** U.S. dirigible *Akron* crashed; 73 died.

1937 **May 6, Lakehurst, N.J.:** German zeppelin *Hindenburg* destroyed by fire at tower mooring; 36 killed.

1945 **July 28, New York City:** U.S. Army bomber B-25 crashed into Empire State Building; 13 dead.

1960 **Dec. 16, New York City:** United DC-8 and Trans World Super Constellation collided then crashed in two boroughs, killing 134 in air and on ground.

1961 **Feb. 15, nr. Brussels, Belgium:** 72 on board and farmer on ground killed in crash of Sabena plane; U.S. figure skating team wiped out.

1966 **Dec. 24, Binh Thai, South Vietnam:** crash of military-chartered CL-44 into village killed 129.

1971 **July 30, Morioka, Japan:** Japanese Boeing 727 and F-86 fighter collided in midair; 162 died.

1972 **Oct. 13, Moscow, Russia:** Aeroflot Ilyushin IL-14 crashed during landing due to pilot fatigue and 176 people perish.

1973 **Jan. 22, Kano, Nigeria:** 171 Nigerian Muslims returning from Mecca and 5 crewmen died in crash.

Feb. 21, Sinai: civilian Libyan Arab Airlines Boeing 727 shot down by Israeli fighters after it had strayed off course; 108 died, 5 survived. Officials claimed that the pilot had ignored fighters' warnings to land.

1974 **March 3, Paris:** Turkish DC-10 jumbo jet crashed in forest shortly after takeoff; all 346 passengers and crew killed.

Dec. 4, Colombo, Sri Lanka: Dutch DC-8 carrying Muslims to Mecca crashed on landing approach, killing all 191 people aboard.

1975 **April 4, nr. Saigon, Vietnam:** Air Force Galaxy C-5A crashed after takeoff, killing 172, mostly Vietnamese children.

Aug. 3, Agadir, Morocco: chartered Boeing 707, returning Moroccan workers home after vacation in France, plunged into mountainside; all 188 aboard killed.

1976 **Sept. 10, Zagreb, Yugoslavia:** midair collision between British Airways Trident and Yugoslav charter DC-9 fatal to all 176 people aboard.

1977 **March 27, Santa Cruz de Tenerife, Canary Islands:** Pan American and KLM Boeing 747s collided on runway. All 249 on KLM plane and 333 of 394 aboard Pan Am jet killed. Total of 582 is highest for any type of aviation disaster.

1978 **Jan. 1, Bombay:** Air India 747 with 213 aboard exploded and plunged into sea minutes after takeoff.

Nov. 15, Colombo, Sri Lanka: chartered Icelandic Airlines DC-8, carrying 249 Muslim pilgrims from Mecca, crashed in thunderstorm during landing approach; 183 killed.

1979 **May 25, Chicago:** American Airlines DC-10 lost left engine upon takeoff and crashed seconds later, killing all 272 people aboard and 3 on the ground in worst U.S. air disaster.

Nov. 26, Jidda, Saudi Arabia: Pakistan International Airlines 707 carrying pilgrims returning from Mecca crashed on takeoff; all 156 aboard killed.

Nov. 28, Mt. Erebus, Antarctica: Air New Zealand DC-10 crashed on sightseeing flight; 257 killed.

1980 Aug. 19, Riyadh, Saudi Arabia: all 301 aboard Saudi Arabian jet killed when burning plane made safe landing but passengers were unable to escape.

1981 Dec. 1, Ajaccio, Corsica: Yugoslav DC-9 Super 80 carrying tourists crashed into mountain on landing approach, killing all 178 aboard.

1983 Aug. 30, nr. island of Sakhalin off Siberia: Korean Air Lines Boeing 747 shot down by Soviet fighter after it strayed off course into Soviet airspace. All 269 aboard killed. Secret Soviet documents released in Oct. 1992 reveal that the plane was flying a straight course for two hours with its navigational lights on and did not take evasive action. The Soviet fighter did not give a warning by firing tracer bullets as originally claimed.

Nov. 27, Madrid: Colombian Avianca Boeing 747 crashed near Mejorada del Campó Airport, killing 181 people aboard. Eleven people survived the accident.

1985 June 23, Atlantic Ocean: Air India 747 exploded over the ocean killing 329. The probable cause was a Sikh terrorist bomb.

Aug. 12, Japan: Japan Air Lines Boeing 747 crashed into a mountain, killing 520 of the 524 aboard. Highest death toll in a single-plane crash in aviation history.

Dec. 12, Gander, Newfoundland: a chartered Arrow Air DC-8 bringing American soldiers home for Christmas crashed on takeoff. All 256 aboard died.

1987 Aug. 16, Romulus, Mich.: Northwest Airlines McDonnell Douglas MD-80 crashed into a highway shortly after takeoff from Detroit Metropolitan Airport, killing 156 (including 2 on the ground). Girl, 4, only survivor.

Nov. 29, Burma: Korean Air Boeing 747 jetliner exploded from bomb planted by North Korean agents and crashed into sea, killing all 115 aboard.

1988 July 3, Persian Gulf: U.S. Navy cruiser *Vincennes* shot down Iran Air Airbus A-300 after mistaking it for an attacking jet fighter; 290 killed.

Aug. 28, Ramstein Air Force Base, West Germany: three jets from Italian Air Force acrobatic team collided in midair during air show and crashed, killing 70 people, including the pilots and spectators on the ground.

Dec. 21, Lockerbie, Scotland: N.Y.-bound Pan-Am Boeing 747 exploded in flight from a terrorist bomb and crashed into Scottish village, killing all 259 aboard and 11 on the ground. For terrorist attacks, *see* pp. 613–614.

1989 June 7, Paramaribo, Suriname: a Surinam Airways DC-8 carrying 174 passengers and 9 crew members crashed into the jungle while making a third attempt to land in a thick fog, killing 168 aboard.

1991 May 26, nr. Bangkok, Thailand: Austrian Lauda Air Boeing 767, en route to Vienna, crashed into jungle hilltop shortly after takeoff from Bangkok airport, killing all 223 aboard. Thailand's worst air disaster.

July 11, Jedda, Saudi Arabia: Canadian-chartered DC-8 carrying pilgrims returning to Nigeria crashed after takeoff, killing 261 people.

1994 April 14, northern Iraq: two American F-15C fighter aircraft mistook two U.S. Army blackhawk helicopters for Russian-made Iraqi MI-24 helicopters and shot them down over no-fly zone, killing all 26 on board.

April 26, Nagoya, Japan: China Airlines Airbus A-300 from Taiwan crash-landed and exploded on the tarmac. Only 7 of the 271 passengers aboard survived.

1995 Dec. 20, nr. Cali, Colombia: 160 people killed when American Airlines Boeing 757 crashed in Andean Mountains.

1996 Jan. 8, Kinshasa, Zaire: Russian-built Antonov-32 cargo plane crashed after takeoff from Kinshasa into the center of the city, killing over 350 people and injuring at least 470.

Feb. 6, off coast of Puerto Plata, Dominican Republic: Dominican Alas Nacionales Boeing 737 crashed into Atlantic Ocean after takeoff, killing 189.

July 17, off coast of Long Island, N.Y.: TWA Boeing 747-100 bound for Paris from N.Y. exploded over waters of eastern L.I. and crashed into Atlantic Ocean, killing all 230 aboard.

Nov. 12, nr. New Delhi, India: shortly after takeoff, Saudi Arabian Airlines Boeing 747 collided in midair with Kazak Airlines Ilyushin 76 plane approaching the New Delhi airport. All 349 passengers and crew were killed; the world's worst midair collision.

1997 Aug. 6, Guam: Korean Air Boeing 747-300 from Seoul crashed into jungle near Agana International Airport, killing 228 people; 26 survived.

Sept. 26, nr. northern Indonesia: Indonesian Garuda Airlines A-300 Airbus jetliner crashed while approaching Medan Airport, Sumatra, killing all 234 people aboard.

1998 Feb. 16, Taipei, Taiwan: China Airlines Airbus A-300 jumbo jet crashed while trying to land in fog at Chiang Kai-shek International Airport, killing all 196 passengers and crew and at least 6 people on the ground.

Sept. 2, off Nova Scotia, Canada: Swissair flight from N.Y. to Geneva crashed off Canadian coast, killing all 229 aboard. 136 Americans were on the McDonnell Douglas MD-11.

1999 Oct. 31, southeast of Nantucket Island: Egypt Air Boeing 767-300 on flight from N.Y. to Cairo crashed into the Atlantic Ocean, killing all 217 aboard.

2000 Jan. 30, off the Ivory Coast: Kenya Airways Airbus A-310, carrying 179 passengers and crew, crashed after takeoff from Abidjan into the Atlantic Ocean. Ten people survived.

July 25, Gonesse, France: Air France Concorde jet en route to N.Y. crashed into a hotel just after taking off from Charles de Gaulle airport near Paris; all 109 aboard and 4 on the ground were killed; first Concorde jet to crash since the plane went into commercial service in 1976.

2001 Sept. 11, New York City, Arlington, Va., and Shanksville, Pa.: For the attacks on the World Trade Center and the Pentagon, *see* p. 614.

Nov. 12, Queens, N. Y.: American Airlines Airbus A-300 bound for Santo Domingo, Dominican Republic, crashed into residential neighborhood minutes after taking off from JFK International Airport. All 260 people aboard and 5 on the ground were killed.

2002 May 25, nr. Pescadores off western Taiwan: China Airlines Boeing 747, bound for Hong Kong with 225 people aboard, broke apart in midair and plunged into sea 20 minutes after takeoff from Taipei. There were no survivors.

July 27, nr. Lviv, Ukraine: Russian-built Sukhoi-27 fighter jet crashed while performing an acrobatic maneuver during an air show. Eighty-three people were killed, including 23 children; the 2 pilots ejected to safety. It is the worst air show disaster in history.

2003 Feb. 19, nr. Shahdad, Iran: Iranian military airplane, Ilyushin Il-76MD, carrying members of Iran's Revolutionary Guards, crashed in the Sirach Mountains. All 276 on board were killed, making this Iran's worst air disaster.

SPACE ACCIDENTS

1967 Jan. 27, *Apollo 1*: a fire aboard the space capsule on the ground at Cape Kennedy, Fla., killed astronauts Virgil I. Grissom, Edward H. White, and Roger Chaffee.

April 23–24, *Soyuz 1*: Vladimir M. Komarov was killed when his craft crashed after its parachute lines, released at 23,000 ft for reentry, became snarled.

1971 June 6–30, *Soyuz 11*: three cosmonauts, Georgi T. Dolrovolsky, Vladislav N. Volkov, and Viktor I. Patsayev, found dead in the craft after its automatic landing. Apparent cause of death was loss of pressurization in the space craft during reentry into the earth's atmosphere.

1980 March 18, USSR: a Vostok rocket exploded on its launch pad while being refueled, killing 50 at the Plesetsk Space Center.

1986 Jan. 28, *Challenger* Space Shuttle: exploded 73 seconds after liftoff, killing all 7 crew members. They were: Francis R. Scobee, Michael J. Smith, Judith A. Resnick, Ronald E. McNair, Ellison S. Onizuka, Gregory B. Jarvis, and schoolteacher Christa McAuliffe. A booster leak ignited the fuel, causing the explosion.

2003 Feb. 1, *Columbia* Space Shuttle: broke up on reentering Earth's atmosphere on its way to Kennedy Space Center, killing all seven crew members. They were: Rick D. Husband, William C. McCool, Michael P. Anderson, David M. Brown, Kalpana Chawla, Laurel Clark, and the first Israeli astronaut, Ilan Ramon. Foam insulation fell from the shuttle during launch, damaging the left wing. On reentry hot gases entered the wing, leading to the destruction of the space craft.

RAILROAD ACCIDENTS

NOTE: Very few passengers were killed in a single U.S. train wreck up until 1853. These early trains ran slowly and made short trips, night travel was rare, and there were not many of them in operation.

1831 June 17, nr. Charleston, S.C.: boiler exploded on America's first passenger locomotive, *The Best Friend of Charleston,* injuring the fireman and the engineer.

1833 Nov. 8, nr. Heightstown, N.J.: world's first train wreck and first passenger fatalities recorded. A 24-passenger Camden & Amboy train derailed due to a broken axle, killing 2 passengers and injuring all others. Former President John Quincy Adams and Cornelius Vanderbilt, who later made a fortune in railroads, were aboard the train.

1853 May 6, Norwalk, Conn.: New Haven Railroad train ran through an open drawbridge and plunged into the Norwalk River. Forty-six passengers were crushed to death or drowned. This was the first major drawbridge accident.

1856 July 17, Camp Hill, nr. Ft. Washington, Pa.: two Northern Penn trains crashed head-on. Approximately 50–60 people died, mostly children on their way to a Sunday school picnic.

1876 Dec. 29, Ashtabula, Ohio: Lake Shore train fell into the Ashtabula River when the bridge it was crossing collapsed; 92 people were killed.

1887 Aug. 10, nr. Chatsworth, Ill.: a burning railroad trestle collapsed while a Toledo, Peoria & Western train was crossing, killing 81 and injuring 372.

1904 Aug. 7, Eden, Colo.: train derailed on bridge during flash flood; 96 killed.

1910 March 1, Wellington, Wash.: two trains swept into canyon by avalanche; 96 dead.

1915 May 22, Gretna, Scotland: two passenger trains and troop train collided; 227 killed.

1917 Dec. 12, Modane, France: nearly 550 killed in derailment of troop train near mouth of Mt. Cenis tunnel.

1918 July 9, Nashville, Tenn.: 101 killed in a 2-train collision near Nashville.

Nov. 1, New York City: derailment of subway train in Malbone St. tunnel in Brooklyn left 92 dead.

1926 March 14, Virilla River Canyon, Costa Rica: an overcrowded train carrying pilgrims derailed while crossing the Colima Bridge, killing over 300 people and injuring hundreds more.

1939 Dec. 22, nr. Magdeburg, Germany: more than 125 killed in collision; 99 killed in another wreck near Friedrichshafen.

1943 Dec. 16, nr. Rennert, N.C.: 72 killed in derailment and collision of 2 Atlantic Coast Line trains.

1944 March 2, nr. Salerno, Italy: 521 suffocated when Italian train stalled in tunnel.

1949 Oct. 22, nr. Nowy Dwor, Poland: more than 200 reported killed in derailment of Danzig-Warsaw express.

1950 Nov. 22, Richmond Hill, N.Y.: 79 died when one Long Island Railroad commuter train crashed into rear of another.

1951 Feb. 6, Woodbridge, N.J.: 85 died when Pennsylvania Railroad commuter train plunged through temporary overpass.

1952 Oct. 8, Harrow-Wealdstone, England: two express trains crashed into commuter train; 112 dead.

1957 Sept. 1, nr. Kendal, Jamaica: about 175 killed when train plunged into ravine.

Sept. 29, nr. Montgomery, West Pakistan: express train crashed into standing oil train; nearly 300 killed.

Dec. 4, St. John's, England: 92 killed and 187 injured as one commuter train crashed into another in fog.

1960 **Nov. 14, Pardubice, Czechoslovakia:** two trains collided; 110 dead, 106 injured.

1962 **May 3, nr. Tokyo:** 163 killed and 400 injured when train crashed into wreckage of collision between inbound freight train and outbound commuter train.

1963 **Nov. 9, nr. Yokohama, Japan:** two passenger trains crashed into derailed freight train, killing 162.

1964 **July 26, Custoias, Portugal:** passenger train derailed; 94 dead.

1970 **Feb. 4, nr. Buenos Aires:** 236 killed when express train crashed into standing commuter train.

1972 **Oct. 6, nr. Saltillo, Mexico:** train carrying religious pilgrims derailed and caught fire, killing 204 and injuring over 1,000.

Oct. 30, Chicago: two Illinois Central commuter trains collided during morning rush hour; 45 dead and over 200 injured.

1974 **Aug. 30, Zagreb, Yugoslavia:** train entering station derailed, killing 153 and injuring over 60.

1981 **June 6, nr. Mansi, India:** driver of train carrying over 500 passengers braked to avoid hitting a cow, causing train to plunge off a bridge into the Baghmati River; 268 passengers were reported killed, but at least 300 more were missing.

1982 **July 11, Tepic, Mexico:** Nogales-Guadalajara train plunged down mountain gorge, killing 120.

1989 **Jan. 15, Maizdi Khan, Bangladesh:** train carrying Muslim pilgrims crashed head-on with a mail train, killing at least 110 people and injuring as many as 1,000.

Aug. 10, nr. Los Mochis, Mexico: a second-class passenger train traveling from Mazatlán to Mexicali, plunged off a bridge at Puente del Rio Bamoa into the river and killed an estimated 85 people and injured 107.

1990 **Jan. 4, Sangi village, Sindh province, Pakistan:** overcrowded 16-car passenger train rammed into a standing freight train. At least 210 people were killed and 700 were believed injured in what is said to be Pakistan's worst train disaster.

1993 **Sept. 22, nr. Mobile, Ala.:** Amtrak's *Sunset Limited,* en route to Miami, jumped rails on weakened bridge and plunged in Big Bayou Canot, killing 47 people.

1995 **Aug. 20, Firozabad, northern India:** a speeding passenger train rammed another train that was stalled after hitting a cow. About 300 people were killed and over 400 injured.

1997 **March 3, Punjab province, Pakistan:** passenger train crashed due to failed brakes, killing 119 and injuring at least 80 people.

1998 **June 3, nr. Eschede, Germany:** Inter City Express passenger train traveling at 125 mph crashed into support pier of overpass, killing 98. Is nation's worst postwar train accident.

1999 **Oct. 5, London:** out-bound Thames commuter train passed a red signal near Paddington Station and collided with London-bound Great Western express, killing 30 people and injuring 245.

2002 **Feb. 20, nr. Ayyat, Egypt:** 361 killed in fire after gas cylinder used for cooking exploded aboard crowded passenger train. Egypt's worst train disaster.

May 25, Muamba, Mozambique: 192 died and dozens more injured when passenger cars rolled for several miles at top speed into freight cars from which they had been disconnected because of mechanical problems.

June 24, nr. Msagali, central Tanzania: runaway passenger train collided with freight train on same track, leaving 200 dead.

OIL SPILLS

1976 **Dec. 15, Buzzards Bay, Mass.:** *Argo Merchant* ran aground and broke apart southeast of Nantucket Island, spilling its entire cargo of 7.7 million gallons of fuel oil.

1978 **March 16, off Portsall, France:** wrecked supertanker *Amoco Cadiz* spilled 68 million gallons, causing widespread environmental damage over 100 mi of Brittany coast—world's largest tanker disaster.

1979 **June 3, Gulf of Mexico:** exploratory oil well Ixtoc 1 blew out, spilling an estimated 140 million gallons of crude oil into the open sea. Although it is the largest known oil spill, it had a low environmental impact.

1989 **Mar. 24, Prince William Sound, Alaska:** tanker *Exxon Valdez* hit an undersea reef and spilled 10 million plus gallons of oil into the waters, causing the worst oil spill in U.S. history.

Dec. 19, off Las Palmas, the Canary Islands: explosion in Iranian supertanker, the *Kharg-5,* caused 19 million gallons of crude oil to spill into Atlantic Ocean about 400 mi north of Las Palmas, forming a 100-square-mile oil slick.

1991 **Jan. 25, southern Kuwait:** during the Persian Gulf War, Iraq deliberately released an estimated 460 million gallons of crude oil into the Persian Gulf from tankers 10 mi off Kuwait. Spill had little military significance. On Jan. 27, U.S. warplanes bombed pipe systems to stop the flow of oil.

1994 **Sept. 8, Russia:** dam built to contain oil burst and spilled oil into Kolva River tributary. U.S. Energy Department estimated spill at 2 million barrels. Russian state-owned oil company claimed spill was only 102,000 barrels.

1996 **Feb. 15, off Welsh coast:** supertanker *Sea Empress* ran aground at port of Milford Haven, Wales, spewed out 70,000 tons of crude oil, and created a 25-mile slick.

SPORTS DISASTERS

1955 **June 11, Le Mans, France:** racing car in Grand Prix hurtled into grandstand, killing 82 spectators.

1964 **May 24, Lima, Peru:** more than 300 soccer fans killed and over 500 injured during riot and panic following unpopular ruling by referee in Peru vs. Argentina soccer game. It is worst soccer disaster on record.

1971 **Jan. 2, Glasgow, Scotland:** 66 killed in crush at Glasgow Rangers home stadium when soccer fans trying to leave encountered fans trying to return to stadium after hearing that a late goal had been scored.

1982 **Oct. 20, Moscow:** according to *Sovietsky Sport,* as many as 340 died at Lenin Stadium when exiting soccer fans collided with returning fans after final goal was scored. All the fans had been crowded into one section of stadium by police.

1985 **May 11, Bradford, England:** 56 burned to death and over 200 injured when fire engulfed main grandstand at Bradford's soccer stadium.

May 29, Brussels, Belgium: group of drunken British soccer fans supporting Liverpool club stormed stand filled with Italian supporters of Juventus team before European Champion's Cup final. While British fans attacked rival spectators at the Heysel Stadium, concrete retaining wall collapsed and 39 people were crushed or trampled to death, 32 of them Italians. More than 400 people were injured.

1988 **March 12, Katmandu, Nepal:** some 80 soccer fans seeking cover during a violent hail storm at the national stadium were trampled to death in a stampede because the stadium doors were locked.

1989 **April 15, Sheffield, England:** 96 people were killed at Hillsborough stadium during a semifinal match between Liverpool and Nottingham Forest. Most of the victims, who were Liverpool fans, were crushed when a barrier collapsed on an overcrowded pen behind one of the goals. It is Britain's worst soccer disaster.

1996 **Oct. 16, Guatemala City:** at least 84 killed and 147 injured by stampeding soccer fans before a 1998 World Cup qualifying match between Guatemala and Costa Rica held at Mateo Flores National Stadium.

2001 **May 9, Accra, Ghana:** at least 120 people were killed in a stampede at a soccer match. It was Africa's worst soccer-related disaster ever.

TERRORIST ATTACKS

(within the United States or against Americans abroad)

1920 **Sept. 16, New York City:** TNT bomb planted in unattended horse-drawn wagon exploded on Wall Street opposite House of Morgan, killing 35 people and injuring hundreds more. Bolshevist or anarchist terrorists believed responsible, but crime never solved.

1975 **Jan. 24, New York City:** bomb set off in historic Fraunces Tavern killed 4 and injured more than 50 people. Puerto Rican nationalist group (FALN) claimed responsibility, and police tied 13 other bombings to the group.

1983 **April 18, Beirut, Lebanon:** U.S. embassy destroyed in suicide car-bomb attack; 63 dead.

Oct. 23, Beirut, Lebanon: Shi'ite suicide bombers exploded truck near U.S. military barracks at Beirut airport, killing 241 Marines. Minutes later a second bomb killed 58 French paratroopers in their barracks in West Beirut.

1988 **Dec. 21, Lockerbie, Scotland:** N.Y.-bound Pan-Am Boeing 747 exploded in flight from a terrorist bomb and crashed into Scottish village, killing all 259 aboard and 11 on the ground. Passengers included 35 Syracuse University students and many U.S. military personnel. Libya formally admitted responsibility 15 years later (Aug. 2003) and offered $2.7 billion compensation to victims' families.

1993 **Feb. 26, New York City:** bomb exploded in basement garage of World Trade Center, killing 6 and injuring at least 1,040 others. In 1995, militant Islamist Sheik Omar Abdel Rahman and 9 others were convicted of conspiracy charges, and in 1998, Ramzi Yousef, believed to have been the mastermind, was convicted of the bombing. Al-Qaeda involvement is suspected.

1995 **April 19, Oklahoma City:** car bomb exploded outside federal office building, collapsing wall and floors. 168 people were killed, including 19 children and 1 person who died in rescue effort. Over 220 buildings sustained damage. Timothy McVeigh and Terry Nichols later convicted in the antigovernment plot to avenge the Branch Davidian standoff in Waco, Tex., exactly two years earlier. (*See* Miscellaneous Disasters.)

1996 **June 25, Dhahran, Saudi Arabia:** truck bomb exploded outside Khobar Towers military complex, killing 19 American servicemen and injuring hundreds of others. Thirteen Saudis and a Lebanese, all alleged members of Islamic militant group Hezbollah, were indicted on charges relating to the attack in June 2001.

1998 **Aug. 7, Nairobi, Kenya, and Dar es Salaam, Tanzania:** truck bombs exploded almost simultaneously near 2 U.S. embassies, killing 224 (213 in Kenya and 11 in Tanzania) and injuring about 4,500. Four men, two of whom had received training at al-Qaeda camps inside Afghanistan, were convicted of the killings in May 2001 and

Suspected al-Qaeda Terrorist Acts

1993 (Feb.): Bombing of World Trade Center (WTC); 6 killed.

1993 (Oct.): Killing of U.S. soldiers in Somalia.

1996 (June): Truck bombing at Khobar Towers barracks in Dhahran, Saudi Arabia, kills 19 Americans.

1998 (Aug.): Bombing of U.S. embassies in East Africa; 224 killed, including 12 Americans.

1999 (Dec.): Plot to bomb millennium celebrations in Seattle foiled when customs agents arrest an Algerian smuggling explosives into the U.S.

2000 (Oct.): Bombing of the USS *Cole* in port in Yemen; 17 U.S. sailors killed.

2001 (Sept.): Destruction of WTC, Pentagon attack. Total dead 3,044.

2002 (Apr.): Explosion at historic synagogue in Tunisia leaves 21 dead, including 14 German tourists.

2002 (May): Car explodes outside hotel in Karachi, Pakistan, killing 14, including 11 French citizens.

2002 (June): Bomb explodes outside American Consulate in Karachi, Pakistan, killing 12.

2002 (Oct.): Nightclub bombings in Bali, Indonesia, kill 202, mostly Australian citizens.

2002 (Nov.): Suicide attack on a hotel in Mombasa, Kenya, kills 16.

2003 (May): Suicide bombers kill 34, including 8 Americans, at housing compounds for Westerners in Riyadh, Saudi Arabia.

2003 (May): Four bombs kill 24 people, targeting Jewish, Spanish, and Belgian sites in Casablanca, Morocco.

2003 (Aug.): Suicide car bomb kills 12, injures 150, at Marriott Hotel in Jakarta, Indonesia.

later sentenced to life in prison. A federal grand jury had indicted 22 men in connection with the attacks, including Saudi dissident Osama bin Laden, who remained at large.

2000 **Oct. 12, Aden, Yemen:** U.S. Navy destroyer USS *Cole* was heavily damaged when a small boat loaded with explosives blew up alongside it. Seventeen sailors were killed in a deliberate terrorist attack. Osama bin Laden, or members of his al-Qaeda terrorist network suspected.

2001 **Sept. 11, New York City, Arlington, Va., and Shanksville, Pa.:** hijackers crashed two commercial jets into twin towers of World Trade Center; two more hijacked jets were crashed into the Pentagon and a field in rural Pa. Total dead and missing numbered 3,044: 2,801 in New York City, 184 at the Pentagon, 40 in Pa., and 19 hijackers. Islamic al-Qaeda terrorist group blamed.

2003 **May 12, Riyadh, Saudi Arabia:** suicide bombers killed 34, including eight Americans, at housing compounds for Westerners. Al-Qaeda suspected.

Total International Terrorist Attacks, 1981-2002

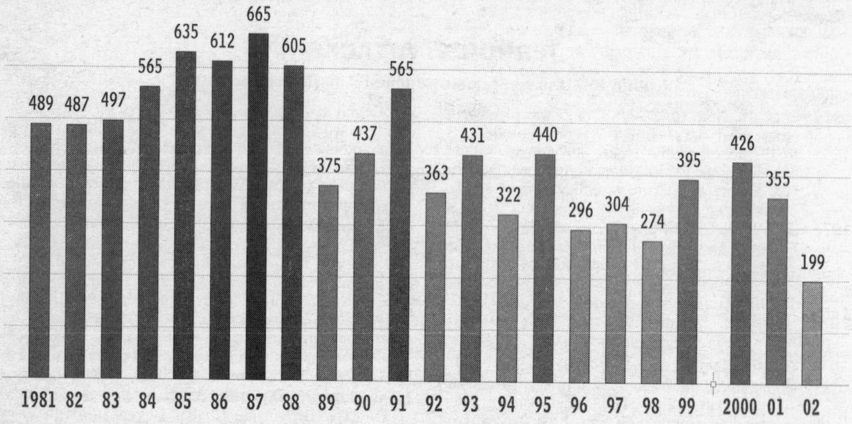

Source: Patterns of Global Terrorism 2002, U.S. Department of State.

MISCELLANEOUS DISASTERS

1952 **Dec. 4–7, London, England:** high-pressure system settled over London, trapping pollution near the ground. Some 4,000 people died in "Great Smog," mostly from respiratory and cardiac distress.

1981 **July 18, Kansas City, Mo.:** suspended walkway in Hyatt Regency Hotel collapsed; 113 dead, 186 injured.

1982–1983 **worldwide:** El Niño caused wildly unusual weather in the U.S. throughout 1983, including severe winter storms in southern Calif., widespread flooding across the South, and unusually mild winter weather in the central and northern parts of the country. Warming ocean currents resulted in failed fishing harvests in Peru and Ecuador, and drought in the western Pacific region led to disastrous forest fires in Indonesia and Australia. Overall loss to world economy was over $8 billion. Similar event in 1997–1998 resulted in estimated loss of $25–33 billion.

1984 **Dec. 3, Bhopal, India:** toxic gas, methyl isocyanate, seeped from Union Carbide insecticide plant, killed more than 2,000, injured about 150,000.

1987 **Sept. 18, Goiânia, Brazil:** 244 people contaminated with cesium-137 that was removed from a steel cylinder taken from a cancer-therapy machine in an abandoned clinic and sold as scrap. Four people died in worst radiation disaster in Western Hemisphere.

1988 **July 6, North Sea off Scotland:** 166 workers killed in explosion and fire on Occidental Petroleum's *Piper Alpha* rig in North Sea; 64 survivors. It is the world's worst offshore oil disaster.

1993 **April 19, Waco, Tex.:** 51-day stalemate between federal agents and members of Christian Branch Davidian cult ended in a fiery tragedy after federal agents botched their assault on the sect's compound. About 80 Branch Davidians, including at least 17 children, died when the compound burned to the ground in a suspicious blaze. Earlier, on Feb. 28, four agents were shot to death in failed attack on heavily armed compound. Jurors in the criminal trial of surviving cult members were unable to determine who fired the first shot. The incident was reopened for investigation in Aug. 1999.

1996 **May 10–11, Mt. Everest, Nepal:** 8 climbers died near summit during storm on mountain. A total of 15 climbers died that season, the worst single loss of life on Everest.

I Want Your Job, Lady!

In a sour economy, men are flocking to nursing, child care, and other "female" professions

By LISA TAKEUCHI CULLEN TIME

Jim Warner always had good jobs, but they never seemed to last. He had been a technical sergeant in Vietnam, and then, after returning to Los Angeles, he worked as an air-traffic controller, a Hughes Aircraft manufacturing coordinator, and a real estate agent. When the cold war ended and Southern California's economy slumped, Warner moved to New Jersey and took a low-wage position as a shoe salesman. He worked hard, but the job didn't really pay off—until he met Mary Del Guidice.

Del Guidice, a director of nursing at Hackensack University Medical Center, liked Warner's way with customers. They got to talking, and, over time, she persuaded him to make yet another career switch. Today Nurse Warner, 53, bustles around the hospital's unit for patients emerging from surgery, his goateed face smiling above a burly frame clad in spotless white scrubs. He earns $65,000 and goes home feeling a sense of satisfaction. "I have finally found my calling in, yes, a women's field."

"Mannies" and "Murses"

More and more men are heeding the call, taking up occupations traditionally dominated by females. Searching for more meaningful work or simply desperate for a paycheck in a sluggish economy, they are applying in increasing numbers for jobs or training in nursing, child care, housekeeping, teaching. The jobs are often crying out for more applicants, and offer solid, if unspectacular, pay. There's a downside, though, including cutesy nicknames like "murses" for male nurses and "mannies" for nannies. And pop-culture stereotyping is hard to shake. Consider Ben Stiller's ridiculed nurse in *Meet the Parents,* Freddie Prinze, Jr.'s fragile nanny on *Friends,* and Eddie Murphy's hapless child-care provider in the film *Daddy Day Care.*

But there may be strength in the shifting numbers. Men account for 5.4% of registered nurses, up from 2.7% in 1980—still a small number, to be sure, but they represent 9% of nursing-school students, and schools say applications have swelled. In public schools, just 26% of teachers are men. But males account for about a third of students in crash training courses for teachers in New York City and Los Angeles; in L.A., 43% of applicants for those courses are men. A rush of men is hitting employment agencies like Help Unlimited in Washington, which says males account for half its placements in secretarial and administrative temp jobs, up from just a few before 2000. Maria Raimo of Elite Nannies in New York City says, "Male applications are way up in the past year, what with all the layoffs. I have people who used to work at IBM and other corporations registering as housemen, companions for the elderly."

Women Face New Competition

For women, the trend is a mixed blessing. Some advocates have long argued that pay in fields like child care and teaching would not rise significantly until men moved into them. But amid today's persistently high unemployment, some women are worried that men are muscling into the last reliable sources of jobs for females—not to mention the management posts. With men around, for women, "it's like being an apprentice who never becomes a journeyman," says Tina Abbott, secretary-treasurer of the AFL-CIO in Michigan. Certainly the job market remains bleak. Job searches for laid-off workers average five months. Half of all job seekers have switched industries over the past year, according to outplacement firm Challenger, Gray & Christmas. Given that the industries with the most openings

Where the Men Aren't

In these occupations—many of them low-paying—women still make up 75% or more of those employed.

Position	Percent female	Position	Percent female	Position	Percent female
Preschool/kindergarten teachers	98%	Occupational therapists	93%	Special-education teachers	86%
Dental hygienists	98	Speech therapists	92	Librarians	86
Secretaries	98	Teachers' aides	92	Legal assistants	84
Child-care workers	97	Dressmakers	92	Telephone operators	83
Cleaners and servants	96	Hairdressers and cosmetologists	90	File clerks	82
Stenographers	95	Bank tellers	87	Apparel-sales workers	78
Typists	95	Dietitians	86	Cashiers	77
Registered nurses	93			Underwriters	76
				Waiters	76

Source: Department of Labor, Bureau of Labor Statistics.

include nursing and teaching, notes CEO John Challenger, "artificial barriers like gender begin to break down when people have to make ends meet."

It isn't always desperation that drives the shift; sometimes it's simply the quest for job satisfaction. Nick Peters, 48, of Des Moines had spent years in hospital administration when he hit a wall. He plans to begin course work to become a "real-time" reporter, the modern moniker for a court reporter. Membership in the National Court Reporters Association is 90% female. Peters will join the other 10% when he starts his reporting course, although no men are enrolled in that course today.

The "female" professions tend to offer more flexible hours. Ron Patrizio, 43, a biotech-firm sales rep in Central Florida, got sick of his old routine. He spent much of his time wining and dining doctors, hoping they would prescribe his firm's drugs. He made as much as $67,000 a year, and constantly accompanied clients to operas and hockey games. On a whim, he took a class in massage therapy. Men make up less than 20% of the profession, but at the Pinellas Park school Patrizio attended, a third of those enrolled were men. In his first year he earned only $18,000, but the job gave him time to meet the woman who is now his wife.

Some men making these choices are perceived to lack ambition. Fraternity brothers were baffled when Michael Strumph chose nursing as his major. Strumph, 27, had his priorities. His volunteer work as a paramedic attracted him to the medical field, but as the single parent of an 8-year-old boy, he wanted the flexible schedule a doctor doesn't have. Plus, he says, "doctors give orders and plan someone's care, but it's nurses who actually make them better." While his frat brothers scrambled for scarce jobs in finance and technology, Strumph had three offers before he graduated in 2001. With extra shifts at his Montclair, N.J., hospital, he earns $90,000 a year.

Stereotypes Raise Eyebrows

While murses don't cause much of a flutter anymore, mannies remain a rarity. When Lloyd Morgan walks around the Upper East Side of Manhattan with his two charges, the sight unhinges strangers' jaws. Morgan, 25, earned his college degree in social work, but took a job as a nanny. Three years later, he finds the hours and duties give him the freedom to pursue other dreams, like acting. Employed by a couple who are both lawyers, Morgan picks up the kids from school, takes them to parks and museums, and supervises their homework. On a snowed-out school day, they made snow forts for hours. Reared by a single mother, Morgan considers his work great training for becoming a dad someday.

Many men who enter female-dominated fields endure winks, nudges, and misunderstandings. In child care, some of the concerns are so serious as to harm job prospects; some nanny-placement agencies refuse to consider men, for fear of hiring a pedophile or turning off parents. But in many cities, parents with hectic schedules and energetic boys are increasingly asking for male nannies. "I have a larger demand than the pool of available male nannies," says Cliff Greenhouse, president of the Pavillion Agency in New York City, which has placed three men in recent months, up from maybe one annually in recent years.

Younger men seem less concerned about gender stereotypes than do their elders, perhaps because many grew up with working mothers, with girls as equals in the classroom, or with female bosses. If women can be police officers or CEOs, they reason, why can't men be kindergarten teachers or librarians?

Men at the Center of Circle Time

Adrian Echevarria, 21, sees no problem going from drumming with his rock band by night to wiping little noses and teaching kids their colors and shapes by day. When parents walk into his preschool in Oak Park, Ill., and see a young man in baggy clothes, some "freak out," he says. But when their children clamber onto his back and call him Mr. A., the moms and dads come around. The job pays Echevarria about $15,000 a year and helps him finance his next goal: earning a degree to teach elementary school.

Teachers, like librarians and bank tellers, weren't always primarily female. Men tended to fill those jobs until poor pay, low prestige, and small chance for advancement drove them out. Today, just 9% of teachers in elementary and middle schools are men, down from 18% in 1981. The absence of male role models in the classroom concerns educators, parents, and policymakers. "When men teach children, people think they couldn't make it in another industry," says Bryan Nelson, director of MenTeach, an advocacy group. That's changing with recruitment programs like Call Me Mister in South Carolina, which focuses on putting young black men at the chalkboard.

As a young man, Reginald Grant, 47, excelled in traditionally male, high-earning fields. A former Marine and defensive back for the New York Jets, he segued smoothly into subsequent careers in financial planning and software sales. During the tech boom, Grant co-founded two sports-related Internet-based companies. But after the tech bubble vaporized, he found himself staring at a billboard advertising a teaching fellowship in Los Angeles. A year later, he's teaching honors English to eighth-graders in the tough Watts neighborhood. He makes $36,000; in tech his base salary alone was $60,000. "My lifestyle has taken a change, but I touch kids nobody else could touch," he says.

Men like Grant are learning what women have known for years. "The secret of these so-called women's jobs is that they do in fact involve a lot of skill and training," says Heidi Hartmann, a labor economist and president of the Institute for Women's Policy Research. Men often require more training and vetting for household positions, but the Pavillion Agency has fielded a "flood" of résumés from out-of-work men believing they can easily nab a post as, say, a personal chef.

Some experts doubt the durability of the male-to-female-job trend. A University of Pennsylvania study found, for example, that within four years of graduating, male nurses leave their profession at twice the rate of women. Another study seemed to determine that gender flexibility is even bad for you: women in top management and men playing Mr. Mom have an increased risk of heart disease. So when the economy recovers, as it someday must, will murses and mannies go back to traditionally male jobs? □

Occupations with the Largest Job Growth, 2000–2010

(by number of new jobs; numbers in thousands of jobs)

Occupation	Employment 2000	Employment 2010	Change Number	Change Percent
Computer software engineers, applications	380	760	380	100%
Computer support specialists	506	996	490	97
Computer software engineers, systems software	317	601	284	90
Network/computer systems administrators	229	416	187	82
Personal/home care aides	414	672	258	62
Computer systems analysts	431	689	258	60
Medical assistants	329	516	187	57
Home health aides	615	907	291	47
Security guards	1,106	1,497	391	35
Customer service representatives	1,946	2,577	631	32

Source: U.S. Department of Labor, Bureau of Labor Statistics, *Monthly Labor Review,* Nov. 2001. Web: www.bls.gov.

Occupations with the Largest Job Decline, 2000–2010

(numbers in thousands of jobs)

Occupation	Employment 2000	Employment 2010	Change Number	Change Percent
Railroad brake, signal, switch operators	22	9	–13	–61%
Telephone operators	54	35	–19	–35
Loan interviewers/ clerks	139	101	–38	–28
Meter readers, utilities	49	36	–13	–26
Farmers/ranchers	1,294	965	–328	–25
Order clerks	348	277	–71	–20
Insurance claims/ policy processing clerks	289	231	–58	–20
Word processors/ typists	297	240	–57	–19
Office machine operators, except computer	84	68	–16	–19
Railroad conductors/ yardmasters	45	36	–8	–19

Source: U.S. Department of Labor, Bureau of Labor Statistics, *Monthly Labor Review,* Nov. 2001. Web: www.bls.gov.

Economic Outlook Through 2010

Source: Bureau of Labor Statistics, *Monthly Labor Review,* Nov. 2001, www.bls.gov/opub/mlr/2001/11/art1abs.htm.

Every two years the Bureau of Labor Statistics (BLS) publishes its latest projections on the structure of the economy, labor force demographics, and future job growth. The following is a summary of the most recent BLS projections, which were released at the end of 2001.

Continued Growth

BLS projections for the U.S. economy during the 2000–2010 decade reflect continued growth. Gross domestic product (GDP) is expected to reach $12.8 trillion in chained 1996 dollars by the end of the decade, an increase of $3.6 trillion over the period. Rising by an average annual rate of 3.4%, GDP is projected to grow faster than the 3.2% annual rate of growth over the preceding 10-year period.

Slower growth of civilian household employment, from 1.3% a year during the 1990–2000 period to 1.1% from 2000–2010, is expected to result in an increase of 16.2 million employees over the latter period, slightly less than the increase of 16.4 million employees between 1990 and 2000. The report assumes an unemployment rate of 4.0% in 2010, the same as in 2000.

Consumer Spending to Grow

Personal consumption spending, which makes up two-thirds of economic activity, is expected to grow at an average annual rate of 3.5% from 2000 to 2010, versus 3.4% from 1990 to 2000.

Consumer spending on long-lasting items, such as motor vehicles, personal computers, and household furnishings, is highly cyclical. Over the coming decade, with a projected rise in family income—a key in determining future spending trends—durable goods are still expected to be the fastest growth sector, increasing at an annual average rate of 5.0% in the 2000–2010 period.

During the past several decades, expenditures on non-durable goods, such as food and clothing, have increased at a significantly slower pace than spending on durable goods. As family income increases, spending on these short-term consumable necessities also rises, up to a point, after which spending tends to increase less rapidly than rises in income, although the latter increases do enhance demand for higher quality products.

Continued Trade Deficit

Globalization and international competition have played an important role in U.S. economic activity. With the world assumed to become more open to trade, the share of GDP accounted for by both exports and imports is expected to grow apace, and the dollar is expected to remain moderately strong throughout the projection period, but not so strong as to significantly weaken anticipated export growth.

Exports are expected to grow at a 7.8% annual rate between 2000 and 2010, compared with 7.0% per year during the 1990–2000 period. Exports of goods are expected to lead the way with an 8.1% annual rate of growth during the coming 10-year period, while exports of services are anticipated to grow at a rate of 7.1%.

Imports are expected to grow at 7.9% annually over the 2000–2010 projection period, 0.1 percentage point higher than the projected growth rate for exports, but lower than the 9.3% annual growth rate for imports over the 1990–2000 span. Imports of goods are expected to grow at 8.4% per year, and a 4.9 annual rate of growth is projected for imports of services during the 2000–2010 period.

As a result, net exports (exports minus imports) are projected to continue to make a negative contribution to the aggregate demand, reaching $889.1 billion in real terms by 2010. Both exports and imports are expected to increase their share of GDP by 2010, to 18.6% and 25.6%, respectively.

Disposable Income on the Rise

On a per capita basis, nominal disposable income is projected to increase at an annual average rate of 4.8% from 2000 to 2010, reaching a level of $40,768 in the latter year, a gain of more than $15,000 over the projection span. In real terms—chained 1996 dollars—per capita income is projected to grow 2.6% per year from 2000 to 2010, up from a 1.7% rate of growth between 1990 and 2000. Thus, the bureau expects its projections to be characterized by a long-term improvement in the real standard of living, at least as measured on the basis of growth of disposable personal income.

Employment Outlook

Civilian household employment is projected to increase by 1.1% per year from 2000 to 2010, or 1.62 million persons per year. The result is that more than 16 million employed persons will be added to the economy over the 10-year projection period. The civilian labor force is projected to grow at a rate of 1.1% per year from 2000 to 2010, the same rate of increase as that attained over the preceding 10-year period. This translates into an increase of almost 17 million over the projection span.

Characteristics of the Civilian Labor Force, 1990–2010

(in thousands)

Group	Level			Percent change			Percent distribution		
	1990	2000	2010*	1980–1990	1990–2000	2000–2010*	1990	2000	2010*
Total	125,840	140,863	157,721	17.7%	11.9%	12.0%	100.0%	100.0%	100.0%
Age									
16 to 24	22,492	22,715	26,081	–11.1	1.0	14.8	17.9	16.1	16.5
25 to 54	88,322	99,974	104,994	32.6	13.2	5.0	70.2	71.0	66.6
55 and older	15,026	18,175	26,646	–0.1	21.0	46.6	11.9	12.9	16.9
Sex									
Men	69,011	75,247	82,221	12.3	9.0	9.3	54.8	53.4	52.1
Women	56,829	65,616	75,500	24.9	15.5	15.1	45.2	46.6	47.9
Race									
White	107,447	117,574	128,043	14.8	9.4	8.9	85.4	83.5	81.2
Black	13,740	16,603	20,041	26.5	20.8	20.7	10.9	11.8	12.7
Asian and other[1]	4,653	6,687	9,636	87.9	43.7	44.1	3.7	4.7	6.1
Hispanic origin	10,720	15,368	20,947	74.4	43.4	36.3	8.5	10.9	13.3
Other than Hispanic origin	115,120	125,495	136,774	14.2	9.0	9.0	91.5	89.1	86.7
White non-Hispanic	97,818	102,963	109,118	11.6	5.3	6.0	77.0	73.1	69.2

NOTE: Data apply to workers age 16 and older. * Projected. 1. The "Asian and other" group includes (1) Asians and Pacific Islanders and (2) American Indians and Alaska Natives. The historical data are derived by subtracting "black" and "white" from the total; projections are made directly, not by subtraction. *Source: Monthly Labor Review,* Nov. 2001.

Employment Status by Race, 1975–2002

(numbers in thousands)

Year	Employment rate	Unemployment rate
White		
1975	56.7%	7.8%
1980	60.0	6.3
1985	61.0	6.2
1990	63.7	4.8
1995	63.8	4.9
2000	65.1	3.5
2001	64.4	4.2
2002	63.4	5.1
Black		
1975	50.1	14.8
1980	52.3	14.3
1985	53.4	15.1
1990	56.7	11.4
1995	57.1%	10.4%
2000	60.8	7.6
2001	59.7	8.7
2002	58.1	10.3
Hispanic[1]		
1975	53.4	12.2
1980	57.6	10.1
1985	57.8	10.5
1990	61.9	8.2
1995	59.7	9.3
2000	64.7	5.7
2001	64.9	6.6
2002	63.9	7.6

NOTE: Data apply to workers age 16 and older. 1. Hispanic persons may be of any race. *Source:* U.S. Department of Labor, Bureau of Labor Statistics. Web: data.bls.gov.

Number of Employed and Unemployed Workers by Sex and Age, 1970–2002
(in thousands)

	2002[1]	2001[1]	2000[1]	1999[1]	1998[1]	1997[1]	1995[1]	1990[2]	1985	1980	1970
Men, 20 years and over											
Employed	69,734	69,776	68,580	67,761	67,134	66,524	64,085	61,678	56,562	53,101	45,581
Unemployed	3,896	3,040	2,350	2,433	2,580	2,826	3,239	3,239	3,715	3,353	1,638
Women, 20 years and over											
Employed	60,420	60,417	59,352	58,655	57,278	57,647	54,396	50,535	44,154	38,492	26,952
Unemployed	3,228	2,599	2,212	2,285	2,424	2,187	2,819	2,596	3,129	2,615	1,349
Total, 16 years and over											
Employed	136,486	136,933	135,208	133,488	131,463	130,785	124,900	118,793	107,150	99,303	78,678
Unemployed	8,377	6,801	5,655	5,880	6,209	5,957	7,404	7,047	8,312	7,637	4,093
Total, 16–19 years											
Employed	6,332	6,740	7,276	7,172	7,051	6,614	6,419	6,581	6,434	7,710	6,144
Unemployed	1,253	1,162	1,093	1,162	1,205	944	1,346	1,212	1,468	1,669	1,106

1. Data beginning in 1994 are not directly comparable with earlier years due to the introduction of a major redesign of the Current Population Survey. 2. Revised; data beginning in 1990 are not directly comparable with earlier years due to the introduction of 1990 census-based population controls, adjusted for the estimated undercount. *Source:* U.S. Department of Labor, Bureau of Labor Statistics. Current Population Survey. Web: data.bls.gov.

Persons in the Labor Force, 1840–2002

	Labor force[1]			Labor force[1]	
Year	Number (thousands)	Percent of working-age population	Year	Number (thousands)	Percent of working-age population
1840	5,420	46.6%	1940	52,789	52.2%
1850	7,697	46.8	1950	60,054	53.5
1860	10,533	47.0	1960	69,877	55.3
1870	12,925	45.8	1970	82,049	58.2
1880	17,392	47.3	1980	106,085	62.0
1890	23,318	49.2	1990	125,182	65.3
1900	29,073	50.2	2000	140,863	67.2
1910	37,371	52.2	2001	141,815	66.9
1920	42,434	51.3	2002	144,863	66.6
1930	48,830	49.5			

1. For 1840 to 1930, the data relate to the population and gainful workers at age 10 and over; for 1940 to 1960, the data relate to the population and labor force at age 14 and over; for 1970 and 1980, the data relate to the population and labor force at age 16 and over. For 1940 to 1980, the data include the Armed Forces. *Source:* U.S. Bureau of the Census and *Monthly Labor Review,* March 2002. Web: data.bls.gov.

Farm and Non-Farm Labor Force, 1940–2001
(number in thousands)

	Civilian labor force employed				Civilian labor force employed		
Year	Total	Agriculture	Nonagricultural industries	Year	Total	Agriculture	Nonagricultural industries
1940	47,520	9,540	37,980	1975	85,846	3,408	82,438
1945	52,820	8,580	44,240	1980	99,303	3,364	95,938
1950	58,918	7,160	51,758	1985	107,150	3,179	103,971
1955	62,170	6,450	55,722	1990[1]	118,793	3,223	115,570
1960[1]	65,778	5,458	60,318	1995	124,900	3,440	121,460
1965	71,088	4,361	66,726	2000[2]	135,208	3,305	131,903
1970	78,678	3,463	75,215	2001	135,073	3,144	131,929

1. Not strictly comparable with data for prior years. 2. Beginning in Jan. 2000, data are not strictly comparable with data for 1999 and earlier years because of the revisions in the population controls used in the household survey. *Source:* U.S. Department of Labor, Bureau of Labor Statistics. Web: www.bls.gov/cps/cpsaat1.pdf.

Unemployment Rate by Race, Age, and Sex, 2001–2002

	2001	2002		2001	2002
White			Men, 20 years and over	8.0%	9.5%
Total, 16 years and over	4.2%	5.1%	Women, 20 years and over	7.0	8.8
Total, 16–19 years	12.7	14.5	**Hispanic or Latino**		
Men, 20 years and over	3.7	4.7	Total, 16 years and over	6.6	7.5
Women, 20 years and over	3.6	4.4	Total, 16–19 years	17.7	20.1
Black			Men, 20 years and over	5.2	6.4
Total, 16 years and over	8.6	10.2	Women, 20 years and over	6.6	7.2
Total, 16–19 years	29.0	29.8			

Source: U.S. Department of Labor, Bureau of Labor Statistics. Web: data.bls.gov.

Employed and Unemployed Persons by Occupation
(in thousands; 16 years and over)

Occupations	Employed 2001	Employed 2002	Unemployed 2001 (number)	Unemployed 2001 (percent)	Unemployed 2002 (number)	Unemployed 2002 (percent)
Total	**136,933**	**136,485**	**6,801**	4.7%	**8,378**	5.8%
Management, professional, and related	47,043	47,180	1,102	2.3	1,482	3.0
Management, business, and financial operations	19,830	19,823	455	2.2	622	3.0
Professional and related	27,213	27,358	647	2.3	859	3.0
Service	21,183	21,766	1,311	5.8	1,544	6.6
Sales and office	35,785	35,408	1,652	4.4	2,110	5.6
Office and administrative support	20,098	19,580	873	4.2	1,112	5.4
Natural resources, construction, and maintenance	13,688	13,562	943	6.4	1,155	7.8
Farming, fishing, and forestry	1,052	1,040	163	13.4	142	12.0
Construction and extraction	7,920	7,898	626	7.3	788	9.1
Installation, maintenance, and repair	4,716	4,623	154	3.2	225	4.6
Production, transportation, and material moving	19,234	18,569	1,318	6.4	1,530	7.6
Production	10,727	10,081	759	6.6	848	7.8
Transportation and material moving	8,507	8,488	559	6.2	682	7.4

Source: U.S. Department of Labor, Bureau of Labor Statistics. Web: data.bls.gov.

Overall Unemployment Rate in the Civilian Labor Force, 1920–2003

Year	Rate	Year	Rate	Year	Rate	Year	Rate	Year	Rate	Year	Rate
1920	5.2%	1944	1.2%	1962	5.5%	1980	7.1%	1992	7.5%	2001	4.8%
1928	4.2	1946	3.9	1964	5.2	1982	9.7	1993	6.9	2002	5.8
1930	8.7	1948	3.8	1966	3.8	1984	7.5	1994	6.1	2003	
1932	23.6	1950	5.3	1968	3.6	1986	7.0	1995	5.6	Jan.	5.7
1934	21.7	1952	3.0	1970	4.9	1987	6.2	1996	5.4	Feb.	5.8
1936	16.9	1954	5.5	1972	5.6	1988	5.5	1997	4.9	March	5.8
1938	19.0	1956	4.1	1974	5.6	1989	5.3	1998	4.5	April	6.0
1940	14.6	1958	6.8	1976	7.7	1990	5.6	1999	4.2	May	6.1
1942	4.7	1960	5.5	1978	6.1	1991	6.8	2000	4.0	June	6.4

NOTES: Estimates prior to 1940 are based on sources other than direct enumeration. Data prior to 1948 are for persons age 14 and over. Data beginning in 1948 are for persons age 16 and over. *Source:* U.S. Department of Labor, Bureau of Labor Statistics. Web: stats.bls.gov.

Mothers in the Labor Force, 1955–2001

Year	Percentage of mothers with children: Under 18 years	6 to 17 years	Under 6 years[1]
1955	27.0%	38.4%	18.2%
1965	35.0	45.7	25.3
1975	47.3	54.8	38.8
1980	56.6	64.3	46.8
1985	62.1	69.9	53.5
1990	66.7	74.7	58.2
1991	66.6	74.4	58.4
1992	67.2	75.9	58.0
1993	67.0	75.4	57.9
1994	68.4	76.0	60.3
1995	69.7	76.4	62.3
1996	70.2	77.2	62.3
1997	72.1	78.1	65.0
1998	71.8	77.6	64.9
1999	72.2	78.2	64.8
2000	72.3	78.7	64.6
2001	72.1	78.3	64.3

1. May also have older children. NOTE: 1955 data are for April; 1965 and 1975–1994 data are for March. Data for 1994 and subsequent years are not directly comparable to previous years because of major revisions to the survey. *Source:* U.S. Department of Labor, Bureau of Labor Statistics. Web: data.bls.gov.

Women in the Labor Force, 1900–2002

Year	Number[1] (thousands)	% female population aged 16 and over[1]	% of labor force population aged 16 and over[1]
1900	5,319	18.8%	18.3%
1910	7,445	21.5	19.9
1920	8,637	21.4	20.4
1930	10,752	22.0	22.0
1940	12,845	25.4	24.3
1950	18,389	33.9	29.6
1960	23,240	37.7	33.4
1970	31,543	43.3	38.1
1980	45,487	51.5	42.5
1990[2]	56,829	57.5	45.2
1995[3]	60,944	58.9	46.1
2000	65,616	60.2	46.6
2001	62,992	60.1	44.4
2002	62,739	59.8	43.3

1. For 1900–1930, data relate to population and labor force aged 10 and over; for 1940, to population and labor force aged 14 and over; beginning 1950, to civilian population and labor force aged 16 and over. 2. Data beginning in 1990 are not strictly comparable with data for prior years because population controls were adjusted. 3. Data beginning 1994 are not strictly comparable with data for prior years because of a major revision to survey methodology. *Source:* U.S. Department of Labor, Women's Bureau.

Work Stoppages (Strikes) Involving 1,000 Workers or More

Year	Work stoppages	Workers involved (thousands)	Days idle (thousands)	Year	Work stoppages	Workers involved (thousands)	Days idle (thousands)
1950	424	1,698	30,390	1991	40	392	4,584
1960	222	896	13,260	1992	35	364	3,989
1970	381	2,468	52,761	1993	35	182	3,981
1975	235	965	17,563	1994	45	322	5,020
1980	187	795	20,844	1995	31	192	5,771
1983	81	909	17,461	1996	37	273	4,889
1984	62	376	8,499	1997	29	339	4,497
1985	54	324	7,079	1998	34	387	5,116
1986	69	533	11,861	1999	17	73	1,996
1987	46	174	4,481	2000	39	394	20,419
1988	40	118	4,381	2001	29	99	1,151
1989	51	452	16,996	2002	19	46	660
1990	44	185	5,926				

NOTE: Refers to stoppages that began in the year. Days idle is total for all stoppages in effect. Workers are counted more than once if they were involved in more than one stoppage during the year. *Source:* U.S. Department of Labor, Bureau of Labor Statistics. Web: data.bls.gov.

Union Membership, by States

Source: Monthly Labor Review Online, Bureau of Labor Statistics. Web: http://www.bls.gov.

In 2002 13.2% of wage and salary workers were union members, down from 13.4% in 2001. The union membership rate has steadily declined from a high of 20.1% in 1983. Union membership among wage and salary workers shows a distinct geographic pattern, according to the Current Population Survey. Union membership is highest in the Northeast, Midwest, and Pacific regions, and lowest in the South.

Four states had union membership rates higher than 20% in 2002: New York, Hawaii, Alaska, and Michigan. These states, along with New Jersey, have been among the most unionized since at least 1995. North Carolina and South Carolina have the lowest rates, 3.2% and 4.9%, respectively. New York has a union membership rate eight times that of North Carolina (25.3% vs. 3.2% of workers).

California (2.5 million), New York (2.0 million), and Illinois (1.1 million) have the greatest number of union members. More than half (8.1 million) of the 16.1 million union members in the United States live in six states, although these states accounted for only 35% of wage and salary employment nationally.

Union Membership Rates by State, 2002 Annual Average

(U.S. Rate = 13.2%)

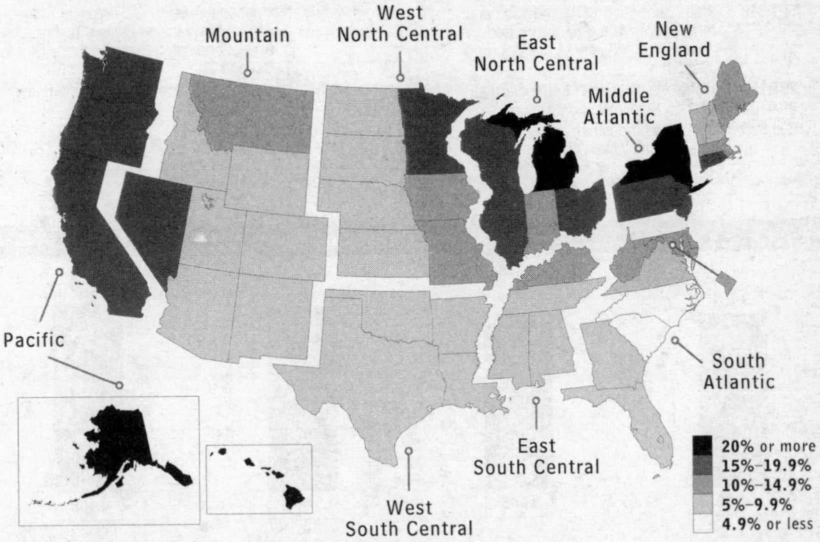

Source: Current Population Survey, Bureau of Labor Statistics. Web: www.bls.gov/cps/unionmem.pdf.

Employed Wage and Salary Workers Represented by Unions, 2002

Occupation	Percent of workers
Precision production, craft, and repair	21.6%
Operators, fabricators, and laborers	20.3
Managerial and professional specialty	15.0
Service occupations	13.8
Technical, sales, and administrative support	9.9
Farming, forestry, and fishing	5.1

Industry	Percent of workers
Government workers	42.0%
Transportation and public utilities	24.3
Manufacturing	15.1
Nonagricultural industries	9.4
Private wage and salary workers	9.3
Wholesale and retail trade	4.9
Agriculture	2.6

Source: U.S. Bureau of Labor Statistics. Web: stats.bls.gov/cps/unionmem.pdf

National Labor Organizations with Membership over 100,000

Members	Union[1]
2,668,925	National Education Association
1,398,412	International Brotherhood of Teamsters
1,385,043	United Food and Commercial Workers International Union
1,376,292	Service Employees International Union
1,300,000	American Federation of State, County, and Municipal Employees
795,335	Laborers' International Union of North America
741,270	American Federation of Teachers
722,987	International Association of Machinists and Aerospace Workers
722,095	International Brotherhood of Electrical Workers
701,818	International Union, United Automobile, Aerospace, and Agricultural Implement Workers of America
589,143	Communications Workers of America
588,790	United Steelworkers of America
538,431	United Brotherhood of Carpenters and Joiners of America
389,173	National Postal Mail Handlers Union
388,526	International Union of Operating Engineers
324,349	United Association of Journeymen and Apprentices of the Plumbing and Pipe-Fitting Industry of the U.S. and Canada
297,150	National Association of Letter Carriers
294,127	American Postal Workers Union
292,395	Paper, Allied-Industrial, and Chemical International Union
255,792	International Association of Fire Fighters
255,137	Hotel Employees and Restaurant Employees International Union
217,604	Union of Needletrades, Industrial, and Textile Employees
198,453	American Federation of Government Employees
179,861	Amalgamated Transit Union
151,257	Sheet Metal Workers International Association
136,586	Office and Professional Employees International Union
135,072	International Association of Bridge, Structural, Ornamental, and Reinforcing Iron Workers
115,218	Bakery, Confectionery, Tobacco Workers, and Grain Millers International Union
110,000	Transport Workers Union of America
109,105	United Mine Workers of America
104,827	Transportation Communications Workers International Union
104,000	American Federation of Musicians of the U.S. and Canada
103,506	International Alliance of Theatrical Stage Employees, Moving Picture Technicians, Artists, and Allied Crafts of the U.S. and Canada
102,402	International Brotherhood of Painters and Allied Trades

1. Unless otherwise noted, unions are AFL-CIO affiliated. *Source:* U.S. Department of Labor.

Median Age of the Labor Force

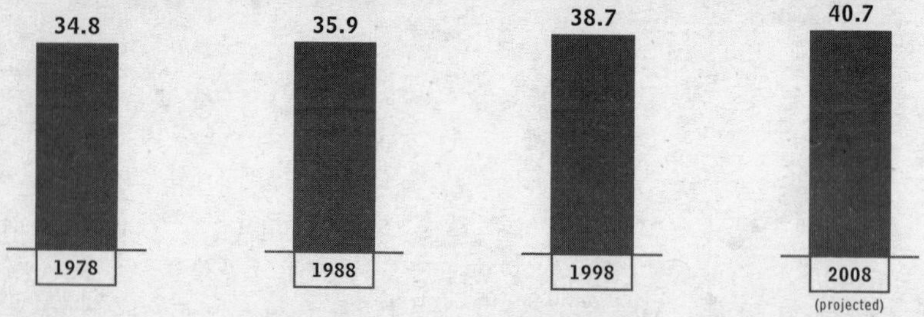

Source: U.S. Department of Labor, Bureau of Labor Statistics. Web: www.bls.gov/opub/working/page2b.htm.

Median Weekly Earnings of Selected Occupations, 2002

Occupation	Both sexes: Number of workers (in thousands)	Both sexes: Median weekly earnings	Men: Number of workers (in thousands)	Men: Median weekly earnings	Women: Number of workers (in thousands)	Women: Median weekly earnings
Total, 16 years and over	**100,204**	**$609**	**56,431**	**$ 680**	**43,773**	**$530**
Managerial and professional specialty	32,288	884	16,014	1,059	16,274	756
Executive, administrative, and managerial	15,890	891	8,343	1,084	7,548	737
Professional specialty	16,398	879	7,672	1,038	8,726	773
Technical, sales, and administrative support	27,446	551	10,709	702	16,737	490
Technicians and related support	3,607	693	1,794	840	1,813	590
Sales occupations	10,055	602	5,666	744	4,389	441
Administrative support, including clerical	13,784	503	3,249	585	10,535	488
Service occupations	11,263	385	5,375	449	5,888	343
Private household	330	277	24	(1)	306	277
Protective service	2,283	647	1,877	690	406	500
Service, except private household and protective	8,650	355	3,474	380	5,175	339
Precision production, craft, and repair	11,518	633	10,603	650	915	482
Mechanics and repairers	4,011	675	3,820	679	192	594
Construction trades	4,390	609	4,297	610	92	577
Other precision production, craft, and repair	3,117	621	2,485	673	631	447
Operators, fabricators, and laborers	14,237	484	11,178	513	3,060	385
Machine operators, assemblers, and inspectors	5,655	476	3,754	523	1,901	387
Transportation and material moving occupations	4,562	581	4,198	592	365	451
Handlers, equipment cleaners, helpers, and laborers	4,020	401	3,226	412	794	360
Farming, forestry, and fishing	1,613	364	1,347	378	266	308

1. Indicates base is less than 50,000 workers, so no data are provided. *Source:* U.S. Department of Labor, Bureau of Labor Statistics. Web: stats.bls.gov.

Youth Employment Trends

Source: U.S. Department of Labor. *Report on the Youth Labor Force,* November 2000. Based on Current Population Survey data. Web: stats.bls.gov/opub/rylf/rylfhome.htm.

How Many Youths Work?

During the 1996–1998 period, 2.9 million youths age 15 to 17 worked during school months, and 4.0 million worked during the summer months.

Among youths, employment increased markedly with age. During the school months of 1996–1998, only 9% of 15-year-olds were employed in an average month, compared with 26% of those a year older and 39% of 17-year-olds. Youths in each age group were more likely to work in the summer, during which employment rates increased to 18%, 36%, and 48% at each age, respectively.

Despite popular perceptions that youths work more than they did in the past, the proportion of 15- to 17-year-olds who work has declined over time. Employment-population ratios declined with economic downturns in the early 1980s and 1990s. After the decline in the early 1990s, however, the rates did not return to earlier levels. During the 1996–1998 period, a quarter of youths worked during the school months, down from 30% in 1977–1979. Just over a third worked during the summer, down from 43% during the late 1970s.

How Much Do Youths Earn?

The minimum wage often is associated with young workers first entering the labor force. CPS data indicate that earnings were above the minimum wage for most youths, with hourly earnings in the school and summer months about the same. The minimum wage was $5.15 in 1998.

In 1998, median earnings of 15- to 17-year-olds combined were $5.57 per hour. In 1998, the earnings increased with age: 15-year-olds earned a median of $5.38 per hour, 16-year-olds earned $5.52, and 17-year-olds earned $5.65 per hour. Earnings varied slightly across sex and race groups. Hispanic and white males had the highest median hourly earnings; Hispanic and black females had the lowest.

Where Do Youths Work?

About 62% of youths age 15 to 17 employed during the school months of the 1996–1998 period worked in retail trade, more than in any other major industry. Within retail trade, eating and drinking places accounted for the greatest share of employed youths, about one-third of all employed 15- to 17-year-olds. Another 1 in 4 youths was employed in service industries. In the summer, youth employment was less concentrated in retail trade and youths were employed in a wider variety of industries than during the school months. Retail trade still accounted for about half, services increased to 30%, and employment in agriculture and goods-producing industries (mining, construction, and manufacturing) increased. This seasonal pattern of employment also was present in earlier periods.

Industries that Employ Largest Share of Youths Age 15–17

Industry	Percent of total employed youths
Male	
Eating and drinking places	31.3%
Grocery stores	13.6
Miscellaneous entertainment and recreation services	4.5
Agricultural production, livestock	3.6
Construction	3.6
Department stores	3.1
Landscape and horticultural services	2.2
Newspaper publishing and printing	1.9
Agricultural production, crops	1.5
Gasoline service stations	1.3
Female	
Eating and drinking places	32.6%
Grocery stores	9.9
Private households	5.7
Department stores	4.4
Miscellaneous entertainment and recreation services	4.0
Stores, apparel and accessory, except shoe	3.6
Drug stores	1.9
Nursing and personal care facilities	1.7
Retail bakeries	1.5
Child day-care services	1.4

NOTE: Figures based on youths working during school months, which are Jan. to May and Sept. to Dec. *Source:* U.S. Department of Labor. *Report on the Youth Labor Force,* Nov. 2000. Web: www.bls.gov/opub/rylf/pdf/chapter4.pdf.

Federal Minimum Wage Rates, 1955–2003

Year	Value of the minimum wage: Current dollars	Constant (1996) dollars[1]
1955	$0.75	$4.39
1956	1.00	5.77
1957	1.00	5.58
1958	1.00	5.43
1959	1.00	5.39
1960	1.00	5.30
1961	1.15	6.03
1962	1.15	5.97
1963	1.25	6.41
1964	1.25	6.33
1965	1.25	6.23
1966	1.25	6.05
1967	1.40	6.58
1968	$1.60	$7.21
1969	1.60	6.84
1970	1.60	6.47
1971	1.60	6.20
1972	1.60	6.01
1973	1.60	5.65
1974	2.00	6.37
1975	2.10	6.12
1976	2.30	6.34
1977	2.30	5.95
1978	2.65	6.38
1979	2.90	6.27
1980	3.10	5.90
1981	$3.35	$5.78
1982	3.35	5.45
1983	3.35	5.28
1984	3.35	5.06
1985	3.35	4.88
1986	3.35	4.80
1987	3.35	4.63
1988	3.35	4.44
1989	3.35	4.24
1990	3.80	4.56
1991	4.25	4.90
1992	4.25	4.75
1993	4.25	4.61
1994	$4.25	$4.50
1995	4.25	4.38
1996	4.75	4.75
1997	5.15	5.03
1998	5.15	4.96
1999	5.15	4.85
2000	5.15	4.72
2001	5.15	4.56
2002	5.15	4.49
2003	5.15	4.40

1. Adjusted for inflation using the CPI-U (Consumer Price Index for All Urban Consumers). *Source:* Web: www.dol.gov/esa/public/minwage.

Median Income of Households by Selected Characteristics, 2001

Characteristic	Number (thousands)	Median income
All households	**109,297**	**$42,228**
Type of household		
Family households	74,329	52,275
Married-couple families	56,747	60,471
Female householder, no husband present	13,143	28,142
Male householder, no wife present	4,438	40,715
Nonfamily households	34,969	25,631
Female householder	19,390	20,264
Male householder	15,579	32,312
Race and Hispanic origin of householder		
White	90,682	44,517
Non-Hispanic	80,818	46,305
Black	13,315	29,470
Asian and Pacific Islander	4,071	53,635
Hispanic origin[1]	10,499	33,565
Age of householder		
15 to 24	6,391	28,196
25 to 34	18,988	45,080
35 to 44	24,031	$53,320
45 to 54	22,208	58,045
55 to 64	15,203	45,864
65 and over	22,476	23,118
Region		
Northeast	21,128	45,716
Midwest	25,755	43,834
South	39,151	38,904
West	23,263	45,087
Earnings of full-time, year-round workers		
Male	58,712	38,275
Female	41,639	29,215
Per capita income		
All races[2]	282,082	22,851
White	230,071	24,127
Non-Hispanic	194,822	26,134
Black	36,023	14,953
Asian and Pacific Islander	12,500	24,277
Hispanic origin[1]	37,438	13,003

1. Persons of Hispanic origin may be of any race. 2. Data for American Indians and Alaska Natives are not shown separately in this table. *Source:* U.S. Bureau of the Census, *Money Income in the United States: 2001.* Web: www.census.gov.

Median Four-Person Family Income
(in current dollars)

Year	Income	Percent change	Year	Income	Percent change	Year	Income	Percent change
2001	$63,278	1.7%	1992	$44,251	2.8%	1983	$29,184	5.7%
2000	62,228	3.7	1991	43,056	3.9	1982	27,619	5.1
1999	59,981	6.9	1990	41,151	1.7	1981	26,274	8.0
1998	56,061	3.5	1989	40,763	4.4	1980	24,332	8.6
1997	53,350	3.6	1988	39,051	6.1	1979	22,395	9.6
1996	51,518	3.7	1987	36,812	6.0	1978	20,428	9.1
1995	49,687	5.7	1986	34,716	5.9	1977	18,723	8.1
1994	47,012	4.1	1985	32,777	5.4	1976	17,315	9.3
1993	45,161	2.1	1984	31,097	6.6	1975	15,848	7.5

Source: Income Statistics Branch/HHES Division, U.S. Bureau of the Census. Web: www.census.gov.

Per Capita Personal Income

Year	Amount	Year	Amount	Year	Amount	Year	Amount	Year	Amount	Year	Amount
1935	$ 474	1970	$ 3,893	1983	$12,352	1989	$18,176	1995	$23,562	2001	$30,413
1945	1,223	1975	5,851	1984	13,585	1990	19,188	1996	24,651	2002	30,941
1950	1,501	1979	8,638	1985	14,427	1991	19,652	1997	25,924		
1955	1,881	1980	9,910	1986	15,122	1992	20,576	1998	27,203		
1960	2,219	1981	10,949	1987	15,968	1993	21,231	1999	28,546		
1965	2,773	1982	11,731	1988	17,052	1994	22,086	2000	29,469		

Source: U.S. Department of Commerce, Bureau of Economic Analysis, *Survey of Current Business.* Web: www.bea.doc.gov/bea/regional/spi/.

Distribution of Household Income by Race

	White			Black			Hispanic origin[1]		
Income range	1972	1985	2001	1972	1985	2001	1972	1985	2001
Number of households (thousands)	60,618	76,576	90,682	6,809	9,797	13,315	2,655	5,213	10,499
Percent distribution									
Under $5,000	3.6%	2.9%	2.4%	8.3%	7.7%	6.8%	3.8%	4.9%	3.9%
$5,000 to $9,999	7.9	7.4	5.2	15.4	17.0	10.9	8.6	11.8	6.7
$10,000 to $14,999	7.5	7.3	6.7	13.0	11.2	8.7	12.1	11.4	8.3
$15,000 to $24,999	14.1	14.7	13.0	20.0	18.7	16.5	20.7	18.8	17.5
$25,000 to $34,999	15.0	13.8	12.2	15.6	13.4	14.3	20.5	15.4	15.4
$35,000 to $49,999	20.9	18.2	15.5	13.7	14.1	14.9	18.9	16.8	17.3
$50,000 to $74,999	19.7	19.2	18.8	10.9	11.4	15.4	11.4	13.1	16.5
$75,000 to $99,999	6.8	9.2	11.4	2.2	4.5	6.8	2.6	5.3	7.5
$100,000 and over	4.6	7.4	14.8	1.0	1.9	5.6	1.5	2.5	7.0
Median income	$36,510	$38,226	$44,517	$21,311	$22,742	$29,470	$27,552	$26,803	$33,565

1. Persons of Hispanic origin may be of any race. *Source:* U.S. Bureau of the Census. *Current Population Reports,* P60-206. Sept. 2001. Web: www.census.gov/hhes/www/income.html.

Consumer Credit Outstanding[1]
(in billions of dollars)

	Total	Commercial banks	Finance companies	Credit unions	Savings institutions	Nonfinancial business	Pools of securitized assets[2]
1975	$ 168.7	$ 82.9	$ 32.7	$ 25.7	n.a.	n.a.	n.a.
1980	302.1	147.0	62.3	44.0	n.a.	n.a.	n.a.
1985	526.3	245.1	111.7	72.7	n.a.	n.a.	n.a.
1990	751.9	347.1	133.3	93.1	n.a.	n.a.	n.a.
1995	1,122.8	502.0	152.1	131.9	$40.1	$85.1	$211.6
1999	1,426.2	499.8	181.6	167.9	61.5	80.3	435.1
2000	1,566.5	541.5	193.2	184.4	64.6	82.7	500.1
2001	1,702.8	558.0	236.5	189.6	69.1	67.9	581.7
2002	1,762.3	587.4	232.3	195.7	68.6	56.9	621.4

1. Covers most short- and intermediate-term credit extended to individuals, excluding loans secured by real estate. 2. Outstanding balances of pools upon which securities have been issued; these balances are no longer carried on the balance sheets of the loan originators. n.a. = not available. *Source:* Federal Reserve Board. Web http://www.federalreserve.gov/default.htm.

Per Capita Personal Income by State

State	1980	1990	2000	2002	State	1980	1990	2000	2002
Alabama	$ 7,465	$14,899	$23,521	$25,128	Montana	$ 8,342	$14,743	$22,518	$25,020
Alaska	13,007	20,887	29,642	32,151	Nebraska	8,895	17,379	27,630	29,771
Arizona	8,854	16,262	24,988	26,183	Nevada	10,848	20,248	29,506	30,180
Arkansas	7,113	13,779	21,995	23,512	New Hampshire	9,150	20,231	33,169	34,334
California	11,021	20,656	32,149	32,996	New Jersey	10,966	24,182	37,118	39,453
Colorado	10,143	18,818	32,434	33,276	New Mexico	7,940	14,213	21,931	23,941
Connecticut	11,532	25,426	40,702	42,706	New York	10,179	22,322	34,689	36,043
Delaware	10,059	19,719	31,012	32,779	North Carolina	7,780	16,284	26,882	27,711
DC	12,251	24,643	38,838	42,120	North Dakota	8,642	15,320	24,708	26,982
Florida	9,246	18,785	27,764	29,596	Ohio	9,399	17,547	27,977	29,405
Georgia	8,021	17,121	27,794	28,821	Oklahoma	9,018	15,117	23,650	25,575
Hawaii	10,129	20,905	27,851	30,001	Oregon	9,309	17,201	27,660	28,731
Idaho	8,105	15,304	23,727	25,057	Pennsylvania	9,353	18,884	29,504	31,727
Illinois	10,454	20,159	31,856	33,404	Rhode Island	9,227	19,035	29,113	31,319
Indiana	8,914	16,815	26,933	28,240	South Carolina	7,392	15,101	24,000	25,400
Iowa	9,226	16,683	26,431	28,280	South Dakota	7,800	15,628	25,958	26,894
Kansas	9,880	17,639	27,374	29,141	Tennessee	7,711	15,903	25,946	27,671
Kentucky	7,679	14,751	24,085	25,579	Texas	9,439	16,747	27,752	28,551
Louisiana	8,412	14,279	23,090	25,446	Utah	7,671	14,063	23,436	24,306
Maine	7,760	17,041	25,380	27,744	Vermont	7,957	17,444	26,848	29,567
Maryland	10,394	22,088	33,482	36,298	Virginia	9,413	19,543	31,120	32,922
Massachusetts	10,103	22,248	37,704	39,244	Washington	10,256	19,268	31,230	32,677
Michigan	9,801	18,239	29,127	30,296	West Virginia	7,764	13,964	21,738	23,688
Minnesota	9,673	18,784	31,935	34,071	Wisconsin	9,364	17,399	28,100	29,923
Mississippi	6,573	12,578	20,900	22,372	Wyoming	11,018	16,905	27,372	30,578
Missouri	8,812	17,407	27,206	28,936	**United States**	**9,494**	**18,667**	**29,469**	**30,941**

NOTE: Per capita personal income was computed using midyear population estimates of the Bureau of the Census. *Source:* U.S. Department of Commerce, Bureau of Economic Analysis, *Survey of Current Business.* Web: www.bea.doc.gov/bea/regional/spi/.

Poverty in the United States

Source: U.S. Bureau of the Census, March 2001 supplement to the Current Population Survey (CPS). Web: www.census.gov.

The poverty rate in 2001 rose to 11.7%, up from 11.3% in 2000. About 32.9 million people were poor in 2001, 1.3 million more than in 2000. The increases coincided with a recession that began in March 2001. The increase in the poverty rate was the first year-to-year increase since 1991–1992.

People ages 18 to 64 accounted for most of the net change between 2000 and 2001. Their poverty rate rose to 10.1%, up from 9.6%, and the number of poor increased to 17.8 million, from 16.7 million in 2000. Children continue to represent a disproportionate share of the poor (35.7%), as they make up only 25.6% of the population. However, at 16.3% and 11.7 million, their poverty rate and number of poor were unchanged from 2000.

The South had the highest poverty rate in 2001 (13.5%), higher than its rate of 12.8% in 2000. The number of poor in the South also increased, from 12.7 million in 2000 to 13.5 million in 2001. The poverty rates in the Northeast, Midwest, and West did not change.

For non-Hispanic whites, the poverty rate rose from 7.4% to 7.8% between 2000 and 2001. The number of poor increased from 14.4 million to 15.3 million. Poverty rates for blacks (22.7%), Hispanics (21.4%), and Asian and Pacific Islanders (10.2%) did not change between 2000 and 2001. However, the number of poor Hispanics rose to 8.0 million in 2001, up from 7.7 million in 2000. Hispanics may be of any race.

The poverty rate for families increased to 9.2% in 2001, up from the 26-year-low measured in 2000 (8.7%). In 2001 6.8 million families were poor, up from 6.4 million in 2000. Families with a female householder and no husband present experienced an increase in the number of poor (from 3.3 million in 2000 to 3.5 million in 2001), but not their poverty rate (26.4%). Of those female-householder families, the number of poor non-Hispanic white and Hispanic families increased, whereas Asian and Pacific Islander families experienced a decrease in their number of poor as well as their poverty rate.

The poverty rate increased in metropolitan areas outside central cities (suburbs), from 7.8% in 2000 to 8.2% in 2001. For people living inside central cities, the poverty rate was 16.5%, unchanged from 2000. A disproportionate share of poor people live inside central cities: 40.7% compared with 28.9% of all people. Among people living outside metropolitan areas, the number of poor rose to 7.5 million, up from 7.0 million in 2000. This increase did not translate into a higher poverty rate (14.2%).

Weighted Average Poverty Thresholds[1] for Families, 1960–2002

Calendar year	Individual[2]	Families of 2 persons or more: 2 persons[2]	3 persons	4 persons	5 persons	6 persons	7 persons
1960	$1,490	$ 1,924	$ 2,359	$ 3,022	$ 3,560	$ 4,002	$ 4,921[3]
1965	1,582	2,048	2,514	3,223	3,797	4,264	5,248[3]
1970	1,954	2,525	3,099	3,968	4,680	5,260	6,468[3]
1975	2,724	3,506	4,293	5,500	6,499	7,316	9,022[3]
1980	4,190	5,363	6,565	8,414	9,966	11,269	12,761
1985	5,469	6,998	8,573	10,989	13,007	14,696	16,656
1990	6,652	8,509	10,419	13,359	15,792	17,839	20,241
1995	7,763	9,933	12,158	15,569	18,408	20,804	23,552
1996	7,995	10,223	12,516	16,036	18,952	21,389	24,268
1997	8,183	10,473	12,802	16,400	19,380	21,886	24,802
1998	8,316	10,634	13,003	16,660	19,680	22,228	25,257
1999	8,501	10,869	13,290	17,029	20,127	22,727	25,912
2000	8,959	11,531	13,470	17,761	21,419	24,636	28,347
2001	9,214	11,859	13,853	18,267	22,029	25,337	29,154
2002	9,359	12,047	14,480	18,244	21,469	24,038	26,924

1. Annual income. 2. Householder under 65 years. 3. For years before 1980, data are for families with seven persons or more. *Source:* U.S. Bureau of the Census. Web: www.census.gov.

Persons Below Poverty Level, 1975–2001

(in thousands)

Year	All persons	Percent	White	Percent	Black	Percent	Hispanic origin[1]	Percent	Asian and Pac. Isl.	Percent
1975	25,877	12.3%	17,770	9.7%	7,545	31.3%	2,991	26.9%	n.a.	n.a.
1980	29,272	13.0	19,699	10.2	8,579	32.5	3,491	25.7	n.a.	n.a.
1985	33,064	14.0	22,860	11.4	8,926	31.3	5,236	29.0	n.a.	n.a.
1990	33,585	13.5	22,326	10.7	9,837	31.9	6,006	28.1	858	12.2%
1995	36,425	13.8	24,423	11.2	9,872	29.3	8,574	30.3	1,411	14.6
2000	31,139	11.3	21,291	9.4	7,901	22.1	7,155	21.2	1,226	10.8
2001	32,907	11.7	22,739	9.9	8,136	22.7	7,997	21.4	1,275	10.2

n.a. = not available. 1. Persons of Hispanic origin may be of any race. *Source:* U.S. Bureau of the Census. Web: www.census.gov.

Percent of People in Poverty by State, 1999–2001

State	3-year average 1999–2001	Average 2000–2001	Average 1999–2000
United States	11.6%	11.5%	11.6%
Alabama	14.8	14.6	14.3
Alaska	7.9	8.1	7.6
Arizona	12.9	13.2	11.9
Arkansas	16.3	17.1	15.6
California	13.1	12.6	13.4
Colorado	9.0	9.2	9.1
Connecticut	7.4	7.5	7.4
Delaware	8.5	7.6	9.4
DC	16.1	16.7	15.0
Florida	12.0	11.9	11.7
Georgia	12.6	12.5	12.5
Hawaii	10.4	10.2	9.9
Idaho	12.7	12.0	13.3
Illinois	10.2	10.4	10.3
Indiana	7.9	8.5	7.6
Iowa	7.7	7.8	7.8
Kansas	10.1	9.1	10.1
Kentucky	12.4	12.6	12.3
Louisiana	17.5	16.7	18.2
Maine	10.3	10.2	10.3
Maryland	7.3	7.3	7.3
Massachusetts	10.2	9.4	10.8
Michigan	9.7	9.6	9.8
Minnesota	6.8	6.5	6.5
Mississippi	16.8	17.1	15.6
Missouri	10.2	9.4	10.4
Montana	14.4	13.7	15.0
Nebraska	9.7	9.0	9.8
Nevada	9.0	7.9	10.0
New Hampshire	6.2	5.5	6.1
New Jersey	7.7	7.7	7.6
New Mexico	18.8	17.7	19.2
New York	14.1	14.0	14.0
North Carolina	12.9	12.5	13.1
North Dakota	12.4	12.1	11.7
Ohio	10.8	10.3	11.0
Oklahoma	14.3	15.0	13.9
Oregon	11.8	11.3	11.7
Pennsylvania	9.2	9.1	9.0
Rhode Island	10.0	9.9	10.1
South Carolina	12.7	13.1	11.4
South Dakota	9.0	9.6	9.2
Tennessee	13.2	13.8	12.7
Texas	15.2	15.2	15.4
Utah	8.0	9.1	6.7
Vermont	9.8	9.9	9.8
Virginia	8.0	8.1	8.1
Washington	10.4	10.8	10.2
West Virginia	15.6	15.6	15.2
Wisconsin	8.6	8.6	8.9
Wyoming	10.3	9.7	11.2

Source: U.S. Census Bureau, Current Population Survey, 2000, 2001, and 2002 Annual Demographic Supplements. Web: www.census.gov.

People and Families in Poverty by Selected Characteristics, 2000 and 2001

Characteristic	2001 Number (thousands)	2001 Percent[1]	2000 Number (thousands)	2000 Percent[1]
INDIVIDUALS				
Total	32,907	11.7%	31,581	11.3%
Race[2] and Hispanic origin				
White	22,739	9.9	21,645	9.5
Non-Hispanic	15,271	7.8	14,366	7.4
Black	8,136	22.7	7,982	22.5
Asian and Pacific Islander	1,275	10.2	1,258	9.9
Hispanic[3]	7,997	21.4	7,747	21.5
Age				
Under 18	11,733	16.3	11,587	16.2
18 to 64	17,760	10.1	16,671	9.6
65 and over	3,414	10.1	3,323	9.9
Region				
Northeast	5,687	10.7	5,474	10.3
Midwest	5,966	9.4	5,916	9.3
South	13,515	13.5	12,705	12.8
West	7,739	12.1	7,485	11.8
FAMILIES				
Total	6,813	9.2	6,400	8.7
White	4,579	7.4	4,333	7.1
Non-Hispanic	3,051	5.7	2,896	5.4
Black	1,829	20.7	1,686	19.3
Asian and Pacific Islander	234	7.8	233	7.8
Hispanic[3]	1,649	19.4	1,540	19.2

1. Percentage of total population. 2. Data for American Indians and Alaska Natives are not shown separately. 3. Hispanics may be of any race. *Source:* U.S. Census Bureau, *Current Population Survey,* 2001 and 2002 Annual Demographic Supplements.

Social Welfare Expenditures Under Public Programs
(in millions of dollars)

Item	1965	1970	1975	1980	1985	1990	1995
Amount							
Gross domestic product	$701,000	$1,023,100	$1,590,800	$2,718,900	$4,108,000	$5,682,900	$7,186,900
Total social welfare expenditures[1]	77,084	145,979	288,967	492,213	731,840	1,048,951	1,505,136
Social insurance	28,123	54,691	123,013	229,754	369,595	513,822	705,483
Public aid	6,283	16,488	41,447	72,703	98,362	146,811	253,530
Health and medical programs	6,155	10,030	16,535	26,762	38,643	61,684	85,507
Veterans' programs	6,031	9,078	17,019	21,466	27,042	30,916	39,072
Education	28,108	50,846	80,834	121,050	172,048	258,332	365,625
Housing	318	701	3,172	6,879	12,598	19,468	29,361
Other social welfare	2,066	4,145	6,947	13,599	13,552	17,918	26,558
All health and medical care[2]	9,302	24,801	51,022	99,145	170,665	274,472	435,075
As percent of gross domestic product							
Gross domestic product	100.0%	100.0%	100.0%	100.0%	100.0%	100.0%	100.0%
Total social welfare expenditures	11.0	14.3	18.2	18.1	17.8	18.5	20.9
Social insurance	4.0	5.3	7.7	8.5	9.0	9.0	9.8
Public aid	.9	1.6	2.6	2.7	2.4	2.6	3.5
Health and medical programs	.9	1.0	1.0	1.0	.9	1.1	1.2
Veterans' programs	.9	.9	1.1	.8	.7	.5	.5
Education	4.0	5.0	5.1	4.5	4.2	4.5	5.1
Housing	(3)	.1	.2	.3	.3	.3	.4
Other social welfare	.3	.4	.4	.5	.3	.3	.4
All health and medical care	1.3	2.4	3.2	3.6	4.2	4.8	6.1

NOTES: Through 1976, fiscal year ended June 30 for federal government, most states, and some localities. Beginning in 1977, federal fiscal year ended Sept. 30. 1. Represents program and administrative expenditures from federal, state, and local public revenues and trust funds under public law. Includes workers' compensation and temporary disability insurance payments made through private carriers and self-insurers. Includes capital outlay and some expenditures abroad. 2. Combines "health and medical programs" with medical services provided in connection with social insurance, public aid, veterans', and "other social welfare" categories. 3. Less than 0.05%. *Source:* Social Security Administration. Web: www.ssa.gov/statistics/Supplement/1999/tables/index.html.

Drop in Welfare Rolls, 1993–2000

	Number of families on welfare Jan. 1993	Number of families on welfare June 2000	Percent reduction 1993–2000
Alabama	51,910	18,677	−64%
Alaska	11,626	7,542	−35
Arizona	68,982	31,897	−54
Arkansas	26,897	12,046	−55
California	844,494	489,054	−42
Colorado	42,445	10,772	−75
Connecticut	56,759	27,149	−52
Delaware	11,315	5,819	−49
DC	24,628	22,397	−09
Florida	256,145	62,805	−75
Georgia	142,040	51,215	−64
Guam	1,406	2,760	96
Hawaii	17,869	14,942	−16
Idaho	7,838	1,382	−82
Illinois	229,308	85,807	−63
Indiana	73,115	35,068	−52
Iowa	36,515	20,082	−45
Kansas	29,818	12,404	−58
Kentucky	83,320	37,471	−55
Louisiana	89,931	25,521	−72
Maine	23,903	10,654	−55
Maryland	80,256	28,895	−64
Massachusetts	113,571	41,682	−63
Michigan	228,377	70,897	−69
Minnesota	63,995	39,295	−39
Mississippi	60,520	14,979	−75
Missouri	88,744	45,912	−48
Montana	11,793	4,467	−62
Nebraska	16,637	10,088	−39%
Nevada	12,892	6,916	−46
New Hampshire	10,805	5,791	−46
New Jersey	126,179	50,126	−60
New Mexico	31,103	22,701	−27
New York	428,191	248,148	−42
North Carolina	128,946	44,731	−65
North Dakota	6,577	2,887	−56
Ohio	257,665	95,835	−63
Oklahoma	50,955	7,251	−86
Oregon	42,409	17,121	−60
Pennsylvania	204,216	87,972	−57
Puerto Rico	60,950	31,273	−49
Rhode Island	21,900	16,324	−25
South Carolina	54,599	15,496	−72
South Dakota	7,262	2,789	−62
Tennessee	112,159	55,491	−51
Texas	279,002	128,289	−54
Utah	18,606	8,157	−56
Vermont	10,081	5,858	−42
Virgin Islands	1,073	778	−27
Virginia	73,446	30,078	−59
Washington	100,568	54,768	−46
West Virginia	41,525	10,661	−74
Wisconsin	81,291	16,410	−80
Wyoming	6,493	565	−91
U.S. total	**4,963,050**	**2,208,095**	**−56**

Source: U.S. Dept. of Health and Human Services, Administration for Children and Families. Web: www.acf.dhhs.gov.

Food Insecurity and Hunger, 2001

(numbers in thousands)

				Food insecure					
		Food secure		Total		Without hunger		With hunger	
Category	Total number[1]	Number	Percent	Number	Percent	Number	Percent	Number	Percent
All households	107,824	96,303	89.3%	11,521	10.7%	8,010	7.4%	3,511	3.3%
Household composition:									
With children < 18	38,330	32,141	83.9	6,189	16.1	4,744	12.4	1,445	3.8
Married couple families	26,182	23,389	89.3	2,793	10.7	2,247	8.6	546	2.1
Female head, no spouse	9,080	6,185	68.1	2,895	31.9	2,101	23.1	794	8.7
Male head, no spouse	2,389	2,009	84.1	380	15.9	298	12.5	82	3.4
Other household with child[2]	678	555	81.9	123	18.1	99	14.6	24	3.5
With no children < 18	69,495	64,163	92.3	5,332	7.7	3,266	4.7	2,066	3.0
More than one adult	40,791	38,328	94.0	2,463	6.0	1,595	3.9	868	2.1
Women living alone	16,513	14,915	90.3	1,598	9.7	952	5.8	646	3.9
Men living alone	12,192	10,922	89.6	1,270	10.4	718	5.9	552	4.5
Households with elderly	24,836	23,458	94.5	1,378	5.5	1,002	4.0	376	1.5
Elderly living alone	10,390	9,758	93.9	632	6.1	426	4.1	206	2.0
Race/ethnicity of households:									
White non-Hispanic	80,337	74,230	92.4	6,107	7.6	4,072	5.1	2,035	2.5
Black non-Hispanic	13,134	10,331	78.7	2,803	21.3	1,986	15.1	817	6.2
Hispanic[3]	9,864	7,717	78.2	2,147	21.8	1,613	16.4	534	5.4
Other non-Hispanic	4,489	4,026	89.7	463	10.3	339	7.6	124	2.8

1. Total households in each category exclude households whose food security status is unknown. 2. Households with children in complex living arrangements, e.g., children of other relatives or unrelated roommate or boarder. 3. Hispanics may be of any race. *Source:* Economic Research Service, U.S. Dept. of Agriculture, *Household Food Security in the United States, 2001*. Web: http://www.ers.usda.gov/publications/fanrr29/fanrr29b.pdf.

Food Stamp Households, 2000
(for year ending Sept. 30)

Household type	Households: Number (1,000)	Households: Percent
Total	**7,335**	**100.0%**
With children	3,955	53.9
Single-parent households	2,704	36.9
Married-couple households	573	7.8
Other	676	9.2
With elderly	1,542	21.0
Living alone	1,226	16.7
Not living alone	316	4.3
Disabled	2,017	27.5
Living alone	1,154	15.6
Not living alone	853	11.8

Sex, race, and Hispanic origin	Participants: Number (1,000)	Participants: Percent
Total	**17,091**	**100.0%**
Male	6,891	40.3
Female	10,198	59.7
White, non-Hispanic	6,837	40.0
Black, non-Hispanic	6,123	35.8
Hispanic	3,168	18.5
Asian	591	3.5
Native American	290	1.7
Other	83	0.5

Source: U.S. Dept. of Agriculture, Food and Nutrition Service, *Characteristics of Food Stamp Households: Fiscal Year 2000,* Oct. 2001. From *Statistical Abstract of the United States, 2002.*

Social Security

Source: Social Security Administration.

The original Social Security Act was passed in 1935 and is administered by the Social Security Administration and other agencies within the Department of Health and Human Services.

What Does Social Security Offer?

The Social Security contribution you pay gives you four different kinds of protection: (1) retirement benefits, (2) survivors' benefits, (3) disability benefits, and (4) Medicare hospital insurance benefits.

Retirement Benefits

Currently, as a worker you become eligible for the full amount of your retirement benefits at age 65. You may retire at age 62 and get 80% of your full benefit. The closer you are to age 65 when you start collecting your benefit, the larger the fraction of your full benefit you will get.

The amount of the retirement benefit you are entitled to at age 65 is the key to all other benefits under the program. The retirement benefit is based on covered earnings, which will be updated (indexed) to reflect the increases in average wages that have occurred since the earnings were paid. Your largest 35 years of adjusted earnings are averaged together and a formula is applied to the adjusted average to figure the benefit rate.

Survivor Benefits

This feature of the Social Security program gives your family valuable life-insurance protection. The amount of protection is again geared to what the worker would be entitled to if he had been age 65 when he died. Your survivors could get:

1. A one-time cash payment of $255 for your spouse or minor children if you have enough work credits.
2. A benefit for each child until he or she reaches 18 (or 19, if the child is in full-time attendance at an elementary or secondary school), or at any age if disabled before 22.
3. A benefit for your widow(er), at any age, if she/he has your entitled children under 16 or disabled in care.
4. Your spouse or divorced spouse can get a widow's, widower's, or surviving divorced spouse's benefit starting at age 60. A widow, or widower, who first becomes entitled at 65 or later will get 100% of his or her deceased spouse's basic amount (or the amount of the deceased spouse's reduced benefits).
5. Dependent parents can sometimes collect survivors' benefits. They are usually eligible if: (a) they were getting at least half their support from the deceased worker; (b) they have reached 62; (c) they are not eligible for a greater retirement benefit based on their own earnings; and (d) they have not married since the worker's death.

Disability Benefits

Disability benefits can be paid to several groups of people:

• Disabled workers under age 65 and their families.

• Persons disabled before age 22 who continue to be disabled. These benefits are payable as early as age 18 when a parent (or step-parent or grandparent under certain circumstances) receives Social Security retirement or disability benefits or when an insured parent dies.

• Disabled widows and widowers and (under certain conditions) disabled, surviving, and divorced spouses of workers who were insured at death. These benefits are payable as early as 50.

The SSA determines whether or not you qualify for disability benefits based on criteria including the severity of your condition and the earnings you continue to receive after you become disabled. To be considered for disability benefits, you should file a claim with a Social Security office as soon as you become disabled.

Medicare Program

Medicare is the nation's largest health insurance program. Generally, you are eligible for Medicare if you or your spouse worked for at least ten years in Medicare-covered employment and you are 65 years old and a citizen or permanent resident of the United States. You might also qualify for coverage if you are a younger person with a disability or with chronic kidney disease.

Medicare-covered services include:

• **Hospital insurance.** Financial assistance is available for necessary medical care and services furnished by Medicare-certified hospitals, skilled nursing facilities, home health agencies, and hospices.

• **Inpatient hospital care.** Medicare helps pay for up to 90 days of inpatient hospital care in each benefit period. Covered services include your semi-private room and meals, general nursing services, operating and recovery room costs, intensive care, drugs, laboratory tests, X rays, and all other necessary medical services and supplies.

• **Skilled nursing facility care.** If you meet certain conditions, Medicare will help pay for up to 100 days in a participating skilled nursing facility in each benefit period.

• **Home health care.** If you meet certain conditions, Medicare pays the full approved cost of covered home health care services. This includes part-time or intermittent skilled nursing services prescribed by a physician for treatment or rehabilitation of homebound patients.

• **Hospice care.** Medicare helps pay for hospice care for terminally ill beneficiaries who select the hospice care benefit.

• **Medical insurance (Part B).** Medicare Part B helps pay for doctor's services, outpatient hospital services (including emergency room visits), ambulance transportation, diagnostic tests, laboratory services, some preventive care like mammography and Pap smear screening, outpatient therapy services, durable medical equipment and supplies, and a variety of other health services.

Average Monthly Social Security Benefits, 1940–2001

	Retired workers			Disabled workers			Non-disabled
Year	Total	Men	Women	Total	Men	Women	widowers
1940	$ 22.71	$ 23.26	$ 18.38	—	—	—	$ 20.36
1945	25.11	25.71	19.99	—	—	—	20.17
1950[1]	29.03	30.16	22.98	—	—	—	21.65
1955	69.74	75.86	56.05	—	—	—	49.68
1960	81.73	92.03	63.26	$ 91.16	$ 94.02	$ 78.91	62.12
1965[1]	82.69	90.89	68.78	93.26	97.89	80.27	73.81
1970	123.82	136.80	103.67	139.79	148.39	115.74	106.95
1975[2]	196.42	220.35	160.50	220.60	241.48	175.27	185.34
1980[2]	321.10	374.00	244.90	352.10	388.80	269.70	277.50
1985[3]	432.00	509.60	322.20	459.20	514.00	345.00	431.10
1990[3]	550.50	654.60	403.30	566.90	637.80	438.90	541.10
1995[3]	671.70	794.30	505.80	675.70	767.30	546.00	662.50
1998[3]	744.70	882.10	577.10	737.00	841.50	610.60	716.70
1999	757.71	904.62	697.50	754.12	846.48	629.63	776.07
2000	844.60	951.50	729.60	787.00	883.00	661.10	811.80
2001	874.50	984.90	755.90	814.90	913.80	688.70	840.80

1. Jan.–Aug. 2. Jan.–May. 3. Jan.–Nov. *Source:* Social Security Administration, *Social Security Bulletin: Annual Statistical Supplement, 2002.*

Gross Domestic Product or Expenditure, 1930–2002

(in billions of dollars)

Item	1930	1940	1950	1960	1970	1980	1990	2000	2002
Gross domestic product	$91.3	$101.3	$294.3	$527.4	$1,039.7	$2,795.6	$5,803.2	$9,872.9	$10,446.2
Personal consumption expenditures	70.2	71.2	192.7	332.2	648.9	1,762.9	3,831.5	6,728.4	7,303.7
Gross private domestic investment	10.8	13.6	54.1	75.7	150.4	484.2	847.2	1,767.5	1,593.2
Exports of goods and services	4.4	4.8	12.3	25.3	57.0	278.9	557.2	1,102.9	1,014.9
Imports of goods and services	4.1	3.4	11.6	22.8	55.8	293.8	628.6	1,466.9	1,438.5
Government[1]	10.0	15.1	46.9	113.8	237.1	569.7	1,181.4	1,741.0	1,972.9

1. Government consumption expenditures and gross investment. *Source:* U.S. Bureau of Economic Analysis. Web: www.bea.gov.

The Public Debt

Year	Gross debt amount	Year	Gross debt amount	Year	Gross debt amount	Year	Gross debt amount
1800	$82,976,294	1855	$ 35,586,957	1910	$ 2,652,665,838	1965	$ 320,904,110,042
1805	82,312,151	1860	64,842,288	1915	3,058,136,873	1970	389,158,403,690
1810	53,173,218	1865	2,680,647,870	1920	25,952,456,406	1975	576,649,000,000[1]
1815	99,833,660	1870	2,480,672,428	1925	20,516,193,888	1980	930,210,000,000[1]
1820	91,015,566	1875	2,232,284,532	1930	16,185,309,831	1985	1,945,941,616,460
1825	83,788,433	1880	2,120,415,371	1935	28,700,892,625	1990	3,233,313,451,777
1830	48,565,407	1885	1,863,964,873	1940	42,967,531,038	1995	4,973,982,900,709
1835	33,733	1890	1,552,140,205	1945	258,682,187,410	1999	5,656,270,901,633
1840	3,573,344	1895	1,676,120,983	1950	257,357,352,351	2000	5,674,178,209,887
1845	15,925,303	1900	2,136,961,092	1955	280,768,553,189	2001	5,807,463,412,200
1850	63,452,774	1905	2,274,615,064	1960	290,216,815,242	2002	6,228,235,965,597

NOTE: Figures as of Jan. 1 for years 1800–1840; as of July 1 for years 1845–1920; as of June 30 for years 1925–1950; as of Dec. 31 for years 1955–1985; as of Sept. 30 for years 1990–present. 1. Rounded to millions. *Source:* U.S. Department of the Treasury, The Public Debt Online. Web: www.publicdebt.treas.gov/opd/opdpdodt.htm.

Receipts and Outlays of the Federal Government, 1789–2005
(in millions of dollars)

1789–1842: federal fiscal year ended Dec. 31; 1844–1976: June 30; 1977–present: Sept. 30.

	Total			On-budget[1]		
Year	Receipts	Outlays	Surplus or deficit (–)	Receipts	Outlays	Surplus or deficit (–)
1789–1849	$ 1,160	$ 1,090	$ 70	$ 1,160	$ 1,090	$ 70
1850–1900	14,462	15,453	–991	14,462	15,453	–991
1905	544	567	–23	544	567	–23
1910	676	694	–18	676	694	–18
1915	683	746	–63	683	746	–63
1920	6,649	6,358	291	6,649	6,358	291
1925	3,641	2,924	717	3,641	2,924	717
1930	4,058	3,320	738	4,058	3,320	738
1935	3,609	6,412	–2,803	3,609	6,412	–2,803
1940	6,548	9,468	–2,920	5,998	9,482	–3,484
1945	45,159	92,712	–47,553	43,849	92,569	–48,720
1950	39,443	42,562	–3,119	37,336	42,038	–4,702
1955	65,451	68,444	–2,933	60,370	64,461	–4,091
1960	92,492	92,191	301	81,851	81,341	510
1965	116,817	118,228	–1,411	100,094	101,699	–1,605
1970	192,807	195,649	–2,842	159,348	168,042	–8,694
1975	279,090	332,332	–53,242	216,633	271,892	–55,260
1980	517,112	590,947	–73,835	403,903	476,618	–72,715
1985	734,088	946,423	–212,334	547,918	769,615	–221,698
1990	1,031,969	1,253,198	–221,229	750,314	1,028,133	–277,819
1995	1,351,830	1,515,837	–164,007	1,000,751	1,227,173	–226,422
2000	2,025,218	1,788,826	236,392	1,544,634	1,458,061	86,573
2001	1,991,194	1,863,895	127,299	1,483,675	1,517,057	–33,382
2002	1,853,173	2,010,975	–157,802	1,337,852	1,655,313	–317,461
2005[2]	2,135,188	2,343,399	–208,211	1,545,685	1,953,094	–407,409

1. Excludes the Social Security surplus. For years prior to 1933, on-budget surplus was not calculated separately. 2. Estimated. *Source:* The Budget for Fiscal Year 2003.

The Federal Budget, 2001–2006
(in billions of dollars)

			Estimates			
Description	Actual 2001	Actual 2002	2003	2004	2005	2006
Receipts by source						
Individual income taxes	$994.3	$858.3	$1006.4	$1,058.6	$1,112.0	$1,157.3
Corporate income taxes	151.1	148.0	205.5	212.0	237.1	241.4
Social insurance and retirement receipts	694.0	700.8	749.2	789.8	835.2	868.7
Excise taxes	66.1	67.0	69.0	71.2	73.6	75.3
Estate and gift taxes	28.4	26.5	23.0	26.6	23.4	26.4
Customs duties and fees	19.4	18.6	19.8	21.9	23.0	24.7
Miscellaneous receipts:	37.8	33.9	40.2	42.8	43.2	44.4
Bipartisan economic security plan	—	—	–65.0	–47.5	–9.5	17.0
Total receipts	**1,991.0**	**1,853.2**	**2,048.1**	**2,175.4**	**2,338.0**	**2,455.3**
Outlays by function						
National defense	308.5	348.6	379.0	393.8	413.5	428.5
International affairs	16.6	22.4	22.5	22.8	23.3	23.9
General science, space, and technology	19.9	20.8	22.2	22.8	23.5	24.0
Energy	0.1	0.5	0.6	0.3	0.8	0.7
Natural resources and environment	26.3	30.2	30.6	31.1	31.7	32.4
Agriculture	26.6	29.5	24.2	22.8	21.3	20.4
Commerce and housing credit	6.0	–0.4	3.7	5.1	3.1	1.2
Transportation	55.2	61.9	59.4	56.3	56.0	56.9
Community and regional development	12.0	13.0	17.4	18.0	17.4	15.6
Education, training, employment, and social services	57.3	70.5	79.0	81.0	82.7	84.2
Health	172.6	196.5	231.9	258.8	277.8	297.0
Medicare	217.5	230.9	234.4	244.3	261.3	281.8
Income security	269.8	312.5	319.7	325.0	334.3	345.2
Social security	433.1	456.4	475.9	495.7	519.7	546.2
Veterans' benefits and services	45.8	51.0	56.6	58.6	63.2	62.9
Administration of justice	30.4	34.3	40.6	43.5	39.5	39.7
General government	15.2	17.4	17.6	19.6	18.6	19.0
Net interest	206.2	171.0	180.7	188.8	190.2	188.3
Allowances	—	—	6.4	0.8	–0.5	–0.3
Undistributed offsetting receipts	–55.2	–47.8	–74.1	–100.2	–100.4	–98.6
Total outlays	**1,863.9**	**2,011.0**	**2,128.2**	**2,189.1**	**2,276.9**	**2,369.1**

Source: Department of the Treasury and Office of Management and Budget.

Summary of Federal Government Expenditure, by State and Territory, Fiscal Year 2002

(in millions of dollars)

State and outlying area	Total	Retirement and disability	Other direct payments	Grants	Procurement	Salaries and wages
United States total	**$1,917,637**	**$612,996**	**$422,239**	**$412,371**	**$270,965**	**$199,066**
Alabama	34,291	11,717	7,086	6,344	6,035	3,109
Alaska	7,562	981	560	3,127	1,396	1,499
Arizona	34,761	11,471	6,193	6,664	7,291	3,142
Arkansas	18,372	6,777	5,202	4,047	1,095	1,251
California	206,401	59,256	45,166	48,084	34,753	19,143
Colorado	26,229	8,073	4,753	4,740	4,526	4,138
Connecticut	25,387	7,348	5,088	5,279	6,216	1,456
Delaware	4,766	1,851	1,121	1,121	207	465
District of Columbia	33,533	1,876	2,130	4,832	10,875	13,821
Florida	104,814	43,709	25,961	16,350	9,757	9,038
Georgia	51,336	15,945	10,160	10,500	7,364	7,366
Hawaii	10,474	2,899	1,435	1,835	1,621	2,684
Idaho	8,378	2,713	1,690	1,837	1,357	781
Illinois	70,275	24,068	20,223	14,975	4,664	6,344
Indiana	34,200	12,877	9,345	6,969	2,802	2,208
Iowa	18,839	6,570	6,169	4,060	955	1,084
Kansas	17,496	5,973	4,614	3,272	1,653	1,984
Kentucky	28,880	9,795	5,906	6,346	3,978	2,854
Louisiana	29,988	9,225	8,092	7,437	2,773	2,461
Maine	9,205	3,267	1,580	2,270	1,240	848
Maryland	49,537	12,789	7,285	6,312	13,488	9,664
Massachusetts	47,480	13,436	11,537	12,339	6,793	3,376
Michigan	55,909	21,241	14,564	13,279	3,539	3,286
Minnesota	27,056	9,225	7,089	6,492	2,228	2,022
Mississippi	21,308	6,688	5,000	5,046	2,734	1,840
Missouri	42,347	13,051	9,916	8,429	7,313	3,637
Montana	6,974	2,199	1,752	1,912	350	760
Nebraska	11,583	3,774	3,767	2,342	591	1,109
Nevada	10,737	4,425	2,126	1,840	1,250	1,096
New Hampshire	6,937	2,726	1,216	1,632	788	574
New Jersey	50,673	17,906	13,131	10,822	4,840	3,974
New Mexico	17,478	4,174	2,154	3,954	5,393	1,802
New York	128,994	39,201	31,389	42,461	7,417	8,526
North Carolina	48,180	17,971	10,369	10,939	2,923	5,978
North Dakota	6,437	1,384	2,643	1,425	329	655
Ohio	65,976	24,599	16,181	14,844	5,243	5,109
Oklahoma	24,355	8,393	5,187	5,108	2,515	3,152
Oregon	19,839	7,687	4,652	4,814	994	1,692
Pennsylvania	85,601	31,194	22,917	18,017	7,415	6,058
Rhode Island	7,503	2,479	1,650	2,094	495	786
South Carolina	26,103	9,708	5,063	5,592	3,105	2,636
South Dakota	6,315	1,702	2,099	1,506	378	631
Tennessee	39,276	13,196	8,309	8,658	5,912	3,200
Texas	123,431	37,324	27,648	24,858	20,581	13,019
Utah	12,302	3,723	1,869	2,697	2,084	1,929
Vermont	4,111	1,304	736	1,281	431	359
Virginia	74,537	18,634	8,515	7,714	26,170	13,504
Washington	40,218	13,063	7,994	8,296	5,586	5,278
West Virginia	13,361	5,460	2,780	3,298	602	1,221
Wisconsin	28,844	11,158	6,830	7,255	1,888	1,713
Wyoming	3,666	1,095	553	1,234	319	465
American Samoa	154	39	2	93	13	6
Micronesia	140	—	13	126	1	—
Guam	1,114	198	78	251	308	279
Marshall Islands	203	1	—	58	144	—
Northern Marianas	102	21	3	66	9	3
Palau	42	—	—	41	1	—
Puerto Rico	14,062	5,282	2,658	4,828	365	930
Virgin Islands	573	138	90	266	29	50
Undistributed	18,996	17	—	65	15,844	3,071

NOTE: Detail may not add to total due to rounding. *Source: U.S. Census Bureau, Consolidated Federal Funds Report for Fiscal Year 2002.* Web: www.census.gov.

National Income by Type
(in billions of dollars)

Type of income	1930	1940	1950	1960	1970	1980	1990	2000	2001	2002
National income	**$75.6**	**$81.1**	**$241.0**	**$427.5**	**$837.5**	**$2,243.0**	**$4,642.1**	**$7,980.9**	**$8,122.0**	**$8,347.9**
Compensation of employees	46.9	52.2	155.4	296.4	617.2	1,651.7	3,351.0	5,715.2	5,874.9	5,977.4
Wage and salary accruals	46.2	49.9	147.2	272.8	551.5	1,377.4	2,754.6	4,837.2	4,950.6	5,003.7
Supplements to wages and salaries	0.7	2.3	8.1	23.6	65.7	274.3	596.4	878.0	924.3	973.7
Proprietors' income[1,2]										
Farm	4.4	4.5	13.5	11.4	14.3	13.1	31.1	30.6	19.0	12.9
Nonfarm	7.3	8.4	25.1	40.4	65.5	164.5	349.9	684.4	708.8	743.7
Rental income[1]	4.9	3.4	8.7	16.2	20.3	31.3	49.1	141.6	137.9	142.4
Corporate profits[1,2]	7.3	9.5	35.4	52.3	81.6	198.5	408.6	876.4	731.6	787.4
Net interest	4.8	3.2	3.0	10.7	38.4	183.9	452.4	532.7	649.8	684.2
Personal income	76.5	78.6	229.9	412.7	841.1	2,323.9	4,903.2	8,319.2	8,685.3	8,929.1
Disposable personal income	74.6	76.7	210.6	366.2	736.5	2,019.8	4,293.6	7,031.0	7,393.2	7,815.5
Personal savings	3.2	4.5	15.2	26.4	69.5	205.6	334.3	67.7	169.7	291.0

1. Includes capital consumption adjustment. 2. Includes inventory valuation adjustment. *Source:* U.S. Department of Commerce, Bureau of Economic Analysis, *Survey of Current Business,* May 2003. Web: www.bea.doc.gov.

U.S. Direct Investment in Other Countries, 2001
(in millions of dollars)

	All industries	Petroleum	Manufacturing	Wholesale trade	Banking	Finance, insurance, real estate	Services	Other industries
All countries	**$113,977**	**$12,668**	**$36,381**	**$9,289**	**$9,925**	**$34,983**	**$7,513**	**$3,217**
Canada	14,440	8,088	3,877	682	–100	1,076	241	576
Europe	56,133	1,217	25,036	4,522	–31	20,648	4,216	524
Austria	766	(D)	524	127	33	139	40	(D)
Belgium	1,279	–19	169	214	53	366	468	27
Denmark	–369	–216	43	–219	0	(D)	–11	(D)
Finland	137	–11	131	35	0	(D)	1	(D)
France	655	(D)	218	12	–140	–142	98	(D)
Germany	11,360	191	11,257	–479	–26	–453	746	124
Greece	41	(D)	34	66	–33	(D)	6	21
Ireland	581	(D)	1,551	176	20	–1,513	1,008	(D)
Italy	1,609	(D)	749	–61	29	351	60	(D)
Luxembourg	4,848	–1	199	267	73	4,208	101	1
Netherlands	16,058	1,263	5,644	1,844	(D)	6,198	608	(D)
Norway	970	113	–4	78	(D)	773	–84	(D)
Portugal	9	(D)	44	83	–1	1	–98	(D)
Spain	496	(D)	214	–305	87	551	–15	(D)
Sweden	–4,106	–27	–4,723	101	(D)	665	–100	(D)
Switzerland	6,629	–4	1,031	2,446	–72	3,550	329	–651
Turkey	29	–29	8	22	45	2	22	–42
United Kingdom	13,231	–1,278	7,757	56	161	4,812	1,011	713
Other	1,909	849	192	57	(D)	1,082	27	(D)
Latin America and other Western Hemisphere	26,510	718	1,668	1,403	10,462	8,016	1,295	2,948
South America	3,887	–12	61	–49	235	1,485	244	1,924
Argentina	–421	–90	–826	–134	60	708	21	–161
Brazil	–17	–45	–31	–14	120	347	–11	–384
Chile	2,834	8	610	13	58	361	–13	1,795
Colombia	–104	–71	116	2	(D)	–22	(D)	(D)
Ecuador	–66	–35	–37	12	(D)	20	(D)	(D)
Peru	120	62	18	5	(D)	15	(*)	(D)
Venezuela	1,360	100	108	51	–14	56	264	795
Other	181	59	101	14	13	–1	–25	18
Central America	(D)	–376	1,115	48	(D)	1,748	227	(D)
Costa Rica	–16	10	48	(D)	0	4	(*)	(D)
Guatemala	–372	–383	1	–4	(D)	7	(*)	(D)
Honduras	–163	(D)	–118	4	(D)	–4	0	(D)
Mexico	(D)	123	1,118	98	(D)	1,303	–66	(D)
Panama	753	–23	21	(D)	(D)	422	293	(D)
Other	–53	(D)	–24	10	(D)	16	0	(D)
Other Western Hemisphere	(D)	1,106	492	1,405	(D)	4,784	824	(D)
Bahamas	–122	(D)	(D)	(D)	–552	362	5	(D)
Barbados	56	(D)	2	75	(D)	(D)	157	(D)
Bermuda	5,865	(D)	(D)	1,196	0	2,951	460	(D)
Dominican Republic	(D)	(D)	21	13	(D)	(*)	(D)	(D)

	All industries	Petroleum	Manufacturing	Wholesale trade	Banking	Finance, insurance, real estate	Services	Other industries
Jamaica	$-44	(D)	$-20	(D)	(D)	$5	$7	(D)
Netherlands Antilles	131	(*)	(D)	$2	$0	131	(D)	$0
Trinidad and Tobago	(D)	$397	60	2	(D)	(D)	(*)	(D)
United Kingdom Islands, Caribbean	697	-76	123	87	-1,284	1,530	222	94
Other	(D)	(D)	(D)	(D)	(D)	(D)	(D)	(D)
Africa	798	1,750	-166	67	-22	-778	-192	139
Egypt	762	1,088	-330	-12	(D)	2	31	(D)
Nigeria	221	955	-2	(D)	(D)	(D)	0	0
South Africa	-4	61	269	10	(D)	(D)	-243	(D)
Other	-181	-354	-103	(D)	16	93	20	(D)
Middle East	1,269	501	466	63	-72	221	21	68
Israel	493	(*)	421	-2	-9	10	-5	77
Saudi Arabia	-75	-2	32	(*)	(D)	-22	36	(D)
United Arab Emirates	196	25	(D)	66	(D)	(D)	16	16
Other	655	478	(D)	(*)	-24	(D)	-26	(D)
Asia and Pacific	15,012	507	5,501	2,552	-313	5,800	1,932	-967
Australia	-423	987	-1,039	10	55	736	-477	-696
China	1,236	-230	1,403	204	101	-175	-67	-1
Hong Kong	2,992	-39	-457	1,913	-593	1,713	149	306
India	289	-6	187	-93	37	43	26	95
Indonesia	291	-14	-13	(D)	13	(D)	(D)	403
Japan	5,474	-135	1,626	456	-140	2,606	2,047	-985
Korea, Republic of	953	2	669	-42	92	137	21	74
Malaysia	-549	-305	-292	32	(D)	51	-38	(D)
New Zealand	235	36	51	104	(D)	-17	(D)	(D)
Philippines	47	-152	264	19	6	89	(*)	-178
Singapore	2,970	58	2,782	-145	30	48	203	-6
Taiwan	955	4	166	90	123	437	25	111
Thailand	668	328	137	(*)	67	231	19	-114
Other	-126	-26	17	(D)	(D)	(D)	-2	(D)

NOTES: Only countries receiving more than ten trillion dollars in 2001 are listed separately. * Less than $500,000 (+/–). (D) Suppressed to avoid disclosure of data of individual companies. *Source:* U.S. Department of Commerce, Bureau of Economic Analysis. Web: www.bea.doc.gov/bea/di/diapos_01.htm.

Federal Outlays by Agency, 2001–2003

(in millions of dollars)

Department or agency	2001	2002	2003 (estimate)
Legislative Branch	$ 3,034	$ 3,218	$ 3,961
The Judiciary	4,405	4,823	5,419
Agriculture	68,144	68,731	72,773
Commerce	5,015	5,314	5,790
Defense—Military	291,015	331,951	358,155
Education	35,721	46,282	59,481
Energy	16,420	17,681	19,796
Health and Human Services	426,392	465,812	502,013
Homeland Security	n.a.	17,476	28,155
Housing and Urban Development	33,939	31,885	37,987
Interior	7,993	9,739	10,357
Justice	21,433	21,112	22,156
Labor	39,755	64,704	70,746
State	7,444	9,453	10,977
Transportation	54,081	56,104	52,280
Treasury	389,300	370,558	368,803
Veterans Affairs	45,050	50,884	56,946
Corps of Engineers	4,726	4,797	4,146
Other Defense—Civil Programs	34,164	35,157	40,148
Environmental Protection Agency	7,391	7,450	7,958
Executive Office of the President	246	451	334
Federal Emergency Management Agency	4,413	n.a.	n.a.
General Services Administration	$ -8	$ -677	$ 424
International Assistance Programs	11,777	13,342	13,020
National Aeronautics and Space Administration	14,095	14,430	14,599
National Science Foundation	3,690	4,188	4,853
Office of Personnel Management	50,914	52,512	55,793
Small Business Administration	-570	493	1,553
Social Security Administration (on-budget)	40,007	45,816	44,506
Social Security Administration (off-budget)	421,257	442,425	465,404
Other Independent Agencies (On-budget)	11,475	16,636	14,994
Other Independent Agencies (Off-budget)	2,302	-651	-4,238
Allowances	n.a.	n.a.	-1,125
Undistributed offsetting receipts	-191,125	-201,121	-207,787
(On-budget)	(-114,404)	(-115,009)	(-114,718)
(Off-budget)	(-76,721)	(-86,112)	(-93,069)
Total outlays	**1,863,895**	**2,010,975**	**2,140,377**

Source: Budget of the United States Government, Fiscal Year 2004.

U.S. Contributions to International Organizations
(in millions of dollars)

Organization	2002	2003 (est.)	2004 (est.)
UN and affiliated agencies:			
Food and Agriculture Organization	$ 73	$ 73	$ 73
International Atomic Energy Agency	47	57	54
International Civil Aviation Organization	12	12	13
International Labor Organization	55	57	50
International Maritime Organization	1	1	1
International Telecommunications Union	6	7	7
United Nations—Regular	251	232	322
UN War Crimes Tribunals	24	27	30
Iraq War Crimes Commission	—	4	2
UN Capital Master Plan	—	8	—
UN Capital Master Plan Task Force	—	1	—
Universal Postal Union	1	1	1
World Health Organization	108	94	94
World Intellectual Property Org.	1	1	1
World Meteorological Org.	8	9	8
UNESCO	—	—	71
Subtotal	*587*	*584*	*727*
Inter-American organizations:			
Inter-American Institute for Cooperation on Agriculture	17	17	17
Organization of American States	54	54	55
Pan American Health Org.	55	56	56
Subtotal	*126*	*127*	*128*
Regional organizations:			
Asia-Pacific Economic Coop.	1	1	1
North Atlantic Assembly	1	1	1
North Atlantic Treaty Org.	42	52	47
Org. for Economic Coop. and Development	53	69	62
South Pacific Commission	1	1	1
Subtotal	*98*	*124*	*112*

Organization	2002	2003 (est.)	2004 (est.)
Other international organizations:			
Org. for Prohibition of Chemical Weapons	$ 11	$ 15	$ 14
OPCW—Title IV & V	2	5	5
World Trade Org./GATT	13	15	15
Other international organizations	8	9	9
Subtotal	*34*	*44*	*43*
UN Buydown	47	19	—
Total	**892**	**898**	**1,010**
International peacekeeping activities:			
UN Disengagement Observer Force	11	8	10
UN Interim Force in Lebanon	24	34	31
UN Iraq–Kuwait Observer Mission	5	4	5
UN Mission for the Referendum in Western Sahara	14	12	11
UN Mission in Bosnia and Herzegovina	24	—	—
UN Mission in Kosovo	83	97	83
UN Mission in Cyprus	7	5	6
UN Observer Mission in Georgia	8	6	9
War Crimes Tribunal—Yugoslavia	18	15	20
War Crimes Tribunal—Rwanda	14	12	19
UN Mission in Sierra Leone	270	146	84
UN Transitional Administration in East Timor	119	58	9
UN Organization Mission in the Dem. Rep. of the Congo	235	280	210
UN Mission in Ethiopia and Eritrea	73	56	53
Strategic Deployment Stocks	—	39	—
Total new obligations	**905**	**772**	**550**

NOTE: All years are fiscal years. *Source:* Budget of the United States Government Fiscal Year 2004.

Producer Price Indexes by Major Commodity Groups

Commodity	2002	2001	2000	1995	1990	1985	1980	1975	1970
All commodities	**131.1**	**134.2**	**132.7**	**124.7**	**116.3**	**103.2**	**89.8**	**58.4**	**38.1**
Farm products	99.0	103.8	99.5	107.4	112.2	95.1	102.9	77.0	45.8
Processed foods and feeds	136.2	137.3	133.1	127.0	121.9	103.5	95.9	72.6	44.6
Textile products and apparel	119.9	121.3	121.4	120.8	114.9	102.9	89.7	67.4	52.4
Hides, skins, and leather products	157.6	158.4	151.5	153.7	141.7	108.9	94.7	56.5	42.0
Fuels and related products and power	93.2	105.3	103.5	78.0	82.2	91.4	82.8	35.4	15.3
Chemicals and allied products	151.9	151.8	151.0	142.5	123.6	103.7	89.0	62.0	35.0
Rubber and plastic products	126.8	127.2	125.5	124.3	113.6	101.9	90.1	62.2	44.9
Lumber and wood products	173.3	174.4	178.2	178.1	129.7	106.6	101.5	62.1	39.9
Pulp, paper, and allied products	185.9	184.8	183.7	172.2	141.3	113.3	86.3	59.0	37.5
Metals and metal products	125.9	125.4	128.1	134.5	123.0	104.4	95.0	61.5	38.7
Machinery and equipment	122.9	123.7	124.0	126.6	120.7	107.2	86.0	57.9	40.0
Furniture and household durables	133.5	133.2	132.6	128.2	119.1	107.1	90.7	67.5	51.9
Nonmetallic mineral products	146.2	144.3	142.5	129.0	114.7	108.6	88.4	54.4	35.3
Transportation equipment	144.6	145.2	143.8	139.7	121.5	107.9	82.9	56.7	41.9

NOTES: 1982 = 100. *Source:* U.S. Department of Labor, Bureau of Labor Statistics, Division of Industrial Prices and Price Indexes. Web: data.bls.gov.

Consumer Price Index for All Urban Consumers

Group	2002	2001	2000	1999	1995	1990	1985	1980	1975	1970	1965	1960	1950
All items	179.9	177.1	172.2	166.6	152.4	130.7	107.6	82.4	53.8	38.8	31.5	29.6	24.1
Food and beverages	176.8	173.6	168.4	164.6	148.9	132.1	105.6	86.7	60.2	40.1	n.a.	n.a.	n.a.
Housing	180.3	176.4	169.6	163.9	148.5	128.5	107.7	81.1	50.7	36.4	n.a.	n.a.	n.a.
Apparel	124.0	127.3	129.6	131.3	132.0	124.1	105.0	90.9	72.5	59.2	47.8	45.7	40.3
Transportation	152.9	154.3	153.3	144.4	139.1	120.5	106.4	83.1	50.1	37.5	31.9	29.8	22.7
Medical care	285.6	272.8	260.8	250.6	220.5	162.8	113.5	74.9	47.5	34.0	25.2	22.3	15.1

NOTES: 1982–1984 = 100. n.a. = not available. *Source:* U.S. Department of Labor, Bureau of Labor Statistics. Web: data.bls.gov.

Average Prices of Selected Fuels and Electricity, 1980–2001

(In dollars per unit, except electricity, in cents per kWh. Represents price to end-users, except as noted.)

Type	1980	1990	1994	1995	1996	1997	1998	1999	2000	2001
Crude oil, composite (bbl)[1]	28.07	22.22	15.59	17.23	20.71	19.04	12.52	17.51	28.26	22.96
Motor gasoline (gal.):[2]										
Unleaded regular	1.25	1.16	1.11	1.15	1.23	1.23	1.06	1.17	1.51	1.46
Unleaded premium	n.a.	1.35	1.31	1.34	1.41	1.42	1.25	1.36	1.69	1.66
No. 2 heating oil (gal.)	0.97	1.06	0.88	0.87	0.99	0.98	0.85	0.88	1.31	1.25
No. 2 diesel fuel (gal.)	0.82	0.73	0.55	0.56	0.68	0.64	0.49	0.58	0.94	0.84
Residual fuel oil (gal.)	0.61	0.44	0.35	0.39	0.46	0.42	0.31	0.37	0.60	0.53
Natural gas, residential (1,000 cu/ft)	3.68	5.80	6.41	6.06	6.34	6.94	6.82	6.69	7.76	n.a.
Electricity, residential (kWh)	5.36	7.83	8.38	8.40	8.36	8.43	8.26	8.16	8.22	8.48

NOTE: n.a. = not available. 1. Refiner acquisition cost. 2. Average, all service. *Source:* U.S. Energy Information Administration, *Monthly Energy Review.* From *Statistical Abstract of the United States, 2002.*

Exports and Imports of Goods and Services, 1980–2010

Category	Billions of chained 1996 dollars				Average annual rate of change		
	1980	1990	2000	2010[1]	1980–1990	1990–2000	2000–2010[1]
Exports of goods and services	**$333.4**	**$575.7**	**$1,133.2**	**$2,393.7**	**5.6%**	**7.0%**	**7.8%**
Goods	238.9	393.2	836.1	1,821.2	5.1	7.8	8.1
Foods, feeds, and beverages	44.7	44.4	60.0	91.4	–0.1	3.1	4.3
Industrial supplies and materials	86.9	111.7	168.2	228.4	2.5	4.2	3.1
Capital goods, except autos	56.0	124.8	394.9	1,123.1	8.3	12.2	11.0
Computers	1.0	12.3	85.6	406.0	28.5	21.4	16.8
Civilian aircraft and parts	26.9	40.9	43.1	78.2	4.3	0.5	6.1
Other	48.5	79.1	271.5	740.4	5.0	13.1	10.6
Autos and parts	28.3	39.8	78.3	154.5	3.5	7.0	7.0
Consumer goods	25.1	48.1	89.8	182.7	6.7	6.4	7.4
Other merchandise exports	14.8	32.4	45.9	103.3	8.1	3.6	8.4
Services	89.0	183.4	299.3	591.7	7.5	5.0	7.1
Residual[2]	–31.8	–16.5	–8.6	–182.9	—	—	—
Imports of goods and services	**$326.3**	**$632.2**	**$1,532.3**	**$3,282.7**	**6.8%**	**9.3%**	**7.9%**
Goods	260.6	497.9	1,315.6	2,954.5	6.7	10.2	8.4
Foods, feeds, and beverages	20.9	30.4	49.4	61.9	3.8	5.0	2.3
Industrial supplies and materials	118.1	142.4	254.5	331.6	1.9	6.0	2.7
Petroleum and products	51.5	59.5	86.0	96.6	1.4	3.8	1.2
Other	55.0	83.6	167.9	234.8	4.3	7.2	3.4
Capital goods, except autos	18.5	88.8	451.7	1,428.6	17.0	17.7	12.2
Computers	0.2	11.6	152.6	670.2	50.1	29.4	15.9
Civilian aircraft and parts	6.0	13.5	23.9	36.7	8.5	5.8	4.4
Other	19.1	68.9	279.3	824.0	13.7	15.0	11.4
Autos and parts	52.5	101.6	192.5	322.8	6.8	6.6	5.3
Consumer goods	49.8	112.8	293.5	858.9	8.5	10.0	11.3
Other merchandise imports	12.4	35.2	80.9	148.0	11.0	8.7	6.2
Services	65.6	136.6	218.7	352.8	7.6	4.8	4.9
Residual[3]	–6.7	–21.5	–12.6	–323.9	—	—	—
Trade Deficit	**$ 7.1**	**$–56.5**	**$ –399.1**	**$ –889.1**	—	**21.6%**	**8.3%**

1. Projected. 2. The residual following the detailed categories for exports is the difference between the aggregate of "exports of goods and services" and the sum of the figures for those separate categories for exports of goods and services. 3. The residual following the detailed categories for imports is the difference between the aggregate of "imports of goods and services" and the sum of the figures for those separate categories for imports of goods and services. *Source:* Bureau of Labor Statistics, *Monthly Labor Review,* Nov. 2001.

Imports and Exports of Leading Commodities

by Principal SITC Groupings (in millions of dollars)

Item	2002 Cumulative Exports	2002 Cumulative Imports
Total balance of payment basis	**$163,810**	**$261,179**
Net adjustments	**–2,662**	**738**
Selected commodities:		
ADP equipment; office machines	7,762	17,994
Airplane parts	3,411	1,403
Airplanes	6,694	3,912
Alcoholic bev.,distilled	94	677
Aluminum	728	1,574
Animal feeds	1,092	142
Basketware, etc.	931	1,477
Cereal flour	369	448
Chemicals—medicinal	3,459	5,151
Chemicals—organic	3,645	7,547
Chemicals—plastics	4,562	2,369
Cigarettes	418	71
Clothing	1,335	13,871
Coal	384	227
Coffee	4	281
Copper	238	910
Cork, wood, lumber	873	2,032
Corn	1,264	45
Cotton, raw and linters	637	9
Crude oil	27	14,446
Electrical machinery	16,064	18,410
Fish and preparations	768	2,064
Footwear	135	3,579
Furniture and bedding	1,013	4,915
Gem diamonds	328	3,048
General industrial machinery	7,252	8,238
Glass	552	500
Glassware	172	394
Gold, nonmonetary	625	501
Hides and skins	363	21
Iron and steel mill products	1,271	3,083
Jewelry	534	1,439
Lighting, plumbing	320	1,119
Liquefied propane/butane	97	308
Live animals	$ 121	$ 580
Meat and preparations	1,584	983
Metal manufactures, n.e.s.	2,731	3,783
Metal ores; scrap	999	667
Metalworking machinery	900	1,134
Mineral fuels, other	510	277
Natural gas	156	2,782
Nickel	124	224
Oils/fats, vegetable	315	236
Optical goods	550	667
Paper and paperboard	2,309	3,332
Petroleum preparations	1,274	3,740
Photographic equipment	815	1,225
Platinum	144	534
Pottery	19	343
Power generating machinery	7,942	8,628
Printed materials	1,048	825
Pulp and waste paper	904	562
Records/magnetic media	1,016	1,048
Rice	196	33
Rubber tires and tubes	523	1,087
Scientific instruments	6,645	4,748
Ships, boats	377	326
Silver and bullion	87	165
Soybeans	1,800	5
Specialized ind. mach.	5,540	4,377
Sugar	1	110
Television, VCR, etc.	4,907	13,274
Textile yarn, fabric	2,385	3,581
Tobacco, unmanufactured	366	175
Toys/games/sporting goods	736	3,534
Vegetables and fruits	1,787	2,905
Vehicles	13,489	39,155
Watches/clocks/parts	54	562
Wheat	801	78
Wood manufactures	365	1,709

NOTES: SITC = Standard International Trade Classification. Details may not equal totals due to rounding. Data not seasonally adjusted. *Source:* U.S. Census Bureau, Foreign Trade Division. Web: http://www.census.gov/foreign-trade/Press-Release/current_press_release/exh15.txt.

Retail Prices of Selected Foods in U.S. Cities, 1890–1970

(in cents per unit indicated)

Year	Flour (5 lbs)	Bread (lb)	Round steak (lb)	Bacon (lb)	Butter (lb)	Eggs (doz.)	Milk (½ gal.)	Oranges (doz.)	Potatoes (10 lbs)	Coffee (lb)	Sugar (5 lbs)
1970	58.9¢	24.3¢	130.2¢	94.9¢	86.6¢	61.4¢	65.9¢	86.4¢	89.7¢	91.1¢	64.8¢
1965	58.1	20.9	108.4	81.3	75.4	52.7	52.6	77.8	93.7	83.3	59.0
1960	55.4	20.3	105.5	65.5	74.9	57.3	52.0	74.8	71.8	75.3	58.2
1955	53.8	17.7	90.3	65.9	70.9	60.6	46.2	52.8	56.4	93.0	52.1
1950	49.1	14.3	93.6	63.7	72.9	60.4	41.2	49.3	46.1	79.4	48.7
1945	32.1	8.8	40.6	41.1	50.7	58.1	31.2	48.5	49.3	30.5	33.4
1940	21.5	8.0	36.4	27.3	36.0	33.1	25.6	29.1	23.9	21.2	26.0
1935	25.3	8.3	36.0	41.3	36.0	37.6	23.4	22.0	19.1	25.7	28.2
1930	23.0	8.6	42.6	42.5	46.4	44.5	28.2	57.1	36.0	39.5	30.5
1925	30.5	9.3	36.2	47.1	55.2	55.4	27.8	57.1	36.0	50.4	35.0
1920	40.5	11.5	39.5	52.3	70.1	68.1	33.4	63.2	63.0	47.0	97.0
1915	21.0	7.0	23.0	26.9	35.8	34.1	17.6	n.a.	15.0	30.0	33.0
1910	18.0	n.a.	17.4	25.5	35.9	33.7	16.8	n.a.	17.0	n.a.	30.0
1905	16.0	n.a.	14.0	18.1	29.0	27.2	14.4	n.a.	17.0	n.a.	30.0
1900	12.5	n.a.	13.2	14.3	26.1	20.7	13.6	n.a.	14.0	n.a.	30.5
1895	12.0	n.a.	12.3	13.0	24.9	20.6	13.6	n.a.	14.0	n.a.	26.5
1890	14.5	n.a.	12.3	12.5	25.5	20.8	13.6	n.a.	16.0	n.a.	34.5

NOTE: n.a. = not available. *Source:* U.S. Bureau of the Census, *Historical Statistics of the United States, Colonial Times to 1970, Bicentennial Edition, Part 2.*

Per Capita Consumption of Principal Foods[1]

(in pounds unless otherwise noted)

Food	1990	1995	1998	1999	2000
Red meats[2,3,4]	112.3	115.1	115.6	117.7	113.5
Beef	63.9	64.4	64.9	65.8	64.4
Veal	0.9	0.8	0.7	0.6	n.a.
Lamb & mutton	1.0	0.9	0.9	0.9	n.a.
Pork	46.4	49.0	49.2	50.5	47.7
Poultry[2,3,4]	56.3	62.9	65.0	68.3	66.5
Chicken	42.4	48.8	50.8	54.2	52.9
Turkey	13.8	14.1	14.2	14.1	13.6
Fish and shellfish	15.0	14.9	14.8	15.2	15.2
Eggs[4]	30.2	30.2	31.8	32.8	250.0[5]
Cheese	24.6	27.3	28.3	29.8	29.8
Cottage cheese	3.4	2.7	2.7	2.7	2.6
Beverage milks	221.8	209.8	204.6	203.8	22.6[6]
Yogurt (excluding frozen)	4.0	5.1	5.1	4.9	9.9
Ice cream	15.8	15.7	16.6	16.8	16.5
Lowfat ice cream[7]	7.7	7.5	8.3	7.9	7.3
All dairy products, milk equivalent, milkfat basis[8]	568.3	583.8	581.7	597.9	593.0
Fats and oils	63.0	66.3	65.6	68.5	74.5
Butter and margarine (product weight)	15.3	13.7	12.8	12.9	12.8
Shortening	22.2	22.5	21.0	21.6	23.1
Lard and beef tallow	2.2	4.3	5.2	5.7	6.0
Salad and cooking oils	25.3	26.9	27.9	29.4	35.2
Fruits and vegetables	656.0	694.3	702.4	719.0	707.7
Fruit	272.6	284.9	284.4	297.9	279.4
Vegetables	383.5	409.4	418.0	421.2	428.3
Peanuts (shelled)	6.0	5.7	5.9	6.4	n.a.
Tree nuts (shelled)	2.4	1.9	2.3	2.7	n.a.
Flour and cereal products[9]	181.0	192.8	198.4	201.9	199.9
Wheat flour	136.0	141.8	146.0	148.4	146.3
Rice (milled basis)	15.8	18.9	18.9	19.4	19.7
Caloric sweeteners[10]	136.9	149.8	155.1	158.4	152.4
Coffee (green bean equiv.)	10.3	8.0	9.5	10.0	n.a.
Cocoa (chocolate liquor equiv.)	4.3	3.6	4.4	4.6	n.a.

1. In pounds, retail weight unless otherwise stated. Consumption normally represents total supply minus exports, nonfood use, and ending stocks. Calendar-year data, except fresh citrus fruits, peanuts, tree nuts, and rice, which are on crop-year basis. 2. Totals may not add up due to rounding. 3. Boneless, trimmed weight. Chicken series revised to exclude amount of ready-to-cook chicken going to pet food as well as some water leakage that occurs when chicken is cut up before packaging. 4. Excludes shipments to the U.S. territories. 5. Number per capita. 6. Gallons. 7. Formerly known as ice milk. 8. Includes condensed and evaporated milk and dry milk products. 9. Includes rye, corn, oats, and barley products. Excludes quantities used in alcoholic beverages, corn sweeteners, and fuel. 10. Dry weight equivalent. *Source:* U.S. Department of Agriculture, Economic Research Service. Web: www.usda.gov.

Output by Major Industry Division, 1990–2010

Industry	Billions of chained 1992 dollars			Percent distribution			Percent change	
	1990	2000	2010*	1990	2000	2010*	1990–2000	2000–2010*
Total	**$11,472.2**	**$16,180.2**	**$22,286.1**	**100.0%**	**100.0%**	**100.0%**	**3.5%**	**3.3%**
Goods producing	3,947.5	5,724.4	7,681.0	34.4	35.4	34.5	3.8	3.0
Mining	205.4	212.1	229.9	1.8	1.3	1.0	0.3	0.8
Construction	730.0	910.1	1,182.1	6.4	5.6	5.3	2.2	2.6
Manufacturing	3,022.0	4,601.4	6,278.6	26.3	28.4	28.2	4.3	3.2
Durable	1,480.8	2,785.2	4,136.4	12.9	17.2	18.6	6.5	4.0
Nondurable	1,553.0	1,834.5	2,219.7	13.5	11.3	10.0	1.7	1.9
Service producing	6,732.3	9,421.9	13,079.1	58.7	58.2	58.7	3.4	3.3
Transportation, communications, and utilities	931.1	1,278.0	1,961.9	8.1	7.9	8.8	3.2	4.4
Wholesale trade	607.7	920.4	1,409.6	5.3	5.7	6.3	4.2	4.4
Retail trade	896.8	1,222.4	1,627.9	7.8	7.6	7.3	3.1	2.9
Finance, insurance, and real estate	1,198.1	1,806.4	2,429.1	10.4	11.2	10.9	4.2	3.0
Services	2,056.7	3,031.5	4,377.9	17.9	18.7	19.6	4.0	3.7
Government	1,043.4	1,161.6	1,287.5	9.1	7.2	5.8	1.1	1.0
Federal government	388.9	353.3	359.8	3.4	2.2	1.6	–1.0	0.2
State and local government	654.5	808.3	927.7	5.7	5.0	4.2	2.1	1.4
Agriculture	257.2	333.7	404.5	2.2	2.1	1.8	2.6	1.9
Private households	12.6	14.7	13.3	0.1	0.1	0.1	1.5	–1.0
Special industries[1]	529.9	706.8	1,102.2	4.6	4.4	4.9	2.9	4.5
Residual[2]	–7.4	–21.3	5.9	–0.1	–0.1	0.0	—	—

*Projected. 1. Consists of nonproducing accounting categories to reconcile input-output system with NIPA accounts. 2. Residual is shown for the first level only. Subcategories do not necessarily add to higher categories as a byproduct of chainweighting. *Source:* U.S. Department of Labor, Bureau of Labor Statistics, *Monthly Labor Review,* Nov. 2001.

Personal Consumption Expenditures

Category	Billions of chained 1996 dollars 1980	1990	2000	2010 (projected)	Average annual rate of change (percent) 1980–90	1990–2000	2000–2010 (projected)
Gross domestic product	$4,900.9	$6,707.9	$9,224.0	$12,835.6	3.2%	3.2%	3.4%
Personal consumption expenditures	3,193.0	4,474.5	6,257.8	8,786.5	3.4	3.4	3.5
Durable goods	279.8	487.1	895.5	1,455.4	5.7	6.3	5.0
New light vehicles	88.3	159.9	218.6	307.3	6.1	3.2	3.5
Other motor vehicles and parts	54.1	86.2	129.3	176.2	4.8	4.1	3.1
Personal computers	.0	1.6	108.8	802.4	(1)	52.1	22.1
Software	.0	.5	17.8	36.3	(1)	43.7	7.4
Furniture	95.5	160.4	294.6	483.2	5.3	6.3	5.1
Ophthalmic products	6.2	16.1	20.4	27.7	10.1	2.4	3.1
Other durable goods	53.5	80.8	152.9	256.1	4.2	6.6	5.3
Nondurable goods	1,065.8	1,369.6	1,849.9	2,635.5	2.5	3.1	3.6
Food and beverages	585.4	722.4	881.3	1,102.8	2.1	2.0	2.3
Clothing and shoes	124.0	197.2	335.3	511.0	4.7	5.5	4.3
Gasoline and motor oil	94.8	113.1	136.6	169.8	1.8	1.9	2.2
Fuel oil and coal	17.7	13.1	13.8	15.5	−3.0	.6	1.1
Tobacco products	65.6	52.0	42.8	46.5	−2.3	−1.9	.8
Drugs and medicines	54.5	80.3	139.9	316.6	4.0	5.7	8.5
Other nondurable goods	138.9	194.3	305.7	497.5	3.4	4.6	5.0
Services	1,858.4	2,616.2	3,527.7	4,784.5	3.5	3.0	3.1
Housing	541.5	696.2	850.1	1,070.2	2.5	2.0	2.3
Household operation	202.9	259.8	377.6	579.2	2.5	3.8	4.4
Electricity	66.7	83.2	103.9	137.7	2.2	2.2	2.9
Natural gas	31.1	29.5	32.8	30.8	−0.5	1.1	−0.6
Telephone	40.0	62.6	141.8	296.2	4.6	8.5	7.6
Other	66.2	85.9	100.8	142.5	2.6	1.6	3.5
Transportation services	124.7	173.4	251.3	318.5	3.4	3.8	2.4
Motor vehicle leases	—	5.5	37.6	49.1	(2)	21.2	2.7
Other	—	168.1	213.6	269.2	(2)	2.4	2.3
Medical services	487.6	710.9	903.9	1,174.9	3.8	2.4	2.7
Recreation services	79.7	145.0	227.0	408.1	6.2	4.6	6.0
Personal business services	242.8	363.2	554.8	759.0	4.1	4.3	3.2
Financial services	94.4	154.2	222.7	292.5	5.0	3.7	2.8
Other	147.4	209.0	332.4	467.4	3.6	4.7	3.5
Other services	170.8	267.0	362.3	488.3	4.6	3.1	3.0
Residual[3]	−35.6	−20.5	−68.7	−789.4			
Personal consumption expenditures + GDP	65.2	66.7	67.8	68.5			

NOTE: (—) Indicates data not available. 1. Undefined because of denominator with value zero. 2. Not applicable. 3. The residual is the difference between the first line and the sum of the most detailed lines. *Source:* Historical data, Bureau of Economic Analsysis; projected data, Bureau of Labor Statistics. *Monthly Labor Review,* Nov. 2002.

Farm Income
(in millions of dollars)

Year	Cash receipts from marketings: Crops	Livestock, livestock products	Government payments	Gross cash income
1930	$ 3,868	$ 5,187	—	$ 9,055
1935	2,977	4,143	$ 573	7,693
1940	3,469	4,913	723	9,105
1945	9,655	12,008	742	22,405
1950	12,356	16,105	283	28,764
1955	13,523	15,967	229	29,842
1960	15,023	18,989	703	34,958
1965	17,479	21,886	2,463	42,215
1970	20,977	29,532	3,717	54,768
1975	45,813	43,089	807	90,707
1980	71,746	67,991	1,285	143,295
1985	74,293	69,822	7,705	157,854
1990	80,131	89,843	9,298	186,824
1991	$82,060	$86,735	$ 8,214	$184,858
1992	84,853	86,350	9,169	188,160
1993	87,500	90,200	13,402	200,100
1994	93,100	88,200	7,900	198,300
1995	101,000	87,100	7,300	205,900
1996	106,200	93,000	7,300	217,400
1997	111,100	96,500	7,500	227,500
1998	101,700	94,100	12,400	225,000
1999	92,600	95,600	21,500	225,000
2000	94,100	99,500	22,900	230,100
2001	95,800	106,100	21,100	n.a.
2002[1]	97,900	106,400	10,700	n.a.

NOTE: n.a. = not available. 1. Forecast. *Source:* U.S. Department of Agriculture, Economic Research Service. *Agricultural Income and Finance.* Web: www.usda.gov.

Farm Indexes

(1990–1992 = 100)

Year	Prices paid by farmers[1]	Prices rec'd by farmers[2]	Ratio[3]	Year	Prices paid by farmers[1]	Prices rec'd by farmers[2]	Ratio[3]
1975	47	73	155	1995	109	102	93
1980	75	98	131	1996	115	112	98
1985	86	91	106	1997	118	107	91
1990	99	104	105	1998	115	102	89
1991	100	100	99	1999	115	96	83
1992	101	98	97	2000	120	96	80
1993	103	101	98	2001	123	102	83
1994	106	100	94	2002	124	98	79

1. Commodities and services, interest, taxes, and wage rates. 2. All farm products. 3. Ratio of index of prices received by farmers to index of prices paid by farmers. May not compute directly due to rounding. *Source:* U.S. Department of Agriculture, National Agricultural Statistics Service. Web: www.usda.gov.

Number of Farms by State, 2000–2002

State	2000	2001	2002	State	2000	2001	2002
Alabama	47,000	47,000	47,000	Nebraska	54,000	53,000	52,000
Alaska	580	580	590	Nevada	3,000	3,000	3,000
Arizona	7,500	7,300	7,300	New Hampshire	3,100	3,100	3,100
Arkansas	48,000	48,000	48,500	New Jersey	9,600	9,600	9,600
California	87,500	85,000	84,000	New Mexico	15,200	15,000	15,000
Colorado	29,500	30,000	30,000	New York	38,000	37,500	37,000
Connecticut	3,900	3,900	3,900	North Carolina	57,000	56,000	56,000
Delaware	2,600	2,500	2,400	North Dakota	30,300	30,300	30,000
Florida	44,000	44,000	44,000	Ohio	80,000	78,000	78,000
Georgia	50,000	50,000	50,000	Oklahoma	85,000	86,000	87,000
Hawaii	5,500	5,300	5,300	Oregon	40,000	40,000	41,000
Idaho	24,500	24,000	24,000	Pennsylvania	59,000	59,000	59,000
Illinois	78,000	76,000	76,000	Rhode Island	700	700	700
Indiana	64,000	63,000	63,000	South Carolina	24,000	24,000	24,500
Iowa	95,000	93,500	92,500	South Dakota	32,500	32,500	32,500
Kansas	64,000	63,000	63,000	Tennessee	90,000	91,000	90,000
Kentucky	90,000	88,000	89,000	Texas	226,000	227,000	230,000
Louisiana	29,500	29,000	29,000	Utah	15,500	15,000	15,000
Maine	6,800	6,700	6,700	Vermont	6,700	6,600	6,600
Maryland	12,400	12,400	12,200	Virginia	49,000	49,000	49,000
Massachusetts	6,100	6,000	6,000	Washington	40,000	39,000	39,000
Michigan	52,000	52,000	52,000	West Virginia	20,500	20,500	20,500
Minnesota	79,000	79,000	79,000	Wisconsin	77,000	77,000	77,000
Mississippi	43,000	42,000	43,000	Wyoming	9,200	9,200	9,200
Missouri	109,000	108,000	107,000	**U.S. total**	**2,172,280**	**2,155,680**	**2,158,090**
Montana	27,600	27,500	28,000				

NOTE: A farm is any establishment from which $1,000 or more of agricultural products were sold or would normally be sold during the year. *Source:* U.S. Department of Agriculture. Web: www.usda.gov.

Number of Farms, Land in Farms, and Average-Size Farm: United States, 1990–2002

Year	Number of farms	Land in farms (1,000 acres)	Average farm size (acres)	Year	Number of farms	Land in farms (1,000 acres)	Average farm size (acres)
1990	2,145,820	986,850	460	1997	2,190,510	956,010	436
1991	2,116,760	981,736	464	1998	2,191,360	953,500	435
1992	2,107,840	978,503	464	1999	2,192,070	947,440	432
1993	2,201,590	968,845	440	2000	2,172,280	943,090	434
1994	2,197,690	965,935	440	2001	2,155,680	941,310	437
1995	2,196,400	962,515	438	2002	2,158,090	941,480	436
1996	2,190,500	958,675	438				

NOTE: A farm is any establishment from which $1,000 or more of agricultural products were sold or would normally be sold during the year. *Source:* U.S. Department of Agriculture. Web: www.usda.gov.

Agricultural Output by State, 2002 Crops

State	Corn (1,000 bu)	Wheat (1,000 bu)	Cotton, ginned (1,000 ba)	Potatoes (1,000 cwt)	Rice (1,000 cwt)	Cattle[1] (1,000 head)	Hogs and pigs[2] (1,000 head)
Alabama	15,840	2,400	575	554		1,440	165
Alaska						11.5	1.2
Arizona	5,180	9,455	576	2,106		820	143
Arkansas	34,840	38,640	1,650		96,752	1,850	305
California	25,500	31,500	2,010	17,695	42,989	5,250	135
Colorado	112,320	38,700		30,189		2,650	790
Connecticut						56	3.8
Delaware	13,861	4,060		936		25	22
Florida	3,264	301	83	9,659		1,750	35
Georgia	33,350	8,200	1,650			1,290	345
Hawaii						150	24
Idaho	8,000	87,660		133,385		2,000	22
Illinois	1,496,0000	31,850		1,984		1,360	4,050
Indiana	631,620	17,490		728		860	3,150
Iowa	1,963,500	800				3,600	15,300
Kansas	290,000	267,300	76	986		6,350	1,530
Kentucky	106,080	18,020				2,430	370
Louisiana	63,320	8,800	750		29,400	860	20
Maine				16,960		93	6
Maryland	32,300	11,880		1,175		240	45
Massachusetts				740		49	16.5
Michigan	232,300	32,830		13,878		990	860
Minnesota	1,051,900	62,240		18,700		2,470	5,900
Mississippi	66,250	9,020	1,980		16,192	1,070	275
Missouri	283,500	34,200	610	1,296	11,011	4,500	2,950
Montana	1,820	109,895		3,224		2,400	185
Nebraska	940,800	48,640		8,611		6,200	2,900
Nevada		405		2,584		510	6.5
New Hampshire						40	3.2
New Jersey	4,060	1,856		689		46	15
New Mexico	8,820	3,740	114	2,336		1,590	3
New York	43,650	7,424		5,500		1,450	86
North Carolina	58,100	20,160	790	3,570		920	9,600
North Dakota	114,425	216,610		23,460		1,880	154
Ohio	252,560	50,220		1,008		1,220	1,440
Oklahoma	24,700	98,000	200			5,400	2,490
Oregon	3,105	34,010		24,936		1,360	31
Pennsylvania	59,160	9,990		2,590		1,630	1,080
Rhode Island				90		5.5	2.9
South Carolina	11,960	7,030	130			435	300
South Dakota	304,000	42,235		330		3,700	1,290
Tennessee	66,340	13,800	813			2,270	220
Texas	205,660	78,300	5,039	5,360	14,616	14,000	930
Utah	2,030	4,892		244		880	670
Vermont						280	2.5
Virginia	20,130	10,710	99	1,386		1,630	400
Washington	13,300	129,695		95,200		1,100	24
West Virginia	3,150	336				405	11
Wisconsin	391,500	10,771		31,125		3,300	520
Wyoming	4,464	2,376				1,290	115
Total U.S.	**9,007,659**	**1,616,441**	**17,145**	**463,214**	**210,960**	**96,106**	**58,943**

NOTE: All figures are for the year 2002, unless otherwise indicated. 1. Inventory as of Jan. 1, 2003. 2. Inventory as of Dec. 1, 2002. *Source:* U.S. Department of Agriculture, National Agricultural Statistics Service. Web: www.usda.gov.

Largest Bankruptcies, 1980–Present

Company	Bankruptcy date	Total assets pre-bankruptcy (in millions)
Worldcom, Inc.[1]	7/21/2002	$103,914
Enron Corp.[2]	12/2/2001	63,392
Conseco, Inc	12/18/02	61,392
Texaco, Inc.	4/12/87	35,892
Financial Corp. of America	9/9/88	33,864
Global Crossing Ltd.	1/28/2002	30,185
UAL Corp.	12/9/2002	25,197
Adelphia Communications	6/25/2002	24,499
Pacific Gas and Electric Co.	4/6/2001	21,470
MCorp	3/31/89	20,228
First Executive Corp.	5/13/91	15,193
Gibraltar Financial Corp.	2/8/90	15,011
Kmart Corp.	1/22/2002	14,600
FINOVA Group, Inc. (The)	3/7/2001	14,050
HomeFed Corp.	10/22/92	13,885
Southeast Banking Corp.	9/20/91	13,390
NTL, Inc.	5/8/2002	13,003
Reliance Group Holdings, Inc.	6/12/2001	12,598
Imperial Corp. of America	2/28/90	12,263
Federal-Mogul Corp.	10/1/2001	10,150
First City Bancorp. of Texas	10/31/92	9,943
First Capital Holdings	5/30/91	9,675
Baldwin-United	9/26/83	9,383

1. Worldcom, Inc. assets taken from the audited annual report dated 12/31/2001. 2. The Enron assets were taken from the tax documents filed on 11/19/2001. The company has announced that the financials were under review at the time of filing for Chapter 11. *Source:* New Generation Research, Inc. Web: www.bankruptcydata.com.

Leading National Advertisers

(in millions; ranked by total U.S. advertising spending)

Rank	Advertiser	2002 ad dollars
1.	General Motors Corp.	$3,652.2
2.	AOL Time Warner	2,922.8
3.	Procter & Gamble Co.	2,673.4
4.	Pfizer	2,566.2
5.	Ford Motor Co.	2,251.8
6.	DaimlerChrysler	2,031.8
7.	Walt Disney Co.	1,803.0
8.	Johnson & Johnson	1,799.0
9.	Sears, Roebuck & Co.	1,661.2
10.	Unilever	1,640.0
11.	Sony Corp.	1,621.1
12.	GlaxoSmithKline	1,554.0
13.	Toyota Motor Corp.	1,552.7
14.	Verizon Communications	$1,527.5
15.	McDonald's Corp.	1,335.7
16.	Viacom	1,259.8
17.	Altria Group	1,206.0
18.	Honda Motor Co.	1,192.8
19.	Merck & Co.	1,158.4
20.	L'Oreal	1,117.7
21.	PepsiCo	1,113.9
22.	J.C. Penney Corp.	1,108.0
23.	SBC Communications	1,091.6
24.	U.S. Government	1,082.8
25.	Nestle	1,073.2

Source: AdAge. Web: adage.com.

World Port Ranking, 2000

Total cargo volume, metric tons (1,000s)

Rank	Port	Country	Tons
1.	Singapore	Singapore	325,591
2.	Rotterdam	Netherlands	319,969
3.	South Louisiana	United States	197,680
4.	Shanghai	China	186,287
5.	Hong Kong	China	174,642
6.	Houston	United States	173,770
7.	Chiba	Japan	169,043
8.	Nagoya	Japan	153,370
9.	Ulsan	South Korea	151,067
10.	Kwangyang	South Korea	139,476
11.	Antwerp	Belgium	130,531
12.	New York/New Jersey	United States	125,885
13.	Inchon	South Korea	120,398
14.	Pusan	South Korea	117,229
15.	Yokohama	Japan	116,994
16.	Kaohsiung	Taiwan	115,287
17.	Guangzhou	China	101,521
18.	Quinhuangdao	China	97,430
19.	Ningbo	China	96,601
20.	Marseilles	France	94,097
21.	Osaka	Japan	92,948
22.	Richards Bay	South Africa	91,519
23.	Kitakyushu	Japan	87,346
24.	Qingdao	China	86,360
25.	Hamburg	Germany	85,863

Container traffic (TEUs)[1]

Rank	Port	Country	TEUs
1.	Hong Kong	China	18,098,000
2.	Singapore	Singapore	17,090,000
3.	Pusan	South Korea	7,540,387
4.	Kaohsiung	Taiwan	7,425,832
5.	Rotterdam	Netherlands	6,274,000
6.	Shanghai	China	5,613,000
7.	Los Angeles	United States	4,879,429
8.	Long Beach	United States	4,600,787
9.	Hamburg	Germany	4,248,247
10.	Antwerp	Belgium	4,082,334
11.	Tanjung Priok	Indonesia	3,368,629
12.	Port Kelang	Malaysia	3,206,753
13.	Dubai	U.A.E.	3,058,866
14.	New York/New Jersey	United States	3,050,036
15.	Tokyo	Japan	2,898,724
16.	Felixstowe	U.K.	2,793,217
17.	Bremer Ports	Germany	2,712,420
18.	Gioia Tauro	Italy	2,652,701
19.	San Juan	United States	2,333,788
20.	Yokohama	Japan	2,317,393
21.	Manila	Philippines	2,288,599
22.	Kobe	Japan	2,265,992
23.	Yantian	China	2,139,680
24.	Qingdao	China	2,120,000
25.	Laem Chabang	Thailand	2,105,262

1. TEU denotes twenty-foot equivalent units. *Source:* American Association of Port Authorities. Web: www.aapa-ports.org.

United States' Largest Banks
(in millions of U.S. dollars)

Rank	Name (city, state)	Consolidated assets
1.	J. P. Morgan Chase & Company (New York, N.Y.)	$621,696
2.	Bank of America Corp. (Charlotte, N.C.)	574,410
3.	Citigroup (New York, N.Y.)	514,803
4.	Wachovia Corp. (Charlotte, N.C.)	323,783
5.	Bank One Corp. (Chicago, Ill.)	226,331
6.	Wells Fargo & Company (San Francisco, Calif.)	196,755
7.	FleetBoston Financial Corp. (Providence, R.I.)	192,100
8.	U.S. BC (Cincinnati, Ohio)	177,979
9.	Suntrust Banks, Inc. (Atlanta, Ga.)	118,315
10.	HSBC North America Inc. (Buffalo, N.Y.)	85,936
11.	Bank of New York Company, Inc. (New York, N.Y.)	76,683
12.	Keycorp (Cleveland, Ohio)	76,669
13.	State Street Corp. (Boston, Mass.)	71,787
14.	BB&T Corp. (Winston-Salem, N.C.)	63,996
15.	PNC Financial Services Group, Inc. (Pittsburgh, Pa.)	62,331
16.	ABN Amro North America Holding Company (Chicago, Ill.)	60,497
17.	Bank One Corp. (Columbus, Ohio)	56,850
18.	MBNA Corp. (Wilmington, Del.)	52,007
19.	Fifth Third Bancorp (Cincinnati, Ohio)	51,761
20.	Southtrust Corp. (Birmingham, Ala.)	51,329
21.	Wells Fargo & Company (Minneapolis, Minn.)	50,105
22.	National City Corp. (Indianapolis, Ind.)	47,656
23.	ABN Amro North America Holding Company (Troy, Mich.)	47,623
24.	Regions Financial Corp. (Birmingham, Ala.)	45,336
25.	National City Corp. (Cleveland, Ohio)	43,814
26.	Charter One Financial, Inc. (Cleveland, Ohio)	43,342
27.	Amsouth Bancorporation (Birmingham, Ala.)	42,090
28.	Comerica (Detroit, Mich.)	41,688
29.	Citigroup (Sioux Falls, S.D.)	41,134
30.	Unionbancal Corp. (San Francisco, Calif.)	39,834

NOTE: As of March 31, 2003. *Source:* Federal Reserve System, National Information Center.

Largest U.S. Businesses

2002 rank	Company	Revenues ($ millions)
1.	Wal-Mart Stores	$246,525.0
2.	General Motors	186,763.0
3.	Exxon Mobil	182,466.0
4.	Ford Motor	163,630.0
5.	General Electric	131,698.0
6.	Citigroup	100,789.0
7.	ChevronTexaco	92,043.0
8.	International Business Machines	83,132.0
9.	American Intl. Group	67,722.8
10.	Verizon Communications	67,625.0
11.	Altria Group	62,182.0
12.	ConocoPhillips	58,394.0
13.	Home Depot	58,247.0
14.	Hewlett-Packard	56,588.0
15.	Boeing	54,069.0
16.	Fannie Mae	52,901.1
17.	Merck	51,790.3
18.	Kroger	51,759.5
19.	Cardinal Health	51,135.7
20.	McKesson	50,006.0
21.	State Farm Insurance	49,653.7
22.	AT&T	46,727.0
23.	Bank of America Corp.	45,732.0
24.	Amerisourcebergen	45,234.8
25.	Target	43,917.0
26.	J.P. Morgan Chase	43,372.0
27.	SBC Communications	43,138.0
28.	Berkshire Hathaway	42,353.0
29.	AOL Time Warner	41,780.0
30.	Sears Roebuck	41,366.0
31.	Procter & Gamble	40,238.0
32.	Freddie Mac	39,663.0
33.	Costco Wholesale	38,762.5
34.	Johnson & Johnson	36,298.0
35.	Albertson's	35,916.0
36.	Dell Computer	35,404.0
37.	Pfizer	35,281.0
38.	MetLife	34,055.0
39.	Kmart	32,765.0
40.	Morgan Stanley	$32,415.0
41.	Safeway	32,399.2
42.	J.C. Penney	32,347.0
43.	United Parcel Service	31,272.0
44.	Allstate	29,579.0
45.	Walgreen	28,681.1
46.	Wells Fargo	28,473.0
47.	Microsoft	28,365.0
48.	Merrill Lynch	28,253.0
49.	United Technologies	28,212.0
50.	ConAgra	27,629.6
51.	Dow Chemical	27,609.0
52.	Marathon Oil	27,470.0
53.	Delphi	27,427.0
54.	Sprint	27,180.0
55.	Valero Energy	26,976.3
56.	Lockheed Martin	26,806.0
57.	Prudential Financial	26,797.0
58.	Intel	26,764.0
59.	Motorola	26,679.0
60.	Lowe's	26,490.9
61.	Walt Disney	25,329.0
62.	PepsiCo	25,112.0
63.	UnitedHealth Group	25,020.0
64.	International Paper	24,976.0
65.	New York Life Insurance	24,720.7
66.	Viacom	24,605.7
67.	DuPont	24,522.0
68.	CVS	24,181.5
69.	American Express	23,807.0
70.	Wachovia Corp.	23,591.0
71.	Archer Daniels Midland	23,453.6
72.	Tyson Foods	23,367.0
73.	Sysco	23,350.5
74.	Georgia-Pacific	23,271.0
75.	Goldman Sachs Group	22,854.0
76.	Ingram Micro	22,459.3
77.	BellSouth	22,440.0

2002 rank	Company	Revenues ($ millions)	2002 rank	Company	Revenues ($ millions)
78.	Honeywell Intl.	22,274.0	90.	HCA	$19,729.0
79.	Bank One Corp.	$22,171.0	91.	Best Buy	19,597.0
80.	Electronic Data Systems	21,782.0	92.	Coca-Cola	19,564.0
81.	Supervalu	20,908.5	93.	Autonation	19,478.5
82.	Alcoa	20,618.0	94.	Washington Mutual	19,037.0
83.	FedEx	20,607.0	95.	Cisco Systems	18,915.0
84.	Mass. Mutual Life Insurance	20,247.1	96.	Weyerhaeuser	18,521.0
85.	Caterpillar	20,152.0	97.	Visteon	18,395.0
86.	Johnson Controls	20,103.4	98.	Bristol-Myers Squibb	18,119.0
87.	Cigna	19,915.0	99.	Northrop Grumman	17,837.0
88.	Aetna	19,878.7	100.	Abbott Laboratories	17,684.7
89.	TIAA-CREF	19,791.0			

Source: Fortune 500, For more detailed information, visit *Fortune* on the Web, www.fortune.com/.

Most and Least Fuel Efficient Vehicles, 2003

Most fuel efficient

Vehicle	MPG City	MPG Hwy.
Overall: Honda Insight	61	68
Two seater: Honda Insight	61	68
Compact car: Toyota Prius	52	45
Midsize car: Honda Accord	26	34
Large car: Chevrolet Impala	21	32
Small station wagon: Volkswagen Jetta Wagon (diesel)	42	50
Midsize station wagon: Ford Focus station wagon	27	36
Small pickup truck: Chevrolet S10 Pickup (Flex-Fuel) 2WD	22	28
Standard pickup truck (tie): Ford Ranger Pickup 2WD and Mazda B2300 2WD	24	28
Sport utility vehicle: Toyota Rav4 2WD	25	31
Minivan (tie): Chrysler Voyager/ Town & Country 2WD and Dodge Caravan 2WD	19	27
Passenger van (tie): Chevrolet Astro 2WD and GMC Safari 2WD	15	20

Least fuel efficient

Vehicle	MPG City	MPG Hwy.
Two seater: Ferrari Enzo Ferrari	8	12
Compact car: Bentley Continental R	11	16
Midsize car: Bentley Arnage	10	14
Large car: Bentlley Arnage LWB	10	14
Small station wagon: BMW 540i Sport Wagon	17	21
Midsize station wagon: Audi S6 Avant	15	21
Small pickup truck (tie): Chevrolet S10 Pickup 2WD and GMC Sonoma 2WD	16	22
Standard pickup truck: Dodge Ram 1500 Pickup 4WD	11	15
Sport utility vehicle: Mercedes-Benz G500 AWD	12	14
Minivan: Kia Sedona	15	20
Passenger van: Dodge Ram Wagon 2500 2WD	12	17

Source: www.Fueleconomy.gov.

Life Insurance in Force

(in millions of dollars)

As of Dec. 31	Ordinary	Group	Industrial	Credit	Total
1900	$ 6,124	—	$ 1,449	—	$ 7,573
1915	16,650	$ 100	4,279	—	21,029
1930	78,576	9,801	17,963	$ 73	106,413
1945	101,550	22,172	27,675	365	151,762
1950	149,116	47,793	33,415	3,844	234,168
1955	216,812	101,345	39,682	14,493	372,332
1960	341,881	175,903	39,563	29,101	586,448
1965	499,638	308,078	39,818	53,020	900,554
1970	734,730	551,357	38,644	77,392	1,402,123
1975	1,083,421	904,695	39,423	112,032	2,139,571
1980	1,760,474	1,579,355	35,994	165,215	3,541,038
1985	3,247,289	2,561,595	28,250	215,973	6,053,107
1990	5,366,982	3,753,506	24,071	248,038	9,392,597
1995	6,872,252	4,604,856	18,134	201,083	11,696,325
1998	8,505,894	5,735,273	17,365	212,917	14,471,449
1999	(1)	6,110,218	(1)	213,453	15,496,069
2000	(1)	6,376,127	(1)	200,770	15,953,267
2001	(1)	6,765,074	(1)	178,851	16,289,648

1. Starting in 1999, the figures for Ordinary and Industrial have been combined as Individual, for a total of $9,172,397 in 1999, $9,376,370 in 2000, and $9,345,723 in 2001. *Source:* American Council of Life Insurers.

Top NYSE Stocks by Dollar Value

2002 Rank	Issue (symbol) (2001 rank)	2002 dollar volume (in millions)
1.	General Electric Company (GE) (2)	$160,473
2.	International Business Machines (IBM) (1)	150,066
3.	Citigroup Inc. (C) (4)	145,161
4.	Tyco International (TYC) (7)	117,919
5.	Pfizer Inc (PFE) (5)	115,292
6.	Wal-Mart Stores (WMT) (12)	103,178
7.	Johnson & Johnson (JNJ) (10)	98,076
8.	Bank of America Corporation (BAC) (15)	96,063
9.	American Int'l Group, Inc. (AIG) (8)	94,698
10.	Exxon Mobil Corporation (XOM) (9)	94,000
11.	Merck & Co. (MRK) (11)	80,928
12.	AOL Time Warner Inc. (AOL) (3)	79,907
13.	Philip Morris Companies (MO) (19)	79,069
14.	Home Depot, Inc. (HD) (21)	78,713
15.	Goldman Sachs Group (GS) (25)	76,766
16.	Procter & Gamble Company (PG) (35)	73,912
17.	Fannie Mae (FNM) (20)	70,004
18.	J.P. Morgan Chase & Co. (JPM) (13)	67,080
19.	Merrill Lynch & Co. (MER) (18)	62,853
20.	3M Company (MMM) (39)	62,794
21.	Viacom Inc. (VIA.B) (27)	60,755
22.	Verizon Communications (VZ) (28)	57,029
23.	Texas Instruments Incorporated (TXN) (14)	56,878
24.	Coca-Cola Company (KO) (40)	56,793
25.	Bristol-Myers Squibb Company (BMY) (22)	56,666
26.	Morgan Stanley (MWD) (16)	56,504
27.	Wells Fargo & Company (WFC) (43)	$55,050
28.	Eli Lilly and Company (LLY) (26)	52,389
29.	Pharmacia Corporation (PHA) (30)	52,097
30.	Pepsico, Inc. (PEP) (42)	51,863
31.	SBC Communications (SBC) (24)	51,571
32.	ChevronTexaco Corporation (CVX)	49,925
33.	General Motors Corporation (GM)	49,626
34.	Freddie Mac (FRE) (38)	49,197
35.	Abbott Laboratories (ABT)	47,030
36.	Wyeth (WYE)	46,712
37.	Royal Dutch Petroleum Company (RD)	46,450
38.	UnitedHealth Group (UNH)	45,137
39.	Nokia Corporation (NOK) (17)	44,621
40.	Household International, Inc. (HI)	44,374
41.	Lowe's Companies, Inc. (LOW)	43,200
42.	Northrop Grumman Corporation (NOC)	42,369
43.	AT&T Corp. (T) (31)	41,868
44.	Micron Technology, Inc. (MU) (23)	41,734
45.	American Express Company (AXP) (37)	41,298
46.	United Parcel Service (UPS)	40,939
47.	Electronic Data Systems (EDS)	39,855
48.	United Technologies Corporation (UTX)	39,307
49.	Schering-Plough Corporation (SGP) (29)	38,664
50.	Capital One Financial Corporation (COF)	38,619

Source: New York Stock Exchange.

50 Most Active Stocks on NYSE

2002 rank	Company name (symbol) (2001 rank)	2002 share volume (in millions)
1.	Lucent Technologies Inc.(LU) (2)	5,572.20
2.	Tyco International (TYC) (15)	5,267.20
3.	General Electric Company (GE) (1)	5,221.60
4.	AOL Time Warner Inc. (AOL)	4,514.50
5.	Nortel Networks Corporation (NT) (4)	4,293.20
6.	Citigroup Inc. (C) (7)	3,823.40
7.	Pfizer Inc (PFE) (8)	3,411.20
8.	EMC Corporation (EMC) (3)	3,204.90
9.	AT&T Corp. (T) (10)	3,093.60
10.	AT&T Wireless Services, Inc. (AWE) (22)	2,711.10
11.	Nokia Corporation (NOK) (6)	2,622.20
12.	Qwest Communications International (Q) (18)	2,594.60
13.	Motorola, Inc. (MOT) (12)	2,526.40
14.	Exxon Mobil Corporation (XOM) (23)	2,523.00
15.	J.P. Morgan Chase & Co. (JPM) (41)	2,438.60
16.	Texas Instruments Inc. (TXN) (13)	2,399.20
17.	Sprint Corporation (PCS Grp.) (PCS) (24)	2,395.90
18.	Home Depot, Inc. (HD) (26)	2,265.80
19.	Ford Motor Company (F) (48)	1,996.60
20.	Corning Incorporated (GLW) (14)	1,922.80
21.	Liberty Media Corporation (L)	1,896.50
22.	Wal-Mart Stores (WMT) (27)	1,881.70
23.	Bristol-Myers Squibb (BMY) (45)	1,838.30
24.	Micron Technology, Inc. (MU) (17)	1,836.20
25.	Int'l Business Machines (IBM) (19)	1,805.40
26.	Johnson & Johnson (JNJ) (31)	1,730.00
27.	SBC Communications (SBC) (30)	1,728.90
28.	Walt Disney Company (DIS) (28)	1,716.40
29.	Philip Morris Companies (MO) (29)	1,706.60
30.	Hewlett-Packard Company (HPQ) (21)	1,659.90
31.	K-Mart (KM)	1,573.90
32.	El Paso Corporation (EP)	1,538.00
33.	Merck & Co. (MRK) (39)	1,517.30
34.	Verizon Communications (VZ) (50)	1,492.40
35.	Schering-Plough Corporation (SGP) (32)	1,491.30
36.	Merrill Lynch & Co. (MER) (37)	1,481.20
37.	Calpine Corporation (CPN) (47)	1,480.20
38.	American Int'l Group, Inc. (AIG) (40)	1,440.90
39.	Bank of America Corporation (BAC) (35)	1,432.10
40.	Viacom Inc. (VIA.B) (38)	1,405.50
41.	Solectron Corporation (SLR) (34)	1,340.00
42.	McDonald's Corporation (MCD)	1,320.00
43.	Cendant Corporation (CD) (25)	1,310.40
44.	Taiwan Semiconductor (TSM)	1,301.00
45.	Pharmacia Corporation (PHA) (43)	1,264.10
46.	Morgan Stanley (MWD) (20)	1,262.00
47.	Agere Systems Inc.(AGRA) (42)	1,254.40
48.	Gap, Inc. (GPS) (49)	1,250.30
49.	Advanced Micro Devices, Inc. (AMD) (33)	1,250.10
50.	Williams Companies (WMB)	1,183.30

Source: New York Stock Exchange.

Top NASDAQ Stocks by Market Value, 2002

Rank	Name	Symbol	Market value (in thousands)
1.	Microsoft Corporation	MSFT	$276,411,465
2.	Intel Corporation	INTC	103,151,250
3.	Cisco Systems, Inc.	CSCO	94,649,242
4.	Dell Computer Corporation	DELL	69,252,375
5.	Amgen Inc.	AMGN	62,216,770
6.	Oracle Corporation	ORCL	57,628,098
7.	Fifth Third Bancorp	FITB	33,829,487
8.	Comcast Corporation	CMCSA	31,942,111
9.	QUALCOMM Incorporated	QCOM	28,569,098
10.	Applied Materials, Inc.	AMAT	21,554,904
11.	eBay Inc.	EBAY	20,938,204
12.	Comcast Corporation	CMCSK	20,685,844
13.	Costco Wholesale Corporation	COST	12,789,467
14.	Nextel Communications, Inc.	NXTL	10,712,128
15.	Maxim Integrated Products, Inc.	MXIM	10,584,496
16.	Paychex, Inc.	PAYX	10,493,246
17.	Bed Bath & Beyond Inc.	BBBY	10,103,513
18.	Sun Microsystems, Inc.	SUNW	9,686,565
19.	Yahoo! Inc.	YHOO	9,661,133
20.	Intuit Inc.	INTU	9,629,767
21.	USA Interactive	USAI	8,809,256
22.	SouthTrust Corporation	SOTR	8,619,073
23.	Staples, Inc.	SPLS	8,611,779
24.	Linear Technology Corporation	LLTC	8,024,460
25.	Starbucks Corporation	SBUX	7,914,390
26.	Cintas Corporation	CTAS	7,785,095
27.	Northern Trust Corporation	NTRS	$7,743,351
28.	Apollo Group, Inc.	APOL	7,654,636
29.	Biomet, Inc.	BMET	7,445,409
30.	Amazon.com, Inc.	AMZN	7,205,874
31.	Chiron Corporation	CHIR	7,073,387
32.	Electronic Arts Inc.	ERTS	7,032,103
33.	Xilinx, Inc.	XLNX	6,944,445
34.	Teva Pharmaceutical Industries Limited	TEVA	6,866,557
35.	MedImmune, Inc.	MEDI	6,819,969
36.	Gilead Sciences, Inc.	GILD	6,687,188
37.	KLA-Tencor Corporation	KLAC	6,673,930
38.	Fiserv, Inc.	FISV	6,497,215
39.	VERITAS Software Corporation	VRTS	6,429,192
40.	Genzyme Corporation	GENZ	6,344,717
41.	Cincinnati Financial Corporation	CINF	6,063,950
42.	Biogen, Inc.	BGEN	5,971,504
43.	Adobe Systems Incorporated	ADBE	5,859,782
44.	Symantec Corporation	SYMC	5,766,680
45.	PeopleSoft, Inc.	PSFT	5,727,662
46.	EchoStar Communications Corporation	DISH	5,394,800
47.	PACCAR Inc.	PCAR	5,345,821
48.	Apple Computer, Inc.	AAPL	5,142,836
49.	IDEC Pharmaceuticals Corporation	IDPH	5,076,105
50.	Microchip Technology Incorporated	MCHP	4,965,404

Source: The NASDAQ Stock Market, Inc.

Most Active NASDAQ Stocks, 2002

Rank	Name	Symbol	Total volume (in thousands)
1.	Cisco Systems, Inc.	CSCO	19,993,758
2.	Sun Microsystems, Inc.	SUNW	17,540,084
3.	Intel Corporation	INTC	14,859,198
4.	Oracle Corporation	ORCL	12,672,133
5.	Microsoft Corporation	MSFT	9,901,385
6.	Applied Materials, Inc.	AMAT	8,635,815
7.	JDS Uniphase Corporation	JDSU	6,933,046
8.	Nextel Communications, Inc.	NXTL	6,249,307
9.	Dell Computer Corporation	DELL	6,172,229
10.	Brocade Communications Systems, Inc.	BRCD	4,332,013
11.	Siebel Systems, Inc.	SEBL	4,177,516
12.	QUALCOMM Incorporated	QCOM	4,009,153
13.	Amgen Inc.	AMGN	3,678,698
14.	Juniper Networks, Inc.	JNPR	3,667,978
15.	KLA-Tencor Corporation	KLAC	3,619,546
16.	QLogic Corporation	QLGC	3,204,959
17.	Broadcom Corporation	BRCM	3,194,437
18.	VERITAS Software Corporation	VRTS	3,136,361
19.	Comcast Corporation	CMCS	2,989,444
20.	Flextronics International Ltd.	FLEX	2,849,305
21.	BEA Systems, Inc.	BEAS	2,829,789
22.	Yahoo! Inc.	YHOO	2,800,545
23.	Xilinx, Inc.	XLNX	2,734,386
24.	CIENA Corporation	CIEN	2,699,401
25.	NVIDIA Corporation	NVDA	2,692,773
26..	Novellus Systems, Inc.	NVLS	2,407,196
27.	Sanmina-SCI Corporation	SANM	2,302,717
28.	Network Appliance, Inc.	NTAP	2,242,141
29.	Atmel Corporation	ATML	2,220,169
30.	i2 Technologies, Inc.	ITWO	2,178,959
31.	PeopleSoft, Inc.	PSFT	2,162,844
32.	Amazon.com, Inc.	AMZN	2,135,781
33.	Applied Digital Solutions, Inc.	ADSX	2,101,885
34.	Maxim Integrated Products, Inc.	MXIM	2,092,626
35.	Altera Corporation	ALTR	2,078,789
36.	RF Micro Devices, Inc.	RFMD	2,021,069
37.	Charter Communications, Inc.	CHTR	1,986,890
38.	ADC Telecommunications, Inc.	ADCT	1,850,159
39.	Vitesse Semiconductor Corporation	VTSS	1,846,726
40.	Linear Technology Corporation	LLTC	1,844,761
41.	PMC - Sierra, Inc.	PMCS	1,799,136
42.	VeriSign, Inc.	VRSN	1,770,000
43.	eBay Inc.	EBAY	1,764,342
44.	Sonus Networks, Inc.	SONS	1,755,494
45.	Check Point Software Technologies Ltd.	CHKP	1,665,146
46.	Applied Micro Circuits Corporation	AMCC	1,648,853
47.	Conexant Systems, Inc.	CNXT	1,465,803
48.	Apple Computer, Inc.	AAPL	1,402,961
49.	Millennium Pharmaceuticals, Inc.	MLNM	1,308,794
50.	Costco Wholesale Corporation	COST	1,294,692

Source: The NASDAQ Stock Market, Inc.

The Backwards Loan

Here's why "reverse" mortgages are the rage—and how they can hurt you

By JEAN CHATZKY TIME

The buzz among homeowners continues to be about mortgage refinancing. Why? Because interest rates are still so low (6% for a typical 30-year loan). But what's more intriguing—and maybe a little scary—is the big surge in people taking out reverse mortgages. These are loans that let homeowners who are 62 or older take cash from their home equity and pay nothing back—not a cent—until they move out or die. Some reverse mortgages guarantee a fixed monthly payment for life (an annuity). By the latest measures available, the pace of new reverse mortgages has leaped 74% in just one year.

Here's a concern: though a reverse mortgage can be a good financial move under the right circumstances, it can also be an unnecessary straitjacket. Many seniors, hurt by falling yield payouts from their retirement accounts, are casting about for ways to maintain their standard of living. At the same time, lenders are marketing reverse mortgages more aggressively—all in all, a recipe for trouble. So here's what you (or your parents) need to know:

The Mechanics

Reverse-mortgage payouts come in three forms: a monthly payment for as long as you or your spouse lives (the annuity), a lump sum, or a line of credit. You can combine these options.

There's no credit or income requirement. The amount you can get depends largely on the value of your house but also on your age. The older you are, the more you can get, but loan caps usually range from $155,000 in rural areas to $281,000 in metropolitan areas.

As an example, consider a 77-year-old Chicago couple with a home worth $250,000. On the basis of life expectancies, they would qualify for a reverse-mortgage lump sum or line of credit of $175,600 or a monthly payout that would add up to that amount by the time they were both expected to be dead, minus loan costs (in this case, they would net $1,069 a month).

The lenders who dreamed up reverse mortgages in the 1950s figured the annuity option would be the most popular, since it gives homeowners a chance to beat the bank (if they live longer than expected). Instead, two-thirds take the line of credit, figuring to use only as much as they need and preserve the rest, according to Ken Scholen, a home-equity expert at the AARP. Any unused portion of the credit line grows with inflation.

When the homeowner moves out of the home or dies, the amount that must be paid back to the bank is the sum of the payouts plus interest (more on the interest later) as well as any fees financed as part of the loan.

The Costs

Reverse mortgages involve costs, just like regular mortgages, that can eat up any financial advantage in the short term. These costs often get swept under the rug in the sales pitch because they are not up-front charges but are subtracted from the amount the borrower eventually receives. Take the house from the example above, with a $175,600 reverse mortgage. Typical costs would include an origination fee of $4,700, mortgage insurance of $4,700, other finance costs of $1,200 and servicing fees (deducted monthly but computed up front) of $4,500—leaving a payout of only $160,500. Live in the house longer than the bank expects, and you are ahead. Leave (or die) much sooner, and you have paid too much.

Other Options

Why not just sell your home and move? Particularly now, you may find that you can get more money than you ever imagined, then scale down close by or relocate to a lower-cost area. Also talk to your grown kids. Often parents mistakenly assume that their kids want the family home (when they don't), or they don't have extra money with which to help their parents (when they do). Believe it or not, federal law requires borrowers to go through financial counseling before taking a reverse mortgage—a paternalistic rule but probably a helpful one. The counseling takes two or three hours and is provided free by federally approved agencies.

The Negotiation

For the vast majority of people, a reverse mortgage insured by the Federal Housing Authority (FHA) is the best deal. This is called a home-equity conversion mortgage, and many of its costs—including interest, which floats with one-year Treasury bills and is now 3.55%—are consistent from lender to lender. So you don't have to shop or dicker. Exceptions include origination fees, which may be as high as 2% of loan value, and servicing fees, generally around $30 or so a month. Non-FHA reverse mortgages with higher loan limits are available from Fannie Mae (the Homekeeper Loan, up to $322,000). Just remember that a reverse mortgage is only for people with compelling reasons to stay in their current home. □

Money Market Interest Rates and Mortgage Rates, 1980–2001

Type	1980	1985	1990	1995	2000	2001
Federal funds, effective rate	13.35%	8.10%	8.10%	5.83%	6.24%	3.88%
Prime rate charged by banks	15.26	9.93	10.01	8.83	9.23	6.94
Discount rate[1]	11.77	7.69	6.98	5.21	5.73	3.40
Large negotiable CDs:						
3-month, secondary market	13.07	8.05	8.15	5.92	6.35	3.71
6-month, secondary market	12.94	8.24	8.17	5.98	6.46	3.66
Taxable money market funds[2]	12.68	7.71	7.82	5.48	5.89	3.67
Tax-exempt money market funds[2]	n.a.	4.90	5.45	3.39	3.54	2.24
Certificates of deposits (CDs):[3]						
6-month	n.a.	8.05	7.79	4.92	5.09	3.43
1-year	n.a.	8.53	7.92	5.39	5.46	3.60
2½-year	n.a.	9.32	7.96	5.69	5.64	3.97
5-year	n.a.	9.99	8.06	6.00	5.97	4.58
U.S. Government securities:						
Secondary market:[4]						
3-month Treasury bill	11.39	7.47	7.50	5.49	5.82	3.40
6-month Treasury bill	11.32	7.65	7.46	5.56	5.90	3.34
1-year Treasury bill	10.85	7.81	7.35	5.60	5.78	3.84
Home mortgages:						
New-home mortgage yields[5]	12.70	11.60	10.05	7.87	7.52	7.00
Conventional, 15-yr. fixed[3]	n.a.	11.48	9.73	7.39	7.76	6.53
Conventional, 30-yr. fixed[3]	n.a.	11.85	9.97	7.86	8.08	7.01

NOTE: n.a. = not available. 1. Rate for the Federal Reserve Bank of New York. 2. 12-month return for period ending Dec. 31. *Source:* iMoneyNet, Inc., Westborough, Mass., *Money Market Insight,* monthly. Web: www.imoneynet.com. 3. Annual averages. *Source:* Bankrate, Inc., North Palm Beach, Fla., *Bank Rate Monitor,* weekly. 4. Averages based on daily closing bid yields in secondary market, bank discount basis. 5. Effective rate (in the primary market) on conventional mortgages, reflecting fees and charges as well as contract rate and assumed, on the average, repayment at end of ten years. *Source:* U.S. Federal Housing Finance Board, *Rates & Terms on Conventional Home Mortgages, Annual Summary. Source:* Except as noted, Board of Governors of the Federal Reserve System, *Federal Reserve Bulletin,* monthly. From *Statistical Abstract of the United States: 2002.*

Financial Documents You Should Have

Financial advisers recommend that your long-term financial plan include the following:

Wills

A will states how you want your property disposed of after your death. Having a will saves time and money for your family, since dying without one—called "intestate"—means more money from your estate will likely go to taxes and requires extra legal fees. In addition, your property will be disposed of according to state law.

Where to store a will can be a problem. In some states safe deposit boxes are automatically sealed upon a person's death, so a copy of your will and letter of instruction should be left where your executor can find it easily.

Executor

The executor of your estate is the person (family member or attorney) or entity (such as a trust company) that carries out the instructions in your will. If you do not name an executor, the court will appoint one.

Letter of Instruction

Some experts recommend leaving a letter of instruction to let your family know: where documents are located, what money you are owed, what burial or funeral arrangements you wish, and who should be notified. This is not a substitute for a will.

Trusts

Trusts are not just for the very rich. You might want to discuss the creation of a trust with your lawyer or financial planner. Assets placed in trusts are automatically given to the beneficiaries, avoiding probate costs. A revocable living trust says who will control your assets while you are alive and after you have died.

Durable Power of Attorney for Health Care

Also called a living trust, this ensures that your affairs will be handled as you wish if you become incapacitated. Unless you specify otherwise, a court could be asked to name a guardian to handle your affairs if you could not do so. In addition to managing your money and supervising any health care arrangements, the durable power of attorney can be called upon to make life and death decisions (such as whether to switch off life support machinery).

As people live longer and need more health care, many financial advisers are also recommending long-term care insurance to cover nursing home costs.

Long-term disability insurance, which will provide for you if you become incapacitated and unable to work for a long period, is also frequently recommended. Remember, many employers offer this type of insurance but it often only applies to on-the-job injuries.

Life Insurance

Life insurance is intended to provide for those who would be hurt financially by your death. Single people with no dependents do not usually need life insurance. On the other hand, if your spouse and children would suffer if your salary came to an abrupt end, then you need life insurance. Consult a financial planner, or review the considerable amount of information available about insurance on the web, at the library, or from consumer groups.

How to Measure the Shrinking Value of the Dollar

The CPI inflation calculator uses the average Consumer Price Index for a given calendar year. This data represents changes in prices of all goods and services purchased for consumption by urban households. This index value has been calculated every year since 1913. For the current year, the latest monthly index value is used. In 2002, for example, it took $17.89 to buy what $1 bought in 1913. Note that in 1920, it cost $2.02, and declined in 1925 and through the 1930s, illustrating the effect of the Great Depression, when prices slumped. Prices did not pass $2 again until 1950.

Year	Amount it took to equal $1 in 1913	Year	Amount it took to equal $1 in 1913	Year	Amount it took to equal $1 in 1913	Year	Amount it took to equal $1 in 1913
1913	$1.00	1940	$1.41	1965	$ 3.18	1990	$13.20
1920	2.02	1945	1.82	1970	3.92	1995	15.39
1925	1.77	1950	2.43	1975	5.43	2000	17.39
1930	1.69	1955	2.71	1980	8.32	2001	17.89
1935	1.38	1960	2.99	1985	10.87	2002	17.89

Source: Bureau of Labor Statistics. Web: http://stats.bls.gov/.

Top 10 Ways to Prepare for Retirement

Source: Department of Labor. Web: http://www.dol.gov/ebsa/Publications/10_ways_to_prepare.html.

1. Know your retirement needs.

Retirement is expensive. Experts estimate that you'll need about 70% of your pre-retirement income—lower earners, 90% or more—to maintain your standard of living when you stop working.

2. Find out about Social Security.

Social Security pays the average retiree about 40% of pre-retirement earnings. Call the Social Security Administration at 1-800-772-1213 for a free Personal Earnings and Benefit Estimate Statement (PEBES).

3. Learn about your employer's pension or profit sharing plan.

If your employer offers a plan, check to see what your benefit is worth. Most employers will provide an individual benefit statement. Before you change jobs, find out what will happen to your pension. Learn what benefits you may have from previous employment. Find out if you will be entitled to benefits from your spouse's plan. For a free booklet on private pensions, call the U.S. Department of Labor at 1-800-998-7542.

4. Contribute to a tax-sheltered plan.

If your employer offers a tax-sheltered savings plan, such as a 401(k), sign up and contribute all you can. Your taxes will be lower, your company may kick in more, and automatic deductions make it easy.

5. Ask your employer to start a plan.

If your employer doesn't offer a retirement plan, suggest that he/she start one. Simplified plans can be set up by certain employers. For information on simplified employee pensions, order Internal Revenue Service Publication 590 by calling 1-800-829-3676.

6. Put money into an IRA.

You can put $2,000 a year into an Individual Retirement Account (IRA) and delay paying taxes on investment earnings until retirement age. If you don't have a retirement plan (or are in a plan and earn less than a certain amount), you can also take a tax deduction for your IRA contributions. IRS Publication 590 contains information about IRAs.

7. Don't touch your savings.

Don't dip into your retirement savings. You'll lose principal and interest, and you may lose tax benefits. If you change jobs, roll over your savings directly into an IRA or your new employer's retirement plan.

8. Start now, set goals, and stick to them.

Start early. The sooner you start saving, the more time your money has to grow.

9. Consider basic investment principles.

How you save can be as important as how much you save. Inflation and the type of investments you make play important roles in how much you'll have saved at retirement. Know how your pension or savings plan is invested.

10. Ask questions.

Talk to your employer, your bank, your union, or a financial adviser.

Retirement Information

The following government organizations offer retirement planning information:

Administration on Aging
www.aoa.dhhs.gov/default.htm
Variety of information

Department of Veteran Affairs
www.va.gov/
Material for veterans

FirstGov for Seniors
www.seniors.gov/index.htm
Federal clearinghouse

Internal Revenue Service
www.irs.gov/
Tax-oriented information

Employee Benefits Security Administration
www.dol.gov/ebsa/welcome.html
Pension plan information

Pension Benefit Guaranty Corporation
www.pbgc.gov/default.htm
Private pension plan information

Railroad Retirement Board www.rrb.gov/
Retirement programs for railroad workers

Social Security Administration
www.ssa.gov/retirement/
Range of material

How to Buy Life Insurance

Source: The American Council of Life Insurers. Web: www.acli.com/public/media/mainframe_med.htm.

Life insurance is intended to provide for your dependents after you die. There is no federal income tax on life insurance benefits.

Evaluate the Need

To determine how much insurance you need, consider ongoing obligations (mortgage payments, school tuition, monthly bills), costs associated with your death (medical bills, burial fees, estate taxes), and your family's readjustment (moving, job hunting expenses).

Generally, you will need a life insurance policy with a **face amount** worth from five to seven times your gross annual income. The face amount is what is paid at your death.

The **cash value** of a policy is what it is worth at any given time, based on how much you have paid in premiums, how long you have had the policy, and your insurance company's financial situation. A policy may have no cash value in its early years.

Types of Life Insurance

TERM LIFE INSURANCE: provides coverage for a specific period of time. Policies can often be renewed at the end of the term, which can last from one to 30 years.

Advantages:

- Lower premiums, allowing you to buy greater protection when you are younger and the need is greatest.
- Provide protection for a specific expense that will end over time, such as mortgage payments.

Disadvantages:

- Premiums usually increase as you age.
- Some policies cannot be renewed; others might become too expensive to keep.
- Policies generally don't offer a cash value.

PERMANENT LIFE INSURANCE: offers lifetime protection as long as the premiums are paid. There are several types of permanent life offering various features. For instance, premiums can either be fixed or flexible. Some permanent life premiums can be invested in stocks or bonds.

Advantages:

- Premiums can be fixed or flexible.
- Policy accumulates a cash value against which you can borrow. (To avoid reduced death benefits for your survivors, you must repay loans with interest.)
- You can surrender part, or all, of the policy and receive the cash value, or convert it into an income-producing annuity.
- You may be able to buy added insurance without taking a medical exam.

Disadvantages:

- Premiums may be expensive.
- It may cost more than term insurance if you don't keep the policy long enough.

Finding an Agent

Most people buy policies through an insurance agent. Get the names of several agents from business associates or family members. Find out what companies they represent, what types of policy they sell, and what licenses they hold.

Choosing a Policy

Your agent's role is to find a policy that is right for you. Be prepared to discuss your financial situation, personal goals, family background, and health. You may have to take a physical exam. Tell the truth. Lying on your application could result in a denial of benefits for your survivors.

The agent should be able to explain various insurance policies. Get a step-by-step explanation. Many companies offer buyer's guides. Consider:

- When does the policy take effect?
- Can you afford the premiums?
- Will the premiums increase?
- What happens if you fail to pay a premium?
- What amounts in the policy are guaranteed?
- Will death benefits be affected by interest rates or other factors?
- Does the policy pay dividends?
- What provisions in the policy could change?
- Will you be notified if there are changes?

Consider Other Provisions

Riders are additional provisions that can be added to a policy. Riders might include additional benefits for accidental death; suspending premium payments if you become disabled; or provisions for "accelerated" or "living benefits," which pay for long-term care for catastrophic or terminal illnesses.

Research the Company

Some 1,700 U.S. companies sell life insurance. Make sure you choose a company in sound financial shape and licensed in your state. Contact your state's insurance department. A number of organizations rate the financial health of insurance companies. Many libraries have publications listing these ratings.

Points to Remember:

- Take your time. Make sure you understand what the policy offers and that you are comfortable with the product, agent, and company.
- Make your check payable to the company issuing the policy, not the agent. Get a receipt.
- When you receive your policy, there is often a cancellation period.
- Notify the company or the agent of any errors in your policy.
- It can be expensive to surrender one policy and buy another.
- Contact the company's customer service department with complaints. If you remain unsatisfied, contact your state insurance commission.
- Review your policy periodically, especially when your situation changes, to ensure adequate coverage.

For More Information:

- American Council of Life Insurers, Web: www.acli.com/public/media/mainframe_med.htm
- National Insurance Consumer Helpline (NICH) 1-800-942-2424
- Books and periodicals on personal finance and insurance in your local library
- Consumer affairs division of your state insurance commission

Understanding Credit Reports

Source: Federal Reserve Bank of Philadelphia. Web: www.phil.frb.org/consumers/creditreport.html.

Just about everyone uses credit, whether it is for car, student, or bank loans; mortgages; or credit cards. Banks and other businesses rely on credit reports, which contain:

• Social Security numbers, current and previous addresses, nicknames, spouse's name, year of birth, plus current and previous employers;

• records of loans, credit cards, bank accounts, and retail store accounts;

• public information on bankruptcy, tax liens, or legal judgments against you;

• names of people who have obtained copies of your credit report within the last six months (two years for employment purposes).

Consumer reporting agencies (credit bureaus) obtain the information from various sources, including retail stores and banks.

The report can only be shown to:

• businesses thinking of extending you credit;
• current or potential employers;
• insurance companies;
• government agencies considering granting you certain licenses or benefits;
• anyone with a legitimate business reason initiated by the consumer.

The decision to grant you a loan or issue you a credit card is made by the business that requested the report, not the credit bureau.

If you are denied credit, the lender must give you the name, address, and telephone number of the company that provided the report.

Even if you have never been denied credit, you have the right to see your report. In making the request include your name, telephone number, addresses for the last five years, Social Security number, and birth date. The agency may charge you for the report, depending on what state you live in.

You should tell the reporting agency if you disagree with anything in your report. Mistakes must be removed. If the reporting agency stands by its original report, however, you have the right to present your side of the story in a short statement that gets attached to your credit report.

Material stays on your report for seven years—ten years if a bankruptcy is involved; it is automatically deleted thereafter. Exceptions are cases of transactions of $150,000 or more (including life insurance), or employment with an annual salary of $75,000 or more.

To obtain your credit report

The three main credit bureaus are:

Equifax Information Services, LLC
P.O. Box 740241
Atlanta, GA 30374
(800) 685-1111
www.equifax.com

Experian National Consumer Assistance Center
P.O. Box 2002
Allen, TX 75013
(888) 397-3742
www.experian.com

TransUnion Consumer Disclosure Center
P.O. Box 1000
Chester, PA 19022
(800) 888-4213
www.tuc.com

Credit Card Use, 1989–1998

General-purpose credit cards include Mastercard, Visa, Optima, and Discover. All dollar figures are given in constant 1998 dollars based on consumer price index data as published by the U.S. Bureau of Labor Statistics.

				Percent of cardholding families who:		
Age of family head and family income[1]	**Percent having a general-purpose credit card**	**Percent having a balance after last month's bills**	**Median balance[2]**	**Almost always pay off the balance**	**Sometimes pay off the balance**	**Hardly ever pay off the balance**
1989 total	56.0%	52.1%	$1,300	52.9%	21.2%	25.8%
1992 total	62.4	52.6	1,100	53.0	19.6	27.4
1995 total	66.4	56.0	1,600	52.4	20.1	27.5
1998 total	67.5	54.7	1,900	53.6	19.3	26.9
Under 35 years old	58.3	71.6	1,500	39.0	22.5	38.5
35 to 44 years old	71.3	62.5	2,000	46.5	19.1	34.4
45 to 54 years old	75.3	59.2	2,000	48.2	22.7	29.1
55 to 64 years old	76.0	48.8	2,300	61.0	20.1	18.9
65 to 74 years old	71.2	33.9	1,000	74.0	14.9	11.1
75 years old and over	50.8	16.7	700	86.3	7.8	5.9
Less than $10,000	23.2	64.0	900	46.4	19.9	33.8
$10,000 to $24,999	50.8	56.9	1,200	52.3	19.3	28.4
$25,000 to $49,999	73.2	58.2	1,700	48.3	20.5	31.2
$50,000 to $99,999	89.6	55.9	2,400	53.9	20.2	25.9
$100,000 and more	97.9	36.4	3,100	72.0	13.8	14.1

1. Families include one-person units. 2. Among families having a balance. *Source:* Board of Governors of the Federal Reserve System, unpublished data. From *Statistical Abstract of the U.S., 2002.*

How to TKO Telemarketers

It's dinnertime and you're afraid to answer your phone. You're not alone. The good news: new gadgets and laws can help fend off those pesky phone pitches

By PERRY BACON, JR. and ERIC ROSTON
TIME

Six-thirty P.M. is a sacred time in American life, but one also often filled with dread. Everyone's home, washed up, and ready to eat. We count on dinner as the family hour, yet know that at any moment it could be punctured by a phone call from some scripted stranger hawking island vacations or aluminum siding.

If the number of intrusive sales calls you receive seems to be on the rise, that's because it is. Revenue from telemarketing pitches increased 250% from 1990 to 2002, to $295 billion, and is growing today even amid an economy that's flat. Salespeople in 2003 will place 100 million calls daily to homes and businesses, and those who get on hot-prospect lists—usually by buying something—can easily get half a dozen calls a day.

New Law Helps—Somewhat

Consumers are buying gadgets with names like Phone Butler and TeleZapper to help keep unwanted salespeople at bay. But the callers keep developing new technologies to defeat the gadgets. Federal and state legislators are passing laws to tighten regulation of telemarketers. In March 2003 President Bush signed a bill authorizing the Federal Trade Commission (FTC) to create a national Do Not Call Registry, which anyone can sign up for online and by phone. But there are big asterisks in the federal law, which, for instance, exempts from regulation telemarketers for charities and political candidates.

You may pride yourself on never buying anything from a telemarketer—or even letting one finish a sentence. But enough of your neighbors and colleagues respond to phone pitches to make it a lucrative business. Home repairers, mortgage refinancers, long-distance providers, and popular magazines have found phone pitches to be among their most cost-effective sales tools. U.S. consumers also unwittingly hand over as much as $50 billion a year to fraudulent callers, who make pleas for phony charities or offer prizes with strings attached or cheap vacations with hidden fees.

Telemarketing has been around almost as long as the telephone, but it didn't take off until the 1980s brought a decline in long-distance prices, along with a powerful technology called the automatic dialer. This device can call hundreds of homes at the same time and then immediately route the unwitting customer to a live telemarketer. When you answer your phone at home and hear nothing but light static, it's often because an automatic dialer has reached you but no agent was free to take the call. An unlisted number used to provide protection, until digital technology allowed marketers to easily gather lists of consumers who have given their numbers to companies with which they do business.

How to sign up for the Do Not Call Registry:

By phone: 1-888-382-1222; (TTY: 1-866-290-4236)
Online: www.donotcall.gov

Consumers Fight Back

While technology has greatly expanded the telemarketers' reach, it has also given consumers weapons to fight back. Caller ID—which is used by 38% of U.S. households today, up from 30% in 1998—at first allowed users to detect calls from salespeople and other pests. But telemarketers learned to mask their numbers so that they read as UNAVAILABLE or OUT OF AREA on caller-ID displays, and users often answer because they think the call might be an urgent one from a friend or colleague—an impulse that's especially prevalent in these days of orange alerts.

Major phone companies offer services like SBC's Privacy Manager, which for $5 a month screens calls that don't register on caller ID. Anyone with an anonymous phone number is required to identify herself, and if she's a telemarketer, you can press a button to activate a pre-recorded message telling her not to call again—a request that telemarketers are required under federal law to respect (but one that many nonetheless ignore). "Clearly this is a privacy war, and many times the phone companies are the arms dealers," says Robert Bulmash of Private Citizen Inc., based in Naperville, Ill., which campaigns against telemarketing. Like many arms dealers, the phone companies work both sides of the conflict: they avidly sell their services by phone and also peddle their customers' phone numbers to other telemarketers.

The phone companies face growing competition, though, from products like the $30 Phone Butler, sold by Morgan-Francis Inc., based in Fort Myers, Fla., which performs a function similar to that of the Privacy Manager. A more aggressive approach is touted by Privacy Technologies, based in Glenwillow, Ohio, which developed the TeleZapper. A small black box that connects to any phone, the $40 TeleZapper greets each incoming call with shrill tones that resemble the sound of a disconnected phone. When automatic dialers detect this sound, they often interpret it to mean the number is disconnected and hang up. A downside of this device, though, is that it might cause your mom to do the same. Another problem: some telemarketers have either changed their software or bought new dialers that stay on the line even when they hear the zapper's tones.

You might think—or hope—that telemarketers would eventually run out of workers willing to endure constant rejection and abuse. Think again. Expanding global trade, combined with falling prices for international calls, has allowed telemarketers to move call centers to countries where more pliant employees line up for such work. "In the U.S., to work in a call center is not a very glorifying job," but in countries such as India and Mexico, the white-collar environment and relatively high wages have job applicants lining up, says Robert Fabro, president of Hispanic Call Centers, which oversees phone banks in 62 countries and specializes in reaching immigrant populations in the U.S.

States Take Action

Lately, the fight against telemarketers has shifted toward Washington and the state capitals. In 1989 Florida adopted a do-not-call plan in which phone companies were required to put an asterisk in the phone book beside the names of people who did not want to hear from telemarketers. This law was soon modified into a formal do-not-call list. But the law didn't completely shield Floridians because out-of-state telemarketers, often unaware of the list, continued to call. And Florida-based firms started annoying residents of neighboring Georgia—and helped inspire Georgians to pass their do-not-call law.

Almost all the 20 states that don't have do-not-call laws are considering them. More than 15 million Americans have signed up for the lists, and states that have lists are seeking to strengthen them. Some ban almost all telemarketing calls, but in most states, certain big industries, such as insurers, have been exempted. One idea being considered in the state legislatures and Congress is a so-called dinner-hour ban that would preclude any telemarketing calls in the early evening, even to people not on do-not-call lists. That includes the usual exemptions, such as the one for politicians, whose solicitations are protected by the First Amendment.

The law President Bush signed allots $16 million to set up a national do-not-call list. The law also instructs the Federal Communications Commission (FCC) to adopt similar rules and make industries that the FCC regulates—banking, telecommunications, and media—subscribe to the national list. The new federal rules require telemarketers to display their phone numbers on caller-ID devices beginning in early 2004; they also combat dead-air calls from autodialers.

Lawsuits filed in Colorado and Oklahoma by telemarketing firms are challenging the FTC's jurisdiction in maintaining a do-not-call registry. But telemarketers might not find much luck in court. In 1986, before the days of anti-telemarketing laws and TeleZappers, Bulmash of Private Citizen won a suit he filed against a persistent telemarketer, which was forced to pay court fees and the 97¢ it would cost Bulmash to have his number unlisted for a month. □

Know Your Telemarketing Rights

Source: Federal Trade Commission. Web: www.ftc.gov/bcp/conline/pubs/tmarkg/ditch.htm.

In its publication "Ditch the Pitch: Hanging Up on Telephone Hucksters," the Federal Trade Commission (FTC) outlines your rights in dealing with telephone solicitation. The following is a synopsis.

Telemarketing fraud costs Americans more than $50 billion a year. The FTC warns consumers to be alert to such common telephone marketing schemes:

• **Credit card protection offers:** Consumers are only liable for $50 in unauthorized credit card charges. Do not buy "insurance" to protect against greater loss. Do not give out personal information, such as credit card or bank account numbers, unless you know whom you are dealing with, and understand why the information is requested. Thieves sometimes claim to be bank security officials and ask for personal information so they can activate "protection features" on your credit card.

• **Advance-fees for "guaranteed" loans:** It is illegal for companies doing business by phone to promise you a loan and ask you for money in advance. Legitimate lenders may charge fees, but these are seldom required before the loan is approved. In addition, banks also consider a loan applicant's credit history. Legitimate lenders do not "guarantee" loans in advance. Legitimate fees are usually paid to the lending institution, not the person who handled the paperwork.

• **International sweepstakes and lotteries:** It is illegal for U.S. citizens to participate in foreign sweepstakes or lotteries whether it is over the phone, by mail, or on the Internet. Mail about foreign lotteries should be turned over to the post office.

FTC Telemarketing Rules:

• Calls are restricted to between 8 A.M. and 9 P.M.

• Telemarketers must tell you it is a sales call, the name of the seller, and what they are selling.

• It is illegal for telemarketers to lie about their products or services.

• Telemarketers must tell you the total cost of whatever they are selling, any restrictions, and if a sale is nonrefundable.

• Callers promoting prizes must tell you the odds of winning, that no purchase or payment is necessary to win, and any restrictions on receiving the prize.

• It is illegal for telemarketers to withdraw money from your bank account without your express, verifiable authorization.

• You do not have to pay for credit services until those services are delivered.

• It is illegal for a telemarketer to call you if you have asked not to be called.

Do not be pressured into making an immediate payment. You can take time to evaluate the offer. If you suspect fraud, contact your local police, state Attorney General's office, or consumer protection agency.

Remember, if an offer seems too good to be true, it probably is.

Stolen Identity: A Consumer Nightmare

Source: Federal Trade Commission (FTC).

A new type of criminal has emerged—one who can wreak havoc with your finances and credit and destroy your good reputation. It's relatively easy for a determined thief to steal your name, your Social Security number, your credit card number, or some other bit of personal information without your knowledge and commit fraud in your name.

Unfortunately, you may not find out that your identity has been stolen until you receive bills for credit card accounts that you never opened, debts that you never incurred, or charges on your bills that you didn't sign for, authorize, or know anything about.

How Can This Happen?

When you make everyday transactions like writing a check at a store, charging purchases, renting a car, mailing your tax return, calling home on your cell phone, ordering new checks, or applying for a credit card, chances are that you don't give this a second thought. But crooks known as "identity thieves" may be paying attention. Each transaction requires you to share your personal information such as your bank and credit card account numbers, your Social Security number, name, address, and phone numbers. Despite your best efforts to control your personal information, skilled thieves can use a variety of methods, low- and high-tech, to gain access to your data.

How Your Identity Is Stolen

The Federal Trade Commission (FTC) has listed the following ways that imposters can get your personal information and take over your identity:

- They steal your wallet and purse containing your identification and credit and bank cards.
- They steal your mail, including your bank and credit card statements, pre-approved credit offers, telephone calling cards, and tax information.
- They complete a "change of address" form to divert your mail to another location.
- They rummage through your trash, or the trash of businesses, for personal data in a practice known as "dumpster diving."
- They fraudulently obtain your credit card report by posing as a landlord, employer, or someone else who may have a legitimate need for, and a legal right to the information.
- They get your business or personnel records at work.
- They find personal information in your home.
- They use personal information you share on the Internet.
- They buy your personal information from "inside" sources. For example, an identity thief may pay a store employee for information about you that appears on an application for goods, services, or credit.

How Your Stolen Identity Is Used

The crooks call your credit card company and, pretending to be you, ask to change the mailing address on your credit card account. The imposter then runs up charges on your account. Because your bills are being sent to the new address, it may take some time before you realize that there is a problem.

Thieves can also open a new credit card account using your name, date of birth, and your Social Security number. When they use the credit card and don't pay the bills, the delinquent account is reported on your credit report.

Other scenarios include: establishing a phone or wireless service in your name, opening a bank account in your name and writing bad checks on it, and buying cars by taking out auto loans in your name.

Minimize Risk

Sign your credit cards upon receipt. Only carry cards that you need. Do not carry your Social Security card. Never write your PIN or Social Security number on anything you are going to throw away. Shred documents containing your Social Security number.

Do not release personal information such as your Social Security or bank account number over the phone unless you made the phone call and understand why the information is necessary.

Obtain an annual copy of your credit report from the three main credit bureaus and ensure the material is correct.

Be aware of credit card billing cycles. If you do not receive a bill on time, contact the company. A thief charging purchases to your account would likely change your billing address, so it takes you longer to discover the fraud.

If You're a Victim

Do these three things immediately:

1) Contact the fraud departments of each of the three major credit bureaus and report that your identity has been stolen. Ask that a "fraud alert" be placed on your file and that no new credit be granted without your approval.

Main Credit Reporting Bureaus:

Equifax, P.O. Box 740241, Atlanta, GA 30374-0241, (800) 525-6285

Experian, P.O. Box 9530, Allen, TX 75013, (888) 397-3742

Trans Union, P.O. Box 2000, Chester, PA, (800) 888-4213

2) For any accounts that have been fraudulently accessed or opened, contact the security departments of the appropriate creditors or financial institutions. Close these accounts. Put passwords (not your mother's maiden name) on any new accounts you open.

3) File a report with your local police or the police where the identity theft took place. Get a copy of the report in case the bank, credit card company, or others need proof of the crime later on.

The Consumer Action Handbook

Source: U.S. Office of Consumer Affairs.

The *2003 Consumer Action Handbook,* published by the Federal Consumer Information Center, is 160 pages of valuable information that no consumer should be without. It provides advice on car repair, purchase and leasing, shopping from home, avoiding consumer and investment fraud, home improvement and financing, and much more. Also included is the *Consumer Assistance Directory* with thousands of useful names, addresses, phone numbers, and websites.

Single copies of the *Consumer Action Handbook* are available free ($2.00 service fee) by writing to: Handbook, Federal Consumer Information Center, Pueblo, CO 81009, or by calling 1-800-688-9889. The handbook can also be viewed on the FCIC website: www.pueblo.gsa.gov.

You've Got Spam: How to "Can" Unwanted Email

Source: Federal Trade Commission.

As more people use email, marketers are increasingly using email messages to pitch their products and services. Some consumers find unsolicited commercial email—also known as "spam"—annoying and time consuming; others have lost money to bogus offers that arrived in their email inbox.

Typically, an email spammer buys a list of email addresses from a list broker, who compiles it by "harvesting" addresses from the Internet. If your email address appears in a newsgroup posting, on a website, in a chat room, or in an online service's membership directory, it may find its way onto these lists. The marketer then uses special software that can send hundreds of thousands—even millions—of email messages to the addresses at the click of a mouse.

The FTC suggests that you treat commercial email solicitations the same way you would treat an unsolicited telemarketing sales call. Don't believe promises from strangers. Greet money-making opportunities that arrive at your inbox with skepticism. Most of the time, these are old-fashioned scams delivered via the newest technology.

Tips to Reduce Spam

Try not to display your email address in public. That includes newsgroup postings, chat rooms, websites, or in an online service's membership directory. You may want to opt out of member directories for your online services; spammers may use them to harvest addresses.

Check the privacy policy when you submit your address to a website. See if it allows the company to sell your address. You may want to opt out of this provision, if possible, or not submit your address at all to websites that won't protect it.

Read and understand the entire form before you transmit personal information through a website. Some websites allow you to opt out of receiving email from their "partners"—but you may have to uncheck a preselected box if you want to opt out.

Decide if you want to use two email addresses—one for personal messages and one for newsgroups and chat rooms. You also might consider using a disposable email address service that creates a separate email address that forwards to your permanent account. If one of the disposable addresses begins to receive spam, you can shut it off without affecting your permanent address.

Use a unique email address. Your choice of email addresses may affect the amount of spam you receive. Spammers use "dictionary attacks" to sort through possible name combinations at large ISPs or email services, hoping to find a valid address. Thus, a common name such as jdoe may get more spam than a more unique name like jd51x02oe. Of course, there is a downside—it's harder to remember an unusual email address.

Use an email filter. Check your email account to see if it provides a tool to filter out potential spam or a way to channel spam into a bulk email folder. You might want to consider these options when you're choosing which Internet Service Provider (ISP) to use.

What Can I Do With the Spam?

Report it to the Federal Trade Commission. Send a copy of unwanted or deceptive messages to uce@ftc.gov. The FTC uses the unsolicited emails stored in this database to pursue law enforcement actions against people who send deceptive spam email.

Let the FTC know if a "remove me" request is not honored. If you want to complain about a removal link that doesn't work or not being able to unsubscribe from a list, you can fill out the FTC's online complaint form at www.ftc.gov. Your complaint will be added to the FTC's Consumer Sentinel database and made available to hundreds of law enforcement and consumer protection agencies. You can also call the FTC toll–free: 1-877-FTC-HELP (1-877-382-4357); TTY: 1-866-653-4261.

Whenever you complain about spam, it's important to include the full email header. The information in the header makes it possible for consumer protection agencies to follow up on your complaint.

Send a copy of the spam to your ISP's abuse desk. By doing this, you can let the ISP know about the spam problem on their system and help them to stop it in the future. Make sure to include a copy of the spam, along with the full email header. At the top of the message, state that you're complaining about being spammed.

Complain to the sender's ISP. Most ISPs want to cut off spammers who abuse their system. Again, make sure to include a copy of the message and header information and state that you're complaining about spam.

Dirty Dozen: 12 Scams Most Likely to Arrive Via Bulk Email

Email boxes are filling up with more offers for business opportunities than any other kind of unsolicited commercial email. That's a problem, according to the Federal Trade Commission, because many of these offers are scams.

The FTC has identified the 12 scams that are most likely to arrive in consumers' email boxes. The "dirty dozen" are:

1. Business opportunities: Many of these are illegal pyramid schemes masquerading as legitimate opportunities to earn money.

2. Bulk email: Sending bulk email violates the terms of service of most Internet service providers. If you use one of the automated email programs, your ISP may shut you down.

3. Chain letters: Chain letters—traditional or high-tech—are almost always illegal, and nearly all of the people who participate in them lose their money.

4. Work-at-home schemes: You'll pay a small fee to get started in the business. Then, you'll learn that the email sender never had real employment to offer. Instead, you'll get instructions on how to send the same ad in your own bulk emailings.

5. Health and diet scams: Most of these gimmicks simply do not work.

6. Effortless income: If these get-rich-quick schemes worked, wouldn't everyone be using them?

7. Free goods: Most of these offers are covering up pyramid schemes, operations that inevitably collapse.

8. Investment opportunities: Many are schemes that eventually collapse because there isn't enough money coming in to continue simulating earnings. Other schemes are a good investment for the promoters, but not for participants.

9. Cable descrambler kits: The devices you use probably won't work. Most of the cable TV systems in the U.S. use technology that these devices can't crack.

10. Guaranteed loans or credit, on easy terms: The loans usually turn out to be useless lists of lenders who will turn you down if you don't meet their qualifications.

11. Credit repair: The scam artists who promote these services can't deliver. Only time, a deliberate effort, and a personal debt repayment plan will improve your credit.

12. Vacation prize promotions: Most unsolicited commercial email goes to thousands or millions of recipients at a time. Often, the cruise ship you're booked on may look more like a tug boat.

National Consumer Organizations

NOTE: For other organizations, *see* Societies & Associations, pp. 660–690.

Alliance Against Fraud in Telemarketing & Electronic Commerce (AAFTEC), c/o National Consumers League, 1701 K St. NW, Suite 1200, Washington, DC 20006; 202-835-3323; 202-835-0747 (fax); Web: www.fraud.org/aaft/aaftset.htm.

Combats telemarketing and Internet fraud through consumer education.

American Association of Retired Persons (AARP), Consumer Affairs Section, 601 E St. NW, Washington, DC 20049; 800-424-3410; Web: www.aarp.org.

Offers information on housing, insurance, funeral practices, eligibility for public benefits, financial security, transportation, and consumer protection issues on behalf of midlife and older consumers.

American Council on Consumer Interests (ACCI), 415 South Duff, Ste. C., Ames, IA 50010-6600; 515-956-4666; 515-233-3101 (fax); Web: http://consumerinterests.org.

Provides research-based information on topics of consumer interest. Provides information about consumer publications, policies, and resources.

American Council on Science and Health (ACSH), 1995 Broadway, 2nd Fl., New York, NY 10023-5860; 212-362-7044; 212-362-4919 (fax); Web: www.acsh.org.

A consumer education consortium concerned with issues related to food, nutrition, chemicals, pharmaceuticals, lifestyle, the environment, and health.

American Savings Education Council, 2121 K Street NW, Suite 600, Washington, DC 20037-1896; 202-659-0670; Web: www.asec.org.

Raises public awareness about what is needed to ensure long-term personal financial independence.

Better Business Bureau (BBB), 4200 Wilson Blvd., Suite 800, Arlington, VA 22203-1838; 703-276-0100; Web: www.bbb.org.

The BBB offers a variety of consumer services including educational materials, information on charities and other organizations seeking public donations, and mediation and arbitration services.

Center for Auto Safety (CAS), 1825 Connecticut Ave. NW, Suite 330, Washington, DC 20009-5708; 202-328-7700; Web: www.autosafety.org.

Founded by Consumers Union and Ralph Nader in 1970 to advocate for auto safety and quality.

Center for Science in the Public Interest (CSPI), 1875 Connecticut Ave. NW, Suite 300, Washington, DC 20009; 202-332-9110; 202-265-4954 (fax); Web: www.cspinet.org.

Provides research, education, and advocacy on nutrition, health, food safety, and related issues.

Center for the Study of Services/Consumers' Checkbook, Consumers' CHECKBOOK Headquarters, 733 15th Street NW, Suite 820, Washington, DC 20005; 800-213-7283; Web: www.checkbook.org.

Aids consumers in selecting doctors, hospitals, health plans, cars, and finding bargains.

Coalition Against Insurance Fraud, 1012 14th St. NW, Suite 200, Washington, DC 20005; 202-393-7330; 202-293-7329 (fax); Web: www.insurancefraud.org.

Organization of consumers, government agencies, and insurers dedicated to combating all forms of insurance fraud.

Consumer Action (CA), 717 Market St., Suite 310, San Francisco, CA 94103-2109; 415-777-9635 (multilingual consumer complaint hotline); 415-777-9456 (voice/ttd); Web: www.consumer-action.org.

Advocate for credit, finance, HMOs, and telecommunications issues.

Consumer Federation of America (CFA), 1424 16th St. NW, Suite 604, Washington, DC 20036; 202-387-6121; Web: www.consumerfed.org.

Composed of more than 260 organizations, CFA is a consumer advocacy and education organization. CFA focuses much of its advocacy in the areas of financial service, utilities, product safety, transportation, health care, and food safety.

Consumers Union of U.S., Inc. (CU), 101 Truman Ave., Yonkers, NY 10703-1057; 914-378-2000; Web: www.consumersunion.org.

Publisher of *Consumer Reports*. Researches and tests consumer goods and services.

Federal Trade Commission (FTC), CRC-240, Washington, DC 20580; 1-877-FTC-HELP or 202-326-2222; Web: www.ftc.gov.

Enforces a variety of federal antitrust and consumer protection laws.

HALT: An Organization of Americans for Legal Reform, 1612 K Street NW, Suite 510, Washington, DC 20006; 202-887-8255, toll-free: 1-888-367-4258; 202-887-9699 (fax); Web: www.halt.org.

Helps consumers handle their legal affairs.

National Community Reinvestment Coalition (NCRC), 733 15th Street NW, Suite 540, Washington, DC 20005; 202-628-8866; 202-628-9800 (fax); Web: www.ncrc.org.

Works toward ending discriminatory banking practices and increasing the flow of private capital and credit into underserved communities.

National Consumer Law Center (NCLC), 77 Summer Street, 10th Fl., Boston, MA 02110-1006; 617-542-8010; 617-542-8028 (fax); Web: www.consumerlaw.org.

Focuses on the interests of low-income consumers in court, before administrative agencies, and before legislatures.

National Consumers League (NCL), 1701 K St. NW, Suite 1200, Washington, DC 20006; 202-835-3323; 202-835-0747 (fax); Web: nclnet.org.

Founded in 1899, NCL is America's pioneer consumer advocacy organization. It focuses on consumer health and safety protection as well as fairness in the marketplace and workplace.

National Council on Aging (NCOA), 300 D St. SW, Suite 801, Washington, DC 20024; 202-479-1200; 202-479-0735 (fax); Web: www.ncoa.org.

Advocates public policies and provides programs and services that serve older persons.

National Foundation for Credit Counseling, Inc. (NFCC), 801 Roeder Rd., Suite 900, Silver Spring, MD 20910; 301-589-5600; 301-495-5623 (fax); Web: www.nfcc.org.

Provides assistance with stressful financial situations.

National Fraud Information Center/Internet Fraud Watch (NFIC/IFW), c/o National Consumers League, 1701 K St. NW, Suite 1200, Washington, DC 20006; 800-876-7060; Web: www.fraud.org.

Help on avoiding telemarketing fraud and online and Internet fraud, and assistance in filing complaints.

National Senior Citizens Law Center, 1101 14th St. NW, Suite 400, Washington, DC 20005; 202-289-6976; 202-289-7224 (fax); Web: www.nsclc.org.

Helps low-income and older Americans with legal services.

Public Citizen, Inc., 1600 20th St. NW, Washington, DC 20009; 202-588-1000; Web: www.citizen.org.

Represents consumer interests in Congress, the courts, government agencies, and the media. Its divisions include Auto Safety, Congress Watch, Critical Mass (Energy & Environment Program), Global Trade Watch, Health Research group, and the Litigation Group.

Scam Watch, U.S. Headquarters, 5977 Honeywell Drive, Indianapolis, IN 48236; 317-823-0377; 317-826-1895 (fax); Web: www.scamwatch.com.

Provides the Internet community with complete fraud protection services. All services are available 24 hours a day and are cost-free. Scam Watch is an agency of InterGov International.

United Seniors Health Cooperative (USHC), 409 Third Street SW, Suite 200, Washington, DC 20024; 202-479-6973; 202-479-6660 (fax); Web: www.unitedseniorshealth.org.

Helps seniors achieve good health, independence, and financial security.

U.S. Public Interest Research Group (U.S. PIRG), 218 D St. SE, Washington, DC 20003; 202-546-9707; 202-546-2461 (fax); Web: www.uspirg.org.

Advocates on issues such as the environment, product safety, financial privacy, and identity theft.

Women's Bureau, Dept. of Labor, 200 Constitution Ave., NW, Room S-3002, Washington, DC 20210; 202-219-5529, 1-800-827-5335, 202-693-6710; 202-693-6725 (fax); Web: www.dol.gov/wb/.

Advocates for work issues such as sexual harassment, pregnancy discrimination, and child care.

Copyrights

Source: Excerpted from *Copyright Basics (Circular 1),* U.S. Copyright Office.

Copyright is a form of protection provided by the laws of the United States to the creators of "original works of authorship," including literary, dramatic, musical, artistic, and certain other intellectual works. This protection is available to both published and unpublished works. The 1976 Copyright Act generally gives the owner of copyright the exclusive right to do and to authorize others to do the following:

• to reproduce the copyrighted work in copies or phonorecords;

• to prepare derivative works based upon the copyrighted work;

• to distribute copies or phonorecords of the copyrighted work to the public by sale or other transfer of ownership, or by rental, lease, or lending;

• to perform and/or display the copyrighted work publicly; and

• in the case of sound recordings, to perform the work publicly by means of a digital audio transmission.

It is illegal for anyone to violate these rights. However, these rights are not unlimited in scope. In some cases they are limited by the doctrine of "fair use," or by a "compulsory license" under which certain limited uses of copyrighted works are permitted in exchange for payment.

What Works Are Protected

Copyright protects "original works of authorship" that are fixed in a tangible form of expression. The fixation need not be directly perceptible so long as it may be communicated with the aid of a machine or device. Categories include:

• literary works;

• musical works, including any accompanying words;

- dramatic works, including any accompanying music;
- pantomimes and choreographic works;
- pictorial, graphic, and sculptural works;
- motion pictures and other audiovisual works;
- sound recordings; and
- architectural works.

These categories should be viewed quite broadly. For example, computer programs and most "compilations" are registrable as "literary works." Maps and architectural plans are registrable as "pictorial, graphic, and sculptural works."

What Is Not Protected

Several categories of material are generally not eligible for federal copyright protection. These include, among others:

- works that have not been fixed in a tangible form of expression. For example, choreographic works that have not been notated or recorded, or improvisational speeches or performances that have not been written or recorded;
- titles, names, short phrases, and slogans; familiar symbols or designs; mere variations of typographic ornamentation, lettering, or coloring; mere listings of ingredients or contents;
- ideas, procedures, methods, systems, processes, concepts, principles, discoveries, or devices, as distinguished from a description, explanation, or illustration;
- works consisting entirely of information that is common property and containing no original authorship. For example, standard calendars, height and weight charts, tape measures and rulers, and lists or tables taken from public documents or other common sources.

Patents

Source: Department of Commerce, Patent and Trademark Office.

A patent, in the most general sense, is a document issued by a government, conferring some special right or privilege. The term is now restricted mainly to patents for inventions, and occasionally, land patents.

The grant of a patent for an invention gives the inventor the privilege, for a limited period of time, of excluding others from making, using, or selling a certain article.

In the United States, the law provides that a patent may be granted, for a term of 20 years from the date of application, to any person who has invented or discovered any new and useful art, machine, manufacture, or composition of matter, as well as any new and useful improvements thereof. A patent may also be granted to a person who has invented or discovered and asexually reproduced a new and distinct variety of plant (other than a tuber-propagated one) or has invented a new, original, and ornamental design for an article of manufacture, for a term of 20 years and 14 years, respectively.

A patent is granted only upon receipt of a complete, regularly filed application and the appropriate fees, and upon determination that the invention is new, useful, and, in view of the prior art, unobvious to one skilled in the art. The disclosure must be of such nature as to enable others to reproduce the invention.

Patents are not granted for printed matter, for methods of doing business, or for devices for which claims contrary to natural laws are made. Applications for a perpetual-motion machine have been made from time to time, but until a working model is presented that actually fulfills the claim, no patent will be issued.

A complete application, which must be addressed to the Commissioner of Patents and Trademarks, Washington, DC 20231, consists of a specification with one or more claims; oath or declaration; drawing (whenever the nature of the case admits of it); and a basic filing fee of $380. The filing fee is not returned to the applicant if the patent is refused. If the patent is allowed, other fees are required. Phone 1-800-786-9199 for the latest fees.

Trademarks

Source: Department of Commerce, Patent and Trademark Office.

A trademark may be defined as a word, letter, device, or symbol, as well as any combination of these, that is used in connection with merchandise and that points distinctly to the origin of the goods.

Certificates of registration of trademarks are issued under the seal of the Patent and Trademark Office and may be registered by the owner if he or she is engaged in interstate or foreign commerce. Federal jurisdiction over trademarks arises under the commerce clause of the Constitution. Effective Nov. 16, 1989, applications to register may also be based on a "bona fide intention to use the mark in commerce." Trademarks may be registered by foreign owners who comply with U.S. law, as well as by citizens of foreign countries with which the United States has treaties relating to trademarks. American citizens may register trademarks in foreign countries by complying with the laws of those countries. The right to registration and protection of trademarks in many foreign countries is guaranteed by treaties.

General jurisdiction in trademark cases involving Federal Registrations is given to federal courts. Adverse decisions of examiners on applications for registration are appealable to the Trademark Trial and Appeal Board, whose affirmances and decisions in *inter partes* proceedings are subject to court review. Before adopting a trademark, a person should make a search of prior marks to avoid unwittingly infringing upon them.

The duration of a trademark registration is ten years, but it may be renewed indefinitely for 10-year periods, provided the trademark is still in use at the time of expiration.

The application fee for registering is $325 per class.

U.S. Societies and Associations

Names are listed alphabetically according to key word in title; figure in parentheses is year of founding; other figure is membership.

The following is a partial list selected for general readership interest. A comprehensive listing of approximately 23,000 national and international organizations can be found in the *Encyclopedia of Associations*, 34th ed., 2000, published by Gale Research Company, 835 Penobscot Building, 645 Griswold St., Detroit, Mich. 48226-4049, available in most public libraries.

AARP (American Association of Retired Persons) (1958): 601 E. St. N.W., Washington, D.C. 20049. 33,000,000. Phone: (800) 424-3410. www.aarp.org.

Abortion Federation, National (1977): 1755 Mass. Ave., Ste. 600, Washington, D.C. 20036. Phone: (202) 667-5881www.prochoice.org.

Accountants, American Institute of Certified Public (1887): 1211 Avenue of the Americas, New York, N.Y. 10036-8775. 330,000. Phone: (212) 596-6200. www.aicpa.org.

ACSM: American Congress on Surveying and Mapping (1941): 6 Montgomery Village Ave., Ste. 403, Gaithersburg, Md. 20879. 8,000. Phone: (240) 632-9716. www.acsm.net.

Actors' Equity Association (1913): 165 W. 46th St., New York, N.Y. 10036. 40,000. Phone: (212) 869-8530. www.actorsequity.org.

Actuaries, Society of (1949): 475 N. Martingale Rd., Ste. 800, Schaumburg, Ill. 60173-2226. 16,500. Phone: (847) 706-3500. www.soa.org.

Adirondack Mountain Club (1922): 814 Goggins Rd., Lake George, N.Y. 12845-4117. 22,000. Phone: (518) 668-4447. www.adk.org.

Aeronautic Association, National (1905): 1815 N. Fort Myer Dr., Ste. 500, Arlington, Va. 22209. 300,000. Phone: (703) 527-0226. www.naa-usa.org.

Africa-American Institute, The (1953): 380 Lexington Ave., New York, N.Y. 10168-4298. Phone: (212) 949-5666. http://www.aaionline.org/

AFS Intercultural Programs—USA (American Field Service) (1947): 71 W. 23rd St., 17th Fl., New York, N.Y. 10010. 100,000. Phone: (212) 807-8686. www.afs.org.

Agricultural History Society (1919): 603 Ross Hall/Dept. of History, Iowa State University, Ames, Iowa 50011. 1,400. Phone: (515) 294-5620. www.iastate.edu/~history_info/aghissoc.htm.

Agronomy, American Society of (1907): 677 S. Segoe Rd., Madison, Wis. 53711-1086. 11,400. Phone: (608) 273-8080; fax: (608) 273-2021. www.agronomy.org.

Air & Waste Management Association (1907): One Gateway Center, 3rd Flr., Pittsburgh, Pa. 15222. 14,000. Phone: (412) 232-3444. www.awma.org.

Aircraft Association, Experimental (1953): EAA Aviation Center, P.O. Box 3086, Oshkosh, Wis. 54903-3086. 170,000. Phone: (920) 426-4800. www.eaa.org.

Aircraft Owners and Pilots Association (1939): 421 Aviation Way, Frederick, Md. 21701-4798. 350,000. Phone: (301) 695-2000; fax: (301) 695-2375. www.aopa.org.

Air Force Association (1946): 1501 Lee Highway, Arlington, Va. 22209-1198. 150,000. Phone: (703) 247-5800. www.afa.org.

Air Line Pilots Association (1931): P.O. Box 1169, Herndon, Va. 20172. 50,000. Phone: (703) 689-2270. www.alpa.org.

Al-Anon Family Group Headquarters, Inc. For families and friends of alcoholics. (1951): 1600 Corporate Landing Pkwy., Virginia Beach, Va. 23454-5617. 33,000 groups worldwide. Phone: (757) 563-1600. www.al-anon.org.

Alcoholics Anonymous (1935): A.A. World Services, Inc., P.O. Box 459, New York, N.Y. 10163. 2,160,013. Phone: (212) 870-3400. www.aa.org.

Alexander Graham Bell Association for the Deaf (1890): 3417 Volta Place N.W., Washington, D.C. 20007-2778. 6,200. Phone: (202) 337-5220 V, 337-5221 TTY; fax: (202) 337-8314. www.agbell.org.

Alzheimer's Association (1980): 225 N. Michigan Ave., Ste. 1700, Chicago, Ill. 60601-7633. 200 chapters. Phone: (312) 335-8700; (800) 272-3900. www.alz.org.

American Academy of Allergy, Asthma and Immunology (1943): 611 E. Wells St., Milwaukee, Wis. 53202. 5,000. Phone: (414) 272-6071. www.aaaai.org.

American Alliance for Health, Physical Education, Recreation and Dance (1885): 1900 Association Dr., Reston, Va. 20191. 26,000. Phone: (800) 213-7193. www.aahperd.org.

American Automobile Association (1902): 1000 AAA Dr., Heathrow, Fla. 32746-5063. Phone: (407) 444-7000. www.aaa.com.

American Civil Liberties Union (1920): 125 Broad St., 18th Flr., New York, N.Y. 10004-2400. 275,000. Phone: (212) 549-2500. www.aclu.org.

American Contract Bridge League (1927): 2990 Airways Blvd., Memphis, Tenn. 38116-3847. Phone: (800) 467-1623; fax: (901) 398-7754. www.acbl.org.

American Federation of Labor and Congress of Industrial Organizations (AFL-CIO) (1955): 815 16th St. N.W., Washington, D.C. 20006. 13,000,000. Phone: (202) 637-5000. www.aflcio.org.

American Federation of Musicians of the United States and Canada (1896): 1501 Broadway, Ste. 600, Paramount Bldg., New York, N.Y. 10036. Phone: (212) 869-1330. www.afm.org.

American Forests (1875): P.O. Box 2000, Washington, D.C. 20013. 115,000. Phone: (202) 955-4500. www.americanforests.org.

American Foundrymen's Society, Inc. (1896): 505 State St., Des Plaines, Ill. 60016-8399. 13,000. Phone: (847) 824-0181; (800) 537-4237. www.afsinc.org.

American Friends Service Committee (1917): 1501 Cherry St., Philadelphia, Pa. 19102-1479. Phone: (215) 241-7000. www.afsc.org.

American Geographical Society, The (1851): 120 Wall St., Ste. 100, New York, N.Y. 10005-3904. 1,500. Phone: (212) 422-5456; fax: (212) 422-5480. email: amgeosoc@earthlink.net. www.amergeog.org.

American Geriatrics Society (1942): 350 Fifth Ave., Ste. 801, New York, N.Y. 10118. 6,000. Phone: (212) 308-1414; fax: (212) 832-8646. www.americangeriatrics.org.

American Heart Association (1924): 7272 Greenville Ave., Dallas, Tex. 75231-4596. 4,200,000 volunteers. Phone: (800) AHA-USA1. www.americanheart.org.

American Historical Association (1884): 400 A St. S.E., Washington, D.C. 20003-3889. 15,000. Phone: (202) 544-2422. email: aha@theaha.org. www.theaha.org.

American Indian Affairs, Association on (1923): Box 268, Sisseton, S.D. 57262. 40,000. Phone: (605) 698-3998. www.indian-affairs.org.
American Jewish Committee (1906): P.O. Box 705, New York, N.Y. 10105. 100,000. Phone: (212) 751-4000. www.ajc.org.
American Kennel Club (1884): 260 Madison Ave., New York, N.Y. 10016. 500+ member clubs. Phone: (212) 696-8200; (919) 233-9767 (customer service). www.akc.org.
American Legion, The (1919): 700 N. Pennsylvania St., Indianapolis, Ind. 46206. 3,000,000. Phone: (317) 630-1200. www.legion.org.
American Legion Auxiliary (1919): 777 N. Meridian St., 3rd Flr., Indianapolis, Ind. 46204. 1,000,000. Phone: (317) 955-3845. www.legion-aux.org.
American Mensa, Ltd. (1960): 1229 Corporate Drive West, Arlington, Tex. 76006–6103. 50,000. Phone: (817) 607-0060. www.us.mensa.org.
American Montessori Society (1960): 281 Park Avenue South, 6th Flr., New York, N.Y. 10010-6102. Phone: (212) 358-1250; fax: (212) 358-1256. www.amshq.org.
American Museum of Natural History (1869): Central Park West at 79th St., New York, N.Y. 10024-5192. 500,000. Phone: (212) 769-5606. www.amnh.org.
American Planning Association (1917) and American Institute of Certified Planners: Administrative Offices: 122 S. Michigan Ave., Chicago, Ill. 60603. 30,000. Phone: (312) 431-9100. www.planning.org.
Americans for Democratic Action, Inc. (1947): 1625 K St. N.W., Ste. 210, Washington, D.C. 20006. 70,000. Phone: (202) 785-5980. www.adaction.org.
American Society for Nutritional Sciences (1928): 9650 Rockville Pike, Ste. 4500, Bethesda, Md. 20814-3990. 3,600. Phone: (301) 530-7050. www.asns.org.
American Society for Public Administration (ASPA) (1939): 1120 G St. N.W., Ste. 700, Washington, D.C. 20005. 12,000. Phone: (202) 393-7878. www.aspanet.org.
American Universities, Association of (1900): 1200 New York Avenue NW, Ste. 550, Washington, D.C. 20005. Phone: (202) 408-7500. www.aau.edu.
American Water Resources Association (1964): 4 W. Federal St., P.O. Box 1626, Middleburg, Va. 20118-1626. Phone: (540) 687-8390. www.awra.org.
Amnesty International USA (1961): 322 Eighth Ave., New York, N.Y. 10001. 300,000. Phone: (212) 807-8400. www.amnesty-usa.org.
AMVETS (American Veterans of World War II, Korea, and Vietnam) (1943): 4647 Forbes Blvd., Lanham, Md. 20706-4380. 250,000. Phone: (877) 7AMVETS. www.amvets.org.
Animals, The American Society for the Prevention of Cruelty to (ASPCA) (1866): 424 E. 92nd St., New York, N.Y. 10128-6804. 400,000+. Phone: (212) 876-7700. www.aspca.org.
Animals, The Fund For, Inc. (1967): 200 W. 57th St., New York, N.Y. 10019. 175,000. Phone: (212) 246-2096. www.fund.org.
Anthropological Association, American (1902): 2200 Wilson Blvd., Ste. 600, Arlington, Va. 22201. 11,500. Phone: (703) 528-1902. www.aaanet.org.
Anti-Defamation League (1913): 823 United Nations Plaza, New York, N.Y. 10017-3560. Phone: (212) 885-7700. www.adl.org.
Anti-Vivisection Society, The American (1883): 801 Old York Rd., #204, Jenkintown, Pa. 19046-1685. 15,000. Phone: (215) 887-0816; fax: (215) 887-2088. www.aavs.org.
Appraisers, American Society of (1936): 555 Herndon Parkway, Ste. 125, Herndon, VA 20170. 6,500. Phone: (703) 478-2228. www.appraisers.org.
Arboriculture, International Society of (1924): P.O. Box 3129, Champaign, Ill. 61826-3129. 8,000. Phone: (217) 355-9411; fax (217) 355-9516. email: isa@isa-arbor.com. www2.champaign.isa-arbor.com.
Archaeological Institute of America (1879): 656 Beacon St., Boston, Mass. 02215-2006. 11,000. Phone: (617) 353-9361. email: aia@aai.bu.edu. www.archaeological.org.
Architects, The American Institute of (1857): 1735 New York Ave. N.W., Washington, D.C. 20006-5292. 59,000. Phone: (202) 626-7300. www.aia.org.
Architectural Historians, Society of (1940): 1365 N. Astor St., Chicago, Ill. 60610-2144. 4,000. Phone: (312) 573-1365; fax: (312) 573-1141. www.sah.org.
Army, Association of the United States (1950): 2425 Wilson Blvd., Arlington, Va. 22201-3385. 100,000+. Phone: (703) 841-4300. www.ausa.org.
Arthritis Foundation (1948): P.O. Box 7669, Atlanta, Ga. 30357-0669. Over 150 local offices. Phone: (800) 283-7800. www.arthritis.org.
Arts, National Endowment for the (1965): 1100 Pennsylvania Ave. N.W., Washington, D.C. 20506. Phone: (202) 682-5400. arts.endow.gov.
ASM International ® (formerly the American Society for Metals) (1913): 9639 Kinsman Rd., Materials Park, Ohio 44073-0002. 44,000. Phone: (440) 338-5151; fax: (440) 338-4634. www.asm-intl.org.
Association for Investment Management and Research (1990): 560 Ray C. Hunt Dr., Charlottesville, Va. 22903-0668. 36,000. Phone: (800) 247-8132. www.aimr.com.
Astronomical Society, American (1899): 2000 Florida Ave., Ste. 400, Washington, D.C. 20009. 6,300. Phone: (202) 328-2010. www.aas.org.
Atheists, American (1963): P.O. Box 5733, Parsippany, N.J. 07054-6733. 40,000 families. Phone: (908) 276-7300. www.atheists.org.
Audubon Society, National (1905): 700 Broadway, New York, N.Y. 10003-9562. 550,000. Phone: (212) 979-3000. www.audubon.org.
Authors League of America (1912): 330 W. 42nd St., 29th Flr., New York, N.Y. 10036-6902. 14,000. Phone: (212) 268-1208.
Autism Society of America (1965): 7910 Woodmont Ave., Ste. 300, Bethesda, Md. 20814-3015. 18,000+. Phone: (301) 657-0881; (800) 3AUTISM. www.autism-society.org.
Automobile Club, National (1924): 1151 East Hillsdale Blvd., Foster City, Calif. 94404. 200,000. Phone: (650) 294-7000. www.nationalautoclub.com.
Bar Association, American (1878): 541 N. Fairbanks Court, Chicago, Ill. 60611. 371,000. Phone: (312) 988-5522. www.abanet.org.
Barber Shop Quartet Singing in America, Society for the Preservation and Encouragement of (SPEBSQSA, Inc.) (1938): 6315 Harmony Lane, Kenosha, Wis. 53143. 34,000. Phone: (800) 876-SING. www.spebsqsa.org.
Better Business Bureaus, Council of (1912): 4200 Wilson Blvd., Ste. 800, Arlington, Va. 22203-1804. Phone: (703) 276-0100; fax: (703) 525-8277. www.bbb.org.
Bible Society, American (1816): 1865 Broadway, New York, N.Y. 10023-7505. Phone: (800) 32-BIBLE; (212) 408-1200. www.americanbible.org.
Biblical Literature, Society of (1880): 825 Houston Mill Road, Ste. 350, Atlanta, Ga. 30329. 7,000 members, 1,200 subscribers. Phone: (404) 727-3100; fax: (404) 727-3101. www.sbl-site.org.
Big Brothers Big Sisters of America (1977): 230 N. 13th St., Philadelphia, Pa. 19107. Phone: (215) 567-7000. www.bbbsa.org.
Biochemistry and Molecular Biology, American Society for (1906): 9650 Rockville Pike, Bethesda, Md. 20814. 10,000. Phone: (301) 530-7145. www.faseb.org/asbmb.
Biological Sciences, American Institute of (1947): 1444 I St. N.W., Ste. 200, Washington, D.C. 20005. 6,000. Phone: (202) 628-1500. www.aibs.org.

Blind, American Council of the (1961): 1155 15th St. N.W., Ste. 1004, Washington, D.C. 20005. 40,000. Phone: (202) 467-5081. www.acb.org.

Blind, National Federation of the (1940): 1800 Johnson St., Baltimore, Md. 21230. 50,000. Phone: (410) 659-9314. www.nfb.org.

B'nai B'rith International (1843): 2020 K St. N.W., Washington, D.C. 20006. 500,000. Phone: (202) 857-6589. www.bbinet.org.

Booksellers Association, American (1900): 828 So. Broadway, Tarrytown, N.Y. 10591. 4,500. Phone: (914) 591-2665, (800) 637-0037. www.bookweb.org.

Boys & Girls Clubs of America (1906): 1230 West Peachtree St. N.W., Atlanta, Ga., 30309. 2,800,000 youth served. Phone: (404) 487-5700. www.bgca.org.

Boy Scouts of America (1910): 1325 W. Walnut Hill Lane, P.O. Box 152079, Irving, Tex. 75015-2079. 4.8 mil. www.scouting.org.

Brady Campaign, The (1974) (formerly Handgun Control, Inc.): 1225 Eye St. N.W., Ste. 1100, Washington, D.C. 20005. 380,000. Phone: (202) 898-0792. www.bradycampaign.org.

Broadcasters, National Association of (1922): 1771 N St. N.W., Washington, D.C. 20036-2891. Phone: (202) 429-5300. www.nab.org.

Brookings Institution, The (1916): 1775 Massachusetts Ave. N.W., Washington, D.C. 20036-2188. Phone: (202) 797-6000. www.brookings.org.

Business Education Association, National (1946): 1914 Association Dr., Reston, Va. 20191-1596. 16,000. Phone: (703) 860-8300; fax: (703) 620-4483. email: nbea@nbea.org; www.nbea.org.

Business Women's Association, American (1949): 9100 Ward Parkway, P.O. Box 8728, Kansas City, Mo. 64114-0728. 80,000. Phone: (800) 228-0007. fax: (816) 361-4991. email: abwa@abwahq.org. www.abwahq.org.

Camp Fire USA (1910): 4601 Madison Ave., Kansas City, Mo. 64112-1278. 629,000. Phone: (816) 756-1950. www.campfire.org.

Camping Association, The American (1910): 5000 State Rd. 67 N., Martinsville, Ind. 46151-7902. 5,500, 2,000+ camps. Phone: (765) 342-8456. www.acacamps.org.

Cancer Society, American (1913): 1599 Clifton Rd. N.E., Atlanta, Ga. 30329. Over 2 million volunteers. Phone: (800) ACS-2345 or check local listings. www.cancer.org.

CARE, Inc. (1945): 151 Ellis St. NE, Atlanta, Ga. 30303-2439. Programs in 62 developing countries. Phone: (404) 681-2552. www.care.org.

Carnegie Endowment for International Peace (1910): 1779 Massachusetts Ave., N.W., Washington, D.C. 20036–2103. Phone: (202) 483-7600; fax: (202) 483-1840. www.ceip.org.

Catholic Charities USA (1910): 1731 King St., Ste. 200, Alexandria, Va. 22314. 1,400 agencies and institutions. Phone: (703) 549-1390. www.catholiccharitiesusa.org.

Catholic Daughters of the Americas (1903): 10 W. 71st St., New York, N.Y. 10023. 115,000. Phone: (212) 877-3041. www.catholicdaughters.org.

Catholic War Veterans of the U.S.A. Inc. (1935): 441 N. Lee St., Alexandria, Va. 22314. 35,000. Phone: (703) 549-3622. www.cwv.org.

Cerebral Palsy Associations, Inc., United (1949): 1660 L St. N.W., Ste. 700, Washington, D.C. 20036. 153 affiliates. Phone: (800) USA-5-UCP, (202) 776-0406, TTY (202) 973-7197. www.ucpa.org.

Chamber of Commerce of the U.S. (1912): 1615 H St. N.W., Washington, D.C. 20062. 220,000. Phone: (202) 659-6000. www.uschamber.com.

Chemical Engineers, American Institute of (1908): 3 Park Ave., New York, N.Y. 10016-5991. 52,000. Phone: (212) 591-8100; (800) 242-4363. www.aiche.org.

Chemical Society, American (1876): 1155 16th St. N.W., Washington, D.C. 20036. 151,024. Phone: (800) 227-5558. www.chemistry.org.

Chess Federation, United States (1939): 3054 NYS Rte. 9W, New Windsor, N.Y. 12553. 50,000+. Phone: (845) 562-8350. www.uschess.org.

Child Labor Committee, National (1904): 1501 Broadway, Ste. 403, New York, N.Y. 10036. Phone: (212) 840-1801. www.kapow.org.

Children's Book Council (1945): 12 W. 37th St., 2nd Fl., New York, N.Y. 10018-7480. Phone: (212) 966-1990; fax: (212) 966-2073. email: staff@cbcbooks.org. www.cbcbooks.org.

Child Welfare League of America (1920): 440 First St. N.W., 3rd Fl., Washington, D.C. 20001-2085. 1,000 agencies. Phone: (202) 638-2952. www.cwla.org.

Chiropractic Association, American (1963): 1701 Clarendon Blvd., Arlington, Va. 22209. 22,000. Phone: (800) 986-4636; fax: (703) 243-2593. www.amerchiro.org.

Cities, National League of (1924): 1301 Pennsylvania Ave. N.W., Washington, D.C. 20004-1763. 18,000 cities and towns. Phone: (202) 626-3000. www.nlc.org.

Civil Air Patrol, National Headquarters (1941): 105 S. Hansell St., Bldg. 714, Maxwell AFB, Ala. 36112-6332. 53,000. Phone: (334) 953-4287. www.capnhq.gov.

Civil Engineers, American Society of (1852): 1801 Alexander Bell Dr., Reston, Va. 20191-4400. 123,000. Phone: (800) 548–ASCE (2723); (703) 295-6300. www.asce.org.

Clinical Pathologists, American Society of (1922): 2100 W. Harrison St., Chicago, Ill. 60612. 77,200. Phone: (312) 738-1336. www.ascp.org.

College Fund, United Negro (UNCF) (1944): 8260 Willow Oaks Corporate Dr., P.O. Box 10444, Fairfax, Va. 22031. 39 member institutions. Phone: (703) 205-3400, (800) 331-2244; fax: (703) 205-3576. www.uncf.org.

Colleges and Employers, National Association of (formerly College Placement Council) (1956): 62 E. Highland Ave., Bethlehem, Pa. 18017. 3,200. Phone: (800) 544-5272. www.naceweb.org.

Common Cause (1970): 1250 Connecticut Ave. N.W., Washington, D.C. 20036. 250,000. Phone: (800) 926-1064. www.commoncause.org.

Composers/USA, National Association of (1933): P.O. Box 49256, Barrington Station, Los Angeles, Calif. 90049. 600. Phone: (310) 541-8213. www.music-usa.org/nacusa/.

Congress of Racial Equality (CORE) (1942): 817 Broadway, 3rd Flr., New York, N.Y. 10003. Nationwide network of chapters. Phone: (212) 598-4000; fax: (212) 598-4141. www.core-online.org.

Conscientious Objectors, Central Committee for (1948): 1515 Cherry St., Philadelphia, Pa. 19102. Phone: (215) 563-8787. 630 20th St., Oakland, Calif. 94612. Phone: (510) 465-1617. www.objector.org.

Conservation Engineers, Association of (1961): John Bruner, 125 W. 25th St., Cheyenne, Wyo. 82002. Phone: (307) 777-6325. www.conservation.state.mo.us/engineering/ace.

Consumer Federation of America (1968): 1424 16th St. N.W., Ste. 604, Washington, D.C. 20036. 260 member organizations. Phone: (202) 387-6121. www.consumerfed.org.

Consumers League, National (1899): 1701 K St. N.W., Ste. 1200, Washington, D.C. 20006. Phone: (202) 835-3323. www.natlconsumersleague.org.

Consumers Union (1936): 101 Truman Ave., Yonkers, N.Y. 10703-1057. 4.6 million subscribers to *Consumer Reports Magazine*. Phone: (914) 378-2000. www.consumersunion.org.

Country Music Association (1958): One Music Circle South, Nashville, Tenn. 37203. 6,000. Phone: (615) 244-2840. www.cmaworld.com.

Credit Management, National Association of (1896): 8840 Columbia 100 Parkway, Columbia, Md. 21045-2158. 30,000+ members. Phone: (410) 740-5560. www.nacm.org.

Credit Union National Association (1934): P.O. Box 431, Madison, Wis. 53701-0431. 51 state leagues representing 12,400 credit unions. Phone: (800) 356-9655. www.cuna.org.

Crime and Delinquency, National Council on (1907): 1970 Broadway, Ste. 500, Oakland, Calif. 94612. Phone: (510) 208-0500. www.nccd-crc.org.

CSA/USA, Celiac Sprue Association/United States of America, Inc., (1978): P.O. Box 31700, Omaha, Neb. 68131-0700. 6 regions in U.S., 74 chapters, 36 active resource units. Phone: (402) 558-0600; fax: (402) 558-1347. www.csaceliacs.org.

Dairy Council, National (1915): 10255 W. Higgins Rd. Ste. 900, Rosemont, Ill. 60018. www.nationaldairycouncil.org.

Daughters of the American Revolution, National Society (1896): 1776 D St. N.W., Washington, D.C. 20006-5303. 172,000. Phone: (202) 628-1776. www.dar.org.

Deaf, National Association of the (1880): 814 Thayer Ave., Silver Spring, Md. 20910-4500. 51 state association affiliates. Phone: (301) 587-1788 V; (301) 587-1789 TTY. www.nad.org.

Defenders of Wildlife (1947): 1130 17th St. N.W., Washington, D.C. 20030. 200,000 members and supporters. Phone: (202) 682-9400. www.defenders.org.

Dental Association, American (1859): 211 E. Chicago Ave., Chicago, Ill. 60611. 141,000. Phone: (312) 440-2500. www.ada.org.

Diabetes Association, American (1940): 1701 N. Beauregard St., Alexandria, Va. 22311. Phone: (703) 549-1500; (800) 342-2383. www.diabetes.org/.

Dignity (1969): 1500 Massachusetts Ave. N.W., Ste. 11, Washington, D.C. 20005. 5,000. Phone: (202) 861-0017 and (800) 877-8797. www.dignityusa.org.

Disabled American Veterans (1920): 3725 Alexandria Pike, Cold Spring, Ky. 41076. 1,400,000. Phone: (859) 441-7300. www.dav.org.

Dowsers, Inc., The American Society of (1961): P.O. Box 24, Danville, Vt. 05828. 5,000. Phone: (800) 711-9530. email: ASD@dowsers.org. www.dowsers.org.

Ducks Unlimited, Inc. (1937): One Waterfowl Way, Memphis, Tenn. 38120. 600,000. Phone: (800) 45DUCKS. www.ducks.org.

Earthwatch (1971): 3 Clock Tower Place, Ste. 100, Box 75, Maynard, Mass. 01754. 75,000. Phone: (978) 461-0081. www.earthwatch.org.

Eastern Star, Order of, General Grand Chapter (1876): 1618 New Hampshire Ave. N.W., Washington, D.C. 20009-2549. 1,207,301. Phone: (202) 667-4737. www.easternstar.org.

Easter Seal Society, The National (1919): 230 W. Monroe, Ste. 1800, Chicago, Ill. 60606. 109 state and local affiliate societies operating 500 service sites. Phone: (312) 726-6200; (312) 726-4258 TTY. www.easter-seals.org.

Economic Association, American (1885): 2014 Broadway, Ste. 305, Nashville, Tenn. 37203. 22,000. 5,500 inst. subscribers. Phone: (615) 322-2595. www.vanderbilt.edu/AEA.

Edison Electric Institute (1933): 701 Pennsylvania Ave. N.W., Washington, D.C. 20004-2696. Phone: (202) 508-5000. www.eei.org.

Education, American Council on (ACE), (1918): One Dupont Circle N.W., Washington, D.C. 20036-1193. 1,600+ colleges and universities and 200+ higher education associations. Phone: (202) 939-9300. www.acenet.edu.

Educational Exchange, Council on International (1947): 7 Custom House St., 3rd Fl., Portland, Maine 04101. Phone: (800) 40-STUDY. www.ciee.org.

Educational Research Association, American (1916): 1230 17th St. N.W., Washington, D.C. 20036-3078. 22,000. Phone: (202) 223-9485. www.aera.net.

Education Association, National (1857): 1201 16th St. N.W., Washington, D.C. 20036-3290. 2.3 million. Phone: (202) 833-4000. www.nea.org.

Electrochemical Society, The (1902): 65 S. Main St., Pennington, N.J. 08534-2839. 7,000. Phone: (609) 737-1902; fax: (609) 737-2743. email: ecs@electrochem.org. www.electrochem.org.

Elks of the U.S.A., Benevolent and Protective Order of the (1868): 2750 N. Lakeview Ave., Chicago, Ill. 60614-1889. 1,300,000. Phone: (773) 755-4700. www.elks.org/default.cfm.

Energy Engineers, Association of (1977): 4025 Pleasantdale Rd., Ste. 420, Atlanta, Ga. 30340. 8,500. Phone: (770) 447-5083; fax: (770) 446-3969. email: info@aeecenter.org. www.aeecenter.org.

English-Speaking Union of the United States (1920): 144 E. 39th St., New York, N.Y. 10016. 18,000. Phone: (212) 817-1200. www.english-speakingunion.org.

Entomological Society of America (1889): 9301 Annapolis Rd., Lanham, Md. 20706-3115. 7,400+. Phone: (301) 731-4535; fax: (301) 731-4538. email: esa@entsoc.org. www.entsoc.org.

Esperanto League for North America, The (1952): P.O. Box 1129, El Cerrito, Calif. 94530. Over 1,000. Phone: (800) 377-3726. www.esperanto-usa.org.

Exceptional Children, The Council for (1922): 1110 N. Glebe Rd., Ste. 300, Arlington, Va. 22201-5704. 54,000. Phone: (703) 620-3660 V; (703) 264-9446 TTY; fax: (703) 264-9494. email: cec@cec.sped.org. www.cec.sped.org.

Exploration Geophysicists, Society of (1930): 8801 South Yale, Tulsa, Okla. 74137-3575. 16,536. Phone: (918) 497-5500. www.seg.org.

Family and Consumer Sciences, American Association of (1909): 1555 King St., Alexandria, Va. 22314. 14,500. Phone: (703) 706-4600. www.aafcs.org.

Family Campers & RVers (1949): 176 Tyler Ave., Englewood, Fla. 34223-3651. 42,000 families. www.fcrv.org.

Family, Career, and Community Leaders of America [evolved from Future Homemakers of America, Inc. (1945)]: 1910 Association Dr., Reston, Va. 20191-1584. 230,000. Phone: (703) 476-4900. www.fcclainc.org.

Family Physicians, American Academy of (1947): 11400 Tomahawk Creek Pkwy., Leawood, Kans. 66211-2672. 88,000. Phone: (913) 906-6000. www.aafp.org.

Family Relations, National Council on (1938): 3989 Central Ave. N.E., #550, Minneapolis, Minn. 55421. 42,000 families. Phone: (888) 781-9331. www.ncfr.com.

Farm Bureau Federation, American (1919): 225 Touhy Ave., Park Ridge, Ill. 60068. 4.7 million member families. Phone: (847) 685-8600. www.fb.com.

Federal Bar Association (1920): 2215 M St. N.W., Washington, D.C. 20037. 15,000. Phone: (202) 785-1614; fax: (202) 785-1568. www.fedbar.org.

Federal Employees, National Federation of (1917): 1016 16th St. N.W., Washington, D.C. 20036. 150,000. Phone: (202) 862-4400. www.nffe.org.

Fellowship of Reconciliation (1915): 521 N. Broadway, Nyack, N.Y. 10960. 20,000. Phone: (845) 358-4601. www.forusa.org.

Female Executives, National Association for (1972): P.O. Box 156, Congers, N.Y. 10920. 150,000+. Phone: (800) 927-NAFE. www.nafe.com.

FFA Organization, National (1928): P.O. Box 68960, 6060 FFA Dr., Indianapolis, Ind. 46268. 457,278. Phone: (317) 802-6060. www.ffa.org.

Fire Protection Association, National (1896): One Batterymarch Park, Quincy, Mass. 02169-7471. 65,000+. Phone: (617) 770-3000. www.nfpa.org.

Flag Foundation, National (1968): Flag Plaza, 1275 Bedford Ave, Pittsburgh, Pa. 15219. 3,000+. Phone: (412) 261-1776. www.americanflags.org.

Fleet Reserve Association (1924): 125 N. West St., Alexandria, Va. 22314-2754. 162,000. Phone: (703) 683-1400. www.fra.org.

Foreign Policy Association (1918): 470 Park Ave. So., New York, N.Y. 10016-6819. Phone: (212) 481-8100. www.fpa.org.

Foreign Relations, Council on (1921): 58 E. 68th St., New York, N.Y. 10021. 3,400. Phone: (212) 434-9400. www.cfr.org.

Foreign Study, American Institute for (1964): River Plaza, 9 W. Broad St., Stamford, Conn. 06902-3788. Phone: (800) 727-2437. www.aifs.org.

Forensic Sciences, American Academy of (1948): 410 N. 21st St., Ste. 203., P.O. Box 669, Colorado Springs, Colo. 80901-0669. 4,315. Phone: (719) 636-1100; fax: (719) 636-1993. www.aafs.org.

Foresters, Society of American (1900): 5400 Grosvenor Lane, Bethesda, Md. 20814. 18,000. Phone: (301) 897-8720. www.safnet.org.

4-H Program (early 1900s): 1400 Independence Ave., S.W., Washington, D.C. 20250. 5.6 million. Phone: (202) 720-2908. www.4-h.org/.

Freedom of Information Center (1958): 133 Neff Annex, Univ. of Missouri, Columbia, Mo. 65211. Phone: (573) 882-4856. www.missouri.edu/~foiwww/

French Institute/Alliance Française (1898): 22 E. 60th St., New York, N.Y. 10022. 9,000. Phone: (212) 355-6100. www.fiaf.org.

Friends of Animals Inc. (1957): 777 Post Rd., Darien, Conn. 06820. 120,000. Phone: (203) 656-1522. www.friendsofanimals.org/.

Friends of the Earth (1969): 1025 Vermont Ave. N.W., Washington, D.C. 20005. 35,000. Phone: (877) 843-8687. www.foe.org.

Gamblers Anonymous: Box 17173, Los Angeles, Calif. 90017. Phone: (213) 386-8789. www.gamblersanonymous.org.

Gay and Lesbian Task Force, National (1973): 1325 Massachusetts Ave. N.W., Ste. 600, Washington, D.C. 20005. 35,000 members. Phone: (202) 393-5177. www.ngltf.org.

Genealogical Society, National (1903): 4527 17th St. N., Arlington, Va. 22207-2399. 17,000+. Phone: (703) 525-0050; fax: (703) 525-0052. www.ngsgenealogy.org.

Geographers, Association of American (1904): 1710 16th St. N.W., Washington, D.C. 20009-3198. 7,000. Phone: (202) 234-1450; fax: (202) 234-2744. email: gaia@aag.org. www.aag.org.

Geographic Education, National Council for (1915): 206A Martin Hall, Jacksonville State University, Jacksonville, Ala. 36265-1602. 3,700. Phone: (256) 782-5293. www.ncge.org.

Geographic Society, National (1888): 1145 17th St. N.W., Washington, D.C. 20036-4688. 9,200,000. Phone: (800) 647-5463. www.nationalgeographic.com.

Geological Institute, American (1948): 4220 King St., Alexandria, Va. 22302-1502. 34 geoscience societies representing 100,000 geoscientists. Phone: (703) 379-2480. www.agiweb.org/.

Geological Society of America, Inc. (1888): P.O. Box 9140, Boulder, Colo. 80301-9140. 15,000. Phone: (303) 447-2020. www.geosociety.org.

German American National Congress, The (Deutsch-Amerikanischer National Kongress—D.A.N.K.) (1958): 4740 N. Western Ave., Executive Office, Chicago, Ill. 60625-2097. Phone: (773) 275-1100. www.dank.org.

Gideons International, The (1889): P.O. Box 140800, Nashville, Tenn. 37214-0800. 130,000. Phone: (615) 883-8533. www.gideons.org.

Gifted, The Association for the (1958): Indiana Academy for Science, Mathematics, and Humanities, Ball State University, Muncie, Ind. 47036. Phone: (765) 285-7455. www.cectag.org

Girl Scouts of the U.S.A. (1912): 420 Fifth Ave., New York, N.Y. 10018-2798. 2,500,000. Phone: (212) 852-8000. www.girlscouts.org.

Girls Incorporated (1945): 120 Wall St., 3rd. Flr., New York, N.Y. 10005. 350,000. Phone: (800) 374-4475. www.girlsinc.org.

Graphoanalysis Society, International (1929): 111 N. Canal St., Ste. 955, Chicago, Ill. 60606. 10,000. Phone: (312) 930-9446; www.igas.com.

Gray Panthers (1970): 733 15th St. N.W., Ste. 437, Washington, D.C. 20005. Over 50 chapters (networks). Phone: (202) 737-1160. www.graypanthers.org.

Greenpeace (1971): 702 H St. N.W., Washington, D.C. 20001. 2.5 million. Phone: (800) 326-0959. www.greenpeaceusa.org.

Guide Dog Foundation for the Blind, Inc.® (1946): 371 E. Jericho Turnpike, Smithtown, N.Y. 11787-2976. 100,000. Phone: (631) 265-2121; (800) 548-4337; fax: (631) 361-5192. www.guidedog.org.

Hadassah, The Women's Zionist Organization of America (1912): 50 W. 58th St., New York, N.Y. 10019. 385,000. Phone: (212) 355-7900. www.hadassah.org.

Heating, Refrigerating and Air-Conditioning Engineers, Inc., American Society of (1959): 1791 Tullie Circle N.E., Atlanta, Ga. 30329. 50,000. Phone: (404) 636-8400. www.ashrae.org.

Helicopter Association International (1948): 1635 Prince St., Alexandria, Va. 22314. Phone: (703) 683-4646. www.rotor.com.

Historians, The Organization of American (1907): 112 N. Bryan St., Bloomington, Ind. 47408-4199. 12,000. Phone: (812) 855-7311. www.oah.org.

Historic Preservation, National Trust for (1949): 1785 Massachusetts Ave. N.W., Washington, D.C. 20036. 275,000. Phone: (202) 588–6000. www.nationaltrust.org.

Horse Council, Inc., American (1969): 1616 H St. N.W., 7th Fl., Washington, D.C. 20006. More than 190 organizations and 2,400 individuals. Phone: (202) 296-4030. www.horsecouncil.org.

Horse Shows Association, Inc., American (1917): 4047 Iron Works Parkway, Lexington, Ky. 40511. 70,000+. Phone: (859) 258-2472. www.ahsa.org.

Horticultural Association, National Junior (1935): 15 Railroad Ave., Homer City, Pa. 15748. Phone: (724) 479-3254. www.njha.org.

Horticultural Society, American (1922): 7931 East Boulevard Dr., Alexandria, Va. 22308. 22,000. Phone: (703) 768-5700 or (800) 777-7931; fax: (703) 768-8700. www.ahs.org.

Hostelling International—American Youth Hostels (1934): 8401 Colesville Rd., Ste. 600, Silver Spring, Md. 20910. 120,000. Phone: (301) 495-1240 for membership and reservations. www.hiayh.org.

Humane Association, American (1877): 63 Inverness Drive East, Englewood, Colo. 80112-5117. Phone: (866) 242-1877. www.americanhumane.org.

Humane Society of the United States (1954): 2100 L St. N.W., Washington, D.C. 20037. 5,000,000. Phone: (202) 452-1100. www.hsus.org.

Humanities, National Endowment for the (1965): 1100 Pennsylvania Ave. N.W., Washington, D.C. 20506. Phone: (202) 606-8400. www.neh.fed.us.

Hydrogen Energy, International Association for (1975): P.O. Box 248266, Coral Gables, Fla. 33124. 2,500. Phone: (305) 284-4666. www.iahe.org.

Industrial Engineers, Institute of (1948): 3577 Parkway Lane, Ste. 200, Norcross, Ga. 30092. 17,000+. Phone: (800) 494-0460. www.iienet.org.
Insurance and Financial Advisors, National Association of (1890): 2901 Telestar Court, Falls Church, Va. 22042–1205. 108,000. Phone: (877) TO-NAIFA. www.naifa.org..
Izaak Walton League of America (1922): 707 Conservation Lane, Gaithersburg, Md. 20878-2983. 50,000+. Phone: (800) 453-5463. www.iwla.org.
Jewish Community Centers Association (JCC) of North America (1917): 15 E. 26th St., New York, N.Y. 10010-1579. 275+ affiliated Jewish Community Centers, YM-YWHAs, and camps serving 1 million+ members. Phone: (212) 532-4958; fax: (212) 481-4174. email: info@jcca.org. www.jcca.org.
Jewish Congress, American (1918): 1001 Connecticut Ave., N.W., Ste. 407, Washington, D.C., 20036. 50,000. Phone: (202) 466–9661. www.ajcongress.org.
Jewish Historical Society, American (1892): 15 W. 16th St., New York, N.Y. 10011. 3,500. Phone: (212) 294-6160; fax: (212) 294-6161. email: ajhs@ajhs.org. www.ajhs.org.
Jewish War Veterans of the U.S.A. (1896): 1811 R St. N.W., Washington, D.C. 20009-1659. Phone: (202) 265-6280. www.jwv.org.
Jewish Women, National Council of (1893): 53 W. 23rd St., New York, N.Y. 10010. 90,000. Phone: (800) 829–NCJW. www.ncjw.org.
John Birch Society (1958): P.O. Box 8040, Appleton, Wis. 54912. Under 100,000. Phone: (920) 749-3780; fax: (920) 749-5062. www.jbs.org.
Journalists, Society of Professional (1909): 3909 N. Meridian St., Indianapolis, Ind. 46208. 13,500. Phone: (317) 927-8000. www.spj.org.
Judaism, American Council for (1943): P.O. Box 9009, Alexandria, Va. 22304. Phone: (703) 836-2546. www.acjna.org
Junior Achievement Inc. (1919): One Education Way, Colorado Springs, Colo. 80906. 5.2 million. Phone: (719) 540-8000; fax: (719) 540-6299. www.ja.org.
Junior Chamber of Commerce, The United States, Jaycees (1920): P.O. Box 7, Tulsa, Okla. 74102-0007. 113,000. Phone: (918) 584-2481; fax: (918) 584-4422. www.usjaycees.org.
Junior Leagues International, Inc., Association of (1921): 132 W. 31st St., 11th flr.; New York, N.Y. 10001-3406. 295 Leagues, 193,000+ members. Phone: (212) 951-8300. www.ajli.org.
Junior State of America (1934): 60 E. Third Ave., Ste. 320, San Mateo, Calif. 94401-4302. 15,000. Phone: (650) 347-1600 or (800) 334-5353. www.jsa.org.
Kiwanis International (1915): 3636 Woodview Trace, Indianapolis, Ind. 46268. 316,000. Phone: (317) 875-8755. email: kiwanismail@kiwanis.org. www.kiwanis.org.
Knights of Columbus (1852): One Columbus Plaza, New Haven, Conn. 06510. 1,600,000. Phone: (203) 752-4000. www.kofc.org.
Knights Templar, Grand Encampment of (1816): 5097 N. Elston Ave., Ste. 101, Chicago, Ill. 60630-2460. 220,000. Phone: (773) 777-3300. www.knightstemplar.org.
La Leche League International (1956): 1400 N. Meacham Rd., Schaumburg, Ill. 60173-4808. 50,000. Phone: (847) 519-7730. www.lalecheleague.org.
Law, American Society of International (1906): 2223 Massachusetts Ave. N.W., Washington, D.C. 20008. 4,300. Phone: (202) 939-6000. www.asil.org.
League of Women Voters of the U.S. (1920): 1730 M St. N.W., Washington, D.C. 20036-4508. Phone: (202) 429-1965; fax: (202) 429-0854. www.lwv.org.
Legal Aid and Defender Association, National (1911): 1140 Connecticut Ave. N.W., Washington, D.C. 20036. 2,400. Phone: (202) 452-0620. www.nlada.org.
Legal Professionals, National Association of (1949): 314 East 3rd St., Ste. 210, Tulsa, Okla. 74120-2409. 6,000. Phone: (918) 582-5188. www.nals.org.
Leukemia & Lymphoma Society (1949): 1311 Mamaroneck Ave., White Plains, NY 10605. Phone: (914) 949-5213. www.leukemia-lymphoma.org.
Library Association, American (1876): 50 E. Huron St., Chicago, Ill. 60611. 57,000. Phone: (800) 545-2433. www.ala.org.
Lions Clubs International (1917): 300 22nd St., Oak Brook, Ill. 60523-8842. 1,419,408. Phone: (630) 571-5466. www.lionsclubs.org.
Lung Association, American (1904): 61 Broadway, New York, N.Y. 10006. 99 constituent and affiliate associations. Phone: (212) 315-8700. www.lungusa.org.
Magazine Editors, American Society of (1963): 919 Third Ave., 22nd Flr., New York, N.Y. 10022. 900. Phone: (212) 872-3737. www.asme.magazine.org
Management Accountants, Institute of (1919): 10 Paragon Dr., Montvale, N.J. 07645-1759. 80,000. Phone: (800) 638-4427. www.imanet.org.
Management Association, American (1923): 1601 Broadway, New York, N.Y. 10019. 700,000. Phone: (212) 586-8100. www.amanet.org.
Management Consultants, Institute of (1968): 2025 M St. N.W., Ste. 800, Washington, D.C. 20036–2557. 25 chapters. Phone: (202) 367-1134. www.imcusa.org.
Manufacturers, National Association of (1895): 1331 Pennsylvania Ave. N.W., Washington, D.C. 20004-1790. Approx. 14,000. Phone: (202) 637-3000. www.nam.org.
Manufacturing Engineers, Society of: One SME Drive, Dearborn, Mich. 48121. Phone: (313) 271–1500 x 1078; fax: (313) 240–8251. www.sme.org.
March of Dimes Birth Defects Foundation (1938): 1275 Mamaroneck Ave., White Plains, N.Y. 10605. 104 chapters. Phone: (888) 663-4637. www.modimes.org.
Marine Conservation, Center for (1972):1725 De Sales St., N.W., Ste. 600, Washington, D.C. 20036. 120,000. Phone: (202) 429-5609. www.cmc-ocean.org.
Marine Corps Association (1913): 715 Broadway, Quantico, Va. 22134. 100,723. Phone: (703) 640-6161; (800) 336-0291. www.mca-marines.org.
Marine Technology Society (1963): 5565 Sterrett Place, Ste. 108, Columbia, Md. 21044. 2,000+. Phone: (410) 884-5330; fax: (202) 429-9417. www.mtsociety.org.
Masons, Ancient and Accepted Scottish Rite, Northern Masonic Jurisdiction, Supreme Council 33 (1813): P.O. Box 519, Lexington, Mass. 02420-0519. 330,000. Phone: (781) 862-4410. www.supremecouncil.org/
Masons, Ancient and Accepted Scottish Rite, Southern Jurisdiction, Supreme Council (1801): 1733 16th St. N.W., Washington, D.C. 20009. 500,000. Phone: (202) 232-3579. www.srmason-sj.org/web
Mathematical Association of America (1915): P.O. Box 91112, Washington, D.C. 20090-1112. Phone: (800) 331-1622. www.maa.org.
Mathematical Society, American (1888): 201 Charles St., Providence, R.I. 02940-6248. Phone: (401) 455-4000. email: ams@ams.org. www.ams.org.
Mayflower Descendants, General Society of (1897): P.O. Box 3297, Plymouth, Mass. 02361. 24,500+. Phone: (508) 746-3188. www.mayflower.org.
Mechanical Engineers, American Society of (1880): 3 Park Ave., New York, N.Y. 10016-5990. 125,000. Phone: (800) 843-2763. www.asme.org.
Medical Association, American (1847): 515 N. State St., Chicago, Ill. 60610. 300,000 physicians. Phone: (312) 464-5000. www.ama-assn.org.

Mental Health Association, National (1909): 2001 N. Beauregard St., 12th Fl., Alexandria, Va., 22311. 340 affiliates. Phone: (703) 684-7722; (800) 969-NMHA; TTY (800) 433-5959; fax: (703) 684-5968. email: nmhainfo@aol.com. www.nmha.org

Meteorological Society, American (1919): 45 Beacon St., Boston, Mass. 02108-3693. 11,000+. Phone: (617) 227-2425. www.ametsoc.org/ams.

Military Chaplains Association of the U.S.A. (1925): P.O. Box 7056, Arlington, Va. 22207-7056. 1,500. Phone: (703) 276-2189. www.mca-usa.org.

Mining, Metallurgical, and Petroleum Engineers, The American Institute of (1871): 8307 Shaffer Parkway, Littleton, Colo. 80127-4012. 4 Member Societies: Society for Mining, Metallurgy and Exploration; The Minerals, Metals & Materials Society; Iron & Steel Society; Society of Petroleum Engineers. Phone: (303) 948-4255; fax: (303) 948-4260. email: aime@aimehq.org. www.aimehq.org.

Model Aeronautics, Academy of (1936): 5161 East Memorial Dr., Muncie, Ind. 47302. 150,000. Phone: (765) 287-1256. www.modelaircraft.org/templates/ama/.

Modern Language Association of America (1883): 26 Broadway, 3rd Fl., New York, N.Y. 10004-1789. 30,000+. Phone: (646) 576-5000. www.mla.org.

Moose International, Inc. (1888): Rte. 31, Mooseheart, Ill. 60539. 1,600,000+. Phone: (630) 859-2000. www.mooseintl.org.

Mothers Against Drunk Driving (MADD) (1980): 511 E. John Carpenter Frwy., Ste. 700, Irving, Tex. 75062. 3 million members and supporters. Victim hotline: (800) GET-MADD. www.madd.org.

Motion Picture Arts & Sciences, Academy of (1927): 8949 Wilshire Blvd., Beverly Hills, Calif. 90211-1972. Phone: (310) 247-3000. www.oscars.org.

Multiple Sclerosis Society, National (1946): 733 Third Ave., New York, N.Y. 10017. 350,000. Phone: (800) FIGHT-MS (344-4867). www.nationalmssociety.org.

Muscular Dystrophy Association (1950): 3300 East Sunrise Dr., Tucson, Ariz. 85718. 2,300,000 volunteers. Phone: (800) 572-1717. www.mdausa.org.

Museums, American Association of (1906): 1575 Eye St. N.W., Ste. 400, Washington, D.C. 20005. 16,000+. Phone: (202) 289-1818; fax: (202) 289-6578, TTY (202) 289-8439. www.aam-us.org.

Muzzle Loading Rifle Association, National (1933): P.O. Box 67, Friendship, Ind. 47021-0067. 25,000. Phone: (812) 667-5131. www.nmlra.org.

NAFSA: Association of International Educators (1948): 1307 New York Ave. N.W., 8th Flr., Washington, D.C. 20005-4701. 8,000+. Phone: (202) 737-3699. www.nafsa.org.

National Abortion and Reproductive Rights Action League (NARAL) (1969): 1156 15th St. N.W., Washington, D.C. 20005. 500,000. Phone: (202) 973-3000. www.naral.org.

National Association for the Advancement of Colored People (1909): 4805 Mt. Hope Dr., Baltimore, Md. 21215. 500,000+. Phone: (877) NAACP-98. www.naacp.org.

National Association of Insurance and Financial Advisors (1890): 2901 Telestar Court, Falls Church, Va. 22042-1205. 80,000. Phone: (703) 770-8100. www.naifa.org/index.html.

National Conference for Community and Justice, The (founded as The Natl. Conf. of Christians & Jews) (1927): 475 Park Avenue South, 19th Flr., New York, N.Y. 10016-6901. Phone: (212) 545-1300. www.nccj.org.

National Cooperative Business Association (formerly Cooperative League of the U.S.A.) (1916): 1401 New York Ave. N.W., Ste. 1100, Washington, D.C. 20005. Phone: (202) 638-6222. www.ncba.org.

National Council of La Raza (1968): 1111 19th St. N.W., Ste. 1000, Washington, D.C. 20036. 20,000+. Phone: (202) 785-1670. www.nclr.org.

National Council of the Churches of Christ in the USA (1950): 475 Riverside Drive, Rm. 850, New York, N.Y. 10115. 35 Protestant and Orthodox communions. Phone: (212) 870-2227. www.ncccusa.org.

National Grange of the Order of Patrons of Husbandry (1867): 1616 H St. N.W., Washington, D.C. 20006-4999. 300,000. Phone: (202) 628-3507; fax: (202) 347-1091. www.nationalgrange.org.

National Press Club (1908): National Press Bldg., 529 14th St. N.W., 13th Flr., Washington, D.C. 20045. 4,500+. Phone: (202) 662-7500. npc.press.org.

National PTA (National Congress of Parents and Teachers) (1897): 330 N. Wabash Ave., Ste. 2100, Chicago, Ill. 60611. 6.5 million. Phone: (800) 307-4782. email: info@pta.org. www.pta.org.

National Rifle Association of America (1871): 11250 Waples Mill Rd., Fairfax, Va. 22030. 3,300,000. Phone: (703) 267-1000. www.nra.org.

National Urban League, Inc. (1910): 120 Wall St., New York, N.Y. 10005. 115 affiliates in 34 states and D.C. Phone: (212) 558-5300. www.nul.org.

National Wildlife Federation (1936): 11100 Wildlife Center Dr., Reston, Va. 20190. 4,000,000+. Phone: (703) 438-6000. www.nwf.org.

Nature Conservancy, The (1951): 4245 N. Fairfax Dr., Ste. 100, Arlington, Va. 22203-1606. 900,000. Phone: (800) 628-6860. http://nature.org.

Naturopathic Physicians, American Association of (1986): 3201 New Mexico Ave. N.W., Ste. 350, Washington, D.C. 20016. 1,700. Phone: (866) 538-2267. www.naturopathic.org.

Naval Architects and Marine Engineers, The Society of (1893): 601 Pavonia Ave., Jersey City, N.J. 07306. 10,000+. Phone: (800) 798-2188; fax: (201) 798-4975. www.sname.org.

Naval Engineers, American Society of (1888): 1452 Duke St., Alexandria, Va. 22314. 6,800. Phone: (703) 836-6727; fax: (703) 836-7491. www.navalengineers.org.

Naval Institute, United States (1873): 291 Wood Rd., Annapolis, Md. 21402. 80,000+. Phone: (410) 268-6110. www.usni.org.

Navigation, The Institute of (1945): 3975 University Dr., Ste. 390, Fairfax, Va. 22030. 3,800. Phone: (703) 383-9688; fax: (703) 383-9689. email: membership@ion.org. www.ion.org.

Navy League of the United States (1902): 2300 Wilson Blvd., Arlington, Va. 22201-3308. 71,500. Phone: (703) 528-1775. www.navyleague.org.

NDIA (National Defense Industrial Association) (1997): 2111 Wilson Blvd., Ste. 400, Arlington, Va. 22201. 28,000 individual, 900 companies. Phone: (703) 522-1820. www.ndia.org.

Neurofibromatosis Foundation, Inc., The National (1978): 95 Pine St., 16th Flr., New York, N.Y. 10005. 38,000. Phone: (800) 323-7938; in N.Y. State (212) 344-NNFF; fax: (212) 747-0004. email: nnff@aol.com. www.nf.org.

Newspaper Association of America (1992): 1921 Gallows Rd., Ste. 600, Vienna, Va. 22182–3900. 70,000+ newspaper executives. Phone (703) 902-1600. www.naa.org.

Nondestructive Testing, Inc., The American Society for (1941): 1711 Arlingate Lane, P.O. Box 28518, Columbus, Ohio 43228-0518. 10,240. Phone: (800) 222-ASNT. www.asnt.org.

Nuclear Society, American (1954): 555 N. Kensington Ave., La Grange Park, Ill. 60526. 13,000. Phone: (708) 352-6611. www.ans.org.

Numismatic Association, American (1891): 818 N. Cascade Ave., Colorado Springs, Colo. 80903-3279. 28,000. Phone: (719) 632-2646. email: ana@money.org. www.money.org.

Nurses Association, American (1897): 600 Maryland Ave. S.W., Ste. 100, Washington, D.C. 20024. 180,000. Phone: (800) 274-4ANA. www.ana.org.

Ocean Conservancy, The (formerly Center for Marine Conservation) (1972): 1725 De Sales St. N.W., Ste. 600, Washington, D.C. 20036. 120,000. Phone: (202) 429-5609. www.oceanconservancy.org/

Odd Fellows, Sovereign Grand Lodge, Independent Order of (1819): 422 Trade St., Winston-Salem, N.C. 27101. 460,000. Phone: (336) 725-5955. www.ioof.org.

Olympic Committee, United States (1921): One Olympic Plaza, Colorado Springs, Colo. 80909-5760. Phone: (719) 866-4500. www.olympic-usa.org.

Optimist International (1919): 4494 Lindell Blvd., St. Louis, Mo. 63108. 130,000+. Phone: (314) 371-6000. www.optimist.org.

Optometric Association, American (1898): 243 N. Lindbergh Blvd., St. Louis, Mo. 63141. 32,000. Phone: (314) 991-4100. www.aoanet.org.

Ornithologists' Union, American (1883): 1313 Dolley Madison Blvd., Ste. 402, McLean, Va 22101. 4,000. Phone: (202) 357-2051. www.aou.org.

Overeaters Anonymous, Inc. (1960): World Service Office, P.O. Box 44020, Rio Rancho, N.M. 87174–4020. 150,000. Phone: (505) 891-2664. www.overeatersanonymous.org.

Parents, Families and Friends of Lesbians and Gays (1981): 1726 M St. N.W., Ste. 400, Washington, D.C. 20036. 77,000 households. Phone: (202) 467-8180. www.pflag.org.

Parents Without Partners (1957): 1650 South Dixie Hwy., Ste. 510, Boca Raton, Fla. 33432. 50,000+. Phone: (561) 391-8833. www.parentswithoutpartners.org.

Peace Action (a merger of SANE and the Nuclear Weapons Freeze Campaign) (1957): 1100 Wayne Ave., Ste. 1020, Silver Spring, Md. 20910. 55,000. Phone: (301) 565-4050. www.webcom.com/peaceact.

People For the American Way (1980): 2000 M St. N.W., Ste. 400, Washington, D.C. 20036. 300,000. Phone: (202) 467-4999. www.pfaw.org.

Petroleum Geologists, American Association of (1917): 1444 South Boulder Ave., Tulsa, Okla. 74119. 31,500. Phone: (918) 584-2555. www.aapg.org.

Pharmaceutical Association, American (1852): 2215 Constitution Ave. N.W., Washington, D.C. 20037-2985. 50,000+. Phone: (202) 628-4410. www.aphanet.org.

Philatelic Society, American (1886): 100 Oakwood Ave., P.O. Box 8000, State College, Pa. 16803. 55,000+. Phone: (814) 237-3803. www.stamps.org.

Photogrammetry and Remote Sensing, American Society for (1934): 5410 Grosvenor Lane, Ste. 210, Bethesda, Md. 20814-2160. 7,000+. Phone: (301) 493-0290; fax: (301) 493-0208. email: asprs@asprs.org. www.asprs.org.

Photographic Society of America (1934): 3000 United Founders Blvd., Ste. 103, Oklahoma City, Okla. 73112-3940. Phone: (405) 843-1437. www.psa-photo.org.

Physical Society, The American (1899): One Physics Ellipse, College Park, Md. 20740-3844. 41,000. Phone: (301) 209-3200. www.aps.org.

Physical Therapy Association, American (APTA) (1921): 1111 N. Fairfax St., Alexandria, Va. 22314-1488. 66,000+. Phone: (703) 684-2782. www.apta.org.

Physics, American Institute of (1931): One Physics Ellipse, College Park, Md. 20740-3843. 125,000. Phone: (301) 209-3100. www.aip.org.

Pilot International (1921): Pilot International Headquarters, 244 College St., P.O. Box 4844, Macon, Ga. 31208-4844. 25,000. Phone: (478) 743-7403. www.pilotinternational.org.

Planetary Society, The (1980): 65 N. Catalina Ave., Pasadena, Calif. 91106-2301. 100,000. Phone: (626) 793-5100. www.planetary.org.

Planned Parenthood® Federation of America, Inc., (1916): 434 West 33rd St. New York, N.Y. 10001. 150 affiliates. Phone: (212) 541-7800; fax: (212) 245-1845. www.plannedparenthood.org.

Plastics Engineers, Society of (1942): P.O. Box 403, 14 Fairfield Dr., Brookfield, Conn. 06804-0403. 32,000+. Phone: (203) 775-0471. www.4spe.org.

Police and Concerned Citizens, American Federation of (1966): Records Center, 3801 Biscayne Blvd., Miami, Fla. 33137. 100,000. Phone: (305) 573-0070. www.aphf.org/p14_afop.html.

Police, International Association of Chiefs of (1893): 515 N. Washington St., Alexandria, Va. 22314-2357. 19,000+. Phone: (703) 836-6767. www.theiacp.org.

Political and Social Science, American Academy of (1889): 3814 Walnut St., Philadelphia, Pa. 19104–6197. Phone: (215) 746-6446. www.aapss.org/.

Political Science, Academy of (1880): 475 Riverside Dr., Ste. 1274, New York, N.Y. 10115-1274. 8,500. Phone: (212) 870-2500. www.psqonline.org.

Prevent Blindness America (1908): 500 E. Remington Rd., Schaumburg, Ill. 60173. 21 affiliates and divisions. Phone: (800) 331-2020. www.preventblindness.org.

Professional Engineers, National Society of (1934): 1420 King St., Alexandria, Va. 22314-2794. 60,000. Phone: (703) 684-2800; fax: (703) 836-4875. www.nspe.org.

Professional Photographers of America, Inc. (1880): 299 Peachtree St. N.W., #2200, Atlanta, Ga. 30303-2206. 14,000. Phone: (404) 522-8600. www.ppa.com.

Psychiatric Association, American (1844): 1000 Wilson Blvd., Ste. 1825, Arlington, Va. 22209-3901. 40,537. Phone: (703) 907-7300. www.psych.org.

Psychoanalytic Association, The American (1911): 309 E. 49th St., New York, N.Y. 10017. 3,000+ psychoanalysts. Phone: (212) 752-0450; fax: (212) 593-0571. www.apsa.org.

Psychological Association, American (1892): 750 First St. N.E., Washington, D.C. 20002–4242. 159,000. Phone: (202) 336 5500; (202) 336-6123 TTY. www.apa.org.

Public Health Association, American (1872): 800 I St. N.W., Washington, D.C. 20001-3710. 50,000+. Phone: (202) 777-2742. www.apha.org.

Puppeteers of America (1937): P.O. Box 29417, Parma, Ohio 44129-0417. Phone: (888) 568-6235. www.puppeteers.org

Quality, The American Society for (1946): 600 N. Plankinton Ave., Milwaukee, Wis. 53203. 135,000+. Phone: (414) 272-8575. www.asq.org.

Railroads, Association of American (1934): 50 F St. N.W., Washington, D.C. 20001-1564. Phone: (202) 639-2100. www.aar.org.

Recording Arts & Sciences, Inc., National Academy of (1957): 3402 Pico Blvd., Santa Monica, Calif. 90405. 13,000. Phone: (310) 392-3777. www.grammy.com.

Red Cross, American (1881): 2025 E Street N.W., Washington, D.C. 20006. Approx. 1,650 chapters. Phone: (202) 303-4498. www.redcross.org.

Rehabilitation Association, National (1925): 633 S. Washington St., Alexandria, Va. 22314. 12,000. Phone: (703) 836-0850; TDD: (703) 836-0849. www.nationalrehab.org.

Reserve Officers Association of the United States (1922): 1 Constitution Ave. N.E., Washington, D.C. 20002-5655. 93,000. Phone: (800) 809-9448. www.roa.org.

Retired Federal Employees, National Association (1921): 606 N. Washington St., Alexandria, Va. 22314. 400,000+. Phone: (703) 838-7760. www.narfe.org.

Reye's Syndrome Foundation, National (1974): P.O. Box 829, Bryan, Ohio 43506-0829. Phone: (800) 233-7393; fax: (419) 636-9897. email: nsrf@reyessyndrome.orgwww.reyessyndrome.org.

RID-USA (Remove Intoxicated Drivers) (1978): Box 520, Schenectady, N.Y. 12301. Phone: (518) 372-0034/(518) 393-HELP; fax: (518) 370-4917. www.crisny.org/not-for-profit/ridusa/.

Right to Life, Committee, Inc., National (1973): 512 10th St. N.W., Washington, D.C. 20004. Phone: (202) 626-8800. www.nrlc.org

Rotary International (1905): One Rotary Center, 1560 Sherman Ave., Evanston, Ill. 60201. 1.2 million in 161 countries and 35 geographical regions. Phone: (847) 866-3000. www.rotary.org.

SAE (Society of Automotive Engineers) (1905): 400 Commonwealth Dr., Warrendale, Pa. 15096-0001. 80,000. Phone: (724) 776-4847. www.sae.org.

Safety Council, National (1913): 1121 Spring Lake Dr., Itasca, Ill. 60143-3201. Phone: (630) 285-1121. www.nsc.org.

Salvation Army, The (1865): National Headquarters, P.O. Box 269, Alexandria, Va. 22313. 453,150. Phone: (703) 684-5500. www.salvationarmy.org.

Save-the-Redwoods League (1918): 114 Sansome St., Rm 1200, San Francisco, Calif. 94104-3823. 45,000. Phone: (415) 362-2352. www.savetheredwoods.org.

Science, American Association for the Advancement of (1848): 1200 New York Ave. N.W., Washington, D.C. 20005. 143,000. Phone: (202) 326-6400. www.aaas.org.

Science and Health, American Council on (1978): 1995 Broadway, 2nd Flr., New York, N.Y. 10023-5860. Phone: (212) 362-7044; fax: (212) 362-4919. email: acsh@acsh.org. www.acsh.org.

Science Fiction Society, World (1939): P.O. Box 426159, Kendall Square Station, Cambridge, Mass. 02142. email: mpc@wsfs.org www.wsfs.org.

Scientists, Federation of American (FAS) (1945): 1717 K St. N.W., Ste. 209, Washington, D.C. 20036. 4,000. Phone: (202) 546-3300. www.fas.org.

SCRABBLE® Association, National (1978): P.O. Box 700, 403 Front Street Garden, Greenport, N.Y. 11944. 10,000. Phone: (631) 477-0033. www.scrabble-assoc.com

Screen Actors Guild (1933): 5757 Wilshire Blvd., Los Angeles, Calif. 90036-3600. 96,000. Phone: (323) 954-1600. www.sag.com.

Sculpture Society, National (1893): 237 Park Ave., New York, N.Y. 10017. 4,000. Phone: (212) 764-5645. www.nationalsculpture.org

Seeing Eye Inc., The (1929): P.O. Box 375, Morristown, N.J. 07963-0375. Phone: (973) 539-4425. www.seeingeye.org.

Senior Citizens, National Alliance of (1974): 2525 Wilson Blvd., Arlington, Va. 22201. 117,000. Fax: (703) 528-4380.

Shrine of North America and Shriners Hospitals for Children, The (1872 and 1922): 2900 Rocky Point Drive, Tampa, Fla. 33607-1460. 525,000. Phone: (813) 281-0300. www.shrinershq.org.

Sierra Club (1892): 85 2nd Street, San Francisco, Calif. 94105-3441. 700,000+. Phone: (415) 977-5500. www.sierraclub.org.

SIETAR INTERNATIONAL (The International Society for Intercultural Education, Training and Research) (1974): c/o ICHEC, Blvd. Brand Whitlock 2, 1150 Brussels, Belgium. 12,500. Phone: (+32-2) 739 3843. www.sietarinternational.org.

Simon Wiesenthal Center (1977): 1399 South Roxbury, Los Angeles, Calif. 90035. 400,000 member families. Phone: (800) 900-9036. www.wiesenthal.org.

Small Business United, National (1937): 1156 15th St. N.W., Washington, D.C. 20005. 65,000+. Phone: (202) 293-8830; fax: (202) 872-8543. email: nsbu@nsbu.org. www.nsbu.org.

Social Work Education, Council on (1952): 1725 Duke St., Ste. 500, Alexandria, Va. 22314. Phone: (703) 683-8080; fax: (703) 683-8099. www.cswe.org.

Social Workers, National Association of (1955): 750 First St. N.E., Ste. 700, Washington, D.C. 20002-4241. Phone: (202) 408-8600. www.naswdc.org.

Society for Integrative and Comparative Biology (formerly the American Society of Zoologists) (1890): 1313 Dolley Madison Blvd. #402, McLean, Va. 22101. 2,100. Phone: (703) 790-1745; (800) 955-1236. email: SICB@BurkInc.com www.sicb.org.

Soil and Water Conservation Society (1945): 945 S.W. Ankeny Rd., Ankeny, Iowa 50021. 10,000. Phone: (515) 289-2331; fax: (515) 289-1227. www.swcs.org.

Songwriters Guild of America, The (1931): 1500 Harbor Blvd., Weehawken, N.J. 07087-6732. Phone: (201) 867-7603. www.songwriters.org.

Sons of Italy in America, Order (1905): 219 E St. N.E., Washington, D.C. 20002. 500,000. Phone: (202) 547-2900. www.osia.org.

Sons of the American Revolution, National Society of the (1889): 1000 S. 4th St., Louisville, Ky. 40203. 26,000. Phone: (502) 589-1776. www.sar.org.

Soroptimist International of the Americas (1921): Two Penn Center Plaza, Ste. 1000, Philadelphia, Pa. 19102-1883. 100,000. Phone: (215) 557-9300. www.soroptimist.org/

Southern Early Childhood Association (formerly SACUS) (1948): P.O. Box 55930, Little Rock, Ark. 72215-5930. 21,000. Phone: (800) 305-7322; fax: (501) 227-5297. email: seca@aristotle.net. www.seca50.org.

Space Society, National (1974): 600 Pennsylvania Ave. S.E., Ste. 201, Washington, D.C. 20003. Phone: (202) 543-1900; fax: (202) 546-4189. www.nss.org/.

Special Olympics International, Inc. (1968): 1325 G St. N.W., Ste. 500, Washington, D.C., 20005. 1,000,000. Phone: (202) 628-3630. www.specialolympics.org.

Speech-Language-Hearing Association, American (1925): 10801 Rockville Pike, Rockville, Md. 20852. 99,000+. Phone & TTY: (800) 638-8255. www.asha.org.

Sports Car Club of America Inc. (1944): P.O. Box 19400, Topeka, Kans. 66619-0400. 55,000. Phone: (785) 357-7222. www.scca.org/index.html.

Statistical Association, American (1839): 1429 Duke St., Alexandria, Va. 22314-3415. 19,000. Phone: (888) 231-3473. www.amstat.org.

Student Association, United States (1947): 1413 K Street N.W., 9th Flr., Washington, D.C. 20005. 350 schools (3.5 million students). Phone: (202) 347-8772. www.usstudents.org.

Surgeons, American College of (1913): 633 North Saint Clair, Chicago, Ill. 60611-3211. 56,000+. Phone: (312) 202-5000. www.facs.org.

Symphony Orchestra League, American (1942): 33 W. 60th St., 5th Fl., New York, N.Y. 10023-7905. 5,500. Phone: (212) 262-5161. www.symphony.org.

TASH: The Association for Persons with Severe Handicaps (1974): 29 W. Susquehanna Ave., Ste. 210, Baltimore, Md. 21204. 8,500. Phone: (410) 828-8274. www.tash.org.

Tax Foundation (1937): 1900 M St. N.W., Ste. 550, Washington, D.C. 20036. Phone: (202) 464-6200; fax: (202) 464-6201. email: taxfnd@intr.net. www.taxfoundation.org

Teachers, American Federation of (1916): 555 New Jersey Ave. N.W., Washington, D.C., 20001. 900,000+. Phone: (202) 879-4400. www.aft.org.

Testing & Materials, American Society for (1898): 100 Barr Harbor Dr., W. Conshohocken, Pa. 19428-2959. 35,000. Phone: (610) 832-9585. www.astm.org.

The Arc (1950): 1010 Wayne Ave., Ste. 650, Silver Spring, Md. 20910. A national organization on mental retardation. 140,000 members, 1,200 state and local chapters. Phone: (301) 565-3842. www.thearc.org.

Theosophical Society in America, The (1875): P.O. Box 270, Wheaton, Ill. 60189-0270. 4,400. Phone: (630) 668-1571. www.theosophical.org.

Tin Can Sailors, Inc. (1976): P.O. Box 100, Somerset, Mass. 02726. 20,900. Phone: (800) 223-5535. www.destroyers.org.

Toastmasters International (1924): P.O. Box 9052, Mission Viejo, Calif. 92690-7052. 170,000. Phone: (949) 858-8255; fax: (949) 858-1207. www.toastmasters.org.

TOUGHLOVE International (1977): P.O. Box 1069, Doylestown, Pa. 18901. 500 registered groups. Phone: (215) 348-7090. www.toughlove.org.

TransAfrica Forum (1981): 1426 21st St. N.W., Washington, D.C. 20036. Phone: (202) 223-1960; fax: (202) 223-1966. www.transafricaforum.org.

Travel Agents, American Society of (ASTA) (1931): 1101 King St., Alexandria, Va. 22314. 26,000. Phone: (703) 739-2782. www.astanet.com.

Travelers Aid International (1851); 1612 K St. N.W., Ste. 506, Washington, D.C. 20006. 45 agencies, 500+ corporate representatives. Phone: (202) 546-1127; fax: (202) 546-9112. www.travelersaid.org.

Tuberous Sclerosis Association, Inc., National (1974): 801 Roeder Rd., Ste. 750, Silver Spring, Md. 20910. 5,000. Phone: (800) 225-6872; fax: (301) 562-9870. www.tsalliance.org.

UFOs, National Investigations Committee on (1967): 14617 Victory Blvd., Ste. 4, Van Nuys, Calif. 91411. Phone: (818) 989-5942. www.nicufo.com.

UNICEF, U.S. Committee for (1947): 333 E. 38th St., New York, N.Y. 10016. 20,000 volunteers. Phone: (800) FOR-KIDS. www.unicefusa.org.

Union of Concerned Scientists (1969): 2 Brattle Square, Cambridge, Mass. 02238. 70,000. Phone: (617) 547-5552. www.ucsusa.org.

United Daughters of the Confederacy® (1894): 328 N. Boulevard, Richmond, Va. 23220-4057. 24,000. Phone: (804) 355-1636. www.hqudc.org.

United Jewish Communities (formerly United Jewish Appeal) (1939): P.O. Box 30, Old Chelsea Station, New York, N.Y. 10113. Phone: (212) 284-6500. www.ujc.org.

United Way of America (1918): 701 N. Fairfax St., Alexandria, Va. 22314-2045. 1,400 local United Ways. Phone: (703) 836-7100; fax: (703) 683-7840. www.unitedway.org.

University Women, American Association of (1881): 1111 16th St. N.W., Washington, D.C. 20036. 150,000. Phone: (800) 326-AAUW (2289); TDD: (202) 785-7777. www.aauw.org.

USO (United Service Organizations) (1941): World Headquarters, Washington Navy Yard, 1008 Eberle Place SE, Ste. 301, Washington, D.C. 20374-5096. 120 centers worldwide. Phone: (202) 610–5700. www.uso.org.

Veterans Committee, American (AVC) (1944): Bethesda, Md. 20817. 15,000. Phone & fax: (301) 320-6490. www.usmm.net/avc-mast45.html

Veterans of Foreign Wars of the U.S. (1899): 406 W. 34th St., Kansas City, Mo. 64111. VFW and Auxiliary, 2.1 million. Phone: (816) 756-3390. www.vfw.org.

Veterinary Medical Association, American (1863): 1931 N. Meacham Rd., Ste. 100, Schaumburg, Ill. 60173. 62,000. Phone: (847) 925-8070. www.avma.org.

Volunteers of America (1896): 1660 Duke St., Alexandria, Va. 22314-3421. 40,000+ volunteers. Phone: (703) 341-5000; (800) 899-0089. www.voa.org.

War Resisters League (1923): 339 Lafayette St., New York, N.Y. 10012. 12,000. Phone: (212) 228-0450; fax: (212) 228-6193. www.warresisters.org.

Washington Legal Foundation (1977): 2009 Massachusetts Ave. N.W., Washington, D.C. 20036. 100,000. Phone: (202) 588-0302. www.wlf.org.

Water Quality Association (1974): 4151 Naperville Rd., Lisle, Ill. 60532. 2,200. Phone: (630) 505-0160. www.wqa.org.

Welding Society, American (1919): 550 N.W. LeJeune Rd., Miami, Fla. 33126. 50,000. Phone: (305) 443-9353; (800) 443-9353. www.aws.org.

Wildlife Fund (U.S.), World (1961): 1250 24th St. N.W., Washington, D.C. 20037. 1.2 million. Phone: (800) 225-5993. www.wwf.org.

Woman's Christian Temperance Union, National (1874): 1730 Chicago Ave., Evanston, Ill. 60201-4585. Under 20,000. Phone: (847) 864-1397. www.wctu.org.

Women, National Organization for (NOW) (1966): 733 15th St. N.W., 2nd fl., Washington, D.C. 20005. 500,000. Phone: (202) 628-8669. www.now.org.

Women Police, The International Association of (1915): RR#1, Box 149, Deer Isle, Me. 04627-9700. 3,000. Phone: (207) 348-6976; fax: (207) 348-6171. www.iawp.org.

Women's American ORT (1927): 250 Park Ave. South, New York, N.Y. 10003. Chapters throughout the U.S. Phone: (800) 51–WAORT. www.waort.org.

Women's Educational and Industrial Union (1877): 356 Boylston St., Boston, Mass. 02116. 1,500. Phone: (617) 536-5651; fax: (617) 247-8826. www.weiu.org.

Women's International League for Peace and Freedom (1915): 1213 Race St., Philadelphia, Pa. 19107–1691. 10,000. Phone: (215) 563-7110. www.wilpf.org.

World Future Society (1966): 7910 Woodmont Ave., Ste. 450, Bethesda, Md. 20814. 30,000. Phone: (301) 656-8274; fax: (301) 951-0394. www.wfs.org.

World Health, American Association for (1953): 1825 K St. N.W., Washington, D.C. 20006. Phone: (202) 466-5883; fax: (202) 466-5896. email: AAWHstaff@aol.com. www.thebody.com/aawh/aawhpage.html.

World Peace, International Association of Educators for (1967): P.O. Box 3282, Mastin Lake Station, Huntsville, Ala. 35810-0282. 102 countries. Phone: (256) 534-5501. www.iaewp.com.

World Peace Foundation (1910): 79 John F. Kennedy St., Cambridge, Mass. 02138. Phone: (617) 496-2258; fax: (617) 491-8588. www.worldpeacefoundation.org

Worldwatch Institute (1974): 1776 Massachusetts Ave. N.W., Washington, D.C. 20036-1904. Global environmental research organization. Phone: (202) 452-1999; fax: (202) 296-7365. email: worldwatch@worldwatch.org. www.worldwatch.org.

Writers Union, National (1981): 113 University Place, 6th Flr., New York, N.Y. 10003. 6,500. Phone: (212) 254-0279. www.nwu.org.

YMCA of the USA (1844): 101 N. Wacker Dr., Chicago, Ill. 60606. 16.9 million. Phone: (312) 977-0031. www.ymca.net.

Young Women's Christian Association of the U.S.A. (1858 in U.S.A., 1855 in England): 1015 18th St., N.W., Ste. 110, Washington, D.C 20036. 2,000,000. Phone: (202) 467 0801. www.ywca.org.

Zero Population Growth (1968): 1400 Sixteenth St. N.W., Ste. 320, Washington, D.C. 20036. 55,000. Phone: (202) 332-2200. www.zpg.org.

Zionist Organization of America (1897): 4 E. 34th St., New York, N.Y. 10016. 50,000. Phone: (212) 481-1500; fax: (212) 481-1515. www.zoa.org.

In any broad overview of history, arbitrary compartmentalization of facts is self-defeating (and makes locating interrelated people, places, and things that much harder). Therefore, Headline History is designed as a "timeline"—a chronology that highlights both the march of time and interesting, sometimes surprising, juxtapositions.

See also related sections of the almanac, particularly Inventions and Discoveries, U.S. Government and History, and Countries of the World.

B.C.

Before Christ (B.C.) or Before the Common Era (B.C.E.)

Ra, Egyptian Sun God (3000–2000 B.C.)

The Great Pyramid at Giza (c. 2680 B.C.)

Stonehenge (c. 3000–1500 B.C.)

4.5 billion B.C. Planet Earth formed.

3 billion B.C. First signs of primeval life (bacteria and blue-green algae) appear in oceans.

600 million B.C. Earliest date to which fossils can be traced.

4.4 million B.C. Earliest known hominid fossils (*Ardipithecus ramidus*) found in Aramis, Ethiopia, 1994.

4.2 million B.C. *Australopithecus anamensis* found in Lake Turkana, Kenya, 1995.

3.2 million B.C. *Australopithecus afarensis* (nicknamed "Lucy") found in Ethiopia, 1974.

2.5 million B.C. *Homo habilis* ("Skillful Man"). First brain expansion; is believed to have used stone tools.

1.8 million B.C. *Homo erectus* ("Upright Man"). Brain size twice that of *Australopithecine* species.

1.7 million B.C. *Homo erectus* leaves Africa.

100,000 B.C. First modern *Homo sapiens* in South Africa.

70,000 B.C. Neanderthal man (use of fire and advanced tools).

35,000 B.C. Neanderthal man replaced by later groups of *Homo sapiens* (i.e., Cro-Magnon man, etc.).

18,000 B.C. Cro-Magnons replaced by later cultures.

15,000 B.C. Migrations across Bering Straits into the Americas.

10,000 B.C. Semi-permanent agricultural settlements in Old World.

10,000–4,000 B.C. Development of settlements into cities and development of skills such as the wheel, pottery, and improved methods of cultivation in Mesopotamia and elsewhere.

5500–3000 B.C. Predynastic Egyptian cultures develop (5500–3100 B.C.); begin using agriculture (c. 5000 B.C.). Earliest known civilization arises in Sumer (4500–4000 B.C.). Earliest recorded date in Egyptian calendar (4241 B.C.). First year of Jewish calendar (3760 B.C.). First phonetic writing appears (c. 3500 B.C.). Sumerians develop a city-state civilization (c. 3000 B.C.). Copper used by Egyptians and Sumerians. Western Europe is neolithic, without metals or written records.

3000–2000 B.C. Pharaonic rule begins in Egypt. King Khufu (Cheops), 4th dynasty (2700–2675 B.C.), completes construction of the Great Pyramid at Giza (c. 2680 B.C.). The Great Sphinx of Giza (c. 2540 B.C.) is built by King Khafre. Earliest Egyptian mummies. Papyrus. Phoenician settlements on coast of what is now Syria and Lebanon. Semitic tribes settle in Assyria. Sargon, first Akkadian king, builds Mesopotamian empire. The Gilgamesh epic (c. 3000 B.C.). Abraham leaves Ur (c. 2000 B.C.). Systematic astronomy in Egypt, Babylon, India, China.

3000–1500 B.C. The most ancient civilization on the Indian subcontinent, the sophisticated and extensive Indus Valley civilization, flourishes in what is today Pakistan. In Britain, Stonehenge erected according to some unknown astronomical rationale. Its three main phases of construction are thought to span c. 3000–1500 B.C.

2000–1500 B.C. Hyksos invaders drive Egyptians from Lower Egypt (17th century B.C.). Amosis I frees Egypt from Hyksos (c. 1600 B.C.). Assyrians rise to power—cities of Ashur and Nineveh. Twenty-four-character alphabet in Egypt. Israelites enslaved in Egypt. Cuneiform inscriptions used by Hittites. Peak of Minoan culture on Isle of Crete—earliest form of written Greek. Hammurabi, king of Babylon, develops oldest existing code of laws (18th century B.C.).

1500–1000 B.C. Ikhnaton develops monotheistic religion in Egypt (c. 1375 B.C.). His successor, Tutankhamen, returns to earlier gods. Moses leads Israelites out of Egypt into Canaan—Ten Commandments. Greeks destroy Troy (c. 1193 B.C.). End of Greek civilization in Mycenae with invasion of Dorians. Chinese civilization develops under Shang Dynasty. Olmec civilization in Mexico—stone monuments; picture writing.

1000–900 B.C. Solomon succeeds King David, builds Jerusalem temple. After Solomon's death, kingdom divided into Israel and Judah. Hebrew elders begin to write Old Testament books of Bible. Phoenicians colonize Spain with settlement at Cadiz.

900–800 B.C. Phoenicians establish Carthage (c. 810 B.C.). The *Iliad* and the *Odyssey,* perhaps composed by Greek poet Homer.

800–700 B.C. Prophets Amos, Hosea, Isaiah. First recorded Olympic games (776 B.C.). Legendary founding of Rome by Romulus (753 B.C.). Assyrian king Sargon II conquers Hittites, Chaldeans, Samaria (end of Kingdom of Israel). Earliest written music. Chariots introduced into Italy by Etruscans.

700–600 B.C. End of Assyrian Empire (616 B.C.)—Nineveh destroyed by Chaldeans (Neo-Babylonians) and Medes (612 B.C.). Founding of Byzantium by Greeks (c. 660 B.C.). Building of the Acropolis in Athens. Solon, Greek lawgiver (640–560 B.C.). Sappho of Lesbos, Greek poet (fl. c. 610–580 B.C.). Lao-tse, Chinese philosopher and founder of Taoism (born c. 604 B.C.).

600–500 B.C. Babylonian King Nebuchadnezzar builds empire, destroys Jerusalem (586 B.C.). Babylonian Captivity of the Jews (starting 587 B.C.). Hanging Gardens of Babylon. Cyrus the Great of Persia creates great empire, conquers Babylon (539 B.C.), frees the Jews. Athenian democracy develops. Aeschylus, Greek dramatist (525–465 B.C.). Pythagoras, Greek philosopher and mathematician (582?–507? B.C.). Confucius (551–479 B.C.) develops ethical and social philosophy in China. The *Analects* or Lun-yü ("collected sayings") are compiled by the second generation of Confucian disciples. Buddha (563?–483? B.C.) founds Buddhism in India.

Pythagoras (582?–507? B.C.)

Buddha (563?–483? B.C.)

SOME ANCIENT CIVILIZATIONS

Name	Approximate dates	Location	Major cities
Akkadian	2350–2230 B.C.	Mesopotamia, parts of Syria, Asia Minor, Iran	Akkad, Ur, Erich
Assyrian	1800–889 B.C.	Mesopotamia, Syria	Assur, Nineveh, Calah
Babylonian	1728–1686 B.C. (old) 625–539 B.C. (new)	Mesopotamia, Syria, Palestine	Babylon
Cimmerian	750–500 B.C.	Caucasus, northern Asia Minor	—
Egyptian	2850–715 B.C.	Nile valley	Thebes, Memphis, Tanis
Etruscan	900–396 B.C.	Northern Italy	—
Greek	900–200 B.C.	Greece	Athens, Sparta, Thebes, Mycenae, Corinth
Hittite	1640–1200 B.C.	Asia Minor, Syria	Hattusas, Nesa
Indus Valley	3000–1500 B.C.	Pakistan, Northwestern India	—
Lydian	700–547 B.C.	Western Asia Minor	Sardis, Miletus
Mede	835–550 B.C.	Iran	Media
Minoan	3000–1100 B.C.	Crete	Knossos
Persian	559–330 B.C.	Iran, Asia Minor, Syria	Persepolis, Pasargadae
Phoenician	1100–332 B.C.	Palestine (colonies: Gibraltar, Carthage, Sardinia)	Tyre, Sidon, Byblos
Phrygian	1000–547 B.C.	Central Asia Minor	Gordion
Roman	500 B.C.–A.D. 300	Italy, Mediterranean region, Asia Minor, western Europe	Rome, Byzantium
Scythian	800–300 B.C.	Caucasus	—
Sumerian	3200–2360 B.C.	Mesopotamia	Ur, Nippur

Confucius
(551–479 B.C.)

Parthenon
(447–432 B.C.)

Plato
(427?–348 or 347 B.C.)

Augustus Caesar
(63 B.C.–A.D. 14)

500–400 B.C. Greeks defeat Persians: battles of Marathon (490 B.C.), Thermopylae (480 B.C.), Salamis (480 B.C.). Peloponnesian Wars between Athens and Sparta (431–404 B.C.)—Sparta victorious. Pericles comes to power in Athens (462 B.C.). Flowering of Greek culture during the Age of Pericles (450–400 B.C.). The Parthenon is built in Athens as a temple of the goddess Athena (447–432 B.C.). Ictinus and Callicrates are the architects and Phidias is responsible for the sculpture. Sophocles, Greek dramatist (496?–406 B.C.). Hippocrates, Greek "Father of Medicine" (born 460 B.C.). Xerxes I, king of Persia (rules 485–465 B.C.).

400–300 B.C. Pentateuch—first five books of the Old Testament evolve in final form. Philip of Macedon, who believed himself to be a descendant of the Greek people, assassinated (336 B.C.) after subduing the Greek city-states; succeeded by son, Alexander the Great (356–323 B.C.), who destroys Thebes (335 B.C.), conquers Tyre and Jerusalem (332 B.C.), occupies Babylon (330 B.C.), invades India, and dies in Babylon. His empire is divided among his generals; one of them, Seleucis I, establishes Middle East empire with capitals at Antioch (Syria) and Seleucia (in Iraq). Trial and execution of Greek philosopher Socrates (399 B.C.). Dialogues recorded by his student, Plato (c. 427–348 or 347 B.C.). Euclid's work on geometry (323 B.C.). Aristotle, Greek philosopher (384–322 B.C.). Demosthenes, Greek orator (384–322 B.C.). Praxiteles, Greek sculptor (400–330 B.C.).

300–251 B.C. First Punic War (264–241 B.C.): Rome defeats the Carthaginians and begins its domination of the Mediterranean. Temple of the Sun at Teotihuacán, Mexico (c. 300 B.C.). Invention of Mayan calendar in Yucatán—more exact than older calendars. First Roman gladiatorial games (264 B.C.). Archimedes, Greek mathematician (287–212 B.C.).

250–201 B.C. Second Punic War (219–201 B.C.): Hannibal, Carthaginian general (246–142 B.C.), crosses the Alps (218 B.C.), reaches gates of Rome (211 B.C.), retreats, and is defeated by Scipio Africanus at Zama (202 B.C.). Great Wall of China built (c. 215 B.C.).

200–151 B.C. Romans defeat Seleucid King Antiochus III at Thermopylae (191 B.C.)—beginning of Roman world domination. Maccabean revolt against Seleucids (167 B.C.).

150–101 B.C. Third Punic War (149–146 B.C.): Rome destroys Carthage, killing 450,000 and enslaving the remaining 50,000 inhabitants. Roman armies conquer Macedonia, Greece, Anatolia, Balearic Islands, and southern France. Venus de Milo (c. 140 B.C.). Cicero, Roman orator (106–43 B.C.).

100–51 B.C. Julius Caesar (100–44 B.C.) invades Britain (55 B.C.) and conquers Gaul (France) (c. 50 B.C.). Spartacus leads slave revolt against Rome (71 B.C.). Romans conquer Seleucid empire. Roman general Pompey conquers Jerusalem (63 B.C.). Cleopatra on Egyptian throne (51–31 B.C.). Chinese develop use of paper (c. 100 B.C.). Virgil, Roman poet (70–19 B.C.). Horace, Roman poet (65–8 B.C.).

50–1 B.C. Caesar crosses Rubicon to fight Pompey (50 B.C.). Herod made Roman governor of Judea (37 B.C.). Caesar murdered (44 B.C.). Caesar's nephew, Octavian, defeats Mark Antony and Cleopatra at Battle of Actium (31 B.C.), and establishes Roman empire as Emperor Augustus; rules 27 B.C.–A.D. 14. Pantheon built for the first time under Agrippa, 27 B.C. Ovid, Roman poet (43 B.C.–A.D. 18).

A.D.

Christian Era (A.D.) or the Common Era (C.E.)

Roman Aqueduct
Montpellier, France

1–49 Birth of Jesus Christ (variously given from 4 B.C. to A.D. 7). After Augustus, Tiberius becomes emperor (dies, A.D. 37), succeeded by Caligula (assassinated, A.D. 41), who is followed by Claudius. Crucifixion of Jesus (probably A.D. 30). Han dynasty in China founded by Emperor Kuang Wu Ti. Buddhism introduced to China.

50–99 Claudius poisoned (A.D. 54), succeeded by Nero (commits suicide, A.D. 68). Missionary journeys of Paul the Apostle (A.D. 34–60). Jews revolt against Rome; Jerusalem destroyed (A.D. 70). Roman persecutions of Christians begin (A.D. 64). Colosseum built in Rome (A.D. 71–80). Trajan (rules A.D. 98–116); Roman empire extends to Mesopotamia, Arabia, Balkans. First Gospels of St. Mark, St. John, St. Matthew.

100–149 Hadrian rules Rome (A.D. 117–138); codifies Roman law, rebuilds Pantheon, establishes postal system, builds wall between England and Scotland. Jews revolt under Bar Kokhba (A.D. 122–135); final Diaspora (dispersion) of Jews begins.

150–199 Marcus Aurelius rules Rome (A.D. 161–180). Oldest Mayan temples in Central America (c. A.D. 200).

200–249 Goths invade Asia Minor (c. A.D. 220). Roman persecutions of Christians increase. Persian (Sassanid) empire re-established. End of Chinese Han dynasty.

250–299 Increasing invasions of the Roman empire by Franks and Goths. Buddhism spreads in China. Classic period of Mayan civilization (A.D. 250–900); develop hieroglyphic writing, advances in art, architecture, science.

300–349 Constantine the Great (rules A.D. 312–337) reunites eastern and western Roman empires, with new capital (Constantinople) on site of Byzantium (A.D. 330); issues Edict of Milan legalizing Christianity (A.D. 313); becomes a Christian on his deathbed (A.D. 337). Council of Nicaea (A.D. 325) defines orthodox Christian doctrine. First Gupta dynasty in India (c. A.D. 320).

350–399 Huns (Mongols) invade Europe (c. A.D. 360). Theodosius the Great (rules A.D. 392–395)—last emperor of a united Roman empire. Roman empire permanently divided in A.D. 395: western empire ruled from Rome; eastern empire ruled from Constantinople.

400–449 Western Roman empire disintegrates under weak emperors. Alaric, king of the Visigoths, sacks Rome (A.D. 410). Attila, Hun chieftain, attacks Roman provinces (A.D. 433). St. Patrick returns to Ireland (A.D. 432) and brings Christianity to the island. St. Augustine's *City of God* (A.D. 411).

450–499 Vandals destroy Rome (A.D. 455). Western Roman empire ends as Odoacer, German chieftain, overthrows last Roman emperor, Romulus Augustulus, and becomes king of Italy (A.D. 476). Ostrogothic kingdom of Italy established by Theodoric the Great (A.D. 493). Clovis, ruler of the Franks, is converted to Christianity (A.D. 496). First schism between western and eastern churches (A.D. 484).

500–549 Eastern and western churches reconciled (519). Justinian I, the Great (483–565), becomes Byzantine emperor (527), issues his first code of civil laws (529), conquers North Africa, Italy, and part of Spain. Plague spreads through Europe (542 *et seq.*). Arthur, semi-legendary king of the Britons (killed, c. 537). Boëthius, Roman scholar (executed, 524).

550–599 Beginnings of European silk industry after Justinian's missionaries smuggle silkworms out of China (553). Mohammed, Muhammadfounder of Islam (570–632). Buddhism in Japan (c. 560). St. Augustine of Canterbury brings Christianity to Britain (597). After killing about half the population, plague in Europe subsides (594).

600–649 Mohammed flees from Mecca to Medina (the *Hegira*); first year of the Muslim calendar (622). Muslim empire grows (634). Arabs conquer Jerusalem (637), destroy Alexandrian library (641), conquer Persians (641). Fatima, Mohammed's daughter (606–632).

650–699 Arabs attack North Africa (670), destroy Carthage (697). Venerable Bede, English monk (672–735).

700–749 Arab empire extends from Lisbon to China (by 716). Charles Martel, Frankish leader, defeats Arabs at Tours/Poitiers, halting Arab advance in Europe (732). Charlemagne (742–814). Introduction of pagodas in Japan from China.

750–799 Charlemagne becomes king of the Franks (771). Caliph Harun al-Rashid rules Arab empire (786–809): the "golden age" of Arab culture. Vikings begin attacks on Britain (790), land in Ireland (795). City of Machu Picchu flourishes in Peru.

800–849 Charlemagne crowned first Holy Roman Emperor in Rome (800). Charlemagne dies (814), succeeded by his son, Louis the Pious, who divides France among his sons (817). Arabs conquer Crete, Sicily, and Sardinia (826–827).

850–899 Norsemen attack as far south as the Mediterranean but are thwarted (859), discover Iceland (861). Alfred the Great becomes king of Britain (871), defeats Danish invaders (878). Russian nation founded by Vikings under Prince Rurik, establishing capital at Novgorod (855–879).

900–949 Beginning of Mayan Post-Classical period (900–1519). Vikings discover Greenland (c. 900). Arab Spain under Abd ar-Rahman III becomes center of learning (912–961). Otto I becomes King of Germany (936).

950–999 Mieczyslâw I becomes first ruler of Poland (960). Eric the Red establishes first Viking colony in Greenland (982). Hugh Capet elected King of France in 987; Capetian dynasty to rule until 1328. Musical notation systematized (c.

Mayan Pyramid at Chichén Itzá

Celtic Cross

Japanese Pagoda

Viking Ship (c. 900)

Mesa Verde Cliff Dwellings (c. 1000–1300)

Cathedral and Tower at Pisa

Chartres Cathedral

King John (1167–1216)

990). Vikings and Danes attack Britain (988–999). Otto I crowned Holy Roman Emperor by Pope John XII (962).

1000–1099 (A.D.)

c. 1000–1300 Classic Pueblo period of Anasazi culture; cliff dwellings.
c. 1000 Hungary and Scandinavia converted to Christianity. Viking raider Leif Eriksson discovers North America, calls it Vinland. *Beowulf,* Old English epic.
c. 1008 Murasaki Shikibu finishes *The Tale of Genji,* the world's first novel.
1009 Muslims destroy Holy Sepulchre in Jerusalem.
1013 Danes control England. Canute takes throne (1016), conquers Norway (1028), dies (1035); kingdom divided among his sons: Harold Harefoot (England), Sweyn (Norway), Hardecanute (Denmark).
1040 Macbeth murders Duncan, king of Scotland.
1053 Robert Guiscard, Norman invader, establishes kingdom in Italy, conquers Sicily (1072).
1054 Final separation between Eastern (Orthodox) and Western (Roman) churches.
1055 Seljuk Turks, Asian nomads, move west, capture Baghdad, Armenia (1064), Syria, and Palestine (1075).
1066 William of Normandy invades England, defeats last Saxon king, Harold II, at Battle of Hastings, crowned William I of England ("the Conqueror").
1068 Construction on the cathedral in Pisa, Italy, begins.
1073 Emergence of strong papacy when Gregory VII is elected. Conflict with English and French kings and German emperors will continue throughout medieval period.
1095 At Council of Clermont, Pope Urban II calls for a holy war to wrest control of Jerusalem from Muslims, which launches the First Crusade (1096), one of at least 8 European military campaigns between 1095 and 1291 to regain the Holy Land.

1100–1199 (A.D.)

1100–1300 Construction of Cathedral at Chartres, France.
1144 Second Crusade begins.
c. 1150 Angkor Wat is completed.
1150–1167 Universities of Paris and Oxford founded in France and England.
1162 Thomas á Becket named Archbishop of Canterbury, murdered by Henry II's men (1170). Troubadours (wandering minstrels) glorify romantic concepts of feudalism.
1169 Ibn-Rushd begins translating Aristotle's works.
1189 Richard I ("the Lionhearted") succeeds Henry II in England, killed in France (1199), succeeded by King John. Third Crusade.

1200–1299 (A.D.)

1200–1204 Fourth Crusade.
1211 Genghis Khan invades China, captures Peking (1214), conquers Persia (1218), invades Russia (1223), dies (1227).
1212 Children's Crusade.
1215 King John forced by barons to sign Magna Carta at Runneymede, limiting royal power.
1217 Fifth Crusade.
1228 Sixth Crusade.

THE CRUSADES (1096–1291)

In 1095 at Council of Clermont, Pope Urban II calls for war to rescue Holy Land from Muslim infidels. The *First Crusade* (1096) is assembled in response to Emperor Alexius I. The Christians capture Antioch (1098) and Jerusalem (1099). They establish the Crusader States, ruled by Europeans. It is the only successful crusade. The *Second Crusade* begins after the Seljuk Turks recapture Edessa, one of the Crusader States, in 1144. It is led by King Louis VIII of France and Holy Roman Emperor Conrad III. Crusaders perish in Asia Minor (1147).

Saladin controls Egypt (1171), unites Islam in holy war *(jihad)* against Christians, recaptures Jerusalem (1187). *Third Crusade* (1189) under kings of France, England, and Germany fails to reduce Saladin's power. *Fourth Crusade* (1200–1204)—French knights sack Greek Christian Constantinople, establish Latin empire in Byzantium. Greeks reestablish Orthodox faith (1262).

Children's Crusade (1212)—only one of 30,000 French children and about 200 of 20,000 German children survive to return home. Other Crusades—*Fifth,* against Egypt (1217), *Sixth* (1228), *Seventh* (1248), *Eighth* (1270). Mamelukes conquer Acre; end of the Crusades (1291).

1231 The Inquisition begins as Pope Gregory IX assigns Dominicans responsibility for combating heresy. Torture used (1252). Ferdinand and Isabella establish Spanish Inquisition (1478). Tourquemada, Grand Inquisitor, forces conversion or expulsion of Spanish Jews (1492). Forced conversion of Moors (1499). Inquisition in Portugal (1531). First Protestants burned at the stake in Spain (1543). Spanish Inquisition abolished (1834).
1241 Mongols defeat Germans in Silesia, invade Poland and Hungary, withdraw from Europe after Ughetai, Mongol leader, dies.
1248 Seventh Crusade.
1251 Kublai Khan governs China, becomes ruler of Mongols (1259), establishes Yuan dynasty in China (1280), invades Burma (1287), dies (1294).
1260 Chartres cathedral consecrated.
1270 Eighth Crusade.
1271 Marco Polo of Venice travels to China, in court of Kublai Khan (1275–1292), returns to Genoa (1295) and writes *Travels.*
1273 Thomas Aquinas stops work on *Summa Theologica,* the basis of all Catholic theological teaching; never completes it.
1295 English King Edward I summons the Model Parliament.

1300–1399 (A.D.)

1312–1337 Mali Empire reaches its height in Africa under King Mansa Musa.
c. 1325 The beginning of the Renaissance in Italy: writers Dante, Petrarch, Boccaccio; painter Giotto. Development of *Noh* drama in Japan. Aztecs establish Tenochtitlán on site of modern Mexico City. Peak of Muslim culture in Spain. Small cannon in use.
1337–1453 Hundred Years' War—English and French kings fight for control of France.
1347–1351 At least 25 million people die in Europe's "Black Death" (bubonic plague).
1368 Ming Dynasty begins in China.
1376–1382 John Wycliffe, pre-Reformation religious reformer, and followers translate Latin Bible into English.
1378 The Great Schism (to 1417)—rival popes in Rome and Avignon, France, fight for control of Roman Catholic Church.
c. 1387 Chaucer's *Canterbury Tales.*
1399 Tamerlane begins last great conquest.

1400–1499 (A.D.)

1407 Casa di San Giorgio, one of the first public banks, founded in Genoa.
1415 Henry V defeats French at Agincourt. Jan Hus, Bohemian preacher and follower of Wycliffe, burned at stake in Constance as heretic.
1418–1460 Portugal's Prince Henry the Navigator sponsors exploration of Africa's coast.
1420 Brunelleschi begins work on the Duomo in Florence.
1428 Joan of Arc leads French against English, captured by Burgundians (1430) and turned over to the English, burned at the stake as a witch after ecclesiastical trial (1431).
1438 Incas rule in Peru.
1450 Florence becomes center of Renaissance arts and learning under the Medicis.
1453 Turks conquer Constantinople, end of the Byzantine empire, beginning of the Ottoman empire.
1455 The Wars of the Roses, civil wars between rival noble factions, begin in England (to 1485). Having invented printing with movable type at Mainz, Germany, Johann Gutenberg completes first Bible.
1462 Ivan the Great rules Russia until 1505 as first czar; ends payment of tribute to Mongols.
1492 Moors conquered in Spain by troops of Ferdinand and Isabella. Columbus becomes first European to encounter Caribbean islands, returns to Spain (1493). Second voyage to Dominica, Jamaica, Puerto Rico (1493–1496). Third voyage to Orinoco (1498). Fourth voyage to Honduras and Panama (1502–1504).
1497 Vasco da Gama sails around Africa and discovers sea route to India (1498). Establishes Portuguese colony in India (1502). John Cabot, employed by England, reaches and explores Canadian coast. Michelangelo's *Bacchus* sculpture.

1500–1599 (A.D.)

1501 First black slaves in America brought to Spanish colony of Santo Domingo.
c. 1503 Leonardo da Vinci paints the *Mona Lisa.* Michelangelo sculpts the *David* (1504).

Thomas Aquinas (1225–1274)

The Duomo in Florence

Joan of Arc (1412–1431)

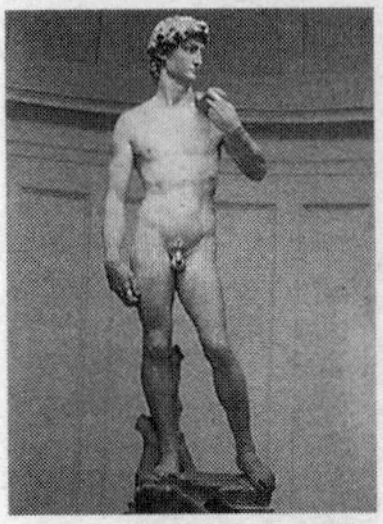
Michelangelo's David (1504)

Balboa (1475–1517)

Martin Luther
(1483–1546)

Henry VIII
(1491–1547)

Queen Elizabeth I
(1533–1603)

William Shakespeare
(1564–1616)

Rembrandt van Rijn
(1606–1669)

1506 St. Peter's Church started in Rome; designed and decorated by such artists and architects as Bramante, Michelangelo, da Vinci, Raphael, and Bernini before its completion in 1626.

1509 Henry VIII ascends English throne. Michelangelo paints the ceiling of the Sistine Chapel.

1513 Balboa becomes the first European to encounter the Pacific Ocean. Machiavelli's *The Prince*.

1517 Turks conquer Egypt, control Arabia. Martin Luther posts his 95 theses denouncing church abuses on church door in Wittenberg—start of the Reformation in Germany.

1519 Ulrich Zwingli begins Reformation in Switzerland. Hernando Cortes conquers Mexico for Spain. Charles I of Spain is chosen Holy Roman Emperor Charles V. Portuguese explorer Ferdinand Magellan sets out to circumnavigate the globe.

1520 Luther excommunicated by Pope Leo X. Suleiman I ("the Magnificent") becomes Sultan of Turkey, invades Hungary (1521), Rhodes (1522), attacks Austria (1529), annexes Hungary (1541), Tripoli (1551), makes peace with Persia (1553), destroys Spanish fleet (1560), dies (1566). Magellan reaches the Pacific, is killed by Philippine natives (1521). One of his ships under Juan Sebastián del Cano continues around the world, reaches Spain (1522).

1524 Verrazano, sailing under the French flag, explores the New England coast and New York Bay.

1527 Troops of the Holy Roman Empire attack Rome, imprison Pope Clement VII—the end of the Italian Renaissance. Castiglione writes *The Courtier.* The Medici family expelled from Florence.

1532 Pizarro marches from Panama to Peru, kills the Inca chieftain, Atahualpa, of Peru (1533). Machiavelli's *The Prince* published posthumously.

1535 Reformation begins as Henry VIII makes himself head of English Church after being excommunicated by Pope. Sir Thomas More executed as traitor for refusal to acknowledge king's religious authority. Jacques Cartier sails up the St. Lawrence River, basis of French claims to Canada.

1536 Henry VIII executes second wife, Anne Boleyn. John Calvin establishes Reformed and Presbyterian form of Protestantism in Switzerland, writes *Institutes of the Christian Religion.* Danish and Norwegian Reformations. Michelangelo's *Last Judgment.*

1541 John Knox leads Reformation in Scotland, establishes Presbyterian church there (1560).

1543 Publication of *On the Revolution of Heavenly Bodies* by Polish scholar Nicolaus Copernicus—giving his theory that the earth revolves around the sun.

1545 Council of Trent to meet intermittently until 1563 to define Catholic dogma and doctrine, reiterate papal authority.

1547 Ivan IV ("the Terrible") crowned as czar of Russia, begins conquest of Astrakhan and Kazan (1552), battles nobles (boyars) for power (1564), kills his son (1580), dies, and is succeeded by his weak and feebleminded son, Fyodor I.

1553 Roman Catholicism restored in England by Queen Mary I.

1556 Akbar the Great becomes Mogul emperor of India, conquers Afghanistan (1581), continues wars of conquest (until 1605).

1558 Queen Elizabeth I ascends the throne (rules to 1603). Restores Protestantism, establishes state Church of England (Anglicanism). Renaissance will reach height in England—Shakespeare, Marlowe, Spenser.

1561 Persecution of Huguenots in France stopped by Edict of Orleans. French religious wars begin again with massacre of Huguenots at Vassy. St. Bartholomew's Day Massacre—thousands of Huguenots murdered (1572). Amnesty granted (1573). Persecution continues periodically until Edict of Nantes (1598) gives Huguenots religious freedom (until 1685).

1568 Protestant Netherlands revolts against Catholic Spain; independence will be acknowledged by Spain in 1648. High point of Dutch Renaissance—painters Rubens, Van Dyck, Hals, and Rembrandt.

1570 Japan permits visits of foreign ships. Queen Elizabeth I excommunicated by Pope. Turks attack Cyprus and war on Venice. Turkish fleet defeated at Battle of Lepanto by Spanish and Italian fleets (1571). Peace of Constantinople (1572) ends Turkish attacks on Europe.

1580 Francis Drake returns to England after circumnavigating the globe; knighted by Queen Elizabeth I (1581). Montaigne's *Essays* published.

1582 Pope Gregory XIII implements the Gregorian calendar.

1583 William of Orange rules the Netherlands; assassinated on orders of Philip II of Spain (1584).
1587 Mary, Queen of Scots, executed for treason by order of Queen Elizabeth I. Monteverdi's *First Book of Madrigals.*
1588 Defeat of the Spanish Armada by English. Henry, King of Navarre and Protestant leader, recognized as Henry IV, first Bourbon king of France. Converts to Roman Catholicism in 1593 in attempt to end religious wars.
1590 Henry IV enters Paris, wars on Spain (1595), marries Marie de Medici (1600), assassinated (1610). Spenser's *The Faerie Queen.* El Greco's *St. Jerome.* Galileo's experiments with falling objects.
1598 Boris Godunov becomes Russian czar. Tycho Brahe describes his astronomical experiments.

1600–1699 (A.D.)

1600 Giordano Bruno burned as a heretic. English East India Company established.
1603 Ieyasu rules Japan, moves capital to Edo (Tokyo). Shakespeare's *Hamlet.*
1605 Cervantes's *Don Quixote de la Mancha,* the first modern novel.
1607 Jamestown, Virginia, established—first permanent English colony on American mainland. Pocahontas, daughter of Chief Powhatan, saves life of John Smith.
1609 Samuel de Champlain establishes French colony of Quebec. The *Relation,* the first newspaper, debuts in Germany.
1610 Galileo sees the moons of Jupiter through his telescope.
1611 Gustavus Adolphus elected King of Sweden. King James Version of the Bible published in England. Rubens paints his *Descent from the Cross.*
1614 John Napier discovers logarithms.
1618 Start of the Thirty Years' War—Protestants revolt against Catholic oppression; Denmark, Sweden, and France will invade Germany in later phases of war. Kepler proposes last of three laws of planetary motion.
1619 A Dutch ship brings the first African slaves to British North America.
1620 Pilgrims, after three-month voyage in *Mayflower,* land at Plymouth Rock. Francis Bacon's *Novum Organum.*
1623 New Netherland founded by Dutch West India Company.
1630 Massachusetts Bay Colony.
1632 Maryland founded by Lord Baltimore.
1633 Inquisition forces Galileo (astronomer) to recant his belief in Copernican theory.
1642 English Civil War. Cavaliers, supporters of Charles I, against Roundheads, parliamentary forces. Oliver Cromwell defeats Royalists (1646). Parliament demands reforms. Charles I offers concessions, brought to trial (1648), beheaded (1649). Cromwell becomes Lord Protector (1653). Rembrandt paints his *Night Watch.*
1643 Taj Mahal completed.
1644 End of Ming Dynasty in China—Manchus come to power. Descartes's *Principles of Philosophy.*
1648 End of the Thirty Years' War. German population about half of what it was in 1618 because of war and pestilence.
1658 Cromwell dies; son Richard resigns and Puritan government collapses.
1660 English Parliament calls for the restoration of the monarchy; invites Charles II to return from France.
1661 Charles II is crowned King of England. Louis XIV begins personal rule as absolute monarch; starts to build Versailles.
1664 British take New Amsterdam from the Dutch. English limit "Nonconformity" with reestablished Anglican Church. Isaac Newton's experiments with gravity.
1665 Great Plague in London kills 75,000.
1666 Great Fire of London. Molière's *Misanthrope.*
1667 Milton's *Paradise Lost,* widely considered the greatest epic poem in English.
1682 Pennsylvania founded by William Penn.
1683 War of European powers against the Turks (to 1699). Vienna withstands three-month Turkish siege; high point of Turkish advance in Europe.
1684 Gottfried Wilhelm Leibniz's calculus published.
1685 James II succeeds Charles II in England, calls for freedom of conscience (1687). Protestants fear restoration of Catholicism and demand "Glorious Revolution." William of Orange invited to England and James II escapes

Catherine de Medici (1519–1589)

Galileo (1564–1642)

Pocahontas (c. 1595–1617)

Taj Mahal

John Milton (1608–1674)

Sir Isaac Newton
(1642–1727)

Frederick the Great
(1712–1786)

Samuel Johnson
(1709–1784)

to France (1688). William III and his wife, Mary, crowned. In France, Edict of Nantes of 1598, granting freedom of worship to Huguenots, is revoked by Louis XIV; thousands of Protestants flee.

1689 Peter the Great becomes Czar of Russia—attempts to westernize nation and build Russia as a military power. Defeats Charles XII of Sweden at Poltava (1709). Beginning of the French and Indian Wars (to 1763), campaigns in America linked to a series of wars between France and England for domination of Europe.

1690 William III of England defeats former king James II and Irish rebels at Battle of the Boyne in Ireland. John Locke's *Human Understanding.*

1700–1799 (A.D.)

1701 War of the Spanish Succession begins—the last of Louis XIV's wars for domination of the continent. The Peace of Utrecht (1714) will end the conflict and mark the rise of the British Empire. Called Queen Anne's War in America, it ends with the British taking New Foundland, Acadia, and Hudson's Bay Territory from France, and Gibraltar and Minorca from Spain.

1704 Deerfield (Mass.) Massacre of English colonists by French and Indians. Bach's first cantata. Jonathan Swift's *Tale of a Tub. Boston News Letter*—first newspaper in America.

1707 United Kingdom of Great Britain formed—England, Wales, and Scotland joined by parliamentary Act of Union.

1729 Bach's *St. Matthew Passion.* Isaac Newton's *Principia* translated from Latin into English.

1732 Benjamin Franklin begins publishing *Poor Richard's Almanack.* James Oglethorpe and others found Georgia.

1735 John Peter Zenger, New York editor, acquitted of libel in New York, establishing press freedom.

1740 Capt. Vitus Bering, Dane employed by Russia, discovers Alaska. Frederick II "the Great" crowned king of Prussia.

1746 British defeat Scots under Stuart Pretender Prince Charles at Culloden Moor. Last battle fought on British soil.

1751 Publication of the *Encyclopédie* begins in France, the "bible" of the Enlightenment.

1755 Samuel Johnson's *Dictionary* first published. Great earthquake in Lisbon, Portugal—over 60,000 die. U.S. postal service established.

1756 Seven Years' War (French and Indian Wars in America) (to 1763), in which Britain and Prussia defeat France, Spain, Austria, and Russia. France loses North American colonies; Spain cedes Florida to Britain in exchange for Cuba. In India, over 100 British prisoners die in "Black Hole of Calcutta."

1757 Beginning of British Empire in India as Robert Clive, British commander, defeats Nawab of Bengal at Plassey.

1759 British capture Quebec from French. Voltaire's *Candide.* Haydn's *Symphony No. 1.*

THE REVOLUTIONARY WAR

Conflicts increase between colonists and Britain on western frontier because of royal edict limiting western expansion (1763) and regulation of colonial trade and increased taxation of colonies (Writs of Assistance allow search for illegal shipments, 1761; Sugar Act, 1764; Currency Act, 1764; Stamp Act, 1765; Quartering Act, 1765; Duty Act, 1767). Boston Massacre (1770). Lord North attempts conciliation (1770). Boston Tea Party (1773), followed by punitive measures passed by Parliament—the "Intolerable Acts."

First Continental Congress (1774) sends "Declaration of Rights and Grievances" to King George III, urges colonies to form Continental Association. Paul Revere's ride and Lexington and Concord battle between Massachusetts Minutemen and British (1775).

Second Continental Congress (1775), while sending "olive branch" to the king, begins to raise army, appoints Washington commander-in-chief, and seeks alliance with France. Some colonial legislatures urge their delegates to vote for independence. Declaration of Independence **(July 4, 1776).**

Major Battles of the Revolutionary War: *Long Island:* Howe defeats Putnam's division of Washington's Army in Brooklyn Heights, but Americans escape across East River (1776). *Trenton and Princeton:* Washington defeats Hessians at Trenton, British at Princeton. Winters at Morristown (1776–1777). Howe winters in Philadelphia; Washington at Valley Forge (1777–1778). Burgoyne surrenders British army to General Gates at *Saratoga* (1777).

France recognizes American independence (1778). The War moves south: Savannah captured by British (1778); Charleston occupied (1780); Americans fight successful guerrilla actions under Marion, Pickens, and Sumter. In the West, George Rogers Clark attacks Forts Kaskaskia and Vincennes (1778–1779), defeating British in the region. Cornwallis surrenders at *Yorktown,* Virginia **(Oct. 19, 1781).** By 1782, Britain is eager for peace because of conflicts with European nations. *Peace of Paris* (1783): Britain recognizes American independence.

1762 Catherine II ("the Great") becomes czarina of Russia. Jean Jacques Rousseau's *Social Contract.* Mozart tours Europe as six-year-old prodigy.

1765 James Watt invents the steam engine. Britain imposes the Stamp Act on the American colonists.

1769 Sir William Arkwright patents a spinning machine—an early step in the Industrial Revolution.

1770 The Boston Massacre.

1772 Joseph Priestley and Daniel Rutherford independently discover nitrogen. Partition of Poland—in 1772, 1793, and 1795, Austria, Prussia, and Russia divide land and people of Poland, end its independence.

1773 The Boston Tea Party.

1774 First Continental Congress drafts "Declaration of Rights and Grievances."

1775 The American Revolution begins with battle of Lexington and Concord. Second Continental Congress. Priestley discovers hydrochloric and sulfuric acids.

1776 Declaration of Independence. Gen. George Washington crosses the Delaware Christmas night. Adam Smith's *Wealth of Nations.* Edward Gibbon's *Decline and Fall of the Roman Empire.* Thomas Paine's *Common Sense.* Fragonard's *Washerwoman.* Mozart's *Haffner Serenade.*

1778 Capt. James Cook discovers Hawaii. Franz Mesmer uses hypnotism.

1781 Immanuel Kant's *Critique of Pure Reason.* Herschel discovers Uranus.

1783 Revolutionary War ends with Treaty of Paris. William Blake's poems. Beethoven's first printed works.

1784 Crimea annexed by Russia. John Wesley's *Deed of Declaration,* the basic work of Methodism.

1785 Russians settle Aleutian Islands.

1787 The Constitution of the United States signed. Lavoisier's work on chemical nomenclature. Mozart's *Don Giovanni.*

1788 French *Parlement* presents grievances to Louis XVI who agrees to convening of Estates-General in 1789—not called since 1613. Goethe's *Egmont.* Laplace's *Laws of the Planetary System.*

1789 French Revolution begins with the storming of the Bastille. In U.S., Washington elected president with all 69 votes of the Electoral College, takes oath of office in New York City. Vice President: John Adams. Secretary of State: Thomas Jefferson. Secretary of Treasury: Alexander Hamilton.

1790 H.M.S. *Bounty* mutineers settle on Pitcairn Island. Aloisio Galvani experiments on electrical stimulation of the muscles. Philadelphia temporary capital of U.S. as Congress votes to establish new capital on Potomac. U.S. population about 3,929,000, including 698,000 slaves. Lavoisier formulates *Table of 31 chemical elements.*

1791 U.S. Bill of Rights ratified. Boswell's *Life of Johnson.*

1792 Mary Wollstonecraft's *Vindication of the Rights of Woman.*

1793 Louis XVI and Marie Antoinette executed. Reign of Terror begins in France. Eli Whitney invents the cotton gin, spurring the growth of the cotton industry and helping to institutionalize slavery in the U.S. South.

1794 Kosciusko's uprising in Poland quelled by the Russians. In U.S., Whiskey Rebellion in Pennsylvania as farmers object to liquor taxes. Reign of Terror ends with execution of Robespierre.

1796 Napoléon Bonaparte, French general, defeats Austrians. In the U.S., Washington's Farewell Address **(Sept. 17);** John Adams elected president; Thomas Jefferson, vice president. Edward Jenner introduces smallpox vaccination.

1798 Napoleon extends French conquests to Rome and Egypt. U.S. Navy Department established.

Benjamin Franklin (1706–1790)

George Washington (1732–1799)

Alexander Hamilton (1755–1804)

Ludwig van Beethoven (1770–1827)

FRENCH REVOLUTION (1789–1799)

Revolution begins when Third Estate (Commons) delegates swear not to disband until France has a constitution. Paris mob storms Bastille, symbol of royal power **(July 14, 1789).** National Assembly votes for Constitution, Declaration of the Rights of Man, a limited monarchy, and other reforms (1789–1790). Legislative Assembly elected, Revolutionary Commune formed, and French Republic proclaimed (1792). War of the First Coalition—Austria, Prussia, Britain, Netherlands, and Spain fight to restore French nobility (1792–1797). Start of series of wars between France and European powers that will last, almost without interruption, for 23 years. Louis XVI and Marie Antoinette executed. Committee of Public Safety begins Reign of Terror as political control measure. Interfactional rivalry leads to mass killings. Danton and Robespierre executed. Third French Constitution sets up Directory government (1795). Napoleon abolishes the Directory, establishes the Consulate, becomes the First Consul of France (1799).

Napoléon Bonaparte (1769–1821)

Edgar Allan Poe (1809–1849)

Richard Wagner (1813–1883)

Harriet Beecher Stowe (1811–1896)

Walt Whitman (1819–1892)

1799 Rosetta Stone discovered in Egypt. Napoleon leads coup that overthrows Directory, establishes the Consulate, becomes First Consul—one of three who rule France together.

1800–1899 (A.D.)

1800 Napoleon conquers Italy, firmly establishes himself as First Consul in France. In the U.S., federal government moves to Washington, D.C. Robert Owen's social reforms in England. William Herschel discovers infrared rays. Alessandro Volta produces electricity.

1801 Austria makes temporary peace with France. United Kingdom of Great Britain and Ireland established with one monarch and one parliament; Catholics excluded from voting.

1803 U.S. negotiates Louisiana Purchase from France: for $15 million, U.S. doubles its domain, increasing its territory by 827,000 sq. mi. (2,144,500 sq km), from Mississippi River to Rockies and from Gulf of Mexico to British North America.

1804 Haiti declares independence from France; first black nation to gain freedom from European colonial rule. Napoleon transforms the Consulate of France into an empire, proclaims himself emperor of France, systematizes French law under *Code Napoleon.* In the U.S., Alexander Hamilton is mortally wounded in duel with Aaron Burr. Lewis and Clark expedition begins exploration of what is now northwest U.S.

1805 Lord Nelson defeats the French-Spanish fleets in the Battle of Trafalgar. Napoleon victorious over Austrian and Russian forces at the Battle of Austerlitz.

1807 Robert Fulton makes first successful steamboat trip on *Clermont* between New York City and Albany.

1808 French armies occupy Rome and Spain, extending Napoleon's empire. Britain begins aiding Spanish guerrillas against Napoleon in Peninsular War. In the U.S., Congress bars importation of slaves. Beethoven's *Fifth* and *Sixth Symphonies* performed.

1812 Napoleon's Grand Army invades Russia in June. Forced to retreat in winter, most of Napoleon's 600,000 men are lost. In the U.S., war with Britain declared over freedom of the seas for U.S. vessels (War of 1812). USS *Constitution* sinks British frigate.

1814 French defeated by allies (Britain, Austria, Russia, Prussia, Sweden, and Portugal) in War of Liberation. Napoleon exiled to Elba, off Italian coast. Bourbon king Louis XVIII takes French throne. George Stephenson builds first practical steam locomotive.

1815 Napoleon returns: "Hundred Days" begin. Napoleon defeated by Wellington at Waterloo, banished again to St. Helena in South Atlantic. Congress of Vienna: victorious allies change the map of Europe. War of 1812 ends with Treaty of Ghent.

1819 Simón Bolívar liberates New Granada (now Colombia, Venezuela, and Ecuador) as Spain loses hold on South American countries; named president of Colombia.

1820 Missouri Compromise—Missouri admitted as slave state but slavery barred in rest of Louisiana Purchase north of 36°30′ N.

1821 Guatemala, Panama, and Santo Domingo proclaim independence from Spain.

1822 Greeks proclaim a republic and independence from Turkey. Turks invade Greece. Russia declares war on Turkey (1828). Greece also aided by France and Britain. War ends and Turks recognize Greek independence (1829). Brazil becomes independent of Portugal. Schubert's *Eighth Symphony* ("The Unfinished").

1823 U.S. Monroe Doctrine warns European nations not to interfere in Western Hemisphere.

1824 Mexico becomes a republic, three years after declaring independence from Spain. Bolívar liberates Peru, becomes its president. Beethoven's *Ninth Symphony.*

1825 First passenger-carrying railroad in England.

1826 Joseph-Nicéphore Niepce takes the world's first photograph.

WAR OF 1812

British interference with American trade, impressment of American seamen, and "War Hawks" drive for western expansion lead to war. American attacks on Canada foiled; U.S. Commodore Perry wins battle of Lake Erie (1813). British capture and burn Washington (1814) but fail to take Fort McHenry at Baltimore. Andrew Jackson repulses assault on New Orleans after Treaty of Ghent ends war (1815). War settles little but strengthens U.S. as independent nation.

1830 French invade Algeria. Louis Philippe becomes "Citizen King" as revolution forces Charles X to abdicate. Mormon church formed in U.S. by Joseph Smith.

1831 Polish revolt against Russia fails. Belgium separates from the Netherlands. In U.S., Nat Turner leads unsuccessful slave rebellion.

1833 Slavery abolished in British Empire.

1834 Charles Babbage invents "analytical engine," precursor of computer. McCormick patents reaper.

1836 Boer farmers start "Great Trek"—Natal, Transvaal, and Orange Free State founded in South Africa. Mexican army besieges Texans in Alamo. Entire garrison, including Davy Crockett and Jim Bowie, wiped out. Texans gain independence from Mexico after winning Battle of San Jacinto. Dickens's *Pickwick Papers.*

1837 Victoria becomes queen of Great Britain. Mob kills Elijah P. Lovejoy, Illinois abolitionist publisher.

1839 First Opium War (to 1842) between Britain and China, over importation of drug into China.

1840 Lower and Upper Canada united.

1841 U.S. President Harrison dies (**April 4**) one month after inauguration; John Tyler becomes first vice president to succeed to presidency.

1842 Crawford Long uses first anesthetic (ether).

1843 Wagner's opera *The Flying Dutchman.*

1844 Democratic convention calls for annexation of Texas and acquisition of Oregon ("Fifty-four-forty-or-fight"). Five Chinese ports opened to U.S. ships. Samuel F. B. Morse patents telegraph.

1845 Congress adopts joint resolution for annexation of Texas. Edgar Allan Poe publishes *The Raven and Other Poems.*

1846 U.S. declares war on Mexico. California and New Mexico annexed by U.S. Brigham Young leads Mormons to Great Salt Lake. W. T. Morton uses ether as anesthetic. Sewing machine patented by Elias Howe. Frederick Douglass launches abolitionist newspaper *The North Star.* Failure of potato crop causes famine in Ireland.

1848 Revolt in Paris: Louis Philippe abdicates; Louis Napoleon elected president of French Republic. Revolutions in Vienna, Venice, Berlin, Milan, Rome, and Warsaw. Put down by royal troops in 1848–1849. U.S.-Mexico War ends; Mexico cedes claims to Texas, California, Arizona, New Mexico, Utah, Nevada. U.S. treaty with Britain sets Oregon Territory boundary at 49th parallel. Karl Marx and Friedrich Engels's *Communist Manifesto.* Harriet Tubman escapes from slavery and joins the Underground Railroad. Women's Rights Convention in Seneca Falls, N.Y.

1849 California gold rush begins.

1850 Henry Clay opens great debate on slavery, warns South against secession.

1851 Herman Melville's *Moby-Dick.*

1852 South African Republic established. Louis Napoleon proclaims himself Napoleon III ("Second Empire"). Harriet Beecher Stowe's *Uncle Tom's Cabin.*

1853 Crimean War begins as Turkey declares war on Russia. Commodore Perry reaches Tokyo.

1854 Britain and France join Turkey in war on Russia. In U.S., Kansas-Nebraska Act permits local option on slavery; rioting and bloodshed. Japanese allow American trade. Antislavery men in Michigan form Republican Party. Tennyson's *Charge of the Light Brigade.* Thoreau's *Walden.*

1855 Armed clashes in Kansas between pro- and anti-slavery forces. Florence Nightingale nurses wounded in Crimea. Walt Whitman's *Leaves of Grass.*

1856 Flaubert's *Madame Bovary.*

1857 Supreme Court, in Dred Scott decision, rules that a slave is not a citizen. Financial crisis in Europe and U.S. Great Mutiny (Sepoy Rebellion) begins in India. India placed under crown rule as a result.

1858 Pro-slavery constitution rejected in Kansas. Abraham Lincoln makes strong antislavery speech in Springfield, Ill.: "This Government cannot endure permanently half slave and half free." Lincoln-Douglas debates. First trans-Atlantic telegraph cable completed by Cyrus W. Field.

1859 John Brown raids Harpers Ferry; is captured and hanged. Work begins on Suez Canal. Unification of Italy starts under leadership of Count Cavour, Sardinian premier. Joined by France in war against Austria. Jean-Joseph-Étienne Lenoir builds first practical internal-combustion engine. Edward Fitzgerald's translation of *The Rubaiyat of Omar Khayyam.* Charles Darwin's *Origin of Species.* J. S. Mill's *On Liberty.*

Dred Scott (1795?–1858)

Charles Darwin (1809–1882)

Frederick Douglass (1817–1895)

Harriet Tubman (c. 1820–1913)

Samuel Clemens (Mark Twain) (1835–1910)

Abraham Lincoln (1809–1865)

Robert E. Lee (1807–1870)

William Tecumseh Sherman (1820–1891)

1860 South Carolina secedes from the Union.

1861 U.S. Civil War begins as attempts at compromise fail. Mississippi, Florida, Alabama, Georgia, Louisiana, and Texas secede; with South Carolina, they form the Confederate States of America, with Jefferson Davis as president. Virginia, Arkansas, Tennessee, North Carolina secede and join Confederacy. First Battle of Bull Run (Manassas). Congress creates Colorado, Dakota, and Nevada territories; adopts income tax; Lincoln inaugurated. Serfs emancipated in Russia. Pasteur's theory of germs. Independent Kingdom of Italy proclaimed under Sardinian king Victor Emmanuel II.

1862 Several major Civil War battles: Battle of Shiloh, Second Battle of Bull Run (Manassas), Battle of Antietam. Salon des Refusés introduces impressionism.

1863 French capture Mexico City; proclaim Archduke Maximilian of Austria emperor. Battle of Gettysburg.

1864 Gen. Sherman's Atlanta campaign and "march to the sea."

1865 Gen. Lee surrenders to Grant at Appomattox; the Civil War is over. Lincoln fatally shot at Ford's Theater by John Wilkes Booth. Vice President Johnson sworn as successor. Booth caught and dies of gunshot wounds; four conspirators are hanged. Joseph Lister begins antiseptic surgery. Gregor Mendel's *Law of Heredity.* Lewis Carroll's *Alice's Adventures in Wonderland.*

1866 Alfred Nobel invents dynamite (patented in Britain, 1867). Seven Weeks' War: Austria defeated by Prussia and Italy.

1867 Austria-Hungary Dual Monarchy established. French leave Mexico; Maximilian executed. Dominion of Canada established. U.S. buys Alaska from Russia for $7,200,000. South African diamond field discovered. Japan ends 675-year shogun rule. Volume I of Marx's *Das Kapital.* Strauss's *Blue Danube.*

1868 Revolution in Spain; Queen Isabella deposed, flees to France. In U.S., Fourteenth Amendment giving civil rights to blacks is ratified. Georgia under military government after legislature expels blacks.

1869 First U.S. transcontinental rail route completed. James Fisk and Jay Gould's attempt to control gold market causes Black Friday panic. Suez Canal opens. Mendeleev's periodic table of elements.

1870 Franco-Prussian War (to 1871): Napoleon III capitulates at Sedan. Revolt in Paris; Third Republic proclaimed.

1871 France surrenders Alsace-Lorraine to Germany; war ends. German Empire proclaimed with Prussian King as Kaiser Wilhelm I. Fighting with Apaches begins in American West. Boss Tweed corruption exposed in New York. The Chicago Fire, with 250 deaths and $196-million damage. Stanley meets Livingstone in Africa.

1872 Congress gives amnesty to most Confederates. Jules Verne's *Around the World in 80 Days.*

THE CIVIL WAR

Apart from the matter of slavery, the Civil War arose out of both the economic and political rivalry between an agrarian South and an industrial North and the issue of the right of states to secede from the Union.

1861 After South Carolina secedes **(Dec. 20, 1860)**, Mississippi, Florida, Alabama, Georgia, Louisiana, and Texas follow, forming the Confederate States of America, with Jefferson Davis as president **(Jan.–March)**. War begins as Confederates fire on Fort Sumter **(April 12)**. Lincoln calls for 75,000 volunteers. Southern ports blockaded by superior Union naval forces. Virginia, Arkansas, Tennessee, and North Carolina secede to complete 11-state Confederacy. Union army advancing on Richmond repulsed at first Battle of Bull Run (Manassas) **(July)**.

1862 Edwin M. Stanton named secretary of war **(Jan.)**. Grant wins first important Union victory in West, at Fort Donelson; Nashville falls **(Feb.)**. Ironclads, Union's *Monitor* and Confederate's *Virginia (Merrimac)* duel at Hampton Roads **(March)**. New Orleans falls to Union fleet under Farragut; city occupied **(April)**. Grant's army escapes defeat at Shiloh. Memphis falls as Union gunboats control upper Mississippi **(June)**. Confederate general Robert E. Lee victorious at second Battle of Bull Run (Manassas) **(Aug.)**. Union army under McClellan halts Lee's attack on Washington in the Battle of Antietam **(Sept.)**. Lincoln removes McClellan for lack of aggressiveness. Burnside's drive on Richmond fails at Fredericksburg **(Dec.)**. Union forces under Rosecrans chase Bragg through Tennessee; battle of Murfreesboro **(Oct.–Jan. 1863)**.

1863 Lee defeats Hooker at Chancellorsville; "Stonewall" Jackson, Confederate general, dies **(May)**. Confederate invasion of Pennsylvania stopped at Gettysburg by George Meade—Lee loses 20,000 men—the greatest battle of the war **(July)**. That and the Union victory at Vicksburg mark the war's turning point. Union general George H. Thomas, the "Rock of Chickamauga," holds Bragg's forces on Georgia-Tennessee border **(Sept.)**. Sherman, Hooker, and Thomas drive Bragg back to Georgia. Tennessee restored to the Union **(Nov.)**.

1864 Ulysses S. Grant named commander-in-chief of Union forces **(March)**. In the Wilderness campaign, Grant forces Lee's Army of Northern Virginia back toward Richmond **(May–June)**. Sherman's Atlanta campaign and "march to the sea" **(May–Sept.)**. Farragut's victory at Mobile Bay **(Aug.)**. Hood's Confederate army defeated at Nashville. Sherman takes Savannah **(Dec.)**.

1865 Sheridan defeats Confederates at Five Forks; Confederates evacuate Richmond **(April)**. On **April 9**, Lee surrenders to Grant at Appomattox.

1873 Economic crisis in Europe. U.S. establishes gold standard.

1875 First Kentucky Derby.

1876 Sioux kill Gen. George A. Custer and 264 troopers at Little Big Horn River. Alexander Graham Bell patents the telephone.

1877 After presidential election of 1876, electoral commission gives disputed electoral college votes to Rutherford B. Hayes despite Tilden's popular majority. Russo-Turkish war (ends in 1878 with power of Turkey in Europe broken). Reconstruction ends in the American South. Thomas Edison patents phonograph. The Nez Perce leader Chief Joseph is forced to surrender. Tchaikovsky's *Swan Lake.*

1878 Congress of Berlin revises Treaty of San Stefano, ending Russo-Turkish War; makes extensive redivision of southeast Europe. First commercial telephone exchange opened in New Haven, Conn.

1879 Thomas A. Edison invents electric light.

1880 U.S.-China treaty allows U.S. to restrict immigration of Chinese labor.

1881 President Garfield fatally shot by assassin; Vice President Arthur succeeds him. Charles J. Guiteau convicted and executed (1882).

1882 Terrorism in Ireland after land evictions. Britain invades and conquers Egypt. Germany, Austria, and Italy form Triple Alliance. In U.S., Congress adopts Chinese Exclusion Act. Rockefeller's Standard Oil Trust is first industrial monopoly. In Berlin, Robert Koch announces discovery of tuberculosis germ.

1883 Congress creates Civil Service Commission. Brooklyn Bridge and Metropolitan Opera House completed.

1884 Berlin West Africa Conference held in Berlin (lasting until **Feb. 1885**), at which the major European nations discuss expansion in Africa.

1885 British general Charles G. "Chinese" Gordon killed at Khartoum in Egyptian Sudan. World's first skyscraper built in Chicago.

1886 Bombing at Haymarket Square, Chicago, kills seven policemen and injures many others. Eight alleged anarchists accused—three imprisoned, one commits suicide, four hanged. (In 1893, Illinois governor Altgeld, critical of trial, pardons three survivors.) Statue of Liberty dedicated. Geronimo, Apache Indian chief, surrenders.

1887 Queen Victoria's Golden Jubilee. Sir Arthur Conan Doyle's first Sherlock Holmes story, *A Study in Scarlet.*

1888 Historic March blizzard in northeast U.S.—many perish, property damage exceeds $25 million. George Eastman's box camera (the Kodak). J. B. Dunlop invents pneumatic tire. Jack the Ripper murders in London.

1889 Second (Socialist) International founded in Paris. Indian Territory in Oklahoma opened to settlement. Thousands die in Johnstown, Pa. flood. Eiffel Tower built for the Paris exposition. Mark Twain's *A Connecticut Yankee in King Arthur's Court.*

1890 Congress votes to pass Sherman Antitrust Act. Sioux chief Sitting Bull arrested and killed by police on Pine Ridge reservation; two weeks later, U.S. troops kill over 200 Sioux at Battle of Wounded Knee.

1892 Battle between steel strikers and Pinkerton guards at Homestead, Pa.; union defeated after militia intervenes. Silver mine strikers in Idaho fight non-union workers; U.S. troops dispatched. Diesel engine patented.

1893 New Zealand becomes first country in the world to grant women the vote.

1894 Sino-Japanese War begins (ends in 1895 with China's defeat). In France, Capt. Alfred Dreyfus convicted on false treason charge (pardoned in 1906). In U.S., Jacob S. Coxey of Ohio leads "Coxey's Army" of unemployed on Washington. Eugene V. Debs calls general strike of rail workers to support Pullman Company strikers; strike broken, Debs jailed for six months. Edison's kinetoscope given first public showing in New York City.

1895 X-rays discovered by German physicist Wilhelm Roentgen. Auguste and Louis Lumière premiere motion pictures at a café in Paris.

Johannes Brahms (1833–1897)

Chief Joseph (c. 1840–1904)

Statue of Liberty

Marie Curie (1867–1934)

SPANISH-AMERICAN WAR (1898–1899)

War fires stoked by "jingo journalism" as American people support Cuban rebels against Spain. American business sees economic gain in Cuban trade and resources and American power zones in Latin America. Outstanding events: Submarine mine sinks U.S. battleship *Maine* in Havana Harbor **(Feb. 15);** 260 killed; responsibility never fixed. Congress declares independence of Cuba **(April 19).** Spain declares war on U.S. **(April 24);** Congress **(April 25)** formally declares nation has been at war with Spain since **April 21.** Commodore George Dewey wins seven-hour battle of Manila Bay **(May 1).** Spanish fleet destroyed off Santiago, Cuba **(July 3);** city surrenders **(July 17).** Treaty of Paris (ratified by Senate 1899) ends war. U.S. given Guam and Puerto Rico and agrees to pay Spain $20 million for Philippines. Cuba independent of Spain; under U.S. military control for three years until **May 20, 1902.** Yellow fever is eradicated and political reforms achieved.

Sigmund Freud (1856–1939)

Carrie Chapman Catt (1859–1947)

Albert Einstein (1879–1955)

Vladimir Lenin (1870–1924)

Robert Peary (1856–1920)

1896 Supreme Court's *Plessy* v. *Ferguson* decision—"separate but equal" doctrine. Alfred Nobel's will establishes prizes for peace, science, and literature. Marconi receives first wireless patent in Britain. William Jennings Bryan delivers "Cross of Gold" speech at Democratic Convention in Chicago. First modern Olympic games held in Athens, Greece.

1897 Theodor Herzl launches Zionist movement.

1898 Chinese "Boxers," anti-foreign organization, established. They stage uprisings against Europeans in 1900; U.S. and other Western troops relieve Peking legations. U.S. Battleship *Maine* is sunk in Havana Harbor. Spanish-American War begins. U.S. destroys Spanish fleet near Santiago, Cuba. Pierre and Marie Curie discover radium and polonium.

1899 Boer War (or South African War): conflict between British and Boers (descendants of Dutch settlers of South Africa). Causes rooted in longstanding territorial disputes and in friction over political rights for English and other "uitlanders" following 1886 discovery of vast gold deposits in Transvaal. (British victorious as war ends in 1902.) Casualties: 5,774 British dead, about 4,000 Boers. Union of South Africa established in 1908 as confederation of colonies; becomes British dominion in 1910.

1900–2002 (A.D.)

1900 Hurricane ravages Galveston, Tex.; 6,000–8,000 dead. Fauvist movement in painting begins, led by Henri Matisse. Sigmund Freud's *The Interpretation of Dreams.* Carrie Chapman Catt succeeds Susan B. Anthony as president of National Woman Suffrage Association.

1901 Queen Victoria dies, and is succeeded by her son, Edward VII. As President McKinley begins second term, he is shot fatally by anarchist Leon Czolgosz. Theodore Roosevelt sworn in as successor.

1902 Enrico Caruso's first gramophone recording. Aswan Dam completed.

1903 Wright brothers, Orville and Wilbur, fly first powered, controlled, heavier-than-air plane at Kitty Hawk, N.C. Henry Ford organizes Ford Motor Company. The Boston Red Sox win the first World Series against the Pittsburgh Pirates. W.E.B. Du Bois publishes *The Souls of Black Folk.*

1904 Russo-Japanese War begins—competition for Korea and Manchuria. *Entente Cordiale:* Britain and France settle their international differences. General theory of radioactivity by Rutherford and Soddy. New York City subway opens.

1905 In Russo-Japanese War, Port Arthur surrenders to Japanese; Russia suffers other defeats. President Roosevelt mediates Treaty of Portsmouth, N.H., which recognizes Japan's control of Korea and restores southern Manchuria to China. The Russian Revolution of 1905 begins on "Bloody Sunday" when troops fire onto a defenseless group of demonstrators in St. Petersburg. Strikes and riots follow. Sailors on battleship *Potemkin* mutiny; reforms, including first Duma (parliament), established by Czar Nicholas II's "October Manifesto." Albert Einstein's special theory of relativity and other key theories in physics. Franz Lehar's *Merry Widow.*

1906 San Francisco earthquake and three-day fire; more than 500 dead. Roald Amundsen, Norwegian explorer, fixes magnetic North Pole.

1907 Second Hague Peace Conference, of 46 nations, adopts 10 conventions on rules of war. Financial panic of 1907 in U.S. Mahler begins work on "Song of the Earth." Oklahoma becomes 46th state. Picasso's *Les Demoiselles d'Avignon* introduces cubism.

1908 Earthquake kills 150,000 in southern Italy and Sicily. U.S. Supreme Court, in Danbury Hatters' case, outlaws secondary union boycotts. Model T produced by Ford Motor Company.

1909 North Pole reportedly reached by American explorers Robert E. Peary and Matthew Henson. The National Association for the Advancement of Colored People is founded in New York by prominent black and white intellectuals and led by W.E.B. Du Bois.

1910 Boy Scouts of America incorporated. Angel Island, in San Francisco Bay, becomes immigration center for Asians entering U.S.

1911 First use of aircraft as offensive weapon in Turkish-Italian War. Italy defeats Turks and annexes Tripoli and Libya. Chinese Republic proclaimed after revolution overthrows Manchu dynasty. Sun Yat-sen named president. Mexican Revolution: Porfirio Diaz, president since 1877, replaced by Francisco Madero. Triangle Shirtwaist Company fire in New York; 146 killed. Amundsen reaches South Pole. Ernest Rutherford discovers the structure of the atom. Richard Strauss's *Der Rosenkavalier.* Irving Berlin's *Alexander's Ragtime Band.*

1912 Balkan Wars (1912–1913) resulting from territorial disputes: Turkey defeated by alliance of Bulgaria, Serbia, Greece, and Montenegro; London peace treaty (1913) partitions most of European Turkey among the victors. In second war (1913), Bulgaria attacks Serbia and Greece and is defeated after Romania intervenes and Turks recapture Adrianople. *Titanic* sinks on maiden voyage; over 1,500 drown. New Mexico and Arizona admitted as states.

1913 Suffragists demonstrate in London. Garment workers strike in New York and Boston; win pay raise and shorter hours. Henry Ford develops first moving assembly line. 16th Amendment (income tax) and 17th (popular election of U.S. senators) adopted. Bill creating U.S. Federal Reserve System becomes law. Stravinsky's *The Rite of Spring*. Woodrow Wilson becomes 28th U.S. president. Armory Show introduces modern art to U.S.; Duchamp's *Nude Descending a Staircase* shocks public.

1914 World War I begins: Austrian Archduke Francis Ferdinand and wife Sophie are assassinated; Austria declares war on Serbia, Germany on Russia and France, Britain on Germany. Panama Canal officially opened. Congress sets up Federal Trade Commission, passes Clayton Antitrust Act. U.S. Marines occupy Veracruz, Mexico, intervening in civil war to protect American interests.

1915 *Lusitania* sunk by German submarine. Second Battle of Ypres. U.S. banks lend $500 million to France and Britain. Genocide of estimated 600,000 to 1 million Armenians by Turkish soldiers. D. W. Griffith's film *Birth of a Nation*. Albert Einstein's *General Theory of Relativity*.

1916 Congress expands armed forces. Battle of Verdun. Battle of the Somme. Tom Mooney arrested for San Francisco bombing (pardoned in 1939). Pershing fails in raid into Mexico in quest of rebel Pancho Villa. U.S. buys Virgin Islands from Denmark for $25 million. President Wilson re-elected with "he kept us out of war" slogan. "Black Tom" explosion at munitions dock in Jersey City, N.J., $40,000,000 damages; traced to German saboteurs. Margaret Sanger opens first birth control clinic. Easter Rebellion in Ireland put down by British troops. Jeannette Rankin becomes first woman elected to Congress.

1917 First U.S. combat troops in France as U.S. declares war on Germany **(April 6)**. Third Battle of Ypres. Russian Revolution of 1917—climax of long unrest under czars. February Revolution—Nicholas II forced to abdicate, liberal government created. Kerensky becomes prime minister and forms provisional government **(July)**. In October Revolution, Bolsheviks seize power in armed coup d'état led by Lenin and Trotsky. Kerensky flees. Balfour Declaration promises Jewish homeland in Palestine. U.S. declares war on Austria-Hungary **(Dec. 7)**. Armistice between

W.E.B. Du Bois (1868–1963)

Woodrow Wilson (1856–1924)

Bessie Smith (1894–1937)

WORLD WAR I (1914–1918)

Imperial, territorial, and economic rivalries led to the "Great War" between the Central Powers (Austria-Hungary, Germany, Bulgaria, and Turkey) and the Allies (U.S., Britain, France, Russia, Belgium, Serbia, Greece, Romania, Montenegro, Portugal, Italy, and Japan). About 10 million combatants killed, 20 million wounded.

1914 Austrian Archduke Francis Ferdinand and wife assassinated in Sarajevo by Serbian nationalist, Gavrilo Princip **(June 28)**. Austria declares war on Serbia **(July 28)**. Germany declares war on Russia **(Aug. 1)**, on France **(Aug. 3)**, invades Belgium **(Aug. 4)**. Britain declares war on Germany **(Aug. 4)**. Germans defeat Russians in Battle of Tannenberg on Eastern Front **(Aug.)**. First Battle of the Marne **(Sept.)**. German drive stopped 25 miles from Paris. By end of year, war on the Western Front is "positional" in the trenches.

1915 German submarine blockade of Great Britain begins **(Feb.)**. Dardanelles Campaign—British land in Turkey **(April)**, withdraw from Gallipoli **(Dec.–Jan. 1916)**. Germans use gas at second Battle of Ypres **(April–May)**. *Lusitania* sunk by German submarine—1,198 lost, including 128 Americans **(May 7)**. On Eastern Front, German and Austrian "great offensive" conquers all of Poland and Lithuania; Russians lose 1 million men (by **Sept. 6**). "Great Fall Offensive" by Allies results in little change from 1914 **(Sept.–Oct.)**. Britain and France declare war on Bulgaria **(Oct. 14)**.

1916 Battle of Verdun—Germans and French each lose about 350,000 men **(Feb.)**. Extended submarine warfare begins **(March)**. British-German sea battle of Jutland **(May)**; British lose more ships, but German fleet never ventures forth again. On Eastern Front, the Brusilov offensive demoralizes Russians, costs them 1 million men **(June–Sept.)**. Battle of the Somme—British lose over 400,000; French, 200,000; Germans, about 450,000; all with no strategic results **(July–Nov.)**. Romania declares war on Austria-Hungary **(Aug. 27)**. Bucharest captured **(Dec.)**.

1917 U.S. declares war on Germany **(April 6)**. Submarine warfare at peak **(April)**. On Italian Front, Battle of Caporetto—Italians retreat, losing 600,000 prisoners and deserters **(Oct.–Dec.)**. On Western Front, Battles of Arras, Champagne, Ypres (third battle), etc. First large British tank attack **(Nov.)**. U.S. declares war on Austria-Hungary **(Dec. 7)**. Armistice between new Russian Bolshevik government and Germans **(Dec. 15)**.

1918 Great offensive by Germans **(March–June)**. Americans' first important battle role at Château-Thierry—as they and French stop German advance **(June)**. Second Battle of the Marne **(July–Aug.)**—start of Allied offensive at Amiens, St. Mihiel, etc. Battles of the Argonne and Ypres panic German leadership **(Sept.–Oct.)**. British offensive in Palestine **(Sept.)**. Germans ask for armistice **(Oct. 4)**. British armistice with Turkey **(Oct.)**. German Kaiser abdicates **(Nov.)**. Hostilities cease on Western Front **(Nov. 11)**.

Mahatma Gandhi (1869–1948)

William Butler Yeats (1865–1939)

Robert Frost (1874–1963)

Pablo Picasso (1881–1973)

Babe Ruth (George Herman Ruth) (1895–1948)

new Russian Bolshevik government and Germans **(Dec. 15).** Sigmund Freud's *Introduction to Psychoanalysis.*

1918 Russian revolutionaries execute the former czar and his family. Russian Civil War between Reds (Bolsheviks) and Whites (anti-Bolsheviks); Reds win in 1920. Allied troops (U.S., British, French) intervene **(March);** leave in 1919. Second Battle of the Marne **(July–Aug.)** German Kaiser abdicates **(Nov.);** hostilities cease on the Western Front. Japanese hold Vladivostok until 1922. Worldwide influenza epidemic strikes; by 1920, nearly 20 million are dead. In U.S. alone, 500,000 perish.

1919 Third International (Comintern) establishes Soviet control over international Communist movements. Paris peace conference. Versailles Treaty, incorporating Woodrow Wilson's draft Covenant of League of Nations, signed by Allies and Germany; rejected by U.S. Senate. Congress formally ends war in 1921. 18th (Prohibition) Amendment adopted. Alcock and Brown make first trans-Atlantic nonstop flight. Mahatma Gandhi initiates satyagraha ("truth force") campaigns, beginning his nonviolent resistance movement against British rule in India.

1920 League of Nations holds first meeting at Geneva, Switzerland. U.S. Dept. of Justice "red hunt" nets thousands of radicals; aliens deported. Women's suffrage (19th) amendment ratified. Treaty of Sèvres dissolves Ottoman Empire. First Agatha Christie mystery. Sinclair Lewis's *Main Street.*

1921 Reparations Commission fixes German liability at 132 billion gold marks. German inflation begins. Major treaties signed at Washington Disarmament Conference limit naval tonnage and pledge to respect territorial integrity of China. In U.S., Nicola Sacco and Bartolomeo Vanzetti, Italian-born anarchists, convicted of armed robbery murder; case stirs worldwide protests; they are executed in 1927.

1922 Mussolini marches on Rome; forms Fascist government. Irish Free State, a self-governing dominion of British Empire, officially proclaimed. Kemal Atatürk, founder of modern Turkey, overthrows last sultan. James Joyce's *Ulysses.*

1923 Adolf Hitler's "Beer Hall Putsch" in Munich fails; in 1924 he is sentenced to five years in prison where he writes *Mein Kampf;* released after eight months. Occupation of Ruhr by French and Belgian troops to enforce reparations payments. Widespread Ku Klux Klan violence in U.S. Earthquake destroys third of Tokyo. George Gershwin's *Rhapsody in Blue.* Bessie Smith, known as "the Empress of the Blues," makes her first record. Irish poet William Butler Yeats wins Nobel Prize in Literature.

1924 Death of Lenin; Stalin wins power struggle, rules as Soviet dictator until death in 1953. Italian Fascists murder Socialist leader Giacomo Matteotti. Interior Secretary Albert B. Fall and oilmen Harry Sinclair and Edward L. Doheny are charged with conspiracy and bribery in the Teapot Dome scandal, involving fraudulent leases of naval oil reserves. In 1931, Fall is sentenced to year in prison; Doheny and Sinclair acquitted of bribery. Nathan Leopold and Richard Loeb convicted in "thrill killing" of Bobby Franks in Chicago; defended by Clarence Darrow; sentenced to life imprisonment. (Loeb killed by fellow convict in 1936; Leopold paroled in 1958, dies in 1971.) Robert Frost wins first of four Pulitzers.

1925 Nellie Tayloe Ross elected governor of Wyoming; first woman governor elected in U.S. Locarno conferences seek to secure European peace by mutual guarantees. John T. Scopes convicted and fined for teaching evolution in a public school in Tennessee "Monkey Trial"; sentence set aside. John Logie Baird, Scottish inventor, transmits human features by television. Hitler publishes Volume I of *Mein Kampf.*

1926 General strike in Britain brings nation's activities to standstill. U.S. marines dispatched to Nicaragua during revolt; they remain until 1933. Gertrude Ederle of U.S. is first woman to swim English Channel. Ernest Hemingway's *The Sun Also Rises.*

1927 German economy collapses. Socialists riot in Vienna; general strike follows acquittal of Nazis for political murder. Trotsky expelled from Russian Communist Party. Charles A. Lindbergh flies first successful solo nonstop flight from New York to Paris. Ruth Snyder and Judd Gray convicted of murder of Albert Snyder; they are executed at Sing Sing prison in 1928. Philo T. Farnsworth demonstrates working television model. Georges Lemaître proposes Big Bang Theory. Babe Ruth hits 60 home runs in the season; record stands for next 34 years. *The Jazz Singer,* with Al Jolson, first part-talking motion picture.

1928 Kellogg-Briand Pact, outlawing war, signed in Paris by 65 nations. Alexander Fleming discovers penicillin. Richard E. Byrd starts expedition to Antarctic; returns in 1930. Anthropologist Margaret Mead publishes *Coming of Age in Samoa. Oxford English Dictionary* published after 44 years of research.

1929 Trotsky expelled from USSR Lateran Treaty establishes independent Vatican City. In U.S., stock market prices collapse, with U.S. securities losing $26 billion—first phase of Depression and world economic crisis. St. Valentine's Day gangland massacre in Chicago. Edwin Powell Hubble proposes theory of expanding universe.

1930 Britain, U.S., Japan, France, and Italy sign naval disarmament treaty. Nazis gain in German elections. Cyclotron developed by Ernest O. Lawrence, U.S. physicist. Pluto discovered by astronomers.

1931 Spain becomes a republic with overthrow of King Alfonso XIII. German industrialists finance 800,000-strong Nazi party. British parliament enacts statute of Westminster, legalizing dominion equality with Britain. Mukden Incident begins Japanese occupation of Manchuria. In U.S., Hoover proposes one-year moratorium of war debts. Harold C. Urey discovers heavy hydrogen. Gangster Al Capone sentenced to 11 years in prison for tax evasion (freed in 1939; dies in 1947). Notorious Scottsboro trial begins, exposing depth of Southern racism. "The Star Spangled Banner" officially becomes national anthem.

1932 Nazis lead in German elections with 230 Reichstag seats. Famine in USSR. In U.S., Congress sets up Reconstruction Finance Corporation to stimulate economy. Veterans march on Washington—most leave after Senate rejects payment of cash bonuses; others removed by troops under Douglas MacArthur. U.S. protests Japanese aggression in Manchuria. Amelia Earhart is first woman to fly Atlantic solo. Charles A. Lindbergh's baby son kidnapped, killed. (Bruno Richard Hauptmann arrested in 1934, convicted in 1935, executed in 1936.)

1933 Hitler appointed German chancellor, gets dictatorial powers. Reichstag fire in Berlin; Nazi terror begins. Germany and Japan withdraw from League of Nations. Giuseppe Zangara executed for attempted assassination of president-elect Roosevelt in which Chicago mayor Cermak is fatally shot. Roosevelt inaugurated ("the only thing we have to fear is fear itself"); launches New Deal. Prohibition repealed. USSR recognized by U.S.

1934 Chancellor Dollfuss of Austria assassinated by Nazis. Hitler becomes führer. USSR admitted to League of Nations. Dionne sisters, first quintuplets to survive beyond infancy, born in Canada. Mao Zedong begins the Long March north with 100,000 soldiers.

1935 Saar incorporated into Germany after plebiscite. Nazis repudiate Versailles Treaty, introduce compulsory military service. Mussolini invades Ethiopia; League of Nations invokes sanctions. Roosevelt opens second phase of

Benito Mussolini (1883–1945)

Joseph Stalin (1879–1953)

Adolf Hitler (1889–1945)

THE HOLOCAUST (1933–1945)

"Holocaust" is the term describing the Nazi annihilation of about 6 million Jews (two thirds of the pre-World War II European Jewish population), including 4,500,000 from Russia, Poland, and the Baltic; 750,000 from Hungary and Romania; 290,000 from Germany and Austria; 105,000 from The Netherlands; 90,000 from France; 54,000 from Greece.

The Holocaust was unique in its being *genocide*—the systematic destruction of a people solely because of religion, race, ethnicity, nationality, or sexual preference—on an unmatched scale. Along with the Jews, another 9 to 10 million people—Gypsies, Slavs (Poles, Ukrainians, and Belarussians), homosexuals, and the disabled—were exterminated.

1933 Hitler named German Chancellor **(Jan.)**. Dachau, first concentration camp, established **(March)**. Boycotts against Jews begin **(April)**.

1935 Anti-Semitic Nuremberg Laws passed by Reichstag; Jews lose citizenship and civil rights **(Sept.)**.

1937 Buchenwald concentration camp opens **(July)**.

1938 Extension of anti-Semitic laws to Austria after annexation **(March)**. *Kristallnacht* (Night of Broken Glass)—anti-Semitic riots and destruction of Jewish institutions in Germany and Austria **(Nov. 9)**. 26,000 Jews sent to concentration camps; Jewish children expelled from schools **(Nov. 9–10)**. Expropriation of Jewish property and businesses **(Dec.)**.

1940 As war continues, Einsatzgruppen (mobile killing squads) follow German army into conquered lands, rounding up and massacring Jews and other "undesirables."

1941 Goering instructs Heydrich to carry out the "final solution to the Jewish question" **(July 31)**. Deportation of German Jews begins; massacres of Jews in Odessa and Kiev **(Nov.)**; and in Riga and Vilna **(Dec.)**.

1942 Mass killings using Zyklon-B begin at Auschwitz-Birkenau **(Jan.)**. Nazi leaders attend Wannsee Conference to coordinate the "final solution" **(Jan. 20)**. 100,000 Jews from Warsaw Ghetto deported to Treblinka death camp **(July)**.

1943 Warsaw Ghetto uprisings **(Jan.** and **April)**; Ghetto exterminated **(May)**.

1944 476,000 Hungarian Jews sent to Auschwitz **(May–June)**. D-day **(June 6)**. Soviet Army liberates Maidanek death camp **(July)**. Nazis try to hide evidence of death camps **(Nov.)**.

1945 As Allies advance, Nazis force concentration camp inmates on death marches. Americans liberate Buchenwald and British liberate Bergen-Belsen camps **(April)**. Nuremberg War Crimes Trial **(Nov. 1945–Oct. 1946)**.

Dorothea Lange's photo "Migrant Mother" (1936) documented the Great Depression (1929–1940)

Amelia Earhart (1897–1937)

New Deal in U.S., calling for social security, better housing, equitable taxation, and farm assistance. Huey Long assassinated in Louisiana.

1936 Germans occupy Rhineland. Italy annexes Ethiopia. Rome-Berlin Axis proclaimed (Japan to join in 1940). Trotsky exiled to Mexico. King George V dies; succeeded by son, Edward VIII, who soon abdicates to marry an American-born divorcée, and is succeeded by brother, George VI. Spanish civil war begins. Hundreds of Americans join the "Lincoln Brigades." (Franco's fascist forces defeat Loyalist forces by 1939, when Madrid falls.) War between China and Japan begins, to continue through World War II. Japan and Germany sign anti-Comintern pact; joined by Italy in 1937.

1937 Hitler repudiates war guilt clause of Versailles Treaty; continues to build German power. Italy withdraws from League of Nations. U.S. gunboat *Panay* sunk by Japanese in Yangtze River. Japan invades China, conquers most of coastal area. Amelia Earhart lost somewhere in Pacific on round-the-world flight. Picasso's *Guernica* mural.

1938 Hitler marches into Austria; political and geographical union of Germany and Austria proclaimed. Munich Pact—Britain, France, and Italy agree to let Germany partition Czechoslovakia. Douglas "Wrong-Way" Corrigan flies from New York to Dublin. Fair Labor Standards Act establishes minimum wage. Orson Welles's radio broadcast *War of the Worlds*.

1939 Germany invades Poland; occupies Bohemia and Moravia; renounces pact with England and concludes 10-year non-aggression pact with USSR. Russo-Finnish War begins; Finns to lose one-tenth of territory in 1940 peace treaty. World War II begins. In U.S., Roosevelt submits $1,319-million defense budget, proclaims U.S. neutrality, and declares limited emergency. Einstein writes FDR about feasibility of atomic bomb. New York World's Fair opens. DAR refuses to allow Marian Anderson to perform. *Gone with the Wind* premieres.

WORLD WAR II (1939–1945)

Axis powers (Germany, Italy, Japan, Hungary, Romania, Bulgaria) *versus* Allies (U.S., Britain, France, USSR, Australia, Belgium, Brazil, Canada, China, Denmark, Greece, Netherlands, New Zealand, Norway, Poland, South Africa, Yugoslavia).

1939 Germany invades Poland and annexes Danzig; Britain and France give Hitler ultimatum **(Sept. 1)**, declare war **(Sept. 3)**. Disabled German pocket battleship *Admiral Graf Spee* blown up off Montevideo, Uruguay, on Hitler's orders **(Dec. 17)**. Limited activity ("Sitzkrieg") on Western Front.

1940 Nazis invade Netherlands, Belgium, and Luxembourg **(May 10)**. Chamberlain resigns as Britain's prime minister; Churchill takes over **(May 10)**. Germans cross French frontier **(May 12)** using air/tank/infantry "Blitzkrieg" tactics. Dunkerque evacuation—about 335,000 out of 400,000 Allied soldiers rescued from Belgium by British civilian and naval craft **(May 26–June 3)**. Italy declares war on France and Britain; invades France **(June 10)**. Germans enter Paris; city undefended **(June 14)**. France and Germany sign armistice at Compiègne **(June 22)**. Nazis bomb Coventry, England **(Nov. 14)**.

1941 Germans launch attacks in Balkans. Yugoslavia surrenders—General Mihajlovic continues guerrilla warfare; Tito leads left-wing guerrillas **(April 17)**. Nazi tanks enter Athens; remnants of British Army quit Greece **(April 27)**. Hitler attacks Russia **(June 22)**. Atlantic Charter—FDR and Churchill agree on war aims **(Aug. 14)**. Japanese attacks on Pearl Harbor, Philippines, Guam force U.S. into war; U.S. Pacific fleet crippled **(Dec. 7)**. U.S. and Britain declare war on Japan. Germany and Italy declare war on U.S.; Congress declares war on those countries **(Dec. 11)**.

1942 British surrender Singapore to Japanese **(Feb. 15)**. Roosevelt orders Japanese and Japanese Americans in western U.S. to be exiled to "relocation centers," many for the remainder of the war **(Feb. 19)**. U.S. forces on Bataan peninsula in Philippines surrender **(April 9)**. U.S. and Filipino troops on Corregidor island in Manila Bay surrender to Japanese **(May 6)**. Village of Lidice in Czechoslovakia razed by Nazis **(June 10)**. U.S. and Britain land in French North Africa **(Nov. 8)**.

1943 Casablanca Conference—Churchill and FDR agree on unconditional surrender goal **(Jan. 14–24)**. German 6th Army surrenders at Stalingrad—turning point of war in Russia **(Feb. 1–2)**. Remnants of Nazis trapped on Cape Bon, ending war in Africa **(May 12)**. Mussolini deposed; Badoglio named premier **(July 25)**. Allied troops land on Italian mainland after conquest of Sicily **(Sept. 3)**. Italy surrenders **(Sept. 8)**. Nazis seize Rome **(Sept. 10)**. Cairo Conference: FDR, Churchill, Chiang Kai-shek pledge defeat of Japan, free Korea **(Nov. 22–26)**. Teheran Conference: FDR, Churchill, Stalin agree on invasion plans **(Nov. 28–Dec. 1)**.

1944 U.S. and British troops land at Anzio on west Italian coast and hold beachhead **(Jan. 22)**. U.S. and British troops enter Rome **(June 4)**. D-Day—Allies launch Normandy invasion **(June 6)**. Hitler wounded in bomb plot **(July 20)**. Paris liberated **(Aug. 25)**. Athens freed by Allies **(Oct. 13)**. Americans invade Philippines **(Oct. 20)**. Germans launch counteroffensive in Belgium—Battle of the Bulge **(Dec. 16)**.

1945 Yalta Agreement signed by FDR, Churchill, Stalin—establishes basis for occupation of Germany, returns to Soviet Union lands taken by Germany and Japan; USSR agrees to friendship pact with China **(Feb. 11)**. Mussolini killed at Lake Como **(April 28)**. Admiral Doenitz takes command in Germany; suicide of Hitler announced **(May 1)**. Berlin falls **(May 2)**. Germany signs unconditional surrender terms at Rheims **(May 7)**. Allies declare V-E Day **(May 8)**. Potsdam Conference—Truman, Churchill, Atlee (after **July 28**), Stalin establish council of foreign ministers to prepare peace treaties; plan German postwar government and reparations **(July 17–Aug. 2)**. A-bomb dropped on Hiroshima by U.S. **(Aug. 6)**. USSR declares war on Japan **(Aug. 8)**. Nagasaki hit by A-bomb **(Aug. 9)**. Japan agrees to surrender **(Aug. 14)**. V-J Day—Japanese sign surrender terms aboard battleship *Missouri* **(Sept. 2)**.

1940 Hitler invades Norway, Denmark (**April 9**), the Netherlands, Belgium, Luxembourg (**May 10**), and France (**May 12**). Churchill becomes Britain's prime minister. Trotsky assassinated in Mexico (**Aug. 20**). Estonia, Latvia, and Lithuania annexed by USSR. U.S. trades 50 destroyers for leases on British bases in Western Hemisphere. Selective Service Act signed. The first official network television broadcast is put out by NBC.

1941 Germany attacks the Balkans and Russia. Japanese surprise attack on U.S. fleet at Pearl Harbor brings U.S. into World War II; U.S. and Britain declare war on Japan. Manhattan Project (atomic bomb research) begins. Roosevelt enunciates "four freedoms," signs Lend-Lease Act, declares national emergency, promises aid to USSR. Orson Welles's *Citizen Kane*.

1942 Declaration of United Nations signed in Washington (**Jan. 1**). Nazi leaders attend Wannsee Conference to coordinate the "final solution to the Jewish question," the systematic genocide of Jews known as the Holocaust. Women's military services established. Enrico Fermi achieves nuclear chain reaction. More than 120,000 Japanese and persons of Japanese ancestry living in western U.S. moved to "relocation centers," some for the duration of the war (Executive Order 9066). Coconut Grove nightclub fire in Boston kills 492 (**Nov. 28**).

1943 Churchill and Roosevelt hold Casablanca Conference (**Jan. 14–23**). Mussolini deposed. President freezes prices, salaries, and wages to prevent inflation. Income tax withholding introduced.

1944 Allies invade Normandy on D-Day (**June 6**). G.I. Bill of Rights enacted. Bretton Woods Conference creates International Monetary Fund and World Bank (**July 1–22**). Dumbarton Oaks Conference—U.S., British Commonwealth, and USSR propose establishment of United Nations (**Aug. 21–Oct. 7**). Battle of the Bulge (**Dec. 16**). Gunnar Myrdal's *An American Dilemma*.

1945 Yalta Conference (Roosevelt, Churchill, Stalin) plans final defeat of Germany (**Feb. 4–11**). FDR dies (**April 12**). Hitler commits suicide (**April 30**); Germany surrenders (**May 7**); **May 8** is declared V-E Day. Potsdam Conference (Truman, Churchill, Stalin) establishes basis of German reconstruction (**July–Aug.**). U.S. drops atomic bombs on Japanese cities of Hiroshima (**Aug. 6**) and Nagasaki (**Aug. 9**). Japan signs official surrender on V-J Day (**Sept. 2**). United Nations established (**Oct. 24**). First electronic computer, ENIAC, built.

1946 First meeting of UN General Assembly opens in London (**Jan. 10**). Winston Churchill's "Iron Curtain" speech warns of Soviet expansion (**March 5**). League of Nations dissolved (**April**). Italy abolishes monarchy (**June**). Verdict in Nuremberg war trial: 12 Nazi leaders (including 1 tried in absentia) sentenced to hang; 7 imprisoned; 3 acquitted (**Oct. 1**). Goering commits suicide a few hours before 10 other Nazis are executed (**Oct. 15**). Juan Perón becomes president of Argentina. Benjamin Spock's childcare classic published.

1947 Britain nationalizes coal mines (**Jan. 1**). Peace treaties for Italy, Romania, Bulgaria, Hungary, Finland signed in Paris (**Feb. 10**). Soviet Union rejects U.S. plan for UN atomic-energy control (**March 4**). Truman proposes Truman Doctrine, which was to aid Greece and Turkey in resisting communist expansion (**March 12**). Marshall Plan for European recovery proposed—a coordinated program to help European nations recover from ravages of war (**June**). (By the time it ended in 1951, this "European Recovery Program" had cost $13 billion.) India and Pakistan gain independence from Britain (**Aug. 15**). U.S. Air Force pilot Chuck Yeager becomes first person to break the sound barrier (**Oct. 14**). Jackie Robinson joins the Brooklyn Dodgers. Anne Frank's *The Diary of a Young Girl* published.

1948 Gandhi assassinated in New Delhi by Hindu fanatic (**Jan. 30**). Burma (**Jan. 4**) and Ceylon (**Feb. 4**) granted independence by Britain. Communists seize power in Czechoslovakia (**Feb. 23–25**). Organization of American States (OAS) Charter signed at Bogotá, Colombia (**April 30**). Nation of Israel proclaimed; British end mandate at midnight; Arab armies attack (**May 14**). Berlin blockade begins (**June 24**), prompting Allied airlift (**June 26**). (Blockade ends **May 12, 1949**; airlift continues until **Sept. 30, 1949**.) Stalin and Tito break (**June 28**). Independent Republic of Korea is proclaimed, following election supervised by UN (**Aug. 15**). Verdict in Japanese war trial: 18 imprisoned (**Nov. 12**); Tojo and six others hanged (**Dec. 23**). United States of Indonesia established as Dutch and Indonesians settle conflict (**Dec. 27**). Alger Hiss, former

Franklin Delano Roosevelt (1882–1945)

Winston Churchill (1874–1965)

Harry S. Truman (1884–1972)

Atomic Bomb

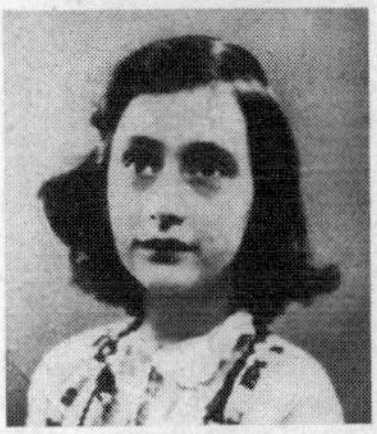

Anne Frank (1929–1945)

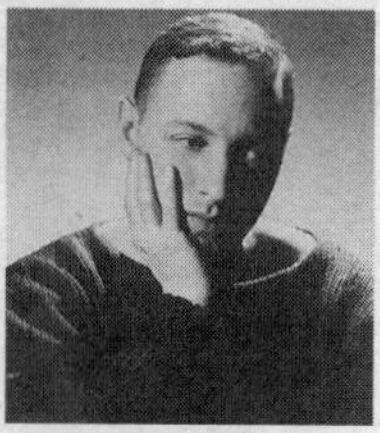

Tennessee Williams (1911–1983)

Woody Guthrie (1912–1967)

Dwight D. Eisenhower (1890–1969)

Dag Hammarskjöld (1905–1961)

U.S. State Department official, indicted on perjury charges after denying passing secret documents to communist spy ring; convicted in second trial (1950) and sentenced to five-year prison term. Truman ends racial segregation in military. Alfred Kinsey publishes *Sexual Behavior in the American Male*. Tennessee Williams's *A Streetcar Named Desire* wins Pulitzer.

1949 Cease-fire in Palestine **(Jan. 7).** Truman proposes Point Four Program to help world's less developed areas **(Jan. 20).** Israel signs armistice with Egypt **(Feb. 24).** Start of North Atlantic Treaty Organization (NATO)—treaty signed by 12 nations **(April 4).** Federal Republic of Germany (West Germany) established **(May 23).** First successful Soviet atomic test **(July 14).** Communist People's Republic of China formally proclaimed by Chairman Mao Zedong **(Oct. 1).** German Democratic Republic (East Germany) established under Soviet rule **(Oct. 7).** South Africa institutionalizes apartheid.

1950 Brink's robbery in Boston; almost $3 million stolen **(Jan. 17).** Truman orders development of hydrogen bomb **(Jan. 31).** Robert Schuman proposes Schuman Plan to pool European coal and steel **(May 9).** Korean War begins when North Korean Communist forces invade South Korea **(June 25).** Assassination attempt on President Truman by Puerto Rican nationalists **(Nov. 1).** McCarthyism begins.

1951 Julius and Ethel Rosenberg sentenced to death for passing atomic secrets to Russians **(March).** Spurred by Schuman Plan, six nations form European Coal and Steel Community **(April);** effective 1952. Japanese peace treaty signed in San Francisco by 49 nations **(Sept. 8).** Color television introduced in U.S. Libya gains independence **(Dec. 24).**

1952 George VI dies; his daughter becomes Elizabeth II **(Feb. 6).** AEC announces "satisfactory" experiments in hydrogen-weapons research; eyewitnesses tell of blasts near Enewetak **(Nov.).** Ralph Ellison's *The Invisible Man*.

1953 Gen. Dwight D. Eisenhower inaugurated president of United States **(Jan. 20).** Stalin dies **(March 5).** Malenkov becomes Soviet premier; Beria, minister of interior; Molotov, foreign minister **(March 6).** Dag Hammarskjöld begins term as UN secretary-general **(April 10).** James Watson and Francis Crick publish their discovery of the molecular model of DNA **(April–May).** Edmund Hillary of New Zealand and Tenzing Norgay of Nepal reach top of Mt. Everest **(May 29).** East Berliners rise against Communist rule; quelled by tanks **(June 17).** Egypt becomes republic ruled by military junta **(June 18).** Julius and Ethel Rosenberg executed in Sing Sing prison **(June 19).** Korean armistice signed **(July 27).** Moscow announces explosion of hydrogen bomb **(Aug. 20).** Tito becomes president of Yugoslavia. James Watson, Francis Crick, and Rosalind Franklin discover structure of DNA. Ernest Hemingway wins Pulitzer for *The Old Man and the Sea*.

1954 First atomic submarine *Nautilus* launched **(Jan. 21).** Five U.S. congressmen shot on floor of House as Puerto Rican nationalists fire from spectators' gallery; all five recover **(March 1).** Soviet Union grants sovereignty to East Germany **(March 23).** *Army* v. *McCarthy* inquiry—Senate subcommittee report blames both sides **(April 22–June 17).** Dien Bien Phu, French military outpost in Vietnam, falls to Vietminh army **(May 7).** U.S. Supreme Court (in *Brown* v. *Board of Education of Topeka*) unanimously bans racial segregation in public schools **(May 17).** Eisenhower launches world atomic pool without Soviet Union **(Sept. 6).** Eight-nation Southeast Asia defense treaty (SEATO) signed at Manila **(Sept. 8).** Dr. Jonas Salk starts inoculating children against polio. Algerian War of Independence against France begins **(Nov.);** France struggles to maintain colonial rule until 1962 when it agrees to Algeria's independence. William Faulkner's *A Fable* wins Pulitzer.

KOREAN WAR (1950–1953)

1950 North Korean Communist forces invade South Korea **(June 25).** UN calls for cease-fire and asks UN members to assist South Korea **(June 27).** Truman orders U.S. forces into Korea **(June 27).** North Koreans capture Seoul **(June 28).** Gen. Douglas MacArthur designated commander of unified UN forces **(July 8).** Pusan Beachhead—UN forces counterattack and capture Seoul **(Aug.–Sept.),** capture Pyongyang, North Korean capital **(Oct.).** Chinese Communists enter war **(Oct. 26),** force UN retreat toward 39th parallel **(Dec.).**

1951 Gen. Matthew B. Ridgway replaces MacArthur after he threatens Chinese with massive retaliation **(April 11).** Armistice negotiations **(July)** continue with interruptions until **June 1953.**

1953 Armistice signed **(July 27).** Chinese troops withdraw from North Korea **(Oct. 26, 1958),** but over 200 violations of armistice noted to **1959.**

1955 Nikolai A. Bulganin becomes Soviet premier, replacing Malenkov **(Feb. 8).** Churchill resigns; Anthony Eden succeeds him **(April 6).** West Germany becomes a sovereign state **(May 5).** Western European Union (WEU) comes into being **(May 6).** Warsaw Pact, east European mutual defense agreement, signed **(May 14).** Argentina ousts Perón **(Sept. 19).** President Eisenhower suffers coronary thrombosis in Denver **(Sept. 24).** Rosa Parks refuses to sit at the back of the bus. Martin Luther King, Jr., leads black boycott of Montgomery, Ala., bus system **(Dec. 1);** desegregated service begins **Dec. 21, 1956.** AFL and CIO become one organization—AFL-CIO **(Dec. 5).** Tennessee Williams's *Cat on a Hot Tin Roof* wins Pulitzer.

1956 Nikita Khrushchev, First Secretary of USSR Communist Party, denounces Stalin's excesses **(Feb. 24).** First aerial H-bomb tested over Namu islet, Bikini Atoll—10 million tons TNT equivalent **(May 21).** Workers' uprising against Communist rule in Poznan, Poland, is crushed **(June 28–30);** rebellion inspires Hungarian students to stage a protest against Communism in Budapest **(Oct. 23).** Egypt takes control of Suez Canal **(July 26).** Hungarian rebellion forces Soviet troops to withdraw from Budapest **(Oct.).** Israel launches attack on Egypt's Sinai peninsula and drives toward Suez Canal **(Oct. 29).** Imre Nagy announces Hungary's withdrawal from Warsaw Pact **(Nov. 1);** Soviet troops enter and reclaim Budapest **(Nov. 4).** British and French invade Port Said on the Suez Canal **(Nov. 5).** Cease-fire forced by U.S. pressure stops British, French, and Israeli advance **(Nov. 6).** Morocco gains independence. Ingmar Bergman's *The Seventh Seal.* Woody Guthrie composes "This Land is Your Land." Allen Ginsberg's *Howl.*

1957 Eisenhower Doctrine calls for aid to Mideast countries which resist armed aggression from Communist-controlled nations **(Jan. 5).** The "Little Rock Nine" integrate Arkansas high school. Eisenhower sends troops to quell mob and protect school integration **(Sept. 24).** Russians launch *Sputnik I,* first Earth-orbiting satellite—the Space Age begins **(Oct. 4).**

1958 European Economic Community (Common Market) becomes effective **(Jan. 1).** Army's Jupiter-C rocket fires first U.S. Earth satellite, *Explorer I,* into orbit **(Jan. 31).** Egypt and Syria merge into United Arab Republic **(Feb. 1).** Khrushchev becomes premier of Soviet Union as Bulganin resigns **(Mar. 27).** Gen. Charles de Gaulle becomes French premier **(June 1),** remaining in power until 1969. Eisenhower orders U.S. Marines into Lebanon at request of President Chamoun, who fears overthrow **(July 15).** New French constitution adopted **(Sept. 28),** de Gaulle elected president of 5th Republic **(Dec. 21).**

1959 Cuban President Batista resigns and flees—Castro takes over **(Jan. 1).** Tibet's Dalai Lama escapes to India **(Mar. 31).** St. Lawrence Seaway opens, allowing ocean ships to reach Midwest **(April 25).** Alaska and Hawaii become states. Leakeys discover hominid fossils.

1960 American U-2 spy plane, piloted by Francis Gary Powers, shot down over Russia **(May 1).** Khrushchev kills Paris summit conference because of U-2 **(May 16).** Top Nazi murderer of Jews, Adolf Eichmann, captured by Israelis in Argentina **(May 23)**—executed in Israel in 1962. Powers sentenced to prison for 10 years **(Aug. 19)**—freed in **February 1962** in exchange for Soviet spy. Communist China and Soviet Union split in conflict over Communist ideology. Senegal, Ghana, Nigeria, Madagascar, and Zaire (Belgian Congo) gain independence. Cuba begins confiscation of $770 million of U.S. property **(Aug. 7).** There are 900 U.S. military advisers in South Vietnam.

1961 U.S. breaks diplomatic relations with Cuba **(Jan. 3).** Robert Frost recites "The Gift Outright" at John F. Kennedy's inauguration as president of U.S. **(Jan. 20).** Moscow announces putting first man in orbit around Earth, Maj. Yuri A. Gagarin **(April 12).** Cuba invaded at Bay of Pigs by an estimated 1,200 anti-Castro exiles aided by U.S.; invasion crushed **(April 17).** First U.S. spaceman, Navy Cmdr. Alan B. Shepard, Jr., rockets 116.5 miles up in 302-mile trip **(May 5).** Virgil Grissom becomes second American astronaut, making 118-mile-high, 303-mile-long rocket flight over Atlantic **(July 21).** Gherman Stepanovich Titov is launched in Soviet spaceship *Vostok II:* makes 17½ orbits in 25 hours, covering 434,960 miles before landing safely **(Aug. 6).** East Germans erect Berlin Wall between East and West Berlin to halt flood of refugees **(Aug. 13).** USSR fires 50-megaton hydrogen bomb, biggest explosion in history **(Oct. 29).** There are 2,000 U.S. military advisers in South Vietnam.

Fidel Castro (1926–)

John H. Glenn, Jr. (1921–)

Martin Luther King, Jr. (1929–1968)

John F. Kennedy (1917–1963)

James H. Meredith
(1933–)

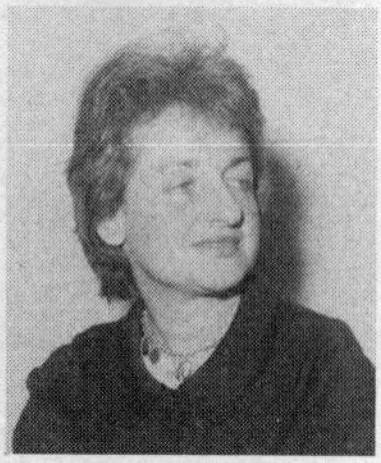

Betty Friedan
(1921–)

1962 Lt. Col. John H. Glenn, Jr., is first American to orbit Earth—three times in 4 hr 55 min **(Feb. 20).** France transfers sovereignty to new republic of Algeria **(July 3).** Cuban missile crisis—USSR to build missile bases in Cuba; Kennedy orders Cuban blockade, lifts blockade after Russians back down **(Aug.–Nov.).** James H. Meredith, escorted by federal marshals, registers at University of Mississippi **(Oct. 1).** Pope John XXIII opens Second Vatican Council **(Oct. 11)**—Council holds four sessions, finally closing **Dec. 8, 1965.** Cuba releases 1,113 prisoners of 1961 invasion attempt **(Dec. 24).** Burundi, Jamaica, Western Samoa, Uganda, and Trinidad and Tobago become independent. William Faulkner wins Pulitzer for *The Reivers.* Rachel Carson's *Silent Spring.*

1963 France and West Germany sign treaty of cooperation ending four centuries of conflict **(Jan. 22).** Michael E. De Bakey implants artificial heart in human for first time at Houston hospital; plastic device functions and patient lives for four days **(April 21).** Pope John XXIII dies **(June 3)**—succeeded **June 21** by Cardinal Montini, who becomes Paul VI. U.S. Supreme Court rules no locality may require recitation of Lord's Prayer or Bible verses in public schools **(June 17).** U.K.'s Profumo scandal **(June).** Civil rights rally held by 200,000 blacks and whites in Washington, D.C.; Martin Luther King delivers "I have a dream" speech **(Aug. 28).** Washington-to-Moscow "hot line" communications link opens, designed to reduce risk of accidental war **(Aug. 30).** President Kennedy shot and killed by sniper in Dallas, Tex. Lyndon B. Johnson becomes president same day **(Nov. 22).** Lee Harvey Oswald, accused assassin of President Kennedy, is shot and killed by Jack Ruby, Dallas nightclub owner **(Nov. 24).** Kenya achieves independence. Betty Friedan publishes *The Feminine Mystique.* There are 15,000 U.S. military advisers in South Vietnam.

VIETNAM WAR (1950–1975)

U.S., South Vietnam, and Allies versus North Vietnam and National Liberation Front (Viet Cong).

1950 President Truman sends 35-man military advisory group to aid French fighting to maintain colonial power in Vietnam.

1954 After defeat of French at Dien Bien Phu, Geneva Agreements **(July)** provide for withdrawal of French and Vietminh to either side of demarcation zone (DMZ) pending reunification elections, which are never held. Presidents Eisenhower and Kennedy (from 1954 onward) send civilian advisers and, later, military personnel to train South Vietnamese.

1960 Communists form National Liberation Front in South.

1960–1963 U.S. military advisers in South Vietnam rise from 900 to 15,000.

1963 Ngo Dinh Diem, South Vietnam's premier, slain in coup **(Nov. 1).**

1964 North Vietnamese torpedo boats reportedly attack U.S. destroyers in Gulf of Tonkin **(Aug. 2).** President Johnson orders retaliatory air strikes. Congress approves Gulf of Tonkin resolution **(Aug. 7)** authorizing president to take "all necessary measures" to win in Vietnam, allowing for the war's expansion.

1965 U.S. planes begin combat missions over South Vietnam. In **June,** 23,000 American advisers committed to combat. By end of year over 184,000 U.S. troops in area.

1966 B-52s bomb DMZ, reportedly used by North Vietnam for entry into South **(July 31).**

1967 South Vietnam National Assembly approves election of Nguyen Van Thieu as president **(Oct. 21).**

1968 U.S. has almost 525,000 men in Vietnam. In Tet offensive **(Jan.–Feb.),** Viet Cong guerrillas attack Saigon, Hue, and some provincial capitals. In My Lai massacre, American soldiers kill 300 Vietnamese villagers **(March 16).** President Johnson orders halt to U.S. bombardment of North Vietnam **(Oct. 31).** Saigon and N.L.F. join U.S. and North Vietnam in Paris peace talks.

1969 President Nixon announces Vietnam peace offer **(May 14)**—begins troop withdrawals **(June).** Viet Cong forms Provisional Revolutionary Government. U.S. Senate calls for curb on commitments **(June 25).** Ho Chi Minh, 79, North Vietnam president, dies **(Sept. 3);** collective leadership chosen. Some 6,000 U.S. troops pulled back from Thailand and 1,000 marines from Vietnam (announced **Sept. 30**). Massive demonstrations in U.S. protest or support war policies **(Oct. 15).**

1970 U.S. troops invade Cambodia in order to destroy North Vietnamese sanctuaries **(May 1).**

1971 Congress bars use of combat troops, but not air power, in Laos and Cambodia **(Jan. 1).** South Vietnamese troops, with U.S. air cover, fail in Laos thrust. Many American ground forces withdrawn from Vietnam combat. *New York Times* publishes Pentagon papers, classified material on expansion of war **(June).**

1972 Nixon responds to North Vietnamese drive across DMZ by ordering mining of North Vietnam ports and heavy bombing of Hanoi-Haiphong area **(April 1).** Nixon orders "Christmas bombing" of North to get North Vietnamese back to conference table **(Dec.).**

1973 President orders halt to offensive operations in North Vietnam **(Jan. 15).** Representatives of North and South Vietnam, U.S., and N.L.F. sign peace pacts in Paris, ending longest war in U.S. history **(Jan. 27).** Last American troops departed in their entirety **(March 29).**

1974 Both sides accuse each other of frequent violations of cease-fire agreement.

1975 Full-scale warfare resumes. South Vietnam premier Nguyen Van Thieu resigns **(April 21).** South Vietnamese government surrenders to North Vietnam; U.S. Marine embassy guards and U.S. civilians and dependents evacuated **(April 30).** More than 140,000 Vietnamese refugees leave by air and sea, many to settle in U.S. Provisional Revolutionary Government takes control **(June 6).**

1976 Election of National Assembly paves way for reunification of North and South.

1964 U.S. Supreme Court rules that congressional districts should be roughly equal in population **(Feb. 17).** Jack Ruby convicted of murder in slaying of Lee Harvey Oswald; sentenced to death by Dallas jury **(March 14)**—conviction reversed **Oct. 5, 1966;** Ruby dies **Jan. 3, 1967,** before second trial can be held. Three civil rights workers—Schwerner, Goodman, and Cheney—murdered in Mississippi **(June).** Twenty-one arrests result in trial and conviction of seven by federal jury. Nelson Mandela sentenced to life imprisonment **(June 11).** Congress approves Gulf of Tonkin resolution **(Aug. 7).** President's Commission on the Assassination of President Kennedy issues Warren Report concluding that Lee Harvey Oswald acted alone. The Beatles appear on *The Ed Sullivan Show.*

1965 Rev. Dr. Martin Luther King, Jr., and more than 2,600 other blacks arrested in Selma, Ala., during three-day demonstrations against voter-registration rules **(Feb. 1).** Malcolm X, black-nationalist leader, shot to death at Harlem rally in New York City **(Feb. 21).** U.S. Marines land in Dominican Republic as fighting persists between rebels and Dominican army **(April 28).** Medicare, senior citizens' government medical assistance program, begins **(July 1).** Blacks riot for six days in Watts section of Los Angeles: 34 dead, over 1,000 injured, nearly 4,000 arrested, fire damage put at $175 million **(Aug. 11–16).** Power failure in Ontario plant blacks out parts of eight states of northeast U.S. and two provinces of southeast Canada **(Nov. 9).** Ralph Nader's *Unsafe at Any Speed.*

1966 Black teenagers riot in Watts, Los Angeles; two men killed and at least 25 injured **(March 15).** Supreme Court decides *Miranda* v. *Arizona.*

1967 Three Apollo astronauts—Col. Virgil I. Grissom, Col. Edward White II, and Lt. Cmdr. Roger B. Chaffee—killed in spacecraft fire during simulated launch **(Jan. 27).** Biafra secedes from Nigeria **(May 30).** Israeli and Arab forces battle; six-day war ends with Israel occupying Sinai Peninsula, Golan Heights, Gaza Strip, and east bank of Suez Canal **(June 5).** Red China announces explosion of its first hydrogen bomb **(June 17).** Racial violence in Detroit; 7,000 National Guardsmen aid police after night of rioting. Similar outbreaks occur in New York City's Spanish Harlem, Rochester, N.Y., Birmingham, Ala., and New Britain, Conn. **(July 23).** Thurgood Marshall sworn in as first black U.S. Supreme Court justice **(Oct. 2).** Dr. Christiaan N. Barnard and team of South African surgeons perform world's first successful human heart transplant **(Dec. 3)**—patient dies 18 days later.

1968 North Korea seizes U.S. Navy ship *Pueblo;* holds 83 on board as spies **(Jan. 23).** Tet offensive, turning point in Vietnam war **(Jan.–Feb.).** My Lai massacre **(March 16).** President Johnson announces he will not seek or accept presidential renomination **(March 31).** Martin Luther King, Jr., civil rights leader, is slain in Memphis **(April 4)**—James Earl Ray, indicted in murder, captured in London on **June 8.** In 1969 Ray pleads guilty and is sentenced to 99 years. Sen. Robert F. Kennedy is shot and critically wounded in Los Angeles hotel after winning California primary **(June 5)**—dies **June 6.** Sirhan B. Sirhan convicted 1969. Czechoslovakia is invaded by Russians and Warsaw Pact forces to crush liberal regime **(Aug. 20).**

1969 Richard M. Nixon is inaugurated 37th president of the U.S. **(Jan. 20).** Stonewall riot in New York City marks beginning of gay rights movement **(June 28).** *Apollo 11* astronauts—Neil A. Armstrong, Edwin E. Aldrin, Jr., and Michael Collins—take man's first walk on moon **(July 20).** Sen. Edward M. Kennedy pleads guilty to leaving scene of fatal accident at Chappaquiddick, Mass. **(July 18),** in which Mary Jo Kopechne was drowned—gets two-month suspended sentence **(July 25).** Woodstock Festival **(Aug. 15–17).** *Sesame Street* debuts. Internet (ARPA) goes online.

1970 Biafra surrenders after 32-month fight for independence from Nigeria **(Jan. 15).** Rhodesia severs last tie with British crown and declares itself a racially segregated republic **(March 1).** U.S. troops invade Cambodia **(May 1).** Four students at Kent State University in Ohio slain by National Guardsmen at demonstration protesting incursion into Cambodia **(May 4).** Senate repeals Gulf of Tonkin resolution **(June 24).**

1971 Supreme Court rules unanimously that busing of students may be ordered to achieve racial desegregation **(April 20).** Anti-war militants attempt to disrupt government business in Washington **(May 3)**—police and military units arrest as many as 12,000; most are later released. *Pentagon Papers* published **(June).** Twenty-sixth Amendment to U.S. Constitution lowers voting age to 18. UN seats Communist China and expels Nationalist China **(Oct. 25).**

The Beatles

Malcolm X
(1925–1965)

Thurgood Marshall
(1908–1993)

Lyndon B. Johnson
(1908–1973)

Richard Nixon
(1913–1994)

Mao Zedong
(1893–1976)

Duke Ellington
(1899–1974)

Gerald R. Ford
(1913–)

Jimmy Carter
(1924–)

1972 President Nixon makes unprecedented eight-day visit to Communist China and meets with Mao Zedong **(Feb. 21–27).** Britain takes over direct rule of Northern Ireland in bid for peace **(March 24).** Gov. George C. Wallace of Alabama is shot by Arthur H. Bremer at Laurel, Md., political rally **(May 15).** Five men are apprehended by police in attempt to bug Democratic National Committee headquarters in Washington, D.C.'s Watergate complex—start of the Watergate scandal **(June 17).** Supreme Court rules that death penalty is unconstitutional **(June 29).** Eleven Israeli athletes at Olympic Games in Munich are killed after eight members of an Arab terrorist group invade Olympic Village; five guerrillas and one policeman are also killed **(Sept. 5).** "Christmas bombing" of North Vietnam **(Dec. 25).**

1973 Great Britain, Ireland, and Denmark enter European Economic Community **(Jan. 1).** Supreme Court rules on *Roe* v. *Wade* **(Jan. 22).** Vietnam War ends with signing of peace pacts **(Jan. 27).** Nixon, on national TV, accepts responsibility, but not blame, for Watergate; accepts resignations of advisers H. R. Haldeman and John D. Ehrlichman, fires John W. Dean III as counsel **(April 30).** Greek military junta abolishes monarchy and proclaims republic **(June 1).** U.S. bombing of Cambodia ends, marking official halt to 12 years of combat activity in Southeast Asia **(Aug. 15).** Chile's Marxist president, Salvadore Allende, is overthrown **(Sept. 11).** Fourth and biggest Arab-Israeli conflict begins as Egyptian and Syrian forces attack Israel as Jews mark Yom Kippur, holiest day in their calendar **(Oct. 6).** Spiro T. Agnew resigns as vice president and then, in federal court in Baltimore, pleads no contest to charges of evasion of income taxes on $29,500 he received in 1967, while governor of Maryland. He is fined $10,000 and put on three years' probation **(Oct. 10).** In the "Saturday Night Massacre," Nixon fires special Watergate prosecutor Archibald Cox and Deputy Attorney General William D. Ruckelshaus; Attorney General Elliot L. Richardson resigns **(Oct. 20).** Egypt and Israel sign U.S.-sponsored cease-fire accord **(Nov. 11).** Duke Ellington's autobiography, *Music Is My Mistress,* is published.

1974 Patricia Hearst, 19-year-old daughter of publisher Randolph Hearst, kidnapped by Symbionese Liberation Army **(Feb. 5).** House Judiciary Committee adopts three articles of impeachment charging President Nixon with obstruction of justice, failure to uphold laws, and refusal to produce material subpoenaed by the committee **(July 30).** Richard M. Nixon announces he will resign the next day, the first president to do so **(Aug. 8).** Vice President Gerald R. Ford of Michigan is sworn in as 38th president of the U.S. **(Aug. 9).** Ford grants "full, free, and absolute pardon" to ex-president Nixon **(Sept. 8).**

1975 John N. Mitchell, H. R. Haldeman, John D. Ehrlichman found guilty of Watergate cover-up **(Jan. 1);** sentenced to 30 months to 8 years in jail **(Feb. 21).** Pol Pot and Khmer Rouge take over Cambodia **(April).** American merchant ship *Mayaguez,* seized by Cambodian forces, is rescued in operation by U.S. Navy and Marines, 38 of whom are killed **(May 15).** *Apollo* and *Soyuz* spacecraft take off for U.S.-Soviet link-up in space **(July 15).** President Ford escapes assassination attempt in Sacramento, Calif. **(Sept. 5).** President Ford escapes second assassination attempt in 17 days **(Sept. 22).**

1976 Supreme Court rules that blacks and other minorities are entitled to retroactive job seniority **(March 24).** Ford signs Federal Election Campaign Act **(May 11).** Supreme Court rules that death penalty is not inherently cruel or unusual and is a constitutionally acceptable form of punishment **(July 3).** Nation celebrates bicentennial **(July 4).** Israeli airborne commandos attack Uganda's Entebbe Airport and free 103 hostages held by pro-Palestinian hijackers of Air France plane; one Israeli and several Ugandan soldiers killed in raid **(July 4).** Mysterious disease that eventually claims 29 lives strikes American Legion convention in Philadelphia **(Aug. 4).** Jimmy Carter elected U.S. president **(Nov. 2).**

1977 First woman Episcopal priest ordained **(Jan. 1).** Scientists identify previously unknown bacterium as cause of mysterious "legionnaire's disease" **(Jan. 18).** Carter pardons Vietnam draft evaders **(Jan. 21).** Scientists report using bacteria in lab to make insulin **(May 23).** Supreme Court rules that states are not required to spend Medicaid funds on elective abortions **(June 20).** Deng Xiaoping, purged Chinese leader, restored to power as "Gang of Four" is expelled from Communist Party **(July 22).** South African activist Stephen Biko dies in police custody

(Sept. 12). Nuclear-proliferation pact, curbing spread of nuclear weapons, signed by 15 countries, including U.S. and USSR **(Sept. 21).**

1978 President chooses Federal Appeals Court Judge William H. Webster as F.B.I. Director **(Jan. 19).** Rhodesia's prime minister Ian D. Smith and three black leaders agree on transfer to black majority rule **(Feb. 15).** U.S. Senate approves Panama Canal neutrality treaty **(March 16);** votes treaty to turn canal over to Panama by year 2000 **(April 18).** Former Italian premier Aldo Moro kidnapped by left wing terrorists, who kill five bodyguards **(March 16);** he is found slain **(May 9).** Californians in referendum approve Proposition 13 for nearly 60% slash in property tax revenues **(June 6).** Supreme Court, in Bakke case, bars quota systems in college admissions but affirms constitutionality of programs giving advantage to minorities **(June 28).** Pope Paul VI, dead at 80, mourned **(Aug. 6);** new Pope, John Paul I, 65, dies unexpectedly after 34 days in office **(Sept. 28);** succeeded by Karol Cardinal Wojtyla of Poland as John Paul II **(Oct. 16).** "Framework for Peace" in Middle East signed by Egypt's president Anwar Sadat and Israeli premier Menachem Begin after 13-day conference at Camp David led by President Carter **(Sept. 17).** Jim Jones's followers commit mass suicide in Jonestown, Guyana **(Nov. 18).**

1979 Oil spills pollute ocean waters in Atlantic and Gulf of Mexico **(Jan. 1, June 8, July 21).** Ohio agrees to pay $675,000 to families of dead and injured in Kent State University shootings **(Jan. 4).** Vietnam and Vietnam-backed Cambodian insurgents announce fall of Phnom Penh, Cambodian capital, and collapse of Pol Pot regime **(Jan. 7).** Shah leaves Iran after year of turmoil **(Jan. 16);** revolutionary forces under Muslim leader, Ayatollah Ruhollah Khomeini, take over (**Feb. 1** *et seq.*). Nuclear power plant accident at Three Mile Island, Pa., releases radiation **(March 28).** Conservatives win British election; Margaret Thatcher new prime minister **(May 3).** Carter and Brezhnev sign SALT II agreement **(June 14).** Nicaraguan president Gen. Anastasio Somoza Debayle resigns and flees to Miami **(July 17);** Sandinistas form government **(July 19).** Earl Mountbatten of Burma, 79, British World War II hero, and three others killed by blast on fishing boat off Irish coast **(Aug. 27);** two I.R.A. members accused **(Aug. 30).** Iranian militants seize U.S. embassy in Teheran and hold hostages **(Nov. 4).** Soviet invasion of Afghanistan stirs world protests **(Dec. 27).**

1980 Six U.S. embassy aides escape from Iran with Canadian help **(Jan. 29).** F.B.I.'s undercover operation "Abscam" (for Arab scam) implicates public officials **(Feb. 2).** U.S. breaks diplomatic ties with Iran **(April 7).** Eight U.S. servicemen are killed and five are injured as helicopter and cargo plane collide in abortive desert raid to rescue American hostages in Teheran **(April 25).** Supreme Court upholds limits on federal aid for abortions **(June 30).** Shah of Iran dies at 60 **(July 27).** Anastasio Somoza Debayle, ousted Nicaragua ruler, and two aides assassinated in Asunción, Paraguay capital **(Sept. 17).** Iraq troops hold 90 square miles of Iran after invasion; 8-year Iran-Iraq war begins **(Sept. 19).** Ronald Reagan elected president in Republican sweep **(Nov. 4).** Three U.S. nuns and lay worker found shot in El Salvador **(Dec. 4).** John Lennon of the Beatles shot dead in New York City **(Dec. 8).** Smallpox eradicated.

1981 Ronald Reagan takes oath as 40th president **(Jan. 20).** U.S.-Iran agreement frees 52 hostages held in Teheran since 1979 **(Jan. 20);** hostages welcomed back in U.S. **(Jan. 25).** President Reagan wounded by gunman, with press secretary and two law-enforcement officers **(March 30).** Pope John Paul II wounded by gunman **(May 14).** Supreme Court rules, 4–4, that former president Nixon and three top aides may be required to pay monetary damages for unconstitutional wiretap of home telephone of former national security aide **(June 22).** Reagan nominates Judge Sandra Day O'Connor, 51, of Arizona, as first woman on Supreme Court **(July 7).** More than 110 die in collapse of aerial walkways in lobby of Hyatt Regency Hotel in Kansas City; 188 injured **(July 18).** Air controllers strike, disrupting flights **(Aug. 3);** government dismisses strikers **(Aug. 11).** AIDS is first identified.

1982 British overcome Argentina in Falklands war **(April 2–June 15).** Israel invades Lebanon in attack on P.L.O. **(June 4).** John W. Hinckley, Jr., found not guilty because of insanity in shooting of President Reagan **(June 21).** Alexander M. Haig, Jr., resigns as secretary of state **(June 25).** Equal Rights Amendment fails ratification **(June 30).** Princess

Pope John Paul II (1920–)

Anwar Sadat (1918–1981)

Ayatollah Ruhollah Khomeini (1900–1989)

Ronald Reagan (1911–)

Sandra Day O'Connor (1930–)

Indira Gandhi
(1917–1984)

Corazon Aquino
(1933–)

Mikhail S. Gorbachev
(1931–)

Margaret Thatcher
(1925–)

Sally K. Ride
(1951–)

Grace, 52, dies of injuries when car plunges off mountain road; daughter Stephanie, 17, suffers serious injuries **(Sept. 14).** Lebanese Christian Phalangists kill hundreds of people in two Palestinian refugee camps in West Beirut **(Sept. 15).** Leonid Brezhnev, Soviet leader, dies at 75 **(Nov. 10).** Yuri V. Andropov, 68, chosen as successor **(Nov. 15).** Permanent artificial heart implanted in human for first time in Dr. Barney B. Clark, 61, at University of Utah Medical Center in Salt Lake City **(Dec. 2).**

1983 Pope John Paul II signs new Roman Catholic code incorporating changes brought about by Second Vatican Council **(Jan. 25).** Second space shuttle, *Challenger,* makes successful maiden voyage, which includes the first U.S. space walk in nine years **(April 4).** U.S. Supreme Court declares many local abortion restrictions unconstitutional **(June 15).** Sally K. Ride, 32, first U.S. woman astronaut in space as a crew member aboard space shuttle *Challenger* **(June 18).** U.S. admits shielding former Nazi Gestapo chief Klaus Barbie, 69, the "butcher of Lyon," wanted in France for war crimes **(Aug. 15).** Benigno S. Aquino, Jr., 50, political rival of Philippines president Marcos, slain in Manila **(Aug. 21).** South Korean Boeing 747 jetliner bound for Seoul apparently strays into Soviet airspace and is shot down by a Soviet SU-15 fighter after it had tracked the airliner for two hours; all 269 aboard are killed, including 61 Americans **(Aug. 30).** Terrorist explosion kills 237 U.S. Marines in Beirut **(Oct. 23).** U.S. and Caribbean allies invade Grenada **(Oct. 25).**

1984 Bell System broken up **(Jan. 1).** France gets first deliveries of Soviet natural gas **(Jan. 1).** Syria frees captured U.S. Navy pilot, Lieut. Robert C. Goodman, Jr. **(Jan. 3).** U.S. and Vatican exchange diplomats after 116-year hiatus **(Jan. 10).** Reagan orders U.S. Marines withdrawn from Beirut international peacekeeping force **(Feb. 7).** Yuri V. Andropov dies at 69; Konstantin U. Chernenko, 72, named Soviet Union leader **(Feb. 9).** Italy and Vatican agree to end Roman Catholicism as state religion **(Feb. 18).** Reagan ends U.S. role in Beirut by relieving Sixth Fleet from peacekeeping force **(March 30).** Congress rebukes President Reagan on use of federal funds for mining Nicaraguan harbors **(April 10).** Soviet Union withdraws from summer Olympic games in U.S., and other bloc nations follow **(May 7** *et seq.*). José Napoleón Duarte, moderate, elected president of El Salvador **(May 11).** Three hundred slain as Indian Army occupies Sikh Golden Temple in Amritsar **(June 6).** Thirty-ninth Democratic National Convention, in San Francisco, nominates Walter F. Mondale and Geraldine A. Ferraro **(July 16–19).** Thirty-third Republican National Convention, at Dallas, renominates President Reagan and Vice President Bush **(Aug. 20–25).** Brian Mulroney and Conservative party win Canadian election in landslide **(Sept. 4).** Indian prime minister Indira Gandhi assassinated by two Sikh bodyguards; 1,000 killed in anti-Sikh riots; son Rajiv succeeds her **(Oct. 31).** President Reagan re-elected in landslide with 59% of vote **(Nov. 6).** Toxic gas leaks from Union Carbide plant in Bhopal, India, killing 2,000 and injuring 150,000 **(Dec. 3).**

1985 Ronald Reagan, 73, takes oath for second term as 40th president **(Jan. 20).** General Westmoreland settles libel action against CBS **(Feb. 18).** Prime Minister Margaret Thatcher addresses Congress, endorsing Reagan's policies **(Feb. 20).** USSR leader Chernenko dies at 73 and is replaced by Mikhail Gorbachev, 54 **(March 11).** Two Shi'ite Muslim gunmen capture TWA airliner with 133 aboard, 104 of them Americans **(June 14);** 39 remaining hostages freed in Beirut **(June 30).** Supreme Court, 5–4, bars public school teachers from parochial schools **(July 1).** Arthur James Walker, 50, retired naval officer, convicted by federal judge of participating in Soviet spy ring operated by his brother, John Walker **(Aug. 9).** P.L.O. terrorists hijack *Achille Lauro,* Italian cruise ship, with 80 passengers, plus crew **(Oct. 7);** American, Leon Klinghoffer, killed **(Oct. 8);** Italian government toppled by political crisis over hijacking **(Oct. 16).** John A. Walker and son, Michael I. Walker, 22, sentenced in Navy espionage case **(Oct. 28).** Reagan and Gorbachev meet at summit **(Nov. 19);** agree to step up arms control talks and renew cultural contacts **(Nov. 21).** Terrorists seize Egyptian Boeing 737 airliner after take-off from Athens **(Nov. 23);** 59 dead as Egyptian forces storm plane on Malta **(Nov. 24).** U.S. budget-balancing bill enacted **(Dec. 12).**

1986 Spain and Portugal join European Economic Community **(Jan. 1).** President freezes Libyan assets in U.S. **(Jan. 8).** Supreme Court bars racial bias in trial jury selection **(Jan. 14).** *Voyager 2* spacecraft reports secrets of Uranus **(Jan. 26).** Space shuttle *Challenger* explodes after launch at Cape Canaveral, Fla., killing all seven aboard **(Jan. 28).** Haiti president

Jean-Claude Duvalier flees to France **(Feb. 7).** President Marcos flees Philippines after ruling 20 years, as newly elected Corazon Aquino succeeds him **(Feb. 26).** Prime Minister Olof Palme of Sweden shot dead **(Feb. 28).** Austrian president Kurt Waldheim's service as Nazi army officer revealed **(March 3).** Union Carbide agrees to settlement with victims of Bhopal gas leak in India **(March 22).** Halley's comet yields information on return visit **(April 10).** U.S. planes attack Libyan "terrorist centers" **(April 14).** Desmond Tutu elected archbishop in South Africa **(April 14).** Major nuclear accident at Soviet Union's Chernobyl power station alarms world **(April 26** *et seq.*). Ex-Navy analyst, Jonathan Jay Pollard, 31, guilty as spy for Israel **(June 4).** Supreme Court reaffirms abortion rights **(June 11).** World Court rules U.S. broke international law in mining Nicaraguan waters **(June 27).** Supreme Court voids automatic provisions of budget-balancing law **(July 7).** Jerry A. Whitworth, ex-Navy radioman, convicted as spy **(July 24);** he is also part of Walker family spy ring. Muslim captors release Rev. Lawrence Martin Jenco **(July 26).** Senate Judiciary Committee approves William H. Rehnquist as chief justice of U.S. **(Aug. 14).** House votes arms appropriations bill rejecting administration's "star wars" policy **(Aug. 15).** Three Lutheran church groups in U.S. set to merge **(Aug. 29).** Congress overrides Reagan veto of stiff sanctions against South Africa **(Sept. 29** and **Oct. 2).** Congress approves immigration bill barring hiring of illegal aliens, with amnesty provision **(Oct. 17).** Reagan signs $11.7-billion budget reduction measure **(Oct. 21).** He approves sweeping revision of U.S. tax code **(Oct. 22).** Democrats triumph in elections, gaining eight seats to win Senate majority **(Nov. 4).** Secret initiative to send arms to Iran revealed **(Nov. 6** *et seq.*); Reagan denies exchanging arms for hostages and halts arms sales **(Nov. 19);** diversion of funds from arms sales to Nicaraguan Contras revealed **(Nov. 25).**

1987 William Buckley, U.S. hostage in Lebanon, reported slain **(Jan. 20).** Supreme Court rules Rotary Clubs must admit women **(May 4).** Iraqi missiles kill 37 in attack on U.S. frigate *Stark* in Persian Gulf **(May 17);** Iraqi president apologizes **(May 18).** Prime Minister Thatcher wins rare third term in Britain **(June 11).** Supreme Court justice Lewis F. Powell, Jr., retires **(June 26).** Klaus Barbie, 73, Gestapo wartime chief in Lyon, sentenced to life by French court for war crimes **(July 4).** Oliver North, Jr., tells congressional inquiry higher officials approved his secret Iran-Contra operations **(July 7–10).** Admiral John M. Poindexter, former National Security Adviser, testifies he authorized use of Iran arms sale profits to aid Contras **(July 15–22).** Secretary of State George P. Shultz testifies he was deceived repeatedly on Iran-Contra affair **(July 23–24).** Defense Secretary Caspar W. Weinberger tells inquiry of official deception and intrigue **(July 31, Aug. 3).** Reagan says Iran arms-Contra policy went astray and accepts responsibility **(Aug. 12).** Severe earthquake strikes Los Angeles, leaving 100 injured and six dead **(Oct. 1).** Senate, 58–42, rejects Robert H. Bork as Supreme Court justice **(Oct. 23).**

1988 U.S. and Canada reach free trade agreement **(Jan. 2).** Robert C. McFarlane, former National Security Adviser, pleads guilty in Iran-Contra case **(March 11).** U.S. Navy ship shoots down Iranian airliner in Persian Gulf, mistaking it for jet fighter; 290 killed **(July 3).** Terrorists kill nine tourists on Aegean cruise **(July 11).** Democratic convention nominates Gov. Michael Dukakis of Massachusetts for president and Texas senator Lloyd Bentsen for vice president **(July 17** *et seq.*). Republicans nominate George Bush for president and Indiana senator Dan Quayle for vice president **(Aug. 15** *et seq.*). Plane blast kills Pakistani president Mohammad Zia ul-Haq **(Aug. 17).** Republicans sweep 40 states in election. Bush beats Dukakis **(Nov. 8).** Benazir Bhutto, first Islamic woman prime minister, chosen to lead Pakistan **(Dec. 1).** Pan-Am 747 explodes from terrorist bomb and crashes in Lockerbie, Scotland, killing all 259 aboard and 11 on ground **(Dec. 21).**

1989 U.S. planes shoot down two Libyan fighters over international waters in Mediterranean **(Jan. 4).** Emperor Hirohito of Japan dead at 87 **(Jan. 7).** George Herbert Walker Bush inaugurated as 41st U.S. president **(Jan. 20).** Iran's Ayatollah Khomeini declares author Salman Rushdie's book *The Satanic Verses* offensive and sentences him to death **(Feb. 14).** Ruptured tanker *Exxon Valdez* sends 11 million gallons of crude oil into Alaska's Prince William Sound **(March 24).** Tens of thousands of Chinese students take over Beijing's Tiananmen Square in rally for democracy **(April 19** *et seq.*). U.S. jury convicts Oliver North in Iran-Contra

William Rehnquist (1924–)

George Bush (1924–)

Benazir Bhutto (1953–)

François Mitterrand
(1916–1996)

General Colin Powell
(1937–)

Saddam Hussein
(1937–)

affair (**May 4**). More than one million in Beijing demonstrate for democracy; chaos spreads across nation (**mid-May** *et seq.*). Mikhail S. Gorbachev named Soviet president (**May 25**). Thousands killed in Tiananmen Square as Chinese leaders take hard line toward demonstrators (**June 4** *et seq.*). Army general Colin R. Powell is first black chairman of Joint Chiefs of Staff (**Aug. 9**). P. W. Botha quits as South Africa's president (**Aug. 14**). *Voyager 2* spacecraft speeds by Neptune after making startling discoveries about the planet and its moons (**Aug. 29**). Deng Xiaoping resigns from China's leadership (**Nov. 9**). After 28 years, Berlin Wall is open to West (**Nov. 11**). Czech Parliament ends Communists' dominant role (**Nov. 30**). Romanian uprising overthrows Communist government (**Dec. 15** *et seq.*); President Ceausescu and wife executed (**Dec. 25**). U.S. troops invade Panama, seeking capture of Gen. Manuel Noriega (**Dec. 20**); resistance to U.S. collapses (**Dec. 24**). Dalai Lama wins Nobel Peace Prize.

1990 World Wide Web debuts, popularizes Internet. Gen. Manuel Noriega surrenders in Panama (**Jan. 3**). Yugoslav Communists end 45-year monopoly of power (**Jan. 22**). Soviet Communists relinquish sole power (**Feb. 7**). South Africa frees Nelson Mandela, imprisoned 27½ years (**Feb. 11**). Violeta Barrios de Chamorro inaugurated as Nicaraguan president. Hubble Space Telescope launched (**April 25**). U.S.-Soviet summit reaches accord on armaments (**June 1**). Western Alliance ends cold war and proposes joint action with Soviet Union and Eastern Europe (**July 6**). U.S. Appeals Court overturns Oliver North's Iran-Contra conviction (**July 20**). Iraqi troops invade Kuwait and seize petroleum reserves, setting off Persian Gulf War (**Aug. 2** *et seq.*). East and West Germany reunited (**Oct. 3**). Republicans set back in midterm elections (**Nov. 8**). Gorbachev assumes emergency powers (**Nov. 17**). Leaders of 34 nations in Europe and North America proclaim a united Europe (**Nov. 21**). Margaret Thatcher resigns as British prime minister (**Nov. 22**); John Major succeeds her (**Nov. 28**). Lech Walesa wins Poland's runoff presidential election (**Dec. 9**). Haiti elects leftist priest as president in first democratic election (**Dec. 17**).

1991 U.S. and Allies at war with Iraq (**Jan. 15**). Warsaw Pact dissolves military alliance (**Feb. 25**). Cease-fire ends Persian Gulf War; UN forces are victorious (**April 3**). Europeans end sanctions on South Africa (**April 15**). Supreme Court limits death row appeals (**April 16**). Winnie Mandela sentenced in kidnapping (**May 13**). William H. Webster retires as director of CIA; Robert H. Gates succeeds him (**May 14**). France agrees to sign 1968 treaty banning spread of atomic weapons (**June 3**). Communist government of Albania resigns (**June 4**). Jiang Qing, widow of Mao, commits suicide (**June 4**). South African Parliament repeals apartheid laws (**June 5**). Warsaw Pact dissolved (**July 1**). Boris N. Yeltsin inaugurated as first freely elected president of Russian Republic (**July 10**). Bush-Gorbachev summit negotiates strategic arms reduction treaty (**July 31**). China accepts nuclear nonproliferation treaty (**Aug. 10**). Lithuania, Estonia, and Latvia win independence (**Aug. 25**); Bush recognizes them (**Sept. 2**). Haitian

THE PERSIAN GULF WAR (Jan. 16, 1991–April 6, 1991)

1990 Iraq invades its tiny neighbor, Kuwait, after talks break down over oil production and debt repayment. Iraqi president Saddam Hussein later annexes Kuwait and declares it a 19th province of Iraq (**Aug. 2**). President Bush believes that Iraq intends to invade Saudi Arabia and take control of the region's oil supplies. He begins organizing a multinational coalition to seek Kuwait's freedom and restoration of its legitimate government. The UN Security Council authorizes economic sanctions against Iraq. Bush orders U.S. troops to protect Saudi Arabia at the Saudis' request and "Operation Desert Shield" begins (**Aug. 6**). 230,000 American troops arrive in Saudi Arabia to take defensive action, but when Iraq continues a huge military buildup in Kuwait, the President orders an additional 200,000 troops deployed to prepare for a possible offensive action by the U.S.-led coalition forces. He subsequently obtains a UN Security Council resolution setting a **Jan. 15, 1991** deadline for Iraq to withdraw unconditionally from Kuwait (**Nov. 8**).

1991 Bush wins congressional approval for his position with the most devastating air assault in history against military targets in Iraq and Kuwait (**Jan. 16**). He rejects a Soviet-Iraq peace plan for a gradual withdrawal that does not comply with all the UN resolutions and gives Iraq an ultimatum to withdraw from Kuwait by noon **Feb. 23** (**Feb. 22**). The president orders the ground war to begin (**Feb. 24**). In a brilliant and lightning-fast campaign, U.S. and coalition forces smash through Iraq's defenses and defeat Saddam Hussein's troops in only four days of combat. Allies enter Kuwait City (**Feb. 26**). Iraqi army sets fire to over 500 of Kuwait's oil wells as final act of destruction to Kuwait's infrastructure. Bush orders a unilateral cease-fire 100 hours after the ground offensive started (**Feb. 27**). Allied and Iraqi military leaders meet on battlefield to discuss terms for a formal cease-fire to end the Gulf War. Iraq agrees to abide by all of the UN resolutions (**Mar. 3**). The first Allied prisoners of war are released (**Mar. 4**). Official cease-fire accepted and signed (**April 6**). 532,000 U.S. forces served in Operation Desert Storm. There were a total of 147 U.S. battle deaths during the Gulf War, 145 nonbattle deaths, and 467 wounded in action.

troops seize president in uprising (**Sept. 30**). U.S. suspends assistance to Haiti (**Oct. 1**). Professor Anita Hill accuses Judge Clarence Thomas of sexual harassment (**Oct. 6**); Senate, 52–48, confirms Thomas for Supreme Court after stormy hearings (**Oct. 15**). Israel and Soviet Union resume relations after 24 years (**Oct. 18**). U.S. indicts two Libyans in 1988 bombing of Pan Am Flight 103 over Lockerbie, Scotland (**Nov. 15**). Anglican envoy Terry Waite and U.S. Prof. Thomas M. Sutherland freed by Lebanese (**Nov. 18**). Last three U.S. hostages freed in Lebanon (**Dec. 2–4**). Soviet Union breaks up after President Gorbachev's resignation; constituent republics form Commonwealth of Independent States (**Dec. 25**).

1992 Yugoslav Federation broken up (**Jan. 15**). Bush and Yeltsin proclaim formal end to cold war (**Feb. 1**). U.S. lifts trade sanctions against China (**Feb. 21**). U.S. recognizes three former Yugoslav republics (**April 7**). Gen. Noriega, former Panama leader, convicted in U.S. court (**April 9**). Four police officers acquitted in Los Angeles beating of Rodney King; rioting erupts in South-Central Los Angeles (**April 29** *et seq.*). Caspar W. Weinberger indicted in Iran-Contra affair (**June 16**). Last Western hostages freed in Lebanon (**June 17**). Supreme Court reaffirms right to abortion (**June 29**). Democrats nominate Bill Clinton and Al Gore (**July 1**). Gen. Noriega sentenced to 40 years on drug charges (**July 10**). Court clears *Exxon Valdez* skipper (**July 10**). Israeli Parliament approves Yitzhak Rabin's coalition government, dominated by Labor Party (**July 13**). Police officers acquitted in April on criminal charges in Rodney King beating are indicted on federal civil rights charges (**Aug. 5**). North American trade compact announced (**Aug. 12**). Republicans renominate Bush and Quayle (**Aug. 20**). UN expels Serbian-dominated Yugoslavia (**Sept. 22**). Senate ratifies second Strategic Arms Limitation Treaty (**Oct. 1**). Top Japanese leader, Shin Kanemaru, resigns in scandal (**Oct. 14**). Bill Clinton elected president, Al Gore vice president; Democrats keep control of Congress (**Nov. 3**). Russian Parliament approves START treaty (**Nov. 4**). U.S. forces leave Philippines, ending nearly a century of American military presence (**Nov. 24**). Czechoslovak Parliament approves separation into two nations (**Nov. 25**). UN approves U.S.-led force to guard food for Somalia (**Dec. 3**). Prince and Princess of Wales agree to separate (**Dec. 9**). Bush pardons former Reagan administration officials involved in Iran-Contra affair (**Dec. 24**).

1993 Vaclav Havel elected as Czech president (**Jan. 26**). Clinton agrees to compromise on military's ban on homosexuals (**Jan. 29**). U.S. begins airlift of supplies to besieged Bosnia towns (**Feb. 28**). Federal agents besiege Texas Branch Davidian religious cult after six are killed in raid (**March 1** *et seq.*). Five arrested, sixth sought in bombing of World Trade Center in New York (**March 29**). Two police officers convicted on federal civil rights charges in Rodney King beating (**April 17**); sentenced (**Aug. 4**). Fire kills 72 as cult standoff in Texas ends with federal assault (**April 19**). President of Sri Lanka assassinated (**May 1**). British Commons approves European unity pact (**May 20**). Twenty-two UN troops killed in Somalia (**June 5**). Ruth Bader Ginsburg appointed to Supreme Court (**June 14**). Iraq accepts UN weapons monitoring (**July 19**). Vincent W. Foster, Jr., senior White House lawyer, commits suicide (**July 22**). Midwest flood damage expected to exceed $10 billion (**July 24**). Israeli-Palestinian accord reached (**Aug. 28**). U.S. agents blamed in Waco, Tex., siege (**Oct. 1**). Yeltsin's forces crush revolt in Russian Parliament (**Oct. 4** *et seq.*). China breaks nuclear test moratorium (**Oct. 5**). Canada's opposition Liberal Party regains power in landslide (**Oct. 25**). Europe's Maastricht Treaty takes effect, creating European Union (**Nov. 1**). Jean Chretien sworn in as Canada's 20th prime minister (**Nov. 4**). House of Representatives approves North American Free Trade Agreement (**Nov. 17**); Senate follows (**Nov. 21**). South Africa adopts majority rule constitution (**Nov. 18**). Clinton signs Brady bill regulating firearms purchases (**Nov. 30**). Toni Morrison wins Nobel prize for literature.

1994 Serbs' heavy weapons pound Sarajevo (**Jan. 5–6**). Olympic figure skater Nancy Kerrigan attacked (**Jan. 6**); three arrested in attack (**Jan. 13**). Major earthquake jolts Los Angeles; 51 dead (**Jan. 17** *et seq.*). Clinton ends trade embargo on Vietnam (**Feb. 9**). Aldrich Ames, high C.I.A. official, charged with spying for Soviets (**Feb. 22**). Four convicted in World Trade Center bombing (**March 4**). Mexican presidential candidate assassinated (**March 23**). Rwandan genocide of Tutsis by Hutus begins; estimated 800,000 slaughtered in c. 100 days (**April 6**). South Africa holds first interracial national election (**April 29**);

Hubble Space Telescope

Lech Walesa
(1943–)

Toni Morrison
(1931–)

Ruth Bader Ginsburg
(1933–)

Boris Yeltsin
(1931–)

Nelson Mandela
(1918–)

Jean-Bertrand Aristide
(1953–)

Dalai Lama
(1935–)

Yitzhak Rabin
(1922–1995)

Seamus Heaney
(1939–)

Nelson Mandela elected president. Israel and Palestinians sign accord **(May 4).** Clinton accused of sexual harassment while governor of Arkansas **(May 6).** Congress votes protection for women's health clinics **(May 12).** O. J. Simpson arrested in killings of wife, Nicole Brown Simpson, and friend, Ronald Goldman **(June 18).** Supreme Court approves limit on abortion protests **(June 30).** Senate confirms Stephen G. Breyer for Supreme Court **(July 29).** Women's health clinic doctor shot dead outside Florida clinic **(July 29).** Major league baseball players strike **(Aug. 13).** "Carlos the Jackal," international terrorist, captured **(Aug. 15).** IRA declares cease-fire in Northern Ireland **(Aug. 31).** Small plane crashes into White House **(Sept. 12).** Baseball owners end season and cancel World Series **(Sept. 14).** Powerful earthquake strikes Japan **(Oct. 4).** Aristide returns to joyous Haiti **(Oct. 4).** U.S. sends forces to Persian Gulf **(Oct. 7).** Ulster Protestants declare cease-fire **(Oct. 13).** Israel and Jordan sign peace treaty **(Oct. 17).** Reagan, 83, reveals he has Alzheimer's disease **(Nov. 6).** G.O.P. wins control of House and Senate **(Nov. 8).** Aristide forms Haitian government with prime minister and full cabinet **(Nov. 9).** Clinton orders Bosnian arms embargo ended **(Nov. 10).** Newt Gingrich named House Speaker **(Dec. 5).** Bentsen resigns as Treasury Secretary **(Dec. 6).** Russians attack secessionist Republic of Chechnya **(Dec. 11** *et seq.*). John Salvi kills two at Massachusetts Planned Parenthood clinic **(Dec. 30).**

1995 Republicans take control of Congress **(Jan. 4).** More than 5,000 dead in Japanese earthquake (**Jan. 17** *et seq.*). Criminal trial of O. J. Simpson opens in California **(Jan. 24).** U.S. rescues Mexico's economy with $20-billion aid program **(Feb. 21).** Senate rejects balanced-budget amendment **(March 2).** Nerve gas attack in Tokyo subway kills eight and injures thousands. The Aum Shinrikyo ("Supreme Truth") cult is to blame **(March 20).** Major League Baseball strike ends **(April 2).** Appeals court upholds woman's plea to enter Citadel military academy **(April 13).** UN Council votes easier sanctions for Iraq **(April 14).** Scores killed as terrorist's car bomb blows up block-long Oklahoma City federal building **(April 19);** Timothy McVeigh, 27, Army veteran, arrested as suspect **(April 21);** authorities seek second suspect, link right-wing paramilitary groups to bombing **(April 22).** Death toll 2,000 in Rwanda massacre **(April 22).** Fighting escalates in Bosnia and Croatia **(May 1).** U.S. shuttle docks with Russian space station **(June 27).** F.B.I. suspends four in Idaho siege inquiry **(Aug. 11).** France explodes nuclear device in Pacific; wide protests ensue **(Sept. 5).** Senator Bob Packwood of Oregon resigns under pressure for sexual and official misconduct **(Sept. 6).** Israelis and Palestinians agree on transferring West Bank to Arabs **(Sept. 24).** Los Angeles jury finds O. J. Simpson not guilty of murder charges **(Oct. 3).** Pope John Paul II visits U.S. on whirlwind tour **(Oct. 4–8).** Warring parties agree on cease-fire in Bosnia **(Oct. 5).** Million Man March draws hundreds of thousands of black men to capital **(Oct. 16).** Quebec narrowly rejects independence from Canada **(Oct. 30).** Israeli prime minister Yitzhak Rabin slain by Jewish extremist at peace rally **(Nov. 4).** U.S. servicemen admit rape of Japanese schoolgirl in Okinawa **(Nov. 7).** Nigeria hangs writer Ken Saro-Wiwa and eight other minority rights advocates **(Nov. 10).** Irish voters approve end to constitutional ban on divorce **(Nov. 24).** Combatants sign Bosnia peace treaty **(Dec. 14).** House move stalls Congress–White House negotiations to avert government shutdown **(Dec. 20).** Seamus Heaney wins Nobel prize for literature.

1996 U.S. budget crisis in fourth month **(Jan 3).** Clinton approves resumption of many government operations **(Jan. 6).** Senate ratifies major arms reduction treaty **(Jan. 26).** France announces end to nuclear tests **(Jan. 29).** At least 73 dead in Sri Lankan suicide bombing **(Feb. 1).** Suicide bombers kill 59 in Israel **(March 4).** Bob Dole sweeps Republican primaries **(March 5).** Britain alarmed by deadly cow disease (**March 20** *et seq.*). UN tribunal charges war crimes by Bosnian Muslims and Croats **(March 22).** Commerce Secretary Ronald H. Brown killed in plane crash **(April 3).** FBI arrests suspected Unabomber **(April 3).** Clinton signs line-item veto bill **(April 9).** President blocks ban on late-term abortions **(April 10).** ValuJet crashes in Everglades; all 110 aboard killed **(May 11).** Chechnya peace treaty signed **(May 27).** Israel elects Benjamin Netanyahu as prime minister **(May 31).** China agrees to world ban on atomic testing (**June 6**). Leaders in Balkans sign accord on arms limits (**June 14**). Jazz great Ella Fitzgerald dies (**June 15**). Truck bomb kills 19 at U.S. base in Saudi Arabia (**June 25**). Boris Yeltsin is reelected in Russian election (**July 3**). Prince Charles and Princess Diana agree on divorce (**July 12**). 747 airliner crashes in Atlantic off Long Island; all 230 aboard perish (**July 17**). Bomb mars Summer Olympic games in Atlanta (**July 25**). Clinton signs bill to raise minimum wage (**Aug. 2**). Congress passes welfare reform bill (**Aug. 2**); approved by Clinton (**Aug. 22**). Republican convention opens in San Diego (**Aug. 12**); Bob Dole and Jack Kemp nominated (**Aug. 14**). Democrats convene in Chicago (**Aug. 26**). Iraqis strike at Kurdish enclave (**Aug. 31**); after warning, U.S. attacks Iraq's southern air defenses (**Sept. 2–3**); Iraq halts attacks on U.S. planes enforcing flight exclusion zones in north and south (**Sept. 13**). Violence flares in Jerusalem over Israel opening tourist tunnel (**Sept. 24**). Taliban Muslim fundamentalists capture Afghan capital (**Sept. 27**). Ethnic violence breaks out in Zairian refugee camps (**Oct. 13**); thousands of refugees from Rwanda and Burundi abandon camps (**Oct. 21**). Clinton-Gore ticket wins national election; Republicans retain control of Congress (**Nov. 5**). Mid-air collision in India kills 342 (**Nov. 12**). Texaco settles racial bias suit (**Nov. 15**). Hundreds of thousands of Hutu refugees return to Rwanda (**Nov. 15–18**). Clinton appoints Madeleine Albright as first female U.S. secretary of state (**Dec. 5**). Kofi Annan named UN secretary-general (**Dec. 13**). FBI agent charged with spying for Moscow (**Dec. 18**). Thousands march in Belgrade in continuing protest against president's annulment of election results (**Dec. 26**).

1997 Two Hutu sentenced to death in Rwandan genocide (**Jan. 3**). Floods cause wide damage in U.S. West (**Jan. 5**). Newt Gingrich reelected as House Speaker (**Jan. 7**). Hebron agreement signed; Israel gives up large part of West Bank city of Hebron (**Jan. 16**). U.S. shuttle joins Russian space station (**Jan. 17**). Gingrich found guilty of ethics violations (**Jan. 17**). President Clinton starts second term (**Jan. 20**). U.S., U.K., and France agree to freeze Nazis' gold loot (**Feb. 3**). O. J. Simpson found liable in civil suit (**Feb. 5**). Deng Xiaoping, Chinese leader, dead at 92 (**Feb. 19**). Israeli government approves establishment of Jewish settlement in East Jerusalem, a setback in Middle East peace process (**Feb. 26**). Tornadoes wreak havoc in Arkansas, Ohio, and Kentucky (**March 3**). State of anarchy in Albania when third of population loses savings because of pyramid schemes (**March 13**). Hale-Bopp comet is the closest it will be to Earth until 4397 (**March 22**). Heaven's Gate cult members commit mass suicide in California (**March 27**). U.S. Appeals Court upholds California ban on affirmative action (**April 8**). U.S. judge upholds California marijuana law (**April 11**). Tiger Woods breaks multiple records in Masters golf tournament (**April 13**). Fire kills 300 pilgrims outside Mecca (**April 15**). Senate, 74–26, approves chemical-weapons treaty (**April 24**). Thousands flee North Dakota flood (**April 27**). Sergeant Major of the Army, Gene C. McKinney, charged in sex cases (**May 7**). Russian president Yeltsin signs Chechnya peace treaty (**May 12**). U.S.-Russian spaceship linkup in orbit ends (**May 21**). U.S. jobless rate for May reported 4.8%, lowest since 1973 (**June 6**). European Union bolsters currency merger (**June 16**). Congress votes major tax cuts (**June 26**). Hong Kong returns to Chinese rule (**June 30**). U.S. spacecraft begins exploration of Mars (**July 4**). Andrew Cunanan murders fashion designer Gianni Versace (**July 15**). Khmer Rouge hold trial of longtime leader Pol Pot (**July 25**). White House and GOP agree on measure to balance budget (**July 28**). U.S. spacecraft transmits thousands of pictures from Mars (**Aug. 8**). Clinton exercises new line-item veto (**Aug. 11**). Timothy J. McVeigh sentenced to death for Oklahoma City bombing (**Aug. 14**). Princess Diana, 36, killed with two others in Paris car crash (**Aug. 31**). Three Islamic suicide bombers kill four persons in Jerusalem (**Sept. 4**). Mother Teresa dead at 87 (**Sept. 5**). Swiss plan first payment to Holocaust victims (**Sept. 17**). Militant Taliban leaders seize Kabul (**Sept. 27**). Iraq expels all U.S. members of UN arms-inspection team (**Oct. 29**). GOP victorious in off-year elections (**Nov. 4**). Pakistani convicted in 1993 CIA killings (**Nov. 10**). Two convicted in New York World Trade Center bombing (**Nov. 12**). Egyptian Islamic militants kill 62 at Luxor tourist site (**Nov. 17**). FBI ends 16-month investigation of crash of Flight 800 off Long Island; denies sabotage (**Nov. 18**). European Union plans to admit six nations (**Dec. 13**). U.S. company launches first commercial spy satellite (**Dec. 24**). Paris court convicts "Carlos the Jackal" of murder (**Dec. 24**).

Ella Fitzgerald (1918–1996)

Madeleine Albright (1937–)

Kofi Annan (1938–)

Hale-Bopp Comet

Princess Diana (1961–1997)

Mother Teresa (1910–1997)

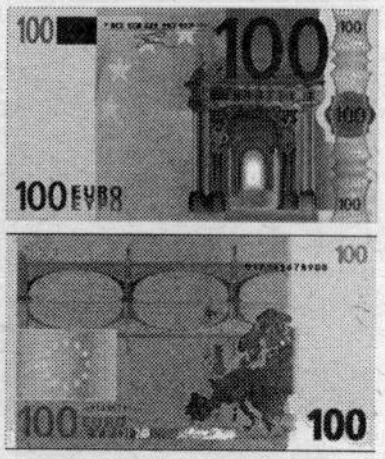

Euro 100

Mars Sojourner Rover

William J. Clinton (1946–)

Gerhard Schröder (1944–)

1998 Ramzi Ahmed Yousef sentenced to life for 1993 World Trade Center bombing **(Jan. 9)**. Pope John Paul II visits Cuba **(Jan. 21–25)**. President accused in White House sex scandal; denies allegations of affair with White House intern, Monica Lewinsky **(Jan. 21** *et seq.*). President outlines first balanced budget in 30 years **(Feb. 3)**. U.S. plane cuts ski cable in Italy and sends car plunging; 20 killed **(Feb. 3)**. Thousands dead in Afghanistan quake **(Feb. 4** *et seq.*). U.S. court rules line-item veto unconstitutional **(Feb. 12)**. Serbs battle ethnic Albanians in Kosovo **(March 5** *et seq.*). U.S. drops condemnation of China's human rights record **(March 13)**. Hindu nationalist Vajpayee becomes India's prime minister **(March 19)**. FDA approves Viagra, male impotence drug **(March 27)**. Federal judge in Arkansas throws out Paula Jones case **(April 1)**. Landmark peace settlement, the Good Friday Accord, reached in Northern Ireland **(April 10)**. U.S. trade deficit biggest in decade **(April 17)**. Europeans agree on single currency, the euro **(May 3)**. Unabomber, Theodore Kaczynski, sentenced to four life terms **(May 4)**. India conducts three atomic tests despite worldwide disapproval **(May 11, 13)**. Indonesian dictator Suharto steps down after 32 years in power **(May 21)**. Pakistan stages five nuclear tests in response to India's **(May 29, 30)**. Serbs renew attack on Kosovo rebels **(June 1)**. Life sentence meted out to Terry Nichols, convicted in Oklahoma City bombing fatal to 168 **(June 4)**. Nigerian dictator Sani Abacha dies **(June 8)**. Congress votes to overhaul IRS **(July 9)**. Iraq ends cooperation with UN arms inspectors **(Aug. 5)**. U.S. embassies in Kenya and Tanzania bombed **(Aug. 7)**. Clinton admits to affair with White House intern in televised address to nation **(Aug. 17)**. Russia fights to avert financial collapse **(Aug. 17)**. U.S. cruise missiles hit suspected terrorist bases in Sudan and Afghanistan **(Aug. 20)**. North Korea fires missile across Japan **(Aug. 31)**. Swissair jet crashes; kills 229 **(Sept. 2)**. Starr Report by independent counsel outlines case for impeachment proceedings against president **(Sept. 11)**. Senate sustains veto of bill to outlaw late-term abortions **(Sept. 18)**. Iran lifts death threat against Salman Rushdie **(Sept. 24)**. German chancellor Helmut Kohl defeated by Gerhard Schröder **(Sept. 27)**. U.S. budget surplus largest in three decades **(Oct. 5)**. Matthew Shepard, gay Wyoming student, fatally beaten in hate crime **(Oct. 6)**. NATO, on verge of air strikes, reaches settlement with Milosevic on Kosovo **(Oct. 12)**. Former Chilean dictator Pinochet arrested in London **(Oct. 16)**. Wye Mills Agreement between Netanyahu and Arafat moves Middle East peace talks forward **(Oct. 23)**. More than 10,000 die in Central American hurricane, Mitch **(Nov. 1)**. Democrats unexpectedly gain five House seats in national election; Republicans keep control of House and Senate **(Nov. 3)**. House Speaker Gingrich to step down **(Nov. 9)**. House panel drafts impeachment charges; votes along party lines to approve four articles **(Dec. 11–12)**. Clinton orders air strikes on Iraq **(Dec. 16–19)**. House impeaches President Clinton along party lines on two charges, perjury and obstruction of justice **(Dec. 19)**.

1999 U.S. agrees to ease restrictions on Cuba **(Jan. 4)**. Dennis Hastert elected to replace Newt Gingrich as Speaker of the House **(Jan. 6)**. NBA ends 191-day labor dispute **(Jan. 6)**. International Olympic Committee expels six members as bribery scandal widens **(Jan. 24)**. King Hussein of Jordan dies **(Feb. 7)**. Senate acquits President Clinton of impeachment charges **(Feb. 12)**. Gen. Olusegun Obasanjo elected president of Nigeria **(Feb. 28)**. First nonstop balloon flight around world completed in 20 days by Bertrand Piccard (Switzerland) and Brian Jones (UK) **(March 1–20)**. Marine pilot acquitted in killing of 20 in 1998 Italian ski gondola accident; Italians outraged **(March 4)**. U.S. accuses China of stealing nuclear secrets **(March 5)**. Joe DiMaggio dies at age 84 **(March 8)**. Czech Republic, Poland, and Hungary join NATO **(March 12)**. NATO launches air strikes on Serbia to end attacks against ethnic Albanians in Kosovo **(March 24)**. Dr. Jack Kevorkian convicted of second-degree murder in assisted-suicide case **(March 26)**. "Melissa" computer virus spreads through the Internet **(March 27)**. Libya hands over two suspects in 1988 Pan Am jet bombing **(April 5)**. Two Colo. students go on shooting spree in Columbine High School, killing 15, including themselves **(April 20)**. NATO bombs mistakenly hit Chinese embassy in Belgrade **(May 7)**. Citadel graduates its first woman **(May 8)**. Crime rate in U.S. falls for seventh consecutive year **(May 16)**. Ehud Barak defeats Benjamin Netanyahu in Israeli prime minister election **(May 17)**. U.S. inspects suspected nuclear weapons site in North Korea, finds nothing **(May 20–24)**. Serbs sign agreement to pull troops out of Kosovo after 11 weeks of NATO air attacks **(June 9)**. Nelson Mandela retires as president of South Africa; succeeded by Thabo Mbeki **(June 16)**. Britain's Prince Edward marries Sophie Rhys-Jones **(June 19)**. Kurd leader Abdullah Ocalan sentenced to death for treason in Turkey **(June 29)**. White supremacist goes on shooting spree in Midwest, killing three including self and wounding eight **(July 2–5)**. U.S. soccer team tops China for women's World Cup **(July 10)**. Taiwanese leader Lee Teng-hui challenges "One China" policy **(July 11)**. Serial killer Rafael Reséndez-Ramirez surrenders himself to U.S. authorities **(July 13)**. John F. Kennedy, Jr., wife Carolyn Bessette Kennedy, and sister-in-law Lauren Bessette killed in plane crash off coast of Martha's Vineyard **(July 16)**. Col. Eileen Collins becomes first female to head a space shuttle mission **(July 16)**. Falun Gong meditation sect banned by Chinese government **(July 22)**. Day-trader kills 9 and wounds 13 in two Atlanta brokerage offices before committing suicide **(July 29)**. Yeltsin replaces Prime Minister Stepashin with Vladimir Putin in fourth government shakeup in 17 months **(Aug. 9)**. Islamic militants declare independence for Dagestan and announce holy war against Russia **(Aug. 10)**. White supremacist opens fire at Jewish community center in LA, wounding five and killing one as he flees **(Aug. 10)**. More than 17,000 people die in 7.4 earthquake in Turkey **(Aug. 17)**. Attorney General Janet Reno reopens investigation of 1993 Waco, Tex., stand-off **(Aug. 25)**. People of East Timor vote for independence from Indonesia **(Aug. 31)**. Israeli prime minister Ehud Barak and PLO leader Yasir Arafat announce peace accord **(Sept. 4)**. Larry Gene Ashbrook goes on rampage in Tex. church, killing seven and himself **(Sept. 15)**. NASA accidentally loses $125 million spacecraft as it orbits Mars **(Sept. 23)**. Dozens of people exposed to radiation in Japan's worst nuclear accident **(Sept. 30)**. Russia sends ground troops to Chechnya as conflict with Islamic militants intensifies **(Oct. 1)**. World population reaches six billion milestone **(Oct. 11)**. Military coup led by Gen. Pervez Musharraf overthrows Pakistani government **(Oct. 12)**. Tobacco companies admit to harm caused by cigarette smoking **(Oct. 13)**. Senate rejects 1996 nuclear test-ban treaty; international leaders upset by U.S. stand **(Oct. 13)**. Indonesia elects Muslim leader Abdurrahman Wahid president **(Oct. 20)**. Pro golfer Payne Stewart and five others killed in plane crash **(Oct. 25)**. EgyptAir flight crashes over Atlantic, killing all 217 on board **(Oct. 31)**. Judge finds Microsoft to be a monopoly **(Nov. 5)**. U.S. and China reach landmark trade agreement **(Nov. 15)**. China launches first spacecraft **(Nov. 21)**. Five-year-old Cuban refugee Elián González gets caught in politically charged custody battle **(Nov. 25)**. World Trade Organization conference disrupted by violent protests in Seattle **(Nov. 29** *et seq.*). New Northern Ireland government begins self-rule for first time in 25 years **(Dec. 2)**. Muslim terrorists hijack Indian Airlines jet with 189 on board **(Dec. 24)**.

2000 Socialist president, Ricardo Lagos, elected in Chile **(Jan. 16)**. George W. Bush and Al Gore take Iowa caucuses in U.S. presidential race **(Jan. 22)**. Austria at center of European dispute after conservative People's Party forms coalition with the far-right Freedom Party, headed by xenophobe Jörg Haider **(Feb. 3)**. First Lady Hillary Clinton officially enters N.Y. Senate race **(Feb. 6)**. Hijackers seize Afghan plane; release hostages in Stansted, England **(Feb. 6–12)**. Britain ends self-rule in Northern Ireland after Irish Republican Army misses disarmament deadline **(Feb. 11)**. NEAR spacecraft becomes first to orbit an asteroid **(Feb. 14)**. Wary investors cause stock plunge; beginning of the end of the Internet stock boom **(Feb. 25)**. Reformists win control of Iranian parliament for first time since 1979 Islamic revolution **(Feb. 26)**. Gun maker Smith & Wesson limits the manufacture and distribution of handguns in light of lawsuits **(March 17)**. Mass murder or suicide of hundreds in Ugandan doomsday cult **(March 18)**. Acting Russian president Vladimir V. Putin formally chosen for post **(March 25)**. Microsoft loses antitrust suit; appeal expected **(April 3)**. Controversial Osprey plane crash kills 19 marines **(April 8)**. Cuban boy Elián González reunited with father after federal raid of Miami relatives' home **(April 22)**. Vermont approves same-sex unions **(April 25)**. "I love you" virus disrupts computers worldwide **(May 4)**. South Carolina removes Confederate battle flag from capitol dome **(May 18)**. Chile ends Augusto Pinochet's immunity, clearing way for trial on murder and torture charges during years as dictator **(May 24)**. Israeli troops withdraw from Lebanese security zone after 22 years of occupation **(May 24)**. Former Indonesian president Suharto under house arrest,

Thabo Mbeki (1942–)

Eileen Collins (1956–)

Hillary Clinton (1947–)

Vladimir Putin (1952–)

Vicente Fox Quesada
(1942–)

Vojislav Kostunica
(1944–)

Yasir Arafat
(1929–)

Ariel Sharon
(1928–)

George W. Bush
(1946–)

charged with corruption and abuse of power **(May 29).** Britain restores parliamentary powers to Northern Ireland after Sinn Fein agrees to disarm **(June 4).** Presidents of North and South Korea sign peace accord, ending half-century of antagonism **(June 15).** British find 58 bodies of illegal Asian immigrants suffocated in Dutch truck that transported them **(June 20).** Elián González returns to Cuba with father **(June 23).** U.S. navy resumes shelling exercises of Puerto Rico's Vieques Island, used as a training site **(June 25).** Human genome deciphered; expected to revolutionize the practice of medicine **(June 26).** Iraq believed to resume missile program **(June 30).** Vicente Fox Quesada elected president of Mexico **(July 2).** Bashar al-Assad succeeds late father, Hafez al-Assad, as Syrian president **(July 10).** Concorde crash kills 113 near Paris **(July 25).** Republican convention picks Texas governor George W. Bush as presidential candidate; Dick Cheney for vice presidential spot **(Aug. 2).** Democratic convention selects Vice President Al Gore and Sen. Joseph I. Lieberman to head ticket **(Aug. 14).** Los Alamos scientist Wen Ho Lee, accused of stealing sensitive nuclear weapons data, freed after serving nine months in prison **(Sept. 13).** Olympic Games open in Australia **(Sept. 15).** Six-year Whitewater investigation of the Clintons ends without indictments **(Sept. 20).** Yugoslav opposition claims victory; incumbent Slobodan Milosevic denies results **(Sept. 25).** Danish voters reject euro **(Sept. 26).** Abortion pill, RU-486, wins U.S. approval **(Sept. 28).** Palestinians and Israelis clash, spurred by visit of right-wing Israeli leader Ariel Sharon to a joint Jewish/Muslim holy site; "Al Aksa intifada" continues unabated **(Sept. 30** *et seq.*). Nationwide uprising overthrows Yugoslavian president Milosevic **(Oct. 5).** Vojislav Kostunica sworn in as Yugoslav president **(Oct. 7).** 17 U.S. sailors on navy destroyer *Cole* die in Yemen terrorist explosion **(Oct. 12).** U.S. presidential election closest in decades; Bush's slim lead in Florida leads to automatic recount in that state **(Nov. 7–8).** Republicans file federal suit to block manual recount of Florida presidential election ballots sought by Democrats **(Nov. 11).** Philippine president Joseph Estrada impeached after receiving gambling payoffs **(Nov. 13).** Florida Supreme Court rules hand count of presidential ballots may continue **(Nov. 21).** Global warming talks collapse at Hague conference **(Nov. 25).** Florida Secretary of State Katherine Harris certifies Bush as winner by 537 votes **(Nov. 26).** Mad Cow disease alarms Europe **(Nov. 30** *et seq.*). Israeli prime minister Ehud Barak resigns **(Dec. 9).** U.S. Supreme Court orders halt to manual recount of presidential votes in Florida **(Dec. 9).** Supreme Court seals Bush victory by 5–4; rules there can be no further recounting **(Dec. 12).**

2001 Congo president Laurent Kabila assassinated by bodyguard **(Jan. 16).** In final days of presidency, Bill Clinton issues controversial pardons, including one for Marc Rich, billionaire fugitive financier **(Jan. 20).** George W. Bush is sworn in as 43rd president **(Jan. 20).** Earthquake kills thousands in India **(Jan. 26** *et seq.*). Libyan convicted in Flight 103 bombing over Lockerbie, Scotland **(Jan. 31).** Right-winger Ariel Sharon wins election in Israel **(Feb. 6).** U.S. submarine *Greeneville* sinks Japanese fishing boat, killing 9 **(Feb. 9).** FBI agent Robert Hanssen is charged with spying for Russia for 15 years **(Feb. 20).** The long-simmering resentment of Macedonia's ethnic Albanians erupts into violence **(March 15** *et seq.*). British livestock epidemic, foot-and-mouth disease, reaches crisis levels **(March 23).** Bush abandons global-warming treaty (Kyoto Protocol), angering European leaders **(March 30).** U.S. spy plane and Chinese jet collide. The 24 crew members of the U.S. plane are detained for 11 days; U.S. issues a formal statement of regret **(April 2** *et seq.*). Race riots in Cincinnati continue for several days following a shooting of an unarmed black man by a white police officer **(April 7** *et seq.*). U.S. millionaire Dennis Tito becomes first space tourist, visiting the International Space Station aboard a Russian booster **(April 28).** Former Klansman Thomas E. Blanton convicted of 1963 murder of four black girls in Birmingham, Ala. **(May 1).** After a Palestinian suicide bomber kills 5 and wounds more than 100 in a Netanya shopping mall, Israeli warplanes retaliate by bombing West Bank and Gaza strip **(May 18).** Four are declared guilty in 1998 terrorist bombings of U.S. embassies in Kenya and Tanzania **(May 29).** Balance of the Senate shifts after Jim Jeffords of Vermont changes his party affiliation from Republican to Independent. The move strips Republicans of control of the Senate and gives Democrats the narrowest of majorities (50–49–1) **(June 5).** Bush signs new tax-cut law, cutting taxes by $1.35 trillion over

11 years, the largest tax cut in 2 decades **(June 7).** Mohammad Khatami, Iran's moderate president, is reelected in a landslide **(June 9).** Oklahoma City bomber Timothy McVeigh executed **(June 11).** Syrian forces evacuate Beirut area after decades of occupation **(June 19).** Former Yugoslav president Slobodan Milosevic is delivered to UN tribunal in The Hague to await war-crimes trial **(June 29).** Without U.S., 178 nations reach agreement on climate accord, which rescues, though dilutes, 1997 Kyoto Protocol **(July 23).** Bush allows stem cell research, approving federal funds for studies using existing strains of stem cells **(Aug. 9).** After six months of fighting, a peace agreement is signed between rebels and the Macedonian government **(Aug. 13).** Budget surplus dwindles; some blame the slowing economy and the Bush tax cut **(Aug. 22).** Terrorists attack United States. Hijackers ram jetliners into twin towers of New York City's World Trade Center and the Pentagon. A fourth hijacked plane crashes 80 mi outside of Pittsburgh. Toll of dead is more than 3,000. Within days, Islamic militant Osama bin Laden and the al-Qaeda terrorist network are identified as the parties behind the attacks **(Sept. 11).** Anthrax scare rivets nation, as anthrax-laced letters are sent to various media and government officials. Several die after handling the letters (**October 5** *et seq.*). In response to Sept. 11 terrorist attacks, U.S. and British forces launch bombing campaign against Taliban government and al-Qaeda terrorist camps in Afghanistan. Bombings continue on a daily basis (**Oct. 7** *et seq.*). Irish Republican Army announces that it has begun to dismantle its weapons arsenal, marking a dramatic leap forward in Northern Ireland peace process **(Oct. 23).** Plane crash kills 260 in Queens, N.Y. **(Nov. 12).** Afghani factions create a post-Taliban government **(Nov. 27).** Enron Corp., one of world's largest energy companies, files bankruptcy **(Dec. 2).** Israel condemns the Palestinian Authority as a "terror-supporting entity" and severs ties with leader Yasir Arafat following mounting violence against Israelis. The Israeli Army begins bombing Palestinian areas (**Dec. 4** *et seq.*). Taliban regime in Afghanistan collapses after two months of bombing by American warplanes and fighting by Northern Alliance ground troops **(Dec. 9).** Hamid Karzai, new interim Afghan leader, is sworn in **(Dec. 22).**

2002 The euro currency debuts in twelve European countries **(Jan. 2).** U.S. takes Taliban and al-Qaeda prisoners to Guantanamo Bay **(Jan. 10).** Defrocked priest John Geoghan convicted of child molestation; church's role in cover-up sparks national outrage **(Jan. 18).** U.S. reporter Daniel Pearl kidnapped in Pakistan **(Jan. 23).** Kenneth L. Lay, chairman of bankrupt energy trader Enron, resigns; company under federal investigation for hiding debt and misrepresenting earnings **(Jan. 24).** President Bush's first State of Union address labels Iran, Iraq, and North Korea "an axis of evil" **(Jan. 29).** Queen Elizabeth II of England marks 50 years as monarch **(Feb 6).** The trial of Slobodan Milosevic on charges of crimes against humanity opens at The Hague **(Feb. 12).** American Taliban soldier John Walker Lindh charged with supporting terrorism **(Feb. 13).** Reporter Pearl confirmed dead in Pakistan **(Feb. 21).** Angolan UNITA rebel leader Jonas Savimbi killed in battle **(Feb. 22).** Tamil Tigers and Sri Lankan government sign a cease-fire agreement **(Feb. 22).** Hundreds in India die in Hindu-Muslim clashes **(March 2).** U.S. and Afghan troops launch Operation Anaconda against remaining al-Qaeda and Taliban fighters in Afghanistan **(March 2).** Saudi peace proposal—offering Israel normal relations with all Arab nations in return for withdrawal from occupied territories—approved at Arab League summit **(March 28).** Israeli tanks and warplanes attack West Bank towns of Nablus, Jenin, Bethlehem, and others in response to string of Palestinian suicide attacks. In the first three months of 2002, 14 suicide bombers killed dozens of Israeli civilians and wounded hundreds **(March 29–April 21).** Israeli prime minister Sharon calls for exile of Palestinian leader Yasir Arafat **(April 2).** UNITA Rebels and Angolan government sign a cease-fire ending 30 years of civil war **(April 4).** International Criminal Court wins UN ratification, but U.S. refuses to ratify **(April 11).** Venezuelan president Hugo Chavez ousted in coup, then reinstated **(April 12, 14).** U.S. and Russia reach landmark arms agreement to cut both countries' nuclear arsenals by up to two-thirds over the next ten years **(May 13).** East Timor becomes a new nation **(May 20).** In letter to Director, FBI lawyer Coleen Rowley criticizes FBI for thwarting terrorist efforts **(May 21).** Dirty bomb plot foiled with arrest of Jose Padilla **(June 10).** U.S. abandons 31-year-old Antiballistic Missile treaty **(June**

Mohammad Khatami
(1943–)

World Trade Center

Hamid Karzai
(1957–)

Jacques Chirac
(1932–)

Tony Blair
(1953–)

Hu Jintao
(1942–)

13). At national conference, U.S. bishops recommend zero tolerance policy for priests who abuse children (**June 14**). Arthur Andersen firm convicted of destroying documents relating to former client Enron Corp. (**June 15**). Bush announces U.S. will not recognize an independent Palestinian state until Yasir Arafat is replaced (**June 24**). WorldCom, after admitting to misstating profits, files for bankruptcy—largest claim in U.S. history (**July 21**). Pennsylvania miners rescued after spending 77 hours in a dark, flooded mine shaft (**July 28**). Bush signs corporate reform bill in response to spate of corporate scandals (**July 30**). Bush addresses United Nations, calls for a "regime change" in Iraq (**Sept. 12**). Tyco executives L. Dennis Kozlowski and Mark Swartz indicted in stock-fraud scheme (**Sept. 12**). Five al-Qaeda terrorist suspects arrested in New York (**Sept. 13**). Terrorist bomb in Bali kills hundreds (**Oct. 12**). Government suspended in Northern Ireland in protest of suspected IRA spy ring (**Oct. 14**). Former ImClone Executive Sam Waksal pleads guilty to charges including fraud and perjury (**Oct. 15**). North Korea admits to developing nuclear arms in defiance of treaty (**Oct. 16**). Vatican calls for softening of U.S. bishops' abuse policy (**Oct. 18**). Chechen rebels take 763 hostages in Moscow theater; Russian authorities release a gas into theater, killing 116 hostages and freeing remaining survivors (**Oct. 23–26**). Snipers prey upon DC suburbs, killing ten and wounding others (**Oct. 2–24**). Police arrest two sniper suspects, John Allen Muhammad and John Lee Malvo (**Oct. 24**). CIA kills six al-Qaeda members in Yemen (**Nov. 4**). Republicans retake the Senate in midterm elections; gain additional House seats (**Nov. 5**). UN Security Council passes unanimous resolution calling on Iraq to disarm or else face "serious consequences" (**Nov. 8**). China's Jiang Zemin officially retires as general secretary; Hu Jintao named as his successor (**Nov. 14**). UN arms inspectors return to Iraq (**Nov. 18**). EPA relaxes Clean Air Act (**Nov. 22**). Bush signs legislation creating cabinet-level Department of Homeland Security (**Nov. 25**). Boston archbishop Cardinal Bernard Law resigns over growing child sexual abuse scandal in the Catholic Church (**Dec. 13**). Trent Lott steps down as Republican leader after furor over prosegregationist remark (**Dec. 20**). Sen. Bill Frist unanimously elected Republican leader of the Senate (**Dec. 23**).

For 2003 chronology, *see* Current Events pp. 33-44.

PICTURE CREDITS

The editors wish to thank the following organizations and individuals who have contributed illustrations to Headline History.

Agence France Press/Archive Photos: **Mao Zedong;** AIP Niels Bohr Library: **Marie Curie, Albert Einstein;** AMW Pressedienst/Archive Photos: **Nelson Mandela;** Archive Photos: **Richard Wagner, William Butler Yeats, Pablo Picasso, Anne Frank, Woody Guthrie, Robert Frost, William Faulkner, The Beatles, Mahatma Gandhi, Duke Ellington, Tennessee Williams, Toni Morrison, Seamus Heaney, Ella Fitzgerald, Lech Walesa, Princess Diana, Pope John Paul, Mother Teresa, Yitzhak Rabin, Malcolm X, William Rehnquist, Anwar Sadat;** Linda J. Barnes: **the Duomo in Florence;** British Information Services: **Margaret Thatcher;** Consolidated News/Archive Photos: **Jean-Bertrand Aristide;** Tina Diodati: **Aqueduct, Parthenon;** Embassy of the Philippines: **Corazon Aquino;** Embassy of Yugoslavia: **Vojislav Kostunica;** The French Consulate, Boston: **François Mitterrand;** Gerald R. Ford Library: **Gerald Ford;** Peter F. Harrington: **Stonehenge;** Erik Hjortshoj: **Pagoda;** Imapress/Archive Photos: **Boris Yeltsin;** INA/Reuters/Archive Photos: **Saddam Hussein;** John Fitzgerald Kennedy Library, Boston: **John F. Kennedy;** Priscilla Lee: **Dalai Lama;** Leo Baeck Inst./Archive Photos: **Sigmund Freud;** Jimmy Carter Library: **Jimmy Carter;** The Library of Congress Picture Collection: **Pocahontas, Taj Mahal, Edgar Allan Poe, Harriet Tubman, Walt Whitman, Dred Scott, Samuel Clemens (Mark Twain), Henri Matisse, W.E.B. Du Bois, Woodrow Wilson, Bessie Smith, Dorothea Lange, Amelia Earhart, Harry S. Truman, John H. Glenn, Jr., James H. Meredith, Betty Friedan, Richard Nixon, Lyndon B. Johnson;** Pete Maio: **Mesa Verde;** Muzammil Paha/Reuters/Archive Photos: **Benazir Bhutto;** National Archives and Records Admin.: **Frederick Douglass, Harriet Beecher Stowe, Abraham Lincoln, Robert E. Lee, William Tecumseh Sherman, Chief Joseph, Benito Mussolini, Franklin Delano Roosevelt, Adolf Hitler, Winston Churchill, Atomic Bomb, Dwight D. Eisenhower, Rev. Martin Luther King, Jr.;** NASA: **Eileen Collins, Hubble Space Telescope;** NASA/JPL/Caltech: **Mars Sojourner Rover;** NOAA: **World Trade Center;** Novosti Photos: **Vladimir Lenin, Mikhail S. Gorbachev;** Elaine Ouellette: **Pantheon in Rome;** The Permanent Mission of India to the UN: **Indira Gandhi;** Permanent Mission of Islamic Republic of Iran to the UN: **Ayatollah Ruhollah Khomeini;** Renée Scott: **Celtic Cross, Mayan Pyramid;** The Republican National Committee: **Ronald Reagan, George Bush;** Kim Storm: **Egyptian Pyramid;** United Nations: **Dag Hammarskjöld, Fidel Castro, Kofi Annan, Hamid Karzai, Yasir Arafat, Ariel Sharon, Gerhard Schröder, Hu Jintao, Jacques Chirac, Mohammad Khatami, Tony Blair, Thabo Mbeki, Vicente Fox Quesada, Vladimir Putin;** U.S. Army Photos: **Joseph Stalin, Yalta Conference, General Colin Powell;** U.S. Senate Photo Office: **Hillary Clinton;** U.S. State Department: **Madeleine Albright;** U.S. Supreme Court: **Ruth Bader Ginsburg, Thurgood Marshall, Sandra Day O'Connor;** Tasha Vincent: **Cathedral and Tower at Pisa, Chartres Cathedral, Michelangelo's David, Statue of Liberty;** The White House: **William J. Clinton, George W. Bush.**

80 Days That Changed the World

TIME magazine first appeared on newsstands in 1923. To mark the publication's 80th anniversary, the editors challenged themselves to an experiment in history: to select from those eight decades 80 specific days that had changed the course of history. Some were easy calls: the attack on Pearl Harbor, D-day, 9/11. But some passed without notice even as they happened: the day the double helix structure of DNA was first decoded; the day oil was discovered in Saudi Arabia; the day the first digital page was posted on the World Wide Web. If you don't agree with our selections—well, challenging you to come up with a list of your own is part of the idea.

1. Oct. 29, 1923 — Ataturk Orders Turkey's Turn to the West

Turning his back on Islamic culture, General Mustafa Kemal—later known as Ataturk—declared Turkey was no longer an empire, but a republic. Ataturk's top-down cultural revolution wrenched his nation into the modern world.

2. Nov. 8, 1923 — Adolf Hitler's Practice Power Grab

With Germany seething over the humiliating terms of the World War I armistice, Adolf Hitler and his Nazi followers launched a putsch in a Munich beer hall, taking three powerful officials hostage. The putsch failed and Hitler went to jail—where, ironically, he wrote the book, *Mein Kampf*, that he later rode to power.

3. Jan. 21, 1924 — V. I. Lenin Dies

The man who oversaw Russia's communist revolution died at only 53. His early passing opened the way for the horrors perpetrated by Joseph Stalin, whose harsh tactics Lenin had questioned.

4. Sept. 25, 1926 — The 40-Hour Revolution

In 1911 Henry Ford perfected the assembly line. Three years later, he began paying the workers in his auto factories $5 a day—believing that well-paid workers would be able to afford his cars. In 1926 he put his workers on a 40-hour week, allowing them more time for leisure; the world soon followed suit.

5. May 21, 1927 — Lindbergh Flies the Atlantic, Alone

Winning the $25,000 prize was beside the point: Lindbergh's heroic solo flight from Long Island to Paris—33½ hours long—thrilled the world, sealed the future of flight, and created one of the 20th century's great heroes.

6. Oct. 6, 1927 — Motion Pictures Get a Voice

"You ain't heard nothin' yet!" boasted singer Al Jolson halfway through *The Jazz Singer.* The movie broke free from silent-screen traditions only for brief dialogue and a few songs. By 1930 virtually every Hollywood film was a talkie, and the movies haven't shut up since.

7. Sept. 3, 1928 — Fleming Discovers Penicillin

Scottish researcher Alexander Fleming happened to glance at some Petri dishes due to be sterilized for reuse—and noticed that the "mold juice" in it was killing off bacterial cultures. He named the juice penicillin; it would be another decade before doctors began fully taking advantage of its powers.

8. Nov. 18, 1928 — Mickey Mouse Bows In

Walt Disney, an unknown 27-year-old animator, had a great idea: marrying the new sound films to his new cartoon character, Mickey Mouse. When the result—*Steamboat Willie*—opened in a New York City theater, crowds rushed to savor the freedom and energy of this radical new form.

9. Oct. 9, 1929 — Wall Street Takes a Fall

The Roaring '20s ended on a dismal note: Wall Street lost 12% of its value on its way to an ultimate decline of 89%. The slump ushered in the Great Depression, which held America in its grip until World War II.

10. March 12, 1930 — Gandhi Begins the Salt March

Mohandas K. Gandhi led a band of followers on the first steps of a 25-day, 240-mile march to Dandi, an oceanside town where he would collect a few grains of salt in defiance of a British tax. It was the beginning of a crusade that would end in independence for India 17 years later.

11. March 4, 1933 — Franklin Roosevelt Launches the New Deal

Nearly a quarter of the U.S. labor force was out of work. Banks had shut their doors; farms were going belly up; breadlines snaked through city streets. But the newly inaugurated president outlined a plan of economic revolution that remade the relationship between Americans and their government.

12. July 1, 1934 — The Movies Crack Down on Morals

When the potent Roman Catholic lobby formed the Legion of Decency to rate films, the industry instituted a code that cracked down on overt sexuality.

13. June 10, 1935 AA Takes Its First Steps

Bill Wilson, a stockbroker and a drunk from Brooklyn, N.Y., hooked up with fellow alcoholic Robert H. Smith on a business trip to Akron, Ohio. Following Bill W.'s strategy, they crafted a simple set of principles—later refined into 12 steps—that became the foundation of America's self-help culture.

14. Aug. 9, 1936 Jesse Owens Triumphs in Berlin

African-American track star Jesse Owens raced to scoop up four medals—and set three world records—at the Berlin Olympics. He became the hero of the Games Adolf Hitler had planned as a showcase for Aryan supremacy.

15. March 3, 1938 Oil Is Discovered in Saudi Arabia

Ibn Saud, the King of Saudi Arabia, authorized a team of U.S. engineers to explore the trackless desert in search of water. At 4,727 ft., they hit the largest supply of crude oil in the world. The tables of world economic might had turned.

16. April 15, 1938 Superman Takes Flight

Cleveland teenagers Jerry Siegel (writer) and Joe Shuster (illustrator) dreamed up the Man of Steel in 1932, but did not succeed in getting him into print until six years later. To Americans mired in the Great Depression, Superman offered both escape and hope—and began the great age of comics.

17. Nov. 9, 1938 Hitler Declares War on the Jews

Nazis and their sympathizers stormed through Germany's cities, smashing the storefronts of shops owned by Jews. The "Night of Broken Glass"—Kristallnacht—was the first time the Nazis incited the entire population against German Jews, and was the first step to the Holocaust.

18. Sept. 1, 1939 Germany Storms into Poland

The long-anticipated European war began when Adolf Hitler launched a bold, unprovoked attack on Poland. Within two days Britain and France jumped to Poland's defense and World War II was under way in Europe.

19. May 10, 1940 Winston Churchill Takes Power in England

In May 1940, as Britain's soldiers were in danger of being trapped before Hitler's blitzkrieg across France, Neville Chamberlain stepped down as prime minister and Winston Churchill took power.

20. Dec. 7, 1941 Japan Attacks Pearl Harbor

Japanese dive bombers launched a surprise attack on America's Pacific fleet, based in Hawaii. Denouncing "a day that will live in infamy," President Franklin D. Roosevelt led the U.S. into war.

21. June 6, 1944 D-Day: The Allies Invade Europe

Four years after Hitler's armies stormed across Europe, the Allies struck back, launching their long-awaited invasion of occupied France along the beaches of Normandy. A massive armada carried troops across the choppy English Channel; they achieved surprise, but still met tough resistance. Hitler and his Third Reich would be dead within a year.

22. Aug. 6, 1945 America Drops an Atom Bomb on Japan

At 8:15 a.m. the *Enola Gay* dropped a single bomb on the Japanese city of Hiroshima; an estimated one-third of the city's 350,000 residents were killed instantly. The bomb was the first to harness the power of atomic fission, and unleashed a new era of dread upon the world.

23. April 15, 1947 Jackie Robinson Breaks Baseball's Color Line

Brooklyn Dodgers president and general manager Branch Rickey aimed to dismantle segregation in baseball, and in former UCLA star Jackie Robinson, he found the right combination of moral fiber and athletic prowess to do the job.

24. Aug. 15, 1947 India Wins Its Independence

"At the stroke of midnight hour . . . India will awake to life and freedom." So declared Jawaharlal Nehru in his speech on the eve of his nation's independence from Britain. But the new nation also awoke to religious turmoil, as majority Hindus battled minority Muslims, and the partition of the Punjab province into Pakistan laid the groundwork for decades of unrest.

25. Oct. 14, 1947 Man Breaks Through the Sound Barrier

Chuck Yeager of the newborn U.S. Air Force had been seeking to fly faster than Mach 1, the never-crossed barrier past which man would fly faster than the speed of sound. On this day, Yeager was dropped in his experimental plane XS-1 from a bomber at 20,000 ft., fired up his craft's four rockets, then flew supersonic for the first time.

26. Jan. 5, 1948 Jackson Pollock Shows His First Action Paintings

The reviews? "Monotonous intensity." The sales? Two canvases. But when Jackson Pollock, America's first painter-pop star, showed his first action paintings—created by flinging, dripping, and hurling paint on the canvas—he opened the doors for the emergence of America's Abstract Expressionist painters as a significant force.

27. May 14, 1948 Israel Becomes a State

David Ben Gurion read a 979-word declaration of independence at the Tel Aviv Art Museum. At midnight, British rule over Palestine lapsed, and the world's first Jewish state was born.

28. Oct. 1, 1949 Mao Zedong's Communists Take Power in China

Communist revolutionary Mao Zedong chose a symbol of ancient power—Beijing's red-lacquered Gate of Eternal Peace, entrance to the 500-year-old palace of China's emperors—to declare the birth of the communist People's Republic of China. The world's largest nation was now a stronghold for Marxist-Leninist doctrine.

29. Feb. 9, 1950 Sen. Joseph McCarthy Begins His Reign of Terror

The obscure backbench senator from Wisconsin told an audience in Wheeling, W. Va.: "I have here in my hand a list of 205 (State Dept. employees) that were made known to the secretary of state as being members of the Communist Party . . . " The list was bogus, as were many of the charges of communist involvement McCarthy leveled at innocent Americans before his star finally fell in 1954.

30. Oct. 20, 1950 The Mau-Mau Revolt Begins in Kenya

The Mau-Mau were a secret society who vowed to drive the white man from the British colony of Kenya. Their first strike was the assassination of Chief Kungu Wauhiu of the Kikuyu tribe, a British sympathizer. The rebellion spread, fanning hopes across Africa of an end to colonialism.

31. Oct. 15, 1951 I Love Lucy Debuts on Television

The first reviews were mixed: TIME called it "a triumph of bounce over bumbling material." But TIME soon came around, and so did Americans—the situation comedy starring Lucille Ball and husband Desi Arnaz soon became the nation's favorite program. Revolutionary in its day, it remains TV's most popular comedy ever.

32. Feb. 28, 1953 The Double Helix Is Described

When American James Watson and Briton Francis Crick succeeded in their attempt to find the structure of DNA, which turned out to be a double helix, they solved one of biology's greatest puzzles and opened the door to a new age of medicine: DNA forensics, testing for genetic diseases, and the development of the biotechnology industry.

33. July 5, 1954 Elvis Presley Makes His First Record

Memphis record producer Sam Phillips was searching for a new sound. In Elvis Presley, only 19, he found what he sought: a singer who could bring the excitement of black music to a larger audience. Phillips let Presley sing through a series of mawkish ballads, until Elvis worked out on an Arthur Crudup number, "That's All Right." Phillips rolled the tape, and a star was born.

34. Dec. 1, 1955 Rosa Parks Sparks the Civil Rights Movement

After a hard day of work as a seamstress in a Montgomery, Ala., department store, African-American Rosa Parks found a seat in the first row of the "colored" section of a city bus. When the driver ordered her to move to accommodate a boarding white passenger—a standard request—Parks refused. She was arrested, sparking a 381-day bus boycott that ended segregation on the city's buses.

35. Oct. 4, 1957 The USSR Launches the First Satellite

The U.S. and the USSR were locked in the cold war, vying for military, scientific, and propaganda victories. When a Soviet rocket successfully placed a 184-lb satellite in orbit around the earth, the achievement rocked the world. The "space race" led directly to the U.S. landing on the moon in 1969.

36. July 17, 1959 A Find in Africa Rewrites Humanity's History

British anthropologists Richard and Mary Leakey unearthed the fragments of a hominid fossil skull later named *Zinjanthropus boisei* in the Olduvai Gorge in Tanganyika (now Tanzania). The age of the skull: 1.75 million years old, stretching the history of humanity by a third.

37. May 9, 1960 The Birth-Control Pill Appears

When the oral contraceptive Enovid was approved by the U.S. Food and Drug Administration, it marked the beginning of a new era in sexuality: for the first time, intercourse without pregnancy was possible, and parenthood could be planned.

38. Sept. 27, 1962 Silent Spring Sparks Environmentalism

Biologist Rachel Carson's eloquent, rigorous attack on the overuse of DDT and other pesticides upset the chemical industry—critics denounced her as a "hysterical woman." But she succeeded in placing humanity's relationship to nature on the world's political agenda.

39. Oct. 11, 1962 Pope John XXIII Shakes Up the Catholic Church

Well into his 70s, Angelo Giuseppe Roncalli was expected to be a "caretaker" pontiff when he was elected pope by his fellow cardinals in 1958. But he turned out to be a revolutionary: calling 2,600 Roman Catholic bishops together in Rome in a Vatican Council, he urged them in a 38-minute speech on this day to update their ancient religion.

40. Oct. 27, 1962 The Cuban Missile Crisis Ramps Up the Cold War

When the U.S. learned that the Soviet Union had placed missiles on Cuban soil, young President John F. Kennedy demanded their removal. On this day, the belligerent Soviet boss, Nikita Khrushchev, backed down and agreed to remove the missiles, under the threat of a U.S. invasion of Cuba.

41. Aug. 28, 1963 American Blacks March on Washington

Crystallizing the growing strength of the civil rights movement, Dr. Martin Luther King and others brought African Americans together at the Lincoln Memorial to call for legislation to end all vestiges of segregation. King electrified the crowd with a soaring address in which he declared "I have a dream" for a better America—one with full rights for all.

42. Nov. 22, 1963 John F. Kennedy Is Assassinated

As President John Kennedy and his wife Jacqueline rode through a motorcade in Dallas, shots rang out. Within an hour, the life of a young president—and his promise of a New Frontier—were dead. Adding to the senselessness of the event, accused assassin Lee Harvey Oswald was then killed live on national television.

43. Feb. 9, 1964 The Beatles Appear on Ed Sullivan

The brash young Brits provided a welcome reprieve from America's recent assassination. Smart, sassy, tuneful, and fun, the quartet from Liverpool conquered America from their first appearance on Ed Sullivan's Sunday night variety show—and opened the door to the groovy '60s.

44. June 30, 1966 NOW Is Founded to Promote Feminism

Betty Friedan and fellow feminists gathered in Washington, DC, at a federal conference on the status of women, but found it to be a sham. On the spot, they began to create NOW, the National Organization for Women, to advance gender equality.

45. Aug. 5, 1966 Mao Zedong Unleashes the Cultural Revolution

Mao Zedong sent fanatical young leftists into the streets, urging them to attack a corrupt, entrenched party bureaucracy. The result was chaos: a reign of terror by radical ideologues that left the country drained, divided, and desperately poor—for years.

46. Dec. 3, 1967 The First Human Heart Is Transplanted

South African surgeon Christiaan Barnard performed the world's first heart transplant on patient Louis Washkansky. The recipient died 18 days later, for the complexities of tissue rejection were not clearly understood at the time. But the dramatic operation opened the door to a new age of organ replacement and transplantation.

47. Jan. 31, 1968 The Tet Offensive Turns the Tide in Vietnam

As Vietnamese celebrated their New Year's holiday, the guerrilla Viet Cong and regular army of North Vietnam launched a massive surprise strike. Though U.S. and South Vietnamese troops were taken by surprise, they recovered quickly, and won a technical victory. But the strike left Americans thinking that the war was an unwinnable folly.

48. April 4, 1968 Dr. Martin Luther King, Jr., Is Assassinated

In Memphis to support a strike by city sanitation workers, the civil rights leader was shot down as he stood on the balcony of a small motel. In the wake of the murder, blacks across the nation rioted, and advocates of King's nonviolent philosophy found themselves losing ground to those who called for more confrontational tactics.

49. June 5, 1968 Robert F. Kennedy Is Murdered

He entered the wide-open Democratic party presidential contest late, and the senator from New York, brother to the slain President, was pushing hard to defeat the front-runner, Vice President Hubert Humphrey. Moments after being declared victor in the important California primary, Kennedy was gunned down by a Palestinian, Sirhan Sirhan.

50. June 28, 1969 The Gay Rights Movement Is Born

Hundreds of people rioted in the streets for hours after eight New York City police officers cracked down on the Stonewall Inn, a dive in Greenwich Village that served a wide variety of mainly gay patrons. The impromptu demonstration was the first time gays had come together to demand respect, and was the starting point for the gay rights movement.

51. July 20, 1969 Man Lands on the Moon

Ohio-born Neil Armstrong, 38, became the first man to set foot on another world after NASA's Lunar Landing Module settled to Earth . . . er, Moon . . . in the Valley of Tranquillity.

52. Nov. 15, 1971 The Microchip Is Designed

Continuing the revolution that began when the first transistor was developed in 1949, engineers at Intel created the first microprocessor—in essence, a computer on a single silicone chip.

53. June 17, 1972 The Watergate Burglary Unravels a Presidency

It was actually the burglars' second break-in at the offices of the Democratic National Comittee in Washington, DC's Watergate complex. When security guard Frank Wills found tape on the door, he called the cops. The burglars were arrested, and their trail led straight to the Oval Office—and to the 1974 fall of President Richard Nixon.

54. Jan. 22, 1973 Abortion Is Legalized in America

In a decision that continues to divide Americans 30 years later, the U.S. Supreme Court declared abortion was legal in the case of *Roe* v. *Wade,* by a vote of 7–2. Justice Harry Blackmun's historic decision stated that women had a constitutional right to make private decisions about whether to continue or terminate a pregnancy.

55. April 30, 1975 Saigon Falls to the Communists

In a final, hectic bug-out, Americans lined up on the roof of a building in the U.S. embassy complex, awaiting rescue by helicopters. It was America's final, pitiful exit from Vietnam—a debacle that took 16 years and claimed 58,000 American lives.

56. April 1, 1976 Apple Begins a New Age of Computers

Most computers in 1976 were monsters with monster price tags. But two young California hackers, visionary Steve Jobs and techie Steve Wozniak, came together to form a new company whose goal was to put a computer on every desktop, in both homes and offices.

57. May 25, 1977 Star Wars Opens

"It wasn't like a movie opening; it was like an earthquake," recalls star Carrie Fisher (Princess Leia). Directed by George Lucas, the film rewrote Hollywood's book with its splashy special effects and ushered in the age of marketing tie-ins, action figures, and endless spin-offs.

58. July 25, 1978 The First Test-Tube Baby Is Born

The world's first test-tube baby was a 5-lb, 12-oz bundle of squealing ethical questions and implications for the future of the species. Louise Brown is now 25, and one of some one million test-tube babies.

59. Feb. 1, 1979 Ayatollah Khomeini Returns to Iran

With Shah Rezah Pahlevi in exile, Prime Minister Shapour Bakhtiar allowed the Shah's nemesis—fundamentalist cleric Ayatollah Khomeini—to return to his native land. Within eight days, Khomeini held the reins of power in Iran. Khomeini's supporters soon seized and held 52 Americans, provoking a 444-day confrontation with the U.S.

60. May 3, 1979 Margaret Thatcher Leads Britain

Routing Labour's James Callaghan and smashing the gender barrier, the tough conservative soon embarked on a program that remade her nation: breaking the unions' stranglehold; energizing the business world; altering the welfare-state mentality; and fighting a war over the Falkland Islands.

61. Dec. 12, 1979 The Soviet Union Invades Afghanistan

Soviet leaders were concerned that their unaligned neighbor was beginning to tilt toward the U.S. So President Leonid Brezhnev sent in troops to take over. The invasion turned into a nearly decade-long quagmire for his nation. Ironically, the U.S. aided the rebel mujahadeen, whose ranks included future terrorist Osama bin Laden.

62. Sept. 20, 1980 A Good Day for Savers

Accountant Ted Benna was redesigning a retirement program for a bank—but he ended up changing the way Americans pay for their later years. A little-noticed section of the newly revised Internal Revenue Code, Section 401(k), he realized, would allow employees to save part of their pay as a retirement plan, and the employer could match the sum. Soon most U.S. companies offered the program.

63. July 27, 1982 A Modern Plague Is Identified

Only 13 months after a mystery disease had first appeared, it was rapidly turning into an epidemic, particularly among gay men and drug addicts; some called it "gay cancer." Yet it was not a cancer, and it wasn't restricted to gays. At a meeting in Washington, DC, a new name was chosen: acquired immunodeficiency syndrome, or AIDS.

64. March 8, 1983 Ronald Reagan Bedevils the Soviets

Speaking before the National Association of Evangelicals in Orlando, Fla., President Reagan denounced "the aggressive impulses of an evil empire." The words shocked many in America, who found them too sweeping—but they touched the hearts of rebels behind the Iron Curtain, who ultimately helped bring it down.

65. March 11, 1985 Mikhail Gorbachev Leads the USSR

The untimely deaths of two Soviet leaders, Yuri Andropov and Konstantin Chernenko, thrust into power a reformer profoundly disillusioned with the status quo. "It's at the top that we must start changes to let the people breathe," Gorbachev recalls thinking. Now in supreme command, he began the revolution-from-above that ushered in the age of *perestroika* and *glasnost.*

66. Dec. 29, 1987 Prozac Is Approved To Treat Depression

Fluoxetine hydrochloride had been approved for use in Belgium the year before, the first in a new class of medications that treated depression by exquisitely controlling the levels of serotonin, a brain chemical involved in mood. Cleared for sale in the U.S. under the name Prozac, it quickly altered the treatment of depression and other disorders.

67. Nov. 9, 1989 The Berlin Wall Comes Down

Responding to weeks of peaceful demonstrations, the East German Politburo announced on Nov. 8 that all citizens could leave East Germany at any crossing "immediately." By dawn, an estimated 100,000 delirious Germans were celebrating and dismantling the hated Wall, which had divided them since August 1961.

68. Nov. 24, 1989 Osama bin Laden Takes Charge

Sheik Abdullah Azzam, 48, was the most prominent advocate of a jihad to save Muslim lands from infidel encroachment. On this day, he was killed by a land mine in the Pakistani frontier city of Peshawar. His deputy, Saudi aristocrat Osama bin Laden, took over the role of first among the jihadis; soon he would found al-Qaeda.

69. Feb. 11, 1990 Nelson Mandela Is Released from Prison

South Africa's anti-apartheid leader was released from prison by the white-minority government after a confinement that lasted 27 years, 6 months, and 7 days. In that time, he had become an unstoppable force; the world had lost patience with white rule in South Africa and had placed its faith in a man whom no one had seen in decades.

70. Aug. 6, 1991 The World Wide Web Is Born

Tim Berners-Lee, a young British scientist at CERN, a high-energy physics lab in Geneva, came up with a new way to send scientific documents over the Internet. His superiors weren't interested, so he posted a message on an Internet newsgroup—a kind of electronic public-access bulletin board—announcing the existence of the "WorldWideWeb (www) project." The message included instructions on how to download the very first Web browser from the very first website. And the Web was born.

71. Feb. 26, 1993 The World Trade Center Is Bombed

Six people were killed and more than a thousand injured when a terrorist bomb exploded in New York City's famed twin towers. Some 20,000 workers were evacuated safely. The bombing highlighted the need to improve security and evacuation procedures in the buildings—steps that would save thousands of lives eight years later.

72. April 19, 1995 A Federal Building in Oklahoma Is Bombed

When a 7,000-lb fertilizer bomb exploded in a rental truck parked outside the Alfred P. Murrah Federal Building in Oklahoma City, 168 died, including 19 children. U.S. Army veteran Timothy McVeigh was tried and found guilty of the bombing; he was put to death in 2001.

73. Aug. 9, 1995 The Dotcom Boom Begins

Illinois student Marc Andreessen designed Mosaic software that created a graphic interface for Internet messages. The product was a hit; now Andreessen had a vastly improved browser, Netscape. When the new company began to sell stock in an initial public offering, it soared. The event touched off a "dot-com" boom that would fuel a huge bull market on Wall Street, until it collapsed early in 2000.

74. Oct. 3, 1995 O. J. Simpson Is Found Not Guilty

Nine blacks, two whites, and one Hispanic rendered their verdict in a Los Angeles courtroom: football legend Orenthal James Simpson was not guilty of the murder of his ex-wife, Nicole Brown Simpson, and her friend, Ronald Goldman. African Americans, convinced Simpson had been framed, celebrated the verdict; white Americans thought the trial had been a sham. Racial divides still ran deep in America.

75. Aug. 3, 1997 Princess Diana Dies in a Car Wreck

Princess Diana was hugely popular in Britain and around the world, even after her divorce from the heir to the throne, Prince Charles. Her new boyfriend was Dodi Fayed, an Egyptian-born multimillionaire. After dinner in Paris, they were being driven home when their Mercedes crashed; the Princess was pronounced dead hours later.

76. March 27, 1998 Viagra Is Approved by the FDA

The drug was originally designed to treat angina, but researchers at Pfizer laboratories found that it could also reverse impotence in men. The FDA approved the drug as expected on the final day of its six-month priority review, offering relief from a problem long considered incurable.

77. Nov. 29, 1999 Protesters Stop the WTO Meeting in Seattle

Leaders of the World Trade Organization were meeting in Seattle on a new round of global trade rules. But the meeting was hijacked by some 50,000 protesters, representing a wide variety of groups: unions, environmental organizations, family farmers, consumers. The dramatic confrontation between civilians and corporate leaders was the first serious opposition to the tide of corporate globalization that began to sweep the world in the 1990s.

78. Dec. 12, 2000 The Supreme Court Names New President

Putting an end to a fiasco—a national election that had gone undecided for 35 days, due to vote-counting problems in Florida—the U.S. Supreme Court handed down a 5–4 decision that put Republican candidate George W. Bush in the White House, rather than Democrat Al Gore.

79. Sept. 11, 2001 Terrorists Strike America

Operatives of the Islamic terrorist group al-Qaeda hijacked four airliners and sent two of them crashing into the twin towers of the World Trade Center in Manhattan, killing almost 3,000 people. A third airliner crashed into the Pentagon, killing 184; a fourth crashed in a field in Pennsylvania, perhaps brought down by heroic passengers. It was the most devastating attack on American soil since the Japanese struck Pearl Harbor in 1941.

80. Jan. 29, 2002 George W. Bush Takes Aim at an "Axis of Evil"

In his State of the Union speech following the 9/11 attacks on America, President Bush denounced what he termed an "axis of evil"—Iran, Iraq, and North Korea. Many found little evidence for such a linkage, but 14 months later the U.S. and Britain launched a war in Iraq that brought down the regime of strongman Saddam Hussein.

Measuring Global Poverty

Traditionally, poverty has been measured by the lack of a minimum income (or consumption level) necessary to meet basic needs. Measuring poverty on a global scale requires establishing a uniform poverty level across extremely divergent economies, which can result in only rough comparisons. The World Bank has defined the international poverty line as U.S. $1 and $2 per day in 1993 Purchasing Power Parity (PPP)[1], which adjusts for differences in the prices of goods and services between countries. The $1 per day level is generally used for the least developed countries, primarily African; the $2-per-day level is used for middle income economies such as those of East Asia and Latin America. By this measure, in 2003 there were 1.2 billion out of the developing world's 4.8 billion people living on $1 per day, while another 2.8 billion were living on less than $2 per day[2]. In 2003, the richest fifth of the world's population received 85% of the total world income, while the poorest fifth received just 1.4% of the global income.

The $1- and $2-per-day measures offer a convenient, albeit crude, way to quantify global poverty. In the last several decades, poverty research has adopted a broader, multidimensional approach, taking into account a variety of social indicators in addition to income. The UN's Human Poverty Index, for example, factors in illiteracy, malnutrition among children, early death, poor health care, and poor access to safe water. Vulnerability to famine or flooding, lack of sanitation, exposure to disease, a diet poor in nutrients, and the absence of education are as much the signs of poverty as material deprivation. Providing the poor with basic social services and infrastructure would in many cases alleviate poverty to a greater extent than simply a rise in income level.

1. Purchasing power parity (PPP), as defined by the World Bank, is "a method of measuring the relative purchasing power of different countries' currencies over the same types of goods and services. Because goods and services may cost more in one country than in another, PPP allows us to make more accurate comparisons of standards of living across countries."
2. The original $1 per day was based on 1985 PPP estimates; currently the poverty line is based on 1993 PPP estimates, which has raised the amount from $1.00 to $1.08. As a convention, "$1 a day" is still widely used when discussing income poverty.

World's Poorest Countries, 2003

UN list of least developed countries[1]

Afghanistan, Angola, Bangladesh, Benin, Bhutan, Burkina Faso, Burundi, Cambodia, Cape Verde, Central African Republic, Chad, Comoros, Democratic Republic of Congo, Djibouti, Equatorial Guinea, Eritrea, Ethiopia, Gambia, Guinea, Guinea-Bissau, Haiti, Kiribati, Lao People's Democratic Republic, Lesotho, Liberia, Madagascar, Malawi, Maldives, Mali, Mauritania, Mozambique, Myanmar, Nepal, Niger, Rwanda, Samoa, Sao Tome and Principe, Senegal, Sierra Leone, Solomon Islands, Somalia, Sudan, Togo, Tuvalu, Uganda, Tanzania, Vanuatu, Yemen, Zambia.

1. The U.N. classifies countries as "least developed" based on three criteria: (1) annual gross domestic product (GDP) below $900 per capita; (2) quality of life, based on life expectancy at birth, per capita calorie intake, primary and secondary school enrollment rates, and adult literacy; and (3) economic vulnerability, based on instability of agricultural productions and exports, inadequate diversification, and economic smallness. Half or more of the population in the 49 least developed countries listed above are estimated to live at or below the absolute poverty line of U.S. $1 dollar per day.

Gap Between Rich and Poor: World Income Inequality

Percentage share of income (poorest and richest 20% of population)

Countries with greatest inequality	Lowest 20%	Highest 20%	Countries with greatest equality	Lowest 20%	Highest 20%
1. Sierra Leone	1.1%	63.4%	1. Slovak Republic	11.9%	31.4%
2. Central African Republic	2.0	65.0	2. Belarus	11.4	33.3
3. Swaziland	2.7	64.4	3. Hungary	10.0	34.4
4. Brazil	2.2	64.1	4. Denmark	9.6	34.5
5. Nicaragua	2.3	63.6	5. Japan	10.6	35.7
6. South Africa	2.9	64.8	6. Sweden	9.6	34.5
7. Paraguay	1.9	60.7	7. Czech Republic	10.3	35.9
8. Colombia	3.0	60.9	8. Finland	10.0	35.8
9. Chile	3.3	61.0	9. Norway	9.7	35.8
10. Honduras	2.2	59.4	10. Bulgaria	10.1	36.8

NOTE: Countries are ranked according to the Gini index (or coefficient), a measure of income inequality within a country. A country's Gini rating is between 0 and 100, with 0 indicating perfect equality and 100 indicating absolute inequality. Sierra Leone, the country with the greatest income inequality in the world is 62.9 on the Gini index; the Slovak Republic, the country with the greatest income equality is 19.5. (The U.S. rates 40.8 on the Gini index—the poorest 20% of its population receive 5.2% of income; the richest 20% receive 46.4%.) *Source: World Development Index 2002,* The World Bank.

Most and Least Livable Countries: UN Human Development Index, 2003

The Human Development Index (HDI), published annually by the UN, ranks nations according to their citizens' quality of life rather than strictly by a nation's traditional economic figures. The criteria for calculating rankings include life expectancy, educational attainment, and adjusted real income.

"Most Livable" Countries, 2003

1. Norway
2. Iceland
3. Sweden
4. Australia
5. Netherlands
6. Belgium
7. United States
8. Canada
9. Japan
10. Switzerland
11. Denmark
12. Ireland
13. United Kingdom
14. Finland
15. Luxembourg
16. Austria
17. France
18. Germany
19. Spain
20. New Zealand
21. Italy
22. Israel
23. Portugal
24. Greece
25. Cyprus

"Least Livable" Countries, 2003

1. Sierra Leone
2. Niger
3. Burkina Faso
4. Mali
5. Burundi
6. Mozambique
7. Ethiopia
8. Central African Republic
9. Congo, Dem. Rep. of the
10. Guinea-Bissau
11. Chad
12. Angola
13. Zambia
14. Malawi
15. Côte d'Ivoire
16. Tanzania
17. Benin
18. Rwanda
19. Guinea
20. Senegal
21. Eritrea
22. Mauritania
23. Djibouti
24. Nigeria
25. Gambia

Source: Human Development Report, 2003, United Nations. Web: www.undp.org/hdr2003.

The 2002 Transparency International Corruption Perceptions Index

According to the annual survey by the Berlin-based organization Transparency International, the world's least corrupt country is Finland and its most corrupt is Bangladesh. The index defines corruption as the abuse of public office for private gain, and measures the degree to which corruption is perceived to exist among a country's public officials and politicians. It is a composite index, drawing on 15 surveys from 9 independent institutions, which gathered the opinions of business people and country analysts. Because of the absence of reliable data, only 102 of the world's countries are included in the survey. The scores range from 10 (squeaky clean) to zero (highly corrupt). A score of 5.5 is the number Transparency International considers the borderline figure distinguishing countries that do and do not have a serious corruption problem.

Country rank	Country	2002 CPI Score
1.	Finland	9.7
2.	Denmark	9.5
	New Zealand	9.5
4.	Iceland	9.4
5.	Singapore	9.3
	Sweden	9.3
7.	Canada	9.0
	Luxembourg	9.0
	Netherlands	9.0
10.	United Kingdom	8.7
11.	Australia	8.6
12.	Norway	8.5
	Switzerland	8.5
14.	Hong Kong	8.2
15.	Austria	7.8
16.	United States	7.7
17.	Chile	7.5
18.	Germany	7.3
	Israel	7.3
20.	Belgium	7.1
	Japan	7.1
	Spain	7.1
23.	Ireland	6.9
24.	Botswana	6.4
25.	France	6.3
	Portugal	6.3
27.	Slovenia	6.0
28.	Namibia	5.7
29.	Estonia	5.6
	Taiwan	5.6
31.	Italy	5.2
32.	Uruguay	5.1
33.	Hungary	4.9
	Malaysia	4.9
	Trinidad & Tobago	4.9
36.	Belarus	4.8
	Lithuania	4.8
	South Africa	4.8
	Tunisia	4.8
40.	Costa Rica	4.5
	Jordan	4.5
	Mauritius	4.5
	South Korea	4.5
44.	Greece	4.2
45.	Brazil	4.0
	Bulgaria	4.0
	Jamaica	4.0
	Peru	4.0
	Poland	4.0
50.	Ghana	3.9
51.	Croatia	3.8
52.	Czech Republic	3.7
	Latvia	3.7
	Morocco	3.7
	Slovak Republic	3.7
	Sri Lanka	3.7
57.	Colombia	3.6
	Mexico	3.6
59.	China	3.5
	Dominican Rep.	3.5
	Ethiopia	3.5
62.	Egypt	3.4
	El Salvador	3.4
64.	Thailand	3.2
	Turkey	3.2
66.	Senegal	3.1
67.	Panama	3.0
68.	Malawi	2.9
	Uzbekistan	2.9
70.	Argentina	2.8
71.	Côte d'Ivoire	2.7
	Honduras	2.7
	India	2.7
	Russia	2.7
	Tanzania	2.7
	Zimbabwe	2.7
77.	Pakistan	2.6
	Philippines	2.6
	Romania	2.6
	Zambia	2.6
81.	Albania	2.5
	Guatemala	2.5
	Nicaragua	2.5
	Venezuela	2.5
85.	Georgia	2.4
	Ukraine	2.4
	Vietnam	2.4
88.	Kazakhstan	2.3
89.	Bolivia	2.2
	Cameroon	2.2
	Ecuador	2.2
	Haiti	2.2
93.	Moldova	2.1
	Uganda	2.1
95.	Azerbaijan	2.0
96.	Indonesia	1.9
	Kenya	1.9
98.	Angola	1.7
	Madagascar	1.7
	Paraguay	1.7
101.	Nigeria	1.6
102.	Bangladesh[1]	1.2

1. The Bangladesh score was based on only three available independent survey sources, which varied greatly. Transparency International stresses that these results need to be viewed with caution. *Source:* Transparency International, 2002. Web: www.transparency.org.

Country Statistics at a Glance

Country rankings of the type presented below cannot pretend to be definitive; instead they aspire only to provide the reader with an approximation of the high and low ends on a particular scale. Country data vary enormously depending on the sources, and the absence of reliable data on some countries requires their omission, which further skews the results.

LARGEST COUNTRIES[1] (in sq mi)*: 2002

1.	Russia	6,592,735
2.	Canada	3,851,788
3.	United States	3,717,792
4.	China	3,705,386
5.	Brazil	3,286,470
6.	Australia	2,967,893
7.	India	1,269,338
8.	Argentina	1,068,296
9.	Kazakhstan	1,049,150
10.	Sudan	967,493

SMALLEST COUNTRIES[1] (in sq mi)*: 2002

1.	Vatican City	0.2
2.	Monaco	0.8
3.	Nauru	8.1
4.	Tuvalu	10.0
5.	San Marino	23.6
6.	Liechtenstein	62.0
7.	Marshall Islands	70.0
8.	St. Kitts & Nevis	101.0
9.	Maldives	116.0
10.	Malta	122.0

HIGHEST POPULATION DENSITY[2] (per sq mi): 2002

1.	Monaco	42,675
2.	Singapore	17,232
3.	Vatican City	5,298
4.	Malta	3,282
5.	Maldives	2,846
6.	Bahrain	2,599
7.	Bangladesh	2,490
8.	Barbados	1,666
9.	Taiwan	1,627
10.	Nauru	1,550

LOWEST POPULATION DENSITY[2] (per sq mi): 2002

1.	Western Sahara	2.5
2.	Mongolia	4.5
3.	Namibia	6.0
4.	Australia	6.6
5.	Botswana	6.8
6.	Suriname	6.9
7.	Iceland	7.1
8.	Mauritania	7.3
9.	Libya	8.1
10.	Canada	8.4

HIGHEST GDP PER CAPITA[3] (PPP in U.S. dollars): 2001

1.	Luxembourg	$44,000
2.	United States	36,300
3.	San Marino	34,600
4.	Norway	31,800
5.	Switzerland	31,700
6.	Canada	29,400
7.	Belgium	29,000
	Denmark	29,000
9.	Ireland	28,500
10.	Japan	28,000

LOWEST GDP PER CAPITA[3] (PPP in U.S. dollars): 2001

1.	East Timor	$500
	Sierra Leone	500
3.	Somalia	550
4.	Congo, Dem. Rep. of	590
5.	Burundi	600
6.	Tanzania	610
7.	Malawi	660
8.	Ethiopia	700
9.	Comoros	710
10.	Eritrea	740

HIGHEST INFLATION[3]: 2001

1.	Congo Dem. Rep. of	358.0%
2.	Angola	110.0
3.	Somalia	+100.0
4.	Zimbabwe	100.0
5.	Iraq	60.0
6.	Suriname	59.0
7.	Belarus	46.1
8.	Turkey	45.2
9.	Romania	34.5
10.	Tajikistan	33.0

LOWEST INFLATION[3]: 2001

1.	Nauru	−3.6%
2.	Japan	−0.9
3.	China	−0.8
4.	St. Vincent and the Grenadines	−0.4
5.	Vietnam	−0.3
6.	Syria	0.3
7.	Antigua and Barbuda	0.4
8.	Lebanon	0.5
	Switzerland	0.5
	Taiwan	0.5

HIGHEST INFANT MORTALITY RATE[2]: 2002 (deaths per 1,000 births)

1.	Mozambique	199.0
2.	Angola	193.8
3.	Sierra Leone	146.9
4.	Afghanistan	142.5
5.	Liberia	132.2
6.	Niger	123.6
7.	Somalia	120.3
8.	Mali	119.2
9.	Tajikistan	113.4
10.	Guinea-Bissau	110.3

LOWEST INFANT MORTALITY RATE[2]: 2002 (deaths per 1,000 births)

1.	Japan	3.3
2.	Sweden	3.4
3.	Iceland	3.5
4.	Singapore	3.6
5.	Finland	3.7
6.	Norway	3.9
7.	Andorra	4.1
8.	Germany	4.2
9.	Austria	4.3
	Netherlands	4.3

HIGHEST LIFE EXPECTANCY[2] (in years): 2002

1.	Andorra	83.5
2.	San Marino	81.4
3.	Japan	80.9
4.	Singapore	80.4
5.	Australia	80.1
6.	Sweden	80.0
	Switzerland	80.0
8.	Canada	79.8
	Iceland	79.8
10.	Italy	79.4

LOWEST LIFE EXPECTANCY[2] (in years): 2002

1.	Mozambique	31.3
2.	Botswana	32.3
3.	Zambia	35.2
4.	Lesotho	36.9
5.	Angola	37.0
6.	Malawi	38.0
7.	Zimbabwe	39.0
8.	Rwanda	39.3
9.	Swaziland	39.5
10.	Ethiopia	41.2

NOTE: Only countries for which statistics were available in sources 1, 2, or 3 figure in these lists. *Size refers to the total area of a country, which includes the land area plus bodies of water. *Sources:* 1. Information Please Database. 2. U.S. Census Bureau, International Database. 3. *The World Factbook, 2002.*

A Profile of the World

Source: The World Factbook, 2002.

Geography

Total area: 510.072 million sq km (316.96 million sq mi). **Land area:** 148.94 million sq km (92.55 million sq mi). **Water area:** 361.132 million sq km (224.41 million sq mi). **Coastline:** 356,000 km (221,208 mi). **Note:** 70.8% of the world is water, 29.2% is land.

Terrain: Highest elevation is Mt. Everest at 8,850 m (29,035 ft) and lowest land depression is the Dead Sea at –411 m (–1,349 ft) below sea level. The greatest ocean depth is the Mariana Trench at 10,924 m (35,840 ft) in the Pacific Ocean.

Land use: *Arable land:* 10%. *Permanent crops:* 1%. *Meadows and pastures:* 26%. *Forests and woodlands:* 32%. *Other:* 31% (1993 est.). *Irrigated land:* 2,481,250 sq km (1,541,849 sq mi).

People

Population: 6,314,869,159 (Sept. 1, 2003, est. from U.S. Census Bureau)

Growth rate: 1.23% (2002 est.)

Birth rate: 21 births/1,000 population (2002 est.)

Death rate: 9 deaths/1,000 population (2002 est.)

Sex ratio (at birth): 1.05 male(s)/female (2002 est.)

Infant mortality rate: 51 deaths/1,000 live births (2002 est.)

Life expectancy at birth: *Total population:* 64 years. *Male:* 62 years. *Female:* 65 years (2002 est.).

Total fertility rate: 2.7 children born/woman (2002 est.)

Literacy: Age 15 and over who can read and write (1995 est.) *Combined:* 77%. *Male:* 83%. *Female:* 71%.

Government and Economy

Political divisions: 193 sovereign nations, 61 dependent areas, and 6 disputed territories.

Economy: Growth in global output (gross world product, GWP) fell from 4.8% in 2000 to 2.2% in 2001. The causes: slowdowns in the U.S. economy (21% of GWP) and in the 15 EU economies (20% of GWP); continued stagnation in the Japanese economy (7.3% of GWP); and spillover effects in the less developed regions of the world. China, the second largest economy in the world (12% of GWP), proved an exception, continuing its rapid annual growth, officially announced as 7.3% but estimated by many observers as perhaps two percentage points lower. Russia (2.6% of GWP), with 5.2% growth, continued to make uneven progress, its GDP per capita still only one-third that of the leading industrial nations.

GWP: (gross world product/purchasing power parity)—$47 trillion (2001 est.)

GWP—real growth rate: 2.2% (2001 est.)

GWP/PPP—per capita: $7,600 (2001 est.)

GWP composition: agriculture 4%, industry 32%, services 64% (2001 est.)

Inflation rate (consumer price index): developed countries 1% to 4% typically; developing countries 5% to 60% typically (2001 est.).

Unemployment rate: 30% combined unemployment and underemployment in many non-industrialized countries; developed countries typically 4%–12% unemployment (2001 est.)

Exports: $6.3 trillion (f.o.b., 2001 est.)

Imports: $6.3 trillion (c.i.f., 2001 est.)

External debt: $2 trillion for less developed nations (2001 est.)

Military expenditures: roughly 2% of GWP (1999 est.)

Territories, Colonies, and Dependencies

Source: The World Factbook, 2002

The following is a list of dependencies—territories under the jurisdiction of another country.

Under Australian Jurisdiction (6)
Ashmore and Cartier Islands
Christmas Island
Cocos (Keeling) Islands
Coral Sea Islands
Heard Island and McDonald Islands
Norfolk Island

Under Danish Jurisdiction (2)
Faeroe Islands
Greenland

Under Dutch Jurisdiction (2)
Aruba
Netherlands Antilles

Under French Jurisdiction (16)
Bassas da India
Clipperton Island
Europa Island
French Guiana
French Polynesia
French Southern and Antarctic Lands
Glorioso Islands
Guadeloupe
Juan de Nova Island
Martinique
Mayotte
New Caledonia
Réunion
Saint Pierre and Miquelon
Tromelin Island
Wallis and Futuna

Under New Zealand Jurisdiction (3)
Cook Islands
Niue
Tokelau

Under Norwegian Jurisdiction (3)
Bouvet Island
Jan Mayen
Svalbard

Under UK Jurisdiction (15)
Anguilla
Bermuda
British Indian Ocean Territory
British Virgin Islands
Cayman Islands
Falkland Islands
Gibraltar
Guernsey
Jersey
Isle of Man
Montserrat
Pitcairn Islands
Saint Helena
South Georgia and the South Sandwich Islands
Turks and Caicos Islands

Under U.S. Jurisdiction (15)
American Samoa
Baker Island
Guam
Howland Island
Iraq
Jarvis Island
Johnston Atoll
Kingman Reef
Midway Islands
Navassa Island
Northern Mariana Islands
Palmyra Atoll
Puerto Rico
Virgin Islands
Wake Island

Disputed Territories (6): Antarctica, Gaza Strip, Paracel Islands, Spratly Islands, West Bank, Western Sahara

Total Population of the World by Decade, 1950–2040

(historical and projected)

Year	Total world population (mid-year figures)	Ten-year growth rate (%)	Year	Total world population (mid-year figures)	Ten-year growth rate (%)
1950	2,556,000,053	18.9%	2000	6,082,966,429	12.6%
1960	3,039,451,023	22.0	2010[1]	6,848,932,929	10.7
1970	3,706,618,163	20.2	2020[1]	7,584,821,144	8.7
1980	4,453,831,714	18.5	2030[1]	8,246,619,341	7.3
1990	5,278,639,789	15.2	2040[1]	8,850,045,889	5.6

1. Projected. *Source:* U.S. Census Bureau, International Database.

World's 50 Most Populous Countries: 2003

Rank	Country	Population	Rank	Country	Population	Rank	Country	Population
1.	China	1,286,975,468	19.	Thailand	64,265,276	35.	Canada	32,207,113
2.	India	1,049,700,118	20.	France	60,180,529	36.	Morocco	31,689,265
3.	United States	290,342,554	21.	United Kingdom	60,094,648	37.	Kenya	31,639,091
4.	Indonesia	234,893,453	22.	Italy	57,998,353	38.	Afghanistan	28,717,213
5.	Brazil	182,032,604	23.	Congo, Dem. Rep. of	56,625,039	39.	Peru	28,409,897
6.	Pakistan	150,694,740	24.	Korea, South	48,289,037	40.	Nepal	26,469,569
7.	Russia	144,526,278	25.	Ukraine	48,055,439	41.	Uzbekistan	25,981,647
8.	Bangladesh	138,448,210	26.	South Africa	42,768,678	42.	Uganda	25,632,794
9.	Nigeria	133,881,703	27.	Burma (Myanmar)	42,510,537	43.	Iraq	24,683,313
10.	Japan	127,214,499	28.	Colombia	41,662,073	44.	Venezuela	24,654,694
11.	Mexico	104,907,991	29.	Spain	40,217,413	45.	Saudi Arabia	24,293,844
12.	Philippines	84,619,974	30.	Argentina	38,740,807	46.	Malaysia	23,092,940
13.	Germany	82,398,326	31.	Poland	38,622,660	47.	Taiwan	22,603,000
14.	Vietnam	81,624,716	32.	Sudan	38,114,160	48.	Korea, North	22,466,481
15.	Egypt	74,718,797	33.	Tanzania	35,922,454	49.	Romania	22,271,839
16.	Iran	68,278,826	34.	Algeria	32,818,500	50.	Ghana	20,467,747
17.	Turkey	68,109,469						
18.	Ethiopia	66,557,553						

Source: U.S. Census Bureau, International Database.

Most Populous Cities of the World: 2003

Rank	City[1]	Population	Rank	City[1]	Population
1.	Mumbai (Bombay), India	12,383,100	11.	Jakarta, Indonesia	8,827,900
2.	Buenos Aires, Argentina	12,116,400	12.	Mexico City, Mexico	8,681,400
3.	Karachi, Pakistan	10,537,200	13.	Moscow, Russia	8,368,200
4.	Manila, Philippines	10,232,900	14.	Lagos, Nigeria	8,349,700
5.	Delhi, India	10,203,700	15.	Tokyo, Japan	8,240,100
6.	Sao Paulo, Brazil	10,195,000	16.	Lima, Peru	8,113,000
7.	Seoul, South Korea	9,630,600	17.	New York City, U.S.	8,084,316
8.	Istanbul, Turkey	9,419,000	18.	Cairo, Egypt	7,937,700
9.	Shanghai, China	9,005,600	19.	Teheran, Iran	7,893,700
10.	Dhaka, Bangladesh	8,942,300	20.	London, United Kingdom	7,417,700

1. Refers to the city proper, as opposed to an urban agglomeration, which would also count the surrounding urban areas in the total. *Source:* © Stefan Helders, World Gazetteer, 2003. Reprinted with permission. Web: www.world-gazetteer.com, U.S. Census Bureau.

Most Populous Urban Agglomerations[1]: 2003

Name	Country	Est. population (in millions)	Name	Country	Est. population (in millions)
1. Tokyo	Japan	31.1	11. Cairo	Egypt	15.9
2. Mexico City	Mexico	21.2	12. Calcutta	India	14.1
3. New York	USA	21.2	13. Manila	Philippines	13.8
4. Seoul	South Korea	20.0	14. Buenos Aires	Argentina	13.1
5. São Paulo	Brazil	18.8	15. Shanghai	China	12.0
6. Jakarta	Indonesia	17.9	16. Moscow	Russia	12.0
7. Osaka–Kobe–Kyoto	Japan	17.6	17. Rio de Janeiro	Brazil	11.4
8. Delhi	India	17.0	16. Paris	France	11.3
9. Mumbai (Bombay)	India	17.0	19. Rhein–Ruhr	Germany	11.3
10. Los Angeles	USA	16.4	20. Teheran	Iran	11.2

NOTE: The definitions of agglomerations vary significantly from city to city, hence the difficulty of compiling an accurate, comparative list of the world's most populous urban areas. 1. Includes metropolitan areas and surrounding urban agglomerations. Agglomerations include a central city and bordering urban areas. Some agglomerations have more than one central city (e.g., Washington, DC, includes Baltimore; Tokyo includes Yokohama and Kawasaki; New York includes Newark and Paterson, N.J.). *Sources:* ©Stefan Helders, *World Gazetteer, 2003.* Reprinted with permission. Web: www.world-gazetteer.com, U.S. Census Bureau.

Area and Population of Countries

(mid-2003 estimates)

Country	Area (in sq km)	Population
Afghanistan	647,500	28,717,213
Albania	28,748	3,582,205
Algeria	2,381,740	32,818,500
Andorra	468	69,150
Angola	1,246,700	10,766,471
Antigua and Barbuda	443	67,897
Argentina	2,766,890	38,740,807
Armenia	29,800	3,326,448
Australia	7,686,850	19,731,984
Austria	83,858	8,188,207
Azerbaijan	86,600	7,830,764
Bahamas, The	13,940	297,477
Bahrain	665	667,238
Bangladesh	144,000	138,448,210
Barbados	431	277,264
Belarus	207,600	10,322,151
Belgium	30,510	10,289,088
Belize	22,966	266,440
Benin	112,620	7,041,490
Bhutan	47,000	2,139,549
Bolivia	1,098,580	8,586,443
Bosnia and Herzegovina	51,129	3,989,018
Botswana	600,370	1,573,267
Brazil	8,511,965	182,032,604
Brunei	5,770	358,098
Bulgaria	110,910	7,537,929
Burkina Faso	274,200	13,228,460
Burundi	27,830	6,096,156
Cambodia	181,040	13,124,764
Cameroon	475,440	15,746,179
Canada	9,976,140	32,207,113
Cape Verde	4,033	412,137
Central African Republic	622,984	3,683,538
Chad	1,284,000	9,253,493
Chile	756,950	15,665,216
China	9,596,960	1,286,975,468
Colombia	1,138,910	41,662,073
Comoros	2,170	632,948
Congo, Democratic Republic of the (formerly Zaire)	342,000	2,954,258
Congo, Republic of the	2,345,410	56,625,039
Costa Rica	51,100	3,896,092
Côte d'Ivoire	322,460	16,962,491
Croatia	56,542	4,422,248
Cuba	110,860	11,263,429
Cyprus	9,250	771,657
Czech Republic	78,866	10,249,216
Denmark	43,094	5,384,384
Djibouti	23,000	457,130
Dominica	754	69,655
Dominican Republic	48,730	8,715,602
East Timor	15,057	997,853
Ecuador	283,560	13,710,234
Egypt	1,001,450	74,718,797
El Salvador	21,040	6,470,379
Equatorial Guinea	28,051	510,473
Eritrea	121,320	4,362,254
Estonia	45,226	1,408,556
Ethiopia	1,127,127	66,557,553
Fiji	18,270	868,531
Finland	337,030	5,190,785
France	547,030	60,180,529
Gabon	267,667	1,321,560
Gambia, The	11,300	1,501,050
Georgia	69,700	4,934,413
Germany	357,021	82,398,326
Ghana	239,460	20,467,747
Greece	131,940	10,665,989

Country	Area (in sq km)	Population
Grenada	344	89,258
Guatemala	108,890	13,909,384
Guinea	245,857	9,030,220
Guinea-Bissau	36,120	1,360,827
Guyana	214,970	702,100
Haiti	27,750	7,527,817
Honduras	112,090	6,669,789
Hungary	93,030	10,045,407
Iceland	103,000	280,798
India	3,287,590	1,049,700,118
Indonesia	1,919,440	234,893,453
Iran	1,648,000	68,278,826
Iraq	437,072	24,683,313
Ireland	70,280	3,924,140
Israel	20,770	6,116,533
Italy	301,230	57,998,353
Jamaica	10,991	2,695,867
Japan	377,835	127,214,499
Jordan	92,300	5,460,265
Kazakhstan	2,717,300	16,763,795
Kenya	582,650	31,639,091
Kiribati	811	98,549
Korea, North	120,540	22,466,481
Korea, South	98,480	48,289,037
Kuwait	17,820	2,183,161
Kyrgyzstan	198,500	4,892,808
Laos	236,800	5,921,545
Latvia	64,589	2,348,784
Lebanon	10,400	3,727,703
Lesotho	30,355	1,861,959
Liberia	111,370	3,317,176
Libya	1,759,540	5,499,074
Liechtenstein	160	33,145
Lithuania	65,200	3,592,561
Luxembourg	2,586	454,157
Macedonia	25,713	2,063,122
Madagascar	587,040	16,979,744
Malawi	118,480	11,651,239
Malaysia	329,750	23,092,940
Maldives	300	329,684
Mali	1,240,000	11,626,219
Malta	316	400,420
Marshall Islands	181.3	56,429
Mauritania	1,030,700	2,912,584
Mauritius	2,040	1,210,447
Mexico	1,972,550	104,907,991
Micronesia, Federated States of	702	136,973
Moldova	33,843	4,439,502
Monaco	1.95	32,130
Mongolia	1,565,000	2,712,315
Morocco	446,550	31,689,265
Mozambique	801,590	17,479,266
Myanmar (Burma)	678,500	42,510,537
Namibia	825,418	1,927,447
Nauru	21	12,570
Nepal	140,800	26,469,569
Netherlands	41,526	16,150,511
New Zealand	268,680	3,951,307
Nicaragua	129,494	5,128,517
Niger	1,267,000	11,058,590
Nigeria	923,768	133,881,703
Norway	324,220	4,546,123
Oman	212,460	2,807,125
Pakistan	803,940	150,694,740
Palau	458	19,717
Panama	78,200	2,960,784
Papua New Guinea	462,840	5,295,816

Country	Area (in sq km)	Population
Paraguay	406,750	6,036,900
Peru	1,285,220	28,409,897
Philippines	300,000	84,619,974
Poland	312,685	38,622,660
Portugal	92,391	10,102,022
Qatar	11,437	817,052
Romania	237,500	22,271,839
Russia	17,075,200	144,526,278
Rwanda	26,338	7,810,056
Saint Kitts and Nevis	261	38,763
Saint Lucia	616	162,157
Saint Vincent and the Grenadines	389	116,812
Samoa	2,944	178,173
San Marino	61	28,119
São Tomé and Príncipe	1,001	175,883
Saudi Arabia	1,960,582	24,293,844
Senegal	196,190	10,580,307
Seychelles	455	80,469
Sierra Leone	71,740	5,732,681
Singapore	693	4,608,595
Slovakia	48,845	5,430,033
Slovenia	20,273	1,935,677
Solomon Islands	28,450	509,190
Somalia	637,657	8,025,190
South Africa	1,219,912	42,768,678
Spain	504,782	40,217,413
Sri Lanka	65,610	19,742,439
Sudan	2,505,810	38,114,160
Suriname	163,270	435,449
Swaziland	17,363	1,161,219
Sweden	449,964	8,878,085
Switzerland	41,290	7,318,638
Syria	185,180	17,585,540
Taiwan	35,980	22,603,000
Tajikistan	143,100	6,863,752
Tanzania	945,087	35,922,454
Thailand	514,000	64,265,276
Togo	56,785	5,429,299
Tonga	748	108,141
Trinidad and Tobago	5,128	1,104,209
Tunisia	163,610	9,924,742
Turkey	780,580	68,109,469
Turkmenistan	488,100	4,775,544
Tuvalu	26	11,305
Uganda	236,040	25,632,794
Ukraine	603,700	48,055,439
United Arab Emirates	82,880	2,484,818
United Kingdom	244,820	60,094,648
United States	9,629,091	290,342,554
Uruguay	176,220	3,413,329
Uzbekistan	447,400	25,981,647
Vanuatu	12,200	199,414
Vatican City	0.44	900
Venezuela	912,050	24,654,694
Vietnam	329,560	81,624,716
Western Sahara	266,000	261,794
Yemen	527,970	19,349,881
Yugoslavia	102,350	10,655,774
Zambia	752,614	10,307,333
Zimbabwe	390,580	12,576,742

Source: U.S. Census Bureau, International Database and *The World Factbook, 2002.*

The Death Penalty Worldwide

According to Amnesty International, during 2002 more than 1,526 people were executed in 31 countries, and more than 3,248 people were sentenced to death in 67 countries. For U.S. figures, *see* p. 385.

Death Penalty Outlawed (year)[1]

Andorra (1990)
Angola (1992)
Australia (1984)
Austria (1950)
Azerbaijan (1998)
Belgium (1996)
Bermuda (1999)
Bulgaria (1998)
Cambodia (1989)
Canada (1976)
Cape Verde (1981)
Colombia (1910)
Costa Rica (1877)
Côte d'Ivoire (2000)
Croatia (1990)
Cyprus (1983)
Czech Republic (1990)
Denmark (1933)
Djibouti (1995)
Dominican Republic (1966)
East Timor (1999)
Ecuador (1906)
Estonia (1998)
Finland (1949)
France (1981)
Georgia (1997)
Germany (1987)
Guinea-Bissau (1993)
Haiti (1987)
Honduras (1956)
Hungary (1990)
Iceland (1928)
Ireland (1990)
Italy (1947)
Kiribati (1979)
Liechtenstein (1987)
Lithuania (1998)
Luxembourg (1979)
Macedonia (n.a.)
Malta (1971)
Marshall Islands (1986)
Mauritius (1995)
Micronesia (1986)
Moldova (1995)
Monaco (1962)
Mozambique (1990)
Namibia (1990)
Nepal (1990)
Netherlands (1870)
New Zealand (1961)
Nicaragua (1979)
Norway (1905)
Palau (n.a.)
Panama (1903)
Paraguay (1992)
Poland (1997)
Portugal (1867)
Romania (1989)
San Marino (1848)
São Tomé and Príncipe (1990)
Serbia and Montenegro (2002)
Seychelles (1993)
Slovak Republic (1990)
Slovenia (1989)
Solomon Islands (1966)
South Africa (1995)
Spain (1978)
Sweden (1921)
Switzerland (1942)
Turkmenistan (1999)
Tuvalu (1978)
Ukraine (1999)
United Kingdom (1973)
Uruguay (1907)
Vanuatu (1980)
Vatican City State (1969)
Venezuela (1863)
Yugoslavia (2002)

Death Penalty Permitted in Exceptional Cases[2]

Albania (2000)
Argentina (1984)
Bolivia (1997)
Bosnia-Herzegovina (n.a.)
Brazil (1979)
Chile (2001)
Cook Islands (n.a.)
El Salvador (1983)
Fiji (1979)
Greece (1993)
Israel (1954)
Latvia (1999)
Mexico (n.a.)
Peru (1979)
Turkey (2002)

De Facto Ban on Death Penalty[3] (year)[4]

Bhutan (1964)
Brunei Darussalam (1957)
Burkina Faso (1988)
Central African Republic (1981)
Congo (Republic) (1982)
Gambia (1981)
Grenada (1978)
Madagascar (1958)
Maldives (1952)
Mali (1980)
Nauru (1968)
Niger (1976)
Papua New Guinea (1950)
Russian Federation (1996)
Samoa (1962)
Senegal (1967)
Sri Lanka (1976)
Suriname (1982)
Togo (n.a.)
Tonga (1982)

Death Penalty Permitted

Afghanistan
Algeria
Antigua and Barbuda
Armenia
Bahamas
Bahrain
Bangladesh
Barbados
Belarus
Belize
Benin
Botswana
Burundi
Cameroon
Chad
China (People's Republic)
Comoros
Congo (Democratic Republic)
Cuba
Dominica
Egypt
Equatorial Guinea
Eritrea
Ethiopia
Gabon
Ghana
Guatemala
Guinea
Guyana
India

Indonesia
Iran
Iraq
Jamaica
Japan
Jordan
Kazakhstan
Kenya
Korea, North
Korea, South
Kuwait
Kyrgyzstan
Laos
Lebanon
Lesotho
Liberia
Libya
Malawi
Malaysia
Mauritania
Mongolia
Morocco
Myanmar
Nigeria
Oman
Pakistan
Palestinian Authority
Philippines
Qatar
Rwanda
St. Kitts and Nevis
St. Lucia
St. Vincent and the Grenadines
Saudi Arabia
Sierra Leone
Singapore
Somalia
Sudan
Swaziland
Syria
Taiwan
Tajikistan
Tanzania
Thailand
Trinidad and Tobago
Tunisia
Uganda
United Arab Emirates
United States of America
Uzbekistan
Vietnam
Yemen
Zambia
Zimbabwe

NOTE: n.a. = date not available. 1. Year death penalty abolished for most, though not necessarily all crimes. 2. Exceptional crimes include some committed under military law or crimes committed in wartime. 3. Death penalty is sanctioned by law but has not been the practice for ten or more years (year of last execution). 4. Date of death penalty abolition for ordinary crimes. *Source:* Amnesty International, Jan. 2003.

Infant Mortality and Life Expectancy for Selected Countries, 2003

Country	Infant mortality[1]	Life expectancy[2]	Country	Infant mortality[1]	Life expectancy[2]	Country	Infant mortality[1]	Life expectancy[2]
Albania	37.3	72.4	Germany	4.2	78.4	Pakistan	76.5	62.2
Angola	193.8	37.0	Greece	6.1	78.9	Panama	21.4	72.3
Australia	4.8	80.1	Guatemala	37.9	65.2	Peru	37.0	70.9
Austria	4.3	78.2	Hungary	8.6	72.2	Poland	8.9	73.9
Bangladesh	66.1	61.3	India	59.6	63.6	Portugal	5.7	76.3
Brazil	31.7	71.1	Iran	44.2	69.3	Russia	19.5	67.7
Canada	4.9	79.8	Ireland	5.3	77.3	Slovakia	8.6	74.4
Chile	8.9	76.3	Israel	7.4	79.0	South Africa	60.8	46.6
China	25.3	72.2	Italy	6.2	79.4	Spain	4.5	79.2
Costa Rica	10.6	76.4	Japan	3.3	80.9	Sri Lanka	15.2	72.6
Cyprus	7.5	77.3	Kenya	63.4	45.2	Sweden	3.4	80.0
Czech Republic	5.4	75.2	Korea, South	7.3	75.4	Switzerland	4.4	80.0
Denmark	4.9	77.1	Mexico	23.7	72.3	Syria	31.7	69.4
Ecuador	32.0	71.9	Mozambique	199.0	31.3	United Kingdom	5.3	78.2
Egypt	35.3	70.4	New Zealand	6.1	78.3	United States	6.8	77.1
Finland	3.7	77.9	Nigeria	71.3	51.0	Venezuela	23.8	73.8
France	4.4	79.3	Norway	3.9	79.1	Zimbabwe	66.5	39.0

1. Infant deaths per 1,000 live births. 2. Life expectancy at birth, in years, both sexes. *Source:* U.S. Census Bureau, International Database.

Crude Birth and Death Rates for Selected Countries
(per 1,000 population)

Country	Birth rate							Death rate						
	2003	2002	2001	1990	1985	1980	1975	2003	2002	2001	1990	1985	1980	1975
Australia	12.6	12.71	12.86	15.4	15.7	15.3	16.9	7.3	7.25	7.18	7.0	7.5	7.4	7.9
Austria	9.4	9.58	9.74	11.6	11.6	12.0	12.5	9.7	9.73	9.80	10.6	11.9	12.2	12.8
Belgium	10.4	10.58	10.74	12.6	11.5	12.7	12.2	10.1	10.08	10.10	10.6	11.2	11.6	12.2
Czech Republic[1]	9.0	9.08	9.11	13.4	14.5	16.4	19.6	10.7	10.76	10.81	11.7	11.8	12.1	11.5
France	12.5	11.94	12.10	13.5	13.9	14.8	14.1	9.1	9.04	9.09	9.3	10.1	10.2	10.6
Germany[2]	8.6	8.99	9.16	11.4	9.6	10.0	9.7	10.3	10.36	10.42	11.2	11.5	11.6	12.1
Greece	9.8	9.82	9.83	10.2	11.7	15.4	15.7	9.9	9.79	9.73	9.3	9.4	9.1	8.9
Ireland	14.6	14.62	14.57	15.1	17.6	21.9	21.5	7.9	8.01	8.07	9.1	9.4	9.7	10.6
Israel	18.7	18.91	19.12	22.2	23.5	24.1	28.2	6.2	6.21	6.22	6.2	6.6	6.7	7.1
Italy	9.2	8.93	9.05	9.8	10.1	11.2	14.8	10.1	10.13	10.07	9.4	9.5	9.7	9.9
Japan	9.6	10.03	10.04	9.9	11.9	13.7	17.2	8.6	8.53	8.34	6.7	6.2	6.2	6.4
Mauritius	16.1	16.34	16.50	21.0	18.8	27.0	25.1	6.8	6.81	6.82	6.5	6.8	7.2	8.1
Netherlands	11.3	11.58	11.85	13.3	12.3	12.8	13.0	8.7	8.67	8.69	8.6	8.5	8.1	8.3
New Zealand	14.1	14.23	14.28	18.0	15.6	—	18.4	7.5	7.55	7.56	7.9	8.4	—	8.1
Norway	12.2	12.39	12.60	14.3	12.3	12.5	14.1	9.7	9.78	9.83	10.7	10.7	10.1	9.9
Panama	20.8	18.60	19.06	23.9	26.6	26.8	32.3	6.2	4.96	4.95	—	—	—	—
Poland	10.5	10.29	10.20	14.3	18.2	19.5	18.9	10.0	9.97	9.98	10.2	10.3	9.8	8.7
Portugal	11.4	11.50	11.51	11.8	12.8	16.4	19.1	10.2	10.21	10.21	10.4	9.6	9.9	10.4
Romania	10.8	10.81	10.80	13.6	15.8	—	—	12.2	12.27	12.28	10.6	10.9	—	—
Switzerland	9.6	9.84	10.12	12.5	11.6	11.3	12.3	8.8	8.79	8.77	9.5	9.2	9.2	8.7
Tunisia	16.5	16.83	17.11	25.8	31.3	35.2	36.6	5.0	5.00	4.99	—	—	—	—
United Kingdom	11.0	11.34	11.54	13.9	13.3	13.5	12.5	10.2	10.30	10.35	11.2	11.8	11.8	11.9
United States	14.1	14.10	14.20	16.7	15.7	16.2	14.0	8.4	8.70	8.70	8.6	8.7	8.9	8.9

1. Data prior to 1994 pertain to the former Czechoslovakia. 2. All data pertaining to Germany prior to 1990 are for West Germany. NOTE: (—) = not available. *Source:* United Nations, *Monthly Bulletin of Statistics, June 1997.* Data for 2001, 2002, 2003 from the U.S. Census Bureau, International Database.

Military Budgets of Selected Countries

(in billions of dollars)

Country	Military budget	Country	Military budget	Country	Military budget	Country	Military budget
United States	$399.1	Brazil[1]	$10.7	Singapore	$4.8	Vietnam	$2.4
Russia[1]	65.0	Taiwan[1]	10.7	Sweden	4.5	North Korea[1]	2.1
China[1]	47.0	Israel	10.6	Egypt[1]	4.4	Czech Republic	1.6
Japan	42.6	Spain	8.4	Norway	3.8	Philippines	1.4
United Kingdom	38.4	Australia	7.6	Greece	3.5	Portugal	1.3
France	29.5	Canada	7.6	Poland	3.5	Libya[1]	1.2
Germany	24.9	Netherlands	6.6	Argentina[1]	3.3	Hungary	1.1
Saudi Arabia	21.3	Turkey	5.8	Colombia[1]	2.9	Syria	1.0
Italy	19.4	Mexico	5.9	Belgium	2.7	Cuba[1]	0.8
India	15.6	Ukraine	5.0	Pakistan[1]	2.6	Sudan[1]	0.6
South Korea	14.1	Iran[1]	4.8	Denmark	2.4	Yugoslavia	0.7

NOTE: Figures are for latest year available, usually 2002. Expenditures are used in a few cases where official budges are significantly lower than actual spending. The figure for the United States is from the annual budget request for Fiscal Year 2004. 1. 2001 funding. *Sources:* Table prepared by Center for Defense Information. International Institute for Strategic Studies, Department of Defense.

Significant Armed Conflicts, 2003

Main warring parties	Year began[1]
Middle East	
Iran vs. Mujahideen Khalq Organization (MKO)	1979
Iraq vs. U.S. & UK	2003
Israel vs. Palestinian Authority/Hamas/Hezbollah/ Palestinian separatists	1948
Asia	
Afghanistan: U.S., UK, Northern Alliance, and Coalition Forces vs. al-Qaeda	2001
India vs. Kashmiri separatist groups/Pakistan	1948
India vs. Assam insurgents (various)	1979
Indonesia vs. Aceh separatists[2]	1976
Indonesia vs. Christians and Muslims in Molucca Islands	1977
Indonesia vs. Irian Jaya separatists	1969
Nepal vs. Maoist rebels	1995
Philippines vs. Mindanaoan separatists (MILF/ASG)	1971
Africa	
Algeria vs. Armed Islamic Group (GIA)	1991
Burundi: Tutsi vs. Hutu	1988
Democratic Republic of Congo and allies vs. Rwanda, Uganda, and indigenous rebels[3]	1997
Somalia vs. rival clans	1991
Sudan vs. Sudanese People's Liberation Army[3]	1983
Uganda vs. Lord's Resistance Army (LRA)	1986
Europe	
Russia vs. Chechen separatists	1994
Latin America	
Colombia vs. National Liberation Army (ELN)	1978
Colombia vs. Revolutionary Armed Forces of Colombia (FARC)	1978
Colombia vs. Autodefensas Unidas de Colombia (AUC)	1990

NOTE: As of Sept. 2003. 1. Where multiple parties and long-standing but sporadic conflict are concerned, date of first combat deaths is given. 2. 2002 ceasefire abandoned; fighting resumed in May 2003. 3. Ceasefire agreements signed in 2002, but violence continues. *Source:* Center for Defense Information, www.cdi.org and Project Ploughshares, www.ploughshares.ca.

Recently Suspended Armed Conflicts

Main warring parties	Year began–year ceasefire declared
Solomon Islands vs. Malaitan Eagle Force and Isatabu Freedom Movement	1998–2003
Liberia vs. LURD rebels	2000–2003
Côte d'Ivoire vs. rebels	2002–2003
Angola vs. UNITA	1975–2002
Sri Lanka vs. Tamil Eelan	1978–2002
Sierra Leone vs. RUF	1991–2002
Chad vs. Muslim separatists (MDJT)	1998–2002
Taliban vs. Northern Alliance	1995–2001
Indonesia vs. East Timor	1975–2000
Tajikistan vs. United Tajik Opposition (UTO)	1992–2000
Ethiopia vs. Eritrea	1998–2000
Fiji vs. insurgents	2000

Sources: Center for Defense Information, www.cdi.org, Project Ploughshares, www.ploughshares.ca, and news sources.

Countries with Nuclear Weapons Capability

Acknowledged: Britain, China, France, India, Pakistan, Russia, United States

Unacknowledged: Israel

Seeking: Iran, North Korea[1]

Abandoned: South Africa—Constructed but then voluntarily dismantled six uranium bombs. Belarus, Kazakhstan, Ukraine—When Soviet Union broke up, these former states possessed nuclear warheads that they have since given up.

1. In Dec. 2002, North Korea revealed that it had violated its 1994 agreement to freeze its nuclear weapons program and has been developing a nuclear bomb. On April 24, 2003, North Korea announced it possessed a nuclear bomb but this claim has not been verified. *Source:* U.S. State Department and *Time* magazine.

See also UN peacekeeping missions, p. 907.

Worldwide Refugees and Asylum Seekers, 2002

Country	Number
Sudan	4,500,000[1]
Afghanistan	4,200,000[1]
Palestinian State	3,275,000[1]
Colombia	2,600,000
Angola	2,500,000–4,000,000
Congo, Dem. Rep. of	2,400,000[1]
Iraq	1,395,000[1]
Burma	1,100,000–1,500,000
Indonesia	600,000–1,000,000[1]
Turkey	425,000–1,000,000[1]
Burundi	800,000[1]
Jordan	800,000
Uganda	625,000–725,000
Côte d'Ivoire	525,000–725,000[1]
Sri Lanka	718,000
Somalia	650,000[1]
India	640,000
Azerbaijan	581,000
Bosnia and Herzegovina	528,000
Russian Federation	430,000
Liberia	380,000–430,000
Eritrea	360,000
Yugoslavia	336,000[1]
Vietnam	302,000
Lebanon	300,000
Georgia	288,000
Croatia	268,000
Cyprus	265,000
Kenya	230,000
El Salvador	203,000
North Korea	200,000[1]
China	178,000
Syria	170,000[1]
Algeria	100,000–200,000[1]
Zimbabwe	100,000–200,000
Nepal	100,000–150,000
Sierra Leone	130,000
Guatemala	129,000
Bhutan	127,000
Congo, Rep. of	125,000[1]
Ethiopia	110,000
Western Sahara	110,000
Philippines	104,000
Nigeria	80,000
Bangladesh	67,000
Armenia	62,000
Rwanda	50,000

NOTE: Countries in which more than 50,000 civilians have fled to become refugees or asylum seekers or have been internally displaced. Estimates of the numbers of uprooted persons are often fragmentary. 1. Sources vary significantly. *Source: World Refugee Survey 2003,* U.S. Committee on Refugees.

Economic Statistics by Country, 2001

Country	GDP/PPP	GDP/PPP per capita	Real growth rate (%)	Inflation (%)
Afghanistan	21 billion[1]	$ 800	n.a.	n.a.
Albania	13.2 billion	3,800	7.3 %	3.0 %
Algeria	177 billion	5,600	3.8	3.0
Andorra	1.3 billion[1]	19,000	3.8	4.3
Angola	13.3 billion	1,330	5.4	110.0
Antigua and Barbuda	674 million[1]	10,000	3.5	0.4
Argentina	453 billion	12,000	–4.6	4.0
Armenia	11.2 billion	3,350	9.6	3.1[1]
Australia	465.9 billion	24,000	2.3	4.3
Austria	220 billion	27,000	1.2	2.6
Azerbaijan	24.3 billion	3,100	9.9	1.6
Bahamas	5 billion	16,800[1]	3.5	1.5
Bahrain	8.4 billion	13,000	4.0	1.5
Bangladesh	230 billion	1,750	5.6	5.8[1]
Barbados	4 billion	14,500	–2.0	3.5
Belarus	84.8 billion	8,200	4.1	46.1
Belgium	267.7 billion	26,100	1.1	2.4
Belize	830 million	3,250	3.0	1.7
Benin	6.8 billion	1,040	5.4	3.0
Bhutan	2.5 billion	1,200	6.0[1]	7.0[1]
Bolivia	21.4 billion	2,600	0.0	2.0
Bosnia and Herzegovina	7 billion	1,800	6.0	5.0
Botswana	12.4 billion	7,800	4.7	6.6
Brazil	1.34 trillion	7,400[1]	1.9	7.7
Brunei Darussalam	6.2 billion	18,000	3.0	1.0[2]
Bulgaria	48 billion	6,200	4.0	7.5
Burkina Faso	12.8 billion	1,040	4.7	3.5
Burundi	3.7 billion	600	1.4	14.0
Cambodia	18.7 billion	1,500	5.3	1.6[1]
Cameroon	26.4 billion	1,700	4.9	2.0[1]
Canada	875 billion	27,700	1.9	2.8
Cape Verde	600 million	1,500	3.0	3.0
Central African Rep.	4.6 billion	1,300	1.8	3.6
Chad	8.9 billion	1,030	8.0	3.0[1]
Chile	153 billion	10,000	3.1	3.5
China	5.56 trillion	$ 4,300	7.3 %	0.8
Colombia	255 billion	6,300	1.5	7.6%
Comoros	424 million	710	1.0	3.5
Congo, Dem. Rep. of	32 billion	590	–4.0	358.0
Congo, Rep. of	2.5 billion	900	4.2	3.0
Costa Rica	31.9 billion	8,500	0.3	12.1
Côte d'Ivoire	25.5 billion	1,550	–1.0	2.5[1]
Croatia	36.1 billion	8,300	4.0	5.0
Cuba	25.5 billion	2,300	3.0	0.5
Cyprus*	9.1 billion	15,000	2.6	1.9
	1.1 billion[1]	7,000	0.8[1]	53.2[1]
Czech Rep.	147.9 billion	14,400	3.4	4.7
Denmark	149.8 billion	28,000	1.1	2.4
Djibouti	586 million	1,400	0.0	2.0
Dominica	262 million	3,700	–3.2	1.0
Dominican Rep.	50 billion	5,800	1.5	5.0
East Timor	415 billion	500	18.0	n.a.
Ecuador	39.6 billion	3,000	4.3	22.0
Egypt	258 billion	3,700	2.5	2.3
El Salvador	28.4 billion	4,600	1.4	3.8
Equatorial Guinea	1.04 billion	2,100	6.0	6.0
Eritrea	3.2 billion	740	7.0	15.0
Estonia	14.3 billion	10,000	4.7	5.8
Ethiopia	46 billion	700	7.3	6.8
Fiji	4.4 billion	5,200	1.0	3.0[1]
Finland	133.5 billion	25,800	0.6	2.6
France	1.51 trillion	25,400	2.1	1.7
Gabon	6.7 billion	5,500	2.5	1.5
Gambia, The	2.5 billion	1,770	5.7	4.0
Georgia	15.5 billion	3,100	8.4	4.6
Germany	2.174 trillion	26,200	0.6	2.4
Ghana	39.4 billion	1,980	3.0	25.0
Greece	189.7 billion	17,900	3.7	3.4
Grenada	424 million	4,750	6.5	2.8
Guatemala	48.3 billion	3,700	2.3	7.6
Guinea	15 billion	1,970	3.3	6.0[1]
Guinea-Bissau	1.2 billion	900	7.2	5.0
Guyana	2.5 billion[1]	3,600	2.8	6.0

Country	GDP/PPP	GDP/PPP per capita	Real growth rate (%)	Inflation (%)
Haiti	12 billion	$ 1,700	–1.2%	14.0%
Honduras	17 billion	2,600	2.1	9.7
Hungary	120.9 billion	12,000	3.9	9.2
Iceland	6.85 billion[1]	24,800	4.3	3.5
India	2.5 trillion	2,500	5.0	3.5[1]
Indonesia	687 billion	3,000	3.3	11.5
Iran	426 billion	6,400	5.0	13.0
Iraq	59 billion	2,500	–5.7	60.0
Ireland	104.7 billion	27,300	5.6	4.9
Israel	119 billion	20,000	–0.6	1.1
Italy	1.402 trillion	24,300	1.8	2.7
Jamaica	9.8 billion	3,700	1.1	6.9
Japan	3.45 trillion	27,200	–0.3	–0.6
Jordan	21.6 billion	4,200	2.8	1.5
Kazakhstan	98.1 billion	5,900	12.2	8.5
Kenya	31 billion	1,000	1.0	3.3
Kiribati	79 million	840	1.5	2.5
Korea, North	21.8 billion	1,000	–3.0	n.a.
Korea, South	865 billion	18,000	3.3	4.3
Kuwait	30.9 billion	15,100	4.0	2.7
Kyrgyzstan	13.5 billion	2,800	5.0	7.0
Laos	9.2 billion	1,630	5.0	10.0
Latvia	18.6 billion	7,800	6.3	2.5
Lebanon	18.8 billion	5,200	1.0	0.5
Lesotho	5.3 billion	2,450	2.6	6.9
Liberia	3.6 billion	1,100	5.0	8.0
Libya	40 billion	7,600	3.0	13.6
Liechtenstein	730 million[3]	23,000	n.a.	1.0
Lithuania	27.4 billion	7,600	4.8	1.3
Luxembourg	19.2 billion	43,400	4.0	2.4
Macedonia	9 billion	4,400	–4.0	5.3
Madagascar	14 billion	870	5.0	7.0
Malawi	7 billion	660	1.7	28.6
Malaysia	200 billion	9,000	0.3	1.5
Maldives	1.2 billion	3,870	7.0	3.0[1]
Malta	5.95 billion	15,000	4.0	2.8
Marshall Is.	115 million	1,600	1.0	1.9[2]
Mauritania	5 billion	1,800	4.0	4.4
Mauritius	12.9 billion	10,800	5.2	4.2
Mexico	920 billion	9,000	–0.3	6.5
Micronesia	269 million	2,000	2.0	2.5
Moldova	11.3 billion	2,550	6.1	9.6
Monaco	870 million[2]	27,000	n.a.	n.a.
Mongolia	4.7 billion	1,770	2.4	11.8[1]
Morocco	112 billion	3,700	5.0	1.0
Mozambique	17.5 billion	900	9.2	10
Myanmar	63 billion	1,500	2.3	20
Namibia	8.1 billion	4,500	4.0	8.8
Nauru	60 million	5,000	n.a.	–3.6[4]
Nepal	35.6 billion	1,400	2.6	2.1[5]
Netherlands	413 billion	25,800	1.1	4.5
New Zealand	75.4 billion	19,500	3.1	2.6
Nicaragua	12.3 billion	2,500	2.5	7.4
Niger	8.4 billion	820	3.1	4.2
Nigeria	105.9 billion	840	3.5	14.9
Norway	138.7 billion	30,800	1.3	3.1
Oman	21.5 billion	8,200	7.4	1.0
Pakistan	299 billion	2,100	3.3	4.0
Palau	174 million	9,000	1.0	3.4[1]
Panama	16.9 billion	5,900	1.4	1.0[1]
Papua New Guinea	12.2 billion	2,400	–2.5	10.3

Country	GDP/PPP	GDP/PPP per capita	Real growth rate (%)	Inflation (%)
Paraguay	26.2 billion	$ 4,600	0.0%	7.2%
Peru	132 billion	4,800	–0.3	1.5
Philippines	335 billion	4,000	2.8	6.0
Poland	339.6 billion	8,800	1.5	5.3
Portugal	174.1 billion	17,300	1.7	4.4
Qatar	16.3 billion	21,200	5.6	2.0
Romania	152.7 billion	6,800	4.8	34.5
Russia	1.2 trillion	8,300	5.2	21.9
Rwanda	7.2 billion	1,000	5.0	5.0
St. Kitts	339 million	8,700	1.0	1.7
St. Lucia	700 million[1]	4,400	–2.5	3.0
St. Vincent	339 million	2,900	–0.8	–0.4
Samoa	618 million	3,500	6.0	2.5
San Marino	940 million	34,600	7.5	3.3
São Tomé	189 million	1,200	4.0	7.0
Saudi Arabia	241 billion	10,600	1.6	1.7
Senegal	16.2 billion	1,580	5.7	3.0
Serbia and Montenegro	24 billion	2,250	5.0	40.0
Seychelles	605 million	7,600	1.5	6.1
Sierra Leone	2.7 billion	500	3.0	15.0
Singapore	106.3 billion	24,700	–2.2	1.5
Slovakia	62 billion	11,500	3.0	7.4
Slovenia	31 billion	16,000	4.0	8.4
Solomon Is.	800 million	1,700	–10.0	7.9
Somalia	4.1 billion	550	3.0	+100.0[1]
South Africa	412 billion	9,400	2.6	5.8
Spain	757 billion	18,900	2.8	3.8
Sri Lanka	62.7 billion	3,250	–1.0	14.2
Sudan	49.3 billion	1,360	5.5	10.0
Suriname	1.5 billion[1]	3,500	–5.5	59.0
Swaziland	4.6 billion	4,200	2.5	7.5
Sweden	219 billion	24,700	1.6	2.7
Switzerland	226 billion	31,100	1.6	1.0
Syria	54.2 billion	3,200	2.0	0.3
Taiwan	386 billion	17,200	–2.0	1.0
Tajikistan	7.5 billion	1,140	8.3	33.0
Tanzania	22.1 billion	610	5.0	500.0
Thailand	410 billion	6,600	1.4	1.6
Togo	7.6 billion	1,500	2.2	2.2
Tonga	225 million[1]	2,200	5.3	9.4
Trinidad	10.6 billion	9,000	4.0	5.6
Tunisia	64.5 billion	6,600	4.8	2.7
Turkey	443 billion	6,700	–6.5	69.0
Turkmenistan	21.5 billion	4,700	10.0	10.0
Tuvalu	12.2 million[1]	1,100	3.0	5.0
Uganda	29 billion	1,200	5.1	3.5
Ukraine	205 billion	4,200	9.0	12.0
UAE	51 billion[1]	21,100	5.6	4.5[1]
UK	1.47 trillion	24,700	2.4	2.8
U.S.	10.082 trillion	36,300	0.3	2.8
Uruguay	31 billion	9,200	–1.5	3.6
Uzbekistan	62 billion	2,500	3.0	23.0
Vanuatu	257 million[1]	1,300	2.7	2.5
Venezuela	146.2 billion	6,100	2.7	12.3
Vietnam	168.1 billion	2,100	4.7	0.0
Yemen	14.8 billion	820	4.0	10.0
Zambia	8.5 billion	870	3.9	21.5
Zimbabwe	28 billion	2,450	–6.5	100.0

NOTES: Definitions: Gross domestic product (GDP): The value of all goods and services produced domestically. Purchasing power parity (PPP): The PPP method involves the use of standardized international dollar price weights, which are applied to the GDP produced in a given economy. The data derived from the 1998 method provide a better comparison of economic well-being between countries than conversions at official currency exchange rates. n.a. = not available. *First line of figures for Greek Cyprus, second for Turkish Cyprus. 1. 2000 est. 2. 1999 est. 3. 1998 est. 4. 1993 est. 5. FY 2000/2001 est. *Source:* U.S. Census Bureau, International Database and *The World Factbook, 2002.*

Kingdoms and Monarchs of the World

Country	Monarch	Type of monarchy
Bahrain	Sheik Hamad bin Isa al-Khalifa	Constitutional
Belgium	King Albert II	Constitutional
Bhutan	King Jigme Singye Wangchuck	Constitutional
Brunei	Sultan Haji Hassanal Bolkiah	Constitutional
Cambodia	King Norodom Sihanouk	Constitutional
Denmark	Queen Margrethe II	Constitutional
Japan	Emperor Akihito	Constitutional
Jordan	King Abdullah II	Constitutional
Kuwait	Sheik Jaber al-Ahmad al-Sabah	Constitutional
Lesotho	King Letsie III	Constitutional
Liechtenstein	Prince Hans Adam II	Constitutional
Luxembourg	Grand Duke Henri	Constitutional
Malaysia	King Syed Sirajuddin	Constitutional
Monaco	Prince Rainier III	Constitutional
Morocco	King Muhammad VI	Constitutional
Nepal	King Gyandendra	Constitutional
Netherlands	Queen Beatrix	Constitutional
Norway	King Harald V	Constitutional
Oman	Sultan Qabus ibn Sa'id	Absolute
Qatar	Emir Sheik Hamad ibn Khalifa al-Thani	Traditional
Samoa	Malietoa Tanumafili II	Constitutional
Saudi Arabia	King Fahd bin 'Abdulaziz	Absolute
Spain	King Juan Carlos I	Parliamentary
Swaziland	King Mswati III	Absolute
Sweden	King Carl XVI Gustaf	Constitutional
Thailand	King Bhumibol Adulyadej	Constitutional
Tonga	King Taufa'ahau Tupou IV	Constitutional
United Kingdom	Queen Elizabeth II[1]	Constitutional[2]

1. Queen Elizabeth II is also the Sovereign of 15 countries in the Commonwealth of Nations: Antigua and Barbuda, Australia, the Bahamas, Barbados, Belize, Canada, Grenada, Jamaica, New Zealand, Papua New Guinea, St. Kitts and Nevis, St. Lucia, St. Vincent and the Grenadines, the Solomon Islands, and Tuvalu. 2. Also parliamentary democracy.

U.S.-Designated Foreign Terrorist Organizations[1]

Name and base of operations	Goals and targets	Current strength	Year founded	Activities
Abu Nidal Organization (ANO) a.k.a. Fatah; Iraq	Targets U.S., UK, France, Israel, moderate Palestinians, the PLO, Arab countries	400	1974	Attacks in 20 countries, killing or injuring 900. Leader Abu Nidal died in 2002
Abu Sayyaf Group (ASG); Philippines, Malaysia	Aims to create Islamic state in Philippines; profit-driven terror	200-500	1991	Kidnappings, bombings, assassinations, and extortion
Al-Aqsa Martyrs Brigade; West Bank, Gaza Strip, Israel	Aims to drive out Israelis and to establish a Palestinian state	Unknown	2000	Shootings, suicide operations (first female suicide bombing)
Armed Islamic Group (GIA); Algeria	Aims to replace Algerian regime with an Islamic state	1,500 or less	1992	Massacred thousands of civilians, targeted foreigners
'Asbat al-Ansar (The League of Followers); Lebanon	Aims to create Islamic state, opposes peace with Israel	300	1990s	Assassinations, bombings of Western targets, failed coup
Aum Supreme Truth (Aum); Japan, Russia	Claims U.S. will start WWIII with Japan, beginning Armageddon	1,500-2,000	1987	Chemical attacks on Tokyo subways, no recent activity
Basque Fatherland and Liberty (ETA); Spain, France	Targets Spanish and French government interests, tourists	Unknown	1959	Since 1960, more than 800 killed, hundreds injured
Communist Party of Philippines/New People's Army (CPP/NPA); Philippines	Targets Philippine security forces, politicians, judges, government informers, NPA rebels	11,500	1969	Assassinations, murders, attacks on U.S. personnel and interests
Al-Gama'a al-Islamiyya (Islamic Group, IG); Egypt	Aims to replace Egypt's government with an Islamic state	Unknown	1973	1993 World Trade Center bombings, attacks on tourists
HAMAS (Islamic Resistance Movement); West Bank, Gaza Strip, Israel	Aims to replace Israel with Palestinian Islamic state using political and violent means	Unknown	1987	Large-scale suicide bombings and attacks against Israelis and Palestinian collaborators
Harakat ul-Mujahidin (HUM); Pakistan	Targets Indian troops, Kashmiri civilians, and Western interests	Unknown	1985	Linked to al-Qaeda, hijacked Indian airliner in 1999
Hezbollah (Party of God); Lebanon, worldwide cells	Dedicated to eliminating Israel, is anti-U.S. and anti-Israel	several thousand	1982	Suicide bombings of U.S. Marine barracks (241 killed), hijacked 1985 TWA Flight 847
Islamic Movement of Uzbekistan (IMU); South Asia, Tajikistan, Iran	Aims to remove Karimov, establish an Islamic state, and to fight anti-Islamic opponents	less than 1,000	1991	Car bombs, taking foreign hostages, most active in Kyrgyzstan and Tajikistan
Jaish-e-Mohammed (JEM) (Army of Mohammed); Pakistan	Aims to unite Kashmir with Pakistan, targets Indian government and political leaders	several hundred	2000	Murder of U.S. journalist, Indian Parliament bombing, anti-Christian attacks

Name and base of operations	Goals and targets	Current strength	Year founded	Activities
Jemaah Islamiya (JI); cells span Southeast Asia	Plotted against tourist spots, U.S., Israeli, British, and Australian diplomatic buildings	5,000	1990s	Bombings in Indonesia and Philippines, 2002 Bali bombings (202 killed, 300 wounded)
Al-Jihad; Cairo, Egypt, Yemen, Afghanistan, Pakistan, Lebanon, UK	Aims to replace the Egyptian government with Islamic state, attack U.S., Israeli interests	Unknown	1970s	Attacks on Egyptian government personnel, assassinated Anwar Sadat
Kahane Chai (Kach); Israel, West Bank	Organizes protests against the Israeli Government	Unknown	1994	Threats made to Arabs, Palestinians, and Israeli officials
Kurdistan Workers' Party (PKK) a.k.a. KADEK; Turkey, Europe, Middle East	Targets Turkish security forces, officials, and villagers who oppose organization	4,000–5,000	1974	Attacked diplomatic and commercial facilities, bombed tourist sites
Lashkar-e-Tayyiba (LT) (Army of the Righteous); Pakistan	Targets Indian troops and civilians in Kashmir	several hundred	1989	Attacks on border security forces and Indian Parliament
Lashkar I Jhangvi (LJ); Pakistan, Afghanistan	Anti-Shi'ite group aims to create a Muslim state in Pakistan.	less than 100	1996	Armed attacks, bombings, attempted assassinations
Liberation Tigers of Tamil Eelam (LTTE); Sri Lanka	Targets key personnel, senior political and military leaders	at least 10,000	1976	Assassinations, suicide bombers: "The Black Tigers"
Mujahedin-e Khalq Organization (MEK or MKO) a.k.a. The National Liberation Army of Iran (NLA); Iraq	Largest armed Iranian opposition to the present government, advocates a secular Iranian regime	several thousand	1960s	Assassinations, terrorist bombings, foreign military-aided assaults, large-scale overseas attacks
National Liberation Army (ELN); Colombia, Venezuela	Targets foreign employees from large corporations	3,000–5,000	1965	Kidnapping, hijacking, bombing, and extortion
Palestine Islamic Jihad (PIJ); Israel, West Bank, Gaza Strip	Targets Israeli military and civilians, opposes secularism	Unknown	1970s	Suicide bombings, attacks on Israeli interests
Palestine Liberation Front (PLF); Iraq	Known for aerial attacks against Israel	Unknown	1970s	Attacked Italian ship *Achille Lauro,* murdered a U.S. citizen
Popular Front for the Liberation of Palestine (PFLP); Syria, Lebanon, Israel, West Bank, Gaza Strip	Targets Israel's "illegal occupation" of Palestine and opposes negotiations with Israel	Unknown	1967	International terrorist acts in the 1970s, attacks against Israel and moderate Arab targets since 1978
Popular Front for the Liberation of Palestine–General Command (PFLP-GC); Syria	Attacks in Europe and the Middle East. Targets Israel, West Bank, and Gaza Strip	several hundred	1968	Unusual attacks: hot air balloons, hang gliders, Lebanese guerrilla operations
Al-Qaeda; Afghanistan until 2001, Southeast Asia, Middle East, worldwide cells	Targets "non-Islamic" regimes and U.S. citizens	several thousand	1980s	Bombings of embassies and *USS Cole;* September 11, 2001, U.S. attacks
Real IRA (RIRA); Northern Ireland, UK, Irish Republic	Targets civilians, military, police, and Protestant communities	100–200 activists	1998	Ignores cease-fire, Omagh bombing, more than 80 attacks since 1999
Revolutionary Armed Forces of Colombia (FARC); Colombia	Targets Colombian political, military, and economic interests, also foreign citizens	9,000–12,000	1964	Bombings, mortar attacks, kidnappings, extortion, guerrilla warfare, and drug trafficking
Revolutionary Nuclei (RN); Athens, Greece	Targets U.S. and European interests and government buildings in Greece	Believed small	1995	Arson attacks, low-level bombings, usually striking in early-morning hours
Revolutionary Organization 17 November; Athens, Greece	Seeks removal of U.S. bases, Turkish military, and the severing of NATO and EU ties	Believed small	1975	Assassinations, bombings, improvised rocket attacks, supported by bank robberies
Revolutionary People's Liberation Party/Front; Turkey	Anti-U.S., anti-NATO, and anti-Turkish establishment group	Unknown	1978	Attacks on U.S. interests, suicide bombings
The Salafist Group for Call and Combat (GSPC); Algeria	Military and government targets, pledges to avoid civilians	Unknown	1992	Attacks military, police, and government convoys
Sendero Luminoso (Shining Path, or SL); Peru	Aims to build communist regime, targets political enemies	400–500 militants	1960s	30,000 dead, assassinations, bombings, village raids
United Self-Defense Forces of Colombia (AUC); Colombia	Targets "insurgents" from FARC and ELN	6,000–8,150	1997	Assassinations, guerrilla warfare, and drug trafficking

1. On April 30, 2003, the U.S. State Department designated these 36 groups as Foreign Terrorist Organizations (FTOs).
Source: U.S. Department of State, Office of Counterterrorism, Center for Defense Information, Terrorism Project.

Major sources: The World Factbook 2002; Center for International Research, U.S. Bureau of the Census; *The Columbia Encyclopedia; The World Book Encyclopedia; Encyclopædia Britannica;* U.S. State Dept.; and various newspapers.
(information as of Sept. 2003)

Definitions: Gross domestic product (GDP): The value of all goods and services produced domestically; purchasing power parity (PPP): The PPP method involves the use of standardized international dollar price weights, which are applied to the GDP produced in a given economy. The data derived from the PPP method provide a better comparison of economic well-being between countries than conversions at official currency exchange rates. Literacy rates and population figures are supplied by the U.S. Census Bureau.

Afghanistan

ISLAMIC EMIRATE OF AFGHANISTAN

National name: Dowlat-e Eslami-ye Afghanestan
President: Hamid Karzai (2002)
Area: 250,000 sq mi (647,500 sq km)
Population (2003 est.): 28,717,213 (growth rate: 2.4%); birth rate: 40.6/1000; infant mortality rate: 142.5/1000; density per sq mi: 115
Capital and largest city (2003 est.): Kabul, 2,206,300. **Other large cities:** Kandahar, 349,300; Mazar-i-Sharif, 246,900; Charikar, 202,600; Herat, 171,500. **Monetary unit:** Afghani. **Languages:** Pushtu, Dari Persian, other Turkic and minor languages. **Ethnicity/race:** Pashtun 44%, Tajik 25%, Hazara 10%, Uzbek 8%, minor ethnic groups (Chahar Aimaks, Turkmen, Baloch, and others). **Religion:** Islam (Sunni 84%, Shi'ite 15%), other 1%. **Literacy rate:** 36% (1999 est.)
Economic summary: GDP/PPP (2000 est.): $21 billion; per capita $800. **Real growth rate:** n.a. **Inflation:** n.a. **Unemployment:** n.a. **Arable land:** 12%. **Agriculture:** wheat, fruits, nuts, wool, mutton, sheepskin, and lambskin. **Labor force** (2000 est): 10 million; agriculture 80%, industry 10%, services 10% (1990 est.). **Natural resources:** natural gas, petroleum, coal, copper, chromite, talc, barites, sulfur, lead, zinc, iron ore, salt, precious and semiprecious stones. **Industries:** small-scale production of textiles, soap, furniture, shoes, fertilizer, and cement; handwoven carpets; natural gas, coal, copper. **Exports:** $1.2 billion (2001 est.): opium, fruits and nuts, handwoven carpets, wool, cotton, hides and pelts, precious and semi-precious gems. **Imports:** $1.3 billion (2001 est.): capital goods, food and petroleum products; most consumer goods. **Major trading partners:** Pakistan, India, Belgium, Germany, Russia, UAE, Japan, Kenya, South Korea, Turkmenistan (1999).

Geography Afghanistan, approximately the size of Texas, is bordered on the north by Turkmenistan, Uzbekistan, and Tajikistan, on the extreme northeast by China, on the east and south by Pakistan, and by Iran on the west. The country is split east to west by the Hindu Kush mountain range, rising in the east to heights of 24,000 ft (7,315 m). With the exception of the southwest, most of the country is covered by high snow-capped mountains and is traversed by deep valleys.

Government In June 2002 a multiparty republic replaced an interim government that had been established in Dec. 2001, following the fall of the Islamic Taliban government.

History Darius I and Alexander the Great were the first to use Afghanistan as the gateway to India. Islamic conquerors arrived in the 7th century, and Genghis Khan and Tamerlane followed in the 13th and 14th centuries.

In the 19th century, Afghanistan became a battleground in the rivalry between imperial Britain and czarist Russia for control of Central Asia. Three Anglo-Afghan wars (1839–1842, 1878–1880, and 1919) ended inconclusively. In 1893 Britain established an unofficial border, the Durand Line, separating Afghanistan from British India, and London granted full independence in 1919. Emir Amanullah founded an Afghan monarchy in 1926.

During the cold war, King Mohammed Zahir Shah developed close ties with the Soviet Union, accepting extensive economic assistance from Moscow. He was overthrown in 1973 by his cousin Mohammed Daoud, who was himself ousted in a 1978 coup by Noor Taraki. Taraki and his successor, Babrak Karmal, attempted to create a Marxist state. However, the new leadership was criticized by armed insurgents who bitterly opposed communism and hoped to create an Islamic state in Afghanistan. Fearing his government was on the verge of collapse, Karmal called for Soviet troops. Moscow responded with a full-scale invasion of the country in Dec. 1979.

The Soviets were met with fierce resistance from groups already energized by opposition to the Karmal government. The guerrilla forces, calling themselves *mujahideen*, pledged a jihad, or holy war, to expel the invaders. Initially armed with outdated weapons, the mujahideen became a focus of U.S. cold war strategy against the Soviet Union, and with Pakistan's help, Washington began funneling sophisticated arms to the resistance. Moscow's troops were soon bogged down in a no-win conflict with determined Afghan fighters. In April 1988 the USSR, U.S., Afghanistan, and Pakistan signed accords calling for an end to outside aid to the warring factions. In return, a Soviet withdrawal took place in Feb. 1989, but the pro-Soviet government of President Najibullah was left in the capital, Kabul.

By mid-April 1992 Najibullah was ousted as Islamic rebels advanced on the capital. Almost immediately, the various rebel groups began fighting one another for control. Amid the chaos of competing factions, a group calling itself the Taliban—consisting of Islamic students—seized control of Kabul in Sept. 1996. It imposed harsh fundamentalist laws, including stoning for adultery and severing hands for theft. Women were prohibited from work and school, and they were required to cover themselves from head to foot in public. By fall 1998 the Taliban controlled about 90% of the country and, with its scorched-earth tactics and human rights abuses, had turned itself into an international pariah. Only three countries, Pakistan, Saudi Arabia, and the UAR, recognized the Taliban as Afghanistan's legitimate government

On Aug. 20, 1998, U.S. cruise missiles struck a terrorist training complex in Afghanistan believed to have been financed by Osama bin Laden, a wealthy Islamic radical sheltered by the Taliban. The U.S. asked for the deportation of Bin Laden, whom they believed was involved in the bombing of the U.S. embassies in

Kenya and Tanzania on Aug. 7, 1998. The UN also demanded the Taliban hand over Bin Laden for trial.

In Sept. 2001, legendary guerrilla leader Ahmed Shah Masoud was killed by suicide bombers, a seeming death knell for the anti-Taliban forces, a loosely connected group referred to as the Northern Alliance. Days later, terrorists attacked New York's World Trade Center Towers and the Pentagon, and Bin Laden emerged as the primary suspect in the tragedy.

On Oct. 7, after the Taliban repeatedly and defiantly refused to turn over Bin Laden, the U.S. and its allies began daily air strikes against Afghan military installations and terrorist training camps. Five weeks later, with the help of U.S. air support, the Northern Alliance managed with breathtaking speed to take the key cities of Mazar-i-Sharif and Kabul, the capital. On Dec. 7, the Taliban regime collapsed entirely when its troops fled their last stronghold, Kandahar. However, al-Qaeda members and other mujahideen from various parts of the Islamic world who had earlier fought alongside the Taliban persisted in pockets of fierce resistance, forcing U.S. and allied troops to maintain a presence in Afghanistan. Osama bin Laden and Taliban leader Mullah Muhammad Omar remained at large.

In Dec. 2001, Hamid Karzai, a Pashtun (the dominant ethnic group in the country) and the leader of the powerful 500,000-strong Populzai clan, was named head of Afghanistan's interim government; in June 2002, he formally became president. The U.S. was one of 31 nations contributing peacekeeping forces to the country in 2002 and 2003, but it also maintained 9,000 additional troops to combat the remnants of the Taliban and al-Qaeda. Fighting persisted into 2003, and in March, in the largest operation in more than a year, about 1,000 soldiers raided Kandahar, seeking out al-Qaeda members. U.S. Secretary of State Donald Rumsfeld declared in May that major combat in Afghanistan had ended, marking the formal transition from military operations to reconstruction. But attacks on American-led forces intensified over the summer, and warlords maintained tight regional control. Indeed, President Karzai had almost no power beyond Kabul. A report released by Human Rights Watch in August accused province leaders, police officers, and even some cabinet ministers of extortion, kidnapping, and assault, and criticized the United States for not cracking down on the abuse. In Aug. 2003, NATO, which had been supplying 90% of the troops policing the country, formally took command of the peacekeeping force.

Albania

THE REPUBLIC OF ALBANIA

National name: Republika E Shqiperise
President: Alfred Moisiu (2002)
Prime Minister: Fatos Nano (2002)
Area: 11,100 sq mi (28,748 sq km)
Population (2003 est.): 3,582,205 (growth rate: 1.2%); birth rate: 18.2/1000; infant mortality rate: 37.3/1000; density per sq mi: 323
Capital and largest city (2003 est.): Tirana, 353,400. **Other large cities:** Durres, 113,900; Elbasan, 97,000. **Monetary unit:** Lek. **Languages:** Albanian (Tosk is the official dialect), Greek. **Ethnicity/race:** Albanian 95%, Greeks 3%, other 2%: Vlachs, Gypsies, Serbs, and Bulgarians (1989 est.). **Religions:** Islam 70%, Albanian Orthodox 20%, Roman Catholic 10%. **Literacy rate:** 93% (1997 est.)
Economic summary: GDP/PPP (2001 est.): $13.2 billion; per capita $3,800. **Real growth rate:** 7.3%. **Inflation:** 3%. **Unemployment:** 17% officially; may be as high as 30%. **Arable land:** 21%. **Agriculture:** wheat, corn, potatoes, vegetables, fruits, sugar beets, grapes; meat, dairy products. **Labor force:** 1.283 million (not including 352,000 emigrant workers and 261,000 domestically unemployed) (2000 est.); agriculture 50%, industry and services 50%. **Industries:** food processing, textiles and clothing; lumber, oil, cement, chemicals, mining, basic metals, hydropower. **Natural resources:** petroleum, natural gas, coal, chromium, copper, timber, nickel, hydropower. **Exports:** $306 million (f.o.b., 2001 est.): textiles and footwear; asphalt, metals and metallic ores, crude oil; vegetables, fruits, tobacco. **Imports:** $1.1 billion (f.o.b., 2001 est.): machinery and equipment, foodstuffs, textiles, chemicals. **Major trading partners:** Italy, Greece, Germany, Macedonia, Austria, Turkey, Bulgaria.

Geography Albania is situated on the eastern shore of the Adriatic Sea, with Montenegro and Serbia to the north, Macedonia to the east, and Greece to the south. Slightly larger than Maryland, Albania may be divided into two major regions: a mountainous highland region (north, east, and south) constituting 70% of the land area, and a western coastal lowland region that contains nearly all of the country's agricultural lands and is the most densely populated part of Albania.

Government Emerging democracy.

History A part of Illyria in ancient times and later of the Roman Empire, Albania was ruled by the Byzantine Empire from 535 to 1204. An alliance (1444–1466) of Albanian chiefs failed to halt the advance of the Ottoman Turks, and the country remained under at least nominal Turkish rule for more than four centuries, until it proclaimed its independence on Nov. 28, 1912.

Largely agricultural, Albania is one of the poorest countries in Europe. A battlefield in World War I, after the war it became a republic in which a conservative Muslim landlord, Ahmed Zogu, proclaimed himself president in 1925, and king (Zog I) in 1928. He ruled until Italy annexed Albania in 1939. Communist guerrillas under Enver Hoxha seized power in 1944, near the end of World War II. Hoxha was a devotee of Stalin, emulating the Soviet leader's repressive tactics, imprisoning or executing landowners and others who did not conform to the socialist ideal. Hoxha eventually broke with Soviet communism in 1961 because of differences with Khrushchev and then aligned himself with Chinese communism, which he also abandoned in 1978 after the death of Mao. From then on Albania went its own way to forge its individual version of the socialist state and became one of the most isolated—and economically underdeveloped—countries in the world. Hoxha was succeeded by Ramiz Alia in 1982.

Elections in March 1991 gave the Communists a decisive majority. But a general strike and street demonstrations soon forced the all-Communist cabinet to resign. In June 1991 the Communist Party of Labor renamed itself the Socialist Party and renounced its past ideology. The opposition Democratic Party won a landslide victory in the 1992 elections, and Sali Berisha, a former cardiologist, became Albania's first elected president. The following year, ex-Communists, including Ramiz Alia and former prime minister Fatos Nano, were imprisoned on corruption charges.

But Albania's experiment with democratic reform and a free-market economy went disastrously awry in March 1997, when large numbers of its citizens invested in shady get-rich-quick pyramid schemes. When five of these schemes collapsed in the beginning of the year, robbing Albanians of an estimated $1.2 billion in savings, their rage turned against the government, which appeared to have sanctioned the nationwide swindle. Rioting broke out, the country's fragile infrastructure collapsed, and gangsters and rebels overran the country, plunging it into virtual anarchy. A multinational protection force eventually restored order and set up the elections that formally ousted President Sali Berisha.

In spring 1999, Albania was heavily involved in the affairs of its fellow ethnic Albanians to the north, in Kosovo. Albania served as an outpost for NATO troops and took in approximately 440,000 Kosovar refugees, about half the total number of ethnic Albanians who were driven from their homes in Kosovo.

Ilir Meta, elected prime minister in 1999, rapidly moved forward in his first years to modernize the economy, privatize business, fight crime, and reform the judiciary and tax systems.He resigned in Jan. 2002, frustrated by political infighting. In June 2002, former general Alfred Moisiu was elected president, endorsed by both the Socialists (headed by Fatos Nano) and the Democrats (led by Sali Berisha) in an effort to end the unproductive political fractiousness that has stalemated the government.

Algeria

DEMOCRATIC AND POPULAR REPUBLIC OF ALGERIA

National name: Al Jumhuriyah al Jaza'iriyah ad Dimuqratiyah ash Shabiyah

President: Abdel-Aziz Bouteflika (1999)

Prime Minister: Ahmed Ouyahia (2003)

Area: 919,590 sq mi (2,381,740 sq km)

Population (2003 est.): 32,818,500 (growth rate: 1.7%); birth rate: 21.9/1000; infant mortality rate: 37.7/1000; density per sq mi: 36

Capital and largest city (2003 est.): Algiers, 3,917,000 (metro. area), 1,742,800 (city proper). **Other large cities:** Oran, 752,200; Constantine, 530,100; Batna, 278,100; Annaba, 246,700. **Monetary unit:** Dinar. **Languages:** Arabic (official), French, Berber dialects. **Ethnicity/race:** Arab-Berber 99%, European less than 1%. **Religion:** 99% Islam (Sunni). **Literacy rate:** 61.6% (1995 est.)

Economic summary: GDP/PPP (2001 est.): $177 billion; per capita $5,600. **Real growth rate:** 3.8%. **Inflation:** 3%. **Unemployment:** 34%. **Arable land:** 3%. **Agriculture:** wheat, barley, oats, grapes, olives, citrus, fruits; sheep, cattle. **Labor force:** 9.4 million; government 29%, agriculture 25%, construction and public works 15%, industry 11%, other 20% (1996 est.). **Industries:** petroleum, natural gas, light industries, mining, electrical, petrochemical, food processing. **Natural resources:** petroleum, natural gas, iron ore, phosphates, uranium, lead, zinc. **Exports:** $20 billion (f.o.b., 2001 est.): petroleum, natural gas, and petroleum products 97%. **Imports:** $1 billion (f.o.b., 2001 est): capital goods, food and beverages, consumer goods. **Major trading partners:** Italy, Spain, U.S., France, Brazil, Germany.

Geography Nearly four times the size of Texas, Algeria is bordered on the west by Morocco and Western Sahara and on the east by Tunisia and Libya. The Mediterranean Sea to the north, and to the south are Mauritania, Mali, and Niger. The Saharan region, which is 85% of the country, is almost completely uninhabited. The highest point is Mount Tahat in the Sahara, which rises 9,850 ft (3,000 m).

Government Parliamentary republic.

History Excavations in Algeria have indicated that *Homo erectus* resided there between 500,000 and 700,000 years ago. Phoenician traders settled on the Mediterranean coast in the 1st millennium B.C. As ancient Numidia, Algeria became a Roman colony, part of what was called Mauretania Caesariensis, at the close of the Punic Wars (145 B.C.). Conquered by the Vandals about A.D. 440, it fell from a high state of civilization to virtual barbarism, from which it partly recovered after an invasion by Arabs about 650. Christian during its Roman period, the indigenous Berbers were then converted to Islam. Falling under the control of the Ottoman Empire by 1536, Algiers served for three centuries as the headquarters of the Barbary pirates. Ostensibly to rid the region of the pirates, the French occupied Algeria in 1830 and made it a part of France in 1848.

Algerian independence movements led to the uprisings of 1954–1955, which developed into full-scale war. In 1962, French president Charles de Gaulle began the peace negotiations, and on July 5, 1962, Algeria was proclaimed independent. In Oct. 1963, Ahmed Ben Bella was elected president, and the country became socialist. He began to nationalize foreign holdings and aroused opposition. He was overthrown in a military coup on June 19, 1965, by Col. Houari Boumediène, who suspended the constitution and sought to restore economic stability.

In Dec. 1991 in the first parliamentary elections ever held in Algeria, the fundamentalist Islamic Salvation Front (Front Islamique du Salut; FIS) won the largest number of votes. To thwart the electoral results, the army cancelled the general election, which plunged the country into a bloody civil war. An estimated 100,000 people have been massacred by Islamic terrorists since war began in Jan. 1992. The undeclared civil war escalated in its brutality and senselessness in 1997–1998. Islamic extremists, who had originally focused their attacks on government officials and then shifted to intellectuals and journalists, abandoned political motivations entirely and targeted defenseless villagers. The mass slaughters were as savage as they were random, and the government was markedly ineffectual in stemming the violence. There is some evidence that the army in fact looked the other way while its civilians were slaughtered. Algeria refused international mediation and kept the outside world largely in the dark about the war within its borders.

Abdel-Aziz Bouteflika's ascension to the presidency in April 1999 was initially expected to bring peace and some economic improvement to this desperate war-torn country. Bouteflika, however, has been locked in power struggles with the military, whose support is crucial. Despite the appearance of democracy, Algeria remains in essence a military dictatorship. Bouteflika's plan of national reconciliation, which included an amnesty for Islamic militants not convicted of murder or rape, has done little to heal wounds. In 2001 violence by Islamic militants was again on the rise, and the long-disaffected Berber minority engaged in several large-scale protests. The Berber-speaking region of Kabylia and other regions continued large protests against the government in 2002.

Algeria's most destructive earthquake in two decades struck near the capital on May 21, 2003. The 6.7 magnitude earthquake killed more than 2,000 people and injured many thousands more.

Andorra

PRINCIPALITY OF ANDORRA

National name: Valls d'Andorra
Head of Government: Marc Forné Molné (1994)
Chiefs of State (Coprinces): Frederic de Saint-Sernin for France and Nemesi Marques Oste for Spain
Area: 181 sq mi (468 sq km)
Population (2003 est.): 69,150 (growth rate: 0.4%); birth rate: 9.7/1000; infant mortality rate: 4.1/1000; density per sq mi: 383
Capital and largest city (2003 est.): Andorra la Vella, 23,000. **Monetary units:** Euro. **Languages:** Catalán (official), French, Castilian, Portuguese. **Ethnicity/race:** Spanish 43%, Andorran 33%, Portuguese 11%, French 7%, other 6%. **Religion:** Roman Catholic. **Literacy rate:** 100%
Economic summary: GDP/PPP (2000 est.): $1.3 billion; per capita $19,000. **Real growth rate:** 3.8%. **Inflation:** 4.3%. **Unemployment:** 0%. **Arable land:** 2%. **Agriculture:** small quantities of tobacco, rye, wheat, barley, oats, vegetables; sheep. **Labor force:** 33,000 (2001 est.); agriculture 1%, industry 21%, services 78% (2000 est.). **Industries:** tourism (particularly skiing), cattle raising, timber, tobacco, banking. **Natural resources:** hydropower, mineral water, timber, iron ore, lead. **Exports:** $58 million (f.o.b., 1998): tobacco products, furniture. **Imports:** $1.077 billion (c.i.f., 1998): consumer goods, food, electricity. **Major trading partners:** France, Spain, U.S.

Geography Andorra is nestled high in the Pyrénées Mountains on the French-Spanish border.

Government A parliamentary coprincipality composed of the bishop of Urgel (Spain) and the president of France. Their representatives are listed above. The principality was internationally recognized as a sovereign state in 1993.

History An autonomous and semi-independent coprincipality, Andorra has been under the joint suzerainty of the French state and the Spanish bishops of Urgel since 1278. It maintains closer ties to Spain, however, and Catalán is its official language. In the late 20th century, Andorra became a popular tourist and winter sports destination and a wealthy international commercial center because of its banking facilities, low taxes, and lack of customs duties. In 1990 Andorra approved a customs union treaty with the EU permitting free movement of industrial goods between the two, but with Andorra applying the EU's external tariffs to third countries. Andorra became a member of the UN in 1993 and a member of the Council of Europe in 1994.

Angola

REPUBLIC OF ANGOLA

President: José Eduardo dos Santos (1979)
Prime Minister: Fernando da Piedade Dias dos Santos (2003)
Area: 481,351 sq mi (1,246,700 sq km)
Population (2003 est.): 10,766,471 (growth rate: 2.0%); birth rate: 45.6/1000; infant mortality rate: 193.8/1000; density per sq mi: 22
Capital and largest city (2003 est.): Luanda, 2,297,200. **Other large cities:** Huambo, 171,000; Lubango, 136,000. **Monetary unit:** New Kwanza. **Languages:** Bantu, Portuguese (official). **Ethnicity/race:** Ovimbundu 37%, Kimbundu 25%, Bakongo 13%, mestico (mixed European and Native African) 2%, European 1%, other 22%. **Religions:** Indigenous 47%, Roman Catholic 38%, Protestant 15% (1998 est.). **Literacy rate:** 42% (1998 est.)
Economic summary: GDP/PPP (2001 est.): $13.3 billion; per capita $1,330. **Real growth rate:** 5.4%. **Inflation:** 110%. **Unemployment:** extensive unemployment and underemployment affecting more than half the population. **Arable land:** 2%. **Agriculture:** bananas, sugarcane, coffee, sisal, corn, cotton, manioc (tapioca), tobacco, vegetables, plantains; livestock; forest products; fish. **Labor force:** 5 million (1997 est.); agriculture 85%, industry and services 15%. **Industries:** petroleum; diamonds, iron ore, phosphates, feldspar, bauxite, uranium, and gold; cement; basic metal products; fish processing; food processing; brewing; tobacco products; sugar; textiles. **Natural resources:** petroleum, diamonds, iron ore, phosphates, copper, feldspar, gold, bauxite, uranium. **Exports:** $7 billion (f.o.b., 2001 est.): crude oil, diamonds, refined petroleum products, gas, coffee, sisal, fish and fish products, timber, cotton. **Imports:** $2.7 billion (f.o.b., 2001 est.): machinery and electrical equipment, vehicles and spare parts; medicines, food, textiles, military goods. **Major trading partners:** U.S., EU, China, South Korea, South Africa, Brazil.

Geography Angola, more than three times the size of California, extends for more than 1,000 mi (1,609 km) along the South Atlantic in southwest Africa. The Democratic Republic of the Congo and the Republic of Congo are to the north and east, Zambia is to the east, and Namibia is to the south. A plateau averaging 6,000 ft (1,829 m) above sea level rises abruptly from the coastal lowlands. Nearly all the land is desert or savanna, with hardwood forests in the northeast.

Government Angola underwent a transition from a one-party socialist state to a nominally multiparty democracy in 1992.

History The original inhabitants of Angola are thought to have been Khoisan speakers. After 1000, large numbers of Bantu speakers migrated to the region and became the dominant group. Angola derives its name from the Bantu kingdom of Ndongo, whose name for its king is *ngola*.

Explored by the Portuguese navigator Diego Cão in 1482, Angola became a link in trade with India and Southeast Asia. Later it was a major source of slaves for Portugal's New World colony of Brazil. Development of the interior began after the Berlin Conference in 1885 fixed the colony's borders, and British and Portuguese investment fostered mining, railways, and agriculture.

Following World War II, independence movements began but were sternly suppressed by Portuguese military force. The major nationalist organizations were the Popular Movement for the Liberation of Angola (MPLA), a Marxist party; National Front for the Liberation of Angola (FNLA); and the National Union for the Total Independence of Angola (UNITA). After 14 years of war, Portugal finally granted independence to Angola in 1975. The MPLA, which had led the independence movement, has controlled the government ever since. But no period of peace followed Angola's long war for independence. UNITA disputed the MPLA's ascendancy, and civil war broke out almost immediately. With the Soviet Union and Cuba supporting the Marxist MPLA, and the United States and South Africa supporting the anticommunist UNITA, the country became a cold war battleground.

With the waning of the cold war and the withdrawal of Cuban troops in 1989, the MPLA began to make the transition to a multiparty democracy. Despite shifting ideologies, the civil war continued, with UNITA's charismatic rebel leader, Jonas Savimbi, armed and sustained by his control of approximately 80% of the country's diamond trade. Free elections took place in

1992, with incumbent president José Eduardo dos Santos and the MPLA winning the UN-certified election over Savimbi and UNITA. Savimbi then withdrew, charging election fraud, and the civil war resumed.

In 1997 Angola played a crucial role in the civil wars of both the Republic of Congo and the Democratic Republic of the Congo. By aiding in the overthrow of these countries' leaders, Pascal Lissouba and Mobutu Sese Seko, the Angolan government was also able to destroy the UNITA strongholds within their borders. Angola again came to the aid of the Democratic Republic of the Congo's new leader, Laurent Kabila, in 1998, helping to fight the rebellion against his shaky year-old administration.

Four years of relative peace took place between 1994 and 1998, when the UN, at a cost of $1.6 billion, oversaw the 1994 Lusaka peace accord. In 1997 it was agreed that a coalition government with UNITA would be implemented. But Savimbi violated the accord repeatedly by refusing to give up his strongholds, failing to demobilize his army, and retaking territory. As a result, the government suspended coalition rule in Sept. 1998, and the country again plunged into civil war. Angola's citizens continued to suffer. The hostilities affected an estimated 4 million people, about a third of the total population, and there were almost 2 million refugees.

On Feb. 22, 2002, government troops killed Jonas Savimbi, and his exhausted troops were ready to lay down their arms. Six weeks later, on April 4, rebel leaders signed a cease-fire deal with the government, signalling the end of 30 years of civil war. Within another five weeks, 80% of the rebels had been disarmed. While peace finally seemed secure, more than a half-million Angolans were faced with starvation. Thousands of Angolan refugees who had fled to Congo, Namibia, Zambia, and other countries began returning to their country in 2003, where their prospects are poor: 80% of Angolans have no access to health care and the average life expectancy is 40 years.

Antigua and Barbuda

Sovereign: Queen Elizabeth II (1952)
Governor-General: James Beethoven Carlisle (1993)
Prime Minister: Lester Bryant Bird (1994)
Land area: 171 sq mi (443 sq km)
Population (2003 est.): 67,897 (growth rate: 1.3%); birth rate: 18.2/1000; infant mortality rate: 20.9/1000; density per sq mi: 397
Capital and largest city (2003 est.): St. John's, 23,500. **Other large cities:** English Harbour, 2,900; Codrington (capital of Barbuda), est. pop. 870. **Monetary unit:** East Caribbean dollar. **Language:** English. **Ethnicity/race:** black, British, Portuguese, Lebanese, Syrian. **Religions:** Anglican and Roman Catholic. **Literacy rate:** 89% (1960 est.)
Economic summary: GDP/PPP (2000 est.): $674 million; per capita $10,000. **Real growth rate:** 3.5%. **Inflation:** 0.4%. **Unemployment:** 7%. **Arable land:** 18%. **Agriculture:** cotton, fruits, vegetables, bananas, coconuts, cucumbers, mangoes, sugarcane; livestock. **Labor force:** 30,000; commerce and services 82%, agriculture 11%, industry 7% (1983). **Industries:** tourism, construction, light manufacturing (clothing, alcohol, household appliances). **Natural resources:** negl; pleasant climate fosters tourism. **Exports:** $40 million (2000 est.): petroleum products, manufactures, machinery and transport equipment, food and live animals. **Imports:** $357 million (2000 est.): food and live animals, machinery and transport equipment, manufactures, chemicals, oil. **Major trading partners:** OECS, Barbados, Guyana, Trinidad and Tobago, U.S., UK, Canada. **Member of Commonwealth of Nations**

Geography Antigua, the larger of the two main islands, is 108 sq mi (280 sq km). The island dependencies of Redonda (an uninhabited rocky islet) and Barbuda (a coral island formerly known as Dulcina) are 0.5 sq mi (1.30 sq km) and 62 sq mi (161 sq km), respectively.

Government Constitutional monarchy.

History Antigua was explored by Christopher Columbus in 1493 and named for the Church of Santa Maria de la Antigua in Seville. Antigua was colonized by Britain in 1632; Barbuda was first colonized in 1678. The country joined the West Indies Federation in 1958. With the breakup of the federation, it became one of the West Indies Associated States in 1967, self-governing its internal affairs. Full independence was granted Nov. 1, 1981.

The Bird family has controlled the islands since Vere C. Bird founded the Antigua Labor Party in the mid-1940s. While tourism and financial services have turned the country into one of the more prosperous in the Caribbean, law enforcement officials have charged that Antigua and Barbuda is a major center of money laundering, drug trafficking, and arms smuggling. Several scandals have tainted the Bird family, especially the 1995 conviction of Lester Bird's brother, Ivor, for cocaine smuggling. In 2000, Antigua and 35 other offshore banking centers agreed to reforms meant to prevent money laundering.

Argentina

ARGENTINE REPUBLIC

National name: República Argentina.
President: Néstor Kirchner (2003)
Area: 1,068,296 sq mi (2,766,890 sq km)
Population (2003 est.): 38,740,807 (growth rate: 1.0%); birth rate: 17.5/1000; infant mortality rate: 16.2/1000; density per sq mi: 36
Capital and largest city (2003 est.): Buenos Aires, 13,076,300 (metro. area), 12,116,400 (city proper). **Other large cities:** Córdoba, 1,486,200; Rosario, 1,276,900; Mendoza, 988,600; Mar del Plata, 683,700. **Monetary unit:** Peso. **Languages:** Spanish (official), English, Italian, German, French. **Ethnicity/race:** European (mostly of Spanish and Italian descent) 97%, other (mostly Indian or mestizo) 3%. **Religions:** Roman Catholic 92%, Protestant 2%, Jewish 2%, other 4%. **Literacy rate:** 96.2% (1995 est.)
Economic summary: GDP/PPP (2001 est.): $453 billion; per capita $12,000. **Real growth rate:** –4.6%. **Inflation:** 4%. **Unemployment:** 25% (yearend 2001). **Arable land:** 9%. **Agriculture:** sunflower seeds, lemons, soybeans, grapes, corn, tobacco, peanuts, tea, wheat; livestock. **Labor force:** 15 million (1999); agriculture n.a., industry n.a., services n.a. **Industries:** food processing, motor vehicles, consumer durables, textiles, chemicals and petrochemicals, printing, metallurgy, steel. **Natural resources:** fertile plains of the pampas, lead, zinc, tin, copper, iron ore, manganese, petroleum, uranium. **Exports:** $26.5 billion (f.o.b., 2000 est.): edible oils, fuels and energy, cereals, feed, motor vehicles. **Imports:** $23.8 billion (f.o.b., 2000 est.): machinery and equipment, motor vehicles, chemicals, metal manufactures, plastics. **Major trading partners:** Brazil, U.S., Chile, Spain, Germany, China.

Geography Second in South America only to Brazil in size and population, Argentina is a plain, rising from the Atlantic to the Chilean border and the towering Andes peaks. Aconcagua (22,834 ft., 6,960 m) is the highest peak in the world outside Asia. Argentina is also bordered by Bolivia and Paraguay on the north, and by Uruguay and Brazil on the east.

Government Republic.

History First explored in 1516 by Juan Díaz de Solis, Argentina developed slowly under Spanish colonial rule. Buenos Aires was settled in 1580; the cattle industry was thriving as early as 1600. Invading British forces were expelled in 1806–1807, and after Napoléon conquered Spain (1808), the Argentinians set up their own government in 1810. On July 9, 1816, independence was formally declared.

As it had in World War I, Argentina proclaimed neutrality at the outbreak of World War II, but in the closing phase declared war on the Axis powers on March 27, 1945. Juan D. Perón, an army colonel, emerged as the strongman of the postwar era, winning the presidential elections of 1946 and 1951. Perón's political strength was reinforced by his second wife—Eva Duarte de Perón (Evita)—and her popularity with the working classes. Although she never held a government post, Evita acted as de facto minister of health and labor, establishing a national charitable organization, and awarding generous wage increases to the unions, who responded with political support for Perón. Opposition to Perón's increasing authoritarianism led to a coup by the armed forces, which sent Perón into exile in 1955, three years after Evita's death. Argentina entered a long period of military dictatorships with brief intervals of constitutional government.

The former dictator returned to power in 1973 and his third wife, Isabel Martínez de Perón, was elected vice president. After Perón's death in 1974, she became the hemisphere's first woman chief of state, assuming control of a nation teetering on economic and political collapse. In 1975, terrorist acts by left- and right-wing groups killed some 700 people. The cost of living rose 355%, while strikes and demonstrations were constant. On March 24, 1976, a military junta led by army commander Lt. Gen. Jorge Rafael Videla seized power and imposed martial law.

The military began the "dirty war" to restore order and eradicate its opponents. The Argentine Commission for Human Rights, in Geneva, has charged the junta with 2,300 political murders, over 10,000 political arrests, and the disappearances of 20,000 to 30,000 people. While violence declined, the economy remained in chaos. In March 1981 Videla was deposed by Field Marshal Roberto Viola, who in turn was succeeded by Lt. Gen. Leopoldo Galtieri.

On April 2, 1982, Galtieri invaded the British-held Falkland Islands, known as Las Islas Malvinas (Malvinas Islands) in Spanish, in what was seen as an attempt to increase his popularity. Great Britain, however, won a decisive victory, and Galtieri resigned in disgrace three days after Argentina's surrender. Maj. Gen. Reynaldo Bignone took over June 14, amid increasing prodemocratic public sentiment. As the 1983 elections approached, inflation hit 900% and Argentina's crippling foreign debt reached unprecedented levels.

In the presidential election of Oct. 1983, Raúl Alfonsín, leader of the Radical Civic Union, handed the Peronist Party its first defeat since its founding. Growing unemployment and quadruple-digit inflation, however, led to a Peronist victory in the elections of May 1989. Alfonsín resigned a month later in the wake of riots over high food prices, in favor of the new Peronist president, Carlos Menem. In 1991, Menem promoted economic austerity measures that deregulated businesses and privatized state-owned industries. But beginning in Sept. 1998, eight years into Menem's two-term presidency, Argentina entered its worst recession in a decade. Menem's economic policies, tolerance of corruption, and pardoning of military leaders involved in the dirty war eventually lost him the support of the poor and the working class who had elected him.

In Dec. 1999 Fernando de la Rua became president. Despite the introduction of several tough economic austerity plans, by 2001 the recession slid into its third year. In March 2001, de la Rua brought back former Peronist economy minister Domingo Cavallo, who had rescued the country from hyperinflation in 1991. The IMF gave Argentina $13.7 billion in emergency aid in Jan. 2001 and $8 billion in Aug. 2001.

The international help was not enough, however, and by the end of 2001, Argentina neared economic collapse. Rioters protesting government austerity measures forced de la Rua to resign in Dec. 2001. Argentina then defaulted on its $155 billion foreign debt payments, the largest such default in history. After a period of instability, Congress named Eduardo Duhalde president on Jan. 1, 2002. Duhalde soon announced an economic plan devaluing the Argentine peso, which had been pegged to the dollar for a decade. The devaluation plunged the banking industry into crisis and wiped out much of the savings of the middle class.

In July 2002, former junta leader Galtieri and 42 other military officers were arrested and charged with the torture and execution of 22 leftist guerrillas during Argentina's 7-year military dictatorship. In recent years, judges have found legal loopholes allowing them to circumvent the blanket amnesty laws passed in 1986 and 1987, which have allowed many accused of atrocities during the dirty war to walk free. In the 2003 presidential elections, Peronist Néstor Kirchner, the former governor of Santa Cruz, became president on May 25 after former president Carlos Menem abandoned the race. Kirchner has vowed to aggressively reform the courts, police, and armed services, and to repeal amnesty laws for perpetrators of the dirty war. He declared within his first months in office, "There can be no impunity in Argentina. . . . A society without justice or memory does not have a destiny."

Armenia

President: Robert Kocharian (1998)
Prime Minister: Andranik Markarian (2000)
Area: 11,506 sq mi (29,800 sq km)
Population (2003 est.): 3,326,448 (growth rate: 0.2%); (Armenian, 93%; others, Kurds, Ukrainians, and Russians); birth rate: 12.6/1000; infant mortality rate: 40.9/1000; density per sq mi: 289
Capital and largest city (2003 est.): Yerevan, 1,462,700 (metro. area), 1,267,600 (city proper). **Other large cities:** Vanadzor, 147,400; Gyumri (Leninakan), 125,300; Abovian, 59,300. **Monetary unit:** Dram. **Language:** Armenian. **Ethnicity/race:** Armenian 93%, Russian 2%, Azeri 1%, other (mostly Yezidi Kurds) 4% (2002). Note: as of the end of 1993, virtually all Azeris had emigrated from Armenia. **Religion:** Armenian Orthodox 94%. **Literacy rate:** 99% (1989 est.)
Economic summary: GDP/PPP (2001 est.): $11.2 billion; per capita $3,350. **Real growth rate:** 9.6%. **Inflation:** 3.1% (2000 est.). **Unemployment:** 20%. Note: official rate is 10.9% for 2000. **Arable land:** 18%. **Agriculture**: fruit (especially grapes), vegetables; livestock. **Labor force:** 1.4 million (2001); agriculture 44%, services 14%, industry 42% (2000 est.). **Industries:**metal-cutting machine tools, forging-pressing machines, electric motors, tires, knitted wear, hosiery, shoes, silk fabric, chemicals, trucks, instruments, microelectronics, gem cutting, jewelry manufacturing, software development, food processing, brandy. **Natural resources:** small deposits of gold, copper, molybdenum, zinc, alumina. **Exports:**

$338.5 million (f.o.b., 2001 est.): diamonds, scrap metal, machinery and equipment, brandy, copper ore. **Imports:** $868.6 million (f.o.b., 2001 est.): natural gas, petroleum, tobacco products, foodstuffs, diamonds. **Major trading partners:** Belgium, Russia, U.S., Iran.

Geography Armenia is located in the southern Caucasus and is the smallest of the former Soviet republics. It is bounded by Georgia on the north, Azerbaijan on the east, Iran on the south, and Turkey on the west. Contemporary Armenia is a fraction of the size of ancient Armenia. A land of rugged mountains and extinct volcanoes, its highest point is Mount Aragats, 13,435 ft (4,095 m).

Government Republic.

History One of the world's oldest civilizations, Armenia once included Mount Ararat, which biblical tradition identifies as the mountain that Noah's ark rested on after the flood. It was the first country in the world to officially embrace Christianity as its religion (c. A.D. 300).

In the 6th century B.C., Armenians settled in the kingdom of Urartu (the Assyrian name for Ararat), which was in decline. Under Tigrane the Great (fl. 95–55 B.C.) the Armenian empire reached its height and became one of the most powerful in Asia, stretching from the Caspian to the Mediterranean Seas. Throughout most of its long history, however, Armenia has been invaded by a succession of empires. Under constant threat of domination by foreign forces, Armenians became both cosmopolitan as well as fierce protectors of their culture and tradition.

Over the centuries Armenia was conquered by Greeks, Romans, Persians, Byzantines, Mongols, Arabs, Ottoman Turks, and Russians. From the 16th century through World War I major portions of Armenia were controlled by their most brutal invader, the Ottoman Turks, under whom the Armenians experienced discrimination, religious persecution, heavy taxation, and armed attacks. In response to Armenian nationalist stirrings, the Turks massacred thousands of Armenians in 1894 and 1896. The most horrific massacre took place in April 1915 during World War I, when the Turks ordered the deportation of the Armenian population to the deserts of Syria and Mesopotamia. According to the majority of historians, between 600,000 and 1.5 million Armenians were murdered or died of starvation. The Armenian massacre is considered the first genocide in the 20th century. Turkey denies that a genocide took place, and claims that a much smaller number died in a civil war.

After the Turkish defeat in World War I, the independent Republic of Armenia was established on May 28, 1918, but survived only until Nov. 29, 1920, when it was annexed by the Soviet Army. On March 12, 1922, the Soviets joined Georgia, Armenia, and Azerbaijan to form the Transcaucasian Soviet Socialist Republic, which became part of the USSR. In 1936, after a reorganization, Armenia became a separate constituent republic of the USSR. Since 1988, Armenia has been involved in a territorial dispute with Azerbaijan over the enclave of Nagorno-Karabakh, to which both lay claim. Also in 1988, a devastating earthquake killed thousands and wreaked economic havoc.

Armenia declared its independence from the collapsing Soviet Union on Sept. 23, 1991. In 1992–1994, Armenia successfully fought Azerbaijan for control of Nagorno-Karabakh. The majority of the enclave are Armenian Christians who want to secede from Azerbaijan and either become part of Armenia or gain full independence. Enormous casualties were involved.

An Armenian diaspora has existed throughout the nation's history, and Armenian emigration has been particularly heavy since independence from the Soviet Union. An estimated 60% of the total 8 million Armenians worldwide live outside the country, with 1 million each in the U.S. and Russia. Significant Armenian communities are located in Georgia, France, Iran, Lebanon, Syria, Argentina, and Canada.

Australia

COMMONWEALTH OF AUSTRALIA

Sovereign: Queen Elizabeth II (1952)
Governor-General: Michael Jeffery (2003)
Prime Minister: John Howard (1996)
Area: 2,967,893 sq mi (7,686,850 sq km)
Population (2003 est.): 19,731,984 (growth rate: 0.5%); birth rate: 12.6/1000; infant mortality rate: 4.8/1000; density per sq mi: 7
Capital (2003 est.): Canberra, 327,700. **Largest cities:** Sydney, 4,250,100; Melbourne, 3,610,800; Brisbane, 1,545,700; Perth, 1,375,200; Adelaide, 1,087,600. **Monetary unit:** Australian dollar. **Language:** English. **Ethnicity/race:** Caucasian 92%, Asian 7%, aboriginal (353,000) and other 1%. **Religions:** Anglican 26.1%, Roman Catholic 26%, other Christian 24.3%. **Literacy rate:** 100% (1980 est.)
Economic summary: GDP/PPP (2001 est.): $465.9 billion; per capita $24,000. **Real growth rate:** 2.3%. **Inflation:** 4.3%. **Unemployment:** 6.7%. **Arable land:** 7%. **Agriculture:** wheat, barley, sugarcane, fruits; cattle, sheep, poultry. **Labor force:** 9.2 million (Dec. 2001); services 73%, industry 22%, agriculture 5% (1997 est.). **Industries:** mining, industrial and transportation equipment, food processing, chemicals, steel. **Natural resources:** bauxite, coal, iron ore, copper, tin, silver, uranium, nickel, tungsten, mineral sands, lead, zinc, diamonds, natural gas, petroleum. **Exports:** $68.8 billion (2001 est.): coal, gold, meat, wool, alumina, iron ore, wheat, machinery and transport equipment. **Imports:** $70.2 billion (2001 est.): machinery and transport equipment, computers and office machines, telecommunication equipment and parts; crude oil and petroleum products. **Major trading partners:** Japan, U.S., South Korea, China, New Zealand, Singapore, UK, Germany, Malaysia. **Member of Commonwealth of Nations**

Geography The continent of Australia, with the island state of Tasmania, is approximately equal in area to the United States (excluding Alaska and Hawaii). Mountain ranges run from north to south along the east coast, reaching their highest point in Mount Kosciusko (7,308 ft; 2,228 m). The western half of the continent is occupied by a desert plateau that rises into barren, rolling hills near the west coast. The Great Barrier Reef, extending about 1,245 mi (2,000 km), lies along the northeast coast. The island of Tasmania (26,178 sq mi; 67,800 sq km) is off the southeast coast.

Government Democracy. Symbolic executive power is vested in the British monarch, who is represented throughout Australia by the governor-general.

History The first inhabitants of Australia were the Aborigines, who migrated there at least 40,000 years ago from Southeast Asia. There may have been between a half million to a full million Aborigines at the time of European settlement; today there are about 350,000.

Dutch, Portuguese, and Spanish ships sighted Australia in the 17th century; the Dutch landed at the Gulf of Carpentaria in 1606. In 1616 the territory became known as New Holland. The British arrived in 1688, but it was not until Captain James Cook's voyage in 1770 that Great Britain claimed possession of the vast island, calling it New South Wales. A British penal colony was set up at Port Jackson (what is now Sydney) in 1788, and about 161,000 transported English convicts were settled there until the system was suspended in 1839.

Free settlers and former prisoners established six colonies: New South Wales (1786), Tasmania (then Van Diemen's Land) (1825), Western Australia (1829), South Australia (1834), Victoria (1851), and Queensland (1859). Various gold rushes attracted settlers, as did the mining of other minerals. Sheep farming and grain soon became important economic enterprises. The six colonies became states and in 1901 federated into the Commonwealth of Australia with a constitution that incorporated British parliamentary and U.S. federal traditions. Australia became known for its liberal legislation: free compulsory education, protected trade unionism with industrial conciliation and arbitration, the secret ballot, women's suffrage, maternity allowances, and sickness and old-age pensions.

Australia fought alongside Britain in World War I, notably with the Australia and New Zealand Army Corps (ANZAC) in the Dardanelles campaign (1915). Participation in World War II brought Australia closer to the United States. Parliamentary power in the second half of the 20th century shifted between three political parties: the Australian Labour Party, the Liberal Party, and the National Party. Australia relaxed its discriminatory immigration laws in the 1960s and 1970s, which favored Northern Europeans. Thereafter, about 40% of its immigrants came from Asia, diversifying a population that was predominantly of English and Irish heritage.

In March 1996 the opposition Liberal Party–National Party coalition easily won the national elections, removing the Labour Party after 13 years in power. Pressure from the new, conservative One Nation Party threatened to reduce the gains made by Aborigines and to limit immigration. An Aboriginal movement had grown in the 1960s that gained full citizenship and improved education for the country's poorest socioeconomic group.

In Sept. 1999, Australia led the international peacekeeping force sent to restore order in East Timor, Indonesia. Pro-Indonesian militias had begun massacring civilians following a UN-sponsored referendum that overwhelmingly called for East Timor's independence.

In Nov. 1999, Australia's 11.6 million voters rejected a referendum that would have ended Australia's formal allegiance to the British Crown. The referendum would have replaced the British governor-general with an Australian president chosen by Parliament. Although the vast majority of Australians do not consider themselves monarchists, they rejected the referendum because it did not provide for direct, popular elections but gave Parliament the power to select the president.

In 2000, Prime Minister Howard instituted a new tax system, lowering income and corporate taxes, and adding sales taxes on goods and services. Sydney hosted the 2000 Summer Olympic games.

John Howard won a third term of office in Nov. 2001, primarily as the result of his policy against illegal immigration, which some have condemned as xenophobic. Howard has dealt with refugees attempting to enter Australia—most of them from Afghanistan, Iran, and Iraq, and numbering about 5,000 annually—by imprisoning them in bleak detention camps and subjecting them to a lengthy immigration process. The asylum-seekers have staged riots and hunger strikes. Howard has also dealt with immigrants through the "Pacific solution," which re-routes boat people from Australian shores to camps in Papua New Guinea and Nauru.

Prime Minister Howard sent 2,000 Australian troops to fight alongside American and British troops in the 2003 Gulf War, despite strong opposition among Australians. There were no Australian casualties. In July, Australia sent a peace-keeping force to the Solomon Islands, which had descended into lawlessness during a brutal civil war.

Australian External Territories

Norfolk Island (13.36 sq mi; 34.6 sq km) was placed under Australian administration in 1914. Population 1,866 (July 2002 est.). Formerly a notorious penal colony, Norfolk Island became home to the entire population of Pitcairn Island in 1856. The 194 residents of tiny Pitcairn—all of whom were the descendants of the mutineers from the HMS *Bounty* and their Tahitian wives—embarked on the 3,700-mile journey to Norfolk because of overpopulation. Many Norfolk residents can trace their genealogy directly to the adventurers from *Bounty*.

The Ashmore and Cartier Islands (1.93 sq mi), situated in the Indian Ocean off the northwest coast of Australia, came under Australian administration in 1934.

Heard Island and the McDonald Islands (159 sq mi; 412 sq km), lying in the sub-Antarctic, were placed under Australian administration in 1947. The islands are uninhabited.

Christmas Island (52 sq mi; 135 sq km) is situated in the Indian Ocean. It came under Australian administration in 1958. Most of the island's residents had been phosphate miners until the 1990s, when the Australian-based Casinos Austria International Ltd. built a $45 million casino on Christmas Island. As a result, the population has more than doubled, to 2,771 (July 2001 est.).

Coral Sea Islands (400,000 sq mi; 1,036,000 sq km, but only a few sq mi of land) became a territory of Australia in 1969. There is no permanent population on the islands.

Cocos (Keeling) Islands are made up of a group of 27 small coral islands in two separate atolls in the Indian Ocean, 1,721 mi (2,768 km) northwest of Perth. West Island is the largest, about 6.2 mi (10 km) long. The islands became an Australian territory in 1955. In April 1984 the residents voted to merge with Australia. The population of the Cocos is 632 (July 2002 est.).

Austria

REPUBLIC OF AUSTRIA

National name: Republik Österreich
President: Thomas Klestil (1992)
Chancellor: Wolfgang Schüssel (2000)
Area: 32,378 sq mi (83,858 sq km)
Population (2003 est.): 8,188,207 (growth rate: –0.03%); birth rate 9.4/1000; infant mortality rate: 4.3/1000; density per sq mi: 253
Capital and largest city (2003 est.): Vienna, 2,041,300 (metro area), 1,523,600 (city proper). **Other large cities:** Graz, 219,500; Linz, 185,300; Salzburg, 145,500; Innsbruck, 115,600. **Monetary units:** Euro (formerly schilling). **Languages:** German 98% (small Slovene, Croatian, and Hungarian-speaking minorities). **Ethnicity/race:** German 88%, non-nationals 9.3% (includes Croatians, Slovenes, Hungarians, Czechs, Slovaks, Roma), naturalized 2%. **Religions:** Roman Catholic 78%, Protestant 5%, Islam and other 17%. **Literacy rate:** 98%
Economic summary: GDP/PPP (2001 est.): $220 billion; per capita $27,000. **Real growth rate:** 1.2%. **Inflation:** 2.6%. **Unemployment:** 4.8%. **Arable land:** 17%. **Agriculture:** grains, potatoes, sugar beets, wine,

fruit; dairy products, cattle, pigs, poultry; lumber. **Labor force:** 4.3 million; services 67%, industry and crafts 29%, agriculture and forestry 4%. **Industries:** construction, machinery, vehicles and parts, food, chemicals, lumber and wood processing, paper and paperboard, communications equipment, tourism. **Natural resources:** iron ore, oil, timber, magnesite, lead, coal, lignite, copper, hydropower. **Exports:** $70 billion (f.o.b., 2001) (2000 est.): machinery and equipment, motor vehicles and parts, paper and paperboard, metal goods, chemicals, iron and steel; textiles, foodstuffs. **Imports:** $73 billion (c.i.f., 2001): machinery and equipment, motor vehicles, chemicals, metal goods, oil and oil products; foodstuffs. **Major trading partners:** EU, Switzerland, U.S., Hungary.

Geography Slightly smaller than Maine, Austria includes much of the mountainous territory of the eastern Alps (about 75% of the area). The country contains many snowfields, glaciers, and snowcapped peaks, the highest being the Grossglockner (12,530 ft; 3,819 m). The Danube is the principal river. Forests and woodlands cover about 40% of the land.

Government Federal republic.

History Settled in prehistoric times, the central European land that is now Austria was overrun in pre-Roman times by various tribes, including the Celts. After the fall of the Roman Empire, of which Austria was part, the area was invaded by Bavarians and Slavic Avars. Charlemagne conquered the area in 788 and encouraged colonization and Christianity. In 1252, Ottokar, king of Bohemia, gained possession, only to lose the territories to Rudolf of Hapsburg in 1278. Thereafter, until World War I, Austria's history was largely that of its ruling house, the Hapsburgs. Austria emerged from the Congress of Vienna in 1815 as the continent's dominant power. The *Ausgleich* of 1867 provided for a dual sovereignty, the empire of Austria and the kingdom of Hungary, under Franz Joseph I, who ruled until his death on Nov. 21, 1916. The Austrian-Hungarian minority rule of this immensely diverse empire became increasingly difficult in an age of emerging nationalist movements. When Archduke Francis Ferdinand was assassinated by a Serbian nationalist in Sarajevo in 1914, World War I, as well as the destruction of the Austro-Hungarian Empire, began.

During World War I, Austria-Hungary was one of the Central powers with Germany, Bulgaria, and Turkey, and the conflict left the country in political chaos and economic ruin. Austria, shorn of Hungary, was proclaimed a republic in 1918, and the monarchy was dissolved in 1919. A parliamentary democracy was set up by the constitution of Nov. 10, 1920. To check the power of Nazis advocating union with Germany, Chancellor Engelbert Dolfuss in 1933 established a dictatorship, but was assassinated by the Nazis on July 25, 1934. Kurt von Schuschnigg, his successor, struggled to keep Austria independent, but on March 12, 1938, German troops occupied the country, and Hitler proclaimed its *Anschluss* (union) with Germany, annexing it to the Third Reich.

After World War II, the U.S. and Britain declared the Austrians a "liberated" people. But the Russians prolonged the occupation. Finally Austria concluded a state treaty with the USSR and the other occupying powers and regained its independence on May 15, 1955. The second Austrian republic, established Dec. 19, 1945, on the basis of the 1920 constitution (amended in 1929), was declared by the federal Parliament to be permanently neutral.

On June 8, 1986, former UN secretary-general Kurt Waldheim was elected to the ceremonial office of president in a campaign marked by controversy over his alleged links to Nazi war crimes in Yugoslavia. Austria became a member of the European Union in 1995, but it retained its strict constitutional neutrality and forbade the stationing of foreign troops on its soil.

In Feb. 2000 the conservative People's Party formed a coalition with the far-right Freedom Party, headed by Jörg Haider. A nationalist against immigration, Haider had made several controversial remarks praising some Nazi policies, which he has since recanted. His gradual rise to power—from 5% in 1983 to 28% in the October 1999 election—was credited to voters weary of decades of stasis under the rule of the Social Democrats. The European Union condemned Austria's new coalition, froze diplomatic contacts, and imposed sanctions, accusing Haider of being a racist, xenophobe, and Nazi-sympathizer. Austria responded angrily by criticizing the EU for interfering in the affairs of a democratically elected government. Given the controversy, Haider chose not to join the government and resigned from the party in May 2000, but he continued to wield influence from the sidelines. In Sept. 2000, the EU lifted sanctions against Austria. The Freedom Party's popularity began to decline markedly in 2001.

In Sept. 2002, the coalition between the People's Party and the Freedom Party dissolved after a shake-up in the Freedom Party, instigated by Haider. In Nov. 2002, the People's Party made large gains in general elections. After failed coalition talks with other parties, the People's Party again formed a government with the Freedom Party in Feb. 2003. A government plan to overhaul the country's pension program led to widespread strikes in May and June 2003—the first national strikes in decades.

Azerbaijan

REPUBLIC OF AZERBAIJAN

President: Heydar Aliyev (1993)
Prime Minister: Ilham Aliyev (2003)
Area: 33,436 sq mi (86,600 sq km)
Population (2003 est.): 7,830,764 (growth rate: 1.0%); birth rate: 19.3/1000; infant mortality rate: 82.4/1000; density per sq mi: 234
Capital and largest city (2003 est.): Baku, 2,118,600 (metro area), 1,235,400 (city proper), a port on the Caspian Sea. **Other large cities (2003 est.):** Ganja, 303,000; Sumgait, 280,500. **Monetary unit:** Manat. **Languages:** Azerbaijani Turkic, Russian, Armenian. **Ethnicity/race:** Azeri 90%, Dagestani 3.2%, Russian 2.5%, Armenian 2%, other 2.3% (1998 est.). Note: almost all Armenians live in the separatist Nagorno-Karabakh region. **Religions:** Islam 93.4%, Russian Orthodox 2.5%, Armenian Orthodox 2.3%, other 1.8% (1995 est.). **Literacy rate:** 97% (1989 est.)
Economic summary: GDP/PPP (2001 est.): $24.3 billion; per capita $3,100. **Real growth rate:** 9.9%. **Inflation:** 1.6%. **Unemployment:** 20% (official rate is 1.3% for 2001) (1999 est.). **Arable land:** 19%. **Agriculture:** cotton, grain, rice, grapes, fruit, vegetables, tea, tobacco; cattle, pigs, sheep, goats. **Labor force:** 2.9 million (1997); agriculture and forestry 32%, industry and construction 15%, services 53% (1997). **Industries:** petroleum and natural gas, petroleum products, oilfield equipment; steel, iron ore, cement; chemicals and petrochemicals; textiles. **Natural resources:** petroleum, natural gas, iron ore, nonferrous metals, alumina. **Exports:** $2 billion (f.o.b., 2001 est.): oil and gas 90%, machinery, cotton, foodstuffs. **Imports:** $1.6 billion (f.o.b., 2001): machinery and equipment, foodstuffs, metals, chemicals. **Major trading partners:** Italy, France, Israel, Turkey, Russia, U.S., Iran, Germany.

Geography Azerbaijan is located on the western shore of the Caspian Sea at the southeast extremity of the Caucasus. The region is a mountainous country. About 7% of it is arable land. The Kura River Valley is the area's major agricultural zone.

Government Constitutional republic.

History Northern Azerbaijan was known as Caucasian Albania in ancient times. The area was the site of many conflicts involving Arabs, Kazars, and Turks. After the 11th century, the territory became dominated by Turks and eventually a stronghold of the Shi'ite Muslim religion and Islamic culture. The territory of Soviet Azerbaijan was acquired by Russia from Persia through the Treaty of Gulistan in 1813 and the Treaty of Turkamanchai in 1828.

After the Bolshevik Revolution, Azerbaijan declared its independence from Russia in May 1918. The republic was reconquered by the Red Army in 1920, and was annexed into the Transcaucasian Soviet Socialist Republic in 1922. It was later reestablished as a separate Soviet Republic on Dec. 5, 1936. Azerbaijan declared independence from the collapsing Soviet Union on Aug. 30, 1991.

Since 1988, Azerbaijan and Armenia have been feuding over the enclave of Nagorno-Karabakh. The majority of the enclave's inhabitants are Armenian Christians agitating to secede from the predominantly Muslim Azerbaijan and join with Armenia. War broke out in 1988 when Nagorno-Karabakh tried to break away and annex itself to Armenia, and 30,000 died before a cease-fire agreement was reached in 1994, with Armenia regaining its hold over the disputed enclave. Final plans on the status of Nagorno-Karabakh have yet to be determined; in April 2001, however, Azerbaijani president Heydar Aliev and Armenian president Robert Kocharian met with American, French, and Russian negotiators, and made significant progress toward a settlement.

The country's economic troubles are expected to be transformed through Western investment in Azerbaijan's oil resources, an untapped reserve whose estimated worth is trillions of dollars. Since 1994, the Azerbaijan state oil company (SOCAR) has signed several billion-dollar agreements with international oil companies. A total of 15 production-sharing agreements have been signed; only one, run by BP-led Azerbaijan International Operating Company (AIOC) is thus far producing crude oil. Azerbaijan's pro-Western stance and its careful economic management have made it the most attractive of the oil-rich Caspian countries for foreign investment. In the years since its independence, the country has undergone rapid privatization and the IMF has given it high marks as one of the most successful economic overhauls ever.

But difficult negotiations over the route of the pipeline stalled Azerbaijan's potential oil boom. Routes through Russia, Turkey, Georgia, and Iran were proposed, and U.S., Russian, British, Iranian, and Chinese contenders in the "pipeline war" vied for dominance. In the volatile Caucasus region the options were complex, since all the proposed routes must pass through an unstable field of political, ethnic, religious, and environmental land mines. In 1999, a route through Georgia and Turkey, ending at the Mediterranean port of Ceyhan (favored by the U.S. because it bypasses Russia and Iran) was selected. In Sept. 2002, construction of the 1,100-mile Baku-Tblisi-Ceyhan pipeline began. Major investors are Britain's BP (33%), Azerbaijan's SOCAR (25%), the U.S.'s Unocal (8.9%), and Norway's Statoil (8.7%).

In 2003, President Aliyev, who is seriously ill, chose his son as the new prime minister, paving the way for his eventual succession. The opposition protested strenuously.

Bahamas

COMMONWEALTH OF THE BAHAMAS

Sovereign: Queen Elizabeth II (1952)
Governor-General: Ivy Dumont (2001)
Prime Minister: Perry Christie (2002)
Area: 5,382 sq mi (13,940 sq km)
Population (2003 est.): 297,477 (growth rate: 1.0%); birth rate: 18.6/1000; infant mortality rate: 26.2/1000; density per sq mi: 55
Capital and largest city (2003 est.): Nassau, 222,200. **Monetary unit:** Bahamian dollar. **Language:** English. **Ethnicity/race:** black 85%, white 12%, Asian and Hispanic 3%. **Religions:** Baptist 32%, Anglican 20%, Roman Catholic 19%, Methodist 6%, Church of God 6%, other Protestant 12%. **Literacy rate:** 98.2% (1995 est.)
Economic summary: GDP/PPP (2001 est.): $5 billion; per capita $16,800 (2000 est.). **Real growth rate:** 3.5%. **Inflation:** 1.5%. **Unemployment:** 6.9% (2001 est.). **Arable land:** 1%. **Agriculture:** citrus, vegetables; poultry. **Labor force:** 156,000 (1999); tourism 40%, other services 50%, industry 5%, agriculture 5% (1995 est.). **Industries:** tourism, banking, cement, oil refining and transshipment, salt, rum, aragonite, pharmaceuticals, spiral-welded steel pipe. **Natural resources:** salt, aragonite, timber, arable land. **Exports:** $535.8 million (2000): fish and crawfish; rum, salt, chemicals; fruit and vegetables (1999). **Imports:** $1.88 billion (2000): machinery and transport equipment, manufactures, chemicals, mineral fuels; food and live animals (1999). **Major trading partners:** U.S., France, Germany, UK, South Korea, Italy, Japan. **Member of Commonwealth of Nations**

Geography The Bahamas are an archipelago of about 700 islands and 2,400 uninhabited islets and cays lying 50 mi off the east coast of Florida. They extend for about 760 mi (1,223 km). Only about 30 of the islands are inhabited; the most important is New Providence (80 sq mi; 207 sq km), on which the capital, Nassau, is situated. Other islands include Grand Bahama, Abaco, Eleuthera, Andros, Cat Island, and San Salvador (or Watling's Island).

Government Parliamentary democracy.

History The Arawak Indians were the first inhabitants of the Bahamas. Columbus's first encounter with the New World was on Oct. 12, 1492, when he landed on the Bahamian island of San Salvador. The British first built settlements on the islands in the 17th century. In the early 18th century, the Bahamas were a favorite pirate haunt.

The Bahamas were a crown colony from 1717 until they were granted internal self-government in 1964. The islands moved toward greater autonomy in 1968 after the overwhelming victory in general elections of the Progressive Liberal Party, led by Prime Minister Lynden O. Pindling, over the predominantly white United Bahamians Party. With its new mandate from the 85% black population, Pindling's government negotiated a new constitution with Britain under which the colony became the Commonwealth of the Bahama Islands in 1969. On July 10, 1973, the Bahamas became an independent nation.

Once heavily reliant on agriculture and fishing, the Bahamas has diversified its economy into tourism, financial services, and international shipping. While it enjoys a per capita income that is among the top 30 in the world, there is a big gap between the urban middle class and poor farmers. In addition, the nation is vulnerable to hurricanes, which regularly inflict serious damage.

Bahrain

STATE OF BAHRAIN

Emir: Sheik Hamad ibn Isa al-Khalifah (1999)
Prime Minister: Sheik Khalifah ibn Sulman al-Khalifah (1970)
Area: 257 sq mi (665 sq km)
Population (2003 est.): 667,238 (growth rate: 1.5%); birth rate: 19.0/1000; infant mortality rate: 18.6/1000; density per sq mi: 2,599
Capital and largest city (2003 est.): Al-Manámah, 527,000 (metro area), 149,900 (city proper). **Monetary unit:** Bahrain dinar. **Languages:** Arabic (official), English, Farsi, Urdu. **Ethnicity/race:** Bahraini 63%, Asian 19%, other Arab 10%, Iranian 8%. **Religion:** Islam (Shi'ite 70%, Sunni 30%). **Literacy rate:** 88.5% (2002 est.)
Economic summary: GDP/PPP (2001 est): $8.4 billion; per capita $13,000. **Real growth rate:** 4%. **Inflation:** 1.5%. **Unemployment:** 15% (1998 est.). **Arable land:** 5%. **Agriculture:** fruit, vegetables; poultry, dairy products; shrimp, fish. **Labor force:** 295,000 (1998 est.); industry, commerce, and service 79%, government 20%, agriculture 1% (1997 est.). **Industries:** petroleum processing and refining, aluminum smelting, offshore banking, ship repairing; tourism. **Natural resources:** oil, associated and nonassociated natural gas, fish, pearls. **Exports:** $5.5 billion (f.o.b., 2001): petroleum and petroleum products, aluminum, textiles. **Imports:** $4.5 billion (f.o.b., 2001): crude oil, machinery, chemicals. **Major trading partners:** India, Saudi Arabia, Japan, South Korea, , U.S., UK, France, Japan.

Geography Bahrain is an archipelago in the Persian Gulf off the coast of Saudi Arabia. The islands for the most part are level expanses of sand and rock. A causeway connects Bahrain to Saudi Arabia.

Government Constitutional monarchy.

History Known in ancient times as Dilmun, Bahrain was an important center of trade by the 3rd millennium B.C. The islands were ruled by the Persians in the 4th century A.D., and then by Arabs until 1541, when the Portuguese invaded them. Persia again claimed Bahrain in 1602. In 1783 Ahmad ibn al-Khalifah took over, and the al-Khalifahs remain the ruling family today. Bahrain became a British protectorate in 1820. It did not gain full independence until Aug. 14, 1971.

Although oil was discovered in Bahrain in the 1930s, it was relatively little compared to other Gulf states, and the wells are expected to be the first in the region to dry up. Sheik Isa ibn-Sulman al-Khalifah, who became emir in 1961, was determined to diversify his country's economy, and set about establishing Bahrain as a major financial center. The country provides its people with free medical care, education, and old-age pensions.

Conflicts between the Shi'ites and Sunnis are a continuing problem in Bahrain. The Sunni minority, to which the ruling al-Khalifah family belongs, controls nearly all the power and wealth in the country. Shi'ite Muslims have continued to agitate for more representation in government, and minor violent clashes have led to about two dozen deaths since 1994.

Bahrain has been an important Western ally, serving as a Western air base during the Persian Gulf War in 1991 and the Iraq war in 2003. It continues to serve as the base of the United States' Fifth Fleet, which patrols the Gulf.

Sheik Isa ibn-Sulman al-Khalifah died in 1999 after four decades of rule. He was succeeded by his son, Sheik Hamad ibn Isa al-Khalifah, who immediately began a sweeping democratization of the country: censorship has been relaxed and draconian laws repealed, exiles have been repatriated, and the stateless Bidoons have been granted citizenship. In a Feb. 2001 referendum, which permitted women to vote for the first time, Bahrainis overwhelmingly supported the transformation of the traditional monarchy into a constitutional one. In Oct. 2002, Bahrain had its first parliamentary election since 1973.

Bangladesh

PEOPLE'S REPUBLIC OF BANGLADESH

President: Iajuddin Ahmed (2002)
Prime Minister: Khaleda Zia (2001)
Area: 55,598 sq mi (144,000 sq km)
Population (2003 est.): 138,448,210 (growth rate: 2.1%); birth rate: 29.9/1000; infant mortality rate: 66.1/1000; density per sq mi: 2,490
Capital and largest city (2003 est.): Dhaka, 10,356,500 (metro.area), 8,942,300 (city proper). **Other large cities:** Chittagong, 2,592,400; Khulna, 1,211,500. **Monetary unit:** Taka. **Principal Languages:** Bangla (official), English. **Ethnicity/race:** Bengali 98%, Biharis 250,000, tribals less than 1 million. **Religions:** Islam 83%, Hindu 16%, other 1%. **Literacy rate:** 56% (2000 est.)
Economic summary: GDP/PPP (2001 est.): $230 billion; per capita $1,750. **Real growth rate:** 5.6%. **Inflation:** 5.8% (2000 est.) **Unemployment:** 35% (2001 est.). **Arable land:** 61%. **Agriculture:** rice, jute, tea, wheat, sugarcane, potatoes, tobacco, pulses, oilseeds, spices, fruit; beef, milk, poultry. **Labor force:** 64.1 million (1998); note: extensive export of labor to Saudi Arabia, Kuwait, UAE, Oman, Qatar, and Malaysia; agriculture, 63%, services 26%, industry 11% (FY95/96). **Industries:** cotton textiles, jute, garments, tea processing, paper newsprint, cement, chemical fertilizer, light engineering, sugar. **Natural resources:** natural gas, arable land, timber, coal. **Exports:** $6.6 billion (2001): garments, jute and jute goods, leather, frozen fish and seafood. **Imports:** $8.7 billion (2001): machinery and equipment, chemicals, iron and steel, textiles, raw cotton, food, crude oil and petroleum products, cement. **Major trading partners:** U.S., Germany, UK, France, Netherlands, Italy, India, EU, Japan, Singapore, China. **Member of Commonwealth of Nations**

Geography Bangladesh, on the northern coast of the Bay of Bengal, is surrounded by India, with a small common border with Myanmar in the southeast. The country is low-lying riverine land traversed by the many branches and tributaries of the Ganges and Brahmaputra Rivers. Tropical monsoons and frequent floods and cyclones inflict heavy damage in the delta region.

Government Parliamentary democracy.

History What is now called Bangladesh is part of the historic region of Bengal, the northeast portion of the Indian subcontinent. The earliest reference to the region was to a kingdom called Vanga, or Banga (c. 1000 B.C.). Buddhists ruled for centuries, but by the 10th century Bengal was primarily Hindu. In 1576,

Bengal became part of the Mogul Empire, and the majority of East Bengalis converted to Islam. Bengal was ruled by British India from 1757 until Britain withdrew in 1947, and Pakistan was founded out of the two predominantly Muslim regions of the Indian subcontinent. West Pakistan and East Pakistan were united by religion (Islam), but their peoples were separated by culture, physical features, and 1,000 miles of Indian territory. Bangladesh consists primarily of East Bengal (West Bengal is part of India and its people are primarily Hindu) plus the Sylhet district of the Indian state of Assam. For almost 25 years after independence from Britain, its history was part of Pakistan's (*see* Pakistan).

Tension between East and West Pakistan developed from the outset because of their vast geographic, economic, and cultural differences. East Pakistan's Awami League, a political party founded by the Bengali nationalist Sheik Mujibur Rahman in 1949, sought independence from West Pakistan. Although 56% of the population resided in East Pakistan, the West held the lion's share of political and economic power. In 1970 East Pakistanis secured a majority of the seats in the National Assembly. President Yahya Khan postponed the opening of the National Assembly in an attempt to circumvent East Pakistan's demand for greater autonomy. As a consequence East Pakistan seceded, and the independent state of Bangladesh, or Bengali nation, was proclaimed on March 26, 1971. Civil war broke out, and with the help of Indian troops in the last few weeks of the war, East Pakistan defeated West Pakistan on Dec. 16, 1971. An estimated 1 million Bengalis were killed in the fighting or later slaughtered. Ten million more took refuge in India. In Feb. 1974, Pakistan agreed to recognize the independent state of Bangladesh.

Founding president Sheikh Mujibur was assassinated in 1975, as was the next president, Zia ur-Rahman. On March 24, 1982, Gen. Hossain Mohammad Ershad, army chief of staff, took control in a bloodless coup but was forced to resign on Dec. 6, 1990, amid violent protests and numerous allegations of corruption. A succession of prime ministers governed in the 1990s, including Khaleda Zia, wife of the assassinated president Zia ur-Rahman and Sheikh Hasina Wazed, the daughter of Sheik Mujibur.

Prime Minister Sheikh Hasina completed her five-year term as prime minister in July 2000—the first leader to do so since the country gained independence from Pakistan in 1974. In Oct. 2001 elections, Khaleda Zia again won the prime ministership.

Bangladesh is facing a catastrophic public-health crisis. Dangerous levels of arsenic have been found in groundwater, the result of a 30-year-old safe-water program. To save people from drinking contaminated river and pond water, between 3 million and 4 million wells were built throughout the country. But arsenic naturally occurring in the ground has seeped into well water, causing slow poisoning. The World Bank has estimated that as many as 35 million people may have been affected, with ailments ranging from cancer to diabetes to skin lesions.

In October 2002, the government began a three-month crackdown on crime, enlisting the army to help stem a rising problem. In all officials arrested more than 8,000 people. Human rights organizations reported abuses, but in Feb. 2003, parliament passed legislation that barred any civil legal action for injuries or other harm inflicted during "Operation Clean Heart."

Barbados

Sovereign: Queen Elizabeth II (1952)
Governor-General: Sir Clifford Husbands (1996)
Prime Minister: Owen Arthur (1994)
Area: 166 sq mi (431 sq km)
Population (2003 est.): 277,264 (growth rate: 0.4%); birth rate: 13.2/1000; infant mortality rate: 12.7/1000; density per sq mi: 1,666
Capital and largest city (2003 est.): Bridgetown, 98,900. **Monetary unit:** Barbados dollar. **Language:** English. **Ethnicity/race:** African 90%, European 4%, other 6%. **Religions:** Anglican 40%, Methodist 7%, Pentecostal 8%, Roman Catholic 4%. **Literacy rate:** 97.4% (1995 est.)
Economic summary: GDP/PPP (2001 est.): $4 billion; per capita: $14,500. **Real growth rate:** –2%. **Inflation:** 3.5%. **Unemployment:** 10%. **Arable land:** 37%. **Agriculture:** sugarcane, vegetables, cotton. **Labor force:** 128,500; services 75%, industry 15%, agriculture 10% (1996 est.). **Industries:** tourism, sugar, light manufacturing, component assembly for export. **Natural resources:** petroleum, fish, natural gas. **Exports:** $272 million (2000): sugar and molasses, rum, other foods and beverages, chemicals, electrical components, clothing. **Imports:** $1.16 billion (2000): consumer goods, machinery, foodstuffs, construction materials, chemicals, fuel, electrical components. **Major trading partners:** Caribbean community, U.S., UK, Japan, Canada. **Member of Commonwealth of Nations**

Geography An island in the Atlantic about 300 mi (483 km) north of Venezuela, Barbados is only 21 mi long (34 km) and 14 mi across (23 km) at its widest point. It is circled by fine beaches and narrow coastal plains. The highest point is Mount Hillaby (1,105 ft; 337 m) in the north-central area.

Government Parliamentary democracy.

History Barbados is thought to have been originally inhabited by Arawak Indians. By the time Europeans explored the island, however, it was uninhabited. The Portuguese were the first Europeans to set foot on the island, but it was the British who first established a colony there in 1627. Colonists first cultivated tobacco and cotton, but by the 1640s they had switched to sugar, which was enormously profitable. Slaves were brought in from Africa to work sugar plantations, and eventually the population was about 90% black. A slave revolt took place in 1816; slavery was abolished in the British Empire in 1834.

Barbados was the administrative headquarters of the Windward Islands until it became a separate colony in 1885. Barbados was a member of the Federation of the West Indies from 1958 to 1962. Britain granted the colony independence on Nov. 30, 1966, and it became a parliamentary democracy within the Commonwealth.

Since independence, Barbados has been politically stable. However, local anger over rulings by the final appeals court, appointed by Queen Elizabeth, led to the creation in 1997 of a constitutional commission to consider abandoning all ties to Great Britain.

Belarus

REPUBLIC OF BELARUS

President: Alyaksandr Lukashenka (1994)
Prime Minister: Syarhey Sidorski (acting) (2003)
Area: 80,154 sq mi (207,600 sq km)
Population (2003 est.): 10,322,151 (growth rate: –0.4%); birth rate: 10.2/1000; infant mortality rate: 13.9/1000; density per sq mi: 129

Capital and largest city (2003 est.): Mensk (Minsk), 1,769,500. **Other large cities:** Gomel, 502,200; Mogilyov, 374,000; Vitebsk, 355,800; Grodno, 314,100; Brest, 306,300; Bobruysk, 228,100. **Monetary unit:** Belorussian ruble. **Language:** Belorussian (White Russian). **Ethnicity/race:** Belorussian 81.2%, Russian 11.4%, Polish, Ukrainian, and other 7.4%. **Religion:** Orthodoxy is predominant. **Literacy rate:** 98% (1989 est.)

Economic summary: GDP/PPP (2001 est.): $84.8 billion; per capita $8,200. **Real growth rate:** 4.1%. **Inflation:** 46.1%. **Unemployment:** 2.1% officially registered unemployed (Dec. 2000); large number of underemployed workers. **Arable land:** 30%. **Agriculture:** grain, potatoes, vegetables, sugar beets, flax; beef, milk. **Labor force:** 4.8 million (2000); industry and construction n.a., agriculture and forestry n.a., services n.a. **Industries:** metal-cutting machine tools, tractors, trucks, earthmovers, motorcycles, television sets, chemical fibers, fertilizer, textiles, radios, refrigerators. **Natural resources:** forests, peat deposits, small quantities of oil and natural gas, granite, dolomitic limestone, marl, chalk, sand, gravel, clay. **Exports:** $7.5 billion (f.o.b., 2001): machinery and equipment, mineral products, chemicals, textiles, foodstuffs, metals. **Imports:** $8.1 billion (f.o.b., 2001): mineral products, machinery and equipment, chemicals, foodstuffs, metals. **Major trading partners:** Russia, Ukraine, Poland, Germany.

Geography Much of Belarus (formerly the Belorussian Soviet Socialist Republic of the USSR, and then Byelorussia) is a hilly lowland with forests, swamps, and numerous rivers and lakes. There are wide rivers emptying into the Baltic and Black Seas. Its forests cover over one-third of the land and its peat marshes are a valuable natural resource. The largest lake is Narach, 31 sq mi (79.6 sq km).

Government Republic.

History In the 5th century A.D., Belarus (also known as White Russia) was colonized by east Slavic tribes. Kiev dominated it from the 9th to 12th centuries. After the destruction of Kiev by the Mongols in the 13th century, the territory was conquered by the dukes of Lithuania, although it retained a degree of autonomy. Belarus became part of the Grand Duchy of Lithuania, which merged with Poland in 1569. Following the partitions of Poland in 1772, 1793, and 1795, in which Poland was divided among Russia, Prussia, and Austria, Belarus became part of the Russian empire.

Following World War I, Belarus proclaimed itself a republic, only to find itself occupied by the Red Army soon after its March 1918 announcement. The Polish-Soviet War of 1918–1921 was fought to decide the fate of Belarus. West Belarus was ceded to Poland; the larger eastern part formed the Belorussian SSR, and was then joined to the USSR in 1922. In 1939, the Soviet Union took back West Belarus from Poland under the secret protocol of the Nazi-Soviet Nonaggression Pact and incorporated it into the Belorussian Soviet Socialist Republic. Occupied by the Nazis in World War II, Belarus was one of the most devastated battlefields.

When the Chernobyl nuclear power plant in Ukraine exploded in 1986, 70% of its radioactivity fell on Belarus. Cancer and other illnesses have multiplied as a result.

Belarus declared its sovereignty in July 1990 and its independence in Aug. 1991. It became a cofounder of the Commonwealth of Independent States (CIS) in Dec. 1991. In Jan. 1994, the country's Parliament ousted its reform-minded leader, Stanislav Shushkevich, in protest against his support for market economics. He was replaced by Alyaksandr Lukashenka, who over the next two years greatly expanded the powers of the presidency. Lukashenka sought to renew ties with Russia, and, with much fanfare, Belarus and Russia signed a treaty in April 1997 aimed at significantly increasing cooperation between the two states, stopping just short of union.

The Russian financial crisis that began in fall 1998 severely affected Belarus's Soviet-style planned economy. Belarus is almost completely dependent on Russia, which buys 70% of its exports.

Critics continue to denounce the increasingly oppressive political atmosphere and human rights violations in Belarus under the Soviet-style authoritarianism of President Lukashenka. In 1999, the year Lukashenka was to step down, he rigged a national referendum allowing him to cancel the elections and remain president. Lukashenka's government has been accused of running a death squad that has killed dozens, including opposition party members and underworld figures. After harassing the opposition and curtailing their campaign activities, Lukashenka won reelection in the Sept. 9, 2001, presidential race.

Belgium

KINGDOM OF BELGIUM

National name: Royaume de Belgique—Koninkrijk België

Sovereign: King Albert II (1993)

Prime Minister: Guy Verhofstadt (1999)

Area: 11,780 sq mi (30,510 sq km)

Population (2003 est.): 10,289,088 (growth rate: 0.04%); birth rate: 10.4/1000; infant mortality rate: 4.6/1000; density per sq mi: 873

Capital and largest city (2003 est.): Brussels, 1,750,600 (metro area), 981,200 (city proper). **Other large cities:** Antwerp, 952,600 (metro area), 450,000 (city proper); Ghent, 226,900; Charleroi, 201,200; Liège, 185,700; Bruges, 117,200. **Monetary units:** Euro (formerly Belgian franc). **Languages:** Dutch (Flemish); French; German; legally bilingual (Dutch and French). **Ethnicity/race:** Fleming 58%, Walloon 31%, mixed or other 11%. **Religion:** Roman Catholic 75%. **Literacy rate:** 99% (1980)

Economic summary: GDP/PPP (2001 est.): $267.7 billion; per capita $26,100. **Real growth rate:** 1.1%. **Inflation:** 2.4%. **Unemployment:** 6.8%. **Arable land:** 25%. **Agriculture:** sugar beets, fresh vegetables, fruits, grain, tobacco; beef, veal, pork, milk. **Labor force:** 4.44 million; services 73%, industry 25%, agriculture 2% (1999 est.). **Industries:** engineering and metal products, motor vehicle assembly, processed food and beverages, chemicals, basic metals, textiles, glass, petroleum, coal. **Natural resources:** coal, natural gas. **Exports:** $160.3 billion (f.o.b., 2001): machinery and equipment, chemicals, diamonds, metals and metal products. **Imports:** $154 billion (f.o.b., 2001): machinery and equipment, chemicals, metals and metal products. **Major trading partners:** EU.

Geography Located in western Europe, Belgium has about 40 mi of seacoast on the North Sea, at the Strait of Dover, and is approximately the size of Maryland. The Meuse and the Schelde, Belgium's principal rivers, are important commercial arteries.

Government Parliamentary democracy under a constitutional monarch. Under the 1994 constitution, autonomy was granted to the Walloon region (Wallonia), the Flemish region (Flanders), and the bilingual Brussels-Capital region; autonomy was also guaranteed for the Flemish-, French-, and German-speaking "communities." The central government retains responsibility for foreign policy, defense, taxation, and social security.

History Belgium occupied part of the Roman province of Belgica, named after the Belgae, a people of ancient Gaul. The area was conquered by Julius Caesar in 57–50 B.C., then was overrun by the Franks in the 5th century A.D. It was part of Charlemagne's empire in the 8th century, then in the next century was absorbed into Lotharingia and later into the duchy of Lower Lorraine. In the 12th century it was partitioned into the duchies of Brabant and Luxembourg, the bishopric of Liège, and the domain of the count of Hainaut, which included Flanders. In the 16th century, Belgium, with most of the area of the low countries, passed to the duchy of Burgundy and was inherited by Charles V, who incorporated it into his Holy Roman Empire. Then, in 1555, the low countries were united with Spain. By the Treaty of Utrecht in 1713, the country's sovereignty passed to Austria. During the wars that followed the French Revolution, Belgium was occupied and later annexed to France. But with the downfall of Napoléon, the Congress of Vienna in 1815 gave the country to the Netherlands. The Belgians revolted in 1830 and declared their independence.

Germany's invasion of Belgium in 1914 set off World War I. The Treaty of Versailles (1919) gave the areas of Eupen, Malmédy, and Moresnet to Belgium. Leopold III succeeded Albert, king during World War I, in 1934. In World War II, Belgium was overwhelmed by Nazi Germany, and Leopold III was held prisoner. When he attempted to return in 1950, socialists and liberals revolted. He abdicated July 16, 1951, and his son, Baudouin, became king. Because of growing opposition to Belgian rule in its African colonies, Belgium granted independence to the Congo (now Democratic Republic of the Congo) in 1960 and to Ruanda-Urundi (now the nations of Rwanda and Burundi) in 1962.

Divisions between Flemings and Walloons grew, and linguistic regionalization increased, culminating in the revised constitution of 1994, which granted more autonomy to Belgium's three regions and language "communities."

In the 1990s the Belgian government was involved in numerous scandals that tainted it with a reputation for incompetence and corruption. In 1991, a deputy prime minister was murdered in a contract killing that remained unsolved. In 1998, Belgian statesman and former NATO secretary-general Willy Claes was convicted of bribery. International relations fared no better. Belgian peacekeeping troops abandoned Rwanda, a former colony, at the height of the 1994 genocide against the Tutsis. The discovery of the Dutroux child-sex-and-murder ring in 1996 led to further national outrage that was compounded by disclosures that official negligence and corruption had resulted in even more children's deaths. As the scandal continued into 1997, it fueled pressure for reform of the political, judicial, and police systems. In 1999, a public health scandal and cover-up involving Dioxin, a cancer-causing chemical, resulted in the resignation of Prime Minister Jean-Luc Dehaene. Dehaene has been credited with a significant upturn in the economy during the same period.

The new prime minister, Guy Verhofstadt of the Liberal Party, cobbled together a coalition of six political parties in June 1999. Verhofstadt has promised a series of reforms aimed at the legal system and the civil service.

Under "universal jurisdiction," Belgian prosecutors may try anyone accused of war crimes, whatever their nationality and wherever the crimes took place. In 2001, Belgian courts convicted four Rwandans, including two nuns, for their role in the massacre of the Tutsi people in Rwanda. In 2003, however, Belgium amended the law, severely limiting its scope—the country found itself overwhelmed with quixotic lawsuits against an assortment of world leaders including George W. Bush, Tony Blair, Ariel Sharon, and Yasir Arafat, among others.

In May 2003, Prime Minister Verhofstadt's coalition of Liberals and Socialists won a large victory in national elections. Verhofstadt has passed extremely liberal social policies, including the legalization of gay marriage, euthanasia, and marijuana.

Belize

Sovereign: Queen Elizabeth II (1952)
Governor-General: Sir Colville Young (1993)
Prime Minister: Said Musa (1998)
Area: 8,867 sq mi (22,966 sq km)
Population (2003 est.): 266,440 (growth rate: 2.4%); birth rate: 30.5/1000; infant mortality rate: 27.1/1000; density per sq mi: 30
Capital (2003 est.): Belmopan, 8,700. **Largest city:** Belize City, 52,600. **Monetary unit:** Belize dollar. **Languages:** English (official), Creole, Spanish, Garifuna, Mayan. **Ethnicity/race:** mestizo 48.7%, Creole 24.9%, Maya 10.6%, Garifuna 6.1%, other 9.7%. **Religions:** Roman Catholic 49.6%, Protestant 27%, other 14%. **Literacy rate:** 70.3% (1991 est.)
Economic summary: GDP/PPP (2001 est.): $830 million; per capita $3,250. **Real growth rate:** 3%. **Inflation:** 1.7%. **Unemployment:** 11.5% (2000). **Arable land:** 3%. **Agriculture:** bananas, coca, citrus, sugarcane; lumber; fish, cultured shrimp. **Labor force:** 90,000; note: shortage of skilled labor and all types of technical personnel (1997 est.); agriculture 27%, industry 18%, services 55%. **Industries:** garment production, food processing, tourism, construction. **Natural resources:** arable land potential, timber, fish, hydropower. **Exports:** $239.6 million (f.o.b., 2001 est.): sugar, bananas, citrus, clothing, fish products, molasses, wood. **Imports:** $505 million (c.i.f., 2001 est.): machinery and transportation equipment, manufactured goods; food, beverages, tobacco; fuels, chemicals, pharmaceuticals. **Major trading partners:** EU, U.S., Caricom, Canada, Mexico, Central America. **Member of Commonwealth of Nations**

Geography Belize is situated on the Caribbean Sea, south of Mexico and east and north of Guatemala in Central America. In area, it is about the size of New Hampshire. Most of the country is heavily forested with various hardwoods. Mangrove swamps and cays along the coast give way to hills and mountains in the interior. The highest point is Victoria Peak, 3,681 ft (1,122 m).

Government Parliamentary democracy within the British Commonwealth.

History The Mayan civilization spread into the area of Belize between 1500 B.C. and A.D. 300 and flourished until about 1200. Several major archeological sites—notably Caracol, Lamanai, Lubaantun, Altun Ha, and Xunantunich—reflect the advanced civilization and much denser population of that period. European contact began in 1502 when Columbus sailed along the coast. The first recorded European settlement was begun by shipwrecked English seamen in 1638. Over the next 150 years, more English settlements were established. This period was also marked by piracy, indiscriminate logging, and sporadic attacks by Indians and neighboring Spanish settlements. Great Britain first sent an official representative to the area in the late 18th century, but Belize was not formally termed the Colony of British Honduras until 1840. It became a Crown colony in 1862. Subsequently, several constitutional changes were enacted to expand representative government. Full internal self-government under a ministerial system was granted in Jan. 1964.

Guatemala had long made claims on Honduran territory. Although the dispute between Guatemala and Great Britain remained unresolved, Belize became independent on Sept. 21, 1981. Guatemala recognized Belize's sovereignty in Sept. 1991. However, Guatemala still claims more than half of Belize's territory. Prime Minister Said Musa was reelected to a second term in March 2003.

Benin

REPUBLIC OF BENIN

National name: Republique du Benin
President: Mathieu Kérékou (1996)
Area: 43,483 sq mi (112,620 sq km)
Population (2003 est.): 7,041,490 (growth rate: 3.0%); birth rate: 43.1/1000; infant mortality rate: 86.8/1000; density per sq mi: 162
Capital (2003 est.): Porto-Novo (official), 231,600. **Largest cities:** Cotonou (de facto capital) 734,600; Parakou 205,300; Djougou, 184,200. **Monetary unit:** CFA Franc. **Languages:** French (official), African languages. **Ethnicity/race:** African 99% (42 ethnic groups, most important being Fon, Adja, Yoruba, Bariba), Europeans 5,500. **Religions:** indigenous 50%, Christian 30%, Islam 20%. **Literacy rate:** 37.5% (2000)
Economic summary: GDP/PPP (2001 est.): $6.8 billion; per capita $1,040. **Real growth rate:** 5.4%. **Inflation:** 3%. **Unemployment:** n.a. **Arable land:** 15%. **Agriculture:** cotton, corn, cassava (tapioca), yams, beans, palm oil, peanuts, livestock. **Labor force:** n.a. **Industries:** textiles, food processing, chemical production, construction materials. **Natural resources:** small offshore oil deposits, limestone, marble, timber. **Exports:** $35.3 million (f.o.b., 2000): cotton, crude oil, palm products, cocoa. **Imports:** $437.6 million (c.i.f., 2000): foodstuffs, capital goods, petroleum products. **Major trading partners:** Brazil, France, Indonesia, Thailand, Morocco, Portugal, Côte d'Ivoire, U.S., China, Netherlands, Japan.

Geography This West African nation on the Gulf of Guinea, between Togo on the west and Nigeria on the east, is about the size of Tennessee. It is bounded also by Burkina Faso and Niger on the north. The land consists of a narrow coastal strip that rises to a swampy, forested plateau and then to highlands in the north. A hot and humid climate blankets the entire country.

Government Republic under a multiparty democratic rule.

History The Abomey kingdom of the Dahomey, or Fon, peoples was established in 1625. A rich cultural life flourished, and Benin's wooden masks, bronze statues, tapestries, and pottery are world renowned. One of the smallest and most densely populated regions in Africa, Benin was annexed by the French in 1893 and incorporated into French West Africa in 1904. It became an autonomous republic within the French Community in 1958, and on Aug. 1, 1960, Dahomey was granted its independence within the Community.

Gen. Christophe Soglo deposed the first president, Hubert Maga, in an army coup in 1963. He dismissed the civilian government in 1965, proclaiming himself chief of state. A group of young army officers seized power in Dec. 1967, deposing Soglo. In Dec. 1969, Benin had its fifth coup of the decade, with the army again taking power. In May 1970, a three-man presidential commission with a six-year term was created to take over the government. In May 1972, yet another army coup ousted the triumvirate and installed Lt. Col. Mathieu Kérékou as president. Between 1974 and 1989 Dahomey embraced socialism, and changed its name to the People's Republic of Benin. The name *Benin* commemorates an African kingdom that flourished from the 15th to the 17th century in what is now southwest Nigeria. In 1990, Benin abandoned Marxist ideology, began moving toward multiparty democracy, and changed its name again, to the Republic of Benin.

By the end of the 1980s, Benin's economy was near collapse. As its oil boom ended, Nigeria expelled 100,000 Beninese migrant workers and closed the border with Benin. Kérékou's socialist collectivization of Benin's agriculture and the ballooning bureaucracy further damaged the economy. By 1988, international financial institutions feared Benin would default on its loans and pressured Kérékou to make financial reforms.

Kérékou subsequently embarked on a major privatization campaign, cut the government payroll, and reduced social services, prompting student and labor union unrest. Fearing a revolution, Kérékou agreed to a new constitution and free elections. In 1991, Nicéphore Soglo, an economist and former director of the International Bank for Reconstruction and Development, was elected president. Although he enjoyed widespread support at first, Soglo gradually became unpopular as austerity measures reduced living standards and a 50% currency devaluation in 1994 caused inflation. Kérékou defeated Soglo in the 1996 elections, and was easily reelected In March 2001.

Bhutan

KINGDOM OF BHUTAN

National name: Druk-yul
Ruler: King Jigme Singye Wangchuck (1972)
Prime Minister: Lyonpo Kinzang Dorji (2002)
Area: 18,147 sq mi (47,000 sq km)
Population (2003 est.): 2,139,549 (growth rate: 2.1%); birth rate: 34.8/1000; infant mortality rate: 104.7/1000; density per sq mi: 118
Capital and largest city (2003 est.): Thimphu (official), 60,200. **Monetary unit:** Ngultrum. **Language:** Dzongkha (official). **Ethnicity/race:** Bhote 50%, ethnic Nepali 35%, indigenous or migrant tribes 15%. **Religions:** Buddhist 75%, Hindu 25%. **Literacy rate:** 42.2% (1995 est.)
Economic summary: GDP/PPP (2001 est.): $2.5 billion; per capita $1,200. **Real growth rate:** 6% (2000 est.). **Inflation:** 7% (2000 est.). **Unemployment:** n.a. **Arable land:** 3%. **Agriculture:** rice, corn, root crops, citrus, foodgrains; dairy products, eggs. **Labor force:** n.a.; note: massive lack of skilled labor; agriculture 93%, services 5%, industry and commerce 2%. **Industries:** cement, wood products, processed fruits, alcoholic beverages, calcium carbide. **Natural resources:** timber, hydropower, gypsum, calcium carbide. **Exports:** $154 million (f.o.b., 2000 est.): electricity (to India), cardamom, gypsum, timber, handicrafts, cement, fruit, precious stones, spices. **Imports:** $196 million (c.i.f., 2000 est.): fuel and lubricants, grain, machinery and parts, vehicles, fabrics, rice. **Major trading partners:** India, Bangladesh, Japan, UK, Germany, U.S.

Geography Mountainous Bhutan, half the size of Indiana, is situated on the southeast slope of the Himalayas, bordered on the north and east by Tibet and on the south and west and east by India. The landscape consists of a succession of lofty and rugged mountains and deep valleys. In the north, towering peaks reach a height of 24,000 ft (7,315 m).

Government In the 1990s, the king gradually gave up absolute rule, transforming his kingdom into a constitutional monarchy.

History Although archeological exploration of Bhutan has been limited, evidence of civilization in the region dates back to at least 2000 B.C. Aboriginal Bhutanese, known as Monpa, are believed to have migrated from Tibet. The traditional name of the country since the 17th century has been Drukyul, Land of the Drokpa (Dragon People), a reference to the dominant branch of Tibetan Buddhism that is still practiced in the Himalayan kingdom.

British troops invaded the region in 1865 and negotiated an agreement under which Britain agreed to pay an annual allowance to the Bhutanese monarchy on condition of good behavior. A treaty between India and the seat of government, Thimphu, in 1949 increased this subsidy and placed Bhutan's foreign affairs under Indian control. Until the 1960s Bhutan was largely isolated from the rest of the world, and its people carried on a tranquil, traditional way of life, farming and trading, which had remained intact for centuries. After China invaded Tibet, however, Bhutan strengthened its ties and contact with India in an effort to avoid Tibet's fate. New roads and other connections to India began to end its isolation. In the 1960s Bhutan also undertook social modernization, abolishing slavery and the caste system, emancipating women, and enacting land reform. In 1985, Bhutan made its first diplomatic links with non-Asian countries.

A pro-democracy campaign emerged in 1991, which the government claimed was composed largely of Nepali immigrants. As a result, some 100,000 Nepali civil servants were either evicted or encouraged to emigrate. Most of them crossed the border back into Nepal, where they were housed in UN-administered refugee camps. Several rounds of talks aimed at deciding which country should claim the refugees have yielded few results, and the refugees have continued to languish in the camps for more than a decade.

In 1998, King Jigme Singye Wangchuck voluntarily curtailed his powerful monarchy by yielding to the formerly rubber-stamp legislature, giving it the right to remove him from leadership and appoint his cabinet. The move was the largest step to date in a gradual program to dilute the monarchy after nearly a century of absolute rule. Bhutan edged closer to becoming a parliamentary democracy in December 2002, with the release of a draft constitution.

Bolivia

REPUBLIC OF BOLIVIA

National name: República de Bolivia
President: Gonzalo Sánchez de Lozada (2002)
Area: 424,162 sq mi (1,098,580 sq km)
Population (2003 est.): 8,586,443 (growth rate: 1.8%); birth rate: 25.5/1000; infant mortality rate: 56.0/1000; density per sq mi: 20
Historic and judicial capital (2003 est.): Sucre, 204,200; **Administrative capital:** La Paz, 1,576,100 (metro. area), 830,500 (city proper). **Other large cities:** Santa Cruz, 1,168,700; Cochabamba, 815,800; El Alto, 728,500; Oruro, 211,700. **Monetary unit:** Boliviano. **Languages:** Spanish (official), Quechua (official), Aymara (official). **Ethnicity/race:** Quechua 30%, Aymara 25%, mestizo (mixed European and Indian ancestry) 30%, European 15%. **Religion:** Roman Catholic 95%, Protestant 5%. **Literacy rate:** 83.1% (1995 est.)
Economic summary: GDP/PPP (2001 est.): $21.4 billion; per capita $2,600. **Real growth rate:** 0%. **Inflation:** 2%. **Unemployment:** 7.6% (2000) with widespread underemployment. **Arable land:** 2%. **Agriculture:** soybeans, coffee, coca, cotton, corn, sugarcane, rice, potatoes; timber. **Labor force:** 2.5 million; agriculture n.a., industry n.a., services n.a. **Industries:** mining, smelting, petroleum, food and beverages, tobacco, handicrafts, clothing. **Natural resources:** tin, natural gas, petroleum, zinc, tungsten, antimony, silver, iron, lead, gold, timber, hydropower. **Exports:** $1.2 billion (2001 est.): soybeans, natural gas, zinc, gold, wood. **Imports:** $1.5 billion (2001 est.): capital goods, raw materials and semi-manufactures, chemicals, petroleum, food. **Major trading partners:** U.S., Colombia, UK, Brazil, Peru, Argentina, Chile.

Geography Landlocked Bolivia is equal in size to California and Texas combined. Brazil forms its eastern border; its other neighbors are Peru and Chile on the west and Argentina and Paraguay on the south. The western part, enclosed by two chains of the Andes, is a great plateau—the Altiplano, with an average altitude of 12,000 ft (3,658 m). Almost half the population lives on the plateau, which contains Oruro, Potosí, and La Paz. At an altitude of 11,910 ft (3,630 m), La Paz is the highest administrative capital city in the world. The Oriente, a lowland region ranging from rain forests to grasslands, comprises the northern and eastern two-thirds of the country. Lake Titicaca, at an altitude of 12,507 ft (3,812 m), is the highest commercially navigable body of water in the world.

Government Republic.

History Famous since Spanish colonial days for its mineral wealth, modern Bolivia was once a part of the ancient Incan empire. After the Spaniards defeated the Incas in the 16th century, Bolivia's predominantly Indian population was reduced to slavery. The remoteness of the Andes helped protect the Bolivian Indians from the European diseases that decimated other South American Indians. But the existence of a large indigenous group forced to live under the thumb of their colonizers created a stratified society of haves and have-nots that continues to this day.

By the end of the 17th century the mineral wealth had begun to dry up. The country won its independence in 1825 and was named after Simón Bolívar, the famous liberator. Hampered by internal strife, Bolivia lost great slices of territory to three neighboring nations. Several thousand square miles and its outlet to the Pacific were taken by Chile after the War of the Pacific (1879–1884). In 1903, a piece of Bolivia's Acre Province, rich in rubber, was ceded to Brazil. And in 1938, after losing the Chaco War of 1932–1935 to Paraguay, Bolivia gave up its claim to nearly 100,000 square mi of the Gran Chaco. Political instability ensued.

In 1965, a guerrilla movement mounted from Cuba and headed by Maj. Ernesto (Ché) Guevara began a revolutionary war. With the aid of U.S. military advisers, the Bolivian army smashed the guerrilla movement, capturing and killing Guevara on Oct. 8, 1967. A string of military coups followed before the military returned the government to civilian rule in 1982, when

Hernán Siles Zuazo became president. At that point, Bolivia was regularly shut down by work stoppages and had the lowest per capita income in South America.

In June 1993, free-market advocate Gonzalo Sánchez de Lozada was elected president. He was succeeded by former general Hugo Bánzer, an ex-dictator-cum-democrat who became president for the second time in Aug. 1997. Bánzer made significant progress in wiping out illicit coca production and drug trafficking, which has pleased the United States. However, the eradication of coca, a major crop in Bolivia since Incan times, has plunged many Bolivian farmers into abject poverty.

In Aug. 2002, Gonzalo Sánchez de Lozada again became president, pledging to continue economic reforms and to create jobs. In Feb. 2003, rioting took place in protest against a proposed income tax, which the government then withdrew.

Bosnia and Herzegovina

THE FEDERATION OF BOSNIA AND HERZEGOVINA

Presidency, Chairman of the (rotating): Dragan Covic (2003)

Prime Minister: Adnan Terzic (2002)

Area: 19,741 sq mi (51,129 sq km)

Population (2003 est.): 3,989,018 (all data dealing with population is subject to considerable error because of the dislocations caused by military action and ethnic cleansing) (growth rate: 0.4%); birth rate: 12.7/1000; infant mortality rate: 22.7/1000; density per sq mi: 202

Capital and largest city (2003 est.): Sarajevo, 581,500 (unofficial). **Other large cities:** Banja Luka, 189,700; Tuzla 119,200; Mostar, 90,800. **Monetary unit:** Marka. **Language:** The language that used to be known as Serbo-Croatian but is now known as Serbian, Croatian, or Bosnian, depending on the speaker's ethnic and political affiliation. It is written in Latin and Cyrillic. **Ethnicity/race:** Serb 37.1%, Bosniak 48%, Croat 14.3%, other 0.5% (2000) . **Religions:** Slavic Muslim 40%, Orthodox 31%, Catholic 15%, Protestant 4%, other 10%. **Literacy rate:** 93% (1999)

Economic summary: GDP/PPP (2001 est.): $7 billion; per capita $1,800 . **Real growth rate:** 6%. **Inflation:** 5%. **Unemployment:** 40%. **Arable land:** 10%. **Agriculture:** wheat, corn, fruits, vegetables; livestock. **Labor force:** 1.026 million; agriculture n.a., industry n.a., services n.a. **Industries:** steel, coal, iron ore, lead, zinc, manganese, bauxite, vehicle assembly, textiles, tobacco products, wooden furniture, tank and aircraft assembly, domestic appliances, oil refining. **Natural resources:** coal, iron, bauxite, manganese, forests, copper, chromium, lead, zinc, hydropower. **Exports:** $1.1 billion (f.o.b., 2001 est.): miscellaneous manufactures, crude materials. **Imports:** $3.1 billion (f.o.b., 2001 est.): machinery and transport equipment, industrial products, foodstuffs. **Major trading partners:** Croatia, Switzerland, Italy, Germany, Slovenia.

Geography Bosnia and Herzegovina make up a triangular-shaped republic, about half the size of Kentucky, on the Balkan peninsula. The Bosnian region in the north is mountainous and covered with thick forests. The Herzegovina region in the south is largely rugged, flat farmland. It has a narrow coastline without natural harbors stretching 13 mi (20 km) along the Adriatic Sea.

Government Emerging democracy.

History Since the time of the Roman Empire, the Balkans has been a crossroads of religions and civilizations. The ethnic groups now known as Bosnians, Croats, and Serbs are largely the result of different religious and cultural identities created by contact with neighboring empires that expanded and contracted in the Balkans over centuries. With minor differences, they speak the same language, called Serbo-Croatian or sometimes Bosnian.

Called Illyricum in ancient times, the Romans conquered the area now called Bosnia and Herzegovina in the 2nd and 1st centuries B.C. and folded it into the Roman province of Dalmatia. In the 4th and 5th centuries A.D. Goths overran that portion of the declining Roman Empire and occupied the area until the 6th century, when the Byzantine Empire claimed it. Slavs began settling the region during the 7th century. Around 1200, Bosnia won independence from Hungary and endured as an independent Christian state for some 260 years.

The expansion of the Ottoman Empire into the Balkans introduced another cultural, political, and religious framework. The Turks defeated the Serbs at the famous battle of Kosovo in 1389. They conquered Bosnia in 1463. During the roughly 450 years Bosnia and Herzegovina were under Ottoman rule, many Christian Slavs became Muslim. A Bosnian Islamic elite gradually developed and ruled the country on behalf of the Turkish overlords. As the borders of the Ottoman Empire began to shrink in the 19th century, Muslims from elsewhere in the Balkans migrated to Bosnia. Bosnia also developed a sizable Jewish population, with many Jews settling in Sarajevo after their expulsion from Spain in 1492. However, through the 19th century the term *Bosnian* commonly included residents of all faiths. A relatively secular society, intermarriage among religious groups was not unknown.

Neighboring Serbia and Montenegro fought against the Ottoman Empire in 1876, and were aided by the Russians, their fellow Slavs. At the Congress of Berlin in 1878, following the end of the Russo-Turkish War (1877–1878), Austria-Hungary was given a mandate to occupy and govern Bosnia and Herzegovina, in an effort by Europe to ensure that Russia did not dominate the Balkans. Although the provinces were still officially part of the Ottoman Empire, they were annexed by the Austro-Hungarian Empire on Oct. 7, 1908. As a result, relations with Serbia, which had claims on Bosnia and Herzegovina, became embittered. The hostility between the two countries climaxed in the assassination of Austrian Archduke Franz Ferdinand in Sarajevo on June 28, 1914, by a Serbian nationalist. This event precipitated the start of World War I (1914–1918). Bosnia and Herzegovina were annexed to Serbia as part of the newly formed Kingdom of Serbs, Croats, and Slovenes on Oct. 26, 1918. The name was later changed to Yugoslavia in 1929.

When Germany invaded Yugoslavia in 1941, Bosnia and Herzegovina were made part of Nazi-controlled Croatia. During the German and Italian occupation, Bosnian and Herzegovinian resistance fighters fought a fierce guerrilla war against the Ustachi, the Croatian Fascist troops. At the end of World War II, Bosnia and Herzegovina were reunited into a single state as one of the six republics of the newly reestablished Communist Yugoslavia under Marshall Tito. His authoritarian control kept the ethnic enmities of his patchwork nation in check. Tito died in 1980, and with growing economic dissatisfaction and the fall of the iron curtain over the next decade, Yugoslavia began to splinter.

In Dec. 1991, Bosnia and Herzegovina declared independence from Yugoslavia and asked for recognition by the European Union (EU). In a March 1992 referendum, Bosnian voters chose independence, and President Izetbegovic declared the nation an independent state.

Unlike the other former Yugoslav states, which were generally composed of a dominant ethnic group, Bosnia was an ethnic tangle of Muslims (44%), Serbs (31%), and Croats (17%), and this mix contributed to the duration and savagery of its fight for independence.

Both the Croatian and Serbian presidents had planned to partition Bosnia between themselves. Attempting to carve out their own enclaves, the Serbian minority, with the help of the Serbian Yugoslav army, took the offensive and laid siege, particularly on Sarajevo, and began its ruthless campaigns of ethnic cleansing, which involved the expulsion or massacre of Muslims. Croats also began carving out their own communities. By the end of Aug. 1992, rebel Bosnian Serbs had conquered over 60% of Bosnia. The war did not begin to wane until NATO stepped in, bombing Serb positions in Bosnia in Aug. and Sept. 1995. Serbs entered the UN safe havens of Tuzla, Zepa, and Srebernica, where they murdered thousands.

U.S.-sponsored peace talks in Dayton, Ohio, led to an agreement in 1995 that called for a Muslim-Croat federation and a Serb entity within the larger federation of Bosnia. Sixty thousand NATO troops were to supervise its implementation. Fighting abated and orderly elections were held in Sept. 1996. President Alija Izetbegovic, a Bosnian Muslim, or Bosniac, won the majority of votes to become the leader of the three-member presidency, each representing one of the three ethnic groups.

But this alliance of unreconstructed enemies had little success in creating a working government or keeping violent clashes in check. The terms of the Dec. 1995 Dayton Peace Accord were largely ignored by Bosnian Serbs, with its former president, arch-nationalist Radovan Karadzic, still in de facto control of the Serbian enclave. Many indicted war criminals, including Karadzic, remain at large. Despite NATO's pledge in Oct. 1997 to remain in Bosnia beyond the 1998 mandate, the largely ineffective peacekeeping force was characterized by chronic ambivalence.

The crucial priorities facing postwar Bosnian leaders were rebuilding the economy, resettling the estimated 1 million refugees still displaced, and establishing a working government. Progress on these goals has been minimal, and a massive corruption scandal uncovered in 1999 severely tested the goodwill of the international community. Millions of dollars from international aid projects earmarked for reconstruction and humanitarian purposes had been pilfered by Bosnian officials, according to an American-led international antifraud unit.

In 1994, the UN's International Criminal Tribunal for the former Yugoslavia opened in The Hague, Netherlands. As of 2001, more than 100 individuals had been indicted. The first genocide conviction was handed down in Aug. 2001. Radislav Drstic, a Bosnian Serb general, was found guilty of genocide in the killing of up to 8,000 Bosnian Muslims in Srebrenica in 1995. It was the first genocide conviction in Europe since the UN genocide treaty was drawn up in 1951. In 2001, the trial of former Serbian president Slobodan Milosevic began. He was charged with crimes against humanity.

In July 2002, the presidents of Bosnia, Croatia, and Yugoslavia met for the first time since war broke out in the Balkans more than a decade ago. The countries pledged to cooperate on the repatriation of refugees, fight organized crime, and assist each other in economic development.

In presidential elections in Oct. 2002, the rotating tripartite presidency was divided between Mirko Sarovic (Serb Democratic Party), Dragan Covic (Croatian Democratic Union), and Sulejman Tihic (Party of Democratic Action, a primarily Muslim party). Adnan Terzic became prime minister in Dec. 2002. Sarovic, the Serb member of the presidency, was forced to resign in April 2003 following a scandal involving illegal military exports to Iraq. Borislav Paravac replaced him.

Botswana

REPUBLIC OF BOTSWANA

President: Festus Mogae (1998)
Area: 231,803 sq mi (600,370 sq km)
Population (2003 est.): 1,573,267 (growth rate: –0.6%); birth rate: 25.5/1000; infant mortality rate: 67.3/1000; density per sq mi: 7
Capital and largest city (2003 est.): Gaborone, 195,000. **Monetary unit:** Pula. **Languages:** English (official), Setswana. **Ethnicity/race:** Tswana (or Setswana) 79%, Kalanga 11%, Basarwa 3%, other (including Kgalagadi and white) 7%. **Religions:** indigenous beliefs 85%, Christian 15%. **Literacy rate:** 69.8% (1995 est.)
Economic summary: GDP/PPP (2001 est.): $12.4 billion; per capita $7,800. **Real growth rate:** 4.7%. **Inflation:** 6.6%. **Unemployment:** 40% (official rate is 21%). **Arable land:** 1%. **Agriculture:** livestock, sorghum, maize, millet, beans, sunflowers, groundnuts. **Labor force:** 264,000 formal sector employees (2000). **Industries:** diamonds, copper, nickel, coal, salt, soda ash, potash; livestock processing; textiles. **Natural resources:** diamonds, copper, nickel, soda ash, meat, textiles. **Exports:** $2.5 billion (f.o.b., 2001 est.): diamonds 80%, copper, nickel, soda ash, meat, textiles (2001). **Imports:** $2.1 billion (f.o.b., 2001 est.): foodstuffs, machinery, electrical goods, transport equipment, textiles, fuel and petroleum products, wood and paper products, metal and metal products (2000). **Major trading partners:** European Free Trade Association (EFTA), Southern African Customs Union (SACU), Zimbabwe. **Member of Commonwealth of Nations**

Geography Twice the size of Arizona, Botswana is in south-central Africa, bounded by Namibia, Zambia, Zimbabwe, and South Africa. Most of the country is near-desert, with the Kalahari occupying the western part of the country. The eastern part is hilly, with salt lakes in the north.

Government Parliamentary republic.

History The earliest inhabitants of the region were the San, who were followed by the Tswana. About half the country today is ethnic Tswana. The term for the country's people, *Batswana,* refers to national rather than ethnic origin.

Encroachment by the Zulu in the 1820s and by Boers from Transvaal in the 1870s and 1880s threatened the peace of the region. In 1885, Britain established the area as a protectorate, then known as Bechuanaland. In 1961, Britain granted a constitution to the country. Self-government began in 1965, and on Sept. 30, 1966, the country became independent. Botswana is Africa's oldest democracy.

The new country maintained good relations with its white-ruled neighbors, but gradually changed its policies, harboring rebel groups from South Rhodesia as well as some from South Africa.

Although Botswana is rich in diamonds, it has high unemployment and stratified socioeconomic classes. In 1999 it suffered its first budget deficit in 16 years because of a slump in the international diamond market. Yet it remains one of the wealthiest as well as most stable countries on the continent.

After 17 years in power, President Ketumile Masire retired in 1997, and Festus Mogae, an Oxford-educated economist, became the new president. Mogae has won high marks from the international financial community for continuing to privatize Botswana's mining and industrial operations.

Although Botswana's economic outlook remains strong, the devastation that AIDS is causing threatens to destroy the country's future. In 2001, Botswana had the highest rate of HIV infection in the world: 350,000 of its 1.6 million people were infected, and half the population between 25 and 29 are dying of the disease. In 2002, however, Botswana, with the help of international donors, launched an ambitious national campaign against AIDS that promises that there will be no new HIV cases by 2016, the 50th anniversary of the country's independence.

Brazil

FEDERATIVE REPUBLIC OF BRAZIL

National name: República Federativa do Brasil
President: Luiz Inácio Lula da Silva (2003)
Area: 3,286,470 sq mi (8,511,965 sq km)
Population (2003 est.): 182,032,604 (growth rate: 1.2%); birth rate: 17.7/1000; infant mortality rate: 31.7/1000; density per sq mi: 55
Capital (2003 est.): Brasília, 2,160,100. **Largest cities:** São Paulo, 18,847,400 (metro. area), 10,195,000 (city proper); Rio de Janeiro, 11,437,100 (metro. area), 6,119,800 (city proper); Salvador, 2,590,400; Belo Horizonte, 2,347,500; Recife, 1,485,500; Porto Alegre, 1,372,700. **Monetary unit:** Real. **Language:** Portuguese. **Ethnicity/race:** white (includes Portuguese, German, Italian, Spanish, Polish) 55%, mixed white and African 38%, African 6%, other (includes Japanese, Arab, Amerindian) 1%. **Religion:** Roman Catholic 80% (nominal). **Literacy rate:** 83.3% (1995 est.)
Economic summary: GDP/PPP (2001 est.): $1.34 trillion; per capita $7,400 (2000 est.). **Real growth rate:** 1.9% (2001 est.). **Inflation:** 7.7%. **Unemployment:** 6.4%. **Arable land:** 6%. **Agriculture:** coffee, soybeans, wheat, rice, corn, sugarcane, cocoa, citrus; beef. **Labor force:** 79 million (1999 est.); services 53%, agriculture 23%, industry 24%. **Industries:** textiles, shoes, chemicals, cement, lumber, iron ore, tin, steel, aircraft, motor vehicles and parts, other machinery and equipment. **Natural resources:** bauxite, gold, iron ore, manganese, nickel, phosphates, platinum, tin, uranium, petroleum, hydropower, timber. **Exports:** $57.8 billion (f.o.b., 2001 est.): manufactures, iron ore, soybeans, footwear, coffee, autos. **Imports:** $57.7 billion (f.o.b., 2001): machinery and equipment, chemical products, oil, electricity, autos and auto parts. **Major trading partners:** U.S., Argentina, Germany, Japan, Italy, Netherlands.

Geography Brazil covers nearly half of South America and is the continent's largest nation. It extends 2,965 mi (4,772 km) north-south, 2,691 mi (4,331 km) east-west, and borders every nation on the continent except Chile and Ecuador. Brazil may be divided into the Brazilian Highlands, or plateau, in the south and the Amazon River Basin in the north. More than a third of Brazil is drained by the Amazon and its more than 200 tributaries. The Amazon is navigable for ocean steamers to Iquitos, Peru, 2,300 mi (3,700 km) upstream. Southern Brazil is drained by the Plata system—the Paraguay, Uruguay, and Paraná Rivers.

Government Federal republic.

History Brazil is the only Latin American nation that derives its language and culture from Portugal. The native inhabitants mostly consisted of the nomadic Tupí-Guaraní Indians. Adm. Pedro Alvares Cabral claimed the territory for Portugal in 1500. The early explorers brought back a wood that produced a red dye, *pau-brasil,* from which the land received its name. Portugal began colonization in 1532 and made the area a royal colony in 1549.

During the Napoleonic Wars, King João VI, fearing the advancing French armies, fled the country in 1808 and set up his court in Rio de Janeiro. João was drawn home in 1820 by a revolution, leaving his son as regent. When Portugal tried to reimpose colonial rule, the prince declared Brazil's independence on Sept. 7, 1822, becoming Pedro I, emperor of Brazil. Harassed by his Parliament, Pedro I abdicated in 1831 in favor of his five-year-old son, who became emperor in 1840 (Pedro II). The son was a popular monarch, but discontent built up and, in 1889, following a military revolt, he abdicated. Although a republic was proclaimed, Brazil was ruled by military dictatorships until a revolt permitted a gradual return to stability under civilian presidents.

President Wenceslau Braz cooperated with the Allies and declared war on Germany during World War I. In World War II, Brazil again cooperated with the Allies, welcoming Allied air bases, patrolling the South Atlantic, and joining the invasion of Italy after declaring war on the Axis powers.

After a military coup in 1964, Brazil had a series of military governments. Gen. João Baptista de Oliveira Figueiredo became president in 1979 and pledged a return to democracy in 1985. The election of Tancredo Neves on Jan. 15, 1985, the first civilian president since 1964, brought a nationwide wave of optimism, but when Neves died several months later, Vice President José Sarney became president. Collor de Mello won the election of late 1989, pledging to lower hyperinflation with free-market economics. When Collor faced impeachment by Congress because of a corruption scandal in Dec. 1992 and resigned, Vice President Itamar Franco assumed the presidency.

A former finance minister, Fernando Cardoso, won the presidency in the Oct. 1994 election with 54% of the vote. Cardoso sold off inefficient government-owned monopolies in the telecommunication, electrical power, port, mining, railway, and banking industries.

In Jan. 1999, the Asian economic crisis spread to Brazil. Rather than prop up the currency through financial markets, Brazil opted to let the currency float, which sent the real plummeting—at one time as much as 40%. Cardoso was highly praised by the international community for quickly turning around his country's economic crisis. Despite his efforts, however, the economy continued to slow throughout 2001, and the country also faced an energy crisis. The IMF offered Brazil an additional aid package in Aug. 2001. And in Aug. 2002, to ensure that Brazil would not be dragged down by neighboring Argentina's catastrophic economic problems, the IMF agreed to lend Brazil a phenomenal $30 billion over fifteen months.

In Jan. 2003, Luiz Inacio Lula da Silva, a former trade union leader and factory worker widely known by the name Lula, became Brazil's first working-class president. As leader of Brazil's only socialist party, the Workers' Party, Lula has pledged to increase social services and improve the lot of the poor. To improve Brazil's economy, however, fiscal austerity will be essential. The president's first major legislative success came in July when his plan to reform the country's debt-ridden pension system—which operates under an annual $20 billion deficit—was approved. Civil servants, however, have staged massive strikes opposing the reforms. But polls in August demonstrated that the majority of Brazilians continued to support Lula's tough economic reform efforts.

Brunei Darussalam

STATE OF BRUNEI DARUSSALAM

Sultan: Haji Hassanal Bolkiah (1967)
Area: 2,228 sq mi (5,770 sq km)
Population (2003 est.): 358,098 (growth rate: 1.6%); birth rate: 19.7/1000; infant mortality rate: 13.5/1000; density per sq mi: 161
Capital and largest city (2003 est.): Bandar Seri Begawan, 78,000. **Other large cities:** Kuala Belait 27,800, Seria 23,400. **Monetary unit:** Brunei dollar. **Languages:** Malay (official), Chinese, English. **Ethnicity/race:** Malay 67%, Chinese 15%, other 18%. **Religions:** Islam (official religion) 67%, Buddhist 13%, Christian 10%, indigenous beliefs and other 10%. **Literacy rate:** 88.2% (1995 est.)
Economic summary: GDP/PPP (2001 est.): $6.2 billion; per capita $18,000. **Real growth rate:** 3%. **Inflation:** 1% (1999 est.). **Unemployment:** 10% (2001 est.). **Arable land:** 1%. **Agriculture:** rice, vegetables, fruits, chickens, water buffalo. **Labor force:** 143,400 (1999 est.); note: includes foreign workers and military personnel; note: temporary residents make up 41% of labor force (1991 est.); government 48%, production of oil, natural gas, services, and construction 42%, agriculture, forestry, and fishing 10% (1999 est.). **Industries:** petroleum, petroleum refining, liquefied natural gas, construction. **Natural resources:** petroleum, natural gas, timber. **Exports:** $3 billion (f.o.b., 2000 est.): crude oil, natural gas, refined products. **Imports:** $1.4 billion (c.i.f., 2000 est.): machinery and transport equipment, manufactured goods, food, chemicals. **Major trading partners:** Japan, U.S., South Korea, Thailand, Singapore, UK, Malaysia.

Geography About the size of Delaware, Brunei is an independent sultanate on the northwest coast of the island of Borneo in the South China Sea, wedged between the Malaysian states of Sabah and Sarawak.

Government Constitutional sultanate.

History Brunei was trading with China during the 6th century, and, through allegiance to the Javanese Majapahit kingdom (13th to 15th century), it came under Hindu influence. In the early 15th century, with the decline of the Majapahit kingdom and widespread conversion to Islam, Brunei became an independent sultanate. It was a powerful state from the 16th to the 19th century, ruling over the northern part of Borneo and adjacent island chains. But it fell into decay and lost Sarawak in 1841, becoming a British protectorate in 1888 and a British dependency in 1905. Japan occupied Brunei during World War II; it was liberated by Australia in 1945.

The sultan regained control over internal affairs in 1959, but Britain retained responsibility for the state's defense and foreign affairs until 1984, when the sultanate became fully independent. Sultan Bolkiah was crowned in 1967 at the age of 22, succeeding his father, Sir Omar Ali Saifuddin, who had abdicated. During his reign, exploitation of the rich Seria oilfield had made the sultanate wealthy. Brunei has one of the highest per capita incomes in Asia, and the sultan is believed to be one of the richest men in the world. In Aug. 1998, Oxford-educated Prince Al-Muhtadee Billah was inaugurated as heir to the 500-year-old monarchy.

Bulgaria

REPUBLIC OF BULGARIA

National name: Republika Bulgariya
President: Georgi Purvanov (2002)
Prime Minister: Simeon Saxe-Coburg Gotha (2001)
Area: 42,822 sq mi (110,910 sq km)
Population (2003 est.): 7,537,929 (growth rate: –0.6%); birth rate: 8.0/1000; infant mortality rate: 13.7/1000; density per sq mi: 176
Capital and largest city (2003 est.): Sofia, 1,088,700. **Other large cities:** Plovdiv, 338,200; Varna, 312,300; Burgas, 192,000; Ruse, 161,000. **Monetary unit:** Lev. **Language:** Bulgarian. **Ethnicity/race:** Bulgarian 83.6%, Turk 9.5%, Roma 4.6%, other (including Macedonian, Armenian, Tatar, Circassian) 2.3%. **Religions:** Bulgarian Orthodox 83.8%, Islam 12.1%, Roman Catholic 1.7%, Jewish 0.1%, Protestant, Gregorian-Armenian, and other 2.3%. **Literacy rate:** 98% (1999)
Economic summary: GDP/PPP (2001 est.): $48 billion; per capita $6,200. **Real growth rate:** 4%. **Inflation:** 7.5%. **Unemployment:** 17.5%. **Arable land:** 39%. **Agriculture:** vegetables, fruits, tobacco, livestock, wine, wheat, barley, sunflowers, sugar beets. **Labor force:** 3.83 million (2000 est.); agriculture 26%, industry 31%, services 43% (1998 est.). **Industries:** electricity, gas and water; food, beverages and tobacco; machinery and equipment, base metals, chemical products, coke, refined petroleum, nuclear fuel. **Natural resources:** bauxite, copper, lead, zinc, coal, timber, arable land. **Exports:** $4.6 billion (f.o.b., 2001 est.): clothing, footwear, iron and steel, machinery and equipment, fuels. **Imports:** $6.2 billion (f.o.b., 2001 est.): fuels, minerals, and raw materials; machinery and equipment; metals and ores; chemicals and plastics; food, textiles. **Major trading partners:** Italy, Turkey, Germany, Greece, Yugoslavia, Russia, France.

Geography Bulgaria shares borders with Serbia, Macedonia, Romania, Greece, and Turkey. Two mountain ranges and two great valleys mark the topography of Bulgaria, a country the size of Tennessee and situated on the Black Sea. The Maritsa is Bulgaria's principal river, and the Danube also flows through the country.

Government Parliamentary democracy.

History The Thracians lived in what is now known as Bulgaria from about 3500 B.C. They were incorporated into the Roman Empire by the first century A.D. At the decline of the empire, the Goths, Huns, Bulgars, and Avars invaded. The Bulgars, who crossed the Danube from the north in 679, took control of the region. Although the country bears the name of the Bulgars, the Bulgar language and culture died out, replaced by a Slavic language, writing, and religion. In 865, Boris I adopted Orthodox Christianity. The Bulgars twice conquered most of the Balkan peninsula between 893 and 1280. But in 1396 they were invaded by the Ottoman Empire, which made Bulgaria a Turkish province until 1878. Ottoman rule was harsh and inescapable, given Bulgaria's proximity to its oppressor. In 1878, Russia forced Turkey to give Bulgaria its independence after the Russo-Turkish War (1877–1878), but the European powers, fearing Russia's and Bulgaria's dominance in the Balkans, intervened at the Congress of Berlin (1878), limited Bulgaria's territory, and fashioned it into a small principality ruled by the nephew of the Russian czar, Alexander of Battenburg.

Alexander was succeeded in 1887 by Prince Ferdinand of Saxe-Coburg-Gotha, who declared a kingdom independent of Russia on Oct. 5, 1908. In the First Balkan War (1912–1913), Bulgaria and the other members of the Balkan League fought against Turkey to regain Balkan territory. Angered by the small portion of Macedonia it received after the battle—it considered Macedonia an integral part of Bulgaria—the country instigated the Second Balkan War (June–Aug. 1913) against Turkey as well as its former allies. Bulgaria lost the war and all the territory it had gained in the First Balkan War. Bulgaria joined Germany in World War I in the hope of again gaining Macedonia. After this second failure, Ferdinand abdicated in favor of his son in 1918. Boris III squandered Bulgaria's resources and assumed dictatorial powers in 1934–1935. Bulgaria fought on the side of the Nazis in World War II, but after Russia declared war on Bulgaria on Sept. 5, 1944, Bulgaria switched sides. Three days later, on Sept. 9, 1944, a Communist coalition took control of the country and set up a government under Kimon Georgiev.

A Soviet-style People's Republic was established in 1947 and Bulgaria acquired the reputation of being the most slavishly loyal to Moscow of all the East European Communist countries. The general secretary of the Bulgarian Communist Party, Todor Zhikov, resigned in 1989 after 35 years in power. His successor, Peter Mladenov, purged the Politburo, ended the Communist monopoly on power, and held free elections in May 1990 that led to a surprising victory for the Communist Party, renamed the Bulgarian Socialist Party (BSP). Mladenov was forced to resign in July 1990.

In Oct. 1991, the Union of Democratic Forces won, forming Bulgaria's first non-Communist government since 1946. Power shifted back and forth between the pro-Western Union of Democratic Forces (UDF) and the BSP during the 1990s. The economy continued to deteriorate amid growing concern over the spread of organized crime. A new UDF government, led by Prime Minister Ivan Kostov, was elected in 1997 to overhaul the economic system and institute reforms aimed at stopping the rise of public corruption. Progress on both fronts remained slow. As a result, the UDF lost the July 2001 election to the former king of Bulgaria, leader of the Simeon II National Movement (SNM). The new prime minister, Simeon Saxe-Coburg Gotha (Simeon II), had been dethroned 55 years earlier (at age nine) during the Communist take-over of the country.

Bulgaria became a member of NATO in 2003. It was one of just four UN Security Council members to support the war in Iraq, and in July 2003 it sent a security force of 500 to help police the country.

Burkina Faso

National name: Burkina Faso
President: Blaise Compaoré (1987)
Prime Minister: Paramanga Ernest Yonli (2000)
Area: 105,869 sq mi (274,200 sq km)
Population (2003 est.): 13,228,460 (growth rate: 2.6%); birth rate: 44.8/1000; infant mortality rate: 99.8/1000; density per sq mi: 125
Capital and largest city (2003 est.): Ouagadougou, 962,100. **Monetary unit:** CFA Franc. **Languages:** French (official), tribal languages. **Ethnicity/race:** Mossi (over 40%), Gurunsi, Senufo, Lobi, Bobo, Mande, Fulani. **Religions:** Islam 50%, Christian (mainly Roman Catholic) 10%, indigenous beliefs 40%. **Literacy rate:** 36% (2001)
Economic summary: GDP/PPP (2001 est.): $12.8 billion; per capita $1,040. **Real growth rate:** 4.7%. **Inflation:** 3.5%. **Unemployment:** n.a. **Arable land:** 13%. **Agriculture:** peanuts, shea nuts, sesame, cotton, sorghum, millet, corn, rice; livestock. **Labor force:** 5 million (1999); note: a large part of the male labor force migrates annually to neighboring countries for seasonal employment; agriculture 90% (2000 est.). **Industries:** cotton lint, beverages, agricultural processing, soap, cigarettes, textiles, gold. **Natural resources:** manganese, limestone, marble; small deposits of gold, antimony, copper, nickel, bauxite, lead, phosphates, zinc, silver. **Exports:** $265 million (f.o.b., 2001 est.): cotton, animal products, gold. **Imports:** $580 million (f.o.b., 2001 est.): capital goods, food products, petroleum. **Major trading partners:** Venezuela, Benelux, Italy, France, Côte d'Ivoire.

Geography Slightly larger than Colorado, Burkina Faso, formerly known as Upper Volta, is a landlocked country in West Africa. Its neighbors are Côte d'Ivoire, Mali, Niger, Benin, Togo, and Ghana. The country consists of extensive plains, low hills, high savannas, and a desert area in the north.

Government Parliamentary.

History Burkina Faso was originally inhabited by the Bobo, Lobi, and Gurunsi peoples, with the Mossi and Gurma peoples immigrating to the region in the 14th century. The lands of the Mossi empire became a French protectorate in 1897, and by 1903 France had subjugated the other ethnic groups. Called Upper Volta by the French, it became a separate colony in 1919, was partitioned among Niger, the Sudan, and Côte d'Ivoire in 1932, and was reconstituted in 1947. An autonomous republic within the French Community, Upper Volta became independent on Aug. 5, 1960.

President Maurice Yameogo was deposed on Jan. 3, 1966, by a military coup led by Col. Sangoulé Lamizana, who dissolved the National Assembly and suspended the constitution. Constitutional rule returned in 1978 with the election of an Assembly and a presidential vote in June in which Gen. Lamizana won by a narrow margin over three other candidates.

On Nov. 25, 1980, Col. Sayé Zerbo led a bloodless coup that toppled Lamizana. In turn, Maj. Jean-Baptist Ouedraogo ousted Zerbo on Nov. 7, 1982. But the real revolutionary change occurred the following year when a 33-year-old flight commander, Thomas Sankara, took control. A Marxist-Leninist, he challenged the traditional Mossi chiefs, advocated women's liberation, and allied the country with North Korea, Libya, and Cuba. To sever ties to the colonial past, Sankara changed the name of the country in 1984 to Burkina Faso, which combines two of the nation's languages and means "the land of upright men."

While Sankara's investments in schools, food production, and clinics brought some improvement in living standards, foreign investment declined, many businesses left the country, and unhappy labor unions began strikes. On Oct. 15, 1987, formerly loyal soldiers assassinated Sankara. His best friend and ally Blaise Compaoré became president. Compaoré immediately set about "rectifying" Sankara's revolution. In 1991 he agreed to economic reforms proposed by the World Bank. A new constitution paved the way for elections in 1991, which Compaoré won easily, although opposition parties boycotted.

Burma (Myanmar)

SEE MYANMAR.

Burundi

REPUBLIC OF BURUNDI

National name: Republika Y'Uburundi
President: Domitien Ndayizeye (2003)
Area: 10,745 sq mi (27,830 sq km)
Population (2003 est.): 6,096,156 (growth rate: 2.2%); birth rate: 39.7/1000; infant mortality rate: 71.5/1000; density per sq mi: 567
Capital and largest city (2003 est.): Bujumbura, 331,700. **Other large city:** Gitega, 45,700. **Monetary unit:** Burundi franc. **Languages:** Kirundi and French (official), Swahili. **Ethnicity/race:** Hutu (Bantu) 85%, Tutsi (Hamitic) 14%, Twa (Pygmy) 1%. **Religions:** Roman Catholic 62%, Protestant 5%, indigenous 23%, Islam 10%. **Literacy rate:** 35.3% (1995 est.)
Economic summary: GDP/PPP (2001 est.): $3.7 billion; per capita $600. **Real growth rate:** 1.4%. **Inflation:** 14%. **Unemployment:** n.a. **Arable land:** 30%. **Agriculture:** coffee, cotton, tea, corn, sorghum, sweet potatoes, bananas, manioc (tapioca); beef, milk, hides. **Labor force:** 1.9 million. **Industries:** light consumer goods such as blankets, shoes, soap; assembly of imported components; public works construction; food processing. **Natural resources:** nickel, uranium, rare earth oxides, peat, cobalt, copper, platinum (not yet exploited), vanadium, arable land, hydropower. **Exports:** $24 million (f.o.b., 2001 est.): coffee, tea, sugar, cotton, hides. **Imports:** $125 million (f.o.b., 2001 est.): capital goods, petroleum products, foodstuffs. **Major trading partners:** EU, U.S., Kenya, Switzerland, Tanzania, Zambia, India, China.

Geography Wedged between Tanzania, the Democratic Republic of the Congo, and Rwanda in east-central Africa, Burundi occupies a high plateau divided by several deep valleys. It is equal in size to Maryland.

Government Republic.

History The original inhabitants of Burundi were the Twa, a Pygmy people who now make up only 1% of the population. Today the population is divided between the Hutu (approximately 85%) and the Tutsi, approximately 14%. While the Hutu and Tutsi are considered to be two separate ethnic groups, scholars point out that they speak the same language, have a history of intermarriage, and share many cultural characteristics. Traditionally, the differences between the two groups were occupational rather than ethnic. Agricultural people were considered Hutu, while the cattle-owning elite were identified as Tutsi. Supposedly Tutsi were tall and thin, while Hutu were short and square, but in fact it is often impossible to tell one from the other. The 1933 requirement by the Belgians that everyone carry an identity card indicating tribal ethnicity as Tutsi or Hutu increased the distinction. Since independence, the land-owning Tutsi aristocracy has dominated Burundi.

Burundi was once part of German East Africa. Belgium won a League of Nations mandate in 1923, and subsequently Burundi, with Rwanda, was transferred to the status of a United Nations trust territory. In 1962, Burundi gained independence and became a kingdom under Mwami Mwambutsa IV, a Tutsi. A Hutu rebellion took place in 1965, leading to brutal Tutsi retaliations. Mwambutsa was deposed by his son, Ntaré V, in 1966. Ntaré in turn was overthrown the same year in a military coup by Premier Michel Micombero, also a Tutsi. In 1970–1971, a civil war erupted, leaving more than 100,000 Hutu dead.

On Nov. 1, 1976, Lt. Col. Jean-Baptiste Bagaza led a coup and assumed the presidency. He suspended the constitution and announced that a 30-member Supreme Revolutionary Council would be the governing body. In Sept. 1987 Bagaza was overthrown by Maj. Pierre Buyoya, who became president. Ethnic hatred again flared in Aug. 1988, and about 20,000 Hutu were slaughtered. Buyoya, however, began reforms to heal the country's ethnic rift. The Burundi Democracy Front's candidate, Melchior Ndadaye, won the country's first democratic presidential elections, held on June 2, 1993. Ndadaye, the first Hutu to assume power in Burundi, was killed within months during a coup. The second Hutu president, Cyprien Ntaryamira, was killed on April 6, 1994, when a plane carrying him and the Rwandan president was shot down. As a result, Hutu youth gangs began massacring Tutsi; the Tutsi-controlled army retaliated by killing Hutus.

The frequency of ethnic clashes increased, developing into a low-intensity civil war. A six-nation regional proposal to send troops into Burundi to maintain peace and order was devised in July 1996. Distrustful of the scheme, the Tutsi-dominated army led a coup deposing the Hutu president and installed Maj. Pierre Buyoya that month. More than 300,000 people have been killed in the civil war since 1993, and both the Tutsi-dominated army and the Hutu rebel forces are responsible for the continuing slaughter. After several aborted ceasefires, a 2001 peace plan included a power-sharing agreement that has been successful: Buyoya, a Tutsi, governed the new transitional government for the first 18 months; then, in April 2003, a Hutu president, Domitien Ndayizeye, assumed power. Ndayizeye will serve as president for 18 months; after which elections will then follow. Despite a new government in place and the promise of a political solution, the fighting has continued to rage.

Cambodia

King: Norodom Sihanouk (1993)
Prime Minister: Hun Sen (1998)
Area: 69,900 sq mi (181,040 sq km)
Population (2003 est.): 13,124,764 (growth rate: 1.8%); birth rate: 27.3/1000; infant mortality rate: 75.9/1000; density per sq mi: 188
Capital and largest city (2003 est.): Phnom Penh, 1,169,800. **Monetary unit:** Riel. **Languages:** Khmer (official), French, English. **Ethnicity/race:** Khmer 90%, Vietnamese 5%, Chinese 1%, other 4%. **Religions:** Theravada Buddhist 95%, others 5%. **Literacy rate:** 35% (1990 est.)
Economic summary: GDP/PPP (2001 est.): $18.7 billion; per capita $1,500. **Real growth rate:** 5.3%. **Inflation:** 1.6% (2000 est.). **Unemployment:** 2.8% (1999 est.). **Arable land:** 21%. **Agriculture:** rice, rubber, corn, vegetables. **Labor force:** 6 million (1998 est.); agriculture 80% (2001 est.). **Industries:** garments, tourism, rice milling, fishing, wood and wood products, rubber, cement, gem mining, textiles. **Natural resources:** timber, gemstones, some iron ore, manganese, phosphates, hydropower potential. **Exports:** $1.05 billion (f.o.b., 2000 est.): timber, garments, rubber, rice, fish. **Imports:** $1.4 billion (f.o.b., 2000 est.): petroleum products, cigarettes, gold, construction materials, machinery, motor vehicles. **Major trading partners:** U.S., Vietnam, Germany, Singapore, UK, Thailand, Hong Kong, China.

Geography Situated on the Indochinese peninsula, Cambodia is bordered by Thailand and Laos on the north and Vietnam on the east and south. The Gulf of Thailand is off the western coast. The size of Missouri, the country consists chiefly of a large alluvial plain ringed by mountains and on the east is the Mekong River. The plain is centered around Lake Tonle Sap, which is a natural storage basin of the Mekong.

Government Multiparty liberal democracy under a constitutional monarchy.

History The area that is present-day Cambodia came under Khmer rule about 600, when the region was at the center of a vast empire that stretched over most of Southeast Asia. Under the Khmers, who were Hindus, a magnificent temple complex was constructed at Angkor. Buddhism was introduced in the 12th century during the rule of Jayavaram VII. However, the kingdom, then known as Kambuja, fell into decline after Jayavaram's reign and was nearly annihilated by Thai and Vietnamese invaders. Its power steadily diminished until 1863, when France colonized the region, joining Cambodia, Laos, and Vietnam into a single protectorate known as French Indochina.

The French quickly usurped all but ceremonial powers from the monarch, Norodom. When he died in 1904, the French passed over his sons and handed the throne to his brother, Sisowath. Sisowath and his son ruled until 1941, when Norodom Sihanouk was elevated to power. Sihanouk's coronation, along with the Japanese occupation during the war, worked to reinforce a sentiment among Cambodians that the region should be free from outside control. After World War II, Cambodians sought independence, but France was reluctant to part with its colony. Cambodia was granted independence within the French Union in 1949. But the French-Indochinese War provided an opportunity for Sihanouk to gain full military control of the country. He abdicated in 1955 in favor of his parents, remaining head of the government, and when his father died in 1960, became chief of state without returning to the throne. In 1963, he sought a guarantee of Cambodia's neutrality from all parties to the Vietnam War.

However, North Vietnamese and Vietcong troops had begun using eastern Cambodia as a safe haven from which to launch attacks into South Vietnam, making it increasingly difficult to stay out of the war. An indigenous Communist guerrilla movement known as the Khmer Rouge also began to put pressure on the government in Phnom Penh. On March 18, 1970, while Sihanouk was abroad, anti-Vietnamese riots broke out and Sihanouk was overthrown by Gen. Lon Nol. The Vietnam peace agreement of 1973 stipulated withdrawal of foreign forces from Cambodia, but fighting continued between Hanoi-backed insurgents and U.S.-supplied government troops.

Combat climaxed in April 1975 when the Lon Nol regime was overthrown by Pol Pot, leader of the Khmer Rouge forces. The four years of nightmarish Khmer Rouge rule led to the state-sponsored extermination of citizens by its own government. Between 1 million and 2 million people were massacred on the "killing fields" of Cambodia or worked to death through forced labor. Pol Pot's radical vision of transforming the country into a Marxist agrarian society led to the virtual extermination of the country's professional and technical class.

Pol Pot was ousted by Vietnamese forces on Jan. 8, 1979, and a new pro-Hanoi government led by Heng Samrin was installed. Pol Pot and 35,000 Khmer Rouge fighters fled into the hills of western Cambodia, where they were joined by forces loyal to the ousted Sihanouk in a guerrilla movement aimed at overthrowing the Heng Samrin government. The Vietnamese plan originally called for a withdrawal by early 1990 and a negotiated political settlement. The talks became protracted, however, and a UN agreement was not signed until 1992, when Sihanouk was appointed leader of an interim Supreme National Council convened to run the country until elections could be held in 1993.

Free elections in May 1993 saw the defeat of Heng Samrin's successor, Hun Sen, who refused to accept the outcome of the vote and insisted instead on a power-sharing agreement. Under the arrangement, Hun Sen and Sihanouk's son, Prince Norodom Ranariddh, would act as co–prime ministers.The Khmer Rouge stronghold in the western jungles splintered in 1997, with factions either battling each other or defecting. Ranariddh and Hun Sen both courted Khmer Rouge factions in an effort to shore up their power. In early July, Hun Sen took advantage of the charged political atmosphere to depose Ranariddh, the country's only popularly elected leader. Hun Sen later launched a brutal purge, executing more than 40 political opponents. Shortly after the July coup, the Khmer Rouge organized a show trial of their notorious leader, Pol Pot, who had not been seen by the West in more than two decades. He was sentenced to house arrest for his crimes against humanity. He died on April 15, 1998. In the July 1998 election, Hun Sen defeated opposition leaders Sam Rainsy and Prince Ranariddh, but the opposition parties accused him of voter fraud. Cambodia was able to regain its UN seat, lost nearly a year earlier as a result of Hun Sen's coup.

In March 2003 the UN and Cambodia announced that after five years they had finally agreed on a system to try senior Khmer Rouge officials on charges of genocide. Both parties were only cautiously optimistic that the breakthrough would ever yield results. Among those expected to stand trial are Ta Mok, alias "the butcher," and Kang Kech Iev, alias Duch, who ran the notorious Tuol Sleng prison. Prime Minister Hun Sen, once a member of the Khmer Rouge himself, has been decidedly unenthusiastic about bringing former Khmer Rouge to justice.

Cameroon

REPUBLIC OF CAMEROON

National name: République du Cameroun
President: Paul Biya (1982)
Prime Minister: Peter Mafany Musonge (1996)
Area: 183,567 sq mi (475,440 sq km)
Population (2003 est.): 15,746,179 (growth rate: 2.0%); birth rate: 35.5/1000; infant mortality rate: 70.1/1000; density per sq mi: 86
Capital: Yaoundé, 1,395,200 (metro. area), 1,154,400 (city proper). **Largest city:** Douala, 1,490,500 (metro.area), 1,274.300 (city proper) . **Monetary unit:** CFA Franc. **Languages:** French and English (both official); 24 major African language groups. **Ethnicity/race:** Cameroon Highlanders 31%, Equatorial Bantu 19%, Kirdi 11%, Fulani 10%, Northwest Bantu 8%, Eastern Nigritic 7%, other African 13%, non-African less than 1%. **Religions:** indigenous beliefs 40%, Christian 40%, Islam 20%. **Literacy rate:** 63.4% (1995 est.)
Economic summary: GDP/PPP (2001 est.): $26.4 billion; per capita $1,700. **Real growth rate:** 4.9%. **Inflation:** 2% (2000 est.). **Unemployment:** 30% (2001 est.). **Arable land:** 13%. **Agriculture:** coffee, cocoa, cotton, rubber, bananas, oilseed, grains, root starches; livestock; timber. **Labor force:** n.a.; agriculture 70%, industry and commerce 13%, other 17%. **Industries:** petroleum production and refining, food processing, light consumer goods, textiles, lumber. **Natural resources:** petroleum, bauxite, iron ore, timber, hydropower. **Exports:** $2.1 billion (f.o.b., 2000 est.): crude oil and petroleum products, lumber, cocoa beans, aluminum, coffee, cotton. **Imports:** $1.5 billion (f.o.b., 2000 est.): machinery, electrical equipment, transport equipment, fuel, food. **Major trading partners:** Italy, France, Netherlands, Germany, U.S., Japan.

Geography Cameroon is a Central African nation on the Gulf of Guinea, bordered by Nigeria, Chad, the Central African Republic, the Republic of Congo, Equatorial Guinea, and Gabon. It is nearly twice the size of Oregon. Mount Cameroon (13,350 ft; 4,069 m), near the coast, is the highest elevation in the country. The main rivers are the Benue, Nyong, and Sanaga.

Government After a 1972 plebiscite, a unitary republic was formed out of East and West Cameroon to replace the former federal republic.

History Bantu speakers were among the first groups to settle Cameroon, followed by the Muslim Fulani in the 18th and 19th centuries. The land escaped colonial rule until 1884, when treaties with tribal chiefs brought the area under German domination. After World War I, the League of Nations gave the French a mandate over 80% of the area, and the British 20% adjacent to Nigeria. After World War II, when the country came under a UN trusteeship in 1946, self-government was granted, and the Cameroon People's Union emerged as the dominant party by campaigning for reunification of French and British Cameroon and for independence. Accused of being under Communist control, the party waged a campaign of revolutionary terror from 1955 to 1958, when it was crushed. In British Cameroon, unification was also promoted by the leading party, the Kamerun National Democratic Party, led by John Foncha.

France set up Cameroon as an autonomous state in 1957, and the next year its legislative assembly voted for independence by 1960. In 1959 a fully autonomous government of Cameroon was formed under Ahmadou Ahidjo. Cameroon became an independent republic on Jan. 1, 1960. In 1961 the southern part of the British territory joined the new Federal Republic of Cameroon and the northern section voted for unification with Nigeria. The president of Cameroon since independence, Ahmadou Ahidjo, was replaced in 1982 by the prime minister, Paul Biya. Both administrations have been authoritarian.

With the expansion of oil, timber, and coffee exports, the economy has continued to improve, although corruption is prevalent, and environmental degradation remains a concern. In June 2000 the World Bank agreed to provide more than $200 million to build a $3.7 billion pipeline connecting the oil fields in neighboring Chad with the Cameroon coast.

Canada

Sovereign: Queen Elizabeth II (1952)
Governor-General: Adrienne Clarkson (1999)
Prime Minister: Jean Chrétien (1993)
Area: 3,851,788 sq mi (9,976,140 sq km)
Population (2003 est.): 32,207,113 (growth rate: 0.3%); birth rate: 11.0/1000; infant mortality rate: 4.9/1000; density per sq mi: 8
Capital (2003 est.): Ottawa, Ontario, 1,089,100 (metro. area), 852,100 (city proper). **Largest cities (metropolitan areas):** Toronto, 5,508,000, 4,494,200 (city proper); Montreal, 3,248,000; Vancouver, 1,865,300; Calgary, 1,089,100; Edmonton, 966,200; Quebec, 689,400; Winnipeg, 675,800; Hamilton, 636,900 (part of Toronto metro. area); London, 439,400; Kitchener, 426,200 . **Monetary unit:** Canadian dollar. **Languages:** English, French (both official). **Ethnicity/race:** British Isles origin 28%, French origin 23%, other European 15%, indigenous Indian and Inuit 2%, other, mostly Asian, African, Arab 6%, mixed background 26%. **Religions:** Roman Catholic 46%, United Church 16%, Anglican 10%.
Literacy rate: 97% (1986 est.)
Economic summary: GDP/PPP (2001 est.): $875 billion; per capita $27,700. **Real growth rate:** 1.9%. **Inflation:** 2.8%. **Unemployment:** 7.2%. **Arable land:** 5%. **Agriculture:** wheat, barley, oilseed, tobacco, fruits, vegetables; dairy products; forest products; fish. **Labor force:** 16.4 million; services 74%, manufacturing 15%, construction 5%, agriculture 3%, other 3% (2000). **Industries**: transportation equipment, chemicals, processed and unprocessed minerals, food products; wood and paper products; fish products, petroleum and natural gas. **Natural resources:** iron ore, nickel, zinc, copper, gold, lead, molybdenum, potash, silver, fish, timber, wildlife, coal, petroleum, natural gas, hydropower. **Exports:** $273.8 billion (f.o.b., 2001 est.): motor vehicles and parts, industrial machinery, aircraft, telecommunications equipment; chemicals, plastics, fertilizers; wood pulp, timber, crude petroleum, natural gas, electricity, aluminum. **Imports:** $238.3 billion (f.o.b., 2001 est.): machinery and equipment, motor vehicles and parts, crude oil, chemicals, electricity, durable consumer goods. **Major trading partners:** U.S., Japan, UK, Germany, South Korea, Netherlands, China.

Geography Covering most of the northern part of the North American continent and with an area larger than that of the United States, Canada has an extremely varied topography. In the east the mountainous maritime provinces have an irregular coastline on the Gulf of St. Lawrence and the Atlantic. The St. Lawrence plain, covering most of southern Quebec and Ontario, and the interior continental plain, covering southern Manitoba and Saskatchewan and most of Alberta, are the principal cultivable areas. They are separated by a forested plateau rising from Lakes Superior and Huron.

Westward toward the Pacific, most of British Columbia, Yukon, and part of western Alberta are covered by parallel mountain ranges, including the Rockies. The Pacific border of the coast range is ragged with fjords and channels. The highest point in Canada is Mount Logan (19,850 ft; 6,050 m), which is in the Yukon. The two principal river systems are the Mackenzie and the St. Lawrence. The St. Lawrence, with its tributaries, is navigable for over 1,900 mi (3,058 km).

Government Canada is a federation of ten provinces (Alberta, British Columbia, Manitoba, New Brunswick, Newfoundland and Labrador, Nova Scotia, Ontario, Prince Edward Island, Quebec, and Saskatchewan) and three territories (Northwest Territories, Yukon, and as of April 1, 1999, Nunavut). Formally considered a constitutional monarchy, Canada is governed by its own House of Commons. While the governor-general is officially the representative of Queen Elizabeth II, in reality the governor-general acts only upon the advice of the Canadian prime minister.

History The first inhabitants of Canada were native Indian peoples, primarily the Inuit (Eskimo). The Norse explorer Leif Eriksson probably reached the shores of Canada (Labrador or Nova Scotia) in 1000, but the history of the white man in the country actually began in 1497, when John Cabot, an Italian in the service of Henry VII of England, reached Newfoundland or Nova Scotia. Canada was taken for France in 1534 by Jacques Cartier. The actual settlement of New France, as it was then called, began in 1604 at Port Royal in what is now Nova Scotia; in 1608, Quebec was founded. France's colonization efforts were not very successful, but French explorers by the end of the 17th century had penetrated beyond the Great Lakes to the western prairies and south along the Mississippi to the Gulf of Mexico. Meanwhile, the English Hudson's Bay Company had been

Canadian Prime Ministers Since 1867

Term	Prime Minister	Party	Term	Prime Minister	Party
1867–1873	Sir John A. Macdonald	Conservative	1926–1930	W. L. Mackenzie King	Liberal
1873–1878	Alexander Mackenzie	Liberal	1930–1935	Richard B. Bennett	Conservative
1878–1891	Sir John A. Macdonald	Conservative	1935–1948	W. L. Mackenzie King	Liberal
1891–1892	Sir John J. C. Abbott	Conservative	1948–1957	Louis S. St. Laurent	Liberal
1892–1894	Sir John S. D. Thompson	Conservative	1957–1963	John G. Diefenbaker	Conservative
1894–1896	Sir Mackenzie Bowell	Conservative	1963–1968	Lester B. Pearson	Liberal
1896	Sir Charles Tupper	Conservative	1968–1979	Pierre Elliott Trudeau	Liberal
1896–1911	Sir Wilfrid Laurier	Liberal	1979–1980	Charles Joseph Clark	Conservative
1911–1917	Sir Robert L. Borden	Conservative	1980–1984	Pierre Elliott Trudeau	Liberal
1917–1920	Sir Robert L. Borden	Unionist	1984	John Turner	Liberal
1920–1921	Arthur Meighen	Unionist	1984–1993	Brian Mulroney	Conservative
1921–1926	W. L. Mackenzie King	Liberal	1993	Kim Campbell	Conservative
1926	Arthur Meighen	Conservative	1993–	Jean Chrétien	Liberal

established in 1670. Because of the valuable fisheries and fur trade, a conflict developed between the French and English; in 1713, Newfoundland, Hudson Bay, and Nova Scotia (Acadia) were lost to England. During the Seven Years' War (1756–1763), England extended its conquest, and the British general James Wolfe won his famous victory over Gen. Louis Montcalm outside Quebec on Sept. 13, 1759. The Treaty of Paris in 1763 gave England control.

At that time the population of Canada was almost entirely French, but in the next few decades, thousands of British colonists emigrated to Canada from the British Isles and from the American colonies. In 1849, the right of Canada to self-government was recognized. By the British North America Act of 1867, the dominion of Canada was created through the confederation of Upper and Lower Canada, Nova Scotia, and New Brunswick. In 1869, Canada purchased from the Hudson's Bay Company the vast middle west (Rupert's Land) from which the provinces of Manitoba (1870), Alberta (1905), and Saskatchewan (1905) were later formed. In 1871, British Columbia joined the dominion, and in 1873, Prince Edward Island followed. The country was linked from coast to coast in 1885 by the Canadian Pacific Railway.

During the formative years between 1866 and 1896, the Conservative Party, led by Sir John A. Macdonald, governed the country, except during the years 1873–1878. In 1896 the Liberal Party took over and, under Sir Wilfrid Laurier, an eminent French Canadian, ruled until 1911. By the Statute of Westminster in 1931 the British dominions, including Canada, were formally declared to be partner nations with Britain, "equal in status, in no way subordinate to each other," and bound together only by allegiance to a common Crown.

Newfoundland became Canada's tenth province on March 31, 1949, following a plebiscite. Canada also includes three territories—the Yukon Territory, the Northwest Territories, and the newest territory, Nunavut. This new territory includes all of the Arctic north of the mainland, Norway having recognized Canadian sovereignty over the Sverdrup Islands in the Arctic in 1931.

The Liberal Party, led by William Lyon Mackenzie King, dominated Canadian politics from 1921 until 1957, when it was succeeded by the Progressive Conservatives. The Liberals, under the leadership of Lester B. Pearson, returned to power in 1963. Pearson remained prime minister until 1968, when he retired and was replaced by a former law professor, Pierre Elliott Trudeau. Trudeau maintained Canada's defensive alliance with the United States but began moving toward a more independent policy in world affairs.

Trudeau's election was considered in part a response to the most serious problem confronting the country, the division between French- and English-speaking Canadians, which had led to a separatist movement in the predominantly French province of Quebec. In 1974, the provincial government, the Parti Québecois (PQ) passed a law making French the official language of Quebec, but in Dec. 1979, the law was voided by the Canadian Supreme Court. In May 1980, Quebec held a referendum on whether the province should seek independence from Canada; it was defeated by 60% of the voters.

Resolving a dispute that had occupied Trudeau since the beginning of his tenure, Queen Elizabeth II signed the Constitution Act (also called the Canada Act) in Ottawa on April 17, 1982, thereby cutting the last legal tie between Canada and Britain. The constitution retains Queen Elizabeth as queen of Canada and keeps Canada's membership in the Commonwealth.

In the national election on Sept. 4, 1984, the Progressive Conservative Party scored an overwhelming victory, fundamentally changing the country's political landscape. The Conservatives, led by Brian Mulroney, won the highest political majority in Canadian history. The dominant foreign issue was a free-trade pact with the U.S., a treaty bitterly opposed by the Liberal and New Democratic Parties. The conflict led to elections in Nov. 1988 that solidly reelected Mulroney and gave him a mandate to proceed with the agreement.

The issue of separatist sentiments in French-speaking Quebec flared up again in 1990 with the failure of the Meech Lake Accord. The accord was designed to ease the Quebecers' fear of losing their identity within the English-speaking majority by giving Quebec constitutional status as a "distinct society." In

Population by Provinces and Territories

Province	2002 (in thousands)	2001 (in thousands)
Alberta	3,098.8	3,064.2
British Columbia	4,131.0	4,095.9
Manitoba	1,149.1	1,150.0
New Brunswick	755.6	757.0
Newfoundland and Labrador	531.7	533.7
Nova Scotia	943.8	942.6
Ontario	12,009.2	11,874.4
Prince Edward Island	139.6	138.5
Quebec	7,444.3	7,410.5
Saskatchewan	1,012.7	1,015.7
Northwest Territories	41.1	40.8
Yukon Territory	29.9	29.8
Nunavut	28.4	28.1

Source: Statistics Canada.

an attempt to keep Canada united, the three major political parties came to an agreement in Feb. 1992 on constitutional reforms. Voters in the Northwest Territories authorized the division of their region in two, creating a homeland for Canadian Eskimos, the Inuits, which in April 1999 became the territory of Nunavut. Also in 1992, Canada announced its decision to withdraw its combat units from NATO command. The economy continued to be mired in a long recession that many blamed on the free-trade agreement. A national referendum was held in Oct. 1992 on the proposal to change the constitution to ensure greater representation in Parliament for the more populous regions and thereby the French-speaking Quebecers. The referendum, however, was defeated.

Brian Mulroney's popularity continued to decline, causing him to resign before the next election. In June 1993 the governing Progressive Conservative Party chose Defense Minister Kim Campbell as its leader, making her the first female prime minister in Canadian history. The national election in Oct. 1993 resulted in the reemergence of the Liberal Party and the installation of Jean Chrétien as prime minister.

The Quebec referendum on secession in Oct. 1995 yielded a narrow rejection of the proposal. But separatists vowed to try again. Since then, however, the Reform Party has replaced the Bloc Québecois as the official opposition.

On April 1, 1999, the Northwest Territories were officially divided to create a new territory in the east that would be governed by Canada's Inuits, who make up 85% of the area's population. Composed of 770,000 sq mi of mostly snow and ice reaching well to the north of the Arctic Circle, the 25,700 residents of Nunavut are governed from the new capital, Iqaluit.

In July 2000, Stockwell Day of the new conservative Canadian Alliance Party unexpectedly emerged as the leader of Canada's opposition. In elections held in Nov. 2000, however, Prime Minister Jean Chrétien of the Liberal Party won a landslide victory of a third five-year term. After the election, the conservatives rapidly lost steam.

Chrétien announced in Aug. 2002 that he would not seek a fourth term and would instead retire from politics in 2004. Conflict between Chrétien and his former finance minister, Paul Martin, has divided and weakened the Liberal Party. Canada legalized medical marijuana for the terminally or chronically ill in 2001; it began legally dispensing marijuana by prescription in July 2003.

Canada-U.S. relations were strained in 2003 when Canada refused to join Washington's coalition supporting the war in Iraq. In Quebec's provincial elections in April 2003, the Liberal party had a surprising win over the separatist Parti Quebecois, who had dominated Quebec for the past nine years. Also in 2003, Ottawa and British Columbia legalized same-sex marriage; sanctioning it on a federal level will be voted on in 2004.

Cape Verde

REPUBLIC OF CAPE VERDE

National name: República de Cabo Verde
President: Pedro Pires (2001)
Prime Minister: José Maria Neves (2001)
Area: 1,557 sq mi (4,033 sq km)
Population (2003 est.): 412,137 (growth rate: 2.0%); birth rate: 26.9/1000; infant mortality rate: 50.5/1000; density per sq mi: 265
Capital and largest city (2003 est.): Praia, 99,400. **Other large city:** Mindelo, 66,100. **Monetary unit:** Cape Verdean escudo. **Languages:** Portuguese, Criuolo. **Ethnicity/race:** Creole (mulatto) 71%, African 28%, European 1%. **Religion:** Roman Catholic fused with indigenous beliefs. **Literacy rate:** 71.6% (1995 est.)
Economic summary: GDP/PPP (2001 est.): $600 million; per capita $1,500. **Real growth rate:** 3%. **Inflation:** 3%. **Unemployment:** 21% (2000 est.). **Arable land:** 10%. **Agriculture:** bananas, corn, beans, sweet potatoes, sugarcane, coffee, peanuts; fish. **Labor force:** n.a. **Industries:** food and beverages, fish processing, shoes and garments, salt mining, ship repair. **Natural resources:** salt, basalt rock, limestone, kaolin, fish. **Exports:** $27.3 million (f.o.b., 2001 est.): fuel, shoes, garments, fish, hides. **Imports:** $218 million (f.o.b., 2001 est.): foodstuffs, industrial products, transport equipment, fuels. **Major trading partners:** Portugal, UK, Germany, Guinea-Bissau, France.

Geography Cape Verde, only slightly larger than Rhode Island, is an archipelago in the Atlantic 385 mi (500 km) west of Senegal.

The islands are divided into two groups: Barlavento in the north, composed of Santo Antão (291 sq mi; 754 sq km), Boa Vista (240 sq mi; 622 sq km), São Nicolau (132 sq mi; 342 sq km), São Vicente (88 sq mi; 246 sq km), Sal (83 sq mi; 298 sq km), and Santa Luzia (13 sq mi; 34 sq km); and Sotavento in the south, consisting of São Tiago (383 sq mi; 992 sq km), Fogo (184 sq mi; 477 sq km), Maio (103 sq mi; 267 sq km), and Brava (25 sq mi; 65 sq km). The islands are mostly mountainous, with the land deeply scarred by erosion. There is an active volcano on Fogo.

Government Republic.

History Uninhabited upon their discovery in 1456, the Cape Verde islands became part of the Portuguese empire in 1495. A majority of today's inhabitants are of mixed Portuguese and African ancestry.

Positioned on the great trade routes between Africa, Europe, and the New World, the islands became a prosperous center for the slave trade but suffered economic decline after the slave trade was abolished in 1876. In the 20th century, Cape Verde served as a shipping port.

In 1951, Cape Verde's status changed from a Portuguese colony to an overseas province, and in 1961 the inhabitants became full Portuguese citizens. An independence movement led by the African Party for the Independence of Guinea-Bissau (another former Portuguese colony) and Cape Verde (PAIGC) was founded in 1956. Following the 1974 coup in Portugal, after which Portugal began abandoning its colonial empire, the islands became independent (July 5, 1975).

The first multiparty elections since independence on Jan. 13, 1991, resulted in the ruling African Party for the Independence of Cape Verde (PAICV) losing its majority to the Movement for Democracy Party (MPD). The MPD candidate, Antonio Monteiro, won the subsequent presidential election. Monteiro was easily reelected in 1996.

In an effort to take advantage of its proximity to cross-Atlantic sea and air lanes, the government has embarked on a major expansion of its port and airport capacities. It is also modernizing the fishing fleet and enhancing its fish processing industry. These projects are being partly paid for by the EU and the World Bank, making Cape Verde one of the largest per capita aid recipients in the world. Disenchantment with the government's privatization program, continued high unemployment, and widespread poverty helped defeat the MPD in elections held in Jan. 2001. The PAICV swept back into power and José Maria Neves became prime minister.

Central African Republic

National name: République Centrafricaine
President: Gen. François Bozizé (2003)
Prime Minister: Abel Goumba (2003)
Area: 240,534 sq mi (622,984 sq km)
Population (2003 est.): 3,683,538 (growth rate: 1.6%); birth rate: 35.9/1000; infant mortality rate: 93.3/1000; density per sq mi: 15
Capital and largest city (2003 est.): Bangui, 810,000 (metro.area), 669,800 (city proper). **Monetary unit:** CFA Franc. **Languages:** French (official), Sangho, Arabic, Hansa, Swahili. **Ethnicity/race:** Baya 33%, Banda 27%, Mandjia 13%, Sara 10%, Mboum 7%, M'Baka 4%, Yakoma 4%, other 2%. **Religions:** indigenous beliefs 35%, Protestant and Roman Catholic with animist influence 50%, Islam 15%. **Literacy rate:** 60% (1995 est.)
Economic summary: GDP/PPP (2001 est.): $4.6 billion; per capita $1,300. **Real growth rate:** 1.8%. **Inflation:** 3.6%. **Unemployment:** 8% (23% for Bangui). **Arable land:** 3%. **Agriculture:** cotton, coffee, tobacco, manioc (tapioca), yams, millet, corn, bananas; timber. **Labor force:** n.a. **Industries:** diamond mining, sawmills, breweries, textiles, footwear, assembly of bicycles and motorcycles. **Natural resources:** diamonds, uranium, timber, gold, oil, hydropower. **Exports:** $166 million (f.o.b., 2000): diamonds, timber, cotton, coffee, tobacco. **Imports:** $154 million (f.o.b., 2000): food, textiles, petroleum products, machinery, electrical equipment, motor vehicles, chemicals, pharmaceuticals, consumer goods, industrial products. **Major trading partners:** Benelux, Côte d'Ivoire, Spain, China, Egypt, France, Cameroon, Germany, Japan.

Geography Situated about 500 mi (805 km) north of the equator, the Central African Republic is a landlocked nation bordered by Cameroon, Chad, the Sudan, the Democratic Republic of the Congo, and the Republic of Congo. The Ubangi and the Shari are the largest of many rivers.

Government Multiparty republic since 1991.

History From the 16th to 19th century, the people of this region were ravaged by slave traders. The Banda, Baya, Ngbandi, and Azande make up the largest ethnic groups.

The French occupied the region in 1894. As the colony of Ubangi-Shari, what is now the Central African Republic was united with Chad in 1905. In 1910 it was joined with Gabon and the Middle Congo to become French Equatorial Africa. After World War II a rebellion in 1946 forced the French to grant self-government. In 1958 the territory voted to become an autonomous republic within the French Community, and on Aug. 13, 1960, President David Dacko proclaimed the republic's independence from France. Dacko moved the country into Beijing's orbit, but was overthrown in a coup on Dec. 31, 1965, by Col. Jean-Bédel Bokassa, army chief of staff.

On Dec. 4, 1976, the Central African Republic became the Central African Empire. Marshal Jean-Bédel Bokassa, who had ruled the republic since he took power in 1965, was declared Emperor Bokassa I. Brutality and excess characterized his regime. He was overthrown in a coup on Sept. 20, 1979. Former president David Dacko returned to power and changed the country's name back to the Central African Republic. An army coup on Sept. 1, 1981, deposed President Dacko again.

In 1991, President André Kolingba, under pressure, announced a move toward parliamentary democracy. In elections held in Aug. 1993, Prime Minister Ange-Félix Patassé defeated Kolingba. Part of Patassé's popularity rested on his pledge to pay the back salaries of the military and civil servants.

A 1994 economic upturn was too small to effectively improve the catastrophic financial condition of the nation. Patassé was unable to pay the salaries due government workers, and the military revolted in 1996. At Patassé's request, French troops suppressed the uprising. In 1998 the United Nations sent an all-African peacekeeping force to the country. In elections held in Sept. 1999, amid widespread charges of massive fraud, Patassé easily defeated Kolingba. Patassé survived a coup attempt in May 2001, but two years later, in March 2003, he was overthrown by Gen. François Bozizé.

Chad

REPUBLIC OF CHAD

National name: République du Tchad
President: Idriss Déby (1990)
Prime Minister: Moussa Faki (2003)
Area: 495,752 sq mi (1,284,000 sq km)
Population (2003 est.): 9,253,493 (growth rate: 3.1%); birth rate: 47.1/1000; infant mortality rate: 95.7/1000; density per sq mi: 19
Capital and largest city (2003 est.): N'Djamena, 609,600. **Monetary unit:** CFA Franc. **Languages:** French and Arabic (official), more than 100 tribal languages. **Ethnicity/race:** North and center: Muslims (Arabs, Toubou, Hadjerai, Fulbe, Kotoko, Kanembou, Baguirmi, Boulala, Zaghawa, and Maba); South: non-Muslims (Sara [the largest ethnic group, 25% of the population], Ngambaye, Mbaye, Goulaye, Moundang, Moussei, Massa). **Religions:** Islam 51%, Christian 35%, animalist 7%, other 7%. **Literacy rate:** 40% (1998)
Economic summary: GDP/PPP (2001 est.): $8.9 billion; per capita $1,030. **Real growth rate:** 8%. **Inflation:** 3% (2000 est.). **Unemployment:** n.a. **Arable land:** 3%. **Agriculture:** cotton, sorghum, millet, peanuts, rice, potatoes, manioc (tapioca); cattle, sheep, goats, camels. **Labor force:** n.a.; agriculture more than 85% (subsistence farming, herding, and fishing). **Industries:** cotton textiles, meatpacking, beer brewing, natron (sodium carbonate), soap, cigarettes, construction materials. **Natural resources:** petroleum (unexploited but exploration under way), uranium, natron, kaolin, fish (Lake Chad). **Exports:** $172 million (f.o.b., 2000 est.): cotton, cattle, gum arabic. **Imports:** $223 million (f.o.b., 2000 est.): machinery and transportation equipment, industrial goods, petroleum products, foodstuffs, textiles. **Major trading partners:** Portugal, Germany, Thailand, Costa Rica, South Africa, France, Nigeria, Cameroon, India.

Geography A landlocked country in north-central Africa, Chad is about 85% the size of Alaska. Its neighbors are Niger, Libya, the Sudan, the Central African Republic, Cameroon, and Nigeria. Lake Chad, from which the country gets its name, lies on the western border with Niger and Nigeria. In the north is a desert that runs into the Sahara.

Government Republic.

History The area around Lake Chad has been inhabited since at least 500 B.C. In the 8th century A.D. Berbers began migrating to the area. Islam arrived in 1085, and by the 16th century a trio of rival kingdoms flourished: the Kanem-Bornu, the Baguirmi, and Ouaddaï. In 1883–1893, all three kingdoms came under the rule of the Sudanese conqueror Rabih al-Zubayr. In 1900, Rabih was overthrown by the

French, who absorbed these kingdoms into the colony of French Equatorial Africa, as part of Ubangi-Shari, in 1910.

France began the country's development after 1920, when it became a separate colony. In 1946, French Equatorial Africa was admitted to the French Community, and in 1958 the Chad territory became an autonomous republic within the French Community. An independence movement led by the first premier and president, François (later Ngarta) Tombalbaye, achieved complete independence on Aug. 11, 1960. Tombalbaye was killed in the 1975 coup and succeeded by Gen. Félix Malloum, who faced a Libyan-financed civil war throughout his tenure in office. In 1977, Libya seized a strip of Chadian land and launched an invasion two years later.

Nine rival groups meeting in Lagos, Nigeria, in March 1979 agreed to form a provisional government headed by Goukouni Oueddei, a former rebel leader. Fighting broke out again in Chad in March 1980, when Defense Minister Hissen Habré challenged Goukouni and seized the capital. Libyan president Muammar al-Qaddafi, in Jan. 1981, proposed a merger of Chad with Libya. The Libyan proposal was rejected and Libyan troops withdrew from Chad that year, but in 1983 they poured back into the northern part of the country in support of Goukouni. France, in turn, sent troops into southern Chad in support of Habré. Government troops then launched an offensive in early 1987 that drove the Libyans out of most of the country.

In 1990, Idriss Déby, a former defense minister and head of a rebel group, the Patriotic Salvation Movement, overthrew Habré, suspended the constitution, and dissolved the legislature. In 1994 a new constitution was drafted and an amnesty for political prisoners was declared. Déby won multiparty elections in 1996 and was reelected in 2001.

The Movement for Democracy and Justice in Chad (MDJC), led by Deby's former defense minister, Youssouf Togoimi, began fighting against the government in 1998. In Jan. 2002 a ceasefire was declared, but clashes persisted.

In June 2000 the World Bank agreed to provide more than $200 million to build a $3.7 billion pipeline connecting the oil fields in Chad to those in Cameroon. Oil revenues are estimated to earn $2.5 billion over the next 30 years. But environmentalists fear the giant project will harm rain forests, and human rights groups are concerned it will only benefit the oil companies and the political elite in Cameroon and Chad. The World Bank, however, has forced Chad to agree to spend 80% of the resulting oil revenues on education, health, infrastructure, and other social welfare projects desperately needed by this impoverished country.

In Jan. 2003, Chad's southeast-based rebels, the National Resistance Army, signed a ceasefire with the government. The insurgency began in 1998, one of a half-dozen rebellions Déby has faced during his rule.

Chile

REPUBLIC OF CHILE

National name: República de Chile
President: Ricardo Lagos (2000)
Area: 292,258 sq mi (756,950 sq km)
Population (2003 est.): 15,665,216 (growth rate: 1.1%); birth rate: 16.1/1000; infant mortality rate: 8.9/1000; density per sq mi: 54
Capital and largest city (2003 est.): Santiago, 5,333,100 (metro.area), 4,372,800 (city proper). **Other large cities:** Viña del Mar, 303,100; Valparaíso, 274,100; Talcahuano, 252,800; Temuco, 247,200; Concepción, 217,600. **Monetary unit:** Chilean Peso. **Language:** Spanish. **Ethnicity/race:** European and European-Indian 95%, Indian 3%, other 2%. **Religions:** Roman Catholic 89%, Protestant 11%, small Jewish and Muslim populations. **Literacy rate:** 95.2% (1995 est.)
Economic summary: GDP/PPP (2001 est.): $153 billion; per capita $10,000. **Real growth rate:** 3.1%. **Inflation:** 3.5%. **Unemployment:** 10.1%. **Arable land:** 3%. **Agriculture:** wheat, corn, grapes, beans, sugar beets, potatoes, fruit; beef, poultry, wool; fish; timber. **Labor force:** 5.9 million (2000 est.); agriculture 14%, industry 27%, services 59% (1997 est.). **Industries:** copper, other minerals, foodstuffs, fish processing, iron and steel, wood and wood products, transport equipment, cement, textiles. **Natural resources:** copper, timber, iron ore, nitrates, precious metals, molybdenum, hydropower. **Exports:** $18.5 billion (f.o.b., 2001): copper, fish, fruits, paper and pulp, chemicals. **Imports:** $18 billion (f.o.b., 2001): consumer goods, chemicals, motor vehicles, fuels, electrical machinery, heavy industrial machinery, food. **Major trading partners:** U.S., Japan, UK, Brazil, China, Argentina, China.

Geography Situated south of Peru and west of Bolivia and Argentina, Chile fills a narrow 1,800-mile (2,897 km) strip between the Andes and the Pacific. One-third of Chile is covered by the towering ranges of the Andes. In the north is the driest place on Earth, the Atacama Desert, and in the center is a 700-mile-long (1,127 km), thickly populated valley with most of Chile's arable land. At the southern tip of Chile's mainland is Punta Arenas, the southernmost city in the world, and beyond that lies the Strait of Magellan and Tierra del Fuego, an island divided between Chile and Argentina. The southernmost point of South America is Cape Horn, a 1,390-foot (424 m) rock on Horn Island in the Wollaston group, which belongs to Chile. Chile also claims sovereignty over 482,628 sq mi (1,250,000 sq km) of Antarctic territory, the Juan Fernández Islands, about 400 mi (644 km) west of the mainland, and Easter Island, about 2,000 mi (3,219 km) west.

Government Republic.

History Chile was originally under the control of the Incas in the north and the nomadic Araucanos in the south. In 1541, a Spaniard, Pedro de Valdivia, founded Santiago. Chile won its independence from Spain in 1818 under Bernardo O'Higgins and an Argentinian, José de San Martin. O'Higgins, dictator until 1823, laid the foundations of the modern state with a two-party system and a centralized government.

The dictator from 1830 to 1837, Diego Portales, fought a war with Peru in 1836–1839 that expanded Chilean territory. Chile fought the War of the Pacific with Peru and Bolivia from 1879 to 1883, winning Antofagasta, Bolivia's only outlet to the sea, and extensive areas from Peru. Pedro Montt led a revolt that overthrew José Balmaceda in 1891 and established a parliamentary dictatorship lasting until a new constitution was adopted in 1925. Industrialization began before World War I and led to the formation of Marxist groups. Juan Antonio Ríos, president during World War II, was originally pro-Nazi but in 1944 led his country into the war on the side of the Allies.

A small abortive army uprising in 1969 raised the fear of military intervention in preventing a Marxist, Salvador Allende Gossens, from taking office after his election to the presidency on Sept. 4, 1970. Allende was the first president in a non-Communist country freely elected on a Marxist-Leninist program. Allende quickly established relations with Cuba and the People's Republic of China and nationalized several American companies. Allende's overthrow and death in an army assault on the presidential palace in Sept. 1973 ended a 46-year era of constitutional government in Chile.

The takeover was led by a four-man junta headed by Army Chief of Staff Augusto Pinochet Ugarte, who assumed the office of president. Committed to "exterminat[ing] Marxism," the junta suspended Parliament, banned political activity, and broke relations with Cuba. It also abolished DINA, the secret police, and decreed an amnesty for political prisoners, while free-market reforms improved the economy. In 1977, Pinochet promised elections by 1985 if conditions warranted. After losing the plebiscite, Pinochet stepped down in Jan. 1990 in favor of Patricio Aylwin, who was elected in Dec. 1989 as the head of a 17-party coalition. In Dec. 1993, Eduardo Frei Ruiz-Tagle, the candidate of a center-left coalition and son of a previous president, was elected president.

In March 1998, Pinochet retired as army commander in chief. In Oct. 1998, he was arrested and detained in England on an extradition request issued by a Spanish judge who sought Pinochet in connection with the disappearance of Spanish citizens during his rule. British courts ultimately denied his extradition, and Pinochet returned to Chile in March 2000, where the courts ultimately ruled that he was mentally unfit to stand trial.

Ricardo Lagos became president in March 2000, the first socialist to run the country since Allende. Chile's economic growth slowed to 3% for 2001, partly the result of a drop in international copper prices and the economic turmoil in neighboring Argentina. In 2003 there were several minor financial scandals involving insider information and bribery. In response, Lagos introduced new reforms promising greater transparency.

China

PEOPLE'S REPUBLIC OF CHINA

National name: Zhonghua Renmin Gongheguo
President: Hu Jintao (2003)
Prime Minister: Wen Jiabao (2003)
Area: 3,705,386 sq mi (9,596,960 sq km)[1]
Population (2003 est.): 1,286,975,468 (growth rate: 0.6%); birth rate: 13.0/1000; infant mortality rate: 25.3/1000; density per sq mi: 347
Capital (2003 est.): Beijing, 9,376,200 (metro. area), 6,619,000 (city proper). **Largest cities:** Shanghai, 12,039,900 (metro. area), 9,005,600 (city proper); Tianjin (Tientsin), 4,333,900; Wuhan, 3,959,700; Shenyang (Mukden), 3,574,100; Guangzhou, 3,473,800; Haerbin, 2,904,900; Xian, 2,642,100; Chungking (Chongquing) 2,370,100; Chengdu, 2,011,000; Hong Kong (Xianggang), 1,361,200. **Monetary unit:** Yuan/Renminbi. **Languages:** Chinese, Mandarin, also local dialects. **Ethnicity/race:** Han Chinese 91.9%, Zhuang, Uygur, Hui, Yi, Tibetan, Miao, Manchu, Mongol, Buyi, Korean, and other nationalities 8.1%. China has 56 ethnic groups. **Religions:** Officially atheist but traditional religion contains elements of Confucianism, Taoism, Buddhism. **Literacy rate:** 81.5% (1995 est.)
Economic summary: GDP/PPP (2001 est.): $5.56 trillion; per capita $4,300. **Real growth rate:** 7.3% (official estimate). **Inflation:** 0.8%. **Unemployment:** urban unemployment roughly 10%; substantial unemployment and underemployment in rural areas. **Arable land:** 13%. **Agriculture:** rice, wheat, potatoes, sorghum, peanuts, tea, millet, barley, cotton, oilseed; pork; fish. **Labor force:** 706 million (2000 est.); agriculture 50%, industry 23%, services 27% (2001 est.). **Industries:** iron and steel, coal, machine building, armaments, textiles and apparel, petroleum, cement, chemical fertilizers, footwear, toys, food processing, automobiles, consumer electronics, telecommunications. **Natural resources:** coal, iron ore, petroleum, natural gas, mercury, tin, tungsten, antimony, manganese, molybdenum, vanadium, magnetite, aluminum, lead, zinc, uranium, hydropower potential (world's largest). **Exports:** $262.1 billion (f.o.b., 2001 est.): machinery and equipment; textiles and clothing, footwear, toys and sporting goods; mineral fuels. **Imports:** $236.2 billion (f.o.b., 2001 est.): machinery and equipment, mineral fuels, plastics, iron and steel, chemicals. **Major trading partners:** U.S., Hong Kong, Japan, South Korea, Germany, Netherlands, UK, Singapore, Taiwan, Russia, Malaysia.

1. Including Manchuria and Tibet.

Geography The greater part of the country is mountainous. Its principal ranges are the Tien Shan, the Kunlun chain, and the Trans-Himalaya. In the southwest is Tibet, which China annexed in 1950. The Gobi Desert lies to the north. China proper consists of three great river systems: the Yellow River (Huang He), 2,109 mi (5,464 km) long; the Yangtze River (Chang Jiang), the third-longest river in the world at 2,432 mi (6,300 km); and the Pearl River (Zhu Jiang), 848 mi (2,197 km) long.

Government Communist state.

History The earliest recorded human settlements in what is today called China were discovered in the Huang Ho basin and date from about 5000 B.C. During the Shang dynasty (1500–1000 B.C.), the precursor of modern China's ideographic writing system developed, allowing the emerging feudal states of the era to achieve an advanced stage of civilization, rivaling in sophistication anything found at the time in Europe, the Middle East, or the Americas. It was following this initial flourishing of civilization, in a period known as the Chou dynasty (1122–249 B.C.), that Lao-tse, Confucius, Mo Ti, and Mencius laid the foundation of Chinese philosophical thought.

The feudal states, often at war with one another, were first united under Emperor Ch'in Shih Huang Ti, during whose reign (246–210 B.C.) work was begun on the Great Wall of China, a monumental bulwark against invasion from the West. Although the Great Wall symbolized China's desire to protect itself from the outside world, under the Han dynasty (206 B.C.–A.D. 220), the civilization conducted extensive commercial trading with the West.

In the T'ang dynasty (618–907)—often called the golden age of Chinese history—painting, sculpture, and poetry flourished, and woodblock printing, which enabled the mass production of books, made its earliest known appearance. The Mings, last of the native rulers (1368–1644), overthrew the Mongol, or Yuan, dynasty (1271–1368) established by Kublai Khan. The Mings in turn were overthrown in 1644 by invaders from the north, the Manchus.

China remained largely isolated from the rest of the world's civilizations, closely restricting foreign activities. By the end of the 18th century only Canton (location of modern-day Hong Kong) and the Portuguese port of Macao were open to European merchants. But with the first Anglo-Chinese War in 1839–1842, a long period of instability and concessions to Western colonial powers began. Following the war, several ports were opened up for trading, and Hong Kong was ceded to Britain. Treaties signed after further hostilities (1856–1860) weakened Chinese sovereignty and gave foreigners immunity from Chinese jurisdiction. European powers took advantage of the disastrous Sino-Japanese War of 1894–1895 to gain further trading concessions from China. Peking's response, the Boxer Rebellion (1900), was suppressed by an international force.

The death of Empress Dowager Tzu Hsi in 1908 and the accession of the infant emperor Hsüan T'ung (Pu-Yi) were followed by a nationwide rebellion led by Dr. Sun Yat-sen, who overthrew the Manchus and became the first president of the Provisional Chinese Republic in 1911. Dr. Sun resigned in favor of Yuan Shih-k'ai, who suppressed the Republicans in a bid to consolidate his power. Yuan's death in June 1916 was followed by years of civil war between rival militarists and Dr. Sun's Republicans. Nationalist forces, led by General Chiang Kai-shek and with the advice of Communist experts, soon occupied most of China, setting up a Kuomintang regime in 1928. Internal strife continued, however, and Chiang eventually broke with the Communists.

On Sept. 18, 1931, Japan launched an invasion of Manchuria, capturing the province. Tokyo set up a puppet state dubbed Manchukuo and installed the last Manchu emperor, Henry Pu-Yi (Hsüan T'ung), as its nominal leader. Japanese troops moved to seize China's northern provinces in July 1937 but were resisted by Chiang, who had been able to use the Japanese invasion to unite most of China behind him. Within two years, however, Japan had seized most of the nation's eastern ports and railways. The Kuomintang government retreated first to Hankow and then to Chungking, while the Japanese set up a puppet government at Nanking, headed by Wang Jingwei.

Japan's surrender to the Western Allies in 1945 touched off civil war between the Kuomintang forces under Chiang and Communists led by Mao Zedong, who had been battling since the 1930s for control of China. Despite U.S. aid, the Kuomintang were overcome by the Soviet-supported Communists, and Chiang and his followers were forced to flee the mainland, establishing a government-in-exile on the island of Formosa (Taiwan). The Mao regime proclaimed the People's Republic of China on Oct. 1, 1949, with Beijing as the new capital and Zhou Enlai as premier.

After the Korean War began in June 1950, China led the Communist bloc in supporting North Korea, and on Nov. 26, 1950, the Mao regime sent troops to assist the North in its efforts to capture the South.

In an attempt to restructure China's primarily agrarian economy, Mao undertook the "Great Leap Forward" campaign in 1958, a disastrous program that aimed to combine the establishment of rural communes with a crash program of village industrialization. The Great Leap forced the abandonment of farming activities, leading to widespread famine in which more than 20 million people died of malnutrition.

In 1959, a failed uprising against China's invasion and occupation of Tibet forced Tibetan Buddhism's spiritual leader, the Dalai Lama, and 100,000 of his followers to flee to India. The invasion of Tibet, as well as border disputes between China and India—with whom Moscow had warm relations—and a perceived rivalry for the leadership of the world Communist movement caused a serious souring of relations between China and the USSR, former allies.

The failure of the Great Leap Forward touched off a power struggle within the Chinese Communist Party between Mao and his supporters and a reformist faction including future premier Deng Xiaoping. Mao moved to Shanghai, and from that base he and his supporters waged what they called the Cultural Revolution. Beginning in the spring of 1966, Mao ordered the closing of schools and the formation of ideologically pure Red Guard units, dominated by youths and students. The Red Guards campaigned against "old ideas, old culture, old habits, and old customs." Millions died as a series of violent purges were carried out. By early 1967, the Cultural Revolution had succeeded in bolstering Mao's position as China's paramount leader.

Anxious to exploit the Sino-Soviet rift, the Nixon administration made a dramatic announcement in July 1971 that National Security Adviser Henry Kissinger had secretly visited Beijing and reached an agreement whereby Nixon would visit China. The movement toward reconciliation, which signaled the end of the U.S. containment policy toward China, provided momentum for China's admission to the UN. Despite U.S. opposition to expelling Taiwan (Nationalist China), the world body overwhelmingly voted to oust Taiwan in favor of Beijing's Communist government.

President Nixon went to Beijing for a week early in 1972, meeting Mao as well as Zhou. The summit ended with a historic communiqué on Feb. 28, in which both nations promised to work toward improved relations. Full diplomatic relations were barred by China as long as the U.S. continued to recognize the legitimacy of Nationalist China.

Following Zhou's death on Jan. 8, 1976, his successor, Vice Premier Deng Xiaoping, was supplanted within a month by Hua Guofeng, former minister of public security. Hua became permanent premier in April. In Oct. he was named successor to Mao as chairman of the Communist Party. But Mao's death on Sept. 10 unleashed the bitter intraparty rivalries that had been suppressed since the Cultural Revolution. Old opponents of Mao launched a campaign against his widow, Jiang Qing, and three of her "radical" colleagues. The so-called Gang of Four was denounced for having undermined the party, the government, and the economy. They were tried and convicted in 1981. Meanwhile, in 1977, Deng Xiaoping was reinstated as deputy premier, chief of staff of the army, and member of the Central Committee of the Politburo.

Beijing and Washington announced full diplomatic relations on Jan. 1, 1979, and the Carter administration abrogated the Taiwan defense treaty. Deputy Premier Deng sealed the agreement with a visit to the U.S. that coincided with the opening of embassies in both capitals on March 1. On Deng's return from the U.S., Chinese troops invaded and briefly occupied an area along Vietnam's northern border. The action was seen as a response to Vietnam's invasion of Cambodia and ouster of the Khmer Rouge government, which China had supported.

In 1981, Deng protégé Hu Yaobang replaced Hua Guofeng as party chairman. Deng became chairman of the committee's military commission, giving him control over the army. The body's 215 members concluded the session with a statement holding Mao Zedong responsible for the "grave blunder" of the Cultural Revolution.

Under Deng Xiaoping's leadership, meanwhile, China's Communist ideology went through a massive reinterpretation, and sweeping economic changes were set in motion in the early 1980s. The Chinese scrapped the personality cult that idolized Mao Zedong, muted Mao's old call for class struggle and exportation of the Communist revolution, and imported Western technology and management techniques to replace the Marxist tenets that had slowed modernization. Deng concluded an agreement for the return of Hong Kong following the expiration of Britain's 99-year lease on the territory on July 1, 1997.

The removal of Hu Yaobang as party chairman in Jan. 1987 signaled a hard-line resurgence within the party. Hu—who had become a hero to many reform-minded Chinese—was replaced by former premier Zhao Ziyang. With the death of Hu in April 1989, the ideological struggle spilled into the streets of the capital, as student demonstrators occupied Beijing's Tiananmen Square in May, calling for democratic reforms. Less than a month later, the demonstrations were crushed in a bloody crackdown as troops and tanks moved into the square and fired on protesters, killing several hundred.

In annual sessions of the rubber-stamp National People's Congress in 1992 and 1993, the government called for accelerating the drive for economic reform, but the sessions were widely seen as an effort to maintain China's moves toward a market economy while retaining political authoritarianism. At the session in 1993, Communist Party leader Jiang Zemin was elected president, while hard-liner Li Peng was reelected to another five-year term as prime minister. Since 1993, the Chinese economy has continued to grow rapidly.

Deng Xiaoping's death in Feb. 1997 left a younger generation in charge of managing the enormous country. In 1998, Prime Minister Zhu Rongji introduced a sweeping program to privatize state-run businesses and further liberalize the nation's economy, a move lauded by Western economists.

On July 1, 1997, when Britain's lease on the New Territories expired, Hong Kong returned to Chinese sovereignty, and in 1999, the Portuguese colony of Macao also was returned to Chinese rule.

In Aug. 1999, China rounded up thousands of members of the Falun Gong sect, a highly popular religious movement that combines elements of Buddhism, Taoism, and martial arts. China, which has now outlawed the sect, was thought to consider the apolitical spiritual group threatening because its numbers exceeded the membership of the Chinese Communist Party.

Tensions between the U.S. and China reached crisis levels in April 2001, when a U.S. Navy EP-3 surveillance plane and a Chinese fighter F-8 jet collided near the Chinese coast. The crew members of the U.S. plane were detained for 11 days and released after the U.S. issued a formal statement of regret.

In Nov. 2001 China was admitted to the World Trade Organization in Nov. 2001. Its entry ended a 15-year debate over whether China is entitled to the full trading rights of capitalist countries.

In Nov. 2002, Vice President Hu Jintao became general secretary of the Communist Party at the 16th Party Congress, succeeding President Jiang. But Jiang retained various positions of power, including head of the Central Military Commission, and filled the Politburo Standing Committee with his protégés. Jiang has thus positioned himself to rule as éminence grise for some time to come. In March 2003, Hu Jintao also assumed the presidency.

In March, the World Health Organization labeled severe acute respiratory syndrome (SARS) a "worldwide health threat." Officials think the potentially deadly virus originated in Guangdong Province. After coming under fire by the WHO for underreporting the extent of the illness, China in April declared about 2,600 known cases of SARS and about 115 deaths from it, numbers many times higher than initially disclosed. In addition, the health minister and the mayor of Beijing were fired in April for the cover-up.

Hong Kong

Status: Special Administrative Region of China
Chief Executive: Tung Chee Hwa (1997)
Area: 422 sq mi (1,092 sq km)
Population (2003 est.): 7,394,170 (growth rate: 0.5%); birth rate: 10.7/1000; infant mortality rate: 5.6/1000; density per sq mi: 17,537

Hong Kong consists of the island of Hong Kong (32 sq mi; 83 sq km), Stonecutters' Island, Kowloon Peninsula, and the New Territories on the adjoining mainland. The island of Hong Kong was ceded to Britain in 1841. Stonecutters' Island and Kowloon were annexed in 1860, and the New Territories, which are mainly agricultural lands, were leased from China in 1898 for 99 years. On July 1, 1997, Hong Kong was returned to China. The vibrant capitalist enclave retains its status as a free port, with its laws to remain unchanged for 50 years. Chief Executive Tung Chee Hwa formulated a policy agenda based upon the concept of "one country, two systems," thus preserving Hong Kong's economic independence.

In a series of massive demonstrations in July 2003, more than 500,000 people took to the streets of Hong Kong to protest proposed anti-subversion laws that curtailed civil rights. Surprisingly, Tung Chee-hwa scrapped the law in September.

Macao

Status: Special Administrative Region of China
Chief Executive: Edmund Ho (1999)
Area: 10 sq mi (25.4 sq km)
Population (2003 est.): 469,903 (average annual growth rate: 0.8%); birth rate: 12.1/1000; infant mortality rate: 4.4/1000; density per sq mi: 47,915

Colonized by the Portuguese in 1557, Macao was the oldest European outpost in China. In 1987, Portugal and China reached an agreement to return Macao to Chinese rule on Dec. 20, 1999. They agreed upon provisions to insure the autonomy of Macao, including its right to elect local leaders, the right of its residents to travel freely, and the right to maintain its way of life for 50 years after the start of Chinese rule.

Colombia

REPUBLIC OF COLOMBIA

National name: República de Colombia
President: Alvaro Uribe (2002)
Area: 439,733 sq mi (1,138,910 sq km)
Population (2003 est.): 41,662,073 (growth rate: 1.6%); birth rate: 21.6/1000; infant mortality rate: 22.5/1000; density per sq mi: 95
Capital and largest city (2003 est.): Santafé de Bogotá, 6,837,800. **Other large cities:** Cali, 2,283,200; Medellín, 1,957,800; Barranquilla, 1,330,400; Cartagena, 901,500. **Monetary unit:** Colombian Peso. **Language:** Spanish. **Ethnicity/race:** mestizo 58%, white 20%, mulatto 14%, black 4%, mixed black-Indian 3%, Indian 1%. **Religion:** Roman Catholic 90%. **Literacy rate:** 91.3% (1995 est.)
Economic summary: GDP/PPP (2001 est.): $255 billion; per capita $6,300. **Real growth rate:** 1.5%. **Inflation:** 7.6%. **Unemployment:** 17%. **Arable land:** 2%. **Agriculture:** coffee, cut flowers, bananas, rice, tobacco, corn, sugarcane, cocoa beans, oilseed, vegetables; forest products; shrimp. **Labor force:** 18.3

million (1999 est.); services 46%, agriculture 30%, industry 24% (1990). **Industries:** textiles, food processing, oil, clothing and footwear, beverages, chemicals, cement; gold, coal, emeralds. **Natural resources:** petroleum, natural gas, coal, iron ore, nickel, gold, copper, emeralds, hydropower. **Exports:** $12.3 billion (f.o.b., 2001 est.): petroleum, coffee, coal, apparel, bananas, cut flowers. **Imports:** $12.7 billion (c.i.f., 2001 est.): industrial equipment, transportation equipment, consumer goods, chemicals, paper products, fuels, electricity. **Major trading partners:** U.S., Andean Community of Nations, EU, Japan.

Geography Colombia is bordered by Panama on the northwest, on the east by Venezuela and Brazil, and on the southwest by Peru and Ecuador. Through the western half of the country, three Andean ranges run north and south. The eastern half is a low, jungle-covered plain, drained by spurs of the Amazon and Orinoco Rivers, inhabited mostly by isolated tropical-forest Indian tribes. The fertile plateau and valley of the eastern range are the most densely populated parts of the country.

Government Republic.

History Little is known about the various Indian tribes who inhabited Colombia before the Spanish arrived. In 1510 Spaniards founded Darien, the first permanent European settlement on the American mainland. In 1538 they established the colony of New Granada, the area's name until 1861.

After a 14-year struggle, in which Simón Bolívar's Venezuelan troops won the battle of Boyacá in Colombia on Aug. 7, 1819, independence was attained in 1824. Bolívar united Colombia, Venezuela, Panama, and Ecuador in the Republic of Greater Colombia (1819–1830), but lost Venezuela and Ecuador to separatists. Two political parties dominated the region: the Conservatives believed in a strong central government and a powerful church; the Liberals believed in a decentralized government, strong regional power, and a less influential role for the church. Bolívar was himself a Conservative, while his vice president, Francisco de Paula Santander, was the founder of the Liberal Party.

Santander served as president between 1832 and 1836, a period of relative stability, but by 1840 civil war erupted. Other periods of Liberal dominance (1849–1857 and 1861–1880), which sought to disestablish the Roman Catholic Church, were marked by insurrection. Nine different governments followed, each rewriting the constitution. In 1861 the country was called the United States of New Granada; in 1863 it became the United States of Colombia; and in 1885, it became the Republic of Colombia.

In 1899 a brutal civil war broke out, the War of a Thousand Days, that lasted until 1902. The following year, Colombia lost its claims to Panama because it refused to ratify the lease to the U.S. of the Canal Zone. Panama declared its independence in 1903.

The Conservatives held power until 1930, when revolutionary pressure put the Liberals back in power. The Liberal administrations of Enrique Olaya Herrera and Alfonso López (1930–1938) were marked by social reforms that failed to solve the country's problems, and in 1946, a period of insurrection and banditry broke out, referred to as La Violencia, which claimed hundreds of thousands of lives by 1958. Laureano Gómez (1950–1953); the army chief of staff, Gen. Gustavo Rojas Pinilla (1953–1956); and a military junta (1956–1957) sought to curb disorder by repression.

Marxist guerrilla groups organized in the 1960s and 1970s, most notably the May 19th Movement (M-19), the National Liberation Army (ELN), and the Revolutionary Armed Forces of Colombia (FARC), plunging the country into violence and instability. In the 1970s and 1980s, Colombia became one of the international centers for illegal drug production and trafficking, and at times the drug cartels (the Medillin and Cali cartels were the most notorious) virtually controlled the country. In the 1990s, numerous right-wing paramilitary groups also formed, made up of drug traffickers and landowners. The umbrella group for these paramilitaries is the United Self-Defense Forces of Colombia (AUC).

Belisario Betancur Cuartas, a Conservative who assumed the presidency in 1982, unsuccessfully attempted to stem the guerrilla violence. In an official war against drug trafficking, Colombia became a public battleground with bombs, killings, and kidnappings. By 1989, homicide had become the leading cause of death in the nation. Elected president in 1990, César Gaviria Trujillo proposed lenient punishment in exchange for surrender by the leading drug dealers. Ernesto Samper of the Liberal Party became president in 1994. In 1996 he was accused of accepting campaign contributions from drug traffickers, but the House of Representatives absolved him of the charges.

Andrés Pastrana Arango was elected president in 1998, pledging to clean up corruption. In Dec. 1999 the Colombian military reported that 2,787 people were kidnapped that year—the largest number in the world—and blamed rebels. The murder rate soared in 1999, with some 23,000 people reported killed by leftist guerrillas, right-wing paramilitaries, drug traffickers, and common criminals. The violence has created more than 100,000 refugees, while 2 million Colombians have fled the country in recent years.

In Aug. 2000, the U.S. government approved "Plan Colombia," a $1.3 billion in antidrug trafficking aid that Pastrana used to undercut drug production and prevent guerrilla groups from benefiting from drug sales. In Aug. 2001, Pastrana signed "war legislation," which expands the rights of the military in dealing with rebels.

Alvaro Uribe of the Liberal party easily won the presidential election in May 2002. He took office in Aug., pledging to get tough on the rebels and drug traffickers by increasing military spending and seeking U.S. military cooperation. An upsurge in violence accompanied his inauguration, and Uribe declared a state of emergency within a week. In his first year, Uribe beefed up Colombia's security forces with the help of U.S. special forces, launched an aggressive campaign against the drug trade, and passed several economic reform bills.

Comoros

UNION OF COMOROS ISLANDS

President: Azali Assoumani (2002)
Area: 838 sq mi (2,170 sq km)
Population (2003 est.): 632,948 (growth rate: 3.0%); birth rate: 38.5/1000; infant mortality rate: 79.5/1000; density per sq mi: 755
Capital and largest city (2003 est.): Moroni (on Grande Comoro), 60,200. **Monetary unit:** Franc. **Languages:** French and Arabic (both official), Shikomoro (a blend of Swahili and Arabic). **Ethnicity/race:** Antalote, Cafre, Makoa, Oimatsaha, Sakalava. **Religions:** Sunni Muslim 98%, Roman Catholic 2%. **Literacy rate:** 57.3% (1995 est.)
Economic summary: GDP/PPP: (2001 est.) $424 million; per capita $710 . **Real growth rate:** 1%. **Inflation:** 3.5%. **Unemployment:** 20% (1996 est.). **Arable land:** 35%. **Agriculture:** vanilla, cloves, perfume essences, copra, coconuts, bananas,

cassava (tapioca). **Labor force:** 144,500 (1996 est.): agriculture 80%. **Industries:** tourism, perfume distillation. **Natural resources:** negl. **Exports:** $35.3 million (f.o.b., 2001 est.): vanilla, ylang-ylang, cloves, perfume oil, copra. **Imports:** $44.9 million (f.o.b., 2001 est.): rice and other foodstuffs, consumer goods; petroleum products, cement, transport equipment. **Major trading partners:** France, U.S., Singapore, Germany, South Africa, Kenya, Pakistan.

Geography The Comoros Islands—Grande Comoro (Ngazidja), Anjouan, Mohéli, and Mayotte (which is not part of the country and retains ties to France)—are an archipelago of volcanic origin in the Indian Ocean, 190 mi off the coast of Mozambique.

Government Emerging republic. Under a new constitution ratified in March 2002, each island will have its own president with a federal president assuming overall authority. The federal presidency will rotate every four years between the three islands.

History Comoros was frequented by travelers from Africa, Madagascar, Indonesia, and Arabia before the first Europeans encountered the islands. Arabic influence has been the strongest.

France colonized Mayotte in 1843 and by 1904 had annexed the remainder of the archipelago. In a 1974 referendum, 95% of the population voted for independence. The exception was Mayotte, which, with its Christian majority, voted against joining the other mainly Islamic islands in independence. Today it remains a French overseas territory.

The remaining Comoros islands declared themselves independent on July 6, 1975, with Ahmed Abdallah as president. A month after independence, he was overthrown by Justice Minister Ali Soilih. This was only the beginning of Comoros's chronic instability: the country has gone through more than 20 coups since independence and has experienced several attempts at secession. Orchestrating at least four of these coups was a group of white mercenaries known as Les Affreux (The Terrible Ones), and their notorious leader, Frenchman "Colonel" Bob Denard. Denard fled Comoros in 1989, when 3,000 French soldiers were sent after him.

The island of Anjouan declared independence on Aug. 3, 1997, after months of protests and clashes with security forces. The secessionists wanted a return to French rule, contending that independence from France has brought economic disaster and political chaos. Mohéli, the smallest island, also seceded. But France refused to support the secession of either island. In Sept. 1997, President Mohamed Taki's forces attempted to retake Anjouan but failed.

In 1999, Col. Azali Assoumani led a coup, overthrowing interim president Tadjidine. He promised interim military rule would end in a year, a pledge the Organization of African Unity would continue to remind him of. After years of aborted peace talks, a new constitution was approved in March 2002, and the three islands were reunited. Each island elected its own president, and in May a federal president was elected from Grand Comoros, former military coup leader Assoumani. In Feb. 2003, a coup against Assoumani was thwarted.

Congo, Republic of

REPUBLIC OF CONGO

National name: République Populaire du Congo
President: Denis Sassou-Nguesso (1997)
Area: 132,046 sq mi (342,000 sq km)
Population (2003 est.): 2,954,258 (growth rate: 1.5%); birth rate: 29.5/1000; infant mortality rate: 95.3/1000; density per sq mi: 22
Capital and largest city (2003 est.): Brazzaville, 1,169,900. **Other large city:** Pointe-Noire, 544,200. **Monetary unit:** CFA Franc. **Languages:** French (official), Lingala, Kikongo, others. **Ethnicity/race:** south: Kongo 48%; north: Sangha 20%, M'Bochi 12%; center: Teke 17%, Europeans 8,500 (mostly French). **Religions:** Christian 50%, animist 48%, Islam 2%. **Literacy rate:** 74.9% (1995 est.)
Economic summary: GDP/PPP (2001 est.): $2.5 billion; per capita $900. **Real growth rate:** 4.2%. **Inflation:** 3%. **Unemployment:** n.a. **Arable land:** 1%. **Agriculture:** cassava (tapioca), sugar, rice, corn, peanuts, vegetables, coffee, cocoa; forest products. **Labor force:** n.a. **Industries:** petroleum extraction, cement, lumber, brewing, sugar, palm oil, soap, flour, cigarettes. **Natural resources**: petroleum, timber, potash, lead, zinc, uranium, copper, phosphates, natural gas, hydropower. **Exports:** $2.6 billion (f.o.b., 2001): petroleum 90%, lumber, plywood, sugar, cocoa, coffee, diamonds. **Imports:** $725 million (f.o.b., 2001): petroleum products, capital equipment, construction materials, foodstuffs. **Major trading partners:** U.S., South Korea, China, Germany, France, Italy, Belgium.

Geography The Congo is situated in west-central Africa astride the equator. It borders Gabon, Cameroon, the Central African Republic, the Democratic Republic of the Congo, and the Angola exclave of Cabinda, with a short stretch of coast on the South Atlantic. Its area is nearly three times that of Pennsylvania. Most of the inland is tropical rain forest, drained by tributaries of the Congo River.

Government Dictatorship.

History In precolonial times, the region now called the Republic of Congo was dominated by three kingdoms: Kongo (originating about 1000), the Loango (flourishing in the 17th century), and Tio. After the Portuguese located the Congo River in 1482, commerce was carried on with the tribes, especially the slave trade.

The Frenchman Pierre Savorgnan de Brazza signed a treaty with Makoko, ruler of the Bateke people, in 1880, thus establishing French control. It was first called French Congo, and after 1905 Middle Congo. With Gabon and Ubangi-Shari, it became the colony of French Equatorial Africa in 1910. Abuse of laborers led to public outcry against the French colonialists as well as rebellions among the Congolese, but the exploitation of the native workers continued until 1930. During World War II the colony joined Chad in supporting the Free French cause against the Vichy government. The Congo proclaimed its independence without leaving the French Community in 1960, calling itself the Republic of Congo.

Congo's second president, Alphonse Massemba-Débat, instituted a Marxist-Leninist government. In 1968, Maj. Marien Ngouabi overthrew him but kept Congo on a socialist course. He was sworn in for a second five-year term in 1975. A four-man commando squad assassinated Ngouabi on March 18, 1977. Col. Joachim Yhombi-Opango, army chief of staff, assumed the presidency on April 4. Yhombi-Opango resigned on Feb. 4, 1979, and was replaced by Col. Denis Sassou-Nguesso.

In July 1990 the leaders of the ruling party voted to end the one-party system. A national political conference, hailed as a model for sub-Saharan Africa, renounced Marxism in 1991, and scheduled the country's first free elections for 1992.

Political and ethnic tensions intensified in 1993 after legislative elections, when the opposition's rejection of the results developed into violence. A peace agreement was signed between the government and the opposition in Aug. 1994. A four-month civil war (June 5–Oct. 15, 1997) devastated Brazzaville, the capital. Buttressed by military aid from Angola, former Marxist dictator Denis Sassou-Nguesso overthrew President Pascal Lissouba, the country's first democratically elected president. In late 1999 a peace agreement was signed between Sassou-Nguesso, who comes from the north, and the rebels representing the populous south. The postwar period has been traumatic: a recurrence of sleeping sickness and other diseases have swept the country, yet 60% of its health centers are out of commission.

In March 2002, President Sassou-Nguesso was reelected with 89.4% of the vote. His opponents were either barred from the country or withdrew from the election.

The so-called Ninja rebels continue to battle government forces, each attempting to gain or maintain control of the country's rich oil reserves and each seemingly unconcerned about the toll this new outbreak of violence is taking on civilians. In May 2003, the government and Ninja rebels signed an agreement to end hostilities.

Congo, Democratic Republic of the

DEMOCRATIC REPUBLIC OF THE CONGO

President: Joseph Kabila (2001)
Area: 905,563 sq mi (2,345,410 sq km)
Population (2003 est.): 56,625,039 (growth rate: 3.0%); birth rate: 45.1/1000; infant mortality rate: 96.6/1000; density per sq mi: 63
Capital and largest city (2003 est.): Kinshasa, 6,541,300. **Other large cities:** Lubumbashi, 1,105,900; Mbuji-Mayi, 938,000; Kolwezi, 832,400; Kisangani, 523,000 . **Monetary unit:** Congolese franc. **Languages:** French (official), Swahili, Lingala, Ishiluba, and Kikongo, others. **Ethnicity/race:** over 200 African ethnic groups, the majority are Bantu; the four largest tribes—Mongo, Luba, Kongo (all Bantu), and the Mangbetu-Azande (Hamitic)—make up about 45% of the population. **Religions:** Roman Catholic 50%, Protestant 20%, Kimbanguist 10%, Islam 10%; syncretic and traditional, 10%. **Literacy rate:** 77.3% (1995 est.)
Economic summary: GDP/PPP (2001 est.): $32 billion; per capita $590. **Real growth rate:** –4%. **Inflation:** 358%. **Unemployment:** n.a. **Arable land:** 3%. **Agriculture:** coffee, sugar, palm oil, rubber, tea, quinine, cassava (tapioca), palm oil, bananas, root crops, corn, fruits; wood products. **Labor force:** 14.51 million (1993 est.); agriculture 65%, industry 16%, services 19% (1991 est.). **Industries:** mining (diamonds, copper, zinc), mineral processing, consumer products (including textiles, footwear, cigarettes, processed foods and beverages), cement. **Natural resources:** cobalt, copper, cadmium, petroleum, industrial and gem diamonds, gold, silver, zinc, manganese, tin, germanium, uranium, radium, bauxite, iron ore, coal, hydropower, timber. **Exports**: $750 million (f.o.b., 2001 est.): diamonds, copper, coffee, cobalt, crude oil. **Imports:** $1.024 billion (f.o.b., 2001 est.): foodstuffs, mining and other machinery, transport equipment, fuels. **Major trading partners:** Benelux, U.S., South Africa, Finland, Italy, Nigeria, Kenya, China.

Geography The Congo, in west-central Africa, is bordered by the Congo Republic, the Central African Republic, the Sudan, Uganda, Rwanda, Burundi, Tanzania, Zambia, Angola, and the Atlantic Ocean. It is one-quarter the size of the U.S. The principal rivers are the Ubangi and Bomu in the north and the Congo in the west, which flows into the Atlantic. The entire length of Lake Tanganyika lies along the eastern border with Tanzania and Burundi.

Government Dictatorship.

History Formerly the Belgian Congo, this territory was inhabited by ancient Negrito peoples (Pygmies), who were pushed into the mountains by Bantu and Nilotic invaders. The American correspondent Henry M. Stanley navigated the Congo River in 1877 and opened the interior to exploration. Commissioned by King Leopold II of the Belgians, Stanley made treaties with native chiefs that enabled the king to obtain personal title to the territory at the Berlin Conference of 1885.

Leopold accumulated a vast personal fortune from ivory and rubber through Congolese slave labor; 10 million people are estimated to have died from forced labor, starvation, and outright extermination during Leopold's colonial rule. His brutal exploitation of the Congo eventually became an international cause célèbre, prompting Belgium to take over administration of the Congo, which remained a colony until agitation for independence forced Brussels to grant freedom on June 30, 1960. In elections that month, two prominent nationalists won: Patrice Lumumba of the leftist Mouvement National Congolais became prime minister and Joseph Kasavubu of the ABAKO party became head of state. But within weeks of independence, the Katanga Province, led by Moise Tshombe, seceded from the new republic, and another mining province, South Kasai, followed. Belgium sent paratroopers to quell the civil war, and with Kasavubu and Lumumba of the national government in conflict, the United Nations flew in a peacekeeping force.

Kasavubu staged an army coup in 1960 and handed Lumumba over to the Katangan forces. A UN investigating commission found that Lumumba had been killed by a Belgian mercenary in the presence of Tshombe, who was then the president of Katanga. U.S. and Belgian involvement in the assassination have been alleged. Dag Hammarskjold, UN secretary-general, died in a plane crash en route to a peace conference with Tshombe on Sept. 17, 1961.

Tshombe rejected a national reconciliation plan submitted by the UN in 1962. Tshombe's troops fired on the UN force in Dec., and in the ensuing conflict Tshombe capitulated on Jan. 14, 1963. The peacekeeping force withdrew, and, in a complete about-face, Kasavubu named Tshombe premier in order to fight a spreading rebellion. Tshombe used foreign mercenaries, and with the help of Belgian paratroops airlifted by U.S. planes, defeated the most serious opposition, a Communist-backed regime in the northeast.

Kasavubu abruptly dismissed Tshombe in 1965, but was then himself ousted by Gen. Joseph-Desiré Mobutu, army chief of staff. The new president nationalized the Union Minière, the Belgian copper mining enterprise that had been a dominant force in the Congo since colonial days. Mobutu eliminated opposition to win the election in 1970. In 1975, he nationalized much of the economy, barred religious instruction in schools, and decreed the adoption of African names. He changed the country's name to Zaire and his own to Mobuto Sese Seko, which means "the all-powerful warrior who, because of his endurance and inflexible will to win, will go from conquest to conquest leaving fire in his wake." In 1977, invaders from Angola calling themselves the Congolese National Liberation Front pushed into Shaba and threatened the important mining center of Kolwezi. France and Belgium provided military aid to defeat the rebels.

Laurent Kabila and his long-standing but little-known guerrilla movement launched a seven-month campaign that ousted Mobutu in May 1997, ending one of the world's most corrupt and megalomaniacal regimes. The last of the CIA-nurtured cold war despots, Mobutu deftly courted France and the U.S., which used Zaire as a launching pad for covert operations against bordering countries, particularly Marxist Angola. Mobutu's disastrous policies drove his country to economic collapse while he siphoned off millions of dollars for himself. Mobutu fled in exile to Morocco on May 16, 1997, where he died of cancer in September.

The country was renamed the Democratic Republic of the Congo, its name before Mobutu changed it to Zaire in 1971. But elation over Mobutu's downfall faded as Kabila's own autocratic style emerged, and he seemed devoid of a clear plan for reconstructing the country. He stymied UN human rights investigations and continued to depend on foreign troops for border skirmishes rather than establish a strong national army. Many Congolese dismissed him as a puppet ruler who allowed his country to be overrun by outsiders, particularly the Rwandans. At the same time, he alienated many of his former supporters who helped him establish power, including Rwanda and Uganda.

In Aug. 1998, Congolese rebel forces, led by ethnic Tutsi in eastern Congo who were backed by Rwanda and Uganda, began attacking Kabila's forces. The rebels gained control of a large portion of the country until Angolan, Namibian, and Zimbabwean troops came to Kabila's aid and pushed the rebels back. In 1999, the Lusaka Accord was signed by all six of the countries involved, as well as by most, but not all, of the various rebel groups.

In Jan. 2001, Kabila was assassinated, allegedly by one of his bodyguards. His young and inexperienced son Joseph became the new president, and demonstrated a willingness to engage in talks to end the civil war. In April 2002, the government agreed to a power-sharing arrangement with Ugandan-supported rebels, and in July, the presidents of the Congo and Rwanda signed an accord: Rwanda promised to withdraw its 35,000 troops from the eastern Congolese border; the Congo would in turn disarm the thousands of Hutu militiamen in its territory, who threatened Rwandan security—many of them supported or participated in the 1994 genocide against Rwandan Tutsis. In Sept. 2002, Uganda also signed a peace accord with the nation. But the warring parties were slow to depart; most had been looting the Congo of its natural resources and had little incentive to end the war. More than 2.5 million people are estimated to have died in the Congo's complex four-year civil war, which has involved 7 foreign armies and numerous rebel groups that often fought among themselves.

Despite the peace agreement and power-sharing plan signed between the main parties in the four-year Congolese war, the fighting and killing continued into 2003. In April 2003, hundreds of civilians were massacred in the eastern province of Ituri in an ethnic conflict. In June a French force with a UN mandate was deployed to defend the population from further tribal fighting. Joseph Kabila signed a new constitution in April, and on July 17, 2003, Congo's new power-sharing government was inaugurated. The new government includes 4 vice presidents and 36 ministers, 16 of which are former rebels.

Costa Rica

REPUBLIC OF COSTA RICA

National name: República de Costa Rica
President: Abel Pacheco (2002)
Area: 19,730 sq mi (51,100 sq km)
Population (2003 est.): 3,896,092 (growth rate: 1.5%); birth rate: 19.4/1000; infant mortality rate: 10.6/1000; density per sq mi: 197
Capital and largest city (2003 est.): San José, 1,527,300 (metro. area), 337,200 (city proper). **Monetary unit:** Colón. **Language:** Spanish. **Ethnicity/race:** white (including mestizo) 94%, black 3%, Indian 1%, Chinese 1%, other 1%. **Religion:** Roman Catholic 76.3%, Evangelical 13.7%. **Literacy rate:** 95.5% (1999 est.)
Economic summary: GDP/PPP (2001 est.): $31.9 billion; per capita $8,500. **Real growth rate:** 0.3%. **Inflation:** 12.1%. **Unemployment:** 5.2% (2000 est.). **Arable land:** 4%. **Agriculture:** coffee, pineapples, bananas, sugar, corn, rice, beans, potatoes; beef; timber. **Labor force:** 1.9 million (1999); agriculture 20%, industry 22%, services 58% (1999 est.). **Industries:** microprocessors, food processing, textiles and clothing, construction materials, fertilizer, plastic products. **Natural resources:** hydropower. **Exports:** $5 billion (2001): coffee, bananas, sugar; pineapples; textiles, electronic components, medical equipment. **Imports:** $6.5 billion (2001): raw materials, consumer goods, capital equipment, petroleum. **Major trading partners:** U.S., EU, Central America, Puerto Rico, Mexico, Venezuela.

Geography This Central American country lies between Nicaragua to the north and Panama to the south. Its area slightly exceeds that of Vermont and New Hampshire combined. It has a narrow Pacific coastal region. Cocos Island (10 sq mi; 26 sq km), about 300 mi (483 km) off the Pacific Coast, is under Costa Rican sovereignty.

Government Democratic republic.

History Costa Rica was inhabited by an estimated 25,000 Indians when Columbus explored it in 1502. Few of the Indians survived the Spanish conquest, which began in 1563. The region grew slowly and was administered as a Spanish province. Costa Rica achieved independence in 1821 but was absorbed for two years by Agustín de Iturbide in his Mexican empire. It became a republic in 1848. Except for the military dictatorship of Tomás Guardia from 1870 to 1882, Costa Rica has enjoyed one of the most democratic governments in Latin America.

In the 1970s, rising oil prices, falling international commodity prices, and inflation hurt the economy. Efforts have since been made to reduce reliance on coffee, banana, and beef exports. Tourism is now a major business. Oscar Arias Sanchez, who became president in 1986, was awarded the Nobel Peace Prize in 1987 for his role in negotiating settlements to both the Nicaraguan and the Salvadoran civil wars.

José Maria Figueres Olsen of the National Liberation Party became president in 1994. He opposed economic suggestions made by the International Monetary Fund, instead favoring greater government intervention in the economy. The World Bank subsequently withheld $100 million of financing. In 1998, Miguel Angel Rodríguez of the Social Christian Unity Party became president, pledging economic reforms, such as privatization. In 2000, Costa Rica and Nicaragua resolved a long-standing dispute over navigation of the San Juan River, which forms their border. A psychiatrist, Abel Pacheco, also of the Social Christian Unity Party, won the presidency in elections held in April 2002. In May

2003, several national strikes took place, by energy and telecommunications workers over privatization, and by teachers over their salaries.

Côte d'Ivoire

REPUBLIC OF CÔTE D'IVOIRE

National name: République de la Côte d'Ivoire
President: Laurent Gbagbo (2000)
Prime Minister: Seydou Diarra (2003)
Area: 124,502 sq mi (322,460 sq km)
Population (2003 est.): 16,962,491 (growth rate: 2.2%); birth rate: 40.0/1000; infant mortality rate: 98.3/1000; density per sq mi: 136
Capital (2003 est.): Yamoussoukro (official), 185,600 . **Largest city:** Abidjan,(administrative capital) 4,113,600 (metro. area), 3,427,500 (city proper). **Monetary unit:** CFA Franc. **Languages:** French (official) and African languages (Diaula esp.). **Ethnicity/race:** Akan 42.1%, Voltaiques (Gur) 17.6%, Northern Mandes 16.5%, Krous 11%, Southern Mandes 10%, other 2.8% (includes 130,000 Lebanese and 20,000 French). **Religions:** indigenous 25%-40%, Islam 35%-40%, Christian 20%-30%. **Literacy rate:** 48.5%
Economic summary:GDP/PPP (2001 est.): $25.5 billion; per capita $1,550. **Real growth rate:** –1%. **Inflation:** 2.5% (2000 est.). **Unemployment:** 13% in urban areas (1998 est.). **Arable land:** 9%. **Agriculture:** coffee, cocoa beans, bananas, palm kernels, corn, rice, manioc (tapioca), sweet potatoes, sugar, cotton, rubber; timber. **Labor force:** 68% agricultural (2000 est.). **Industries:** foodstuffs, beverages; wood products, oil refining, truck and bus assembly, textiles, fertilizer, building materials, electricity. **Natural resources:** petroleum, natural gas, diamonds, manganese, iron ore, cobalt, bauxite, copper, hydropower. **Exports:** $3.6 billion (f.o.b., 2001 est.): cocoa 33%, coffee, tropical woods, petroleum, bananas, pineapples, palm oil, cotton, fish (1999). **Imports:** $2.4 billion (f.o.b., 2001 est.): food, consumer goods; capital goods, fuel, transport equipment, raw materials. **Major trading partners:** France, U.S., Netherlands, Germany, Italy, Nigeria, China.

Geography Côte d'Ivoire (also known as the Ivory Coast), in western Africa on the Gulf of Guinea is a little larger than New Mexico. Its neighbors are Liberia, Guinea, Mali, Burkina Faso, and Ghana. The country consists of a coastal strip in the south, dense forests in the interior, and savannas in the north.

Government Presidential/parliamentary democracy until Dec. 1999, when a coup installed a military dictatorship.

History Côte d'Ivoire was originally made up of numerous isolated settlements; today it represents more than sixty distinct tribes, including the Baoule, Bete, Senoufou, Agni, Malinke, Dan, and Lobi. Côte d'Ivoire attracted both French and Portuguese merchants in the 15th century who were in search of ivory and slaves. French traders set up establishments early in the 19th century, and in 1842, the French obtained territorial concessions from local tribes, gradually extending their influence along the coast and inland. The area was organized as a territory in 1893, became an autonomous republic in the French Union after World War II, and achieved independence on Aug. 7, 1960. Côte d'Ivoire formed a customs union in 1959 with Dahomey (Benin), Niger, and Burkina Faso. The nation's economy is one of the most developed in sub-Saharan Africa. It is the world's largest exporter of cocoa and one of the largest exporters of coffee.

From independence until his death in 1993, Felix Houphouët-Boigny served as president. Massive protests by students, farmers, and professionals forced the president to legalize opposition parties and hold the first contested presidential election in Oct. 1990, which Houphouët-Boigny won with 81% of the vote.

Beginning in Sept. 1998, thousands of demonstrators protested a constitutional revision that granted President Henri Konan Bédié greatly enhanced powers. Bédié has also promoted the concept of *ivoirité,* which, roughly translated, means "pure Ivoirian pride." Although its defenders describe *ivoirité* as a term of positive national pride, it has led to a dangerous xenophobia, with numerous ethnic Malians and Burkinans being driven out of the country in 1999.

President Bédié was overthrown in the country's first military coup in Dec. 1999, and Gen. Robert Guei assumed control of the country. As a result, the majority of foreign aid to the country has ceased.

In what were seen as the first steps toward reasserting democracy, voters overwhelmingly approved a draft constitution in July 2000. However, the document requires both parents of a potential presidential candidate to have been Ivorian, thereby excluding the nearly 40% of the population and increasing the possibility of ethnic tension. Guei, who had promised to stay in power only to "sweep the house clean," instead decided to run for president in October 2000 elections. Gen. Guei ran against a civilian opposition candidate, Laurent Gbagbo. Each declared victory in an election most believe to have been rife with fraud. Popular outcry against Guei soon turned violent, forcing him to leave the country, and Gbagbo assumed the presidency. Many observers questioned his mandate, however, since the popular opposition leader Alassane Ouattara had been excluded from the election on the specious grounds that he was not a pure-blooded Ivoirian. It was not until June 2002 that Ouattara was finally granted full Ivoirian citizenship, which will allow him to run in the next presidential election in 2005. Hundreds have died in violence sparked by the dispute.

Mutineering soldiers attempted a coup on Sept. 19, 2002. Guei and Interior Minister Doudou were killed in fighting between government soldiers and the rebels. President Gbagbo accused Guei of staging the coup. Fighting continued, even after a French-brokered peace accord was signed on Jan. 25, 2003, calling for the government to share power with the rebels. President Gbagbo's supporters found such a plan unacceptable, and there was rioting in the capital. Finally, the power-sharing plan was agreed on in March, a full cease-fire was signed in May, and the war was declared officially over in July.

Croatia

REPUBLIC OF CROATIA

President: Stipe Mesic (2000)
Prime Minister: Ivica Racan (2000)
Area: 21,831 sq mi (56,542 sq km)
Population (2003 est.): 4,422,248 (growth rate: 0.2%); birth rate: 12.8/1000; infant mortality rate: 6.9/1000; density per sq mi: 203
Capital and largest city (2003 est.): Zagreb, 685,500. **Other large cities:** Split, 173,600; Rijeka, 142,500; Osijek, 89,600. **Monetary unit:** Kuna. **Language:** What was once known as Serbo-Croatian is now known as Serbian, Croatian, or Bosnian, depending on the speaker's political and ethnic affiliation. **Ethnicity/race:** Croat 78.1%, Serb 12.2%, Bosniak 0.9%, Hungarian 0.5%, Slovenian 0.5%, others 8.1% (1991). **Religions:** Catholic 76.5%, Orthodox 11.1%, Slavic Muslim 1.2%, Protestant 0.4%, others 10.8%. **Literacy**

rate: 97% (1991 est.)
Economic summary: GDP/PPP (2001 est.): $36.1 billion; per capita $8,300. **Real growth rate:** 4%. **Inflation:** 5%. **Unemployment:** 23% (Dec. 2001). **Arable land:** 24%. **Agriculture:** wheat, corn, sugar beets, sunflower seed, barley, alfalfa, clover, olives, citrus, grapes, soybeans, potatoes; livestock, dairy products. **Labor force:** 1.7 million; agriculture n.a., industry n.a., services n.a. **Industries:** chemicals and plastics, machine tools, fabricated metal, electronics, pig iron and rolled steel products, aluminum, paper, wood products, construction materials, textiles, shipbuilding, petroleum and petroleum refining, food and beverages; tourism. **Natural resources:** oil, some coal, bauxite, low-grade iron ore, calcium, natural asphalt, silica, mica, clays, salt, hydropower. **Exports:** $4.5 billion (f.o.b., 2001): transport equipment, textiles, chemicals, foodstuffs, fuels. **Imports:** $8.4 billion (c.i.f., 2001): machinery, transport and electrical equipment, chemicals, fuels and lubricants, foodstuffs. **Major trading partners:** Italy, Germany, Bosnia and Herzegovina, Slovenia, Austria, Russia.

Geography Croatia is a former Yugoslav republic on the Adriatic Sea. It is about the size of West Virginia. Part of Croatia is a barren, rocky region lying in the Dinaric Alps. The Zagorje region north of the capital, Zagreb, is a land of rolling hills, and the fertile agricultural region of the Pannonian Plain is bordered by the Drava, Danube, and Sava Rivers in the east. Over one-third of Croatia is forested.

Government Presidential/parliamentary democracy.

History Croatia, at one time the Roman province of Pannonia, was settled in the 7th century by the Croats. They converted to Christianity between the 7th and 9th centuries and adopted the Roman alphabet under the suzerainty of Charlemagne. In 925, the Croats defeated Byzantine and Frankish invaders and established their own independent kingdom, which reached its peak during the 11th century. A civil war ensued in 1089, which later led to the country being conquered by the Hungarians in 1091. The signing of the *Pacta Conventa* by Croatian tribal chiefs and the Hungarian king in 1102 united the two nations politically under the Hungarian monarch, but Croatia retained its autonomy.

Following the defeat of the Hungarians by the Turks at the battle of Mohács in 1526, Croatia (along with Hungary) elected Austrian Archduke Ferdinand of Hapsburg as their king. After the establishment of the Austro-Hungarian kingdom in 1867, Croatia became part of Hungary until the collapse of Austria-Hungary in 1918 following its defeat in World War I. On Oct. 29, 1918, Croatia proclaimed its independence and joined in union with Montenegro, Serbia, and Slovenia to form the Kingdom of Serbs, Croats, and Slovenes. The name was changed to Yugoslavia in 1929.

When Germany invaded Yugoslavia in 1941, Croatia became a Nazi puppet state. Croatian Fascists, the Ustachi, slaughtered countless Serbs and Jews during the war. After Germany was defeated in 1945, Croatia was made into a republic of the newly reestablished Communist nation of Yugoslavia. In June 1991, the Croatian Parliament passed a declaration of independence from Yugoslavia. A six-month civil war followed with the Serbian-dominated Yugoslavian army. The war claimed thousands of lives and wrought mass destruction.

A UN cease-fire was arranged on Jan. 2, 1992. The Security Council in Feb. approved sending a 14,000-member peacekeeping force to monitor the cease-fire and protect the minority Serbs in Croatia. In a 1993 referendum the Serb-occupied portion of Croatia (Krajina) resoundingly voted for integration with Serbs in Bosnia and Serbia proper. Although the Zagreb government and representatives of Krajina signed a cease-fire in March 1994, further negotiations broke down. In a lightning-quick operation, the Croatian army retook western Slavonia in May 1995. Similarly, in Aug., the central Croatian region of Krajina, held by Serbs, was returned to Zagreb's control.

Announcing on television in 1999 that "national issues are more important than democracy," President Tudjman continued to alienate Croatians with his authoritarian rule, out-of-touch nationalism, and disastrous handling of the war-shattered economy. In Dec. 1999, Tudjman died and was succeeded by Stipe Mesic, a reformer. One of his first acts in office was to invite back the 300,000 ethnic Serbs who had been banished from the country under Tudjman.

In July 2002, Mesic met with the presidents of Bosnia and Yugoslavia for the first time since war broke out between Croatia and Yugoslavia more than a decade ago. The three countries pledged to cooperate on the repatriation of refugees, to fight organized crime, and to assist each other economically. In 2003, Croatia formally submitted its application to join the EU.

Cuba

REPUBLIC OF CUBA

National name: República de Cuba
President: Fidel Castro (1976)
Area: 42,803 sq mi (110,860 sq km)
Population (2003 est.): 11,263,429 (growth rate: 0.5%); birth rate: 11.9/1000; infant mortality rate: 7.2/1000; density per sq mi: 263
Capital and largest city (2003 est.): Havana, 2,686,000 (metro. area), 2,343,700 (city proper). **Other large cities:** Santiago de Cuba, 554,400; Camagüey, 354,400; Holguin, 319,300; Guantánamo, 274,300; Santa Clara, 251,800. **Monetary unit:** Cuban Peso. **Language:** Spanish. **Ethnicity/race:** mulatto 51%, white 37%, black 11%, Chinese 1%. **Religion:** at least 85% nominally Roman Catholic before Castro assumed power. **Literacy rate:** 95.7% (1995 est.)
Economic summary: GDP/PPP (2001 est.): $25.5 billion; per capita $2,300. **Real growth rate:** 3%. **Inflation:** 0.5%. **Unemployment:** 4.1%. **Arable land:** 33%. **Agriculture:** sugar, tobacco, citrus, coffee, rice, potatoes, beans; livestock. **Labor force:** 4.3 million (2000 est.); agriculture 24%, industry 25%, services 51% (1999). **Industries:** sugar, petroleum, tobacco, chemicals, construction, services, nickel, steel, cement, agricultural machinery, biotechnology. **Natural resources:** cobalt, nickel, iron ore, copper, manganese, salt, timber, silica, petroleum, arable land. **Exports:** $1.7 billion (f.o.b., 2001 est.): sugar, nickel, tobacco, fish, medical products, citrus, coffee. **Imports:** $4.9 billion (f.o.b., 2001 est.): petroleum, food, machinery, chemicals, semifinished goods, transport equipment, consumer goods. **Major trading partners:** Russia, Canada, Netherlands, Spain, Venezuela, Italy.

Geography The largest island of the West Indies group (equal in area to Pennsylvania), Cuba is also the westernmost—just west of Hispaniola (Haiti and the Dominican Republic), and 90 mi (145 km) south of Key West, Fla., at the entrance to the Gulf of Mexico. The island is mountainous in the southeast and south-central area (Sierra Maestra). It is flat or rolling elsewhere. Cuba also includes numerous smaller islands, islets, and cays.

Government Communist state.

History Arawak (or Taino) Indians inhabiting Cuba when Columbus landed on the island in 1492 died from diseases brought by sailors and settlers. By 1511, Spaniards under Diego Velásquez had established settlements. Havana's superb harbor made it a common transit point to and from Spain.

In the early 1800s, Cuba's sugarcane industry boomed, requiring massive numbers of black slaves. A simmering independence movement turned into open warfare from 1867 to 1878. Slavery was abolished in 1886. In 1895, the poet José Marti led the struggle that finally ended Spanish rule, thanks largely to U.S. intervention in 1898 after the sinking of the battleship *Maine* in Havana harbor.

An 1899 treaty made Cuba an independent republic under U.S. protection. The U.S. occupation, which ended in 1902, suppressed yellow fever and brought large American investments. The 1901 Platt Amendment allowed the U.S. to intervene in Cuba's affairs, which it did four times from 1906 to 1920. Cuba terminated the amendment in 1934.

In 1933 a group of army officers, including army sergeant Fulgencio Batista, overthrew President Gerado Machado. Batista became president in 1940, running a corrupt police state.

In 1956, Fidel Castro Ruz launched a revolution from his camp in the Sierra Maestra mountains. Castro's brother Raul, and Ernesto (Ché) Guevara, an Argentine physician, were his top lieutenants. Many anti-Batista landowners supported the rebels. The U.S. ended military aid to Cuba in 1958, and on New Year's Day 1959, Batista fled into exile and Castro took over the government.

The U.S. initially welcomed what looked like a democratic Cuba, but a rude awakening came within a few months when Castro established military tribunals for political opponents and jailed hundreds. Castro disavowed Cuba's 1952 military pact with the U.S., confiscated U.S. assets, and established Soviet-style collective farms. The U.S. broke relations with Cuba on Jan. 3, 1961, and Castro formalized his alliance with the Soviet Union. Thousands of Cubans fled the country.

In 1961 a U.S.-backed group of Cuban exiles invaded Cuba. Planned during the Eisenhower administration, the invasion was given the go-ahead by President John Kennedy, although he refused to give U.S. air support. The landing at the Bay of Pigs on April 17, 1961, was a fiasco. The invaders did not receive popular Cuban support and were easily repulsed by the Cuban military.

A Soviet attempt to install medium-range missiles in Cuba—capable of striking targets in the United States with nuclear warheads—provoked a crisis in 1962. Denouncing the Soviets for "deliberate deception," on Oct. 22 Kennedy said that the U.S. would blockade Cuba so the missiles could not be delivered. Six days later Soviet premier Nikita Khrushchev ordered the missile sites dismantled and returned to the USSR, in return for a U.S. pledge not to attack Cuba.

The U.S. established limited diplomatic ties with Cuba on Sept. 1, 1977, making it easier for Cuban-Americans to visit the island. Contact with the more affluent Cuban Americans prompted a wave of discontent in Cuba, producing a flood of asylum seekers. In response, Castro opened the port of Mariel to a "freedom flotilla" of boats from the U.S., allowing 125,000 to flee to Miami. After the refugees arrived, it was discovered their ranks were swelled with prisoners, mental patients, homosexuals, and others unwanted by the Cuban government.

Cuba fomented Communist revolution around the world, especially in Angola, where thousands of Cuban troops were sent in the 1980s.

Russian aid, which had long supported Cuba's failing economy, ended when communism collapsed in eastern Europe in 1990. Cuba's foreign trade also plummeted, producing a severe economic crisis. In 1993, Castro permitted limited private enterprise, allowed Cubans to possess convertible currencies, and encouraged foreign investment in its tourist industry. In March 1996, the U.S. tightened its embargo with the Helms-Burton Act.

Christmas became an official holiday in 1997, for the first time since the revolution, in response to Pope John Paul II's 1998 visit to Cuba, which raised hopes for greater religious freedom.

In June 2000, Castro won a publicity bonanza when the Clinton administration sent Elian Gonzalez, a young boy found clinging to an inner tube, back to Cuba. The U.S. Cuban community had demanded that the boy remain in Miami rather than be returned to his father in Cuba. By many accounts, the influential Cuban-Americans lost public sympathy by pitting political ideology against familial bonds.

In March and April 2003, Castro sent nearly 80 dissidents to prison with long sentences, prompting an international condemnation of Cuba's harsh crackdown on human rights.

Cyprus

REPUBLIC OF CYPRUS

National name: Kypriaki Dimokratia—Kibris Cumhuriyeti
President: Tassos Papadopoulos (2003)
Area: 3,571 sq mi (9,250 sq km)
Population (2003 est.): 771,657 (growth rate: 0.5%); birth rate: 12.8/1000; infant mortality rate: 7.5/1000; density per sq mi: 216
Capital and largest city (2003 est.): Lefkosia (Nicosia) (in government-controlled area), 197,600. **Monetary unit:** Cyprus pound. **Languages:** Greek, Turkish (official), English is widely spoken. **Ethnicity/race:** total: Greek 85.2% (99.5% of the Greeks live in the Greek area, 0.5% live in the Turkish area), Turkish 11.6% (1.3% live in the Greek area, 98.7% live in the Turkish area), other 3.2% (2000). **Religions:** Greek Orthodox 78%, Sunni Muslim 18%, Maronite, Armenian, Apostolic, Latin, and others 4% (1993 est.). **Literacy rate:** 97% (1999)
Economic summary: GDP/PPP: Greek Cypriot area (2001 est.): $9.1 billion; $15,000 per capita; Turkish Cypriot area (2000 est.): $1.1 billion; $7,000 per capita. **Real growth rate:** Greek Cypriot area: 2.6% (2001 est.); Turkish Cypriot area: 0.8% (2000 est.). **Inflation:** Greek Cypriot area: 1.9% (2001 est.); Turkish Cypriot area: 53.2% (2000 est.). **Unemployment:** Greek Cypriot area: 3% (2001 est.); Turkish Cypriot area: 5.6% (1999 est.). **Arable land:** 10%. **Agriculture:** potatoes, citrus, vegetables, barley, grapes, olives, vegetables. **Labor force** (2000): Greek Cypriot area: 291,000; Turkish Cypriot area: 86,300 (2000); Greek Cypriot area: services 73%, industry 22%, agriculture 5% (2000); Turkish Cypriot area: services 56.4%, industry 22.8%, agriculture 20.8% (1998). **Industries:** food, beverages, textiles, chemicals, metal products, tourism, wood products. **Natural resources:** copper, pyrites, asbestos, gypsum, timber, salt, marble, clay earth pigment. **Exports:** Greek Cypriot area: $851 million (f.o.b., 2001 est.): citrus, potatoes, grapes, wine, cement, clothing and shoes; Turkish Cypriot area: $50.7 million (f.o.b., 2000): citrus, potatoes, textiles. **Imports:** Greek Cypriot area: $3.5 billion (f.o.b., 2001 est.): consumer goods, petroleum and lubricants, food and feed grains,

machinery; Turkish Cypriot area: $424.9 million (f.o.b., 2000): food, minerals, chemicals, machinery. **Major trading partners:** Greek Cypriot area: UK, Greece, Russia, Syria, Lebanon, U.S., Italy, Germany; Turkish Cypriot area: Turkey, UK, other EU. **Member of Commonwealth of Nations**

Geography The third-largest island in the Mediterranean (one and one-half times the size of Delaware), Cyprus lies off the southern coast of Turkey and the western shore of Syria. The highest peak is Mount Olympus at 6,406 ft (1,953 m).

Government Republic. Mediation efforts by the UN seek to achieve reunification of the island under one federated system of government.

History Cyprus was the site of early Phoenician and Greek colonies. For centuries its rule passed through many hands. It fell to the Turks in 1571, and a large Turkish colony settled on the island.

In World War I, at the outbreak of hostilities with Turkey, Britain annexed the island. It was declared a Crown colony in 1925. For centuries the Greek population, regarding Greece as its mother country, has sought self-determination and reunion with Greece *(enosis)*. The resulting quarrel with Turkey threatened NATO. Cyprus became an independent nation on Aug. 16, 1960, with Britain, Greece, and Turkey as guarantor powers.

Archbishop Makarios, president since 1959, was overthrown on July 15, 1974, by a military coup led by the Cypriot National Guard. The new regime named Nikos Giorgiades Sampson as president and Bishop Gennadios as head of the Cypriot Church to replace Makarios. Diplomacy failed to resolve the crisis. Turkey invaded Cyprus by sea and air on July 20, 1974, asserting its right to protect the Turkish Cypriot minority. Geneva talks involving Greece, Turkey, Britain, and the two Cypriot factions failed in mid-Aug., and the Turks subsequently gained control of 40% of the island. Some 180,000 Greek Cypriots were uprooted by the Turkish troops. Greece made no armed response to the superior Turkish force but bitterly suspended military participation in the NATO alliance. The tension continued after Makarios returned to become president on Dec. 7, 1974. He offered self-government to the Turkish minority, but rejected any solution "involving transfer of populations and amounting to partition of Cyprus."

Turkish Cypriots proclaimed a separate state under Rauf Denktash in the northern part of the island on Nov. 15, 1983, naming it the "Turkish Republic of Northern Cyprus." The UN Security Council, in its Resolution 541 of Nov. 18, 1983, declared this action illegal and called for withdrawal. No country except Turkey has recognized this illegal entity.

In 1988, George Vassiliou, a conservative and critic of UN proposals to reunify Cyprus, became president. The purchase of missiles capable of reaching the Turkish coast evoked threats of retaliation from Turkey in 1997, and Cyprus's plans to deploy more missiles in Aug. 1999 again raised Turkey's ire.

The continued strife between Greek Cypriots and Turkish Cypriots threatened Cyprus's potential EU membership—it had in fact met all the economic standards—and provided a great incentive to both sides to resolve their differences. UN-sponsored talks between the Greek and Turkish leaders, Kleridas and Denktash, continued intensively in 2002, but without resolution. In Dec. 2002, the EU invited Cyprus to join in 2004, provided the UN plan was accepted by February 2003. But just weeks before the UN deadline, Kleridas was defeated by right-wing candidate Tassos Papadopoulos in presidential elections. Papadopoulos has a reputation as a hard-liner on reunification—he's rejected all previous UN attempts to reunify Cyprus. The UN deadline passed, and by mid-March, the UN declared that the talks had failed, and it appeared that only the Greek side of the island would join the EU in 2004.

Czech Republic

President: Vaclav Klaus (2003)
Prime Minister: Vladimír Spidla (2002)
Area: 30,450 sq mi (78,866 sq km)
Population (2003 est.): 10,249,216 (growth rate: –0.2%); birth rate: 9.0/1000; infant mortality rate: 5.4/1000; density per sq mi: 337
Capital and largest city (2003 est.): Prague, 1,378,700 (metro. area), 1,169,800 (city proper). **Other large cities:** Brno, 376,400; Ostrava, 317,700; Plzen, 164,900; Olomouc, 102,900. **Monetary unit:** Koruna. **Languages:** Czech; Slovak minority. **Ethnicity/race:** Czech 81.2%, Moravian 13.2%, Slovak 3%.1, Polish 0.6%, German 0.5%, Roma (Gypsy) 0.3%, Hungarian 0.2%, other 0.5%. **Religions:** atheist 39.8%, Roman Catholic 39.2%, Protestant 4.6%, Orthodox 3%, other 13.4%. **Literacy rate:** 99.9% (1999 est.)
Economic summary: GDP/PPP (2001 est.): $147.9 billion; per capita $14,400. **Real growth rate:** 3.4%. **Inflation:** 4.7%. **Unemployment:** 8.5%. **Arable land:** 40%. **Agriculture:** wheat, potatoes, sugar beets, hops, fruit; pigs, poultry. **Labor force:** 5.203 million (1999 est.); agriculture 5%, industry 40%, services 55% (2000 est.). **Industries:** metallurgy, machinery and equipment, motor vehicles, glass, armaments. **Natural resources:** hard coal, soft coal, kaolin, clay, graphite, timber. **Exports:** $32.7 billion (f.o.b., 2000): machinery and transport equipment 44%, intermediate manufactures 25%, chemicals 7%, raw materials and fuel 7% (2000). **Imports:** $37.4 billion (f.o.b., 2000): machinery and transport equipment 40%, intermediate manufactures 21%, raw materials and fuels 13%, chemicals 11% (2000). **Major trading partners:** Germany, Slovakia, Austria, Poland, UK, France.

Geography The Czech Republic's central European landscape is dominated by the Bohemian Massif, which rises to heights of 3,000 ft (900 m) above sea level. This ring of mountains encircles a large elevated basin, the Bohemian Plateau. The principal rivers are the Elbe and the Vltava.

Government Parliamentary democracy.

History Probably about the 5th century A.D., Slavic tribes from the Vistula basin settled in the region of Bohemia, Moravia, and Silesia. The Czechs founded the kingdom of Bohemia and the Premyslide dynasty, which ruled Bohemia and Moravia from the 10th to the 16th century. One of the Bohemian kings, Charles IV, Holy Roman emperor, made Prague an imperial capital and a center of Latin scholarship. The Hussite movement founded by Jan Hus (1369?–1415) linked the Slavs to the Reformation and revived Czech nationalism, previously under German domination. A Hapsburg, Ferdinand I, ascended the throne in 1526. The Czechs rebelled in 1618, precipitating the Thirty Years' War (1618–1648). Defeated in 1620, they were ruled for the next 300 years as part of the Austrian empire. Full independence from the Hapsburgs was not achieved until the end of World War I, following the collapse of the Austrian-Hungarian Empire.

A union of the Czech lands and Slovakia was proclaimed in Prague on Nov. 14, 1918, and the Czech nation became one of the two component parts of the newly formed Czechoslovakian state. In March 1939, German troops occupied Czechoslovakia, and Czech

Bohemia and Moravia became German protectorates for the duration of World War II. The former government returned in April 1945 when the war ended and the country's pre-1938 boundaries were restored. When elections were held in 1946, Communists became the dominant political party and gained control of the Czechoslovakian government in 1948. Thereafter, the former democracy was turned into a Soviet-style state.

Nearly 42 years of Communist rule ended with the nearly bloodless "velvet revolution" in 1989. Václav Havel, a leading playwright and dissident, was elected president of Czechoslovakia in 1989. Havel, imprisoned twice by the Communist regime and his plays banned, became an international symbol for human rights, democracy, and peaceful dissent. The return of democratic political reform saw a strong Slovak nationalist movement emerge by the end of 1991, which sought independence for Slovakia. When the general elections of June 1992 failed to resolve the continuing coexistence of the two republics within the federation, Czech and Slovak political leaders agreed to separate their states into two fully independent nations. On Jan. 1, 1993, the Czechoslovakian federation was dissolved and two separate independent countries were established—the Czech Republic and Slovakia.

In March 1999, the Czech Republic joined NATO, and it was invited to join the EU in May 2004.

In Aug. 2002, severe flooding caused 70,000 people in Prague and 200,000 nationwide to be evacuated.

President Václav Havel left office in Feb. 2003, after 13 years as president. Over the years, Havel lost some of his immense popularity with Czechs, who became disenchanted with his failings as a political leader. But internationally, Havel has remained a towering figure of moral authority and courage. In March, Vaclav Klaus became the Czech Republic's second president. A conservative economist, he and Havel often clashed.

Denmark

KINGDOM OF DENMARK

National name: Kongeriget Danmark
Sovereign: Queen Margrethe II (1972)
Prime Minister: Anders Fogh Rasmussen (2001)
Area: 16,639 sq mi (43,094 sq km)[1]
Population (2003 est.): 5,384,384 (growth rate: 0.1%); birth rate: 11.5/1000; infant mortality rate: 4.9/1000; density per sq mi: 324
Capital and largest city (2003 est.): Copenhagen, 1,094,400. **Other large cities:** Århus, 220,700; Odense, 144,600; Ålborg, 120,600. **Monetary unit:** Krone. **Languages:** Danish, Faeroese, Greenlandic (an Inuit dialect), small German-speaking minority. **Ethnicity/race:** Scandinavian, Eskimo, Faeroese, German. **Religions:** Evangelical Lutheran 95%, other Protestant and Roman Catholic 3%, other 2%. **Literacy rate:** 100%
Economic summary: GDP/PPP (2001 est.): $149.8 billion; per capita $28,000. **Real growth rate:** 1.1%. **Inflation:** 2.4%. **Unemployment:** 5.3% (2000). **Arable land:** 56%. **Agriculture:** barley, wheat, potatoes, sugar beets; pork, dairy products; fish. **Labor:** 2.856 million; services 79%, industry 17%, agriculture 4% (2000 est.). **Industries:** food processing, machinery and equipment, textiles and clothing, chemical products, electronics, construction, furniture, and other wood products, shipbuilding, windmills. **Natural resources:** petroleum, natural gas, fish, salt, limestone, stone, gravel and sand. **Exports:** $52.4 billion (f.o.b., 2001): machinery and instruments, meat and meat products, dairy products, fish, chemicals, furniture, ships, windmills. **Imports:** $44.1 billion (f.o.b., 2001): machinery and equipment, raw materials and semimanufactures for industry, chemicals, grain and foodstuffs, consumer goods. **Major trading partners:** EU, U.S., Norway.

1. Excluding Faeroe Islands and Greenland.

Geography Smallest of the Scandinavian countries (half the size of Maine), Denmark occupies the Jutland peninsula, a lowland area. The country also consists of several islands in the Baltic Sea; the two largest are Sjælland, the site of Copenhagen, and Fyn.

Government Constitutional monarchy.

History From 10,000 to 1500 B.C., the population of present-day Denmark evolved from a society of hunters and fishers into an agricultural one. Called Jutland by the end of the 8th century, its mariners were among the Vikings, or Norsemen, who raided western Europe and the British Isles from the 9th to 11th century.

The country was Christianized by Saint Ansgar and Harald Blaatand (Bluetooth)—the first Christian king—in the 10th century. Harald's son, Sweyn, conquered England in 1013. Sweyn's son, Canute the Great, who reigned from 1014 to 1035, united Denmark, England, and Norway under his rule; the southern tip of Sweden was part of Denmark until the 17th century. On Canute's death, civil war tore apart the country until Waldemar I (1157–1182) reestablished Danish hegemony over the north.

In 1282, the nobles won the Great Charter, and Eric V was forced to share power with Parliament and a Council of Nobles. Waldemar IV (1340–1375) restored Danish power, checked only by the Hanseatic League of north German cities allied with ports from Holland to Poland. Denmark, Norway, and Sweden united under the rule of his daughter Margrethe in 1397. But Sweden later achieved autonomy and in 1523, under Gustavus I, independence.

Denmark supported Napoléon, for which it was punished at the Congress of Vienna in 1815 by the loss of Norway to Sweden. In 1864, the Prussians under Bismarck and the Austrians made war on Denmark as an initial step in the unification of Germany. Denmark was neutral in World War I.

In 1940, Denmark was invaded by the Nazis. King Christian X reluctantly cautioned his fellow Danes to accept the occupation, but there was widespread resistance against the Nazis. Denmark was the only occupied country in World War II to save all its Jews from extermination, by smuggling them out of the country.

Beginning in 1944, Denmark's relationship with its territories changed substantially. In that year, Iceland declared its independence from Denmark, ending a union that had existed since 1380. In 1948, the Faeroe Islands, which had also belonged to Denmark since 1380, were granted home rule, and in 1953, Greenland officially became a territory of Denmark.

Immigration to Denmark fell dramatically in 2002, after Denmark's center-right government instituted more restrictive laws for asylum-seekers. Because of Denmark's social welfare benefits, it had become a much sought-after haven for refugees.

Outlying Territories of Denmark

Faeroe Islands

Status: Autonomous part of Denmark
Chief of State: Queen Margrethe II (1972)
High Commissioner: Birgit Kleis (2001)
Prime Minister: Anfinn Kallsberg (1998)
Area: 540 sq mi (1,399 sq km)
Population (2003 est.): 46,345 (average annual growth rate: 0.5%); birth rate: 13.8/1000; infant mortality rate:

6.5/1000; density per sq mi: 86
Capital and largest city (2003 est.): Tórshavn, 17,300. **Monetary unit:** Faeroese krone. **Languages:** Faeroese, Danish (both official). **Ethnicity/race:** Scandinavian. **Literacy rate:** 99%

This group of 18 islands, of which 17 are inhabited, is located in the North Atlantic about 200 mi (322 km) northwest of the Shetland Islands. They were settled by the Vikings, the ancestors of the modern-day Faeroese, in the 8th century. The Faeroese language is derived from Old Norse. The islands joined Denmark in 1386 and have been part of the Danish kingdom ever since. The Faeroes have had home rule, under Danish authority, since 1948.

Greenland

Status: Autonomous part of Denmark
Chief of State: Queen Margrethe II (1972)
High Commissioner: Gunnar Martens (1995)
Premier: Jonathan Motzfeldt (1997)
Area: 836,326 sq mi (incl. 677,851 sq mi covered by icecap) (2,166,086 sq km)
Population (2003 est.): 56,385 (average annual growth rate: 0.8%); birth rate: 16.1/1000; infant mortality rate: 16.8/1000; density per sq mi: 0.07
Capital and largest city (2003 est.): Godthaab, 14,100. **Monetary unit:** Krone. **Ethnicity/race:** Greenlander 88% (Eskimos and Greenland-born whites), Danish and other 12% (2000). **Literacy rate:** 99%

The Inuit are believed to have crossed from North America to northwest Greenland, the world's largest island, between 4000 B.C. and A.D. 1000. Greenland was colonized in 985–986 by Eric the Red. The Norse settlements declined in the 14th century, however, mainly as a result of a cooling in Greenland's climate, and in the 15th century they became extinct. In 1721, Greenland was recolonized by the Royal Greenland Trading Company of Denmark.

Greenland was under U.S. protection during World War II, but maintained Danish sovereignty. A definitive agreement for the joint defense of Greenland within the framework of NATO was signed in 1951. A large U.S. air base at Thule in the far north was completed in 1953.

Under 1953 amendments to the Danish constitution, Greenland became part of Denmark, with two representatives in the Danish Folketing. On May 1, 1979, Greenland gained home rule, with its own local Parliament (Landsting). In Feb. 1982, Greenlanders voted to withdraw from the European Union, which they had joined as part of Denmark in 1973.

Djibouti

REPUBLIC OF DJIBOUTI

National name: Jumhouriyya Djibouti
President: Ismail Omar Guelleh (1999)
Prime Minister: Dileita Mohamed Dileita (2001)
Area: 8,880 sq mi (23,000 sq km)
Population (2003 est.): 457,130 (growth rate: 2.1%); birth rate: 40.8/1000; infant mortality rate: 107.0/1000; density per sq mi: 51
Capital (2003 est.): Djibouti, 547,100. **Monetary unit:** Djibouti franc. **Languages:** Arabic and French (both official), Afar, Somali. **Ethnicity/race:** Somali 60%, Afar 35%, French, Arab, Ethiopian, and Italian 5%. **Religions:** Islam 94%, Christian 6%. **Literacy rate:** 46.2% (1995 est.)
Economic summary: GDP/PPP (2001 est.): $586 million; per capita $1,400. **Real growth rate:** 0%. **Inflation:** 2%. **Unemployment:** 50% (2000 est.). **Arable land:** 0%. **Agriculture:** fruits, vegetables; goats, sheep, camels. **Labor:** 282,000. **Industries:** construction, agricultural processing. **Natural resources:** geothermal areas. **Exports:** $260 million (f.o.b., 1999 est.): reexports, hides and skins, coffee (in transit). **Imports:** $440 million (f.o.b., 1999 est.): foods, beverages, transport equipment, chemicals, petroleum products. **Major trading partners:** Somalia, Yemen, Ethiopia, France, Italy, Saudi Arabia, UK.

Geography Djibouti lies in northeast Africa on the Gulf of Aden at the southern entrance to the Red Sea. It borders on Ethiopia, Eritrea, and Somalia. The country, the size of Massachusetts, is mainly a stony desert, with scattered plateaus and highlands.

Government Republic with a unicameral legislature.

History Ablé immigrants from Arabia migrated to what is now Djibouti in about the 3rd century B.C. Their descendants are the Afars, one of the two main ethnic groups that make up Djibouti today. Somali Issas arrived thereafter. Islam came to the region in 825.

Djibouti was acquired by France between 1843 and 1886 by treaties with the Somali sultans. Small, arid, and sparsely populated, it is important chiefly because of the capital city's port, the terminal of the Djibouti–Addis Ababa railway that carries 60% of Ethiopia's foreign trade. Originally known as French Somaliland, the colony voted in 1958 and 1967 to remain under French rule. It was renamed the Territory of the Afars and Issas in 1967 and took the name of its capital city on June 27, 1977, when France transferred sovereignty to the new independent nation of Djibouti. On Sept. 4, 1992, voters approved in referendum a new multiparty constitution. In 1991, conflict between the Afars and the Issa-dominated government erupted and the continued warfare has ravaged the country.

The dictatorial president, Hassan Gouled Aptidon, who had run the country since its independence, finally stepped aside in 1999, and Ismail Omar Guelleh was elected president. In March 2000, the main Afars rebel group signed a peace accord with the government. The fighting, severe drought, and the presence of tens of thousands of refugees from its war-torn neighbors, Ethiopia and Somalia, have severely strained Djibouti's agricultural capacity.

In April 2000 experts estimated some 150,000 people, or more than one-quarter of the population, needed food aid. The United Nations agreed to spend $2.7 million to increase the city of Djibouti's port facilities since it is a crucial regional grain terminus. Djibouti also agreed to let the Port Authority in the nearby Arab nation of Dubai run the port for 20 years to increase efficiency. In 2002, Djibouti became a key U.S. military base used to combat terrorism.

Dominica

COMMONWEALTH OF DOMINICA

President: Vernon Shaw (1998)
Prime Minister: Pierre Charles (2000)
Area: 291 sq mi (754 sq km)
Population (2003 est.): 69,655 (growth rate: 1.0%); birth rate: 16.8/1000; infant mortality rate: 15.3/1000; density per sq mi: 239
Capital and largest city (2003 est.): Roseau, 20,000. **Monetary unit:** East Caribbean dollar. **Languages:** English (official) and French patois. **Ethnicity/race:** black, Carib Indians. **Religions:** Roman Catholic 77%, Protestant 15%. **Literacy rate:** 94% (1970 est.)
Economic summary: GDP/PPP (2001 est.): $262 million; per capita $3,700. **Real growth rate:** –3.2%. **Inflation:** 1%. **Unemployment:** 23% (2000 est.). **Arable land:** 4%. **Labor force:** 25,000; agriculture 40%, industry and commerce 32%, services 28%.

Agriculture: bananas, citrus, mangoes, root crops, coconuts, cocoa; forest and fishery potential not exploited. **Industries:** soap, coconut oil, tourism, copra, furniture, cement blocks, shoes. **Natural resources:** timber, hydropower, arable land. **Exports:** $49 million (f.o.b., 2000 est.): bananas, soap, bay oil, vegetables, grapefruit, oranges. **Imports:** $132 million (c.i.f., 2000 est.): manufactured goods, machinery and equipment, food, chemicals. **Major trading partners:** Caricom countries, UK, U.S., Netherlands, Canada. **Member of Commonwealth of Nations**

Geography Dominica (pronounced Dom-in-EEK-a) is a mountainous island of volcanic origin of the Lesser Antilles in the Caribbean, south of Guadeloupe and north of Martinique.

Government Parliamentary democracy.

History Explored by Columbus in 1493, Dominica was claimed by Britain and France until 1763, when it was formally ceded to Britain. Along with other Windward Isles, it became a self-governing member of the West Indies Associated States in free association with Britain in 1967.

Dissatisfaction over the slow pace of reconstruction after Hurricane David devastated the island in Sept. 1979 brought a landslide victory to Mary Eugenia Charles of the Freedom Party in July 1980. The Freedom Party won again in 1985 and 1990, and the government sold state enterprises. The opposition United Workers' Party won in June 1995. In 1997 Dominica became the first Caribbean country to participate in the work of Green Globe, aiming to make Dominica a model ecotourism destination. Although the island is poorer than some of its Caribbean neighbors, Dominica has a relatively low crime rate and does not have the extremes of wealth and poverty evident on other islands. Economic austerity measures, including higher taxes, were introduced in 2002. Massive protests followed.

Dominican Republic

National name: República Dominicana
President: Hipólito Mejía (2000)
Area: 18,815 sq mi (48,730 sq km)
Population (2003 est.): 8,715,602 (growth rate: 1.7%); birth rate: 23.9/1000; infant mortality rate: 34.2/1000; density per sq mi: 463
Capital and largest city (2003 est.): Santo Domingo, 2,851,300 (metro.area), 2,252,400 (city proper). **Other large city:** Santiago de los Caballeros, 501,800. **Monetary unit:** Dominican Peso. **Languages:** Spanish, English widely spoken. **Ethnicity/race:** white 16%, black 11%, mixed 73%. **Religion:** Roman Catholic 95%. **Literacy rate:** 82.1% (1995 est.)
Economic summary: GDP/PPP (2001 est.): $50 billion; per capita $5,800. **Real growth rate:** 1.5%. **Inflation:** 5%. **Unemployment:** 15%. **Arable land:** 21%. **Agriculture:** sugarcane, coffee, cotton, cocoa, tobacco, rice, beans, potatoes, corn, bananas; cattle, pigs, dairy products, beef, eggs. **Labor force:** 2.3 million to 2.6 million; services and government 58.7%, industry 24.3%, agriculture 17% (1998 est.). **Industries:** tourism, sugar processing, ferronickel and gold mining, textiles, cement, tobacco. **Natural resources:** nickel, bauxite, gold, silver. **Exports:** $5.5 billion (f.o.b., 2001): ferronickel, sugar, gold, silver, coffee, cocoa, tobacco, meats, consumer goods. **Imports:** $8.7 billion (f.o.b., 2001 est.): foodstuffs, petroleum, cotton and fabrics, chemicals and pharmaceuticals. **Major trading partners:** U.S., Netherlands, Canada, France, Japan, Mexico, Venezuela.

Geography The Dominican Republic in the West Indies occupies the eastern two-thirds of the island of Hispaniola, which it shares with Haiti. Its area equals that of Vermont and New Hampshire combined. Duarte Peak, at 10,417 ft (3,175 m), is the highest point in the West Indies.

Government Representative democracy.

History The Dominican Republic was explored by Columbus on his first voyage in 1492. He named it La Española, and his son, Diego, was its first viceroy. The capital, Santo Domingo, founded in 1496, is the oldest European settlement in the Western Hemisphere.

Spain ceded the colony to France in 1795, and Haitian blacks under Toussaint L'Ouverture conquered it in 1801. In 1808 the people revolted and captured Santo Domingo the next year, setting up the first republic. Spain regained title to the colony in 1814. In 1821 Spanish rule was overthrown, but in 1822 the colony was reconquered by the Haitians. In 1844 the Haitians were thrown out, and the Dominican Republic was established, headed by Pedro Santana. Uprisings and Haitian attacks led Santana to make the country a province of Spain from 1861 to 1865.

President Buenaventura Báez, faced with an economy in shambles, attempted to have the country annexed to the U.S. in 1870, but the U.S. Senate refused to ratify a treaty of annexation. Disorder continued until the dictatorship of Ulíses Heureaux; in 1916, when chaos broke out again, the U.S. sent in a contingent of marines, who remained until 1934.

A sergeant in the Dominican army trained by the marines, Rafaél Leonides Trujillo Molina overthrew Horacio Vásquez in 1930 and established a dictatorship that lasted until his assassination 31 years later.

Leftists rebelled on April 24, 1965, and U.S. president Lyndon Johnson sent in marines and troops. After a cease-fire on May 6, a compromise installed Hector Garcia-Godoy as provisional president. Joaquin Balaguer won in free elections in 1966 against Bosch, and U.S. and other foreign troops withdrew. Balaguer restored political and economic stability.

In 1978 the army suspended the counting of ballots when Balaguer trailed in a fourth-term bid. After a warning from President Jimmy Carter, however, Balaguer accepted the victory of Antonio Guzmán of the Dominican Revolutionary Party. Salvador Jorge Blanco of the Dominican Revolutionary Party was elected president on May 16, 1982, defeating Balaguer and Bosch. Balaguer was again elected president in May 1986 and remained in office for the next ten years.

In 1996, U.S.-raised Leonel Fernandez secured more than 51% of the vote through an alliance with Balaguer. The first item on the president's agenda was the partial sale of some state-owned enterprises. Fernandez was praised for ending decades of isolationism and improving ties with other Caribbean countries, but he was criticized for not fighting corruption and alleviating the poverty that affects 60% of the population.

In Aug. 2000 the center-left Hipólito Mejía was elected president amid popular discontent over power outages in the recently privatized electric industry. In 2001 the army was deployed in major cities to fight rising crime.

East Timor

EAST TIMOR

President: José Alexandre (Xanana) Gusmão (2002)
Prime Minister: Mari Alkatiri (2002)
Area: 5,814 sq mi (15,057 sq km)
Population (2003 est.): 997,853 (growth rate: 2.1%); birth rate: 27.8/1000; infant mortality rate: 50.5/1000; density per sq mi: 172
Capital and largest city (2003 est.): Dili, 50,800.

Monetary unit: U.S. dollar. **Languages:** Tetum, Portuguese (official), Bahasa Indonesia, English. **Ethnicity/race:** Malay and Papuan descent. **Religions:** Roman Catholic 90%, Islam 4%, Protestant 3%, Hindu 0.5%, Buddhist, animist. **Literary rate:** 48% (2001)

Economic summary: GDP/PPP (2001 est.): $415 billion; per capita $500. **Real growth rate:** 18%. **Inflation:** n.a. **Unemployment:** 50% (including underemployment). **Arable land:** n.a. **Agriculture:** coffee, rice, maize, cassava, sweet potatoes, soybeans, cabbage, mangoes, bananas, vanilla. **Labor force:** n.a. **Industries:** printing, soap manufacturing, handicrafts, woven cloth. **Natural resources:** gold, petroleum, natural gas, manganese, marble. **Exports:** $8 million (2001 est.): coffee, sandalwood, marble; note - the potential for oil and vanilla exports. **Imports:** $237 million (2001 est.).

Geography East Timor is located in the eastern part of Timor, an island in the Indonesian archipelago that lies between the South China Sea and the Indian Ocean. East Timor includes the enclave of Oecussi, which is located within West Timor (Indonesia). After Indonesia, East Timor's closest neighbor is Australia, 400 mi to the south. It is semi-arid and mountainous.

Government Republic.

History Timor was first colonized by the Portuguese in 1520. The Dutch, who claimed many of the surrounding islands, took control of the western portion of the island in 1613. Portugal and the Netherlands fought over the island until an 1860 treaty divided Timor, granting Portugal the eastern half of the island as well as the western enclave of Oecussi (the first Portuguese settlement on the island). Australia and Japan fought each other on the island during World War II; nearly 50,000 East Timorese died during the subsequent Japanese occupation.

In 1949, the Netherlands gave up its colonies in the Dutch West Indies, including West Timor, and the nation of Indonesia was born. East Timor remained under Portuguese control until 1975, when the Portuguese abruptly pulled out after 400 years of colonization. The sudden Portuguese withdrawal left the island vulnerable. Nine days after the Democratic Republic of East Timor was declared an independent nation, it was invaded by Indonesia and annexed on July 16, 1976. Although no country except Australia officially recognized the annexation, Indonesia's invasion was sanctioned by the United States and other western countries, who had cultivated Indonesia as a trading partner and cold-war ally (Fretilin, the East Timorese political party spearheading independence, was Marxist at the time).

Indonesia's invasion and its brutal occupation of East Timor—small, remote, and poor—largely escaped international attention. East Timor's resistance movement was violently suppressed by Indonesian military forces, and more than 200,000 Timorese were reported to have died from famine, disease, and fighting since the annexation. Indonesia's human rights abuses finally began receiving international notice in the 1990s, and in 1996 two East Timorese activists, Bishop Carlos Filipe Ximenes Belo and José Ramos-Horta, received the Nobel Peace Prize for their efforts to gain freedom peacefully for East Timor.

After Indonesia's hard-line president Suharto left office in 1998, his successor, B. J. Habibie, unexpectedly announced his willingness to hold a referendum on East Timorese independence, reversing 25 years of Indonesian intransigence. As the referendum on self-rule drew closer, fighting between separatist guerrillas and pro-Indonesian paramilitary forces in East Timor intensified. The UN-sponsored referendum had to be rescheduled twice because of violence. On Aug. 30, 1999, 78.5% of the population voted to secede from Indonesia. In the days following the referendum, pro-Indonesian militias and Indonesian soldiers retaliated by razing towns, slaughtering civilians, and forcing a third of the population out of the province. After enormous international pressure, Indonesia finally agreed to allow UN forces into East Timor on Sept. 12. Led by Australia, an international peacekeeping force began restoring order to the ravaged region.

The UN Transitional Authority in East Timor (UNTAET) then governed the territory for nearly three years. A parliament was elected in 2001 and a constitution assembled, and on May 20, 2002, nationhood was declared. Charismatic rebel leader José Alexandre Gusmão, who was imprisoned by Indonesia from 1992 to 1999, was overwhelmingly elected the nation's first president on April 14, 2002. The president has a largely symbolic role; real power rests with the parliament and Prime Minister Mari Alkatiri, also a former guerrilla leader.

The first new country of the millennium, East Timor is also one of the world's poorest. Its meager infrastructure was destroyed by the Indonesian militias in 1999 and the economy, primarily made up of subsistence farming and fishing, is in shambles. As-of-yet-untapped off-shore gas and oil reserves, however, promise to bolster the economy in the next few years.

Indonesia has convicted only a meager number of militia officers in the deadly rampage after the 1999 independence referendum.

Ecuador

REPUBLIC OF ECUADOR

National name: República del Ecuador
President: Lucio Gutiérrez (2003)
Area: 109,483 sq mi (283,560 sq km)
Population (2003 est.): 13,710,234 (growth rate: 2.0%); birth rate: 24.9/1000; infant mortality rate: 32.0/1000; density per sq mi: 125
Capital (2003 est.): Quito, 1,780,700 (metro.area), 1,443,900 (city proper). **Largest cities:** Guayaquil, 2,597,600 (metro area), 2,013,500 (city proper); Cuenca, 285,700. **Monetary unit:** U.S. dollar. **Languages:** Spanish (official), Quechua. **Ethnicity/race:** mestizo (mixed Indian and Spanish) 65%, Indian 25%, Spanish 7%, black 3%. **Religion:** Roman Catholic 95%. **Literacy rate:** 90.1% (1995 est.)
Economic summary: GDP/PPP (2001 est.): $39.6 billion; per capita $3,000. **Real growth rate:** 4.3%. **Inflation:** 22%. **Unemployment:** 14% with widespread underemployment. **Arable land:** 6%. **Agriculture:** bananas, coffee, cocoa, rice, potatoes, manioc (tapioca), plantains, sugarcane; cattle, sheep, pigs, beef, pork, dairy products; balsa wood; fish, shrimp . **Labor force:** 3.7 million (urban); agriculture 30%, industry 25%, services 45% (2001 est.). **Industries:** petroleum, food processing, textiles, metal work, paper products, wood products, chemicals, plastics, fishing, lumber. **Natural resources:** petroleum, fish, timber, hydropower. **Exports:** $4.8 billion (2001 est.): petroleum, bananas, shrimp, coffee, cocoa, cut flowers, fish. **Imports:** $4.8 billion (2001 est.): machinery and equipment, chemicals, raw materials, fuels; consumer goods. **Major trading partners:** U.S., Peru, Chile, Italy, Japan, Venezuela, Brazil.

Geography Ecuador, about equal in area to Nevada, is in the northwest part of South America fronting on the Pacific. To the north is Colombia and to the east and south is Peru. Two high and parallel ranges of the

Andes, traversing the country from north to south, are topped by tall volcanic peaks. The highest is Chimborazo at 20,577 ft (6,272 m). The Galápagos Islands (or Colón Archipelago; 3,029 sq mi; 7,845 sq km), in the Pacific Ocean about 600 mi (966 km) west of the South American mainland, became part of Ecuador in 1832.

Government Republic.

History The tribes in the northern highlands of Ecuador formed the Kingdom of Quito around 1000. It was absorbed, by conquest and marriage, into the Inca empire. Spanish conquistador Francisco Pizarro conquered the land in 1532, and through the 17th century a Spanish colony thrived by exploitation of the Indians. The first revolt against Spain occurred in 1809. Ecuador then joined Venezuela, Colombia, and Panama in a confederacy known as Greater Colombia.

When Greater Colombia collapsed in 1830, Ecuador became independent. Revolts and dictatorships followed; it had 48 presidents during the first 131 years of the republic. Conservatives ruled until the revolution of 1895 ushered in nearly a half century of Radical Liberal rule, during which the church was disestablished and freedom of worship, speech, and press was introduced. Although it was under military rule in the 1970s, the country did not experience the violence and repression characteristic of other Latin American military regimes. Its last 30 years of democracy, however, have been largely ineffectual because of a weak executive branch and a strong, fractious Congress.

Peru invaded Ecuador in 1941 and seized a large tract of Ecuadorian territory in the disputed Amazon. In 1981 and 1995 war broke out again. In May 1999, Ecuador and Peru signed a treaty ending a nearly 60-year border dispute involving the stretch of Amazon jungle.

In 1998, Ecuador experienced one of its worst economic crises. El Niño caused $3 billion in damage, the price of its principal export, oil, plunged, and its inflation rate, 43%, was the highest in Latin America. In 1999, the government was near bankruptcy, the currency lost 40% of its value against the dollar, and the poverty rate soared to 70%, doubling in five years. The president's economic austerity plan was protested with massive strikes in March 1999.

President Jamil Mahuad was overthrown in Jan. 2000, in the first military coup in Latin America in a decade. The junta gave power to the vice president, Gustavo Noboa. Faced with the worst economic crisis in Ecuador's history, Noboa restructured Ecuador's foreign debt, adopted the U.S. dollar as the national currency, and continued privatization of state-owned industries, generating enormous opposition. In Feb. 2001, the government cut fuel prices after violent protests by Indians, who are among Ecuador's most disadvantaged people.

Within two years, Ecuador's economy had rebounded from the brink of collapse. The economy grew by 5.4% for 2001, the highest rate in Latin America. Inflation was 22%, down from 91% in 2000, and the budget was balanced. But chronic corruption among senior government officials, as well as among the courts and the judiciary, has continued. According to Quito's chamber of commerce, Ecuador annually loses $2 billion (11.2% of the GDP) a year to corruption.

Lucio Gutiérrez, a leftist colonel best known for orchestrating the 2000 coup against President Jamil Mahuad, was elected to the presidency in 2003 on an anti-corruption platform. His attempts to introduce austere fiscal reforms, however, quickly alienated his political base, and numerous national strikes took place over 2003. In August Gutiérrez broke with the powerful Andean Indian party, Pachakutik, after it .rejected a labor bill required under Ecuador's loan deal with the International Monetary Fund.

Egypt

ARAB REPUBLIC OF EGYPT

President: Hosni Mubarak (1981)
Prime Minister: Atef Ebeid (1999)
Area: 386,660 sq mi (1,001,450 sq km)
Population (2003 est.): 74,718,797 (growth rate: 1.9%); birth rate: 24.4/1000; infant mortality rate: 35.3/1000; density per sq mi: 193
Capital and largest city (2003 est.): Cairo, 15,892,400 (metro.area), 7,937,700 (city proper). **Other large cities:** Alexandria, 3,891,000; Giza, 2,597,600 (part of Cairo metro. area); Shubra el Khema, 1,018,000 (part of Cairo metro. area); El Mahalla el Kubra, 462,300. **Monetary unit:** Egyptian pound. **Language:** Arabic. **Ethnicity/race:** Eastern Hamitic stock (Egyptians, Bedouins, and Berbers) 99%, Greek, Nubian, Armenian, other European (primarily Italian and French) 1%. **Religions:** Islam 94%, Christian (mostly Coptic) 6%. **Literacy rate:** 51.4% (1995 est.)
Economic summary: GDP/PPP (2001 est.): $258 billion; per capita $3,700. **Real growth rate:** 2.5%. **Inflation:** 2.3%. **Unemployment:** 12%. **Arable land:** 3%. **Agriculture:** cotton, rice, corn, wheat, beans, fruits, vegetables; cattle, water buffalo, sheep, goats. **Labor force:** 20.6 million; agriculture 29%, industry 22%, services 49% (2000 est.). **Industries:** textiles, food processing, tourism, chemicals, hydrocarbons, construction, cement, metals. **Natural resources:** petroleum, natural gas, iron ore, phosphates, manganese, limestone, gypsum, talc, asbestos, lead, zinc. **Exports:** $7.1 billion (f.o.b., 2001 est.): crude oil and petroleum products, cotton, textiles, metal products, chemicals. **Imports:** $164 billion (f.o.b., 2001 est.): machinery and equipment, foodstuffs, chemicals, wood products, fuels. **Major trading partners:** EU, U.S., Middle East, Asian countries.

Geography Egypt, at the northeast corner of Africa on the Mediterranean Sea, is bordered on the west by Libya, on the south by the Sudan, and on the east by the Red Sea and Israel. It is nearly one and one-half times the size of Texas. Egypt is divided into two unequal, extremely arid regions by the landscape's dominant feature, the northward-flowing Nile River. The Nile starts 100 mi (161 km) south of the Mediterranean and fans out to a sea front of 155 mi between the cities of Alexandria and Port Said.

Government Republic.

History Egyptian history dates back to about 4000 B.C., when the kingdoms of upper and lower Egypt, already highly sophisticated, were united. Egypt's golden age coincided with the 18th and 19th dynasties (16th to 13th century B.C.), during which the empire was established. Persia conquered Egypt in 525 B.C., Alexander the Great subdued it in 332 B.C., and then the dynasty of the Ptolemies ruled the land until 30 B.C., when Cleopatra, last of the line, committed suicide and Egypt became a Roman, then Byzantine, province. Arab caliphs ruled Egypt from 641 until 1517, when the Turks took it for their Ottoman Empire.

Napoléon's armies occupied the country from 1798 to 1801. In 1805, Mohammed Ali, leader of a band of Albanian soldiers, became pasha of Egypt. After completion of the Suez Canal in 1869, the French and British took increasing interest in Egypt. British troops occupied Egypt in 1882, and British resident agents became its actual administrators, though it remained under nominal Turkish sovereignty. In 1914, this fiction was ended, and Egypt became a protectorate of Britain.

Egyptian nationalism forced Britain to declare Egypt an independent sovereign state on Feb. 28, 1922, although the British reserved rights for the protection of the Suez Canal and the defense of Egypt. In 1936, by an Anglo-Egyptian treaty of alliance, all British troops and officials were to be withdrawn, except from the Suez Canal Zone. When World War II started, Egypt remained neutral. British imperial troops finally ended the Nazi threat to Suez in 1942 in the battle of El Alamein, west of Alexandria. In 1951, Egypt abrogated the 1936 treaty and the 1899 Anglo-Egyptian condominium of the Sudan. Rioting and attacks on British troops in the Suez Canal Zone followed, reaching a climax in Jan. 1952. The army, led by Gen. Mohammed Naguib, seized power on July 23, 1952. Three days later, King Farouk abdicated in favor of his infant son. The monarchy was abolished and a republic proclaimed on June 18, 1953, with Naguib holding the posts of provisional president and premier. He relinquished the latter in 1954 to Gamal Abdel Nasser, leader of the ruling military junta, who was confirmed as president in a referendum on June 23, 1956.

Nasser's policies embroiled his country in continual conflict. In 1956, the U.S. and Britain withdrew their pledges of financial aid for the building of the Aswan High Dam. In response, Nasser nationalized the Suez Canal and expelled British oil and embassy officials. Israel, barred from the canal and exasperated by terrorist raids, invaded the Gaza Strip and the Sinai Peninsula. Britain and France, after demanding Egyptian evacuation of the canal zone, attacked Egypt on Oct. 31, 1956. Worldwide pressure forced Britain, France, and Israel to halt the hostilities. A UN emergency force occupied the canal zone, and all troops were evacuated in the spring of 1957.

From 1956 to 1961, Egypt and Syria united to form a single country called the United Arab Republic (UAR). Syria ended this relationship in 1961 after a military coup, but Egypt continued to call itself the UAR until 1971.

On June 5, 1967, Israel invaded the Sinai Peninsula, the East Bank of the Jordan River, and the zone around the Gulf of Aqaba. A UN cease-fire on June 10 saved the Arabs from complete rout. Nasser declared the 1967 cease-fire void along the canal in April 1969 and began a war of attrition. The U.S. peace plan of June 19, 1970, resulted in Egypt's agreement to reinstate the cease-fire for at least three months (from Aug.) and to accept Israel's existence within "recognized and secure" frontiers that might emerge from UN-mediated talks. In return, Israel accepted the principle of withdrawing from occupied territories. On Sept. 28, 1970, Nasser died of a heart attack. Anwar el-Sadat, an associate of Nasser and a former newspaper editor, became the next president.

In July 1972, Sadat ordered the expulsion of Soviet "advisers and experts" from Egypt because the Russians had not provided the sophisticated weapons he felt were needed to retake territory lost to Israel in 1967. The fourth Arab-Israeli War broke out on Oct. 6, 1973, during the Jewish holiday of Yom Kippur. Egypt swept deep into the Sinai, while Syria strove to throw Israel off the Golan Heights. A UN-sponsored truce was accepted on Oct. 22. In Jan. 1974, both sides agreed to a settlement negotiated by U.S. secretary of state Henry A. Kissinger that gave Egypt a narrow strip along the entire Sinai bank of the Suez Canal. In June, President Nixon made the first visit by a U.S. president to Egypt and full diplomatic relations were established. The Suez Canal was cleared and reopened on June 5, 1975.

In the most audacious act of his career, Sadat flew to Jerusalem at the invitation of Prime Minister Menachem Begin and pleaded before Israel's Knesset on Nov. 20, 1977, for a permanent peace settlement. The Arab world reacted with fury—only Morocco, Tunisia, Sudan, and Oman approved. Egypt and Israel signed a formal peace treaty on March 26, 1979. The pact ended 30 years of war and established diplomatic and commercial relations.

Egyptian and Israeli officials met in the Sinai desert on April 26, 1979, to implement the peace treaty calling for the phased withdrawal of occupation forces from the peninsula. By mid-1980, two-thirds of the Sinai was transferred, but progress was not matched elsewhere—the negotiation of Arab autonomy in the Gaza Strip and the West Bank remained stymied. Sadat halted further talks in Aug. 1980 because of continued Israeli settlement of the West Bank. On Oct. 6, 1981, Sadat was assassinated by extremist Muslim soldiers at a parade in Cairo. Vice President Hosni Mubarak, a former air force chief of staff, succeeded him. Israel completed the return of the Sinai to Egyptian control on April 25, 1982. Israel's invasion of Lebanon in June brought a marked cooling in Egyptian-Israeli relations, but not a disavowal of the peace treaty.

The government has concentrated much of its time and attention in recent years on combating Islamic extremism, particularly attacks against Copts (Egyptian Christians).

El Salvador

REPUBLIC OF EL SALVADOR

National name: República de El Salvador
President: Francisco Flores (1999)
Area: 8,124 sq mi (21,040 sq km)
Population (2003 est.): 6,470,379 (growth rate: 2.2%); birth rate: 27.9/1000; infant mortality rate: 26.8/1000; density per sq mi: 796
Capital and largest city (2003 est.): San Salvador, 1,791,700 (metro. area), 504,700 (city proper). **Other large cities:** Santa Ana, 167,200; San Miguel, 145,100; Zacatecoluca, 36,700. **Monetary unit:** Colón; U.S. dollar. **Language:** Spanish. **Ethnicity/race:** mestizo 90%, Indian 1%, white 9%. **Religion:** Roman Catholic. **Literacy rate:** 71.5% (1995 est.)
Economic summary: GDP/PPP (2001 est.): $28.4 billion; per capita $4,600. **Real growth rate:** 1.4%. **Inflation:** 3.8%. **Unemployment:** 10%. **Arable land:** 27%. **Agriculture:** coffee, sugar, corn, rice, beans, oilseed, cotton, sorghum; shrimp; beef, dairy products. **Labor force:** 2.35 million (1999); agriculture 30%, industry 15%, services 55% (1999 est.). **Industries:** food processing, beverages, petroleum, chemicals, fertilizer, textiles, furniture, light metals. **Natural resources:** hydropower, geothermal power, petroleum, arable land. **Exports:** $2.9 billion (2001): offshore assembly exports, coffee, sugar, shrimp, textiles, chemicals, electricity. **Imports:** $5 billion (2001): raw materials, consumer goods, capital goods, fuels, foodstuffs, petroleum, electricity. **Major trading partners:** U.S., Guatemala, Honduras, EU, Mexico.

Geography Situated on the Pacific coast of Central America, El Salvador has Guatemala to the west and Honduras to the north and east. It is the smallest of the Central American countries, its area equal to that of Massachusetts, and the only one without an Atlantic coastline. Most of the country is on a fertile volcanic plateau about 2,000 ft (607 m) high.

Government Republic.

History The Pipil Indians, descendants of the Aztecs, likely migrated to the region in the 11th century. In 1525, Pedro de Alvarado, a lieutenant of Cortés, conquered El Salvador.

El Salvador, with the other countries of Central America, declared its independence from Spain on Sept. 15, 1821, and was part of a federation of Central American states until that union dissolved in 1838. For decades after its independence, El Salvador experienced numerous revolutions and wars against other Central American republics. From 1931 to 1979 El Salvador was ruled by a series of military dictatorships.

In 1969, El Salvador invaded Honduras after Honduran landowners deported several thousand Salvadorans. Five thousand people ultimately died in what became known as the "football war" because it broke out during a soccer game between the two countries.

In the 1970s discontent with societal inequalities, a poor economy, and the repressive measures of dictatorship led to civil war between the government, the right-wing Nationalist Republican Alliance (ARENA) party, and leftist antigovernment guerrilla units, whose leading group was the Farabundo Martí National Liberation Front (FMLN). The U.S. intervened on the side of the military, despite its scores of human rights violations. The presidency of José Napoleón Duarte, a moderate civilian, from 1984–1989, offered an alternative to the political extremes of right and left, but Duarte was unable to end the war and in 1989, Alfredo Cristiani of ARENA was elected.

On Jan. 16, 1992, the government signed a peace treaty with the guerrilla forces, formally ending the 12-year civil war that had killed 75,000. El Salvador's subsequent presidents have all belonged to ARENA, including the current president, Francisco Flores, who took office in 1999. In 1998, Hurricane Mitch devastated the country, leaving 200 dead and over 30,000 homeless. In Jan. and Feb. 2001, major earthquakes struck El Salvador, damaging about 20% of the nation's housing. An even worse disaster beset the country in the summer when a severe drought destroyed 80% of the country's crops, causing famine in the countryside.

Equatorial Guinea

REPUBLIC OF EQUATORIAL GUINEA

National name: Républica de Guinea Ecuatorial
President: Col. Teodoro Obiang Nguema Mbasogo (1979)
Prime Minister: Cándido Muatetema Rivas (2001)
Area: 10,830 sq mi (28,051 sq km)
Population (2003 est.): 510,473 (growth rate: 2.4%); birth rate: 36.9/1000; infant mortality rate: 89.0/1000; density per sq mi: 47
Capital and largest city (2003 est.): Malabo, 92,900. **Monetary unit:** CFA Franc. **Languages:** Spanish (official), French (2nd official), pidgin English, Fang, Bubi, Creole. **Ethnicity/race:** Bioko (primarily Bubi, some Fernandinos), Río Muni (primarily Fang), Europeans less than 1,000, mostly Spanish. **Religions:** Roman Catholic, Protestant, traditional. **Literacy rate:** 78.5% (1995 est.)
Economic summary: GDP/PPP (2001 est.): $1.04 billion; per capita $2,100. **Real growth rate:** 6%. **Inflation:** 6%. **Unemployment:** 30% (1998 est.). **Arable land:** 5%. **Agriculture:** coffee, cocoa, rice, yams, cassava (tapioca), bananas, palm oil nuts; livestock; timber. **Labor force:** n.a. **Industries:** petroleum, fishing, sawmilling, natural gas. **Natural resources:** oil, petroleum, timber, small unexploited deposits of gold, manganese, uranium. **Exports:** $2.1 billion (f.o.b., 2001 est.): petroleum, timber, cocoa. **Imports:** $736 million (f.o.b., 2001): petroleum sector equipment, manufactured goods and equipment. **Major trading partners:** China, Japan, U.S., South Korea, France, Spain, Italy.

Geography Equatorial Guinea, formerly Spanish Guinea, consists of Río Muni (10,045 sq mi; 26,117 sq km), on the western coast of Africa, and several islands in the Gulf of Guinea, the largest of which is Bioko (formerly Fernando Po) (785 sq mi; 2,033 sq km). The other islands are Annobón, Corisco, Elobey Grande, and Elobey Chico. The total area is twice that of Connecticut.

Government Presidential republic with a 17-member Supreme Military Council since a 1979 coup.

History The mainland was originally inhabited by Pygmies. The Fang and Bubi migrated there in the 17th century and to the main island of Fernando Po (now called Bioko) in the 19th century. In the 18th century, the Portuguese ceded land to the Spanish that included Equatorial Guinea. From 1827 to 1844, Britain administered Fernando Po, but it was then reclaimed by Spain. Río Muni, the mainland, was not occupied by the Spanish until 1926. Spanish Guinea, as it was then called, gained independence from Spain on Oct. 12, 1968. It is Africa's only Spanish-speaking country.

From the outset, President Francisco Macías Nguema, considered the father of independence, began a brutal reign, destroying the economy of the fledgling country and abusing human rights. Calling himself the "Unique Miracle," Nguema is considered one of the worst despots in African history. In 1971, the U.S. State Department reported that his regime was "characterized by abandonment of all government functions except internal security, which was accomplished by terror; this led to the death or exile of up to one-third of the population." On Aug. 3, 1979, Nguema was overthrown and executed by his nephew, Lieut. Col. Teodoro Obiang Nguema Mbasogo. Obiang has been gradually modernizing the country but has retained many of his uncle's dictatorial practices, including the amassing of personal wealth by siphoning it from the public coffers.

A recent off-shore oil boom resulted in the economy's growth by 71.2% in 1997, the first year of the petroleum bonanza, and has sustained this phenomenal rate of growth. It is unlikely, however, that the country's new wealth will benefit the average citizen—the president's family and cronies control the industry.

Eritrea

President: Isaias Afwerki (1993)
Area: 46,842 sq mi (121,320 sq km)
Population (2003 est.): 4,362,254 (growth rate: 2.6%); birth rate: 39.4/1000; infant mortality rate: 76.3/1000; density per sq mi: 93
Capital and largest city (2003 est.): Asmara, 899,000 (metro. area), 400,000 (city proper). **Other large cities:** the ports of Massawa, 30,700; and Assab, 56,300. **Monetary unit:** Nakfa. **Languages:** Afar, Bilen, Kunama, Nara, Arabic, Tobedawi, Saho, Tigre, Tigrinya. **Ethnicity/race:** ethnic Tigrinya 50%, Tigre and Kunama 40%, Afar 4%, Saho (Red Sea coast dwellers) 3%. **Religions:** Islam and Eritrean Orthodox

Christianity. **Literacy rate:** 25%

Economic summary: GDP/PPP (2001 est.): $3.2 billion; per capita $740. **Real growth rate:** 7%. **Inflation:** 15%. **Unemployment:** n.a. **Arable land:** 4%. **Agriculture**: sorghum, lentils, vegetables, corn, cotton, tobacco, coffee, sisal; livestock, goats; fish. **Labor force:** n.a.; agriculture 80%, industry and services 20%. **Industries:** food processing, beverages, clothing and textiles. **Natural resources:** gold, potash, zinc, copper, salt, possibly oil and natural gas, fish. **Exports:** $34.8 million (f.o.b., 2000): livestock, sorghum, textiles, food, small manufactures. **Imports:** $470.5 million (c.i.f., 2000): machinery, petroleum products, food, manufactured goods. **Major trading partners:** Sudan, Ethiopia, Japan, UAE, Italy, Germany, UK, Korea.

Geography Eritrea was formerly the northernmost province of Ethiopia and is about the size of Indiana. Much of the country is mountainous. Its narrow Red Sea coastal plain is one of the hottest and driest places in Africa. The cooler central highlands have fertile valleys that support agriculture. Eritrea is bordered by the Sudan on the north and west, the Red Sea on the north and east, and Ethiopia and Djibouti on the south.

Government A transitional government committed to a democratic system.

History Eritrea was part of the first Ethiopian kingdom of Aksum until its decline in the 8th century. It came under the control of the Ottoman Empire in the 16th century, and later of the Egyptians. The Italians captured the coastal areas in 1885, and the Treaty of Uccialli (May 2, 1889) gave Italy sovereignty over part of Eritrea. The Italians named their colony after the Roman name for the Red Sea, *Mare Erythraeum,* and ruled it up until World War II. The British captured Eritrea in 1941 and later administered it as a UN Trust Territory until it became federated with Ethiopia on Sept. 15, 1952. It was made an Ethiopian province on Nov. 14, 1962. A civil war broke out against the Ethiopian government, led by rebel groups who opposed the union and wanted independence for Eritrea. Fighting continued over the next 32 years.

In 1991, the Ethiopian People's Revolutionary Democratic Front deposed the country's hardline communist dictator Mengistu. Without Mengistu's troops to battle, the Eritrean People's Liberation Front was able to gain control of Asmara, the Eritrean capital, and form a provisional government. In 1993, a referendum on Eritrean independence was held, supported by the UN and the new Ethiopian government. Eritrean voters almost unanimously opted for an independent republic. Ethiopia recognized Eritrea's sovereignty on May 3, 1993, and sought a new era of cooperation between the two countries.

The cooperation did not last long. Following Eritrea's independence, Eritrea and Ethiopia disagreed about the exact demarcation of their borders, and in May 1998 border clashes broke out. After an eight-month lull that both sides used to reinforce their 600-mile common border, war broke out in earnest. Both impoverished countries spent millions of dollars on warplanes and weapons, about 80,000 people were killed, and refugees were legion. Eritrea eventually lost the war against its more populous and powerful neighbor, and a formal peace agreement was signed in Dec. 2000. The United Nations has supplied more than four-thousand troops to continue patrolling the buffer zone between the two nations. An international boundary commission ruled on the disputed border between the two countries on April 13, 2002. Ethiopia disputed the new border, escalating tensions once again.

Estonia

REPUBLIC OF ESTONIA

National name: Eesti
President: Arnold Rüütel (2001)
Prime Minister: Juhan Parts (2003)
Area: 17,462 sq mi (45,226 sq km)
Population (2003 est.): 1,408,556 (growth rate: –0.4%); birth rate: 9.2/1000; infant mortality rate: 12.0/1000; density per sq mi: 81
Capital and largest city (2003 est.): Tallinn, 379,000. **Other large city:** Tartu, 100,100. **Monetary unit:** Kroon. **Languages:** Estonian (official), Russian, Finnish, English. **Ethnicity/race:** Estonian 65.3%, Russian 28.1%, Ukrainian 2.5%, Belorussian 1.5%, Finn 1%, other 1.6% (1998). **Religions:** Lutheran 78%, Orthodox 19%. **Literacy:** 100% (1998 est.)
Economic summary: GDP/PPP (2001 est.): $14.3 billion; per capita $10,000. **Real growth rate:** 4.7%. **Inflation:** 5.8%. **Unemployment:** 12.4%. **Arable land:** 27%. **Agriculture:** potatoes, vegetables; livestock and dairy products; fish. **Labor force:** 608,600; industry 20%, agriculture 11%, services 69% (1999 est.). **Industries:** engineering, electronics, wood and wood products, textile; services; transit, information technology, telecommunications. **Natural resources:** oil shale, peat, phosphorite, clay, limestone, sand, dolomite, arable land, sea mud. **Exports:** $3.4 billion (f.o.b., 2001): machinery and equipment 24%, wood products 20%, textiles 17%, food products 9%, metals, chemical products (1999). **Imports:** $4.1 billion (f.o.b., 2001): machinery and equipment 38.5%, chemical products 11.2%, textiles 9.5%, foodstuffs 8.6%, metals 8.1% (2000). **Major trading partners:** Finland, Sweden, Russia, Latvia, Germany, U.S.

Geography Estonia is mainly a lowland country that is bordered by the Baltic Sea, Latvia, and Russia. It has numerous lakes and forests and many rivers, most draining northward into the Gulf of Finland or eastward into Lake Peipus, its largest lake.

Government Parliamentary democracy.

History Estonians resisted the assaults of Vikings, Danes, Swedes, and Russians before the 13th century. In 1346, the Danes, who possessed northern Estonia, sold the land to the Teutonic Knights of Germany, who already possessed Livonia (southern Estonia and Latvia). The Teutonic Knights reduced the Estonians to serfdom. In 1526, the Swedes took over, and the power of the German (Balt) landowning class was reduced. But after 1721, when Russia succeeded Sweden as the ruling power under the Peace of Nystad, the Estonians were subject to a double bondage—the Balts and the czarist officials. The oppression lasted until the closing months of World War I, when Estonia finally achieved independence after a victorious war (1918–1920). But shortly after the start of World War II, the nation was occupied by Russian troops and incorporated as the 16th republic of the USSR in 1940. Germany occupied the nation from 1941 to 1944, when it was retaken by the Soviets.

Estonia declared independence from the Soviet Union in March 1990. Soviet resistance ensued, but after recognition by European and other countries, the Soviet Union acknowledged Estonian nationhood on Sept. 6, 1991. UN membership followed on Sept. 17, 1991. The newly independent nation embraced free-market reforms. Fueled by foreign investments, economic advances continued unabated in 1997. At the end of 1998, Estonia relaxed the strict citizenship requirements that kept the country's Russian speakers—about one-third of the population—from gaining citizenship. This reform eased the way for Estonia's entry into the European Union, which will take place in 2004, the year it will also join NATO.

Ethiopia

FEDERAL DEMOCRATIC REPUBLIC OF ETHIOPIA

President: Girma Woldegiorgis (2001)
Prime Minister: Meles Zenawi (1995)
Area: 435,184 sq mi (1,127,127 sq km)
Population (2003 est.): 66,557,553 (growth rate: 2.0%); birth rate: 39.8/1000; infant mortality rate: 103.2/1000; density per sq mi: 153
Capital and largest city (2003 est.): Addis Ababa, 2,716,200. **Monetary unit:** Birr. **Languages:** Amharic (official), English, Orominga, Tigrigna, over 70 languages spoken. **Ethnicity/race:** Oromo 40%, Amhara and Tigrean 32%, Sidamo 9%, Shankella 6%, Somali 6%, Afar 4%, Gurage 2%, other 1%. **Religions:** Islam 45%–50%, Ethiopian Orthodox 35%–40%, animist 12%, other 3%-8%. **Literacy rate:** 35.5% (1995 est.)
Economic summary: GDP/PPP (2001 est.): $46 billion; per capita $700. **Real growth rate:** 7.3%. **Inflation:** 6.8%. **Unemployment:** n.a. **Arable land:** 10%. **Agriculture:** cereals, pulses, coffee, oilseed, sugarcane, potatoes, qat; hides, cattle, sheep, goats. **Labor force:** n.a; agriculture and animal husbandry 80%, government and services 12%, industry and construction 8% (1985). **Industries:** food processing, beverages, textiles, chemicals, metals processing, cement. **Natural resources:** small reserves of gold, platinum, copper, potash, natural gas, hydropower. **Exports:** $442 million (f.o.b., 2000 est.): coffee, qat, gold, leather products, oilseeds. **Imports:** $1.54 billion (f.o.b., 2001 est.): food and live animals, petroleum and petroleum products, chemicals, machinery, motor vehicles, cereals, textiles. **Major trading partners:** Germany, Japan, Djibouti, Saudi Arabia, U.S., Italy, Russia.

Geography Ethiopia is in east-central Africa, bordered on the west by the Sudan, the east by Somalia and Djibouti, the south by Kenya, and the northeast by Eritrea. It has several high mountains, the highest of which is Ras Dashan at 15,158 ft (4,620 m). The Blue Nile, or Abbai, rises in the northwest and flows in a great semicircle before entering the Sudan. Its chief reservoir, Lake Tana, lies in the northwest.

Government Federal republic.

History Archeologists have found the oldest known human ancestors in Ethiopia, including *Ardipithecus ramidus kadabba* (c. 5.8–5.2 million years old) and *Australopithecus anamensis* (c. 4.2 million years old). Originally called Abyssinia, Ethiopia is sub-Saharan Africa's oldest state, and its Solomonic dynasty claims descent from King Menelik I, traditionally believed to have been the son of the queen of Sheba and King Solomon. The current nation is a consolidation of smaller kingdoms that owed feudal allegiance to the Ethiopian emperor.

Hamitic peoples migrated to Ethiopia from Asia Minor in prehistoric times. Semitic traders from Arabia penetrated the region in the 7th century B.C. Its Red Sea ports were important to the Roman and Byzantine Empires. Coptic Christianity was brought to the region in A.D. 341, and a variant of it became Ethiopia's state religion. Ancient Ethiopia reached its peak in the 5th century, then was isolated by the rise of Islam and weakened by feudal wars.

Modern Ethiopia emerged under Emperor Menelik II, who established its independence by routing an Italian invasion in 1896. He expanded Ethiopia by conquest. Disorders that followed Menelik's death brought his daughter to the throne in 1917, with his cousin, Tafari Makonnen, as regent and heir apparent. When the empress died in 1930, Tafari was crowned Emperor Haile Selassie I.

Haile Selassie, called the "Lion of Judah," outlawed slavery and tried to centralize his scattered realm, in which 70 languages were spoken. In 1931, he created a constitution, revised in 1955, that called for a Parliament with an appointed senate and an elected chamber of deputies, and a system of courts. But basic power remained with the emperor.

Fascist Italy invaded Ethiopia on Oct. 3, 1935, forcing Haile Selassie into exile in May 1936. Ethiopia was annexed to Eritrea, then an Italian colony, and to Italian Somaliland, forming Italian East Africa. In 1941, British troops routed the Italians, and Haile Selassie returned to Addis Ababa. In 1952, Eritrea was incorporated into Ethiopia.

On Sept. 12, 1974, Haile Selassie was deposed, the constitution suspended, and Ethiopia proclaimed a socialist state under a collective military dictatorship called the Provisional Military Administrative Council (PMAC), also known as the Derg. U.S. aid stopped, and Cuban and Soviet aid began. Lt. Col. Mengistu Haile Mariam became head of state in 1977. During this period Ethiopia fought against Eritrean secessionists as well as Somali rebels, and the government fought against its own people in a campaign called the "red terror." Thousands of political opponents were killed. Mengistu remained leader until 1991, when his greatest supporter, the Soviet Union, dismantled itself.

A group called the Ethiopian People's Revolutionary Democratic Front seized the capital in 1991, and in May a separatist guerrilla organization, the Eritrean People's Liberation Front, took control of the province of Eritrea. The two groups agreed that Eritrea would have an internationally supervised referendum on independence. This election took place in April 1993 with almost unanimous support for Eritrean independence. Ethiopia accepted and recognized Eritrea as an independent state within a few days. Sixty-eight leaders of the former military government were put on trial in April 1996 on charges that included genocide and crimes against humanity.

Since Eritrea's independence, Eritrea and Ethiopia had disagreed about the exact demarcation of their borders, and in May 1998 Eritrea initiated border clashes that developed into a full-scale war that left more than 80,000 dead and further destroyed both countries' ailing economies. After a costly and bloody two-year war, a permanent cease-fire was reached in June 2000—Ethiopia had the upper hand when the fighting ceased—and a formal peace agreement was signed in Dec. 2000. The United Nations has provided more than four thousand peacekeeping forces to patrol the buffer zone between the two nations. An international commission defined a new border between the two countries in April 2002. Ethiopia disputed the new border, escalating tensions between the two countries once again.

Fiji

REPUBLIC OF THE FIJI ISLANDS

President: Ratu Josefa Iloilo (2000)
Prime Minister: Laisenia Qarase (2001)
Area: 7,054 sq mi (18,270 sq km)
Population (2003 est.): 868,531 (growth rate: 1.7%); birth rate: 23.1/1000; infant mortality rate: 13.3/1000; density per sq mi: 123
Capital and largest city (2003 est.): Suva (on Viti Levu), 177,300. **Monetary unit:** Fiji dollar. **Languages:** Fijian, Hindustani, English (official). **Ethnicity/race:** Fijian 51%, Indian 44%, European,

other Pacific Islanders, overseas Chinese, and other 5% (1998). **Religions:** Christian 52%, Hindu 38%, Islam 8%, other 2%. **Literacy rate:** 92.5% (1999 est.)
Economic summary: GDP/PPP (2001 est.): $4.4 billion; per capita $5,200. **Real growth rate:** 1%. **Inflation:** 3% (2000 est.). **Unemployment:** 7.6% (1999). **Arable land:** 11%. **Agriculture:** sugarcane, coconuts, cassava (tapioca), rice, sweet potatoes, bananas; cattle, pigs, horses, goats; fish. **Labor force:** 137,000 (1999); agriculture, including subsistence agriculture 70% (2001 est.). **Industries:** tourism, sugar, clothing, copra, gold, silver, lumber, small cottage industries. **Natural resources:** timber, fish, gold, copper, offshore oil potential, hydropower. **Exports:** $572 million (f.o.b., 2000): sugar, garments, gold, timber, fish, molasses, coconut oil. **Imports:** $833 million (c.i.f., 2000): manufactured goods, machinery and transport equipment, petroleum products, food, chemicals. **Major trading partners:** Australia, U.S., UK, Japan, other Pacific island countries, New Zealand, Singapore, Hong Kong, Taiwan.

Geography Fiji consists of 332 islands in the southwest Pacific Ocean about 1,960 mi (3,152 km) from Sydney, Australia. About 110 of these islands are inhabited. The two largest are Viti Levu (4,109 sq mi; 10,642 sq km) and Vanua Levu (2,242 sq mi; 5,807 sq km).

Government Republic until May 2000, when coup installed interim military dictatorship.

History Fiji, which had been inhabited since the second millennium B.C., was explored by the Dutch and the British in the 17th and 18th centuries. In 1874, an offer of cession by the Fijian chiefs was accepted, and Fiji was proclaimed a possession and dependency of the British Crown. In the 1880s large-scale cultivation of sugarcane began. Over the next 40 years, more than 60,000 indentured laborers from India were brought to the island to work the plantations. By 1920, all indentured servitude had ended. Racial conflict between Indians and the indigenous Fijians has been central to the small island's history.

Fiji became independent on Oct. 10, 1970. In Oct. 1987, Brig. Gen. Sitiveni Rabuka staged a coup to prevent an Indian-dominated coalition party from taking power. The military coup caused an exodus of thousands of Fijians of Indian origin who suffered ethnic discrimination at the hands of the government.

A new constitution, which took effect in July 1998, provided for a multiracial cabinet and raised the prospect of a coalition government. The previous constitution had guaranteed dominance to ethnic Fijians. In 1999, Fiji's first ethnic Indian prime minister, Mahendra Chaudhry, took office.

Continuing ethnic tensions, partly fueled by economic problems, plunged Fiji into a national nightmare in 2000. On May 19, a group of armed soldiers entered the Parliament and took three dozen people hostage, including President Chaudhry. George Speight, a part-Fijian businessman, led the insurrection, and demanded that the 1997 constitution be rewritten to allow dominance of ethnic Fijians. The standoff lasted two months. In July 2000, Speight and other coup leaders were taken into custody and charged with treason. In Feb. 2002, Speight was sentenced to death, but his sentence was commuted.

Although the coup was eventually foiled, deposed prime minister Chaudhry and his democratically elected government were not restored to power. Instead, the military and the Great Council of Chiefs, a group of 50 traditional Fijian leaders, appointed an interim government dominated by ethnic Fijians. Elections were held in Aug.–Sept. 2001, but no party achieved a majority. Interim prime minister Laisenia Qarase's Fijian United Party won 31 of 71 seats, and Qarase was sworn in as prime minister in September. His cabinet consisted entirely of ethnic Fijians, but a court ruled in 2002 that ethnic Indians must be included. In July 2003, Fiji's Supreme Court unanimously upheld that decision, declaring Qarase's government unconstitutional.

Finland

REPUBLIC OF FINLAND

National name: Suomen Tasavalta—Republiken Finland
President: Tarja Halonen (2000)
Prime Minister: Matti Vanhanen (2003)
Area: 130,127 sq mi (337,030 sq km)
Population (2003 est.): 5,190,785 (growth rate: 0.1%); birth rate: 10.5/1000; infant mortality rate: 3.7/1000; density per sq mi: 40
Capital and largest city (2003 est.): Helsinki, 1,162,900 (metro.area), 582,600 (city proper). **Other large cities:** Espoo, 229,500; Tampere, 201,200; Vantaa, 189,200; Turku, 178,100. **Monetary units:** Euro (formerly markka). **Languages:** Finnish, Swedish (both official); small Sami- (Lapp) and Russian-speaking minorities. **Ethnicity/race:** Finn 93%, Swede 6%, Sami (Lapp) 0.11%, Romany (Gypsy) 0.12%, Tatar 0.02%. **Religions:** Evangelical Lutheran 89%, Greek Orthodox 1%, none 9%, other 1%. **Literacy rate:** 100% (1980)
Economic summary: GDP/PPP (2001 est.): $133.5 billion; per capita $25,800. **Real growth rate:** 0.6%. **Inflation:** 2.6%. **Unemployment:** 9.4%. **Arable land**: 7%. **Agriculture:** barley, wheat, sugar beets, potatoes; dairy cattle; fish. **Labor force:** 2.6 million (2000 est.); public services 32%, industry 22%, commerce 14%, finance, insurance, and business services 10%, agriculture and forestry 8%, transport and communications 8%, construction 6%. **Industries:** metal products, electronics, shipbuilding, pulp and paper, copper refining, foodstuffs, chemicals, textiles, clothing. **Natural resources:** timber, copper, zinc, iron ore, silver. **Exports:** $40.1 billion (f.o.b., 2001): machinery and equipment, chemicals, metals; timber, paper, pulp. **Imports:** $31.2 billion (f.o.b., 2001): foodstuffs, petroleum and petroleum products, chemicals, transport equipment, iron and steel, machinery, textile yarn and fabrics, grains. **Major trading partners:** Germany, Sweden, UK, U.S., France, Italy, Russia, Japan.

Geography Finland is three times the size of Ohio. It is heavily forested and contains thousands of lakes, numerous rivers, and extensive areas of marshland. Except for a small highland region in the extreme northwest, the country is a lowland less than 600 ft (180 m) above sea level. Off the southwest coast are the Swedish-populated Åland Islands (581 sq mi; 1,505 sq km), which have had an autonomous status since 1921.

Government Republic.

History The first inhabitants of Finland were the Sami (Lapp) people. When Finnish speakers migrated to Finland in the first millennium B.C., the Sami were forced to move northward to the arctic regions, with which they are traditionally associated. The Finns' repeated raids on the Scandinavian coast impelled Eric IX, the Swedish king, to conquer the country in 1157. It was made a part of the Swedish kingdom and converted to Christianity.

By 1809 the whole of Finland was conquered by Alexander I of Russia, who set up Finland as a grand duchy. The period of Russification (1809–1914) sapped Finnish political power and made Russian the country's official language. When Russia became engulfed by the March Revolution of 1917, Finland seized the opportunity to declare independence on Dec. 6, 1917.

The USSR attacked Finland on Nov. 30, 1939, after Finland refused to give into Soviet territorial demands. The Finns staged a strong defense for three months before capitulating. They were forced to cede the Soviets 16,000 sq mi (41,440 sq km). Under German pressure, the Finns joined the Nazis against Russia in 1941, but were defeated again and forced to cede the Petsamo area to the USSR. In 1948, a treaty of friendship and mutual assistance was signed by the two nations. Finland continued to pursue a foreign policy of nonalignment throughout the cold war era.

Running on a platform to revitalize the economy, Ahtisaari, a Social Democrat, won the country's first direct presidential election in a runoff in Feb. 1994. Previously, presidents had been chosen by electors. Finland became a member of the European Union in Jan. 1995. Showing concern over NATO expansion eastward, Russian president Yeltsin in March 1997 iterated his view that Finnish membership in the military alliance was unacceptable. On Jan. 1, 1999, Finland, along with ten other European countries, adopted the euro as its currency. In 2000, Tarja Halonen, who had been Finland's foreign minister, became its first woman president.

For three years in a row beginning in 2000, Finland was judged to be the world's least corrupt country, according to the annual corruption survey by the Berlin-based organization Transparency International. In April 2003, Finland appointed its first female prime minister, making it the only country in Europe with both a female president and prime minister. But Prime Minister Jaatteenmaki resigned after only two months in office when it was revealed that she had used leaked classified information against her rival in the election. In June, Defense Minister Matti Vanhanen was selected by Parliament to replace her.

France

FRENCH REPUBLIC

National name: République Française
President: Jacques Chirac (1995)
Prime Minister: Jean-Pierre Raffarin (2002)
Area: 211,208 sq mi (547,030 sq km)
Population (2003 est.): 60,180,529 (growth rate: 0.4%); birth rate: 12.5/1000; infant mortality rate: 4.4/1000; density per sq mi: 285
Capital and largest city (2003 est.): Paris, 11,330,700 (metro.area), 2,110,400 (city proper). **Other large cities:** Marseille, 820,700; Lyon, 443,900; Toulouse, 411,800; Nice, 332,000; Nantes, 282,300; Strasbourg, 272,600; Bordeaux, 217,000. **Monetary units:** Euro (formerly French franc). **Languages:** French, declining regional dialects (Provençal, Breton, Alsatian, Corsican). **Ethnicity/race:** Celtic and Latin with Teutonic, Slavic, North African, Southeast Asian, and Basque minorities. **Religions:** Roman Catholic 83%-88%, Protestant 2%, Islam 5%-10%, Jewish 1%. **Literacy rate:** 99% (1980 est.)
Economic summary: GDP/PPP (2001 est.): $1.51 trillion; per capita $25,400. **Real growth rate:** 2.1%. **Inflation:** 1.7%. **Unemployment:** 8.9%. **Arable land:** 33%. **Agriculture:** wheat, cereals, sugar beets, potatoes, wine grapes; beef, dairy products; fish. **Labor force:** 26.6 million; services 71%, industry 25%, agriculture 4% (1997). **Industries:** machinery, chemicals, automobiles, metallurgy, aircraft, electronics; textiles, food processing; tourism. **Natural resources:** coal, iron ore, bauxite, zinc, potash, timber, fish. **Exports:** $293.3 billion (f.o.b., 2001): machinery and transportation equipment, aircraft, plastics, chemicals, pharmaceutical products, iron and steel, beverages. **Imports:** $292.6 billion (f.o.b., 2001): machinery and equipment, vehicles, crude oil, aircraft, plastics, chemicals. **Major trading partners:** EU, U.S.

Geography France is about 80% the size of Texas. In the Alps near the Italian and Swiss borders is western Europe's highest point—Mont Blanc (15,781 ft; 4,810 m). The forest-covered Vosges Mountains are in the northeast, and the Pyrénées are along the Spanish border. Except for extreme northern France, the country may be described as four river basins and a plateau. Three of the streams flow west—the Seine into the English Channel, the Loire into the Atlantic, and the Garonne into the Bay of Biscay. The Rhône flows south into the Mediterranean. For about 100 mi (161 km), the Rhine is France's eastern border. In the Mediterranean, about 115 mi (185 km) east-southeast of Nice, is the island of Corsica (3,367 sq mi; 8,721 sq km).

Government Fifth republic.

History Archeological excavations indicate that France has been continuously settled since Paleolithic times. The Celts, who were later called *Gauls* by the Romans, migrated from the Rhine valley into what is now France. In about 600 B.C. Greeks and Phoenicians established settlements along the Mediterranean, most notably at Marseille. Julius Caesar conquered part of Gaul in 57–52 B.C., and it remained Roman until Franks invaded in the 5th century A.D.

The Treaty of Verdun (843) divided the territories corresponding roughly to France, Germany, and Italy among the three grandsons of Charlemagne. Charles the Bald inherited *Francia Occidentalis,* which became an increasingly feudalized kingdom. By 987, the crown passed to Hugh Capet, a princeling who controlled only the Ile-de-France, the region surrounding Paris. For 350 years, an unbroken Capetian line added to its domain and consolidated royal authority until the accession in 1328 of Philip VI, first of the Valois line. France was then the most powerful nation in Europe, with a population of 15 million.

The missing pieces in Philip Valois's domain were the French provinces still held by the Plantagenet kings of England, who also claimed the French crown. Beginning in 1338, the Hundred Years' War eventually settled the contest. After France's victory in the final battle, Castillon (1453), the Valois were the ruling family, and the English had no French possessions left except Calais. Once Burgundy and Brittany were added, the Valois dynasty's holdings resembled modern France. Protestantism spread throughout France in the 16th century and led to civil wars. Henry IV, of the Bourbon dynasty, issued the Edict of Nantes (1598), granting religious tolerance to the Huguenots (French Protestants). Absolute monarchy reached its apogee in the reign of Louis XIV (1643–1715), the Sun King, whose brilliant court was the center of the Western world.

After a series of costly foreign wars that weakened the government, the French Revolution plunged France into a bloodbath beginning in 1789 with the establishment of the First Republic and ending with a new authoritarianism under Napoléon Bonaparte, who had successfully defended the infant republic from foreign attack and then made himself first consul in 1799 and emperor in 1804. The Congress of Vienna (1815) sought to restore the pre-Napoléonic order in the person of Louis XVIII, but industrialization and the middle class, both fostered under Napoléon, built pressure for change, and a revolution in 1848 drove Louis

Rulers of France

Name	Born	Ruled[1]
Carolingian Dynasty		
Pepin the Short	c. 714	751–768
Charlemagne[2]	742	768–814
Louis I the Pious[3]	778	814–840
Charles I the Bald[4]	823	840–877
Louis II the Stammerer	846	877–879
Louis III[5]	c. 863	879–882
Carloman[5]	?	879–884
Charles II the Fat[6]	839	884–887[7]
Eudes (Odo), count of Paris	?	888–898
Charles III the Simple[8]	879	893–923[9]
Robert I[10]	c. 865	922–923
Rudolf (Raoul), duke of Burgundy	?	923–936
Louis IV d'Outremer	c. 921	936–954
Lothair	941	954–986
Louis V the Sluggard	c. 967	986–987
Capetian Dynasty		
Hugh Capet	c. 940	987–996
Robert II the Pious[11]	c. 970	996–1031
Henry I	1008	1031–1060
Philip I	1052	1060–1108
Louis VI the Fat	1081	1108–1137
Louis VII the Young	c.1121	1137–1180
Philip II (Philip Augustus)	1165	1180–1223
Louis VIII the Lion	1187	1223–1226
Louis IX (St. Louis)	1214	1226–1270
Philip III the Bold	1245	1270–1285
Philip IV the Fair	1268	1285–1314
Louis X the Quarreler	1289	1314–1316
John I[12]	1316	1316
Philip V the Tall	1294	1316–1322
Charles IV the Fair	1294	1322–1328
House of Valois		
Philip VI	1293	1328–1350
John II the Good	1319	1350–1364
Charles V the Wise	1337	1364–1380
Charles VI the Well-Beloved	1368	1380–1422
Charles VII	1403	1422–1461
Louis XI	1423	1461–1483
Charles VIII	1470	1483–1498
Louis XII the Father of the People	1462	1498–1515
Francis I	1494	1515–1547
Henry II	1519	1547–1559
Francis II	1544	1559–1560
Charles IX	1550	1560–1574
Henry III	1551	1574–1589
House of Bourbon		
Henry IV of Navarre	1553	1589–1610
Louis XIII	1601	1610–1643
Louis XIV the Great	1638	1643–1715
Louis XV the Well-Beloved	1710	1715–1774
Louis XVI	1754	1774–1792[13]
Louis XVII (Louis Charles de France)[14]	1785	1793–1795
First Republic		
National Convention	—	1792–1795
Directory (Directoire)	—	1795–1799
Consulate		
Napoléon Bonaparte[15]	1769	1799–1804
First Empire		
Napoléon I	1769	1804–1815[16]
Restoration of House of Bourbon		
Louis XVIII le Désiré	1755	1814–1824
Charles X	1757	1824–1830[17]
Bourbon-Orleans Line		
Louis Philippe ("Citizen King")	1773	1830–1848[18]
Second Republic		
Louis Napoléon[19]	1808	1848–1852
Second Empire		
Napoléon III (Louis Napoléon)	1808	1852–1870[20]
Third Republic (Presidents)		
Louis Adolphe Thiers	1797	1871–1873
Marie E. P. M. de MacMahon	1808	1873–1879
François P. J. Grévy	1807	1879–1887
Sadi Carnot	1837	1887–1894
Jean Casimir-Périer	1847	1894–1895
François Félix Faure	1841	1895–1899
Émile Loubet	1838	1899–1906
Clement Armand Fallières	1841	1906–1913
Raymond Poincaré	1860	1913–1920
Paul E. L. Deschanel	1856	1920–1920
Alexandre Millerand	1859	1920–1924
Gaston Doumergue	1863	1924–1931
Paul Doumer	1857	1931–1932
Albert Lebrun	1871	1932–1940
Vichy Government (Chief of State)		
Henri Philippe Pétain	1856	1940–1944
Provisional Government (Presidents)		
Charles de Gaulle	1890	1944–1946
Félix Gouin	1884	1946–1946
Georges Bidault	1899	1946–1947
Fourth Republic (Presidents)		
Vincent Auriol	1884	1947–1954
René Coty	1882	1954–1959
Fifth Republic (Presidents)		
Charles de Gaulle	1890	1959–1969
Georges Pompidou	1911	1969–1974
Valéry Giscard d'Estaing	1926	1974–1981
François Mitterrand	1916	1981–1995
Jacques Chirac	1932	1995–

1. For kings and emperors through the Second Empire, year of end of rule is also that of death, unless otherwise indicated. 2. Crowned Emperor of the West in 800. His brother, Carloman, ruled as king of the Eastern Franks from 768 until his death in 771. 3. Holy Roman Emperor, 814–840. 4. Holy Roman Emperor, 875–877 as Charles II. 5. Ruled jointly, 879–882. 6. Holy Roman Emperor, 881–887, as Charles III. 7. Died 888. 8. King, 893–898, in opposition to Eudes. 9. Died 929. 10. Not counted in regular line of kings of France by some authorities. Elected by nobles but killed in Battle of Soissons. 11. Sometimes called Robert I. 12. Posthumous son of Louis X; lived for only five days. 13. Executed 1793. 14. Titular king only. He died in prison according to official reports, but many pretenders appeared during the Bourbon restoration. 15. As first consul, Napoléon held the power of government. In 1804, he became emperor. 16. Abdicated first time, June 1814. Reentered Paris, March 1815, after escape from Elba; Louis XVIII fled to Ghent. Abdicated second time, June 1815. He named as his successor his son, Napoléon II, who was not acceptable to the Allies. He died 1821. 17. Died 1836. 18. Died 1850. 19. President; became emperor in 1852. 20. Died 1873.

Philippe, last of the Bourbons, into exile. Prince Louis Napoléon, a nephew of Napoléon I, declared the Second Empire in 1852 and took the throne as Napoléon III. His opposition to the rising power of Prussia ignited the Franco-Prussian War (1870–1871), which ended in his defeat, his abdication, and the creation of the Third Republic.

A new France emerged from World War I as the continent's dominant power. But four years of hostile occupation had reduced northeast France to ruins. Beginning in 1919, French foreign policy aimed at keeping Germany weak through a system of alliances, but it failed to halt the rise of Adolf Hitler and the Nazi war machine. On May 10, 1940, Nazi troops attacked, and, as they approached Paris, Italy joined with Germany. The Germans marched into an undefended Paris and Marshal Henri Philippe Pétain signed an armistice on June 22. France was split into an occupied north and an unoccupied south, Vichy France, which became a totalitarian German puppet state with Pétain as its chief. Allied armies liberated France in Aug. 1944, and a provisional government in Paris headed by Gen. Charles de Gaulle was established. The Fourth Republic was born on Dec. 24, 1946. The empire became the French Union; the National Assembly was strengthened and the presidency weakened; and France joined NATO. A war against Communist insurgents in French Indochina, now Vietnam, was abandoned after the defeat of French forces at Dien Bien Phu in 1954. A new rebellion in Algeria threatened a military coup, and on June 1, 1958, the Assembly invited de Gaulle to return as premier with extraordinary powers. He drafted a new constitution for a Fifth Republic, adopted on Sept. 28, which strengthened the presidency and reduced legislative power. He was elected president on Dec. 21, 1958.

France next turned its attention to decolonialization in Africa; the French protectorates of Morocco and Tunisia had received independence in 1956. French West Africa was partitioned and the new nations were granted independence in 1960. Algeria, after a long civil war, finally became independent in 1962. Relations with most of the former colonies remained amicable. De Gaulle took France out of the NATO military command in 1967 and expelled all foreign-controlled troops from the country. De Gaulle's government was weakened by massive protests in May 1968 when student rallies became violent and millions of factory workers engaged in wildcat strikes across France. After normalcy was reestablished in 1969, de Gaulle's successor, Georges Pompidou, modified Gaullist policies to include a classical laissez-faire attitude toward domestic economic affairs. The conservative, pro-business climate contributed to the election of Valéry Giscard d'Estaing as president in 1974.

Socialist François Mitterrand attained a stunning victory in the May 10, 1981, presidential election. The victors immediately moved to carry out campaign pledges to nationalize major industries, halt nuclear testing, suspend nuclear power plant construction, and impose new taxes on the rich. The Socialists' policies during Mitterrand's first two years created a 12% inflation rate, a huge trade deficit, and devaluations of the franc. In March 1986, a center-right coalition led by Jacques Chirac won a slim majority in legislative elections. Chirac became prime minister, initiating a period of "cohabitation" between him and the Socialist president, Mitterrand. Mitterrand's decisive reelection in 1988 led to Chirac being replaced as premier by Michel Rocard, a Socialist. Relations, however, cooled with Rocard, and in May 1991 he was replaced with Edith Cresson, France's first female prime minister and, like Mitterrand, a Socialist. But Cresson's unpopularity forced Mitterrand to replace Cresson with a more well-liked Socialist, Pierre Bérégovoy, who eventually was embroiled in a scandal and committed suicide. Mitterrand did succeed in helping draft the Maastricht Treaty and, after winning a slim victory in a referendum, confirming close economic and security ties between France and the European Union (EU).

On his third try Chirac won the presidency in May 1995, campaigning vigorously on a platform to reduce unemployment. Elections for the National Assembly in 1997 gave the Socialist coalition a majority. Shortly after becoming president, Chirac resumed France's nuclear testing in the South Pacific, despite widespread international protests as well as rioting in the countries affected by it. Socialist leader Lionel Jospin became prime minister in 1997. In the spring of 1999, the country took part in the NATO airstrikes in Kosovo, despite some internal opposition.

In the fall of 1999, Britain and France argued heatedly about France's refusal to allow the importation of British beef. France remained leery of the possibility of infection from bovine spongiform encephalopathy (BSE), commonly known as mad cow disease, despite the fact that the EU had lifted the three-year ban on British beef in Aug. 1999.

Jean-Marie Le Pen, leader of the right-wing, anti-immigrant National Front party, shocked France in April 2002 with his second-place finish in the first round of France's presidential election. He took 17% of the vote, eliminating Lionel Jospin, the Socialist prime minister, who tallied 16%. Jospin, stunned by the result, announced that he was retiring from politics and threw his support behind incumbent President Jacques Chirac, who won with an overwhelming 82.2% of the vote in the run-off election. Chirac's center-right coalition won an absolute majority in Parliament. In July 2002, Chirac survived an assassination attempt by a right-wing extremist.

During the fall 2002/winter 2003 diplomatic wrangling at the United Nations over Iraq, France repeatedly defied the U.S. and Britain by calling for more weapons inspections and diplomacy before resorting to war. Relations between the U.S. and France were severely strained. In March 2003, France indicated it would veto a UN resolution permitting the use of force against Iraq. President Chirac stated: "We refuse to follow a path that will lead automatically to war as long as the inspectors don't say to us, 'We can't go any further.'"

France sent peacekeeping forces to assist two African countries in 2002 and 2003, Cote d'Ivoire and the Democratic Republic of the Congo.

Prime Minister Raffarin's plan to overhaul the national pension system sparked numerous strikes across France in May and June 2003, including tens of thousands of sanitation workers, teachers, transportation workers, and air traffic controllers. In August, a deadly heat wave killed an estimated 10,000 people, mostly elderly. The catastrophe occurred during two weeks of 104°F (40°C) temperatures.

Overseas Departments

Overseas Departments elect representatives to the National Assembly, and the same administrative organization as that of continental France applies to them.

French Guiana (including Inini)

Status: Overseas Department
Prefect: Henri Masse (1999)
Area: 35,135 sq mi (91,000 sq km)
Population (2003 est.): 186,917 (growth rate: 1.7%); birth rate 21.3/1000; infant mortality rate 12.8/1000; density per sq mi: 5
Capital and largest city (2003 est.): Cayenne, 60,500. **Monetary unit:** Franc. **Language:** French. **Ethnicity/race:** black or mulatto 66%, white 12%, East Indian, Chinese, Amerindian 12%, other 10%. **Religion:** Roman Catholic. **Literacy rate:** 83% (1982 est.)
Economic summary: GDP/PPP (1998 est.): $1 billion; per capita $6,000. **Real growth rate:** n.a. **Inflation:** 2.5% (1992). **Unemployment:** 21.4% (1998). **Arable land:** negl. **Agriculture:** rice, manioc (tapioca), sugar, cocoa, vegetables, bananas; cattle, pigs, poultry. **Labor force:** 58,800 (1997); services, government,

and commerce 60.6%, industry 21.2%, agriculture 18.2% (1980). **Industries:** construction, shrimp processing, forestry products, rum, gold mining. **Natural resources:** bauxite, timber, gold (widely scattered), cinnabar, kaolin, fish. **Exports:** $155 million (f.o.b., 1997): shrimp, timber, gold, rum, rosewood essence, clothing. **Imports:** $625 million (c.i.f., 1997): food (grains, processed meat), machinery and transport equipment, fuels and chemicals. **Major trading partners:** France, Switzerland, U.S., Trinidad and Tobago.

French Guiana, lying north of Brazil and east of Suriname on the northeast coast of South America, was variously settled by the Spanish, Dutch, and French. The Treaty of Breda awarded France the territory in 1667. The French used it as a penal colony between 1852 and 1939, which included the infamous Devil's Island. In 1947 it became an overseas department of France. Since then, many indigenous French Guianians have called for increased autonomy, although only around 5% favor independence from France, partly due to the vast subsidies from the French government. The European Space Center at Kourou has brought a corner of French Guiana into the modern world and attracted a sizable expatriate workforce.

Guadeloupe

Status: Overseas Department
Prefect: Dominique Vian (2002)
Area: 687 sq mi (1,780 sq km)
Population (2003 est.): 440,189 (growth rate: 1.0%); birth rate: 16.2/1000; infant mortality rate: 9.1/1000; density per sq mi: 641
Capital (2003 est.): Basse-Terre, 12,900. **Largest city:** Abymes, 65,700. **Monetary unit:** Franc. **Languages:** French, Creole patois. **Ethnicity/race:** black or mulatto 90%, white 5%, East Indian, Lebanese, Chinese less than 5%. **Religion:** Roman Catholic. **Literacy rate:** 90% (1982 est.)
Economic summary: GDP/PPP (1996 est.): $3.7 billion; per capita $9,000. **Real growth rate:** n.a. **Inflation:** n.a. **Unemployment:** 27.8% (1998). **Arable land:** 11%. **Agriculture:** bananas, sugarcane, tropical fruits and vegetables; cattle, pigs, goats. **Labor force:** 125,900 (1997). **Industries:** construction, cement, rum, sugar, tourism. **Natural resources:** cultivable land, beaches and climate that foster tourism. **Exports:** $140 million (f.o.b., 1997): bananas, sugar, rum. **Imports:** $1.7 billion (c.i.f., 1997): foodstuffs, fuels, vehicles, clothing and other consumer goods, construction materials. **Major trading partners:** France, Martinique, U.S., Germany, Japan, Netherlands Antilles.

Guadeloupe, in the West Indies about 300 mi (483 km) southeast of Puerto Rico, was explored by Columbus in 1493. It consists of the twin islands of Basse-Terre and Grande-Terre and five dependencies—Marie-Galante, Les Saintes, La Désirade, St. Barthélemy, and the northern three-fifths of St. Martin. The volcano Soufrière (4,813 ft; 1,467 m), also called La Grande Soufrière, is the highest point on Guadeloupe. Violent activity in 1976 and 1977 caused thousands to flee their homes.

French colonization began in 1635, and in 1674 Guadeloupe became part of the domain of France. In 1946, it became an overseas department of France.

Martinique

Status: Overseas Department
Prefect: Michel Cadot (2000)
Area: 425 sq mi (1,100 sq km)
Population (2003 est.): 425,966 (growth rate: 0.9%); birth rate: 15.0/1000; infant mortality rate: 7.4/1000; density per sq mi: 1,003
Capital and largest city (2003 est.): Fort-de-France, 170,300 (metro. area), 96,400 (city proper). **Other large cities:** Le Lamentin, 36,400; Schoelcher, 21,400; Sainte-Marie, 20,600. **Monetary unit:** Franc. **Languages:** French, Creole patois. **Ethnicity/race:** African and African-white-Indian mixture 90%, white 5%, East Indian, Lebanese, Chinese less than 5%. **Religion:** Roman Catholic. **Literacy rate:** 100% (1983)
Economic summary: GDP/PPP (1997 est.): $4.39 billion; per capita $11,000 (1997 est.). **Real growth rate:** n.a. **Inflation:** 3.9% (1990). **Unemployment:** 27.2% (1998). **Arable land:** 10%. **Agriculture:** pineapples, avocados, bananas, flowers, vegetables, sugarcane. **Labor force:** 170,000 (1997); agriculture 10%, industry 17%, services 73% (1997). **Industries:** construction, rum, cement, oil refining, sugar, tourism. **Natural resources:** coastal scenery and beaches, cultivable land. **Exports:** $250 million (f.o.b., 1997): refined petroleum products, bananas, rum, pineapples. **Imports:** $2 billion (c.i.f., 1997): petroleum products, crude oil, foodstuffs, construction materials, vehicles, clothing and other consumer goods. **Major trading partners:** France, Guadeloupe, Venezuela, Germany, Italy, U.S.

Martinique, a mountainous island lying in the Lesser Antilles about 300 mi (483 km) northeast of Venezuela, was probably explored by Columbus in 1502 and was taken for France in 1635. Martinique became a domain of the French crown in 1674. It became an overseas department of France in 1946.

Réunion

Status: Overseas Department
Prefect: Jean Doubigny (1998)
Area: 970 sq mi (2,512 sq km)
Population (2003 est.): 755,171 (growth rate: 1.5%); birth rate: 20.2/1000; infant mortality rate: 8.1/1000; density per sq mi: 779
Capital and largest city (2003 est.): Saint-Denis, 142,600. **Other large cities:** Saint-Paul, 95,100; Saint-Pierre, 74,700; Le Tampon, 65,400. **Monetary unit:** Franc. **Languages:** French, Creole. **Ethnicity/race:** French, African, Malagasy, Chinese, Pakistani, Indian. **Religion:** Roman Catholic 86%. **Literacy rate:** 79% (1982 est.)
Economic summary: GDP/PPP (1998 est.): $3.4 billion; per capita $4,800. **Real growth rate:** 3.8%. **Inflation:** n.a. **Unemployment:** 42.8%. **Arable land:** 13%. **Agriculture:** sugarcane, vanilla, tobacco, tropical fruits, vegetables, corn. **Labor force:** 261,000 (1995); agriculture 8%, industry 19%, services 73% (1990). **Industries:** sugar, rum, cigarettes, handicraft items, flower oil extraction. **Natural resources:** fish, arable land, hydropower. **Exports:** $214 million (f.o.b., 1997): sugar, rum and molasses, perfume essences, lobster. **Imports:** $2.5 billion (c.i.f., 1997): manufactured goods, food, beverages, tobacco, machinery and transportation equipment, raw materials, and petroleum products. **Major trading partners:** France, Japan, Comoros, Bahrain, Germany, Italy.

Of volcanic origin, Réunion consists mostly of rugged mountains and short torrential rivers. It is located about 450 mi (724 km) east of Madagascar, in the Indian Ocean. First explored by Portuguese navigators in the 16th century, the island of Réunion, then uninhabited, was taken as a French possession in 1642. African slaves were imported first to work coffee and then sugar plantations; with the abolition of slavery in 1848, indentured laborers from Indochina, India, and East Africa were brought in. In 1947, Réunion became an overseas department of France.

Overseas Territories

Overseas Territories are comparable to Departments except that their administrative organization includes a locally elected government.

French Polynesia

Status: Overseas Territory
High Commissioner: Jean Aribaud (1999)
Area: 1,609 sq mi (4,167 sq km)
Population (2003 est.): 262,125 (growth rate: 1.3%); birth rate: 17.7/1000; infant mortality rate: 8.8/1000; density per sq mi: 163
Capital (2003 est.): Papeete (on Tahiti), 111,400 (metro. area), 30,200 (city proper). **Monetary unit:** Pacific financial community franc. **Language:** French. **Ethnicity/race:** Polynesian 78%, Chinese 12%, local French 6%, metropolitan French 4%. **Religions:** Protestant 54%, Roman Catholic 30%, other 16%. **Literacy rate:** 98% (1977)
Economic summary: GDP/PPP (2001 est.): $1.3 billion; per capita $5,000 . **Real growth rate:** 4%. **Inflation:** 1.5% (1994). **Unemployment:** n.a. **Arable land:** 2%. **Agriculture:** coconuts, vanilla, vegetables, fruits; poultry, beef, dairy products. **Labor force:** 70,000 (1996); agriculture 13%, industry 19%, services 68% (1997). **Industries:** tourism, pearls, agricultural processing, handicrafts. **Natural resources:** timber, fish, cobalt, hydropower. **Exports:** $205 million (f.o.b., 1999): cultured pearls, coconut products, mother-of-pearl, vanilla, shark meat (1997). **Imports:** $749 million (f.o.b., 1999): fuels, foodstuffs, equipment. **Major trading partners:** Japan, U.S., France, Australia.

The term *French Polynesia* is applied to the scattered French possessions in the South Pacific—Mangareva (Gambier), Makatea, the Marquesas Islands, Rapa, Rurutu, Rimatara, the Society Islands, the Tuamotu Archipelago, Tubuai, Raivavae, and the island of Clipperton—which were organized into a single colony in 1903. There are 120 islands, of which 25 are uninhabited. The principal and most populous island—Tahiti, in the Society group—was claimed by the French in 1768. The indigenous people are mostly Maoris.

The Pacific Nuclear Test Center on the atoll of Mururoa, 744 mi (1,200 km) from Tahiti, was completed in 1966. In 1975 worldwide opposition forced the French to move the testing underground on Fangataufa. To compensate the residents for the nuclear weapons tests in 1995–1996, France offered a 10-year $194-million annual compensation package. An independence movement continues to flourish in French Polynesia.

New Caledonia and Dependencies

Status: Overseas Territory
President: Pierre Frogier (2001)
High Commissioner: Thierry Lataste (1998)
Area: 7,359 sq mi (19,060 sq km)
Population (2003 est.): 210,798 (growth rate: 1.4%); birth rate: 19.4/1000; infant mortality rate: 8.1/1000; density per sq mi: 29
Capital (2003 est.): Nouméa, 134,500 (metro. area), 86,400 (city proper). **Monetary unit:** Pacific financial community franc. **Languages:** French, Melanesian and Polynesian dialects. **Ethnicity/race:** Kanak (Melanesian) 42.5%, European 37.1%, Wallisian 8.4%, Polynesian 3.8%, Indonesian 3.6%, Vietnamese 1.6%, other 3%. **Religions:** Roman Catholic 60%, Protestant 30%. **Literacy rate**: 91% (1976)
Economic summary: GDP/PPP (2000 est.): $3.1 billion; per capita $15,000. **Real growth rate:** 2.1%. **Inflation:** 2.3%. **Unemployment:** 19% (1996). **Arable land:** 1%. **Agriculture:** vegetables; beef, deer, other livestock products. **Labor force:** 79,395 (including 15,018 unemployed, 1996); agriculture 7%, industry 23%, services 70% (1999 est.). **Industries:** nickel mining and smelting. **Natural resources:** nickel, chrome, iron, cobalt, manganese, silver, gold, lead, copper. **Exports:** $400 million (f.o.b., 2000): ferronickels, nickel ore, fish. **Imports:** $1 billion (f.o.b., 2000): transport equipment, machinery and electrical equipment, fuels, minerals, wine, sugar, rice. **Major trading partners:** Japan, France, Taiwan, Australia, U.S., Singapore, New Zealand.

New Caledonia (6,466 sq mi; 16,747 sq km), about 1,070 mi (1,722 km) northeast of Sydney, Australia, was explored by Capt. James Cook in 1774 and annexed by France in 1853. The government also administers the Isle of Pines, the Loyalty Islands (Uvéa, Lifu, and Maré), the Belep Islands, the Huon Island group, and Chesterfield Islands. The native people are Melanesians called the Kanak. In 1984, the French National Assembly passed a law that granted internal autonomy to New Caledonia. In 1998 the Nouméa Accords postponed discussions about independence for the territory until at least 2013.

Southern and Antarctic Lands

Status: Overseas Territory
Administrator: François Garde (2000)
Area: 3,004 sq mi (7,781 sq km, excluding Adélie Land)
Capital: Port-au-Français

This territory is uninhabited except for the personnel of scientific bases. It consists of Adélie Land (166,752 sq mi; 431,888 sq km) on the Antarctic mainland (which the U.S. does not recognize) and the following islands in the southern Indian Ocean: the Kerguelen and Crozet archipelagos and the islands of Saint-Paul and New Amsterdam.

Wallis and Futuna Islands

Status: Overseas Territory
Administrator: Christian Job (2002)
Area: 106 sq mi (274 sq km)
Population (2003 est.): 15,734 (growth rate: n.a.); birth rate: n.a./1000; infant mortality rate: n.a./1000; density per sq mi: 149
Capital (2003 est.): Mata-Utu, 1,300. **Languages:** French, Wallisian. **Ethnicity/race:** Polynesian. **Religion:** Roman Catholic. **Literacy rate:** 50% (1969 est.)
Economic summary: GDP/PPP (1997 est.): $30 million; per capita $2,000. **Real growth rate:** n.a. **Inflation:** n.a. **Unemployment:** n.a. **Arable land:** 5%. **Agriculture:** breadfruit, yams, taro, bananas; pigs, goats. **Labor force:** n.a.; agriculture, livestock, and fishing 80%, government 4% (2001 est.). **Industries:** copra, handicrafts, fishing, lumber. **Natural resources:** negl. **Exports:** $250,000 (f.o.b., 1999): copra, chemicals, construction materials. **Imports:** $300,000 (f.o.b., 1999): chemicals, machinery, passenger ships, consumer goods. **Major trading partners:** Italy, Croatia, U.S., Denmark, France, Australia, New Zealand.

The two island groups in the South Pacific between Fiji and Samoa were settled by French missionaries at the beginning of the 19th century. A protectorate was established in the 1880s. There is a French-appointed high administrator, a 20-member Territorial Assembly, and a deputy and a senator to the French national Parliament. The three traditional Polynesian kings also help decide internal policy matters. Following a referendum by the Polynesian inhabitants, the status was changed to that of an Overseas Territory in 1961.

Territorial Collectivities

The Territorial Collectivity status was created in 1976 for Mayotte; it was conceived as being midway between an Overseas Territory and an Overseas Department.

Saint Pierre and Miquelon

Status: Territorial Collectivity
Prefect: Claude Valleix (2002)
Area: 93 sq mi (242 sq km)
Population (2003 est.): 6,976 (growth rate: 0.8%); birth rate: 14.6/1000; infant mortality rate: 8.0/1000; density per sq mi: 75
Capital (2003 est.): Saint Pierre, 5,900. **Ethnicity/race:** Basques and Bretons (French fishermen). **Literacy rate:** 99% (1982 est.)
Economic summary: GDP/PPP (1996 est.): $74 million, supplemented by annual payments from France of about $60 million; per capita $11,000. **Real growth rate:** n.a. **Inflation:** 2.1% (1991–96 average). **Unemployment:** 9.8% (1997). **Arable land:** 13%. **Agriculture:** vegetables; poultry, cattle, sheep, pigs; fish. **Labor force:** 3,000 (1997); fishing 18%, industry (mainly fish processing) 41%, services 41% (1996 est.). **Industries:** fish processing and supply base for fishing fleets; tourism. **Natural resources:** fish, deepwater ports. **Exports:** $12 million (f.o.b., 1999): fish and fish products, soybeans, animal feed, mollusks and crustaceans, fox and mink pelts. **Imports:** $55 million (f.o.b., 1999): meat, clothing, fuel, electrical equipment, machinery, building materials. **Major trading partners:** U.S., Egypt, Japan, Colombia, France, Canada.

The sole remnant of the French colonial empire in North America, these islands were first occupied by the French in 1604. Their importance arises from their proximity to the Grand Banks, located 10 mi south of Newfoundland, making them the center of the French Atlantic cod fisheries.

Mayotte

Status: Territorial Collectivity
Prefect: Pierre Bayle (1998)
Area: 144 sq mi (374 sq km)
Population (2003 est.): 178,437 (growth rate: 3.5%); birth rate: 42.9/1000; infant mortality rate: 66.0/1000; density per sq mi: 1,236
Capital (2003 est.): Dzaoudzi 15,100. **Largest City:** Mamoudzou, 45,700
Economic summary: GDP/PPP (1998 est.): $85 million; per capita $600. **Real growth rate:** n.a. **Inflation:** n.a. **Unemployment:** 45% (1997). **Arable land:** n.a. **Agriculture:** vanilla, ylang-ylang (perfume essence), coffee, copra. **Labor force:** n.a. **Industries:** newly created lobster and shrimp industry, construction. **Natural resources:** negl. **Exports:** $3.44 million (f.o.b., 1997): ylang-ylang (perfume essence), vanilla, copra, coconuts, coffee, cinnamon. **Imports:** $141.3 million (f.o.b., 1997): food, machinery and equipment, transportation equipment, metals, chemicals. **Major trading partners:** France, Comoros, Réunion, Africa, Southeast Asia.

France gained colonial control over Mayotte in 1843. It is the most populous of the four Comoros Islands in the Indian Ocean off Mozambique in Africa. Mayotte chose to remain a French dependency rather than join the other Comoran islands in declaring independence in 1975. Comoros laid claim to Mayotte shortly after independence and continues to do so. In July 2000, 70% of voters opted to accept greater autonomy but remain a part of France.

Gabon

GABONESE REPUBLIC

National name: République Gabonaise
President: Omar Bongo (1967)
Premier: Jean-François Ntoutoume (1999)
Area: 103,346 sq mi (267,667 sq km)
Population (2003 est.): 1,321,560 (growth rate: 2.5%); birth rate: 36.5/1000; infant mortality rate: 55.0/1000; density per sq mi: 13
Capital and largest city (2003 est.): Libreville, 661,600. **Other large cities:** Port-Gentil, 116,200; Franceville, 41,300. **Monetary unit:** CFA Franc. **Languages:** French (official), Fang, Myene, Bateke, Bapounou/Eschira, Bandjabi. **Ethnicity/race:** Bantu tribes, including four major tribal groupings: Fang, Punu, Nzeiby, Mbede (Obamba/Bateke); Pygmies 0.7%, naturalized population 0.3%, foreigners 15%. **Religions:** Christian 55%-75%, Animist, Islam less than 1%. **Literacy rate:** 63.2% (1995 est.)
Economic summary: GDP/PPP (2001 est.): $6.7 billion; per capita $5,500. **Real growth rate:** 2.5%. **Inflation:** 1.5%. **Unemployment:** 21% (1997 est.). **Arable land:** 1%. **Agriculture:** cocoa, coffee, sugar, palm oil, rubber; cattle; okoume (a tropical softwood); fish. **Labor force:** 600,000; agriculture 60%, services and government 25%, industry and commerce 15%. **Industries:** food and beverage; textile; lumbering and plywood; cement; petroleum extraction and refining; manganese, and gold mining; chemicals; ship repair. **Natural resources:** petroleum, manganese, uranium, gold, timber, iron ore, hydropower. **Exports:** $2.5 billion (f.o.b., 2001 est.): crude oil 81%, timber, manganese, uranium (2000). **Imports:** $921 million (f.o.b., 2001 est.): machinery and equipment, foodstuffs, chemicals, construction materials. **Major trading partners:** U.S., France, China, Netherlands Antilles, Côte d'Ivoire, Belgium. **Member of French Community**

Geography This West African country with the Atlantic as its western border is also bounded by Equatorial Guinea, Cameroon, and the Congo. Its area is slightly less than Colorado's. Most of the country is covered by a dense tropical forest.

Government Republic.

History The earliest humans in Gabon were believed to be the Babinga, or Pygmies, dating back to 7000 B.C., who were later followed by Bantu groups from southern and eastern Africa. Now there are many tribal groups in the country, the largest being the Fang peoples, who constitute 25% of the population.

Gabon was first explored by the Portuguese navigator Diego Cam in the 15th century. In 1472, the Portuguese explorers encountered the mouth of the Como River, and named it "Rio de Gabao," river of Gabon, which later became the name of the country. The Dutch began arriving in 1593, and the French in 1630. In 1839, the French founded their first settlement on the left bank of the Gabon estuary and gradually occupied the hinterland during the second half of the 19th century. The land became a French territory in 1888, an autonomous republic within the French Union after World War II, and an independent republic on Aug. 17, 1960.

After his conversion to Islam in 1973, President Bongo changed his given name, Albert Bernard, to Omar. He has been reelected every five years since 1967. Strikes and riots led to a transitional constitution in May 1990 legalizing political parties and calling for free elections. In its first multiparty election in Dec. 1993, the incumbent president received just over 51% of the vote, while the opposition candidate refused to accept defeat; he alleged fraud and tried to establish a rival government.

In Dec. 1998, President Bongo, who had ruled the country for 31 years, was elected for an additional seven. Gabon lacks roads, schools, and adequate health care, yet the oil-rich country has lined the pockets of its ruler, who, according to the French weekly *L'Autre Afrique,* is said to own more real estate in Paris than any other foreign leader. Despite his reputation for corruption and authoritarianism, Bongo has a strong national following. In July 2003, the country's constitution was changed, allowing Bongo to remain in power indefinitely.

Gambia, The

REPUBLIC OF THE GAMBIA

President: Yahya Jammeh (1994)
Area: 4,363 sq mi (11,300 sq km)
Population (2003 est.): 1,501,050 (growth rate: 2.8%); birth rate: 40.8/1000; infant mortality rate: 74.9/1000; density per sq mi: 344
Capital (2003 est.): Banjul, 46,700. **Largest city:** Serekunda, 344,100. **Monetary unit:** Dalasi. **Languages:** Native tongues, English (official). **Ethnicity/race:** African 99% (Mandinka 42%, Fula 18%, Wolof 16%, Jola 10%, Serahuli 9%, other 4%), non-Gambian 1%. **Religions:** Islam 90%, Christian 9%, traditional 1%. **Literacy rate:** 47.5% (2001 est.)
Economic summary: GDP/PPP (2001 est.): $2.5 billion; per capita $1,770. **Real growth rate:** 5.7%. **Inflation:** 4%. **Unemployment:** n.a. **Arable land:** 19%. **Agriculture:** peanuts, millet, sorghum, rice, corn, sesame, cassava (tapioca), palm kernels; cattle, sheep, goats; forest and fishery resources not fully exploited. **Labor force:** 400,000; agriculture 75%, industry, commerce, and services 19%, government 6%. **Industries:** processing peanuts, fish, and hides; tourism; beverages; agricultural machinery assembly, woodworking, metalworking; clothing. **Natural resources:** fish. **Exports:** $139.2 million (f.o.b., 2001): peanuts and peanut products, fish, cotton lint, palm kernels. **Imports:** $200.3 million (f.o.b., 2001): foodstuffs, manufactures, fuel, machinery and transport equipment. **Major trading partners:** Benelux, Japan, UK, Brazil, Spain, China, Netherlands, France. **Member of Commonwealth of Nations**

Geography Situated on the Atlantic coast in westernmost Africa and surrounded on three sides by Senegal, Gambia is twice the size of Delaware. The Gambia River flows for 200 mi (322 km) through Gambia on its way to the Atlantic. The country, the smallest on the continent, averages only 20 mi (32 km) in width.

Government Republic.

History Since the 13th century, the Wolof, Malinke, and Fulani peoples settled in what is now The Gambia. The Portuguese were the first European explorers, encountering the Gambia River in 1455, and in 1681 the French founded an enclave at Albredabut. During the 17th century, Gambia was settled by various companies of English merchants. Slavery was the chief source of revenue before it was abolished in 1807. Gambia became a Crown colony in 1843 and an independent nation within the Commonwealth of Nations on Feb. 18, 1965. Full independence was approved in a 1970 referendum, and on April 24 of that year Gambia proclaimed itself a republic.

Elections on April 29, 1992, returned President Jawara for a fifth term. His People's Progressive Party won 25 of the 36 seats in the House of Representatives. A military coup led by Capt. Yahya Jammeh deposed the president in July 1994, suspended the constitution, and banned existing political parties. Jammeh promised new elections, which were held in Sept. 1996, and he won 55% of the vote against his nearest rival, Ousseynou Darboe. In April 1997, he completed the promised return to civilian rule. Censorship of the press and other repressive measures continue to mar the country's transition to democracy.

Unrest plagued Gambia throughout much of 2000. In January Jammeh crushed a coup attempt staged by some of his own bodyguards, and in April violent student protests rocked the country. The peanut export system collapsed in the same year from mismanagement, leaving farmers unpaid and unable to sell a bumper crop of the country's main commodity. In 2001, Jammeh lifted the ban against various opposition parties he had outlawed after his 1994 coup. He was reelected in Oct. 2001 with 53% of the vote.

Georgia

GEORGIA

National Name: Sakartvelo
President: Eduard Shevardnadze (1992)
Minister of State: Avtandil Jorbenadze (2001)
Area: 26,911 sq mi (69,700 sq km)
Population (2003 est.): 4,934,413 (growth rate: –0.3%); birth rate: 11.8/1000; infant mortality rate: 51.2/1000; density per sq mi: 183
Capital and largest city (2003 est.): Tbilisi, 1,440,000 (metro.area), 1,240,200 (city proper). **Other large cities:** Kutaisi, 268,800; Batoumi, 145,400; and Sokhumi, 110,300. **Monetary unit:** Lari. **Languages:** Georgian (official); Russian; Armenian; Azerbaijani. **Ethnicity/race:** Georgian 70.1%, Armenian 8.1%, Russian 6.3%, Azeri 5.7%, Ossetian 3%, Abkhaz 1.8%, other 5%. **Religions:** Georgian Orthodox 65%, Islam 11%, Russian Orthodox 10%, Armenian Orthodox 8%, . **Literacy rate:** 99% (1989 est.)
Economic summary: GDP/PPP (2001 est.): $15.5 billion; per capita $3,100. **Real growth rate:** 8.4%. **Inflation:** 4.6%. **Unemployment:** 17%. **Arable land:** 11%. **Agriculture:** citrus, grapes, tea, vegetables, potatoes; livestock. **Labor force:** 2.1 million; industry 20%, agriculture 40%, services 40% (1999 est.). **Industries:** steel, aircraft, machine tools, electrical appliances, mining (manganese), chemicals, wood products, wine. **Natural resources:** forests, hydropower, manganese deposits, iron ore, copper, minor coal and oil deposits; coastal climate and soils allow for important tea and citrus growth. **Exports:** $450 million (2001 est.): citrus, grapes, tea, vegetables, potatoes; livestock. **Imports:** $723 million (2001 est.): fuels, machinery and parts, transport equipment, grain and other foods, pharmaceuticals. **Major trading partners:** Turkey, Russia, Germany, Azerbaijan, Armenia, U.S., EU.

Geography Georgia is bordered by the Black Sea in the west, by Turkey and Armenia in the south, by Azerbaijan in the east, and Russia in the north. The republic also includes the Abkhaz and Adzhar autonomous republics and the Yugo-Ossetian Autonomous Oblast.

Government Republic.

History Georgia became a kingdom about 4 B.C. and Christianity was introduced in A.D. 337. During the reign of Queen Tamara (1184–1213), its territory included the whole of Transcaucasia. During the 13th century, Tamerlane and the Mongols decimated its population. From the 16th century on, the country was the scene of a struggle between Persia and Turkey. In the 18th century it became a vassal to Russia in exchange for protection from the Turks and Persians.

Georgia joined Azerbaijan and Armenia in 1917 to establish the anti-Bolshevik Transcaucasian Federation, and upon its dissolution, proclaimed its independence in 1918. In 1922, Georgia, Armenia, and Azerbaijan were annexed by the USSR and formed the Transcaucasian Soviet Socialist Republic. In 1936, it became a separate Soviet republic. Under Soviet rule Georgia was transformed from an agrarian country to a largely industrial, urban society.

Georgia proclaimed its independence from the USSR on April 6, 1991. In Jan. 1992, its leader, Zviad Gamsakhurdia, was sacked and later accused of dictatorial policies, the jailing of opposition leaders, human rights abuses, and clamping down on the media. A ruling military council was established by the opposition until a civilian authority could be restored. In 1992, Eduard Shevardnadze, the Soviet Union's foreign minister under Gorbachev, became president.

In 1992–1993, the government engaged in armed conflict with separatists in the breakaway province of Abkhazia. In 1994, Russia and Georgia signed a cooperation treaty that authorized Russia to keep three military bases in Georgia and allowed Russians to train and equip the Georgian army. In 1996, Georgia and its breakaway region of South Ossetia agreed to a cessation of hostilities in their six-year conflict. With little progress in resolving the Abkhazia situation, however, Parliament in April 1997 voted overwhelmingly to threaten Russia with loss of its military bases should it fail to extend Russian military control over the separatist region. In 1998, the U.S. and Britain began an operation to remove nuclear material from Georgia, dangerous remains from its Soviet years. A darling of the West since his days as the Soviet Union's foreign minister, Shevardnadze is viewed far less favorably by his own people, who are frustrated by unemployment, poverty, cronyism, and rampant corruption. In the 2000 presidential elections, Shevardnadze was reelected with 80% of the vote, though international observers have determined the election was marred by irregularities.

In 2002, U.S. troops trained Georgia's military in antiterrorism measures. The U.S. hopes that Georgian troops will subdue Muslim rebels fighting in the country, who are believed to be linked to al-Qaeda.

Tensions between Georgia and Russia have increased over the Pankisi Gorge, a lawless region of Georgia that Russia says has become a haven for Islamic militants and Chechen rebels.

In May 2003, work began on the Georgian section of the enormously ambitious Baku-Tblisi-Ceyhan oil pipeline, which runs from Azerbaijan through Georgia to Turkey.

Germany

FEDERAL REPUBLIC OF GERMANY

National name: Bundesrepublik Deutschland
President: Johannes Rau (1999)
Chancellor: Gerhard Schröder (1998)
Area: 137,846 sq mi (357,021 sq km)
Population (2003 est.): 82,398,326 (growth rate: –0.2%); birth rate: 8.6/1000; infant mortality rate: 4.2/1000; density per sq mi: 598
Capital and largest city (2003 est.): Berlin (capital since Oct. 3, 1990), 3,933,300 (metro.area), 3,274,500 (city proper). **Other large cities:** Hamburg, 1,686,100; Munich, 1,185,400; Cologne, 965,300; Frankfurt, 648,000; Essen, 588,800; Dortmund, 587,600; Stuttgart, 581,100; Düsseldorf, 568,900; Bremen, 527,900; Hanover, 516,300; Duisberg, 513,400. **Monetary units:** Euro (formerly Deutsche mark). **Language:** German. **Ethnicity/race:** German 91.5%, Turkish 2.4%, Italians 0.7%, Greeks 0.4%, Poles 0.4%, other 4.6%. **Religions:** Protestant 34%, Roman Catholic 34%, Islam 3.7%, Unaffiliated or other 28.3%.
Literacy rate: 99% (1977 est.)
Economic summary GDP/PPP (2001 est.): $2.174 trillion; per capita $26,200. **Real growth rate:** 0.6%. **Inflation:** 2.4%. **Unemployment:** 9.4%. **Arable land:** 34%. **Agriculture:** potatoes, wheat, barley, sugar beets, fruit, cabbages; cattle, pigs, poultry. **Labor force:** 41.9 million; industry 33.4%, agriculture 2.8%, services 63.8% (1999). **Industries:** among the world's largest and most technologically advanced producers of iron, steel, coal, cement, chemicals, machinery, vehicles, machine tools, electronics, food and beverages; shipbuilding; textiles. **Natural resources:** iron ore, coal, potash, timber, lignite, uranium, copper, natural gas, salt, nickel, arable land. **Exports:** $560.7 billion (f.o.b., 2001 est.): machinery, vehicles, chemicals, metals and manufactures, foodstuffs, textiles. **Imports:** $472.9 billion (f.o.b., 2001 est.): machinery, vehicles, chemicals, foodstuffs, textiles, metals. **Major trading partners:** EU, U.S., Japan.

Geography Located in central Europe, Germany is made up of the North German Plain, the Central German Uplands (Mittelgebirge), and the Southern German Highlands. The Bavarian plateau in the southwest averages 1,600 ft (488 m) above sea level, but it reaches 9,721 ft (2,962 m) in the Zugspitze Mountains, the highest point in the country. Germany's major rivers are the Danube, the Elbe, the Oder, the Weser, and the Rhine. Germany is about the size of Montana.

Government Federal republic.

History The Celts are believed to have been the first inhabitants of Germany. They were followed by German tribes at the end of the 2nd century B.C. German invasions destroyed the declining Roman Empire in the 4th and 5th centuries A.D. One of the tribes, the Franks, attained supremacy in western Europe under Charlemagne, who was crowned Holy Roman Emperor in 800. By the Treaty of Verdun (843), Charlemagne's lands east of the Rhine were ceded to the German Prince Louis. Additional territory acquired by the Treaty of Mersen (870) gave Germany approximately the area it maintained throughout the Middle Ages. For several centuries after Otto the Great was crowned king in 936, German rulers were also usually heads of the Holy Roman Empire.

By the 14th century, the Holy Roman Empire was little more than a loose federation of the German princes who elected the Holy Roman emperor. In 1438, Albert of Hapsburg became emperor, and for the next several centuries the Hapsburg line ruled the Holy Roman Empire until its decline in 1806. Relations between state and church were changed by the Reformation, which began with Martin Luther's 95 theses, and came to a head in 1547, when Charles V scattered the forces of the Protestant League at Mühlberg. The Counter Reformation followed. A dispute over the succession to the Bohemian throne brought on the Thirty Years' War (1618–1648), which devastated Germany and left the empire divided into hundreds of small principalities virtually independent of the emperor.

Meanwhile, Prussia was developing into a state of considerable strength. Frederick the Great (1740–1786) reorganized the Prussian army and defeated Maria Theresa of Austria in a struggle over Silesia. After the defeat of Napoléon at Waterloo (1815), the struggle between Austria and Prussia for supremacy in Germany continued, reaching its climax in the defeat of Austria in the Seven Weeks' War (1866) and the formation of the Prussian-dominated North German Confederation (1867). The architect of this new German unity was Otto von Bismarck, a conservative, monarchist, and militaristic Prussian prime minister.

He unified all of Germany in a series of three wars against Denmark (1864), Austria (1866), and France (1870–1871). On Jan. 18, 1871, King Wilhelm I of Prussia was proclaimed German emperor in the Hall of Mirrors at Versailles. The North German Confederation, created in 1867, was abolished, and the Second German Reich, consisting of the North and South German states, was born. With a powerful army, an efficient bureaucracy, and a loyal bourgeoisie, Chancellor Bismarck consolidated a powerful centralized state.

Wilhelm II dismissed Bismarck in 1890 and embarked upon a "New Course," stressing an intensified colonialism and a powerful navy. His chaotic foreign policy culminated in the diplomatic isolation of Germany and the disastrous defeat in World War I (1914–1918). The Second German Empire collapsed following the defeat of the German armies in 1918, the naval mutiny at Kiel, and the flight of the kaiser to the Netherlands. The Social Democrats, led by Friedrich Ebert and Philipp Scheidemann, crushed the Communists and established a moderate state, known as the Weimar Republic, with Ebert as president. President Ebert died on Feb. 28, 1925, and on April 26, Field Marshal Paul von Hindenburg was elected president. The mass of Germans regarded the Weimar Republic as a child of defeat, imposed upon a Germany whose legitimate aspirations to world leadership had been thwarted by a world conspiracy. Added to this were a crippling currency debacle, a tremendous burden of reparations, and acute economic distress.

Adolf Hitler, an Austrian war veteran and a fanatical nationalist, fanned discontent by promising a Greater Germany, abrogation of the Treaty of Versailles, restoration of Germany's lost colonies, and the destruction of the Jews, whom he scapegoated as the reason for Germany's downfall and depressed economy. When the Social Democrats and the Communists refused to combine against the Nazi threat, President von Hindenburg made Hitler the chancellor on Jan. 30, 1933. With the death of von Hindenburg on Aug. 2, 1934, Hitler repudiated the Treaty of Versailles and began full-scale rearmament. In 1935, he withdrew Germany from the League of Nations, and the next year he reoccupied the Rhineland and signed the Anti-Comintern pact with Japan, at the same time strengthening relations with Italy. Austria was annexed in March 1938. By the Munich agreement in Sept. 1938, he gained the Czech Sudetenland, and in violation of this agreement he completed the dismemberment of Czechoslovakia in March 1939. His invasion of Poland on Sept. 1, 1939, precipitated World War II.

Hitler established death camps to carry out "the final solution to the Jewish question." By the end of the war, Hitler's Holocaust had killed 6 million Jews, as well as Gypsies, homosexuals, Communists, the handicapped, and others not fitting the Aryan ideal. After some dazzling initial successes in 1939–1942, Germany surrendered unconditionally to Allied and Soviet military commanders on May 8, 1945. On June 5 the four-nation Allied Control Council became the de facto government of Germany.

(For details of World War II and of the Holocaust, *see* Headline History, World War II.)

At the Berlin (or Potsdam) Conference (July 17–Aug. 2, 1945) President Truman, Premier Stalin, and Prime Minister Clement Attlee of Britain set forth the guiding principles of the Allied Control Council: Germany's complete disarmament and demilitarization, destruction of its war potential, rigid control of industry, and decentralization of the political and economic structure. Pending final determination of territorial questions at a peace conference, the three victors agreed to the ultimate transfer of the city of Königsberg (now Kaliningrad) and its adjacent area to the USSR and to the administration by Poland of former German territories lying generally east of the Oder-Neisse Line. For purposes of control, Germany was divided into four national occupation zones.

The Western powers were unable to agree with the USSR on any fundamental issues. Work of the Allied Control Council was hamstrung by repeated Soviet vetoes; and finally, on March 20, 1948, Russia walked out of the Council. Meanwhile, the U.S. and Britain had taken steps to merge their zones economically (Bizone); on May 31, 1948, the U.S., Britain, France, and the Benelux countries agreed to set up a German state comprising the three Western zones. The USSR reacted by clamping a blockade on all ground communications between the Western zones and West Berlin, an enclave in the Soviet zone. The Western Allies countered by organizing a gigantic airlift to fly supplies into the beleaguered city. The USSR was finally forced to lift the blockade on May 12, 1949.

The Federal Republic of Germany was proclaimed on May 23, 1949, with its capital at Bonn. In free elections, West German voters gave a majority in the Constituent Assembly to the Christian Democrats, with the Social Democrats largely making up the opposition. Konrad Adenauer became chancellor, and Theodor Heuss of the Free Democrats was elected first president.

The East German states adopted a more centralized constitution for the Democratic Republic of Germany, put into effect on Oct. 7, 1949. The USSR thereupon dissolved its occupation zone but Soviet troops remained. The Western Allies declared that the East German Republic was a Soviet creation undertaken without self-determination and refused to recognize it. Soviet forces created a state controlled by the secret police with a single party, the Socialist Unity (Communist) Party.

Agreements in Paris in 1954 giving the Federal Republic full independence and complete sovereignty came into force on May 5, 1955. Under the agreement, West Germany and Italy became members of the Brussels treaty organization created in 1948 and renamed the Western European Union. West Germany also became a member of NATO. In 1955, the USSR recognized the Federal Republic. The Saar territory, under an agreement between France and West Germany, held a plebiscite and despite economic links to France, elected to rejoin West Germany on Jan. 1, 1957.

The division between West Germany and East Germany was intensified when the Communists erected the Berlin Wall in 1961. In 1968, the East German Communist leader, Walter Ulbricht, imposed restrictions on West German movements into West Berlin. The Soviet-bloc invasion of Czechoslovakia in Aug. 1968 added to the tension. West Germany signed a treaty with Poland in 1970, renouncing force and setting Poland's western border as the Oder-Neisse Line. It subsequently resumed formal relations with Czechoslovakia in a pact that "voided" the Munich treaty that gave Nazi Germany the Sudetenland. By 1973, normal relations were established between East and West Germany and the two states entered the United Nations.

West German chancellor Willy Brandt, winner of a Nobel Peace Prize for his foreign policies, was forced to resign in 1974 when an East German spy was discovered to be one of his top staff members. Succeeding him was a moderate Social Democrat, Helmut Schmidt. Schmidt staunchly backed U.S. military strategy in Europe, staking his political fate on placing U.S. nuclear missiles in Germany unless the Soviet Union reduced its arsenal of intermediate missiles. He also strongly opposed nuclear freeze proposals.

Helmut Kohl of the Christian Democrat Party became chancellor in 1982. An economic upswing in 1986 led to Kohl's reelection. The fall of the Communist government in East Germany left only Soviet objections to German reunification to be dealt with. On the night of Nov. 9, 1989, the Berlin Wall was opened, making reunification all but inevitable. In July 1990, Kohl asked Soviet leader Gorbachev to drop his objections in exchange for financial aid from (West) Germany. Gorbachev agreed, and on Oct. 3, 1990, the German Democratic Republic acceded to the Federal Republic and Germany became a united and sovereign state for the first time since 1945.

A reunited Berlin serves as the official capital of unified Germany, although the government would continue to have administrative functions in Bonn during the 12-year transition period. The issue of the cost of reunification and the modernization of the former East Germany were serious considerations facing the reunified nation.

In its most important election in decades, on Sept. 27, 1998, Germans chose Social Democrat Gerhard Schröder as chancellor over Christian Democrat incumbent Helmut Kohl, ending a 16-year-long rule that oversaw the reunification of Germany and symbolized the end of the cold war in Europe. A centrist, Schröder campaigned for "the new middle" and promised to rectify Germany's high unemployment rate of 10.6%.

Tension between the old-style left-wing and the more probusiness pragmatists within Schröder's government came to a head with the abrupt resignation of Finance Minister Oskar Lafontaine in March 1999, who was also chairman of the ruling Social Democratic Party. Lafontaine's plans to raise taxes on industry and raise German wages—already nearly the highest in the world—went against the more centrist policies of Schröder. Hans Eichel was chosen to become the next finance minister.

Germany joined the other NATO allies in the military conflict in Kosovo in 1999. Before the Kosovo crisis, Germans had not participated in an armed conflict since World War II. Germany agreed to take 40,000 Kosovar refugees, the most of any NATO country.

In Dec. 1999, former chancellor Helmut Kohl and other high officials in the Christian Democrat Party admitted accepting tens of millions of dollars in illegal donations during the 1980s and 1990s. The enormity of the scandal led to the virtual dismemberment of the CDU in early 2000, a party that had long been a stable conservative force in German politics.

In July 2000, Schröder managed to pass significant tax reforms that would lower the top income-tax rate from 51% to 42% by 2005. He also eliminated the capital gains tax on companies selling shares in other companies, a measure that was expected to spur mergers. In May 2001, the German Parliament authorized the payment of $4.4 billion in compensation to 1.2 million surviving Nazi-era slave laborers.

Schröder was narrowly reelected in Sept. 2002, defeating conservative businessman Edmund Stoiber. Schröder's Social Democrats and coalition partner, the Greens, won a razor-thin majority in parliament. Stoiber held an early lead in the polls, but Schröder's deft handling of Germany's catastrophic floods in Aug. and his tough stance against U.S. plans for a preemptive attack on Iraq buoyed him in the weeks leading up to the election. Germany's continued reluctance to support the U.S.'s call for military action against Iraq severely strained its relations with Washington.

Germany's recession continued in 2003—for the past three years Europe's biggest economy has had the lowest growth rate among EU countries. In Aug. 2003, Schröder unfurled an ambitious fiscal reform package, and called his proposal "the most significant set of structural reforms in the social history of Germany."

Ghana

REPUBLIC OF GHANA

President: John Agyekum Kufuor (2001)
Area: 92,456 sq mi (239,460 sq km)
Population (2003 est.): 20,467,747 (growth rate: 1.5%); birth rate: 25.8/1000; infant mortality rate: 53.0/1000; density per sq mi: 221
Capital and Largest City (2003 est.): Accra, 2,825,800 (metro.area), 1,661,400 (city proper). **Other large cities:**Kumasi, 645,100; Tamale, 279,600. **Monetary unit:** Cedi. **Languages:** English (official), Native tongues (Brong Ahafo, Twi, Fanti, Ga, Ewe, Dagbani). **Ethnicity/race:** black African 98.5% (major tribes: Akan 44%, Moshi-Dagomba 16%, Ewe 13%, Ga 8%, Gurma 3%, Yoruba 1%), European and other 1.5% (1998). **Religions:** Christian 63%, indigenous beliefs 21%, Islam 16%. **Literacy rate:** 64.5% (1995 est.)
Economic summary: GDP/PPP (2001 est.): $39.4 billion; per capita $1,980. **Real growth rate:** 3%. **Inflation:** 25%. **Unemployment:** 20% (1997 est.). **Arable land:** 16%. **Agriculture:** cocoa, rice, coffee, cassava (tapioca), peanuts, corn, shea nuts, bananas; timber. **Labor force:** 9 million (2000 est.); agriculture 60%, industry 15%, services 25% (1999 est.). **Industries:** mining, lumbering, light manufacturing, aluminum smelting, food processing. **Natural resources:** gold, timber, industrial diamonds, bauxite, manganese, fish, rubber, hydropower. **Exports:** $1.94 billion (f.o.b., 2000): gold, cocoa, timber, tuna, bauxite, aluminum, manganese ore, diamonds. **Imports:** $2.83 billion (f.o.b., 2000): capital equipment, petroleum, foodstuffs. **Major trading partners:** Togo, UK, Italy, Netherlands, Germany, U.S., France, Nigeria, Spain. **Member of Commonwealth of Nations**

Geography A West African country bordering on the Gulf of Guinea, Ghana is bounded by Côte d'Ivoire to the west, Burkina Faso to the north, Togo to the east, and the Atlantic Ocean to the south. It compares in size to Oregon, and its largest river is the Volta.

Government Constitutional democracy.

History Several major civilizations flourished in the general region of what is now Ghana. The ancient empire of Ghana (located 500 mi northwest of the contemporary state) reigned until the 13th century. The Akan peoples established the next major civilization, beginning in the 13th century, and then the Ashanti empire flourished in the 18th and 19th centuries.

Called the Gold Coast, the area was first seen by Portuguese traders in 1470. They were followed by the English (1553), the Dutch (1595), and the Swedes (1640). British rule over the Gold Coast began in 1820, but it was not until after quelling the severe resistance of the Ashanti in 1901 that it was firmly established. British Togoland, formerly a colony of Germany, was incorporated into Ghana by referendum in 1956. Created as an independent country on March 6, 1957, Ghana, as the result of a plebiscite, became a republic on July 1, 1960.

Premier Kwame Nkrumah attempted to take leadership of the Pan-African Movement, holding the All-African People's Congress in his capital, Accra, in 1958 and organizing the Union of African States with Guinea and Mali in 1961. But he oriented his country toward the Soviet Union and China and built an autocratic rule over all aspects of Ghanaian life. In Feb.

1966, while Nkrumah was visiting Beijing and Hanoi, he was deposed by a military coup led by Gen. Emmanuel K. Kotoka.

A series of military coups followed and on June 4, 1979, Flight Lt. Jerry Rawlings overthrew Lt. Gen. Frederick Akuffo's military rule. Rawlings permitted the election of a civilian president to go ahead as scheduled the following month, and Hilla Limann, candidate of the People's National Party, took office. Charging the civilian government with corruption and repression, Rawlings staged another coup on Dec. 31, 1981. As chairman of the Provisional National Defense Council, Rawlings instituted an austerity program and reduced budget deficits. Rawlings was reelected in 1982 and again in 1996.

A major cocoa producer, Ghana has been hurt by slumps in cocoa prices. In July 2000, Ghana and neighboring countries began destroying massive amounts of cocoa to drive up the price. Together they produce 70% of the world's cocoa. Since gold is Ghana's largest source of foreign exchange, fluctuating prices have hammered the economy, and mining companies cut 10,000 jobs in 1999. Saudi Arabian investors rescued Ashanti Goldfields, the largest company in sub-Saharan Africa, from near collapse in Feb. 2000.

In Jan. 2001, John Agyekum Kufuor took office, becoming Ghana's first democratically elected president since independence.

Greece

HELLENIC REPUBLIC

National name: Elliniki Dimokratia
President: Kostis Stephanopoulos (1995)
Prime Minister: Kostas Simitis (1996)
Area: 50,942 sq mi (131,940 sq km)
Population (2003 est.): 10,665,989 (growth rate: –0.01%); birth rate: 9.8/1000; infant mortality rate: 6.1/1000; density per sq mi: 209
Capital (2003 est.): Athens, Athens, 3,247,000 (metro. area), 747,300 (city proper). **Other large cities:** Thessaloníki, 361,200; Piraeus, 179,300; Patras, 167,000. **Monetary unit:** Euro (formerly drachma). **Language:** Greek. **Ethnicity/race:** Greek 98%, other 2%; note: the Greek government states there are no ethnic divisions in Greece. **Religions:** Greek Orthodox 98%, Islam 1.3%, other 0.7%. **Literacy rate:** 97% (1999)
Economic summary: GDP/PPP (2001 est.): $189.7 billion; per capita $17,900. **Real growth rate:** 3.7%. **Inflation:** 3.4%. **Unemployment:** 11%. **Arable land:** 22%. **Agriculture:** wheat, corn, barley, sugar beets, olives, tomatoes, wine, tobacco, potatoes; beef, dairy products. **Labor force:** 4.32 million (1999 est.); industry 21%, agriculture 20%, services 59% (2000 est.). **Industries:** tourism; food and tobacco processing, textiles; chemicals, metal products; mining, petroleum. **Natural resources:** bauxite, lignite, magnesite, petroleum, marble, hydropower potential. **Exports:** $12.5 billion (f.o.b., 2001): food and beverages, manufactured goods, petroleum products, chemicals, textiles. **Imports:** $30.3 billion (f.o.b., 2001): machinery, transport equipment, fuels, chemicals. **Major trading partners:** EU, U.S.

Geography Located in southern Europe, Greece forms an irregular-shaped peninsula in the Mediterranean with two additional large peninsulas projecting from it: the Chalcidice and the Peloponnese. The Greek Islands are generally subdivided into two groups, according to location: the Ionian Islands (including Corfu, Cephalonia, and Leucas) west of the mainland and the Aegean Islands (including Euboea, Samos, Chios, Lesbos, and Crete) to the east and south. North-central Greece, Epirus, and western Macedonia are all mountainous. The main chain of the Pindus Mountains extends from northwest Greece to the Peloponnese. Mount Olympus, rising to 9,570 ft (2,909 m), is the highest point in the country.

Government Parliamentary republic.

History Indo-European peoples, including the Mycenaeans, began entering Greece about 2000 B.C. and set up sophisticated civilizations. About 1200 B.C., the Dorians, another Indo-European people, invaded Greece, and a dark age followed, known mostly through the Homeric epics. At the end of this time, classical Greece began to emerge (c. 750 B.C.) as a loose composite of city-states with a heavy involvement in maritime trade and a devotion to art, literature, politics, and philosophy. Greece reached the peak of its glory in the 5th century B.C., but the Peloponnesian War (431–404 B.C.) weakened the nation, and it was conquered by Philip II and his son Alexander the Great of Macedonia, who considered themselves Greek. By the middle of the 2nd century B.C., Greece had declined to the status of a Roman province. It remained within the eastern Roman Empire until Constantinople fell to the Crusaders in 1204. In 1453, the Turks took Constantinople and by 1460, Greece was a Turkish province with its Orthodox Church intact. Greece won independence with sovereignty guaranteed by Britain, France, and Russia.

The protecting powers chose Prince Otto of Bavaria as the first king of modern Greece in 1832 to reign over an area only slightly larger than the Peloponnese peninsula. Chiefly under the next king, George I, chosen by the protecting powers in 1863, Greece acquired much of its present territory. During his 57-year reign, a period in which he encouraged parliamentary democracy, Thessaly, Epirus, Macedonia, Crete, and most of the Aegean islands were added from the disintegrating Turkish empire. Unfavorable economic conditions forced about one-sixth of the entire Greek population to emigrate (mostly to the U.S.) in the late 19th and early 20th centuries. An unsuccessful war against Turkey after World War I brought down the monarchy, which was replaced by a republic in 1923.

Two military dictatorships and a financial crisis brought George II back from exile, but only until 1941, when Italian and German invaders defeated tough Greek resistance. After British and Greek troops liberated the country in Oct. 1944, Communist guerrillas staged a long military campaign against the government; the Greek civil war, infamous for its brutality, began in Dec. 1944 and continued until Oct. 16, 1949, when the Communist guerrillas conceded defeat. The Greek government received U.S. aid under the Truman Doctrine, the predecessor of the Marshall Plan, to fight against the Communists.

Greece was a charter member of the UN, and became a member of the North Atlantic Treaty Organization (NATO) in 1951. A military junta seized power in April 1967, sending young King Constantine II into exile. Col. George Papadopoulos, a leader of the junta, gradually attempted to revamp his hardline, right-wing image: first, by giving up his military post for that of prime minister in 1973, and later, as president, by ending martial law. A coup ousted Papadopoulos in Nov. 1973. The seven-year regime of the "colonels," infamous for torturing and exiling opponents and scoffing at human rights, collapsed entirely a year later, after having bungled an attempt to seize Cyprus.

A referendum in Dec. 1974, five months after the demise of the military dictatorship, ended the Greek monarchy and established a republic. Former premier Karamanlis returned from exile to become premier of Greece's first civilian government since 1967. Greece has continued to be ruled by freely elected civilian governments ever since. On Jan. 1, 1981, Greece became the 10th member of the European Union. Andreas Papandreou, son of former premier George Papandreou, founded the Panhellenic Socialist Movement (PASOK) and became Greece's first socialist premier (1981–1989).

The Greeks were the most vocal dissenters within the NATO alliance regarding the 1999 intervention in Kosovo. They were both wary of the economic and political instability that would accompany a large influx of refugees and reluctant to ignore an Eastern Orthodox religious history shared with the Serbs.

Greece continued to experience tensions with Turkey over a disputed, unpopulated 10-acre island and over Cyprus, which is divided into Greek and Turkish sectors.

The pro-Westerm socialist prime minister Kostas Simitis is credited with reviving the Greek economy. Still, *The Economist* magazine estimates it will be at least another 15 years before the per capita GDP in Greece comes close to the current EU average.

In the summer of 2002, the government was finally able to crack down on the 17 November (17N) terrorist organization, which had entirely eluded the Greek authorities for the past 27 years. The radical leftist group is responsible for more than 20 assassinations of American, British, and Greek diplomats, military personnel, and businessmen. Greece has been criticized for decades by the international community for being soft on terrorism, and confidence in its ability to provide adequate security when it hosts the 2004 Olympics has never been strong.

Grenada

STATE OF GRENADA

Sovereign: Queen Elizabeth II (1952)
Governor-General: Sir Daniel Williams (1996)
Prime Minister: Keith C. Mitchell (1995)
Area: 133 sq mi (344 sq km)
Population (2003 est.): 89,258 (growth rate 1.5%); birth rate: 22.9/1000; infant mortality rate: 14.6/1000; density per sq mi: 672
Capital and largest city (2003 est.): St. George's, 4,300. **Monetary unit:** East Caribbean dollar. **Language:** English. **Ethnicity/race:** black African descent 82%, mixed 13%, white, other 5%. **Religions:** Roman Catholic 53%, Anglican 13.8%, other Protestant 33..2%. **Literacy rate:** 98% (1970 est.)
Economic summary: GDP/PPP (2001 est.): $424 million; per capita $4,750. **Real growth rate:** 6.5%. **Inflation:** 2.8%. **Unemployment:** 11.5% (1999). **Arable land:** 6%. **Agriculture:** bananas, cocoa, nutmeg, mace, citrus, avocados, root crops, sugarcane, corn, vegetables. **Labor force:** 42,300 (1996); services 62%, agriculture 24%, industry 14% (1999 est.). **Industries:** food and beverages, textiles, light assembly operations, tourism, construction. **Natural resources:** timber, tropical fruit, deepwater harbors. **Exports:** $78 million (2000 est.): bananas, cocoa, nutmeg, fruit and vegetables, clothing, mace. **Imports:** $270 million (2000 est.): food, manufactured goods, machinery, chemicals, fuel (1989). **Major trading partners:** Caricom, UK, U.S., Netherlands, Japan. **Member of Commonwealth of Nations**

Geography Grenada (the first "a" is a long vowel) is the most southerly of the Windward Islands, about 100 mi (161 km) from the Venezuelan coast. It is a volcanic island traversed by a mountain range, the highest peak of which is Mount St. Catherine (2,756 ft; 840 m).

Government Constitutional monarchy. A governor-general represents the sovereign, Elizabeth II.

History The Arawak Indians were the first to inhabit Grenada, but they were all eventually massacred by the belligerent Carib Indians. When Columbus arrived in 1498 he encountered the Caribs, who continued to rule over the island for another 150 years. The French gained control of the island in 1672 and held on to it until 1762, when the British invaded. Black slaves were granted freedom in 1833. After more than 200 years of British rule, most recently as part of the West Indies Associated States, Grenada became independent on Feb. 7, 1974, with Eric M. Gairy as prime minister.

In 1979, the Marxist New Jewel Movement staged a coup, and its leader, Maurice Bishop, became prime minister. Bishop, a protégé of Cuba's President Castro, was killed in a military coup on Oct. 19, 1983.

In an effort to establish order on the island and eliminate the Cuban military presence, U.S. president Ronald Reagan ordered an invasion of Grenada on Oct. 25 involving over 1,900 U.S. troops and a small military force from Barbados, Dominica, Jamaica, St. Lucia, and St. Vincent. The troops met strong resistance from Cuban military personnel on the island but soon occupied it. After a gradual withdrawal of peacekeeping forces, a centrist coalition led by Herbert A. Blaize won a parliamentary majority in 1984. The New National Party (NNP), led by Keith C. Mitchell, won a majority in the 1995 parliamentary elections.

Guatemala

REPUBLIC OF GUATEMALA

National name: República de Guatemala
President: Alfonso Portillo Cabrera (2000)
Area: 42,042 sq mi (108,890 sq km)
Population (2003 est.): 13,909,384 (growth rate: 2.8%); birth rate: 35.0/1000; infant mortality rate: 37.9/1000; density per sq mi: 331
Capital and largest city (2003 est.): Guatemala City, 2,655,900 (metro. area), 1,128,800 (city proper). **Other large cities:** Mixco, 287,600; Villa Nueva, 138,900. **Monetary unit:** Quetzal. **Languages:** Spanish, Indian languages. **Ethnicity/race:** Mestizo—mixed Amerindian-Spanish ancestry (in local Spanish called Ladino) 55%, Amerindian or predominantly Amerindian 43%. **Religions:** Roman Catholic, Protestant, Mayan. **Literacy rate:** 63.6% (2000 est.)
Economic summary: GDP/PPP (2001 est.): $48.3 billion; per capita $3,700. **Real growth rate:** 2.3%. **Inflation:** 7.6%. **Unemployment:** 7.5% (1999 est.). **Arable land:** 13%. **Agriculture:** sugarcane, corn, bananas, coffee, beans, cardamom; cattle, sheep, pigs, chickens. **Labor force:** 4.2 million (1999 est.); agriculture 50%, industry 15%, services 35% (1999 est.). **Industries:** sugar, textiles and clothing, furniture, chemicals, petroleum, metals, rubber, tourism. **Natural resources:** petroleum, nickel, rare woods, fish, chicle, hydropower. **Exports:** $2.9 billion (f.o.b., 2001): coffee, sugar, bananas, fruits and vegetables, cardamom, meat, apparel, petroleum, electricity. **Imports:** $4.9 billion (f.o.b., 2001): fuels, machinery and transport equipment, construction materials, grain, fertilizers, electricity. **Major trading partners:** U.S., El Salvador, Costa Rica, Nicaragua, Germany, Mexico, South Korea, Venezuela.

Geography The northernmost of the Central American nations, Guatemala is the size of Tennessee. Its neighbors are Mexico on the north and west, and Belize, Honduras, and El Salvador on the east. The country consists of three main regions—the cool highlands with the heaviest population, the tropical area along the Pacific and Caribbean coasts, and the tropical jungle in the northern lowlands (known as the Petén).

Government Constitutional democratic republic.

History Once the site of the impressive ancient Mayan civilization, Guatemala was conquered by Spanish conquistador Pedro de Alvarado in 1524 and became a republic in 1839 after the United Provinces of Central America collapsed. From 1898 to 1920, dictator Manuel Estrada Cabrera ran the country, and from 1931 to 1944, Gen. Jorge Ubico Castaneda served as strongman.

After Ubico's overthrow in 1944, liberal-democratic coalitions led by Juan José Arévalo (1945–1951) and Jacobo Arbenz Guzmán (1951–1954) instituted social and political reforms that strengthened the peasantry and urban workers at the expense of the military and big landowners like the U.S.-owned United Fruit Company. With covert U.S. backing, Col. Carlos Castillo Armas led a coup in 1954, and Arbenz took refuge in Mexico.

A series of repressive regimes followed, and the country was plunged into a 36-year civil war between military governments and leftist rebels. Death squads murdered an estimated 50,000 leftists and political opponents during the 1970s. The U.S. ended military aid in 1978.

After several other military governments, civilian Marco Vinicio Cerezo Arévalo took office in 1986. He was followed by Jorge Serrano Elías in 1991. In 1993, Serrano moved to dissolve Congress and the Supreme Court and suspend constitutional rights, but the military deposed Serrano and allowed the inauguration of de Leon Carpio, the former attorney general for human rights. A peace agreement was signed in Dec. 1996, ending the longest civil war in Latin American history, which had left some 200,000 dead. In June 1997, the new president Álvaro Arzú Irigoyen and the guerrilla movement leader Ricardo Ramirez received the UNESCO Houphouet-Boigny Peace Prize.

In 1999, a Guatemalan truth commission blamed the army for 93% of the atrocities and the rebels (the Guatemalan National Revolutionary Unit) for 3%. The former guerrillas apologized for their crimes, and President Clinton apologized for U.S. support of the right-wing military governments. The army has not acknowledged its guilt. Alfonso Portillo Cabrera became president in Jan. 2000. In Aug. 2000, Portillo apologized for the former government's human rights abuses and pledged to prosecute those responsible and compensate victims.

In July 2003, the country's highest court ruled that former coup leader and military dictator Efrain Rios Montt, responsible for a massacre of tens of thousands of civilians during the civil war, was eligible to run for president in November. The ruling conflicts with the constitution, which bans anyone who seized power in a coup from running for the presidency.

Guinea

REPUBLIC OF GUINEA

National name: République de Guinée
President: Lansana Conté (1984)
Premier: Lamine Sidimé (1999)
Area: 94,925 sq mi (245,857 sq km)
Population (2003 est.): 9,030,220 (growth rate: 2.7%); birth rate: 42.5/1000; infant mortality rate: 93.3/1000; density per sq mi: 95
Capital and largest city (2003 est.): Conakry, 1,767,200. **Monetary unit:** Guinean franc. **Languages:** French (official), native tongues (Malinké, Susu, Fulani). **Ethnicity/race:** Peuhl 40%, Malinke 30%, Susu 20%, smaller tribes 10%. **Religions:** Islam 85%, Christian 8%, indigenous 7%. **Literacy rate:** 35.9% (1995 est.)
Economic summary: GDP/PPP (2001 est.): $15 billion; per capita $1,970. **Real growth rate:** 3.3%. **Inflation:** 6% (2000 est.). **Unemployment:** n.a. **Arable land:** 4%. **Agriculture:** rice, coffee, pineapples, palm kernels, cassava (tapioca), bananas, sweet potatoes; cattle, sheep, goats; timber. **Labor force:** 3 million (1999); agriculture 80%, industry and services 20% (2000 est.). **Industries:** bauxite, gold, diamonds; alumina refining; light manufacturing and agricultural processing industries. **Natural resources:** bauxite, iron ore, diamonds, gold, uranium, hydropower, fish. **Exports:** $694.5 million (f.o.b., 2000): bauxite, alumina, gold, diamonds, coffee, fish, agricultural products. **Imports:** $555.2 million (f.o.b., 2000): petroleum products, metals, machinery, transport equipment, textiles, grain and other foodstuffs. **Major trading partners:** Belgium, U.S., Ireland, Russia, France, Côte d'Ivoire.

Geography Guinea, in West Africa on the Atlantic, is also bordered by Guinea-Bissau, Senegal, Mali, Côte d'Ivoire, Liberia, and Sierra Leone. Slightly smaller than Oregon, the country consists of a coastal plain, a mountainous region, a savanna interior, and a forest area in the Guinea Highlands. The highest peak is Mount Nimba at 5,748 ft (1,752 m).

Government Republic.

History Beginning in 900, the Susu migrated from the north and began settling in the area that is now Guinea. The Susu civilization reached its height in the 13th century. Today the Susu make up about 20% of Guinea's population. From the 16th to the 19th century, the Fulani empire dominated the region. In 1849, the French claimed it as a protectorate. First called Rivières du Sud, the protectorate was rechristened French Guinea, and finally, in 1895, it became part of French West Africa.

Guinea achieved independence on Oct. 2, 1958, and became an independent state with Sékou Touré as president. Under Touré, the country became the first avowedly Marxist state in Africa. Diplomatic relations with France were suspended in 1965, with the Soviet Union replacing France as the country's chief source of economic and technical assistance.

Prosperity came in 1960 after the start of exploitation of bauxite deposits. Touré was reelected to a seven-year term in 1974 and again in 1981. Touré died after 26 years as president in March 1984. A week later, a military regime headed by Col. Lansana Conté took power.

In 1989, President Conté announced that Guinea would move to a multiparty democracy, and in 1991, voters approved a new constitution. In Dec. 1993 elections, the president's Unity and Progress Party took almost 51% of the vote. In 2001, a government referendum was passed doing away with presidential term limits, which would allow Conté to run for a third term in 2003. Despite the trappings of multiparty rule, Conté has ruled the country with an iron fist.

Guinea had ongoing difficulties with its neighbor Liberia, which was embroiled in a long civil war during the 1990s and again in 2000–2003. Guinea had taken sides against rebel leader Charles Taylor in Liberia's civil war and was part of the Nigerian-led

ECOMOG forces that intervened in the crisis. As a consequence, President Conté's relations with Taylor remained sour after Taylor became Liberia's president in 1997. The fighting in Liberia spilled over the border into Guinea on several occasions. Sierra Leone's recent civil war also caused problems for neighboring Guinea. Already burdened by an inadequate infrastructure and a weak economy, an influx of nearly 300,000 refugees from Sierra Leone has overwhelmed the country.

Guinea-Bissau

REPUBLIC OF GUINEA-BISSAU

National name: Républica da Guiné-Bissau
President: Henrique Rosa (interim) (2003)
Prime Minister: Antonio Artur Sanhá (2003)
Area: 13,946 sq mi (36,120 sq km)
Population (2003 est.): 1,360,827 (growth rate: 2.2%); birth rate: 38.4/1000; infant mortality rate: 110.3/1000; density per sq mi: 98
Capital and largest city (2003 est.): Bissau, 296,900. **Monetary unit:** CFA Franc. **Languages:** Portuguese, Criolo, African languages. **Ethnicity/race:** African 99% (Balanta 30%, Fula 20%, Manjaca 14%, Mandinga 13%, Papel 7%), European and mulatto less than 1%. **Religions:** traditional 50%, Islam 45%, Christian 5%. **Literacy rate:** 34% (2000 est.)
Economic summary: GDP/PPP (2001 est.): $1.2 billion; per capita $900. **Real growth rate:** 7.2%. **Inflation:** 5%. **Unemployment:** n.a. **Arable land:** 11%. **Agriculture:** rice, corn, beans, cassava (tapioca), cashew nuts, peanuts, palm kernels, cotton; timber; fish. **Labor force:** 480,000; agriculture 82% (2000 est.). **Industries:** agricultural products processing, beer, soft drinks. **Natural resources:** fish, timber, phosphates, bauxite, unexploited deposits of petroleum. **Exports:** $80 million (f.o.b., 2000 est.): cashew nuts 70%, shrimp, peanuts, palm kernels, sawn lumber. **Imports:** $55.2 million (f.o.b., 2000 est.): foodstuffs, machinery and transport equipment, petroleum products. **Major trading partners:** India, Italy, South Korea, Belgium, Portugal, Senegal, Thailand, China.

Geography A neighbor of Senegal and Guinea in West Africa, on the Atlantic coast, Guinea-Bissau is about half the size of South Carolina. The country is a low-lying coastal region of swamps, rain forests, and mangrove-covered wetlands, with about 25 islands off the coast.

Government Republic.

History The land now known as Guinea-Bissau was once the kingdom of Gabú, which was part of the larger Mali empire. After 1546 Gabú became more autonomous, and at least portions of the kingdom existed until 1867. The first European to encounter Guinea-Bissau was the Portuguese explorer Nuño Tristão in 1446; colonists in the Cape Verde Islands obtained trading rights in the territory, and it became a center of the Portuguese slave trade. In 1879, the connection with the islands was broken.

The African Party for the Independence of Guinea-Bissau and Cape Verde (another Portuguese colony) was founded in 1956, and guerrilla warfare by nationalists grew increasingly effective. By 1974 the rebels controlled most of the countryside, where they formed a government that was soon recognized by scores of countries. The military coup in Portugal in April 1974 brightened the prospects for freedom, and in Aug. the Lisbon government signed an agreement granting independence to the province. The new republic took the name Guinea-Bissau.

In Nov. 1980, Premier João Bernardo Vieira headed a military coup that deposed Luis Cabral, president since 1974. In his 19 years of rule, Vieira was criticized for crony capitalism and corruption and for failing to alleviate the poverty of Guinea-Bissau, one of the world's poorest countries. Vieira also brought in troops from Senegal and the Republic of Guinea to help fight against an insurgency movement, a highly unpopular move. In May 1999 rebels deposed Vieira.

Following a period of military rule, Kumba Yalá, a former teacher and popular leader of Guinea-Bissau's independence movement, was elected president in 2000.

In Sept. 2003 he was deposed in a military coup by Gen. Verissimo Correia Seabra, who then appointed an interim president and a prime minister. Yalá's increasingly repressive measures and refusal to hold elections were cited as the cause.

Guyana

COOPERATIVE REPUBLIC OF GUYANA

President: Bharrat Jagdeo (1999)
Prime Minister: Samuel Hinds (1999)
Area: 83,000 sq mi (214,970 sq km)
Population (2003 est.): 702,100 (growth rate: 0.9%); birth rate: 17.9/1000; infant mortality rate: 37.5/1000; density per sq mi: 8
Capital and largest city (2003 est.): Georgetown, 227,700. **Monetary unit:** Guyanese dollar. **Languages:** English (official), Amerindian dialects. **Ethnicity/race:** East Indian 50%, black 36%, Amerindian 7%, European and Chinese and mixed 7%. **Religions:** Christian 50%, Hindu 35%, Islam 10%, other 5%. **Literacy rate:** 98.1% (1995 est.)
Economic summary: GDP/PPP (2000 est.): $2.5 billion; per capita $3,600. **Real growth rate:** 2.8% (2001 est.). **Inflation:** 6% (2001 est.). **Unemployment:** 9.1% (2000) (understated). **Arable land:** 2%. **Labor force:** 418,000 (2001 est.); agriculture n.a., industry n.a., services n.a. **Agriculture:** sugar, rice, wheat, vegetable oils; beef, pork, poultry, dairy products; fish (shrimp). **Industries:** bauxite, sugar, rice milling, timber, textiles, gold mining. **Natural resources:** bauxite, gold, diamonds, hardwood timber, shrimp, fish. **Exports:** $505 million (f.o.b., 2000): sugar, gold, bauxite/alumina, rice, shrimp, molasses, rum, timber. **Imports:** $585 million (c.i.f., 2000): manufactures, machinery, petroleum, food. **Major trading partners:** Canada, U.S., UK, Netherlands Antilles, Trinidad and Tobago. **Member of Commonwealth of Nations**

Geography Guyana is the size of Idaho and is situated on the northern coast of South America east of Venezuela, west of Suriname, and north of Brazil. A tropical forest covers more than 80% of the country.

Government Republic.

History The Dutch, English, and French established colonies in what is now known as Guyana, but by the early 17th century the majority of the settlements were Dutch. During the Napoleonic wars Britain took over the Dutch colonies of Berbice, Demerara, and Essequibo, which became British Guiana in 1831.

Slavery was outlawed in 1834, and the great need for plantation workers led to a large wave of immigration, primarily of East Indians. Today, about half of the population is of East Indian descent and about 43% are of African descent.

British Guiana was made a Crown colony in 1928, and in 1953 it was granted home rule. In 1950, Forbes Burnham, who was Afro-Guyanese, and Cheddi Jagan, who was Indian-Guyanese, created the colony's first political party, which was dedicated to gaining the colony's independence. The two leaders split in 1955, creating separate parties. The leftist Jagan and the more moderate Burnham were to dominate Guyanan politics for decades to come. On May 26, 1966, the country gained independence, and resumed its traditional name, Guyana.

Burnham and his People's National Congress ruled Guyana for 21 years, until Burnham's death in 1985. In 1992, Jagan's People's Progressive Party won a majority in the general election. Jagan, who had served as prime minister in the 1960s while Guyana was still a colony, became president. Former finance minister Bharrat Jagdeo assumed the presidency in Aug. 1999.

Guyana's potential economic development was hurt in 2000 as border disputes with both Venezuela to the west and Suriname to the east heated up. Suriname and Guyana have been unable to resolve the border dispute in an oil-rich coastal area. Venezuela's president Hugo Chavez has revived a 19th-century claim to more than half of Guyana's territory.

In March 2001, Bharrat Jagdeo won a second term in elections that underscored Guyana's bitter racial tensions. The reelection of Jagdeo, an ethnic East Indian, caused rioting among Afro-Guyanese, who claimed widespread election fraud.

Haiti

REPUBLIC OF HAITI

National name: République d'Haïti
President: Jean-Bertrand Aristide (2000)
Prime Minister: Yvon Neptune (2002)
Area: 10,714 sq mi (27,750 sq km)
Population (2003 est.): 7,527,817 (growth rate: 2.1%); birth rate: 34.1/1000; infant mortality rate: 76.0/1000; density per sq mi: 703
Capital and largest city (2003 est.): Port-au-Prince, 1,764,000 (metro. area), 1,119,000 (city proper). **Monetary unit:** Gourde. **Languages:** Creole and French (both official). **Ethnicity/race:** black 95%, mulatto and European 5%. **Religions:** Roman Catholic 80%, Protestant 16%, Vaudou 95%. **Literacy rate:** 45% (1995 est.)
Economic summary: GDP/PPP (2001 est.): $12 billion; per capita $1,700. **Real growth rate:** –1.2%. **Inflation:** 14%. **Unemployment:** widespread unemployment and underemployment; more than two-thirds of the labor force do not have formal jobs (2001). **Arable land:** 20%. **Agriculture:** coffee, mangoes, sugarcane, rice, corn, sorghum; wood. **Labor force:** 3.6 million (1995); note: shortage of skilled labor, unskilled labor abundant (2001); agriculture 66%, services 25%, industry 9%. **Industries:** sugar refining, flour milling, textiles, cement, light assembly industries based on imported parts. **Natural resources:** bauxite, copper, calcium carbonate, gold, marble, hydropower. **Exports:** $326.6 million (f.o.b., 2001): manufactures, coffee, oils, mangoes. **Imports:** $977.5 million (c.i.f., 2001): food, manufactured goods, machinery and transport equipment, fuels, raw materials. **Major trading partners:** U.S., EU, Dominican Republic.

Geography Haiti, in the West Indies, occupies the western third of the island of Hispaniola, which it shares with the Dominican Republic. About the size of Maryland, Haiti is two-thirds mountainous, with the rest of the country marked by great valleys, extensive plateaus, and small plains.

Government Republic with an elected government.

History Explored by Columbus on Dec. 6, 1492, Haiti's native Arawaks fell victim to Spanish rule. In 1697, Haiti became the French colony of Saint-Dominique, which became a leading sugarcane producer dependent on slaves. In 1791, an insurrection erupted among the slave population of 480,000, resulting in a declaration of independence by Pierre-Dominique Toussaint l'Ouverture in 1801. Napoléon Bonaparte suppressed the independence movement, but it eventually triumphed in 1804 under Jean-Jacques Dessalines, who gave the new nation the Arawak name *Haiti*.

The revolution wrecked Haiti's economy. Years of strife between the light-skinned mulattos who dominated the economy and the majority black population, plus disputes with neighboring Santo Domingo, continued to hurt the nation's development. After a succession of dictatorships a bankrupt Haiti accepted a U.S. customs receivership from 1905 to 1941. Occupation by U.S. Marines from 1915 to 1934 brought stability. Haiti's high population growth made it the most densely populated nation in the hemisphere.

In 1949, after four years of democratic rule by President Dumarsais Estimé, dictatorship returned under Gen. Paul Magloire, who was succeeded by François Duvalier, nicknamed "Papa Doc," in 1957. Duvalier's secret police, the "Tontons Macoutes," ensured political stability with brutal efficiency. Duvalier's son, Jean-Claude, or "Baby Doc," succeeded his father in 1971 as ruler of the poorest nation in the Western Hemisphere. In the early 1980s, Haiti became one of the first countries to face an AIDS epidemic. Fear of the disease caused tourists to stay away, and the tourist industry collapsed, causing rising unemployment. Unrest generated by the economic crisis forced Duvalier to flee the country in 1986.

Throughout the 1990s the international community tried to establish democracy in Haiti. The country's first elected chief executive, Jean-Bertrand Aristide, a Roman Catholic priest, took office on Feb. 7, 1991. The military, however, soon took control. A UN peacekeeping force, led by the U.S.—Operation Uphold Democracy—arrived in 1994. Aristide was restored to office and René Preval became his successor in 1996 elections. U.S. soldiers and UN peacekeepers left in 2000. Haiti's government is ineffectual and the economy is in ruins. With 50% unemployment, Haiti produces a steady flow of refugees to the U.S.

In 2000, former president Aristide was reelected president in elections boycotted by the opposition and questioned by many foreign observers. The U.S. and other countries have threatened Haiti, already one of the world's poorest countries, with sanctions unless democratic procedures are strengthened.

Honduras

REPUBLIC OF HONDURAS

National name: República de Honduras
President: Ricardo Maduro (2002)
Area: 43,278 sq mi (112,090 sq km)
Population (2003 est.): 6,669,789 (growth rate: 2.5%); birth rate: 31.7/1000; infant mortality rate: 30.0/1000; density per sq mi: 154
Capital and largest city (2003 est.): Tegucigalpa, 1,436,000 (metro. area), 1,248,300 (city proper). **Monetary unit:** Lempira. **Languages:** Spanish (official), English widely spoken in business. **Ethnicity/race:** mestizo (mixed Indian and European) 90%, Indian 7%, black 2%, white 1%. **Religions:** Roman Catholic 97%, Protestant minority. **Literacy rate:** 74% (1999)
Economic summary: GDP/PPP (2001 est.): $17 billion; per capita $2,600. **Real growth rate:** 2.1%. **Inflation:** 9.7%. **Unemployment:** 28%. **Arable land:** 15%. **Agriculture:** bananas, coffee, citrus; beef; timber; shrimp. **Labor force:** 2.3 million (1997 est.);

agriculture 34%, industry 21%, services 45% (2001 est.). **Industries:** sugar, coffee, textiles, clothing, wood products. **Natural resources:** timber, gold, silver, copper, lead, zinc, iron ore, antimony, coal, fish, hydropower. **Exports:** $2 billion (f.o.b., 2001 est.): coffee, bananas, shrimp, lobster, meat; zinc, lumber. **Imports:** $2.7 billion (f.o.b., 2001 est.): machinery and transport equipment, industrial raw materials, chemical products, fuels, foodstuffs. **Major trading partners:** U.S., El Salvador, Germany, Belgium, Guatemala, Mexico, Japan.

Geography Honduras, in the north-central part of Central America, has a Caribbean as well as a Pacific coastline. Guatemala is to the west, El Salvador to the south, and Nicaragua to the east. The second-largest country in Central America, Honduras is slightly larger than Tennessee. Generally mountainous, the country is marked by fertile plateaus, river valleys, and narrow coastal plains.

Government Democratic constitutional republic.

History During the first millennium, Honduras was inhabited by the Maya. Columbus explored the country in 1502. Honduras, with four other Central American nations, declared its independence from Spain in 1821 to form a federation of Central American states. In 1838, Honduras left the federation and became independent. Political unrest rocked Honduras in the early 1900s, resulting in an occupation by U.S. Marines. Dictator Gen. Tiburcio Carias Andino established a strong government in 1932.

In 1969, El Salvador invaded Honduras after Honduran landowners deported several thousand Salvadorans. Five thousand people ultimately died in what is called "the football war," because it broke out during a soccer game between the two countries. By threatening economic sanctions and military intervention, the OAS induced El Salvador to withdraw. After a decade of military rule, parliamentary democracy returned with the election of Roberto Suazo Córdova as president in 1982. However, Honduras faced severe economic problems and tensions along its border with Nicaragua. "Contra" rebels, waging a guerrilla war against the Sandinista regime in Nicaragua, used Honduras as a training and staging area. The U.S. also used Honduras for military exercises and built bases to train Honduran and Salvadoran troops.

In 1997, Carlos Flores Facussé of the Liberal Party was elected president. He began to reform the economy and modernize the government. In recent years, Honduras has faced high unemployment, inflation, and over-dependence on coffee and bananas. In Oct. 1998, Hurricane Mitch killed some 13,000 Hondurans, left 2 million homeless, and caused more than $5 billion in damage.

In 2002, Ricardo Maduro became president, promising to lessen crime and corruption, but his hardline efforts, growing increasingly more repressive, have not improved the problem. A prison riot in April 2003 left 86 prisoners dead.

Hungary

REPUBLIC OF HUNGARY

National name: Magyar Köztársaság
President: Ferenc Mádl (2000)
Prime Minister: Péter Medgyessy (2002)
Area: 35,919 sq mi (93,030 sq km)
Population (2003 est.): 10,045,407 (growth rate: –0.4%); birth rate: 9.3/1000; infant mortality rate: 8.6/1000; density per sq mi: 280
Capital and largest city (2003 est.): Budapest, 2,597,000 (metro. area), 1,769,500 (city proper). **Other large cities:** Debrecen, 210,500; Miskolc, 182,600; Szeged, 173,200; Pécs, 163,900. **Monetary unit:** Forint. **Languages:** Magyar (Hungarian), 98.2%; other, 1.8%. **Ethnicity/race:** Hungarian 89.9%, Gypsy 4%, German 2.6%, Serb 2%, Slovak 0.8%, Romanian 0.7%. **Religions:** Roman Catholic 67.5%, Protestant 25%, atheist and others 7.5%. **Literacy rate:** 99% (1980 est.)
Economic summary: GDP/PPP (2001 est.): $120.9 billion; per capita $12,000. **Real growth rate:** 3.9%. **Inflation:** 9.2%. **Unemployment:** 6.5%. **Arable land:** 52%. **Agriculture:** wheat, corn, sunflower seed, potatoes, sugar beets; pigs, cattle, poultry, dairy products. **Labor force:** 4.2 million (1997); services 65%, industry 27%, agriculture 8% (1996). **Industries:** mining, metallurgy, construction materials, processed foods, textiles, chemicals (especially pharmaceuticals), motor vehicles. **Natural resources:** bauxite, coal, natural gas, fertile soils, arable land. **Exports:** $27.9 billion (f.o.b., 2001): machinery and equipment, other manufactures, food products, raw materials, fuels and electricity (2000). **Imports:** $29.5 billion (f.o.b., 2001): machinery and equipment, other manufactures, fuels and electricity, food products, raw materials. **Major trading partners:** Germany, Austria, Italy, Netherlands, Russia.

Geography This central European country is the size of Indiana. Most of Hungary is a fertile, rolling plain lying east of the Danube River and drained by the Danube and Tisza Rivers. In the extreme northwest is the Little Hungarian Plain. South of that area is Lake Balaton (250 sq mi; 648 sq km).

Government Parliamentary democracy.

History By 14 B.C., western Hungary was part of the Roman Empire's provinces of Pannonia and Dacia. The area east of the Danube was never a part of the Roman Empire and was largely occupied by various Germanic and Asiatic peoples. In 896 all of Hungary was invaded by the Magyars, who founded a kingdom. Christianity was accepted during the reign of Stephen I (Saint Stephen), 977–1038. A devastating invasion by the Mongols killed half of Hungary's population in 1241. The peak of Hungary's great period of medieval power came during the reign of Louis I the Great (1342–1382), whose dominions touched the Baltic, Black, and Mediterranean seas. War with the Turks broke out in 1389, and for more than 100 years the Turks advanced through the Balkans. When the Turks smashed a Hungarian army in 1526, western and northern Hungary accepted Hapsburg rule to escape Turkish occupation. Transylvania became independent under Hungarian princes. Intermittent war with the Turks was waged until a peace treaty was signed in 1699.

After the suppression of the 1848 revolt against Hapsburg rule, led by Louis Kossuth, the dual monarchy of Austria-Hungary was set up in 1867. The dual monarchy was defeated with the other Central Powers in World War I. After a short-lived republic in 1918, the chaotic Communist rule of 1919 under Béla Kun ended with the Romanians occupying Budapest on Aug. 4, 1919. When the Romanians left, Adm. Nicholas Horthy entered the capital with a national army. The Treaty of Trianon of June 4, 1920, by which the Allies parceled out Hungarian territories, cost Hungary 68% of its land and 58% of its population. Meanwhile, the National Assembly had restored the legal continuity of the old monarchy and, on March 1, 1920, Horthy was elected regent.

In World War II, Hungary allied with Germany, which aided the country in recovering lost territories.

Following the German invasion of Russia on June 22, 1941, Hungary joined the attack against the Soviet Union, but withdrew in defeat from the eastern front by May 1943. Germany occupied the country for the remainder of the war and set up a puppet government. Hungarian Jews and gypsies were sent to death camps. The German regime was driven out by the Soviets in 1944–1945.

By the Treaty of Paris (1947), Hungary had to give up all territory it had acquired since 1937 and to pay $300 million reparations to the USSR, Czechoslovakia, and Yugoslavia. In 1948, the Communist Party, with the support of Soviet troops, seized control. Hungary was proclaimed a People's Republic and one-party state in 1949. Industry was nationalized, the land collectivized into state farms, and the opposition terrorized by the secret police. The terror, modeled after that of the USSR, reached its height with the trial and life imprisonment of József Cardinal Mindszenty, the leader of Hungary's Roman Catholics, in 1948. On Oct. 23, 1956, an anti-Communist revolution broke out in Budapest. To cope with it, the Communists set up a coalition government and called former premier Imre Nagy back to head the government. But he and most of his ministers were swept by the logic of events into the anti-Communist opposition, and he declared Hungary a neutral power, withdrawing from the Warsaw Treaty and appealing to the United Nations for help. One of his ministers, János Kádár, established a counterregime and asked the USSR to send in military power. Soviet troops and tanks suppressed the revolution in bloody fighting after 190,000 people had fled the country. Under Kádár (1956–1988), Communist Hungary henceforth maintained more liberal policies in the economic and cultural spheres, and Hungary became the most liberal of the Soviet-bloc nations of eastern Europe. Continuing his program of national reconciliation, Kádár emptied prisons, reformed the secret police, and eased travel restrictions.

Hungary's Communists abandoned their monopoly on power in 1989 voluntarily, and the constitution was amended in Oct. 1989 to allow for a multiparty state. The last Soviet troops left Hungary in June 1991, thereby ending almost 47 years of military presence. The transition to a market economy proved difficult.

In April 1999, Hungary became part of NATO, and it will join the EU in 2004. In 2003, Hungary sent about 300 troops to support the peacekeeping effort in Iraq.

Iceland

REPUBLIC OF ICELAND

National name: Lydveldid Island
President: Ólafur Ragnar Grímsson (1996)
Prime Minister: David Oddsson (1991)
Area: 39,768 sq mi (103,000 sq km)[1]
Population (2003 est.): 280,798 (growth rate: 0.7%); birth rate: 14.1/1000; infant mortality rate: 3.5/1000; density per sq mi: 7
Capital and largest city (2003 est.): Reykjavik, 184,200 (metro. area), 114,800 (city proper). **Monetary unit:** Icelandic króna. **Language:** Icelandic. **Ethnicity/race:** homogeneous mixture of descendants of Norwegians and Celts. **Religions:** Church of Iceland (Evangelical Lutheran) 87.1%, other Protestant and Roman Catholic 5.8%, other 7.1%. **Literacy rate:** 99.9% (1997 est.)
Economic summary: GDP/PPP (2000 est.): $6.85 billion; per capita $24,800. **Real growth rate:** 4.3%. **Inflation:** 3.5%. **Unemployment:** 1% (Apr. 2001 est.). **Arable land:** negl. **Agriculture:** potatoes, turnips; cattle, sheep; fish. **Labor force:** 159,000 (2000); agriculture 5.1%, fishing and fish processing 11.8%, manufacturing 12.9%, construction 10.7%, other services 59.5% (1999). **Industries:** fish processing; aluminum smelting, ferrosilicon production, geothermal power; tourism. **Natural resources:** fish, hydropower, geothermal power, diatomite. **Exports:** $2 billion (f.o.b., 2000): fish and fish products 70%, animal products, aluminum, diatomite and ferrosilicon. **Imports**: $2.2 billion (f.o.b., 2000): machinery and equipment, petroleum products; foodstuffs, textiles. **Major trading partners:** EU, U.S., Japan.

1. Including some offshore islands.

Geography Iceland, an island about the size of Kentucky, lies in the north Atlantic Ocean east of Greenland and just touches the Arctic Circle. It is one of the most volcanic regions in the world. More than 13% is covered by snowfields and glaciers, and most of the people live in the 7% of the island that is made up of fertile coastland. The Gulf Stream keeps Iceland's climate milder than one would expect from an island near the Arctic Circle.

Government Constitutional republic.

History The earliest inhabitants of Iceland were Irish hermits, who left the island upon the arrival of the pagan Norse people in the late 9th century. A constitution drawn up c. 930 created a form of democracy and provided for an *Althing*, the world's oldest practicing legislative assembly. The island's early history was preserved in the Icelandic sagas of the 13th century.

In 1262–1264, Iceland came under Norwegian rule and passed to ultimate Danish control through the unification of the kingdoms of Norway, Sweden, and Denmark (the Kalmar Union) in 1397.

In 1874, Icelanders obtained their own constitution, and in 1918, Denmark recognized Iceland, via the Act of Union, as a separate state with unlimited sovereignty. It remained, however, nominally under the Danish monarchy.

During the German occupation of Denmark in World War II, British, then American, troops occupied Iceland and used it for a strategic air base. While officially neutral, Iceland cooperated with the Allies throughout the conflict. On June 17, 1944, after a popular referendum, the Althing proclaimed Iceland an independent republic.

The country joined the North Atlantic Treaty Organization in 1949, and subsequently received an American air force base in 1951. In 1970, it was admitted to the European Free Trade Association. Iceland unilaterally extended its territorial fishing limit from 3 to 200 nautical mi in 1972, precipitating a dispute with the UK known as the "cod wars," which ended in 1976, when the UK recognized the new limits. In 1980, the Icelanders elected a woman to the office of the presidency, the first elected female chief of state (i.e., president as distinct from prime minister) in the world. After the recession of the early 1990s, Iceland's economy rebounded.

At the International Whaling Commission meeting in July 2001, Iceland refused to agree to the continuation of the moratorium on commercial whaling that has been in effect since 1986, and in 2003, after a 14-year lull, it began hunting whales for scientific research. In May 2003, David Oddsson was reelected, making him the longest-serving prime minister in Europe.

India

REPUBLIC OF INDIA

National name: Bharat
President: A.P.J. Abdul Kalam (2002)
Prime Minister: Atal Bihari Vajpayee (1998)
Area: 1,269,338 sq mi (3,287,590 sq km)
Population (2003 est.): 1,049,700,118 (growth rate: 1.5%); birth rate: 23.3/1000; infant mortality rate: 59.6/1000; density per sq mi: 827
Capital (2003 est.): Delhi, 17,037,900 (metro.area), 10,203,700 (city proper). **Largest cities:** Bombay (Mumbai), 17,012,100 (metro.area), 12,383,100 (city proper); Calcutta (Kolkata), 14,090,200 (metro.area), 4,760,800 (city proper); Bangalore, 4,461,100; Madras (Chennai), 4,382,100; Ahmedabad, 3,653,700; Hyderabad, 3,585,600; Kanpur, 2,631,800. **Monetary unit:** Rupee. **Principal languages:** Hindi (official), English (official), Bengali, Gujarati, Kashmiri, Malayalam, Marathi, Oriya, Punjabi, Tamil, Telugu, Urdu, Kannada, Assamese, Sanskrit, Sindhi (all recognized by the constitution). Dialects, 1,652. **Ethnicity/race:** Indo-Aryan 72%, Dravidian 25%, Mongoloid and other 3% (2000). **Religions:** Hindu 81.3%, Islam 12%, Christian 2.3%, Sikh 1.9%, other (including Buddhists and Jains) 2.5%. **Literacy rate:** 52% (1995 est.)
Economic summary: GDP/PPP (2001 est.): $2.5 trillion; per capita $2,500. **Real growth rate:** 5%. **Inflation:** 3.5% (2000 est.). **Unemployment:** 4.4% (1999). **Arable land:** 54%. **Agriculture:** rice, wheat, oilseed, cotton, jute, tea, sugarcane, potatoes; cattle, water buffalo, sheep, goats, poultry; fish. **Labor force:** 406 million (1999); agriculture 60%, services 23%, industry 17% (1999). **Industries:** textiles, chemicals, food processing, steel, transportation equipment, cement, mining, petroleum, machinery, software. **Natural resources:** coal (fourth-largest reserves in the world), iron ore, manganese, mica, bauxite, titanium ore, chromite, natural gas, diamonds, petroleum, limestone, arable land. **Exports:** $44.5 billion (f.o.b., 2001): textile goods, gems and jewelry, engineering goods, chemicals, leather manufactures. **Imports:** $53.8 billion (f.o.b., 2001): crude oil, machinery, gems, fertilizer, chemicals. **Major trading partners:** U.S., Hong Kong, Japan, UK, Germany, Saudi Arabia. **Member of Commonwealth of Nations**

Geography One-third the area of the United States, the Republic of India occupies most of the subcontinent of India in southern Asia. It borders on China in the northeast. Other neighbors are Pakistan on the west, Nepal and Bhutan on the north, and Burma and Bangladesh on the east.

The country can be divided into three distinct geographic regions: the Himalayan region in the north, which contains some of the highest mountains in the world, the Gangetic Plain, and the plateau region in the south and central part. Its three great river systems have extensive deltas and all rise in the Himalayas: the Ganges, 1,540 mi (2,478 km), the Indus, and the Brahmaputra.

Government Federal republic.

History One of the earliest civilizations, the Indus Valley civilization flourished on the Indian subcontinent from c. 2600 B.C. to c. 2000 B.C. The Aryans who invaded India c. 1500 B.C. from the northwest found a land that was already home to an advanced civilization. They introduced Sanskrit and the Vedic religion, a forerunner of Hinduism, to the area. Buddhism was founded in the 6th century B.C. and was spread throughout northern India, most notably by one of the great ancient kings of the Mauryan dynasty, Asoka (c. 269–232 B.C.), who also unified most of the Indian subcontinent for the first time.

In 1526, Muslim invaders founded the great Mogul empire, centered on Delhi, which lasted, at least in name, until 1857. Akbar the Great (1542–1605) strengthened and consolidated this empire. The long reign of his great-grandson, Aurangzeb (1618–1707), represents both the greatest extent of the Mogul empire and the beginning of its decay.

Vasco da Gama, the Portuguese explorer, visited India first in 1498, and for the next 100 years the Portuguese had a virtual monopoly on trade with the subcontinent. Meanwhile, the English founded the East India Company, which set up its first factory at Surat in 1612 and began expanding its influence, fighting the Indian rulers and the French, Dutch, and Portuguese traders simultaneously.

Bombay, taken from the Portuguese, became the seat of English rule in 1687. The defeat of French and Mogul armies by Lord Clive in 1757 laid the foundation of the British Empire in India. The East India Company continued to suppress native uprisings and extend British rule until 1858, when the administration of India was formally transferred to the British Crown following the Sepoy Mutiny of native troops in 1857–1858.

After World War I, in which the Indian states sent more than 6 million troops to fight beside the Allies, Indian nationalist unrest rose to new heights under the leadership of a Hindu lawyer, Mohandas K. Gandhi, called Mahatma Gandhi. His philosophy of civil disobedience called for nonviolent noncooperation against British authority. He soon became the leading spirit of the Indian National Congress Party, which was the spearhead of revolt. In 1919, the British gave added responsibility to Indian officials, and in 1935, India was given a federal form of government and a measure of self-rule.

In 1942, with the Japanese pressing hard on the eastern borders of India, the British War Cabinet tried and failed to reach a political settlement with nationalist leaders. The Congress Party took the position that the British must quit India. In 1942, fearing mass civil disobedience, the government of India carried out widespread arrests of Congress leaders, including Gandhi.

Gandhi was released in 1944 and negotiations for a settlement were resumed. Finally, in Aug. 1947, India gained full independence. The victory was soured, however, by the partitioning of the predominantly Muslim regions of the north into the separate nation of Pakistan. The Muslim League, led by Mohammed Ali Jinnah, demanded a separate nation for the Muslim minority to prevent Hindu political and social domination. Indian Hindus, however, had hoped for a unified rather than balkanized Indian subcontinent. Lord Mountbatten as viceroy partitioned India along religious lines and split the provinces of Bengal and the Punjab, which both nations claimed. The partition of Pakistan and India led to the largest migration in human history, with 17 million people fleeing across the borders in both directions to escape the bloody riots occurring among sectarian groups. Armed conflict also broke out over rival claims to the princely states of Jammu and Kashmir.

Jawaharlal Nehru, nationalist leader and head of the Congress Party, was made prime minister. In 1949, a constitution was approved, making India a sovereign republic. Under a federal structure the states were organized on linguistic lines. The dominance of the Congress Party contributed to stability. In 1956, the republic absorbed former French settlements. Five years later, the republic forcibly annexed the Portuguese enclaves of Goa, Damao, and Diu.

Nehru died in 1964. His successor, Lal Bahadur Shastri, died on Jan. 10, 1966. Nehru's daughter, Indira Gandhi, became prime minister, and she continued his policy of nonalignment.

In 1971, the Pakistani army moved in to quash the independence movement in East Pakistan that was supported by India, and some 10 million Bengali refugees poured across the border into India, creating social, economic, and health problems. After numerous border incidents, India invaded East Pakistan and in two weeks forced the surrender of the Pakistani army. East Pakistan was established as an independent state and renamed Bangladesh.

In May 1975, the 300-year-old kingdom of Sikkim became a full-fledged Indian state. Situated in the Himalayas, Sikkim was a virtual dependency of Tibet until the early 19th century. Under an 1890 treaty between China and Great Britain, it became a British protectorate, and was made an Indian protectorate after Britain quit the subcontinent.

In the summer of 1975, the world's largest democracy veered suddenly toward authoritarianism when a judge in Allahabad, Indira Gandhi's home constituency, found Gandhi's landslide victory in the 1971 elections invalid because civil servants had illegally aided her campaign. Amid demands for her resignation, Gandhi decreed a state of emergency on June 26 and ordered mass arrests of her critics, including all opposition party leaders except the Communists.

Despite strong opposition to her repressive measures, particularly resentment against compulsory birth control programs, Gandhi, in 1977, announced parliamentary elections for March. At the same time, she freed most political prisoners. The landslide victory of Morarji R. Desai unseated Gandhi, but she staged a spectacular comeback in the elections of Jan. 1980.

In 1984, Gandhi ordered the Indian army to root out a band of Sikh holy men and gunmen who were using the most sacred shrine of the Sikh religion, the Golden Temple in Amritsar, as a base for terrorist raids in a violent campaign for greater political autonomy in the strategic Punjab border state. The perceived sacrilege to the Golden Temple kindled outrage among many of India's 14 million Sikhs and brought a spasm of mutinies and desertions by Sikh officers and soldiers in the army.

On Oct. 31, 1984, Indira Gandhi was assassinated by two men identified by police as Sikh members of her bodyguard. The ruling Congress Party chose her older son, Rajiv Gandhi, to succeed her as prime minister for four years. While running for reelection, former prime minister Rajiv Gandhi was assassinated on May 22, 1991, by Tamil militants who objected to India's mediation of the civil war in Sri Lanka.

The ruling Congress Party lost the parliamentary elections of May 1996, and its waning resulted in a period of political instability. The Hindu nationalist Bharatiya Janata Party (BJP) then became the dominant force in politics, with Atal Bihari Vajpayee becoming prime minister twice in two years.

In May 1998, India set off five nuclear tests, surprising the international community, which widely condemned India's pronuclear stance. Despite international urging for restraint, Pakistan responded by conducting several nuclear tests of its own two weeks later. India has resisted signing the Comprehensive Test Ban Treaty for nuclear weapons and has been slapped with sanctions by the U.S. and other countries. Less than a year later, in April 1999, both India and Pakistan tested nuclear-capable ballistic missiles.

India and Pakistan have held various talks about the disputed territory of Kashmir, which is the issue at the base of their chronic antagonism and their displays of nuclear strength. India controls two-thirds of this Himalayan region, which is the only Indian state that is predominantly Muslim.

The Indian Air Force launched air strikes on May 26, 1999, and later sent in ground troops against Islamic guerrilla forces in Kashmir. India blamed Pakistan for orchestrating violence in Kashmir by sending soldiers and mercenaries across the so-called Line of Control that divides Kashmir between India and Pakistan. Pakistan countered that the guerrillas are independent Kashmiri freedom fighters struggling for India's ouster from the region. Most international sources agreed with India's assumption that Pakistan was arming the soldiers. In Aug. 1999, Pakistan was forced to withdraw, but fighting continued sporadically during the coming year.

In Oct. 2001, violence again broke out in the region when a suicide bombing by a Pakistan-based militant organization killed 38 in India-controlled Kashmir. India retaliated with heavy shelling across the Line of Control. India, angered by Washington's sudden coziness to Pakistan following Sept. 11, took the opportunity to point out that while Pakistan might be helping the U.S. fight terrorism on the Afghan front, it was simultaneously supporting terrorism on its own borders with India. On Dec. 13, 2001, suicide bombers attacked the Indian parliament, killing 14 people. Indian officials blamed the deadly attack on Islamic militants supported by Pakistan.

After six months of steadily escalating tensions that brought the two countries to the brink of war—the threat of nuclear confrontation loomed large—India and Pakistan made modest gestures in the summer of 2002 to thwart disaster. More than 1 million troops, however, remained stationed along the Line of Control, and any resolution in the conflict over the disputed territory remained elusive.

Violent clashes between Muslims and Hindus rocked the state of Gujarat in late February and early March 2002 after a Muslim mob fire-bombed a train, killing 58 Hindu activists. Hindus retaliated, and more than 500 people died in the bloodshed.

Hope for a peaceful solution to the conflict in Kashmir was raised Nov. 2002, when a newly elected coalition government in India-controlled Jammu and Kashmir vowed to reach out to separatists and to improve conditions in the state. But hopes were dashed in March 2003, following the slaughter of 24 Hindus in Indian-controlled Kashmir. Officials blamed the massacre on Islamic militants. Days after the violence, both India and Pakistan test-fired short-range missiles capable of carrying nuclear warheads. Violence in Kashmir resumed in June, when 12 Indian soldiers were killed. Two bombs exploded in Bombay in August, killing more than 50 people and injuring about 150. Indian officials blamed Lashkar-e-Taiba, a Pakistan-based militant Islamic group.

Indonesia

REPUBLIC OF INDONESIA

National name: Republik Indonesia
President: Megawati Sukarnoputri (2001)
Area: 741,096 sq mi (1,919,440 sq km)
Population (2003 est.): 234,893,453 (growth rate: 1.5%); birth rate: 21.5/1000; infant mortality rate: 38.1/1000; density per sq mi: 317
Capital and largest city (2003 est.): Jakarta, 17,891,000 (metro. area), 8,827,900 (city proper).
Other large cities: Surabaya, 3,038,800; Bandung, 2,733,500; Medan, 2,204,300; Semarang, 1,267,100.
Monetary unit: Rupiah. **Languages:** Bahasa

Indonesia (official), Dutch, English, and more than 583 languages and dialects. **Ethnicity/race:** Javanese 45%, Sundanese 14%, Madurese 7.5%, coastal Malays 7.5%, other 26%. **Religions:** Islam 88%, Christian 9%, Hindu 2%, other 1%. **Literacy rate:** 83.8% (1995 est.)

Economic summary: GDP/PPP (2001 est.): $687 billion; per capita $3,000. **Real growth rate:** 3.3%. **Inflation:** 11.5%. **Unemployment:** 8%. **Arable land:** 10%. **Agriculture:** rice, cassava (tapioca), peanuts, rubber, cocoa, coffee, palm oil, copra; poultry, beef, pork, eggs. **Labor force:** 99 million (1999); agriculture 45%, industry 16%, services 39% (1999 est.) **Industries:** petroleum and natural gas; textiles, apparel, and footwear; mining, cement, chemical fertilizers, plywood; rubber; food; tourism. **Natural resources:** petroleum, tin, natural gas, nickel, timber, bauxite, copper, fertile soils, coal, gold, silver. **Exports:** $56.5 billion (f.o.b., 2001 est.): oil and gas, electrical appliances, plywood, textiles, rubber. **Imports:** $38.1 billion (f.o.b., 2001 est.): machinery and equipment; chemicals, fuels, foodstuffs. **Major trading partners:** Japan, U.S., Singapore, South Korea, China, Malaysia, Australia.

Geography Indonesia is an archipelago in Southeast Asia consisting of 17,000 islands (6,000 inhabited) and straddling the equator. The largest islands are Sumatra, Java (the most populous), Bali, Kalimantan (Indonesia's part of Borneo), Sulawesi (Celebes), the Nusa Tenggara islands, the Moluccas Islands, and Irian Jaya (also called West Papua), the western part of New Guinea. Its neighbor to the north is Malaysia and to the east is Papua New Guinea.

Indonesia, part of the "ring of fire," has the largest number of active volcanoes in the world. Earthquakes are frequent. The "Wallace Line," a zoological demarcation between Asian and Australian flora and fauna, divides Indonesia.

Government Republic.

History The 17,000 islands that make up Indonesia were home to a diversity of cultures and indigenous beliefs when the islands came under the influence of Hindu priests and traders in the first and second centuries A.D. Muslim invasions began in the 13th century, and most of the archipelago had converted to Islam by the 15th. Portuguese traders arrived early in the next century but were ousted by the Dutch around 1595. The Dutch United East India Company established posts on the island of Java, in an effort to control the spice trade.

After Napoléon subjugated the Netherlands in 1811, the British seized the islands but returned them to the Dutch in 1816. In 1922, Indonesia was made an integral part of the Dutch kingdom. During World War II, Japan seized the islands. Tokyo was primarily interested in Indonesia's oil, which was vital to the war effort, and tolerated fledgling nationalists such as Sukarno and Mohammed Hatta. After Japan's surrender, Sukarno and Hatta proclaimed Indonesian independence on Aug. 17, 1945. Allied troops, mostly British Indian forces, fought nationalist militia to reassert the prewar status quo until the arrival of Dutch troops.

In Nov. 1946, a draft agreement on forming a Netherlands-Indonesian Union was reached, but differences in interpretation resulted in more fighting between Dutch and nationalist forces. Following a bitter war for independence, leaders on both sides agreed to terms of a union on Nov. 2, 1949. The transfer of sovereignty took place in Amsterdam on Dec. 27, 1949. In Feb. 1956, Indonesia abrogated the union, and began seizing Dutch property in the islands.

In 1963, Netherlands New Guinea (the Dutch portion of the island of New Guinea) was transferred to Indonesia and renamed West Irian, which became Irian Jaya in 1973 and West Papua in 2000. Hatta and Sukarno, the cofathers of Indonesian independence, split over Sukarno's concept of "guided democracy," and under Sukarno's rule the Indonesian Communist Party (PKI) steadily increased its influence.

Three years later, Sukarno was named president for life. Sukarno enjoyed mass support for his policies, but a growing power struggle between the military and the PKI loomed over his government. After an attempted military coup was put down by army chief of staff General Suharto and officers loyal to him, Suharto's forces killed hundreds of thousands of suspected Communists in a massive purge aimed at undermining Sukarno's rule.

Suharto took over the reins of government and gradually eased Sukarno out of office, completing his consolidation of power in 1967. Under Suharto the military assumed an overarching role in national affairs, and relations with the West were enhanced. Indonesia's economy improved dramatically and national elections were permitted, although the opposition was so tightly controlled as to virtually choke off dissent.

In 1975, Indonesia invaded the former Portuguese half of the island of Timor and seized the territory in 1976. A separatist movement developed at once. Unlike the rest of Indonesia, which had been a Dutch colony, East Timor was governed by the Portuguese for 400 years, and while 90% of Indonesians are Muslim, the East Timorese are primarily Catholic. More than 200,000 Timorese are reported to have died from famine, disease, and fighting since the annexation. In 1996, two East Timorese resistance activists, Bishop Carlos Filipe Ximenes Belo and José Ramos-Horta, received the Nobel Peace Prize.

In the summer of 1997, Indonesia suffered a major economic setback along with most other Asian economies. Banks failed and the value of Indonesia's currency, the rupiah, plummeted. Antigovernment demonstrations and riots broke out, directed mainly at the country's prosperous ethnic Chinese. As the economic crisis deepened, student demonstrators occupied the national Parliament, demanding Suharto's ouster. On May 21, 1998, Suharto stepped down, ending 32 years of rule, and handed over power to Vice President B. J. Habibie.

June 7, 1999, marked Indonesia's first free parliamentary election since 1955. The ruling Golkar Party took a backseat to the Indonesian Democratic Party-Struggle (PDI-P), led by Megawati Sukarnoputri, the daughter of Sukarno, Indonesia's first president.

The ethnic, religious, and political tensions kept in check during former President Suharto's 32 years of authoritarian rule ruptured in the months following his downfall. Rioting and violence shook the provinces of Aceh, Ambon (in the Moluccas), Borneo, and Irian Jaya. But nowhere was the violence more brutal and unjust than in East Timor. Habibie unexpectedly ended 25 years of Indonesian intransigence by announcing in Feb. 1999 that he was willing to hold a referendum on East Timorese independence. Twice rescheduled because of violence, a UN-organized referendum took place on Aug. 30, 1999, with 78.5% of the population voting to secede from Indonesia. In the days following the election, pro-Indonesian militias and Indonesian soldiers massacred civilians and forced a third of the population out of the region. After enormous international pressure, the government, which was either unwilling or unable to stop the violent rampage, finally agreed to allow UN forces into East Timor on Sept. 12, 1999. East Timor finally achieved independence on May 20, 2002.

In a surprising upset, the Indonesian parliament elected Abdurrahman Wahid as the new president of Indonesia on Oct. 20, 1999, defeating Megawati Sukarnoputri, the popular leader of the Indonesian Democratic Party-Struggle. Wahid was a Sufi cleric as well as an adept politician with a reputation for honesty and moderation.

The northern Sumatran province of Aceh, a devoutly Muslim province of 4.5 million people, became the next troubled region of Indonesia, with Aceh separatists stepping up protests and demands for independence. Wahid proposed a referendum on permitting Islamic law in Aceh, but staunchly refused to discuss independence for the oil-rich province.

Rioting, bombing, and growing unrest continued to plague Indonesia in 2000. On June 4, 2000, separatists declared Irian Jaya (also called West Papua) an independent state. Wahid flatly opposed independence for the province, which contains sizable copper and gold mines. Unlike East Timor, there is little international support for an independent Irian Jaya.

In fall 2000, Suharto failed twice to show up in court to face corruption charges of embezzling $570 million in state funds, but his lawyers insisted he was too ill to stand trial.

In the fall of 2000 and winter of 2001, President Wahid came under increasing criticism for corruption and incompetence. He was blamed for not stopping the continuing ethnic clashes and loss of life in Aceh, Irian Jaya, the Moluccas Islands, and especially in Borneo, where the Dayak people turned against Madurese immigrants, slaughtering hundreds. Wahid was forced from power in July 2001, and Vice President Megawati Sukarnoputri assumed the helm. Popular among the poor, Megawati's retiring nature and lack of political experience led some to question her abilities to govern this fledgling democracy beleaguered by separatist movements and continuous violence.

A terrorist bombing on Oct. 12, 2002, at a night club in Bali killed more than 200 people, mostly tourists. In Aug.–Sept. 2003, Amrozi bin Nurhasyim and Imam Samudra, members of Jemaah Islamiyah, an Islamic terrorist group linked with al-Qaeda, were sentenced to death for their roles in the bombing. But the radical Muslim cleric Abu Bakar Bashir, believed to be the head of Jemaah Islamiyah, was only given a light four-year sentence on lesser charges, causing parts of the international community to question Indonesia's commitment to fighting terrorism.

In May 2003, President Megawati declared military rule in Aceh and launched an offensive intended to destroy the Free Aceh Movement. The invasion marked the end of a cease-fire that was signed in Dec. 2002 between the Indonesian government and Aceh separatists. Some 12,000 have been killed in the conflict since 1976.

A car bomb exploded at Jakarta's Marriott Hotel in Aug. 2003, killing at least 16 people and injuring more than 150. Officials blamed Jemaah Islamiyah.

Iran

ISLAMIC REPUBLIC OF IRAN

Chief of State: Ayatollah Khamenei (1989)
President: Mohammad Khatami (1997)
Area: 636,293 sq mi (1,648,000 sq km)
Population (2003 est.): 68,278,826 (growth rate: 1.2%); birth rate: 17.2/1000; infant mortality rate: 44.2/1000; density per sq mi: 107
Capital and largest city (2003 est.): Teheran, 11,224,800 (metro. area), 7,893,700 (city proper). **Other large cities:** Mashad, 2,061,100; Isfahan, 1,378,600; Tabriz, 1,213,400. **Monetary unit:** Rial. **Languages:** Farsi (Persian), Azari, Kurdish, Arabic. **Ethnicity/race:** Persian 51%, Azerbaijani 24%, Gilaki and Mazandarani 8%, Kurd 7%, Arab 3%, Lur 2%, Baloch 2%, Turkmen 2%, other 1%. **Religions:** Shi'ite Muslim 89%, Sunni Muslim 10%. **Literacy rate:** 72.1% (1994 est.)
Economic summary: GDP/PPP (2001 est.): $426 billion; per capita $6,400. **Real growth rate:** 5%. **Inflation:** 13%. **Unemployment:** 14% (1999 est.). **Arable land:** 10%. **Agriculture:** wheat, rice, other grains, sugar beets, fruits, nuts, cotton; dairy products, wool; caviar. **Labor force:** 18 million; note: shortage of skilled labor (1998); agriculture 30%, industry 25%, services 45% (2001 est.). **Industries:** petroleum, petrochemicals, textiles, cement and other construction materials, food processing (particularly sugar refining and vegetable oil production), metal fabricating, armaments. **Natural resources:** petroleum, natural gas, coal, chromium, copper, iron ore, lead, manganese, zinc, sulfur. **Exports:** $27.4 billion (f.o.b., 2001 est.): petroleum 85%, carpets, fruits and nuts, iron and steel, chemicals. **Imports:** $17.2 billion (f.o.b., 2001 est.): industrial raw materials and intermediate goods, capital goods, foodstuffs and other consumer goods, technical services, military supplies. **Major trading partners:** Japan, Italy, UAE, France, China, Germany.

Geography Iran, a Middle Eastern country south of the Caspian Sea and north of the Persian Gulf, is three times the size of Arizona. It shares borders with Iraq, Turkey, Azerbaijan, Turkmenistan, Armenia, Afghanistan, and Pakistan.

The Elburz Mountains in the north rise to 18,603 ft (5,670 m) at Mount Damavend. From northwest to southeast, the country is crossed by a desert 800 mi (1,287 km) long.

Government Iran has been an Islamic theocracy since the Pahlavi monarchy regime was overthrown on Feb. 11, 1979.

History The region now called Iran was occupied by the Medes and the Persians in the 1500s B.C., until the Persian king Cyrus the Great overthrew the Medes and became ruler of the Achaemenid (Persian) Empire, which reached from the Indus to the Nile at its zenith in 525 B.C. Persia fell to Alexander in 331–330 B.C., and a succession of other rulers: the Seleucids (312–302 B.C.), the Greek-speaking Parthians (247 B.C.–A.D. 226), the Sasanians, and the Arab Muslims (in 641). By the mid-800s Persia had become an international scientific and cultural center. In the 12th century it was invaded by the Mongols. The Safavid dynasty (1501–1722), under whom the dominant religion became Shi'ite Islam, followed, and was then replaced by the Qajar dynasty (1794–1925).

During the Qajar dynasty, the Russians and the British fought for economic control of the area, and during World War I, Iran's neutrality did not stop it from becoming a battlefield for Russian and British troops. A coup in 1921 brought Reza Kahn to power. In 1925, he became shah and changed his name to Reza Shah Pahlavi. He subsequently did much to modernize the country and abolished all foreign extraterritorial rights.

The country's pro-Axis allegiance in World War II led to Anglo-Russian occupation of Iran in 1941 and deposition of the shah in favor of his son, Mohammed Reza Pahlavi. Pahlavi's Westernization programs alienated the clergy, and his authoritarian rule led to massive demonstrations during the 1970s, to which the shah responded with the imposition of martial law in Sept. 1978. The shah and his family fled Iran on Jan. 16, 1979, and the exiled cleric Ayatollah Ruhollah Khomeini returned to establish an Islamic theocracy. Khomeini proceeded with his plans for revitalizing Islamic traditions. He urged women to return to the veil; banned alcohol, Western music, and mixed bathing; shut down the media; closed universities, and eliminated political parties.

Revolutionary militants invaded the U.S. embassy in Teheran on Nov. 4, 1979, seized staff members as hostages, and precipitated an international crisis. Khomeini refused all appeals, even a unanimous vote by the UN Security Council demanding immediate release of the hostages. Iranian hostility toward Washington was reinforced by the Carter administration's economic boycott and deportation order against Iranian students in the U.S., the break in diplomatic relations, and ultimately an aborted U.S. raid in April aimed at rescuing the hostages.

As the first anniversary of the embassy seizure neared, Khomeini and his followers insisted on their original conditions: guarantee by the U.S. not to interfere in Iran's affairs, cancellation of U.S. damage claims against Iran, release of $8 billion in frozen Iranian assets, an apology, and the return of the assets held by the former imperial family. These conditions were largely met and the 52 American hostages were released on Jan. 20, 1980, ending 444 days in captivity.

The sporadic war with Iraq regained momentum in 1982, as Iran launched an offensive in March and regained much of the border area occupied by Iraq in late 1980. The stalemated war with Iraq dragged on well into 1988. Although Iraq expressed its willingness to cease fighting, Iran stated that it would not stop the war until Iraq agreed to pay for war damages and to punish the Iraqi government leaders involved in the conflict. On July 20, 1988, Khomeini, after a series of Iranian military reverses, agreed to cease-fire negotiations with Iraq. A cease-fire went into effect on Aug. 20, 1988. Khomeini died in June 1989 and Ayatollah Khamenei succeeded him as the supreme leader.

By early 1991 the Islamic revolution appeared to have lost much of its militancy. Attempting to revive a stagnant economy, President Rafsanjani took measures to decentralize the command system and introduce free-market mechanisms.

Mohammad Khatami, a little-known moderate cleric, former newspaperman, and national librarian, won the presidential election with 70% of the vote on May 23, 1997, a stunning victory over the conservative ruling elite. Khatami has supported greater social and political freedoms, and has made overtures for friendlier relations with the West. But his steps toward liberalizing the strict clerical rule governing the country have put him at odds with the supreme leader, Ayatollah Khamenei.

Signaling a seismic change in Iran's political environment, reform candidates won the overwhelming majority of seats in Feb. 2000 parliamentary elections, thereby wresting control from hard-liners, who had dominated the Parliament since the 1979 Islamic revolution. The Parliament's reformist transformation greatly buttressed the efforts of Khatami in constructing a nation of "lasting pluralism and Islamic democracy." Khatami has walked a jittery tightrope between student groups and other liberals pressuring him to introduce bolder freedoms, and Iran's military and conservative clerical elite (including Iran's supreme leader, Ayatollah Khamenei), who have expressed growing impatience with the president's liberalizing measures.

In June 2001 elections, Mohammad Khatami demonstrated the overwhelming popularity of his reforms by winning reelection with 77% of the vote. Khatami's new cabinet, composed of 20 moderates, disappointed liberals who hoped he would step up the pace of reform. Friction between Iran's reformers and conservatives increased in 2002.

Iran cooperated in the fight against global terrorism after the Sept. 11 bombings, capturing and turning over al-Qaeda suspects and assisting its war-torn neighbor Afghanistan in restoring peace. Yet U.S. President Bush, who announced in Jan. 2002 that Iran was part of an "axis of evil," has discounted Iran's efforts. After the U.S.-led war in Iraq, the Bush administration aggressively accused Iran of pursuing an illegal nuclear program and harboring suspected al-Qaeda terrorists, fanning Iran's suspicions that the U.S. may be targeting it for an attack in the future. In June 2003, the International Atomic Energy Agency (IAEA) criticized Iran's concealment of much of its nuclear facilities and called on the country to permit more rigorous inspections of its nuclear sites. Iran has denied using its civilian nuclear resources to develop nuclear weapons, but much of the international community has serious doubts. In Aug. 2003, the IAEA found traces of highly enriched uranium in a nuclear facility; in face of this evidence, Iran is under intense pressure to cooperate more fully with the IAEA.

Iraq

REPUBLIC OF IRAQ

National name: Jumhouriyat Al Iraq
President: none—country under U.S. control
Area: 168,753 sq mi (437,072 sq km)
Population (2003 est.): 24,683,313 (growth rate: 2.8%); birth rate: 33.7/1000; infant mortality rate: 55.2/1000; density per sq mi: 146
Capital and largest city (2003 est.): Baghdad, 6,777,300 (metro. area), 5,772,000 (city proper). **Largest cities:** Mosul, 1,791,600; Basra, 1,377,000; Irbil, 864,900; Karkuk (Kirkuk), 755,700. **Monetary unit:** U.S. dollar . **Languages:** Arabic (official) and Kurdish. **Ethnicity/race:** Arab 75%–80%, Kurdish 15%–20%, Turkoman, Assyrian, or other 5%. **Religions:** Islam 97% (Shi'ite 60%–65%, Sunni 32%–37%), Christian or other 3%. **Literacy rate:** 58% (1995 est.)
Economic summary: GDP/PPP (2001 est.): $59 billion; per capita $2,500. **Real growth rate:** –5.7%. **Inflation:** 60%. **Unemployment:** n.a. **Arable land:** 12%. **Agriculture:** wheat, barley, rice, vegetables, dates, cotton; cattle, sheep. **Labor force:** 4.4 million (1989); agriculture n.a., industry n.a., services n.a. **Industries:** petroleum, chemicals, textiles, construction materials, food processing. **Natural resources:** petroleum, natural gas, phosphates, sulfur. **Exports:** $15.8 billion (f.o.b., 2001 est.): crude oil. **Imports:** $11 billion (f.o.b., 2001 est.): food, medicine, manufactures. **Major trading partners:** U.S., Italy, France, Spain, Australia, China, Russia (2000).

Geography Iraq, a triangle of mountains, desert, and fertile river valley, is bounded on the east by Iran, on the north by Turkey, on the west by Syria and Jordan, and on the south by Saudi Arabia and Kuwait. It is twice the size of Idaho. The country has arid desert land west of the Euphrates, a broad central valley between the Euphrates and Tigris, and mountains in the northeast.

Government The government of Saddam Hussein collapsed on April 9 after U.S. and British forces invaded the country. American diplomat Paul Bremer serves as the civil administrator of the country. An Iraqi interim governing council with limited powers was inaugurated in July. Twenty-five Iraqis, representative of Iraq's various ethnic and religious groups, sit on the council. The presidency will rotate alphabetically among nine of the members, changing each month.

History From earliest times Iraq was known as Mesopotamia—the land between the rivers—for it embraces a large part of the alluvial plains of the Tigris and Euphrates Rivers.

An advanced civilization existed by 4000 B.C. Sometime after 2000 B.C. the land became the center of the ancient Babylonian and Assyrian Empires. Mesopotamia was conquered by Cyrus the Great of Persia in 538 B.C., and by Alexander in 331 B.C. After an Arab conquest in 637–640, Baghdad became capital of the ruling caliphate. The country was cruelly pillaged by the Mongols in 1258, and during the 16th, 17th, and 18th centuries was the object of repeated Turkish-Persian competition.

Nominal Turkish suzerainty imposed in 1638 was replaced by direct Turkish rule in 1831. In World War I, Britain occupied most of Mesopotamia and was given a mandate over the area in 1920. The British renamed the area Iraq and recognized it as a kingdom in 1922. In 1932, the monarchy achieved full independence. Britain again occupied Iraq during World War II because of its pro-Axis stance in the initial years of the war.

Iraq became a charter member of the Arab League in 1945, and Iraqi troops took part in the Arab invasion of Palestine in 1948.

At age 3, King Faisal II succeeded his father, Ghazi I, who was killed in an automobile accident in 1939. Faisal and his uncle, Crown Prince Abdul-Illah, were assassinated in July 1958 in a swift revolutionary coup that ended the monarchy and brought to power a military junta headed by Abdul Karem Kassim. Kassim reversed the monarchy's pro-Western policies, attempted to rectify the economic disparities between rich and poor, and began to form alliances with Communist countries.

Kassim was overthrown and killed in a coup staged on March 8, 1963, by the military and the Ba'ath Socialist Party. The Ba'ath Party advocated secularism, pan-Arabism, and socialism. The following year, the new leader, Abdel Salam Arif, consolidated his power by driving out the Ba'ath Party. He adopted a new constitution in 1964. In 1966, he died in a helicopter crash. His brother, Gen. Abdel Rahman Arif, assumed the presidency, crushed the opposition, and won an indefinite extension of his term in 1967.

Arif's regime was ousted in July 1968 by a junta led by Maj. Gen. Ahmed Hassan al-Bakr of the Ba'ath Party. Bakr and his second-in-command, Saddam Hussein, imposed authoritarian rule in an effort to end the decades of political instability that followed World War II. One of the world's leading producers of oil, Iraq's oil revenues were used to develop one of the strongest military forces in the region.

On July 16, 1979, President Bakr was succeeded by Saddam Hussein, whose regime steadily developed an international reputation for repression, human rights abuses, and terrorism.

A long-standing territorial dispute over control of the Shatt-al-Arab waterway between Iraq and Iran broke into full-scale war on Sept. 20, 1980, when Iraq invaded western Iran. The eight-year war cost the lives of an estimated 1.5 million people, and finally ended in a UN-brokered ceasefire in 1988. Poison gas was used by both Iran and Iraq.

In July 1990, President Hussein asserted spurious territorial claims on Kuwaiti land. A mediation attempt by Arab leaders failed, and on Aug. 2, 1990, Iraqi troops invaded Kuwait and set up a puppet government. The UN unsuccessfully imposed trade sanctions against Iraq to pressure it to withdraw. On Jan. 18, 1991, UN forces, under the leadership of U.S. general Norman Schwarzkopf, launched Gulf War (Operation Desert Storm), liberating Kuwait in less than a week.

The war did little to dwarf Iraq's resilient dictator. Rebellions by both Shi'ites and Kurds, encouraged by the U.S., were brutally crushed. In 1991, the UN set up a northern no-fly zone to protect Iraq's Kurdish population; in 1992 a southern no-fly zone was established as a buffer between Iraq and Kuwait and to protect Shi'ites.

The UN Security Council imposed sanctions beginning in 1990, which barred Iraq from selling oil except in exchange for food and medicine. The sanctions against Iraq have failed to crush its leader but have caused catastrophic suffering among its people—the country's infrastructure is in ruins, and disease, malnutrition, and the infant mortality rate have skyrocketed.

The UN weapons inspections team mandated to ascertain that Iraq had destroyed all its nuclear, chemical, biological, and ballistic arms after the war was continually thwarted by Saddam Hussein. In Nov. 1997, he expelled the American members of the UN inspections team, a standoff that stretched on until Feb. 1998. But in Aug. 1998, Hussein again put a halt to the inspections. On Dec. 16, the United States and Britain began Operation Desert Fox, four days of intensive air strikes. From then on, the U.S. and Britain conducted hundreds of air strikes on Iraqi targets within the no-fly zones. The sustained, low-level warfare continued unabated into 2003.

After the Sept. 11, 2001, terrorist attacks, President Bush began calling for a "regime change" in Iraq, describing the nation as part of an "axis of evil." The alleged existence of weapons of mass destruction, the thwarting of UN weapons inspections, Iraq's links to terrorism, and Saddam Hussein's despotism and human rights abuses were the major reasons cited for necessitating a preemptive strike against the country. Foreign and domestic critics expressed skepticism about the Bush administration's allegations and whether military means were the only way to resolve them. The Bush administration also presented action against Iraq as part of the U.S. war on terrorism, but it repeatedly failed to conclusively link Iraq to al-Qaeda. Critics warned that a focus on Iraq would deflect attention away from the real threat of terrorism and thwart the chance for a resolution in the Israeli-Palestinian conflict. The Arab world and much of Europe condemned the hawkish and unilateral U.S. stance. Only the UK declared its intention to support the U.S. in military action. In response to the mounting U.S. threats, Hussein continued to refuse UN weapons inspections and engaged in his characteristic defiant bluster. On Sept. 12, 2002, Bush addressed the UN, challenging the organization to swiftly enforce its own resolutions against Iraq, or else the U.S. would have no choice but to act on its own. On Nov. 8, the UN Security Council unanimously approved a resolution imposing tough new arms inspections on Iraq. On Nov. 26, new inspections of Iraq's military holdings began.

The UN's formal report at the end of Jan. 2003 was not promising, with chief weapons inspector Hans Blix lamenting that "Iraq appears not to have come to a genuine acceptance, not even today, of the disarmament that was demanded of it." While the Bush administration felt the report cemented its claim that a military solution was imperative, several permanent members of the UN Security Council did not find it conclusive: France, Russia, and China urged that the UN inspectors be given more time to complete its task. U.S. diplomatic relations with France and Germany—both highly critical of what they saw as Bush's rush to war before exhausting the alternatives of inspections and containment—were severely strained.

The U.S. began sending troops to the region in early 2003; by March, about 225,000 soldiers were deployed. Britain also sent about 45,000 troops. In a February UN report, Blix indicated that modest progress had been made in Iraq's cooperation. Both pro- and anti-war nations felt the report supported their point of view. Massive, worldwide anti-war demonstrations took place on Feb. 15.

On Feb. 24, the U.S. introduced a draft resolution to the UN proposing an ultimatum to Iraq, one authorizing military action unless Iraq demonstrated by March 17 that it had disarmed. France and Russia, permanent members of the Security Council with veto power, made it clear that they would not support the resolution. The U.S. and Britain's intense lobbying efforts among the other UN Security Council members yielded only two other supporters, Spain and Bulgaria. George W. Bush, backed by Britain's Tony Blair (who faced increasing pressure from his Labor Party to avoid military action without UN approval), continued to call for war, insisting that they would go ahead with a "coalition of the willing" if not with UN support. All diplomatic efforts ceased by March 17, when President Bush delivered an ultimatum to Saddam Hussein to leave the country within 48 hours or else face an attack.

On March 20, the war against Iraq began with the launch of Operation Iraqi Freedom. In the coming days, the U.S. and Britain met greater-than-expected resistance as they attempted to march on Baghdad. But by April 9, U.S. forces took control of Baghdad, signalling the collapse of Saddam Hussein's regime. On April 14, after taking control of the city of Tikrit, the Pentagon declared that the major fighting of the war was over. Saddam Hussein's whereabouts remained unknown.

Post-war reconstruction went far less smoothly than the war itself. The country was enveloped in violence and chaos, and coalition forces continued to meet Iraqi resistance and fighting. Many essential services, such as electricity and water, have yet to be restored. Within the first month following the war, the U.S. sacked its civil administrator, Gen. Jay Garner, because of his inability to curb the country's lawlessness, and replaced him with a diplomat, Paul Bremer. Iraqis have strongly protested against the delay in self-rule and the absence of a timetable to end the U.S. occupation. In May, the UN Security Council approved a resolution lifting the economic sanctions against Iraq and supporting the U.S.-led administration in Iraq. In July, Bremer appointed an Iraqi governing council, a first step in turning over power to the Iraqis, though the council has limited power. On Sept. 1, the Iraq Governing Council appointed a 25-member cabinet to begin running the government, a significant step in transferring authority to Iraqis.

Months of searching for Iraq's weapons of mass destruction—one of the prime reasons the Bush and Blair administrations cited for launching to war—yielded no hard evidence, and both administrations and their intelligence agencies came under fire. There were also mounting allegations that the existence of these weapons was exaggerated or distorted as a pretext to justify the war.

Organized guerrilla attacks by forces loyal to Saddam Hussein continued on a daily basis. The U.S. launched several tough military campaigns to subdue the remaining Iraqi resistance, which also had the effect of further alienating the populace. The Pentagon has estimated that the war costs $4 billion a month. 140,000 American and 11,000 British troops remain in Iraq, as well as about 10,000 coalition troops. Given Iraq's continued instability and the small, but steady number of American casualties (by August, more soldiers had died in the aftermath of the war than during the official period of combat), some lawmakers on both sides of the aisle have questioned whether more troops should be deployed. Guerrilla attacks increased in late summer. Several oil pipelines were sabotaged; on Aug. 7 the Jordanian embassy was bombed; and on Aug. 19 a suicide bombing destroyed UN headquarters in Baghdad, killing top UN envoy Sérgio Vieira de Mello and 22 others. Just ten days later, on Aug. 29, a car bomb at a holy shrine in Najaf killed one of Iraq's most important Shi'ite leaders, Ayatollah Muhammad Bakr al-Hakim, as well as about 80 others, and wounded 125. An attempted assassination of a member of the Iraqi governing council narrowly failed in September. It is unclear who was responsible for these guerrilla-style attacks.

In September, President Bush announced he would ask Congress for $87 billion in additional military and construction spending for Iraq. He also recast the rationale for war, no longer citing the danger of weapons of mass destruction, but instead describing Iraq as "the central front" in the war against terrorism—a free and democratic Iraq would serve as a model for the rest of the Middle East. In a cooly received speech at the UN in September, Bush asked the international community to provide more troops and money for Iraq, but made it clear that decision-making would remain with the U.S.

Ireland

National name: Ireland, or Eire in the Irish language
President: Mary McAleese (1997)
Taoiseach (Prime Minister): Bertie Ahern (1997)
Area: 27,135 sq mi (70,280 sq km)
Population (2003 est.): 3,924,140 (growth rate: 0.7%); birth rate: 14.6/1000; infant mortality rate: 5.3/1000; density per sq mi: 145
Capital (2003 est.): Dublin, 1,018,500. **Other large cities:**Cork, 193,400; Limerick, 84,900; Galway, 67,200. **Monetary units:** Euro (formerly Irish pound [punt]). **Languages:** English, Irish Gaelic. **Ethnicity/race:** Celtic, English. **Religions:** Roman Catholic 91.6%, Anglican 2.5%, other 5.9%. **Literacy rate:** 98% (1981 est.)
Economic summary: GDP/PPP (2001 est.): $104.7 billion; per capita $27,300. **Real growth rate:** 5.6%. **Inflation:** 4.9%. **Unemployment:** 4.3%. **Arable land:** 20%. **Agriculture:** turnips, barley, potatoes, sugar beets, wheat; beef, dairy products. **Labor force:** 1.8 million (2001); services 64%, industry 28%, agriculture 8% (2000 est.). **Industries:** food products, brewing, textiles, clothing; chemicals, pharmaceuticals, machinery, transportation equipment, glass and crystal; software. **Natural resources:** zinc, lead, natural gas, barite, copper, gypsum, limestone, dolomite, peat, silver. **Exports:** $75.9 billion (f.o.b., 2001): machinery and equipment, computers, chemicals, pharmaceuticals; live animals, animal products. **Imports:** $49.5 billion (f.o.b., 2001): data processing equipment, other machinery and equipment, chemicals; petroleum and petroleum products, textiles, clothing. **Major trading partners:** EU, U.S., Japan.

Geography Ireland is situated in the Atlantic Ocean and separated from Great Britain by the Irish Sea. Half the size of Arkansas, it occupies the entire island except for the six counties that make up Northern Ireland. Ireland resembles a basin—a central plain rimmed with mountains, except in the Dublin region. The mountains are low, with the highest peak, Carrantuohill in County Kerry, rising to 3,415 ft (1,041 m). The principal river is the Shannon, which begins in the north-central area, flows south and southwest for about 240 mi (386 km), and empties into the Atlantic.

Government Republic.

History In the Stone and Bronze Ages, Ireland was inhabited by Picts in the north and a people called the Erainn in the south, the same stock, apparently, as in all the isles before the Anglo-Saxon invasion of Britain. About the 4th century B.C., tall, red-haired Celts arrived from Gaul or Galicia. They subdued and assimilated the inhabitants and established a Gaelic civilization. By the beginning of the Christian Era, Ireland was divided into five kingdoms—Ulster, Connacht, Leinster, Meath, and Munster. Saint Patrick introduced Christianity in 432, and the country developed into a center of Gaelic and Latin learning. Irish monasteries, the equivalent of universities, attracted intellectuals as well as the pious and sent out missionaries to many parts of Europe and, some believe, to North America.

Norse depredations along the coasts, starting in 795, ended in 1014 with Norse defeat at the Battle of Clontarf by forces under Brian Boru. In the 12th century, the pope gave all of Ireland to the English Crown as a papal fief. In 1171, Henry II of England was acknowledged "Lord of Ireland," but local sectional rule continued for centuries, and English control over the whole island was not reasonably absolute until the 17th century. In the Battle of the Boyne (1690), the Catholic King James II and his French supporters were defeated by the Protestant King William III (of Orange). An era of Protestant political and economic supremacy began.

By the Act of Union (1801), Great Britain and Ireland became the "United Kingdom of Great Britain and Ireland." A steady decline in the Irish economy followed in the next decades. The population had reached 8.25 million when the great potato famine of 1846–1848 took many lives and drove more than 2 million people to immigrate to North America.

In the meantime, anti-British agitation continued along with demands for Irish home rule. The advent of World War I delayed the institution of home rule and resulted in the Easter Rebellion in Dublin (April 24–29, 1916), in which Irish nationalists unsuccessfully attempted to throw off British rule. Guerrilla warfare against British forces followed proclamation of a republic by the rebels in 1919. The Irish Free State was established as a dominion on Dec. 6, 1922, with six northern counties remaining as part of the United Kingdom. A civil war ensued between those supporting the Anglo-Irish Treaty that established the Irish Free State and those repudiating it because it led to the partitioning of the island. The Irish Republican Army (IRA), led by Eamon de Valera, fought against the partition but lost. De Valera joined the government in 1927 and became prime minister in 1932. In 1937 a new constitution changed the nation's name to Éire. Ireland remained neutral in World War II.

In 1948, De Valera was defeated by John A. Costello, who demanded final independence from Britain. The Republic of Ireland was proclaimed on April 18, 1949, and withdrew from the Commonwealth. From the 1960s onwards, two antagonistic currents dominated Irish politics. One sought to bind the wounds of the rebellion and civil war. The other was the effort of the outlawed Irish Republican Army and more moderate groups to bring Northern Ireland into the republic. The "troubles"—the violence and terrorist acts between Republicans and Unionists in both the Republic of Ireland and Northern Ireland—would plague the island for the remainder of the century.

Under the First Programme for Economic Expansion (1958–1963), economic protection was dismantled and foreign investment encouraged. This prosperity brought profound social and cultural changes to what had been one of the poorest and least technologically advanced countries in Europe. Ireland joined the European Economic Community (now the EU) in 1973. In the 1990 presidential election, Mary Robinson was elected the republic's first woman president. The election of a candidate with socialist and feminist sympathies was regarded as a watershed in Irish political life, reflecting the changes taking place in Irish society. Irish voters approved the Maastricht Treaty, which paved the way for the establishment of the EU, by a large majority in a referendum held in 1992. In 1993, the Irish and British governments signed a joint peace initiative (the Downing Street Declaration), in which they pledged to seek mutually agreeable political structures in Northern Ireland and between the two islands. A referendum on allowing divorce under certain conditions—hitherto constitutionally forbidden—was narrowly passed in Nov. 1995.

In 1998 hope for a solution to the troubles in Northern Ireland seemed palpable. A landmark settlement, the Good Friday Agreement of April 10, 1998, called for Protestants to share political power with the minority Catholics, and gave the Republic of Ireland a voice in Northern Irish affairs. The resounding commitment to the settlement was demonstrated in a dual referendum on May 22: the North approved the accord by a vote of 71% to 29%, and in the Irish Republic 94% favored it. After numerous stops and starts, the new government in Northern Ireland was formed on Dec. 2, 2000, but it has been suspended several times since then because of Sinn Fein's (which holds two seats in the parliament) refusal to disarm, a key stipulation of the Good Friday Accord. Ireland has continued to call for Sinn Fein to comply.

In June 2001, Ireland voted against expansion of the EU to include other countries, which came as a shock to the 14 other EU members. To the relief of the EU, in Oct. 2002 Ireland endorsed the expansion (the Nice Treaty).

Despite a number of recent corruption and bribery scandals, most of which involved the centrist Fianna Fáil party of Prime Minister Bertie Ahern, the party won 81 of 166 seats in May 2002. Ahern became the first Irish prime minister in 33 years to be elected to a second successive term.

In Aug. 2003, Michael McKevitt, leader of the Real IRA, was sentenced to 20 years in prison. The Real IRA split from the IRA because it opposed the Northern Irish peace process.

See also Northern Ireland, under United Kingdom.

Israel

STATE OF ISRAEL

National name: Medinat Yisra'el
President: Moshe Katsav (2000)
Prime Minister: Ariel Sharon (2001)
Area: 8,019 sq mi (20,770 sq km)
Population (2003 est.): 6,116,533 (growth rate: 1.3%); birth rate: 18.7/1000; infant mortality rate: 7.4/1000; density per sq mi: 763

Capital and largest city (2003 est.): Jerusalem, 695,500. **Other large cities:** Tel Aviv, 365,300; Haifa, 280,200. **Monetary unit:** Shekel. **Languages:** Hebrew (official), Arabic, English. **Ethnicity/race:** Jewish 80.1% (Europe/Americas/Oceania-born 32.1%, Israel-born 20.8%, Africa-born 14.6%, Asia-born 12.6%), non-Jewish 19.9% (mostly Arab) (1996 est.). **Religions:** Judaism 80.1%, Islam 14.6%, Christian 2.1%, others 3.2%. **Literacy rate:** 95% (1992 est.)

Economic summary: GDP/PPP (2001 est.): $119 billion; per capita $20,000. **Real growth rate:** –0.6%. **Inflation:** 1.1%. **Unemployment:** 9%. **Arable land:** 17%. **Agriculture:** citrus, vegetables, cotton; beef, poultry, dairy products. **Labor force:** 2.4 million (2000 est.); public services 31.2%, manufacturing 20.2%, finance and business 13.1%, commerce 12.8%, construction 7.5%, personal and other services 6.4%, transport, storage, and communications 6.2%, agriculture, forestry, and fishing 2.6% (1996). **Industries:** high-technology projects (including aviation, communications, computer-aided design and manufactures, medical electronics), wood and paper products, potash and phosphates, food, beverages, and tobacco, caustic soda, cement, diamond cutting. **Natural resources:** timber, potash, copper ore, natural gas, phosphate rock, magnesium bromide, clays, sand. **Exports:** $26.5 billion (f.o.b., 2001 est.): machinery and equipment, software, cut diamonds, agricultural products, chemicals, textiles and apparel. **Imports:** $30.6 billion (f.o.b., 2001 est.): raw materials, military equipment, investment goods, rough diamonds, fuels, consumer goods. **Major trading partners:** U.S., Benelux, Germany, Hong Kong, UK, Netherlands, Switzerland, Italy.

1. Israel proclaimed Jerusalem as its capital in 1950, but the U.S., like nearly all other countries, maintains its embassy in Tel Aviv.

Geography Israel, slightly larger than Massachusetts, lies at the eastern end of the Mediterranean Sea. It is bordered by Egypt on the west, Syria and Jordan on the east, and Lebanon on the north. Its maritime plain is extremely fertile. The southern Negev region, which comprises almost half the total area, is largely a desert. The Jordan, the only important river, flows from the north through Lake Hule (Waters of Merom) and Lake Kinneret (Sea of Galilee or Sea of Tiberias), finally entering the Dead Sea, 1,349 ft (411 m) below sea level—the world's lowest land elevation.

Government Parliamentary democracy.

History Palestine, considered a holy land by Jews, Muslims, and Christians, and homeland of the modern state of Israel, was known as Canaan to the ancient Hebrews. Palestine's name derives from the Philistines, a people who occupied the southern coastal part of the country in the 12th century B.C.

A Hebrew kingdom established in 1000 B.C. was later split into the kingdoms of Judah and Israel; they were subsequently invaded by Assyrians, Babylonians, Egyptians, Persians, Romans, and Alexander the Great of Macedonia. By A.D. 135, few Jews were left in Palestine; most lived in the scattered and tenacious communities of the Diaspora. Palestine became a center of Christian pilgrimage after the emperor Constantine converted to that faith. The Arabs took Palestine from the Byzantine empire in 634–40. Interrupted only by Christian Crusaders, Muslims ruled Palestine until the 20th century. During World War I, British forces defeated the Turks in Palestine and governed the area under a League of Nations mandate from 1923.

As part of the 19th-century Zionist movement, Jews had begun settling in Palestine as early as 1820. This effort to establish a Jewish homeland received British approval in the Balfour Declaration of 1917. During the 1930s, Jews persecuted by the Hitler regime poured into Palestine. The postwar acknowledgment of the Holocaust—Hitler's genocide of 6 million Jews—increased international interest in and sympathy for the cause of Zionism. However, Arabs in Palestine and surrounding countries bitterly opposed prewar and postwar proposals to partition Palestine into Arab and Jewish sectors. The British mandate to govern Palestine ended after the war, and, in 1947, the UN voted to partition Palestine. When the British officially withdrew on May 14, 1948, the Jewish National Council proclaimed the State of Israel.

U.S. recognition came within hours. The next day, Arab forces from Egypt, Jordan, Syria, Lebanon, and Iraq invaded the new nation. By the cease-fire on Jan. 7, 1949, Israel had increased its original territory by 50%, taking western Galilee, a broad corridor through central Palestine to Jerusalem, and part of modern Jerusalem. Chaim Weizmann and David Ben-Gurion became Israel's first president and prime minister. The new government was admitted to the UN on May 11, 1949.

The next clash with Arab neighbors came when Egypt nationalized the Suez Canal in 1956 and barred Israeli shipping. Coordinating with an Anglo-French force, Israeli troops seized the Gaza Strip and drove through the Sinai to the east bank of the Suez Canal, but withdrew under U.S. and UN pressure. In the Six-Day War of 1967, Israel made simultaneous air attacks against Syrian, Jordanian, and Egyptian air bases, totally defeating the Arabs. Expanding its territory by 200%, Israel at the cease-fire held the Golan Heights, the West Bank of the Jordan River, Jerusalem's Old City, and all of the Sinai and the east bank of the Suez Canal.

In the face of Israeli reluctance even to discuss the return of occupied territories, the fourth Arab-Israeli War erupted on Oct. 6, 1973, with a surprise Egyptian and Syrian assault on the Jewish high holy day of Yom Kippur. Initial Arab gains were reversed when a cease-fire took effect two weeks later, but Israel suffered heavy losses.

A dramatic breakthrough in the tortuous history of Mideast peace efforts occurred on Nov. 9, 1977, when Egypt's president Anwar Sadat declared his willingness to talk peace. Prime Minister Menachem Begin, on Nov. 15, extended an invitation to the Egyptian leader to address the Knesset in Jerusalem. Sadat's arrival in Israel four days later raised worldwide hopes, but a peace agreement between Egypt and Israel was long in coming. On March 14, 1979, the Knesset approved a final peace treaty, and 12 days later, Begin and Sadat signed the document, together with President Jimmy Carter, in a White House ceremony. Israel began its withdrawal from the Sinai, which it had annexed from Egypt, on May 25.

Although Israel withdrew its last settlers from the Sinai in April 1982, the fragile Mideast peace was shattered on June 9, 1982, by a massive Israeli assault on southern Lebanon, where the Palestinian Liberation Organization was entrenched. The PLO had long plagued Israelis with terrorist actions. Israel destroyed PLO strongholds in Tyre and Sidon and reached the suburbs of Beirut on June 10. A U.S.-mediated accord between Lebanon and Israel, signed on May 17, 1983, provided for Israeli withdrawal from Lebanon. Israel eventually withdrew its troops from the Beirut area but kept them in southern Lebanon, where occasional skirmishes would continue. Lebanon, under pressure from Syria, canceled the accord in March 1984.

A continual source of tension has been the relationship between the Jews and the Palestinians living within Israeli territories. Most Arabs fled the region when the state of Israel was declared, but those who remain now make up almost one-fifth of the population of Israel. They are about two-thirds Muslim, as well as Christian and Druze. Palestinians living on the West Bank and the Gaza Strip fomented the riots begun in 1987, known as the *intifada*. Violence heightened as Israeli police cracked down and Palestinians retaliated. Continuing Jewish settlement of lands designated for Palestinians has added to the unrest.

In 1989, the leader of the PLO, Yasir Arafat, reversed decades of PLO polemic by acknowledging Israel's right to exist. He stated his willingness to enter negotiations to create a Palestinian political entity that would coexist with the Israeli state.

In 1991, Israel was struck by Iraqi missiles during the Persian Gulf War. The Israelis did not retaliate in order to preserve the international coalition against Iraq. In 1992, Yitzhak Rabin became prime minister. He halted the disputed Israeli settlement of the occupied territories.

Highly secretive talks in Norway resulted in the landmark Oslo Accord between the PLO and the Israeli government in 1993. The accord stipulated a five-year plan in which Palestinians of the West Bank and the Gaza Strip would gradually become self-governing. Arafat became president of the new Palestinian Authority. In 1994, Israel signed a peace treaty with Jordan; Israel still has no formal peace agreement with Syria or Lebanon.

On Nov. 4, 1995, Prime Minister Rabin was slain by a Jewish extremist, jeopardizing the tenuous progress toward peace. Shimon Peres succeeded him until May 1996 elections for the Knesset gave Israel a new hardline prime minister, Benjamin Netanyahu, by a razor-thin margin. Netanyahu reversed or stymied much of the Oslo Agreement, contending that it offered too many concessions too fast and jeopardized Israelis' safety.

Israeli-Palestinian peace negotiations in 1997 were repeatedly undermined by both sides. Although the Hebron Accord was signed in Jan., calling for the withdrawal of Israeli troops from the city, the construction of new Jewish settlements on the West Bank in March profoundly upset progress toward peace.

Terrorism erupted again in 1997 when radical Hamas suicide bombers claimed the lives of more than 20 Israeli civilians. Netanyahu, accusing Palestinian Authority president Arafat of lax security, retaliated with draconian sanctions against Palestinians working in Israel, including the withholding of millions of dollars in tax revenue, a blatant violation of the Oslo Agreement. Netanyahu also persisted in authorizing right-wing Israelis to build new settlements in mostly Arab East Jerusalem. Arafat, meanwhile, seemed unwilling or unable to curb the violence of extremist Arabs.

An Oct. 1998 summit at Wye Mills, Md., generated the first real progress in the stymied Middle East peace talks in 19 months, with Israeli prime minister Benjamin Netanyahu and Palestinian president Yasir Arafat settling several important interim issues called for by the 1993 Oslo Peace Agreement. The peace accord, however, began unraveling almost immediately. By the end of April 1999, Israel had made 41 air raids on Hezbollah guerrillas in Lebanon. The guerrillas were fighting against Israeli troops and their allies, the South Lebanon Army militia, who occupied a security zone set up in 1985 to guard Israel's borders. Public pressure in Israel to withdraw the troops grew.

Labour Party leader Ehud Barak won the 1999 election and announced that he planned not only to pursue peace with the Palestinians, but to establish relations with Syria and end the low-grade war in Southern Lebanon with the Iranian-armed Hezbollah guerrillas. In Dec. 1999, Israeli-Syrian talks resumed after a nearly four-year hiatus. By Jan. 2000, however, talks had broken down when Syria demanded a detailed discussion of the return of all of the Golan Heights. In Feb., new Hezbollah attacks on Israeli troops in southern Lebanon led to Israel's retaliatory bombing as well as Barak's decision to pull out of Lebanon. Israeli troops pulled out of Lebanon on May 24, 2000, after 22 years of occupation.

Peace talks in July 2000 at Camp David between Ehud Barak and Yasir Arafat ended unsuccessfully, despite President Clinton's strongest efforts—the status of Jerusalem was the primary sticking point. In September, Likud leader Ariel Sharon visited the compound called Temple Mount by Jews and Haram al Sharif by Muslims, a fiercely contested site that is sacred to both Jews and Muslims. The visit set off the worst violence in years, killing around 400 people, mostly Palestinians. The violence (dubbed the Al-Aksa intifada) and the stalled peace process fueled growing concerns about Israeli security, paving the way for hard-liner Sharon's stunning landslide victory over Barak in Feb. 2001. Violence on both sides continued at an alarming rate. Palestinians carried out some of the most horrific suicide bombings and terrorist attacks in years (Hamas and the Al-Aksa Martyr Brigade claimed responsibility for the majority of them), killing Israeli civilians in cafés, bus stops, and supermarkets. In retaliation, Israel unleashed bombing raids on Palestinian territory and sent troops and tanks to occupy West Bank and Gaza cities.

In Dec. 2001, Sharon announced that Arafat was "irrelevant," and called for his expulsion from the territories. Israeli troops surrounded him at Palestinian Authority headquarters for the first half of 2002. Under strong U.S. pressure, Arafat eventually appointed a prime minister, Mahmoud Abbas. Well-respected internationally, Abbas had only a small political base among Palestinians. On May 1, a day after Abbas was sworn in as prime minister, the Bush administration unfurled its "road map" for peace in the Middle East, calling on both sides to make concessions and end the wave of deadly violence that had claimed more than 2,400 Palestinians and about 800 Israelis in the previous 33 months. It ultimately envisioned the creation of a Palestinian state by 2005. Sharon publicly acknowledged the need for a Palestinian state and Abbas committed himself to ending terrorism, but the road map led nowhere, with neither side honoring their obligations: Abbas, with little real political power, did not disable terrorist organizations, and Israel did not dismantle settlements, much less prevent new ones from cropping up. Sharon continued to build the controversial security fence/wall—the term itself is contentious—that divides Israeli and Palestinian areas. Three militant Palestinian groups (Hamas, Islamic Jihad, and Fatah) declared a cease-fire on killing Israelis on June 29, but attacks resumed just weeks later. By Aug. 2003, the assassination of senior Hamas leader Abu Shanab by Israel and the suicide bombing of an Israeli bus that killed 20, including 6 children, ended hope for the short-lived road map. As the assassinations and retaliations continued, Mahmoud Abbas resigned out of frustration with the peace process and with continued power wrangling with Arafat. In September, further exacerbating tensions, Israel announced that it was prepared to "remove" Arafat, much to the dismay of the international community.

Italy

ITALIAN REPUBLIC

National name: Repubblica Italiana
President: Carlo Azeglio Ciampi (1999)
Prime Minister: Silvio Berlusconi (2001)
Area: 116,305 sq mi (301,230 sq km)
Population (2003 est.): 57,998,353 (growth rate: –0.1%); birth rate: 9.2/1000; infant mortality rate: 6.2/1000; density per sq mi: 499
Capital and largest city (2003 est.): Rome, 3,550,900 (metro. area), 2,455,600 (city proper). **Other large cities:** Milan, 1,180,700; Naples, 991,700; Turin, 856,000; Palermo, 651,500; Genoa, 602,500; Bologna, 369,300; Florence, 351,600; Bari, 311,900; Catania, 305,900; Venice, 265,700. **Monetary units:** Euro (formerly lira). **Languages:** Italian; small German-, French-, and Slovene-speaking minorities. **Ethnicity/race:** Italian (includes small clusters of German-, French-, and Slovene-Italians in the north and Albanian-Italians and Greek-Italians in the south), Sicilians, Sardinians. **Religions:** Roman Catholic 98%, other 2%. **Literacy rate:** 98% (1998)
Economic summary: GDP/PPP (2001 est.): $1.402 trillion; per capita $24,300. **Real growth rate:** 1.8%. **Inflation:** 2.7%. **Unemployment:** 10%. **Arable land:** 28.%. **Agriculture:** fruits, vegetables, grapes, potatoes, sugar beets, soybeans, grain, olives; beef, dairy products; fish. **Labor force:** 23.6 million; services 63%, industry 32%, agriculture 5%. **Industries:** tourism, machinery, iron and steel, chemicals, food processing, textiles, motor vehicles, clothing, footwear, ceramics. **Natural resources:** mercury, potash, marble, sulfur, natural gas and crude oil reserves, fish, coal, arable land. **Exports:** $243 billion (f.o.b., 2001 est.): engineering products, textiles and clothing, production machinery, motor vehicles, transport equipment, chemicals; food, beverages and tobacco; minerals and nonferrous metals. **Imports:** $226 billion (f.o.b., 2001 est.): engineering products, chemicals, transport equipment, energy products, minerals and nonferrous metals, textiles and clothing; food, beverages and tobacco. **Major trading partners:** EU, U.S.

Geography Italy, slightly larger than Arizona, is a long peninsula shaped like a boot surrounded on the west by the Tyrrhenian Sea and on the east by the Adriatic. It is bounded by France, Switzerland, Austria, and Slovenia to the north. The Apennine Mountains form the peninsula's backbone; the Alps form its northern boundary. The largest of its many northern lakes is Garda (143 sq mi; 370 sq km); the Po, its principal river, flows from the Alps on Italy's western border and crosses the Lombard plain to the Adriatic Sea. Several islands form part of Italy, the largest of which are Sicily (9,926 sq mi; 25,708 sq km) and Sardinia (9,301 sq mi; 24,090 sq km).

Government Republic.

History The migrations of Indo-European peoples into Italy probably began about 2000 B.C. and continued down to 1000 B.C. From about the 9th century B.C. until it was overthrown by the Romans in the 3rd century B.C., the Etruscan civilization dominated the area. By 264 B.C. all Italy south of Cisalpine Gaul was under the leadership of Rome. For the next seven centuries, until the barbarian invasions destroyed the western Roman Empire in the 4th and 5th centuries A.D., the history of Italy is largely the history of Rome. From 800 on, the Holy Roman Emperors, Roman Catholic popes, Normans, and Saracens all vied for control over various segments of the Italian peninsula. Numerous city-states, such as Venice and Genoa, whose political and commercial rivalries were intense, and many small principalities flourished in the late Middle Ages. Although Italy remained politically fragmented for centuries, it became the cultural center of the Western world from the 13th to the 16th century.

In 1713, after the War of the Spanish Succession, Milan, Naples, and Sardinia were handed over to the Hapsburgs of Austria, which lost some of its Italian territories in 1735. After 1800, Italy was unified by Napoléon, who crowned himself king of Italy in 1805; but with the Congress of Vienna in 1815, Austria once again became the dominant power in a disunited Italy. Austrian armies crushed Italian uprisings in 1820–1821 and 1831. In the 1830s, Giuseppe Mazzini, a brilliant liberal nationalist, organized the Risorgimento (Resurrection), which laid the foundation for Italian unity. Disappointed Italian patriots looked to the House of Savoy for leadership. Count Camille di Cavour (1810–1861), premier of Sardinia in 1852 and the architect of a united Italy, joined England and France in the Crimean War (1853–1856), and in 1859, helped France in a war against Austria, thereby obtaining Lombardy. By plebiscite in 1860, Modena, Parma, Tuscany, and the Romagna voted to join Sardinia. In 1860, Giuseppe Garibaldi conquered Sicily and Naples and turned them over to Sardinia. Victor Emmanuel II, king of Sardinia, was proclaimed king of Italy in 1861. The annexation of Venetia in 1866 and of papal Rome in 1870 marked the complete unification of peninsular Italy into one nation under a constitutional monarchy.

Italy declared its neutrality upon the outbreak of World War I on the ground that Germany had embarked upon an offensive war. In 1915, Italy entered the war on the side of the Allies but obtained less territory than it expected in the postwar settlement. Benito ("Il Duce") Mussolini, a former socialist, organized discontented Italians in 1919 into the Fascist Party to "rescue Italy from Bolshevism." He led his Black Shirts in a march on Rome and, on Oct. 28, 1922, became premier. He transformed Italy into a dictatorship, embarking on an expansionist foreign policy with the invasion and annexation of Ethiopia in 1935 and allying himself with Adolf Hitler in the Rome-Berlin Axis in 1936. When the Allies invaded Italy in 1943, Mussolini's dictatorship collapsed; he was executed by Partisans on April 28, 1945, at Dongo on Lake Como. Following the armistice with the Allies (Sept. 3, 1943), Italy joined the war against Germany as a cobelligerent. A June 1946 plebiscite rejected monarchy and a republic was proclaimed. The peace treaty of Sept. 15, 1947, required Italian renunciation of all claims in Ethiopia and Greece and the cession of the Dodecanese to Greece and of five small Alpine areas to France. The Trieste area west of the new Yugoslav territory was made a free territory (until 1954, when the city and a 90-square-mile zone were transferred to Italy and the rest to Yugoslavia).

Italy became an integral member of NATO and the European Economic Community (later the EU) as it successfully rebuilt its postwar economy. A prolonged outbreak of terrorist activities by the left-wing Red Brigades threatened domestic stability in the 1970s, but by the early 1980s the terrorist groups had been suppressed. "Revolving door" governments, political instability, scandal, and corruption characterized Italian politics in the 1980s and 1990s.

Italy adopted the euro as its currency in Jan. 1999. Treasury Secretary Carlo Ciampi, who is credited with the economic reforms that permitted Italy to enter the European Monetary Union, was elected president in May 1999. Italy joined its NATO partners in the

Kosovo crisis. Aviano Air Base in northern Italy was a crucial base for launching air strikes into Kosovo and Yugoslavia.

In June 2001, Silvio Berlusconi, the conservative billionaire, was sworn in as prime minister. He pledged to reduce unemployment, cut taxes, revamp the educational system, and reform the bureaucracy. His critics are alarmed by the apparent massive conflict of interest of a prime minister who also owns 90% of Italy's media. He has also been accused of Mafia connections and was under indictment for tax fraud and bribery. Found guilty in three out of four of his trials, he was acquitted in all of them on appeal. Several other cases are pending.

In Nov. 2002, Giulio Andreotti, who served as Italy's prime minister numerous times between 1972 and 1992, was sentenced to 24 years for ordering the Mafia to murder a journalist in 1979. At 84, however, he was deemed too old for prison.

In 2003, Parliament passed an immunity law for top government officials that meant the latest corruption trial involving Berlusconi—he is accused of bribing judges in 1985—would be suspended while he remained in office. The law was passed just weeks before Berlusconi took over the rotating EU presidency in July, meant in part to help Italy save face while their president held a high-profile international position. His first day on the EU job, Berlusconi caused a diplomatic furor when he compared a German European Parliament member to a Nazi concentration-camp guard.

Jamaica

Sovereign: Queen Elizabeth II (1952)
Governor-General: Sir Howard Cooke (1991)
Prime Minister: Percival J. Patterson (1992)
Area: 4,244 sq mi (10,991 sq km)
Population (2003 est.): 2,695,867 (growth rate: 1.2%); birth rate: 17.4/1000; infant mortality rate: 13.3/1000; density per sq mi: 635
Capital and largest city (2003 est.): Kingston, 937,700 (metro. area), 590,500 (city proper). **Monetary unit:** Jamaican dollar. **Languages:** English, Jamaican Creole. **Ethnicity/race:** African 76.3%, Afro-European 15.1%, East Indian and Afro-East Indian 3%, white 3.2%, Chinese and Afro-Chinese 1.2%, other 1.2%. **Religions:** Protestant 61.3%, Roman Catholic 4%, other 39.1%. **Literacy rate:** 85% (1995 est.)
Economic summary: GDP/PPP (2001 est.): $9.8 billion; per capita $3,700. **Real growth rate:** 1.1%. **Inflation:** 6.9%. **Unemployment:** 16% (2000 est.). **Arable land:** 16%. **Agriculture:** sugarcane, bananas, coffee, citrus, potatoes, vegetables; poultry, goats, milk. **Labor force:** 1.13 million (1998); services 60%, agriculture 21%, industry 19% (1998). **Industries:** tourism, bauxite, textiles, food processing, light manufactures, rum, cement, metal, paper, chemical products. **Natural resources:** bauxite, gypsum, limestone. **Exports:** $1.6 billion (f.o.b., 2001 est.): alumina, bauxite; sugar, bananas, rum. **Imports:** $3.1 billion (f.o.b., 2001 est.): machinery and transport equipment, construction materials, fuel, food, chemicals, fertilizers. **Major trading partners:** U.S., EU, UK, Canada, Caricom countries, Latin America. **Member of Commonwealth of Nations**

Geography Jamaica is an island in the West Indies, 90 mi (145 km) south of Cuba and 100 mi (161 km) west of Haiti. It is a little smaller than Connecticut. The island is made up of coastal lowlands, a limestone plateau, and the Blue Mountains, a group of volcanic hills, in the east.

Government Constitutional parliamentary democracy.

History Jamaica was inhabited by Arawak Indians when Columbus explored it in 1494 and named it St. Iago. It remained under Spanish rule until 1655, when it became a British possession. Buccaneers operated from Port Royal, also the capital, until it fell into the sea in an earthquake in 1692. Disease decimated the Arawaks, so black slaves were imported to work on the sugar plantations. During the 17th and 18th centuries the British were consistently harassed by the Maroons, armed bands of freed slaves roaming the countryside. Abolition of the slave trade (1807), emancipation of the slaves (1833), and a drop in sugar prices eventually led to a depression that resulted in an uprising in 1865. The following year Jamaica became a Crown colony, and conditions improved considerably. Introduction of bananas reduced dependence on sugar.

On May 5, 1953, Jamaica gained internal autonomy, and, in 1958, it led in organizing the West Indies Federation. A nationalist labor leader, Sir Alexander Bustamente, later campaigned to withdraw from the federation. After a referendum, Jamaica became independent on Aug. 6, 1962. Michael Manley, of the socialist People's National Party, became prime minister in 1972.

The Labour Party defeated Manley in 1980 and its capitalist-oriented leader, Edward P. G. Seaga, became prime minister. He encouraged private investment and began an austerity program. Like other Caribbean countries, Jamaica was hard-hit by the 1981–1982 recession. Devaluation of the Jamaican dollar made Jamaican products more competitive on the world market and the country achieved record growth in tourism and agriculture. While manufacturing also grew, food prices rose as much as 75% and thousands of Jamaicans fell deeper into poverty.

In 1989, Manley was reelected, but he resigned in 1992 and was replaced by P. J. Patterson. In May 1997, the government signed a "Ship-Rider Agreement," allowing U.S. authorities to enter Jamaican waters and search vessels with the Jamaican government's permission, to fight drug trafficking. In 2001, violence between politically connected gangs escalated in Kingston, promoting fears that the tourist industry could suffer. In Oct. 2002, Patterson won his third term in office.

Japan

National name: Nippon
Emperor: Akihito (1989)
Prime Minister: Junichiro Koizumi (2001)
Area: 145,882 sq mi (377,835 sq km)
Population (2003 est.): 127,214,499 (growth rate: 0.1%); birth rate: 9.6/1000; infant mortality rate: 3.3/1000; density per sq mi: 872
Capital and largest city (2003 est.): Tokyo, 31,139,900 (metro.area), 8,240,100 (city proper). **Other large cities:** Yokohama, 3,494,900 (part of Tokyo metro. area); Osaka, 2,597,000; Nagoya, 2,189,700; Sapporo, 1,848,000; Kobe, 1,529,900 (part of Osaka metro. area); Kyoto, 1,470,600 (part of Osaka metro. area); Fukuoka, 1,368,900; Kawasaki, 1,276,200 (part of Tokyo metro. area); Hiroshima, 1,132,700. **Monetary unit:** Yen. **Language:** Japanese. **Ethnicity/race:** Japanese 99%, other 1% (mostly Korean). **Religions:** Shintoist, Buddhist, Christian. **Literacy rate:** 99% (1970 est.)
Economic summary: GDP/PPP (2001 est.): $3.45 trillion; per capita $27,200. **Real growth rate:** –0.3%. **Inflation:** –0.6%. **Unemployment:** 4.9%. **Arable land:** 12%. **Agriculture:** rice, sugar beets, vegetables, fruit; pork, poultry, dairy products, eggs; fish. **Labor force:** 67.7 million (Dec. 2000); services 65%, industry 30%,

agriculture 5%. **Industries:** among world's largest and technologically advanced producers of motor vehicles, electronic equipment, machine tools, steel and nonferrous metals, ships, chemicals; textiles, processed foods. **Natural resources:** negligible mineral resources, fish. **Exports:** $404.6 billion (f.o.b., 2001 est.): motor vehicles, semiconductors, office machinery, chemicals. **Imports:** $331.6 billion (f.o.b., 2001 est.): fuels, foodstuffs, chemicals, textiles, office machinery. **Major trading partners:** U.S., Taiwan, South Korea, China, Hong Kong, Indonesia, Australia.

Geography An archipelago in the Pacific, Japan is separated from the east coast of Asia by the Sea of Japan. It is approximately the size of Montana. Japan's four main islands are Honshu, Hokkaido, Kyushu, and Shikoku. The Ryukyu chain to the southwest was U.S.-occupied from 1945 to 1972, when it reverted to Japanese control, and the Kurils to the northeast are Russian-occupied.

Government Constitutional monarchy with a parliamentary government.

History Legend attributes creation of Japan to the sun goddess, from whom the emperors were descended. The first of them was Jimmu, supposed to have ascended the throne in 660 B.C., a tradition that constituted official doctrine until 1945.

Recorded Japanese history begins in approximately A.D. 400, when the Yamato clan, eventually based in Kyoto, managed to gain control of other family groups in central and western Japan. Contact with Korea introduced Buddhism to Japan at about this time. Through the 700s Japan was much influenced by China, and the Yamato clan set up an imperial court similar to that of China. In the ensuing centuries, the authority of the imperial court was undermined as powerful gentry families vied for control.

At the same time, warrior clans were rising to prominence as a distinct class known as samurai. In 1192, the Minamoto clan set up a military government under their leader, Yoritomo. He was designated shogun (military dictator). For the following 700 years, shoguns from a succession of clans ruled in Japan, while the imperial court existed in relative obscurity.

First contact with the West came in about 1542, when a Portuguese ship off course arrived in Japanese waters. Portuguese traders, Jesuit missionaries, and Spanish, Dutch, and English traders followed. Suspicious of Christianity and of Portuguese support of a local Japanese revolt, the shoguns of the Tokugawa period (1603–1867) prohibited all trade with foreign countries; only a Dutch trading post at Nagasaki was permitted. Western attempts to renew trading relations failed until 1853, when Commodore Matthew Perry sailed an American fleet into Tokyo Bay. Trade with the West was forced upon Japan under terms less than favorable to the Japanese. Strife caused by these actions brought down the feudal world of the shoguns. In 1868, the emperor Meiji came to the throne, and the shogun system was abolished.

Japan quickly made the transition from a medieval to a modern power. An imperial army was established with conscription, and parliamentary government was formed in 1889. The Japanese began to take steps to extend their empire. After a brief war with China in 1894–1895, Japan acquired Formosa (Taiwan), the Pescadores Islands, and part of southern Manchuria. China also recognized the independence of Korea (Chosen), which Japan later annexed (1910).

In 1904–1905, Japan defeated Russia in the Russo-Japanese War, gaining the territory of southern Sakhalin (Karafuto) and Russia's port and rail rights in Manchuria. In World War I, Japan seized Germany's Pacific islands and leased areas in China. The Treaty of Versailles then awarded Japan a mandate over the islands.

At the Washington Conference of 1921–1922, Japan agreed to respect Chinese national integrity, but, in 1931, invaded Manchuria. The following year, Japan set up this area as a puppet state, "Manchukuo," under Emperor Henry Pu-Yi, the last of China's Manchu dynasty. On Nov. 25, 1936, Japan joined the Axis. The invasion of China came the next year, followed by the Pearl Harbor attack on the U.S. on Dec. 7, 1941. Japan won its first military engagements during the war, extending its power over a vast area of the Pacific. Yet, after 1942, the Japanese were forced to retreat, island by island, to their own country. The dropping of atomic bombs on the cities of Hiroshima and Nagasaki in 1945 by the United States finally brought the government to admit defeat. Japan surrendered formally on Sept. 2, 1945, aboard the battleship *Missouri* in Tokyo Bay. Southern Sakhalin and the Kuril Islands reverted to the USSR, and Formosa (Taiwan) and Manchuria to China. The Pacific islands remained under U.S. occupation.

Gen. Douglas MacArthur was appointed supreme commander of the U.S. occupation of postwar Japan (1945–1952). In 1947, a new constitution took effect. The emperor became largely a symbolic head of state. The U.S. and Japan signed a security treaty in 1951, allowing for U.S. troops to be stationed in Japan. In 1952, Japan regained full sovereignty, and, in 1972, the U.S. returned to Japan the Ryuku Islands, including Okinawa.

Japan's postwar economic recovery was nothing short of remarkable. New technologies and manufacturing were undertaken with great success. A shrewd trade policy gave Japan larger shares in many Western markets, an imbalance that caused some tensions with the U.S. The close involvement of Japanese government in the country's banking and industry produced accusations of protectionism. Yet economic growth continued through the 1970s and 1980s, eventually making Japan the world's second-largest economy (after the U.S.).

During the 1990s, Japan suffered an economic downturn prompted by scandals involving government officials, bankers, and leaders of industry. Japan succumbed to the Asian economic crisis in 1998, experiencing its worst recession since World War II. These setbacks led to the resignation of Prime Minister Ryutaro Hashimoto in July 1998. He was replaced by Keizo Obuchi. In 1999, Japan seemed to make slight progress in an economic recovery. Prime Minister Obuchi died of a stroke in May 2000 and was succeeded by Yoshiro Mori, whose administration was dogged by scandal and blunders from the outset.

Despite attempts to revive the economy, fears that Japan would slide back into recession increased in early 2001. The embattled Mori resigned in April 2001 and was replaced by Liberal Democrat Junichiro Koizumi—the country's 11th prime minister in 13 years. Koizumi's plans to revitalize the country's tattered economy with painful reforms were buoyed in July elections, when his coalition dominated parliamentary elections. Koizumi's popularity was fleeting, however, and after two years in office the economy remained in a slump and his attempts at reform were thwarted.

At an unprecedented summit meeting in North Korea in Sept. 2002, President Kim Jong Il apologized to Koizumi for North Korea's kidnapping of Japanese citizens during the 1970s and 1980s, and Koizumi pledged a generous aid package—both significant steps toward normalizing relations.

Koizumi was overwhelmingly reelected in Sept. 2003 and promised to push ahead with tough econonic reforms.

Jordan

THE HASHEMITE KINGDOM OF JORDAN

National name: Al Mamlaka al Urduniya al Hashemiyah
Ruler: King Abdullah II (1999)
Prime Minister: Ali Abu al-Ragheb (2000)
Area: 35,637 sq mi (92,300 sq km) excludes West Bank
Population (2003 est.): 5,460,265 (growth rate: 2.1%); birth rate: 23.7/1000; infant mortality rate: 18.9/1000; density per sq mi: 153
Capital and largest city (2003 est.): Amman, 2,677,500 (metro. area), 1,293,200. **Other large cities:** Zarka, 512,200; Irbid, 267,200; As-Salt, 200,400. **Monetary unit:** Jordanian dinar. **Languages:** Arabic (official), English. **Ethnicity/race:** Arab 98%, Circassian 1%, Armenian 1%. **Religions:** Islam 92%, Christian 6%, other 2%. **Literacy rate:** 86.6% (1995 est.)
Economic summary: GDP/PPP (2001 est.): $21.6 billion; per capita $4,200. **Real growth rate:** 2.8%. **Inflation:** 1.5%. **Unemployment:** 16% official rate; actual rate is 25%–30% (2001 est.). **Arable land:** 3%. **Agriculture:** wheat, barley, citrus, tomatoes, melons, olives; sheep, goats, poultry. **Labor force:** 1.26 million; note: in addition, at least 300,000 workers are employed abroad (2001); services 82.5%, industry 12.5%, agriculture 5% (2001 est.). **Industries:** phosphate mining, petroleum refining, cement, potash, light manufacturing, tourism. **Natural resources:** phosphates, potash, shale oil. **Exports:** $2.2 billion (f.o.b., 2001 est.): phosphates, fertilizers, potash, agricultural products, manufactures, pharmaceuticals. **Imports:** $4.6 billion (f.o.b., 2001 est.): crude oil, machinery, transport equipment, food, live animals, manufactured goods. **Major trading partners:** India, Iraq, Saudi Arabia, EU, U.S., Indonesia, UAE, Lebanon, Kuwait, Syria, Ethiopia, Germany, Japan, UK, Italy, Turkey, Malaysia, China.

Geography The Middle East kingdom of Jordan is bordered on the west by Israel and the Dead Sea, on the north by Syria, on the east by Iraq, and on the south by Saudi Arabia. It is comparable in size to Indiana. Arid hills and mountains make up most of the country. The southern section of the Jordan River flows through the country.

Government Constitutional hereditary monarchy.

History In biblical times, the country that is now Jordan contained the lands of Edom, Moab, Ammon, and Bashan. Together with other Middle Eastern territories, Jordan passed in turn to the Assyrians, the Babylonians, the Persians, and, about 330 B.C., the Seleucids. Conflict between the Seleucids and the Ptolemies enabled the Arabic-speaking Nabataeans to create a kingdom in southeast Jordan. In A.D. 106 it became part of the Roman province of Arabia and in 633–636 was conquered by the Arabs. In the 16th century, Jordan submitted to Ottoman Turkish rule and was administered from Damascus. Taken from the Turks by the British in World War I, Jordan (formerly known as Transjordan) was separated from the Palestine mandate in 1920, and in 1921, placed under the rule of Abdullah ibn Hussein.

In 1923, Britain recognized Jordan's independence, subject to the mandate. In 1946, grateful for Jordan's loyalty in World War II, Britain abolished the mandate. That part of Palestine occupied by Jordanian troops was formally incorporated by action of the Jordanian Parliament in 1950. King Abdullah was assassinated in 1951. His son Talal, who was mentally ill, was deposed the next year. Talal's son Hussein, born on Nov. 14, 1935, succeeded him.

From the beginning of his reign, Hussein had to steer a careful course between his powerful neighbor to the west, Israel, and rising Arab nationalism, frequently a direct threat to his throne. Riots erupted when he joined the Central Treaty Organization (the Baghdad Pact) in 1955, and he incurred further unpopularity when Britain, France, and Israel attacked the Suez Canal in 1956, forcing him to place his army under nominal command of the United Arab Republic of Egypt and Syria. The 1961 breakup of the UAR eased Arab national pressure on Hussein, who was the first to recognize Syria after it reclaimed its independence. Jordan was swept into the 1967 Arab-Israeli War, however, and lost the old city of Jerusalem and all of its territory west of the Jordan River, the West Bank. Embittered Palestinian guerrilla forces virtually took over sections of Jordan in the aftermath of defeat, and open warfare broke out between the Palestinians and government forces in 1970.

Despite intervention of Syrian tanks, Hussein's Bedouin army defeated the Palestinians. The Jordanians drove out the Syrians and 12,000 Iraqi troops who had been in the country since the 1967 war. Ignoring protests from other Arab states, Hussein, by mid-1971, crushed Palestinian strength in Jordan and shifted the problem to Lebanon, where many of the guerrillas had fled. As Egypt and Israel neared final agreement on a peace treaty early in 1979, Hussein met with Yasir Arafat, the PLO leader, on March 17, and issued a joint statement of opposition. Although the U.S. pressed Jordan to break Arab ranks on the issue, Hussein elected to side with the great majority, cutting ties with Cairo and joining the boycott against Egypt.

Jordan's stance during the Persian Gulf War strained relations with the U.S. and led to the termination of U.S. aid. The signing of a national charter by King Hussein and leaders of the main political groups in June 1991 meant political parties were permitted in exchange for acceptance of the constitution and the monarchy. King Hussein's decision to join the Middle East peace talks in mid-1991 helped restore his country's relations with the U.S.

In July 1994, King Hussein and the Israeli prime minister Yitzhak Rabin signed a declaration ending the state of belligerency between the two countries. A peace agreement between the two countries was signed on Oct. 26, 1994, although a clause in it calling the king the "custodian" of Islamic holy shrines in Jerusalem angered the PLO. In the wake of the agreement Jordan's relations with the U.S. and with the moderate Arab states, including Saudi Arabia, warmed. In 1997, Jordan began negotiating with the United States about membership in the World Trade Organization, determined to attract foreign investment. On Feb. 7, 1999, King Hussein died of cancer after 46 years on the throne, sending the Middle East and much of the world into mourning for the influential Middle East statesman. Just weeks earlier, on Jan. 26, King Hussein unexpectedly deposed his brother, Prince Hassan, who had been heir apparent for 34 years, and named his eldest son, Abdullah, 37, as the new crown prince. King Abdullah II, a popular military leader with little political experience, became king on Feb. 7, 2000. In June, King Abdullah dismissed conservative prime minister Abdul Raouf al-Rawabdeh and replaced him with Ali Abu al-Ragheb, a liberal with strong business ties.

In 2002–2003, Jordan found itself caught in the middle of the mounting hostility between the U.S. and Iraq; much of Jordan's oil is imported from its neighbor, and a war next door could ignite political instability in the country—many of Jordan's 5 million Palestinians are Iraqi supporters. But at the same time, Jordan did not want to anger its superpower benefactor—the U.S. is its largest aid donor.

Kazakhstan

REPUBLIC OF KAZAKHSTAN

President: Nursultan A. Nazarbayev (1990)
Prime Minister: Daniyal Akhmetov (2003)
Area: 1,049,150 sq mi (2,717,300 sq km)
Population (2003 est.): 16,763,795 (growth rate: 0.8%); birth rate: 18.4/1000; infant mortality rate: 58.7/1000; density per sq mi: 16
Capital (2003 est.): Astana, 288,200 (formerly Aqmola; capital since 1997). **Largest cities:** Almaty (former capital), 1,045,900; Karaganda, 404,600; Shymkent, 333,500; Taraz, 305,700; Pavlodar, 299,500; Ust-Kamenogorsk, 288,000; Aqtöbe, 234,400. **Monetary unit:** Tenge. **Languages:** Kazak (Qazaq), state language spoken by 64.4% of population; Russian, official language spoken by 95% of population and used in everyday business. **Ethnicity/race:** Kazak (Qazaq) 53.4%, Russian 30%, Ukrainian 3.7%, Uzbek 2.5%, German 2.4%, Tatar 1.4%, other 6.6% (1999). **Religions:** Islam, 47%; Russian Orthodox, 44%; Protestant, 2%; other, 7%. **Literacy rate:** 98.4% (1999 est.)
Economic summary: GDP/PPP (2001 est.): $98.1 billion; per capita $5,900. **Real growth rate:** 12.2%. **Inflation:** 8.5%. **Unemployment:** 10%. **Arable land:** 11%. **Agriculture:** grain (mostly spring wheat), cotton; wool, livestock. **Labor force:** 8.4 million (1999); industry 30%, agriculture 20%, services 50% (2001 est.). **Industries:** oil, coal, iron ore, manganese, chromite, lead, zinc, copper, titanium, bauxite, gold, silver, phosphates, sulfur, iron and steel, tractors and other agricultural machinery, electric motors, construction materials. **Natural resources:** major deposits of petroleum, natural gas, coal, iron ore, manganese, chrome ore, nickel, cobalt, copper, molybdenum, lead, zinc, bauxite, gold, uranium. **Exports:** $10.5 billion (f.o.b., 2001 est.): oil and oil products 52.8%, ferrous metals 12.9%, machinery, chemicals, grain, wool, meat, coal (2000). **Imports:** $8.2 billion (f.o.b., 2001 est.): machinery and parts 29.5%, energy and fuels 11.3%, electrical equipment 8.8%, vehicles 8.7%, ferrous metals 6.4% (2000). **Major trading partners:** Russia, China, Germany, U.S.

Geography Kazakhstan lies in the north of the central Asian republics and is bounded by Russia in the north, China in the east, the Kyrgyzstan and Uzbekistan in the south, and the Caspian Sea and part of Turkmenistan in the west. It has almost 1,177 mi (1,894 km) of coastline on the Caspian Sea. Kazakhstan is slightly more than twice the size of Texas. The territory is mostly steppe land with hilly plains and plateaus.

Government Republic.

History The indigenous Kazakhs were a nomadic Turkic people who belonged to several divisions of Kazakh hordes. They grouped together in settlements and lived in dome-shaped tents made of felt called "yurts." Their tribes migrated seasonally to find pastures for their herds of sheep, horses, and goats. Although they had chiefs, the Kazakhs were rarely united as a single nation under one great leader. Their tribes fell under Mongol rule in the 13th century and they were dominated by Tartar khanates until the area was conquered by Russia in the 18th century.

The area became part of the Kirgiz Autonomous Republic formed by the Soviet authorities in 1920, and in 1925 this entity's name was changed to the Kazakh Autonomous Soviet Socialist Republic (Kazakh ASSR). After 1927, the Soviet government began forcing the nomadic Kazakhs to settle on collective and state farms, and the Soviets continued the czarist policy of encouraging large numbers of Russians and other Slavs to settle in the region.

Owing to the region's intensive agricultural development and its use as a testing ground for nuclear weapons by the Soviet government, serious environmental problems developed by the late 20th century. Along with the other central Asian republics, Kazakhstan obtained its independence from the collapsing Soviet Union in 1991. Kazakhstan proclaimed its membership in the Commonwealth of Independent States on Dec. 21, 1991, along with ten other former Soviet republics. In 1993, the country overwhelmingly approved the Nuclear Non-Proliferation Treaty. President Nursultan Nazarbayev restructured and consolidated many operations of the government in 1997, eliminating a third of the government ministries and agencies. In 1997, the national capital was changed from Almaty, the largest city, to Astana (formerly Aqmola).

In Jan. 1999, Nazarbayev was sworn into office for another seven years, although the election was widely criticized because an opposition leader was disqualified from running on a technicality. Despite his authoritarianism, Nazarbayev, who has ruled Kazakhstan since 1989 when it was still part of the Soviet Union, is a widely popular leader. Kazakhstan has the potential for becoming one of central Asia's richest countries because of its huge mineral and oil resources and its liberalized economy, which encourages Western investment. In 2000, oil was discovered in Kazakhstan's portion of the Caspian Sea—it is believed to be the largest oil find in 30 years. In March 2001, a pipeline opened to transport oil from the Tengiz fields to the Russian Black Sea port of Novorossiysk.

But as its economic outlook blossoms, Kazakhstan's scarce democratic principles continues to wither. In the past several years, the president has harassed the independent media, arrested opposition leaders, and passed a law making it virtually impossible for new political parties to form.

Kenya

REPUBLIC OF KENYA

National name: Jamhuri ya Kenya
President: Mwai Kibaki (2002)
Area: 224,961 sq mi (582,650 sq km)
Population (2003 est.): 31,639,091 (growth rate: 1.3%); birth rate: 28.8/1000; infant mortality rate: 63.4/1000; density per sq mi: 141
Capital and largest city (2003 est.): Nairobi, 3,064,800 (metro. area), 2,411,900 (city proper). **Other large city:** Mombasa, 712,600. **Monetary unit:** Kenya shilling. **Languages:** English (official), Swahili (national), and several other languages spoken by 25 ethnic groups. **Ethnicity/race:** Kikuyu 22%, Luhya 14%, Luo 13%, Kalenjin 12%, Kamba 11%, Kisii 6%, Meru 6%, Asian, European, and Arab 1%, other 15%. **Religions:** Protestant, 45%; Roman Catholic, 33%; traditional, 10%; Islam, 10%; others, 2%. **Literacy rate:** 78.1% (1995 est.)
Economic summary: GDP/PPP (2001 est.): $31 billion; per capita $1,000. **Real growth rate:** 1%. **Inflation:** 3.3%. **Unemployment:** 40%. **Arable land:** 7%. **Agriculture:** coffee, tea, corn, wheat, sugarcane, fruit, vegetables; dairy products, beef, pork, poultry, eggs. **Labor force:** 10 million; agriculture 75%–80%. **Industries:** small-scale consumer goods (plastic,

furniture, batteries, textiles, soap, cigarettes, flour), agricultural products processing; oil refining, cement; tourism. **Natural resources:** gold, limestone, soda ash, salt barites, rubies, fluorspar, garnets, wildlife, hydropower. **Exports:** $1.8 billion (f.o.b., 2001 est.): tea, horticultural products, coffee, petroleum products, fish, cement. **Imports:** $3.1 billion (f.o.b., 2001 est.): machinery and transportation equipment, petroleum products, motor vehicles, iron and steel, resins and plastics. **Major trading partners:** UK, Tanzania, Uganda, Germany, UAE, Japan, India. **Member of Commonwealth of Nations**

Geography Kenya lies across the equator in east-central Africa, on the coast of the Indian Ocean. It is twice the size of Nevada. Kenya borders Somalia to the east, Ethiopia to the north, Tanzania to the south, Uganda to the west, and Sudan to the northwest. In the north, the land is arid; the southwest corner is in the fertile Lake Victoria Basin; and a length of the eastern depression of the Great Rift Valley separates western highlands from those that rise from the lowland coastal strip.

Government Republic.

History Paleontologists believe people may first have inhabited Kenya about 2 million years ago. In the 700s, Arab seafarers established settlements along the coast, and the Portuguese took control of the area in the early 1500s. More than 40 ethnic groups reside in Kenya. Its largest group, the Kikuyu, migrated to the region at the beginning of the 18th century.

The land became a British protectorate in 1890 and a Crown colony in 1920, when it went by the name British East Africa. Nationalist stirrings began in the 1940s, and in 1952 the Mau Mau movement, made up of Kikuyu militants, rebelled against the government. The fighting lasted until 1956.

On Dec. 12, 1963, Kenya became fully independent. Jomo Kenyatta, a nationalist leader during the independence struggle who had been jailed by the British, became its first president. From 1964 to 1992, the country was ruled as a one-party state by the Kenya African National Union (KANU), first under Kenyatta and then under Daniel arap Moi. Demonstrations and riots pressured Moi to allow for multiparty elections in 1992.

The economy did not flourish under Daniel arap Moi's rule. In the 1990s, Kenya's infrastructure began disintegrating and official graft was rampant, contributing to the withdrawal of much foreign aid. In early 1995, President Moi moved against the opposition and ordered the arrest of anyone who insulted him.

A series of disasters plagued Kenya in 1997 and 1998: severe flooding destroyed roads, bridges, and crops; epidemics of malaria and cholera overwhelmed the ineffectual health care system; and ethnic clashes erupted between the Kikuyu and Kalenjin ethnic groups in the Rift Valley.

On Aug. 7, 1998, the U.S. embassy in Nairobi was bombed by terrorists, killing 243 and injuring more than 1,000. The embassy in neighboring Tanzania was bombed the same day, killing ten.

In a successful effort to win back IMF and World Bank funding, which had been suspended because of Kenya's corruption and poor economic practices, President Moi appointed his high-profile critic and political opponent, Richard Leakey, as head of the civil service in 1999. The third-generation white Kenyan, son of paleontologists Louis and Mary Leakey, he had been a highly effective reformer as head of the Kenya Wildlife Service. But after 20 months during which he made a promising start at cleaning up Kenya's corrupt bureaucracy, Leakey was sacked by Moi. Kenya is regularly ranked among the ten most corrupt countries in the world, according to the watchdog group Transparency International.

An anticorruption law, sponsored by the ruling party, failed to pass in Parliament in Aug. 2001, and imperiled Kenya's chances for international aid. Opposition leaders called the law a cynical ploy meant to give the appearance of reform—the proposed law, they contended, was in fact too weak and full of loopholes to make a dent in corruption.

Opposition leader Mwai Kibaki won the Dec. 2002 presidential election, defeating Moi's protégé, Uhuru Kenyatta (term limits prevented Moi, in power for 24 years, from running again). Kibaki has promised to put an end to the country's rampant corruption.

Kiribati

REPUBLIC OF KIRIBATI

President: Anote Tong (2003)
Area: 313 sq mi (811 sq km)
Population (2003 est.): 98,549 (growth rate: 2.3%); birth rate: 31.2/1000; infant mortality rate: 51.3/1000; density per sq mi: 315
Capital and largest city (2003 est.): Tarawa, 26,600. **Monetary unit:** Australian dollar. **Languages:** English (official), I-Kiribati (Gilbertese). **Ethnicity/race:** Micronesian. **Religions:** Roman Catholic 52%, Protestant 40%. **Literacy rate:** 90%
Economic summary: GDP/PPP (2001 est.): $79 million, supplemented by a nearly equal amount from external sources; per capita $840. **Real growth rate:** 1.5%. **Inflation:** 2.5%. **Unemployment:** 2%; underemployment 70% (1992 est.). **Arable land:** 0%. **Agriculture:** copra, taro, breadfruit, sweet potatoes, vegetables; fish. **Labor force:** 7,870 economically active, not including subsistence farmers (1985 est.). **Industries:** fishing, handicrafts. **Natural resources:** phosphate (production discontinued in 1979). **Exports:** $6 million (f.o.b., 1998): copra 62%, seaweed, fish. **Imports:** $44 million (c.i.f., 1999): foodstuffs, machinery and equipment, miscellaneous manufactured goods, fuel. **Major trading partners:** Japan, Bangladesh, U.S., Australia, Brazil, Poland, Fiji. **Member of Commonwealth of Nations**

Geography Kiribati, formerly the Gilbert Islands, consists of three widely separated main groups of southwest Pacific islands, the Gilberts on the equator, the Phoenix Islands to the east, and the Line Islands farther east. Ocean Island, producer of phosphates until it was mined out in 1981, is also included in the 2 million square miles of ocean. Most of the islands of Kiribati are low-lying coral atolls built on a submerged volcanic chain and encircled by reefs.

Government Republic.

History Kiribati was first settled by early Austronesian-speaking peoples long before the 1st century A.D. Fijians and Tongans arrived about the 14th century and subsequently merged with the older groups to form the traditional I-Kiribati Micronesian society and culture. The islands were first sighted by British and American ships in the late 18th and early 19th centuries, and the first British settlers arrived in 1837. A British protectorate since 1892, the Gilbert and Ellice Islands became a Crown colony in 1915–1916. Kiritimati (Christmas) Atoll became a part of the colony in 1919; the Phoenix Islands in 1937.

Tarawa and others of the Gilbert group were occupied by Japan during World War II. Tarawa was the site of one of the bloodiest battles in U.S. Marine Corps history when Marines landed in Nov. 1943 to dislodge the Japanese defenders. The Gilbert Islands and Ellice

Islands (now Tuvalu) were separated in 1975 and granted internal self-government by Britain. Kiribati became independent on July 12, 1979.

Kiribati's 1995 act of moving the international date line far to the east, so that it encompassed Kiribati's Line Islands group, courted controversy. The move, which fulfilled one of President Tito's campaign promises, was intended to enable Kiribati to become the first country to see the dawn on Jan. 1, 2000, and welcome the new millennium—an event of significance for tourism. In 1999, Kiribati gained UN membership.

In 2002, Kiribati passed a controversial law enabling it to shut down newspapers. The legislation followed the launching of Kiribati's first successful nongovernment-run newspaper. Anote Tong of the opposition party Boutokaan Te Koaua was elected president in 2003.

Korea, North

DEMOCRATIC PEOPLE'S REPUBLIC OF KOREA

National name: Choson Minjujuui Inmin Konghwaguk
Head of State: Kim Jong Il (1994)
Premier: Hong Song Nam (1997)
Area: 46,540 sq mi (120,540 sq km)
Population (2003 est.): 22,466,481 (growth rate: 1.1%); birth rate: 17.6/1000; infant mortality rate: 25.7/1000; density per sq mi: 483
Capital and largest city (2003): Pyongyang, 3,222,000 (metro. area), 2,767,900. **Monetary unit:** Won. **Language:** Korean. **Ethnicity/race:** racially homogeneous. **Religions:** Buddhism and Confucianism; religious activities almost nonexistent. **Literacy rate:** 99% (1990 est.)
Economic summary: GDP/PPP (2001 est.): $21.8 billion; per capita $1,000. **Real growth rate:** –3%. **Inflation:** n.a. **Unemployment:** n.a. **Arable land:** 14%. **Agriculture:** rice, corn, potatoes, soybeans, pulses; cattle, pigs, pork, eggs. **Labor force:** 9.6 million; agricultural 36%, nonagricultural 64%. **Industries:** military products; machine building, electric power, chemicals; mining (coal, iron ore, magnesite, graphite, copper, zinc, lead, and precious metals), metallurgy; textiles, food processing; tourism. **Natural resources:** coal, lead, tungsten, zinc, graphite, magnesite, iron ore, copper, gold, pyrites, salt, fluorspar, hydropower. **Exports:** $708 million (f.o.b., 2000 est.): minerals, metallurgical products, manufactures (including armaments); agricultural and fishery products. **Imports:** $1.686 billion (c.i.f., 2000 est.): petroleum, coking coal, machinery and equipment; consumer goods, grain. **Major trading partners:** Japan, South Korea, Hong Kong, China, France, Germany.

Geography Korea is a 600-mile (966 km) peninsula jutting out from Manchuria and China (and a small portion of the USSR) into the Sea of Japan and the Yellow Sea off eastern Asia. North Korea occupies an area slightly smaller than Pennsylvania north of the 38th parallel.

The country is almost completely covered by a series of north-south mountain ranges separated by narrow valleys. The Yalu River forms part of the northern border with Manchuria.

Government Authoritarian socialist; one-man dictatorship.

History The ancient history of the Korean peninsula can be traced to the Neolithic Age, when Turkic-Manchurian-Mongol peoples migrated into the region from China. The first agriculturally based settlements appeared around 6000 B.C. Some of the larger communities of this era were established along the Han-gang River near modern-day Seoul, others near Pyongyang and Pusan. According to ancient lore, Korea's earliest civilization, known as Choson, was founded in 2333 B.C. by Tan-gun.

In the 17th century, Korea became a vassal state of China and was cut off from outside contact until the Sino-Japanese War of 1894–1895. Following Japan's victory, Korea was granted independence. By 1910, Korea had been annexed by Japan, which developed the country but never won over the Korean nationalists, who continued to agitate for independence.

After Japan's surrender at the conclusion of World War II, the Korean peninsula was partitioned into two occupation zones, divided at the 38th parallel. The USSR controlled the north, with the U.S. taking charge of the south. In 1948, the division was made permanent with the establishment of the separate regimes of North and South Korea. The Democratic People's Republic of Korea (North Korea) was established on May 1, 1948, with Kim Il Sung as president.

Hoping to unify the Koreas under a single Communist government, the North launched a surprise invasion of South Korea on June 25, 1950. In the following days, the UN Security Council condemned the attack and demanded an immediate withdrawal.

President Harry S. Truman ordered U.S. air and naval units into action to enforce the UN order. The British government followed suit, and soon a UN multinational command was set up to aid the South Koreans.

The North Korean invaders swiftly seized Seoul and surrounded the allied forces in the peninsula's southeast corner near Pusan. In a desperate bid to reverse the military situation, UN Commander Gen. Douglas MacArthur ordered an amphibious landing at Inchon on Sept. 15 and routed the North Korean army. MacArthur's forces pushed north across the 38th parallel, approaching the Yalu River.

Prompted by this successful counteroffensive, Communist China entered the war, forcing the UN troops into a headlong retreat. Seoul was lost again, then regained. Ultimately, the war stabilized near the 38th parallel, but dragged on for two years while negotiations took place. An armistice was agreed to on July 27, 1953.

By early 1994, tensions had mounted over international inspection of North Korea's nuclear sites. Kim Il Sung's death on July 8, 1994, introduced a period of uncertainty, as his son, Kim Jong Il, assumed the leadership mantle. Negotiations over the country's suspected atomic weapons dragged on, but an agreement was reached in June 1995 that included a provision for providing the North with a South Korean nuclear reactor.

The nuclear crises that characterized the mid-1990s were overshadowed when famine struck the nation's 24 million inhabitants in 1998 and 1999. Two years of floods were followed by severe droughts in 1997 and 1998, causing devastating crop failures. Because of lack of fuel and machinery parts, and weather conditions that have encouraged parasites, only 10% of North Korea's rice fields could be worked. Despite the staggering food crisis that necessitated foreign aid, North Korea remains one of the world's few remaining hermetic hard-line Communist regimes.

In Sept. 1998, North Korea launched a test missile over Japan, claiming it was simply a scientific satellite. This launch alarmed Japan, and much of the rest of the world, about North Korea's intentions regarding reentry into the nuclear arms race. In 1999, North Korea agreed to allow the United States to conduct ongoing inspections of a suspected nuclear development site, Kumchangri, which North Korea admitted had been devised for "a sensitive military purpose." In exchange, the U.S. would increase food aid and initiate a program for bringing potato production to the country.

Antagonism between North and South Korea erupted into open aggression twice within six months in late 1998 and 1999, with South Korea hitting one North Korean vessel and sinking two others that were discovered trespassing in South Korean waters.

In the fall of 1999, North Korea's four years of severe famine, which claimed an estimated 2 million to 3 million lives between 1995 and 1998, had begun to wane. Tension with South Korea eased dramatically in June 2000, when South Korea's president, Kim Dae Jung, met with North Korea's President Kim Jong Il in Pyongyang. The summit marked the first ever meeting of the two countries' leaders. But efforts toward reconciliation fizzled thereafter, and various minor military skirmishes followed over the next years.

In Jan. 2002, President Bush described North Korea as part of an "axis of evil." Such open hostility marked a dramatic shift in U.S. policy toward North Korea from the Clinton administration's policy of engagement.

In July 2002, North Korea began a series of radical economic initiatives aimed at reforming the devastated economy and introducing free-market policies. The country devalued its currency, raised food prices by as much as 50%, and increased wages.

The reclusive and secretive North Korea stunned the world in late 2002 with two shocking admissions. In September, the government unexpectedly acknowledged that it had kidnapped about a dozen Japanese in the 1970s and 1980s for the purposes of training North Korean spies. In October, confronted with U.S. intelligence, North Korea admitted that it had violated a 1994 agreement freezing its nuclear-weapons program and had in fact been developing nuclear bombs.

In late December, North Korea expelled UN weapons inspectors from the country and announced it could no longer agree to the terms of the nuclear Non-Proliferation Treaty (NPT), officially withdrawing from it in January 2003. Kim continued to provoke the international community into the spring, reactivating a plant at Yongbyon that converts nuclear waste into weapons-grade plutonium, test-launching missiles, and taunting the U.S. by intercepting an air force spy plane. During talks with China and the U.S. in April, North Korea announced that it had already produced nuclear weapons and threatened to test or export them. In July North Korean officials reported that the country had reprocessed enough plutonium to build six nuclear bombs. This news was followed by a report in the *New York Times* that North Korea has built a second plutonium-processing plant. Kim's motives for this bellicose stance have mystified much of the world, but in the past Kim has regularly confused diplomacy with extortion, using threats and hostile acts to wring aid and food from the international community for his starving, impoverished country. Officials from the U.S., North Korea, China, Russia, South Korea, and Japan met in August in Beijing to discuss North Korea's nuclear weapons program, but nothing substantive resulted.

Korea, South

REPUBLIC OF KOREA

National name: Taehan Min'guk
President: Roh Moo Hyun (2003)
Prime Minister: Goh Kun (2003)
Area: 38,023 sq mi (98,480 sq km)
Population (2003 est.): 48,289,037 (growth rate: 0.7%); birth rate: 12.6/1000; infant mortality rate: 7.3/1000; density per sq mi: 1,270
Capital and largest city (2003 est.): Seoul, 19,969,100 (metro.area), 9,630,600 (city proper). **Other large cities:** Pusan, 3,504,900; Inchon, 2,479,600 (part of Seoul metro. area); Taegu, 2,369,800. **Monetary unit:** Won. **Language:** Korean. **Ethnicity/race:** homogeneous (except for about 20,000 Chinese). **Religions:** Christian, 49%; Buddhist, 47%; Confucianist, 3%; Chondogyo (religion of the Heavenly Way) and other, 1% (1996 est.). **Literacy rate:** 98% (1995 est.)
Economic summary: GDP/PPP (2001 est.): $865 billion; per capita $18,000. **Real growth rate:** 3.3%. **Inflation:** 4.3%. **Unemployment:** 3.9%. **Arable land:** 17%. **Agriculture:** rice, root crops, barley, vegetables, fruit; cattle, pigs, chickens, milk, eggs; fish. **Labor force:** 22 million; services 69%, industry 21.5%, agriculture 9.5%. **Industries:** electronics, automobile production, chemicals, shipbuilding, steel, textiles, clothing, footwear, food processing. **Natural resources:** coal, tungsten, graphite, molybdenum, lead, hydropower potential. **Exports:** $168.3 billion (f.o.b., 2001): electronic products, machinery and equipment, motor vehicles, steel, ships; textiles, clothing, footwear; fish. **Imports:** $152.3 billion (f.o.b., 2001): machinery, electronics and electronic equipment, oil, steel, transport equipment, textiles, organic chemicals, grains. **Major trading partners:** U.S., Japan, China, Hong Kong, Taiwan, Saudi Arabia, Australia.

Geography Slightly larger than Indiana, South Korea lies below the 38th parallel on the Korean peninsula, bordering the East Sea and the Yellow Sea. It is mountainous in the east; in the west and south are many harbors on the mainland and offshore islands.

Government Republic.

History South Korea came into being after World War II, the result of a 1945 agreement reached by the Allies at the Potsdam Conference, making the 38th parallel the boundary between a northern zone of the Korean peninsula to be occupied by the USSR and southern zone to be controlled by U.S. forces. (For details, *see* Korea, North.)

Elections were held in the U.S. zone in 1948 for a national assembly, which adopted a republican constitution and elected Syngman Rhee as the nation's president. The new republic was proclaimed on Aug. 15 and was recognized as the legal government of Korea by the UN on Dec. 12, 1948.

On June 25, 1950, North Korean Communist forces launched a massive surprise attack on South Korea, quickly overrunning the capital, Seoul. U.S. armed intervention was ordered on June 27 by President Harry S. Truman, and on the same day the UN invoked military sanctions against North Korea. Gen. Douglas MacArthur was named commander of the UN forces. U.S. and South Korean troops fought a heroic holding action, but by the first week of Aug. were forced back to a 4,000-square-mile beachhead in southeast Korea. There they stood off superior North Korean forces until Sept. 15, when a major UN amphibious assault was launched deep behind Communist lines at Inchon, the port of Seoul.

By Sept. 30, UN forces were in complete control of South Korea. They then crossed the 38th parallel and pursued retreating Communist forces into North Korea. In late October, as UN forces neared the Sino-Korean border, several hundred thousand Chinese Communist troops entered the conflict, pushing MacArthur's forces back to the border between North and South Korea. By the time truce talks began on July 10, 1951, UN forces had crossed over the parallel again and were driving back into North Korea. Cease-fire negotiations dragged on for two years before an armistice was finally signed at Panmunjom on July 27, 1953, leaving a devastated Korea in need of large-scale rehabilitation. No official peace treaty has ever been signed between the former combatants.

President Syngman Rhee, after 12 years in office, was forced to resign in 1960 amid rising discontent with his autocratic leadership. Po Sun Yun was elected to succeed him, but political instability continued. In 1961, Gen. Park Chung Hee seized power and subsequently began a program of economic reforms designed to stimulate the nation's economy. The U.S. stepped up military aid, strengthening South Korea's armed forces to 600,000 men. Park's assassination on Oct. 26, 1979, by Kim Jae Kyu, head of the Korean Central Intelligence Agency, brought a liberalizing trend as new president Choi Kyu Hah freed imprisoned dissidents.

The release of opposition leader Kim Dae Jung in Feb. 1980 sparked antigovernment demonstrations that turned into riots, which were brutally suppressed by authorities. Kim, the most visible leader of the opposition, was imprisoned again. Choi resigned on Aug. 16. Chun Doo Hwan, head of a military Special Committee for National Security Measures, was the sole candidate as the electoral college confirmed him as president on Aug. 27. In 1986–1987, South Korea's opposition demanded the president be selected by direct popular vote. After weeks of protest and rioting, Chun agreed to the demand. A split in the opposition led to Roh Tae Woo's election on Dec. 16, 1987.

In Aug. 1996 Roh was convicted on bribery charges and Chun was convicted for bribery as well as his role in the 1979 coup and the 1980 crackdown on rioters. In 1997, an accumulation of corrupt business practices and bad loans led to a series of bankruptcies and a massive devaluation of South Korea's currency. The political instability that followed helped former dissident Kim Dae Jung become the first South Korean president ever to be elected from the political opposition.

In 1998 the Asian economic crisis bottomed out in South Korea, and it began rebounding in 1999—the only sizable Asian economy to do so.

Antagonism between North and South Korea erupted into open aggression twice in 1998 and 1999. Tensions eased dramatically in June 2000, when President Kim Dae Jung met with the North's president, Kim Jong Il, in Pyongyang. The summit marked the first ever meeting of the countries' leaders. President Kim Dae Jung won the Nobel Peace Prize in Oct. 2000, for his "Sunshine Policy," which included initiating peace and reconciliation with North Korea. Cross-border discussions stalled after President George W. Bush told President Kim Dae Jung in a March 2001 meeting that he would not discuss missile negotiations any time soon with North Korea, shelving President Clinton's efforts toward normalizing relations. Bush's identification of North Korea as part of an "axis of evil" in 2002 served as a further obstacle to South-North discussions.

Roh Moo Hyun of the ruling Millennium Democratic Party became president in February 2003 and promptly faced daunting problems. His vow to pursue his predecessor's Sunshine Policy toward North Korea was put to the test as the North continued to taunt the world with boasts about its nuclear capabilities. In addition, many South Koreans began to resent the United States' dominant influence over their country. In May Roh faced a corruption investigation related to a real-estate transaction.

Kuwait

STATE OF KUWAIT

National name: Dawlat al Kuwayt
Emir: Sheik Jaber al-Ahmad al-Sabah (1977)
Prime Minister: Sheik Sabah al-Ahmed al-Sabah (2003)
Area: 6,880 sq mi (17,820 sq km)
Population (2003 est.): 2,183,161 (growth rate: 1.9%); birth rate: 21.8/1000; infant mortality rate: 10.6/1000; density per sq mi: 317
Capital (2003 est.): Kuwait, 1,709,800 (metro.area), 32,600 (city proper). **Largest city:** as-Salimiyah, 146,900. **Monetary unit:** Kuwaiti dinar. **Languages:** Arabic (official), English. **Ethnicity/race:** Kuwaiti 45%, other Arab 35%, South Asian 9%, Iranian 4%, other 7%. **Religions:** Islam, 85% (Shi'ite 30%, Sunni 70%), Christian, Hindu, Parsi, and other, 15%. **Literacy rate:** 78.6% (1995 est.)
Economic summary: GDP/PPP (2001 est.): $30.9 billion; per capita $15,100. **Real growth rate:** 4%. **Inflation:** 2.7%. **Unemployment:** 1.8% (official 1996 est.). **Arable land:** 0.34%. **Agriculture:** practically no crops; fish. **Labor force:** 1.3 million (1998 est.); note: 68% of the population in the 15–64 age group is non-national (July 1998 est.); agriculture n.a., industry n.a., services n.a. **Industries:** petroleum, petrochemicals, desalination, food processing, construction materials. **Natural resources:** petroleum, fish, shrimp, natural gas. **Exports:** $16.2 billion (f.o.b., 2001 est.): oil and refined products, fertilizers. **Imports:** $7.4 billion (f.o.b., 2001 est.): food, construction materials, vehicles and parts, clothing. **Major trading partners:** Japan, U.S., South Korea, Singapore, Netherlands, Pakistan, Indonesia, UK, Germany, China, France, Australia.

Geography Kuwait is situated northeast of Saudi Arabia at the northern end of the Persian Gulf, south of Iraq. It is slightly larger than Hawaii. The low-lying desert land is mainly sandy and barren.

Government Kuwait is a constitutional monarchy, governed by the al-Sabah family.

History Kuwait is believed to have been part of an early civilization in the 3rd millennium B.C. and to have traded with Mesopotamian cities. Archeological and historical traces disappeared around the first millennium B.C. At the beginning of the 18th century A.D., the 'Anizah tribe of central Arabia founded Kuwait City, which became an autonomous sheikdom by 1756. 'Abd Rahim of the al-Sabah became the first sheik, and his descendants continue to rule Kuwait today. In the late 18th and early 19th centuries, the sheikdom belonged to the fringes of the Ottoman Empire. Kuwait obtained British protection in 1897 when the sheik feared that the Turks would expand their hold over the area. In 1961, Britain ended the protectorate, giving Kuwait independence, but agreed to give military aid on request. Iraq immediately threatened to occupy the area, and the British sent troops to defend Kuwait. Soon afterward the Arab League sent in troops, replacing the British. Iraq's claim was dropped when the Arab League recognized Kuwait's independence on July 20, 1961. Kuwait typically followed a neutral and mediatory policy among Arab states.

Oil was discovered there in the 1930s, and Kuwait proved to have 20% of the world's known oil resources. Since 1946 it has been the world's second-largest oil exporter. The sheik, who receives half the profits, devotes most of them to the education, welfare, and modernization of his kingdom. In 1966, Sheik Sabah designated a relative, Jaber al-Ahmad al-Sabah, as his successor. By 1968, the sheikdom had established a model welfare state, and it sought to establish dominance among the sheikdoms and emirates of the Persian Gulf.

In July 1990, Iraqi president Saddam Hussein blamed Kuwait for falling oil prices. After a failed Arab mediation attempt to solve the dispute peacefully, Iraq invaded Kuwait on Aug. 2, 1990, set up a pro-Iraqi provisional government, and drained Kuwait of its economic resources. A coalition of Arab and Western military forces drove Iraqi troops from Kuwait in a mere four days, from Feb. 23–27, ending the Persian Gulf War. The emir returned to his country from Saudi Arabia in mid-March. Martial law, in effect since the end of the Gulf War, ended in late June. The U.S. sent 2,400 troops to the country in Aug. 1992 as part of a training exercise but this was widely interpreted as a show of strength to Saddam Hussein.

The general election of Oct. 1992 was a success for supporters of a return to Islamic law. A political independent was named speaker of the Parliament, and the opposition held 31 of the 50 seats. Iraqi "training" maneuvers near the Kuwaiti border in Oct. 1994 renewed fears of aggression in the country. A Kuwaiti appeal brought the quick deployment of U.S. and British troops and equipment. In 1999, the emir gave women the right to vote and run for Parliament. Later in 1999, however, Parliament defeated the ruler's decree. Kuwaiti society has grown increasingly conservative under the influence of Islamic fundamentalists. In 2003, traditionalists won a sweeping victory in parliamentary elections. The emir and crown prince (who served as prime minister) are elderly and ailing; in July 2003, the country's de facto leader, foreign minister Sabah al-Ahmed al-Sabah, replaced the crown prince as prime minister.

Kyrgyzstan

THE KYRGYZ REPUBLIC

President: Askar Akayev (1990)
Prime Minister: Nikolay Tanayev (2002)
Area: 76,641 sq mi (198,500 sq km)
Population (2003 est.): 4,892,808; (Kyrgyz, 52.4%; Russian, 18%; Uzbek, 12.9%; Ukrainian, 2.5%; German, 2.4%; other, 11.8%) (growth rate: 1.7%); birth rate: 26.1/1000; infant mortality rate: 75.3/1000; density per sq mi: 64
Capital and largest city (2003 est.): Bishkek (formerly Frunze), 824,900. **Other large city:** Osh 225,600. **Monetary unit:** Som. **Languages:** Kyrgyz (official); Russian is de facto second language of communication. **Ethnicity/race:** Kyrgyz 52.4%, Russian 18%, Uzbek 12.9%, Ukrainian 2.5%, German 2.4%, other 11.8%. **Religions:** Islam, 75%; Russian Orthodox, 20%; other, 5%. **Literacy rate:** 97% (1989 est.)
Economic summary: GDP/PPP (2001 est.): $13.5 billion; per capita $2,800. **Real growth rate:** 5%. **Inflation:** 7%. **Unemployment:** 7.2% (1999 est.). **Arable land:** 7%. **Agriculture:** tobacco, cotton, potatoes, vegetables, grapes, fruits and berries; sheep, goats, cattle, wool. **Labor force:** 2.7 million (2000); agriculture 55%, industry 15%, services 30% (2000 est.). **Industries:** small machinery, textiles, food processing, cement, shoes, sawn logs, refrigerators, furniture, electric motors, gold, rare earth metals. **Natural resources:** abundant hydropower; significant deposits of gold and rare earth metals; locally exploitable coal, oil, and natural gas; other deposits of nepheline, mercury, bismuth, lead, and zinc. **Exports:** $475 million (f.o.b., 2001 est.): cotton, wool, meat, tobacco; gold, mercury, uranium, hydropower; machinery; shoes. **Imports:** $420 million (f.o.b., 2001 est.): oil and gas, machinery and equipment, foodstuffs. **Major trading partners:** Germany, Uzbekistan, Russia, China, Kazakhstan, U.S., Turkey.

Geography Kyrgyzstan (formerly Kirghizia) is a rugged country with the Tien Shan mountain range covering approximately 95% of the whole territory. The mountaintops are covered with perennial snow and glaciers. Kyrgyzstan borders Kazakhstan on the north and northwest, Uzbekistan in the southwest, Tajikistan in the south, and China in the southeast. The republic is the same size in area as the state of Nebraska.

Government Constitutional republic.

History The native Kyrgyz are a Turkic people who in ancient times first settled in the Tien Shan mountains. They were traditionally pastoral nomads. There was extensive Russian colonization in the 1900s and Russian settlers were given much of the best agricultural land. This led to an unsuccessful and disastrous revolt by the Kyrgyz people in 1916. Kyrgyzstan became part of the Soviet Federated Socialist Republic in 1924, and was made an autonomous republic in 1926. It became a constituent republic of the USSR in 1936. The Soviets forced the Kyrgyz to abandon their nomadic culture and brought modern farming and industrial production techniques into their society. It has greatly changed their traditional way of life.

Kyrgyzstan proclaimed its independence from the Soviet Union on Aug. 31, 1991. On Dec. 21, 1991, Kyrgyzstan joined the Commonwealth of Independent States. The country joined the UN and the IMF in 1992 and adopted a shock-therapy economic program. Voters endorsed market reforms in a referendum held in Jan. 1994, and in 1996, referendum voters overwhelmingly endorsed proposed constitutional changes that enhanced the power of the president. Representatives of the country along with those of Russia, China, Kazakhstan, and Tajikistan signed a nonaggression agreement in April 1996. In March 1997, Russian border control was extended until the end of the year as authorities in Kyrgyzstan grew increasingly concerned about the growth of the illegal narcotics trade in the country.

Since 1999, several groups of radical Islamic gunmen, believed to be from Uzbekistan or Tajikistan, have led raids and kidnappings from camps in Kyrgyzstan's mountains.

In elections held Oct. 30, 2000, President Askar Akayev easily won reelection with nearly 75% of the vote. The election, however, was marred by allegations of fraud, diminishing Kyrgyzstan's claim to be the centerpiece of Central Asian democracy.

In 2001, Kyrgyzstan permitted troops from the U.S. and seven other nations to be stationed in the country in support of efforts to fight against the Taliban and al-Qaeda in neighboring Afghanistan. In 2002, construction of a large U.S. airbase began outside of Bishkek.

In Feb. 2003, a controversial referendum expanded Akayev's powers, and in June Parliament granted him lifelong immunity from prosecution.

Laos

LAO PEOPLE'S DEMOCRATIC REPUBLIC

President: Khamtai Siphandon (2001)
Prime Minister: Boungnang Vorachith (2001)
Area: 91,428 sq mi (236,800 sq km)
Population (2003 est.): 5,921,545 (growth rate: 2.5%); birth rate: 36.9/1000; infant mortality rate: 88.9/1000; density per sq mi: 65

Capital and largest city (2003 est.): Vientiane, 194,200. **Monetary unit:** New Kip. **Languages:** Lao (official), French, English. **Ethnicity/race:** Lao Loum (lowland) 68%, Lao Theung (upland) 22%, Lao Soung (highland) including the Hmong ("Meo") and the Yao (Mien) 9%, ethnic Vietnamese/Chinese 1%. **Religions:** Buddhist 60%, animist and other 40%. **Literacy rate:** 57% (1999 est.)

Economic summary: GDP/PPP (2001 est.): $9.2 billion; per capita $1,630 . **Real growth rate:** 5%. **Inflation:** 10%. **Unemployment:** 5.7% (1997 est.). **Arable land:** 4%. **Agriculture:** sweet potatoes, vegetables, corn, coffee, sugarcane, tobacco, cotton; tea, peanuts, rice; water buffalo, pigs, cattle, poultry. **Labor force:** 2.4 million (1999). **Industries:** tin and gypsum mining, timber, electric power, agricultural processing, construction, garments, tourism. **Natural resources:** timber, hydropower, gypsum, tin, gold, gemstones. **Exports:** $325 million (2001 est.): wood products, garments, electricity, coffee, tin. **Imports:** $540 million (f.o.b., 2000 est.): machinery and equipment, vehicles, fuel. **Major trading partners:** Thailand, France, Germany, UK, Belgium, Singapore, Japan, Hong Kong, China.

Geography A landlocked nation in Southeast Asia occupying the northwest portion of the Indochinese peninsula, Laos is surrounded by China, Vietnam, Cambodia, Thailand, and Burma. It is twice the size of Pennsylvania. Laos is a mountainous country, especially in the north, where peaks rise above 9,000 ft (2,800 m). Dense forests cover the northern and eastern areas. The Mekong River, which forms the boundary with Burma and Thailand, flows entirely through the country for 932 mi (1,500 km) of its course.

Government Communist state.

History The Lao people migrated into Laos from southern China from the 8th century onward. In the 14th century, the first Laotian state was founded, the Lan Xang kingdom, which ruled Laos until it split into three separate kingdoms in 1713. During the 18th century the three kingdoms came under Siamese (Thai) rule, and, in 1893, became a French protectorate. Its territory was incorporated into the union of Indochina. A strong nationalist movement developed during World War II, but France reestablished control in 1946 and made the king of Luang Prabang constitutional monarch of all Laos. France granted semiautonomy in 1949 and then, spurred by the Viet Minh rebellion in Vietnam, full independence within the French Union in 1950.

In 1951, Prince Souphanouvong organized the Pathet Lao, a Communist independence movement, in North Vietnam. Viet Minh and Pathet Lao forces invaded central Laos, and civil war resulted. By the Geneva agreements of 1954 and an armistice of 1955, two northern provinces were given to the Pathet Lao: the rest went to the royal regime. Full sovereignty was given to the kingdom by the Paris agreements of Dec. 29, 1954. In 1957, Prince Souvanna Phouma, the royal premier, and Pathet Lao leader Prince Souphanouvong, the premier's half-brother, agreed to reestablishment of a unified government, with Pathet Lao participation and integration of Pathet Lao forces into the royal army. The agreement broke down in 1959, and armed conflict began anew.

In 1960, the struggle became three-way as Gen. Phoumi Nosavan, controlling the bulk of the royal army, set up in the south a pro-Western revolutionary government headed by Prince Boun Oum. General Phoumi took Vientiane in December, driving Souvanna Phouma into exile in Cambodia. The Soviet bloc supported Souvanna Phouma. In 1961, a ceasefire was arranged and the three princes agreed to a coalition government headed by Souvanna Phouma.

But North Vietnam, the U.S. (in the form of CIA personnel), and China remained active in Laos after the settlement. North Vietnam used a supply line (Ho Chi Minh Trail) running down the mountain valleys of eastern Laos into Cambodia and South Vietnam, particularly after the U.S.–South Vietnamese incursion into Cambodia in 1970 stopped supplies via Cambodian seaports.

An agreement reached in 1973 revived the coalition government. The Communist Pathet Lao seized complete power in 1975, installing Souphanouvong as president and Kaysone Phomvihane as premier. Since then other parties and political groups have been moribund and most of their leaders have fled the country. The monarchy was abolished on Dec. 2, 1975, when the Pathet Lao ousted a coalition government and King Sisavang Vatthana abdicated.

The Supreme People's Assembly in Aug. 1991 adopted a new constitution that dropped all references to socialism but retained the one-party state. In addition to implementing market-oriented policies, the country has passed laws governing property, inheritance, and contracts.

During the 1990s, the country began making more diplomatic overtures toward its neighbors. In 1995, the U.S. announced a lifting of its ban on aid to the nation. By most international estimates, Laos is one of the ten poorest countries in the world. The subsistence farmers who make up more than 80% of the population have been plagued with bad agricultural conditions—alternately flood or drought—since 1993.

Since March 2000, Vientiane has been rocked by a series of unexplained blasts. The activity has been widely attributed to a group of Hmong tribesmen based in the north. The anti-Communist rebel group has been protesting the government's reluctance to embrace democratic reforms. Others attribute the bombs to rival factions in the government or military.

In June 2003, two foreign journalists and an American pastor of Lao descent were sentenced to 15 years in prison for obstructing police officers and possessing weapons and explosives, charges related to the death of a security guard. The defendants and human rights groups contend they were punished for covering the Hmong rebellion, which the government has refused to acknowledge. Facing international criticism, the Lao government released the prisoners in July.

Latvia

THE REPUBLIC OF LATVIA

National name: Latvija
President: Vaira Vike-Freiberga (1999)
Prime Minister: Einars Repse (2002)
Area: 24,938 sq mi (64,589 sq km)
Population (2003 est.): 2,348,784 (growth rate: –0.6%); birth rate: 8.6/1000; infant mortality rate: 14.6/1000; density per sq mi: 94

Capital and largest city (2003 est.): Riga, 867,700 (metro. area), 706,200 (city proper). **Other large cities:** Daugavpils, 111,700; Liepaja, 82,300. **Monetary unit:** Lats. **Language:** Latvian. **Ethnicity/race:** Latvian 57.7%, Russian 29.6%, Belorussian 4.1%, Ukrainian 2.7%, Polish 2.5%, other 3.4%. **Religions:** Lutheran, Roman Catholic, and Russian Orthodox. **Literacy:** 99.8%

Economic summary: GDP/PPP (2001 est.): $18.6 billion; per capita $7,800. **Real growth rate:** 6.3%. **Inflation:** 2.5%. **Unemployment:** 7.6%. **Arable land:** 29%. **Agriculture:** grain, sugar beets, potatoes, vegetables; beef, pork, milk, eggs; fish. **Labor force:** 1.1 million; agriculture 15%, industry 25%, services 60% (2000 est.). **Industries:** buses, vans, street and railroad cars, synthetic fibers, agricultural machinery, fertilizers, washing machines, radios, electronics, pharmaceuticals, processed foods, textiles; note—dependent on imports for energy and raw materials. **Natural resources:** peat, limestone, dolomite, hydropower, wood, arable land, minimal; amber. **Exports:** $2.2 billion (f.o.b., 2001): wood and wood products, machinery and equipment, metals, textiles, foodstuffs. **Imports:** $3.3 billion (f.o.b., 2001): machinery and equipment, chemicals, fuels, vehicles. **Major trading partners:** Germany, UK, Sweden, Lithuania, Russia, Finland.

Geography Latvia borders Estonia on the north, Lithuania in the south, the Baltic Sea with the Gulf of Riga in the west, Russia in the east, and Belarus in the southeast. Latvia is largely a fertile lowland with numerous lakes and hills to the east.

Government Parliamentary democracy.

History Baltic tribespeople settled along the Baltic Sea, and lacking a centralized government, fell prey to more powerful peoples. In the 13th century they were overcome by the Livonian Brothers of the Sword, a German order of knights whose mission was to conquer and Christianize the Baltic region. The land became part of the state of Livonia until 1561. Germans made up the ruling class of Livonia and Baltic tribes made up the peasantry. German became the official language of the region.

Poland conquered the territory in 1562, until Sweden took over the land in 1629, and ruled over it until 1721. Then the land passed to Russia. From 1721 until 1918, the Latvians remained Russian subjects, although they preserved their language, customs, and folklore.

The Russian Revolution of 1917 gave them their opportunity for freedom, and the Latvian republic was proclaimed on Nov. 18, 1918. The republic lasted little more than 20 years. Plagued by political instability, Latvia essentially became a dictatorship under President Karlis Ulmanis. It was occupied by Russian troops in 1939 and incorporated into the Soviet Union in 1940. Latvia allied itself with Germany in World War II, and German armies occupied the nation from 1941 to 1944. Of the 70,000 Jews living in Latvia during the war, 95% were massacred. In 1944, Russia again took control of Latvia.

Latvia was one of the most economically well-off and industrialized parts of the Soviet Union. When a coup against Soviet president Mikhail Gorbachev failed in 1991, the Baltic nations saw an opportunity to free themselves from Soviet domination and, following the actions of Lithuania and Estonia, Latvia declared its independence on Aug. 21, 1991. European and most other nations quickly recognized their independence, and on Sept. 2, 1991, President Bush announced full diplomatic recognition for Latvia, Estonia, and Lithuania. The Soviet Union recognized Latvia's independence on Sept. 6, and UN membership followed on Sept. 17, 1991.

Because Latvians' ethnic identity had been quashed throughout its history by foreign rulers, the new Latvian republic set up strict citizenship laws, limiting citizenship to ethnic Latvians and to those who had lived in the region before Soviet rule in 1940. This denied about 452,000 of the country's 740,000 ethnic Russians of citizenship.

Latvia's bid to join the European Union was not accepted in talks that began in 1997. In addition to improving its administrative systems, Latvia was told that it had to speed up naturalization of minorities, in particular its large number of Russians. In 1998, a referendum passed easing the citizenship rules, although it was still necessary to be competent in the Latvian language, which many believe is unreasonable to expect of older or poorly educated ethnic Russians. To aid in admission to NATO, Parliament in 2002 passed a law no longer requiring parliamentary candidates to speak Latvian. Latvia has been invited to become a member of both the EU and NATO in May 2004. In June 2003, Prime Minister Vike-Freiberga easily won reelection.

Lebanon

REPUBLIC OF LEBANON

National name: Al-Joumhouriya al-Lubnaniya
President: Émile Lahoud (1998)
Premier: Rafiq al-Hariri (2000)
Area: 4,015 sq mi (10,400 sq km)
Population (2003 est.): 3,727,703 (growth rate: 1.3%); birth rate: 19.7/1000; infant mortality rate: 26.4/1000; density per sq mi: 928
Capital and largest city (2003 est.): Beirut, 1,916,100 (metro. area), 1,171,000 (city proper). **Other large cities:** Tripoli, 212,900; Sidon, 149,000. **Monetary unit:** Lebanese pound. **Languages:** Arabic (official), French, English. **Ethnicity/race:** Arab 95%, Armenian 4%, other 1%. **Religions:** Islam 70%, Christian 30% (17 recognized sects), Judaism negl. (1 sect). **Literacy rate:** 86.4% (1997 est.)
Economic summary: GDP/PPP (2001 est.): $18.8 billion; per capita $5,200. **Real growth rate:** 1%. **Inflation:** 0.5%. **Unemployment:** 18% (1997 est.). **Arable land:** 18%. **Agriculture:** citrus, grapes, tomatoes, apples, vegetables, potatoes, olives, tobacco; sheep, goats. **Labor force:** 1.5 million; note: in addition, there are as many as 1 million foreign workers (1999 est.); services n.a., industry n.a., agriculture n.a. **Industries:** banking; food processing; jewelry; cement; textiles; mineral and chemical products; wood and furniture products; oil refining; metal fabricating. **Natural resources:** limestone, iron ore, salt, water-surplus state in a water-deficit region, arable land. **Exports:** $700 million (f.o.b., 2001 est.): foodstuffs, machinery and transport equipment, consumer goods, chemicals, textiles, metals, fuels, agricultural foods. **Imports:** $6.6 billion (f.o.b., 2001 est.): foodstuffs, machinery and transport equipment, consumer goods, chemicals, textiles, metals, fuels, agricultural foods. **Major trading partners:** Saudi Arabia, UAE, Switzerland, U.S., France, Iraq, Jordan, Kuwait, Syria, Italy, Germany, China, UK.

Geography Lebanon lies at the eastern end of the Mediterranean Sea north of Israel and west of Syria. It is four-fifths the size of Connecticut.

The Lebanon Mountains, which parallel the coast on the west, cover most of the country, while on the eastern border is the Anti-Lebanon range. Between the two lies the Bekaa Valley, the principal agricultural area.

Government Republic.

History After World War I, France was given a League of Nations mandate over Lebanon and its neighbor Syria, which together had previously been a single political unit in the Ottoman Empire. France divided them in 1920 into separate colonial administrations, drawing a border that separated predominantly Muslim Syria from the kaleidoscope of religious communities in Lebanon, where Maronite Christians were then dominant. After 20 years of the French mandate regime, Lebanon's independence was proclaimed on Nov. 26, 1941, but full independence came in stages. Under an agreement between representatives of Lebanon and the French National Committee of Liberation, most of the powers exercised by France were transferred to the Lebanese government on Jan. 1, 1944. The evacuation of French troops was completed in 1946.

According to the National Pact, different religious communities are represented in the government by having a Maronite Christian president, a Sunni Muslim prime minister, and a Shi'ite National Assembly speaker. The arrangement worked for two decades. Civil war broke out in 1958, with Muslim factions led by Kamal Jumblat and Saeb Salam rising in insurrection against the Lebanese government headed by President Camille Chamoun, a Maronite Christian favoring close ties to the West. At Chamoun's request, President Eisenhower, on July 15, sent U.S. troops to reestablish the government's authority.

Clan warfare between various religious factions in Lebanon goes back centuries. The hodgepodge includes Maronite Christians, who since independence have dominated the government; Sunni Muslims, who have prospered in business and shared political power; the Druze, who hold a faith incorporating aspects of Islam and Gnosticism; and Shi'ite Muslims.

A new—and bloodier—Lebanese civil war that broke out in 1975 resulted in the addition of still another ingredient in the brew—the Syrians. In the fighting between Lebanese factions, 40,000 Lebanese were estimated to have been killed and 100,000 wounded between March 1975 and Nov. 1976. At that point, a Syrian-dominated Arab Deterrent Force intervened and brought large-scale fighting to a halt.

Palestinian guerrillas staging raids on Israel from Lebanese territory drew punitive Israeli raids on Lebanon and two large-scale Israeli invasions, in 1978 and again in 1982. The Israelis withdrew in June 1978 after the UN Security Council created a 6,000-man peacekeeping force for the area, called UNIFIL. As they departed, the Israelis turned their strongholds over to a Christian militia that they had organized, instead of to the UN force.

The second Israeli invasion came on June 6, 1982, after an assassination attempt by Palestinian terrorists on the Israeli ambassador in London. As a base of the PLO, Lebanon became the Israelis' target. Nearly 7,000 Palestinians were dispersed to other Arab nations, and Israel pulled back some of its forces. The violence seemed to have come to an end when, on Sept. 14, Bashir Gemayel, the 34-year-old president-elect, was killed by a bomb that destroyed the headquarters of his Christian Phalangist Party.

The day after Gemayel's assassination, Israeli troops moved into West Beirut in force. On Sept. 17, it was revealed that Christian militiamen had massacred hundreds of Palestinians in two refugee camps, but Israel denied responsibility. On Sept. 20, Amin Gemayel, older brother of Bashir Gemayel, was elected president by the Parliament.

The massacre in the refugee camps prompted the return of a multinational peacekeeping force. Its mandate was to support the central Lebanese government, but it soon found itself drawn into the struggle for power between different Lebanese factions. During their stay in Lebanon, 260 U.S. Marines and about 60 French soldiers were killed, most of them in suicide bombings of the Marine and French army compounds on Oct. 23, 1983. The multinational force left in the spring of 1984.

In July 1986, Syrian observers took a position in Beirut to monitor a peacekeeping agreement. The agreement broke down and fighting between Shi'ite and Druze militia in West Beirut became so intense that Syrian troops mobilized in Feb. 1987, suppressing militia resistance.

In early 1991, the Lebanese government, backed by Syria, attempted to regain control over the south and disband all private militias, thereby ending the 16-year civil war. These conflicts destroyed much of the infrastructure and industry of Lebanon.

In the general elections of Aug. 1992 most Christians abstained from voting, demanding that Syrian forces first leave the country. The new legislature consisted of mostly pro-Syrian members. The largest Christian party was further weakened when in Jan. 1993 it appeared to split into two factions.

In June 1999, just before Israeli prime minister Benjamin Netanyahu left office, Israel bombed Southern Lebanon, its most severe attack on the country since 1996. In May 2000, the new prime minister, Ehud Barak, withdrew Israeli troops after 22 years of occupation.

In Sept. 2000, opposition party candidates allied with former prime minister Rafiq al-Hariri won a landslide victory in parliamentary elections, in which Lebanon's severe recession was a major issue. Hariri became prime minister a month later.

In the summer of 2001, Syria withdrew nearly all of its 25,000 troops from Beirut and surrounding areas. Troops, however, remain in the countryside. With the continuation of Israeli-Palestinian violence in 2002, Hezbollah began again building up forces along the Lebanese-Israeli border.

Lesotho

KINGDOM OF LESOTHO

Sovereign: King Letsie III (1996)
Prime Minister: Pakalitha Mosisili (1998)
Area: 11,720 sq mi (30,355 sq km)
Population (2003 est.): 1,861,959 (growth rate: 0.3%); birth rate: 27.3/1000; infant mortality rate: 86.2/1000; density per sq mi: 159
Capital and largest city (2003 est.): Maseru 173,700. **Monetary unit:** Maluti. **Languages:** English and Sesotho (official); also Zulu and Xhosa. **Ethnicity/race:** Sotho 99.7%, Europeans 1,600, Asians 800. **Religions:** Christian 80%, indigenous beliefs, Islam, and Bahai. **Literacy rate:** 83% (1999 est.)
Economic summary: GDP/PPP (2001 est.): $5.3 billion; per capita $2,450. **Real growth rate:** 2.6%. **Inflation:** 6.9%. **Unemployment:** 45% (2000 est.). **Arable land:** 11%. **Agriculture:** corn, wheat, pulses, sorghum, barley; livestock. **Labor force:** 700,000 economically active; 86% of resident population engaged in subsistence agriculture; roughly 35% of the active male wage earners work in South Africa. **Industries:** food, beverages, textiles, apparel assembly, handicrafts; construction; tourism. **Natural resources:** water, agricultural and grazing land, some diamonds and other minerals. **Exports:** $250 million (f.o.b., 2001 est.): manufactures 75% (clothing, footwear, road vehicles), wool and mohair, food and live animals. **Imports:** $720 million (f.o.b., 2001 est.): food; building materials, vehicles, machinery, medicines, petroleum products. **Major trading partners:** South African Customs Union, North America, Asia. **Member of Commonwealth of Nations**

Geography Mountainous Lesotho, the size of Maryland, is surrounded by the Republic of South Africa in the east-central part of that country except for short borders on the east and south with two discontinuous units of the Republic of Transkei.

Government Parliamentary constitutional monarchy.

History Lesotho (formerly Basutoland) was constituted a native state under British protection by a treaty signed with the native chief Moshoeshoe in 1843. It was annexed to Cape Colony in 1871, but in 1884 it was restored to direct control by the Crown. The colony of Basutoland became the independent nation of Lesotho on Oct. 4, 1966, with King Moshoeshoe II as sovereign.

In the 1970 elections, Ntsu Mokhehle, head of the Basutoland Congress Party, claimed a victory, but Prime Minister Leabua Jonathan declared a state of emergency, suspended the constitution, and arrested Mokhehle. King Moshoeshoe II returned after a compromise with Jonathan in which the new constitution would name him head of state but forbid his participation in politics.

After the king refused to approve the replacement in Feb. 1990 of individuals dismissed by Justin Metsino Lekhanya, the chairman of the Military Council, the latter stripped the king of his executive power. Then in early March, Lekhanya sent the king into exile. In Nov., the king was dethroned, and his son was sworn in as King Letsie III.

Lekhanya was himself forced to resign in April 1991, and Col. Ramaema became the new chairman in May. In Jan. 1995, the crown reverted to the father of Letsie III, Moshoeshoe II. Letsie again became crown prince. In 1996, however, King Moshoeshoe died in an automobile accident, and Letsie again assumed the throne.

In fall 1998, hundreds of demonstrators protested for weeks in front of the king's palace, claiming voting fraud in the May elections that put Prime Minister Pakalitha Mosisili in power. They demanded that the government step down and hold new elections. Troops from South Africa and Botswana entered the country to stop the riots and put down an army mutiny.

In parliamentary elections in 2002, the ruling Lesotho Congress for Democracy won 54% of the vote.

Liberia

REPUBLIC OF LIBERIA

President: Gyude Bryant (2003)
Area: 43,000 sq mi (111,370 sq km)
Population (2003 est.): 3,317,176 (growth rate: 2.7%); birth rate: 45.3/1000; infant mortality rate: 132.2/1000; density per sq mi: 77
Capital and largest city (2003 est.): Monrovia, 1,348,900 (metro. area), 550,200 (city proper). **Monetary unit:** Liberian dollar. **Languages:** English (official) and tribal dialects. **Ethnicity/race:** indigenous African tribes 95% (including Kpelle, Bassa, Gio, Kru, Grebo, Mano, Krahn, Gola, Gbandi, Loma, Kissi, Vai, and Bella), Americo-Liberians 5% (descendants of former slaves). **Religions:** traditional 40%, Christian 40%, Islam 20%. **Literacy rate:** 38.3% (1995 est.)
Economic summary: GDP/PPP (2001 est.): $3.6 billion; per capita $1,100. **Real growth rate:** 5%. **Inflation:** 8%. **Unemployment:** 70%. **Arable land:** 2%. **Agriculture:** rubber, coffee, cocoa, rice, cassava (tapioca), palm oil, sugarcane, bananas; sheep, goats; timber. **Labor force:** agriculture 70%, industry 8%, services 22% (2000 est.). **Industries:** rubber processing, palm oil processing, timber, diamonds. **Natural resources:** iron ore, timber, diamonds, gold, hydropower. **Exports:** $55 million (f.o.b., 2000 est.): rubber, timber, iron, diamonds, cocoa, coffee. **Imports:** $170 million (f.o.b., 2000 est.): fuels, chemicals, machinery, transportation equipment, manufactured goods; rice and other foodstuffs. **Major trading partners:** Belgium, Germany, Italy, U.S., France, South Korea, Japan, Singapore.

Geography Lying on the Atlantic in the southern part of West Africa, Liberia is bordered by Sierra Leone, Guinea, and Côte d'Ivoire. It is comparable in size to Tennessee. Most of the country is a plateau covered by dense tropical forests, which thrive under an annual rainfall of about 160 in. a year.

Government Republic.

History Africa's first republic, Liberia was founded in 1822 as a result of the efforts of the American Colonization Society to settle freed American slaves in West Africa. The society contended that the immigration of blacks to Africa was an answer to the problem of slavery as well as to what it felt was the incompatibility of the races. Over the course of forty years, about 12,000 slaves were voluntarily relocated. Originally called Monrovia, the colony became the Free and Independent Republic of Liberia in 1847.

The English-speaking Americo-Liberians, descendants of former American slaves, make up only 5% of the population, but have historically dominated the intellectual and ruling class. Liberia's indigenous population is composed of 16 different ethnic groups.

The government of Africa's first republic was modeled after that of the United States, and Joseph Jenkins Roberts of Virginia was elected the first president. Ironically, Liberia's constitution denied indigenous Liberians equal rights with the lighter-skinned American emigrants and their descendants.

After 1920, considerable progress was made toward opening up the interior, a process that was spurred in 1951 by the establishment of a 43-mile (69-km) railroad to the Bomi Hills from Monrovia. In July 1971, while serving his sixth term as president, William V. S. Tubman died following surgery and was succeeded by his long-time associate, Vice President William R. Tolbert, Jr.

Tolbert was ousted in a military coup on April 12, 1980, by Master Sgt. Samuel K. Doe, backed by the U.S. government. Doe's rule was characterized by corruption and brutality. A rebellion led by Charles Taylor, a former Doe aide, and the National Patriotic Front of Liberia (NPFL), started in Dec. 1989; the following year, Doe was assassinated. The Economic Community of West African States (ECOWAS) negotiated with the government and the rebel factions and attempted to restore order, but the civil war raged on. By April 1996, factional fighting by the country's warlords had destroyed any last vestige of normalcy and civil society. The civil war finally ended in 1997.

In what was considered by international observers to be a free election, Charles Taylor won 75% of the presidential vote in July 1997. Taylor's government focused more on armed security rather than reconstruction of the country after its long civil war. While Taylor attempted to fashion himself into a democratic political leader, his behavior was that of a militia rebel. The country has next to no health care system, and the capital is without electricity and running water. Taylor supported Sierra Leone's brutal Revolutionary United Front (RUF) in the hopes of toppling his neighbor's government, and in exchange for diamonds, which enriched his personal coffers. As a consequence, the UN issued sanctions.

Between 2000 and 2002, fighting at the junction of the border between Liberia, Sierra Leone, and Guinea occurred between a jumble of warring factions, including the armies of Liberia and Guinea, rebel Guineans and Liberians, and the RUF. Taylor charged neighboring Guinea with aiding the rebels, who were operating from within Guinean territory. In 2002, rebels—Liberians United for Reconciliation and Democracy

(LURD)—intensified their attacks on Taylor's government. By June 2003, LURD and other rebel groups controlled two-thirds of the country. Taylor signed a cease-fire accord in June, and agreed to rebel demands to give up the presidency—an offer he quickly rescinded. In July rebel groups moved into Monrovia, and the increased fighting intensified an already dire humanitarian crisis. In August, ECOWAS, the West African peacekeeping troops led by Nigeria, entered the country, along with a handful of American marines. Finally, on Aug. 11, Taylor stepped down and went into exile in Nigeria. Gyude Bryant, a businessman seen as a coalition-builder, was selected by the various factions as the new president.

Libya

SOCIALIST PEOPLE'S LIBYAN ARAB JAMAHIRIYA

National name: Socialist People's Libyan Arab Jamahiriya
Chief of State: Col. Muammar al-Qaddafi (1969)
Prime Minister: Mubarak Abdallah al-Shamikh (2000)
Area: 679,358 sq mi (1,759,540 sq km)
Population (2003 est.): 5,499,074 (growth rate: 2.4%); birth rate: 27.4/1000; infant mortality rate: 26.8/1000; density per sq mi: 8
Capital and largest city (2003 est.): Tripoli, 2,357,800 (metro. area), 1,269,700 (city proper). **Other large city:**Benghazi, 734,900. **Monetary unit:** Libyan dinar. **Languages:** Arabic, Italian and English widely understood in major cities. **Ethnicity/race:** Berber and Arab 97%, Greeks, Maltese, Italians, Egyptians, Pakistanis, Turks, Indians, Tunisians. **Religion:** Islam. **Literacy rate:** 76.2% (1995 est.)
Economic summary: GDP/PPP (2001 est.): $40 billion; per capita $7,600. **Real growth rate:** 3%. **Inflation:** 13.6%. **Unemployment:** 30% (2000 est.). **Arable land:** 1%. **Agriculture:** wheat, barley, olives, dates, citrus, vegetables, peanuts, soybeans; cattle. **Labor force:** 1.5 million (2000 est.); services and government 54%, industry 29%, agriculture 17% (1997 est.). **Industries:** petroleum, food processing, textiles, handicrafts, cement. **Natural resources:** petroleum, natural gas, gypsum. **Exports:** $13.1 billion (f.o.b., 2001 est.): crude oil, refined petroleum products. **Imports:** $8.7 billion (f.o.b., 2001 est.): machinery, transport equipment, food, manufactured goods. **Major trading partners:** Italy, Germany, Spain, Turkey, France, Switzerland, UK, Tunisia, South Korea.

Geography Libya stretches along the northeast coast of Africa between Tunisia and Algeria on the west and Egypt on the east; to the south are the Sudan, Chad, and Niger. It is one-sixth larger than Alaska. A greater part of the country lies within the Sahara. Along the Mediterranean coast and farther inland is arable plateau land.

Government Military dictatorship.

History The first inhabitants of Libya were Berber tribes. In the 7th century B.C., Phoenicians colonized the eastern section of Libya, called Cyrenaica, and Greeks colonized the western portion, called Tripolitania. Tripolitania was for a time under Carthaginian control. It became part of the Roman Empire from 46 B.C. to A.D. 436, after which it was sacked by the Vandals. Cyrenaica belonged to the Roman Empire from the 1st century B.C. until its decline, after which it was invaded by Arab forces in 642. Beginning in the 16th century, both Tripolitania and Cyrenaica nominally became part of the Ottoman Empire.

Tripolitania was one of the outposts for the Barbary pirates who raided Mediterranean merchant ships or required them to pay tribute. In 1801, the pasha of Tripoli raised the price of tribute, which led to the Tripolitan war with the United States. When the peace treaty was signed on June 4, 1805, U.S. ships no longer had to pay tribute to Tripoli.

Following the outbreak of hostilities between Italy and Turkey in 1911, Italian troops occupied Tripoli. Italian sovereignty was recognized in 1912. Libyans continued to fight the Italians until 1914, by which time Italy controlled most of the land. Italy formally united Tripolitania and Cyrenaica in 1934 as the colony of Libya.

Libya was the scene of much desert fighting during World War II. After the fall of Tripoli on Jan. 23, 1943, it came under Allied administration. In 1949, the UN voted that Libya should become independent, and in 1951 it became the United Kingdom of Libya. Oil was discovered in the impoverished country in 1958, and eventually transformed its economy.

On Sept. 1, 1969, 27-year-old Col. Muammar al-Qaddafi deposed the king and revolutionized the country, making it a pro-Arabic, anti-Western, Islamic republic with socialist leanings. It was also rabidly anti-Israeli. A notorious firebrand, Qaddafi aligned himself with dictators, such as Uganda's Idi Amin, and fostered anti-Western terrorism.

On Aug. 19, 1981, two U.S. Navy F-14s shot down two Soviet-made SU-22s of the Libyan air force that had attacked them in air space above the Gulf of Sidra. On March 24, 1986, U.S. and Libyan forces skirmished in the Gulf of Sidra, and two Libyan patrol boats were sunk. Qaddafi's troops also supported rebels in Chad but suffered major military reverses in 1987. A two-year-old U.S. covert policy to destabilize the Libyan government ended in failure in Dec. 1990.

On Dec. 21, 1988, a Boeing 747 exploded in flight over Lockerbie, Scotland, the result of a terrorist bomb, killing all 259 people aboard and 11 on the ground. This and other acts of terrorism, including the bombing of a Berlin discoteque in 1986, and the downing of a French UTA airliner in 1989 that killed 170, turned Libya into a pariah in the eyes of the west. Two Libyan intelligence agents were indicted in the Lockerbie bombing, but Qaddafi refused to hand them over, leading to UN-approved trade and air traffic embargoes in 1992. On April 5, 1999, after years of negotiations, Libya surrendered the two men. The suspects, Abdel Basset Ali al-Megrahi and Lamen Khalifa Fhimah, were tried in the Netherlands in 2000–2001. Megrahi was found guilty of mass murder; the other defendant was found innocent. Libya had hoped its faint-hearted cooperation would lead to suspended sanctions, which had severely affected the Libyan economy. The UN did suspend its sanctions, but they were not formally removed for another four years, until Sept. 2003, when Libya finally admitted its guilt and agreed to pay $2.7 billion to the families.

Qaddafi has also sought to play a leading role in African affairs, promoting a united Africa. The policy suffered a severe setback, however, in Sept. 2000, when Libyan resentment over the 1 million black Africans living in the country of 6 million people erupted into violence. Rampaging mobs killed hundreds of blacks, prompting several African nations to launch airlifts to repatriate thousands of citizens.

In Jan. 2003, Libya was chosen to chair the UN Human Rights Commission over the objections of the United States and numerous human rights organizations, who cited Libya's egregious human rights record.

Liechtenstein

PRINCIPALITY OF LIECHTENSTEIN

Ruler: Prince Hans Adam II (1989)
Head of Government: Otmar Hasler (2001)
Area: 62 sq mi (160 sq km)
Population (2003 est.): 33,145 (growth rate: 0.4%); birth rate: 10.9/1000; infant mortality rate: 4.8/1000; density per sq mi: 537
Capital and largest city (2003 est.): Vaduz, 5,300. **Monetary unit:** Swiss franc. **Languages:** German (official), Alemmanic dialect. **Ethnicity/race:** Alemannic 86%; Italian, Turkish, and other 14%. **Religions:** Roman Catholic, 76.2%, Protestant, 7%; unknown, 10.6%; other, 6.2%. **Literacy rate:** 100% (1981)
Economic summary: GDP/PPP (1998 est.): $730 million; per capita $23,000. **Real growth rate:** n.a. **Inflation:** 1% (2001). **Unemployment:** 1.8% (Feb. 1999). **Arable land:** 25%. **Agriculture:** wheat, barley, corn, potatoes; livestock, dairy products. **Labor force:** 22,891 of which 13,847 are foreigners; 8,231 commute from Austria and Switzerland to work each day; industry, trade, and building 45%, services 53%, agriculture, fishing, forestry, and horticulture 2% (1997 est.). **Industries:** electronics, metal manufacturing, textiles, ceramics, pharmaceuticals, food products, precision instruments, tourism. **Natural resources:** hydroelectric potential, arable land. **Exports:** $2.47 billion (1996):small specialty machinery, dental products, stamps, hardware, pottery. **Imports:** $917.3 million (1996): machinery, metal goods, textiles, foodstuffs, motor vehicles. **Major trading partners:** EU and EFTA countries.

Geography Tiny Liechtenstein, not quite as large as Washington, D.C., lies on the east bank of the Rhine River south of Lake Constance between Austria and Switzerland. It consists of low valley land and Alpine peaks. Falknis (8,401 ft; 2,561 m) and Naafkopf (8,432 ft; 2,570 m) are the tallest.

Government Hereditary constitutional monarchy.

History The Liechtensteiners are descended from the Alemanni tribe that came into the region after A.D. 500. Founded in 1719, Liechtenstein was a member of the German Confederation from 1815 to 1866, when it became an independent principality. It abolished its army in 1868 and has managed to stay neutral and undamaged in all European wars since then. Liechtenstein still claims 1,600 sq km of Czech territory (the royal family's ancestral home) confiscated in 1918; the Czech Republic insists that restitution does not go back before Feb. 1948, when the Communists seized power. In a referendum on July 1, 1984, male voters granted women the right to vote in national (but not local) elections—a victory for Prince Hans Adam. A treaty negotiated between EFTA (European Free Trade Association) and the EU linking the two as the European Economic Area was ratified by Liechtenstein in a Dec. 1993 vote, but Switzerland rejected it. After renegotiation the treaty was again subjected to a referendum in April 1995 and approved. Liechtenstein won a special concession limiting immigration.

Blacklisted in 2000 as a center for money laundering, Liechtenstein toughened its laws and made major efforts to clean up its financial practices. In 2002, the country was removed from the OECD's (Organization of Economic Cooperation and Development's) money-laundering blacklist.

In March 2003, Liechtenstein's people overwhelmingly voted to give its prince more powers, including the right to dismiss governments and approve judicial nominees. Prince Hans Adam II had threatened to leave the country if his demands for more authority were not met. Before the vote, he had already possessed more power than any other European monarch. In August he announced he would give up the throne in one year's time, passing it on to his son, Prince Alois.

Lithuania

REPUBLIC OF LITHUANIA

National name: Lietuva
President: Rolandas Paksas (2003)
Prime Minister: Algirdas Brazauskas (2001)
Area: 25,174 sq mi (65,200 sq km)
Population (2003 est.): 3,592,561 (growth rate: –0.2%); birth rate: 10.5/1000; infant mortality rate: 14.2/1000; density per sq mi: 143
Capital and largest city (2003 est.): Vilnius, 543,500. **Other large cities:** Kaunas, 379,800; Klaipéda, 193,400. **Monetary unit:** Litas. **Languages:** Lithuanian (official), Polish, Russian. **Ethnicity/race:** Lithuanian 80.6%, Russian 8.7%, Polish 7%, Belorussian 1.6%, other 2.1%. **Religions:** Catholic 85%, others include Lutheran, Russian Orthodox, Protestant, evangelical Christian Baptist, Islam, Judaism. **Literacy:** 98% (1989 est.)
Economic summary: GDP/PPP (2001 est.): $27.4 billion; per capita $7,600. **Real growth rate:** 4.8%. **Inflation:** 1.3%. **Unemployment:** 12.5%. **Arable land:** 45%. **Agriculture:** grain, potatoes, sugar beets, flax, vegetables; beef, milk, eggs; fish. **Labor force:** 1.5 million; industry 30%, agriculture 20%, services 50% (1997 est.). **Industries:** metal-cutting machine tools, electric motors, television sets, refrigerators and freezers, petroleum refining, shipbuilding (small ships), furniture making, textiles, food processing, fertilizers, agricultural machinery, optical equipment, electronic components, computers, amber. **Natural resources:** peat, arable land. **Exports:** $4.8 billion (f.o.b., 2001): mineral products 21%, textiles and clothing 19%, machinery and equipment 11%, chemicals 8%, wood and wood products 6%, foodstuffs 4% (2000). **Imports:** $5.7 billion (f.o.b., 2001): mineral products 23%, machinery and equipment 16%, chemicals 9%, textiles and clothing 9%, transport equipment 9% (2000). **Major trading partners:** Latvia, Germany, Russia, Ukraine, Poland, France, UK.

Geography Lithuania is situated on the eastern shore of the Baltic Sea and borders Latvia on the north, Belarus on the east and south, and Poland and the Kaliningrad region of Russia on the southwest. It is a country of gently rolling hills, many forests, rivers and streams, and lakes. Its principal natural resource is agricultural land.

Government Parliamentary democracy.

History The Liths, or Lithuanians, united in the 12th century under the rule of Mindaugas, who became king in 1251. Through marriage, one of the later Lithuanian rulers became the king of Poland (Ladislaus II) in 1386, uniting the countries. In 1410, the Poles and Lithuanians defeated the powerful Teutonic Knights at Tannenberg. From the 14th to the 16th century, Poland and Lithuania made up one of medieval Europe's largest empires, stretching from the Black Sea almost to Moscow. The two countries formed a confederation for almost 200 years, and in 1569 they formally united. Russia, Prussia, and Austria partitioned Poland in 1772, 1792, and 1795. As a consequence, Lithuania came under Russian rule after the last partition. Russia attempted to immerse Lithuania in Russian culture and language, but anti-Russian sentiment continued to grow. Following World War I and the collapse of Russia, Lithuania declared independence (1918), under German protection.

The republic was then annexed by the Soviet Union in 1940. From June 1941 to 1944, it was occupied by

German troops, with whom Lithuania served in World War II. Some 240,000 Jews were massacred in Lithuania during the Nazi years. In 1944, the Soviets again annexed Lithuania.

The Lithuanian independence movement reemerged in 1988. In 1990, Vytautas Landsbergis, the non-Communist head of the largest Lithuanian popular movement (Sajudis), was elected president. On the same day, the Supreme Council rejected Soviet rule and declared the restoration of Lithuania's independence, the first Baltic republic to take this action. Confrontation with the Soviet Union ensued along with economic sanctions, but they were lifted after both sides agreed to a face-saving compromise.

Lithuania's independence was quickly recognized by major European and other nations, including the United States. The Soviet Union finally recognized the independence of the Baltic states on Sept. 6, 1991. UN admittance followed on Sept. 17, 1991. Successful implementation of structural and legislative reforms in Lithuania attracted greater foreign direct investments by the mid-1990s.

In late 2002, Lithuania was accepted for membership in both the EU and NATO (effective 2004). In Jan. 2003 Rolandas Paksas defeated the incumbent, Valdas Adamkus, in the presidential election, a surprising upset, given that Adamkus had helped bring about his country's entry into NATO and the European Union.

Luxembourg

GRAND DUCHY OF LUXEMBOURG

National name: Grand-Duché de Luxembourg
Ruler: Grand Duke Henri (2000)
Premier: Jean-Claude Juncker (1995)
Area: 998 sq mi (2,586 sq km)
Population (2003 est.): 454,157 (growth rate: 0.3%); birth rate: 11.9/1000; infant mortality rate: 4.7/1000; density per sq mi: 455
Capital and largest city (2003 est.): Luxembourg, 78,800. **Monetary units:** Euro (formerly Luxembourg franc). **Languages:** Luxermbourgish, French, German. **Ethnicity/race:** Celtic base (with French and German blend), Portuguese, Italian, and European (guest and worker residents). **Religions:** Roman Catholic 97%, Protestant and Jewish 3%. **Literacy rate:** 100% (2000 est.)
Economic summary: GDP/PPP (2001 est.): $19.2 billion; per capita $43,400. **Real growth rate:** 4%. **Inflation:** 2.4%. **Unemployment:** 2.4%. **Arable land:** 25%. **Agriculture:** barley, oats, potatoes, wheat, fruits, wine grapes; livestock products. **Labor force:** 262,300 (of whom 87,400 are foreign cross-border workers primarily from France, Belgium, and Germany) (2000); services 90.1%, industry 8%, agriculture 1.9% (1999 est.). **Industries:** banking, iron and steel, food processing, chemicals, metal products, engineering, tires, glass, aluminum. **Natural resources:** iron ore (no longer exploited), arable land. **Exports:** $7.85 billion (f.o.b., 2000): machinery and equipment, steel products, chemicals, rubber products, glass. **Imports:** $10.25 billion (c.i.f., 2000): minerals, metals, foodstuffs, quality consumer goods. **Major trading partners:** EU, U.S.

Geography Luxembourg is about half the size of Delaware. The Ardennes Mountains extend from Belgium into the northern section of Luxembourg. The rolling plateau of the fertile Bon Pays is in the south.

Government Constitutional monarchy.

History Luxembourg, once part of Charlemagne's empire, became an independent state in 963, when Siegfried, count of Ardennes, became sovereign of Lucilinburhuc ("Little Fortress"). In 1060, Conrad, a descendant of Siegfried, took the title count of Luxembourg. From the 15th to the 18th century, Spain, France, and Austria held the duchy in turn. The Congress of Vienna in 1815 made it a Grand Duchy and gave it to William I, king of the Netherlands. In 1839, the Treaty of London ceded the western part of Luxembourg to Belgium. The eastern part, continuing in personal union with the Netherlands and a member of the German Confederation, became autonomous in 1848 and a neutral territory by decision of the London Conference of 1867, governed by its grand duke. Germany occupied the duchy in World Wars I and II. Allied troops liberated the enclave in 1944.

Luxembourg joined NATO in 1949, the Benelux Economic Union (with Belgium and the Netherlands) in 1948, and the European Economic Community (later the EU) in 1957. In 1961, Prince Jean, son and heir of Grand Duchess Charlotte, was made head of state, acting for his mother. She abdicated in 1964, and Prince Jean became grand duke. Grand Duchess Charlotte died in 1985. Luxembourg's Parliament approved the Maastricht Accord, paving the way for the economic unity of the EU in July 1992. Crown Prince Henri was sworn in as grand duke in Oct. 2000, replacing his father, Jean, who had been head of state for 26 years. In 2002, the euro became the country's new currency.

Macedonia

REPUBLIC OF MACEDONIA[1]

National Name: Republika Makedonija
President: Boris Trajkovski (1999)
Prime Minister: Branko Crvenkovski (2002)
Area: 9,928 sq mi (25,713 sq km)
Population (2003 est.): 2,063,122 (growth rate: 0.5%); birth rate: 13.2/1000; infant mortality rate: 12.1/1000; density per sq mi: 211
Capital and largest city (2003 est.): Skopje, 587,300 (metro. area), 452,500 (city proper). **Other large cities:** Bitola, 84,400; Kumanovo, 78,900; Prilep, 56,900. **Monetary unit:** Denar. **Languages:** Macedonian (official), which uses the Cyrillic alphabet, Albanian (official), Turkish, other. **Ethnicity/race:** Macedonian 66.6%, Albanian 22.7%, Turkish 4%, Rom (Gypsy) 2.2%, Serb 2.1%, other 2.4%. **Religions:** Eastern Orthodox 67%, Islam 30% (1994)
Economic summary: GDP/PPP (2001 est.): $9 billion; per capita $4,400. **Real growth rate:** –4%. **Inflation:** 5.3%. **Unemployment:** 39%. **Arable land:** 24%. **Agriculture:** rice, tobacco, wheat, corn, millet, cotton, sesame, mulberry leaves, citrus, vegetables; beef, pork, poultry, mutton. **Labor force:** 1.1 million (2000 est.); agriculture n.a., industry n.a., services n.a. **Industries:** coal, metallic chromium, lead, zinc, ferronickel, textiles, wood products, tobacco, food processing, buses. **Natural resources:** chromium, lead, zinc, manganese, tungsten, nickel, low-grade iron ore, asbestos, sulfur, timber, arable land. **Exports:** $1.2 billion (f.o.b., 2001 est.): food, beverages, tobacco; miscellaneous manufactures, iron and steel. **Imports:** $1.5 billion (f.o.b., 2001 est.): machinery and equipment, chemicals, fuels; food products. **Major trading partners:** Yugoslavia, Germany, U.S., Italy, Greece, Ukraine, Russia.

1. The UN recognized the Republic of Macedonia on April 8, 1993, under the temporary name the Former Yugoslav Republic of Macedonia. The U.S. recognized Macedonia as a state in Feb. 1994.

Geography Macedonia is a landlocked state in the heart of the Balkans and is slightly smaller than the state of Vermont. It is a mountainous country with small basins of agricultural land. The Vardar is the largest and most important river.

Government Parliamentary democracy.

History The Republic of Macedonia occupies the western half of the ancient Kingdom of Macedonia. Historic Macedonia was defeated by Rome and became a Roman province in 148 B.C. After the Roman Empire was divided in A.D. 395, Macedonia was intermittently ruled by the Byzantine Empire until Turkey took possession of the land in 1371. The Ottoman Turks dominated Macedonia for the next five centuries, until 1913. During the 19th and 20th centuries, there was a constant struggle by the Balkan powers to possess Macedonia for its economic wealth and its strategic military corridors. The Treaty of San Stefano in 1878, ending the Russo-Turkish War, gave the largest part of Macedonia to Bulgaria. Bulgaria lost much of its Macedonian territory when it was defeated by the Greeks and Serbs in the Second Balkan War of 1913. Most of Macedonia went to Serbia and the remainder was divided among Greece and Bulgaria.

In 1918, Serbia, which included Macedonia, joined in union with Croatia, Slovenia, and Montenegro to form the Kingdom of Serbs, Croats, and Slovenes, which was renamed Yugoslavia in 1929. Bulgaria joined the Axis powers in World War II and occupied parts of Yugoslavia, including Macedonia, in 1941. During the occupation of their country, Macedonian resistance fighters fought a guerrilla war against the invading troops. The Yugoslavian federation was reestablished after the defeat of Germany in 1945, and in 1946, the government removed the Vardar territory of Macedonia from Serbian control and made it an autonomous Yugoslavian republic. Later, when President Tito recognized the Macedonian people as a separate nation, Macedonia's distinct culture and language were able to flourish, no longer suppressed by outside rule.

On Sept. 8, 1991, Macedonia declared its independence from Yugoslavia and asked for recognition from the European Union nations. It became a member of the UN in 1993 under the provisional name of the Former Yugoslav Republic of Macedonia (FYROM) because Greece vociferously protested Macedonia's right to the name, which is also the name of a large northern province of Greece. To Greece, the use of the name implies Macedonia's interest in territorial expansion into the Greek province. Greece has imposed two trade embargoes against the country as a result.

The Macedonian government, in 1997, urged NATO to extend its peacekeeping role in the Balkans beyond its mid-1998 mandate, saying NATO troops provided a stabilizing role. Ethnic tensions between ethnic Albanians and Macedonians continued to rise during the Kosovo crisis, during which more than 140,000 refugees streamed into the country from neighboring Kosovo. Most of the refugees returned to Kosovo in 2000.

The long-simmering resentment of Macedonia's ethnic Albanians erupted into violence in March 2001, prompting the government to send troops into the heavily Albanian western section of the country. The rebels sought greater autonomy within Macedonia. The more radical aspired to create a greater Albania, one that would unite the ethnic Albanians of Macedonia, Kosovo, and Albania proper, but there was little enthusiasm for pan-Albanianism among Macedonia's war-weary neighbors. On Aug. 13, after six months of fighting, the rebels and the Macedonian government signed a peace agreement that allowed a British-led NATO force to enter the country and disarm the guerrillas. In Nov. 2001, Macedonia's Parliament agreed to constitutional amendments giving broader rights to its Albanian minority. Albanian became one of the country's two official languages.

In Sept. 2002 elections, a center-left coalition ousted the governing coalition, which had been embroiled in previous years' guerrilla insurgency. Branko Crvenkovski of the Together for Macedonia coalition became the new prime minister.

Madagascar

REPUBLIC OF MADAGASCAR

National name: Repoblikan'i Madagasikara
President: Marc Ravalomanana (2002)
Prime Minister: Jacques Sylla(2002)
Area: 226,656 sq mi (587,040 sq km)
Population (2003 est.): 16,979,744 (growth rate: 3.0%); birth rate: 42.2/1000; infant mortality rate: 80.2/1000; density per sq mi: 75
Capital and largest city (2003 est.): Antananarivo, 1,390,800. **Monetary unit:** Malagasy franc. **Languages:** Malagasy and French (both official). **Ethnicity/race:** Malayo-Indonesian (Merina and related Betsileo), Cotiers (mixed African, Malayo-Indonesian, and Arab ancestry—Betsimisaraka, Tsimihety, Antaisaka, Sakalava), French, Indian, Creole, Comoran. **Religions:** traditional 52%, Christian 41%, Islam 7%. **Literacy rate:** 80% (1990 est.)
Economic summary: GDP/PPP (2001 est.): $14 billion; per capita $870. **Real growth rate:** 5%. **Inflation:** 7%. **Unemployment:** n.a. **Arable land:** 4%. **Agriculture:** coffee, vanilla, sugarcane, cloves, cocoa, rice, cassava (tapioca), beans, bananas, peanuts; livestock products. **Labor force:** 7 million (1999). **Industries:** meat processing, soap, breweries, tanneries, sugar, textiles, glassware, cement, automobile assembly plant, paper, petroleum, tourism. **Natural resources:** graphite, chromite, coal, bauxite, salt, quartz, tar sands, semiprecious stones, mica, fish, hydropower. **Exports:** $680 million (f.o.b., 2000): coffee, vanilla, shellfish, sugar; cotton cloth, chromite, petroleum products. **Imports:** $919 million (f.o.b., 2000): intermediate manufactures, capital goods, petroleum, consumer goods, food. **Major trading partners:** France, U.S., Germany, Japan, UK, Hong Kong, China, Singapore.

Geography Madagascar lies in the Indian Ocean off the southeast coast of Africa opposite Mozambique. The world's fourth-largest island, it is twice the size of Arizona. The country's low-lying coastal area gives way to a central plateau. The once densely wooded interior has largely been cut down.

Government Multiparty republic.

History The Malagasy are of mixed Malayo-Indonesian and African-Arab ancestry. Indonesians are believed to have migrated to the island about 700. King Andrianampoinimerina (1787–1810) ruled the major kingdom on the island, and his son, Radama I (1810–1828) unified much of the island. The French made the island a protectorate in 1885, and then, in 1894–1895, ended the monarchy, exiling Queen Rànavàlona III to Algiers. A colonial administration was set up, to which the Comoro Islands were attached in 1908, and other territories later. In World War II, the British occupied Madagascar, which retained ties to Vichy France.

An autonomous republic within the French Community since 1958, Madagascar became an independent member of the community in 1960. In May 1973, an army coup led by Maj. Gen. Gabriel Ramanantsoa ousted Philibert Tsiranana, president since 1959. Comdr. Didier Ratsiraka, named president on June 15, 1975, announced that he would follow a socialist course and, after nationalizing banks and insurance companies, declared all mineral resources nationalized. Repression and censorship characterized his regime. Ratsiraka was reelected in 1989 in a suspicious election that led to riots as well as the formation of a multiparty system in 1990. In 1991, Ratsiraka agreed to share power with the democratically minded opposition leader, Albert Zafy, who then overwhelmingly won the presidential elections in Feb. 1993. But Zafy was impeached by Parliament for abusing his constitutional powers during an economic crisis and lost the 1996 presidential election to Ratsiraka, who became president in Feb. 1997.

The Dec. 2001 presidential election between incumbent president Didier Ratsiraka and Marc Ravalomanana, the mayor of Antananarivo, proved inconclusive and a run-off vote was scheduled. But Ravalomanana claimed the election was rigged, and on Feb. 22, 2002, declared himself president. In response, Ratsiraka declared martial law and set up a rival capital in Toamasina, and Madagascar in effect found itself with two presidents and two capitals. After a recount in April, the High Constitutional Court declared Ravalomanana was the winner with 51.5% of the vote. Ratsiraka, however, refused to accept the outcome. Finally, after some minor skirmishes between rival army factions, Ratsiraka fled to France in July, and Madagascar's six-month civil war ended. In Aug. 2003, he was sentenced in absentia to ten years hard labor, accused of embezzlement.

Malawi

REPUBLIC OF MALAWI

President: Bakili Muluzi (1994)
Area: 45,745 sq mi (118,480 sq km)
Population (2003 est.): 11,651,239 (growth rate: 2.2%); birth rate: 44.7/1000; infant mortality rate: 105.2/1000; density per sq mi: 255
Capital (2003 est.): Lilongwe, 499,200. **Largest city:** Blantyre, 547,500. **Monetary unit:** Kwacha. **Languages:** English and Chichewa (both official). **Ethnicity/race:** Chewa, Nyanja, Tumbuko, Yao, Lomwe, Sena, Tonga, Ngoni, Ngonde, Asian, European. **Religions:** Christian 75%, Islam 20%. **Literacy rate:** 58% (1999 est.)
Economic summary: GDP/PPP (2001 est.): $7 billion; per capita $660. **Real growth rate:** 1.7%. **Inflation:** 28.6%. **Unemployment:** n.a. **Arable land:** 20%. **Agriculture:** tobacco, sugarcane, cotton, tea, corn, potatoes, cassava (tapioca), sorghum, pulses; cattle, goats, groundnuts, Macadamia nuts. **Labor force:** 4.5 million; agriculture 86% (1997 est.). **Industries:** tobacco, tea, sugar, sawmill products, cement, consumer goods. **Natural resources:** limestone, arable land, hydropower, unexploited deposits of uranium, coal, and bauxite. **Exports:** $415.5 million (f.o.b., 2001): tobacco, tea, sugar, cotton, coffee, peanuts, wood products, apparel. **Imports:** $463.6 million (f.o.b., 2001): food, petroleum products, semimanufactures, consumer goods, transportation equipment. **Major trading partners:** South Africa, Germany, U.S., UK, Japan, Netherlands, Zimbabwe, Zambia. **Member of Commonwealth of Nations**

Geography Malawi is a landlocked country the size of Pennsylvania in southeast Africa, surrounded by Mozambique, Zambia, and Tanzania. Lake Malawi, formerly Lake Nyasa, occupies most of the country's eastern border. The north-south Rift Valley is flanked by mountain ranges and high plateau areas.

Government Multiparty democracy.

History Early human inhabitants of what is now Malawi date to 8000–2000 B.C. Bantu-speaking peoples migrated there between the 1st and 4th centuries A.D. A large slave trade took place in the 18th and 19th centuries and brought Islam to the region. At the same time, missionaries introduced Christianity. Several major kingdoms were established in the precolonial period: the Maravi in 1480, the Ngonde in 1600, and the Chikulamayembe in the 18th century.

The first European to make extensive explorations in the area was David Livingstone in the 1850s and 1860s. In 1884, Cecil Rhodes's British South African Company received a charter to develop the country. The company came into conflict with the Arab slavers in 1887–1889. Britain annexed what was then called the Nyasaland territory in 1891 and made it a protectorate in 1892. Sir Harry Johnstone, the first high commissioner, used Royal Navy gunboats to wipe out the slavers.

Between 1951 and 1953, Britain combined Nyasaland with the colonies of Northern and Southern Rhodesia to form a federation, a move protested by black Africans who were wary of alignment with the ultra conservative white-minority rule in South Rhodesia.

On July 6, 1964, Nyasaland became the independent nation of Malawi. Two years later, it became a republic within the Commonwealth of Nations. Dr. Hastings K. Banda became Malawi's first prime minister (a title later changed to president). In his first month as ruler, he declared, "one party, one leader, one government, and no nonsense about it." In 1971, he became president for life, further consolidating his authoritarian rule. In addition to allowing former colonialists to retain considerable power in the country, he maintained warm relations with the white-minority government of South Africa. These policies drew heavy criticism from Malawian citizens and other African nations. In 1992, Banda faced violent protests.

Bakili Muluzi of the United Democratic Front (UDF) won the country's first free election in May 1994, ending Banda's 30-year rule. In 1999, Muluzi was reelected. While Malawi is no longer the repressive society it was under Banda, Muluzi's government has been tainted by corruption scandals. Senior officials are believed to have sold off 160,000 tons of reserve maize in 2000, despite the signs of a coming famine. In 2002 and 2003, the country faced severe food shortages, with more than 3 million people close to starvation.

Malaysia

Head of State: King Syed Sirajuddin Syed Putra Jamalullail
Prime Minister: Mahathir bin Mohamad (1981)
Area: 127,316 sq mi (329,750 sq km)
Population (2003 est.): 23,092,940 (growth rate: 1.9%); birth rate: 23.7/1000; infant mortality rate: 19.0/1000; density per sq mi: 181
Capital and largest city (2003 est.): Kuala Lumpur, 3,688,200 (metro.area), 1,403,400. **Other large cities:** Kelang, 683,200; Johor Bharu, 682,100. **Monetary unit:** Ringgit. **Languages:** Malay (official), Chinese, Tamil, English. **Ethnicity/race:** Malay and other indigenous 58%, Chinese 24%, Indian 8%, others 10%. **Religions:** Malays (all Muslims), Chinese (predominantly Buddhists), Indians (predominantly Hindus). **Literacy rate:** 83.5% (1995 est.)
Economic summary: GDP/PPP (2001 est.): $200 billion; per capita $9,000. **Real growth rate:** 0.3%. **Inflation:** 1.5%. **Unemployment:** 3.7%. **Arable land:** 5%. **Agriculture:** Peninsular Malaysia—rubber, palm oil, cocoa, rice; Sabah—subsistence crops, rubber, timber, coconuts, rice; Sarawak—rubber, pepper; timber. **Labor force:** 9.9 million; local trade and tourism 28%, manufacturing 27%, agriculture, forestry,

and fisheries 16%, services 10%, government 10%, construction 9% (2000 est.). **Industries:** Peninsular Malaysia—rubber and oil palm processing and manufacturing, light manufacturing industry, electronics, tin mining and smelting, logging and processing timber; Sabah—logging, petroleum production; Sarawak—agriculture processing, petroleum production and refining, logging. **Natural resources:** tin, petroleum, timber, copper, iron ore, natural gas, bauxite. **Exports:** $94.4 billion (f.o.b., 2001 est.): electronic equipment, petroleum and liquefied natural gas, wood and wood products, palm oil, rubber, textiles, chemicals. **Imports:** $76.9 billion (f.o.b., 2001 est.): electronics, machinery, petroleum products, plastics, vehicles, iron and steel and iron and steel products, chemicals. **Major trading partners:** U.S., Singapore, Japan, Hong Kong, Netherlands, China, Thailand, Germany. **Member of Commonwealth of Nations**

Geography Malaysia is on the Malay Peninsula in southeast Asia. The nation also includes Sabah and Sarawak on the island of Borneo to the east. Its area slightly exceeds that of New Mexico.

Most of Malaysia is covered by forest, with a mountain range running the length of the peninsula. Extensive forests provide ebony, sandalwood, teak, and other woods.

Government Constitutional monarchy.

History The ancestors of the people that now inhabit the Malaysian peninsula first migrated to the area between 2500 and 1500 B.C. Those living in the coastal regions had early contact with Chinese and Indians; seafaring traders from India brought with them Hinduism, which was blended with the local animist beliefs. As Muslims conquered India, they spread the religion of Islam to Malaysia. In the 15th century A.D., Islam acquired a firm hold on the region when the Hindu ruler of the powerful city-state of Malacca, Parameswara Dewa Shah, converted to Islam.

British and Dutch interest in the region grew in the 1800s, with the British East India Company establishing a trading settlement on the island of Singapore. Trade soared, with Singapore's population growing from only 5,000 in 1820 to nearly 100,000 in just 50 years. In the 1880s, Britain formally established protectorates in Malaysia. At about the same time, rubber trees were introduced from Brazil. With the mass production of automobiles, rubber became a valuable export, and laborers were brought in from India to work the rubber plantations.

Following the Japanese occupation of Malaysia during World War II, a growing nationalist movement prompted the British to establish the semi-autonomous Federation of Malaya in 1948. But Communist guerrillas took to the jungles to begin a war of national liberation against the British, who declared a state of emergency to quell the insurgency, which lasted until 1960.

The independent state of Malaysia came into existence on Sept. 16, 1963, as a federation of Malaya, Singapore, Sabah (North Borneo), and Sarawak. In 1965, Singapore withdrew from the federation to become a separate nation. Since 1966, the 11 states of former Malaya have been known as West Malaysia, and Sabah and Sarawak have been known as East Malaysia.

By the late 1960s Malaysia was torn by communal rioting directed against Chinese and Indians, who controlled a disproportionate share of the country's wealth. Beginning in 1968, the government moved to achieve greater economic balance through a national economic policy.

Malaysia was significantly affected in 1978 by the "boat people" fleeing Vietnam. Because the refugees were mostly ethnic Chinese, the government was apprehensive about any increase in a minority that previously had been the source of internal conflict in the country. In April 1988, it announced that within the year it would cease accepting refugees.

In the 1980s, Dr. Mohamad Mahathir succeeded Datuk Hussein as prime minister. Mahathir instituted economic reforms that would transform Malaysia into one of the so-called Asian Tigers. Throughout the 1990s, Mahathir embarked on a massive project to build a new capital from scratch in an attempt to bypass congested Kuala Lumpur.

Beginning in 1997 and continuing through the next year, Malaysia suffered from the Asian currency crisis. Instead of following the economic prescriptions of the International Monetary Fund and World Bank, the prime minister opted for fixed exchange rates and capital controls. In late 1999, Malyasia was on the road to economic recovery, and it appeared Mahathir's measures were working.

Mahathir sacked his heir apparent, Anwar Ibrahim, from his posts as deputy prime minister and finance minister in Sept. 1998, after a disagreement over how to deal with the country's economic problems. In defiance, Anwar launched a reform movement attacking the government. The prime minister then jailed Anwar, who was beaten and convicted of trumped-up corruption and sex crimes. The prime minister announced plans to retire in late 2003. He named Abdullah Ahmad Badawi, deputy prime minister, as his successor.

In early 2002, Malaysia passed stringent immigration laws that called for stiff fines, imprisonment, or caning for foreigners caught working in the country without proper permits. By the time the law was enacted at the end of July, more than 300,000 domestic, farm, and factory workers had left the country. There had been about 600,000 foreign laborers in Malaysia, mostly from Indonesia and the Philippines, who performed primarily menial tasks. Malaysian officials blame the country's crime problems on the foreigners.

Maldives

REPUBLIC OF MALDIVES

President: Maumoon Abdul Gayoom (1978)
Area: 116 sq mi (300 sq km)
Population (2003 est.): 329,684 (growth rate: 2.9%); birth rate: 36.7/1000; infant mortality rate: 60.1/1000; density per sq mi: 2,846
Capital and largest city (2003 est.): Malé, 81,600. **Monetary unit:** Rufiya. **Languages:** Dhivehi (official); Arabic, Hindi, and English are also spoken. **Ethnicity/race:** Sinhalese, Dravidian, Arab, African. **Religion:** Islam (Sunni Muslim). **Literacy rate:** 93.2% (1995 est.)
Economic summary: GDP/PPP (2001 est.): $1.2 billion; per capita $3,870. **Real growth rate:** 7%. **Inflation:** 3% (2000 est.). **Unemployment:** negl. **Arable land:** 3%. **Agriculture:** coconuts, corn, sweet potatoes; fish. **Labor force:** 67,000 (1995); agriculture 22%, industry 18%, services 60% (1995). **Industries:** fish processing, tourism, shipping, boat building, coconut processing, garments, woven mats, rope, handicrafts, coral and sand mining. **Natural resources:** fish. **Exports:** $88 million (f.o.b., 2000 est.): fish, clothing. **Imports:** $372 million (f.o.b., 2000 est.): consumer goods, intermediate and capital goods, petroleum products. **Major trading partners:** U.S., UK, Sri Lanka, Japan, Singapore, India, Canada.

Geography The Republic of Maldives is a group of atolls in the Indian Ocean about 417 mi (671 km) southwest of Sri Lanka. Its 1,190 coral islets stretch over an area of 35,200 square mi (90,000 sq km). With concerns over global warming and the shrinking of the polar ice caps, Maldives feels directly threatened, as none of its islands rises more than six feet above sea level.

Government Republic.

History The Maldives (formerly called the Maldive Islands) were first settled in the 5th century B.C. by Buddhist seafarers from India and Sri Lanka. According to tradition, Islam was adopted in A.D. 1153. Originally the islands were under the suzerainty of Ceylon (now Sri Lanka). They came under British protection in 1887 and were a dependency of the then-colony of Ceylon until 1948. The independence agreement with Britain was signed July 26, 1965. For centuries a sultanate, the islands adopted a republican form of government in 1952, but the sultanate was restored in 1954. In 1968, however, as the result of a referendum, a republic was again established in the recently independent country. Ibrahim Nasir, the authoritarian president since 1968, was removed from office and replaced by the more progressive Maumoon Abdul Gayoom in 1978. Gayoom was elected to a fifth, five-year term in 1998. In presidential elections, parliament selects one candidate, and the people vote yes or no for him in a referendum.

Mali

REPUBLIC OF MALI

National name: République de Mali
President: Amadou Toumani Touré (2002)
Prime Minister: Ahmed Mohamed Ag Hamani (2002)
Area: 478,764 sq mi (1,240,000 sq km)
Population (2003 est.): 11,626,219 (growth rate: 2.9%); birth rate: 47.8/1000; infant mortality rate: 119.2/1000; density per sq mi: 24
Capital and largest city (2003 est.): Bamako, 1,323,200 (metro. area), 935,400. **Monetary unit:** CFA Franc. **Languages:** French (official), African languages. **Ethnicity/race:** Mande 50% (Bambara, Malinke, Sarakole), Peul 17%, Voltaic 12%, Songhai 6%, Tuareg and Moor 10%, other 5%. **Religions:** Islam 90%, traditional 9%, Christian 1%. **Literacy rate:** 38% (1998 est.)
Economic summary: GDP/PPP (2001 est.): $9.2 billion; per capita $840. **Real growth rate:** –1.2%. **Inflation:** 4.5%. **Unemployment:** 14.6% urban areas; 5.3% rural areas. **Arable land:** 4%. **Agriculture:** cotton, millet, rice, corn, vegetables, peanuts; cattle, sheep, goats. **Labor force:** 3.93 million; agriculture and fishing 80%. **Industries:** food processing; construction; phosphate and gold mining. **Natural resources:** gold, phosphates, kaolin, salt, limestone, uranium, hydropower note: bauxite, iron ore, manganese, tin, and copper deposits are known but not exploited. **Exports:** $575 million (f.o.b., 2001 est.): cotton 43%, gold 40%, livestock (2001 est.). **Imports:** $600 million (f.o.b., 2001 est.): machinery and equipment, construction materials, petroleum, foodstuffs, textiles. **Major trading partners:** Brazil, South Korea, Italy, Canada, Côte d'Ivoire, France, Senegal, Germany, Benelux.

Geography Most of Mali, in West Africa, lies in the Sahara. A landlocked country four-fifths the size of Alaska, it is bordered by Guinea, Senegal, Mauritania, Algeria, Niger, Burkina Faso, and the Côte d'Ivoire. The only fertile area is in the south, where the Niger and Senegal Rivers provide irrigation.

Government Republic.

History Caravan routes have passed through Mali since A.D. 300. The Malinke empire ruled regions of Mali from the 12th to 16th centuries, and the Songhai empire reigned over the Timbuktu-Gao region in the 15th century. Morocco conquered Timbuktu in 1591, and ruled over it for two centuries. Subjugated by France by the end of the 19th century, the land became a colony in 1904 (named French Sudan in 1920) and in 1946 became part of the French Union. On June 20, 1960, it became independent and, under the name of Sudanese Republic, was federated with the Republic of Senegal in the Mali federation. However, Senegal seceded from the federation on Aug. 20, 1960, and the Sudanese Republic then changed its name to the Republic of Mali on Sept. 22.

In the 1960s, Mali concentrated on economic development, continuing to accept aid from both Soviet bloc and Western nations, as well as international agencies. In the late 1960s, it began retreating from close ties with China. But a purge of conservative opponents brought greater power to President Modibo Keita, and in 1968, the influence of the Chinese and their Malian sympathizers increased. The army overthrew the government on Nov. 19, 1968, and for the next than 20 years, Mali was under military rule. Mali and Burkina Faso fought a brief border war from Dec. 25th to 29th, 1985. In 1991, dictator Moussa Traoré was overthrown, and Mali made a peaceful transition to democracy. In 1992, Alpha Konaré became Mali's first democratically elected president.

Mali's second multiparty national elections took place in May 1997, with President Konaré winning reelection.

Konaré has won international praise for his efforts to revive Mali's faltering economy. His adherence to International Monetary Fund guidelines has increased foreign investment and helped make Mali the second-largest cotton producer in Africa. Konaré is also the chairman of the 15-nation ECOWAS (the Economic Community of West African States), which in recent years has concentrated on brokering peace in Sierra Leone, Liberia, and Guinea. Konaré retired after serving the two five-year terms permitted by the constitution.

In June 2002, Amadou Toumani Touré became president. A highly popular and respected public figure, he engineered the 1991 coup that freed the country from military rule. In Aug. 2003, Mali helped secure the release of 14 European tourists who had been held hostage for 6 months by Islamic militants in Algeria.

Malta

MALTA

President: Guido de Marco (1999)
Prime Minister: Eddie Fenech Adami (1998)
Area: 122 sq mi (316 sq km)
Population (2003 est.): 400,420 (growth rate: 0.5%); birth rate: 12.8/1000; infant mortality rate: 5.6/1000; density per sq mi: 3,282
Capital (2003 est.): Valletta, 194,200 (metro. area) 6,900 (city proper). **Largest city:** Birkirkara, 21,600. **Monetary unit:** Maltese lira. **Languages:** Maltese and English (both official). **Ethnicity/race:** Maltese (descendants of ancient Carthaginians and Phoenicians, with strong elements of Italian and other Mediterranean stock), Spanish, English, Arab. **Religion:** Roman Catholic 98%. **Literacy rate:** 88.8% (1995 census)

Economic summary: GDP/PPP (2001 est.): $5.95 billion; per capita $15,000. **Real growth rate:** 4%. **Inflation:** 2.8%. **Unemployment:** 4.5% (2000). **Arable land:** 31%. **Agriculture:** potatoes, cauliflower, grapes, wheat, barley, tomatoes, citrus, cut flowers, green peppers; pork, milk, poultry, eggs. **Labor force:** 147,700 (2000); industry 24%, services 71%, agriculture 5% (1999 est.). **Industries:** tourism; electronics, ship building and repair, construction; food and beverages, textiles, footwear, clothing, tobacco. **Natural resources:** limestone, salt, arable land. **Exports:** $2.5 billion (f.o.b., 2000): machinery and transport equipment, manufactures. **Imports:** $3.1 billion (f.o.b., 2000): machinery and transport equipment, manufactured and semi-manufactured goods; food, drink, and tobacco. **Major trading partners:** U.S., Germany, France, UK, Italy. **Member of Commonwealth of Nations**

Geography The five Maltese islands—Malta, Gozo, Comino, Comminotto, and Filflawith—have a combined land area smaller than Philadelphia. Malta is located in the Mediterranean Sea, about 60 mi (97 km) south of the southeast tip of Sicily.

Government Republic.

History The strategic importance of Malta was recognized by the Phoenicians, who occupied it, as did, in turn, the Greeks, Carthaginians, and Romans. The apostle Paul was shipwrecked there in A.D. 60. With the division of the Roman Empire in A.D. 395, Malta was assigned to the eastern portion dominated by Constantinople. Between 870 and 1090, it came under Arab rule. In 1091, the Norman noble Roger I, then ruler of Sicily, came to Malta with a small retinue and defeated the Arabs. The Knights of St. John (Malta), who obtained the three habitable Maltese islands of Malta, Gozo, and Comino from Charles V in 1530, reached their highest fame when they withstood an attack by superior Turkish forces in 1565. Napoléon seized Malta in 1798, but the French forces were ousted by British troops the next year, and British rule was confirmed by the Treaty of Paris in 1814.

Malta was heavily attacked by German and Italian aircraft during World War II but was never invaded by the Axis powers. It became an independent nation on Sept. 21, 1964, and a republic on Dec. 13, 1974, but remained in the British Commonwealth. In 1979, when its alliance with Great Britain ended, Malta sought to guarantee its neutrality through agreements with other countries. Although Malta applied for membership in the European Union, when the Labour Party won the election in Oct. 1996, it froze Malta's EU application and withdrew from the NATO Partnership for Peace program in an effort to maintain its neutrality. When the Nationalist Party won the Sept. 1998 elections, however, it revived the EU accession bid. The EU invited Malta to join its ranks in 2004, and in a 2003 referendum, Malta accepted.

Marshall Islands

REPUBLIC OF THE MARSHALL ISLANDS

President: Kessai H. Note (2000)
Total land area: 70 sq mi (181.3 sq km), includes the atolls of Bikini, Eniwetok, and Kwajalein
Population (2003 est.): 56,429 (growth rate: 2.9%); birth rate: 34.2/1000; infant mortality rate: 31.6/1000; density per sq mi: 806
Capital and largest city (2003 est.): Majuro, 20,500.
Languages: Both Marshallese and English are official languages. Marshallese is a language in the Malayo-Polynesian family. **Ethnicity/race:** Micronesian. **Religions:** predominantly Christian, mostly Protestant. **Literacy rate:** 93.7% (1999)
Economic summary: GDP/PPP (2001 est.): $115 million; per capita $1,600. **Real growth rate:** 1%. **Inflation:** 1.9% (1999 est.). **Unemployment:** 30.9% (1999 est.). **Arable land:** 17%. **Agriculture:** coconuts, tomatoes, melons, taro, breadfruit, fruits; pigs, chickens. **Labor force:** 28,698; agriculture 21.4%, industry 20.9%, services 57.7%. **Industries:** copra, fish, tourism, craft items from shell, wood, and pearls. **Natural resources:** coconut products, marine products, deep seabed minerals. **Exports:** $9 million (f.o.b., 2000): copra cake, coconut oil, handicrafts. **Imports:** $54 million (f.o.b., 2000): foodstuffs, machinery and equipment, fuels, beverages and tobacco. **Major trading partners:** U.S., Japan, Australia, New Zealand, Singapore, Fiji, China, Philippines.

Geography The Marshall Islands, east of the Carolines, are divided into two chains: the western, or Ralik, group, including the atolls Jaluit, Kwajalein, Wotho, Bikini, and Eniwetok; and the eastern, or Ratak, group, including the atolls Mili, Majuro, Maloelap, Wotje, and Likiep. The islands are of the coral-reef type and rise only a few feet above sea level. The Marshall Islands comprise an area slightly larger than Washington, DC.

Government Constitutional government in free association with the U.S.

History Micronesian peoples were the first inhabitants of the archipelago. The islands were explored by the Spanish in the 16th century and were named for a British captain in 1788. Germany unsuccessfully attempted to colonize the islands in 1885. Japan claimed them in 1914, but after several battles during World War II, the U.S. seized them from the Japanese. In 1947, the UN made the island group, along with the Mariana and Caroline archipelagos, a U.S. trust territory.

U.S. nuclear testing took place between 1946 and 1958 on the islands of Bikini and Enewetak. The people of Bikini were removed to another island, and a total of 23 U.S. atomic and hydrogen bomb tests were conducted. Despite clean-up attempts, the islands remain uninhabited today because of nuclear contamination. The U.S. paid the islands $183.7 million in damages in 1983, and in 1999, the U.S. approved a one-time $3.8-million payment to the relocated people of Bikini atoll.

The United States and the Marshall Islands signed a Compact of Free Association in 1986, which meant the islands became self-governing but would receive U.S. military and economic aid, roughly $65 million a year. The Marshall Islands were admitted to the UN on Sept. 17, 1991.

Kwajalein atoll is the site of an American military base, and has been used for missile defense testing since the 1960s.

In 2000, Kessai Note became the first commoner to become president—his predecessors had been island chiefs. He ran on an anticorruption ticket and is attempting to make his small nation more self-sufficient. In 2003, the U.S. and the Marshall Islands agreed on a new Compact of Free Association, an extension of the lease to use the Kwajalein military base in exchange for economic aid.

Mauritania

ISLAMIC REPUBLIC OF MAURITANIA

National name: République Islamique de Mauritanie
President: Col. Maaouye Ould Sidi Ahmed Taya (1992)
Prime Minister: Sghair Ould M'Bareck (2003)
Area: 397,953 sq mi (1,030,700 sq km)
Population (2003 est.): 2,912,584 (growth rate: 2.9%); birth rate: 42.2/1000; infant mortality rate: 73.8/1000; density per sq mi: 7
Capital and largest city (2003 est.): Nouakchott, 661,400. **Monetary unit:** Ouguiya. **Languages:** Arabic and Wolof (official); French. **Ethnicity/race:** mixed Maur/black 40%, Maur 30%, black 30%. **Religion:** Islam. **Literacy rate:** 41.2% (2002 est.)
Economic summary: GDP/PPP (2001 est.): $5 billion; per capita $1,800. **Real growth rate:** 4%. **Inflation:** 4.4%. **Unemployment:** 21% (1999 est.). **Arable land:** 0.5%. **Agriculture:** dates, millet, sorghum, rice, corn, dates; cattle, sheep. **Labor force:** 786,000; agriculture 50%, services 40%, industry 10%. **Industries:** fish processing, mining of iron ore and gypsum. **Natural resources:** iron ore, gypsum, copper, phosphate, diamonds, gold, oil; fish. **Exports:** $359 million (f.o.b., 2000): iron ore, fish and fish products, gold. **Imports:** $335 million (f.o.b., 2000): machinery and equipment, petroleum products, capital goods, foodstuffs, consumer goods. **Major trading partners:** France Japan, Italy, Spain, U.S., Algeria, Germany, Benelux.

Geography Mauritania, three times the size of Arizona, is situated in northwest Africa with about 350 mi (592 km) of coastline on the Atlantic Ocean. It is bordered by Morocco on the north, Algeria and Mali on the east, and Senegal on the south. The country is mostly desert, with the exception of the fertile Senegal River valley in the south and grazing land in the north.

Government Republic under military government. The legal system is based on Islam.

History Mauritania was first inhabited by blacks and Berbers, and it became a center for the Berber Almoravid movement in the 11th century, which sought to spread Islam through western Africa. It was first explored by the Portuguese in the 15th century, but by the 19th century the French gained control. They organized the area into a territory in 1904, and in 1920 it became one of the colonies that comprised French West Africa. In 1946, it became a French Overseas territory.

Mauritania became an independent nation on Nov. 28, 1960, and was admitted to the United Nations in 1961 over the strenuous opposition of Morocco, which claimed the territory. In the late 1960s, the government sought to make Arab culture dominant. Racial and ethnic tensions between Moors, Arabs, Berbers, and blacks were frequent.

Mauritania and Morocco divided the territory of Spanish Sahara (later called Western Sahara) between them after the Spanish departed in 1975, with Mauritania controlling the southern third. The Polisario Front, indigenous Saharawi rebels, fought for the territory against both Mauritania and Morocco. Increased military spending and rising casualties in the region helped bring down the civilian government of Ould Daddah in 1978. A succession of military rulers followed. In 1979, Mauritania withdrew from Western Sahara.

In 1984, Col. Maaouye Ould Sidi Ahmed Taya took control of the government. He relaxed Islamic law, fought corruption, instituted economic reforms urged by the International Monetary Fund, and held the country's first multiparty parliamentary elections in 1986. Although the 1991 constitution set up a multiparty democracy, politics remains based on ethnic and racial lines. The primary conflict is between blacks that dominate southern regions, and the Moorish-Arabic north, which runs the country. Racial tensions reached a peak in 1989 when Mauritania went to war with Senegal in a dispute over the border. As each country repatriated citizens of the other, critics accused Mauritania of taking the opportunity to expel thousands of blacks.

Although Mauritania officially abolished slavery in 1980, the nation continues to tolerate the enslavement of blacks by North African Arabs. In 1993, the U.S. State Department estimated that there were more than 90,000 chattel slaves in the country.

In 1992, Taya won the nation's first multiparty presidential election, which opponents charged was rigged. Taya's attempts to restructure the economy provoke periodic protests, the most serious of which were the bread riots in Nouakchott in 1995.

In 2002, the government banned a political party, Action for Change (AC), which has campaigned for greater rights for blacks, calling it racist and violent. Two other opposition parties have been banned in the past few years. The IMF granted Mauritania debt relief in June 2002, wiping out $1.1 billion, half of Mauritania's overall debt.

A coup attempt in June 2003 was thwarted. President Taya's crackdown on Islamists is believed to have sparked the attempt to overthrow him.

Mauritius

President: Karl Offman (2002)
Prime Minister: Sir Anerood Jugnauth (2000)
Area: 788 sq mi (2,040 sq km)
Population (2003 est.): 1,210,447 (growth rate: 0.9%); birth rate: 16.1/1000; infant mortality rate: 16.1/1000; density per sq mi: 1,537
Capital and largest city (2003 est.): Port Louis, 577,200 (metro. area), 143,800 (city proper). **Monetary unit:** Mauritian rupee. **Languages:** English, French (official); Creole, Hindi, Urdu, Hakka, Bojpoori. **Ethnicity/race:** Indo-Mauritian 68%, Creole 27%, Sino-Mauritian 3%, Franco-Mauritian 2%. **Religions:** Hindu 52%, Christian 28.3%, Islam 16.6%, other 3.1%. **Literacy rate:** 82.9% (1995 est.)
Economic summary: GDP/PPP (2001 est.): $12.9 billion; per capita $10,800. **Real growth rate:** 5.2%. **Inflation:** 4.2%. **Unemployment:** 8.6%. **Arable land:** 49%. **Agriculture:** sugarcane, tea, corn, potatoes, bananas, pulses; cattle, goats; fish. **Labor force:** 514,000 (1995); construction and industry 36%, services 24%, agriculture and fishing 14%, trade, restaurants, hotels 16%, transportation and communication 7%, finance 3% (1995). **Industries:** food processing (largely sugar milling), textiles, clothing; chemicals, metal products, transport equipment, nonelectrical machinery; tourism. **Natural resources:** arable land, fish. **Exports:** $1.6 billion (f.o.b., 2001 est.): clothing and textiles, sugar, cut flowers, molasses. **Imports:** $2 billion (f.o.b., 2001 est.): manufactured goods, capital equipment, foodstuffs, petroleum products, chemicals (1996). **Major trading partners:** UK, France, U.S., South Africa, Germany, Italy, India, Hong Kong. **Member of Commonwealth of Nations**

Geography Mauritius is a mountainous island in the Indian Ocean east of Madagascar.

Government Parliamentary democracy within the British Commonwealth.

History After a brief Dutch settlement, French immigrants who came in 1715 named the island Île de France and established the first road and harbor infrastructure, as well as the sugar industry, under the leadership of Gov. Mahe de Labourdonnais. Blacks from Africa and Madagascar came as slaves to work in the cane fields. In 1810, the British captured the island and in 1814, by the Treaty of Paris, it was ceded to Great Britain along with its dependencies.

Indian immigration, which followed the abolition of slavery in 1835, rapidly changed the fabric of Mauritian society, and the country flourished with the increased cultivation of sugarcane. The opening of the Suez Canal in 1869 heralded the decline of Mauritius as a port of call for ships rounding the southern tip of Africa, bound for South and East Asia. The economic instability of the price of sugar, the main crop, in the first half of the 20th century brought civil unrest, then economic, administrative, and political reforms. Mauritius became independent on March 12, 1968.

The effects of Cyclone Claudette in 1979, and of falling world sugar prices in the early 1980s, led the government to initiate a vigorous program of agricultural diversification and to develop the processing of imported goods for the export market. The country formally broke ties with the British Crown in March 1992, becoming a republic within the Commonwealth.

In addition to sugarcane, textile production and tourism are the leading industries. Primary education is free, and Mauritius boasts one of the highest literacy rates in sub-Saharan Africa.

With a complicated ethnic mix—about 30% of the population is of African descent, the remainder is of Indian descent, both Hindu and Muslim—racial unrest continually gnaws at the country.

In Feb. 2002, Mauritius went through four successive presidents. Two resigned within days of each other, each after refusing to sign a controversial anti-terrorism law that severely curtails the rights of suspects. The law, supported by the prime minister, was ultimately signed by a third, interim president. At the end of February, a fourth president, Karl Offman, was elected by Parliament.

Mexico

UNITED MEXICAN STATES

Official name: Estados Unidos Mexicanos
President: Vicente Fox Quesada (2000)
Area: 761,602 sq mi (1,972,550 sq km)
Population (2003 est.): 104,907,991 (growth rate: 1.7%); birth rate: 21.9/1000; infant mortality rate: 23.7/1000; density per sq mi: 138
Capital and largest city (2003 est.): Mexico City, 21,233,900 (metro. area), 8,681,400 (city proper). **Other large cities:** Ecatepec, 1,731,900 (part of Mexico City metro. area); Guadalajara, 1,665,800; Puebla, 1,345,500; Nezahualcóyotl, 1,250,700 (part of Mexico City metro. area); Monterrey, 1,135,000. **Monetary unit:** Mexican peso. **Languages:** Spanish, Indian languages. **Ethnicity/race:** mestizo (Indian-Spanish) 60%, Amerindian or predominantly Amerindian 30%, Caucasian or predominantly Caucasian 9%, other 1%. **Religions:** nominally Roman Catholic 89%, Protestant 6%, other 5%. **Literacy rate:** 89.6% (1995 est.)
Economic summary: GDP/PPP (2001 est.): $920 billion; per capita $9,000. **Real growth rate:** –0.3%. **Inflation:** 6.5%. **Unemployment:** urban—3% plus considerable underemployment. **Arable land:** 13%. **Agriculture:** corn, wheat, soybeans, rice, beans, cotton, coffee, fruit, tomatoes; beef, poultry, dairy products; wood products. **Labor force:** 39.8 million (2000); agriculture 20%, industry 24%, services 56% (1998). **Industries:** food and beverages, tobacco, chemicals, iron and steel, petroleum, mining, textiles, clothing, motor vehicles, consumer durables, tourism. **Natural resources:** petroleum, silver, copper, gold, lead, zinc, natural gas, timber. **Exports:** $159 billion (f.o.b., 2001): manufactured goods, oil and oil products, silver, fruits, vegetables, coffee, cotton. **Imports:** $168 billion (f.o.b., 2001): metalworking machines, steel mill products, agricultural machinery, electrical equipment, car parts for assembly, repair parts for motor vehicles, aircraft, and aircraft parts. **Major trading partners:** U.S., Canada, Germany, Spain, Netherlands Antilles, Japan, UK, Venezuela, China, South Korea, Taiwan, Italy, Brazil.

Geography Mexico is bordered by the United States to the north, and Belize and Guatemala to the southeast. Mexico is about one-fifth the size of the United States. Baja California in the west is an 800-mile (1,287-km) peninsula and forms the Gulf of California. In the east are the Gulf of Mexico and the Bay of Campeche, which is formed by Mexico's other peninsula, the Yucatán. The center of Mexico is a great, high plateau, open to the north, with mountain chains on the east and west and with ocean-front lowlands lying outside of them.

Government Federal republic.

History At least three great civilizations—the Mayas, the Olmecs, and later the Toltecs—preceded the wealthy Aztec empire, conquered in 1519–1521 by the Spanish under Hernando Cortés. Spain ruled Mexico as part of the viceroyalty of New Spain for the next 300 years until Sept. 16, 1810, when the Mexicans first revolted. They won independence in 1821.

From 1821 to 1877, there were two emperors, several dictators, and enough presidents and provisional executives to make a new government on the average of every nine months. Mexico lost Texas (1836), and after defeat in the war with the U.S. (1846–1848) it lost the area that is now California, Nevada, and Utah, most of Arizona and New Mexico, and parts of Wyoming and Colorado under the Treaty of Guadalupe Hidalgo. In 1855, the Indian patriot Benito Juárez began a series of reforms, including the disestablishment of the Catholic Church, which owned vast property. The subsequent civil war was interrupted by the French invasion of Mexico (1861) and the crowning of Maximilian of Austria as emperor (1864). He was overthrown and executed by forces under Juárez, who again became president in 1867.

The years after the fall of the dictator Porfirio Diaz (1877–1880 and 1884–1911) were marked by bloody political-military strife and trouble with the U.S., culminating in the punitive U.S. expedition into northern Mexico (1916–1917) in unsuccessful pursuit of the revolutionary Pancho Villa. Since a brief civil war in 1920, Mexico has enjoyed a period of gradual agricultural, political, and social reforms. The Partido Nacional Revolucionario (PNR; National Revolutionary Party), dominated by revolutionary and reformist politicians from northern Mexico, was established in 1929; it continued to control Mexico throughout the 20th century and was renamed the Partido Revolucionario Institucional (PRI; Institutional Revolutionary Party) in 1946. Relations with the U.S. were disturbed in 1938 when all foreign oil wells were expropriated, but a compensation agreement was reached in 1941.

Following World War II, the government emphasized economic growth. During the mid-1970s, under the leadership of President José López Portillo, Mexico became a major petroleum-producer. By the end of Portillo's term, however, Mexico had accumulated a huge external debt because of the government's unrestrained borrowing on the strength of its petroleum revenues. The collapse of oil prices in 1986 cut Mexico's export earnings. In Jan. 1994, Mexico joined Canada and the United States in the North American Free Trade Agreement (NAFTA), which will phase out all tariffs over a 15-year period, and in Jan. 1996, it became a founding member of the World Trade Organization (WTO).

In 1995, the U.S. agreed to prevent the collapse of Mexico's private banks. In return, the U.S. won virtual veto power over much of Mexico's economic policy. In 1997, in what observers called the freest elections in Mexico's history, the PRI lost control of the lower legislative house and the mayoralty of Mexico City in a stunning upset. To increase democracy, President Ernesto Zedillo said in 1999 that he would break precedent and not personally choose the next PRI presidential nominee. Several months later, Mexico held its first presidential primary, which was won by former interior secretary Francisco Labastida, Zedillo's closest ally among the candidates.

In elections held July 2, 2000, the PRI lost the presidency, ending 71 years of one-party rule. Vicente Fox Quesada, of the conservative National Action Party (PAN), took 43% of the vote to Labastida's 36%. Fox vowed tax reform, an overhaul of the legal system, and a reduction in power of the central government. By 2002, however, Fox had made little headway on his ambitious reform agenda. Disfavor with Fox was evident in 2003 parliamentary elections, when the PRI rebounded, winning 224 of the 500 seats in the lower house. In August, Fox admitted publicly that many Mexicans were disappointed with his government thus far.

Micronesia

FEDERATED STATES OF MICRONESIA

President: Joseph J. Urusemal (2003)
Total area: 271 sq mi (702 sq km). Land area, same (includes islands of Pohnpei, Yap, Chuuk, and Kosrae)
Population (2003 est.): 136,973 (growth rate: n.a.); birth rate: n.a./1000; infant mortality rate: n.a./1000; density per sq mi: 505
Capital: (2003 est.) Palikir 11,600. **Languages:** English is the official and common language; major indigenous languages are Chukese, Pohnpeian, Yapase, and Kosrean. **Ethnicity/race:** nine ethnic Micronesian and Polynesian groups. **Literacy rate:** 89% (1980 est.)
Economic summary: GDP/PPP (2001 est.): $269 million; note: GDP is supplemented by grant aid, averaging perhaps $100 million annually; per capita $2,000. **Real growth rate:** 2%. **Inflation:** 2.5%. **Unemployment:** 16% (1999 est.). **Arable land:** 6%. **Agriculture:** black pepper, tropical fruits and vegetables, coconuts, cassava (tapioca), sweet potatoes; pigs, chickens. **Labor force:** n.a.; two-thirds are government employees. **Industries:** tourism, construction, fish processing, craft items from shell, wood, and pearls. **Natural resources:** forests, marine products, deep-seabed minerals. **Exports:** $22 million (f.o.b., FY99/00 est.): fish, garments, bananas, black pepper. **Imports:** $149 million (f.o.b., FY99/00 est.): food, manufactured goods, machinery and equipment, beverages. **Major trading partners:** Japan, U.S., Guam, Australia.

Geography The Federated States of Micronesia is composed of the island states of Yap, Chuuk (Truk), Pohnpei (Ponape), and Kosrae, all in the Caroline Islands. The islands vary geologically from high mountainous islands to low coral atolls, with volcanic outcroppings on Pohnpei, Kosrae, and Chuuk. They are located 3,200 mi (5,150 km) west-southwest of Hawaii, in the north Pacific Ocean.

Government Constitutional government in free association with the United States since Nov. 1986.

History The islands, inhabited by Micronesian and Polynesian peoples, were colonized by Spain in the 17th century. Germany purchased them from Spain in 1898. They were occupied by the Japanese in 1914, but American forces seized them from the Japanese during World War II. On April 2, 1947, the United Nations Security Council created the Trust Territory of the Pacific Islands. The trust placed the Northern Mariana, Caroline, and Marshall Islands under the administration of the United States.

The Micronesian Federation (FMA) became self-governing in 1979. In 1983, the FMA voted to accept a Compact of Free Association with the U.S., and in Nov. 1986, the U.S. government declared the Trust Territory agreements no longer in effect—thereby granting the Federated States of Micronesia full independence. In Nov. 2002, the Compact was renewed for another 20 years.

The FMA was admitted to the United Nations on Sept. 17, 1991. In July 1993, the country became a member of the International Monetary Fund. Micronesia, as well as many other South Pacific countries, is alarmed by the effect continued global warming will have on their islands—the consequent rise in the level of the oceans threatens low-lying islands with flooding and, eventually, with submergence.

Moldova

REPUBLIC OF MOLDOVA

President: Vladimir Voronin (2001)
Prime Minister: Vasile Tarlev (2001)
Area: 13,067 sq mi (33,843 sq km)
Population (2003 est.): 4,439,502 (growth rate: 0.2%); birth rate: 14.3/1000; infant mortality rate: 41.6/1000; density per sq mi: 340
Capital and largest city (2003 est.): Chisinau, 772,500 (metro. area), 709,900 (city proper). **Other large cities:** Tiraspol, 209,800; Beltsy, 175,400; Bendery (Tighina), 144,900. **Monetary unit:** Leu. **Languages:** Moldovan (official; virtually the same as Romanian), Russian, Gagauz (a Turkish dialect). **Ethnicity/race:** Moldavian/Romanian 64.5%, Ukrainian 13.8%, Russian 13%, Gagauz 3.5%, Jewish 1.5%, Bulgarian 2%, other 1.7% (1989 figures). **Religions:** Eastern Orthodox 98%, Jewish 1.5%, Baptist and other 0.5% (2000). **Literacy rate:** 96% (1989 est.)
Economic summary: GDP/PPP (2001 est.): $11.3 billion; per capita $2,550. **Real growth rate:** 6.1%. **Inflation:** 9.6%. **Unemployment:** 1.9% (includes only officially registered unemployed; large numbers of underemployed workers) (Nov. 2000). **Arable land:** 54%. **Agriculture:** vegetables, fruits, wine, grain, sugar beets, sunflower seed, tobacco; beef, milk. **Labor force:** 1.7 million (1998); agriculture 40%, industry 14%, services 46% (1998). **Industries:** food processing, agricultural machinery, foundry equipment, refrigerators and freezers, washing machines, hosiery, sugar, vegetable oil, shoes, textiles. **Natural resources:** lignite, phosphorites, gypsum, arable land, limestone. **Exports:** $580 million (f.o.b., 2001): foodstuffs 42%, textiles and footwear, machinery (2000). **Imports:** $865 million (f.o.b., 2001): mineral products and fuel 32%, machinery and equipment, chemicals, textiles (2000). **Major trading partners:** Russia, Romania, Germany, Ukraine, Italy.

Geography Moldova (formerly Moldavia) is a landlocked republic of hilly plains lying west of the Carpathian Mountains between the Prut and Dneister (Dnestr) Rivers. The country is sandwiched between Romania and Ukraine. The area is a very fertile region with rich black soil (chernozem) covering three-quarters of the territory.

Government Democratic republic.

History Most of what is now Moldova was the independent principality of Moldavia in the 14th century. In the 16th century it came under Ottoman Turkish rule. Russia acquired Moldavian territory in 1791, and again in 1812 (the Treaty of Bucharest) when Turkey gave up the province of Bessarabia[1] to Russia. Turkey held the rest of Moldavia but it was passed to Romania in 1918. Russia did not recognize the cession of this territory.

In 1924, the USSR established Moldavia as an Autonomous Soviet Socialist Republic. As a result of the Nazi-Soviet Nonaggression Pact of 1939, Romania was forced to cede all of Bessarabia to the Soviet Union in 1940. The Soviets merged the Moldavia ASSR with the Romanian-speaking districts of Bessarabia to form the Moldavian Soviet Socialist Republic. During World War II, Romania joined Germany in the attack on the Soviet Union and reconquered Bessarabia. But Soviet troops retook the territory in 1944 and reestablished the Moldavian SSR.

For many years, Romania and the USSR disputed each other's territorial claims over Bessarabia. Following the aborted coup against Soviet president Mikhail Gorbachev, Moldavia proclaimed its independence in Sept. 1991, and changed its name to the Romanian spelling, Moldova.

Conflict between ethnic Romanians and the Russian-Ukrainian majority in Trans-Dniester erupted upon independence. Trans-Dniester separatists (primarily ethnic Russians and Ukrainians) fought for independence from Moldova in 1992; progress on resolving the conflict has been slow. In the south, Gagauz, which is composed mostly of Turkic Christians, has also attempted secession.

The Russian financial crisis in fall 1998 severely affected Moldova, which relies on Russia for 60% of its foreign trade. Economic disaster caused an exodus of an estimated 600,000 Moldovans since then—Moldova is considered the poorest country in Europe. In Feb. 2001, the Communist Party won an overwhelming victory in parliamentary elections, and their leader, Vladimir Voronin, became prime minister. Voronin has attempted to forge closer relations with Moscow, which has sparked protests among those who advocate for closer cultural and ethnic ties to Romania.

1. The area between the Prut and Dniester Rivers.

Monaco

PRINCIPALITY OF MONACO

National name: Principauté de Monaco
Ruler: Prince Rainier III (1949)
Minister of State: Patrick Leclercq (2000)
Area: 0.75 sq mi (465 acres) (1.95 sq km)
Population (2003 est.): 32,130 (growth rate: –0.3%); birth rate: 9.5/1000; infant mortality rate: 5.6/1000; density per sq mi: 42,675
Capital (2003 est.): Monaco, 1,400. **Largest city:** Monte Carlo, 15,400. **Monetary unit:** Euro. **Languages:** French (official), English, Italian, Monégasque. **Ethnicity/race:** French 47%, Monegasque 16%, Italian 16%, other 21%. **Religion:** Roman Catholic 90%. **Literacy rate:** 99%

Economic summary: GDP/PPP (1999 est.): $870 million; $27,000 per capita. **Real growth rate:** n.a. **Inflation:** n.a. **Unemployment:** 3.1% (1998). **Arable land:** 0%. **Agriculture:** none. **Labor force:** 30,540 (Jan. 1994). **Natural resources:** none. **Industries:** tourism, construction, small-scale industrial and consumer products. **Exports:** n.a. **Imports:** n.a. Full customs integration with France, which collects and rebates Monegasque trade duties; also participates in EU.

Geography Monaco is a tiny, hilly wedge driven into the French Mediterranean coast; it is 9 mi east of Nice, France.

Government Constitutional monarchy.

History The Phoenicians, and after them the Greeks, had a temple on the Monacan headland honoring Hercules. From *Monoikos*, the Greek surname for this mythological strong man, the principality took its name. After being independent for 800 years, Monaco was annexed to France in 1793 and was placed under Sardinia's protection in 1815. By the Franco-Monegasque treaty of 1861, Monaco went under French guardianship but continued to be independent. A treaty made with France in 1918 contained a clause providing that, in the event that the male Grimaldi dynasty should die out, Monaco would become an autonomous state under French protection.

Monaco has a tourist business that runs as high as 1.5 million visitors a year and is famous for its beaches and casinos. It had gaming tables as early as 1856. Five years later, a 50-year concession to operate the games was granted to François Blanc, of Bad Homburg. This concession passed into the hands of a private company in 1898.

Prince Rainier III, born on May 31, 1923, succeeded his grandfather, Louis II, on the latter's death, May 9, 1949. Rainier was married, in 1956, to U.S. actress Grace Kelly and they subsequently had three children. Their son, Prince Albert Louis Pierre (b. 1958) is heir to the throne. Immensely popular, Princess Grace died on Sept. 14, 1982, of injuries received in a car accident near Monte Carlo. She was 52.

Monaco's practice of providing a tax shelter for French businessmen resulted in a 1962 dispute between the countries. A compromise was reached by which French citizens with less than five years' residence in Monaco were taxed at French rates, and taxes were imposed on Monegasque companies doing more than 25% of their business outside the principality. In 1967, Rainier took control of the Société des Bains de Mer, operator of the famous Monte Carlo gambling casino, in a program to increase hotel and convention space. The country was admitted to the UN in May 1993, making it the smallest country represented there. It celebrated the 700th anniversary of the Grimaldi reign during 1997.

Mongolia

MONGOLIA

President: Natsagiyn Bagabandi (1997)
Prime Minister: Nambaryn Enkhbayar (2000)
Area: 604,247 sq mi (1,565,000 sq km)
Population (2003 est.): 2,712,315 (growth rate: 1.4%); birth rate: 21.4/1000; infant mortality rate: 57.2/1000; density per sq mi: 4
Capital and largest city (2003 est.): Ulaan Baatar, 804,200. **Monetary unit:** Tugrik. **Languages:** Mongolian, 90%; also Turkic, Russian, and Chinese. **Ethnicity/race:** Mongol 85%, Kazak 7%, Tungusic 4.6% other (including Chinese and Russian) 3.4%. **Religions:**

predominantly Tibetan Buddhist; Islam about 4%. **Literacy rate:** 97.8% (2000)

Economic summary: GDP/PPP (2001 est.): $4.7 billion; per capita $1,770. **Real growth rate:** 2.4%. **Inflation:** 11.8% (2000 est.). **Unemployment:** 20% (2000). **Arable land:** 1%. **Agriculture:** wheat, barley, potatoes, forage crops; sheep, goats, cattle, camels, horses. **Labor force:** 1.4 million (2000); primarily herding/agricultural. **Industries:** construction materials, mining (coal, copper, molybdenum, fluorspar, and gold); oil; food and beverages, processing of animal products. **Natural resources:** oil, coal, copper, molybdenum, tungsten, phosphates, tin, nickel, zinc, wolfram, fluorspar, gold, silver, iron, phosphate. **Exports:** $466.1 million (f.o.b., 2000): copper, livestock, animal products, cashmere, wool, hides, fluorspar, other nonferrous metals. **Imports:** $614.5 million (c.i.f., 2000): machinery and equipment, fuels, food products, industrial consumer goods, chemicals, building materials, sugar, tea. **Major trading partners:** China, U.S., Russia, Japan, South Korea.

Geography Mongolia lies in central Asia between Siberia on the north and China on the south. It is slightly larger than Alaska.

The productive regions of Mongolia—a tableland ranging from 3,000 to 5,000 ft (914 to 1,524 m) in elevation—are in the north, which is well drained by numerous rivers, including the Hovd, Onon, Selenga, and Tula. Much of the Gobi Desert falls within Mongolia.

Government Parliamentary republic now in transition from Communism.

History Nomadic tribes that periodically plundered agriculturally based China from the west are recorded in Chinese history dating back more than 2,000 years. It was to protect China from these marauding peoples that the Great Wall was constructed around 200 B.C. The name *Mongol* comes from a small tribe whose leader, Ghengis Khan, began a conquest that would eventually encompass an enormous empire stretching from Asia to Europe, as far west as the Black Sea and as far south as India and the Himalayas. However, by the 14th century, the kingdom was in serious decline, with invasions from a resurgent China and internecine warfare.

The State of Mongolia was formerly known as Outer Mongolia. It contains the original homeland of the historic Mongols, whose power reached its zenith during the 13th century under Kublai Khan. The area accepted Manchu rule in 1689, but after the Chinese Revolution of 1911 and the fall of the Manchus in 1912, the northern Mongol princes expelled the Chinese officials and declared independence under the Khutukhtu, or "Living Buddha."

In 1921, Soviet troops entered the country, and facilitated the establishment of a republic by Mongolian revolutionaries in 1924. China also made a claim to the region, but was too weak to assert it. Under the 1945 Chinese-Russian Treaty, China agreed to give up Outer Mongolia, which, after a plebiscite, became a nominally independent country.

Allied with the USSR in its dispute with China, Mongolia began mobilizing troops along its borders in 1968 when the two powers became involved in border clashes on the Kazakh-Sinkiang frontier to the west and at the Amur and Ussuri Rivers. A 20-year treaty of friendship and cooperation, signed in 1966, entitled Mongolia to call upon the USSR for military aid in the event of invasion.

In 1989, the Mongolian democratic revolution began, led by Sanjaasurengiyn Zorig. Free elections held in Aug. 1990 produced a multiparty government, though it was still largely Communist. As a result, Mongolia has moved only gradually toward a market economy. With the collapse of the USSR, however, Mongolia was deprived of Soviet aid. Many of the country's factories were forced to shut down, and unemployment rose to 30%. Primarily in reaction to the economic turmoil, the Communist Mongolian People's Revolutionary Party (MPRP) won a significant majority in parliamentary elections in 1992. In 1996, however, the Democratic Alliance, an electoral coalition, defeated the MPRP, breaking with Communist rule for the first time since 1921. But in 1997, a former Communist and chairman of the People's Revolutionary Party, Natsagiyn Bagabandi, was elected president, further strengthening the hand of the antireformers.

Disagreement within Mongolia's ruling coalition over the pace and direction of market reforms in April 1998 caused a shakeup that thrust Tsakhiagiyn Elbegdorj, a proreform politician, into the prime minister's position. But parliamentary cross-purposes led to his resignation, and a succession of prime ministers followed.

In July 2000, and again in May 2001, the Mongolian People's Revolutionary Party (formerly the Communist Party) nearly swept parliamentary elections, winning 72 out of 76 seats. Natsagiyn Bagabandi was reelected in the 2001 elections, giving the MPRP control of both the presidency and Parliament, as well as a mandate to bolster the sluggish economy and dismal living standards. Former Communists, Bagabandi and the MPRP now support radical reform.

Morocco

KINGDOM OF MOROCCO

National name: al-Mamlaka al-Maghrebia
Ruler: King Muhammad VI (1999)
Prime Minister: Driss Jettou (2002)
Area: 172,413 sq mi (446,550 sq km)
Population (2003 est.): 31,689,265 (growth rate: 1.8%); birth rate: 23.3/1000; infant mortality rate: 44.9/1000; density per sq mi: 184
Capital (2003 est.): Rabat, 1,636,600. **Largest cities:** Casablanca, 3,397,000; Fez, 941,800; Marrakech, 755,200. **Monetary unit:** Dirham. **Languages:** Arabic (official), French, Berber dialects, Spanish. **Ethnicity/race:** Arab-Berber 99.1%, other 0.7%, Jewish 0.2%. **Religions:** Islam 98.7%, Christian 1.1%, Jewish 0.2%. **Literacy rate:** 43.7% (1995 est.)
Economic summary: GDP/PPP (2001 est.): $112 billion; per capita $3,700. **Real growth rate:** 5%. **Inflation:** 1%. **Unemployment:** 23% (1999 est.). **Arable land:** 20%. **Agriculture:** barley, wheat, citrus, wine, vegetables, olives; livestock. **Labor force:** 11 million (1997 est.); agriculture 50%, services 35%, industry 15% (1999 est.). **Industries:** phosphate rock mining and processing, food processing, leather goods, textiles, construction, tourism. **Natural resources:** phosphates, iron ore, manganese, lead, zinc, fish, salt. **Exports:** $8.2 billion (f.o.b., 2001 est.): phosphates and fertilizers, food and beverages, minerals. **Imports:** $12.4 billion (f.o.b., 2001 est.): semiprocessed goods, machinery and equipment, food and beverages, consumer goods, fuel. **Major trading partners:** France, Spain, UK, Italy, Germany, India, U.S.

Geography Morocco, about one-tenth larger than California, lies across the Strait of Gibraltar on the Mediterranean and looks out on the Atlantic from the northwest shoulder of Africa. Algeria is to the east and Mauritania to the south. On the Atlantic coast there is a fertile plain. The Mediterranean coast is mountainous. The Atlas Mountains, running northeastward from the south to the Algerian frontier, average 11,000 ft (3,353 m) in elevation.

Government Constitutional monarchy.

History Morocco has been the home of the Berbers since the second millennium B.C. In A.D. 46, Morocco was annexed by Rome as part of the province of Mauritania until the Vandals overran this portion of the declining empire in the 5th century. The Arabs invaded circa 685, bringing Islam. The Berbers joined them in invading Spain in 711, but then revolted against the Arabs, resenting their secondary status. In 1086, Berbers took control of large areas of Moorish Spain until they were expelled in the 13th century.

The land was rarely unified and was usually ruled by small tribal states. Conflicts between Berbers and Arabs were chronic. Portugal and Spain began invading Morocco, which helped to unify the land in defense. In 1660, Morocco came under the control of the Alawite dynasty. It is a sherif dynasty—descended from the prophet Muhammad—and rules Morocco to this day.

During the 17th and 18th centuries Morocco was one of the Barbary states, the headquarters of pirates who pillaged Mediterranean traders. European powers became interested in colonizing the country beginning in 1840, and there were frequent clashes with the French and Spanish. Finally, in 1904, France and Spain concluded a secret agreement that divided Morocco into zones of French and Spanish influence, with France controlling almost all of Morocco and Spain controlling the small southwest portion, which became known as Spanish Sahara. Morocco became an even greater object of European rivalry by the turn of the century, leading almost to a European war in 1905 when Germany attempted to gain a foothold in the mineral-rich country. By the terms of the Algeciras Conference (1906), the sultan of Morocco maintained control of his lands and France's privileges were curtailed. The conference was a telling indication of what was to come in World War I, with Germany and Austria-Hungary lining up on one side of the territorial dispute, and France, Britain, and the United States on the other.

In 1912, the sultan of Morocco, Moulay Abd al-Hafid, permitted the French protectorate status. Nationalism began to grow during World War II. Sultan Mohammed V was deposed by the French in 1953 and replaced by his uncle, but nationalist agitation forced his return in 1955. On his death on Feb. 26, 1961, his son, Hassan, became king. France and Spain recognized the independence and sovereignty of Morocco in 1956. Sultan Sidi Muhammad formed a constitutional government, and in 1961 Moulay Hassan succeeded his father as Hassan II.

Maintaining excellent relations with the West, King Hassan became the second Arab leader to meet with an Israeli leader when, on July 21, 1986, Prime Minister Shimon Peres came to Morocco. Morocco was also the first Arab state to condemn the 1990 Iraqi invasion of Kuwait. In the 1990s, King Hassan promulgated "Hassanian democracy," which allowed for significant political freedom while at the same time retaining ultimate power for the monarch. In Aug. 1999, King Hassan II died after 38 years on the throne and his son, Prince Sidi Muhammad, was crowned King Muhammad VI. Since then Muhammad VI has pledged to make the political system more open, to allow freedom of expression, and to support economic reform. He has also advocated giving more rights to women, which has been opposed by Islamic fundamentalists. The entrenched political elite and the military have also been leery of some reform proposals. With about 20% of the population living in dire poverty, economic expansion is a prime goal.

Morocco's occupation of Western Sahara (formerly Spanish Sahara) has been repeatedly criticized by the international community. In the 1970s, tens of thousands of Moroccans crossed the border into Spanish Sahara to back their government's contention that the northern part of the territory was historically part of Morocco. Spain, which had controlled the territory since 1912, withdrew in 1976, creating a power vacuum that was filled by Morocco in the north and Mauritania in the south. When Mauritania withdrew in Aug. 1979, Morocco overran the remainder of the territory. A rebel group, the Polisario Front, has fought against Morocco since 1976 for the independence of Western Sahara on behalf of the indigenous Saharawis. The Polisario and Morocco agreed in Sept. 1991 to a UN-negotiated cease-fire, which was contingent on a referendum regarding independence. For the past decade, however, the UN has failed to hold the referendum; disputes over voter eligibility have been the major stumbling block, as well as Morocco's opposition to the referendum. In 2002, King Mohammed VI reasserted that he "will not renounce an inch of" Western Sahara.

In July 2002, Morocco invaded a tiny, uninhabited island claimed by Spain off its Mediterranean coast. Spain promptly seized back the island.

On May 16, 2003, terrorists, believed to be associated with al-Qaeda, killed 24 people in several simultaneous attacks. Four bombs targeted Jewish, Spanish, and Belgian buildings in Casablanca.

Mozambique

REPUBLIC OF MOZAMBIQUE

National name: República de Moçambique
President: Joaquim Chissanó (1986)
Prime Minister: Pascoal Mocumbi (1994)
Area: 309,494 sq mi (801,590 sq km)
Population (2003 est.): 17,479,266 (growth rate: 0.8%); birth rate: 38.2/1000; infant mortality rate: 199.0/1000; density per sq mi: 56
Capital and largest city (2003 est.): Maputo, 1,691,000 (metro. area), 1,114,000 (city proper). **Monetary unit:** Metical. **Languages:** Portuguese (official), Bantu languages. **Ethnicity/race:** indigenous tribal groups 99.6% (Shangaan, Chokwe, Manyika, Sena, Makua, and others), Europeans 0.06%, Euro-Africans 0.2%, Indians 0.08%. **Religions:** traditional 50%, Christian 30%, Islam 20%. **Literacy rate:** 42.3% (1998 est.)
Economic summary: GDP/PPP (2001 est.): $17.5 billion; per capita $900. **Real growth rate:** 9.2%. **Inflation:** 10%. **Unemployment:** 21% (1997 est.). **Arable land:** 4%. **Agriculture:** cotton, cashew nuts, sugarcane, tea, cassava (tapioca), corn, coconuts, sisal, citrus and tropical fruits, potatoes, sunflowers; beef, poultry. **Labor force:** 7.4 million (1997 est.); agriculture 81%, industry 6%, services 13% (1997 est.). **Industries:** food, beverages, chemicals (fertilizer, soap, paints), petroleum products, textiles, cement, glass, asbestos, tobacco. **Natural resources:** coal, titanium, natural gas, hydropower, tantalum, graphite. **Exports:** $746 million (f.o.b., 2001 est.): prawns 40%, cashews, cotton, sugar, citrus, timber; bulk electricity (2000). **Imports:** $1.254 billion (c.i.f., 2001 est.): machinery and equipment, mineral products, chemicals, metals, foodstuffs, textiles (2000). **Major trading partners:** South Africa, Zimbabwe, Spain, Portugal, India, U.S., Australia.

Geography Mozambique stretches for 1,535 mi (2,470 km) along Africa's southeast coast. It is nearly twice the size of California. Tanzania is to the north;

Malawi, Zambia, and Zimbabwe to the west; and South Africa and Swaziland to the south.

The country is generally a low-lying plateau broken up by 25 sizable rivers that flow into the Indian Ocean. The largest is the Zambezi, which provides access to central Africa. The principal ports are Maputo, Beira, and Nacala.

Government Multiparty republic.

History Bantu-speakers migrated to Mozambique in the first millennium, and Arab and Swahili traders settled the region thereafter. It was explored by Vasco da Gama in 1498, and first colonized by Portugal in 1505. By 1510, the Portuguese had control of all the former Arab sultanates on the east African coast. Mozambique was administered as part of Goa, in India, until 1752, when it received its own captain-general. Portuguese colonial rule was repressive.

Guerrilla activity began in 1963 and became so effective by 1973 that Portugal was forced to dispatch 40,000 troops to fight the rebels. A cease-fire was signed in Sept. 1974, and after having been under Portuguese colonial rule for 470 years, Mozambique became independent on June 25, 1975. The first president, Samora Moises Machel, had been the head of the National Front for the Liberation of Mozambique (FRELIMO) in its ten-year guerrilla war for independence. He died in a plane crash on Oct. 19, 1986, and was succeeded by his foreign minister, Joaquim Chissanó.

On Jan. 25, 1985, after a decade of independence, the government was locked in a paralyzing war with antigovernment guerrillas, the Mozambique National Resistance (MNR or Renamo), who were backed by the white minority government in South Africa. The guerrilla movement weakened President Chissanó's attempts to institute socialism, which he then decided to abandon in 1989. A new constitution was drafted calling for three branches of government and granting civil liberties. A cease-fire agreement was signed in Oct. 1992 between the government and the MNR, ending 16 years of civil war.

In multiparty elections in 1994 President Chissanó won. In Nov. 1995 the country was the first non-former British colony to become a member of the British Commonwealth. The president's disciplined economic plan has been extremely successful, winning the country foreign confidence and aid. While Mozambique posted some of the world's largest economic growth rates in the late 1990s, it has suffered enormous setbacks because of natural disaster—the enormous damage caused by severe flooding in the winters of 2000 and 2001. Hundreds have died and thousands were displaced by the flooding.

In 2002 Chissanó announced he would not seek a third term in the 2004 presidential elections. FRELIMO selected independence hero Armando Guebuza as their new candidate.

Myanmar

UNION OF MYANMAR

National name: Pyidaungsu Myanmar Naingngandau
Head of State: Senior Gen. Than Shwe (1992)
Prime Minister: Gen. Khin Nyunt (2003)
Area: 261,969 sq mi (678,500 sq km)
Population (2003 est.): 42,510,537 (growth rate: 0.7%); birth rate: 19.1/1000; infant mortality rate: 70.3/1000; density per sq mi: 162
Capital and largest city (2003 est.): Rangoon (Yangon), 4,344,100. **Other large city:**Mandalay, 1,147,400. **Monetary unit:** Kyat. **Languages:** Burmese, minority languages. **Ethnicity/race:** Burman 68%, Shan 9%, Karen 7%, Rakhine 4%, Chinese 3%, Mon 2%, Indian 2%, other 5%. **Religions:** Buddhist 89%, Christian 4%, Islam 4%, Animist 1%, other 2%. **Literacy rate:** 83.1% (1995 est.)
Economic summary: GDP/PPP (2001 est.): $63 billion; per capita $1,500. **Real growth rate:** 2.3%. **Inflation:** 20%. **Unemployment:** 5.1%. **Arable land:** 14%. **Agriculture:** rice, pulses, beans, sesame, groundnuts, sugarcane; hardwood; fish and fish products. **Labor force:** 23.7 million (1999 est.); agriculture 65%, industry 10%, services 25% (1999 est.). **Industries:** agricultural processing; knit and woven apparel; wood and wood products; copper, tin, tungsten, iron; construction materials; pharmaceuticals; fertilizer. **Natural resources:** petroleum, timber, tin, antimony, zinc, copper, tungsten, lead, coal, some marble, limestone, precious stones, natural gas, hydropower. **Exports:** $1.8 billion (f.o.b., 2001): apparel 55%, foodstuffs 18%, wood products 13%, precious stones 2% (2000). **Imports:** $2.2 billion (f.o.b., 2001): machinery, transport equipment, construction materials, food products, textile fabrics, petroleum products. **Major trading partners:** U.S., India, China, Japan, Singapore, South Korea, Taiwan.

Geography Slightly smaller than Texas, Myanmar occupies the Thailand/Cambodia portion of the Indochinese peninsula. India lies to the northwest and China to the northeast. Bangladesh, Laos, and Thailand are also neighbors. The Bay of Bengal touches the southwest coast. The fertile delta of the Irrawaddy River in the south contains a network of intercommunicating canals and nine principal river mouths.

Government Military regime. In 1989, the military government changed the name of Burma to Myanmar. The U.S. State Department does not recognize the name Myanmar or the military regime that represents it.

History The ethnic origins of modern Myanmar (known historically as Burma) are a mixture of Indo-Aryans, who began pushing into the area around 700 B.C., and the Mongolian invaders under Kublai Khan who penetrated the region in the 13th century. Anawrahta (1044–1077) was the first great unifier of Myanmar.

In 1612, the British East India Company sent agents to Burma, but the Burmese doggedly resisted efforts of British, Dutch, and Portuguese traders to establish posts along the Bay of Bengal. Through the Anglo-Burmese War in 1824–1826 and two subsequent wars, the British East India Company expanded to the whole of Burma. By 1886, Myanmar was annexed to India, then became a separate colony in 1937.

During World War II, Burma was a key battleground; the 800-mile Burma Road was the Allies' vital supply line to China. The Japanese invaded the country in Dec. 1941, and by May 1942 had occupied most of it, cutting off the Burma Road. After one of the most difficult campaigns of the war, Allied forces liberated most of Burma prior to the Japanese surrender in Aug. 1945.

Burma became independent on Jan. 4, 1948. In 1962, left-wing general Ne Win staged a coup, banned political opposition, suspended the constitution, and introduced the "Burmese way of socialism." After 25 years of economic hardship and repression, the Burmese people held massive demonstrations in 1987 and 1988. These were brutally quashed by the State Law and Order Council (SLORC). In 1989, the military government officially changed the name of the country to Myanmar.

In May 1990 elections, the opposition National League for Democracy (NLD) won in a landslide. But the military, or SLORC, refused to recognize the election results. The leader of the opposition, Aung San Suu Kyi, was awarded the Nobel Peace Prize in 1991, which focused world attention on SLORC's repressive policies. Daughter of the assassinated general Aung San, who was revered as the father of Burmese independence, Suu Kyi remained under house arrest from 1989 until 1995. A new constitution was drafted in 1994 that called for an elected executive branch but appeared designed specifically to forbid Suu Kyi from becoming president. Suu Kyi continued to protest against the government, but almost every move she made was answered with a counterblow from SLORC.

Although the ruling junta has maintained a tight grip on Myanmar since 1988, it has not been able to subdue an insurgency in the country's south that has gone on for decades. The ethnic Karen movement has sought an independent homeland along Myanmar's southern border with Thailand. The economy has been in a state of collapse except for the junta-controlled heroin trade, the universities have remained closed, and the AIDS epidemic, unrecognized by the junta, has gripped the country.

From 2000 to 2002, Suu Kyi was again placed under house arrest. During this time the military regime and Suu Kyi began unprecedented talks, though signs of democratic reforms remain elusive. In spring 2003, the government cracked down once again on the democracy movement, detaining Suu Kyi and shuttering NLD headquarters.

Namibia

REPUBLIC OF NAMIBIA

President: Sam Nujoma (1990)
Prime Minister: Theo-Ben Gurirab (2002)
Status: Independent Country
Area: 318,694 sq mi (825,418 sq km)
Population (2003 est.): 1,927,447 (growth rate: 1.5%); birth rate: 34.1/1000; infant mortality rate: 68.4/1000; density per sq mi: 6
Capital and largest city (2003 est.): Windhoek, 221,000
Summer capital: Swakopmund, 26,200. **Monetary unit:** Namibian dollar. **Languages:** Afrikaans, German, English (official), several indigenous. **Ethnicity/race:** black 87.5%, white 6%, mixed 6.5%. Note: about 50% of the population belong to the Ovambo tribe and 9% to the Kavangos tribe; other ethnic groups are: Herero 7%, Damara 7%, Nama 5%, Caprivian 4%, Bushmen 3%, Baster 2%, Tswana 0.5%. **Religion:** Predominantly Christian. **Literacy rate:** 38% (1960 est.)
Economic summary: GDP/PPP (2001 est.): $8.1 billion; per capita $4,500. **Real growth rate:** 4%. **Inflation:** 8.8%. **Unemployment:** 30% to 40%, including underemployment (1997 est.). **Arable land:** 1%. **Agriculture:** millet, sorghum, peanuts; livestock; fish. **Labor force:** 500,000; agriculture 47%, industry 25%, services, 28% (1999 est.). **Industries:** meatpacking, fish processing, dairy products; mining (diamond, lead, zinc, tin, silver, tungsten, uranium, copper). **Natural resources:** diamonds, copper, uranium, gold, lead, tin, lithium, cadmium, zinc, salt, vanadium, natural gas, hydropower, fish; note: suspected deposits of oil, coal, and iron ore. **Exports:** $1.58 billion (f.o.b., 2001 est.): diamonds, copper, gold, zinc, lead, uranium; cattle, processed fish, karakul skins. **Imports:** $1.71 billion (f.o.b., 2001 est.): foodstuffs; petroleum products and fuel, machinery and equipment, chemicals. **Major trading partners:** UK, South Africa, Spain, France, Japan, U.S., Germany.

Geography Namibia is bounded on the north by Angola and Zambia, on the east by Botswana, and on the east and south by South Africa. It is for the most part a portion of the high plateau of southern Africa, with a general elevation of from 3,000 to 4,000 ft.

Government Republic.

History The San peoples may have inhabited what is now Namibia more than 2,000 years ago. The Bantu-speaking Herero migrated there in the 1600s. The Ovambo, the largest ethnic group today, migrated there in the 1800s.

In the late 15th century, the Portuguese explorer Bartolomeu Dias became the first European to visit Namibia. Formerly called South-West Africa, the territory became a German colony in 1884. In 1908, German troops massacred the majority of the Herero population. The land was taken by South African forces in 1915, becoming a South African mandate by the terms of the Treaty of Versailles in 1920.

South Africa's application for incorporation of the territory was rejected by the UN General Assembly in 1946, and South Africa was invited to prepare a trusteeship agreement instead. By a law passed in 1949, however, the territory was brought into much closer association with South Africa—including representation in its Parliament.

In 1968, the UN called for South Africa's withdrawal from the territory, which was given the name *Namibia.* When South Africa refused, the UN Security Council and the International Court of Justice condemned it. Under a 1974 Security Council resolution, South Africa was required to begin the transfer of power to the Namibians by May 30, 1975, or face UN action. Prime Minister Balthazar J. Vorster rejected UN supervision, claiming that his government was prepared to negotiate Namibian independence, but not with the South-West African People's Organization (SWAPO), the principal black separatist group. Meanwhile, the all-white legislature of South-West Africa eased several laws on apartheid in public places.

Despite international opposition, the Turnhalle Conference in Windhoek drafted a constitution to organize an interim government based on racial divisions, a proposal overwhelmingly endorsed by white voters in the territory in 1977. At the urging of ambassadors of the five Western members of the Security Council, South Africa on June 11 announced rejection of the Turnhalle constitution and acceptance of the Western proposal to include the South-West African People's Organization in negotiations.

As policemen wielding riot sticks charged demonstrators in a black South-West Africa township, South Africa handed over limited powers to a new, multiracial administration in the former German colony on June 17, 1985. Installation of the new government ended South Africa's direct rule, but South Africa retained an effective veto over the new government's decisions along with responsibility for the territory's defense and foreign policy. An agreement between South Africa, Angola, and Cuba arranged for elections in Nov. 1989 to establish a new government. SWAPO leader Sam Nujoma was elected president, and on March 21, 1990, Namibia achieved independence.

Nujoma was reelected in 1994, and again in 1999, after the constitution was amended to allow him to seek a third term. In Sept. 1999, fighting took place between Namibian troops and separatists from the Caprivi Strip, a narrow corridor jutting out of Namibia that provides the country with access to the Zambezi River.

In Jan. 2001, Nujoma ordered police to arrest, deport, and imprison gays. Home Affairs Minister Jerry Ekandjo had made similar remarks in 2000, telling new police officers to "eliminate gays and lesbians from the face of Namibia."

Nujoma announced in Nov. 2001 that he would not seek reelection when his term expires in 2004.

Nauru

REPUBLIC OF NAURU

President: René Harris (2003)
Area: 8.11 sq mi (21 sq km)
Population (2003 est.): 12,570 (growth rate: 1.9%); birth rate: 26.1/1000; infant mortality rate: 10.3/1000; density per sq mi: 1,550
Capital and largest city (2003 est.): Yaren, 4,900. **Monetary unit:** Australian dollar. **Languages:** Nauruan (official) and English. **Ethnicity/race:** Nauruan 58%, other Pacific Islander 26%, Chinese 8%, European 8%. **Religions:** Protestant 58%, Roman Catholic 24%, Confucian and Taoist 8%. **Literacy rate:** 99%
Economic summary: GDP/PPP (2001 est.): $60 million; per capita $5,000. **Real growth rate:** n.a. **Inflation:** –3.6% % (1993). **Unemployment:** 0%. **Arable land:** 0%. **Agriculture:** coconuts. **Labor force:** employed in mining phosphates, public administration, education, and transportation. **Industries:** phosphate mining, financial services, coconut products. **Natural resources:** phosphates, fish. **Exports:** $25.3 million (f.o.b., 1991): phosphates. **Imports:** $21.1 million (c.i.f., 1991): food, fuel, manufactures, building materials, machinery. **Major trading partners:** New Zealand, Australia, South Korea, U.S., UK, Indonesia, India. **Special relationship within the Commonwealth of Nations**

Geography Nauru (pronounced NAH-oo-roo) is an island in the Pacific just south of the equator, about 2,500 mi (4,023 km) southwest of Honolulu. Phosphate mining has virtually destroyed the tiny nation's ecology, turning its tropical vegetation into a barren, rocky wasteland.

Government Republic.

History In 1798, a British navigator became the first European to visit the island. Germany annexed it in 1888, and by the turn of the century, phosphate, a lucrative fertilizer, began to be mined. The island was placed under joint Australian, New Zealand, and British mandate after World War I. The Japanese occupied the island during World War II, and forced 1,200 Nauruans—roughly two-thirds of the population—to relocate. In 1947, it became a UN trusteeship administered by Australia. By 1967, the phosphate mining industry finally came under control of the islanders, and on Jan. 31, 1968, Nauru became one of the world's smallest independent republics.

Devastated by almost a century of phosphate strip-mining by foreign companies, Nauru appealed to the International Court of Justice. In 1993, Australia offered Nauru an out-of-court settlement for damages, agreeing to pay $2.5 million Australian dollars annually for 20 years. New Zealand and the UK additionally agreed to pay a one-time settlement of $12 million each. Declining phosphate prices, the high cost of maintaining an international airline, and the government's financial mismanagement combined to make the economy collapsed in the late 1990s. By the millennium it was virtually bankrupt.

In 2000, the G7 nations put pressure on the country to review its banking system, which is used by Russian criminals for money laundering.

Since Sept. 2001, Nauru has accepted three boatloads of Asian refugees destined for Australia. Australia compensated the island with $20 million and other financial incentives for taking this refugee problem off their hands. The detention camps, which held more than 400 asylum seekers in 2003, are said to be extremely bleak and lack medical care.

Bernard Dowiyogo, elected in 2003 as president for the seventh time (nonsequentially), died on March 9 following emergency heart surgery. Ludwig Scotty, a senior cabinet minister, was elected in May elections. But in August, Scotty was sacked in a no-confidence vote, and René Harris, who has twice served as president, was elected to the post.

Nepal

KINGDOM OF NEPAL

Ruler: King Gyanendra Bir Bikram Shah Deva (2001)
Prime Minister: Surya Bahadur Thapa (2003)
Area: 54,363 sq mi (140,800 sq km)
Population (2003 est.): 26,469,569 (growth rate: 2.3%); birth rate: 32.5/1000; infant mortality rate: 70.6/1000; density per sq mi: 487
Capital and largest city (2003 est.): Kathmandu, 1,203,100 (metro. area), 729,000 (city proper). **Other large cities:** Biratnagar, 174,600; Lalitpur, 169,100. **Monetary unit:** Nepalese rupee. **Languages:** Nepali (official), Newari, Bhutia, Maithali. **Ethnicity/race:** Newars, Indians, Tibetans, Gurungs, Magars, Tamangs, Bhotias, Rais, Limbus, Sherpas. **Religions:** Hindu 86.2%, Buddhist 7.8%, Islam 3.8%, other 2.2%. **Literacy rate:** 27.5% (1995 est.)
Economic summary: GDP/PPP (2001 est.): $35.6 billion; per capita $1,400. **Real growth rate:** 2.6%. **Inflation:** 2.1% (FY00/01 est.). **Unemployment:** 47%. **Arable land:** 20%. **Agriculture:** rice, corn, wheat, sugarcane, root crops; milk, water buffalo meat. **Labor force:** 10 million (1996 est.); note: severe lack of skilled labor; agriculture 81%, services 16%, industry 3%. **Industries:** tourism, carpet, textile; small rice, jute, sugar, and oilseed mills; cigarette; cement and brick production. **Natural resources:** quartz, water, timber, hydropower, scenic beauty, small deposits of lignite, copper, cobalt, iron ore. **Exports:** $757 million (f.o.b., FY00/01 est.), but does not include unrecorded border trade with India: carpets, clothing, leather goods, jute goods, grain. **Imports:** $1.6 billion (f.o.b., FY00/01 est.): gold, machinery and equipment, petroleum products, fertilizer. **Major trading partners:** India, U.S., Germany, Singapore, China/Hong Kong.

Geography A landlocked country the size of Arkansas, lying between India and the Tibetan Autonomous Region of China, Nepal contains Mount Everest (29,035 ft; 8,850 m), the tallest mountain in the world. Along its southern border, Nepal has a strip of level land that is partly forested, partly cultivated. North of that is the slope of the main section of the Himalayan range, including Everest and many other peaks higher than 8,000 m.

Government In Nov. 1990, King Birendra promulgated a new constitution and introduced a multiparty parliamentary democracy in Nepal.

History The first civilizations in Nepal, which flourished around the 6th century B.C., were confined to the fertile Kathmandu Valley where the present-day capital of the same name is located. It was in this region that Prince Siddhartha Gautama was born circa 563 B.C. Gautama achieved enlightenment as Buddha, and spawned Buddhist belief.

Nepali rulers' early patronage of Buddhism largely gave way to Hinduism, reflecting the increased influence of India, around the 12th century. Though the successive dynasties of the Gopalas, the Kiratis, and the Licchavis expanded their rule, it was not until the reign of the Malla kings from 1200–1769 that Nepal assumed the approximate dimensions of the modern state.

The kingdom of Nepal was unified in 1768 by King Prithvi Narayan Shah, who had fled India following the Moghul conquests of the subcontinent. Under Shah and his successors Nepal's borders expanded as far west as Kashmir and as far east as Sikkim (now part of India). A commercial treaty was signed with Britain in 1792, and again in 1816 after more than a year of hostilities with the British East India Company.

In 1923, Britain recognized the absolute independence of Nepal. Between 1846 and 1951, the country was ruled by the Rana family, which always held the office of prime minister. In 1951, however, the king took over all power and proclaimed a constitutional monarchy. Mahendra Bir Bikram Shah became king in 1955. After Mahendra died of a heart attack in 1972, Prince Birendra, at 26, succeeded to the throne.

In 1990, a prodemocracy movement forced King Birendra to lift the ban on political parties. The first free election in three decades provided a victory for the liberal Nepali Congress Party in 1991, although the Communists made a strong showing. A small but growing Maoist guerrilla movement, seeking to overthrow the constitutional monarchy and install a Communist government, began operating in the countryside in 1996.

On June 1, 2001, King Birendra was shot and killed by his equally popular son, Dipendra. Crown Prince Dipendra, angered by his family's disapproval of his choice of a bride, also killed his mother and several other members of the royal family before shooting himself. Dipendra was crowned king while in a coma; upon his death on June 4, Prince Gyanendra, the younger brother of Birendra, succeeded him.

The Maoist guerrillas agreed to a cease-fire with the government in July. Peace talks broke down, however, when the government refused to abolish the constitutional monarchy and establish an assembly. The rebels launched a deadly offensive against security targets, and King Gyanendra declared a state of emergency in November and ordered the army to crack down on the group. The rebels stepped up their campaign in western Nepal in April and May 2002, and the government responded with equal intensity, killing hundreds of Maoists, the largest toll since the insurgency began in 1996.

In August 2003, the Maoist rebels withdrew from peace talks with the government and ended a cease-fire signed in January.

The Netherlands

KINGDOM OF THE NETHERLANDS

National name: Koninkrijk der Nederlanden
Sovereign: Queen Beatrix (1980)
Prime Minister: Jan Peter Balkenende (2002)
Area: 16,033 sq mi (41,526 sq km)
Population (2003 est.): 16,150,511 (growth rate: 0.3%); birth rate: 11.3/1000; infant mortality rate: 4.3/1000; density per sq mi: 1,007
Capital and largest city (2003 est.): Amsterdam (official), 737,900; The Hague (administrative capital), 465,900. **Other large cities:** Rotterdam, 600,700; Utrecht, 263,900; Eindhoven, 206,900. **Monetary units:** Euro (formerly guilder). **Language:** Dutch, Frisian. **Ethnicity/race:** Dutch 83%, Moroccans, Turks, and other 17% (1988). **Religions:** Roman Catholic 31%, Protestant 21%, Islam 4.4%, other 3.6%, unaffiliated 40%. **Literacy rate:** 99% (2000 est.)
Economic summary: GDP/PPP (2001 est.): $413 billion; per capita $25,800. **Real growth rate:** 1.1%. **Inflation:** 4.5%. **Unemployment:** 2.4%. **Arable land:** 27%. **Agriculture:** grains, potatoes, sugar beets, fruits, vegetables; livestock. **Labor force:** 7.2 million (2000); services 73%, industry 23%, agriculture 4% (1998 est.). **Industries:** agroindustries, metal and engineering products, electrical machinery and equipment, chemicals, petroleum, construction, microelectronics, fishing. **Natural resources:** natural gas, petroleum, arable land. **Exports:** $214 billion (f.o.b., 2001): machinery and equipment, chemicals, fuels; foodstuffs. **Imports:** $195 billion (f.o.b., 2001 est.): machinery and transport equipment, chemicals, fuels; foodstuffs, clothing. **Major trading partners:** EU, Central and Eastern Europe, U.S.

Geography The Netherlands, on the coast of the North Sea, is twice the size of New Jersey. Part of the great plain of north and west Europe, the Netherlands has maximum dimensions of 190 by 160 mi (360 by 257 km) and is low and flat except in Limburg in the southeast, where some hills rise to 300 ft (92 m). About half the country's area is below sea level, making the famous Dutch dikes a requisite for the use of much land. Reclamation of land from the sea through dikes has continued through recent times. All drainage reaches the North Sea, and the principal rivers—Rhine, Maas (Meuse), and Schelde—have their sources outside the country.

Government Constitutional monarchy.

History Julius Caesar found the low-lying Netherlands inhabited by Germanic tribes—the Nervii, Frisii, and Batavi. The Batavi on the Roman frontier did not submit to Rome's rule until 13 B.C., and then only as allies.

The Franks controlled the region from the 4th to the 8th century, and it became part of Charlemagne's empire in the 8th and 9th centuries. The area later passed into the hands of Burgundy and the Austrian Hapsburgs, and finally in the 16th century came under Spanish rule.

When Philip II of Spain suppressed political liberties and the growing Protestant movement in the Netherlands, a revolt led by William of Orange broke out in 1568. Under the Union of Utrecht (1579), the seven northern provinces became the United Provinces of the Netherlands. War between the United Provinces and Spain continued into the 17th century, but in 1648 Spain finally recognized Dutch independence.

The Dutch East India Company was established in 1602, and by the end of the 17th century Holland was one of the great sea and colonial powers of Europe.

The nation's independence was not completely established until after the Thirty Years' War (1618–1648), when the country's rise as a commercial and maritime power began. In 1688, the English Parliament invited William of Orange, stadtholder, and his wife, Mary Stuart, to rule England as William III and Mary II. William then used the combined resources of England and the Netherlands to wage war on Louis XIV's France. In 1814, all the provinces of Holland and Belgium were merged into one kingdom, but in 1830 the southern provinces broke away to form the kingdom of Belgium. A liberal constitution was adopted by the Netherlands in 1848. The country remained neutral during World War I.

In spite of its neutrality in World War II, the Netherlands was invaded by the Nazis in May 1940, and the Dutch East Indies were later taken by the Japanese. The nation was liberated in May 1945. In 1948, after a reign of 50 years, Queen Wilhelmina abdicated and was succeeded by her daughter Juliana.

In 1949, after a four-year war, the Netherlands granted independence to the Dutch East Indies, which became the Republic of Indonesia. The Netherlands also joined NATO that year. The Netherlands joined the European Economic Community (later, the EU) in 1958. In 1999, it adopted the single European currency, the euro.

In 1963, it turned over the western half of New Guinea to Indonesia, ending 300 years of Dutch presence in Asia. Attainment of independence by Suriname on Nov. 25, 1975, left the Netherlands Antilles and Aruba as the country's only overseas territories.

Although prostitution is legal, the government moved in July 1997 to permit the operation of brothels as a means of regulating the former. Only those with a valid resident's permit would be permitted to be employed in the brothels. In 1999, the Netherlands again defied convention by preparing to legalize euthanasia. In Sept. 2000, the Netherlands became the first nation in the world to legalize same-sex marriages.

Wim Kok's government resigned in April 2002 after a report concluded that Dutch UN troops failed to prevent a massacre of Bosnian Muslims by Bosnian Serbs in a UN safe haven near Srebrenica in 1995. Explaining his action, the popular prime minister said, "The international community is big and anonymous. We are taking the consequences of the international community's failure in Srebrenica."

The country's normally bland political scene was further rocked with the May 2002 assassination of Pim Fortuyn, a right-wing, anti-immigrant politician. Days later, his party, Lijst Pim Fortuyn, placed second in national elections, behind Jan Peter Balkenende's Christian Democrats. Leading the country into a marked shift to the right, Balkenende formed a three-way center-right coalition government with his Christian Democrats, Pim Fortuyn List, and the People's Party for Freedom and Democracy. Balkenende became prime minister in July. In 2003, the Netherlands agreed to send 1,100 troops to Iraq to relieve the U.S. troops stationed there.

Netherlands Autonomous Countries

Netherlands Antilles

Status: Part of the Kingdom of the Netherlands
Governor: Frits Goedgedrag (2002)
Prime Minister: Mirna Louisa-Godett (2003)
Area: 371 sq mi (960 sq km)
Population (2003 est.): 216,226 (growth rate: 0.9%); birth rate: 15.8/1000; infant mortality rate: 10.7/1000; density per sq mi: 583
Capital and largest city (2003 est.): Willemstad, 60,100. **Ethnicity/race:** mixed African 85%, Carib Indian, European, Latin, Asian. **Literacy rate:** 98% (1981 est.)
Economic summary: GDP/PPP (2000 est.): $2.4 billion; per capita $11,400. **Real growth rate:** –3.5%. **Inflation:** 5.8%. **Unemployment:** 15% (1998 est.). **Arable land:** 10%. **Agriculture:** aloes, sorghum, peanuts, vegetables, tropical fruit. **Labor force:** 89,000; agriculture 1%, industry 13%, services 86% (1994 est.). **Industries:** tourism (Curacao, Sint Maarten, and Bonaire), petroleum refining (Curacao), petroleum transshipment facilities (Curacao and Bonaire), light manufacturing (Curacao). **Natural resources:** phosphates (Curacao only), salt (Bonaire only). **Exports:** $276 million (f.o.b., 2000): petroleum products. **Imports:** $1.5 billion (f.o.b., 2000): crude petroleum, food, manufactures. **Major trading partners:** U.S., Guatemala, Venezuela, France, Singapore, Mexico, Gabon, Italy, Netherlands.

The Netherlands Antilles are composed of two groups of Caribbean islands 500 mi (805 km) apart: Curaçao (173 sq mi; 448 sq km) and Bonaire (95 sq mi; 246 sq km) are located about 40 mi (64 km) off the Venezuelan coast.

Originally inhabited by Arawak Indians, these two islands as well as Aruba were claimed by Spain in 1527, and then by the Dutch in 1643. The Dutch Lesser Antilles to the north—Sint Eustatius, the southern part of Saint Martin (Dutch: Sint Maarten), and Saba—make up the remainder of the island federation. First inhabited by the Carib Indians, Saint Martin was explored by Columbus in 1493. In 1845, the six islands (then including Aruba) officially formed the Netherlands Antilles. In 1994, the islands voted to preserve their federation with the Netherlands.

Aruba

Status: Part of the Kingdom of the Netherlands
Governor: Olindo Koolman (1992)
Prime Minister: Nelson O. Oduber (2001)
Area: 75 sq mi (193 sq km)
Population (2003 est.): 70,844 (growth rate: 0.6%); birth rate: 11.9/1000; infant mortality rate: 6.1/1000; density per sq mi: 951
Capital and largest city (2003 est.): Oranjestad, 20,700. **Ethnicity/race:** mixed European/Caribbean Indian 80%. **Literacy rate:** 97%
Economic summary: GDP/PPP (2000 est.): $1.94 billion; per capita $28,000. **Real growth rate:** 2.5%. **Inflation:** 4%. **Unemployment:** 0.6% (1999 est.). **Arable land:** 11% aloe plantations included (0.01%). **Agriculture:** aloes; livestock; fish. **Labor force:** 41,501 (1997 est.); most employment is in wholesale and retail trade and repair, followed by hotels and restaurants (1997 est.). **Industries:** tourism, transshipment facilities, oil refining. **Natural resources:** negl.; white sandy beaches. **Exports:** $2.58 billion (including oil reexports) (f.o.b., 2000): live animals and animal products, art and collectibles, machinery and electrical equipment, transport equipment. **Imports:** $2.61 billion (f.o.b., 2000): machinery and electrical equipment, crude oil for refining and reexport, chemicals; foodstuffs. **Major trading partners:** U.S., Colombia, Netherlands, Netherlands Antilles, Japan.

Aruba, an island slightly larger than Washington, DC, lies 18 mi (28.9 km) off the coast of Venezuela in the southern Caribbean.

The Arawak Indians were the first inhabitants of Aruba. Spain explored the island in 1499, and more than a century later the Netherlands (1636) claimed the island. After a brief rule by the British, the Dutch again took control of the island in 1816, and it officially became part of the Netherlands Antilles in 1846.

On Jan. 1, 1986, Aruba seceded from the federation, but decided in 1994 to indefinitely postpone the transition to full independence. The Netherlands controls Aruba's defense and foreign affairs, but all internal affairs are handled by an island government directing its own civil service, judiciary, revenue, and currency.

New Zealand

Sovereign: Queen Elizabeth II (1952)
Governor-General: Dame Silvia Cartwright (2001)
Prime Minister: Helen Clark (1999)
Area: 103,737 sq mi (268,680 sq km) (excluding dependencies)
Population (2003 est.): 3,951,307 (growth rate: 0.7%); birth rate: 14.1/1000; infant mortality rate: 6.1/1000; density per sq mi: 38
Capital (2003 est.): Wellington, 342,500 (metro.area),

165,100 (city proper). **Largest cities:** Auckland, 369,300 (metro. area), 359,500 (city proper); Christchurch, 334,100. **Monetary unit:** New Zealand dollar. **Languages:** English (official), Maori. **Ethnicity/race:** European 79.1%, Maori 9.7%, Pacific Islander 3.8%, Asian and other 7.4%. **Religions:** Christian 81%, none or unspecified 18%, Hindu, Confucian, and other 1%. **Literacy rate:** 99% (1980 est.)

Economic summary: GDP/PPP (2001 est.): $75.4 billion; per capita $19,500. **Real growth rate:** 3.1%. **Inflation:** 2.6%. **Unemployment:** 5.5%. **Arable land:** 6%. **Agriculture:** wheat, barley, potatoes, pulses, fruits, vegetables; wool, beef, dairy products; fish. **Labor force:** 1.92 million: services 65%, industry 25%, agriculture 10% (1995). **Industries:** food processing, wood and paper products, textiles, machinery, transportation equipment, banking and insurance, tourism, mining. **Natural resources:** natural gas, iron ore, sand, coal, timber, hydropower, gold, limestone. **Exports:** $14.2 billion (2001 est.): dairy products, meat, wood and wood products, fish, machinery. **Imports:** $12.5 billion (2001 est.): machinery and equipment, vehicles and aircraft, petroleum, electronics, textiles, plastics. **Major trading partners:** Australia, U.S., Japan, UK, South Korea, China, Germany. **Member of Commonwealth of Nations**

Geography New Zealand, about 1,250 mi (2,012 km) southeast of Australia, consists of two main islands and a number of smaller, outlying islands so scattered that they range from the tropical to the antarctic. The country is the size of Colorado. New Zealand's two main components are the North Island and the South Island, separated by Cook Strait. The North Island (44,281 sq mi; 115,777 sq km) is 515 mi (829 km) long and volcanic in its south-central part. This area contains many hot springs and beautiful geysers. South Island (58,093 sq mi; 151,215 sq km) has the Southern Alps along its west coast, with Mount Cook (12,283.3 ft; 3,754 m) the highest point. Other inhabited islands include Stewart Island, the Chatham Islands, and Great Barrier Island.

Government Parliamentary democracy.

History Maoris were the first inhabitants of New Zealand, arriving on the islands in about 1000. Maori oral history maintains the Maoris came to the island in seven canoes from other parts of Polynesia. In 1642, New Zealand was explored by Abel Tasman, a Dutch navigator. British captain James Cook made three voyages to the islands, beginning in 1769. Britain formally annexed the islands in 1840.

The Treaty of Waitangi (Feb. 6, 1840) between the British and several Maori tribes promised to protect Maori land if the Maoris recognized British rule. Encroachment upon the land by European settlers was relentless, however, and skirmishes between the two groups intensified.

From the outset, the country has been in the forefront in instituting social welfare legislation. New Zealand was the world's first country to give women the right to vote (1893). It adopted old-age pensions (1898); a national child welfare program (1907); social security for the aged, widows, and orphans, along with family benefit payments; minimum wages; a 40-hour workweek and unemployment and health insurance (1938); and socialized medicine (1941).

New Zealand fought with the Allies in both world wars as well as in Korea. In 1999, it became part of the UN peacekeeping force sent to East Timor. In June 2002, Prime Minister Helen Clark apologized to Samoans for the unfair treatment they received during colonial rule. The Labor Party's Clark was elected to a second term as prime minister in July 2002. In June 2003, Parliament legalized prostitution 60–59.

Cook Islands and Overseas Territories

The Cook Islands (93 sq mi; 241 sq km) were placed under New Zealand administration in 1901. They achieved self-governing status in association with New Zealand in 1965. **Population (July 2002 est.):** 21,008.

Niue (100 sq mi; 259 sq km) was formerly administered as part of the Cook Islands. It was placed under separate New Zealand administration in 1901 and achieved self-governing status in association with New Zealand in 1974. The capital is Alofi. **Population (2002 est.):** 2,124.

Tokelau (3.86 sq mi; 10 sq km) was formerly administered as part of the Gilbert and Ellice Islands colony. It was placed under New Zealand administration in 1925. **Population (2002 est.):** 1,445.

Nicaragua

REPUBLIC OF NICARAGUA

National name: República de Nicaragua
President: Enrique Bolaños (2002)
Area: 49,998 sq mi (129,494 sq km)
Population (2003 est.): 5,128,517 (growth rate: 2.2%); birth rate: 26.3/1000; infant mortality rate: 31.4/1000; density per sq mi: 103
Capital and largest city (2003 est.): Managua, 1,390,500 (metro. area), 1,146,000 (city proper). **Monetary unit:** Gold cordoba. **Language:** Spanish. **Ethnicity/race:** mestizo (mixed Amerindian and white) 69%, white 17%, black 9%, Indian 5%. **Religions:** Roman Catholic 85%, Protestant 15%. **Literacy rate:** 68.2% (1999)

Economic summary: GDP/PPP (2001 est.): $12.3 billion; per capita $2,500. **Real growth rate:** 2.5%. **Inflation:** 7.4%. **Unemployment:** 23% plus considerable underemployment (2001 est.). **Arable land:** 20%. **Agriculture:** coffee, bananas, sugarcane, cotton, rice, corn, tobacco, sesame, soya, beans; beef, veal, pork, poultry, dairy products. **Labor force:** 1.7 million (1999); services 43%, agriculture 42%, industry 15% (1999 est.). **Industries:** food processing, chemicals, machinery and metal products, textiles, clothing, petroleum refining and distribution, beverages, footwear, wood. **Natural resources:** gold, silver, copper, tungsten, lead, zinc, timber, fish. **Exports:** $609.5 million (f.o.b., 2001 est.): coffee, shrimp and lobster, cotton, tobacco, beef, sugar, bananas; gold. **Imports:** $1.6 billion (f.o.b., 2001 est.): machinery and equipment, raw materials, petroleum products, consumer goods. **Major trading partners:** U.S., Germany, Canada, Costa Rica, Honduras, Venezuela, Guatemala, Mexico,

Geography Largest but most sparsely populated of the Central American nations, Nicaragua borders on Honduras to the north and Costa Rica to the south. It is slightly larger than New York State. Nicaragua is mountainous in the west, with fertile valleys. A plateau slopes eastward toward the Caribbean. Two big lakes—Nicaragua, about 100 mi long (161 km), and Managua, about 38 mi long (61 km)—are connected by the Tipitapa River. The Pacific coast is volcanic and very fertile. The Caribbean coast, swampy and indented, is aptly called the "Mosquito Coast."

Government Republic.

History Nicaragua, which derives its name from the chief of the area's leading Indian tribe at the time of the Spanish Conquest, was first settled by the Spanish in 1522. The country won independence in 1838. For the next century, Nicaragua's politics were dominated by the competition for power between the Liberals, who were centered in the city of León, and the Conservatives, centered in Granada.

To back up its support of the new Conservative government in 1909, the U.S. sent a small detachment of Marines to Nicaragua from 1912 to 1925. The Bryan-Chamorro Treaty of 1916 (terminated in 1970) gave the U.S. an option on a canal route through Nicaragua and naval bases. U.S. Marines were sent again to quell disorder after the 1924 elections. A guerrilla leader, Gen. César Augusto Sandino, fought the U.S. troops from 1927 until their withdrawal in 1933.

After ordering Sandino's assassination, Gen. Anastasio Somoza García was dictator from 1936 until his own assassination in 1956. He was succeeded by his son Luis, who alternated with trusted family friends in the presidency until his death in 1967. He was succeeded by his brother, Maj. Gen. Anastasio Somoza Debayle. The Somozas ruled Nicaragua with an iron fist, reducing its dependence on banana exports, exiling political foes, and amassing a family fortune.

Sandinista guerrillas, leftists who took their name from Sandino, launched an offensive in 1979. After seven weeks of fighting, Somoza fled the country on July 17, 1979. The Sandinistas assumed power two days later. On Jan. 23, 1981, the Reagan administration suspended U.S. aid, charging that Nicaragua, with the aid of Cuba and the Soviet Union, was supplying arms to rebels in El Salvador. The Sandinistas denied the charges. Later that year, Nicaraguan guerrillas known as "Contras," began a war to overthrow the Sandinistas. Elections were finally held on Nov. 4, 1984, with Daniel Ortega, the Sandinista junta coordinator, winning the presidency. The war intensified in 1986–1987. Negotiations sponsored by the Contadora (neutral Latin American) nations foundered, but Costa Rican president Oscar Arias promoted a treaty signed by Central American leaders in Aug. 1987.

Violetta Barrios de Chamorro, owner of the opposition paper *La Prensa,* led a broad anti-Sandinista coalition to victory in the 1990 elections, ending 11 years of Sandinista rule. Enthusiasm for Chamorro gradually faded. Business groups were dissatisfied with the pace of reforms; Sandinistas, upset with what they regarded as the dismantling of their earlier achievements, threatened to take up arms again; and many people were disillusioned over governmental corruption and the continuing influence of the Sandinistas on the government and the army. Former Managua mayor and Conservative candidate Arnoldo Alemán won the 1996 election. Ortega was his closest rival.

In 1998, Hurricane Mitch killed more than 9,000 people, left 2 million people homeless, and caused $10 billion in damages. Many people fled to the U.S., which offered Nicaraguans an immigration amnesty program until July 1999.

Nicaragua remains one of the poorest countries in the Western Hemisphere. Property is often caught in a three-way battle between those who owned it before the Sandinistas came to power; cooperatives set up by the Sandinistas; and former Contras who claim they were promised land for joining the anti-Sandinista forces.

In Nov. 2001 presidential elections, Enrique Bolaños, the ruling Liberal party leader, defeated Daniel Ortega, the Sandinista leader who had attempted a comeback after his defeat in 1990. The Sandinistas elected Ortega as party head in March 2002, despite his series of losses in recent presidential elections.

Former president Arnoldo Aleman was charged with fraud and embezzlement in Aug. 2002, and jailed a year later pending his trial. Prosecutors allege that he stole $100 million in state funds during his presidency.

Niger

REPUBLIC OF NIGER

National name: République du Niger
President: Tandja Mamadou (1999)
Prime Minister: Hama Amadou (1999)
Area: 489,189 sq mi (1,267,000 sq km)
Population (2003 est.): 11,058,590 (growth rate: 2.8%); birth rate: 49.5/1000; infant mortality rate: 123.6/1000; density per sq mi: 23
Capital and largest city (2003 est.): Niamey, 748,600. **Other large cities:** Zinder, 202,300; Maradi, 189,000. **Monetary unit:** CFA Franc. **Languages:** French (official); Hausa; Songhai; Arabic. **Ethnicity/race:** Hausa 56%, Djerma 22%, Fula 8.5%, Tuareg 8%, Beri Beri (Kanouri) 4.3%, Arab, Toubou, and Gourmantche 1.2%, about 4,000 French expatriates. **Religions:** Islam 80%, Animist and Christian 20%. **Literacy rate:** 15.3% (2002)
Economic summary: GDP/PPP (2001 est.): $8.4 billion; per capita $820. **Real growth rate:** 3.1%. **Inflation:** 4.2%. **Unemployment:** n.a. **Arable land:** 4%. **Agriculture:** cowpeas, cotton, peanuts, millet, sorghum, cassava (tapioca), rice; cattle, sheep, goats, camels, donkeys, horses, poultry. **Labor force:** 70,000 receive regular wages or salaries; agriculture 90%, industry and commerce 6%, government 4%. **Industries:** uranium mining, cement, brick, textiles, food processing, chemicals, slaughterhouses. **Natural resources:** uranium, coal, iron ore, tin, phosphates, gold, petroleum. **Exports:** $246 million (f.o.b., 2001 est.): uranium ore 65%, livestock products, cowpeas, onions (1998 est.). **Imports:** $331 million (f.o.b., 2001 est.): consumer goods, primary materials, machinery, vehicles and parts, petroleum, cereals. **Major trading partners:** France, Nigeria, Spain, U.S., Côte d'Ivoire, Nigeria.

Geography Niger, in West Africa's Sahara region, is four-fifths the size of Alaska. It is surrounded by Mali, Algeria, Libya, Chad, Nigeria, Benin, and Burkina Faso. The Niger River in the southwest flows through the country's only fertile area. Elsewhere the land is semiarid.

Government Republic, emerging from military rule.

History The nomadic Tuaregs were the first inhabitants in the Sahara region. The Hausa (14th century), the Zerma (17th century), the Gobir (18th century), and Fulani (19th century) also established themselves in the region now called Niger.

Niger was incorporated into French West Africa in 1896. There were frequent rebellions, but when order was restored in 1922, the French made the area a colony. In 1958, the voters approved the French constitution and voted to make the territory an autonomous republic within the French Community. The republic adopted a constitution in 1959 but the next year withdrew from the Community, proclaiming its independence.

During the 1970s, the country's economy flourished from uranium production, but when uranium prices fell in the 1980s, its brief period of prosperity ended. The 1974 army coup ousted President Hamani Diori, who had held office since 1960. An estimated 2 million people were starving in Niger, but 200,000 tons of imported food, half U.S.-supplied, substantially ended famine conditions by the year's end. The new president, Lt. Col. Seyni Kountché, chief of staff of the army, installed a 12-man military government. A predominantly civilian government was formed by Kountché in 1976.

In 1993, the country's first multiparty election resulted in the presidency of Ousmane Mahamane, who was then deposed in a Jan. 1996 coup. In July, the military leader of the coup, Ibrahim Baré Maïnassara, was declared president in a rigged election. Considered a corrupt and ineffectual president, Maïnassara was assassinated in April 1999 by his own guards. The National Reconciliation Council, responsible for the coup, kept its promise and held democratic elections; in Nov. 1999, Tandja Mamadou was elected president. As a result, foreign aid, primarily from France, was restored.

The nomadic Tuaregs of the north, of Berber and Arab descent, have a fiercely insular culture and share little affinity with the black African majority of Niger. Conflict between the Tuaregs and the other tribes of Niger first surfaced in the early 20th century. A cease-fire between the government and Tuareg rebels (Revolutionary Armed Forces of the Sahara) went into effect in 1995, and in June 1997, the Democratic Renewal Front, a holdout Tuareg rebel group, also agreed to sign a peace accord. The impoverished Tuaregs have received little of the economic aid they were promised, which is not surprising given Niger's political instability and desperate poverty.

Niger found itself an unwitting pawn in the war against Iraq when both the U.S. and Britain used the now-discredited claim that Iraq sought to buy uranium from Niger as a casus belli. To the embarrassment of the Bush administration, the Iraq-Niger uranium intelligence was quickly exposed as a forgery, but British PM Tony Blair continued to insist on the veracity of the claim. In July 2003, Prime Minister Amadou demanded that "If Britain has evidence to support its claim then it has only to produce it for everybody to see. . . . Everybody knows that the claims are untrue."

Nigeria

FEDERAL REPUBLIC OF NIGERIA

President: Olusegun Obasanjo (1999)
Area: 356,667 sq mi (923,768 sq km)
Population (2003 est.): 133,881,703 (growth rate: 2.5%); birth rate: 38.8/1000; infant mortality rate: 71.3/1000; density per sq mi: 375
Capital (2003 est.): Abuja, 590,400 (metro. area), 165,700 (city proper). **Largest cities:** Lagos (2003 est.), 9,529,700 (metro. area), 8,349,700 (city proper); Kano, 3,329,900; Ibadan, 3,139,500; Kaduna, 1,510,300. **Monetary unit:** Naira. **Languages:** English (official), Hausa, Yoruba, Ibo, and more than 200 others. **Ethnicity/race:** Hausa, Fulani, Yoruba, Ibo, Kanuri, Ibibio, Tiv, Ijaw. **Religions:** Islam 50%, Christian 40%, indigenous 10%. **Literacy rate:** 57.1% (1995 est.)
Economic summary: GDP/PPP (2001 est.): $105.9 billion; per capita $840. **Real growth rate:** 3.5%. **Inflation:** 14.9%. **Unemployment:** 28% (1992 est.). **Arable land:** 31%. **Agriculture:** cocoa, peanuts, palm oil, corn, rice, sorghum, millet, cassava (tapioca), yams, rubber; cattle, sheep, goats, pigs; timber; fish. **Labor force:** 66 million; agriculture 70%, industry 10%, services 20% (1999 est.). **Industries:** crude oil, coal, tin, columbite, palm oil, peanuts, cotton, rubber, wood, hides and skins, textiles, cement and other construction materials, food products, footwear, chemicals, fertilizer, printing, ceramics, steel. **Natural resources:** natural gas, petroleum, tin, columbite, iron ore, coal, limestone, lead, zinc, arable land. **Exports:** $20.3 billion (f.o.b., 2001 est.): petroleum and petroleum products 95%, cocoa, rubber. **Imports:** $13.7 billion (f.o.b., 2001 est.): machinery, chemicals, transport equipment, manufactured goods, food and live animals. **Major trading partners:** U.S., Spain, India, France, Brazil, UK, Germany, China. **Member of Commonwealth of Nations**

Geography Nigeria, one-third larger than Texas and the most populous country in Africa, is situated on the Gulf of Guinea in West Africa. Its neighbors are Benin, Niger, Cameroon, and Chad. The lower course of the Niger River flows south through the western part of the country into the Gulf of Guinea. Swamps and mangrove forests border the southern coast; inland are hardwood forests.

Government Multiparty government transitioning from military to civilian rule.

History The first inhabitants of what is now Nigeria were thought to have been the Nok people (500 B.C.–c. A.D. 200). The Kanuri, Hausa, and Fulani peoples subsequently migrated there. Islam was introduced in the 13th century, and the empire of Kanem controlled the area from the end of the 11th century to the 14th.

The Fulani empire ruled the region from the beginning of the 19th century until the British annexed Lagos in 1851 and seized control of the rest of the region by 1886. It formally became the Colony and Protectorate of Nigeria in 1914. During World War I, native troops of the West African frontier force joined with French forces to defeat the German garrison in the Cameroons.

On Oct. 1, 1960, Nigeria gained independence, becoming a member of the Commonwealth of Nations and joining the United Nations. Organized as a loose federation of self-governing states, the independent nation faced an overwhelming task of unifying a country with 250 ethnic and linguistic groups.

Rioting broke out in 1966, and military leaders, primarily of Ibo ethnicity, seized control. In July, a second military coup put Col. Yakubu Gowon in power, a choice unacceptable to the Ibos. Also in that year, the Muslim Hausas in the north massacred the predominantly Christian Ibos in the east, many of whom had been driven from the north. Thousands of Ibos took refuge in the eastern region, which declared its independence as the Republic of Biafra on May 30, 1967. Civil war broke out. In Jan. 1970, after 31 months of civil war, Biafra surrendered to the federal government.

Gowon's nine-year rule was ended in 1975 by a bloodless coup that made Army Brig. Muritala Rufai Mohammed the new chief of state. The return of civilian leadership was established with the election of Alhaji Shehu Shagari as president in 1979. An oil boom in the 1970s buoyed the economy and by the 1980s Nigeria was considered an exemplar of African democracy and economic well-being.

The military again seized power in 1984, only to be followed by another military coup the following year. Maj. Gen. Ibrahim Babangida announced that the country would be returned to civilian rule, but after the presidential election of June 12, 1993, he voided the results. Nevertheless, Babangida resigned as president in Aug. In Nov. the military, headed by defense minister Sani Abacha, seized power again.

Corruption and notorious governmental inefficiency as well as a harshly repressive military regime characterized Abacha's reign over this oil-rich country. A UN fact-finding mission in 1996 reported that Nigeria's "problems of human rights are terrible and the political problems are terrifying." During the 1970s, Nigeria had the 33rd highest per-capita income in the world, but by 1997 it had dropped to the 13th poorest.

As leader of the multination peacekeeping force ECOMOG, Nigeria has established itself as West Africa's superpower, intervening militarily in the civil wars of Liberia and Sierra Leone. But Nigeria's costly war efforts have been unpopular with its own people, who feel Nigeria's limited economic resources are being unnecessarily drained.

Under military rule for all but ten years since independence from Britain, the military has reneged on its promises to give up power eight times. Despite international pressure to institute democratic rule, the notoriously authoritarian Gen. Sani Abacha, whose formidable security forces kept a tight rein over the country, refused to loosen his absolute grip on political and military power. Abacha's repressive rule turned Nigeria into an international pariah. The hanging of writer Ken Saro-Wiwa in 1995 because he protested against the government was condemned around the world.

Abacha died of a heart attack on June 8, 1998, and was succeeded by another military ruler, Gen. Abdulsalam Abubakar, who pledged to step aside for an elected leader by May 1999. Abubakar's freeing of political prisoners and other gestures of easing the military's iron-clad rule were signs of hope, but the suspicious death of opposition leader Mashood Abiola, who had been imprisoned by the military ever since he legally won the 1993 presidential election, was a crushing blow to democratic proponents. In Feb. 1999, free presidential elections led to an overwhelming victory for Gen. Olusegun Obasanjo, a former member of the military elite who was imprisoned for three years for criticizing the military rule, and released just eight months before his election. Obasanjo's commitment to democracy, his anticorruption drives, and his desire to recover billions allegedly stolen by the family and cronies of Abacha initially gained him high praise from the populace as well as the international community. But within two years, the hope of reform seemed doomed as economic mismanagement and rampant corruption persisted. Obasanjo's priorities in 2001 were symbolized by his plans to build a $330 million national soccer stadium, an extravagance that exceeded the combined budget for both health and education.

Nigeria's stability has been repeatedly threatened by fighting between fundamentalist Muslims and Christians over the spread of Islamic law (sharia) across the heavily Muslim north. About one-third of Nigeria's 36 states are ruled by sharia law. More than 10,000 people have died in religious clashes since military rule ended in 1999.

In April 2003 elections, incumbent president Obasanjo won 61.9% of the vote; election fraud has been confirmed by international observers, though it is likely Obasanjo would have won anyway, simply not with such a high margin.

Norway

KINGDOM OF NORWAY

National name: Kongeriket Norge
Sovereign: King Harald V (1991)
Prime Minister: Kjell Magne Bondevik (2001)
Area: 125,181 sq mi (324,220 sq km)
Population (2003 est.): 4,546,123 (growth rate: 0.2%); birth rate: 12.2/1000; infant mortality rate: 3.9/1000; density per sq mi: 36
Capital and largest city (2003 est.): Oslo, 791,500. **Other large cities:** Bergen, 211,200; Stavanger, 168,600; Trondheim, 144,000. **Monetary unit:** Norwegian krone. **Languages:** Two official forms of Norwegian: Bokmål and Nynorsk. **Ethnicity/race:** Germanic (Nordic, Alpine, Baltic), Lapps (Sami). **Religions:** Evangelical Lutheran 86% (state church), other Protestant and Roman Catholic 36%, other 1%, none and unknown 10%. **Literacy rate:** 100%
Economic summary: GDP/PPP (2001 est.): $138.7 billion; per capita $30,800. **Real growth rate:** 1.3%. **Inflation:** 3.1%. **Unemployment:** 3.6%. **Arable land:** 3%. **Agriculture:** barley, wheat, potatoes; pork, beef, veal, milk; fish. **Labor force:** 2.4 million (2000 est.); services 74%, industry 22%, agriculture, forestry, and fishing 4% (1995). **Industries:** petroleum and gas, food processing, shipbuilding, pulp and paper products, metals, chemicals, timber, mining, textiles, fishing. **Natural resources:** petroleum, copper, natural gas, pyrites, nickel, iron ore, zinc, lead, fish, timber, hydropower. **Exports:** $58 billion (f.o.b., 2001 est.): petroleum and petroleum products, machinery and equipment, metals, chemicals, ships, fish. **Imports:** $33.5 billion (f.o.b., 2001 est.): machinery and equipment, chemicals, metals, foodstuffs. **Major trading partners:** EU, U.S., Japan.

Geography Norway is situated in the western part of the Scandinavian peninsula. It extends about 1,100 mi (1,770 km) from the North Sea along the Norwegian Sea to more than 300 mi (483 km) above the Arctic Circle, the farthest north of any European country. It is slightly larger than New Mexico. Nearly 70% of Norway is uninhabitable and covered by mountains, glaciers, moors, and rivers. The hundreds of deep fjords that cut into the coastline give Norway an overall oceanfront of more than 12,000 mi (19,312 km). Galdhø Peak, at 8,100 ft (2,469 m), is Norway's highest point and the Glåma (Glomma) is the principal river, at 372 mi (598 km) long.

Government Constitutional monarchy.

History Norwegians, like the Danes and Swedes, are of Teutonic origin. The Norsemen, also known as Vikings, ravaged the coasts of northwest Europe from the 8th to the 11th century and were ruled by local chieftains. Olaf II Haraldsson became the first effective king of all Norway in 1015 and began converting the Norwegians to Christianity. After 1442, Norway was ruled by Danish kings until 1814, when it was united with Sweden—although retaining a degree of independence and receiving a new constitution—in an uneasy partnership. In 1905, the Norwegian Parliament arranged a peaceful separation and invited a Danish prince to the Norwegian throne—King Haakon VII. A treaty with Sweden provided that all disputes be settled by arbitration and that no fortifications be erected on the common frontier.

When World War I broke out, Norway joined with Sweden and Denmark in a decision to remain neutral and to cooperate in the joint interest of the three countries. In World War II, Norway was invaded by the Germans on April 9, 1940. It resisted for two months before the Nazis took complete control. King Haakon and his government fled to London, where they established a government-in-exile. Maj. Vidkun Quisling, who served as Norway's premier during the war, was the most notorious of the Nazi collaborators. The word for traitor, *quisling,* bears his name. He was executed by the Norwegians on Oct. 24, 1945.

Despite severe losses in the war, Norway recovered quickly as its economy expanded. The country led the world in social experimentation. It entered the North Atlantic Treaty Organization in 1949. In the late 20th century, the Labor Party and the Conservative Party seesawed for control, each sometimes having to lead minority governments. An important debate has been over Norway's membership in the European Union. In an advisory referendum held in Nov. 1994, voters rejected seeking membership for their nation in the EU. The country became the second-largest net oil exporter after Saudi Arabia in 1995. Norway continued to experience rapid economic growth into the new millennium.

In March 2000, Prime Minister Kjell Magne Bondevik resigned after parliament voted to build the country's first gas-fired power stations. Bondevik had objected to the project, asserting that the plants would emit too much carbon dioxide. Labor Party leader Jens Stoltenberg succeeded Bondevik. Stoltenberg and the Labor Party were defeated in Sept. 2001 elections, and no party emerged with a clear majority. After a month of talks, the Conservatives, the Christian People's Party, and the Liberals formed a coalition with Bondevik as prime minister. The governing coalition was backed by the far-right Progress Party.

Tension mounted between Norway and Australia in Aug. 2001, when Australia refused to allow a Norwegian ship, the *Tampa,* which had rescued 460 mainly Afghan refugees from a sinking ferry off Indonesia, to dock on Australia's Christmas Island. New Zealand and Nauru stepped in and offered to process the refugees' asylum claims.

Dependencies of Norway

Svalbard (23,957 sq mi; 62,049 sq km), in the Arctic Ocean about 360 mi north of Norway, consists of the Spitsbergen group and several smaller islands, including Bear Island, Hope Island, King Charles Land, and White Island (or Gillis Land). The capital is Longyearbyen. It came under Norwegian administration in 1925. **Population:** 2,868 (July 2002 est.). 62% of the population is Russian and Ukrainian; 38% are Norwegian. Coal mining is the major economic activity. **Bouvet Island** (23 sq mi; 58.5 sq km), an island nature reserve in the South Atlantic about 1,600 mi south-southwest of the Cape of Good Hope, came under Norwegian administration in 1928. It is uninhabited.

Jan Mayen Island (144 sq mi; 373 sq km), in the Arctic Ocean between Norway and Greenland, came under Norwegian administration in 1929. There are no permanent inhabitants, just workers at the navigation base and weather/radio station.

Oman

SULTANATE OF OMAN

National name: Saltonat Uman
Sultan: Qabus ibn Sa'id (1970)
Area: 82,031 sq mi (212,460 sq km)[1]
Population (2003 est.): 2,807,125 (growth rate: 3.4%); birth rate: 37.5/1000; infant mortality rate: 21.0/1000; density per sq mi: 34
Capital (2003 est.): Muscat, 797,000 (metro.area), 54,800 (city proper). **Monetary unit:** Omani rial. **Languages:** Arabic (official); also English and Indian languages. **Ethnicity/race:** Arab, Baluchi, South Asian (Indian, Pakistani, Sri Lankan, Bangladeshi), African. **Religion:** Islam 95%. **Literacy rate:** 80%
Economic summary: GDP/PPP (2001 est.): $21.5 billion; per capita $8,200. **Real growth rate:** 7.4%. **Inflation:** 1%. **Unemployment:** n.a. **Arable land:** 0%. **Agriculture:** dates, limes, bananas, alfalfa, vegetables; camels, cattle; fish. **Labor force:** 920,000 (2002 est.); agriculture n.a., industry n.a., services n.a. **Industries:** crude oil production and refining, natural gas production, construction, cement, copper. **Natural resources:** petroleum, copper, asbestos, some marble, limestone, chromium, gypsum, natural gas. **Exports:** $10.9 billion (f.o.b., 2001 est.): petroleum, reexports, fish, metals, textiles. **Imports:** $5.4 billion (f.o.b., 2001 est.): machinery and transport equipment, manufactured goods, food, livestock, lubricants. **Major trading partners:** Japan, Thailand, China, South Korea, UAE, U.S., UK, Italy, Germany.

1. Excluding the Kuria Muria Islands.

Geography Oman is a 1,000-mile-long (1,700-km) coastal plain at the southeast tip of the Arabian peninsula lying on the Arabian Sea and the Gulf of Oman. It is bordered by the United Arab Emirates, Saudi Arabia, and Yemen. The country is the size of Kansas.

Government Absolute monarchy.

History Arabs migrated to Oman from the 9th century B.C. onward, and conversion to Islam occurred in the 7th century A.D. Muscat, the capital of the geographical area known as Oman, was occupied by the Portuguese from 1508 to 1648. Then it fell to Ottoman Turks, but in 1741 Ahmad ibn Sa'id forced them out. The descendants of Sultan Ahmad rule Oman today.

Ahmad expanded his empire to East Africa, and for a time the Omani capital was in Zanzibar. After 1861, however, Zanzibar fell from Omani control.

The sultans and imams of Oman clashed continuously throughout the 20th century until 1959, when the last Ibadi imam was evicted from the country. In a palace coup on July 23, 1970, the sultan, Sa'id bin Taimur, who had ruled since 1932, was overthrown by his son, who promised to establish a modern government and use newfound oil wealth to aid the people of this very isolated state. Oman joined the Arab League and the United Nations in 1971.

A long border dispute with Yemen was resolved in Oct. 1992; in 1997, the countries agreed to new maps defining the border.

In 1997, Sultan Qabus granted women the right to be elected to the country's consultative body, the Shura Council (Majlis al-Shura). The council has no formal powers, but it advises the sultan on economic matters and public policy. Two women were elected to the council in 1997 as well as in 2000. In 2003, the sultan extended voting rights to everyone over 21; previously, voters were selected from among the elite—about a quarter of the population was allowed to vote.

Pakistan

ISLAMIC REPUBLIC OF PAKISTAN

President: Gen. Pervez Musharraf (2001)
Prime minister: Mir Zafarullah Khan Jamali (2002)
Area: 310,401 sq mi (803,940 sq km)[1]
Population (2003 est.): 150,694,740 (growth rate: 2.1%); birth rate: 29.6/1000; infant mortality rate: 76.5/1000; density per sq mi: 485
Capital (2003 est.): Islamabad, 601,600. **Largest cities:** Karachi, 10,573,200; Lahore, 5,756,100; Faisalabad (Lyallpur), 2,247,700; Rawalpindi, 1,598,600; Gujranwala, 1,384,100. **Monetary unit:** Pakistan rupee. **Principal languages:** Punjabi 48%, Sindhi 12%, Siraiki (a Punjabi variant) 10%, Pashtu 8%, Urdu (official) 8%, Balochi 3%, Hindko 2%, Brahui 1%, English, Burushaski, and others. **Ethnicity/race:** Punjabi, Sindhi, Pashtun (Pathan), Baloch, Muhajir (immigrants from India and their descendants). **Religions:** Islam 97%, Hindu, Christian, Buddhist, Parsi. **Literacy rate:** 42.7% (1998)
Economic summary GDP/PPP (2001 est.): $299 billion; per capita $2,100. **Real growth rate:** 3.3%. **Inflation:** 4%. **Unemployment:** 6.3%. **Arable land:** 28%. **Agriculture:** cotton, wheat, rice, sugarcane, fruits, vegetables; milk, beef, mutton, eggs. **Labor force:** 40.4 million; note: extensive export of labor, mostly to the Middle East, and use of child labor (2000 est.); agriculture 44%, industry 17%, services 39% (1999 est.). **Industries:** textiles, food processing, beverages, construction materials, clothing, paper products, shrimp. **Natural resources:** land, extensive natural gas reserves, limited petroleum, poor quality coal, iron ore, copper, salt, limestone. **Exports:** $8.8 billion (f.o.b.,

2001): textiles (garments, cotton cloth, and yarn), rice, other agricultural products. **Imports:** $9.2 billion (f.o.b., 2001): machinery, petroleum, petroleum products, chemicals, transportation equipment, edible oils, grains, pulses, flour. **Major trading partners:** U.S., UK, Germany, UAE, Hong Kong, Germany, Kuwait, Saudi Arabia, Japan.

1. Excluding Kashmir and Jammu.

Geography Pakistan is situated in the western part of the Indian subcontinent, with Afghanistan and Iran on the west, India on the east, and the Arabian Sea on the south. The name *Pakistan* is derived from the Urdu words *Pak* (meaning pure) and *stan* (meaning country). It is nearly twice the size of California.

The northern and western highlands of Pakistan contain the towering Karakoram and Pamir mountain ranges, which include some of the world's highest peaks: K2 (28,250 ft; 8,611 m) and Nanga Parbat (26,660 ft; 8,126 m). The Baluchistan Plateau lies to the west, and the Thar Desert and an expanse of alluvial plains, the Punjab and Sind, lie to the east. The 1,000-mile-long (1,609 km) Indus River and its tributaries flow through the country from the Kashmir region to the Arabian Sea.

Government Military rule was instituted Oct. 1999; a nominal democracy was declared in June 2001 by the ruling military leader, Pervez Musharraf.

History Pakistan was one of the two original successor states to British India, which was partitioned along religious lines in 1947. For almost 25 years following independence, it consisted of two separate regions, East and West Pakistan, but now is made up only of the western sector. Both India and Pakistan have laid claim to the Kashmir region, and this territorial dispute led to war in 1949, and again in 1965, 1971, and 1999, and remains unresolved today.

What is now Pakistan was in prehistoric times the Indus Valley civilization (c. 2500–1700 B.C.). A series of invaders—Aryans, Persians, Greeks, Arabs, Turks, and others—controlled the region for the next several thousand years. Islam, the dominant religion, was introduced in 711. In 1526, the land became part of the Mogul Empire, which ruled most of the Indian subcontinent from the 16th to the mid-18th century. By 1857, the British became the dominant power in the region. With Hindus holding most of the economic, social, and political advantages, the Muslim minority's dissatisfaction grew, leading to the formation of the nationalist Muslim League in 1906 by Mohammed Ali Jinnah (1876–1949). The league supported Britain in the Second World War while the Hindu nationalist leaders, Nehru and Gandhi, refused. In return for the league's support of Britain, Jinnah expected British backing for Muslim autonomy. Britain agreed to the formation of Pakistan as a separate dominion within the Commonwealth in Aug. 1947, a bitter disappointment to India's dream of a unified subcontinent. Jinnah became governor-general. The partition of Pakistan and India along religious lines resulted in the largest migration in human history, with 17 million people fleeing across the borders in both directions to escape the sectarian violence accompanying the partition.

Pakistan became a republic on March 23, 1956, with Maj. Gen. Iskander Mirza becoming the first president. Military rule prevailed for the next two decades. Tensions between East and West Pakistan existed from the outset. Separated by more than a thousand miles, the two regions shared few cultural and social traditions other than religion. To the growing resentment of East Pakistan, the West monopolized the country's political and economic power. In 1970, East Pakistan's Awami League, led by the Bengali leader Sheik Mujibur Rahman, secured a majority of the seats in the National Assembly. President Yahya Khan postponed the opening of the National Assembly to skirt East Pakistan's demand for greater autonomy, provoking civil war. The independent state of Bangladesh, or Bengali nation, was proclaimed on March 26, 1971. Indian troops entered the war in its last weeks fighting on the side of the new state. Pakistan was defeated on Dec. 16, 1971, and President Yahya Khan stepped down. Zulfikar Ali Bhutto took over Pakistan and accepted Bangladesh as an independent entity. In 1976, formal relations between India and Pakistan resumed.

Pakistan's first elections under civilian rule took place in March 1977, and the overwhelming victory of Bhutto's Pakistan People's Party (PPP) was denounced as fraudulent. A rising tide of violent protest and political deadlock led to a military takeover on July 5 by Gen. Mohammed Zia ul-Haq. Bhutto was tried and convicted for the 1974 murder of a political opponent, and despite worldwide protests was executed on April 4, 1979, touching off riots by his supporters. Zia declared himself president on Sept. 16, 1978, and ruled by martial law until Dec. 30, 1985, when a measure of representative government was restored. On Aug. 19, 1988, President Zia was killed in a midair explosion of a Pakistani Air Force plane. Elections at the end of 1988 brought longtime Zia opponent Benazir Bhutto, daughter of Zulfikar Bhutto, into office as prime minister.

In the 1990s, Pakistan saw a shaky succession of governments—Benazir Bhutto was prime minister twice and Nawaz Sharif three times, until he was deposed in a coup on Oct. 12, 1999, by Gen. Pervez Musharraf. The Pakistani public, familiar with military rule for 25 of the nation's 52-year history, generally viewed the coup as a positive step, and hoped it would bring a badly needed economic upswing.

India went ahead with five nuclear tests in May 1998 near Pakistan's borders, which further deteriorated fragile relations between Pakistan and India. In an act of nuclear brinkmanship, Pakistan conducted its own nuclear tests in late May. Fighting with India again broke out in the disputed territory of Kashmir in May 1999.

Close ties with Afghanistan's Taliban government thrust Pakistan into a difficult position following the Sept. 11 terrorist attacks on the U.S. Under U.S. pressure, Pakistan broke with its neighbor to become the United States' chief ally in the region. In return, President Bush ended sanctions (instituted after Pakistan's testing of nuclear weapons in 1998), rescheduled its debt, and helped to bolster the legitimacy of Pervez Musharraf's rule, who appointed himself president in 2001.

On Dec. 13, 2001, suicide bombers attacked the Indian parliament, killing 14 people, including 5 assailants. Indian officials blamed the attack on Islamic militants supported by Pakistan. Both sides assembled hundreds of thousands of troops along the Indian-Pakistani border, bringing the two nuclear powers to the brink of war.

In April 2002, voters overwhelmingly approved a referendum to extend Musharraf's presidency for another five years. The vote, however, outraged opposing political parties and human rights groups that said the process was rigged. In Aug., he unveiled 29 constitutional amendments that strengthened his grip on the country.

Pakistani officials dealt a heavy blow to al-Qaeda in March 2003, arresting Khalid Shaikh Mohammed, the top aide to Osama bin Laden, who organized the 2001 terrorist attacks against the U.S. The search for bin Laden intensified in northern Pakistan following Mohammed's arrest.

The strain between Pakistan and India intensified once again in March 2003, following the slaughter of 24 Hindus in Indian-controlled Kashmir. Officials blamed the massacre on Islamic militants. Days after the violence, both India and Pakistan test-fired short-range missiles capable of carrying nuclear warheads.

At a June meeting at Camp David, President Bush offered President Musharraf a $3 billion aid package, but indicated he will not sell Pakistan the F-16 fighters it has been seeking for 14 years. In order to receive the money, Pakistan must continue to assist the U.S. in its fight against terrorism and stop helping North Korea assemble a nuclear-weapons program.

Palau

REPUBLIC OF PALAU

President: Tommy Remengesau (2001)
Total area: 177 sq mi (458 sq km)
Population (2003 est.): 19,717 (growth rate: 1.2%); birth rate: 19.0/1000; infant mortality rate: 15.8/1000; density per sq mi: 112
Capital and largest city (2003 est.): Koror, 11,100. **Monetary unit:** U.S. dollar used. **Languages:** Palauan, English (official). **Ethnicity/race:** Palauans are a composite of Polynesian, Malayan, and Melanesian races. **Religions:** Christian. About one-third of the islanders observe Modekngei religion, indigenous to Palau. **Literacy rate:** 92% (1980 est.)
Economic summary: GDP/PPP (2001 est.): $174 million; note: GDP numbers reflect U.S. spending; per capita $9,000. **Real growth rate:** 1%. **Inflation:** 3.4% (2000 est.). **Unemployment:** 2.3% (2000 est.). **Arable land:** 22%. **Agriculture:** coconuts, copra, cassava (tapioca), sweet potatoes. **Labor force:** 8,300 (1999); agriculture 20%, industry n.a., services n.a. **Industries:** tourism, craft items (from shell, wood, pearls), construction, garment making. **Natural resources:** forests, minerals (especially gold), marine products, deep-seabed minerals. **Exports:** $11 million (f.o.b., 1999): shellfish, tuna, copra, garments. **Imports:** $126 million (f.o.b., 1999): machinery and equipment, fuels, metals; foodstuffs. **Major trading partners:** U.S., Japan, Singapore.

Geography The Palau island chain consists of about 200 islands located in the western Pacific Ocean, 528 mi (650 km) southeast of the Philippines. Only eight of the islands are permanently inhabited.

Government Constitutional republic.

History The original settlers of Palau are believed to have arrived from Indonesia as early as 2500 B.C. The Palau islands' position on the western threshold of Oceania and their proximity to Southeast Asia have led to the population being a mixture of Malay, Melanesian, Filipino, and Polynesian ancestry.

Explored by the Spanish navigator Ruy López de Villalobos in 1543, the islands remained under nominal Spanish ownership for more than 300 years before Spain sold them to Germany in 1899. Japan occupied Palau during World War I and received a mandate over them from the League of Nations in 1920. They remained in Japanese control and served as an important naval base until the U.S. seized them during World War II. After the war they became a UN trusteeship (1947), administered by the United States. Palau signed a Compact of Free Association with the U.S. in 1992, requiring the United States to provide economic aid in exchange for the right to build and maintain U.S. military facilities in Palau. Palau became a sovereign state in 1994.

Palestinian State (proposed)

WEST BANK AND GAZA STRIP

President: Yasir Arafat (1994)
Area: West Bank: 2,263 sq mi (5,860 sq km); Gaza Strip: 139 sq mi (360 sq km)
Population (2003 est.): West Bank: 2,237,194, Gaza Strip: 1,274,868 (growth rate: West Bank: 3.0%, Gaza Strip: 3.7%); birth rate: West Bank: 34.1/1000, Gaza Strip: 41.2/1000; infant mortality rate: West Bank: 20.7/1,000, Gaza Strip: 24.1/1000; density per sq mi: West Bank: 989, Gaza Strip: 9,172
Capital: Undetermined. **Large cities (2003 est.):** Gaza, 1,331,600 (metro. area), 407,600 (city proper), Hebron, 137,000; Nablus, 115,400. **Monetary units:** New Israeli shekels, Jordanian dinars, U.S. dollars. **Languages:** Arabic, Hebrew, English, French. **Ethnicity/race:** West Bank: Palestinian Arab and other 83%, Jewish 17%; Gaza Strip: Palestinian Arab and other 99.4%, Jewish 0.6%. **Religions:** West Bank: Islam 75%, Jewish 17%, Christian and other 8%; Gaza Strip: Islam 98.7%, Christian 0.7%, Jewish 0.6%
Economic summary: Gaza Strip: GDP/PPP (2001 est.): $750 million; $625 per capita. **Real growth rate:** –35%. **Inflation:** 1% (includes West Bank). **Unemployment:** 26% (includes West Bank). **Arable land:** 26%. **Agriculture:** olives, citrus, vegetables; beef, dairy products. **Labor force:** n.a.; services 66%, industry 21%, agriculture 13% (1996). **Industries:** generally small family businesses that produce textiles, soap, olive-wood carvings, and mother-of-pearl souvenirs; the Israelis have established some small-scale modern industries in an industrial center. **Natural resources:** arable land, natural gas. **Exports:** $603 million (f.o.b., 2001 est.) (includes West Bank): citrus, flowers. **Imports:** $1.9 billion (c.i.f., 2001 est.) (includes West Bank): food, consumer goods, construction materialss. **Major trading partners:** Israel, Egypt, West Bank. **West Bank: GDP/PPP** (2001 est.): $2.1 billion; $1,000 per capita. **Real growth rate:** –35%. **Arable land:** negl. **Agriculture:** olives, citrus, vegetables; beef, dairy products. **Labor force:** n.a.; agriculture 13%; industry 13%, commerce, restaurants, and hotels 12%, construction 8%, other services 54% (1996). **Natural resources:** arable land. **Major trading partners:** Israel, Jordan, Gaza Strip.

Geography The West Bank is mostly composed of limestone hills (conventionally called the Samarian Hills north of Jerusalem and the Judaean Hills south of Jerusalem) having an average height of 2,300 to 3,000 ft (700 to 900 m). The Gaza Strip is located between Israel and Egypt on the Mediterranean coast. It is a flat to rolling sand- and dune-covered coastal plain.

Government The Palestinian Authority (PA), with Arafat its elected leader, took control of the newly non-Israeli-occupied areas, assuming governmental duties in 1994.

History The history of the proposed modern Palestinian state, which is expected to be formed from the territories of the West Bank and Gaza Strip, began with the British Mandate of Palestine. From Sept. 29, 1923, until May 14, 1948, Britain controlled the region, but by 1947, Britain had appealed to the UN to solve the complex problem of competing Palestinian and Jewish claims to the land. In Aug. 1947, the UN proposed dividing Palestine into a Jewish state, an Arab state, and a small international zone. Arabs rejected the idea. As soon as Britain pulled out of Palestine in 1948, neighboring Arab nations invaded, intent on crushing the newly declared State of Israel. Israel emerged victorious, affirming its sovereignty. The remaining areas of Palestine were divided between Transjordan (now Jordan), which annexed the West Bank, and Egypt, which gained control of the Gaza Strip.

Through a series of political and social policies, Jordan sought to consolidate its control over the political future of Palestinians and to become their speaker. Jordan even extended citizenship to Palestinians in 1949—Palestinians constituted about two-thirds of the country's population. In the Gaza Strip, administered by Egypt from 1948–1967, poverty and unemployment were high, and most of the Palestinians lived in refugee camps.

In the Arab-Israeli war of 1967, Israel, over a period of six days, defeated the military forces of Egypt, Syria, and Jordan, and annexed the territories of East Jerusalem, the Golan Heights, the West Bank, the Gaza Strip, and all of the Sinai peninsula. The Palestinian Liberation Organization (PLO), formed in 1964, was a terrorist organization bent on Israel's annihilation. Palestinian rioting, demonstrations, and terrorist acts against Israelis became chronic. In 1974, PLO leader Yasir Arafat addressed the UN General Assembly, the first stateless government to do so. Violence again escalated in 1987 during the *intifada* ("shaking off"), a new era in Palestinian mass mobilization. In 1988, Yasir Arafat publicly eschewed terrorism and officially recognized the state of Israel.

In 1993, highly secretive talks in Norway between the PLO and the Israeli government resulted in the Oslo Agreement. The accord stipulated a five-year plan in which Palestinians of the West Bank and the Gaza Strip would gradually become self-governing. On Sept. 13, 1993, Arafat and Israeli prime minister Yitzak Rabin signed the historic "Declaration of Principles." As part of the agreement, Israel pulled out of the Gaza Strip and Jericho in the West Bank in 1994. The Palestinian Authority (PA), with Arafat as its elected leader, took control of the newly non-Israeli-occupied areas, assuming all governmental duties.

Intensive negotiations between Ehud Barak and Arafat in 2000 remained deadlocked over Israeli-occupied East Jerusalem, which Arafat insisted must be the capital of the future Palestinian state. Arafat, however, allowed his Sept. 13 deadline for declaring a Palestinian state to pass in the interest of continued negotiations with Israel. At the end of Sept., however, the stalemate disintegrated into the worst violence between Israelis and Palestinians in years, provoked by Likud hardliner Ariel Sharon's visit to the compound called Temple Mount by Jews and Haram al Sharif by Muslims, a fiercely contested site that is sacred to both Jews and Muslims. The continuing violence, dubbed the Al Aksa intifada, fueled growing concerns about Israeli security, paving the way for the right-wing Sharon's stunning landslide victory over Barak in Feb. 2001, which outraged Palestinians and much of the Arab world. In late March 2002, Israeli troops invaded Palestinian-controlled territories in the West Bank in response to the growing number of suicide bombers. Israeli troops razed several major Palestinian cities and refugee camps, vowing to destroy the "terrorist infrastructure."

For five months in 2002, Israeli troops surrounded Yasir Arafat at the Palestinian Authority headquarters in Ramallah, and Prime Minister Sharon, blaming Arafat directly for inciting terror, called for his expulsion from the territories. Washington echoed Israel's view that Arafat had become "irrelevant," and announced hat the U.S. would not recognize an independent Palestinian state until Arafat was replaced. Throughout the summer, Palestinian suicide bombings (Hamas and the Al-Aksa Martyr Brigade claimed responsibility for the majority of them) and Israeli reprisals continued. Israeli troops killed several top Hamas leaders and imposed strict 24-hour curfews on West Bank towns, allowing residents only brief windows of time to shop and seek medical treatment. The move created a humanitarian crisis and coincided with the release of a U.S. Agency for International Development report that found that 30% of Palestinian children under age 5 suffer chronic malnutrition.

'In March 2003, Arafat agreed to political reforms that included sharing power with a prime minister. Mahmoud Abbas (also called Abu Mazan), second-in-command of the Palestine Liberation Organization, assumed the post on April 30. Unlike Arafat, Abbas emphatically rejects the Palestinian intifada, but he had no influence or control over Palestinian militant groups the way Arafat does. Abbas had strong relationships with Israeli and American officials, but little popular support among Palestinians. On May 1, the Bush administration unfurled its "road map" for peace in the Middle East, which called on both sides to make concessions and end the wave of deadly violence that has claimed more than 2,000 Palestinians and about 800 Israelis in the past two-and-a-half years. Sharon publicly acknowledged the need for a Palestinian state and Abbas committed himself to ending terrorism, but the road map has led nowhere, with neither side honoring their obligations: Abbas, with little real political power, did not disable terrorist organizations, and Israel did not dismantle settlements, much less prevent new ones from cropping up. Sharon continued to build the controversial security fence/wall—the term itself is contentious—that divides Israeli and Palestinian areas. Three militant Palestinian groups (Hamas, Islamic Jihad, and Fatah) declared a cease-fire on killing Israelis on June 29, but attacks resumed just weeks later. By Aug. 2003, the assassination of senior Hamas leader Abu Shanab by Israel and the suicide bombing of an Israeli bus that killed 20, including 6 children, ended hope for the short-lived road map. As the killings and retaliations continued, Mahmoud Abbas resigned out of frustration with the peace process and with continued power wrangling with Arafat. In September, Arafat appointed a new prime minister, Ahmed Qurei. The situation deteriorated further when Israel announced it was prepared to "remove" Arafat from power, a measure condemned by much of the international community.

Panama

REPUBLIC OF PANAMA

National name: República de Panamá
President: Mireya Moscoso (1999)
Area: 30,193 sq mi (78,200 sq km)
Population (2003 est.): 2,960,784 (growth rate: 1.5%); birth rate: 20.8/1000; infant mortality rate: 21.4/1000; density per sq mi: 98
Capital and largest city (2003 est.): Panama City, 1,053,500 (metro.area), 437,200 (city proper). **Other large cities:** San Miguelito, 309,500; Colón, 44,400. **Monetary unit:** balboa; U.S. dollar. **Languages:** Spanish (official); many bilingual in English. **Ethnicity/race:** mestizo (mixed Indian and European ancestry) 70%, West Indian 14%, white 10%, Indian 6%. **Religions:** Roman Catholic 85%, Protestant 15%. **Literacy rate:** 90.8% (1995 est.)
Economic summary: GDP/PPP (2001 est.): $16.9 billion; per capita $5,900. **Real growth rate:** 1.4%. **Inflation:** 1% (2000 est.). **Unemployment:** 13% (2000 est.). **Arable land:** 7%. **Agriculture:** bananas, rice,

corn, coffee, sugarcane, vegetables; livestock; shrimp. **Labor force:** 1.1 million (2000 est.); note: shortage of skilled labor, but an oversupply of unskilled labor; agriculture 20.8%, industry 18%, services 61.2% (1995 est.). **Industries:** construction, petroleum refining, brewing, cement and other construction materials, sugar milling. **Natural resources:** copper, mahogany forests, shrimp, hydropower. **Exports:** $5.9 billion (f.o.b., 2001 est.): bananas, shrimp, sugar, coffee, clothing. **Imports:** $6.7 billion (f.o.b., 2001 est.): capital goods, crude oil, foodstuffs, consumer goods, chemicals. **Major trading partners:** U.S., Sweden, Benelux, Costa Rica, Ecuador, Venezuela, Japan.

Geography The southernmost of the Central American nations, Panama is south of Costa Rica and north of Colombia. The Panama Canal bisects the isthmus at its narrowest and lowest point, allowing passage from the Caribbean Sea to the Pacific Ocean. Panama is slightly smaller than South Carolina. It is marked by a chain of mountains in the west, moderate hills in the interior, and a low range on the east coast. There are extensive forests in the fertile Caribbean area.

Government Constitutional democracy.

History Explored by Columbus in 1502 and by Balboa in 1513, Panama was the principal shipping point to and from South and Central America in colonial days. In 1821, when Central America revolted against Spain, Panama joined Colombia, which had already declared its independence. For the next 82 years, Panama attempted unsuccessfully to break away from Colombia. Between 1850 and 1900 Panama had 40 administrations, 50 riots, 5 attempted secessions, and 13 U.S. interventions. After a U.S. proposal for canal rights over the narrow isthmus was rejected by Colombia, Panama proclaimed its independence with U.S. backing in 1903.

For canal rights in perpetuity, the U.S. paid Panama $10 million and agreed to pay $250,000 each year, which was increased to $430,000 in 1933. It was increased again in 1955. In exchange, the U.S. got the Canal Zone—a 10-mile-wide strip across the isthmus—and considerable influence in Panama's affairs. On Sept. 7, 1977, President Omar Torrijos Herrera and President Jimmy Carter signed treaties giving Panama gradual control of the canal, phasing out U.S. military bases, and guaranteeing the canal's neutrality.

Nicolas Ardito Barletta, Panama's first directly elected president in 16 years, was inaugurated on Oct. 11, 1984, for a five-year term. He was a puppet of strongman Gen. Manuel Noriega, a former CIA operative and head of the secret police. Noriega replaced Barletta with vice president Eric Arturo Delvalle a year later. In 1988, Noriega was indicted in the U.S. for drug trafficking, but when Delvalle attempted to fire him, Noriega forced the National Assembly to replace Delvalle with Manuel Solis Palma. In Dec. 1989, the assembly named Noriega "maximum leader" and declared the U.S. and Panama to be in a state of war. In Dec. 1989, 24,000 U.S. troops seized control of Panama City in an attempt to capture Noriega after a U.S. soldier was killed in Panama. On Jan. 3, 1990, Noriega surrendered himself to U.S. custody and was transported to Miami, where he was later convicted of drug trafficking. Guillermo Endara, who probably would have won an election suppressed earlier by Noriega, was installed as president.

On Dec. 31, 1999, the U.S. formally handed over control of the Panama Canal to Panama. Meanwhile, Colombian rebels and paramilitary forces have made periodic incursions into Panamanian territory, raising security concerns. Panama has also faced increased drug and arms smuggling.

Panama Canal. In 1524, King Charles V of Spain ordered a survey of a waterway across the isthmus in consideration of building a canal. In 1878, the Colombian government gave a construction concession to the French Canal Company. The effort ended in bankruptcy nine years later, and the United States ultimately paid the French $40 million for their rights and assets. The U.S. project, built on territory controlled by the United States, began in 1904 and was completed in 1914.

Papua New Guinea

Sovereign: Queen Elizabeth II (1952)
Governor-General: Sir Albert Kipalan (2003)
Prime Minister: Sir Michael Somare (2002)
Area: 178,703 sq mi (462,840 sq km)
Population (2003 est.): 5,295,816 (growth rate: 2.3%); birth rate: 31.1/1000; infant mortality rate: 54.8/1000; density per sq mi: 30
Capital and largest city (2003 est.): Port Moresby, 324,900. **Monetary unit:** Kina. **Languages:** English, Tok Pisin (a Melanesian Creole English), Hiri Motu, and 717 distinct native languages. **Ethnicity/race:** Papuan, Melanesian, Negrito, Micronesian, Polynesian. **Religions:** over half are Christian, remainder indigenous. **Literacy rate:** 64.5% (2000)
Economic summary: GDP/PPP (2001 est.): $12.2 billion; per capita $2,400. **Real growth rate:** –2.5%. **Inflation:** 10.3%. **Unemployment:** n.a. **Arable land:** 0%. **Agriculture:** coffee, cocoa, coconuts, palm kernels, tea, rubber, sweet potatoes, fruit, vegetables; poultry, pork. **Labor force:** 2.3 million (1999); agriculture 85%, industry n.a., services n.a. **Industries:** copra crushing, palm oil processing, plywood production, wood chip production; mining of gold, silver, and copper; crude oil production; construction, tourism. **Natural resources:** gold, copper, silver, natural gas, timber, oil, fisheries. **Exports:** $1.8 billion (f.o.b., 2001 est.): oil, gold, copper ore, logs, palm oil, coffee, cocoa, crayfish, prawns. **Imports:** $1.024 billion (f.o.b., 2001 est.): machinery and transport equipment, manufactured goods, food, fuels, chemicals. **Major trading partners:** Australia, Japan, China, Germany, South Korea, UK, Philippines, U.S., Singapore, New Zealand, Indonesia, Malaysia. **Member of Commonwealth of Nations**

Geography Papua New Guinea occupies the eastern half of the island of New Guinea, just north of Australia, and many outlying islands. The Indonesian province of West Papua (Irian Jaya) is to the west. To the north and east are the islands of Manus, New Britain, New Ireland, and Bougainville, all part of Papua New Guinea. About one-tenth larger than California, its mountainous interior has only recently been explored. Two major rivers, the Sepik and the Fly, are navigable for shallow-draft vessels.

Government Constitutional monarchy with parliamentary democracy.

History The first inhabitants of the island New Guinea were Papuan, Melanesian, and Negrito tribes, who altogether spoke more than 700 distinct languages. The eastern half of New Guinea was first explored by Spanish and Portuguese explorers in the 16th century. In 1828, the Dutch formally took possession of the western half of the island (now the province of West Papua [Irian Jaya], Indonesia). In 1885, Germany formally annexed the northern coast and

Britain took similar action in the south. In 1906, Britain transferred its rights to British New Guinea to a newly independent Australia, and the name of the territory was changed to the Territory of Papua. Australian troops invaded German New Guinea (called Kaiser-Wilhelmsland) in World War I and gained control of the territory under a League of Nations mandate. New Guinea and some of Papua were invaded by Japanese forces in 1942. After being liberated by the Australians in 1945, it became a United Nations trusteeship, administered by Australia. The territories were combined and called the Territory of Papua and New Guinea.

Australia granted limited home rule in 1951. Autonomy in internal affairs came nine years later, and in Sept. 1975, Papua New Guinea achieved complete independence from Britain.

A violent nine-year secessionist movement took place on the island of Bougainville. In 1989, guerrillas of the Bougainville Revolutionary Army (BRA) shut down the island's Australian-owned copper mine, a major source of revenue for the country. The rebels believed that Bougainville deserved a greater share of the earnings for its copper. In 1990, the BRA declared Bougainville's independence, whereupon the government blockaded the island until Jan. 1991, when a peace treaty was signed. In 1997, Papua New Guinea's government hired South African mercenary soldiers to fight on Bougainville in order to end the long-running crisis, but this action led to massive demonstrations and the mercenary contract was rescinded. In April 1998, a cease-fire was declared.

On July 17, 1998, an earthquake-triggered tsunami (tidal wave) off the northern coast of Papua New Guinea killed at least 1,500 people and left thousands more injured and homeless.

Paraguay

REPUBLIC OF PARAGUAY

National name: República del Paraguay
President: Nicanor Duarte Frutos (2003)
Area: 157,046 sq mi (406,750 sq km)
Population (2003 est.): 6,036,900 (growth rate: 2.6%); birth rate: 30.1/1000; infant mortality rate: 27.7/1000; density per sq mi: 38
Capital and largest city (2003 est.): Asunción, 1,482,200 (metro. area), 525,100. **Other large cities:** Ciudad del Este, 239,500; San Lorenzo, 210,000. **Monetary unit:** Guaraní. **Languages:** Spanish (official), Guaraní. **Ethnicity/race:** mestizo (mixed Spanish and Indian) 95%, whites plus Amerindians 5%. **Religion:** Roman Catholic 90%. **Literacy rate:** 92.1% (1995 est.)
Economic summary: GDP/PPP (2001 est.): $26.2 billion; per capita $4,600. **Real growth rate:** 0%. **Inflation:** 7.2%. **Unemployment:** 17.8%. **Arable land:** 6%. **Agriculture:** cotton, sugarcane, soybeans, corn, wheat, tobacco, cassava (tapioca), fruits, vegetables; beef, pork, eggs, milk; timber. **Labor force:** 2 million (2000 est.); agriculture 45%. **Industries:** sugar, cement, textiles, beverages, wood products. **Natural resources:** hydropower, timber, iron ore, manganese, limestone. **Exports:** $2.2 billion (f.o.b., 2001 est.): electricity, soybeans, feed, cotton, meat, edible oils. **Imports:** $2.7 billion (f.o.b., 2001 est.): road vehicles, consumer goods, tobacco, petroleum products, electrical machinery. **Major trading partners:** Brazil, Uruguay, Argentina. **International conflicts:** none.

Geography California-size Paraguay is surrounded by Brazil, Bolivia, and Argentina in south-central South America. Eastern Paraguay, between the Paraná and Paraguay Rivers, is upland country with the thickest population settled on the grassy slope that inclines toward the Paraguay River. The greater part of the Chaco region to the west is covered with marshes, lagoons, dense forests, and jungles.

Government Constitutional republic.

History Indians speaking Guaraní—the most common language in Paraguay today, after Spanish—were the country's first inhabitants. In 1526 and again in 1529, Sebastian Cabot explored Paraguay when he sailed up the Paraná and Paraguay Rivers. From 1608 until their expulsion from the Spanish dominions in 1767, the Jesuits maintained an extensive establishment in the south and east of Paraguay. In 1811, Paraguay revolted against Spanish rule and became a nominal republic under two consuls.

Paraguay was governed by three dictators during the first 60 years of independence. The third, Francisco López, waged war against Uruguay, Brazil, and Argentina in 1865–1870, a conflict in which half the male population was killed. A new constitution in 1870, designed to prevent dictatorships and internal strife, failed to do so, and not until 1912 did a period of comparative economic and political stability begin. The Chaco War (1932–1935) with Bolivia won Paraguay more western territory.

After World War II, politics became particularly unstable. Alfredo Stroessner was dictator from 1954 until 1989, during which he was accused of the torture and murder of thousands of political opponents. Despite Paraguay's human rights record, the U.S. continuously supported Stroessner.

Stroessner was overthrown by army leader Gen. Andres Rodriguez in 1989. Rodriguez went on to win Paraguay's first multicandidate election in decades. Paraguay's new constitution went into effect in 1992. In 1993, Juan Carlos Wasmosy, a wealthy businessman and the candidate of the governing Colorado Party, won a five-year term in free elections.

Raúl Cubas Grau was elected president in May 1998. In 1999, Cubas was forced from office for his alleged involvement in the assassination of Vice President Luis María Argaña. The vice president had criticized Cubas for refusing to jail his mentor, Gen. Lino Oviedo, who had been convicted of leading a failed 1996 coup against Wasmosy.

The new president, Luis Ángel González Macchi, undertook a governmental overhaul, and for the first time since Stroessner was overthrown, political and economic power was no longer entirely within the hands of the corrupt and military-backed Colorado Party. The U.S. has accused the Colorado Party of smuggling, money laundering, trafficking Bolivian cocaine, and supporting international terrorist organizations.

In Aug. 2000, the opposition Liberal Party won its first major victory in more than 50 years with the election of Julio Cesar Franco as vice president. He narrowly defeated the son of the previous vice president, Argaña. Paraguay's government sought to clean up the political system by bringing to trial political and military figures suspected of human rights violations, corruption, or other crimes.

In 2002, anti-government rioters demanded that President Macchi resign, blaming him for Paraguay's protracted recession since the late 1990s. In Dec. 2002, Macchi was accused of mishandling $16 million in state funds. He was acquitted in an impeachment trial in Feb. 2003. Former journalist Nicanor Duarte Frutos became president on August 15, 2003. He has pledged to clean up the pervasive corruption in his nearly bankrupt country.

Peru

REPUBLIC OF PERU

National name: República del Perú
President: Alejandro Toledo (2001)
Prime Minister: Beatriz Merino (2003)
Area: 496,223 sq mi (1,285,220 sq km)
Population (2003 est.): 28,409,897 (growth rate: 1.7%); birth rate: 22.8/1000; infant mortality rate: 37.0/1000; density per sq mi: 57
Capital and largest city (2003 est.): Lima, 8,113,000 (metro. area). **Other large cities:** Arequipa, 837,300; Trujillo, 725,200; Chiclayo, 598,400. **Monetary unit:** Nuevo sol (1991). **Languages:** Spanish and Quéchua (both official), Aymara, and other native languages. **Ethnicity/race:** Indian 45%, mestizo (mixed Indian and European ancestry) 37%, white 15%, black, Japanese, Chinese, and other 3%. **Religion:** Roman Catholic (90%). **Literacy rate:** 88.3% (1995 est.)
Economic summary: GDP/PPP (2001 est.): $132 billion; per capita $4,800. **Real growth**: –0.3%. **Inflation:** 1.5%. **Unemployment:** 9%; widespread underemployment. **Arable land:** 3%. **Agriculture:** coffee, cotton, sugarcane, rice, wheat, potatoes, corn, plantains, coca; poultry, beef, dairy products, wool; fish. **Labor force:** 7.5 million (2000 est.); agriculture, mining and quarrying, manufacturing, construction, transport, services. **Industries:** mining of metals, petroleum, fishing, textiles, clothing, food processing, cement, auto assembly, steel, shipbuilding, metal fabrication. **Natural resources:** copper, silver, gold, petroleum, timber, fish, iron ore, coal, phosphate, potash, hydropower, natural gas. **Exports:** $7.3 billion (f.o.b., 2001 est.): fish and fish products, gold, copper, zinc, crude petroleum and byproducts, lead, coffee, sugar, cotton. **Imports:** $7.4 billion (f.o.b., 2001 est.): machinery, transport equipment, foodstuffs, petroleum, iron and steel, chemicals, pharmaceuticals. **Major trading partners:** U.S., UK, Switzerland, China, Japan, Chile, Brazil, Spain, Venezuela, Colombia.

Geography Peru, in western South America, extends for nearly 1,500 mi (2,414 km) along the Pacific Ocean. Colombia and Ecuador are to the north, Brazil and Bolivia to the east, and Chile to the south. Five-sixths the size of Alaska, Peru is divided by the Andes Mountains into three sharply differentiated zones. To the west is the coastline, much of it arid, extending 50 to 100 mi (80 to 160 km) inland. The mountain area, with peaks over 20,000 ft (6,096 m), lofty plateaus, and deep valleys, lies centrally. Beyond the mountains to the east is the heavily forested slope leading to the Amazonian plains.

Government Constitutional republic.

History Peru was once part of the great Incan empire and later the major vice-royalty of Spanish South America. It was conquered in 1531–1533 by Francisco Pizarro. On July 28, 1821, Peru proclaimed its independence, but the Spanish were not finally defeated until 1824. For a hundred years thereafter, revolutions were frequent; a new war was fought with Spain in 1864–1866, and an unsuccessful war was fought with Chile from 1879 to 1883 (the War of the Pacific).

Peru emerged from 20 years of dictatorship in 1945 with the inauguration of President José Luis Bustamente y Rivero after the first free election in many decades. But he served for only three years and was succeeded in turn by Gen. Manual A. Odria, Manuel Prado y Ugarteche, and Fernando Belaúnde Terry. On Oct. 3, 1968, Belaúnde was overthrown by Gen. Juan Velasco Alvarado. In 1975, Velasco was replaced in a bloodless coup by his premier, Gen. Francisco Morales Bermudez, who promised to restore civilian government. In elections held on May 18, 1980, Belaúnde Terry, the last civilian president, was elected president again. Maoist guerrilla group Shining Path, or Sendero Luminoso, began their brutal campaign to overthrow the government. The military's subsequent crackdown led to further civilan human rights abuses and disappearances. A smaller rebel group, Tupac Amaru, also fought against the government.

Peru's fragile democracy survived. In 1985, Belaúnde Terry was the first elected president to turn over power to a constitutionally elected successor since 1945. Alberto Fujimori won the 1990 elections. Citing continuing terrorism, drug trafficking, and corruption, Fujimori dissolved Congress, suspended the constitution, and imposed censorship in April 1992. By September, most of Shining Path had been vanquished. A new constitution was approved in 1993.

Fujimori was reelected in 1995, and again in May 2000 to a third five-year term, after his opponent, Alejandro Toledo, withdrew from the contest, charging fraud. In Sept. 2000, Fujimori's intelligence chief, Vladimiro Montesinos, was videotaped bribing a congressman. Fujimori announced he would dismantle the powerful National Intelligence Service, which has been accused of human rights violations. Two months later, he stunned his nation by resigning during a trip to Japan. Revelations that Fujimori secretly held Japanese citizenship—and could not be extradited to face corruption charges—enraged the populace.

In 2001, the centrist Alejandro Toledo was elected president with 53% of the vote, narrowly defeating former president Alan García. His rags-to-riches story and mixed Indian and Latino heritage made him popular among the poor. Inheriting a country wracked by economic troubles and corruption, Toledo did little, however, to restore confidence in the government. Early in his presidency, he gave himself a significant pay raise while at the same time calling for economic austerity. In June 2002, a popular revolt took place in the cities of Arequipa, Tacna, and other areas of southern Peru after the sale of two state-run electricity firms to a Belgian company Tractebel—Toledo had specifically promised during his campaign not to sell these firms. Opinion polls have revealed that more than 60% of Peruvians are adamantly opposed to privatization and foreign investment, which in the past has led to price increases, mass layoffs, corruption, and few discernible benefits for the populace. To quell the rioting, Toledo suspended the decision to privatize, apologized publicly, and reshuffled his government.

In Aug. 2003, a truth commission report revealed that 69,000 people were killed during the 1980–2000 wars between rebel groups and the government, about twice the original estimate. The deaths were carried out by the rebels (54%) as well as the military (30%); other militias were responsible for the remainder.

The Philippines

REPUBLIC OF THE PHILIPPINES

National name: Republika ng Pilipinas
President: Gloria Macapagal Arroyo (2001)
Area: 115,830 sq mi (300,000 sq km)
Population (2003 est.): 84,619,974 (growth rate: 2.1%); birth rate: 26.3/1000; infant mortality rate: 25.0/1000; density per sq mi: 731
Capital and largest city (2003 est.): Manila, 13,790,900 (metro. area), 10,232,900 (city proper). **Other large cities:** Quezon City (2000 est.), 1,669,776 (part of Manila metro. area); Cebu (2003 est.), 761,900. **Monetary unit:** Peso. **Languages:** Filipino (based on Tagalog) and English (both official); regional languages: Tagalog, Ilocano, Cebuano, others.

Ethnicity/race: Christian Malay 91.5%, Muslim Malay 4%, Chinese 1.5%, other 3%. **Religions:** Roman Catholic 83%, Protestant 9%, Islam 5%, Buddhist and other 3%. **Literacy rate:** 94.6% (1995 est.)

Economic summary: GDP/PPP (2001 est.): $335 billion; per capita $4,000. **Real growth rate:** 2.8%. **Inflation:** 6%. **Unemployment:** 10% (2001). **Arable land:** 18%. **Agriculture:** rice, coconuts, corn, sugarcane, bananas, pineapples, mangoes; pork, eggs, beef; fish. **Labor force:** 32 million (2000); agriculture 39.8%, government and social services 19.4%, services 17.7%, manufacturing 9.8%, construction 5.8%, other 7.5% (1998 est.). **Industries:** textiles, pharmaceuticals, chemicals, wood products, food processing, electronics assembly, petroleum refining, fishing. **Natural resources:** timber, petroleum, nickel, cobalt, silver, gold, salt, copper. **Exports:** $37 billion (f.o.b., 2000): electronic equipment, machinery and transport equipment, garments, coconut products. **Imports:** $30 billion (f.o.b., 2000): raw materials and intermediate goods, capital goods, consumer goods, fuels. **Major trading partners:** U.S., Japan, Netherlands, Singapore, Taiwan, Hong Kong, EU, South Korea.

Geography The Philippine Islands are an archipelago of over 7,000 islands lying about 500 mi (805 km) off the southeast coast of Asia. The overall land area is comparable to that of Arizona. Only about 7% of the islands are larger than one square mile, and only one-third have names. The largest are Luzon in the north (40,420 sq mi; 104,687 sq km), Mindanao in the south (36,537 sq mi; 94,631 sq km), and Samar (5,124 sq mi; 13,271 sq km). The islands are of volcanic origin, with the larger ones crossed by mountain ranges. The highest peak is Mount Apo (9,690 ft; 2,954 m) on Mindanao.

Government Republic.

History Ferdinand Magellan, the Portuguese navigator in the service of Spain, explored the Philippines in 1521. Twenty-one years later, a Spanish exploration party named the group of islands in honor of Prince Philip, who was later to become Philip II of Spain. Spain retained possession of the islands for the next 350 years.

The Philippines were ceded to the U.S. in 1899 by the Treaty of Paris after the Spanish-American War. Meanwhile, the Filipinos, led by Emilio Aguinaldo, had declared their independence. They initiated guerrilla warfare against U.S. troops that persisted until the capture of Aguinaldo in 1901. By 1902, peace was established except among the Islamic Moros on the southern island of Mindanao.

The first U.S. civilian governor-general was William Howard Taft (1901–1904). The Jones Law (1916) provided for the establishment of a Philippine Legislature composed of an elective Senate and House of Representatives. The Tydings-McDuffie Act (1934) provided for a transitional period until 1946, at which time the Philippines would become completely independent. Under a constitution approved by the people of the Philippines in 1935, the Commonwealth of the Philippines came into being with Manuel Quezon y Molina as president.

On Dec. 8, 1941, the islands were invaded by Japanese troops. Following the fall of Gen. Douglas MacArthur's forces at Bataan and Corregidor, Quezon established a government-in-exile that he headed until his death in 1944. He was succeeded by Vice President Sergio Osmeña. U.S. forces under MacArthur reinvaded the Philippines in Oct. 1944 and, after the liberation of Manila in Feb. 1945, Osmeña reestablished the government.

The Philippines achieved full independence on July 4, 1946. Manual A. Roxas y Acuña was elected its first president, succeeded by Elpidio Quirino (1948–1953), Ramón Magsaysay (1953–1957). Carlos P. García (1957–1961), Diosdado Macapagal (1961–1965), and Ferdinand E. Marcos (1965–1986).

Under Marcos, civil unrest broke out in opposition to the leader's despotic rule. Martial law was declared on Sept. 21, 1972, and Marcos proclaimed a new constitution that ensconced himself as president. Martial law was officially lifted on Jan. 17, 1981, but Marcos and his wife, Imelda, retained broad powers.

Despite warnings that his life would be endangered, opposition leader Benigno S. Aquino returned to the Philippines from self-exile on Aug. 21, 1983. He was shot to death as he was being escorted from his plane by military police at Manila International Airport. There was widespread suspicion that Marcos had ordered Aquino's assassination. The event became a watershed in modern Filipino political history, acting as a catalyst for opposition groups and the "People Power" movement, led by the late leader's widow, Corazon Aquino.

In an attempt to resecure American support, Marcos set presidential elections for Feb. 7, 1986. With the support of the Catholic Church, Corazon Aquino declared her candidacy. Marcos was declared the official winner, but independent observers reported widespread election fraud and vote-rigging. Anti-Marcos protests exploded in the capital Manila, Defense Minister Juan Enrile and Lt. Gen. Fidel Ramos defected to the opposition, and Marcos lost virtually all support; he was forced to flee into exile and entered the U.S. on Feb. 25, 1986.

The Aquino government survived coup attempts by Marcos supporters and other right-wing elements, including one in November by Enrile. Legislative elections on May 11, 1987, gave pro-Aquino candidates a large majority. Negotiations on renewal of leases for U.S. military bases threatened to sour relations between the two countries. Volcanic eruptions from Mount Pinatubo, however, severely damaged Clark Air Base, and in July 1991, the U.S. decided simply to abandon it.

In elections in May 1992, Gen. Fidel Ramos, who had the support of outgoing Aquino, won the presidency in a seven-way race. In Sept. 1992, the U.S. Navy turned over the Subic Bay naval base to the Philippines, ending its long-standing U.S. military presence.

Meanwhile, the separatist Moro National Liberation Front was fighting a protracted war for an Islamic homeland on Mindanao, the southernmost of the two main islands. In 1996, the group agreed to a government plan designed to grant it a greater degree of political autonomy. Frequent and violent clashes continued, however. The army also battled another rebel group, the Moro Islamic Liberation Front. In Aug. 2001, both rebel groups signed unity agreements with the Philippine government. The cease-fire between the government and the Moro Islamic Liberation Front temporarily broke down in February 2003 but was reinstated in July. About 120,000 people have died in the conflict, and more than 3 million have been displaced.

In May 1998, 61-year-old former action film star Joseph Estrada was elected president of the Philippines. Within two years, however, the Philippine Senate began to impeach Estrada on corruption charges. Massive street demonstrations and the loss of political support eventually forced Estrada from office. Vice

President Gloria Macapagal Arroyo, daughter of former president Diosdado Macapagal, became president in Jan. 2001.

Abu Sayyaf, a small group of guerrillas that has been fighting since the 1970s for an independent Islamic state and reportedly has links to Osama bin Laden, gained international notoriety throughout 2000 and 2001 with its spree of kidnappings that resulted in dozens of deaths. The group's leader, Abu Sabaya, was killed in June 2002 during a clash with government troops. The Philippine military then began to focus on eliminating the New People's Army, a group of communist guerrillas that has targeted Philippine security forces since 1969 and opposes any U.S. presence in the Philippines. In March 2003, a bomb that killed 21 people, the country's worst terrorist attack in nearly three years, was thought to be the work of the Moro Islamic Liberation Front. International officials reported in June 2003 that Jemaah Islamiyah, an affiliate of al-Qaeda, was training recruits in Mindanao, in the southern Philippines. The Moro Islamic Liberation Front controls the area.

In July 2003, dozens of mutinous soldiers took over a Manila housing complex, protesting low pay and demanding the resignation of President Arroyo and the defense secretary. The demonstration ended peacefully.

Poland

REPUBLIC OF POLAND

National name: Rzeczpospolita Polska
President: Aleksander Kwasniewski (1995)
Premier: Leszek Miller (2001)
Area: 120,728 sq mi (312,685 sq km)
Population (2003 est.): 38,622,660 (growth rate: 0.1%); birth rate: 10.5/1000; infant mortality rate: 8.9/1000; density per sq mi: 320
Capital and largest city (2003 est.): Warsaw, 2,201,900 (metro. area), 1,607,600 (city proper). **Other large cities:** Lodz, 778,200; Krakow, 733,100; Wroclaw, 632,200; Poznan, 581,200; Gdansk, 456,700; Szczecin, 415,700. **Monetary unit:** Zloty. **Language:** Polish. **Ethnicity/race:** Polish 97.6%, German 1.3%, Ukrainian 0.6%, Belorussian 0.5% (1990 est.). **Religions:** Roman Catholic 95% (about 75% practicing), Russian Orthodox, Protestant, and other 5%. **Literacy rate:** 99% (1978 est.)
Economic summary: GDP/PPP (2001 est.): $339.6 billion; per capita $8,800. **Real growth rate:** 1.5%. **Inflation:** 5.3%. **Unemployment:** 16.7%. **Arable land:** 46%. **Agriculture:** potatoes, fruits, vegetables, wheat; poultry, eggs, pork. **Labor force:** 17.6 million (2000 est.); industry 22.1%, agriculture 27.5%, services 50.4% (1999). **Industries:** machine building, iron and steel, coal mining, chemicals, shipbuilding, food processing, glass, beverages, textiles. **Natural resources:** coal, sulfur, copper, natural gas, silver, lead, salt, arable land. **Exports:** $30.8 billion (f.o.b., 2001): machinery and transport equipment 30.2%, intermediate manufactured goods 25.5%, miscellaneous manufactured goods 20.9%, food and live animals 8.5% (1999). **Imports:** $41.7 billion (f.o.b., 2001): machinery and transport equipment 38.2%, intermediate manufactured goods 20.8%, chemicals 14.3%, miscellaneous manufactured goods 9.5% (1999). **Major trading partners:** Germany, Italy, France, Netherlands, UK, Czech Republic, Russia, U.S.

Geography Poland, a country the size of New Mexico, is in north-central Europe. Most of the country is a plain with no natural boundaries except the Carpathian Mountains in the south and the Oder and Neisse Rivers in the west. Other major rivers, which are important to commerce, are the Vistula, Warta, and Bug.

Government Democratic republic.

History Great (north) Poland was founded in 966 by Mieszko I, who belonged to the Piast dynasty. The tribes of southern Poland then united to form Little Poland. In 1047, both Great Poland and Little Poland united under the rule of Casimir I the Restorer. Poland merged with Lithuania by royal marriage in 1386. The Polish-Lithuanian state reached the peak of its power between the 14th and 16th century, scoring military successes against the (Germanic) Knights of the Teutonic Order, the Russians, and the Ottoman Turks.

Lack of a strong monarchy enabled Russia, Prussia, and Austria to carry out a first partition of the country in 1772, a second in 1792, and a third in 1795. For more than a century thereafter, there was no Polish state, just Austrian, Prussian, and Russian sectors, but the Poles never ceased their efforts to regain their independence. The Polish people revolted against Russian, Prussian, and Austrian dominance throughout the 19th century. Poland was formally reconstituted in Nov. 1918, with Marshal Josef Pilsudski as chief of state. In 1919, Ignace Paderewski, the famous pianist and patriot, became the first premier. In 1926, Pilsudski seized complete power in a coup and ruled dictatorially until his death on May 12, 1935.

Despite a ten-year nonaggression pact signed in 1934, Hitler attacked Poland on Sept. 1, 1939. Soviet troops invaded from the east on Sept. 17, and on Sept. 28, a German-Soviet agreement divided Poland between the USSR and Germany. Wladyslaw Raczkiewicz formed a government-in-exile in France, which moved to London after France's defeat in 1940. All of Poland was occupied by Germany after the Nazi attack on the USSR in June 1941. Nazi Germany's occupation policy in Poland was designed to eradicate Polish culture through mass executions and to exterminate the country's large Jewish minority.

The Polish government-in-exile was replaced with the Communist-dominated Polish Committee of National Liberation by the Soviet Union in 1944. Moving to Lublin after that city's liberation, it proclaimed itself the Provisional Government of Poland. Some former members of the Polish government in London joined with the Lublin government to form the Polish Government of National Unity, which Britain and the U.S. recognized. On Aug. 2, 1945, in Berlin, President Harry S. Truman, Joseph Stalin, and Prime Minister Clement Attlee of Britain established a new de facto western frontier for Poland along the Oder and Neisse Rivers. (The border was finally agreed to by West Germany in a nonaggression pact signed on Dec. 7, 1970.) On Aug. 16, 1945, the USSR and Poland signed a treaty delimiting the Soviet-Polish frontier. Under these agreements, Poland was shifted westward. In the east, it lost 69,860 sq mi (180,934 sq km); in the west, it gained (subject to final peace-conference approval) 38,986 sq mi (100,973 sq km).

A new constitution in 1952 made Poland a "people's democracy" of the Soviet type. In 1955, Poland became a member of the Warsaw Treaty Organization, and its foreign policy became identical to that of the USSR. The government undertook persecution of the Roman Catholic Church as a remaining source of opposition. Wladyslaw Gomulka was elected leader of the United Workers (Communist) Party in 1956. He denounced the Stalinist terror, ousted many Stalinists, and improved relations with the church. Most collective farms were dissolved, and the press became freer.

A strike that began in shipyards and spread to other industries in Aug. 1980 produced a stunning victory for workers when the economically hard-pressed government accepted for the first time in a Marxist state the right of workers to organize in independent unions.

Led by Solidarity, a free union founded by an electrician, Lech Walesa, workers launched a drive for liberty and improved conditions. A national strike for a five-day workweek in Jan. 1981 led to the dismissal of Premier Pinkowski and the naming of the fourth premier in less than a year, Gen. Wojciech Jaruzelski. Martial law was declared on Dec. 13, when Walesa and other Solidarity leaders were arrested. It formally ended in 1984 but the government retained emergency powers. Increasing opposition to the government because of the failing economy led to a new wave of strikes in 1988. Unable to totally quell the dissent, the government re-legalized Solidarity and allowed it to compete in elections.

Solidarity members won a stunning victory in 1989, taking almost all the seats in the Senate and all of the 169 seats they were allowed to contest in the Sejm. This gave them substantial influence in the new government. Tadeusz Mazowiecki was appointed prime minister. Lech Walesa won the presidential election of 1990 with 74% of the vote. In 1991, the first fully free parliamentary election since World War II resulted in representation for 29 political parties. Efforts to turn Poland into a market economy, however, led to economic difficulties and widespread discontent. In the second democratic parliamentary election of Sept. 1993, voters returned power to ex-Communists and their allies. Solidarity's popularity and influence continued to wane. In 1995, Aleksander Kwasniewski, leader of the successor to the Communist Party, the Democratic Left, won the presidency over Walesa in a landslide.

In 1999, Poland became part of NATO, along with the Czech Republic and Hungary. Poland was invited to join the European Union (EU), effective May 2004.

In Sept. 2001 parliamentary elections, former Communists, reconstituted as the center-left Democratic Left Alliance, won 41% of the vote. The election seemed to mark the demise of Solidarity, which did not win a single seat.

Poland was a staunch supporter of the United States and Britain during the 2003 Iraq war, and sent 200 troops to Iraq (60 were combat soldiers). In Sept. 2003, Poland became the leader of a 9,000-strong, multinational stabilizing force in Iraq. It contributed 2,000 of its own soldiers.

Portugal

REPUBLIC OF PORTUGAL

National name: República Portuguesa
President: Jorge Sampaio (1996)
Prime Minister: José Manuel Durão Barroso (2002)
Area: 35,672 sq mi (92,391 sq km)
Population (2003 est.): 10,102,022 (growth rate: 0.1%); birth rate: 11.4/1000; infant mortality rate: 5.7/1000; density per sq mi: 283
Capital and largest city (2003 est.): Lisbon, 2,618,100 (metro. area), 559,400. **Other large city:** Oporto, 264,200. **Monetary units:** Euro (formerly escudo). **Language:** Portuguese. **Ethnicity/race:** Homogeneous Mediterranean stock in mainland, Azores, Madeira Islands; citizens of black African descent who immigrated to mainland during decolonization number less than 100,000. **Religions:** Roman Catholic 94%, Protestant. **Literacy rate:** 87.4%
Economic summary: GDP/PPP (2001 est.): $174.1 billion; per capita $17,300. **Real growth rate:** 1.7%. **Inflation:** 4.4%. **Unemployment:** 4.4%. **Arable land:** 21%. **Agriculture:** grain, potatoes, olives, grapes; sheep, cattle, goats, poultry, beef, dairy products. **Labor force:** 5.1 million (2000); services 60%, industry 30%, agriculture 10% (1999 est.). **Industries:** textiles and footwear; wood pulp, paper, and cork; metalworking; oil refining; chemicals; fish canning; wine; tourism. **Natural resources:** fish, forests (cork), tungsten, iron ore, uranium ore, marble, arable land, hydropower. **Exports:** $24.8 billion (f.o.b., 2001): clothing and footwear, machinery, chemicals, cork and paper products, hides. **Imports:** $37.8 billion (f.o.b., 2001): machinery and transport equipment, chemicals, petroleum, textiles, agricultural products. **Major trading partners:** EU, U.S., Japan.

Geography Portugal occupies the western part of the Iberian Peninsula and is slightly smaller than Indiana. The country is crossed by three large rivers that rise in Spain, flow into the Atlantic, and divide the country into three geographic areas. The Minho River, part of the northern boundary, cuts through a mountainous area that extends south to the vicinity of the Douro River. South of the Douro, the mountains slope to the plains around the Tejo River. The remaining division is the southern one of Alentejo. The Azores stretch over 340 mi (547 km) in the Atlantic, and consist of nine islands with a total area of 902 square mi (2,335 sq km). Madeira, consisting of two inhabited islands, Madeira and Porto Santo, and two groups of uninhabited islands, lie in the Atlantic about 535 mi (861 km) southwest of Lisbon.

Government Parliamentary democracy.

History An early Celtic tribe, the Lusitanians, are believed to have been the first inhabitants of Portugal. The Roman Empire conquered the region in about 140 B.C. Toward the end of the Roman Empire, the Visigoths had invaded the entire Iberian peninsula.

Portugal won its independence from Moorish Spain in 1143. King John I (1385–1433) unified his country at the expense of the Castilians and the Moors of Morocco. The expansion of Portugal was brilliantly coordinated by John's son, Prince Henry the Navigator. In 1488, Bartolomeu Dias reached the Cape of Good Hope, proving that Asia was accessible by sea. In 1498, Vasco da Gama reached the west coast of India. By the middle of the 16th century, the Portuguese Empire extended to West and East Africa, Brazil, Persia, Indochina, and Malaya.

In 1581, Philip II of Spain invaded Portugal and held it for 60 years, precipitating a catastrophic decline in Portuguese commerce. Courageous and shrewd explorers, the Portuguese proved to be inefficient and corrupt colonizers. By the time the Portuguese monarchy was restored in 1640, Dutch, English, and French competitors began to seize the lion's share of the world's colonies and commerce. Portugal retained Angola and Mozambique in Africa, and Brazil (until 1822).

The corrupt King Carlos, who ascended the throne in 1889, made Joao Franco the premier with dictatorial power in 1906. In 1908, Carlos and his heir were shot dead on the streets of Lisbon. The new king, Manoel II, was driven from the throne in the revolution of 1910, and Portugal became a French-style republic. Traditionally friendly to Britain, Portugal fought in World War I on the Allied side in Africa as well as on the Western Front. Weak postwar governments and a revolution in 1926 brought Antonio Oliveira Salazar to power. As minister of finance (1928–1940) and premier (1932–1968), Salazar ruled Portugal as a virtual dictator. He kept Portugal neutral in World War II but gave the Allies naval and air bases after 1943. Portugal joined NATO as a founding member in 1949 but did not gain admission to the United Nations until 1955.

Portugal's foreign and colonial policies met with increasing difficulty both at home and abroad beginning in the 1950s—the bloodiest and most protracted wars against colonialism in Africa were fought against the Portuguese. Portugal lost the tiny remnants of its Indian empire—Goa, Daman, and Diu—to Indian military occupation in 1961, the year an insurrection broke out in Angola. For the next 13 years, Salazar, who died in 1970, and his successor, Marcello Caetano, fought independence movements amid growing world criticism. Leftists in the armed forces, weary of a losing battle, launched a successful revolution on April 25, 1974. After the 1974 revolution, the new military junta gave up its territories, beginning with Portuguese Guinea in Sept. 1974, which became the Republic of Guinea-Bissau. The decolonization of the Cape Verde Islands and Mozambique was effected in July 1975. Angola achieved independence later that same year, thus ending a colonial involvement in that continent that had begun in 1415. Full-scale, internationalized civil war, however, followed Portugal's departure from Angola, and Indonesia forcibly annexed independent East Timor. Also in that year, the government nationalized banking, transport, heavy industries, and the media. Portugal continued to experience social, economic, and political upheavals for the next decade.

Portugal was admitted to the European Economic Community (now European Union) on Jan. 1, 1986, and on Feb. 16, Mario Soares became the country's first civilian president in 60 years. Aníbal Cavaço Silva, an advocate of free-market economics and the Social Democratic candidate, was elected as prime minister in 1985, signaling a more politically stable era. General elections in Oct. 1995 went to the Socialist Party, which fell just short of an absolute majority in the assembly. Lisbon mayor Jorge Sampaio, a Socialist, won the race for president in Jan. 1996. Portugal's Socialist government continued to take advantage of rosy economic conditions in 1997, and in 1999, it became a founding member of the European Economic and Monetary Union (EMU).

After Portugal's former territory, East Timor, was plunged into violence when its people voted to separate from Indonesia in Aug. 1999, Portugal was in the forefront of urging the UN to send in an armed, international peacekeeping force to protect the East Timorese from pro-Indonesian militia groups. Portugal gave up its last colony, Macao, on Dec. 20, 1999, turning the small Asian seaport over to China.

In 2002, center-right Social Democrat leader José Manuel Durão Barroso became prime minister, after the Socialist Party suffered defeats. In July and Aug. 2003, more than a thousand people died during an unprecedented heat wave that caused fires to ravage Portugal's forests.

Qatar

STATE OF QATAR

Emir: Sheik Hamad bin Khalifa al-Thani (1995)
Prime Minister: Abdullah bin Khalifa al-Thani (1996)
Area: 4,416 sq mi (11,437 sq km)
Population (2003 est.): 817,052 (growth rate: 1.1%); birth rate: 15.7/1000; infant mortality rate: 20.0/1000; density per sq mi: 185
Capital (2003 est.): Doha, 550,700 (metro. area), 318,500 (city proper). **Monetary unit:** Qatari riyal. **Languages:** Arabic (official); English is also widely spoken. **Ethnicity/race:** Arab 40%, Pakistani 18%, Indian 18%, Iranian 10%, other 14%. **Religion:** Islam 95%. **Literacy rate:** 79% (1995 est.)
Economic summary: GDP/PPP (2001 est.): $16.3 billion; per capita $21,200. **Real growth rate:** 5.6%. **Inflation:** 2%. **Unemployment:** 2.7%. **Arable land:** 1%. **Agriculture:** fruits, vegetables; poultry, dairy products, beef; fish. **Labor force:** 280,122 (1997 est.). **Industries:** crude oil production and refining, fertilizers, petrochemicals, steel reinforcing bars, cement. **Natural resources:** petroleum, natural gas, fish. **Exports:** $11 billion (f.o.b., 2001 est.): petroleum products 80%, fertilizers, steel. **Imports:** $3.5 billion (f.o.b., 2001 est.): machinery and transport equipment, food, chemicals. **Major trading partners:** Japan, Singapore, South Korea, U.S., UAE, UK, Germany, Italy.

Geography Qatar (pronounced KAH-tar) occupies a small peninsula that extends into the Persian Gulf from the east side of the Arabian Peninsula. Saudi Arabia is to the west and the United Arab Emirates to the south. The country is mainly barren.

Government Traditional monarchy.

History Qatar was once controlled by the sheikhs of Bahrain, but in 1867, war broke out between the people and their absentee rulers. To keep the peace in the Gulf, the British installed Muhammad ibn Thani Al Thani, head of a leading Qatari family, as the region's ruler. In 1893, the Ottoman Turks made incursions into Qatar, but the emir successfully deflected them. In 1916, the emir agreed to allow Qatar to become a British protectorate.

Oil was discovered in the 1940s, bringing wealth to the country in the 1950s and 1960s. About 85% of Qatar's income from exports comes from oil. Its people have one of the highest per capita incomes in the world. In 1971, Qatar was to join the other emirates of the Trucial Coast to become part of the United Arab Emirates. But both Qatar and Bahrain decided against the merger and instead became independent nations.

Qatar permitted the international forces to use Qatar as a base during the 1991 Persian Gulf War. A border dispute erupted with Saudi Arabia that was settled in Dec. 1992. A territorial dispute with Bahrain over the Hawar Islands remains unresolved, however. In 1994, Qatar signed a defense pact with the U.S., becoming the third Gulf state to do so.

In June 1995, Crown Prince Hamad bin Khalifa al-Thani deposed his father, primarily because the king was out of step with the country's economic reforms. The emir was not stripped of his title, and much of the power was already in his son's hands. The new emir lifted press censorship and instituted other liberal reforms, including the first democratic election in its history. Although the 1999 election—for the 29-member municipal council—was a minor election, it involved major political change: women were permitted to vote in the election as well as run for office. In 2003 Crown Prince Jassim, who declared he had never wanted to be king, abdicated in favor of his younger brother, Prince Tamim.

Qatar is the home of Al Jazeera, the Arabic satellite television network that has broadcast exclusive video footage of and statements by Osama bin Laden. The independent station is immensely popular in the Middle East, but has been criticized by many Arab countries for running interviews with controversial and opposition figures.

Qatar served as the headquarters for U.S. Central Command (CENTCOM) during the 2003 war in Iraq.

Romania

REPUBLIC OF ROMANIA

President: Ion Iliescu (2000)
Prime Minister: Adrian Nastase (2000)
Area: 91,699 sq mi (237,500 sq km)
Population (2003 est.): 22,271,839 (growth rate: –0.2%); birth rate: 10.8/1000; infant mortality rate: 18.4/1000; density per sq mi: 243
Capital and largest city (2003 est.): Bucharest, 2,210,800 (metro. area), 1,906,800 (city proper). **Other large cities:** Iasi, 320,000; Cluj-Napoca, 316,400; Timisoara, 316,100; Constanta, 309,000; Craiova, 301,100, Galati, 297,100; Brasov, 282,500. **Monetary unit:** Leu. **Languages:** Romanian (official); Hungarian- and German-speaking minorities. **Ethnicity/race:** Romanian 89.5%, Hungarian 6.6%, German 0.4%, Ukrainian, Serb, Croat, Russian, Turk, and Gypsy 3.9%. **Religions:** Romanian Orthodox 87%, Protestant 6.8%, Roman Catholic 5.6%, other 0.4%, unaffiliated 0.2%. **Literacy rate:** 97% (1992)
Economic summary: GDP/PPP (2001 est.): $152.7 billion; per capita $6,800. **Real growth rate:** 4.8%. **Inflation:** 34.5%. **Unemployment:** 9.1%. **Arable land:** 41%. **Agriculture:** wheat, corn, sugar beets, sunflower seed, potatoes, grapes; eggs, sheep. **Labor force:** 9.9 million (1999 est.); agriculture 40%, industry 25%, services 35% (1998). **Industries:** textiles and footwear, light machinery and auto assembly, mining, timber, construction materials, metallurgy, chemicals, food processing, petroleum refining. **Natural resources:** petroleum (reserves declining), timber, natural gas, coal, iron ore, salt, arable land, hydropower. **Exports:** $11.5 billion (f.o.b., 2001 est.): textiles and footwear 26%, metals and metal products 15%, machinery and equipment 11%, minerals and fuels 6% (1999). **Imports:** $14.4 billion (f.o.b., 2001 est.): machinery and equipment 23%, fuels and minerals 12%, chemicals 9%, textile and products 19% (1999). **Major trading partners:** Italy, Germany, France, Turkey, U.S., Russia.

Geography Romania is in southeast Europe and is slightly smaller than Oregon. The Carpathian Mountains divide Romania's upper half from north to south and connect near the center of the country with the Transylvanian Alps, running east and west. North and west of these ranges lies the Transylvanian plateau, and to the south and east are the plains of Moldavia and Walachia. In its last 190 mi (306 km), the Danube River flows through Romania only. It enters the Black Sea in northern Dobruja, just south of the border with the Ukraine.

Government Republic.

History Most of Romania was the Roman province of Dacia from about A.D. 100 to 271. From the 3rd to the 12th century, wave after wave of barbarian conquerors overran the native Daco-Roman population. Subjection to the first Bulgarian empire (8th–10th century) brought Eastern Orthodox Christianity to the Romanians. In the 11th century, Transylvania was absorbed into the Hungarian empire. By the 16th century, the main Romanian principalities of Moldavia and Walachia had become satellites within the Ottoman Empire, although they retained much independence. After the Russo-Turkish War of 1828–1829, they became Russian protectorates. The nation became a kingdom in 1881 after the Congress of Berlin.

At the start of World War I, Romania proclaimed its neutrality, but later joined the Allied side and in 1916 declared war on the Central Powers. The armistice of Nov. 11, 1918, gave Romania vast territories from Russia and the Austro-Hungarian Empire, doubling its size. The areas acquired included Bessarabia, Transylvania, and Bukovina. The Banat, a Hungarian area, was divided with Yugoslavia. King Carol II was crowned in 1930 and transformed the throne into a royal dictatorship. In 1938, he abolished the democratic constitution of 1923. In 1940, the country was reorganized along Fascist lines, and the Fascist Iron Guard became the nucleus of the new totalitarian party. On June 27, the Soviet Union occupied Bessarabia and northern Bukovina. King Carol II dissolved Parliament, granted the new premier, Ion Antonescu, full power, abdicated his throne, and went into exile.

Romania subsequently signed the Axis Pact on Nov. 23, 1940, and the following June joined in Germany's attack on the Soviet Union, reoccupying Bessarabia. About 270,000 Jews were massacred in Fascist Romania. Following the invasion of Romania by the Red Army in Aug. 1944, King Michael led a coup that ousted the Antonescu government. An armistice with the Soviet Union was signed in Moscow on Sept. 12, 1944. A Communist-dominated government bloc won elections in 1946, Michael abdicated on Dec. 30, 1947, and in 1955 Romania joined the Warsaw Treaty Organization and the United Nations.

Running a neo-Stalinist police state from 1967–1989, Nicolae Ceausescu wound the iron curtain tightly around Romania, turning a moderately prosperous country into one at the brink of starvation. To repay his $10 billion foreign debt in 1982, he ransacked the Romanian economy of everything that could be exported, leaving the country with desperate shortages of food, fuel, and other essentials. An army-assisted rebellion in Dec. 1989 led to Ceausescu's overthrow, trial, and execution.

An ex-Communist, Ion Iliescu of the National Salvation Front, served as president from 1990–1995. Emil Constantinescu of the Democratic Convention Party served as president from 1996–2000. The post-Communist governments' conflicted and half-hearted attempts to change to a free-market economy have been largely unrealized. In 2000 former president Iliescu returned to power with a landslide victory, easily defeating a xenophobic nationalist opponent. Discrimination against the Magyars (ethnic Hungarians) and the Roma (gypsies) continues, fueled by several ultranationalist political parties.

The country applied for membership in the EU in June 1995, but it is doubtful that Romania will be able to join the Union before at least 2007. Economic reform has proceeded at a glacial pace, and growing dissatisfaction with the government's inefficiencies and economic policies led to a wave of protests by workers, students, and others that peaked in 1997, and again in 1999, when coal miners striked.

Romania was invited to join NATO in 2004, and deployed 650 peacekeeping forces to Iraq in 2003.

Russia

RUSSIAN FEDERATION

President: Vladimir Putin (2000)
Prime Minister: Mikhail Kasyanov (2000)
Area: 6,592,735 sq mi (17,075,200 sq km)
Population (2003 est.): 144,526,278 (growth rate: –0.4%); birth rate: 10.1/1000; infant mortality rate: 19.5/1000; density per sq mi: 22
Capital and largest city (2003 est.): Moscow, 11,970,500 (metro. area), 8,368,200 (city proper). **Other large cities:** St. Petersburg, 4,582,300; Novosibirsk, 1,395,500; Nizhny Novgorod, 1,340,900; Yekaterinburg, 1,256,600; Samara, 1,146,800; Kazan, 1,113,600; Ufa, 1,096,600; Chelyabinsk, 1,080,000;

Perm, 998,800; Volgograd, 984,200. **Monetary unit:** Ruble. **Languages:** Russian, others. **Ethnicity/race:** Russian 81.5%, Tatar 3.8%, Ukrainian 3%, Chuvash 1.2%, Bashkir 0.9%, Byelorussian 0.8%, Moldavian 0.7%, other 8.1%. **Religions:** Russian Orthodox, Islam, others. **Literacy rate:** 98% (1989 est.)

Economic summary: GDP/PPP (2001 est.): $1.2 trillion; per capita $8,300. **Real growth rate:** 5.2%. **Inflation:** 21.9%. **Unemployment:** 8.7%, plus considerable underemployment. **Arable land:** 8%. **Agriculture:** grain, sugar beets, sunflower seed, vegetables, fruits; beef, milk. **Labor force:** 71.3 million; agriculture 10.8%, industry 27.8%, services 61.4%. **Industries:** complete range of mining and extractive industries producing coal, oil, gas, chemicals, and metals; all forms of machine building from rolling mills to high-performance aircraft and space vehicles; shipbuilding; road and rail transportation equipment; communications equipment; agricultural machinery, tractors, and construction equipment; electric power generating and transmitting equipment; medical and scientific instruments; consumer durables, textiles, foodstuffs, handicrafts. **Natural resources:** wide natural resource base including major deposits of oil, natural gas, coal, and many strategic minerals, timber; note: formidable obstacles of climate, terrain, and distance hinder exploitation of natural resources. **Exports:** $103.3 billion (2001 est.): petroleum and petroleum products, natural gas, wood and wood products, metals, chemicals, and a wide variety of civilian and military manufactures. **Imports:** $51.7 billion (2001 est.): machinery and equipment, consumer goods, medicines, meat, grain, sugar, semifinished metal products. **Major trading partners:** Germany, U.S., Italy, Belarus, China, Ukraine, Netherlands, Kazakhstan.

Geography The Russian Federation is the largest republic of the Commonwealth of Independent States. It occupies an area about one and four-fifths of the size of the United States and occupies most of eastern Europe and north Asia. Russia stretches from the Baltic Sea in the west to the Pacific Ocean in the east and from the Arctic Ocean in the north to the Black Sea and the Caucasus, the Altai, and Sayan Mountains, and the Amur and Ussuri Rivers in the south. It is bordered by Norway and Finland in the northwest, Estonia, Latvia, Belarus, Ukraine, Poland, and Lithuania in the west, Georgia and Azerbaijan in the southwest, and Kazakhstan, Mongolia, China, and North Korea along the southern border. The federation is composed of 21 republics.

Government Constitutional federation.

History Tradition says the Viking Rurik came to Russia in 862 and founded the first Russian dynasty in Novgorod. The various tribes were united by the spread of Christianity in the 10th and 11th centuries; Vladimir "the Saint" was converted in 988. During the 11th century, the grand dukes of Kiev held such centralizing power as existed. In 1240, Kiev was destroyed by the Mongols, and the Russian territory was split into numerous smaller dukedoms. Early dukes of Moscow extended their dominion over other Russian cities through their office of tribute collector for the Mongols and because of Moscow's role as an administrative and trade center.

In the late 15th century, Duke Ivan III acquired Novgorod and Tver and threw off the Mongol yoke. Ivan IV, the Terrible (1533–1584), first Muscovite czar, is considered to have founded the Russian state. He crushed the power of rival princes and boyars (great landowners), but Russia remained largely medieval until the reign of Peter the Great (1689–1725), grandson of the first Romanov czar, Michael (1613–1645). Peter made extensive reforms aimed at westernization and, through his defeat of Charles XII of Sweden at the Battle of Poltava in 1709, he extended Russia's boundaries to the west. Catherine the Great (1762–1796) continued Peter's westernization program and also expanded Russian territory, acquiring the Crimea, Ukraine, and part of Poland. During the reign of Alexander I (1801–1825), Napoléon's attempt to subdue Russia was defeated (1812–1813), and new territory was gained, including Finland (1809) and Bessarabia (1812). Alexander originated the Holy Alliance, which for a time crushed Europe's rising liberal movement.

Alexander II (1855–1881) pushed Russia's borders to the Pacific and into central Asia. Serfdom was abolished in 1861, but heavy restrictions were imposed on the emancipated class. Revolutionary strikes, following Russia's defeat in the war with Japan, forced Nicholas II (1894–1917) to grant a representative national body (Duma), elected by narrowly limited suffrage. It met for the first time in 1906, little influencing Nicholas in his reactionary course.

World War I demonstrated czarist corruption and inefficiency, and only patriotism held the poorly equipped army together for a time. Disorders broke out in Petrograd (renamed Leningrad and now St. Petersburg) in March 1917, and defection of the Petrograd garrison launched the revolution. Nicholas II was forced to abdicate on March 15, 1917, and he and his family were killed by revolutionists on July 16, 1918. A provisional government under the successive premierships of Prince Lvov and a moderate, Alexander Kerensky, lost ground to the radical, or Bolshevik, wing of the Socialist Democratic Labor Party. On Nov. 7, 1917, the Bolshevik Revolution, engineered by N. Lenin[1] and Leon Trotsky, overthrew the Kerensky government and authority was vested in a Council of People's Commissars, with Lenin as premier.

The humiliating Treaty of Brest-Litovsk (March 3, 1918) concluded the war with Germany, but civil war and foreign intervention delayed Communist control of all Russia until 1920. A brief war with Poland in 1920 resulted in Russian defeat.

Emergence of the USSR The Union of Soviet Socialist Republics was established as a federation on Dec. 30, 1922. The death of Lenin on Jan. 21, 1924, precipitated an intraparty struggle between Joseph Stalin, general secretary of the party, and Trotsky, who favored swifter socialization at home and fomentation of revolution abroad. Trotsky was dismissed as commissar of war in 1925 and banished from the Soviet Union in 1929. He was murdered in Mexico City on Aug. 21, 1940, by a political agent. Stalin further consolidated his power by a series of purges in the late 1930s, liquidating prominent party leaders and military officers. Stalin assumed the premiership on May 6, 1941.

Soviet foreign policy, at first friendly toward Germany and antagonistic toward Britain and France and then, after Hitler's rise to power in 1933, becoming anti-Fascist and pro–League of Nations, took an abrupt turn on Aug. 24, 1939, with the signing of a nonaggression pact with Nazi Germany. The next month, Moscow joined in the German attack on Poland, seizing territory later incorporated into the Ukrainian and Belorussian SSRs. The Russo-Finnish War (1939–1940) added territory to the Karelian SSR set up on March 31, 1940; the annexation of Bessarabia and

1. N. Lenin was the pseudonym taken by Vladimir Ilich Ulyanov. It is sometimes given as Nikolai Lenin or V. Lenin.

Rulers of Russia Since 1533

Name	Born	Ruled[1]
Ivan IV the Terrible	1530	1533–1584
Theodore I	1557	1584–1598
Boris Godunov	c.1551	1598–1605
Theodore II	1589	1605–1605
Demetrius I[2]	?	1605–1606
Basil IV Shuiski	?	1606–1610[3]
"Time of Troubles"	—	1610–1613
Michael Romanov	1596	1613–1645
Alexis I	1629	1645–1676
Theodore III	1656	1676–1682
Ivan V[4]	1666	1682–1689[5]
Peter I the Great[4]	1672	1682–1725
Catherine I	c.1684	1725–1727
Peter II	1715	1727–1730
Anna	1693	1730–1740
Ivan VI	1740	1740–1741[6]
Elizabeth	1709	1741–1762
Peter III	1728	1762–1762
Catherine II the Great	1729	1762–1796
Paul I	1754	1796–1801
Alexander I	1777	1801–1825
Nicholas I	1796	1825–1855
Alexander II	1818	1855–1881
Alexander III	1845	1881–1894
Nicholas II	1868	1894–1917[7]
PROVISIONAL GOVERNMENT (PREMIERS)		
Prince Georgi Lvov	1861	1917–1917
Alexander Kerensky	1881	1917–1917
POLITICAL LEADERS OF USSR		
Vladimir Ilyich Lenin	1870	1917–1924
Aleksei Rykov	1881	1924–1930
Vyacheslav Molotov	1890	1930–1941
Joseph Stalin[8]	1879	1941–1953
Georgi M. Malenkov	1902	1953–1955
Nikolai A. Bulganin	1895	1955–1958
Nikita S. Khrushchev	1894	1958–1964
Leonid I. Brezhnev	1906	1964–1982
Yuri V. Andropov	1914	1982–1984
Konstantin U. Chernenko	1912	1984–1985
Mikhail S. Gorbachev	1931	1985–1991
PRESIDENT OF RUSSIA		
Boris Yeltsin	1931	1991–1999
Vladimir Putin	1952	2000–

1. For czars through Nicholas II, year of end of rule is also that of death, unless otherwise indicated. 2. Also known as Pseudo-Demetrius. 3. Died 1612. 4. Ivan V and Peter I the Great ruled jointly until 1689, when Ivan was deposed. 5. Died 1696. 6. Died 1764. 7. Killed 1918. 8. General secretary of Communist Party, 1924–1953.

Bukovina from Romania became part of the new Moldavian SSR on Aug. 2, 1940; and the annexation of the Baltic republics of Estonia, Latvia, and Lithuania in June 1940 created the 14th, 15th, and 16th Soviet republics. The illegal annexation of the Baltic republics was never acknowledged by the U.S. for the 51 years leading up to Soviet recognition of Estonia, Latvia, and Lithuania's independence on Sept. 6, 1991. The Soviet-German collaboration ended abruptly with a lightning attack by Hitler on June 22, 1941, which seized 500,000 sq mi of Russian territory before Soviet defenses, aided by U.S. and British arms, could halt it. The Soviet resurgence at Stalingrad from Nov. 1942 to Feb. 1943 marked the turning point in a long battle, ending in the final offensive of Jan. 1945. Then, after denouncing a 1941 nonaggression pact with Japan in April 1945, when Allied forces were nearing victory in the Pacific, the Soviet Union declared war on Japan on Aug. 8, 1945, and quickly occupied Manchuria, Karafuto, and the Kuril Islands.

The USSR built a cordon of Communist states running from Poland in the north to Albania and Bulgaria in the south, including East Germany, Czechoslovakia, Hungary, and Romania, which composed the territories the Soviet troops occupied at the war's end. With its eastern front solidified, the Soviet Union launched a political offensive against the non-Communist West, moving first to block the Western access to Berlin. The Western powers countered with an airlift, completed unification of West Germany, and organized the defense of western Europe in the North Atlantic Treaty Organization (NATO). Stalin died on March 6, 1953, and was succeeded the next day by G. M. Malenkov as premier.

The new power in the Kremlin was Nikita S. Khrushchev, first secretary of the party. Khrushchev formalized the eastern European system into a Council for Mutual Economic Assistance (Comecon) and a Warsaw Pact Treaty Organization as a counterweight to NATO. The Soviet Union exploded a hydrogen bomb in 1953, developed an intercontinental ballistic missile by 1957, sent the first satellite into space (Sputnik I) in 1957, and put Yuri Gagarin in the first orbital flight around Earth in 1961. Khrushchev's downfall stemmed from his decision to place Soviet nuclear missiles in Cuba and then, when challenged by the U.S., backing down and removing the weapons. He was also blamed for the ideological break with China after 1963. Khrushchev was forced into retirement on Oct. 15, 1964, and was replaced by Leonid I. Brezhnev as first secretary of the party and Aleksei N. Kosygin as premier.

U.S. president Jimmy Carter and Brezhnev signed the SALT II treaty in Vienna on June 18, 1979, setting ceilings on each nation's arsenal of intercontinental ballistic missiles. The U.S. Senate refused to ratify the treaty because of the invasion of Afghanistan by Soviet troops on Dec. 27, 1979. On Nov. 10, 1982, Soviet radio and television announced the death of Leonid Brezhnev. Yuri V. Andropov, who had formerly headed the KGB, became his successor, but died less than two years later, in Feb. 1984. Konstantin U. Chernenko, a 72-year-old party stalwart who had been close to Brezhnev, succeeded him.

In the months following Chernenko's assumption of power, the Kremlin took on a hostile attitude toward the West of a kind rarely seen since the height of the cold war 30 years before. Led by Moscow, all the Soviet bloc countries except Romania boycotted the 1984 Summer Olympic Games in Los Angeles—tit-for-tat for the U.S.-led boycott of the 1980 Moscow Games, in the view of most observers. After 13 months in office, Chernenko died on March 10, 1985. He had been ill much of the time and left only a minor imprint on Soviet history. Chosen to succeed him as Soviet leader was Mikhail S. Gorbachev, who led the Soviet Union in its long-awaited shift to a new generation of leadership. Unlike his immediate predecessors, Gorbachev did not also assume the title of president but wielded power from the post of party general secretary.

The Soviet Union took much criticism in early 1986 over the April 24 meltdown at the Chernobyl nuclear plant and its reluctance to give out any information on the accident.

In June 1987, Gorbachev obtained the support of the Central Committee for proposals that would loosen some government controls over the economy and in June 1988, an unusually open party conference approved several resolutions reforming the Soviet system. These included a shift of some power from the party to local soviets, and a ten-year limit on the terms of elected government and party officials. Gorbachev was elected president in 1989. The elections to the Duma were the first competitive elections in the Soviet Union since 1917. Dissident candidates won a surprisingly large minority although pro-government deputies maintained a strong lock on the Supreme Soviet.

Dissolution of the USSR The possible beginning of the fragmentation of the Communist Party took place when Boris Yeltsin, leader of the Russian SSR who urged faster reform, left the Communist Party along with other radicals. In March 1991, the Soviet people were asked to vote in a referendum on national unity engineered by Gorbachev. The resultant victory for the federal government was tempered by the separate approval in Russia for the creation of a popularly elected presidency of the Russian republics. The bitter election contest for the Russian presidency, principally between Yeltsin and a Communist loyalist, resulted in a major victory for Yeltsin. He took the oath of office for the new position on July 10, 1991.

Reversing his relative hard-line position, Gorbachev together with leaders of nine Soviet republics signed an accord called the Union Treaty, which was meant to preserve the unity of the nation. In exchange the federal government would have turned over control of industrial and natural resources to the individual republics. An attempted coup d'état took place on Aug. 19, 1991, orchestrated by a group of eight senior officials calling itself the State Committee on the State of Emergency. Boris Yeltsin, barricaded in the Russian Parliament building, defiantly called for a general strike. The next day huge crowds demonstrated in Leningrad, and Yeltsin supporters fortified barricades surrounding the Parliament building. On Aug. 21 the coup committee disbanded, and at least some of its members attempted to flee Moscow. The Soviet Parliament formally reinstated Gorbachev as president. Two days later he resigned from his position as general-secretary of the Communist Party and recommended that its Central Committee be disbanded. On Aug. 29 the Parliament approved the suspension of all Communist Party activities pending an investigation of its role in the failed coup. At the time of the attempted coup, the republic's president, Boris Yeltsin, was the most popular political figure in the former Soviet Union. A leading reformer, he became the first directly elected leader in Russian history and received 60% of the vote for president of the Russian Republic.

Yeltsin championed the cause for national reconstruction and the adoption of a Union Treaty with the other republics to create a free-market economic association. On Dec. 12, 1991, the Russian Parliament ratified Yeltsin's plea to establish a new commonwealth of independent nations open to all former members of the Soviet Union. The new union was created with the governments of Ukraine and Belarus who along with Russia were the three original cofounders of the Soviet Union in 1922. After the end of the Soviet Union, Russia and ten other Soviet republics joined in a Commonwealth of Independent States on Dec. 21, 1991.

At the start of 1992, Russia embarked on a series of dramatic economic reforms, including the freeing of prices on most goods, which led to an immediate downturn. A national referendum on confidence in Yeltsin and his economic program took place in April 1993. To the surprise of many, the president and his shock-therapy program won by a resounding margin. In September, Yeltsin dissolved the legislative bodies left over from the Soviet era. The impasse between the executive and the legislature resulted in an armed conflict on Oct. 3. Yeltsin prevailed largely through the support of the military and other forces.

The southern republic of Chechnya's president accelerated his region's drive for independence in 1994. In December, Russian troops closed the borders and sought to squelch the independence drive. The Russian military forces met firm and costly resistance. In May 1997, the two-year war formally ended with the signing of a peace treaty that adroitly avoided the issue of Chechen independence.

In March 1998 Yeltsin dismissed his entire government and replaced Prime Minister Viktor Chernomyrdin with the young and little known fuel and energy minister Sergei Kiriyenko. On Aug. 28, 1998, amid the Russian stock market's free fall, the Russian government halted trading of the ruble on international currency markets. This financial crisis led to a long-term economic downturn and to political upheaval. President Boris Yeltsin then sacked Prime Minister Kiriyenko and reappointed Chernomyrdin. The Duma rejected Chernomyrdin and on Sept. 11 elected foreign minister Yevgeny Primakov as prime minister. The repercussions of Russia's financial emergency were felt throughout the Commonwealth of Independent States.

Impatient with Yeltsin's chronic illnesses and increasingly erratic behavior, the Duma attempted to impeach him in May 1999 on five charges: provoking the 1991 fall of the Soviet Union, using force to dissolve the Parliament in 1993, starting the ill-conceived 1994–1996 war in Chechnya, ruining the nation's military, and impoverishing the Russian people through ruinous economic policies—the charge regarding Chechnya was considered the only one with a chance of approval. But the impeachment motion was quickly quashed and soon Yeltsin was on the ascendancy again. In keeping with his capricious style, Yeltsin dismissed Prime Minister Yevgeny Primakov and replaced him with Interior Minister Sergei Stepashin. Just three months later, however, Yeltsin ousted Stepashin and replaced him with Vladimir Putin on Aug. 9, 1999, announcing that in addition to serving as prime minister, the former KGB agent was his choice as a successor in the 2000 presidential election.

In a decision that took Russia and the world by surprise, Boris Yeltsin resigned on Dec. 31, 1999, and Vladimir Putin became the acting president. One of Putin's first acts was to grant Yeltsin immunity from prosecution (Yeltsin and family members had been accused of corruption and financial misconduct). On March 26, 2000, Putin won the presidential election with about 53% of the vote. Since then Putin has moved to centralize power in Moscow and has attempted to limit the power and influence of both the regional governors and wealthy business leaders. Although Russia remains economically stagnant, Putin has brought his nation a measure of political stability it never had under the mercurial and erratic Yeltsin.

Just three years after the bloody 1994–1996 Chechen-Russian war ended in devastation and stalemate, the fighting started again in 1999, with Russia launching air strikes and following up with ground troops. By the end of November, Russian troops had surrounded Chechnya's capital, Grozny, and about 215,000 Chechen refugees had fled to neighboring Ingushetia. Russia maintained that a political solution was impossible until Islamic militants in Chechnya had been vanquished. In Feb. 2000, after almost five months of fighting, Russian troops captured Grozny, the Chechen capital. The control of Grozny was a political as well as a military victory for Putin, whose hard-line stance against Chechnya has greatly contributed to his political popularity. Despite repeated Russian claims of victory, the war continued to drag on in 2002.

In 1999, the former Russian satellites of Poland, Hungary, and the Czech Republic joined NATO, raising Russia's hackles. The desire of Lithuania, Latvia, and Estonia, all of which were once part of the Soviet Union, to join the organization in the future has further alarmed Russia.

In Aug. 2000 the Russian government was severely criticized for its handling of the *Kursk* disaster, a nuclear submarine accident that left 118 sailors dead.

Russia was initially alarmed in 2001 when the U.S. announced its rejection of the Anti-Ballistic Missile Treaty of 1972, which for 30 years had been viewed as a crucial force in keeping the nuclear arms race at bay. But Putin was eventually placated by Bush's reassurances, and in May 2002, the U.S. and Russian leaders announced a landmark pact to cut both countries' nuclear arsenals by up to two-thirds over the next ten years.

On Oct. 23, Chechen rebels seized a crowded Moscow theater and detained 763 people, including 3 Americans. Armed and wired with explosives, the rebels demanded that Russian government end the war in Chechnya. Government forces stormed the theater the next day, after releasing a gas into the theater, which killed not only all the rebels but more than 100 hostages.

During the fall 2002–winter 2003 diplomatic wrangling at the United Nations over Iraq, Russia sided with the majority of western European nations in calling for more weapons inspections and diplomacy before resorting to war. Russia's UN ambassador stated: "We see no reason whatsoever to interrupt the inspections and any resolution which contains ultimatums and which contains automaticity for the use of force is not acceptable to us."

In March Chechens voted in a referendum that approved a new regional constitution making Chechnya a separatist republic within Russia. Agreeing to the constitution meant abandoning claims for complete independence. While Moscow has presented the referendum as a way of bringing peace to the war-ravaged region, it is unclear how much power Russia would actually grant the separatist republic. A spate of Chechen suicide bombings followed throughout the year.

In April 2003 reformist politician Sergei Yushenkov became the third outspoken critic of the Kremlin to be assassinated in the last five years. Just hours before he was gunned down, Yushenkov had officially registered his new political party, Liberal Russia.

Rwanda

RWANDESE REPUBLIC

National name: Repubulika y'u Rwanda
President: Paul Kagame (2000)
Prime Minister: Bernard Makuza (2000)
Area: 10,169 sq mi (26,338 sq km)
Population (2003 est.): 7,810,056 (growth rate: 1.8%); birth rate: 40.1/1000; infant mortality rate: 102.6/1000; density per sq mi: 768
Capital and largest city (2003 est.): Kigali, 298,100. **Monetary unit:** Rwanda franc. **Languages:** Kinyarwanda, French, and English (all official). **Ethnicity/race:** Hutu 84%, Tutsi 15%, Twa (Pygmoid) 1%. **Religions:** Roman Catholic 56.5%, Protestant 26%, Adventist 11.1%, Islam 4.6%, Animist 0.1%. **Literacy rate:** 48% (1995 est.)
Economic summary: GDP/PPP (2001 est.): $7.2 billion; per capita $1,000. **Real growth rate:** 5%. **Inflation:** 5%. **Unemployment:** n.a. **Arable land:** 32%. **Agriculture:** coffee, tea, pyrethrum (insecticide made from chrysanthemums), bananas, beans, sorghum, potatoes; livestock. **Labor force:** 3.6 million; agriculture 90%. **Industries:** cement, agricultural products, small-scale beverages, soap, furniture, shoes, plastic goods, textiles, cigarettes. **Natural resources:** gold, cassiterite (tin ore), wolframite (tungsten ore), methane, hydropower, arable land. **Exports:** $61 million (f.o.b., 2001 est.): coffee, tea, hides, tin ore. **Imports:** $248 million (f.o.b., 2001 est.): foodstuffs, machinery and equipment, steel, petroleum products, cement and construction material. **Major trading partners:** EU, Pakistan, U.S., China, Malaysia, Kenya, India, Tanzania.

Geography Rwanda, in east-central Africa, is surrounded by Congo, Uganda, Tanzania, and Burundi. It is slightly smaller than Maryland. Steep mountains and deep valleys cover most of the country. Lake Kivu in the northwest, at an altitude of 4,829 ft (1,472 m) is the highest lake in Africa. Extending north of it are the Virunga Mountains, which include the volcano Karisimbi (14,187 ft; 4,324 m), Rwanda's highest point.

Government Republic.

History The original inhabitants of Rwanda were the Twa, a Pygmy people who now make up only 1% of the population. While the Hutu and Tutsi are often considered to be two separate ethnic groups, scholars point out that they speak the same language, have a history of intermarriage, and share many cultural characteristics. Traditionally, the differences between the two groups were occupational rather than ethnic. Agricultural people were considered Hutu, while the cattle-owning elite were identified as Tutsi. Supposedly Tutsi were tall and thin, while Hutu were short and square, but it is often impossible to tell one from the other. The 1933 requirement by the Belgians that everyone carry an identity card indicating tribal ethnicity as Tutsi or Hutu increased the distinction. Since independence, repeated violence in both Rwanda and Burundi has increased ethnic differentiation between the groups.

Rwanda, which became a part of German East Africa in 1890, was first visited by European explorers in 1854. During World War I, it was occupied in 1916 by Belgian troops. After the war, it became a Belgian League of Nations mandate, along with Burundi, under the name of Ruanda-Urundi. The mandate was made a UN trust territory in 1946. Until the Belgian Congo achieved independence in 1960, Ruanda-Urundi was administered as part of that colony. Belgium at first maintained Tutsi dominance but eventually encouraged power sharing between Hutu and Tutsi. Ethnic tensions led to civil war, forcing many Tutsi into exile. When Ruanda became the independent nation of Rwanda on July 1, 1962, it was under Hutu rule.

In Oct. 1990, the Rwandan Patriotic Front (RPF), Tutsi rebels in exile in Uganda, invaded in an attempt to overthrow the Hutu-led Rwandan government. Peace accords were signed in Aug. 1993, calling for a coalition government. But after the downing of a plane in April 1994 that killed the presidents of both Rwanda and Burundi, deep-seated ethnic violence erupted. (It is now believed that the plane was shot down by Hutu extremists who rejected the Hutu-Tutsi power-sharing plan proposed by President Juvénal Habyarimana, a Hutu moderate.)

The presidential guard began murdering Tutsi opposition leaders, and soon policemen and soldiers began attempting to murder the entire Tutsi population. In 100 days, beginning in April 1994, Hutus rampaged through the country, slaughtered an estimated 800,000 Tutsi and their moderate Hutu sympathizers. A 30,000-member militia group, the Interahamwe, led much of the murderous spree, but, goaded by radio propaganda, ordinary Hutus joined in massacring their Tutsi neighbors. Although the genocidal slaughter seemed a spontaneous eruption of hatred, it has in fact been shown to have been carefully orchestrated by the Hutu government.

In response, the Tutsi rebel force, the Rwandan Patriotic Front, swept across the country in a 14-week civil war, routing the largely Hutu government. Despite horrific reports of genocide, no country came to the Tutsi's assistance. The UN, already stationed in Rwanda at the time of the killing, withdrew entirely after ten of its soldiers were killed.

In the aftermath of the genocide, an estimated 1.7 million Hutus fled across the border into neighboring Zaire (now the Democratic Republic of the Congo). Although Tutsi rebels took control of the government, they permitted a Hutu, Pasteur Bizimungu, to serve as president, attempting to deflect accusations of a resurgence in Tutsi elitism and to foster national unity. Paul Kagame, the Tutsi rebel leader, became vice president and minister of defense.

Amid the legitimate refugees from the genocide were Hutu militiamen, who began waging guerrilla warfare from refugee camps in Zaire. The Hutu guerrillas in Zaire, as well as Zaire's threat to exile their own ethnic Tutsi, led to Rwanda's support of rebel forces, headed by Laurent Kabila, bent on overthrowing Zaire's Mobutu Sese Seko. But Rwanda soon grew disenchanted with the new regime of Kabila. The Kabila government was not able to prevent the raids from Hutu guerrillas that continued to traumatize the country and destabilize the region. In Aug. 1998, a little more than a year after Kabila took over, a rebellion began against his reign, instigated by Rwanda and Uganda.

Refugee problems, continued massacres, and the horrific legacy of genocide continued to haunt the national psyche. In Sept. 1998, a UN tribunal sentenced Jean Kambanda, a former prime minister of Rwanda, to life in prison for his part in the 1994 genocide. He became the first person in history to be convicted for the crime of genocide, first defined in the 1948 Genocide Convention after World War II. By 2001, eight others had also been convicted of the same charge. The UN tribunal, however, has been criticized for its inefficiency and slow pace. In Dec. 1999, an independent report, commissioned by the UN, took Kofi Annan and other UN officials to task for not intervening effectively in the genocide.

In April 2000, President Bizimungu resigned and Vice President Paul Kagame became the first Tutsi president of the nation. It was Kagame's rebel force that seized Rwanda's capital and put an end to the genocide in 1994.

Rwanda continued fighting against Congo throughout its four-year civil war. Finally, in July 2002, Kagame and Joseph Kabila, who became president of Congo after his father was assassinated in 1999, signed a peace accord: Rwanda promised to withdraw its 35,000 troops from the eastern Congolese border; Congo would in turn disarm the thousands of Hutu militiamen in its territory, who threaten Rwandan security—many of them supported or participated in the Rwandan genocide.

In May 2003, 93% of Rwandans voted to approve a new constitution that institutes the balance of political power between Hutu and Tutsi—no party, for example, can hold more than half the seats in parliament. It also outlaws the incitement of ethnic hatred. In Aug. 26 presidential elections, the first since the Rwandan genocide, Paul Kagame, who has served as president since 2000, won a landslide victory.

St. Kitts and Nevis

FEDERATION OF ST. KITTS AND NEVIS

Sovereign: Queen Elizabeth II (1952)
Governor-General: Sir Cuthbert Sebastian (1996)
Prime Minister: Denzil Douglas (1995)
Area: St. Kitts 65 sq mi (168 sq km); Nevis 36 sq mi (93 sq km)
Population (2003 est.): 38,763 (growth rate: 1.0%); birth rate: 18.4/1000; infant mortality rate: 15.4/1000; density per sq mi: 385
Capital (2003 est.): Basseterre (on St. Kitts), 11,500. **Largest town on Nevis:** Charlestown, 1,300. **Monetary unit:** East Caribbean dollar. **Languages:** English. **Ethnicity/race:** black African. **Literacy rate:** 97% (1980 est.)
Economic summary: GDP/PPP (2001 est.): $339 million; per capita $8,700. **Real growth rate:** 1%. **Inflation:** 1.7%. **Unemployment:** 4.5% (1997). **Arable land:** 17%. **Agriculture**: sugarcane, rice, yams, vegetables, bananas; fish. **Labor force:** 18,172 (June 1995). **Industries:** sugar processing, tourism, cotton, salt, copra, clothing, footwear, beverages. **Natural resources:** arable land. **Exports:** $51.7 million (2000 est.): machinery, food, electronics, beverages, tobacco. **Imports:** $141.3 million (2000 est.): machinery, manufactures, food, fuels. **Major trading partners:** U.S., UK, Caricom countries.

Geography St. Kitts, the larger of the two islands, is roughly oval in shape except for a long, narrow peninsula to the southeast. Its highest point is Mount Liamuiga (3,792 ft [1,156 m]). The Narrows, a 2-mile- (3-km-) wide channel, separates the two islands. The circularly shaped Nevis is surrounded by coral reefs and the island is almost entirely a single mountain, Nevis Peak (3,232 ft [985 m]). A volcanic mountain chain dominates the center of both islands.

Government Constitutional monarchy.

History When Christopher Columbus explored the islands in 1493, they were inhabited by the Carib people. Today, most of the inhabitants are the descendants of African slaves. St. Kitts, formerly St. Christopher, was settled by the British in 1623; Nevis in 1628. The French settled on St. Kitts in 1627, and an Anglo-French rivalry lasted for more than 100 years. After a decisive British victory over the French at Brimstone Hill in 1782, the islands came under permanent British control. The islands, including nearby Anguilla, were united in 1882. They joined the West Indies federation in 1958 and remained in that association until its dissolution in 1962. St. Kitts-Nevis-Anguilla became an associated state of the United Kingdom in 1967. Anguilla seceded in 1980, and St. Kitts and Nevis became independent on Sept. 19, 1983.

A drop in world sugar prices hurt the nation's economy through the mid-1980s, and the government sought to reduce the islands' dependence on sugar production and to diversify the economy, promoting tourism and financial services. In 1990, the premier of Nevis announced that he intended to seek an end to the federation with St. Kitts by 1992, but a local election in June 1992 postponed the idea. In Aug. 1998, 62% of the population voted for Nevis to secede, but the vote fell short of the two-thirds majority required.

The country had been blacklisted by various international financial agencies for improprieties in its offshore financial services industry, but by 2002 it had been removed from all such lists.

St. Lucia

Sovereign: Queen Elizabeth II (1952)
Governor-General: Dame Pearlette Louisy (1997)
Prime Minister: Kenny D. Anthony (1997)
Area: 238 sq mi (616 sq km)
Population (2003 est.): 162,157 (growth rate: 1.6%); birth rate: 20.9/1000; infant mortality rate: 14.4/1000; density per sq mi: 682
Capital and largest city (2003 est.): Castries, 60,300. **Monetary unit:** East Caribbean dollar. **Languages:** English (official) and patois. **Ethnicity/race:** African descent 90%, mixed 6%, East Indian 3%, white 1%. **Religions:** Roman Catholic 90%, Protestant 7%, Anglican 3%. **Literacy rate:** 67% (1980 est.)
Economic summary: GDP/PPP (2000 est.): $700 million; per capita $4,400 (2001 est.). **Real growth rate:** –2.5% (2001 est.). **Inflation:** 3% (2001 est.). **Unemployment:** 15% (1996 est.). **Arable land:** 5%. **Agriculture:** bananas, coconuts, vegetables, citrus, root crops, cocoa. **Labor force:** 43,800; agriculture 43.4%, services 38.9%, industry and commerce 17.7% (1983 est.). **Industries:** clothing, assembly of electronic components, beverages, corrugated cardboard boxes, tourism, lime processing, coconut processing. **Natural resources:** forests, sandy beaches, minerals (pumice), mineral springs, geothermal potential. **Exports:** $68.3 million (2000 est.): bananas 41%, clothing, cocoa, vegetables, fruits, coconut oil. **Imports:** $319.4 million (2000 est.): food 23%, manufactured goods 21%, machinery and transportation equipment 19%, chemicals, fuels. **Major trading partners:** UK, U.S., Caricom countries, Japan, Canada. **Member of Commonwealth of Nations**

Geography One of the Windward Islands of the eastern Caribbean, St. Lucia lies just south of Martinique. It is of volcanic origin. A chain of wooded mountains runs from north to south, and from them flow many streams into fertile valleys.

Government Parliamentary democracy. A governor-general represents the sovereign, Queen Elizabeth II.

History The first inhabitants of St. Lucia were the Arawak Indians, who were forced off the island by the Caribs. Explored by Spain and then France, St. Lucia became a British territory in 1814 and one of the Windward Islands in 1871. With other Windward Islands, St. Lucia was granted home rule in 1967 as one of the West Indies Associated States. On Feb. 22, 1979, St. Lucia achieved full independence in ceremonies boycotted by the opposition St. Lucia Labour Party, which had advocated a referendum before cutting ties with Britain. The United Workers Party (UWP), then in power, called for new elections and was defeated by the St. Lucia Labour Party (SLP). The UWP was returned to power in the elections of 1982, 1987, and 1992.

Kenny Anthony became prime minister in 1997, when his St. Lucia Labour Party won 16 of the 17 parliamentary seats.

The 1999 European Union decision to end its preferential treatment of bananas imported from former colonies has led St. Lucia to try to diversify its agricultural crops. In 2002, tropical storm Lili devasted the banana crop.

St. Vincent and the Grenadines

Sovereign: Queen Elizabeth II (1952)
Governor-General: Frederick Ballantyne (2002)
Prime Minister: Ralph Gonsalves (2001)
Area: 150 sq mi (389 sq km)
Population (2003 est.): 116,812 (growth rate: 1.1%); birth rate: 17.2/1000; infant mortality rate: 15.7/1000; density per sq mi: 778
Capital and largest city (2003 est.): Kingstown, 17,600. **Monetary unit:** East Caribbean dollar. **Languages:** English (official), French patois. **Ethnicity/race:** African descent, white, East Indian, Carib Indian. **Religions:** Anglican 47%, Methodist 28%, Roman Catholic 13%. **Literacy rate:** 96% (1970 est.)
Economic summary: GDP/PPP (2001 est.): $339 million; per capita $2,900. **Real growth rate:** –0.8%. **Inflation:** –0.4%. **Unemployment:** 22% (1997 est.). **Arable land:** 10%. **Agriculture:** bananas, coconuts, sweet potatoes, spices; small numbers of cattle, sheep, pigs, goats; fish. **Labor force:** 67,000 (1984 est.); agriculture 26%, industry 17%, services 57% (1980 est.). **Industries:** food processing, cement, furniture, clothing, starch. **Natural resources:** hydropower, cropland. **Exports:** $53.7 million (2000 est.): bananas 39%, eddoes and dasheen (taro), arrowroot starch, tennis racquets. **Imports**: $185.6 million (2000 est.): foodstuffs, machinery and equipment, chemicals and fertilizers, minerals and fuels. **Major trading partners:** Caricom countries, UK, U.S. **Member of Commonwealth of Nations**

Geography St. Vincent, chief island of the chain, is 18 mi (29 km) long and 11 mi (18 km) wide, and is located 100 mi (161 km) west of Barbados. The island is mountainous and well forested. St. Vincent is dominated by the volcano Mount Soufrière, which rises to 4,048 ft (1,234 m). The Grenadines, a chain of nearly 600 islets with a total area of only 17 sq mi (27 sq km), extend for 60 mi (96 km) between St. Vincent and Grenada. The main islands in the Grenadines are Bequia, Balliceau, Canouan, Mayreau, Mustique, Isle D'Quatre, Petit Saint Vincent, and Union Island.

Government Parliamentary democracy.

History The Carib Indians inhabited St. Vincent before the Europeans arrived, and the island still sports a sizable number of Carib artifacts. Explored by Columbus in 1498, and alternately claimed by Britain and France, St. Vincent became a British colony by the Treaty of Paris in 1763. In 1773, the island was divided between the Caribs and the British, but conflicts between the groups persisted. In 1776, the Caribs revolted and were subdued. Thereafter the British deported most of them to islands in the Gulf of Honduras. Sugarcane cultivation brought thousands of African slaves and, later, Portuguese and East Indian laborers.

The islands belonged to the West Indies Federation from 1958 until its dissolution in 1962, won home rule in 1969 as part of the West Indies Associated States, and achieved full independence Oct. 26, 1979. Prime Minister Milton Cato's government quelled a brief rebellion on Dec. 8, 1979, attributed to economic problems following the eruption of La Soufrière in April 1979 (which had caused the evacuation of the northern two-thirds of the island). The eruption, followed by Hurricane Allen in 1980, seriously damaged the nation's economy, particularly the important banana crop, in the 1980s. But by the 1990s the economy had begun to rebound, and the small tourism industry began to grow. In 1996, St. Vincent and the Grenadines signed agreements with the U.S. that allowed U.S.

Coast Guard personnel to pursue suspected drug smugglers into their territorial waters and provided for extradition of criminals. In 1997, the country's permanent representative to the Organization of American States assumed the chairmanship of that body's Permanent Council.

With the 1999 decision by the European Union to end its preferential treatment of bananas imported from former colonies, St. Vincent and the Grenadines has sought to diversify its economy, primarily through expanding tourism. In March 2001 elections, the Unity Labour Party (ULP) won a landslide upset, capturing 12 of the 15 contested parliamentary seats. Ralph Gonsalves, a lawyer, became the new prime minister.

Samoa

INDEPENDENT STATE OF SAMOA

Head of State: Malietoa Tanumafili II (1963)
Prime Minister: Tuilaepa Sailele Malielegaoi (1998)
Area: 1,137 sq mi (2,944 sq km)
Population (2003 est.): 178,173 (growth rate: 0.9%); birth rate: 15.4/1000; infant mortality rate: 29.7/1000; density per sq mi: 157
Capital and largest city (2003 est.): Apia, 35,900. **Monetary unit:** Tala. **Languages:** Samoan and English. **Ethnicity/race:** Samoan 92.6%, Euronesians 7% (persons of European and Polynesian blood), Europeans 0.4%. **Religion:** Christian 99.7%. **Literacy rate:** 80% (1999)
Economic summary: GDP/PPP (2001 est.): $618 million; per capita $3,500. **Real growth rate:** 6%. **Inflation:** 2.5%. **Unemployment:** n.a.; note: substantial underemployment. **Arable land:** 19%. **Agriculture:** coconuts, bananas, taro, yams. **Labor force:** 90,000 (2000 est.); agriculture 65%, services 30%, industry 5% (1995 est.). **Industries:** food processing, building materials, auto parts. **Natural resources:** hardwood forests, fish, hydropower. **Exports:** $17 million (f.o.b., 2000): fish, coconut oil and cream, copra, taro, garments, beer. **Imports:** $90 million (f.o.b., 2000): machinery and equipment, industrial supplies, foodstuffs. **Major trading partners:** Australia, Indonesia, American Samoa, New Zealand, U.S., Fiji, Japan.

Geography Samoa, formerly Western Samoa, is in the South Pacific Ocean about 2,200 mi (3,540 km) south of Hawaii. The larger islands in the Samoan chain, Upolu and Savai'i, are mountainous and of volcanic origin. There is little level land except in the coastal areas, where most cultivation takes place.

Government Constitutional monarchy under a native chief.

History Polynesians, possibly from Tonga, first settled in the Samoan islands about 1000 B.C. Samoa was explored by Dutch and French traders in the 18th century. Toward the end of the 19th century, conflicting interests of the U.S., Britain, and Germany resulted in an 1899 treaty that recognized the paramount interests of the U.S. in those islands west of 171°W (American Samoa) and Germany's interests in the other islands (Western Samoa).

New Zealand seized Western Samoa from Germany in 1914, and in 1946 it became a UN trust territory administered by New Zealand. A resistance movement to both German and New Zealand rule, known as the *Mau* ("strongly held view") movement, helped to edge the islands toward independence on Jan. 1, 1962. A constitutional monarchy, Samoa has a legislative assembly whose members are from the *matai,* or titled class.

Barraged regularly by cyclones that have wreaked havoc on the country's primarily agrarian economy, Samoa has begun stepping up its tourism industry—not such a difficult undertaking in this archetypical South Pacific paradise.

A referendum in 1990 gave most women the right to vote for the first time. In 1997, a new constitutional amendment changed the country's name to Samoa. In 2002, the prime minister of New Zealand apologized to Samoa for the injustices that occurred under New Zealand rule.

San Marino

MOST SERENE REPUBLIC OF SAN MARINO

National name: Repubblica di San Marino
Captains Regent: Pier Marino Menicucci and Giovanni Giannoni (2003)
Area: 24 sq mi (61.2 sq km)
Population (2003 est.): 28,119 (growth rate: 0.3%); birth rate: 10.5/1000; infant mortality rate: 6.0/1000; density per sq mi: 1,190
Capital (2003 est.): San Marino, 4,300. **Largest city:** Serravalle, 8,700. **Monetary unit:** Euro. **Language:** Italian. **Ethnicity/race:** Sammarinese, Italian. **Religion:** Roman Catholic. **Literacy rate:** 96% (1976 est.)
Economic summary: GDP/PPP (2001 est.): $940 million; per capita $34,600. **Real growth rate:** 7.5%. **Inflation:** 3.3%. **Unemployment:** 2.6%. **Arable land:** 17%. **Agriculture:** wheat, grapes, corn, olives; cattle, pigs, horses, beef, cheese, hides. **Labor force:** 18,500 (1999); services 57%, industry 42%, agriculture 1% (2000 est.). **Industries:** tourism, banking, textiles, electronics, ceramics, cement, wine. **Natural resources:** building stone. **Exports:** trade data are included with the statistics for Italy: building stone, lime, wood, chestnuts, wheat, wine, baked goods, hides, ceramics. **Imports:** trade data are included with the statistics for Italy: wide variety of consumer manufactures, food.

Geography One-tenth the size of New York City, San Marino is surrounded by Italy. It is situated in the Apennines, a little inland from the Adriatic Sea near Rimini.

Government Republic.

History According to tradition, San Marino was founded about A.D. 350 and had the good luck for centuries to stay out of the many wars and feuds on the Italian peninsula. It is the oldest republic in the world. San Marino has survived, completely intact, attacks by other self-governing Italian city-states, the Napoleonic Wars, the unification of Italy, and two world wars. Those born in San Marino remain citizens and can vote no matter where they live. Throughout the 1990s San Marino has taken a more active role in international diplomacy, establishing strong diplomatic and economic ties to a host of other countries. It joined the United Nations in 1992.

São Tomé and Príncipe

DEMOCRATIC REPUBLIC OF SÃO TOMÉ AND PRÍNCIPE

President: Fradique de Menezes (2003)
Prime Minister: Maria das Neves (2002)
Area: 386 sq mi (1,001 sq km)
Population (2003 est.): 175,883 (growth rate: 3.5%); birth rate: 41.9/1000; infant mortality rate: 46.0/1000; density per sq mi: 455
Capital and largest city (2003 est.): São Tomé, 53,300. **Monetary unit:** Dobra. **Language:** Portuguese. **Ethnicity/race:** mestico, angolares (descendants of Angolan slaves), forros (descendants of freed slaves),

servicais (contract laborers from Angola, Mozambique, and Cape Verde), tongas (children of servicais born on the islands), Europeans (primarily Portuguese). **Religions:** Roman Catholic, Evangelical Protestant, Seventh-Day Adventist. **Literacy rate:** 79.3% (1991 est.)

Economic summary: GDP/PPP (2001 est.): $189 million; per capita $1,200. **Real growth rate:** 4%. **Inflation:** 7%. **Unemployment:** n.a. **Arable land:** 2%. **Agriculture:** cocoa, coconuts, palm kernels, copra, cinnamon, pepper, coffee, bananas, papayas, beans; poultry; fish. **Labor force:** n.a.; population mainly engaged in subsistence agriculture and fishing; note: shortages of skilled workers. **Industries:** light construction, textiles, soap, beer; fish processing; timber. **Natural resources:** fish, hydropower. **Exports:** $4.1 million (f.o.b., 2000 est.): cocoa 90%, copra, coffee, palm oil. **Imports:** $40 million (f.o.b., 2000 est.): machinery and electrical equipment, food products, petroleum products. **Major trading partners:** Portugal, Netherlands, Spain, France, UK.

Geography The tiny volcanic islands of São Tomé and Príncipe lie in the Gulf of Guinea about 150 mi (240 km) off West Africa. São Tomé (about 330 sq mi; 859 sq km) is covered by a dense mountainous jungle, out of which have been carved large plantations. Príncipe (about 40 sq mi; 142 sq km) consists of jagged mountains. Other islands in the republic are Pedras Tinhosas and Rolas. About 95% of the population lives on São Tomé.

Government Republic.

History São Tomé and Príncipe, believed to have been originally uninhabited, were explored by Portuguese navigators in 1471 and settled by the end of the century. Intensive cultivation by slave labor made the islands a major producer of sugar during the 17th century but output declined until the introduction of coffee and cocoa in the 19th century brought new prosperity. The island of São Tomé was the world's largest producer of cocoa in 1908, and the crop is still its most important. Working conditions for laborers, however, were horrendous, and in 1909 British and German chocolate manufacturers boycotted São Tomé cocoa in protest. An exile liberation movement was formed in 1953 after Portuguese landowners quelled labor riots by killing several hundred African workers.

The Portuguese revolution of 1974 brought the end of the overseas empire, and on July 12, 1975, Lisbon granted São Tomé independence. Manuel Pinto da Costa, leader of the only legal political party (Movement for the Liberation of São Tomé and Principe [MLSTP]) became president and Miguel Trovoada served as prime minister. After a 1978 coup attempt failed, Trovoada was accused of participating in the conspiracy and exiled. In 1990 a new constitution instituted multi-party rule. Trovoada returned and in March 1991 became president in the country's first free elections. Príncipe became autonomous in 1995. Protests and unrest erupted throughout the 1990s over unemployment and soaring inflation. One of Africa's poorest countries, São Tomé has what is believed to be enormous untapped off-shore oil reserves—an estimated 6 billion barrels that are expected to begin flowing by 2007 or 2008. Businessman Fradique de Menezes won the presidential election in 2001. In July 2003, a military coup deposed Menezes while he was out of the country. Major Fernando Pereira, head of the country's military school, seized power, but relinquished it a week later under international pressure. Menezes again assumed the presidency.

Saudi Arabia

KINGDOM OF SAUDI ARABIA

National name: Al-Mamlaka al-'Arabiya as-Sa'udiya
Sovereign: King Fahd bin 'Abdulaziz (1982)
Area: 756,981 sq mi (1,960,582 sq km)
Population (2003 est.): 24,293,844 (growth rate: 3.1%); birth rate: 37.2/1000; infant mortality rate: 47.9/1000; density per sq mi: 32
Capital and largest city (2003 est.): Riyadh, 3,724,100. **Other large cities:** Jeddah, 2,745,000; Makkah (Mecca), 1,614,800. **Monetary unit:** Riyal. **Languages:** Arabic, English widely spoken. **Ethnicity/race:** Arab 90%, Afro-Asian 10%. **Religion:** Islam 100%. **Literacy rate:** 78% (2002 est.)

Economic summary: GDP/PPP (2001 est.): $241 billion; per capita $10,600. **Real growth rate:** 1.6%. **Inflation:** 1.7%. **Unemployment:** n.a. **Arable land:** 2%. **Agriculture**: wheat, barley, tomatoes, melons, dates, citrus; mutton, chickens, eggs, milk. **Labor force:** 7 million; note: 35% of the population in the 15–64 age group is non-national (July 1998 est.); agriculture 12%, industry 25%, services 63% (1999 est.). **Industries:** crude oil production, petroleum refining, basic petrochemicals, cement, construction, fertilizer, plastics. **Natural resources:** petroleum, natural gas, iron ore, gold, copper. **Exports:** $66.9 billion (f.o.b., 2001): petroleum and petroleum products 90%. **Imports:** $29.7 billion (f.o.b., 2001): machinery and equipment, foodstuffs, chemicals, motor vehicles, textiles. **Major trading partners:** U.S., Japan, South Korea, Singapore, India, Germany, Italy, UK.

Geography Saudi Arabia occupies most of the Arabian Peninsula, with the Red Sea and the Gulf of Aqaba to the west, and the Arabian Gulf to the east. Neighboring countries are Jordan, Iraq, Kuwait, Qatar, the United Arab Emirates, the Sultanate of Oman, Yemen, and Bahrain, connected to the Saudi mainland by a causeway. Saudi Arabia contains the world's largest continuous sand desert, the Rub Al-Khali, or Empty Quarter. Its oil region lies primarily in the eastern province along the Arabian Gulf.

Government Saudi Arabia was an absolute monarchy until 1992, at which time the Sa'ud royal family introduced the country's first constitution. The legal system is based on the *sharia* (Islamic law).

History Saudi Arabia is not only the homeland of the Arab peoples—it is thought that the first Arabs originated on the Arabian peninsula—but also the homeland of Islam, the world's second-largest religion. Muhammad founded Islam there, and it is the location of the two holy pilgrimage cities of Mecca and Medina. The Islamic calendar begins in 622, the year of the hegira, or Muhammad's flight from Mecca. A succession of invaders attempted to control the peninsula, but by 1517 the Ottoman Empire dominated, and in the middle of the 18th century, it was divided into separate principalities. In 1745 Muhammad ibn 'Abd al-Wahhab began calling for the purification and reform of Islam, and the Wahhabi movement swept across Arabia. By 1811, Wahhabi leaders had waged a *jihad*—a holy war—against other forms of Islam on the peninsula, and succeeded in uniting much of it. By 1818, however, the Wahhabis had been driven out of power again by the Ottomans and their Egyptian allies.

The kingdom of Saudi Arabia is almost entirely the creation of King Ibn Saud (1882–1953). A descendant of Wahhabi leaders, he seized Riyadh in 1901 and set himself up as leader of the Arab nationalist movement. By 1906 he had established Wahhabi dominance in Nejd and conquered Hejaz in 1924–1925. Hejaz and Nejd were merged to form the kingdom of Saudi Arabia in 1932, which was an absolute monarchy ruled by sharia, Islamic law. A year later the region of Asir was incorporated into the kingdom.

Oil was discovered in 1936, and commercial production began during World War II. Its wealth allowed the country to provide free health care and education while not collecting any taxes from its people. Saudi Arabia was neutral until nearly the end of the war, but it was permitted to be a charter member of the United Nations. The country joined the Arab League in 1945 and took part in the 1948–1949 war against Israel. Saudi Arabia still does not recognize the state of Israel. On Ibn Saud's death in 1953, his eldest son, Saud, began an 11-year reign marked by an increasing hostility toward the radical Arabism of Egypt's Gamal Abdel Nasser. In 1964, the ailing Saud was deposed and replaced by the premier, Crown Prince Faisal, who gave vocal support but no military help to Egypt in the 1967 Arab-Israeli war.

Faisal's assassination by a deranged kinsman in 1975 shook the Middle East, but it failed to alter his kingdom's course. His successor was his brother, Prince Khalid. Khalid gave influential support to Egypt during negotiations on Israeli withdrawal from the Sinai Desert. King Khalid died of a heart attack in 1982, and was succeeded by his half-brother, Prince Fahd bin 'Abdulaziz, who had exercised the real power throughout Khalid's reign. King Fahd, a pro-Western modernist, chose his 58-year-old half-brother, Abdullah, as crown prince.

Saudi Arabia and the smaller, oil-rich Arab states on the Persian Gulf, fearful that they might become Ayatollah Ruhollah Khomeini's next targets if Iran conquered Iraq, made large financial contributions to the Iraqi war effort during the 1980s. At the same time, cheating by other members of the Organization of Petroleum Exporting Countries (OPEC), competition from nonmember oil producers, and conservation efforts by consuming nations combined to drive down the world price of oil. Saudi Arabia has one-third of all known oil reserves, but falling demand and rising production outside OPEC combined to reduce its oil revenues from $120 billion in 1980 to less than $25 billion in 1985, threatening the country with domestic unrest and undermining its influence in the Gulf area.

At the start of 1996, King Fahd passed authority to Crown Prince Abdullah, saying he needed rest. Although not an abdication, it was unclear how long the king would be absent. In 1998 the country's oil income fell by 40% because of a worldwide decline in prices, and it entered its first recession in 6 years.

In 2000, Saudi Arabia, along with other OPEC nations experiencing a recession, decided to reduce production to raise oil prices. In 2001, OPEC cut oil production three additional times.

Saudi Arabia's relations with the U.S. were strained after the Sept. 11, 2001, terrorist attacks—15 of the suicide bombers involved were Saudis. Despite the monarchy's close ties to the West, much of the extremely influential religious establishment has supported anti-Americanism and Islamic militancy.

In March 2002, Crown Prince Abdullah of Saudi Arabia offered a Middle East peace plan at the annual Arab summit: all Arab governments would offer "normal relations and the security of Israel in exchange for a full Israeli withdrawal from all occupied Arab lands, recognition of an independent Palestinian state with noble Jerusalem as its capital, and the return of the Palestinian refugees." An extraordinary offer because it promised the backing of the entire Arab world, the Saudi plan nevertheless seemed unrealistic in the concessions it expected from Israel. And without a ceasefire, much less an agreement to negotiate between the Israelis and Palestinians, the plan languished.

In Aug. 2003, following the U.S.-led war on Iraq in March and April 2003, the United States withdrew its troops stationed in Saudi Arabia. The U.S. had maintained troops in the country for the past decade, a source of great controversy in the strongly conservative Islamic country. One of the major reasons for the Sept. 11 attacks, according to Saudi terrorist Osama bin Laden, was the presence of U.S. troops in the home of Islam's holiest sites, Medina and Mecca. On May 12, suicide bombers killed 34, including 8 Americans, at housing compounds for Westerners in Riyadh. Al-Qaeda was suspected. Saudi Arabia's commitment to antiterrorist measures was again called into question by the U.S. and other countries. In July, the U.S. Congress bitterly criticized Saudi Arabia's alleged financing of terrorist organizations and for harboring a civil servant who had ties to two of the Sept. 11 hijackers. While the government has arrested a sizeable number of suspected terrorists in the past year, it remains a hotbed of Islamic militancy.

Senegal

REPUBLIC OF SENEGAL

National name: République du Sénegal
President: Abdoulaye Wade (2000)
Prime Minister: Idrissa Seck (2002)
Area: 75,749 sq mi (196,190 sq km)
Population (2003 est.): 10,580,307 (growth rate: 2.5%); birth rate: 36.2/1000; infant mortality rate: 57.6/1000; density per sq mi: 140
Capital and largest city (2003 est.): Dakar, 2,476,400. **Monetary unit:** CFA Franc. **Languages:** French (official); Wolof, Serer, other ethnic dialects. **Ethnicity/race:** Wolof 36%, Fulani 17%, Serer 17%, Toucouleur 9%, Diola 9%, Mandingo 9%, European and Lebanese 1%, other 2%. **Religions:** Islam 94%, Christian 5%, indigenous 1% . **Literacy rate:** 39.1% (2001 est.)
Economic summary: GDP/PPP (2001 est.): $16.2 billion; per capita $1,580. **Real growth rate:** 5.7%. **Inflation:** 3%. **Unemployment:** 48% (urban youth 40%). **Arable land:** 12%. **Agriculture:** peanuts, millet, corn, sorghum, rice, cotton, tomatoes, green vegetables; cattle, poultry, pigs; fish. **Labor force:** n.a.; agriculture 70%. **Industries:** agricultural and fish processing, phosphate mining, fertilizer production, petroleum refining, construction materials. **Natural resources:** fish, phosphates, iron ore. **Exports:** $1 billion (f.o.b., 2001): fish, groundnuts (peanuts), petroleum products, phosphates, cotton. **Imports:** $1.3 billion (f.o.b., 2001): foods and beverages, consumer goods, capital goods, petroleum products. **Major trading partners:** France, India, Italy, Spain, Côte d'Ivoire, Nigeria, Germany, U.S.

Geography The capital of Senegal, Dakar, is the westernmost point in Africa. The country, slightly smaller than South Dakota, surrounds Gambia on three sides and is bordered on the north by Mauritania, on the east by Mali, and on the south by Guinea and Guinea-Bissau.

Senegal is mainly a low-lying country, with a semidesert area in the north and northeast and forests in the southwest. The largest rivers include the Senegal in the north and the Casamance in the south tropical climate region.

Government Multiparty democractic republic.

History The Toucouleur people, among the early inhabitants of Senegal, converted to Islam in the 11th century, although their religious beliefs retained strong elements of animism. The Portuguese had some stations on the banks of the Senegal River in the 15th century, and the first French settlement was made at Saint-Louis in 1659. Gorée Island became a major center for the Atlantic slave trade through the 1700s, and millions of Africans were shipped from there to the New World. The British took parts of Senegal at various times, but the French gained possession in 1840 and made it part of French West Africa in 1895. In 1946, together with other parts of French West Africa, Senegal became an overseas territory of France. On June 20, 1960, it became an independent republic federated with Mali, but the federation collapsed within four months.

Although Senegal is neither a large nor a strategically located country, it has nonetheless played a prominent role in African politics since its independence. As a black nation that is more than 90% Muslim, Senegal has been a diplomatic and cultural bridge between the Islamic and black African worlds. Senegal has also maintained closer economic, political, and cultural ties to France than probably any other former French African colony.

Senegal's first president, Léopold Sédar Senghor, towered over the country's political life until his voluntary retirement in 1981. He replaced multiparty democracy with an authoritarian regime. An acclaimed poet, Senghor sought to become a "black-skinned Frenchman," a quest he ultimately discovered to be impossible. An advocate of "African socialism," Senghor increased government involvement in the economy through a series of four-year plans.

In 1973 Senegal and six other nations created the West African Economic Community. When rising oil prices and fluctuations in the price of peanuts, a major export crop, ruined the economy in the 1970s, Senghor reversed course. He emphasized new industries such as tourism and fishing. Politically, the so-called passive revolution allowed limited opposition.

When the economy continued to stagnate, and with it Senghor's popularity, he resigned after 20 years at the helm in favor of his protégé, Abdou Diouf. Diouf, who led the country for the next 20 years, initiated further economic and political liberalization, including the sale of government companies and permitting the existence of political parties. In March 2000, opposition party challenger Abdoulaye Wade won 60% of the vote in multiparty elections. Diouf stepped aside in what was hailed as a rare smooth transition of power in Africa. In Jan. 2001, the Senegalese voted in a new constitution that legalized opposition parties and granted women equal property rights with men. In Sept. 2002, more than 1,100 passengers were killed when the state-owned *Joola* ferry sank. The government accepted responsibility for the disaster.

Serbia and Montenegro

SERBIA AND MONTENEGRO

President: Svetozar Marovic (2003)
Prime Minister: Dragisa Pesic (2001)
Area: 39,517 sq mi (102,350 sq km)
Population (2003 est.): 10,655,774 (growth rate: 0.2%); birth rate: 12.7/1000; infant mortality rate: 16.9/1000; density per sq mi: 95
Capital and largest city (2003 est.): Belgrade, 1,717,800 (metro. area), 1,285,200 (city proper). **Other large cities:** Pristina, 204,500; Novi Sad, 191,300; Nis, 174,000. **Monetary unit:** Yugoslav new dinar. **Languages:** Serbian 95%, Albanian 5%. What was once known as Serbo-Croatian is now known as Serbian, Croatian, or Bosnian, depending on the speaker's political and ethnic affiliation. It is written in Latin and Cyrillic. **Ethnicity/race:** Serbs 62.6%, Albanians 16.5%, Montenegrins 5%, Hungarians 3.3%, other 12.6%. **Religions:** Orthodox 65%, Islam 19%, Roman Catholic 4%, Protestant 1%, other 11%. **Literacy rate:** 93% (1991)
Economic summary: GDP/PPP (2001 est.): $24 billion; per capita $2,250. **Real growth rate:** 5%. **Inflation:** 40%. **Unemployment:** 30%. **Arable land:** 36%. **Agriculture:** cereals, fruits, vegetables, tobacco, olives; cattle, sheep, goats. **Labor force:** 3 million (2001 est.); agriculture n.a., industry n.a., services n.a. **Industries:** machine building (aircraft, trucks, and automobiles; tanks and weapons; electrical equipment; agricultural machinery); metallurgy (steel, aluminum, copper, lead, zinc, chromium, antimony, bismuth, cadmium); mining (coal, bauxite, nonferrous ore, iron ore, limestone); consumer goods (textiles, footwear, foodstuffs, appliances); electronics, petroleum products, chemicals, and pharmaceuticals. **Natural resources:** oil, gas, coal, antimony, copper, lead, zinc, nickel, gold, pyrite, chrome, hydropower, arable land. **Exports:** $2 billion (f.o.b., 2001 est.): manufactured goods, food and live animals, raw materials. **Imports:** $4.5 billion (f.o.b., 2001 est.): machinery and transport equipment, fuels and lubricants, manufactured goods, chemicals, food and live animals, raw materials. **Major trading partners:** Bosnia and Herzegovina, Italy, the Former Yugoslav Republic of Macedonia, Germany, Russia.

Geography Serbia and Montenegro together are about the size of the state of Kentucky and largely mountainous. The northeast section of Serbia is part of the rich, fertile Danubian Plain drained by the Danube, Tisa, Sava, and Morava River systems. Montenegro is a jumbled mass of mountains, containing also some grassy slopes and fertile river valleys.

Government In Feb. 2003, the Federal Republic of Yugoslavia was renamed Serbia and Montenegro. The former Yugoslavia, once an often volatile union of six republics, splintered in the 1990s from a brutal ten-year civil war. The renaming reflects the two remaining republics, Serbia and Montenegro. The new government will be a loose union, linked only by a small joint administration in charge of defense and foreign affairs.

History Renamed Serbia and Montenegro in 2003, the former Yugoslavia was formed on Dec. 4, 1918, from the patchwork of Balkan states and territories. World War I began there with the assassination of Archduke Franz Ferdinand of Austria at Sarajevo on June 28, 1914. The new kingdom of Serbs, Croats, and Slovenes included the former kingdoms of Serbia and Montenegro; Bosnia-Herzegovina, previously administered jointly by Austria and Hungary; Croatia-Slavonia, a semiautonomous region of Hungary; and Dalmatia, formerly administered by Austria. King Peter I of Serbia became the first monarch; his son, Alexander I, succeeded him on Aug. 16, 1921. Croatian demands for a federal state forced Alexander to assume dictatorial powers in 1929 and to change the country's name to Yugoslavia. Serbian dominance continued despite his efforts, amid the resentment of other regions. A Macedonian associated with Croatian dissidents assassinated Alexander in Marseilles, France, on Oct. 9, 1934, and his cousin, Prince Paul, became regent for the king's son, Prince Peter.

Paul's pro-Axis policy brought Yugoslavia to sign the Axis Pact on March 25, 1941, and opponents overthrew the government two days later. On April 6 the

Nazis occupied the country, and the young king and his government fled. Two guerrilla armies—the Chetniks under Draza Mihajlovic supporting the monarchy, and the Partisans under Tito (Josip Broz) leaning toward the USSR—fought the Nazis for the duration of the war. In 1943, Tito established an Executive National Committee of Liberation to function as a provisional government. Tito won the election held in the fall of 1945, as monarchists boycotted the vote. A new Assembly abolished the monarchy and proclaimed the Federal People's Republic of Yugoslavia, with Tito as prime minister. Tito ruthlessly eliminated the opposition and broke with the Soviet bloc in 1948. Yugoslavia followed a middle road, combining orthodox Communist control of politics and general overall economic policy with a varying degree of freedom in the arts, travel, and individual enterprise. Tito became president in 1953 and president-for-life under a revised constitution adopted in 1963.

After Tito's death on May 4, 1980, a rotating presidency designed to avoid internal dissension was put into effect immediately, and the feared clash of Yugoslavia's multiple nationalities and regions appeared to have been averted. In May 1991 Croatian voters supported a referendum calling for their republic to become an independent nation. A similar referendum passed in December in Slovenia. In June the respective Parliaments in both republics passed declarations of independence. Ethnic violence flared almost immediately. The largely Serbian-led Yugoslav military pounded breakaway Bosnia and Herzegovina, leading the UN Security Council in May 1992 to impose economic sanctions on the Belgrade government.

Despite rampant inflation reaching approximately 3,000% per month in Dec. 1993, the Serbian government of Slobodan Milosevic maintained its effective control over the rump Yugoslavia. Trade sanctions were lifted in Dec. 1995 following the signing of the Dayton Accords. In June 1996, the UN Security Council lifted its heavy weapons embargo. Large groups of demonstrators in 1996–1997 engaged in several months of daily protests after Slobodan Milosevic refused to recognize opposition victories in local elections and in elections in Montenegro. Constitutionally barred from another term as president of Serbia, Milosevic became president of the Federal Republic of Yugoslavia (Serbia and Montenegro) in July 1997.

The situation in Serbia's provinces of Montenegro and Kosovo grew divisive in 1997 and 1998. In May 1998, Montenegro elected the reform-minded Milo Djukanovic as president. Not only was he an outspoken critic of Yugoslav president Milosevic but he has openly contemplated secession.

In Feb. 1998 the Yugoslav army and Serbian police began fighting against the separatist Kosovo Liberation Army, but their scorched-earth tactics were concentrated on ethnic Albanian civilians—Muslims who make up 90% of Kosovo's population. More than 900 Kosovars were killed in the fighting, and the hundreds of thousands forced to flee their homes were without adequate food and shelter. Although Serbs make up only 10% of Kosovo's population, the region figures strongly in Serbian nationalist mythology.

NATO was reluctant to intervene because Kosovo—unlike Bosnia in 1992—was legally a province of Yugoslavia. The proof of civilian massacres finally gave NATO the impetus to intervene for the first time ever in the dealings of a sovereign nation with its own people. After months of negotiations led nowhere, on March 24, 1999, NATO began launching air strikes. Weeks of daily bombings destroyed significant Serbian military targets, yet Milosevic showed no signs of relenting. In fact, Serbian militia stepped up civilian massacres and deportations in Kosovo—by the end of the conflict, the UN high commissioner for refugees estimated that at least 850,000 people had fled Kosovo. The refugee crisis put a heavy burden on neighboring countries such as Albania and Macedonia. As effective as NATO airpower might be against Serbian targets, it was utterly helpless in preventing Serb soldiers and paramilitaries from wreaking havoc on Kosovo's civilians. The initial reason NATO gave for involvement in Kosovo was to avoid a wider Balkan war, but once Serbia began accelerating its campaign of ethnic cleansing in Kosovo, NATO's reason for fighting changed to preventing a human rights calamity. Yet without a concomitant change in military strategy—sending in ground troops—many wondered whether there would be any Kosovars left to save. NATO's hesitation in committing to a land battle—and therefore putting its troops at greater risk—ultimately paid off. Serbia finally agreed to sign a UN-approved peace agreement with NATO on June 3, ending the 11-week war.

In Sept. 2000, federal elections in Yugoslavia formally ended the autocratic rule of Milosevic, who had entangled his country in almost continuous war, first with the breakaway republics of Croatia and Bosnia (1991–1995) and then in the Serbian province of Kosovo in 1998. Despite dragging Yugoslavia into economic collapse and relegating it to pariah status throughout much of the world, Milosevic had managed to hold fast to the presidency after the Kosovo debacle.

In the Sept. 24 elections, Vojislav Kostunica, a constitutional law professor and political outsider, won the presidency in spite of widespread reports of fraud and voter intimidation. When Milosevic refused to honor the results and demanded a runoff election, the country erupted in massive public demonstrations, ultimately forcing Milosevic to step down on Oct. 5. But Kostunica was quick to assert himself as a true-believing Serb nationalist with no plans for becoming the darling of the West. He faced a daunting task in revitalizing the nation's shattered economy and in rebuilding the infrastructure destroyed during the NATO bombing.

Milosevic was arrested on April 1, 2001, by Yugoslavian authorities and charged with corruption and abuse of power, and in June he was turned over to the United Nations International Criminal Tribunal for the former Yugoslavia in The Hague, where he has been on trial throughout 2003, charged with genocide and crimes against humanity. The UN Security Council lifted the arms embargo on Yugoslavia in Sept. 2001, removing the last sanction by the international community against the country.

In March 2002, the nation agreed to form a new state, replacing Yugoslavia with a loose federation called Serbia and Montenegro, which went into effect Feb. 2003. The new arrangement was made to placate Montenegro's restive stirrings for independence and will allow Montenegro to hold a referendum on independence in three years' time. The loose federation will be linked only by a small joint administration in charge of defense and foreign affairs. On March 7, parliament elected a president of the new federation, Svetozar Marovic. In May 2003, Filip Vujanovic, a strong advocate of Montenegran independence, was elected Montenegro's president.

The prime minister of the Serbian state, Zoran Djindjic, a reformer who helped bring about the fall of Slobodan Milosevic, was assassinated on March 12. Extreme nationalists, organized crime, and Serbia's own police and security services were implicated.

Seychelles

REPUBLIC OF SEYCHELLES

President: France-Albert René (1977)
Area: 176 sq mi (455 sq km)
Population (2003 est.): 80,469 (growth rate: 1.0%); birth rate: 16.9/1000; infant mortality rate: 16.4/1000; density per sq mi: 458
Capital and largest city (2003 est.): Victoria, 23,000. **Monetary unit:** Seychelles rupee. **Languages:** English and French (both official), and Seselwa (a creole). **Ethnicity/race:** Seychellois (mixture of Asians, Africans, Europeans). **Religions:** Roman Catholic 86.6%, Anglican 6.8%, other Christian 2.5%, other 4.1%. **Literacy rate:** 58% (1971 est.)
Economic summary: GDP/PPP (2001 est.): $605 million; per capita $7,600. **Real growth rate:** 1.5%. **Inflation:** 6.1%. **Unemployment:** n.a. **Arable land:** 2%. **Agriculture:** coconuts, cinnamon, vanilla, sweet potatoes, cassava (tapioca), bananas; broiler chickens; tuna fish. **Labor force:** 30,900 (1996); industry 19%, services 71%, agriculture 10% (1989). **Industries:** fishing; tourism; processing of coconuts and vanilla, coir (coconut fiber) rope, boat building, printing, furniture; beverages. **Natural resources:** fish, copra, cinnamon trees. **Exports:** $182.6 million (f.o.b., 2001): canned tuna, cinnamon bark, copra, petroleum products (reexports). **Imports:** $360.2 million (f.o.b., 2001): machinery and equipment, foodstuffs, petroleum products, chemicals. **Major trading partners:** UK, Italy, France, Netherlands, South Africa, Singapore. **Member of Commonwealth of Nations**

Geography Seychelles consist of an archipelago of about 100 islands in the Indian Ocean northeast of Madagascar. The principal islands are Mahé (55 sq mi; 142 sq km), Praslin (15 sq mi; 38 sq km), and La Digue (4 sq mi; 10 sq km). The Aldabra, Farquhar, and Desroches groups are included in the territory of the republic.

Government Socialist multiparty republic.

History The Seychelles were uninhabited when the British East India Company became the first visitors to the archipelago in 1609. Thereafter, they became a favorite pirate haven. The French claimed the islands in 1756 and administered them as part of the colony of Mauritius. The British gained control of the islands through the Treaty of Paris (1814), and changed the islands' name from the French Séchelles to the Anglicized Seychelles.

The islands became self-governing in 1975 and independent on June 29, 1976. They have remained a member of the Commonwealth of Nations. Their first president, James Mancham, was overthrown in 1977 by the prime minister, France-Albert René. At first René created a socialist state with a one-party system, but later he reintroduced a multiparty system as well as various reforms.

To increase revenue the government in 1996 quietly initiated an Economic Citizenship Program that provides foreigners with the opportunity to obtain a Seychelles passport upon payment of $25,000. A new law in late 1995 granted immunity from criminal prosecution to anyone investing $10 million in the country.

In elections held in March 1998, President France-Albert René was reelected with 66.6% of the vote.

In Sept. 2001, President René was reelected for another five years, defeating Wavel Ramkalawan, an Anglican priest.

Sierra Leone

REPUBLIC OF SIERRA LEONE

President: Ahmad Tejan Kabbah (1998)
Area: 27,699 sq mi (71,740 sq km)
Population (2003 est.): 5,732,681, (growth rate: 2.3%); birth rate: 43.9/1000; infant mortality rate: 146.9/1000; density per sq mi: 207
Capital and largest city (2003 est.): Freetown, 1,051,000. **Monetary unit:** Leone. **Languages:** English (official), Mende, Temne, Krio. **Ethnicity/race:** 20 native African tribes 90% (Temne 30%, Mende 30%, other 30%), Creole, European, Lebanese, and Asian 20%. **Religions:** Islam 60%, Indigenous 30%, Christian 10%. **Literacy rate:** 31.4% (1995 est.)
Economic summary: GDP/PPP (2001 est.): $2.7 billion; per capita $500. **Real growth rate:** 3%. **Inflation:** 15%. **Unemployment:** n.a. **Arable land:** 7%. **Agriculture:** rice, coffee, cocoa, palm kernels, palm oil, peanuts; poultry, cattle, sheep, pigs; fish. **Labor force:** 1.369 million (1981 est.); note: only about 65,000 wage earners (1985). **Industries:** mining (diamonds); small-scale manufacturing (beverages, textiles, cigarettes, footwear); petroleum refining. **Natural resources:** diamonds, titanium ore, bauxite, iron ore, gold, chromite. **Exports:** $65 million (f.o.b., 2000 est.): diamonds, rutile, cocoa, coffee, fish. **Imports:** $145 million (f.o.b., 2000 est.): foodstuffs, machinery and equipment, fuels and lubricants, chemicals. **Major trading partners:** New Zealand, Belgium, U.S., France, Czech Republic, UK, Netherlands. **Member of Commonwealth of Nations**

Geography Sierra Leone, on the Atlantic Ocean in West Africa, is half the size of Illinois. Guinea, in the north and east, and Liberia, in the south, are its neighbors. Mangrove swamps lie along the coast, with wooded hills and a plateau in the interior. The eastern region is mountainous.

Government Constitutional democracy.

History The Bulom people were thought to have been the earliest inhabitants of Sierra Leone, followed by the Mende and Temne peoples in the 15th century, and thereafter the Fulani. The Portuguese were the first Europeans to explore the land and gave Sierra Leone its name, which means "lion mountains." Freetown, on the coast, was ceded to English settlers in 1787 as a home for blacks discharged from the British armed forces and also for runaway slaves who had found asylum in London. In 1808 the coastal area became a British colony, and in 1896 a British protectorate was proclaimed over the hinterland.

Sierra Leone became an independent nation on April 27, 1961. A military coup overthrew the civilian government in 1967, which was in turn replaced by civilian rule a year later. The country declared itself a republic on April 19, 1971.

A coup attempt early in 1971 led to then prime minister Siaka Stevens calling in troops from neighboring Guinea's army, which remained for two years. Stevens turned the government into a one-party state under the aegis of the All People's Congress Party in April 1978. In 1992 rebel soldiers overthrew Stevens's successor, Joseph Momoh, calling for a return to a multiparty system. In 1996, another military coup ousted the country's military leader and president. Nevertheless, a multiparty presidential election proceeded in 1996, and People's Party candidate Ahmad Tejan Kabbah won with 59.4% of the vote, becoming Sierra Leone's first democratically elected president.

But a violent military coup ousted President Kabbah's civilian government in May 1997. The leader of the coup, Lieut. Col. Johnny Paul Koroma, assumed the title "Head of the Armed Forces Revolutionary Council" (AFRC). Koroma began a reign of terror, destroying the economy and murdering enemies. The Commonwealth of Nations demanded the reinstatement of Kabbah, and ECOMOG, the Nigerian-led peacekeeping force, intervened. On March 10, 1998, after ten months in exile, Kabbah resumed his rule over Sierra Leone. The ousted junta and other rebel forces continued to wage attacks, many of which included the torture, rape, and brutal maimings of thousands of civilians, including countless children—amputation by machete is the horrific signature of the rebels. In addition to political power, the rebels are after control of Sierra Leone's rich diamond fields.

In Jan. 1999, rebels and Liberian mercenaries stormed the capital, demanding the release of the imprisoned Revolutionary United Front (RUF) leader, Foday Sankoh. ECOMOG regained control of Freetown, but President Kabbah later released Sankoh so he could participate in peace negotiations. Pressured by Nigeria and the U.S., among other countries, Kabbah agreed to an untenable power-sharing agreement in July 1999, which made Sankoh vice president of the country—and in charge of the diamond mines. The accord dissolved in May 2000 after the RUF abducted about 500 UN peacekeepers and attacked Freetown. Sankoh was captured and died in government custody in 2003, while awaiting trial for war crimes.

The conflict was officially declared over in Jan. 2002. An estimated 50,000 people were killed in the decade-long civil war. The UN installed its largest peacekeeping force in the country (17,000 troops). In May, President Kabbah was reelected with 70% of the vote.

Singapore

REPUBLIC OF SINGAPORE

President: S. R. Nathan (1999)
Prime Minister: Goh Chok Tong (1990)
Area: 267 sq mi (692.7 sq km)
Population (2003 est.): 4,608,595 (growth rate: 0.8%); birth rate: 12.8/1000; infant mortality rate: 3.6/1000; density per sq mi: 17,232
Capital and largest city (2003 est.): Singapore, 3,438,600. **Monetary unit:** Singapore dollar. **Languages:** Malay, Chinese (Mandarin), Tamil, English (all official). **Ethnicity/race:** Chinese 76.7%, Malay 14%, Indian 7.9%, other 1.4%. **Religions:** Islam, Christian, Buddhist, Hindu, Taoist. **Literacy rate:** 93.5% (1999)
Economic summary: GDP/PPP (2001 est.): $106.3 billion; per capita $24,700. **Real growth rate:** –2.2%. **Inflation:** 1.5%. **Unemployment:** 4.5%. **Arable land:** 2%. **Agriculture:** rubber, copra, fruit, orchids, vegetables; poultry, eggs, fish, ornamental fish. **Labor force:** 2.19 million (2000); financial, business, and other services 35%, manufacturing 21%, construction 13%, transportation and communication 9%, other 22%. **Industries:** electronics, chemicals, financial services, oil drilling equipment, petroleum refining, rubber processing and rubber products, processed food and beverages, ship repair, entrepot trade, biotechnology. **Natural resources:** fish, deepwater ports. **Exports:** $122 billion (f.o.b., 2001 est.): machinery and equipment (including electronics), consumer goods, chemicals, mineral fuels. **Imports:** $116 billion (2001 est.): machinery and equipment, mineral fuels, chemicals, foodstuffs. **Major trading partners:** Malaysia, U.S., Hong Kong, Japan, Taiwan, Thailand, China, South Korea, Germany, Netherlands, Saudi Arabia. **Member of Commonwealth of Nations**

Geography The Republic of Singapore consists of the main island of Singapore, off the southern tip of the Malay Peninsula between the South China Sea and the Indian Ocean, and 58 nearby islands.

Government Parliamentary republic.

History Inhabitants of the Malaysian peninsula and the island of Singapore first migrated to the area between 2500 and 1500 B.C. (*see* Malaysia). British and Dutch interest in the region grew with the spice trade, and the trading post of Singapore was founded in 1819 by Sir Stamford Raffles. It was made a separate Crown colony of Britain in 1946, when the former colony of the Straits Settlements was dissolved. The other two settlements on the peninsula—Penang and Malacca—became part of the Union of Malaya, and the small island of Labuan was transferred to North Borneo. The Cocos (or Keeling) Islands and Christmas Island were transferred to Australia in 1955 and in 1958, respectively.

Singapore attained full internal self-government in 1959, and Lee Kwan Yew, an economic visionary with an authoritarian streak, took the helm as prime minister. On Sept. 16, 1963, Singapore joined Malaya, Sabah (North Borneo), and Sarawak in the Federation of Malaysia. It withdrew from the Federation on Aug. 9, 1965, and a month later proclaimed itself a republic.

Under Lee, Singapore developed into one of the cleanest, safest, and most economically prosperous cities in Asia. However, Singapore's strict rules of civil obedience also drew criticism from those who said the nation's prosperity was achieved at the expense of individual freedoms.

S. R. Nathan was declared president without an election when he was certified as the only candidate eligible to run in 1999 elections. In Aug. 2003, Prime Minister Goh announced plans to resign, but said he would remain in office until the economy, which suffered a sharp downturn during the SARS outbreak, recovered.

Slovakia

REPUBLIC OF SLOVAKIA

President: Rudolf Schuster (1999)
Prime Minister: Mikulás Dzurinda (1998)
Area: 18,859 sq mi (48,845 sq km)
Population (2003 est.): 5,430,033 (growth rate: 0.1%); birth rate: 10.1/1000; infant mortality rate: 8.6/1000; density per sq mi: 288
Capital and largest city (2003 est.): Bratislava, 428,800. **Other large city:** Kosice, 233,600. **Monetary unit:** Koruna. **Languages:** Slovak (official), Hungarian. **Ethnicity/race:** Slovak 85.7%, Hungarian 10.6%, Roma 1.6%, Czech 1%, Ruthenian 0.3%, Ukrainian 0.3%, German 0.1%, Polish 0.1%. **Religions:** Roman Catholic 60.3%, atheist 9.7%, Protestant 8.4%, Orthodox 4.1%, other 17.5%. **Literacy rate:** 99%
Economic summary: GDP/PPP (2001 est.): $62 billion; per capita $11,500. **Real growth rate:** 3%. **Inflation:** 7.4%. **Unemployment:** 19.8%. **Arable land:** 31%. **Agriculture:** grains, potatoes, sugar beets, hops, fruit; pigs, cattle, poultry; forest products. **Labor force:** 3 million (1999); industry 29.3%, agriculture 8.9%, construction 8%, transport and communication 8.2%, services 45.6% (1994). **Industries:** metal and metal products; food and beverages; electricity, gas, coke, oil, nuclear fuel; chemicals and manmade fibers; machinery; paper and printing; earthenware and ceramics; transport vehicles; textiles; electrical and optical apparatus; rubber products. **Natural resources:** brown coal and lignite; small amounts of iron ore, copper and manganese ore; salt; arable land.

Exports: $12.5 billion (f.o.b., 2001 est.): machinery and transport equipment 39.4%, intermediate manufactured goods 27.5%, miscellaneous manufactured goods 13%, chemicals 8% (1999). **Imports:** $14.4 billion (f.o.b., 2001 est.): machinery and transport equipment 37.7%, intermediate manufactured goods 18%, fuels 13%, chemicals 11%, miscellaneous manufactured goods 9.5% (1999). **Major trading partners:** EU, Czech Republic, Russia (2000).

Geography Slovakia is located in central Europe. The land has rugged mountains, rich in mineral resources, with vast forests and pastures. The Carpathian Mountains dominate the topography of Slovakia, with lowland areas in the southern region. Slovakia is about twice the size of the state of Maryland.

Government Parliamentary democracy.

History Present-day Slovakia was settled by Slavic Slovaks about the 6th century. They were politically united in the Moravian empire in the 9th century. In 907, the Germans and the Magyars conquered the Moravian state, and the Slovaks fell under Hungarian control from the 10th century up until 1918. When the Hapsburg-ruled empire collapsed in 1918 following World War I, the Slovaks joined the Czech lands of Bohemia, Moravia, and part of Silesia to form the new joint state of Czechoslovakia. In March 1939, Germany occupied Czechoslovakia, established a German "protectorate," and created a puppet state out of Slovakia with Monsignor Josef Tiso as premier. The country was liberated from the Germans by the Soviet army in the spring of 1945, and Slovakia was restored to its prewar status and rejoined to a new Czechoslovakian state.

After the Communist Party took power in Feb. 1948, Slovakia was again subjected to a centralized Czech-dominated government, and antagonism between the two republics developed. On Jan. 1969, the nation became the Slovak Socialist Republic of Czechoslovakia.

Nearly 42 years of Communist rule for Slovakia ended when Vaclav Havel became president of Czechoslovakia in 1989 and democratic political reform began. However, with the demise of Communist power, a strong Slovak nationalist movement resurfaced, and the rival relationship between the two states increased. By the end of 1991, discussions between Slovak and Czech political leaders turned to whether the Czech and Slovak republics should continue to coexist within the federal structure or be divided into two independent states.

After the general election in June 1992, it was decided that two fully independent republics would be created. The Republic of Slovakia came into existence on Jan. 1, 1993. The Parliament in February elected Michal Kovac as president.

Vladimir Meciar, who served three times as Slovakia's prime minister, exhibited increasingly authoritarian behavior, and was cited as the reason Slovakia was eliminated from consideration for both the EU and NATO. A referendum in May 1997 on whether the country should join NATO was boycotted by 90% of the electorate after it turned into a showdown between the prime minister and the president, who wanted a question about direct election of the president placed on the ballot. For more than a year, Slovakia was without a president after Michal Kovac finished his term. Finally, the constitution was changed to allow for direct vote, and Rudolf Schuster was elected in May 1999.

Populist prime minister Meciar was unseated in 1998 elections by the reformist government of Mikulás Dzurinda. Meciar has been blamed for Slovakia's very low influx of foreign capital because of his government's lack of transparency. In April 2000 Meciar was arrested and charged with paying illegal bonuses to his cabinet ministers while in office. A three-week standoff with police preceded the arrest, ending only when police commandos blew open the door on Meciar's house and seized him. He was also questioned about his alleged involvement in the 1995 kidnapping of the son of Slovakia's former president, Michal Kovac.

Dzurinda has improved Slovakia's reputation in the West. The country will become both an EU and a NATO member in 2004. But Dzurinda's tough economic measures have made him unpopular within the country. In Sept. 2002 elections, the ruling coalition held onto power, despite Meciar coming out ahead in the vote.

Slovenia

REPUBLIC OF SLOVENIA

President: Janez Drnovsek (2002)
Prime Minister: Anton Rop (2002)
Area: 7,827 sq mi (20,273 sq km)
Population (2003 est.): 1,935,677 (growth rate: –0.1%); birth rate: 9.2/1000; infant mortality rate: 4.4/1000; density per sq mi: 247
Capital and largest city (2003 est.): Ljubljana, 258,000. **Other large city:** Maribor, 92,400. **Monetary unit:** Slovenian tolar. **Languages:** Slovenian; most can also speak Serbo-Croatian. **Ethnicity/race:** Slovene 88%, Serbo-Croatian 5%, Bosniak 1%, other 6%. **Religions:** Roman Catholic 70.8% (including 2% Uniate), Lutheran 1%, Islam 1%, other 27.2%. **Literacy rate:** 99%
Economic summary: GDP/PPP (2001 est.): $31 billion; per capita $16,000. **Real growth rate:** 4%. **Inflation:** 8.4%. **Unemployment:** 11.5%. **Arable land:** 11%. **Agriculture:** potatoes, hops, wheat, sugar beets, corn, grapes; cattle, sheep, poultry. **Labor force:** 857,400; agriculture n.a., industry n.a., services n.a. **Industries:** ferrous metallurgy and rolling mill products, aluminum reduction and rolled products, lead and zinc smelting, electronics (including military electronics), trucks, electric power equipment, wood products, textiles, chemicals, machine tools. **Natural resources:** lignite coal, lead, zinc, mercury, uranium, silver, hydropower, forests. **Exports:** $9.2 billion (f.o.b., 2001): manufactured goods, machinery and transport equipment, chemicals, food. **Imports:** $9.9 billion (f.o.b., 2001): machinery and transport equipment, manufactured goods, chemicals, fuels and lubricants, food. **Major trading partners:** Germany, Italy, Croatia, Austria, France, Hungary, Russia.

Geography Slovenia occupies an area about the size of the state of Massachusetts. It is largely a mountainous republic and almost half of the land is forested, with hilly plains spread across the central and eastern regions. Mount Triglav, the highest peak, rises to 9,393 ft (2,864 m).

Government Parliamentary democractic republic.

History Slovenia was originally settled by Illyrian and Celtic peoples. It became part of the Roman empire in the first century B.C.

The Slovenes were a south Slavic group that settled in the region during the 6th century A.D. During the 7th century, the Slavs established the Slavic state of Samu, which owed its allegiance to the Avars, who dominated the Hungarian plain until Charlemagne defeated them in the late 8th century.

When the Hungarians were defeated by the Turks in 1526, Hungary accepted Austrian Hapsburg rule in order to escape Turkish domination; the Hapsburg monarchy was the first to include all of the Slovene regions. Thus, Slovenia and Croatia became part of the Austro-Hungarian kingdom when the dual-monarchy was established in 1867. Like Croatia and unlike the other Balkan states, it is primarily Roman Catholic.

Following the defeat and collapse of Austria-Hungary in World War I, Slovenia declared its independence. It formally joined with Montenegro, Serbia, and Croatia on Dec. 4, 1918, to form the new nation called the Kingdom of the Serbs, Croats, and Slovenes. The name was later changed to Yugoslavia in 1929.

During World War II, Germany occupied Yugoslavia, and Slovenia was divided among Germany, Italy, and Hungary. For the duration of the war many Slovenes fought a guerrilla war against the Nazis under the leadership of the Croatian-born Communist resistance leader, Marshal Tito. After the final defeat of the Axis powers in 1945, Slovenia was again made into a republic of the newly established Communist nation of Yugoslavia.

In the 1980s, Slovenia agitated for greater autonomy and occasionally threatened to secede. It introduced a multiparty system and in 1990 elected a non-Communist government. Slovenia declared its independence from Yugoslavia on June 25, 1991. The Serbian-dominated Yugoslavian army tried to keep Slovenia in line and some brief fighting took place, but the army then withdrew its forces. Unlike Croatia and Bosnia, Slovenia was able to sever itself from Yugoslavia with relatively little violence. With recognition of its independence granted by the European Community in 1992, the country began realigning its economy and society toward western Europe. Slovenia will join the EU and NATO in 2004.

Solomon Islands

Sovereign: Queen Elizabeth II (1952)
Governor-General: Sir John Lapli (1999)
Prime Minister: Sir Allan Kemakeza (2001)
Area: 10,985 sq mi (28,450 sq km)
Population (2003 est.): 509,190 (growth rate: 2.8%); birth rate: 32.5/1000; infant mortality rate: 22.9/1000; density per sq mi: 46
Capital and largest city (2003 est.): Honiara (on Guadalcanal), 54,600. **Monetary unit:** Solomon Islands dollar. **Languages:** English, Solomon Pijin (an English pidgin), over 60 indigenous Melanesian languages. **Ethnicity/race:** Melanesian 93%, Polynesian 4%, Micronesian 1.5%, European 0.8%, Chinese 0.3%, other 0.4%. **Religions:** Anglican, Roman Catholic, South Seas Evangelical, Seventh-Day Adventist, United (Methodist) Church, other Protestant. **Literacy rate:** 30%
Economic summary: GDP/PPP (2001 est.): $800 million; per capita $1,700. **Real growth rate:** –10%. **Inflation:** 7.9%. **Unemployment:** n.a. **Arable land:** 1%. **Agriculture:** cocoa, beans, coconuts, palm kernels, rice, potatoes, vegetables, fruit; cattle, pigs; timber; fish. **Labor force:** 26,842; agriculture 75%, industry 5%, services 20% (2000 est.). **Industries:** fish (tuna), mining, timber. **Natural resources:** fish, forests, gold, bauxite, phosphates, lead, zinc, nickel. **Exports:** $165 million (f.o.b., 1999 est.): timber, fish, copra, palm oil, cocoa. **Imports**: $152 million (f.o.b., 1999 est.): plant and equipment, manufactured goods, food and live animals, fuels, chemicals. **Major trading partners:** Japan, China, Philippines, South Korea, UK, Thailand, Australia, New Zealand, U.S. **Member of British Commonwealth**

Geography A scattered archipelago of about 1,000 mountainous islands and low-lying coral atolls, the Solomon Islands lie east of Papua New Guinea and northeast of Australia in the south Pacific. The islands include Guadalcanal, Malaita, Santa Isabel, San Cristóbal, Choiseul, New Georgia, and the Santa Cruz group.

Government Parliamentary democracy.

History It is thought that people have lived in the Solomon Islands since at least 2000 B.C. Explored in 1568 by Alvaro de Mendana of Spain, the Solomons were not visited again for about 200 years. In 1886, Great Britain and Germany divided the islands between them, but later Britain was given control of the entire territory. The Japanese invaded the islands in World War II, and they became the scene of some of the bloodiest battles in the Pacific theater, most famously the battle of Guadalcanal. The British gained control of the island again in 1945. In 1976 the islands became self-governing, and gained independence in 1978.

Since early 1999, the Isatabu Freedom Movement, a militia group made up of indigenous Isatabus from Guadalcanal, have expelled more than 20,000 Malaitans from the island. The Malaitans had migrated from nearby Malaita, and many secured jobs in the capital, Honiara, stirring resentment among Isatabus that has grown steadily since independence. In response to the ethnic violence and expulsions, a rival Malaitan militia group was founded, the Malaita Eagle Force. In June 2000, the Malaita Eagle Force stole police weapons, forced Prime Minister Bartholomew Ulufa'alu to resign, and seized control of Honiara. The rival groups agreed to a cease-fire in June 2000, barely averting a civil war. Although a peace agreement has been signed and elections have taken place, the country continues to suffer from lawlessness. In July 2003, at the request of the prime minister, a 2,250-strong international peace-keeping force led by Australia arrived on the island to restore order, disarm the militias, and expel the "thieves, drunkards, and extortionists" from the notoriously corrupt police force. The warlord Harold Keke surrendered to Australian forces in August.

Somalia

SOMALI DEMOCRATIC REPUBLIC

National name: Jamhuuriyadda Soomaaliya
Prime Minister: Hassan Abshir Farah (2001)
Area: 246,199 sq mi (637,657 sq km)
Population (2003 est.): 8,025,190 (growth rate: 2.9%); birth rate: 46.4/1000; infant mortality rate: 120.3/1000; density per sq mi: 33
Capital and largest city (2003 est.): Mogadishu, 1,208,800. **Monetary unit:** Somali shilling. **Languages:** Somali (official), Arabic, English, Italian. **Ethnicity/race:** Somali 85%, Bantu, Arabs. **Religion:** Islam (Sunni). **Literacy rate:** 37.8% (2001 est.)
Economic summary: GDP/PPP (2001 est.): $4.1 billion; per capita $550. **Real growth rate:** 3%. **Inflation:** over 100% (businesses print their own money) (2000 est.). **Unemployment:** n.a. **Arable land:** 2%. **Agriculture:** cattle, sheep, goats; bananas, sorghum, corn, coconuts, rice, sugarcane, mangoes, sesame seeds, beans; fish. **Labor force:** 3.7 million (very few are skilled laborers) (1993 est.); agriculture (mostly pastoral nomadism) 71%, industry and services 29%. **Industries:** a few light industries, including sugar refining, textiles, petroleum refining (mostly shut down), wireless communication. **Natural resources:**

uranium and largely unexploited reserves of iron ore, tin, gypsum, bauxite, copper, salt, natural gas, likely oil reserves. **Exports:** $186 million (f.o.b., 1999 est.): livestock, bananas, hides, fish, charcoal, scrap metal (1999). **Imports:** $314 million (f.o.b.): manufactures, petroleum products, foodstuffs, construction materials, qat (1995). **Major trading partners:** Saudi Arabia, UAE, Yemen, Djibouti, Kenya, India.

Geography Somalia, situated in the Horn of Africa, lies along the Gulf of Aden and the Indian Ocean. It is bounded by Djibouti in the northwest, Ethiopia in the west, and Kenya in the southwest. In area it is slightly smaller than Texas. Generally arid and barren, Somalia has two chief rivers, the Shebelle and the Juba.

Government Between Jan. 1991 and Aug. 2000, Somalia had no working government. A fragile parliamentary government was formed Aug. 22, 2000.

History From the 7th to the 10th century, Arab and Persian trading posts were established along the coast of present-day Somalia. Nomadic tribes occupied the interior, occasionally pushing into Ethiopian territory. In the 16th century, Turkish rule extended to the northern coast, and the Sultans of Zanzibar gained control in the south.

After British occupation of Aden in 1839, the Somali coast became its source of food. The French established a coal mining station in 1862 at the site of Djibouti, and the Italians planted a settlement in Eritrea. Egypt, which for a time claimed Turkish rights in the area, was succeeded by Britain. By 1920, a British protectorate and an Italian protectorate occupied what is now Somalia. The British ruled the entire area after 1941, with Italy returning in 1950 to serve as United Nations trustee for its former territory.

By 1960, Britain and Italy granted independence to their respective sectors, enabling the two to join as the Republic of Somalia on July 1, 1960. Somalia broke diplomatic relations with Britain in 1963 when the British granted the Somali-populated Northern Frontier District of Kenya to the Republic of Kenya.

On Oct. 15, 1969, President Abdi Rashid Ali Shermarke was assassinated and the army seized power, dissolving the legislature and arresting all government leaders. Maj. Gen. Mohamed Siad Barre, as president of a renamed Somali Democratic Republic, leaned heavily toward the USSR. In 1977, Somalia openly backed rebels in the easternmost area of Ethiopia, the Ogaden Desert, which had been seized by Ethiopia at the turn of the century. Somalia acknowledged defeat in an eight-month war against the Ethiopians that year, having lost much of its 32,000-man army and most of its tanks and planes. President Siad Barre fled the country in late Jan. 1991. His departure left Somalia in the hands of a number of clan-based guerrilla groups, none of which trusted each other.

Africa's worst drought occurred in 1992, and coupled with the devastation of civil war, Somalia was plunged into a severe famine—an estimated one-third of the population was in danger of dying from starvation. U.S. troops were sent in to protect the delivery of food in Dec. 1992. In May the UN took control of the relief efforts from the U.S. The warlord Mohamed Farah Aidid ambushed UN troops and dragged American bodies through the streets, causing an about-face in America's willingness to involve itself in the fate of this anarchic country. Peace talks in Kenya appeared to be moving slowly but steadily toward an agreement on an interim government, at least in principle, when on March 23, 1994, they collapsed. The last of the U.S. troops left in late March, leaving 19,000 UN troops behind.

Since 1991 Somalia has been engulfed in anarchy. Years of peace negotiations between the various factions have been fruitless, and warlords and militias rule over individual swathes of land. In 1991, a breakaway nation, the Somaliland Republic, proclaimed its independence. Since then several warlords have set up their own ministates—Colonel Jama Ali Jama is president of breakaway Puntland, and Mohamed "General Morgan" Said Hersi has ruled Jubaland since the fall of 1998. Although internationally unrecognized, these states have been peaceful and stable.

In Aug. 2000, a parliament convened in nearby Djibouti and elected Somalia's first government in nearly a decade. After its first year in office, the new government still controlled only 10% of the country. But it had made significant advances for a country starting over: a national police force and army are in place and half of the 20,000 militias roaming the country have been demobilized.

In Nov. 2001, the U.S. froze the assets of Somalia's largest financial company, al-Barakaat, because of its alleged association with al-Qaeda terrorists. The company is a money-wiring business that transfers millions of dollars annually from Somali immigrants abroad to their relatives in Somalia. The freeze has severely damaged the fragile Somalian economy.

South Africa

REPUBLIC OF SOUTH AFRICA

National name: Republic of South Africa
President: Thabo Mbeki (1999)
Area: 471,008 sq mi (1,219,912 sq km)
Population (2003 est.): 42,768,678 (growth rate: 0%); birth rate: 18.9/1000; infant mortality rate: 60.8/1000; density per sq mi: 91
Administrative capital (2003 est.): Pretoria, 1,541,300 (metro. area), 1,249,700 (city proper); **Legislative capital and largest city:** Cape Town, 3,140,600 (metro. area), 2,733,000 (city proper); **Judicial capital:** Bloemfontein, 378,000. No decision has been made to relocate the seat of government. South Africa is demarcated into nine provinces, consisting of the Gauteng, Northern Province, Mpumalanga, North West, KwaZulu/Natal, Eastern Cape, Western Cape, Northern Cape, and Free State. Each province has its own capital. **Other large cities:** Durban/Pinetown, 2,396,100; Johannesburg, 1,675,200; East Rand, 1,378,792 (part of Johannesburg metro. area, 2000 est.). **Monetary unit:** Rand. **Languages:** Xhosa and Zulu (official), English, Afrikaans, Ndebele, Sesotho sa Leboa, Sesotho, Swati, Xitsonga, Setswana, Tshivenda. **Ethnicity/race:** black 75.2%, white 13.6%, Colored 8.6%, Indian 2.6%. **Religions:** Christian; Hindu; Islam. **Literacy rate:** 85% (2000 est.)
Economic summary: GDP/PPP (2001 est.): $412 billion; per capita $9,400. **Real growth rate:** 2.6%. **Inflation:** 5.8%. **Unemployment:** 37%. **Arable land:** 12%. **Agriculture:** corn, wheat, sugarcane, fruits, vegetables; beef, poultry, mutton, wool, dairy products. **Labor force:** 17 million economically active (2000); agriculture 30%, industry 25%, services 45%. **Industries:** mining (world's largest producer of platinum, gold, chromium), automobile assembly, metalworking, machinery, textile, iron and steel, chemicals, fertilizer, foodstuffs. **Natural resources:** gold, chromium, antimony, coal, iron ore, manganese, nickel, phosphates, tin, uranium, gem diamonds, platinum, copper, vanadium, salt, natural gas.

Exports: $32.3 billion (f.o.b., 2001 est.): gold, diamonds, platinum, other metals and minerals, machinery and equipment. **Imports:** $28.1 billion (f.o.b., 2001 est.): machinery, foodstuffs and equipment, chemicals, petroleum products, scientific instruments. **Major trading partners:** EU, U.S., Japan, Mozambique, Saudi Arabia.

Geography South Africa, on the continent's southern tip, is bordered by the Atlantic Ocean on the west and by the Indian Ocean on the south and east. Its neighbors are Namibia in the northwest, Zimbabwe and Botswana in the north, and Mozambique and Swaziland in the northeast. The kingdom of Lesotho forms an enclave within the southeast part of South Africa, which occupies an area nearly three times that of California.

The southernmost point of Africa is Cape Agulhas, located in the Western Cape Province about 100 mi (161 km) southeast of the Cape of Good Hope.

Government Republic.

History The San people were the first settlers. The Dutch East India Company landed the first European settlers on the Cape of Good Hope in 1652, launching a colony that by the end of the 18th century numbered only about 15,000. Known as Boers or Afrikaners, speaking a Dutch dialect known as Afrikaans, the settlers as early as 1795 tried to establish an independent republic.

After occupying the Cape Colony in that year, Britain took permanent possession in 1814 at the end of the Napoleonic Wars, bringing in 5,000 settlers. Anglicization of government and the freeing of slaves in 1833 drove about 12,000 Afrikaners to make the "great trek" north and east into African tribal territory, where they established the republics of the Transvaal and the Orange Free State.

The discovery of diamonds in 1867 and gold nine years later brought an influx of "outlanders" into the republics and spurred Cape Colony prime minister Cecil Rhodes to plot annexation. Rhodes's scheme of sparking an "outlander" rebellion, to which an armed party under Leander Starr Jameson would ride to the rescue, misfired in 1895, forcing Rhodes to resign. What British expansionists called the "inevitable" war with the Boers eventually broke out on Oct. 11, 1899. The defeat of the Boers in 1902 led in 1910 to the Union of South Africa, composed of four provinces, the two former republics, and the old Cape and Natal colonies. Louis Botha, a Boer, became the first prime minister. Organized political activity among Africans started with the establishment of the African National Congress in 1912.

Jan Christiaan Smuts brought the nation into World War II on the Allied side against Nationalist opposition, and South Africa became a charter member of the United Nations in 1945, but refused to sign the Universal Declaration of Human Rights. Apartheid—racial separation—dominated domestic politics as the Nationalists gained power and imposed greater restrictions on Bantus, Asians, and Coloreds (in South Africa the term meant any nonwhite person). African voters were removed from the voter rolls in 1936.

Afrikaner hostility to Britain triumphed in 1961 with the declaration on May 31 of the Republic of South Africa and the severing of ties with the Commonwealth. Nationalist prime minister H. F. Verwoerd's government in 1963 asserted the power to restrict the freedom of those who opposed rigid racial laws. Three years later, amid increasing racial tension and criticism from the outside world, Verwoerd was assassinated. His Nationalist successor, Balthazar J. Vorster, launched a campaign of conciliation toward conservative black African states, offering development loans and trade concessions.

Elections on May 7, 1987, increased the power of President P. W. Botha's Nationalist Party while enabling the far-right Conservative Party to replace the liberal Progressives as the official opposition. The results of the whites-only vote indicated a strong conservative reaction against Botha's policy of limited reform.

A stroke led Botha to step down as leader of his party in 1989 in favor of F. W. de Klerk. De Klerk accelerated the pace of reform. He removed the ban from the African National Congress, the principal anti-apartheid organization, and released Nelson Mandela, the ANC deputy president, after 27 years of imprisonment. Negotiations between the government and the ANC commenced.

On June 5, 1991, the Parliament scrapped the country's apartheid laws concerning property ownership. On June 17 the Parliament did the same for the Population Registration Act of 1950, which classified all South Africans at birth by race. In Feb. 1993 the ANC approved a plan that would allow minority parties to participate in the government for five years after the end of white rule. Also in February, the first nonwhites entered the cabinet in an apparent bid to broaden the base of the ruling National Party.

The 1994 election, the country's first multiracial one, resulted in a massive victory for Mandela and his ANC. The new government included six ministers from the National Party and three from the Inkatha Freedom Party.

In 1997 the Truth and Reconciliation Commission, chaired by Desmond Tutu, began hearings regarding human rights violations between 1960 and 1993. The commission promised amnesty to those who confessed their crimes under the apartheid system. In 1998 F. W. de Klerk, P. W. Botha, and leaders of the ANC appeared before the commission, and the nation continued to grapple with its enlightened but often painful and divisive process of national recovery.

Nelson Mandela, whose term as president cemented his reputation as one of the world's most enlightened statesmen, retired in 1999. On June 2, 1999, Thabo Mbeki, the pragmatic deputy president of South Africa and leader of the African National Congress, was elected president in a landslide, having already assumed many of Mandela's governing responsibilities.

In 2000 and 2001, Mbeki wrestled with a slumping economy, a skyrocketing crime rate, and the country's rising AIDS epidemic. South Africa, which has the highest number of HIV-positive people in the world (nearly 5 million), has been hampered in fighting the epidemic by its president's highly controversial views. Mbeki has denied the link between HIV and AIDS, claimed that the West has exaggerated the epidemic to sell drugs, and charged that Western AIDS activists consider "Africans to be germ carriers and human beings of a lower order." The international community as well as most South African leaders, including Nelson Mandela and Desmond Tutu, have admonished Mbeki on his lack of leadership in combating AIDS. Finally, in Aug. 2003, after years of delay, Mbeki reversed himself on his hands-off AIDS policy, promising a nationwide antiretroviral drug program that will prolong the life of AIDS victims.

Spain

KINGDOM OF SPAIN

National name: Reino de España
Ruler: King Juan Carlos I (1975)
Prime Minister: José María Aznar (1996)
Area: 194,896 sq mi (504,782 sq km)[1]
Population (2003 est.): 40,217,413 (growth rate: 0.1%); birth rate: 10.1/1000; infant mortality rate: 4.5/1000; density per sq mi: 206
Capital and largest city (2003 est.): Madrid, 5,130,000 (metro. area), 3,169,400 (city proper). **Other large cities:** Barcelona, 1,528,800; Valencia, 741,100; Seville, 679,100. **Monetary units:** Euro (formerly peseta). **Languages:** Castilian Spanish (official), Catalan, Galician, Basque. **Ethnicity/race:** composite of Mediterranean and Nordic types. **Religion:** Roman Catholic 94%. **Literacy rate:** 97%
Economic summary: GDP/PPP (2001 est.): $757 billion; per capita $18,900. **Real growth rate:** 2.8%. **Inflation:** 3.8%. **Unemployment:** 13%. **Arable land:** 28%. **Agriculture:** grain, vegetables, olives, wine grapes, sugar beets, citrus; beef, pork, poultry, dairy products; fish. **Labor force:** 17.1 million (2001); services 64%, manufacturing, mining, and construction 29%, agriculture 7% (2001 est.). **Industries:** textiles and apparel (including footwear), food and beverages, metals and metal manufactures, chemicals, shipbuilding, automobiles, machine tools, tourism. **Natural resources:** coal, lignite, iron ore, uranium, mercury, pyrites, fluorspar, gypsum, zinc, lead, tungsten, copper, kaolin, potash, hydropower, arable land. **Exports:** $118.6 billion (f.o.b., 2001 est.): machinery, motor vehicles; foodstuffs, other consumer goods. **Imports:** $150.5 billion (f.o.b., 2001 est.): machinery and equipment, fuels, chemicals, semifinished goods; foodstuffs, consumer goods (1997). **Major trading partners:** EU, Latin America, U.S., OPEC, Japan.

1. Including the Balearic and Canary Islands.

Geography Spain occupies 85% of the Iberian Peninsula, which it shares with Portugal, in southwest Europe. Africa is less than 10 mi (16 km) south at the Strait of Gibraltar. A broad central plateau slopes to the south and east, crossed by a series of mountain ranges and river valleys. Principal rivers are the Ebro in the northeast, the Tajo in the central region, and the Guadalquivir in the south. Off Spain's east coast in the Mediterranean are the Balearic Islands (1,936 sq mi; 5,014 sq km), the largest of which is Majorca. Sixty mi (97 km) west of Africa are the Canary Islands (2,808 sq mi; 7,273 sq km).

Government Parliamentary monarchy.

History Spain, originally inhabited by Celts, Iberians, and Basques, became a part of the Roman Empire in 206 B.C., when it was conquered by Scipio Africanus. In A.D. 412, the barbarian Visigothic leader Ataulf crossed the Pyrenees and ruled Spain, first in the name of the Roman emperor and then independently. In 711, the Muslims under Tariq entered Spain from Africa and within a few years completed the subjugation of the country. In 732, the Franks, led by Charles Martel, defeated the Muslims near Poitiers, thus preventing the further expansion of Islam in southern Europe. Internal dissension of Spanish Islam invited a steady Christian conquest from the north.

Aragon and Castile were the most important Spanish states from the 12th to the 15th century, consolidated by the marriage of Ferdinand II and Isabella I in 1469. The last Muslim stronghold, Granada, was captured in 1492. Roman Catholicism was established as the official state religion and most Jews (1492) and Muslims (1502) were expelled. In the era of exploration, discovery, and colonization, Spain amassed tremendous wealth and a vast colonial empire through the conquest of Peru by Pizarro (1532–1533) and of Mexico by Cortés (1519–1521). The Spanish Hapsburg monarchy became for a time the most powerful in the world. In 1588, Philip II sent his invincible Armada to invade England, but its destruction cost Spain its supremacy on the seas and paved the way for England's colonization of America. Spain then sank rapidly to the status of a second-rate power under the rule of weak Hapsburg kings, and never again played a major role in European politics. The War of the Spanish Succession (1701–1714) resulted in Spain's loss of Belgium, Luxembourg, Milan, Sardinia, and Naples. Its colonial empire in the Americas and the Philippines vanished in wars and revolutions during the 18th and 19th centuries.

In World War I, Spain maintained a position of neutrality. In 1923, Gen. Miguel Primo de Rivera became dictator. In 1930, King Alfonso XIII revoked the dictatorship, but a strong antimonarchist and republican movement led to his leaving Spain in 1931. The new constitution declared Spain a workers' republic, broke up the large estates, separated church and state, and secularized the schools. The elections held in 1936 returned a strong Popular Front majority, with Manuel Azaña as president.

On July 18, 1936, a conservative army officer in Morocco, Francisco Franco Bahamonde, led a mutiny against the government. The civil war that followed lasted three years and cost the lives of nearly a million people. Franco was aided by Fascist Italy and Nazi Germany, while Soviet Russia helped the Loyalist side. Several hundred leftist Americans served in the Abraham Lincoln Brigade on the side of the republic. The war ended when Franco took Madrid on March 28, 1939. Franco became head of the state, national chief of the Falange Party (the governing party), and premier and caudillo (leader). In a referendum in 1947, the Spanish people approved a Franco-drafted succession law declaring Spain a monarchy again. Franco, however, continued as chief of state.

In 1969, Franco and the Cortes (states) designated Prince Juan Carlos Alfonso Victor María de Borbón (who married Princess Sophia of Greece on May 14, 1962) to become king of Spain when the provisional government headed by Franco came to an end. Franco died of a heart attack on Nov. 20, 1975, after more than a year of ill health, and Juan Carlos was proclaimed king seven days later.

Under pressure from Catalonian and Basque nationalists, Premier Adolfo Suárez granted home rule to these regions in 1979. Basque separatists committed hundreds of terrorist bombings and kidnappings that continue to the present. With the overwhelming election of Prime Minister Felipe González Márquez and his Spanish Socialist Workers Party in the Oct. 20, 1982, parliamentary elections, the Franco past was finally buried.

Spain entered NATO in 1982. A treaty admitting Spain, along with Portugal, to the European Economic Community, now the European Union, took effect on Jan. 1, 1986. Later that year, Spain voted to remain in NATO but outside of its military command. General elections in March 1996 produced a victory for the conservative Popular Party, and its leader, José María Aznar, became prime minister. He and his party easily won reelection in 2000.

On Oct. 16, 1998, Spain issued a warrant for the extradition of former Chilean dictator Augusto Pinochet, charging him with the genocide, torture, and kidnapping of thousands of people, including Spanish nationals, during his 17-year rule. Eventually, Pinochet was returned to Chile where he was deemed unfit to stand trial.

In Aug. 2002, Batasuna, the political wing of the Basque terrorist organization ETA, was banned. The wisdom of driving the party underground instead of permitting it a legitimate political outlet has been questioned.

Aznar's backing of the U.S. war in Iraq was highly unpopular—90% of Spaniards opposed the war. (Spain sent no troops to Iraq during the war, but contributed 1,300 peacekeeping forces during the reconstruction period.) Yet his People's Party did extremely well in municipal elections in May 2003. The country's relative prosperity and the prime minister's tough stance against the ETA were thought to be responsible for the strong showing.

Sri Lanka

DEMOCRATIC SOCIALIST REPUBLIC OF SRI LANKA

President: Chandrika B. Kumaratunga (1994)
Prime Minister: Ranil Wickremesinghe (2001)
Area: 25,332 sq mi (65,610 sq km)
Population (2003 est.): 19,742,439 (growth rate: 1.0%); birth rate: 16.1/1000; infant mortality rate: 15.2/1000; density per sq mi: 779
Capital and largest city (2003 est.): Colombo, 2,436,000 (metro. area), 656,100 (city proper); **Legislative and Judicial capital:** Sri Jayawardenepura Kotte, 118,300. **Other large cities:** Dehiwala-Mount Lavinia 214,300; Moratuwa, 181,000; Kandy, 112,400. **Monetary unit:** Sri Lanka rupee. **Languages:** Sinhala (official), Tamil, English. **Ethnicity/race:** Sinhalese 74%, Tamil 18%, Moor 7%, Burgher, Malay, and Vedda 1%. **Religions:** Buddhist 70%, Hindu 15%, Christian 8%, Islam 7%. **Literacy rate:** 90.2% (1995 est.)
Economic summary: GDP/PPP (2001 est.): $62.7 billion; per capita $3,250. **Real growth rate:** –1%. **Inflation:** 14.2%. **Unemployment:** 7.7%. **Arable land:** 13%. **Agriculture:** rice, sugarcane, grains, pulses, oilseed, spices, tea, rubber, coconuts; milk, eggs, hides, beef. **Labor force:** 6.6 million (1998); services 45%, agriculture 38%, industry 17% (1998 est.). **Industries:** rubber processing, tea, coconuts, and other agricultural commodities; clothing, cement, petroleum refining, textiles, tobacco. **Natural resources:** limestone, graphite, mineral sands, gems, phosphates, clay, hydropower. **Exports:** $4.9 billion (f.o.b., 2001): textiles and apparel, tea, diamonds, coconut products, petroleum products. **Imports:** $6 billion (f.o.b., 2001): machinery and equipment, textiles, petroleum, foodstuffs. **Major trading partners:** U.S., UK, Middle East, Germany, Japan, India, Hong Kong, Singapore, South Korea. **Member of Commonwealth of Nations**

Geography An island in the Indian Ocean off the southeast tip of India, Sri Lanka is about half the size of Alabama. Most of the land is flat and rolling; mountains in the south-central region rise to over 8,000 ft (2,438 m).

Government Republic.

History Indo-Aryan emigration from India in the 5th century B.C. came to form the largest ethnic group on Sri Lanka today, the Sinhalese. Tamils, the second-largest ethnic group on the island, were originally from the Tamil region of India, and emigrated between the 3rd century B.C. and A.D. 1200. Until colonial powers controlled Ceylon (the country's name until 1972), Sinhalese and Tamil rulers fought for dominance over the island. The Tamils, primarily Hindus, claimed the northern section of the island and the Sinhalese, who are predominantly Buddhist, controlled the south. In 1505 the Portuguese took possession of Ceylon until the Dutch India Company usurped control (1658–1796). The British took over in 1796, and Ceylon became an English Crown colony in 1802. The British developed coffee, tea, and rubber plantations. On Feb. 4, 1948, after pressure from Ceylonese nationalist leaders (which briefly unified the Tamil and Sinhalese), Ceylon became a self-governing dominion of the Commonwealth of Nations.

S. W. R. D. Bandaranaike became prime minister in 1956 and championed Sinhalese nationalism, making Sinhala the country's only official language and including state support of Buddhism, further marginalizing the Tamil minority. He was assassinated in 1959 by a Buddhist monk. His widow, Sirimavo Bandaranaike, became the world's first female prime minister in 1960. The name *Ceylon* was changed to Sri Lanka on May 22, 1972, which was its original name and means "resplendent island."

The Tamil minority's mounting resentment toward the Sinhalese majority's monopoly on political and economic power, exacerbated by cultural and religious differences, erupted in bloody violence in 1983. By the end of 2001, the civil war, showing no signs of ceasing, had claimed 62,000 lives. Tamils make up about 18% of the population in Sri Lanka, whereas approximately three-quarters of Sri Lanka's 18 million people are Sinhalese. Tamil rebel groups, the strongest of which are the Liberation Tigers of Tamil Eelam, or Tamil Tigers, are fighting for a separate nation.

India had sent a peacekeeping force in July 1987 to help maintain an accord granting the Tamil minority limited autonomy. The agreement failed, and Indian troops withdrew at the end of 1989.

President Ranasinghe Premadasa was assassinated at a May Day political rally in 1993, when a Tamil rebel detonated explosives strapped to himself. Tamil extremists have frequently resorted to terrorist attacks against civilians and are renowned for suicide bombers that target government officials. The next president, Chandrika Kumaratunga, vowed to restore peace to the country. In Dec. 1999, she was herself wounded in a terrorist attack. By early 2000, 18 years of war had claimed the lives of more than 64,000, mostly civilians.

After Dec. 2001 elections, Ranil Wickremesinghe, a longtime bitter rival of President Kumaratunga, was sworn in as prime minister. Wickremesinghe's victory precipitated a formal cease-fire with the Tamil rebels. Norway brokered the fragile peace agreement, which was signed in Feb. 2002 by Wickremesinghe and rebel leader Velupillai Prabhakaran. In September talks, the government lifted its ban on the group, and the Tigers dropped their demand for an independent Tamil state. Another significant breakthrough came in December when the Tigers and the government struck a power-sharing deal that would give the rebels regional autonomy. But negotiations in 2003 achieved little. In June, a group of international donors pledged $4.5 billion in reconstruction aid to Sri Lanka on the condition that progress be made in the peace talks.

Sudan

REPUBLIC OF THE SUDAN

National name: Jamhuryat es-Sudan
President: Lt. Gen. Omar Hassan Ahmad al-Bashir (1989)
Area: 967,493 sq mi (2,505,810 sq km)
Population (2003 est.): 38,114,160 (growth rate: 2.7%); birth rate: 36.5/1000; infant mortality rate: 65.6/1000; density per sq mi: 39
Capital (2003 est.): Khartoum, 5,717,300 (metro. area),

1,397,900 (city proper). **Largest cities:** Omdurman, 2,103,900; Port Sudan, 450,400. **Monetary unit:** Dinar. **Languages:** Arabic (official), English, tribal dialects. **Ethnicity/race:** black 52%, Arab 39%, Beja 6%, foreigners 2%, other 1%. **Religions:** Islam (Sunni) 70%, indigenous 20%, Christian 5%. **Literacy rate:** 46.1% (1995 est.)

Economic summary: GDP/PPP (2001 est.): $49.3 billion; per capita $1,360. **Real growth rate:** 5.5%. **Inflation:** 10%. **Unemployment:** 18.7% (2002 est.). **Arable land:** 7%. **Agriculture:** cotton, groundnuts (peanuts), sorghum, millet, wheat, gum arabic, sugarcane, cassava (tapioca), mangos, papaya, bananas, sweet potatoes, sesame; sheep, livestock. **Labor force:** 11 million; agriculture 80%, industry and commerce 7%, government 13% (1998 est.). **Industries:** oil, cotton ginning, textiles, cement, edible oils, sugar, soap distilling, shoes, petroleum refining, pharmaceuticals, armaments, automobile/light truck assembly. **Natural resources:** petroleum; small reserves of iron ore, copper, chromium ore, zinc, tungsten, mica, silver, gold, hydropower. **Exports:** $2.1 billion (f.o.b.): oil and petroleum products, cotton, sesame, livestock, groundnuts, gum arabic, sugar. **Imports:** $1.6 billion (f.o.b.): foodstuffs, manufactured goods, refinery and transport equipment, medicines and chemicals, textiles, wheat. **Major trading partners:** Japan, China, Saudi Arabia, Germany, UK.

Geography The Sudan, in northeast Africa, is the largest country on the continent, measuring about one-fourth the size of the United States. Its neighbors are Chad and the Central African Republic on the west, Egypt and Libya on the north, Ethiopia and Eritrea on the east, and Kenya, Uganda, and Democratic Republic of the Congo on the south. The Red Sea washes about 500 mi of the eastern coast. It is traversed from north to south by the Nile.

Government Military government.

History What is now northern Sudan was in ancient times the kingdom of Nubia, which came under Egyptian rule after 2600 B.C. An Egyptian and Nubian civilization called Kush flourished until A.D. 350. Missionaries converted the region to Christianity in the 6th century, but an influx of Muslim Arabs, who had already conquered Egypt, eventually controlled the area and replaced Christianity with Islam. During the 1500s a people called the Funj conquered much of Sudan, and several other black African groups settled in the south, including the Dinka, Shilluk, Nuer, and Azande. Egyptians again conquered the Sudan in 1874, and after Britain occupied Egypt in 1882, it took over Sudan in 1898, ruling the country in conjunction with Egypt. It was known as the Anglo-Egyptian Sudan between 1898 and 1955.

The 20th century saw the growth of Sudanese nationalism, and in 1953 Egypt and Britain granted the Sudan self-government. Independence was proclaimed on Jan. 1, 1956. Since independence, the Sudan has been ruled by a series of unstable parliamentary governments and military regimes. Under Maj. Gen. Gaafar Mohamed Nimeiri, the Sudan instituted fundamentalist Islamic law in 1983. This exacerbated the rift between the Arab North, the seat of the government, and the black African animists and Christians in the South. Differences in language, religion, ethnicity, and political power erupted in an unending civil war between government forces, strongly influenced by the National Islamic Front (NIF), and the southern rebels, whose most influential faction is the Sudan People's Liberation Army (SPLA). Human rights violations, religious persecution, and allegations that the Sudan had been a safe haven for terrorists isolated the country from most of the international community. In 1995, the UN imposed sanctions against it.

On Aug. 20, 1998, the United States launched cruise missiles that destroyed a pharmaceutical manufacturing facility in Khartoum that allegedly manufactured chemical weapons. The U.S. contended that the Sudanese factory was financed by Islamic militant Osama bin Laden.

Since 1999 international attention has been focused on evidence that slavery is widespread throughout Sudan. Arab raiders from the north of the country have enslaved thousands of southerners, who are black. The Dinka people have been the hardest hit. Some sources point out that the raids intensified in the 1980s along with the civil war between north and south. Since the early 1990s, several international human rights organizations have engaged in the controversial practice of buying back slaves from the traders. Some contend this may inadvertently encourage slavery since slave redemption has become profitable. The antislavery organizations counter that in the absence of a political solution, buying back slaves is the only hope for thousands of Sudanese.

Ever since Bashir's military coup in 1989, the de facto ruler of Sudan had been Hassan el-Turabi, a cleric and political leader who is a major figure in the pan-Arabic Islamic fundamentalist resurgence. In 1999, however, Bashir ousted Turabi and placed him under house arrest. Since then Bashir has made overtures to the West, and in Sept. 2001, the UN lifted its five-year-old sanctions. The U.S., however, still officially considers it a terrorist state.

A cease-fire was declared between the Sudanese government and the Sudan People's Liberation Army (SPLA) in July 2002. During peace talks, which continued through 2003, the government agreed to a power-sharing government for six years, to be followed by a referendum on self-determination for the south. Much skepticism remains whether the government will make good on its promises—it has violated agreements made in 1997 and 1998 and seems determined to hold on to Sudan's oil fields, 75% of which are located in the south. Fighting on both sides continued throughout the peace negotiations. After 20 years of brutal civil war, more than 2 million people have died, mostly the result of starvation and disease.

Suriname

REPUBLIC OF SURINAME

President: Ronald Venetiaan (2000)
Prime Minister: Jules Ajodhia (2000)
Area: 63,039 sq mi (163,270 sq km)
Population (2003 est.): 435,449 (growth rate: 1.3%); birth rate: 19.4/1000; infant mortality rate: 24.7/1000; density per sq mi: 7
Capital and largest city (2003 est.): Paramaribo, 217,300. **Monetary unit:** Surinamese dollar . **Languages:** Dutch (official), Surinamese (lingua franca), English widely spoken. **Ethnicity/race:** East Indians, also known locally as Hindustanis (their ancestors emigrated from northern India in the latter part of the 19th century) 37%, Creole (mixed European and African ancestry) 31%, Javanese 15%, "Bush Negroes," also known as Maroons (their ancestors were brought to the country in the 17th and 18th centuries as slaves) 10%, Amerindian 2%, Chinese 2%, Europeans 1%, other 2%. **Religions:** Hindu 27.4%, Protestant 25.2%, Roman Catholic 22.8%, Islam 19.6%, indigenous about 5%. **Literacy rate:** 93% (1995 est.)
Economic summary: GDP/PPP (2000 est.): $1.5 billion; per capita $3,500. **Real growth rate:** –5.5%. **Inflation:** 59%. **Unemployment:** 20% (1997). **Arable land:** 0%.

Agriculture: paddy rice, bananas, palm kernels, coconuts, plantains, peanuts; beef, chickens; forest products; shrimp. **Labor force:** 100,000; agriculture n.a., industry n.a., services n.a. **Industries:** bauxite and gold mining, alumina production, oil, lumbering, food processing, fishing. **Natural resources:** timber, hydropower, fish, kaolin, shrimp, bauxite, gold, and small amounts of nickel, copper, platinum, iron ore. **Exports:** $399 million (f.o.b., 2000): alumina, crude oil, lumber, shrimp and fish, rice, bananas. **Imports:** $525 million (f.o.b., 1999): capital equipment, petroleum, foodstuffs, cotton, consumer goods. **Major trading partners:** U.S., Norway, Netherlands, France, Japan, UK, Trinidad and Tobago, Brazil.

Geography Suriname lies on the northeast coast of South America, with Guyana to the west, French Guiana to the east, and Brazil to the south. It is about one-tenth larger than Michigan. The principal rivers are the Corantijn on the Guyana border, the Marowijne in the east, and the Suriname, on which the capital city of Paramaribo is situated.

Government Constitutional democracy.

History Suriname's earliest inhabitants were the Surinen Indians, after whom the country is named. By the 16th century they had been supplanted by other South American Indians. Spain explored Suriname in 1593, but by 1602 the Dutch began to settle the land, followed by the English. The English transferred sovereignty to the Dutch in 1667 (the Treaty of Breda) in exchange for New Amsterdam (New York). Colonization was confined to a narrow coastal strip, and until the abolition of slavery in 1863, African slaves furnished the labor for the coffee and sugarcane plantations. Escaped African slaves fled into the interior, reconstituted their western African culture, and came to be called "Bush Negroes" by the Dutch. After 1870, East Indian laborers were imported from British India and Javanese from the Dutch East Indies.

Known as Dutch Guiana, the colony was integrated into the kingdom of the Netherlands in 1948. Two years later Dutch Guiana was granted home rule, except for foreign affairs and defense. After race rioting over unemployment and inflation, the Netherlands granted Suriname complete independence on Nov. 25, 1975. A coup d'état in 1980 brought military rule. During much of the 1980s Suriname was under the repressive control of Lieut. Col. Dési Bouterse. The Netherlands stopped all aid in 1982 when Suriname soldiers killed 15 journalists, politicians, lawyers, and union officials. Defense spending increased significantly, and the economy suffered. A guerrilla insurgency by the Jungle Commando (a Bush Negro guerrilla group) threatened to destabilize the country and was harshly suppressed by Bouterse. Free elections were held on May 25, 1991, depriving the military of much of its political power. In 1992 a peace treaty was signed between the government and several guerrilla groups. In March 1997, the president announced new economic measures, including eliminating import tariffs on most basic goods coupled with strict price controls. Later that year, the Netherlands said it would prosecute Bouterse for cocaine trafficking.

Public discontent over the 70% inflation rate prompted President Jules Wijdenbosch to hold elections in May 2000, one year ahead of schedule. The New Front for Democracy and Development, a coalition led by former president Ronald Venetiaan, won the election. Suriname has earned a reputation as a center for drug trafficking; in 1998, former dictator Bouterse was sentenced in absentia in the Netherlands for transporting cocaine. As of Jan. 2004, Suriname changed the name of its currency from the guilder to the dollar.

Swaziland

KINGDOM OF SWAZILAND

Ruler: King Mswati III (1986)
Prime Minister: Barnabas Sibusiso Dlamini (1996)
Area: 6,704 sq mi (17,363 sq km)
Population (2003 est.): 1,161,219 (growth rate: 0.8%); birth rate: 29.4/1000; infant mortality rate: 67.4/1000; density per sq mi: 173
Capital (2003 est.): Mbabane 69,000. **Largest city:** Manzini, 75,000. **Monetary unit:** Lilangeni. **Languages:** English and Swazi (official). **Ethnicity/race:** African 97%, European 3%. **Religions:** Christian 60%, indigenous 40%. **Literacy rate:** 78.3% (1999 est.)
Economic summary: GDP/PPP (2001 est.): $4.6 billion; per capita $4,200. **Real growth rate:** 2.5%. **Inflation:** 7.5%. **Unemployment:** 34% (2000 est.). **Arable land:** 10%. **Agriculture:** sugarcane, cotton, corn, tobacco, rice, citrus, pineapples, sorghum, peanuts; cattle, goats, sheep. **Labor force:** n.a. **Industries:** mining (coal), wood pulp, sugar, soft drink concentrates, textile and apparel. **Natural resources:** asbestos, coal, clay, cassiterite, hydropower, forests, small gold and diamond deposits, quarry stone, and talc. **Exports:** $702 million (f.o.b., 2001): soft drink concentrates, sugar, wood pulp, cotton yarn, refrigerators, citrus and canned fruit. **Imports:** $850 million (f.o.b., 2001): motor vehicles, machinery, transport equipment, foodstuffs, petroleum products, chemicals. **Major trading partners:** South Africa, EU, UK, Mozambique, U.S., Japan, Singapore. **Member of Commonwealth of Nations**

Geography Swaziland, which is about 85% the size of New Jersey, is surrounded by South Africa and Mozambique. The country consists of a high veld in the west and a series of plateaus descending from 6,000 ft (1,829 m) to a low veld of 1,500 ft (457 m).

Government Absolute monarchy.

History Bantu peoples migrated southwest to the area of Mozambique in the 16th century. A number of clans broke away from the main body in the 18th century and settled in Swaziland. In the 19th century these clans organized as a tribe, partly because they were in constant conflict with the Zulu. Their ruler, Mswazi, appealed to the British in the 1840s for help against the Zulu. The British and the Transvaal governments guaranteed the independence of Swaziland in 1881.

South Africa held Swaziland as a protectorate from 1894 to 1899, but after the Boer War, in 1902, Swaziland was transferred to British administration. The paramount chief was recognized as the native authority in 1941. In 1963, the territory was constituted a protectorate, and on Sept. 6, 1968, it became the independent nation of Swaziland.

Since 1986, King Mswati III has ruled as sub-Saharan Africa's last absolute monarch. Political parties are banned and the king appoints 10 of the 65 members of Parliament as well as the prime minister. King Mswati can veto any law passed by the legislature and frequently rules by decree.

With a modern infrastructure, Swaziland boasts one of the largest per capita manufacturing sectors in Africa. It is one of the few countries on the continent never to face an economic crisis severe enough to warrant imposition of a World Bank adjustment program. Many of the businesses in Swaziland moved there from South Africa in the 1980s in an effort to avoid international sanctions against apartheid.

In 2002, hundreds of thousands of Swazis faced starvation. Two years of drought as well as bad planning and agricultural practices were blamed for the crisis. The government came under criticism for buying the king a $50 million-dollar luxury jet—a quarter of the national budget—while famine loomed. In 2002, the country's judges resigned en masse in protest of the government's refusal to comply with court decisions. In April 2003, the government information minister announced that the media was banned from making negative remarks about the government—criticism of the king's new luxury jet in particular would not be tolerated.

Sweden

KINGDOM OF SWEDEN

National name: Konungariket Sverige
Sovereign: King Carl XVI Gustaf (1973)
Prime Minister: Göran Persson (1996)
Area: 173,731 sq mi (449,964 sq km)
Population (2003 est.): 8,878,085 (growth rate: –0.1%); birth rate: 9.7/1000; infant mortality rate: 3.4/1000; density per sq mi: 51
Capital and largest city (2003 est.): Stockholm, 1,622,300 (metro. area), 1,251,900 (city proper). **Other large cities:** Göteborg, 506,600; Malmö, 245,300; Uppsala, 127,300. **Monetary unit:** Krona. **Language:** Swedish. **Ethnicity/race:** white 88%, Lapp (Sami), foreign-born or first-generation immigrants (Finns, Yugoslavs, Danes, Norwegians, Greeks, Turks) 12%. **Religions:** Evangelical Lutheran 87%, Roman Catholic 1.5%, Pentecostal 1%, other 3.5%. **Literacy rate:** 99% (1979 est.)
Economic summary: GDP/PPP (2001 est.): $219 billion; per capita $24,700. **Real growth rate:** 1.6%. **Inflation:** 2.7%. **Unemployment:** 3.9. **Arable land:** 7%. **Agriculture:** barley, wheat, sugar beets; meat, milk. **Labor force:** 4.4 million; agriculture 2%, industry 24%, services 74% (2000 est.). **Industries:** iron and steel, precision equipment (bearings, radio and telephone parts, armaments), wood pulp and paper products, processed foods, motor vehicles. **Natural resources:** zinc, iron ore, lead, copper, silver, timber, uranium, hydropower. **Exports:** $96 billion (f.o.b., 2001 est.): machinery 35%, motor vehicles, paper products, pulp and wood, iron and steel products, chemicals. **Imports:** $89.2 billion (f.o.b., 2001 est.): machinery, petroleum and petroleum products, chemicals, motor vehicles, iron and steel; foodstuffs, clothing. **Major trading partners:** EU, U.S., Norway.

Geography Sweden, which occupies the eastern part of the Scandinavian peninsula, is the fourth-largest country in Europe, and is one-tenth larger than California. The country slopes eastward and southward from the Kjólen Mountains along the Norwegian border, where the peak elevation is Kebnekaise at 6,965 ft (2,123 m) in Lapland. In the north are mountains and many lakes. To the south and east are central lowlands and south of them are fertile areas of forest, valley, and plain. Along Sweden's rocky coast, chopped up by bays and inlets, are many islands, the largest of which are Gotland and Öland.

Government Constitutional monarchy.

History The earliest historical mention of Sweden is found in Tacitus's *Germania,* where reference is made to the powerful king and strong fleet of the Sviones. In the 11th century, Olaf Sköttkonung became the first Swedish king to be baptized as a Christian. Around 1400, an attempt was made to unite Sweden, Norway, and Denmark into one kingdom, but this led to bitter strife between the Danes and the Swedes. In 1520, the Danish king Christian II conquered Sweden and in the "Stockholm Bloodbath" put leading Swedish personages to death. Gustavus Vasa (1523–1560) broke away from Denmark and fashioned the modern Swedish state. He also confiscated property from the Roman Catholic Church in Sweden to pay Sweden's war debts. The king justified his actions on the basis of Martin Luther's doctrines, which were being accepted nationwide with royal encouragement. The Lutheran Swedish church was eventually adopted as the state church.

Sweden played a leading role in the second phase (1630–1635) of the Thirty Years' War (1618–1648). By the Treaty of Westphalia (1648), Sweden obtained western Pomerania and some neighboring territory on the Baltic. In 1700, a coalition of Russia, Poland, and Denmark united against Sweden and by the Peace of Nystad (1721) forced it to relinquish Livonia, Ingria, Estonia, and parts of Finland. Sweden emerged from the Napoleonic Wars with the acquisition of Norway from Denmark and with a new royal dynasty stemming from Marshal Jean Bernadotte of France, who became King Charles XIV (1818–1844). The artificial union between Sweden and Norway led to an uneasy relationship, and the union was finally dissolved in 1905. Sweden maintained a position of neutrality in both world wars.

An elaborate structure of welfare legislation, imitated by many larger nations, began with the establishment of old-age pensions in 1911. Economic prosperity based on its neutralist policy enabled Sweden, together with Norway, to pioneer in public health, housing, and job security programs. Forty-four years of Socialist government were ended in 1976 with the election of a conservative coalition headed by Thorbjörn Fälldin. The Socialists were returned to power in the election of 1982, but Prime Minister Olof Palme, a Socialist, was assassinated by a gunman on Feb. 28, 1986, leaving Sweden stunned. Palme's Socialist domestic policies were carried out by his successor, Ingvar Carlsson. Elections in Sept. 1991 ousted the Social Democrats (Socialists) from power. The new coalition of four conservative parties pledged to reduce taxes and cut back on the welfare state but not alter Sweden's traditional neutrality. In Sept. 1994 the Social Democrats emerged again after three years as the opposition party.

In a 1994 referendum voters approved joining the European Union. Although supportive of a European monetary union, Sweden decided not to adopt the euro when it debuted in 1999 and rejected it again overwhelmingly in a referendum in Sept. 2003.

The Social Democrat party, and its leader, Prime Minister Persson, easily won the Sept. 2002 elections. The center-left Social Democrats have run the government for 61 out of the last 71 years.

In Sept. 2003, Foreign Minister Anna Lindh, the highly popular foreign minister, was stabbed and killed by an unknown attacker.

Switzerland

SWISS CONFEDERATION

National name: Schweiz/Suisse/Svizzera/Svizra
President: Pascal Couchepin (2003)
Area: 15,942 sq mi (41,290 sq km)
Population (2003 est.): 7,318,638 (growth rate: 0.1%); birth rate: 9.6/1000; infant mortality rate: 4.4/1000; density per sq mi: 459
Capital (2003 est.): Bern, 122,700. **Largest cities:** Zurich, 971,800 (metro. area), 348,100 (city proper); Geneva, 178,900; Basel, 162,800; Lausanne, 117,400. **Monetary unit:** Swiss franc. **Languages:** German, French, Italian (all official), Romansch. **Ethnicity/race:**

German 65%, French 18%, Italian 10%, Romansch 1%, other 6%. **Religions:** Roman Catholic 46.1%, Protestant 40%, other 5%, no religion 8.9%. **Literacy rate:** 99% (1980 est.)

Economic summary: GDP/PPP (2001 est.): $226 billion; per capita $31,100. **Real growth rate:** 1.6%. **Inflation:** 1%. **Unemployment:** 1.8%. **Arable land:** 10%. **Agriculture:** grains, fruits, vegetables; meat, eggs. **Labor force:** 4 million; services 69%, industry 26%, agriculture 5% (1998). **Industries:** machinery, chemicals, watches, textiles, precision instruments. **Natural resources:** hydropower potential, timber, salt. **Exports:** $91.4 billion (f.o.b., 2001): machinery, chemicals, metals, watches, agricultural products. **Imports:** $91.4 billion (f.o.b., 2001): machinery, chemicals, vehicles, metals; agricultural products, textiles. **Major trading partners:** EU, U.S., Japan.

Geography Switzerland, in central Europe, is the land of the Alps. Its tallest peak is the Dufourspitze at 15,203 ft (4,634 m) on the Swiss side of the Italian border, one of 10 summits of the Monte Rose massif. The tallest peak in all of the Alps, Mont Blanc (15,771 ft; 4,807 m), is actually in France. Most of Switzerland is composed of a mountainous plateau bordered by the great bulk of the Alps on the south and by the Jura Mountains on the northwest. The country's largest lakes—Geneva, Constance (Bodensee), and Maggiore—straddle the French, German-Austrian, and Italian borders, respectively. The Rhine, navigable from Basel to the North Sea, is the principal inland waterway.

Government Federal republic.

History Called Helvetia in ancient times, Switzerland in 1291 was a league of cantons in the Holy Roman Empire. Fashioned around the nucleus of three German forest districts of Schwyz, Uri, and Unterwalden, the Swiss Confederation slowly added new cantons. In 1648 the Treaty of Westphalia gave Switzerland its independence from the Holy Roman Empire.

French revolutionary troops occupied the country in 1798 and named it the Helvetic Republic, but Napoleon in 1803 restored its federal government. By 1815, the French- and Italian-speaking peoples of Switzerland had been granted political equality.

In 1815, the Congress of Vienna guaranteed the neutrality and recognized the independence of Switzerland. In the revolutionary period of 1847, the Catholic cantons seceded and organized a separate union called the *Sonderbund*, but they were defeated and rejoined the federation.

In 1848, the new Swiss constitution established a union modeled upon that of the U.S. The federal constitution of 1874 established a strong central government while giving large powers of control to each canton. National unity and political conservatism grew as the country prospered from its neutrality. Its banking system became the world's leading repository for international accounts.

Strict neutrality was its policy in both world wars. Geneva was the seat of the League of Nations (later the European headquarters of the United Nations) and of a number of international organizations.

Allegations in the 1990s concerning secret assets of Jewish Holocaust victims deposited in Swiss banks led to international criticism and the establishment of a fund to reimburse the victims and their families.

Surprisingly, women were not given the right to vote or to hold office until 1971. Switzerland's first woman president—as well as the first Jew to assume the position—was Ruth Dreifuss in 1999.

In Sept. 2000, the Swiss voted against a plan to cut the number of foreigners in the country to 18% of the population (in 2000 foreigners made up 19.3%). Since 1970, four similar anti-immigration plans have failed. With unemployment at 1.8%, the lowest in eight years, few Swiss feel threatened by the economic repercussions of foreign workers.

On Sept 10, 2002, the Swiss abandoned their long-held neutrality to become the 190th member of the UN.

Syria

SYRIAN ARAB REPUBLIC

National name: Al-Jamhouriya al Arabiya As-Souriya
President: Bashar al-Assad (2000)
Prime Minister: Muhammad Naji al-Otari (2003)
Area: 71,498 sq mi (185,180 sq km)
Population (2003 est.): 17,585,540 (growth rate: 2.5%); birth rate: 29.5/1000; infant mortality rate: 31.7/1000; density per sq mi: 246
Capital (2003 est.): Damascus, 2,381,800 (metro. area), 1,861,900. **Largest cities:** Aleppo, 2,492,100 (metro. area), 1,933,700 (city proper); Homs, 751,500; Latakia, 417,100; Hama, 380,200. **Monetary unit:** Syrian pound. **Languages:** Arabic (official), French and English widely understood. **Ethnicity/race:** Arab 90.3%, Kurds, Armenians, and other 9.7%. **Religions:** Islam 90%, Christian 10%. **Literacy rate:** 70.8% (1997 est.)
Economic summary: GDP/PPP (2001 est.): $54.2 billion; per capita $3,200. **Real growth rate:** 2%. **Inflation:** 0.3%. **Unemployment:** 20% (2000 est.). **Arable land:** 26%. **Agriculture:** wheat, barley, cotton, lentils, chickpeas, olives, sugar beets; beef, mutton, eggs, poultry, milk. **Labor force:** 4.7 million; agriculture 40%, industry 20%, services 40% (1996 est.). **Industries:** petroleum, textiles, food processing, beverages, tobacco, phosphate rock mining. **Natural resources:** petroleum, phosphates, chrome and manganese ores, asphalt, iron ore, rock salt, marble, gypsum, hydropowerr. **Exports:** $5 billion (f.o.b., 2001 est.): crude oil 68%, textiles 7%, fruits and vegetables 6%, raw cotton 4% (1998 est.). **Imports:** $4 billion (f.o.b., 2001 est.): machinery and transport equipment 21%, food and livestock 18%, metal and metal products 15%, chemicals and chemical products 10% (2000 est.). **Major trading partners:** Germany, Italy, France, Turkey, Saudi Arabia, Lebanon, China, South Korea, U.S.

Geography Slightly larger than North Dakota, Syria lies at the eastern end of the Mediterranean Sea. It is bordered by Lebanon and Israel on the west, Turkey on the north, Iraq on the east, and Jordan on the south. Coastal Syria is a narrow plain, in back of which is a range of coastal mountains, and still farther inland a steppe area. In the east is the Syrian Desert, and in the south is the Jebel Druze Range. The highest point in Syria is Mount Hermon (9,232 ft; 2,814 m) on the Lebanese border.

Government Republic under a military regime since March 1963.

History Ancient Syria was conquered by Egypt about 1500 B.C., and after that by Hebrews, Assyrians, Chaldeans, Persians, and Alexander the Great of Macedonia. From 64 B.C. until the Arab conquest in A.D. 636, it was part of the Roman Empire except during brief periods. The Arabs made it a trade center for their extensive empire, but it suffered severely from the Mongol invasion in 1260 and fell to the Ottoman Turks in 1516. Syria remained a Turkish province until World War I.

A secret Anglo-French pact of 1916 put Syria in the French zone of influence. The League of Nations gave France a mandate over Syria after World War I, but the French were forced to put down several nationalist uprisings. In 1930, France recognized Syria as an independent republic but still subject to the mandate. After nationalist demonstrations in 1939, the French high commissioner suspended the Syrian constitution. In 1941, British and Free French forces invaded Syria to eliminate Vichy control. During the rest of World War II, Syria was an Allied base. Again in 1945, nationalist demonstrations broke into actual fighting, and British troops had to restore order. Syrian forces met a series of reverses while participating in the Arab invasion of Palestine in 1948. In 1958, Egypt and Syria formed the United Arab Republic, with Gamal Abdel Nasser of Egypt as president. However, Syria became independent again on Sept. 29, 1961, following a revolution.

In the Arab-Israeli War of 1967, Israel quickly vanquished the Syrian army. Before acceding to the UN cease-fire, the Israeli forces took control of the fortified Golan Heights. Syria joined Egypt in attacking Israel in Oct. 1973 in the fourth Arab-Israeli war, but was pushed back from initial successes on the Golan Heights and ended up losing more land. However, in the settlement worked out by U.S. secretary of state Henry A. Kissinger in 1974, the Syrians recovered all the territory lost in 1973 and a token amount of land, including the deserted town of Quneitra, lost in 1967.

In the mid-1970s Syria sent some 20,000 troops to support Muslim Lebanese in their armed conflict with Christian militants supported by Israel during the civil war in Lebanon. Syrian troops frequently clashed with Israeli troops during Israel's 1982 invasion of Lebanon and remained thereafter as occupiers of large portions of Lebanon.

The first Arab country to condemn Iraq's invasion of Kuwait, Syria sent troops to help defend Saudi Arabia from possible Iraqi attack.

In 1990, President Assad ruled out any possibility of legalizing opposition political parties. In Dec. 1991 voters approved a fourth term for Assad, giving him 99.98% of the vote.

In the 1990s, the slowdown in the Israeli-Palestinian peace process was echoed in the lack of progress in Israeli-Syrian relations. Confronted with a steadily strengthening strategic partnership between Israel and Turkey, Syria took steps to construct a countervailing alliance by improving relations with Iraq, strengthening ties with Iran, and collaborating more closely with Saudi Arabia. In Dec. 1999, Israeli-Syrian talks resumed after a nearly four-year hiatus, with the aging Assad (who would die seven months later) attempting to shore up his legacy. From Syria's point of view, normalization of relations between the two countries largely depended on Israel's withdrawal from the Golan Heights, which was territory that Israel had captured from Syria during the Arab-Israeli War of 1967. By Jan. 2000, however, talks broke down over just that issue.

On June 10, 2000, President Hafez al-Assad died. He had ruled with an iron fist since taking power in a military coup in 1970. His son, Bashar al-Assad, an ophthalmologist by training, succeeded him. He has emulated his father's autocratic rule.

In the summer of 2001, Syria withdrew nearly all of its 25,000 troops from Beirut. Syrian soldiers, however, remain in the Lebanese countryside.

In April 2003, shortly after the Iraq war wound down, the Bush administration turned its ire on Syria, calling the country a rogue nation that harbored members of Saddam Hussein's regime and possessed chemical weapons. The U.S. threatened diplomatic, economic, and unspecified "other" sanctions.

In Sept. 2003, the president appointed a new reformist prime minister, Muhammad Naji al-Otari, signaling a possible shift in Syria's political and economic policies.

Taiwan

REPUBLIC OF CHINA

President: Chen Shui-bian (2000)
Prime Minister: Yu Shyi-kun (2002)
Area: 13,892 sq mi (35,980 sq km)
Population (2003 est.): 22,603,000 (growth rate: 0.7%); birth rate: 12.7/1000; infant mortality rate: 6.7/1000; density per sq mi: 1,627
Capital and largest city (2003 est.): Taipei, 7,871,900 (metro. area), 2,722,600 (city proper). **Other large cities:** Kaohsiung, 1,514,900; Tai Chung, 1,069,900; Tainan, 755,800; Keelung, 410,500. **Monetary unit:** Taiwan dollar. **Language:** Chinese (Mandarin). **Ethnicity/race:** Taiwanese 84%, mainland Chinese 14%, aborigine 2%. **Religions:** mixture of Buddhist, Confucian, and Taoist 93%, Christian 4.5%, other 2.5%. **Literacy rate:** 94% (1998 est.)
Economic summary: GDP/PPP (2001 est.): $386 billion; per capita $17,200. **Real growth rate:** –2%. **Inflation:** 1%. **Unemployment:** 5%. **Arable land:** 24%. **Agriculture:** rice, corn, vegetables, fruit, tea; pigs, poultry, beef, milk; fish. **Labor force:** 9.8 million; services 56%, industry 36%, agriculture 8%. **Industries:** electronics, petroleum refining, chemicals, textiles, iron and steel, machinery, cement, food processing. **Natural resources:** small deposits of coal, natural gas, limestone, marble, and asbestos. **Exports:** $122 billion (f.o.b., 2001): machinery and electrical equipment 55%, metals, textiles, plastics, chemicals. **Imports:** $109 billion (f.o.b., 2001): machinery and electrical equipment 50%, minerals, precision instruments. **Major trading partners:** U.S., Hong Kong, Europe, Association of Southeast Asian Nations, Japan, South Korea.

Geography The Republic of China today consists of the island of Taiwan, an island 100 mi (161 km) off the Asian mainland in the Pacific; two off-shore islands, Kinmen (Quemoy) and Matsu; and the nearby islets of the Pescadores chain. It is slightly larger than the combined areas of Massachusetts and Connecticut. Taiwan is divided by a central mountain range that runs from north to south, rising sharply on the east coast and descending gradually to a broad western plain, where cultivation is concentrated.

Government Multiparty democracy.

History Taiwan was inhabited by aborigines of Malayan descent when Chinese from the areas now designated as Fukien and Kwangtung began settling it in the 7th century, becoming the majority. The Portuguese explored the area in 1590, naming it "the Beautiful" (Formosa). In 1624 the Dutch set up forts in the south, the Spanish in the north. The Dutch forced out the Spanish in 1641 and controlled the island until 1661, when Chinese general Koxinga took it over and established an independent kingdom. The Manchus seized the island in 1683 and held it until 1895, when it passed to Japan after the first Sino-Japanese War. Japan developed and exploited Formosa. It was the target of heavy American bombing during World War II, and at the close of the war the island was restored to China.

After the defeat of its armies on the mainland, the Nationalist government of Generalissimo Chiang Kai-shek retreated to Taiwan in Dec. 1949. Chiang dominated the island, even though only 15% of the population consisted of the 1949 immigrants, the Kuomintang. He maintained a 600,000-man army in the hope of eventually recovering the mainland. Beijing viewed the Taiwanese government with suspicion and anger, referring to Taiwan as a breakaway province of China.

The UN seat representing all of China was held by the Nationalists for over two decades before being lost in Oct. 1971, when the People's Republic of China was admitted and Taiwan was forced to abdicate its seat to Beijing.

Chiang died at 87 of a heart attack on April 5, 1975. His son, Chiang Ching-kuo, continued as premier and was a dominant figure in the Taipei regime. In April 1991, President Lee Teng-hui formally declared an end to emergency rule, which had existed since Chiang's forces originally occupied the island. In the first full election in many decades, the governing Kuomintang in Dec. 1991 won 71% of the vote, affirming the island's opposition to reunification with China. In Feb. 1993 the president, himself a native Taiwanese, nominated Lien Chan, another native, to be prime minister, marking a further generational shift away from the mainland exiles.

In the island's first free presidential election, voters defied mainland intimidation and gave 54% of the vote to incumbent president Lee Teng-hui. The second-place finisher, with 21%, advocated complete independence from China.

In 1998, Taiwan renewed its push for a separate UN seat—its sixth attempt in recent years. The move has been blocked each time by the Beijing government.

President Lee Teng-hui rankled mainland China by announcing in July 1999 that he was abandoning the longstanding "One China" policy that has kept the peace between the small island and its powerful neighbor, and would from now on deal with China on a "state-to-state basis." China, which has vowed to someday unite Taiwan with the mainland, has threatened to use force against Taiwan, and in late August conducted submarine warfare exercises and missile tests near the island in an effort to intimidate its tiny brazen neighbor, as it had once before in 1996.

In March 2000 elections voters elected pro-independence candidate Chen Shui-bian of the Democratic Progressive Party, ending more than 50 years of Nationalist rule.

Taiwan joined the World Trade Organization in Jan. 2002, just one day after China gained entry. In August President Chen outraged China when he asserted that Taiwan and China are separate countries and that a referendum on independence for Taiwan is a "basic human right."

Tajikistan

REPUBLIC OF TAJIKISTAN

President: Imomali Rakhmonov (1992)
Prime Minister: Akil Akilov (1999)
Area: 55,251 sq mi (143,100 sq km)
Population (2003 est.): 6,863,752 (growth rate: 2.4%); birth rate: 32.8/1000; infant mortality rate: 113.4/1000; density per sq mi: 124
Capital and largest city (2003 est.): Dushanbe, 817,100 (metro. area), 590,300 (city proper). **Other large city:** Khodzhent (Leninabad), 156,500. **Monetary unit:** Tajik ruble. **Language:** Tajik. **Ethnicity/race:** Tajik 64.9%, Uzbek 25%, Russian 3.5% (declining because of emigration), other 6.6%. **Religion:** Sunni Muslim 85%. **Literacy rate:** 98% (1989 est.)
Economic summary: GDP/PPP (2001 est.): $7.5 billion; per capita $1,140. **Real growth rate:** 8.3%. **Inflation:** 33%. **Unemployment:** 20%. **Arable land:** 5%. **Agriculture:** cotton, grain, fruits, grapes, vegetables; cattle, sheep, goats. **Labor force:** 3.187 million (2000); agriculture 67%, industry 8%, services 25% (2000 est.). **Industries:** aluminum, zinc, lead, chemicals and fertilizers, cement, vegetable oil, metal-cutting machine tools, refrigerators and freezers. **Natural resources:** hydropower, some petroleum, uranium, mercury, brown coal, lead, zinc, antimony, tungsten, silver, gold. **Exports:** $640 million (f.o.b., 2001 est.): aluminum, electricity, cotton, fruits, vegetable oil, textiles. **Imports:** $700 million (f.o.b., 2001 est.): electricity, petroleum products, aluminum oxide, machinery and equipment, foodstuffs. **Major trading partners:** Europe, Russia, Uzbekistan.

Geography Ninety-three percent of Tajikistan's territory is mountainous, and the mountain glaciers are the source of its rivers. Tajikistan is an earthquake-prone area. The republic is bounded by China in the east, Afghanistan to the south, Uzbekistan and Kyrgyzstan to the west and north. The central Asian republic also includes the Gorno-Badakh Shan Autonomous region. Tajikistan is slightly larger than the state of Illinois.

Government Republic.

History The Tajiks, whose language is nearly identical with Persian, were part of the ancient Persian empire that was ruled by Darius I and later conquered by Alexander the Great (333 B.C.). In the 7th and 8th centuries, Arabs conquered the region and brought Islam. The Tajiks were successively ruled by Uzbeks and then Afghans until claimed by Russia in the 1860s. In 1924, Tajikistan was consolidated into a newly formed Tajik Autonomous Soviet Socialist Republic, which was administratively part of the Uzbek SSR until the Tajik ASSR gained full-fledged republic status in 1929.

Tajikistan declared its sovereignty in Aug. 1990. In 1991, the republic's Communist leadership supported the attempted coup against Soviet president Mikhail Gorbachev. Tajikistan joined with ten other former Soviet republics in the Commonwealth of Independent States on Dec. 21, 1991. A parliamentary republic was proclaimed and presidential rule abolished in Nov. 1992. After independence, Tajikistan experienced sporadic conflict as the Communist-dominated government struggled to combat an insurgency by Islamic and democratic opposition forces. Despite continued international efforts to end the civil war, periodic fighting continued. About 60,000 people lost their lives in Tajikistan's civil war. The conflict ended officially on June 27, 1997, with the signing in Moscow of peace accords between the government of President Imomali Rakhmonov and the United Tajik Opposition (UTO), a coalition of largely Islamic groups. Since then, however, peace has been tenuous, marred regularly by killing sprees by various opposition groups.

In 2000, Tajikistan allowed approximately 25,000 Russian troops into the country to help stem the violence by helping to patrol the long border with Taliban-run Afghanistan. The Tajiks had long supported Afghanistan's Northern Alliance fighters in their battle against the militantly Islamist Taliban, and the Taliban's fall in Dec. 2001 has returned a measure of security to this war-ravaged and impoverished country.

A referendum in June 2003 extended the president's term in office for an additional 14 years. Opposition parties cried foul.

Tanzania

UNITED REPUBLIC OF TANZANIA

President: Benjamin William Mkapa (1995)
Prime Minister: Frederick Tluway Sumaye (1995)
Area: 364,898 sq mi (945,087 sq km)[1]
Population (2003 est.): 35,922,454 (growth rate: 2.2%); birth rate: 39.5/1000; infant mortality rate: 103.7/1000; density per sq mi: 98
Administrative capital and largest city (2003 est.): Dar es Salaam, 2,489,800; **Official capital:** Dodoma, 164,500. **Monetary unit:** Tanzanian shilling. **Languages:** Swahili and English (both official), local languages. **Ethnicity/race:** mainland: native African (95% Bantu, consisting of well over 100 tribes) 99%, Asian, European, and Arab 1%. Zanzibar: Arab, mixed Arab and native African, native African. **Religions:** mainland: Christian 30%, Islam 35%, indigenous 35%; Zanzibar: Islam, 99% . **Literacy rate:** 67.8% (1995 est.)
Economic summary: GDP/PPP (2001 est.): $22.1 billion; per capita $610. **Real growth rate:** 5%. **Inflation:** 5% **Unemployment:** n.a. **Arable land:** 4%. **Agriculture:** coffee, sisal, tea, cotton, pyrethrum (insecticide made from chrysanthemums), cashew nuts, tobacco, cloves (Zanzibar), corn, wheat, cassava (tapioca), bananas, fruits, vegetables; cattle, sheep, goats. **Labor force:** 13.495 million; agriculture 80%, industry and commerce 20% (2000 est.). **Industries:** primarily agricultural processing (sugar, beer, cigarettes, sisal twine), diamond and gold mining, oil refining, shoes, cement, textiles, wood products, fertilizer, salt. **Natural resources:** hydropower, tin, phosphates, iron ore, coal, diamonds, gemstones, gold, natural gas, nickel. **Exports:** $827 million (f.o.b., 2001): gold, coffee, cashew nuts, manufactures, cotton (2000). **Imports:** $1.55 billion (f.o.b., 2001): consumer goods, machinery and transportation equipment, industrial raw materials, crude oil. **Major trading partners:** UK, India, Germany, Netherlands, South Africa, Japan, Australia. **Member of Commonwealth of Nations**

1. Including Zanzibar.

Geography Tanzania is in East Africa on the Indian Ocean. To the north are Uganda and Kenya; to the west, Burundi, Rwanda, and Congo; and to the south, Mozambique, Zambia, and Malawi. Its area is three times that of New Mexico. Tanzania contains three of Africa's best-known lakes—Victoria in the north, Tanganyika in the west, and Nyasa in the south. Mount Kilimanjaro in the north, 19,340 ft (5,895 m), is the highest point on the continent. The island of Zanzibar is separated from the mainland by a 22-mile channel.

Government Republic.

History Arab traders first began to colonize the area in 700. Portuguese explorers reached the coastal regions in 1500 and held some control until the 17th century, when the sultan of Oman took power. With what are now Burundi and Rwanda, Tanganyika became the colony of German East Africa in 1885. After World War I, it was administered by Britain under a League of Nations mandate and later as a UN trust territory.

Although not mentioned in old histories until the 12th century, Zanzibar was always believed to have had connections with southern Arabia. The Portuguese made it one of their tributaries in 1503 and later established a trading post, but they were driven from Oman by Arabs in 1698. Zanzibar was declared independent of Oman in 1861 and, in 1890, it became a British protectorate.

Tanganyika became independent on Dec. 9, 1961; Zanzibar on Dec. 10, 1963. On April 26, 1964, the two nations merged into the United Republic of Tanganyika and Zanzibar. The name was changed to Tanzania six months later.

An invasion by Ugandan troops in Nov. 1978 was followed by a counterattack in Jan. 1979, in which 5,000 Tanzanian troops were joined by 3,000 Ugandan exiles opposed to President Idi Amin. Within a month, full-scale war developed. Tanzanian president Julius Nyerere kept troops in Uganda in open support of former Ugandan president Milton Obote, despite protests from opposition groups, until the national elections in Dec. 1980.

In Nov. 1985, Nyerere stepped down as president. Ali Hassan Mwinyi, his vice president, succeeded him. Running unopposed, Mwinyi was elected president in October. Shortly thereafter plans were announced to study the benefits of instituting a multiparty democracy, and in Oct. 1995 the country's first multiparty elections since independence took place.

On Aug. 7, 1998, the U.S. embassy in Dar es Salaam was bombed by terrorists, killing ten. The same day an even more devastating explosion destroyed the U.S. embassy in neighboring Kenya.

Since taking office in 1995 President Benjamin William Mkapa has sought to increase economic productivity while dealing with serious pollution problems and deforestation. With more than one million people infected with HIV, AIDS care and prevention have been major public health issues. On foreign policy, Tanzania has taken a leading diplomatic role in East Africa, hosting peace talks for the factions fighting in neighboring Burundi. The UN International Criminal Tribunal for Rwanda (ICTR) is located in the town of Arusha. In Oct. 2000, Mkapa was easily reelected.

Thailand

KINGDOM OF THAILAND

Ruler: King Bhumibol Adulyadej (1946)
Prime Minister: Thaksin Shinawatra (2001)
Area: 198,455 sq mi (514,000 sq km)
Population (2003 est.): 64,265,276 (growth rate: 1.0%); birth rate: 16.4/1000; infant mortality rate: 21.8/1000; density per sq mi: 324
Capital and largest city (2003 est.): Bangkok, 8,838,500 (metro. area), 6,610,800 (city proper). **Other large cities:** Nonthanburi, 304,700; Chiang Mai, 175,500. **Monetary unit:** baht. **Languages:** Thai (Siamese), Chinese, English. **Ethnicity/race:** Thai 75%, Chinese 14%, other 11%. **Religions:** Buddhist 95%, Islam 3.8%, Christian 0.5%, Hindu 0.1%, other 0.6%. **Literacy rate:** 93.8% (1995 est.)
Economic summary: GDP/PPP (2001 est.): $410 billion; per capita $6,600. **Real growth rate:** 1.4%. **Inflation:** 1.6%. **Unemployment:** 3.9%. **Arable land:** 33%. **Agriculture:** rice, cassava (tapioca), rubber, corn, sugarcane, coconuts, soybeans. **Labor force:** 33.4 million; agriculture 54%, industry 15%, services 31%. **Industries:** tourism; textiles and garments, agricultural processing, beverages, tobacco, cement, light manufacturing, such as jewelry; electric appliances and components, computers and parts, integrated circuits, furniture, plastics; world's second-largest tungsten producer and third-largest tin producer. **Natural resources:** tin, rubber, natural gas, tungsten, tantalum, timber, lead, fish, gypsum, lignite, fluorite, arable land. **Exports:** $65.3 billion (f.o.b., 2001 est.): computers, transistors, seafood, clothing, rice. **Imports:** $62.3 billion (f.o.b., 2001 est.): capital goods, intermediate goods and raw materials, consumer goods, fuels. **Major trading partners:** U.S., Japan, Singapore, China, Hong Kong, Malaysia, Netherlands, Taiwan.

Geography Thailand occupies the western half of the Indochinese peninsula and the northern two-thirds of the Malay Peninsula in southeast Asia. Its neighbors are Burma (Myanmar) on the north and west, Laos on the north and northeast, Cambodia on the east, and Malaysia on the south. Thailand is about the size of France.

Government Constitutional monarchy.

History The Thais first began settling their present homeland in the 6th century, and by the end of the 13th century ruled most of the western portion. During the next 400 years, they fought sporadically with the Cambodians to the east and Burmese to the west. Formerly called Siam, Thailand has never experienced foreign rule. The British gained a colonial foothold in the region in 1824, but by 1896 an Anglo-French accord guaranteed the independence of Thailand. A coup in 1932 demoted the monarchy to titular status and established representative government with universal suffrage.

At the outbreak of World War II, Japanese forces attacked Thailand. After five hours of token resistance Thailand yielded to Japan on Dec. 8, 1941, subsequently becoming a staging area for the Japanese campaign against Malaya. Following the demise of a pro-Japanese puppet government in July 1944, Thailand repudiated the declaration of war it had been forced to make in 1942 against Britain and the U.S.

By the late 1960s the nation's problems largely stemmed from conflicts brewing in neighboring Cambodia and Vietnam. Although Thailand had received $2 billion in U.S. economic and military aid since 1950, and had sent troops (paid by the U.S.) to Vietnam while permitting U.S. bomber bases on its territory, the collapse of South Vietnam and Cambodia in spring 1975 brought rapid changes in the country's diplomatic posture. At the Thai government's insistence, the U.S. agreed to withdraw all 23,000 U.S. military personnel remaining in Thailand by March 1976.

Three years of civilian government ended with a military coup on Oct. 6, 1976. Political parties, banned after the coup, gained limited freedom in 1980. The same year, the National Assembly elected Gen. Prem Tinsulanonda as prime minister. Prem continued as prime minister following 1983 and 1986 elections.

Fleeing from Laos, Vietnam, and the murderous regime of Cambodia's Pol Pot, refugees flooded into Thailand in 1978 and 1979. Despite efforts by the United States and other Western countries to resettle them, a total of 130,000 Laotians and Vietnamese were living in camps along the Cambodian border in mid-1980.

On April 3, 1981, a military coup against the Prem government failed. Another coup attempt on Sept. 9, 1985, was crushed by loyal troops after ten hours of fighting in Bangkok. In Feb. 1991, yet another coup yielded another junta, which declared a state of emergency and abolished the constitution. A scandal over a land-reform program caused the fall of the government in May 1995. A succession of governments followed.

Following several years of unprecedented economic growth, Thailand's economy, once one of the strongest in the region, collapsed under the weight of foreign debt in 1997. The Thai economy's downfall set off a chain reaction in the region, sparking the Asian currency crisis. The Thai government quickly accepted restructuring guidelines as a condition of the International Monetary Fund's $17 billion bailout. Thailand's economy, while far from completely recovered, continued to improve over the next several years. The Thai Rak Thai ("Thais Love Thais") party won elections in Jan. 2001 and formed a coalition government with the Chart Thai and New Aspiration Parties. Thaksin Shinawatra became prime minister. The hugely popular Thaksin, a billionaire telecommunications mogul, was indicted in Dec. 2000 on corruption charges but was acquitted in August 2001.

In Feb. 2003, Thaksin announced plans to eliminate the drug trade from Thailand within three months. When the operation concluded at the end of April, nearly 2,300 people had been killed. Government officials claimed responsibility for about 35 of the casualties, blaming drug dealers and gang members for the other deaths. Human rights activists, however, suspected police forces had been overly aggressive in their campaign.

A high-ranking member of al-Qaeda, Riduan Isamuddin, known as Hambali, was captured in August in Thailand in a joint operation between the CIA and Thai police. Officials believe Hambali, an Indonesian, organized the 2002 bombing of a Bali nightclub and the Aug. 2003 attack on the Marriott hotel in Jakarta.

Togo

REPUBLIC OF TOGO

National name: République Togolaise
President: Gen. Gnassingbé Eyadema (1967)
Prime Minister: Koffi Sama (2002)
Area: 21,925 sq mi (56,785 sq km)
Population (2003 est.): 5,429,299 (growth rate: 2.4%); birth rate: 35.2/1000; infant mortality rate: 68.7/1000; density per sq mi: 248
Capital and largest city (2003 est.): Lomé, 749,700 (metro. area), 676,400 (city proper). **Monetary unit:** CFA Franc. **Languages:** French (official), Ewé, Mina (south), Kabyé, Cotocoli (north), and many dialects. **Ethnicity/race:** native African (37 tribes; largest and most important are Ewe, Mina, and Kabre) 99%, European and Syrian-Lebanese less than 1%. **Religions:** Indigenous beliefs 51%, Christian 29%, Islam 20%. **Literacy rate:** 51.7% (1995 est.)
Economic summary: GDP/PPP (2001 est.): $7.6 billion; per capita $1,500. **Real growth rate:** 2.2%. **Inflation:** 2.2%. **Unemployment:** n.a. **Arable land:** 41%. **Agriculture:** coffee, cocoa, cotton, yams, cassava (tapioca), corn, beans, rice, millet, sorghum; livestock; fish. **Labor force:** 1.74 million (1996); agriculture 65%, industry 5%, services 30% (1998 est.). **Industries:** phosphate mining, agricultural processing, cement; handicrafts, textiles, beverages. **Natural resources:** phosphates, limestone, marble, arable land. **Exports:** $306 million (f.o.b., 2001): cotton, phosphates, coffee, cocoa. **Imports:** $420 million (f.o.b., 2001): machinery and equipment, foodstuffs, petroleum products. **Major trading partners:** Benin, Nigeria, Belgium, Ghana, France, China, Côte d'Ivoire.

Geography Togo, twice the size of Maryland, is on the south coast of West Africa bordering on Ghana to the west, Burkina Faso to the north, and Benin to the east. The Gulf of Guinea coastline, only 32 mi long (51 km), is low and sandy. The only port is at Lomé. The Togo hills traverse the central section.

Government Republic transitioning to multiparty democratic rule.

History The Voltaic peoples and the Kwa were the earliest known inhabitants. The Ewe followed in the 14th century, and the Ane in the 18th century. The Danish claimed the land in the 18th century, but by 1884 it was established as a German colony (Togoland). The area was split between the British and the French under League of Nations mandates after World

War I and subsequently administered as UN trusteeships. The British portion voted for incorporation with Ghana. The French portion became Togo, which declared its independence on April 27, 1960.

Togo's first democratically elected president, Sylvano Olympius, was overthrown in 1963. He was shot by Sgt. Etienne Eyadema while he attempted to scale the walls of the American Embassy to seek asylum. The government of Nicolas Grunitzky was overthrown in a bloodless coup on Jan. 13, 1967, led by Lt. Col. Etienne Eyadema (now called Gen. Gnassingbé Eyadema). A National Reconciliation Committee was set up to rule the country, but in April, Eyadema dissolved the committee and took over as president. He suspended the constitution, banned political parties, and created a cult of personality around his presidency—his official biography describes him as a "force of nature." Under pressure from the West, Eyadema legalized opposition parties in 1993, but the first multiparty presidential election in Aug. 1993 (which gave Eyadema more than 96% of the vote) was considered fraudulent, as was his 1998 reelection. In 2003, Eyadema was reelected, continuing his tenure as the longest-serving ruler in Africa—36 years.

Tonga

KINGDOM OF TONGA

Sovereign: King Taufa'ahau Tupou IV (1965)
Prime Minister: Prince Lavaka Ata Ulukalala (2000)
Area: 289 sq mi (748 sq km)
Population (2003 est.): 108,141 (growth rate: 1.9%); birth rate: 24.5/1000; infant mortality rate: 13.3/1000; density per sq mi: 374
Capital and largest city (2003 est.): Nuku'alofa, 24,500. **Monetary unit:** Pa'anga. **Languages:** Tongan (an Austronesian language), English. **Ethnicity/race:** Polynesian, European (about 300). **Religions:** Christian; Free Wesleyan Church claims over 30,000 adherents. **Literacy rate:** 98.5% (1996 est.)
Economic summary: GDP/PPP (2000 est.): $225 million; per capita $2,200. **Real growth rate:** 5.3%. **Inflation:** 9.4% (2001 est.). **Unemployment:** 13.3% (1996 est.). **Arable land:** 24%. **Agriculture:** squash, coconuts, copra, bananas, vanilla beans, cocoa, coffee, ginger, black pepper; fish. **Labor force:** 33,908 (1996); agriculture 65% (1997 est.). **Industries:** tourism, fishing. **Natural resources:** fish, fertile soil. **Exports:** $9.3 million (f.o.b., 2000): squash, fish, vanilla beans, root crops. **Imports:** $70 million (c.i.f., 2000): foodstuffs, machinery and transport equipment, fuels, chemicals. **Major trading partners:** Japan, U.S., New Zealand, Australia, Fiji. **Member of Commonwealth of Nations**

Geography Situated east of the Fiji Islands in the South Pacific, Tonga (also called the Friendly Islands) consists of some 150 islands, of which 36 are inhabited. Most of the islands contain active volcanic craters; others are coral atolls.

Government Hereditary constitutional monarchy.

History Polynesians have lived on Tonga for at least 3,000 years. The Dutch were the first to explore the islands, landing on Tafahi in 1616. British explorer James Cook landed on islands in 1773 and 1777, and dubbed them the Friendly Islands. The current royal dynasty of Tonga was founded in 1831 by Taufa'ahau Tupou, who took the name George I. He consolidated the kingdom by conquest and in 1875 granted a constitution. In 1900, his great-grandson, George II, signed a treaty of friendship with Britain, and the country became a British protected state. The treaty was revised in 1959. Tonga became independent on June 4, 1970.

The government is largely controlled by the king, his nominees, and a small group of hereditary nobles. In the 1990s a movement began aimed at curtailing the powers of the monarchy, and the Tongan Pro-Democracy Movement (TPDM) has continued to gain in popular support. In 1999, Tonga gained UN membership.

The king's official court jester, American Jesse Bogdonoff, a former salesman of magnets to relieve back pain, will go to trial in 2004 for squandering $26 million of the government's money in unsound investment schemes. The king, who celebrated his 85th birthday in 2003, has grown increasingly authoritarian and has curtailed press freedom.

Trinidad and Tobago

REPUBLIC OF TRINIDAD AND TOBAGO

President: Maxwell Richards (2003)
Prime Minister: Patrick Manning (2001)
Area: 1,980 sq mi (5,128 sq km)
Population (2003 est.): 1,104,209 (growth rate: 0.4%); birth rate: 12.7/1000; infant mortality rate: 25.0/1000; density per sq mi: 558
Capital and largest city (2003 est.): Port-of-Spain, 263,800 (metro. area), 45,300 (city proper). **Monetary unit:** Trinidad and Tobago dollar. **Languages:** English (official), Hindi, French, Spanish. **Ethnicity/race:** black 39.5%, East Indian (a local term—primarily immigrants from northern India) 40.3%, mixed 18.4%, white 0.6%, Chinese and other 1.2%. **Religions:** Roman Catholic 29.4%, Hindu 23.8%, Anglican 10.9%, Islam 5.8%, Presbyterian 3.4%, other 26.7%. **Literacy rate:** 94% (2000)
Economic summary: GDP/PPP (2001 est.): $10.6 billion; per capita $9,000. **Real growth rate:** 4%. **Inflation:** 5.6%. **Unemployment:** 11.8%. **Arable land:** 15%. **Agriculture:** cocoa, sugarcane, rice, citrus, coffee, vegetables; poultry. **Labor force:** 564,000 (2000); construction and utilities 12%, manufacturing, mining, and quarrying 14%, agriculture 10%, services 64%. **Industries:** petroleum, chemicals, tourism, food processing, cement, beverage, cotton textiles. **Natural resources:** petroleum, natural gas, asphalt. **Exports:** $4.1 billion (f.o.b., 2001 est.): petroleum and petroleum products, chemicals, steel products, fertilizer, sugar, cocoa, coffee, citrus, flowers. **Imports:** $3.5 billion (f.o.b., 2001 est.): machinery, transportation equipment, manufactured goods, food, live animals. **Major trading partners:** U.S., Caricom countries, Latin America, EU. **Member of Commonwealth of Nations**

Geography Trinidad and Tobago lie in the Caribbean Sea off the northeast coast of Venezuela. Trinidad, the larger at 1,864 sq mi (4,828 sq km), is mainly flat and rolling, with mountains in the north that reach a height of 3,085 ft (940 m) at Mount Aripo. Tobago, at just 116 sq mi (300 sq km), is heavily forested with hardwood trees.

Government Parliamentary democracy.

History When Trinidad was explored by Columbus in 1498, it was inhabited by the Arawaks; Carib Indians inhabited Tobago. Trinidad remained in Spanish possession, despite raids by other European nations, until it was ceded to Britain in 1802. Tobago passed between Britain and France several times, but it was ultimately given to Britain in 1814.

Slavery was abolished in 1834. Between 1845 and 1917, thousands of indentured workers were brought from India to work on sugarcane plantations. In 1889 Trinidad and Tobago were made a single colony.

Partial self-government was instituted in 1925, and from 1958 to 1962 the nation was part of the West Indies Federation. On Aug. 31, 1962, it became independent and on Aug. 1, 1976, Trinidad and Tobago became a republic, remaining within the Commonwealth. While the country is a stable democracy and enjoys the highest living standards in the Caribbean thanks to oil revenue, tension between East Indians and blacks has underlined much of political life. In 1970 rioting and an army mutiny against the East Indian population prompted a state of emergency, which lasted for two years.

Eric Williams, "Father of the Nation" and leader of the People's National Movement (PNM), which is largely supported by blacks, governed from 1956 until his death in 1981. In Dec. 1986 the multiracial National Alliance for Reconstruction (NAR), based in Tobago, won a parliamentary majority, promising to sell most state-owned companies, reorganize the civil service, and reduce dependence on oil.

In 1990, to protest the NAR government, some 100 radical black Muslims blew up the police station in an attempted coup, in which the prime minister and other officials were held hostage for six days. The NAR was defeated in 1991, and the PNM returned to power. In 1995, the East Indian–based party, the United National Congress (UNC), led by Basdeo Panday, formed a coalition government with the NAR. In 2000, Panday narrowly won another term.

In Dec. 2001 elections, both the governing UNC party and the People's National Movement (PNM) party gained 18 seats each. The two parties agreed to allow President Robinson to select the prime minister to end the impasse. But when Robinson selected Patrick Manning of the PNM because of his "moral and spiritual values," the opposition angrily called for new elections. In Oct. 2002 elections, Manning's party declared victory. Maxwell Richards, a university dean, was selected president by Parliament in 2003.

Tunisia

REPUBLIC OF TUNISIA

National name: Al-Joumhouria Attunisia
President: Zine al-Abidine Ben Ali (1987)
Prime Minister: Mohamed Ghannouchi (1999)
Area: 63,170 sq mi (163,610 sq km)
Population (2003 est.): 9,924,742 (growth rate: 1.2%); birth rate: 16.5/1000; infant mortality rate: 26.9/1000; density per sq mi: 157
Capital and largest city (2003 est.): Tunis, 1,660,300 (metro. area), 699,700 (city proper). **Monetary unit:** Tunisian dinar. **Languages:** Arabic (official), French. **Ethnicity/race:** Arab-Berber 98%, European 1%, Jewish less than 1%. **Religions:** Islam (Sunni) 98%, Christian 1%, Jewish, less than 1%. **Literacy rate:** 66.7% (1995 est.)
Economic summary: GDP/PPP (2001 est.): $64.5 billion; per capita $6,600. **Real growth rate:** 4.8%. **Inflation:** 2.7%. **Unemployment:** 15.6% (2000 est.). **Arable land:** 19%. **Agriculture:** olives, olive oil, grain, dairy products, tomatoes, citrus fruit, beef, sugar beets, dates, almonds. **Labor force:** 2.69 million; note: shortage of skilled labor; services 55%, industry 23%, agriculture 22%. **Industries:** petroleum, mining (particularly phosphate and iron ore), tourism, textiles, footwear, agribusiness, beverages. **Natural resources:** petroleum, phosphates, iron ore, lead, zinc, salt. **Exports:** $6.6 billion (f.o.b., 2001 est.): textiles, mechanical goods, phosphates and chemicals, agricultural products, hydrocarbons. **Imports**: $8.9 billion (f.o.b., 2001 est.): machinery and equipment, hydrocarbons, chemicals, food. **Major trading partners:** France, Italy, Germany, Belgium, Libya, Spain.

Geography Tunisia, at the northernmost bulge of Africa, thrusts out toward Sicily to mark the division between the eastern and western Mediterranean Sea. Twice the size of South Carolina, it is bordered on the west by Algeria and by Libya on the south. Coastal plains on the east rise to a north-south escarpment that slopes gently to the west. The Sahara Desert lies in the southernmost part. Tunisia is more mountainous in the north, where the Atlas range continues from Algeria.

Government Republic.

History Tunisia was settled by the Phoenicians in the 12th century B.C. By the sixth and fifth centuries B.C., the great city-state of Carthage (derived from the Phoenician name for "new city") dominated much of the western Mediterranean. The three Punic Wars between Rome and Carthage (the second was the most famous, pitting the Roman general Scipio Africanus against Carthage's Hannibal) led to the complete destruction of Carthage by 146 B.C.

Except for an interval of Vandal conquest in A.D. 439–533, Carthage was part of the Roman Empire until the Arab conquest of 648–669. It was then ruled by various Arab and Berber dynasties, followed by the Turks, who took it in 1570–1574 and made it part of the Ottoman Empire until the 19th century. In the late 16th century, it was a stronghold for the Barbary pirates. French troops occupied the country in 1881, and the bey, the local Tunisian ruler, signed a treaty acknowledging it as a French protectorate.

Nationalist agitation forced France to recognize Tunisian independence and sovereignty in 1956. The Constituent Assembly deposed the bey on July 25, 1957, declared Tunisia a republic, and elected Habib Bourguiba as president. Bourguiba maintained a pro-Western foreign policy that earned him enemies. Tunisia refused to break relations with the U.S. during the Arab-Israeli War in June 1967. Concerned with Islamic fundamentalist plots against the state, the government stepped up efforts to eradicate the movement, including censorship and frequent detention of suspects.

In 1987, the aged Bourguiba was declared mentally unfit to continue as president and was removed from office in a bloodless coup. He was succeeded by General Zine al-Abidine Ben Ali, whose tenure was marked by a rise in Islamic fundamentalism and growing anti-Western sentiments among the populace. Ben Ali was reelected in Oct. 1999 with 99% of the vote in an election criticized by many human rights observers. In May 2000 Ben Ali's Constitutional Democratic Assembly Party swept local elections with 92% of the vote, in a contest many opposition leaders boycotted. However, Tunisia's economy continued to improve in the late 1990s, making the country one of the most attractive in Africa for foreign investors. In May 2002, a referendum passed that ended the three-term limit for the presidency. It permitted Ben Ali, who has served as president for the past 15 years, to run for two more terms. Opposition parties protested.

Turkey

REPUBLIC OF TURKEY

National name: Türkiye Cumhuriyeti
President: Ahmet Necdet Sezer (2000)
Prime Minister: Recep Tayyip Erdogan (2003)
Area: 301,382 sq mi (incl. 9,121 in Europe) (780,580 sq km)
Population (2003 est.): 68,109,469 (growth rate: 1.2%); birth rate: 17.6/1000; infant mortality rate: 44.2/1000; density per sq mi: 226
Capital (2003 est.): Ankara, 3,582,000 (metro. area), 3,456,100 (city proper). **Largest cities:** Istanbul, 10,048,900 (metro. area), 9,419,000 (city proper); Izmir, 2,398,200; Bursa, 1,288,900; Adana, 1,219,900; Gaziantep, 979,500. **Monetary unit:** Turkish lira. **Language:** Turkish. **Ethnicity/race:** Turkish 80%, Kurdish 20%. **Religion:** Islam (mostly Sunni) 99.8%. **Literacy rate:** 85% (2000)
Economic summary: GDP/PPP (2001 est.): $443 billion; per capita $6,700. **Real growth rate:** –6.5%. **Inflation:** 69%. **Unemployment:** 10.6% (plus underemployment of 6.1%) (2001). **Arable land:** 35%. **Agriculture:** tobacco, cotton, grain, olives, sugar beets, pulse, citrus; livestock. **Labor force:** 23.8 million (2001 3rd quarter); note: about 1.2 million Turks work abroad (1999); agriculture 40%, services 38%, industry 22% (2001). **Industries:** textiles, food processing, autos, mining (coal, chromite, copper, boron), steel, petroleum, construction, lumber, paper. **Natural resources:** antimony, coal, chromium, mercury, copper, borate, sulfur, iron ore, arable land, hydropower. **Exports:** $33.8 billion (f.o.b., 2001): apparel 24.8%, foodstuffs 12.8%, textiles 12.7%, metal manufactures 8.8%, transport equipment 8.5% (2000). **Imports:** $39.7 billion (c.i.f., 2001 est.): machinery 25.4%, chemicals 13.4%, semi-finished goods 13.7%, fuels 14.0%, transport equipment 12.4% (2000). **Major trading partners:** Germany, U.S., Italy, France, Russia.

Geography Turkey is at the northeast end of the Mediterranean Sea in southeast Europe and southwest Asia. To the north is the Black Sea and to the west is the Aegean Sea. Its neighbors are Greece and Bulgaria to the west, Russia and Ukraine to the north (through the Black Sea), Georgia, Armenia, Azerbaijan, and Iran to the east, and Syria and Iraq to the south. The Dardanelles, the Sea of Marmara, and the Bosporus divide the country. Turkey in Europe comprises an area about equal to the state of Massachusetts. Turkey in Asia is about the size of Texas. Its center is a treeless plateau rimmed by mountains.

Government Republican parliamentary democracy.

History Anatolia (Turkey in Asia) was occupied in about 1900 B.C. by the Indo-European Hittites and, after the Hittite empire's collapse in 1200 B.C., by Phrygians and Lydians. The Persian Empire occupied the area in the 6th century B.C., giving way to the Roman Empire, then later the Byzantine Empire. The Ottoman Turks first appeared in the early 13th century, subjugating Turkish and Mongol bands pressing against the eastern borders of Byzantium and making the Christian Balkan states their vassals. They gradually spread through the Near East and Balkans, capturing Constantinople in 1453 and storming the gates of Vienna two centuries later. At its height, the Ottoman Empire stretched from the Persian Gulf to western Algeria. Lasting for 600 years, the Ottoman Empire was not only one of the most powerful empires in the history of the Mediterranean region, but it generated a great cultural outpouring of Islamic art, architecture, and literature.

After the reign of Sultan Süleyman I the Magnificent (1494–1566), the Ottoman Empire began to decline politically, administratively, and economically. By the 18th century, Russia was seeking to establish itself as the protector of Christians in Turkey's Balkan territories. Russian ambitions were checked by Britain and France in the Crimean War (1854–1856), but the Russo-Turkish War (1877–1878) gave Bulgaria virtual independence and Romania and Serbia liberation from their nominal allegiance to the sultan. Turkish weakness stimulated a revolt of young liberals known as the Young Turks in 1909. They forced Sultan Abdul Hamid to grant a constitution and install a liberal government. However, reforms were no barrier to further defeats in a war with Italy (1911–1912) and the Balkan Wars (1912–1913). Turkey sided with Germany in World War I, and, as a result, lost territory at the conclusion of the war.

Turkey's current boundaries were drawn in 1923 at the Conference of Lausanne, and Turkey became a republic with Kemal Atatürk as the first president. The Ottoman sultanate and caliphate were abolished, and modernization, reform, and industrialization began under Atatürk's direction. He secularized Turkish society, reducing Islam's dominant role and replacing Arabic with the Latin alphabet for writing the Turkish language. After Atatürk's death in 1938, parliamentary government and a multiparty system gradually took root in Turkey, despite periods of instability and brief intervals of military rule. Neutral during most of World War II, Turkey, on Feb. 23, 1945, declared war on Germany and Japan, but it took no active part in the conflict. Turkey became a full member of NATO in 1952, was a signatory in the Balkan Entente (1953), joined the Baghdad Pact (1955; later CENTO), joined the Organization for European Economic Cooperation (OEEC) and the Council of Europe, and became an associate member of the European Common Market in 1963.

Turkey invaded Cyprus by sea and air on July 20, 1974, following the failure of diplomatic efforts to resolve conflicts between Turkish and Greek Cypriots. Turkey unilaterally announced a cease-fire on Aug. 16, after having gained control of 40% of the island. Turkish Cypriots established their own state in the north on Feb. 13, 1975. In July 1975, after a 30-day warning, Turkey took control of all the U.S. installations except the joint defense base at Incirlik, which it reserved for "NATO tasks alone."

The establishment of military government in Sept. 1980 stopped the slide toward anarchy and brought some improvement in the economy. A Constituent Assembly, consisting of the six-member National Security Council and members appointed by them, drafted a new constitution that was approved by an overwhelming (91.5%) majority of the voters in a Nov. 6, 1982, referendum. Martial law was gradually lifted. The military, however, effectively continues to control the country.

About 12 million Kurds, roughly 20% of Turkey's population, live in the southeast region of Turkey. Turkey, however, does not officially recognize Kurds as a minority group and is therefore exempted from protecting their rights. Oppression of Kurds and Kurdish culture led to the emergence in 1984 of the Kurdistan Workers' Party (PKK), a militant Kurdish terrorist campaign under the leadership of Abdullah Ocalan. Although the guerrilla movement sought independence at first, by the late 1980s the rebel Kurds were willing to accept an autonomous state or a federation with Turkey. About 35,000 have died in clashes between the military and the PKK during the 1980s and '90s. On

Feb. 16, 1999, Ocalan was captured. He was tried and convicted of treason and separatism on June 2, 1999, and sentenced to death.

On Aug. 17, 1999, western Turkey was devastated by an earthquake (magnitude 7.4) that left more than 17,000 dead and 200,000 homeless. Another huge earthquake struck in November.

Construction on a $3 billion, 1,000-mile oil pipeline running from Baku, Azerbaijan, to the Mediterranean port city of Cyan began in Sept. 2002, which is expected to bolster the economy.

In the summer of 2002, Prime Minister Bülent Ecevit, despite grave illness, refused to step down or pave the way for a successor. His intransigence led to the resignations of numerous key officials in his three-party coalition government. The prime minister finally relented, and in Nov. 3 elections, the recently formed Justice and Development Party (AK) won. Its leader, Recep Tayyip Erdogan, was barred from becoming prime minister, however, because of a conviction for "inciting religious hatred" by reciting an Islamic poem at a rally in 1998. Another popular AK leader, Abdullah Gul, became prime minister. In March 2003, Erdogan, after a change in Turkish law, was permitted to run for a seat in parliament again, and easily won. Gul resigned as prime minister, making way for Erdogan.

In March 2003, U.S.-Turkish relations were severely strained when Turkey's parliament narrowly failed to pass a resolution permitting the U.S. to use Turkish bases as a launching pad for the pending war against Iraq. Turkish opinion polls reported that an overwhelming 90% of Turks were against war in Iraq, but the U.S. had promised the country much-needed economic aid.

In an effort to make itself more attractive for potential EU membership, Turkey has begun revamping some of its repressive laws and policies. In 2003, its parliament passed a law reducing the military's role in political life, and offered partial amnesty to PKK members, many of whom have sought refuge in northern Iraq.

Turkmenistan

TURKMENISTAN

President-for-Life: Saparmurad A. Niyazov (1990)
Area: 188,455 sq mi (488,100 sq km)
Population (2003 est.): 4,775,544 (growth rate: 1.9%); birth rate: 28.0/1000; infant mortality rate: 73.2/1000; density per sq mi: 25
Capital and largest city (2003 est.): Ashgabat, 727,700. **Other large cities:** Chardzhou, 213,500; Tashauz, 160,400. **Monetary unit:** Manat. **Languages:** Turkmen, 72%; Russian, 12%; Uzbek, 9%. **Ethnicity/race:** Turkmen 77%, Uzbek 9.2%, Russian 6.7%, Kazak 2%, other 5.1% (1995). **Religions:** Islam 89%, Eastern Orthodox 9%, unknown 2%. **Literacy rate:** 98% (1989 est.)
Economic summary: GDP/PPP (2001 est.): $21.5 billion; per capita $4,700. **Real growth rate:** 10%. **Inflation:** 10%. **Unemployment:** n.a. **Arable land:** 4%. **Agriculture:** cotton, grain; livestock. **Labor force:** 2.34 million (1996); agriculture 48%, industry 15%, services 37% (1998 est.). **Industries:** natural gas, oil, petroleum products, textiles, food processing. **Natural resources:** petroleum, natural gas, coal, sulfur, salt. **Exports:** $2.7 billion (f.o.b., 2001 est.): gas 33%, oil 30%, cotton fiber 18%, textiles 8% (1999). **Imports:** $2.3 billion (c.i.f., 2001 est.): machinery and equipment 60%, foodstuffs 15% (1999). **Major trading partners:** Ukraine, Iran, Turkey, Italy, Switzerland, Russia, UAE, France.

Geography Turkmenistan (formerly Turkmenia) is bounded by the Caspian Sea in the west, Kazakhstan in the north, Uzbekistan in the east, and Iran and Afghanistan in the south. About nine-tenths of Turkmenistan is desert, chiefly the Kara-Kum. One of the world's largest sand deserts, it is approximately 138,966 sq mi (360,000 sq km).

Government One-party republic.

History Turkmenistan was once part of the ancient Persian Empire. The Turkmen people were originally pastoral nomads and some of them continued this way of life up into the 20th century, living in transportable dome-shaped felt tents. The territory was ruled by the Seljuk Turks in the 11th century. The Mongols of Ghenghis Khan conquered the land in the 13th century and dominated the area for the next two centuries until they were deposed in the late 15th century by invading Uzbeks. Prior to the 19th century, Turkmenia was divided into two lands, one belonging to the khanate of Khiva and the other belonging to the khanate of Bukhara. In 1868, the khanate of Khiva was made part of the Russian empire and Turkmenia became known as the Transcaspia Region of Russian Turkistan. Turkmenistan was later formed out of the Turkistan Autonomous Soviet Socialist Republic, founded in 1922, and was made an independent Soviet Socialist Republic on May 13, 1925. It was the poorest of the Soviet republics.

Turkmenistan declared its sovereignty in Aug. 1990 and became a member of the Commonwealth of Independent States on Dec. 21, 1991, together with ten other former Soviet republics. It established a government more authoritarian than those functioning in the other newly independent central Asian republics. President Saparmurad A. Niyazov, also called the Turkmenbashi (Leader of All Turkmens), has attempted to create a cult of personality through extravagant self-promotion. Cities, aftershave, and a meteor now bear his name. In 2002, he renamed all the months of the calendar. January is now called by his preferred name, Turkmenbashi; April is named after his mother. Protests against his authoritarian rule and practices notwithstanding, Niyazov was voted president-for-life by his rubber-stamp Parliament in 1999.

In the 1990s, Turkmenistan exported gas through a Russian pipeline, bringing in about $1 billion per year. But in 1993, Russia closed down Turkmenistan's only pipeline because it competed with Russia's own gas exportation. Turkmenistan was limited to exporting gas to its impoverished central Asian neighbors, who were unable to pay their bills. The nation then opened a pipeline route to Iran, generally agreed to be the most economical route for exporting Caspian oil, and thus ruffled the feathers of Iran's enemy, the U.S. So far, the new plan has not brought in money, and the country is living off loans from Western countries such as Germany who hope to partner with the oil-rich, money-poor country.

An alleged assassination attempt against Niyazov in Nov. 2002 (thought by outsiders to have been staged) resulted in the conviction of 46 opposition leaders and critics of the government.

Tuvalu

Sovereign: Queen Elizabeth II (1952)
Governor-General: Faimalaga Luka (2003)
Prime Minister: Saufatu Sopoanga (2002)
Area: 10 sq mi (26 sq km)
Population (2003 est.): 11,305 (growth rate: 1.4%); birth rate: 21.6/1000; infant mortality rate: 21.3/1000; density per sq mi: 1,126
Capital and largest city (2003 est.): Funafuti, 5,300. **Monetary unit:** Australian dollar. **Languages:** Tuvaluan, English. **Ethnicity/race:** Polynesian 96%.

Religion: Church of Tuvalu (Congregationalist) 97%. **Literacy rate:** 55% (1996)

Economic summary: GDP/PPP (2000 est.): $12.2 million; per capita $1,100. **Real growth rate:** 3%. **Inflation:** 5%. **Unemployment:** n.a. **Arable land:** 0%. **Agriculture:** coconuts; fish. **Labor force:** 7,000 (2001 est.); people make a living mainly through exploitation of the sea, reefs, and atolls and from wages sent home by those working abroad (mostly workers in the phosphate industry and sailors). **Industries:** fishing, tourism, copra. **Natural resources:** fish. **Exports:** $276,000 (f.o.b., 1997): copra, fish. **Imports:** $7.2 million (c.i.f., 1998): food, animals, mineral fuels, machinery, manufactured goods. **Major trading partners:** Sweden, Fiji, Iceland, Germany, Greece, Australia, Portugal, New Zealand. **Member of Commonwealth of Nations**

Geography Tuvalu consists of nine small islands scattered over 500,000 sq mi of the western Pacific, just south of the equator. The islands include Niulakita, Nukulaelae, Funafuti, Nukufetau, Vaitupu, Nui, Niutao, Nanumaga (Nanumanga), and Nanumea.

Government Constitutional monarchy with a parliamentary democracy.

History Formerly the Ellice Islands, Tuvalu's first Polynesian settlers were probably Samoans or Tongans. The Ellice Islands became a British protectorate in 1892 and were annexed by Britain in 1915–1916 as part of the Gilbert and Ellice Islands Colony. The Ellice Islands were separated from the Gilberts in 1975, given home rule, and renamed Tuvalu. Full independence was granted on Sept. 30, 1978, but it remained part of the Commonwealth. In 1979, the U.S. gave Tuvalu four islands that had been U.S. territory.

In 1997, the government adopted a strong stance on the need to control emissions of greenhouse gases in order to ensure the survival of low-lying island nations, which are threatened by rising sea levels—Tuvalu's highest point is just 16 ft above sea level. In 2000, Tuvalu became a member of the United Nations.

Uganda

REPUBLIC OF UGANDA

President: Yoweri Museveni (1986)
Prime Minister: Apolo Nsibambi (1999)
Area: 91,135 sq mi (236,040 sq km)
Population (2003 est.): 25,632,794 (growth rate: 3.0%); birth rate: 46.6/1000; infant mortality rate: 87.9/1000; density per sq mi: 281
Capital and largest city (2003 est.): Kampala, 1,461,600 (metro. area), 1,244,000 (city proper). **Monetary unit:** Ugandan new shilling. **Languages:** English (official), Swahili, Luganda, Ateso, Luo. **Ethnicity/race:** Baganda 17%, Karamojong 12%, Basogo 8%, Iteso 8%, Langi 6%, Rwanda 6%, Bagisu 5%, Acholi 4%, Lugbara 4%, Bunyoro 3%, Batobo 3%, European, Asian, Arab 1%, other 23%. **Religions:** Christian 66%, Islam 16%. **Literacy rate:** 62.7% (2000 est.)

Economic summary: GDP/PPP (2001 est.): $29 billion; per capita $1,200. **Real growth rate:** 5.1%. **Inflation:** 3.5%. **Unemployment:** n.a. **Arable land:** 25%. **Agriculture:** coffee, tea, cotton, tobacco, cassava (tapioca), potatoes, corn, millet, pulses; beef, goat meat, milk, poultry, cut flowers. **Labor force:** 12 million; agriculture 82%, industry 5%, services 13% (1999 est.). **Industries:** sugar, brewing, tobacco, cotton textiles, cement. **Natural resources:** copper, cobalt, hydropower, limestone, salt, arable land. **Exports:** $367 million (f.o.b., 2001): coffee, fish and fish products, tea; gold, cotton, flowers, horticultural products. **Imports:** $1.26 billion (f.o.b., 2001): capital equipment, vehicles, petroleum, medical supplies; cereals. **Major trading partners:** Germany, Netherlands, U.S., Spain, Belgium, Kenya, India, South Africa, Japan. **Member of the Commonwealth of Nations**

Geography Uganda, twice the size of Pennsylvania, is in East Africa. It is bordered on the west by Congo, on the north by the Sudan, on the east by Kenya, and on the south by Tanzania and Rwanda. The country, which lies across the equator, is divided into three main areas—swampy lowlands, a fertile plateau with wooded hills, and a desert region. Lake Victoria forms part of the southern border.

Government Multiparty democractic republic.

History About 500 B.C. Bantu-speaking peoples migrated to the area now called Uganda. By the 14th century, three kingdoms dominated, Buganda (meaning "state of the Gandas"), Bunyoro, and Ankole. Uganda was first explored by Europeans as well as Arab traders in 1844. An Anglo-German agreement of 1890 declared it to be in the British sphere of influence in Africa, and the Imperial British East Africa Company was chartered to develop the area. The company did not prosper financially, and in 1894 a British protectorate was proclaimed. Few Europeans permanently settled in Uganda, but it attracted many Indians, who became important players in Ugandan commerce.

Uganda became independent on Oct. 9, 1962. Sir Edward Mutesa, the king of Buganda (Mutesa II), was elected the first president, and Milton Obote the first prime minister, of the newly independent country. With the help of a young army officer, Col. Idi Amin, Prime Minister Obote seized control of the government from President Mutesa four years later.

On Jan. 25, 1971, Colonel Amin deposed President Obote. Obote went into exile in Tanzania. Amin expelled Asian residents and launched a reign of terror against Ugandan opponents, torturing and killing tens of thousands. In 1976, he had himself proclaimed "President for Life." In 1977, Amnesty International estimated that 300,000 may have died under his rule, including church leaders and recalcitrant cabinet ministers.

After Amin held military exercises on the Tanzanian border in 1978, angering Tanzania's president, Julius Nyerere, a combined force of Tanzanian troops and Ugandan exiles loyal to former president Obote invaded Uganda and chased Amin into exile in Saudi Arabia in 1979. After a series of interim administrations, President Obote led his People's Congress Party to victory in 1980 elections that opponents charged were rigged. On July 27, 1985, army troops staged a coup and took over the government. Obote fled into exile. The military regime installed Gen. Tito Okello as chief of state.

The National Resistance Army (NRA), an anti-Obote group led by Yoweri Museveni, kept fighting after it had been excluded from the new regime. It seized Kampala on Jan. 29, 1986, and Museveni was declared president. Museveni has transformed the ruins of Idi Amin and Milton Obote's Uganda into an economic miracle, preaching a philosophy of self-sufficiency and anticorruption. Western countries have flocked to assist him in the country's transformation. Nevertheless, it remains one of Africa's poorest countries. A ban on political parties was lifted in 1996, and the incumbent Museveni won 72% of the vote, reflecting his popularity due to the country's economic recovery.

Uganda has waged an enormously successful campaign against AIDS, dramatically reducing the rate of new infections through an intensive public health and education campaign. Museveni won reelection in March 2001 with 70% of the vote, following a nasty and spirited campaign.

Close ties with Rwanda (many Rwandan Tutsi exiles helped Museveni come to power) led to the cooperation of Uganda and Rwanda in the ousting of Zaire's Mobutu Sese Seko in 1997, and a year later, in efforts to unseat his successor, Laurent Kabila, whom both countries originally supported but from whom they grew estranged. But in 1999, Uganda and Rwanda quarreled over strategy in the Congo, and began fighting each other. The two countries mended their differences in 2002. Uganda also signed a peace accord with the Congo in Sept. 2002, finally withdrawing its remaining troops from the country in May 2003.

Throughout 2002, Uganda continued its 15-year battle against the extremist rebel group, the Lord's Resistance Army (LRA), based in Sudan. Between 8,000 and 10,000 children have been abducted by the LRA and form the army of "prophet" Joseph Kony, whose aim is to take over Uganda and run it according to his vision of Christianity.

In Aug. 2003, former dictator Idi Amin died in exile in Saudi Arabia.

Ukraine

UKRAINE

President: Leonid D. Kuchma (1994)
Prime Minister: Viktor Yanukovich (2002)
Area: 233,089 sq mi (603,700 sq km)
Population (2003 est.): 48,055,439 (growth rate: –0.7%); birth rate: 9.9/1000; infant mortality rate: 20.9/1000; density per sq mi: 206
Capital (2003 est.): Kyiv (Kiev), 3,296,100 (metro. area), 2,588,400 (city proper). **Other large cities:** Kharkiv, 1,435,200; Odessa, 1,022,300; Donetske, 984,900; Lviv, 700,100. **Monetary unit:** Hryvna. **Language:** Ukrainian. **Ethnicity/race:** Ukrainian 77.8%, Russian 17.3%, other 4.9%. **Religions:** Orthodox 76%, Ukrainian Catholic (Uniate) 13.5%, Jewish 2.3%, Baptist, Mennonite, Protestant, and Islam 8.2%. **Literacy rate:** 98% (1989 est.)
Economic summary: GDP/PPP (2001 est.): $205 billion; per capita $4,200. **Real growth rate:** 9%. **Inflation:** 12%. **Unemployment:** 3.6% officially registered; large number of unregistered or underemployed workers (Nov. 2001). **Arable land:** 57%. **Agriculture:** grain, sugar beets, sunflower seeds, vegetables; beef, milk. **Labor force:** 22.8 million (year-end 1997); industry 32%, agriculture 24%, services 44% (1996). **Industries:** coal, electric power, ferrous and nonferrous metals, machinery and transport equipment, chemicals, food processing (especially sugar). **Natural resources:** iron ore, coal, manganese, natural gas, oil, salt, sulfur, graphite, titanium, magnesium, kaolin, nickel, mercury, timber, arable land. **Exports:** $17.3 billion (2001 est.): ferrous and nonferrous metals, fuel and petroleum products, machinery and transport equipment, food products. **Imports:** $17.1 billion (2001 est.): energy, machinery and parts, transportation equipment, chemicals. **Major trading partners:** Russia, Turkey, Germany, Turkmenistan, U.S.

Geography Located in southeast Europe, the country consists largely of fertile black soil steppes. Mountainous areas include the Carpathians in the southwest and the Crimean chain in the south. There are forest lakes in the north. Ukraine is bordered by Belarus on the north, by Russia on the north, northeast, and east, by the Sea of Azov and the Black Sea on the south, by Moldova and Romania on the southwest, and by Hungary, Slovakia, and Poland on the west.

Government Constitutional republic.

History Ukraine was known as "Kievan Rus" (from which *Russia* is a derivative) up until the 16th century. In the 9th century, Kiev was the major political and cultural center in eastern Europe. Kievan Rus reached the height of its power in the 10th century and adopted Byzantine Christianity, the Church Slavonic written language, and the Cyrillic alphabet during that period. The Mongol conquest in 1240 ended Kievan power. From the 13th to the 16th century, Kiev was under the influence of Poland and western Europe. The negotiation of the Union of Brest-Litovsk in 1596 divided the Ukrainians into Orthodox and Ukrainian Catholic faithful. In 1654, Ukraine asked the czar of Moscovy for protection against Poland, and the Treaty of Pereyasav signed that year recognized the suzerainty of Moscow. The agreement was interpreted by Moscow as an invitation to take over Kiev, and the Ukrainian state was eventually absorbed into the Russian empire.

After the Russian Revolution, Ukraine declared its independence from Russia on Jan. 28, 1918, and several years of warfare ensued with several groups. The Red Army finally was victorious over Kiev, and in 1920 Ukraine became a Soviet republic. In 1922, Ukraine became one of the founders of the Union of Soviet Socialist Republics. In the 1930s, the Soviet government's enforcement of collectivization met with peasant resistance, which in turn prompted the confiscation of grain from Ukrainian farmers by Soviet authorities; the resulting famine took an estimated 5 million lives. Ukraine was one of the most devastated Soviet republics after World War II. (For details on World War II, *see* Headline History, World War II.) On April 26, 1986, the nation's nuclear power plant at Chernobyl was the site of the world's worst nuclear accident. On Oct. 29, 1991, the Ukrainian Parliament voted to shut down the reactor within two years' time and asked for international assistance in dismantling it.

When President Leonid Kravchuk was elected by the Ukrainian Parliament in 1990, he vowed to seek Ukrainian sovereignty. Ukraine declared its independence on Aug. 24, 1991. In Dec. 1991, Ukrainian, Russian, and Belorussian leaders cofounded a new Commonwealth of Independent States with the new capital to be situated in Minsk, Belarus. The new country's government was slow to reform the Soviet-era state-run economy, which was plagued by declining production, rising inflation, and widespread unemployment in the years following independence. The U.S. announced in Jan. 1994 that an agreement had been reached with Russia and Ukraine for the destruction of Ukraine's entire nuclear arsenal. In Oct. 1994, Ukraine began a program of economic liberalization and moved to reestablish central authority over Crimea. In 1995, Crimea's separatist leader was removed and the Crimean constitution revoked.

In June 1996, the last strategic nuclear warhead was removed to Russia. Also that month Parliament approved a new constitution that allowed for private ownership of land. An agreement was signed in May 1997 on the future of the Black Sea fleet, by which Ukrainian and Russian ships will share the port of Sevastopol for 20 years. Ukraine and Russia also signed a ten-year political treaty three days later, by which, among other provisions, Russia recognized the political and territorial integrity of Ukraine, including the Crimean Peninsula.

The Russian financial crisis in fall 1998 led to severe problems for the Ukrainian economy, which is dependent on Russia for 40% of its foreign trade. Ukraine remains saddled with its Soviet-era economy, and most of its major industries are still under state control. Corruption is rampant, and as a result, Western investors have shown only minimal interest. The election of the reform-minded Viktor Yushchenko as prime minister in Dec. 1999, however, was greeted with optimism by the West. He was also highly popular among ordinary Ukrainians. But in April 2001, he was dismissed in a no-confidence vote engineered by Communist hardliners and Ukrainian big business.

In the winter of 2001 violent demonstrations rocked Ukraine, with protesters demanding the resignation and impeachment of authoritarian president Leonid Kuchma. Critics accused Kuchma of involvement in the murder of a journalist critical of government corruption. Kuchma was recorded on tape urging that the journalist be disposed of. The president is also believed to have shipped military equipment to Iraq despite the international embargo, raising the ire of the U.S. But by the summer of 2003, the U.S. had muzzled its objections to Kuchma when the Ukraine promised to send 1,600 soldiers to support peacekeeping efforts in Iraq.

United Arab Emirates

President: Sheikh Zayed bin Sultan al-Nahyan (1971)
Prime Minister: Sheikh Maktoum bin Rashid al-Maktoum (1990)
Area: 32,000 sq mi (82,880 sq km)
Population (2003 est.): 2,484,818 (growth rate: 1.5%); birth rate: 18.5/1000; infant mortality rate: 15.6/1000; density per sq mi: 78
Capital (2003 est.): Abu Dhabi, 539,800. **Largest city:** Dubai, 1,511,700 (metro. area), 906,100 (city proper). **Monetary unit:** U.A.E. dirham. **Languages:** Arabic (official), English as a second language. **Ethnicity/race:** Emiri 19%, other Arab and Iranian 23%, South Asian 50%, other expatriates (includes Westerners and East Asians) 8% (1982). **Religions:** Islam (Sunni 80%, Shi'ite 16%), others 4%. **Literacy rate:** 79.2% (1995 est.)
Economic summary: GDP/PPP (2000 est.): $51 billion; per capita $21,100. **Real growth rate:** 5.6%. **Inflation:** 4.5% (2000 est.). **Unemployment:** n.a. **Arable land:** 0%. **Agriculture:** dates, vegetables, watermelons; poultry, eggs, dairy products; fish. **Labor force:** 1.6 million; note: 73.9%% of the population in the 15-64 age group is non-national (July 2002 est.); services 78%, industry 15%, agriculture 7%. **Industries:** petroleum, fishing, petrochemicals, construction materials, some boat building, handicrafts, pearling. **Natural resources:** petroleum, natural gas. **Exports:** $47.6 billion (f.o.b., 2000 est.): crude oil 45%, natural gas, reexports, dried fish, dates. **Imports:** $28.6 billion (f.o.b., 2000 est.): machinery and transport equipment, chemicals, food. **Major trading partners:** Japan, India, Singapore, South Korea, Oman, Iran, UK, U.S., Italy, Germany.

Geography The United Arab Emirates, in the eastern part of the Arabian Peninsula, extends along part of the Gulf of Oman and the southern coast of the Persian Gulf. The nation is the size of Maine. Its neighbors are Saudi Arabia to the west and south, Qatar to the north, and Oman to the east. Most of the land is barren and sandy.

Government Federation formed in 1971 by seven emirates known as the Trucial States—Abu Dhabi (the largest), Dubai, Sharjah, Ajman, Fujairah, Ras al Khaimah, and Umm al-Qaiwain.

History Originally the area was inhabited by a seafaring people who were converted to Islam in the 7th century. Later, a dissident sect, the Carmathians, established a powerful sheikdom, and its army conquered Mecca. After the sheikdom disintegrated, its people became pirates. Threatening the Sultanate of Muscat and Oman early in the 19th century, the pirates provoked the intervention of the British, who in 1820 enforced a partial truce and in 1853 a permanent truce. Thus what had been called the Pirate Coast was renamed the Trucial Coast. The British provided the nine Trucial states with protection but did not formally administer them as a colony.

The British withdrew from the Persian Gulf in 1971, and the Trucial states became a federation called the United Arab Emirates (UAE). Two of the Trucial states, Bahrain and Oman, chose not to join the federation, reducing the number of states to seven.

The country signed a military defense agreement with the U.S. in 1994 and one with France in 1995. In 1997, UAE officials protested Iranian military activities in the Persian Gulf, especially in regard to the ownership of three Gulf islands, which had been the subject of disputes for many years.

In 2000, one of the biggest arms deals in history took place, with the United Arab Emirates buying 80 fighter jets and missiles from Lockheed Martin for nearly $8 billion.

After the Sept. 11 terrorist attacks on New York and Washington, DC, the UAE was identified as a major financial center used by al-Qaeda in transferring money to the hijackers. The nation immediately cooperated with the U.S., freezing accounts tied to suspected terrorists and strongly clamping down on money laundering. The U.S. stationed troops in the UAE during the 2003 Iraq war, and the country provided significant humanitarian aid to Iraq in the aftermath.

United Kingdom

UNITED KINGDOM OF GREAT BRITAIN AND NORTHERN IRELAND

Sovereign: Queen Elizabeth II (1952)
Prime Minister: Tony Blair (1997)
Area: 94,525 sq mi (244,820 sq km)
Population (2003 est.): 60,094,648 (growth rate: 0.1%); birth rate: 11.0/1000; infant mortality rate: 5.3/1000; density per sq mi: 636
Capital and largest city (2003 est.): London, 11,219,000 (metro. area), 7,417,700 (city proper). **Other large cities:** Glasgow, 1,099,400; Birmingham, 971,800; Liverpool, 461,900; Edinburgh, 460,000; Leeds, 417,000; Bristol, 406,500; Manchester, 390,700; Bradford, 288,400. **Monetary unit:** Pound sterling (£). **Languages:** English, Welsh, Scots Gaelic. **Ethnicity/race:** English 81.5%; Scottish 9.6%; Irish 2.4%; Welsh 1.9%; Ulster 1.8%; West Indian, Indian, Pakistani, and other 2.8%. **Religions:** Church of England (established church), Church of Wales (disestablished), Church of Scotland (established church—Presbyterian), Church of Ireland (disestablished), Roman Catholic, Methodist, Congregational, Baptist, Jewish. **Literacy rate:** 99% (2000 est.)
Economic summary: GDP/PPP (2001 est.): $1.47 trillion; per capita $24,700. **Real growth rate:** 2.4%. **Inflation:** 2.8%. **Unemployment:** 5.1%. **Arable land:** 26%. **Agriculture:** cereals, oilseed, potatoes, vegetables; cattle, sheep, poultry; fish. **Labor force:** 29.7 million; agriculture 1%, industry 25%, services 74% (1999). **Industries:** machine tools, electric power equipment, automation equipment, railroad equipment,

shipbuilding, aircraft, motor vehicles and parts, electronics and communications equipment, metals, chemicals, coal, petroleum, paper and paper products, food processing, textiles, clothing, and other consumer goods. **Natural resources:** coal, petroleum, natural gas, tin, limestone, iron ore, salt, clay, chalk, gypsum, lead, silica, arable land. **Exports:** $287 billion (f.o.b., 2001): manufactured goods, fuels, chemicals; food, beverages, tobacco. **Imports:** $337 billion (c.i.f., 2001): manufactured goods, machinery, fuels; foodstuffs. **Major trading partners:** EU, U.S., Japan.

Geography The United Kingdom, consisting of Great Britain (England, Wales, and Scotland) and Northern Ireland, is twice the size of New York State. England, in the southeast part of the British Isles, is separated from Scotland on the north by the granite Cheviot Hills; from them the Pennine chain of uplands extends south through the center of England, reaching its highest point in the Lake District in the northwest. To the west along the border of Wales—a land of steep hills and valleys—are the Cambrian Mountains, while the Cotswolds, a range of hills in Gloucestershire, extend into the surrounding shires.

Important rivers flowing into the North Sea are the Thames, Humber, Tees, and Tyne. In the west are the Severn and Wye, which empty into the Bristol Channel and are navigable, as are the Mersey and Ribble.

Government The United Kingdom is a constitutional monarchy and parliamentary democracy, with a queen and a Parliament that has two houses: the House of Lords, with 574 life peers, 92 hereditary peers, 26 bishops, and the House of Commons, which has 651 popularly elected members. Supreme legislative power is vested in Parliament, which sits for five years unless sooner dissolved. The House of Lords was stripped of most of its power in 1911, and now its main function is to revise legislation. In Nov. 1999 hundreds of hereditary peers were expelled in an effort to make the body more democratic. The executive power of the Crown is exercised by the cabinet, headed by the prime minister.

Ruler Queen Elizabeth II, born April 21, 1926, elder daughter of King George VI and Queen Elizabeth, succeeded to the throne on the death of her father on Feb. 6, 1952. On Nov. 20, 1947, she married Prince Philip, duke of Edinburgh, born June 10, 1921. Their children are Prince Charles[1] (heir apparent), born Nov. 14, 1948; Princess Anne, born Aug. 15, 1950; Prince Andrew, born Feb. 19, 1960; and Prince Edward, born March 10, 1964. Prince William Arthur Philip Louis, son of Prince Charles and the late princess of Wales and second in line to the throne, was born June 21, 1982. A second son, Prince Henry Charles Albert David, was born Sept. 15, 1984, and is third in line.

History Stonehenge and other examples of prehistoric culture are what remains of the earliest inhabitants of Britain. Celtic peoples followed. Roman invasions of the 1st century B.C. brought Britain into contact with continental Europe. When the Roman legions withdrew in the 5th century A.D., Britain fell easy prey to the invading hordes of Angles, Saxons, and Jutes from Scandinavia and the Low Countries. The invasions had little effect on the Celtic peoples of Wales and Scotland. Seven large Anglo-Saxon kingdoms were established, and the original Britons were forced into Wales and Scotland. It was not until the 10th century that the country finally became united under the kings of Wessex. Following the death of Edward the Confessor (1066), a dispute about the succession arose, and William, duke of Normandy, invaded England, defeating the Saxon king, Harold II, at the Battle of Hastings (1066). The Norman conquest introduced Norman French law and feudalism.

The reign of Henry II (1154–1189), first of the Plantagenets, saw an increasing centralization of royal power at the expense of the nobles, but in 1215 King John (1199–1216) was forced to sign the Magna Carta, which awarded the people, especially the nobles, certain basic rights. Edward I (1272–1307) continued the conquest of Ireland, reduced Wales to subjection, and made some gains in Scotland. In 1314, however, English forces led by Edward II were ousted from Scotland after the Battle of Bannockburn. The late 13th and early 14th centuries saw the development of a separate House of Commons with tax-raising powers. Edward III's claim to the throne of France led to the Hundred Years' War (1338–1453) and the loss of almost all the large English territory in France. In England, the great poverty and discontent caused by the war were intensified by the Black Death, a plague that reduced the population by about one-third. The Wars of the Roses (1455–1485), a struggle for the throne between the House of York and the House of Lancaster, ended in the victory of Henry Tudor (Henry VII) at Bosworth Field (1485).

During the reign of Henry VIII (1509–1547), the church in England asserted its independence from the Roman Catholic Church. Under Edward VI and Mary, the two extremes of religious fanaticism were reached, and it remained for Henry's daughter, Elizabeth I (1558–1603), to set up the Church of England on a moderate basis. In 1588, the Spanish Armada, a fleet sent out by Catholic King Philip II of Spain, was defeated by the English and destroyed during a storm. During Elizabeth's reign, England became a world power. Elizabeth's heir was a Stuart—James VI of Scotland—who joined the two crowns as James I (1603–1625). The Stuart kings incurred large debts and were forced either to depend on Parliament for taxes or to raise money by illegal means. In 1642, war broke out between Charles I and a large segment of the Parliament; Charles was defeated and executed in 1649, and the monarchy was then abolished. After the death in 1658 of Oliver Cromwell, the lord protector, the Puritan Commonwealth fell to pieces and Charles II was placed on the throne in 1660. The struggle between the king and Parliament continued, but Charles II knew when to compromise. His brother, James II (1685–1688), possessed none of his ability and was ousted by the Revolution of 1688, which confirmed the primacy of Parliament. James's daughter, Mary, and her husband, William of Orange, then became the rulers.

Queen Anne's reign (1702–1714) was marked by the duke of Marlborough's victories over France at Blenheim, Oudenarde, and Malplaquet in the War of the Spanish Succession. England and Scotland meanwhile were joined by the Act of Union (1707). Upon the death of Anne, the distant claims of the elector of Hanover were recognized, and he became king of Great Britain and Ireland as George I. The unwillingness of the Hanoverian kings to rule resulted in the formation by the royal ministers of a cabinet, headed by a prime minister, which directed all public business. Abroad, the constant wars with France expanded the British Empire all over the globe, particularly in North America and India. This imperial

1. The title Prince of Wales, which is not inherited, was conferred on Prince Charles by his mother on July 26, 1958. The investiture ceremony took place on July 1, 1969. The previous Prince of Wales was Prince Edward Albert, who held the title from 1911 to 1936 before he became Edward VIII.

Rulers of England and Great Britain

Name	Born	Ruled[1]
SAXONS[2]		
Egbert[3]	c. 775	802–839
Ethelwulf	?	839–858
Ethelbald	?	858–860
Ethelbert	?	860–865
Ethelred I	?	865–871
Alfred the Great	849	871–899
Edward the Elder	c. 870	899–924
Athelstan	895	924–939
Edmund I the Deed-doer	921	939–946
Edred	c. 925	946–955
Edwy the Fair	c. 943	955–959
Edgar the Peaceful	943	959–975
Edward the Martyr	c. 962	975–978
Ethelred II the Unready	968	978–1016
Edmund II Ironside	c. 993	1016
DANES		
Canute	995	1016–1035
Harold I Harefoot	c.1016	1035–1040
Hardecanute	c.1018	1040–1042
SAXONS		
Edward the Confessor	c.1004	1042–1066
Harold II	c.1020	1066
HOUSE OF NORMANDY		
William I the Conqueror	1027	1066–1087
William II Rufus	c.1056	1087–1100
Henry I Beauclerc	1068	1100–1135
Stephen of Boulogne	c.1100	1135–1154
HOUSE OF PLANTAGENET		
Henry II	1133	1154–1189
Richard I Coeur de Lion	1157	1189–1199
John Lackland	1167	1199–1216
Henry III	1207	1216–1272
Edward I Longshanks	1239	1272–1307
Edward II	1284	1307–1327
Edward III	1312	1327–1377
Richard II	1367	1377–1399[4]
HOUSE OF LANCASTER		
Henry IV Bolingbroke	1367	1399–1413
Henry V	1387	1413–1422

Name	Born	Ruled[1]
Henry VI	1421	1422–1461[5]
HOUSE OF YORK		
Edward IV	1442	1461–1483[5]
Edward V	1470	1483–1483
Richard III	1452	1483–1485
HOUSE OF TUDOR		
Henry VII	1457	1485–1509
Henry VIII	1491	1509–1547
Edward VI	1537	1547–1553
Jane (Lady Jane Grey)[6]	1537	1553–1553
Mary I ("Bloody Mary")	1516	1553–1558
Elizabeth I	1533	1558–1603
HOUSE OF STUART		
James I[7]	1566	1603–1625
Charles I	1600	1625–1649
COMMONWEALTH		
Council of State	—	1649–1653
Oliver Cromwell[8]	1599	1653–1658
Richard Cromwell[8]	1626	1658–1659[9]
RESTORATION OF HOUSE OF STUART		
Charles II	1630	1660–1685
James II	1633	1685–1688[10]
William III[11]	1650	1689–1702
Mary II[11]	1662	1689–1694
Anne	1665	1702–1714
HOUSE OF HANOVER		
George I	1660	1714–1727
George II	1683	1727–1760
George III	1738	1760–1820
George IV	1762	1820–1830
William IV	1765	1830–1837
Victoria	1819	1837–1901
HOUSE OF SAXE-COBURG[12]		
Edward VII	1841	1901–1910
HOUSE OF WINDSOR[12]		
George V	1865	1910–1936
Edward VIII	1894	1936[13]
George VI	1895	1936–1952
Elizabeth II	1926	1952–

1. Year of end of rule is also that of death, unless otherwise indicated. 2. Dates for Saxon kings are still subject of controversy. 3. Became king of West Saxons in 802; considered (from 828) first king of all England. 4. Died 1400. 5. Henry VI reigned again briefly 1470–1471. 6. Nominal queen for 9 days; not counted as queen by some authorities. She was beheaded in 1554. 7. Ruled in Scotland as James VI (1567–1625). 8. Lord Protector. 9. Died 1712. 10. Died 1701. 11. Joint rulers (1689–1694). 12. Name changed from Saxe-Coburg to Windsor in 1917. 13. Was known after his abdication as the duke of Windsor, died 1972.

growth was checked by the revolt of the American colonies (1775–1781). Struggles with France broke out again in 1793 and during the Napoleonic Wars, which ended at Waterloo in 1815.

The Victorian era, named after Queen Victoria (1837–1901), saw the growth of a democratic system of government that had begun with the Reform Bill of 1832. The two important wars in Victoria's reign were the Crimean War against Russia (1853–1856) and the Boer War (1899–1902), the latter enormously extending Britain's influence in Africa. Increasing uneasiness at home and abroad marked the reign of Edward VII (1901–1910). Within four years after the accession of George V in 1910, Britain entered World War I when Germany invaded Belgium. The nation was led by coalition cabinets, headed first by Herbert Asquith and then, starting in 1916, by the Welsh statesman David Lloyd George. Postwar labor unrest culminated in the general strike of 1926.

King Edward VIII succeeded to the throne on Jan. 20, 1936, at his father's death, but abdicated on Dec. 11, 1936 (in order to marry an American divorcée, Wallis Warfield Simpson), in favor of his brother, who became George VI.

The efforts of Prime Minister Neville Chamberlain to stem the rising threat of Nazism in Germany failed with the German invasion of Poland on Sept. 1, 1939, which was followed by Britain's entry into World War II on Sept. 3. Allied reverses in the spring of 1940 led to Chamberlain's resignation and the formation of another coalition war cabinet by the Conservative leader, Winston Churchill, who led Britain through most of World War II. Churchill resigned shortly after V-E Day, May 8, 1945, but then formed a "caretaker" government that remained in office until after the parliamentary elections in July, which the Labour Party won overwhelmingly. The new government, formed by Clement R. Attlee, began a moderate socialist program.

In 1951, Churchill again became prime minister at the head of a Conservative government. George VI died on Feb. 6, 1952, and was succeeded by his daughter, Elizabeth II. Churchill stepped down in 1955 in favor of Sir Anthony Eden, who resigned on grounds of ill health in 1957 and was succeeded by Harold

British Prime Ministers Since 1770

Name	Term	Name	Term
Lord North (Tory)	1770–1782	William E. Gladstone (Liberal)	1886–1886
Marquis of Rockingham (Whig)	1782–1782	Marquis of Salisbury (Conservative)	1886–1892
Earl of Shelburne (Whig)	1782–1783	William E. Gladstone (Liberal)	1892–1894
Duke of Portland (Coalition)	1783–1783	Earl of Rosebery (Liberal)	1894–1895
William Pitt, the Younger (Tory)	1783–1801	Marquis of Salisbury (Conservative)	1895–1902
Henry Addington (Tory)	1801–1804	Arthur James Balfour (Conservative)	1902–1905
William Pitt, the Younger (Tory)	1804–1806	Sir H. Campbell-Bannerman (Liberal)	1905–1908
Baron Grenville (Whig)	1806–1807	Herbert H. Asquith (Liberal)	1908–1915
Duke of Portland (Tory)	1807–1809	Herbert H. Asquith (Coalition)	1915–1916
Spencer Perceval (Tory)	1809–1812	David Lloyd George (Coalition)	1916–1922
Earl of Liverpool (Tory)	1812–1827	Andrew Bonar Law (Conservative)	1922–1923
George Canning (Tory)	1827–1827	Stanley Baldwin (Conservative)	1923–1924
Viscount Goderich (Tory)	1827–1828	James Ramsay MacDonald (Labour)	1924–1924
Duke of Wellington (Tory)	1828–1830	Stanley Baldwin (Conservative)	1924–1929
Earl Grey (Whig)	1830–1834	James Ramsay MacDonald (Labour)	1929–1931
Viscount Melbourne (Whig)	1834–1834	James Ramsay MacDonald (Coalition)	1931–1935
Sir Robert Peel (Tory)	1834–1835	Stanley Baldwin (Coalition)	1935–1937
Viscount Melbourne (Whig)	1835–1841	Neville Chamberlain (Coalition)	1937–1940
Sir Robert Peel (Tory)	1841–1846	Winston Churchill (Coalition)	1940–1945
Earl Russell (Whig)	1846–1852	Clement R. Attlee (Labour)	1945–1951
Earl of Derby (Tory)	1852–1852	Sir Winston Churchill (Conservative)	1951–1955
Earl of Aberdeen (Coalition)	1852–1855	Sir Anthony Eden (Conservative)	1955–1957
Viscount Palmerston (Liberal)	1855–1858	Harold Macmillan (Conservative)	1957–1963
Earl of Derby (Conservative)	1858–1859	Sir Alec Frederick Douglas-Home (Conservative)	1963–1964
Viscount Palmerston (Liberal)	1859–1865	Harold Wilson (Labour)	1964–1970
Earl Russell (Liberal)	1865–1866	Edward Heath (Conservative)	1970–1974
Earl of Derby (Conservative)	1866–1868	Harold Wilson (Labour)	1974–1976
Benjamin Disraeli (Conservative)	1868–1868	James Callaghan (Labour)	1976–1979
William E. Gladstone (Liberal)	1868–1874	Margaret Thatcher (Conservative)	1979–1990
Benjamin Disraeli (Conservative)	1874–1880	John Major (Conservative)	1990–1997
William E. Gladstone (Liberal)	1880–1885	Tony Blair (Labour)	1997–
Marquis of Salisbury (Conservative)	1885–1886		

Macmillan and Sir Alec Douglas-Home. In 1964, Harold Wilson led the Labour Party to victory. A lagging economy brought the Conservatives back to power in 1970. Prime Minister Edward Heath won Britain's admission to the European Community. Margaret Thatcher became Britain's first woman prime minister as the Conservatives won 339 seats on May 3, 1979.

An Argentine invasion of the Falkland Islands on April 2, 1982, involved Britain in a war 8,000 mi from the home islands. Argentina had long claimed the Falklands, known as the *Malvinas* in Spanish, which had been occupied by the British since 1832. Britain won a decisive victory within six weeks when more than 11,000 Argentine troops on the Falklands surrendered on June 14, 1982.

Although there were continuing economic problems and foreign policy disputes, an upswing in the economy in 1986–1987 led Thatcher to call elections in June, and she won a near-unprecedented third consecutive term. The unpopularity of Thatcher's poll tax together with an uncompromising position toward further European integration eroded support within her own party. When John Major won the Conservative Party leadership in November, Thatcher resigned, paving the way for Major to form a government.

Eighteen years of Conservative rule ended in May 1997 when Tony Blair and the Labour Party triumphed in the British elections. Blair has been compared to former U.S. president Bill Clinton for his youthful, telegenic personality and centrist views. He produced constitutional reform that partially decentralized the UK, leading to the formation of separate Parliaments in Wales and Scotland by 1999. Britain turned over its colony Hong Kong to China in July 1997.

Blair's controversial meeting in Oct. 1997 with Sinn Fein's president, Gerry Adams, was the first meeting in 76 years between a British prime minister and a Sinn Fein leader. It infuriated numerous factions but was a symbolic gesture in support of the nascent peace talks in Northern Ireland. In 1998 the Good Friday Agreement, strongly supported by Tony Blair, led to the first promise of peace between Catholics and Protestants since the beginning of the so-called Troubles.

Along with the U.S., Britain launched air strikes against Iraq in Dec. 1998 after Saddam Hussein expelled UN arms inspectors. In the spring of 1999, Britain spearheaded the NATO operation in Kosovo, which resulted in Yugoslavian president Slobodan Milosevic's withdrawal from the territory.

In the fall of 1999, Britain and France argued heatedly about France's refusal to allow the importation of British beef. France remained leery of the possibility of infection from bovine spongiform encephalopathy (BSE), commonly known as mad cow disease, despite the fact that the EU had lifted the three-year ban on British beef in August.

In Feb. 2001, foot-and-mouth disease broke out among British livestock, prompting other nations to ban British meat import and forcing the slaughter of thousands of cattle, pigs, and sheep in an effort to stem the highly contagious disease. The episode cost farmers and the tourist industry billions of dollars.

In June 2001, Blair won a second landslide victory, with the Labour Party capturing 413 seats in Parliament.

Britain became the U.S.'s staunchest ally after the Sept. 11 attacks on New York and Washington, DC. British troops joined the U.S. in the bombing campaign against Afghanistan in Oct. 2001, after the Taliban-led government refused to turn over the prime suspect in the terrorist attacks, Osama bin Laden. After the Taliban was toppled two months later, the UK led the peacekeeping forces stationed in Afghanistan, the International Security Assistance Force (ISAF), from Jan. to June 2002. The UK also sent additional troops to fight against remaining Taliban and al-Qaeda troops.

Blair again proved himself to be the U.S.'s strongest international supporter in Sept. 2002, when he became President Bush's major ally in calling for a war against Iraq. Blair maintained that military action was justified because Iraq was developing weapons of mass destruction that were a direct threat to its enemies. Blair continued to support the Bush administration's hawkish policies despite great opposition in his own party. The British public was also largely opposed to a war on Iraq: in March 2003, a *Times of London* newspaper poll indicated that only 19% of respondents approved of military action without a UN mandate. As the inevitability of the U.S. strike on Iraq grew nearer, Blair announced that he would join the U.S. in fighting Iraq with or without a second UN resolution. Three of his ministers resigned as a result. Britain entered the war on March 20, supplying 45,000 troops who fought mostly in Basra, in the southern portion of the country. In the aftermath of the war, Blair came under fire from government officials for allegedly exaggerating Iraq's possession of weapons of mass destruction. Critics were particularly skeptical of Blair's Sept. 2002 intelligence dossier claiming that Iraq's chemical and biological weapons "are deployable within 45 minutes of an order to use them." Foreign Secretary Jack Straw acknowledged publicly that the "white paper," which contained plagiarized material from a graduate student's thesis written 12 years ago, was "an embarrassment," but the Blair government has staunchly defended the veracity of all British intelligence regarding Iraq. The arguments grew so vociferous between the Blair government and the BBC that a prominent weapons scientist caught in the middle committed suicide. In July Blair announced that "history would forgive" the UK and U.S. "if we are wrong"—the end to the "inhuman carnage and suffering" caused by Saddam Hussein was justification enough for the war, he said.

Northern Ireland

Status: Part of United Kingdom
First Minister: (suspended Oct. 14, 2002)
Area: 5,452 sq mi (14,121 sq km)
Population (1998 est.): 1,688,600
Capital and largest city (2003 est.): Belfast, 484,800 (metro. area), 246,200 (city proper). **Monetary unit:** British pound sterling (£). **Language:** English. **Religions:** Presbyterian, Church of Ireland, Roman Catholic, Methodist.

Geography Northern Ireland is composed of 26 districts, derived from the boroughs of Belfast and Londonderry and the counties of Antrim, Armagh, Down, Fermanagh, Londonderry, and Tyrone. Together they are commonly called Ulster, though the territory does not include the entire ancient province of Ulster. It is slightly larger than Connecticut.

Government Northern Ireland is an integral part of the United Kingdom (it has 12 representatives in the British House of Commons), but under the terms of the Government of Ireland Act in 1920, it had a semiautonomous government. In 1972, however, after three years of sectarian violence between Protestants and Catholics that resulted in more than 400 dead and thousands injured, Britain suspended the Ulster Parliament. The Ulster counties were governed directly from London after an attempt to return certain powers to an elected assembly in Belfast.

As a result of the Good Friday Agreement of 1998, a new coalition government was formed on Dec. 2, 1999, with the British government formally transferring governing power to the Northern Irish Parliament. David Trimble, Protestant leader of the Ulster Unionist Party (UUP) and winner of the 1998 Nobel Peace Prize, became first minister. The government has been suspended four times since then; it has remained suspened since Oct. 14, 2002.

History Ulster was part of Catholic Ireland until the reign of Elizabeth I (1558–1603) when, after suppressing three Irish rebellions, the Crown confiscated lands in Ireland and settled the Scots Presbyterians in Ulster. Another rebellion in 1641–1651, brutally crushed by Oliver Cromwell, resulted in the settlement of Anglican Englishmen in Ulster. Subsequent political policy favoring Protestants and disadvantaging Catholics encouraged further Protestant settlement in Northern Ireland.

Northern Ireland did not separate from the South until William Gladstone presented, in 1886, his proposal for home rule in Ireland. The Protestants in the North feared domination by the Catholic majority. Industry, moreover, was concentrated in the North and dependent on the British market. When World War I began, civil war threatened between the regions. Northern Ireland, however, did not become a political entity until the six counties accepted the Home Rule Bill of 1920. This set up a semiautonomous Parliament in Belfast and a Crown-appointed governor advised by a cabinet of the prime minister and 8 ministers, as well as a 12-member representation in the House of Commons in London.

When the Republic of Ireland gained sovereignty in 1922, relations improved between North and South, although the Irish Republican Army (IRA), outlawed in recent years, continued the struggle to end the partition of Ireland. In 1966–1969, rioting and street fighting between Protestants and Catholics occurred in Londonderry, fomented by extremist nationalist Protestants, who feared the Catholics might attain a local majority, and by Catholics demonstrating for civil rights. These confrontations became known as "the Troubles."

The religious communities, Catholic and Protestant, became hostile armed camps. British troops were brought in to separate them, but themselves became a target of Catholics, particularly by the IRA, which by this time had turned into a full-fledged terrorist movement. The goal of the IRA was to eject the British and unify Northern Ireland with the Irish Republic to the south. The Protestants remained tenaciously loyal to the United Kingdom, and various Protestant terrorist organizations pursued the Unionist cause through violence. Various attempts at representational government and power-sharing foundered during the 1970s, and both sides were further polarized. Direct rule from London and the presence of British troops failed to stop the violence.

In Oct. 1977, the 1976 Nobel Peace Prize was awarded to Mairead Corrigan and Betty Williams, founders of the Community of Peace People, a nonsectarian organization dedicated to creating peace in Northern Ireland. Intermittent violence continued, however, and on Aug. 27, 1979, an IRA bomb killed Lord Mountbatten as he was sailing off southern Ireland, heightening tensions. Catholic protests over the death of IRA hunger striker Bobby Sands in 1981 fueled more violence. Riots, sniper fire, and terrorist attacks killed more than 3,200 people between 1969 and 1998. Among the attempts at reconciliation undertaken during the 1980s was the Anglo-Irish Agreement (1985), which, to the dismay of Unionists, marked the first time the Republic of Ireland had been given an official consultative role in the affairs of the province.

In 1997, Northern Ireland made a significant step in the direction of stemming sectarian strife. The first formal peace talks began on Oct. 6 with representatives of eight major Northern Irish political parties participating, a feat that in itself required three years of negotiations. Two smaller Protestant parties, including hard-liner Ian Paisley's Democratic Unionists, boycotted the talks. For the first time, Sinn Fein, the political wing of the IRA, won two seats in the British Parliament, which went to Sinn Fein president Gerry Adams and second-in-command, Martin McGuinness. Although the election strengthened the IRA's political legitimacy, it was the IRA's resumption of the 17-month cease-fire, which had collapsed in Feb. 1996, that gained them a place at the negotiating table.

A landmark settlement, the Good Friday Agreement of April 10, 1998, came after 19 months of intensive negotiations that involved 8 of the 10 Northern Irish political parties. The accord called for Protestants to share political power with the minority Catholics, and it gave the Republic of Ireland a voice in Northern Irish affairs. In turn, Catholics were to suspend the goal of a united Ireland—a territorial claim that was the raison d'être of the IRA and was written into the Irish Republic's constitution—unless the largely Protestant North voted in favor of such an arrangement, an unlikely occurrence.

The resounding commitment to the settlement was demonstrated in a dual referendum on May 22, 1998: the North approved the accord by a vote of 71% to 29%, and in the Irish Republic 94% favored it. In October, the Nobel Peace Prize was awarded to John Hume and David Trimble, leaders of the largest Catholic and Protestant political parties, an incentive for all sides to ensure that this time the peace would last.

In Dec. 1998 the rival Northern Ireland politicians agreed on the organization and contents of the new coalition government, but in June 1999 the peace process again hit an impasse when the IRA refused to disarm prior to the assembly of Northern Ireland's new provincial cabinet. Sinn Fein insisted the IRA would only begin giving up its illegal weapons after the formation of the new government; Unionists demanded disarmament first. As a result, the Ulster Unionists boycotted the assembly session that would have nominated the cabinet to run the new coalition government. The nascent Northern Irish government was stillborn in July 1999.

Subsequent talks on the agreement, which would have ended three decades of direct rule from London, seemed to go nowhere. Finally, at the end of November, David Trimble, leader of the Ulster Unionists, abandoned the seemingly sacrosanct "no guns, no government" position, and took a difficult leap of faith in agreeing to form a government prior to Sinn Fein's disarmament. If the IRA did not begin the destruction of their weapons by Jan. 31, 2000, however, the Ulster Unionists threatened they would withdraw from the Northern Irish Parliament, shutting down the new government. With this compromise in place, the new government was quickly formed, and on Dec. 2, 1999, the British government formally transferred governing power to the Northern Irish Parliament. David Trimble became first minister. Two leaders of Sinn Fein, Gerry Adams and Martin McGuinness, received seats in the 4-party, 12-member Parliament. But by the deadline, Sinn Fein had made little progress toward disarmament, and claimed it had not made any such commitment. As a result, the British government suspended Parliament on Feb. 12, 2000, and once again imposed direct rule. In July 2001, after issuing one last ultimatum to the IRA to begin destroying its weapons stores, Ulster Unionist leader David Trimble resigned his post as first minister.

Following Trimble's departure, the IRA offered another vague and open-ended disarmament plan, only to withdraw it. But on Oct. 23, days before Britain was to suspend the assembly, Sinn Fein leader Gerry Adams dramatically announced that the IRA had indeed begun disarming. Partially in response to the Sept. 11 attacks, which made the IRA's claim to weapons of terror seem even more senselessly brutal, Sinn Fein chose to embrace the promise of a political solution to the Northern Irish troubles. On Nov. 6, David Trimble was reelected as first minister.

On April 8, 2002, international weapons inspectors announced that the IRA had put more stockpiled munitions "beyond use," the euphemistic phrase used in the negotiations to mean disarmament. British and Irish leaders hoped that Protestant guerrilla groups would also begin to surrender their weapons. However, in mid-June British and Irish political leaders called emergency talks to stem the rising tide of violence in Belfast. On July 16, the IRA issued a public apology to the families of the 650 civilians killed by the IRA since the late 1960s.

On Oct. 14, the British government again assumed direct rule of Northern Ireland, after the Unionists threatened to quit the Assembly in protest of suspected spying activity by the IRA. In March and April 2003, negotiations were again underway to reinstate the Northern Ireland assembly. But Sinn Fein's vague language, weakly pledging that its "strategies and disciplines will not be inconsistent with the Good Friday Agreement," caused Tony Blair to challenge Sinn Fein to once and for all make a clear, unambiguous pledge to renounce paramilitary for political means. According to the *New York Times* (April 24, 2003), "virtually every newspaper in Britain and Ireland has editorialized in favor of full disarmament, and the Irish government, traditionally sympathetic to Sinn Fein, is almost as adamant about the matter as London is."

Scotland

Status: Part of United Kingdom
First Minister: Jack McConnell (2001)
Area: 30,414 sq mi (78,772 sq km)
Population (1996 est.): 5,128,000; density per sq mi: 168.6
Capital (2003 est.): Edinburgh, 663,700 (metro. area), 460,000 (city proper). **Largest city:** Glasgow, 1,361,000 (metro. area), 1,099,400 (city proper). **Monetary unit:** British pound sterling (£). **Languages:** English, Scots Gaelic. **Religions:** Church of Scotland (established church—Presbyterian), Roman Catholic, Scottish Episcopal Church, Baptist, Methodist

Geography Scotland occupies the northern third of the island of Great Britain. It is bounded by England in the south and on the other three sides by water: by the Atlantic Ocean on the west and north and by the North Sea on the east. Scotland is divided into three physical regions—the Highlands; the Central Lowlands, containing two-thirds of the population; and the Southern Uplands. The western Highland coast is intersected throughout by long, narrow sea lochs, or fjords. Scotland also includes the Outer and Inner Hebrides and other islands off the west coast and the Orkney and Shetland Islands off the north coast.

Government England and Scotland have shared a monarch since 1603 and a Parliament since 1707, but in May 1999, Scotland elected its own Parliament for the first time in three centuries. The new Scottish legislature was in part the result of British prime minister Tony Blair's campaign promise to permit devolution, the transfer of local powers from London to Edinburgh. In a Sept. 1997 referendum, 74% of Scotland voted in favor of their own Parliament, which controls most domestic affairs, including health, education, and transportation, and has powers to legislate and raise taxes. Queen Elizabeth opened the new Parliament on July 2, 1999.

History The first inhabitants of Scotland were the Picts, a Celtic tribe. Between A.D. 82 and A.D. 208, the Romans invaded Scotland, naming it Caledonia. Roman influence over the land, however, was minimal.

The Scots, a Celtic tribe from Ireland, migrated to the west coast of Scotland in about 500. Kenneth McAlpin, King of the Scots, ascended the throne of the Pictish kingdom in about 843, thereby uniting the various Scots and Pictish tribes under one kingdom called Dal Riada. By the 11th century, the monarchy had extended its borders to include much of what is Scotland today.

English influence in the region expanded when Malcolm III, king of Scotland from 1057–1093, married an English princess. England's appetite for Scottish land began to grow over the 12th and 13th centuries, and in 1296 King Edward I of England successfully invaded Scotland. The following year Robert the Bruce led a revolt for independence, was crowned king of Scotland (Robert I) in 1306, and after years of battle defeated the English in 1314 at the Battle of Bannockburn. In 1328 the English finally recognized Scottish independence.

In the 16th century John Knox introduced the Scottish reformation, and the Presbyterian church replaced Catholicism as the official religion. In 1567, Mary, Queen of Scots, a Catholic, was forced to abdicate the Scottish throne, and was later executed by Elizabeth I of England. Mary's son, James VI, was raised as a Protestant, and in 1603 he succeeded Elizabeth on the English throne as King James I of England. James thus became ruler of both Scotland and England, though the countries remained separate. In 1707, after a century of turmoil, Scotland and England passed the Act of Union, which united Scotland, England, and Wales under one rule as the Kingdom of Great Britain. The House of Hanover replaced the Stuart lineage on the throne in 1714, which caused a rebellion among Scots who still supported the Stuarts. The Jacobites, as the rebels were called, led two uprisings, in 1715 and again in 1745.

With the advent of the Industrial Revolution, Scotland, whose chief product had been textiles, began developing the industries of shipbuilding, coal mining, iron, and steel. In the late 20th century Scotland concentrated on electronics and high-tech industries. The North Sea has also become an important source of oil and gas.

In May 1999, Scotland elected its first separate Parliament in three centuries. Labour won the largest number of seats, defeating the Scottish National Party (SNP), which supports Scotland's independence from Britain.

Wales

Status: Part of United Kingdom
First Secretary: Rhodri Morgan (2000)
Area: 8,019 sq mi (20,768 sq km)
Population (1993 est.): 2,906,500
Capital and largest city (2003 est.): Cardiff, 676,400 (metro. area), 280,800 (city proper). **Monetary unit:** British pound sterling (£). **Languages:** English, Welsh. **Religions:** Calvinistic Methodist, Church of Wales (disestablished—Anglican), Roman Catholic

Geography Wales lies west of England and is separated from England by the Cambrian Mountains. It is bordered on the northwest, west, and south by the Irish Sea and on the northeast and east by England. Wales is generally hilly; the Snowdon range in the northern part culminates in Mount Snowdon (3,560 ft, 1,085 m), Wales's highest peak.

Government Until 1999, Wales was ruled solely by the UK government and a secretary of state. In the referendum of Sept. 18, 1997, Welsh citizens voted to establish a National Assembly. Wales will remain part of the UK, and the secretary of state for Wales and members of Parliament from Welsh constituencies will continue to have seats in Parliament. Unlike Scotland, which in 1999 voted to have its own Parliament, the National Assembly will not be able to legislate and raise taxes. Wales will, however, control most of its local affairs. The Welsh assembly officially opened on July 1, 1999.

History The prehistoric peoples of Wales left behind megaliths and other impressive monuments. They were followed by settlements of Celts in the region. The Romans occupied the region from the 1st to the 5th century A.D. Thereafter Angles, Saxons, and Jutes invaded the British island, but they left Wales virtually untouched. Beginning in the 8th century, the various Welsh tribes fought with their Anglo-Saxon neighbors to the east, but the Welsh were able to thwart attempted invasions. After William the Conqueror subdued England in 1066, however, his Norman armies marched into Wales in 1093 and occupied portions of it. By 1282, the English conquest of Wales was complete, and in 1284, the Statute of Rhuddlan formalized England's sovereignty over Wales. In 1301, King Edward I gave his son, who later became Edward II, the title Prince of Wales, a gesture meant to indicate the unity and relationship between the two lands. With the exception of Edward II, all subsequent British monarchs have given this title to their eldest son.

In 1400, the Welsh prince Owen Glendower led a revolt against the English, expelling them from much of Wales in just four years. By 1410, however, his rebellion was crushed. In 1485, Henry VII became king of England. A Welshman and the first in the Tudor line, Henry's reign, and that of subsequent Tudors, made English rule more palatable to the Welsh. His son, King Henry VIII, joined England and Wales under the Act of Union in 1536.

The Industrial Revolution of the 19th century transformed Wales and threatened the traditional livelihood of farmers and shepherds. In the 20th century, the economy of Wales was based primarily on coal production. After World War I, coal prices dropped; this, coupled with the Great Depression, fueled high unemployment rates and economic uncertainty.

In recent years, a resurgence of the Welsh language and culture has demonstrated a stronger national identity among the Welsh, and politically the country moved toward greater self-government (devolution). In 1999, with the strong support of Britain's prime minister, Tony Blair, Wales opened the Welsh National

Assembly, the first real self-government Wales has had in more than six hundred years.

Overseas Territories and Crown Dependencies of the United Kingdom

Anguilla

Status: Overseas territory
Governor: Peter Johnstone (2000)
Chief Minister: Osbourne Fleming (2000)
Area: 39.38 sq mi (102 sq km)
Population (2003 est.): 12,738; (growth rate: 0.9%); birth rate: 14.7/1000; infant mortality rate: 22.8/1000; density per sq mi: 323
Capital (2003 est.): The Valley, 830. **Monetary unit:** East Caribbean dollar. **Ethnicity/race:** black African. **Literacy:** 95% (1984 est.)
Economic summary: GDP/PPP (2001 est.): $104 million; per capita $8,600. **Real growth rate:** 0%. **Inflation:** 2.3%. **Unemployment:** 8% (1999). **Arable land:** 0%. **Agriculture:** small quantities of tobacco, vegetables; cattle raising. **Labor force:** 6,735 (1999); commerce 36%, services 29%, construction 18%, transportation and utilities 10%, manufacturing 3%, agriculture/fishing/forestry/mining 4%. **Industries:** tourism, boat building, offshore financial services. **Natural resources:** salt, fish, lobster. **Exports:** $2.6 million (1999): lobster, fish, livestock, salt, concrete blocks, rum. **Imports:** $80.9 million (1999); fuels, foodstuffs, manufactures, chemicals, textiles. **Major trading partners:** U.S., UK, Puerto Rico.

Anguilla was first colonized in 1650 by English settlers from St. Christopher (St. Kitts) and has since remained a British territory. It was originally part of the West Indies Associated States as a component of the St. Kitts-Nevis-Anguilla Federation. In 1967, Anguilla declared its independence from the federation but Britain did not recognize this action. In Feb. 1969, Anguilla voted to cut all ties with Britain and become an independent republic. In March, Britain landed troops on the island and, on March 30, a truce was signed. In July 1971, Anguilla became a dependency of Britain and two months later Britain ordered the withdrawal of all its troops. A new constitution for Anguilla, effective in Feb. 1976, provided for separate administration and a government of elected representatives. The Associated State of St. Kitts-Nevis-Anguilla ended in 1980, and in 1982 a new Anguillan constitution took effect.

Bermuda

Status: Overseas territory
Governor: Sir John Vereker (2002)
Premier: Alex Scott (2003)
Area: 21 sq mi (53.3 sq km)
Population (2003 est.): 64,482; (growth rate: 0.5%); birth rate: 12.1/1000; infant mortality rate: 9.1/1000; density per sq mi: 3,133
Capital (2003 est.): Hamilton, 970. **Monetary unit:** Bermuda dollar. **Ethnicity/race:** black African 58%, white and other 42%. **Literacy rate:** 98% (1970 est.)
Economic summary: GDP/PPP (2001 est.): $2.2 billion; per capita $34,800. **Real growth rate:** 2.9%. **Inflation:** 3% (July 2001) . **Unemployment:** 4.5% (1993). **Arable land:** 6%. **Agriculture:** bananas, vegetables, citrus, flowers; dairy products. **Labor force:** 37,472 (2000); clerical 22%, services 20%, laborers 17%, professional and technical 17%, administrative and managerial 13%, sales 8%, agriculture and fishing 3%. **Industries:** tourism, international business, light manufacturing. **Natural resources:** limestone, pleasant climate fostering tourism. **Exports:** $51 million (2000): reexports of pharmaceuticals. **Imports:** $719 million (2000): machinery and transport equipment, construction materials, chemicals, food and live animals. **Major trading partners:** EU, UK, U.S., Russia.

Bermuda is an archipelago of about 360 small islands, 580 mi (934 km) east of North Carolina. The largest is (Great) Bermuda, or Main Island. Explored by Juan de Bermúdez, a Spaniard, the islands were settled in 1612 by an offshoot of the Virginia Company. Bermuda became a Crown colony in 1684.

In 1968, Bermuda was granted a new constitution, its first prime minister, and autonomy, except for foreign relations, defense, and internal security. The predominantly white United Bermuda Party has retained power in four elections against the opposition—the black-led Progressive Labour Party—although Bermuda's population is 58% black. U.S. air and navy bases, which had been leased in 1941 for 99-year terms, closed in 1995, along with Canadian, British army, and Royal Navy bases. In a referendum held in Aug. 1995, nearly three-fourths of those voting opposed independence. The prime minister's unexpected resignation in March 1997 led the ruling United Bermuda Party to name Pamela Gordon the country's first female and youngest premier. She was succeeded in 1998 by Jennifer Smith. Smith resigned in July 2003, after her party revolted against her following a narrow victory in parliamentary elections. Alex Scott became the new leader of the Progressive Labor Party and Bermuda's premier.

British Indian Ocean Territory

Status: Overseas territory
Commissioner: John White (1998)
Administrative headquarters: Victoria, Seychelles
Area: 85 sq mi (220 sq km)

This territory, consisting of the Chagos Archipelago and other small island groups, was formed in 1965 by agreement with Mauritius and the Seychelles. One of its islands, Diego Garcia (17 sq mi), is a joint U.S.-UK refueling and support station that was used during the Persian Gulf War (1991), the war against Afghanistan (1991), and the second Iraq war (1993). The island's small native population, known as the Ilois, were forced to relocate (1967–1973) to Mauritius and the Seychelles, where the majority of these former agricultural workers live in poverty in urban slums. In 2000, a British court ruled that the immigration order was invalid, but upheld the island's military status. The Ilois are currently suing the British government for compensation and the right of return.

British Virgin Islands

VIRGIN ISLANDS
Status: Overseas territory
Governor: Tom Macan (2002)
Chief Minister: Orlando Smith (2003)
Area: 59 sq mi (153 sq km)
Population (2003 est.): 21,730; (growth rate: 1.1%); birth rate: 15.0/1000; infant mortality rate: 18.8/1000; density per sq mi: 368
Capital (2003 est.): Road Town (on Tortola): 9,100. **Monetary unit:** U.S. dollar. **Literacy rate:** 97.8% (1991 est.)
Economic summary: GDP/PPP (2000 est.): $311 million; per capita $16,000. **Real growth rate:** 4.4%. **Inflation:** 3.3%. **Unemployment:** 3% (1995). **Arable land:** 20%. **Agriculture:** fruits, vegetables; livestock, poultry; fish. **Labor force:** 4,911 (1980). **Industries:** tourism, light industry, construction, rum, concrete

block, offshore financial center. **Natural resources:** negl. **Exports:** $6.2 million (2000 est.): rum, fresh fish, fruits, animals; gravel, sand. **Imports:** $230 million (2000 est.): building materials, automobiles, foodstuffs, machinery. **Major trading partners:** U.S. Virgin Islands., Puerto Rico, U.S.

Some 36 islands (more than 20 are uninhabited) in the Caribbean Sea northeast of Puerto Rico and west of the Leeward Islands, the British Virgin Islands are economically interdependent with the U.S. Virgin Islands to the south. The principal islands are Tortola, Virgin Gorda, Anegada, and Jost Van Dyke. When Christopher Columbus explored the islands in 1493, he found the Carib people living there. By 1596 most of the Caribs had fled or been killed.

The British Virgin Islands were annexed in 1672. The English planters' slave-based sugar plantations declined after slavery was abolished in the first half of the 19th century. The islands received a separate administration in 1956 as a Crown colony. Tourism is the islands' mainstay.

Cayman Islands

Status: Overseas territory
Governor: Bruce Dinwiddy (2002)
Area: 101 sq mi (262 sq km)
Population (2003 est.): 41,934 (growth rate: 0.9%); birth rate: 13.3/1000; infant mortality rate: 8.6/1000; density per sq mi: 415
Capital (2003 est.): George Town (on Grand Cayman), 29,400. **Monetary unit:** Cayman Islands dollar. **Literacy rate:** 98% (1970 est.)
Economic summary: GDP/PPP (1999 est.): $1.18 billion; per capita $30,000. **Real growth rate:** 4.5% (2000). **Inflation:** 2.3% (2000). **Unemployment:** 4.1% (1997). **Arable land:** 0%. **Agriculture:** vegetables, fruit; livestock, turtle farming. **Labor force:** 19,820 (1995); agriculture 1.4%, industry 12.6%, services 86% (1995). **Industries:** tourism, banking, insurance and finance, construction, construction materials, furniture. **Natural resources:** fish, climate and beaches that foster tourism. **Exports:** $1.2 million (1999): turtle products, manufactured consumer goods. **Imports:** $457.4 million (1999): foodstuffs, manufactured goods. **Major trading partners:** U.S., Trinidad and Tobago, UK, Netherlands Antilles, Japan.

The Caymans consist of three islands—Grand Cayman (76 sq mi; 197 sq km), Cayman Brac (22 sq mi; 57 sq km), and Little Cayman (20 sq mi; 52 sq km)—situated about 180 mi (290 km) northwest of Jamaica. They were dependencies of Jamaica until 1959, when they became a unit territory within the Federation of the West Indies. In 1962, upon the dissolution of the federation, the Cayman Islands became a British dependency, and a new constitution approved in 1972 provided for a greater degree of autonomy. Tourism and finance are the Cayman Islands' major industries. For a time, the Cayman Islands were blacklisted by the Paris-based Financial Action Task Force (FATF) for its alleged loose policy concerning money laundering. It was removed from the list in 2001.

Channel Islands: Jersey and Guernsey

Status: Crown dependencies
Lieutenant Governor of Jersey: Sir Michael Wilkes (1995)
Lieutenant Governor of Guernsey: Vice Adm. Sir John Coward (1994)
Area: 45 sq mi (116 sq km) (Jersey), 30 sq mi (78 sq km) (Guernsey)
Populations (2003 est.): Jersey, 90,156; Guernsey, 64,818
Capital of Jersey (2003 est.): St. Helier, 28,600
Capital of Guernsey (2003 est.): St. Peter Port, 16,600. **Monetary units:** Guernsey pound; Jersey pound

This group of islands, lying in the English Channel off the northwest coast of France, belonged to the Duchy of Normandy until it passed to the English Crown with the Norman conquest of 1066. It was the only British possession occupied by Germany during World War II. English and French are commonly spoken (though use of the latter is declining), and a Norman-French patois survives.

For administrative purposes, the islands are divided into the Bailiwick of Jersey (45 sq mi; 116 sq km), including the Ecrehous rocks and Les Minquiers, and the Bailiwick of Guernsey (30 sq mi; 78 sq km), including Alderney (3 sq mi; 7.8 sq km), Sark (2 sq mi; 5.2 sq km), Herm, Jethou, Brechou, and other smaller islands. The Channel Islands enjoy tax sovereignty, and their exports are protected by British tariff barriers. Financial services, tourism, market gardening, and dairy farming are important industries.

Falkland Islands

Status: Overseas territory
Governor: Howard Pearce (2002)
Chief Executive: A. M. Gurr
Area: 4,700 sq mi (12,173 sq km)
Population (July 2002 est.): 2,967
Capital (2003 est.): Stanley (on East Falkland), 2,100. **Monetary unit:** Falkland Island pound
Economic summary: GDP/PPP (1996 est.): $52 million; per capita $19,000. **Real growth rate:** 1%. **Inflation:** 3.6% (1998). **Unemployment:** full employment; labor shortage. **Arable land:** 0%. **Agriculture:** fodder and vegetable crops; sheep, dairy products. **Labor force:** 1,100 (est.); agriculture 95% (mostly sheepherding and fishing). **Industries:** wool and fish processing; sale of stamps and coins; tourism. **Natural resources:** fish, wildlife. **Exports:** $7.6 million (1995): wool, hides, meat. **Imports:** $24.7 million (1995): fuel, food and drink, building materials, clothing. **Major trading partners:** UK, Japan, Chile, New Zealand.

This sparsely inhabited dependency consists of a group of islands in the South Atlantic, about 250 mi (402 km) east of the South American mainland. The largest islands are East Falkland and West Falkland. The English captain John Strong made the first recorded landing in the Falklands in 1690. The islands passed between the French, Spanish, and British until 1820, when the Argentine government proclaimed its sovereignty. In 1833 a British force expelled the few remaining Argentine officials from the island without firing a shot, and in 1841 a British civilian lieutenant-governor was appointed for the Falklands. Colonial status was granted to the Falklands in 1892. Argentina, calling the islands *Las Islas Malvinas*, regularly protested Britain's occupation of the islands. On April 2, 1982, Argentina's military government invaded the Falklands. The Falkland Islands war ended ten weeks later with the surrender of the Argentine forces at Stanley to British troops, who had forcibly reoccupied the islands. Argentina still claims the islands. But an agreement between Argentina and the United Kingdom in 1995 sought to defuse licensing and sovereignty conflicts that would dampen foreign interest in exploiting the Falkland Islands' potential oil reserves.

Gibraltar

Status: Overseas territory
Governor: Francis Richards (2003)
Chief Minister: Peter Caruana (1996)
Area: 2.51 sq mi (6.5 sq km)
Population (2003 est.): 27,776 (growth rate: 0.2%); birth

rate: 11.1/1000; infant mortality rate: 5.3/1000; density per sq mi: 11,068. **Monetary unit:** Gibraltar pound. **Literacy rate:** 99%

Economic summary: GDP/PPP (1997 est.): $500 million; per capita $17,500. **Real growth rate:** n.a. **Inflation:** 1.5% (1998). **Unemployment:** 13.5% (1996). **Arable land:** 0%. **Agriculture:** none. **Labor force:** 14,800 (including non-Gibraltar laborers); services 60%, industry 40%, agriculture negl. **Industries:** tourism, banking and finance, ship-building and repairing; tobacco, mineral water, beer. **Natural resources:** negl. **Exports:** $81.1 million (f.o.b., 1997): (principally reexports) petroleum 51%, manufactured goods 41%, other 8%. **Imports:** $492 million (c.i.f., 1997): fuels, manufactured goods, and foodstuffs. **Major trading partners:** UK, Morocco, Portugal, Netherlands, Spain, U.S., Germany, Japan.

Gibraltar, at the south end of the Iberian Peninsula, is a rocky promontory commanding the western entrance to the Mediterranean. Aside from its strategic importance, it is also a free port, naval base, and coaling station. It was captured by the Moorish leader Tarik, crossing from Africa into Spain in 711, and its name is derived from the Arabic, *Jabal-al-Tarik* (Mount of Tarik). In the 15th century, it passed to the Moorish ruler of Granada and later became Spanish. It was captured by an Anglo-Dutch force in 1704 during the War of the Spanish Succession and passed to Great Britain by the Treaty of Utrecht in 1713. Since then Spain has continually laid claims to it. Most of the inhabitants of Gibraltar are of Spanish, Italian, and Maltese descent, and in 1981 Gibraltarians were granted full British citizenship. Spanish efforts to recover Gibraltar culminated in a referendum in 1967, in which the residents voted overwhelmingly to retain their link with Britain. In response, Spain sealed Gibraltar's land border between 1969 and 1985. In 2002, Britain and Spain discussed sharing the sovereignty of Gibraltar. In response, the government of Gibraltar held a referendum in Nov. 2002 in which the population voted almost unanimously against shared sovereignty.

Isle of Man

Status: Crown dependency
Lieutenant Governor: Ian David Macfadyen (2000)
Chief Minister: Donald James Gelling (1996)
Area: 221 sq mi (572 sq km)
Population (2003 est.): 74,261 (growth rate: –1.3%); birth rate: 11.4/1000; infant mortality rate: 6.2/1000; density per sq mi: 336
Capital (2003 est.): Douglas, 25,400. **Monetary unit:** Isle of Man pound

The Isle of Man is situated in the Irish Sea, equidistant from Scotland, Ireland, and England. Among its earliest inhabitants were Celts, and their language, Manx, which is closely related to Irish and Scottish Gaelic, remained the everyday speech of the people until the first half of the 19th century. Manx now has no native speakers. Norse (Viking) invasions began about 800, and the island was a dependency of Norway until 1266. During this period the Isle of Man came under a Scandinavian system of government that has remained practically unchanged ever since. The island came under the control of England in 1341. After allowing a succession of feudal lords to rule the island, the British Parliament purchased sovereignty over the island in 1765. The Isle of Man continues to be administered according to its own laws by a government composed of the lieutenant governor, a legislative council, and a House of Keys, one of the most ancient legislative assemblies in the world.

Montserrat

Status: Overseas territory
Governor: Tony Longrigg (2001)
Chief Minister: John Osborne (2001)
Area: 39 sq mi (102 sq km)
Population (2003 est.): 8,995 (growth rate: 1.0%); birth rate: 17.6/1000; infant mortality rate: 7.8/1000; density per sq mi: 228
Capital (2003 est.): Plymouth. The city was abandoned in 1997 due to volcanic activity. Interim government buildings have been built at Brades Estate, in the Carr's Bay/Little Bay vicinity at the northwest end of Montserrat. **Monetary unit:** East Caribbean dollar
Economic summary: GDP/PPP (1999 est.): $31 million; per capita $2,400. **Real growth rate:** –1.5%. **Inflation:** 5% (1998). **Unemployment:** 6%. **Arable land:** 20%. **Agriculture:** cabbages, carrots, cucumbers, tomatoes, onions, peppers; livestock products. **Labor force:** 4,521 (1992); note—recently lowered by flight of people from volcanic activity; agriculture n.a., industry n.a., services n.a. **Industries:** tourism, rum, textiles, electronic appliances. **Natural resources:** negl. **Exports:** $1.5 million (1998): electronic components, plastic bags, apparel, hot peppers, live plants, cattle. **Imports:** $26 million (1998): machinery and transportation equipment, foodstuffs, manufactured goods, fuels, lubricants, and related materials. **Major trading partners:** U.S., Antigua and Barbuda, UK, Trinidad and Tobago, Japan, Canada.

The island of Montserrat is in the Lesser Antilles of the West Indies. Until 1956, it was a division of the Leeward Islands. In 1958 Montserrat joined the Federation of the West Indies, remaining a member until that organization's dissolution in 1962. Unlike most other British West Indies possessions, Montserrat, with its weak economy, has not vigorously sought independence. The Soufrière Hills volcano began erupting in 1995, and the situation continued to worsen through 1998, with the capital, Plymouth, destroyed and the southern and central parts of the British colony having been evacuated. Thousands had moved to nearby Antigua, Britain, or other parts of the Caribbean. The volcano continued to erupt throughout 2003.

Pitcairn Island

Status: Overseas territory
Governor: Richard Fell (nonresident) (2001)
Island Mayor: Steve Christian (1999)
Area: 18.15 sq mi (47 sq km)
Population (July 2003 est.): 48; density per sq mi: 3
Capital: Adamstown

Pitcairn Island, in the South Pacific about midway between Australia and South America, consists of the island of Pitcairn and the three uninhabited islands of Henderson, Duicie, and Oeno. Pitcairn was settled in 1790 by British mutineers from the ship *Bounty,* commanded by Capt. William Bligh. One of the most remote islands in the world, it was annexed as a British colony in 1838. Overpopulation forced removal of the settlement to Norfolk Island in 1856, but about 40 persons soon returned.

The descendants of First Mate Fletcher Christian, the eight other mutineers, and the dozen or so Tahitians who accompanied them still inhabit the island. In addition to English, the residents of Pitcairn speak a dialect that is a mixture of Tahitian and 18th-century English.

St. Helena

Status: Overseas territory
Governor: David Hollamby (1999)
Area: 158 sq mi (410 sq km)
Population (2003 est.): 7,367 (growth rate: 0.7%); birth

rate: 12.9/1000; infant mortality rate: 20.7/1000; density per sq mi: 47
Capital (2003 est.): Jamestown, 1,500. **Monetary unit:** Pound sterling. **Literacy rate:** 97% (1987 est.)

St. Helena is a remote volcanic island in the South Atlantic about 1,100 mi (1,770 km) from the west coast of Africa. It is famous as Napoleon's place of exile (1815–1821). The island was discovered in 1502 by João da Nova, a Spanish navigator in the service of Portugal. It was taken for England in 1659 by the East India Company and was brought under the direct government of the Crown in 1834. After the opening of the Suez Canal in 1870, St. Helena's importance as a port of call diminished. About two-thirds of the colony's budget is provided by the United Kingdom in the form of a subsidy.

St. Helena has two dependencies: Ascension (34 sq mi; 88 sq km), an island about 700 mi (1,127 km) northwest of St. Helena; and Tristan da Cunha (40 sq mi; 104 sq km), a group of six islands about 1,500 mi (2,414 km) south-southwest of St. Helena.

South Georgia and the South Sandwich Islands

Status: Overseas territory
Commissioner: Donald A. Lamont (1999)
Area: 1,506 sq mi (3,903 sq km)
Population: no indigenous inhabitants

The islands are located in the South Atlantic Ocean, east of the tip of South America, approximately 1,000 km east of the Falkland Islands, from which they are administered. In addition to South Georgia Island and the nine South Sandwich Islands, the island group includes Shag Rocks, Black Rock, Clerke Rocks, and Bird Island. A small military garrison on South Georgia withdrew in March 2001 and was replaced by a permanent group of scientists of the British Antarctic Survey.

Turks and Caicos Islands

Status: Overseas territory
Governor: Jim Poston (2002)
Chief Minister: Derek H. Taylor (1995)
Area: 166 sq mi (430 sq km)
Population (2003 est.): 19,350 (growth rate: 1.9%); birth rate: 23.5/1000; infant mortality rate: 16.9/1000; density per sq mi: 117
Capital (2003 est.): Cockburn Town, 5,000. **Monetary unit:** U.S. dollar. **Literacy rate:** 98% (1970 est.)
Economic summary: GDP/PPP (1999 est.): $128 million; per capita $7,300. **Real growth rate:** 8.7%. **Inflation:** 4% (1995). **Unemployment:** 10%. **Arable land**: 2%. **Agriculture:** corn, beans, cassava (tapioca), citrus fruits; fish. **Labor force:** 4,848 (1990); about 33% in government and 20% in agriculture and fishing; significant numbers in tourism, financial, and other services (1997 est.). **Industries:** tourism, offshore financial services. **Natural resources:** spiny lobster, conch. **Exports:** $13.7 million (1999): lobster, dried and fresh conch, conch shells. **Imports:** $175.6 million (1999): food and beverages, tobacco, clothing, manufactures, construction materials. **Major trading partners:** U.S., UK.

These two groups of islands are near the Bahamas in the Caribbean. The principal islands in the Turks group are Grand Turk and Salt Cay; the principal islands in the Caicos group are South Caicos, East Caicos, Middle (or Grand) Caicos, North Caicos, Providenciales, and West Caicos. The islands were not settled by Europeans until 1678, when British colonists from Bermuda established a salt-panning industry. The islands were at first placed under the Bahamian government, but in 1874 they became dependencies of the colony of Jamaica. Following Jamaica's independence, they became a British Crown colony. The salt production industry, the islands' economic mainstay, ceased in 1964 and gave way to tourism, offshore financial services, and fishing.

United States

THE UNITED STATES OF AMERICA

President: George W. Bush (2001)
Vice President: Richard B. Cheney (2001)
Area (2003): 3,717,792 sq mi (9,629,091 sq km)
Population (2003 est.): 291,950,153 (Sept. 1)
Population (2000 census): 280,562,489 (change 1990–2000: 13.2%) (growth rate: 0.5%); birth rate: 14.1/1000; infant mortality rate: 6.7/1000; density per sq mi: 79.6
Capital (2003 est.): Washington, DC, 570,898. **Largest cities:** New York, city proper, 8,084,316; Los Angeles, 3,798,981; Chicago, 2,886,251; Houston, 2,009,834; Philadelphia, 1,492,231; Phoenix, 1,371,960; San Diego, 1,259,532; Dallas, 1,211,467; San Antonio, 1,194,222; Detroit, 925,051. **Monetary unit:** dollar. **Languages:** English, sizable Spanish-speaking minority. **Ethnicity/race:** White: 211,460,626 (75.1%); Black: 34,658,190 (12.3%); American Indian and Alaska Native: 2,475,956 (0.9%); Asian: 10,242,998 (3.6%); Native Hawaiian and Other Pacific Islander: 398,835 (0.1%); Other race: 15,359,073 (5.5%); Hispanic origin:[1] 35,305,818 (12.5%). **Religions:** Protestant, 56%; Roman Catholic, 28%; Jewish, 2%; other, 4%; none, 10%. **Literacy rate:** 97% (1979 est.)
Economic summary: GDP/PPP (2001 est.): $10.082 trillion; per capita $36,300. **Real growth rate:** 0.3%. **Inflation:** 2.8%. **Unemployment:** 5% (2002). **Arable land:** 19%. **Agriculture:** wheat, other grains, corn, fruits, vegetables, cotton; beef, pork, poultry, dairy products; forest products; fish. **Labor force:** 144.9 million (includes unemployed) (2002); managerial and professional 31.1%, technical, sales and administrative support 28.6%, services 14.1%, manufacturing, mining, transportation, and crafts 23.7%, farming, forestry, and fishing 2.5% (2002) note: figures exclude the unemployed. **Industries:** leading industrial power in the world, highly diversified and technologically advanced; petroleum, steel, motor vehicles, aerospace, telecommunications, chemicals, electronics, food processing, consumer goods, lumber, mining. **Natural resources:** coal, copper, lead, molybdenum, phosphates, uranium, bauxite, gold, iron, mercury, nickel, potash, silver, tungsten, zinc, petroleum, natural gas, timber. **Exports:** $723 billion (f.o.b., 2001 est.): capital goods, automobiles, industrial supplies and raw materials, consumer goods, agricultural products. **Imports:** $1.148 trillion (f.o.b., 2001 est.): crude oil and refined petroleum products, machinery, automobiles, consumer goods, industrial raw materials, food and beverages. **Major trading partners:** Canada, Mexico, Japan, UK, Germany, France, Netherlands, China, Taiwan.

1. Persons of Hispanic origin can be of any race.

Government Federal republic.

The president is elected for a four-year term and may be reelected only once. The bicameral Congress consists of the 100-member Senate, elected to a six-year term with one-third of the seats becoming vacant every two years, and the 435-member House of Representatives, elected every two years. The minimum voting age is 18. (*See also* Profile of the United States, U.S. States, U.S. Cities, U.S. Statistics, and U.S. Government and History.)

U.S. Territories and Outlying Areas

Puerto Rico

COMMONWEALTH OF PUERTO RICO

Status: Commonwealth
Governor: Sila María Calderón (2001)
Capital and largest city (2002 est.): San Juan, 433,412. **Other large cities:** Bayamón, 224,670; Ponce, 186,112; Carolina, 187,468
Land area: 3,515 sq mi (9,104 sq km)
Population (est. 2003): 3,885,877 (growth rate: 0.7%); birth rate: 15.0/1000; infant mortality rate: 9.4/1000; density per sq mi: 1,105. **Currency:** U.S. dollars. **Languages:** Spanish and English (both official). **Ethnicity/race:** Almost entirely Hispanic. **Religions:** Roman Catholic 85%, Protestant denominations and other 15%. **Literacy rate:** 89% (1980 est.)
Economic summary: GDP/PPP (2001 est.): $43.9 billion; per capita $11,200. **Real growth rate:** 2.2%. **Inflation:** 5.7%. **Unemployment:** 9.5% (2000). **Arable land:** 4%. **Agriculture:** sugarcane, coffee, pineapples, plantains, bananas; livestock products, chickens. **Labor force:** 1.3 million (2000); agriculture 3%, industry 20%, services 77% (2000 est.). **Industries:** pharmaceuticals, electronics, apparel, food products; tourism. **Natural resources:** some copper and nickel; potential for onshore and offshore oil. **Exports:** $38.5 billion (f.o.b., 2000): pharmaceuticals, electronics, apparel, canned tuna, rum, beverage concentrates, medical equipment. **Imports:** $27 billion (c.i.f., 2000): chemicals, machinery and equipment, clothing, food, fish, petroleum products. **Major trading partner:** U.S.

The Commonwealth of Puerto Rico is located in the Caribbean Sea, about 1,000 mi east-southeast of Miami, Fla. A possession of the United States, it consists of the island of Puerto Rico plus the adjacent islets of Vieques, Culebra, and Mona. Puerto Rico has a mountainous, tropical ecosystem with very little flat land and few mineral resources.

Puerto Rico's governor is elected directly for a four-year term. A bicameral legislature consists of a 27-member Senate and a 51-member House of Representatives, all elected for four-year terms. From 1940 to 1968, Puerto Rican politics was dominated by a party advocating voluntary association with the U.S. Since then, the New Progressive Party, a party favoring U.S. statehood, has won five of the last eight gubernatorial elections. Puerto Ricans have twice voted to determine their political status. In 1967, the outcome was Commonwealth 60%; statehood 39%; independence 1%. In 1993, Commonwealth dropped to 48.6%; statehood rose to 46.3%; independence polled 4.4%; and 0.6% of the ballots were blank or spoiled.

Under the Commonwealth formula, residents of Puerto Rico lack voting representation in Congress and do not participate in presidential elections. As U.S. citizens, Puerto Ricans are subject to military service and most federal laws. Residents of the Commonwealth pay no federal income tax on locally generated earnings, but Puerto Rico government income-tax rates are set at a level that closely parallels federal-plus-state levies on the mainland.

When Christopher Columbus arrived there in 1493, the island was inhabited by the peaceful Arawak Indians, who were being challenged by the warlike Carib Indians. Puerto Rico remained economically undeveloped until 1830, when sugarcane, coffee, and tobacco plantations were gradually developed. After Puerto Ricans began to press for independence, Spain granted the island broad powers of self-government in 1897. But during the Spanish-American War of 1898 American troops invaded the island and Spain ceded it to the U.S. Since then, Puerto Rico has remained an unincorporated U.S. territory. Its people were granted American citizenship under the Jones Act in 1917; were permitted to elect their own governor, beginning in 1948; and now fully administer their internal affairs under a constitution approved by the U.S. Congress in 1952. In spite of broad popular support for the autonomy of the Commonwealth government and a rapidly modernizing industrial society, there were expressions of dissatisfaction. Puerto Rican extremists dramatized their desire for independence with an attempt to assassinate President Truman on Nov. 1, 1950, and on March 1, 1954, they wounded five congressmen in an attack on the U.S. Capitol.

A self-help program of economic development and social welfare (called "Operation Bootstrap") was forged in the 1940s by four-time governor Luis Muñoz Marín. In a little more than four decades, much of the island's crushing poverty was eliminated. This was done partly through the development of manufacturing and service industries, the latter related to an enormous growth in tourism. Also, many Puerto Ricans migrated to large cities on the mainland U.S.

Puerto Rico is a major hub of Caribbean commerce, finance, tourism, and communications. San Juan is one of the world's busiest cruise-ship ports, and Puerto Rico's standard of living continues to be among the highest in the hemisphere. Its future political status, however, remains unclear. On March 4, 1998, the U.S. House of Representatives passed a bill that called for binding elections in Puerto Rico to decide the island's permanent political status.

Since the 1940s, the U.S. Navy has used Vieques island as a bombing range. Protests against the exercises grew in recent years, and in a July 2001 referendum residents of the island voted overwhelmingly to close the base. The navy withdrew from Vieques in May 2003.

Guam

TERRITORY OF GUAM

Status: Territory
Governor: Felix Camacho (2003)
Capital (2000 est.): Agaña, 1,100
Land area: 212 sq mi (549 sq km)
Population (2003 est.): 163,941 (growth rate :1.9%); birth rate: 23.2/1000; infant mortality rate: 6.5/1000; density per sq mi: 773. **1996 est. net migration:** 3 migrants per 1,000 population. **Languages:** English and Chamorro; note: most residents are bilingual; Japanese also widely spoken. **Ethnicity/race:** Chamorro 37%, Filipino 26%, Caucasian 10%, Chinese, Japanese, Korean, and other, 27%. **Religions:** Roman Catholic 85%, other 15% (1999 est.). **Literacy rate:** 99% (1990 est.). **Currency:** U.S. dollars
Economic summary: GDP/PPP (2000 est.): $3.2 billion; per capita $21,000. **Real growth rate:** n.a. **Inflation:** 0% (1999 est.). **Unemployment:** 15% (2000 est.). **Arable land:** 11%. **Agriculture:** fruits, copra, vegetables; eggs, pork, poultry, beef. **Labor force:** 60,000 (2000 est.); federal and territorial government 26%, private 74% (trade 24%, other services 40%, industry 10%) (2000 est.). **Industries:** US military, tourism, construction, transshipment services, concrete products, printing and publishing, food processing, textiles. **Natural resources:** fishing (largely undeveloped), tourism (especially from Japan). **Exports:** $75.7 million (f.o.b., 1999 est.): mostly transshipments of refined petroleum products; construction materials, fish, food and beverage products. **Imports:** $203 million (f.o.b., 1999 est.): petroleum and petroleum products, food, manufactured goods. **Major trading partners:** U.S., Japan.

Guam is the largest and southernmost island in the Marianas Archipelago. The island is divided into a northern coralline limestone plateau and a southern chain of volcanic hills. Today Guam is an unincorporated, organized territory of the United States. The people of Guam have been U.S. citizens since 1950. They have been represented in the U.S. Congress since 1973 by a nonvoting delegate, but do not participate in presidential elections. The executive branch includes a popularly elected governor, who serves a four-year term. The legislative branch is a 21-member unicameral legislature whose members are elected every two years.

Guam was probably explored by the Portuguese navigator Ferdinand Magellan (sailing for Spain) in 1521. The island was formally claimed by Spain in 1565, and its people were forced into submission and conversion to Roman Catholicism beginning in 1668. After the Spanish-American War of 1898, Spain ceded Guam to the United States. From 1899 to 1949, the U.S. Navy administered Guam, except during the Japanese occupation from 1941–1944. Guam was liberated by American military forces in the summer of 1944. Guam's economy is based on tourism and U.S. military spending (U.S. naval and air force bases occupy one-third of the land on Guam).

U.S. Virgin Islands

VIRGIN ISLANDS OF THE UNITED STATES

Status: Territory
Governor: Charles Turnbull (1999)
Capital (2000 est.): Charlotte Amalie (on St. Thomas), 11,004
Land area: 136 sq mi (352 sq km)
Population (est. 2003): 124,778 (growth rate: 1.0%); birth rate: 15.8/1000; infant mortality rate: 9.0/1000; density per sq mi: 918. **Languages:** English (official), but Spanish and French are also spoken. **Ethnicity/race:** West Indian 74% (45% born in the Virgin Islands and 29% born elsewhere in the West Indies), U.S. mainland 13%, Puerto Rican 5%, other 8%, black 80%, white 15%, other 5%, 14% of Hispanic origin. **Religions:** Baptist 42%, Roman Catholic 34%, Episcopalian 17%, other 7%. **Literacy rate:** 90%. **Currency:** U.S. dollars
Economic summary: GDP/PPP (2000 est.): $1.8 billion; per capita $15,000. **Real growth rate:** n.a. **Inflation:** n.a. **Unemployment:** 5% (March 1999). **Arable land:** 15%. **Agriculture:** fruit, vegetables, sorghum; Senepol cattle. **Labor force:** 48,356; agriculture 1%, industry 20%, services 79%. **Industries:** tourism, petroleum refining, watch assembly, rum distilling, construction, pharmaceuticals, textiles, electronics. **Natural resources:** sun, sand, sea, surf. **Exports:** $n.a.: refined petroleum products. **Imports:** $n.a.: crude oil, foodstuffs, consumer goods, building materials. **Major trading partners:** U.S., Puerto Rico.

The Virgin Islands, consisting of nine main islands and some 75 islets, were explored by Columbus in 1493. They were originally inhabited by the Carib Indians. Since 1666, England has held six of the main islands; the remaining three (St. Croix, St. Thomas, and St. John), as well as about 50 of the islets, were eventually acquired by Denmark, which named them the Danish West Indies. In 1917, these islands were purchased by the U.S. from Denmark for $25 million.

Congress granted U.S. citizenship to Virgin Islanders in 1927. Universal suffrage was given in 1936 to all persons who could read and write English. The governor was elected by popular vote for the first time in 1970; previously he had been appointed by the U.S. president. A unicameral 15-person legislature serves the Virgin Islands, and congressional legislation gave the islands a nonvoting representative in Congress. Residents of the islands substantially enjoy the same rights as those enjoyed by mainlanders, but they may not vote in presidential elections.

Tourism is the primary economic activity, accounting for most of the GDP and 70% of employment. All goods made in the Virgin Islands qualify for duty-free entry into the United States.

American Samoa

TERRITORY OF AMERICAN SAMOA

Status: Territory
Governor: Togiola Tulafono (2003)
Capital (2003 est.): Pago Pago, 4,100
Land area: 77 sq mi (199 sq km)
Population (2003 est.): 70,260 (growth rate: 1.9%); birth rate: 23.3/1000; infant mortality rate: 9.8/1000; density per sq mi: 914. **Languages:** Samoan (closely related to Hawaiian and other Polynesian languages) and English; most people are bilingual. **Ethnicity/race:** Samoan (Polynesian) 89%, Tongan 4%, Caucasian 2%, other 5%. **Religions:** Christian Congregationalist 50%, Roman Catholic 20%, Protestant denominations and other 30%. **Literacy rate:** 97% (1980 est.). **Currency:** U.S. dollars
Economic summary: GDP/PPP (2000 est.): $500 million; per capita $8,000. **Real growth rate:** n.a. **Inflation:** n.a. **Unemployment:** 6% (2000). **Arable land:** 5%. **Agriculture:** bananas, coconuts, vegetables, taro, breadfruit, yams, copra, pineapples, papayas; dairy products, livestock. **Labor force:** 14,000 (1996); government 33%, tuna canneries 34%, other 33% (1990). **Industries:** tuna canneries (largely dependent on foreign fishing vessels), handicrafts. **Natural resources:** pumice, pumicite. **Exports:** $345 million (1999): canned tuna 93%. **Imports:** $452 million (1999): materials for canneries 56%, food 8%, petroleum products 7%, machinery and parts 6%. **Major trading partners:** U.S., Australia, Japan, New Zealand, Fiji.

American Samoa, a group of five volcanic islands and two coral atolls located some 2,600 mi south of Hawaii in the South Pacific, is an unincorporated, unorganized territory of the U.S. It includes the eastern Samoan islands of Tutuila, Aunu'u, and Rose; three islands (Ta'u, Olosega, and Ofu) of the Manu'a group; and Swains Island. Around 1000 B.C. Proto-polynesians established themselves in the islands, and their descendants are one of the few remaining Polynesian societies. The Dutch navigator Jacob Roggeveen sighted the Manu'a Islands in 1722. American Samoa has been a territory of the United States since April 17, 1900, when the High Chiefs of Tutuila signed the first of two Deeds of Cession for the islands to the U.S. (Congress ratified the Deeds in 1929.) Swains Island, which is privately owned, came under U.S. administration in 1925.

Until World War II the United States operated a coaling station and naval base in Pago Pago. During the war, the islands were an important U.S. Marines staging area. In 1960 American Samoa ratified its territorial constitution and has since developed a modern, self-governing political system. American Samoans elect a governor, lieutenant governor, and legislature. The legislature (Fono) consists of two houses: the Senate, selected by village chiefs (matai) for four-year terms, and the House of Representatives, elected by the general population for two-year terms. The people of American Samoa are U.S. nationals, not U.S. citizens, but many have become naturalized American citizens. American Samoa does 80%–90% of its foreign trade with the U.S. Canned tuna is the primary export, earning $300 million annually. Transfers from the U.S. government add substantially to American Samoa's economic well-being.

Northern Mariana Islands

THE COMMONWEALTH OF THE NORTHERN MARIANA ISLANDS, OR CNMI

Status: Commonwealth
Governor: Juan N. Babautu (2002)
Capital: Chalan Kanoa (on Saipan)
Total area: 184 sq mi (477 sq km)
Population (2003 est.): 80,006 (growth rate: 1.8%); birth rate: 20.0/1000; infant mortality: 5.5/1000; density per sq mi: 434. **Languages:** English (official), Chamorro, Carolinian. **Ethnicity/race:** Chamorro, Carolinians, other Micronesians, Caucasian, Japanese, Chinese, Korean. **Religion:** Primarily Roman Catholic. **Literacy rate:** 97% (1980 est.). **Currency:** U.S. dollars
Economic summary: GDP/PPP (2000 est.): $900 million; note: GDP numbers reflect U.S. spending; per capita $12,500. **Real growth rate:** n.a. **Inflation:** 1.2%. **Unemployment:** n.a. **Arable land:** 15%. **Agriculture:** coconuts, fruits, vegetables; cattle. **Labor force:** 6,006 total indigenous labor force; 2,699 unemployed; 28,717 foreign workers (1995). **Industries:** tourism, construction, garments, handicrafts. **Natural resources:** arable land, fish. **Exports:** $n.a.: garments. **Imports:** $n.a.: food, construction equipment and materials, petroleum products. **Major trading partners:** U.S., Japan.

The Northern Mariana Islands, east of the Philippines and south of Japan, include the islands of Rota, Saipan, Tinian, Pagan, Guguan, Agrihan, and Aguijan. Although sighted by Ferdinand Magellan in 1521 as he sailed for Spain, the islands were not settled by Europeans until 1668, when missionaries converted the indigenous Chamorro people to Catholicism. They were ruled successively by Spain, Germany, and Japan before they became a UN Trusteeship (administered by the U.S.) after World War II. The Commonwealth of the Northern Mariana Islands (CNMI) became part of the United States in Nov. 1986. Spanish cultural traditions remain strong.

In recent years, Saipan's garment industry has been accused of exploiting thousands of Asian immigrants. Saipan's territorial status enables its employers to claim their clothing is "Made in the USA," while paying workers low wages and sidestepping import duties and tariffs.

Midway Islands

Status: Territory
Total area: 2 sq mi (5 sq km)
Population (1995 est.): no indigenous inhabitants; 453 U.S. military personnel.

The Midway Islands consist of a circular atoll, 6 mi in diameter, that encloses two islands. Lying about 1,150 mi west-northwest of Hawaii, the islands were first explored by Captain N. C. Brooks on July 5, 1859, in the name of the U.S. The atoll was declared a U.S. possession in 1867, and in 1903 Theodore Roosevelt made it a naval reservation. The island was renamed "Midway" by the U.S. Navy in recognition of its geographic location on the route between California and Japan. Air traffic across the Pacific increased the island's importance in the mid-1930s; the San Francisco–Manila mail route included a regular stop on Midway. Its military importance was soon recognized, and the navy began building an air and submarine base there in 1940. The Battle of Midway, which took place from June 3–6, 1942, was considered a turning point in World War II. After the war, the strategic importance of the island declined; the Midway stop for commercial air traffic was eliminated in 1950, and the air base closed in 1992.

Wake Island

Status: Territory
Total area: 2.51 sq mi (6.5 sq km)
Comparative size: about 11 times the size of the Mall in Washington, DC
Population (1995 est.): no indigenous inhabitants; 302 U.S. military personnel and civilian contractors.
Economy: The economic activity is limited to providing services to U.S. military personnel and contractors on the island. All food and manufactured goods must be imported.

Wake Island, about halfway between Midway and Guam, is an atoll consisting of the three islets of Wilkes, Peale, and Wake. They were discovered by the British in 1796 and annexed by the U.S. in 1899. In 1938, Pan American Airways established a seaplane base, and Wake Island was used as a commercial base for several years. On Dec. 8, 1941, it was attacked by the Japanese, who finally took possession on Dec. 23. It was surrendered by the Japanese on Sept. 4, 1945.

Johnston Atoll

Status: Territory
Land area: 1.08 sq mi (2.8 sq km); density per sq mi: 1,111
Population (July 1997 est.): no indigenous inhabitants; 1,200 U.S. military and civilian personnel

Johnston is a coral atoll about 700 mi southwest of Hawaii. It consists of four small islands—Johnston Island, Sand Island, Hikina Island, and Akau Island—which lie on a 9-mile-long reef. The atoll was discovered by Capt. Charles James Johnston of HMS *Cornwallis* in 1807. In 1858 it was claimed by Hawaii, and later became a U.S. possession. Johnston Atoll was used by the U.S. Air Force to conduct test launchings of nuclear missiles and contains a landfill of plutonium-contaminated waste. In 2004, the military will depart and the atoll will be turned into a wildlife refuge. However, the U.S. Fish and Wildlife Service, the atoll's inheritor, is concerned about the possibility of eventual radioactive leakage.

Baker, Howland, and Jarvis Islands

Status: Territory

These Pacific islands were claimed by the United States under the Guano Act of 1856 on May 13, 1936. Guano, composed of phosphates, was used as fertilizer in the 19th century, and its collection was highly lucrative. Through the Guano Act the U.S. gained 79 tiny territories around the world; it still controls eight of them. Baker Island is a saucer-shaped atoll with an area of approximately one square mile about 1,650 mi from Hawaii. Howland Island, 36 mi to the northwest, is 1 mile long and half a mile wide. On their round-the-world flight in 1937, Amelia Earhart and Fred J. Noonan were headed for Howland when they disappeared. Jarvis Island is several hundred mi to the east.

Kingman Reef

Status: Territory

Kingman Reef, located about 1,000 mi south of Hawaii, was discovered by Capt. E. Fanning in 1798, but named for Capt. W. E. Kingman, who rediscovered it in 1853. Triangular in shape, it is about 9.5 mi long. A U.S. possession since 1922, Kingman Reef is a Naval Defensive Sea Area and Airspace Reservation, and is closed to the public.

Navassa Island

Status: Territory

Navassa Island is located in the Caribbean Sea, 99.4 mi (160 km) south of the U.S. naval base at Guantanamo, Cuba, between Cuba, Haiti, and Jamaica. The island has a total area of 2.01 sq mi (5.2 sq km). It was claimed for the U.S. under the Guano Act in 1857. The Navassa Phosphate Company mined the island until 1900, enlisting hundreds of freed American slaves to dig out several tons of guano. Working conditions were so brutal that the laborers finally revolted in 1889, killing their supervisors. The island is also claimed by Haiti.

Palmyra Atoll

Status: Territory

Palmyra Atoll is an incorporated territory of the U.S. and privately owned. The atoll has a total area of 4.6 sq mi (11.9 sq km) and is located in the North Pacific Ocean, 994 mi (1,600 km) southwest of Honolulu. It was a U.S. military base during World War II but was not attacked.

Uruguay

ORIENTAL REPUBLIC OF URUGUAY

National name: República Oriental del Uruguay
President: Jorge Batlle (2000)
Area: 68,039 sq mi (176,220 sq km)
Population (2003 est.): 3,413,329 (growth rate: 0.8%); birth rate: 17.2/1000; infant mortality rate: 13.8/1000; density per sq mi: 50
Capital and largest city (2003 est.): Montevideo, 1,745,100 (metro. area), 1,347,600 (city proper). **Monetary unit:** Uruguay peso. **Language:** Spanish. **Ethnicity/race:** white 88%, mestizo 8%, black 4%. **Religions:** Roman Catholic 66%, Protestant 2%, Jewish 1%. **Literacy rate:** 97.3% (1995 est.)
Economic summary: GDP/PPP (2001 est.): $31 billion; per capita $9,200. **Real growth rate:** –1.5%. **Inflation:** 3.6%. **Unemployment:** 15.2%. **Arable land:** 7%. **Agriculture:** rice, wheat, corn, barley; livestock; fish. **Labor force:** 1.2 million; agriculture 14%, industry 16%, services 70%. **Industries:** food processing, electrical machinery, transportation equipment, petroleum products, textiles, chemicals, beverages. **Natural resources:** arable land, hydropower, minor minerals, fisheries. **Exports:** $2.24 billion (f.o.b., 2001 est.): meat, rice, leather products, wool, vehicles, dairy products. **Imports:** $2.9 billion (f.o.b., 2001 est.): machinery, chemicals, road vehicles, crude petroleum. **Major trading partners:** Mercosur partners, EU, U.S.

Geography Uruguay, on the east coast of South America south of Brazil and east of Argentina, is comparable in size to Oklahoma. The country consists of a low, rolling plain in the south and a low plateau in the north. It has a 120-mile (193 km) Atlantic shoreline, a 235-mile (378 km) frontage on the Rio de la Plata, and 270 mi (435 km) on the Uruguay River, its western boundary.

Government Constitutional republic.

History Prior to European settlement, Uruguay was inhabited by indigenous people, the Charrúas. Juan Díaz de Solis, a Spaniard, visited Uruguay in 1516, but the Portuguese were first to settle it when they founded the town of Colonia del Sacramento in 1680. After a long struggle, Spain wrested the country from Portugal in 1778, by which time almost all of the indigenous people had been exterminated. Uruguay revolted against Spain in 1811, only to be conquered in 1817 by the Portuguese from Brazil. Independence was reasserted with Argentine help in 1825, and the republic was set up in 1828.

A revolt in 1836 touched off nearly 50 years of factional strife, including an inconclusive civil war (1839–1851) and a war with Paraguay (1865–1870), accompanied by occasional armed intervention by Argentina and Brazil. Uruguay, made prosperous by meat and wool exports, founded a welfare state early in the 20th century under President José Batlle y Ordóñez, who ruled from 1903 to 1929. A decline began in the 1950s as successive governments struggled to maintain a large bureaucracy and costly social benefits. Economic stagnation and left-wing terrorist activity followed.

A military coup ousted the civilian government in 1973. The military dictatorship that followed used fear and terror to demoralize the population, taking thousands of political prisoners. After ruling for 12 years, the brutal military regime permitted election of a civilian government in Nov. 1984 and relinquished rule in March 1985; full political and civil rights were then restored.

Subsequent leaders contended with high inflation and a mammoth national debt. Presidential and legislative elections in Nov. 1994 resulted in a narrow victory for the center-right Colorado Party and its presidential candidate, Julio Sanguinetti Cairolo, who had been president in 1985–1990. He pushed for constitutional and economic reforms aimed at reducing inflation and the size of the public sector, including tax increases and privatization. In Nov. 1999 Jorge Batlle, of the center-right Colorado Party, won the presidency. In Aug. 2000 a commission began investigating the disappearances of 160 people who vanished during the military regime.

In 2002, Uruguay entered its fourth year of recession. Economic troubles in neighboring Argentina caused a staggering 90% drop in tourists, devastating Uruguay's important tourism industry. Agricultural exports were hurt by the 2001 foot-and-mouth outbreak among cattle. Batlle also faced a sizable budget deficit, a growing public debt, and a weakening of the peso on international markets. The country's economic outlook began improving in 2003.

Uzbekistan

REPUBLIC OF UZBEKISTAN

National name: Uzbekiston Respublikasi
President: Islam A. Karimov (1990)
Prime Minister: Otkir Sultonov (1995)
Area: 172,741 sq mi (447,400 sq km)
Population (2003 est.): 25,981,647 (growth rate: 1.8%); birth rate: 26.1/1000; infant mortality rate: 71.5/1000; density per sq mi: 150
Capital and largest city (2003 est.): Tashkent, 3,457,500 (metro. area), 2,155,400 (city proper). **Other large cities:** Samarkand, 374,900; Andijon, 354,500. **Monetary unit:** Uzbekistani sum. **Languages:** Uzbek, Russian, Tajik, other. **Ethnicity/race:** Uzbek 80%, Russian 5.5%, Tajik 5%, Kazak 3%, Karakalpak 2.5%, Tatar 1.5%, other 2.5% (1996 est.). **Religions:** Islam (mostly Sunnis) 88%, Eastern Orthodox 9%, other 3%. **Literacy rate:** 99% (1996)
Economic summary: GDP/PPP (2001 est.): $62 billion; per capita $2,500. **Real growth rate:** 3%. **Inflation:** 23%. **Unemployment:** 10% plus another 20%

underemployed (1999 est.). **Arable land:** 11%. **Agriculture:** cotton, vegetables, fruits, grain; livestock. **Labor force:** 11.9 million (1998 est.); agriculture 44%, industry 20%, services 36% (1995). **Industries:** textiles, food processing, machine building, metallurgy, natural gas, chemicals. **Natural resources:** natural gas, petroleum, coal, gold, uranium, silver, copper, lead and zinc, tungsten, molybdenum. **Exports:** $2.8 billion (f.o.b., 2001 est.): cotton 41.5%, gold 9.6%, energy products 9.6%, mineral fertilizers, ferrous metals, textiles, food products, automobiles (1998 est.). **Imports:** $2.5 billion (f.o.b., 2001 est.): machinery and equipment 49.8%, foodstuffs 16.4%, chemicals, metals (1998 est.). **Major trading partners:** Russia, Switzerland, UK, Ukraine, South Korea, Kazakhstan, Germany.

Geography Uzbekistan is situated in central Asia between the Amu Darya and Syr Darya Rivers, the Aral Sea, and the slopes of the Tien Shan Mountains. It is bounded by Kazakhstan in the north and northwest, Kyrgyzstan and Tajikistan in the east and southeast, Turkmenistan in the southwest, and Afghanistan in the south. The republic also includes the Karakalpakstan Autonomous Republic, with its capital, Nukus (1992 est. pop., 182,000). The country is about one-tenth larger in area than the state of California.

Government Republic; authoritarian presidential rule.

History The Uzbekistan land was once part of the ancient Persian empire and was later conquered by Alexander the Great in the 4th century B.C. During the 8th century, the nomadic Turkic tribes living there were converted to Islam by invading Arab forces who dominated the area. The Mongols under Ghengis Khan took over the region from the Seljuk Turks in the 13th century, and it later became part of Tamerlane the Great's empire and that of his successors until the 16th century. The Uzbeks invaded the territory in the early 16th century and merged with the other inhabitants in the area. Their empire broke up into separate Uzbek principalities, the khanates of Khiva, Bukhara, and Kokand. These city-states resisted Russian expansion into the area but were conquered by the Russian forces in the mid-19th century.

The territory was made into the Uzbek Republic in 1924 and became the independent Uzbekistan Soviet Socialist Republic in 1925. Under Soviet rule, Uzbekistan concentrated on growing cotton with the help of irrigation, mechanization, and chemical fertilizers and pesticides, causing serious environmental damage.

In June 1990, Uzbekistan became the first central Asian republic to declare that its own laws had sovereignty over those of the central Soviet government. Uzbekistan became fully independent and joined with ten other former Soviet republics on Dec. 21, 1991, in the Commonwealth of Independent States.

Vozrozhdeniye, an island in the Aral Sea, was a secret test site for biological weapons during the Soviet era. In 1988, the Soviets attempted to bury the evidence on the island, a frightening legacy that Uzbekistan inherited upon independence. U.S. scientists have confirmed that the island contains live anthrax and other deadly poisons.

In Feb. 1992, President Karimov, a former Communist Party boss, affirmed his commitment to democracy and human rights, but he effectively suppressed opposition parties in mid-1993. The criminal code was amended to impose stricter penalties for antigovernment activity. Opposition groups were largely excluded in future elections while the ruling party continued to post decisive victories.

In 1999, the country battled against militant Islamic groups bent on the overthrow of the secular government. In Feb. 1999, a series of bomb blasts killed 16 and injured hundreds in the capital, Tashkent. Militant Islamic gunmen remain stationed across the border in southern Kyrgyzstan, and Uzbek fighter planes have been unable to rout them. In 2000, Russia offered to help Uzbekistan "liquidate" the Islamic extremists, and Russia has also offered to send at least $30 million worth of weapons.

In 2001, Uzbekistan provided the United States with a base to fight against Taliban and al-Qaeda forces in neighboring Afghanistan. About 1,000 U.S. soldiers were stationed there in 2002.

Vanuatu

REPUBLIC OF VANUATU

President: John Bani (1999)
Prime Minister: Edward Natapei (2001)
Area: 4,710 sq mi (12,200 sq km)
Population (2003 est.): 199,414 (growth rate: 1.6%); birth rate: 24.3/1000; infant mortality rate: 58.1/1000; density per sq mi: 42
Capital and largest city (2003 est.): Port Vila, 35,300. **Monetary unit:** Vatu. **Languages:** Bislama (a Melanesian pidgin English), English, French (all 3 official). **Ethnicity/race:** indigenous Melanesian 98%, French, Vietnamese, Chinese, other Pacific Islanders. **Religions:** Presbyterian 36.7%, Roman Catholic 15%, Anglican 15%, other Christian 10%, indigenous beliefs 7.6%, other 15.7%. **Literacy rate:** 53% (1979 est.)
Economic summary: GDP/PPP (2000 est.): $257 million; per capita $1,300. **Real growth rate:** 2.7%. **Inflation:** 2.5%. **Unemployment:** n.a. **Arable land:** 3%. **Agriculture:** copra, coconuts, cocoa, coffee, taro, yams, coconuts, fruits, vegetables; fish, beef. **Labor force:** n.a.; agriculture 65%, services 30%, industry 5% (2000 est.). **Industries:** food and fish freezing, wood processing, meat canning. **Natural resources:** manganese, hardwood forests, fish. **Exports**: $22.8 million (f.o.b., 2000): copra, kava, beef, cocoa, timber, coffee. **Imports:** $87.5 million (f.o.b., 2000): machinery and equipment, foodstuffs, fuels. **Major trading partners:** Japan, Belgium, U.S., Germany, Australia, Singapore, New Zealand.

Geography Vanuatu is an archipelago of 83 islands lying between New Caledonia and Fiji in the South Pacific. Largest of the islands is Espiritu Santo (875 sq mi; 2,266 sq km); others are Efate, Malekula, Malo, Pentecost, and Tanna.

Government Republic.

History The first settlers were believed to have arrived approximately 3,500 years ago from New Guinea and the Solomon Islands by canoe. The islands were sighted by Pedro Fernandes de Queiros of Portugal in 1606 and were charted by the British navigator James Cook in 1774, who named the archipelago New Hebrides, after the northern Scottish islands. Competing British and French claims to the islands led to the formation of a condominium government, allowing for joint British-French rule in 1906. The islands' plantation economy, based on imported Vietnamese labor, was prosperous until the 1920s, when markets for its products declined. Diseases brought by missionaries, sandalwood traders, and others helped reduce the population from approximately 1 million in 1800 to 45,000 in 1935. The islands served as a major Allied base in World

War II. After World War II, the indigenous Melanesians began lobbying for independence. In 1980 the country achieved independence and was renamed Vanuatu.

A brief rebellion by French settlers and plantation workers on Espiritu Santo took place in May 1980. Britain, France, and Papua New Guinea sent soldiers, who quelled the revolt, which the new government said was financed by the Phoenix Foundation, a right-wing U.S. group.

Vatican City (Holy See)

National name: Stato della Città del Vaticano
Ruler: Pope John Paul II (1978)
Area: 0.17 sq mi (0.44 sq km)
Population (July 2002 est.): 900; population growth rate: 1.2%; density per sq mi: 5,298. **Monetary unit:** Euro. **Languages:** Latin, Italian, and various other languages. **Ethnicity/race:** Italians, Swiss. **Religion:** Roman Catholic.
Labor force: dignitaries, priests, nuns, guards, and 3,000 lay workers who live outside the Vatican.
Budget (1997): Revenues: $209.6 million; expenditures: $198.5 million, including capital expenditures.

Geography The Vatican City State is situated on the Vatican hill, on the right bank of the Tiber River, within the city of Rome.

Government The pope has full legal, executive, and judicial powers. Executive power over the area is in the hands of a commission of cardinals appointed by the pope. The College of Cardinals is the pope's chief advisory body, and upon his death the cardinals elect his successor for life.

History The Vatican City State, sovereign and independent, is the survivor of the papal states that in 1859 comprised an area of some 17,000 sq mi (44,030 sq km). During the struggle for Italian unification, from 1860 to 1870, most of this area became part of Italy. By an Italian law of May 13, 1871, the temporal power of the pope was abrogated, and the territory of the papacy was confined to the Vatican and Lateran palaces and the villa of Castel Gandolfo. The popes consistently refused to recognize this arrangement. The Lateran Treaty of Feb. 11, 1929, between the Vatican and the kingdom of Italy established the autonomy of the Holy See.

The first session of Ecumenical Council Vatican II was opened by John XXIII on Oct. 11, 1962, to plan and set policies for the modernization of the Roman Catholic Church. Pope Paul VI continued the council, presiding over the last three sessions. Vatican II, as it is called, revolutionized some of the church's practices. Power was decentralized, giving bishops a larger role, the liturgy was vernacularized, and laymen were given a larger part in church affairs.

On Aug. 26, 1978, Cardinal Albino Luciani was chosen by the College of Cardinals to succeed Paul VI, who had died of a heart attack on Aug. 6. The new pope took the name John Paul I. Only 34 days after his election, John Paul I died of a heart attack, ending the shortest reign in 373 years. On Oct. 16, Cardinal Karol Wojtyla, 58, was chosen pope and took the name John Paul II. Pope John Paul II became the first Polish pope and the first non-Italian pope since the 16th century. His rule has been characterized by conservatism regarding church doctrine. He has been the Vatican's greatest ambassador, traveling to more than 115 countries.

On May 13, 1981, a Turkish terrorist shot the pope in St. Peter's Square, the first assassination attempt against the pontiff in modern times. On June 3, 1985, the Vatican and Italy ratified a new church-state treaty, known as a concordat, replacing the Lateran Pact of 1929. The new accord affirmed the independence of Vatican City but ended a number of privileges the Catholic Church had in Italy, including its status as the state religion. The treaty ended Rome's status as a "sacred city."

In March 2000, the pope issued an apology for sins committed by Catholics over the past 2,000 years, including religious persecutions and discrimination against women. Several groups criticized the vagueness of the apology, wishing the pope had specified the church's particularly egregious sins. The pope also remained circumspect about the U.S. church's sexual abuse scandals in 2002. In 2003, the Vatican launched an international campaign against legalizing same-sex marriage.

For a list of all the popes, *see* pp. 339–341.

Venezuela

REPUBLIC OF VENEZUELA

National name: Republica de Venezuela
President: Hugo Chavez (1999)
Area: 352,143 sq mi (912,050 sq km)
Population (2003 est.): 24,654,694 (growth rate: 1.5%); birth rate: 19.8/1000; infant mortality rate: 23.8/1000; density per sq mile: 70
Capital (2003 est.): Caracas, 3,517,300 (metro area), 1,741,400 (city proper). **Largest cities:** Maracaibo, 1,889,000 (metro. area), 1,854,300 (city proper); Valencia, 1,515,400; Barquisimeto, 948,900. **Monetary unit:** bolivar. **Languages:** Spanish (official), various indigenous languages in the remote interior. **Ethnicity/race:** mestizo 67%, white 21%, black 10%, Amerindian 2%. **Religions:** Roman Catholic 96%, Protestant 2%. **Literacy rate:** 91.1% (1995 est.)
Economic summary: GDP/PPP (2001 est.): $146.2 billion; per capita $6,100. **Real growth rate:** 2.7%. **Inflation:** 12.3%. **Unemployment:** 14.1%. **Arable land:** 3%. **Agriculture:** corn, sorghum, sugarcane, rice, bananas, vegetables, coffee; beef, pork, milk, eggs; fish. **Labor force:** 9.9 million (1999); services 64%, industry 23%, agriculture 13%. **Industries:** petroleum, iron ore mining, construction materials, food processing, textiles, steel, aluminum, motor vehicle assembly. **Natural resources:** petroleum, natural gas, iron ore, gold, bauxite, other minerals, hydropower, diamonds. **Exports:** $29.5 billion (f.o.b., 2001): petroleum, bauxite and aluminum, steel, chemicals, agricultural products, basic manufactures. **Imports:** $18.4 billion (f.o.b., 2001): raw materials, machinery and equipment, transport equipment, construction materials. **Major trading partners:** U.S., Brazil, Colombia, Italy, Spain, Germany.

Geography Venezuela, a third larger than Texas, occupies most of the northern coast of South America on the Caribbean Sea. It is bordered by Colombia to the west, Guyana to the east, and Brazil to the south. Mountain systems break Venezuela into four distinct areas: (1) the Maracaibo lowlands; (2) the mountainous region in the north and northwest; (3) the Orinoco basin, with the llanos (vast grass-covered plains) on its northern border and great forest areas in the south and southeast; and (4) the Guiana Highlands, south of the Orinoco, accounting for nearly half the national territory.

Government Federal republic.

History When Columbus explored Venezuela on his third voyage in 1498, the area was inhabited by Arawak, Carib, and Chibcha Indians. A subsequent Spanish explorer gave the country its name, meaning "Little Venice." Caracas was founded in 1567. Simón Bolívar, who led the liberation of much of the continent from Spain, was born in Caracas in 1783. With Bolívar taking part, Venezuela was one of the first South American colonies to revolt in 1810, winning independence in 1821. Federated at first with Colombia and Ecuador as the Republic of Greater Colombia, Venezuela became a republic in 1830. A period of unstable dictatorships followed. Antonio Guzman Blanco governed from 1870 to 1888, developing an infrastructure, expanding agriculture, and welcoming foreign investment.

Gen. Juan Vicente Gómez was dictator from 1908 to 1935, when Venezuela became a major oil exporter. A military junta ruled after his death. Leftist Dr. Rómulo Betancourt and the Democratic Action Party won a majority of seats in a constituent assembly to draft a new constitution in 1946. A well-known writer, Rómulo Gallegos, candidate of Betancourt's party, became Venezuela's first democratically elected president in 1947. Within eight months, Gallegos was overthrown by a military-backed coup led by Marcos Peréz Jiménez, who was ousted himself in 1958. Since 1959, Venezuela has been one of the most stable democracies in Latin America. Betancourt served from 1959–1964, while Rafael Caldera Rodríguez, president from 1969 to 1974, legalized the Communist Party and established diplomatic relations with Moscow.

Venezuela benefited from the oil boom of the early 1970s. In 1974, President Carlos Andrés Pérez took office, and in 1976 Venezuela nationalized foreign-owned oil and steel companies, offering compensation. Luis Herrera Campíns took office in 1978. Declining world oil prices sent Venezuela's economy into a tailspin, increasing the country's foreign debt. Pérez was reelected to a nonconsecutive term in 1988 and launched an unpopular austerity program. Military officers staged two unsuccessful coup attempts in 1992, while the following year Congress impeached Pérez on corruption charges. President Rafael Caldera Rodríguez was elected in Dec. 1993 to face the 1994 collapse of half of the country's banking sector, falling oil prices, foreign debt repayment, and inflation. In 1997, the government announced an expansion of gold and diamond mining to reduce reliance on oil.

Leftist president Hugo Chavez took office in 1999, pledging political and economic reforms to give the poor a greater share of the country's oil wealth. A constituent assembly was formed to rewrite the constitution in July 1999, followed by the creation of a constitutional assembly made up of Chavez's allies that replaced the democratically elected Congress. Chavez's assumption of greater power prompted charges that he is establishing a left-wing dictatorship.

Chavez was reelected to a six-year term in July 2000. Troops were called in to quell serious protests over the election in several cities. In 2000 Chavez visited other OPEC countries, becoming the first foreign head of state to visit Iraq since the 1991 Gulf War. He is close to President Fidel Castro of Cuba, which receives Venezuelan oil at reduced prices.

In Dec. 2001, business and labor organizations held a work stoppage to protest Chavez's increasingly authoritarian government. In April 2002, tensions reached a boiling point as workers reduced oil production to protest Chavez policies. Following a massive anti-Chavez demonstration during which 12 people were killed, a coalition of business and military leaders forced Chavez from power for two days, hoping to install an interim government leading to elections. However, international criticism of the coup, especially from Latin America, and an outpouring of support for Chavez from Venezuela's poor, returned Chavez to power. After the coup, Chavez remained highly popular among the poor, despite the desperate state of the economy. Venezuelan labor unions, business organizations, the media, and a good part of the military were far less enchanted with his continued rule.

Beginning in early Dec. 2002, a general strike was called by business and labor leaders. By January it had virtually brought the economy, including the oil industry, to a halt. Strike leaders pledged to continue until Chavez resigned or agreed to early elections. But in Feb. 2003, after nine weeks, the strikers conceded defeat. In Aug. 2003, a petition with 3.2 million signatures was delivered to the country's election commission demanding a recall referendum on Chavez. Chavez (who held on to a 34% approval rating in August) was expected to challenge the referendum process every step of the way. In September, the National Election Board rejected the petition as invalid; opposition leaders vowed to launch a new one.

Vietnam

SOCIALIST REPUBLIC OF VIETNAM

National name: Công Hòa Xa Hôi Chú Nghia Viêt Nam
President: Tran Duc Luong (1997)
Prime Minister: Phan Van Khai (1997)
Area: 127,243 sq mi (329,560 sq km)
Population (2003 est.): 81,624,716 (growth rate: 1.3%); birth rate: 19.6/1000; infant mortality rate: 30.8/1000; density per sq mi: 641
Capital (2003 est.): Hanoi, 2,543,700 (metro. area), 1,396,500 (city proper). **Largest cities:** Ho Chi Minh City (Saigon), 5,894,100 (metro. area), 3,415,300 (city proper); Haiphong, 581,600; Da Nang, 452,700; Hué 271,900; Nha Trang, 270,100; Qui Nho'n, 199,700. **Monetary unit:** Dong. **Languages:** Vietnamese (official), French, English, Khmer, Chinese. **Ethnicity/race:** Vietnamese 85%–90%, Chinese 3%, Muong, Thai, Meo, Khmer, Man, Cham. **Religions:** Buddhist, Roman Catholic, Islam, Taoist, Confucian, Animist. **Literacy rate:** 93.7% (1995 est.)
Economic summary: GDP/PPP (2001 est.): $168.1 billion; per capita $2,100. **Real growth rate:** 4.7%. **Inflation:** 0%. **Unemployment:** 25%. **Arable land:** 17%. **Agriculture:** paddy rice, corn, potatoes, rubber, soybeans, coffee, tea, bananas, sugar; poultry, pigs; fish. **Labor force:** 38.2 million; agriculture 67%, industry and services 33%. **Industries:** food processing, garments, shoes, machine building, mining, cement, chemical fertilizer, glass, tires, oil, coal, steel, paper. **Natural resources:** phosphates, coal, manganese, bauxite, chromate, offshore oil and gas deposits, forests, hydropower. **Exports:** $15.1 billion (f.o.b., 2001 est.): crude oil, marine products, rice, coffee, rubber, tea, garments, shoes. **Imports:** $15.3 billion (f.o.b., 2001 est.): machinery and equipment, petroleum products, fertilizer, steel products, raw cotton, grain, cement, motorcycles. **Major trading partners:** Japan, China, Australia, Singapore, Taiwan, Germany, U.S., South Korea, Thailand, Hong Kong.

Geography Vietnam occupies the eastern and southern part of the Indochinese peninsula in Southeast Asia, with the South China Sea along its entire coast. China is to the north and Laos and Cambodia to the west. Long and narrow on a north-south axis, Vietnam is about twice the size of Arizona. The Mekong River delta lies in the south.

Government Communist state.

History The Vietnamese are descendants of nomadic Mongols from China and migrants from Indonesia. According to mythology, the first ruler of Vietnam was Hung Vuong, who founded the nation in 2879 B.C. China ruled the nation then known as Nam Viet as a vassal state from 111 B.C. until the 15th century, an era of nationalistic expansion, when Cambodians were pushed out of the southern area of what is now Vietnam.

A century later, the Portuguese were the first Europeans to enter the area. France established its influence early in the 19th century, and within 80 years conquered the three regions into which the country was then divided—Cochin-China in the south, Annam in the central region, and Tonkin in the north.

France first unified Vietnam in 1887, when a single governor-generalship was created, followed by the first physical links between north and south—a rail and road system. Even at the beginning of World War II, however, there were internal differences among the three regions. Japan took over military bases in Vietnam in 1940, and a pro-Vichy French administration remained until 1945. Veteran Communist leader Ho Chi Minh organized an independence movement known as the Vietminh to exploit the confusion surrounding France's weakened influence in the region. At the end of the war, Ho's followers seized Hanoi and declared a short-lived republic, which ended with the arrival of French forces in 1946.

Paris proposed a unified government within the French Union under the former Annamite emperor, Bao Dai. Cochin-China and Annam accepted the proposal, and Bao Dai was proclaimed emperor of all Vietnam in 1949. Ho and the Vietminh withheld support, and the revolution in China gave them the outside help needed for a war of resistance against French and Vietnamese troops armed largely by a United States worried about cold war Communist expansion.

A bitter defeat at Dien Bien Phu in northwest Vietnam on May 5, 1954, broke the French military campaign and resulted in the division of Vietnam. In the new South, Ngo Dinh Diem, premier under Bao Dai, deposed the monarch in 1955 and made himself president. Diem used strong U.S. backing to create an authoritarian regime that suppressed all opposition but could not eradicate the Northern-supplied Communist Viet Cong.

Skirmishing grew into a full-scale war, with escalating U.S. involvement. A military coup, U.S.-inspired in the view of many, ousted Diem on Nov. 1, 1963, and a kaleidoscope of military governments followed. The most savage fighting of the war occurred in early 1968 during the Vietnamese New Year, known as Tet. Although the so-called Tet Offensive ended in a military defeat for the North, its psychological impact changed the course of the war.

U.S. bombing and an invasion of Cambodia in the summer of 1970—an effort to destroy Viet Cong bases in the neighboring state—marked the end of major U.S. participation in the fighting. Most American ground troops were withdrawn from combat by mid-1971 when the U.S. conducted heavy bombing raids on the Ho Chi Minh Trail—a crucial North Vietnamese supply line. In 1972, secret peace negotiations led by Secretary of State Henry A. Kissinger took place, and a peace settlement was signed in Paris on Jan. 27, 1973.

By April 9, 1975, Hanoi's troops marched within 40 miles of Saigon, the South's capital. South Vietnam's president Thieu resigned on April 21 and fled. Gen. Duong Van Minh, the new president, surrendered Saigon on April 30, ending a war that claimed the lives of 1.3 million Vietnamese and 58,000 Americans.

In 1977, border clashes between Vietnam and Cambodia intensified, as well as accusations by its former ally Beijing that Chinese residents of Vietnam were being subjected to persecution. Beijing cut off all aid and withdrew 800 technicians.

Hanoi was also preoccupied with a continuing war in Cambodia, where 60,000 Vietnamese troops had invaded and overthrown the country's Communist leader Pol Pot and his pro-Chinese regime. In early 1979, Vietnam was conducting a two-front war: defending its northern border against a Chinese invasion, and supporting its army in Cambodia, which was still fighting Pol Pot's Khmer Rouge guerrillas. Hanoi's Marxist policies combined with the destruction of the country's infrastructure during the decades of fighting devastated Vietnam's economy. However, it started to pick up in 1986 under *do Maui* (economic renovation), an effort at limited privatization. Vietnamese troops began limited withdrawals from Laos and Cambodia in 1988, and Vietnam supported the Cambodian peace agreement signed in Oct. 1991.

The U.S. lifted a Vietnamese trade embargo in Feb. 1994 that had been in place since U.S. involvement in the war. Full diplomatic relations were announced between the two countries in July 1995. In April 1997, a pact was signed with the U.S. concerning repayment of the $146 million wartime debt incurred by the South Vietnamese government, and the following year the nation began a drive to eliminate inefficient bureaucrats and streamline the approval process for direct foreign investment. Efforts of reform-minded officials toward political and economic change have been thwarted by Vietnam's ruling Communist Party. In April 2001, however, reform-minded Nong Duc Manh was appointed general secretary of the ruling Communist Party, succeeding Le Kha Phieu. Even with a reformer at the helm of the party, change has been slow and cautious.

In Nov. 2001, Vietnam's National Assembly approved a trade agreement that opened U.S. markets to Vietnam's goods and services. Tariffs on Vietnam's products dropped to about 4% from rates as high as 40%. Vietnam in return opened its state markets to foreign competition and agreed to meet international standards on copyright and investment issues. The pact took effect in early December.

In July 2002, the National Assembly reappointed President Tran Duc Luong and Prime Minister Phan Van Khai.

The government highlighted its efforts to crack down on corruption and crime with the June 2003 conviction of notorious criminal syndicate boss Truong Van Cam, known as Nam Cam. He, along with 155 other defendants, was sentenced to death.

(For a Vietnam War chronology, *see* Headline History.)

Western Sahara (proposed state)

WESTERN SAHARA

Area: 102,703 sq mi (266,000 sq km)
Population (2003 est.): 261,794 (growth rate: n.a.%); birth rate: n.a./1000; infant mortality rate: n.a./1000; density per sq mi: 3
Largest cities (2003 est.): El Aaiun 198,200. **Monetary unit:** Tala. **Languages:** Hassaniya Arabic, Moroccan Arabic. **Ethnicity/race:** Saharawi, Arab, Berber. **Religion:** Islam
Economic summary: GDP/PPP: n.a. **Arable land:** 0%. **Agriculture:** fruits and vegetables (grown in the few

oases); camels, sheep, goats (kept by nomads). **Labor force:** 12,000; animal husbandry and subsistence farming 50%. **Industries:** phosphate mining, handicrafts. **Natural resources:** phosphates, iron ore. **Exports:** n.a.: phosphates 62%. **Imports:** n.a.: fuel for fishing fleet, foodstuffs. **Major trading partners:** Morocco claims and administers Western Sahara, so trade partners are included in overall Moroccan accounts.

Geography Located in northern Africa on the Atlantic Ocean, Western Sahara is surrounded by Algeria to the east, Morocco to the north, and Mauritania to the south. About the size of Colorado, it is mostly low, flat desert with some small mountains in the south and northeast.

Government Legal status of the territory is disputed and sovereignty unresolved; a UN referendum on the issue is planned. The territory is contested by Morocco and the Polisario Front, which in Feb. 1976 formally proclaimed a government-in-exile of the Saharawi Arab Democratic Republic, now officially recognized by about 55 countries.

History Little is known about Western Sahara before the 4th century B.C., when trade with Europe began. During the Middle Ages it was occupied first by Berbers and then by the Arabic-speaking Muslim Bedouins. In the 19th century the Spanish laid claim to the southern coastal region, called Rio de Oro, and later occupied the northern interior region, Saguia el Hamra, in 1934. The Spanish formally united the two regions, and it became known as Spanish Sahara in 1958. Both Morocco and Mauritania sought to control the territory, and when the Spanish departed in 1976 they divided the territory between them. In the meantime, the indigenous Saharawis began fighting for independence. In 1976, the insurgents, called the Polisario Front, declared a government-in-exile (the Saharawi Arab Democratic Republic) from their base in Algeria. Mauritania reached a peace agreement with the Polisario in 1979, but Morocco then seized the land given up by Mauritania and now exerts administrative control over the entire region. The Polisario Front fought Morocco to a stalemate, and agreed in Sept. 1991 to a cease-fire, which was contingent on a referendum regarding independence. For the past decade, however, the UN has failed to hold the referendum; disputes over voter eligibility have been the major stumbling block, as well as Morocco's opposition to the referendum. In Aug. 2001, former secretary of state James A. Baker III, special UN envoy to the Western Sahara, proposed that instead of a referendum on independence, Western Sahara consider becoming an autonomous region of Morocco. The Western Sahara government rejected the new proposal, which it saw as a reversal of the UN's decade-old promise to hold a referendum on self-determination. In 2002, King Mohammed VI of Morocco reasserted that he "will not renounce an inch of" the Western Sahara.

In August 2003, a UN Security Council resolution adopted a new peace plan that would turn Western Sahara into a semi-autonomous region of Morocco for up to five years, after which a referendum would be held to determine independence, autonomy, or integration into Morocco. The Polisario agreed to the plan; Morocco refused to consider it. The Polisario also released 243 Moroccan prisoners, some of who had been imprisoned for decades; 914 Moroccan prisoners remain.

Yemen

REPUBLIC OF YEMEN

National name: Al Jumhuriyahal Yamaniyah
President: Ali Abdullah Saleh (1990)
Prime Minister: Abdul Qader Bajamal (2001)
Area: 203,849 sq mi (527,970 sq km)
Population (2003 est.): 19,349,881 (growth rate: 3.4%); birth rate: 43.2/1000; infant mortality rate: 65.0/1000; density per sq mi: 95
Capital and largest city (2003 est.): Sanaá, 1,778,900. **Other large cities:** Aden, 568,700; Hodiedah, 426,100; Tiaz, 317,600. **Monetary unit:** Rial. **Language:** Arabic. **Ethnicity/race:** predominantly Arab; Afro-Arab concentrations in western coastal locations; South Asians in southern regions; small European communities in major metropolitan areas. **Religion:** Islam (Sunni and Shi'ite). **Literacy rate:** 38% (1990 est.)
Economic summary: GDP/PPP (2001 est.): $14.8 billion; per capita $820. **Real growth rate:** 4%. **Inflation:** 10%. **Unemployment:** 30%. **Arable land:** 3%. **Agriculture:** grain, fruits, vegetables, pulses, qat (mildly narcotic shrub), coffee, cotton; dairy products, livestock (sheep, goats, cattle, camels), poultry; fish. **Labor force:** n.a.; most people are employed in agriculture and herding or as expatriate laborers; services, construction, industry, and commerce account for less than one-half of the labor force. **Industries:** crude oil production and petroleum refining; small-scale production of cotton textiles and leather goods; food processing; handicrafts; small aluminum products factory; cement. **Natural resources:** petroleum, fish, rock salt, marble, small deposits of coal, gold, lead, nickel, and copper, fertile soil in west. **Exports:** $3.9 billion (f.o.b., 2001 est.): crude oil, coffee, dried and salted fish. **Imports:** $3 billion (f.o.b., 2001 est.): food and live animals, machinery and equipment. **Major trading partners:** Thailand, China, South Korea, Singapore, Japan, Saudi Arabia, UAE, France, U.S., Italy.

Geography Formerly divided into two nations, the People's Democratic Republic of Yemen and the Yemen Arab Republic, the Republic of Yemen occupies the southwest tip of the Arabian Peninsula on the Red Sea opposite Ethiopia, and extends along the southern part of the Arabian Peninsula on the Gulf of Aden and the Indian Ocean. Saudi Arabia is to the north and Oman is to the east. The country is about the size of France. A 700-mile (1,130-km) narrow coastal plain in the south gives way to a mountainous region and then a plateau area.

Government Parliamentary republic.

History The history of Yemen dates back to the Minaean (1200–650 B.C.) and Sabaean (750–115 B.C.) kingdoms. Ancient Yemen (centered around the port of Aden) engaged in the lucrative myrrh and frankincense trade. It was invaded by the Romans (1st century A.D.) as well as the Ethiopians and Persians (6th century A.D.). In A.D. 628 it converted to Islam and in the 10th century came under the control of the Rassite dynasty of the Zaidi sect, which remained involved in North Yemeni politics until 1962. The Ottoman Turks nominally occupied the area from 1538 to the decline of their empire in 1918.

The northern portion of Yemen was ruled by imams until a pro-Egyptian military coup took place in 1962. The junta proclaimed the Yemen Arab Republic, and after a civil war in which Egypt's Nasser and the USSR supported the revolutionaries, and King Saud of Saudi Arabia and King Hussein of Jordan supported the royalists, the royalists were finally defeated in mid-1969.

The southern port of Aden, strategically located at the opening of the Red Sea, was colonized by Britain in 1839, and by 1937, with an expansion of its territory, it was known as the Aden Protectorate. In the 1960s the Nationalist Liberation Front (NLF) fought against British rule, which led to the establishment of the People's Republic of Southern Yemen on Nov. 30, 1967. In 1979, under strong Soviet influence, the country became the only Marxist state in the Arab world.

The Republic of Yemen was established on May 22, 1990, when pro-Western Yemen and the Marxist Yemen Arab Republic merged after 300 years of separation to form the new nation. The poverty and decline in Soviet economic support in the south was an important incentive for the merger. The new president, Ali Abdullah Saleh, was elected by the Parliaments of both countries.

Differences over power sharing and the pace of integration between the north and the south came to a head in 1994, resulting in a civil war. The north's superior forces quickly overwhelmed the south in May and early June despite the south's brief declaration of succession. The victorious north presented a reconciliation plan providing for a general amnesty and pledges to protect political democracy.

The president's party, the General People's Congress, won an enormous victory in the April 1997 parliamentary elections, the first since the civil war. In 1998–1999, a militant Islamic group, the Aden-Abyan Islamic Army, kidnapped several groups of Western tourists, which led to the deaths of several during a poorly orchestrated rescue attempt. The group's leader, Zein Al-Abidine al-Mihdar, threatened to continue attacks on tourists and government officials. The goal of the militants is to overthrow the government and turn Yemen into an Islamic state.

On Oct. 12, 2000, 17 Americans died and 37 were wounded when suicide bombers attacked the U.S. Navy destroyer *Cole,* which was refueling in Aden, Yemen. The U.S. has had numerous clashes with Yemeni authorities during the investigation of the terrorist act. After the Sept. 11 terrorist attacks on the U.S., however, Yemen increased its cooperation with the U.S. and assisted in antiterrorism measures. In Oct. 2002, a French tanker, the *Limburg,* was the apparent victim of a terrorist attack off the coast of Yemen.

Yugoslavia

SEE SERBIA AND MONTENEGRO.

Zaire

SEE CONGO, DEMOCRATIC REPUBLIC OF.

Zambia

REPUBLIC OF ZAMBIA

President: Levy Mwanawasa (2002)
Area: 290,584 sq mi (752,614 sq km)
Population (2003 est.): 10,307,333 (growth rate: 1.5%); birth rate: 39.5/1000; infant mortality rate: 99.3/1000; density per sq mi: 35
Capital and largest city (2003 est.): Lusaka, 1,773,300 (metro. area), 1,265,000 (city proper). **Other large cities:**Ndola, 349,300; Kitwe, 306,200; Kabwe, 219,600, Chingola, 151,100. **Monetary unit:** Kwacha. **Languages:** English (official) and local dialects. **Ethnicity/race:** African 98.7%, European 1.1%, other 0.2%. **Religions:** Christian 50%–75%, Islam and Hindu 24%–49%, remainder indigenous beliefs. **Literacy rate:** 78.9%

Economic summary: GDP/PPP (2001 est.): $8.5 billion; per capita $870. **Real growth rate:** 3.9%. **Inflation:** 21.5%. **Unemployment:** 50% (2000 est.). **Arable land:** 7%. **Agriculture:** corn, sorghum, rice, peanuts, sunflower seed, vegetables, flowers, tobacco, cotton, sugarcane, cassava (tapioca); cattle, goats, pigs, poultry, milk, eggs, hides; coffee. **Labor force:** 3.4 million; agriculture 85%, industry 6%, services 9%. **Industries:** copper mining and processing, construction, foodstuffs, beverages, chemicals, textiles, fertilizer, horticulture. **Natural resources:** copper, cobalt, zinc, lead, coal, emeralds, gold, silver, uranium, hydropower. **Exports:** $876 million (f.o.b., 2001 est.): copper 55%, cobalt, electricity, tobacco, flowers, cotton. **Imports:** $12.05 billion (f.o.b., 2001 est.): machinery, transportation equipment, petroleum products, electricity, fertilizer; foodstuffs, clothing. **Major trading partners:** UK, South Africa, Switzerland, Malawi, Zimbabwe, U.S. **International conflicts:** none.

Geography Zambia, a landlocked country in south-central Africa, is about one-tenth larger than Texas. It is surrounded by Angola, Zaire, Tanzania, Malawi, Mozambique, Zimbabwe, Botswana, and Namibia. The country is mostly a plateau that rises to 8,000 ft (2,434 m) in the east.

Government Republic.

History Early humans inhabited present-day Zambia between one and two million years ago. Today the country is made up almost entirely of Bantu-speaking peoples. Empire builder Cecil Rhodes obtained mining concessions in 1889 from King Lewanika of the Barotse and sent settlers to the area soon thereafter. The region was ruled by the British South Africa Company, which he established, until 1924, when the British government took over the administration.

From 1953 to 1964, Northern Rhodesia was federated with Southern Rhodesia (now Zimbabwe) and Nyasaland (now Malawi) in the Federation of Rhodesia and Nyasaland. On Oct. 24, 1964, Northern Rhodesia became the independent nation of Zambia.

Kenneth Kaunda, the first president, kept Zambia within the Commonwealth of Nations. The country's economy, dependent on copper exports, was threatened when Rhodesia declared its independence from British rule in 1965 and defied UN sanctions, which Zambia supported, an action that deprived Zambia of its trade route through Rhodesia. The U.S., Britain, and Canada organized an airlift in 1966 to ship gasoline into Zambia.

In 1972 Kaunda outlawed all opposition political parties. The world copper market collapsed in 1975. The Zambian economy was devastated—it had been the third-largest miner of copper in the world after the United States and Soviet Union. With a soaring debt and inflation rate in 1991, riots took place in Lusaka, resulting in a number of killings. Mounting domestic pressure forced Kaunda to move Zambia toward multiparty democracy. National elections on Oct. 31, 1991, brought a stunning defeat to Kaunda. The new president, Frederick Chiluba, called for sweeping economic reforms, including privatization and the establishment of a stock market. He was reelected in Nov. 1996. Chiluba declared martial law in 1997 and arrested Kaunda following a failed coup attempt. The 1999 slump in world copper prices again depressed the economy since copper provides 80% of Zambia's export earnings.

In 2001 Chiluba contemplated changing the constitution to allow him to run for another presidential term. After protests he relented, and selected Levy Mwanawasa, a former vice president with whom he had fallen out, as his successor. Mwanawasa became president in

Jan. 2002; opposition parties protested over alleged fraud. In June 2002, Mwanawasa, once seen as a pawn of Chiluba, accused the former president of stealing millions from the government while in office. Chiluba was arrested and charged in Feb. 2003.

Although the country faced the threat of famine in 2002, the president refused to accept any international donations of food that had been genetically modified, which Mwanawasa considered "poison."

In Aug. 2003, impeachment proceedings against the president for corruption were unsuccessful. More than 120,000 civil servants held two nationwide strikes in August to protest the government's failure to pay housing allowances.

Zimbabwe

REPUBLIC OF ZIMBABWE

President: Robert Mugabe (1987)
Area: 150,803 sq mi (390,580 sq km)
Population (2003 est.): 12,576,742 (growth rate: 0.8%); birth rate: 30.3/1000; infant mortality rate: 66.5/1000; density per sq mi: 83
Capital and largest city (2003 est.): Harare, 2,331,400 (metro. area), 1,919,700 (city proper). **Other large cities:** Bulawayo, 965,000; Chitungwiza, 411,700. **Monetary unit:** Zimbabwean dollar. **Languages:** English (official), Ndebele, Shona (85%). **Ethnicity/race:** African 98% (Shona 82%, Ndebele 14%, other 2%), white 1%, mixed and Asian 1%. **Religions:** Christian 25%, Animist 24%, Syncretic 50%. **Literacy rate:** 85% (1995 est.)
Economic summary: GDP/PPP (2001 est.): $28 billion; per capita $2,450. **Real growth rate:** –6.5%. **Inflation:** 100%. **Unemployment:** 60%. **Arable land:** 8%. **Agriculture:** corn, cotton, tobacco, wheat, coffee, sugarcane, peanuts; cattle, sheep, goats, pigs. **Labor force:** 5.5 million (2000 est.); agriculture 66%, services 24%, industry 10% (1996 est.). **Industries:** mining (coal, gold, copper, nickel, tin, clay, numerous metallic and nonmetallic ores), steel, wood products, cement, chemicals, fertilizer, clothing and footwear, foodstuffs, beverages. **Natural resources:** coal, chromium ore, asbestos, gold, nickel, copper, iron ore, vanadium, lithium, tin, platinum group metals. **Exports:** $2.1 billion (f.o.b., 2001 est.): tobacco 30%, gold 11%, ferroalloys 9%, textile/clothing 3% (2000). **Imports:** $1.5 billion (f.o.b., 2001 est.): machinery and transport equipment 34%, other manufactures 18%, chemicals 17%, fuels 11% (1999). **Major trading partners:** South Africa, UK, Japan, Germany, China.

Geography Zimbabwe, a landlocked country in south-central Africa, is slightly smaller than California. It is bordered by Botswana on the west, Zambia on the north, Mozambique on the east, and South Africa on the south.

Government Parliamentary democracy.

History The remains of early humans, dating back 500,000 years, have been discovered in present-day Zimbabwe. The land's earliest settlers, the Khoisan, date back to 200 B.C. After a period of Bantu domination, the Shona people ruled, followed by the Nguni and Zulu peoples. By the mid-19th century the descendants of the Nguni and Zulu, the Ndebele, had established a powerful warrior kingdom.

The first British explorers, colonists, and missionaries arrived in the 1850s, and the massive influx of foreigners led to the establishment of the territory Rhodesia, named after Cecil Rhodes of the British South Africa Company. In 1923, European settlers voted to become the self-governing British colony of Southern Rhodesia. After a brief federation with Northern Rhodesia (now Zambia) and Nyasaland (now Malawi) in the post–World War II period, Southern Rhodesia (also known as Rhodesia) chose to remain a colony when its two partners voted for independence in 1963.

On Nov. 11, 1965, the conservative white-minority government of Rhodesia declared its independence from Britain. The country resisted the demands of black Africans, and Prime Minister Ian Smith withstood British pressure, economic sanctions, and guerrilla attacks to uphold white supremacy. On March 1, 1970, Rhodesia formally proclaimed itself a republic. Heightened guerrilla war and a withdrawal of South African military aid in 1976 marked the beginning of the collapse of Smith's 11 years of resistance.

Black nationalist movements were led by Bishop Abel Muzorewa of the African National Congress and Ndabaningi Sithole, who were moderates, and guerrilla leaders Robert Mugabe of the Zimbabwe African National Union (ZANU) and Joshua Nkomo of the Zimbabwe African People's Union (ZAPU), who advocated revolution.

On March 3, 1978, Smith, Muzorewa, Sithole, and Chief Jeremiah Chirau signed an agreement to transfer power to the black majority by Dec. 31, 1978. They constituted themselves an Executive Council, with chairmanship rotating but with Smith retaining the title of prime minister. Blacks were named to each cabinet ministry, serving as coministers with the whites already holding these posts. African nations and rebel leaders immediately denounced the action, but Western governments were more reserved, although none granted recognition to the new regime.

The white minority finally consented to hold multiracial elections in 1980, and Robert Mugabe won a landslide victory. The country achieved independence on April 17, 1980, under the name Zimbabwe. Mugabe eventually established a one-party socialist state, but by 1990 he had instituted multiparty elections and in 1991 deleted all references to Marxism-Leninism and scientific socialism from the constitution. Parliamentary elections in April 1995 gave Mugabe's party a stunning victory with 63 of the 65 contested seats, and in 1996 Mugabe won another six-year term as president.

In 2000, veterans of Zimbabwe's war for independence in the 1970s began squatting on land owned by white farmers in an effort to reclaim land taken under British colonization—one-third of Zimbabwe's arable land was owned by 4,000 whites. In Feb. 2000, President Mugabe's government lost a referendum on a constitutional amendment that would have allowed the seizure of land owned by white farmers without paying them compensation. Despite the defeat, the government supported the land-taking. In Aug. 2002, Mugabe ordered all white commercial farmers to leave their land without compensation; by November most of the 4,000 farmers had been forced to leave. Mugabe's support for the squatters and his repressive rule has led to foreign sanctions against Zimbabwe. Once heralded as a champion of the anticolonial movement, Mugabe is now viewed by much of the international community as an authoritarian responsible for egregious human rights abuses and for running the economy of his country into the ground.

In March 2002, Mugabe was reelected president for another six years in a blatantly rigged election whose results were enforced by the president's militia. Since the election inflation has hit 300%, farming has been destroyed, and the country faces severe food shortages. In March 2003, a nationwide strike was held; a brutal crackdown followed.

United Nations

Preamble of the United Nations Charter

The Charter of the United Nations was adopted at the San Francisco Conference of 1945. The complete text is available on the UN website, www.un.org/aboutun/charter.

We the peoples of the United Nations determined to save succeeding generations from the scourge of war, which twice in our lifetime has brought untold sorrow to mankind, and

To reaffirm faith in fundamental human rights, in the dignity and worth of the human person, in the equal rights of men and women and of nations large and small, and

To establish conditions under which justice and respect for the obligations arising from treaties and other sources of international law can be maintained, and

To promote social progress and better standards of life in larger freedom, and for these ends

To practice tolerance and live together in peace with one another as good neighbors, and

To unite our strength to maintain international peace and security, and

To insure, by the acceptance of principles and the institution of methods, that armed force shall not be used, save in the common interest, and

To employ international machinery for the promotion of the economic and social advancement of all peoples, have resolved to combine our efforts to accomplish these aims.

Accordingly, our respective Governments, through representatives assembled in the city of San Francisco, who have exhibited their full powers found to be in good and due form, have agreed to the present Charter of the United Nations and do hereby establish an international organization to be known as the United Nations.

Principal Organs of the United Nations

Secretariat

This is the directorate on UN operations, apart from political decisions. The staff works under the secretary-general, whom it assists and advises.

Secretaries-General

Kofi Annan, Ghana, Jan. 1, 1997.

Boutros Boutros-Ghali, Egypt, Jan. 1, 1992–Dec. 31, 1996.

Javier Pérez de Cuéllar, Peru, Jan. 1, 1982–Dec. 31, 1991.

Kurt Waldheim, Austria, Jan. 1, 1972–Dec. 31, 1981.

U Thant, Burma (Myanmar), Nov. 3, 1961–Dec. 31, 1971.

Dag Hammarskjöld, Sweden, April 11, 1953–Sept. 17, 1961.

Trygve Lie, Norway, Feb. 1, 1946–April 10, 1953.

General Assembly

The General Assembly is the world's forum for discussing matters affecting world peace and security, and for making recommendations concerning them. It has no power of its own to enforce decisions. It is composed of the 51 original member nations and those admitted since, a total of 191. On important questions including international peace and security, a two-thirds majority of those present and voting is required. Decisions on other questions are made by a simple majority. Emphasis is given on questions relating to international peace and security brought before it by any member, the Security Council, or nonmembers. It also maintains a broad program of international cooperation in economic, social, cultural, educational, and health fields, and for assisting in human rights and freedoms.

International Court of Justice

The International Court of Justice is the UN's principal judicial organ. Based in The Hague, Netherlands, the Court pursues two primary objectives: (1) settling legal disputes submitted by states in accordance with international law, and (2) advising on legal questions brought by authorized international organs and agencies. The Court consists of 15 judges elected to nine-year terms by the United Nations General Assembly and the Security Council during independent sittings.

Security Council

The Security Council is the primary instrument for establishing and maintaining international peace. Its main purpose is to prevent war by settling disputes between nations. Under the charter, the council is permitted to dispatch a UN force to stop aggression. All member nations undertake to make available armed forces, assistance, and facilities to maintain international peace and security (*see* p. 907 for list of UN Peacekeeping Operations).

The Security Council has 15 members. There are five permanent members: the United States, the Russian Federation, Britain, France, and China; and ten temporary members elected by the General Assembly for two-year terms, from five different regions of the world. Voting on procedural matters requires a nine-vote majority to carry. However, on questions of substance, the vote of each of the five permanent members is required. As of Jan. 2003, the ten elected nonpermanent members were Angola, Chile, Germany, Pakistan, Spain, Bulgaria, Cameroon, Guinea, Mexico, and Syria.

Economic and Social Council

This council is composed of 54 members elected by the General Assembly to three-year terms. It works under the authority of the General Assembly and seeks to promote progress in terms of higher standards of living, full employment, and economic and social viability; it also seeks solutions to international socioeconomic, health, and other problems through international and cultural cooperation. Finally, it advocates for the universal respect for and observance of human rights and fundamental freedoms for all.

Trusteeship Council

The UN charter originally established the Trusteeship Council as a main organ of the UN and entrusted it with the administration of territories placed under the trusteeship system.

The Trusteeship Council suspended operations on Nov. 1, 1994, after the October independence of Palau, the last UN territory.

UN Peacekeeping Missions

Since 1948 there have been 56 UN peacekeeping operations. Forty-three of these operations have been created by the United Nations Security Council since 1988. Thus far, close to 130 nations have contributed personnel at various times; 89 are currently providing peacekeepers. As of Aug. 31, 2003, the top contributors of military and civilian personnel to current missions were: Pakistan (4,180), Bangladesh (3,925), India (2,933), and Ghana (2,027). In 2003, there were 15 peacekeeping operations underway with a total of 36,948 personnel. The latest peace-keeping operation, a 16,000-strong force deployed to Liberia on Oct. 1, is not included in that total.

Current UN Peacekeeping Operations

Region/Country	Duration
AFRICA	
Western Sahara	April 1991–present
Sierra Leone	Oct. 1999–present
Democratic Republic of the Congo	Nov. 1999–present
Ethiopia and Eritrea	July 2000–present
Côte d'Ivoire	May 2003–present
Liberia	Oct. 2003–present
ASIA	
India/Pakistan	Jan. 1949–present
East Timor	May 2002–present
EUROPE	
Cyprus	March 1964–present
Georgia	Aug. 1993–present
Kosovo	June 1999–present
MIDDLE EAST	
Middle East	May 1948–present
Golan Heights	June 1974–present
Lebanon	March 1978–present
Iraq/Kuwait	April 1991–present

Completed UN Peacekeeping Operations

Region/Country	Duration
AFRICA	
Congo	July 1960–June 1964
Angola	Dec. 1988–May 1991
Namibia	April 1989–March 1990
Angola	May 1991–Feb. 1995
Somalia	April 1992–March 1993
Mozambique	Dec. 1992–Dec. 1994
Somalia	March 1993–March 1995
Rwanda/Uganda	June 1993–Sept. 1994
Liberia	Sept. 1993–Sept. 1997
Rwanda	Oct. 1993–March 1996
Chad/Libya	May–June 1994
Angola	Feb. 1995–June 1997
Angola	June 1997–Feb. 1999
Sierra Leone	July 1998–Oct. 1999
Central African Republic	April 1998–Feb. 2000
MIDEAST	
Middle East—1st UN Emergency Force	Nov. 1956–June 1967
Lebanon	June–Dec. 1958
Yemen	July 1963–Sept. 1964
Middle East—2nd UN Emergency Force	Oct. 1973–July 1979
Iran/Iraq	Aug. 1988–Feb. 1991
AMERICAS	
Dominican Republic	May 1965–Oct. 1966
Central America Observer Group	Nov. 1989–Jan. 1992
El Salvador	July 1991–April 1995
Haiti	Sept. 1993–June 1996
Haiti	July 1996–July 1997
Guatemala	Jan.–May 1997
Haiti	Aug.–Nov. 1997
Haiti	Dec. 1997–March 2000
ASIA	
West New Guinea	Oct. 1962–April 1963
India/Pakistan	Sept. 1965–March 1966
Afghanistan/Pakistan	May 1988–March 1990
Cambodia	Oct. 1991–March 1992
Cambodia	March 1992–Sept. 1993
Tajikistan	Dec. 1994–May 2000
East Timor	Oct. 1999–May 2002
EUROPE	
Former Yugoslavia	Feb. 1992–March 1995
Croatia	March 1995–Jan. 1996
Former Yugoslavia Rep. of Macedonia	March 1995–Feb. 1999
Bosnia & Herzegovina	Dec. 1995–Dec. 2002
Croatia	Jan. 1996–Jan. 1998
Croatia	Jan. 1998–Oct. 1998

Source: United Nations Dept. of Public Information.

Members of the United Nations (191 nations)

Country	Joined UN[1]
Afghanistan	1946
Albania	1955
Algeria	1962
Andorra	1993
Angola	1976
Antigua and Barbuda	1981
Argentina	1945
Armenia	1992
Australia	1945
Austria	1955
Azerbaijan	1992
Bahamas	1973
Bahrain	1971
Bangladesh	1974
Barbados	1966
Belarus	1945
Belgium	1945
Belize	1981
Benin	1960
Bhutan	1971
Bolivia	1945
Bosnia and Herzegovina	1992
Botswana	1966
Brazil	1945
Brunei Darussalam	1984
Bulgaria	1955
Burkina Faso	1960
Burma (Myanmar)	1948
Burundi	1962
Cambodia	1955
Cameroon	1960
Canada	1945
Cape Verde	1975
Central African Republic	1960
Chad	1960
Chile	1945
China[2]	1945
Colombia	1945
Comoros	1975
Congo	1960
Congo, Dem. Rep.	1960
Costa Rica	1945
Côte d'Ivoire	1960
Croatia	1992
Cuba	1945
Cyprus	1960
Czech Republic[3]	1993
Denmark	1945
Djibouti	1977
Dominica	1978
Dominican Republic	1945
East Timor[4]	2002
Ecuador	1945
Egypt	1945
El Salvador	1945
Equatorial Guinea	1968
Eritrea	1993
Estonia	1991
Ethiopia	1945
Fiji	1970
Finland	1955
France	1945
Gabon	1960
Gambia	1965
Georgia	1992
Germany	1973
Ghana	1957
Greece	1945
Grenada	1974
Guatemala	1945
Guinea	1958
Guinea-Bissau	1974
Guyana	1966
Haiti	1945
Honduras	1945
Hungary	1955
Iceland	1946
India	1945
Indonesia	1950
Iran	1945
Iraq	1945
Ireland	1955
Israel	1949
Italy	1955
Jamaica	1962
Japan	1956
Jordan	1955
Kazakhstan	1992
Kenya	1963
Kiribati	1999
North Korea	1991
South Korea	1991
Kuwait	1963
Kyrgyzstan	1992
Laos	1955
Latvia	1991
Lebanon	1945
Lesotho	1966
Liberia	1945
Libya	1955
Liechtenstein	1990
Lithuania	1991
Luxembourg	1945
Macedonia[5]	1993
Madagascar	1960
Malawi	1964
Malaysia	1957
Maldives	1965
Mali	1960
Malta	1964
Marshall Islands	1991
Mauritania	1961
Mauritius	1968
Mexico	1945
Micronesia	1991
Moldova	1992
Monaco	1993
Mongolia	1961
Morocco	1956
Mozambique	1975
Namibia	1990
Nauru	1999
Nepal	1955
Netherlands	1945
New Zealand	1945
Nicaragua	1945
Niger	1960
Nigeria	1960
Norway	1945
Oman	1971
Pakistan	1947
Palau	1994
Panama	1945
Papua New Guinea	1975
Paraguay	1945
Peru	1945
Philippines	1945
Poland	1945
Portugal	1955
Qatar	1971
Romania	1955
Russian Federation	1945
Rwanda	1962
St. Kitts and Nevis	1983
St. Lucia	1979
St. Vincent and the Grenadines	1980
Samoa, Western	1976
San Marino	1992
São Tomé and Príncipe	1975
Saudi Arabia	1945
Senegal	1960
Serbia and Montenegro[6]	2000
Seychelles	1976
Sierra Leone	1961
Singapore	1965
Slovakia[3]	1993
Slovenia	1992
Solomon Islands	1978
Somalia	1960
South Africa	1945
Spain	1955
Sri Lanka	1955
Sudan	1956
Suriname	1975
Swaziland	1968
Sweden	1946
Switzerland[4]	2002
Syria	1945
Tajikistan	1992
Tanzania	1961
Thailand	1946
Togo	1960
Tonga	1999
Trinidad and Tobago	1962
Tunisia	1956
Turkey	1945
Turkmenistan	1992
Tuvalu	2000
Uganda	1962
Ukraine	1945
United Arab Emirates	1971
United Kingdom	1945
United States	1945
Uruguay	1945
Uzbekistan	1992
Vanuatu	1981
Venezuela	1945
Vietnam	1977
Yemen, Republic of	1947
Zambia	1964
Zimbabwe	1980

1. The UN officially came into existence on Oct. 24, 1945. 2. On Oct. 25, 1971, the UN voted membership to the People's Republic of China, which replaced the Republic of China (Taiwan) in the world body. 3. Czechoslovakia was an original member of the United Nations from Oct. 24, 1945. As of Dec. 31, 1992, it ceased to exist and the Czech Republic and Slovakia as successor states were admitted Jan. 19, 1993. 4. Newest members. 5. The General Assembly on April 8, 1993, decided to admit the state provisionally being referred to as "The Former Yugoslav Republic of Macedonia" pending settlement of the difference that has arisen over its name. 6. The Socialist Federal Republic of Yugoslavia was a charter member; after its dissolution, the Federal Republic of Yugoslavia was admitted Nov. 1, 2000. On Feb. 4, 2003, the name of the Federal Republic of Yugoslavia was changed to Serbia and Montenegro

U.S. Representatives to the United Nations

Year	Ambassador	Year	Ambassador
1946	Edward R. Stettinius, Jr.	1975–1976	Daniel P. Moynihan
1946–1947	Herschel V. Johnson (acting)	1976–1977	William W. Scranton
1947–1953	Warren R. Austin	1977–1979	Andrew Young
1953–1960	Henry Cabot Lodge, Jr.	1979–1981	Donald McHenry
1960–1961	James J. Wadsworth	1981–1985	Jeane J. Kirkpatrick
1961–1965	Adlai E. Stevenson	1985–1989	Vernon A. Walters
1965–1968	Arthur J. Goldberg	1989–1992	Thomas J. Pickering
1968	George W. Ball	1992–1993	Edward J. Perkins
1968–1969	James Russell Wiggins	1993–1996	Madeleine K. Albright
1969–1971	Charles W. Yost	1997–1998	Bill Richardson
1971–1973	George Bush	1999–2001	Richard Holbrooke
1973–1975	John A. Scali	2001–	John D. Negroponte

Selected International Organizations

Arab League (AL)
Members: (21 plus the Palestine Liberation Organization) Algeria, Bahrain, Comoros, Djibouti, Egypt, Iraq, Jordan, Kuwait, Lebanon, Libya, Mauritania, Morocco, Oman, Qatar, Saudi Arabia, Somalia, Sudan, Syria, Tunisia, UAE, Yemen, Palestine Liberation Organization

Association of Southeast Asian Nations (ASEAN)
Members: (10) Brunei, Burma, Cambodia, Indonesia, Laos, Malaysia, Philippines, Singapore, Thailand, Vietnam
Associate Member: (1) Papua New Guinea

Group of 8 (G-8)
Members: (9) Canada, EU (as one member), France, Germany, Italy, Japan, Russia, UK, U.S.

Commonwealth of Nations
Members: (54) Antigua and Barbuda, Australia, the Bahamas, Bangladesh, Barbados, Belize, Botswana, Brunei, Cameroon, Canada, Cyprus, Dominica, Fiji, the Gambia, Ghana, Grenada, Guyana, India, Jamaica, Kenya, Kiribati, Lesotho, Malawi, Malaysia, Maldives, Malta, Mauritius, Mozambique, Namibia, Nauru, New Zealand, Nigeria, Pakistan (suspended), Papua New Guinea, Saint Kitts and Nevis, Saint Lucia, Saint Vincent and the Grenadines, Samoa, Seychelles, Sierra Leone, Singapore, Solomon Islands, South Africa, Sri Lanka, Swaziland, Tanzania, Tonga, Trinidad and Tobago, Tuvalu, Uganda, UK, Vanuatu, Zambia, Zimbabwe

Commonwealth of Independent States (CIS)
Members: (12) Armenia, Azerbaijan, Belarus, Georgia, Kazakhstan, Kyrgyzstan, Moldova, Russia, Tajikistan, Turkmenistan, Ukraine, Uzbekistan

European Union (EU)
Members: (15) Austria, Belgium, Denmark, Finland, France, Germany, Greece, Ireland, Italy, Luxembourg, Netherlands, Portugal, Spain, Sweden, UK **New Members in 2004:** (10) Cyprus, Czech Republic, Estonia, Hungary, Latvia, Lithuania, Malta, Poland, Slovakia, Slovenia

North Atlantic Treaty Organization (NATO)
Members: (19) Belgium, Canada, Czech Republic, Denmark, France, Germany, Greece, Hungary, Iceland, Italy, Luxembourg, Netherlands, Norway, Poland, Portugal, Spain, Turkey, UK, U.S. **New members in 2004:** (7) Bulgaria, Estonia, Latvia, Lithuania, Romania, Slovakia, Slovenia

African Union (AU)[1]
Members: (53) Algeria, Angola, Benin, Botswana, Burkina Faso, Burundi, Cameroon, Cape Verde, Central African Republic, Chad, Comoros, Congo, Côte d'Ivoire, Democratic Republic of the Congo, Djibouti, Egypt, Equatorial Guinea, Eritrea, Ethiopia, Gabon, The Gambia, Ghana, Guinea, Guinea-Bissau, Kenya, Lesotho, Liberia, Libya, Madagascar, Malawi, Mali, Mauritania, Mauritius, Mozambique, Namibia, Niger, Nigeria, Rwanda, São Tomé and Príncipe, Senegal, Seychelles, Sierra Leone, Somalia, South Africa, Sudan, Swaziland, Tanzania, Togo, Tunisia, Uganda, Western Sahara, Zambia, Zimbabwe

Organization of Petroleum Exporting Countries (OPEC)
Members: (11) Algeria, Indonesia, Iran, Iraq, Kuwait, Libya, Nigeria, Qatar, Saudi Arabia, UAE, Venezuela

1. The Organization of African Unity (OAU), the African Union's predecessor, was formally disbanded on July 8, 2002. The AU was inaugurated July 9, 2002. The 53 member nations remain the same.

Foreign Embassies in the United States

Source: U.S. Department of State

Embassy of Afghanistan, 2341 Wyoming Ave., N.W.,Washington, D.C. 20008. Phone: 202-483-6410.

Embassy of the Republic of Albania, 2100 S St., N.W., Washington, D.C. 20008. Phone: 202-223-4942.

Embassy of the Democratic & Popular Republic of Algeria, 2118 Kalorama Rd., N.W., Washington, D.C. 20008. Phone: 202-265-2800.

Embassy of Andorra/Permanent Mission to the UN, 2 United Nations Plaza, 25th flr. New York, N.Y. 10017. Phone: 212-750-8064.

Embassy of the Republic of Angola, 1615 M St., N.W., Suite 900, Washington, D.C. 20036. Phone: 202-785-1156.

Embassy of Antigua & Barbuda, 3216 New Mexico Ave., N.W., Washington, D.C. 20016. Phone: 202-362-5211.

Embassy of the Argentine Republic, 1600 New Hampshire Ave., N.W., Washington, D.C. 20009. Phone: 202-238-6400.

Embassy of the Republic of Armenia, 2225 R Street, N.W., Washington, D.C. 20008. Phone: 202-319-1976.

Embassy of Australia, 1601 Massachusetts Ave., N.W., Washington, D.C. 20036. Phone: 202-797-3000.

Embassy of Austria, 3524 International Court, N.W., Washington, D.C. 20008-3027. Phone: 202-895-6700.

Embassy of the Republic of Azerbaijan, 2741 34th St., N.W., Washington, D.C. 20008. Phone: 202-337-3500.

Embassy of the Commonwealth of the Bahamas, 2220 Massachusetts Ave., N.W., Washington, D.C. 20008. Phone: 202-319-2660.

Embassy of the Kingdom of Bahrain, 3502 International Dr., N.W., Washington, D.C. 20008. Phone: 202-342-0741.

Embassy of the People's Republic of Bangladesh, 3510 International Drive, N.W., Washington, D.C. 20008. Phone: 202-244-0183.

Embassy of Barbados, 2144 Wyoming Ave., N.W., Washington, D.C. 20008. Phone: 202-939-9200 to 9202.

Embassy of the Republic of Belarus, 1619 New Hampshire Ave., N.W., Washington, D.C. 20009. Phone: 202-986-1604.

Embassy of Belgium, 3330 Garfield St., N.W., Washington, D.C. 20008. Phone: 202-333-6900.

Embassy of Belize, 2535 Massachusetts Ave., N.W., Washington, D.C. 20008. Phone: 202-332-9636.

Embassy of the Republic of Benin, 2124 Kalorama Road, N.W., Washington, D.C. 20008. Phone: 202-232-6656 to 6658.

Embassy of Bolivia, 3014 Massachusetts Ave., N.W., Washington, D.C. 20008. Phone: 202-483-4410.

Embassy of Bosnia and Herzegovina, 2109 E St. N.W., Washington, D.C. 20037. Phone: 202-337-1500.

Embassy of Botswana, 1531-1533 New Hampshire Ave., N.W., Washington, D.C. 20036. Phone: 202-244-4990.

Brazilian Embassy, 3006 Massachusetts Ave., N.W., Washington, D.C. 20008. Phone: 202-238-2700.

Embassy of Brunei Darussalam, 3520 International Court, N.W., Washington, D.C. 20008. Phone: 202-237-1838.

Embassy of the Republic of Bulgaria, 1621 22nd St., N.W., Washington, D.C. 20008. Phone: 202-387-0174.

Embassy of Burkina Faso, 2340 Massachusetts Ave., N.W., Washington, D.C. 20008. Phone: 202-332-5577.

Embassy of the Union of Burma (Myanmar), 2300 S St., N.W., Washington, D.C. 20008. Phone: 202-332-9044.

Embassy of the Republic of Burundi, 2233 Wisconsin Ave., N.W., Suite 212, Washington, D.C. 20007. Phone: 202-342-2574.

Embassy of the Kingdom of Cambodia, 4500 16th St., N.W., Washington, D.C. 20011. Phone: 202-726-7742.

Embassy of the Republic of Cameroon, 2349 Massachusetts Ave., N.W., Washington, D.C. 20008. Phone: 202-265-8790.

Embassy of Canada, 501 Pennsylvania Ave., N.W., Washington, D.C. 20001. Phone: 202-682-1740.

Embassy of the Republic of Cape Verde, 3415 Massachusetts Ave., N.W., Washington, D.C. 20007. Phone: 202-965-6820.

Embassy of Central African Republic, 1618 22nd St. N.W., Washington, D.C. 20008. Phone: 202-483-7800.

Embassy of the Republic of Chad, 2002 R St., N.W., Washington, D.C. 20009. Phone: 202-462-4009.

Embassy of Chile, 1732 Massachusetts Ave., N.W., Washington, D.C. 20036. Phone: 202-785-1746.

Embassy of the People's Republic of China, 2300 Connecticut Ave., N.W., Washington, D.C. 20008. Phone: 202-328-2500 (to 2502).

Embassy of Colombia, 2118 Leroy Pl., N.W., Washington, D.C. 20008. Phone: 202-387-8338.

Embassy of the Federal and Islamic Republic of Comoros, c/o Permanent Mission of the Federal and Islamic Republic of Comoros to the United Nations, 420 E. 50th St., New York, N.Y. 10022. Phone: 212-972-8010.

Embassy of the Democratic Republic of Congo, 1800 New Hampshire Ave., N.W., Washington, D.C. 20009. Phone: 202-234-7690.

Embassy of the Republic of Congo, 4891 Colorado Ave., N.W., Washington, D.C. 20011. Phone: 202-726-0825.

Embassy of Costa Rica, 2114 S St., N.W., Washington, D.C. 20008. Phone: 202-234-2945.

Embassy of the Republic of Côte d'Ivoire, 3421 Massachusetts Ave., N.W., Washington, D.C. 20007. Phone: 202-797-0300.

Embassy of the Republic of Croatia, 2343 Massachusetts Ave., N.W., Washington, D.C. 20008-2853. Phone: 202-588-5899.

Cuban Interests Section, 2630 16th St., N.W., Washington, D.C. 20009. Phone: 202-797-8518.

Embassy of the Republic of Cyprus, 2211 R St. N.W., Washington, D.C. 20008. Phone: 202-462-5772.

Embassy of the Czech Republic, 3900 Spring of Freedom St., N.W., Washington, D.C. 20008. Phone: 202-274-9100.

Royal Danish Embassy, 3200 Whitehaven St., N.W., Washington, D.C. 20008. Phone: 202-234-4300.

Embassy of the Republic of Djibouti, 1156 15th St., N.W., Suite 515, Washington, D.C. 20005. Phone: 202-331-0270.

Embassy of the Commonwealth of Dominica, 3216 New Mexico Ave., N.W., Washington, D.C. 20016. Phone: 202-364-6781/2.

Embassy of the Dominican Republic, 1715 22nd St., N.W., Washington, D.C. 20008. Phone: 202-332-6280.

Embassy of Ecuador, 2535 15th St., N.W., Washington, D.C. 20009. Phone: 202-234-7200.

Embassy of the Arab Republic of Egypt, 3521 International Court, N.W., Washington, D.C. 20008. Phone: 202-895-5400.

Embassy of El Salvador, 2308 California St., N.W., Washington, D.C. 20008. Phone: 202-265-9671.

Embassy of Equatorial Guinea, 2020 16th Street, N.W., Washington, D.C. 20009. Phone: 202-518-5700.

Embassy of the State of Eritrea, 1708 New Hampshire Ave., N.W., Washington, D.C., 20009. Phone: 202-319-1991.

Embassy of Estonia, 1730 M Street N.W., Washington, D.C. 20036. Phone: 202-588-0101.

Embassy of Ethiopia, 3506 International Dr., N.W., Washington, D.C. 20008. Phone: 202-364-1200.

European Union Delegation, 2300 M St., N.W., Washington, D.C. 20037. Phone: 202-862-9500.

Embassy of Fiji, 2233 Wisconsin Ave., N.W., Suite 240, Washington, D.C. 20007. Phone: 202-337-8320.

Embassy of Finland, 3301 Massachusetts Ave., N.W., Washington, D.C. 20008. Phone: 202-298-5800.

Embassy of France, 4101 Reservoir Rd., N.W., Washington, D.C. 20007. Phone: 202-944-6000.

Embassy of the Gabonese Republic, 2034 20th St., N.W., Suite 200, Washington, D.C. 20009. Phone: 202-797-1000.

Embassy of the Republic of the Gambia, 1155 15th St., N.W., Suite 1000, Washington, D.C. 20005-2076. Phone: 202-785-1399.

Embassy of the Republic of Georgia, 1615 New Hampshire Ave., N.W., Suite 300, Washington, D.C. 20009. Phone: 202-387-2390.

Embassy of Germany, 4645 Reservoir Rd., N.W., Washington, D.C. 20007-1998. Phone: 202-298-4000.

Embassy of Ghana, 3512 International Dr., N.W., Washington, D.C. 20008. Phone: 202-686-4520 to 4026.

Embassy of Greece, 2221 Massachusetts Ave., N.W., Washington, D.C. 20008. Phone: 202-939-5800.

Embassy of Grenada, 1701 New Hampshire Ave., N.W., Washington, D.C. 20009. Phone: 202-265-2561.

Embassy of Guatemala, 2220 R St., N.W., Washington, D.C. 20008. Phone: 202-745-4952 to 4954.

Embassy of the Republic of Guinea, 2112 Leroy Pl., N.W., Washington, D.C. 20008. Phone: 202-483-9420.

Embassy of the Republic of Guinea-Bissau, 1511 K Street, N.W., Suite 519, Washington, D.C. 20005. Phone: 202-347-3950.

Embassy of Guyana, 2490 Tracy Pl., N.W., Washington, D.C. 20008. Phone: 202-265-6900.

Embassy of the Republic of Haiti, 2311 Massachusetts Ave., N.W., Washington, D.C. 20008. Phone: 202-332-4090 to 4092.

Apostolic Nunciature of the Holy See, 3339 Massachusetts Ave., N.W., Washington, D.C. 20008. Phone: 202-333-7121.

Embassy of Honduras, 3007 Tilden St., N.W., Suite 4-M, Washington, D.C. 20008. Phone: 202-966-7702.

Embassy of the Republic of Hungary, 3910 Shoemaker St., N.W., Washington, D.C. 20008. Phone: 202-364-8218.

Embassy of Iceland, 1156 15th St., N.W., Suite 1200, Washington, D.C. 20005-1704. Phone: 202-265-6653 to 6655.

Embassy of India, 2107 Massachusetts Ave., N.W., Washington, D.C. 20008. Phone: 202-939-7000.

Embassy of the Republic of Indonesia, 2020 Massachusetts Ave., N.W., Washington, D.C. 20036. Phone: 202-775-5200.

Iranian Interests Section, 2209 Wisconsin Ave., N.W., Washington, D.C. 20007. Phone: 202-965-4990.

Iraqi Interests Section, 1801 P St., N.W., Washington, D.C. 20036. Phone: 202-483-7500.

Embassy of Ireland, 2234 Massachusetts Ave., N.W., Washington, D.C. 20008. Phone: 202-462-3939.

Embassy of Israel, 3514 International Dr., N.W., Washington, D.C. 20008. Phone: 202-364-5500.

Embassy of Italy, 3000 Whitehaven St., N.W., Washington, D.C. 20008. Phone: 202-612-4400.

Embassy of Jamaica, 1520 New Hampshire Ave., N.W., Washington, D.C. 20036. Phone: 202-452-0660.

Embassy of Japan, 2520 Massachusetts Ave., N.W., Washington, D.C. 20008. Phone: 202-238-6700.

Embassy of the Hashemite Kingdom of Jordan, 3504 International Dr., N.W., Washington, D.C. 20008. Phone: 202-966-2664.

Embassy of the Republic of Kazakhstan, (temporary) 1401 16th St., N.W., Washington, D.C. 20036. Phone: 202-232-5488.

Embassy of the Republic of Kenya, 2249 R St., N.W., Washington, D.C. 20008. Phone: 202-387-6101.

Embassy of the Republic of Korea, 2450 Massachusetts Ave., N.W., Washington, D.C. 20008. Phone: 202-939-5600.

Embassy of the State of Kuwait, 2904 Tilden St., N.W., Washington, D.C. 20008. Phone: 202-966-0702.

Embassy of the Kyrgyz Republic, 1732 Wisconsin Ave., Washington, D.C. 20007. Phone: 202-338-5141.

Embassy of the Lao People's Democratic Republic, 2222 S St., N.W., Washington, D.C. 20008. Phone: 202-332-6416.

Embassy of Latvia, 4325 17th St., N.W., Washington, D.C. 20011. Phone: 202-726-8213.

Embassy of Lebanon, 2560 28th St., N.W., Washington, D.C. 20008. Phone: 202-939-6300.

Embassy of the Kingdom of Lesotho, 2511 Massachusetts Ave., N.W., Washington, D.C. 20008. Phone: 202-797-5533 to 5536.

Embassy of the Republic of Liberia, 5201 16th St., N.W., Washington, D.C. 20011. Phone: 202-723-0437.

Embassy of the Republic of Lithuania, 2622 16th St., N.W., Washington, D.C. 20009. Phone: 202-234-5860.

Embassy of Luxembourg, 2200 Massachusetts Ave., N.W., Washington, D.C. 20008. Phone: 202-265-4171.

Embassy of the Republic of Macedonia, 1101 30th St., N.W., Suite 302, Washington, D.C. 20007. Phone: 202-337-3063.

Embassy of the Republic of Madagascar, 2374 Massachusetts Ave., N.W., Washington, D.C. 20008. Phone: 202-265-5525, 5526.

Embassy of Malawi, 2408 Massachusetts Ave., N.W., Washington, D.C. 20008. Phone: 202-797-2007.

Embassy of Malaysia, 2401 Massachusetts Ave., N.W., Washington, D.C. 20008. Phone: 202-328-2700.

Embassy of the Republic of Mali, 2130 R St., N.W., Washington, D.C. 20009. Phone: 202-332-2249.

Embassy of Malta, 2017 Connecticut Ave., N.W., Washington, D.C. 20008. Phone: 202-462-3611.

Embassy of the Republic of the Marshall Islands, 2433 Massachusetts Ave., N.W., Washington, D.C. 20008. Phone: 202-234-5414.

Embassy of the Islamic Republic of Mauritania, 2129 Leroy Pl., N.W., Washington, D.C. 20008. Phone: 202-232-5700, 5701.

Embassy of the Republic of Mauritius, 4301 Connecticut Ave., N.W., Suite 441, Washington, D.C. 20008. Phone: 202-244-1491.

Embassy of Mexico, 1911 Pennsylvania Ave., N.W., Washington, D.C. 20006. Phone: 202-728-1600.

Embassy of the Federated States of Micronesia, 1725 N St., N.W., Washington, D.C. 20036. Phone: 202-223-4383.

Embassy of the Republic of Moldova, 2101 S St., N.W., Washington, D.C. 20008. Phone: 202-667-1130, 1131, 1137.

Embassy of Mongolia, 2833 M St., N.W., Washington, D.C. 20007. Phone: 202-333-7117.

Embassy of the Kingdom of Morocco, 1601 21st St., N.W., Washington, D.C. 20009. Phone: 202-462-7979 to 7982, inclusive.

Embassy of the Republic of Mozambique, 1990 M St., N.W., Suite 570, Washington, D.C. 20036. Phone: 202-293-7146.

Embassy of the Republic of Namibia, 1605 New Hampshire Ave., N.W., Washington, D.C. 20009. Phone: 202-986-0540.

Embassy of Nepal, 2131 Leroy Pl., N.W., Washington, D.C. 20008. Phone: 202-667-4550.

Embassy of the Netherlands, 4200 Linnean Ave., N.W., Washington, D.C. 20008. Phone: 202-244-5300.

Embassy of New Zealand, 37 Observatory Circle, N.W., Washington, D.C. 20008. Phone: 202-328-4800.

Embassy of Nicaragua, 1627 New Hampshire Ave., N.W., Washington, D.C. 20009. Phone: 202-939-6570.

Embassy of the Republic of Niger, 2204 R St., N.W., Washington, D.C. 20008. Phone: 202-483-4224 to 4227, inclusive.

Embassy of the Federal Republic of Nigeria, 1333 16th St., N.W., Washington, D.C. 20036. Phone: 202-986-8400.

Royal Embassy of Norway, 2720 34th St., N.W., Washington, D.C. 20008. Phone: 202-333-6000.

Embassy of the Sultanate of Oman, 2535 Belmont Rd., N.W., Washington, D.C. 20008. Phone: 202-387-1980.

Embassy of the Islamic Republic of Pakistan, 2315 Massachusetts Ave., N.W., Washington, D.C. 20008. Phone: 202-939-6200.

Embassy of the Republic of Palau, 1150 18th St., N.W., #750, Washington, D.C. 20036. Phone: 202-452-6814.

Embassy of the Republic of Panama, 2862 McGill Terrace, N.W., Washington, D.C. 20008. Phone: 202-483-1407.

Embassy of Papua New Guinea, 1779 Massachusetts Ave., N.W., Suite 805, Washington, D.C. 20036. Phone: 202-745-3680.

Embassy of Paraguay, 2400 Massachusetts Ave., N.W., Washington, D.C. 20008. Phone: 202-483-6960.

Embassy of Peru, 1700 Massachusetts Ave., N.W., Washington, D.C. 20036. Phone: 202-833-9860 to 9869.

Embassy of the Philippines, 1600 Massachusetts Ave., N.W., Washington, D.C. 20036. Phone: 202-467-9300.

Embassy of the Republic of Poland, 2640 16th St., N.W., Washington, D.C. 20009. Phone: 202-234-3800 to 3802.

Embassy of Portugal, 2125 Kalorama Rd., N.W., Washington, D.C. 20008. Phone: 202-328-8610.

Embassy of the State of Qatar, 4200 Wisconsin Ave., N.W., Washington, D.C. 20016. Phone: 202-274-1600.

Embassy of Romania, 1607 23rd St., N.W., Washington, D.C. 20008. Phone: 202-332-2879.

Embassy of the Russian Federation, 2650 Wisconsin Ave., N.W., Washington, D.C. 20007. Phone: 202-298-5700.

Embassy of the Republic of Rwanda, 1714 New Hampshire Ave., N.W., Washington, D.C. 20009. Phone: 202-232-2882.

Embassy of Saint Kitts and Nevis, 3216 New Mexico Ave., N.W., Washington, D.C. 20016. Phone: 202-686-2636.

Embassy of Saint Lucia, 3216 New Mexico Ave., N.W., Washington, D.C. 20016. Phone: 202-364-6792 to 6795.

Embassy of Saint Vincent and the Grenadines, 3216 New Mexico Ave., N.W., Washington, D.C. 20016. Phone: 202-364-6730.

Royal Embassy of Saudi Arabia, 601 New Hampshire Ave., N.W., Washington, D.C. 20037. Phone: 202-337-4076/4134.

Embassy of the Republic of Senegal, 2112 Wyoming Ave., N.W., Washington, D.C. 20008. Phone: 202-234-0540/0541.

Embassy of Serbia and Montenegro, 2134 Kalorama Rd., N.W., Washington, D.C. 20008. Phone: 202-462-6566.

Embassy of the Republic of Seychelles, 800 Second Ave., Suite 400C, New York, N.Y. 10017. Phone: 212-687-9766.

Embassy of Sierra Leone, 1701 19th St., N.W., Washington, D.C. 20009. Phone: 202-939-9261.

Embassy of the Republic of Singapore, 3501 International Pl., N.W., Washington, D.C. 20008. Phone: 202-537-3100.

Embassy of the Slovak Republic, 3523 International Court, N.W., Washington, D.C. 20008. Phone: 202-237-1054.

Embassy of the Republic of Slovenia, 1525 New Hampshire Ave., N.W., Washington, D.C. 20036. Phone: 202-667-5363.

Embassy of the Republic of South Africa, 3051 Massachusetts Ave., N.W., Washington, D.C. 20008. Phone: 202-232-4400.

Embassy of Spain, 2375 Pennsylvania Ave., N.W., Washington, D.C. 20037. Phone: 202-728-2330.

Embassy of Sri Lanka, 2148 Wyoming Ave., N.W., Washington, D.C. 20008. Phone: 202-483-4025 to 4028.

Embassy of the Republic of the Sudan, 2210 Massachusetts Ave., N.W., Washington, D.C. 20008. Phone: 202-338-8565.

Embassy of the Republic of Suriname, 4301 Connecticut Ave., N.W., Suite 460, Washington, D.C. 20008. Phone: 202-244-7488.

Embassy of the Kingdom of Swaziland, 3400 International Drive, N.W., Washington, D.C. 20008. Phone: 202-362-6683.

Embassy of Sweden, 1501 M St., N.W., Washington, D.C. 20005. Phone: 202-467-2600.

Embassy of Switzerland, 2900 Cathedral Ave., N.W., Washington, D.C. 20008. Phone: 202-745-7900.

Embassy of the Syrian Arab Republic, 2215 Wyoming Ave., N.W., Washington, D.C. 20008. Phone: 202-232-6313.

The Republic of China on Taiwan, 4201 Wisconsin Ave., N.W., Washington, D.C. 20016. Phone: 202-895-1800.

Embassy of the United Republic of Tanzania, 2139 R St., N.W., Washington, D.C. 20008. Phone: 202-884-1080.

Royal Thai Embassy, 1024 Wisconsin Ave., N.W., Washington, D.C. 20007. Phone: 202-944-3600.

Embassy of the Republic of Togo, 2208 Massachusetts Ave., N.W., Washington, D.C. 20008. Phone: 202-234-4212.

Embassy of the Republic of Trinidad and Tobago, 1708 Massachusetts Ave., N.W., Washington, D.C. 20036. Phone: 202-467-6490.

Embassy of Tunisia, 1515 Massachusetts Ave., N.W., Washington, D.C. 20005. Phone: 202-862-1850.

Embassy of the Republic of Turkey, 2525 Massachusetts Ave., N.W., Washington, D.C. 20008. Phone: 202-612-6700.

Embassy of Turkmenistan, 2207 Massachusetts Ave., N.W., Washington, D.C. 20008. Phone: 202-588-1500.

Embassy of the Republic of Uganda, 5911 16th St., N.W., Washington, D.C. 20011. Phone: 202-726-7100.

Embassy of Ukraine, 3350 M St., N.W., Washington, D.C. 20007. Phone: 202-333-0606.

Embassy of the United Arab Emirates, 3522 International Court, N.W., #300, Washington, D.C. 20008. Phone: 202-328-4536.

United Kingdom of Great Britain & Northern Ireland—British Embassy, 3100 Massachusetts Ave., N.W., Washington, D.C. 20008. Phone: 202-588-6500.

Embassy of Uruguay, 1913 I St., N.W., Washington, D.C. 20006. Phone: 202-331-1313.

Embassy of the Republic of Uzbekistan, 1746 Massachusetts Ave., N.W., Washington, D.C. 20036. Phone: 202-887-5300.

Embassy of the Republic of Venezuela, 1099 30th St., N.W., Washington D.C. 20007. Phone: 202-342-2214.

Embassy of the Socialist Republic of Vietnam, 1233 20th St., N.W., Suite 400, Washington, D.C. 20036. Phone: 202-861-0737.

Embassy of the Republic of Yemen, 2600 Virginia Ave., N.W., Suite 705, Washington, D.C. 20037. Phone: 202-965-4760.

Embassy of the Republic of Zambia, 2419 Massachusetts Ave., N.W., Washington, D.C. 20008. Phone: 202-265-9717.

Embassy of the Republic of Zimbabwe, 1608 New Hampshire Ave., N.W., Washington, D.C. 20009. Phone: 202-332-7100.

Diplomatic Personnel to and from the U.S.

Country	U.S. Representative to[1]	Rank	Representative from[1]	Rank
Afghanistan	Robert P. Finn	Amb.	Ishaq Shahryar	Amb.
Albania	James F. Jeffrey	Amb.	Fatos Tarifa	Amb.
Algeria	Janet A. Sanderson	Amb.	Idriss Jazairy	Amb.
Andorra	George Argyros	Amb.	Jelena Pia Comella	Cd'A
Angola	Christopher Dell	Amb.	Josefina Pitra Diakité	Amb.
Antigua and Barbuda[2]	Earl N. Phillips, Jr.	Amb.	Lionel Alexander Hurst	Amb.
Argentina	James D. Walsh	Amb.	Eduardo Amadeo	Amb.
Armenia	John M. Ordway	Amb.	Arman Kirakossian	Amb.
Australia	John Thomas Schieffer	Amb.	Michael J. Thawley	Amb.
Austria	William Lyons Brown, Jr.	Amb.	Peter Moser	Amb.
Azerbaijan	Ross L. Wilson	Amb.	Elmar Mamedyarov	Cd'A
Bahamas	Richard Blankenship	Amb.	Joshua Sears	Amb.
Bahrain	Ronald Neumann	Amb.	Khalifa bin Ali Al-Khalifa	Amb.
Bangladesh	Mary Ann Peters	Amb.	Syed Hasan Ahmad	Amb.
Barbados[2]	Earl N. Phillips, Jr.	Amb.	Michael King	Amb.
Belarus	Michael G. Kozak	Amb.	Valeriy V. Tsepaklo	Amb.
Belgium	Stephen F. Brauer	Amb.	Franciskus van Daele	Amb.
Belize	Russell Freeman	Amb.	Lisa Shoman	Amb.
Benin	Pamela Bridgewater	Amb.	Segbe Cyrille Oguin	Amb.
Bolivia	David N. Greenlee	Amb.	Jaime Aparico Otero	Amb.
Bosnia-Herzegovina	Clifford G. Bond	Amb.	Igor Davidovic	Amb.
Botswana	Joseph Hugging	Amb.	Kgosi Seepapitso IV	Amb.
Brazil	Donna Hrinak	Amb.	Rubens Antonio Barbosa	Amb.
Brunei	Gene B. Christy	Amb.	Pengiran Anak Dato Puteh	Amb.
Bulgaria	James W. Pardew	Amb.	Elena Poptodorova	Amb.
Burkina Faso	Anthony Holmes	Amb.	Tertius Zongo	Amb.
Burma (Myanmar)	Carmen M. Martinez	Cd'A	Tin Winn	Amb.
Burundi	James Howard Yellin	Amb.	Thomas Ndikumana	Amb.
Cambodia	Charles Aaron Ray	Amb.	Roland Eng	Amb.
Cameroon	George M. Staples	Amb.	Raymond Epote	Cd'A.
Canada	Paul Cellucci	Amb.	Michael Kergin	Amb.
Cape Verde	Donald C. Johnson	Amb.	Jose Brito	Amb.
Central African Republic	Mattie Sharpless	Amb.	Emmanual Touaboy	Amb.
Chad	Christopher E. Goldthwait	Amb.	Hassaballah Ahmat Soubiane	Amb.
Chile	William R. Brownfield	Amb.	Andrés Bianchi	Amb.
China	Clark J. Randt, Jr.	Amb.	Yang Jiechi	Amb.
Colombia	Anne W. Patterson	Amb.	Luis Alberto Moreno	Amb.
Comoros	John Price	Amb.	Ahmed Djabir	Amb.
Congo, Dem. Rep. of	Aubrey Hooks	Amb.	Faida Mitifu	Amb.
Congo, Rep. of	Robin R. Sanders	Amb.	Serge Mombouli	Amb.
Costa Rica	John J. Danilovich	Amb.	Jaime Daremblum	Amb.
Côte d'Ivoire	Arlene Render	Amb.	Pascal Daso Kokora	Amb.
Croatia	Lawrence G. Rossin	Amb.	Ivan Grdesic	Amb.
Cuba	James C. Cason	P.O.	Dagoberto Rodriguez Barrera	P.O.
Cyprus	Michael Klossen	Amb.	Erato Kozakou-Marcoullis	Amb.
Czech Republic	Craig R. Stapleton	Amb.	Martin Palous	Amb.
Denmark	Stuart Bernsein	Amb.	Ulrik Andreas Federspiel	Amb.
Djibouti	Donald Yamamoto	Amb.	Roble Olhaye Oudine	Amb.
Dominica[2]	Earl N. Phillips, Jr.	Amb.	Swinbourne Lestrade	Amb.
Dominican Republic	Hans R. Hertell	Amb.	Hugo Guiliani Cury	Amb.
East Timor	Grover Joseph Rees	Amb.	Jose Luis Guterrés	Amb.
Ecuador	Kristie Anne Kenney	Amb.	Ivonne A-Baki	Amb.
Egypt	C. David Welch	Amb.	M. Nabil Fahmy	Amb.
El Salvador	Rose M. Likins	Amb.	Rene A. Rodriguez	Amb.
Equatorial Guinea	George M. Staples	Amb.	Micha Ondo Bile	Amb.
Eritrea	Donald McConnell	Amb.	Girma Asmerom	Amb.
Estonia	Joseph DeThomas	Amb.	Sven Juergenson	Amb.
Ethiopia	Aurelia A. Brazeal	Amb.	Kassahun Ayele	—
EU Delegation	Rockwell Schnabel	Amb.	Günther Burghardt	Amb.
Fiji[3]	David L. Lyon	Amb.	Anare Jale	Amb.

Country	U.S. Representative to[1]	Rank	Representative from[1]	Rank
Finland	Bonnie McElveen-Hunter	Amb.	Jukka Valtasaari	Amb.
France	Howard A. Leach	Amb.	John-David Levitte	Amb.
Gabon	Kenneth P. Moorefield	Amb.	Jules Marius Ogouebandja	Amb.
Gambia, The	Jackson McDonald	Amb.	Essa Bokar Sey	Amb.
Georgia	Richard Miles	Amb.	Levan Mikeladze	Amb.
Germany	Daniel R. Coats	Amb.	Wolfgang Ischinger	Amb.
Ghana	Mary Carlin Yates	Amb.	Alan Kyerematen	Amb.
Greece	Thomas J. Miller	Amb.	Yeoryious Sawaides	Amb.
Grenada[2]	Earl N. Phillips, Jr.	Amb.	Denis G. Antoine	Amb.
Guatemala	John Randle Hamilton	Amb.	Antonio F. Arenales Forno	Amb.
Guinea	R. Barrie Walkley	Amb.	Raflou Alpha Oumar Barry	Amb.
Guinea-Bissau	—	—	Henrique Adriano Da Silva	Cd'A.
Guyana	Ronald D. Godard	Amb.	Dr. Odeen Ishmael	Amb.
Haiti	Roger Noriega	Amb.	Harry Frantz Leo	Cd'A
Holy See	Jim Nicholson	Amb.	Gabriel Montalvo	Pap. Nun.
Honduras	Larry Leon Palmer	Amb.	Mario Miguel Cunahuati	Amb.
Hong Kong	Michael Klosson	C.G.	—	—
Hungary	Nancy Goodman Brinker	Amb.	Andras Simonyi	Amb.
Iceland	James I. Gadsen	Amb.	Helgi Agustsson	Amb.
India	Robert D. Blackwill	Amb.	Lalit Mansingh	Amb.
Indonesia	Ralph L. Boyce	Amb.	Soemadi D. M. Brotodiningrat	Amb.
Iran	—	—	—	—
Ireland	Richard Egan	Amb.	Noel Fahey	Amb.
Israel	Daniel C. Kurtzer	Amb.	Daniel Ayalon	Amb.
Italy	Mel Sembler	Amb.	Ferdinando Salleo	Amb.
Jamaica	Sue McCourt Cobb	Amb.	Seymour Mullings	Amb.
Japan	Howard S. Baker	Amb.	Ryozo Kato	Amb.
Jordan	Edward Gnehm, Jr.	Amb.	Karim Tawiq Kawar	Amb.
Kazakhstan	Larry C. Napper	Amb.	Kanat Saudabayev	Amb.
Kenya	Johnnie Carson	Amb.	Yusuf A. Nzibo	Amb.
Kiribati, Republic of	Michael J. Senko	Amb.	—	—
Korea	Thomas C. Hubbard	Amb.	Sung-Chul Yang	Amb.
Kuwait	Richard H. Jones	Amb.	Salem Abdullah Al-Jaber Al-Sabah	Amb.
Kyrgyz Republic	John M. O'Keefe	Amb.	Baktybek Abdrisaev	Amb.
Laos	Douglas A. Hartwick	Amb.	Phanthong Phommahaxay	Amb.
Latvia	Brian E. Carlson	Amb.	Aivis Ronis	Amb.
Lebanon	Vincent Battle	Amb.	Farid Abboud	Amb.
Lesotho	Robert D. Loftis	Amb.	Dr. Lebohang K. Moleko	Amb.
Liberia	John William Blaney III	Amb.	William Bull	Amb.
Liechtenstein	Mercer Reynolds III	Amb.	Claudia Fritsche	Amb.
Lithuania	John F. Tefft	Amb.	Vygaudas Usackas	Amb.
Luxembourg	Peter Terpeluk, Jr.	Amb.	Arlette Conzemius-Paccourd	Amb.
Macedonia	Lawrence Butler	Amb.	Nikola Dimitrov	Amb.
Madagascar	Wanda L. Nesbitt	Amb.	Zina Andrianarivelo-Razafy	Amb.
Malawi	Roger A. Meece	Amb.	Tony Kandiero	Amb.
Malaysia	Marie T. Huhtala	Amb.	Ghazzali bin Sheikh Abdul Khalid	Amb.
Mali	Vicki Huddlestone	Amb.	Cheick Oumar Diarrah	Amb.
Malta	Anthony Gioia	Amb.	John Lowell	Amb.
Marshall Islands	Michael J. Senko	Amb.	Banny de Brum	Amb.
Mauritania	John W. Limbert	Amb.	Mohamedou Ould Michel	Amb.
Mauritius	John Price	Amb.	Usha Jeetah	Amb.
Mexico	Antonio O. Garza	Amb.	Juan José Bremer Martino	Amb.
Micronesia	Larry Miles Dinger	Amb.	Jesse B. Marehalau	Amb.
Moldova	Pamela Hyde Smith	Amb.	Mihai Manoli	Amb.
Mongolia	John Dinger	Amb.	Jalbuu Choinhor	Amb.
Morocco	Margaret DeB. Tutwiler	Amb.	Aziz Mekouar	Amb.
Mozambique	Sharon Wilkinson	Amb.	Armando A. Panguene	Amb.
Namibia	Kevin J. McGuire	Amb.	Leonard Nangolo Iipumbu	Amb.
Nauru[3]	David L. Lyon	Amb.	—	—
Nepal	Michael Malinowski	Amb.	Jai Pratap Rana	Amb.
Netherlands	Clifford Sobel	Amb.	Boudewijn Johannes Van Eenennaam	Amb.
New Zealand	Charles J. Swindells	Amb.	John Wood	Amb.
Nicaragua	Barbara Calandra Moore	Amb.	Carlos Ulvert	Amb.
Niger	Gail Dennise Thomas Mathieu	Amb.	Joseph Diatta	Amb.
Nigeria	Howard Jeter	Amb.	Jibril Muhammad Aminu	Amb.
Norway	John Doyle Ong	Amb.	Knut VolleBaek	Amb.

Country	U.S. Representative to[1]	Rank	Representative from[1]	Rank
Oman	Richard Lewis Baltimore III	Amb.	Mohamed Ali Al-Khusaiby	Amb.
Pakistan	Nancy J. Powell	Amb.	Ashraf Jehangir Qazi	Amb.
Palau	Francis Ricciardone, Jr.	Amb.	Hersey Kyota	Amb.
Panama	Linda Ellen Watt	Amb.	Roberto Alfaro	Amb.
Papua New Guinea	Susan Jacobs	Amb.	Nagora Y. Bogan, KBE	Amb.
Paraguay	John F. Keane	Amb.	Leila Rachid-Cowles	Amb.
Peru	John R. Dawson	Amb.	Robert Danino	Amb.
Philippines	Francis Ricciardone, Jr.	Amb.	Albert Del Rosario	Amb.
Poland	Christopher R. Hill	Amb.	Przemyslaw Grudzinski	Amb.
Portugal	John N. Palmer	Amb.	Pedro M. Dos Reis Alves Catarino	Amb.
Qatar	Maureen Quinn	Amb.	Baderomar al-Dafa	Amb.
Romania	Michael Guest	Amb.	Sorin Ducaru	Amb.
Russia	Alexander Vershbow	Amb.	Yuriy Viktorovich Ushakov	Amb.
Rwanda	Margaret K. McMillion	Amb.	Dr. Richard Sezibera	Amb.
Saint Kitts and Nevis[2]	Earl N. Phillips, Jr.	Amb.	Osbert Liburd	Amb.
Saint Lucia[2]	Earl N. Phillips, Jr.	Amb.	Sonia Merlyn Johnny	Amb.
Saint Vincent and the Grenadines[2]	Earl N. Phillips, Jr.	Amb.	Ellsworth John	Amb.
Samoa, Western	Charles Swindells	Amb.	Tuiloma Slade	Amb.
São Tomé and Príncipe, Dem. Rep. of	Kenneth P. Moorefield	Amb.	Domingos Augusto Ferreira	UN PM
Saudi Arabia	Robert Jordan	Amb.	Prince Bandar Bin Sultan	Amb.
Senegal	Harriet L. Elam-Thomas	Amb.	Amadou L. Ba	Amb.
Serbia and Montenegro	William D. Montgomery	Amb.	Ivan Zivkovic	Cd'A
Seychelles	John Price	Amb.	Claude Morel	Amb.
Sierra Leone	Peter Chaveas	Amb.	Ibrahim M. Kamara	Amb.
Singapore	Franklin Lavin	Amb.	Heng Chee Chan	Amb.
Slovakia	Ronald Weiser	Amb.	Martin Butora	Amb.
Slovenia	Johnny Young	Amb.	Davorin Kracun	Amb.
Solomon Islands	Susan Jacobs	Amb.	Jeremiah Manele	Cd'A
South Africa	Cameron R. Hume	Amb.	Thandabantu Nhlapo	Cd'A
Spain	George Argyros	Amb.	Javier Ruperez	Amb.
Sri Lanka	E. Ashley Wills	Amb.	Devinda R Subasinghe	Amb.
Sudan	—	Amb.	Khidr Haroun Ahmed	Cd'A interim
Suriname	Daniel A. Johnson	Amb.	Henry Illes	Amb.
Swaziland	James D. McGee	Amb.	Mary Madzandza Kanya	Amb.
Sweden	Charles Heimbold, Jr.	Amb.	Jan Eliasson	Amb.
Switzerland	Mercer Reynolds III	Amb.	Christian Blickenstorfer	Amb.
Syria	Theodore Kattouf	Amb.	Dr. Rostom Al Zoubi	Cd'A
Tajikistan	Franklin Huddle	Amb.	Khamrokhon Zaripov	UN PM
Tanzania	Robert V. Royall	Amb.	Andrew Mhando Daraja	Amb.
Thailand	Darryl N. Johnson	Amb.	Sakthip Krairiksh	Amb.
Togo	Karl Hofmann	Amb.	Akousso Lelou Bodjona	Amb.
Tonga[3]	David L. Lyon	Amb.	Sonatane T. T. Tupou	Amb.
Trinidad and Tobago	Roy L. Austin	Amb.	Mackisack A. Logie	Cd'A
Tunisia	Rust Deming	Amb.	Hatem Atallah	Amb.
Turkey	W. Robert Pearson	Amb.	O. Faruk Logoglu	Amb.
Turkmenistan	Laura E. Kennedy	Amb.	Meret Orazov	Amb.
Tuvalu[3]	David L. Lyon	Amb.	—	—
Uganda	Jimmy Kolker	Amb.	Edith Grace Ssempala	Amb.
Ukraine	Carlos E. Pascual	Amb.	Kostyantyn Gryshchenko	Amb.
United Arab Emirates	Marcelle Wahba	Amb.	Al Asri Saeed Al Dhahri	Amb.
United Kingdom	William Farish	Amb.	Sir Christopher Meyer	Amb.
Uruguay	Martin J. Silverstein	Amb.	Hugo Fernandez Faingold	Amb.
Uzbekistan	John Edward Herbst	Amb.	Shavkat S. Khamrakulov	Amb.
Vanuatu	Susan Jacobs	Amb.	—	—
Venezuela	Charles S. Shapiro	Amb.	Luís Hererra Marcano	Cd'A
Vietnam	Raymond Burghardt	Amb.	Nguyen Tam Chien	Amb.
Yemen	Edmund J. Hull	Amb.	Abdulwahab Al-Hajjri	Amb.
Zambia	Martin George Brennan	Amb.	Dunstan Weston Kamana	Amb.
Zimbabwe	Joseph G. Sullivan	Amb.	Simbi Yeke Mubako	Amb.

1. As of June 2003. 2. The U.S. embassy in Barbados currently serves seven independent nations of the Eastern Caribbean (Barbados, Antigua and Barbuda, Dominica, Grenada, St. Kitts and Nevis, St. Lucia, and St. Vincent and the Grenadines) and provides consular services to American citizens in the nearby European dependent territories. 3. Ambassador to Fiji, Nauru, Tonga, and Tuvalu. 4. Head of Interests Section in U.S. NOTE: Amb.=Ambassador; Cd'A=Charge d'Affaires; C.G.=Consul General; Pap. Nun.=Papal Nuncio; P.O.=Principal Officer. *Source:* U.S. Department of State.

The Olympic Games

1896	Athens, Greece
1900	Paris, France
1904	St. Louis, United States
1906	Athens, Greece
1908	London, Great Britain
1912	Stockholm, Sweden
1920	Antwerp, Belgium
1924	Chamonix, France (W)
1924	Paris, France (S)
1928	St. Moritz, Switzerland (W)
1928	Amsterdam, Netherlands (S)
1932	Lake Placid, United States (W)
1932	Los Angeles, United States (S)
1936	Garmisch-Partenkirchen, Germany (W)
1936	Berlin, Germany (S)
1948	St. Moritz, Switzerland (W)
1948	London, Great Britain (S)
1952	Oslo, Norway (W)
1952	Helsinki, Finland (S)
1956	Cortina d'Ampezzo, Italy (W)
1956	Melbourne, Australia (S)
1960	Squaw Valley, United States (W)
1960	Rome, Italy (S)
1964	Innsbruck, Austria (W)
1964	Tokyo, Japan (S)
1968	Grenoble, France (W)
1968	Mexico City, Mexico (S)
1972	Sapporo, Japan (W)
1972	Munich, Germany (S)
1976	Innsbruck, Austria (W)
1976	Montreal, Canada (S)
1980	Lake Placid, United States (W)
1980	Moscow, USSR (S)
1984	Sarajevo, Yugoslavia (W)
1984	Los Angeles, United States (S)
1988	Calgary, Canada (W)
1988	Seoul, South Korea (S)
1992	Albertville, France (W)
1992	Barcelona, Spain (S)
1994	Lillehammer, Norway (W)
1996	Atlanta, United States (S)
1998	Nagano, Japan (W)
2000	Sydney, Australia (S)
2002	Salt Lake City, United States (W)
2004	Athens, Greece (S)
2006	Turin, Italy (W)
2008	Beijing, China (S)
2010	Vancouver, Canada (W)

(W)—Site of Winter Games. (S)—Site of Summer Games

The first Olympic Games of which there is record were held in 776 B.C., and consisted of one event, a great foot race of about 200 yards held on a plain by the River Alpheus (now the Ruphia) just outside the little town of Olympia in Greece. It was from that date the Greeks began to keep their calendar by "Olympiads," the four-year spans between the celebrations of the famous games.

The modern Olympic Games, which started in Athens in 1896, are the result of the devotion of a French educator, Baron Pierre de Coubertin, to the idea that, since young people and athletics have gone together through the ages, education and athletics might go hand-in-hand toward a better international understanding.

The principal organization responsible for the staging of the Games is the International Olympic Committee (IOC). Other important roles are played by the National Olympic Committees in each participating country, international sports federations, and the organizing committee of the host city.

The Olympic motto is "Citius, Altius, Fortius,"—"Faster, Higher, Stronger." The Olympic symbol is five interlocking circles colored blue, yellow, black, green, and red, on a white background, representing the five continents. At least one of those colors appears in the national flag of every country.

Beginning in 1994, the IOC decided to change the format of having both the Summer and Winter Games in the same year. Summer and Winter Olympics now alternate every two years.

In Feb. 1998 the IOC announced that new sports added to the games must include women's events.

Winter Games: Gold Medals

FIGURE SKATING–MEN

1908	Ulrich Salchow, Sweden
1920	Gillis Grafström, Sweden
1924	Gillis Grafström, Sweden
1928	Gillis Grafström, Sweden
1932	Karl Schäfer, Austria
1936	Karl Schäfer, Austria
1948	Dick Button, United States
1952	Dick Button, United States
1956	Hayes Alan Jenkins, United States
1960	David Jenkins, United States
1964	Manfred Schnelldorfer, Germany
1968	Wolfgang Schwarz, Austria
1972	Ondrej Nepela, Czechoslovakia
1976	John Curry, Great Britain
1980	Robin Cousins, Great Britain
1984	Scott Hamilton, United States
1988	Brian Boitano, United States
1992	Viktor Petrenko, Unified Team*
1994	Alexei Urmanov, Russia
1998	Ilia Kulik, Russia
2002	Alexei Yagudin, Russia

*Former Soviet Union team.

FIGURE SKATING–WOMEN

1908	Madge Syers, Britain
1920	Magda Julin-Mauroy, Sweden
1924	Herma Planck-Szabö, Austria
1928	Sonja Henie, Norway
1932	Sonja Henie, Norway
1936	Sonja Henie, Norway
1948	Barbara Ann Scott, Canada
1952	Jeanette Altwegg, Great Britain
1956	Tenley Albright, United States
1960	Carol Heiss, United States
1964	Sjoukje Dijkstra, Netherlands
1968	Peggy Fleming, United States
1972	Beatrix Schuba, Austria
1976	Dorothy Hamill, United States
1980	Anett Pötzsch, East Germany
1984	Katarina Witt, East Germany
1988	Katarina Witt, East Germany
1992	Kristi Yamaguchi, United States
1994	Oksana Baiul, Ukraine
1998	Tara Lipinski, United States
2002	Sarah Hughes, United States

SPEED SKATING–MEN

(U.S. winners only)

500 Meters

1924	Charles Jewtraw	44.00
1932	Jack Shea	43.40
1952	Ken Henry	43.20
1964	Terry McDermott	40.10
1980	Eric Heiden	38.03
2002	Casey FitzRandolph	69.23[1]

1,000 Meters

1976	Peter Mueller	1:19.32
1980	Eric Heiden	1:15.18
1994	Dan Jansen	1:12.43[2]

1,500 Meters

1932	Jack Shea	2:57.50
1980	Eric Heiden	1:55.44
2002	Derek Parra	1:43.95[2]

5,000 Meters

1932	Irving Jaffee	9:40.80
1980	Eric Heiden	7:02.29

10,000 Meters

1932	Irving Jaffee	19:13.60
1980	Eric Heiden	14:28.13

1. Combined time of two races. 2. World record.

SPEED SKATING–WOMEN

(U.S. winners only)

500 Meters

1972	Anne Henning	43.33
1976	Sheila Young	42.76
1988	Bonnie Blair	39.10
1992	Bonnie Blair	40.33
1994	Bonnie Blair	39.25

1,000 Meters

1992	Bonnie Blair	1:21.90
1994	Bonnie Blair	1:18.74
2002	Chris Witty	1:13.83[1]

1,500 Meters

1972	Dianne Holum	2:20.85

1. World record.

SKIING, ALPINE–MEN

Downhill

1948	Henri Oreiller, France	2:55.00
1952	Zeno Colò, Italy	2:30.80
1956	Toni Sailer, Austria	2:52.20
1960	Jean Vuarnet, France	2:06.00
1964	Egon Zimmermann, Austria	2:18.16
1968	Jean-Claude Killy, France	1:59.85
1972	Bernhard Russi, Switzerland	1:51.43
1976	Franz Klammer, Austria	1:45.73
1980	Leonhard Stock, Austria	1:45.50
1984	Bill Johnson, United States	1:45.59
1988	Pirmin Zurbriggen, Switzerland	1:59.63
1992	Patrick Ortlieb, Austria	1:50.37
1994	Tommy Moe, United States	1:45.75
1998	Jean-Luc Cretier, France	1:50.11
2002	Fritz Strobl, Austria	1:39.13

Slalom

1948	Edi Reinalter, Switzerland	2:10.30
1952	Othmar Schneider, Austria	2:00.00
1956	Toni Sailer, Austria	3:14.70
1960	Ernst Hinterseer, Austria	2:08.90
1964	Pepi Stiegler, Austria	2:11.13
1968	Jean-Claude Killy, France	1:39.73
1972	Francisco Ochoa, Spain	1:49.27
1976	Piero Gros, Italy	2:03.29
1980	Ingemar Stenmark, Sweden	1:44.26
1984	Phil Mahre, United States	1:39.41
1988	Alberto Tomba, Italy	1:39.47
1992	Finn Christian Jagge, Norway	1:44.39
1994	Thomas Stangassinger, Austria	2:02.02
1998	Hans-Petter Buraas, Norway	1:49.31
2002	Jean-Pierre Vidal, France	1:41.06

Giant Slalom

1952	Stein Eriksen, Norway	2:25.00
1956	Toni Sailer, Austria	3:00.10
1960	Roger Staub, Switzerland	1:48.30
1964	François Bonlieu, France	1:46.71
1968	Jean-Claude Killy, France	3:29.28
1972	Gustav Thöni, Italy	3:09.62
1976	Heini Hemmi, Switzerland	3:26.97
1980	Ingemar Stenmark, Sweden	2:40.74
1984	Max Julen, Switzerland	2:41.18
1988	Alberto Tomba, Italy	2:06.37
1992	Alberto Tomba, Italy	2:06.98
1994	Markus Wasmeier, Germany	2:52.46
1998	Hermann Maier, Austria	2:38.51
2002	Stephan Eberharter, Austria	2:23.28

Super Giant Slalom

1988	Frank Piccard, France	1:39.66
1992	Kjetil Andre Aamadt, Norway	1:13.04
1994	Markus Wasmeier, Germany	1:32.53
1998	Hermann Maier, Austria	1:34.84
2002	Kjetil Andre Aamodt, Norway	1:21.58

Men's Combined (Downhill and Slalom)

		Points
1936	Franz Pfnür, Germany	99.25
1948	Henri Oreiller, France	3.27
1952–1984	Not held	
1988	Hubert Strolz, Austria	36.55
1992	Josef Polig, Italy	14.58
		Time
1994	Lasse Kjus, Norway	3:17.53
1998	Mario Reiter, Austria	3:08.06
2002	Kjetil Andre Aamodt, Norway	3:17.56

SKIING, ALPINE–WOMEN

Downhill

1948	Hedy Schlunegger, Switzerland	2:28.30
1952	Trude Jochum-Beiser, Austria	1:47.10
1956	Madeleine Berthod, Switzerland	1:40.70
1960	Heidi Biebl, Germany	1:37.60
1964	Christl Haas, Austria	1:55.39
1968	Olga Pall, Austria	1:40.87
1972	Marie-Theres Nadig, Switzerland	1:36.68
1976	Rosi Mittermaier, West Germany	1:46.16
1980	Annemarie Moser-Pröll, Austria	1:37.52
1984	Michela Figini, Switzerland	1:13.36
1988	Marina Kiehl, West Germany	1:25.86
1992	Kerrin Lee-Gartner, Canada	1:52.55
1994	Katja Seizinger, Germany	1:35.93
1998	Katja Seizinger, Germany	1:28.89
2002	Carole Montillet, France	1:39.56

Slalom

1948	Gretchen Fraser, United States	1:57.20
1952	Andrea Mead Lawrence, United States	2:10.60
1956	Renée Colliard, Switzerland	1:52.30
1960	Anne Heggtveit, Canada	1:49.60
1964	Christine Goitschel, France	1:29.86
1968	Marielle Goitschel, France	1:25.86
1972	Barbara Cochran, United States	1:31.24
1976	Rosi Mittermaier, West Germany	1:30.54
1980	Hanni Wenzel, Liechtenstein	1:25.09
1984	Paoletta Magoni, Italy	1:36.47
1988	Vreni Schneider, Switzerland	1:36.69
1992	Petra Kronberger, Austria	1:32.68
1994	Vreni Schneider, Switzerland	1:56.01
1998	Hilde Gerg, Germany	1:32.40
2002	Janica Kostelic, Croatia	1:46.10

Giant Slalom

1952	Andrea Mead Lawrence, United States	2:06.80
1956	Ossi Reichert, Germany	1:56.50
1960	Yvonne Rügg, Switzerland	1:39.90
1964	Marielle Goitschel, France	1:52.24

1968	Nancy Greene, Canada	1:51.97
1972	Marie-Theres Nadig, Switzerland	1:29.90
1976	Kathy Kreiner, Canada	1:29.13
1980	Hanni Wenzel, Liechtenstein	2:41.66
1984	Debbie Armstrong, United States	2:20.98
1988	Vreni Schneider, Switzerland	2:06.49
1992	Pernilla Wiberg, Sweden	2:12.74
1994	Deborah Compagnoni, Italy	2:30.97
1998	Deborah Compagnoni, Italy	2:50.59
2002	Janica Kostelic, Croatia	2:30.01

Super Giant Slalom

1988	Sigrid Wolf, Austria	1:19.03
1992	Deborah Compagnoni, Italy	1:21.22
1994	Diann Roffe-Steinrotter, United States	1:22.15
1998	Picabo Street, United States	1:18.02
2002	Daniela Ceccarelli, Italy	1:13.59

Combined (Downhill and Slalom)

		Points
1936	Christl Cranz, Germany	97.06
1948	Trude Beiser, Austria	6.58
1952-84	Not held	
1988	Anita Wachter, Austria	29.25
1992	Petra Kronberger, Austria	2.55
		Time
1994	Pernilla Wiberg, Sweden	3:05.16
1998	Katja Seizinger, Germany	2:40.74
2002	Janica Kostelic, Croatia	2:43.28

ICE HOCKEY

MEN

1920 Canada
1924 Canada
1928 Canada
1932 Canada
1936 Great Britain
1948 Canada
1952 Canada
1956 USSR
1960 United States
1964 USSR
1968 USSR
1972 USSR
1976 USSR
1980 United States
1984 USSR
1988 USSR
1992 Unified Team*
1994 Sweden
1998 Czech Republic
2002 Canada

WOMEN

1998 United States
2002 Canada

*Former Soviet Union team.

2002 Men's Championship
Canada 5, United States 2
2002 Women's Championship
Canada 3, United States 2

FREESTYLE SKIING—MEN

Moguls

1992 Edgar Grospiron, France
1994 Jean-Luc Brassard, Canada
1998 Jonny Moseley, United States
2002 Janne Lahtela, Finland

Aerials

1994 Andreas Schoenbaechler, Switzerland
1998 Eric Bergoust, United States
2002 Ales Valenta, Czech Republic

FREESTYLE SKIING—WOMEN

Moguls

1992 Donna Weinbrecht, United States
1994 Stine Lise Hattestad, Norway
1998 Tae Satoya, Japan
2002 Kari Traa, Norway

Aerials

1994 Lina Cherjazova, Uzbekistan
1998 Nikki Stone, United States
2002 Alisa Camplin, Australia

DISTRIBUTION OF MEDALS 2002 WINTER OLYMPIC GAMES

(Salt Lake City, Utah)

	Gold	Silver	Bronze	Total
Germany	12	16	7	35
United States	10	13	11	34
Norway	11	7	6	24
Canada	6	3	8	17
Austria	2	4	10	16
Russia	6	6	4	16
Italy	4	4	4	12
France	4	5	2	11
Switzerland	3	2	6	11
China	2	2	4	8
Netherlands	3	5	0	8
Finland	4	2	1	7
Sweden	0	2	4	6
Croatia	3	1	0	4
Korea	2	2	0	4
Bulgaria	0	1	2	3
Estonia	1	1	1	3
Great Britain	1	0	2	3
Australia	2	0	0	2
Czech Republic	1	0	1	2
Japan	0	1	1	2
Poland	0	1	1	2
Spain	0	0	1	1
Belarus	0	0	1	1
Slovenia	0	0	1	1

2002 UNITED STATES MEDALISTS

Alpine Skiing

Men's Combined—SILVER—Bode Miller
Men's Giant Slalom—SILVER—Bode Miller

Bobsleigh

Four-Man—SILVER—Todd Hayes, Bill Schuffenhauer, Garrett Hines, Randy Jones
Four-Man—BRONZE—Mike Kohn, Doug Sharp, Brian Shimer, Dan Steele
Women—GOLD—Jill Bakken, Vonetta Flowers

Figure Skating

Women—GOLD—Sarah Hughes
Women—BRONZE—Michelle Kwan
Men—BRONZE—Timothy Goebel

Freestyle Skiing

Men's Aerials—SILVER—Joe Pack
Men's Moguls—SILVER—Travis Mayer
Women's Moguls—SILVER—Shannon Bahrke

Hockey

Men—SILVER—Tom Barrasso, Brian Rolston, Mike York, Tony Amonte, Chris Chelios, Chris Drury, Mike Dunham, Bill Guerin, Brett Hull, John LeClair, Brian Leetch, Mike Modano, Brian Rafalski, Jeremy Roenick, Gary Suter, Keith Tkachuk, Doug Weight, Scott Young, Tom Poti, Mike Richter, Phil Housley, Adam Deadmarsh, Aaron Miller
Women—Silver—Chris Bailey, Laurie Baker, Karyn Bye, Julie Chu, Natalie Darwitz, Sara DeCosta, Tricia Dunn, Cammi Granato, Courtney Kennedy, Andrea Kilbourne, Katie King, Shelley Looney, Sue Merz, Allison Mleczko, Tara Mounsey, Jenny Potter, Angela Ruggiero, Sara Tueting, Lyndsay Wall, Krissy Wendell

Luge

Men's Doubles—SILVER—Brian Martin, Mark Grimmette
Men's Doubles—BRONZE—Clay Ives

Short Track Speed Skating

Men's 1,000 m—SILVER—Apolo Anton Ohno
Men's 1,500 m—GOLD—Apolo Anton Ohno
Men's 500 m—BRONZE—Rusty Smith

Skeleton

Men—GOLD—Jim Shea
Women—GOLD—Tristan Gale
Women—SILVER—Lea Ann Parsley

Snowboarding

Men's Halfpipe—GOLD—Ross Powers
Men's Halfpipe—SILVER—Danny Kass
Men's Halfpipe—BRONZE—Jarret Thomas
Men's Parallel Giant Slalom—BRONZE—Chris Klug
Women's Halfpipe—GOLD—Kelly Clark

Speed Skating

Women's 1,000 m—GOLD—Chris Witty
Women's 1,000 m—BRONZE—Jennifer Rodriguez
Women's 1,500 m—BRONZE—Jennifer Rodriguez
Men's 1,000 m—BRONZE—Joey Cheek
Men's 1,500 m—GOLD—Derek Parra
Men's 500 m—GOLD—Casey FitzRandolph
Men's 500 m—BRONZE—Kip Carpenter
Men's 5,000 m—SILVER—Derek Parra

Other 2002 Winter Olympic Games Champions

Biathlon

Men's 10 km Sprint—Ole Einar Bjoerndalen, Norway
Men's 12.5 km Pursuit—Ole Einar Bjoerndalen, Norway
Men's 20 km Individual—Ole Einar Bjoerndalen, Norway
Men's 4 × 7.5 km Relay—Norway
Women's 10 km Pursuit—Olga Pyleva, Russia
Women's 15 km Individual—Andrea Henkel, Germany
Women's 4 × 7.5 km Relay—Germany
Women's 7.5 km Sprint—Kati Wilhelm, Germany

Bobsledding

2-man—Germany
4-man—Germany
Women—United States

Cross-Country Skiing

Men's 10 km Free Pursuit—Johann Muehlegg, Spain
Men's 15 km Classical—Andrus Veerpalu, Estonia
Men's 30 km Free Mass Start—Johann Muehlegg, Spain
Men's 4 × 10 km Relay—Norway
Men's 50 km Classical—Mikhail Ivanov, Russia
Men's Sprint—Tor Arne Hetland, Norway
Women's 10 km Classical—Bente Skari, Norway
Women's 15 km Free Mass Start—Stefania Belmondo, Italy
Women's 30 km Classical—Gabriella Paruzzi, Italy
Women's 4 × 5 km Relay—Germany
Women's 5 km Free Pursuit—Olga Danilova, Russia
Women's Sprint—Julija Tchepalova, Russia

Curling

Men—Norway
Women—Germany

Figure Skating

Pairs—David Pelletier and Jamie Sale, Canada; Elena Berezhnaya and Anton Sikharulidze, Russia
Ice dancing—Marina Anissina and Gwendal Peizerat, France

Skeleton

Men—Jim Shea, United States
Women—Tristan Gale, United States

Luge

Men's Doubles—Germany
Men's Singles—Armin Zoeggeler, Italy
Women's Singles—Sylke Otto, Germany

Nordic Combined

Individual 15 km—Samppa Lajunen, Finland
Sprint 7.5 km—Samppa Lajunen, Finland
Team 4 × 5 km Relay—Finland

Short Track Speed Skating

Women's 1,000 km—Yang Yang (A), China
Women's 1,500 km—Gi-Hyun Ko, Korea
Women's 3,000 km Relay—Korea
Women's 500 m—Yang Yang (A), China
Men's 1,000 m—Steven Bradbury, Australia
Men'1 1,500 m—Apolo Anton Ohno, United States
Men's 500 m—Marc Gagnon, Canada
Men's 5,000 m Relay—Canada

Ski Jumping

Individual K120—Simon Ammann, Switzerland
Individual K90—Simon Ammann, Switzerland
Team K120-Germany

Snowboarding

Men's Halfpipe—Ross Powers, United States
Men' Parallel Giant Slalom—Philipp Schoch, Switzerland
Women's Halfpipe—Kelly Clark, United States
Women's Parallel Giant Slalom—Isabelle Blanc, France

Speed Skating

Women's 1,500 m—Anni Friesinger, Germany
Women's 3,000 m—Claudia Pechstein, Germany
Women's 500 m—Catriona LeMay Doan, Canada
Women's 5,000 m—Claudia Pechstein, Germany
Men's 1,000 m—Gerard van Velde, Netherlands
Men's 10,000 m—Jochem Uytdehaage, Netherlands
Men's 5,000 m—Jochem Uytdehaage, Netherlands

Summer Games: Gold Medals

TRACK AND FIELD–MEN

100-Meter Dash

1896	Thomas Burke, United States	12.00
1900	Francis W. Jarvis, United States	10.80
1904	Archie Hahn, United States	11.00
1906	Archie Hahn, United States	11.20
1908	Reginald Walker, South Africa	10.80
1912	Ralph Craig, United States	10.80
1920	Charles Paddock, United States	10.80
1924	Harold Abrahams, Great Britain	10.60
1928	Percy Williams, Canada	10.80
1932	Eddie Tolan, United States	10.30
1936	Jesse Owens, United States	10.30[1]
1948	Harrison Dillard, United States	10.30
1952	Lindy Remigino, United States	10.40
1956	Bobby Morrow, United States	10.50
1960	Armin Hary, Germany	10.20
1964	Robert Hayes, United States	10.00
1968	James Hines, United States	09.90
1972	Valery Borzow, USSR	10.14
1976	Hasely Crawford, Trinidad and Tobago	10.06
1980	Allan Wells, Britain	10.25
1984	Carl Lewis, United States	09.99
1988	Carl Lewis, United States	09.92[2]
1992	Linford Christie, Great Britain	09.96
1996	Donovan Bailey, Canada	09.84[3]
2000	Maurice Greene, United States	09.87

1. Wind assisted. 2. Lewis was awarded the gold medal when Ben Johnson of Canada, the original winner in 09.79s, was stripped of the medal after testing positive for steroid use. 3. World record.

200-Meter Dash

1900	John Tewksbury, United States	22.20
1904	Archie Hahn, United States	21.60
1908	Robert Kerr, Canada	22.60
1912	Ralph Craig, United States	21.70
1920	Allan Woodring, United States	22.00
1924	Jackson Scholz, United States	21.60
1928	Percy Williams, Canada	21.80
1932	Eddie Tolan, United States	21.20
1936	Jesse Owens, United States	20.70
1948	Melvin E. Patton, United States	21.10
1952	Andrew Stanfield, United States	20.70
1956	Bobby Morrow, United States	20.60
1960	Livio Berruti, Italy	20.50
1964	Henry Carr, United States	20.30
1968	Tommie Smith, United States	19.80
1972	Vallery Borzov, USSR	20.00
1976	Don Quarrie, Jamaica	20.23
1980	Pietro Mennea, Italy	20.19
1984	Carl Lewis, United States	19.80
1988	Joe DeLoach, United States	19.75
1992	Mike Marsh, United States	20.01
1996	Michael Johnson, United States	19.32[1]
2000	Konstantinos Kenteris, Greece	20.09

1. World record.

400-Meter Dash

1896	Thomas Burke, United States	54.20
1900	Maxwell Long, United States	49.40
1904	Harry Hillman, United States	49.20
1906	Paul Pilgrim, United States	53.20
1908	Wyndham Halswelle, Great Britain (walkover)	50.00
1912	Charles Reidpath, United States	48.20
1920	Bevil Rudd, South Africa	49.60
1924	Eric Liddell, Great Britain	47.60
1928	Ray Barbuti, United States	47.80
1932	William Carr, United States	46.20
1936	Archie Williams, United States	46.50
1948	Arthur Wint, Jamaica, B.W.I.	46.20
1952	George Rhoden, Jamaica, B.W.I.	45.90
1956	Charles Jenkins, United States	46.70
1960	Otis Davis, United States	44.90
1964	Mike Larrabee, United States	45.10
1968	Lee Evans, United States	43.80
1972	Vincent Matthews, United States	44.66
1976	Alberto Juantorena, Cuba	44.26
1980	Viktor Markin, USSR	44.60
1984	Alonzo Babers, United States	44.27
1988	Steve Lewis, United States	43.87
1992	Quincy Watts, United States	43.50
1996	Michael Johnson, United States	43.49
2000	Michael Johnson, United States	43.84

800-Meter Run

1896	Edwin Flack, Australia	2:11.00
1900	Alfred Tysoe, Great Britain	2:01.40
1904	James Lightbody, United States	1:56.00
1906	Paul Pilgrim, United States	2:01.20
1908	Mel Sheppard, United states	1:52.80
1912	Ted Meredith, United States	1:51.90
1920	Albert Hill, Great Britain	1:53.40
1924	Douglas Lowe, Great Britain	1:52.40
1928	Douglas Lowe, Great Britain	1:51.80
1932	Thomas Hampson, Great Britain	1:49.80
1936	John Woodruff, United States	1:52.90
1948	Malvin Whitfield, United States	1:49.20
1952	Malvin Whitfield, United States	1:49.20
1956	Tom Courtney, United States	1:47.70
1960	Peter Snell, New Zealand	1:46.30
1964	Peter Snell, New Zealand	1:45.10
1968	Ralph Doubell, Australia	1:44.30
1972	David Wottle, United States	1:45.90
1976	Alberto Juantorena, Cuba	1:43.50
1980	Steve Ovett, Britain	1:45.40
1984	Joaquin Cruz, Brazil	1:43.00
1988	Paul Ereng, Kenya	1:43.45
1992	William Tanui, Kenya	1:43.66
1996	Vebjoern Rodal, Norway	1:42.58
2000	Nils Schumann, Germany	1:45.08

1,500-Meter Run

1896	Edwin Flack, Australia	4:33.20
1900	Charles Bennett, Great Britain	4:06.00
1904	James Lightbody, United States	4:05.40
1906	James Lightbody, United States	4:12.00
1908	Mel Sheppard, United States	4:03.40
1912	Arnold Jackson, Great Britain	3:56.80
1920	Albert Hill, Great Britain	4:01.80
1924	Paavo Nurmi, Finland	3:53.60
1928	Harry Larva, Finland	3:53.20
1932	Luigi Becali, Italy	3:51.20
1936	Jack Lovelock, New Zealand	3:47.80
1948	Henri Eriksson, Sweden	3:49.80
1952	Joseph Barthel, Luxembourg	3:45.20
1956	Ron Delany, Ireland	3:41.20
1960	Herb Elliott, Australia	3:35.60
1964	Peter Snell, New Zealand	3:38.10
1968	Kipchoge Keino, Kenya	3:34.90
1972	Pekka Vasala, Finland	3:36.30
1976	John Walker, New Zealand	3:39.17
1980	Sebastian Coe, Britain	3:38.40
1984	Sebastian Coe, Britain	3:32.53
1988	Peter Rono, Kenya	3:35.96
1992	Fermin Cacho Ruiz, Spain	3:40.12
1996	Noureddine Morceli, Algeria	3:35.78
2000	Noah Ngeny, Kenya	3:32.07

5,000-Meter Run

1912	Hannes Kolehmainen, Finland	14:36.60
1920	Joseph Guillemot, France	14:55.60
1024	Paavo Nurmi, Finland	14:31.20
1928	Willie Ritola, Finland	14:38.00
1932	Lauri Lehtinen, Finland	14:30.00
1936	Gunnar Hockert, Finland	14:22.20
1948	Gaston Reiff, Belgium	14:17.60
1952	Emil Zatopek, Czechoslovakia	14:06.60
1956	Vladimir Kuts, USSR	13:39.60
1960	Murray Halberg, New Zealand	13:43.40
1964	Bob Schul, United States	13:48.80
1968	Mohamed Gammoudi, Tunisia	14:05.00
1972	Lasse Viren, Finland	13:26.40
1976	Lasse Viren, Finland	13:24.76
1980	Miruts Yifter, Ethiopia	13:21.00
1984	Saud Aouita, Morocco	13:05.59
1988	John Ngugi, Kenya	13:11.70
1992	Dieter Baumann, Germany	13:12.52
1996	Venuste Niyongabo, Burundi	13:07.96
2000	Millon Wolde, Ethiopia	13:35.49

10,000-Meter Run

1912	Hannes Kolehmainen, Finland	31:20.80
1920	Paavo Nurmi, Finland	31:45.80
1924	Willie Ritola, Finland	30:23.20
1928	Paavo Nurmi, Finland	30:18.80
1932	Janusz Kusocinski, Poland	30:11.40
1936	Ilmari Salminen, Finland	30:15.40
1948	Emil Zatopek, Czechoslovakia	29:59.60
1952	Emil Zatopek, Czechoslovakia	29:17.00
1956	Vladimir Kuts, USSR	28:45.60
1960	Peter Bolotnikov, USSR	28:32.20
1964	Billy Mills, United States	28:24.40
1968	Nartali Temu, Kenya	29:27.40
1972	Lasse Viren, Finland	27:38.40
1976	Lasse Viren, Finland	27:40.38
1980	Miruts Yifter, Ethiopia	27:42.70
1984	Alberto Cova, Italy	27:47.50
1988	Mly Brahim Boutaib, Morocco	27:21.46
1992	Khalid Skah, Morocco	27:47.70
1996	Haile Gebrselassie, Ethiopia	27:07.34
2000	Haile Gebrselassie, Ethiopia	21:18.20

Marathon

1896	Spiridon Loues, Greece	2:58:50.00
1900	Michel Teato, France	2:59:45.00
1904	Thomas Hicks, United States	3:28:53.00
1906	William J. Sherring, Canada	2:51:23.65
1908	John J. Hayes, United States	2:55:18.40
1912	Kenneth McArthur, South Africa	2:36:54.80
1920	Hannes Kolehmainen, Finland	2:32:35.80
1924	Albin Stenroos, Finland	2:41:22.60
1928	A. B. El Quafi, France	2:32:57.00
1932	Juan Zabala, Argentina	2:31:36.00
1936	Kitei Son, Japan	2:29:19.20
1948	Delfo Cabrera, Argentina	2:34:51.60
1952	Emil Zatopek, Czechoslovakia	2:23:30.20
1956	Alain Mimoun, France	2:25:00.00
1960	Abebe Bikila, Ethiopia	2:15:16.20
1964	Abebe Bikila, Ethiopia	2:12:11.20
1968	Mamo Wold, Ethiopia	2:20:26.40
1972	Frank Shorter, United States	2:12:19.80
1976	Walter Cierpinski, East Germany	2:09:55.00
1980	Walter Cierpinski, East Germany	2:11:30.00
1984	Carlos Lopes, Portugal	2:09:21.00
1988	Gelindo Bordin, Italy	2:10:47.00
1992	Hwang Young-Cho, South Korea	2:13:23.00
1996	Josia Thugwane, South Africa	2:12:36.00
2000	Gezahgne Abera, Ethiopia	2:10:11.00

110-Meter Hurdles

1896	Thomas Curtis, United States	17.60
1900	Alvin Kraenzlein, United States	15.40
1904	Frederick Schule, United States	16.00
1906	R.G. Leavitt, United States	16.20
1908	Forrest Smithson, United States	15.00
1912	Frederick Kelly, United States	15.10
1920	Earl Thomson, Canada	14.80
1924	Daniel Kinsey, United States	15.00
1928	Sydney Atkinson, South Africa	14.80
1932	George Saling, United States	14.60
1936	Forrest Towns, United States	14.20
1948	William Porter, United States	13.90
1952	Harrison Dillard, United States	13.70
1956	Lee Calhoun, United States	13.50
1960	Lee Calhoun, United States	13.80
1964	Hayes Jones, United States	13.60
1968	Willie Davenport, United States	13.30
1972	Rodney Milburn, United States	13.24
1976	Guy Drut, France	13.30
1980	Thomas Munkett, East Germany	13.20
1984	Roger Kingdom, United States	13.20
1988	Roger Kingdom, United States	12.98
1992	Mark McCoy, Canada	13.12
1996	Allen Johnson, United States	12.95
2000	Anier Garcia, Cuba	13.00

200-Meter Hurdles

1900	Alvin Kraenzlein, United States	25.40
1904	Harry Hillman, United States	24.60

400-Meter Hurdles

1900	John Tewksbury, United States	57.60
1904	Harry Hillman, United States	53.00
1908	Charles Bacon, United States	55.00
1920	Frank Loomis, United States	54.00
1924	F. Morgan Taylor, United States	52.60
1928	Lord David Burghley, Great Britain	53.40
1932	Robert Tisdall, Ireland	51.80[1]
1936	Glenn Hardin, United States	52.40
1948	Roy Cochran, United States	51.10
1952	Charles Moore, United States	50.80
1956	Glenn Davis, United States	50.10
1960	Glenn Davis, United States	49.30
1964	Rex Cawley, United States	49.60
1968	David Hemery, Great Britain	48.10
1972	John Akii-Bua, Uganda	47.80
1976	Edwin Moses, United States	47.64
1980	Volker Beck, East Germany	48.70
1984	Edwin Moses, United States	47.75
1988	Andre Phillips, United States	47.19
1992	Kevin Young, United States	46.78
1996	Derrick Adkins, United States	47.54
2000	Angelo Taylor, United States	47.50

1. Record not allowed.

2,500-Meter Steeplechase

1900	George Orton, United States	7:34.00
1904	James Lightbody, United States	7:39.60

3,000-Meter Steeplechase

1920	Percy Hodge, Great Britain	10:00.40
1924	Willie Ritola, Finland	09:33.60
1928	Toivo Loukola, Finland	09:21.80
1932	Volmari Iso-Hollo, Finland	10:33.40[1]
1936	Volmari Iso-Hollo, Finland	09:03.80
1948	Thure Sjoestrand, Sweden	09:04.60
1952	Horace Ashenfelter, United States	08:45.40
1956	Chris Brasher, Great Britain	08:41.20
1960	Zdzislaw Krzyskowiak, Poland	08:34.20
1964	Gaston Roelants, Belgium	08:30.80
1968	Amos Biwott, Kenya	08:51.00
1972	Kipchoge Keino, Kenya	08:23.60
1976	Anders Gardervd, Sweden	08:08.02
1980	Bronislaw Malinowski, Poland	08:09.70
1984	Julius Korir, Kenya	08:11.80
1988	Julius Karluki, Kenya	08:05.51
1992	Matthew Birir, Kenya	08:08.84
1996	Joseph Keter, Kenya	08:07.12
2000	Reuben Kosgei, Kenya	08:21.43

1. About 3,450 meters-extra lap by error.

10,000-Meter Walk

1912	George Goulding, Canada	46:28.40
1920	Ugo Frigerio, Italy	48:06.20
1924	Ugo Frigerio, Italy	47:49.00
1948	John Mikaelsson, Sweden	45:13.20
1952	John Mikaelsson, Sweden	45:02.80

20,000-Meter Walk

1956	Leonid Spirin, USSR	1:31:27.40
1960	Vladimir Golubnichy, USSR	1:34:07.20
1964	Ken Mathews, Great Britain	1:29:34.00
1968	Vladimir Golubnichy, USSR	1:33:58.40
1972	Peter Frenkel, East Germany	1:26:42.40
1976	Daniel Bautista, Mexico	1:24:40.60
1980	Maurizio Damiliano, Italy	1:23:35.50
1984	Ernesto Conto, Mexico	1:23.13.00
1988	Jozef Pribilinec, Czechoslovakia	1:19:57.00
1992	Daniel Plaza, Spain	1:21:45.00
1996	Jefferson Perez, Ecuador	1:20:07.00
2000	Robert Korzeniowski, Poland	1:18.59.00

50,000-Meter Walk

1932	Thomas W. Green, Great Britain	4:50:10.00
1936	Harold Whitlock, Great Britain	4:30:41.10
1948	John Ljunggren, Sweden	4:41:52.00
1952	Giuseppe Dordoni, Italy	4:28:07.80
1956	Norman Read, New Zealand	4:30:42.80
1960	Donald Thompson, Great Britain	4:25:30.00
1964	Abdon Pamich, Italy	4:11:12.40
1968	Christoph Hohne, East Germany	4:20:13.60
1972	Bern Kannernberg, West Germany	3:56:11.60
1980	Hartwig Guader, East Germany	3:49:24.00
1984	Raul Gonzalez, Mexico	3:37:26.00
1988	Viacheslau Ivanenko, USSR	3:48:29.00
1992	Andrei Perlov, Unified Team[1]	3:50:13.00
1996	Robert Korzeniowski, Poland	3:43:30.00
2000	Robert Korzeniowski, Poland	3:42.22.00

1. Former Soviet Union team.

400-Meter Relay (4x100)

1912	Great Britain	42.40
1920	United States	42.20
1924	United States	41.00
1928	United States	41.00
1932	United States	40.00
1936	United States	39.80

1948	United States	40.60
1952	United States	40.10
1956	United States	39.50
1960	Germany	39.50
1964	United States	39.00
1968	United States	38.20
1972	United States	38.19
1976	United States	38.33
1980	USSR	38.26
1984	United States	37.83
1988	USSR	38.19
1992	United States	37.40[1]
1996	Canada	37.69
2000	United States	37.61

1. World record.

1,600-Meter Relay (4x400)

1912	United States	3:16.60
1920	Great Britain	3:22.20
1924	United States	3:16.00
1928	United States	3:14.20
1932	United States	3:08.20
1936	Great Britain	3:09.00
1948	United States	3:10.40
1952	Jamaica, B.W.I.	3:03.90
1956	United States	3:04.80
1960	United States	3:02.20
1964	United States	3:00.70
1968	United States	2:56.10
1972	Kenya	2:59.80
1976	United States	2:58.65
1980	USSR	3:01.10
1984	United States	2:57.91
1988	United States	2:56.16
1992	United States	2:55.74[1]
1996	United States	2:55.99
2000	United States	2:56.35

1. World record.

Team Race

		Pts
1900	Great Britain (5,000 meters)	26
1904	United States (4 miles)	27
1908	Great Britain (3 miles)	6
1912	United States (3,000 meters)	9
1920	United States (3,000 meters)	10
1924	Finland (3,000 meters)	9

Standing High Jump

1900	Ray Ewry, United States	5 ft 5 in
1904	Ray Ewry, United States	4 ft 11 in
1906	Ray Ewry, United States	5 ft 1⅝ in
1908	Ray Ewry, United States	5 ft 2 in
1912	Platt Adams, United States	5 ft 4⅛ in

Running High Jump

1896	Ellery Clark, United States	5 ft 11¼ in
1900	Irving Baxter, United States	6 ft 2¾ in
1904	Samuel Jones, United States	5 ft 11 in
1906	Con Leahy, Ireland	5 ft 9⅞ in
1908	Harry Porter, United States	6 ft 3 in
1912	Alma Richards, United States	6 ft 4 in
1920	Richmond Landon, United States	6 ft 4¼ in
1924	Harold Osborn, United States	6 ft 5 15/16 in
1928	Robert W. King, United States	6 ft 4⅜ in
1932	Duncan McNaughton, Canada	6 ft 5⅝ in
1936	Cornelius Johnson, United States	6 ft 7 15/16 in
1948	John Winter, Australia	6 ft 6 in
1952	Walter David, United States	6 ft 8 15/16 in
1956	Charles Damas, United States	6 ft 11¼ in
1960	Robert Shavlakadze, USSR	7 ft 1 in
1964	Valeri Brumel, USSR	7 ft 1¾ in
1968	Dick Fosbury, United States	7 ft 4¼ in
1972	Yuri Tarmak, USSR	7 ft 3¾ in
1976	Jacek Wszola, Poland	7 ft 4½ in
1980	Gerd Wessig, East Germany	7 ft 8¾ in
1984	Dietmar Mogenburg, West Germany	7 ft 8½ in
1988	Guennadi Avdeenko, USSR	7 ft ½ in
1992	Javier Sotomayer, Cuba	7 ft 8½ in
1996	Charles Austin, United States	7 ft 10 in
2000	Sergey Kliugin, Russia	7 ft 8½ in

Long Jump

1896	Ellery Clark, United States	20 ft 9¾ in
1900	Alvin Kraenzlein, United States	23 ft 6⅞ in
1904	Myer Prinstein, United States	24 ft 1 in
1906	Myer Prinstein, United States	23 ft 7½ in
1908	Frank Irons, United States	24 ft 6½ in
1912	Albert Gutterson, United States	24 ft 11¼ in
1920	William Petterssen, Sweden	23 ft 5½ in
1924	DeHart Hubbard, United States	24 ft 5⅛ in
1928	Edward B. Hamm, United States	25 ft 4¾ in
1932	Edward Gordon, United States	25 ft ¾ in
1936	Jesse Owens, United States	26 ft 5 5/16 in
1948	Willie Steele, United States	25 ft 8 in
1952	Jerome Biffle, United States	24 ft 10 in
1956	Gregory Bell, United States	25 ft 8¼ in
1960	Ralph Boston, United States	26 ft 7¾ in
1964	Lynn Davies, Great Britain	26 ft 5¾ in
1968	Bob Beamon, United States	29 ft 2½ in
1972	Randy Williams, United States	27 ft ½ in
1976	Arnie Robinson, United States	24 ft 7¾ in
1980	Lutz Dombrowski, E. Germany	28 ft ¼ in
1984	Carl Lewis, United States	28 ft ¼ in
1988	Carl Lewis, United States	28 ft 7¼ in
1992	Carl Lewis, United States	28 ft 5½ in
1996	Carl Lewis, United States	27 ft 10¾ in
2000	Ivan Pedroso, Cuba	28 ft ¾ in

Triple Jump

1896	James B. Connolly, United States	45 ft
1900	Myer Prinstein, United States	47 ft 4¼ in
1904	Myer Prinstein, United States	47 ft
1906	P.G. O'Connor, Ireland	46 ft 2 in
1908	Timothy Ahearne, Great Britain	48 ft 1¼ in
1912	Gustaf Lindblom, Sweden	48 ft 5⅛ in
1920	Vilho Tuulos, Finland	47 ft 6⅞ in
1924	Archie Winter, Australia	50 ft 11⅛ in
1928	Mikio Oda, Japan	49 ft 10 13/16 in
1932	Chuhei Nambu, Japan	51 ft 7 in
1936	Naoto Tajima, Japan	52 ft 5⅞ in
1948	Arne Ahman, Sweden	50 ft 6¼ in
1952	Adhemar da Silva, Brazil	53 ft 2½ in
1956	Adhemar da Silva, Brazil	53 ft 7½ in
1960	Jozef Schmidt, Poland	55 ft 1¾ in
1964	Jozef Schmidt, Poland	55 ft 3¼ in
1968	Viktor Saneyev, USSR	57 ft ¾ in
1972	Viktor Saneyev, USSR	56 ft 11 in
1976	Viktor Saneyev, USSR	56 ft 8¾ in
1980	Jaak Uudmae, USSR	56 ft 11⅛ in
1984	Al Joyner, United States	56 ft 7½ in
1988	Hristo Markov, Bulgaria	57 ft 9¼ in
1992	Mike Conley, United States	59 ft 7½ in
1996	Kenny Harrison, United States	59 ft 4¼ in
2000	Jonathan Edwards, Great Britain	58 ft 1¼ in

Pole Vault

1896	William Hoyt, United States	10 ft 9¾ in
1900	Irving Baxter, United States	10 ft 9⅞ in
1904	Charles Dvorak, United States	11 ft 6 in
1906	Fernand Gouder, France	11 ft 6 in
1908	Alfred Gilbert, United States, and Edward Cook, United States (tie)	12 ft 2 in
1912	Harry Babcock, United States	12 ft 11½ in
1920	Frank Foss, United States	13 ft 5 9/16 in
1924	Lee Barnes, United States	12 ft 11½ in
1928	Sabin W. Carr, United States	13 ft 9⅜ in
1932	William Miller, United States	14 ft 1⅞ in
1936	Earle Meadows, United States	14 ft 3¼ in
1948	Guinn Smith, United States	14 ft ¼ in
1952	Robert Richards, United States	14 ft 11⅛ in
1956	Robert Richards, United States	14 ft 11½ in
1960	Don Bragg, United States	15 ft 5⅛ in
1964	Fred Hansen, United States	16 ft 8¾ in

1968	Bob Seagren, United States	17 ft 8½ in
1972	Wolfgang Nordwig, East Germany	18 ft ½ in
1976	Tadeusz Slusarski, Poland	18 ft ½ in
1980	Wladyslaw Kozakiewics, Poland	18 ft 11½ in
1984	Pierre Quinon, France	18 ft 10¼ in
1988	Sergei Bubka, USSR	19 ft 4¼ in
1992	Maxim Tarassov, Unified Team[1]	19 ft 0¼ in
1996	Jean Galfione, France	19 ft 5¼ in
2000	Nick Hysong, United States	19 ft 4¼ in

1. Former Soviet Union team.

16-lb Shot-Put

1896	Robert Garrett, United States	36 ft 9¾ in
1900	Richard Sheldon, United States	46 ft 3⅛ in
1904	Ralph Rose, United States	48 ft 7 in
1906	Martin Sheridan, United States	40 ft 4 4/5 in
1908	Ralph Rose, United States	46 ft 7½ in
1912	Pat McDonald, United States	50 ft 4 in
1920	Ville Porhola, Finland	48 ft 7⅛ in
1924	Clarence Houser, United States	49 ft 2½ in
1928	John Kuck, United States	52 ft 11 11/16 in
1932	Leo Sexton, United States	52 ft 6 3/16 in
1936	Hans Woellke, Germany	53 ft 1¾ in
1948	Wilbur Thompson, United States	56 ft 2 in
1952	Parry O'Brien, United States	57 ft 1½ in
1956	Parry O'Brien, United States	60 ft 11 in
1960	Bill Nieder, United States	64 ft 6¾ in
1964	Dallas Long, United States	66 ft 8¼ in
1968	Randy Matson, United States	67 ft 4¾ in
1972	Wladyslaw Komar, Poland	69 ft 6 in
1976	Udo Beyer, East Germany	69 ft ¾ in
1980	Vladmir Klselyov, USSR	70 ft ½ in
1984	Alessandro Andrei, Italy	69 ft 9 in
1988	Uhf Timmerman, East Germany	73 ft 8¾ in
1992	Michael Stulze, United States	71 ft 2½ in
1996	Randy Barnes, United States	70 ft 11¼ in
2000	Arsi Harju, Finland	69 ft 10¼ in

Discus Throw

1896	Robert Garrett, United States	95 ft 7½ in
1900	Rudolf Bauer, Hungary	118 ft 2⅞ in
1904	Martin Sheridan, United States	128 ft 10½ in
1906	Martin Sheridan, United States	136 ft ⅓ in
1908	Martin Sheridan, United States	134 ft 2 in
1912	Armas Taipale, Finland	145 ft 9/16 in
1920	Elmer Niklander, Finland	146 ft 7 in
1924	Clarence Houser, United States	151 ft 5¼ in
1928	Clarence Houser, United States	155 ft 2 2/5 in
1932	John Anderson, United States	162 ft 4⅞ in
1936	Ken Carpenter, United States	165 ft 7⅜ in
1948	Adolfo Consolini, Italy	173 ft 2 in
1952	Simeon Iness, United States	180 ft 6½ in
1956	Al Oerter, United States	184 ft 10½ in
1960	Al Oerter, United States	194 ft 2 in
1964	Al Oerter, United States	200 ft 1½ in
1968	Al Oerter, United States	212 ft 6 in
1972	Ludvik Danek, Czechoslovakia	211 ft 3 in
1976	Mac Wilkins, United States	221 ft 5 in
1980	Viktor Rashchupkin, USSR	218 ft 8 in
1984	Rolf Dannenberg, West Germany	218 ft 6 in
1988	Jurgen Schult, East Germany	225 ft 9¼ in
1992	Romas Ubartas, Lithuania	213 ft 7¾ in
1996	Lars Riedel, Germany	227 ft 8 in
2000	Virgilijus Alekna, Lithuania	227 ft 4in

Javelin Throw

1906	Eric Lemming, Sweden	175 ft 6 in
1908	Eric Lemming, Sweden	179 ft 10½ in
1912	Eric Lemming, Sweden	198 ft 11¼ in
1920	Jonni Myyra, Finland	215 ft 9¾ in
1924	Jonni Myyra, Finland	206 ft 6¾ in
1928	Eric Lundquist, Sweden	218 ft 6⅛ in
1932	Matti Jarvinen, Finland	238 ft 7 in
1936	Gerhard Stoeck, Germany	235 ft 8 5/16 in
1948	Kaj Rautavaara, Finland	228 ft 10½ in
1952	Cy Young, United States	242 ft¾ in
1956	Egil Danielsen, Norway	281 ft 2¼ in
1960	Viktor Tsibuelnko, USSR	277 ft 8⅜ in
1964	Pauli Nevala, Finland	271 ft 2¼ in
1968	Janis Lusis, USSR	295 ft 7 in
1972	Klaus Wolfermann, West Germany	296 ft 10 in
1976	Miklos Nemeth, Hungary	310 ft 4 in
1980	Dainis Kula, USSR	299 ft 2⅜ in
1984	Arto Haerkoenen, Finland	284 ft 8 in
1988	Tapio Korjus, Finland	276 ft 6 in
1992	Jan Zelezny, Czechoslovakia	294 ft 2 in
1996	Jan Zelezny, Czech Republic	289 ft 3 in
2000	Jan Zelezny, Czech Republic	295 ft 9½ in

16-lb Hammer Throw

1900	John Flanagan, United States	167 ft 4 in
1904	John Flanagan, United States	168 ft 1 in
1908	John Flanagan, United States	170 ft 4¼ in
1912	Matt McGrath, United States	179 ft 7⅛ in
1920	Pat Ryan, United States	173 ft 5⅝ in
1924	Fred Tootell, United States	174 ft 10¼ in
1928	Patrick O'Callaghan, Ireland	168 ft 7½ in
1932	Patrick O'Callaghan, Ireland	176 ft 11⅛ in
1936	Karl Hein, Germany	185 ft 4 in
1948	Imre Nemeth, Hungary	183 ft 11½ in
1952	Jozsef Csermak, Hungary	197 ft 11 9/16 in
1956	Harold Connolly, United States	207 ft 2¾ in
1960	Vasily Rudenkov, USSR	220 ft 1⅝ in
1964	Romuald Klim, USSR	228 ft 9½ in
1968	Gyula Zsivotzky, Hungary	240 ft 8 in
1972	Anatoly Bondarchuk, USSR	247 ft 8½ in
1976	Yuri Sedykh, USSR	254 ft 4 in
1980	Yuri Sedykh, USSR	(81.80m) 268 ft 4½ in
1984	Juha Tiainen, Finland	256 ft 2 in
1988	Sergei Litvinov, USSR	278 ft 2½ in
1992	Andrey Abduvaliyev, Unified Team[1]	270 ft 9½ in
1996	Balazs Kiss, Hungary	266 ft 6 in
2000	Szymon Ziolkowski, Poland	262 ft 6 in

1. Former Soviet Union team.

Decathlon

1912	Jim Thorpe, United States	—
	Hugo Wieslander, Sweden	—
1920	Helge Lovland, Norway	6,804.35 pts.
1924	Harold Osborn, United States	7,710.775 pts.
1928	Paavo Yrjola, Finland	8,053.29 pts.
1932	James Bausch, United States	8,462.23 pts.
1936	Glenn Morris, United States	7,900 pts.[1]
1948	Robert B. Mathias, United States	7,139 pts.
1952	Robert B. Mathias, United States	7,887 pts.
1956	Milton Campbell, United States	7,937 pts.
1960	Rafer Johnson, United States	8,392 pts.
1964	Willi Holdorf, Germany	7,887 pts.[1]
1968	Bill Toomey, United States	8,193 pts.
1972	Nikolai Avilov, USSR	8,454 pts.
1976	Bruce Jenner, United States	8,618 pts.
1980	Daley Thompson, Great Britain	8,495 pts.
1984	Daley Thompson, Great Britain	8,797 pts.
1988	Christian Schenk, East Germany	8,488 pts.
1992	Robert Zmelik, Czechoslovakia	8,611 pts.
1996	Dan O'Brien, United States	8,824 pts.
2000	Erki Nool, Estonia	8,641 pts.

1. Point system revised.

TRACK AND FIELD–WOMEN

100-Meter Dash

1928	Elizabeth Robinson, United States	12.20
1932	Stella Walsh, Poland	11.90
1936	Helen Stephens, United States	11.50
1948	Fanny Blankers-Koen, Netherlands	11.90
1952	Marjorie Jackson, Australia	11.50
1956	Betty Cuthbert, Australia	11.50
1960	Wilma Rudolph, United States	11.00
1964	Wyomia Tyus, United States	11.40
1968	Wyomia Tyus, United States	11.00
1972	Renate Stecher, East Germany	11.07

1976	Annegret Richter, West Germany	11.08
1980	Lyudmila Kondratyeva, USSR	11.06
1984	Evelyn Ashford, United States	10.97
1988	Florence Griffith-Joyner, United States	10.54
1992	Gail Devers, United States	10.82
1996	Gail Devers, United States	10.94
2000	Marion Jones, United States	10.75

200-Meter Dash

1948	Fanny Blankers-Koen, Netherlands	24.40
1952	Marjorie Jackson, Australia	23.70
1956	Betty Cuthbert, Australia	23.40
1960	Wilma Rudolph, United States	24.00
1964	Edith McGuire, United States	23.00
1968	Irena Szewinska, Poland	22.50
1972	Renate Stecher, East Germany	22.40
1976	Baerbel Eckert, East Germany	22.37
1980	Barbara Wockel, East Germany	22.03
1984	Valerie Brisco-Hooks, United States	21.81
1988	Florence Griffith-Joyner, United States	21.34
1992	Gwen Torrence, United States	21.81
1996	Marie-Jose Perec, France	22.12
2000	Marion Jones, United States	21.84

400-Meter Dash

1964	Betty Cuthbert, Australia	52.00
1968	Colette Besson, France	52.00
1972	Monika Zehrt, East Germany	51.08
1976	Irena Szewinska, Poland	49.29
1980	Marita Koch, East Germany	48.88
1984	Valerie Brisco-Hooks, United States	48.83
1988	Olga Bryzguina, USSR	48.65
1992	Marie Jose-Perec, France	48.83
1996	Marie Jose-Perec, France	48.25
2000	Cathy Freeman, Australia	49.11

800-Meter Run

1928	Lina Radke, Germany	2:16.80
1960	Ljudmila Shevcova, USSR	2:04.30
1964	Ann Packer, Great Britain	2:01.10
1968	Madeline Manning, United States	2:00.90
1972	Hildegard Falck, West Germany	1:58.60
1976	Tatiana Kazankina, USSR	1:54.94
1980	Nadezhda Olizarenko, USSR	1:53.50
1984	Doina Melinte, Romania	1:57.60
1988	Sigrun Wodars, East Germany	1:56.10
1992	Ellen Van Langen, Netherlands	1:55.54
1996	Svetlana Masterkova, Russia	1:57.73
2000	Maria Mutola, Mozambique	1:56.15

1,500-Meter Run

1972	Ludmila Bragina, USSR	4:01.40
1976	Tatiana Kazankina, USSR	4:05.48
1980	Tatiana Kazankina, USSR	3:56.60
1984	Gabriella Dorio, Italy	4:03.25
1988	Paula Ivan, Romania	3:53.96
1992	Hassiba Boulmerka, Algeria	3:55.30
1996	Svetlana Masterkova, Russia	4:00.83
2000	Nouria Merah-Benida, Algeria	4:05.10

5,000-Meter Run

1996	Wang, Jun-Xia, China	14:59.88
2000	Gabriela Szabo, Romania	14:40.79

10,000-Meter Run

1992	Derartu Tulu, Ethiopia	31:60.02
1996	Fernanda Ribeiro, Portugal	31:01.63
2000	Derartu Tulu, Ethiopia	30:17.49

80-Meter Hurdles

1932	Mildred Didrikson, United States	11.70
1936	Trebisonda Valla, Italy	11.70
1948	Fanny Blankers-Koen, Netherlands	11.20
1952	Shirley S. de la Hunty, Australia	10.90
1956	Shirley S. de la Hunty, Australia	10.70
1960	Irina Press, USSR	10.80
1964	Karin Balzer, Germany	10.50[1]
1968	Maureen Caird, Australia	10.30

1. Wind assisted.

100-Meter Hurdles

1972	Annelie Ehrhardt, East Germany	12.59
1976	Johanna Schaller, East Germany	12.77
1980	Vera Komisova, USSR	12.56
1984	Benita Fitzgerald-Brown, United States	12.84
1988	Jordanka Donkova, Bulgaria	12.38
1992	Paraskevi Patoulidou, Greece	12.64
1996	Ludmila Engquist, Sweden	12.58
2000	Olga Shishigina, Kazakhstan	12.65

400-Meter Hurdles

1984	Nawai El Moutawakel, Morocco	54.61
1988	Debra Flintoff-King, Australia	53.17
1992	Sally Gunnell, Great Britain	53.23
1996	Deon Hemmings, Jamaica	52.82
2000	Irina Privalova, Russia	53.02

400-Meter Relay

1928	Canada	48.40
1932	United States	47.00
1936	United States	46.90
1948	Netherlands	47.50
1952	United States	45.90
1956	Australia	44.50
1960	United States	44.50
1964	Poland	43.60
1968	United States	42.80
1972	West Germany	42.81
1976	East Germany	42.50
1980	East Germany	41.60
1984	United States	41.65
1988	United States	41.98
1992	United States	42.11
1996	United States	41.95
2000	Bahamas	41.95

1,600-Meter Relay

1972	East Germany	3:23.00
1976	East Germany	3:19.23
1980	USSR	3:20.20
1984	United States	3:18.29
1988	USSR	3:15.18
1992	Unified Team[1]	3:20.20
1996	United States	3:20.91
2000	United States	3:22.62

1. Former Soviet Union team.

10,000-Meter Walk

1992	ChenYue-Ling, China	44:32
1996	Yelena Nikolayeva, Russia	41:49

20,000-Meter Walk

2000	Liping Wang, China	1:29.05

Marathon

1984	Joan Benoit, United States	2:24:52
1988	Rose Mota, Portugal	2:25.40
1992	Valentina Yegorova, Unified Team	2:32.41
1996	Fatuma Roba, Ethiopia	2:26.05
2000	Naoko Takahashi, Japan	2:23.14

Running High Jump

1928	Ethel Catherwood, Canada	5 ft 3 in
1932	Jean Shiley, United States	5 ft 5¼ in
1936	Ibolya Csak, Hungary	5 ft 3 in
1948	Alice Coachman, United States	5 ft 6⅛ in
1952	Ester Brand, South Africa	5 ft 5¾ in
1956	Mildred McDaniel, United States	5 ft 9¼ in
1960	Iolanda Balas, Romania	6 ft ¾ in
1964	Iolanda Balas, Romania	6 ft 2¾ in
1968	Miloslava Rezkova, Czechoslovakia	5 ft 11¾ in
1972	Ulrike Meyfarth, West Germany	6 ft 3⅝ in
1976	Rosemarie Ackerman, E. Germany	6 ft 4 in
1980	Sara Simeoni, Italy	6 ft 5½ in
1984	Ulrike Meyfarth, West Germany	6 ft 7½ in
1988	Louise Ritter, United States	6 ft 8 in
1992	Heike Henkel, Germany	6 ft 7½ in
1996	Stefka Kostadinova, Bulgaria	6 ft 8¾ in
2000	Yelena Yelesina, Russia	6 ft 7 in

Long Jump

1948	Olga Gyarmati, Hungary	18 ft 8¼ in
1952	Yvette Williams, New Zealand	20 ft 5¾ in
1956	Elzbieta Krzesinska, Poland	20 ft 9¾ in
1960	Vera Krepkina, USSR	20 ft 10¾ in
1964	Mary Rand, Great Britain	22 ft 2 in
1968	Viorica Ciscopoleanu, Romania	22 ft 4½ in
1972	Heidemarie Rosendahl, West Germany	22 ft 3 in
1976	Angela Voigt, East Germany	22 ft ½ in
1980	Tatiana Kolpakova, USSR	23 ft 2 in
1984	Anisoara Stanciu, Romania	22 ft 10 in
1988	Jackie Joyner-Kersee, United States	24 ft 3½ in
1992	Heike Drechsler, Germany	23 ft 5¼ in
1996	Chioma Ajunwa, Nigeria	23 ft 4½ in
2000	Heike Drechsler, Germany	22 ft 11¼ in

Triple Jump

1996	Inessa Kravets, Ukraine	50 ft 3½ in
2000	Tereza Marinova, Belarus	49 ft 10 ½ in

Shot-Put

1948	Micheline Ostermeyer, France	45 ft 1½ in
1952	Galina Zybina, USSR	50 ft 1½ in
1956	Tamara Tishkyevich, USSR	54 ft 5 in
1960	Tamara Press, USSR	56 ft 9⅞ in
1964	Tamara Press, USSR	59 ft 6 in
1968	Margitta Gummel, East Germany	64 ft 4 in
1972	Nadezhda Chizhova, USSR	69 ft
1976	Ivanka Christova, Bulgaria	69 ft 5 in
1980	Ilona Sluplanek, East Germany	73 ft 6 in
1984	Claudia Losch, West Germany	67 ft 2¼ in
1988	Natalya Lisovskaya, USSR	72 ft 11½ in
1992	Svetlana Kriveleva, Unified Team[1]	69 ft 1¼ in
1996	Astrid Kumbernuss, Germany	67 ft 5½ in
2000	Yanina Korolchik, Belarus	67 ft 5½ in

1. Former Soviet Union team.

Discus Throw

1928	Helena Konopacka, Poland	129 ft 11⅞ in
1932	Lillian Copeland, United States	133 ft 2 in
1936	Gisela Mauermayer, Germany	156 ft 3 3/16 in
1948	Micheline Ostermeyer, France	137 ft 6½ in
1956	Olga Fikotova, Czechoslovakia	176 ft 1½ in
1960	Nina Ponomareva, USSR	180 ft 8¼ in
1964	Tamara Press, USSR	187 ft 10¾ in
1968	Lia Manoliu, Romania	191 ft 2½ in
1972	Faina Melnik, USSR	218 ft 7 in
1976	Evelin Schlaak, East Germany	226 ft 4 in
1980	Evelin Jahl, East Germany	229 ft 6½ in
1984	Ria Stalman, Netherlands	214 ft 5 in
1988	Martina Hellmann, East Germany	237 ft 2¼ in
1992	Maritza Marten, Cuba	229 ft 10¼ in
1996	Ilke Wyludda, Germany	228 ft 6½ in
2000	Ellina Zvereva, Belarus	224 ft 5 in

Javelin Throw

1932	Mildred Didrikson, United States	143 ft 4 in
1936	Tilly Fleischer, Germany	148 ft 2¾ in
1948	Herma Bauma, Austria	149 ft 6 in
1952	Dana Zatopek, Czechoslovakia	165 ft 7 in
1956	Inessa Janzeme, USSR	176 ft 8 in
1960	Elvira Ozolina, USSR	183 ft 8 in
1964	Mihaela Penes, Romania	198 ft 7½ in
1968	Angela Nemeth, Hungary	198 ft
1972	Ruth Fuchs, East Germany	209 ft 7 in
1976	Ruth Fuchs, East Germany	216 ft 4 in
1980	Maria Colon, Cuba	224 ft 5 in
1984	Tessa Sanderson, Britain	228 ft 2 in
1988	Petra Felke, East Germany	245 ft
1992	Silke Renke, Germany	224 ft 2½ in
1996	Heli Rantanen, Finland	222 ft 11 in
2000	Trine Hattestad, Norway	226 ft 1 in

Hammer Throw

2000	Kamila Skolimowska, Poland	233 ft 5 ¾ in

Pole Vault

2000	Stacy Dragila, United States	15 ft 1 in

Pentathlon

1964	Irina Press, USSR	5,246 pts.
1968	Ingrid Becker, West Germany	5,098 pts.
1972	Mary Peters, Britain	4,801 pts.
1976	Siegrun Siegl, East Germany	4,745 pts.
1980	Nadyeszhda Tkachenko, USSR	5,083 pts.
1984	Daniele Masala, Italy	5,469 pts.
1988	Jackie Joyner-Kersee, United States	7,291 pts.

Heptathlon

1992	Jackie Joyner-Kersee, United States	7,044 pts.
1996	Ghada Shouaa, Syria	6,780 pts.
2000	Denise Lewis, Great Britain	6,584 pts.

SWIMMING–MEN

50-Meter Freestyle

1988	Matt Biondi, United States	22.14
1992	Alexander Popov, Unified Team[1]	21.91
1996	Alexander Popov, Russia	22.13
2000	Anthony Ervin and Gary Hall, Jr., United States	21.98

1. Former Soviet Union team.

100-Meter Freestyle

1896	Alfred Hajos, Hungary	1:22.20
1904	Zoltan de Halmay, Hungary	1:02.80[1]
1906	Charles Daniels, United States	1:13.00
1908	Charles Daniels, United States	1:05.60
1912	Duke P. Kahanamoku, United States	1:03.40
1920	Duke P. Kahanamoku, United States	1:01.40
1924	John Weissmuller, United States	0:59.00
1928	John Weissmuller, United States	0:58.60
1932	Yasuji Miyazaki, Japan	0:58.20
1936	Ferenc Csik, Hungary	0:57.60
1948	Walter Ris, United States	0:57.30
1952	Clarke Scholes, United States	0:57.40
1956	Jon Henricks, Australia	0:55.40
1960	John Devitt, Australia	0:55.20
1964	Don Schollander, United States	0:53.40
1968	Michael Wenden, Australia	0:52.20
1972	Mark Spitz, United States	0:51.22
1976	Jim Montgomery, United States	0:49.99
1980	Jorg Woithe, East Germany	0:50.40
1984	Rowdy Gaines, United States	0:49.80
1988	Matt Biondi, United States	0:48.63
1992	Alexander Popov, Unified Team[2]	0:49.02
1996	Alexander Popov, Russia	0:48.74
2000	Pieter van den Hoogenband, Netherlands	0:48.30

1. 100 yards. 2. Former Soviet Union team.

200-Meter Freestyle

1900	Frederick Lane, Australia	2:25.20
1904	Charles Daniels, United States	2:44.20[1]
1968	Michael Wenden, Australia	1:55.20
1972	Mark Spitz, United States	1:52.78
1976	Bruce Furniss, United States	1:50.29
1980	Sergei Kopiliakov, USSR	4:49.81
1984	Michael Gross, West Germany	1:47.44
1988	Duncan Armstrong, Australia	1:47.25
1992	Evgueni Sadovyi, Unified Team[2]	1:46.70
1996	Danyon Loader, New Zealand	1:47.63
2000	Pieter van den Hoogenband, Netherlands	1:45.35[3]

1. 220 yards 2. Former Soviet Union team. 3. World record.

400-Meter Freestyle

1896	Paul Neumann, Austria	8:12.60[1]
1904	Charles Daniels, United States	6:16.20[2]
1906	Otto Sheff, Austria	6:23.80
1908	Henry Taylor, Great Britain	5:36.80
1912	George Hodgson, Canada	5:24.40
1920	Norman Ross, United States	5:26.80
1926	John Weissmuller, United States	5:04.20
1928	Albert Zorilla, Argentina	5:01.60
1932	Clarence Crabbe, United States	4:48.40

1936	Jack Medica, United States	4:44.50
1948	William Smith, United States	4:41.00
1952	Jean Boiteux, France	4:30.70
1956	Murray Rose, Australia	4:27.30
1960	Murray Rose, Australia	4:18.30
1964	Don Schollander, United States	4:12.20
1968	Mike Burton, United States	4:09.00
1972	Bradford Cooper, Australia	4:00.27[3]
1976	Brian Goodell, United States	3:51.93
1980	Vladimir Salnikov, USSR	3:51.31
1984	George DiCarlo, United States	3:51.23
1988	Uwe Dassier, East Germany	3:46.95
1992	Evgueni Sadovyi, Unified Team	3:45.00[4]
1996	Danyon Loader, New Zealand	3:47.97
2000	Ian Thorpe, Australia	3:40.59[4]

1. 500 meters. 2. 440 yards. 3. Rich DeMont, United States, won but was disqualified following day for medical reasons. 4. World record.

1,500-Meter Freestyle

1904	Emil Rausch, Germany	27:18.20[1]
1906	Henry Taylor, Great Britain	28:28.00[2]
1908	Henry Taylor, Great Britain	22:48.40
1912	George Hodgson, Canada	22:00.00
1920	Norman Ross, United States	22:23.20
1924	Andrew Charlton, Australia	20:06.60
1928	Arne Borg, Sweden	19:51.80
1932	Kusuo Kitamura, Japan	19:12.40
1936	Noboru Terada, Japan	19:13.70
1948	James McLane, United States	19:18.50
1952	Ford Konno, United States	18:30.00
1956	Murray Rose, Australia	17:58.90
1960	Jon Konrads, Australia	17:19.60
1964	Robert Windle, Australia	17:01.70
1968	Michael Burton, United States	16:38.90
1972	Michael Burton, United States	15:52.58
1976	Brian Goodell, United States	15:02.40
1980	Vladimir Salnikov, USSR	14:58.27
1984	Michael O'Brien, United States	15:05.20
1988	Vladimir Salnikov, USSR	15:00.40
1992	Kieren Perkins, Australia	14:43.48
1996	Kieren Perkins, Australia	14:56.40
2000	Grant Hackett, Australia	14:48.33

1. One mile. 2. 1,600 meters

100-Meter Backstroke

1904	Walter Brack, Germany	1:16.80[1]
1908	Arno Bieberstein, Germany	1:24.60
1912	Harry Hebner, United States	1:21.20
1920	Warren Kealoha, United States	1:15.20
1924	Warren Kealoha, United States	1:13.20
1928	George Kojac, United States	1:08.20
1932	Masaji Kiyokawa, Japan	1:08.60
1936	Adolph Kiefer, United States	1:05.90
1948	Allen Stack, United States	1:06.40
1952	Yoshinobu Oyakawa, United States	1:05.40
1956	David Thiele, Australia	1:02.20
1960	David Thiele, Australia	1:01.90
1968	Roland Matthes, East Germany	0:58.70
1972	Roland Matthes, East Germany	0:56.58
1976	John Naber, United States	0:55.49
1980	Bengt Baron, Sweden	0:56.53
1984	Rick Carey, United States	0:55.79
1988	Daichi Suzuki, Japan	0:55.05
1992	Mark Tewksbury, Canada	0:53.98
1996	Jeff Rouse, United States	0:54.10
2000	Lenny Krayzelburg, United States	0:53.72

1. 100 yards

200-Meter Backstroke

1900	Ernst Hoppenberg, Germany	2:47.00
1964	Jed Graef, United States	2:10.30
1968	Roland Matthes, East Germany	2:09.60
1972	Roland Matthes, East Germany	2:02.82
1976	John Naber, United States	1:59.19
1980	Sandor Wladar, Hungary	2:01.93
1984	Rick Carey, United States	2:00.23
1988	Igor Polianski, USSR	1:59.37
1992	Martin Lopez Zubero, Spain	1:58.47
1996	Brad Bridgewater, United States	1:58.54
2000	Lenny Krayzelburg, United States	1:56.76

100-Meter Breaststroke

1968	Donald McKenzie, United States	1:07.70
1972	Nobutaka Taguchi, Japan	1:04.94
1976	John Hencken, United States	1:03.11
1980	Duncan Goodhew, Britain	1:03.34
1984	Steve Lindquist, United States	1:01.65
1988	Adrian Moorhouse, Great Britain	1:02.04
1992	Nelson Diebel, United States	1:01.50
1996	Fred Deburghgraeve, Belgium	1:00.60[1]
2000	Domenico Fioravanti, Italy	1:00.46

1. World record.

200-Meter Breaststroke

1908	Frederick Holman, Great Britain	3:09.20
1912	Walter Bathe, Germany	3:01.80
1920	Haken Malmroth, Sweden	3:04.40
1924	Robert Skelton, United States	2:56.60
1928	Yoshiyuki Tsuruta, Japan	2:48.80
1932	Yoshiyuki Tsuruta, Japan	2:45.40
1936	Tetsuo Hamuro, Japan	2:41.50
1948	Joseph Verdeur, United States	2:39.30
1952	John Davies, Australia	2:34.40
1956	Masaura Furukawa, Japan	2:34.70
1960	Bill Muliken, United States	2:37.40
1964	Ian O'Brien, Australia	2:07.80
1968	Felipe Munoz, Mexico	2:28.70
1972	John Hencken, United States	2:21.55
1976	David Willkie, Britain	2:15.11
1980	Robertas Zulpa, USSR	2:15.85
1984	Victor Davis, Canada	2:13.34
1988	Jozef Szabo, Hungary	2:13.52
1992	Mike Barrowman, United States	2:10.16
1996	Norbert Rozsa, Hungary	2:12.57
2000	Domenico Fioravanti, Italy	2:10.87

100-Meter Butterfly

1968	Douglas Russell, United States	55.90
1972	Mark Spitz, United States	54.27
1976	Matt Vogel, United States	54.35
1980	Par Arvidsson, Sweden	54.92
1984	Michael Gross, West Germany	53.08
1988	Anthony Nesty, Surinam	53.00
1992	Pablo Morales, United States	53.32
1996	Denis Pankratov, Russia	52.27[1]
2000	Lars Froelander, Sweden	52.00

1. World record.

200-Meter Butterfly

1956	Bill Yorzyk, United States	2:19.30
1960	Mike Troy, United States	2:12.80
1964	Kevin Berry, Australia	2:06.60
1968	Carl Robie, United States	2:08.70
1972	Mark Spitz, United States	2:00.70
1976	Mike Bruner, United States	1:59.23
1980	Sergei Fesenko, USSR	1:59.76
1984	Jon Sieben, Australia	1:57.00
1988	Michael Gross, East Germany	1:56.94
1992	Mel Stewart, United States	1:56.26
1996	Denis Pankratov, Russia	1:56.51
2000	Tom Malchow, United States	1:55.35

200-Meter Individual Medley

1968	Charles Hickcox, United States	2:12.00
1972	Gunnar Larsson, Sweden	2:07.17
1988	Tamas Darnyi, Hungary	2:00.17
1992	Tamas Darnyi, Hungary	2:00.76
1996	Attila Czene, Hungary	1:59.91
2000	Massimiliano Rosolino, Italy	1:58.98

400-Meter Individual Medley

1964	Dick Roth, United States	4:45.40
1968	Charles Hickox, United States	4:48.40
1972	Gunnar Larsson, Sweden	4:31.98

1976 Rod Strachan, United States 4:23.68
1980 Aleksandr Sidorenko, USSR 4:22.80
1984 Alex Baumann, Canada 4:17.41
1988 Tamas Darnyi, Hungary 4:14.75
1992 Tamas Darnyi, Hungary 4:14.23
1996 Tom Dolan, United States 4:14.90
2000 Tom Dolan, United States 4:11.76[1]
1. World record.

400-Meter Freestyle Relay
1964 United States 3:32.20
1968 United States 3:31.70
1972 United States 3:26.42
1988 United States 3:16.52
1992 United States 3:16.74
1996 United States 3:15.41
2000 Australia 3:13.67[1]
1. World record.

800-Meter Freestyle Relay
1908 Great Britain 10:55.60
1912 Australia 10:11.20
1920 United States 10:04.40
1924 United States 09:53.40
1928 United States 09:36.20
1932 Japan 08:58.40
1936 Japan 08:51.50
1948 United States 08:46.10
1952 United States 08:31.10
1956 Australia 08:23.60
1960 United States 08:10.20
1964 United States 07:52.10
1968 United States 07:52.30
1972 United States 07:35.78
1976 United States 07:23.22
1980 USSR 07:23.50
1984 United States 07:16.59
1988 United States 07:12.51
1992 Unified Team[1] 07:11.95
1996 United States 07:14.84
2000 Australia 07:07.05[2]
1. Former Soviet Union team. 2. World record.

400-Meter Medley Relay
1960 United States 4:05.40
1964 United States 3:58.40
1968 United States 3:54.90
1972 United States 3:48.16
1976 United States 3:42.22
1980 Australia 3:45.70
1984 United States 3:39.30
1988 United States 3:36.93
1992 United States 3:36.93
1996 United States 3:34.84
2000 United States 3:33.73[1]
1. World record.

Springboard Dive **Points**
1908 Albert Zuerner, Germany 85.50
1912 Paul Guenther, Germany 79.23
1920 Louis Kuehn, United States 675.00
1924 Albert White, United States 696.40
1928 Pete Desjardins, United States 185.04
1932 Michael Galitzen, United States 161.38
1936 Richard Degener, United States 163.57
1948 Bruce Harlan, United States 163.64
1952 David Browning, United States 205.59
1956 Robert Clotworthy, United States 159.56
1960 Gary Tobian, United States 170.00
1964 Ken Sitzberger, United States 159.90
1968 Bernard Wrightson, United States 170.15
1972 Vladimir Vasin, USSR 594.09
1976 Phil Boggs, United States 619.05
1980 Alexsandr Portnov, USSR 905.02
1984 Greg Louganis, United States 754.41
1988 Greg Louganis, United States 730.80
1992 Mark Lenzi, United States 676.53
1996 Xiong Ni, China 701.46
2000 Xiong Ni, China 708.72

Platform Dive **Points**
1904 G.E. Sheldon, United States 12.75
1906 Gottlob Walz, Germany 156.00
1908 Hialmar Johansson, Sweden 83.75
1912 Erik Adlerz, Sweden 73.94
1920 Clarence Pinkston, United States 100.67
1924 Albert White, United States 487.30
1928 Pete Desjardins, United States 98.74
1932 Harold Smith, United States 124.80
1936 Marshall Wayne, United States 113.58
1948 Samuel Lee, United States 130.05
1952 Samuel Lee, United States 156.28
1956 Joaquin Capilla, Mexico 152.44
1960 Bob Webster, United States 165.56
1964 Bob Webster, United States 148.58
1968 Klaus Dibiasi, Italy 164.18
1972 Klaus Dibiasi, Italy 504.12
1976 Klaus Dibiasi, Italy 600.51
1980 Falk Hoffman, E. Germany 835.65
1984 Greg Louganis, United States 710.91
1988 Greg Louganis, United States 638.61
1992 Sun, Shu-Wei, China 677.31
1996 Dmitri Saoutine, Russia 692.34
2000 Tian Liang, China 724.53

Synchronized 3m Springboard Dive **Points**
2000 Xiao Hailiang and Xiong Ni, China 365.58

Synchronized 10m Platform Dive **Points**
2000 Igor Loukachine and Dmitri Saoutine, Russia 365.04

SWIMMING–WOMEN

50-Meter Freestyle
1988 Kristin Otto, East Germany 25.49
1992 Yang, Wen-Yi, China 24.79
1996 Amy Van Dyken, United States 24.87
2000 Inge de Bruijn, Netherlands 24.32

100-Meter Freestyle
1912 Fanny Durack, Australia 1:22.20
1920 Ethelda Bleibtrey, United States 1:13.60
1924 Ethel Lackie, United States 1:12.40
1928 Albina Osipowich, United States 1:11.00
1932 Helene Madison, United States 1:06.80
1936 Hendrika Mastenbroek, Netherlands 1:05.90
1948 Greta Andersen, Denmark 1:06.30
1952 Katalin Szoke, Hungary 1:06.80
1956 Dawn Fraser, Australia 1:02.00
1960 Dawn Fraser, Australia 1:01.20
1964 Dawn Fraser, Australia 0:59.50
1968 Marge Jan Henne, United States 1:00.00
1972 Sandra Neilson, United States 0:58.59
1976 Kornelia Ender, East Germany 0:55.65
1980 Barbara Krause, East Germany 0:54.79
1984 Carrie Steinseifer, United States 0:55.92
1988 Kristin Otto, East Germany 0:54.93
1992 Zhuang Yong, China 0:54.64
1996 Le Jingyi, China 0:54.50
2000 Inge de Bruijn, Netherlands 0:58.83

200-Meter Freestyle
1968 Debbie Meyer, United States 2:10.50
1972 Shane Gould, Australia 2:03.56
1976 Kornelia Ender, East Germany 1:59.26
1980 Barbara Krause, East Germany 1:58.33
1984 Mary Wayle, United States 1:59.23
1988 Heike Friedrich, East Germany 1:57.65
1992 Nicole Haislett, United States 1:57.90
1996 Claudia Poll, Costa Rica 1:58.16
2000 Susie O'Neill, Australia 1:58.24

400-Meter Freestyle
1920 Ethelda Bleibtrey, United States 4:34.00[1]
1924 Martha Norelius, United States 6:02.20
1928 Martha Norelius, United States 5:42.80

1932	Helene Madison, United States	5:28.50
1936	Hendrika Mastenbroek, Netherlands	5:26.40
1948	Ann Curtis, United States	5:17.80
1952	Valerie Gyenge, Hungary	5:12.10
1956	Lorraine Crapp, Australia	4:54.60
1960	Chris von Saltza, United States	4:50.60
1964	Ginny Duenkel, United States	4:43.30
1968	Debbie Meyer, United States	4:31.80
1972	Shane Gould, Australia	4:19.04
1976	Petra Thumer, East Germany	4:09.89
1980	Ines Diers, East Germany	4:08.76
1984	Tiffany Cohen, United States	4:07.10
1988	Janet Evans, United States	4:03.85
1992	Dagmar Hase, Germany	4:07.18
1996	Michelle Smith, Ireland	4:07.25
2000	Brooke Bennett, United States	4:05.80

1. 300 meters.

800-Meter Freestyle

1968	Debbie Meyer, United States	9:24.00
1972	Keena Rothhammer, United States	8:53.68
1976	Petra Thumer, East Germany	8:37.14
1980	Michelle Ford, Australia	8:28.90
1984	Tiffany Cohen, United States	8:24.95
1988	Janet Evans, United States	8:20.20
1992	Janet Evans, Unites States	8:25.52
1996	Brooke Bennett, Unites States	8:27.89
2000	Brooke Bennett, United States	8:19.67

100-Meter Backstroke

1924	Sybil Bauer, United States	1:23.20
1928	Marie Braun, Netherlands	1:22.00
1932	Eleanor Holm, United States	1:19.40
1936	Dina Senff, Netherlands	1:18.90
1948	Karen Harup, Denmark	1:14.40
1952	Joan Harrison, South Africa	1:14.30
1956	Judy Grinham, Great Britain	1:12.90
1960	Lynn Burke, United States	1:09.30
1964	Cathy Ferguson, United States	1:07.70
1968	Kaye Hall, United States	1:06.20
1972	Melissa Belote, United States	1:05.78
1976	Ulrike Richter, East Germany	1:01.83
1980	Rica Reinisch, East Germany	1:00.86
1984	Theresa Andrews, United States	1:02.55
1988	Kristin Otto, East Germany	1:00.89
1992	Krisztina Egerszegi, Hungary	1:00.68
1996	Beth Botsford, United States	1:01.19
2000	Diana Mocanu, Romania	1:00.21

200-Meter Backstroke

1968	Pokey Watson, United States	2:24.80
1972	Melissa Belote, United States	2:19.19
1976	Ulrike Richter, East Germany	2:13.43
1980	Rica Reinisch, East Germany	2:11.77
1984	Jolanda DeRover, Netherlands	2:12.38
1988	Krisztina Egerszegi, Hungary	2:09.29
1992	Krisztina Egerszegi, Hungary	2:07.06
1996	Krisztina Egerszegi, Hungary	2:07.83
2000	Diana Mocanu, Romania	2:08.16

100-Meter Breaststroke

1968	Djurdjica Bjedov, Yugoslavia	1:15.80
1972	Catherine Carr, United States	1:13.58
1976	Hannelore Anke, East Germany	1:11.16
1980	Ute Geweniger, East Germany	1:10.22
1984	Petra Van Staveren, Netherlands	1:09.88
1988	Tainia Dangalakova, Bulgaria	1:07.95
1992	Elena Roudkovskaia, Unified Team	1:08.00
1996	Penny Heyns, South Africa	1:07.73
2000	Megan Quann, United States	1:07.05

200-Meter Breaststroke

1924	Lucy Morton, Great Britain	3:33.20
1928	Hilde Schrader, Germany	3:12.60
1932	Clare Dennis, Australia	3:06.30
1936	Hideko Maehata, Japan	3:03.60
1948	Nel van Vliet, Netherlands	2:57.20
1952	Eva Szekely, Hungary	2:51.70
1956	Ursala Happe, Germany	2:53.10
1960	Anita Lonsbrough, Great Britain	2:49.50
1964	Galina Prozumenschikova, USSR	2:46.40
1968	Sharon Wichman, United States	2:44.40
1972	Beverly Whitfield, Australia	2:41.71
1976	Marina Koshevaia, USSR	2:33.35
1980	Lina Kachushite, USSR	2:29.54
1984	Anne Ottenbrite, Canada	2:30.38
1988	Silke Hoerner, East Germany	2:26.71
1992	Kyoko Iwasaki, Japan	2:26.65
1996	Penny Heyns, South Africa	2:25.41
2000	Agnes Kovacs, Hungary	2:24.35

100-Meter Butterfly

1956	Shelley Mann, United States	1:11.00
1960	Carolyn Schuler, United States	1:09.50
1964	Sharon Stouder, United States	1:04.70
1968	Lynn McClements, Australia	1:05.50
1972	Mayumi Aoki, Japan	1:03.34
1976	Kornelia Ender, East Germany	1:00.13
1980	Caren Metschuck, East Germany	1:00.42
1984	Mary Meagher, United States	0:59.26
1988	Kristin Otto, East Germany	0:59.00
1992	Qian Hong, China	0:58.62
1996	Amy Van Dyken, United States	0:59.13
2000	Inge de Bruijn, Netherlands	0:56.61[1]

1. World record.

200-Meter Butterfly

1968	Ada Kok, Netherlands	2:24.70
1972	Karen Moe, United States	2:15.57
1976	Andrea Pollack, East Germany	2:11.41
1980	Ines Geissler, East Germany	2:10.44
1984	Mary Meagher, United States	2:06.90
1988	Kathleen Nord, East Germany	2:09.51
1992	Summer Sanders, United States	2:06.67
1996	Susan O'Neill, Australia	2:07.76
2000	Misty Hyman, United States	2:05.88

200-Meter Individual Medley

1968	Claudia Kolb, United States	2:24.70
1972	Shane Gould, Australia	2:23.07
1984	Tracy Caulkins, United States	2:12.64
1988	Daniela Hunger, East Germany	2:12.59
1992	Lin Lee, China	2:11.55[1]
1996	Michelle Smith, Ireland	2:13.93
2000	Yana Klochkova, Ukraine	2:10.68

1. World record.

400-Meter Individual Medley

1964	Donna de Varona, United States	5:18.70
1968	Claudia Kolk, United States	5:08.50
1972	Gail Neall, Australia	5:02.97
1976	Ulrike Tauber, East Germany	4:42.77
1980	Petra Schneider, East Germany	4:36.29
1984	Tracy Caulkins, United States	4:39.21
1988	Janet Evans, United States	4:37.76
1992	Krisztina Egerszegi, Hungary	4:36.54
1996	Michelle Smith, Ireland	4:39.18
2000	Yana Klochkova, Ukraine	4:33.59[1]

1. World record.

400-Meter Freestyle Relay

1912	Great Britain	5:52.80
1920	United States	5:11.60
1924	United States	4:58.80
1928	United States	4:47.60
1932	United States	4:38.00
1936	Netherlands	4:36.00
1948	United States	4:29.20
1952	Hungary	4:24.40
1956	Australia	4:17.10
1960	United States	4:08.90
1964	United States	4:03.80
1968	United States	4:02.50
1972	United States	3:55.19

1976	United States	3:44.82
1980	East Germany	3:42.71
1984	United States	3:44.43
1988	East Germany	3:40.63
1992	United States	3:39.46
1996	United States	3:39.29
2000	United States	3:36.61[1]

1. World record.

800-Meter Freestyle Relay

1996	United States	7:59.87
2000	United States	7:57.80

400-Meter Medley Relay

1960	United States	4:41.10
1964	United States	4:33.90
1968	United States	4:28.30
1972	United States	4:20.75
1976	East Germany	4:07.95
1980	East Germany	4:06.67
1984	United States	4:08.34
1988	East Germany	4:03.74
1992	United States	4:02.54
1996	United States	4:02.88
2000	United States	3:58.30[1]

1. World record.

Springboard Dive		Points
1920	Aileen Riggin, United States	539.90
1924	Elizabeth Becker, United States	474.50
1928	Helen Meany, United States	78.62
1932	Georgia Coleman, United States	87.52
1936	Marjorie Gestring, United States	89.27
1948	Victoria M. Draves, United States	108.74
1952	Patricia McCormick, United States	147.30
1956	Patricia McCormick, United States	142.36
1960	Ingrid Kramer, Germany	155.81
1964	Ingrid Kramer Engel, Germany	145.00
1968	Sue Gossick, United States	150.77
1972	Micki King, United States	450.03
1976	Jennifer Chandler, United States	506.19
1980	Irina Kalinina, USSR	725.91
1984	Sylvie Bernier, Canada	530.70
1988	Gao Min, China	580.23
1992	Gao Min, China	572.40
1996	Fu Ming-Xia, China	547.68
2000	Fu Ming-Xia, China	609.42

Platform Dive		Points
1912	Greta Johansson, Sweden	39.90
1920	Stefani Fryland, Denmark	34.60
1924	Caroline Smith, United States	166.00
1928	Elizabeth B. Pinkston, United States	31.60
1932	Dorothy Poynton, United States	40.26
1936	Dorothy Poynton Hill, United States	33.92
1948	Victoria M. Draves, United States	68.87
1952	Patricia McCormick, United States	79.37
1956	Patricia McCormick, United States	84.85
1960	Ingrid Kramer, Germany	91.28
1964	Lesley Bush, United States	99.80
1968	Milena Duchkova, Czechoslovakia	109.59
1972	Ulrika Knape, Sweden	390.00
1976	Elena Vaytsekhovskaia, USSR	406.59
1980	Martina Jaschke, East Germany	596.25
1984	Zhou Ji-Hong, China	435.51
1988	Xu Yan-Mei, China	445.20
1992	Fu Ming-Xia, China	461.43
1996	Fu Ming-Xia, China	521.58
2000	Laura Wilkinson, United States	543.75

Synchronized 3m Springboard Dive		Points
2000	Vera Ilina and Ioulia Pakhalina, Russia	332.64

Synchronized 10m Platform Dive		Points
2000	Li Na and Sang Xue, China	345.12

BASKETBALL–MEN

1904	United States	1972	USSR
1936	United States	1976	United States
1948	United States	1980	Yugoslavia
1952	United States	1984	United States
1956	United States	1988	USSR
1960	United States	1992	United States
1964	United States	1996	United States
1968	United States	2000	United States

BASKETBALL–WOMEN

1976	USSR	1992	Unified Team[1]
1980	USSR	1996	United States
1984	United States	2000	United States
1988	United States		

1. Former Soviet Union team.

BOXING

(U.S. winners only)

NOTE: U.S. boycotted Olympics in 1980.

Flyweight-112 pounds (51 kg)

1904	George Finnegan	1952	Nate Brooks
1920	Frank De Genaro	1976	Leo Randolph
1924	Fidel La Barba	1984	Steve McCrory

Bantamweight-119 (54 kg)

1904	O.L. Kirk	1988	Kennedy McKinney

Featherweight-126 pounds (57 kg)

1904	O.L. Kirk	1984	Meldrick Taylor
1924	Jackie Fields		

Lightweight-132 pounds (60 kg)

1904	H.J. Spanger	1976	Howard Davis
1920	Samuel Mosberg	1984	Pernell Whitaker
1968	Ronnie Harris	1992	Oscar De La Hoya

Light Welterweight-140 pounds (63.5 kg)

1952	Charles Adkins	1976	Ray Leonard
1972	Ray Seales	1984	Jerry Page

Welterweight-148 pounds (67 kg)

1904	Al Young	1984	Mark Breland
1932	Edward Flynn		

Light Middleweight-157 pounds (71 kg)

1960	Wilbert McClure	1996	David Reid
1984	Frank Tate		

Middleweight-165 pounds (75 kg)

1904	Charles Mayer	1960	Eddie Cook
1932	Carmen Barth	1976	Michael Spinks
1952	Floyd Patterson		

Light Heavyweight-179 pounds (81 kg)

1920	Edward Eagan	1960	Cassius Clay
1952	Norvel Lee	1976	Leon Spinks
1956	James Boyd	1988	Andrew Maynard

Heavyweight-201 pounds (91 kg)

1904	Sam Berger	1968	George Foreman
1952	Edward Sanders	1984	Henry Tilman
1956	Pete Rademacher	1988	Ray Mercer
1964	Joe Frazier		

Super Heavyweight (unlimited)

1984	Tyrell Biggs

DISTRIBUTION OF MEDALS—2000 SUMMER GAMES

Country	Gold	Silver	Bronze	Total
United States	39	25	33	97
Russia	32	28	28	88
China	28	16	15	59
Australia	16	25	17	58
Germany	14	17	26	57
France	13	14	11	38
Italy	13	8	13	34
Cuba	11	11	7	29
Great Britain	11	10	7	28
Korea	8	9	11	28
Romania	11	6	9	26
Netherlands	12	9	4	25
Ukraine	3	10	10	23
Japan	5	8	5	18
Hungary	8	6	3	17
Belarus	3	3	11	17
Poland	6	5	3	14
Canada	3	3	8	14
Bulgaria	5	6	2	13
Greece	4	6	3	13
Sweden	4	5	3	12
Brazil	0	6	6	12
Spain	3	3	5	11
Norway	4	3	3	10
Switzerland	1	6	2	9
Ethiopia	4	1	3	8
Czech Republic	2	3	3	8
Kazakhstan	3	4	0	7
Kenya	2	3	2	7
Jamaica	0	4	3	7
Denmark	2	3	1	6
Indonesia	1	3	2	6
Mexico	1	2	3	6
Georgia	0	0	6	6
Lithuania	2	0	3	5
Slovakia	1	3	1	5
Algeria	1	1	3	5
Belgium	0	2	3	5
South Africa	0	2	3	5
Morocco	0	1	4	5
Chinese Taipei	0	1	4	5
Iran	3	0	1	4
Turkey	3	0	1	4
Finland	2	1	1	4
Uzbekistan	1	1	2	4
New Zealand	1	0	3	4
Argentina	0	2	2	4
Korea	0	1	3	4
Austria	2	1	0	3
Azerbaijan	2	0	1	3
Latvia	1	1	1	3
Yugoslavia	1	1	1	3
Estonia	1	0	2	3
Thailand	1	0	2	3
Nigeria	0	3	0	3
Slovenia	2	0	0	2
Bahamas	1	1	0	2
Croatia	1	0	1	2
Saudi Arabia	0	1	1	2
Moldova	0	1	1	2
Trinidad & Tobago	0	1	1	2
Costa Rica	0	0	2	2
Portugal	0	0	2	2
Cameroon	1	0	0	1
Colombia	1	0	0	1
Mozambique	1	0	0	1
Ireland	0	1	0	1
Uruguay	0	1	0	1
Vietnam	0	1	0	1
Armenia	0	0	1	1
Barbados	0	0	1	1
Chile	0	0	1	1
India	0	0	1	1
Iceland	0	0	1	1
Israel	0	0	1	1
Kyrgyzstan	0	0	1	1
Kuwait	0	0	1	1
Macedonia	0	0	1	1
Qatar	0	0	1	1
Sri Lanka	0	0	1	1
Total	**301**	**299**	**328**	**928**

Other 2000 Summer Olympic Games Champions

Archery

Women's individual—Yun Mi-jin, South Korea
Women's team—South Korea
Men's individual—Simon Fairweather, Australia
Men's team—South Korea

Badminton

Men's singles—Ji Xinpeng, China
Men's doubles—Indonesia (Tony Gunawan, Candra Wijaya)
Women's singles—Gong Zhichao, China
Women's doubles—China (Ge Fei, Gu Jun)
Mixed doubles—China (Jun Zhang, Ling Gao)

Baseball

Men—United States

Beach Volleyball

Women—Australia (Natalie Cook, Kerri Pottharst)
Men—United States (Dain Blanton, Eric Fonoimoana)

Boxing

Light flyweight—Brahim Asloum, France
Flyweight—Wijan Ponlid, Thailand
Bantamweight—Guillermo Rigondeaux, Cuba
Featherweight—Bekzat Sattarkhanov, Kazakhstan
Lightweight—Mario Kindelan, Cuba
Light welterweight—Mahamadkadyz Abdullaev, Uzbekistan
Welterweight—Oleg Saitov, Russia
Light middleweight—Yermakhan Ibraimov, Kazakhstan
Middleweight—Jorge Gutierrez, Cuba
Light heavyweight—Alexander Lebziak, Russia
Heavyweight—Felix Savon, Cuba
Super heavyweight—Audley Harrison, Great Britain

Cycling—Men

1 km time trial (track)—Jason Queally, Great Britain
Individual pursuit (track)—Robert Bartko, Germany
Team pursuit (track)—Germany
Individual points race (track)—Juan Llaneras, Spain
Individual sprint (track)—Marty Nothstein, United States
Olympic sprint (track)—France
Madison (track)—Australia
Keirin (track)—Florian Rousseau, France
Mountain bike—Miguel Martinez, France
Individual road race—Jan Ullrich, Germany
Individual time trial (road)—Viacheslav Ekimov, Russia

Cycling—Women

500m time trial (track)—Felicia Ballanger, France
Individual pursuit (track)—Leontien Zijlaard, Netherlands
Sprint (track)—Felicia Ballanger, France
Points race (track)—Antonella Bellutti, Italy

Mountain bike—Paola Pezzo, Italy
Road race—Leontien Zijlaard, Netherlands
Individual time trial (road)—Leontien Zijlaard, Netherlands

Equestrian
Individual three-day—David O'Connor, United States
Three-day team event—Australia
Individual dressage—Anky van Grunsven, Netherlands
Team dressage—Germany
Individual jumping—Jeroen Dubbeldam, Netherlands
Team jumping—Germany

Fencing—Men
Individual epee—Pavel Kolobkov, Russia
Individual foil—Kim Young-ho, South Korea
Individual sabre—Mihai Claudiu Covaliu, Romania
Team epee—Italy
Team foil—France
Team sabre—Russia

Fencing—Women
Individual epee—Timea Nagy, Hungary
Individual foil—Valentina Vezzali, Italy
Team epee—Russia
Team foil—Italy

Field Hockey
Men—Netherlands
Women—Australia

Gymnastics—Men
All-around—Alexei Nemov, Russia
Floor exercise—Igors Vihrovs, Latvia
Pommel horse—Marius Urzica, Romania
Rings—Szilveszter Csollany, Hungary
Horizontal bar—Alexei Nemov, Russia
Parallel bars—Li Xiaopeng, China
Vault—Gervasio Deferr, Spain
Team—China

Gymnastics—Women
All-around—Simona Amanar, Romania
Uneven bars—Svetlana Khorkina, Russia
Balance beam—Liu Xuan, China
Floor exercise—Elena Zamolodtchikova, Russia
Vault—Elena Zamolodtchikova, Russia
Team—Romania

Judo—Men
Extra-lightweight (60kg)—Tadahiro Nomura, Japan
Half-lightweight (66kg)—Huseyin Ozkan, Turkey
Lightweight (73kg)—Giuseppe Maddaloni, Italy
Half-middleweight (81kg)—Makoto Takimoto, Japan
Middleweight (90kg)—Mark Huizinga, Netherlands
Half-heavyweight (100kg)—Kosei Inoue, Japan
Heavyweight (100kg+)—David Douillet, France

Judo—Women
Extra-lightweight (48kg)—Ryoko Tamura, Japan
Half-lightweight (52kg)—Legna Verdecia, Cuba
Lightweight (57kg)—Isabel Fernandez, Spain
Half-middleweight (63kg)—Severine Vandenhende, France
Middleweight (70kg)—Sibelis Veranes, Cuba
Half-heavyweight (78kg)—Tang Lin, China
Heavyweight (78kg+)—Yuar lua, China

Kayak-Canoe—Men
Canoe singles 500m—Gyorgy Kolonics, Hungary
Canoe pairs 500m—Hungary
Kayak singles 500m—Knut Holmann, Norway
Kayak pairs 500m—Hungary
Kayak singles 1,000m—Knut Holmann, Norway
Canoe singles 1,000m—Andreas Dittmer, Germany
Kayak pairs 1,000m—Italy
Canoe pairs 1,000m—Romania
Kayak fours 1,000m—Hungary
Canoe slalom singles—Tony Estanguet, France
Canoe slalom pairs—Slovakia
Kayak slalom singles—Thomas Schmidt, Germany

Kayak—Women
500m singles—Josefa Idem Guerrini, Italy
500m pairs—Germany
500m fours—Germany
Single slalom—Stepanka Hilgertova, Czech Republic

Modern Pentathlon
Men—Dmitri Svatkovsky, Russia
Women—Stephanie Cook, Great Britain

Rhythmic Gymnastics
Individual—Yulia Barslukova, Russia
Team—Russia

Rowing—Men
Single sculls—Rob Waddell, New Zealand
Lightweight double sculls—Poland
Heavyweight double sculls—Slovenia
Quadruple sculls—Italy
Coxless pair—France
Lightweight coxless four—France
Heavyweight coxless four—Great Britain
Eight—Great Britain

Rowing—Women
Single sculls—Ekaterina Karsten, Belarus
Lightweight double sculls—Romania
Heavyweight double sculls—Germany
Quadruple sculls—Germany
Coxless pair—Romania
Eight—Romania

Sailing
Open Tornado—Austria
Open 49er—Finland
Open Laser—Ben Ainslie, Great Britain
Open Star—United States
Open Soling—Denmark
Men's Mistral—Christoph Sieber, Austria
Men's 470 fleet—Australia
Men's Finn—Iain Percy, Great Britain
Women's Mistral—Alessandra Sensini, Italy
Women's 470 fleet—Australia
Women's Europe—Shirley Robertson, Great Britain

Shooting—Men
Air pistol—Franck Dumoulin, France
Free pistol—Tanyu Kiriakov, Bulgaria
Rapid fire pistol—Serguei Alifirenko, Russia
Trap—Michael Diamond, Australia
Double trap—Richard Faulds, Great Britain
Air rifle—Cai Yalin, China
Running target—Yang Ling, China
Rifle prone—Jonas Edman, Sweden
Rifle 3-position—Rajmond Debevec, Slovenia
Skeet shooting—Mykola Milchev, Ukraine

Shooting—Women
Air pistol—Tao Luna, China
Sport pistol—Maria Grozdeva, Bulgaria
Air rifle—Nancy Johnson, United States
Rifle three position—Renata Maier-Rozanska, Poland
Trap—Daina Gudzineviciute, Lithuania
Double trap—Pia Hansen, Sweden
Skeet—Zemfira Meftakhetdinova, Azerbaijan

Soccer
Men—Cameroon
Women—Norway

Softball
United States

Synchronized Swimming
Duet—Russia
Team—Russia

Table Tennis
Men's singles—Kong Linghui, China
Men's doubles—China
Women's singles—Wang Nan, China
Women's doubles—China

Taekwondo
Men 58kg—Michail Mouroutsos, Greece
Men 68kg—Steven Lopez, United States
Men 80kg—Angel Matos Fuentes, Cuba
Men 80kg+—Kim Kyong-hun, South Korea
Women 49kg—Lauren Burns, Australia
Women 57kg—Jung Jae-eun, South Korea
Women 67kg—Lee Sun-Hee, South Korea
Women 67kg+—Chen Zhong, China

Team Handball
Men—Russia
Women—Denmark

Tennis
Men's singles—Yevgeny Kafelnikov, Russia
Men's doubles—Canada
Women's singles—Venus Williams, United States
Women's doubles—United States

Trampoline
Men—Alexandre Moskalenko, Russia
Women—Irina Karavaeva, Russia

Triathlon
Men—Simon Whitfield, Canada
Women—Brigitte McMahon, Switzerland

Volleyball
Men—Yugoslavia
Women—Cuba

Water Polo
Men—Hungary
Women—Australia

Weightlifting—Men
56kg—Halil Mutlu, Turkey
62kg—Nikolay Pechalov, Croatia
69kg—Galabin Boevski, Bulgaria
77kg—Zhan Xugang, China
85kg—Pyrros Dimas, Greece
94kg—Akakios Kakiasvilis, Greece
105kg—Hossein Tavakoli, Iran
105kg+—Hossein Rezazadeh, Iran

Weightlifting—Women
48kg—Tara Nott, United States
53kg—Yang Xia, China
58kg—Soraya Jimenez, Mexico
63kg—Xiaomin Chen, China
69kg—Lin Weining, China
75kg—Maria Urrutia, Colombia
75kg+—Ding Meiyuan, China

Wrestling—Freestyle
54kg—Namig Abdullayev, Azerbaijan
63kg—Mourad Oumakhanov, Russia
58kg—Alireza Dabir, Iran
69kg—Daniel Igali, Canada
76kg—Alexander Leipold, Germany
85kg—Adam Saitiev, Russia
97kg—Saghid Mourtasaliyev, Russia
130kg—David Moussoulbes, Russia

Wrestling—Greco-Roman
54kg—Sim Kwon Ho, South Korea
58kg—Armen Nazarian, Bulgaria
63kg—Varteres Samourgachev, Russia
69kg—Filiberto Azcuy, Cuba
76kg—Mourat Kardanov, Russia
85kg—Hamza Yerlikaya, Turkey
97kg—Mikael Ljungberg, Sweden
130kg—Rulon Gardner, United States

Football

The pastime of kicking around a ball goes back beyond the limits of recorded history. Ancient savage tribes played football of a primitive kind. There was a ball-kicking game played by Athenians, Spartans, and Corinthians 2,500 years ago, which the Greeks called *Episkuros*. The Romans had a somewhat similar game called *Harpastum* and are supposed to have carried the game with them when they invaded the British Isles in the first century B.C.

Undoubtedly the game known in the United States as football traces directly to the English game of rugby, though the modifications have been many. Informal football was played on college lawns well over a century ago, and an annual freshman-sophomore series of "scrimmages" began at Yale in 1840. The first formal intercollegiate football game was the Princeton-Rutgers contest at New Brunswick, N.J., on Nov. 6, 1869, with Rutgers winning by 6 goals to 4.

In those days, games were played with 25, 20, 15, or 11 men on a side. In 1880, there was a convention at which Walter Camp of Yale persuaded the delegates to agree to 11 players on a side.

The first professional game was played in 1895 at Latrobe, Pa. The National Football League was founded in 1921. The All-American Conference went into action in 1946. At the end of the 1949 season the two circuits merged, retaining the name of the older league. In 1960, the American Football League began operations. In 1970, the leagues merged. The United States Football League played its first season in 1983, from March to July. It suspended spring operations after the 1985 season, and planned a 1986 move to fall, but suspended operations again.

In March 1991, another effort at spring football was launched. This time the ten-team World League of American Football had the backing of the National Football League. After two seasons it was suspended. The league returned in 1995, with six teams in Europe. In 1998, it was renamed the NFL Europe League.

In 2002 the NFL divisions were realigned. National and American Conferences were split into four divisions with four teams per division. Scheduling has also been changed and every team will meet every other team at least once every four years.

College Football

NATIONAL COLLEGE FOOTBALL CHAMPIONS

The "National Collegiate Athletic Association Football Guide" recognizes as unofficial national champion the team selected each year by press association polls of writers and coaches.

1936 Minnesota
1937 Pittsburgh
1938 Texas Christian
1939 Texas A & M
1940 Minnesota
1941 Minnesota
1942 Ohio State
1943 Notre Dame
1944 Army
1945 Army
1946 Notre Dame
1947 Notre Dame
1948 Michigan
1949 Notre Dame
1950 Oklahoma
1951 Tennessee
1952 Mich. State
1953 Maryland
1954 Ohio State and UCLA
1955 Oklahoma
1956 Oklahoma
1957 Auburn and Ohio State
1958 Louisiana State
1959 Syracuse
1960 Minnesota
1961 Alabama
1962 So. Calif.
1963 Texas
1964 Alabama
1965 Alabama and Mich. State
1966 Notre Dame
1967 So. Calif.
1968 Ohio State
1969 Texas
1970 Texas and Nebraska
1971 Nebraska
1972 So. Calif.
1973 Notre Dame and U. of Ala.
1974 Oklahoma and So. Calif.
1975 Oklahoma
1976 Pittsburgh
1977 Notre Dame
1978 Alabama and So. Calif.
1979 Alabama
1980 Georgia
1981 Clemson
1982 Penn State
1983 Miami (Fla.)
1984 Brigham Young
1985 Oklahoma
1986 Penn State
1987 Miami (Fla.)
1988 Notre Dame
1989 Miami (Fla.)
1990 Colorado and Georgia Tech
1991 Miami (Fla.) and Washington
1992 Alabama
1993 Florida State
1994 Nebraska
1995 Nebraska
1996 Univ. of Florida
1997 Michigan and Nebraska
1998 Tennessee
1999 Florida State
2000 Oklahoma
2001 Miami (Fla.)
2002 Ohio State

RECORD OF ANNUAL MAJOR COLLEGE FOOTBALL BOWL GAMES

Rose Bowl (At Pasadena, Calif.)

1902 Michigan 49, Stanford 0
1916 Washington State 14, Brown 0
1917 Oregon 14, Pennsylvania 0
1918 Mare Island Marines 19, Camp Lewis 7
1919 Great Lakes 17, Mare Island Marines 0
1920 Harvard 7, Oregon 6
1921 California 28, Ohio State 0
1922 Washington and Jefferson 0, California 0
1923 So. Calif. 14, Penn State 3
1924 Navy 14, Washington 14
1925 Notre Dame 27, Stanford 10
1926 Alabama 20, Washington 19
1927 Alabama 7, Stanford 7
1928 Stanford 7, Pittsburgh 6
1929 Georgia Tech 8, California 7
1930 So. Calif. 47, Pittsburgh 14
1931 Alabama 24, Wash. State 0
1932 So. Calif. 21, Tulane 12
1933 So. Calif. 35, Pittsburgh 0
1934 Columbia 7, Stanford 0
1935 Alabama 29, Stanford 13
1936 Stanford 7, So. Methodist 0
1937 Pittsburgh 21, Washington 0
1938 California 13, Alabama 0
1939 So. Calif. 7, Duke 3
1940 So. Calif. 14, Tennessee 0
1941 Stanford 21, Nebraska 13
1942 Oregon State 20, Duke 16[1]
1943 Georgia 9, UCLA 0
1944 So. Calif. 29, Washington 0
1945 So. Calif. 25, Tennessee 0
1946 Alabama 34, So. Calif. 14
1947 Illinois 45, UCLA 14
1948 Michigan 49, So. Calif. 0
1949 Northwestern 20, California 14
1950 Ohio State 17, California 14
1951 Michigan 14, California 6
1952 Illinois 40, Stanford 7
1953 So. Calif. 7, Wisconsin 0
1954 Michigan State 28, UCLA 20
1955 Ohio State 20, So. Calif. 7
1956 Michigan State 17, UCLA 14
1957 Iowa 35, Oregon State 19
1958 Ohio State 10, Oregon 7
1959 Iowa 38, California 12
1960 Washington 44, Wisconsin 8
1961 Washington 17, Minnesota 7
1962 Minnesota 21, UCLA 3
1963 So. Calif. 42, Wisconsin 37
1964 Illinois 17, Washington 7
1965 Michigan 34, Oregon State 7
1966 UCLA 14, Michigan State 12
1967 Purdue 14, So. Calif. 13
1968 So. Calif. 14, Indiana 3
1969 Ohio State 27, So. Calif. 16
1970 So. Calif. 10, Michigan 3
1971 Stanford 27, Ohio State 17
1972 Stanford 13, Michigan 12
1973 So. Calif. 42, Ohio State 17
1974 Ohio State 42, So. Calif. 21
1975 So. Calif. 18, Ohio State 17
1976 UCLA 23, Ohio State 10
1977 So. Calif. 14, Michigan 6
1978 Washington 27, Michigan 20
1979 So. Calif. 17, Michigan 10
1980 So. Calif. 17, Ohio State 16
1981 Michigan 23, Washington 6
1982 Washington 28, Iowa 0
1983 UCLA 24, Michigan 14
1984 UCLA 45, Illinois 9
1985 So. Calif. 20, Ohio St. 17
1986 UCLA 45, Iowa 28
1987 Arizona State 22, Michigan 15
1988 Michigan State 20, So. Calif. 17
1989 Michigan 22, So. Calif. 14
1990 So. Calif. 17, Michigan 10
1991 Washington 46, Iowa 34
1992 Washington 34, Michigan 14
1993 Michigan 38, Washington 31
1994 Wisconsin 21, UCLA 16
1995 Penn State 38, Oregon 20
1996 So. Calif. 41, Northwestern 32
1997 Ohio State 20, Arizona State 17
1998 Michigan 21, Washington State 16
1999 Wisconsin 38, UCLA 31
2000 Wisconsin 17, Stanford 9
2001 Washington 34, Purdue 24
2002 Miami 37, Nebraska 14
2003 Oklahoma 34, Washington State 14

1. Played at Durham, N.C.

Orange Bowl (At Miami)

1933 Miami (Fla.) 7, Manhattan 0
1934 Duquesne 33, Miami (Fla.) 7
1935 Bucknell 26, Miami (Fla.) 0
1936 Catholic 20, Mississippi 19
1937 Duquesne 13, Mississippi State 12
1938 Auburn 6, Michigan State 0
1939 Tennessee 17, Oklahoma 0
1940 Georgia Tech 21, Missouri 7
1941 Mississippi State 14, Georgetown 7
1942 Georgia 40, Texas Christian 26
1943 Alabama 37, Boston College 21
1944 Louisiana State 19, Texas A & M 14
1945 Tulsa 26, Georgia Tech 12
1946 Miami (Fla.) 13, Holy Cross 6
1947 Rice 8, Tennessee 0
1948 Georgia Tech 20, Kansas 14
1949 Texas 41, Georgia 28
1950 Santa Clara 21, Kentucky 13
1951 Clemson 15, Miami (Fla.) 14
1952 Georgia Tech 17, Baylor 14
1953 Alabama 61, Syracuse 6
1954 Oklahoma 7, Maryland 0
1955 Duke 34, Nebraska 7
1956 Oklahoma 20, Maryland 6
1957 Colorado 27, Clemson 21
1958 Oklahoma 48, Duke 21
1959 Oklahoma 21, Syracuse 6
1960 Georgia 14, Missouri 0
1961 Missouri 21, Navy 14
1962 Louisiana State 25, Colorado 7
1963 Alabama 17, Oklahoma 0
1964 Nebraska 13, Auburn 7
1965 Texas 21, Alabama 17
1966 Alabama 39, Nebraska 28
1967 Florida 27, Georgia Tech 12
1968 Oklahoma 26, Tennessee 24
1969 Penn State 15, Kansas 14
1970 Penn State 10, Missouri 3
1971 Nebraska 17, Louisiana State 12
1972 Nebraska 38, Alabama 6
1973 Nebraska 40, Notre Dame 6
1974 Penn State 16, Louisiana State 9
1975 Notre Dame 13, Alabama 11
1976 Oklahoma 14, Michigan 6
1977 Ohio State 27, Colorado 10
1978 Arkansas 31, Oklahoma 6
1979 Oklahoma 31, Nebraska 24
1980 Oklahoma 24, Florida State 7
1981 Oklahoma 18, Florida State 17
1982 Clemson 22, Nebraska 15
1983 Nebraska 21, Louisiana State 20
1984 Miami (Fla.) 31, Nebraska 30
1985 Washington 28, Oklahoma 17
1986 Oklahoma 25, Penn State 10
1987 Oklahoma 42, Arkansas 8
1988 Miami (Fla.) 20, Oklahoma 14
1989 Miami (Fla.) 23, Nebraska 3
1990 Notre Dame 21, Colorado 6
1991 Colorado 10, Notre Dame 9
1992 Miami (Fla.) 22, Nebraska 0
1993 Florida State 27, Nebraska 14
1994 Florida State 18, Nebraska 16
1995 Nebraska 24, Miami (Fla.) 17
1996 Florida State 31, Notre Dame 26
1997 Nebraska 41, Virginia Tech 21
1998 Nebraska 42, Tennessee 17
1999 Florida 31, Syracuse 10
2000 Michigan 35, Alabama 34
2001 Oklahoma 13, Florida State 2
2002 Florida 56, Maryland 23
2003 So. Calif. 38, Iowa 17

Sugar Bowl (At New Orleans)

1935 Tulane 20, Temple 14
1936 Texas Christian 3, Louisiana State 2
1937 Santa Clara 21, Louisiana State 14
1938 Santa Clara 6, Louisiana State 0
1939 Texas Christian 15, Carnegie Tech 7
1940 Texas A & M 14, Tulane 13
1941 Boston College 19, Tennessee 13
1942 Fordham 2, Missouri 0
1943 Tennessee 14, Tulsa 7
1944 Georgia Tech 20, Tulsa 18
1945 Duke 29, Alabama 26
1946 Oklahoma A & M 33, St. Mary's (Calif.) 13
1947 Georgia 20, North Carolina 10
1948 Texas 27, Alabama 7
1949 Oklahoma 14, North Carolina 6
1950 Oklahoma 35, Louisiana State 0
1951 Kentucky 13, Oklahoma 7
1952 Maryland 28, Tennessee 13
1953 Georgia Tech 24, Mississippi 7
1954 Georgia Tech 42, West Virginia 19
1955 Navy 21, Mississippi 0

1956 Georgia Tech 7, Pittsburgh 0
1957 Baylor 13, Tennessee 7
1958 Mississippi 39, Texas 7
1959 Louisiana State 7, Clemson 0
1960 Mississippi 21, Louisiana State 0
1961 Mississippi 14, Rice 6
1962 Alabama 10, Arkansas 3
1963 Mississippi 17, Arkansas 13
1964 Alabama 12, Mississippi 7
1965 Louisiana State 13, Syracuse 10
1966 Missouri 20, Florida 18
1967 Alabama 34, Nebraska 7
1968 Louisiana State 20, Wyoming 13
1969 Arkansas 16, Georgia 2
1970 Mississippi 27, Arkansas 22
1971 Tennessee 34, Air Force Academy 13
1972 Oklahoma 40, Auburn 22
1973 Oklahoma 14, Penn State 0
1974 Notre Dame 24, Alabama 23
1975 Nebraska 13, Florida 10
1976 Alabama 13, Penn State 6
1977 Pittsburgh 27, Georgia 3
1978 Alabama 35, Ohio State 6
1979 Alabama 14, Penn State 7
1980 Alabama 24, Arkansas 9
1981 Georgia 17, Notre Dame 10
1982 Pittsburgh 24, Georgia 20
1983 Penn State 27, Georgia 23
1984 Auburn 9, Michigan 7
1985 Nebraska 28, Louisiana State 10
1986 Tennessee 35, Miami (Fla.) 7
1987 Nebraska 30, Louisiana State 15
1988 Syracuse 16, Auburn 16 (tie)
1989 Florida State 13, Auburn 7
1990 Miami (Fla.) 33, Alabama 25
1991 Tennessee 23, Virginia 22
1992 Notre Dame 39, Florida 28
1993 Alabama 34, Miami (Fla.) 13
1994 Florida 41, West Virginia 7
1995 Florida State 23, Florida 17
1996 Virginia Tech 28, Texas 10
1997 Florida 52, Florida State 20
1998 Florida State 31, Ohio State 14
1999 Ohio State 24, Texas A & M 14
2000 Florida State 46, Virginia Tech. 29
2001 Miami (Fla.) 37, Florida 20
2002 Louisiana State 47, Illinois 34
2003 Georgia 26, Florida State 13

Cotton Bowl (At Dallas)

1937 Texas Christian 16, Marquette 6
1938 Rice 28, Colorado 14
1939 St. Mary's (Calif.) 20, Texas Tech. 13
1940 Clemson 6, Boston College 3
1941 Texas A & M 13, Fordham 12
1942 Alabama 29, Texas A & M 21
1943 Texas 14, Georgia Tech 7
1944 Randolph Field 7, Texas 7
1945 Oklahoma A & M 34, Texas Christian 0
1946 Texas 40, Missouri 27
1947 Louisiana State 0, Arkansas 0
1948 So. Methodist 13, Penn State 13
1949 So. Methodist 21, Oregon 13
1950 Rice 27, North Carolina 13
1951 Tennessee 20, Texas 14
1952 Kentucky 20, Texas Christian 7
1953 Texas 16, Tennessee 0
1954 Rice 28, Alabama 6
1955 Georgia Tech 14, Arkansas 6
1956 Mississippi 14, Texas Christian 13
1957 Texas Christian 28, Syracuse 27
1958 Navy 20, Rice 7
1959 Air Force 0, Texas Christian 0
1960 Syracuse 23, Texas 14
1961 Duke 7, Arkansas 6
1962 Texas 12, Mississippi 7
1963 Louisiana State 13, Texas 0
1964 Texas 28, Navy 6
1965 Arkansas 10, Nebraska 7
1966 Louisiana State 14, Arkansas 7
1967 Georgia 24, So. Methodist 9
1968 Texas A & M 20, Alabama 16
1969 Texas 36, Tennessee 13
1970 Texas 21, Notre Dame 17
1971 Notre Dame 24, Texas 11
1972 Penn State 30, Texas 6
1973 Texas 17, Alabama 13
1974 Nebraska 19, Texas 3
1975 Penn State 41, Baylor 20
1976 Arkansas 31, Georgia 10
1977 Houston 30, Maryland 21
1978 Notre Dame 38, Texas 10
1979 Notre Dame 35, Houston 34
1980 Houston 17, Nebraska 14
1981 Alabama 30, Baylor 2
1982 Texas 14, Alabama 12
1983 So. Meth. 7, Pittsburgh 3
1984 Georgia 10, Texas 9
1985 Boston College 45, Houston 28
1986 Texas A & M 36, Auburn 16
1987 Ohio State 28, Texas A & M 12
1988 Texas A & M 35, Notre Dame 10
1989 UCLA 17, Arkansas 3
1990 Tennessee 31, Arkansas 27
1991 Miami (Fla.) 46, Texas 3
1992 Florida State 10, Texas A & M 2
1993 Notre Dame 28, Texas A & M 3
1994 Notre Dame 24, Texas A & M 21
1995 So. Calif. 55, Texas Tech 14
1996 Colorado 38, Oregon 6
1997 Brigham Young 19, Kansas State 15
1998 UCLA 29, Texas A & M 23
1999 Texas 38, Mississippi State 11
2000 Arkansas 27, Texas 6
2001 Kansas State 35, Tennessee 21
2002 Oklahoma 10, Arkansas 3
2003 Texas 35, Louisiana State 20

Gator Bowl (At Jacksonville, Fla.)

1953 Florida 14, Tulsa 13
1954 Texas Tech 35, Auburn 13
1955 Auburn 33, Baylor 13
1956 Vanderbilt 25, Auburn 13
1957 Georgia Tech 21, Pittsburgh 14
1958 Tennessee 3, Texas A & M 0
1959 Mississippi 7, Florida 3
1960 Arkansas 14, Georgia Tech 7
1961 Florida 13, Baylor 12
1962 Penn State 30, Georgia Tech 15
1963 Florida 17, Penn State 7
1964 No. Carolina 35, Air Force 0
1965 Florida State 36, Oklahoma 19
1966 Georgia Tech 31, Texas Tech 21
1967 Tennessee 18, Syracuse 12
1968 Penn State 17, Florida State 17 (tie)
1969 Missouri 35, Alabama 10
1970 Florida 14, Tennessee 13
1971 Auburn 35, Mississippi 28
1972 Georgia 7, North Carolina 3
1973 Auburn 24, Colorado 3
1974 Texas Tech 28, Tennessee 19
1975 Auburn 27, Texas 3
1976 Maryland 13, Florida 0
1977 Notre Dame 20, Penn State 9
1978 Pittsburgh 34, Clemson 3
1979 Clemson 17, Ohio State 15
1980 North Carolina 17, Michigan 15
1981 Pittsburgh 37, South Carolina 9
1982 North Carolina 31, Arkansas 27
1983 Florida State 31, West Virginia 12
1984 Florida 14, Iowa 6
1985 Oklahoma State 21, South Carolina 14
1986 Florida State 34, Oklahoma State 23
1987 Clemson 27, Stanford 21
1988 Louisiana State 30, South Carolina 13
1989 Georgia 34, Mich. State 27
1990 Clemson 27, West Virginia 7
1991 Michigan 35, Mississippi 3
1992 Oklahoma 38, Virginia 14
1993 Florida 27, No. Carolina St. 10
1994 Alabama 24, No. Carolina 10
1995 Tennessee 45, Virginia Tech 23
1996 Syracuse 41, Clemson 0
1997 North Carolina 20, West Virginia 13
1998 North Carolina 42, Virginia Tech 3
1999 Georgia Tech 35, Notre Dame 28
2000 Miami (Fla.) 28, Georgia Tech 13
2001 Virginia Tech 41, Clemson 20
2002 Florida State 30, Virginia Tech 17
2003 North Carolina State 28, Notre Dame 6

RESULTS OF OTHER 2002–2003 BOWL GAMES

Tostitos Fiesta Bowl—Ohio State 31, Miami 24
New Orleans Bowl—North Texas 24, Cincinnati 19
Mazda Tangerine Bowl—Texas Tech 55, Clemson 15
Conagra Foods Hawaii Bowl—Tulane 36, Hawaii 28
Insight Bowl—Pittsburgh 38, Oregon State 13
Mainstay Independence Bowl—Mississippi 27, Nebraska 23
Continental Tire Bowl—Virginia 48, West Virginia 22
Gaylord Hotels Music City Bowl—Minnesota 29, Arkansas 14
Crucial.com Humanitarian Bowl—Boise State 34, Iowa State 16
Axa Liberty Bowl—Texas Christian 17, Colorado State 3
Chick-Fil-A Peach Bowl—Maryland 30, Tennessee 3
Outback Bowl—Michigan 38, Florida 30
GMAC Bowl—Marshall 38, Louisville 15
Las Vegas Bowl—UCLA 27, New Mexico 13
Motor City Bowl—Boston College 51, Toledo 25
Houston Bowl—Oklahoma State 33, Southern Miss 23
Pacific Life Holiday Bowl—Kansas State 34, Arizona State 27
Alamo Bowl—Wisconsin 31, Colorado 28
Seattle Bowl—Wake Forest 38. Oregon 17
Wells Fargo Sun Bowl—Purdue 34, Washington 24
Silicon Valley Football Classic—Fresno State 30, Georgia Tech 21
Diamond Walnut San Francisco Bowl—Virginia Tech 20, Air Force 13
Capital One Bowl—Auburn 13, Penn State 9

HEISMAN MEMORIAL TROPHY WINNERS

The Heisman Memorial Trophy is presented annually by the Downtown Athletic Club of New York City to the nation's outstanding college football player, as determined by a poll of sportswriters and sportscasters.

1935 Jay Berwanger, Chicago
1936 Larry Kelley, Yale
1937 Clinton Frank, Yale
1938 Davey O'Brien, Texas Christian
1939 Nile Kinnick, Iowa
1940 Tom Harmon, Michigan
1941 Bruce Smith, Minnesota
1942 Frank Sinkwich, Georgia
1943 Angelo Bertelli, Notre Dame
1944 Leslie Horvath, Ohio State
1945 Felix Blanchard, Army
1946 Glenn Davis, Army
1947 Johnny Lujack, Notre Dame
1948 Doak Walker, So. Methodist
1949 Leon Hart, Notre Dame
1950 Vic Janowicz, Ohio State
1951 Dick Kazmaier, Princeton
1952 Billy Vessels, Oklahoma
1953 Johnny Lattner, Notre Dame
1954 Alan Ameche, Wisconsin
1955 Howard Cassady, Ohio State
1956 Paul Hornung, Notre Dame
1957 John Crow, Texas A & M
1958 Pete Dawkins, Army
1959 Billy Cannon, Louisiana State
1960 Joe Bellino, Navy
1961 Ernie Davis, Syracuse
1962 Terry Baker, Oregon State
1963 Roger Staubach, Navy
1964 John Huarte, Notre Dame
1965 Mike Garrett, So. Calif.
1966 Steve Spurrier, Florida
1967 Gary Beban, UCLA
1968 O. J. Simpson, So. Calif.
1969 Steve Owens, Oklahoma
1970 Jim Plunkett, Stanford
1971 Pat Sullivan, Auburn
1972 Johnny Rodgers, Nebraska
1973 John Cappelletti, Penn State
1974-75 Archie Griffin, Ohio State
1976 Tony Dorsett, Pittsburgh
1977 Earl Campbell, Texas
1978 Billy Sims, Oklahoma
1979 Charles White, So. Calif.
1980 George Rogers, South Carolina
1981 Marcus Allen, So. Calif.
1982 Herschel Walker, Georgia
1983 Mike Rozier, Nebraska
1984 Doug Flutie, Boston College
1985 Bo Jackson, Auburn
1986 Vinny Testaverde, Miami
1987 Tim Brown, Notre Dame
1988 Barry Sanders, Oklahoma State
1989 Andre Ware, Houston
1990 Ty Detmer, Brigham Young
1991 Desmond Howard, Michigan
1992 Gino Torretta, Miami
1993 Charlie Ward, Florida State
1994 Rashaan Salaam, Colorado
1995 Eddie George, Ohio State
1996 Danny Wuerffel, Florida
1997 Charles Woodson, Michigan
1998 Ricky Williams, Texas
1999 Ron Dayne, Wisconsin
2000 Chris Weinke, Florida State
2001 Eric Crouch, University of Nebraska
2002 Carson Palmer, University of Southern California

2002 NCAA CHAMPIONSHIP PLAYOFFS

DIVISION I-AA

Quarterfinals
(Dec. 7, 2002)
McNeese State 24, Montana 20
Villanova 24, Fordham 10
Western Kentucky 31, Western Illinois 28
Georgia Southern 31, Maine 7

Semifinals
(Dec. 14, 2002)
McNeese State 39, Villanova 28
Western Kentucky 31, Georgia Southern 28

Championship
(Dec. 21, 2002)
Western Kentucky 34, McNeese State 14

DIVISION II

Quarterfinals
(Nov. 30, 2002)
Valdosta State 31, Carson-Newman 28
Texas A&M-Kingsville 27, Univ. of California-Davis 20 (OT)
Grand Valley State 62, Indiana (Pa.) 21
Northern Colorado 23, Northwest Missouri State 12

Semifinals
(Dec. 7, 2002)
Valdosta State 21, Texas A&M-Kingsville 12
Grand Valley State 44, Northern Colorado 7

Championship
(Dec. 14, 2002)
Grand Valley State 31, Valdosta State 24

DIVISION III

Quarterfinals
(Dec. 7, 2002)
Mount Union 45, Wabash 16
John Carroll 16, Brockport State 10 (OT)
St. John's (Minn.) 21, Linfield 14
Trinity (Texas) 38, Bridgewater 32

Semifinals
(Dec. 14, 2002)
Mount Union 57, John Carroll 19
Trinity (Texas) 41, St. John's (Minn.) 34

Championship
(Dec. 21, 2002)
Mount Union 48, Trinity (Texas) 7

2002 NATIONAL ASSOCIATION OF INTERCOLLEGIATE ATHLETICS CHAMPIONSHIPS

Quarterfinals
(Nov. 30, 2002)
Georgetown (Ky.) 24, St. Francis (Ind.) 0
Sioux Falls (S.D.) 13, Mary (N.D.) 10
McKendree (Ill.) 32, Northwestern Oklahoma State 27
Carroll (Mont.) 35, Southern Oregon 31

Semifinals
(Dec. 7, 2003)
Carroll (Mont.) 20, Sioux Falls (S.D.) 17
Georgetown (Ky.) 35, McKendree (Ill.) 19

Championship
(Dec. 21, 2002)
Carroll (Mont.) 28, Georgetown (Ky.) 7

COLLEGE FOOTBALL HALL OF FAME

(P.O. Box 11146, South Bend, Indiana)

NOTE: Date given is player's last year of competition.

Players

Abell, Earl—Colgate, 1915
Agase, Alex—Purdue/Illinois, 1946
Agganis, Harry—Boston Univ., 1952
Albert, Frank—Stanford, 1941
Aldrich, Chas. (Ki)—Texas Christian, 1938
Aldrich, Malcolm—Yale, 1921
Alexander, Joseph—Syracuse, 1920
Allen, Marcus—So. Calif., 1981
Alworth, Lance—Arkansas, 1961
Ameche, Alan (Horse)—Wisconsin, 1954
Amling, Warren—Ohio State, 1946
Anderson, Dick—Colorado, 1967
Anderson, Donny—Texas Tech, 1965
Anderson, H. (Hunk)—Notre Dame, 1921
Arnett, Jon—So. Calif., 1956
Atkins, Doug—Tennessee, 1952
Babich, Bob—Miami-Ohio, 1968
Bacon, C. Everett—Wesleyan, 1912
Bagnell, Francis (Reds)—Pennsylvania, 1950
Bailey, Johnny—Texas A&M, 1989
Baker, Hobart (Hobey)—Princeton, 1913
Baker, John—So. Calif., 1931
Baker, Terry—Oregon State, 1962
Ballin, Harold—Princeton, 1914
Banker, Bill—Tulane, 1929
Banonis, Vince—Detroit, 1941
Barnes, Stanley—So. Calif., 1921
Barrett, Charles—Cornell, 1915
Baston, Bert—Minnesota, 1916
Battles, Cliff—W. Va. Wesleyan, 1931
Baugh, Sammy—Texas Christian, 1936
Baughan, Maxie—Georgia Tech, 1959
Bausch, James—Kansas, 1930
Beagle, Ron—Navy, 1955
Beasley, Terry—Auburn, 1971
Beban, Gary—UCLA, 1967
Bechtol, Hub—Texas Tech, 1946
Beck, Ray—Georgia Tech, 1951
Beckett, John—Oregon, 1913
Bednarik, Chuck—Pennsylvania 1948
Behm, Forrest—Nebraska, 1940
Bell, Bobby—Minnesota, 1962
Bell, Ricky—Southern California, 1976
Bellino, Joe—Navy, 1960
Below, Marty—Wisconsin, 1923
Benbrook, A.—Michigan, 1911
Bentrim, Jeff—North Dakota State, 1986
Bertelli, A.—Notre Dame, 1943
Berry, Charlie—Lafayette, 1924
Berwanger, John (Jay)—Chicago, 1935
Bettencourt, Larry—St. Mary's, 1927
Biletnikoff, Fred—Florida State, 1964
Blanchard, Felix (Doc)—Army, 1946
Blazine, Tony—Ill. Wesleyan, 1934
Bock, Ed—Iowa State, 1938
Bomar, Lynn—Vanderbilt, 1924
Bomeisler, Doug (Bo)—Yale, 1913
Booth, Albie—Yale, 1931
Bork, George—Northern Illinois, 1963
Borries, Fred—Navy, 1934
Bosely, Bruce—West Virginia, 1955
Bosseler, Don—Miami (Fla.), 1956
Bottari, Vic—California, 1939
Bowden, Murry—Dartmouth, 1970
Boynton, Ben—Williams, 1920
Bozis, Al—Georgetown, 1941
Bradshaw, Terry—Louisiana Tech, 1969
Brewer, Charles—Harvard, 1895
Bright, John—Drake, 1951
Brodie, John—Stanford, 1956
Brooke, George—Pennsylvania, 1895
Brosky, Al—Illinois, 1952
Brown, Bob—Nebraska, 1963
Brown, George—Navy/San Diego State, 1947
Brown, Gordon—Yale, 1900
Brown, Jim—Syracuse, 1956
Brown, John, Jr.—Navy, 1913
Brown, Johnny Mack—Alabama, 1925
Brown, Raymond (Tay)—So. Calif., 1932
Brown, Tom—Minnesota, 1960
Browner, Ross—Notre Dame, 1977
Bruner, Teel—Centre College (Ky.), 1985
Buchanan, Buck—Grambling State, 1962
Budde, Brad—So. Calif., 1979
Bunker, Paul—Army, 1902
Burford, Chris—Stanford, 1959
Burris, Kurt—Oklahoma, 1954
Burton, Ron—Northwestern, 1956
Butkus, Dick—Illinois, 1964
Butler, Kevin—Georgia, 1984
Butler, Robert—Wisconsin, 1912
Cafego, George—Tennessee, 1939
Cagle, Chris—SW La./Army, 1929
Cain, John—Alabama, 1932
Calip, Brad—East Central (Okla.), 1984
Cameron, Eddie—Wash. & Lee, 1924
Campbell, David C.—Harvard, 1901
Campbell, Earl—Texas, 1977
Cannon, Billy—Louisiana State, 1959
Cannon, Jack—Notre Dame, 1929
Cappelletti, John—Penn State, 1973
Carideo, Frank—Notre Dame, 1930
Caroline, J.C.—Illinois, 1954
Carney, Charles—Illinois, 1921
Carpenter, Bill—Army, 1959
Carpenter, C. Hunter—VPI, 1905
Carroll, Charles—Washington, 1928
Carson, Harry—So. Carolina State, 1975
Carter, Anthony—Michigan, 1982
Casanova, Tommy—Louisiana State, 1971
Casey, Edward L.—Harvard, 1919
Cason, Rod—Angelo State, 1971
Cassady, Howard—Ohio State, 1955
Chamberlain, Guy—Nebraska, 1915
Chapman, Sam—Cal.-Berkeley, 1938
Chappuis, Bob—Michigan, 1947
Christman, Paul—Missouri, 1940
Cichy, Joe—North Dakota State, 1970
Clark, Earl (Dutch)—Colo. College, 1929
Cleary, Paul—So. Calif., 1947
Clevenger, Zora—Indiana, 1903
Cloud, Jack—William & Mary, 1948
Cochran, Gary—Princeton, 1895
Cody, Josh—Vanderbilt, 1920
Coleman, Don—Mich. State, 1951
Conerly, Chuck—Mississippi, 1947
Connor, George—Notre Dame, 1947
Cooper, Bill—Muskingum (Ohio), 1960
Corbin, W.—Yale, 1888
Corbus, William—Stanford, 1933
Cowan, Hector—Princeton, 1889
Covert, Jimbo—Pittsburgh, 1983
Coy, Edward H. (Tad)—Yale, 1909
Crawford, Brad—Franklin (Ind.), 1977
Crawford, Fred—Duke, 1933
Crow, John D.—Texas A & M, 1957
Crowley, James—Notre Dame, 1924
Csonka, Larry—Syracuse, 1967
Cutter, Slade—Navy, 1934
Czarobski, Ziggie—Notre Dame, 1947
Dale, Carroll—Virginia Tech, 1959
Dalrymple, Gerald—Tulane, 1931
Dalton, John—Navy, 1912
Daly, Charles—Harvard/Army, 1902
Daniell, Averell—Pittsburgh, 1936
Daniell, James—Ohio State, 1941
Davies, Tom—Pittsburgh, 1921
Davis, Ernest—Syracuse, 1961
Davis, Glenn—Army, 1946
Davis, Robert T.—Georgia Tech, 1947
Dawkins, Pete—Army, 1958
Delaney, Joe—Northwestern State, 1980
Deery, Tom—Widener, 1981
DeLong, Steve—Tennessee, 1964
Dement, Kenneth—SE Missouri, 1954
Den Herder, Vern—Central (Iowa), 1970
De Rogatis, Al—Duke, 1940
DesJardien, Paul—Chicago 1914
Devino, Aubrey—Iowa, 1921
DeWitt, John—Princeton, 1903
Dial, Buddy—Rice, 1958
Dicus, Chuck—Arkansas, 1970
Dierdorf, Dan—Michigan, 1970
Ditka, Mike—Pittsburgh, 1960
Dobbs, Glenn—Tulsa, 1942
Dodd, Bobby—Tennessee, 1930
Donan, Holland—Princeton, 1950
Donchess, Joseph—Pittsburgh, 1929
Dorsett, Tony—Pittsburgh, 1976
Dougherty, Nathan—Tennessee, 1909
Dove, Bob—Notre Dame, 1942
Drahos, Nick—Cornell, 1940
Driscoll, Paddy—Northwestern, 1917
Drury, Morley—So. Calif., 1927
Dryer, Fred—San Diego State, 1968
Dudek, Joe—Plymouth State, 1985
Duden, Dick—Navy, 1945
Dudley, William (Bill)—Virginia, 1941
Duncan, Randy—Iowa, 1958
Easley, Ken—UCLA, 1980
Eckersall, Walter—Chicago, 1906
Edwards, Turk—Washington State, 1931
Edwards, William—Princeton, 1900
Eichenlaub, R.—Notre Dame, 1913
Eisenhauer, Steve—Navy, 1953
Elking, Larry—Baylor, 1964
Elliott, Chalmers—Purdue, 1944 & Mich., 1947
Elliott, Pete—Michigan, 1948
Elmendorf, Dave—Texas A & M, 1970
Elway, John—Stanford, 1982
Evans, Ray—Kansas, 1947
Exendine, Albert—Carlisle, 1908
Falaschi, Nello—Santa Clara, 1937
Fears, Tom—Santa Clara/UCLA, 1947
Feathers, Beattie—Tennessee, 1933
Fenimore, Robert—Oklahoma State, 1947
Fenton, G.E. (Doc)—Louisiana State, 1910
Ferguson, Bob—Ohio State, 1961
Ferraro, John—So. Calif., 1944
Fesler, Wesley—Ohio State, 1930
Fincher, Bill—Georgia Tech, 1920
Fischer, Bill—Notre Dame, 1948
Fish, Hamilton—Harvard, 1909
Fisher, Robert—Harvard, 1911
Flowers, Abe—Georgia Tech, 1920
Flowers, Charlie—Mississippi, 1959
Floyd, George—Eastern Kentucky, 1981
Fortmann, Daniel—Colgate, 1935
Fralic, Bill—Pittsburgh, 1984
Francis, Sam—Nebraska, 1936
Franck, George (Sonny)—Minnesota, 1940
Franco, Edmund (Ed)—Fordham, 1937
Frank, Clint—Yale, 1937
Franz, Rodney—California, 1949
Frederickson, Tucker—Auburn, 1964
Friedman, Benny—Michigan, 1926
Gabriel, Roman—North Carolina St., 1961
Gain, Bob—Kentucky, 1950
Galiffa, Arnold—Army, 1949
Galimore, Willie—Florida A & M, 1956
Gallarneau, Hugh—Stanford, 1941

Gamble, Kenny—Colgate, 1987
Garbisch, Edgar—Army, 1924
Garrett, Mike—So. Calif., 1965
Gelbert, Charles—Pennsylvania, 1896
Geyer, Forest—Oklahoma, 1915
Gibbs, Jake—Mississippi, 1960
Giel, Paul—Minnesota, 1953
Gifford, Frank—So. Calif., 1951
Gilbert, Chris—Texas, 1968
Gilbert, Walter—Auburn, 1936
Gilmer, Harry—Alabama, 1947
Gipp, George—Notre Dame, 1920
Gladchuk, Chet—Boston College, 1940
Glass, Bill—Baylor, 1956
Glover, Rich—Nebraska, 1972
Goldberg, Marshall—Pittsburgh, 1938
Goodreault, Gene—Boston College, 1940
Gordon, Walter—California, 1918
Governale, Paul—Columbia, 1942
Grabowski, Jim—Illinois, 1965
Graham, Otto—Northwestern, 1943
Gradishar, Randy—Ohio State, 1973
Grange, Harold (Red)—Illinois, 1925
Grayson, Roberty—Stanford, 1935
Green, Charles—Wittenberg, 1964
Green, Hugh—Pittsburgh, 1980
Green, Joe—North Texas State, 1968
Green, Tim—Syracuse, 1985
Griese, Bob—Purdue, 1966
Griffin, Archie—Ohio State, 1975
Grinnell, William—Tufts, 1934
Groom, Jerry—Notre Dame, 1950
Guglielmi, Ralph—Notre Dame, 1954
Gulick, Merel—Hobart, 1929
Guyon, Joe—Georgia Tech, 1919
Hadl, John—Kansas, 1961
Hale, Edwin—Mississippi Col., 1921
Hall, Parker—Mississippi, 1938
Ham, Jack—Penn State, 1970
Hamilton, Robert (Bones)—Stanford, 1935
Hamilton, Tom—Navy, 1925
Hannah, John—Alabama, 1972
Hanson, Vic—Syracuse, 1926
Harder, Pat—Wisconsin, 1942
Hardwick, H. (Tack)—Harvard, 1914
Hare, T. Truxton—Pennsylvania, 1900
Harley, Chick—Ohio State, 1919
Harmon, Tom—Michigan, 1940
Harpster, Howard—Carnegie Tech, 1928
Hart, Edward J. Princeton, 1911
Hart, Leon—Notre Dame, 1949
Hartman, Bill—Georgia, 1937
Haslett, Jim—Indiana (Pa.), 1978
Hawkins, Frank—Nevada, 1980
Haynes, Michael—Arizona State, 1975
Hazel, Homer—Rutgers, 1924
Healey, Ed—Dartmouth, 1916
Heffelfiner, W. (Pudge)—Yale, 1891
Hein, Mel—Washington State, 1930
Heinrich, Don—Washington, 1952
Hendricks, Ted—Miami, 1968
Henry, Wilbur—Wash. & Jefferson, 1919
Herschberger, Clarence—Chicago, 1899
Herwig, Robert—California, 1937
Heston, Willie—Michigan, 1904
Hickman, Herman—Tennessee, 1931
Hickok, William—Yale, 1895
Hicks, John—Ohio State, 1973
Hill, Dan—Duke, 1938
Hillebrand, A.R. (Doc)—Princeton, 1900
Hinkey, Frank—Yale, 1894
Hinkle, Carl—Vanderbilt, 1937
Hinkle, Clark—Bucknell, 1932
Hirsch, Elroy—Wisconsin/Michigan, 1943
Hitchcock, James—Auburn, 1932
Hoage, Terry—Georgia, 1983
Hoffman, Frank—Notre Dame, 1931
Hogan, James J.—Yale, 1904
Holland, Jerome (Brud)—Cornell, 1938
Holleder, Don—Army, 1955
Hollenbeck, William—Pennsylvania, 1908
Holovak, Michael—Boston College, 1942
Holt, Pierce—Angelo State, 1980
Holub, E.J.—Texas Tech, 1960
Hornung, Paul—Notre Dame, 1956
Horrell, Edwin—California, 1924
Horvath, Les—Ohio State, 1944
Howe Arthur—Yale, 1911
Howell, Millard (Dixie)—Alabama, 1934
Hubbard, Cal—Centenary, 1926
Hubbard, John—Amherst, 1906
Hubert, Allison—Alabama, 1925
Huff, Robert Lee (Sam)—W. Va., 1955
Humble, Weldon G.—Rice, 1946
Hunley, Ricky—Arizona, 1983
Hunt, Joel—Texas A & M, 1927
Huntington, Ellery—Colgate, 1914
Hutson, Don—Alabama, 1934
Ingram, James—Navy, 1906
Iacavazzi, Cosmo—Princeton, 1964
Isbell, Cecil—Purdue, 1937
Jablonsky, Harvey—Wash. U./Army, 1933
Jackson, Bo—Auburn, 1985
Jackson, Keith—Oklahoma, 1987
Janowicz, Vic—Ohio State, 1951
Jefferson, John—Arizona State, 1977
Jenkins, Darold—Missouri, 1941
Jensen, Jack—Cal.-Berkeley, 1948
Joesting, Herbert—Minnesota, 1927
Johnson, Billy—Widener, 1973
Johnson, Gary—Grambling State, 1974
Johnson, James—Carlisle, 1903
Johnson, Robert—Tennessee, 1967
Johnson, Ron—Michigan, 1968
Jones, Brent—Santa Clara, 1985
Jones, Calvin—Iowa, 1955
Jones, Gormer—Ohio State, 1935
Jones, Stan—Maryland, 1953
Jordan, Lee Roy—Alabama, 1962
Juhan, Frank—Univ. of South, 1910
Justice, Charlie—North Carolina, 1949
Kaer, Mort—So. Calif., 1926
Karras, Alex—Iowa, 1957
Kavanaugh, Kenneth—Louisiana State, 1939
Kaw, Edgar—Cornell, 1922
Kazmaier, Richard—Princeton, 1951
Keck, James—Princeton, 1921
Kelley, Larry—Yale, 1936
Kelly, William—Montana, 1926
Kenna, Ed—Syracuse, 1966
Kern, George—Boston College, 1941
Ketcham, Henry—Yale, 1913
Keyes, Leroy—Purdue, 1968
Killinger, William—Penn State, 1922
Kilmer, Billy—UCLA, 1960
Kimbrough, John—Texas A & M, 1940
Kinard, Frank—Mississippi, 1937
Kinard, Terry—Clemson, 1982
Kiner, Steve—Tennessee, 1969
King, Philip—Princeton, 1893
Kinnick, Nile—Iowa, 1939
Kipke, Harry—Michigan, 1923
Kirkpatrick, John Reed—Yale, 1910
Kitzmiller, John—Oregon, 1929
Koch, Barton—Baylor, 1931
Kitner, Malcolm—Texas, 1942
Kramer, Ron—Michigan, 1956
Kroll, Alex—Rutgers, 1961
Krueger, Charlie—Texas A & M, 1957
Kwalick, Ted—Penn State, 1968
Lach, Steve—Duke, 1941
Lane, Myles—Dartmouth, 1927
Lanier, Sr., Willie—Morgan State, 1966
Lattner, Joseph J.—Notre Dame, 1953
Lauricella, Hank—Tennessee, 1952
Lautenschlaeger—Tulane, 1925
Layden, Elmer—Notre Dame, 1924
Layne, Bobby—Texas, 1947
Lea, Langdon—Princeton, 1895
LeBaron, Eddie—Univ. of Pacific, 1949
LeClair, Jim—North Dakota, 1971
Leech, James—Va. Mil. Inst., 1920
Lester, Darrell—Texas Christian, 1935
Levias, Jerry—Southern Methodist, 1968
Lewis, D. D.—Mississippi State, 1968
Lilly, Bob—Texas Christian, 1960
Little, Floyd—Syracuse, 1966
Lio, Augie—Georgetown, 1940
Lockbaum, Gordie—Holy Cross, 1987
Locke, Gordon—Iowa, 1922
Lomax, Neil—Portland (Ore.) State, 1980
Long, Chuck—Iowa, 1985
Long, Mel—Toledo, 1971
Loria, Frank—Virginia Tech, 1967
Lott, Ronnie—So. Calif., 1980
Lourie, Don—Princeton, 1921
Lucas, Richard—Penn State, 1959
Luckman, Sid—Columbia, 1938
Lujack, John—Notre Dame, 1947
Lund, J. L. (Pug)—Minnesota, 1934
Lynch, Jim—Notre Dame, 1966
MacAfee, Ken—Notre Dame, 1977
Macomber, Bart—Illinois, 1915
MacLeod, Robert—Dartmouth, 1938
Maegle, Dick—Rice, 1954
Mahan, Edward W.—Harvard, 1915
Majors, John—Tennessee, 1956
Mallory, William—Yale, 1893
Mancha, Vaughn—Alabama, 1947
Mann, Gerald—So. Methodist, 1927
Manning, Archie—Mississippi, 1970
Manske, Edgar—Northwestern, 1933
Marinaro, Ed—Cornell, 1971
Marino, Dan—Pittsburgh, 1982
Markov, Vic—Washington, 1937
Marshall, Robert—Minnesota, 1907
Martin, Jim—Notre Dame, 1949
Matson, Ollie—San Fran. U., 1952
Matthews, Ray—Texas Christian, 1928
Maulbetsch, John—Michigan, 1914
Mauthe, J. L. (Pete)—Penn State, 1912
Maxwell, Robert—Chicago/Swarthmore, 1906
McAfee, George—Duke, 1939
McCallum, Napoleon—Navy, 1985
McCauley, Don—North Carolina, 1970
McClung, Thomas L.—Yale, 1891
McColl, William F.—Stanford, 1951
McCormick, James B.—Princeton, 1907
McDonald, Tom—Oklahoma, 1956
McDowall, Jack—No. Carolina State, 1927
McElhenny, Hugh—Washington, 1951
McEver, Gene—Tennessee, 1931
McEwan, John—Minn./Army, 1916
McFadden, J. B.—Clemson, 1939
McFadin, Bud—Texas, 1950
McGee, Mike—Duke, 1959
McGinley, Edward—Pennsylvania, 1924
McGovern, J.—Minnesota, 1910
McGraw, Thurman—Colorado State, 1949
McGriff, Tyrone—Florida A & M, 1979
McKeever, Mike—So. Calif., 1960
McKenzie, Reggie—Michigan, 1971
McLaren, George—Pittsburgh, 1918
McMahon, Jim—Brigham Young, 1981
McMillan, Dan—So. Calif./California, 1922
McMillin, A. N. (Bo)—Centre, 1921
McWhorter, Robert—Georgia, 1913
Mercer, Leroy—Pennsylvania, 1912
Meredith, Don—So. Methodist, 1959
Merritt, Frank—Army, 1943
Metzger, Bert—Notre Dame, 1930
Meyland, Wayne—Nebraska, 1967
Michaels, Lou—Kentucky, 1957
Michels, John—Tennessee, 1952
Mickal, Abe—Louisiana State, 1935
Miller, Creighton—Notre Dame, 1943
Miller, Don—Notre Dame, 1925
Miller, Edgar (Rip)—Notre Dame, 1924
Miller, Eugene—Penn State, 1913
Miller, Fred—Notre Dame, 1928
Millner, Wayne—Notre Dame, 1935

Milstead, Century—Wabash/Yale, 1923
Minds, John—Pennsylvania, 1897
Minisi, Anthony—Navy/Pennsylvania, 1947
Modzelewski, Dick—Maryland, 1952
Moffatt, Alex—Princeton, 1884
Molinski, Ed—Tennessee, 1940
Montgomery, Cliff—Columbia, 1933
Montgomery, Wilbert—Abilene Christian, 1976
Moomaw, Donn—UCLA, 1952
Morley, William—Columbia, 1903
Morris, George—Georgia Tech, 1952
Morris, Larry—Georgia Tech, 1954
Morton, Craig—California, 1964
Morton, William—Dartmouth, 1931
Moscrip, Monk—Stanford, 1935
Muller, Harold (Brick)—Calif., 1922
Musso, Johnny—Alabama, 1971
Nagurski, Bronko—Minnesota, 1929
Neighbors, Billy—Alabama, 1961
Nevers, Ernie—Stanford, 1925
Newell, Marshall—Harvard, 1893
Newman, Harry—Michigan, 1932
Newsome, Ozzie—Alabama, 1977
Nielsen, Gifford—Brigham Young, 1976
Nix, Dwayne, Texas A&M-Kingsville, 1968
Nobis, Tommy—Texas, 1965
Nomellini, Leo—Minnesota, 1949
Oberland, Andrew—Dartmouth, 1925
O'Brien, Davey—Texas Christian, 1938
O'Brien, Ken—Cal.-Davis, 1982
O'Dea, Pat—Wisconsin, 1899
Odell, Robert—Pennsylvania, 1943
O'Hearn, J.—Cornell, 1915
Olds, Robin—Army, 1942
Oliphant, Elmer—Purdue/Army, 1917
Olsen, Merlin—Utah State, 1961
Onkotz, Dennis—Penn State, 1969
Oosterbaan, Ben—Michigan, 1927
O'Rourke, Charles—Boston College, 1940
Orsi, John—Colgate, 1931
Osgood, W. D.—Cornell/Pennsylvania, 1895
Osmanski, William—Holy Cross, 1938
Outland, John—Kansas/Pennsylvania, 1899
Owen, George—Harvard, 1922
Owens, Jim—Oklahoma, 1949
Owens, Steve—Oklahoma, 1969
Page, Alan—Notre Dame, 1966
Palumbo, Joe—U. of Virginia, 1951
Pardee, Jack—Texas A & M, 1956
Parilli, Vito (Babe)—Kentucky, 1951
Parker, Clarence (Ace)—Duke, 1936
Parker, Jackie—Miss. State, 1953
Parker, James—Ohio State, 1956
Payton, Walter—Jackson State, 1974
Pazzetti, V. J.—Wesleyan/Lehigh, 1912
Peabody, Endicott—Harvard, 1941
Peck, Robert—Pittsburgh, 1916
Pellegrini, Bob—Maryland, 1955
Pennock, Stanley B.—Harvard, 1914
Pfann, George—Cornell, 1923
Phillips, H. D.—Univ. of South, 1904
Phillips, Loyd—Arkansas, 1966
Pingel, John—Michigan State, 1938
Pihos, Pete—Indiana, 1945
Pinckert, Ernie—So. Calif., 1931
Plunkett, Jim—Stanford, 1970
Poe, Arthur—Princeton, 1899
Pollard, Fritz—Brown, 1916
Poole, Barney—Miss./Army, 1947
Powell, Marvin—So. Calif., 1976
Pregulman, Merv—Michigan, 1943
Price, Eddie—Tulane, 1949
Pritchard, Ron—Arizona State, 1968
Pruitt, Greg—Oklahoma, 1972
Pugh, Larry—Westminster, Pa., 1964
Pund, Henry—Georgia Tech, 1928
Ramsey, Gerrard—Wm. & Mary, 1942
Rauch, John—Georgia, 1948
Reasons, Gary—Northwestern State (La.), 1983
Redell, Bill—Occidental, 1963
Redman, Rick—Washington, 1964
Reeds, Claude—Oklahoma, 1913
Reid, Mike—Penn State, 1970
Reid, Steve—Northwestern, 1936
Reid, William—Harvard, 1900
Reifsnyder, Bob—Navy, 1958
Renfro, Mel—Oregon, 1963
Rentner, Ernest—Northwestern, 1932
Reppert, Scott—Lawrence (Wis.), 1982
Ressler, Glenn—Penn State, 1964
Reynolds, Robert—Nebraska, 1952
Reynolds, Robert—Stanford, 1935
Rhino, Randy—Georgia Tech, 1974
Rhome, Jerry—Tulsa, 1964
Richardson, Willie—Jackson State (Miss.), 1962
Richter, Les—California, 1951
Richter, Pat—Wisconsin, 1962
Riley, John—Northwestern, 1931
Rimington, Dave—Nebraska, 1982
Rinehart, Charles—Lafayette, 1897
Ritchie, Richard—Texas A & M, 1977
Ritcher, Jim—No. Carolina St., 1979
Roberts, Calvin—Gustavus Adolphus (Minn.), 1952
Roberts, J. D.—Oklahoma, 1953
Robeson, Paul—Rutgers, 1918
Robinson, Dave—Penn State, 1962
Robinson, Jerry—UCLA, 1978
Rodgers, Ira—West Virginia, 1919
Rodgers, Johnny—Nebraska, 1972
Rogers, Edward L.—Minnesota, 1903
Rogers, George—South Carolina, 1980
Roland, Johnny—Missouri, 1965
Romig, Joe—Colorado, 1961
Rosenberg, Aaron—So. Calif., 1934
Rote, Kyle—So. Methodist, 1950
Routt, Joe—Texas A & M, 1937
Salmon, Louis—Notre Dame, 1904
Sanders, Barry—Oklahoma State, 1988
Sarkisian, Alex—Northwestern, 1948
Sauer, George—Nebraska, 1933
Savitsky, George—Pennsylvania, 1947
Saxon, Jimmy—Texas, 1961
Sayers Gale—Kansas, 1964
Scarbath, Jack—Maryland, 1952
Scarlett, Hunter—Pennsylvania, 1909
Schloredt, Bob—Washington, 1960
Schmidt, Joe—Pittsburgh, 1952
Schoonover, Wear—Arkansas, 1929
Schreiner, Dave—Wisconsin, 1942
Schultz, Adolf (Germany)—Mich., 1908
Schwab, Frank—Lafayette, 1922
Schwartz, Marchmont—Notre Dame, 1931
Schwegler, Paul—Washington, 1931
Scott, Clyde—Arkansas, 1949
Scott, Freddie—Amherst, 1973
Scott, Richard—Navy, 1947
Scott, Tom—Virginia, 1953
Seibels, Henry—Sewanee, 1899
Sellers, Ron—Florida State, 1968
Selmon, Lee Roy—Oklahoma, 1975
Sewell, Harley—Texas, 1952
Shakespeare, Bill—Notre Dame, 1935
Shell, Donnie—So. Carolina St., 1973
Shelton, Murray—Cornell, 1915
Shevlin, Tom—Yale, 1905
Shively, Bernie—Illinois, 1926
Simons, Claude—Tulane, 1934
Sims, Billy—Oklahoma, 1979
Simpson, O. J.—So. Calif., 1968
Singletary, Mike—Baylor, 1980
Sington, Fred—Alabama, 1930
Sinkwich, Frank—Georgia, 1942
Sisemore, Jerry—Texas, 1972
Sitko, Emil—Notre Dame, 1949
Skladany, Joe—Pittsburgh, 1933
Slater, F.F. (Duke)—Iowa, 1921
Smith, Billy Ray—Arkansas, 1982
Smith, Bruce—Minnesota, 1941
Smith, Bubba—Michigan State, 1966
Smith, Ernie—So. Calif., 1932
Smith, Harry—So. Calif., 1939
Smith, Jim Ray—Baylor, 1954
Smith, John (Clipper)—Notre Dame, 1927
Smith, Riley—Alabama, 1935
Smith, Vernon—Georgia, 1931
Snow, Neil—Michigan, 1901
Spani, Gary—Kansas State, 1977
Sparlis, Al—UCLA, 1945
Spears, Clarence W.—Dartmouth, 1915
Spears, W.D.—Vanderbilt, 1927
Sprackling, William—Brown, 1911
Sprague, M. (Bud)—Texas/Army, 1928
Spurrier, Steve—Florida, 1966
Stafford, Harrison—Texas, 1932
Stagg, Amos Alonzo—Yale, 1889
Stanfill, Bill—Georgia, 1968
Starcevich, Max—Washington, 1936
Staubach, Roger—Navy, 1963
Steffen, Walter—Chicago, 1908
Steffy, Joe—Army, 1947
Stein, Herbert—Pittsburgh, 1921
Steuber, Robert—Missouri, 1943
Stevens, Mal—Yale, 1923
Stevenson, Ben—Tuskegee (Ala.), 1930
Stevenson, Vincent—Pennsylvania, 1905
Stillwagon, Jim—Ohio State, 1970
Stinchcomb, Gaylord—Ohio State, 1920
Strom, Brock—Air Force, 1959
Strong, Ken—New York Univ., 1928
Strupper, George—Georgia Tech, 1917
Stuhldreher, Harry—Notre Dame, 1924
Stydahar, Joe—West Virginia, 1935
Suffridge, Robert—Tennessee, 1940
Suhey, Steve—Penn State, 1947
Sullivan, Pat—Auburn, 1971
Sundstrom, Frank—Cornell, 1923
Swann, Lynn—So. Calif., 1973
Swanson, Clarence—Nebraska, 1921
Swiacki, Bill—Holy Cross/Colombia, 1947
Swink, Jim—Texas Christian, 1956
Talboom, Eddie—Wyoming, 1950
Taliafarro, George—Indiana, 1948
Tarkenton, Fran—Georgia, 1960
Tavener, John—Indiana, 1944
Taylor, Bruce—Boston Univ., 1969
Taylor, Charles—Stanford, 1942
Theismann, Joe—Notre Dame, 1970
Thomas, Aurelius—Ohio State, 1957
Thompson, Joe—Pittsburgh, 1907
Thomsen, Lynn—Austana, 1986
Thorne, Samuel B.—Yale, 1906
Thorpe, Jim—Carlisle, 1912
Ticknor, Ben—Harvard, 1930
Tigert, John—Vanderbilt, 1904
Tinsley, Gaynell—Louisiana State, 1936
Tipton, Eric—Duke, 1938
Tonnemaker, Clayton—Minnesota, 1949
Torrey, Robert—Pennsylvania, 1906
Trautman, Randy—Boise State, 1981
Travis, Ed Tarkio—Missouri, 1920
Trippi, Charles—Georgia, 1946
Tryon, J. Edward—Colgate, 1925
Tubbs, Jerry—Oklahoma, 1956
Utay, Joe—Texas A & M, 1907
Van Brocklin, Norm—Oregon, 1948
Van Pelt, Brad—Michigan State, 1972
Van Sickel, Dale—Florida, 1929
Van Surdam, Henderson—Wesleyan, 1905
Very, Dexter—Penn State, 1912
Vessels, Billy—Oklahoma, 1952
Vick, Ernie—Michigan, 1921
Wagner, Huber—Pittsburgh, 1913
Walker, Doak—So. Methodist, 1949
Walker, Herschel—Georgia, 1982
Wallace, Bill—Rice, 1935
Walsh, Adam—Notre Dame, 1924
Warburton, I. (Cotton)—So. Calif., 1934

Ward, Robert (Bob)—Maryland, 1951
Warner, William—Cornell, 1903
Washington, Ken—UCLA, 1939
Weatherall, Jim—Oklahoma, 1951
Webster, George—Mich. State, 1966
Wedemeyer, Herman J.—St. Mary's, 1947
Weekes, Harold—Columbia, 1902
Wehrli, Roger—Missouri, 1968
Weiner, Art—North Carolina, 1949
Weir, Ed—Nebraska, 1925
Welch, Gus—Carlisle, 1914
Weller, John—Princeton, 1935
Wendell, Percy—Harvard, 1913
West, D. Belford—Colgate, 1919
Westfall, Bob—Michigan, 1941
Weyand, Alex—Army, 1915
Wharton, Charles—Pennsylvania, 1896
Wheeler, Arthur—Princeton, 1894
White, Byron (Whizzer)—Colorado, 1937
White, Charles—So. Calif., 1979
White, Danny—Arizona State, 1973
White, Ed—California-Berkeley, 1968
White, Randy—Maryland, 1974
White, Reggie—Tennessee, 1983
Whitmire, Don—Alabama/Navy, 1944
Wickhorst, Frank—Navy, 1926
Widseth, Ed—Minnesota, 1936
Wildung, Richard—Minnesota, 1942
Williams, Bob—Notre Dame, 1950
Williams, Doug—Grambling, 1977
Williams, James—Rice, 1949
Willis, William—Ohio State, 1945
Wilson, George—Washington, 1925
Wilson, George—Lafayette, 1928
Wilson, Harry—Penn State/Army, 1923
Wilson, Marc—Brigham Young, 1979
Winslow, Kellen—Missouri, 1978
Wistert, Albert A.—Michigan, 1942
Wistert, Al—Michigan, 1942
Wistert, Frank (Whitey)—Michigan, 1933
Wood, Barry—Harvard, 1931
Wojciechowicz, Alex—Fordham, 1936
Wyant, Andrew—Bucknell/Chicago, 1894
Wyatt, Bowden—Tennessee, 1938
Wyckoff, Clint—Cornell, 1896
Yarr, Tom—Notre Dame, 1931
Yary, Ron—So. Calif., 1968
Yoder, Lloyd—Carnegie Tech, 1926
Young, Claude (Buddy)—Illinois, 1946
Young, Harry—Wash. & Lee, 1916
Young, Steve—Brigham Young, 1983
Young, Walter—Oklahoma, 1938
Youngblood, Jack—Florida, 1970
Youngblood, Jim—Tennessee, 1972
Zarnas, Gus—Ohio State, 1937

Coaches

Bill Alexander
Dr. Ed Anderson
Ike Armstrong
Chris Ault
Earl Banks
Harry Baujan
Matty Bell
Hugo Bezdek
Dana X. Bible
Bernie Bierman
Bob Blackman
Earl (Red) Blaik
Frank Broyles
Earle Bruce
Paul "Bear" Bryant
Harold Burry
Jim Butterfield
James "Wally" Butts
Charles W. Caldwell
Walter Camp
Len Casanova
Marino Casem
Frank Cavanaugh
Jerry Claiborne
Richard Colman
Don Coryell
Carmen Cozza
Fritz Crisler
Duffy Daugherty
Bob Devaney
Dan Devine
Doug Dickey
Gil Dobie
Bobby Dodd
Terry Donahue
Michael Donohue
Vince Dooley
Gus Dorais
Bill Edwards
Charles (Rip) Engle
Forest Evashevski
Don Faurot
Hayden Fry
Joseph Fusco
Jake Gaither
Sid Gillman
Ernest Godfrey
Ray Graves
Andy Gustafson
Jack Harding
Edward K. Hall
Richard Harlow
Jesse Harper
Percy Haughton
Woody Hayes
John W. Heisman
R.A. (Bob) Higgins
Paul Hoernemann
Orin E. Hollingberry
Frank Howard
Marcelino (Chelo) Huerta
William Ingram
Don James
Morley Jennings
Howard Jones
L. (Biff) Jones
Thomas (Tad) Jones
Ralph (Shug) Jordan
Bob Keade
Andy Kerr
Roy Kidd
Chuck Klausing
Frank Kush
Frank Leahy
George E. Little
Lou Little
El (Slip) Madigan
Fred Martinelli
Dave Maurer
Charley McClendon
Herbert McCracken
Daniel McGugin
John McKay
Allyn McKeen
DeOrmond (Tuss) McLaughry
John Merritt
L.R. (Dutch) Meyer
Bernie Moore
Scrappy Moore
Jack Mollenkopf
Ray Morrison
Darrell Mudra
Arnett "Ace" Mumford
George A. Munger
Clarence Munn
Frank Murray
William Murray
Ed (Hooks) Mylin
Earle (Greasy) Neale
Jess Neely
David Nelson
Robert Neyland
Billy Nicks
Homer Norton
Frank (Buck) O'Neill
Tom Osborne
Bennie Owen
Ara Parseghian
Doyt Perry
James Phalea
Tommy Prothro
John Ralston
Harold "Tubby" Raymond
E.N. Robinson
Knute Rockne
E. L. (Dick) Romney
William W. Roper
Darrell Royal
Ad Rutschman
Henry (Red) Sanders
George F. Sanford
Bo Schembechler
Ron Schipper
Francis A. Schmidt
Floyd (Ben) Schwartzwalder
Clark Shaughnessy
Buck Shaw
Edgar Sherman
Andrew L. Smith
Carl Snavely
Jim Sochor
Amos A. Stagg
Gilbert Steinke
Jock Sutherland
Barry Switzer
James Tatum
Grant Teaff
Frank W. Thomas
Lee Tressell
Thad Vann
John H. Vaught
Wallace Wade
Lynn Waldorf
Glenn (Pop) Warner
Frank Waters
E.E. (Tad) Wieman
John W. Wilce
Bud Wilkinson
Henry L. Williams
George W. Woodruff
Warren Woodson
Bowden Wyatt
Bill Yeoman
Fielding H. Yost
Jim Young
Robert Zuppke

Professional Football

SUPER BOWLS I-XXXVII

Game	Date	Winner	Loser	Site	Attendance
XXXVII	Jan. 26, 2003	Tampa Bay (NFC) 48	Oakland Raiders (AFC) 21	Qualcomm Stadium, San Diego, Calif.	67,603
XXXVI	Feb. 3, 2002	New England (AFC) 20	St. Louis (NFC) 17	Superdome, New Orleans	72,922
XXXV	Jan. 28, 2001	Baltimore (AFC) 34	New York Giants (NFC) 7	Raymond James Stadium, Tampa, Fla.	71,921
XXXIV	Jan. 30, 2000	St. Louis (NFC) 23	Tennessee (AFC) 16	Georgia Dome, Atlanta, Ga.	72,625
XXXIII	Jan. 31, 1999	Denver (AFC) 34	Atlanta (NFC) 19	Pro Player Stadium, Miami, Fla.	74,803
XXXII	Jan. 25, 1998	Denver (AFC) 31	Green Bay (NFC) 24	Qualcomm Stadium, San Diego, Calif.	68,912
XXXI	Jan. 26, 1997	Green Bay (NFC) 35	New England (AFC) 21	Superdome, New Orleans, La.	72,301
XXX	Jan. 28, 1996	Dallas (NFC) 27	Pittsburgh (AFC) 17	Sun Devil Stadium, Tempe, Ariz.	76,347
XXIX	Jan. 29, 1995	San Francisco (NFC) 49	San Diego (AFC) 26	Joe Robbie Stadium, Miami, Fla.	74,107
XXVIII	Jan. 30, 1994	Dallas (NFC) 30	Buffalo (AFC) 13	Georgia Dome, Atlanta, Ga.	72,817
XXVII	Jan. 31, 1993	Dallas (NFC) 52	Buffalo (AFC) 17	Rose Bowl, Pasadena, Calif.	98,374
XXVI	Jan. 26, 1992	Washington (NFC) 37	Buffalo (AFC) 24	Metrodome, Minneapolis, Minn.	63,130
XXV	Jan. 27, 1991	Giants (NFC) 20	Buffalo (AFC) 19	Tampa Stadium, Tampa, Fla.	73,813
XXIV	Jan. 28, 1990	San Francisco (NFC) 55	Denver (AFC) 10	Superdome, New Orleans	72,919
XXIII	Jan. 22, 1989	San Francisco (NFC) 20	Cincinnati (AFC) 16	Joe Robbie Stadium, Miami, Fla.	75,179
XXII	Jan. 31, 1988	Washington (NFC) 42	Denver (AFC) 10	Jack Murphy Stadium, San Diego, Calif.	73,302
XXI	Jan. 25, 1987	Giants (NFC) 39	Denver (AFC) 20	Rose Bowl, Pasadena, Calif.	101,063
XX	Jan. 26, 1986	Chicago (NFC) 46	New England (AFC) 10	Superdome, New Orleans	73,818
XIX	Jan. 20, 1985	San Francisco (NFC) 38	Miami (AFC) 16	Stanford Stadium, Palo Alto, Calif.	84,059

Game	Date	Winner	Loser	Site	Attendance
XVIII	Jan. 22, 1984	Los Angeles Raiders (AFC) 38	Washington (NFC) 9	Tampa Stadium, Tampa, Fla	72,920
XVII	Jan. 30, 1983	Washington (NFC) 27	Miami (AFC) 17	Rose Bowl, Pasadena, Calif.	103,667
XVI	Jan. 24, 1982	San Francisco (NFC) 26	Cincinnati (AFC) 21	Silverdome, Pontiac, Mich.	81,270
XV	Jan. 25, 1981	Oakland (AFC) 27	Philadelphia (NFC) 10	Superdome, New Orleans	75,500
XIV	Jan. 20, 1980	Pittsburgh (AFC) 31	Los Angeles (NFC) 19	Rose Bowl, Pasadena	103,985
XIII	Jan. 21, 1979	Pittsburgh (AFC) 35	Dallas (NFC) 31	Orange Bowl, Miami	79,484
XII	Jan. 15, 1978	Dallas (NFC) 27	Denver (AFC) 10	Superdome, New Orleans	75,583
XI	Jan. 9, 1977	Oakland (AFC) 32	Minnesota (NFC) 14	Rose Bowl, Pasadena	103,424
X	Jan. 18, 1976	Pittsburgh (AFC) 21	Dallas (NFC) 17	Orange Bowl, Miami	80,187
IX	Jan. 12, 1975	Pittsburgh (AFC) 16	Minnesota (NFC) 6	Tulane Stadium, New Orleans	80,997
VIII	Jan. 13, 1974	Miami (AFC) 24	Minnesota (NFC) 7	Rice Stadium, Houston	71,882
VII	Jan. 14, 1973	Miami (AFC) 14	Washington (NFC) 7	Memorial Coliseum, Los Angeles	90,182
VI	Jan. 16, 1972	Dallas (NFC) 24	Miami (AFC) 3	Tulane Stadium, New Orleans	81,591
V	Jan. 17, 1971	Baltimore (AFC) 16	Dallas (NFC) 13	Orange Bowl, Miami	79,204
IV	Jan. 11, 1970	Kansas City (AFL) 23	Minnesota (NFL) 7	Tulane Stadium, New Orleans	80,562
III	Jan. 12, 1969	New York (AFL) 16	Baltimore (NFL) 7	Orange Bowl, Miami	75,389
II	Jan. 14, 1968	Green Bay (NFL) 33	Oakland (AFL) 14	Orange Bowl, Miami	75,546
I	Jan. 15, 1967	Green Bay (NFL) 35	Kansas City (AFL) 10	Memorial Coliseum, Los Angeles	61,946

NOTE: Super Bowls I to IV were played before the American Football League and National Football League merged into the NFL, which was divided into two conferences, the NFC and AFC.

NATIONAL FOOTBALL LEAGUE FINAL STANDINGS 2002

AMERICAN FOOTBALL CONFERENCE

	W	L	T	Pct	PF	PA
East						
New York Jets[1]	9	7	0	.562	359	336
New England Patriots	9	7	0	.562	381	346
Miami Dolphins	9	7	0	.562	378	301
Buffalo Bills	8	8	0	.500	379	397
North						
Pittsburgh Steelers[1]	10	5	1	.656	390	345
Cleveland Browns[2]	9	7	0	.562	344	320
Baltimore Ravens	7	9	0	.438	316	354
Cincinnati Bengals	2	14	0	.125	279	456
South						
Tennessee Titans[1]	11	5	0	.688	367	324
Indianapolis Colts[2]	10	6	0	.625	349	313
Jacksonville Jaguars	6	10	0	.375	328	315
Houston Texans	4	12	0	.250	213	356
West						
Oakland Raiders[1]	11	5	0	.688	450	304
Denver Broncos	9	7	0	.562	392	344
San Diego Chargers	8	8	0	.500	333	367
Kansas City Chiefs	8	8	0	.500	467	399

1. Division champion. 2. Wild card qualifier for playoffs. **Wild card:** N.Y. Jets 41, Indianapolis 0; Pittsburgh 36, Cleveland 33. **Division:** Tennessee 34, Pittsburgh 31; Oakland 30, N.Y. Jets 10. **Conference:** Oakland 41, Tennessee 24.

NATIONAL FOOTBALL CONFERENCE

	W	L	T	Pct	PF	PA
East						
Philadelphia Eagles[1]	12	4	0	.750	415	241
New York Giants[2]	10	6	0	.625	320	279
Washington Redskins	7	9	0	.438	307	365
Dallas Cowboys	5	11	0	.312	217	329
North						
Green Bay Packers[1]	12	4	0	.750	398	328
Minnesota Vikings	6	10	0	.375	390	442
Chicago Bears	4	12	0	.250	281	379
Detroit Lions	3	13	0	.188	306	451
South						
Tampa Bay Buccaneers[1]	12	4	0	.750	346	196
Atlanta Falcons[2]	9	6	1	.594	402	314
New Orleans Saints	9	7	0	.562	432	388
Carolina Panthers	7	9	0	.438	258	302
West						
San Francisco 49ers[1]	10	6	0	.625	367	351
St. Louis Rams	7	9	0	.438	316	369
Seattle Seahawks	7	9	0	.438	355	369
Arizona Cardinals	5	11	0	.312	262	417

1. Division champion. 2. Wild card qualifier for playoffs. **Wild card:** Atlanta 27, Green Bay 7; San Francisco 39, N.Y. Giants 38. **Division:** Tampa Bay 31, San Francisco 6; Philadelphia 20, Atlanta 6. **Conference:** Tampa Bay 27, Philadelphia 10.

LEAGUE CHAMPIONSHIP—SUPER BOWL XXXVII

(Jan. 26, 2003, Qualcomm Stadium, San Diego, Calif. Attendance: 67,603. Time: 3:50)

Scoring

	1st Q	2nd Q	3rd Q	4th Q	Final
Oakland	3	0	6	12	**21**
Tampa Bay	3	17	14	14	**48**

1st: OAK—Janikowski 40-yd field goal, 4:20. Key plays: C. Woodson 12-yd interception return to TB 36. Gannon 8-yd pass to Garner to TB 28. Gannon 9-yd pass to Brown to TB 19. TB—Gramatica 31-yd field goal, 7:09. Key plays: B. Johnson 11-yd pass to Jurevicius to TB 40. B. Johnson 23-yd pass to Jurevicius to OAK 37. Pittman 23-yd run to OAK 14.

2nd: TB—Gramatica 43-yd field goal, 3:44. Key plays: Jackson 9-yd interception return to TB 49. B. Johnson 11-yd pass to K. Johnson to OAK 39. B. Johnson 9-yd pass to K. Johnson to OAK 27. TD: Alstott 2-yd run (Gramatica kick), 8:36. Key plays: Williams 25-yd punt return to OAK 27. Pittman 19-yd run to OAK 2. TD: McCardell 5-yd pass from B. Johnson (Gramatica kick), 14:30. Key plays: Pittman 9-yd run to TB 42. B. Johnson 16-yd pass to Alstott to OAK 42. Pittman 3-yd run plus 5-yd illegal use of hands penalty on OAK Grant to OAK 29. B. Johnson 10-yd pass to K. Johnson to OAK 20. Alstott 3-yd run to OAK 17. B. Johnson 12-yd pass to Alstott to OAK 5.

3rd: TB—TD: McCardell 8-yd pass from B. Johnson (Gramatca kick), 9:30. Key plays: B. Johnson 10-yd run to TB 29. B. Johnson 9-yd pass to K. Johnson to TB 40. B. Johnson 11-yd pass to Jurevicius to OAK 46. B. Johnson 33-yd pass to Jurevicius to OAK 14. B. Johnson 12-yd pass to Dilger to OAK 1. TD: D. Smith 44-yd interception return (Gramatica kick), 10:13. OAK—TD: Porter 39-yd pass from Gannon, 12:46. Key plays: Gannon 25-yd pass to Jolley to OAK 42. 6-yd pass interference on TB's Quarles to TB 46. Gannon 7-yd pass to Ritchie to TB 39.

4th: OAK—TD: E. Johnson 13-yd return of blocked punt, 0:44. TD: Rice 48-yd pass from Gannon, 8:54. Key plays: OAK take over at OAK 22 after TB FG attempt. Gannon 9-yd pass to Jolley to OAK 31. Gannon 7-yd pass to Wheatley to OAK 38. Gannon 14-yd pass to Jolley to TB 45. TB—TD: Brooks 44-yd interception return (Gramatica kick), 13:42. TD—D. Smith 50-yd interception return (Gramatica kick), 14:58.

Individual Statistics

Passing: OAK—Gannon 24–44 for 272 yds. TB—B. Johnson 18–34 for 215 yds.
Rushing: OAK—Garner 7–10, Crockett 2–6, Gannon 2–3. TB—Pittman 29–124, Alstott 10–15, B. Johnson 1–10, Stecker 1–1, Tupa 1–0.
Receiving: OAK—Rice 5–77, Porter 4–62, Jolley 5–59, Garner 7–51, T. Brown 1–9, Wheatley 1–7, Ritchie 1–7. TB—Jurevicius 4–78, K. Johnson 6–69, Alstott 5–43, McCardell 2–13, Dilger 1–12..
Field goals: OAK—Janikowski 1–1. TB—Gramatica 2–2.
Punting: OAK—Lechler 5. TB—Tupa 4.
Kick/Punt Returns: OAK—Knight 8, Gordon 3, Cooper 1. TB—Stecker 3, Williams 1, D. Smith 1.
Interceptions: OAK—Gannon 5. TB—B. Johnson 1.

MVP: Dexter Jackson, Tampa Bay defensive back.

Statistics of the Game

	Raiders	Buccaneers
First downs	11	24
3rd down efficiency	7/16	6/15
Total offense (net yards)	269	365
Plays	60	76
Average gain	4.5	4.8
Rushing yards (net)	19	150
Rushes	11	42
Average per rush	1.7	3.6
Passing yards (net)	250	215
Completions/attempts	24/44	18/34
Yards per pass	5.1	6.3
Yards lost to sacks	22	0
Had intercepted	5	1
Punts/average	5/39	5/31
Penalties/yards	7/51	5/41
Fumbles/lost	1/0	1/0
Time of possession	22:46	37:14

NATIONAL LEAGUE CHAMPIONS

Year	Champion	(W-L-T)
1920	Akron Pros	(6–0–3)
1921	Chicago Bears (Staley's)	(10-1-1)
1922	Canton Bulldogs	(10-0-2)
1923	Canton Bulldogs	(11-0-1)
1924	Cleveland Indians	(7-1-1)
1925	Chicago Cardinals	(11-2-1)
1926	Frankford Yellow Jackets	(14-1-1)
1927	New York Giants	(11-1-1)
1928	Providence Steamrollers	(8-1-2)
1929	Green Bay Packers	(12-0-1)
1930	Green Bay Packers	(10-3-1)
1931	Green Bay Packers	(12-2-0)
1932	Chicago Bears	(7-1-6)

Year	Eastern Conference winners (W-L-T)	Western Conference winners (W-L-T)	League champion playoff results
1933	New York Giants (11-3-0)	Chicago Bears (10-2-1)	Chicago Bears 23, New York 21
1934	New York Giants (8-5-0)	Chicago Bears (13-0-0)	New York 30, Chicago Bears 13
1935	New York Giants (9-3-0)	Detroit Lions (7-3-2)	Detroit 26, New York 7
1936	Boston Redskins (7-5-0)	Green Bay Packers (10-1-1)	Green Bay 21, Boston 6
1937	Washington Redskins (8-3-0)	Chicago Bears (9-1-1)	Washington 28, Chicago Bears 21
1938	New York Giants (8-2-1)	Green Bay Packers (8-3-0)	New York 23, Green Bay 17
1939	New York Giants (9-1-1)	Green Bay Packers (9-2-0)	Green Bay 27, New York 0
1940	Washington Redskins (9-2-0)	Chicago Bears (8-3-0)	Chicago Bears 73, Washington 0
1941	New York Giants (8-3-0)	Chicago Bears (10-1-1)[2]	Chicago Bears 37, New York 9
1942	Washington Redskins (10-1-1)	Chicago Bears (11-0-0)	Washington 14, Chicago Bears 6
1943	Washington Redskins (6-3-1)[2]	Chicago Bears (8-1-1)	Chicago Bears 41, Washington 21
1944	New York Giants (8-1-1)	Green Bay Packers (8-2-0)	Green Bay 14, New York 7
1945	Washington Redskins (8-2-0)	Cleveland Rams (9-1-0)	Cleveland 15, Washington 14
1946	New York Giants (7-3-1)	Chicago Bears (8-2-1)	Chicago Bears 24, New York 14
1947	Philadelphia Eagles (8-4-0)[2]	Chicago Cardinals (9-3-0)	Chicago Cardinals 28, Philadelphia 21
1948	Philadelphia Eagles (9-2-1)	Chicago Cardinals (11-1-0)	Philadelphia 7, Chicago Cardinals 0
1949	Philadelphia Eagles (11-1-0)	Los Angeles Rams (8-2-2)	Philadelphia 14, Los Angeles 0
1950[1]	Cleveland Browns (10-2-0)[2, 3]	Los Angeles Rams (9-3-0)[2]	Cleveland 30, Los Angeles 28
1951[1]	Cleveland Browns (11-1-0)	Los Angeles Rams (8-4-0)	Los Angeles 24, Cleveland 17
1952[1]	Cleveland Browns (8-4-0)	Detroit Lions (9-3-0)[2]	Detroit 17, Cleveland 7
1953	Cleveland Browns (11-1-0)	Detroit Lions (10-2-0)	Detroit 17, Cleveland 16
1954	Cleveland Browns (9-3-0)	Detroit Lions (9-2-1)	Cleveland 56, Detroit 10
1955	Cleveland Browns (9-2-1)	Los Angeles Rams (8-3-1)	Cleveland 38, Los Angeles 14
1956	New York Giants (8-3-1)	Chicago Bears (9-2-1)	New York 47, Chicago Bears 7
1957	Cleveland Browns (9-2-1)	Detroit Lions (8-4-0)[2]	Detroit 59, Cleveland 14
1958	New York Giants (9-3-0)[2]	Baltimore Colts (9-3-0)	Baltimore 23, New York 17[4]
1959	New York Giants (10-2-0)	Baltimore Colts (9-3-0)	Baltimore 31, New York 16
1960	Philadelphia Eagles (10-2-0)	Green Bay Packers (8-4-0)	Philadelphia 17, Green Bay 13
1961	New York Giants (10-3-1)	Green Bay Packers (11-3-0)	Green Bay 37, New York 0
1962	New York Giants (12-2-0)	Green Bay Packers (13-1-0)	Green Bay 16, New York 7
1963	New York Giants (11-3-0)	Chicago Bears (11-1-2)	Chicago 14, New York 10
1964	Cleveland Browns (10-3-1)	Baltimore Colts (12-2-0)	Cleveland 27, Baltimore 0
1965	Cleveland Browns (11-3-0)	Green Bay Packers (11-3-1)[2]	Green Bay 23, Cleveland 12
1966	Dallas Cowboys (10-3-1)	Green Bay Packers (12-2-0)	Green Bay 34, Dallas 27
1967	Dallas Cowboys (9-5-0)[2]	Green Bay Packers (9-4-1)[2]	Green Bay 21, Dallas 17
1968	Cleveland Browns (10-4-0)[2]	Baltimore Colts (13-1-0)[2]	Baltimore 34, Cleveland 0
1969	Cleveland Browns (10-3-1)[2]	Minnesota Vikings (12-2-0)[2]	Minnesota 27, Cleveland 7

1. League was divided into American and National Conferences, 1950-52 and again in 1970, when leagues merged. 2. Won divisional playoff. 3. Cleveland Browns and San Francisco 49ers joined league after All-America Football Conference (1946–1949) folded. 4. Won at 8:15 of sudden death overtime period.

NATIONAL CONFERENCE CHAMPIONS

Year	Eastern Division	Central Division	Western Division	Champion
1970	Dallas Cowboys (10-4-0)	Minnesota Vikings (12-2-0)	San Francisco 49ers (10-3-1)	Dallas
1971	Dallas Cowboys (11-3-0)	Minnesota Vikings (11-3-0)	San Francisco 49ers (9-5-0)	Dallas
1972	Washington Redskins (11-3-0)	Green Bay Packers (10-4-0)	San Francisco 49ers (8-5-1)	Washington
1973	Dallas Cowboys (10-4-0)	Minnesota Vikings (12-2-0)	Los Angeles Rams (12-2-0)	Minnesota
1974	St. Louis Cardinals (10-4-0)	Minnesota Vikings (10-4-0)	Los Angeles Rams (10-4-0)	Minnesota
1975	St. Louis Cardinals (11-3-0)	Minnesota Vikings (12-2-0)	Los Angeles Rams (10-4-0)	Dallas[1]
1976	Dallas Cowboys (11-3-0)	Minnesota Vikings (11-2-1)	Los Angeles Rams (10-3-1)	Minnesota
1977	Dallas Cowboys (12-2-0)	Minnesota Vikings (9-5-0)	Los Angeles Rams (10-4-0)	Dallas
1978	Dallas Cowboys (12-4-0)	Minnesota Vikings (8-7-1)	Los Angeles Rams (12-4-0)	Dallas
1979	Dallas Cowboys (11-5-0)	Tampa Bay Buccaneers (10-6-0)	Los Angeles Rams (9-7-0)	Los Angeles
1980	Philadelphia Eagles (12-4-0)	Minnesota Vikings (9-7-0)	Atlanta Falcons (12-4-0)	Philadelphia
1981	Dallas Cowboys (12-4-0)	Tampa Bay Buccaneers (9-7-0)	San Francisco 49ers (13-3-0)	San Francisco
1982[2]				Washington
1983	Washington Redskins (14-2-0)	Detroit Lions (8-8-0)	San Francisco 49ers (10-6-0)	Washington
1984	Washington Redskins (11-5-0)	Chicago Bears (10-6-0)	San Francisco 49ers (15-1-0)	San Francisco
1985	Dallas Cowboys (10-6-0)	Chicago Bears (15-1-0)	Los Angeles Rams (11-5-0)	Chicago
1986	New York Giants (14-2-0)	Chicago Bears (14-2-0)	San Francisco 49ers (10-5-1)	New York
1987	Washington Redskins (11-4-0)	Chicago Bears (11-4-0)	San Francisco 49ers (13-2-0)	Washington
1988	Philadelphia Eagles (10-6-0)	Chicago Bears (12-4-0)	San Francisco 49ers (10-6-0)	San Francisco
1989	New York Giants (12-4-0)	Minnesota Vikings (10-6-0)	San Francisco 49ers (14-2-0)	San Francisco
1990	New York Giants (13-3-0)	Chicago Bears (11-5-0)	San Francisco 49ers (14-2-0)	New York
1991	Washington (14-2-0)	Detroit Lions (12-4-0)	New Orleans Saints (11-5-0)	Washington
1992	Dallas Cowboys (13-3-0)	Minnesota Vikings (11-5-0)	San Francisco 49ers (14-2-0)	Dallas
1993	Dallas Cowboys (12-4-0)	Detroit Lions (10-6-0)	San Francisco 49ers (10-6-0)	Dallas
1994	Dallas Cowboys (12-4-0)	Minnesota Vikings (10-6-0)	San Francisco 49ers (13-3-0)	San Francisco
1995	Dallas Cowboys (12-4-0)	Green Bay Packers (11-5-0)	San Francisco 49ers (11-5-0)	Dallas
1996	Dallas Cowboys (10-6-0)	Green Bay Packers (13-3-0)	Carolina Panthers (12-4-0)	Green Bay
1997	New York Giants (10-5-1)	Green Bay Packers (13-3-0)	San Francisco 49ers (13-3-0)	Green Bay
1998	Dallas Cowboys (10-6-0)	Minnesota Vikings (15-1-0)	Atlanta Falcons (14-2-0)	Atlanta
1999	Washington Redskins (10-6-0)	Tampa Bay Buccaneers (11-5-0)	St. Louis Rams (13-3-0)	St. Louis
2000	New York Giants (12-4-0)	Minnesota Vikings (11-5-0)	New Orleans Saints (10-6-0)	New York
2001	Philadelphia Eagles (11-5-0)	Chicago Bears (13-3-0)	St. Louis Rams (14-2-0)	St. Louis

Year	East	North	South	West	Champion
2002	Philadelphipa (12-4-0)	Green Bay (12-4-0)	Tampa Bay (12-4-0)	San Francisco (10-6-0)	Tampa Bay

1. Wild card. 2. Schedule reduced to 9 games from usual 16, with no standings kept in Eastern, Central, and Western Divisions, because of 57-day player strike. Washington Redskins won conference title and also had best regular-season record (8-1-0).

AMERICAN LEAGUE CHAMPIONS

Year	Eastern Division (W-L-T)	Western Division (W-L-T)	League champion, playoff results
1960	Houston Oilers (10-4-0)	Los Angeles Chargers (10-4-0)	Houston 24, Los Angeles 16
1961	Houston Oilers (10-3-1)	San Diego Chargers (12-2-0)	Houston 10, San Diego 3
1962	Houston Oilers (11-3-0)	Dallas Texans (11-3-0)	Dallas 20, Houston 17[1]
1963	Boston Patriots (8-6-1)[2]	San Diego Chargers (11-3-0)	San Diego 51, Boston 10
1964	Buffalo Bills (12-2-0)	San Diego Chargers (8-5-1)	Buffalo 20, San Diego 7
1965	Buffalo Bills (10-3-1)	San Diego Chargers (9-2-3)	Buffalo 23, San Diego 0
1966	Buffalo Bills (9-4-1)	Kansas City Chiefs (11-2-1)	Kansas City 31, Buffalo 7
1967	Houston Oilers (9-4-1)	Oakland Raiders (13-1-0)	Oakland 40, Houston 7
1968	New York Jets (11-3-0)	Oakland Raiders (12-2-0)[2]	New York 27, Oakland 23
1969	New York Jets (10-4-0)	Oakland Raiders (12-1-1)	Kansas City 17, Oakland 7[3]

1. Won at 2:45 of second sudden death overtime period. 2. Won divisional playoff. 3. Kansas City defeated New York, 13-6, and Oakland defeated Houston, 56-7, in interdivisional playoffs.

AMERICAN CONFERENCE CHAMPIONS

Year	Eastern Division	Central Division	Western Division	Champion
1970	Baltimore Colts (11-2-1)	Cincinnati Bengals (8-6-0)	Oakland Raiders (8-4-2)	Baltimore
1971	Miami Dolphins (10-3-1)	Cleveland Browns (9-5-0)	Kansas City Chiefs (10-3-1)	Miami
1972	Miami Dolphins (14-0-0)	Pittsburgh Steelers (11-3-0)	Oakland Raiders (10-3-1)	Miami
1973	Miami Dolphins (12-2-0)	Cincinnati Bengals (10-4-0)	Oakland Raiders (9-4-1)	Miami
1974	Miami Dolphins (11-3-0)	Pittsburgh Steelers (10-3-1)	Oakland Raiders (12-2-0)	Pittsburgh
1975	Baltimore Colts (10-4-0)	Pittsburgh Steelers (12-2-0)	Oakland Raiders (12-2-0)	Pittsburgh
1976	Baltimore Colts (11-3-0)	Pittsburgh Steelers (10-4-0)	Oakland Raiders (13-1-0)	Oakland
1977	Baltimore Colts (10-4-0)	Pittsburgh Steelers (9-5-0)	Denver Broncos (12-2-0)	Denver
1978	New England Patriots (11-5-0)	Pittsburgh Steelers (14-2-0)	Denver Broncos (10-6-0)	Pittsburgh
1979	Miami Dolphins (10-6-0)	Pittsburgh Steelers (12-4-0)	San Diego Chargers (12-4-0)	Pittsburgh
1980	Buffalo Bills (11-5-0)	Cleveland Browns (11-5-0)	San Diego Chargers (11-5-0)	Oakland[1]

Year	Eastern Division	Central Division	Western Division	Champion
1981	Miami Dolphins (11-4-1)	Cincinnati Bengals (12-4-0)	San Diego Chargers (10-6-0)	Cincinnati
1982[2]	Miami Dolphins won the conference title, but the Los Angeles Raiders had best regular-season record (8-1-0).			
1983	Miami Dolphins (12-4-0)	Pittsburgh Steelers (10-6-0)	Los Angeles Raiders (12-4-0)	Los Angeles
1984	Miami Dolphins (14-2-0)	Pittsburgh Steelers (9-7-0)	Denver Broncos (13-3-0)	Miami
1985	Miami Dolphins (12-4-0)	Cleveland Browns (8-8)	Los Angeles Raiders (12-4-0)	New England[1]
1986	New England Patriots (11-5-0)	Cleveland Browns (12-4-0)	Denver Broncos (11-5-0)	Denver
1987	Indianapolis Colts (9-6-0)	Cleveland Browns (10-5-0)	Denver Broncos (10-4-1)	Denver
1988	Buffalo Bills (12-4-0)	Cincinnati Bengals (12-4-0)	Seattle Seahawks (9-7-0)	Cincinnati
1989	Buffalo Bills (9-7-0)	Cleveland Browns (9-6-1)	Denver Broncos (11-5-0)	Denver
1990	Buffalo Bills (13-3-0)	Cincinnati Bengals (9-7-0)	Los Angeles Raiders (12-4-0)	Buffalo
1991	Buffalo Bills (13-3-0)	Houston Oilers (11-5-0)	Denver Broncos (12-4-0)	Buffalo
1992	Miami Dolphins (11-5-0)	Pittsburgh Steelers (11-5-0)	San Diego Chargers (11-5-0)	Buffalo[1]
1993	Buffalo Bills (12-4-0)	Houston Oilers (12-4-0)	Kansas City Chiefs (11-5-0)	Buffalo
1994	Miami Dolphins (10-6-0)	Pittsburgh Steelers (12-4-0)	San Diego Chargers (11-5-0)	San Diego
1995	Buffalo Bills (10-6-0)	Pittsburgh Steelers (11-5-0)	Kansas City Chiefs (13-3-0)	Pittsburgh
1996	New England Patriots (11-5-0)	Pittsburgh Steelers (10-6-0)	Denver Broncos (13-3-0)	New England
1997	New England Patriots (10-6-0)	Pittsburgh Steelers (11-5-0)	Kansas City Chiefs (13-3-0)	Denver[1]
1998	New York Jets (12-4-0)	Jacksonville Jaguars (11-5-0)	Denver Broncos (14-2-0)	Denver
1999	Indianapolis Colts (13-3-0)	Jacksonville Jaguars (14-2-0)	Seattle Seahawks (9-7-0)	Tennessee[1]
2000	Miami Dolphins (11-5-0)	Tennessee Titans (13-3-0)	Oakland Raiders (12-4-0)	Baltimore[1]
2001	New England Patriots (11-5-0)	Pittsburgh Steelers (13-3-0)	Oakland Raiders (10-6-0)	New England

Year	East	North	South	West	Champion
2002	N.Y. Jets (9-7-0)	Pittsburgh (10-5-1)	Tennessee (11-5-0)	Oakland (11-5-0)	Oakland

1. Wild card. 2. Schedule reduced to 9 games from usual 16, with no standings kept in Eastern, Central, and Western Divisions, because of 57-day player strike.

NFL INDIVIDUAL LIFETIME, SEASON, AND GAME RECORDS

(American Football League records were incorporated into NFL records after merger of the leagues.)

Players listed in boldface were active during the 2002 season. The NFL does not recognize records from the All-American Football Conference (AAFC) which existed from 1946 to 1949. The 49ers, Browns, and Colts merged with the NFL in 1949.

All-Time Scoring Leaders (Through 2002)

Rank	Player	Touchdowns	Player	Points
1.	**Jerry Rice**	203	**Gary Anderson**	2,225
2.	**Emmitt Smith**	162	**Morten Andersen**	2,131
3.	Marcus Allen	145	George Blanda	2,002
4.	**Cris Carter**	129	Norm Johnson	1,736
5.	Jim Brown	126	Nick Lowery	1,711
6.	Walter Payton	125	Jan Stenerud	1,699
7.	**Marshall Faulk**	120	Eddie Murray	1,594
8.	John Riggins	116	Al Del Greco	1,584
9.	Lenny Moore	113	Pat Leahy	1,470
10.	Barry Sanders	109	Jim Turner	1,439

All-Time Leading Receivers (Through 2002)

Rank	Player	Number of receptions	Player	Yards
1.	**Jerry Rice**	1,456	**Jerry Rice**	21,597
2.	**Cris Carter**	1,115	**Tim Brown**	14,167
3.	**Tim Brown**	1,018	James Lofton	14,004
4.	Andre Reed	951	**Cris Carter**	13,899
5.	Art Monk	940	Henry Ellard	13,777
6.	Irving Fryar	851	Andre Reed	13,198
7.	Steve Largent	819	Steve Largent	13,089
8.	Henry Ellard	814	Irving Fryar	12,785
9.	**Larry Centers**	808	Art Monk	12,721
10.	James Lofton	764	Charlie Joiner	12,146

All-Time Leading Passers (Through 2002)

Rank	Player	Yards	Player	Number completed	Player	Number of touchdowns
1.	Dan Marino	61,361	Dan Marino	4,967	Dan Marino	420
2.	John Elway	51,475	John Elway	4,123	Fran Tarkenton	342
3.	Warren Moon	49,247	Warren Moon	3,985	**Brett Favre**	314
4.	Fran Tarkenton	47,003	Fran Tarkenton	3,686	John Elway	300
5.	Dan Fouts	43,040	**Brett Favre**	3,652	Warren Moon	291
6.	**Brett Favre**	42,285	Joe Montana	3,409	Johnny Unitas	290
7.	Joe Montana	40,551	Dan Fouts	3,297	Joe Montana	273
8.	Johnny Unitas	40,239	**Vinny Testaverde**	3,211	Dave Krieg	261
9.	**Vinny Testaverde**	39,558	Dave Krieg	3,105	Sonny Jurgensen	255
10.	Dave Krieg	38,151	Boomer Esiason	2,969	Dan Fouts	254

All-Time Interception Leaders (Through 2002)

		Amount
1.	Paul Krause	81
2.	Emlen Tunnell	79
3.	**Rod Woodson**	69
4.	Dick Lane	68
5.	Ken Riley	65
6.	Ronnie Lott	63
7.	Dave Brown	62
	Dick LeBeau	62
9.	Emmitt Thomas	58
10.	Mel Blount	57
	Bobby Boyd	57
	Johnny Robinson	57
	Everson Walls	57
	Eugene Robinson	57

All-Time Sack Leaders (Through 2002)

		Amount
1.	Reggie White	196.5
2.	**Bruce Smith**	195.0
3.	Kevin Greene	157.0
4.	Chris Doleman	149.5
5.	Richard Dent	137.5
6.	Lawrence Taylor	132.5
	Leslie O'Neal	132.5
8.	**John Randle**	132.0
9.	Rickey Jackson	128.0
10.	Derrick Thomas	126.5

All-Time Leading Rushers (Through 2002)

		Yards
1.	**Emmitt Smith**	17,162
2.	Walter Payton	16,726
3.	Barry Sanders	15,269
4.	Eric Dickerson	13,259
5.	Tony Dorsett	12,739
6.	Jim Brown	12,312
7.	Marcus Allen	12,243
8.	Franco Harris	12,120
9.	Thurman Thomas	23,074
10.	**Jerome Bettis**	11,542

Scoring

Most points scored, lifetime—2,225, Gary Anderson, Pittsburgh, 1982–94; Philadelphia, 1995–96; San Francisco, 1997; Minnesota, 1998–2002.

Most points, season—176, Paul Hornung, Green Bay, 1960 (15 td, 41 pat, 15 fg).

Most points, game—40, Ernie Nevers, Chicago Cardinals, 1929 (6 td, 4 pat).

Most touchdowns, lifetime—203, Jerry Rice, San Francisco, 1985–2000; Oakland 2001–2002.

Most points after touchdown, lifetime—943, George Blanda, Chicago Bears, 1949–58; Baltimore, 1950; Houston, 1960–66; Oakland, 1967–75.

Most field goals, lifetime—494, Gary Anderson, Pittsburgh, 1982–94; Philadelphia, 1995–96; San Francisco, 1997; Minnesota, 1998–2002.

Most field goals, season—39, Olindo Mare, Miami, 1999.

Most field goals, game—7, Jim Bakken, St. Louis, 1967; Rich Karlis, Minnesota, 1989; and Chris Boniol, Dallas, 1996.

Longest field goal—63 yards, Tom Dempsey, New Orleans, 1970; Jason Elam, Denver, 1998.

Rushing

Most yards gained, lifetime—17,162, Emmitt Smith, Dallas Cowboys, 1990–2002.

Most yards gained, season—2,105, Eric Dickerson, Los Angeles, 1984.

Most yards gained, game—278, Corey Dillon, Cincinnati, 2000.

Most touchdowns, lifetime—153, Emmitt Smith, Dallas, 1990–2002.

Most touchdowns, season—25, Emmitt Smith, Dallas, 1995.

Most touchdowns, game—6, Ernie Nevers, Chicago Cardinals, 1929.

Longest run from scrimmage—99 yards, Tony Dorsett, Dallas, 1983.

Receiving

Most pass receptions, lifetime—1,456, Jerry Rice, San Francisco, 1985–2000; Oakland 2001–2002.

Most pass receptions, season—123, Herman Moore, Detroit, 1995.

Most pass receptions, game—20, Terrell Owens, San Francisco, 2000.

Most yards gained, pass receptions, lifetime—21,597, Jerry Rice, San Francisco, 1985–2000; Oakland 2001–2002.

Most yards gained, receptions, season—1,848, Jerry Rice, San Francisco, 1995.

Most yards gained, receptions, game—336, Flipper Anderson, Los Angeles Rams, 1989.

Most touchdown receptions, lifetime—192, Jerry Rice, San Francisco, 1985–2000; Oakland 2001–2002.

Most touchdown pass receptions, season—22, Jerry Rice, San Francisco, 1987.

Most touchdown pass receptions, game—5, Bob Shaw, Chicago Cards, 1950; Kellen Winslow, San Diego, 1981; Jerry Rice, San Francisco, 1990.

Interceptions

Most pass interceptions, lifetime—81, Paul Krause, Washington, 1964-67; Minnesota, 1968–79.

Most pass interceptions, season—14, Richard (Night Train) Lane, Detroit, 1952.

Most pass interceptions, game—4, by 18 players.

Longest pass interception return—104 yards, James Willis, Philadelphia, 1996.

Kicking

Highest average punting, lifetime—45.1 yards, Sammy Baugh, Washington, 1937–52.

Longest punt return—103 yards, Robert Bailey, L.A. Rams, 1994.

Longest kick-off return—106 yards, Roy Green, St. Louis, 1979; Al Carmichael, Green Bay, 1956; Noland Smith, Kansas City, 1967.

Passing

Most touchdown passes, lifetime—420, Dan Marino, Miami, 1983–99.

Most touchdown passes, season—48, Dan Marino, Miami, 1984.

Most touchdown passes, game—7, Sid Luckman, Chicago Bears, 1943; Adrian Burk, Philadelphia, 1954; George Blanda, Houston, 1961; Y. A. Tittle, N.Y. Giants, 1962; Joe Kapp, Minnesota, 1969.

Longest pass completion—99 yards, Frank Filchock (to Andy Farkas), Washington, 1939; George Izo (to Bob Mitchell), Washington, 1963; Karl Sweetan (to Pat Studstill), Detroit, 1966; Sonny Jurgensen (to Gerry Allen), Washington, 1968; Jim Plunkett (to Cliff Branch) L.A. Raiders, 1983; Ron Jaworski (to Mike Quick), Philadelphia, 1985; Stan Humphries (to Tony Martin), San Diego, 1994; Brett Favre (to Robert Brooks), Green Bay, 1995.

Most passes completed, lifetime—4,967, Dan Marino, Miami, 1983–99.

Most passes completed, season—404, Warren Moon, 1991.

Most passes completed, game—45, Drew Bledsoe, New England, 1994.

Most yards gained, lifetime—61,361, Dan Marino, Miami, 1983–99.

Most yards gained, season—5,084, Dan Marino, Miami, 1984.

Most yards gained, game—554, Norm Van Brocklin, Los Angeles, 1951.

PRO FOOTBALL HALL OF FAME

(National Football Museum, Canton, Ohio)

Teams named are those with which player is best identified; figures in parentheses indicate number of playing seasons.

Adderley, Herb, defensive back, Packers, Cowboys (12)	1961–72
Allen, George, coach, Rams, Redskins (12)	1966–77
Allen, Marcus, running back, Raiders, Chiefs (16)	1982–97
Alworth, Lance, wide receiver, Chargers, Cowboys (12)	1961–72
Atkins, Doug, defensive end, Browns, Bears, Saints (17)	1953–69
Badgro, Morris, end, N.Y. Yankees, Giants, Brooklyn Dodgers (8)	1927, 1930–36
Barney, Lem, defensive back, Lions (11)	1967–78
Battles, Cliff, back, Redskins (6)	1932–37
Baugh, Sammy, quarterback, Redskins (16)	1936–52
Bednarik, Chuck, center-lineback, Eagles (14)	1949–62
Bell, Bert, NFL founder, Eagles and Steelers, NFL Commissioner	1946–59
Bell, Bobby, linebacker, Chiefs (12)	1963–74
Berry, Raymond, end, Colts (13)	1955–67
Bethea, Elvin, defensive end, Oilers (16)	1968–83
Bidwell, Charles W., owner, Chicago Cardinals	1933–47
Biletnikoff, Fred, wide receiver, Raiders (14)	1965–78
Blanda, George, quarterback-kicker, Bears, Oilers, Raiders (27)	1949–75
Blount, Mel, cornerback, Pittsburgh Steelers (14)	1970–83
Bradshaw, Terry, quarterback, Pittsburgh Steelers (14)	1970–83
Brown, Jim, fullback, Browns (9)	1957–65
Brown, Paul E., coach, Browns (1946–62), Bengals (1968–75)	1946–75
Brown, Roosevelt, tackle, Giants (13)	1953–65
Brown, Willie, cornerback, Broncos, Raiders (16)	1963–78
Buchanan, Buck, tackle, Chiefs (11)	1963–73
Buoniconti, Nick, linebacker, Patriots, Dolphins (14)	1962–74, 1976
Butkus, Dick, linebacker, Bears (9)	1965–73
Campbell, Earl, running back, Oilers, Saints (8)	1978–85
Canadeo, Tony, back, Packers (11)	1941–52
Carr, Joe, NFL president (18)	1921–39
Casper, Dave, tight end, Raiders, Oilers, Vikings (11)	1974–84
Chamberlin, Guy, end, 4 teams (9)	1919–27
Christiansen, Jack, defensive back, Lions (8)	1951–58
Clark, Earl (Dutch), quarterback, Spartans, Lions (7)	1931–38
Connor, George, tackle, linebacker, Bears (8)	1948–55
Conzelman, Jimmy, quarterback, 5 teams (10), owner, Detroit Panthers	1921–48
Creekmur, Lou, offensive tackle/guard, Lions (10)	1950–59
Csonka, Larry, back, Dolphins, Giants (11)	1968–79
Davis, Al, owner, Raiders, coach, general manager	1963–
Davis, Willie, defensive end, Packers (10)	1960–69
Dawson, Len, quarterback, Steelers, Browns, Texans, Chiefs (19)	1957–75
DeLamielleure, guard, Bills, Browns (13)	1973–84
Dickerson, Eric, running back, Rams, Colts, Raiders, Falcons (11)	1983–93
Dierdorf, Dan, tackle/center, Cardinals (13)	1971–83
Ditka, Mike, tight end, Bears, Eagles, Cowboys (12)	1961–72
Donovan, Art, defensive tackle, Colts (12)	1950–61
Dorsett, Tony, running back, Cowboys, Broncos (12)	1977–88
Driscoll, John (Paddy), quarterback, Cards, Bears (11)	1919–29
Dudley, Bill, back, Steelers, Lions, Redskins (9)	1942–53
Edwards, Albert Glen (Turk), tackle, Redskins (9)	1932–40
Ewbank, Weeb, coach, Colts, Jets (20)	1954–73
Fears, Tom, end, Rams (9); coach, Saints	1948–56
Finks, Jim, administrator/general manager, Vikings, Bears, Saints	1964–93
Flaherty, Ray, end, Yankees, Giants (9); coach, Redskins, Yankees (14)	1928–49
Ford, Len, end, defensive end, Browns, Packers (11)	1948–58
Fouts, Dan, quarterback, Chargers (15)	1973–87
Fortmann, Daniel J., guard, Bears (8)	1936–43
Gatski, Frank, offensive lineman, Browns (12)	1946–57
George, Bill, linebacker, Bears, Rams (15)	1952–66
Gibbs, Joe, coach, Redskins (11)	1981–92
Gifford, Frank, back, Giants (12)	1952–64
Gillman, Sid, coach, Rams, Chargers, Oilers (18)	1955–70, 73–74
Graham, Otto, quarterback, Browns (10)	1946–55
Grange, Harold (Red), back, Bears, Yankees (9)	1925–34
Grant, Bud, coach, Vikings (18)	1967–85
Greene, Joe, defensive tackle, Steelers (13)	1968–81
Gregg, Forrest, tackle, Packers (15)	1956–71
Griese, Bob, quarterback, Dolphins (14)	1967–80
Groza, Lou, place-kicker, tackle, Browns (21)	1946–67
Guyon, Joe, back, 6 teams (8)	1919–27
Halas, George, NFL founder, owner and coach, Staleys and Bears, end (11)	1919–27
Ham, Jack, linebacker, Steelers (13)	1970–82
Hampton, Dan, defensive end, defensive tackle, Bears (12)	1979–90
Hannah, John, guard, Patriots (13)	1973–85
Harris, Franco, running back, Steelers, Seahawks (13)	1972–84
Haynes, Mike, defensive back, Patriots, Raiders (10)	1976–85
Healey, Ed, tackle, Bears (8)	1920–27
Hein, Mel, center, Giants (15)	1931–45
Hendricks, Ted, linebacker, Colts, Packers, Raiders (15)	1969–83
Henry, Wilbur (Pete), tackle, Bulldogs, Giants (8)	1920–28
Herber, Arnie, quarterback, Packers, Giants (13)	1930–45
Hewitt, Bill, end, Bears, Eagles (9)	1932–43
Hinkle, Clarke, fullback, Packers (10)	1932–41
Hirsch, Elroy (Crazy Legs), back, end, Rams (12)	1946–57
Hornung, Paul, running back, Packers (9)	1957–62, 64–66
Houston, Ken, defensive back, Oilers, Redskins (14)	1967–80
Hubbard, R. (Cal), tackle, Giants, Packers (9)	1927–36
Huff, Sam, linebacker, Giants, Redskins (13)	1956–67, 1969
Hunt, Lamar, founder A.F.L., owner Texans, Chiefs	1959–
Hutson, Don, end, Packers (11)	1935–45
Johnson, John Henry, back, 49ers, Lions, Steelers, Oilers (13)	1954–66
Johnson, Jimmy, cornerback, 49ers (16)	1961–76
Joiner, Charlie, receiver, Oilers, Bengals, Chargers (18)	1969–86
Jones, David (Deacon), defensive end, Rams, Chargers, Redskins (14)	1961–74
Jones, Stan, defensive tackle, Bears, Redskins (13)	1954–66
Jordan, Henry, defensive tackle, Browns, Packers (13)	1957–69
Jurgensen, Sonny, quarterback, Eagles, Redskins (18)	1957–74
Kelly, Jim, quaterback, Bills (11)	1986–96
Kelly, Leroy, running back, Browns (10)	1964–73
Kiesling, Walt, guard, 6 teams (13)	1926–38
Kinard, Frank (Bruiser), tackle, Dodgers (9)	1938–47
Krause, Paul, safety, Redskins, Vikings (16)	1964–79
Lambeau, Earl (Curly), NFL founder, coach, end, back, Packers (11)	1919–53
Lambert, Jack, linebacker, Steelers (11)	1974–84
Landry, Tom, coach, Cowboys (29)	1960–88
Lane, Richard (Night Train), defensive back, Rams, Cardinals, Lions (14)	1952–65
Langer, Jim, center, Dolphins, Vikings (12)	1970–81
Lanier, Willie, linebacker, Chiefs (11)	1967–77
Largent, Steve, receiver, Seahawks (14)	1976–89
Lary, Yale, defensive back, punter, Lions (11)	1952–64
Laveill, Dante, end, Browns (11)	1946–56
Layne, Bobby, quarterback, Bears, Lions, Steelers (15)	1948–62
Leemans, Alphonse (Tuffy), back, Giants (8)	1936–43
Levy, Marv, coach, Chiefs, Bills (17)	1978–97
Lilly, Bob, defensive tackle, Cowboys (14)	1961–74
Little, Larry, guard, Dolphins, Chargers (14)	1967–80
Lofton, James, wide receiver, Packers, Raiders, Bills, Rams, Eagles (16)	1978–93
Lombardi, Vince, coach, Packers, Redskins (11)	1959–70
Long, Howie, defensive end, Raiders (13)	1981–93
Lott, Ronnie, cornerback, safety, 49ers, Raiders, Jets (14)	1981–94
Luckman, Sid, quarterback, Bears (12)	1939–50
Lyman, Roy (Link), tackle, Bulldogs, Bears (11)	1922–34
Mack, Tom, guard, Rams (13)	1966–78
Mackey, John, tight end, Colts, Chargers (10)	1963–72
Mara, Tim, NFL founder, owner, Giants	1925–59
Mara, Wellington, NFL executive, owner, Giants	1937–
Marchetti, Gino, defensive end, Colts (14)	1952–66
Marshall, George P., NFL founder, owner, Redskins	1932–65
Matson, Ollie, back, Cardinals, Rams, Lions, Eagles (14)	1952–66
Maynard, Don, receiver, Giants, Jets, Cardinals (15)	1958–73
McAfee, George, back, Bears (8)	1940–50

McCormack, Mike, tackle, N.Y. Yanks, Cleveland Browns (10)	1951–62
McDonald, Tommy, wide receiver, Eagles, Cowboys, Rams, Falcons, Browns (12)	1957–68
McElhenny, Hugh, back, 49ers, Vikings, Giants (13)	1952–64
McNally, John (Blood), back, 7 teams (15)	1925–39
Michalske, August, guard, Yankees, Packers (11)	1926–37
Millner, Wayne, end, Redskins (7)	1936–45
Mitchell, Bobby, wide receiver, Browns, Redskins (11)	1958–68
Mix, Ron, tackle, Chargers (11)	1960–71
Montana, Joe, quarterback, 49ers, Chiefs (15)	1979–94
Moore, Lenny, back, Colts (12)	1956–67
Motley, Marion, fullback, Browns, Steelers (9)	1946–55
Munchak, Mike, guard, Oilers (12)	1982–93
Munoz, Anthony, tackle, Bengals (13)	1980–92
Musso, George, guard-tackle, Bears (12)	1933–44
Nagurski, Bronko, fullback, Bears (9)	1930–43
Namath, Joe, quarterback, Jets, Rams (13)	1965–77
Neale, Earle (Greasy), coach, Eagles	1941–50
Nevers, Ernie, fullback, Chicago Cardinals (5)	1926–31
Newsome, Ozzie, tight end, Browns (13)	1978–90
Nitschke, Ray, linebackers, Packers (15)	1958–72
Noll, Chuck, coach, Steelers (23)	1969–81
Nomellini, Leo, defensive tackle, 49ers (14)	1950–63
Olsen, Merlin, defensive tackle, Rams (15)	1962–76
Otto, Jim, center, Raiders (15)	1960–74
Owen, Steve, tackle, Giants (9), coach, Giants (13)	1924–53
Page, Alan, defensive tackle, Vikings, Bears (15)	1967–81
Parker, Clarence (Ace), quarterback, Dodgers (7)	1937–46
Parker, Jim, guard, tackle, Colts (11)	1957–67
Payton, Walter, running back, Bears (13)	1977–89
Perry, Joe, fullback, 49ers, Colts (16)	1948–63
Pihos, Pete, end, Eagles (9)	1947–55
Ray, Hugh (Shorty), NFL advisor	1938–52
Reeves, Dan, owner, Rams	1941–71
Renfro, Mel, cornerback, safety, Cowboys (14)	1964–77
Riggins, John, running back, Jets, Redskins (14)	1971–84
Ringo, Jim, center, Packers (15)	1953–67
Robustelli, Andy, defensive end, Rams, Giants (14)	1951–64
Rooney, Art, NFL founder, owner, Steelers	1933–88
Rooney, Dan, contributor, Steelers	1955–
Rozelle, Pete, commissioner, NFL	1960–89
St. Claire, Bob, tackle, 49ers (11)	1953–63
Sayers, Gale, back, Bears (7)	1965–71
Schmidt, Joe, linebacker, Lions (13)	1953–65
Schramm, Tex, administrator, Rams, Cowboys (42)	1947–89
Selmon, Lee Roy, defensive end, Buccaneers (13)	1976–84
Shaw, Billy, guard, Bills (9)	1961–69
Shell, Art, tackle, Raiders (15)	1968–82
Shula, Don, coach, Colts, Dolphins (33)	1963–95
Simpson, O.J., back, Bills, 49ers (11)	1969–79
Singletary, Mike, linebacker, Bears (12)	1981–92
Slater, Jackie, tackle, Rams (20)	1976–95
Smith, Jackie, tight end, Cardinals, Cowboys (16)	1963–78
Stallworth, John, wide receiver, Steelers (14)	1974–87
Starr, Bart, quarterback, coach, Packers (16)	1956–71
Staubach, Roger, quarterback, Cowboys (11)	1969–79
Stautner, Ernie, defensive tackle, Steelers (14)	1950–63
Stenerud, Jan, placekicker, Chiefs, Packers, Vikings (19)	1967–85
Stephenson, Dwight, center, Dolphins (8)	1980–87
Stram, Hank, coach, Texans/Chiefs, Saints (17)	1960–74, 1976–77
Strong, Ken, back, Giants, Yankees (14)	1929–47
Stydahar, Joe, tackle, Bears (9); coach, Rams, Cardinals (5)	1936–54
Swann, Lynn, wide receiver, Steelers (9)	1974–82
Tarkenton, Fran, quarterback, Vikings, Giants (18)	1961–78
Taylor, Charlie, wide receiver, Redskins (14)	1964–77
Taylor, Jim, fullback, Packers, Saints (10)	1958–67
Taylor, Lawrence, linebacker, Giants (13)	1981–93
Thorpe, Jim, back, 7 teams (12)	1915–28
Tittle, Y.A., quarterback, Colts, 49ers, Giants (17)	1948–64
Trafton, George, center, Bears (13)	1920–32
Trippi, Charley, back, Chicago Cardinals (9)	1947–55
Tunnell, Emlen, defensive back, Giants, Packers (14)	1948–61
Turner, Clyde (Bulldog), center, Bears (13)	1940–52
Unitas, John, quarterback, Colts (18)	1956–73
Upshaw, Gene, guard, Raiders (15)	1967–81
Van Brocklin, Norm, quarterback, Rams, Eagles (12)	1949–60
Van Buren, Steve, back, Eagles (8)	1944–51
Walker, Doak, running back, def. back, kicker, Lions (6)	1950–55
Walsh, Bill, coach, 49ers (10)	1979–88
Warfield, Paul, wide receiver, Browns, Dolphins (13)	1964–74, 76–77
Waterfield, Bob, quarterback, Rams (8)	1945–52
Webster, Mike, center, Steelers, Chiefs (17)	1974–90
Weinmeister, Arnie, tackle, N.Y. Yankees, Giants (6)	1948–53
White, Randy, defensive tackle, Cowboys (14)	1975–88
Wilcox, Dave, linebacker, 49ers (11)	1964–74
Willis, Bill, guard, Browns (8)	1946–53
Wilson, Larry, defensive back, Cardinals (13)	1960–72
Winslow, Kellen, tight end, Chargers (9)	1979–87
Wood, Willie, safety, Packers (12)	1960–71
Wojciechowicz, Alex, center, Lions, Eagles (13)	1938–50
Yary, Ron, tackle, Vikings, Rams (15)	1968–82
Youngblood, Jack, defensive end, Rams (14)	1971–84

Basketball

Basketball is one of the few sports whose exact origin is definitely known. In the winter of 1891–1892, Dr. James Naismith, an instructor in the YMCA Training College (now Springfield College) at Springfield, Mass., deliberately invented the game of basketball in order to provide indoor exercise and competition for the students between the closing of the football season and the opening of the baseball season. He affixed peach baskets overhead on the walls at opposite ends of the gymnasium and organized teams to play his new game in which the purpose was to toss an association (soccer) ball into one basket and prevent the opponents from tossing the ball into the other basket. Because Dr. Naismith had eighteen available players when he invented the game, the first rule was: "There shall be nine players on each side." Later the number of players became optional, depending upon the size of the available court, but the five-player standard was adopted when the game spread over the country. U.S. soldiers brought basketball to Europe in World War I, and it soon became a worldwide sport.

College Basketball

NCAA CHAMPIONS

1939	Oregon
1940	Indiana & USC
1941	Wisconsin
1942	Stanford
1943	Wyoming
1944	Utah
1945	Oklahoma A & M
1946	Oklahoma A & M
1947	Holy Cross
1948	Kentucky
1949	Kentucky
1950	C.C.N.Y.
1951	Kentucky
1952	Kansas
1953	Indiana
1954	La Salle
1955	San Francisco
1956	San Francisco
1957	North Carolina
1958	Kentucky
1959	California
1960	Ohio State
1961	Cincinnati
1962	Cincinnati
1963	Loyola (Chicago)
1964	UCLA
1965	UCLA
1966	Texas Western
1967–73	UCLA
1974	North Carolina State
1975	UCLA
1976	Indiana
1977	Marquette
1978	Kentucky
1979	Michigan State
1980	Louisville
1981	Indiana
1982	North Carolina
1983	North Carolina State

1984	Georgetown	1988	Kansas	1992	Duke	1996	Kentucky	2000	Michigan State
1985	Villanova	1989	Michigan	1993	North Carolina	1997	Arizona	2001	Duke
1986	Louisville	1990	UNLV	1994	Arkansas	1998	Kentucky	2002	Maryland
1987	Indiana	1991	Duke	1995	UCLA	1999	Connecticut	2003	Syracuse

NATIONAL INVITATION TOURNAMENT (NIT) CHAMPIONS

1938	Temple	1953	Seton Hall	1965	St. John's (N.Y.C.)	1978	Texas	1992	Virginia
1939	Long Island U.	1954	Holy Cross	1966	Brigham Young	1979	Indiana	1993	Minnesota
1940	Colorado	1955	Duquesne	1967	So. Illinois	1980	Virginia	1994	Villanova
1941	Long Island U.	1956	Louisville	1968	Dayton	1981	Tulsa	1995	Virginia Tech
1942	West Virginia	1957	Bradley	1969	Temple	1982	Bradley	1996	Nebraska
1943–44	St. John's (N.Y.C.)	1958	Xavier (Cincinnati)	1970	Marquette	1983	Fresno State	1997	Michigan
1945	DePaul	1959	St. John's (N.Y.C.)	1971	North Carolina	1984	Michigan	1998	Minnesota
1946	Kentucky	1960	Bradley	1972	Maryland	1985	UCLA	1999	California
1947	Utah	1961	Providence	1973	Virginia Tech	1986	Ohio State	2000	Wake Forest
1948	St. Louis	1962	Dayton	1974	Purdue	1987	So. Mississippi	2001	Tulsa
1949	San Francisco	1963	Providence	1975	Princeton	1988	Connecticut	2002	Memphis
1950	C.C.N.Y.	1964	Bradley	1976	Kentucky	1989	St. John's (N.Y.C.)	2003	St. John's (N.Y.C.)
1951	Brigham Young			1977	St. Bonaventure	1990	Vanderbilt		
1952	La Salle					1991	Stanford		

MEN'S NCAA BASKETBALL CHAMPIONSHIPS, 2003

Division I

First Round—East
No. Carolina 74, California 76 (OT)
So. Carolina St. 54, Oklahoma 71
Manhattan 65, Syracuse 76
Pennsylvania 63, Oklahoma State 77
Auburn 65, St. Joseph's 63 (OT)
East Tenn. St. 73, Wake Forest 76
Austin Peay 64, Louisville 86
Butler 47, Mississippi St. 46

First Round—Midwest
Holy Cross 68, Marquette 72
Southern Illinois 71, Missouri 72
Weber State 74, Wisconsin 81
Tulsa 84, Dayton 71
Indiana Purdue 64, Kentucky 95
Utah 60, Oregon 58
Wagner 61, Pittsburgh 87
Alabama 62, Indiana 67

First Round—South
Brigham Young 53, Connecticut 58
San Diego 69, Stanford 77
UNC-Asheville 61, Texas 82
Purdue 80, Louisiana State 56
Sam Houston 55, Florida 85
Colorado 64, Michigan State 79
Troy State 59, Xavier 71
UNC-Wilmington 73, Maryland 75

First Round—West
Gonzaga 74, Cincinnati 69
Vermont 51, Arizona 80
Western Kentucky 60, Illinois 65
Arizona State 84, Memphis 71
Central Michigan 79, Creighton 73
Utah State 61, Kansas 64
Colorado State 57, Duke 67
Wisc. Milwaukee 69, Notre Dame 70

Second Round—East
California 65, Oklahoma 74
Butler 79, Louisville 71
Oklahoma State 56, Syracuse 68
Auburn 68, Wake Forest 62

Second Round—Midwest
Missouri 92, Marquette 101 (OT)
Indiana 52, Pittsburgh 74
Tulsa 60, Wisconsin 61
Utah 54, Kentucky 74

Second Round—South
Connecticut 85, Stanford 74
Maryland 77, Xavier 64
Purdue 67, Texas 77
Michigan State 68, Florida 46

Second Round—West
Notre Dame 68, Illinois 60
Gonzaga 95, Arizona 96
Arizona State 76, Kansas 108
Central Michigan 60, Duke 86

Third Round—East
Butler 54, Oklahoma 65
Auburn 78, Syracuse 79

Third Round—Midwest
Wisconsin 57, Kentucky 63
Marquette 77, Pittsburgh 74

Third Round—South
Connecticut 78, Texas 82
Michigan State 60, Maryland 58

Third Round—West
Notre Dame 71, Arizona 88
Duke 65, Kansas 69

Regional Finals
East—Syracuse 63, Oklahoma 47
Midwest—Marquette 83, Kentucky 69
South—Michigan State 76, Texas 85
West—Kansas 78, Arizona 75

Final Four
(April 5, 2003, New Orleans, La.)
Marquette 61, Kansas 94
Syracuse 95, Texas 84

National Final
(April 7, 2003, New Orleans, La.)
Syracuse 81, Kansas 78

Division II

Semifinals
Kentucky Wesleyan 84, Bowie State 64
Northeastern State 84, Queens (N.C.) 69

Championship
Northeastern State 75, Kentucky Wesleyan 64

LEADING NCAA DIVISION I MEN, 2002–2003

POINTS PER GAME

	FGM	3FG	FT	PTS	PPG
Ruben Douglas, New Mexico	218	94	253	783	28.0
Henry Domercant, Eastern Ill.	252	84	222	810	27.9
Mike Helms, Oakland	241	74	196	752	26.9
Michael Watson, Univ. of Mo.-KC	247	118	128	740	25.5
Troy Bell, Boston College	224	106	227	781	25.2

FIELD-GOAL PERCENTAGE

	G	FGM	FGA	FG%
Adam Mark, Belmont	28	199	297	67.0%
Rickey White, Maine	24	131	198	66.2
Matt Nelson, Colorado St.	31	205	319	64.3
Armond Williams, Ill.-Chicago	30	168	263	63.9
Michael Harris, Rice	28	172	276	62.3

REBOUNDING

	G	REB	RPG
Brandon Hunter, Ohio	30	378	12.6
Amien Hicks, Morris Brown	24	298	12.4
Adam Sonn, Belmont	29	352	12.1
Chris Kaman, Central Michigan	31	373	12.0
David West, Xavier	32	379	11.8

ASSISTS

	G	AST	APG
Martell Bailey, Ill.-Chicago	30	244	8.1
Marques Green, St. Bonaventure	27	216	8.0
T. J. Ford, Texas	33	254	7.7
Elliott Prasse-Freeman, Harvard	27	207	7.7
Antawn Dobie, Long Island	26	193	7.4

FREE-THROW PERCENTAGE

	G	FT	FTA	FT%
Steve Drabyn, Belmont	29	78	82	95.1%
Matt Logie, Lehigh	28	91	96	94.8
Hollis Price, Oklahoma	34	130	140	92.9
Brian Dux, Canisius	28	115	125	92.0
J. J. Redick, Duke	33	102	111	91.9

THREE-PT FIELD-GOAL PERCENTAGE

	G	3FG	3FGA	3FG%
Jeff Schiffner, Pennsylvania	28	74	150	49.3%
Kyle Korver, Creighton	34	129	269	48.0
Terrence Woods, Florida A&M	28	139	304	45.7
Chez Marks, Morehead St.	29	82	180	45.6
Tyson Dorsey, Samford	27	75	165	45.5

NCAA DIVISION I SINGLE-GAME SCORING MARKS

	Year	Pts
Kevin Bradshaw, US Int'l vs. Loyola-CA	1991	72
Pete Maravich, LSU vs. Alabama	1970	69
Calvin Murphy, Niagara vs. Syracuse	1969	68
Jay Handlan, Wash. & Lee vs. Furman	1951	66
Pete Maravich, LSU vs. Tulane	1969	66
Anthony Roberts, Oral Rbts. vs. N.C. A.&T.	1977	66
Anthony Roberts, Oral Rbts. vs. Oregon	1977	65
Scott Haffner, Evansville vs. Dayton	1989	65
Pete Maravich, LSU vs. Kentucky	1970	64
Johnny Neumann, Ole Miss vs. LSU	1971	63
Hersey Hawkins, Bradley vs. Detroit	1988	63

NCAA DIVISION I INDIVIDUAL CAREER RECORDS

SCORING—TOTAL POINTS

	Yrs	Last	Gm	Pts
Pete Maravich, LSU	3	1970	83	3,667
Freeman Williams, Port. St.	4	1978	106	3,249
Lionel Simmons, La Salle	4	1990	131	3,217
Alphonso Ford, Miss. Val. St.	4	1993	109	3,165
Harry Kelly, Texas Southern	4	1983	110	3,066
Hersey Hawkins, Bradley	4	1988	125	3,008
Oscar Robertson, Cincinnati	3	1960	88	2,973
Danny Manning, Kansas	4	1988	147	2,951
Alfredrick Hughes, Loyola-Ill.	4	1985	120	2,914
Elvin Hayes, Houston	3	1968	93	2,884

SCORING—AVERAGE POINTS

	Yrs	Last	Pts	Avg
Pete Maravich, LSU	3	1970	3,667	44.2
Austin Carr, Notre Dame	3	1971	2,560	34.6
Oscar Robertson, Cinn.	3	1960	2,973	33.8
Calvin Murphy, Niagara	3	1970	2,548	33.1
Dwight Lamar, SW La.	2	1973	1,862	32.7
Frank Selvy, Furman	3	1954	2,538	32.5
Rick Mount, Purdue	3	1970	2,323	32.3
Darrell Floyd, Furman	3	1956	2,281	32.1
Nick Werkman, Seton Hall	3	1964	2,273	32.0
Willie Humes, Idaho St.	2	1971	1,510	31.5

BLOCKED SHOTS—AVERAGE

	Yrs	Last	No	Avg
Keith Closs, Cen. Conn. St.	2	1996	317	5.87
Adonal Foyle, Colgate	3	1997	492	5.66
David Robinson, Navy	2	1987	351	5.24
Wojciech Mydra, La.-Monroe	4	2002	535	4.65
Shaquille O'Neal, LSU	3	1992	412	4.58

Note: minimum 225 blocked shots.

ASSISTS—TOTAL

	Yrs	Last	Gm	No
Bobby Hurley, Duke	4	1993	140	1,076
Chris Corchiani, N.C. State	4	1991	124	1,038
Ed Cota, N. Carolina	4	2000	138	1,030
Keith Jennings, E. Tenn. St.	4	1991	127	983
Sherman Douglas, Syracuse	4	1989	138	960
Tony Miller, Marquette	4	1995	123	956
Greg Anthony, Portland/UNLV	4	1991	138	950
Doug Gottlieb, ND/Okla St.	4	2000	124	947
Gary Payton, Oregon St.	4	1990	120	938
Orlando Smart, San Fran.	4	1994	116	902

STEALS—AVERAGE

	Yrs	Last	No	Avg
Desmond Cambridge, Alabama A&M	3	2002	330	3.93
Mookie Blaylock, Oklahoma	2	1989	281	3.80
Ronn McMahon, Eastern Wash.	3	1990	225	3.52
Eric Murdock, Providence	4	1991	376	3.21
Van Usher, Tennessee Tech	3	1992	270	3.18

Note: minimum 225 steals.

REBOUNDS—TOTAL, SINCE 1973

	Yrs	Last	Gm	No
Tim Duncan, Wake Forest	4	1997	128	1,570
Derrick Coleman, Syracuse	4	1990	143	1,537
Malik Rose, Drexel	4	1996	120	1,514
Ralph Sampson, Virginia	4	1983	132	1,511
Pete Padgett, Nevada-Reno	4	1976	104	1,464
Lionel Simmons, La Salle	4	1990	131	1,429
Anthony Bonner, St. Louis	4	1990	133	1,424
Tyrone Hill, Xavier-Ohio	4	1990	126	1,380
Popeye Jones, Murray St.	4	1992	123	1,374
Michael Brooks, La Salle	4	1980	114	1,372

WOMEN'S NCAA CHAMPIONSHIPS, 2003

Division I

First Round—Mideast
Tennessee 95, Alabama State 43
Virginia 72, Illinois 56
South Carolina 68, Chattanooga 54
Penn State 64, Holy Cross 33
Colorado 84, Brigham Young 45
North Carolina 72, Austin Peay 70
George Washington 71, Oklahoma 61
Villanova 51, St. Francis (Pa.) 36

First Round—Midwest
Duke 66, Georgia State 48
Utah 73, DePaul 64
Georgia 80, Charlotte 61
Rutgers 64, Western Ky. 52
New Mexico 91, Miami (Fla.) 85
Mississippi State 73, Manhattan 47
UC-Santa Barbara 71, Xavier 62
Texas Tech 67, SW Missouri State 59

First Round—East
Connecticut 91, Boston Univ. 44
Michigan State 47, Texas Christian 50
Boston College 73, Old Dominion 72
Vanderbilt 54, Liberty 44
Arizona 47, Notre Dame 59
Kansas State 79, Harvard 69
Virginia Tech 61, Georgia Tech 59
Purdue 66, Valparaiso 51

First Round—West
Louisiana State 86, SW Texas State 50
Wis.-Green Bay 78, Washington 65
Louisiana Tech 94, Pepperdine 60
Ohio State 66, Weber State 44
Minnesota 68, Tulane 48
Stanford 82, W. Michigan 66
Arkansas 71, Cincinnati 57
Texas 90, Hampton 46

Second Round—Mideast
Tennessee 81, Virginia 51
South Carolina 67, Penn State 77
Colorado 86, North Carolina 67
George Washington 57, Villanova 70

Second Round—Midwest
Duke 65, Utah 54
Georgia 74, Rutgers 64
New Mexico 73, Mississippi State 61
UC-Santa Barbara 68, Texas Tech 72

Second Round—East
Connecticut 81, Texas Christian 66
Boston College 86, Vanderbilt 85
Notre Dame 59, Kansas State 53
Virginia Tech 62, Purdue 80

Second Round—West
Louisiana State 80, Wis.-Green Bay 69
Louisiana Tech 74, Ohio State 61
Minnesota 68, Stanford 56
Arkansas 50, Texas 67

Third Round—Mideast
Tennessee 86, Penn State 58
Colorado 51, Villanova 53

Third Round—Midwest
Duke 66, Georgia 63
New Mexico 48, Texas Tech 71

Third Round—East
Connecticut 70, Boston College 49
Notre Dame 47, Purdue 66

Third Round—West
Louisiana State 69, Louisiana Tech 63
Minnesota 60, Texas 73

Regional Finals
Mideast—Tennessee 73, Villanova 49
Midwest—Duke 57, Texas Tech 51
East—Connecticut 73, Purdue 64
West—Louisiana State 60, Texas 78

Final Four
(April 6, 2003, Atlanta, Ga.)
Tennessee 66, Duke 56
Texas 69, Connecticut 71

National Championship
(April 8, 2003, Atlanta, Ga.)
Tennessee 68, Connecticut 73

Division II

Semifinals
California (Pa.) 43, Northern Kentucky 45
Bentley 62, South Dakota State 69 (OT)

Championship
Northern Kentucky 50, South Dakota State 65

LEADING NCAA DIVISION I WOMEN, 2002–2003

POINTS PER GAME

	FGM	3FG	FT	PTS	PPG
Chandi Jones, Houston	275	52	168	770	27.5
Molly Creamer, Bucknell	239	62	219	759	27.1
LaToya Thomas, Mississippi State	297	18	182	794	25.6
Tiffany Webb, Wright State	246	50	132	674	24.1
Kelly Mazzante, Penn State	292	98	155	837	23.9

FIELD-GOAL PERCENTAGE

	G	FGM	FGA	FG%
Courtney Coleman, Ohio State	32	184	278	66.2%
Janel McCarville, Minnesota	30	155	236	65.7
Chantelle Anderson, Vanderbilt	32	217	341	63.6
Gerlonda Hardin, Austin Peay	31	198	312	63.5
Jocelyn Penn, South Carolina	30	282	449	62.8

THREE-POINT FIELD-GOAL PERCENTAGE

	G	3FG	3FGA	3FG%
Sinnamonn Garrett, New Mexico State	28	68	137	49.6%
Jess Hansen, UC-Santa Barbara	32	67	142	47.2
Kate Bulger, West Virginia	28	77	164	47.0
Lindsay Bowen, Michigan State	29	77	166	46.4
Laura Spanheimer, Creighton	33	77	168	45.8

FREE-THROW PERCENTAGE

	G	FT	FTA	FT%
Jill Marano, La Salle	29	88	93	94.6%
Kandi Brown, Morehead State	28	104	111	93.7
Kim McDonough, St. Peter's	28	81	88	92.0
Erin Thorn, Brigham Young	31	87	95	91.6
Carey Sauer, San Francisco	29	112	123	91.1

REBOUNDS PER GAME

	G	REB	RPG
Jennifer Butler, Massachusetts	28	412	14.7
Angela Buckner, Wichita State	28	366	13.1
Cheryl Ford, Louisiana Tech	34	438	12.9
Ashlee Kelly, Quinnipiac	28	338	12.1
Tori Talbert, Southwest Texas State	32	385	12.0

ASSISTS PER GAME

	G	AST	APG
La'Terrica Dobin, Northwestern State	28	298	10.6
Latesha Lee, Jackson St.	29	214	7.4
Laura Ingham, Nevada	29	212	7.3
Ashley McElhiney, Vanderbilt	30	219	7.3
Ivelina Vrancheva, Florida Int'l.	30	217	7.2

OTHER TOURNAMENTS, 2002–2003

MEN

NIT—St. John's 70, Georgetown 67
NAIA Div. I—Concordia (Calif.) 88, Mountain State (W. Va.) 84 (OT)
NAIA Div. II—Northwestern (Iowa) 77, Bethany (Kans.) 57

WOMEN

NIT—Auburn 64, Baylor 63
NAIA Div. I—Southern Nazarene 71, Oklahoma City 70
NAIA Div. II—Hastings (Nebr.) 59, Dakota Wesleyan (S.D.) 53

Professional Basketball

NATIONAL BASKETBALL ASSOCIATION CHAMPIONS

The National Basketball Association was originally the Basketball Association of America. It took its current name in 1949 when it merged with the National Basketball League.

Year	Eastern Conference	Western Conference	Winner (Series)
1947	Philadelphia Warriors	Chicago Stags	Philadelphia Warriors (4–1)
1948	Philadelphia Warriors	Baltimore Bullets	Baltimore Bullets (4–2)
1949	Washington Capitols	Minneapolis Lakers	Minneapolis Lakers (4–2)
1950	Syracuse Nationals	Minneapolis Lakers	Minneapolis Lakers (4–2)
1951	New York Knickerbockers	Rochester Royals	Rochester Royals (4–3)
1952	New York Knickerbockers	Minneapolis Lakers	Minneapolis Lakers (4–3)
1953	New York Knickerbockers	Minneapolis Lakers	Minneapolis Lakers (4–1)
1954	Syracuse Nationals	Minneapolis Lakers	Minneapolis Lakers (4–3)
1955	Syracuse Nationals	Ft. Wayne Pistons	Syracuse Nationals (4–3)
1956	Philadelphia Warriors	Ft. Wayne Pistons	Philadelphia Warriors (4–1)
1957	Boston Celtics	St. Louis Hawks	Boston Celtics (4–3)
1958	Boston Celtics	St. Louis Hawks	St. Louis Hawks (4–2)
1959	Boston Celtics	Minneapolis Lakers	Boston Celtics (4–0)
1960	Boston Celtics	St. Louis Hawks	Boston Celtics (4–3)
1961	Boston Celtics	St. Louis Hawks	Boston Celtics (4–1)
1962	Boston Celtics	Los Angeles Lakers	Boston Celtics (4–3)
1963	Boston Celtics	Los Angeles Lakers	Boston Celtics (4–2)
1964	Boston Celtics	San Francisco Warriors	Boston Celtics (4–1)
1965	Boston Celtics	Los Angeles Lakers	Boston Celtics (4–1)
1966	Boston Celtics	Los Angeles Lakers	Boston Celtics (4–3)
1967	Philadelphia 76ers	San Francisco Warriors	Philadelphia 76ers (4–2)
1968	Boston Celtics	Los Angeles Lakers	Boston Celtics (4–2)
1969	Boston Celtics	Los Angeles Lakers	Boston Celtics (4–3)
1970	New York Knickerbockers	Los Angeles Lakers	New York Knickerbockers (4–3)
1971	Baltimore Bullets	Milwaukee Bucks	Milwaukee Bucks (4–0)
1972	New York Knickerbockers	Los Angeles Lakers	Los Angeles Lakers (4–1)
1973	New York Knickerbockers	Los Angeles Lakers	New York Knickerbockers (4–1)
1974	Boston Celtics	Milwaukee Bucks	Boston Celtics (4–3)
1975	Washington Bullets	Golden State Warriors	Golden State Warriors (4–0)
1976	Boston Celtics	Phoenix Suns	Boston Celtics (4–2)
1977	Philadelphia 76ers	Portland Trail Blazers	Portland Trail Blazers (4–2)
1978	Washington Bullets	Seattle SuperSonics	Washington Bullets (4–3)
1979	Washington Bullets	Seattle SuperSonics	Seattle SuperSonics (4–1)
1980	Philadelphia 76ers	Los Angeles Lakers	Los Angeles Lakers (4–2)
1981	Boston Celtics	Houston Rockets	Boston Celtics (4–2)
1982	Philadelphia 76ers	Los Angeles Lakers	Los Angeles Lakers (4–2)
1983	Philadelphia 76ers	Los Angeles Lakers	Philadelphia 76ers (4–0)
1984	Boston Celtics	Los Angeles Lakers	Boston Celtics (4–3)
1985	Boston Celtics	Los Angeles Lakers	Los Angeles Lakers (4–2)
1986	Boston Celtics	Houston Rockets	Boston Celtics (4–2)
1987	Boston Celtics	Los Angeles Lakers	Los Angeles Lakers (4–2)
1988	Detroit Pistons	Los Angeles Lakers	Los Angeles Lakers (4–3)
1989	Detroit Pistons	Los Angeles Lakers	Detroit Pistons (4–0)
1990	Detroit Pistons	Portland Trail Blazers	Detroit Pistons (4–1)
1991	Chicago Bulls	Los Angeles Lakers	Chicago Bulls (4–1)
1992	Chicago Bulls	Portland Trail Blazers	Chicago Bulls (4–2)
1993	Chicago Bulls	Phoenix Suns	Chicago Bulls (4–2)
1994	New York Knickerbockers	Houston Rockets	Houston Rockets (4–3)
1995	Orlando Magic	Houston Rockets	Houston Rockets (4–0)
1996	Chicago Bulls	Seattle SuperSonics	Chicago Bulls (4–2)
1997	Chicago Bulls	Utah Jazz	Chicago Bulls (4–2)
1998	Chicago Bulls	Utah Jazz	Chicago Bulls (4–2)
1999	New York Knickerbockers	San Antonio Spurs	San Antonio Spurs (4–1)
2000	Indiana Pacers	Los Angeles Lakers	Los Angeles Lakers (4–2)
2001	Philadelphia 76ers	Los Angeles Lakers	Los Angeles Lakers (4–1)
2002	New Jersey Nets	Los Angeles Lakers	Los Angeles Lakers (4–0)
2003	New Jersey Nets	San Antonio Spurs	San Antonio Spurs (4–2)

INDIVIDUAL NBA SCORING CHAMPIONS

Season	Player, Team	G	FG	FT	Pts	Avg
1953–54	Neil Johnston, Philadelphia Warriors	72	591	577	1,759	24.4
1954–55	Neil Johnston, Philadelphia Warriors	72	521	589	1,631	22.7
1955–56	Bob Pettit, St. Louis Hawks	72	646	557	1,849	25.7
1956–57	Paul Arizin, Philadelphia Warriors	71	613	591	1,817	25.6

Season	Player, Team	G	FG	FT	Pts	Avg
1957–58	George Yardley, Detroit Pistons	72	673	655	2,001	27.8
1958–59	Bob Pettit, St. Louis Hawks	72	719	667	2,105	29.2
1959–60	Wilt Chamberlain, Philadelphia Warriors	72	1,065	577	2,707	37.6
1960–61	Wilt Chamberlain, Philadelphia Warriors	79	1,251	531	3,033	38.4
1961–62	Wilt Chamberlain, Philadelphia Warriors	80	1,597	835	4,029	50.4
1962–63	Wilt Chamberlain, San Francisco Warriors	80	1,463	660	3,586	44.8
1963–64	Wilt Chamberlain, San Francisco Warriors	80	1,204	540	2,948	36.9
1964–65	Wilt Chamberlain, San Francisco Warriors/Phila. 76ers	73	1,063	408	2,534	34.7
1965–66	Wilt Chamberlain, Philadelphia 76ers	79	1,074	501	2,649	33.5
1966–67	Rick Barry, San Francisco Warriors	78	1,011	753	2,775	35.6
1967–68	Dave Bing, Detroit Pistons	79	835	472	2,142	27.1
1968–69	Elvin Hayes, San Diego Rockets	82	930	467	2,327	28.4
1969–70	Jerry West, Los Angeles Lakers	74	831	647	2,309	31.2
1970–71	Lew Alcindor,[1] Milwaukee Bucks	82	1,063	470	2,596	31.7
1971–72	Kareem Abdul-Jabbar, Milwaukee Bucks	81	1,159	504	2,822	34.8
1972–73	Nate Archibald, Kansas City/Omaha Kings	80	1,028	663	2,719	34.0
1973–74	Bob McAdoo, Buffalo Braves	74	901	459	2,261	30.8
1974–75	Bob McAdoo, Buffalo Braves	82	1,095	641	2,831	34.5
1975–76	Bob McAdoo, Buffalo Braves	78	934	559	2,427	31.1
1976–77	Pete Maravich, New Orleans Jazz	73	886	501	2,273	31.1
1977–78	George Gervin, San Antonio Spurs	82	864	504	2,232	27.2
1978–79	George Gervin, San Antonio Spurs	80	947	471	2,365	29.6
1979–80	George Gervin, San Antonio Spurs	78	1,024	505	2,585	33.1
1980–81	Adrian Dantley, Utah Jazz	80	909	632	2,452	30.7
1981–82	George Gervin, San Antonio Spurs	79	993	555	2,551	32.3
1982–83	Alex English, Denver Nuggets	82	959	406	2,326	28.4
1983–84	Adrian Dantley, Utah Jazz	79	802	813	2,418	30.6
1984–85	Bernard King, New York Knicks	55	691	426	1,809	32.9
1985–86	Dominique Wilkins, Atlanta Hawks	78	888	527	2,366	30.3
1986–87	Michael Jordan, Chicago Bulls[2]	82	1,098	833	3,041	37.1
1987–88	Michael Jordan, Chicago Bulls[3]	82	1,069	723	2,868	35.0
1988–89	Michael Jordan, Chicago Bulls[4]	81	966	674	2,633	32.5
1989–90	Michael Jordan, Chicago Bulls[5]	82	1,034	593	2,753	33.6
1990–91	Michael Jordan, Chicago Bulls[6]	82	990	571	2,580	31.5
1991–92	Michael Jordan, Chicago Bulls[7]	80	943	491	2,404	30.1
1992–93	Michael Jordan, Chicago Bulls[8]	78	992	476	2,541	32.6
1993–94	David Robinson, San Antonio Spurs[9]	80	840	693	2,383	29.8
1994–95	Shaquille O'Neal, Orlando Magic[10]	79	930	455	2,315	29.3
1995–96	Michael Jordan, Chicago Bulls[11]	82	916	548	2,491	30.4
1996–97	Michael Jordan, Chicago Bulls[11]	82	920	480	2,431	29.6
1997–98	Michael Jordan, Chicago Bulls[12]	82	881	565	2,357	28.7
1998–99	Allen Iverson, Philadelphia 76ers[13]	48	435	356	1,284	26.8
1999–2000	Shaquille O'Neal, L.A. Lakers	79	956	432	2,344	29.7
2000–01	Allen Iverson, Philadelphia 76ers[14]	71	762	585	2,207	31.1
2001–02	Allen Iverson, Philadelphia 76ers[15]	60	665	475	1,883	31.4
2002–03	Tracy McGrady, Orlando Magic	75	829	576	2,407	32.1

1. (Kareem Abdul-Jabbar). 2. Also had 12 3-point field goals. 3. Also had 7 3-point field goals. 4. Also had 27 3-point field goals. 5. Also had 92 3-point field goals. 6. Also had 29 3-point field goals. 7. Attempted 27 3-point field goals. 8. Also had 81 3-point field goals. 9. Also had 10 3-point field goals. 10. O'Neal scored no 3-point field goals in 1994–1995. 11. Also had 111 3-point field goals in both 1995–1996 and 1996–1997. 12. Also had 30 3-point field goals. 13. Also had 58 3-point field goals. 14. Also had 98 3-point field goals. 15. Also had 78 3-point field goals.

NBA MOST VALUABLE PLAYERS

1956 Bob Pettit, St. Louis
1957 Bob Cousy, Boston
1958 Bill Russell, Boston
1959 Bob Pettit, St. Louis
1960 Wilt Chamberlain, Philadelphia
1961–63 Bill Russell, Boston
1964 Oscar Robertson, Cincinnati
1965 Bill Russell, Boston
1966–68 Wilt Chamberlain, Philadelphia
1969 Wes Unseld, Baltimore
1970 Willis Reed, New York
1971–72 Lew Alcindor (Kareem Abdul-Jabbar), Milwaukee
1973 Dave Cowens, Boston
1974 Kareem Abdul-Jabbar, Milwaukee
1975 Bob McAdoo, Buffalo
1976–77 Kareem Abdul-Jabbar, L.A. Lakers
1978 Bill Walton, Portland
1979 Moses Malone, Houston
1980 Kareem Abdul-Jabbar, L.A. Lakers
1981 Julius Erving, Philadelphia
1982 Moses Malone, Houston
1983 Moses Malone, Philadelphia
1984 Larry Bird, Boston
1985 Larry Bird, Boston
1986 Larry Bird, Boston
1987 Magic Johnson, L.A. Lakers
1988 Michael Jordan, Chicago
1989 Magic Johnson, L.A. Lakers
1990 Magic Johnson, L.A. Lakers
1991 Michael Jordan, Chicago
1992 Michael Jordan, Chicago
1993 Charles Barkley, Phoenix
1994 Hakeem Olajuwon, Houston
1995 David Robinson, San Antonio
1996 Michael Jordan, Chicago
1997 Karl Malone, Utah
1998 Michael Jordan, Chicago
1999 Karl Malone, Utah
2000 Shaquille O'Neal, L.A. Lakers
2001 Allen Iverson, Philadelphia
2002 Tim Duncan, San Antonio
2003 Tim Duncan, San Antonio

NBA LIFETIME LEADERS

(through 2003 season)

Players in bold face active in 2002–2003 season

POINTS

	Yrs	Gm	Pts	Avg
Kareem Abdul-Jabbar	20	1,560	38,387	24.6
Karl Malone	18	1,434	36,374	25.4
Michael Jordan	15	1,072	32,292	30.1
Wilt Chamberlain	14	1,045	31,419	30.1
Moses Malone	19	1,329	27,409	20.6
Elvin Hayes	16	1,303	27,313	21.0
Hakeem Olajuwon	18	1,238	26,946	21.8
Oscar Robertson	14	1,040	26,710	25.7
Dominique Wilkins	15	1,074	26,668	24.8
John Havlicek	16	1,270	26,395	20.8

SCORING AVERAGE

Minimum of 400 games or 10,000 points

	Yrs	Gm	Pts	Avg
Michael Jordan	15	1,071	32,292	30.1
Wilt Chamberlain	14	1,045	31,419	30.1
Shaquille O'Neal	11	742	20,475	27.6
Elgin Baylor	14	846	23,149	27.4
Allen Iverson	7	487	13,170	27.0
Jerry West	14	932	25,192	27.0
Bob Pettit	11	792	20,880	26.4
George Gervin	10	791	20,708	26.2
Oscar Robertson	14	1,040	26,710	25.7
Karl Malone	18	1,434	36,374	25.4

FIELD GOALS MADE

	Yrs	FG	Att	Pct
Kareem Abdul-Jabbar	20	15,837	28,307	.559
Karl Malone	18	13,335	25,810	.517
Wilt Chamberlain	14	12,681	23,497	.540
Michael Jordan	15	12,192	24,537	.497
Elvin Hayes	16	10,976	24,272	.452
Hakeem Olajuwon	18	10,749	20,991	.512
Alex English	15	10,659	21,036	.507
John Havlicek	16	10,513	23,930	.439
Dominique Wilkins	15	9,963	21,589	.461
Patrick Ewing	15	9,702	19,241	.504

FREE THROWS

	Yrs	FT	Att	Pct
Karl Malone	18	9,619	12,963	.742
Moses Malone	19	8,531	11,090	.769
Oscar Robertson	14	7,694	9,185	.838
Michael Jordan	15	7,327	8,772	.835
Jerry West	14	7,160	8,801	.814
Dolph Schayes	16	6,979	8,274	.843
Adrian Dantley	15	6,832	8,351	.818
Kareem Abdul-Jabbar	20	6,712	9,304	.721
Charles Barkley	16	6,349	8,643	.735
Bob Pettit	11	6,182	8,119	.761

3–PT FIELD GOALS MADE

Reggie Miller	2,330
Dale Ellis	1,719
Glen Rice	1,554
Tim Hardaway	1,542
Dan Majerle	1,360

TOTAL MINUTES PLAYED

Kareem Abdul-Jabbar	57,446
Karl Malone	53,479
Elvin Hayes	50,000
Wilt Chamberlain	47,859
John Stockton	47,764

BLOCKED SHOTS

Hakeem Olajuwon	3,830
Kareem Abdul-Jabbar	3,189
Mark Eaton	3,064
David Robinson	2,954
Patrick Ewing	2,894

STEALS

John Stockton	3,265
Michael Jordan	2,514
Maurice Cheeks	2,310
Scottie Pippen	2,286
Clyde Drexler	2,207

REBOUNDS

Wilt Chamberlain	23,924	Robert Parish	14,715
Bill Russell	21,620	**Karl Malone**	14,601
Kareem Abdul-Jabbar	17,440	Nate Thurmond	14,464
Elvin Hayes	16,279	Walt Bellamy	14,241
Moses Malone	16,212	Wes Unseld	13,769

ASSISTS

John Stockton	15,806	**Rod Strickland**	7,704
Mark Jackson	10,215	**Gary Payton**	7,590
Magic Johnson	10,141	Maurice Cheeks	7,392
Oscar Robertson	9,887	Lenny Wilkens	7,211
Isiah Thomas	9,061	**Terry Porter**	7,160

NBA INDIVIDUAL RECORDS, GAME

(Through 2002–2003 season)

Most points, game—100, Wilt Chamberlain, Philadelphia vs. New York, 1962

Most free throws, game—28, Wilt Chamberlain, Philadelphia vs. New York, 1962; 28, Adrian Dantley, Utah vs. Houston, 1984

Most field goals, game—36, Wilt Chamberlain, Philadelphia vs. New York, 1962

Most assists, game—30, Scott Skiles, Orlando vs. Denver, 1990

Most rebounds, game—55, Wilt Chamberlain, Philadelphia vs. Boston, 1960

Most 3-pt. field goals, game—11, Dennis Scott, Orlando vs. Atlanta, 1996

Most blocked shots, game—17, Elmore Smith, Los Angeles vs. Portland, 1973

Most steals, game—11, Larry Kenon, San Antonio vs. Kansas City, 1976; 11, Kendall Gill, New Jersey vs. Miami, 1999

NATIONAL BASKETBALL ASSOCIATION FINAL STANDINGS, 2002–2003

EASTERN CONFERENCE

Atlantic Division	W	L	Pct	GB
New Jersey Nets[1]	49	33	.598	—
Philadelphia 76ers[2]	48	34	.585	1
Boston Celtics[2]	44	38	.537	5
Orlando Magic[2]	42	40	.512	7
Washington Wizards	37	45	.451	12
New York Knicks	37	45	.451	12
Miami Heat	25	57	.305	24

1. Division champion. 2. Playoff qualifier.

Central Division	W	L	Pct	GB
Detroit Pistons[1]	50	32	.610	—
Indiana Pacers[2]	48	34	.585	2
New Orleans Hornets[2]	47	35	.573	3
Milwaukee Bucks[2]	42	40	.512	8
Atlanta Hawks	35	47	.427	15
Chicago Bulls	30	52	.366	20
Toronto Raptors	24	58	.293	26
Cleveland Cavaliers	17	65	.207	33

WESTERN CONFERENCE

Midwest Division	W	L	Pct	GB
San Antonio Spurs[1]	60	22	.732	—
Dallas Mavericks[2]	60	22	.732	—
Minnesota Timberwolves[2]	51	31	.622	9
Utah Jazz[2]	47	35	.573	13
Houston Rockets	43	39	.524	17
Memphis Grizzlies	28	54	.341	32
Denver Nuggets	17	65	.207	43

Pacific Division	W	L	Pct	GB
Sacramento Kings[1]	59	23	.720	—
L.A. Lakers[2]	50	32	.610	9
Portland Trail Blazers[2]	50	32	.610	9
Phoenix Suns[2]	44	38	.537	15
Seattle SuperSonics	40	42	.488	19
Golden State Warriors	38	44	.463	21
L.A. Clippers	27	55	.329	32

1. Division champion. 2. Playoff qualifier.

NBA PLAYOFFS, 2003

EASTERN CONFERENCE

First Round
(Best of 7)
Detroit Pistons defeated Orlando Magic, 4 games to 3
New Jersey Nets defeated Milwaukee Bucks, 4 games to 2
Boston Celtics defeated Indiana Pacers, 4 games to 2
Philadelphia 76ers defeated New Orleans Hornets, 4 games to 2

Conference Semifinals
(Best of 7)
Detroit Pistons defeated Philadelphia 76ers, 4 games to 2
New Jersey Nets defeated Boston Celtics, 4 games to 0

Conference Finals
(Best of 7)
New Jersey Nets defeated Detroit Pistons, 4 games to 0

WESTERN CONFERENCE

First Round
(Best of 7)
San Antonio Spurs defeated Phoenix Suns, 4 games to 2
Sacramento Kings defeated Utah Jazz, 4 games to 1
Dallas Mavericks defeated Portland Trail Blazers, 4 games to 3
L.A. Lakers defeated Minnesota Timberwolves, 4 games to 2

Conference Semifinals
(Best of 7)
San Antonio Spurs defeated L.A. Lakers, 4 games to 2
Dallas Mavericks defeated Sacramento Kings, 4 games to 3

Conference Finals
(Best of 7)
San Antonio Spurs defeated Dallas Mavericks, 4 games to 2

NBA CHAMPIONSHIPS

San Antonio Spurs defeated New Jersey Nets, 4 games to 2
Tim Duncan, San Antonio, named Finals MVP

June 4—San Antonio 101, New Jersey 89
June 6—New Jersey 87, San Antonio 85
June 8—San Antonio 84, New Jersey 79
June 11—New Jersey 77, San Antonio 76
June 13—San Antonio 93, New Jersey 83
June 15—San Antonio 88, New Jersey 77

NBA INDIVIDUAL LEADERS, 2002–2003 SEASON

POINTS PER GAME
Minimum of 49 games played

	Gm	Pts	Avg
Tracy McGrady, Orlando	75	2,407	32.1
Kobe Bryant, L.A. Lakers	82	2,461	30.0
Allen Iverson, Philadelphia	82	2,262	27.6
Shaquille O'Neal, L.A. Lakers	67	1,841	27.5
Paul Pierce, Boston	79	2,048	25.9
Dirk Nowitzki, Dallas	80	2,011	25.1
Tim Duncan, San Antonio	81	1,884	23.3
Chris Webber, Sacramento	67	1,542	23.0
Kevin Garnett, Minnesota	82	1,883	23.0
Ray Allen, Seattle	76	1,713	22.5
Allan Houston, New York	82	1,845	22.5

REBOUNDS PER GAME
Minimum of 49 games played

	Gm	Reb	RPG
Ben Wallace, Detroit	73	1,126	15.4
Kevin Garnett, Minnesota	82	1,102	13.4
Tim Duncan, San Antonio	81	1,043	12.9
Jermaine O'Neal, Indiana	77	796	10.3
Brian Grant, Miami	82	837	10.2
Troy Murphy, Golden State	79	806	10.2
Dirk Nowitzki, Dallas	80	791	9.9
Shawn Marion, Phoenix	81	773	9.5
Jerome Williams, Toronto	71	650	9.2
P. J. Brown, New Orleans	78	701	9.0
Donyell Marshall, Chicago	78	699	9.0

ASSISTS PER GAME
Minimum of 49 games played

	Gm	Ast	Avg
Jason Kidd, New Jersey	80	711	8.9
Jason Williams, Memphis	76	631	8.3
Gary Payton, Milwaukee	80	663	8.3
Stephon Marbury, Phoenix	81	654	8.1
John Stockton, Utah	82	629	7.7
Jamaal Tinsley, Indiana	73	548	7.5
Jason Terry, Atlanta	81	600	7.4
Steve Nash, Dallas	82	598	7.3
Andre Miller, L.A. Clippers	80	537	6.7
Eric Snow, Philadelphia	82	544	6.6

FIELD GOAL PERCENTAGE
Minimum of 288 field goals made

	FGM	FGA	Pct
Eddy Curry, Chicago	335	573	.585
Shaquille O'Neal, L.A. Lakers	695	1,211	.574
Carlos Boozer, Cleveland	331	618	.536
P. J. Brown, New Orleans	319	601	.531
Radoslav Nesterovic, Minnesota	400	762	.525
Nene Hilario, Denver	321	619	.519
Tim Duncan, San Antonio	714	1,392	.513
Matt Harpring, Utah	521	1,020	.511
Pau Gasol, Memphis	569	1,116	.510
Brian Grant, Miami	344	676	.509

FREE-THROW PERCENTAGE
Minimum of 120 free throws made

	FTM	FTA	Pct
Allan Houston, New York	363	395	.919
Ray Allen, Seattle	316	345	.916
Steve Nash, Dallas	308	339	.909
Troy Hudson, Minnesota	208	231	.900
Reggie Miller, Indiana	207	230	.900
Jason Terry, Atlanta	259	292	.887
Dirk Nowitzki, Dallas	483	548	.881
Chauncey Billups, Detroit	318	362	.878
Jerry Stackhouse, Washington	455	518	.878
Darrell Armstrong, Orlando	165	188	.878

3-POINT FIELD GOAL PERCENTAGE
Minimum of 55 3-point field goals made

	3FGM	3FGA	Pct
Bruce Bowen, San Antonio	101	229	.441
Michael Redd, Milwaukee	182	416	.438
Wesley Person, Memphis	100	231	.433
David Wesley, New Orleans	134	316	.424
Wally Szczerbiak, Minnesota	61	145	.421
Steve Nash, Dallas	111	269	.413
Matt Harpring, Utah	66	160	.413
Anthony Peeler, Minnesota	87	212	.410
Mike Bibby, Sacramento	56	137	.409
Eddie Jones, Miami	98	241	.407
Jon Barry, Detroit	87	214	.407

BLOCKED SHOTS PER GAME
Minimum of 49 games played or 96 block shots

	Gm	Blk	BPG
Theo Ratliff, Atlanta	81	262	3.23
Ben Wallace, Detroit	73	230	3.15
Tim Duncan, San Antonio	81	237	2.93
Elton Brand, L.A. Clippers	62	158	2.55
Adonal Foyle, Golden State	82	205	2.50
Shaquille O'Neal, L.A. Lakers	67	159	2.37
Jermaine O'Neal, Indiana	77	178	2.31
Andrei Kirilenko, Utah	80	175	2.19
Shawn Bradley, Dallas	81	170	2.10
Erick Dampier, Golden State	82	154	1.88
Zydrunas Ilgauskas, Cleveland	81	152	1.88
Keon Clark, Sacramento	80	150	1.88

STEALS PER GAME
Minimum of 49 games played or 120 steals

	Gm	Stl	SPG
Allen Iverson, Philadelphia	82	225	2.74
Ron Artest, Indiana	69	159	2.30
Shawn Marion, Phoenix	81	185	2.28
Doug Christie, Sacramento	80	180	2.25
Jason Kidd, New Jersey	80	179	2.24
Kobe Bryant, L.A. Lakers	82	181	2.21
Paul Pierce, Boston	79	139	1.76
Caron Butler, Miami	78	137	1.76
Steve Francis, Houston	81	141	1.74
Jamaal Tinsley, Indiana	73	125	1.71

Women's Professional Basketball

WOMEN'S NATIONAL BASKETBALL ASSOCIATION, 2003 SEASON

Eastern Conference

	W	L	Pct	GB	Home	Road
Detroit Shock[1]	25	9	.735	—	13–4	12–5
Charlotte Sting[1]	18	16	.529	7	13–4	5–12
Connecticut Sun[1]	18	16	.529	7	10–7	8–9
Cleveland Rockers[1]	17	17	.500	8	11–6	6–11
Indiana Fever	16	18	.471	9	11–6	5–12
New York Liberty	16	16	.471	9	11–6	5–12
Washington Mystics	9	25	.265	16	3–14	6–11

Western Conference

	W	L	Pct	GB	Home	Road
Los Angeles Sparks[1]	24	10	.706	—	11–6	13–4
Houston Comets[1]	20	14	.588	4	14–3	6–11
Sacramento Monarchs [1]	19	15	.559	5	12–5	7–10
Minnesota Lynx[1]	18	16	.529	6	11–6	7–10
Seattle Storm	18	16	.529	6	13–4	5–12
San Antonio Silver Stars	12	22	.353	12	9–8	3–14
Phoenix Mercury	8	26	.235	16	6–11	2–15

NOTE: GB refers to Games Behind leader. 1. Playoff qualifier.

Conference Championship Series (Best of 3)

EASTERN CONFERENCE

Date	Result
Sept. 5	Detroit 73, Connecticut 63
Sept. 7	Detroit 79, Connecticut 73

Detroit wins series, 2–0

WESTERN CONFERENCE

Date	Result
Sept. 5	Sacramento 77, Los Angeles 69
Sept. 7	Los Angeles 79, Sacramento 54
Sept. 8	Los Angeles 66, Sacramento 63

Los Angeles wins series, 2–1

League Championship Series (Best of 3)
Detroit wins championship, 2 games to 1

Date	Result
Sept. 12	Los Angeles 75, Detroit 63
Sept. 14	Detroit 62, Los Angeles, 61
Sept. 16	Detroit 83, Los Angeles 78

WNBA ANNUAL AWARDS, 2003 SEASON

Most Valuable Player: Lauren Jackson, Seattle

Rookie of the Year: Cheryl Ford, Detroit

Coach of the Year: Bill Laimbeer, Detroit

Defensive Player of the Year: Sheryl Swoopes, Houston

Most Improved Player of the Year: Michelle Snow, Houston

Kim Perrot Sportsmanship Award: Edna Campbell, Saramento

Cascade Dish and Assist Award: Ticha Penicheiro, Sacramento

Bud Light Peak Performers: Lauren Jackson, Seattle, and Chamique Holdsclaw, Washington

2003 WNBA LEAGUE LEADERS

POINTS PER GAME

	Gm	Pts	PPG
Lauren Jackson, Seattle	33	698	21.2
Chamique Holdsclaw, Washington	27	554	20.5
Tamika Catchings, Indiana	34	671	19.7
Lisa Leslie, Los Angeles	23	424	18.4
Katie Smith, Minnesota	34	620	18.2

REBOUNDS PER GAME

	Gm	Reb	RPG
Chamique Holdsclaw, Washington	27	294	10.9
Cheryl Ford, Detroit	32	334	10.4
Lisa Leslie, Los Angeles	23	231	10.0
Lauren Jackson, Seattle	33	307	9.3
Tari Philliips, New York	33	280	8.5

ASSISTS PER GAME

	Gm	Ast	APG
Ticha Penicheiro, Sacramento	34	229	6.7
Sue Bird, Seattle	34	221	6.5
Nikki Teasley, Los Angeles	34	214	6.3
Shannon Johnson, Orlando	34	196	5.8
Dawn Staley, Charlotte	34	174	5.1

BLOCKS PER GAME

	Gm	Blk	BPG
Margo Dydek, San Antonio	34	100	2.94
Lisa Leslie, Los Angeles	23	63	2.74
Lauren Jackson, Seattle	33	64	1.94
Michelle Snow, Houston	34	62	1.82
Ruth Riley, Detroit	34	58	1.71

STEALS PER GAME

	Gm	Stl	SPG
Sheryl Swoopes, Houston	31	77	2.48
Tamika Catchings, Indiana	34	72	2.12
Ticha Penicheiro, Sacramento	34	61	1.79
Marie Ferdinand, San Antonio	34	58	1.71
Tari Phillips, New York	33	56	1.70

FIELD GOAL PERCENTAGE

	FGM	FGA	FG%
Tamika Williams, Minnesota	129	193	.668
Michelle Snow, Houston	126	253	.498
Ruth Riley, Detroit	115	231	.498
Yolanda Griffith, Sacramento	161	332	.485
Natalie Williams, Indiana	176	363	.485

3-POINT FIELD GOAL PERCENTAGE

	3FGM	3FGA	3FG%
Becky Hammon, New York	23	49	.469
Sandy Brondello, Seattle	21	48	.438
Nikki Teasley, Los Angeles	70	165	.424
Kelly Miller, Charlotte	22	52	.423
Deanna Nolan, Detroit	48	114	.421

FREE THROW PERCENTAGE

	FTM	FTA	FT%
Becky Hammon, New York	39	41	.951
Stephanie White, Indiana	45	48	.938
Chamique Holdsclaw, Washington	140	155	.903
Sheryl Swoopes, Houston	110	124	.887
Sue Bird, Seattle	61	69	.884

Sports Personalities

A name in parentheses is the original name or form of name. Localities are places of birth. Dates of birth appear as month/day/year. **Boldface** years in parentheses are dates of **(birth–death)**.

Information has been gathered from many sources, including the individuals themselves. However, the almanac cannot guarantee the accuracy of every individual item.

Aaron, Hank (Henry) (baseball); Mobile, Ala., 2/5/34
Abdul-Jabbar, Kareem (Lewis Ferdinand Alcindor, Jr.) (basketball); New York City, 4/16/47
Affleck, Francis (auto racing) **(1951–1985)**
Agassi, Andre (tennis); Las Vegas, Nev., 4/29/70
Aikman, Troy (football); Henryetta, Okla., 11/21/66
Ali, Muhammad (Cassius Clay) (boxing); Louisville, Ky., 1/18/42
Allen, Dick (Richard Anthony) (baseball); Wampum, Pa., 3/8/42
Allen, George (football) **(1918–1990)**
Allison, Bobby (Robert Arthur) (auto racing); Hueytown, Ala., 12/3/37
Allison, Davey (auto racing); Hueytown, Ala. **(1961–1993)**
Alston, Walter (baseball); Venice, Ohio **(1911–1984)**
Alworth, Lance (football); Houston, 8/3/40
Ameche, Alan (football); Houston, Tex. **(1933–1988)**
Anderson, Sparky (George) (baseball); Bridgewater, S.D., 2/22/34
Andretti, Mario (auto racing); Montona, Trieste, Italy, 2/28/40
Anthony, Earl (bowling); Kent, Wash. **(1939–2001)**
Appling, Luke (baseball); High Point, N.C. **(1907–1990)**
Arcaro, Eddie (George Edward) (jockey); Cincinnati **(1916–1997)**
Armstrong, Lance (bicycling); Plano, Tex., Sept. 18, 1971
Ashe, Arthur (tennis); Richmond, Va. **(1943–1993)**
Ashford, Evelyn (track & field); Shreveport, La., 4/15/57
Austin, Tracy (tennis); Rolling Hills, Calif., 12/2/62
Averill, Earl (baseball); Everett, Wash. **(1915–1983)**
Babashoff, Shirley (swimming); Whittier, Calif., 1/31/57
Baer, Max (boxing); Omaha, Neb. **(1909–1959)**
Bailey, Donovan (track); Canada, 12/16/67
Banks, Ernie (baseball); Dallas, 1/31/31
Bannister, Roger (runner); Harrow, England, 3/24/29
Barkley, Charles (basketball); Leeds, Ala., 2/20/63
Barry, Rick (Richard) (basketball); Elizabeth, N.J., 3/28/44
Bauer, Hank (Henry) (baseball); East St. Louis, Ill., 7/31/22
Baugh, Sammy (football); Temple, Tex., 3/17/14
Baylor, Elgin (basketball); Washington, D.C., 9/16/34
Beamon, Bob (long jumper); New York City, 8/2/46
Becker, Boris (tennis); Leiman, W. Germany, 11/22/67
Beckham, David (soccer); Leytonstone, England, 5/2/75
Bee, Clair (basketball); Cleveland, Ohio **(1896–1983)**
Beliveau, Jean (hockey); Three Rivers, Quebec, Canada, 8/31/31
Belle, Albert (baseball); Shreveport, La., 8/25/66
Beman, Deane (golf); Washington, D.C., 4/22/38
Bench, Johnny (Johnny Lee) (baseball); Oklahoma City, 12/7/47
Berg, Patty (Patricia Jane) (golf); Minneapolis, 2/13/18
Berra, Yogi (Lawrence) (baseball); St. Louis, 5/12/25
Biletnikoff, Frederick (football); Erie, Pa., 2/23/43
Bing, Dave (basketball); Washington, D.C., 11/24/43
Bird, Larry (basketball); French Lick, Ind., 12/7/56
Blaik, Earl H. (football); Detroit **(1897–1989)**
Blanda, George Frederick (football); Youngwood, Pa., 9/17/27
Bledsoe, Drew (football); Walla Walla, Wash., 2/14/72
Blue, Vida (baseball); Mansfield, La., 7/28/49
Bodine, Brett (auto racing); Chemung, N.Y., 1/11/59
Bodine, Geoff (auto racing); Chemung, N.Y., 4/18/49
Boggs, Wade (baseball); Omaha, Neb., 6/15/58
Bonds, Barry (baseball); Riverside, Calif., 7/24/64
Borg, Björn (tennis); Stockholm, Sweden, 6/6/56
Boros, Julius (golf); Fairfield, Conn. **(1920–1994)**
Bossy, Mike (hockey); Montreal, 1/22/57
Boston, Ralph (long jumper); Laurel, Miss., 5/9/39
Bourque, Ray (hockey); Montreal, Que., 12/28/60
Bradley, Bill (William Warren) (basketball); Crystal City, Mo., 7/28/43
Bradley, Pat (golf); Westford, Mass., 3/24/51
Bradshaw, Terry (football); Shreveport, La., 9/2/48
Breedlove, Craig (Norman) (speed driving); Los Angeles, 3/23/38
Brett, George (baseball); Glendale, W. Va., 5/15/53
Brock, Louis Clark (baseball); El Dorado, Ark., 6/18/39
Brown, Jim (football); St. Simon Island, Ga., 2/17/36
Brumel, Valeri (high jumper); Tolbuzino, Siberia, 4/14/42
Bryant, Paul "Bear" (football); Morro Bottom, Ark. **(1913–1983)**
Bryant, Rosalyn Evette (track); Chicago, 1/7/56
Burton, Michael (swimming); Des Moines, Iowa, 7/3/47
Butkus, Dick (Richard Marvin) (football); Chicago, 12/9/42
Calipari, John (basketball); Moon, Pa., 2/10/59
Campanella, Roy (baseball); Homestead, Pa. **(1921–1993)**

Campbell, Earl (football); Tyler, Tex., 3/29/55
Canseco, Jose (baseball); Havana, Cuba, 7/2/64
Caponi, Donna Maria (golf); Detroit, 1/29/45
Cappelletti, Gino (football); Keewatin, Minn., 3/26/34
Capriati, Jennifer (tennis); New York, N.Y., 3/29/76
Carew, Rod (Rodney Cline) (baseball); Gatun, Panama, 10/1/45
Carlos, John (sprinter); New York City, 6/5/45
Carlton, Steven Norman (baseball); Miami, Fla., 12/22/44
Carner, Joanne Gunderson, Mrs. Don (golf); Kirkland, Wash., 3/4/39
Casals, Rosemary (tennis); San Francisco, 9/16/48
Casper, Billy (golf); San Diego, Calif., 6/24/31
Caulkins, Tracy (swimming); Winona, Minn., 1/11/63
Cauthen, Steve (jockey); Covington, Ky., 5/1/60
Chamberlain, Wilt (Wilton) (basketball); Philadelphia **(1936–1999)**
Chandler, A. B. (Happy) (baseball); Louisville, Ky. **(1899–1991)**
Chandler, Spud (baseball); Commerce, Ga. **(1907–1990)**
Chang, Michael (tennis); Hoboken, N.J., 2/22/72
Chapot, Frank (equestrian); Camden, N.J., 2/24/34
Chastain, Brandi (soccer); San Jose, Calif., 7/21/68
Chinaglia, Giorgio (soccer); Carrara, Italy, 1/24/47
Clarke, Bobby (Robert Earle) (hockey); Flin Flon, Manitoba, Canada, 8/13/49
Clemens, Roger (baseball); Dayton, Ohio, 8/4/62
Clemente, Roberto Walker (baseball); Carolina, Puerto Rico **(1934–1972)**
Cobb, Ty (Tyrus Raymond) (baseball); Narrows, Ga. **(1886–1961)**
Cochran, Barbara Ann (skiing); Claremont, N.H., 1/14/51
Cochran, Marilyn (skiing); Burlington, Vt., 2/7/50
Cochran, Robert (skiing); Claremont, N.H., 12/11/51
Coe, Sebastian Newbold (track); London, England, 9/29/56
Coffey, Paul (hockey); Weston, Ont., 6/1/61
Colavito, Rocky (Rocco Domenico) (baseball); New York City, 8/10/33
Coleman, Derrick (basketball); Mobile, Ala., 6/21/67
Comaneci, Nadia (gymnast); Onesti, Romania, 11/12/61
Conigliaro, Tony (baseball); Revere, Mass. **(1945–1990)**
Connors, Jimmy (James Scott) (tennis); East St. Louis, Ill., 9/2/52
Cooper, Cynthia (basketball); Chicago, Ill., 4/14/63
Cordero, Angel (jockey); Santurce, Puerto Rico, 5/8/42
Cosell, Howard (broadcaster); Winston-Salem, N.C. **(1918–1995)**
Courier, Jim (tennis); Sanford, Fla., 8/17/70
Cournoyer, Yvan Serge (hockey); Drummondville, Quebec, Canada, 11/22/43
Court, Margaret Smith (tennis); Albury, New South Wales, Australia, 7/16/42
Cousy, Bob (basketball); New York City, 8/9/28
Crabbe, Buster (swimming); Scottsdale, Ariz. **(1908–1983)**
Crenshaw, Ben (golf); Austin, Tex., 1/11/52
Cronin, Joe (baseball executive); San Francisco **(1906–1984)**
Cruyff, Johan (soccer); Amsterdam, Netherlands, 4/25/47
Csonka, Larry (Lawrence Richard) (football); Stow, Ohio, 12/25/46
Dancer, Stanley (harness racing); New Egypt, N.J., 7/25/27
Dark, Alvin (baseball); Comanche, Okla., 1/7/22
Davenport, Willie (track); Troy, Ala. **(1943–2002)**
Dawson, Andre (baseball); Miami, Fla., 7/10/54
Dawson, Leonard Ray (football); Alliance, Ohio, 6/20/35
Dean, Dizzy (Jay Hanna) (baseball); Lucas, Ark. **(1911–1974)**
DeBusschere, Dave (basketball); Detroit **(1940–2003)**
De La Hoya, Oscar (boxing); East Los Angeles, Calif., 2/4/73
Delvecchio, Alex Peter (hockey); Fort William, Ontario, Canada, 12/4/31
Demaret, Jim (golf); Houston **(1910–1983)**
Dempsey, Jack (William H.) (boxing); Manassa, Colo. **(1895–1983)**
DeVicenzo, Roberto (golf); Buenos Aires, 4/14/23
Dibbs, Edward George (tennis); Brooklyn, New York, 2/23/51
Dietz, James W. (rowing); New York, N.Y., 1/12/49
DiMaggio, Joe (baseball); Martinez, Calif. **(1914–1999)**
Dionne, Marcel (hockey); Drummondville, Quebec, Canada, 8/3/51
Dorsett, Tony (football); Rochester, Pa., 4/7/54
Dryden, Kenneth (hockey); Hamilton, Ontario, Canada, 8/4/47
Drysdale, Don (baseball); Van Nuys, Calif. **(1936–1993)**
Duran, Roberto (boxing); Panama City, 6/16/51
Durocher, Leo (baseball); West Springfield, Mass. **(1906–1991)**
Durr, Francois (tennis); Algiers, Algeria, 12/25/42
Earnhardt, Dale (auto racing); Concord, N.C. **(1951–2001)**
Eckersley, Dennis (baseball); Oakland, Calif., 10/3/54
Elder, Lee (golf); Dallas, 7/14/34
Elway, John (football); Port Angeles, Wash., 6/28/60
Emerson, Roy (tennis); Kingsway, Australia, 11/3/36
Ender, Kornelia (swimming); Plauen, East Germany, 10/25/58
Erving, Julius ("Dr. J") (basketball); Roosevelt, N.Y., 2/22/50
Esposito, Phil (Philip Anthony) (hockey); Sault Ste. Marie, Ontario, Canada, 2/20/42
Evans, Lee (runner); Mandena, Calif., 2/25/47
Evert, Chris (Christine Marie) (tennis); Fort Lauderdale, Fla., 12/21/54
Ewbank, Weeb (football); Richmond, Ind. **(1907–1998)**
Ewing, Patrick (basketball); Kingston, Jamaica, 8/5/62
Favre, Brett (football); Gulfport, Miss., 10/10/69
Feller, Robert (Bob) (baseball); Van Meter, Iowa, 11/3/18
Feuerbach, Allan Dean (track); Preston, Iowa, 1/12/48
Finley, Charles O. (sportsman); Ensley, Ala. **(1918–1996)**
Fischer, Bobby (chess); Chicago, 3/9/43
Fitzsimmons, Bob (Robert Prometheus) (boxing); Cornwall, England **(1862–1917)**
Fleming, Peggy Gale (ice skating); San Jose, Calif., 7/27/48
Ford, Whitey (Edward) (baseball); New York City, 10/21/28
Foreman, George (boxing); Marshall, Tex., 1/10/49
Fosbury, Richard (high jumper); Portland, Ore., 3/6/47
Fox, Nellie (Jacob Nelson) (baseball); St. Thomas, Pa. **(1927–1975)**
Foxx, James Emory (baseball); Sudlersville, Md. **(1907–1967)**
Foyt, A. J. (auto racing); Houston, 1/16/35
Frazier, Joe (boxing); Beauford, S.C., 1/17/44
Frazier, Walt (basketball); Atlanta, 3/29/45
Freeman, Cathy (track & field); Mackay, Queensland, Australia, 2/16/73
Frick, Ford C. (baseball); Wawaka, Ind. **(1894–1978)**
Furniss, Bruce (swimming); Fresno, Calif., 5/27/57
Gable, Dan (wrestling); Waterloo, Iowa, 10/25/45
Gabriel, Roman (football); Wilmington, N.C., 8/5/40
Gallagher, Michael Donald (skiing); Yonkers, N.Y., 10/3/41
Garvey, Steve (baseball); Tampa, Fla., 12/22/48
Gehrig, Lou (Henry Louis) (baseball); New York City **(1903–1941)**
Gehringer, Charlie (baseball); Fowlerville, Mich. **(1903–1993)**
Geoffrion, "Boom Boom" (Bernie) (hockey); Montreal, 2/14/31
Gerulaitis, Vitas (tennis); Brooklyn, N.Y. **(1954–1994)**
Gervin, George (basketball); Long Beach, Calif., 4/27/52
Giacomin, Ed (hockey); Sudbury, Ontario, Canada, 6/6/39
Giamatti, A. Bartlett (baseball); South Hadley, Mass. **(1938–1989)**
Gibson, Bob (baseball); Omaha, Neb., 11/9/35
Gifford, Frank (football); Santa Monica, Calif., 8/16/30
Gilbert, Rod (Rodrique) (hockey); Montreal, 7/1/41
Gilmore, Artis (basketball); Chipley, Fla., 9/21/49
Glance, Harvey (track); Phenix City, Ala., 3/28/57
Gonzalez, Pancho (tennis); Los Angeles **(1928–1995)**
Goodell, Brian Stuart (swimming); Stockton, Calif., 4/2/59
Gooden, Dwight (baseball); Tampa, Fla., 11/16/64
Goodrich, Gail (basketball); Los Angeles, 4/23/43
Goolagong, Cawley, Evonne (tennis); Griffith, Australia, 7/31/51
Gordon, Jeff (auto racing); Vallejo, Calif., 8/4/71
Gossage, "Goose" (Rich) (baseball); Colorado Springs, Colo., 4/5/51
Graf, Steffi (tennis); Mannheim, W. Germany, 6/14/69
Graham, David (golf); Windson, Australia, 5/23/46
Graham, Otto Everett (football); Waukegan, Ill., 12/6/21
Grange, Red (Harold) (football); Forksville, Pa. **(1904–1991)**
Green, Hubert (golf); Birmingham, Ala., 12/28/46
Greene, Charles E. (sprinter); Pine Bluff, Ark., 3/21/45
Greene, "Mean" (Joe) (football); Temple, Tex., 9/24/46
Gretzky, Wayne (hockey); Brantford, Ont., 1/26/61
Griese, Bob (Robert Allen) (football); Evansville, Ind., 2/3/45
Griffey, Ken, Jr. (baseball); Donora, Pa., 11/21/69
Grove, Lefty (Robert Moses) (baseball); Lonaconing, Md. **(1900–1975)**
Groza, Lou (football); Martins Ferry Ohio **(1924–2000)**
Guidry, Ronald Ames (baseball); Lafayette, La., 8/28/50
Gwynn, Tony (baseball); Los Angeles, Calif., 5/9/60
Halas, George (football); Chicago **(1895–1983)**
Hall, Gary (swimming); Fayetteville, N.C., 8/7/51
Hamill, Dorothy (figure skating); Chicago, 7/26/56
Hamilton, Scott (figure skating); Bowling Green, Ohio, 8/28/58
Hamm, Mia (soccer); Selma, Ala., 3/17/72
Hammond, Kathy (runner); Sacramento, Calif., 11/2/51
Hardaway, Anfernee (basketball); Memphis, Tenn., 7/18/72
Harding, Tonya (figure skating); Portland, Ore., 11/12/70
Harris, Franco (football); Ft. Dix, N.J., 3/7/50
Hartack, William, Jr. (jockey); Colver, Pa., 12/9/32
Hasek, Dominik (hockey); Pardubice, Czechoslovakia, 1/29/65
Haughton, William (harness racing); Gloversville, N.Y. **(1923–1986)**
Havlicek, John (basketball); Martins Ferry, Ohio, 4/8/40
Hayes, Elvin (basketball); Rayville, La., 11/17/45
Hayes, Woody (football); Upper Arlington, Ohio **(1913–1987)**
Heiden, Eric (speed skating); Madison, Wis., 6/14/58
Hencken, John (swimming); Culver City, Calif., 5/29/54
Henderson, Rickey (baseball); Chicago, 12/25/58
Henie, Sonja (ice skater); Oslo **(1912–1969)**
Herman, Floyd Caves (Babe) (baseball); Buffalo, N.Y. **(1903–1987)**
Hernandez, Keith (baseball); San Francisco, 10/20/53
Hershiser, Orel (baseball); Buffalo, N.Y., 9/16/58
Hickcox, Charles (swimming); Phoenix, Ariz., 2/6/47
Hines, James (sprinter); Dumas, Ark., 9/10/46
Hingis, Martina (tennis); Kosice, Slovakia, 9/30/80
Hodges, Gil (baseball); Princeton, Ind. **(1924–1972)**
Hogan, Ben (golf); Dublin, Tex. **(1912–1997)**
Holmes, Larry (boxing); Cuthert, Ga., 11/3/49
Holyfield, Evander (boxing); Atlanta, Ga., 10/19/62
Hornsby, Rogers (baseball); Winters, Tex. **(1896–1963)**
Hornung, Paul (football); Louisville, Ky., 12/23/35
Houk, Ralph (baseball); Lawrence, Kan., 8/9/19

Howard, Elston (baseball); St. Louis **(1929–1980)**
Howe, Gordon (hockey); Floral, Sask., Canada, 3/31/28
Howell, Jim Lee (football); Lonoke, Ark. **(1914–1995)**
Howser, Dick (baseball); Miami, Fla. **(1937–1987)**
Hubbell, Carl (baseball); Carthage, Mo. **(1903–1988)**
Huff, Sam (Robert Lee) (football); Morgantown, W. Va., 10/4/34
Hull, Bobby (hockey); Point Anne, Ontario, Canada, 1/3/39
Hunter, "Catfish" (Jim) (baseball); Hertford, N.C. **(1946–1999)**
Hutson, Donald (football); Pine Bluff, Ark. **(1913–1997)**
Irwin, Hale (golf); Joplin, Mo., 6/3/45
Jacobs, Helen Hull (tennis); Globe, Ariz. **(1908–1997)**
Jackson, Phil (basketball coach); Deer Lodge, Mont., 9/17/45
Jackson, Reggie (baseball); Wyncote, Pa., 5/18/46
Jagr, Jaromir (hockey); Kladno, Czechoslovakia, 2/15/72
Jeffries, James J. (boxing); Carroll, Ohio **(1875–1953)**
Jenkins, Ferguson Arthur (baseball); Chatham, Ontario, Canada, 12/13/43
Jenner, (W.) Bruce (track); Mt. Kisco, N.Y., 10/28/49
Jezek, Linda (swimming); Palo Alto, Calif., 3/10/60
Johnson, Anthony (rowing); Washington, D.C., 11/16/40
Johnson, Jack (John Arthur) (boxing); Galveston, Tex. **(1876–1946)**
Johnson, Jimmy (football); Port Arthur, Tex., 8/14/43
Johnson, "Magic" (Earvin) (basketball); E. Lansing, Mich., 8/14/59
Johnson, Michael (track); Dallas, Tex., 9/13/67
Johnson, Rafer (decathlon); Hillsboro, Tex., 8/18/35
Johnson, Randy (baseball); Walnut Creek, Calif., 9/10/63
Johnson, Wilham Julius (Judy) (baseball); Wilmington, Del. **(1899–1989)**
Jones, Cobi (soccer); Detroit, Mich., 6/16/70
Jones, Deacon (David) (football); Eatonville, Fla., 12/9/38
Jones, Marion (track & field); Los Angeles, Calif., 10/12/75
Jordan, Michael (basketball); Brooklyn, N.Y., 2/17/63
Joyner, Florence Griffith (sprinter); Mojave Desert, Calif. **(1959–1998)**
Joyner-Kersee, Jackie (track); East St. Louis, Ill., 3/3/62
Juantoreno, Alberto (track); Santiago, Cuba, 12/3/51
Jurgensen, Sonny (football); Wilmington, N.C., 8/23/34
Justice, Dave (baseball); Cincinnati, Ohio, 4/14/66
Kaat, Jim (baseball); Zeeland, Mich., 11/7/38
Kaline, Al (Albert) (baseball); Baltimore, 12/19/34
Keino, Kipchoge (runner); Kapchemoiymo, Kenya, 1/17/40
Kelly, Leroy (football); Philadelphia, 5/20/42
Kelly, Red (Leonard Patrick) (hockey); Simcoe, Ontario, Canada, 7/9/27
Kerrigan, Nancy (figure skating); Woburn, Mass., 10/13/69
Killebrew, Harmon (baseball); Payette, Idaho, 6/29/36
Killy, Jean-Claude (skiing); Saint-Cloud, France, 8/30/43
Kilmer, Bill (William Orland) (football); Topeka, Kan., 9/5/39
King, Bille Jean (Bille Jean Moffitt) (tennis); Long Beach, Calif., 11/22/43
Kinsella, John (swimming); Oak Park, Ill., 8/26/52
Kluszewski, Ted (baseball); Argo, Ill. **(1924–1988)**
Kodes, Jan (tennis); Prague, 3/1/46
Kolb, Claudia (swimming); Hayward, Calif., 12/19/49
Korbut, Olga (gymnast); Grodno, Byelorussia, USSR, 5/16/55
Koufax, Sandy (Sanford) (baseball); Brooklyn, N.Y., 12/30/35
Kramer, Jack (tennis); Las Vegas, Nev., 8/1/21
Kramer, Jerry (football); Jordan, Mont., 1/23/36
Krayzelburg, Lenny (swimming); Odessa, Ukraine, 9/28/75
Kuenn, Harvey (baseball); West Allis, Wis. **(1930–1988)**
Kuhn, Bowie Kent (baseball); Takoma Park, Md., 10/28/26
Kwan, Michelle (figure skating); Torrance, Calif., 7/7/80
Lafleur, Guy Damien (hockey); Thurson, Quebec, Canada, 8/20/51
Laird, Ronald (walker); Louisville, Ky., 5/31/35
Lalas, Alexi (soccer); Birmingham, Mich., 6/1/70
Lamonica, Daryle (football); Fresno, Calif., 7/17/41
Landis, Kenesaw Mountain (1st baseball commissioner); Millville, Ohio **(1866–1944)**
Landry, Tom (football); Mission, Tex. **(1924–2000)**
Landy, John (runner); Australia, 4/4/30
Larrieu, Francie (track); Palo Alto, Calif., 11/28/52
La Russa, Tony (baseball); Tampa, Fla., 10/4/44
Lasorda, Tom (baseball); Norristown, Pa., 9/22/27
Laver, Rod (tennis); Rockhampton, Australia, 8/9/38
Layne, Bobby (football); Lubbock, Texas **(1927–1986)**
Leetch, Brian (hockey); Corpus Christi, Tex., 3/3/68
Lemieux, Mario (hockey); Montreal, Quebec, Canada, 10/5/65
Lendl, Ivan (tennis); Prague, 3/7/60
Leonard, Benny (Benjamin Leiner) (boxing); New York City **(1896–1947)**
Leonard, Sugar Ray (boxing); Wilmington, N.C., 5/17/56
Lewis, Carl (track); Willingboro, N.J., 7/1/61
Lindros, Eric (hockey); London, Ont., 2/28/73
Lipinski, Tara (figure skating); Philadelphia, Pa., 6/10/82
Liquori, Marty (runner); Montclair, N.J., 9/11/49
Little, Lou (football); Leominster, Mass. **(1893–1979)**
Littler, Gene (golf); La Jolla, Calif., 7/21/30
Lobo, Rebecca (basketball); Southwick, Mass., 10/6/73
Lombardi, Vince (football); Brooklyn, N.Y. **(1913–1970)**
Longden, Johnny (horse racing); Wakefield, England **(1907–2003)**
Lopat, Eddie (baseball); New York, N.Y. **(1918–1992)**
Lopez, Al (baseball); Tampa, Fla., 8/20/08
Lopez, Nancy (golf); Torrance, Calif., 1/6/57
Louis, Joe (Joe Louis Barrow) (boxing); Lafayette, Ala. **(1914–1981)**
Lukas, D. Wayne (horse racing); Antigo, Wis., 9/2/35
Lynn, Frederic Michael (baseball); Chicago, Ill., 2/3/52
Lynn, Janet (figure skating); Rockford, Ill., 4/6/53
Mack, Connie (Cornelius Alexander McGillicuddy) (baseball executive); East Brookfield, Mass. **(1862–1956)**
Mackey, John (football); New York City, 9/24/41
Maddux, Greg (baseball); San Angelo, Texas, 4/14/66
Mahovlich, Frank (Francis William) (hockey); Timmins, Ontario, Canada, 1/10/38
Mahre, Phil (skiing); White Pass, Wash., 5/10/57
Malone, Karl (basketball); Summerfield, La., 7/24/63
Malone, Moses (basketball); Petersburg, Va., 3/23/55
Mandlikova, Hana (tennis); Prague, Czechoslovakia, 2/62
Mann, Carol (golf); Buffalo, N.Y., 2/3/41
Manning, Madeline (runner); Cleveland, 1/11/48
Mantle, Mickey Charles (baseball); Spavinaw, Okla. **(1931–1995)**
Maravich, "Pistol Pete" (Peter) Aliquippa, Pa. **(1948–1988)**
Marble, Alice (tennis); Palm Springs, Calif. **(1913–1990)**
Marciano, Rocky (boxing); Brockton, Mass. **(1923–1969)**
Marichal, Juan (baseball); Laguna Verde, Montecristi, Dominican Republic, 10/20/37
Marino, Dan (football); Pittsburgh, Pa., 9/15/61
Maris, Roger (baseball); Hibbing, Minn. **(1934–1985)**
Martin, Billy (Alfred Manuel) (baseball); Berkeley, Calif. **(1928–1989)**
Martin, Christy (boxing); Mullers, W.Va., 6/12/68
Martin, Rick (Richard Lionel) (hockey); Verdun, Quebec, Canada, 7/26/51
Martinez, Pedro (baseball); Manoguayabo, Dominican Republic, 10/25/71
Mathews, Ed (Edwin) (baseball); Texarkana, Tex. **(1931–2001)**
Mattingly, Don (baseball); Evansville, Ind., 4/20/61
Matson, Randy (shot putter); Kilgore, Tex., 3/5/45
Mays, Willie (baseball); Westfield, Ala., 5/6/31
McAdoo, Bob (basketball); Greensboro, N.C., 9/25/51
McCarthy, Joe (Joseph Vincent) (baseball); Philadelphia **(1887–1978)**
McCovey, Willie Lee (baseball); Mobile, Ala., 1/10/38
McDonald, Lanny (hockey); Hanna, Alberta, Canada, 2/16/53
McDowell, Jack (baseball); Van Nuys, Calif., 1/16/66
McEnroe, John Patrick, Jr. (tennis); Wiesbaden, Germany, 2/16/59
McGraw, John Joseph (baseball); Truxton, N.Y. **(1873–1934)**
McGwire, Mark (baseball); Pomona, Calif., 10/1/63
McLain, Dennis (baseball); Chicago, 3/24/44
McMillan, Kathy Laverne (track); Raeford, N.C., 11/7/57
Merrill, Janice (track); New London, Conn., 6/18/62
Messier, Mark (hockey); Edmonton, Alberta, Canada, 1/18/61
Meyer, Deborah (swimming); Haddonfield, N.J., 8/14/52
Meyers, Ann (basketball); San Diego, Calif., 3/26/55
Middlecoff, Cary (golf); Halls, Tenn. **(1921–1998)**
Mikita, Stan (hockey); Sokolce, Czechoslovakia, 5/20/40
Milburn, Rodney, Jr. (hurdler); Opelousas, La., 5/18/50
Miller, Cheryl (basketball); Riverside, Calif., 1/3/64
Miller, Johnny (golf); San Francisco, 4/29/47
Miller, Reggie (basketball); Riverside, Calif., 8/24/65
Montana, Joe (football); New Eagle, Pa., 6/11/56
Montgomery, Jim (swimming); Madison, Wis., 1/24/55
Montgomery, Tim (track); Gaffney, S.C., 1/25/75
Moody, Helen Wills (tennis); Centerville, Calif. **(1906–1998)**
Moore, Archie (boxing); Benoit, Miss. **(1916–1998)**
Morgan, Joe Leonard (baseball); Bonham, Tex., 9/19/43
Morrall, Earl (football); Muskegon, Mich., 5/17/34
Morton, Craig L. (football); Flint, Mich., 2/5/43
Mosconi, Wilie (pocket billiards); Philadelphia **(1913–1993)**
Moses, Edwin Corley (track); Dayton, Ohio, 8/31/58
Mungo, Van Lingo (baseball); Pageland, S.C. **(1911–1985)**
Munson, Thurman (baseball); Akron, Ohio **(1947–1979)**
Murphy, Calvin (basketball); Norwalk, Conn., 5/9/48
Murray, Eddie (baseball); Los Angeles, Calif., 2/24/56
Musial, Stan (baseball); Donora, Pa., 11/21/20
Myers, Linda (archery); York, Pa., 6/19/47
Naber, John (swimming); Evanston, Ill., 1/20/56
Namath, Joe (Joseph William) (football); Beaver Falls, Pa., 5/31/43
Nastase, Ilie (tennis); Bucharest, 7/19/46
Navratilova, Martina (tennis); Prague, 10/18/56
Nehemiah, Renaldo (track); Newark, N.J., 3/24/59
Nelson, Cindy (skiing); Lutsen, Minn., 8/19/55
Newcombe, John (tennis); Sydney, Australia, 5/23/43
Niekro, Phil (baseball); Lansing, Ohio, 4/1/39
Nicklaus, Jack (golf); Columbus, Ohio, 1/21/40
Norman, Gregory (golf); Mount Isa, Australia, 2/10/55
Oerter, Al (discus thrower); New York City, 9/19/36
Olajuwon, Hakeem (basketball); Lagos, Nigeria, 1/21/63
Oldfield, Barney (racing driver); Fulton County, Ohio **(1878–1946)**

Oliva, Tony (Pedro) (baseball); Pinar Del Rio, Cuba, 7/20/40
Olsen, Merlin Jay (football); Logan, Utah, 9/15/40
O'Malley, Walter (baseball executive); New York City **(1903–1979)**
O'Neal, Shaquille (basketball); Newark, N.J., 3/6/72
Orantes, Manuel (tennis); Granada, Spain, 2/6/49
Orr, Bobby (hockey); Parry Sound, Ontario, Canada, 3/20/48
Ovett, Steve (track); Brighton, England, 10/9/55
Owens, Jesse (track); Decatur, Ala. **(1914–1980)**
Paige, Satchel (Leroy) (baseball); Mobile, Ala. **(1906–1982)**
Palmer, Arnold (golf); Latrobe, Pa., 9/10/29
Palmer, James Alvin (baseball); New York City, 10/15/45
Parcells, Bill (football coach); Englewood, N.J., 8/22/41
Parent, Bernard Marcel (hockey); Montreal, 4/3/45
Park, Brad (Douglas Bradford) (hockey); Toronto, Ontario, Canada, 7/6/48
Parseghian, Ara (football); Akron, Ohio, 5/21/23
Pasarell, Charles (tennis); San Juan, Puerto Rico, 2/12/44
Patterson, Floyd (boxing); Waco, N.C., 1/4/35
Peete, Calvin (golf); Detroit, Mich., 7/18/43
Pelé (Edson Arantes do Nascimento) (soccer); Tres Coracoes, Brazil, 10/23/40
Perry, Gaylord (baseball); Williamston, N.C., 9/15/38
Perry, Jim (baseball); Williamston, N.C., 10/30/36
Pettit, Bob (basketball); Baton Rouge, La., 12/12/32
Petty, Richard Lee (auto racing); Randleman, N.C., 7/2/37
Pincay, Laffit, Jr. (jockey); Panama City, Panama, 12/29/46
Pippen, Scottie (basketball); Trenton, N.J., 9/25/65
Plager, Barclay (ice hockey); Kirkland Lake, Ontario **(1941–1988)**
Plante, Jacques (hockey); Sahwinigan Falls, Quebec, Canada **(1929–1986)**
Player, Gary (golf); Johannesburg, South Africa, 11/1/35
Plunkett, Jim (football); San Jose, Calif., 12/5/47
Potvin, Denis Charles (hockey); Hull, Quebec, Canada, 10/29/53
Powell, Boog (John) (baseball); Lakeland, Fla., 8/17/41
Powell, Mike (track); Philadelphia, 11/10/63
Prefontaine, Steve Roland (runner); Coos Bay, Ore. **(1951–1975)**
Prince, Bob (baseball announcer); Pittsburgh **(1917–1985)**
Proell, Annemarie Moser (Alpine skier); Kleinarl, Austria, 3/27/53
Rafter, Patrick (tennis); Brisbane, Australia, 12/28/72
Ralston, Dennis (tennis); Bakersfield, Calif., 7/27/42
Rankin, Judy Torluemke (golf); St. Louis, Mo., 2/18/45
Raschi, Vic (baseball); West Springfield, Mass. **(1919–1988)**
Ratelle, Jean (Joseph Gilbert Yvon Jean) (hockey); St. Jean, Quebec, Canada, 10/29/53
Rawis, Betsy (Elizabeth Earle) (golf); Spartanburg, S.C., 5/4/28
Reed, Willis (basketball); Hico, La., 6/25/42
Reese, Pee Wee (Harold) (baseball); Ekron, Ky. **(1919–1999)**
Resch, Glenn "Chico" (hockey); Moose Jaw, Saskatchewan, Canada, 7/10/48
Rice, Jerry (football); Crawford, Miss., 10/13/62
Richard, Maurice (hockey); Montreal, 8/14/24
Riessen, Martin (tennis); Hinsdale, Ill., 12/4/41
Rigney, William (baseball); Alameda, Calif. **(1918–2001)**
Rios, Marcelo (tennis); Santiago, Chile, 12/26/75
Ripken, Cal, Jr. (baseball); Havre de Grace, Md., 8/24/60
Rizzuto, Phil (baseball); New York City, 9/25/18
Robertson, Oscar (basketball); Charlotte, Tenn., 11/24/38
Robinson, Arnie (track); San Diego, Calif., 4/7/48
Robinson, Brooks (baseball); Little Rock, Ark., 5/18/37
Robinson, David (basketball); Key West, Fla., 8/6/65
Robinson, Frank (baseball); Beaumont, Tex., 8/31/35
Robinson, Jackie (baseball); Cairo, Ga. **(1919–1972)**
Robinson, Larry Clark (hockey); Marvelville, Ontario, Canada, 6/2/51
Robinson, "Sugar" Ray (boxing); Detroit **(1920–1989)**
Rockne, Knute Kenneth (football); Voss, Norway **(1888–1931)**
Rockwell, Martha (skiing); Providence, R.I., 4/26/44
Rodman, Dennis (basketball); Trenton, N.J., 5/13/61
Ronaldo (soccer); Bento Ribeiro, Brazil, 9/22/76
Rono, Henry (track); Kiptaragon, Kenya, 2/12/52
Rooney, Art (football); Pittsburgh, Pa. **(1901–1988)**
Rose, Pete (Peter Edward) (baseball); Cincinnati, 4/14/41
Rosenbloom, Maxie (boxing); New York City **(1904–1976)**
Rosewall, Ken (tennis); Sydney, Australia, 11/2/34
Rote, Kyle (football); San Antonio **(1928–2002)**
Roush, Edd (baseball); Oakland City, Ind. **(1893–1988)**
Rozelle, Pete (Alvin Ray) (commissioner of National Football League); South Gate, Calif. **(1926–1996)**
Rudolph, Wilma Glodean (sprinter); St. Bethlehem, Tenn. **(1940–1994)**
Russell, Bill (basketball); Monroe, La., 2/12/34
Ruth, Babe (George Herman Ruth) (baseball); Baltimore **(1895–1948)**
Rutherford, Johnny (auto racing); Fort Worth, 3/12/38
Ryan, Nolan (Lynn Nolan, Jr.) (baseball); Refugio, Tex., 1/31/47
Ryon, Luann (archery); Long Beach, Calif., 1/13/53
Ryun, Jim (runner); Wichita, Kan., 4/29/47
Salazar, Alberto (track); Havana, 8/7/58
Sampras, Pete (tennis); Washington, D.C., 8/12/71
Samuels, Howard (horse racing soccer); New York City **(1920–1984)**
Sanders, Barry (football); Wichita, Kan., 7/16/68
Sanders, Deion (baseball/football); Ft. Myers, Fla., 8/9/67
Santana, Manuel (Manuel Santana Martinez) (tennis); Chamartin, Spain, 5/10/38
Sayers, Gale (football); Wichita, Kan., 5/30/43
Schmidt, Mike (baseball); Dayton, Ohio, 9/27/49
Schoendienst, Red (Albert) (baseball); Germantown, Ill., 2/2/23
Schollander, Donald (swimming); Charlotte, N.C., 4/30/46
Scurry, Briana (soccer); Minneapolis, Minn., 9/7/71
Seagren, Bob (Robert Lloyd) (pole vaulter); Pomona, Calif., 10/17/46
Seau, Junior (football); Oceanside, Calif., 1/19/69
Seaver, Tom (baseball); Fresno, Calif., 11/17/44
Seidler, Maren (track); Brooklyn, N.Y., 6/11/51
Seles, Monica (tennis); Novi Sad, Yugoslavia, 12/2/73
Selke, Frank (ice hockey); Canada **(1893–1985)**
Sewell, Joe (baseball); Titus, Ala. **(1898–1990)**
Shepherd, Lee (auto racing) **(1945–1985)**
Shero, Fred (hockey); Camden, N.J. **(1925–1990)**
Shoemaker, Willie (jockey); Fabens, Tex., 8/19/31
Shore, Eddie (ice hockey); Saskatchewan, Canada **(1902–1985)**
Shorter, Frank (runner); Munich, Germany, 10/31/47
Shriver, Pam (tennis); Baltimore, 7/4/62
Shula, Don (Donald Francis) (football); Grand River, Ohio, 1/4/30
Silvester, Jay (discus thrower); Tremonton, Utah, 2/27/37
Simpson, O.J. (Orenthal James) (football); San Francisco, 7/9/47
Sims, Billy (football); St. Louis, 9/18/55
Smith, Bubba (Charles Aaron) (football); Orange, Tex., 2/28/45
Smith, Emmitt (football); Pensacola, Fla., 5/15/69
Smith, Ozzie (baseball); Mobile, Ala., 12/26/54
Smith, Ronnie Ray (sprinter); Los Angeles, 3/28/49
Smith, Stanley Roger (tennis); Pasadena, Calif., 12/14/46
Smith, Tommie (sprinter); Clarksville, Tex., 6/5/44
Smoke, Marcia Jones (canoeing); Oklahoma City, 7/18/41
Snead, Sam (golf); Hot Springs, Va. **(1912–2002)**
Sneva, Tom (auto racing); Spokane, Wash., 6/1/48
Snider, Duke (Edwin) (baseball); Los Angeles, 9/19/26
Solomon, Harold (tennis); Washington, D.C., 9/17/52
Sosa, Sammy (Samuel) (baseball); San Pedro de Macoris, Dominican Republic, 11/12/68
Spahn, Warren (baseball); Buffalo, N.Y., 4/23/21
Speaker, Tristram (baseball); Hubbard City, Tex. **(1888–1958)**
Spencer, Brian (ice hockey); Fort St. James, British Columbia **(1949–1988)**
Spinks, Leon (boxing); St. Louis, 7/11/53
Spitz, Mark (swimming); Modesto, Calif., 2/10/50
Stabler, Kenneth (football); Foley, Ala., 12/25/45
Stagg, Amos Alonzo (football); West Orange, N.J. **(1862–1965)**
Stargell, Willie (Wilver Dornell) (baseball); Earlsboro, Okla. **(1941–2001)**
Starr, Bart (football); Montgomery, Ala., 1/9/34
Staub, "Rusty" (Daniel) (baseball); New Orleans, 4/4/44
Staubach, Roger (football); Cincinnati, 2/5/42
Steinkraus, William C. (equestrian); Cleveland, 10/12/25
Stenerud, Jan (football); Fetsund, Norway, 11/26/42
Stengel, Casey (Charles Dillon) (baseball); Kansas City, Mo. **(1891–1975)**
Stenmark, Ingemar (Alpine skier); Tarnaby, Sweden, 3/18/56
Stevens, Scott (hockey); Completon, New Brunswick, 5/4/66
Stockton, Richard LaClede (tennis); New York City, 2/18/51
Stones, Dwight Edwin (track); Los Angeles, 12/6/53
Strawberry, Darryl (baseball); Los Angeles, 3/12/62
Street, Picabo (skiing); Triumph, Idaho, 4/3/71
Sullivan, John Lawrence (boxing); Boston **(1858–1918)**
Summitt, Pat (basketball); Henrietta, Tenn., 6/14/52
Sutton, Don (Donald Howard) (baseball); Clio, Ala., 4/2/45
Swann, Lynn (football); Alcoa, Tenn., 3/7/52
Swoopes, Sheryl (basketball); Brownfield, Tex., 3/25/71
Tanner, Leonard Roscoe III (tennis); Chattanooga, Tenn., 10/15/51
Tarkenton, Fran (Francis) (football); Richmond, Va., 2/3/40
Tebbetts, Birdie (George R.) (baseball); Nashua, N.H. **(1914–1999)**
Theismann, Joe (football); New Brunswick, N.J., 9/9/46
Thomas, Frank (baseball); Columbus, Ga., 5/27/68
Thomas, Isiah (basketball); Chicago, Ill., 4/30/61
Thomas, Thurman (football); Houston, Texas, 5/16/66
Thompson, David (basketball); Shelby, N.C., 7/13/54
Thorpe, Ian (swimming); Sydney, New South Wales, Australia, 10/13/82
Thorpe, Jim (James Francis) (all-around athlete); nr. Prague, Okla. **(1888–1953)**
Tilden, William Tatem II (tennis); Philadelphia **(1893–1953)**
Tittle, Y. A. (Yelberton Abraham) (football); Marshall, Tex., 10/24/26
Toomey, William (decathlon); Philadelphia, 1/10/39
Trevino, Lee (golf); Dallas, 12/1/39
Trottier, Bryan (hockey); Val Marie, Sask., Canada, 7/17/56
Tunney, Gene (James J.) (boxing); New York City **(1898–1978)**
Tyson, Mike (boxing); Brooklyn, N.Y., 6/30/66
Tyus, Wyomia (runner); Griffin, Ga., 8/29/45
Ueberroth, Peter (baseball); Evanston, Ill., 9/2/37
Unitas, John (football); Pittsburgh **(1933–2002)**

Unser, Al (auto racing); Albuquerque, N. Mex., 5/29/39
Unser, Bobby (auto racing); Albuquerque, N. Mex., 2/20/34
Valenzuela, Fernando (baseball); Sonora, Mexico, 11/1/60
Valvano, Jim (basketball); New York, N.Y. **(1946–1993)**
Van Brocklin, Norm (football); Eagle Butte, S. Dak. **(1926–1983)**
Vaughn, Mo (baseball); Norwalk, Conn., 12/15/67
Vilas, Guillermo (tennis); Mar del Plata, Argentina, 8/17/52
Viola, Frank (baseball); Hempstead, N.Y., 4/19/60
Viren, Lasse (track); Myrskyla, Finland, 7/12/49
Vitale, Dick (basketball); E. Rutherford, N.J., 6/9/39
Wade, Virginia (tennis); Bournemouth, England, 7/10/45
Wagner, Honus (John Peter Honus) (baseball); Carnegie, Pa. **(1867–1955)**
Waitz, Grete (Andersen) (running); Oslo, Norway, 10/1/53
Walcott, Jersey Joe (Arnold Cream) (boxing); Merchantville, N.J. **(1914–1994)**
Wallace, Rusty (auto racing); St. Louis, Mo., 8/14/56
Walsh, Adam (football) **(1902–1985)**
Walton, Bill (basketball); La Mesa, Calif., 11/5/52
Waterfield, Bob (football); Burbank, Calif **(1921–1983)**
Watson, Martha Rae (track); Long Beach, Calif., 8/19/46
Watson, Tom (golf); Kansas City, Mo., 9/4/49
Weaver, Earl (baseball); St. Louis, 8/14/30
Weiskopf, Tom (golf); Massillon, Ohio, 11/9/42
Weiss, George (baseball executive); New Haven, Conn. **(1895–1972)**
Weissmuller, Johnny (swimmer and actor); Windber, Pa. **(1904–1984)**
West, Jerry (basketball); Cheylan, W. Va., 5/28/38
White, Reggie (football); Chattanooga, Tenn., 12/19/61
White, Willye B. (long jumper); Money, Miss., 1/1/36
Whitworth, Kathy (golf); Monahans, Tex., 9/27/39
Wilkens, Mac Maurice (track); Eugene, Ore., 11/15/50
Wilkins, Lennie (basketball) 11/25/37
Wilkinson, Bud (football); Minneapolis **(1916–1994)**
Williams, Dick (baseball); St. Louis, 5/7/29
Williams, Serena (tennis); Saginaw, Mich., 9/26/81
Williams, Ted (baseball); San Diego, Calif. **(1918–2002)**
Williams, Venus (tennis); Lynnwood, Calif., 6/17/80
Wills, Maury (baseball); Washington, D.C., 10/2/32
Winfield, Dave (baseball); St. Paul, Minn., 10/3/51
Wohlhuter, Richard C. (runner); Geneva, Ill., 12/23/45
Wood, "Smokey Joe" (Joseph) (baseball); Kansas City, Mo. **(1890–1985)**
Woods, Tiger (Eldrick) (golf); Long Beach, Calif., 12/30/75
Wottle, David James (runner); Canton, Ohio, 8/7/50
Wright, Mickey (Mary Kathryn) (golf); San Diego, Calif., 2/14/35
Yarborough, Cale (William Caleb) (auto racing); Timmonsville, S.C., 3/27/39
Yastrzemski, Carl (baseball); Southampton, N.Y., 8/22/39
Young, Cy (Denton True) (baseball); Gilmore, Ohio **(1867–1955)**
Young, Sheila (speed skater, bicycle racer); Detroit, 10/14/50
Young, Steve (football); Salt Lake City, Utah, 10/11/61
Zaharias, Babe Didrikson (golf); Port Arthur, Tex. **(1913–1956)**

Hockey

Ice hockey, by birth and upbringing a Canadian game, is an offshoot of field hockey. Some historians say that the first ice hockey game was played in Montreal in Dec. 1879 between two teams composed almost exclusively of McGill University students, but others assert that earlier hockey games took place in Kingston, Ontario, or Halifax, Nova Scotia. In the Montreal game of 1879, there were fifteen players on a side, who used an assortment of crude sticks to keep the puck in motion. Early rules allowed nine men on a side, but the number was reduced to seven in 1886 and later to six.

The first governing body of the sport was the Amateur Hockey Association of Canada, organized in 1887. In the winter of 1894–1895, a group of college students from the United States visited Canada and saw hockey played. They became enthusiastic about the game and introduced it as a winter sport when they returned home. The first professional league was the International Hockey League, which operated in northern Michigan in 1904–1906.

Until 1910, professionals and amateurs were allowed to play together on "mixed teams," but this arrangement ended with the formation of the first "big league," the National Hockey Association, in eastern Canada in 1910. The Pacific Coast League was organized in 1911 for western Canadian hockey. The league included Seattle and later other American cities. The National Hockey League replaced the National Hockey Association in 1917. Boston, in 1924, was the first American city to join that circuit. The league expanded to include western cities in 1967. The Stanley Cup was competed for by "mixed teams" from 1894 to 1910, thereafter by professionals. It was awarded to the winner of the NHL playoffs from 1926–1967 and now to the league champion. The World Hockey Association was organized in Oct. 1972 and was dissolved after the 1978–1979 season when the NHL absorbed four of the teams.

Rule changes have been implemented to steer the league from its violent reputation in order to better showcase the world's most talented stars.

Hockey, once considered a cold-weather sport, has taken major strides in increasing its fan base to the southern and western part of the United States as well. In the 1995–1996 season, Florida and Colorado battled in the Stanley Cup Finals, the San Jose Sharks sold out all 41 of their home games, and the second team in two years (Winnipeg) migrated from Canada to the Southwest region of the U.S. (Phoenix).

The NHL continued to expand when the Nashville Predators joined the league in the 1998–1999 season. The 1999–2000 season included the new Atlanta Thrashers and the 2000–2001 season introduced the Columbus Blue Jackets and the Minnesota Wild.

STANLEY CUP WINNERS

Emblematic of World Professional Championship; NHL Championship after 1967

1893 Montreal A.A.A.
1894 Montreal A.A.A.
1895 Montreal Victorias
1896 (Feb.) Winnipeg Victorias
1896 (Dec.) Montreal Victorias
1897–99 Montreal Victorias
1899–1900 Montreal Shamrocks
1901 Winnipeg Victorias
1902 Montreal A.A.A.
1903–05 Ottawa Silver Seven
1906 Montreal Wanderers
1907 (Jan.) Kenora Thistles
1907 (March) Montreal Wanderers
1908 Montreal Wanderers
1909 Ottawa Senators
1910 Montreal Wanderers
1911 Ottawa Senators
1912–13 Quebec Bulldogs
1914 Toronto Blueshirts
1915 Vancouver Millionaries
1916 Montreal Canadiens
1917 Seattle Metropolitans
1918 Toronto Arenas
1919 No champion
1920–21 Ottawa Senators
1922 Toronto St. Patricks
1923 Ottawa Senators
1924 Montreal Canadiens
1925 Victoria Cougars
1926 Montreal Maroons
1927 Ottawa Senators
1928 N.Y. Rangers
1929 Boston Bruins
1930–31 Montreal Canadiens
1932 Toronto Maple Leafs
1933 N.Y. Rangers
1934 Chicago Blackhawks
1935 Montreal Maroons
1936–37 Detroit Red Wings
1938 Chicago Red Hawks
1939 Boston Bruins
1940 N.Y. Rangers

1941 Boston Bruins
1942 Toronto Maple Leafs
1943 Detroit Red Wings
1944 Montreal Canadiens
1945 Toronto Maple Leafs
1946 Montreal Canadiens
1947–49 Toronto Maple Leafs
1950 Detroit Red Wings
1951 Toronto Maple Leafs
1952 Detroit Red Wings
1953 Montreal Canadiens
1954–55 Detroit Red Wings
1956–60 Montreal Canadiens
1961 Chicago Blackhawks
1962–64 Toronto Maple Leafs
1965–66 Montreal Canadiens
1967 Toronto Maple Leafs
1968–69 Montreal Canadiens
1970 Boston Bruins
1971 Montreal Canadiens
1972 Boston Bruins
1973 Montreal Canadiens
1974–75 Philadelphia Flyers
1976–79 Montreal Canadiens
1980–83 N.Y. Islanders
1984–85 Edmonton Oilers
1986 Montreal Canadiens
1987–88 Edmonton Oilers
1989 Calgary Flames
1990 Edmonton Oilers
1991–92 Pittsburgh Penguins
1993 Montreal Canadiens
1994 N.Y. Rangers
1995 N.J. Devils
1996 Colorado Avalanche
1997–98 Detroit Red Wings
1999 Dallas Stars
2000 N.J. Devils
2001 Colorado Avalanche
2002 Detroit Red Wings
2003 N.J. Devils

NHL CHAMPIONS

Wales Trophy
1939–41 Boston
1942 New York
1943 Detroit
1944–47 Montreal
1948 Toronto
1948–55 Detroit
1956 Montreal
1957 Detroit
1958–62 Montreal
1963 Toronto
1964 Montreal
1965 Detroit
1966 Montreal
1967 Chicago

Eastern Division
1968–69 Montreal
1970 Chicago
1971–72 Boston
1973 Montreal
1974 Boston

Eastern Conference[1]
1975 Buffalo
1976–79 Montreal
1980 Buffalo
1981 Montreal
1982–84 N.Y. Islanders
1985 Philadelphia
1986 Montreal
1987 Philadelphia
1988 Boston
1989 Montreal
1990 Boston
1991–92 Pittsburgh
1993 Montreal
1994 N.Y. Rangers
1995 New Jersey
1996 Florida
1997 Philadelphia
1998 Washington
1999 Buffalo
2000–01 New Jersey
2002 Carolina
2003 New Jersey

1. Prior to 1994 was the Wales Conference.

CAMPBELL BOWL

Western Division
1968–70 St. Louis
1971–73 Chicago
1974 Philadelphia

Western Conference[2]
1975–77 Philadelphia
1978–79 N.Y. Islanders
1980 Philadelphia
1981 N.Y. Islanders
1982–85 Edmonton
1986 Calgary
1987–88 Edmonton
1989 Calgary
1990 Edmonton
1991 Minnesota
1992 Chicago
1993 Los Angeles
1994 Vancouver
1995 Detroit
1996 Colorado
1997–98 Detroit
1999–2000 Dallas
2001 Colorado
2002 Detroit
2003 Anaheim

2. Prior to 1994 was the Campbell Conference.

NATIONAL HOCKEY LEAGUE YEARLY TROPHY WINNERS

The Hart Trophy—Most Valuable Player
1924 Frank Nighbor, Ottawa
1925 Billy Burch, Hamilton
1926 Nels Stewart, Montreal Maroons
1927 Herb Gardiner, Montreal Canadiens
1928 Howie Morenz, Montreal Canadiens
1929 Roy Worters, N.Y. Americans
1930 Nels Stewart, Montreal Maroons
1931–32 Howie Morenz, Montreal Canadiens
1933 Eddie Shore, Boston
1934 Aurel Joliat, Montreal Canadiens
1935–36 Eddie Shore, Boston
1937 Babe Siebert, Montreal Canadiens
1938 Eddie Shore, Boston
1939 Toe Blake, Montreal Canadiens
1940 Ebbie Goodfellow, Detroit
1941 Bill Cowley, Boston
1942 Tommy Anderson, N.Y. Americans
1943 Bill Cowley, Boston
1944 Babe Pratt, Toronto
1945 Elmer Lach, Montreal Canadiens
1946 Max Bentley, Chicago
1947 Maurice Richard, Montreal Canadiens
1948 Buddy O'Connor, N.Y. Rangers
1949 Sid Abel, Detroit
1950 Chuck Rayner, N.Y. Rangers
1951 Milt Schmidt, Boston
1952–53 Gordie Howe, Detroit
1954 Al Rollins, Chicago
1955 Ted Kennedy, Toronto
1956 Jean Belveau, Montreal Canadiens
1957–58 Gordie Howe, Detroit
1959 Andy Bathgate, N.Y. Rangers
1960 Gordie Howe, Detroit
1961 Bernie Geoffrion, Montreal Canadiens
1962 Jacques Plante, Montreal Canadiens
1963 Gordon Howe, Detroit
1964 Jean Beliveau, Montreal Canadiens
1965–66 Bobby Hull, Chicago
1967–68 Stan Mikita, Chicago
1969 Phil Esposito, Boston
1970–72 Bobby Orr, Boston
1973 Bobby Clarke, Philadelphia
1974 Phil Esposito, Boston
1975–76 Bobby Clarke, Philadelphia
1977–78 Guy Lafleur, Montreal
1979 Bryan Trottier, N.Y. Islanders
1980–87 Wayne Gretzky, Edmonton
1988 Mario Lemieux, Pittsburgh
1989 Wayne Gretzky, Los Angeles
1990 Mark Messier, Edmonton
1991 Brett Hull, St. Louis
1992 Mark Messier, N.Y. Rangers
1993 Mario Lemieux, Pittsburgh
1994 Sergei Fedorov, Detroit
1995 Eric Lindros, Philadelphia
1996 Mario Lemieux, Pittsburgh
1997–98 Dominik Hasek, Buffalo
1999 Jaromir Jagr, Pittsburgh
2000 Chris Pronger, St. Louis
2001 Joe Sakic, Colorado
2002 Jose Theodore, Montreal
2003 Peter Forsberg, Colorado

Vezina Trophy—Leading Goalkeeper
1956–60 Jacques Plante, Montreal
1961 Johnny Bower, Toronto
1962 Jacques Plante, Montreal
1963 Glenn Hall, Chicago
1964 Charlie Hodge, Montreal
1965 Terry Sawchuk—Johnny Bower, Toronto
1966 Gump Worsley—Charlie Hodge, Montreal
1967 Glen Hall—Denis Dejordy, Chicago
1968 Gump Worsley—Rogie Vachon, Montreal
1969 Glenn Hall—Jacques Plante, St. Louis
1970 Tony Esposito, Chicago
1971 Ed Giacomin—Gilles Villemure, N.Y. Rangers

1972 Tony Esposito—Gary Smith, Chicago
1973 Ken Dryden, Montreal
1974 Bernie Parent, Philadelphia and Tony Esposito, Chicago
1975 Bernie Parent, Philadelphia
1976 Ken Dryden, Montreal
1977–79 Ken Dryden—Bunny Larocque, Montreal
1980 Bob Sauve—Don Edwards, Buffalo
1981 Richard Sevigny—Denis Herron—Bunny Larocque, Montreal
1982 Billy Smith, N.Y. Islanders
1983 Pete Peeters, Boston
1984 Tom Barrasso, Buffalo
1985 Pelle Lindbergh, Philadelphia
1986 John Vanbiesbrouck, N.Y. Rangers
1987 Ron Hextall, Philadelphia
1988 Grant Fuhr, Edmonton
1989–90 Patrick Roy, Montreal
1991 Ed Belfour, Chicago
1992 Patrick Roy, Montreal
1993 Ed Belfour, Chicago
1994–95 Dominik Hasek, Buffalo
1996 Jim Carey, Washington
1997–99 Dominik Hasek, Buffalo
2000 Olaf Kolzig, Washington
2001 Dominik Hasek, Buffalo
2002 Jose Theodore, Montreal
2003 Martin Brodeur, New Jersey

James Norris Trophy—Defenseman

1954 Red Kelly, Detroit
1955–58 Doug Harvey, Montreal
1959 Tom Johnson, Montreal
1960–62 Doug Harvey, Montreal, N.Y. Rangers (62)
1963–65 Pierre Pilote, Chicago
1966 Jacques Laperriere, Montreal
1967 Harry Howell, N.Y. Rangers
1968–75 Bobby Orr, Boston
1976 Denis Potvin, N.Y. Islanders
1977 Larry Robinson, Montreal
1978–79 Denis Potvin, N.Y. Islanders
1980 Larry Robinson, Montreal
1981 Randy Carlyle, Pittsburgh
1982 Doug Wilson, Chicago
1983–84 Rod Langway, Washington
1985–86 Paul Coffey, Edmonton
1987–88 Ray Bourque, Boston
1989 Chris Chelios, Montreal
1990–91 Ray Bourque, Boston
1992 Brian Leetch, N.Y. Rangers
1993 Chris Chelios, Chicago
1994 Ray Bourque, Boston
1995 Paul Coffey, Detroit
1996 Chris Chelios, Chicago
1997 Brian Leetch, N.Y. Rangers
1998 Rob Blake, Los Angeles
1999 Al MacInnis, St. Louis
2000 Chris Pronger, St. Louis
2001–2003 Nicklas Lidstrom, Detroit

Lady Byng Trophy—Sportsmanship

1960 Don McKenney, Boston
1961 Red Kelly, Toronto
1962–63 Dave Keon, Toronto
1964 Ken Wharram, Chicago
1965 Bobby Hull, Chicago
1966 Alex Delvecchio, Detroit
1967–68 Stan Mikita, Chicago
1969 Alex Delvecchio, Detroit
1970 Phil Goyette, St. Louis
1971 Johnny Bucyk, Boston
1972 Jean Ratelle, N.Y. Rangers
1973 Gilbert Perreault, Buffalo
1974 Johnny Bucyk, Boston
1975 Marcel Dionne, Detroit
1976 Jean Ratelle, N.Y. Rangers, Boston
1977 Marcel Dionne, Los Angeles
1978 Butch Goring, Los Angeles
1979 Bob MacMillan, Atlanta
1980 Wayne Gretzky, Edmonton
1981 Rick Kehoe, Pittsburgh
1982 Rick Middleton, Boston
1983–84 Mike Bossy, N.Y. Islanders
1985 Jari Kurri, Edmonton
1986 Mike Bossy, N.Y. Islanders
1987 Joey Mullen, Calgary
1988 Mats Naslund, Montreal
1989 Joey Mullen, Calgary
1990 Brett Hull, St. Louis
1991–92 Wayne Gretzky, Los Angeles
1993 Pierre Turgeon, N.Y. Islanders
1994 Wayne Gretzky, Los Angeles
1995 Ron Francis, Pittsburgh
1996–97 Paul Kariya, Anaheim
1998 Ron Francis, Pittsburgh
1999 Wayne Gretzky, N.Y. Rangers
2000 Pavol Demitra, St. Louis
2001 Joe Sakic, Colorado
2002 Ron Francis, Carolina
2003 Alexander Mogilny, Toronto

Calder Trophy—Rookie

1962 Bobby Rousseau, Montreal
1963 Kent Douglas, Toronto
1964 Jacques Laperriere, Montreal
1965 Roger Crozier, Detroit
1966 Brit Selby, Toronto
1967 Bobby Orr, Boston
1968 Derek Sanderson, Boston
1969 Danny Grant, Minnesota
1970 Tony Esposito, Chicago
1971 Gilbert Perreault, Buffalo
1972 Ken Dryden, Montreal
1973 Steve Vickers, N.Y. Rangers
1974 Denis Potvin, N.Y. Islanders
1975 Eric Vail, Atlanta
1976 Bryan Trottier, N.Y. Islanders
1977 Willi Plett, Atlanta
1978 Mike Bossy, N.Y. Islanders
1979 Bobby Smith, Minnesota
1980 Ray Bourque, Boston
1981 Peter Stastny, Quebec
1982 Dale Hawerchuk, Winnipeg
1983 Steve Larmer, Chicago
1984 Tom Barrasso, Buffalo
1985 Mario Lemieux, Pittsburgh
1986 Gary Suter, Calgary
1987 Luc Robitaille, Los Angeles
1988 Joe Nieuwendyk, Calgary
1989 Brian Leetch, N.Y. Rangers
1990 Sergei Makarov, Calgary
1991 Ed Belfour, Chicago
1992 Pavel Bure, Vancouver
1993 Teemu Selanne, Winnipeg
1994 Martin Brodeur, N.J. Devils
1995 Peter Forsberg, Quebec
1996 Daniel Alfredsson, Ottawa
1997 Bryan Berard, N.Y. Islanders
1998 Sergei Samsonov, Boston
1999 Chris Drury, Colorado
2000 Scott Gomez, New Jersey
2001 Evgeni Nabokov, San Jose
2002 Dany Heatley, Atlanta
2003 Barret Jackman, St. Louis

Art Ross Trophy—Leading Scorer

1955 Bernie Geoffrion, Montreal
1956 Jean Beliveau, Montreal
1957 Gordie Howe, Detroit
1958–59 Dickie Moore, Montreal
1960 Bobby Hull, Chicago
1961 Bernie Geoffrion, Montreal
1962 Bobby Hull, Chicago
1963 Gordie Howe, Detroit
1964–65 Stan Mikita, Chicago
1966 Bobby Hull, Chicago
1967–68 Stan Mikita, Chicago
1969 Phil Esposito, Boston
1970 Bobby Orr, Boston
1971–74 Phil Esposito, Boston
1975 Bobby Orr, Boston
1976–78 Guy Lafleur, Montreal
1979 Bryan Trottier, N.Y. Islanders
1980 Marcel Dionne, Los Angeles
1981–87 Wayne Gretzky, Edmonton
1988–89 Mario Lemieux, Pittsburgh
1990–91 Wayne Gretzky, Los Angeles
1992–93 Mario Lemieux, Pittsburgh
1994 Wayne Gretzky, Los Angeles
1995 Jaromir Jagr, Pittsburgh
1996–97 Mario Lemieux, Pittsburgh
1998–2001 Jaromir Jagr, Pittsburgh
2002 Jarome Iginla, Calgary
2003 Peter Forsberg, Colorado

OTHER NHL AWARDS—2003

Frank Selke Trophy (Top defensive forward)—Jere Lehtinen, Dallas

King Clancy Trophy (Humanitarian community involvement)—Brendan Shanahan, Detroit

Jack Adams Award (Coach of the Year)—Jacques Lemaire, Minnesota

Bill Masterson Trophy (Perseverance, sportsmanship, and dedication to hockey)—Steve Yzerman, Detroit

STANLEY CUP PLAYOFFS—2003

NOTE: Home teams are in capitals.

EASTERN CONFERENCE

Quarterfinals

Ottawa Senators defeated New York Islanders, 4 games to 1
New Jersey Devils defeated Boston Bruins, 4 games to 1
Tampa Bay Lightning defeated Washington Capitals, 4 games to 2
Philadelphia Flyers defeated Toronto Maple Leafs, 4 games to 3

Semifinals

Ottawa Senators defeated Philadelphia Flyers, 4 games to 2
New Jersey Devils defeated Tampa Bay Lightning, 4 games to 1

Finals

New Jersey Devils defeated Ottawa Senators, 4 games to 3
May 10—OTTAWA 3, New Jersey 2 (OT)
May 13—New Jersey 4, OTTAWA 1
May 15—NEW JERSEY 1, Ottawa 0
May 17—NEW JERSEY 5, Ottawa 2
May 19—OTTAWA 3, New Jersey 1
May 21—Ottawa 2, NEW JERSEY 1 (OT)
May 23—New Jersey 3, OTTAWA 2

WESTERN CONFERENCE

Quarterfinals

Dallas Stars defeated Edmonton Oilers, 4 games to 2
Anaheim Mighty Ducks defeated Detroit Red Wings, 4 games to 0
Minnesota Wild defeated Colorado Avalanche, 4 games to 3
Vancouver Canucks defeated St. Louis Blues, 4 games to 3

Semifinals

Anaheim Mighty Ducks defeated Dallas Stars, 4 games to 2
Minnesota Wild defeated Vancouver Canucks, 4 games to 3

Finals

Anaheim Mighty Ducks defeated Minnesota Wild, 4 games to 0
May 10—Anaheim 1, MINNESOTA 0 (2OT)
May 12—Anaheim 2, MINNESOTA 0
May 14—ANAHEIM 4, Minnesota 0
May 16—ANAHEIM 2, Minnesota 1

STANLEY CUP CHAMPIONSHIP FINALS

New Jersey Devils defeated Anaheim Mighty Ducks, 4 games to 3.

May 27—NEW JERSEY 3, Anaheim 0
May 29—NEW JERSEY 3, Anaheim 0
May 31—ANAHEIM 3, New Jersey 2 (OT)
June 2—ANAHEIM 1, New Jersey 0 (OT)
June 5—NEW JERSEY 6, Anaheim 3
June 7—ANAHEIM 5, New Jersey 2
June 9—NEW JERSEY 3, Anaheim 0

Conn Smythe Trophy for most valuable player in the playoffs: John-Sebasien Giguere, Anaheim

NATIONAL HOCKEY LEAGUE FINAL STANDINGS OF THE CLUBS: 2002–2003

EASTERN CONFERENCE

Northeast Division

	W	L	T	Pts	GF	GA
Ottawa Senators[1]	52	21	8	113	263	182
Toronto Maple Leafs[2]	44	28	7	98	236	208
Boston Bruins[2]	36	31	11	87	245	237
Montreal Canadiens	30	35	8	77	206	234
Buffalo Sabres	27	37	10	72	190	219

Atlantic Division

	W	L	T	Pts	GF	GA
New Jersey Devils[1]	46	20	10	108	216	166
Philadelphia Flyers[2]	45	20	13	107	211	166
N.Y. Islanders[2]	35	34	11	83	224	231
N.Y. Rangers	32	36	10	78	210	231
Pittsburgh Penguins	27	44	6	65	189	255

Southeast Division

	W	L	T	Pts	GF	GA
Tampa Bay Lightning[1]	35	25	16	93	219	210
Washington Capitals[2]	39	29	8	92	224	220
Atlanta Thrashers	31	39	7	74	226	284
Florida Panthers	24	36	13	70	176	237
Carolina Hurricanes	22	43	11	61	171	240

WESTERN CONFERENCE

Central Division

	W	L	T	Pts	GF	GA
Detroit Red Wings[1]	48	20	10	110	269	203
St. Louis Blues[2]	41	24	11	99	253	222
Chicago Blackhawks	30	33	13	79	207	226
Nashville Predators	27	35	13	74	183	206
Columbus Blue Jackets	29	42	8	69	213	263

Pacific Division

	W	L	T	Pts	GF	GA
Dallas Stars[1]	46	17	15	111	245	169
Anaheim Mighty Ducks[2]	40	27	9	95	203	193
Los Angeles Kings	33	37	6	78	203	221
Phoenix Coyotes	31	35	11	78	204	230
San Jose Sharks	28	37	9	73	214	239

Northwest Division

	W	L	T	Pts	GF	GA
Colorado Avalanche[1]	42	19	13	105	251	194
Vancouver Canucks[2]	45	23	13	104	264	208
Minnesota Wild[2]	42	29	10	95	198	178
Edmonton Oilers[2]	36	26	11	92	231	230
Calgary Flames	29	36	13	75	186	228

1. Best record in conference. 2. Playoff qualifier.

NHL LEADING SCORERS: 2002–2003

	Gm	G	A	Pts
Peter Forsberg, Colorado	75	29	77	106
Markus Naslund, Vancouver	82	48	56	104
Joe Thornton, Boston	77	36	65	101
Milan Hejduk, Colorado	82	50	48	98
Todd Bertuzzi, Vancouver	82	46	51	97
Pavol Demitra, St. Louis	78	36	57	93
Glen Murray, Boston	82	44	48	92
Mario Lemieux, Pittsburgh	67	28	63	91
Dany Heatley, Atlanta	77	41	48	89
Mike Modano, Dallas	79	28	57	85

NHL CAREER SCORING LEADERS

(Through 2002–2003 season)

		Yrs	Gm	G	A	Pts
1.	Wayne Gretzky	20	1,487	894	1,963	2,857
2.	Gordie Howe	26	1,767	801	1,049	1,850
3.	**Mark Messier**	24	1,680	676	1,168	1,844
4.	Marcel Dionne	18	1,348	731	1,040	1,771
5.	**Ron Francis**	23	1,651	536	1,222	1,758
6.	**Mario Lemieux**	15	879	682	1,011	1,692
7.	**Steve Yzerman**	20	1,378	660	1,010	1,670
8.	Phil Esposito	18	1,282	717	873	1,590
9.	Ray Bourque	22	1,612	410	1,169	1,579
10.	Paul Coffey	21	1,409	396	1,135	1,531

Players active during 2002–2003 season in **bold** type.

NHL LEADING GOALTENDERS: 2002–2003

(Minimum 26 games played)

	Gm	W	L	T	GAA
Marty Turco, Dallas	55	31	10	10	1.72
Roman Cechmanek, Philadelphia	58	33	15	10	1.83
Dwayne Roloson, Minnesota	50	23	16	8	2.00
Martin Brodeur, New Jersey	73	41	23	9	2.02
Patrick Lalime, Ottawa	67	39	20	7	2.16
Patrick Roy, Colorado	63	35	15	13	2.18
Robert Esche, Philadelphia	30	12	9	3	2.20
Tomas Vokoun, Nashville	69	25	31	11	2.20
Emmanuel Fernandez, Minnesota	35	19	13	2	2.24
Ed Belfour, Toronto	62	37	20	5	2.26

NHL CAREER GOALTENDING WINS LEADERS

(Through 2002–2003 season)

		Yrs	Gm	W	L	T
1.	**Patrick Roy**	20	1,029	551	315	131
2.	Terry Sawchuk	21	971	447	330	172
3.	Jacques Plante	18	837	435	247	146
4.	Tony Esposito	16	886	423	306	152
5.	Glenn Hall	18	906	407	326	163
6.	Grant Fuhr	19	868	403	295	114
7.	**Ed Belfour**	15	797	401	262	105
8.	Mike Vernon	19	781	385	273	92
9.	**Curtis Joseph**	14	767	380	279	87
10.	J. Vanbiesbrouck	20	882	374	346	119

Players active during 2002–2003 season in **bold** type.

Bowling

The game of bowling in the United States is an indoor development of the more ancient outdoor game that survives as lawn bowling. The outdoor game is prehistoric in origin and probably goes back to primitive man and round stones that were rolled at some target. It is believed that a game something like nine-pins was popular among the Dutch, Swiss, and Germans as long ago as A.D. 1200. The game was played outdoors with an alley consisting of a single plank 12 to 18 inches wide, along which a ball was rolled toward three rows of three pins each placed at the far end of the alley. When the first indoor alleys were built and how the game was modified from time to time are matters of dispute.

It is supposed that the early settlers of New Amsterdam (New York City), being Dutch, brought their two bowling games with them. About a century ago the game of nine-pins was flourishing in the United States but was so corrupted by gambling on matches that it was barred by law in New York and Connecticut. Since the law specifically barred "nine-pins," it was eventually evaded by adding another pin and thus legally making it a new game.

Various organizations were formed to make rules for bowling and supervise competition in the United States, but none was successful until the American Bowling Congress, organized Sept. 9, 1895, became the ruling body.

AMERICAN BOWLING CONGRESS CHAMPIONS

Year	Singles	All events
1959	Ed Lubanski	Ed Lubanski
1960	Paul Kulbaga	Vince Lucci
1961	Lyle Spooner	Luke Karen
1962	Andy Renaldo	Billy Young
1963	Fred Delello	Bus Owalt
1964	Jim Stefanich	Les Zikes, Jr.
1965	Ken Roeth	Tom Hathaway
1966	Don Chapman	John Wilcox
1967	Frank Perry	Gary Lewis
1968	Wayne Kowalski	Vince Mazzanti
1969	Greg Campbell	Eddie Jackson
1970	Jake Yoder	Mike Berlin
1971	Al Cohn	Al Cohn
1972	Bill Pointer	Mac Lowry
1973	Ed Thompson	Ron Woolet
1974	Gene Krause	Bob Hart
1975	Jim Setser	Bobby Meadows
1976	Mike Putzer	Jim Lindquist
1977	Frank Gadaleto	Bud Debenham
1978	Rich Mersek	Chris Cobus
1979	Rick Peters	Bob Basacchi
1980	Mike Eaton	Steve Fehr
1981	Rob Vital	Rod Toft
1982	Bruce Bohm	Rich Wonders
1983	Rick Kendrick	Tony Cariello
1984	Bob Antczak and Neal Young (tie)	Bob Goike
1985	Glen Harbison	Barry Asher

Year	Singles	All events
1986	Jess Mackey	Ed Marazka
1987	Terry Taylor	Ryan Schafer
1988	Steve Hutkowski	Rick Steelsmith
1989	Paul Tetreault	George Hall
1990	Bob Hochrein	Mike Neumann
1991	Ed Deines	Tom Howery
1992	Bob Youker and Gary Blatchford (tie)	Mike Tucker
1993	Dan Bock	Jeff Nimke
1994	John Weltzien	Thomas Holt
1995	Matt Surina	Jeff Kwiatkowski
1996	Donald Scudder, Jr.	Scott Kurtz
1997	John Socha	Jeff Richgels
1998	John Gaines	Chris Barnes
1999	Dan Winter	Thomas A. Jones
2000	Garran Hein	Roy Daniels
2001	Nicholas Hoagland	D. J. Archer
2002	Mark Millsap	Stephen A. Hardy
2003	Ron R. Bahr	Steve P. Kloempken

PROFESSIONAL BOWLERS ASSOCIATION

PBA World Championship[1]

1960	Don Carter
1961	Dave Soutar
1962	Carmen Salvino
1963	Billy Hardwick
1964	Bob Strampe
1965	Dave Davis
1966	Wayne Zahn
1967	Dave Davis
1968	Wayne Zahn
1969	Mike McGrath
1970	Mike McGrath
1971	Mike Lemongello
1972	Johnny Guenther
1973	Earl Anthony
1974	Earl Anthony
1975	Earl Anthony
1976	Paul Colwell
1977	Tommy Hudson
1978	Warren Nelson
1979	Mike Aulby
1980	Johnny Petraglia
1981	Earl Anthony
1982	Earl Anthony
1983	Earl Anthony
1984	Bob Chamberlain
1985	Mike Aulby
1986	Tom Crites
1987	Randy Pedersen
1988	Brian Voss
1989	Pete Weber
1990	Jim Pencak
1991	Mike Miller
1992	Eric Forkel
1993	Ron Palombi
1994	David Traber
1995	Scott Alexander
1996	Butch Soper
1997	Rich Steelsmith
1998	Pete Weber
1999	Tim Criss
2000	Norm Duke
2001	Walter Ray Williams, Jr.
2002	Doug Kent
2003	Walter Ray Williams, Jr.

1. Formerly National Championship Tournament.

BOWLING PROPRIETORS' ASSOCIATION OF AMERICA—MEN

United States Open[1]

1971	Mike Lemongello
1972	Don Johnson
1973	Mike McGrath
1974	Larry Laub
1975	Steve Neff
1976	Paul Moser
1977	Johnny Petraglia
1978	Nelson Burton, Jr.
1979	Joe Berardi
1980	Steve Martin
1981	Marshall Holman
1982	Dave Husted
1983	Gary Dickinson
1984	Mark Roth
1985	Marshall Holman
1986	Steve Cook
1987	Del Ballard
1988	Pete Weber
1989	Mike Aulby
1990	Ron Palumbi, Jr.
1991	Pete Weber
1992	Robert Lawrence
1993	Del Ballard, Jr.
1994	Justin Hromek
1995	Dave Husted
1996	Dave Husted
1997	Not held
1998	Walter Ray Williams, Jr.
1999	Bob Learn, Jr.
2000	Robert Smith
2001	Mika Koivuniemi
2002–2003[2]	Walter Ray Williams, Jr.

1. Replaced All-Star tournament and is rolled as part of PBA tour. 2. 2002 and 2003 tournaments combined.

WOMEN'S INTERNATIONAL BOWLING CONGRESS CHAMPIONS

Year	Singles	All events
1959	Mae Bolt	Pat McBride
1960	Marge McDaniels	Judy Roberts
1961	Elaine Newton	Evelyn Teal
1962	Martha Hoffman	Flossie Argent
1963	Dot Wilkinson	Helen Shablis
1964	Jean Havlish	Jean Havlish
1965	Doris Rudell	Donna Zimmerman
1966	Gloria Bouvia	Kate Helbig
1967	Gloria Paeth	Carol Miller
1968	Norma Parks	Susie Reichley
1969	Joan Bender	Helen Duval
1970	Dorothy Fothergill	Dorothy Fothergill
1971	Mary Scruggs	Lorrie Nichols
1972	D. D. Jacobson	Mildred Martorella
1973	Bobby Buffaloe	Toni Calvery
1974	Shirley Garms	Judy C. Soutar
1975	Barbara Leicht	Virginia Norton
1976	Bev Shonk	Betty Morris
1977	Akiko Yamaga	Akiko Yamaga
1978	Mae Bolt	Annese Kelly
1979	Betty Morris	Betty Morris
1980	Betty Morris	Cheryl Robinson
1981	Virginia Norton	Virginia Norton
1982	Gracie Freeman	Aleta Rzepecki
1983	Aleta Rzepecki	Virginia Norton
1984	Freida Gates	Shinobu Saitoh
1985	Polly Schwarzel	Aleta Sill
1986	Dana Stewart	Robin Romeo and Maria Lewis (tie)
1987	Regi Junak	Leanne Barrette
1988	Michelle Meyer-Welty	Lisa Wagner
1989	Lorraine Anderson	Nancy Fehn
1990	Dana Miller-Mackie and Paula Carter (tie)	Carol Norman
1991	Debbie Kuhn	Debbie Kuhn
1992	Patty Ann	Mitsuko Tokimoto
1993	Karen Collurs and Kari Murph (tie)	Bertha Blackshur and Sharon Davis (tie)
1994	Vicki Fifield	Wendy Macpherson-Papanos
1995	Beth Owen	Beth Owen
1996	Cindy Berlanga	Lorrie Nichols
1997	Jean Schmidt	Kendra Cameron
1998	Nellie Glandon	Liz Johnson
1999	Maggie Matheson	Marlene Walls
2000	Cathy Krasner	Carolyn Dorin-Ballard
2001	Lisa Wagner	Jonquay Armon
2002	Theresa Smith	Cara Honeychurch
2003	Michelle Feldman	Michelle Feldman

BOWLING PROPRIETORS' ASSOCIATION OF AMERICA—WOMEN

United States Open[1]

1971 Paula Carter
1972 Lorrie Nichols
1973 Mildred Martorella
1974 Pat Costello (Calif.)
1975 Paula Carter
1976 Patty Costello (Pa.)
1977 Betty Morris
1978 Donna Adamek
1979 Diana Silva
1980 Pat Costello (Calif.)
1981 Donna Adamek
1982 Shinobu Saitoh
1983 Dana Miller
1984 Karen Ellingsworth
1985 Pat Mercatanti
1986 Wendy Macpherson
1987 Carol Nurman
1988 Lisa Wagner
1989 Robin Romeo
1990 Dana Miller-Mackie
1991 Anne Marie Duggan
1992 Tish Johnson
1993 Dede Davidson
1994 Aleta Sill
1995 Tish Johnson
1996 Liz Johnson
1997 Not held
1998 Aleta Sill
1999 Kim Adler
2000 Tennelle Grijalva
2001 Kim Terrell
2002–2003[2] Kelly Kulick

1. Rolled as part of PWBA tour. 2. 2002 and 2003 tournaments combined.

WIBC QUEENS TOURNAMENT CHAMPIONS

1961 Janet Harman
1962 Dorothy Wilkinson
1963 Irene Monterosso
1964 D.D. Jacobson
1965 Betty Kuczynski
1966 Judy Lee
1967 Mildred Martorella
1968 Phyllis Massey
1969 Ann Feigel
1970 Mildred Martorella
1971 Mildred Martorella
1972 Dorothy Fothergill
1973 Dorothy Fothergill
1974 Judy Soutar
1975 Cindy Powell
1976 Pamela Buckner
1977 Dana Stewart
1978 Loa Boxberger
1979 Donna Adamek
1980 Donna Adamek
1981 Katsuko Sugimoto
1982 Katsuko Sugimoto
1983 Aleta Rzepecki
1984 Kazue Inahashi
1985 Aleta Sill
1986 Cora Fiebig
1987 Cathy Almeida
1988 Wendy Macpherson
1989 Carol Gianotti
1990 Patty Ann
1991 Dede Davidson
1992 Cindy Coburn-Carroll
1993 Jan Schmidt
1994 Anne Marie Duggan
1995 Sandy Postma
1996 Lisa Wagner
1997 Sandra-Jo Shiery-Odom
1998 Lynda Norry
1999 Leanne Barrette
2000 Wendy Macpherson
2001 Carolyn Dorin-Ballard
2002 Kim Terrell
2003 Wendy Macpherson

PBA WORLD CHAMPIONSHIP—2003

(March 3–9, 2003, Taylor, Mich.)

Winner—Walter Ray Williams, Jr., Ocala, Fla., defeated Brian Kretzer, Dayton, Ohio, 226–205 in title match.

3. Parker Bohn III, Jackson, N.J.

4. Pete Weber, St. Ann, Mo.

AMERICAN BOWLING CONGRESS TOURNAMENT—2003

(Feb. 8–June 22, 2003, Knoxville, Tenn.)

Singles—Ron R. Bahr, Topeka, Kans.	837
Doubles—Sean Rash, Wichita, Kans., and Derek S. Sapp, Macomb, Ill.	1,540
Team—Bowler Edge Pro Shop, Menasha, Wis.	3,294
All events—Steve P. Kloempken, Ogden, Utah	2,215

WOMEN'S INTERNATIONAL BOWLING CONGRESS TOURNAMENT—2003

(March 20–July 9, 2003, Reno, Nev.)

Singles—Michelle Feldman, Skaneateles, N.Y.	764
Doubles—Karen Collura, Toronto, Ontario, and Connie Ward, Hamilton, Ontario	1,496
Team—Barry Asher's Embroidery, Yorba Linda, Calif.	3,220
All events—Michelle Feldman, Skaneateles, N.Y.	2,048

WOMEN'S INTERNATIONAL BOWLING CONGRESS QUEENS TOURNAMENT—2003

(April 7–11, 2003, Reno, Nev.)

Winner—Wendy Macpherson, Henderson, Nev., defeated Kendra Gaines, Orlando, Fla., 218–193 in title match.
3. Tish Johnson, Northridge, Calif.
4. Robin Romeo, Newhall, Calif.
5. Lisa Bishop, Bellevilile, Mich.

Skiing

HISTORY OF SKIING IN THE UNITED STATES

Skis were devised for utility, to aid those who had to travel over snow. The Norwegians, Swedes, Lapps, and other inhabitants of northern lands used skis for many centuries before skiing became a sport. Emigrants from these countries brought skis to the United States with them. The first skier of record in the United States was a mailman by the name of "Snowshoe" Thompson, born and raised in Telemarken, Norway, who came to the United States and, beginning in 1850, used skis through 20 successive winters in carrying mail from northern California to Carson Valley, Idaho.

Ski clubs sprang up over 100 years ago where there were Norwegian and Swedish settlers in Wisconsin and Minnesota, and ski contests were held in that territory in 1886. On Feb. 21, 1904, at Ishpenning, Mich., a small group of skiers organized the National Ski Association. In 1961 it was renamed the United States Ski Association. In the 1990s it became the United States Ski and Snowboard Association and included freestyle and disabled skiing.

ALPINE SKIING

2003 Chevy Truck U.S. Alpine Championships
(March 19–25, 2003, Whiteface Mountain, Lake Placid, N.Y.)

Men

Downhill—1. Steve Nyman, Sundance, Utah; 2. Kevin Francis, Bend, Ore.; 3. Scott Macartney, Redmond, Wash.

Slalom—1. Bode Miller, Franconia, N.H.; 2. Erik Schlopy, Park City, Utah; 3. Jesse Marshall, Pittsfield, Vt.

Super G—1. Bode Miller, Franconia, N.H.; 2. Jake Fiala, Frisco, Colo.; 3. (tie) Scott Macartney, Redmond, Wash., and Marco Sullivan, Squaw Valley, Calif.

Giant Slalom—1. Erik Schlopy, Park City, Utah; 2. Bode Miller, Franconia, N.H.; 3. Jesse Marshall, Pittsfield, Vt.

Combined—1. Bode Miller, Franconia, N.H.; 2. Scott Macartney, Redmond, Wash.; 3. Nick Baker, Gilford, N.H.

Women

Downhill—1. Julia Mancuso, Olympic Valley, Calif.; 2. Lindsey C. Kildow, Vail, Colo.; 3. Jonna Mendes, Heavenly, Calif.

Slalom—1. Kristina Koznick, Burnsville, Minn.; 2. Katie Hitchcock, Carmichael, Calif.; 3. Sarah Schleper, Vail, Colo.

Super G—1. Julia Mancuso, Olympic Valley, Calif.; 2. Jonna Mendes, Heavenly, Calif.; 3. Lindsey C. Kildow, Vail, Colo.

Giant Slalom—1. Julia Mancuso, Olympic Valley, Calif.; 2. Jessica Kelley, Starksboro, Vt.; 3. (tie) Jonna Mendes, Heavenly, Calif.; and Kristina Koznick, Burnsville, Minn.

Combined —1. Lindsey C. Kildow, Vail, Colo.; 2. Sarah Schleper, Vail, Colo.; 3. Resi Stiegler, Jackson Hole, Wyo.

2003 Alpine World Cup Champions

Men	Pts
Overall—Stephan Eberharter, Austria	1,333
Downhill—Stephan Eberharter, Austria	790
Slalom—Kalle Palander, Finland	658
Giant Slalom—Michael von Gruenigen, Switzerland	542
Super G—Stephan Eberharter, Austria	356
Combined—Bode Miller, United States	125

Women	Pts
Overall—Janica Kostelic, Croatia	1,570
Downhill—Michaela Dorfmeister, Austria	372
Slalom—Janica Kostelic, Croatia	710
Giant Slalom—Anja Paerson, Sweden	514
Super G—Carole Montillet, France	493
Combined—Janica Kostelic, Croatia	100

2003 Disabled World Cup

Skiers are placed in categories appropriate to their disability. There are 3 blind classes, 11 standing classes, and 5 sitting classes. When several classes combine in competition, a factor system is used to calculate results.

Men

Downhill—**Blind:** Bart Bunting/Nathan Chivers, Australia. **Sitting:** Harald Eder, Austria. **Standing:** Michael Milton, Australia

Slalom—**Blind:** Jon Santacana/Miguel Galindo, Spain. **Sitting:** Martin Braxenthaler, Germany. **Standing:** Hubert Mandl, Austria

Giant Slalom—**Blind:** Jon Santacana/Miguel Galindo, Spain. **Sitting:** Martin Braxenthaler, Germany. **Standing:** Romain Riboud, France

Super G—**Blind:** Bart Bunting/Nathan Chivers, Australia. **Sitting:** Martin Braxenthaler, Germany. **Standing:** Michael Milton, Australia

Combined—**Blind:** Jon Santacana/Miguel Galindo, Spain. **Sitting:** Martin Braxenthaler, Germany. **Standing:** Romain Riboud, France

Women

Downhill—**Blind:** Pascale Casanova/Michael Gelin, France. **Sitting:** Sarah Will, United States. **Standing:** Danja Haslacher, Austria

Slalom—**Blind:** Katerina Tepla/R. Karamanova, Czech Republic. **Sitting:** Stephani Victor, United States. **Standing:** Karolina Wisniewska, Canada

Giant Slalom—**Blind:** Katerina Tepla/R. Karamanova, Czech Republic. **Sitting:** Lacey Heward, United States. **Standing:** Danja Haslacher, Austria

Super G—**Blind:** Katerina Tepla/R. Karamanova, Czech Republic. **Sitting:** Lacey Heward, United States. **Standing:** Lauren Woolstencroft, Canada

Combined—**Blind:** Katerina Tepla/R. Karamanova, Czech Republic. **Sitting:** Lacey Heward, United States. **Standing:** Lauren Woolstencroft, Canada

NORDIC SKIING/SKI JUMPING/CROSS COUNTRY

2003 Chevy Truck U.S. Ski Jumping/Nordic Combined Championships
(Feb. 12–13, 2003, Steamboat Springs, Colo.)

Men

Nordic Combined (K114m jumping–7.5k race)—1. Todd Lodwick, Steamboat Springs, Colo.; 2. Johnny Spillane, Steamboat Springs, Colo.; 3. Jed Hinkley, Andover, N.H.

Normal Hill (K88m)—1. Alan Alborn, Anchorage, Alaska; 2. Johnny Spillane, Steamboat Springs, Colo.; 3. Todd Lodwick, Steamboat Springs, Colo.

Large Hill (K114m)—1. Johnny Spillane, Steamboat Springs, Colo.; 2. Alan Alborn, Anchorage, Alaska; 3. Clint Jones, Steamboat Springs, Colo.

Women

Normal Hill (K88m)—1. Jessica Jerome, Park City, Utah; 2. (tie) Alissa Johnson, Park City, Utah; and Lindsey Van, Park City, Utah; 4. Brenna Ellis, Park City, Utah

2003 Chevy Truck U.S. Cross Country Championships
(Jan. 4–12, 2003, Rumford, Maine)

Men

30km Classic—Kris Freeman, Andover, N.H.
10km Free—Carl Swenson, Boulder, Colo.
10km Classic—Kris Freeman, Andover, N.H.
Free Sprints—Carl Swenson, Boulder, Colo.

Women

15km Classic—Wendy Wagner, Park City, Utah
5km Free—Katja Ivanova, Jericho, Vt.
5km Classic—Wendy Wagner, Park City, Utah
Free Sprints—Katja Ivanova, Jericho, Vt.

FREESTYLE SKIING

2003 Freestyle Skiing World Cup Champions

Men

Aerials—Dmitri Arkhipov, Russia
Moguls—Travis Cabral, United States
Dual Moguls—Janne Lahtela, Finland
Ski-Cross—Hiroomi, Takizawa, Japan
Overall—Dmitri Arkhipov, Russia

Women

Aerials—Alisa Camplin, Australia
Moguls—Shannon Bahrke, United States
Dual Moguls—Margarita Marbler, Austria
Ski-Cross—Valentine Scuotto, France
Overall—Kari Traa, Norway

2003 Chevy Truck U.S. Freestyle Championships

(March 21–23, 2003, Missoula, Mont.)

Men

Aerials—Ryan St. Onge, Winter Park, Colo.
Moguls—Luke Westerlund, Breckenridge, Colo.
Dual Moguls—Travis Mayer, Steamboat Springs, Colo.

Women

Aerials—Christina Craddock, West Newton, Mass.
Moguls—Hannah Kearney, Norwich, Vt.
Dual Moguls—Shannon Bahrke, Tahoe City, Calif.

SNOWBOARDING

2003 World Cup Snowboard Champions

Men

Big Air—Jukka Eratuli, Finland
Halfpipe—Xaver Hoffmann, Germany
Parallel Slalom—Mathieu Bozzetto, France
Snowboard Cross—Xavier Delerue, France
Overall—Jasey Jay Anderson, Canada

Women

Halfpipe—Manuela Laura Pesko, Switzerland
Parallel Slalom—Ursula Bruhin, Switzerland
Snowboard Cross—Karine Ruby, France
Overall—Karine Ruby, France

2003 Chevy Trucks U.S. Snowboard Championships

(April 3–6, 2003, Aspen, Colo.)

Men

Slalom—Adam Smith, Tangent, Ore.
Parallel Giant Slalom—Pete Thorndike, Meredith, N.H.
Snowboard Cross—Seth Wescott, Farmington, Maine
Superpipe—Steve Fisher, St. Louis Park, Minn.

Women

Slalom—Lisa Kosglow, Boulder, Colo.
Parallel Giant Slalom—Stacia Hookom, Edwards, Colo.
Snowboard Cross—Lindsey Jacobellis, Bondville, Vt.
Superpipe—Gretchen Bleiler, Snowmass Village, Colo.

JAMES E. SULLIVAN MEMORIAL AWARD WINNERS

(Amateur Athlete of the Year Chosen in Amateur Athletic Union Poll)

1930	Robert Tyre Jones, Jr.	Golf
1931	Bernard E. Berlinger	Track and field
1932	James A. Bausch	Track and field
1933	Glenn Cunningham	Track and field
1934	William R. Bonthron	Track and field
1935	W. Lawson Little, Jr.	Golf
1936	Glenn Morris	Track and field
1937	J. Donald Budge	Tennis
1938	Donald R. Lash	Track and field
1939	Joseph W. Burk	Rowing
1940	J. Gregory Rice	Track and field
1941	Leslie MacMitchell	Track and field
1942	Cornelius Warmerdam	Track and field
1943	Gilbert L. Dodds	Track and field
1944	Ann Curtis	Swimming
1945	Felix (Doc) Blanchard	Football
1946	Y. Arnold Tucker	Football
1947	John B. Kelly, Jr.	Rowing
1948	Robert B. Mathias	Track and field
1949	Richard T. Button	Figure skating
1950	Fred Wilt	Track and field
1951	Robert E. Richards	Track and field
1952	Horace Ashenfelter	Track and field
1953	Sammy Lee	Diving
1954	Malvin Whitfield	Track and field
1955	Harrison Dillard	Track and field
1956	Patricia McCormick	Diving
1957	Bobby Jo Morrow	Track and field
1958	Glenn Davis	Track and field
1959	Parry O'Brien	Track and field
1960	Rafer Johnson	Track and field
1961	Wilma Rudolph Ward	Track and field
1962	Jim Beatty	Track and field
1963	John Pennel	Track and field
1964	Don Schollander	Swimming
1965	Bill Bradley	Basketball
1966	Jim Ryun	Track and field
1967	Randy Matson	Track and field
1968	Debbie Meyer	Swimming
1969	Bill Toomey	Decathlon
1970	John Kinsella	Swimming
1971	Mark Spitz	Swimming
1972	Frank Shorter	Marathon
1973	Bill Walton	Basketball
1974	Rick Wohlhuter	Track and field
1975	Tim Shaw	Swimming
1976	Bruce Jenner	Track and field
1977	John Naber	Swimming
1978	Tracy Caulkins	Swimming
1979	Kurt Thomas	Gymnastics
1980	Eric Heiden	Speed skating
1981	Carl Lewis	Track and field
1982	Mary Decker Tabb	Track and field
1983	Edwin Moses	Track and field
1984	Greg Louganis	Diving
1985	Joan Benoit-Samuelson	Marathon
1986	Jackie Joyner-Kersee	Heptathlon
1987	Jim Abbott	Baseball
1988	Florence Griffith-Joyner	Track and field
1989	Janet Evans	Swimming
1990	John Smith	Wrestling
1991	Mike Powell	Track and field
1992	Bonnie Blair	Speed skating
1993	Charles Ward	Football/Basketball
1994	Dan Jansen	Speed skating
1995	Bruce Baumgartner	Wrestling
1996	Michael Johnson	Track and field
1997	Peyton Manning	Football
1998	Chamique Holdsclaw	Basketball
1999	Kelly and Coco Miller	Basketball
2000	Rulon Gardner	Wrestling
2001	Michelle Kwan	Figure skating
2002	Sarah Hughes	Figure skating

Speed Skating

WORLD SPEED SKATING RECORDS (LONG TRACK)

Distance	Time	Skater	Place	Date
Men				
500 m	34.32	Hiroyasu Shimizu, Japan	Salt Lake City	March 10, 2001
1,000 m	1:07.18	Gerard van Velde, Netherlands	Salt Lake City	Feb. 16, 2002
1,500 m	1:43.95	Derek Parra, United States	Salt Lake City	Feb. 19, 2002
3,000 m	3:42.75	Gianni Romme, Netherlands	Calgary, Canada	Aug. 11, 2000
5,000 m	6:14.66	Jochem Uytdehaage, Netherlands	Salt Lake City	Feb. 9, 2002
10,000 m	12:58.92	Jochem Uytdehaage, Netherlands	Salt Lake City	Feb. 22, 2002
Women				
500 m	37.22	Catriona LeMay Doan, Canada	Calgary, Canada	Dec. 9, 2001
1,000 m	1:13.83	Chris Witty, United States	Salt Lake City	Feb. 17, 2002
1,500 m	1:54.02	Anna "Anni" Friesinger, Germany	Salt Lake City	Feb. 20, 2002
3,000 m	3:57.70	Claudia Pechstein, Germany	Salt Lake City	Feb. 10, 2002
5,000 m	6:46.91	Claudia Pechstein, Germany	Salt Lake City	Feb. 23, 2002

WORLD SPEED SKATING RECORDS (SHORT TRACK)

Distance	Time	Skater	Place	Date
Men				
500 m	41.514	Jeffrey Scholten, Canada	Calgary, Canada	Oct. 13, 2001
1,000 m	1:25.985	Steve Robillard, Canada	Calgary, Canada	Oct. 14, 2001
1,500 m	2:12.234	Steve Robillard, Canada	Calgary, Canada	Nov. 13, 2002
3,000 m	4:38.061	Steve Robillard, Canada	Calgary, Canada	Nov. 13, 2002
5,000 m relay	6:43.730	Canada	Calgary, Canada	Oct. 14, 2001
Women				
500 m	43.671	Evgenia Radanova, Bulgaria	Calgary, Canada	Oct. 19, 2001
1,000 m	1:30.483	Chun-Sa Byun, Korea	Budapest, Hungary	Jan. 12, 2003
1,500 m	2:21.069	Eun-Kyung Choi, Korea	Salt Lake City, Utah	Feb. 13, 2002
3,000 m	5:01.976	Eun-Kyung Choi, Korea	Calgary, Canada	Oct. 22, 2000
3,000 m relay	4:12.793	Republic of Korea	Salt Lake City, Utah	Feb. 20, 2002

WORLD SINGLE DISTANCE SPEED SKATING CHAMPIONSHIPS—2003

(March 14–16, 2003, Berlin, Germany)

Men	Time
500 m—Jeremy Wotherspoon, Canada	69.97[1]
1,000 m—Erben Wennemars, Netherlands	1:09.71
1,500 m—Erben Wennemars, Netherlands	1:47.80
5,000 m—Jochem Uytdehaage, Netherlands	6:25.29
10,000 m—Bob de Jong, Netherlands	13:21.33

Women	Time
500 m—Monique Garbrecht-Enfeldt, Germany	77.17[1]
1,000 m—Anni Friesinger, Germany	1:16.85
1,500 m—Anni Friesinger, Germany	1:57.43
3,000 m—Anni Friesinger, Germany	4:06.07
5,000 m—Claudia Pechstein, Germany	7:04.52

1. Combined times.

WORLD SHORT TRACK CHAMPIONSHIPS—2003

(March 21–23, 2003, Warsaw, Poland)

Men	Time
500 m—Jiajun Li, China	43.210
1,000 m—Jiajun Li, China	1:28.391
1,500 m—Hyun-Soo Ahn, Korea	2:25.271
3,000 m—Hyun-Soo Ahn, Korea	4:58.297
Overall—Hyun-Soo Ahn, Korea	89.0 pts
Relay—Korea	6:55.975

Women	Time
500 m—Yang Yang (A), China	46.270
1,000 m—Evgenia Radanova, Bulgaria	1:31.594
1,500 m—Eun-Kyung Choi, Korea	2:24.866
3,000 m—Min-Jee Kim, Korea	5:31.650
Overall—Eun-Kyung Choi, Korea	76.0 pts
Relay—China	4:22.030

Figure Skating

WORLD CHAMPIONS

Men

1960	Alain Giletti, France
1961	No competition
1962	Donald Jackson, Canada
1963	Don McPherson, Canada
1964	Manfred Schnelldorfer, West Germany
1965	Alain Calmat, France
1966–68	Emmerich Danzer, Austria
1969–70	Tim Wood, United States
1971–73	Ondrej Nepela, Czechoslovakia
1974	Jan Hoffman, East Germany
1975	Sergei Yolkov, USSR
1976	John Curry, Britain
1977	Vladimir Kovalev, USSR
1978	Charles Tickner, United States
1979	Vladimir Kovalev, USSR
1980	Jan Hoffman, East Germany
1981–84	Scott Hamilton, United States
1985	Alexandr Fadeev, USSR
1986	Brian Boitano, United States
1987	Brian Orser, Canada
1988	Brian Boitano, United States
1989–91	Kurt Browning, Canada
1992	Viktor Petrenko, Unified Team
1993	Kurt Browning, Canada
1994–95	Elvis Stojko, Canada
1996	Todd Eldredge, United States
1997	Elvis Stojko, Canada
1998–2000	Alexei Yagudin, Russia
2001	Evgeni Plushenko, Russia
2002	Alexei Yagudin, Russia
2003	Evgeni Plushenko, Russia

Women

1956–60	Carol Heiss, United States
1961	No competition
1962–64	Sjoukje Dijkstra, Netherlands
1965	Petra Burka, Canada
1966–68	Peggy Fleming, United States
1969–70	Gabriele Seyfert, East Germany
1971–72	Beatrix Schuba, Austria
1973	Karen Magnusson, Canada
1974	Christine Errath, East Germany
1975	Dianne de Leeuw, Netherlands
1976	Dorothy Hamill, United States
1977	Linda Fratianne, United States
1978	Anett Poetzsch, East Germany
1979	Linda Fratianne, United States
1980	Anett Poetzsch, East Germany
1981	Denise Beillmann, Switzerland
1982	Elaine Zayak, United States
1983	Rosalynn Sumners, United States
1984–85	Katarina Witt, East Germany
1986	Debi Thomas, United States
1987–88	Katarina Witt, East Germany
1989	Midori Ito, Japan
1990	Jill Trenary, United States
1991–92	Kristi Yamaguchi, United States
1993	Oksana Baiul, Ukraine
1994	Yuka Sato, Japan
1995	Chen Lu, China
1996	Michelle Kwan, United States
1997	Tara Lipinski, United States
1998	Michelle Kwan, United States
1999	Maria Butyrskaya, Russia
2000–01	Michelle Kwan, United States
2002	Irina Slutskaya, Russia
2003	Michelle Kwan, United States

U.S. CHAMPIONS

Men

1946–52	Richard Button
1953–56	Hayes Jenkins
1957–60	David Jenkins
1961	Bradley Lord
1962	Monty Hoyt
1963	Tommy Liz
1964	Scott Allen
1965	Gary Visconti
1966	Scott Allen
1967	Gary Visconti
1968–70	Tim Wood
1971	John M. Petkevich
1972	Ken Shelley
1973–75	Gordon McKellen
1976	Terry Kubicka
1977–80	Charles Tickner
1981–84	Scott Hamilton
1985–88	Brian Boitano
1989	Christopher Bowman
1990–91	Todd Eldredge
1992	Christopher Bowman
1993–94	Scott Davis
1995	Todd Eldredge
1996	Rudy Galindo
1997–98	Todd Eldredge
1999–2000	Michael Weiss
2001	Timothy Goebel
2002	Todd Eldredge
2003	Michael Weiss

Women

1943–48	Gretchen Merrill
1949–50	Yvonne Sherman
1951	Sonya Klopfer
1952–56	Tenley Albright
1957–60	Carol Heiss
1961	Laurence Owen
1962	Barbara Roles Pursley
1963	Lorraine Hanlon
1964–68	Peggy Fleming
1969–73	Janet Lynn
1974–76	Dorothy Hamill
1977–80	Linda Fratianne
1981	Elaine Zayak
1982–84	Rosalynn Sumners
1985	Tiffany Chin
1986	Debi Thomas
1987	Jill Trenary
1988	Debi Thomas
1989–90	Jill Trenary
1991	Tonya Harding
1992	Kristi Yamaguchi
1993	Nancy Kerrigan
1994	Tonya Harding
1995	Nicole Bobek
1996	Michelle Kwan
1997	Tara Lipinski
1998–2003	Michelle Kwan

2003 UNITED STATES CHAMPIONSHIPS
(Jan. 12–19, 2003, Dallas, Tex.)

Men's singles
1. Michael Weiss, Fairfax, Va.
2. Timothy Goebel, Rolling Meadow, Ill.
3. Ryan Jahnke, Grosse Pointe Farms, Mich.

Pairs
1. Tiffany Scott, Hanson, Mass., and Philip Dulebohn, Germantown, Md.
2. Kathryn Orscher, Glastonbury, Conn., and Garrett Lucash, Granby, Conn.
3. Rena Inoue and John Baldwin, both Santa Monica, Calif.

Women's singles
1. Michelle Kwan, Manhattan Beach, Calif.
2. Sarah Hughes, Great Neck, N.Y.
3. Sasha Cohen, Laguna Niguel, Calif.

Dance
1. Naomi Lang, Allegan, Mich., and Peter Tchernyshev, St. Petersburg, Russia
2. Tanith Belbin and Benjamin Agosto, both Bloomfield Hills, Mich.
3. Melissa Gregory and Denis Petukhov, both Northbrook, Ill.

2003 WORLD CHAMPIONSHIPS

(March 24–30, Washington, DC)

Men's singles
1. Evgeni Plushenko, Russia
2. Timothy Goebel, United States
3. Takeshi Honda, Japan

Women's singles
1. Michelle Kwan, United States
2. Elena Sokolova, Russia
3. Fumie Suguri, Japan

Pairs
1. Xue Shen and Hongbo Zhao, China
2. Tatiana Totmianina and Maxim Marinin, Russia
3. Maria Petrova and Alexi Tikhonov, Russia

Dance
1. Shae-Lynn Bourne and Victor Kraatz, Canada
2. Irina Lobacheva and Ilia Averbukh, Russia
3. Albena Denkova and Maxim Staviyski, Bulgaria

Swimming

WORLD LONG COURSE RECORDS—MEN

(Through Aug. 28, 2003)

Distance	Record	Holder	Country	Date
Freestyle				
50 m	0:21.64	Alexander Popov	Russia	June 16, 2000
100 m	0:47.84	Pieter van den Hoogenband	Netherlands	Sept. 19, 2000
200 m	1:44.06	Ian Thorpe	Australia	July 25, 2001
400 m	3:40.08	Ian Thorpe	Australia	July 30, 2002
800 m	7:39.16	Ian Thorpe	Australia	July 24, 2001
1,500 m	14:34.56	Grant Hackett	Australia	July 29, 2001
Backstroke				
50 m	0:24.80[1]	Thomas Rupprath	Germany	July 27, 2003
100 m	0:53.60	Lenny Krayzelburg	United States	Aug. 24, 1999
200 m	1:55.15	Aaron Peirsol	United States	March 20, 2002
Breaststroke				
50 m	0:27.18	Oleg Lisog0r	Ukraine	Aug. 2, 2002
100 m	0:59.78[1]	Kosuke Kitajima	Japan	July 21, 2003
200 m	2:09.42[1]	Kosuke Kitajima	Japan	July 24, 2003
Butterfly				
50 m	0:23.43[1]	Matthew Welsh	Australia	July 21, 2003
100 m	0:50.98[1]	Ian Crocker	United States	July 26, 2003
200 m	1:53.93[1]	Michael Phelps	United States	July 22, 2003
Individual medley				
200 m	1:55.94[1]	Michael Phelps	United States	Aug. 9, 2003
400 m	4:09.09[1]	Michael Phelps	United States	July 27, 2003
Medley relay				
400 m	3:31.54[1]	National Team	United States	July 27, 2003
Freestyle relay				
400 m	3:13.67	Olympic Team	Australia	Sept. 16, 2000
800 m	7:04.66	National Team	Australia	July 27, 2001

NOTE: International Swimming Federation (FINA) discontinued acceptance of records in yards in 1968. 1. Awaiting FINA ratification. *Source:* FINA.

WORLD LONG COURSE RECORDS—WOMEN

(Through Aug. 28, 2003)

Distance	Record	Holder	Country	Date
Freestyle				
50 m	0:24.13	Inge de Bruijn	Netherlands	Sept. 22, 2000
100 m	0:53.77	Inge de Bruijn	Netherlands	Sept. 20, 2000
200 m	1:56.64	Franziska van Almsick	Germany	Aug. 3, 2002
400 m	4:03.85	Janet Evans	United States	Sept. 22, 1988
800 m	8:16.22	Janet Evans	United States	Aug. 20, 1989
1,500 m	15:52.10	Janet Evans	United States	March 26, 1988
Backstroke				
50 m	0:28.25	Sandra Voelker	Germany	June 17, 2000
100 m	0:59.58[1]	Natalie Coughlin	United States	Aug. 13, 2002
200 m	2:06.62	Kristina Egerszegi	Hungary	Aug. 25, 1991
Breaststroke				
50 m	0:30.57	Zoe Baker	Great Britain	July 30, 2002
100 m	1:06.37[1]	Jones Leisel	Australia	July 21, 2003
200 m	2:22.99	Hui Qi	China	April 13, 2001
	(tie)[1]	Amanda Beard	United States	July 25, 2003
Butterfly				
50 m	0:25.57	Anna-Karin Kammerling	Sweden	July 30, 2000
100 m	0:56.61	Inge de Bruijn	Netherlands	Sept. 17, 2000
200 m	2:05.78	Otylia Jedrzejczak	Poland	Aug. 4, 2002

Distance	Record	Holder	Country	Date
Individual medley				
200 m	2:09.72	Yanyan Wu	China	Oct. 17, 1997
400 m	4:33.59	Yana Klochkova	Ukraine	Sept. 16, 2000
Medley relay				
400 m	3:58.30	Olympic Team	United States	Sept. 23, 2000
Freestyle relay				
400 m	3:36.00	National Team	Germany	July 29, 2002
800 m	7:55.47	National Team	East Germany	Aug. 18, 1987

NOTE: International Swimming Federation (FINA) discontinued acceptance of records in yards in 1968. 1. Awaiting FINA ratification. *Source:* FINA.

AMERICAN LONG COURSE SWIMMING RECORDS
(Through Aug. 28, 2003)

MEN

Distance	Record	Holder	Date
Freestyle			
50 m	0:21.76	Gary Hall, Jr.	Aug. 15, 2000
100 m	0:48.33	Anthony Ervin	July 27, 2001
200 m	1:45.99	Michael Phelps	Aug. 7, 2003
400 m	3:46.73	Michael Phelps	Aug. 8, 2003
800 m	7:48.09	Larsen Jensen	July 25, 2003
1,500 m	14:56.81	Chris Thompson	Sept. 23, 2000
Backstroke			
50 m	0:24.99	Lenny Krayzelburg	Aug. 28, 1999
100 m	0:53.60	Lenny Krayzelburg	Aug. 24, 1999
200 m	1:55.15	Aaron Peirsol	March 20, 2002
Breaststroke			
50 m	0:27.39	Ed Moses	March 31, 2001
100 m	1:00.21	Ed Moses	April 4, 2003
200 m	2:10.16	Mike Barrowman	July 29, 1992
Butterfly			
50 m	0:23.85	Ian Crocker	July 28, 2001
100 m	0:50.98	Ian Crocker	July 26, 2003
200 m	1:53.93	Michael Phelps	July 23, 2003
Individual medley			
200 m	1:55.94	Michael Phelps	Aug. 9, 2003
400 m	4:09.09	Michael Phelps	July 27, 2003
Medley relay			
400 m	3:33.48	U.S. National Team	Aug. 29, 2002
Freestyle relay			
400 m	3:13.86	U.S. Olympic Team	Sept. 16, 2000
800 m	7:10.26	U.S. National Team	July 23, 2003

WOMEN

Distance	Record	Holder	Date
Freestyle			
50 m	0:24.63	Dara Torres	Sept. 23, 2000
100 m	0:53.99	Natalie Coughlin	Aug. 29, 2002
200 m	1:57.41	Lindsay Benko	July 24, 2003
400 m	4:03.85	Janet Evans	Sept. 22, 1988
800 m	8:16.22	Janet Evans	Aug. 20, 1989
1,500 m	15:52.10	Janet Evans	March 26, 1988
Backstroke			
50 m	0:28.49	Natalie Coughlin	July 23, 2001
100 m	0:59.58	Natalie Coughlin	Aug. 13, 2002
200 m	2:08.53	Natalie Coughlin	Aug. 16, 2002
Breaststroke			
50 m	0:31.34	Megan Quann	Aug. 11, 2000
100 m	1:07.05	Megan Quann	Sept. 18, 2000
200 m	2:22.99	Amanda Beard	July 25, 2003
Butterfly			
50 m	0:26.50	Dara Torres	Aug. 9, 2000
100 m	0:57.58	Dara Torres	Aug. 9, 2000
200 m	2:05.88	Misty Hyman	Sept. 20, 2000
Individual medley			
200 m	2:11.91	Summer Sanders	July 30, 1992
400 m	4:37.58	Summer Sanders	July 26, 1992
Medley relay			
400 m	3:58.30	U.S. Olympic Team	Sept. 23, 2000
Freestyle relay			
400 m	3:36.61	U.S. Olympic Team	Sept. 16, 2000
800 m	7:55.70	U.S. National Team	July 24, 2003

Source: United States Swim Team, FINA.

UNITED STATES NATIONAL CHAMPIONSHIPS
(College Park, Md., Aug. 5–9, 2003)

Men	Time
50 m freestyle—Neil Walker	0:22.59
100 m freestyle—Michael Phelps	0:49.19
200 m freestyle—Michael Phelps	1:45.99
400 m freestyle—Michael Phelps	3:46.73
800 m freestyle—Larsen Jensen	7:57.35
1500 m freestyle—Larsen Jensen	15:11.81
100 m backstroke—Randall Bal	0:54.63
200 m backstroke—Michael Phelps	1:56.10
100 m breaststroke—Glenn Moses	1:01.11
200 m breaststroke—Gary Marshall	2:13.28
100 m butterfly—Eugene Botes	0:53.20
200 m butterfly—Brian Johns	1:59.29
200 m individual medley—Michael Phelps	1:55.94
400 m individual medley—Brian Johns	4:17.04
400 m medley relay—Circle C Swimming	3:42.61
400 m freestyle relay—Circle C Swimming	3:21.25
800 m freestyle relay—Mission Viejo	7:24.43

Women	Time
50 m freestyle—Malia Metella	0:25.18
100 m freestyle—Sarah Wanezek	0:55.73
200 m freestyle—Brittany Reimer	2:00.62
400 m freestyle—Kalyn Keller	4:10.68
800 m freestyle—Kalyn Keller	8:31.54
1500 m freestyle—Kalyn Keller	16:08.64
100 m backstroke—Lauren Rogers	1:02.50
200 m backstroke—Jennifer Fratesi	2:12.47
100 m breaststroke—Megan Quann	1:08.80
200 m breaststroke—Caroline Bruce	2:27.88
100 m butterfly—Emily Goetsch	0:59.87
200 m butterfly—Kaitlin Sandeno	2:08.78
200 m individual medley—Kaitlin Sandeno	2:12.97
400 m individual medley—Kaitlin Sandeno	4:40.82
400 m medley relay—Novaquatics, Inc.	4:12.11
400 m freestyle relay—Texas Aquatics	3:44.97
800 m freestyle relay—Trojan Swim Club	8:10.79

FINA WORLD CHAMPIONSHIPS, 2003

(Barcelona, Spain, July 13–27, 2003)

Men	Time
50 m freestyle—Alexander Popov, Russia	0:21.92
100 m freestyle—Alexander Popov, Russia	0:48.42
200 m freestyle—Ian Thorpe, Australia	1:45.14
400 m freestyle—Ian Thorpe, Australia	3:42.58
800 m freestyle—Grant Hackett, Australia	7:43.82
1500 m freestyle—Grant Hackett, Australia	14:43.14
50 m backstroke—Thomas Rupprath, Germany	0:24.80
100 m backstroke—Aaron Peirsol, United States	0:53.61
200 m backstroke—Aaron Peirsol, United States	1:55.92
50 m breaststroke—James Gibson, Great Britain	0:27.56
100 m breaststroke—Kosuke Kitajima, Japan	0:59.78
200 m breaststroke—Kosuke Kitajima, Japan	2:09.42
50 m butterfly—Matt Welsh, Australia	0:23.43
100 m butterfly—Ian Crocker, United States	0:50.98
200 m butterfly—Michael Phelps, United States	1:54.35
200 m individual medley—Michael Phelps, United States	1:56.04
400 m individual medley—Michael Phelps, United States	4:09.09
4×100 m medley relay—United States	3:31.54
4×100 m freestyle relay—Russia	3:14.06
4×200 m freestyle relay—Australia	7:08.58

Women	Points
50 m freestyle—Inge de Bruijn, Netherlands	0:24.47
100 m freestyle—Hanna-M. Seppala, Finland	0:54.37
200 m freestyle—Alena Popchenko, Belarus	1:58.32
400 m freestyle—Hannah Stockbauer, Germany	4:06.75
800 m freestyle—Hannah Stockbauer, Germany	8:23.66
1500 m freestyle—Hannah Stockbauer, Germany	16:00.18
50 m backstroke—Nina Zhivanevskaya, Spain	0:28.48
100 m backstroke—Antje Buschschulte, Germany	1:00.50
200 m backstroke—Katy Sexton, Great Britain	2:08.74
50 m breaststroke—Xuejuan Luo, China	0:30.67
100 m breaststroke—Xuejuan Luo, China	1:06.80
200 m breaststroke—Amanda Beard, United States	2:22.99
50 m butterfly—Inge de Bruijn, Netherlands	0:25.84
100 m butterfly—Jenny Thompson, United States	0:57.96
200 m butterfly—Otylia Jedrzejczak, Poland	2:07.56
200 m individual medley—Yana Klochkova, Ukraine	2:10.75
400 m individual medley—Yana Klochkova, Ukraine	4:36.74
4×100 m medley relay—China	3:59.89
4×100 m freestyle relay—United States	3:38.09
4×200 m freestyle relay—United States	7:55.70

Boxing

Whether it be called pugilism, prize fighting, or boxing, there is no tracing "the Sweet Science" to any definite source. Tales of rivals exchanging blows for fun, fame, or money go back to earliest recorded history and classical legend. There was a mixture of boxing and wrestling called the "pancratium" in the ancient Olympic Games; in such contests rivals belabored one another with hands fortified by heavy leather wrappings that were sometimes studded with metal. More than one Olympic competitor lost his life in this brutal exercise.

There was little law or order in pugilism until Jack Broughton, one of the early champions of England, drew up a set of rules for the game in 1743. Broughton, called "the father of English boxing," also is credited with having invented boxing gloves. However, these gloves—or "mufflers" as they were called—were used only in teaching "the manly art of self-defense" or in training bouts. All professional championship fights were contested with bare knuckles until 1892, when John L. Sullivan lost the heavyweight championship of the world to James J. Corbett in New Orleans in a bout in which both contestants wore regulation gloves.

The Broughton Rules were superseded by the London Prize Ring Rules of 1838. In 1884 the eighth marquis of Queensberry, with the help of John G. Chambers, put forward the Queensberry Rules, a code that called for gloved contests. Amateurs took to the Queensberry Rules more quickly than the professionals did.

HISTORY OF WORLD HEAVYWEIGHT CHAMPIONSHIP FIGHTS (WBC, WBA, IBF)

(Bouts in which a new champion was crowned)

Date	Where held	Winner, weight (age)	Loser, weight (age)	Rounds
Sept. 7, 1892	New Orleans, La.	James J. Corbett, 178 (26)	John L. Sullivan, 212 (33)	21
March 17, 1897	Carson City, Nev.	Bob Fitzsimmons, 167 (34)	James J. Corbett, 183 (30)	KO 14
June 9, 1899	Coney Island, N.Y.	James J. Jeffries, 206 (24)[1]	Bob Fitzsimmons, 167 (37)	KO 11
Feb. 23, 1906	Los Angeles	Tommy Burns, 180 (24)[2]	Marvin Hart, 188 (29)	20
Dec. 26, 1908	Sydney, Australia	Jack Johnson, 196 (30)	Tommy Burns, 176 (27)	KO 14
April 5, 1915	Havana, Cuba	Jess Willard, 230 (33)	Jack Johnson, 205½ (37)	KO 26
July 4, 1919	Toledo, Ohio	Jack Dempsey, 187 (24)	Jess Willard, 245 (37)	KO 3
Sept. 23, 1926	Philadelphia	Gene Tunney, 189 (28)[3]	Jack Dempsey, 190 (31)	10
June 12, 1930	New York	Max Schmeling, 188 (24)	Jack Sharkey, 197 (27)	WF 4
June 21, 1932	Long Island City	Jack Sharkey, 205 (29)	Max Schmeling, 188 (26)	15
June 29, 1933	Long Island City	Primo Carnera, 260½ (26)	Jack Sharkey, 201 (30)	KO 6
June 14, 1934	Long Island City	Max Baer, 209½ (25)	Primo Carnera, 263¼ (27)	KO 11
June 13, 1935	Long Island City	Jim Braddock, 193¾ (29)	Max Baer, 209½ (26)	15
June 22, 1937	Chicago	Joe Louis, 197¼ (23)	Jim Braddock, 197 (31)	KO 8
June 22, 1949	Chicago	Ezzard Charles, 181¾ (27)[4]	Joe Walcott, 195½ (35)	15
Sept. 27, 1950	New York	Ezzard Charles, 184½ (29)[5]	Joe Louis, 218 (36)	15

Date	Where held	Winner, weight (age)	Loser, weight (age)	Rounds
July 18, 1951	Pittsburgh	Joe Walcott, 194 (37)	Ezzard Charles, 182 (30)	KO 7
Sept. 23, 1952	Philadelphia	Rocky Marciano, 184 (29)[6]	Joe Walcott, 196 (38)	KO13
Nov. 30, 1956	Chicago	Floyd Patterson, 182¼ (21)	Archie Moore, 187¾ (42)	KO 5
June 26, 1959	New York	Ingemar Johansson, 196 (26)	Floyd Patterson, 182 (24)	KO 3
June 20, 1960	New York	Floyd Patterson, 190 (25)	Ingemar Johansson, 194¾ (27)	KO 5
Sept. 25, 1962	Chicago	Sonny Liston, 214 (28)	Floyd Patterson, 189 (27)	KO 1
Feb. 25, 1964	Miami Beach, Fla.	Cassius Clay (Muhammad Ali), 210 (22)[7]	Sonny Liston, 218 (30)	KO 7
March 4, 1968	New York	Joe Frazier, 204½ (24)[8]	Buster Mathis, 243½ (23)	KO 11
April 27, 1968	Oakland, Calif.	Jimmy Ellis, 197 (28)[9]	Jerry Quarry, 195 (22)	15
Feb. 16, 1970	New York	Joe Frazier, 205 (26)[10]	Jimmy Ellis, 201 (29)	KO 5
Jan. 22, 1973	Kingston, Jamaica	George Foreman, 217½ (24)	Joe Frazier, 214 (29)	KO 2
Oct. 30, 1974	Kinshasa, Zaire	Muhammad Ali, 216½ (32)	George Foreman, 220 (26)	KO 8
Feb. 15, 1978	Las Vegas, Nev.	Leon Spinks, 197 (25)	Muhammad Ali, 224½ (36)	15
June 9, 1978	Las Vegas, Nev.	Larry Holmes, 212 (28)[11]	Ken Norton, 220 (32)	15
Sept. 15, 1978	New Orleans	Muhammad Ali, 221 (36)[12]	Leon Spinks, 201 (25)	15
Oct. 20, 1979	Pretoria, S. Africa	John Tate, 240 (24)[13]	Gerrie Coetzee, 222 (24)	15
March 31, 1980	Knoxville, Tenn.	Mike Weaver, 207½ (27)	John Tate, 232 (25)	KO 15
Dec. 10, 1982	Las Vegas, Nev.	Michael Dokes, 216 (24)	Mike Weaver, 209½ (30)	KO 1
Sept. 23, 1983	Richfield, Ohio	Gerrie Coetzee, 215 (28)	Michael Dokes, 217 (25)	KO 10
March 9, 1984	Las Vegas, Nev.	Tim Witherspoon, 220½ (26)[14]	Greg Page, 239½ (25)	12
Aug. 31, 1984	Las Vegas, Nev.	Pinklon Thomas, 216 (26)	Tim Witherspoon, 217 (26)	12
Nov. 9, 1984	Las Vegas, Nev.	Larry Holmes, 221½ (35)[15]	James Smith, 227 (31)	KO 12
Dec. 1, 1984	Sun City, S. Africa	Greg Page, 236 (25)[16]	Gerry Coetzee, 217 (29)	KO 8
April 29, 1985	Buffalo, N.Y.	Tony Tubbs, 229 (26)[16]	Greg Page, 239½ (26)	15
Sept. 21,1985	Las Vegas, Nev.	Michael Spinks, 200 (29)	Larry Holmes, 221 (35)	15
Jan. 17, 1986	Atlanta, Ga.	Tim Witherspoon, 227 (28)	Tony Tubbs, 229 (27)	15
Nov. 23, 1986	Las Vegas, Nev.	Mike Tyson, 217 (20)[17]	Trevor Berbick, 220 (29)	KO 2
Dec. 12, 1986	New York, N.Y.	James Smith, 230 (33)[16]	Tim Witherspoon, 218 (29)	KO 1
March 7, 1987	Las Vegas, Nev.	Mike Tyson, 217 (20)[16]	James Smith, 230 (33)	12
Feb. 10, 1990	Tokyo	James "Buster" Douglas, 231½ (29)[18]	Mike Tyson, 220 (23)	KO 10
Oct. 25, 1990	Las Vegas, Nev.	Evander Holyfield, 208 (28)	James "Buster" Douglas, 246 (30)	KO 3
Nov. 13, 1992	Las Vegas, Nev.	Riddick Bowe,[19] 235 (25)	Evander Holyfield, 205 (30)	12
Nov. 6, 1993	Las Vegas, Nev.	Evander Holyfield, 217 (30)	Riddick Bowe, 246 (26)	12
April 22, 1994	Las Vegas, Nev.	Michael Moorer, 214 (26)	Evander Holyfield,[20] 214 (31)	12
Sept 24, 1994	London	Oliver McCall,[21] 228 (29)	Lennox Lewis, 238 (28)	2
Nov. 5, 1994	Las Vegas, Nev.	George Foreman,[22] 250 (45)	Michael Moorer, 222 (26)	10
April 8, 1995	Las Vegas, Nev.	Bruce Seldon,[23] 232 (28)	Tony Tucker, 238 (36)	7
Dec.9, 1995	Stuttgart, Ger.	Frans Botha,[24] 227 (28)	Axel Schulz, 222 (27)	12
March 16, 1996	Las Vegas, Nev.	Mike Tyson,[25] 220 (29)	Frank Bruno, 247 (34)	3
June 22, 1996	Dortmund, Ger.	Michael Moorer, 222 (28)	Axel Schulz, 222 (27)	12
Sept. 7, 1996	Las Vegas, Nev.	Mike Tyson, 219 (30)	Bruce Seldon, 229 (29)	1
Nov. 9, 1996	Las Vegas, Nev.	Evander Holyfield,[23] 215 (34)	Mike Tyson, 222 (30)	11
Feb. 7, 1997	Las Vegas, Nev.	Lennox Lewis,[25] 251 (31)	Oliver McCall, 237 (30)	5
Nov. 8, 1997	Las Vegas, Nev.	Evander Holyfield,[26] 214 (35)	Michael Moorer, 223 (30)	8
Nov. 13, 1999	Las Vegas, Nev.	Lennox Lewis,[23, 27] 240 (33)	Evander Holyfield, 217 (36)	12
Aug. 12, 2000	Las Vegas, Nev.	Evander Holyfield,[23] 221 (37)	John Ruiz, 224 (24)	12
March 3, 2001	Las Vegas, Nev.	John Ruiz,[23] 227 (27)	Evander Holyfield, 217 (38)	12
Apr. 21, 2001	South Africa	Hasim Rahman, [25, 26] 237 (28)	Lennox Lewis, 253 (35)	KO 5
Nov. 17, 2001	Las Vegas, Nev.	Lennox Lewis,[25, 26, 28] 246 (36)	Hasim Rahman, 236 (29)	KO 4
Dec. 14, 2002	Atlantic City, N.J.	Chris Byrd[26], 214 (32)	Evander Holyfield, 220 (40)	12
March 1, 2003	Las Vegas, Nev.	Roy Jones, Jr., 34[23] (193)	John Ruiz, 31 (226)	12

1. Jeffries retired as champion in March 1905. He named Marvin Hart and Jack Root as leading contenders and agreed to referee their fight in Reno, Nev., on July 3, 1905, with the stipulation that he would term the winner the champion. Hart, 190 (28), knocked out Root, 171 (29), in the 12th round. 2. Burns claimed the title after defeating Hart. 3. Tunney retired as champion after defeating Tom Heeney on July 26, 1928. 4. After Louis announced his retirement as champion on March 1, 1949, Charles won recognition from the National Boxing Association as champion by defeating Walcott. 5. Charles gained undisputed recognition as champion by defeating Louis, who came out of retirement. 6. Retired as champion April 27, 1956. 7. The World Boxing Association (WBA) later withdrew its recognition of Clay as champion and declared the winner of a bout between Ernie Terrell and Eddie Machen would gain its version of the title. Terrell, 199 (25), won a 15-round decision from Machen, 192 (32), in Chicago on March 5, 1965. Clay, 212¼ (25) and Terrell, 212½ (27), met in Houston on Feb. 6, 1967, Clay winning a 15-round decision. 8. Winner recognized by N.Y., Mass., Maine, Ill., Tex. and Pa. to fill vacated title when Clay was stripped of championship for failing to accept U.S. Induction. 9. Bout was final of eight-man tournament to fill Clay's place and is recognized by World Boxing Association. 10. Bout settled controversy over title. 11. Holmes won World Boxing Council title after WBC had withdrawn recognition of Spinks, March 18, 1978, and awarded its title to Norton. WBC said Spinks had reneged on agreement to fight Norton. 12. Ali regained World Boxing Association championship. 13. Tate won WBA title after Ali retired and left it vacant. 14. Tim Witherspoon and Greg Page fought for the WBC heavyweight title vacated by Larry Holmes, who could not come to agreement on a deal to fight Page, the No. 1 contender. Holmes declared he would fight under the banner of the International Boxing Federation (IBF). Several dates were set and postponed for fights between Holmes and Gerry Coetzee, the WBA champ, the latest being Nov. 16, 1984. 15. First fight under banner of International Boxing Federation. 16. New WBA champion. 17. New WBC champion. 18. New undisputed champion. 19. The WBC stripped Bowe of its version of the title in December 1992 and named Lennox Lewis champion. 20. After the loss, Holyfield retired. 21. New WBC champion. Lennox Lewis had been named champion in 1992 and had won three title defenses before losing to McCall. 22. For combined WBA/IBF titles. Later WBA stripped Foreman of title for failing to fight no. 1 contender Tony Tucker. IBF also stripped Foreman on June 29, 1995. 23. New WBA champion. 24. Botha later tested positive for steroids and was stripped of the title. 25. New WBC champion. 26. New IBF champion. 27. Surrendered WBA title to fight Michael Grant in unsanctioned bout. 28. Lewis surrendered his IBF title in 2002.

OTHER WORLD BOXING TITLEHOLDERS

(Through Aug. 13, 2003)

Light Heavyweight

1903	Jack Root, George Gardner
1903–05	Bob Fitzsimmons
1905–12	Philadelphia Jack O'Brien[1]
1912–16	Jack Dillon
1916–20	Battling Levinsky
1920–22	Georges Carpentier
1923	Battling Siki
1923–25	Mike McTigue
1925–26	Paul Berlenbach
1926–27	Jack Delaney[2]
1927	Mike McTigue
1927–29	Tommy Loughran
1930	Jimmy Slattery
1930–34	Maxie Rosenbloom
1934–35	Bob Olin
1935–39	John Henry Lewis
1939	Melio Bettina
1939–41	Billy Conn[2]
1941	Anton Christoforidis (NBA)
1941–48	Gus Lesnevich
1948–50	Freddie Mills
1950–52	Joey Maxim
1952–61	Archie Moore[3]
1961–63	Harold Johnson
1963–65	Willie Pastrano
1965–66	José Torres
1966–67	Dick Tiger
1968	Dick Tiger, Bob Foster
1969–70	Bob Foster
1971	Vicente Rondon (WBA), Bob Foster (WBC)
1972–73	Bob Foster (WBA, WBC)
1974	John Conteh (WBA), Bob Foster (WBC)[1, 4]
1975–76	Victor Galindez (WBA), John Conteh (WBC)
1977	Victor Galindez (WBA), John Conteh (WBC),[4] Miguel Cuello (WBC)
1978	Victor Galindez (WBA), Mike Rossman (WBA), Miguel Cuello (WBC), Mate Parlov (WBC), Marvin Johnson (WBC)
1979	Mike Rossman (WBA), Victor Galindez (WBA), Marvin Johnson (WBC), Matthew (Franklin) Saad Muhammad (WBC)
1980	Matthew Saad Muhammad (WBC), Marvin Johnson (WBA), Eddie (Gregory) Mustafa Muhammad (WBA)
1981	Matthew Saad Muhammad (WBC), Eddie Mustafa Muhammad (WBA), Michael Spinks (WBA), Dwight Braxton (WBC)
1982	Dwight Braxton (WBC), Michael Spinks (WBA)
1983	Michael Spinks (undisputed)
1984	Michael Spinks (undisputed)
1985	Michael Spinks (undisputed)[5]
1986	Marvin Johnson (WBA), Dennis Andries (WBC)
1987	Thomas Hearns (WBC), Virgil Hill (WBA), Bobby Czyz (IBF)
1988	Charles Williams (IBF), Virgil Hill (WBA), Donny LaLonde (WBC), Sugar Ray Leonard (WBC)
1989	Dennis Andries (WBC), Virgil Hill (WBA), Charles Williams (IBF), Jeff Harding (WBC)
1990	Virgil Hill (WBA), Charles Williams (IBF), Jeff Harding (WBC), Dennis Andries (WBC)
1991	Virgil Hill (WBA), Thomas Hearns (WBA), Dennis Andries (WBC), Charles Williams (IBF)
1992	Charles Williams (IBF), James Waring (IBF), Jeff Harding (WBC)
1993	Virgil Hill (WBA), Jeff Harding (WBC), Henry Maske (IBF)
1994	Virgil Hill (WBA), Mike McCallum (WBC), Henry Maske (IBF)
1995	Virgil Hill (WBA), Fabio Tiozzo (WBC), Henry Maske (IBF)
1996–97	Virgil Hill (WBA), Fabio Tiozzo (WBC), Henry Maske (IBF)
1998	Roy Jones (WBA, WBC), Reggie Johnson (IBF)
1999–2001	Roy Jones (WBA, WBC, IBF)
2002	Bruno Girard (WBA), Roy Jones (WBC, IBF)
2003	Vacant (WBA), Antonio Tarver (WBC, IBF)

1. Retired. 2. Abandoned title. 3. NBA withdrew recognition in 1961, New York Commission in 1962; recognized thereafter only by California and Europe. 4. WBC withdrew recognition. 5. Spinks relinquished title in 1985 to fight for heavyweight title.

Middleweight

1867–72	Tom Chandler
1872–81	George Rooke
1881–82	Mike Donovan[1]
1884–91	Jack (Nonpareil) Dempsey
1891–97	Bob Fitzsimmons[2]
1908	Stanley Ketchel, Billy Papke
1908–10	Stanley Ketchel[3]
1913	Frank Klaus
1913–14	George Chip
1914–17	Al McCoy
1917–20	Mike O'Dowd
1920–23	Johnny Wilson
1923–26	Harry Greb
1926	Tiger Flowers
1926–31	Mickey Walker[2]
1931–41	Gorilla Jones, Ben Jeby, Marcel Thil, Lou Brouillard, Vince Dundee, Teddy Yarosz, Babe Risko, Freddy Steele, Al Hostak, Solly Kreiger, Fred Apostoli, Cerferino Garcia, Ken Overlin, Billy Soose, Tony Zale[4]
1941–47	Tony Zale
1947–48	Rocky Graziano
1948	Tony Zale
1948–49	Marcel Cerdan
1949–51	Jake LaMotta
1951–52	Ray Robinson[1]
1952	Ray Robinson, Randy Turpin
1953–55	Carl Olson
1955–57	Ray Robinson[5]
1957	Gene Fullmer, Ray Robinson
1957–58	Carmen Basilio
1958–60	Ray Robinson[6]
1959–62	Gene Fullmer (NBA)
1960–61	Paul Pender[7]
1961–62	Terry Downes[1]
1962	Paul Pender[1]
1962–63	Dick Tiger
1963–65	Joey Giardello
1965–66	Dick Tiger
1966	Emile Griffith
1967	Nino Benvenuti, Emile Griffith
1968	Emile Griffith, Nino Benvenuti
1969	Nino Benvenuti
1970	Nino Benvenuti, Carlos Monzon
1971–73	Carlos Monzon
1974–75	Carlos Monzon (WBA), Rodrigo Valdez (WBC)
1976	Carlos Monzon (WBA, WBC), Rodrigo Valdez (WBC)
1977	Carlos Monzon (WBA, WBC),[1] Rodrigo Valdez (WBA, WBC)
1978	Rodrigo Valdez, Hugo Corro
1979	Hugo Corro, Vito Antuofermo
1980	Vito Antuofermo, Alan Minter, Marvin Hagler
1981	Marvin Hagler
1982–86	Marvin Hagler (undisputed)
1987	Marvin Hagler (undisputed), Sugar Ray Leonard (undisputed)
1988	Sumbu Kalambay (WBA), Thomas Hearns (WBC), Iran Barkley (WBC), Frank Tate (IBF), Michael Nunn (IBF), James Kinchen (NABF)
1989	Michael Nunn (IBF), Mike McCallum (WBA), Iran Barkley (WBC), Roberto Duran (WBC)
1990	Michael McCallum (WBA), Michael Nunn (IBF), Iran Barkley (WBC)
1991	Michael Nunn (IBF), James Toney (IBF), Michael McCallum (WBA)
1992	James Toney (IBF), Julian Jackson (WBC), Reggie Johnson (WBA)
1993	Reggie Johnson (WBA), Gerald McClellan (WBA), Roy Jones (IBF)
1994	Julian Jackson (WBA), Gerald McClellan (WBA), Roy Jones (IBF)
1995	Jorge Castro (WBA), Julian Jackson (WBC), Bernard Hopkins (IBF)
1996	William Joppy (WBA), Keith Holmes (WBC), Bernard Hopkins (IBF)

1997	Shinji Takehara (WBA), Quincy Taylor (WBC), Bernard Hopkins (IBF)
1998	William Joppy (WBA), Hassine Cherifi (WBC), Bernard Hopkins (IBF)
1999–2000	William Joppy (WBA), Keith Holmes (WBC), Bernard Hopkins (IBF)
2001	Felix Trinidad (WBA), Bernard Hopkins (WBC, IBF)
2002	William Joppy (WBA), Bernard Hopkins (WBC, IBF)
2003	Bernard Hopkins (WBA, WBC, IBF)

1. Retired. 2. Abandoned title. 3. Died. 4. National Boxing Association and New York Commission disagreed on champions. Those listed were accepted by one or the other until Zale gained world-wide recognition. 5. Ended retirement in 1954. 6. NBA withdrew recognition. 7. Recognized by New York, Massachusetts, and Europe.

Welterweight

1892–94	Mysterious Billy Smith
1894–96	Tommy Ryan
1896	Kid McCoy[1]
1896–1900	Mysterious Billy Smith
1900	Rube Ferns
1900–01	Matty Matthews
1901	Ruby Ferns
1901–04	Joe Walcott
1904	Dixie Kid[1]
1904–06	Joe Walcott
1906–07	Honey Mellody
1907	Mike (Twin) Sullivan[1]
1915–19	Ted Lewis
1919–22	Jack Britton
1922–26	Mickey Walker
1926–27	Pete Latzo
1927–29	Joe Dundee
1929–30	Jackie Fields
1930	Young Jack Thompson
1930–31	Tommy Freeman
1931	Young Jack Thompson
1931–32	Lou Brouillard
1932–33	Jackie Fields
1933	Young Corbett 3rd
1933–34	Jimmy McLarnin, Barney Ross
1934–35	Jimmy McLarnin
1935–38	Barney Ross
1938–40	Henry Armstrong
1940–41	Fritzie Zivic
1941–46	Freddie Cochrane
1946	Marty Servo[2]
1946–51	Ray Robinson[1]
1951	Johnny Bratton (NBA)
1951–54	Kid Gavilan
1954–55	Johnny Saxton
1955	Tony DeMarco
1955–56	Carmen Basilio
1956	Johnny Saxton
1956–57	Carmen Basilio[1]
1958	Virgil Akins
1959–60	Don Jordan
1960–61	Benny (Kid) Paret
1961	Emile Griffith
1961–62	Benny (Kid) Paret
1962–63	Emile Griffith, Luis Rodriguez
1963–66	Emile Griffith[1]
1966–69	Curtis Cokes
1969	Curtis Cokes, José Napoles
1970	José Napoles, Billy Backus
1971	Billy Backus, José Napoles
1972–74	José Napoles
1975	José Napoles (WBA, WBC),[3] Angel Espada (WBA), John Stracey (WBC)
1976	Angel Espada (WBA), José Cuevas (WBA), John Stracey (WBC), Carlos Palomino
1977–78	José Cuevas (WBA), Carlos Palomino (WBC)
1979	José Cuevas (WBA), Carlos Palomino (WBC), Wilfredo Benitez (WBC)
1980	José Cuevas (WBA), Ray Leonard (WBC), Roberto Duran (WBC), Thomas Hearns (WBA)
1981	Ray Leonard (WBC), Thomas Hearns (WBA), Ray Leonard (WBC, WBA)
1982	Ray Leonard
1983–85	Donald Curry (WBA), Milton McCrory (WBC)
1985–86	Donald Curry (undisputed)
1987	Mark Breland (WBA), Marlon Starling (WBA), Lloyd Honeyghan (IBF)
1988	Marlon Starling (WBA), Tomas Molinares (WBA), Lloyd Honeyghan (WBC), Simon Brown (IBF)
1989	Mark Breland (WBA), Marlon Starling (WBC), Simon Brown (IBF)
1990	Mark Breland (WBA), Aaron Davis (WBA), Simon Brown (IBF), Marlon Starling (WBC), Maurice Blocker (WBC)
1991	Meldrick Taylor (WBA), Simon Brown (IBF, WBC)
1992	Meldrick Taylor (WBA), James "Buddy" McGirt (WBC), Maurice Blocker (IBF)
1993	Cristianto Espana (WBA), Pernell Whitaker (WBC), Felix Trinidad (IBF)
1994	Ike Quartey (WBA), Pernell Whitaker (WBC), Felix Trinidad (IBF)
1995	Ike Quartey (WBA), Pernell Whitaker (WBC), Felix Trinidad (IBF)
1996–97	Ike Quartey (WBA), Pernell Whitaker (WBC), Felix Trinidad (IBF)
1998	Ike Quartey (WBA), Oscar De La Hoya (WBC), Felix Trinidad (IBF)
1999	James Page (WBA), Oscar De La Hoya (WBC), Felix Trinidad (IBF, WBC)
2000	James Page (WBA), Shane Mosley (WBC), Vacant (IBF)
2001	Andrew Lewis (WBA), Shane Mosley (WBC), Vernon Forrest (IBF)
2002	Ricardo Mayorga (WBA), Vernon Forrest (WBC), Michele Piccirillo (IBF)
2003	Ricardo Mayorga (WBA, WBC), Cory Spinks (IBF)

1. Retired. 2. Abandoned title. 3. WBA withdrew recognition.

Lightweight

1869–99	Kid Lavigne
1899–1902	Frank Erne
1902–08	Joe Gans
1908–10	Battling Nelson
1910–12	Ad Wolgast
1912–14	Willie Ritchie
1914–17	Freddy Welsh
1917–25	Benny Leonard[1]
1925	Jimmy Goodrich
1925–26	Rocky Kansas
1926–30	Sammy Mandell
1930	Al Singer
1930–33	Tony Canzoneri
1933–35	Barney Ross[2]
1935–36	Tony Canzoneri
1936–38	Lou Ambers
1938–39	Henry Armstrong
1939–40	Lou Ambers
1940–41	Lew Jenkins
1941–42	Sammy Angott[1]
1943–47	Beau Jack (N.Y.), Bob Montgomery (N.Y.), Sammy Angott (NBA), Juan Zurita (NBA), Ike Williams (NBA)
1947–51	Ike Williams
1951–52	James Carter
1952	Lauro Salas
1952–54	James Carter
1954	Paddy DeMarco
1954–55	James Carter
1955–56	Wallace Smith
1956–62	Joe Brown
1962–65	Carlos Ortiz
1965	Ismael Laguna
1965–68	Carlos Ortiz
1968	Teo Cruz
1969	Teo Cruz, Mando Ramos
1970	Mando Ramos, Ismael Laguna, Ken Buchanan
1971	Ken Buchanan (WBA), Mando Ramos (WBC), Pedro Carrasco (WBC)
1972	Ken Buchanan (WBA), Roberto Duran (WBA), Pedro Carrasco (WBC), Mando Ramos (WBC), Chango Carmona (WBC), Rodolfo Gonzalez (WBC)
1973	Roberto Duran (WBA), Rodolfo Gonzalez (WBC)
1974	Roberto Duran (WBA), Rodolfo Gonzalez (WBC), Guts Ishimatsu (WBC)
1975	Roberto Duran (WBA), Guts Ishimatsu (WBC)
1976	Roberto Duran (WBA), Guts Ishimatsu (WBC), Esteban De Jesus (WBC)
1977	Roberto Duran (WBA), Esteban De Jesus (WBC)
1978	Roberto Duran (WBA, WBC)
1979	Roberto Duran,[2] Jim Watt (WBC), Ernesto Espana (WBA)
1980	Ernesto Espana (WBA), Hilmer Kenty (WBA), Jim Watt (WBC)
1981	Hilmer Kenty (WBA), Sean O'Grady (WBA), James Watt (WBC), Alexis Arguello (WBC), Arturo Frias (WBA)
1982	Arturo Frias (WBA), Ray Mancini (WBA), Alexis Arguello (WBC)

1983	Edwin Rosario (WBC), Ray Mancini (WBA)
1984	Edwin Rosario (WBC), Livingstone Bramble (WBA)
1985	Jose Luis Ramirez (WBC), Hector Camacho (WBC), Livingstone Bramble (WBA)
1986	Hector Camacho (WBC), Livingstone Bramble (WBA), Jim Paul (IBF)
1987	Edwin Rosario (WBA), Jose Luis Ramirez (WBC), Greg Haugen (IBF)
1988	Jose Luis Ramirez (WBC), Julio Cesar Chavez (WBA), Greg Haugen (IBF), Julio Cesar Chavez (WBC & WBA title unified)
1989	Pernell Whitaker (IBF, WBC), Edwin Rosario (WBA)
1990	Pernell Whitaker (IBF, WBC), Juan Nazario (WBA)
1991	Pernell Whitaker (IBF, WBA, WBC)
1992	Pernell Whitaker (IBF, WBA, WBC),[3] Joey Gamache (WBA)
1993	Dingaan Thobela (WBA), Angel Gonzalez (WBC), Freddie Pendleton (IBF)
1994	Orzubek Nazarov (WBA), Angel Gonzalez (WBC), Rafael Ruelas (IBF)
1995	Orzubek Nazarov (WBA), Angel Gonzalez (WBC), Oscar De La Hoya (IBF)
1996	Gusshie Nazarov (WBA), Jean Baptiste Mendy (WBC), Phillip Holiday (IBF)
1997	Orzubek Nazarov (WBA), Jean Baptiste Mendy (WBC), Philip Holiday (IBF)
1998	Jean Baptiste Mendy (WBA), Cesar Bazan (WBC), Shane Mosley (IBF)
1999	Stefano Zoff (WBA), Stevie Johnston (WBC), Paul Spadafora (IBF)
2000	Takanori Hatakeyama (WBA), Jose Luis Castillo (WBC), Paul Spadafora (IBF)
2001	Julien Lorcy (WBA), Jose Luis Castillo (WBC), Paul Spadafora (IBF)
2002	Leonard Dorin (WBA), Floyd Mayweather (WBC), Paul Spadafora (IBF)
2003	Leonard Dorin (WBA), Floyd Mayweather (WBC), Vacant (IBF)

1. Retired. 2. Abandoned title. 3. Moving up in weight class, so resigned titles.

Featherweight

1889	Dal Hawkins[1]
1890	Billy Murphy
1892–1900	George Dixon
1900–01	Terry McGovern
1901	Young Corbett[1]
1901–12	Abe Attell
1912–23	Johnny Kilbane
1923	Eugene Criqui
1923–25	Johnny Dundee[1]
1925–27	Louis (Kid) Kaplan[1]
1927–28	Benny Bass
1928	Tony Canzoneri
1928–29	Andre Routis
1929–32	Battling Battalino[1]
1932	Tommy Paul (NBA), Kid Chocolate (N.Y.)
1933–36	Freddie Miller
1936–37	Petey Sarron
1937–38	Henry Armstrong[1]
1938–40	Joey Archibald
1940–41	Harry Jefra, Joey Archibald
1941–42	Chalky Wright
1942–48	Willie Pep
1948–49	Sandy Saddler[2]
1949–50	Willie Pep
1950–57	Sandy Saddler
1957–59	Kid Bassey
1959–63	Davey Moore
1963–64	Sugar Ramos
1964–67	Vicente Saldivar[2]
1968	Howard Winstone, José Legra,[3] Paul Rojas (WBA), Sho Saijo (WBA)
1969	Sho Saijo (WBA), Johnny Famechon[3]
1970	Sho Saijo (WBA), Johnny Famechon,[3] Vicente Salvidar,[3] Kuniaki Shibata[3]
1971	Sho Saijo (WBA), Antonio Gomez (WBA), Kuniaki Shibata (WBC)
1972	Antonio Gomez (WBA), Ernesto Marcel (WBA), Kuniaki Shibata (WBC), Clemente Sanchez (WBC), José Legra (WBC)
1973	Ernesto Marcel (WBA), José Legra (WBC), Eder Jofre (WBC)
1974	Ernesto Marcel (WBA),[2] Ruben Olivares (WBA), Alexis Arguello (WBA), Eder Jofre (WBC), Bobby Chacon (WBC)
1975	Alexis Arguello (WBA), Bobby Chacon (WBC), Ruben Olivares (WBC), David Kotey (WBC)
1976	Alexis Arguello (WBA),[2] David Kotey (WBC), Danny Lopez (WBC)
1977	Rafael Ortega (WBA), Danny Lopez (WBC)
1978	Rafael Ortega (WBA), Cecilio Lastra (WBA), Eusebio Pedroza (WBA), Danny Lopez (WBC)
1979	Eusebio Pedroza (WBA), Danny Lopez (WBC)
1980	Eusebio Pedroza (WBA), Danny Lopez (WBC), Salvador Sanchez (WBC)
1981	Eusebio Pedroza (WBA), Salvador Sanchez (WBC)
1982	Eusebio Pedroza (WBA), Salvador Sanchez (WBC)[4]
1983	Juan Laporte (WBC), Eusebio Pedroza (WBA)
1984	Wilfred Gomez (WBC), Eusebio Pedroza (WBA)
1985	Eusebio Pedroza (WBA), Barry McGuigan (WBA), Azumah Nelson (WBC)
1986	Barry McGuigan (WBA), Stevie Cruz (WBA), Azumah Nelson (WBC)
1987	Azumah Nelson (WBC), Antonio Esparragoza (WBA)
1988	Calvin Grove (IBF), Jorge Paez (IBF), Antonio Esparragoza (WBA), Jeff Fenech (WBC)
1989	Jorge Paez (IBF), Antonio Esparragoza (WBA), Jeff Fenech (WBC)
1990	Marcos Villasana (WBC), Antonio Esparragoza (WBA), Jorge Paez (IBF)
1991	Yung-Kyun Park (WBA), Troy Dorsey (IBF), Marcos Villagana (WBC)
1992	Paul Hodkinson (WBC), Manuel Medina (IBF), Yung-Kyun Park (WBA)
1993	Yung-Kyun Park (WBA), Goyo Vargas (WBC), Tom Johnson (IBF)
1994	Eloy Rojas (WBA), Kevin Kelley (WBC), Tom Johnson (IBF)
1995	Eloy Rojas (WBA), Alejandro Gonzalez (WBC), Tom Johnson (IBF)
1996	Wilfredo Vázquez (WBA), Luisto Espinoza (WBC), Tom Johnson (IBF)
1997	Elroy Rojas (WBA), Luisito Espinoza (WBC), Tom Johnson (IBF)
1998	vacant (WBA), Luisito Espinoza (WBC), Manuel Medina (IBF)
1999	Freddie Norwood (WBA), Cesar Soto (WBC), Manuel Medina (IBF)
2000	Freddie Norwood (WBA), Guty Espadas (WBC), Paul Ingle (IBF)
2001	Derrick Gainer (WBA), Erik Morales (WBC), Frankie Toledo (IBF)
2002	Derrick Gainer (WBA), vacant (WBC), Johnny Tapia (IBF)
2003	Derrick Gainer (WBA), Erik Morales (WBC), Manuel Marquez (IBF)

1. Abandoned title. 2. Retired. 3. Recognized in Europe, Mexico, and Asia. 4. Killed in auto accident.

Bantamweight

1890–92	George Dixon[1]
1894–99	Jimmy Barry[2]
1899–1900	Terry McGovern[1]
1901	Harry Harris[1]
1902–03	Harry Forbes
1903–04	Frankie Neil
1904	Joe Bowker[1]
1905–07	Jimmy Walsh[1]
1910–14	Johnny Coulon
1914–17	Kid Williams
1917–20	Pete Herman
1920	Joe Lynch
1920–21	Joe Lynch, Pete Herman, Johnny Buff
1922	Johnny Buff, Joe Lynch
1923	Joe Lynch
1924	Joe Lynch, Abe Goldstein, Eddie "Cannonball" Martin

1925	Eddie "Cannonball" Martin, Charlie (Phil) Rosenberg[3]
1927–28	Bud Taylor (NBA)[1]
1929–34	Al Brown
1935	Al Brown, Baltazar Sangchili
1936	Baltazar Sangchili, Tony Marino, Sixto Escobar
1937	Sixto Escobar, Harry Jeffra
1938	Harry Jeffra, Sixto Escobar
1939–40	Sixto Escobar[2]
1940–42	Lou Salica
1942–46	Manuel Ortiz
1947	Manuel Ortiz, Harold Dade
1948–50	Manuel Ortiz
1950–52	Vic Toweel
1952–54	Jimmy Carruthers[2]
1954–55	Robert Cohen
1956	Robert Cohen, Mario D'Agata, Raul Macias (NBA)
1957	Mario D'Agata, Alphonse Halimi
1958–59	Alphonse Halimi
1959–60	Jose Becerra[2]
1960–61	Alphonse Halimi[4]
1961–62	Johnny Caldwell[4]
1961–65	Eder Jofre
1965–68	Masahika "Fighting" Harada
1968	Masahika "Fighting" Harada, Lionel Rose
1969	Lionel Rose, Ruben Olivares
1970	Ruben Olivares, Chucho Castillo
1971	Chucho Castillo, Ruben Olivares
1972	Ruben Olivares, Rafael Herrera, Enrique Pinder
1973	Enrique Pinder (WBA), Romeo Anaya (WBA), Arnold Taylor (WBA), Rodolfo Martinez (WBC), Rafael Herrera
1974	Arnold Taylor (WBA), Soo Hwan Hong (WBA), Rafael Herrera (WBC), Rodolfo Martinez (WBC)
1975	Soo Hwan Hong (WBA), Alfonso Zamora (WBA), Rodolfo Martinez (WBC)
1976	Alfonso Zamora (WBA), Rodolfo Martinez (WBC), Carlos Zarate (WBC)
1977	Alfonso Zamora (WBA), Jorge Lujan (WBA), Carlos Zarate (WBC)
1978	Jorge Lujan (WBA), Carlos Zarate (WBC)
1979	Jorge Lujan (WBA), Carlos Zarate (WBC), Lupe Pintor (WBC)
1980	Jorge Lujan (WBA), Lupe Pintor (WBC), Julian Solis (WBA), Jeff Chandler (WBA)
1981	Lupe Pintor (WBC), Jeff Chandler (WBA)
1982	Lupe Pintor (WBC), Jeff Chandler (WBA)
1983	Jeff Chandler (WBA), Albert Dauila (WBC)
1984	Richie Sandqual (WBA), Albert Dauila (WBC)
1985	Richard Sandoval (WBA), Daniel Zaragoza (WBC), Miguel Lora (WBC)
1986	Richard Sandoval (WBA), Bernardo Pinango (WBA), Jeff Fenech (IBF)
1987	Bernardo Pinango (WBA), Takuya Muguruma (WBA), Miguel Lora (WBC)
1988	Wilfredo Vásquez (WBA), Jibaro Perez (WBC), Moon Sung-gil (WBA), Orlando Canizales (IBF)
1989	Jibaro Perez (WBC), Moon Sung-gil (WBA), Orlando Canizales (IBF), Kaokor Galaxy (WBA), Luis Espinosa (WBA)
1990	Orlando Canizales (IBF), Jibaro Perez (WBC), Luis Espinosa (WBA)
1991	Greg Richardson (WBC), Orlando Canizales (IBF), Luis Espinosa (WBA)
1992	Joichiro Tatsuyoshi (WBC), Victor Manuel Rabanales (WBC), Eddie Cook (WBA), Orlando Gonzales (IBF)
1993	Jorge Julio (WBA), Byun-Jong-il (WBC), Orlando Canizales (IBF)
1994	John Michael Johnson (WBA), Yasuei Yakushiji (WBC), Orlando Canizales (IBF)
1995	Daorun Chuwatang (WBA), Yasuei Yakushiji (WBC), Mbulelo Botile (IBF)
1996–97	Nana Konadu (WBA), Wayne McCullough (WBC), Mbulelo Botile (IBF)
1998	Nana Konadu (WBA), Joichiro Tatsuyoshi (WBC), Tim Austin (IBF)
1999–2001	Paulie Ayala (WBA), Veeraphol Sahaprom (WBC), Tim Austin (IBF)
2002	Johnny Bredahl (WBA), Veeraphol Sahaprom (WBC), Tim Austin (IBF)
2003	Johnny Bredahl (WBA), Veerapol Sahaprom (WBC), Rafael Marquez (IBF)

1. Abandoned title. 2. Retired. 3. Deprived of title for failing to make weight. 4. Recognized in Europe.

Horse Racing

Ancient drawings on stone and bone prove that horse racing is at least 3,000 years old, but thoroughbred racing is a modern development. Practically every thoroughbred in training today traces its registered ancestry back to one or more of three sires that arrived in England about 1728 from the Near East and became known, from the names of their owners, as the Byerly Turk, the Darley Arabian, and the Godolphin Arabian. The Jockey Club (English) was founded at Newmarket in 1750 or 1751 and became the custodian of the Stud Book as well as the court of last resort in deciding turf affairs.

Horse racing took place in this country before the Revolution, but the great lift to the breeding industry came with the importation in 1798, by Col. John Hoomes of Virginia, of Diomed, winner of the Epsom Derby of 1780. Diomed's lineal descendants included such famous 19th-century stars of the American turf as American Eclipse, Sir Archy, and Lexington. From 1800 to the time of the Civil War there were race courses and breeding establishments plentifully scattered through Virginia, North Carolina, South Carolina, Tennessee, Kentucky, and Louisiana.

The oldest stake event in North America is the Queen's Plate, a Canadian fixture that was first run in the Province of Quebec in 1836. The oldest stake event in the United States is the Travers, which was first run at Saratoga in 1864. The gambling that goes with horse racing and trickery by jockeys, trainers, owners, and track officials caused attacks on the sport by reformers and a demand among horse racing enthusiasts for an honest and effective control of some kind, but nothing of lasting value to racing came of this until the formation in 1894 of the Jockey Club (American).

"TRIPLE CROWN" WINNERS IN THE UNITED STATES

(Kentucky Derby, Preakness, and Belmont Stakes)

Year	Horse	Owner	Year	Horse	Owner
1919	Sir Barton	J. K. L. Ross	1946	Assault	Robert J. Kleberg
1930	Gallant Fox	William Woodward	1948	Citation	Warren Wright
1935	Omaha	William Woodward	1973	Secretariat	Meadow Stable
1937	War Admiral	Samuel D. Riddle	1977	Seattle Slew	Karen Taylor
1941	Whirlaway	Warren Wright	1978	Affirmed	Louis Wolfson
1943	Count Fleet	Mrs. John Hertz			

KENTUCKY DERBY

Churchill Downs; 3-year-olds; 1¼ mi

Year	Winner	Jockey	Year	Winner	Jockey	Year	Winner	Jockey
1875	Aristides	O. Lewis	1920	Paul Jones	T. Rice	1964	Northern Dancer	W. Hartack
1876	Vagrant	R. Swim	1921	Behave Yourself	C. Thompson	1965	Lucky Debonair	W. Shoemaker
1877	Baden Baden	W. Walker	1922	Morvich	A. Johnson	1966	Kauai King	D. Brumfield
1878	Day Star	J. Carter	1923	Zev	E. Sande	1967	Proud Clarion	R. Ussery
1879	Lord Murphy	C. Shauer	1924	Black Gold	J. D. Mooney	1968	Forward Pass[1]	I. Valenzuela
1880	Fonso	G. Lewis	1925	Flying Ebony	E. Sande	1969	Majestic Prince	W. Hartack
1881	Hindoo	J. McLaughlin	1926	Bubbling Over	A. Johnson	1970	Dust Commander	M. Manganello
1882	Apollo	B. Hurd	1927	Whiskery	L. McAtee	1971	Canonero II	G. Avila
1883	Leonatus	W. Donohue	1928	Reigh Count	C. Lang	1972	Riva Ridge	R. Turcotte
1884	Buchanan	I. Murphy	1929	Clyde Van Dusen	L. McAtee	1973	Secretariat	R. Turcotte
1885	Joe Cotton	B. Henderson	1930	Gallant Fox	E. Sande	1974	Cannonade	A. Cordero, Jr.
1886	Ben Ali	P. Duffy	1931	Twenty Grand	C. Kurtsinger	1975	Foolish Pleasure	J. Vasquez
1887	Montrose	I. Lewis	1932	Burgoo King	E. James	1976	Bold Forbes	A. Cordero, Jr.
1888	Macbeth II	G. Covington	1933	Brokers Tip	D. Meade	1977	Seattle Slew	J. Cruguet
1889	Spokane	T. Kiley	1934	Cavalcade	M. Garner	1978	Affirmed	S. Cauthen
1890	Riley	I. Murphy	1935	Omaha	W. Saunders	1979	Spectacular Bid	R. Franklin
1891	Kingman	I. Murphy	1936	Bold Venture	I. Hanford	1980	Genuine Risk	J. Vasquez
1892	Azra	L. Clayton	1937	War Admiral	C. Kurtsinger	1981	Pleasant Colony	J. Velasquez
1893	Lookout	E. Kunze	1938	Lawrin	E. Arcaro	1982	Gato del Sol	E. Delahoussaye
1894	Chant	F. Goodale	1939	Johnstown	J. Stout	1983	Sunny's Halo	E. Delahoussaye
1895	Halma	S. Perkins	1940	Gallahadion	C. Bierman	1984	Swale	L. Pincay, Jr.
1896	Ben Brush	W. Simms	1941	Whirlaway	E. Arcaro	1985	Spend a Buck	A. Cordero, Jr.
1897	Typhoon II	B. Garner	1942	Shut Out	W. D. Wright	1986	Ferdinand	W. Shoemaker
1898	Plaudit	W. Simms	1943	Count Fleet	J. Longden	1987	Alysheba	C. McCarron
1899	Manuel	F. Taral	1944	Pensive	C. McCreary	1988	Winning Colors	G. Stevens
1900	Lieut. Gibson	J. Boland	1945	Hoop Jr.	E. Arcaro	1989	Sunday Silence	P. Valenzuela
1901	His Eminence	J. Winkfield	1946	Assault	W. Mehrtens	1990	Unbridled	C. Perret
1902	Alan-a-Dale	J. Winkfield	1947	Jet Pilot	E. Guerin	1991	Strike the Gold	C. Antley
1903	Judge Himes	H. Booker	1948	Citation	E. Arcaro	1992	Lil E. Tee	P. Day
1904	Elwood	F. Prior	1949	Ponde	S. Brooks	1993	Sea Hero	J. Bailey
1905	Agile	J. Martin	1950	Middleground	W. Boland	1994	Go For Gin	C. McCarron
1906	Sir Huon	R. Troxler	1951	Count Turf	C. McCreary	1995	Thunder Gulch	G. Stevens
1907	Pink Star	A. Minder	1952	Hill Gail	E. Arcaro	1996	Grindstone	J. Bailey
1908	Stone Street	A. Pickens	1953	Dark Star	H. Moreno	1997	Silver Charm	G. Stevens
1909	Wintergreen	V. Powers	1954	Determine	R. York	1998	Real Quiet	K. Desormeaux
1910	Donau	F. Herbert	1955	Swaps	W. Shoemaker	1999	Charismatic	C. Antley
1911	Meridian	G. Archibald	1956	Needles	D. Erb	2000	Fusaichi Pegasus	K. Desormeaux
1912	Worth	C. H. Shilling	1957	Iron Liege	W. Hartack	2001	Monarchos	J. Chavez
1913	Donerail	R. Goose	1958	Tim Tam	I. Valenzuela	2002	War Emblem	V. Espinoza
1914	Old Rosebud	J. McCabe	1959	Tomy Lee	W. Shoemaker	2003	Funny Cide	J. Santos
1915	Regret	J. Notter	1960	Venetian Way	W. Hartack			
1916	George Smith	J. Loftus	1961	Carry Back	J. Sellers			
1917	Omar Khayyam	C. Borel	1962	Decidedly	W. Hartack			
1918	Exterminator	W. Knapp	1963	Chateauguay	B. Baeza			
1919	Sir Barton	J. Loftus						

1. Dancer's Image finished first but was disqualified after traces of drugs were found in his system.

PREAKNESS STAKES

Pimlico; 3-year-olds; 1³⁄₁₆ mi

Year	Winner	Jockey
1873	Survivor	G. Barbee
1874	Culpepper	W. Donohue
1875	Tom Ochiltree	L. Hughes
1876	Shirley	G. Barbee
1877	Cloverbrook	C. Holloway
1878	Duke of Magenta	C. Holloway
1879	Harold	L. Hughes
1880	Grenada	L. Hughes
1881	Saunterer	T. Costello
1882	Vanguard	T. Costello
1883	Jacobus	G. Barbee
1884	Knight of Ellerslie	S. Fisher
1885	Tecumseh	J. McLaughlin
1886	The Bard	S. Fisher
1887	Dunboyne	W. Donohue
1888	Refund	F. Littlefield
1889	Buddhist	W. Anderson
1890	Montague	W. Martin
1891-93	Not held	
1894	Assignee	F. Taral
1895	Belmar	F. Taral
1896	Margrave	H. Griffin
1897	Paul Kauvar	T. Thorpe
1898	Sly Fox	W. Simms
1899	Half Time	R. Clawson
1900	Hindus	H. Spencer
1901	The Parader	F. Landry
1902	Old England	L. Jackson
1903	Flocarline	W. Gannon
1904	Bryn Mawr	E. Hildebrand
1905	Cairngorm	W. Davis
1906	Whimsical	W. Miller
1907	Don Enrique	G. Mountain
1908	Royal Tourist	E. Dugan
1909	Effendi	W. Doyle
1910	Layminster	R. Estep
1911	Watervale	E. Dugan
1912	Colonel Holloway	C. Turner
1913	Buskin	J. Butwell
1914	Holiday	A. Schuttinger
1915	Rhine Maiden	D. Hoffman
1916	Damrosch	L. McAtee
1917	Kalitan	E. Haynes
1918	War Cloud	J. Loftus
1918	Jack Hare Jr.	C. Peak
1919	Sir Barton	J. Loftus
1920	Man o' War	C. Kummer
1921	Broomspun	F. Coltiletti
1922	Pillory	L. Morris
1923	Vigil	B. Marinelli
1924	Nellie Morse	J. Merimee
1925	Coventry	C. Kummer
1926	Display	J. Maiben
1927	Bostonian	W. Abel
1928	Victorian	S. Workman
1929	Dr. Freeland	L. Schaefer
1930	Gallant Fox	E. Sande
1931	Mate	G. Ellis
1932	Burgoo King	E. James
1933	Head Play	C. Kurtsinger
1934	High Quest	R. Jones
1935	Omaha	W. Saunders
1936	Bold Venture	G. Woolf
1937	War Admiral	C. Kurtsinger
1938	Dauber	M. Peters
1939	Challedon	G. Seabo
1940	Bimelech	F.A. Smith
1941	Whirlaway	E. Arcaro
1942	Alsab	B. James
1943	Count Fleet	J. Longden
1944	Pensive	C. McCreary
1945	Polynesian	W.D. Wright
1946	Assault	W. Mehrtens
1947	Faultless	D. Dodson
1948	Citation	E. Arcaro
1949	Capot	T. Atkinson
1950	Hill Prince	E. Arcaro
1951	Bold	E. Arcaro
1952	Blue Man	C. McCreary
1953	Native Dancer	E. Guerin
1954	Hasty Road	J. Adams
1955	Nashua	E. Arcaro
1956	Fabius	W. Hartack
1957	Bold Ruler	E. Arcaro
1958	Tim Tam	I. Valenzuela
1959	Royal Orbit	W. Harmatz
1960	Bally Ache	R. Ussery
1961	Carry Back	J. Sellers
1962	Greek Money	J. Rotz
1963	Candy Spots	W. Shoemaker
1964	Northern Dancer	W. Hartack
1965	Tom Rolfe	R. Turcotte
1966	Kauai King	D. Brumfield
1967	Damascus	W. Shoemaker
1968	Forward Pass	I. Valenzuela
1969	Majestic Prince	W. Hartack
1970	Personality	E. Belmonte
1971	Canonero II	G. Avila
1972	Bee Bee Bee	E. Nelson
1973	Secretariat	R. Turcotte
1974	Little Current	M. Rivera
1975	Master Derby	D. McHargue
1976	Elocutionist	J. Lively
1977	Seattle Slew	J. Cruguet
1978	Affirmed	S. Cauthen
1979	Spectacular Bid	R. Franklin
1980	Codex	A. Cordero
1981	Pleasant Colony	J. Velasquez
1982	Aloma's Ruler	J. Kaenel
1983	Deputed Testamony	D. Miller
1984	Gate Dancer	A. Cordero
1985	Tank's Prospect	P. Day
1986	Snow Chief	A. Solis
1987	Alysheba	C. McCarron
1988	Risen Star	E. Delahoussaye
1989	Sunday Silence	P. Valenzuela
1990	Summer Squall	P. Day
1991	Hansel	J. Bailey
1992	Pine Bluff	C. McCarron
1993	Prairie Bayou	M. Smith
1994	Tabasco Cat	P. Day
1995	Timber Country	P. Day
1996	Louis Quatorze	P. Day
1997	Silver Charm	G. Stevens
1998	Real Quiet	K. Desormeaux
1999	Charismatic	C. Antley
2000	Red Bullet	J. Bailey
2001	Point Given	G. Stevens
2002	War Emblem	V. Espinoza
2003	Funny Cide	J. Santos

BELMONT STAKES

Belmont Park; 3-year-olds; 1½ mi

Run at Jerome Park 1867 to 1890; at Morris Park 1890–94; at Belmont Park 1905–62; at Aqueduct 1963–67. Distance 1⅝ mi prior to 1874; reduced to 1½ mi, 1874; reduced to 1¼ mi, 1890; reduced to 1⅛ mi, 1893; increased to 1¼ mi, 1895; increased to 1⅜ mi, 1896; reduced to 1¼ mi in 1904; increased to 1½ mi, 1926.

Year	Winner	Jockey
1867	Ruthless	J. Gilpatrick
1868	General Duke	B. Swim
1869	Fenian	C. Miller
1870	Kingfisher	W. Dick
1871	Harry Bassett	W. Miller
1872	Joe Daniels	J. Roe
1873	Springbok	J. Roe
1874	Saxon	G. Barbee
1875	Calvin	B. Swim
1876	Algerine	B. Donohue
1877	Cloverbrook	C. Holloway
1878	Duke of Magenta	L. Hughes
1879	Spendthrift	G. Evans
1880	Grenada	L. Hughes
1881	Saunterer	T. Costello
1882	Forester	J. McLaughlin
1883	George Kinney	J. McLaughlin
1884	Panique	J. McLaughlin
1885	Tyrant	P. Duffy
1886	Inspector B	J. McLaughlin
1887	Hanover	J. McLaughlin
1888	Sir Dixon	J. McLaughlin
1889	Eric	W. Hayward
1890	Burlington	P. Barnes
1891	Foxford	E. Garrison
1892	Patron	W. Hayward
1893	Commanche	W. Simms
1894	Henry of Navarre (11/2)	W. Simms
1895	Belmar	F. Taral
1896	Hastings	H. Griffin
1897	Scottish Chieftain	J. Scherrer
1898	Bowling Brook	F. Littlefield

Year	Winner	Jockey
1899	Jean Beraud	R. Clawson
1900	Ildrim	N. Turner
1901	Commando	H. Spencer
1902	Masterman	J. Bullman
1903	Africander	J. Bullman
1904	Delhi	G. Odom
1905	Tanya	E. Hildebrand
1906	Burgomaster	L. Lyne
1907	Peter Pan	G. Mountain
1908	Colin	J. Notter
1909	Joe Madden	E. Dugan
1910	Sweep	J. Butwell
1911-12	Not held	
1913	Prince Eugene	R. Troxler
1914	Luke McLuke	M. Buxton
1915	The Finn	G. Byrne
1916	Friar Rock	E. Haynes
1917	Hourless	J. Butwell
1918	Johren	F. Robinson
1919	Sir Barton	J. Loftus
1920	Man o' War	C. Kummer
1921	Grey Lag	E. Sande
1922	Pillory	C.H. Miller
1923	Zev	E. Sande
1924	Mad Play	E. Sande
1925	American Flag	A. Johnson
1926	Crusader	A. Johnson
1927	Chance Shot	E. Sande
1928	Vito	C. Kummer
1929	Blue Larkspur	M. Garner
1930	Gallant Fox	E. Sande
1931	Twenty Grand	C. Kurtsinger
1932	Faireno	T. Malley
1933	Hurryoff	M. Garner
1934	Peace Chance	W. D. Wright
1935	Omaha	W. Saunders
1936	Granville	J. Stout
1937	War Admiral	C. Kurtsinger
1938	Pasteurized	J. Stout
1939	Johnstown	J. Stout
1940	Bimelech	F.A. Smith
1941	Whirlaway	E. Arcaro
1942	Shut Out	E. Arcaro
1943	Count Fleet	J. Longden
1944	Bounding Home	G.L. Smith
1945	Pavot	E. Arcaro
1946	Assault	W. Mehrtens
1947	Phalanx	R. Donoso
1948	Citation	E. Arcaro
1949	Capot	T. Atkinson
1950	Middleground	W. Boland
1951	Counterpoint	D. Gorman
1952	One Count	E. Arcaro
1953	Native Dancer	E. Guerin
1954	High Gun	E. Guerin
1955	Nashua	E. Arcaro
1956	Needles	D. Erb
1957	Gallant Man	W. Shoemaker
1958	Cavan	P. Anderson
1959	Sword Dancer	W. Shoemaker
1960	Celtic Ash	W. Hartack
1961	Sherluck	B. Baeza
1962	Jaipur	W. Shoemaker
1963	Chateauguay	B. Baeza
1964	Quadrangle	M. Ycaza
1965	Hail to All	J. Sellers
1966	Amberoid	W. Boland
1967	Damascus	W. Shoemaker
1968	Stage Door Johnny	H. Gustines
1969	Arts and Letters	B. Baeza
1970	High Echelon	J. Rotz
1971	Pass Catcher	R. Blum
1972	Riva Ridge	R. Turcotte
1973	Secretariat	R. Turcotte
1974	Little Current	M. Rivera
1975	Avatar	W. Shoemaker
1976	Bold Forbes	A. Cordero, Jr.
1977	Seattle Slew	J. Cruguet
1978	Affirmed	S. Cauthen
1979	Coastal	R. Hernandez
1980	Temperence Hill	E. Maple
1981	Summing	G. Martens
1982	Conquistador Cielo	L. Pincay, Jr.
1983	Caveat	L. Pincay, Jr.
1984	Swale	L. Pincay, Jr.
1985	Creme Fraiche	E. Maple
1986	Danzig Connection	C. McCarron
1987	Bet Twice	C. Perret
1988	Risen Star	E. Delahoussaye
1989	Easy Goer	P. Day
1990	Go And Go	M. Kinane
1991	Hansel	J. Bailey
1992	A.P. Indy	E. Delahoussaye
1993	Colonial Affair	J. Krone
1994	Tabasco Cat	P. Day
1995	Thunder Gulch	G.Stevens
1996	Editor's Note	R. Douglas
1997	Touch Gold	C. McCarron
1998	Victory Gallop	G. Stevens
1999	Lemon Drop Kid	J. Santos
2000	Commendable	P. Day
2001	Point Given	G. Stevens
2002	Sarava	E. Prado
2003	Empire Maker	J. Bailey

TRIPLE CROWN RACES—2003

Kentucky Derby (Churchill Downs, Louisville, Ky., May 3, 2003.) Purse: $1,000,000. Distance: $1\frac{1}{4}$ mi. Order of finish: 1. Funny Cide (Santos), mutuel returns: $27.60, $12.40, $8.20. 2. Empire Maker (Bailey), $5.80, $4.40. 3. Peace Rules (Prado), $6.00. 4. Atswhatimtalknbout (Flores). 5. Eye of the Tiger (Coa). 6. Buddy Gil (Stevens). 7. Outta Here (Desormeaux). 8. Ten Cents a Shine (Borel). 9. Ten Most Wanted (Day). 10. Domestic Dispute (Solis). 11. Scrimshaw (Velasquez). 12. Offlee Wild (Albarado). 13. Supah Blitz (Homeister, Jr.). 14. Indian Express (Baze). 15. Lone Star Sky (Sellers). 16. Brancusi (Farina). Winner's purse: $800,200. Margin of victory: $1\frac{3}{4}$ lengths. Time of race: 2:01.19.

Preakness Stakes (Pimlico, Baltimore, Md., May 17, 2003.) Purse: $1,000,000. Distance: $1\frac{3}{16}$ mi. Order of finish: 1. Funny Cide (Santos), mutuel returns: $5.80, $4.60, $3.40. 2. Midway Road (Albarado), $15.40, $9.00. 3. Scrimshaw (Stevens), $4.00. 4. Peace Rules (Prado). 5. Señor Swinger (Day). 6. New York Hero (Chavez). 7. Foufa's Warrior (Dominguez). 8. Cherokee's Boy (Fogelsonger). 9. Ten Cents a Shine (Bailey). 10. Kissin Saint (Migliore). Winner's purse: $650,000. Margin of victory: $9\frac{3}{4}$ lengths. Time of race: 1:55.61.

Belmont Stakes (Belmont Park, Elmont, N.Y., June 7, 2003.) Gross purse: $1,000,000. Distance: $1\frac{1}{2}$ mi. Order of finish: 1. Empire Maker (Bailey), mutuel returns: $6.00, $3.70, $2.80. 2. Ten Most Wanted (Day), $5.80, $3.20. 3. Funny Cide (Santos), $2.70. 4. Dynever (Prado). 5. Supervisor (Velazquez). 6. Scrimshaw (Stevens). Winner's purse: $600,000. Margin of victory: $\frac{3}{4}$ length. Time of race: 2:28.26.

ECLIPSE AWARDS—2002

(Presented on Jan. 27, 2003)

Horse of the Year	Azeri
2-year-old colt	Vindication
2-year-old filly	Storm Flag Flying
3-year-old colt	War Emblem
3-year-old filly	Farda Amiga
Older male	Left Bank
Older female	Azeri
Sprinter	Orientate
Male turf	High Chaparral
Female turf	Golden Apples
Steeplechase	Flat Top
Owner	Richard Englander
Breeder	Juddmonte Farms
Jockey	Jerry Bailey
Apprentice jockey	Ryan Fogelsonger
Trainer	Robert Frankel

(Based on vote by the Thoroughbred Racing Associations, the *Daily Racing Form,* and the National Turf Writers Association.)

Track and Field

WORLD OUTDOOR RECORDS—MEN

(Through Aug. 31, 2003)

Recognized by the International Athletic Federation. The IAAF decided late in 1976 not to recognize records in yards except for the one-mile run. The IAAF also requires automatic timing for all records for races of 400 meters or less.

Event	Record	Holder	Home country	Where made	Date
Running					
100 m	0:09.78	Tim Montgomery	United States	Paris, France	Sept. 14, 2002
200 m	0:19.32	Michael Johnson	United States	Atlanta, Ga.	Aug. 1, 1996
400 m	0:43.18	Michael Johnson	United States	Seville, Spain	Aug. 26, 1999
800 m	1:41.11	Wilson Kipketer	Denmark	Köln, Germany	Aug. 24, 1997
1,000 m	2:11.96	Noah Ngeny	Kenya	Rieti, Italy	Sept. 5, 1999
1,500 m	3:26.00	Hicham El Guerrouj	Morocco	Rome, Italy	July 14, 1998
1 mile	3:43.13	Hicham El Guerrouj	Morocco	Rome, Italy	July 7, 1999
2,000 m	4:44.79	Hicham El Guerrouj	Morocco	Berlin, Germany	Sept. 7, 1999
3,000 m	7:20.67	Daniel Komen	Kenya	Rieti, Italy	Sept. 1, 1996
3,000 m steeplechase	7:53.17	Brahim Boulami	Morocco	Zürich, Switzerland	Aug. 16, 2002
5,000 m	12:39.36	Haile Gebrselassie	Ethiopia	Helsinki, Finland	June 13, 1998
10,000 m	26:22.75	Haile Gebrselassie	Ethiopia	Hengelo, Netherlands	June 1, 1998
20,000 m	56:55.60	Arturo Barrios	Mexico	La Fleche, France	March 30, 1991
25,000 m	1:13:55.80	Toshihiko Seko	Japan	Christchurch, N.Z.	March 22, 1981
30,000 m	1:29:18.80	Toshihiko Seko	Japan	Christchurch, N.Z.	March 22, 1981
1 hour	21,101 m	Arturo Barrios	Mexico	La Fleche, France	March 30, 1991
Marathon[1]	2:05.38	Khalid Khannouchi	United States	London, England	April 14, 2002
Walking					
20,000 m	1:17:25.60	Bernardo Segura	Mexico	Bergen, Norway	May 7, 1994
30,000 m	2:01:44.10	Maurizio Damilano	Italy	Cuneo, Italy	Oct. 3, 1992
50,000 m	3:40:57.90	Thierry Toutain	France	Héricourt, France	Sept. 29, 1996
2 hours	29,572 m	Maurizio Damilano	Italy	Cuneo, Italy	Oct. 3, 1992
Hurdles					
110 m	0:12.91	Colin Jackson	Great Britain	Stuttgart, Germany	Aug. 20, 1993
400 m	0:46.78	Kevin Young	United States	Barcelona, Spain	Aug. 6, 1992
Relay races					
400 m (4 × 100)	0:37.40	National Team	United States	Barcelona, Spain	Aug. 8, 1992
	0:37.40	National Team	United States	Stuttgart, Germany	Aug. 21, 1993
800 m (4 × 200)	1:18.68	Santa Monica T.C.	United States	Walnut, Calif.	April 17, 1994
1,600 m (4 × 400)	2:54.20	National Team	United States	New York, N.Y.	July 22, 1998
3,200 m (4 × 800)	7:03.89	National Team	Britain	London, England	Aug. 30, 1982
6,000 m	14:38.80	National Team	West Germany	Köln, Germany	Aug. 17, 1977
Field events					
High jump	2.45 m	Javier Sotomayor	Cuba	Salamanca, Spain	July 27, 1993
Long jump	8.95 m	Mike Powell	United States	Tokyo, Japan	Aug. 30, 1991
Triple jump	18.29 m	Jonathan Edwards	Great Britain	Goteborg, Sweden	Aug. 7, 1995
Pole vault	6.14 m	Sergey Bubka	Ukraine	Sestriere, Italy	July 31, 1994
Shot-put	23.12 m	Randy Barnes	United States	Los Angeles, Calif.	May 20, 1990
Discus throw	74.08 m	Jürgen Schult	East Germany	Neubrandenburg, E. Germany	June 6, 1986
Hammer throw	86.74 m	Yuriy Sedykh	USSR	Stuttgart, Germany	Aug. 30, 1986
Javelin throw	98.48 m	Jan Zelezny	Czech Republic	Jena, Germany	May 25, 1996
Decathlon	9,026 pts.	Roman Sebrle	Czech Republic	Götzis, Austria	May 27, 2001

1. Not recognized by IAAF as world record, but considered to be "world-best performance." *Source:* IAAF.

WORLD OUTDOOR RECORDS—WOMEN

(Through Aug. 31, 2003)

Event	Record	Holder	Home country	Where made	Date
Running					
100 m	0:10.49	Florence Griffith-Joyner	United States	Indianapolis, Ind.	July 16, 1988
200 m	0:21.34	Florence Griffith-Joyner	United States	Seoul, South Korea	Sept. 29, 1988
400 m	0:47.60	Martina Koch	East Germany	Canberra, Australia	Oct. 6, 1985
800 m	1:53.28	Jarmila Kratochvilova	Czechoslovakia	Munich, W. Germany	July 26, 1983
1000 m	2:28.98	Svetlana Masterkova	Russia	Brussels, Belgium	Aug. 23, 1996
1,500 m	3:50.46	Qu Yunxia	China	Beijing, China	Sept. 11, 1993
1 mile	4:12.56	Svetlana Masterkova	Russia	Zurich, Switzerland	Aug. 14, 1996

Event	Record	Holder	Home country	Where made	Date
2,000 m	5:25.36	Sonia O'Sullivan	Ireland	Edinburgh, Scotland	July 8, 1994
3,000 m	8:06.11	Wang Junxia	China	Beijing, China	Sept. 13, 1993
5,000 m	14:28.09	Jiang Bo	China	Shanghai, China	Oct. 23, 1997
10,000 m	29:31.78	Wang Junxia	China	Beijing, China	Sept. 8, 1993
20,000 m	1:05:26.60	Tegla Loroupe	Kenya	Borgholzhausen, Germany	Sept. 3, 2000
25,000 m	1:27:05.90	Tegla Loroupe	Kenya	Mengerskirchen, Germany	Sept. 21, 2002
30,000 m	1:45:50.00[1]	Tegla Loroupe	Kenya	Warstein, Germany	June 6, 2003
1 hour	18.340	Tegla Loroupe	Kenya	Borgholzhausen, Germany	July 8, 1998
3,000 m steeplechase	9:08.33[1]	Gulnara Samitova	Russia	Tula, Russia	Aug. 10, 2003
Marathon[1,2]	2:15:25[1]	Paula Radcliffe	Great Britain	London, England	April 13, 2003
Walking					
5,000 m	20:02.60	Gillian O'Sullivan	Ireland	Dublin, Ireland	July 13, 2002
10,000 m	41:56.23	Nadezhda Ryashkina	Russia	Seattle, Wash.	July 24, 1990
20,000 m	1:26:52.30	Olimpiada Ivanova	Russia	Brisbane, Australia	Sept. 6, 2001
Hurdles					
100 m	0:12.21	Yordanka Donkova	Bulgaria	Stara Zagora, Bulgaria	Aug. 20, 1988
400 m	0:52.34	Yuliya Pechonkina	Russia	Tula, Russia	Aug. 8, 2003
Relay races					
400 m (4 × 100)	0:41.37	East Germany	E. Germany	Canberra, Australia	Oct. 6, 1985
800 m (4 × 200)	1:27.46	United States "Blue"	United States	Philadelphia, Pa.	April 29, 2000
1,600 m (4 × 400)	3:15.17	USSR	USSR	Seoul, South Korea	Oct. 1, 1988
3,200 m (4 × 800)	7:50.17	USSR	USSR	Moscow, USSR	Aug. 5, 1984
Field events					
High jump	2.09 m	Stefka Kostadinova	Bulgaria	Rome, Italy	Aug. 30, 1987
Pole vault	4.82 m[1]	Yelena Isinbayeva	Russia	Gateshead, England	July 13, 2003
Long jump	7.52 m	Galina Chistyakova	USSR	Leningrad, Russia	June 11, 1988
Triple jump	15.50 m	Inessa Kravets	Ukraine	Goteborg, Sweden	Aug. 10, 1995
Shot-put	22.63 m	Natalya Lisovskaya	USSR	Moscow, Russia	June 7, 1987
Discus throw	76.80 m	Gabriele Reinsch	East Germany	Neubrandenburg, E. Ger.	July 9, 1988
Hammer throw	76.07 m	Mihaela Melinte	Romania	Rüdlingen, Switzerland	Aug. 29, 1999
Javelin throw	71.54 m	Osleidys Menéndez	Cuba	Réthymno, Greece	July 1, 2001
Heptathlon	7,291 pts	Jackie Joyner-Kersee	United States	Seoul, South Korea	Sept. 24, 1988

1. Awaiting IAAF ratification. 2. Not recognized by IAAF as world record, but considered to be "world-best performance." *Source:* IAAF.

AMERICAN OUTDOOR RECORDS—MEN

(Through Aug. 31, 2003)

Event	Record	Holder	Where made	Date
Running				
100 m	0:09.78	Tim Montgomery	Paris, France	Sept. 14, 2002
200 m	0:19.32	Michael Johnson	Atlanta, Ga.	Aug. 1, 1996
400 m	0:43.18	Michael Johnson	Seville, Spain	Aug. 26, 1999
800 m	1:42.60	Johnny Gray	Koblenz, W. Germany	Aug. 29, 1985
1,000 m	2:13.90	Richard Wohlhuter	Oslo, Norway	July 30, 1974
1,500 m	3:29.77	Sydney Maree	Cologne, W. Germany	Aug. 25, 1985
1 mile	3:47.69	Steve Scott	Oslo, Norway	July 7, 1982
2,000 m	4:52.44	Jim Spivey	Lausanne, Switzerland	Sept. 15, 1987
3,000 m	7:30.84	Bob Kennedy	Monaco	Aug. 8, 1998
5,000 m	12:58.21	Bob Kennedy	Zurich, Switzerland	Aug. 14, 1996
10,000 m	27:13.98	Meb Keflezighi	Stanford, Calif.	May 4, 2001
3,000-m steeplechase	8:09.17	Henry Marsh	Koblenz, W. Ger.	Aug. 29, 1985
Marathon	2:05:38	Khalid Khannouchi	London, England	April 14, 2002
Hurdles				
110 m	0:12.92	Roger Kingdom	Berlin, Germany	Aug. 16, 1989
		Allen Johnson	Atlanta, Ga.	June 23, 1996
400 m	0:46.78	Kevin Young	Barcelona	Aug. 6, 1992
Relay races				
400 m (4 × 100)	0:37.40	Olympic Team	Barcelona, Spain	Aug. 8, 1992
		USA National Team	Stuttgart, Germany	Aug. 21, 1993
800 m (4 × 200)	1:18.68	Santa Monica T.C.	Walnut, Calif.	April 17, 1994
1,600 m (4 × 400)	2:54.20	USA National Team	New York, N.Y.	July 22, 1998
3,200 m (4 × 800)	7:06.50	Santa Monica T.C.	Walnut, Calif.	Apr. 26, 1986
6,000 m (4 × 1,500)	14:46.30	National Team	Bourges, France	June 24, 1979

Event	Record	Holder	Where made	Date
Field events				
High jump	7 ft. 10½ in.	Charles Austin	Zurich, Switzerland	Aug. 7, 1991
Long jump	29 ft. 4½ in.	Mike Powell	Tokyo, Japan	Aug. 30, 1991
Triple jump	59 ft. 4 in.	Kenny Harrison	Atlanta, Ga.	July 27, 1996
Pole vault	19 ft. 9 ¼in.	Jeff Hartwig	Jonesboro, Ark.	June 14, 2000
Shot-put	75 ft. 10¼ in.	Randy Barnes	Los Angeles	May 20, 1990
Discus throw	237 ft. 4 in.	Ben Plucknett	Stockholm, Swe.	July 7, 1981
Javelin throw	285 ft. 10 in.	Tom Pukstys	Jena, Germany	May 25, 1997
Hammer throw	270 ft. 9 in.	Lance Deal	Milan, Italy	July 9, 1996
Decathlon	8,891 pts	Dan O'Brien	Talence, France	Sept. 4–5, 1992

AMERICAN OUTDOOR RECORDS—WOMEN

(Through Aug. 31, 2003)

Event	Record	Holder	Where made	Date
Running				
100 m	0:10.49	Florence Griffith Joyner	Indianapolis, Ind.	July 16, 1988
200 m	21.34	Florence Griffith Joyner	Seoul, South Korea	Sept. 29, 1988
400 m	0:48.83	Valerie Brisco	Los Angeles, Calif.	Aug. 6, 1984
800 m	1:56.40	Jearl Miles-Clark	Zurich, Switzerland	Aug. 11, 1999
1,000 m	2:31.80	Regina Jacobs	Brunswick, Maine	July 3, 1999
1,500 m	3:57.12	Mary Slaney	Stockholm, Sweden.	July 26, 1983
2,000 m	5:32.70	Mary Slaney	Eugene, Ore.	Aug. 3, 1984
1 mile	4:16.71	Mary Decker Slaney	Zurich, Switzerland	Aug. 21, 1985
3,000 m	8:29.69	Mary Decker Slaney	Cologne, Germany	Aug. 25, 1985
5,000 m	14:45.35	Regina Jacobs	Sacramento, Calif.	July 21, 2000
10,000 m	30:50.32	Deena Drossin	Palo Alto, Calif.	May 3, 2002
3,000 m steeplechase	9:41.94	Elizabeth Jackson	Brisbane, Australia	Sept. 4, 2001
Marathon	2:21:16	Deena Drossin	London, England	April 13, 2003
Hurdles				
100 m	0:12.33	Gail Devers	Sacramento, Calif.	July 23, 2000
400 m	0:52.61	Kim Batten	Gotebörg, Sweden	Aug. 11, 1995
Relay races				
400 m (4 × 100)	41.47	U.S.A. National Team	Athens, Greece	Aug. 9, 1997
800 m (4 × 200)	1:27.46	United States Blue Team	Philadelphia, Pa.	April 29, 2000
1,600 m (4 × 400)	3:15.51	U.S. Olympic Team	Seoul, South Korea	Oct. 1, 1988
Field events				
Pole vault	15 ft 9¼ in.	Stacy Dragila	Stanford, Calif.	June 9, 2001
High jump	6 ft 8 in.	Louise Ritter	Austin, Tex.	July 9, 1988
Long jump	24 ft 7 in.	Jackie Joyner-Kersee	New York, N.Y.	May 22, 1994
Triple jump	47 ft 3½ in.	Sheila Hudson	Stockholm, Sweden	July 8, 1996
Shot-put	66 ft 2½ in.	Ramona Pagel	San Diego, Calif.	June 25, 1988
Discus throw	227 ft 10 in.	Suzy Powell	La Jolla, Calif.	April 27, 2002
Hammer throw	236 ft 3in.	Anna Norgren-Mahon	Walnut, Calif.	July 27, 2002
Javelin throw (old)	227 ft 5 in.	Kate Schmidt	Fürth, W. Ger.	Sept. 10, 1977
Javelin throw (new)	199 ft 8 in.	Kim Kreiner	Santo Domingo, Dom. Rep.	Aug. 7, 2003
Heptathlon	7,291 pts	Jackie Joyner-Kersee	Seoul, South Korea	Sept. 23–24, 1988

HISTORY OF THE RECORD FOR THE MILE RUN

(Under 4 minutes)

Time	Athlete	Country	Year	Location
3:59.4	Roger Bannister	England	1954	Oxford, England
3:58.0	John Landy	Australia	1954	Turku, Finland
3:57.2	Derek Ibbotson	England	1957	London
3:54.5	Herb Elliott	Australia	1958	Dublin
3:54.4	Peter Snell	New Zealand	1962	Wanganui, N.Z.
3:54.1	Peter Snell	New Zealand	1964	Auckland, N.Z.
3:53.6	Michel Jazy	France	1965	Rennes, France
3:51.3	Jim Ryun	United States	1966	Berkeley, Calif.
3:51.1	Jim Ryun	United States	1967	Bakersfield, Calif.
3:51.0	Filbert Bayi	Tanzania	1975	Kingston, Jamaica
3:49.4	John Walker	New Zealand	1975	Goteborg, Sweden
3:49.0	Sebastian Coe	England	1979	Oslo
3:48.8	Steve Ovett	England	1980	Oslo
3:48.53	Sebastian Coe	England	1981	Zurich, Switzerland
3:48.40	Steve Ovett	England	1981	Koblenz, W. Ger.
3:47.33	Sebastian Coe	England	1981	Brussels
3:46.31	Steve Cram	England	1985	Oslo
3:44.39	Noureddine Morceli	Algeria	1993	Rieti, Italy
3:43.13	Hicham El Guerrouj	Morocco	1999	Rome, Italy

Source: USA Track & Field.

2003 IAAF WORLD CHAMPIONSHIPS

(Aug. 23–31, 2003, Paris, France)

Men's Events

Event, athlete, country	Results
100 m—Kim Collins, St. Kitts and Nevis	10.07
200 m—John Capel, United States	20.30
400 m—Jerome Young, United States	44.50
800 m—Djabir Saïd-Guerni, Algeria	1:44.81
1,500 m—Hicham El Guerrouj, Morocco	3:31.77
5,000 m—Eliud Kipchoge, Kenya	12:52.79
10,000 m—Kenenisa Bekele, Ethiopia	26:49.57
Marathon—Jaouad Gharib, Morocco	2:08:31
3,000 m steeplechase—Saif Saaeed Shaheen, Qatar	8:04.39
110 m hurdles—Allen Johnson, United States	13.12
400 m hurdles—Felix Sánchez, Dominican Republic	47.25
High jump—Jacques Freitag, Republic of South Africa	2.35
Pole vault—Giuseppe Gibilisco, Italy	5.90 m
Long jump—Dwight Phillips, United States	8.32 m
Triple jump—Christian Olsson, Sweden	17.72 m
Shot put—Andrei Mikhnevich, Belarus	21.69 m
Discus throw—Virgilijus Alekna, Lithuania	69.69 m
Hammer throw—Ivan Tikhon, Belarus	83.05 m
Javelin throw—Sergey Makarov, Russia	85.44 m
20 km walk—Jefferson Pérez, Ecuador	1:17:21
50 km walk—Robert Korzeniowski, Poland	3:36:03
4 × 100 m relay—United States	38.06
4 × 400 m relay—United States	2:58.88
200 m amputee—Marlon Shirley, United States	22.93
400 m blind—Carlos Lopes, Portugal	52.41
400 m cerebral palsy—Mohamed Allek, Algeria	55.33
1,500 m wheelchair—Joël Jeannot, France	3:13.03
Decathlon—Tom Pappas, United States	8,750 pts.

Women's Events

Event, athlete, country	Results
100 m—Kelli White, United States[1]	10.85
200 m—Kelli White, United States[1]	22.05
400 m—Ana Guevara, Mexico	48.89
800 m—Maria de Lourdes Mutola, Mozambique	1:59.89
1,500 m—Tatyana Tomashova, Russia	3:58.52
5,000 m—Tirunesh Dibaba, Ethiopia	14:51.72
10,000 m—Berhane Adere, Ethiopia	30:04.18
Marathon—Catherine Ndereba, Kenya	2:23:55
100 m hurdles—Perdita Felicien, Canada	12.53
400 m hurdles—Jana Pittman, Australia	53.22
High jump—Hestrie Cloete, Republic of South Africa	2.06 m
Pole vault—Svetlana Feofanova, Russia	4.75 m
Long jump—Eunice Barber, France	6.99 m
Triple jump—Tatyana Lebedeva, Russia	15.18 m
Shot put—Svetlana Krivelyova, Russia	20.63 m
Discus throw—Irina Yatchenko, Belarus	67.32 m
Hammer throw—Yipsi Moreno, Cuba	73.33 m
Javelin throw—Miréla Manjani, Greece	66.52 m
20 km walk—Yelena Nikolayeva, Russia	1:26:52
4 × 100 m relay—France	41.78
4 × 400 m relay—United States	3:22.63
200 m blind—Adria Rocha Santos, Brazil	25.22
800 m wheelchair—Louise Sauvage, Australia	1:57.15
Heptathlon—Carolina Klüft, Sweden	7,001 pts

1. In early Sept. 2003, the IAAF found Kelli White guilty of doping charges and sent the case to the U.S. Anti-Doping Agency for disciplinary action. Should White be stripped of her medals, Torri Edwards (U.S.) would win the 100 m and Anastasiya Kapachinskaya (Russia) would be awarded the 200 m.

Tennis

Lawn tennis is a comparatively modern modification of the ancient game of court tennis. Maj. Walter Clopton Wingfield thought that something like court tennis might be played outdoors on lawns, and in Dec. 1873, at Nantclwyd, Wales, he introduced his new game under the name of *Sphairistike* at a lawn party. The game was a success and spread rapidly, but the name was a total failure and almost immediately disappeared when all the players and spectators began to refer to the new game as *lawn tennis.* In the early part of 1874, a young lady named Mary Ewing Outerbridge returned from Bermuda to New York, bringing with her the implements and necessary equipment of the new game, which she had obtained from a British Army supply store in Bermuda. Miss Outerbridge and friends played the first game of lawn tennis in the United States on the grounds of the Staten Island Cricket and Baseball Club in the spring of 1874.

For a few years, the new game went along in haphazard fashion until about 1880, when standard measurements for the court and standard equipment within definite limits became the rule. In 1881, the U.S. Lawn Tennis Association (whose name was changed in 1975 to the U.S. Tennis Association) was formed and conducted the first national championship at Newport, R.I. The international matches for the Davis Cup began with a series between the British and U.S. players on the courts of the Longwood Cricket Club, Chestnut Hill, Mass., in 1900, with the home players winning.

Professional tennis, which got its start in 1926 when the French star Suzanne Lenglen was paid $50,000 for a tour, received full recognition in 1968. Staid old Wimbledon, the London home of what are considered the world championships, let the pros compete. This decision ended a long controversy over open tennis and changed the format of the competition. The U.S. championships were also opened to the pros and the site of the event, long held at Forest Hills, N.Y., was shifted to the National Tennis Center in Flushing Meadows, N.Y., in 1978. Pro tours for men and women became worldwide in play that continued throughout the year.

DAVIS CUP CHAMPIONSHIPS

No matches in 1901, 1910, 1915–1918, and 1940–1945

1900 United States 3, British Isles 0
1902 United States 3, British Isles 2
1903 British Isles 4, United States 1
1904 British Isles 5, Belgium 0
1905 British Isles 5, United States 0
1906 British Isles 5, United States 0
1907 Australasia 3, British Isles 2
1908 Australasia 3, United States 2
1909 Australasia 5, United States 0
1911 Australasia 5, United States 0
1912 British Isles 3, Australasia 2
1913 United States 3, British Isles 2
1914 Australasia 3, United States 2
1919 Australasia 4, British Isles 1
1920 United States 5, Australasia 0
1921 United States 5, Japan 0
1922 United States 4, Australasia 1
1923 United States 4, Australasia 1
1924 United States 5, Australasia 0
1925 United States 5, France 0
1926 United States 4, France 1
1927 France 3, United States 2
1928 France 4, United States 1
1929 France 3, United States 2
1930 France 4, United States 1
1931 France 3, Great Britain 2
1932 France 3, United States 2
1933 Great Britain 3, France 2
1934 Great Britain 4, United States 1
1935 Great Britain 5, United States 0
1936 Great Britain 3, Australia 2
1937 United States 4, Great Britain 1
1938 United States 3, Australia 2
1939 Australia 3, United States 2
1946 United States 5, Australia 0
1947 United States 4, Australia 1
1948 United States 5, Australia 0
1949 United States 4, Australia 1
1950 Australia 4, United States 1
1951 Australia 3, United States 2
1952 Australia 4, United States 1
1953 Australia 3, United States 2
1954 United States 3, Australia 2
1955 Australia 5, United States 0
1956 Australia 5, United States 0
1957 Australia 3, United States 2
1958 United States 3, Australia 2
1959 Australia 3, United States 2
1960 Australia 4, Italy 1
1961 Australia 5, Italy 0
1962 Australia 5, Mexico 0
1963 United States 3, Australia 2
1964 Australia 3, United States 2
1965 Australia 4, Spain 1
1966 Australia 4, India 1
1967 Australia 4, Spain 1
1968 United States 4, Australia 1
1969 United States 5, Romania 0
1970 United States 5, West Germany 0
1971 United States 3, Romania 2
1972 United States 3, Romania 2
1973 Australia 5, United States 0
1974 South Africa (Default by India)
1975 Sweden 3, Czechoslovakia 2
1976 Italy 4, Chile 1
1977 Australia 3, Italy 1
1978 United States 4, Britain 1
1979 United States 5, Italy 0
1980 Czechoslovakia 3, Italy 2
1981 United States 3, Argentina 1
1982 United States 3, France 0
1983 Australia 3, Sweden 2
1984 Sweden 4, United States 1
1985 Sweden 3, West Germany 2
1986 Australia 3, Sweden 2
1987 Sweden 5, India 0
1988 West Germany 4, Sweden 1
1989 West Germany 3, Sweden 2
1990 United States 3, Australia 2
1991 France 3, United States 1
1992 United States 3, Switzerland 1
1993 Germany 4, Australia 1
1994 Sweden 4, Russia 1
1995 United States 3, Russia 1
1996 France 3, Sweden 2
1997 Sweden 5, United States 0
1998 Sweden 4, Italy 1
1999 Australia 3, France 2
2000 Spain 3, Australia 1
2001 France 3, Australia 2
2002 Russia 3, France 2

FEDERATION CUP CHAMPIONSHIPS

World team competition for women conducted by International Lawn Tennis Federation

1963 United States 2, Australia 1
1964 Australia 2, United States 1
1965 Australia 2, United States 1
1966 United States 3, West Germany 0
1967 United States 2, Britain 0
1968 Australia 3, Netherlands 0
1969 United States 2, Australia 1
1970 Australia 3, West Germany 0
1971 Australia 3, Britain 0
1972 South Africa 2, Britain 1
1973 Australia 3, South Africa 0
1974 Australia 2, United States 1
1975 Czechoslovakia 3, Australia 0
1976 United States 2, Australia 1
1977 United States 2, Australia 1
1978 United States 2, Australia 1
1979 United States 3, Australia 0
1980 United States 3, Australia 0
1981 United States 3, Britain 0
1982 United States 3, West Germany 0
1983 Czechoslovakia 2, West Germany 1
1984 Czechoslovakia 2, Australia 1
1985 Czechoslovakia 2, United States 1
1986 United States 3, Czechoslovakia 0
1987 West Germany 2, United States 1
1988 Czechoslovakia 2, Soviet Union 1
1989 United States 3, Spain 0
1990 United States 2, Soviet Union 1
1991 Spain 2, United States 1
1992 Germany 2, Spain 1
1993 Spain 3, Australia 0
1994 Spain 3, United States 0
1995 Spain 3, United States 2
1996 United States 5, Spain 0
1997 France 4, Netherlands 1
1998 Spain 3, Switzerland 2
1999 United States 4, Russia 1
2000 United States 5, Spain 0
2001 Belgium 2, Russia 1
2002 Slovak Republic 3, Spain 1

U.S. NATIONAL AND OPEN CHAMPIONS

SINGLES—MEN

NATIONAL

1881–87 Richard D. Sears
1888–89 Henry Slocum, Jr.
1890–92 Oliver S. Campbell
1893–94 Robert D. Wrenn
1895 Fred H. Hovey
1896–97 Robert D. Wrenn
1898–1900 Malcolm Whitman
1901–02 William A. Larned
1903 Hugh L. Doherty
1904 Holcombe Ward
1905 Beals C. Wright
1906 William J. Clothier
1907–11 William A. Larned
1912–13 Maurice McLoughlin[1]
1914 R. N. Williams II
1915 William Johnston
1916 R. N. William II
1917–18 R. Lindley Murray[2]
1919 William Johnston
1920–25 Bill Tilden
1926–27 Jean Rene Lacoste
1928 Henri Cochet
1929 Bill Tilden
1930 John H. Doeg
1931–32 Ellsworth Vines
1933–34 Fred J. Perry
1935 Wilmer L. Allison
1936 Fred J. Perry
1937–38 Don Budge
1939 Robert L. Riggs
1940 Donald McNeill
1941 Robert L. Riggs
1942 Fred Schroeder
1943 Joseph Hunt
1944–45 Frank Parker
1946–47 Jack Kramer
1948–49 Richard Gonzales
1950 Arthur Larsen
1951–52 Frank Sedgman
1953 Tony Trabert
1954 Vic Seixas
1955 Tony Trabert
1956 Ken Rosewall
1957 Mal Anderson
1958 Ashley Cooper
1959–60 Neale Fraser
1961 Roy Emerson
1962 Rod Laver
1963 Rafael Osuna
1964 Roy Emerson
1965 Manuel Santana

1966 Fred Stolle
1967 John Newcombe
1968 Arthur Ashe
1969 Rod Laver

OPEN
1968 Arthur Ashe
1969 Rod Laver
1970 Ken Rosewall
1971 Stan Smith
1972 Ilie Nastase
1973 John Newcombe
1974 Jimmy Connors
1975 Manuel Orantes
1976 Jimmy Connors
1977 Guillermo Vilas
1978 Jimmy Connors
1979 John McEnroe
1980–81 John McEnroe
1982 Jimmy Connors
1983 Jimmy Connors
1984 John McEnroe
1985–87 Ivan Lendl
1988 Mats Wilander
1989 Boris Becker
1990 Pete Sampras
1991 Stefan Edberg
1992 Stefan Edberg
1993 Pete Sampras
1994 Andre Agassi
1995 Pete Sampras
1996 Pete Sampras
1997–98 Patrick Rafter
1999 Andre Agassi
2000 Marat Safin
2001 Lleyton Hewitt
2002 Pete Sampras
2003 Andy Roddick

1. Challenge Round abandoned in 1912. 2. Patriotic Tournament in 1917.

SINGLES—WOMEN

NATIONAL
1887 Ellen F. Hansel
1888–89 Bertha Townsend
1890 Ellen C. Roosevelt
1891–92 Mabel E. Cahill
1893 Aline M. Terry
1894 Helen R. Helwig
1895 Juliette P. Atkinson
1896 Elisabeth H. Moore
1897–98 Juliette P. Atkinson
1899 Marion Jones
1900 Myrtle McAteer
1901 Elisabeth H. Moore
1902 Marion Jones
1903 Elisabeth H. Moore
1904 May Sutton
1905 Elisabeth H. Moore
1906 Helen Homans
1907 Evelyn Sears
1908 Maud Bargar-Wallach
1909–11 Hazel V. Hotchkiss
1912–14 Mary K. Browne
1915–18 Molla Bjurstedt
1919 Hazel Hotchkiss Wightman
1920–22 Molla Bjurstedt Mallory
1923–25 Helen N. Wills
1926 Molla B. Mallory
1927–29 Helen N. Wills
1930 Betty Nuthall
1931 Helen Wills Moody
1932–35 Helen Jacobs
1936 Alice Marble
1937 Anita Lizana
1938–40 Alice Marble
1941 Sarah Palfrey Cooke
1942–44 Pauline Betz
1945 Sarah Cooke
1946 Pauline Betz
1947 Louise Brough
1948–50 Margaret Osborne duPont
1951–53 Maureen Connolly
1954–55 Doris Hart
1956 Shirley Fry
1957–58 Althea Gibson
1959 Maria Bueno
1960–61 Darlene Hard
1962 Margaret Smith
1963–64 Maria Bueno
1965 Margaret Smith
1966 Maria Bueno
1967 Billie Jean King
1968–69 Margaret Smith Court[1]

OPEN
1968 Virginia Wade
1969–70 Margaret Court
1971–72 Billie Jean King
1973 Margaret Court
1974 Billie Jean King
1975–78 Chris Evert
1979 Tracy Austin
1980 Chris Evert-Lloyd
1981 Tracy Austin
1982 Chris Evert-Lloyd
1983–84 Martina Navratilova
1985 Hana Mandlikova
1986–87 Martina Navratilova
1988 Steffi Graf
1989 Steffi Graf
1990 Grabriela Sabatini
1991 Monica Seles
1992 Monica Seles
1993 Steffi Graf
1994 Arantxa Sanchez Vicario
1995 Steffi Graf
1996 Steffi Graf
1997 Martina Hingis
1998 Lindsay Davenport
1999 Serena Williams
2000–01 Venus Williams
2002 Serena Williams
2003 Justine Henin-Hardenne

1. With the inaugural of the Open Tournament in 1968, the United States Lawn Tennis Association held a championship at Longwood, Chestnut Hill, Mass., which barred contract professionals in 1968 and 1969.

DOUBLES—MEN

NATIONAL
1920 Bill Johnston–C. J. Griffin
1921–22 Bill Tilden–Vincent Richards
1923 Bill Tilden–B. I. C. Norton
1924 H. O. Kinsey–R. G. Kinsey
1925–26 Vincent Richards–R. N. Williams II
1927 Bill Tilden–Frank Hunter
1928 G. M. Lott, Jr.–V. Hennessy
1929–30 G. M. Lott, Jr.–J. H. Doeg
1931 W. L. Allison–John Van Ryn
1932 E. H. Vines, Jr.–Keith Gledh
1933–34 G. M. Lott, Jr.–L. R. Stoefen
1935 W. L. Allison–John Van Ryn
1936 Don Budge–Gene Mako
1937 G. von Cramm–H. Henkel
1938 Don Budge–Gene Mako
1939 A. K. Quist–J. E. Bromwich
1940–41 Jack Kramer–F. R. Schroeder
1942 Gardnar Mulloy–Bill Talbert
1943 Jack Kramer–Frank Parker
1944 Don McNeill–Bob Falkenburg
1945 Gardnar Mulloy–Bill Talbert
1946 Gardnar Mulloy–Bill Talbert
1947 Jack Kramer–Fred Schroeder
1948 Gardnar Mulloy–Bill Talbert
1949 John Bromwich–William Sidwell
1950 John Bromwich–Frank Sedgman
1951 Frank Sedgman–Ken McGregor
1952 Vic Seixas–Mervyn Rose
1953 Mervyn Rose–Rex Hartwig
1954 Vic Seixas–Tony Trabert
1955 Kosei Kamo–Atsushi Miyagi
1956 Lewis Hoad–Ken Rosewall
1957 Ashley Cooper–Neale Fraser
1958 Ham Richardson–Alex Olmedo
1959–60 Neale Fraser–Roy Emerson
1961 Chuck McKinley–Dennis Ralston
1962 Rafael Osuna–Antonio Palafox
1963–64 Chuck McKinley–Dennis Ralston
1965–66 Fred Stolle–Roy Emerson
1967 John Newcombe–Tony Roche
1968 Stan Smith–Bob Lutz[1]
1969 Richard Crealy–Allan Stone[1]

OPEN
1968 Stan Smith–Bob Lutz
1969 Fred Stolle–Ken Rosewall
1970 Nikki Pilic–Fred Barthes
1971 John Newcombe–Roger Taylor
1972 Cliff Drysdale–Roger Taylor
1973 John Newcombe–Owen Davidson
1974 Bob Lutz–Stan Smith
1975 Jimmy Connors–Ilie Nastase
1976 Marty Riessen–Tom Okker
1977 Frew McMillan–Bob Hewitt
1978 Bob Lutz–Stan Smith
1979 John McEnroe–Peter Fleming
1980 Stan Smith–Bob Lutz
1981 John McEnroe–Peter Fleming
1982 Kevin Curren–Steve Denton
1983 John McEnroe–Peter Fleming
1984 John Fitzgerald–Tomas Smid
1985 Ken Flach–Robert Seguso
1986 Andres Gomez–Slobodan Zivojinovic
1987 Stefan Edberg–Anders Jarryd
1988 Sergio Casal–Emilio Sanchez
1989 John McEnroe–Mark Woodforde
1990 Pieter Aldrich–Danie Visser
1991 John Fitzgerald–Anders Jarryd
1992 Jim Grabb–Richey Reneberg
1993 Ken Flach–Rick Leach

1994	Jacco Hingh–Paul Haarhuis
1995–96	Todd Woodbridge–Mark Woodforde
1997	Yevgeny Kafelnikov–Daniel Vacek
1998	Sandon Stolle–Cyril Zuk
1999	Sebastien Lareau–Alex O'Brien
2000	Lleyton Hewitt–Max Mirnyi
2001	Wayne Black–Kevin Ullyett
2002	Mahesh Bhupathi–Max Mirnyi
2003	Jonas Bjorkman–Todd Woodbridge

1. With the inaugural of the Open Tournament in 1968, the United States Lawn Tennis Association held a national championship at Longwood, Chestnut Hill, Mass., which barred contract professionals in 1968 and 1969.

DOUBLES—WOMEN

NATIONAL

1924	G. W. Wightman–Helen Wills
1925	Mary K. Browne–Helen Wills
1926	Elizabeth Ryan–Eleanor Goss
1927	L. A. Godfree–Ermyntrude Harvey
1928	Hazel Hotchkiss Wightman–Helen Wills
1929	Phoebe Watson–L. R. C. Michell
1930	Betty Nuthall–Sarah Palfrey
1931	Betty Nuthall–E. B. Wittingstall
1932	Helen Jacobs–Sarah Palfrey
1933	Betty Nuthall–Freda James
1934	Helen Jacobs–Sarah Palfrey
1935	Helen Jacobs–Sarah Palfrey Fabyan
1936	Marjorie G. Van Ryn–Carolin Babcock
1937–40	Sarah Palfrey Fabyan–Alice Marble
1941	Sarah Palfrey Cooke–Margaret Osborne
1942–47	A. Louise Brough–Margaret Osborne
1948–50	A. Louise Brough–Margaret O. duPont
1951–54	Doris Hart–Shirley Fry
1955–57	A. Louise Brough–Margaret O. duPont
1958–59	Darlene Hard–Jeanne Arth
1960	Darlene Hard–Maria Bueno
1961	Darlene Hard–Lesley Turner
1962	Darlene Hard–Maria Bueno
1963	Margaret Smith–Robyn Ebbern
1964	Karen Hantze Susman–Billie Jean Moffitt
1965	Nancy Richey–Carole Caldwell Graebner
1966	Nancy Richey–Maria Bueno
1967	Billie Jean King–Rosemary Casals
1968	Margaret Court–Maria Bueno[1]
1969	Margaret Court–Virginia Wade[1]

OPEN

1968	Maria Bueno–Margaret Court
1969	Darlene Hard–Francoise Durr
1970	Margaret Court–Judy Dalton
1971	Rosemary Casals–Judy Dalton
1972	Francoise Durr–Betty Stove
1973	Margaret Court–Virginia Wade
1974	Billie Jean King–Rosemary Casals
1975	Margaret Court–Virginia Wade
1976	Linky Boshoff–Ilana Kloss
1977	Martina Navratilova–Betty Stove
1978	Billie Jean King–Martina Navratilova
1979	Betty Stove–Wendy Turnbull
1980	Billie Jean King–Martina Navratilova
1981	Kathy Jordan–Anne Smith
1982	Rosemary Casals–Wendy Turnbull
1983–84	Martina Navratilova–Pam Shriver
1985	Claudia Khode-Kilsch–Helena Sukova
1986–87	Martina Navratilova–Pam Shriver
1988	Gigi Fernandez–Robin White
1989	Hana Mandlikova–Martina Navratilova
1990	Gigi Fernandez–Martina Navratilova
1991	Pam Shriver–Natalia Zvereva
1992	Gigi Fernandez–Natalia Zvereva
1993	Arantxa Sanchez Vicario–Helena Sukova
1994	Jana Novotna–Arantxa Sanchez Vicario
1995	Gigi Fernandez–Natasha Zvereva
1996	Gigi Fernandez–Natasha Zvereva
1997	Lindsay Davenport–Jana Novotna
1998	Martina Hingis–Jana Novotna
1999	Serena Williams–Venus Williams
2000	Julie-Halard Decugis–Ai Sugiyama
2001	Lisa Raymond–Renae Stubbs
2002–03	Virginia Ruano Pascual–Paola Suarez

1. With the inaugural of the Open Tournament in 1968, the United States Lawn Tennis Association held a national championship at Longwood, Chestnut Hill, Mass., which barred contract professionals in 1968 and 1969.

U.S. OPEN, 2003
(Flushing Meadow, N.Y., Aug. 25–Sept. 7, 2003)

Men's singles—Andy Roddick defeated Juan Carlos Ferrero, 6–3, 7–6, 6–3.

Women's singles—Justine Henin-Hardenne defeated Kim Clijsters, 7–5, 6–1.

Men's doubles—Jonas Bjorkman and Todd Woodbridge defeated Bob and Mike Bryan, 5–7, 6–0, 7–5.

Women's doubles—Virginia Ruano Pascual and Paola Suarez defeated Martina Navratilova and Svetlana Kuznetsova, 6–2, 6–2.

Mixed doubles—Katrina Srebotnik and Bob Bryan defeated Lina Krasnoroutskaya and Daniel Nestor, 5–7, 7–5, 7–6 (10–5).

BRITISH (WIMBLEDON) CHAMPIONS
(Amateur from inception in 1877 through 1967)
SINGLES—MEN

1908–09	Arthur Gore
1910–13	A. F. Wilding
1914	N. E. Brookes
1919	G. L. Patterson
1920–21	Bill Tilden
1922	G. L. Patterson
1923	William Johnston
1924	Jean Borotra
1925	Rene Lacoste
1926	Jean Borotra
1927	Henri Cochet
1928	Rene Lacoste
1929	Jean Cochet
1930	Bill Tilden
1931	S. B. Wood
1932	Ellsworth Vines
1933	J. H. Crawford
1934–36	Fred Perry
1937–38	Don Budge
1939	Robert L. Riggs
1946	Yvon Petra
1947	Jack Kramer
1948	R. Falkenburg
1949	Fred Schroeder
1950	Budge Patty
1951	Richard Savitt
1952	Frank Sedgman
1953	Vic Siexas
1954	Jaroslav Drobny
1955	Tony Trabert
1956–57	Lewis Hoad
1958	Ashley Cooper

1959	Alex Olmedo
1960	Neale Fraser
1961–62	Rod Laver
1963	Chuck McKinley
1964–65	Roy Emerson
1966	Manuel Santana
1967	John Newcombe
1968–69	Rod Laver
1970–71	John Newcombe
1972	Stan Smith
1973	Jan Kodes
1974	Jimmy Connors
1975	Arthur Ashe
1976–80	Bjorn Borg
1981	John McEnroe
1982	Jimmy Connors
1983–84	John McEnroe
1985–86	Boris Becker
1987	Pat Cash
1988	Stefan Edberg
1989	Boris Becker
1990	Stefan Edberg
1991	Michael Stich
1992	Andre Agassi
1993–95	Pete Sampras
1996	Richard Krajicek
1997–2000	Pete Sampras
2001	Goran Ivanisevic
2002	Lleyton Hewitt
2003	Roger Federer

SINGLES—WOMEN

1919–23	Suzanne Lenglen
1924	Kathleen McKane
1925	Suzanne Lenglen
1926	Kathleen Godfree
1927–29	Helen Wills
1930	Helen Wills Moody
1931	Cilly Aussem
1932–33	Helen Wills Moody
1934	D. E. Round
1935	Helen Wills Moody
1936	Helen Jacobs
1937	D. E. Round
1938	Helen Wills Moody
1939	Alice Marble
1946	Pauline M. Betz
1947	Margaret Osborne
1948–50	A. Louise Brough
1951	Doris Hart
1952–54	Maureen Connolly
1955	A. Louise Brough
1956	Shirley Fry
1957–58	Althea Gibson
1959–60	Maria Bueno
1961	Angela Mortimer
1962	Karen Susman
1963	Margaret Smith
1964	Maria Bueno
1965	Margaret Smith
1966–68	Billie Jean King
1969	Ann Jones
1970	Margaret Court
1971	Evonne Goolagong
1972–73	Billie Jean King
1974	Chris Evert
1975	Billie Jean King
1976	Chris Evert
1977	Virginia Wade
1978–79	Martina Navratilova
1980	Evonne Goolagong Cawley
1981	Chris Evert-Lloyd
1982–87	Martina Navratilova
1988–89	Steffi Graf
1990	Martina Navratilova
1991–93	Steffi Graf
1994	Conchita Martinez
1995–96	Steffi Graf
1997	Martina Hingis
1998	Jana Novotna
1999	Lindsay Davenport
2000–01	Venus Williams
2002–03	Serena Williams

DOUBLES—MEN

1953	K. Rosewall–L. Hoad
1954	R. Hartwig–M. Rose
1955	R. Hartwig–L. Hoad
1956	L. Hoad–K. Rosewall
1957	Gardnar Mulloy–Budge Patty
1958	Sven Davidson–Ulf Schmidt
1959	Roy Emerson–Neale Fraser
1960	Dennis Ralston–Rafael Osuna
1961	Roy Emerson–Neale Fraser
1962	Fred Stolle–Bob Hewitt
1963	Rafael Osuna–Antonio Palafox
1964	Fred Stolle–Bob Hewitt
1965	John Newcombe–Tony Roche
1966	John Newcombe–Ken Fletcher
1967	Bob Hewitt–Frew McMillan
1968–70	John Newcombe–Tony Roche
1971	Rod Laver–Roy Emerson
1972	Bob Hewitt–Frew McMillan
1973	Jimmy Connors–Ilie Nastase
1974	John Newcombe–Tony Roche
1975	Vitas Gerulaitis–Sandy Mayer
1976	Brian Gottfried–Raul Ramirez
1977	Ross Case–Geoff Masters
1978	Fred McMillan–Bob Hewitt
1979	Peter Fleming–John McEnroe
1980	Peter McNamara–Paul McNamee
1981	John McEnroe–Peter Fleming
1982	Paul McNamee–Peter McNamara
1983–84	John McEnroe–Peter Fleming
1985	Heinz Gunthardt–Balazs Taroczy
1986	Joakim Nystrom–Mats Wilander
1987	Ken Flach–Robert Seguso
1988	Ken Flach–Robert Seguso
1989	John Fitzgerald–Anders Jarryd
1990	Rick Leach–Jim Pugh
1991	Anders Jarryd–John Fitzgerald
1992	John McEnroe–Michael Stich
1993–97	Todd Woodbridge–Mark Woodforde
1998	Jacco Eltingh–Paul Haarhuis
1999	Mahesh Bhupathi–Leander Paes
2000	Todd Woodbridge–Mark Woodforde
2001	Donald Johnson–Jared Palmer
2002–03	Todd Woodbridge–Jonas Bjorkman

DOUBLES—WOMEN

1956	Althea Gibson–Angela Buxton
1957	Althea Gibson–Darlene Hard
1958	Althea Gibson–Maria Bueno
1959	Darlene Hard–Jeanne Arth
1960	Darlene Hard–Maria Bueno
1961	Karen Hantze–Billie Jean Moffitt
1962	Karen Hantze Susman–Billie Jean Moffitt
1963	Darlene Hard–Maria Bueno
1964	Margaret Smith–Les Turnerley
1965	Billie Jean Moffitt–Maria Bueno
1966	Nancy Richey–Maria Bueno
1967–68	Billie Jean King–Rosemary Casals
1969	Margaret Court–Judy Tegart
1970–71	Billie Jean King–Rosemary Casals
1972	Billie Jean King–Betty Stove
1973	Billie Jean King–Rosemary Casals
1974	Evonne Goolagong–Peggy Michel
1975	Ann Kiyomura–Kazuko Sawamatsu
1976	Chris Evert–Martina Navratilova
1977	Helen Cawley–JoAnne Russell
1978	Wendy Turnbull–Kerry Reid
1979	Billie Jean King–Martina Navratilova
1980	Kathy Jordan–Anne Smith
1981	Martina Navratilova–Pam Shriver
1982–84	Pam Shriver–Martina Navratilova
1985	Kathy Jordan–Elizabeth Smylie
1986	Pam Shriver–Martina Navratilova
1987	Claudia Khode-Kilsch–Helena Sukova
1988	Steffi Graf–Gabriela Sabatini
1989	Jana Novotna–Helena Sukova
1990	Jana Novotna–Helena Sukova
1991	Pam Shriver–Natalia Zvereva
1992	Gigi Fernandez–Natalia Zvereva
1993	Gigi Fernandez–Natalia Zvereva
1994	Gigi Fernandez–Natalia Zvereva
1995	Jana Novotna–Arantxa Sanchez Vicario
1996	Martina Hingis–Helena Sukova
1997	Gigi Fernandez–Natasha Zvereva

1998	Martina Hingis–Jana Novotna	2000	Venus Williams–Serena Williams	2002	Serena Williams–Venus Williams
1999	Lindsay Davenport–Corina Morariu	2001	Lisa Raymond–Rennae Stubbs	2003	Kim Clijsters–Ai Sugiyama

WIMBLEDON CHAMPIONS, 2003

(Wimbledon, England, June 23–July 6, 2003)

Men's singles—Roger Federer defeated Mark Philippoussis, 7–6 (5), 6–2, 7–6 (3).

Women's singles—Serena Williams defeated Venus Williams, 4–6, 6–5, 6–2.

Men's doubles—Todd Woodbridge and Jonas Bjorkman defeated Mahesh Bhupathi and Max Mirnyi, 3–6, 6–3, 7–6 (4), 6–3.

Women's doubles—Kim Clijsters and Ai Sugiyama defeated Virginia Ruano Pascual and Paola Suarez, 6–4, 6–4.

Mixed doubles—Leander Paes and Martina Navratilova defeated Andy Ram and Anastassia Rodionova, 6–3, 6–3.

OTHER 2003 GRAND SLAM CHAMPIONS

French Open

(Paris, May 26–June 8, 2003)

Men's singles—Juan Carlos Ferrero defeated Martin Verkerk, 6–1, 6–3, 6–2.

Women's singles—Justine Henin-Hardenne defeated Kim Clijsters, 6–0, 6.4.

Men's doubles—Bob Bryan and Mike Bryan defeated Paul Haarhuis and Yevgeny Kafelnikov, 7–6 (7–3), 6–3.

Women's doubles—Kim Clijsters and Ai Sugiyama defeated Virginia Ruano Pascual and Paola Suarez, 6–7)5–7), 6–2, 9–7).

Mixed doubles—Mike Bryan and Lisa Raymond defeated Elena Likhovtseva abnd Mahesh Bhupathi, 6–3, 6–4.

Australian Open

(Melbourne, Australia, Jan. 13–26, 2003)

Men's singles—Andre Agassi defeated Rainer Schuettler, 6–2, 6–2, 6–1.

Women's singles—Serna Williams defeated Venus Williams, 7–6 (7–4), 3–6, 6–4.

Men's doubles—Michael Liodra and Fabrice Santoro defeated Mark Knowles and Daniel Nestor, 6–4, 3–6, 6–3.

Women's doubles—Serena Williams and Venus Williams defeated Virginia Ruano Pascual and Paola Suarez, 4–6, 6–4, 6–3.

Mixed doubles—Leander Paes and Martina Navratilova defeated Todd Woodbridge and Eleni Daniilidou, 6–4, 7–5.

OTHER WTA TOURNAMENTS, 2003

Tournament	Singles champion
adidas International, Sydney, Australia	Kim Clijsters
Toray Pan Pacific Open, Tokyo, Japan	Lindsay Davenport
Open Gaz de France, Paris, France	Serena Williams
Proximus Diamond Games, Antwerp, Belgium	Venus Williams
Dubai Duty Free, UAE	Justine Henin-Hardenne
State Farm Women's Tennis Classic, Scottsdale, Ariz.	Ai Sugiyama
Pacific Life Open, Indian Wells, Calif.	Kim Clijsters
NASDAQ-100 Open, Miami, Fla.	Serena Williams
Family Circle Cup, Charleston, S.C.	Justine Henin-Hardenne
Bausch & Lomb Championships, Amelia Island, Fla.	Elena Dementieva
J&S Cup, Warsaw, Poland	Amelie Mauresmo
MasterCard German Open, Berlin, Germany	Justine Henin-Hardenne
Telecom Italia Masters, Rome, Italy	Kim Clijsters
Open de España, Madrid, Spain	Chanda Rubin
Hastings Direct Int'l Championships, Eastbourne, England	Chanda Rubin
Bank of the West Classic, Stanford, Calif.	Kim Clijsters
Acura Classic, San Diego, Calif.	Justine Henin-Hardenne
Idea Prokom Open, Sopot, Poland	Anna Pistolesi

Source: www.wtatour.com.

WOMEN'S TOP 5 MONEY WINNERS, 2003

1.	Justine Henin-Hardenne	$2,985,764
2.	Kim Clijsters	2,785,264
3.	Serena Williams	2,249,038
4.	Lindsay Davenport	1,278,593
5.	Venus Williams	998,222

As of Sept. 15, 2003. *Source:* www.wtatour.com.

OTHER ATP TOURNAMENTS, 2003

Tournament	Singles champion
Marseille, France	Roger Federer
Rotterdam, Netherlands	Max Mirnyi
Memphis, Tenn.	Taylor Dent
Acapulco, Mexico	Agustin Calleri
Dubai, UAE	Roger Federer
Indian Wells, Calif.	Lleyton Hewitt
Miami, Fla.	Andre Agassi
Monte Carlo, Monaco	Juan Carlos Ferrero
Barcelona, Spain	Carlos Moya
Rome, Italy	Felix Mantilla
Hamburg, Germany	Guillermo Coria
Halle, Germany	Roger Federer
London/Queen's Club, England	Andy Roddick
Gstaad, Switzerland	Jiri Novak
Stuttgart, Germany	Guillermo Coria
Indianapolis, Ind.	Andy Roddick
Kitzbuhel, Austria	Guillermo Coria
Washington, DC	Tim Henman
Montreal, Canada	Andy Roddick
Cincinnati, Ohio	Andy Roddick

Source: www.atptennis.com.

MEN'S TOP 5 MONEY WINNERS, 2003

1.	Andy Roddick	$2,705,662
2.	Juan Carlos Ferrero	2,413,330
3.	Roger Federer	2,147,580
4.	Andre Agassi	1,830,929
5.	Guillermo Coria	1,588,982

As of Sept. 15, 2003. *Source:* www.atptennisr.com.

Harness Racing

Oliver Wendell Holmes, the famous Autocrat of the Breakfast Table, wrote that the running horse was a gambling toy but the trotting horse was useful and, furthermore, "horse-racing is not a republican institution; horse-trotting is." Oliver Wendell Holmes was a born-and-bred New Englander, and New England was the nursery of the harness racing sport in America. Pacers and trotters were matters of local pride and prejudice in colonial New England, and, shortly after the Revolution, the Messenger and Justin Morgan strains produced many winners in harness racing "matches" along the turnpikes of New York, Connecticut, Rhode Island, Massachusetts, Vermont, and New Hampshire.

There was English thoroughbred blood in Messenger and Justin Morgan, and, many years later, it was blended in Rysdyk's Hambletonian, foaled in 1849. Hambletonian was not particularly fast under harness but his descendants have had almost a monopoly of prizes, titles, and records in the harness racing game. Hambletonian was purchased as a foal with its dam for a total of $124 by William Rysdyk of Goshen, N.Y., and made a modest fortune for the purchaser.

Trotters and pacers often were raced under saddle in the old days, and, in fact, the custom still survives in some places in Europe. Dexter, the great trotter that lowered the mile record from 2:19¾ to 2:17 ¼ in 1867, was said to handle just as well under saddle as when pulling a sulky. But as sulkies were lightened in weight and improved in design, trotting under saddle became less common and finally faded out in this country.

HISTORY OF TRADITIONAL HARNESS RACING STAKES

THE HAMBLETONIAN

Year	Winner	Driver	Best time	Total purse
1967	Speedy Streak	Del Cameron	2:00	$122,650
1968	Nevele Pride	Stanley Dancer	1:59.2	116,190
1969	Lindy's Pride	Howard Beissinger	1:57 .3	124,910
1970	Timothy T.	John Simpson, Jr.	1:58.2[1]	143,630
1971	Speedy Crown	Howard Beissinger	1:57.2	129,770
1972	Super Bowl	Stanley Dancer	1:56.2	119,090
1973	Flirth	Ralph Baldwin	1:57.1	144,710
1974	Christopher T	Billy Haughton	1:58.3	160,150
1975	Bonefish	Stanley Dancer	1:59[2]	232,192
1976	Steve Lobell	Billy Haughton	1:56.2	263,524
1977	Green Speed	Billy Haughton	1:55.3	284,131
1978	Speedy Somolli	Howard Beissinger	1:55[3]	241,280
1979	Legend Hanover	George Sholty	1:56.1	300,000
1980	Burgomeister	Billy Haughton	1:56.3	293,570
1981	Shiaway St. Pat	Ray Remmen	2:01.1[4]	838,000
1982	Speed Bowl	Tommy Haughton	1:56.4	875,750
1983	Duenna	Stanley Dancer	1:57.2	1,000,000
1984	Historic Freight	Ben Webster	1:56.2[5]	1,219,000
1985	Prakas	Bill O'Donnell	1:54.3	1,272,000
1986	Nuclear Kosmos	Ulf Thoresen	1:55.2[6]	1,172,082
1987	Mack Lobell	John Campbell	1:53.3	1,046,300
1988	Armbro Goal	John Campbell	1:54.3	1,156,800
1989	Park Avenue Joe and Probe*	Ron Wayples Bill Fahy	1:54.3	1,131,000
1990	Harmonious	John Campbell	1:54.1	1,346,000
1991	Giant Victory	Jack Moiseyev	1:54.4	1,238,000
1992	Alf Palema	Mickey McNichol	1:56.2[7]	1,288,000
1993	American Winner	Ron Pierce	1:53.1	1,200,000
1994	Victory Dream	Mike Lachance	1:53.4	1,200,000
1995	Tagliabue	John Campbell	1:54.4	1,200,000
1996	Continentalvictory	Mike Lachance	1:52.1	1,200,000
1997	Malabar Man	Malvern Burroughs	1:53.4	1,000,000
1998	Muscles Yankee	John Campbell	1:52.2	1,000,000
1999	Self Possessed	Mike Lachance	1:51.3	1,000,000
2000	Yankee Paco	Travor Ritchie	1:53.2	1,000,000
2001	Scarlet Knight	Stefan Melander	1:53.4	1,000,000
2002	Chip Chip Hooray	Eric Ledford	1:53.3	1,000,000
2003	Amigo Hall	Mike Lachance	1:54.0	1,000,000

Three-year-old trotters. One mile. Guy McKinney won first race at Syracuse in 1926; held at Goshen, N.Y., 1930–1942, 1944–1956; at Yonkers, N.Y., 1943; at Du Quoin, Ill., 1957–1980. Since 1981, the race has been held at The Meadowlands in East Rutherford, N.J. *Cowinners. Fastest heat won by: 1. By Formal Notice. 2. By Yankee Bambino. 3. By Speedy Somolli and Florida Pro. 4. By Super Juan. 5. Delvin G. Hanover. 6. Royal Prestige. 7. Baltic Sonata.

LITTLE BROWN JUG

Year	Winner	Driver	Best time	Total purse
1967	Best of All	Jim Hackett	1:59[1]	$84,778
1968	Rum Customer	Billy Haughton	1:59.3	104,226
1969	Laverne Hanover	Billy Haughton	2:00.2	109,731
1970	Most Happy Fella	Stanley Dancer	1:57.1	100,110
1971	Nansemond	Herve Filion	1:57.2	102,994
1972	Strike Out	Keith Waples	1:56.3	104,916
1973	Melvin's Woe	Joe O'Brien	1:57.3	120,000
1974	Ambro Omaha	Billy Haughton	1:57	132,630
1975	Seatrain	Ben Webster	1:57[2]	147,813
1976	Keystone Ore	Stanley Dancer	1:56.4[3]	153,799
1977	Governor Skipper	John Chapman	1:56.1	150,000
1978	Happy Escort	William Popfinger	1:55.2[4]	186,760
1979	Hot Hitter	Herve Filion	1:55.3	226,455
1980	Niatross	Clint Galbraith	1:54.4	207,361
1981	Fan Hanover	Glen Garnsey	1:56[5]	243,799
1982	Merger	John Campbell	1:56.3	328,900
1983	Ralph Hanover	Ron Waples	1:55.3	358,800
1984	Colt 46	Norman Boring	1:53.3	366,717
1985	Nihilator	Bill O'Donnell	1:52.1	350,730
1986	Barberry Spur	Bill O'Donnell	1:52.4	407,684
1987	Jaguar Spur	Richard Stillings	1:55.3	412,330
1988	B.J. Scoot	Mike Lachance	1:52.3	486,050
1989	Goalie Jeff	Mike Lachance	1:54.1	500,200
1990	Beach Towel	Ray Remmen	1:53.3	253,049
1991	Precious Bunny	Jack Moiseyev	1:54.1	575,150
1992	Fake Left	Ron Waples	1:54.2	556,210
1993	Life Sign	John Campbell	1:52	465,500
1994	Magical Mike	Mike Lachance	1:52.3	512,830
1995	Nick's Fantasy	John Campbell	1:51.2	543,670
1996	Armbro Operative	Jack Moiyesev	1:52.3	542,220
1997	Western Dreamer	Mike Lachance	1:51.1	605,210
1998	Shady Character	Ron Pierce	1:52.3	566,630
1999	Blissfull Hall	Ron Pierce	1:55.3	543,980
2000	Astreos	Chris Christoforou	1:55.3	547,972
2001	Bettor's Delight	Mike Lachance	1:51.4	646,050
2002	Million Dollar Cam	Luc Ouellette	1:50.2	618,625
2003	No Pan Intended	David Miller	1:50.0	605,050

Three-year-old pacers. One Mile. Raced at Delaware County Fair Grounds, Delaware, Ohio. 1. By Nardin's Byrd. 2. By Albert's Star. 3. By Armbro Ranger. 4. By Falcon Almahurst. 5. By Seahawk Hanover.

HARNESS HORSE OF THE YEAR

1959	Bye Bye Byrd, Pacer
1960–61	Adios Butler, Pacer
1962	Su Mac Lad, Trotter
1963	Speedy Scot, Trotter
1964–66	Bret Hanover, Pacer
1967–69	Nevele Pride, Trotter
1970	Fresh Yankee, Trotter
1971–72	Albatross, Pacer
1973	Sir Dalrae, Pacer
1974	Delmonica Hanover, Trotter
1975	Savoir, Trotter
1976	Keystone Ore, Pacer
1977	Green Speed, Trotter
1978	Abercrombie, Pacer
1979–80	Niatross, Pacer
1981	Fan Hanover, Pacer
1982–83	Cam Fella, Pacer
1984	Fancy Crown, Trotter
1985	Nihilator, Trotter
1986	Forrest Skipper
1987–88	Mack Lobell
1989	Matt's Scooter
1990	Beach Towell
1991	Precious Bunny
1992	Artsplace
1993	Staying Together
1994	Cam's Card Shark
1995	CR Kay Suzie
1996	Continentalvictory
1997	Malabar Man
1998–99	Moni Maker
2000	Gallo Blue Chip
2001	Bunny Lake
2002	Real Desire

Chosen in poll conducted by U.S. Trotting Association in conjunction with the U.S. Harness Writers Association.

Golf

It may be that golf originated in Holland—historians believe it did—but certainly Scotland fostered the game and is famous for it. In fact, in 1457 the Scottish Parliament, disturbed because football and golf had lured young Scots from the more soldierly exercise of archery, passed an ordinance that "futeball and golf be utterly cryit doun and nocht usit." James I and Charles I of the royal line of Stuarts were golf enthusiasts, whereby the game came to be known as "the royal and ancient game of golf."

The golf balls used in the early games were leather-covered and stuffed with feathers. Clubs of all kinds were fashioned by hand to suit individual players. The great step in spreading the game came with the change from the feather ball to the gutta-percha ball about 1850. In 1860, formal competition began with the establishment of an annual tournament for the British Open championship. There are records of "golf clubs" in the United States as far back as colonial days but no proof of actual play before John Reid and some friends laid out six holes on the Reid lawn in Yonkers, N.Y., in 1888 and played there with golf balls and clubs brought over from Scotland by Robert Lockhart. This group then formed the St. Andrews Golf Club of Yonkers, and golf was established in this country.

However, it remained a rather sedate and almost aristocratic pastime until a 20-year-old ex-caddy, Francis Ouimet of Boston, defeated two great British professionals, Harry Vardon and Ted Ray, in the United States Open championship at Brookline, Mass., in 1913. This feat put the game and Francis Ouimet on the front pages of the newspapers and stirred a wave of enthusiasm for the sport. The greatest feat so far in golf history is that of Robert Tyre Jones, Jr., of Atlanta, who won the British Open, the British Amateur, the U.S. Open, and the U.S. Amateur titles in one year, 1930.

THE MASTERS TOURNAMENT WINNERS

Augusta National Golf Club, Augusta, Ga.

Year	Winner	Score	Year	Winner	Score	Year	Winner	Score
1934	Horton Smith	284	1959	Art Wall, Jr.	284	1982	Craig Stadler[1]	284
1935	Gene Sarazen[1]	282	1960	Arnold Palmer	282	1983	Severiano Ballesteros	280
1936	Horton Smith	285	1961	Gary Player	280	1984	Ben Crenshaw	277
1937	Byron Nelson	283	1962	Arnold Palmer[1]	280	1985	Bernhard Langer	282
1938	Henry Picard	285	1963	Jack Nicklaus	286	1986	Jack Nicklaus	279
1939	Ralph Guldahl	279	1964	Arnold Palmer	276	1987	Larry Mize[1]	285
1940	Jimmy Demaret	280	1965	Jack Nicklaus	271	1988	Sandy Lyle	281
1941	Craig Wood	280	1966	Jack Nicklaus[1]	288	1989	Nick Faldo[1]	283
1942	Byron Nelson[1]	280	1967	Gay Brewer, Jr.	280	1990	Nick Faldo	278
1943–45	No Tournaments		1968	Bob Goalby	277	1991	Ian Woosnam	277
1946	Herman Keiser	282	1969	George Archer	281	1992	Fred Couples	275
1947	Jimmy Demaret	281	1970	Billy Casper[1]	279	1993	Bernard Langer	277
1948	Claude Harmon	279	1971	Charles Coody	279	1994	Jose Maria Olazabal	279
1949	Sam Snead	282	1972	Jack Nicklaus	286	1995	Ben Crenshaw	274
1950	Jimmy Demaret	283	1973	Tommy Aaron	283	1996	Nick Faldo	276
1951	Ben Hogan	280	1974	Gary Player	278	1997	Tiger Woods	270
1952	Sam Snead	286	1975	Jack Nicklaus	276	1998	Mark O'Meara	279
1953	Ben Hogan	274	1976	Ray Floyd	271	1999	Jose Maria Olazabal	280
1954	Sam Snead[1]	289	1977	Tom Watson	276	2000	Vijay Singh	278
1955	Cary Middlecoff	279	1978	Gary Player	277	2001	Tiger Woods	272
1956	Jack Burke	289	1979	Fuzzy Zoeller[1]	280	2002	Tiger Woods	276
1957	Doug Ford	283	1980	Severiano Ballesteros	275	2003	Mike Weir	281
1958	Arnold Palmer	284	1981	Tom Watson	280			

1. Winner in playoff.

U.S. OPEN CHAMPIONS

Year	Winner	Score	Where played	Year	Winner	Score	Where played
1895	Horace Rawlins	173	Newport	1912	John McDermott	294	Buffalo
1896	James Foulis	152	Shinnecock Hills	1913	Francis Ouimet[1, 2]	304	Brookline
1897	Joe Lloyd	162	Chicago	1914	Walter Hagen	290	Midlothian
1898[3]	Fred Herd	328	Myopia	1915	Jerome D. Travers[2]	297	Baltusrol
1899	Willie Smith	315	Baltimore	1916	Charles Evans, Jr.[2]	286	Minikahda
1900	Harry Vardon	313	Chicago	1917–18	No tournaments[4]		
1901	Willie Anderson[1]	331	Myopia	1919	Walter Hagen[2]	301	Brae Burn
1902	Laurie Auchterlonie	307	Garden City	1920	Edward Ray	295	Inverness
1903	Willie Anderson[1]	307	Baltusrol	1921	Jim Barnes	289	Columbia
1904	Willie Anderson	303	Glen View	1922	Gene Sarazen	288	Skokie
1905	Willie Anderson	314	Myopia	1923	R. T. Jones, Jr.[1, 2]	296	Inwood
1906	Alex Smith	295	Onwentsia	1924	Cyril Walker	297	Oakland Hills
1907	Alex Ross	302	Philadelphia	1925	Willie Macfarlane[1]	291	Worcester
1908	Fred McLeod[1]	322	Myopia	1926	R. T. Jones, Jr.[2]	293	Scioto
1909	George Sargent	290	Englewood	1927	Tommy Armour[1]	301	Oakmont
1910	Alex Smith[1]	298	Philadelphia	1928	Johnny Farrell[1]	294	Olympia Fields
1911	John McDermott[1]	307	Chicago	1929	R. T. Jones, Jr.[1, 2]	294	Winged Foot

Year	Winner	Score	Where played
1930	R. T. Jones, Jr.[2]	287	Interlachen
1931	Billy Burke[1]	292	Inverness
1932	Gene Sarazen	286	Fresh Meadow
1933	John Goodman[2]	287	North Shore
1934	Olin Dutra	293	Merion
1935	Sam Parks, Jr.	299	Oakmont
1936	Tony Manero	282	Baltusrol
1937	Ralph Guldahl	281	Oakland Hills
1938	Ralph Guldahl	284	Cherry Hills
1939	Byron Nelson[1]	284	Philadelphia
1940	Lawson Little[1]	287	Canterbury
1941	Craig Wood	284	Colonial
1942–45	No tournaments[5]		
1946	Lloyd Mangrum[1]	284	Canterbury
1947	Lew Worsham[1]	282	St. Louis
1948	Ben Hogan	276	Riviera
1949	Cary Middlecoff	286	Medinah
1950	Ben Hogan[1]	287	Merion
1951	Ben Hogan	287	Oakland Hills
1952	Julius Boros	281	Northwood
1953	Ben Hogan	283	Oakmont
1954	Ed Furgol	284	Baltusrol
1955	Jack Fleck[1]	287	Olympic
1956	Cary Middlecoff	281	Oak Hill
1957	Dick Mayer[1]	298	Inverness
1958	Tommy Bolt	283	Southern Hills
1959	Bill Casper, Jr.	282	Winged Foot
1960	Arnold Palmer	280	Cherry Hills
1961	Gene Littler	281	Oakland Hills
1962	Jack Nicklaus[1]	283	Oakmont
1963	Julius Boros[1]	293	Country Club
1964	Ken Venturi	278	Congressional
1965	Gary Player[1]	282	Bellerive
1966	Bill Casper[1]	278	Olympic
1967	Jack Nicklaus	275	Baltusrol
1968	Lee Trevino	275	Oak Hill
1969	Orville Moody	281	Champions G.C.
1970	Tony Jacklin	281	Hazeltine
1971	Lee Trevino[1]	280	Merion
1972	Jack Nicklaus	290	Pebble Beach
1973	Johnny Miller	279	Oakmont
1974	Hale Irwin	287	Winged Foot
1975	Lou Graham[1]	287	Medinah
1976	Jerry Pate	277	Atlanta A.C.
1977	Hubert Green	278	Southern Hills
1978	Andy North	285	Cherry Hills
1979	Hale Irwin	284	Inverness
1980	Jack Nicklaus	272	Baltusrol
1981	David Graham	273	Merion
1982	Tom Watson	282	Pebble Beach
1983	Larry Nelson	280	Oakmont
1984	Fuzzy Zoeller[1]	276	Winged Foot
1985	Andy North	279	Oakland Hills
1986	Ray Floyd	279	Shinnecock Hills
1987	Scott Simpson	277	Olympic Golf Club
1988	Curtis Strange[1]	278	The Country Club
1989	Curtis Strange	278	Oak Hill Country Club
1990	Hale Irwin[1]	280	Medinah C.C.
1991	Payne Stewart[1]	282	Hazeltine
1992	Tom Kite	285	Pebble Beach
1993	Lee Janzen	272	Baltusrol
1994	Ernie Els	279	Oakmont
1995	Corey Pavin	280	Shinnecock Hills
1996	Steve Jones	278	Oakland Hills
1997	Ernie Els	276	Congressional C.C.
1998	Lee Janzen	280	Olympic Country Club
1999	Payne Stewart	279	Pinehurst
2000	Tiger Woods	272	Pebble Beach
2001	Retief Goosen	276	Southern Hills
2002	Tiger Woods	277	Bethpage Black
2003	Jim Furyk	272	Olympia Fields

1. Winner in playoff. 2. Amateur. 3. In 1898, competition was extended to 72 holes. 4. In 1917, Jock Hutchison, with a 292, won an Open Patriotic Tournament for the benefit of the American Red Cross at Whitemarsh Valley Country Club. 5. In 1942, Ben Hogan, with a 271, won a Hale American National Open Tournament for the benefit of the Navy Relief Society and USO at Ridgemoor Country Club.

U.S. AMATEUR CHAMPIONS

1895	Charles B. Macdonald
1896–97	H. J. Whigham
1898	Findlay S. Douglas
1899	H. M. Harriman
1900–01	Walter J. Travis
1902	Louis N. James
1903	Walter J. Travis
1904–05	H. Chandler Egan
1906	Eben M. Byers
1907–08	Jerome D. Travers
1909	Robert A. Gardner
1910	W. C. Fownes, Jr.
1911	Harold H. Hilton
1912–13	Jerome D. Travers
1914	Francis Ouimet
1915	Robert A. Gardner
1916	Charles Evans, Jr.
1919	S. D. Herron
1920	Charles Evans, Jr.
1921	Jesse P. Guilford
1922	Jess W. Sweetser
1923	Max R. Marston
1924–25	R. T. Jones, Jr.
1926	George Von Elm
1927–28	R. T. Jones, Jr.
1929	H. R. Johnston
1930	R. T. Jones, Jr.
1931	Francis Ouimet
1932	Ross Somerville
1933	G. T. Dunlap, Jr.
1934–35	Lawson Little
1936	John W. Fischer
1937	John Goodman
1938	Willie Turnesa
1939	Marvin H. Ward
1940	R. D. Chapman
1941	Marvin H. Ward
1946	Ted Bishop
1947	Robert Riegel
1948	Willie Turnesa
1949	Charles Coe
1950	Sam Urzetta
1951	Billy Maxwell
1952	Jack Westland
1953	Gene Littler
1954	Arnold Palmer
1955–56	Harvie Ward
1957	Hillman Robbins
1958	Charles Coe
1959	Jack Nicklaus
1960	Deane Beman
1961	Jack Nicklaus
1962	Labron Harris, Jr.
1963	Deane Beman
1964	Bill Campbell
1965[2]	Robert Murphy, Jr.
1966	Gary Cowan[1]
1967	Bob Dickson
1968	Bruce Fleisher
1969	Steven Melnyk
1970	Lanny Wadkins
1971	Gary Cowan
1972	Vinny Giles 3d
1973[3]	Craig Stadler
1974	Jerry Pate
1975	Fred Ridley
1976	Bill Sander
1977	John Fought
1978	John Cook
1979	Mark O'Meara
1980	Hal Sutton
1981	Nathaniel Crosby
1982	Jay Sigel
1983	Jay Sigel
1984	Scott Verplank
1985	Sam Randolph
1986	Buddy Alexander
1987	Bill Mayfair
1988	Eric Meeks
1989	Chris Patton
1990	Phil Mickelson
1991	Mitch Voges
1992	Justin Leonard
1993	John Harris
1994–96	Tiger Woods
1997	Matthew Kuchar
1998	Hank Kuehne
1999	David Gossett
2000	Jeff Quinney
2001	Bubba Dickerson
2002	Ricky Barnes
2003	Nick Flanagan

1. Winner in playoff. 2. Tourney switched to medal play through 1972. 3. Return to match play.

U.S. PGA CHAMPIONS

1916	Jim Barnes
1919	Jim Barnes
1920	Jock Hutchison
1921	Walter Hagen
1922–23	Gene Sarazen
1924–27	Walter Hagen
1928–29	Leo Diegel
1930	Tommy Armour
1931	Tom Creavy
1932	Olin Dutra
1933	Gene Sarazen
1934	Paul Runyan
1935	Johnny Revolta
1936–37	Denny Shute
1938	Paul Runyan
1939	Henry Picard
1940	Byron Nelson
1941	Victor Ghezzi
1942	Sam Snead
1944	Bob Hamilton
1945	Byron Nelson
1946	Ben Hogan
1947	Jim Ferrier
1948	Ben Hogan
1949	Sam Snead
1950	Chandler Harper
1951	Sam Snead
1952	Jim Turnesa
1953	Walter Burkemo
1954	Chick Harbert
1955	Doug Ford
1956	Jack Burke, Jr.
1957	Lionel Hebert
1958[2]	Dow Finsterwald
1959	Bob Rosburg
1960	Jay Hebert
1961	Jerry Barber[1]
1962	Gary Player
1963	Jack Nicklaus
1964	Bobby Nichols
1965	Dave Marr
1966	Al Geiberger
1967	Don January[1]
1968	Julius Boros
1969	Ray Floyd
1970	Dave Stockton
1971	Jack Nicklaus
1972	Gary Player
1973	Jack Nicklaus
1974	Lee Trevino
1975	Jack Nicklaus
1976	Dave Stockton
1977	Lanny Wadkins[1]
1978	John Mahaffey
1979	David Graham[1]
1980	Jack Nicklaus
1981	Larry Nelson
1982	Ray Floyd
1983	Hal Sutton
1984	Lee Trevino
1985	Hubert Green
1986	Bob Tway
1987	Larry Nelson
1988	Jeff Sluman
1989	Payne Stewart
1990	Wayne Grady
1991	John Daly
1992	Nick Price
1993	Paul Azinger[1]
1994	Nick Price
1995	Steve Elkington
1996	Mark Brooks[1]
1997	Davis Love III
1998	Vijay Singh
1999–2000	Tiger Woods
2001	David Toms
2002	Rich Beem
2003	Shaun Micheel

1. Winner in playoff. 2. Switched to medal play.

U.S. WOMEN'S AMATEUR CHAMPIONS

1916	Alexa Stirling
1919–20	Alexa Stirling
1921	Marion Hollins
1922	Glenna Collett
1923	Edith Cummings
1924	Dorothy Campbell Hurd
1925	Glenna Collett
1926	Helen Stetson
1927	Mrs. M. B. Horn
1928–30	Glenna Collett
1931	Helen Hicks
1932–34	Virginia Van Wie
1935	Glenna Collett Vare
1936	Pamela Barton
1937	Mrs. J. A. Page, Jr.
1938	Patty Berg
1939–40	Betty Jameson
1941	Mrs. Frank Newell
1946	Mildred Zaharias
1947	Louise Suggs
1948	Grace Lenczyk
1949	Mrs. D. G. Porter
1950	Beverly Hanson
1951	Dorothy Kirby
1952	Jacqueline Pung
1953	Mary Lena Faulk
1954	Barbara Romack
1955	Patricia Lesser
1956	Marlene Stewart
1957	JoAnne Gunderson
1958	Anne Quast
1959	Barbara McIntire
1960	JoAnne Gunderson
1961	Anne Quast Decker
1962	JoAnne Gunderson
1963	Anne Quast Welts
1964	Barbara McIntire
1965	Jean Ashley
1966	JoAnne Gunderson
1967	Lou Dill
1968	JoAnne G. Carner
1969	Catherine LaCoste
1970	Martha Wilkinson
1971	Laura Baugh
1972	Mary Ann Budke
1973	Carol Semple
1974	Cynthia Hill
1975	Beth Daniel
1976	Donna Horton
1977	Beth Daniel
1978	Cathy Sherk
1979	Carolyn Hill
1980	Juli Inkster
1981	Juli Inkster
1982	Juli Inkster
1983	Joanne Pacillo
1984	Deb Richard
1985	Michiko Hattori
1986	Kay Cockerill
1987	Kay Cockerill
1988	Pearl Sinn
1989	Vicki Goetze
1990	Pat Hurst
1991	Amy Fruhwirth
1992	Vicki Goetze
1993	Jill McGill
1994	Wendy Ward
1995	Kelli Kuehne
1996	Kelli Kuehne
1997	Silvia Cavalleri
1998	Grace Park
1999	Dorothy Delasin
2000	Marcy Newton
2001	Meredith Duncan
2002	Becky Lucidi
2003	Virada Nirapathpongporn

U.S. WOMEN'S OPEN CHAMPIONS

Year	Winner	Score
1946	Patty Berg (match play)	—
1947	Betty Jameson	295
1948	Mildred D. Zaharias	300
1949	Louise Suggs	291
1950	Mildred D. Zaharias	291
1951	Betsy Rawls	293
1952	Louise Suggs	284
1953	Betsy Rawls[1]	302
1954	Mildred D. Zaharias	291
1955	Fay Crocker	299
1956	Katherine Cornelius[1]	302
1957	Betsy Rawls	299
1958	Mickey Wright	290
1959	Mickey Wright	287
1960	Betsy Rawls	291
1961	Mickey Wright	293
1962	Murle Lindstrom	301
1963	Mary Mills	289
1964	Mickey Wright[1]	290
1965	Carol Mann	290
1966	Sandra Spuzich	297
1967	Catherine LaCoste[2]	294
1968	Susie Berning	289
1969	Donna Caponi	294
1970	Donna Caponi	287
1971	JoAnne Carner	288
1972	Susie Berning	299
1973	Susie Berning	290
1974	Sandra Haynie	295
1975	Sandra Palmer	295
1976	JoAnne Carner[1]	292
1977	Hollis Stacy	292
1978	Hollis Stacy	289
1979	Jerilyn Britz	284
1980	Amy Alcott	280
1981	Pat Bradley	279
1982	Janet Alex	283
1983	Jan Stephenson	290
1984	Hollis Stacy	290
1985	Kathy Baker	280
1986	Jane Geddes[1]	287
1987	Laura Davies[1]	285
1988	Liselotte Neumann	277
1989	Betsy King	278
1990	Betsy King	284
1991	Meg Mallon	283
1992	Patty Sheehan	280
1993	Lauri Merten	280
1994	Patty Sheehan	277
1995	Annika Sorenstam	278
1996	Annika Sorenstam	272
1997	Alison Nicholas	274
1998	Se Ri Pak	290
1999	Juli Inkster	272
2000	Karrie Webb	282
2001	Karrie Webb	273
2002	Juli Inkster	276
2003	Hilary Lunke[1]	353

1. Winner in playoff. 2. Amateur.

BRITISH OPEN CHAMPIONS

(First tournament, held in 1860, was won by Willie Park, Sr.)

Year	Winner	Score	Year	Winner	Score	Year	Winner	Score
1920	George Duncan	303	1952	Bobby Locke	287	1978	Jack Nicklaus	281
1921	Jock Hutchison	296	1953	Ben Hogan	282	1979	Severiano Ballesteros	283
1922	Walter Hagen	300	1954	Peter Thomson	283	1980	Tom Watson	271
1923	A. G. Havers	295	1955	Peter Thomson	281	1981	Bill Rogers	276
1924	Walter Hagen	301	1956	Peter Thomson	286	1982	Tom Watson	284
1925	Jim Barnes	300	1957	Bobby Locke	279	1983	Tom Watson	275
1926	R. T. Jones, Jr.	291	1958	Peter Thomson	278	1984	Severiano Ballesteros	276
1927	R. T. Jones, Jr.	285	1959	Gary Player	284	1985	Sandy Lyle	282
1928	Walter Hagen	292	1960	Kel Nagle	278	1986	Greg Norman	280
1929	Walter Hagen	292	1961	Arnold Palmer	284	1987	Nick Faldo	279
1930	R. T. Jones, Jr.	291	1962	Arnold Palmer	276	1988	Seve Ballesteros	273
1931	Tommy Armour	296	1963	Bob Charles	277	1989	Mark Calcavecchia	275
1932	Gene Sarazen	283	1964	Tony Lema	279	1990	Nick Faldo	270
1933	Denny Shute	292	1965	Peter Thomson	285	1991	Ian Baker-Finch	272
1934	Henry Cotton	283	1966	Jack Nicklaus	282	1992	Nick Faldo	272
1935	A. Perry	283	1967	Roberto de Vicenzo	278	1993	Greg Norman	267
1936	A. H. Padgham	287	1968	Gary Player	289	1994	Nick Price	268
1937	Henry Cotton	290	1969	Tony Jacklin	280	1995	John Daly	282
1938	R. A. Whitcombe	295	1970	Jack Nicklaus	283	1996	Tom Lehman	271
1939	R. Burton	290	1971	Lee Trevino	278	1997	Justin Leonard	272
1940	Sam Snead	290	1972	Lee Trevino	278	1998	Mark O'Meara	280
1947	Fred Daly	294	1973	Tom Weiskopf	276	1999	Paul Lawrie	290
1948	Henry Cotton	283	1974	Gary Player	282	2000	Tiger Woods	269
1949	Bobby Locke	283	1975	Tom Watson	279	2001	David Duval	274
1950	Bobby Locke	279	1976	Johnny Miller	279	2002	Ernie Els	278
1951	Max Faulkner	285	1977	Tom Watson	268	2003	Ben Curtis	283

OTHER 2003 PGA TOUR WINNERS

(Through Sept. 28, 2003)

Tournament—winner	First place prize money
Mercedes Championship—Ernie Els	$1,060,000
Sony Open in Hawaii—Ernie Els	864,000
Bob Hope Chrysler Classic—Mike Weir	810,000
AT&T Pebble Beach National Pro-Am—Davis Love III	900,000
Buick Invitational—Tiger Woods	810,000
WGC-Accenture Match Play Championship—Tiger Woods	1,050,000
Ford Championship at Doral—Scott Hoch	900,000
The Honda Classic—Justin Leonard	900,000
THE PLAYERS Championship—Davis Love III	1,170,000
BellSouth Classic—Ben Crane	720,000
MCI Heritage—Davis Love III	810,000
Shell Houston Open—Fred Couples	810,000
HP Classic of New Orleans—Steve Flesch	900,000
Wachovia Championship—David Toms	1,008,000
EDS Byron Nelson Championship—Vijay Singh	1,008,000
Bank of America Colonial—Kenny Perry	900,000
Booz Allen Open—Rory Sabbatini	810,000
Buick Classic—Jonathan Kaye	945,000
FedEx St. Jude Classic—David Toms	810,000
Western Open—Tiger Woods	810,000
Greater Hartford Open—Peter Jacobsen	720,000
The INTERNATIONAL—Davis Love III	900,000
Deutsche Bank Championship—Adam Scott	900,000
Bell Canadian Open—Bob Tway	756,000
John Deere Classic—Vijay Singh	630,000
84 Lumber Classic of Pennsylvania—J. L. Lewis	720,000
Valero Texas Open—Tommy Armour III	630,000

Source: www.pgatour.com.

OTHER 2003 LPGA TOUR WINNERS

(Through Sept. 28, 2003)

Tournament—winner	First place prize money
Welch's/Fry's Championship—Wendy Doolan	$120,000
Safeway Ping—Se Ri Pak	150,000
Kraft Nabisco Championship—Patricia Meunier-Lebouc	240,000
The Office Depot—Annika Sorenstam	225,000
LPGA Takefuji Classic—Candie Kung	165,000
Chick-fil-A Charity Championship—Se Ri Pak	202,500
Michelob Light Open—Grace Park	240,000
Asahi Ryokuken International—Rosie Jones	195,000
LPGA Corning Classic—Juli Inkster	150,000
Kellogg-Keebler Classic—Annika Sorenstam	180,000
McDonald's LPGA Championship—Annika Sorenstam	240,000
Giant Eagle LPGA Classic—Rachel Teske	150,000
Wegman's Rochester LPGA—Rachel Teske	180,000
Shoprite LPGA Classic—Angela Stanford	195,000
BMO Financial Group Canadian Women's Open—Beth Daniel	195,000
Sybase Big Apple Classic—Hee-Won Han	142,500
Evian Masters—Juli Inkster	315,000
Weetabix Women's British Open—Annika Sorenstam	240,000
Wendy's Championship for Chldren—Hee-Won Han	165,000
Jamie Farr Kroger Classic—Se Ri Pak	150,000
Wachovia LPGA Classic—Candie Kung	180,000
State Farm Classic—Candie Kung	180,000
John Q, Hammons Hotel Classic—Karrie Webb	150,000
The Solheim Cup—Europe	
Safeway Classic—Annika Sorenstam	180,000

Source: Ladies Professional Golf Association. Web: www.lpga.com.

Auto Racing

INDIANAPOLIS 500

Year	Winner	Car	Time	mph	Second place
1911	Ray Harroun	Marmon	6:42:08.000	74.590	Ralph Mulford
1912	Joe Dawson	National	6:21:06.000	78.720	Teddy Tetzloff
1913	Jules Goux	Peugeot	6:35:05.000	75.930	Spencer Wishart
1914	René Thomas	Delage	6:03:45.000	82.470	Arthur Duray
1915	Ralph DePalma	Mercedes	5:33:55.510	89.840	Dario Resta
1916[1]	Dario Resta	Peugeot	3:34:17.000	84.000	Wilbur D'Alene
1919	Howard Wilcox	Peugeot	5:40:42.870	88.050	Eddie Hearne
1920	Gaston Chevrolet	Monroe	5:38:32.000	88.620	René Thomas
1921	Tommy Milton	Frontenac	5:34:44.650	89.620	Roscoe Sarles
1922	Jimmy Murphy	Murphy Special	5:17:30.790	94.480	Harry Hartz
1923	Tommy Milton	H. C. S. Special	5:29.50.170	90.950	Harry Hartz
1924	L. L. Corum-Joe Boyer	Dusenberg Special	5:05:23.510	98.230	Earl Cooper
1925	Peter DePaolo	Dusenberg Special	4:56:39.450	101.130	Dave Lewis
1926[2]	Frank Lockhart	Miller Special	4:10:14.950	95.904	Harry Hartz
1927	George Souders	Dusenberg Special	5:07:33.080	97.540	Earl DeVore
1928	Louis Meyer	Miller Special	5:01:33.750	99.480	Lou Moore
1929	Ray Keech	Simplex Special	5:07:25.420	97.580	Louis Meyer
1930	Billy Arnold	Miller-Hartz Special	4:58:39.720	100.448	Shorty Cantlon
1931	Louis Schneider	Bowes Special	5:10:27.930	96.629	Fred Frame
1932	Fred Frame	Miller-Hartz Special	4:48:03.790	104.144	Howard Wilcox
1933	Louis Meyer	Tydol Special	4:48:00.750	104.162	Wilbur Shaw
1934	Bill Cummings	Boyle Products Special	4:46:05.200	104.863	Mauri Rose
1935	Kelly Petillo	Gilmore Special	4:42:22.710	106.240	Wilbur Shaw
1936	Louis Meyer	Ring Free Special	4:35:03.390	109.069	Ted Horn
1937	Wilbur Shaw	Shaw-Gilmore Special	4:24:07.800	113.580	Ralph Hepburn
1938	Floyd Roberts	Burd Piston Ring Special	4:15:58.400	117.200	Wilbur Shaw
1939	Wilbur Shaw	Boyle Special	4:20:47.390	115.035	Jimmy Snyder
1940	Wilbur Shaw	Boyle Special	4:22:31.170	114.277	Rex Mays
1941	Floyd Davis-Mauri Rose	Noc-Out Hose Clamp Special	4:20:36.240	115.117	Rex Mays
1946	George Robson	Thorne Engineering Special	4:21:26.710	114.820	Jimmy Jackson
1947	Mauri Rose	Blue Crown Special	4:17:52.170	116.338	Bill Holland
1948	Mauri Rose	Blue Crown Special	4:10:23.330	119.814	Bill Holland
1949	Bill Holland	Blue Crown Special	4:07:15.970	121.327	Johnny Parsons
1950[3]	Johnnie Parsons	Wynn's Friction Proof Special	2:46:55.970	124.002	Bill Holland
1951	Lee Wallard	Belanger Special	3:57:38.050	126.244	Mike Nazaruk
1952	Troy Ruttman	Agajanian Special	3:52:41.880	128.922	Jim Rathmann
1953	Bill Vukovich	Fuel Injection Special	3:53:01.690	128.740	Art Cross
1954	Bill Vukovich	Fuel Injection Special	3:49:17.270	130.840	Jim Bryan
1955	Bob Sweikert	John Zink Special	3:53:59.130	128.209	Tony Bettenhausen
1956	Pat Flaherty	John Zink Special	3:53:28.840	128.490	Sam Hanks
1957	Sam Hanks	Belond Exhaust Special	3:41:14.250	135.601	Jim Rathmann
1958	Jimmy Bryan	Belond A-P Special	3:44:13.800	133.791	George Amick
1959	Rodger Ward	Leader Card 500 Roadster	3:40:49.200	135.857	Jim Rathmann
1960	Jim Rathmann	Ken-Paul Special	3:36:11.360	138.767	Rodger Ward
1961	A. J. Foyt	Bowes Special	3:35:37.490	139.130	Eddie Sachs
1962	Rodger Ward	Leader Card Special	3:33:50.330	140.293	Len Sutton
1963	Parnelli Jones	Agajanian Special	3:29:35.400	143.137	Jim Clark
1964	A. J. Foyt	Sheraton-Thompson Spl.	3:23:35.830	147.350	Rodger Ward
1965	Jim Clark	Lotus-Ford	3:19:05.340	150.686	Parnelli Jones
1966	Graham Hill	Red Ball Lola-Ford	3:27:52.530	144.317	Jim Clark
1967[4]	A. J. Foyt	Sheraton-Thompson Coyote-Ford	3:18:24.220	151.207	Al Unser
1968	Bobby Unser	Rislone Eagle-Offenhauser	3:16:13.760	152.882	Dan Gurney
1969	Mario Andretti	STP Hawk-Ford	3:11:14.710	156.867	Dan Gurney
1970	Al Unser	Johnny Lightning P. J. Colt-Ford	3:12:37.040	155.749	Mark Donohue
1971	Al Unser	Johnny Lightning P. J. Colt-Ford	3:10:11.560	157.735	Peter Revson
1972	Mark Donohue	Sunoco McLaren-Offenhauser	3:04:05.540	162.962	Al Unser
1973[5]	Gordon Johncock	STP Eagle-Offenhauser	2:05:26.590	159.036	Bill Vukovich, Jr.
1974	Johnny Rutherford	McLaren-Offenhauser	3:09:10.060	158.589	Bobby Unser
1975[6]	Bobby Unser	Jorgensen Eagle-Offenhauser	2:54:55.080	149.213	Johnny Rutherford
1976[7]	Johnny Rutherford	Hy-gain McLaren-Offenhauser	1:42:52.000	148.725	A. J. Foyt
1977	A. J. Foyt	Gilmore Coyote-Foyt	3:05:57.160	161.331	Tom Sneva
1978	Al Unser	1st Nat'l City Lola-Cosworth	3:05:54.990	161.363	Tom Sneva
1979	Rick Mears	Gould Penske-Cosworth	3:08:47.970	158.899	A. J. Foyt
1980	Johnny Rutherford	Pennzoil Chaparral-Cosworth	3:29:59.560	142.862	Tom Sneva
1981[8]	Bobby Unser	Norton Penske-Cosworth	3:35:41.780	139.029	Mario Andretti
1982	Gordon Johncock	STP Wildcat-Cosworth	3:05:09.140	162.084	Rick Mears
1983	Tom Sneva	Texaco Star March-Cosworth	3:05:03.066	162.117	Al Unser
1984	Rick Mears	Pennzoil March-Cosworth	3:03:21.660	163.612	Roberto Guerrero
1985	Danny Sullivan	Miller March-Cosworth	3:16:06.069	152.982	Mario Andretti
1986	Bobby Rahal	Budweiser March-Cosworth	2:55:43.480	170.722	Kevin Cogan

Year	Winner	Car	Time	mph	Second place
1987	Al Unser, Sr.	Cummins March-Cosworth	3:04:59.147	162.175	Roberto Guerrero
1988	Rick Mears	Pennzoil Penske P.C.17-Chevrolet	3:27:10.204	144.809	Emerson Fittipaldi
1989	Emerson Fittipaldi	Marlboro Penske-Cosworth	2:59:01.049	167.581	Al Unser, Jr.
1990	Arie Luyendyk	Domino's Pizza Lola-Cosworth	2:41:18.404	185.981	Bobby Rahal
1991	Rick Mears	Marlboro Penske-Cosworth	2:50:00.791	176.457	Michael Andretti
1992	Al Unser, Jr.	Valvoline-Chevrolet	3:43.05.148	134.477	Scott Goodyear
1993	Emerson Fittipaldi	Penske-Chevrolet	3:10:49.860	157.207	Arie Luyendyk
1994	Al Unser, Jr.	Penske-Mercedes	3:06:29.006	160.872	Jacques Villeneuve
1995	Jacques Villeneuve	Reynard-Ford	3:15:17.561	153.616	Christian Fittipaldi
1996	Buddy Lazier	Reynard-Ford	3:22:45.753	147.956	Davy Jones
1997	Arie Luyendyk	G Force-Aurora	3:25:43.388	145.827	Scott Goodyear
1998	Eddie Cheever	Dallara-Aurora	3:26:40.524	145.155	Buddy Lazier
1999	Kenny Brack	Dallara-Aurora-Goodyear	3:15:51.182	153.176	Jeff Ward
2000	Juan Montoya	GForce-Aurora-Firestone	2:58:59.431	167.607	Buddy Lazier
2001	Helio Castroneves	Dallara-Aurora-Firestone	3:31:54.180	141.574	Gil de Ferran
2002	Helio Castroneves	Dallara-Chevrolet-Firestone	3:00:10.871	166.499	Paul Tracy
2003	Gil de Ferran	Panoz G Force-Toyota-Firestone	3:11:56.989	156.291	Helio Castroneves

1. 300 miles. 2. Race ended at 400 miles because of rain. 3. Race ended at 345 miles because of rain. 4. Race, postponed after 18 laps because of rain on May 30, was finished on May 31. 5. Race postponed May 28 and 29 was cut to 332.5 miles because of rain, May 30. 6. Race ended at 435 miles because of rain. 7. Race ended at 255 miles because of rain. 8. Andretti was awarded the victory the day after the race after Bobby Unser, whose car finished first, was penalized one lap and dropped from first place to second for passing other cars illegally under a yellow caution flag. Unser appealed the decision to the U.S. Auto Club but it was upheld. A panel ruled the penalty was too severe and instead fined Unser $40,000, but restored the victory to him.

2003 NASCAR WINSTON CUP RACES

Date	Race	Raceway	Winner
Feb. 16	Daytona 500	Daytona International Speedway	Michael Waltrip
Feb. 23	Subway 400	North Carolina Speedway	Dale Jarrett
March 2	UAW-DaimlerChrysler 400	Las Vegas Motor Speedway	Matt Kenseth
March 9	Bass Pro Shops MBNA 500	Atlanta Motor Speedway	Bobby Labonte
March 16	Carolina Dodge Dealers 400	Darlington Raceway	Ricky Craven
March 23	Food City 500	Bristol Motor Speedway	Kurt Busch
March 30	Samsung/RadioShack 500	Texas Motor Speedway	Ryan Newman
April 6	Aaron's 499	Talladega Superspeedway	Dale Earnhardt, Jr.
April 13	Virginia 500	Martinsville Speedway	Jeff Gordon
April 27	Auto Club 500	California Speedway	Kurt Busch
May 3	Pontiac Excitement 400	Richmond International Raceway	Joe Nemechek
May 17	Winston Open	Lowe's Motor Speedway	Jeff Burton
May 17	The Winston	Lowe's Motor Speedway	Jimmie Johnson
May 25	Coca-Cola 600	Lowe's Motor Speedway	Jimmie Johnson
June 1	MBNA Armed Forces Family 400	Dover International Speedway	Ryan Newman
June 8	Pocono 500	Pocono Raceway	Tony Stewart
June 15	Sirius 400	Michigan International Speedway	Kurt Busch
June 22	Dodge/Save Mart 350	International Infineon Raceway	Robby Gordon
July 5	Pepsi 400	Daytona International Speedway	Greg Biffle
July 13	Tropicana 400	Chicagoland Speedway	Ryan Newman
July 20	New England 300	New Hampshire International Speedway	Jimmie Johnson
July 27	Pennsylvania 500	Pocono Raceway	Ryan Newman
Aug. 3	Brickyard 400	Indianapolis Motor Speedway	Kevin Harvick
Aug. 10	Sirius at The Glen	Watkins Glen International	Robby Gordon
Aug. 17	GFS Marketplace 400	Michigan International Speedway	Ryan Newman
Aug. 23	Sharpie 500	Bristol Motor Speedway	Kurt Busch
Aug. 31	Mountain Dew Southern 500	Darlington Raceway	Terry Labonte
Sept. 6	Chevy Rock & Roll 400	Richmond International Raceway	Ryan Newman
Sept. 14	Sylvania 300	New Hampshire International Speedway	Jimmie Johnson
Sept. 21	MBNA America 400	Dover International Speedway	Ryan Newman
Sept. 28	EA Sports 500	Talladega Superspeedway	Michael Waltrip

NASCAR WINSTON CUP CHAMPIONS

1949	Red Byron	1964	Richard Petty	1981	Darrell Waltrip	1993	Dale Earnhardt
1950	Bill Rexford	1965	Ned Jarrett	1982	Darrell Waltrip	1994	Dale Earnhardt
1951	Herb Thomas	1966	David Pearson	1983	Bobby Allison	1995	Jeff Gordon
1952	Tim Flock	1967	Richard Petty	1984	Terry Labonte	1996	Terry Labonte
1953	Herb Thomas	1968–69	David Pearson	1985	Darrell Waltrip	1997–98	Jeff Gordon
1954	Lee Petty	1970	Bobby Isaac	1986	Dale Earnhardt	1999	Dale Jarrett
1955	Tim Flock	1971–72	Richard Petty	1987	Dale Earnhardt	2000	Bobby Labonte
1956–57	Buck Baker	1973	Benny Parsons	1988	Bill Elliott	2001	Jeff Gordon
1958–59	Lee Petty	1974–75	Richard Petty	1989	Rusty Wallace	2002	Tony Stewart
1960	Rex White	1976–78	Cale Yarborough	1990	Dale Earnhardt	2003	Matt Kenseth[1]
1961	Ned Jarrett	1979	Richard Petty	1991	Dale Earnhardt		
1962–63	Joe Weatherly	1980	Dale Earnhardt	1992	Alan Kulwicki		

1. As of Sept. 28, 2003.

2003 NASCAR LEADING POINT STANDINGS[1]

Driver	Pts	Winnings	Driver	Pts	Winnings
1. Matt Kenseth	4,227	$3,469,580	11. Michael Waltrip	3,386	$3,948,820
2. Kevin Harvick	3,873	4,153,770	12. Robby Gordon	3,321	3,151,390
3. Dale Earnhardt, Jr.	3,843	4,095,210	13. Jeff Burton	3,245	3,182,340
4. Jimmie Johnson	3,751	4,587,660	14. Rusty Wallace	3,239	3,123,300
5. Ryan Newman	3,738	3,948,990	15. Bill Elliott	3,202	3,314,100
6. Jeff Gordon	3,707	4,067,830	16. Mark Martin	3,131	3,413,400
7. Bobby Labonte	3,528	3,782,460	17. Jamie McMurray[2]	3,089	2,252,120
8. Kurt Busch	3,527	4,413,020	18. Sterling Marlin	3,019	3,259,440
9. Tony Stewart	3,456	4,101,560	19. Greg Biffle[2]	2,984	2,014,600
10. Terry Labonte	3,396	3,041,900	20. Elliott Sadler	2,955	3,041,420

1. As of Sept. 28, 2003. Seven races left in season. 2. Rookie.

INDYCAR/CART CHAMPIONS

1910	Ray Harroun	1933	Louis Meyer	1962	Rodger Ward	1986–87	Bobby Rahal
1911	Ralph Mulford	1934	Bill Cummings	1963–64	A. J. Foyt	1988	Danny Sullivan
1912	Ralph DePalma	1935	Kelly Petillo	1965–66	Mario Andretti	1989	Emerson Fittipaldi
1913	Earl Cooper	1936	Mauri Rose	1967	A. J. Foyt	1990	Al Unser, Jr.
1914	Ralph DePalma	1937	Wilbur Shaw	1968	Bobby Unser	1991	Michael Andretti
1915	Earl Cooper	1938	Floyd Roberts	1969	Mario Andretti	1992	Bobby Rahal
1916	Dario Resta	1939	Wilbur Shaw	1970	Al Unser	1993	Nigel Mansell
1917	Earl Cooper	1940–41	Rex Mays	1971–72	Joe Leonard	1994	Al Unser, Jr.
1918	Ralph Mulford	1946–48	Ted Horn	1973	Roger McCluskey	1995	Jacques Villeneuve
1919	Howard Wilcox	1949	Johnnie Parsons	1974	Bobby Unser	1996	Jimmy Vasser
1920	Gaston Chevrolet	1950	Henry Banks	1975	A. J. Foyt	1997–98	Alessandro Zanardi
1921	Tommy Milton	1951	Tony Bettenhausen	1976	Gordon Johncock	1999	Juan Montoya
1922	James Murphy	1952	Chuck Stevenson	1977–78	Tom Sneva	2000	Gil de Ferran
1923	Eddie Hearne	1953	Sam Hanks	1979	Rick Mears (CART), A. J. Foyt (USAC)[1]	2001	Kenny Brack
1924	James Murphy	1954	Jimmy Bryan	1980	Johnny Rutherford	2002	Cristiano da Matta
1925	Peter DePaolo	1955	Bob Sweikert	1981–82	Rick Mears	2003	Paul Tracy[2]
1926	Harry Hartz	1956–57	Jimmy Bryan	1983	Al Unser		
1927	Peter DePaolo	1958	Tony Bettenhausen	1984	Mario Andretti		
1928–29	Louis Meyer	1959	Rodger Ward	1985	Al Unser		
1930	Billy Arnold	1960–61	A. J. Foyt				
1931	Louis Schneider						
1932	Bob Carey						

NOTE: There have been three sanctioning bodies for the series: the Automobile Association of America (1909–1955), the U.S. Auto Club (1956–1979), and the Championship Auto Racing Team (CART), 1979–present. 1. Two separate series were held in 1979. 2. As of Sept. 28, 2003. Three races left in season.

2003 INDY RACING LEAGUE POINT STANDINGS[1]

Driver	Pts	Driver	Pts	Driver	Pts
1. Scott Dixon	467	9. Scott Sharp	323	17. Alex Barron	206
2. Helio Castroneves	467	10. Tora Takagi	291	18. Buddy Lazier	201
3. Tony Kanaan	460	11. Roger Yasukawa	281	19. Sarah Fisher	193
4. Sam Hornish, Jr.	448	12. Dan Wheldon	277	20. A. J. Foyt IV	190
5. Gil de Ferran	437	13. Bryan Herta	247	21. Felipe Giaffone	188
6. Al Unser, Jr.	352	14. Robbie Buhl	242	22. Vitor Meira	138
7. Tomas Scheckter	341	15. Greg Ray	229	23. Jaques Lazier	120
8. Kenny Brack	328	16. Buddy Rice	229	24. Michael Andretti	80

1. As of Sept. 28, 2003. One race left in season.

WORLD GRAND PRIX DRIVER CHAMPIONS

1950	Giuseppe Farina, Italy, Alfa Romeo	1965	Jim Clark, Scotland, Lotus-Ford
1951	Juan Fangio, Argentina, Alfa Romeo	1966	Jack Brabham, Australia, Brabham-Repco
1952	Alberto Ascari, Italy, Ferrari	1967	Denis Hulme, New Zealand, Brabham-Repco
1953	Alberto Ascari, Italy, Ferrari	1968	Graham Hill, England, Lotus-Ford
1954	Juan Fangio, Argentina, Maserati, Mercedes-Benz	1969	Jackie Stewart, Scotland, Matra-Ford
1955	Juan Fangio, Argentina, Mercedes-Benz	1970	Jochen Rindt, Austria, Lotus-Ford
1956	Juan Fangio, Argentina, Lancia-Ferrari	1971	Jackie Stewart, Scotland, Tyrrell-Ford
1957	Juan Fangio, Argentina, Masserati	1972	Emerson Fittipaldi, Brazil, Lotus-Ford
1958	Mike Hawthorn, England, Ferrari	1973	Jackie Stewart, Scotland, Tyrrell-Ford
1959	Jack Brabham, Australia, Cooper	1974	Emerson Fittipaldi, Brazil, McLaren-Ford
1960	Jack Brabham, Australia, Cooper	1975	Niki Lauda, Austria, Ferrari
1961	Phil Hill, United States, Ferrari	1976	James Hunt, Britain, McLaren-Ford
1962	Graham Hill, England, BRM	1977	Niki Lauda, Austria, Ferrari
1963	Jim Clark, Scotland, Lotus-Ford	1978	Mario Andretti, United States, Lotus
1964	John Surtees, England, Ferrari	1979	Jody Scheckter, South Africa, Ferrari

1980 Alan Jones, Australia, Williams-Ford
1981 Nelson Piquet, Brazil, Brabham-Ford
1982 Keke Rosberg, Finland, Williams-Ford
1983 Nelson Piquet, Brazil. Brabham-BMW
1984 Niki Lauda, Austria, McLaren-Porsche
1985 Alain Prost, France, McLaren-Porsche
1986 Alain Prost, France, McLaren-Porsche
1987 Nelson Piquet, Brazil, Williams-Honda
1988 Aryton Senna, Brazil, McLaren-Honda
1989 Alain Prost, France, McLaren-Honda
1990 Ayrton Senna, Brazil, McLaren-Honda
1991 Aryton Senna, Brazil, McLaren-Honda
1992 Nigel Mansell, Britain, Williams-Renault
1993 Alain Prost, France, Williams-Renault
1994 Michael Schumacher, Germany, Benetton
1995 Michael Schumacher, Germany, Benetton Renault
1996 Damon Hill, Britain, Williams
1997 Jacques Villeneuve, Canada, Williams-Renault
1998 Mika Hakkinen, Finland, McLaren-Mercedes
1999 Mika Hakkinen, Finland, McLaren-Mercedes
2000 Michael Schumacher, Germany, Ferrari
2001 Michael Schumacher, Germany, Ferrari
2002 Michael Schumacher, Germany, Ferrari
2003 Michael Schumacher, Germany, Ferrari[1]

1. As of Sept. 28, 2003. One race left in season.

Yachting

AMERICA'S CUP RECORD

First race in 1851 around Isle of Wight, Cowes, England. First defense and all others through 1920 held 30 miles off New York Bay. Races since 1930 held 30 miles off Newport, R.I. Conducted as one race only in 1851 and 1870; best four-of-seven basis, 1871; best two-of-three, 1876–1887; best three-of-five, 1893–1901; best four-of-seven, since 1930.

Year	Winner and owner	Loser and owner
1851	AMERICA, John C. Stevens, U.S.	AURORA, T. Le Marchant, England[1]
1870	MAGIC, Franklin Osgood, U.S.	CAMBRIA, James Ashbury, England[2]
1871	COLUMBIA, Franklin Osgood, U.S.[3] SAPPHO, William P. Douglas, U.S.	LIVONIA, James Ashbury, England
1876	MADELEINE, John S. Dickerson, U.S.	COUNTESS OF DUFFERIN, Chas. Gifford, Canada
1881	MISCHIEF, J. R. Busk, U.S.	ATALANTA, Alexander Cuthbert, Canada
1885	PURITAN, J. M. Forbes-Gen. Charles Paine, U.S.	GENESTA, Sir Richard Sutton, England
1886	MAYFLOWER, Gen. Charles Paine, U.S.	GALATEA, Lt. William Henn, England
1887	VOLUNTEER, Gen. Charles Paine, U.S.	THISTLE, James Bell et al., Scotland
1893	VIGILANT, C. Oliver Iselin et al., U.S.	VALKYRIE II, Lord Dunraven, England
1895	DEFENDER, C. O. Iselin–W. K. Vanderbilt–E. D. Morgan, U.S.	VALKYRIE III, Lord Dunraven–Lord Lonsdale–Lord Wolverton, England
1899	COLUMBIA, J. P. Morgan–C. O. Iselin, U.S.	SHAMROCK I, Sir Thomas Lipton, Ireland
1901	COLUMBIA, Edwin D. Morgan, U.S.	SHAMROCK II, Sir Thomas Lipton, Ireland
1903	RELIANCE, Cornelius Vanderbilt et al., U.S.	SHAMROCK III, Sir Thomas Lipton, Ireland
1920	RESOLUTE, Henry Walters et al., U.S.	SHAMROCK IV, Sir Thomas Lipton, Ireland
1930	ENTERPRISE, Harold S. Vanderbilt et al., U.S.	SHAMROCK V, Sir Thomas Lipton, Ireland
1934	RAINBOW, Harold S. Vanderbilt, U.S.	ENDEAVOUR, T. O. M. Sopwith, England
1937	RANGER, Harold S. Vanderbilt, U.S.	ENDEAVOUR II, T. O. M. Sopwith, England
1958	COLUMBIA, Henry Sears et al., U.S.	SCEPTRE, Hugh Goodson et al., England
1962	WEATHERLY, Henry D. Mercer et al., U.S.	GRETEL, Sir Frank Packer et al., Australia
1964	CONSTELLATION, New York Y.C. Syndicate, U.S.	SOVEREIGN, J. Anthony Bowden, England
1967	INTREPID, New York Y.C. Syndicate, U.S.	DAME PATTIE, Sydney (Aust.) Syndicate
1970	INTREPID, New York Y.C. Syndicate, U.S.	GRETEL II, Sydney (Aust.) Syndicate
1974	COURAGEOUS, New York, N.Y. Syndicate, U.S.	SOUTHERN CROSS, Sydney (Aust.) Syndicate
1977	COURAGEOUS, New York, N.Y. Syndicate, U.S.	AUSTRALIA, Sun City (Aust.) Syndicate
1980	FREEDOM, New York, N.Y. Syndicate, U.S.	AUSTRALIA, Alan Bond et al, Australia
1983	AUSTRALIA II, Alan Bond et al., Australia	LIBERTY, New York, N.Y. Syndicate, U.S.
1987	STARS & STRIPES, Dennis Conner et al., United States	KOOKABURRA III, Iain Murray et al., Australia
1988[4]	STARS & STRIPES, Dennis Conner, et al., United States	NEW ZEALAND, Michael Fay, et al., New Zealand
1992	AMERICA 3, Bill Koch, et al., United States	IL MORO DI VENEZIA, Paul Cayard, et al., Italy
1995	BLACK MAGIC, Peter Blake, et al., New Zealand	YOUNG AMERICA, Dennis Conner, et al., United States
2000	NEW ZEALAND, Peter Blake, et al., New Zealand	LUNA ROSSA, Patrizio Bertelli, et al., Italy
2003	ALINGHI, Erenesto Bertarelli, et al., Switzerland	NEW ZEALAND, Ross Blackman, et al., New Zealand

1. Fourteen British yachts started against America; *Aurora* finished second. 2. *Cambria* sailed against 23 U.S. yachts and finished tenth. 3. *Columbia* was disabled in the third race, after winning the first two; *Sappho* substituted and won the fourth and fifth. 4. Shortly after Dennis Conner and his 60-foot, twin-hulled catamaran easily defeated the challenge of the *New Zealand,* a 133-foot, single-hulled yacht in the waters off San Diego in early September 1988, a New York State Supreme Court judge ruled that the Americans did not live up to the America's Cup Deed of Gift, which means competing boats must be similar. The judge ruled that the Americans had an unfair advantage over the monohulled ship, and awarded the Cup to New Zealand. However, an appeal awarded the Cup to the United States.

Bicycling

TOUR DE FRANCE–2003

(July 5–27, 2003)

		Team	Behind
1.	Lance Armstrong, United States	U.S. Postal	(1)
2.	Jan Ullrich, Germany	Bianchi	01:01
3.	Alexandre Vinokourov, Kazakhstan	Team Telekom	04:14
4.	Tyler Hamilton, United States	Team CSC	06:17
5.	Haimar Zubeldia, Spain	Euskaltel-Euskadi	06:51
6.	Iban Mayo, Spain	Euskaltel-Euskadi	07:06
7.	Ivan Basso, Italy	Fassa Bortolo	10:12
8.	Christophe Moreau, France	Credit Agricole	12:28
9.	Carlos Sastre, Spain	Team CSC	18:49
10.	Francisco Mancebo, Spain	ibanesto.com	19:15

1. Completed course in 83 hours, 41 minutes, 12 seconds.

Marathons

BOSTON MARATHON

(April 21, 2003)

Men	Time
Robert Kipkoech Cheruiyot, Kenya	2:10:11
Wheelchair—Ernst Van Dyk, South Africa	1:28:32

Women	Time
Svetlana Zakharova, Russia	2:25:20
Wheelchair—Christina Ripp, United States	1:54:47

OTHER 2003 MARATHONS

Antarctica (March 2, 2003)

Men	Time
Bogdan Barewski, Poland	3:33:20
Women	
Jane Baldwin, United States	4:11:10

Los Angeles (March 2, 2003)

Men	Time
Mark Yatich, Kenya	2:09:52
Wheelchair—Saul Mendoza, United States	1:27:07
Women	
Tatyana Pozdnyakora, Ukraine	2:29:40
Wheelchair—Cheri Blauwet, United States	1:50:06

Paris (April 6, 2003)

Men	Time
Mike Rotich, Kenya	2:06:33
Wheelchair—Joël Jeannot, France	1:28:05
Women	
Béatrice Omwanza, Kenya	2:27:44

London (April 13, 2003)

Men	Time
Gezaghegne Abera, Ethiopia	2:07:56
Wheelchair—Joël Jeannot, France	1:32:02
Women	
Paula Radcliffe, Great Britain	2:15:25*
Wheelchair—Francesca Porcellato, Italy	2:04:21

*World record

Little League

LITTLE LEAGUE WORLD SERIES CHAMPIONS

Year	Champion	Runner-up	Score
1947	Williamsport, Pa.	Lock Haven, Pa.	16–7
1948	Lock Haven, Pa.	St. Petersburg, Fla.	6–5
1949	Hammontown, N.J.	Pensacola, Fla.	5–0
1950	Houston, Tex.	Bridgeport, Conn.	2–1
1951	Stamford, Conn.	Austin, Tex.	3–0
1952	Norwalk, Conn.	Monongahela, Pa.	4–3
1953	Birmingham, Ala.	Schenectady, N.Y.	1–0
1954	Schenectady, N.Y.	Colton, Calif.	7–5
1955	Morrisville, Pa.	Merchantville, N.J.	4–3
1956	Roswell, N.M.	Merchantville, N.J.	3–1
1957	Monterrey, Mex.	LaMesa, Calif.	4–0
1958	Monterrey, Mex.	Kankakee, Ill.	10–1
1959	Hamtramck, Mich.	Auburn, Calif.	12–0
1960	Levittown, Pa.	Ft. Worth, Tex.	5–0
1961	El Cajon, Calif.	El Campo, Tex.	4–2
1962	San Jose, Calif.	Kankakee, Ill.	3–0
1963	Granada Hills, Calif.	Stratford, Conn.	2–1
1964	Staten Island, N.Y.	Monterrey, Mex.	4–0
1965	Windsor Locks, Conn.	Stoney Creek, Can.	3–1
1966	Houston, Tex.	W. New York, N.J.	8–2
1967	West Tokyo, Japan	Chicago, Ill.	4–1
1968	Osaka, Japan	Richmond, Va.	1–0
1969	Taipei, Taiwan	Santa Clara, Calif.	5–0
1970	Wayne, N.J.	Campbell, Calif.	2–0
1971	Tainan, Taiwan	Gary, Ind.	12–3
1972	Taipei, Taiwan	Hammond, Ind.	6–0
1973	Tainan City, Taiwan	Tucson, Ariz.	12–0
1974	Kao Hsiung, Taiwan	El Cajon, Calif.	7–2
1975	Lakewood, N.J.	Tampa, Fla.	4–3
1976	Tokyo, Japan	Campbell, Calif.	10–3
1977	Kao Hsiung, Taiwan	El Cajon, Calif.	7–2
1978	Pin-Tung, Taiwan	Danville, Calif.	11–1
1979	Hsien, Taiwan	Campbell, Calif.	2–1
1980	Hua Lian, Taiwan	Tampa, Fla.	4–3
1981	Tai-Chung, Taiwan	Tampa, Fla.	4–2
1982	Kirkland, Wash.	Hsien, Taiwan	6–0
1983	Marietta, Ga.	Barahona, Dom. Rep.	3–1
1984	Seoul, S. Korea	Altamonte Springs, Fla.	6–2
1985	Seoul, S. Korea	Mexicali, Mex.	7–1

Year	Champion	Runner-up	Score
1986	Tianan Park, Taiwan	Tucson, Ariz.	12–0
1987	Hua Lian, Taiwan	Irvine, Calif.	21–1
1988	Tai-Chung, Taiwan	Pearl City, Haw.	10–0
1989	Trumbull, Conn.	Kaohsiung, Taiwan	5–2
1990	Taipei, Taiwan	Shippensburg, Pa.	9–0
1991	Tai-Chung, Taiwan	San Ramon Valley, Calif.	11–0
1992*	Long Beach, Calif.	Zamboanga, Phil.	6–0
1993	Long Beach, Calif.	David Chiriqui, Pan.	3–2
1994	Maracaibo, Venezuela	Northridge, Calif.	4–3
1995	Tainan, Taiwan	Spring, Texas	17–3
1996	Kao-Hsuing City, Taipei	Cranston, R.I.	13–3
1997	Guadalupe, Mexico	South Mission Viejo, Calif.	5–4
1998	Toms River, N.J.	Kashima, Japan	12–9
1999	Hirakata, Osaka, Japan	Phenix City, Ala.	5–0
2000	Maracaibo, Venezuela	Bellaire, Tex.	3–2
2001	Tokyo Kitasuna, Tokyo, Japan	Apopka, Fla.	2–1
2002	Louisville, Ky.	Sendai, Japan	1–0
2003	Musashi-Fuchu, Tokyo, Japan	East Boynton Beach, Fla.	10–1

* Long Beach declared a 6–0 winner after the international tournament committee determined that Zamboanga City had used players that were not within its city limits.

Baseball

The popular tradition that baseball was invented by Abner Doubleday at Cooperstown, N.Y., in 1839 has been enshrined in the Hall of Fame and National Museum of Baseball erected in that town, but research has proved that a game called "Base Ball" was played in this country and England before 1839. The first team baseball as we know it was played at the Elysian Fields, Hoboken, N.J., on June 19, 1846, between the Knickerbockers and the New York Nine. The next fifty years saw a gradual growth of baseball and an improvement of equipment and playing skill.

Historians have it that the first pitcher to throw a curve was William A. (Candy) Cummings in 1867. The Cincinnati Red Stockings were the first all-professional team, and in 1869 they played 64 games without a loss. The standard ball of the same size and weight, still the rule, was adopted in 1872. The first catcher's mask was worn in 1875. The National League was organized in 1876. The first chest protector was worn in 1885. The three-strike rule was put on the books in 1887, and the four-ball ticket to first base was instituted in 1889. The pitching distance was lengthened to 60 feet 6 inches in 1893, and the rules have been modified only slightly since that time.

The American League, under the vigorous leadership of B. B. Johnson, became a major league in 1901. Judge Kenesaw Mountain Landis, by action of the two major leagues, became Commissioner of Baseball in 1921.

MAJOR LEAGUE ALL-STAR GAME

Year	Date	Winning league (manager)	Runs	Losing league (manager)	Runs	Winning pitcher	Losing pitcher	Site	Paid attendance
1933	July 6	A.L. (Mack)	4	N.L. (McGraw)	2	Gomez	Hallahan	Chicago A.L.	47,595
1934	July 10	A.L. (Cronin)	9	N.L. (Terry)	7	Harder	Mungo	New York N.L.	48,363
1935	July 8	A.L. (Cochrane)	4	N.L. (Frisch)	1	Gomez	Walker	Cleveland A.L.	69,831
1936	July 7	N.L. (Grimm)	4	A.L. (McCarthy)	3	J. Dean	Grove	Boston N.L.	25,556
1937	July 7	A.L. (McCarthy)	8	N.L. (Terry)	3	Gomez	J. Dean	Washington A.L.	31,391
1938	July 6	N.L. (Terry)	4	A.L. (McCarthy)	1	Vander Meer	Gomez	Cincinnati N.L.	27,067
1939	July 11	A.L. (McCarthy)	3	N.L. (Hartnett)	1	Bridges	Lee	New York A.L.	62,892
1940	July 9	N.L. (McKechnie)	4	A.L. (Cronin)	0	Derringer	Ruffing	St. Louis N.L.	32,373
1941	July 8	A.L. (Baker)	7	N.L. (McKechnie)	5	E. Smith	Passeau	Detroit A.L.	54,674
1942	July 6	A.L. (McCarthy)	3	N.L. (Durocher)	1	Chandler	Cooper	New York N.L.	34,178
1943	July 13	A.L. (McCarthy)	5	N.L. (Southworth)	3	Leonard	Cooper	Philadelphia A.L.	31,938
1944	July 11	N.L. (Southworth)	7	A.L. (McCarthy)	1	Raffensberger	Hughson	Pittsburgh N.L.	29,589
1946	July 9	A.L. (O'Neill)	12	N.L. (Grimm)	0	Feller	Passeau	Boston A.L.	34,906
1947	July 8	A.L. (Cronin)	2	N.L. (Dyer)	1	Shea	Sain	Chicago N.L.	41,123
1948	July 13	A.L. (Harris)	5	N.L. (Durocher)	2	Raschi	Schmitz	St. Louis A.L.	34,009
1949	July 12	A.L. (Boudreau)	11	N.L. (Southworth)	7	Trucks	Newcombe	Brooklyn N.L.	32,577
1950	July 11	N.L. (Shotton)	4	A.L. (Stengel)	3[1]	Blackwell	Gray	Chicago A.L.	46,127
1951	July 10	N.L. (Sawyer)	8	A.L. (Stengel)	3	Maglie	Lopat	Detroit A.L.	52,075
1952	July 8	N.L. (Durocher)	3	A.L. (Stengel)	2[2]	Rush	Lemon	Philadelphia N.L.	32,785
1953	July 14	N.L. (Dressen)	5	A.L. (Stengel)	1	Spahn	Reynolds	Cincinnati N.L.	30,846
1954	July 13	A.L. (Stengel)	11	N.L. (Alston)	9	Stone	Conley	Cleveland A.L.	68,751
1955	July 12	N.L. (Durocher)	6	A.L. (Lopez)	5[3]	Conley	Sullivan	Milwaukee N.L.	45,643
1956	July 10	N.L. (Alston)	7	A.L. (Stengel)	3	Friend	Pierce	Washington A.L.	28,843
1957	July 9	A.L. (Stengel)	6	N.L. (Alston)	5	Bunning	Simmons	St. Louis N.L.	30,693
1958	July 8	A.L. (Stengel)	4	N.L. (Haney)	3	Wynn	Friend	Baltimore A.L.	48,829
1959[4]	July 7	N.L. (Haney)	5	A.L. (Stengel)	4	Antonelli	Ford	Pittsburgh N.L.	35,277
	Aug. 3	A.L. (Stengel)	5	N.L. (Haney)	3	Walker	Drysdale	Los Angeles N.L.	55,105
1960[4]	July 11	N.L. (Alston)	5	A.L. (Lopez)	3	Friend	Monbouquette	Kansas City A.L.	30,619
	July 13	N.L. (Alston)	6	A.L. (Lopez)	0	Law	Ford	New York A.L.	38,362
1961[4]	July 11	N.L. (Murtaugh)	5	A.L. (Richards)	4[5]	Miller	Wilhelm	San Francisco N.L.	44,115
	July 31	N.L. (Murtaugh)	1	A.L. (Richards)	1[6]	—	—	Boston A.L.	31,851

Year	Date	Winning league (manager)	Runs	Losing league (manager)	Runs	Winning pitcher	Losing pitcher	Site	Paid attendance
1962[4]	July 10	N.L. (Hutchinson)	3	A.L. (Houk)	1	Marichal	Pascual	Washington A.L.	45,480
	July 30	A.L. (Houk)	9	N.L. (Hutchinson)	4	Herbert	Mahaffey	Chicago N.L.	38,359
1963	July 9	N.L. (Dark)	5	A.L. (Houk)	3	Jackson	Bunning	Cleveland A.L.	44,160
1964	July 7	N.L. (Alston)	7	A.L. (Lopez)	4	Marichal	Radatz	New York N.L.	50,850
1965	July 13	N.L. (March)	6	A.L. (Lopez)	5	Koufax	McDowell	Minnesota A.L.	46,706
1966	July 12	N.L. (Alston)	2	A.L. (Mele)	1[5]	Perry	Rickert	St. Louis N.L.	49,926
1967	July 11	N.L. (Alston)	2	A.L. (Bauer)	1[7]	Drysdale	Hunter	Anaheim A.L.	46,309
1968	July 9	N.L. (Schoendienst)	1	A.L. (Williams)	0	Drysdale	Tiant	Houston N.L.	48,321
1969	July 23	N.L. (Schoendienst)	9	A.L. (M. Smith)	3	Carlton	Stottlemyre	Washington A.L.	45,259
1970	July 14	N.L. (Hodges)	5	A.L. (Weaver)	4	Osteen	Wright	Cincinnati N.L.	51,838
1971	July 13	A.L. (Weaver)	6	N.L. (Anderson)	4	Blue	Ellis	Detroit A.L.	53,559
1972	July 25	N.L. (Murtaugh)	4	A.L. (Weaver)	3[5]	McGraw	McNally	Atlanta N.L.	53,107
1973	July 24	N.L. (Anderson)	7	A.L. (Williams)	1	Wise	Blyleven	Kansas City A.L.	40,849
1974	July 23	N.L. (Berra)	7	A.L. (Williams)	2	Brett	Tiant	Pittsburgh N.L.	50,706
1975	July 15	N.L. (Alston)	6	A.L. (Dark)	3	Matlack	Hunter	Milwaukee A.L.	51,540
1976	July 13	N.L. (Anderson)	7	A.L. (D. Johnson)	1	R. Jones	Fidrych	Philadelphia N.L.	63,974
1977	July 19	N.L. (Anderson)	7	A.L. (Martin)	5	Sutton	Palmer	New York A.L.	56,683
1978	July 11	N.L. (Lasorda)	7	A.L. (Martin)	3	Sutter	Gossage	San Diego N.L.	51,549
1979	July 17	N.L. (Lasorda)	7	A.L. (Lemon)	6	Sutter	Kern	Seattle A.L.	58,905
1980	July 8	N.L. (Tanner)	4	A.L. (Weaver)	2	Reuss	John	Los Angeles N.L.	56,088
1981[8]	Aug. 9	N.L. (Green)	5	A.L. (Frey)	4	Blue	Fingers	Cleveland A.L.	72,086
1982	July 13	N.L. (Lasorda)	4	A.L. (Martin)	1	Rogers	Eckersley	Montreal N.L.	59,057
1983	July 6	A.L. (Kuenn)	13	N.L. (Herzog)	3	Steib	Soto	Chicago A.L.	43,801
1984	July 11	N.L. (Owens)	3	A.L. (Altobelli)	1	Leg	Steib	San Francisco N.L.	57,756
1985	July 16	N.L. (Williams)	6	A.L. (Anderson)	1	Hoyt	Morris	Minneapolis A.L.	54,960
1986	July 15	A.L. (Howser)	3	N.L. (Herzog)	2	Clemens	Gooden	Houston N.L.	45,774
1987	July 14	N.L. (Johnson)	2	A.L. (McNamara)	0[9]	Smith	Howell	Oakland A.L.	49,671
1988	July 12	A.L. (Kelly)	2	N.L. (Herzog)	1	Viola	Gooden	Cincinnati, N.L	55,837
1989	July 11	A.L. (LaRussa)	5	N.L. (Lasorda)	3	Ryan	Smoltz	California A.L.	64,036
1990	July 10	A.L. (LaRussa)	2	N.L. (Craig)	0	Saberhagen	Brantley	Chicago N.L.	39,071
1991	July 9	A.L. (LaRussa)	4	N.L. (Piniella)	2	Key	Martinez	Toronto A.L.	52,383
1992	July 14	A.L. (Kelly)	13	N.L. (Cox)	6	Brown	Glavine	San Diego N.L.	59,372
1993	July 13	A.L. (Gaston)	9	N.L. (Cox)	3	McDowell	Burkett	Baltimore A.L.	48,147
1994	July 12	N.L. (Fregosi)	8	A.L. (Gaston)	7[5]	Jones	Bere	Pittsburgh N.L.	59,568
1995	July 11	N.L. (Alou)	3	A.L. (Showalter)	2	Slocumb	Rogers	Texas A.L.	50,920
1996	July 9	N.L. (Cox)	6	A.L. (Hargrove)	0	Smoltz	Nagy	Philadelphia N.L.	62,670
1997	July 8	A.L. (Torre)	3	N.L. (Cox)	1	Johnson	Maddux	Cleveland A.L.	44,916
1998	July 7	A.L. (Hargrove)	13	N.L. (Leyland)	3	Colon	Urbina	Denver N.L.	51,267
1999	July 13	A.L. (Torre)	4	N.L. (Bochy)	1	P. Martinez	Schilling	Boston A.L.	34,187
2000	July 11	A.L. (Torre)	6	N.L. (Cox)	3	Baldwin	Leiter	Atlanta N.L.	51,323
2001	July 10	A.L. (Torre)	4	N.L. (Valentine)	1	Garcia	Park	Seattle A.L.	47,364
2002	July 9	7–7 tie after 11 innings. Bob Brenley, N.L. manager, Joe Torre, A.L. manager						Milwaukee N.L.	41,871
2003	July 15	A.L. (Scioscia)	7	N.L. (Baker)	6	Donnelly	Gagne	Chicago A.L.	47,609

1. Fourteen innings. 2. Five innings, rain. 3. Twelve innings. 4. Two games. 5. Ten innings. 6. Called because of rain after nine innings. 7. Fifteen innings. 8. Game was originally scheduled for July 14, but was put off because of players' strike. 9. Thirteen innings. NOTE: No game in 1945.

NATIONAL BASEBALL HALL OF FAME

Cooperstown, N.Y.

Fielders

Member	Active years
Aaron, Henry (Hank)	1954–1976
Anson, Adrian (Cap)	1876–1897
Aparicio, Luis	1956–1973
Appling, Lucius (Luke)	1930–1950
Ashburn, Richie	1948–1962
Averill, H. Earl	1929–1941
Baker, J. Frank (Home Run)	1908–1922
Bancroft, David	1915–1930
Banks, Ernest	1953–1971
Beckley, Jacob	1888–1907
Bell, James (Cool Papa)[1]	1920–1947
Bench, John	1967–1983
Berra, Lawrence (Yogi)	1946–1965
Bottomley, James	1922–1937
Boudreau, Louis	1938–1952
Bresnahan, Roger	1897–1915
Brett, George	1973–1993
Brock, Lou	1961–1980
Brouthers, Dennis	1879–1896

Member	Active years
Burkett, Jesse	1890–1905
Campanella, Roy	1948–1957
Carew, Rod	1967–1985
Carey, Max	1910–1929
Carter, Gary	1974–1991
Cepeda, Orlando	1958–1974
Chance, Frank	1898–1914
Charleston, Oscar[1]	1915–1954
Clarke, Fred	1894–1915
Clemente, Roberto	1955–1972
Cobb, Tyrus	1905–1928
Cochrane, Gordon (Mickey)	1925–1937
Collins, Edward	1906–1930
Collins, James	1895–1908
Comiskey, Charles	1882–1894
Combs, Earle	1924–1935
Connor, Roger	1880–1897
Crawford, Samuel	1899–1917
Cronin, Joseph	1926–1945

Member	Active years
Cuyler, Hazen (Kiki)	1921–1938
Dandridge, Ray[1]	1933–1953
Davis, George	1890–1909
Delahanty, Edward	1888–1903
Dickey, William	1928–1946
Dihigo, Martin[1]	1923–1945
DiMaggio, Joseph	1936–1951
Doby, Larry	1947–1959
Doerr, Bobby	1937–1951
Duffy, Hugh	1888–1906
Ewing, William	1880–1897
Evers, John	1902–1919
Ferrell, Rick	1929–1947
Fisk, Carlton	1969–1991
Flick, Elmer	1898–1910
Fox, Nellie	1947–1965
Foxx, James	1925–1945
Frisch, Frank	1919–1937
Gehrig, H. Louis (Lou)	1923–1939
Gehringer, Charles	1924–1942

Member	Active years
Gibson, Josh[1]	1929–1946
Goslin, Leon (Goose)	1921–1938
Greenberg, Henry (Hank)	1933–1947
Hafey, Charles (Chick)	1924–1937
Hamilton, William	1888–1901
Hartnett, Charles (Gabby)	1922–1941
Heilmann, Harry	1914–1932
Herman, William	1931–1947
Hooper, Harry	1909–1925
Hornsby, Rogers	1915–1937
Irvin, Monford (Monte)[1]	1939–1956
Jackson, Reggie	1967–1987
Jackson, Travis	1922–1936
Jennings, Hugh	1891–1918
Johnson, William (Judy)[1]	1921–1937
Kaline, Albert W.	1953–1974
Keeler, William (Wee Willie)	1892–1910
Kell, George	1943–1957
Kelley, Joseph	1891–1908
Kelly, George	1915–1932
Kelly, Michael (King)	1878–1893
Killebrew, Harmon	1954–1975
Kiner, Ralph	1946–1955
Klein, Charles H. (Chuck)	1928–1944
Lajoie, Napoleon	1896–1916
Lazzeri, Tony	1926–1939
Leonard, Walter (Buck)[1]	1933–1955
Lindstrom, Frederick	1924–1936
Lloyd, John Henry (Pop)[1]	1905–1931
Lombardi, Ernie	1932–1947
Mantle, Mickey	1951–1968
Manush, Henry (Heinie)	1923–1939
Maranville, Walter (Rabbit)	1912–1935
Matthews, Edwin	1952–1968
Mays, Willie	1951–1973
Mazeroski, William Stanley (Maz)	1956–1972
McCarthy, Thomas	1884–1896
McCovey, Willie	1959–1980
McGraw, John J.	1891–1906
McPhee, John Alexander (Bid)	1882–1899
Medwick, Joseph (Ducky)	1932–1948
Mize, John (The Big Cat)	1936–1953
Morgan, Joe	1963–1984
Murray, Eddie	1977–1997
Musial, Stanley	1941–1963
O'Rourke, James	1876–1894
Ott, Melvin	1926–1947
Perez, Tony	1964–1983
Puckett, Kirby	1984–1995
Reese, Harold (Pee Wee)	1940–1958
Rice, Edgar (Sam)	1915–1934
Rizzuto, Phil	1941–1956
Robinson, Brooks	1955–1977
Robinson, Frank	1956–1976
Robinson, Jack	1947–1956
Robinson, Wilbert	1886–1902
Roush, Edd	1913–1931
Ruth, Babe	1914–1935
Schalk, Raymond	1912–1929
Schoendienst, Red	1945–1963
Schmidt, Mike	1973–1989
Sewell, Joseph	1920–1933
Simmons, Al	1924–1944
Sisler, George	1915–1930
Slaughter, Enos	1938–1959
Smith, Ozzie	1978–1996
Snider, Edwin D. (Duke)	1947–1964
Speaker, Tristram	1907–1928
Stargell, Willie	1962–1982
Stearnes, Norman (Turkey)	1921–1942
Terry, William	1923–1936
Thompson, Samuel	1885–1906
Tinker, Joseph	1902–1916
Traynor, Harold (Pie)	1920–1937
Vaughan, Arky	1932–1948
Wagner, John (Honus)	1897–1917
Wallace, Roderick (Bobby)	1894–1918
Waner, Lloyd	1927–1945
Waner, Paul	1926–1945
Ward, John (Monte)	1878–1894
Wells, Willie	1924–1949
Wheat, Zachariah	1909–1927
Williams, Billy	1959–1976
Williams, Theodore	1939–1960
Wilson, Lewis R. (Hack)	1923–1934
Winfield, David Mark	1973–1995
Yastrzemski, Carl	1961–1983
Youngs, Ross (Pep)	1917–1926
Yount, Robin	1974–1993

1. Negro League player selected by special committee.

Pitchers

Alexander, Grover	1911–1930
Bender, Charles (Chief)	1903–1925
Brown, Mordecai (3-Finger)	1903–1916
Bunning, Jim	1955–1971
Carlton, Steve	1965–1988
Chesbro, John	1899–1909
Clarkson, John	1882–1894
Coveleski, Stanley	1912–1928
Day, Leon	1935–1955
Dean, Jerome (Dizzy)	1930–1947
Drysdale, Don	1956–1969
Faber, Urban (Red)	1914–1933
Feller, Robert	1936–1956
Fingers, Rollie	1968–1985
Ford, Edward (Whitey)	1950–1967
Foster, Andrew (Rube)	1897–1926
Foster, Bill	1923–1937
Galvin, James (Pud)	1876–1892
Gibson, Bob	1959–1975
Gomez, Vernon (Lefty)	1930–1943
Griffith, Clark	1891–1914
Grimes, Burleigh	1916–1934
Grove, Robert (Lefty)	1925–1941
Haines, Jesse	1918–1937
Hoyt, Waite	1918–1938
Hubbell, Carl	1928–1943
Hunter, Jim (Catfish)	1965–1979
Jenkins, Ferguson	1965–1983
Johnson, Walter	1907–1927
Joss, Adrian	1902–1910
Keefe, Timothy	1880–1893
Koufax, Sanford (Sandy)	1955–1966
Lemon, Robert	1946–1958
Lyons, Theodore	1923–1946
Marichal, Juan	1960–1975
Marquard, Richard (Rube)	1908–1924
Mathewson, Christopher	1900–1916
McGinnity, Joseph	1899–1908
Newhouser, Hal	1939–1955
Nichols, Charles (Kid)	1890–1906
Niekro, Phil	1959–1987
Paige, Leroy (Satchel)[1]	1926–1965
Palmer, Jim	1965–1984
Pennock, Herbert	1912–1934
Perry, Gaylord	1962–1983
Plank, Edward	1901–1917
Radbourn, Charles (Hoss)	1880–1891
Rixey, Eppa	1912–1933
Roberts, Robert (Robin)	1948–1966
Rogan, Wilber	1920–1938
Ruffing, Charles (Red)	1924–1947
Rusie, Amos	1889–1901
Ryan, Nolan, Jr.	1966–1993
Seaver, Tom	1967–1986
Smith, Hilton Lee	1932–1948
Spahn, Warren	1942–1965
Sutton, Don	1966–1988
Vance, Arthur (Dazzy)	1915–1935
Waddell, Rube	1897–1910
Walsh, Edward	1904–1917
Welch, Michael (Mickey)	1880–1892
Wilhelm, Hoyt	1952–1972
Williams, Joseph	1910–1932
Willis, Vic	1898–1910
Wynn, Early	1939–1963
Young, Denton (Cy)	1890–1911

1. Negro League player selected by special committee.

Officials and Others

Alston, Walter[1]
Anderson, Sparky[1]
Barlick, Al[2]
Barrow, Edward[1, 3]
Bulkeley, Morgan G.[3]
Cartwright, Alexander[3]
Chadwick, Henry[4]
Chandler, A. B.[5]
Chylak, Nestor, Jr.[2]
Comiskey, Charles[1]
Conlan, John[3]
Connolly, Thomas[2]
Cummings, William A.[6]
Durocher, Leo[1]
Evans, William G.[2, 3]
Foster, Rube[3]
Frick, Ford C.[3, 5]
Giles, Warren C.[3]
Hanlon, Ned[3]
Harridge, William[3]
Harris, Stanley R.[7]
Hubbard, R. Calvin[2]
Huggins, Miller J.[1]
Hulbert, William[3]
Johnson, B. Bancroft[3]
Klem, William[2]
Landis, Kenesaw M.[5]
Lasorda, Tommy[1]
Lopez, Alfonso R.[7]
Mack, Connie[1, 3]
MacPhail, Lee, Jr.[3]
MacPhail, Leland S.[3]
McCarthy, Joseph V.[1]
McGowan, Bill[2]
McKechnie, William B.[1]
Rickey, W. Branch[1, 3]
Selee, Frank G.[1]
Spalding, Albert G.[2]
Stengel, Charles D.[7]
Veeck, Bill[3]
Weaver, Earl[1]
Weiss, George M.[3]
Wright, George[6]
Wright, Harry[1, 6]
Yawkey, Thomas[3]

1. Manager. 2. Umpire. 3. Executive. 4. Writer-statistician. 5. Commissioner. 6. Early player. 7. Player-manager.

BASEBALL'S PERFECTLY PITCHED GAMES[1]
(no opposing runner reached base)

- Lee Richmond—Worcester vs. Cleveland (N.L.) June 12, 1880 (1–0)
- John M. Ward—Providence vs. Buffalo (N.L.) June 17, 1880 (5–0)
- Cy Young—Boston vs. Philadelphia (A.L.) May 5, 1904 (3–0)
- Addie Joss—Cleveland vs. Chicago (A.L.) Oct. 2, 1908 (1–0)
- Ernest Shore[2]—Boston vs. Washington (A.L.) June 23, 1917 (4–0)
- Charles Robertson—Chicago vs. Detroit (A.L.) April 30, 1922 (2–0)
- Don Larsen[3]—New York (A.L.) vs. Brooklyn (N.L.) Oct. 8, 1956 (2–0)
- Jim Bunning—Philadelphia vs. New York (N.L.) June 21, 1964 (6–0)
- Sandy Koufax—Los Angeles vs. Chicago (N.L.) Sept. 9, 1965 (1–0)
- Jim Hunter—Oakland vs. Minnesota (A.L.) May 8, 1968 (4–0)
- Len Barker—Cleveland vs. Toronto (A.L.) May 15, 1981 (3–0)
- Mike Witt—California vs. Texas (A.L.) Sept. 30, 1984 (1–0)
- Tom Browning—Cincinnati vs. Los Angeles (N.L.) Sept. 16, 1988 (1–0)
- Dennis Martinez—Montreal vs. Los Angeles (N.L.) July 28, 1991 (2–0)
- Kenny Rogers—Texas vs. California (A.L.) July 28, 1994 (4–0)
- David Wells—New York vs. Minnesota (A.L.) May 17, 1998 (4–0)
- David Cone[4]—New York (A.L.) vs. Montreal (N.L.) July 18, 1999 (6–0)

1. Harvey Haddix, of Pittsburgh, pitched 12 perfect innings against Milwaukee (N.L.), May 26, 1959, but lost game in 13th on error and hit. Montreal's Pedro Martinez pitched nine perfect innings against the San Diego Padres on June 3, 1995 before surrendering a leadoff double to Bip Roberts in the 10th. Mel Rojas finished the game, which Montreal won, 1–0. 2. Shore, relief pitcher for Babe Ruth who walked first batter before being ejected by umpire, retired 26 batters who faced him and base-runner was out stealing. 3. World Series. 4. Interleague game.

LIFETIME BATTING, PITCHING, AND BASE-RUNNING RECORDS
(Records through 2002. Boldface indicates player active in 2002 season.)

Hits (3,000+)

Pete Rose	4,256
Ty Cobb	4,189
Hank Aaron	3,771
Stan Musial	3,630
Tris Speaker	3,514
Carl Yastrzemski	3,419
Cap Anson	3,418
Honus Wagner	3,415
Paul Molitor	3,319
Eddie Collins	3,315
Willie Mays	3,283
Eddie Murray	3,255
Nap Lajoie	3,242
Cal Ripken, Jr.	3,184
George Brett	3,154
Paul Waner	3,152
Robin Yount	3,142
Tony Gwynn	3,141
Dave Winfield	3,110
Rickey Henderson	**3,055**
Rod Carew	3,053
Lou Brock	3,023
Wade Boggs	3,010
Al Kaline	3,007
Roberto Clemente	3,000

Earned Run Average (Minimum 1,500 innings pitched)

Ed Walsh	1.82
Addie Joss	1.89
Al Spalding	2.04
Mordecai Brown	2.06
John Ward	2.10
Christy Mathewson	2.13
Tommy Bond	2.14
Rube Waddell	2.16
Walter Johnson	2.17
Ed Reulbach	2.28
Will White	2.28
Ed Plank	2.35
Larry Corcoran	2.36
Ed Cicotte	2.38
Candy Cummings	2.39
Doc White	2.39
Nap Rucker	2.42
George Bradley	2.43
Jim McCormick	2.43

Runs Scored

Rickey Henderson	**2,295**
Ty Cobb	2,246
Hank Aaron	2,174
Babe Ruth	2,174
Pete Rose	2,165
Willie Mays	2,062
Cap Anson	1,996
Stan Musial	1,949
Barry Bonds	**1,941**
Lou Gehrig	1,888
Tris Speaker	1,882
Mel Ott	1,859
Frank Robinson	1,829
Eddie Collins	1,821
Carl Yastrzemski	1,816
Ted Williams	1,798
Paul Molitor	1,782
Charlie Gehringer	1,774
Jimmie Foxx	1,751
Honus Wagner	1,736
Jim O'Rourke	1,729
Jesse Burkett	1,720
Willie Keeler	1,719
Billy Hamilton	1,691
Bid McPhee	1,678
Mickey Mantle	1,677
Dave Winfield	1,669
Joe Morgan	1,650

Strikeouts, Pitching

Nolan Ryan	5,714
Steve Carlton	4,136
Roger Clemens	**4,099**
Randy Johnson	**3,871**
Bert Blyleven	3,701
Tom Seaver	3,640
Don Sutton	3,574
Gaylord Perry	3,534
Walter Johnson	3,508
Phil Niekro	3,342
Ferguson Jenkins	3,192
Bob Gibson	3,117
Jim Bunning	2,855
Mickey Lolich	2,832
Cy Young	2,803
Frank Tanana	2,773
Greg Maddux	**2,765**
David Cone	2,668
Chuck Finley	**2,610**
Warren Spahn	2,583
Bob Feller	2,581
Tim Keefe	2,564
Jerry Koosman	2,556

Home Runs

Hank Aaron	755
Babe Ruth	714
Willie Mays	660
Barry Bonds	**658**
Frank Robinson	586
Mark McGwire	583
Harmon Killebrew	573
Reggie Jackson	563
Mike Schmidt	548
Sammy Sosa	**539**
Mickey Mantle	536
Jimmie Foxx	534
Rafael Palmeiro	**528**
Willie McCovey	521
Ted Williams	521
Ernie Banks	512
Eddie Mathews	512
Mel Ott	511
Eddie Murray	504
Lou Gehrig	493
Fred McGriff	**491**
Ken Griffey, Jr.	**481**
Stan Musial	475
Willie Stargell	475
Dave Winfield	465
Jose Canseco	462
Carl Yastrzemski	452
Dave Kingman	442
Andre Dawson	438
Cal Ripken, Jr.	431
Juan Gonzalez	**429**
Billy Williams	426
Jeff Bagwell	**419**
Frank Thomas	**418**
Darrell Evans	414
Duke Snider	407
Al Kaline	399
Andres Galarraga	**398**
Dale Murphy	398
Joe Carter	396
Graig Nettles	390
Johnny Bench	389
Dwight Evans	385
Harold Baines	384
Frank Howard	382
Jim Rice	382
Albert Belle	**381**
Jim Thome	**381**
Orlando Cepeda	379
Tony Perez	379
Gary Sheffield	**379**

Shutouts

Walter Johnson	110
Grover Alexander	90
Christy Mathewson	79
Cy Young	76
Ed Plank	69
Warren Spahn	63
Nolan Ryan	61
Tom Seaver	61
Bert Blyleven	60
Don Sutton	58
Pud Galvin	57
Ed Walsh	57
Bob Gibson	56
Mordecai Brown	55
Steve Carlton	55
Jim Palmer	53
Gaylord Perry	53

Strikeouts, Batting

Reggie Jackson	2,597
Andres Galarraga	**2,000**
Sammy Sosa	**1,977**
Jose Canseco	1,942
Willie Stargell	1,936
Mike Schmidt	1,883
Tony Perez	1,867
Fred McGriff	**1,863**
Dave Kingman	1,816
Bobby Bonds	1,757
Dale Murphy	1,748
Lou Brock	1,730
Mickey Mantle	1,710
Harmon Killebrew	1,699
Chili Davis	1,698
Dwight Evans	1,697
Rickey Henderson	**1,694**
Dave Winfield	1,686
Gary Gaetti	1,602
Mark McGwire	1,596
Lee May	1,570
Jim Thome	**1,559**
Dick Allen	1,556
Willie McCovey	1,550
Dave Parker	1,537
Frank Robinson	1,532
Lance Parrish	1,527

Walks

Rickey Henderson	**2,190**
Barry Bonds	**2,070**
Babe Ruth	2,062
Ted Williams	2,019
Joe Morgan	1,865
Carl Yastrzemski	1,845
Mickey Mantle	1,733
Mel Ott	1,708
Eddie Yost	1,614
Darrell Evans	1,605
Stan Musial	1,599
Pete Rose	1,566
Harmon Killebrew	1,559
Lou Gehrig	1,508
Mike Schmidt	1,507
Eddie Collins	1,499
Willie Mays	1,464
Jimmie Foxx	1,452
Eddie Mathews	1,444
Frank Robinson	1,420
Wade Boggs	1,412
Hank Aaron	1,402

RECORD OF WORLD SERIES GAMES
(through 2002)

Figures in parentheses for winning pitchers (WP) and losing pitchers (LP) indicate the game number in the series.

1903—Boston A.L. 5 (Jimmy Collins); Pittsburgh N.L. 3 (Fred Clarke). WP—Boston: Dinneen (2, 6, 8), Young (5, 7); Pittsburgh: Phillippe (1, 3, 4). LP—Boston: Young (1), Hughes (3), Dinneen (4); Pittsburgh: Leever (2, 6), Kennedy (5), Phillippe (7, 8).

1904—No series.

1905—New York N.L. 4 (John J. McGraw); Philadelphia A.L. 1 (Connie Mack). WP—New York: Mathewson (1, 3, 5); McGinnity (4); Phila.: Bender (2). LP—New York: McGinnity (2); Phila.: Plank (1, 4), Coakley (3), Bender (5).

1906—Chicago A.L. 4 (Fielder Jones); Chicago N.L. 2 (Frank Chance). WP—Chicago: A.L.: Altrock (1), Walsh (3, 5), White (6); Chicago: N.L.: Reulbach (2), Brown (4). LP—Chicago A.L.: White (2), Altrock. (4); Chicago: N.L.: Brown (1, 6), Pfeister (3, 5).

1907—Chicago N.L. 4 (Frank Chance); Detroit A.L. 0 (Hugh Jennings). First game tied 3–3, 12 innings. WP—Pfeister (2), Reulbach (3), Overall (4), Brown (5). LP—Mullin (2, 5), Siever (3), Donovan (4).

1908—Chicago N.L. 4 (Frank Chance); Detroit A.L. 1 (Hugh Jennings). WP—Chicago: Brown (1, 4), Overall (2, 5); Det.: Mullin (3). LP—Chicago: Pfeister (3); Det.: Summers (1, 4), Donovan (2, 5).

1909—Pittsburgh N.L. 4 (Fred Clarke); Detroit A.L. 3 (Hugh Jennings). WP—Pittsburgh: Adams (1, 5, 7), Maddox (3); Det.: Donovan (2), Mullin (4, 6). LP—Pittsburgh: Camnitz (2), Leifield (4), Willis (6); Det.: Mullin (1), Summers (3, 5), Donovan (7).

1910—Philadelphia A.L. 4 (Connie Mack); Chicago N.L. 1 (Frank Chance). WP—Phila.: Bender (1), Coombs (2, 3, 5); Chicago: Brown (4). LP—Phila.: Bender (4); Chicago: Overall (1), Brown (2, 5), McIntyre (3).

1911—Philadelphia A.L. 4 (Connie Mack); New York N.L. 2 (John J. McGraw). WP—Phila.: Plank (2), Coombs (3), Bender (4, 6); New York: Mathewson (1), Crandall (5). LP—Phila.: Bender (1), Plank (5); New York: Marquard (2), Mathewson (3, 4), Ames (6).

1912—Boston A.L. 4 (J. Garland Stahl); New York N.L. 3 (John J. McGraw). Second game tied, 6–6, 11 innings. WP—Boston: Wood (1, 4, 8), Bedient (5); New York: Marquard (3, 6), Tesreau (7). LP—Boston: O'Brien (3, 6), Wood (7); New York: Tesreau (1, 4), Mathewson (5, 8).

1913—Philadelphia A.L. 4 (Connie Mack); New York N.L. 1 (John J. McGraw). WP—Phila.: Bender (1, 4), Bush (3), Plank (5); New York: Mathewson (2); LP—Phila.: Plank (2); New York: Marquard (1), Tesreau (3), Demaree (4), Mathewson (5).

1914—Boston N.L. 4 (George Stallings); Philadelphia A.L. 0 (Connie Mack). WP—Rudolph (1, 4), James (2, 3). LP—Bender (1), Plank (2), Bush (3), Shawkey (4).

1915—Boston A.L. 4 (Bill Carrigan); Philadelphia N.L. 1 (Pat Moran). WP—Boston: Foster (2, 5), Leonard (3), Shore (4); Phila.: Alexander (1). LP—Boston: Shore (1); Phila.: Mayer (2), Alexander (3), Chalmers (4), Rixey (5).

1916—Boston A.L. 4 (Bill Carrigan); Brooklyn N.L. 1 (Wilbert Robinson). WP—Boston: Shore (1, 5), Ruth (2), Leonard (4); Brooklyn: Coombs (3). LP—Boston: Mays (3); Brooklyn: Marquard (1, 4), Smith (2), Pfeffer (5).

1917—Chicago A.L. 4 (Clarence Rowland); New York N.L. 2 (John J. McGraw). WP—Chicago: Cicotte (1), Faber (2, 5, 6); New York: Benton (3), Schupp (4), LP—Chicago: Cicotte (3), Faber (4); New York: Sallee (1, 5), Anderson (2), Benton (6).

1918—Boston A.L. 4 (Ed Barrow); Chicago N.L. 2 (Fred Mitchell). WP—Boston: Ruth (1, 4), Mays (3, 6); Chicago: Tyler (2), Vaughn (5). LP—Boston: Bush (2), Jones (5); Chicago: Vaughn (1, 3), Douglas (4), Tyler (6).

1919—Cincinnati N.L. 5 (Pat Moran); Chicago A.L. 3 (William Gleason). WP—Cincinnati: Ruether (1), Sallee (2), Ring (4), Eller (5, 8); Chicago: Kerr (3, 6), Cicotte (7). LP—Cincinnati: Fisher (3), Ring (6), Sallee (7); Chicago: Cicotte (1, 4), Williams (2, 5, 8).

1920—Cleveland A.L. 5 (Tris Speaker); Brooklyn N.L. 2 (Wilbert Robinson). WP—Cleve.: Coveleski (1, 4, 7), Bagby (5), Mails (6); Brooklyn: Grimes (2), Smith (3). LP—Cleve.: Bagby (2), Caldwell (3). Brooklyn: Marquard (1), Cadore (4), Grimes (5, 7), Smith (6).

1921—New York N.L. 5 (John J. McGraw); New York A.L. 3 (Miller Huggins). WP—New York N.L.: Barnes (3, 6), Douglas (4, 7), Nehf (8); New York A.L.: Mays (1), Hoyt (2, 5). LP—New York N.L.: Nehf (2, 5), Douglas (1). New York A.L.: Quinn (3), Mays (4, 7), Shawkey (6), Hoyt (8).

1922—New York N.L. 4 (John J. McGraw); New York A.L. 0 (Miller Huggins). Second game tied 3–3, 10 innings. WP—Ryan (1), Scott (3), McQuillan (4), Nehf (5); LP—Bush (1, 5), Hoyt (3), Mays (4).

1923—New York A.L. 4 (Miller Huggins); New York N.L. 2 (John J. McGraw). WP—New York A.L.: Pennock (2, 6), Shawkey (4), Bush (5); New York N.L.: Ryan (1), Nehf (3). LP—New York A.L.: Bush (1), Jones (3); New York N.L.: McQuillan (2), Scott (4), Bentley (5), Nehf (6).

1924—Washington A.L. 4 (Bucky Harris); New York N.L. 3 (John J. McGraw). WP—Washington: Zachary (2, 6), Mogridge (4), Johnson (7); New York: Nehf (1), McQuillan (3), Bentley (5). LP—Washington: Johnson (1, 5), Marberry (3); New York: Bentley (2, 7), Barnes (4), Nehf (6).

1925—Pittsburgh N.L. 4 (Bill McKechnie); Washington A.L. 3 (Bucky Harris). WP—Pittsburgh: Aldridge (2, 5), Kremer (6, 7); Washington: Johnson (1, 4), Ferguson (3). LP—Pittsburgh: Meadows (1), Kremer (3), Yde (4); Washington: Coveleski (2, 5), Ferguson (6), Johnson (7).

1926—St. Louis N.L. 4 (Rogers Hornsby); New York A.L. 3 (Miller Huggins). WP—St. Louis: Alexander (2, 6), Haines (3, 7); New York: Pennock (1, 5), Hoyt (4). LP—St. Louis: Sherdel (1, 5), Reinhart (4); New York: Shocker (2),

Ruether (3), Shawkey (6), Hoyt (7).

1927—New York A.L. 4 (Miller Huggins); Pittsburgh N.L. 0 (Donie Bush). WP—Hoyt (1), Pipgras (2), Pennock (3), Moore (4). LP—Kremer (1), Aldridge (2), Meadows (3), Miljus (4).

1928—New York A.L. 4 (Miller Huggins); St. Louis N.L. 0 (Bill McKechnie). WP—Hoyt (1, 4), Pipgras (2), Zachary (3). LP—Sherdel (1, 4), Alexander (2), Haines (3).

1929—Philadelphia A.L. 4 (Connie Mack); Chicago N.L. 1 (Joe McCarthy). WP—Phila.: Ehmke (1), Earnshaw (2), Rommel (4), Walberg (5); Chicago: Bush (3). LP—Phila.: Earnshaw (3) Chicago: Root (1), Malone (2, 5), Blake (4).

1930—Philadelphia A.L. 4 (Connie Mack); St. Louis N.L. 2 (Gabby Street). WP—Phila.: Grove (1, 5), Earnshaw (2, 6); St. Louis: Hallahan (3), Haines (4). LP—Phila.: Walberg (3), Grove (4); St. Louis: Grimes (1, 5), Rhem (2), Hallahan (6).

1931—St. Louis N.L. 4 (Gabby Street); Philadelphia A.L. 3 (Connie Mack). WP—St. Louis: Hallahan (2, 5), Grimes (3, 7); Phila.: Grove (1, 6), Earnshaw (4). LP—St. Louis: Derringer (1, 6), Johnson (4); Phila.: Earnshaw (2, 7), Grove (3), Hoyt (5).

1932—New York A.L. (Joe McCarthy); Chicago N.L. 0 (Charles Grimm). WP—Ruffing (1), Gomez (2), Pipgras (3), Moore (4). LP—Bush (1), Warneke (2), Root (3), May (4).

1933—New York N.L. 4 (Bill Terry); Washington A.L. 1 (Joe Cronin.). WP—New York: Hubbell (1, 4), Schumacher (2), Luque (5); Washington: Whitehill (3). LP—New York: Fitzsimmons (3); Washington: Stewart (1), Crowder (2), Weaver (4), Russell (5).

1934—St. Louis N.L. 4 (Frank Frisch); Detroit A.L. 3 (Mickey Cochrane). WP—St. Louis: J. Dean (1, 7), P. Dean (3, 6); Det.: Rowe (2), Auker (4), Bridges (5). LP—St. Louis: W. Walker (2, 4), J. Dean (5); Det.: Crowder (1), Bridges (3), Rowe (6), Auker (7).

1935—Detroit A.L. 4 (Mickey Cochrane); Chicago N.L. 2 (Charles Grimm). WP—Det.: Bridges (2, 6), Rowe (3), Crowder (4); Chicago: Warneke (1, 5); LP—Det.: Rowe (1, 5), Chicago: Root (2), French (3, 6), Carleton (4).

1936—New York A.L. 4 (Joe McCarthy); New York N.L. 2 (Bill Terry). WP—New York A.L.: Gomez (2, 6), Hadley (3), Pearson (4); New York N.L.: Hubbell (1), Schumacher (5); LP—New York A.L.: Ruffing (1), Malone (5); New York N.L.: Schumacher (2), Fitzsimmons (3, 6), Hubbell (4).

1937—New York A.L. 4 (Joe McCarthy); New York N.L. 1 (Bill Terry). WP—New York A.L.: Gomez (1, 5), Ruffing (2), Pearson (3); New York N.L.: Hubbell (4). LP—New York A.L.: Hadley (4); New York N.L.: Hubbell (1), Melton (2, 5), Schumacher (3).

1938—New York A.L. 4 (Joe McCarthy); Chicago N.L. 0 (Gabby Hartnett). WP—Ruffing (1, 4), Gomez (2), Pearson (3) LP—Lee (1, 4), Dean (2), Bryant (3).

1939—New York A.L. 4 (Joe McCarthy); Cincinnati N.L. 0 (Bill McKechnie). WP—Ruffing (1), Pearson (2), Hadley (3), Murphy (4). LP—Derringer (1), Walters (2, 4), Thompson (3).

1940—Cincinnati N.L. 4 (Bill McKechnie); Detroit A.L. 3 (Del Baker). WP—Cincinnati: Walters (2, 6), Derringer (4, 7); Det.: Newsom (1, 5), Bridges (3). LP—Cincinnati: Derringer (1), Turner (3), Thompson (5); Det.: Rowe (2, 6), Trout (4), Newsom (7).

1941—New York A.L. 4 (Joe McCarthy); Brooklyn N.L. 1 (Leo Durocher). WP—New York: Ruffing (1), Russo (3), Murphy (4), Bonham (5); Bklyn: Wyatt (2). LP—New York: Chandler (2); Bklyn: Davis (1), Casey (3, 4), Wyatt (5).

1942—St. Louis N.L. 4 (Billy Southworth); New York A.L. 1 (Joe McCarthy). WP—St. Louis: Beazley (2, 5), White (3), Lanier (4); New York: Ruffing (1). LP—St. Louis: Cooper (1); New York: Bonham (2), Chandler (3), Donald (4), Ruffing (5).

1943—New York A.L. 4 (Joe McCarthy); St. Louis N.L. 1 (Billy Southworth). WP—New York: Chandler (1, 5), Borowy (3), Russo (4); St. Louis: Cooper (2). LP—New York: Bonham (2); St. Louis: Lanier (1), Brazle (3), Brecheen (4), Cooper (5).

1944—St. Louis N.L. 4 (Billy Southworth); St. Louis A.L. 2 (Luke Sewell). WP—St. Louis N.L.: Donnelly (2), Brecheen (4), Cooper (5), Lanier (6); St. Louis A.L.: Galehouse (1), Kramer (3). LP—St. Louis N.L.: Cooper (1), Wilks (3); St. Louis A.L.: Muncrief (2), Jakucki (4), Galehouse (5), Potter (6).

1945—Detroit A.L. 4 (Steve O'Neill); Chicago N.L. 3 (Charles Grimm). WP—Det.: Trucks (2), Trout (4), Newhouser (5, 7); Chicago: Borowy (1, 6), Passeau (3). LP—Det.: Newhouser (1), Overmire (3), Trout (6); Chicago: Wyse (2), Prim (4), Borowy (5, 7).

1946—St. Louis N.L. 4 (Eddie Dyer); Boston A.L. 3 (Joe Cronin). WP—St. Louis: Brecheen (2, 6, 7), Munger (4); Boston: Johnson (1), Ferriss (3), Dobson (5). LP—St. Louis: Pollet (1), Dickson (3), Brazle (5); Boston: Harris (2, 6), Hughson (4), Klinger (7).

1947—New York A.L. 4 (Bucky Harris); Brooklyn N.L. 3 (Burt Shotton). WP—New York: Shea (1, 5), Reynolds (2), Page (7); Brooklyn: Casey (3, 4), Branca (6). LP—New York: Newsom (3), Bevens (4), Page (6); Brooklyn: Branca (1), Lombardi (2), Barney (5), Gregg (7).

1948—Cleveland A.L. 4 (Lou Boudreau); Boston N.L. 2 (Billy Southworth). WP—Cleve.: Lemon (2, 6), Bearden (3), Gromek (4); Boston: Sain (1), Spahn (5). LP—Cleve.: Feller (1, 5); Boston: Spahn (2), Bickford (3), Sain (4), Voiselle (6).

1949—New York A.L. 4 (Casey Stengel); Brooklyn N.L. 1 (Burt Shotton). WP—New York: Reynolds (1), Page (3), Lopat (4), Raschi (5); Brooklyn: Roe (2). LP—New York: Raschi (2); Brooklyn: Newcombe (1, 4), Branca (3), Barney (5).

1950—New York A.L. 4 (Casey Stengel); Philadelphia N.L. 0 (Eddie Sawyer). WP—Raschi (1), Reynolds (2), Ferrick (3), Ford (4). LP—Konstanty (1), Roberts (2), Meyer (3), Miller (4).

1951—New York A.L. 4 (Casey Stengel); New York N.L. 2 (Leo Durocher). WP—New York A.L.: Lopat (2, 5), Reynolds (4), Raschi (6); New York N.L.: Koslo (1), Hearn (3). LP—New York A.L.: Reynolds (1), Raschi (3); New York N.L.: Jansen (2, 5), Maglie (4), Koslo (6).

1952—New York A.L. 4 (Casey Stengel); Brooklyn N.L. 3 (Chuck Dressen). WP—New York: Raschi (2, 6), Reynolds (4, 7); Brooklyn: Black (1), Roe (3), Erskine (5). LP—New York: Reynolds (1), Lopat (3), Sain (5); Brooklyn: Erskine (2), Black (4, 7), Loes (6).

1953—New York A.L. 4 (Casey Stengel); Brooklyn N.L. 2 (Chuck Dressen). WP—New York: Sain (1), Lopat (2), McDonald (5), Reynolds (6); Brooklyn: Erskine (3), Loes (4). LP—New York: Raschi (3), Ford (4); Brooklyn: Labine (1, 6), Roe (2), Podres (5).

1954—New York N.L. 4 (Leo Durocher); Cleveland A.L. 0 (Al Lopez). WP—Grissom (1), Antonelli (2), Gomez (3), Liddie (4). LP—Lemon (1, 4), Wynn (2), Garcia (3).

1955—Brooklyn N.L. 4 (Walter Alston); New York A.L. 3 (Casey Stengel). WP—Brooklyn: Podres (3, 7), Labine (4), Craig (5); New York: Ford (1, 6), Byrne (2). LP—Brooklyn: Newcombe (1), Loes (2), Spooner (6); New York: Turley (3), Larsen (4), Grim (5), Byrne (7).

1956—New York A.L. 4 (Casey Stengel); Brooklyn N.L. 3 (Walter Alston). WP—New York: Ford (3), Sturdivant (4), Larsen (5), Kucks (7); Brooklyn: Maglie (1), Bessent (2), Labine (6). LP—New York: Ford (1), Morgan (2), Turley (6); Brooklyn: Craig (3), Erskine (4), Maglie (5), Newcombe (7).

1957—Milwaukee N.L. 4 (Fred Haney); New York A.L. 3 (Casey Stengel). WP—Milwaukee: Burdette (2, 5, 7), Spahn (4); New York: Ford (1), Larsen (3), Turley (6). LP—Milwaukee: Spahn (1), Buhl (3), Johnson (6); New York: Shantz (2), Grim (4), Ford (5), Larsen (7).

1958—New York A.L. 4 (Casey Stengel); Milwaukee N.L. 3 (Fred Haney). WP—New York: Larsen (3), Turley (5, 7), Duren (6); Milwaukee: Spahn (1, 4), Burdette (2). LP—New York: Duren (1), Turley (2), Ford (4); Milwaukee: Rush (3), Burdette (5, 7), Spahn (6).

1959—Los Angeles N.L. 4 (Walter Alston); Chicago A.L. 2 (Al Lopez). WP—Los Angeles: Podres (2), Drysdale (3), Sherry (4, 6); Chicago: Wynn (1), Shaw (5). LP—Los Angeles: Craig (1), Koufax (5); Chicago: Shaw (2), Donovan (3), Staley (4), Wynn (6).

1960—Pittsburgh N.L. 4 (Danny Murtaugh); New York A.L. 3 (Casey Stengel). WP—Pittsburgh: Law (1, 4), Haddix (5, 7); New York: Turley (2), Ford (3, 6). LP—Pittsburgh: Friend (2, 6), Mizell (3); New York: Ditmar (1, 5), Terry (4, 7).

1961—New York A.L. 4 (Ralph Houk); Cincinnati N.L. 1 (Fred Hutchinson). WP—New York: Ford (1, 4), Arroyo (3), Daley (5); Cincinnati: Jay (2). LP—New York: Terry (2); Cincinnati: O'Toole (1, 4), Purkey (3), Jay (5).

1962—New York A.L. 4 (Ralph Houk); San Francisco N.L. 3 (Al Dark). WP—New York: Ford (1), Stafford (3), Terry (5, 7); San Francisco Sanford (2), Larsen (4), Pierce (6). LP—New York: Terry (2), Coates (4), Ford (6); San Francisco: O'Dell (1), Pierce (3), Sanford (5, 7).

1963—Los Angeles N.L. 4 (Walter Alston); New York A.L. 0 (Ralph Houk). WP—Koufax (1, 4), Podres (2), Drysdale (3). LP—Ford (1, 4), Downing (2), Bouton (3).

1964—St. Louis N.L. 4 (Johnny Keane); New York A.L. 3 (Yogi Berra). WP—St. Louis: Sadecki (1), Craig (4), Gibson (5, 7); New York: Stottlemyre (2), Bouton (3, 6). LP—St. Louis: Gibson (2), Schultz (3), Simmons (6); New York: Ford (1), Downing (4), Mikkelsen (5), Stottlemyre (7).

1965—Los Angeles N.L. 4 (Walter Alston); Minnesota A.L. 3 (Sam Mele). WP—Los Angeles: Osteen (3), Drysdale (4), Koufax (5, 7); Minnesota: Grant (1, 6), Kaat (2). LP—Los Angeles: Drysdale (1), Koufax (2), Osteen (6); Minnesota: Pascual (3), Grant (4), Kaat (5, 7).

1966—Baltimore A.L. 4 (Hank Bauer); Los Angeles N.L. 0 (Walter Alston). WP—Drabowsky (1), Palmer (2), Bunker (3), McNally (4). LP—Drysdale (1, 4), Koufax (2), Osteen (3).

1967—St. Louis N.L. 4 (Red Schoendienst); Boston A.L. 3 (Dick Williams). WP—St. Louis: Gibson (1, 4, 7), Briles (3); Boston: Lonborg (2, 5); Wyatt (6). LP—St. Louis: Hughes (2), Carlton (5), Lamabe (6); Boston: Santiago (1, 4), Bell (3), Lonborg (7).

1968—Detroit A.L. 4 (Mayo Smith); St. Louis N.L. 3 (Red Schoendienst). WP—Det.: Lolich (2, 5, 7), McLain (6); St. Louis: Gibson (1, 4), Washburn (3), LP—Det.: McLain (1, 4), Wilson (3); St. Louis: Briles (2), Hoerner (5), Washburn (6), Gibson (7).

1969—New York N.L. 4 (Gil Hodges); Baltimore A.L. 1 (Earl Weaver). WP—New York: Koosman (2, 5), Gentry (3), Seaver (4); Baltimore: Cuellar (1). LP—New York: Seaver (1); Baltimore: McNally (2), Palmer (3), Hall (4), Watt (5).

1970—Baltimore A.L. 4 (Earl Weaver); Cincinnati N.L. 1 (Sparky Anderson) 1. WP—Baltimore: Palmer (1), Phoebus (2), McNally (3), Cuellar (5); Cincinnati: Carroll (4). LP—Cincinnati: Nolan (1), Wilcox (2), Cloninger (3), Merritt (5); Baltimore: Watt (4).

1971—Pittsburgh N.L. 4 (Danny Murtaugh); Baltimore A.L. 3 (Earl Weaver). WP—Pittsburgh: Blass (3, 7), Kison (4), Briles (5); Baltimore: McNally (1, 6), Palmer (2). LP—Pittsburgh: Ellis (1), R. Johnson (2), Miller (6); Baltimore: Cuellar (3, 7), Watt (4) McNally (5).

1972—Oakland A.L. 4 (Dick Williams); Cincinnati N.L. (Sparky Anderson) 3. WP—Oakland: Holtzman (1), Hunter (2, 7), Fingers (4); Cincinnati: Billingham (3), Grimsley (5, 6). LP—Oakland: Odom (3), Fingers (5), Blue (6); Cincinnati: Nolan (1), Grimsley (2), Carroll (4), Borbon (7).

1973—Oakland A.L. 4 (Dick Williams): New York N.L. 3 (Yogi Berra). WP—Oakland: Holtzman (1, 7), Lindblad (3), Hunter (6). New York: McGraw (2), Matlack (4), Koosman (5). LP—Oakland: Fingers (2), Holtzman (4), Blue (5). New York: Matlack (1, 7) Parker (3), Seaver (6).

1974—Oakland A.L. 4 (Al Dark); Los Angeles N.L. 1 (Walter Alston). WP—Oakland: Fingers (1), Hunter (3), Holtzman (4), Odom (5). Los Angeles: Sutton (2). LP—Oakland: Blue (2), Los Angeles: Messersmith (1, 4), Downing (3), Marshall (5).

1975—Cincinnati N.L. 4 (Sparky Anderson); Boston A.L. 3 (Darrell Johnson). WP—Cincinnati: Eastwick (2, 3), Gullett (5), Carroll (7); Boston: Tiant (1, 4), Wise (6). LP—Cincinnati: Gullett (1), Norman (4), Darcy (6); Boston: Drago (2), Willoughby (3), Cleveland (5), Burton (7).

1976—Cincinnati N.L. 4 (Sparky Anderson); New York A.L. 0 (Billy Martin). WP—Gullett (1), Billingham (2), Zachry (3), Nolan (4). LP—Alexander (1), Hunter (2), Ellis (3), Figueroa (4).

1977—New York A.L. 4 (Billy Martin); Los Angeles N.L. 2 (Tom Lasorda). WP—New York: Lyle (1), Torrez (3, 6), Guidry (4); Los Angeles: Hooton (2), Sutton (5). LP—New York: Hunter (2), Gullett (5); Los Angeles: Rhoden (1), John (3), Rau (4), Hooton (6).

1978—New York A.L. 4 (Bob Lemon), Los Angeles N.L. 2 (Tom Lasorda); WP—New York: Guidry (3), Gossage (4); Beattie (5), Hunter (6); Los Angeles: John (1), Hooton (2). LP—New York: Figueroa (1), Hunter (2); Los Angeles: Sutton (3, 6), Welch (4), Hooton (5).

1979—Pittsburgh N.L. 4 (Chuck Tanner), Baltimore A.L. 3 (Earl Weaver); WP—Pittsburgh: D. Robinson (2), Blyleven (5), Candelaria (6), Jackson (7); Baltimore: Flanagan (1), McGregor (3), Stoddard (4). LP—Pittsburgh: Kison (1), Candelaria (3), Tekulve (4); Baltimore: Stanhouse (2), Flanagan (5), Palmer (6), McGregor (7).

1980—Philadelphia N.L. 4 (Dallas Green), Kansas City A.L. 2 (Jim Frey); WP—Philadelphia: Walk (1), Carlton (2), McGraw (5), Carlton (6); Kansas City: Quisenberry (3), Leonard (4). LP—Philadelphia: McGraw (3), Christenson (4); Kansas City: Leonard (1), Quisenberry (2), Quisenberry (5), Gale (6).

1981—Los Angeles N.L. 4 (Tom Lasorda), New York A.L. 2 (Bob Lemon); WP—Los Angeles: Valenzuela (3), Howe (4), Reuss (5), Hooton (6); New York: Guidry (1), John (2). LP—Los Angeles: Reuss (1), Hooton (2); New York: Frazier (3), Frazier (4), Guidry (5), Frazier (6).

1982—St. Louis N.L. 4 (Whitey Herzog), Milwaukee A.L. 3 (Harvey Kuenn); WP—St. Louis: Sutter (2), Andujar (3), Stuper (6), Andujar (7). Milwaukee: Caldwell (1), Slaton (4), Caldwell (5). LP—St. Louis: Forsch (1), Bair (4), Forsch (5). Milwaukee: McClure (2), Vuckovich (3), Sutton (6), McClure (7).

1983—Baltimore A.L. 4 (Joe Altobelli), Philadelphia N.L. 1 (Paul Owens); WP—Baltimore: Boddicker (2), Palmer (3), Davis (4), McGregor (5). Philadelphia: Denny (1).

1984—Detroit A.L. 4 (Sparky Anderson), San Diego N.L. 1 (Dick Williams); WP—Det.: Morris (1,4), Wilcox (3), Lopez (5), San Diego: Hawkins (2). LP—Det.: Petry (2), San Diego: Thurmond (1), Lollar (3), Show (4), Hawkins (5).

1985—Kansas City A.L. 4 (Dick Howser), St. Louis N.L. 3 (Whitey Herzog); WP—KC: Saberhagen (3,7) Quisenberry (6), Jackson (5). St. Louis: Tudor (1,4) Dayley (2). LP—KC: Jackson (1), Leibrandt (2), Black (4); St. Louis: Andujar (3), Forsch (5), Worrell (6), Tudor (7).

1986—New York N.L. 4 (Dave Johnson); Boston A.L. (John McNamara) 3 WP—New York—Ojeda (3), Darling (4), Aguilera (6), McDowell (7), Bos: Hurst (1), (5), Crawford (2). LP—New York Darling (1), Gooden (2, 5).

1987—Minnesota A.L. 4 (Tom Kelly); St. Louis N.L. (Whitey Herzog) 3. WP—Minnesota Viola (1, 7), Blyleven (2), Schatzeder (6), St. Louis: Tudor (3), Forsch (4), Cox (5). LP—Minnesota Berenguer (3), Viola (4), Blyleven (5); St. Louis: Magrane (1), Cox (2, 7), Tudor (6).

1988—Los Angeles N.L. 4 (Tommy Lasorda); Oakland A.L.

(Tony LaRussa) 1. WP—Los Angeles: Hershiser (2, 5), Pena (1), Belcher (4); Oakland: Honeycutt (3). LP—Los Angeles: Howell (3); Oakland: Davis (2, 5), Eckersley (1), Stewart (4).

1989—Oakland A.L. 4 (Tony LaRussa); San Francisco N.L. 0 (Roger Craig). WP—Oakland: Dave Stewart (1, 3), Mike Moore (2, 4). LP—San Francisco: Scott Garrelts (1, 3), Don Robinson (4), Rick Reuschel (2).

1990—Cincinnati N.L. 4 (Lou Piniella); Oakland A.L. 0 (Tony LaRussa). WP—Cincinnati: Jose Rijo (1, 4), Rob Dibble (2), Tom Browning (3). LP—Oakland: Dave Stewart (1, 4), Dennis Eckersley (2), Mike Moore (3).

1991—Minnesota A.L. 4 (Tom Kelly); Atlanta N.L. 3 (Bobby Cox). WP—Minnesota: Morris (1,7), Tapani (2), Aguilera (6). Atlanta: Clancy (3), Stanton (4), Glavine (5). LP—Minnesota: Aguilera (3), Gurhtie (4), Tapani (5). Atlanta: Leibrandt (1, 6), Glavine (2), Pena (7).

1992—Toronto A.L. 4 (Cito Gaston); Atlanta N.L. 2 (Bobby Cox). WP—Toronto: Ward (2, 3), Key (4, 6). Atlanta: Glavine (1), Smoltz (5). LP—Toronto: Morris (1, 5). Atlanta: Leibrandt (6), Reardon (2), Avery (3), Glavine (4).

1993—Toronto A.L. 4 (Cito Gaston); Philadelphia N.L. 2 (Jim Fregosi). WP—Toronto: Leiter (1), Hentgen (3), Castillo (4), Ward (6). Philadelphia: Mullholland (2), Schilling (5). LP—Toronto: Stewart (2), Guzman (5). Philadelphia: Schilling (1), Jackson (3), Williams (4, 6).

1994—World Series cancelled due to players' strike.

1995—Atlanta N.L. 4 (Bobby Cox); Cleveland A.L. 2 (Mike Hargrove). WP—Atlanta: Maddux (1), Glavine (2,6), Avery (4). Cleveland: Mesa (3), Hershiser (5). LP—Atlanta: Pena (3), Maddux (5). Cleveland: Hershiser (1), Martinez (2), Hill (4), Poole (6).

1996—New York A.L. 4 (Joe Torre); Atlanta N.L. 2 (Bobby Cox). WP—New York: Cone (3), Lloyd (4), Pettitte (5), Key (6). Atlanta: Smoltz (1), Maddux (2). LP—New York: Pettitte (1), Key (2). Atlanta: Glavine (3), Avery (4), Smoltz (5), Maddux (6).

1997—Florida N.L. 4 (Jim Leyland); Cleveland A.L. 3 (Mike Hargrove). WP—Florida: Hernandez (1, 5), Cook (3), Powell (7). Cleveland: Ogea (2, 6), Wright (4). LP—Florida: Brown (2, 6), Saunders (4). Cleveland: Hershiser (1, 5), Plunk (3), Nagy (7).

1998—New York A.L. 4 (Joe Torre); San Diego N.L. 0 (Bruce Bochy). WP—New York: Wells (1), Hernandez (2), Mendoza (3), Pettitte (4). LP—San Diego: Wall (1), Ashby (2), Hoffman (3), Brown (4).

1999—New York A.L. 4 (Joe Torre); Atlanta N.L. 0 (Bobby Cox). WP—New York: Hernandez (1), Cone (2), Rivera (3), Clemens (4). LP—Atlanta: Maddux (1), Millwood (2), Remlinger (3), Smoltz (4).

2000—New York Yankees A.L. 4 (Joe Torre); New York Mets N.L. 1 (Bobby Valentine). WP—Yankees: Stanton (1, 5), Clemens (2), Nelson (4). Mets: Franco (3). LP—Wendell (1), Hampton (2), Jones (4), Leiter (5). Yankees: Hernandez (3).

2001—Arizona Diamondbacks N.L. 4 (Bob Brenly); New York Yankees A.L. 3 (Joe Torre). WP—Arizona: Schilling (1), Johnson (2, 6, 7). New York: Clemens (3), Rivera (4), Hitchcock (5). LP—New York: Mussina (1), Pettitte (2, 6), Rivera (7). Arizona: Anderson (3), Kim (4), Lopez (5).

2002—Anaheim Angels A.L. 4 (Scioscia); San Francisco Giants N.L. (Baker). WP—Anaheim: Rodriguez (2), Ortiz (3), Donnelly (6), Lackey (7). San Francisco: Schmidt (1), Worrell (4), Zerbe (5). LP—Anaheim: Washburn (1, 5), Rodriguez (4). San Francisco: Rodriguez (2), Hernandez (3, 7), Worrell (6).

WORLD SERIES CLUB STANDINGS

(through 2002)

	Series	Won	Lost	Pct.
Toronto (A)	2	2	0	1.000
Florida (N)	1	1	0	1.000
Arizona (N)	1	1	0	1.000
Anaheim (A)	1	1	0	1.000
Pittsburgh (N)	7	5	2	.714
New York (A)	38	26	12	.684
Oakland (A)	6	4	2	.667
Minnesota (A)	3	2	1	.667
Philadelphia (A)	8	5	3	.625
St. Louis (N)	15	9	6	.600
Boston (A)	9	5	4	.556
Los Angeles (N)	9	5	4	.556
Cincinnati (N)	9	5	4	.556
New York (N-Mets)	4	2	2	.500
Milwaukee (N)	2	1	1	.500
Boston (N)	2	1	1	.500
Chicago (A)	4	2	2	.500
Baltimore (A)	6	3	3	.500
Kansas City (A)	2	1	1	.500
Detroit (A)	9	4	5	.444
Cleveland (A)	5	2	3	.400
New York (N-Giants)	14	5	9	.357
Washington (A)	3	1	2	.333
Atlanta (N)	5	1	4	.200
Philadelphia (N)	5	1	4	.200
Chicago (N)	10	2	8	.200
Brooklyn (N)	9	1	8	.111
St. Louis (A)	1	0	1	.000
San Francisco (N)	3	0	3	.000
Milwaukee (A)	1	0	1	.000
San Diego (N)	2	0	2	.000

Recapitulation	Won
American League	57
National League	39

AMERICAN LEAGUE CHAMPIONSHIP SERIES—2002

Anaheim Angels defeated Minnesota Twins, 4 games to 1

Oct. 8—Minnesota 2, Anaheim 1
Oct. 9—Anaheim 6, Minnesota 3
Oct. 11—Anaheim 2, Minnesota 1
Oct. 12—Anaheim 7, Minnesota 1
Oct. 13—Anaheim 13, Minnesota 5

NATIONAL LEAGUE CHAMPIONSHIP SERIES—2002

San Francisco Giants defeated St. Louis Cardinals, 4 games to 1

Oct. 9—San Francisco 9, St. Louis 6
Oct. 10—San Francisco 4, St. Louis 1
Oct. 12—St. Louis 5, San Francisco 4
Oct. 13—San Francisco 4, St. Louis 3
Oct. 14—San Francisco 2, St. Louis 1

WORLD SERIES—2002

Anaheim Angels win series, 4 games to 3
Series MVP—Troy Glaus

1st Game, at Anaheim, Oct. 19, 2002

					R	H	E
San Francisco	020	002	000	—	4	6	0
Anaheim	010	002	000	—	3	9	0

Pitchers—San Francisco: Schmidt (W), Rodriguez, Worrell, Nen (S, 1). Anaheim: Washburn (L), Donnelly, Schoeneweis, Weber. Attendance: 44,603.

2nd Game, at Anaheim, Oct. 20, 2002

					R	H	E
San Francisco	041	040	001	—	10	12	1
Anaheim	520	011	02x	—	11	16	1

Pitchers—San Francisco: Ortiz, Zerbe, Witasick, Fultz, Rodriguez (L), Worrell. Anaheim: Appier, Lackey, Weber, Rodriguez (W), Percival (S, 1). Attendance: 44,584.

3rd Game, at San Francisco, Oct. 22, 2002

					R	H	E
Anaheim	004	401	010	—	10	16	0
San Francisco	100	030	000	—	4	6	2

Pitchers—Anaheim: Ortiz (W), Donnelly, Schoeneweis. San Francisco: Hernandez (L), Witasick, Fultz, Rodriguez, Eyre. Attendance: 42,707.

4th Game, at San Francisco, Oct. 23, 2002

					R	H	E
Anaheim	012	000	000	—	3	10	1
San Francisco	000	030	01x	—	4	12	1

Pitchers—Anaheim: Lackey, Weber, Rodriguez (L). San Francisco: Rueter, Rodriguez, Worrell (W), Nen (S, 2). Attendance: 42,703.

5th Game, at San Francisco, Oct. 24, 2002

					R	H	E
Anaheim	000	031	000	—	4	10	2
San Francisco	330	002	44x	—	16	16	0

Pitchers—Anaheim: Washburn (L), Donnelly, Weber, Shields. San Francisco: Schmidt, Zerbe (W), Rodriguez, Worrell, Eyre. Attendance: 42,713.

6th Game, at Anaheim, Oct. 26, 2002

					R	H	E
San Francisco	000	031	100	—	5	8	1
Anaheim	000	000	33x	—	6	10	1

Pitchers—San Francisco: Ortiz, Rodriguez, Eyre, Worrell (L), Nen. Anaheim: Appier, Rodriguez, Donnelly (W), Percival (S, 2). Attendance: 44,506.

7th Game, at Anaheim, Oct. 27, 2002

					R	H	E
San Francisco	010	000	000	—	1	6	0
Anaheim	013	000	00x	—	4	5	0

Pitchers—San Francisco: Hernandez (L), Zerbe, Rueter, Worrell. Anaheim: Lackey (W), Donnelly, Rodriguez, Percival (S, 3). Attendance: 44,598.

WORLD SERIES SINGLE GAME AND SINGLE SERIES RECORDS

(through 2002)

Most hits game—5, Paul Molitor, Milwaukee A.L., first game vs. St. Louis N.L., 1982.

Most 4-hit games, series—2, Robin Yount, Milwaukee A.L., first and fifth games vs. St. Louis N.L., 1982.

Most hits inning—2, held by 17 players.

Most hits series—13 (7 games) Bobby Richardson, New York A.L., 1964; Lou Brock, St. Louis N.L., 1968; Marty Barrett, Boston A.L., 1986.

Most home runs, series—5 (6 games) Reggie Jackson, New York A.L., 1977; 4 (4 games) Lou Gehrig, New York A.L., 1928; 4 (6 games) Willie Aikens, Kansas City A.L., 1980; 4 (7 games) Babe Ruth, New York A.L., 1926; Duke Snider, Brooklyn N.L., 1952, 1955; Hank Bauer, New York A.L., 1958; Gene Tenace, Oakland A.L., 1972; 4 Barry Bonds, San Francisco N.L., 2002.

Most home runs, game—3, Babe Ruth, New York A.L., 1926 and 1928; Reggie Jackson, New York A.L., 1977.

Most strikeouts, series—12 (6 games) Willie Wilson, Kansas City A.L., 1980; 11 (7 games) Ed Mathews, Milwaukee N.L., 1958; Wayne Garrett, New York N.L., 1973; 9 (5 games) Carmelo Martinez, San Diego N.L., 1984; 7 (4 games) Bob Muesel, New York A.L., 1927; Ken Caminiti, San Diego N.L., 1998.

Most stolen bases, game—3, Honus Wagner, Pittsburgh N.L., 1909; Willie Davis, Los Angeles N.L., 1965; Lou Brock, St. Louis N.L., 1967 and 1968.

Most strikeouts by pitcher, game—17, Bob Gibson, St. Louis N.L. 1968.

Most strikeouts by pitcher in succession—6, Horace Eller, Cincinnati N.L., 1919; Moe Drabowsky, Baltimore A.L., 1966.

Most strikeouts by pitcher, series—35 (7 games) Bob Gibson, St. Louis N.L., 1968; 23 (4 games) Sandy Koufax, Los Angeles, 1963; 20 (6 games) Chief Bender, Philadelphia A.L., 1911; 18 (5 games) Christy Mathewson, New York N.L., 1905.

Most bases on balls, series—13 (7 games) Barry Bonds, San Francisco N.L., 2002; 11 (7 games) Babe Ruth, New York A.L., 1926; Gene Tenace, Oakland A.L., 1973; 9 (6 games) Willie Randolph, New York A.L., 1981; 7 (5 games) James Sheckard, Chicago N.L., 1910; Mickey Cochrane, Philadelphia A.L., 1929; Joe Gordon, New York A.L., 1941; 7 (4 games) Hank Thompson, New York N.L., 1954.

Most consecutive scoreless innings one series—27, Christy Mathewson, New York N.L., 1905.

LIFETIME WORLD SERIES RECORDS
(through 2002)

Most hits—71, Yogi Berra, New York A.L., 1947, 1949–53, 1955–58, 1960–63.
Most runs—42, Mickey Mantle, New York A.L., 1951–53, 1955–58, 1960–64.
Most runs batted in—40, Mickey Mantle, New York A.L., 1951–53, 1955–58, 1960–64.
Most home runs—18, Mickey Mantle, New York A.L., 1951–53, 1955–58, 1960–64.
Most bases on balls—43, Mickey Mantle, New York A.L., 1951–53, 1955–58, 1960–64.
Most strikeouts—54, Mickey Mantle, New York A.L., 1951–53, 1955–58, 1960–64.
Most stolen bases—14, Eddie Collins, Philadelphia A.L. 1910–11, 13–14; Chicago A.L., 1917, 1919. Lou Brock, St. Louis N.L., 1964, 67–68.
Most victories, pitcher—10, Whitey Ford, New York A.L., 1950, 1953, 1955–58, 1960–64.
Most times member of winning team—10, Yogi Berra, New York A.L., 1947, 1949–53, 1956, 1958, 1961–62.
Most victories, no defeats—6, Vernon Gomez, New York A.L., 1932, 1936(2), 1937(2), 1938.
Most shutouts—4, Christy Mathewson, New York N.L., 1905 (3), 1913.
Most innings pitched—146, Whitey Ford, New York A.L., 1950, 1953, 1955–58, 1960–1964
Most consecutive scoreless innings—33⅔, Whitey Ford, New York A.L., 1960 (18), 1961 (14), 1962 (1⅔).
Most strikeouts by pitcher—94, Whitey Ford, New York A.L., 1950, 1953, 1955–58, 1960–64.

AMERICAN LEAGUE HOME RUN CHAMPIONS

Year	Player, team	No.
1901	Nap Lajoie, Philadelphia	13
1902	Ralph Seybold, Philadelphia	16
1903	Buck Freeman, Boston	13
1904	Harry Davis, Philadelphia	10
1905	Harry Davis, Philadelphia	8
1906	Harry Davis, Philadelphia	12
1907	Harry Davis, Philadelphia	8
1908	Sam Crawford, Detroit	7
1909	Ty Cobb, Detroit	9
1910	J. Garland Stahl, Boston	10
1911	Franklin Baker, Philadelphia	9
1912	Franklin Baker, Philadelphia	10
1913	Franklin Baker, Philadelphia	12
1914	Franklin Baker, Philadelphia; Sam Crawford, Detroit	8
1915	Robert Roth, Chicago-Cleveland	7
1916	Wally Pipp, New York	12
1917	Wally Pipp, New York	9
1918	Babe Ruth, Boston; Clarence Walker, Philadelphia	11
1919	Babe Ruth, Boston	29
1920	Babe Ruth, New York	54
1921	Babe Ruth, New York	59
1922	Ken Williams, St. Louis	39
1923	Babe Ruth, New York	41
1924	Babe Ruth, New York	46
1925	Bob Meusel, New York	33
1926	Babe Ruth, New York	47
1927	Babe Ruth, New York	60
1928	Babe Ruth, New York	54
1929	Babe Ruth, New York	46
1930	Babe Ruth, New York	49
1931	Lou Gehrig, New York; Babe Ruth, New York	46
1932	Jimmie Foxx, Philadelphia	58
1933	Jimmie Foxx, Philadelphia	48
1934	Lou Gehrig, New York	49
1935	Jimmie Foxx, Philadelphia; Hank Greenberg, Detroit	36
1936	Lou Gehrig, New York	49
1937	Joe DiMaggio, New York	46
1938	Hank Greenberg, Detroit	58
1939	Jimmie Foxx, Boston	35
1940	Hank Greenberg, Detroit	41
1941	Ted Williams, Boston	37
1942	Ted Williams, Boston	36
1943	Rudy York, Detroit	34
1944	Nick Etten, New York	22
1945	Vern Stephens, St. Louis	24
1946	Hank Greenberg, Detroit	44
1947	Ted Williams, Boston	32
1948	Joe DiMaggio, New York	39
1949	Ted Williams, Boston	43
1950	Al Rosen, Cleveland	37
1951	Gus Zernial, Chicago-Philadelphia	33
1952	Larry Doby, Cleveland	32
1953	Al Rosen, Cleveland	43
1954	Larry Doby, Cleveland	32
1955	Mickey Mantle, New York	37
1956	Mickey Mantle, New York	52
1957	Roy Sievers, Washington	42
1958	Mickey Mantle, New York	42
1959	Rocky Colavito, Cleveland; Harmon Killebrew, Washington	42
1960	Mickey Mantle, New York	40
1961	Roger Maris, New York	61
1962	Harmon Killebrew, Minnesota	48
1963	Harmon Killebrew, Minnesota	45
1964	Harmon Killebrew, Minnesota	49
1965	Tony Conigliaro, Boston	32
1966	Frank Robinson, Baltimore	49
1967	Carl Yastrzemski, Boston; Harmon Killebrew, Minnesota	44
1968	Frank Howard, Washington	44
1969	Harmon Killebrew, Minnesota	49
1970	Frank Howard, Washington	44
1971	Bill Melton, Chicago	33
1972	Dick Allen, Chicago	37
1973	Reggie Jackson, Oakland	32
1974	Dick Allen, Chicago	32
1975	Reggie Jackson, Oakland; George Scott, Milwaukee	36
1976	Graig Nettles, New York	32
1977	Jim Rice, Boston	39
1978	Jim Rice, Boston	46
1979	Gorman Thomas, Milwaukee	45
1980	Reggie Jackson, New York; Ben Oglivie, Milwaukee	41
1981[1]	Tony Armas, Oakland; Dwight Evans, Boston; Bobby Grich, California; Eddie Murray, Baltimore (tie)	22
1982	Gorman Thomas, Milwaukee; Reggie Jackson, California	39
1983	Jim Rice, Boston	39
1984	Tony Armas, Boston	43
1985	Darrell Evans, Detroit	40
1986	Jesse Barfield, Toronto	40
1987	Mark McGwire, Oakland	49
1988	Jose Canseco, Oakland	42
1989	Fred McGriff, Toronto	36
1990	Cecil Fielder, Detroit	51
1991	Jose Canseco, Oakland; Cecil Fielder, Detroit (tie)	44
1992	Juan Gonzalez, Texas	43
1993	Juan Gonzalez, Texas	46
1994[2]	Ken Griffey, Jr., Seattle	40
1995	Albert Belle, Cleveland	50
1996	Mark McGwire, Oakland	52
1997	Ken Griffey, Jr., Seattle	56
1998	Ken Griffey, Jr., Seattle	56
1999	Ken Griffey, Jr., Seattle	48
2000	Tony Glaus, Anaheim	47
2001	Alex Rodriguez, Texas	52
2002	Alex Rodriguez, Texas	57
2003	Alex Rodriguez, Texas	47

1. Split season because of players' strike. 2. Season ended on Aug. 12 because of players' strike.

AMERICAN LEAGUE BATTING CHAMPIONS

Year	Player, team	Avg.
1901	Nap Lajoie, Philadelphia	.422
1902	Ed Delahanty, Washington	.376
1903	Nap Lajoie, Cleveland	.355
1904	Nap Lajoie, Cleveland	.381
1905	Elmer Flick, Cleveland	.306
1906	George Stone, St. Louis	.358
1907	Ty Cobb, Detroit	.350
1908	Ty Cobb, Detroit	.324
1909	Ty Cobb, Detroit	.377
1910	Ty Cobb, Detroit	.385
1911	Ty Cobb, Detroit	.420
1912	Ty Cobb, Detroit	.410
1913	Ty Cobb, Detroit	.390
1914	Ty Cobb, Detroit	.368
1915	Ty Cobb, Detroit	.369
1916	Tris Speaker, Cleveland	.386
1917	Ty Cobb, Detroit	.383
1918	Ty Cobb, Detroit	.382
1919	Ty Cobb, Detroit	.384
1920	George Sisler, St. Louis	.407
1921	Harry Heilmann, Detroit	.394
1922	George Sisler, St. Louis	.420
1923	Harry Heilmann, Detroit	.403
1924	Babe Ruth, New York	.378
1925	Harry Heilmann, Detroit	.393
1926	Heinie Manush, Detroit	.378
1927	Harry Heilmann, Detroit	.398
1928	Goose Goslin, Washington	.379
1929	Lew Fonseca, Cleveland	.369
1930	Al Simmons, Philadelphia	.381
1931	Al Simmons, Philadelphia	.390
1932	Dale Alexander, Detroit-Boston	.367
1933	Jimmie Foxx, Philadelphia	.356
1934	Lou Gehrig, New York	.363
1935	Buddy Myer, Washington	.349
1936	Luke Appling, Chicago	.388
1937	Charley Gehringer, Detroit	.371
1938	Jimmie Foxx, Boston	.349
1939	Joe DiMaggio, New York	.381
1940	Joe DiMaggio, New York	.352
1941	Ted Williams, Boston	.406
1942	Ted Williams, Boston	.356
1943	Luke Appling, Chicago	.328
1944	Lou Boudreau, Cleveland	.327
1945	George Sternweiss, New York	.309
1946	Mickey Vernon, Washington	.353
1947	Ted Williams, Boston	.343
1948	Ted Williams, Boston	.369
1949	George Kell, Detroit	.343
1950	Billy Goodman, Boston	.354
1951	Ferris Fain, Philadelphia	.344
1952	Ferris Fain, Philadelphia	.327
1953	Mickey Vernon, Washington	.337
1954	Bobby Avila, Cleveland	.341
1955	Al Kaline, Detroit	.340
1956	Mickey Mantle, New York	.353
1957	Ted Williams, Boston	.388
1958	Ted Williams, Boston	.328
1959	Harvey Kuenn, Detroit	.353
1960	Pete Runnels, Boston	.320
1961	Norman Cash, Detroit	.361
1962	Pete Runnels, Boston	.326
1963	Carl Yastrzemski, Boston	.321
1964	Tony Oliva, Minnesota	.323
1965	Tony Oliva, Minnesota	.321
1966	Frank Robinson, Baltimore	.316
1967	Carl Yastrzemski, Boston	.326
1968	Carl Yastrzemski, Boston	.301
1969	Rod Carew, Minnesota	.332
1970	Alex Johnson, California	.329
1971	Tony Oliva, Minnesota	.337
1972	Rod Carew, Minnesota	.318
1973	Rod Carew, Minnesota	.350
1974	Rod Carew, Minnesota	.364
1975	Rod Carew, Minnesota	.359
1976	George Brett, Kansas City	.333
1977	Rod Carew, Minnesota	.388
1978	Rod Carew, Minnesota	.333
1979	Fred Lynn, Boston	.333
1980	George Brett, Kansas City	.390
1981[1]	Carney Lansford, Boston	.336
1982	Willie Wilson, Kansas City	.332
1983	Wade Boggs, Boston	.361
1984	Don Mattingly, New York	.343
1985	Wade Boggs, Boston	.368
1986	Wade Boggs, Boston	.357
1987	Wade Boggs, Boston	.363
1988	Wade Boggs, Boston	.366
1989	Kirby Puckett, Minnesota	.339
1990	George Brett, Kansas City	.328
1991	Julio Franco, Texas	.341
1992	Edgar Martinez, Seattle	.343
1993	John Olerud, Toronto	.363
1994[2]	Paul O'Neill, New York	.359
1995	Edgar Martinez, Seattle	.356
1996	Alex Rodriguez, Seattle	.358
1997	Frank Thomas, Chicago	.347
1998	Bernie Williams, New York	.339
1999	Nomar Garciaparra, Boston	.357
2000	Nomar Garciaparra, Boston	.372
2001	Ichiro Suzuki, Seattle	.350
2002	Manny Ramirez, Boston	.349
2003	Bill Mueller, Boston	.326

1. Split season because of players' strike. 2. Season ended on Aug. 12 because of players' strike.

NATIONAL LEAGUE HOME RUN CHAMPIONS

Year	Player, team	No.
1876	George Hall, Philadelphia Athletics	5
1877	George Shaffer, Louisville	3
1878	Paul Hines, Providence	4
1879	Charles Jones, Boston	9
1880	James O'Rourke, Boston; Harry Stovey, Worcester	6
1881	Dan Brouthers, Buffalo	8
1882	George Wood, Detroit	7
1883	William Ewing, New York	10
1884	Ed Williamson, Chicago	27
1885	Abner Dalrymple, Chicago	11
1886	Arthur Richardson, Detroit	11
1887	Roger Connor, New York; Wm. O'Brien, Washington	17
1888	Roger Connor, New York	14
1889	Sam Thompson, Philadelphia	20
1890	Tom Burns, Brooklyn; Mike Tiernan, New York	13
1891	Harry Stovey, Boston; Mike Tiernan, New York	16
1892	Jim Holliday, Cincinnati	13
1893	Ed Delahanty, Philadelphia	19
1894	Hugh Duffy, Boston; Robert Lowe, Boston	18
1895	Bill Joyce, Washington	17
1896	Ed Delahanty, Philadelphia; Sam Thompson, Philadelphia	13
1897	Nap Lajoie, Philadelphia	10
1898	James Colins, Boston	14
1899	John Freeman, Washington	25
1900	Herman Long, Boston	12
1901	Sam Crawford, Cincinnati	16
1902	Tom Leach, Pittsburgh	6
1903	James Sheckard, Brooklyn	9
1904	Harry Lumley, Brooklyn	9
1905	Fred Odwell, Cincinnati	9
1906	Tim Jordan, Brooklyn	12
1907	David Brain, Boston	10
1908	Tim Jordan, Brooklyn	12
1909	John Murray, New York	7
1910	Fred Beck, Boston; Frank Schulte, Chicago	10
1911	Frank Schulte, Chicago	21
1912	Henry Zimmerman, Chicago	14
1913	Cliff Cravath, Philadelphia	19
1914	Cliff Cravath, Philadelphia	19
1915	Cliff Cravath, Philadelphia	24
1916	Davis Robertson, New York; Fred Williams, Chicago	12
1917	Davis Robertson, New York; Cliff Cravath, Philadelphia	12
1918	Cliff Cravath, Philadelphia	8
1919	Cliff Cravath, Philadelphia	12
1920	Cy Williams, Philadelphia	15
1921	George Kelly, New York	23
1922	Rogers Hornsby, St. Louis	42
1923	Cy Williams, Philadelphia	41
1924	Jacques Fournier, Brooklyn	27
1925	Rogers Hornsby, St. Louis	39
1926	Hack Wilson, Chicago	21
1927	Hack Wilson, Chicago; Cy Williams, Philadelphia	30
1928	Hack Wilson, Chicago; Jim Bottomley, St. Louis	31
1929	Chuck Klein, Philadelphia	43
1930	Hack Wilson, Chicago	56
1931	Chuck Klein, Philadelphia	31
1932	Chuck Klein, Philadelphia; Mel Ott, New York	38
1933	Chuck Klein, Philadelphia	28
1934	Mel Ott, New York; Rip Collins, St. Louis	35
1935	Wally Berger, Boston	34
1936	Mel Ott, New York	33
1937	Mel Ott, New York; Joe Medwick, St. Louis	31
1938	Mel Ott, New York	36
1939	John Mize, St. Louis	28
1940	John Mize, St. Louis	43
1941	Dolph Camilli, Brooklyn	34
1942	Mel Ott, New York	30
1943	Bill Nicholson, Chicago	29

Year	Player, team	No.
1944	Bill Nicholson, Chicago	33
1945	Tommy Holmes, Boston	28
1946	Ralph Kiner, Pittsburgh	23
1947	Ralph Kiner, Pittsburgh; John Mize, New York	51
1948	Ralph Kiner, Pittsburgh; John Mize, New York	40
1949	Ralph Kiner, Pittsburgh	54
1950	Ralph Kiner, Pittsburgh	47
1951	Ralph Kiner, Pittsburgh	42
1952	Ralph Kiner, Pittsburgh; Hank Sauer, Chicago	37
1953	Ed Mathews, Milwaukee	47
1954	Ted Kluszewski, Cincinnati	49
1955	Willie Mays, New York	51
1956	Duke Snider, Brooklyn	43
1957	Hank Aaron, Milwaukee	44
1958	Ernie Banks, Chicago	47
1959	Ed Mathews, Milwaukee	46
1960	Ernie Banks, Chicago	41
1961	Orlando Cepeda, San Francisco	46
1962	Willie Mays, San Francisco	49
1963	Hank Aaron, Milwaukee; Willie McCovey, San Francisco	44
1964	Willie Mays, San Francisco	47
1965	Willie Mays, San Francisco	52
1966	Hank Aaron, Atlanta	44
1967	Hank Aaron, Atlanta	39
1968	Willie McCovey, San Francisco	36
1969	Willie McCovey, San Francisco	45
1970	Johnny Bench, Cincinnati	45
1971	Willie Stargell, Pittsburgh	48
1972	Johnny Bench, Cincinnati	40
1973	Willie Stargell, Pittsburgh	44
1974	Mike Schmidt, Philadelphia	36
1975	Mike Schmidt, Philadelphia	38
1976	Mike Schmidt, Philadelphia	38
1977	George Foster, Cincinnati	52
1978	George Foster, Cincinnati	40
1979	Dave Kingman, Chicago	48
1980	Mike Schmidt, Philadelphia	48
1981[1]	Mike Schmidt, Philadelphia	31
1982	Dave Kingman, New York	37
1983	Mike Schmidt, Philadelphia	40
1984	Mike Schmidt, Philadelphia; Dale Murphy, Atlanta	36
1985	Dale Murphy, Atlanta	37
1986	Mike Schmidt, Philadelphia	37
1987	Andre Dawson, Chicago	49
1988	Darryl Strawberry, New York	39
1989	Kevin Mitchell, San Francisco	47
1990	Ryne Sandberg, Chicago	40
1991	Howard Johnson, New York	38
1992	Fred McGriff, San Diego	35
1993	Barry Bonds, San Francisco	46
1994[2]	Matt Williams, San Francisco	43
1995	Dante Bichette, Colorado	40
1996	Andres Galarraga, Colorado	40
1997	Larry Walker, Colorado	49
1998	Mark McGwire, St. Louis	70
1999	Mark McGwire, St. Louis	65
2000	Sammy Sosa, Chicago	50
2001	Barry Bonds, San Francisco	73
2002	Sammy Sosa, Chicago	49
2003	Jim Thome, Philadelphia	47

1. Split season because of players' strike. 2. Season ended on Aug. 12 because of players' strike.

NATIONAL LEAGUE BATTING CHAMPIONS

Year	Player, team	Avg.
1876	Roscoe Barnes, Chicago	.404
1877	Jim White, Boston	.385
1878	Abner Dalrymple, Milwaukee	.356
1879	Cap Anson, Chicago	.407
1880	George Gore, Chicago	.365
1881	Cap Anson, Chicago	.399
1882	Dan Brouthers, Buffalo	.367
1883	Dan Brouthers, Buffalo	.371
1884	James O'Rourke, Buffalo	.350
1885	Roger Connor, New York	.371
1886	King Kelly, Chicago	.388
1887	Cap Anson, Chicago	.421
1888	Cap Anson, Chicago	.343
1889	Dan Brouthers, Boston	.373
1890	John Glasscock, New York	.336
1891	William Hamilton, Philadelphia	.338
1892	Dan Brouthers, Brooklyn; Clarence Childs, Cleveland	.335
1893	Hugh Duffy, Boston	.378
1894	Hugh Duffy, Boston	.438
1895	Jesse Burkett, Cleveland	.423
1896	Jesse Burkett, Cleveland	.410
1897	Willie Keeler, Baltimore	.432
1898	Willie Keeler, Baltimore	.379
1899	Ed Delahanty, Philadelphia	.408
1900	Honus Wagner, Pittsburgh	.381
1901	Jesse Burkett, St. Louis	.382
1902	Clarence Beaumont, Pittsburgh	.357
1903	Honus Wagner, Pittsburgh	.355
1904	Honus Wagner, Pittsburgh	.349
1905	Cy Seymour, Cincinnati	.377
1906	Honus Wagner, Pittsburgh	.339
1907	Honus Wagner, Pittsburgh	.350
1908	Honus Wagner, Pittsburgh	.354
1909	Honus Wagner, Pittsburgh	.339
1910	Sherwood Magee, Philadelphia	.331
1911	Honus Wagner, Pittsburgh	.334
1912	Henry Zimmerman, Chicago	.372
1913	Jake Daubert, Brooklyn	.350
1914	Jake Daubert, Brooklyn	.329
1915	Larry Doyle, New York	.320
1916	Hal Chase, Cincinnati	.339
1917	Edd Roush, Cincinnati	.341
1918	Zack Wheat, Brooklyn	.335
1919	Edd Roush, Cincinnati	.321
1920	Rogers Hornsby, St. Louis	.370
1921	Rogers Hornsby, St. Louis	.397
1922	Rogers Hornsby, St. Louis	.401
1923	Rogers Hornsby, St. Louis	.384
1924	Rogers Hornsby, St. Louis	.424
1925	Rogers Hornsby, St. Louis	.403
1926	Gene Hargrave, Cincinnati	.353
1927	Paul Waner, Pittsburgh	.380
1928	Rogers Hornsby, Boston	.387
1929	Lefty O'Doul, Philadelphia	.398
1930	Bill Terry, New York	.401
1931	Chick Hafey, St. Louis	.349
1932	Lefty O'Doul, Brooklyn	.368
1933	Chuck Klein, Philadelphia	.368
1934	Paul Waner, Pittsburgh	.362
1935	Arky Vaughan, Pittsburgh	.385
1936	Paul Waner, Pittsburgh	.373
1937	Joe Medwick, St. Louis	.374
1938	Ernie Lombardi, Cincinnati	.342
1939	John Mize, St. Louis	.349
1940	Debs Garms, Pittsburgh	.355
1941	Pete Reiser, Brooklyn	.343
1942	Ernie Lombardi, Boston	.330
1943	Stan Musial, St. Louis	.357
1944	Dixie Walker, Brooklyn	.357
1945	Phil Cavarretta, Chicago	.355
1946	Stan Musial, St. Louis	.365
1947	Harry Walker, St. Louis-Philadelphia	.363
1948	Stan Musial, St. Louis	.376
1949	Jackie Robinson, Brooklyn	.342
1950	Stan Musial, St. Louis	.346
1951	Stan Musial, St. Louis	.355
1952	Stan Musial, St. Louis	.336
1953	Carl Furillo, Brooklyn	.344
1954	Willie Mays, New York	.345
1955	Richie Ashburn, Philadelphia	.338
1956	Hank Aaron, Milwaukee	.328
1957	Stan Musial, St. Louis	.351
1958	Richie Ashburn, Philadelphia	.350
1959	Hank Aaron, Milwaukee	.355
1960	Dick Groat, Pittsburgh	.325
1961	Roberto Clemente, Pittsburgh	.351
1962	Tommy Davis, Los Angeles	.346
1963	Tommy Davis, Los Angeles	.326
1964	Roberto Clemente, Pittsburgh	.339
1965	Roberto Clemente, Pittsburgh	.329
1966	Matty Alou, Pittsburgh	.342
1967	Roberto Clemente, Pittsburgh	.357
1968	Pete Rose, Cincinnati	.335
1969	Pete Rose, Cincinnati	.348
1970	Rico Carty, Atlanta	.366
1971	Joe Torre, St. Louis	.363
1972	Billy Williams, Chicago	.333
1973	Pete Rose, Cincinnati	.338
1974	Ralph Garr, Atlanta	.353
1975	Bill Madlock, Chicago	.354
1976	Bill Madlock, Chicago	.339
1977	Dave Parker, Pittsburgh	.338
1978	Dave Parker, Pittsburgh	.334
1979	Keith Hernandez, St. Louis	.344
1980	Bill Buckner, Chicago	.324
1981[1]	Bill Madlock, Pittsburgh	.341
1982	Al Oliver, Montreal	.331
1983	Bill Madlock, Pittsburgh	.323
1984	Tony Gwynn, San Diego	.351
1985	Willie McGee, St. Louis	.353
1986	Tim Raines, Montreal	.334
1987	Tony Gwynn, San Diego	.370
1988	Tony Gwynn, San Diego	.313

Year	Player, team	Avg.	Year	Player, team	Avg.	Year	Player, team	Avg.
1989	Tony Gwynn, San Diego	.336	1994[2]	Tony Gwynn, San Diego	.394	1999	Larry Walker, Colorado	.379
1990	Willie McGee, St. Louis	.335	1995	Tony Gwynn, San Diego	.368	2000	Todd Helton, Colorado	.372
1991	Terry Pendleton, Atlanta	.319	1996	Tony Gwynn, San Diego	.353	2001	Larry Walker, Colorado	.350
1992	Gary Sheffield, San Diego	.330	1997	Tony Gwynn, San Diego	.372	2002	Barry Bonds, San Francisco	.370
1993	Andres Galarraga, Colorado	.370	1998	Larry Walker, Colorado	.363	2003	Albert Pujols, St. Louis	.359

1. Split season because of players' strike. 2. Season ended on Aug. 12 because of players' strike.

MOST VALUABLE PLAYERS
(Baseball Writers' Association selections)

American League

1931	Lefty Grove, Philadelphia
1932–33	Jimmie Foxx, Philadelphia
1934	Mickey Cochrane, Detroit
1935	Hank Greenberg, Detroit
1936	Lou Gehrig, New York
1937	Charlie Gehringer, Detroit
1938	Jimmie Foxx, Boston
1939	Joe DiMaggio, New York
1940	Hank Greenberg, Detroit
1941	Joe DiMaggio, New York
1942	Joe Gordon, New York
1943	Spurgeon Chandler, New York
1944–45	Hal Newhouser, Detroit
1946	Ted Williams, Boston
1947	Joe DiMaggio, New York
1948	Lou Boudreau, Cleveland
1949	Ted Williams, Boston
1950	Phil Rizzuto, New York
1951	Yogi Berra, New York
1952	Bobby Shantz, Philadelphia
1953	Al Rosen, Cleveland
1954–55	Yogi Berra, New York
1956–57	Mickey Mantle, New York
1958	Jackie Jensen, Boston
1959	Nellie Fox, Chicago
1960–61	Roger Maris, New York
1962	Mickey Mantle, New York
1963	Elston Howard, New York
1964	Brooks Robinson, Baltimore
1965	Zoilo Versalles, Minnesota
1966	Frank Robinson, Baltimore
1967	Carl Yastrzemski, Boston
1968	Dennis McLain, Detroit
1969	Harmon Killebrew, Minnesota
1970	John (Boog) Powell, Baltimore
1971	Vida Blue, Oakland
1972	Dick Allen, Chicago
1973	Reggie Jackson, Oakland
1974	Jeff Burroughs, Texas
1975	Fred Lynn, Boston
1976	Thurman Munson, New York
1977	Rod Carew, Minnesota
1978	Jim Rice, Boston
1979	Don Baylor, California
1980	George Brett, Kansas City
1981	Rollie Fingers, Milwaukee
1982	Robin Yount, Milwaukee
1983	Cal Ripken, Jr., Baltimore
1984	Willie Hernandez, Detroit
1985	Don Mattingly, New York
1986	Roger Clemens, Boston
1987	George Bell, Toronto
1988	Jose Canseco, Oakland
1989	Robin Yount, Milwaukee
1990	Rickey Henderson, Oakland
1991	Cal Ripken, Jr., Baltimore
1992	Dennis Eckersley, Oakland
1993	Frank Thomas, Chicago
1994	Frank Thomas, Chicago
1995	Mo Vaughn, Boston
1996	Juan Gonzalez, Texas
1997	Ken Griffey, Jr., Seattle
1998	Juan Gonzalez, Texas
1999	Ivan Rodriguez, Texas
2000	Jason Giambi, Oakland
2001	Ichiro Suzuki, Seattle
2002	Miguel Tejada, Oakland

National League

1931	Frank Frisch, St. Louis
1932	Chuck Klein, Philadelphia
1933	Carl Hubbell, New York
1934	Dizzy Dean, St. Louis
1935	Gabby Hartnett, Chicago
1936	Carl Hubbell, New York
1937	Joe Medwick, St. Louis
1938	Ernie Lombardi, Cincinnati
1939	Bucky Walters, Cincinnati
1940	Frank McCormick, Cincinnati
1941	Dolph Camilli, Brooklyn
1942	Mort Cooper, St. Louis
1943	Stan Musial, St. Louis
1944	Marty Marion, St. Louis
1945	Phil Cavarretta, Chicago
1946	Stan Musial, St. Louis
1947	Bob Elliott, Boston
1948	Stan Musial, St. Louis
1949	Jackie Robinson, Brooklyn
1950	Jim Konstanty, Philadelphia
1951	Roy Campanella, Brooklyn
1952	Hank Sauer, Chicago
1953	Roy Campanella, Brooklyn
1954	Willie Mays, New York
1955	Roy Campanella, Brooklyn
1956	Don Newcombe, Brooklyn
1957	Hank Aaron, Milwaukee
1958–59	Ernie Banks, Chicago
1960	Dick Groat, Pittsburgh
1961	Frank Robinson, Cincinnati
1962	Maury Wills, Los Angeles
1963	Sandy Koufax, Los Angeles
1964	Ken Boyer, St. Louis
1965	Willie Mays, San Francisco
1966	Roberto Clemente, Pittsburgh
1967	Orlando Cepeda, St. Louis
1968	Bob Gibson, St. Louis
1969	Willie McCovey, San Francisco
1970	Johnny Bench, Cincinnati
1971	Joe Torre, St. Louis
1972	Johnny Bench, Cincinnati
1973	Pete Rose, Cincinnati
1974	Steve Garvey, Los Angeles
1975–76	Joe Morgan, Cincinnati
1977	George Foster, Cincinnati
1978	Dave Parker, Pittsburgh
1979	Willie Stargell, Pittsburgh
1979	Keith Hernandez, St. Louis
1980	Mike Schmidt, Philadelphia
1981	Mike Schmidt, Philadelphia
1982	Dale Murphy, Atlanta
1983	Dale Murphy, Atlanta
1984	Ryne Sandberg, Chicago
1985	Willie McGee, St. Louis
1986	Mike Schmidt, Philadelphia
1987	Andre Dawson, Chicago
1988	Kirk Gibson, Los Angeles
1989	Kevin Mitchell, San Francisco
1990	Barry Bonds, Pittsburgh
1991	Terry Pendleton, Atlanta
1992	Barry Bonds, Pittsburgh
1993	Barry Bonds, San Francisco
1994	Jeff Bagwell, Houston
1995	Barry Larkin, Cincinnati
1996	Ken Caminiti, San Diego
1997	Larry Walker, Colorado
1998	Sammy Sosa, Chicago
1999	Chipper Jones, Atlanta
2000	Jeff Kent, San Francisco
2001–02	Barry Bonds, San Francisco

CY YOUNG AWARD

1956	Don Newcombe, Brooklyn N.L.
1957	Warren Spahn, Milwaukee N.L.
1958	Bob Turley, New York A.L.
1959	Early Wynn, Chicago A.L.
1960	Vernon Law, Pittsburgh N.L
1961	Whitey Ford, New York A.L.
1962	Don Drysdale, Los Angeles N.L.
1963	Sandy Koufax, Los Angeles N.L.
1964	Dean Chance, Los Angeles A.L.
1965	Sandy Koufax, Los Angeles N.L.
1966	Sandy Koufax, Los Angeles N.L.
1967	Jim Lonborg, Boston A.L.; Mike McCormick, San Francisco N.L.
1968	Dennis McLain, Detroit A.L.; Bob Gibson, St. Louis N.L.
1969	Mike Cuellar, Baltimore A.L. and Dennis McLain, Detroit A.L. (tied); Tom Seaver, New York N.L.
1970	Jim Perry, Minnesota A.L.; Bob Gibson, St. Louis N.L.

1971 Vida Blue, Oakland A.L.; Ferguson Jenkins, Chicago N.L.
1972 Gaylord Perry, Cleveland A.L.; Steve Carlton, Philadelphia N.L.
1973 Jim Palmer, Baltimore A.L.; Tom Seaver, New York N.L.
1974 Catfish Hunter, Oakland A.L.; Mike Marshall, Los Angeles N.L.
1975 Jim Palmer, Baltimore A.L.; Tom Seaver, New York N.L.
1976 Jim Palmer, Baltimore A.L.; Randy Jones, San Diego N.L.
1977 Sparky Lyle, New York A.L.; Steve Carlton, Philadelphia N.L.
1978 Ron Guidry, New York A.L.; Gaylord Perry, San Diego N.L.
1979 Mike Flanagan, Baltimore A.L.; Bruce Sutter, Chicago N.L.
1980 Steve Stone, Baltimore A.L.; Steve Carlton, Philadelphia N.L.
1981 Rollie Fingers, Milwaukee A.L.; Fernando Valenzuela, Los Angeles N.L.
1982 Pete Vuckovich, Milwaukee A.L.; Steve Carlton, Philadelphia N.L.
1983 LaMarr Hoyt, Chicago A.L.; John Denny, Philadelphia N.L.
1984 Willie Hernandez, Detroit A.L.; Rick Sutcliffe, Chicago N.L.
1985 Bret Saberhagen, Kansas City A.L.; Dwight Gooden, New York N.L.
1986 Roger Clemens, Boston A.L.; Mike Scott, Houston N.L.
1987 Roger Clemens, Boston A.L.; Steve Bedrosian, Philadelphia N.L.
1988 Frank Viola, Minnesota A.L.; Orel Hershiser, Los Angeles, N.L.
1989 Bret Saberhagen, Kansas A.L.; Mark Davis, San Diego N.L.
1990 Bob Welch, Oakland A.L.; Doug Drabek, Pittsburgh N.L.
1991 Roger Clemens, Boston A.L.; Tom Glavine, Atlanta N.L.
1992 Dennis Eckersley, Oakland A.L.; Greg Maddux, Atlanta N.L.
1993 Jack McDowell, Chicago A.L.; Greg Maddux, Atlanta N.L.
1994 David Cone, Kansas A.L.; Greg Maddux, Atlanta N.L.
1995 Randy Johnson, Seattle A.L.; Greg Maddux, Atlanta N.L.
1996 Pat Hentgen, Toronto A.L.; John Smoltz, Atlanta N.L.
1997 Roger Clemens, Toronto A.L.; Pedro Martinez, Montreal N.L.
1998 Roger Clemens, Toronto A.L.; Tom Glavine, Atlanta N.L.
1999– Pedro Martinez, Boston A.L.;
2000 Randy Johnson, Arizona N.L.
2001 Roger Clemens, New York A.L.; Randy Johnson, Arizona N.L.
2002 Barry Zito, Oakland A.L.; Randy Johnson, Arizona N.L.

MAJOR LEAGUE LIFETIME RECORDS

(through 2003)

Pitching Wins
(Boldface indicates player active in 2003)

		W	L	ERA	G
1.	Cy Young	511	316	2.63	906
2.	Walter Johnson	417	279	2.17	802
3.	Grover Alexander	373	208	2.56	696
4.	Christy Mathewson	373	188	2.13	635
5.	Pud Galvin	365	310	2.85	705
6.	Warren Spahn	363	245	3.09	750
7.	Kid Nichols	361	208	2.95	620
8.	Tim Keefe	342	225	2.62	600
9.	Steve Carlton	329	244	3.22	741
10.	John Clarkson	328	178	2.81	531
11.	Eddie Plank	326	194	2.35	623
12.	Nolan Ryan	324	292	3.19	807
13.	Don Sutton	324	256	3.26	774
14.	Phil Niekro	318	274	3.35	864
15.	Gaylord Perry	314	265	3.11	777
16.	Tom Seaver	311	205	2.86	656
17.	**Roger Clemens**	**310**	**160**	**3.19**	**607**
18.	Charley Radbourn	309	195	2.67	528
19.	Mickey Welch	307	210	2.71	565
20.	Lefty Grove	300	141	3.06	616
21.	Early Wynn	300	244	3.54	691
22.	Bobby Mathews	297	248	2.85	578
23.	**Greg Maddux**	**289**	**163**	**2.89**	**575**
24.	Tommy John	288	231	3.34	760
25.	Bert Blyleven	287	250	3.31	692

Pitchers Active in 2003

		W	L	ERA	G
1.	Roger Clemens	310	160	3.19	607
2.	Greg Maddux	289	163	2.89	575
3.	Tom Glavine	251	157	3.43	537
4.	Randy Johnson	230	114	3.10	454
5.	Chuck Finley	200	173	3.85	524
6.	David Wells	200	128	4.06	557
7.	Mike Mussina	199	110	3.53	386
8.	Kevin Brown	197	131	3.16	451
9.	Jamie Moyer	185	132	4.07	472
10.	Kevin Appier	169	136	3.72	412

Leading Batters, by Batting Average

		G	AB	H	Avg.
1.	Ty Cobb	3,035	11,429	4,191	.367
2.	Rogers Hornsby	2,259	8,173	2,930	.358
3.	Ed Delahanty	1,835	7,505	2,596	.346
4.	Tris Speaker	2,789	10,195	3,514	.345
5.	Billy Hamilton	1,591	6,269	2,159	.344
5.	Ted Williams	2,292	7,706	2,654	.344
7.	Dan Brouthers	1,673	6,711	2,296	.342
7.	Harry Heilmann	2,147	7,787	2,660	.342
7.	Babe Ruth	2,503	8,399	2,873	.342
10.	Willie Keeler	2,123	8,591	2,932	.341
10.	Bill Terry	1,721	6,428	2,193	.341
12.	Lou Gehrig	2,164	8,001	2,721	.340
13.	George Sisler	2,055	8,267	2,812	.340
14.	Jesse Burkett	2,066	8,421	2,850	.338
15.	Tony Gwynn	2,440	9,288	3,141	.338
16.	Nap Lajoie	2,480	9,589	3,242	.338
17.	Al Simmons	2,215	8,759	2,927	.334
18.	Cap Anson	2,523	10,278	3,418	.333
19.	Eddie Collins	2,826	9,949	3,315	.333
20.	Paul Waner	2,549	9,459	3,152	.333
21.	Stan Musial	3,026	10,972	3,630	.331
22.	Sam Thompson	1,407	5,984	1,979	.331
23.	Heinie Manush	2,008	7,654	2,524	.330
24.	Wade Boggs	2,440	9,180	3,010	.328
25.	Rod Carew	2,469	9,315	3,053	.328

Players Active in 2003 (3,000 at-bats minimum)

		G	AB	H	Avg.
1.	Todd Helton	981	3,504	1,182	.337
2.	Nomar Garciaparra	928	3,812	1,231	.323
3.	Vladimir Guerrero	1,004	3,763	1,215	.323
4.	Mike Piazza	1,461	5,350	1,708	.319
5.	Derek Jeter	1,212	4,870	1,546	.317
6.	Manny Ramirez	1,383	5,004	1,585	.317
7.	Edgar Martinez	1,914	6,727	2,119	.315
8.	Larry Walker	1,806	6,334	1,992	.314
9.	Frank Thomas	1,851	6,611	2,048	.310
10.	Chipper Jones	1,405	5,144	1,588	.309

MAJOR LEAGUE ALL-TIME PITCHING RECORDS

(through 2003)

Most Games Won—511, Cy Young, Cleveland N.L., 1890–98, St. Louis N.L., 1899–1900, Boston A.L., 1901–08, Cleveland A.L., 1909–11, Boston N.L., 1911.

Most Games Won, Season—54, Al Spalding, Boston N.A., 1875. (Since 1900—41, Jack Chesbro, New York A.L., 1904.)

Most Consecutive Games Won—24, Carl Hubbell, New York N.L., 1936 (16) and 1937 (8).

Most Consecutive Games Won, Season—19, Tim Keefe, New York N.L., 1888; Rube Marquard, New York N.L., 1912.

Most Years Won 20 or More Games—16, Cy Young, Cleveland N.L., 1891–98, St. Louis N.L., 1899–1900, Boston A.L., 1901–04, 1907–08.

Most Shutouts—110, Walter Johnson, Washington A.L., 1907–27.

Most Shutouts, Season—16, Grover Alexander, Philadelphia N.L., 1916.

Most Consecutive Shutouts—6, Don Drysdale, Los Angeles N.L., 1968.

Most Consecutive Scoreless Innings—59, Orel Hershiser, Los Angeles Dodgers, 1988.

Most Strikeouts—5,714, Nolan Ryan, New York N.L., California A.L., Houston N.L., 1968–1988 Texas, 1989–93.

Most Strikeouts, Season—513, Matthew Kilroy, Baltimore A.A., 1886. (Since 1900—383, Nolan Ryan, California A.L., 1973.)

Most Strikeouts, Game—21, Tom Cheney, Washington A.L., 1962, 16 innings. 20, Roger Clemens, Boston A.L., 1986, nine innings; Kerry Wood, Chicago N.L., 1998, nine innings.

Most Consecutive Strikeouts—10, Tom Seaver, New York N.L. vs. San Diego, April 22, 1970.

Most Games, Season—106, Mike Marshall, Los Angeles N.L., 1974.

Most Complete Games, Season—75, William White, Cincinnati N.L., 1879. (Since 1900—48, Jack Chesbro, New York A.L., 1904.)

MAJOR LEAGUE INDIVIDUAL ALL-TIME HITTING RECORDS

(through 2003)

Highest Batting Average, Season—.440, Hugh Duffy, Boston N.L., 1894;.435, Tip O'Neill, St. Louis, A.A., 1887. (Since 1900—.426, Nap Lajoie, Phil. A.L., 1901); 424, Rogers Hornsby, St. Louis N.L., 1924.

Most Times at Bat—14,053, Pete Rose, Cincinnati N.L., 1963–78; Philadelphia N.L., 1979–83; Montreal N.L., 1984; Cincinnati N.L., 1984–86.

Most Years Batted .300 or Better—23, Ty Cobb, Detroit A.L., 1906–26, Philadelphia A.L., 1927–28.

Most Hits—4,256, Pete Rose, Cincinnati 1963–79, Philadelphia 1980–83, Montreal 1984, Cincinnati 1984–86.

Most Hits, Season—257, George Sisler, St. Louis A.L., 1920.

Most Hits in Succession—12, Mike Higgins, Boston A.L., in four games, 1938; Walt Dropo, Detroit A.L., in three games, 1952.

Most Consecutive Games Batted Safely—56, Joe DiMaggio, New York A.L., 1941.

Most Runs—2,295, Rickey Henderson, Oakland A.L., 1979–84, 1989–93, 1994–95, 1998; New York A.L., 1985–89; Toronto A.L., 1993; San Diego N.L., 1996, 1997, 2001; Anaheim A.L., 1997; New York N.L., 1999–2000; Seattle A.L., 2000; Boston A.L., 2002; Los Angeles N.L., 2003.

Most Runs, Season—196, William Hamilton, Philadelphia N.L., 1894. (Since 1900—177, Babe Ruth, New York A.L., 1921.)

Most Runs Batted in—2,297, Hank Aaron, Milwaukee N.L., 1954–1965; Atlanta N.L., 1966–74; Milwaukee A.L., 1975–76.

Most Runs Batted in, Season—191, Hack Wilson, Chicago N.L., 1930.

Most Home Runs—755, Hank Aaron, Milwaukee N.L., 1954–1965; Atlanta N.L., 1966–74; Milwaukee A.L., 1975–76.

Most Home Runs, Season—162-game season: 73, Barry Bonds, San Francisco N.L., 2001; 70, Mark McGwire, St. Louis N.L., 1998; 66, Sammy Sosa, Chicago N.L., 1998; 65, Mark McGwire, St. Louis N.L., 1999; 64, Sammy Sosa, Chicago N.L., 2001; 63, Sammy Sosa, Chicago N.L., 1999; 61, Roger Maris, New York A.L., 1961. 154-game season: 60, Babe Ruth, New York A.L., 1927.

Most Home Runs with Bases Filled—23, Lou Gehrig, New York A.L., 1927–39.

Most 2-Base Hits—792, Tris Speaker, Boston A.L., 1907–15, Cleveland A.L., 1916–26, Washington A.L., 1927, Philadelphia A.L., 1928.

Most 2-Base Hits, Season—67, Earl Webb, Boston A.L., 1931.

Most 3-Base Hits—309, Sam Crawford, Cincinnati N.L., 1899–1902, Detroit A.L., 1903–17.

Most 3-Base Hits, Season—36, Owen Wilson, Pittsburgh N.L., 1912.

Most Games Played—3,562, Pete Rose, Cincinnati N.L., Philadelphia N.L., Montreal N.L., 1964–86.

Most Consecutive Games Played—2,632, Cal Ripken, Jr., Baltimore Orioles A.L., 1981–1998.

Most Bases on Balls—2,190, Rickey Henderson, Oakland A.L., 1979–84, 1989–93, 1994–95, 1998; New York A.L., 1985–89; Toronto A.L., 1993; San Diego N.L., 1996, 1997, 2001; Anaheim A.L., 1997; New York N.L., 1999–2000; Seattle A.L., 2000; Boston A.L., 2002; Los Angeles N.L., 2003.

Most Bases on Balls, Season—198, Barry Bonds, San Francisco N.L., 2002.

Most Strikeouts, Season—189, Bobby Bonds, San Francisco N.L., 1970.

Most Stolen Bases, Lifetime—1,406, Rickey Henderson, Oakland A.L., 1979–84, 1989–93, 1994–95, 1998; New York A.L., 1985–89; Toronto A.L., 1993; San Diego N.L., 1996, 1997, 2001; Anaheim A.L., 1997; New York N.L., 1999–2000; Seattle A.L., 2000; Boston A.L., 2002; Los Angeles, 2003.

Most Stolen Bases, Season—138, Hugh Nicol, Cincinnati A.A., 1887. Since 1900: 130, Rickey Henderson, Oakland A.L., 1982; 118, Lou Brock, St. Louis N.L., 1974.

Most Stolen Bases, Game—7, George Gore, Chicago N.L. 1881; William Hamilton, Philadelphia N.L. 1894. (Since 1900—6, Eddie Collins, Philadelphia A.L., 1912.) and Otis Nixon, Atlanta N.L., 1991.

Most Times Stealing Home, Lifetime—50, Ty Cobb, Detroit-Phil. A.L., 1905–28.

ROOKIE OF THE YEAR

(Baseball Writers' Association selections)

American League

1949	Roy Sievers, St. Louis
1950	Walt Dropo, Boston
1951	Gil McDougald, New York
1952	Harry Byrd, Philadelphia
1953	Harvey Kuenn, Detroit
1954	Bob Grim, New York
1955	Herb Score, Cleveland
1956	Luis Aparicio, Chicago
1957	Tony Kubek, New York
1958	Albie Pearson, Washington
1959	Bob Allison, Washington
1960	Ron Hansen, Baltimore
1961	Don Schwall, Boston
1962	Tom Tresh, New York
1963	Gary Peters, Chicago
1964	Tony Oliva, Minnesota
1965	Curt Blefary, Baltimore
1966	Tommy Agee, Chicago
1967	Rod Carew, Minnesota
1968	Stan Bahnsen, New York
1969	Lou Piniella, Kansas City
1970	Thurman Munson, New York
1971	Chris Chambliss, Cleveland
1972	Carlton Fisk, Boston
1973	Alonzo Bumbry, Baltimore
1974	Mike Hargrove, Texas
1975	Fred Lynn, Boston
1976	Mark Fidrych, Detroit
1977	Eddie Murray, Baltimore
1978	Lou Whitaker, Detroit
1979	Alfredo Griffin, Toronto
1979	John Castino, Minnesota
1980	Joe Charboneau, Cleveland
1981	Dave Righetti, New York
1982	Cal Ripken, Jr., Baltimore
1983	Ron Kittle, Chicago
1984	Alvin Davis, Seattle
1985	Ozzie Guillen, Chicago
1986	Jose Canseco, Oakland
1987	Mark McGwire, Oakland
1988	Walter Weiss, Oakland
1989	Gregg Olson, Baltimore
1990	Sandy Alomar Jr., Cleveland
1991	Chuck Knoblauch, Minnesota
1992	Pat Listach, Milwaukee
1993	Tim Salmon, California
1994	Bob Hamelin, Kansas City
1995	Marty Cordova, Minnesota
1996	Derek Jeter, New York
1997	Nomar Garciaparra, Boston
1998	Ben Grieve, Oakland
1999	Carlos Beltran, Kansas City
2000	Kazuhiro Sasaki, Seattle
2001	Ichiro Suzuki, Seattle
2002	Eric Hinske, Toronto

National League

1949	Don Newcombe, Brooklyn
1950	Sam Jethroe, Boston
1951	Willie Mays, New York
1952	Joe Black, Brooklyn
1953	Jim Gilliam, Brooklyn
1954	Wally Moon, St. Louis
1955	Bill Virdon, St. Louis
1956	Frank Robinson, Cincinnati
1957	Jack Sanford, Philadelphia
1958	Orlando Cepeda, San Francisco
1959	Willie McCovey, San Francisco
1960	Frank Howard, Los Angeles
1961	Billy Williams, Chicago
1962	Ken Hubbs, Chicago
1963	Pete Rose, Cincinnati
1964	Richie Allen, Philadelphia
1965	Jim Lefebvre, Los Angeles
1966	Tommy Helms, Cincinnati
1967	Tom Seaver, New York
1968	Johnny Bench, Cincinnati
1969	Ted Sizemore, Los Angeles
1970	Carl Morton, Montreal
1971	Earl Williams, Atlanta
1972	Jon Matlack, New York
1973	Gary Matthews, San Francisco
1974	Bake McBride, St. Louis
1975	John Montefusco, San Francisco
1976	Pat Zachry, Cincinnati
1976	Bruce Metzger, San Diego
1977	Andre Dawson, Montreal
1978	Bob Horner, Atlanta
1979	Rick Sutcliffe, Los Angeles
1980	Steve Howe, Los Angeles
1981	Fernando Valenzuela, Los Angeles
1982	Steve Sax, Los Angeles
1983	Darryl Strawberry, New York
1984	Dwight Gooden, New York
1985	Vince Coleman, St. Louis
1986	Todd Worrell, St. Louis
1987	Benito Santiago, San Diego
1988	Chris Sabo, Cincinnati
1989	Jerome Walton, Chicago
1990	Dave Justice, Atlanta
1991	Jeff Baguell, Houston
1992	Eric Karros, Los Angeles
1993	Mike Piazza, Los Angeles
1994	Raul Mondesi, Los Angeles
1995	Hideo Nomo, Los Angeles
1996	Todd Hollandsworth, Los Angeles
1997	Scott Rolen, Philadelphia
1998	Kerry Wood, Chicago
1999	Scott Williamson, Cincinnati
2000	Rafael Furcal, Atlanta
2001	Albert Pujols, St. Louis
2002	Jason Jennings, Colorado

MOST HOME RUNS IN ONE SEASON—45 OR MORE

HR	Player/Team	Year
73	Barry Bonds, San Francisco (N.L.)	2001
70	Mark McGwire, St. Louis (N.L.)	1998
66	Sammy Sosa, Chicago (N.L.)	1998
65	Mark McGwire, St. Louis (N.L.)	1999
64	Sammy Sosa, Chicago (N.L.)	2001
63	Sammy Sosa, Chicago (N.L.)	1999
61	Roger Maris, New York (A.L.)	1961
60	Babe Ruth, New York (A.L.)	1927
59	Babe Ruth, New York (A.L.)	1921
58	Jimmie Foxx, Philadelphia (A.L.)	1932
58	Hank Greenberg, Detroit (A.L.)	1938
58	Mark McGwire, Oakland (A.L.), St. Louis (N.L.)	1997
57	Luis Gonzalez. Arizona (N.L.)	2001
57	Alex Rodriguez, Texas (A.L.)	2002
56	Hack Wilson, Chicago (N.L.)	1930
56	Ken Griffey, Jr., Seattle (A.L.)	1997
56	Ken Griffey, Jr., Seattle (A.L.)	1998
54	Babe Ruth, New York (A.L.)	1920
54	Babe Ruth, New York (A.L.)	1928
54	Ralph Kiner, Pittsburgh (N.L.)	1949
54	Mickey Mantle, New York (A.L.)	1961
52	Mickey Mantle, New York (A.L.)	1956
52	Willie Mays, San Francisco (N.L.)	1965
52	George Foster, Cincinnati (N.L.)	1977
52	Mark McGwire, Oakland (A.L.)	1996
52	Alex Rodriguez, Texas (A.L.)	2001
52	Jim Thome, Cleveland (A.L.)	2002
51	Ralph Kiner, Pittsburgh (N.L.)	1947
51	John Mize, New York (N.L.)	1947
51	Willie Mays, New York (N.L.)	1955
51	Cecil Fielder (A.L.)	1990
50	Jimmie Foxx, Boston (A.L.)	1938
50	Albert Belle, Cleveland (A.L.)	1995
50	Brady Anderson, Baltimore (A.L.)	1996
50	Sammy Sosa, Chicago (N.L.)	2000
50	Greg Vaughn, San Diego (N.L.)	1998
49	Babe Ruth, New York (A.L.)	1930
49	Lou Gehrig, New York (A.L.)	1934
49	Lou Gehrig, New York (A.L.)	1936
49	Ted Kluszewski, Cincinnati (N.L.)	1954
49	Willie Mays, San Francisco (N.L.)	1962
49	Harmon Killebrew, Minnesota (A.L.)	1964
49	Frank Robinson, Baltimore (A.L.)	1966
49	Harmon Killebrew, Minnesota (A.L.)	1969
49	Mark McGwire, Oakland (A.L.)	1987
49	Andre Dawson, Chicago (N.L.)	1987
49	Ken Griffey, Jr., Seattle (A.L.)	1996
49	Larry Walker, Colorado (N.L.)	1997
49	Albert Belle, Chicago (A.L.)	1998
49	Barry Bonds, San Francisco (N.L.)	2000
49	Shawn Green, Los Angeles (N.L.)	2001
49	Todd Helton, Colorado (N.L.)	2001
49	Jim Thome, Cleveland (A.L.)	2001
49	Sammy Sosa, Chicago (N.L.)	2002

HR	Player/Team	Year
48	Jimmie Foxx, Philadelphia (A.L.)	1933
48	Harmon Killebrew, Minnesota (A.L.)	1962
48	Frank Howard, Washington (A.L.)	1969
48	Willie Stargell, Pittsburgh (N.L.)	1971
48	Dave Kingman, Chicago (N.L.)	1979
48	Mike Schmidt, Philadelphia (N.L.)	1980
48	Albert Belle, Cleveland (A.L.)	1996
48	Ken Griffey, Jr., Seattle (A.L.)	1999
47	Babe Ruth, New York (A.L.)	1926
47	Ralph Kiner, Pittsburgh (N.L.)	1950
47	Ed Mathews, Milwaukee (N.L.)	1953
47	Ernie Banks, Chicago (N.L.)	1958
47	Willie Mays, San Francisco (N.L.)	1964
47	Hank Aaron, Atlanta (N.L.)	1971
47	Reggie Jackson, Oakland (A.L.)	1969
47	George Bell, Toronto (A.L.)	1987
47	Kevin Mitchell, San Francisco (N.L.)	1989
47	Andres Galarraga, Colorado (N.L.)	1996
47	Juan Gonzalez, Texas (A.L.)	1996
47	Rafael Palmeiro, Texas (A.L.)	1999
47	Jeff Bagwell, Houston (N.L.)	2000
47	Troy Glaus, Anaheim (A.L.)	2000
47	Rafael Palmeiro, Texas (A.L.)	2001
47	Alex Rodriguez, Texas (A.L.)	2003
47	Jim Thome, Philadelphia (N.L.)	2003
46	Babe Ruth, New York (A.L.)	1924
46	Babe Ruth, New York, (A.L.)	1929
46	Babe Ruth, New York (A.L.)	1931
46	Lou Gehrig, New York (A.L.)	1931
46	Joe DiMaggio, New York (A.L.)	1937
46	Ed Mathews, Milwaukee (N.L.)	1959
46	Orlando Cepeda, San Francisco (N.L.)	1961
46	Jim Rice, Boston (A.L.)	1978
46	Juan Gonzalez, Texas (A.L.)	1993
46	Barry Bonds, San Francisco (N.L.)	1993
46	Jose Canseco, Toronto (A.L.)	1998
46	Vinnie Castilla, Colorado (N.L.)	1998
46	Barry Bonds, San Francisco (N.L.)	2002
45	Ernie Banks, Chicago (N.L.)	1959
45	Harmon Killebrew, Minnesota (A.L.)	1963
45	Willie McCovey, San Francisco (N.L.)	1969
45	Johnny Bench, Cincinnati (N.L.)	1970
45	Gorman Thomas, Milwaukee (A.L.)	1979
45	Hank Aaron, Milwaukee (N.L.)	1962
45	Ken Griffey, Jr., Seattle (A.L.)	1993
45	Juan Gonzalez, Texas (A.L.)	1998
45	Manny Ramirez, Cleveland (A.L.)	1998
45	Chipper Jones, Atlanta (N.L.)	1999
45	Greg Vaughn, Cincinnati (N.L.)	1999
45	Barry Bonds, San Francisco (N.L.)	2003
45	Richie Sexson, Milwaukee (N.L.)	2003

MAJOR LEAGUE BASEBALL—2003

AMERICAN LEAGUE FINAL STANDINGS

EASTERN DIVISION

Team	W	L	Pct	GB
New York Yankees	101	61	.623	—
Boston Red Sox[1]	95	67	.586	6.0
Toronto Blue Jays	86	76	.531	15.0
Baltimore Orioles	71	91	.438	30.0
Tampa Bay Devil Rays	63	99	.389	38.0

CENTRAL DIVISION

Team	W	L	Pct	GB
Minnesota Twins	90	72	.556	—
Chicago White Sox	86	76	.531	4.0
Kansas City Royals	83	79	.512	7.0
Cleveland Indians	68	94	.420	22.0
Detroit Tigers	43	119	.265	47.0

WESTERN DIVISION

Team	W	L	Pct	GB
Oakland Athletics	96	66	.593	—
Seattle Mariners	93	69	.574	3.0
Anaheim Angels	77	85	.475	19.0
Texas Rangers	71	91	.438	25.0

1. Wild card.

AMERICAN LEAGUE LEADERS, 2003

Batting—Bill Mueller, Boston	.326
Home runs—Alex Rodriguez, Texas	47
Runs batted in—Carlos Delgado, Toronto	145
Runs—Alex Rodriguez, Texas	124
Hits—Vernon Wells, Toronto	215
Stolen bases—Carl Crawford, Tampa Bay	55
Doubles—Garret Anderson, Anaheim	49
Triples—Cristian Guzman, Minnesota	14
Slugging percentage—Alex Rodriguez, Texas	.600

A.L. Pitching

Wins—Roy Halladay, Toronto	22
Earned run average—Pedro Martinez, Boston	2.22
Strikeouts—Esteban Loaiza, Chicago	207
Innings pitched—Roy Halladay, Toronto	266
Complete games—Bartolo Colon, Chicago	9
Shutouts—Roy Halladay, Toronto	2
Saves—Keith Foulke, Oakland	43

NATIONAL LEAGUE FINAL STANDINGS

EASTERN DIVISION

Team	W	L	Pct	GB
Atlanta Braves	101	61	.623	—
Florida Marlins[1]	91	71	.562	10.0
Philadelphia Phillies	86	76	.531	15.0
Montreal Expos	83	79	.512	18.0
New York Mets	66	95	.410	34.5

CENTRAL DIVISION

Team	W	L	Pct	GB
Chicago Cubs	88	74	.543	—
Houston Astros	87	75	.537	1.0
St. Louis Cardinals	85	77	.525	3.0
Pittsburgh Pirates	75	87	.463	13.0
Cincinnati Reds	69	93	.426	19.0
Milwaukee Brewers	68	94	.420	20.0

WESTERN DIVISION

Team	W	L	Pct	GB
San Francisco Giants	100	61	.621	—
Los Angeles Dodgers	85	77	.525	15.5
Arizona Diamondbacks	84	78	.519	16.5
Colorado Rockies	74	88	.457	26.5
San Diego Padres	64	98	.395	36.5

1. Wild card.

NATIONAL LEAGUE LEADERS, 2003

Batting—Albert Pujols, St. Louis	.359
Home runs—Jim Thome, Philadelphia	47
Runs batted in—Preston Wilson, Colorado	141
Runs—Albert Pujols, St. Louis	137
Hits—Albert Pujols, St. Louis	212
Stolen bases—Juan Pierre, Florida	65
Doubles—Albert Pujols, St. Louis	51
Triples—Steve Finley, Arizona	10
Slugging percentage—Barry Bonds, San Francisco	.749

N.L. Pitching

Wins—Russ Ortiz, Atlanta	21
Earned run average—Jason Schmidt, San Francisco	2.34
Strikeouts—Kerry Wood, Chicago	266
Innings pitched—Livan Hernandez, Montreal	233
Complete games–Livan Hernandez, Montreal	8
Shutouts—Kevin Millwood, Philadelphia	3
Saves—Eric Gagne, Los Angeles	55

AMERICAN LEAGUE AVERAGES, 2003

Team Pitching

	W	L	ERA	SHO	H	R	SO
Oakland	96	66	3.63	14	1,336	643	1,018
Seattle	93	69	3.76	15	1,340	637	1,001
New York	101	61	4.02	12	1,512	716	1,119
Chicago	86	76	4.17	4	1,364	715	1,056
Cleveland	68	94	4.21	7	1,477	778	943
Anaheim	77	85	4.28	9	1,444	743	980
Minnesota	90	72	4.41	8	1,526	758	997
Boston	95	67	4.48	6	1,503	809	1,141
Toronto	86	76	4.69	6	1,560	826	984
Baltimore	71	91	4.76	3	1,579	820	981
Tampa Bay	63	99	4.93	7	1,454	852	877
Kansas City	83	79	5.05	10	1,569	867	865
Detroit	43	119	5.30	5	1,616	928	764
Texas	71	91	5.67	3	1,625	969	1,009

Team Batting

	Avg.	AB	R	H	HR	RBI
Boston	.289	5,769	961	1,667	238	932
Toronto	.279	5,661	894	1,580	190	853
Minnesota	.277	5,655	801	1,567	155	755
Kansas City	.274	5,568	836	1,526	162	781
New York	.271	5,605	877	1,518	230	845
Seattle	.271	5,561	795	1,509	139	759
Anaheim	.268	5,487	736	1,473	150	687
Baltimore	.268	5,665	743	1,516	152	695
Texas	.266	5,664	826	1,506	239	799
Tampa Bay	.265	5,654	715	1,501	137	678
Chicago	.263	5,487	791	1,445	220	766
Cleveland	.254	5,572	699	1,413	158	660
Oakland	.254	5,497	768	1,398	176	742
Detroit	.240	5,466	591	1,312	153	553

Individual Pitching
(based on 10 decisions)

	W	L	ERA	IP	H	BB	SO
R. Halladay, Toronto	22	7	3.25	266.0	253	32	204
E. Loaiza, Chicago	21	9	2.90	226.1	196	56	207
J. Moyer, Seattle	21	7	3.27	215.0	199	66	129
A. Pettitte, New York	21	8	4.02	208.1	227	50	180
R. Clemens, New York	17	9	3.91	211.2	199	58	190
D. Lowe, Boston	17	7	4.47	203.1	216	72	110
M. Mussina, New York	17	8	3.40	214.2	192	40	195
T. Hudson, Oakland	16	7	2.70	240.0	197	61	162
R. Ortiz, Anaheim	16	13	5.20	180.0	209	63	94
J. Pineiro, Seattle	16	11	3.78	211.2	192	76	151
B. Colon, Chicago	15	13	3.87	242.0	223	67	173
G. Meche, Seattle	15	13	4.59	186.1	187	63	130
M. Mulder, Oakland	15	9	3.13	186.2	180	40	128
D. Wells, New York	15	7	4.14	213.0	242	20	101
B. Anderson, Kansas City	14	11	3.78	197.2	212	43	87
M. Buehrle, Chicago	14	14	4.14	230.1	250	61	119
K. Lohse, Minnesota	14	11	4.61	201.0	211	45	130
P. Martinez, Boston	14	4	2.22	186.2	147	47	206
S. Ponson, Baltimore	14	6	3.77	148.0	147	43	100
B. Radke, Minnesota	14	10	4.49	212.1	242	28	120

Individual Batting
(based on 300 plate appearances)

	Avg.	AB	R	H	HR	RBI
B. Mueller, Boston	.326	524	85	171	19	85
M. Ramirez, Boston	.325	569	117	185	37	104
D. Jeter, New York	.324	482	87	156	10	52
M. Ordonez, Chicago	.317	606	95	192	29	99
V. Wells, Toronto	.317	678	118	215	33	117
G. Anderson, Anaheim	.315	638	80	201	29	116
A. Pierzynski, Minnesota	.312	487	63	152	11	74
I. Suzuki, Seattle	.312	679	111	212	13	62
A. Huff, Tampa Bay	.311	636	91	198	34	107
C. Beltran, Kansas City	.307	521	102	160	26	100
T. Nixon, Boston	.306	441	81	135	28	87
M. Young, Texas	.306	666	106	204	14	72
J. Jones, Minnesota	.304	517	76	157	16	69
C. Delgado, Toronto	.302	570	117	172	42	145
N. Garciaparra, Boston	.301	658	120	198	28	105
H. Blalock, Texas	.300	567	89	170	29	90
D. Mientkiewicz, Minnesota	.300	487	67	146	11	65
F. Catalanotto, Toronto	.299	489	83	146	13	59
A. Rodriguez, Texas	.298	607	124	181	47	118
D. Young, Detroit	.297	562	78	167	29	85

NATIONAL LEAGUE AVERAGES, 2003

Team Pitching

	W	L	ERA	SHO	H	R	SO
Los Angeles	85	77	3.16	17	1,254	556	1,289
San Francisco	100	61	3.73	10	1,349	638	1,006
Chicago	88	74	3.83	14	1,304	683	1,404
Arizona	84	78	3.84	11	1,379	685	1,291
Houston	87	75	3.86	5	1,350	677	1,139
Montreal	83	79	4.01	10	1,467	716	1,028
Florida	91	71	4.04	11	1,415	692	1,132
Philadelphia	86	76	4.04	13	1,386	697	1,060
Atlanta	101	61	4.10	7	1,425	740	992
New York	66	95	4.48	10	1,497	754	907
St. Louis	85	77	4.60	10	1,544	796	969
Pittsburgh	75	87	4.64	10	1,527	801	926
San Diego	64	98	4.87	10	1,458	831	1,091
Milwaukee	68	94	5.02	3	1,590	873	1,034
Cincinnati	69	93	5.09	5	1,578	886	932
Colorado	74	88	5.20	4	1,629	892	866

Team Batting

	Avg.	AB	R	H	HR	RBI
Atlanta	.284	5,670	907	1,608	235	872
St. Louis	.279	5,672	876	1,580	196	827
Colorado	.267	5,518	853	1,472	198	814
Pittsburgh	.267	5,581	753	1,492	163	711
Florida	.266	5,490	751	1,459	157	709
San Francisco	.264	5,456	755	1,440	180	713
Arizona	.263	5,570	717	1,467	152	696
Houston	.263	5,583	805	1,466	191	763
Philadelphia	.261	5,543	791	1,448	166	757
San Diego	.261	5,531	678	1,442	128	642
Chicago	.259	5,519	724	1,431	172	691
Montreal	.258	5,437	711	1,404	144	682
Milwaukee	.256	5,548	714	1,423	196	685
New York	.247	5,341	642	1,317	124	607
Cincinnati	.245	5,509	694	1,349	182	669
Los Angeles	.243	5,458	574	1,328	124	544

Individual Pitching (based on 10 decisions)

	W	L	ERA	IP	H	BB	SO
R. Ortiz, Atlanta	21	7	3.81	212.1	177	102	149
M. Prior, Chicago	18	6	2.43	211.1	183	50	245
W. Williams, St. Louis	18	9	3.87	220.2	220	55	153
J. Schmidt, San Francisco	17	5	2.34	207.2	152	46	208
G. Maddux, Atlanta	16	11	3.96	218.1	225	33	124
H. Nomo, Los Angeles	16	13	3.09	218.1	175	98	177
S. Trachsel, New York	16	10	3.78	204.2	204	65	111
R. Wolf, Philadelphia	16	10	4.23	200.0	176	78	177
L. Hernandez, Montreal	15	10	3.20	233.1	225	57	178
A. Leiter, New York	15	9	3.99	180.2	176	94	139
J. Robertson, Houston	15	9	5.10	160.2	180	64	99
K. Brown, Los Angeles	14	9	2.39	211.0	184	56	185
M. Clement, Chicago	14	12	4.11	201.2	169	79	171
M. Hampton, Atlanta	14	8	3.84	190.0	186	78	110
W. Miller, Houston	14	13	4.13	187.1	168	77	161
K. Millwood, Philadelphia	14	12	4.01	222.0	210	68	169
B. Myers, Philadelphia	14	9	4.43	193.0	205	76	143
V. Padilla, Philadelphia	14	12	3.62	208.2	196	62	133
B. Penny, Florida	14	10	4.13	196.1	195	56	138
M. Redman, Florida	14	9	3.59	190.2	172	61	151
D. Willis, Florida	14	6	3.30	160.2	148	58	142
K. Wood, Chicago	14	11	3.20	211.0	152	100	266

Individual Batting (based on 300 plate appearances)

	Avg.	AB	R	H	HR	RBI
A. Pujols, St. Louis	.359	591	137	212	43	124
T. Helton, Colorado	.358	583	135	209	33	117
B. Bonds, San Francisco	.341	390	111	133	45	90
E. Renteria, St. Louis	.330	587	96	194	13	100
G. Sheffield, Atlanta	.330	576	126	190	39	132
J. Kendall, Pittsburgh	.325	587	84	191	6	58
M. Giles, Atlanta	.316	551	101	174	21	69
L. Castillo, Florida	.314	595	99	187	6	39
M. Grudzielanek, Chicago	.314	481	73	151	3	38
M. Loretta, San Diego	.314	589	74	185	13	72
S. Podsednik, Milwaukee	.314	558	100	175	9	58
M. Lieberthal, Philadelphia	.313	508	68	159	13	81
J. Vidro, Montreal	.310	509	77	158	15	65
R. Hidalgo, Houston	.309	514	91	159	28	88
C. Jones, Atlanta	.305	555	103	169	27	106
J. Pierre, Florida	.305	668	100	204	1	41
L. Gonzalez, Arizona	.304	579	92	176	26	104
M. Byrd, Philadelphia	.303	495	86	150	7	45
J. Payton, Colorado	.302	600	93	181	28	89
B. Abreu, Philadelphia	.300	577	99	173	20	101
M. Grissom, San Francisco	.300	587	82	176	20	79

AMERICAN LEAGUE PENNANT WINNERS

Year	Club	Manager	Won	Lost	Pct
1901	Chicago	Clark C. Griffith	83	53	.610
1902	Philadelphia	Connie Mack	83	53	.610
1903	Boston[1]	Jimmy Collins	91	47	.659
1904	Boston[2]	Jimmy Collins	95	59	.617
1905	Philadelphia	Connie Mack	92	56	.622
1906	Chicago[1]	Fielder A. Jones	93	58	.616
1907	Detroit	Hugh A. Jennings	92	58	.613
1908	Detroit	Hugh A. Jennings	90	63	.588
1909	Detroit	Hugh A. Jennings	98	54	.645
1910	Philadelphia[1]	Connie Mack	102	48	.680
1911	Philadelphia[1]	Connie Mack	101	50	.669
1912	Boston[1]	J. Garland Stahl	105	47	.691
1913	Philadelphia[1]	Connie Mack	96	57	.627
1914	Philadelphia	Connie Mack	99	53	.651
1915	Boston[1]	William F. Carrigan	101	50	.669
1916	Boston[1]	William F. Carrigan	91	63	.591
1917	Chicago[1]	Clarence H. Rowland	100	54	.649
1918	Boston[1]	Ed Barrow	75	51	.595
1919	Chicago	William Gleason	88	52	.629
1920	Cleveland[1]	Tris Speaker	98	56	.636
1921	New York	Miller J. Huggins	98	55	.641
1922	New York	Miller J. Huggins	94	60	.610
1923	New York[1]	Miller J. Huggins	98	54	.645
1924	Washington[1]	Stanley R. Harris	92	62	.597
1925	Washington	Stanley R. Harris	96	55	.636
1926	New York	Miller J. Huggins	91	63	.591
1927	New York[1]	Miller J. Huggins	110	44	.714
1928	New York[1]	Miller J. Huggins	101	53	.656
1929	Philadelphia[1]	Connie Mack	104	46	.693
1930	Philadelphia[1]	Connie Mack	102	52	.662
1931	Philadelphia	Connie Mack	107	45	.704
1932	New York[1]	Joseph V. McCarthy	107	47	.695
1933	Washington	Joseph E. Cronin	99	53	.651
1934	Detroit	Gordon Cochrane	101	53	.656
1935	Detroit[1]	Gordon Cochrane	93	58	.616
1936	New York[1]	Joseph V. McCarthy	102	51	.667
1937	New York[1]	Joseph V. McCarthy	102	52	.662
1938	New York[1]	Joseph V. McCarthy	99	53	.651
1939	New York[1]	Joseph V. McCarthy	106	45	.702
1940	Detroit	Delmar D. Baker	90	64	.584
1941	New York[1]	Joseph V. McCarthy	101	53	.656
1942	New York	Joseph V. McCarthy	103	51	.669
1943	New York[1]	Joseph V. McCarthy	98	56	.636
1944	St. Louis	Luke Sewell	89	65	.578
1945	Detroit[1]	Steve O'Neill	88	65	.575
1946	Boston	Joseph E. Cronin	104	50	.675
1947	New York[1]	Stanley R. Harris	97	57	.630
1948	Cleveland[1]	Lou Boudreau	97	58	.626
1949	New York[1]	Casey Stengel	97	57	.630
1950	New York[1]	Casey Stengel	98	56	.636
1951	New York[1]	Casey Stengel	98	56	.636
1952	New York[1]	Casey Stengel	95	59	.617
1953	New York[1]	Casey Stengel	99	52	.656
1954	Cleveland	Al Lopez	111	43	.721
1955	New York	Casey Stengel	96	58	.623
1956	New York[1]	Casey Stengel	97	57	.630
1957	New York	Casey Stengel	98	56	.636
1958	New York[1]	Casey Stengel	92	62	.597
1959	Chicago	Al Lopez	94	60	.610
1960	New York	Casey Stengel	97	57	.630
1961	New York[1]	Ralph Houk	109	53	.673
1962	New York[1]	Ralph Houk	96	66	.593
1963	New York	Ralph Houk	104	57	.646
1964	New York	Yogi Berra	99	63	.611
1965	Minnesota	Sam Mele	102	60	.630
1966	Baltimore[1]	Hank Bauer	97	53	.606
1967	Boston	Dick Williams	92	70	.568
1968	Detroit[1]	Mayo Smith	103	59	.636
1969	Baltimore[3]	Earl Weaver	109	53	.673
1970	Baltimore[1,3]	Earl Weaver	108	54	.667
1971	Baltimore[4]	Earl Weaver	101	57	.639
1972	Oakland[1,5]	Dick Williams	93	62	.600
1973	Oakland[1,6]	Dick Williams	94	68	.580
1974	Oakland[1,6]	Alvin Dark	90	72	.556
1975	Boston[4]	Darrell Johnson	95	65	.594
1976	New York[7]	Billy Martin	97	62	.610
1977	New York[1,7]	Billy Martin	100	62	.617
1978	New York[1,7]	Billy Martin and Bob Lemon	100	63	.613
1979	Baltimore[8]	Earl Weaver	102	57	.642
1980	Kansas City[9]	Jim Frey	97	65	.599
1981*	New York[4]	Gene Michaeland Bob Lemon	59	48	.551
1982	Milwaukee[8]	Harvey Kuenn	95	67	.586
1983	Baltimore[1,10]	Joe Altobelli	98	64	.605
1984	Detroit[1,7]	Sparky Anderson	104	58	.642
1985	Kansas City[1,11]		91	71	.562
1986	Boston[8]	John McNamara	95	66	.590

Year	Club	Manager	Won	Lost	Pct
1987	Minnesota[5]	Tom Kelly	85	77	.525
1988	Oakland[12]	Tony LaRussa	104	58	.642
1989	Oakland[1,11]	Tony LaRussa	99	63	.611
1990	Oakland[12]	Tony LaRussa	103	59	.636
1991	Minnesota[1,11]	Tom Kelly	95	67	.586
1992	Toronto[1,4]	Cito Gaston	96	66	.593
1993	Toronto[1,10]	Cito Gaston	95	67	.586
1994	Strike ended season Aug. 11. No playoffs, no pennant winner.				
1995	Cleveland[13]	Mike Hargrove	100	44	.694
1996	New York[1,6]	Joe Torre	92	70	.568
1997	Cleveland[6]	Mike Hargrove	86	75	.534
1998	New York[1, 14]	Joe Torre	114	48	.704
1999	New York[1, 15]	Joe Torre	98	64	.605
2000	New York[1, 16]	Joe Torre	87	74	.540
2001	New York[13]	Joe Torre	95	65	.594
2002	Anaheim[17]	Mike Scioscia	99	63	.611

*Split season because of players' strike. 1. World Series winner. 2. No World Series. 3. Defeated Minnesota, Western Division winner, in playoff. 4. Defeated Oakland, Western Division Leader, in playoff. 5. Defeated Detroit, Eastern Division winner, in playoff. 6. Defeated Baltimore, Eastern Division winner, in playoff. 7. Defeated Kansas City, Western Division winner, in playoff. 8. Defeated California, Western Division winner, in playoff. 9. Defeated New York, Eastern Division winner, in playoff. 10. Defeated Chicago, Western Division winner, in playoff. 11. Defeated Toronto, Eastern Division winner, in playoff. 12. Defeated Boston, Eastern division winner, in playoffs. 13. Defeated Seattle Mariners, Western Division winner, in playoff. 14. Defeated Cleveland Indians, Central Division winner, in playoff. 15. Defeated Boston Red Sox, Eastern Division wild-card team, in playoffs. 16. Defeated Seattle Mariners, Western Division wild-card team, in playoff. 17. Defeated Minnesota Twins, Central Division winner, in playoff.

NATIONAL LEAGUE PENNANT WINNERS

Year	Club	Manager	Won	Lost	Pct
1876	Chicago	Albert G. Spalding	52	14	.788
1877	Boston	Harry Wright	31	17	.646
1878	Boston	Harry Wright	41	19	.683
1879	Providence	George Wright	55	23	.705
1880	Chicago	Adrian C. Anson	67	17	.798
1881	Chicago	Adrian C. Anson	56	28	.667
1882	Chicago	Adrian C. Anson	55	29	.655
1883	Boston	John F. Morrill	63	35	.643
1884	Providence	Frank C. Bancroft	84	28	.750
1885	Chicago	Adrian C. Anson	87	25	.777
1886	Chicago	Adrian C. Anson	90	34	.726
1887	Detroit	W. H. Watkins	79	45	.637
1888	New York	James J. Mutrie	84	47	.641
1889	New York	James J. Mutrie	83	43	.659
1890	Brooklyn	Wm. H. McGunnigle	86	43	.667
1891	Boston	Frank G. Selee	87	51	.630
1892	Boston	Frank G. Selee	102	48	.680
1893	Boston	Frank G. Selee	86	44	.662
1894	Baltimore	Edward H. Hanlon	89	39	.695
1895	Baltimore	Edward H. Hanlon	87	43	.669
1896	Baltimore	Edward H. Hanlon	90	39	.698
1897	Boston	Frank G. Selee	93	39	.705
1898	Boston	Frank G. Selee	102	47	.685
1899	Brooklyn	Edward H. Hanlon	88	42	.677
1900	Brooklyn	Edward H. Hanlon	82	54	.603
1901	Pittsburgh	Fred C. Clarke	90	49	.647
1902	Pittsburgh	Fred C. Clarke	103	36	.741
1903	Pittsburgh	Fred C. Clarke	91	49	.650
1904	New York[1]	John J. McGraw	106	47	.693
1905	New York[2]	John J. McGraw	105	48	.686
1906	Chicago	Frank L. Chance	116	36	.763
1907	Chicago[2]	Frank L. Chance	107	45	.704
1908	Chicago[2]	Frank L. Chance	99	55	.643
1909	Pittsburgh[2]	Fred C. Clarke	110	42	.724
1910	Chicago	Frank L. Chance	104	50	.675
1911	New York	John J. McGraw	99	54	.647
1912	New York	John J. McGraw	103	48	.682
1913	New York	John J. McGraw	101	51	.664
1914	Boston[2]	George T. Stallings	94	59	.614
1915	Philadelphia	Patrick J. Moran	90	62	.592
1916	Brooklyn	Wilbert Robinson	94	60	.610
1917	New York	John J. McGraw	98	56	.636
1918	Chicago	Fred L. Mitchell	84	45	.651
1919	Cincinnati[2]	Patrick J. Moran	96	44	.686
1920	Brooklyn	Wilbert Robinson	93	61	.604
1921	New York[2]	John J. McGraw	94	59	.614
1922	New York[2]	John J. McGraw	93	61	.604
1923	New York	John J. McGraw	95	58	.621
1924	New York	John J. McGraw	93	60	.608
1925	Pittsburgh[2]	Wm. B. McKechnie	95	58	.621
1926	St. Louis[2]	Rogers Hornsby	89	65	.578
1927	Pittsburgh	Donie Bush	94	60	.610
1928	St. Louis	Wm. B. McKechnie	95	59	.617
1929	Chicago	Joseph V. McCarthy	98	54	.645
1930	St. Louis	Gabby Street	92	62	.597
1931	St. Louis[2]	Gabby Street	101	53	.656
1932	Chicago	Charles J. Grimm	90	64	.584
1933	New York[2]	William H. Terry	91	61	.599
1934	St. Louis[2]	Frank F. Frisch	95	58	.621
1935	Chicago	Charles J. Grimm	100	54	.649
1936	New York	William H. Terry	92	62	.597
1937	New York	William H. Terry	95	57	.625
1938	Chicago	Gabby Hartnett	89	63	.586
1939	Cincinnati	Wm. B. McKechnie	97	57	.630
1940	Cincinnati[2]	Wm. B. McKechnie	100	53	.654
1941	Brooklyn	Leo E. Durocher	100	54	.649
1942	St. Louis[2]	Wm. H. Southworth	106	48	.688
1943	St. Louis	Wm. H. Southworth	105	49	.682
1944	St. Louis[2]	Wm. H. Southworth	105	49	.682
1945	Chicago	Charles J. Grimm	98	56	.636
1946	St. Louis[2]	Edwin H. Dyer	98	58	.628
1947	Brooklyn	Burton E. Shotton	94	60	.610
1948	Boston	Wm. H. Southworth	91	62	.595
1949	Brooklyn	Burton E. Shotton	97	57	.630
1950	Philadelphia	Edwin M. Sawyer	91	63	.591
1951	New York	Leo E. Durocher	98	59	.624
1952	Brooklyn	Charles W. Dressen	96	57	.630
1953	Brooklyn	Charles W. Dressen	105	49	.682
1954	New York[2]	Leo E. Durocher	97	57	.630
1955	Brooklyn[2]	Walter Alston	98	55	.641
1956	Brooklyn	Walter Alston	93	61	.604
1957	Milwaukee[2]	Fred Haney	95	59	.617
1958	Milwaukee	Fred Haney	92	62	.597
1959	Los Angeles[2]	Walter Alston	88	68	.564
1960	Pittsburgh[2]	Danny Murtaugh	95	59	.617
1961	Cincinnati	Fred Hutchinson	93	61	.604
1962	San Francisco	Alvin Dark	103	62	.624
1963	Los Angeles[2]	Walter Alston	99	63	.611
1964	St. Louis[2]	Johnny Keane	93	69	.574
1965	Los Angeles[2]	Walter Alston	97	65	.599
1966	Los Angeles	Walter Alston	95	67	.586
1967	St. Louis[2]	Red Schoendienst	101	60	.627
1968	St. Louis	Red Schoendienst	97	65	.599
1969	New York[2,3]	Gil Hodges	100	62	.617
1970	Cincinnati[4]	Sparky Anderson	102	60	.630
1971	Pittsburgh[2,3]	Danny Murtaugh	97	65	.599
1972	Cincinnati[4]	Sparky Anderson	95	59	.617
1973	New York[6]	Yogi Berra	82	79	.509

Year	Club	Manager	Won	Lost	Pct
1974	Los Angeles[4]	Walter Alston	102	60	.630
1975	Cincinnati[2,4]	Sparky Anderson	108	54	.667
1976	Cincinnati[2,7]	Sparky Anderson	102	60	.630
1977	Los Angeles[7]	Tom Lasorda	98	64	.605
1978	Los Angeles[7]	Tom Lasorda	95	67	.586
1979	Pittsburgh[2,6]	Chuck Tanner	98	64	.605
1980	Philadelphia[2,8]	Dallas Green	91	71	.562
1981*	Los Angeles[2,9]	Tom Lasorda	63	47	.573
1982	St. Louis[2,3]	Whitey Herzog	92	70	.568
1983	Philadelphia[10]	Paul Owens	90	72	.556
1984	San Diego[11]	Dick Williams	92	70	.568
1985	St. Louis[11]	Whitey Herzog	101	61	.623
1986	New York[2,8]	Dave Johnson	108	54	.667
1987	St. Louis[5]	Whitey Herzog	95	67	.586
1988	Los Angeles[2,12]	Tom Lasorda	94	67	.584
1989	San Francisco[12]	Roger Craig	92	70	.568
1990	Cincinnati[2,4]	Lou Piniella	91	71	.562
1991	Atlanta[4]	Bobby Cox	94	68	.580
1992	Atlanta[4]	Bobby Cox	98	64	.605
1993	Philadelphia[3]	Jim Fregosi	97	65	.599
1994	Strike ended season Aug. 11. No playoffs, no pennant winner.				
1995	Atlanta[2,13]	Bobby Cox	90	54	.625
1996	Atlanta[14]	Bobby Cox	96	66	.593
1997	Florida[2,15]	Jim Leyland	92	70	.568
1998	San Diego[16]	Bruce Bochy	98	64	.605
1999	Atlanta[17]	Bobby Cox	103	59	.636
2000	New York[18]	Bobby Valentine	94	68	.580
2001	Arizona[16]	Bob Brenly	92	70	.568
2002	San Francisco[14]	Dusty Baker	95	66	.590

*Split season because of players' strike. 1. No World Series. 2. World Series winner. 3. Defeated Atlanta, Western Division winner, in playoff. 4. Defeated Pittsburgh, Eastern Division winner, in playoff. 5. Defeated San Francisco, Western Division winner, in playoff. 6. Defeated Cincinnati, Western Division winner, in playoff. 7. Defeated Philadelphia, Eastern Division winner, in playoff. 8. Defeated Houston, Western Division winner, in playoff. 9. Defeated Montreal, Eastern Division winner, in playoff. 10. Defeated Los Angeles, Western Division winner, in playoff. 11. Defeated Chicago, Eastern Division champion, in playoff. 12. Defeated New York, Eastern Division winner, in playoff. 13. Defeated Cincinnati, Central Division winner, in playoff. 14. Defeated St. Louis, Central Division winner, in playoff. 15. Eastern Division wildcard Florida defeated Atlanta, Eastern Division winner, in playoff. 16. Defeated Atlanta, Eastern Division winner, in playoff. 17. Defeated New York, Eastern Division wild card team, in playoff. 18. Eastern Division wild card New York defeated Central Division winner St. Louis in playoff.

Extreme Sports

2003 SUMMER EXTREME GAMES
(Los Angeles, Calif., Aug. 14–17, 2003)

Bike Stunt: Ryan Nyquist (dirt), Jamie Bestwick (vert), Ryan Nyquist (park), Simon O'Brien (flatland)
BMX: Brandon Meadows (downhill)
Agressive Inline: Bruno Lowe (men's park), Elto Yasutoko (men's vert), Fabiola de Silva (women's park)
Motocross: Travis Pastrana (freestyle), Brian Deegan (big air), Matt Buyten (step up)
Skateboarding: Ryan Sheckler (men's park), Vanessa Torres (women's park), Bucky Lasek (vert), Bucky Lasek and Bob Burnquist (vert doubles), Tony Hawk (vert best trick), Eric Koston (street), Chad Muska (street best trick)
Surfing: East Coast
Wakeboarding: Danny Harf (men), Dallas Friday (women)

2003 WINTER EXTREME GAMES
(Aspen, Colo., Jan. 29–Feb. 2, 2003)

Snowboard: Shaun White (men's slopestyle), Janna Meyen (women's slopestyle), Shaun White (men's superpipe), Gretchen Bleiler (women's superpipe), Ueli Kestenholz (men' X), Lindsey Jacobellis (women's X)
Motocross: Mike Metzger (big air)
Snowmobile: T. J. Gulla (hillcross), Blair Morgan (SnoCross)
Skiing: Candide Thovex (superpipe), Lars Lewen (men's X), Aleisha Cline (women's X), Tanner Hall (slopestyle)
Ultracross: Xavier Delerue and Kaj Zackrisson

Gymnastics

2003 WORLD CHAMPIONSHIPS
(Aug. 16–24, 2003, Anaheim, Calif.)

MEN	Points
Team finals—China	171.996
All-around—Paul Hamm, United States	57.774
Floor—Paul Hamm, United States	9.762
Pommel Horse—Haibin Teng, China	9.762
Still Rings—Jordan Jovtchev, Bulgaria	9.787
Vault—Xiao-Peng Li, China	9.818
Parallel Bars—Xiao-Peng Li, China	9.825
High Bar—Takehiro Kashina, Japan	9.775

WOMEN	Points
Team Finals—United States	112.573
All-around—Svetlana Khorkina, Russia	38.124
Vault—Oksana Chusovitina, Uzbekistan	9.481
Uneven Bars—Hollie Vise, United States	9.612
Balance Beam—Ye Fan, China	9.812
Floor Exercise—Daiane Dos Santos, Brazil	9.737

Soccer

The early history of the sport is uncertain. A form of the game in which a leather ball was dribbled was played in China as early as the 4th century B.C. The Romans played a variation of soccer which eventually spread throughout Europe. British schools and universities played soccer (known as football) during the 1800s, however, each school used different sets of rules and the number of players varied. This difficulty was corrected on Oct. 26, 1863, when the Football Association (FA) was formed in London for the purpose of unifying the rules of the game.

The Federation of International Football Associations (FIFA) was created in 1913 as a world governing body to coordinate all of the national associations in the world. The FIFA held the first World Cup Championship tournament in 1930 in Montevideo, Uruguay. Today, soccer is the world's most popular sport. The first FIFA Women's World Cup was held in 1991 with the United States winning the title. The 2003 Women's World Cup was moved from China to the United States because of concern about a Chinese outbreak of Severe Acute Respiratory Syndrome.

WORLD CUP

(W) indicates Women's World Cup

1930 Uruguay
1934 Italy
1938 Italy
1942 No competition
1946 No competition
1950 Uruguay
1954 West Germany
1958 Brazil
1962 Brazil
1966 England
1970 Brazil
1974 West Germany
1978 Argentina
1982 Italy
1986 Argentina
1990 West Germany
1991 United States (W)
1994 Brazil
1995 Norway (W)
1998 France
1999 United States (W)
2002 Brazil

WORLD CUP—2002

QUARTERFINALS
Brazil 2, England 1
Germany 1, United States 0
South Korea 0, Spain 0 (South Korea won 5–3 in shootout)
Turkey 1, Senegal 0

SEMIFINALS
Germany 1, South Korea 0
Brazil 1, Turkey 0

THIRD PLACE
Turkey 3, South Korea 2

CHAMPIONSHIP
Brazil 2, Germany 0
Goals scored: Ronaldo 2 (67th min and 79th min)

Championship game statistics

Statistics	Brazil	Germany
Shots	9	12
Shots on goal	7	4
Fouls	19	21
Corner kicks	3	13
Free kicks	1	2
Penalty kicks	0	0
Offsides	0	1
Own goals	0	0
Cautions	1	1
Expulsions	0	0
Ball possession percentage	44%	56%
Actual playing time	22	28

WORLD CUP

All-Time Top Ten

Country	App	Gm	Record (W–L–T)	Pts	GF	GA
1. Brazil	17	87	60–13–14	141	191	82
2. Germany	15	85	50–17–18	123	176	106
3. Italy	15	70	39–14–17	96	110	67
4. Argentina	13	60	30–19–11	72	102	71
5. England	11	50	26–13–15	61	68	45
6. Spain	11	45	20–15–10	54	71	53
7. France	11	44	21–16–7	49	86	61
8. Sweden	10	42	15–16–10	42	71	65
9. Russia	9	37	17–14–6	41	64	44
10. Yugoslavia	9	37	16–13–8	40	60	46
Uruguay	10	40	15–15–10	40	65	57

WOMEN'S WORLD CUP—1999

(The 2003 Women's World Cup final was held in Oct. 2003, after the Time Almanac went to press.)

SEMIFINALS
United States 2, Brazil 0
China 5, Norway 0

THIRD PLACE
Brazil 0, Norway 0 (Brazil won 5–4 on penalty kicks)

CHAMPIONSHIP
United States 0, China 0 (The United States won 5–4 on penalty kicks)

MAJOR LEAGUE SOCCER 2003 STANDINGS

As of Sept. 28, 2003. The GF and GA columns refer to Goals For and Goals Against in regulation play.

EASTERN CONFERENCE

Team	W	L	T	Pts	GF	GA
Chicago Fire[1]	12	6	7	43	42	33
MetroStars	10	8	8	38	35	33
DC United	10	9	7	37	34	30
New England Revolution	8	9	9	33	43	43
Columbus Crew	8	11	7	31	34	37

1. Clinched playoffs.

WESTERN CONFERENCE

Team	W	L	T	Pts	GF	GA
San Jose Earthquakes[1]	14	5	7	49	44	29
Colorado Rapids[1]	11	9	5	38	31	32
Kansas City Wizards[1]	8	10	8	32	40	40
Los Angeles Galaxy[1]	8	10	8	32	30	30
Dallas Burn	5	17	4	19	30	56

1. Clinched playoffs.

2002 MLS CUP

Oct. 20, 2002, at Foxboro, Mass.
Los Angeles Galaxy 1, New England Revolution 0

	1st	2nd	OT	Total
Los Angeles Galaxy	0	0	1	1
New England Revolution	0	0	0	0

Scoring: Los Angeles: Carlos Ruiz, 113th min. **MVP:** Carlos Ruiz.

2003 REGULAR SEASON

(as of Sept. 28, 2003)

LEADING SCORERS

	Gm	G	A	Pts
Preki, Kansas City	26	11	13	35
Carlos Ruiz, Los Angeles	22	14	3	31
Landon Donovan, San Jose	19	12	6	30
Taylor Twellman, New England	21	13	4	30
Ante Razov, Chicago	21	12	5	29

GOAL SCORING LEADERS

	Gm	No
Carlos Ruiz, Los Angeles	22	14
Taylor Twellman, New England	21	13
Landon Donovan, San Jose	19	12
Ante Razov, Chicago	21	12
John Spencer, Colorado	24	12

LEADING GOALKEEPERS

	Gm	Shts	Svs	GA	GAA
Pat Onstad, San Jose	24	117	94	23	0.93
Jonny Walker, MetroStars	11	62	50	12	1.03
Kevin Hartman, Los Angeles	26	158	128	30	1.11
Nick Rimando, DC	25	128	99	29	1.13
Scott Garlick, Colorado	21	94	69	25	1.17

ASSIST LEADERS

	Gm	No
Preki, Kansas City	26	13
Amado Guevara, MetroStars	22	9
Mark Lisi, MetroStars	22	9
Brian Mullan, San Jose	26	9
Marco Etcheverry, DC	22	7

WOMEN'S UNITED SOCCER ASSOCIATION 2003 FINAL STANDINGS

The WUSA announced its dissolution in Sept. 2003.

Team	W	L	T	Pts	GF	GA	Home	Road
Boston Breakers	10	4	7	37	33	29	5–2–4	5–2–3
Atlanta Beat	9	4	8	35	34	19	7–2–2	2–2–6
San Diego Spirit	8	6	7	31	27	26	6–2–3	2–4–4
Washington Freedom	9	8	4	31	40	31	6–2–2	3–6–2
New York Power	7	9	5	26	33	43	3–4–3	4–5–2
San Jose CyberRays	7	10	4	25	23	30	4–3–3	3–7–1
Carolina Courage	7	10	4	25	31	33	3–6–2	4–4–2
Philadelphia Charge	5	11	5	20	30	40	3–4–3	2–7–2

WUSA PLAYOFFS

Aug. 16—Washington 0, Boston 0 (3–1 penalty kicks)
Aug. 17—Atlanta 2, San Diego 1 (OT)

Championship
Aug. 24, San Diego, Calif.—Washington 2, Atlanta 1

2003 REGULAR SEASON

POINTS LEADERS

	Gm	G	A	Pts
Mia Hamm, Washington	19	11	11	33
Abby Wambach, Washington	18	13	7	33
Marinette Pichon, Philadelphia	18	14	3	31
Dagny Mellgren, Boston	20	14	2	30
Charmaine Hooper, Atlanta	21	11	7	29

ASSISTS LEADERS

	Gm	Assists
Mia Hamm, Washington	19	11
Maren Meinert, Boston	21	10
Shannon Boxx, New York	21	8
Abby Wambach, Washington	18	7
Charmaine Hooper, Atlanta	21	7

GOALS LEADERS

	Gm	Goals
Marinette Pichon, Philadelphia	18	14
Dagny Mellgren, Boston	20	14
Abby Wambach, Washington	18	13
Mia Hamm, Washington	19	11
Charmaine Hooper, Atlanta	21	11
Julie Fleeting, San Diego	18	11
Birgit Prinz, Carolina	20	11

SHOTS LEADERS

	Gm	Shots
Marinette Pichon, Philadelphia	18	77
Julie Fleeting San Diego	18	67
Birgit Prinz, Carolina	20	64
Maren Meinert, Boston	21	62
Abby Wambach, Washington	18	51
Tiffeny Milbrett, New York	17	51
Charmaine Hooper, Atlanta	21	51

History of the Income Tax in the United States

Source: Scott Moody, senior economist, the Tax Foundation.

The nation had few taxes in its early history. From 1791 to 1802, the United States government was supported by internal taxes on distilled spirits, carriages, refined sugar, tobacco and snuff, property sold at auction, corporate bonds, and slaves. The high cost of the War of 1812 brought about the nation's first sales taxes on gold, silverware, jewelry, and watches. In 1817, however, Congress did away with all internal taxes, relying on tariffs on imported goods to provide sufficient funds for running the government.

In 1862, in order to support the Civil War effort, Congress enacted the nation's first income tax law. It was a forerunner of our modern income tax in that it was based on the principles of graduated, or progressive, taxation and of withholding income at the source. During the Civil War, a person earning from $600 to $10,000 per year paid tax at the rate of 3%. Those with incomes of more than $10,000 paid taxes at a higher rate. Additional sales and excise taxes were added, and an "inheritance" tax also made its debut. In 1866, internal revenue collections reached their highest point in the nation's 90-year history—more than $310 million, an amount not reached again until 1911.

The Act of 1862 established the office of Commissioner of Internal Revenue. The Commissioner was given the power to assess, levy, and collect taxes, and the right to enforce the tax laws through seizure of property and income and through prosecution. The powers and authority remain very much the same today.

In 1868, Congress again focused its taxation efforts on tobacco and distilled spirits and eliminated the income tax in 1872. It had a short-lived revival in 1894 and 1895. In the latter year, the U.S. Supreme Court decided that the income tax was unconstitutional because it was not apportioned among the states in conformity with the Constitution.

In 1913, the 16th Amendment to the Constitution made the income tax a permanent fixture in the U.S. tax system. The amendment gave Congress legal authority to tax income and resulted in a revenue law that taxed incomes of both individuals and corporations. In fiscal year 1918, annual internal revenue collections for the first time passed the billion-dollar mark, rising to $5.4 billion by 1920. With the advent of World War II, employment increased, as did tax collections—to $7.3 billion. The withholding tax on wages was introduced in 1943 and was instrumental in increasing the number of taxpayers to 60 million and tax collections to $43 billion by 1945.

In 1981, Congress enacted the largest tax cut in U.S. history, approximately $750 billion over six years. The tax reduction, however, was partially offset by two tax acts, in 1982 and 1984, that attempted to raise approximately $265 billion.

On Oct. 22, 1986, President Reagan signed into law the Tax Reform Act of 1986, one of the most far-reaching reforms of the United States tax system since the adoption of the income tax. In an attempt to remain revenue neutral, the act called for a $120 billion increase in business taxation and a corresponding decrease in individual taxation over a five-year period.

Following what seemed to be a yearly tradition of new tax acts that began in 1986, the Revenue Reconciliation Act of 1990 was signed into law on Nov. 5, 1990. As with the '87, '88, and '89 acts, the 1990 act, while providing a number of substantive provisions, was small in comparison with the 1986 act. The emphasis of the 1990 act was increased taxes on the wealthy.

On Aug. 10, 1993, President Clinton signed the Revenue Reconciliation Act of 1993 into law. The act's purpose was to reduce by approximately $496 billion the federal deficit that would otherwise accumulate in fiscal years 1994 through 1998. In 1997, Clinton signed another tax act. The act, which cut taxes by $152 billion, included a cut in capital-gains tax for individuals, a $500 per child tax credit, and tax incentives for education.

President George W. Bush signed tax acts in 2001, 2002, and 2003. The Job Creation and Workers Assistance Act of 2002 provided tax relief to businesses and included a 13-week extension on unemployment insurance and tax breaks for taxpayers affected by the Sept. 11, 2001, terrorist attacks. Overall, the act projected tax relief of $41.9 billion over the 2003–2012 period. The Jobs and Growth Tax Relief and Reconciliation Act of 2003, a 10-year $350 billion tax package—the third-largest tax cut in U.S. history, temporarily reduced dividend taxes, reduced capitals gains taxes, and increased child credit for most taxpayers.

Internal Revenue Service

The Internal Revenue Service (IRS), a bureau of the U.S. Treasury Department, is the federal agency charged with the administration of the tax laws passed by Congress.

Operations involving most taxpayers are carried out in district offices and service centers. District offices are organized into Resources Management, Examination, Collection, Taxpayer Service, Employee Plans and Exempt Organizations, and Criminal Investigation. All tax returns are filed with the service centers, where the IRS computer operations are located.

Prior to 1987, all tax return processing was performed by hand. In an attempt to improve the speed and efficiency of the manual processing procedure, the IRS began testing an electronic return filing system beginning with the filing of 1985 returns.

Internal Revenue Service

	2002	2001	1996	1995	1994	1970
U.S. population (in thousands)	289,437	285,791	266,210	263,717	261,348	204,878
Number of IRS employees	100,229	97,707	106,642	112,024	110,665	68,683
Cost to govt. of collecting $100 in taxes	$0.45	$0.41	$0.49	$0.54	$0.57	$0.45
Tax per capita	$6,967.40	$7,448.90	$5,584.11	$5,216.70	$4,884.17	$955.31
Collections by principal sources (in thousands of dollars)						
Total IRS collections	$2,016,627,269	$2,128,831,182	$1,486,546,674	$1,375,731,835	$1,276,466,776	$195,722,096
Income and profits taxes						
Individual	$1,037,733,908	$1,178,209,880	$745,313,276	$675,779,337	$619,819,153	$103,651,585
Corporation	$211,437,773	$186,731,643	$189,054,791	$174,422,173	$154,204,684	$35,036,983
Employment taxes	$688,077,238	$682,222,895	$492,365,178	$465,405,305	$443,831,352	$37,449,188
Estate and gift taxes	$27,241,515	$29,247,916	$17,591,817	$15,144,394	$15,606,793	$3,680,076
Alcohol taxes	(1)	(1)	(1)	(1)	(1)	$4,746,382
Tobacco taxes	(1)	(1)	(1)	(1)	(1)	$2,094,212
Excise taxes[2]	$52,136,835	$52,418,848	$42,221,611	$44,980,627	$43,004,794	$2,380,609

NOTE: For fiscal year ending Sept. 30th. 1. Alcohol and tobacco tax collections are now collected and reported by the Bureau of Alcohol, Tobacco, and Firearms. 2. Includes principal and interest paid on refunds. Represents overpayment refunds resulting from examination activity, and other refunds (except earned income credit refunds) required by law, including $35.51 billion in advance individual income tax refunds. *Source:* 2002 IRS Data Book.

The two most significant results of the test were that refunds for the electronically filed returns were issued more quickly and the tax processing error rate was significantly lower when compared to paper returns. Electronic filing of individual income tax returns with refunds became an operational program in selected areas for the 1987 processing year.

Auditing Tax Returns

Most taxpayers' contacts with the IRS arise through the auditing of their tax returns. The service has been empowered by Congress to inquire about all persons who may be liable for any tax and to obtain for review the books and/or records pertinent to those taxpayers' returns.

In 2002 the IRS announced a new auditing policy that focuses less on wage earners—particularly those earning less than $100,000, and instead looks more closely at the very wealthy and business owners, as well as on complex business partnerships, tax shelters, and offshore accounts. A computer program will help to determine which returns have the potential for hidden or unreported income and thus merit an audit.

The Appeals Process

Taxpayers who, after audit of their tax returns, disagree with a proposed change in their tax liabilities are entitled to an independent review of their cases. Taxpayers are able to seek an immediate, informal appeal with the Appeals Office. If, however, the dispute arises from a field audit and the amount in question exceeds $10,000, a taxpayer must submit a written protest. Alternatively, the taxpayer can wait for the examiner's report and then request consideration by the Appeals Office and file a protest if necessary. Taxpayers may represent themselves or be represented by an attorney, accountant, or any other adviser authorized to practice before the IRS. Taxpayers can forgo their right to the above process and await receipt of a deficiency notice. At this juncture, taxpayers can either (1) not pay the deficiency and petition the Tax Court by a required deadline or (2) pay the deficiency and file a claim for refund with the District Director's office. If the claim is not allowed, a suit for refund may be brought either in the District Court or the Claims Court.

Percentages of Income Earned and Federal Individual Income Taxes Paid

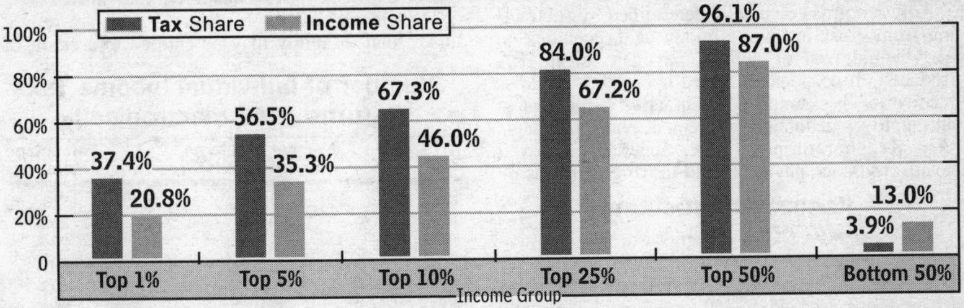

NOTE: Figures for 2000. *Source:* Tax Foundation, Special Report, No. 118, Nov. 2002. Web: http://taxfoundation.org.

Federal Individual Income Tax

Tax Brackets—2003 Taxable Income

Joint return	Single taxpayer	Rate
$0–$14,000	$0–$7,000	10.0%
14,000–56,800	7,000–28,400	15.0
56,800–114,650	28,400–68,800	25.0
114,650 -174,700	68,800–143,500	28.0
174,700–311,950	143,500–311,950	33.0
311,950 and up	311,950 and up	35.0

Source: Tax Foundation.

The federal individual income tax is levied on the worldwide income of U.S. citizens and resident aliens and on certain types of U.S. source income of nonresidents. For a nonitemizer, "tax table income" is adjusted gross income less $3,000 for each personal exemption and the standard deduction. If a taxpayer itemizes, tax table income is adjusted gross income minus total itemized deductions and personal exemptions. In addition, individuals may also be subject to the alternative minimum tax.

Who Must File a Return[1]

If your filing status is:	Age at end of 2002	Gross income at least
Single	Under 65	$7,700
	65 or older	8,850
Married filing jointly	Under 65 (both spouses)	13,850
	65 or older (one spouse)	14,750
	65 or older (both spouses)	15,650
Married filing separately	Any age	3,000
Head of household	Under 65	9,900
	65 or older	11,050
Qualifying widower with dependent child	Under 65	10,850
	65 or older	11,750

1. In 2002.

Adjusted Gross Income

Gross income consists of wages and salaries, unemployment compensation, tips and gratuities, interest, dividends, annuities, rents and royalties, up to 85% of Social Security benefits if the recipient's income exceeds a base amount, and certain other types of income. Among the items excluded from gross income, and thus not subject to tax, are public assistance benefits and interest on exempt securities (mostly state and local bonds).

Adjusted gross income is determined by subtracting from gross income: alimony paid, penalties on early withdrawal of savings, payments to an IRA (reduced proportionately based upon adjusted gross income levels if taxpayer is an active participant in an employer maintained retirement plan), payments to a Keogh retirement plan, and self-employed health insurance payments and moving expenses.

Itemized Deductions

Taxpayers may itemize deductions or take the standard deduction. The standard deduction amounts for 2002 were as follows: $4,700 for single persons, $6,900 for heads of household, $7,850 for married filing jointly or qualifying widower, and $3,925 for married filing separately. Taxpayers 65 and older or blind are entitled to an additional standard deduction of $900.

In itemizing deductions, the following are major items that may be deducted in 2002: state and local income and property taxes, charitable contributions, employee moving expenses, medical expenses (exceeding 7.5% of adjusted gross income), casualty losses (only the amount over the $100 floor which exceeds 10% of adjusted gross income), mortgage interest, and miscellaneous deductions (deductible only to the extent by which cumulatively they exceed 2% of adjusted gross income).

Personal Exemptions

Personal exemptions are available to the taxpayer for himself, his spouse, and his dependents. The 2002 amount was $3,000 for each individual. No exemption is allowed to a taxpayer who can be claimed as a dependent on another taxpayer's return.

Credits

Taxpayers can reduce their income tax liability by claiming the benefit of certain tax credits. Each dollar of tax credit offsets a dollar of tax liability. The following are a few of the available tax credits.

Certain low income households may claim an Earned Income Credit. The maximum Earned Income Credit for 2002 was $376 for taxpayers with no qualifying children, $2,506 for taxpayers with one qualifying child, $4,140 for taxpayers with two or more qualifying children. The maximum credit is reduced if earned income or adjusted gross income exceeds $14,500 for taxpayers with one or more children, or exceeds $6,150 for taxpayers with no children. For families with no qualifying children, the credit is zero if earned income or adjusted gross income exceeds $11,050; for families with one qualifying child, the credit is zero if earned income or adjusted gross income exceeds $29,200; and for taxpayers with two or more qualifying children, the credit is zero if earned income or adjusted gross income exceeds $34,178. The earned income credit is a refundable credit.

A credit for Child and Dependent Care Expenses is available for amounts paid to care for a qualifying child or other dependent so that the taxpayer can work or look for work. The credit is up to 30% (depending on adjusted gross income) of up to $2,400 of employment-related expenses for one qualifying child or dependent and up to $4,800 of employment-related expenses for two qualifying individuals.

The elderly and those under 65 who are retired under total disability may be entitled to a credit of

Number of Individual Income Tax Returns Filed Electronically

Year	Number of returns (in thousands)	Percentage increase
1995	11,807	n.a.
1996	14,968	26.8%
1997	19,136	27.8
1998	24,580	28.4
1999	29,349	19.4
2000	35,394	20.6
2001	40,245	13.7
2002	46,890	16.5

Source: 2002 IRS Data Book.

State Taxes on Individuals

(as of Dec. 31, 2002)

State	Sales/use tax (percent)[1]	Income tax (percent)[2]
Alabama	4%	2.0% – 5.0%
Alaska	none	none
Arizona	5.6	2.87 – 5.04
Arkansas	5.125	1.0 – 6.5[3]
California	7.25	1.0 – 9.3[3]
Colorado	2.9	4.63
Connecticut	6	3.0 – 4.5
Delaware	none	2.2 – 5.95
Florida	6	none
Georgia	4	1.0 – 6.0
Hawaii	4	1.4 – 8.5
Idaho	5	1.6 – 7.8
Illinois	6.25	3.0
Indiana	6	3.4
Iowa	5	0.36 – 8.98
Kansas	5.3	3.5 – 6.45
Kentucky	6	2.0 – 6.0
Louisiana	4	2.0 – 6.0
Maine	5	2.0 – 8.5
Maryland	5	2.0 – 4.75
Massachusetts	5	5.3
Michigan	6	4.0
Minnesota	6.5	5.35 – 7.85
Mississippi	7	3.0 – 5.0
Missouri	4.225	1.5 – 6.0
Montana	none	2.0 – 11.0
Nebraska	5.5%	2.61% – 6.84%
Nevada	6.5	none
New Hampshire	none	([4])
New Jersey	6	1.4 – 6.37
New Mexico	5	1.7 – 8.2
New York	4	4.0 – 6.85
North Carolina	4.5	6.0 – 8.25
North Dakota	5	2.1 – 5.54
Ohio	5	0.743 – 7.5
Oklahoma	4.5	0.5 – 7.0
Oregon	none	5.0 – 9.0
Pennsylvania	6	2.8
Rhode Island	7	25.0[5]
South Carolina	5	2.5 – 7.0
South Dakota	4	none
Tennessee	7	([4])
Texas	6.25	none
Utah	4.75	2.3 – 7.0
Vermont	5	3.6 – 9.5
Virginia	4.5	2.0 – 5.75
Washington	6.5	none
West Virginia	6	3.0 – 6.5
Wisconsin	5	4.6 – 6.75
Wyoming	4	none
District of Columbia	5.75	4.5 – 8.7

1. Local and county taxes, if any, are additional. 2. Tax rate for individuals; unless otherwise noted, range denotes progressive structure; higher income pays higher rate. 3. Indexed for inflation. 4. State income tax is limited to dividends and interest. 5. Percentage of federal tax liability. *Source:* The Federation of Tax Administrators.

up to $750 (if single) or $1,125 (if married and filing jointly). No credit is available if the taxpayer is single and has adjusted gross income of $17,500 or more. Similarly, the credit is unavailable to a married couple filing jointly if their adjusted gross income exceeds $25,000.

Effective for tax years beginning after Dec. 1, 1997, taxpayers who have qualifying children for whom the taxpayer may claim a dependency exemption and who are less than 17 years old as of the close of the tax year are entitled to the child tax credit. The amount of the credit for 2000 was $500. The child credit begins to phase out when AGI reaches $110,000 for joint filers and $75,000 for singles. Taxpayers who have three or more qualifying children may also be entitled to an additional credit.

Federal Estate and Gift Taxes

A Federal Estate Tax Return must generally be filed for the estate of every U.S. citizen or resident whose gross estate, taxable gifts, and specific exemptions exceed $1,000,000 for decedents dying in 2003, and according to the following table if dying in succeeding years:

Decedent dying in	Exclusion amount
2003	$1,000,000
2004 and 2005	1,500,000
2006, 2007, and 2008	2,000,000
2009	3,500,000

The Economic Growth and Tax Relief Reconciliation Act of 2001 completely phases out the federal estate and gift tax by 2010. The tax rates are lowered and the exemption is raised between 2002 and 2009, and the tax is completely eliminated in 2010. However, the post-act law will bring the Estate and Gift Tax back into existence in 2011.

A unified credit of $202,050 is available to offset both estate and gift taxes. Any part of the credit used to offset gift taxes is not available to offset estate taxes. As a result, although they are still taxable as gifts, lifetime taxable transfers no longer cushion the impact of progressive estate tax rates. Lifetime transfers and transfers made at death are combined for estate tax rate purposes.

Gift taxes are computed by applying the uniform rate schedule to lifetime taxable transfers (after deducting the unified credit) and subtracting the taxes payable for prior taxable periods. In general, estate taxes are computed by applying the uniform rate schedule to cumulative transfers and subtracting the gift taxes paid. An appropriate adjustment is made for taxes on lifetime transfers—such as certain gifts within three years of death—in a decedent's estate.

For 2003, an annual gift tax exclusion is provided that permits tax-free gifts to each donee of $11,000 for each year. A husband and wife who agree to treat gifts to third persons as joint gifts can exclude up to $22,000 a year to each donee. An unlimited exclusion for medical expenses and school tuition both paid directly to the institution for the benefit of any donee is also available in addition to the annual gift tax exclusion.

Federal Corporation Taxes

Corporations are taxed under a graduated tax rate structure. If a corporation has taxable income in excess of $100,000, the amount of tax shall be increased by the lesser of 5% of such excess or $11,750. When a corporation has taxable income in excess of $15,000,000, the amount of tax shall be increased by an additional amount equal to the lesser of 3% of such excess or $100,000.

If the corporation qualifies, it may elect to be an S corporation. If it makes this election, the corporation will not (with certain exceptions) pay corporate tax on its income. Its income is instead passed through and taxed to its shareholders. There are several requirements a corporation must meet to qualify as an S corporation, including having 75 or fewer shareholders and having only one class of stock.

Corporate Tax Rates

Taxable income	Tax rate
$0–$50,000	15%
$50,001–$75,000	25%
$75,001–$10,000,000	34%
$10,000,001 and up	35%

State Corporation Income and Franchise Taxes

All states except Texas, Nevada, South Dakota, Washington, and Wyoming impose a tax on corporation net income. The majority of states impose the tax at flat rates ranging from 2.3% to approximately 10.75%. Several states have adopted a graduated basis of rates for corporations.

Nearly all states follow the federal law in defining net income. However, many states provide for varying exclusions and adjustments.

A state is empowered to tax all of the net income of its domestic corporations. With regard to nonresident corporations, however, it may only tax the net income on business carried on within its boundaries. Corporations are, therefore, required to apportion their incomes among the states where they do business, and pay a tax to each of these states. Nearly all states provide an apportionment to their domestic corporations, too, in order that they not be unduly burdened. Several states tax unincorporated businesses separately.

Federal Expenditures for Every Dollar of Taxes Sent to Washington

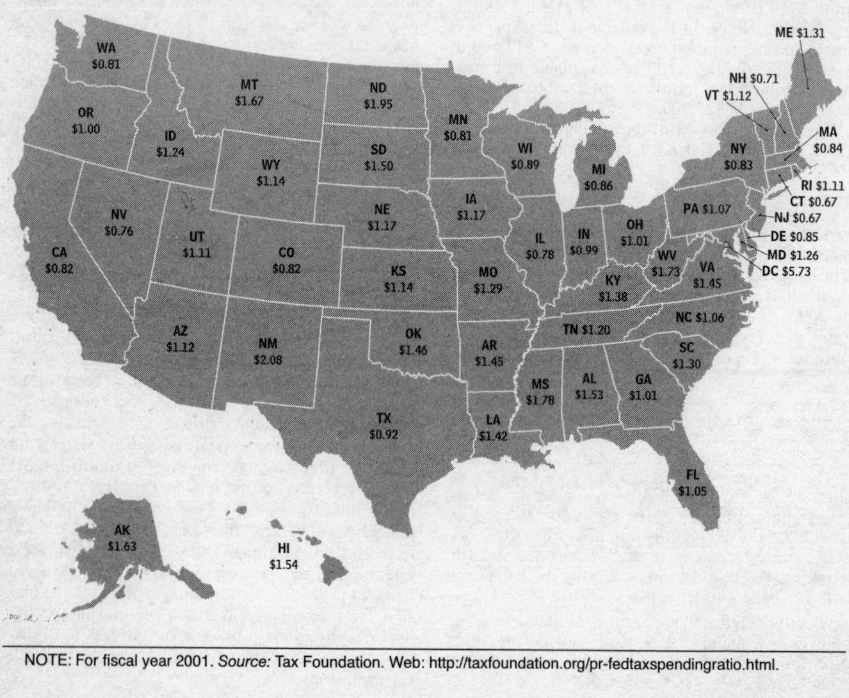

NOTE: For fiscal year 2001. *Source:* Tax Foundation. Web: http://taxfoundation.org/pr-fedtaxspendingratio.html.

The Person of the Year

How "Lucky Lindy"—and a slow week for news—gave birth to a memorable annual tradition

The founders of TIME Magazine, Henry Luce and Briton Haddon, were strong believers in the idea that history is shaped by the deeds of extraordinary men and women. This thesis, most memorably advanced by the British writer Thomas Carlyle, was well-suited to the American vision of the two Yale graduates, since it ran counter to the assertions of Karl Marx and others that history is made by impersonal economic and social forces.

TIME's insistence on the primacy of the individual finds its most memorable form in the magazine's annual designation of a Person of the Year—the individual whose actions most affected the course of the news within the last 12 months. But the magazine's signature annual tribute was not the result of high-level philosophizing: rather, it was driven by something far more important to journalists—a deadline.

The year was 1927; it was the last week in December. During the holiday season, the normal flow of public events had temporarily ebbed to a trickle. Looking to 1928, the editors at TIME were having trouble finding a newsworthy cover subject for the first issue of the new year. At the same time, they realized that they had passed up several opportunities during the year to put aviator Charles Lindbergh on its cover. Since his nonstop flight from New York to Paris in late May, the young pilot had been idolized—yet he had never appeared on the magazine's cover. So the editors came up with a new concept: instead of highlighting a personality of the week, it was decided that the cover for Jan. 2, 1928, would feature Lindbergh, and that beneath his likeness would be the words "Man of the Year."

A year later, the cover for TIME's first issue of 1929 revealed that its editors had named car magnate Walter P. Chrysler as Man of the Year for 1928—and it was obvious that an annual tradition had been born. Though TIME named a number of Women of the Year in the decades that followed, the editors eventually settled on the non-gender-specific term Person of the Year for the magazine's annual citation.

The term "Person of the Year"—redolent of countless Chamber of Commerce dinners—suggests to many people that it is awarded as an accolade. It is not. Rather, it designates the person who, in the editors' opinion, has most affected the course of history in the past twelve months—for good or for ill.

In 1938, for instance, Adolf Hitler completed his Anschluss of Austria and brokered the tragic agreement at Munich that put Czechoslovakia into his hands. However reluctantly, the editors concluded that Hitler's actions had most affected history's course, and he became the 1938 Man of the Year. Similarly, in 1979, Ayatullah Khomeini was named Man of the Year, even while he held Americans hostage in Teheran. TIME received more than 14,000 letters complaining about the choice.

After 75 years, the Person of the Year has become an institution: whereas in one sense it is a sort of intellectual parlor game, it also challenges TIME's editors and readers to reflect on the events of the past year critically, dispassionately, and rigorously. □

1927	Charles Lindbergh
1928	Walter P. Chrysler
1929	Owen D. Young
1930	Mahatma Gandhi
1931	Pierre Laval
1932	Franklin D. Roosevelt
1933	Hugh S. Johnson
1934	Franklin D. Roosevelt
1935	Haile Selassie
1936	Wallis Warfield Simpson
1937	Gen. and Mrs. Chiang Kai-shek
1938	Adolf Hitler
1939	Joseph Stalin
1940	Winston Churchill
1941	Franklin D. Roosevelt
1942	Joseph Stalin
1943	Gen. George C. Marshall
1944	Gen. Dwight D. Eisenhower
1945	Harry S. Truman
1946	James F. Byrnes
1947	Gen. George C. Marshall
1948	Harry S. Truman
1949	Winston Churchill
1950	G.I. Joe
1951	Mohammed Mossadegh
1952	Queen Elizabeth II
1953	Konrad Adenauer
1954	John Foster Dulles
1955	Harlow H. Curtice
1956	Hungarian Patriot
1957	Nikita Khrushchev
1958	Charles DeGaulle
1959	Dwight D. Eisenhower
1960	U.S. Scientists
1961	John F. Kennedy
1962	Pope John XXIII
1963	Rev. Martin Luther King, Jr.
1964	Lyndon B. Johnson
1965	Gen. William Westmoreland
1966	Americans under 25
1967	Lyndon B. Johnson
1968	Astronauts Anders, Borman, Lovell
1969	The Middle Americans
1970	Willy Brandt
1971	Richard M. Nixon
1972	Richard M. Nixon and Henry Kissinger
1973	Judge John J. Sirica
1974	King Faisal
1975	American Women
1976	Jimmy Carter
1977	Anwar Sadat
1978	Deng Xiaoping
1979	Ayatollah Khomeini
1980	Ronald Reagan
1981	Lech Walesa
1982	The Personal Computer
1983	Ronald Reagan and Yuri Andropov
1984	Peter Ueberroth
1985	Deng Xiaoping
1986	Corazon Aquino
1987	Mikhail Gorbachev
1988	Endangered Earth
1989	Mikhail Gorbachev
1990	George Bush
1991	Ted Turner
1992	Bill Clinton
1993	The Peacemakers: Rabin, Arafat, Mandela, De Klerk
1994	Pope John Paul II
1995	Newt Gingrich
1996	Dr. David Ho
1997	Andrew Grove
1998	Bill Clinton and Kenneth Starr
1999	Jeff Bezos
2000	George W. Bush
2001	Rudolph Giuliani
2002	The Whistleblowers

People in the News, 2003

Mahmoud Abbas (Abu Mazen), Palestinian politician, was named prime minister in March by President Yasir Arafat. Palestinian reformists lauded the appointment, while the militant groups Hamas and Islamic Jihad said Arafat was playing into the hands of Israel and the U.S. In June, Abbas and Israeli prime minister Ariel Sharon agreed to begin implementing the road map to peace, but a series of suicide attacks on Israeli targets by Palestinian militants and the assassination of Hamas leaders by Israeli troops thwarted any real progress. Abbas resigned in September, saying Sharon and Arafat had undermined his government.

John Abizaid, U.S. general, replaced Tommy Franks in July as the commander of allied forces in the Persian Gulf. Abizaid, an Arab-American, is fluent in Arabic. Days after he assumed the post, Abizaid said coalition troops in Iraq were confronting "a classical guerrilla-type campaign" by forces loyal to Saddam Hussein and by terrorist groups. The statement departed from defense secretary Donald Rumsfeld's earlier assessments, which said the attacks were random and unorganized.

Peter Arnett, broadcast journalist, was dismissed by NBC in March after he criticized the U.S.-led operation in Iraq in an interview on Iraqi state TV. "The first war plan has failed because of Iraqi resistance," he said. NBC, which had hired Arnett as a freelance journalist, initially supported Arnett but changed course after only hours of further deliberation. Arnett earned praise for his fearless—and ubiquitous—coverage of the 1991 Persian Gulf War for CNN.

John Ashcroft, U.S. attorney general, was widely criticized for seeking sweeping new powers to track down terrorists. Civil libertarians and increasingly, the courts, have condemned the compromise on civil rights and due process in the name of national security. In June, days after an internal review by the Justice Department's inspector general said the detention of 762 illegal immigrants was highly problematic, Ashcroft testified before the House Judiciary Committee that the roundup was necessary to protect the country and that law-enforcement officials should have even broader powers. He toured the country in September to promote the proposed revision of the Patriot Act, which includes wider subpoena powers, an expanded federal death penalty statute, and provisions that allow judges to deny bail for suspects in terrorism cases.

Tariq Aziz, deputy prime minister of Iraq, acted as Saddam Hussein's spokesman in the months leading up to the U.S.-led invasion of Iraq, repeatedly denying that Iraq possessed—or was developing—weapons of mass destruction. In April, he turned himself over to U.S. officials in Baghdad.

Steve Bechler, 23, Baltimore Orioles pitcher, died in February of multi-organ failure caused by complications from heatstroke. He collapsed during a spring-training workout. An autopsy later revealed that the weight-loss supplement ephedra contributed to his death. The finding renewed a controversy over the safety of the herb, which is banned by the National Football League, the International Olympic Committee, and the National Collegiate Athletic Association, but not Major League Baseball.

David Beckham, celebrity British soccer player, was traded from Manchester United to Real Madrid in June. The Spanish team paid Manchester $41 million for the star midfielder. Beckham and his wife, Victoria, a former Spice Girl, rival the royal family in popularity and adoration. Beckham helped to popularize the term "metrosexual," which refers to straight men who take pleasure in primping and shopping.

William Bennett, moral crusader and former public official, admitted in May that he had lost about $8 million gambling in casinos over about a 10-year period. Bennett, a former U.S. secretary of education and director of the National Drug Control Policy as well as the author of *The Book of Virtues,* said he planned to quit gambling.

Silvio Berlusconi, Italian prime minister, created a diplomatic furor on the day he became president of the European Union (a rotating position) when he compared a German legislator to a Nazi concentration-camp guard. Earlier in the year, the Italian Parliament spared Berlusconi from a corruption trial when it passed a law granting Italy's top leaders, including the prime minister, immunity from prosecution. He'll face trial for allegedly bribing judges in 1985 when he leaves office.

Ladan and Laleh Bijani, Iranian conjoined twins, died after a 50-hour surgical procedure in Singapore. The operation to separate the 29-year-old women was the first ever performed on adults. The pair, who had studied law in Teheran, said they were willing to risk dying for the chance to be separated.

Jayson Blair, *New York Times* reporter, resigned in May when confronted by his editors with proof that he had plagiarized and fabricated sources, stories, and quotes in dozens of stories. The scandal traumatized the venerable paper, which ran a 4-page, 7,200-word story chronicling Blair's missteps during his 5-year tenure at the *Times.* "It's a huge black eye," said publisher Arthur Ochs Sulzberger, Jr. Editors who pored over his work found 36 errors in the 73 stories he wrote in a 6-month period.

Tony Blair, prime minister of the United Kingdom, risked his political career by offering the Bush administration unwavering support for military action in Iraq. Blair paid dearly when three members of his cabinet resigned in protest. During the summer, critics accused Blair of exaggerating Iraq's weapons capabilities to justify his case for war. Blair stood by his intelligence reports, including one that stated Hussein could launch biological and chemical weapons in 45 minutes. The prime minister faced additional criticism in July, after David Kelly, a former weapons inspector in Iraq, committed suicide shortly after testifying before the House of Commons Select Committee on Foreign Affairs about whether he told a BBC reporter that the British government had "sexed up" intelligence documents about Iraq's arsenal. In his August testimony in the inquiry into Kelly's death, Blair said he would have resigned if the BBC report had been true.

Hans Blix, chief UN weapons inspector, delivered several reports to the UN Security Council on his team's search for chemical and biological weapons inside Iraq. In his first report, Blix said, "Iraq appears not to have come to a genuine acceptance, not even today, of the disarmament that was demanded of it." Once Iraq began to show signs of cooperation, Blix urged the members of the Security Council to give the inspectors more time to complete the task. President Bush was repeatedly angered by Blix's measured, circumspect reports that failed to provide the president with a "smoking gun" to help build the case for war in Iraq. He retired in June.

L. Paul Bremer, former diplomat and counterterrorism official, took over as the top civilian administrator of

Iraq in May, replacing Lt. Gen. Jay Garner. He oversaw the selection of the Iraqi Governing Council, and faced the daunting task of restoring order to an Iraq mired in unrest and lawlessness.

Kobe Bryant, professional basketball player, was charged with sexual assault in July. He's accused of raping a 19-year-old receptionist and concierge at a Vail, Colorado, spa. He denied the allegation, but did admit to having sex with her. Bryant, who plays for the Los Angeles Lakers, had enjoyed a squeaky-clean reputation and was considered one of basketball's most decent players.

William Bulger, politician and public official, resigned as president of the University of Massachusetts in August, after months of intense pressure and criticism from Massachusetts governor Mitt Romney. Bulger's brother, James "Whitey" Bulger, a local mob leader under indictment for murder and racketeering, has been a fugitive since 1994. In June, William Bulger testified before the U.S. House Government Reform Committee about his brother. Romney charged that the testimony was evasive and defiant, and said it proved Bulger was unfit to run the university. One of the most powerful and prominent politicians in the state, Bulger, a Democrat, served as the president of the state senate for 17 years.

Martha Burk, chair of the National Council of Women's Organizations, led the much-publicized campaign against Augusta National Golf Club, Georgia's exclusive, all-male enclave that hosts the Masters tournament each April. After the tournament, Augusta chairman Hootie Johnson defiantly said, "There never will be a female member, six months after the Masters, a year, ten years, or ever."

Donald Carty, airline executive, resigned as American Airlines chief executive officer in April, after facing intense criticism for his handling of negotiations with airline unions. Unionized workers agreed to steep wage cuts and later learned that the company had arranged to pay several executives, including Carty, lavish retention bonuses.

Steve Case, executive, resigned as chairman of AOL Time Warner in January amid falling stock prices and the attendant dissatisfaction of shareholders. Case had masterminded the 2001 merger of AOL and Time Warner, which at the time confirmed the dominance of new media over traditional outlets. But the honeymoon was brief, and the AOL division became a drain on the once profitable Time Warner empire. In addition, the Securities and Exchange Commission opened an inquiry in July 2002 into AOL's accounting procedures.

Jacques Chirac, president of France, remained steadfast in his opposition to the U.S.-led attack on Iraq. Throughout the diplomatic process in late 2002 and into 2003, France repeatedly called for more weapons inspections before resorting to war. France's refusal to vote for a UN resolution authorizing war in Iraq contributed to Bush's decision to act without a UN mandate. The U.S. was infuriated by what it saw as France's obdurate obstructionism, and relations between the countries plummeted.

Wesley Clark, retired four-star general, threw his hat into the race for the Democratic presidential nomination in September. The former supreme allied commander of NATO has never held elective office. He led U.S. and allied troops in NATO's war in Kosovo in 1999, and retired from the military in 2000 after 34 years of service.

Hillary Rodham Clinton, U.S. senator and former first lady, increased her already high profile with the immensely publicized June release of her not-so-revealing memoir, *Living History.* Clinton made the rounds on the network talk shows and gave dozens of print interviews to promote the book.

Ben Curtis, 26, professional golfer, stunned the world in July when he won the British Open. Curtis's win ranks as one of the biggest upsets in sports history. Curtis had played in only 14 other PGA Tour Tournaments, and he had never finished in the top 10. He shot a 283 in four rounds of play.

Gray Davis, governor of California, faced mounting troubles during the summer as the state's deficit ballooned to a record-setting $38 billion, his opponents gathered enough signatures for a recall vote, his approval ratings plummeted, and credit-rating agencies lowered the state's credit rating. In July Lieutenant Governor Cruz Bustamante set the recall vote for October. Voters will be asked if they favor the recall and who they support as a replacement.

Howard Dean, former governor of Vermont, emerged as a the frontrunner in the crowded field of Democratic presidential hopefuls. In the third quarter of 2003, he raised $14.8 million, more than each of his rivals. Much of Dean's take came from donations through the Internet. Many of Dean's supporters have used the website Meetup.com to organize rallies and letter-writing campaigns.

Dixie Chicks, country music band, faced unexpected backlash after singer Natalie Maines said during a March concert in London, "We're ashamed that the president of the United States is from Texas." Bandmate Emily Robinson added, "We support the troops 100%." Nevertheless, sales of their album *Home* plummeted, and radio stations virtually banished the band from the airwaves.

Mohamed ElBaradei, head of the International Atomic Energy Agency, delivered several reports to the UN Security Council on his team's search for nuclear weapons inside Iraq. ElBaradei reported in February that although Iraq had not cooperated fully, his team had "found no evidence of ongoing prohibited nuclear activities in Iraq." He urged the members of the Security Council to give the inspectors more time to complete the task. President Bush refused, however, and expressed skepticism about the accuracy of ElBaradei's report. In March ElBaradei told the Security Council that documents that said Iraq tried to procure uranium from Niger were crude forgeries. The Bush administration had used the evidence to help justify the war against Iraq.

Tommy Franks, the commander of allied forces in the Persian Gulf, directed the war in Iraq from the high-tech U.S. Central Command (Centcom) near Doha, Qatar. President Bush called on the four-star army general in early 2002 to begin planning the ouster of Saddam Hussein. He worked closely with Defense Secretary Donald Rumsfeld throughout 2002 and during the 2003 offensive. Franks retired in July and was succeeded by Gen. John Abizaid.

Bill Frist, politician and physician from Tennessee, became U.S. Senate majority leader in January, after Trent Lott resigned the post amid a furor over racially provocative remarks he made in December at Strom Thurmond's 100th birthday celebration. President Bush looked to Frist, a relative newcomer to politics who is known for his calm demeanor and his organizational skills, to promote Medicare reform.

Jay Garner, retired U.S. Army general, was appointed in January by President Bush to serve as civil administrator in charge of reconstruction and humanitarian aid in post–Saddam Hussein Iraq. L. Paul Bremer, a former State Department counterterrorism official, replaced Garner in May, when it became clear that Garner had failed to stem the rise of civil unrest and restore order in Iraq.

John Geoghan, defrocked priest, was killed in a Massachusetts prison in August by fellow inmate Joseph Druce, a self-proclaimed homophobe. Geoghan was convicted in 2002 of indecent assault and battery for fondling a young boy in 1991. He was also accused of sexually molesting about 130 children during his 30-year tenure as a priest.

Richard Grasso, chairman and chief executive of the New York Stock Exchange, resigned in September, after enduring weeks of harsh criticism over his compensation package, which included a payout of $140 million in deferred salary and retirement benefits. He had worked for the exchange for 36 years, starting as a clerk in 1968.

Stephen Hadley, deputy national security adviser, took some of the blame in July for the unsubstantiated claim in President Bush's State of the Union address that Iraq had attempted to buy uranium from Niger. Bush used the information to push for a preemptive attack in Iraq. The CIA had warned Hadley twice in October 2002 that intelligence did not back up the claim.

Hambali (Riduan Isamuddin), Indonesian terror suspect, was captured in Thailand in August in a joint operation between the CIA and the Thai police. Hambali, Asia's most-wanted terrorist, served as the operations chief of Jemaah Islamiyah, which has ties to al-Qaeda. Officials believe Hambali organized the 2002 bombing of a Bali nightclub and the attack on the J. W. Marriott hotel in Jakarta, and was involved in the bombing of the U.S.S. *Cole* and the Sept. 11, 2001, terrorist attacks.

Hu Jintao, Chinese politician, assumed the presidency in March, succeeding President Jiang Zemin. Hu had become general secretary of the Communist Party at the 16th Party Congress in November 2002. Although he had served in China's politburo for more than ten years, little is know about Hu's governing style.

Qusay Hussein, second son of Saddam Hussein, was killed in July by U.S. troops after a fierce gunfight in Mosul. Qusay, Saddam's heir apparent, served as supervisor of the Republican Guard and the head of the powerful Iraqi Special Security Organization, which oversees domestic security and intelligence. Though less flamboyant than his father and brother Uday, Quasay was considered equally diabolical.

Saddam Hussein, despotic president of Iraq, brought war upon his country in March with his arrogant refusal to cooperate with the international community and disarm. He also stirred bitter discord in the UN, a role he clearly relished. After the war, troops discovered several mass graves and torture chambers, evidence of rampant human rights abuses at the hands of Hussein. His whereabouts after the conflict remained unknown, but he released several taped messages urging Iraqis to resist the U.S.-led occupation.

Uday Hussein, eldest son of Saddam Hussein, was killed in July by U.S. troops after a brutal firefight in Mosul. Uday had earned a reputation inside Iraq and beyond as a reckless thug. He served a prison sentence in 1988 for murdering one of his father's bodyguards. Eight years later he was nearly crippled in an assassination attempt. In the U.S.-led war against Iraq, Uday commanded a group of fedayeen fighters, militia troops that fight independently of the military.

David Kelly, British weapons inspector, committed suicide in July, shortly after testifying before the House of Commons Select Committee on Foreign Affairs about whether he been the source for a BBC story that asserted the British government had "sexed up" intelligence documents about Iraq's arsenal. The committee relentlessly grilled Kelly, who acknowledged that while he did meet with BBC reporter Andrew Gilligan, who wrote the story, he didn't think he was the "main source." The report led to a major dispute between the BBC and the government.

Katrina Leung, prominent Chinese-American businesswoman, was indicted in May on espionage-related charges. Authorities think that while she was working as an informant to the FBI, she was a double agent, passing on highly sensitive documents to Beijing. She and her FBI contact, James Smith, had a 20-year affair, during which time Leung accessed the classified information. The FBI paid Leung about $1.7 million for her 20 years of service. Smith was indicted on charges of wire fraud and gross negligence.

Daniel Libeskind, architect, in February won the contest to design the site at the World Trade Center, which was destroyed in the September 11, 2001, terrorist attacks. His plans, which he has revised, include a hanging garden, a memorial, a cultural center, and a spiral tower reaching 1,776 feet tall, which will make it the tallest building in the world. He estimates the project, called the "Freedom Tower," will cost about $320 million and take ten years to complete. But Larry Silverstein, the developer who owns the lease to the World Trade Center, has hinted that his rebuilding plan may deviate from Libeskind's.

Luiz Inacio "Lula" da Silva, Brazilian politician, became the country's first working-class president in January. As leader of Brazil's only socialist party, the Workers' Party, Lula pledged to increase social services and improve the lot of the poor. His first major legislative success came in July when his plan to reform the country's debt-ridden pension system—which operates under an annual $20 billion deficit—was approved. Civil servants and union members—his core supporters—took to the streets to protest the reforms. But polls in August demonstrated that the majority of Brazilians continued to support Lula's tough economic reform efforts.

Pfc. Jessica Lynch, American prisoner of war, was rescued in April from a hospital in Nasiriya, Iraq. She was one of 12 members of the 507th Ordnance Maintenance Company captured by Iraqi troops in March. She suffered several broken bones and other injuries in the ordeal. The U.S. military was criticized for exaggerating the heroism involved in Lynch's rescue, and the BBC called its presentation "one of the most stunning pieces of news management ever conceived." The Pentagon countered that the BBC report was "void of all facts and absolutely ridiculous." Lynch returned to her home in rural West Virginia in July to an onslaught of offers from television networks, book publishers, and movie companies, all seeking exclusive rights to her story. In September, she signed a $1 million book deal with Knopf.

Khalid Shaikh Mohammed, suspected terrorist, was captured and arrested in Rawalpindi, Pakistan, in March. He was turned over to U.S. officials, who believe he is one of Osama bin Laden's top deputies and a mastermind of the September 11, 2001, terrorist attacks against the United States.

Roy Moore, chief justice of the Alabama Supreme Court, defiantly refused to remove a 5,280-pound monument of the Ten Commandments from the state courthouse. The state supreme court and a federal judge had ruled that Moore had violated the separation of church and state when he installed the piece. Workers moved "Roy's rock" in August.

Sean Patrick O'Malley, Franciscan friar, was named archbishop of Boston in June by the pope. He replaced Cardinal Bernard Law, who resigned the post in December 2002 amid outrage over his handling of the ongoing sexual-abuse scandal. O'Malley played an integral role in the $85 million settlement reached in September between the archdiocese and abuse victims. Often called a people's bishop, O'Malley is widely considered more down-to-earth and compassionate than his predecessor.

Eli Pariser and Wes Boyd, activists, used their advocacy group, MoveOn, to launch a massive online antiwar campaign in January. The group collected more than 700,000 signatures for a petition that urged President Bush to allow the UN weapons inspectors to complete their task before attacking Iraq. MoveOn also organized the protests against the war that drew millions of people worldwide. Boyd and

Joan Blades created the group in 1998 in response to the "continuing obsession" of conservatives with the President Clinton and Monica Lewinsky scandal.

Richard Perle, government adviser, resigned in March as chairman of the Defense Policy Board, an independent committee that counsels the Pentagon, after being widely criticized for a glaring conflict of interest. Perle was hired as a consultant to Global Crossing, a bankrupt telecommunications company that owns fiber optics networks, to advise the firm on how to gain Defense Department and FBI approval for its joint-venture sale to companies in Hong Kong and Singapore. Perle served as assistant secretary of defense in the Reagan administration and is among the hawks in Defense Secretary Donald Rumsfeld's inner circle who have long argued for a foreign policy of preemption and regime change in Iraq.

John Poindexter, retired rear admiral and former national security adviser, resigned as head of the Pentagon's Defense Advanced Research Projects Agency (DARPA) after July's embarrassing disclosure that the group had organized a terrorism futures market, called the Policy Analysis Market, which would have enabled investors to bet on the likelihood of future terrorist attacks, assassinations, and coups.

Colin Powell, U.S. secretary of state, was one of the only doves and committed multilateralists among top Bush officials during the pre-war period. However, in January 2003, he joined the hawkish faction of the Bush administration, and argued for a preemptive attack on Iraq. As the post-war violence surged and the projected cost of the occupation of Iraq increased, Powell resumed his multilateralist stance, trying—with limited success—to win support at the UN for broader international aid in Iraq.

Muammar al-Qaddafi, Libya's rogue president, finally admitted guilt in Libya's role in the 1988 terrorist bombing of a Boeing 747 over Lockerbie, Scotland, and agreed to pay $2.7 billion to the families of the 270 victims. To the outrage of many, Libya was elected chair of the UN Human Rights Commission earlier in the year.

Howell Raines and Gerald Boyd, executive editor and managing editor, respectively, of the *New York Times,* resigned in June, five weeks after reporter Jayson Blair stepped down. Blair had admitted to fabricating dozens of stories. Several reporters and editors at the *Times* publicly criticized Raines's management style and said he had created an unpleasant work environment. They also expressed outrage that Blair had been allowed to continue writing for the paper after several of his editors complained about his sloppiness and high error rate. In July Bill Keller, a *New York Times* columnist, was selected as executive editor of the paper.

Tom Ridge, former governor of Pennsylvania, was sworn in as the country's first secretary of homeland security in January. The department, established in 2002 in response to the terrorist attacks on September 11, 2001, seeks to protect the country against terrorism and includes 22 agencies and 170,000 employees.

V. Gene Robinson, Episcopalian minister, was approved as the church's first openly gay bishop in August. Diocesan bishops voted 62–45 in favor of his confirmation following an eleventh-hour accusation of sexual misconduct that delayed the vote. An investigation quickly exonerated Robinson. Conservative Anglican church leaders denounced the decision, saying it could split the denomination.

Eric Rudolph, fugitive accused in the bombings of Atlanta's Centennial Olympic Park in 1996, an abortion clinic in Atlanta, and a gay nightclub in Birmingham, Ala., was captured and arrested in North Carolina in June. He had been on the lam since 1998. Police think that since he was relatively clean and healthy that he had been sheltered by supporters. Rudolph had been on the FBI's Ten Most Wanted Fugitives list.

Donald Rumsfeld, U.S. secretary of defense, maintained—and strengthened—his role as one of the Bush administration's most fervent hawks during the war in Iraq. Blunt and outspoken, he ruffled feathers with disparaging remarks about "old Europe." When significant post-war difficulties arose in Iraq, Rumsfeld argued against sending more troops, in keeping with his reformist vision of a streamlined, efficient military.

George Ryan, Republican governor of Illinois, commuted the sentences of 167 inmates on death row, calling capital punishment fundamentally flawed. He announced the move in January, two days before leaving office. "Our capital system is haunted by the demon of error—error in determining guilty, and error in determining who among the guilty deserves to die," he said. In 2000, Ryan had imposed a moratorium on executions.

Mohammed Saeed al-Sahaf, Iraqi information minister, gained a cult following among Americans for his bravado and often outrageous proclamations about the status of the war in Iraq. As coalition troops stormed Baghdad, he declared, "The infidels are committing suicide by the hundreds on the gates of Baghdad." He frequently unleashed unabashed invective against President Bush and British prime minister Tony Blair, calling them "blood-sucking bastards."

Jésica Santillán, 17-year-old Mexican girl, died in February after a second heart and lung transplant. She nearly died after the first procedure, when doctors at Duke University Hospital accidentally used organs from a donor with the wrong blood type.

Rick Santorum, conservative senator from Pennsylvania, outraged many Democrats and activists for his blunt condemnation of homosexuality. In an interview with the Associated Press, he equated gay sex with incest and polygamy. "If the Supreme Court says you have the right to consensual sex within your home, then you have the right to bigamy, you have the right to polygamy, you have the right to incest, you have the right to adultery," he said.

Gerhard Schröder, chancellor of Germany, was an outspoken foe of war in Iraq without the backing of the UN Security Council. He said he considered the weapons inspections to be effective, and favored using diplomacy to disarm Iraq. His stance severely strained relations with Washington.

Arnold Schwarzenegger, Austrian-born actor and body builder, used an August appearance on Jay Leno's *Tonight Show* to announce his plans to run in California's recall election. About 130 other hopefuls entered the fray, hoping to replace Gray Davis. Throughout the campaign, Schwarzenegger, a Republican, remained vague on issues and policy.

Ariel Sharon, Israeli prime minister, halfheartedly began to take the first steps in implementing a U.S.-led peace initiative, called the road map, in May. Sharon outraged right-wing Israelis when he said Israel's policy toward Palestinians amounted to an occupation. But his efforts ultimately rang hollow: Israel did not dismantle settlements, much less prevent new ones from cropping up, and Sharon continued to build the controversial security barrier that divides Israeli and Palestinian areas. By September, a spate of Palestinian suicide bombings and Israeli retaliations dashed hopes for peace.

Elizabeth Smart, Utah teenager, was reunited with her family in March, nine months after being kidnapped at knifepoint from her Salt Lake City bedroom by Brian Mitchell, a 49-year-old self-proclaimed prophet. During her prolonged ordeal, Smart lived an itinerant life with her abductors, Mitchell and his wife, Wanda

Barzee. The trio spent the winter months in San Diego and returned to Utah in early March, when a number of people recognized the 15 year old and tipped off police.

John Snow, public official, was confirmed as treasury secretary in February, replacing Paul H. O'Neill, whom the president felt had not been an effective spokesman for the administration's economic policies. Before assuming the post, Snow was the chairman of CSX, the country's largest railroad, and served as an undersecretary in the Department of Transportation during the Ford administration.

Annika Sorenstam, Swedish professional golfer, created a media frenzy when she competed in the men's PGA Tour's Bank of America Colonial open in May. She missed making the cut into the final round by four shots. Sorenstam was the first woman to play in a men's PGA tournament since 1945, when Babe Didrikson Zaharias played in the Los Angeles Open. In August Sorenstam won the British Open to complete a career Grand Slam. She's the sixth woman golfer to do so. Sorenstam, the best woman golfer in the world, has won 43 LPGA events and nearly $12 million in prize money.

Sammy Sosa, Chicago Cubs slugger, was ejected from a game in June after umpires found cork in his bat. League officials confiscated more than 70 of his bats, and none of them had been altered. He was suspended for seven games. Sosa is the only player in Major League Baseball history with three 60-home run seasons (1998, 1999, and 2001).

Martha Stewart, diva of domesticity, was indicted in June on nine charges of obstruction of justice and securities fraud. The charges stem from her December 2001 sale of 3,928 shares of the biotech stock ImClone. She made the trade the day before the FDA announced it had declined to review ImClone's new cancer drug—news that sent shares tumbling. Authorities accuse her of lying to investigators and altering evidence in their investigation. She resigned as CEO of Martha Stewart Omnimedia after the indictment. The charges tarnished her meticulously cultivated image.

Aung San Suu Kyi, Burmese opposition leader, was taken into "protective custody" in May, after several people died in clashes between her supporters and members of the military junta. The government also cracked down on her group, the National League for Democracy, shuttering regional offices. She was freed from 19 months of house arrest in May 2002.

Charles Taylor, president of Liberia, was indicted on war crimes charges by a special war crimes court in Sierra Leone in March. The 17-count indictment was unsealed in June. The court accused him of "bearing the greatest responsibility" for the prolonged wars that have devastated West Africa. After promising to do so for several months, Taylor resigned in August and went into exile in Nigeria. In September the UN reported that Taylor left the country with about $3 million donated to the country for disarming rebels. Taylor and Slobodan Milosevic are the only two sitting presidents to have been indicted by the tribunal.

George Tenet, director of the CIA, came under fire for his agency's handling of intelligence concerning Iraq as well as the Sept. 11, 2001, attacks. A Congressional report released in June revealed that the CIA and the FBI grossly underestimated warnings of an imminent terrorist attack against the U.S. in 2001. In July, he took responsibility for allowing unsubstantiated claims about Iraq's pursuit of uranium to be included in President Bush's State of the Union address. President Bush, however, continued to support Tenet—and the intelligence generated by his agency.

Texas Democratic legislators bolted the state to boycott a vote on a redistricting measure orchestrated by U.S. representative Tom Delay that would have increased the number of Republican seats in Congress. In May, 51 House Democrats skipped off to Oklahoma, successfully killing a vote on the controversial issue. Eleven state senate Democrats fled to New Mexico in July to block a special session vote. They returned in September to try to resolve the issue on the floor.

Sérgio Vieira de Mello, diplomat, was appointed UN special representative to Iraq in May. Vieira de Mello was charged with coordinating aid from the UN and nongovernmental organizations, returning refugees to their homes, and overseeing human rights. He was killed in August when a suicide bomber demolished UN headquarters in Baghdad. Prior to assuming the post in Iraq, Vieira de Mello, a Brazilian, had been UN high commissioner for human rights and oversaw East Timor's development into a fledgling democracy.

Dominique de Villepin, French foreign minister, emerged as one of the most outspoken critics of President Bush's pursuit of war in Iraq. He earned rare applause at a UN Security Council meeting in February, when he urged council members to give weapons inspectors and diplomacy more time. "No one can say today that the path of war would be shorter than the path of inspections. No one can claim either that it might lead to a safer, more just, and more stable world," he said. He infuriated many in the Bush administration, who considered his protestations inflexible and arrogant.

Christine Todd Whitman, public official, stepped down as the administrator of the Environmental Protection Agency in May. Although she said she missed her husband and home in New Jersey, she was continually at odds with the Bush administration, which favored loosening environmental regulations, and environmentalists, who frequently complained that she deferred to Bush's agenda.

Joseph Wilson, former ambassador, discredited President Bush's claim—and a justification for war in Iraq—that Saddam Hussein was pursuing a nuclear weapons program by seeking to obtain uranium from Niger. Wilson visited Niger in February 2002 to investigate the accusation, and he reported back that it was unsubstantiated. He went public with his findings in July, after months of silence by the Bush administration. In July, columnist Robert Novack identified Wilson's wife, Valerie Plame, as a CIA agent who specializes in weapons of mass destruction. Wilson believes the Bush administration leaked his wife's name as retribution. In September, the Justice Department announced an investigation into the leak.

Paul Wolfowitz, deputy defense secretary, began making a case for an invasion of Iraq shortly after the September 11, 2001, terrorist attacks against the U.S. He said Saddam Hussein should be ousted before he could pass on weapons of mass destruction to terrorist groups such as al-Qaeda. Known for his sharp intelligence and his archly hawkish views, Wolfowitz has worked for every president since 1973, except President Clinton. In 1992, he recommended to the first President Bush that the U.S. launch unilateral, preemptive military strikes against hostile countries seeking to develop or acquire weapons of mass destruction. The proposal was then deemed reckless and overly aggressive, but in the context of the war against terrorism, it became the course President George W. Bush charted with the U.S.-led invasion of Iraq.

2003 Deaths

(through October 1, 2003)

Ivan Allen, 92: former mayor of Atlanta who deftly guided the racial integration of the city in the turbulent 1960s. July 2, 2003

Idi Amin, 80: mercurial Ugandan military dictator whose brutal, tyrannical rule left his country economically and socially devastated. Human rights groups estimate that he ordered the deaths of about 300,000 people. Amin was ousted in 1979, and died in exile in Saudi Arabia. Aug. 16, 2003

Cholly Atkins, 89: tap dancer and choreographer who worked with Motown stars Marvin Gaye, the Temptations, and the Supremes. April 19, 2003

Robert Atkins, 72: cardiologist whose controversial weight-loss plan helped millions of dieters shed pounds, but generated criticism from several health experts, who called the low-carbohydrate regimen extreme and potentially dangerous. April 17, 2003

George Axelrod, 81: screenwriter whose saucy scripts, including *The Seven Year Itch, Breakfast at Tiffany's,* and *The Manchurian Candidate,* satirized the morals of the 1950s and '60s. June 21, 2003

Hank Ballard, 75: rhythm-and-blues singer and songwriter whose racy lyrics were often banned from radio in the 1950s. Ballard wrote the song "The Twist," which Chubby Checker made famous in 1959. March 2, 2003

David Bloom, 39: broadcast journalist who was covering the war in Iraq for NBC, MSNBC, and CNBC when he died of a blood clot. April 6, 2003

Bobby Bonds, 57: All-Star baseball player who, in his 14 seasons in the major leagues, hit 332 home runs and stole 461 bases. He played for the San Francisco Giants for seven years. His son is slugger Barry Bonds. Aug. 23, 2003

Linda Braidwood, 93, and Robert Braidwood, 95: husband-and-wife archaeologist team that in 1947 discovered the earliest-known village, which dated to 6800 B.C., near the Iran-Iraq border. In 1964 they found the earliest-known building, dating from 7250 to 6750 B.C., in southwestern Turkey. They died within hours of each other. Jan. 15, 2003

David Brinkley, 82: pioneering journalist who, with Chet Huntley, hosted NBC's influential *Huntley-Brinkley Report.* Known for his clipped voice and candid, often skeptical comments, Brinkley went on to anchor NBC's *Nightly News.* In 1981, he left NBC for ABC, where he hosted the Sunday morning talk show *This Week with David Brinkley.* His 1995 memoir summed up his career: *David Brinkley: 11 Presidents, 4 Wars, 22 Political Conventions, 1 Moon Landing, 3 Assassinations, 2,000 Weeks of News, and Other Stuff on Television and 18 Years of Growing Up in North Carolina.* June 11, 2003

Charles Bronson, 81: actor who played steely-eyed, impassive tough guys in such films as *Death Wish* and *Once Upon a Time in the West.* Aug. 30, 2003

Herb Brooks, 66: coach who led the U.S. hockey "Miracle on Ice" team to a gold medal at the 1980 Winter Olympics. Under Brooks, a former Olympian himself, the University Minnesota hockey team won three NCAA titles (1974, 1976, and 1978). He died in a car accident. Aug. 11, 2003

Felice Bryant, 77: lyricist who, with her husband, Boudleaux Bryant, wrote more than 800 songs, including the hits "Bye Bye Love" and "Wake Up Little Susie." April 22, 2003

Benny Carter, 95: jazz arranger, bandleader, and composer who is considered one of the three top alto saxophonists of all time. (He shares the honor with Johnny Hodges and Charlie Parker.) Known for his meticulous performances and refined style, Carter influenced generations of jazz musicians. His hits include "Cow-Cow Boogie" and "Only Trust Your Heart." July 12, 2003

Nell Carter, 54: flamboyant singer and actress who won a Tony and an Emmy Award for her performance in *Ain't Misbehavin'.* She starred in the television series *Gimme a Break!* Jan. 23, 2003

Johnny Cash, 71: highly influential and singular country music singer and songwriter who was known as the "Man in Black." In his gritty baritone, Cash typically sang about temptation, flawed yet conscientious characters, and the working poor. He was inducted into both the Country Music and Rock and Roll Halls of Fame and won 11 Grammy Awards. He recorded more than 1,500 songs, which include "I Walk the Line," "Ring of Fire," and "Folsom Prison Blues." Sept. 12, 2003

June Carter Cash, 73: country music singer and songwriter who co-wrote the 1963 hit "Ring of Fire," a dark love song about Johnny Cash, whom she married in 1968. She began performing at age six with her family in the Carter Family band. May 15, 2003

Janet Collins, 86: pioneering prima ballerina of the Metropolitan Opera House who danced in Cole Porter's 1950 Broadway musical *Out of This World* and in *Aida* and *Carmen.* She was the first black artist to perform at the Met. May 28, 2003

Joe Connelly, 85: television writer and producer who, with Bob Mosher, created the series *Leave It to Beaver.* His other credits include *The Munsters* and *Tammy.* Feb. 13, 2003

Richard Crenna, 76: prolific character actor who began his 65-year show-business career as a child in radio. Known for his broad range, Crenna played a squeaky-voiced teen in *Our Miss Brooks,* an army colonel in the *Rambo* movies, and a card shark in *The Flamingo Kid.* Jan. 17, 2003

Hume Cronyn, 91: respected stage and screen character actor whose outstanding performances in plays by Shakespeare, Chekhov, Albee, and Beckett revealed his versatility. He was nominated for five Tony Awards, and won for *Hamlet.* His other Broadway successes include *A Delicate Balance* and *Gin Game.* He also won acclaim for his roles in more than 40 films, including *Cocoon.* He frequently appeared in plays with his wife, Jessica Tandy, who died in 1994. June 15, 2003

Celia Cruz, 77: Cuban singer whose rich contralto voice, persistently upbeat songs, and effusive stage presence earned her the title of Queen of Salsa. Cuban-born, Cruz arrived in the U.S. in 1961 and became a star, performing with dozens of Latin musicians, including Johnny Pacheco and Tito Puente. July 16, 2003

Donald Davidson, 86: one of the foremost philosophers of the twentieth century, Davidson produced revolutionary studies on the philosophy of language, mind, and action. He taught at a variety universities, finishing his career at the University of California, Berkeley. Aug. 30, 2003

Dave DeBusschere, 62: Hall of Fame basketball forward who played for the New York Knicks when the team won NBA Championship titles in 1970 and 1973. He started his career in 1962 with the Detroit

Pistons. The Pistons named him player-coach in 1964, and at age 24 he became the youngest coach in NBA history. May 14, 2003

Harry Ellis Dickson, 94: musician and conductor who played first violin for the Boston Symphony Orchestra for nearly 50 years and was a conductor of the Boston Pops for more than 40 years. March 29, 2003

C. Douglas Dillon, 93: financier and government official who, although he was a lifelong Republican, served as treasury secretary under presidents Kennedy and Johnson. Jan. 10, 2003

Larry Doby, 79: Hall of Fame baseball player who, in 1947, became the first black player in the American League. He joined the Cleveland Indians just 11 weeks after Jackie Robinson debuted as a Brooklyn Dodger. In his 13 seasons as a pro, Doby was an All-Star seven times. June 18, 2003

Robert Donovan, 90: newspaper reporter turned best-selling author who wrote *PT-109,* the chronicle of John F. Kennedy's war experiences. He also wrote a biography of President Truman. Aug. 8, 2003

Buddy Ebsen, 95: actor who danced in films and on Broadway for decades before landing the role as Jed Clampett in 1962 on *The Beverly Hillbillies.* He was cast as the Tin Man in *The Wizard of Oz,* but had to give up the part to Jack Haley because of an allergy to the aluminum-based makeup. July 6, 2003

Jinx Falkenburg, 84: model and actress who, with her husband Tex McCrary, defined the radio and television talk-show format. A film actress, Falkenburg turned to broadcasting in 1946, when she and McCrary hosted the pioneering talk-radio show *Hi Jinx.* Aug. 27, 2003

Howard Fast, 88: prolific writer whose historical novels often involved themes of social justice and rebellion. A member of the Communist Party, he was jailed and blacklisted in 1950 for refusing to cooperate with the House Committee on Un-American Activities. He drew on the experiences in his book *Spartacus,* which became an Oscar-winning film. His other books include *Citizen Tom Payne, Freedom Road,* and his memoir, *Being Red.* March 12, 2003

Orville Freeman, 84: Democratic politician who served as governor of Minnesota from 1954 to 1960. As secretary of agriculture under presidents Kennedy and Johnson, Freeman helped to create the food-stamp program and promoted the export of U.S. farm products. Feb. 20, 2003

Leopoldo Galtieri, 76: repressive general and military dictator of Argentina who ordered the ill-fated 1982 invasion of the British-held Falkland Islands. The move led to a 74-day war with England, in which Galtieri's regime was soundly defeated. After the British regained control of the island, Galtieri was convicted of negligence and imprisoned. Jan. 12, 2003

Jack Gelber, 71: playwright whose award-winning *The Connection* broke ground with its realistic, haunting portrait of drug addicts. The 1959 Off-Broadway play won three Obie Awards. May 9, 2003

Maurice Gibb, 53: songwriter and singer of the influential disco band the Bee Gees. The band, which has sold more than 120 million albums, included Maurice's twin brother, Robin, and another brother, Barry. Three of the band's songs from the *Saturday Night Fever* soundtrack topped the charts. Jan. 12, 2003

Althea Gibson, 76: professional tennis player who was the first black person to play in and win Wimbledon and the United States national tennis championship. She won both tournaments twice, in 1957 and 1958. In all, Gibson won 56 tournaments, including five Grand Slam singles events. Sept. 28, 2003

Tom Glazer, 88: folk singer who, with Pete Seeger, Leadbelly, and Burl Ives, helped to popularize the genre in the 1940s. Feb. 21, 2003

Robert Good, 81: a founder of modern immunology who, in 1968, performed the world's first successful bone marrow transplant. Good's research identified the importance of the thymus in fighting infection. He was a founder of the National Institutes of Medicine. June 13, 2003

Martha Griffiths, 91: politician and women's-rights activist who served as a member of the U.S. House of Representatives from 1955 to 1974, as a Democrat from Michigan. She successfully argued for the inclusion of "sex" in the 1964 Civil Rights Act and long fought for the Equal Rights Amendment, which, although it passed in the House and Senate, was never ratified. April 22, 2003

Arthur Guyton, 83: researcher whose 1956 *Textbook of Medical Physiology,* remains one of the most widely used texts. April 3, 2003

Buddy Hackett, 78: comedian whose cherubic face and brash delivery delighted stage, film, and television audiences for more than 50 years. He began his career in the Borscht Belt and proved himself a versatile actor, appearing in Broadway's *Lunatics and Lovers,* in the film *God's Little Acre,* and as a frequent guest on popular talk shows. June 30, 2003

Albert Hakim, 66: Iranian-born California businessman who, through a complicated web of bank accounts and transactions, financed and helped to organize the Iran-Contra affair of the 1980s. He served two years probation and paid a $5,000 fine for his involvement in the scandal. April 25, 2003

Najeeb Halaby, 87: airline executive, lawyer, and test pilot who served as CEO of Pan American World Airways in the late 1960s and early 1970s. He also headed the Federal Aviation Administration under President Kennedy. His daughter is Queen Noor of Jordan. July 2, 2003

Sue Sally Hale, 65: athlete who broke the gender barrier in the male-dominated world of polo. She played in tournaments disguised as a man for about 20 years before finally winning admission in the U.S. Polo Association in 1972. April 29, 2003

Conrad Hall, 76: Academy Award–winning cinematographer known for his naturalistic style. He won Oscars for *Butch Cassidy and the Sundance Kid* and *American Beauty.* His other credits include *In Cold Blood* and *Road to Perdition,* which also earned him an Oscar nomination. Jan. 4, 2003

Marion Hargrove, 83: U.S. Army G.I. who parlayed his exploits in basic training into 1942's best-selling *See Here, Private Hargrove.* The book and its 1944 sequel were adapted for film. Aug. 23, 2003

Vance Hartke, 84: three-term Democratic senator (1958–1977) from Indiana who was an early critic of the war in Vietnam. July 27, 2003

Andrew Heiskell, 87: executive and philanthropist who worked for Time Inc. for 43 years. He started with the media empire in 1937 as an editor at age 22 and retired as chairman and CEO in 1980. He was influential in the launching of *Money* and *People* magazines. July 6, 2003

Katharine Hepburn, 96: independent, sophisticated film, stage, and television actress whose career spanned nearly 70 years. Spencer Tracy was Hepburn's leading man and romantic partner, and they appeared in nine films together including *State of the Union* and *Adam's Rib.* Hepburn's roles as strong-willed, dry-witted women mirrored her real-life personality. Her other films include *Morning Glory, African Queen, The Philadelphia Story,* and *On Golden Pond.* June 29, 2003

Wendy Hiller, 90: celebrated British stage and film actress best known for her roles as Eliza Doolittle in the 1938 film *Pygmalion* and as the title character in 1941's *Major Barbara.* She won an Oscar for *Separate Tables.* May 14, 2003

Gregory Hines, 57: versatile performer who began his career as a tap dancer and successfully crossed over into acting. He received four Tony nominations, and won for Best Actor in a Musical for *Jelly's Last*

Jam. His film roles include *The Cotton Club* and *White Nights,* opposite Mikhail Baryshnikov. He starred in the sitcom *The Gregory Hines Show.* He died of cancer. Aug. 9, 2003

Jerome Hines, 81: bass who was the Metropolitan Opera's longest-performing vocalist. He played 45 characters in his 41 years with the Met. Feb. 4, 2003

Al Hirschfeld, 99: singular graphic artist whose caricatures of theater personalities graced dozens of publications for more than 75 years. His work most often appeared in the drama section of the *New York Times.* He included the word "Nina," the name of his daughter, in most of his line drawings. His subjects ranged from David Merrick to the Marx brothers to Gwyneth Paltrow. Jan. 20, 2003

Bob Hope, 100: legendary comedian, American icon, and master of the one-liner who used his quick delivery and brash, topical wit to entertain generations of fans, including U.S. troops stationed overseas. Hope began his career in vaudeville and burst onto the national scene in 1938, with the debut of his radio show for Pepsodent toothpaste and with his first feature film, *The Big Broadcast of 1938.* He appeared in several "Road" films with Bing Crosby and Dorothy Lamour. July 27, 2003

Riley Housewright, 89: microbiologist who, as scientific director of the U.S. Army Biological Laboratories from 1956 to 1970, helped to develop anthrax spores, botulinum toxin, and other viruses to use as weapons in war. Jan. 11, 2003

Maynard Jackson, 65: influential former mayor of Atlanta, Ga., who transformed the city into a power base for the black middle class by advocating for the city's black majority and establishing affirmative-action programs. June 23, 2003

Josephine Jacobsen, 94: poet and short-story writer known for her insightful yet spare verse. Her works frequently pondered the human experience. She served as consultant in poetry to the Library of Congress from 1971 to 1973. The post is now called U.S. poet laureate. July 9, 2003

Roy Jenkins, 82: progressive British politician whose long career in public service began in 1948, when he was elected to Parliament as a member of the Labour Party. He served as minister of aviation, home secretary, chancellor of the exchequer, and president of the European Commission. Jenkins cofounded the Social Democratic party in 1981. Jan. 5, 2003

Alfred Kantor, 79: artist whose works chronicled the unimaginable horrors of concentration camps at Auschwitz, Theresienstadt, and Schwarzheide. He destroyed most of the works he created in the camps and recreated them from memory after World War II. Jan. 16, 2003

Bernard Katz, 92: German-born physiologist who won a 1970 Nobel Prize in Physiology or Medicine for his research on how messages are received and transmitted between nerves and muscles. April 20, 2003

Elia Kazan, 94: one of the most influential and talented theater and film directors, Kazan won Best Director Oscars for *Gentleman's Agreement* and *On the Waterfront,* and Tony Awards for directing *All My Sons, Death of a Salesman,* and *J. B.* He was ostracized by many of his colleagues after he testified as a cooperative witness before the House Committee on Un-American Activities in 1952. He cofounded and codirected the Actors Studio. Sept. 28, 2003

Craig Kelly, 36: world champion snowboarder who helped to popularize the sport. He died in an avalanche in Canada. Jan. 20, 2003

Michael Kelly, 46: journalist and editor who was killed while covering the war in Iraq as an embedded reporter. He served as editor in chief of *Atlantic Monthly* magazine from 1999 to 2002 and had also worked for the *New York Times,* the *New Yorker,* and the *New Republic.* April 4, 2003

Rachel Kempson, 92: actress and matriarch of the Redgrave family of actors. She was a respected stage actress in England, appearing in several Shakespeare plays, including *The Tempest* and *Macbeth.* May 24, 2003

Jean Kerr, 80: writer and playwright whose witty observations about the annoyances of life and show business were best illustrated in the book *Please Don't Eat the Daisies* and the play *Mary, Mary.* She was the widow of *New York Times* drama critic Walter Kerr. Jan. 5, 2003

Charles Kindleberger, 92: economist whose 1978 book, *Manias, Panics, and Crashes,* chronicled the history of bubbles in the stock market. He theorized that when investors buy stock in hot new products or industries, the prices become artificially inflated, and eventually the prices tumble. His book was often reprinted after such occurrences, most recently in 2000 after the dot-com bust. July 7, 2003

Larry LeSueur, 93: journalist who covered the German blitz of London for CBS. LeSueur was one of the Murrow Boys, an elite group of journalists hired by Edward R. Murrow to cover World War II in Europe. In 1944, he made the first radio report of the liberation of Paris. He chronicled his experience covering the Russian front in the book *Twelve Months That Changed the World.* Feb. 5, 2003

Felice Lippert, 73: entrepreneur who cofounded Weight Watchers in 1963. Feb. 22, 2003

Russell Long, 84: politician who served as a Democratic senator from Louisiana from 1948 to 1986. He was the son of legendary Louisiana governor Huey Long. May 9, 2003

Lester Maddox, 87: restaurant owner and former governor of Georgia who, in 1964, defiantly refused to serve three black college students at his Pickrick Restaurant, a violation of the Civil Rights Act. He sold his restaurant rather than comply with the law. He was elected governor in 1966, and maintained his segregationist agenda. June 25, 2003

Burke Marshall, 80: public official who served as assistant attorney general in charge of civil rights in the Kennedy and Johnson administrations. A former antitrust lawyer, Marshall helped to write the Civil Rights Act of 1964. June 2, 2003

Bill Mauldin, 81: army sergeant and cartoonist who won a Pulitzer Prize for his works featuring Willie and Joe, two bedraggled World War II infantrymen who battled not only the Germans, but also the boredom and indignities of war. He won a second Pulitzer Prize in 1959 for a cartoon he drew about imprisoned writer Boris Pasternak for the St. Louis *Post-Dispatch.* Jan. 22, 2003

Robert McCloskey, 88: children's book writer and illustrator whose Caldecott Medal–winning *Make Way for Ducklings* remains a classic. He won a second Caldecott Medal for *Time of Wonder.* June 30, 2003

Mark McCormack, 72: founder and CEO of International Management Group (IMG), the sports management conglomerate that represents Tiger Woods, Wayne Gretzky, Arnold Palmer, and Andre Agassi. *Sports Illustrated* called McCormack "the most powerful man in sports." May 16, 2003

Tex McCrary, 93: publicist and political strategist who, with his wife, Jinx Falkenburg, virtually invented the talk-show genre. The pair starred together in several radio and TV shows in the 1940s and '50s. In 1952, McCrary launched a successful campaign to convince Gen. Dwight Eisenhower to run for president on the Republican ticket. July 29, 2003

Robert Merton, 92: sociologist who studied subjects ranging from the mass media to the behavior of scientists. He developed the concepts "self-fulfilling prophecy" and "deviant behavior." He's also credited with creating the focus group. He was the first sociologist to win the National Medal of Science, in 1994. Feb. 23, 2003

Doug Michels, 59: avant-garde artist and architect who, with Chip Lord, created Ant Farm, an "underground" architectural firm. The group created "Cadillac Ranch," an installation of 10 Cadillacs partially buried nose-down in the dirt. June 12, 2003

Paul Monash, 85: film producer whose credits include *Butch Cassidy and the Sundance Kid* and *Slaughterhouse-Five.* He also wrote, directed, and produced television's *Peyton Place.* Jan. 14, 2003

Daniel Patrick Moynihan, 76: sociologist and politician who served four terms as a Democratic senator from New York, as ambassador to the United Nations and India, and as an aide to presidents Kennedy, Johnson, Nixon, and Ford. He was first elected to the Senate in 1976. Mar. 23, 2003

Elizabeth Neuffer, 46: award-winning journalist who worked as a foreign correspondent for the *Boston Globe.* She died in a car accident in Iraq while covering the fallout from the war. May 9, 2003

Frank O'Bannon, 73: career Democratic politician who was governor of Indiana when he died of a stroke. First elected governor in 1996, O'Bannon was reelected in 2000. September 13, 2003

Donald O'Connor, 78: acrobatic dancer, singer, and actor whose solo performance to "Make 'Em Laugh" in *Singin' in the Rain* remains one of the most memorable in film history. His other films include *Beau Geste* and the *Francis* series. Sept. 27, 2003

Robert Palmer, 54: dapper rock musician who played with several British rock groups before launching a successful solo career in the 1980s with such hits as "Addicted to Love" and "Simply Irresistible." He died of a heart attack. Sept. 26, 2003

Suzy Parker, 69: model and actress who many consider the first supermodel. She favored Coco Chanel designs and posed for the photographers Richard Avedon and Horst. Her film credits include *Funny Face* and *Kiss Them for Me.* May 3, 2003

Johnny Paycheck (Donald Lytle), 64: influential outlaw country singer who was as famous for his legal and personal troubles as he was for his music. His hits include "Take This Job and Shove It" and "(Don't Take Her) She's All I Got." Feb. 19, 2003

Gregory Peck, 87: distinguished Oscar-winning actor who often played dignified yet vulnerable characters, such as Atticus Finch in *To Kill a Mockingbird,* a crusading journalist in *Gentleman's Agreement,* and the title character in *MacArthur.* His other roles include *Spellbound* and *Twelve O'Clock High.* June 12, 2003

Sam Phillips, 80: legendary record producer whose Sun Records in Memphis launched the careers of Elvis Presley, Howlin' Wolf, B. B. King, Roy Orbison, Jerry Lee Lewis, and Carl Perkins, and popularized rock and roll. He made a fortune with his early investment in Holiday Inn. July 30, 2003

George Plimpton, 76: urbane writer, editor, and actor who frequently drew upon his own experiences—often his less-than-stellar exploits on the athletic field—in his works. He cofounded *The Paris Review*—the widely respected, but not widely read, literary journal—in 1953. In 1963, he joined the Detroit Lions football team, an experience captured in the book *Paper Lion.* He appeared in several films, including *Reds* and *Goodwill Hunting.* Sept. 25, 2003

Vera Hruba Ralston, 79: skater who competed in the 1936 Olympics and went on to appear in the films *Ice-Capades* and *I, Jane Doe.* Feb. 9, 2003

Donald Regan, 84: financier who resigned as chairman of Merrill Lynch in 1981 to become President Reagan's treasury secretary. Immensely popular and influential with the president, Regan was instrumental in the passage of 1981's tax cuts and drafted the sweeping Tax Reform Act of 1986. He became Reagan's chief of staff in 1985, but ran afoul of First Lady Nancy Reagan. He was forced to resign in 1987, and he and the first lady subsequently traded barbs in their memoirs. June 10, 2003

Natalya Reshetovskaya, 84: Russian pianist and chemist who was married two times to dissident author Aleksandr Solzhenitsyn. May 28, 2003

Leni Riefenstahl, 101: German documentary filmmaker widely praised for her innovative techniques and vilified for her role as a Nazi propagandist. In her 1935 film *Triumph of the Will,* she chronicled a huge Nazi rally at Nuremberg. The film led to 1938's *Olympia,* a two-part documentary about the 1936 Berlin Olympics. Her later works include documentaries and photography books about the Nuba of southern Sudan. Sept. 8, 2003

John Ritter, 54: actor who played the quirky ladies' man Jack Tripper on television's *Three's Company.* Ritter won an Emmy Award and a Golden Globe Award for the role. He also starred in ABC's current hit, *8 Simple Rules for Dating My Teenage Daughter,* and he appeared in the film *Sling Blade.* He died of an aortic dissection. Sept. 11, 2003

Fred Rogers, 74: host of the Emmy Award–winning children's show *Mister Rogers' Neighborhood.* His gentle demeanor and comforting advice entertained millions of children during its 33-year run on PBS. Feb. 27, 2003

Walt Rostow, 86: hawkish economist and historian who, as an adviser to presidents Kennedy and Johnson, advocated U.S. aggressive involvement in the Vietnam War. He believed that the fall of Communism in Southeast Asia would spark modernization. Rostow coined Kennedy's 1960 slogan, "Let's Get This Country Moving." Feb. 13, 2003

Peter Safar, 79: pioneering anesthesiologist who developed the lifesaving technique cardiopulmonary resuscitation (CPR), a combination of mouth-to-mouth resuscitation and closed-chest cardiac compression. Aug. 3, 2003

Edward Said, 67: scholar and literary critic who championed a Palestinian homeland and railed against U.S. and Israeli policy toward Palestinians and Arab nations. In his book *Orientalism,* Said argued the relationship between the West and East is one of "power, of domination of varying degrees of a complex hegemony," with the West using colonization to dominate and demean the East. He taught comparative literature at Columbia University. Sept. 24, 2003

Mongo Santamaria, 85: Cuban-born percussionist whose music fused American jazz and funk with Cuban sounds. He wrote the song "Afro Blue," recorded by John Coltrane, and his version of Herbie Hancock's "Watermelon Man" became a top-10 hit. Feb. 1, 2003

John Schlesinger, 77: British film director whose 1969 film *Midnight Cowboy*—his first Hollywood project—is the only X-rated film to have won a best-picture Academy Award. Schlesinger's films typically featured fully realized yet flawed characters. His other films include *Darling, The Day of the Locust,* and *Marathon Man.* July 25, 2003

Tex Schramm, 83: professional football executive who, as general manager of the Dallas Cowboys, hired coach Tom Landry. The pair led the team to 20 straight winning seasons and two Super Bowl wins. He was the first general manager inducted into the Pro Football Hall of Fame. July 15, 2003

Martha Scott, 88: actress who played Emily in the original Broadway production of Thornton Wilder's *Our Town.* She earned an Oscar nomination for her role in the film adaptation. Her other film credits include *Ben-Hur* and *In Old Oklahoma.* May 28, 2003

Belding Scribner, 82: doctor and researcher whose invention, the Scribner shunt, allowed kidney dialysis patients to survive for years. He won the Albert Lasker Award for Clinical Medical Research in 2002. June 19, 2003

Compay Segundo, 95: Cuban musician who was an accomplished traditional balladeer in the 1920s, '30s, and '40s but gained wide fame in the late 1990s, after he formed a band, the Buena Vista Social Club, with other aging Cuban musicians. The band released an eponymous album and Wim Wenders directed a film about the musicians. July 13, 2003

Hartley Shawcross (Lord Shawcross), 101: British attorney general who was chief prosecutor at the International Military Tribunal at Nuremburg in 1945. He also prosecuted the spies Klaus Fuchs and Alan Nunn May, who were convicted of passing on atomic secrets to the Soviet Union, and William Joyce (Lord Haw-Haw), who broadcast Nazi propaganda during World War II. July 10, 2003

Carol Shields, 68: novelist and poet who frequently and eloquently wrote about ordinary women facing ordinary lives. She won a 1995 Pulitzer Prize for *The Stone Diaries.* July 16, 2003

Nina Simone (Eunice Kathleen Waymoa), 70: sultry chanteuse whose difficult-to-classify music combined jazz, classical, folk, and gospel. Her biggest hit was "My Baby Just Cares for Me." A civil rights activist, she recorded "Mississippi Goddam" after the murder of Medgar Evers. April 21, 2003

Howard "Sandman" Sims, 86: famed Apollo Theater tap dancer who taught his fancy footwork to Gregory Hines, Ben Vereen, Muhammad Ali, and Sugar Ray Robinson. May 20, 2003

Walter Sisulu, 90: South African politician and anti-apartheid crusader who was a longtime mentor to Nelson Mandela. Together, Sisulu and Mandela led the African National Congress, established its Youth League, and served 26 years in prison on Robben Island. May 5, 2003

Alberto Sordi, 82: Italian-born comic actor who appeared in the films *The White Sheik* and *I Vitelloni.* Feb. 24, 2003

Robert Stack, 84: rugged actor whose film and television career spanned 60 years. He's most famous for his role as Eliot Ness in the television series *The Untouchables.* His film credits include *The Bullfighter and the Lady.* May 14, 2003

Edwin Starr, 61: soul singer best known for his Grammy-winning 1970 hit, "War." April 2, 2003

Peter Stone, 73: playwright and screenwriter who was the first scribe to win an Oscar, an Emmy Award, and a Tony Award. His credits include Broadway's *1776* and the films *Father Goose* and *Charade.* April 26, 2003

Edward Teller, 95: Hungarian-born atomic physicist who helped to establish the nuclear era with his advocacy for and work on the atomic bomb and later the hydrogen bomb. He was widely criticized in scientific circles for his testimony that implied that J. Robert Oppenheimer was a security risk. In the 1980s he championed a space-based antimissile system, widely known as the Star Wars program. He won the 1962 Enrico Fermi Award and a 2003 Presidential Medal of Freedom. Sept. 9, 2003

Wallace Terry, 65: black journalist who covered the civil rights movement and the Vietnam War for the *Washington Post* and *TIME* magazine. His 1984 book *Bloods: An Oral History of the Vietnam War by Black Veterans* became a bestseller. May 29, 2003

Sir Denis Thatcher, 88: husband of England's former prime minister Margaret Thatcher. June 26, 2003

Lynne Thigpen, 54: actress who won a Tony Award for her role in *An American Daughter.* She starred in the CBS drama *The District.* March 12, 2003

Strom Thurmond, 100: South Carolina politician who was the longest-serving U.S. senator in history, holding the office from 1954 to 2003. Early in his career Thurmond was an avowed segregationist; he ran for president in 1948 as the nominee of the Dixiecrat States' Rights Party. Before being elected to the Senate, Thurmond was a state senator, a circuit-court judge, and governor of South Carolina. Thurmond eventually moderated his views on race; he hired a black aid who worked for him for about 25 years, and he voted to expand the Voting Rights Act. June 26, 2003

Hugh Trevor-Roper, 89: British historian and prolific writer whose best-selling book *The Last Days of Hitler* remains the definitive account of the fall of the Third Reich. His reputation was marred in 1983, when, as chair of modern history at Oxford, he validated dozens of volumes of Hitler's diaries, which were later revealed to be forgeries. Jan. 26, 2003

Evelyn Trout, 97: pioneering female aviator who was the first woman to complete an all-night flight. She also participated in the first All-Women's Transcontinental Air Race, dubbed the Powder Puff Derby, in 1929. Jan. 24, 2003

Leon Uris, 78: novelist whose fictional account of the creation of modern Israel, 1958's *Exodus,* became one of the all-time top bestsellers. He often wrote about war, and his other novels include *Battle Cry, Mila 18,* and *The Haj.* June 21, 2003

Felix de Weldon, 96: sculptor who created the Marine Corps War Memorial in Arlington, Va., which depicts marines raising the flag on Iwo Jima. Weldon crafted more than 2,000 other sculptures, including busts of Presidents Truman, Kennedy, and Eisenhower. June 2, 2003

Barry White, 58: Grammy Award–winning R&B singer and disco icon known for his lush baritone bass voice. His soulful, seductive songs include "Can't Get Enough of Your Love, Babe" and "You're the First, the Last, My Everything." July 4, 2003

Bernard Williams, 73: one of the 20th century's most brilliant philosophers, Williams was best known for his influential critiques of both Kant and utilitarianism and for defending the centrality of truth in modern thought. He taught at the universities of London, Cambridge, Berkeley, and Oxford. Williams, who was knighted in 1999, also served on a variety of government committees in England and was a Spitfire pilot for the RAF. June 10, 2003

Sloan Wilson, 83: novelist whose 1955 book *The Man in the Gray Flannel Suit* defined the postwar suburban and career angst experienced by countless Americans. Gregory Peck and Jennifer Jones starred in the 1956 film adaptation. May 25, 2003

Kathleen Winsor, 83: writer whose 1944 novel *Forever Amber* introduced the genre of romantic bestseller. The book about the sexual exploits of a woman in Restoration England sold about 100,000 copies in its first week of publication. May 26, 2003

Warren Zevon, 56: rock musician whose wry lyrics often delved into violence and death, as in "Excitable Boy" and "Werewolves of London." But he was equally skilled at crafting love songs, such as "Hasten Down the Wind." He died of cancer. Sept. 7, 2003

Ronald Ziegler, 63: President Nixon's White House press secretary who loyally—and naively—defended the president to the skeptical media during the Watergate crisis. He called the break-in at Watergate a "third-rate burglary." He's credited with coining the term "photo opportunity." Feb. 10, 2003

Paul Zindel, 66: playwright and novelist whose Pulitzer-Prize–winning play *The Effect of Gamma Rays on Man-in-the-Moon Marigolds* recounted growing up in a troubled home dominated by a paranoid mother. He wrote young adult novels *The Pigman* and *Confessions of a Teenage Baboon.* March 27, 2003

Vera Zorina, 86: dancer and actress who frequently collaborated with her first husband, George Balanchine in films and ballets of the 1930s and '40s. Her film credits include *The Goldwyn Follies* and *Louisiana Purchase.* April 9, 2003

See first page of book for additional tabs.